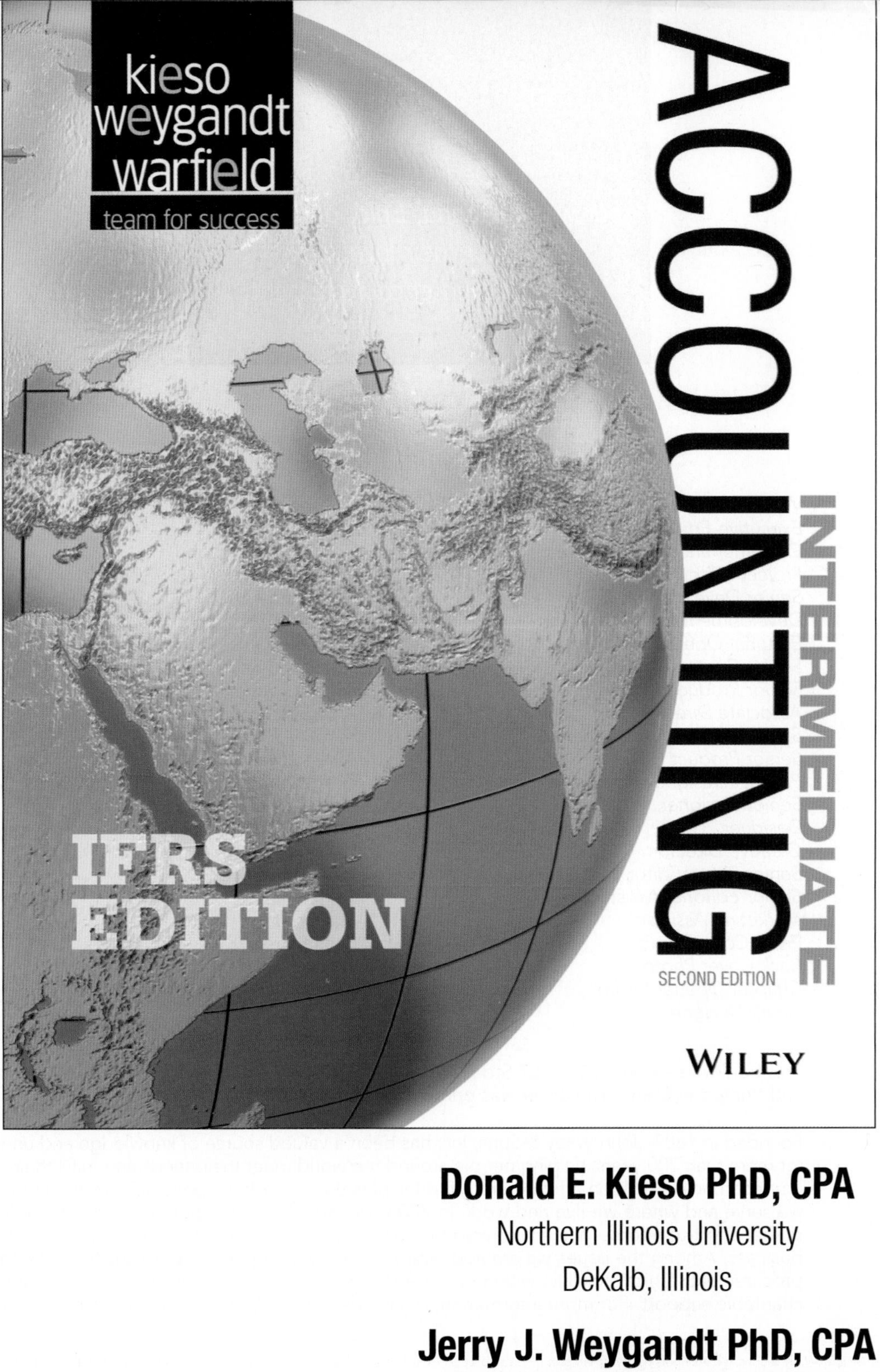
kieso
weygandt
warfield
team for success
ACCOUNTING
INTERMEDIATE
SECOND EDITION
IFRS
EDITION
WILEY

Donald E. Kieso PhD, CPA
Northern Illinois University
DeKalb, Illinois

Jerry J. Weygandt PhD, CPA
University of Wisconsin—Madison
Madison, Wisconsin

Terry D. Warfield, PhD
University of Wisconsin—Madison
Madison, Wisconsin

WILEY

Dedicated to
our wives, **Donna, Enid, and Mary,**
for their love,
support, and encouragement

Vice President & Executive Publisher	George Hoffman
Executive Editor	Joel Hollenbeck
Customer and Market Development Manager	Christopher DeJohn
Project Editor	Ed Brislin
Senior Development Editor	Terry Ann Tatro
Development Editor	Margaret Thompson
Editorial Operations Manager	Yana Mermel
Senior Content Manager	Dorothy Sinclair
Senior Production Editor	Sandra Dumas
Associate Director of Marketing	Amy Scholz
Senior Marketing Manager	Karolina Zarychta Honsa
Senior Product Designer	Allie K. Morris
Product Designer	Greg Chaput
Senior Designer	Maureen Eide
Designer	Kristine Carney
Creative Director	Harry Nolan
Senior Photo Editor	Mary Ann Price
Senior Editorial Assistant	Tai Harriss
Marketing Assistant	Mia Brady
Front Cover Photo	Baris Simsek/E+/Getty Images
Back Cover Photo	©zhang bo/iStockphoto
Chapter Opener Photo	©Anthony Roman/Shutterstock
Cover Designer	Maureen Eide

This book was set in Palatino LT Std by Aptara®, Inc. and printed and bound by Printplus Limited and Printed in China. The cover was printed by Printplus Limited and Printed in China.

Founded in 1807, John Wiley & Sons, Inc. has been a valued source of knowledge and understanding for more than 200 years, helping people around the world meet their needs and fulfill their aspirations. Our company is built on a foundation of principles that include responsibility to the communities we serve and where we live and work. In 2008, we launched a Corporate Citizenship Initiative, a global effort to address the environmental, social, economic, and ethical challenges we face in our business. Among the issues we are addressing are carbon impact, paper specifications and procurement, ethical conduct within our business and among our vendors, and community and charitable support. For more information, please visit our website: *www.wiley.com/go/citizenship*.

To order books or for customer service, please call 1-800-CALL WILEY (225-5945).

ISBN-13   978-1-118-44396-5

10 9 8 7 6 5 4 3 2 1

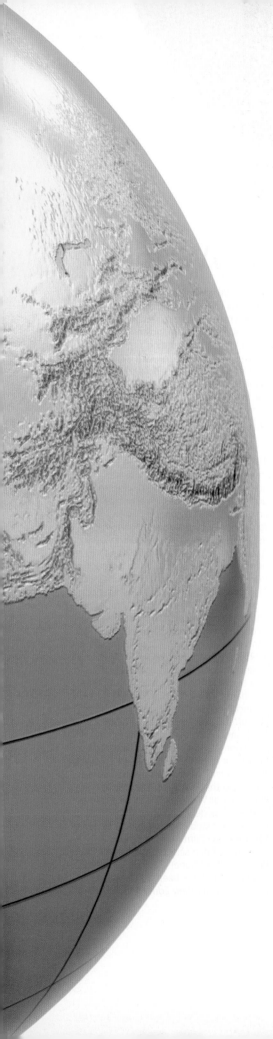

Brief Contents

Author
Commitment

Don **Kieso**

Donald E. Kieso, PhD, CPA, received his bachelor's degree from Aurora University and his doctorate in accounting from the University of Illinois. He has served as chairman of the Department of Accountancy and is currently the KPMG Emeritus Professor of Accountancy at Northern Illinois University. He has public accounting experience with Price Waterhouse & Co. (San Francisco and Chicago) and Arthur Andersen & Co. (Chicago) and research experience with the Research Division of the American Institute of Certified Public Accountants (New York). He has done post-doctorate work as a Visiting Scholar at the University of California at Berkeley and is a recipient of NIU's Teaching Excellence Award and four Golden Apple Teaching Awards. Professor Kieso is the author of other accounting and business books and is a member of the American Accounting Association, the American Institute of Certified Public Accountants, and the Illinois CPA Society. He has served as a member of the Board of Directors of the Illinois CPA Society, then AACSB's Accounting Accreditation Committees, the State of Illinois Comptroller's Commission, as Secretary-Treasurer of the Federation of Schools of Accountancy, and as Secretary-Treasurer of the American Accounting Association. Professor Kieso is currently serving on the Board of Trustees and Executive Committee of Aurora University, as a member of the Board of Directors of Kishwaukee Community Hospital, and as Treasurer and Director of Valley West Community Hospital. From 1989 to 1993, he served as a charter member of the National Accounting Education Change Commission. He is the recipient of the Outstanding Accounting Educator Award from the Illinois CPA Society, the FSA's Joseph A. Silvoso Award of Merit, the NIU Foundation's Humanitarian Award for Service to Higher Education, a Distinguished Service Award from the Illinois CPA Society, and in 2003 an honorary doctorate from Aurora University.

Jerry **Weygandt**

Jerry J. Weygandt, PhD, CPA, is Arthur Andersen Alumni Emeritus Professor of Accounting at the University of Wisconsin—Madison. He holds a Ph.D. in accounting from the University of Illinois. Articles by Professor Weygandt have appeared in the *Accounting Review, Journal of Accounting Research, Accounting Horizons, Journal of Accountancy,* and other academic and professional journals. These articles have examined such financial reporting issues as accounting for price-level adjustments, pensions, convertible securities, stock option contracts, and interim reports. Professor Weygandt is author of other accounting and financial reporting books and is a member of the American Accounting Association, the American Institute of Certified Public Accountants, and the Wisconsin Society of Certified Public Accountants. He has served on numerous committees of the American Accounting Association and as a member of the editorial board of the Accounting Review; he also has served as President and Secretary-Treasurer of the American Accounting Association. In addition, he has been actively involved with the American Institute of Certified Public Accountants and has been a member of the Accounting Standards Executive Committee (AcSEC) of that organization. He has served on the FASB task force that examined the reporting issues related to accounting for income taxes and served as a trustee of the Financial Accounting Foundation. Professor Weygandt has received the Chancellor's Award for Excellence in Teaching and the Beta Gamma Sigma Dean's Teaching Award. He is on the board of directors of M & I Bank of Southern Wisconsin. He is the recipient of the Wisconsin Institute of CPA's Outstanding Educator's Award and the Lifetime Achievement Award. In 2001, he received the American Accounting Association's Outstanding Educator Award.

Terry **Warfield**

Terry D. Warfield, PhD, is the PwC Professor in Accounting at the University of Wisconsin—Madison. He received a B.S. and M.B.A. from Indiana University and a Ph.D. in accounting from the University of Iowa. Professor Warfield's area of expertise is financial reporting, and prior to his academic career, he worked for five years in the banking industry. He served as the Academic Accounting Fellow in the Office of the Chief Accountant at the U.S. Securities and Exchange Commission in Washington, D.C. from 1995–1996. Professor Warfield's primary research interests concern financial accounting standards and disclosure policies. He has published scholarly articles in *The Accounting Review, Journal of Accounting and Economics, Research in Accounting Regulation,* and *Accounting Horizons,* and he has served on the editorial boards of *The Accounting Review, Accounting Horizons,* and *Issues in Accounting Education*. He has served as president of the Financial Accounting and Reporting Section, the Financial Accounting Standards Committee of the American Accounting Association (Chair 1995–1996), and on the AAA-FASB Research Conference Committee. He also served on the Financial Accounting Standards Advisory Council of the Financial Accounting Standards Board. He currently serves as a trustee on the Financial Accounting Foundation. Professor Warfield has received teaching awards at both the University of Iowa and the University of Wisconsin, and he was named to the Teaching Academy at the University of Wisconsin in 1995. Professor Warfield has developed and published several case studies based on his research for use in accounting classes. These cases have been selected for the AICPA Professor-Practitioner Case Development Program and have been published in *Issues in Accounting Education*.

From the Authors

Globalization is occurring rapidly. As economic and other interactions increase among countries, capital markets must provide high-quality financial information. A need therefore exists for high-quality financial reporting standards that meet this objective. Fortunately, **International Financial Reporting Standards (IFRS)** has broad international acceptance, being used in some form by more than 115 countries around the world. One securities regulator noted that IFRS is best positioned to serve as the single set of high-quality accounting standards.

Change Is the Only Constant

Most countries want rapid action related to the acceptance of IFRS. A number of countries have already switched from their own version of accounting standards to IFRS. Students and instructors need educational materials related to IFRS in order to meet this new challenge. Our objective in revising *Intermediate Accounting*, IFRS Edition, was therefore to continue to provide the tools needed to understand what IFRS is and how it is applied in practice. The emphasis on fair value, the proper accounting for financial instruments, and the new developments related to leasing, revenue recognition, and financial statement presentation are examined in light of current practice. In addition, given the rapid changes taking place, we provide and discuss the new Conceptual Framework to understand how these issues will likely be resolved in the future.

> "If this textbook helps you appreciate the challenges, worth, and limitations of financial reporting, if it encourages you to evaluate critically and understand financial accounting concepts and practice, and if it prepares you for advanced study, professional examinations, and the successful and ethical pursuit of your career in accounting or business in a global economy, then we will have attained our objectives."

A Look at Global Accounting

While IFRS has achieved broad acceptance, not all countries have adopted it. For example, U.S. companies still follow U.S. generally accepted accounting principles (U.S. GAAP) in preparing their financial statements. In fact, the differences between IFRS and U.S. GAAP may provide certain companies with a competitive advantage, so understanding these differences may be important in analyzing company performance. In addition, the IASB and the FASB are working together to converge their standards as appropriate. Accordingly, we have included a **Global Accounting Insights** section at the end of selected chapters, to highlight the important differences that remain between IFRS and U.S. GAAP, as well as the ongoing joint convergence efforts to resolve them. As a result, students truly gain a global accounting education by studying this textbook.

Intermediate Accounting Works

Intermediate Accounting, Fifteenth Edition (based on U.S. GAAP) is the market-leading textbook in providing the tools needed to understand what U.S. GAAP is and how it is applied in practice. With this IFRS Second Edition, we strive to continue to provide the material needed to understand this subject area using IFRS. The book is comprehensive and up-to-date, and provides the instructor with flexibility in the topics to cover. We also include proven pedagogical tools, designed to help students learn more effectively and to answer the changing needs of this course.

We are excited about *Intermediate Accounting*, IFRS Second Edition. We believe it meets an important objective of providing useful information to educators and students interested in learning about IFRS. Suggestions and comments from users of this textbook will be appreciated. Please feel free to e-mail any one of us at *AccountingAuthors@yahoo.com*.

Donald E. Kieso
Somonauk, Illinois

Jerry J. Weygandt
Madison, Wisconsin

Terry D. Warfield
Madison, Wisconsin

What's New?

The Second Edition expands our emphasis on student learning and improves upon a teaching and learning package that instructors and students have rated the highest in customer satisfaction. We have developed a number of new pedagogical features and content changes, designed both to help students learn more effectively and to answer the changing needs of the course.

Evolving Issues

As we continue to strive to reflect the constant changes in the accounting environment, we have added a new feature to the Second Edition, **Evolving Issue** boxes, which highlight and discuss areas in which the profession may be encountering controversy or nearing resolution. Our hope is that these high-interest boxes will increase student engagement, as well as serve as classroom discussion points. For another source of high-interest material, see the **What Do the Numbers Mean?** boxes, most of which are new to this edition.

Global Accounting Insights

We have updated the end-of-chapter section, **Global Accounting Insights** (previously known as the Convergence Corner), throughout the textbook. In addition, we now present *Similarities* as well as *Differences* between U.S. GAAP and IFRS to increase student understanding.

Major Content Revisions

In response to the changing environment, we have significantly revised several chapters.

Chapter 2   Conceptual Framework for Financial Reporting
* Updated discussion on the IASB's guidance related to the use of fair value in financial statements, including the establishment of the fair value hierarchy.
* New illustration on the five steps of revenue recognition.
* Revised Constraints section, as now only cost constraint is included in the Conceptual Framework.

Chapter 4   Income Statement and Related Information
* New sections on the one statement and two statement formats for reporting components of other comprehensive income.
* Rewrote the Allocating to Non-Controlling Interest section to increase student understanding.

Chapter 18   Revenue Recognition
* Completely new chapter reflecting the very recent IFRS on revenue recognition.
* Numerous new illustrations providing case examples for correctly applying the new IFRS on revenue recognition.

Chapter 20   Accounting for Pensions and Postretirement Benefits
* New sections on the net defined benefit obligations and how to report changes for it.
* Updated section on past service cost, including discussion of curtailments.

Chapter 23   Statement of Cash Flows
* Reorganized chapter, to present the indirect method through preparation of the statement of cash flows first, followed by the discussion of the direct method as well as the advantages and disadvantages of both methods.
* New Evolving Issue, "Direct versus Indirect Controversy," on the arguments in favor of each method.

See the next two pages for a complete list of content revisions by chapter.

Supplementary Materials

The Solutions Manual, Test Bank, PowerPoint, Instructor's Manual, and all other materials were updated to reflect changes in the Second Edition. Instructor resources and additional student resources, such as online self-tests, are available at **www.wiley.com/college/kieso**. Supplementary materials are also available in *WileyPLUS* where additional resources can help instructors create assignments and track student progress. Additional Course Management Resources are available.

Content Changes by Chapter

Chapter 1 Financial Accounting and Accounting Standards
- Revised opening story, to include more recent commentaries on IFRS.
- New WDNM box, on recent progress toward global adoption of IFRS.
- Updated and expanded discussion of the IASB's standard-setting structure.
- Revised International Convergence section, to include recent developments.
- Moved Appendix 1A, The U.S. Standard-Setting Environment, to book's companion website.

Chapter 2 Conceptual Framework for Financial Reporting
- Updated Conceptual Framework discussion to reflect recent IASB discussion paper, e.g., materiality no longer considered a separate constraint.
- Updated discussion on fair value, including the establishment of the fair value hierarchy, and the revenue recognition principle.
- New WDNM boxes, on the importance of faithful representation, as exemplified by the scandal at **Olympus Corp.**, and the concept of prudence.
- Updated discussion plus added an illustration on the five steps of revenue recognition.
- Updated Constraints section as now only cost constraint is included in the Conceptual Framework.

Chapter 3 The Accounting Information System
- New opening story on impact of global economic crime.
- Enhanced Adjusting Entries section, to provide additional explanation and visuals to students.
- New WDNM box, on companies' need to update their accounting information systems yet unwillingness to interrupt their operations to do so.

Chapter 4 Income Statement and Related Information
- Updated opening story, to discuss recent IASB project on financial statement presentation.
- New sections on the one statement and two statement formats for reporting components of other comprehensive income.
- Rewrote Allocation to Non-Controlling Interest section, to increase student understanding.
- New WDNM boxes, on a recent study that reinforces concerns about earnings management and the use of pro forma earnings measures.
- New Evolving Issue on income reporting.

Chapter 5 Statement of Financial Position and Statement of Cash Flows
- New WDNM box, on presentation order of assets on the statement of financial position.
- New Evolving Issue, on statement of financial position reporting.
- Moved **M&S**'s financial statements from Appendix 5B to Appendix A at end of textbook.

Chapter 6 Accounting and the Time Value of Money
- New opening story, about developing fair value estimates and applying fair value guidance to specific examples.

Chapter 7 Cash and Receivables
- Revised opening story, about banks' bad debt allowances.
- New WDNM box, on consequences of requiring companies to value their securities at fair value.
- New Evolving Issue, on the three-bucket approach of classifying loans and impairment stages.

Chapter 8 Valuation of Inventories: A Cost-Basis Approach
- New opening story, about the difficulties in determining the point at which inventory is considered to be sold.
- Moved Appendix 8B (Special Issues Related to LIFO) and related assignment material to book's companion website.
- Deleted material on sales on installment in Special Sales Agreements section.

Chapter 9 Inventories: Additional Valuation Issues
- New opening story, about why investors need comparable information about inventory when evaluating retailers' financial statements.

Chapter 10 Acquisition and Disposition of Property, Plant, and Equipment
- New opening story, about importance of capital expenditures and how they can affect a company's income.

Chapter 11 Depreciation, Impairments, and Depletion
- New WDNM box, on why some companies do not use revaluation accounting.

Chapter 12 Intangible Assets
- New opening story, on increasing amount of sustainable information provided by companies.
- New Underlying Concepts note about surrounding controversy for R&D accounting.
- New WDNM boxes: (1) how companies protect their intangible assets, (2) the patent battles between e-tailers and cell phone companies, and (3) global R&D incentives.
- New Evolving Issue, on the recognition of R&D and internally generated intangibles.

Chapter 13 Current Liabilities, Provisions, and Contingencies
- Revised Unearned Revenues section, to correspond to recent revenue recognition standard.
- New section on value-added tax (VAT).
- New sections on assurance-type and service-type warranties.
- New Evolving Issue, on how to account for greenhouse gases.

Chapter 14 Non-Current Liabilities
- New opening story, about the impact of long-term debt on governments and companies.
- New WDNM box, on why companies issue 100-year bonds.
- Updated Fair Value Option section, on how to treat changes in liability value due to credit risk changes.
- New footnote on IASB consolidation guidance for whether an off-balance-sheet entity should be on-balance-sheet.

Chapter 15 Equity
- Updated opening story, on the global IPO market.
- New WDNM boxes, on whether buybacks signal good or bad news about companies, and an analysis of recent company dividend payouts.
- Significantly enhanced Share Dividends and Share Splits sections to reflect recent information and pronouncements.

Chapter 16 Dilutive Securities and Earnings per Share
- Updated WDNM box on convertible bonds, to include more recent offerings from Asian companies.
- New illustration on company equity grants.

Chapter 17 Investments
- Revised WDNM box on fair value, to discuss controversial valuation of Greek government bond holdings.
- New illustration to clarify how to determine the adjustment to the carrying value of an investment.
- New Evolving Issue, on fair value controversy.
- New Appendix 17B on required fair value disclosures; deleted discussion of reclassification adjustments (old Appendix 17A).

Chapter 18 Revenue Recognition
- Completely rewritten chapter to reflect recently issued revenue recognition standard, including an overview and discussion of the five-step process.
- New opening story, featuring **Rolls-Royce**, **Qwest Communications**, **Sinovel Wind Group**, and **iGo**, to demonstrate challenges of recognizing revenue properly.
- New Evolving Issue, on the implementation of the recently issued revenue recognition standard.

Chapter 19 Accounting for Income Taxes
- Updated opening story, to include the most recent tax system recommendations by the G20.
- Updated footnotes on determining true cost of taxes and deferred tax assets (**Sony**'s experience in post-quake Japan).
- Expanded discussion of the components of income tax expense on the income statement.
- New WDNM box, on how a reduction in tax rates can be a double-edged sword for companies that have large deferred tax asset balances.

Chapter 20 Accounting for Pensions and Postretirement Benefits
- Chapter has been significantly revised to reflect recent IASB standards. Details are given below.
- Updated opening story, to include recent information about swings in pension plans' status.

- Updated WDNM box, to highlight increased popularity of defined contribution plans with employers as well as differences between countries in which plans are offered.
- New section on Net Defined Benefit Obligation (Asset).
- Rewrote Components of Pension Expense as new section, Reporting Changes in the Defined Benefit Obligation (Asset) to reflect recent IFRS.
- Expanded and updated section on Past Service Cost to reflect recent IASB rulings, including discussion of curtailments.
- New section on Remeasurements, replacing outdated discussion of corridor amortization.

Chapter 21 Accounting for Leases
- Updated opening story on aircraft leasing data and added information about IASB's work on new lease standard.
- New Evolving Issue, on proposal to address off-balance-sheet reporting of leases.

Chapter 22 Accounting Changes and Error Analysis
- New WDNM box, on how accounting changes create comparability challenges.
- Revised WDNM box, on need to protect company statements from negative effects of fraud.
- Reformatted examples of counterbalancing and non-counterbalancing errors as illustrations, for improved student understanding.

Chapter 23 Statement of Cash Flows
- Reorganized chapter, to present indirect method through preparation of the statement of cash flows first, followed by discussion of the direct method and advantages and disadvantages of both methods.
- New WDNM box, on COROA (cash operating return on assets), a new measure of profitability.
- Reformatted "Direct versus Indirect Controversy" as new Evolving Issue box, to highlight the arguments in favor of each method.
- New Underlying Concepts, on how statement of cash flows information and disclosures relate to the objective of financial reporting and the full disclosure principle.

Chapter 24 Presentation and Disclosure in Financial Reporting
- New opening story, about IASB survey of criticisms of current financial statement disclosures and how the Board plans to respond.
- New WDNM boxes: (1) requirements for disclosing collateral arrangements in repurchase agreements, (2) how note disclosure requirements can positively affect securities markets, and (3) differences in British forecasted information.
- New Evolving Issue, on anticipated increase in note disclosure requirements as IFRS and U.S. GAAP converge.
- New graphs on types and trends of economic crime and fraud.

Appendices A-C (New!)
Financial statements for **Marks & Spencer**, **adidas**, and **Puma**.

Contents

Acknowledgments

Second Edition Reviewers

Hsin-Tsai Liu, *National Taiwan University*; Daphne Main, *Loyola University—New Orleans*; Hannah Pantaran, *Silliman University, Philippines*; Fernando Penalva, *IESE Business School*; Dr. Charlie Sohn, *University of Macau*; Nai Hui Su (Suzanne), *National Chung Hsing University*; Professor Ting-Wong, *National Chengchi University*; Rita Yip, *Lingnan University*; Stephen Zeff, *Rice University*.

Ancillary Authors, Contributors, Proofers, and Accuracy Checkers

LuAnn Bean, *Florida Institute of Technology*; John C. Borke, *University of Wisconsin—Platteville*; Jack Cathey, *University of North Carolina—Charlotte*; Jim Emig, *Villanova University*; Larry Falcetto, *Emporia State University*; Coby Harmon, *University of California, Santa Barbara*; Mark Kohlbeck, *Florida Atlantic University*; Steven Lifland, *High Point University*; Jill Misuraca, *University of Tampa*; Barbara Muller, *Arizona State University*;

Yvonne Phang, *Borough of Manhattan Community College*; Laura Prosser, *Black Hills State University*; Lynn Stallworth, *Appalachian State University*; Dick D. Wasson, *Southwestern College*.

Practicing Accountants and Business Executives

From the fields of corporate and public accounting, we owe thanks to the following practitioners for their technical advice and for consenting to interviews.

Mike Crooch, *FASB (retired)*; Tracy Golden, *Deloitte LLP*; John Gribble, *PricewaterhouseCoopers (retired)*; Darien Griffin, *S.C. Johnson & Son*; Michael Lehman, *Sun Microsystems, Inc.*; Tom Linsmeier, *FASB*; Michele Lippert, *Evoke.com*; Sue McGrath, *Vision Capital Management*; David Miniken, *Sweeney Conrad*; Robert Sack, *University of Virginia*; Clare Schulte, *Deloitte LLP*; Willie Sutton, *Mutual Community Savings Bank, Durham, NC*; Lynn Turner, *former SEC Chief Accountant*; Rachel Woods, *PricewaterhouseCoopers*; Arthur Wyatt, *Arthur Andersen & Co., and the University of Illinois—Urbana*.

Finally, we appreciate the exemplary support and professional commitment given us by the development, marketing, production, and editorial staffs of John Wiley & Sons, including the following: Joel Hollenbeck, Chris DeJohn, Karolina Zarychta, Ed Brislin, Sandra Dumas, Brian Kamins, Tai Harriss, Allie Morris, Greg Chaput, Harry Nolan, Maureen Eide, and Kristine Carney. Thanks, too, to Jackie Henry and the staff at Aptara®, Inc. for their work on the textbook, Cyndy Taylor, and to Rebecca Sage and the staff at Integra Publishing Services for their work on the solutions manual.

Suggestions and comments from users of this book will be appreciated. Please feel free to e-mail any one of us at *AccountingAuthors@yahoo.com*.

Donald E. Kieso
Somonauk, Illinois

Jerry J. Weygandt
Madison, Wisconsin

Terry D. Warfield
Madison, Wisconsin

1 Financial Reporting and Accounting Standards

CHAPTER 1

LEARNING OBJECTIVES

After studying this chapter, you should be able to:

1 Describe the growing importance of global financial markets and its relation to financial reporting.

2 Identify the major financial statements and other means of financial reporting.

3 Explain how accounting assists in the efficient use of scarce resources.

4 Explain the need for high-quality standards.

5 Identify the objective of financial reporting.

6 Identify the major policy-setting bodies and their role in the standard-setting process.

7 Explain the meaning of IFRS.

8 Describe the challenges facing financial reporting.

Revolution in International Financial Reporting

The age of free trade and the interdependence of national economies is now with us. Many of the largest companies in the world often do more of their business in foreign lands than in their home country. Companies now access not only their home capital markets for financing but others as well. As this globalization takes place, companies are recognizing the need to have one set of financial reporting standards. For globalization to be efficient, what is reported for a transaction in Beijing should be reported the same way in Paris, New York, or London.

A revolution is therefore occurring in financial reporting. In the past, many countries used their own set of standards or followed standards set by larger countries, such as those in Europe or in the United States. However, that situation is changing rapidly. A single set of rules, called International Financial Reporting Standards (IFRS), is now being used by over 115 countries. Here is what some are saying about IFRS.

- "The global financial crisis that began in 2007 and continues today provides a very clear illustration of the globally connected nature of financial markets and the pressing need for a single set of high quality global accounting standards. That is why the G20 . . . has supported the work of the IASB and called for a rapid move towards global accounting." [Michael Prada, chairman of the IFRS Foundation.]

- "Large multi-national companies stand to realize great benefits from a move to a single set of standards. Companies will have more streamlined IT, easier training, and there will be better communication with outside parties. In fact, the move to IFRS is not so much about the accounting but about the economics of a shrinking world." [Sir David Tweedie, former chairman of the IASB.]

- "The added costs from having to use this complex hodgepodge (different country reporting standards) of financial information can run in the tens of millions of dollars annually. In the international arena, they can act as a barrier to forming and allocating capital efficiently. Thus, there are growing demands for the development of a single set of high quality international accounting standards." [Robert Herz, former chairman of the FASB.]

INTERNATIONAL FOCUS

> Read the **Global Accounting Insights** on pages 17–18 for a discussion of international financial reporting.

- "The current and growing breadth of IFRS adoption across the world suggests that IFRS has become the most practical approach to achieving the objective of having a single set of high-quality, generally accepted standards for financial reporting. Those who share this belief are influenced by the fact that the IASB's structure and due-process procedures are open, accessible, responsive, and marked by extensive consultation." [KPMG Defining Issues.]

- "Developments such as the shocks of the Asian financial crisis, the Enron and WorldCom scandals, and Europe's creation of a unified financial market helped build consensus for global accounting standards. Every relevant international organization has expressed its support for our work to develop a global language for financial reporting." [Hans Hoogervorst, chairman of the IASB, June 2013.]

What these statements suggest is that the international standard-setting process is rapidly changing. And with these changes, it is hoped that a more effective system of reporting will develop, which will benefit all.

PREVIEW OF CHAPTER **1**   As the opening story indicates, countries are moving quickly to adopt International Financial Reporting Standards (IFRS). It is estimated that as many as 310 of the 500 largest global companies are using IFRS. However, the accounting profession faces many challenges in establishing these standards, such as developing a sound conceptual framework, use of fair value measurements, proper consolidation of financial results, off-balance-sheet financing, and proper accounting for leases and pensions. This chapter discusses the international financial reporting environment and the many factors affecting it, as follows.

Financial Reporting and Accounting Standards

Global Markets	Objective of Financial Reporting	Standard-Setting Organizations	Financial Reporting Challenges
• Financial statements and financial reporting • Accounting and capital allocation • High-quality standards	• General-purpose financial statements • Equity investors and creditors • Entity perspective • Decision-usefulness	• IOSCO • IASB • Hierarchy of IFRS	• Political environment • Expectations gap • Significant financial reporting issues • Ethics • International convergence

GLOBAL MARKETS

LEARNING OBJECTIVE 1
Describe the growing importance of global financial markets and its relation to financial reporting.

World markets are becoming increasingly intertwined. International consumers drive Japanese cars, wear Italian shoes and Scottish woolens, drink Brazilian coffee and Indian tea, eat Swiss chocolate bars, sit on Danish furniture, watch U.S. movies, and use Arabian oil. The tremendous variety and volume of both exported and imported goods indicates the extensive involvement in international trade—for many companies, the world is their market.

To provide some indication of the extent of globalization of economic activity, Illustration 1-1 provides a listing of the top 20 global companies in terms of sales.

Rank	Company	Country	Revenues ($ millions)	Rank	Company	Country	Revenues ($ millions)
1	Royal Dutch Shell	Netherlands	484,489	11	Total	France	231,580
2	ExxonMobil	U.S.	452,926	12	Volkswagen	Germany	221,551
3	Wal-Mart Stores	U.S.	446,950	13	Japan Post Holdings	Japan	211,019
4	BP	U.K.	386,463	14	Glencore International	Switzerland	186,152
5	Sinopec Group	China	375,214	15	Gazprom	Russia	157,831
6	China National Petroleum	China	352,338	16	E.ON	Germany	157,057
7	State Grid	China	259,142	17	ENI	Italy	153,676
8	Chevron	U.S.	245,621	18	ING Group	Netherlands	150,571
9	ConocoPhillips	U.S.	237,272	19	General Motors	U.S.	150,276
10	Toyota Motor	Japan	235,364	20	Samsung Electronics	South Korea	148,944

Source: http://money.cnn.com/magazines/fortune/global500/2012/full_list/index.html.

ILLUSTRATION 1-1
Top 20 Global Companies in Terms of Sales

In addition, due to technological advances and less onerous regulatory requirements, investors are able to engage in financial transactions across national borders and to make investment, capital allocation, and financing decisions involving many foreign companies. Also, many investors, in attempts to diversify their portfolio risk, have invested more heavily in international markets. As a result, an increasing number of investors are holding securities of foreign companies. For example, over a recent seven-year period, estimated investments in foreign equity securities by U.S. investors increased over 20-fold, from $200 billion to $4,200 billion.

An indication of the significance of these international investment opportunities can be found when examining the number of foreign registrations on various securities exchanges. As shown in Illustration 1-2, a significant number of foreign companies are found on national exchanges.

ILLUSTRATION 1-2
International Exchange Statistics

Exchange (Location)	Total Share Trading ($ billions)	Total Listings	Domestic Listings	Foreign Listings	Foreign %
NYSE Euronext (U.S.)	18,027,080	2,308	1,788	520	22.5
NASDAQ OMX	12,723,520	2,680	2,383	297	11.1
Tokyo SE Group	3,986,204	2,291	2,280	11	0.5
London SE Group	2,825,662	2,886	2,288	598	20.7
NYSE Euronext (Europe)	2,125,422	1,112	969	143	12.9
Korea Exchange	2,022,640	1,816	1,799	17	0.9
Deutsche Börse (Germany)	1,750,853	746	670	76	10.2
Hong Kong Exchanges	1,444,712	1,496	1,472	24	1.6
Australian Securities Exchange	1,194,163	2,079	1,983	96	4.6
Taiwan SE Corporation	887,520	824	772	52	6.3
Singapore Exchange	284,289	773	462	311	40.2

Source: Focus: The Monthly Newsletter of Regulated Exchanges (September 2011).

As indicated, capital markets are increasingly integrated and companies have greater flexibility in deciding where to raise capital. In the absence of market integration, there can be company-specific factors that make it cheaper to raise capital and list/trade securities in one location versus another. With the integration of capital markets, the automatic linkage between the location of the company and location of the capital market is loosening. As a result, companies have expanded choices of where to raise capital, either equity or debt. The move toward adoption of global accounting standards has and will continue to facilitate this trend.

Financial Statements and Financial Reporting

Accounting is the universal language of business. One noted economist and politician indicated that the single-most important innovation shaping capital markets was the development of sound accounting principles. The essential characteristics of accounting are (1) the identification, measurement, and communication of financial information about (2) economic entities to (3) interested parties. **Financial accounting** is the process that culminates in the preparation of financial reports on the enterprise for use by both internal and external parties. Users of these financial reports include investors, creditors, managers, unions, and government agencies. In contrast, **managerial accounting** is the process of identifying, measuring, analyzing, and communicating financial information needed by management to plan, control, and evaluate a company's operations.

2 LEARNING OBJECTIVE

Identify the major financial statements and other means of financial reporting.

Financial statements are the principal means through which a company communicates its financial information to those outside it. These statements provide a company's history quantified in money terms. The **financial statements** most frequently provided are (1) the statement of financial position, (2) the income statement (or statement of comprehensive income), (3) the statement of cash flows, and (4) the statement of changes in equity. Note disclosures are an integral part of each financial statement.

Some financial information is better provided, or can be provided only, by means of **financial reporting** other than formal financial statements. Examples include the president's letter or supplementary schedules in the corporate annual report, prospectuses, reports filed with government agencies, news releases, management's forecasts, and social or environmental impact statements. Companies may need to provide such information because of authoritative pronouncements, regulatory rule, or custom. Or, they may supply it because management wishes to disclose it voluntarily.

In this textbook, we focus on the development of two types of financial information: (1) the basic financial statements and (2) related disclosures.

Accounting and Capital Allocation

Resources are limited. As a result, people try to conserve them and ensure that they are used effectively. Efficient use of resources often determines whether a business thrives. This fact places a substantial burden on the accounting profession.

3 LEARNING OBJECTIVE

Explain how accounting assists in the efficient use of scarce resources.

Accountants must measure performance accurately and fairly on a timely basis, so that the right managers and companies are able to attract investment capital. For example, relevant financial information that faithfully represents financial results allows investors and creditors to compare the income and assets employed by such companies as **Nokia** (FIN), **McDonald's** (USA), **Air China Ltd.** (CHN), and **Toyota Motor** (JPN). Because these users can assess the relative return and risks associated with investment opportunities, they channel resources more effectively. Illustration 1-3 (on page 6) shows how this process of capital allocation works.

ILLUSTRATION 1-3
Capital Allocation
Process

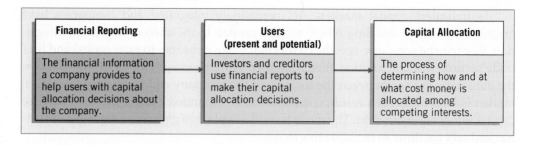

An effective process of capital allocation is critical to a healthy economy. It promotes productivity, encourages innovation, and provides an efficient and liquid market for buying and selling securities and obtaining and granting credit. Unreliable and irrelevant information leads to poor capital allocation, which adversely affects the securities markets.

High-Quality Standards

LEARNING OBJECTIVE **4**

Explain the need for high-quality standards.

To facilitate efficient capital allocation, investors need relevant information and a faithful representation of that information to enable them to make comparisons across borders. For example, assume that you were interested in investing in the telecommunications industry. Four of the largest telecommunications companies in the world are **Nippon Telegraph and Telephone** (JPN), **Deutsche Telekom** (DEU), **Telefonica** (ESP and PRT), and **AT&T** (USA). How do you decide which, if any, of these telecommunications companies you should invest in? How do you compare, for example, a Japanese company like Nippon Telegraph and Telephone with a German company like Deutsche Telekom?

A single, widely accepted set of high-quality accounting standards is a necessity to ensure adequate comparability. Investors are able to make better investment decisions if they receive financial information from Nippon Telegraph and Telephone that is comparable with Deutsche Telekom. Globalization demands a single set of high-quality international accounting standards. But how is this to be achieved? Here are some elements:

1. Single set of high-quality accounting standards established by a single standard-setting body.
2. Consistency in application and interpretation.
3. Common disclosures.
4. Common high-quality auditing standards and practices.
5. Common approach to regulatory review and enforcement.
6. Education and training of market participants.
7. Common delivery systems (e.g., eXtensible Business Reporting Language—XBRL).
8. Common approach to corporate governance and legal frameworks around the world.[1]

Fortunately, as indicated in the opening story, significant changes in the financial reporting environment are taking place, which hopefully will lead to a single, widely accepted set of high-quality accounting standards. The major standard-setters of the world, coupled with regulatory authorities, now recognize that capital formation and investor understanding is enhanced if a single set of high-quality accounting standards is developed.

[1]Robert H. Herz, "Towards a Global Reporting System: Where Are We and Where Are We Going?" *AICPA National Conference on SEC and PCAOB Reporting Developments* (December 10, 2007).

OBJECTIVE OF FINANCIAL REPORTING

What is the objective **(or purpose)** of financial reporting? The objective of general-purpose financial reporting is to **provide financial information about the reporting entity that is useful to present and potential equity investors, lenders, and other creditors in making decisions about providing resources to the entity**. Those decisions involve buying, selling, or holding equity and debt instruments, and providing or settling loans and other forms of credit. **[1]** Information that is decision-useful to capital providers (investors) may also be useful to other users of financial reporting who are not investors. Let's examine each of the elements of this objective.

5 LEARNING OBJECTIVE
Identify the objective of financial reporting.

IFRS

See the Authoritative Literature section (page 19).

General-Purpose Financial Statements

General-purpose financial statements provide financial reporting information to a wide variety of users. For example, when Nestlé (CHE) issues its financial statements, these statements help shareholders, creditors, suppliers, employees, and regulators to better understand its financial position and related performance. Nestlé's users need this type of information to make effective decisions. To be cost-effective in providing this information, general-purpose financial statements are most appropriate. In other words, general-purpose financial statements provide at the **least cost the most useful information possible**.

Equity Investors and Creditors

The objective of financial reporting identifies investors and creditors as the primary user group for general-purpose financial statements. Identifying investors and creditors as the primary user group provides an important focus of general-purpose financial reporting. For example, when Nestlé issues its financial statements, its primary focus is on investors and creditors because they have the most critical and immediate need for information in financial reports. Investors and creditors need this financial information to assess Nestlé's ability to generate net cash inflows and to understand management's ability to protect and enhance the assets of the company, which will be used to generate future net cash inflows. As a result, the primary user groups are not management, regulators, or some other non-investor group.

What do the numbers mean? **DON'T FORGET STEWARDSHIP**

In addition to providing decision-useful information about future cash flows, management also is accountable to investors for the custody and safekeeping of the company's economic resources and for their efficient and profitable use. For example, the management of Nestlé has the responsibility for protecting its economic resources from unfavorable effects of economic factors, such as price changes, and technological and social changes. Because Nestlé's performance in discharging its responsibilities (referred to as its **stewardship** responsibilities) usually affects its ability to generate net cash inflows, financial reporting may also provide decision-useful information to assess management performance in this role. **[2]**

Entity Perspective

As part of the objective of general-purpose financial reporting, an entity perspective is adopted. Companies are viewed as separate and distinct from their owners (present shareholders) using this perspective. The assets of Nestlé are viewed as assets of the company and not of a specific creditor or shareholder. Rather, these investors have claims on Nestlé's assets in the form of liability or equity claims. The entity perspective is consistent with the present business environment where most companies engaged in financial reporting have substance distinct from their investors (both shareholders and creditors). Thus, a perspective that financial reporting should be focused only on the needs of shareholders—often referred to as the **proprietary perspective**—is not considered appropriate.

Decision-Usefulness

Investors are interested in financial reporting because it provides information that is useful for making decisions (referred to as the decision-usefulness approach). As indicated earlier, when making these decisions, investors are interested in assessing (1) the company's ability to generate net cash inflows and (2) management's ability to protect and enhance the capital providers' investments. Financial reporting should therefore help investors assess the amounts, timing, and uncertainty of prospective cash inflows from dividends or interest, and the proceeds from the sale, redemption, or maturity of securities or loans. In order for investors to make these assessments, the economic resources of an enterprise, the claims to those resources, and the changes in them must be understood. Financial statements and related explanations should be a primary source for determining this information.

The emphasis on "assessing cash flow prospects" does not mean that the cash basis is preferred over the accrual basis of accounting. Information based on accrual accounting generally better indicates a company's present and continuing ability to generate favorable cash flows than does information limited to the financial effects of cash receipts and payments.

Recall from your first accounting course the objective of accrual-basis accounting: It ensures that a company records events that change its financial statements in the periods in which the events occur, rather than only in the periods in which it receives or pays cash. Using the accrual basis to determine net income means that a company recognizes revenues when it provides the goods or performs the services rather than when it receives cash. Similarly, it recognizes expenses when it incurs them rather than when it pays them. Under accrual accounting, a company generally recognizes revenues when it makes sales. The company can then relate the revenues to the economic environment of the period in which they occurred. Over the long run, trends in revenues and expenses are generally more meaningful than trends in cash receipts and disbursements.[2]

STANDARD-SETTING ORGANIZATIONS

LEARNING OBJECTIVE ◾6

Identify the major policy-setting bodies and their role in the standard-setting process.

For many years, many nations have relied on their own standard-setting organizations. For example, Canada has the Accounting Standards Board, Japan has the Accounting Standards Board of Japan, Germany has the German Accounting Standards Committee, and the United States has the Financial Accounting Standards Board (FASB). The standards issued by these organizations are sometimes principles-based, rules-based, tax-oriented, or business-based. In other words, they often differ in concept and objective.

The main international standard-setting organization is based in London, United Kingdom, and is called the **International Accounting Standards Board (IASB)**. The IASB issues **International Financial Reporting Standards (IFRS)**, which are used on most foreign exchanges. As indicated earlier, IFRS is presently used or permitted in over 115 countries and is rapidly gaining acceptance in other countries as well.

[2]As used here, cash flow means "cash generated and used in operations." The term *cash flows* also frequently means cash obtained by borrowing and used to repay borrowing, cash used for investments in resources and obtained from the disposal of investments, and cash contributed by or distributed to owners.

IFRS has the best potential to provide a common platform on which companies can report and investors can compare financial information. As a result, our discussion focuses on IFRS and the organization involved in developing these standards—the International Accounting Standards Board (IASB). (A detailed discussion of the U.S. system is provided at the book's companion website, *www.wiley.com/college/kieso*.) The two organizations that have a role in international standard-setting are the **International Organization of Securities Commissions** (IOSCO) and the IASB.

International Organization of Securities Commissions (IOSCO)

The **International Organization of Securities Commissions (IOSCO)** is an association of organizations that regulate the world's securities and futures markets. Members are generally the main financial regulator for a given country. IOSCO does not set accounting standards. Instead, this organization is dedicated to ensuring that the global markets can operate in an efficient and effective basis. The member agencies (such as from France, Germany, New Zealand, and the United States) have resolved to:

- Cooperate together to promote high standards of regulation in order to maintain just, efficient, and sound markets.
- Exchange information on their respective experiences in order to promote the development of domestic markets.
- Unite their efforts to establish standards and an effective surveillance of international securities transactions.
- Provide mutual assistance to promote the integrity of the markets by a rigorous application of the standards and by effective enforcement against offenses.

IOSCO supports the development and use of IFRS as the single set of high-quality international standards in cross-border offerings and listings. It recommends that its members allow multinational issuers to use IFRS in cross-border offerings and listings, as supplemented by reconciliation, disclosure, and interpretation where necessary to address outstanding substantive issues at a national or regional level. (For more information, go to *http://www.iosco.org/*.)

What do the numbers mean? HOW IS IT GOING?

How much progress has been made toward the goal of one single set of global accounting standards? To answer this question, the IASB conducted a major survey on IFRS adoption. The survey indicates that there is almost universal support (95 percent) for IFRS as the single set of global accounting standards. This includes those jurisdictions that have yet to make a decision on adopting IFRS, such as the United States.

More than 80 percent of the jurisdictions report IFRS adoption for all (or in five cases, almost all) public companies. Most of the remaining 11 non-adopters have made significant progress toward IFRS adoption. In addition, those jurisdictions that have adopted IFRS have made very few modifications to the standards. More than 40 percent of the IFRS adopters do so automatically, without an endorsement process. Moreover, where modifications have occurred, they are regarded as temporary arrangements to assist in the migration from national accounting standards to IFRS. It is expected that most of these transitional adjustments will ultimately disappear.

Admittedly, a few large and important economies have not yet (fully) adopted IFRS. But even in such countries, more progress is being made than many people are aware of. Japan already permits the use of full IFRS and has recently widened the scope of companies that are allowed to adopt it. In the United States, non-U.S. companies are allowed to use IFRS for listings on their exchanges. Today, more than 450 foreign private issuers are reporting using IFRS in U.S. regulatory filings, which represents trillions of dollars in market capitalization. In short, much progress has been made by countries in using IFRS.

Source: Adapted from Hans Hoogervorst, "Breaking the Boilerplate," IFRS Foundation Conference (June 13, 2013).

International Accounting Standards Board (IASB)

The standard-setting structure internationally is composed of the following four organizations:

1. The **IFRS Foundation** provides oversight to the IASB, IFRS Advisory Council, and IFRS Interpretations Committee. In this role, it appoints members, reviews effectiveness, and helps in the fundraising efforts for these organizations.
2. The **International Accounting Standards Board (IASB)** develops, in the public interest, a single set of high-quality, enforceable, and global international financial reporting standards for general-purpose financial statements.[3]
3. The **IFRS Advisory Council** (the Advisory Council) provides advice and counsel to the IASB on major policies and technical issues.
4. The **IFRS Interpretations Committee** assists the IASB through the timely identification, discussion, and resolution of financial reporting issues within the framework of IFRS.

In addition, as part of the governance structure, a **Monitoring Board** was created. The purpose of this board is to establish a link between accounting standard-setters and those public authorities (e.g., IOSCO) that generally oversee them. The Monitoring Board also provides political legitimacy to the overall organization. Illustration 1-4 shows the organizational structure for the setting of international accounting standards.

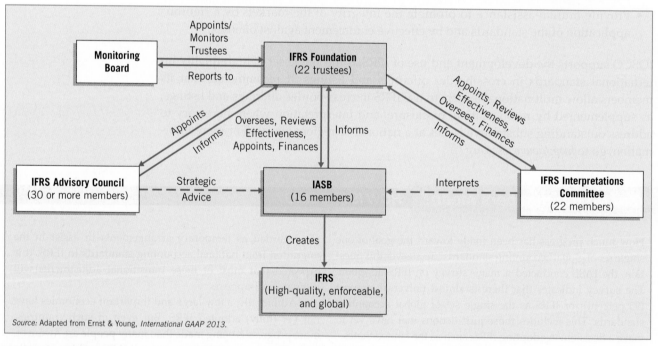

Source: Adapted from Ernst & Young, *International GAAP 2013*.

ILLUSTRATION 1-4
International Standard-
Setting Structure

[3]The IASB was preceded by the International Accounting Standards Committee (IASC), which came into existence on June 29, 1973, as a result of an agreement by professional accountancy bodies in Australia, Canada, France, Germany, Japan, Mexico, the Netherlands, the United Kingdom and Ireland, and the United States. A revised agreement and constitution was signed in November 1982 and has been updated most recently in 2009. The constitution mandates that all standards and interpretations issued under previous constitutions continue to be applicable unless and until they are amended or withdrawn. When the term *IFRS* is used in this textbook, it includes standards and interpretations approved by the IASB, and International Accounting Standards (IAS) and SIC interpretations issued under previous constitutions.

Due Process

In establishing financial accounting standards, the IASB has a thorough, open, and transparent **due process**. The IASB due process has the following elements: (1) an independent standard-setting board overseen by a geographically and professionally diverse body of trustees; (2) a thorough and systematic process for developing standards; (3) engagement with investors, regulators, business leaders, and the global accountancy profession at every stage of the process; and (4) collaborative efforts with the worldwide standard-setting community.

To implement its due process, the IASB follows specific steps to develop a typical IFRS, as Illustration 1-5 shows.

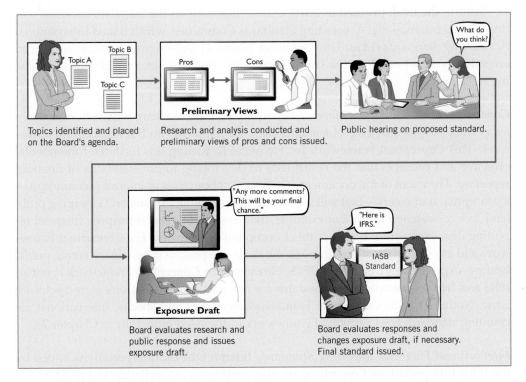

ILLUSTRATION 1-5
IASB Due Process

Furthermore, the characteristics of the IASB, as shown below, reinforce the importance of an open, transparent, and independent due process.

- *Membership.* The Board consists of 16 members. Members are well-paid and appointed for five-year renewable terms. The 16 members come from different countries.[4]
- *Autonomy.* The IASB is not part of any other professional organization. It is appointed by and answerable only to the IFRS Foundation.
- *Independence.* Full-time IASB members must sever all ties from their past employer. The members are selected for their expertise in standard-setting rather than to represent a given country.
- *Voting.* Nine of 16 votes are needed to issue a new IFRS.

With these characteristics, the IASB and its members will be insulated as much as possible from the political process, favored industries, and national or cultural bias.

---

[4]IASB membership reflects geographical representation, generally with four members each from Asia/Oceania, Europe, and North America, and one member each from Africa and South America. Two members are appointed from any area to maintain geographical balance.

Types of Pronouncements

The IASB issues three major types of pronouncements:

1. International Financial Reporting Standards.
2. Conceptual Framework for Financial Reporting.
3. International Financial Reporting Standards Interpretations.

International Financial Reporting Standards. Financial accounting standards issued by the IASB are referred to as International Financial Reporting Standards (IFRS). The IASB has issued 13 of these standards to date, covering such subjects as business combinations and share-based payments.

Prior to the IASB (formed in 2001), standard-setting on the international level was done by the International Accounting Standards Committee, which issued International Accounting Standards (IAS). The committee issued 41 IASs, many of which have been amended or superseded by the IASB. Those still remaining are considered under the umbrella of IFRS.

Conceptual Framework for Financial Reporting. As part of a long-range effort to move away from the problem-by-problem approach, the IASB uses an IFRS conceptual framework. This **Conceptual Framework for Financial Reporting** sets forth the fundamental objective and concepts that the Board uses in developing future standards of financial reporting. The intent of the document is to form a cohesive set of interrelated concepts— a conceptual framework—that will serve as tools for solving existing and emerging problems in a consistent manner. For example, the objective of general-purpose financial reporting discussed earlier is part of this Conceptual Framework. The Conceptual Framework and any changes to it pass through the same due process (preliminary views, public hearing, exposure draft, etc.) as an IFRS. However, this Conceptual Framework is not an IFRS and hence does not define standards for any particular measurement or disclosure issue. Nothing in this Conceptual Framework overrides any specific international accounting standard. The Conceptual Framework is discussed more fully in Chapter 2.

International Financial Reporting Standards Interpretations. **Interpretations** issued by the **IFRS Interpretations Committee** are also considered authoritative and must be followed. These interpretations cover (1) newly identified financial reporting issues not specifically dealt with in IFRS and (2) issues where unsatisfactory or conflicting interpretations have developed, or seem likely to develop, in the absence of authoritative guidance. The IFRS Interpretations Committee has issued over 20 of these interpretations to date.

In keeping with the IASB's own approach to setting standards, the IFRS Interpretations Committee applies a principles-based approach in providing interpretative guidance. To this end, the IFRS Interpretations Committee looks first to the Conceptual Framework as the foundation for formulating a consensus. It then looks to the principles articulated in the applicable standard, if any, to develop its interpretive guidance and to determine that the proposed guidance does not conflict with provisions in IFRS.

The IFRS Interpretations Committee helps the IASB in many ways. For example, emerging issues often attract public attention. If not resolved quickly, these issues can lead to financial crises and scandal. They can also undercut public confidence in current reporting practices. The next step, possible governmental intervention, would threaten the continuance of standard-setting in the private sector. The IFRS Interpretations Committee can address controversial accounting problems as they arise. It determines whether it can resolve them or whether to involve the IASB in solving them. In essence, it becomes a "problem filter" for the IASB. Thus, the IASB will hopefully work on more pervasive long-term problems, while the IFRS Interpretations Committee deals with short-term emerging issues.

Hierarchy of IFRS

Because it is a private organization, the IASB has no regulatory mandate and therefore no enforcement mechanism. As a result, the Board relies on other regulators to enforce the use of its standards. For example, the European Union requires publicly traded member country companies to use IFRS.

7 **LEARNING OBJECTIVE**
Explain the meaning of IFRS.

Any company indicating that it is preparing its financial statements in conformity with IFRS must use all of the standards and interpretations. The following hierarchy is used to determine what recognition, valuation, and disclosure requirements should be used. Companies first look to:

1. International Financial Reporting Standards, International Accounting Standards (issued by the predecessor to the IASB), and IFRS interpretations originated by the IFRS Interpretations Committee (and its predecessor, the IAS Interpretations Committee);
2. The Conceptual Framework for Financial Reporting; and
3. Pronouncements of other standard-setting bodies that use a similar conceptual framework (e.g., U.S. GAAP).

In the absence of a standard or an interpretation in item 1 above, companies look to the Conceptual Framework for Financial Reporting and then to most recent pronouncements of other standard-setting bodies that use a similar conceptual framework to develop accounting standards (or other accounting literature and accepted industry practices to the extent they do not conflict with the above). The overriding requirement of IFRS is that the financial statements provide a fair presentation (often referred to as a "true and fair view"). Fair representation is assumed to occur if a company follows the guidelines established in IFRS.[5] **[3]**

FINANCIAL REPORTING CHALLENGES

Much is right about international financial reporting. One reason for this success is that financial statements and related disclosures capture and organize financial information in a useful and reliable fashion. However, much still needs to be done. Here are some of the major challenges.

8 **LEARNING OBJECTIVE**
Describe the challenges facing financial reporting.

IFRS in a Political Environment

User groups are possibly the most powerful force influencing the development of IFRS. User groups consist of those most interested in or affected by accounting rules. Various participants in the financial reporting environment may want particular economic events accounted for or reported in a particular way, and they fight hard to get what they want. They know that the most effective way to influence IFRS is to participate in the formulation of these rules or to try to influence or persuade the formulators of them.[6]

These user groups often target the IASB, to pressure it to change the existing rules and develop new ones. In fact, these pressures have been multiplying. Some influential groups

---

[5]However, as IASB chairman Hans Hoogervorst noted, "It is not always obvious what is lobbying by vested interests and what is public interest feedback whose purpose is to help us deliver a high quality standard. More often than not the vested interest is packaged in public interest arguments. Sometimes even users do not want change. Analysts are so much in love with their own models that they do not want our standards to shed light on complex issues." See "Strengthening Institutional Relationships," *www.IASB.org* (September 23, 2013).

[6]In rare cases, compliance with a standard or interpretation is judged to be misleading when it conflicts with the objective of financial reporting. In this case, it is possible to have what is referred to as a "true and fair override." If this occurs, extensive disclosure is required to explain the rationale for this unusual exception.

demand that the accounting profession act more quickly and decisively to solve its problems. Other groups resist such action, preferring to implement change more slowly, if at all. Illustration 1-6 shows the various user groups that apply pressure.

ILLUSTRATION 1-6
User Groups that
Influence the Formulation
of Accounting Standards

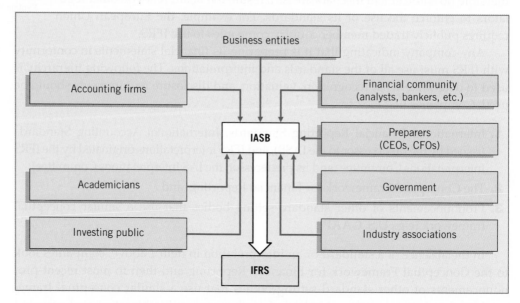

Should there be politics in establishing IFRS for financial accounting and reporting? Why not? We have politics at home, school, the office, church, temple, and mosque. Politics is everywhere. IFRS is part of the real world, and it cannot escape politics and political pressures.

That is not to say that politics in establishing IFRS is a negative force. Considering the **economic consequences** of many accounting rules, special interest groups are expected to vocalize their reactions to proposed rules.[7] What the Board should *not* do is issue standards that are primarily politically motivated. While paying attention to its constituencies, the Board should base IFRS on sound research and a conceptual framework that has its foundation in economic reality.

What do the numbers mean?   *FAIR CONSEQUENCES?*

No recent accounting issue better illustrates the economic consequences of accounting than the current debate over the use of fair value accounting for financial assets. The IASB has had long-standing standards requiring the use of fair value accounting for financial assets, such as investments and other financial instruments. Fair value provides the most relevant and reliable information for investors about these assets and liabilities. However, in the wake of the credit crisis of 2008, some countries, their central banks, and bank regulators wanted to suspend fair value accounting based on concerns that use of fair value accounting, which calls for recording significant losses on poorly performing loans and investments, would scare investors and depositors and lead to a "run on the bank."

Most notable was the lobbying of then French President Nicolas Sarkozy in urging his European Union counterparts to back changes to accounting rules and give banks and insurers some breathing space amid the market turmoil. Mr. Sarkozy sought agreement to new regulations, including changes to the mark-to-market accounting rules that have been blamed for aggravating the crisis. International regulators also have conducted studies of fair value accounting and its role in the credit crisis. It is unclear whether these political pressures will have an effect on fair value accounting, but there is no question that the issue has stirred significant worldwide political debate. In short, the numbers have consequences.

Source: Adapted from Ben Hall and Nikki Tait, "Sarkozy Seeks EU Accounting Change," *The Financial Times Limited* (September 30, 2008).

---

[7]*Economic consequences* means the impact of accounting reports on the wealth positions of issuers and users of financial information and the decision-making behavior resulting from that impact. The resulting behavior of these individuals and groups could have detrimental financial effects on the providers of the financial information. See Stephen A. Zeff, "The Rise of 'Economic Consequences'," *Journal of Accountancy* (December 1978), pp. 56–63.

The Expectations Gap

Accounting scandals at companies like Parmalat (ITA) and Siemens (DEU) have attracted the attention of regulators, investors, and the general public. Due to the size and the number of fraudulent reporting cases, some question whether the accounting profession is doing enough. The expectations gap—what the public thinks accountants should do and what accountants think they can do—is difficult to close.

Although the profession can argue rightfully that accounting cannot be responsible for every financial catastrophe, it must continue to strive to meet the needs of society. However, efforts to meet these needs will become more costly to society. The development of highly transparent, clear, and reliable systems to meet public expectations requires considerable resources.

Significant Financial Reporting Issues

While our reporting model has worked well in capturing and organizing financial information in a useful and reliable fashion, much still needs to be done. For example, if we would move ahead to the year 2025 and look back at financial reporting today, we might read the following.

- *Non-financial measurements.* Financial reports failed to provide some key performance measures widely used by management, such as customer satisfaction indexes, backlog information, and reject rates on goods purchased.

- *Forward-looking information.* Financial reports failed to provide forward-looking information needed by present and potential investors and creditors. One individual noted that financial statements in 2015 should have started with the phrase, "Once upon a time," to signify their use of historical cost and accumulation of past events.

- *Soft assets.* Financial reports focused on hard assets (inventory, plant assets) but failed to provide much information about a company's soft assets (intangibles). The most valuable assets are often intangible. Consider Sony's (JPN) expertise in electronics and Ikea's (NLD) brand image.

- *Timeliness.* Companies only prepared financial statements quarterly and provided audited financials annually. Little to no real-time financial statement information was available.

We believe each of these challenges must be met for the accounting profession to provide the type of information needed for an efficient capital allocation process. We are confident that changes will occur, based on these positive signs:

- Already, some companies voluntarily disclose information deemed relevant to investors. Often such information is non-financial. For example, banking companies now disclose data on loan growth, credit quality, fee income, operating efficiency, capital management, and management strategy.

- Initially, companies used the Internet to provide limited financial data. Now, most companies publish their annual reports in several formats on the Web. The most innovative companies offer sections of their annual reports in a format that the user can readily manipulate, such as in an electronic spreadsheet format. Companies also format their financial reports using eXtensible Business Reporting Language (XBRL), which permits quicker and lower-cost access to companies' financial information.

- More accounting standards now require the recording or disclosing of fair value information. For example, companies either record investments in shares and bonds, debt obligations, and derivatives at fair value, or companies show information related to fair values in the notes to the financial statements.

Changes in these directions will enhance the relevance of financial reporting and provide useful information to financial statement readers.

Ethics in the Environment of Financial Accounting

A noted commentator on the subject of accounting ethics observed, "Based on my experience, new graduates tend to be idealistic . . . thank goodness for that! Still it is very dangerous to think that your armor is all in place and say to yourself, 'I would have never given in to that.' The pressures don't explode on us; they build, and we often don't recognize them until they have us." These observations are particularly appropriate for anyone entering the business world.

In accounting, as in other areas of business, we frequently encounter ethical dilemmas. Some of these dilemmas are simple and easy to resolve. However, many are not, requiring difficult choices among allowable alternatives. Companies that concentrate on "maximizing the bottom line," "facing the challenges of competition," and "stressing short-term results" place accountants in an environment of conflict and pressure. Basic questions such as, "Is this way of communicating financial information good or bad?" "Is it right or wrong?" and "What should I do in the circumstance?" cannot always be answered by simply adhering to IFRS or following the rules of the profession. Technical competence is not enough when encountering ethical decisions.

Doing the right thing is not always easy or obvious. The pressures "to bend the rules," "to play the game," or "to just ignore it" can be considerable. For example, "Will my decision affect my job performance negatively?" "Will my superiors be upset?" or "Will my colleagues be unhappy with me?" are often questions businesspeople face in making a tough ethical decision. The decision is more difficult because there is no comprehensive ethical system to provide guidelines. Time, job, client, personal, and peer pressures can complicate the process of ethical sensitivity and selection among alternatives. Throughout this textbook, **we present ethical considerations to help sensitize you** to the type of situations you may encounter in the performance of your professional responsibility.

International Convergence

As discussed in the opening story, convergence to a single set of high-quality financial reporting standards is a real possibility. Here are some examples of how convergence is occurring:

1. China is reforming its financial reporting system through an approach called a continuous convergence process. The goal is to eliminate differences between its standards and IFRS.

2. Japan now permits the use of IFRS for domestic companies. The number of companies electing to use IFRS is expected to increase substantially in the near future.

3. The IASB and the FASB (of the United States) have spent the last 12 years working to converge their standards. The two Boards just issued a new standard on revenue recognition and will soon follow with other substantial standards on financial instruments and lease accounting.

4. Recently, Malaysia was instrumental in helping to amend the accounting for agricultural assets.

5. Italy's standard-setting group has provided advice and counsel on the accounting for business combinations under common control.

In addition, U.S. and European regulators have agreed to recognize each other's standards for listing on the various world securities exchanges. As a result, costly reconciliation requirements have been eliminated and hopefully will lead to greater comparability and transparency. Because international accounting issues are so important, we provide in each chapter of this textbook **Global Accounting Insights**, which highlight non-IFRS standards, mostly those from the United States. This feature will help you to understand the changes that are taking place in the financial reporting area as we move to one set of global accounting standards.

CONCLUSION

International convergence is underway. Many projects already are completed and differences eliminated. Others are on the drawing board. It appears to be only a matter of time until we have one set of global standards that will be established by the IASB. However, as one international regulator indicates, "the ultimate question remains whether IFRS will in fact function as the single set of high-quality, global accounting standards that the world has been seeking for so long. At least, when it comes to satisfying investors' concerns, there is no question of the attractiveness of the promise of a truly global accounting standard. The only real question is not whether this is good for investors, but how quickly both the accounting standards and the process by which they are established and developed can be globally recognized as world-class."

 # GLOBAL ACCOUNTING INSIGHTS

INTERNATIONAL FINANCIAL REPORTING

Most agree that there is a need for one set of international accounting standards. Here is why:

- *Multinational corporations.* Today's companies view the entire world as their market. For example, many companies find their largest market is not in their home country.
- *Mergers and acquisitions.* The mergers that led to international giants **Kraft/Cadbury** (USA and GBR) and **Vodafone/ Mannesmann** (GBR and DEU) suggest that we will see even more such mergers in the future.

- *Information technology.* As communication barriers continue to topple through advances in technology, companies and individuals in different countries and markets are becoming comfortable buying and selling goods and services from one another.
- *Financial markets.* Financial markets are some of the most significant international markets today. Whether it is currency, equity securities (shares), bonds, or derivatives, there are active markets throughout the world trading these types of instruments.

Relevant Facts

Following are the key similarities and differences between U.S. GAAP (the standards issued by the Financial Accounting Standards Board) and IFRS related to the financial reporting environment.

Similarities

- Generally accepted accounting principles (GAAP) for U.S. companies are developed by the Financial Accounting Standards Board (FASB). The FASB is a private organization. The U.S. Securities and Exchange Commission (SEC) exercises oversight over the actions of the FASB. The IASB is also a private organization. Oversight over the actions of the IASB is regulated by IOSCO.
- Both the IASB and the FASB have essentially the same governance structure, that is, a Foundation that provides oversight, a Board, an Advisory Council, and an Interpretations Committee. In addition, a general body

that involves the public interest is part of the governance structure.

- The FASB relies on the U.S. SEC for regulation and enforcement of its standards. The IASB relies primarily on IOSCO for regulation and enforcement of its standards.
- Both the IASB and the FASB are working together to find common grounds for convergence. A good example is the recent issuance of a new standard on revenue recognition that both organizations support. Also, the Boards are working together on other substantial projects such as the measurement and classification of financial instruments.

Differences

- U.S. GAAP is more detailed or rules-based. IFRS tends to simpler and more flexible in the accounting and disclosure requirements. The difference in approach has resulted in a debate about the merits of principles-based versus rules-based standards.

• Differences between U.S. GAAP and IFRS should not be surprising because standard-setters have developed standards in response to different user needs. In some coun-

tries, the primary users of financial statements are private investors. In others, the primary users are tax authorities or central government planners. In the United States, investors and creditors have driven accounting-standard formulation.

About the Numbers

The FASB and its predecessor organizations have been developing standards for nearly 70 years. The IASB is a relatively new organization (formed in 2001). As a result, it has looked to the United States to determine the structure it should

follow in establishing IFRS. Thus, the international standard-setting structure (presented on page 10) is very similar to the U.S. standard-setting structure. Presented below is a chart of the FASB's standard-setting structure.

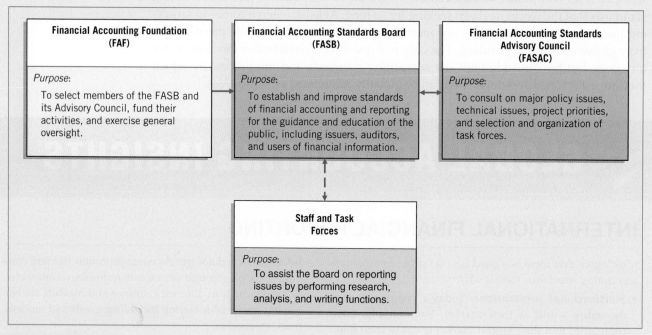

On the Horizon

Both the IASB and the FASB are hard at work developing standards that will lead to the elimination of major differences in the way certain transactions are accounted for and reported. In fact, beginning in 2010, the IASB (and the FASB on its joint projects with the IASB) started its policy of phasing in adoption of new major standards over several years. The major

reason for this policy is to provide companies time to translate and implement international standards into practice.

Much has happened in a very short period of time in the international accounting environment. It now appears likely that in a fairly short period of time, companies around the world will be close to using a single set of high-quality accounting standards.

SUMMARY OF LEARNING OBJECTIVES

1 Describe the growing importance of global financial markets and its relation to financial reporting. World markets are becoming increasingly intertwined. With the integration of capital markets, the automatic linkage between the location of the company and the location of the capital market is loosening. As a result, companies have expanded choices of where to raise capital, either equity or debt. The move toward adoption of global accounting standards has and will continue to facilitate this trend.

2 Identify the major financial statements and other means of financial reporting. Companies most frequently provide (1) the statement of financial position, (2) the income statement or statement of comprehensive income, (3) the statement of cash flows, and (4) the statement of changes in equity. Financial reporting other than financial statements may take various forms. Examples include the president's letter and supplementary schedules in the corporate annual report, prospectuses, reports filed with government agencies, news releases, management's forecasts, and descriptions of a company's social or environmental impact.

3 **Explain how accounting assists in the efficient use of scarce resources.** Accounting provides reliable, relevant, and timely information to managers, investors, and creditors to allow resource allocation to the most efficient enterprises. Accounting also provides measurements of efficiency (profitability) and financial soundness.

4 **Explain the need for high-quality standards.** A single, widely accepted set of high-quality accounting standards is a necessity to ensure adequate comparability. Investors are increasingly making investing decisions across international jurisdictions. As a result, investors need financial information that is comparable across national boundaries. But what are high-quality accounting standards, how should they be developed, and how should they be enforced is still a much debated issue.

5 **Identify the objective of financial reporting.** The objective of general-purpose financial reporting is to provide financial information about the reporting entity that is useful to present and potential equity investors, lenders, and other creditors in making decisions about providing resources to the entity. Information that is decision-useful to investors may also be useful to other users of financial reporting who are not investors.

6 **Identify the major policy-setting bodies and their role in the standard-setting process.** The International Organization of Securities Commissions (IOSCO) does not set accounting standards but is dedicated to ensuring that the global markets can operate in an efficient and effective manner. The International Accounting Standards Board (IASB) is the leading international accounting standard-setting organization. Its mission is to develop, in the public interest, a single set of high-quality and understandable International Financial Reporting Standards (IFRS) for general-purpose financial statements. Standards issued by the IASB have been adopted by over 115 countries worldwide, and all publicly traded European companies must use IFRS.

7 **Explain the meaning of IFRS.** IFRS is comprised of (a) International Financial Reporting Standards, (b) International Accounting Standards, and (c) interpretations issued by the IFRS Interpretations Committee or the former Standing Interpretations Committee (SIC). In the absence of a standard or an interpretation, other accounting literature, including that contained in the Conceptual Framework for Financial Reporting and recent pronouncements of other standard-setting bodies that use a similar conceptual framework, can be applied.

8 **Describe the challenges facing financial reporting.** Challenges include (1) IFRS in a political environment; (2) the expectations gap; (3) financial reporting issues related to key performance measures widely used by management, forward-looking information needed by investors and creditors, sufficient information on a company's soft assets (intangibles), and real-time financial information, including fair values; (4) ethics in accounting; and (5) international convergence.

IFRS AUTHORITATIVE LITERATURE

[1] The Conceptual Framework for Financial Reporting, "Chapter 1, The Objective of General Purpose Financial Reporting" (London, U.K.: IASB, September 2010), par. OB2.

[2] The Conceptual Framework for Financial Reporting, "Chapter 1, The Objective of General Purpose Financial Reporting" (London, U.K.: IASB, September 2010), par. OB4.

[3] International Accounting Standard 8, *Accounting Policies, Changes in Accounting Estimates and Errors* (London, U.K.: IASB, 1993), par. 12.

QUESTIONS

1. What is happening to world markets, and what are the implications for financial reporting?

2. Differentiate broadly between financial accounting and managerial accounting.

3. What are the major financial statements, and what is the difference between financial statements and financial reporting?

4. How does accounting help in the capital allocation process?

5. What is the benefit of a single set of high-quality accounting standards?

6. What is the objective of financial reporting?

7. What is meant by general-purpose financial statements?

8. Who is the primary user group for general-purpose financial statements?

9. Comment on the following statement: A perspective that financial reporting should be focused only on the needs of the shareholders—often referred to as the *proprietary perspective*—is considered appropriate.

10. Comment on the following statement: The objective of financial reporting is primarily to provide decision-useful information for assessing the performance of management.

11. Who are the two key organizations in the development of international accounting standards? Explain their role.

12. What is IOSCO?

13. What is the mission of the IASB?

14. What is the purpose of the Monitoring Board?

15. How are IASB preliminary views and IASB exposure drafts related to IASB standards?

16. Distinguish between IASB standards and the Conceptual Framework for Financial Reporting.

17. Rank from most authoritative to least authoritative the following three items: Conceptual Framework for Financial Reporting, International Financial Reporting Standards, and International Financial Reporting Standards Interpretations.

18. Explain the role of the IFRS Interpretations Committee.

19. What are some of the major challenges facing the accounting profession?

20. What are the sources of pressure that change and influence the development of IFRS?

21. Some individuals have indicated that the IASB must be cognizant of the economic consequences of its pronouncements. What is meant by "economic consequences"? What dangers exist if politics play too much of a role in the development of IFRS?

22. If you were given complete authority in the matter, how would you propose that IFRS should be developed and enforced?

23. One writer recently noted that a high percentage of all companies prepare statements that are in accordance with IFRS. Why then is there such concern about fraudulent financial reporting?

24. What is the "expectations gap"? What is the profession doing to try to close this gap?

25. How are financial accountants challenged in their work to make ethical decisions? Is technical mastery of IFRS not sufficient to the practice of financial accounting?

CONCEPTS FOR ANALYSIS

CA1-1 (IFRS and Standard-Setting) Presented below are five statements that you are to identify as true or false. If false, explain why the statement is incorrect.

1. IFRS is the term used to indicate the whole body of IASB authoritative literature.

2. Any company claiming compliance with IFRS must follow most standards and interpretations but not the disclosure requirements.

3. The primary governmental body that has influence over the IASB is the IFRS Advisory Council.

4. The overriding requirement of IFRS is for the financial statements to give a fair presentation (or true and fair view).

5. The IASB has a government mandate and therefore does not have to follow due process in issuing an IFRS.

CA1-2 (IFRS and Standard-Setting) Presented below are four statements that you are to identify as true or false. If false, explain why the statement is incorrect.

1. The objective of financial statements emphasizes a stewardship approach for reporting financial information.

2. The objective of financial reporting is to prepare a statement of financial position, a statement of comprehensive income, a statement of cash flows, and a statement of changes in equity.

3. The difference between International Accounting Standards and IFRS is that International Accounting Standards are more authoritative.

4. The objective of financial reporting uses an entity rather than a proprietary approach in determining what information to report.

CA1-3 (Financial Reporting and Accounting Standards) Answer the following multiple-choice questions.

1. IFRS stands for:
   (a) International Federation of Reporting Services.
   (b) Independent Financial Reporting Standards.
   (c) International Financial Reporting Standards.
   (d) Integrated Financial Reporting Services.

2. The major key organizations on the international side are the:
   (a) IASB and IFRS Advisory Council.
   (b) IOSCO and the U.S. SEC.
   (c) London Stock Exchange and International Securities Exchange.
   (d) IASB and IOSCO.

3. Which governmental body is most influential in enforcing IFRS?
   (a) Monitoring Board.   (c) IOSCO.
   (b) IFRS Advisory Council.   (d) IFRS Foundation.

4. Accounting standard-setters use the following process in establishing international standards:
   (a) Research, exposure draft, discussion paper, standard.
   (b) Discussion paper, research, exposure draft, standard.
   (c) Research, preliminary views, discussion paper, standard.
   (d) Research, preliminary views, exposure draft, standard.

5. IFRS is comprised of:
   (a) International Financial Reporting Standards and FASB financial reporting standards.
   (b) International Financial Reporting Standards, International Accounting Standards, and International Accounting Standards Interpretations.
   (c) International Accounting Standards and International Accounting Standards Interpretations.
   (d) FASB financial reporting standards and International Accounting Standards.

6. The authoritative status of the Conceptual Framework for Financial Reporting is as follows:
   (a) It is used when there is no standard or interpretation related to the reporting issues under consideration.
   (b) It is not as authoritative as a standard but takes precedence over any interpretation related to the reporting issue.
   (c) It takes precedence over all other authoritative literature.
   (d) It has no authoritative status.

7. The objective of financial reporting places most emphasis on:
   (a) reporting to capital providers.
   (b) reporting on stewardship.
   (c) providing specific guidance related to specific needs.
   (d) providing information to individuals who are experts in the field.

8. General-purpose financial statements are prepared primarily for:
   (a) internal users.   (c) auditors.
   (b) external users.   (d) government regulators.

9. Economic consequences of accounting standard-setting means:
   (a) standard-setters must give first priority to ensuring that companies do not suffer any adverse effect as a result of a new standard.
   (b) standard-setters must ensure that no new costs are incurred when a new standard is issued.
   (c) the objective of financial reporting should be politically motivated to ensure acceptance by the general public.
   (d) accounting standards can have detrimental impacts on the wealth levels of the providers of financial information.

10. The expectations gap is the difference between:
    (a) what financial information management provides and what users want.
    (b) what the public thinks accountants should do and what accountants think they can do.
    (c) what the governmental agencies want from standard-setting and what the standard-setters provide.
    (d) what the users of financial statements want from the government and what is provided.

CA1-4 (Financial Accounting) Omar Morena has recently completed his first year of studying accounting. His instructor for next semester has indicated that the primary focus will be the area of financial accounting.

Instructions

    (a) Differentiate between financial accounting and managerial accounting.

    (b) One part of financial accounting involves the preparation of financial statements. What are the financial statements most frequently provided?

    (c) What is the difference between financial statements and financial reporting?

CA1-5 (Need for IASB) Some argue that having various organizations establish accounting principles is wasteful and inefficient. Rather than mandating accounting rules, each company could voluntarily disclose the type of information it considered important. In addition, if an investor wants additional information, the investor could contact the company and pay to receive the additional information desired.

Instructions

Comment on the appropriateness of this viewpoint.

CA1-6 (IASB Role in Standard-Setting) A press release announcing the appointment of the trustees of the new IFRS Foundation stated that the International Accounting Standards Board (to be appointed by the trustees) ". . . will become the established authority for setting accounting Standards."

Instructions

    (a) Identify the sponsoring organization of the IASB and the process by which the IASB arrives at a decision and issues an accounting standard.

    (b) Indicate the major types of pronouncements issued by the IASB and the purposes of each of these pronouncements.

CA1-7 (Accounting Numbers and the Environment) Hardly a day goes by without an article appearing on the crises affecting many of our financial institutions. It is estimated that the financial institution debacle of 2008, for example, caused a deep recession. Some argue that if financial institutions had been required to report their investments at fair value instead of cost, large losses would have been reported earlier, which would have signaled regulators to close these financial institutions and, therefore, minimize the losses to many investors.

Instructions

Explain how reported accounting numbers might affect an individual's perceptions and actions. Cite two examples.

CA1-8 (Politicization of IFRS) Some accountants have said that politicization in the development and acceptance of International Financial Reporting Standards (IFRS) is taking place. Some use the term "politicization" in a narrow sense to mean the influence by governmental agencies, such as the European Union and the U.S. Securities and Exchange Commission, on the development of IFRS. Others use it more broadly to mean the compromise that results when the bodies responsible for developing IFRS are pressured by interest groups, businesses through their various organizations, financial analysts, bankers, lawyers, academics, auditors, and so on.

Instructions

    (a) What arguments can be raised to support the "politicization" of accounting rule-making?

    (b) What arguments can be raised against the "politicization" of accounting rule-making?

CA1-9 (Models for Setting IFRS) Presented below are three models for setting IFRS.

    1. The purely political approach, where national legislative action decrees IFRS.

    2. The private, professional approach, where IFRS is set and enforced by private professional actions only.

    3. The public/private mixed approach, where IFRS is basically set by private-sector bodies that behave as though they were public agencies and whose standards to a great extent are enforced through governmental agencies.

Instructions

    (a) Which of these three models best describes international standard-setting? Comment on your answer.

    (b) Why do companies, financial analysts, labor unions, industry trade associations, and others take such an active interest in standard-setting?

CA1-10 (Economic Consequences) Several years ago, then French President Nicolas Sarkozy urged his European Union counterparts to put pressure on the IASB to change accounting rules to give banks and insurers some relief from fair value accounting rules amid market turmoil. Mr. Sarkozy sought changes to the mark-to-market accounting rules that have been blamed for aggravating the crisis.

Instructions

Explain how government intervention could possibly affect capital markets adversely.

CA1-11 (Rule-Making Issues) When the IASB issues new pronouncements, the implementation date is usually delayed for several months from date of issuance, with early implementation encouraged. Karen Weller, controller, discusses with her financial vice president the need for early implementation of a rule that would result in a fairer presentation of the company's financial condition and earnings. When the financial vice president determines that early implementation of the rule will adversely affect the reported net income for the year, he discourages Weller from implementing the rule until it is required.

Instructions
Answer the following questions.

    (a) What, if any, is the ethical issue involved in this case?
    (b) Is the financial vice president acting improperly or immorally?
    (c) What does Weller have to gain by advocacy of early implementation?
    (d) Which stakeholders might be affected by the early implementation decision?

CA1-12 (Financial Reporting Pressures) Presented below is abbreviated testimony from Troy Normand in the WorldCom (USA) case. He was a manager in the corporate reporting department and is one of five individuals who pleaded guilty. He is testifying in hopes of receiving no prison time when he is ultimately sentenced.

Q. Mr. Normand, if you could just describe for the jury how the meeting started and what was said during the meeting?

A. I can't recall exactly who initiated the discussion, but right away Scott Sullivan acknowledged that he was aware we had problems with the entries, David Myers had informed him, and we were considering resigning.

He said that he respected our concerns but that we weren't being asked to do anything that he believed was wrong. He mentioned that he acknowledged that the company had lost focus quite a bit due to the preparations for the Sprint merger, and that he was putting plans in place and projects in place to try to determine where the problems were, why the costs were so high.

He did say he believed that the initial statements that we produced, that the line costs in those statements could not have been as high as they were, that he believes something was wrong and there was no way that the costs were that high.

I informed him that I didn't believe the entry we were being asked to do was right, that I was scared, and I didn't want to put myself in a position of going to jail for him or the company. He responded that he didn't believe anything was wrong, nobody was going to be going to jail, but that if it later was found to be wrong, that he would be the person going to jail, not me.

He asked that I stay, don't jump off the plane, let him land it softly, that's basically how he put it. And he mentioned that he had a discussion with Bernie Ebbers asking Bernie to reduce projections going forward and that Bernie had refused.

Q. Mr. Normand, you said that Mr. Sullivan said something about don't jump out of the plane. What did you understand him to mean when he said that?

A. Not to quit.

Q. During this meeting, did Mr. Sullivan say anything about whether you would be asked to make entries like this in the future?

A. Yes, he made a comment that from that point going forward we wouldn't be asked to record any entries, high-level late adjustments, that the numbers would be the numbers.

Q. What did you understand that to be mean, the numbers would be the numbers?

A. That after the preliminary statements were issued, with the exception of any normal transaction, valid transaction, we wouldn't be asked to be recording any more late entries.

Q. I believe you testified that Mr. Sullivan said something about the line cost numbers not being accurate. Did he ask you to conduct any analysis to determine whether the line cost numbers were accurate?

A. No, he did not.

Q. Did anyone ever ask you to do that?

A. No.

Q. Did you ever conduct any such analysis?

A. No, I didn't.

Q. During this meeting, did Mr. Sullivan ever provide any accounting justification for the entry you were asked to make?

A. No, he did not.

Q. Did anything else happen during the meeting?

A. I don't recall anything else.

Q. How did you feel after this meeting?

A. Not much better actually. I left his office not convinced in any way that what we were asked to do was right. However, I did question myself to some degree after talking with him wondering whether I was making something more out of what was really there.

Instructions

Answer the following questions.

    (a) What appears to be the ethical issue involved in this case?

    (b) Is Troy Normand acting improperly or immorally?

    (c) What would you do if you were Troy Normand?

    (d) Who are the major stakeholders in this case?

USING YOUR JUDGMENT

FINANCIAL REPORTING

Financial Reporting Problem

Lola Otero, a new staff accountant, is confused because of the complexities involving accounting standard-setting. Specifically, she is confused by the number of bodies issuing financial reporting standards of one kind or another and the level of authoritative support that can be attached to these reporting standards. Lola decides that she must review the environment in which accounting standards are set, if she is to increase her understanding of the accounting profession.

Lola recalls that during her accounting education there was a chapter or two regarding the environment of financial accounting and the development of IFRS. However, she remembers that her instructor placed little emphasis on these chapters.

Instructions

    (a) Help Lola by identifying key organizations involved in accounting rule-making at the international level.

    (b) Lola asks for guidance regarding authoritative support. Please assist her by explaining what is meant by authoritative support.

 ### International Reporting Case

The following comments were made at an Annual Conference of the Financial Executives Institute (FEI).

There is an irreversible movement toward a single set of rules for financial reporting throughout the world. The international capital markets require an end to:

1. The confusion caused by international companies announcing different results depending on the set of accounting standards applied.

2. Companies in some countries obtaining unfair commercial advantages from the use of particular national accounting standards.

3. The complications in negotiating commercial arrangements for international joint ventures caused by different accounting requirements.

4. The inefficiency of international companies having to understand and use a myriad of different accounting standards depending on the countries in which they operate and the countries in which they raise capital and debt. Executive talent is wasted on keeping up to date with numerous sets of accounting standards and the never-ending changes to them.

5. The inefficiency of investment managers, bankers, and financial analysts as they seek to compare financial reporting drawn up in accordance with different sets of accounting standards.

Instructions

    (a) What is the International Accounting Standards Board?

    (b) What stakeholders might benefit from the use of international accounting standards?

    (c) What do you believe are some of the major obstacles to convergence?

Accounting, Analysis, and Principles

The founders of Oslo Company, Finn Elo and Vender Hakala, are about to realize their dream of taking their company public. They are trying to better understand the various legal and accounting issues they will face as a public company.

Accounting

    (a) What are some of the reporting requirements that their company will have to comply with when they offer securities to investors and creditors?

(b) Identify the two entities that are primarily responsible for establishing IFRS, which will be applied when preparing their financial statements. Explain the relationship of these two organizations to one another.

Analysis

(a) What is decision-usefulness?

(b) Briefly describe how the financial statements that Oslo prepares for its investors and creditors will contribute to decision-usefulness.

Principles

Oslo will prepare its statements in conformity with IFRS. Finn and Vender have heard about an IFRS hierarchy. Briefly explain this hierarchy and advise them on how the hierarchy affects the application of IFRS.

IFRS BRIDGE TO THE PROFESSION

Professional Research

As a newly enrolled accounting major, you are anxious to better understand accounting institutions and sources of accounting literature. As a first step, you decide to explore the IASB's Conceptual Framework for Financial Reporting.

Instructions

Access the Conceptual Framework at the IASB website (*http://eifrs.iasb.org/*) (you may register for free eIFRS access at this site). When you have accessed the document, you can use the search tool in your Internet browser to respond to the following items. (Provide paragraph citations.)

(a) What is the objective of financial reporting?

(b) What other means are there of communicating information, besides financial statements?

(c) Indicate some of the users and the information they are most directly concerned with in economic decision-making.

Professional Simulation

In this simulation, you are asked questions regarding accounting standards. Prepare responses to all parts.

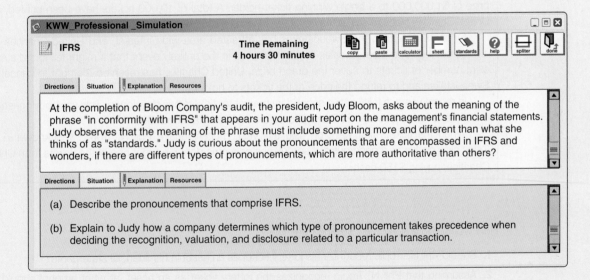

Remember to check the book's companion website, at **www.wiley.com/college/kieso**, to find additional resources for this chapter.

Conceptual Framework for Financial Reporting

After studying this chapter, you should be able to:

1 Describe the usefulness of a conceptual framework.

2 Describe efforts to construct a conceptual framework.

3 Understand the objective of financial reporting.

4 Identify the qualitative characteristics of accounting information.

5 Define the basic elements of financial statements.

6 Describe the basic assumptions of accounting.

7 Explain the application of the basic principles of accounting.

8 Describe the impact that the cost constraint has on reporting accounting information.

What Is It?

Everyone agrees that accounting needs a framework—a conceptual framework, so to speak—that will help guide the development of standards. To understand the importance of developing this framework, let's see how you would respond in the following two situations.

Situation 1: "Taking a Long Shot . . . "

To supplement donations collected from its general community solicitation, Tri-Cities United Charities holds an Annual Lottery Sweepstakes. In this year's sweepstakes, United Charities is offering a grand prize of $1,000,000 to a single winning ticket holder. A total of 10,000 tickets have been printed, and United Charities plans to sell all the tickets at a price of $150 each.

Since its inception, the Sweepstakes has attracted area-wide interest, and United Charities has always been able to meet its sales target. However, in the unlikely event that it might fail to sell a sufficient number of tickets to cover the grand prize, United Charities has reserved the right to cancel the Sweepstakes and to refund the price of the tickets to holders.

In recent years, a fairly active secondary market for tickets has developed. This year, buying–selling prices have varied between $75 and $95 before stabilizing at about $90.

When the tickets first went on sale this year, multimillionaire Phil N. Tropic, well-known in Tri-Cities civic circles as a generous but sometimes eccentric donor, bought one of the tickets from United Charities, paying $150 cash.

How would you answer the following questions?

1. Should Phil N. Tropic recognize his lottery ticket as an asset in his financial statements?

2. Assuming that Phil N. Tropic recognizes the lottery ticket as an asset, at what amount should it be reported? Some possible answers are $150, $100, and $90.

Situation 2: The $20 Million Question

The Hard Rock Mining Company has just completed the first year of operations at its new strip mine, the Lonesome Doe. Hard Rock spent $10 million for the land and $20 million in preparing the site for mining operations. The mine is expected to operate for 20 years. Hard Rock is subject to environmental statutes requiring it to restore the Lonesome Doe mine site on completion of mining operations.

Based on its experience and industry data, as well as current technology, Hard Rock forecasts that restoration will cost about $10 million when it is undertaken. Of those costs, about $4 million is for restoring the topsoil that was removed in preparing the site for mining operations (prior to opening the mine); the rest is directly proportional to the depth of the mine, which in turn is directly proportional to the amount of ore extracted.

How would you answer the following questions?

1. Should Hard Rock recognize a liability for site restoration in conjunction with the opening of the Lonesome Doe Mine? If so, what is the amount of that liability?

2. After Hard Rock has operated the Lonesome Doe Mine for 5 years, new technology is introduced that reduces Hard Rock's estimated future restoration costs to $7 million, $3 million of which relates to restoring the topsoil. How should Hard Rock account for this change in its estimated future liability?

The answer to the questions on the two situations depends on how assets and liabilities are defined and how they should be valued. Hopefully, this chapter will provide you with a framework to resolve questions like these.

Source: Adapted from Todd Johnson and Kim Petrone, *The FASB Cases on Recognition and Measurement,* Second Edition (New York: John Wiley and Sons, Inc., 1996).

PREVIEW OF CHAPTER **2**

As our opening story indicates, users of financial statements can face difficult questions about the recognition and measurement of financial items. To help develop the type of financial information that can be used to answer these questions, financial accounting and reporting relies on a conceptual framework. In this chapter, we discuss the basic concepts underlying the conceptual framework, as follows.

Conceptual Framework for Financial Reporting

Conceptual Framework	First Level: Basic Objective	Second Level: Fundamental Concepts	Third Level: Recognition, Measurement, and Disclosure Concepts
• Need • Development • Overview		• Qualitative characteristics • Basic elements	• Basic assumptions • Basic principles • Cost constraint • Summary of the structure

CONCEPTUAL FRAMEWORK

LEARNING OBJECTIVE ❶

Describe the usefulness of a conceptual framework.

A **conceptual framework** establishes the concepts that underlie financial reporting. A conceptual framework is a coherent system of concepts that flow from an objective. The objective identifies the purpose of financial reporting. The other concepts provide guidance on (1) identifying the boundaries of financial reporting; (2) selecting the transactions, other events, and circumstances to be represented; (3) how they should be recognized and measured; and (4) how they should be summarized and reported.[1]

Need for a Conceptual Framework

Why do we need a conceptual framework? First, to be useful, rule-making should build on and relate to an established body of concepts. A soundly developed conceptual framework thus enables the IASB to issue **more useful and consistent pronouncements over time**, and a coherent set of standards should result. Indeed, without the guidance provided by a soundly developed framework, standard-setting ends up being based on individual concepts developed by each member of the standard-setting body. The following observation by a former standard-setter highlights the problem.

> "As our professional careers unfold, each of us develops a technical conceptual framework. Some individual frameworks are sharply defined and firmly held; others are vague and weakly held; still others are vague and firmly held.... At one time or another, most of us have felt the discomfort of listening to somebody buttress a preconceived conclusion by building a convoluted chain of shaky reasoning. Indeed, perhaps on occasion we have voiced such thinking ourselves.... My experience ... taught me many lessons. A major one was that most of us have a natural tendency and an incredible talent for processing new facts in such a way that our prior conclusions remain intact."[2]

In other words, standard-setting that is based on personal conceptual frameworks will lead to different conclusions about identical or similar issues than it did previously. As a result, standards will not be consistent with one another, and past decisions may not be indicative of future ones. Furthermore, the framework should increase financial statement users' understanding of and confidence in financial reporting. It should enhance comparability among companies' financial statements.

Second, as a result of a soundly developed conceptual framework, the profession should be able to more quickly solve new and emerging **practical problems by referring to an existing framework of basic theory**. For example, assume that **Aphrodite Gold Ltd.** (AUS) sold two issues of bonds. It can redeem them either with $2,000 in cash or with 5 ounces of gold, whichever is worth more at maturity. Both bond issues have a stated interest rate of 8.5 percent. At what amounts should Aphrodite or the buyers of the bonds record them? What is the amount of the premium or discount on the bonds? And how should Aphrodite amortize this amount, if the bond redemption payments are to be made in gold (the future value of which is unknown at the date of issuance)? Consider that Aphrodite cannot know, at the date of issuance, the value of future gold bond redemption payments.

It is difficult, if not impossible, for the IASB to prescribe the proper accounting treatment quickly for situations like this or like those represented in our opening story.

I F R S

See the Authoritative Literature section (page 50).

[1]Recall from our discussion in Chapter 1 that while the Conceptual Framework and any changes to it pass through the same due process (discussion paper, preliminary views, public hearing, exposure draft, etc.) as do the IFRSs, the Conceptual Framework is not an IFRS. That is, the Conceptual Framework does not define standards for any particular measurement or disclosure issue, and nothing in the Conceptual Framework overrides any specific IFRS. **[1]**

[2]C. Horngren, "Uses and Limitations of a Conceptual Framework," *Journal of Accountancy* (April 1981), p. 90.

Practicing accountants, however, must resolve such problems on a daily basis. How? Through good judgment and with the help of a universally accepted conceptual framework, practitioners can quickly focus on an acceptable treatment.

What do the numbers mean? **WHAT'S YOUR PRINCIPLE?**

The need for a conceptual framework is highlighted by accounting scandals such as those at **Royal Ahold** (NLD), **Enron** (USA), and **Satyan Computer Services** (IND). To restore public confidence in the financial reporting process, many have argued that regulators should move toward principles-based rules. They believe that companies exploited the detailed provisions in rules-based pronouncements to manage accounting reports, rather than report the economic substance of transactions. For example, many of the off–balance-sheet arrangements of Enron avoided transparent reporting by barely achieving 3 percent outside equity ownership, a requirement in an obscure accounting rule interpretation. Enron's financial engineers were able to structure transactions to achieve a desired accounting treatment, even if that accounting treatment did not reflect the transaction's true nature. Under principles-based rules, hopefully top management's financial reporting focus will shift from demonstrating compliance with rules to demonstrating that a company has attained financial reporting objectives.

Development of a Conceptual Framework

The IASB issued "Conceptual Framework for Financial Reporting 2010" (the Conceptual Framework) in 2010. The Conceptual Framework is a work in progress in that the IASB has not yet completed updating the previous version of it. Presently, the Conceptual Framework comprises an introduction and four chapters as follows.

2 LEARNING OBJECTIVE
Describe efforts to construct a conceptual framework.

- Chapter 1: The Objective of General Purpose Financial Reporting
- Chapter 2: The Reporting Entity (not yet issued)
- Chapter 3: Qualitative Characteristics of Useful Financial Information
- Chapter 4: The Framework (this material was developed prior to the creation of the IASB but is considered part of the Conceptual Framework until changed or updated), comprised of the following:
    1. Underlying assumption—the going concern assumption;
    2. The elements of financial statements;
    3. Recognition of the elements of financial statements;
    4. Measurement of the elements of financial statements; and
    5. Concepts of capital and capital maintenance.

Chapters 1 and 3 were recently completed. However, much work still needs to be done on the remaining parts of the Conceptual Framework. The IASB has given priority to its completion as the Board recognizes the need for such a document to serve its set of diverse users. It should be emphasized that the Conceptual Framework is not an IFRS and therefore an IFRS always takes precedence even if it appears to be in conflict with the Conceptual Framework. Nonetheless, the Conceptual Framework should provide guidance in many situations where an IFRS does not cover the issue under consideration.[3] **[2]**

---

[3]Working together, the IASB and the FASB developed converged concepts statements on the objective of financial reporting and qualitative characteristics of accounting information. The Boards are working on their own schedules to address the remaining elements of the conceptual framework project. The IASB has issued a discussion paper exploring additional possible changes to the Conceptual Framework for Financial Reporting. The discussion paper seeks input on issues such as the definitions of assets and liabilities, measurement, recognition, presentation and disclosure, and other comprehensive income. See *http://www.ifrs.org/Current-Projects/IASB-Projects/Conceptual-Framework/Pages/Conceptual-Framework-Summary.aspx*.

Overview of the Conceptual Framework

Illustration 2-1 provides an overview of the IASB's Conceptual Framework for Financial Reporting, also referred to simply as the Conceptual Framework.

ILLUSTRATION 2-1
Conceptual Framework
for Financial Reporting

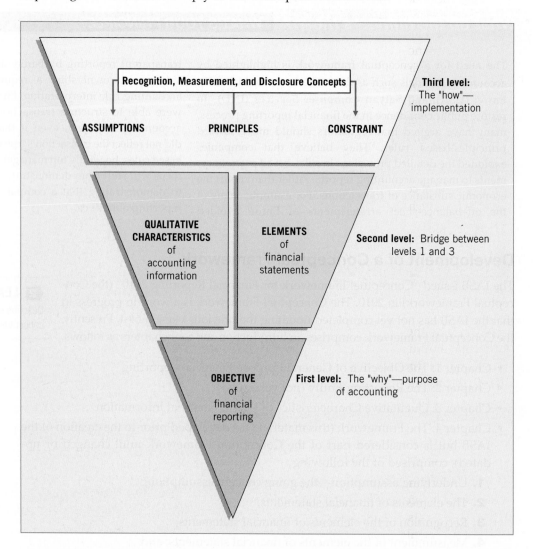

The first level identifies the **objective of financial reporting**—that is, the purpose of financial reporting. The second level provides the **qualitative characteristics** that make accounting information useful and the **elements of financial statements** (assets, liabilities, and so on). The third level identifies the **recognition, measurement, and disclosure** concepts used in establishing and applying accounting standards and the specific concepts to implement the objective. These concepts include assumptions, principles, and a cost constraint that describe the present reporting environment. We examine these three levels of the Conceptual Framework next.

FIRST LEVEL: BASIC OBJECTIVE

LEARNING OBJECTIVE **3**

Understand the objective of financial reporting.

The objective of financial reporting is the foundation of the Conceptual Framework. Other aspects of the Conceptual Framework—qualitative characteristics, elements of financial statements, recognition, measurement, and disclosure—flow logically from the objective. Those aspects of the Conceptual Framework help to ensure that financial reporting achieves its objective.

The objective of general-purpose financial reporting is to provide financial information about the reporting entity that is **useful to present and potential equity investors, lenders, and other creditors** in making decisions about providing resources to the entity. **[3]** Those decisions involve buying, selling, or holding equity and debt instruments, and providing or settling loans and other forms of credit. Information that is decision-useful to capital providers may also be helpful to other users of financial reporting who are not capital providers.

As indicated in Chapter 1, to provide information to decision-makers, companies prepare general-purpose financial statements. **General-purpose financial reporting** helps users who lack the ability to demand all the financial information they need from an entity and therefore must rely, at least partly, on the information provided in financial reports. However, an implicit assumption is that users need reasonable knowledge of business and financial accounting matters to understand the information contained in financial statements. This point is important. It means that financial statement preparers assume a level of competence on the part of users. This assumption impacts the way and the extent to which companies report information.

SECOND LEVEL: FUNDAMENTAL CONCEPTS

The objective (first level) focuses on the purpose of financial reporting. Later, we will discuss the ways in which this purpose is implemented (third level). What, then, is the purpose of the second level? The second level provides conceptual building blocks that explain the qualitative characteristics of accounting information and define the elements of financial statements. **[4]** That is, the second level forms a bridge between the **why** of accounting (the objective) and the **how** of accounting (recognition, measurement, and financial statement presentation).

4 LEARNING OBJECTIVE

Identify the qualitative characteristics of accounting information.

Qualitative Characteristics of Accounting Information

Should companies like **Marks and Spencer plc** (GBR) or **Samsung Electronics Ltd.** (KOR) provide information in their financial statements on how much it costs them to acquire their assets (historical cost basis) or how much the assets are currently worth (fair value basis)? Should **PepsiCo** (USA) combine and show as one company the four main segments of its business, or should it report PepsiCo Beverages, Frito Lay, Quaker Foods, and PepsiCo International as four separate segments?

How does a company choose an acceptable accounting method, the amount and types of information to disclose, and the format in which to present it? The answer: By determining **which alternative provides the most useful information for decision-making purposes (decision-usefulness)**. The IASB identified the qualitative characteristics of accounting information that distinguish better (more useful) information from inferior (less useful) information for decision-making purposes. In addition, the IASB identified a cost constraint as part of the Conceptual Framework (discussed later in the chapter). As Illustration 2-2 (on page 32) shows, the characteristics may be viewed as a hierarchy.

As indicated by Illustration 2-2, qualitative characteristics are either fundamental or enhancing characteristics, depending on how they affect the decision-usefulness of information. Regardless of classification, each qualitative characteristic contributes to the decision-usefulness of financial reporting information. However, providing useful financial information is limited by a pervasive constraint on financial reporting—cost should not exceed the benefits of a reporting practice.

ILLUSTRATION 2-2
Hierarchy of Accounting
Qualities

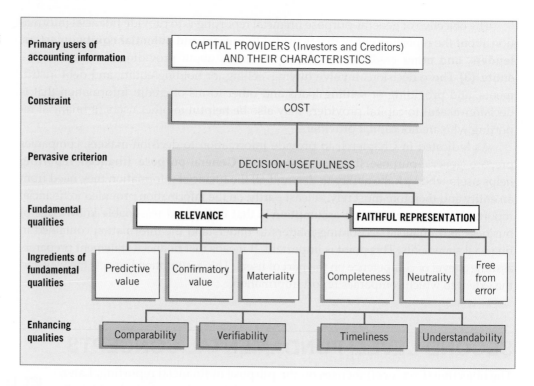

Fundamental Quality—Relevance

Relevance is one of the two fundamental qualities that make accounting information useful for decision-making. Relevance and related ingredients of this fundamental quality are shown below.

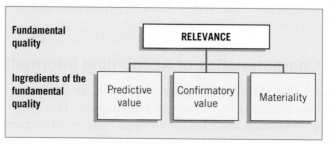

To be **relevant**, accounting information must be capable of making a difference in a decision. Information with no bearing on a decision is irrelevant. Financial information is capable of making a difference when it has predictive value, confirmatory value, or both.

Financial information has **predictive value** if it has value as an input to predictive processes used by investors to form their own expectations about the future. For example, if potential investors are interested in purchasing ordinary shares in **Nippon** (JPN), they may analyze its current resources and claims to those resources, its dividend payments, and its past income performance to predict the amount, timing, and uncertainty of Nippon's future cash flows.

Relevant information also helps users confirm or correct prior expectations; it has **confirmatory value**. For example, when Nippon issues its year-end financial statements, it confirms or changes past (or present) expectations based on previous evaluations. It follows that predictive value and confirmatory value are interrelated. For example, information about the current level and structure of Nippon's assets and liabilities helps users predict its ability to take advantage of opportunities and to react to adverse situations. The same information helps to confirm or correct users' past predictions about that ability.

Materiality is a company-specific aspect of relevance. Information is material if omitting it or misstating it could influence decisions that users make on the basis of the reported financial information. An individual company determines whether information is material because both the nature and/or magnitude of the item(s) to which the information relates must be considered in the context of an individual company's financial report. Information is *immaterial*, and therefore irrelevant, if it would have no impact on a decision-maker. In short, it **must make a difference** or a company need not disclose it.

Assessing materiality is one of the more challenging aspects of accounting because it requires evaluating both the **relative size and importance** of an item. However, it is difficult to provide firm guidelines in judging when a given item is or is not material. Materiality varies both with relative amount and with relative importance. For example, the two sets of numbers in Illustration 2-3 indicate relative size.

	Company A	Company B
Sales	$10,000,000	$100,000
Costs and expenses	9,000,000	90,000
Income from operations	$ 1,000,000	$ 10,000
Unusual gain	$ 20,000	$ 5,000

ILLUSTRATION 2-3
Materiality Comparison

During the period in question, the revenues and expenses, and therefore the net incomes of Company A and Company B, are proportional. Each reported an unusual gain. In looking at the abbreviated income figures for Company A, it appears insignificant whether the amount of the unusual gain is set out separately or merged with the regular operating income. The gain is only 2 percent of the operating income. If merged, it would not seriously distort the income figure. Company B has had an unusual gain of only $5,000. However, it is relatively much more significant than the larger gain realized by Company A. For Company B, an item of $5,000 amounts to 50 percent of its income from operations. Obviously, the inclusion of such an item in operating income would affect the amount of that income materially. Thus, we see the importance of the **relative size** of an item in determining its materiality.

Companies and their auditors generally adopt the rule of thumb that anything under 5 percent of net income is considered immaterial. However, much can depend on specific rules. For example, one market regulator indicates that a company may use this percentage for an initial assessment of materiality, but it must also consider other factors. For example, companies can no longer fail to record items in order to meet consensus analysts' earnings numbers, preserve a positive earnings trend, convert a loss to a profit or vice versa, increase management compensation, or hide an illegal transaction like a bribe. In other words, **companies must consider both quantitative and qualitative factors in determining whether an item is material**.

Thus, it is generally not feasible to specify uniform quantitative thresholds at which an item becomes material. Rather, materiality judgments should be made in the context of the nature and the amount of an item. Materiality factors into a great many internal accounting decisions, too. Examples of such judgments that companies must make include the amount of classification required in a subsidiary expense ledger, the degree of accuracy required in allocating expenses among the departments of a company, and the extent to which adjustments should be made for accrued and deferred items. Only by **the exercise of good judgment and professional expertise** can reasonable and appropriate answers be found, which is the materiality concept sensibly applied.

Fundamental Quality—Faithful Representation

Faithful representation is the second fundamental quality that makes accounting information useful for decision-making. Faithful representation and related ingredients of this fundamental quality are shown below.

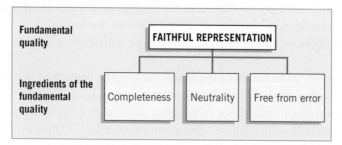

Faithful representation means that the numbers and descriptions match what really existed or happened. Faithful representation is a necessity because most users have neither the time nor the expertise to evaluate the factual content of the information. For example, if Siemens AG's (DEU) income statement reports sales of €60,510 million when it had sales of €40,510 million, then the statement fails to faithfully represent the proper sales amount. To be a faithful representation, information must be complete, neutral, and free of material error.

Completeness. Completeness means that all the information that is necessary for faithful representation is provided. An omission can cause information to be false or misleading and thus not be helpful to the users of financial reports. For example, when Société Générale (FRA) fails to provide information needed to assess the value of its subprime loan receivables (toxic assets), the information is not complete and therefore not a faithful representation of their values.

Neutrality. Neutrality means that a company cannot select information to favor one set of interested parties over another. Providing neutral or unbiased information must be the overriding consideration. For example, in the notes to financial statements, tobacco companies such as British American Tobacco (GBR) should not suppress information about the numerous lawsuits that have been filed because of tobacco-related health concerns—even though such disclosure is damaging to the company.

Neutrality in rule-making has come under increasing attack. Some argue that the IASB should not issue pronouncements that cause undesirable economic effects on an industry or company. We disagree. Accounting rules (and the standard-setting process) must be free from bias, or we will no longer have credible financial statements. Without credible financial statements, individuals will no longer use this information. An analogy demonstrates the point: Many individuals bet on boxing matches because such contests are assumed not to be fixed. But nobody bets on wrestling matches. Why? Because the public assumes that wrestling matches are rigged. If financial information is biased (rigged), the public will lose confidence and no longer use it.

Free from Error. An information item that is free from error will be a more accurate (faithful) representation of a financial item. For example, if UBS (CHE) misstates its loan losses, its financial statements are misleading and not a faithful representation of its financial results. However, faithful representation does not imply total freedom from error. This is because most financial reporting measures involve estimates of various types that incorporate management's judgment. For example, management must estimate the amount of uncollectible accounts to determine bad debt expense. And determination of depreciation expense requires estimation of useful lives of plant and equipment, as well as the residual value of the assets.

What do the numbers mean? UNFAITHFUL—FOR 20 YEARS

The importance of faithful representation is illustrated by the fraud at Olympus Corporation (JPN). Here's what happened, as revealed in a recent report on the fraud by an investigative committee. In transactions dating back nearly 20 years, Olympus was hiding losses related to export sales. The losses arose when the exchange rate between the dollar and yen moved in an unfavorable direction for Olympus, which negatively impacted investments related to the export sales. However, the losses were not reported; that is, the financial statements were not faithful representations.

How could such a loss be hidden? At the time, accounting rules in Japan, as well as in other countries, allowed investments to be carried at cost. Theoretically, there should eventually have been a write-down, but there never was. Rather, management hoped that with additional risky investments, the losses could somehow be made up. They were not, and eventually the losses grew to more than $1 billion. Olympus seems to have been content to sit on the losses until 1997, when accounting rules changed and some investments had to be marked to market.

Olympus then dug the hole deeper; it developed a plan to "sell" the losing investments, at original cost, to shell companies set up by Olympus for that purpose. Under lenient accounting rules, those shell companies would not have to be consolidated with Olympus, so the losses could remain hidden. That all ended when the investigation uncovered the sham adjustments and the losses were finally revealed.

The scandal highlights the importance of accounting rules that result in faithful representation of company performance and financial position. That is, until accounting rulemakers finally started to require fair value accounting for some financial instruments in 1997—seven years after the fraud began—covering up the losses was easy. Furthermore, subsequent rule changes (in the wake of the Enron (USA) scandal) forced companies to stop hiding losses in off-balance-sheet entities. Indeed, the Olympus scandal might never have occurred if the accounting kept a focus on faithful representation.

Source: F. Norris, "Deep Roots of Fraud at Olympus," *The New York Times* (December 8, 2011).

Enhancing Qualities

Enhancing qualitative characteristics are complementary to the fundamental qualitative characteristics. These characteristics distinguish more-useful information from less-useful information. Enhancing characteristics, shown below, are comparability, verifiability, timeliness, and understandability.

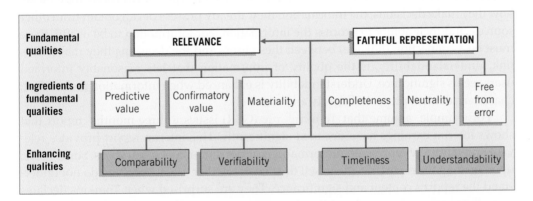

Comparability. Information that is measured and reported in a similar manner for different companies is considered comparable. Comparability enables users to identify the real similarities and differences in economic events between companies. For example, historically the accounting for pensions in Japan differed from that in the United States. In Japan, companies generally recorded little or no charge to income for these costs. U.S. companies recorded pension cost as incurred. As a result, it is difficult to compare and evaluate the financial results of Toyota (JPN) or Honda (JPN) to General Motors (USA) or Ford (USA). Investors can only make valid evaluations if comparable information is available.

Another type of comparability, **consistency**, is present when a company applies the same accounting treatment to similar events, from period to period. Through such application, the company shows consistent use of accounting standards. The idea of consistency does not mean, however, that companies cannot switch from one accounting method to another. A company can change methods, but it must first demonstrate that the newly adopted method is preferable to the old. If approved, the company must then disclose the nature and effect of the accounting change, as well as the justification for it, in the financial statements for the period in which it made the change.[4] When a change in accounting principles occurs, the auditor generally refers to it in an explanatory paragraph of the audit report. This paragraph identifies the nature of the change and refers the reader to the note in the financial statements that discusses the change in detail.

Verifiability. Verifiability occurs when independent measurers, using the same methods, obtain similar results. Verifiability occurs in the following situations.

1. Two independent auditors count **Tata Motors'** (IND) inventory and arrive at the same physical quantity amount for inventory. Verification of an amount for an asset therefore can occur by simply counting the inventory (referred to as *direct verification*).
2. Two independent auditors compute Tata Motors' inventory value at the end of the year using the FIFO method of inventory valuation. Verification may occur by checking the inputs (quantity and costs) and recalculating the outputs (ending inventory value) using the same accounting convention or methodology (referred to as *indirect verification*).

Timeliness. Timeliness means having information available to decision-makers before it loses its capacity to influence decisions. Having relevant information available sooner can enhance its capacity to influence decisions, and a lack of timeliness can rob information of its usefulness. For example, if **Lenovo Group** (CHN) waited to report its interim results until nine months after the period, the information would be much less useful for decision-making purposes.

Understandability. Decision-makers vary widely in the types of decisions they make, how they make decisions, the information they already possess or can obtain from other sources, and their ability to process the information. For information to be useful, there must be a connection (linkage) between these users and the decisions they make. This link, **understandability**, is the quality of information that lets reasonably informed users see its significance. Understandability is enhanced when information is classified, characterized, and presented clearly and concisely.

For example, assume that **Tomkins plc** (GBR) issues a three-months' report that shows interim earnings have declined significantly. This interim report provides relevant and faithfully represented information for decision-making purposes. Some users, upon reading the report, decide to sell their shares. Other users, however, do not understand the report's content and significance. They are surprised when Tomkins declares a smaller year-end dividend and the share price declines. Thus, although Tomkins presented highly relevant information that was a faithful representation, it was useless to those who did not understand it.

Users of financial reports are assumed to have a reasonable knowledge of business and economic activities. In making decisions, users also should review and analyze the

---

[4]Surveys indicate that users highly value consistency. They note that a change tends to destroy the comparability of data before and after the change. Some companies assist users to understand the pre- and post-change data. Generally, however, users say they lose the ability to analyze over time. IFRS guidelines (discussed in Chapter 22) on accounting changes are designed to improve the comparability of the data before and after the change.

information with reasonable diligence. Information that is relevant and faithfully represented should not be excluded from financial reports solely because it is too complex or difficult for some users to understand without assistance.[5]

Basic Elements

An important aspect of developing any theoretical structure is the body of **basic elements** or definitions to be included in it. Accounting uses many terms with distinctive and specific meanings. These terms constitute the language of business or the jargon of accounting.

5 **LEARNING OBJECTIVE**
Define the basic elements of financial statements.

One such term is **asset**. Is it merely something we own? Or is an asset something we have the right to use, as in the case of leased equipment? Or is it anything of value used by a company to generate revenues—in which case, should we also consider the managers of a company as an asset?

As this example and the lottery ticket example in the opening story illustrate, it is necessary, therefore, to develop basic definitions for the elements of financial statements. The Conceptual Framework defines the five interrelated elements that most directly relate to measuring the performance and financial status of a business enterprise. We list them below for review and information purposes; you need not memorize these definitions at this point. We will explain and examine each of these elements in more detail in subsequent chapters.

ELEMENTS OF FINANCIAL STATEMENTS

The elements directly related to the measurement of financial position are assets, liabilities, and equity. These are defined as follows.

ASSET. A resource controlled by the entity as a result of past events and from which future economic benefits are expected to flow to the entity.

LIABILITY. A present obligation of the entity arising from past events, the settlement of which is expected to result in an outflow from the entity of resources embodying economic benefits.

EQUITY. The residual interest in the assets of the entity after deducting all its liabilities.

The elements of income and expenses are defined as follows.

INCOME. Increases in economic benefits during the accounting period in the form of inflows or enhancements of assets or decreases of liabilities that result in increases in equity, other than those relating to contributions from equity participants.

EXPENSES. Decreases in economic benefits during the accounting period in the form of outflows or depletions of assets or incurrences of liabilities that result in decreases in equity, other than those relating to distributions to equity participants.

As indicated, the IASB classifies the elements into two distinct groups. **[5]** The first group of three elements—assets, liabilities, and equity—describes amounts of resources and claims to resources at a **moment in time**. The second group of two elements describes transactions, events, and circumstances that affect a company during a **period of time**. The first class, affected by elements of the second class, provides at any time the cumulative result of all changes. This interaction is referred to as "articulation." That is, key figures in one financial statement correspond to balances in another.

[5]The Conceptual Framework for Financial Reporting, "Chapter 3, Qualitative Characteristics of Useful Financial Information" (London, U.K.: IASB, September 2010), paras. QC30–QC31.

THIRD LEVEL: RECOGNITION, MEASUREMENT, AND DISCLOSURE CONCEPTS

The third level of the Conceptual Framework consists of concepts that implement the basic objectives of level one. These concepts explain how companies should recognize, measure, and report financial elements and events. Here, we identify the concepts as basic assumptions, principles, and a cost constraint. Not everyone uses this classification system, so focus your attention more on **understanding the concepts** than on how we classify and organize them. These concepts serve as guidelines in responding to controversial financial reporting issues.

Basic Assumptions

As indicated earlier, the Conceptual Framework specifically identifies only one assumption—the going concern assumption. Yet, we believe there are a number of other assumptions that are present in the reporting environment. As a result, for completeness, we discuss each of these five basic assumptions in turn: (1) **economic entity**, (2) **going concern**, (3) **monetary unit**, (4) **periodicity**, and (5) **accrual basis**.

Economic Entity Assumption

The economic entity assumption **means that economic activity can be identified with a particular unit of accountability.** In other words, a company keeps its activity separate and distinct from its owners and any other business unit.[6] At the most basic level, the economic entity assumption dictates that Sappi Limited (ZAF) record the company's financial activities separate from those of its owners and managers. Equally important, financial statement users need to be able to distinguish the activities and elements of different companies, such as Volvo (SWE), Ford (USA), and Volkswagen AG (DEU). If users could not distinguish the activities of different companies, how would they know which company financially outperformed the other?

The entity concept does not apply solely to the segregation of activities among competing companies, such as Toyota (JPN) and Hyundai (KOR). An individual, department, division, or an entire industry could be considered a separate entity if we choose to define it in this manner. Thus, **the entity concept does not necessarily refer to a legal entity**. A parent and its subsidiaries are separate **legal** entities, but merging their activities for accounting and reporting purposes does not violate the **economic entity** assumption.[7]

---

[6]In 2010, the IASB issued an exposure draft entitled "Conceptual Framework for Financial Reporting—The Reporting Entity." The IASB proposal indicates that a reporting entity has three features: (1) economic activities have been, are being, or will be conducted; (2) those activities can be distinguished from those of other entities; and (3) financial information about the entity's economic activities has the potential to be of value in making decisions about providing resources to that entity. See IASB, "Conceptual Framework for Financial Reporting—The Reporting Entity," Exposure Draft (March 2010).

[7]The concept of the entity is changing. For example, defining the "outer edges" of companies is now harder. Public companies often consist of multiple public subsidiaries, each with joint ventures, licensing arrangements, and other affiliations. Increasingly, companies form and dissolve joint ventures or customer-supplier relationships in a matter of months or weeks. These "virtual companies" raise accounting issues about how to account for the entity. See Steven H. Wallman, "The Future of Accounting and Disclosure in an Evolving World: The Need for Dramatic Change," *Accounting Horizons* (September 1995). The IASB is addressing these issues in the entity phase of its conceptual framework project (see *http://www.iasb.org/Current+Projects/IASB+Projects/Conceptual+Framework/Conceptual+Framework.htm*) and in its project on consolidations (see *http://www.iasb.org/Current%20Projects/IASB%20Projects/Consolidation/Consolidation.htm*).

Going Concern Assumption

Most accounting methods rely on the going concern assumption—**that the company will have a long life**. Despite numerous business failures, most companies have a fairly high continuance rate. As a rule, we expect companies to last long enough to fulfill their objectives and commitments.

This assumption has significant implications. The historical cost principle would be of limited usefulness if we assume eventual liquidation. Under a liquidation approach, for example, a company would better state asset values at fair value than at acquisition cost. **Depreciation and amortization policies are justifiable and appropriate only if we assume some permanence to the company.** If a company adopts the liquidation approach, the current/non-current classification of assets and liabilities loses much of its significance. Labeling anything a long-lived or non-current asset would be difficult to justify. Indeed, listing liabilities on the basis of priority in liquidation would be more reasonable.

The going concern assumption applies in most business situations. **Only where liquidation appears imminent is the assumption inapplicable.** In these cases a total revaluation of assets and liabilities can provide information that closely approximates the company's fair value. You will learn more about accounting problems related to a company in liquidation in advanced accounting courses.

Monetary Unit Assumption

The monetary unit assumption means that money is the common denominator of economic activity and provides an appropriate basis for accounting measurement and analysis. That is, the monetary unit is the most effective means of expressing to interested parties changes in capital and exchanges of goods and services. Application of this assumption depends on the even more basic assumption that quantitative data are useful in communicating economic information and in making rational economic decisions.

Furthermore, accounting generally ignores price-level changes (inflation and deflation) and assumes that the unit of measure—euros, dollars, or yen—remains reasonably stable. We therefore use the monetary unit assumption to justify adding 1985 pounds to 2015 pounds without any adjustment. It is expected that the pound or other currency, unadjusted for inflation or deflation, will continue to be used to measure items recognized in financial statements. Only if circumstances change dramatically (such as high inflation rates similar to that in some South American countries) will "inflation accounting" be considered.[8]

Periodicity Assumption

To measure the results of a company's activity accurately, we would need to wait until it liquidates. Decision-makers, however, cannot wait that long for such information. Users need to know a company's performance and economic status on a timely basis so that they can evaluate and compare companies, and take appropriate actions. Therefore, companies must report information periodically.

The periodicity (or time period) assumption implies that a company can divide its economic activities into artificial time periods. These time periods vary, but the most common are monthly, quarterly, and yearly.

The shorter the time period, the more difficult it is to determine the proper net income for the period. A month's results usually prove less reliable than a quarter's

---

[8]As noted in the Conceptual Framework (Chapter 4, par. 63), this approach reflects adoption of a financial capital approach to capital maintenance under which the change in capital or a company's net assets is measured in nominal monetary units without adjusting for changes in prices. **[6]** There is a separate IFRS (*IFRS No. 29*, "Financial Reporting in Hyperinflationary Economies") that provides guidance on how to account for adjustments to the purchasing power of the monetary unit. **[7]**

results, and a quarter's results are likely to be less reliable than a year's results. Investors desire and demand that a company quickly process and disseminate information. Yet the quicker a company releases the information, the more likely the information will include errors. **This phenomenon provides an interesting example of the trade-off between relevance and faithful representation in preparing financial data.**

The problem of defining the time period becomes more serious as product cycles shorten and products become obsolete more quickly. Many believe that, given technology advances, companies need to provide more online, real-time financial information to ensure the availability of relevant information.

Accrual Basis of Accounting

Companies prepare financial statements using the accrual basis of accounting. Accrual-basis accounting means that transactions that change a company's financial statements are recorded in the periods in which the events occur. [8] For example, using the accrual basis means that companies recognize revenues when it is probable that future economic benefits will flow to the company and reliable measurement is possible (the revenue recognition principle). This is in contrast to recognition based on receipt of cash. Likewise, under the accrual basis, companies recognize expenses when incurred (the expense recognition principle) rather than when paid.

An alternative to the accrual basis is the cash basis. Under cash-basis accounting, companies record revenue only when cash is received. They record expenses only when cash is paid. The cash basis of accounting is prohibited under IFRS. Why? Because it does not record revenue according to the revenue recognition principle (discussed in the next section). Similarly, it does not record expenses when incurred, which violates the expense recognition principle (discussed in the next section).

Financial statements prepared on the accrual basis inform users not only of past transactions involving the payment and receipt of cash but also of obligations to pay cash in the future and of resources that represent cash to be received in the future. Hence, they provide the type of information about past transactions and other events that is most useful in making economic decisions.

Basic Principles of Accounting

LEARNING OBJECTIVE
Explain the application of the basic principles of accounting.

We generally use four basic principles of accounting to record and report transactions: (1) measurement, (2) revenue recognition, (3) expense recognition, and (4) full disclosure. We look at each in turn.

Measurement Principles

We presently have a "mixed-attribute" system in which one of two measurement principles is used. The most commonly used measurements are based on historical cost and fair value. Selection of which principle to follow generally reflects a trade-off between relevance and faithful representation. Here, we discuss each measurement principle.

Historical Cost. IFRS requires that companies account for and report many assets and liabilities on the basis of acquisition price. This is often referred to as the historical cost principle. Cost has an important advantage over other valuations: **It is generally thought to be a faithful representation of the amount paid for a given item.**

To illustrate this advantage, consider the problems if companies select current selling price instead. Companies might have difficulty establishing a value for unsold items. Every member of the accounting department might value the assets differently. Further, how often would it be necessary to establish sales value? All companies close their accounts at least annually. But some compute their net income every month. Those companies would have to place a sales value on every asset each time they wished to determine income. Critics raise similar objections against current cost (replacement cost, present value of future cash flows) and any other basis of valuation **except historical cost**.

What about liabilities? Do companies account for them on a cost basis? Yes, they do. Companies issue liabilities, such as bonds, notes, and accounts payable, in exchange for assets (or services), for an agreed-upon price. **This price, established by the exchange transaction, is the "cost" of the liability.** A company uses this amount to record the liability in the accounts and report it in financial statements. Thus, many users prefer historical cost because it provides them with a **verifiable benchmark** for measuring historical trends.

Fair Value. **Fair value** is defined as "the price that would be received to sell an asset or paid to transfer a liability in an orderly transaction between market participants at the measurement date." Fair value is therefore a market-based measure. **[9]** Recently, IFRS has increasingly called for use of fair value measurements in the financial statements. This is often referred to as the fair value principle. Fair value information may be more useful than historical cost for certain types of assets and liabilities and in certain industries. For example, companies report many financial instruments, including derivatives, at fair value. Certain industries, such as brokerage houses and mutual funds, prepare their basic financial statements on a fair value basis. At initial acquisition, historical cost equals fair value. In subsequent periods, as market and economic conditions change, historical cost and fair value often diverge. Thus, fair value measures or estimates often provide more relevant information about the expected future cash flows related to the asset or liability. For example, when long-lived assets decline in value, a fair value measure determines any impairment loss.

The IASB believes that fair value information is more relevant to users than historical cost. Fair value measurement, it is argued, provides better insight into the value of a company's assets and liabilities (its financial position) and a better basis for assessing future cash flow prospects. Recently, the Board has taken the additional step of giving companies the option to use fair value (referred to as the fair value option) as the basis for measurement of financial assets and financial liabilities. **[10]** The Board considers fair value more relevant than historical cost because it reflects the current cash equivalent value of financial instruments. As a result, companies now have the option to record fair value in their accounts for most financial instruments, including such items as receivables, investments, and debt securities.

Use of fair value in financial reporting is increasing. However, measurement based on fair value introduces increased subjectivity into accounting reports when fair value information is not readily available. To increase consistency and comparability in fair value measures, the IASB established a fair value hierarchy that provides insight into the priority of valuation techniques to use to determine fair value. As shown in Illustration 2-4, the fair value hierarchy is divided into three broad levels.

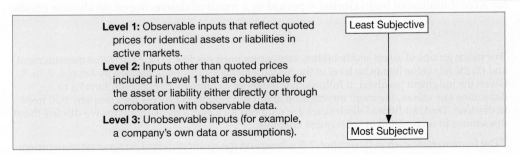

ILLUSTRATION 2-4
Fair Value Hierarchy

As Illustration 2-4 indicates, Level 1 is the least subjective because it is based on quoted prices, like a closing share price in the *Financial Times*. Level 2 is more subjective and would rely on evaluating similar assets or liabilities in active markets. At the most subjective level, Level 3, much judgment is needed, based on the best information available, to arrive at a relevant and representationally faithful fair value measurement.[9]

It is easy to arrive at fair values when markets are liquid with many traders, but fair value answers are not readily available in other situations. For example, how do you value the mortgage assets of a subprime lender such as New Century (USA) given that the market for these securities has essentially disappeared? A great deal of expertise and sound judgment will be needed to arrive at appropriate answers. IFRS also provides guidance on estimating fair values when market-related data is not available. In general, these valuation issues relate to Level 3 fair value measurements. These measurements may be developed using expected cash flow and present value techniques, as described in Chapter 6.

As indicated above, we presently have a "mixed-attribute" system that permits the use of historical cost and fair value. Although the historical cost principle continues to be an important basis for valuation, recording and reporting of fair value information is increasing. The recent measurement and disclosure guidance should increase consistency and comparability when fair value measurements are used in the financial statements and related notes.

Revenue Recognition Principle

When a company agrees to perform a service or sell a product to a customer, it has a **performance obligation**. When the company satisfies this performance obligation, it recognizes revenue. The revenue recognition principle therefore requires that companies recognize revenue in the accounting period in which the performance obligation is satisfied.

To illustrate, assume that Klinke Cleaners cleans clothing on June 30 but customers do not claim and pay for their clothes until the first week of July. Klinke should record revenue in June when it performed the service (satisfied the performance obligation) rather than in July when it received the cash. At June 30, Klinke would report a receivable on its statement of financial position and revenue in its income statement for the service performed. To illustrate the revenue recognition principle in more detail, assume that Airbus (DEU) signs a contract to sell airplanes to British Airways (GBR) for €100 million. To determine when to recognize revenue, Airbus uses the five steps shown in Illustration 2-5.[10]

Many revenue transactions pose few problems because the transaction is initiated and completed at the same time. However, when to recognize revenue in other certain situations is often more difficult. The risk of errors and misstatements is significant. Chapter 18 discusses revenue recognition issues in more detail.

Expense Recognition Principle

Expenses are defined as outflows or other "using up" of assets or incurring of liabilities (or a combination of both) during a period as a result of delivering or producing goods

---

[9]For major groups of assets and liabilities, companies must disclose (1) the fair value measurement and (2) the fair value hierarchy level of the measurements as a whole, classified by Level 1, 2, or 3. Given the judgment involved, it follows that the more a company depends on Level 3 to determine fair values, the more information about the valuation process the company will need to disclose. Thus, additional disclosures are required for Level 3 measurements; we discuss these disclosures in more detail in subsequent chapters.

[10]The framework shown in Illustration 2-5 is based on the recent standard on revenue recognition.

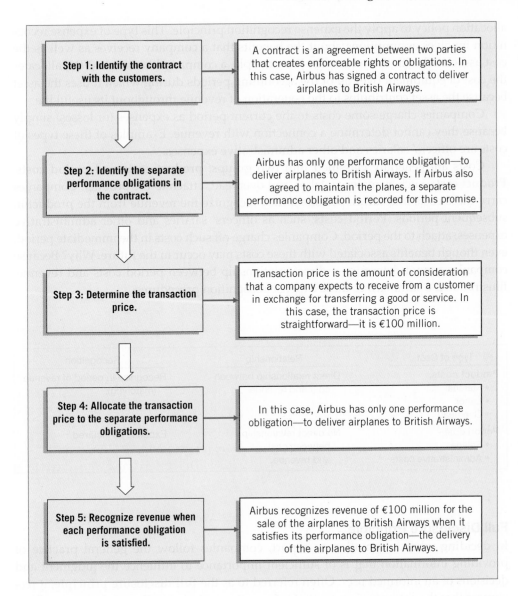

ILLUSTRATION 2-5
The Five Steps of
Revenue Recognition

and/or rendering services. It follows then that recognition of expenses is related to net changes in assets and earning revenues. In practice, the approach for recognizing expenses is, "Let the expense follow the revenues." This approach is the **expense recognition principle**.

To illustrate, companies recognize expenses not when they pay wages or make a product, but when the work (service) or the product actually contributes to revenue. Thus, companies tie expense recognition to revenue recognition. That is, by matching **efforts (expenses) with accomplishment (revenues), the expense recognition principle is implemented** in accordance with the definition of expense (outflows or other using up of assets or incurring of liabilities).[11]

Some costs, however, are difficult to associate with revenue. As a result, some other approach must be developed. Often, companies use a "rational and systematic"

[11]This approach is commonly referred to as the **matching principle**. However, there is some debate about the conceptual validity of the matching principle. A major concern is that matching permits companies to defer certain costs and treat them as assets on the statement of financial position. In fact, these costs may not have future benefits. If abused, this principle permits the statement of financial position to become a "dumping ground" for unmatched costs.

allocation policy to apply the expense recognition principle. This type of expense recognition involves assumptions about the benefits that a company receives as well as the cost associated with those benefits. For example, a company like Nokia (FIN) allocates the cost of equipment over all of the accounting periods during which it uses the asset because the asset contributes to the generation of revenue throughout its useful life.

Companies charge some costs to the current period as expenses (or losses) simply because they cannot determine a connection with revenue. Examples of these types of costs are officers' salaries and other administrative expenses.

Costs are generally classified into two groups: **product costs** and **period costs**. Product costs, such as material, labor, and overhead, attach to the product. Companies carry these costs into future periods if they recognize the revenue from the product in subsequent periods. Period costs, such as officers' salaries and other administrative expenses, attach to the period. Companies charge off such costs in the immediate period, even though benefits associated with these costs may occur in the future. Why? Because companies cannot determine a direct relationship between period costs and revenue. Illustration 2-6 summarizes these expense recognition procedures.

ILLUSTRATION 2-6
Expense Recognition
Procedures for Product
and Period Costs

Type of Cost	Relationship	Recognition
Product costs: • Material • Labor • Overhead	Direct relationship between cost and revenue.	Recognize in period of revenue (matching).
Period costs: • Salaries • Administrative costs	No direct relationship between cost and revenue.	Expense as incurred.

Full Disclosure Principle

In deciding what information to report, companies follow the general practice of providing information that is of sufficient importance to influence the judgment and decisions of an informed user. Often referred to as the full disclosure principle, it recognizes that the nature and amount of information included in financial reports reflects a series of judgmental trade-offs. These trade-offs strive for (1) sufficient detail to disclose matters that **make a difference** to users, yet (2) sufficient condensation to make the **information understandable**, keeping in mind costs of preparing and using it.

Users find information about financial position, income, cash flows, and investments in one of three places: (1) within the main body of financial statements, (2) in the notes to those statements, or (3) as supplementary information.

As discussed in Chapter 1, the **financial statements** are the statement of financial position, income statement (or statement of comprehensive income), statement of cash flows, and statement of changes in equity. They are a structured means of communicating financial information. An item that meets the definition of an element should be recognized if (a) it is probable that any future economic benefit associated with the item will flow to or from the entity; and (b) the item has a cost or value that can be measured with reliability. [11]

Disclosure is not a substitute for proper accounting. As a noted accountant indicated, "Good disclosure does not cure bad accounting any more than an adjective or adverb can be used without, or in place of, a noun or verb." Thus, for example, cash-basis accounting for cost of goods sold is misleading, even if a company discloses accrual-basis amounts in the notes to the financial statements.

The **notes to financial statements** generally amplify or explain the items presented in the main body of the statements. If the main body of the financial statements gives an incomplete picture of the performance and position of the company, the notes should provide the additional information needed. Information in the notes does not have to be quantifiable, nor does it need to qualify as an element. Notes can be partially or totally narrative. Examples of notes include descriptions of the accounting policies and methods used in measuring the elements reported in the statements, explanations of uncertainties and contingencies, and statistics and details too voluminous for presentation in the financial statements. The notes can be essential to understanding the company's performance and position.

Supplementary information may include details or amounts that present a different perspective from that adopted in the financial statements. It may be quantifiable information that is high in relevance but low in reliability. For example, oil and gas companies typically provide information on proven reserves as well as the related discounted cash flows.

Supplementary information may also include management's explanation of the financial information and its discussion of the significance of that information. For example, many business combinations have produced financing arrangements that demand new accounting and reporting practices and principles. In each of these situations, the same problem must be faced: making sure the company presents enough information to ensure that the **reasonably prudent investor** will not be misled.[12]

We discuss the content, arrangement, and display of financial statements, along with other facets of full disclosure, in Chapters 4, 5, and 24.

Cost Constraint

In providing information with the qualitative characteristics that make it useful, companies must consider an overriding factor that limits (constrains) the reporting. This is referred to as the **cost constraint**. That is, companies must weigh the costs of providing the information against the benefits that can be derived from using it. Rule-making bodies and governmental agencies use cost-benefit analysis before making final their informational requirements. In order to justify requiring a particular measurement or disclosure, the benefits perceived to be derived from it must exceed the costs perceived to be associated with it.

8 LEARNING OBJECTIVE

Describe the impact that the cost constraint has on reporting accounting information.

A corporate executive made the following remark to a standard-setter about a proposed rule: "In all my years in the financial arena, I have never seen such an absolutely ridiculous proposal. . . . To dignify these 'actuarial' estimates by recording them as assets and liabilities would be virtually unthinkable except for the fact that the FASB has done equally stupid things in the past. . . . For God's sake, use common sense just this once."[13] Although extreme, this remark indicates the frustration expressed by members of the business community about accounting standard-setting, and whether the benefits of a given pronouncement exceed the costs.

The difficulty in cost-benefit analysis is that the costs and especially the benefits are not always evident or measurable. The costs are of several kinds: costs of collecting and processing, of disseminating, of auditing, of potential litigation, of disclosure

---

[12]To provide guidance for management disclosures, the IASB issued an IFRS practice statement entitled "Management Commentary—A Framework for Presentation." The IASB notes that this practice statement is neither an IFRS nor part of the Conceptual Framework. However, the guidance is issued on the basis that management commentary meets the definition of other financial reporting as referenced in the Conceptual Framework.

[13]"Decision-Usefulness: The Overriding Objective," *FASB Viewpoints* (October 19, 1983), p. 4.

to competitors, and of analysis and interpretation. Benefits to preparers may include greater management control and access to capital at a lower cost. Users may receive better information for allocation of resources, tax assessment, and rate regulation. As noted earlier, benefits are generally more difficult to quantify than are costs.

The implementation of the provisions of the Sarbanes-Oxley Act in the United States illustrates the challenges in assessing costs and benefits of standards. One study estimated the increased costs of complying with the new internal-control standards related to the financial reporting process to be an average of $7.8 million per company. However, the study concluded that ". . . quantifying the benefits of improved more reliable financial reporting is not fully possible."[14]

Despite the difficulty in assessing the costs and benefits of its rules, the IASB attempts to determine that each proposed pronouncement will fill a significant need and that the costs imposed to meet the standard are justified in relation to overall benefits of the resulting information. In addition, they seek input on costs and benefits as part of their due process.

What do the numbers mean?   LET'S BE PRUDENT

Sometimes, in practice, it has been acceptable to invoke the additional constraint of prudence or conservatism as a justification for an accounting treatment under conditions of uncertainty. Prudence or conservatism means when in doubt, choose the solution that will be least likely to overstate assets or income and/or understate liabilities or expenses. The Conceptual Framework indicates that prudence or conservatism generally is in conflict with the quality of neutrality. This is because being prudent or conservative likely leads to a bias in the reported financial position and financial performance.

In fact, introducing biased understatement of assets (or overstatement of liabilities) in one period frequently leads to overstating financial performance in later periods—a result that cannot be described as prudent. This is inconsistent with neutrality, which encompasses freedom from bias. Accordingly, the Conceptual Framework does not include prudence or conservatism as desirable qualities of financial reporting information.

The role of conservatism or prudence may not be fully settled. Recently, the European Parliament (EP) called for the IASB to reintroduce a specific reference to "prudence" in its Conceptual Framework. The EP argues that such a tenet puts pressure on accountants to err on the side of caution when scrutinizing losses. The lawmakers argue that a prudence guideline could help avoid a repeat of the 2007–2009 financial crisis in which European taxpayers had to put billions of euros into struggling banks. Some in the Parliament are linking continued funding for the IFRS to a change in the prudence guidelines.

In response, IASB chairman Hans Hoogervorst described the Parliament's stance as "highly worrisome," noting that pressuring the IASB on this issue will raise concern about its independence. Thus, just as the use of prudence can lead to a lack of neutrality of the reported numbers, the EP's stand on prudence could negatively impact the perceived neutrality of the IASB's standard-setting process.

Source: H. Jones, "IASB Accounting Body Rejects EU Parliament's Funding Conditions," *Reuters* (October 14, 2013), *http://uk.reuters.com/article/2013/10/14/uk-accounting-iasb-idUKBRE99D0KQ20131014.*

Summary of the Structure

Illustration 2-7 presents the Conceptual Framework for Financial Reporting discussed in this chapter. It is similar to Illustration 2-1 (on page 30) except that it provides additional information for each level. We cannot overemphasize the usefulness of this conceptual framework in helping to understand many of the problem areas that we examine in later chapters.

[14]Charles Rivers and Associates, "Sarbanes-Oxley Section 404: Costs and Remediation of Deficiencies," letter from Deloitte and Touche, Ernst and Young, KPMG, and Pricewaterhouse-Coopers to the SEC (April 11, 2005).

ILLUSTRATION 2-7
Conceptual Framework
for Financial Reporting

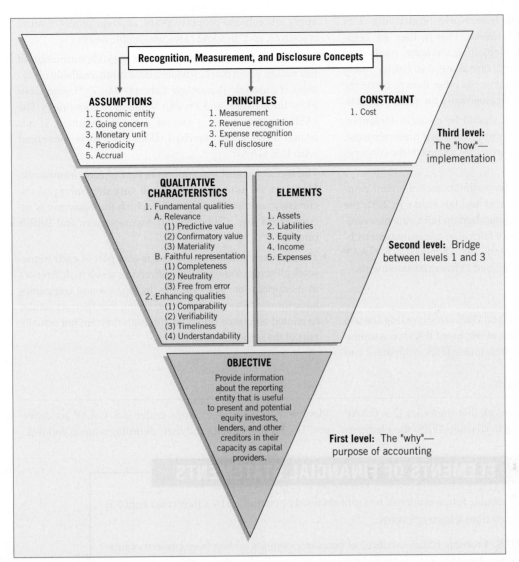

GLOBAL ACCOUNTING INSIGHTS

THE CONCEPTUAL FRAMEWORK

The IASB and the FASB have been working together to develop a common conceptual framework. This framework is based on the existing conceptual frameworks underlying U.S. GAAP and IFRS. The objective of this joint project is to develop a conceptual framework consisting of standards that are principles-based and internally consistent, thereby leading to the most useful financial reporting.

Relevant Facts

Following are the key similarities and differences between U.S. GAAP and IFRS related to the Conceptual Framework for Financial Reporting.

Similarities

• In 2010, the IASB and FASB completed the first phase of a jointly created conceptual framework. In this first phase, they agreed on the objective of financial reporting and a common set of desired qualitative characteristics. These were presented in the Chapter 2 discussion. Note that prior to this converged phase, the Conceptual Framework gave more emphasis to the objective of providing information on management's performance (stewardship).

- The existing conceptual frameworks underlying U.S. GAAP and IFRS are very similar. That is, they are organized in a similar manner (objective, elements, qualitative characteristics, etc.). There is no real need to change many aspects of the existing frameworks other than to converge different ways of discussing essentially the same concepts.

- The converged framework should be a single document, unlike the two conceptual frameworks that presently exist. It is unlikely that the basic structure related to the concepts will change.

- Both the IASB and FASB have similar measurement principles, based on historical cost and fair value. In 2011, the Boards issued a converged standard on fair value measurement so that the definition of fair value, measurement techniques, and disclosures are the same between U.S. GAAP and IFRS when fair value is used in financial statements.

Differences

- Although both U.S. GAAP and IFRS are increasing the use of fair value to report assets, at this point IFRS has adopted it more broadly. As examples, under IFRS, companies can apply fair value to property, plant, and equipment; natural resources; and, in some cases, intangible assets.

- U.S. GAAP has a concept statement to guide estimation of fair values when market-related data is not available (*Statement of Financial Accounting Concepts No. 7, "Using Cash Flow Information and Present Value in Accounting"*). The IASB has not issued a similar concept statement; it has issued a fair value standard *(IFRS 13)* that is converged with U.S. GAAP.

- The monetary unit assumption is part of each framework. However, the unit of measure will vary depending on the currency used in the country in which the company is incorporated (e.g., Chinese yuan, Japanese yen, and British pound).

- The economic entity assumption is also part of each framework although some cultural differences result in differences in its application. For example, in Japan many companies have formed alliances that are so strong that they act similar to related corporate divisions although they are not actually part of the same company.

About the Numbers

While the conceptual framework that underlies U.S. GAAP is very similar to that used to develop IFRS, the elements identified and their definitions under U.S. GAAP are different. The FASB elements and their definitions are as follows.

ELEMENTS OF FINANCIAL STATEMENTS

ASSETS. Probable future economic benefits obtained or controlled by a particular entity as a result of past transactions or events.

LIABILITIES. Probable future sacrifices of economic benefits arising from present obligations of a particular entity to transfer assets or provide services to other entities in the future as a result of past transactions or events.

EQUITY. Residual interest in the assets of an entity that remains after deducting its liabilities. In a business enterprise, the equity is the ownership interest.

INVESTMENTS BY OWNERS. Increases in net assets of a particular enterprise resulting from transfers to it from other entities of something of value to obtain or increase ownership interests (or equity) in it. Assets are most commonly received as investments by owners, but that which is received may also include services or satisfaction or conversion of liabilities of the enterprise.

DISTRIBUTIONS TO OWNERS. Decreases in net assets of a particular enterprise resulting from transferring assets, rendering services, or incurring liabilities by the enterprise to owners. Distributions to owners decrease ownership interests (or equity) in an enterprise.

COMPREHENSIVE INCOME. Change in equity (net assets) of an entity during a period from transactions and other events and circumstances from non-owner sources. It includes all changes in equity during a period except those resulting from investments by owners and distributions to owners.

REVENUES. Inflows or other enhancements of assets of an entity or settlement of its liabilities (or a combination of both) during a period from delivering or producing goods, rendering services, or other activities that constitute the entity's ongoing major or central operations.

EXPENSES. Outflows or other using up of assets or incurrences of liabilities (or a combination of both) during a period from delivering or producing goods, rendering services, or carrying out other activities that constitute the entity's ongoing major or central operations.

GAINS. Increases in equity (net assets) from peripheral or incidental transactions of an entity and from all other transactions and other events and circumstances affecting the entity during a period except those that result from revenues or investments by owners.

LOSSES. Decreases in equity (net assets) from peripheral or incidental transactions of an entity and from all other transactions and other events and circumstances affecting the entity during a period except those that result from expenses or distributions to owners.

Source: "Elements of Financial Statements," *Statement of Financial Accounting Concepts No. 6* (Stamford, Conn.: FASB, December 1985), pp. ix and x.

On the Horizon

The IASB and the FASB face a difficult task in attempting to update, modify, and complete a converged conceptual framework. There are many challenging issues to overcome. For example, how do we trade off characteristics such as highly relevant information that is difficult to verify? How do we define control when we are developing a definition of an asset? Is a liability the future sacrifice itself or the obligation to make the sacrifice? Should a single measurement method, such as historical cost or fair value, be used, or does it depend on whether it is an asset or liability that is being measured? We are optimistic that the new converged conceptual framework will be a significant improvement over its predecessors and will lead to standards that will help financial statement users to make better decisions.

SUMMARY OF LEARNING OBJECTIVES

1 Describe the usefulness of a conceptual framework. The accounting profession needs a conceptual framework to (1) build on and relate to an established body of concepts and objectives, (2) provide a framework for solving new and emerging practical problems, (3) increase financial statement users' understanding of and confidence in financial reporting, and (4) enhance comparability among companies' financial statements.

2 Describe efforts to construct a conceptual framework. The IASB's conceptual framework, The Conceptual Framework for Financial Reporting, is described in one document. The FASB's conceptual framework is developed in a series of concept statements. The IASB and the FASB are now working on a joint project to develop an improved common conceptual framework that provides a sound foundation for developing future accounting standards.

3 Understand the objective of financial reporting. The objective of general-purpose financial reporting is to provide financial information about the reporting entity that is **useful to present and potential equity investors, lenders, and other creditors** in making decisions about providing resources to the entity. Those decisions involve buying, selling, or holding equity and debt instruments, and providing or settling loans and other forms of credit. Information that is decision-useful to capital providers may also be helpful to other users of financial reporting who are not capital providers.

4 **Identify the qualitative characteristics of accounting information.** The overriding criterion by which accounting choices can be judged is decision-usefulness—that is, providing information that is most useful for decision-making. Relevance and faithful representation are the two fundamental qualities that make information decision-useful. Relevant information makes a difference in a decision by having predictive or confirmatory value and by being material. Faithful representation is characterized by completeness, neutrality, and being free from error. Enhancing qualities of useful information are (1) comparability, (2) verifiability, (3) timeliness, and (4) understandability.

5 **Define the basic elements of financial statements.** The basic elements of financial statements are (1) assets, (2) liabilities, (3) equity, (4) income, and (5) expenses. We define these elements on page 37.

6 **Describe the basic assumptions of accounting.** Five basic assumptions underlying financial accounting are as follows. (1) *Economic entity:* The activity of a company can be kept separate and distinct from its owners and any other business unit. (2) *Going concern:* Without information to the contrary, the company will have a long life. (3) *Monetary unit:* Money is the common denominator by which economic activity is conducted, and the monetary unit provides an appropriate basis for measurement and analysis. (4) *Periodicity:* The economic activities of a company can be divided into artificial time periods. (5) *Accrual basis:* Transactions that change a company's financial statements are recorded in the periods in which the events occur, rather than when cash is paid or received.

7 **Explain the application of the basic principles of accounting.** (1) *Measurement principle:* IFRS requires the use of historical cost or fair value depending on the situation. Although the historical cost principle (measurement based on acquisition price) continues to be an important basis for valuation, recording and reporting of fair value information is increasing. (2) *Revenue recognition principle:* A company generally recognizes revenue when it is probable that future economic benefits will flow to the entity, and reliable measurement of the amount of revenue is possible. (3) *Expense recognition principle:* As a general rule, companies recognize expenses when the service or the product actually makes its contribution to revenue (commonly referred to as *matching*). (4) *Full disclosure principle:* Companies generally provide information that is of sufficient importance to influence the judgment and decisions of an informed user.

8 **Describe the impact that the cost constraint has on reporting accounting information.** The cost of providing the information must be weighed against the benefits that can be derived from using the information.

IFRS   AUTHORITATIVE LITERATURE

Authoritative Literature References

[1] International Accounting Standard 8, *Accounting Policies, Changes in Accounting Estimates, and Errors* (London, U.K.: International Accounting Standards Committee Foundation, 2001).

[2] The Conceptual Framework for Financial Reporting (London, U.K.: IASB, 2010).

[3] The Conceptual Framework for Financial Reporting, "Chapter 1, The Objective of General Purpose Financial Reporting" (London, U.K.: IASB, September 2010).

[4] The Conceptual Framework for Financial Reporting, "Chapter 3, Qualitative Characteristics of Useful Financial Information" (London, U.K.: IASB, September 2010).

[5] The Conceptual Framework for Financial Reporting, "Chapter 4, The 1989 *Framework:* The Remaining Text" (London, U.K.: IASB, 2010), paras. 4.2–4.35.

[6] The Conceptual Framework for Financial Reporting, "Chapter 4, The 1989 *Framework:* The Remaining Text," (London, U.K.: IASB, September 2010), par. 43.

[7] International Accounting Standard No. 29, *Financial Reporting in Hyperinflationary Economies* (London, U.K.: IASB, 2001).

[8] The Conceptual Framework for Financial Reporting, "Chapter 1: The Objective of General Purpose Financial Reporting" (London, U.K.: IASB, 2010), par. OB 17.

[9] International Financial Reporting Standard 13, *Fair Value Measurement* (London, U.K.: IASB, 2011), par. 9.

[10] International Financial Reporting Standard 9, "Financial Instruments, Chapter 4: Classification" (London, U.K.: IASB 2010), paras. 4.1.5–4.1.6 and 4.2.2–4.2.3.

[11] The Conceptual Framework for Financial Reporting, "Chapter 4, The 1989 *Framework*: The Remaining Text" (London, U.K.: IASB, 2010), paras. 4.37–4.39.

QUESTIONS

1. What is a conceptual framework? Why is a conceptual framework necessary in financial accounting?

2. What is the primary objective of financial reporting?

3. What is meant by the term "qualitative characteristics of accounting information"?

4. Briefly describe the two fundamental qualities of useful accounting information.

5. How are materiality (and immateriality) related to the proper presentation of financial statements? What factors and measures should be considered in assessing the materiality of a misstatement in the presentation of a financial statement?

6. What are the enhancing qualities of the qualitative characteristics? What is the role of enhancing qualities in the Conceptual Framework?

7. According to the Conceptual Framework, the objective of financial reporting for business enterprises is based on the needs of the users of financial statements. Explain the level of sophistication that the IASB assumes about the users of financial statements.

8. What is the distinction between comparability and consistency?

9. Why is it necessary to develop a definitional framework for the basic elements of accounting?

10. What are the basic elements of the Conceptual Framework? Briefly describe the relationship between the "moment in time" and "period of time" elements.

11. What are the five basic assumptions that underlie the financial accounting structure?

12. The life of a business is divided into specific time periods, usually a year, to measure results of operations for each such time period and to portray financial conditions at the end of each period.

    (a) This practice is based on the accounting assumption that the life of the business consists of a series of time periods and that it is possible to measure accurately the results of operations for each period. Comment on the validity and necessity of this assumption.

    (b) What has been the effect of this practice on accounting? What is its relation to the accrual basis of accounting? What influence has it had on accounting entries and practices?

13. What is the basic accounting problem created by the monetary unit assumption when there is significant inflation? What appears to be the IASB position on a stable monetary unit?

14. The chairman of the board of directors of the company for which you are chief accountant has told you that he has little use for accounting figures based on historical cost. He believes that fair values are of far more significance to the board of directors than "out-of-date costs." Present some arguments to convince him that accounting data should still be based on historical cost.

15. What is the definition of fair value?

16. What is the fair value option? Explain how use of the fair value option reflects application of the fair value principle.

17. Briefly describe the fair value hierarchy.

18. Explain the revenue recognition principle.

19. What is a performance obligation, and how is it used to determine when revenue should be recognized?

20. What are the five steps used to determine the proper time to recognize revenue?

21. Selane Eatery operates a catering service specializing in business luncheons for large corporations. Selane requires customers to place their orders 2 weeks in advance of the scheduled events. Selane bills its customers on the tenth day of the month following the date of service and requires that payment be made within 30 days of the billing date. Conceptually, when should Selane recognize revenue related to its catering service?

22. Mogilny Company paid $135,000 for a machine. The Accumulated Depreciation account has a balance of $46,500 at the present time. The company could sell the machine today for $150,000. The company president believes that the company has a "right to this gain." What does the president mean by this statement? Do you agree?

23. Three expense recognition methods (associating cause and effect, systematic and rational allocation, and immediate recognition) were discussed in the chapter under the expense recognition principle. Indicate the basic nature of each of these expense recognition methods and give two examples of each.

24. Under what conditions should an item be recognized in the financial statements?

25. Briefly describe the types of information concerning financial position, income, and cash flows that might be provided (a) within the main body of the financial statements, (b) in the notes to the financial statements, or (c) as supplementary information.

26. In January 2015, Janeway Inc. doubled the amount of its outstanding shares by selling an additional 10,000 shares to finance an expansion of the business. You propose that this information be shown by a footnote to the statement of financial position as of December 31, 2015. The president objects, claiming that this sale took place after December 31, 2015, and, therefore, should not be shown. Explain your position.

27. Describe the major constraint inherent in the presentation of accounting information.

28. What are some of the costs of providing accounting information? What are some of the benefits of accounting information? Describe the cost-benefit factors that should be considered when new accounting standards are being proposed.

29. Do the IASB and U.S. GAAP conceptual frameworks differ in terms of fair value measurement? Explain.

30. How do the FASB and IASB conceptual frameworks differ in terms of the elements of financial statements?

31. What are some of the challenges to the FASB and IASB in developing a converged conceptual framework?

BRIEF EXERCISES

BE2-1 Match the qualitative characteristics below with the following statements.

1. Relevance
2. Faithful representation
3. Predictive value
4. Confirmatory value
5. Comparability
6. Completeness
7. Neutrality
8. Timeliness

(a) Quality of information that permits users to identify similarities in and differences between two sets of economic phenomena.
(b) Having information available to users before it loses its capacity to influence decisions.
(c) Information about an economic phenomenon that has value as an input to the processes used by capital providers to form their own expectations about the future.
(d) Information that is capable of making a difference in the decisions of users in their capacity as capital providers.
(e) Absence of bias intended to attain a predetermined result or to induce a particular behavior.

BE2-2 Match the qualitative characteristics below with the following statements.

1. Timeliness
2. Completeness
3. Free from error
4. Understandability
5. Faithful representation
6. Relevance
7. Neutrality
8. Confirmatory value

(a) Quality of information that assures users that information represents the economic phenomena that it purports to represent.
(b) Information about an economic phenomenon that changes past or present expectations based on previous evaluations.
(c) The extent to which information is accurate in representing the economic substance of a transaction.
(d) Includes all the information that is necessary for a faithful representation of the economic phenomena that it purports to represent.
(e) Quality of information that allows users to comprehend its meaning.

BE2-3 Discuss whether the changes described in each of the situations below require recognition in the audit report as to consistency. (Assume that the amounts are material.)

(a) The company changed its inventory method to FIFO from weighted-average, which had been used in prior years.
(b) The company disposed of one of the two subsidiaries that had been included in its consolidated statements for prior years.
(c) The estimated remaining useful life of plant property was reduced because of obsolescence.
(d) The company is using an inventory valuation method that is different from those used by all other companies in its industry.

4 **BE2-4** Identify which qualitative characteristic of accounting information is best described in each item below. (Do not use relevance and faithful representation.)

(a) The annual reports of **Best Buy Co.** (USA) are audited by certified public accountants.

(b) **Motorola** (USA) and **Nokia** (FIN) both use the FIFO cost flow assumption.

(c) **Starbucks Corporation** (USA) has used straight-line depreciation since it began operations.

(d) **Heineken Holdings** (NLD) issues its quarterly reports immediately after each quarter ends.

5 **BE2-5** Explain how you would decide whether to record each of the following expenditures as an asset or an expense. Assume all items are material.

(a) Legal fees paid in connection with the purchase of land are €1,500.

(b) Eduardo, Inc. paves the driveway leading to the office building at a cost of €21,000.

(c) A meat market purchases a meat-grinding machine at a cost of €3,500.

(d) On June 30, Monroe and Meno, medical doctors, pay 6 months' office rent to cover the month of July and the next 5 months.

(e) Smith's Hardware Company pays €9,000 in wages to laborers for construction on a building to be used in the business.

(f) Alvarez's Florists pays wages of €2,100 for November to an employee who serves as driver of their delivery truck.

5 **BE2-6** For each item below, indicate to which category of elements of financial statements it belongs.

(a) Retained earnings.

(b) Sales.

(c) Share Premium.

(d) Inventory.

(e) Depreciation.

(f) Loss on sale of equipment.

(g) Interest payable.

(h) Dividends.

(i) Gain on sale of investment.

(j) Issuance of ordinary shares.

6 **BE2-7** If the going concern assumption is not made in accounting, discuss the differences in the amounts shown in the financial statements for the following items.

(a) Land.

(b) Depreciation expense on equipment.

(c) Inventory.

(d) Prepaid insurance.

6 **BE2-8** Identify which basic assumption of accounting is best described in each of the following items.

(a) The economic activities of **FedEx Corporation** (USA) are divided into 12-month periods for the purpose of issuing annual reports.

(b) **Total S.A.** (FRA) does not adjust amounts in its financial statements for the effects of inflation.

(c) **Barclays** (GBR) reports current and non-current classifications in its statement of financial position.

(d) The economic activities of **Tokai Rubber Industries** (JPN) and its subsidiaries are merged for accounting and reporting purposes.

7 **BE2-9** Identify which basic principle of accounting is best described in each item below.

(a) **Parmalat** (ITA) reports revenue in its income statement when it delivers goods instead of when the cash is collected.

(b) **Google** (USA) recognizes depreciation expense for a machine over the 2-year period during which that machine helps the company earn revenue.

(c) **Oracle Corporation** (USA) reports information about pending lawsuits in the notes to its financial statements.

(d) **Fuji Film** (JPN) reports land on its statement of financial position at the amount paid to acquire it, even though the estimated fair value is greater.

7 **BE2-10** Vande Velde Company made three investments during 2015. (1) It purchased 1,000 shares of Sastre Company, a start-up company. Vande Velde made the investment based on valuation estimates from an internally developed model. (2) It purchased 2,000 shares of **Fuji Film** (JPN), which trades on the Nikkei. (3) It invested $10,000 in local development authority bonds. Although these bonds do not trade on an active market, their value closely tracks movements in U.S. Treasury bonds. Rank these three investments in terms of the verifiability of fair value.

4 **BE2-11** Presented below are three different transactions related to materiality. Explain whether you would classify these transactions as material.

(a) Blair Co. has reported a positive trend in earnings over the last 3 years. In the current year, it reduces its bad debt expense to ensure another positive earnings year. The impact of this adjustment is equal to 3% of net income.

(b) Hindi Co. has a gain of €3.1 million on the sale of plant assets and a €3.3 million loss on the sale of investments. It decides to net the gain and loss because the net effect is considered immaterial. Hindi Co.'s income for the current year was €10 million.

(c) Damon Co. expenses all capital equipment under €2,500 on the basis that it is immaterial. The company has followed this practice for a number of years.

6 7 BE2-12 What accounting assumption, principle, or constraint would Marks and Spencer plc (M&S) (GBR)
8 use in each of the situations below?

(a) M&S records expenses when incurred, rather than when cash is paid.

(b) M&S was involved in litigation over the last year. This litigation is disclosed in the financial statements.

(c) M&S allocates the cost of its depreciable assets over the life it expects to receive revenue from these assets.

(d) M&S records the purchase of a new Lenovo (CHN) PC at its cash equivalent price.

3 4 BE2-13 Fill in the blanks related to the following statements.

8 1. Financial reporting imposes _____; the benefits of financial reporting should justify those _____.

2. The information provided by _____ _____ _____ _____ focuses on the needs of all capital providers, not just the needs of a particular group.

3. A depiction of economic phenomena is _____ if it includes all the information that is necessary for faithful representation of the economic phenomena that it purports to represent.

4. _____ is the quality of information that allows users to comprehend its meaning.

5. _____ is the quality of information that permits users to identify similarities in and differences between two sets of economic phenomena.

6. Information about economic phenomena has _____ _____ if it confirms or changes past or present expectations based on previous evaluations.

EXERCISES

1 3 E2-1 (Usefulness, Objective of Financial Reporting) Indicate whether the following statements about the Conceptual Framework are true or false. If false, provide a brief explanation supporting your position.

(a) Accounting rule-making that relies on a body of concepts will result in useful and consistent pronouncements.

(b) General-purpose financial reports are most useful to company insiders in making strategic business decisions.

(c) Accounting standards based on individual conceptual frameworks generally will result in consistent and comparable accounting reports.

(d) Capital providers are the only users who benefit from general-purpose financial reporting.

(e) Accounting reports should be developed so that users without knowledge of economics and business can become informed about the financial results of a company.

(f) The objective of financial reporting is the foundation from which the other aspects of the framework logically result.

1 3 E2-2 (Usefulness, Objective of Financial Reporting, Qualitative Characteristics) Indicate whether the
4 following statements about the Conceptual Framework are true or false. If false, provide a brief explanation supporting your position.

(a) The fundamental qualitative characteristics that make accounting information useful are relevance and verifiability.

(b) Relevant information has predictive value, confirmatory value, or both.

(c) Conservatism, a prudent reaction to uncertainty, is considered a constraint of financial reporting.

(d) Information that is a faithful representation is characterized as having predictive or confirmatory value.

(e) Comparability pertains only to the reporting of information in a similar manner for different companies.

(f) Verifiability is solely an enhancing characteristic for faithful representation.

(g) In preparing financial reports, it is assumed that users of the reports have reasonable knowledge of business and economic activities.

4 **8** **E2-3 (Qualitative Characteristics)** The Conceptual Framework identifies the qualitative characteristics that make accounting information useful. Presented below are a number of questions related to these qualitative characteristics and underlying constraint.

    (a) What is the quality of information that enables users to confirm or correct prior expectations?

    (b) Identify the overall or pervasive constraint developed in the Conceptual Framework.

    (c) A noted accountant once remarked, "If it becomes accepted or expected that accounting principles are determined or modified in order to secure purposes other than economic measurement, we assume a grave risk that confidence in the credibility of our financial information system will be undermined." Which qualitative characteristic of accounting information should ensure that such a situation will not occur? (Do not use faithful representation.)

    (d) Muruyama Group switches from FIFO to average-cost and then back to FIFO over a 2-year period. Which qualitative characteristic of accounting information is not followed?

    (e) Assume that the profession permits the savings and loan industry to defer losses on investments it sells, because immediate recognition of the loss may have adverse economic consequences on the industry. Which qualitative characteristic of accounting information is not followed? (Do not use relevance or faithful representation.)

    (f) What are the two fundamental qualities that make accounting information useful for decision-making?

    (g) Watteau Inc. does not issue its first-quarter report until after the second quarter's results are reported. Which qualitative characteristic of accounting is not followed? (Do not use relevance.)

    (h) Predictive value is an ingredient of which of the two fundamental qualities that make accounting information useful for decision-making purposes?

    (i) Duggan, Inc. is the only company in its industry to depreciate its plant assets on a straight-line basis. Which qualitative characteristic of accounting information may not be present?

    (j) Nadal Company has attempted to determine the replacement cost of its inventory. Three different appraisers arrive at substantially different amounts for this value. The president, nevertheless, decides to report the middle value for external reporting purposes. Which qualitative characteristic of information is lacking in these data? (Do not use reliability or representational faithfulness.)

4 **E2-4 (Qualitative Characteristics)** The qualitative characteristics that make accounting information useful for decision-making purposes are as follows.

Relevance	Neutrality	Verifiability
Faithful representation	Completeness	Understandability
Predictive value	Timeliness	Comparability
Confirmatory value	Materiality	Free from error

Instructions

Identify the appropriate qualitative characteristic(s) to be used given the information provided below.

    (a) Qualitative characteristic being displayed when companies in the same industry are using the same accounting principles.

    (b) Quality of information that confirms users' earlier expectations.

    (c) Imperative for providing comparisons of a company from period to period.

    (d) Ignores the economic consequences of a standard or rule.

    (e) Requires a high degree of consensus among individuals on a given measurement.

    (f) Predictive value is an ingredient of this fundamental quality of information.

    (g) Four qualitative characteristics that enhance both relevance and faithful representation.

    (h) An item is not reported because its effect on income would not change a decision.

    (i) Neutrality is a key ingredient of this fundamental quality of accounting information.

    (j) Two fundamental qualities that make accounting information useful for decision-making purposes.

    (k) Issuance of interim reports is an example of what enhancing ingredient?

5 **E2-5 (Elements of Financial Statements)** Five interrelated elements that are most directly related to measuring the performance and financial status of an enterprise are provided below.

Assets	Income
Liabilities	Expenses
Equity	

Instructions

Identify the element or elements associated with the following nine items.

    (a) Obligation to transfer resources arising from a past transaction.

    (b) Increases ownership interest by issuance of shares.

    (c) Declares and pays cash dividends to owners.

    (d) Increases in net assets in a period from non-owner sources.

 (e) Items characterized by service potential or future economic benefit.
 (f) Equals increase in assets less liabilities during the year, after adding distributions to owners and subtracting investments by owners.
 (g) Residual interest in the assets of the enterprise after deducting its liabilities.
 (h) Increases assets during a period through sale of product.
 (i) Decreases assets during the period by purchasing the company's own shares.

6 7 8 E2-6 (Assumptions, Principles, and Constraint) Presented below are the assumptions, principles, and constraint used in this chapter.

1. Economic entity assumption	**6.** Historical cost principle	**10.** Revenue recognition principle
2. Going concern assumption	**7.** Fair value principle	
3. Monetary unit assumption	**8.** Expense recognition principle	**11.** Cost constraint
4. Periodicity assumption	**9.** Full disclosure principle	
5. Accrual-basis assumption		

Instructions
Identify by number the accounting assumption, principle, or constraint that describes each situation below. Do not use a number more than once.

 (a) Allocates expenses to revenues in the proper period.
 (b) Indicates that fair value changes subsequent to purchase are not recorded in the accounts. (Do not use revenue recognition principle.)
 (c) Ensures that all relevant financial information is reported.
 (d) Rationale why plant assets are not reported at liquidation value. (Do not use historical cost principle.)
 (e) Generally records revenue at the point of sale.
 (f) Indicates that personal and business record keeping should be separately maintained.
 (g) Separates financial information into time periods for reporting purposes.
 (h) Permits the use of fair value valuation in certain situations.
 (i) Assumes that the yen is the "measuring stick" used to report on financial performance of a Japanese company.

6 7 8 E2-7 (Assumptions, Principles, and Constraint) Presented below are a number of operational guidelines and practices that have developed over time.

Instructions
Select the assumption, principle, or constraint that most appropriately justifies these procedures and practices. (Do not use qualitative characteristics.)

 (a) Fair value changes are not recognized in the accounting records.
 (b) Accounts receivable are recorded for sales on account rather than waiting until cash is received.
 (c) Financial information is presented so that investors will not be misled.
 (d) Intangible assets are capitalized and amortized over periods benefited.
 (e) Brokerage companies use fair value for purposes of valuing financial securities.
 (f) Each enterprise is kept as a unit distinct from its owner or owners.
 (g) All significant post-statement of financial position events are reported.
 (h) Revenue is recorded at point of sale.
 (i) All important aspects of bond indentures are presented in financial statements.
 (j) Rationale for accrual accounting.
 (k) The use of consolidated statements is justified.
 (l) Reporting must be done at defined time intervals.
 (m) An allowance for doubtful accounts is established.
 (n) All payments out of petty cash are charged to Miscellaneous Expense.
 (o) Goodwill is recorded only at time of purchase.
 (p) Cash received and paid is not the basis used to recognize revenues and expenses.
 (q) A company charges its sales commission costs to expense.

7 E2-8 (Full Disclosure Principle) The following facts relate to Weller, Inc. Assume that no mention of these facts was made in the financial statements and the related notes.

Instructions
Assume that you are the auditor of Weller, Inc. and that you have been asked to explain the appropriate accounting and related disclosure necessary for each of these items.

 (a) The company decided that, for the sake of conciseness, only net income should be reported on the income statement. Details as to revenues, cost of goods sold, and expenses were omitted.

(b) Equipment purchases of €170,000 were partly financed during the year through the issuance of a €110,000 notes payable. The company offset the equipment against the notes payable and reported plant assets at €60,000.

(c) Weller has reported its ending inventory at €2,100,000 in the financial statements. No other information related to inventories is presented in the financial statements and related notes.

(d) The company changed its method of valuing inventories from weighted-average to FIFO. No mention of this change was made in the financial statements.

7 ▶ **E2-9 (Accounting Principles—Comprehensive)** Presented below are a number of business transactions that occurred during the current year for Gonzales, Inc.

Instructions

In each of the situations, discuss the appropriateness of the journal entries.

(a) The president of Gonzales, Inc. used his expense account to purchase a new Suburban solely for personal use. The following journal entry was made.

Miscellaneous Expense	29,000	
Cash		29,000

(b) Merchandise inventory that cost €620,000 is reported on the statement of financial position at €690,000, the expected selling price less estimated selling costs. The following entry was made to record this increase in value.

Inventory	70,000	
Sales Revenue		70,000

(c) The company is being sued for €500,000 by a customer who claims damages for personal injury apparently caused by a defective product. Company attorneys feel extremely confident that the company will have no liability for damages resulting from the situation. Nevertheless, the company decides to make the following entry.

Loss from Lawsuit	500,000	
Liability for Lawsuit		500,000

(d) Because the general level of prices increased during the current year, Gonzales, Inc. determined that there was a €16,000 understatement of depreciation expense on its equipment and decided to record it in its accounts. The following entry was made.

Depreciation Expense	16,000	
Accumulated Depreciation—Equipment		16,000

(e) Gonzales, Inc. has been concerned about whether intangible assets could generate cash in case of liquidation. As a consequence, goodwill arising from a purchase transaction during the current year and recorded at €800,000 was written off as follows.

Retained Earnings	800,000	
Goodwill		800,000

(f) Because of a "fire sale," equipment obviously worth €200,000 was acquired at a cost of €155,000. The following entry was made.

Equipment	200,000	
Cash		155,000
Sales Revenue		45,000

7 ▶ **E2-10 (Accounting Principles—Comprehensive)** The following information relates to Wang Group.

Instructions

Comment on the appropriateness of the accounting procedures followed by Wang Group.

(a) Depreciation expense on the building for the year was ¥60,000. Because the building was increasing in value during the year, the controller decided to charge the depreciation expense to retained earnings instead of to net income. The following entry is recorded.

Retained Earnings	60,000	
Accumulated Depreciation—Buildings		60,000

(b) Materials were purchased on January 1, 2015, for ¥120,000 and this amount was entered in the Materials account. On December 31, 2015, the materials would have cost ¥141,000, so the following entry is made.

Inventory	21,000	
Gain on Inventories		21,000

(c) During the year, the company purchased equipment through the issuance of ordinary shares. The shares had a par value of ¥135,000 and a fair value of ¥450,000. The fair value of the equipment was not easily determinable. The company recorded this transaction as follows.

Equipment	135,000	
Share Capital		135,000

(d) During the year, the company sold certain equipment for ¥285,000, recognizing a gain of ¥69,000. Because the controller believed that new equipment would be needed in the near future, she decided to defer the gain and amortize it over the life of any new equipment purchased.

(e) An order for ¥61,500 has been received from a customer for products on hand. This order was shipped on January 9, 2015. The company made the following entry in 2014.

Accounts Receivable	61,500	
Sales Revenue		61,500

CONCEPTS FOR ANALYSIS

CA2-1 (Conceptual Framework—General) Wayne Cooper has some questions regarding the theoretical framework in which IFRS is established. He knows that the IASB has attempted to develop a conceptual framework for accounting theory formulation. Yet, Wayne's supervisors have indicated that these theoretical frameworks have little value in the practical sense (i.e., in the real world). Wayne did notice that accounting rules seem to be established after the fact rather than before. He thought this indicated a lack of theory structure but never really questioned the process at school because he was too busy doing the homework.

Wayne feels that some of his anxiety about accounting theory and accounting semantics could be alleviated by identifying the basic concepts and definitions accepted by the profession and considering them in light of his current work. By doing this, he hopes to develop an appropriate connection between theory and practice.

Instructions
(a) Help Wayne recognize the purpose of a conceptual framework.
(b) Identify the benefits that arise from a conceptual framework.

CA2-2 (Conceptual Framework—General) The IASB's Conceptual Framework for Financial Reporting sets forth the objective and fundamentals that will be the basis for developing financial accounting and reporting standards. The objective identifies the purpose of financial reporting. The fundamentals are the underlying concepts of financial accounting that guide the selection of transactions, events, and circumstances to be accounted for; their recognition and measurement; and the means of summarizing and communicating them to interested parties.

The characteristics or qualities of information discussed in the Conceptual Framework are the concepts that make information useful and the qualities to be sought when accounting choices are made.

Instructions
(a) Identify and discuss the benefits that can be expected to be derived from the Conceptual Framework.
(b) What is the most important quality for accounting information as identified in the Conceptual Framework? Explain why it is the most important.
(c) Briefly discuss the importance of any three of the fundamental characteristics or enhancing qualities of accounting information.

CA2-3 (Objective of Financial Reporting) Homer Winslow and Jane Alexander are discussing various aspects of the Conceptual Framework. Homer indicates that this pronouncement provides little, if any, guidance to the practicing professional in resolving accounting controversies. He believes that the Conceptual Framework provides such broad guidelines that it would be impossible to apply the objective(s) to present-day reporting problems. Jane concedes this point but indicates that objective(s) are still needed to provide a starting point for the IASB in helping to improve financial reporting.

Instructions
(a) Indicate the basic objective established in the Conceptual Framework.
(b) What do you think is the meaning of Jane's statement that the IASB needs a starting point to resolve accounting controversies about how to improve financial reporting?

CA2-4 (Qualitative Characteristics) Accounting information provides useful information about business transactions and events. Those who provide and use financial reports must often select and evaluate accounting alternatives. The Conceptual Framework examines the characteristics of accounting information that make it useful for decision-making. It also points out that various limitations inherent in the measurement and reporting process may necessitate trade-offs or sacrifices among the characteristics of useful information.

Instructions

(a) Describe briefly the following characteristics of useful accounting information.
   - **(1)** Relevance.
   - **(2)** Faithful representation.
   - **(3)** Understandability.
   - **(4)** Comparability (consistency).
   - **(5)** Neutrality.

(b) For each of the following pairs of information characteristics, give an example of a situation in which one of the characteristics may be sacrificed in return for a gain in the other.
   - **(1)** Relevance and faithful representation.
   - **(2)** Relevance and consistency.
   - **(3)** Comparability and consistency.
   - **(4)** Relevance and understandability.

(c) What criterion should be used to evaluate trade-offs between information characteristics?

CA2-5 (Revenue Recognition Principle) After the presentation of your report on the examination of the financial statements to the board of directors of Piper Publishing Company, one of the new directors expresses surprise that the income statement assumes that an equal proportion of the revenue is earned with the publication of every issue of the company's magazine. She feels that the "crucial event" in the process of recognizing revenue in the magazine business is the cash sale of the subscription. She says that she does not understand why most of the revenue cannot be recognized in the period of the sale.

Instructions

Discuss the propriety of timing the recognition of revenue in Piper Publishing Company's accounts with respect to the following.

(a) The cash sale of the magazine subscription.

(b) The publication of the magazine every month.

(c) Both events, by recognizing a portion of the revenue with the cash sale of the magazine subscription and a portion of the revenue with the publication of the magazine every month.

CA2-6 (Expense Recognition Principle) An accountant must be familiar with the concepts involved in determining earnings of a business entity. The amount of earnings reported for a business entity is dependent on the proper recognition, in general, of revenue and expense for a given time period. In some situations, costs are recognized as expenses at the time of product sale. In other situations, guidelines have been developed for recognizing costs as expenses or losses by other criteria.

Instructions

(a) Explain the rationale for recognizing costs as expenses at the time of product sale.

(b) What is the rationale underlying the appropriateness of treating costs as expenses of a period instead of assigning the costs to an asset? Explain.

(c) In what general circumstances would it be appropriate to treat a cost as an asset instead of as an expense? Explain.

(d) Some expenses are assigned to specific accounting periods on the basis of systematic and rational allocation of asset cost. Explain the underlying rationale for recognizing expenses on the basis of systematic and rational allocation of asset cost.

(e) Identify the conditions under which it would be appropriate to treat a cost as a loss.

CA2-7 (Expense Recognition Principle) Daniel Barenboim sells and erects shell houses, that is, frame structures that are completely finished on the outside but are unfinished on the inside except for flooring, partition studding, and ceiling joists. Shell houses are sold chiefly to customers who are handy with tools and who have time to do the interior wiring, plumbing, wall completion and finishing, and other work necessary to make the shell houses livable dwellings.

Barenboim buys shell houses from a manufacturer in unassembled packages consisting of all lumber, roofing, doors, windows, and similar materials necessary to complete a shell house. Upon commencing operations in a new area, Barenboim buys or leases land as a site for his local warehouse, field office, and display houses. Sample display houses are erected at a total cost of $30,000 to $44,000 including the cost of the unassembled packages. The chief element of cost of the display houses is the unassembled packages, inasmuch as erection is a short, low-cost operation. Old sample models are torn down or altered into new models every 3 to 7 years. Sample display houses have little salvage value because dismantling and moving costs amount to nearly as much as the cost of an unassembled package.

Instructions

(a) A choice must be made between (1) expensing the costs of sample display houses in the periods in which the expenditure is made and (2) spreading the costs over more than one period. Discuss the advantages of each method.

(b) Would it be preferable to amortize the cost of display houses on the basis of (1) the passage of time or (2) the number of shell houses sold? Explain.

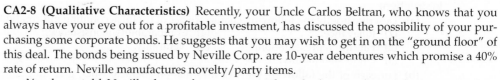

CA2-8 (Qualitative Characteristics) Recently, your Uncle Carlos Beltran, who knows that you always have your eye out for a profitable investment, has discussed the possibility of your purchasing some corporate bonds. He suggests that you may wish to get in on the "ground floor" of this deal. The bonds being issued by Neville Corp. are 10-year debentures which promise a 40% rate of return. Neville manufactures novelty/party items.

You have told Neville that, unless you can take a look at its financial statements, you would not feel comfortable about such an investment. Believing that this is the chance of a lifetime, Uncle Carlos has procured a copy of Neville's most recent, unaudited financial statements which are a year old. These statements were prepared by Mrs. Andy Neville. You peruse these statements, and they are quite impressive. The statement of financial position showed a debt to equity ratio of 0.10 and, for the year shown, the company reported net income of €2,424,240.

The financial statements are not shown in comparison with amounts from other years. In addition, no significant note disclosures about inventory valuation, depreciation methods, loan agreements, etc. are available.

Instructions

Write a letter to Uncle Carlos explaining why it would be unwise to base an investment decision on the financial statements that he has provided to you. Be sure to explain why these financial statements are neither relevant nor a faithful representation.

CA2-9 (Expense Recognition Principle) Anderson Nuclear Power Plant will be "mothballed" at the end of its useful life (approximately 20 years) at great expense. Accountants Ana Alicia and Ed Bradley argue whether it is better to allocate the expense of mothballing over the next 20 years or ignore it until mothballing occurs.

Instructions

Answer the following questions.

(a) What stakeholders should be considered?

(b) What ethical issue, if any, underlies the dispute?

(c) What alternatives should be considered?

(d) Assess the consequences of the alternatives.

(e) What decision would you recommend?

CA2-10 (Cost Constraint) A Special Committee on Financial Reporting proposed the following constraints related to financial reporting.

1. Business reporting should exclude information outside of management's expertise or for which management is not the best source, such as information about competitors.

2. Management should not be required to report information that would significantly harm the company's competitive position.

3. Management should not be required to provide forecasted financial statements. Rather, management should provide information that helps users forecast for themselves the company's financial future.

4. Other than for financial statements, management need report only the information it knows. That is, management should be under no obligation to gather information it does not have, or does not need, to manage the business.

5. Companies should present certain elements of business reporting only if users and management agree they should be reported—a concept of flexible reporting.

6. Companies should not have to report forward-looking information unless there are effective deterrents to unwarranted litigation that discourages companies from doing so.

Instructions

For each item, briefly discuss how the proposed constraint addresses concerns about the costs and benefits of financial reporting.

USING YOUR JUDGMENT

FINANCIAL REPORTING

Financial Reporting Problem

Marks and Spencer plc (M&S)

The financial statements of **M&S** (GBR) are presented in Appendix A. The company's complete annual report, including the notes to the financial statements, is available online.

Instructions

Refer to M&S's financial statements and the accompanying notes to answer the following questions.

(a) Using the notes to the consolidated financial statements, determine M&S's revenue recognition policies.

(b) Give two examples of where historical cost information is reported in M&S's financial statements and related notes. Give two examples of the use of fair value information reported in either the financial statements or related notes.

(c) How can we determine that the accounting principles used by M&S are prepared on a basis consistent with those of last year?

(d) What is M&S's accounting policy related to refunds and loyalty schemes? Why does M&S include the accounting for refunds and loyalty schemes in its Critical accounting estimates and judgments?

Comparative Analysis Case

adidas and Puma

The financial statements of **adidas** (DEU) and **Puma** (DEU) are presented in Appendices B and C, respectively. The complete annual reports, including the notes to the financial statements, are available online.

Instructions

Use the companies' financial information to answer the following questions.

(a) Briefly discuss the currency used by each company in its financial statements. Does the currency used affect the comparability of their reports? Briefly explain.

(b) What are the primary segments or product groups of these two companies as shown in their notes to the financial statements?

(c) How are inventories for these two companies valued? What cost allocation method is used to report inventory? How does their accounting for inventories affect comparability between the two companies?

(d) Which company changed its accounting policies, which then affected the consistency of the financial results from the previous year? What were these changes?

Financial Statement Analysis Case

Nokia (FIN) provided the following disclosure in a recent annual report.

Use of Estimates (Partial)

The preparation of financial statements in conformity with IFRS requires the application of judgment by management in selecting appropriate assumptions for calculating financial estimates, which inherently contain some degree of uncertainty. . . . (below and on the next page) are areas requiring significant judgment and estimation that may have an impact on reported results and the financial position.

Revenue Recognition

Sales from the majority of the Group are recognized when the significant risks and rewards of ownership have transferred to the buyer, continuing managerial involvement usually associated with ownership and effective control have ceased, the amount of revenue can be measured reliably, it is probable that economic benefits associated with the transaction will flow to the Group and the costs incurred or to be incurred in respect of the transaction can be measured reliably. Sales may materially change if management's assessment of such criteria was determined to be inaccurate. The Group makes price protection adjustments based on estimates of future price reductions and certain agreed customer inventories at the date of the price adjustment. Possible changes in these estimates could result in revisions to the sales in future periods.

Revenue from contracts involving solutions achieved through modification of complex telecommunications equipment is recognized on the percentage of completion basis when the outcome of the contract can be estimated reliably. Recognized revenues and profits are subject to revisions during the project in the event that the assumptions regarding the overall project outcome are revised. Current sales and profit estimates for projects may materially change due to the early stage of a longterm project, new technology, changes in the project scope, changes in costs, changes in timing, changes in customers' plans, realization of penalties, and other corresponding factors.

Instructions

(a) Briefly discuss how Nokia's revenue recognition policies are consistent with the revenue recognition principle. Evaluate both:
   1. Sales.
   2. Revenue from contracts.
(b) Briefly discuss how estimates inherent in Nokia's revenue recognition policies can result in reported revenue numbers that are not relevant and faithful representations.
(c) Assume that Nokia's competitors use similar revenue recognition policies for their sales. What are some of the judgments inherent in applying those policies that could raise concerns with respect to the qualitative characteristic of comparability?

Accounting, Analysis, and Principles

William Murray achieved one of his life-long dreams by opening his own business, The Caddie Shack Driving Range, on May 1, 2015. He invested $20,000 of his own savings in the business. He paid $6,000 cash to have a small building constructed to house the operations and spent $800 on golf clubs, golf balls, and yardage signs. Murray leased 4 acres of land at a cost of $1,000 per month. (He paid the first month's rent in cash.) During the first month, advertising costs totaled $750, of which $150 was unpaid at the end of the month. Murray paid his three nephews $400 for retrieving golf balls. He deposited in the company's bank account all revenues from customers ($4,700). On May 15, Murray withdrew $800 in cash for personal use. On May 31, the company received a utility bill for $100 but did not immediately pay it. On May 31, the balance in the company bank account was $15,100.

Murray is feeling pretty good about results for the first month, but his estimate of profitability ranges from a loss of $4,900 to a profit of $2,450.

Accounting

Prepare a statement of financial position at May 31, 2015. (Murray appropriately records any depreciation expense on a quarterly basis.) How could Murray have determined that the business operated at a profit of $2,450? How could Murray conclude that the business operated at a loss of $4,900?

Analysis

Assume Murray has asked you to become a partner in his business. Under the partnership agreement, after paying him $10,000, you would share equally in all future profits. Which of the two income measures above would be more useful in deciding whether to become a partner? Explain.

Principles

What is income according to IFRS? What concepts do the differences in the three income measures for The Caddie Shack Driving Range illustrate?

IFRS BRIDGE TO THE PROFESSION

Professional Research

Your aunt recently received the annual report for a company in which she has invested. The report notes that the statements have been prepared in accordance with IFRS. She has also heard that certain terms have special meanings in accounting relative to everyday use. She would like you to explain the meaning of terms she has come across related to accounting.

Instructions

Access the Conceptual Framework at the IASB website (*http://eifrs.iasb.org/*) (you may register for free eIFRS access at this site). When you have accessed the documents, you can use the search tool in your Internet browser to prepare responses to the following items. (Provide paragraph citations.)

(a) How is "materiality" defined in the Conceptual Framework?

(b) Briefly discuss the role of completeness as it relates to faithful representation.

(c) Your aunt observes that under IFRS, the financial statements are prepared on the accrual basis. According to the Conceptual Framework, what does the "accrual basis" mean?

Professional Simulation

In this simulation, you are asked to address questions regarding the Conceptual Framework. Prepare responses to all parts.

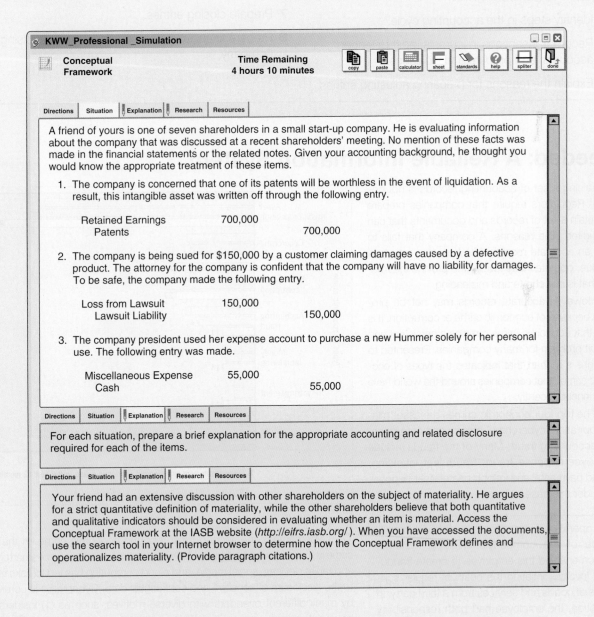

KWW_Professional_Simulation

Conceptual Framework

Time Remaining
4 hours 10 minutes

copy | paste | calculator | sheet | standards | help | spliter | done

Directions | Situation | Explanation | Research | Resources

A friend of yours is one of seven shareholders in a small start-up company. He is evaluating information about the company that was discussed at a recent shareholders' meeting. No mention of these facts was made in the financial statements or the related notes. Given your accounting background, he thought you would know the appropriate treatment of these items.

1. The company is concerned that one of its patents will be worthless in the event of liquidation. As a result, this intangible asset was written off through the following entry.

| Retained Earnings | 700,000 | |
| Patents | | 700,000 |

2. The company is being sued for $150,000 by a customer claiming damages caused by a defective product. The attorney for the company is confident that the company will have no liability for damages. To be safe, the company made the following entry.

| Loss from Lawsuit | 150,000 | |
| Lawsuit Liability | | 150,000 |

3. The company president used her expense account to purchase a new Hummer solely for her personal use. The following entry was made.

| Miscellaneous Expense | 55,000 | |
| Cash | | 55,000 |

Directions | Situation | Explanation | Research | Resources

For each situation, prepare a brief explanation for the appropriate accounting and related disclosure required for each of the items.

Directions | Situation | Explanation | Research | Resources

Your friend had an extensive discussion with other shareholders on the subject of materiality. He argues for a strict quantitative definition of materiality, while the other shareholders believe that both quantitative and qualitative indicators should be considered in evaluating whether an item is material. Access the Conceptual Framework at the IASB website (*http://eifrs.iasb.org/*). When you have accessed the documents, use the search tool in your Internet browser to determine how the Conceptual Framework defines and operationalizes materiality. (Provide paragraph citations.)

Remember to check the book's companion website, at www.wiley.com/college/kieso, to find additional resources for this chapter.

3 The Accounting Information System

Needed: A Reliable Information System

Maintaining a set of accounting records is not optional. Regulators require that companies prepare and retain a set of records and documents that can be audited. The reasons: A company that fails to keep an accurate record of its business may lose revenue, operate ineffectively, and provide information that is inaccurate and misleading.

However, accurate records may not be provided because of economic crime or corruption. It is clear that economic crime remains a persistent and difficult problem for many companies. Presented to the right is a chart that indicates the types of economic crimes that companies around the world have experienced recently.

The top four economic crimes are asset misappropriation, cybercrime, bribery and corruption, and accounting fraud. Many of the frauds include employee expense fraud, fraudulent invoicing, related payments, and inappropriate asset disposal. Consider this case example:

An operational manager had detailed knowledge of the company's invoicing systems, which enabled this employee to create fraudulent invoices inflating the costs of regular supplies of goods and services from a third party. In addition, the employee had both responsibility for the management of asset disposal and the ability to write down the asset to minimal value. The asset was then sold on the secondary market for a significant profit for the manager.

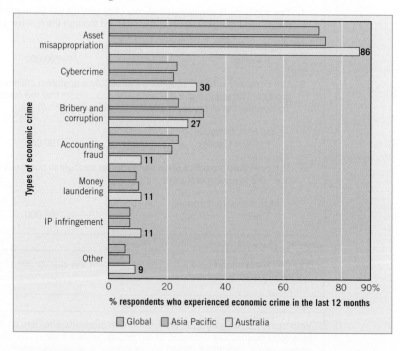

Cybercrime is the second most reported economic crime. In the past, crime in this area was negligible. However, the increased usage of smartphones and tablet devices, social media, and cloud computing has led to risks related to the disclosure of sensitive and confidential data. Cybercrime is committed by many different offenders with diverse motives, such as (1) insiders who have authorized access and then abuse this access for personal gain; (2) competitors seeking unfair advantage; (3) foreign governments committing espionage for political or economic gain; (4) transnational criminal enterprises stealing or extorting information to generate income; and (5) activists protesting organizational actions or policies.

Here is a second case study:

Fraudsters at offshore locations produced a spoofed email from a computer, compromised a website, distributed malicious PDF documents and other URL links, and downloaded software to the company's network without approval. This software gave the fraudsters access to the company's corporate network.

🔍 **CONCEPTUAL FOCUS**

> See the **Underlying Concepts** on pages 72, 73, and 79.

INTERNATIONAL FOCUS

> Read the **Global Accounting Insights** on pages 99–100 for a discussion of accounting information systems worldwide and international auditing standards.

Finally, although the situations are much rarer, large companies sometimes fail to keep an accurate record of their business transactions. Consider **Adecco** (USA), the largest international employment services company, which confirmed existence of weaknesses in its internal controls systems and Adecco staffing operations in certain countries. Manipulation involved such matters as reconciliation of payroll bank accounts, accounts receivable, and documentation in revenue recognition. These irregularities forced an indefinite delay in reporting the company's income figures, which led to significant decline in its share price. Or, consider **Nortel Networks Corp.** (CAN), which overstated and understated its reserve accounts to manage its earnings. This eventually led to the liquidation of the company.

What this all means is that internal controls must be in place to ensure that relevant and accurate information is provided. To do otherwise leaves a company open to fraud or information systems that are often susceptible to errors and other irregularities.

Sources: Adapted from "Cybercrime: Out of Obscurity and into Reality," *Sixth Annual Global Economic Crime Survey* (PricewaterhouseCoopers, 2012); and "Cybercrime: Protecting against the Growing Threat," *Global Economic Crime Survey* (PricewaterhouseCoopers, 2012).

PREVIEW OF CHAPTER | **3**

As the opening story indicates, a reliable information system is a necessity for all companies. The purpose of this chapter is to explain and illustrate the features of an accounting information system. The content and organization of this chapter are as follows.

The Accounting Information System		
Accounting Information System	**The Accounting Cycle**	**Financial Statements for Merchandisers**
• Basic terminology • Debits and credits • Accounting equation • Financial statements and ownership structure	• Identifying and recording • Journalizing • Posting • Trial balance • Adjusting entries • Adjusted trial balance • Preparing financial statements • Closing • Post-closing trial balance • Reversing entries	• Income statement • Retained earnings statement • Statement of financial position • Closing entries

---

ACCOUNTING INFORMATION SYSTEM

An **accounting information system** collects and processes transaction data and then disseminates the financial information to interested parties. Accounting information systems vary widely from one business to another. Various factors shape these systems: the nature of the business and the transactions in which it engages, the size of the firm, the volume of data to be handled, and the informational demands that management and others require.

As we discussed in the opening story, companies are placing a renewed focus on their accounting systems to ensure relevant and representationally faithful information is reported in financial statements. A good accounting information system helps management answer such questions as:

- How much and what kind of debt is outstanding?
- Were our sales higher this period than last?
- What assets do we have?
- What were our cash inflows and outflows?
- Did we make a profit last period?
- Are any of our product lines or divisions operating at a loss?
- Can we safely increase our dividends to shareholders?
- Is our rate of return on net assets increasing?

Management can answer many other questions with the data provided by an efficient accounting system. A well-devised accounting information system benefits every type of company.

Basic Terminology

Financial accounting rests on a set of concepts (discussed in Chapters 1 and 2) for identifying, recording, classifying, and interpreting transactions and other events relating to enterprises. You therefore need to understand the **basic terminology employed in collecting accounting data**.

BASIC TERMINOLOGY

EVENT. A happening of consequence. An event generally is the source or cause of changes in assets, liabilities, and equity. Events may be external or internal.

TRANSACTION. An **external event** involving a transfer or exchange between two or more entities.

ACCOUNT. A systematic arrangement that shows the effect of transactions and other events on a specific element (asset, liability, and so on). Companies keep a separate account for each asset, liability, revenue, and expense, and for capital (owners' equity). Because the format of an account often resembles the letter T, it is sometimes referred to as a **T-account**. (See Illustration 3-3, p. 69.)

REAL AND NOMINAL ACCOUNTS. **Real** (permanent) **accounts** are asset, liability, and equity accounts; they appear on the statement of financial position. **Nominal** (temporary) **accounts** are revenue, expense, and dividend accounts; except for dividends, they appear on the income statement. Companies periodically close nominal accounts; they do not close real accounts.

LEDGER. The book (or electronic records) containing the accounts. A **general ledger** is a collection of all the asset, liability, equity, revenue, and expense accounts. A **subsidiary ledger** contains the details related to a given general ledger account.

JOURNAL. The "book of original entry" where the company initially records transactions and selected other events. Various amounts are transferred from the book of original entry, the journal, to the ledger. Entering transaction data in the journal is known as **journalizing**.

POSTING. The process of transferring the essential facts and figures from the book of original entry to the ledger accounts.

TRIAL BALANCE. The list of all open accounts in the ledger and their balances. The trial balance taken immediately after all adjustments have been posted is called an **adjusted trial balance**. A trial balance taken immediately after closing entries have been posted is called a **post-closing** (or **after-closing**) **trial balance**. Companies may prepare a trial balance at any time.

ADJUSTING ENTRIES. Entries made at the end of an accounting period to bring all accounts up to date on an accrual basis, so that the company can prepare correct financial statements.

FINANCIAL STATEMENTS. Statements that reflect the collection, tabulation, and final summarization of the accounting data. Four statements are involved: (1) The **statement of financial position** shows the financial condition of the enterprise at the end of a period. (2) The **income statement** (or statement of comprehensive income) measures the results of operations during the period. (3) The **statement of cash flows** reports the cash provided and used by operating, investing, and financing activities during the period. (4) The **statement of retained earnings** (or retained earnings statement) reconciles the balance of the retained earnings account from the beginning to the end of the period.

CLOSING ENTRIES. The formal process by which the enterprise reduces all nominal accounts to zero and determines and transfers the net income or net loss to an equity account. Also known as "closing the ledger," "closing the books," or merely "closing."

Debits and Credits

The terms **debit** (Dr.) and **credit** (Cr.) mean left and right, respectively. These terms do not mean increase or decrease, but instead describe *where* a company makes entries in the recording process. That is, when a company enters an amount on the left side of an account, it **debits** the account. When it makes an entry on the right side, it **credits** the account. When comparing the totals of the two sides, an account shows a **debit balance** if the total of the debit amounts exceeds the credits. An account shows a **credit balance** if the credit amounts exceed the debits.

2 LEARNING OBJECTIVE
Explain double-entry rules.

The positioning of debits on the left and credits on the right is simply an accounting custom. We could function just as well if we reversed the sides. However, countries adopted the custom, now the rule, of having debits on the left side of an account and credits on the right side, similar to the custom of driving on one side of the road or the other. This rule applies to all accounts.

The equality of debits and credits provides the basis for the double-entry system of recording transactions (sometimes referred to as double-entry bookkeeping). Under the universally used **double-entry accounting** system, a company records the dual (two-sided) effect of each transaction in appropriate accounts. This system provides a logical method for recording transactions. It also offers a means of proving the accuracy of the recorded amounts. If a company records every transaction with equal debits and credits, then the sum of all the debits to the accounts must equal the sum of all the credits.

Illustration 3-1 presents the basic guidelines for an accounting system. Increases to all asset and expense accounts occur on the left (or debit side) and decreases on the right (or credit side). Conversely, increases to all liability and revenue accounts occur on the right (or credit side) and decreases on the left (or debit side). A company increases equity accounts, such as Share Capital and Retained Earnings, on the credit side, but increases Dividends on the debit side.

ILLUSTRATION 3-1
Double-Entry (Debit and Credit) Accounting System

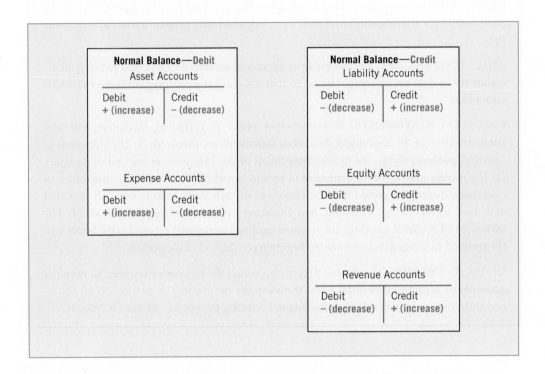

The Accounting Equation

In a double-entry system, for every debit there must be a credit, and vice versa. This leads us, then, to the basic equation in accounting (Illustration 3-2).

ILLUSTRATION 3-2
The Basic Accounting Equation

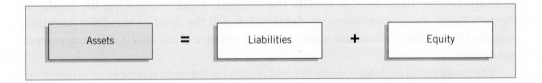

Illustration 3-3 expands this equation to show the accounts that make up equity. The figure also shows the debit/credit rules and effects on each type of account. Study this diagram carefully. It will help you understand the fundamentals of the double-entry system. Like the basic equation, the expanded equation must also balance (total debits equal total credits).

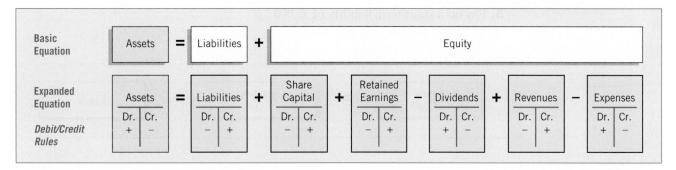

ILLUSTRATION 3-3
Expanded Equation and
Debit/Credit Rules and
Effects

Every time a transaction occurs, the elements of the accounting equation change. However, the basic equality remains. To illustrate, consider the following eight different transactions for Perez Inc.

1. Owners invest $40,000 in exchange for ordinary shares.

Assets + 40,000	=	Liabilities	+	Equity + 40,000

2. Disburse $600 cash for secretarial wages.

Assets − 600	=	Liabilities	+	Equity − 600 (expense)

3. Purchase office equipment priced at $5,200, giving a 10 percent promissory note in exchange.

Assets + 5,200	=	Liabilities +5,200	+	Equity

4. Receive $4,000 cash for services performed.

Assets + 4,000	=	Liabilities	+	Equity + 4,000 (revenue)

5. Pay off a short-term liability of $7,000.

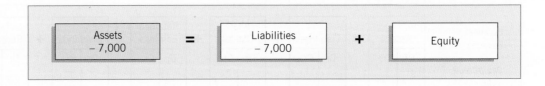

6. Declare a cash dividend of $5,000.

7. Convert a non-current liability of $80,000 into ordinary shares.

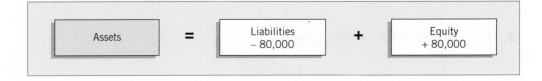

8. Pay cash of $16,000 for a delivery van.

Financial Statements and Ownership Structure

The equity section of the statement of financial position reports share capital and retained earnings. The income statement reports revenues and expenses. The retained earnings statement reports dividends. Because a company transfers dividends, revenues, and expenses to retained earnings at the end of the period, a change in any one of these three items affects equity. Illustration 3-4 shows the equity relationships.

The company's ownership structure dictates the types of accounts that are part of or affect the equity section. A corporation commonly uses Share Capital, Share Premium, Dividends, and Retained Earnings accounts. A proprietorship or a partnership uses a Capital account and a Drawing account. A Capital account indicates the owner's or owners' investment in the company. A Drawing account tracks withdrawals by the owner(s).

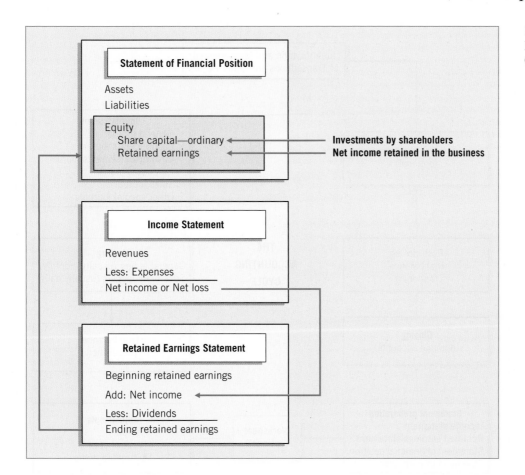

ILLUSTRATION 3-4
Financial Statements and
Ownership Structure

Illustration 3-5 summarizes and relates the transactions affecting equity to the nominal (temporary) and real (permanent) classifications and to the types of business ownership.

ILLUSTRATION 3-5
Effects of Transactions
on Equity Accounts

| | | Ownership Structure | | | |
| | | Proprietorships and Partnerships | | Corporations | |
Transactions Affecting Equity	Impact on Equity	Nominal (Temporary) Accounts	Real (Permanent) Accounts	Nominal (Temporary) Accounts	Real (Permanent) Accounts
Investment by owner(s)	Increase		Capital		Share Capital and related accounts
Revenues recognized	Increase	Revenue ⎫		Revenue ⎫	
Expenses incurred	Decrease	Expense ⎬ Capital		Expense ⎬	Retained Earnings
Withdrawal by owner(s)	Decrease	Drawing ⎭		Dividends ⎭	

THE ACCOUNTING CYCLE

Illustration 3-6 (on page 72) shows the steps in the **accounting cycle**. An enterprise normally uses these accounting procedures to record transactions and prepare financial statements.

3 LEARNING OBJECTIVE
Identify steps in the accounting cycle.

ILLUSTRATION 3-6
The Accounting Cycle

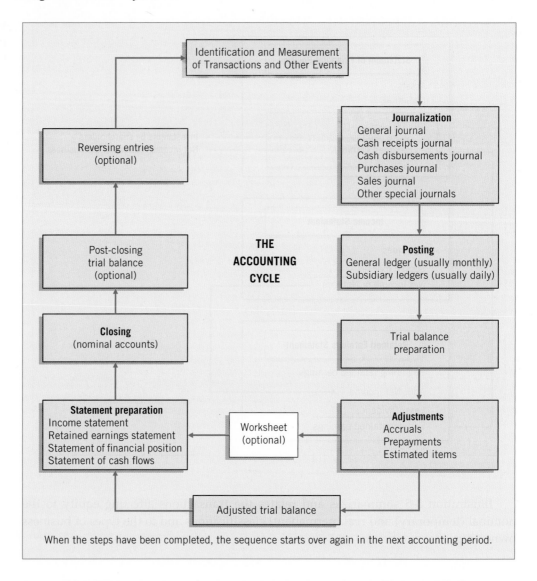

When the steps have been completed, the sequence starts over again in the next accounting period.

Identifying and Recording Transactions and Other Events

The first step in the accounting cycle is analysis of transactions and selected other events. The first problem is to determine what to record. Although IFRS provides guidelines, no simple rules exist that state which events a company should record. Although changes in a company's personnel or managerial policies may be important, the company should not record these items in the accounts. On the other hand, a company should record all cash sales or purchases—no matter how small.

The concepts we presented in Chapter 2 determine what to recognize in the accounts. An item should be recognized in the financial statements if it (1) meets the definition of an element, (2) is probable that any future economic benefit associated with the item will flow to or from the entity, and (3) has a cost or value that can be measured reliably. For example, should we value employees for statement of financial position and income statement purposes? Certainly skilled employees are an important asset (highly relevant), but the problems of determining their value and measuring it reliably have not yet been solved. Consequently, human resources are not recorded. Perhaps when measurement techniques become more sophisticated and accepted, such information will be presented, if only in supplemental form.

🔍 Underlying Concepts

Assets are probable economic benefits controlled by a particular entity as a result of a past transaction or event. Do human resources of a company meet this definition?

Transactions recorded may be an exchange between two entities where each receives and sacrifices value, such as purchases and sales of goods or services. Or, transactions may be transfers in one direction only. For example, an entity may incur a liability without directly receiving value in exchange, such as charitable contributions. Other examples include investments by owners, distributions to owners, payment of taxes, gifts, casualty losses, and thefts.

In short, a company records as many transactions as possible that affect its financial position. As discussed earlier in the case of human resources, it omits some events because of tradition and others because of complicated measurement problems. Recently, however, the accounting profession shows more receptiveness to accepting the challenge of measuring and reporting events previously viewed as too complex and immeasurable.

Journalizing

A company records in **accounts** those transactions and events that affect its assets, liabilities, and equities. The general ledger contains all the asset, liability, and equity accounts. An account (see Illustration 3-3, on page 69) shows the effect of transactions on particular asset, liability, equity, revenue, and expense accounts.

4 LEARNING OBJECTIVE
Record transactions in journals, post to ledger accounts, and prepare a trial balance.

In practice, companies do not record transactions and selected other events originally in the ledger. A transaction affects two or more accounts, each of which is on a different page in the ledger. Therefore, in order to have a complete record of each transaction or other event in one place, a company uses a **journal** (also called "the book of original entry"). In its simplest form, a general journal chronologically lists transactions and other events, expressed in terms of debits and credits to accounts.

As an example, Illustration 3-7 depicts the technique of journalizing, using two transactions for Softbyte, Inc. These transactions are:

September 1 Shareholders invested ₺15,000 cash in the corporation in exchange for ordinary shares.
Purchased computer equipment for ₺7,000 cash.

The J1 indicates these two entries are on the first page of the general journal.

Date	Account Titles and Explanation	Ref.	Debit	Credit
GENERAL JOURNAL				**J1**
2015 Sept. 1	Cash		15,000	
	Share Capital—Ordinary			15,000
	(Issued ordinary shares for cash)			
1	Equipment		7,000	
	Cash			7,000
	(Purchased equipment for cash)			

ILLUSTRATION 3-7
Technique of Journalizing

Each **general journal entry** consists of four parts: (1) a date, (2) the accounts and amounts to be debited (Dr.), (3) the accounts and amounts to be credited (Cr.), and (4) an explanation. A company enters debits first, followed by the credits (slightly indented). The explanation begins below the name of the last account to be credited and may take one or more lines. A company completes the "Ref." column at the time it posts to the accounts.

In some cases, a company uses special journals in addition to the general journal. Special journals summarize transactions possessing a common characteristic (e.g., cash receipts, sales, purchases, cash payments). As a result, using them reduces bookkeeping time.

Posting

The procedure of transferring journal entries to the ledger accounts is called posting. Posting involves the following steps.

1. In the ledger, enter in the appropriate columns of the debited account(s) the date, journal page, and debit amount shown in the journal.
2. In the reference column of the journal, write the account number to which the debit amount was posted.
3. In the ledger, enter in the appropriate columns of the credited account(s) the date, journal page, and credit amount shown in the journal.
4. In the reference column of the journal, write the account number to which the credit amount was posted.

Illustration 3-8 diagrams these four steps, using the first journal entry of Softbyte, Inc. The illustration shows the general ledger accounts in **standard account form**. Some companies call this form the **three-column form of account** because it has three money columns—debit, credit, and balance. The balance in the account is determined after each transaction. The explanation space and reference columns provide special information about the transaction. The boxed numbers indicate the sequence of the steps.

ILLUSTRATION 3-8
Posting a Journal Entry

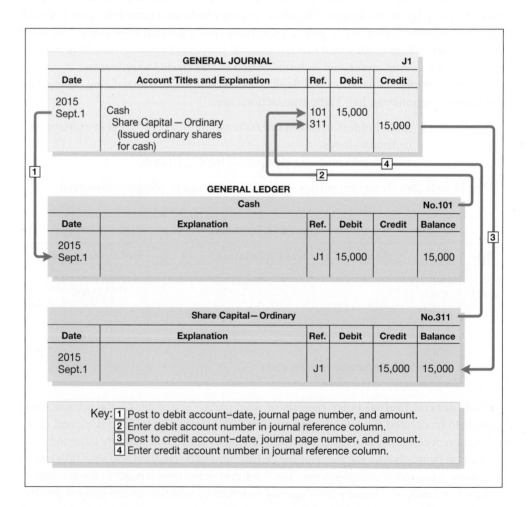

The numbers in the "Ref." column of the general journal refer to the ledger accounts to which a company posts the respective items. For example, the "101" placed in the column to the right of "Cash" indicates that the company posted this ₺15,000 item to Account No. 101 in the ledger.

The posting of the general journal is completed when a company records all of the posting reference numbers opposite the account titles in the journal. Thus, the number in the posting reference column serves two purposes: (1) It indicates the ledger account number of the account involved. (2) It indicates the completion of posting for the particular item. Each company selects its own numbering system for its ledger accounts. Many begin numbering with asset accounts and then follow with liabilities, equity, revenue, and expense accounts, in that order.

The ledger accounts in Illustration 3-8 show the accounts after completion of the posting process. The reference J1 (General Journal, page 1) indicates the source of the data transferred to the ledger account.

An Expanded Example

To show an expanded example of the basic steps in the recording process, we use the October transactions of Pioneer Advertising Agency Inc. Pioneer's accounting period is one month. Illustrations 3-9 through 3-18 show the journal entry and posting of each transaction. For simplicity, we use a T-account form instead of the standard account form. Study the transaction analyses carefully.

The purpose of transaction analysis is (1) to identify the type of account involved, and (2) to determine whether a debit or a credit is required. You should always perform this type of analysis before preparing a journal entry. Doing so will help you understand the journal entries discussed in this chapter as well as more complex journal entries in later chapters. Keep in mind that every journal entry affects one or more of the following items: assets, liabilities, equity, revenues, or expenses.

1. October 1: Shareholders invest ₺100,000 cash in an advertising venture to be known as Pioneer Advertising Agency Inc.

Journal Entry	Oct. 1	Cash	101	100,000	
		Share Capital—Ordinary	311		100,000
		(Issued ordinary shares for cash)			

Posting

Cash 101	
Oct. 1, 100,000	

Share Capital—Ordinary 311	
	Oct. 1, 100,000

ILLUSTRATION 3-9
Investment of Cash by Shareholders

2. October 1: Pioneer purchases office equipment costing ₺50,000 by signing a 3-month, 12%, ₺50,000 note payable.

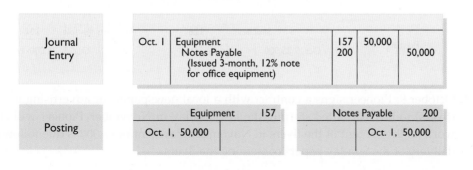

Journal Entry	Oct. 1	Equipment	157	50,000	
		Notes Payable	200		50,000
		(Issued 3-month, 12% note for office equipment)			

Posting

Equipment 157	
Oct. 1, 50,000	

Notes Payable 200	
	Oct. 1, 50,000

ILLUSTRATION 3-10
Purchase of Office Equipment

3. October 2: Pioneer receives a ₺12,000 cash advance from R. Knox, a client, for advertising services that are expected to be completed by December 31.

ILLUSTRATION 3-11
Receipt of Cash for
Future Service

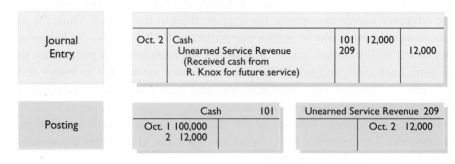

4. October 3: Pioneer pays ₺9,000 office rent, in cash, for October.

ILLUSTRATION 3-12
Payment of Monthly
Rent

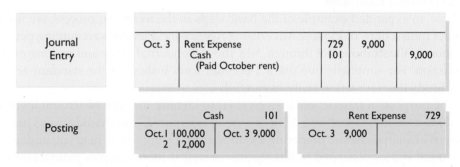

5. October 4: Pioneer pays ₺6,000 for a one-year insurance policy that will expire next year on September 30.

ILLUSTRATION 3-13
Payment for Insurance

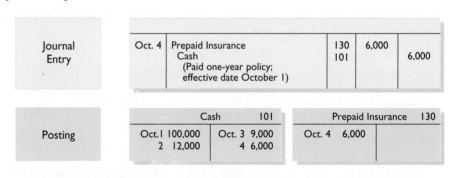

6. October 5: Pioneer purchases, for ₺25,000 on account, an estimated 3-month supply of advertising materials from Aero Supply.

ILLUSTRATION 3-14
Purchase of Supplies on
Account

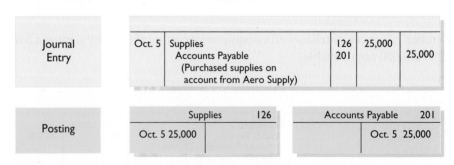

7. October 9: Pioneer signs a contract with a local newspaper for advertising inserts (flyers) to be distributed starting the last Sunday in November. Pioneer will start work on the content of the flyers in November. Payment of ₺7,000 is due following delivery of the Sunday papers containing the flyers.

A business transaction has not occurred. There is only an agreement between Pioneer Advertising and the newspaper for the services to be provided in November. Therefore, no journal entry is necessary in October.

ILLUSTRATION 3-15
Signing a Contract

8. October 20: Pioneer's board of directors declares and pays a ₺5,000 cash dividend to shareholders.

ILLUSTRATION 3-16
Declaration and Payment of Dividend by Corporation

Journal Entry	Oct. 20	Dividends	332	5,000	
		Cash	101		5,000
		(Declared and paid a cash dividend)			

Posting

Cash		101	
Oct.1 100,000	Oct. 3 9,000		
2 12,000	4 6,000		
	20 5,000		

Dividends	332
Oct. 20 5,000	

9. October 26: Pioneer pays employee salaries and wages in cash. Employees are paid once a month, every four weeks. The total payroll is ₺10,000 per week, or ₺2,000 per day. In October, the pay period began on Monday, October 1. As a result, the pay period ended on Friday, October 26, with salaries and wages of ₺40,000 being paid.

ILLUSTRATION 3-17
Payment of Salaries

Journal Entry	Oct. 26	Salaries and Wages Expense	726	40,000	
		Cash	101		40,000
		(Paid salaries to date)			

Posting

Cash		101	
Oct.1 100,000	Oct. 3 9,000		
2 12,000	4 6,000		
	20 5,000		
	26 40,000		

Salaries and Wages Expense	726
Oct. 26 40,000	

10. October 31: Pioneer receives ₺28,000 in cash and bills Copa Company ₺72,000 for advertising services of ₺100,000 performed in October.

Journal Entry	Oct. 31	Cash	101	28,000	
		Accounts Receivable	112	72,000	
		Service Revenue	400		100,000
		(Recognize revenue for services performed)			

Posting

Cash		101	
Oct.1 100,000	Oct. 3 9,000		
2 12,000	4 6,000		
31 28,000	20 5,000		
	26 40,000		

Accounts Receivable	112
Oct. 31 72,000	

Service Revenue	400
	Oct. 31 100,000

ILLUSTRATION 3-18
Recognize Revenue for Services Performed

Trial Balance

A **trial balance** lists accounts and their balances at a given time. A company usually prepares a trial balance at the end of an accounting period. The trial balance lists the accounts in the order in which they appear in the ledger, with debit balances listed in the left column and credit balances in the right column. The totals of the two columns must agree.

The trial balance proves the mathematical equality of debits and credits after posting. Under the double-entry system this equality occurs when the sum of the debit account balances equals the sum of the credit account balances. A trial balance also uncovers errors in journalizing and posting. In addition, it is useful in the preparation of financial statements. The procedures for preparing a trial balance consist of:

1. Listing the account titles and their balances.

2. Totaling the debit and credit columns.

3. Proving the equality of the two columns.

Illustration 3-19 presents the trial balance prepared from the ledger of Pioneer Advertising Agency Inc. Note that the total debits (₺287,000) equal the total credits (₺287,000). A trial balance also often shows account numbers to the left of the account titles.

ILLUSTRATION 3-19
Trial Balance
(Unadjusted)

PIONEER ADVERTISING AGENCY INC.
TRIAL BALANCE
OCTOBER 31, 2015

	Debit	Credit
Cash	₺ 80,000	
Accounts Receivable	72,000	
Supplies	25,000	
Prepaid Insurance	6,000	
Equipment	50,000	
Notes Payable		₺ 50,000
Accounts Payable		25,000
Unearned Service Revenue		12,000
Share Capital—Ordinary		100,000
Dividends	5,000	
Service Revenue		100,000
Salaries and Wages Expense	40,000	
Rent Expense	9,000	
	₺287,000	₺287,000

A trial balance does not prove that a company recorded all transactions or that the ledger is correct. Numerous errors may exist even though the trial balance columns agree. For example, the trial balance may balance even when a company (1) fails to journalize a transaction, (2) omits posting a correct journal entry, (3) posts a journal entry twice, (4) uses incorrect accounts in journalizing or posting, or (5) makes offsetting errors in recording the amount of a transaction. In other words, as long as a company posts equal debits and credits, even to the wrong account or in the wrong amount, the total debits will equal the total credits.

What do the numbers mean? CHANGE MANAGEMENT

For companies considering adoption of IFRS, extensive planning is required to ensure that accounting information system issues are addressed. Identifying the implications of required or elected accounting changes, such as adopting a new set of accounting standards, takes time. And the impact can be broad and vary in significance. The interrelationship of accounting changes with information technology (IT) systems, business processes, taxes, and general operations extends the time required to address all identified issues. In general, this process may require a three- or four-year lead time to prepare the various accounting and reporting systems for first-time adoption of IFRS.

Sources: Adapted from *Mapping the Change: IFRS Implementation Guide* (PricewaterhouseCoopers, 2008); and *IFRS and US GAAP: Similarities and Differences, 2013 Edition* (PricewaterhouseCoopers, 2013).

Adjusting Entries

In order for revenues to be recorded in the period in which services are performed and for expenses to be recognized in the period in which they are incurred, companies make **adjusting entries**. In short, adjustments ensure that companies, like **SAP** (DEU), **Cathay Pacific Airways** (HKG), and **Nokia** (FIN), follow the revenue recognition and expense recognition principles.

5 **LEARNING OBJECTIVE**

Explain the reasons for preparing adjusting entries.

The use of adjusting entries makes it possible to report on the statement of financial position the appropriate assets, liabilities, and equity at the statement date. Adjusting entries also make it possible to report on the income statement the proper revenues and expenses for the period. However, the trial balance—the first pulling together of the transaction data—may not contain up-to-date and complete data. This occurs for the following reasons.

1. Some events are not journalized daily because it is not expedient. Examples are the consumption of supplies and the earning of salaries and wages by employees.

2. Some costs are not journalized during the accounting period because these costs expire with the passage of time rather than as a result of recurring daily transactions. Examples of such costs are building and equipment depreciation and rent and insurance.

3. Some items may be unrecorded. An example is a utility service bill that will not be received until the next accounting period.

Adjusting entries are required every time a company, such as **Sony** (JPN), prepares financial statements. At that time, Sony must analyze each account in the trial balance to determine whether it is complete and up-to-date for financial statement purposes. The analysis requires a thorough understanding of Sony's operations and the interrelationship of accounts. Because of this involved process, usually a skilled accountant prepares the adjusting entries. In gathering the adjustment data, Sony may need to make inventory counts of supplies and repair parts. Further, it may prepare supporting schedules of insurance policies, rental agreements, and other contractual commitments. Companies often prepare adjustments after the statement of financial position date. However, they date the entries as of the statement of financial position date.

Underlying Concepts 🔍

Preparation of financial statements for subperiods such as quarters or months improves the timeliness of the information but raises verifiability concerns due to estimates in preparing adjusting entries.

Types of Adjusting Entries

Adjusting entries are classified as either deferrals or accruals. Each of these classes has two subcategories, as Illustration 3-20 shows.

Deferrals:

1. Prepaid expenses: Expenses paid in cash before they are used or consumed.

2. Unearned revenues: Cash received before services are performed.

Accruals:

1. Accrued revenues: Revenues for services performed but not yet received in cash or recorded.

2. Accrued expenses: Expenses incurred but not yet paid in cash or recorded.

ILLUSTRATION 3-20
Categories of Adjusting Entries

We review specific examples and explanations of each type of adjustment in subsequent sections. We base each example on the October 31 trial balance of Pioneer Advertising Agency Inc. (Illustration 3-19). We assume that Pioneer uses an accounting period of one month. Thus, Pioneer will make monthly adjusting entries, dated October 31.

Adjusting Entries for Deferrals

To defer means to postpone or delay. **Deferrals** are expenses or revenues that are recognized at a date later than the point when cash was originally exchanged. The two types of deferrals are prepaid expenses and unearned revenues.

If a company does not make an adjustment for these deferrals, the asset and liability are overstated, and the related expense and revenue are understated. For example, in Pioneer Advertising's trial balance (Illustration 3-19), the balance in the asset Supplies shows only supplies purchased. This balance is overstated; the related expense account, Supplies Expense, is understated because the cost of supplies used has not been recognized. Thus the adjusting entry for deferrals will decrease a statement of financial position account and increase an income statement account. Illustration 3-21 shows the effects of adjusting entries for deferrals.

ILLUSTRATION 3-21
Adjusting Entries for
Deferrals

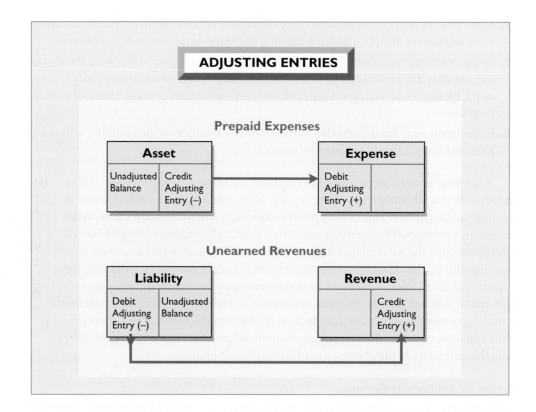

Prepaid Expenses. Assets paid for and recorded before a company uses them are called prepaid expenses. When expenses are prepaid, a company debits an asset account to show the service or benefit it will receive in the future. Examples of common prepayments are insurance, supplies, advertising, and rent. In addition, companies make prepayments when they purchase buildings and equipment.

Prepaid expenses are costs that expire either with the passage of time (e.g., rent and insurance) or through use and consumption (e.g., supplies). The expiration of these costs does not require daily entries, an unnecessary and impractical task. Accordingly, a company like **Louis Vuitton (LVMH Group) (FRA)** usually postpones the recognition of such cost expirations until it prepares financial statements. At each statement date, Louis Vuitton makes adjusting entries to record the expenses that apply to the current accounting period and to show the remaining amounts in the asset accounts.

As shown above, prior to adjustment, assets are overstated and expenses are understated. **Thus, an adjusting entry for prepaid expenses results in a debit to an expense account and a credit to an asset account.**

Supplies. A business enterprise may use several different types of supplies. For example, a public accounting firm will use office supplies such as stationery, envelopes, and accounting paper. An advertising firm will stock advertising supplies such as graph paper, video film, and poster paper. Supplies are generally debited to an asset account when they are acquired. Recognition of supplies used is generally deferred until the adjustment process. At that time, a physical inventory (count) of supplies is taken. The difference between the balance in the Supplies (asset) account and the cost of supplies on hand represents the supplies used (expense) for the period.

For example, Pioneer Advertising purchased advertising supplies costing ₺25,000 on October 5. Pioneer therefore debited the asset Supplies. This account shows a balance of ₺25,000 in the October 31 trial balance (see Illustration 3-19). An inventory count at the close of business on October 31 reveals that ₺10,000 of supplies are still on hand. Thus, the cost of supplies used is ₺15,000 (₺25,000 − ₺10,000). The analysis and adjustment for Supplies is summarized in Illustration 3-22.

Supplies

Oct. 5

Supplies purchased; record asset

Oct. 31

Supplies used; record supplies expense

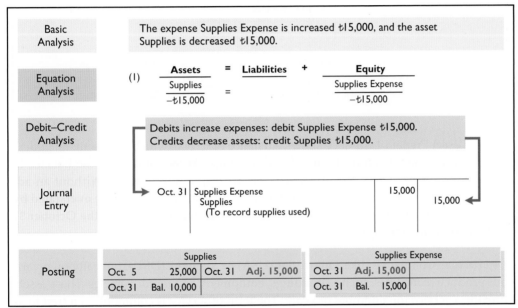

Basic Analysis	The expense Supplies Expense is increased ₺15,000, and the asset Supplies is decreased ₺15,000.

ILLUSTRATION 3-22
Adjustment for Supplies

Equation Analysis

(1)

	Assets	=	**Liabilities**	+	**Equity**
	Supplies				Supplies Expense
	−₺15,000	=			−₺15,000

Debit–Credit Analysis

Debits increase expenses: debit Supplies Expense ₺15,000.
Credits decrease assets: credit Supplies ₺15,000.

Journal Entry

Oct. 31	Supplies Expense	15,000	
	Supplies		15,000
	(To record supplies used)		

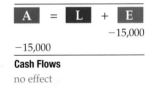

A	=	L	+	E
				−15,000
−15,000				

Cash Flows
no effect

Posting

Supplies			
Oct. 5	25,000	Oct. 31 Adj. 15,000	
Oct. 31 Bal. 10,000			

Supplies Expense	
Oct. 31 Adj. 15,000	
Oct. 31 Bal. 15,000	

After adjustment, the asset account Supplies now shows a balance of ₺10,000, which equals the cost of supplies on hand at the statement date. In addition, Supplies Expense shows a balance of ₺15,000, which equals the cost of supplies used in October. **Without an adjusting entry, October expenses are understated and net income overstated by ₺15,000. Moreover, both assets and equity are overstated by ₺15,000 on the October 31 statement of financial position.**

Insurance. Most companies maintain fire and theft insurance on merchandise and equipment, personal liability insurance for accidents suffered by customers, and automobile insurance on company cars and trucks. The extent of protection against loss determines the cost of the insurance (the amount of the premium to be paid). The insurance policy specifies the term and coverage. The minimum term usually covers one year, but three- to five-year terms are available and may offer lower annual premiums. A company usually debits insurance premiums to the asset account Prepaid Insurance when paid. At the financial statement date, it then debits Insurance Expense and credits Prepaid Insurance for the cost that expired during the period.

For example, on October 4, Pioneer Advertising paid ₺6,000 for a one-year fire insurance policy, beginning October 1. Pioneer debited the cost of the premium to Prepaid

Insurance

Oct. 1

FIRE INSURANCE
1 year
insurance policy
₺6,000

Insurance purchased; record asset

Insurance Policy			
Oct ₺500	Nov ₺500	Dec ₺500	Jan ₺500
Feb ₺500	March ₺500	April ₺500	May ₺500
June ₺500	July ₺500	Aug ₺500	Sept ₺500
1 YEAR ₺6,000			

Oct. 31

Insurance expired; record insurance expense.

Insurance at that time. This account still shows a balance of ₺6,000 in the October 31 trial balance. An analysis of the policy reveals that ₺500 (₺6,000 ÷ 12) of insurance expires each month. The analysis and adjustment for insurance is summarized in Illustration 3-23.

ILLUSTRATION 3-23
Adjustment for Insurance

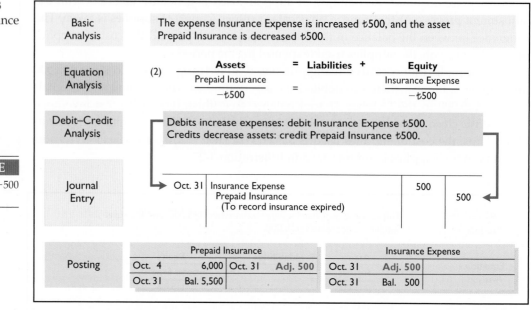

A	**=**	**L**	**+**	**E**
				−500
−500				

Cash Flows
no effect

The asset Prepaid Insurance shows a balance of ₺5,500, which represents the unexpired cost for the remaining 11 months of coverage. At the same time, the balance in Insurance Expense equals the insurance cost that expired in October. **Without an adjusting entry, October expenses are understated by ₺500 and net income overstated by ₺500. Moreover, both assets and equity also are overstated by ₺500 on the October 31 statement of financial position.**

Depreciation. Companies, like Caterpillar (USA) or Siemens (DEU), typically own various productive facilities, such as buildings, equipment, and motor vehicles. These assets provide a service for a number of years. The term of service is commonly referred to as the useful life of the asset. Because Siemens, for example, expects an asset such as a building to provide service for many years, Siemens records the building as an asset, rather than an expense, in the year the building is acquired. Siemens records such assets at cost, as required by the historical cost principle.

To follow the expense recognition principle, Siemens should report a portion of the cost of a long-lived asset as an expense during each period of the asset's useful life. Depreciation is the process of allocating the cost of an asset to expense over its useful life in a rational and systematic manner.

Need for depreciation adjustment. Under IFRS, the acquisition of productive facilities is viewed as a long-term prepayment for services. The need for making periodic adjusting entries for depreciation is therefore the same as we described for other prepaid expenses. That is, a company recognizes the expired cost (expense) during the period and reports the unexpired cost (asset) at the end of the period. The primary causes of depreciation of a productive facility are actual use, deterioration due to the elements, and obsolescence. For example, at the time Siemens acquires an asset, the effects of these factors cannot be known with certainty. Therefore, Siemens must estimate them. **Thus, depreciation is an estimate rather than a factual measurement of the expired cost.**

To estimate depreciation expense, Siemens often divides the cost of the asset by its useful life. For example, if Siemens purchases equipment for ₺10,000 and expects its useful life to be 10 years, Siemens records annual depreciation of ₺1,000.

In the case of Pioneer Advertising, it estimates depreciation on its office equipment to be ₺4,800 a year (cost ₺50,000 less residual value ₺2,000 divided by useful life of 10 years), or ₺400 per month. The analysis and adjustment for depreciation is summarized in Illustration 3-24.

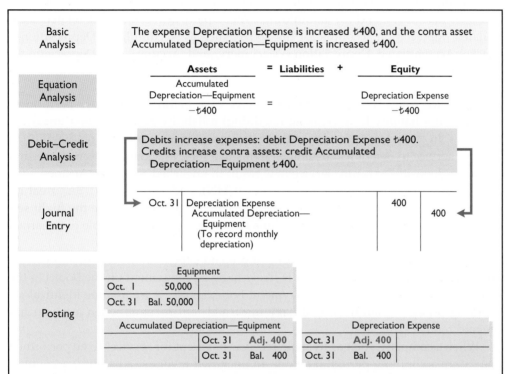

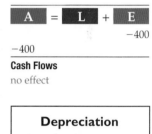

ILLUSTRATION 3-24
Adjustment for Depreciation

The balance in the Accumulated Depreciation—Equipment account will increase ₺400 each month. Therefore, after journalizing and posting the adjusting entry at November 30, the balance will be ₺800.

Statement presentation. Accumulated Depreciation—Equipment is a contra asset account. A **contra asset account** offsets an asset account on the statement of financial position. This means that the Accumulated Depreciation—Equipment account offsets the Equipment account on the statement of financial position. Its normal balance is a credit. Pioneer Advertising uses this account instead of crediting Equipment in order to disclose both the original cost of the equipment and the total expired cost to date. In the statement of financial position, Pioneer deducts Accumulated Depreciation—Equipment from the related asset account as follows.

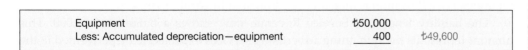

ILLUSTRATION 3-25
Statement of Financial Position Presentation of Accumulated Depreciation

The **book value** (or **carrying value**) of any depreciable asset is the difference between its cost and its related accumulated depreciation. In Illustration 3-25, the book value of the equipment at the statement of financial position date is ₺49,600. Note that the asset's book value generally differs from its fair value. The reason: **Depreciation is an allocation concept, not a valuation concept.** That is, depreciation **allocates an asset's cost to the periods in which it is used. Depreciation does not attempt to report the actual change in the value of the asset.**

Depreciation expense identifies that portion of the asset's cost that expired during the period (in this case, October). **Without this adjusting entry, total assets, total equity, and net income are overstated, and depreciation expense is understated.**

A company records depreciation expense for each piece of equipment, such as trucks or machinery, and for all buildings. A company also establishes related accumulated depreciation accounts for the above, such as Accumulated Depreciation— Trucks, Accumulated Depreciation—Machinery, and Accumulated Depreciation— Buildings.

Unearned Revenues. When companies receive cash before services are performed, they record a liability by increasing (crediting) a liability account called **unearned revenues**. In other words, a company now has a performance obligation (liability) to provide service to one of its customers. Items like rent, magazine subscriptions, and customer deposits for future service may result in unearned revenues. Airlines, such as **Ryanair** (IRL), **China Southern Airlines** (CHN), and **Southwest** (USA), treat receipts from the sale of tickets as unearned revenue until they provide the flight service. Tuition received prior to the start of a semester is another example of unearned revenue.

Unearned revenues are the opposite of prepaid expenses. Indeed, unearned revenue on the books of one company is likely to be a prepayment on the books of the company that made the advance payment. For example, if we assume identical accounting periods, a landlord will have unearned rent revenue when a tenant has prepaid rent.

When a company, such as Ryanair, receives payment for services to be performed in a future accounting period, it credits an unearned revenue (a liability) account to recognize the liability that exists. Ryanair subsequently recognizes revenue when it performs the service. However, making daily recurring entries to record this revenue is impractical. Therefore, Ryanair delays recognition of revenue until the adjustment process. Then, Ryanair makes an adjusting entry to record the revenue for services performed during the period and to show the liability that remains at the end of the accounting period. In the typical case, liabilities are overstated and revenues are understated prior to adjustment. **Thus, the adjusting entry for unearned revenues results in a debit (decrease) to a liability account and a credit (increase) to a revenue account.**

For example, Pioneer Advertising received ₺12,000 on October 2 from R. Knox for advertising services expected to be completed by December 31. Pioneer credited the payment to Unearned Service Revenue. This liability account shows a balance of ₺12,000 in the October 31 trial balance. Based on an evaluation of the service Pioneer performed for Knox during October, the company determines that it should recognize ₺4,000 of revenue in October. The liability (Unearned Service Revenue) is therefore decreased and equity (Service Revenue) is increased, as shown in Illustration 3-26.

The liability Unearned Service Revenue now shows a balance of ₺8,000. This amount represents the remaining advertising services expected to be performed in the future. At the same time, Service Revenue shows total revenue recognized in October of ₺104,000. **Without this adjustment, revenues and net income are understated by ₺4,000 in the income statement. Moreover, liabilities are overstated and equity is understated by ₺4,000 on the October 31 statement of financial position.**

Unearned Revenues

Oct. 2

Thank you in advance for your work

I will finish by Dec. 31

₺12,000

Cash is received in advance; liability is recorded

Oct. 31

Some service has been performed; some revenue is recorded

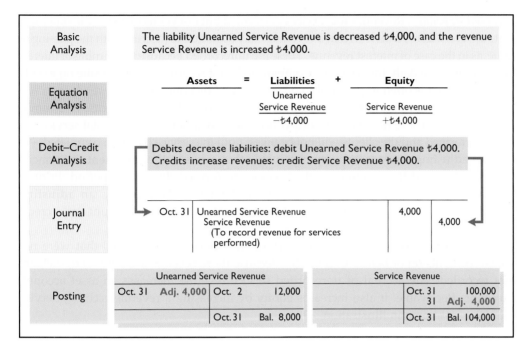

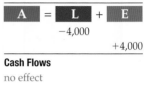

ILLUSTRATION 3-26
Adjustment for Unearned
Service Revenue

Adjusting Entries for Accruals

The second category of adjusting entries is accruals. Companies make adjusting entries for accruals to record revenues for services performed and expenses incurred in the current accounting period. Without an accrual adjustment, the revenue account (and the related asset account) or the expense account (and the related liability account) are understated. Thus, the adjusting entry for accruals **will increase both a statement of financial position and an income statement account**. Illustration 3-27 shows adjusting entries for accruals.

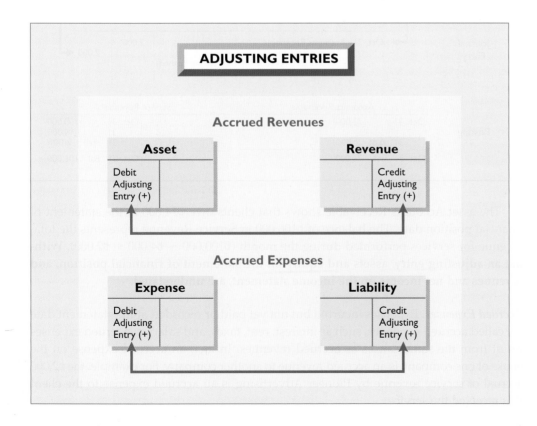

ILLUSTRATION 3-27
Adjusting Entries for
Accruals

Accrued Revenues. Revenues for services performed but not yet recorded at the statement date are accrued revenues. Accrued revenues may accumulate (accrue) with the passing of time, as in the case of interest revenue. These are unrecorded because the earning of interest does not involve daily transactions. Companies do not record interest revenue on a daily basis because it is often impractical to do so. Accrued revenues also may result from services that have been performed but not yet billed nor collected, as in the case of commissions and fees. These may be unrecorded because only a portion of the total service has been performed and the clients will not be billed until the service has been completed.

An adjusting entry records the receivable that exists at the statement of financial position date and the revenue for the services performed during the period. Prior to adjustment, both assets and revenues are understated. Accordingly, **an adjusting entry** for accrued revenues results in a debit (increase) to an asset account and a credit (increase) to a revenue account.

In October, Pioneer Advertising performed services worth ₺2,000 that were not billed to clients on or before October 31. Because these services are not billed, they are not recorded. The accrual of unrecorded service revenue increases an asset account, Accounts Receivable. It also increases equity by increasing a revenue account, Service Revenue, as shown in Illustration 3-28.

Accrued Revenues

My fee is ₺2,000

Revenue and receivable are recorded for unbilled services

ILLUSTRATION 3-28
Accrual Adjustment for Receivable and Revenue Accounts

A	=	L	+	E
+2,000				
				+2,000

Cash Flows
no effect

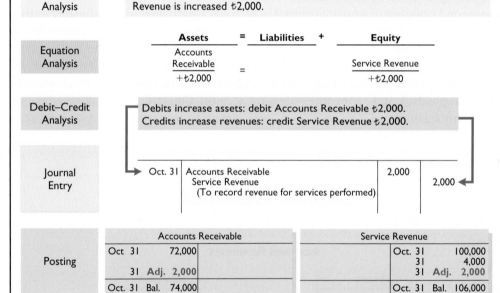

| Basic Analysis | The asset Accounts Receivable is increased ₺2,000, and the revenue Service Revenue is increased ₺2,000. |

Equation Analysis

	Assets	=	Liabilities	+	Equity
	Accounts Receivable				Service Revenue
	+₺2,000	=			+₺2,000

Debit–Credit Analysis

Debits increase assets: debit Accounts Receivable ₺2,000.
Credits increase revenues: credit Service Revenue ₺2,000.

Journal Entry

Oct. 31	Accounts Receivable	2,000	
	Service Revenue		2,000
	(To record revenue for services performed)		

Posting

Accounts Receivable			Service Revenue	
Oct 31	72,000		Oct. 31	100,000
			31	4,000
31 Adj.	2,000		31 Adj.	2,000
Oct. 31 Bal.	74,000		Oct. 31 Bal.	106,000

The asset Accounts Receivable shows that clients owe ₺74,000 at the statement of financial position date. The balance of ₺106,000 in Service Revenue represents the total revenue for services performed during the month (₺100,000 + ₺4,000 + ₺2,000). **Without an adjusting entry, assets and equity on the statement of financial position, and revenues and net income on the income statement, are understated.**

Accrued Expenses. Expenses incurred but not yet paid or recorded at the statement date are called accrued expenses, such as interest, rent, taxes, and salaries. Accrued expenses result from the same causes as accrued revenues. In fact, an accrued expense on the books of one company is an accrued revenue to another company. For example, the ₺2,000 accrual of service revenue by Pioneer Advertising is an accrued expense to the client that received the service.

Adjustments for accrued expenses record the obligations that exist at the statement of financial position date and recognize the expenses that apply to the current accounting period. Prior to adjustment, both liabilities and expenses are understated. Therefore, the adjusting entry for accrued expenses results in a debit (increase) to an expense account and a credit (increase) to a liability account.

Accrued interest. Pioneer Advertising signed a three-month note payable in the amount of ₺50,000 on October 1. The note requires interest at an annual rate of 12 percent. Three factors determine the amount of the interest accumulation: (1) the face value of the note; (2) the interest rate, which is always expressed as an annual rate; and (3) the length of time the note is outstanding. For Pioneer, the total interest due on the ₺50,000 note at its maturity date three months in the future is ₺1,500 (₺50,000 × 12% × 3/12), or ₺500 for one month. Illustration 3-29 shows the formula for computing interest and its application to Pioneer. Note that the formula expresses the time period as a fraction of a year.

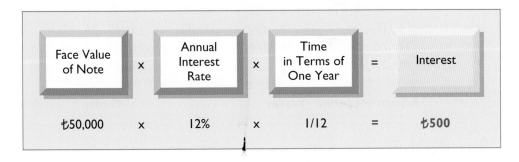

ILLUSTRATION 3-29
Formula for Computing Interest

As Illustration 3-30 shows, the accrual of interest at October 31 increases a liability account, Interest Payable. It also decreases equity by increasing an expense account, Interest Expense.

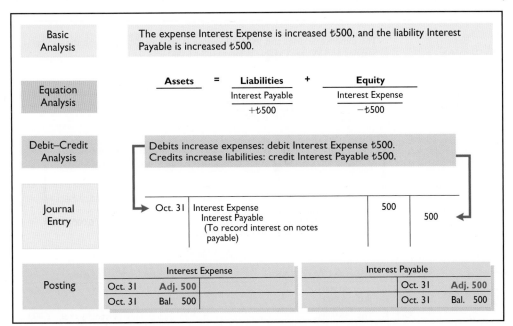

ILLUSTRATION 3-30
Adjustment for Interest

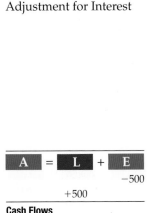

Interest Expense shows the interest charges for the month of October. Interest Payable shows the amount of interest owed at the statement date. Pioneer will not pay this amount until the note comes due at the end of three months. Why does Pioneer use the Interest Payable account instead of crediting Notes Payable? By recording interest payable separately, Pioneer discloses the two types of obligations (interest and principal) in the accounts and statements. **Without this adjusting entry, both liabilities and interest expense are understated, and both net income and equity are overstated.**

Accrued salaries and wages. Companies pay for some types of expenses, such as employee salaries and wages, after the services have been performed. For example, Pioneer Advertising last paid salaries and wages on October 26. It will not pay salaries and wages again until November 23. However, as shown in the calendar below, three working days remain in October (October 29–31).

At October 31, the salaries and wages for these days represent an accrued expense and a related liability to Pioneer. The employees receive total salaries and wages of ₺10,000 for a five-day work week, or ₺2,000 per day. Thus, accrued salaries and wages at October 31 are ₺6,000 (₺2,000 × 3). The analysis and adjustment process is summarized in Illustration 3-31.

ILLUSTRATION 3-31
Adjustment for Salaries and Wages Expense

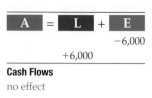

Cash Flows
no effect

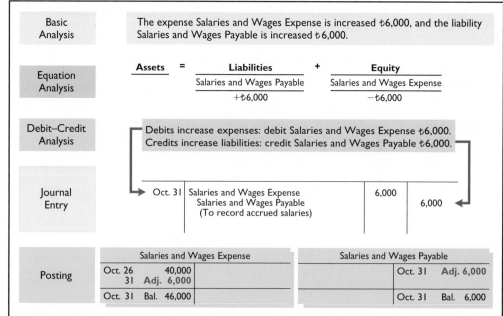

After this adjustment, the balance in Salaries and Wages Expense of ₺46,000 (23 days × ₺2,000) is the actual salaries and wages expense for October. The balance in Salaries and Wages Payable of ₺6,000 is the amount of the liability for salaries and wages owed as of

October 31. **Without the ₺6,000 adjustment for salaries and wages, both Pioneer's expenses and liabilities are understated by ₺6,000.**

Pioneer pays salaries and wages every four weeks. Consequently, the next payday is November 23, when it will again pay total salaries and wages of ₺40,000. The payment consists of ₺6,000 of salaries and wages payable at October 31 plus ₺34,000 of salaries and wages expense for November (17 working days as shown in the November calendar × ₺2,000). Therefore, Pioneer makes the following entry on November 23.

November 23

Salaries and Wages Payable	6,000	
Salaries and Wages Expense	34,000	
Cash		40,000
(To record November 23 payroll)		

This entry eliminates the liability for Salaries and Wages Payable that Pioneer recorded in the October 31 adjusting entry. This entry also records the proper amount of Salaries and Wages Expense for the period between November 1 and November 23.

Bad debts. Proper recognition of revenues and expenses dictates recording bad debts as an expense of the period in which a company recognize revenue for services performed instead of the period in which the company writes off the accounts or notes. The proper valuation of the receivable balance also requires recognition of uncollectible receivables. Proper recognition and valuation require an adjusting entry.

At the end of each period, a company, such as **Marks and Spencer plc (M&S)** (GBR), estimates the amount of receivables that will later prove to be uncollectible. M&S bases the estimate on various factors: the amount of bad debts it experienced in past years, general economic conditions, how long the receivables are past due, and other factors that indicate the extent of uncollectibility. To illustrate, assume that, based on past experience, Pioneer Advertising reasonably estimates a bad debt expense for the month of ₺1,600. The analysis and adjustment process for bad debts is summarized in Illustration 3-32.

Bad Debts

Oct. 31
Uncollectible accounts;
record bad debt expense

ILLUSTRATION 3-32
Adjustment for Bad Debt Expense

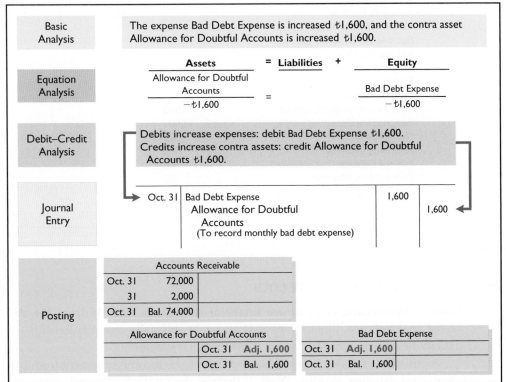

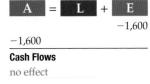

Cash Flows
no effect

Without this adjustment, assets will be overstated, and expenses will be understated. The Allowance for Doubtful Accounts is a contra asset account and is shown on the statement of financial position, similar to Accumulated Depreciation—Equipment.

A company often expresses bad debts as a percentage of the revenue on account for the period. Or, a company may compute bad debts by adjusting the Allowance for Doubtful Accounts to a certain percentage of the trade accounts receivable and trade notes receivable at the end of the period.

Adjusted Trial Balance

After journalizing and posting all adjusting entries, Pioneer Advertising prepares another trial balance from its ledger accounts (shown in Illustration 3-33). This trial balance is called an adjusted trial balance. The purpose of an adjusted trial balance is to **prove the equality** of the total debit balances and the total credit balances in the ledger after all adjustments. Because the accounts contain all data needed for financial statements, the adjusted trial balance is the **primary basis for the preparation of financial statements**.

ILLUSTRATION 3-33
Adjusted Trial Balance

PIONEER ADVERTISING AGENCY INC.
ADJUSTED TRIAL BALANCE
OCTOBER 31, 2015

	Debit	Credit
Cash	ŧ 80,000	
Accounts Receivable	74,000	
Allowance for Doubtful Accounts		ŧ 1,600
Supplies	10,000	
Prepaid Insurance	5,500	
Equipment	50,000	
Accumulated Depreciation—Equipment		400
Notes Payable		50,000
Accounts Payable		25,000
Unearned Service Revenue		8,000
Salaries and Wages Payable		6,000
Interest Payable		500
Share Capital—Ordinary		100,000
Dividends	5,000	
Service Revenue		106,000
Salaries and Wages Expense	46,000	
Supplies Expense	15,000	
Rent Expense	9,000	
Insurance Expense	500	
Interest Expense	500	
Depreciation Expense	400	
Bad Debt Expense	1,600	
	ŧ297,500	ŧ297,500

Preparing Financial Statements

LEARNING OBJECTIVE 6
Prepare financial statements from the adjusted trial balance.

Pioneer Advertising can prepare financial statements directly from the adjusted trial balance. Illustrations 3-34 and 3-35 show the interrelationships of data in the adjusted trial balance and the financial statements.

As Illustration 3-34 shows, Pioneer prepares the income statement from the revenue and expense accounts. Next, it derives the retained earnings statement

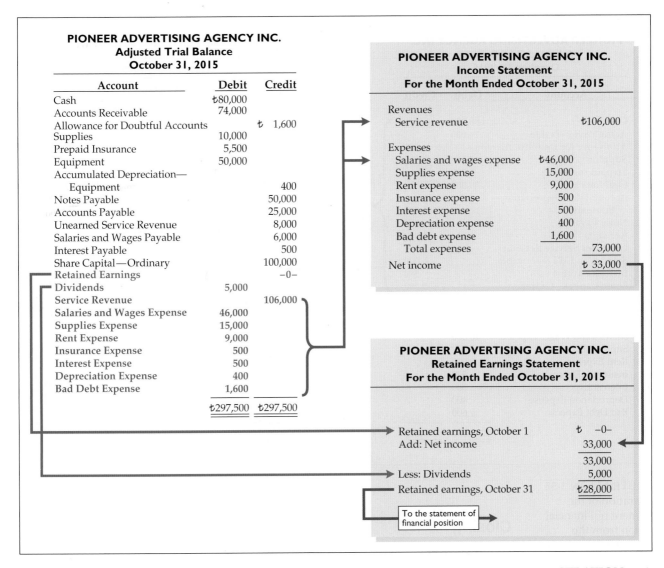

ILLUSTRATION 3-34
Preparation of the Income Statement and Retained Earnings Statement from the Adjusted Trial Balance

from the retained earnings and dividends accounts and the net income (or net loss) shown in the income statement. As Illustration 3-35 (on page 92) shows, Pioneer then prepares the statement of financial position from the asset and liability accounts, the Share Capital—Ordinary account, and the ending retained earnings balance as reported in the retained earnings statement.

What do the numbers mean? 24/7 ACCOUNTING

To achieve the vision of "24/7 accounting," a company must be able to update revenue, income, and statement of financial position numbers every day within the quarter (and potentially publish them on the Internet). Such real-time reporting responds to the demand for more timely financial information made available to all investors—not just to analysts with access to company management.

Two obstacles typically stand in the way of 24/7 accounting: having the necessary accounting systems to close the books on a daily basis, and reliability concerns associated with unaudited real-time data. Only a few companies have the necessary accounting capabilities.

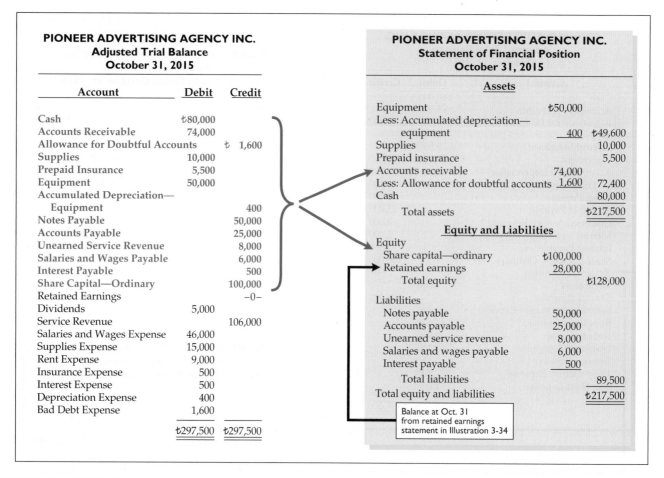

PIONEER ADVERTISING AGENCY INC.
Adjusted Trial Balance
October 31, 2015

Account	Debit	Credit
Cash	₺80,000	
Accounts Receivable	74,000	
Allowance for Doubtful Accounts		₺ 1,600
Supplies	10,000	
Prepaid Insurance	5,500	
Equipment	50,000	
Accumulated Depreciation—		
Equipment		400
Notes Payable		50,000
Accounts Payable		25,000
Unearned Service Revenue		8,000
Salaries and Wages Payable		6,000
Interest Payable		500
Share Capital—Ordinary		100,000
Retained Earnings		–0–
Dividends	5,000	
Service Revenue		106,000
Salaries and Wages Expense	46,000	
Supplies Expense	15,000	
Rent Expense	9,000	
Insurance Expense	500	
Interest Expense	500	
Depreciation Expense	400	
Bad Debt Expense	1,600	
	₺297,500	₺297,500

PIONEER ADVERTISING AGENCY INC.
Statement of Financial Position
October 31, 2015

Assets

Equipment	₺50,000	
Less: Accumulated depreciation—		
equipment	400	₺49,600
Supplies		10,000
Prepaid insurance		5,500
Accounts receivable	74,000	
Less: Allowance for doubtful accounts	1,600	72,400
Cash		80,000
Total assets		₺217,500

Equity and Liabilities

Equity		
Share capital—ordinary	₺100,000	
Retained earnings	28,000	
Total equity		₺128,000
Liabilities		
Notes payable	50,000	
Accounts payable	25,000	
Unearned service revenue	8,000	
Salaries and wages payable	6,000	
Interest payable	500	
Total liabilities		89,500
Total equity and liabilities		₺217,500

Balance at Oct. 31 from retained earnings statement in Illustration 3-34

ILLUSTRATION 3-35
Preparation of the Statement of Financial Position from the Adjusted Trial Balance

Closing

Basic Process

LEARNING OBJECTIVE
Prepare closing entries.

The **closing process** reduces the balance of nominal (temporary) accounts to zero in order to prepare the accounts for the next period's transactions. In the closing process Pioneer Advertising transfers all of the revenue and expense account balances (income statement items) to a clearing or suspense account called Income Summary. The Income Summary account matches revenues and expenses.

Pioneer uses this clearing account only at the end of each accounting period. The account represents the net income or net loss for the period. It then transfers this amount (the net income or net loss) to an equity account. (For a corporation, the equity account is retained earnings; for proprietorships and partnerships, it is a capital account.) Companies post all such **closing entries** to the appropriate general ledger accounts.

Closing Entries

In practice, companies generally prepare closing entries only at the end of a company's annual accounting period. However, to illustrate the journalizing and posting of closing entries, we will assume that Pioneer Advertising closes its books monthly. Illustration 3-36 shows the closing entries at October 31.

A couple of cautions about preparing closing entries: (1) Avoid unintentionally doubling the revenue and expense balances rather than zeroing them. (2) Do not close

	GENERAL JOURNAL		J3
Date	**Account Titles and Explanation**	**Debit**	**Credit**
	Closing Entries		
	(1)		
Oct. 31	Service Revenue	106,000	
	Income Summary		106,000
	(To close revenue account)		
	(2)		
31	Income Summary	73,000	
	Supplies Expense		15,000
	Depreciation Expense		400
	Insurance Expense		500
	Salaries and Wages Expense		46,000
	Rent Expense		9,000
	Interest Expense		500
	Bad Debt Expense		1,600
	(To close expense accounts)		
	(3)		
31	Income Summary	33,000	
	Retained Earnings		33,000
	(To close net income to retained earnings)		
	(4)		
31	Retained Earnings	5,000	
	Dividends		5,000
	(To close dividends to retained earnings)		

ILLUSTRATION 3-36
Closing Entries Journalized

Dividends through the Income Summary account. **Dividends are not expenses, and they are not a factor in determining net income.**

Posting Closing Entries

Illustration 3-37 (on page 94) shows the posting of closing entries and the underlining (ruling) of accounts. All temporary accounts have zero balances after posting the closing entries. In addition, note that the balance in Retained Earnings represents the accumulated undistributed earnings of Pioneer Advertising at the end of the accounting period. Pioneer reports this amount in the statement of financial position and as the ending amount reported on the retained earnings statement. As noted above, **Pioneer uses the Income Summary account only in closing**. It does not journalize and post entries to this account during the year.

As part of the closing process, Pioneer totals, balances, and double-underlines the **temporary accounts**—revenues, expenses, and dividends—as shown in T-account form in Illustration 3-37. It does not close the **permanent accounts**—assets, liabilities, and equity (Share Capital—Ordinary and Retained Earnings). Instead, Pioneer draws a single underline beneath the current period entries for the permanent accounts. The account balance is then entered below the single underline and is carried forward to the next period (see, for example, Retained Earnings).

After the closing process, each income statement account and the dividend account have zero balances and are ready for use in the next accounting period.

Post-Closing Trial Balance

Recall that a trial balance is prepared after posting the regular transactions of the period, and that a second trial balance (the adjusted trial balance) occurs after posting the

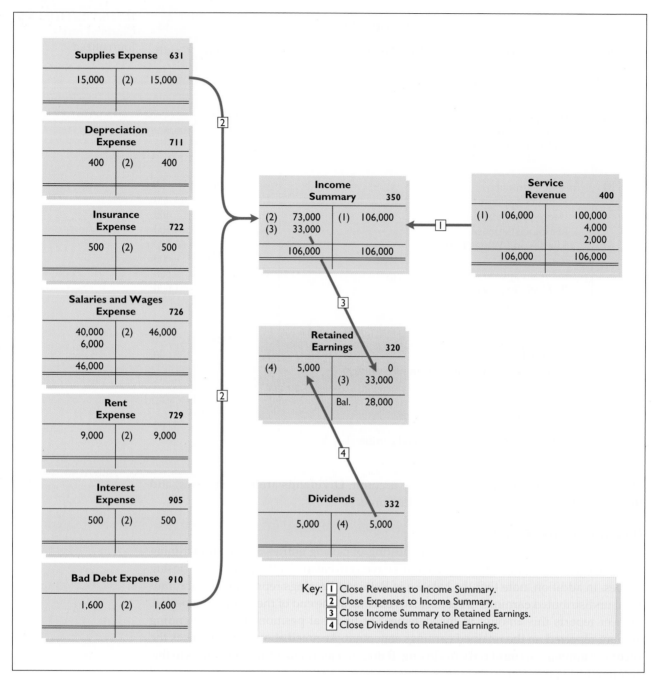

ILLUSTRATION 3-37
Posting of Closing
Entries

adjusting entries. A company may take a third trial balance after posting the closing entries. The trial balance after closing is called the **post-closing trial balance**. The purpose of the post-closing trial balance is **to prove the equality of the permanent account balances that the company carries forward into the next accounting period.** Since all temporary accounts will have zero balances, **the post-closing trial balance will contain only permanent (real)—statement of financial position—accounts**.

Illustration 3-38 shows the post-closing trial balance of Pioneer Advertising Agency Inc.

A post-closing trial balance provides evidence that the company has properly journalized and posted the closing entries. It also shows that the accounting equation is in balance at the end of the accounting period. However, like the other trial balances, it does not prove that Pioneer has recorded all transactions or that the ledger is correct. For example, the post-closing trial balance will balance if a transaction is not journalized and posted, or if a transaction is journalized and posted twice.

ILLUSTRATION 3-38
Post-Closing Trial
Balance

PIONEER ADVERTISING AGENCY INC.
POST-CLOSING TRIAL BALANCE
OCTOBER 31, 2015

Account	Debit	Credit
Cash	₺ 80,000	
Accounts Receivable	74,000	
Allowance for Doubtful Accounts		₺ 1,600
Supplies	10,000	
Prepaid Insurance	5,500	
Equipment	50,000	
Accumulated Depreciation—Equipment		400
Notes Payable		50,000
Accounts Payable		25,000
Unearned Service Revenue		8,000
Salaries and Wages Payable		6,000
Interest Payable		500
Share Capital—Ordinary		100,000
Retained Earnings		28,000
	₺219,500	₺219,500

Reversing Entries—An Optional Step

Some accountants prefer to reverse certain adjusting entries by making a **reversing entry** at the beginning of the next accounting period. A reversing entry is the exact opposite of the adjusting entry made in the previous period. **Use of reversing entries is an optional bookkeeping procedure; it is not a required step in the accounting cycle.** Accordingly, we have chosen to cover this topic in Appendix 3B at the end of the chapter.

What do the numbers mean? HEY, IT'S COMPLICATED

The economic volatility of the past few years has left companies hungering for more timely and uniform financial information to help them react quickly to fast-changing conditions. As one expert noted, companies were extremely focused on trying to reduce costs as well as better plan for the future, but a lot of them discovered that they didn't have the information they needed and they didn't have the ability to get that information. The unsteady recession environment also made it risky for companies to interrupt their operations to get new systems up to speed.

So what to do? Try to piecemeal upgrades each year or start a major overhaul of their internal systems? One company, for example, has standardized as many of its systems as possible and has been steadily upgrading them over the past decade. Acquisitions can also wreak havoc on reporting systems. This company is choosy about when to standardize for companies it acquires, but it sometimes has to implement new systems after international deals.

In other situations, a major overhaul is needed. For example, it is common for companies with a steady stream of acquisitions to have 50 to 70 general ledger systems. In those cases, a company cannot react well unless its systems are made compatible. So is it the big bang (major overhaul) or the piecemeal approach? It seems to depend. One thing is certain—good accounting systems are a necessity. Without one, the risk of failure is high.

Source: Emily Chasan, "The Financial-Data Dilemma," *Wall Street Journal* (July 24, 2012), p. B4.

The Accounting Cycle Summarized

A summary of the steps in the accounting cycle shows a logical sequence of the accounting procedures used during a fiscal period:

1. Enter the transactions of the period in appropriate journals.

2. Post from the journals to the ledger (or ledgers).

3. Prepare an unadjusted trial balance (trial balance).

4. Prepare adjusting journal entries and post to the ledger(s).

5. Prepare a trial balance after adjusting (adjusted trial balance).

6. Prepare the financial statements from the adjusted trial balance.

7. Prepare closing journal entries and post to the ledger(s).

8. Prepare a trial balance after closing (post-closing trial balance).

9. Prepare reversing entries **(optional)** and post to the ledger(s).

A company normally completes all of these steps in every fiscal period.

FINANCIAL STATEMENTS FOR A MERCHANDISING COMPANY

LEARNING OBJECTIVE  **8**

Prepare financial statements for a merchandising company.

Pioneer Advertising Agency Inc. is a service company. In this section, we show a detailed set of financial statements for a merchandising company, Uptown Cabinet Corp. The financial statements, below and on the next page, are prepared from the adjusted trial balance.

Income Statement

The income statement for Uptown, shown in Illustration 3-39, is self-explanatory. The income statement classifies amounts into such categories as gross profit on sales, income from operations, income before taxes, and net income. Although earnings per share information is required to be shown on the face of the income statement for a corporation, we omit this item here; it will be discussed more fully later in the textbook. *(For homework purposes, do not present earnings per share information unless required to do so.)*

ILLUSTRATION 3-39
Income Statement for a
Merchandising Company

UPTOWN CABINET CORP.
INCOME STATEMENT
FOR THE YEAR ENDED DECEMBER 31, 2015

Net sales		₺400,000
Cost of goods sold		316,000
Gross profit on sales		84,000
Selling expenses		
Salaries and wages expense (sales)	₺20,000	
Advertising expense	10,200	
Total selling expenses	30,200	
Administrative expenses		
Salaries and wages expense (general)	₺19,000	
Depreciation expense	6,700	
Property tax expense	5,300	
Rent expense	4,300	
Bad debt expense	1,000	
Telephone and Internet expense	600	
Insurance expense	360	
Total administrative expenses	37,260	
Total selling and administrative expenses		67,460
Income from operations		16,540
Other revenues and gains		
Interest revenue		800
		17,340
Other expenses and losses		
Interest expense		1,700
Income before income taxes		15,640
Income tax		3,440
Net income		₺ 12,200

Retained Earnings Statement

A corporation may retain the net income earned in the business, or it may distribute it to shareholders by payment of dividends. In Illustration 3-40, Uptown added the net income earned during the year to the balance of retained earnings on January 1, thereby increasing the balance of retained earnings. Deducting dividends of ₱2,000 results in the ending retained earnings balance of ₱26,400 on December 31.

ILLUSTRATION 3-40
Retained Earnings
Statement for a
Merchandising Company

UPTOWN CABINET CORP. RETAINED EARNINGS STATEMENT FOR THE YEAR ENDED DECEMBER 31, 2015	
Retained earnings, January 1	₱16,200
Add: Net income	12,200
	28,400
Less: Dividends	2,000
Retained earnings, December 31	₱26,400

Statement of Financial Position

The statement of financial position for Uptown is a classified statement of financial position. In the property, plant, and equipment section, Uptown deducts Accumulated

ILLUSTRATION 3-41
Statement of Financial
Position for a
Merchandising Company

UPTOWN CABINET CORP. STATEMENT OF FINANCIAL POSITION AS OF DECEMBER 31, 2015			
Assets			
Non-current assets			
Property, plant, and equipment			
Equipment		₱67,000	
Less: Accumulated depreciation—equipment		18,700	
Total property, plant, and equipment			₱ 48,300
Current assets			
Inventory		40,000	
Prepaid insurance		540	
Prepaid rent		500	
Notes receivable	₱16,000		
Accounts receivable	41,000		
Interest receivable	800		
Less: Allowance for doubtful accounts	3,000	54,800	
Cash		1,200	
Total current assets			97,040
Total assets			₱145,340
Equity and Liabilities			
Equity			
Share capital—ordinary, ₱5.00 par value, issued and outstanding, 10,000 shares		₱50,000	
Retained earnings		26,400	
Total equity			₱ 76,400
Non-current liabilities			
Bonds payable, due June 30, 2022		30,000	
Current liabilities			
Notes payable	₱20,000		
Accounts payable	13,500		
Property taxes payable	2,000		
Income taxes payable	3,440		
Total current liabilities		38,940	
Total liabilities			68,940
Total equity and liabilities			₱145,340

Depreciation—Equipment from the cost of the equipment. The difference represents the book or carrying value of the equipment.

Interest receivable, inventory, prepaid insurance, and prepaid rent are included as current assets. Uptown considers these assets current because they will be converted into cash or used by the business within a relatively short period of time. Uptown deducts the amount of Allowance for Doubtful Accounts from the total of accounts, notes, and interest receivable because it estimates that only ₺54,800 of ₺57,800 will be collected in cash.

Because Uptown is a corporation, the equity section in the illustration differs somewhat from the capital section for a proprietorship. Total equity consists of share capital—ordinary, which is the original investment by shareholders, and the earnings retained in the business. *For homework purposes, unless instructed otherwise, prepare an unclassified statement of financial position.*

The bonds payable, due in 2022, are non-current liabilities. As a result, the statement of financial position shows the account in a separate section. (The company paid interest on the bonds on December 31.)

The statement of financial position shows property taxes payable as a current liability because it is an obligation that is payable within a year. The statement of financial position also shows other short-term liabilities such as accounts payable.

Closing Entries

Uptown makes closing entries as follows.

General Journal
December 31, 2015

Interest Revenue	800	
Sales Revenue	400,000	
Income Summary		400,800
(To close revenues to Income Summary)		
Income Summary	388,600	
Cost of Goods Sold		316,000
Salaries and Wages Expense (sales)		20,000
Advertising Expense		10,200
Salaries and Wages Expense (general)		19,000
Depreciation Expense		6,700
Rent Expense		4,300
Property Tax Expense		5,300
Bad Debt Expense		1,000
Telephone and Internet Expense		600
Insurance Expense		360
Interest Expense		1,700
Income Tax Expense		3,440
(To close expenses to Income Summary)		
Income Summary	12,200	
Retained Earnings		12,200
(To close Income Summary to Retained Earnings)		
Retained Earnings	2,000	
Dividends		2,000
(To close Dividends to Retained Earnings)		

GLOBAL ACCOUNTING INSIGHTS

ACCOUNTING INFORMATION SYSTEMS

As indicated in this chapter, companies must have an effective accounting system. In the wake of accounting scandals at U.S. companies like **Sunbeam**, **Rite-Aid**, **Xerox**, and **WorldCom**, U.S. lawmakers demanded higher assurance on the quality of accounting reports. Since the passage of the Sarbanes-Oxley Act of 2002 (SOX), companies that trade on U.S. exchanges are required to place renewed focus on their accounting systems to ensure accurate reporting.

Relevant Facts

Following are the key similarities and differences between U.S. GAAP and IFRS related to accounting information systems.

Similarities

- International companies use the same set of procedures and records to keep track of transaction data. Thus, the material in Chapter 3 dealing with the account, general rules of debit and credit, and steps in the recording process—the journal, ledger, and chart of accounts—is the same under both U.S. GAAP and IFRS.

- Transaction analysis is the same under U.S. GAAP and IFRS but, as you will see in later chapters, different standards sometimes impact how transactions are recorded.

- Both the FASB and IASB go beyond the basic definitions provided in this textbook for the key elements of financial statements, that is, assets, liabilities, equity, revenues, and expenses.

- A trial balance under U.S. GAAP follows the same format as shown in the textbook. As shown in the textbook, currency signs are typically used only in the trial balance and the financial statements. The same practice is followed under U.S. GAAP.

Differences

- Rules for accounting for specific events sometimes differ across countries. For example, European companies rely less on historical cost and more on fair value than U.S. companies. Despite the differences, the double-entry accounting system is the basis of accounting systems worldwide.

- Internal controls are a system of checks and balances designed to prevent and detect fraud and errors. While most public U.S. companies have these systems in place, many non-U.S. companies have never completely documented them nor had an independent auditor attest to their effectiveness. Both of these actions are required under SOX. Enhanced internal control standards apply only to large public companies listed on U.S. exchanges.

About the Numbers

Debate about requiring foreign companies to comply with SOX centers on whether the higher costs of a good information system are making the U.S. securities markets less competitive. Presented below are statistics for initial public offerings (IPOs) in the years since the passage of SOX.

Share of IPO proceeds: U.S., Europe, and China (U.S. $, billions)

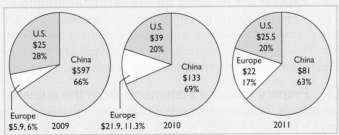

	2009 IPOs	2010 IPOs	2011 IPOs
U.S.	69	168	134
Europe	126	380	430
China	208	502	432

Source: PricewaterhouseCoopers, U.S. IPO Watch: 2011 Analysis and Trends.

Note the U.S. share of IPOs has steadily declined, and some critics of the SOX provisions attribute the decline to the increased cost of complying with the internal control rules.

Others, looking at these same trends, are not so sure about SOX being the cause of the relative decline of U.S. IPOs. These commentators argue that growth in non-U.S. markets is a natural consequence of general globalization of capital flows.

On the Horizon

High-quality international accounting requires both high-quality accounting standards and high-quality auditing. Similar to the convergence of U.S. GAAP and IFRS, there is a movement to improve international auditing standards. The International Auditing and Assurance Standards Board (IAASB) functions as an independent standard-setting body. It works to establish high-quality auditing and assurance and quality-control standards throughout the world. Whether the IAASB adopts internal control provisions similar to those in SOX remains to be seen. You can follow developments in the international audit arena at *http://www.ifac.org/iaasb/*.

KEY TERMS

SUMMARY OF LEARNING OBJECTIVES

1 **Understand basic accounting terminology.** Understanding the following 11 terms helps in understanding key accounting concepts. (1) Event. (2) Transaction. (3) Account. (4) Real and nominal accounts. (5) Ledger. (6) Journal. (7) Posting. (8) Trial balance. (9) Adjusting entries. (10) Financial statements. (11) Closing entries.

2 **Explain double-entry rules.** The left side of any account is the debit side; the right side is the credit side. All asset and expense accounts are increased on the left or debit side, and decreased on the right or credit side. Conversely, all liability and revenue accounts are increased on the right or credit side, and decreased on the left or debit side. Equity accounts, Share Capital—Ordinary and Retained Earnings, are increased on the credit side. Dividends is increased on the debit side.

3 **Identify steps in the accounting cycle.** The basic steps in the accounting cycle are (1) identifying and measuring transactions and other events, (2) journalizing, (3) posting, (4) preparing an unadjusted trial balance, (5) making adjusting entries, (6) preparing an adjusted trial balance, (7) preparing financial statements, and (8) closing.

4 **Record transactions in journals, post to ledger accounts, and prepare a trial balance.** The simplest journal form chronologically lists transactions and events expressed in terms of debits and credits to particular accounts. The items entered in a general journal must be transferred (posted) to the general ledger. Companies should prepare an unadjusted trial balance at the end of a given period after they have recorded the entries in the journal and posted them to the ledger.

5 **Explain the reasons for preparing adjusting entries.** Adjustments achieve a proper recognition of revenues and expenses, so as to determine net income for the current period and to achieve an accurate statement of end-of-the-period balances in assets, liabilities, and equity accounts. The major types of adjusting entries are deferrals (prepaid expenses and unearned revenues) and accruals (accrued revenues and accrued expenses).

6 **Prepare financial statements from the adjusted trial balance.** Companies can prepare financial statements directly from the adjusted trial balance. The income statement is prepared from the revenue and expense accounts. The retained earnings statement is prepared from the retained earnings account, dividends, and net income (or net loss). The statement of financial position is prepared from the asset, liability, and equity accounts.

7 **Prepare closing entries.** In the closing process, the company transfers all of the revenue and expense account balances (income statement items) to a clearing account called Income Summary, which is used only at the end of the fiscal year. Revenues and expenses are matched in the Income Summary account. The net result of this matching represents the net income or net loss for the period. That amount is then transferred to an equity account (Retained Earnings for a corporation and capital accounts for proprietorships and partnerships).

8 **Prepare financial statements for a merchandising company.** The financial statements for a merchandiser differ from those for a service company, as a merchandiser must account for gross profit on sales. The accounting cycle, however, is performed the same.

APPENDIX **3A**	CASH-BASIS ACCOUNTING VERSUS ACCRUAL-BASIS ACCOUNTING

Most companies use **accrual-basis accounting**: They recognize revenue when the performance obligation is satisfied and expenses in the period incurred, without regard to the time of receipt or payment of cash.

9 LEARNING OBJECTIVE
Differentiate the cash basis of accounting from the accrual basis of accounting.

Some small companies and the average individual taxpayer, however, use a strict or modified cash-basis approach. Under the **strict cash basis**, companies record revenue only when they receive cash, and they record expenses only when they disperse cash. Determining income on the cash basis rests upon collecting revenue and paying expenses. The cash basis ignores two principles: the revenue recognition principle and the expense recognition principle. Consequently, cash-basis financial statements are not in conformity with IFRS.

An illustration will help clarify the differences between accrual-basis and cash-basis accounting. Assume that Quality Contractor signs an agreement to construct a garage for ₺22,000. In January, Quality begins construction, incurs costs of ₺18,000 on credit, and by the end of January delivers a finished garage to the buyer. In February, Quality collects ₺22,000 cash from the customer. In March, Quality pays the ₺18,000 due the creditors. Illustrations 3A-1 and 3A-2 show the net incomes for each month under cash-basis accounting and accrual-basis accounting.

ILLUSTRATION 3A-1
Income Statement—
Cash Basis

QUALITY CONTRACTOR
INCOME STATEMENT—CASH BASIS
FOR THE MONTH OF

	January	February	March	Total
Cash receipts	₺–0–	₺22,000	₺ –0–	₺22,000
Cash payments	–0–	–0–	18,000	18,000
Net income (loss)	₺–0–	₺22,000	₺(18,000)	₺ 4,000

ILLUSTRATION 3A-2
Income Statement—
Accrual Basis

QUALITY CONTRACTOR
INCOME STATEMENT—ACCRUAL BASIS
FOR THE MONTH OF

	January	February	March	Total
Revenues	₺22,000	₺–0–	₺–0–	₺22,000
Expenses	18,000	–0–	–0–	18,000
Net income (loss)	₺ 4,000	₺–0–	₺–0–	₺ 4,000

For the three months combined, total net income is the same under both cash-basis accounting and accrual-basis accounting. The difference is in the **timing** of revenues and expenses. The basis of accounting also affects the statement of financial position.

Illustrations 3A-3 and 3A-4 show Quality Contractor's statements of financial position at each month-end under the cash basis and the accrual basis.

ILLUSTRATION 3A-3
Statements of Financial
Position—Cash Basis

QUALITY CONTRACTOR STATEMENTS OF FINANCIAL POSITION—CASH BASIS AS OF			
	January 31	February 28	March 31
Assets			
Cash	₺–0–	₺22,000	₺4,000
Total assets	₺–0–	₺22,000	₺4,000
Equity and liabilities			
Equity	₺–0–	₺22,000	₺4,000
Total equity and liabilities	₺–0–	₺22,000	₺4,000

ILLUSTRATION 3A-4
Statements of Financial
Position—Accrual Basis

QUALITY CONTRACTOR STATEMENTS OF FINANCIAL POSITION—ACCRUAL BASIS AS OF			
	January 31	February 28	March 31
Assets			
Accounts receivable	₺22,000	₺ –0–	₺ –0–
Cash	–0–	22,000	4,000
Total assets	₺22,000	₺22,000	₺4,000
Equity and liabilities			
Equity	₺ 4,000	₺ 4,000	₺4,000
Accounts payable	18,000	18,000	–0–
Total equity and liabilities	₺22,000	₺22,000	₺4,000

Analysis of Quality's income statements and statements of financial position shows the ways in which cash-basis accounting is inconsistent with basic accounting theory:

1. The cash basis understates revenues and assets from the construction and delivery of the garage in January. It ignores the ₺22,000 of accounts receivable, representing a near-term future cash inflow.

2. The cash basis understates expenses incurred with the construction of the garage and the liability outstanding at the end of January. It ignores the ₺18,000 of accounts payable, representing a near-term future cash outflow.

3. The cash basis understates equity in January by not recognizing the revenues and the asset until February. It also overstates equity in February by not recognizing the expenses and the liability until March.

In short, cash-basis accounting violates the accrual concept underlying financial reporting.

The **modified cash basis** is a mixture of the cash basis and the accrual basis. It is based on the strict cash basis but with modifications that have substantial support, such as capitalizing and depreciating plant assets or recording inventory. This method is often followed by professional services firms (doctors, lawyers, accountants, consultants) and by retail, real estate, and agricultural operations.[1]

[1]Companies in the following situations might use a cash or modified cash basis.
(1) A company that is primarily interested in cash flows (for example, a group of physicians that distributes cash-basis earnings for salaries and bonuses).
(2) A company that has a limited number of financial statement users (small, closely held company with little or no debt).
(3) A company that has operations that are relatively straightforward (small amounts of inventory, long-term assets, or long-term debt).

CONVERSION FROM CASH BASIS TO ACCRUAL BASIS

Not infrequently, companies want to convert a cash basis or a modified cash basis set of financial statements to the accrual basis for presentation to investors and creditors. To illustrate this conversion, assume that Dr. Diane Windsor, like many small business owners, keeps her accounting records on a cash basis. In the year 2015, Dr. Windsor received ₺300,000 from her patients and paid ₺170,000 for operating expenses, resulting in an excess of cash receipts over disbursements of ₺130,000 (₺300,000 − ₺170,000). At January 1 and December 31, 2015, she has accounts receivable, unearned service revenue, accrued liabilities, and prepaid expenses as shown in Illustration 3A-5.

	January 1, 2015	December 31, 2015
Accounts receivable	₺12,000	₺9,000
Unearned service revenue	–0–	4,000
Accrued liabilities	2,000	5,500
Prepaid expenses	1,800	2,700

ILLUSTRATION 3A-5
Financial Information Related to Dr. Diane Windsor

Service Revenue Computation

To convert the amount of cash received from patients to service revenue on an accrual basis, we must consider changes in accounts receivable and unearned service revenue during the year. Accounts receivable at the beginning of the year represents revenues recognized last year that are collected this year. Ending accounts receivable indicates revenues recognized this year that are not yet collected. Therefore, to compute revenue on an accrual basis, we subtract beginning accounts receivable and add ending accounts receivable, as the formula in Illustration 3A-6 shows.

Cash Receipts from Customers { − **Beginning Accounts Receivable** + **Ending Accounts Receivable** } = **Revenue on an Accrual Basis**

ILLUSTRATION 3A-6
Conversion of Cash Receipts to Revenue— Accounts Receivable

Similarly, beginning unearned service revenue represents cash received last year for revenues recognized this year. Ending unearned service revenue results from collections this year that will be recognized as revenue next year. Therefore, to compute revenue on an accrual basis, we add beginning unearned service revenue and subtract ending unearned service revenue, as the formula in Illustration 3A-7 shows.

Cash Receipts from Customers { + **Beginning Unearned Service Revenue** − **Ending Unearned Service Revenue** } = **Revenue on an Accrual Basis**

ILLUSTRATION 3A-7
Conversion of Cash Receipts to Revenue— Unearned Service Revenue

Therefore, for Dr. Windsor's dental practice, to convert cash collected from customers to service revenue on an accrual basis, we would make the computations shown in Illustration 3A-8.

Cash receipts from customers		₺300,000
− Beginning accounts receivable	₺(12,000)	
+ Ending accounts receivable	9,000	
+ Beginning unearned service revenue	–0–	
− Ending unearned service revenue	(4,000)	(7,000)
Service revenue (accrual)		₺293,000

ILLUSTRATION 3A-8
Conversion of Cash Receipts to Service Revenue

Operating Expense Computation

To convert cash paid for operating expenses during the year to operating expenses on an accrual basis, we must consider changes in prepaid expenses and accrued liabilities. First, we need to recognize as this year's expenses the amount of beginning prepaid expenses. (The cash payment for these occurred last year.) Therefore, to arrive at operating expense on an accrual basis, we add the beginning prepaid expenses balance to cash paid for operating expenses.

Conversely, ending prepaid expenses result from cash payments made this year for expenses to be reported next year. (Under the accrual basis, Dr. Windsor would have deferred recognizing these payments as expenses until a future period.) To convert these cash payments to operating expenses on an accrual basis, we deduct ending prepaid expenses from cash paid for expenses, as the formula in Illustration 3A-9 shows.

ILLUSTRATION 3A-9
Conversion of Cash Payments to Expenses—Prepaid Expenses

Cash Paid for Operating Expenses	{ + Beginning Prepaid Expenses − Ending Prepaid Expenses }	Expenses = on an Accrual Basis

Similarly, beginning accrued liabilities result from expenses recognized last year that require cash payments this year. Ending accrued liabilities relate to expenses recognized this year that have not been paid. To arrive at expense on an accrual basis, we deduct beginning accrued liabilities and add ending accrued liabilities to cash paid for expenses, as the formula in Illustration 3A-10 shows.

ILLUSTRATION 3A-10
Conversion of Cash Payments to Expenses—Accrued Liabilities

Cash Paid for Operating Expenses	{ − Beginning Accrued Liabilities + Ending Accrued Liabilities }	Expenses = on an Accrual Basis

Therefore, for Dr. Windsor's dental practice, to convert cash paid for operating expenses to operating expenses on an accrual basis, we would make the computations shown in Illustration 3A-11.

ILLUSTRATION 3A-11
Conversion of Cash Paid to Operating Expenses

Cash paid for operating expenses		₺170,000
+ Beginning prepaid expense	₺ 1,800	
− Ending prepaid expense	(2,700)	
− Beginning accrued liabilities	(2,000)	
+ Ending accrued liabilities	5,500	2,600
Operating expenses (accrual)		₺172,600

This entire conversion can be completed in worksheet form, as shown in Illustration 3A-12.

	Diane Windsor.xls				
	Home Insert Page Layout Formulas Data Review View				
	P18 *fx*				
	A	B	C	D	E
1					
2	**DIANE WINDSOR, D.D.S.**				
3	**Conversion of Income Statement Data from Cash Basis to Accrual Basis**				
4	**For the Year 2015**				
5					
6		Cash	Adjustments		Accrual
7	Account Titles	Basis	Add	Deduct	Basis
8	Collections from customers	₺300,000			
9	– Accounts receivable, Jan. 1			₺12,000	
10	+ Accounts receivable, Dec. 31		₺9,000		
11	+ Unearned service revenue, Jan. 1		—	—	
12	– Unearned service revenue, Dec. 31			4,000	
13	Service revenue				₺293,000
14	Disbursement for expenses	170,000			
15	+ Prepaid expenses, Jan. 1		1,800		
16	– Prepaid expenses, Dec. 31			2,700	
17	– Accrued liabilities, Jan. 1			2,000	
18	+ Accrued liabilities, Dec. 31		5,500		
19	Operating expenses				172,600
20	Excess of cash collections over disbursements—cash basis	₺130,000			
21	Net income—accrual basis				₺120,400
22					

Using this approach, we adjust collections and disbursements on a cash basis to revenue and expense on an accrual basis, to arrive at accrual net income. In any conversion from the cash basis to the accrual basis, depreciation or amortization is an additional expense in arriving at net income on an accrual basis.

THEORETICAL WEAKNESSES OF THE CASH BASIS

The cash basis reports exactly when cash is received and when cash is disbursed. To many people that information represents something concrete. Isn't cash what it is all about? Does it make sense to invent something, design it, produce it, market and sell it, if you aren't going to get cash for it in the end? Many frequently say, "Cash is the real bottom line," and also, "Cash is the oil that lubricates the economy." If so, then what is the merit of accrual accounting?

Today's economy is considerably more lubricated by credit than by cash. The accrual basis, not the cash basis, recognizes all aspects of the credit phenomenon. Investors, creditors, and other decision-makers seek timely information about a company's *future* cash flows. Accrual-basis accounting provides this information by reporting the cash inflows and outflows associated with earnings activities as soon as these companies can estimate these cash flows with an acceptable degree of certainty. Receivables and payables are forecasters of future cash inflows and outflows. In other words, accrual-basis accounting aids in predicting future cash flows by reporting transactions and other events with cash consequences at the time the transactions and events occur, rather than when the cash is received and paid.

SUMMARY OF LEARNING OBJECTIVE FOR APPENDIX 3A

9 **Differentiate the cash basis of accounting from the accrual basis of accounting.** The cash basis of accounting records revenues when cash is received and expenses when cash is paid. The accrual basis recognizes revenue when the performance obligation is satisfied and expenses in the period incurred, without regard to the time of the receipt or payment of cash. Accrual-basis accounting is theoretically preferable because it provides information about future cash inflows and outflows associated with earnings activities as soon as companies can estimate these cash flows with an acceptable degree of certainty. Cash-basis accounting is not in conformity with IFRS.

APPENDIX 3B   **USING REVERSING ENTRIES**

LEARNING OBJECTIVE **10**

Identify adjusting entries that may be reversed.

Use of reversing entries simplifies the recording of transactions in the next accounting period. The use of reversing entries, however, does not change the amounts reported in the financial statements for the previous period.

ILLUSTRATION OF REVERSING ENTRIES—ACCRUALS

A company most often uses reversing entries to reverse two types of adjusting entries: accrued revenues and accrued expenses. To illustrate the optional use of reversing entries for accrued expenses, we use the following transaction and adjustment data.

1. October 24 (initial salaries and wages entry): Paid ₺4,000 of salaries and wages incurred between October 10 and October 24.

2. October 31 (adjusting entry): Incurred salaries and wages between October 25 and October 31 of ₺1,200, to be paid in the November 8 payroll.

3. November 8 (subsequent salaries and wages entry): Paid salaries and wages of ₺2,500. Of this amount, ₺1,200 applied to accrued salaries and wages payable at October 31 and ₺1,300 to salaries and wages payable for November 1 through November 8.

Illustration 3B-1 (on page 107) shows the comparative entries.

The comparative entries show that the first three entries are the same whether or not the company uses reversing entries. The last two entries differ. The November 1 reversing entry eliminates the ₺1,200 balance in Salaries and Wages Payable, created by the October 31 adjusting entry. The reversing entry also creates a ₺1,200 credit balance in the Salaries and Wages Expense account. As you know, it is unusual for an expense account to have a credit balance. However, the balance is correct in this instance. Why? Because the company will debit the entire amount of the first salaries and wages payment in the new accounting period to Salaries and Wages Expense. This debit eliminates the credit balance. The resulting debit balance in the expense account will equal the salaries and wages expense incurred in the new accounting period (₺1,300 in this example).

REVERSING ENTRIES NOT USED			REVERSING ENTRIES USED		
Initial Salary Entry					
Oct. 24 Salaries and Wages Expense	4,000		Oct. 24 Salaries and Wages Expense	4,000	
Cash		4,000	Cash		4,000
Adjusting Entry					
Oct. 31 Salaries and Wages Expense	1,200		Oct. 31 Salaries and Wages Expense	1,200	
Salaries and Wages Payable		1,200	Salaries and Wages Payable		1,200
Closing Entry					
Oct. 31 Income Summary	5,200		Oct. 31 Income Summary	5,200	
Salaries and Wages Expense		5,200	Salaries and Wages Expense		5,200
Reversing Entry					
Nov. 1 No entry is made.			Nov. 1 Salaries and Wages Payable	1,200	
			Salaries and Wages Expense		1,200
Subsequent Salary Entry					
Nov. 8 Salaries and Wages Payable	1,200		Nov. 8 Salaries and Wages Expense	2,500	
Salaries and Wages Expense	1,300		Cash		2,500
Cash		2,500			

ILLUSTRATION 3B-1
Comparison of Entries for Accruals, with and without Reversing Entries

When a company makes reversing entries, it debits all cash payments of expenses to the related expense account. This means that on November 8 (and every payday) the company debits Salaries and Wages Expense for the amount paid without regard to the existence of any accrued salaries and wages payable. Repeating the same entry simplifies the recording process in an accounting system.

ILLUSTRATION OF REVERSING ENTRIES—DEFERRALS

Up to this point, we assumed the recording of all deferrals as prepaid expense or unearned revenue. In some cases, though, a company records deferrals directly in expense or revenue accounts. When this occurs, a company may also reverse deferrals.

To illustrate the use of reversing entries for prepaid expenses, we use the following transaction and adjustment data.

1. December 10 (initial entry): Purchased ₺20,000 of supplies with cash.
2. December 31 (adjusting entry): Determined that ₺5,000 of supplies are on hand.

Illustration 3B-2 (on page 108) shows the comparative entries.

After the adjusting entry on December 31 (regardless of whether using reversing entries), the asset account Supplies shows a balance of ₺5,000, and Supplies Expense shows a balance of ₺15,000. If the company initially debits Supplies Expense when it purchases the supplies, it then makes a reversing entry to return to the expense account the cost of unconsumed supplies. The company then continues to debit Supplies Expense for additional purchases of office supplies during the next period.

Deferrals are generally entered in real accounts (assets and liabilities), thus making reversing entries unnecessary. This approach is used because it is advantageous for items that a company needs to apportion over several periods (e.g., supplies and parts inventories). However, for other items that do not follow this regular pattern and that may or may not involve two or more periods, a company ordinarily enters

REVERSING ENTRIES NOT USED				REVERSING ENTRIES USED			
Initial Purchase of Supplies Entry							
Dec. 10	Supplies	20,000		Dec. 10	Supplies Expense	20,000	
	Cash		20,000		Cash		20,000
Adjusting Entry							
Dec. 31	Supplies Expense	15,000		Dec. 31	Supplies	5,000	
	Supplies		15,000		Supplies Expense		5,000
Closing Entry							
Dec. 31	Income Summary	15,000		Dec. 31	Income Summary	15,000	
	Supplies Expense		15,000		Supplies Expense		15,000
Reversing Entry							
Jan. 1	No entry			Jan. 1	Supplies Expense	5,000	
					Supplies		5,000

ILLUSTRATION 3B-2
Comparison of Entries for Deferrals, with and without Reversing Entries

them initially in revenue or expense accounts. The revenue and expense accounts may not require adjusting, and the company thus systematically closes them to Income Summary.

Using the nominal accounts adds consistency to the accounting system. It also makes the recording more efficient, particularly when a large number of such transactions occur during the year. For example, the bookkeeper knows to expense invoice items (except for capital asset acquisitions). He or she need not worry whether an item will result in a prepaid expense at the end of the period, because the company will make adjustments at the end of the period.

SUMMARY OF REVERSING ENTRIES

We summarize guidelines for reversing entries as follows.

1. All accruals should be reversed.
2. All deferrals for which a company debited or credited the original cash transaction to an expense or revenue account should be reversed.
3. Adjusting entries for depreciation and bad debts are not reversed.

Recognize that reversing entries do not have to be used. Therefore, some accountants avoid them entirely.

SUMMARY OF LEARNING OBJECTIVE FOR APPENDIX 3B

10 **Identify adjusting entries that may be reversed.** Reversing entries are most often used to reverse two types of adjusting entries: accrued revenues and accrued expenses. Deferrals may also be reversed if the initial entry to record the transaction is made to an expense or revenue account.

APPENDIX **3C**	USING A WORKSHEET: THE ACCOUNTING CYCLE REVISITED

In this appendix, we provide an additional illustration of the end-of-period steps in the accounting cycle and illustrate the use of a worksheet in this process. Using a **worksheet** often facilitates the end-of-period (monthly, quarterly, or annually) accounting and reporting process. Use of a worksheet helps a company prepare the financial statements on a more timely basis. How? With a worksheet, a company need not wait until it journalizes and posts the adjusting and closing entries.

> **11 LEARNING OBJECTIVE**
>
> Prepare a 10-column worksheet.

A company prepares a worksheet either on columnar paper or within a computer spreadsheet. In either form, a company uses the worksheet to adjust account balances and to prepare financial statements.

The worksheet does not replace the financial statements. Instead, it is an informal device for accumulating and sorting information needed for the financial statements. Completing the worksheet provides considerable assurance that a company properly handled all of the details related to the end-of-period accounting and statement preparation. The 10-column worksheet in Illustration 3C-1 (on page 110) provides columns for the first trial balance, adjustments, adjusted trial balance, income statement, and statement of financial position.

WORKSHEET COLUMNS

Trial Balance Columns

Uptown Cabinet Corp., shown in Illustration 3C-1, obtains data for the trial balance from its ledger balances at December 31. The amount for Inventory, ₺40,000, is the year-end inventory amount, which results from the application of a perpetual inventory system.

Adjustments Columns

After Uptown enters all adjustment data on the worksheet, it establishes the equality of the adjustment columns. It then extends the balances in all accounts to the adjusted trial balance columns.

ADJUSTMENTS ENTERED ON THE WORKSHEET

Items (a) through (g) below serve as the basis for the adjusting entries made in the worksheet for Uptown shown in Illustration 3C-1.

(a) Depreciation of equipment at the rate of 10% per year based on original cost of ₺67,000.
(b) Estimated bad debts of one-quarter of 1 percent of sales (₺400,000).
(c) Insurance expired during the year ₺360.
(d) Interest accrued on notes receivable as of December 31, ₺800.
(e) The Rent Expense account contains ₺500 rent paid in advance, which is applicable to next year.
(f) Property taxes accrued December 31, ₺2,000.
(g) Income taxes payable estimated ₺3,440.

UPTOWN CABINET CORP.
Ten-Column Worksheet
For the Year Ended December 31, 2015

Account Titles	Trial Balance Dr.	Cr.	Adjustments Dr.	Cr.	Adjusted Trial Balance Dr.	Cr.	Income Statement Dr.	Cr.	Statement of Financial Position Dr.	Cr.
Cash	1,200				1,200				1,200	
Notes receivable	16,000				16,000				16,000	
Accounts receivable	41,000				41,000				41,000	
Allowance for doubtful accounts		2,000		(b) 1,000		3,000				3,000
Inventory	40,000				40,000				40,000	
Prepaid insurance	900			(c) 360	540				540	
Equipment	67,000				67,000				67,000	
Accumulated depreciation—equipment		12,000		(a) 6,700		18,700				18,700
Notes payable		20,000				20,000				20,000
Accounts payable		13,500				13,500				13,500
Bonds payable		30,000				30,000				30,000
Share capital—ordinary		50,000				50,000				50,000
Retained earnings, Jan. 1, 2015		16,200				16,200				16,200
Dividends	2,000				2,000				2,000	
Sales revenue		400,000				400,000		400,000		
Cost of goods sold	316,000				316,000		316,000			
Salaries and wages expense (sales)	20,000				20,000		20,000			
Advertising expense	10,200				10,200		10,200			
Salaries and wages expense (general)	19,000				19,000		19,000			
Telephone and Internet expense	600				600		600			
Rent expense	4,800			(e) 500	4,300		4,300			
Property tax expense	3,300		(f) 2,000		5,300		5,300			
Interest expense	1,700				1,700		1,700			
Totals	543,700	543,700								
Depreciation expense			(a) 6,700		6,700		6,700			
Bad debt expense			(b) 1,000		1,000		1,000			
Insurance expense			(c) 360		360		360			
Interest receivable			(d) 800		800				800	
Interest revenue				(d) 800		800		800		
Prepaid rent			(e) 500		500				500	
Property taxes payable				(f) 2,000		2,000				2,000
Income tax expense			(g) 3,440		3,440		3,440			
Income taxes payable				(g) 3,440		3,440				3,440
Totals			14,800	14,800	557,640	557,640	388,600	400,800		
Net income							12,200			12,200
Totals							400,800	400,800	169,040	169,040

ILLUSTRATION 3C-1
Use of a Worksheet

The adjusting entries shown on the December 31, 2015, worksheet are as follows.

(a)

Depreciation Expense	6,700	
Accumulated Depreciation—Equipment		6,700

(b)

Bad Debt Expense	1,000	
Allowance for Doubtful Accounts		1,000

(c)

Insurance Expense	360	
Prepaid Insurance		360

(d)

Interest Receivable	800	
Interest Revenue		800

(e)

Prepaid Rent	500	
Rent Expense		500

(f)

Property Tax Expense	2,000	
Property Taxes Payable		2,000

(g)

Income Tax Expense	3,440	
Income Taxes Payable		3,440

Uptown Cabinet transfers the adjusting entries to the Adjustments columns of the worksheet, often designating each by letter. The trial balance lists any new accounts resulting from the adjusting entries, as illustrated on the worksheet. (For example, see the accounts listed in rows 32 through 40 in Illustration 3C-1.) Uptown then totals and balances the Adjustments columns.

Adjusted Trial Balance

The adjusted trial balance shows the balance of all accounts after adjustment at the end of the accounting period. For example, Uptown adds the ₺2,000 shown opposite Allowance for Doubtful Accounts in the Trial Balance Cr. column to the ₺1,000 in the Adjustments Cr. column. The company then extends the ₺3,000 total to the Adjusted Trial Balance Cr. column. Similarly, Uptown reduces the ₺900 debit opposite Prepaid Insurance by the ₺360 credit in the Adjustments column. The result, ₺540, is shown in the Adjusted Trial Balance Dr. column.

Income Statement and Statement of Financial Position Columns

Uptown extends all the debit items in the Adjusted Trial Balance columns into the Income Statement or Statement of Financial Position columns to the right. It similarly extends all the credit items.

The next step is to total the Income Statement columns. Uptown needs the amount of net income or loss for the period to balance the debit and credit columns. The net income of ₺12,200 is shown in the Income Statement Dr. column because revenues exceeded expenses by that amount.

Uptown then balances the Income Statement columns. The company also enters the net income of ₺12,200 in the Statement of Financial Position Cr. column as an increase in retained earnings.

PREPARING FINANCIAL STATEMENTS FROM A WORKSHEET

The worksheet provides the information needed for preparation of the financial statements without reference to the ledger or other records. In addition, the worksheet sorts that data into appropriate columns, which facilitates the preparation of the statements. The financial statements of Uptown Cabinet are shown in Chapter 3, pages 96–97.

KEY TERMS

worksheet, *109*

SUMMARY OF LEARNING OBJECTIVE FOR APPENDIX 3C

11 **Prepare a 10-column worksheet.** The 10-column worksheet provides columns for the first trial balance, adjustments, adjusted trial balance, income statement, and statement of financial position. The worksheet does not replace the financial statements. Instead, it is an informal device for accumulating and sorting information needed for the financial statements.

Note: All asterisked Questions, Exercises, and Problems relate to material in the appendices to the chapter.

QUESTIONS

1. Give an example of a transaction that results in:

   (a) a decrease in an asset and a decrease in a liability.
   (b) a decrease in one asset and an increase in another asset.
   (c) a decrease in one liability and an increase in another liability.

2. Do the following events represent business transactions? Explain your answer in each case.

   (a) A computer is purchased on account.
   (b) A customer returns merchandise and is given credit on account.
   (c) A prospective employee is interviewed.
   (d) The owner of the business withdraws cash from the business for personal use.
   (e) Merchandise is ordered for delivery next month.

3. Name the accounts debited and credited for each of the following transactions.

   (a) Billing a customer for work done.
   (b) Receipt of cash from customer on account.
   (c) Purchase of office supplies on account.
   (d) Purchase of 15 gallons of gasoline for the delivery truck.

4. Why are revenue and expense accounts called temporary or nominal accounts?

5. Andrea Pafko, a fellow student, contends that the double-entry system means that each transaction must be recorded twice. Is Andrea correct? Explain.

6. Is it necessary that a trial balance be prepared periodically? What purpose does it serve?

7. Indicate whether each of the items below is a real or nominal account and whether it appears in the statement of financial position or the income statement.

   (a) Prepaid Rent.
   (b) Salaries and Wages Payable.
   (c) Inventory.
   (d) Accumulated Depreciation—Equipment.
   (e) Equipment.
   (f) Service Revenue.
   (g) Salaries and Wages Expense.
   (h) Supplies.

8. Employees are paid every Saturday for the preceding work week. If a statement of financial position is prepared on Wednesday, December 31, what does the amount of salaries and wages earned during the first three days of the week (12/29, 12/30, 12/31) represent? Explain.

9. (a) How do the components of revenues and expenses differ between a merchandising company and a service enterprise? (b) Explain the income measurement process of a merchandising company.

10. What differences are there between the trial balance before closing and the trial balance after closing with respect to the following accounts?

(a) Accounts Payable.
(b) Expense accounts.
(c) Revenue accounts.
(d) Retained Earnings account.
(e) Cash.

11. What are adjusting entries, and why are they necessary?

12. What are closing entries, and why are they necessary?

13. Carlo Avardo, maintenance supervisor for Lisbon Insurance Co., has purchased a riding lawnmower and accessories to be used in maintaining the grounds around corporate headquarters. He has sent the following information to the accounting department.

Cost of mower and accessories	€4,000	Date purchased	7/1/15
Estimated useful life	5 yrs	Monthly salary of groundskeeper	€1,100
Residual value	€0	Estimated annual fuel cost	€150

Compute the amount of depreciation expense (related to the mower and accessories) that should be reported on Lisbon's December 31, 2015, income statement. Assume straight-line depreciation.

14. Chen Enterprises made the following entry on December 31, 2015.

Interest Expense	10,000	
Interest Payable		10,000
(To record interest expense due on loan from Hibernia Bank)		

What entry would Hibernia Bank make regarding its outstanding loan to Chen Enterprises? Explain why this must be the case.

15. Are all international companies subject to the same internal control standards? Explain.

16. What are some of the consequences of international differences in internal control standards?

17. Briefly describe the key elements of international auditing convergence.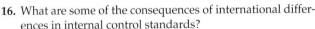

***18.** Distinguish between cash-basis accounting and accrual-basis accounting. Why is accrual-basis accounting acceptable for most business enterprises and the cash-basis unacceptable in the preparation of an income statement and a statement of financial position?

***19.** When salaries and wages expense for the year on an accrual basis is computed, why are beginning accrued salaries and wages subtracted from, and ending accrued salaries and wages added to, salaries and wages paid during the year?

***20.** Explain the distinction between accounting using strict cash-basis accounting and a modified cash basis.

***21.** What are reversing entries, and why are they used?

***22.** "A worksheet is a permanent accounting record, and its use is required in the accounting cycle." Do you agree? Explain.

BRIEF EXERCISES

❹ BE3-1 Transactions for Mehta Company for the month of May are presented below. Prepare journal entries for each of these transactions. (You may omit explanations.)

May 1 B.D. Mehta invests €4,000 cash in exchange for ordinary shares in a small welding corporation.
3 Buys equipment on account for €1,100.
13 Pays €400 to landlord for May rent.
21 Bills Noble Corp. €500 for welding work done.

❹ BE3-2 Agazzi Repair Shop had the following transactions during the first month of business as a proprietorship. Journalize the transactions. (Omit explanations.)

Aug. 2 Invested €12,000 cash and €2,500 of equipment in the business.
7 Purchased supplies on account for €500. (Debit asset account.)
12 Performed services for clients, for which €1,300 was collected in cash and €670 was billed to the clients.
15 Paid August rent €600.
19 Counted supplies and determined that only €270 of the supplies purchased on August 7 are still on hand.

❹ ❺ BE3-3 On July 1, 2015, Crowe Co. pays €15,000 to Zubin Insurance Co. for a 3-year insurance policy. Both companies have fiscal years ending December 31. For Crowe Co. journalize the entry on July 1 and the adjusting entry on December 31.

❹ ❺ BE3-4 Using the data in BE3-3, journalize the entry on July 1 and the adjusting entry on December 31 for Zubin Insurance Co. Zubin uses the accounts Unearned Insurance Revenue and Insurance Revenue.

❹ ❺ BE3-5 Assume that on February 1, **Marks and Spencer plc (M&S)** (GBR) paid £72,000 in advance for 2 years' insurance coverage. Prepare M&S's February 1 journal entry and the annual adjusting entry on June 30.

4 5 BE3-6 LaBouche Corporation owns a warehouse. On November 1, it rented storage space to a lessee (tenant) for 3 months for a total cash payment of €2,400 received in advance. Prepare LaBouche's November 1 journal entry and the December 31 annual adjusting entry.

4 5 BE3-7 Dresser Company's weekly payroll, paid on Fridays, totals €8,000. Employees work a 5-day week. Prepare Dresser's adjusting entry on Wednesday, December 31, and the journal entry to record the €8,000 cash payment on Friday, January 2.

5 BE3-8 Included in Gonzalez Company's December 31 trial balance is a note receivable of €12,000. The note is a 4-month, 10% note dated October 1. Prepare Gonzalez's December 31 adjusting entry to record €300 of accrued interest, and the February 1 journal entry to record receipt of €12,400 from the borrower.

4 BE3-9 Prepare the following adjusting entries at August 31 for Nokia (FIN).

    (a) Interest on notes payable of €300 is accrued.
    (b) Unbilled fees for services performed total €1,400.
    (c) Salaries and wages earned by employees of €700 have not been recorded.
    (d) Bad debt expense for year is €900.

Use the following account titles: Service Revenue, Accounts Receivable, Interest Expense, Interest Payable, Salaries and Wages Expense, Salaries and Wages Payable, Allowance for Doubtful Accounts, and Bad Debt Expense.

5 BE3-10 At the end of its first year of operations, the trial balance of Alonzo Company shows Equipment €30,000 and zero balances in Accumulated Depreciation—Equipment and Depreciation Expense. Depreciation for the year is estimated to be €2,000. Prepare the adjusting entry for depreciation at December 31, and indicate the statement of financial position presentation for the equipment at December 31.

7 BE3-11 Side Kicks has year-end account balances of Sales Revenue €808,900; Interest Revenue €13,500; Cost of Goods Sold €556,200; Operating Expenses €189,000; Income Tax Expense €35,100; and Dividends €18,900. Prepare the year-end closing entries.

9 *BE3-12 Kelly Company had cash receipts from customers in 2015 of €142,000. Cash payments for operating expenses were €97,000. Kelly has determined that at January 1, accounts receivable was €13,000, and prepaid expenses were €17,500. At December 31, accounts receivable was €18,600, and prepaid expenses were €23,200. Compute (a) service revenue and (b) operating expenses.

10 *BE3-13 Assume that GlaxoSmithKline (GBR) made a December 31 adjusting entry to debit Salaries and Wages Expense and credit Salaries and Wages Payable for £4,200 for one of its departments. On January 2, Glaxo paid the weekly payroll of £7,000. Prepare Glaxo's (a) January 1 reversing entry; (b) January 2 entry (assuming the reversing entry was prepared); and (c) January 2 entry (assuming the reversing entry was not prepared).

EXERCISES

4 E3-1 (Transaction Analysis—Service Company) Kai Edo is a licensed public accountant. During the first month of operations of her business (a sole proprietorship), the following events and transactions occurred (amounts in thousands).

April	2	Invested ¥30,000 cash and equipment valued at ¥14,000 in the business.
	2	Hired a secretary-receptionist at a salary of ¥290 per week payable monthly.
	3	Purchased supplies on account ¥700. (Debit an asset account.)
	7	Paid office rent of ¥600 for the month.
	11	Completed a tax assignment and billed client ¥1,100 for services rendered. (Use Service Revenue account.)
	12	Received ¥3,200 advance on a management consulting engagement.
	17	Received cash of ¥2,300 for services completed for Ferengi Co.
	21	Paid insurance expense ¥110.
	30	Paid secretary-receptionist ¥1,160 for the month.
	30	A count of supplies indicated that ¥120 of supplies had been used.
	30	Purchased a new computer for ¥5,100 with personal funds. (The computer will be used exclusively for business purposes.)

Instructions

Journalize the transactions in the general journal. (Omit explanations.)

4 **E3-2 (Corrected Trial Balance)** The trial balance of Geronimo Company does not balance. Your review of the ledger reveals the following. (a) Each account had a normal balance. (b) The debit footings in Prepaid Insurance, Accounts Payable, and Property Tax Expense were each understated €1,000. (c) A transposition error was made in Accounts Receivable and Service Revenue; the correct balances for Accounts Receivable and Service Revenue are €2,750 and €6,690, respectively. (d) A debit posting to Advertising Expense of €300 was omitted. (e) A €3,200 cash drawing by the owner was debited to Geronimo, Capital, and credited to Cash.

GERONIMO COMPANY
TRIAL BALANCE
APRIL 30, 2015

	Debit	Credit
Cash	€ 2,100	
Accounts Receivable	2,570	
Prepaid Insurance	700	
Equipment		€ 8,000
Accounts Payable		4,500
Property Taxes Payable	560	
Geronimo, Capital		11,200
Service Revenue	6,960	
Salaries and Wages Expense	4,200	
Advertising Expense	1,100	
Property Tax Expense		800
	€18,190	€24,500

Instructions
Prepare a correct trial balance.

4 **E3-3 (Corrected Trial Balance)** The trial balance of Scarlatti Corporation does not balance.

SCARLATTI CORPORATION
TRIAL BALANCE
APRIL 30, 2015

	Debit	Credit
Cash	$ 5,912	
Accounts Receivable	5,240	
Supplies	2,967	
Equipment	6,100	
Accounts Payable		$ 7,044
Share Capital—Ordinary		8,000
Retained Earnings		2,000
Service Revenue		5,200
Office Expense	4,320	
	$24,539	$22,244

An examination of the ledger shows these errors.

1. Cash received from a customer on account was recorded (both debit and credit) as $1,580 instead of $1,850.
2. The purchase on account of a computer costing $1,900 was recorded as a debit to Office Expense and a credit to Accounts Payable.
3. Services were performed on account for a client, $2,250, for which Accounts Receivable was debited $2,250 and Service Revenue was credited $225.
4. A payment of $95 for telephone charges was entered as a debit to Office Expense and a debit to Cash.
5. The Service Revenue account was totaled at $5,200 instead of $5,280.

Instructions
From this information prepare a corrected trial balance.

4 **E3-4 (Corrected Trial Balance)** The trial balance of Oakley Co. does not balance.

OAKLEY CO.
TRIAL BALANCE
JUNE 30, 2015

	Debit	Credit
Cash		€ 2,870
Accounts Receivable	€ 3,231	
Supplies	800	
Equipment	3,800	
Accounts Payable		2,666
Unearned Service Revenue	1,200	
Share Capital—Ordinary		6,000
Retained Earnings		3,000
Service Revenue		2,380
Salaries and Wages Expense	3,400	
Office Expense	940	
	€13,371	€16,916

Each of the listed accounts should have a normal balance per the general ledger. An examination of the ledger and journal reveals the following errors.

1. Cash received from a customer on account was debited for €370, and Accounts Receivable was credited for the same amount. The actual collection was for €730.

2. The purchase of a computer printer on account for €500 was recorded as a debit to Supplies for €500 and a credit to Accounts Payable for €500.

3. Services were performed on account for a client for €890. Accounts Receivable was debited for €890 and Service Revenue was credited for €89.

4. A payment of €65 for telephone charges was recorded as a debit to Office Expense for €65 and a debit to Cash for €65.

5. When the Unearned Service Revenue account was reviewed, it was found that service revenue amounting to €225 was performed prior to June 30.

6. A debit posting to Salaries and Wages Expense of €670 was omitted.

7. A payment on account for €206 was credited to Cash for €206 and credited to Accounts Payable for €260.

8. A dividend of €575 was debited to Salaries and Wages Expense for €575 and credited to Cash for €575.

Instructions
Prepare a correct trial balance. (*Note:* It may be necessary to add one or more accounts to the trial balance.)

5 **E3-5 (Adjusting Entries)** The ledger of Chopin Rental Agency on March 31 of the current year includes the following selected accounts before adjusting entries have been prepared.

	Debit	Credit
Prepaid Insurance	€ 3,600	
Supplies	2,800	
Equipment	25,000	
Accumulated Depreciation—Equipment		€ 8,400
Notes Payable		20,000
Unearned Rent Revenue		6,300
Rent Revenue		60,000
Interest Expense	–0–	
Salaries and Wages Expense	14,000	

An analysis of the accounts shows the following.

1. The equipment depreciates €250 per month.

2. One-third of the unearned rent was earned during the quarter.

3. Interest of €500 is accrued on the notes payable.

4. Supplies on hand total €650.

5. Insurance expires at the rate of €300 per month.

Instructions

Prepare the adjusting entries at March 31, assuming that adjusting entries are made quarterly. Additional accounts are Depreciation Expense, Insurance Expense, Interest Payable, and Supplies Expense. (Omit explanations.)

5 ▶ **E3-6 (Adjusting Entries)** Stephen King, D.D.S., opened a dental practice on January 1, 2015. During the first month of operations, the following transactions occurred.

1. Performed services for patients who had dental plan insurance. At January 31, $750 of such services was performed but not yet billed to the insurance companies.

2. Utility expenses incurred but not paid prior to January 31 totaled $520.

3. Purchased dental equipment on January 1 for $80,000, paying $20,000 in cash and signing a $60,000, 3-year note payable. The equipment depreciates $400 per month. Interest is $500 per month.

4. Purchased a one-year malpractice insurance policy on January 1 for $15,000.

5. Purchased $1,600 of dental supplies. On January 31, determined that $400 of supplies were on hand.

Instructions

Prepare the adjusting entries on January 31. (Omit explanations.) Account titles are Accumulated Depreciation—Equipment, Depreciation Expense, Service Revenue, Accounts Receivable, Insurance Expense, Interest Expense, Interest Payable, Prepaid Insurance, Supplies, Supplies Expense, Utilities Expense, and Accounts Payable.

5 ▶ **E3-7 (Analyze Adjusted Data)** A partial adjusted trial balance of Safin Company at January 31, 2015, shows the following.

SAFIN COMPANY		
ADJUSTED TRIAL BALANCE		
JANUARY 31, 2015		
	Debit	Credit
Supplies	£ 900	
Prepaid Insurance	2,400	
Salaries and Wages Payable		£ 800
Unearned Service Revenue		750
Supplies Expense	950	
Insurance Expense	400	
Salaries and Wages Expense	1,800	
Service Revenue		2,000

Instructions

Answer the following questions, assuming the year begins January 1.

(a) If the amount in Supplies Expense is the January 31 adjusting entry and £850 of supplies was purchased in January, what was the balance in Supplies on January 1?

(b) If the amount in Insurance Expense is the January 31 adjusting entry and the original insurance premium was for one year, what was the total premium and when was the policy purchased?

(c) If £2,700 of salaries and wages were paid in January, what was the balance in Salaries and Wages Payable at December 31, 2014?

(d) If £1,600 was received in January for services performed in January, what was the balance in Unearned Service Revenue at December 31, 2014?

5 ▶ **E3-8 (Adjusting Entries)** William Bryant is the new owner of Ace Computer Services. At the end of August 2015, his first month of ownership, Bryant is trying to prepare monthly financial statements. Below is some information related to unrecorded expenses that the business incurred during August.

1. At August 31, Bryant owed his employees $2,900 in salaries and wages that will be paid on September 1.

2. At the end of the month, he had not yet received the month's utility bill. Based on past experience, he estimated the bill would be approximately $600.

3. On August 1, Bryant borrowed $60,000 from a local bank on a 15-year mortgage. The annual interest rate is 8%.

4. A telephone bill in the amount of $117 covering August charges is unpaid at August 31 (use Telephone and Internet Expense account).

Instructions

Prepare the adjusting journal entries as of August 31, 2015, suggested by the information provided.

5 **E3-9** **(Adjusting Entries)** Selected accounts of Leno Company are shown below.

Supplies			
Beg. Bal.	800	10/31	470

Accounts Receivable			
10/17	2,100		
10/31	1,650		

Salaries and Wages Expense		
10/15	800	
10/31	600	

Salaries and Wages Payable		
	10/31	600

Unearned Service Revenue			
10/31	400	10/20	650

Supplies Expense		
10/31	470	

Service Revenue		
	10/17	2,100
	10/31	1,650
	10/31	400

Instructions

From an analysis of the T-accounts, reconstruct (a) the October transaction entries, and (b) the adjusting journal entries that were made on October 31, 2015. Prepare explanations for each journal entry.

5 **E3-10 (Adjusting Entries)** Uhura Resort opened for business on June 1 with eight air-conditioned units. Its trial balance on August 31 is as follows (in thousands).

UHURA RESORT
TRIAL BALANCE
AUGUST 31, 2015

	Debit	Credit
Cash	¥ 19,600	
Prepaid Insurance	4,500	
Supplies	2,600	
Land	20,000	
Buildings	120,000	
Equipment	16,000	
Accounts Payable		¥ 4,500
Unearned Rent Revenue		4,600
Mortgage Payable		50,000
Share Capital—Ordinary		100,000
Retained Earnings		0
Dividends	5,000	
Rent Revenue		86,200
Salaries and Wages Expense	44,800	
Utilities Expense	9,200	
Maintenance and Repairs Expense	3,600	
	¥245,300	¥245,300

Other data:

1. The balance in prepaid insurance is a one-year premium paid on June 1, 2015.
2. An inventory count on August 31 shows ¥650 of supplies on hand.
3. Annual depreciation rates are buildings (4%) and equipment (10%). Residual value is estimated to be 10% of cost.
4. Unearned rent revenue of ¥3,800 was earned prior to August 31.
5. Salaries and wages of ¥375 were unpaid at August 31.
6. Rentals of ¥800 were due from tenants at August 31.
7. The mortgage note is dated 1/1/2015. The mortgage interest rate is 8% per year.

Instructions

(a) Journalize the adjusting entries on August 31 for the 3-month period June 1–August 31. (Omit explanations.)
(b) Prepare an adjusted trial balance on August 31.

6 **E3-11 (Prepare Financial Statements)** The adjusted trial balance of Cavamanlis Co. as of December 31, 2015, contains the following.

CAVAMANLIS CO. ADJUSTED TRIAL BALANCE DECEMBER 31, 2015		
Account Titles	Dr.	Cr.
Cash	$18,972	
Accounts Receivable	6,920	
Prepaid Rent	2,280	
Equipment	18,050	
Accumulated Depreciation—Equipment		$ 4,895
Notes Payable		5,700
Accounts Payable		4,472
Share Capital—Ordinary		20,000
Retained Earnings		11,310
Dividends	3,000	
Service Revenue		12,590
Salaries and Wages Expense	6,840	
Rent Expense	2,760	
Depreciation Expense	145	
Interest Expense	83	
Interest Payable		83
	$59,050	$59,050

Instructions

(a) Prepare an income statement.

(b) Prepare a retained earnings statement.

(c) Prepare a classified statement of financial position.

6 **E3-12 (Prepare Financial Statements)** Flynn Design Agency was founded by Kevin Flynn in January 2011. Presented below is the adjusted trial balance as of December 31, 2015.

FLYNN DESIGN AGENCY ADJUSTED TRIAL BALANCE DECEMBER 31, 2015		
	Dr.	Cr.
Cash	€ 10,000	
Accounts Receivable	21,500	
Supplies	5,000	
Prepaid Insurance	2,500	
Equipment	60,000	
Accumulated Depreciation—Equipment		€ 35,000
Accounts Payable		8,000
Interest Payable		150
Notes Payable		5,000
Unearned Service Revenue		5,600
Salaries and Wages Payable		1,300
Share Capital—Ordinary		10,000
Retained Earnings		3,500
Service Revenue		58,500
Salaries and Wages Expense	12,300	
Insurance Expense	850	
Interest Expense	500	
Depreciation Expense	7,000	
Supplies Expense	3,400	
Rent Expense	4,000	
	€127,050	€127,050

Instructions

(a) Prepare an income statement and a retained earnings statement for the year ending December 31, 2015, and an unclassified statement of financial position at December 31.

(b) Answer the following questions.

(1) If the note has been outstanding 6 months, what is the annual interest rate on that note?

(2) If the company paid €17,500 in salaries and wages in 2015, what was the balance in Salaries and Wages Payable on December 31, 2014?

7 E3-13 (Closing Entries) The adjusted trial balance of Faulk Company shows the following data pertaining to sales at the end of its fiscal year, October 31, 2015: Sales Revenue £800,000; Delivery Expense £12,000; Sales Returns and Allowances £24,000; and Sales Discounts £12,000.

Instructions

(a) Prepare the revenues section of the income statement.

(b) Prepare separate closing entries for (1) sales revenue and (2) the contra accounts to sales revenue.

7 E3-14 (Closing Entries) Presented below is information related to Russell Corporation for the month of January 2015.

Cost of goods sold	€202,000	Salaries and wages expense	€ 61,000
Delivery expense	7,000	Sales discounts	8,000
Insurance expense	12,000	Sales returns and allowances	13,000
Rent expense	20,000	Sales revenue	340,000

Instructions

Prepare the necessary closing entries.

8 E3-15 (Missing Amounts) Presented below is financial information for two different companies.

	Shabbona Company	Jenkins Company
Sales revenue	$90,000	(d)
Sales returns and allowances	(a)	$ 5,000
Net sales	85,000	90,000
Cost of goods sold	56,000	(e)
Gross profit	(b)	38,000
Operating expenses	15,000	23,000
Net income	(c)	15,000

Instructions

Compute the missing amounts.

7 E3-16 (Closing Entries for a Corporation) Presented below are selected account balances for Alistair Co. as of December 31, 2015.

Inventory 12/31/15	$ 60,000	Cost of Goods Sold	$235,700
Share Capital—Ordinary	75,000	Selling Expenses	16,000
Retained Earnings	45,000	Administrative Expenses	38,000
Dividends	18,000	Income Tax Expense	30,000
Sales Returns and Allowances	12,000		
Sales Discounts	15,000		
Sales Revenue	390,000		

Instructions

Prepare closing entries for Alistair Co. on December 31, 2015. (Omit explanations.)

4 E3-17 (Transactions of a Corporation, Including Investment and Dividend) Snyder Miniature Golf and Driving Range Inc. was opened on March 1 by Mickey Snyder. The following selected events and transactions occurred during March.

Mar. 1 Invested £60,000 cash in the business in exchange for ordinary shares.

3 Purchased Michelle Wie's Golf Land for £38,000 cash. The price consists of land £10,000, building £22,000, and equipment £6,000. (Make one compound entry.)

5 Advertised the opening of the driving range and miniature golf course, paying advertising expenses of £1,600.

6 Paid cash £1,480 for a one-year insurance policy.

10 Purchased golf equipment for £2,500 from Young Company, payable in 30 days.

18	Received golf fees of £1,200 in cash.
25	Declared and paid a £1,000 cash dividend.
30	Paid salaries and wages of £900.
30	Paid Young Company in full.
31	Received £750 of fees in cash.

Snyder uses the following accounts: Cash, Prepaid Insurance, Land, Buildings, Equipment, Accounts Payable, Share Capital—Ordinary, Dividends, Service Revenue, Advertising Expense, and Salaries and Wages Expense.

Instructions
Journalize the March transactions. (Provide explanations for the journal entries.)

9 *E3-18 (Cash to Accrual Basis)** Corinne Dunbar, M.D., maintains the accounting records of Dunbar Clinic on a cash basis. During 2015, Dr. Dunbar collected €142,600 from her patients and paid €60,470 in expenses. At January 1, 2015, and December 31, 2015, she had accounts receivable, unearned service revenue, accrued expenses, and prepaid expenses as follows. (All long-lived assets are rented.)

	January 1, 2015	December 31, 2015
Accounts receivable	€11,250	€15,927
Unearned service revenue	2,840	4,111
Accrued expenses	3,435	2,108
Prepaid expenses	1,917	3,232

Instructions
Prepare a schedule that converts Dr. Dunbar's "excess of cash collected over cash disbursed" for the year 2015 to net income on an accrual basis for the year 2015.

9 *E3-19 (Cash and Accrual Basis)** Nalezny Corp. maintains its financial records on the cash basis of accounting. Interested in securing a long-term loan from its regular bank, Nalezny Corp. requests you to convert its cash-basis income statement data to the accrual basis. You are provided with the following summarized data covering 2014, 2015, and 2016.

	2014	2015	2016
Cash receipts from sales:			
On 2014 sales	$290,000	$160,000	$ 30,000
On 2015 sales	–0–	355,000	90,000
On 2016 sales			408,000
Cash payments for expenses:			
On 2014 expenses	185,000	67,000	25,000
On 2015 expenses	40,000[a]	170,000	55,000
On 2016 expenses		45,000[b]	218,000

[a]Prepayments of 2015 expenses.
[b]Prepayments of 2016 expenses.

Instructions
(a) Using the data above, prepare abbreviated income statements for the years 2014 and 2015 on the cash basis.
(b) Using the data above, prepare abbreviated income statements for the years 2014 and 2015 on the accrual basis.

5 **10** *E3-20 (Adjusting and Reversing Entries)** When the accounts of Constantine Inc. are examined, the adjusting data listed below are uncovered on December 31, the end of an annual fiscal period.

1. The prepaid insurance account shows a debit of ₺6,000, representing the cost of a 2-year fire insurance policy dated August 1 of the current year.

2. On November 1, Rent Revenue was credited for ₺2,400, representing revenue from a subrental for a 3-month period beginning on that date.

3. Purchase of advertising materials for ₺800 during the year was recorded in the Supplies Expense account. On December 31, advertising materials of ₺290 are on hand.

4. Interest of ₺770 has accrued on notes payable.

Instructions
Prepare the following in general journal form.
(a) The adjusting entry for each item.
(b) The reversing entry for each item where appropriate.

11 *E3-21 (Worksheet)** Presented below are selected accounts for Acevedo Company as reported in the worksheet at the end of May 2015.

	Acevedo Company.xls						
	Home Insert Page Layout Formulas Data Review View						
	P18 *fx*						
	A	B	C	D	E	F	G
		Adjusted Trial Balance		Income Statement		Statement of Financial Position	
1	Account Titles	Dr.	Cr.	Dr.	Cr.	Dr.	Cr.
2	Cash	15,000					
3	Inventory	80,000					
4	Sales Revenue		470,000				
5	Sales Returns and Allowances	10,000					
6	Sales Discounts	5,000					
7	Cost of Goods Sold	250,000					

Instructions

Complete the worksheet by extending amounts reported in the adjusted trial balance to the appropriate columns in the worksheet. Do not total individual columns.

11 *E3-22 (Worksheet and Statement of Financial Position Presentation)** The adjusted trial balance for Madrasah Co. (in euros) is presented in the following worksheet for the month ended April 30, 2015.

	Madrasah Co.xls						
	Home Insert Page Layout Formulas Data Review View						
	P18 *fx*						
	A	B	C	D	E	F	G
1							
2		**MADRASAH CO.**					
3		**Worksheet (PARTIAL)**					
4		**For the Month Ended April 30, 2015**					
5		Adjusted Trial Balance		Income Statement		Statement of Financial Position	
6							
7	Account Titles	Dr.	Cr.	Dr.	Cr.	Dr.	Cr.
8	Cash	18,972					
9	Accounts Receivable	6,920					
10	Prepaid Rent	2,280					
11	Equipment	18,050					
12	Accumulated Depreciation—Equipment		4,895				
13	Notes Payable		5,700				
14	Accounts Payable		4,472				
15	Madrasah, Capital		34,960				
16	Madrasah, Drawing	6,650					
17	Service Revenue		12,590				
18	Salaries and Wages Expense	6,840					
19	Rent Expense	2,760					
20	Depreciation Expense	145					
21	Interest Expense	83					
22	Interest Payable		83				

Instructions

Complete the worksheet and prepare a classified statement of financial position.

11 *E3-23 (Partial Worksheet Preparation)** Letterman Co. prepares monthly financial statements from a worksheet. Selected portions of the January worksheet showed the following data.

	Letterman Co.xls						
Home Insert Page Layout Formulas Data Review View							
P18 *fx*							
	A	B	C	D	E	F	G
1							
2		**LETTERMAN CO.**					
3		Worksheet (PARTIAL)					
4		For the Month Ended January 31, 2015					
5						Adjusted	
6		Trial Balance		Adjustments		Trial Balance	
7	Account Titles	Dr.	Cr.	Dr.	Cr.	Dr.	Cr.
8	Supplies	3,256			(a) 1,500	1,756	
9	Accumulated Depreciation—Equipment		7,710		(b) 257		7,967
10	Interest Payable		100		(c) 50		150
11	Supplies Expense			(a) 1,500		1,500	
12	Depreciation Expense			(b) 257		257	
13	Interest Expense			(c) 50		50	

During February, no events occurred that affected these accounts. But at the end of February, the following information was available.

(a) Supplies on hand	€515
(b) Monthly depreciation	€257
(c) Accrued interest	€ 50

Instructions
Reproduce the data that would appear in the February worksheet and indicate the amounts that would be shown in the February income statement.

PROBLEMS

4 6 7 **P3-1 (Transactions, Financial Statements—Service Company)** Listed below are the transactions of Yasunari Kawabata, D.D.S., for the month of September (amounts in thousands).

Sept. 1 Kawabata begins practice as a dentist and invests ¥20,000 cash.
2 Purchases equipment on account from Green Jacket Co. for ¥17,280.
4 Pays rent for office space, ¥680 for the month.
4 Employs a receptionist, Michael Bradley.
5 Purchases dental supplies for cash, ¥942.
8 Receives cash of ¥1,690 from patients for services performed.
10 Pays miscellaneous office expenses, ¥430.
14 Bills patients ¥5,820 for services performed.
18 Pays Green Jacket Co. on account, ¥3,600.
19 Withdraws ¥3,000 cash from the business for personal use.
20 Receives ¥980 from patients on account.
25 Bills patients ¥2,110 for services performed.
30 Pays the following expenses in cash: office salaries ¥1,800; miscellaneous office expenses ¥85.
30 Dental supplies used during September, ¥330.

Instructions

(a) Enter the transactions shown above in appropriate general ledger accounts (use T-accounts). Use the following ledger accounts: Cash; Accounts Receivable; Supplies; Equipment; Accumulated Depreciation—Equipment; Accounts Payable; Yasunari Kawabata, Capital; Service Revenue; Rent Expense; Office Expense; Salaries and Wages Expense; Supplies Expense; Depreciation Expense; and Income Summary. Allow 10 lines for the Cash and Income Summary accounts, and 5 lines for each of the other accounts needed. Record depreciation using a 5-year life on the equipment, the straight-line method, and no residual value. Do not use a drawing account.

(b) Prepare a trial balance.

(c) Prepare an income statement, a statement of owner's equity, and an unclassified statement of financial position.

(d) Close the ledger.

(e) Prepare a post-closing trial balance.

5 **6** **P3-2 (Adjusting Entries and Financial Statements)** Mason Advertising Agency was founded in January 2011. Presented below are adjusted and unadjusted trial balances as of December 31, 2015.

<table>
<tr><td colspan="5" align="center">MASON ADVERTISING AGENCY
TRIAL BALANCE
DECEMBER 31, 2015</td></tr>
<tr><td></td><td colspan="2" align="center">Unadjusted</td><td colspan="2" align="center">Adjusted</td></tr>
<tr><td></td><td align="center">Dr.</td><td align="center">Cr.</td><td align="center">Dr.</td><td align="center">Cr.</td></tr>
<tr><td>Cash</td><td>€ 11,000</td><td></td><td>€ 11,000</td><td></td></tr>
<tr><td>Accounts Receivable</td><td>20,000</td><td></td><td>23,500</td><td></td></tr>
<tr><td>Supplies</td><td>8,400</td><td></td><td>3,000</td><td></td></tr>
<tr><td>Prepaid Insurance</td><td>3,350</td><td></td><td>2,500</td><td></td></tr>
<tr><td>Equipment</td><td>60,000</td><td></td><td>60,000</td><td></td></tr>
<tr><td>Accumulated Depreciation—Equipment</td><td></td><td>€ 28,000</td><td></td><td>€ 33,000</td></tr>
<tr><td>Accounts Payable</td><td></td><td>5,000</td><td></td><td>5,000</td></tr>
<tr><td>Interest Payable</td><td></td><td>–0–</td><td></td><td>150</td></tr>
<tr><td>Notes Payable</td><td></td><td>5,000</td><td></td><td>5,000</td></tr>
<tr><td>Unearned Service Revenue</td><td></td><td>7,000</td><td></td><td>5,600</td></tr>
<tr><td>Salaries and Wages Payable</td><td></td><td>–0–</td><td></td><td>1,300</td></tr>
<tr><td>Share Capital—Ordinary</td><td></td><td>10,000</td><td></td><td>10,000</td></tr>
<tr><td>Retained Earnings</td><td></td><td>3,500</td><td></td><td>3,500</td></tr>
<tr><td>Service Revenue</td><td></td><td>58,600</td><td></td><td>63,500</td></tr>
<tr><td>Salaries and Wages Expense</td><td>10,000</td><td></td><td>11,300</td><td></td></tr>
<tr><td>Insurance Expense</td><td></td><td></td><td>850</td><td></td></tr>
<tr><td>Interest Expense</td><td>350</td><td></td><td>500</td><td></td></tr>
<tr><td>Depreciation Expense</td><td></td><td></td><td>5,000</td><td></td></tr>
<tr><td>Supplies Expense</td><td></td><td></td><td>5,400</td><td></td></tr>
<tr><td>Rent Expense</td><td>4,000</td><td></td><td>4,000</td><td></td></tr>
<tr><td></td><td>€117,100</td><td>€117,100</td><td>€127,050</td><td>€127,050</td></tr>
</table>

Instructions

(a) Journalize the annual adjusting entries that were made. (Omit explanations.)

(b) Prepare an income statement and a retained earnings statement for the year ending December 31, 2015, and an unclassified statement of financial position at December 31.

(c) Answer the following questions.

(1) If the note has been outstanding 3 months, what is the annual interest rate on that note?

(2) If the company paid €12,500 in salaries in 2015, what was the balance in Salaries and Wages Payable on December 31, 2014?

5 **P3-3 (Adjusting Entries)** A review of the ledger of Baylor Company at December 31, 2015, produces the following data pertaining to the preparation of annual adjusting entries.

1. Salaries and Wages Payable $0. There are eight employees. Salaries and wages are paid every Friday for the current week. Five employees receive $700 each per week, and three employees earn $600 each per week. December 31 is a Tuesday. Employees do not work weekends. All employees worked the last 2 days of December.

2. Unearned Rent Revenue $429,000. The company began subleasing office space in its new building on November 1. Each tenant is required to make a $5,000 security deposit that is not refundable until occupancy is terminated. At December 31, the company had the following rental contracts that are paid in full for the entire term of the lease.

Date	Term (in months)	Monthly Rent	Number of Leases
Nov. 1	6	$6,000	5
Dec. 1	6	$8,500	4

3. Prepaid Advertising $13,200. This balance consists of payments on two advertising contracts. The contracts provide for monthly advertising in two trade magazines. The terms of the contracts are as shown below.

Contract	Date	Amount	Number of Magazine Issues
A650	May 1	$6,000	12
B974	Oct. 1	$7,200	24

The first advertisement runs in the month in which the contract is signed.

4. Notes Payable $60,000. This balance consists of a note for one year at an annual interest rate of 12%, dated June 1.

Instructions

Prepare the adjusting entries at December 31, 2015. (Show all computations.)

4 5
6 7 **P3-4 (Financial Statements, Adjusting and Closing Entries)** The trial balance of Bellemy Fashion Center contained the following accounts at November 30, the end of the company's fiscal year.

BELLEMY FASHION CENTER TRIAL BALANCE NOVEMBER 30, 2015	Debit	Credit
Cash	€ 28,700	
Accounts Receivable	33,700	
Inventory	45,000	
Supplies	5,500	
Equipment	133,000	
Accumulated Depreciation—Equipment		€ 24,000
Notes Payable		51,000
Accounts Payable		48,500
Share Capital—Ordinary		90,000
Retained Earnings		8,000
Sales Revenue		757,200
Sales Returns and Allowances	4,200	
Cost of Goods Sold	495,400	
Salaries and Wages Expense	140,000	
Advertising Expense	26,400	
Utilities Expense	14,000	
Maintenance and Repairs Expense	12,100	
Delivery Expense	16,700	
Rent Expense	24,000	
	€978,700	€978,700

Adjustment data:

1. Supplies on hand totaled €1,500.

2. Depreciation is €15,000 on the equipment.

3. Interest of €11,000 is accrued on notes payable at November 30.

Other data:

1. Salaries and wages expense is 70% selling and 30% administrative.

2. Rent expense and utilities expense are 80% selling and 20% administrative.

3. €30,000 of notes payable are due for payment next year.

4. Maintenance and repairs expense is 100% administrative.

Instructions

    (a) Journalize the adjusting entries.

    (b) Prepare an adjusted trial balance.

    (c) Prepare an income statement and retained earnings statement for the year and a classified statement of financial position as of November 30, 2015.

    (d) Journalize the closing entries.

    (e) Prepare a post-closing trial balance.

5 **P3-5 (Adjusting Entries)** The accounts listed below appeared in the December 31 trial balance of the Savard Theater.

	Debit	Credit
Equipment	€192,000	
Accumulated Depreciation—Equipment		€ 60,000
Notes Payable		90,000
Admissions Revenue		380,000
Advertising Expense	13,680	
Salaries and Wages Expense	57,600	
Interest Expense	1,400	

Instructions

    (a) From the account balances listed above and the information given below, prepare the annual adjusting entries necessary on December 31. (Omit explanations.)

        (1) The equipment has an estimated life of 16 years and a residual value of €24,000 at the end of that time. (Use straight-line method.)

        (2) The note payable is a 90-day note given to the bank October 20 and bearing interest at 8%. (Use 360 days for denominator.)

        (3) In December, 2,000 coupon admission books were sold at €30 each. They could be used for admission any time after January 1. The proceeds were recorded as Admissions Revenue.

        (4) Advertising expense paid in advance and included in Advertising Expense €1,100.

        (5) Salaries and wages accrued but unpaid €4,700.

    (b) What amounts should be shown for each of the following on the income statement for the year?

        (1) Interest expense.   (3) Advertising expense.

        (2) Admissions revenue.   (4) Salaries and wages expense.

5 **6** **P3-6 (Adjusting Entries and Financial Statements)** The following are the trial balance and other information related to Yorkis Perez, a consulting engineer.

YORKIS PEREZ, CONSULTING ENGINEER
TRIAL BALANCE
DECEMBER 31, 2015

	Debit	Credit
Cash	R$ 29,500	
Accounts Receivable	49,600	
Allowance for Doubtful Accounts		R$ 750
Supplies	1,960	
Prepaid Insurance	1,100	
Equipment	25,000	
Accumulated Depreciation—Equipment		6,250
Notes Payable		7,200
Yorkis Perez, Capital		35,010
Service Revenue		100,000
Rent Expense	9,750	
Salaries and Wages Expense	30,500	
Utilities Expense	1,080	
Office Expense	720	
	R$149,210	R$149,210

1. Fees received in advance from clients R$6,000.

2. Services performed for clients that were not recorded by December 31, R$4,900.

3. Bad debt expense for the year is R$1,430.

4. Insurance expired during the year R$480.

5. Equipment is being depreciated at 10% per year.

6. Yorkis Perez gave the bank a 90-day, 10% note for R$7,200 on December 1, 2015.

7. Rent of the building is R$750 per month. The rent for 2015 has been paid, as has that for January 2016.

8. Salaries and wages earned but unpaid December 31, 2015, R$2,510.

Instructions

(a) From the trial balance and other information given, prepare annual adjusting entries as of December 31, 2015. (Omit explanations.)

(b) Prepare an income statement for 2015, a statement of owner's equity, and a classified statement of financial position. Yorkis Perez withdrew R$17,000 cash for personal use during the year.

5 6 P3-7 (Adjusting Entries and Financial Statements) Sorenstam Advertising Corp. was founded in January 2011. Presented below are the adjusted and unadjusted trial balances as of December 31, 2015.

SORENSTAM ADVERTISING CORP.
TRIAL BALANCE
DECEMBER 31, 2015

	Unadjusted Dr.	Unadjusted Cr.	Adjusted Dr.	Adjusted Cr.
Cash	€ 7,000		€ 7,000	
Accounts Receivable	19,000		20,000	
Supplies	8,500		3,500	
Prepaid Insurance	3,250		2,500	
Equipment	60,000		60,000	
Accumulated Depreciation—Equipment		€ 27,000		€ 35,750
Accounts Payable		5,000		5,000
Interest Payable				150
Notes Payable		5,000		5,000
Unearned Service Revenue		7,000		5,600
Salaries and Wages Payable				1,500
Share Capital—Ordinary		10,000		10,000
Retained Earnings		4,500		4,500
Service Revenue		58,600		61,000
Salaries and Wages Expense	10,000		11,500	
Insurance Expense			750	
Interest Expense	350		500	
Depreciation Expense			8,750	
Supplies Expense	5,000		10,000	
Rent Expense	4,000		4,000	
	€117,100	€117,100	€128,500	€128,500

Instructions

(a) Journalize the annual adjusting entries that were made. (Omit explanations.)

(b) Prepare an income statement and a retained earnings statement for the year ending December 31, 2015, and an unclassified statement of financial position at December 31, 2015.

(c) Answer the following questions.

(1) If the useful life of equipment is 6 years, what is the expected residual value?

(2) If the note has been outstanding 3 months, what is the annual interest rate on that note?

(3) If the company paid €12,500 in salaries and wages in 2015, what was the balance in Salaries and Wages Payable on December 31, 2014?

4 5 6 7 **P3-8 (Adjusting and Closing)** Presented below is the trial balance of the Ko Golf Club, Inc. as of December 31. The books are closed annually on December 31.

KO GOLF CLUB, INC.
TRIAL BALANCE
DECEMBER 31

	Debit	Credit
Cash	£ 15,000	
Accounts Receivable	13,000	
Allowance for Doubtful Accounts		£ 1,100
Prepaid Insurance	9,000	
Land	350,000	
Buildings	120,000	
Accumulated Depreciation—Buildings		38,400
Equipment	150,000	
Accumulated Depreciation—		
Equipment		70,000
Share Capital—Ordinary		400,000
Retained Earnings		82,000
Dues Revenue		200,000
Green Fees Revenue		5,900
Rent Revenue		17,600
Utilities Expense	54,000	
Salaries and Wages Expense	80,000	
Maintenance and Repairs Expense	24,000	
	£815,000	£815,000

Instructions

(a) Enter the balances in ledger accounts. Allow five lines for each account.

(b) From the trial balance and the information given below, prepare annual adjusting entries and post to the ledger accounts. (Omit explanations.)

(1) The buildings have an estimated life of 30 years with no residual value (straight-line method).

(2) The equipment is depreciated at 10% per year.

(3) Insurance expired during the year £3,500.

(4) The rent revenue represents the amount received for 11 months for dining facilities. The December rent has not yet been received.

(5) It is estimated that 12% of the accounts receivable will be uncollectible.

(6) Salaries and wages earned but not paid by December 31, £3,600.

(7) Dues received in advance from members £8,900.

(c) Prepare an adjusted trial balance.

(d) Prepare closing entries and post.

4 5 6 7 8 **P3-9 (Adjusting and Closing)** Presented on page 129 is the December 31 trial balance of New York Boutique.

NEW YORK BOUTIQUE
TRIAL BALANCE
DECEMBER 31

	Debit	Credit
Cash	€ 18,500	
Accounts Receivable	32,000	
Allowance for Doubtful Accounts		€ 700
Inventory, December 31	80,000	
Prepaid Insurance	5,100	
Equipment	84,000	
Accumulated Depreciation—Equipment		35,000
Notes Payable		28,000
Share Capital—Ordinary		80,600
Retained Earnings		10,000
Sales Revenue		600,000
Cost of Goods Sold	408,000	
Salaries and Wages Expense	115,000	
Advertising Expense	6,700	
Office Expense	5,000	
	€754,300	€754,300

Instructions

(a) Construct T-accounts and enter the balances shown.

(b) Prepare adjusting journal entries for the following and post to the T-accounts. (Omit explanations.) Open additional T-accounts as necessary. (The books are closed yearly on December 31.)

(1) Bad debt expense is estimated to be €1,400.

(2) Equipment is depreciated based on a 7-year life (no residual value).

(3) Insurance expired during the year €2,550.

(4) Interest accrued on notes payable €3,360.

(5) Salaries and wages earned but not paid €2,400.

(6) Advertising paid in advance €700.

(7) Office supplies on hand €1,500, charged to Office Expense when purchased.

(c) Prepare closing entries and post to the accounts.

9 *P3-10 (Cash and Accrual Basis)** On January 1, 2015, Norma Smith and Grant Wood formed a computer sales and service enterprise in Manchester, U.K., by investing £90,000 cash. The new company, Lakeland Sales and Service, has the following transactions during January.

1. Pays £6,000 in advance for 3 months' rent of office, showroom, and repair space.

2. Purchases 40 personal computers at a cost of £1,500 each, 6 graphics computers at a cost of £2,500 each, and 25 printers at a cost of £300 each, paying cash upon delivery.

3. Sales, repair, and office employees earn £12,600 in salaries and wages during January, of which £3,000 was still payable at the end of January.

4. Sells 30 personal computers at £2,550 each, 4 graphics computers for £3,600 each, and 15 printers for £500 each; £75,000 is received in cash in January, and £23,400 is sold on a deferred payment basis.

5. Other operating expenses of £8,400 are incurred and paid for during January; £2,000 of incurred expenses are payable at January 31.

Instructions

(a) Using the transaction data above, prepare for the month of January (1) a cash-basis income statement, and (2) an accrual-basis income statement.

(b) Using the transaction data above, prepare as of January 31, 2015, (1) a cash-basis statement of financial position and (2) an accrual-basis statement of financial position.

(c) Identify the items in the cash-basis financial statements that make cash-basis accounting inconsistent with the theory underlying the elements of financial statements.

5 6 7 11 *P3-11 (Worksheet, Statement of Financial Position, Adjusting and Closing Entries) Cooke Company has a fiscal year ending on September 30. Selected data from the September 30 worksheet are presented below.

	Cooke Co.xls				
Home Insert Page Layout Formulas Data Review View					
P18	fx				
	A	B	C	D	E
1					
2	**COOKE COMPANY**				
3	Worksheet				
4	For the Month Ended September 30, 2015				
5		Trial Balance		Adjusted Trial Balance	
6	Account Titles	Dr.	Cr.	Dr.	Cr.
7	Cash	37,400		37,400	
8	Supplies	18,600		4,200	
9	Prepaid Insurance	31,900		3,900	
10	Land	80,000		80,000	
11	Equipment	120,000		120,000	
12	Accumulated Depreciation—Equipment		36,200		42,000
13	Accounts Payable		14,600		14,600
14	Unearned Service Revenue		2,700		700
15	Mortgage Payable		50,000		50,000
16	Cooke, Capital		109,700		109,700
17	Cooke, Drawing	14,000		14,000	
18	Service Revenue		278,500		280,500
19	Salaries and Wages Expense	109,000		109,000	
20	Maintenance and Repairs Expense	30,500		30,500	
21	Advertising Expense	9,400		9,400	
22	Utilities Expense	16,900		16,900	
23	Property Tax Expense	18,000		21,000	
24	Interest Expense	6,000		12,000	
25	Totals	491,700	491,700		
26	Insurance Expense			28,000	
27	Supplies Expense			14,400	
28	Interest Payable				6,000
29	Depreciation Expense			5,800	
30	Property Taxes Payable				3,000
31	Totals			506,500	506,500

Instructions

(a) Prepare a complete worksheet.

(b) Prepare a classified statement of financial position. (*Note:* €10,000 of the mortgage payable is due for payment in the next fiscal year.)

(c) Journalize the adjusting entries using the worksheet as a basis.

(d) Journalize the closing entries using the worksheet as a basis.

(e) Prepare a post-closing trial balance.

USING YOUR JUDGMENT

FINANCIAL REPORTING

Financial Reporting Problem

Marks and Spencer plc (M&S)

The financial statements of M&S (GBR) are presented in Appendix A. The company's complete annual report, including the notes to the financial statements, is available online.

Instructions

- **(a)** What were M&S's total assets at March 30, 2013? At March 31, 2012?
- **(b)** How much cash (and cash equivalents) did M&S have on March 30, 2013?
- **(c)** What were M&S's selling and administrative expenses in 2013? In 2012?
- **(d)** What were M&S's revenues in 2013? In 2012?
- **(e)** Using M&S's financial statements and related notes, identify items that may result in adjusting entries for prepayments and accruals.
- **(f)** What were the amounts of M&S's depreciation and amortization expense in 2012 and 2013?

Comparative Analysis Case

adidas and Puma

The financial statements of adidas (DEU) and Puma (DEU) are presented in Appendices B and C, respectively. The complete annual reports, including the notes to the financial statements, are available online.

Instructions

Use the companies' financial information to answer the following questions.

- **(a)** Which company had the greater percentage increase in total assets from 2011 to 2012?
- **(b)** Did either company report the effect of a discontinued operation in its income statement? If so, briefly describe how the reporting of a discontinued operation can affect comparisons between the companies.
- **(c)** Which company had more depreciation and amortization expense, as a percentage of operating cash flow, for 2012? What are some reasons that there would be a difference in these amounts between the two companies?

Financial Statement Analysis Case

Vodafone Group plc

Vodafone is based in the United Kingdom. Selected data from Vodafone's 2012 annual report follows (pounds in millions).

	2012	2011	2010
Revenues	£46,417	£45,884	£44,472
Gross profit %	32.04%	32.84%	33.80%
Operating profit	£11,187	£5,596	£9,480
Operating cash flow less capital expenditures	8,459	9,173	9,145
Profit (loss)	7,003	7,870	8,618

In its 2012 annual report, Vodafone states, "Our leading performance is based on 3 core strengths . . . . The successful implementation of our strategy to generate liquidity or free cash flow from non-controlled interests."

Instructions

- **(a)** Compute the percentage change in sales, operating profit, net cash flow, and net earnings from year to year for the years presented.
- **(b)** Evaluate Vodafone's performance. Which trend seems most favorable? Which trend seems least favorable? What are the implications of these trends for Vodafone's strategy? Explain.

Accounting, Analysis, and Principles

The Amato Theater is nearing the end of the year and is preparing for a meeting with its bankers to discuss the renewal of a loan. The accounts listed on page 132 appeared in the December 31, 2015, trial balance.

	Debit	Credit
Prepaid Advertising	£ 6,000	
Equipment	192,000	
Accumulated Depreciation—Equipment		£ 60,000
Notes Payable		90,000
Unearned Service Revenue		17,500
Service Revenue		360,000
Advertising Expense	18,680	
Salaries and Wages Expense	67,600	
Interest Expense	1,400	

Additional information is available as follows.

1. The equipment has an estimated useful life of 16 years and a residual value of £40,000 at the end of that time. Amato uses the straight-line method for depreciation.

2. The note payable is a one-year note given to the bank January 31 and bearing interest at 10%. Interest is calculated on a monthly basis.

3. The theater sold 350 coupon ticket books at £50 each. Two hundred ticket books were used in 2015. One hundred fifty of these ticket books can be used only for admission any time after January 1, 2016. The cash received was recorded as Unearned Service Revenue.

4. Advertising paid in advance was £6,000 and was debited to Prepaid Advertising. The company has used £2,500 of the advertising as of December 31, 2015.

5. Salaries and wages accrued but unpaid at December 31, 2015, were £3,500.

Accounting

Prepare any adjusting journal entries necessary for the year ended December 31, 2015.

Analysis

Determine Amato's income before and after recording the adjusting entries. Use your analysis to explain why Amato's bankers should be willing to wait for Amato to complete its year-end adjustment process before making a decision on the loan renewal.

Principles

Although Amato's bankers are willing to wait for the adjustment process to be completed before they receive financial information, they would like to receive financial reports more frequently than annually or even quarterly. What trade-offs, in terms of relevance and faithful representation, are inherent is preparing financial statements for shorter accounting time periods?

IFRS BRIDGE TO THE PROFESSION

Professional Research

Recording transactions in the accounting system requires knowledge of the important characteristics of the elements of financial statements, such as assets and liabilities. In addition, accountants must understand the inherent uncertainty in accounting measures and distinctions between related accounting concepts that are important in evaluating the effects of transactions on the financial statements.

Instructions

Access the Conceptual Framework at the IASB website (*http://eifrs.iasb.org/*) (you may register for free eIFRS access at this site). When you have accessed the document, you can use the search tool in your Internet browser to respond to the following items. (Provide paragraph citations.)

(a) Provide the definition of an asset and discuss how the economic benefits embodied in an asset might flow to a company.

(b) Provide the definition of a liability and discuss how a company might satisfy a liability.

(c) What is "accrual basis"? How do adjusting entries illustrate application of the accrual basis?

Professional Simulation

The professional simulation for this chapter asks you to address questions related to the accounting information system.

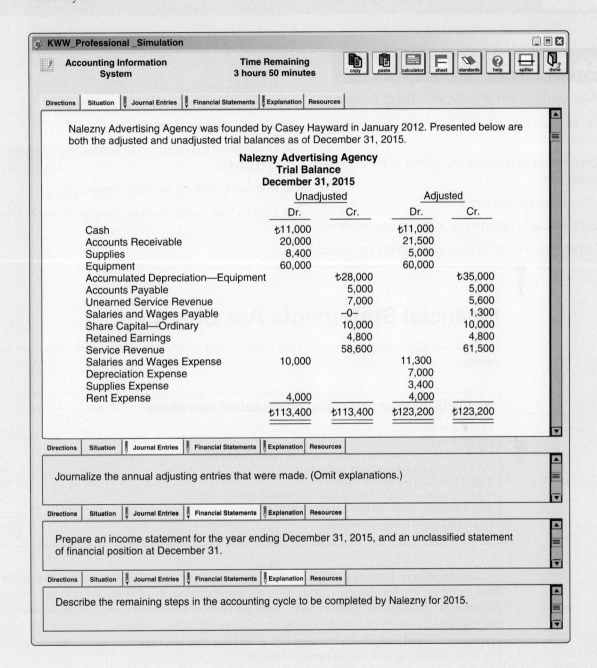

KWW_Professional _Simulation

| Accounting Information System | Time Remaining 3 hours 50 minutes | copy | paste | calculator | sheet | standards | help | splitter | done |

Directions | Situation | Journal Entries | Financial Statements | Explanation | Resources

Nalezny Advertising Agency was founded by Casey Hayward in January 2012. Presented below are both the adjusted and unadjusted trial balances as of December 31, 2015.

Nalezny Advertising Agency
Trial Balance
December 31, 2015

	Unadjusted Dr.	Unadjusted Cr.	Adjusted Dr.	Adjusted Cr.
Cash	₺11,000		₺11,000	
Accounts Receivable	20,000		21,500	
Supplies	8,400		5,000	
Equipment	60,000		60,000	
Accumulated Depreciation—Equipment		₺28,000		₺35,000
Accounts Payable		5,000		5,000
Unearned Service Revenue		7,000		5,600
Salaries and Wages Payable		–0–		1,300
Share Capital—Ordinary		10,000		10,000
Retained Earnings		4,800		4,800
Service Revenue		58,600		61,500
Salaries and Wages Expense	10,000		11,300	
Depreciation Expense			7,000	
Supplies Expense			3,400	
Rent Expense	4,000		4,000	
	₺113,400	₺113,400	₺123,200	₺123,200

Directions | Situation | Journal Entries | Financial Statements | Explanation | Resources

Journalize the annual adjusting entries that were made. (Omit explanations.)

Directions | Situation | Journal Entries | Financial Statements | Explanation | Resources

Prepare an income statement for the year ending December 31, 2015, and an unclassified statement of financial position at December 31.

Directions | Situation | Journal Entries | Financial Statements | Explanation | Resources

Describe the remaining steps in the accounting cycle to be completed by Nalezny for 2015.

Remember to check the book's companion website, at www.wiley.com/ college/kieso, to find additional resources for this chapter.

Income Statement and Related Information

After studying this chapter, you should be able to:

1 Understand the uses and limitations of an income statement.

2 Understand the content and format of the income statement.

3 Prepare an income statement.

4 Explain how to report items in the income statement.

5 Identify where to report earnings per share information.

6 Explain intraperiod tax allocation.

7 Understand the reporting of accounting changes and errors.

8 Prepare a retained earnings statement.

9 Explain how to report other comprehensive income.

Financial Statements Are Changing

Tesco Group (GBR) recently presented the following additional supplemental information in its income statement.

Non-IFRS measure: underlying profits before income tax	
Profit before tax	£2,954
Adjustments for:	
IAS 32 and IAS 39 "Financial instruments"—fair value re-measurement	88
IAS 19 income statement charge for pensions	403
"Normal" cash contribution for pensions	(376)
IAS 17 "Leases"—impact of annual uplifts in rent and rent-free periods	27
IFRS 3 Amortization charge from intangible assets arising on acquisition	32
Underlying profit before income tax	**£3,128**

The directors of Tesco commented in their report to shareholders that they believe the "Underlying profit before income tax" provides additional useful information to shareholders on company trends and performance. They note that these measures are used for internal performance analysis and that underlying profit as defined by IFRS may not be directly comparable with other companies' adjusted profit measures (sometimes referred to as pro forma measures). In addition, they state that it is not intended to be a substitute for, or superior to, IFRS measurements of profit.

Why do companies make these additional adjustments? One major reason is that companies believe the items on the income statement are not representative of operating results. Here is another example using **Marks and Spencer plc (M&S)** (GBR). M&S at one time reported in a separate schedule adjustments to net income for items such as strategic programme costs, restructuring costs, and impairment charges. All these adjustments made the adjusted income measure higher than reported income.

Skeptics of these practices note that these adjustments generally lead to higher adjusted net income. In addition, they note that it is difficult to compare these adjusted or pro forma numbers as one company may have a different view as to what it believes is fundamental to the business. In many ways, the pro forma reporting practices by Tesco and M&S represent implied criticisms of certain financial reporting standards, including how the information is presented on the income statement.

Recently, the IASB initiated a project on financial statement presentation to address users' concerns about these practices. Users believe too many alternatives for classifying and reporting income statement information exist. They note that information is often highly aggregated and inconsistently presented. As a result, it is difficult to assess the financial performance of the company and compare its results with other companies.

Take the income statement as an example. Some companies disaggregate product costs (such as materials and labor) as well as general and administrative costs (such as rent and utilities) in their income statements. Other companies simply report product costs and general and administrative costs in the aggregate. It is difficult to understand the nature of these costs (recurring or non-recurring, fixed or variable) if the costs are aggregated. In other words, two different companies can comply with existing standards for income statement presentation but vary considerably in the detail provided.

What is needed is a common set of principles to be followed when income statement information is presented. The IASB's work on financial statement presentation has been on the "back burner" as the Board focused instead on the major projects of revenue, leases, insurance, and financial instruments. However, input from IASB stakeholders indicate that the project on financial statement presentation and, in particular, income reporting should be a high priority. Hopefully, a restarted project on financial statement presentation will provide those necessary principles.

Sources: "Staff Draft of Exposure Draft: Financial Statement Presentation" (IASB: July 10, 2010); and H. Hoogervorst, "The Imprecise World of Accounting," Speech to the International Association for Accounting Education and Research (June 20, 2012).

CONCEPTUAL FOCUS

> See the **Underlying Concepts** on page 153.
> Read the **Evolving Issue** on page 158 for a discussion of income reporting.

INTERNATIONAL FOCUS

> Read the **Global Accounting Insights** on pages 159–160 for a discussion of non-IFRS financial reporting regarding the income statement.

PREVIEW OF CHAPTER 4

As indicated in the opening story, companies are attempting to provide income statement information they believe is useful for decision-making. Investors need complete and comparable information on income and its components to assess company profitability correctly. In this chapter, we examine the many different types of revenues, expenses, gains, and losses that affect the income statement and related information, as follows.

Income Statement and Related Information

Income Statement	Format of the Income Statement	Reporting within the Income Statement	Other Reporting Issues
• Usefulness • Limitations • Quality of earnings	• Elements • Intermediate components • Illustration • Condensed income statements	• Gross profit • Income from operations • Income before income tax • Net income • Non-controlling interest • Earnings per share • Discontinued operations • Intraperiod tax allocation • Summary	• Accounting changes and errors • Retained earnings statement • Comprehensive income • Statement of changes in equity

INCOME STATEMENT

LEARNING OBJECTIVE 1
Understand the uses and limitations of an income statement.

The **income statement** is the report that measures the success of company operations for a given period of time. (It is also often called the statement of income or statement of earnings.[1]) The business and investment community uses the income statement to determine profitability, investment value, and creditworthiness. It provides investors and creditors with information that helps them predict the **amounts, timing, and uncertainty of future cash flows**.

Usefulness of the Income Statement

The income statement helps users of financial statements predict future cash flows in a number of ways. For example, investors and creditors use the income statement information to:

Which company did better last year?

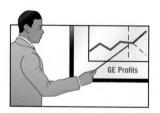

Hmmm... Where am I headed?

1. *Evaluate the past performance of the company.* Examining revenues and expenses indicates how the company performed and allows comparison of its performance to its competitors. For example, analysts use the income data provided by **Hyundai** (KOR) to compare its performance to that of **Toyota** (JPN).

2. *Provide a basis for predicting future performance.* Information about past performance helps to determine important trends that, if continued, provide information about future performance. For example, **General Electric (GE)** (USA) at one time reported consistent increases in revenues. Obviously, past success does not necessarily translate into future success. However, analysts can better predict future revenues, and hence earnings and cash flows, if a reasonable correlation exists between past and future performance.

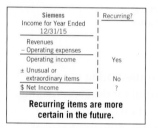

Recurring items are more certain in the future.

3. *Help assess the risk or uncertainty of achieving future cash flows.* Information on the various components of income—revenues, expenses, gains, and losses—highlights the relationships among them. It also helps to assess the risk of not achieving a particular level of cash flows in the future. For example, investors and creditors often segregate **Siemens AG**'s (DEU) operating performance from discontinued operations because Siemens primarily generates revenues and cash through its operations. Thus, results from continuing operations have greater significance for predicting future performance than do results from discontinued operations.

In summary, information in the income statement—revenues, expenses, gains, and losses—helps users evaluate past performance. It also provides insights into the likelihood of achieving a particular level of cash flows in the future.

Limitations of the Income Statement

Because net income is an estimate and reflects a number of assumptions, income statement users need to be aware of certain limitations associated with its information. Some of these limitations include:

You left something out!

1. *Companies omit items from the income statement that they cannot measure reliably.* Current practice prohibits recognition of certain items from the determination of income even though the effects of these items can arguably affect the company's performance. For example, a company may not record unrealized gains and losses on certain

[1]We will use the term *income statement* except in situations where a company reports other comprehensive income (discussed later in the chapter). In that case, we will use the term **statement of comprehensive income.**

investment securities in income when there is uncertainty that it will ever realize the changes in value. In addition, more and more companies, like **L'Oréal** (FRA) and **Daimler AG** (DEU), experience increases in value due to brand recognition, customer service, and product quality. A common framework for identifying and reporting these types of values is still lacking.

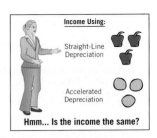

2. *Income numbers are affected by the accounting methods employed.* One company may depreciate its plant assets on an accelerated basis; another chooses straight-line depreciation. Assuming all other factors are equal, the first company will report lower income. In effect, we are comparing apples to oranges.

3. *Income measurement involves judgment.* For example, one company in good faith may estimate the useful life of an asset to be 20 years while another company uses a 15-year estimate for the same type of asset. Similarly, some companies may make optimistic estimates of future warranty costs and bad debt write-offs, which results in lower expense and higher income.

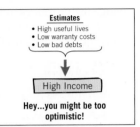

In summary, several limitations of the income statement reduce the usefulness of its information for predicting the amounts, timing, and uncertainty of future cash flows.

Quality of Earnings

So far, our discussion has highlighted the importance of information in the income statement for investment and credit decisions, including the evaluation of the company and its managers.[2] Companies try to meet or beat market expectations so that the market price of their shares and the value of management's compensation increase. As a result, companies have incentives to manage income to meet earnings targets or to make earnings look less risky.

Regulators have expressed concern that the motivations to meet earnings targets may override good business practices. This erodes the quality of earnings and the quality of financial reporting. As a former regulator noted, "Managing may be giving way to manipulation; integrity may be losing out to illusion."[3]

What is **earnings management**? It is often defined as the planned timing of revenues, expenses, gains, and losses to smooth out bumps in earnings. In most cases, companies use earnings management to increase income in the current year at the expense of income in future years. For example, they prematurely recognize sales in order to boost earnings. As one commentator noted, ". . . it's like popping a cork in [opening] a bottle of wine before it is ready."

Companies also use earnings management to decrease current earnings in order to increase income in the future. The classic case is the use of "cookie jar" reserves. Companies establish these reserves by using unrealistic assumptions to estimate liabilities for such items as loan losses, restructuring charges, and warranty returns. The companies then reduce these reserves to increase reported income in the future.

Such earnings management negatively affects the **quality of earnings** if it distorts the information in a way that is less useful for predicting future earnings and cash flows. Markets rely on trust. The bond between shareholders and the company must remain strong. Investors or others losing faith in the numbers reported in the financial statements will damage capital markets.

---

[2]In support of the usefulness of income information, accounting researchers have documented an association between the market prices of companies and reported income. See W. H. Beaver, "Perspectives on Recent Capital Markets Research," *The Accounting Review* (April 2002), pp. 453–474.

[3]A. Levitt, "The Numbers Game." Remarks to NYU Center for Law and Business, September 28, 1998 (Securities and Exchange Commission, 1998).

Managing earnings up or down adversely affects the quality of earnings. Why do companies engage in such practices? Some recent research concludes that many companies tweak quarterly earnings to meet investor expectations. How do they do it? Research findings indicate that companies tend to nudge their earnings numbers up by a 10th of a cent or two. That lets them round results up to the highest cent, as illustrated in the following chart.

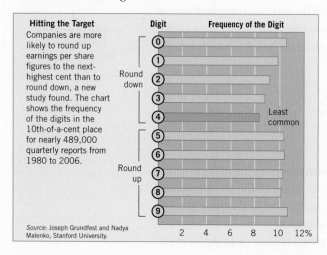

Hitting the Target

Companies are more likely to round up earnings per share figures to the next-highest cent than to round down, a new study found. The chart shows the frequency of the digits in the 10th-of-a-cent place for nearly 489,000 quarterly reports from 1980 to 2006.

Source: Joseph Grundfest and Nadya Malenko, Stanford University.

What the research shows is that the number "4" appeared less often in the 10th's place than any other digit and significantly less often than would be expected by chance. This effect is called "quadrophobia." For the typical company in the study, an increase of $31,000 in quarterly net income would boost earnings per share by a 10th of a cent. A more recent analysis of quarterly results for more than 2,600 companies found that rounding up remains more common than rounding down.

Another recent study reinforces the concerns about earnings management. Based on a survey of 169 public-company chief financial officers (and with in-depth interviews of 12), the study concludes that high-quality earnings are sustainable when backed by actual cash flows and "avoiding unreliable long-term estimates." However, about 20 percent of firms manage earnings to misrepresent their economic performance. And when they do manage earnings, it could move EPS by an average of 10 percent.

Is such earnings management a problem for investors? It is if they cannot determine the impact on earnings quality. Indeed, the surveyed CFOs "believe that it is difficult for outside observers to unravel earnings management, especially when such earnings are managed using subtle unobservable choices or real actions." What's an investor to do? The survey authors say the CFOs "advocate paying close attention to the key managers running the firm, the lack of correlation between earnings and cash flows, significant deviations between firm and peer experience, and unusual behavior in accruals."

Sources: S. Thurm, "For Some Firms, a Case of 'Quadrophobia'," *Wall Street Journal* (February 14, 2010); and H. Greenberg, "CFOs Concede Earnings Are 'Managed'," *www.cnbc.com* (July 19, 2012). The study referred to is by I. Dichev, J. Graham, C. Harvey, and S. Rajgopal, "Earnings Quality: Evidence from the Field," Emory University Working Paper (July 2012).

FORMAT OF THE INCOME STATEMENT

Elements of the Income Statement

LEARNING OBJECTIVE **2**

Understand the content and format of the income statement.

Net income results from revenue, expense, gain, and loss transactions. The income statement summarizes these transactions. This method of income measurement, the **transaction approach**, focuses on the income-related activities that have occurred during the period.[4] The statement can further classify income by customer, product line, or function; by operating and non-operating; and by continuing and discontinued. The two major elements of the income statement are as follows.

[4]The most common alternative to the transaction approach is the **capital maintenance approach** to income measurement. Under this approach, a company determines income for the period based on the change in equity, after adjusting for capital contributions (e.g., investments by owners) or distributions (e.g., dividends). The main drawback associated with the capital maintenance approach is that the components of income are not evident in its measurement. Various tax authorities use the capital maintenance approach to identify unreported income and refer to this approach as the "net worth check."

ELEMENTS OF FINANCIAL STATEMENTS

INCOME. Increases in economic benefits during the accounting period in the form of inflows or enhancements of assets or decreases of liabilities that result in increases in equity, other than those relating to contributions from shareholders.

EXPENSES. Decreases in economic benefits during the accounting period in the form of outflows or depletions of assets or incurrences of liabilities that result in decreases in equity, other than those relating to distributions to shareholders. **[1]**

See the Authoritative Literature section (page 162).

The definition of income includes both revenues and gains. Revenues arise from the ordinary activities of a company and take many forms, such as sales, fees, interest, dividends, and rents. Gains represent other items that meet the definition of income and may or may not arise in the ordinary activities of a company. Gains include, for example, gains on the sale of long-term assets or unrealized gains on trading securities.

The definition of expenses includes both expenses and losses. Expenses generally arise from the ordinary activities of a company and take many forms, such as cost of goods sold, depreciation, rent, salaries and wages, and taxes. Losses represent other items that meet the definition of expenses and may or may not arise in the ordinary activities of a company. Losses include losses on restructuring charges, losses related to sale of long-term assets, or unrealized losses on trading securities.[5]

When gains and losses are reported on an income statement, they are generally separately disclosed because knowledge of them is useful for assessing future cash flows. For example, when **McDonald's** (USA) sells a hamburger, it records the selling price as revenue. However, when McDonald's sells land, it records any excess of the selling price over the book value as a gain. This difference in treatment results because the sale of the hamburger is part of McDonald's regular operations. The sale of land is not.

We cannot overemphasize the importance of reporting these elements. Most decision-makers find the *parts* of a financial statement to be more useful than the whole. As we indicated earlier, investors and creditors are interested in predicting the amounts, timing, and uncertainty of future income and cash flows. Having income statement elements shown in some detail and in comparison with prior years' data allows decision-makers to better assess future income and cash flows.[6]

Intermediate Components of the Income Statement

Companies generally present some or all of the following sections and totals within the income statement, as shown in Illustration 4-1 (on page 140).

---

[5]The IASB takes the position that income includes both revenues and gains because they both reflect increases in economic benefits. Similarly, expenses include both expenses and losses because they both reflect decreases in economic benefits.

[6]If a company prepares a statement of comprehensive income, then disclosure is required for (1) other comprehensive income classified by nature, (2) comprehensive income of associates and joint ventures, and (3) total comprehensive income. The statement of comprehensive income is discussed in more detail later in the chapter.

ILLUSTRATION 4-1
Income Statement
Format

1. **Sales or Revenue Section.** Presents sales, discounts, allowances, returns, and other related information. Its purpose is to arrive at the net amount of sales revenue.
2. **Cost of Goods Sold Section.** Shows the cost of goods sold to produce the sales.

   Gross Profit. Revenue less cost of goods sold.

3. **Selling Expenses.** Reports expenses resulting from the company's efforts to make sales.
4. **Administrative or General Expenses.** Reports expenses of general administration.
5. **Other Income and Expense.** Includes most other transactions that do not fit into the revenues and expenses categories provided above. Items such as gains and losses on sales of long-lived assets, impairments of assets, and restructuring charges are reported in this section. In addition, revenues such as rent revenue, dividend revenue, and interest revenue are often reported.

   Income from Operations. Company's results from normal operations.

6. **Financing Costs.** A separate item that identifies the financing cost of the company, hereafter referred to as *interest expense*.

   Income before Income Tax. The total income before income tax.

7. **Income Tax.** A short section reporting taxes levied on income before income tax.

   Income from Continuing Operations. A company's results before any gain or loss on discontinued operations. If the company does not have any gain or loss on discontinued operations, this section is not reported and this amount is reported as net income.

8. **Discontinued Operations.** Gains or losses resulting from the disposition of a component of a company.

   Net Income. The net results of the company's performance over a period of time.

9. **Non-Controlling Interest.** Presents an allocation of net income to the controlling shareholders and to the non-controlling interest (also referred to as *minority interest*).
10. **Earnings per Share.** Per share amounts that are reported.

Illustration

LEARNING OBJECTIVE
Prepare an income statement.

Illustration 4-2 presents an income statement for Boc Hong Company. Boc Hong's income statement includes all of the major items in the list above, except for discontinued operations. In arriving at net income, the statement presents the following subtotals and totals: gross profit, income from operations, income before income tax, and net income.

Condensed Income Statements

In some cases, an income statement cannot possibly present all the desired expense detail. To solve this problem, a company includes only the totals of components in the statement of income. It then also prepares supplementary schedules to support the totals. This format may thus reduce the income statement itself to a few lines on a single sheet. For this reason, readers who wish to study all the reported data on operations must give their attention to the supporting schedules.

ILLUSTRATION 4-2
Income Statement

BOC HONG COMPANY
INCOME STATEMENT
FOR THE YEAR ENDED DECEMBER 31, 2015

Sales			
Sales revenue			$3,053,081
Less: Sales discounts		$ 24,241	
Sales returns and allowances		56,427	80,668
Net sales			2,972,413
Cost of goods sold			1,982,541
Gross profit			989,872
Selling expenses			
Sales salaries and commissions	$202,644		
Sales office salaries	59,200		
Travel and entertainment	48,940		
Advertising expense	38,315		
Delivery expense	41,209		
Shipping supplies and expense	24,712		
Postage and stationery	16,788		
Telephone and Internet expense	12,215		
Depreciation of sales equipment	9,005	453,028	
Administrative expenses			
Officers' salaries	186,000		
Office salaries	61,200		
Legal and professional services	23,721		
Utilities expense	23,275		
Insurance expense	17,029		
Depreciation of building	18,059		
Depreciation of office equipment	16,000		
Stationery, supplies, and postage	2,875		
Miscellaneous office expenses	2,612	350,771	803,799
Other income and expense			
Dividend revenue		98,500	
Rent revenue		42,910	
Gain on sale of plant assets		30,000	171,410
Income from operations			357,483
Interest on bonds and notes			126,060
Income before income tax			231,423
Income tax			66,934
Net income for the year			$ 164,489
Attributable to:			
Shareholders of Boc Hong			$ 120,000
Non-controlling interest			44,489
Earnings per share			$1.74

For example, consider the income statement shown in Illustration 4-3 (on page 142) for Boc Hong Company. This statement is a condensed version of the more detailed income statement presented in Illustration 4-2. It is more representative of the type found in practice. Illustration 4-4 (on page 142) shows an example of a supporting schedule, cross-referenced as Note D and detailing the selling expenses.

How much detail should a company include in the income statement? On the one hand, a company wants to present a simple, summarized statement so that readers can readily discover important factors. On the other hand, it wants to disclose the results of all activities and to provide more than just a skeleton report. As a result, the income statement always includes certain basic elements, but companies can present them in various formats.

ILLUSTRATION 4-3
Condensed Income
Statement

BOC HONG COMPANY
INCOME STATEMENT
FOR THE YEAR ENDED DECEMBER 31, 2015

Net sales		$2,972,413
Cost of goods sold		1,982,541
Gross profit		989,872
Selling expenses (see Note D)	$453,028	
Administrative expenses	350,771	803,799
Other income and expense		171,410
Income from operations		357,483
Interest expense		126,060
Income before income tax		231,423
Income tax		66,934
Net income for the year		$ 164,489
Attributable to:		
Shareholders of Boc Hong		$ 120,000
Non-controlling interest		44,489
Earnings per share		$1.74

ILLUSTRATION 4-4
Sample Supporting
Schedule

Note D: Selling expenses	
Sales salaries and commissions	$202,644
Sales office salaries	59,200
Travel and entertainment	48,940
Advertising expense	38,315
Delivery expense	41,209
Shipping supplies and expense	24,712
Postage and stationery	16,788
Telephone and Internet expense	12,215
Depreciation of sales equipment	9,005
Total selling expenses	$453,028

What do the numbers mean? YOU MAY NEED A MAP

Many companies increasingly promote their performance through the reporting of various "pro forma" earnings measures. A recent study of the top 40 New Zealand companies documented an increase in pro forma reporting from just 10 percent of companies in 2004 to 45 percent in 2010. A similar study of French companies showed that 79 percent of the sample companies reported pro forma numbers that are higher than unadjusted (IFRS) numbers, suggesting that managers have significant motives for reporting a profit that would be higher than under IFRS-based numbers and higher than in analysts' forecasts.

A good example is that of Vivendi Universal (FRA), which has been announcing its annual earnings on a pro forma basis for a few years. The corporation then reconciles its pro forma and IFRS earnings in its financial statements. Its pro forma earnings measures, called "adjusted net income,

group share," are systematically higher than earnings computed under IFRS. The most astonishing point is the type of items excluded. The reconciliation statement included in the annual report conspicuously excluded important operational and economic expenses such as "non-recurring expenses," "gains/losses on disposals," "financial provisions," and even "goodwill amortization and income tax."

One regulator calls such earnings measures EBS— "Everything but Bad Stuff." Indeed, public companies in the United States are required to reconcile non-U.S. GAAP financial measures to U.S. GAAP, thereby giving investors a roadmap to analyze adjustments companies make to their U.S. GAAP numbers to arrive at pro forma results. This provides investors a more complete picture of company profitability, not the story preferred by management. A similar rule might be in order internationally.

Sources: Gaynor B, "Crisis of Accounting's Double Standards," *The New Zealand Herald* (November 27, 2010); and F. Aubert, "The Relative Informativeness of GAAP and *Pro Forma* Earnings Announcements in France," *Journal of Accounting and Taxation*, Vol. 2(1) (June 2010), pp. 1–14. See also SEC Regulation G, "Conditions for Use of Non-GAAP Financial Measures," Release No. 33–8176 (March 28, 2003).

REPORTING WITHIN THE INCOME STATEMENT

Gross Profit

Boc Hong Company's gross profit is computed by deducting cost of goods sold from net sales. The disclosure of net sales is useful because Boc Hong reports regular sales revenue as a separate item. It discloses unusual or incidental revenues in other income and expense. As a result, analysts can more easily understand and assess trends in revenue from continuing operations.

4 **LEARNING OBJECTIVE**
Explain how to report items in the income statement.

Similarly, the reporting of gross profit provides a useful number for evaluating performance and predicting future earnings. Statement readers may study the trend in gross profits to understand how competitive pressure affected profit margins.

Income from Operations

Boc Hong Company determines income from operations by deducting selling and administrative expenses as well as other income and expense from gross profit. Income from operations highlights items that affect regular business activities. As such, it is a metric often used by analysts in helping to predict the amount, timing, and uncertainty of future cash flows.

Expense Classification

Companies are required to present an analysis of expenses classified either by their nature (such as cost of materials used, direct labor incurred, delivery expense, advertising expense, employee benefits, depreciation expense, and amortization expense) or their function (such as cost of goods sold, selling expenses, and administrative expenses).

An advantage of the **nature-of-expense method** is that it is simple to apply because allocations of expense to different functions are not necessary. For manufacturing companies that must allocate costs to the product produced, using a nature-of-expense approach permits companies to report expenses without making arbitrary allocations.

The **function-of-expense method**, however, is often viewed as more relevant because this method identifies the major cost drivers of the company and therefore helps users assess whether these amounts are appropriate for the revenue generated. As indicated, a disadvantage of this method is that the allocation of costs to the varying functions may be arbitrary and therefore the expense classification becomes misleading.

To illustrate these two methods, assume that the accounting firm of Telaris Co. performs audit, tax, and consulting services. It has the following revenues and expenses.

Service revenues	€400,000
Cost of services	
Staff salaries (related to various services performed)	145,000
Supplies expense (related to various services performed)	10,000
Selling expenses	
Advertising costs	20,000
Entertainment expense	3,000
Administrative expenses	
Utilities expense	5,000
Depreciation on building	12,000

If Telaris Group uses the nature-of-expense approach, its income statement presents each expense item but does not classify the expenses into various subtotals. This approach is shown in Illustration 4-5 (on page 144).

ILLUSTRATION 4-5
Nature-of-Expense
Approach

TELARIS CO. INCOME STATEMENT FOR THE MONTH OF JANUARY 2015	
Service revenues	€400,000
Staff salaries	145,000
Supplies expense	10,000
Advertising costs	20,000
Utilities expense	5,000
Depreciation on building	12,000
Entertainment expense	3,000
Net income	€205,000

If Telaris uses the function-of-expense approach, its income statement is as follows.

ILLUSTRATION 4-6
Function-of-Expense
Approach

TELARIS CO. INCOME STATEMENT FOR THE MONTH OF JANUARY 2015	
Service revenues	€400,000
Cost of services	155,000
Selling expenses	23,000
Administrative expenses	17,000
Net income	€205,000

The function-of-expense method is generally used in practice although many companies believe both approaches have merit. These companies use the function-of-expense approach on the income statement but provide detail of the expenses (as in the nature-of-expense approach) in the notes to the financial statements. For example, Boc Hong's condensed income statement, shown in Illustrations 4-3 and 4-4, indicates how this information might be reported.[7] The IASB-FASB discussion paper on financial statement presentation also recommends the dual approach used in the Boc Hong illustrations. *For homework purposes, use the function-of-expense approach shown in the Boc Hong example in Illustration 4-3 (on page 142), unless directed otherwise.*

Gains and Losses

What should be included in net income is controversial. For example, should companies report gains and losses, and corrections of revenues and expenses of prior years, as part of retained earnings? Or, should companies first present them in the income statement and then carry them to retained earnings?

This issue is extremely important because the number and magnitude of these items are substantial. For example, Illustration 4-7 identifies the most common types and number of gains and losses reported in a survey of 500 large companies. Notice that more than 40 percent of the surveyed firms reported restructuring charges, which often contain write-offs and other one-time items. A survey of 200 IFRS adopters indicates that about 27 percent of the surveyed firms reported a discontinued operation charge.[8]

---

[7]Manufacturing companies that follow the nature-of-expense method generally report direct labor, raw materials used, and changes in inventory related to work in process and finished goods. The overhead items are listed as basic expenses. If the function-of-expense method is used, depreciation expense, amortization expense, and labor costs must also be disclosed because this information is considered useful for predicting future cash flows.

[8]*Accounting Trends and Techniques—2012* (New York: AICPA) and *IFRS Accounting Trends and Techniques—2011* (New York: AICPA).

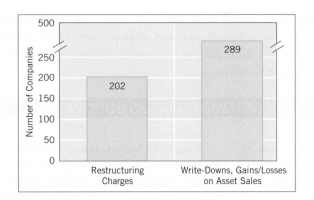

ILLUSTRATION 4-7
Number of Unusual
Items Reported in a
Recent Year by 500 Large
Companies

As our opening story discusses, we need consistent and comparable income reporting practices to avoid "promotional" information reported by companies. Developing a framework for reporting these gains and losses is important to ensure reliable income information.[9] Some users argue that the most useful income measure reflects only regular and recurring revenue and expense elements. Unusual, non-recurring items do not reflect a company's future earning power.

In contrast, others warn that a focus on income that excludes these items potentially misses important information about a company's performance. Any gain or loss experienced by the company, whether directly or indirectly related to operations, contributes to its long-run profitability. As one analyst notes, "write-offs matter. . . . They speak to the volatility of past earnings."[10]

In general, the IASB takes the position that both revenues and expenses and other income and expense should be reported as part of income from operations. For example, it would be inappropriate to exclude items clearly related to operations (such as inventory write-downs and restructuring and relocation expenses) because they occur irregularly or infrequently, or are unusual in amount. Similarly, it would be inappropriate to exclude items on the grounds that they do not involve cash flows, such as depreciation and amortization expenses. **However, companies can provide additional line items, headings, and subtotals when such presentation is relevant to an understanding of the entity's financial performance.**

IFRS indicates additional items that may need disclosure on the income statement to help users predict the amount, timing, and uncertainty of future cash flows. Examples of these unusual items are as follows.

- Losses on write-downs of inventories to net realizable value or of property, plant, and equipment to recoverable amount, as well as reversals of such write-downs.
- Losses on restructurings of the activities of a company and reversals of any provisions for the costs of restructuring.
- Gains or losses on the disposal of items of property, plant, and, equipment or investments.
- Litigation settlements.
- Other reversals of liabilities.

Most companies therefore report these items as part of operations and disclose them in great detail if material in amount. Some, for example, simply show each item as a separate item on the income statement before income from operations. Others use the caption

---

[9]As indicated in the opening story, the IASB is working on a project on financial statement presentation, on how to best report income as well as information presented in the statement of financial position and the statement of cash flows.

[10]D. McDermott, "Latest Profit Data Stir Old Debate Between Net and Operating Income," *Wall Street Journal* (May 3, 1999).

Other income and expense and then itemize them in this section or in the notes to the financial statements. *For homework purposes, itemize gains, losses, revenues, and expenses that are not reported as part of the revenue and expense sections of the income statement in the "Other income and expense" section.*

What do the numbers mean?   ARE ONE-TIME CHARGES BUGGING YOU?

It is an age-old question: which number—net income or income from operations—should an analyst use in evaluating companies that have unusual items? Some argue that operating income better represents what will happen in the future. Others note that special items are often no longer special. For example, one study noted that in 2001, companies in the Standard & Poor's 500 index wrote off items totaling $165 billion—more than in the prior five years combined.

A more recent study indicates that companies continue to make adjustments for one-time or unusual items. And the trend is increasing, with 36 percent of large companies making adjustments for one-time or unusual items in 2012 compared to 20 percent in 2011.

A study by Multex.com and the *Wall Street Journal* indicated that analysts should not ignore these charges. Based on data for companies taking unusual charges, the study documented that companies reporting the largest unusual charges had more negative share price performance following the charge, compared to companies with smaller charges. Thus, rather than signaling the end of bad times, these unusual charges indicated poorer future earnings.

In fact, some analysts use these charges to weed out companies that may be headed for a fall. Following the "cockroach theory," any charge indicating a problem raises the probability of more problems. Thus, investors should be wary of the increasing use of restructuring and other one-time charges, which may bury expenses that signal future performance declines.

Sources: Adapted from J. Weil and S. Liesman, "Stock Gurus Disregard Most Big Write-Offs, but They Often Hold Vital Clues to Outlook," *Wall Street Journal Online* (December 31, 2001); and R. Walters, "Exceptional Costs Becoming Business as Usual for Tech Groups," *Financial Times* (November 14, 2013).

Income before Income Tax

Boc Hong computes income before income tax by deducting interest expense (often referred to as *financing costs*) from income from operations. Under IFRS, companies must report their financing costs on the income statement. The reason for this requirement is to differentiate between a company's business activities (how it uses capital to create value) and its financing activities (how it obtains capital).

In most cases, the financing costs involve interest expense. In other situations, companies offset against interest expense, items such as interest revenue. Illustration 4-8 indicates how **Network Rail** (GBR) presents its financing costs involving only interest expense.

ILLUSTRATION 4-8
Presentation of Finance Costs

Network Rail

On its income statement:
(in thousands)

Finance costs	Note 10	£1,014

10 Finance costs

Interest on bank loans and overdrafts	£ 71
Interest on bonds issued under the debt issuance programme	672
Interest on debt issued under the medium term note programme	253
Interest on commercial paper	12
Interest on obligations under finance leases	16
Other interest	82
Total borrowing costs	1,106
Less: Amounts included in the cost of qualifying assets	92
Total finance costs	£1,014

Borrowing costs are included in the costs of qualifying assets to the extent that the asset is financed by the Group. The average rate used during the year was 5.0%.

As indicated, some companies offset interest revenue and interest expense, and identify it as either finance costs or interest expense and interest revenue, net. *For homework purposes, consider only interest expense as financing costs. Interest revenue (income) should be reported as part of "Other income and expense."*

Net Income

Boc Hong deducts income tax from income before income tax to arrive at net income. Net income represents the income after all revenues and expenses for the period are considered. It is viewed by many as the most important measure of a company's success or failure for a given period of time.

Income tax is reported on the income statement right before net income because this expense cannot be computed until all revenues and expenses are determined. In practice, an understanding of how the company arrived at the income tax for the period is important. For example, some of the revenue items may have different tax rates associated with them. In other cases, expense items may not be deductible for income tax purposes. Understanding these situations enables users to better predict what the future holds for the company. As a result, there is often extensive disclosure related to how the number for income tax expense is determined. Chapter 19 discusses this subject in detail.

Allocation to Non-Controlling Interest

A company like **Siemens** (DEU) owns substantial interests in other companies. Siemens generally consolidates the financial results of these companies into its own financial statements. In these cases, Siemens is referred to as the parent, and the other companies are referred to as subsidiaries. Non-controlling interest is then the portion of equity (net assets) interest in a subsidiary not attributable to the parent company.

To illustrate, assume that Boc Hong acquires 70 percent of the outstanding shares of LTM Group. Because Boc Hong owns more than 50 percent of LTM, it consolidates LTM's financial results with its own. Consolidated net income is then allocated to the controlling (Boc Hong) and non-controlling shareholders' percentage of ownership in LTM. In other words, under this arrangement, the ownership of LTM is divided into two classes: (1) the majority interest represented by shareholders who own the controlling interest and (2) the non-controlling interest (sometimes referred to as the minority interest) represented by shareholders who are not part of the controlling group. When Boc Hong prepares a consolidated income statement, IFRS requires that net income be allocated to the controlling and non-controlling interest. This allocation is reported at the bottom of the income statement, after net income. An example of how Boc Hong reports its non-controlling interest is shown in Illustration 4-9.

Net income	$164,489
Attributable to:	
Shareholders of Boc Hong	$120,000
Non-controlling interest	44,489

ILLUSTRATION 4-9
Presentation of Non-Controlling Interest

These amounts are to be presented as allocations of net income or net loss, not as an item of income or expense.

Earnings per Share

LEARNING OBJECTIVE **5**
Identify where to report earnings per share information.

A company customarily sums up the results of its operations in one important figure: net income. However, the financial world has widely accepted an even more distilled and compact figure as the most significant business indicator—**earnings per share** (EPS).

The computation of earnings per share is usually straightforward. Earnings per share is net income minus preference dividends (income available to ordinary shareholders), divided by the weighted average of ordinary shares outstanding.[11]

To illustrate, assume that Lancer, Inc. reports net income of $350,000. It declares and pays preference dividends of $50,000 for the year. The weighted-average number of ordinary shares outstanding during the year is 100,000 shares. Lancer computes earnings per share of $3, as shown in Illustration 4-10.

ILLUSTRATION 4-10
Equation Illustrating
Computation of Earnings
per Share

$$\frac{\text{Net Income} - \text{Preference Dividends}}{\text{Weighted Average of Ordinary Shares Outstanding}} = \text{Earnings per Share}$$

$$\frac{\$350,000 - \$50,000}{100,000} = \$3$$

Note that EPS measures the number of dollars earned by each ordinary share. It does not represent the dollar amount paid to shareholders in the form of dividends.

Prospectuses, proxy material, and annual reports to shareholders commonly use the "net income per share" or "earnings per share" ratio. The financial press and securities analysts also highlight EPS. Because of its importance, **companies must disclose earnings per share on the face of the income statement**.

Many corporations have simple capital structures that include only ordinary shares. For these companies, a presentation such as "Earnings per share" is appropriate on the income statement. In many instances, however, companies' earnings per share are subject to dilution (reduction) in the future because existing contingencies permit the issuance of additional shares. **[3]**[12]

In summary, the simplicity and availability of EPS figures lead to their widespread use. Because of the importance that the public, even the well-informed public, attaches to earnings per share, companies must make the EPS figure as meaningful as possible.

Discontinued Operations

As Illustration 4-7 (on page 145) shows, one of the most common types of unusual items is discontinued operations. The IASB defines a discontinued operation as a component of an entity that either has been disposed of, or is classified as held-for-sale, and:

1. Represents a major line of business or geographical area of operations, or

2. Is part of a single, co-coordinated plan to dispose of a major line of business or geographical area of operations, or

3. Is a subsidiary acquired exclusively with a view to resell. **[4]**

---

[11]In calculating earnings per share, companies deduct preference dividends from net income if the dividends are declared or if they are cumulative though not declared. In addition, any amount allocated to the non-controlling interest should be deducted from net income in determining earnings per share.

[12]We discuss the computational problems involved in accounting for these dilutive securities in earnings per share computations in Chapter 16.

To illustrate a **component**, **Unilever plc** (GBR) manufactures and sells consumer products. It has several product groups, each with different product lines and brands. For Unilever, a product group is the lowest level at which it can clearly distinguish the operations and cash flows from the rest of the company's operations. Therefore, each product group is a component of the company. If a component were disposed of, Unilever would classify it as a discontinued operation.

Here is another example. Assume that Softso Inc. has experienced losses with certain brands in its beauty-care products group. As a result, Softso decides to sell that part of its business. It will discontinue any continuing involvement in the product group after the sale. In this case, Softso eliminates the operations and the cash flows of the product group from its ongoing operations, and reports it as a discontinued operation.

On the other hand, assume Softso decides to remain in the beauty-care business but will discontinue the brands that experienced losses. Because Softso cannot differentiate the cash flows from the brands from the cash flows of the product group as a whole, it cannot consider the brands a component. Softso does not classify any gain or loss on the sale of the brands as a discontinued operation.

Companies report as discontinued operations (in a separate income statement category) the gain or loss from **disposal of a component of a business**. In addition, companies report the **results of operations of a component that has been or will be disposed of** separately from continuing operations. Companies show the effects of discontinued operations net of tax as a separate category, after continuing operations.

To illustrate, Multiplex Products, Inc., a highly diversified company, decides to discontinue its electronics division. During the current year, the electronics division lost £300,000 (net of tax). Multiplex sold the division at the end of the year at a loss of £500,000 (net of tax). Illustration 4-11 shows the reporting of discontinued operations for Multiplex.

Income from continuing operations		£20,000,000
Discontinued operations		
Loss from operation of discontinued electronics division (net of tax)	£300,000	
Loss from disposal of electronics division (net of tax)	500,000	800,000
Net income		£19,200,000

ILLUSTRATION 4-11
Income Statement
Presentation of
Discontinued Operations

Companies use the phrase **"Income from continuing operations"** only when gains or losses on discontinued operations occur.[13]

A company that reports a discontinued operation must report per share amounts for the line item either on the face of the income statement or in the notes to the financial statements. **[5]** To illustrate, consider the income statement for Poquito Industries Inc., shown in Illustration 4-12 (on page 150). Notice the order in which Poquito shows the data, with per share information at the bottom. Assume that the company had 100,000 shares outstanding for the entire year. The Poquito income statement, as Illustration 4-12 shows, is highly condensed. Poquito would need to describe items such as "Other income and expense" and "Discontinued operations" fully and appropriately in the statement or related notes.

---

[13]In practice, a company will generally report only one line on the income statement, such as "Loss on discontinued operations," and then in the notes explain the two loss components that total £800,000. *For homework purposes, report both amounts on the face of the income statement, net of tax, if both amounts are provided.*

ILLUSTRATION 4-12
Income Statement

POQUITO INDUSTRIES INC.
INCOME STATEMENT
FOR THE YEAR ENDED DECEMBER 31, 2015

Sales revenue		R$1,420,000
Cost of goods sold		600,000
Gross profit		820,000
Selling and administrative expenses		320,000
Other income and expense		
Interest revenue	R$ 10,000	
Loss on disposal of part of Textile Division	(5,000)	
Loss on sale of investments	(30,000)	(25,000)
Income from operations		475,000
Interest expense		15,000
Income before income tax		460,000
Income tax		184,000
Income from continuing operations		276,000
Discontinued operations		
Income from operations of Pizza Division, less		
applicable income tax of R$24,800	54,000	
Loss on disposal of Pizza Division, less		
applicable income tax of R$41,000	(90,000)	(36,000)
Net income		R$240,000
Per share		
Income from continuing operations		R$2.76
Income from operations of discontinued division, net of tax		0.54
Loss on disposal of discontinued operation, net of tax		(0.90)
Net income		R$2.40

Intraperiod Tax Allocation

LEARNING OBJECTIVE ▣ 6
Explain intraperiod tax allocation.

Companies report discontinued operations on the income statement net of tax. The allocation of tax to this item is called intraperiod tax allocation, that is, allocation within a period. It relates the income tax expense (sometimes referred to as the income tax provision) of the fiscal period to the **specific items** that give rise to the amount of the income tax provision.

Intraperiod tax allocation helps financial statement users better understand the impact of income taxes on the various components of net income. For example, readers of financial statements will understand how much income tax expense relates to "income from continuing operations." This approach should help users to better predict the amount, timing, and uncertainty of future cash flows. In addition, intraperiod tax allocation discourages statement readers from using pretax measures of performance when evaluating financial results, and thereby recognizes that income tax expense is a real cost.

Companies use intraperiod tax allocation on the income statement for the following items: (1) income from continuing operations and (2) discontinued operations. The general concept is "**let the tax follow the income.**"

To compute the income tax expense attributable to "Income from continuing operations," a company would find the income tax expense related to both the revenue and expense transactions as well as other income and expense used in determining this income subtotal. (In this computation, the company does not consider the tax consequences of items excluded from the determination of "Income from continuing operations.") Companies then associate a separate tax effect (e.g., for discontinued operations). Here, we look in more detail at calculation of intraperiod tax allocation for discontinued gain or discontinued loss.

Discontinued Operations (Gain)

In applying the concept of intraperiod tax allocation, assume that Schindler Co. has income before income tax of €250,000. It has a gain of €100,000 from a discontinued operation. Assuming a 30 percent income tax rate, Schindler presents the following information on the income statement.

Income before income tax		€250,000
Income tax		75,000
Income from continuing operations		175,000
Gain on discontinued operations	€100,000	
Less: Applicable income tax	30,000	70,000
Net income		€245,000

ILLUSTRATION 4-13
Intraperiod Tax Allocation, Discontinued Operations Gain

Schindler determines the income tax of €75,000 (€250,000 × 30%) attributable to "Income before income tax" from revenue and expense transactions related to this income. Schindler omits the tax consequences of items excluded from the determination of "Income before income tax." The company shows a separate tax effect of €30,000 related to the "Gain on discontinued operations."

Discontinued Operations (Loss)

To illustrate the reporting of a loss from discontinued operations, assume that Schindler Co. has income before income tax of €250,000. It suffers a loss from discontinued operations of €100,000. Assuming a 30 percent tax rate, Schindler presents the income tax on the income statement as shown in Illustration 4-14. In this case, the loss provides a positive tax benefit of €30,000. Schindler, therefore, subtracts it from the €100,000 loss.

Income before income tax		€250,000
Income tax		75,000
Income from continuing operations		175,000
Loss from discontinued operations	€100,000	
Less: Applicable income tax reduction	30,000	70,000
Net income		€105,000

ILLUSTRATION 4-14
Intraperiod Tax Allocation, Discontinued Operations Loss

Companies may also report the tax effect of a discontinued item by means of a note disclosure, as illustrated below.

Income before income tax		€250,000
Income tax		75,000
Income from continuing operations		175,000
Loss on discontinued operations, less applicable income tax reduction (Note 1)		70,000
Net income		€105,000

Note 1: During the year the Company suffered a loss on discontinuing operations of €70,000, net of applicable income tax reduction of €30,000.

ILLUSTRATION 4-15
Note Disclosure of Intraperiod Tax Allocation

Summary

Illustration 4-16 (on page 152) provides a summary of the primary income items.

Type of Situation	Criteria	Examples	Placement on Income Statement
Sales or service revenues	Revenues arising from the ordinary activities of the company	Sales revenue, service revenue	Sales or revenue section
Cost of goods sold	Expense arising from the cost of inventory sold or services provided	In a merchandising company, Cost of goods sold; in a service company, Cost of services	Deduct from sales (to arrive at gross profit) or service revenue
Selling and administrative expenses	Expenses arising from the ordinary activities of the company	Sales salaries, Freight-out, Rent, Depreciation, Utilities	Deduct from gross profit; if the function-of-expense approach is used, depreciation and amortization expense and labor costs must be disclosed
Other income and expense	Gains and losses and other ancillary revenues and expenses	Gain on sale of long-lived assets, Impairment loss on intangible assets, Investment revenue, Dividend and Interest revenue, Casualty losses	Report as part of income from operations
Financing costs	Separates cost of financing from operating costs	Interest expense	Report in a separate section between income from operations and income before income tax
Income tax	Levies imposed by governmental bodies on the basis of income	Taxes computed on income before income tax	Report in separate section between income before income tax and net income
Discontinued operations	A component of a company that has either been disposed of or is classified as held-for-sale	A sale by a diversified company of a major division representing its only activities in the electronics industry Food distributor that sells wholesale to supermarkets decides to discontinue the division in a major geographic area	Report gains or losses on discontinued operations net of tax in a separate section between income from continuing operations and net income
Non-controlling interest	Allocation of net income or loss divided between two classes: (1) the majority interest represented by the shareholders who own the controlling interest, and (2) the non-controlling interest (often referred to as the *minority interest*)	Net profit (loss) attributable to non-controlling shareholders	Report as a separate item below net income or loss as an allocation of the net income or loss (not as an item of income or expense)

ILLUSTRATION 4-16
Summary of Income Items

As indicated, companies report all revenues, gains, expenses, and losses on the income statement and, at the end of the period, close them to Income Summary. They provide useful subtotals on the income statement, such as gross profit, income from operations, income before income tax, and net income. Companies classify discontinued operations of a component of a business as a separate item in the income statement, after "Income from continuing operations." Companies present other income and expense in a separate section, before income from operations. Providing intermediate income figures helps readers evaluate earnings information in assessing the amounts, timing, and uncertainty of future cash flows.

What do the numbers mean?   DIFFERENT INCOME CONCEPTS

As indicated in the opening story, the IASB is working on a project related to presentation of financial statements. In 2008, the IASB (and FASB) issued an exposure draft that presented examples of what these new financial statements might look like. Recently, they conducted field tests on two groups: preparers and users. Preparers were asked to recast their financial statements and then comment on the results.

Users examined the recast statements and commented on their usefulness.

One part of the field test asked analysts to indicate which primary performance metric they use or create from a company's income statement. They were provided with the following options: (a) Net income; (b) Pretax income; (c) Income before interest and taxes (EBIT); (d) Income before interest, taxes, depreciation, and amortization (EBITDA); (e) Operating income; (f) Comprehensive income; and (g) Other. Presented below is a chart that highlights their responses.

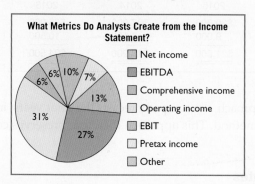

Source: "FASB-IASB Report on Analyst Field Test Results," Financial Statement Presentation Informational Board Meeting (September 21, 2009).

As indicated, Operating income (31%) and EBITDA (27%) were identified as the two primary performance metrics that respondents use or create from a company's income statement. A majority of the respondents identified a primary performance metric that uses net income as its foundation (pretax income would be in this group). Clearly, users and preparers look at more than just the bottom line income number, which supports the IFRS requirement to provide subtotals within the income statement.

OTHER REPORTING ISSUES

In this section, we discuss reporting issues related to (1) accounting changes and errors, (2) retained earnings statement, (3) comprehensive income, and (4) statement of changes in equity.

> **7 LEARNING OBJECTIVE**
> Understand the reporting of accounting changes and errors.

Accounting Changes and Errors

Changes in accounting principle, changes in estimates, and corrections of errors require unique reporting provisions.

Changes in Accounting Principle

Changes in accounting occur frequently in practice because important events or conditions may be in dispute or uncertain at the statement date. One type of accounting change results when a company adopts a different accounting principle. **Changes in accounting principle** include a change in the method of inventory pricing from FIFO to average-cost, or a change in accounting for construction contracts from the percentage-of-completion to the completed-contract method. [6][14]

> **Underlying Concepts** 🔍
>
> Companies can change principles, but they must demonstrate that the newly adopted principle is preferable to the old one. Such changes result in lost consistency from period to period.

A company recognizes a change in accounting principle by making a **retrospective adjustment** to the financial statements. Such an adjustment recasts the prior years' statements on a basis consistent with the newly adopted principle. The company records the cumulative effect of the change for prior periods as an adjustment to beginning retained earnings of the earliest year presented.

To illustrate, Gaubert Inc. decided in March 2015 to change from FIFO to weighted-average inventory pricing. Gaubert's income before income tax, using the new weighted-average method in 2015, is $30,000. Illustration 4-17 presents the pretax income data for 2013 and 2014 for this example.

Year	FIFO	Weighted-Average Method	Excess of FIFO over Weighted-Average Method
2013	$40,000	$35,000	$5,000
2014	30,000	27,000	3,000
Total			$8,000

ILLUSTRATION 4-17
Calculation of a Change in Accounting Principle

[14]In Chapter 22, we examine in greater detail the problems related to accounting changes, and changes in estimates (discussed in the next section).

Illustration 4-18 shows the information Gaubert presented in its comparative income statements, based on a 30 percent tax rate.

ILLUSTRATION 4-18
Income Statement
Presentation of a Change
in Accounting Principle

	2015	2014	2013
Income before income tax	$30,000	$27,000	$35,000
Income tax	9,000	8,100	10,500
Net income	$21,000	$18,900	$24,500

Thus, under the retrospective approach, the company recasts the prior years' income numbers under the newly adopted method. This approach therefore preserves comparability across years.

Changes in Accounting Estimates

Changes in accounting estimates are inherent in the accounting process. For example, companies estimate useful lives and residual values of depreciable assets, uncollectible receivables, inventory obsolescence, and the number of periods expected to benefit from a particular expenditure. Not infrequently, due to time, circumstances, or new information, even estimates originally made in good faith must be changed. A company accounts for such changes in the period of change if they affect only that period, or in the period of change and future periods if the change affects both.

To illustrate a change in estimate that affects only the period of change, assume that DuPage Materials Corp. consistently estimated its bad debt expense at 1 percent of credit sales. In 2015, however, DuPage determines that it must revise upward the estimate of bad debts for the current year's credit sales to 2 percent, or double the prior years' percentage. The 2 percent rate is necessary to reduce accounts receivable to net realizable value. Using 2 percent results in a bad debt charge of CHF240,000, or double the amount using the 1 percent estimate for prior years. DuPage records the bad debt expense and related allowance at December 31, 2015, as follows.

Bad Debt Expense	240,000	
Allowance for Doubtful Accounts		240,000

DuPage includes the entire change in estimate in 2015 income because the change does not affect future periods. **Companies do not handle changes in estimate retrospectively.** That is, such changes are not carried back to adjust prior years. (We examine changes in estimate that affect both the current and future periods in greater detail in Chapter 22.) **Changes in estimate are not considered errors.**

Corrections of Errors

Errors occur as a result of mathematical mistakes, mistakes in the application of accounting principles, or oversight or misuse of facts that existed at the time financial statements were prepared. In recent years, many companies have corrected for errors in their financial statements. The errors involved such items as improper reporting of revenue, accounting for share options, allowances for receivables, inventories, and other provisions.

Companies correct errors by making proper entries in the accounts and reporting the corrections in the financial statements. Corrections of errors are treated as prior period adjustments, similar to changes in accounting principles. Companies record a correction of an error in the year in which it is discovered. They report the error in the financial statements as an adjustment to the beginning balance of retained earnings. If a company prepares comparative financial statements, it should restate the prior statements for the effects of the error.

To illustrate, in 2015, Tsang Co. determined that it incorrectly overstated its accounts receivable and sales revenue by NT$100,000 in 2014. In 2015, Tsang makes the following entry to correct for this error (ignore income taxes).

Retained Earnings	100,000	
Accounts Receivable		100,000

Retained Earnings is debited because sales revenue, and therefore net income, was overstated in a prior period. Accounts Receivable is credited to reduce this overstated balance to the correct amount.

Summary

The impact of changes in accounting principle and error corrections are debited or credited directly to retained earnings, if related to a prior period. Illustration 4-19 summarizes the basic concepts related to these two items, as well as the accounting and reporting for changes in estimates. Although simplified, the chart provides a useful framework for determining the treatment of special items affecting the income statement.

ILLUSTRATION 4-19
Summary of Accounting Changes and Errors

Type of Situation	Criteria	Examples	Placement on Income Statement
Changes in accounting principle	Change from one generally accepted accounting principle to another.	Change in the basis of inventory pricing from FIFO to average-cost.	Recast prior years' income statements on the same basis as the newly adopted principle.
Changes in accounting estimates	Normal, recurring corrections and adjustments.	Changes in the realizability of receivables and inventories; changes in estimated lives of equipment, intangible assets; changes in estimated liability for warranty costs, income taxes, and salary payments.	Show change only in the affected accounts (not shown net of tax) and disclose the nature of the change.
Corrections of errors	Mistake, misuse of facts.	Error in reporting income and expense.	Restate prior years' income statements to correct for error.

Retained Earnings Statement

Net income increases retained earnings. A net loss decreases retained earnings. Both cash and share dividends decrease retained earnings. Changes in accounting principle (generally) and prior period adjustments may increase or decrease retained earnings. Companies charge or credit these adjustments (net of tax) to the opening balance of retained earnings.

8 LEARNING OBJECTIVE
Prepare a retained earnings statement.

Companies may show retained earnings information in different ways. For example, some companies prepare a separate retained earnings statement, as Illustration 4-20 shows.

ILLUSTRATION 4-20
Retained Earnings Statement

CHOI INC.		
RETAINED EARNINGS STATEMENT		
FOR THE YEAR ENDED DECEMBER 31, 2015		
Retained earnings, January 1, as reported		₩1,050,000
Correction for understatement of net income in prior period (inventory error)		50,000
Retained earnings, January 1, as adjusted		1,100,000
Add: Net income		360,000
		1,460,000
Less: Cash dividends	₩100,000	
Share dividends	200,000	300,000
Retained earnings, December 31		₩1,160,000

The reconciliation of the beginning to the ending balance in retained earnings provides information about why net assets increased or decreased during the year. The association of dividend distributions with net income for the period indicates what management is doing with earnings: It may be "plowing back" into the business part or all of the earnings, distributing all current income, or distributing current income plus the accumulated earnings of prior years.

Restrictions of Retained Earnings

Companies often restrict retained earnings to comply with contractual requirements, board of directors' policy, or current necessity. Generally, companies disclose in the notes to the financial statements the amounts of restricted retained earnings. In some cases, companies transfer the amount of retained earnings restricted to an account titled **Appropriated Retained Earnings**. The retained earnings section may therefore report two separate amounts: (1) retained earnings free (unrestricted) and (2) retained earnings appropriated (restricted). The total of these two amounts equals the total retained earnings.

Comprehensive Income

LEARNING OBJECTIVE ◗**9**

Explain how to report other comprehensive income.

Companies generally include in income all revenues, expenses, and gains and losses recognized during the period. These items are classified within the income statement so that financial statement readers can better understand the significance of various components of net income. Changes in accounting principle and corrections of errors are excluded from the calculation of net income because their effects relate to prior periods.

In recent years, use of fair values for measuring assets and liabilities has increased. Furthermore, possible reporting of gains and losses related to changes in fair value has placed a strain on income reporting. Because fair values are continually changing, some argue that recognizing these gains and losses in net income is misleading. The IASB agrees and has identified a limited number of transactions that should be recorded directly to equity. One example is unrealized gains and losses on non-trading equity securities.[15] These gains and losses are excluded from net income, thereby reducing volatility in net income due to fluctuations in fair value. At the same time, disclosure of the potential gain or loss is provided.

Companies include these items that bypass the income statement in a measure called comprehensive income. Comprehensive income includes all changes in equity during a period *except* those resulting from investments by owners and distributions to owners. Comprehensive income, therefore, includes the following: all revenues and gains, expenses and losses reported in net income, and all gains and losses that bypass net income but affect equity. These items—non-owner changes in equity that bypass the income statement—are referred to as other comprehensive income.

Companies must display the components of other comprehensive income in one of two ways: (1) a single continuous statement (**one statement approach**) or (2) two separate but consecutive statements of net income and other comprehensive income (**two statement approach**). The one statement approach is often referred to as the statement of comprehensive income. The two statement approach uses the traditional term income statement for the first statement and the comprehensive income statement for the second statement.

[15]We further discuss non-trading equity securities in Chapter 17. Additional examples of other comprehensive items are translation gains and losses on foreign currency, unrealized gains and losses on certain hedging transactions (Chapter 17 Appendix), actuarial gains and losses in certain situations (Chapter 20), and changes in revaluation surplus (Chapters 11 and 12).

Under either approach, companies display each component of net income and each component of other comprehensive income. In addition, net income and comprehensive income are reported. Companies are not required to report earnings per share information related to comprehensive income.[16]

We illustrate these two alternatives in the next two sections. In each case, assume that V. Gill Inc. reports the following information for 2015: sales revenue €800,000, cost of goods sold €600,000, operating expenses €90,000, and an unrealized holding gain on non-trading equity securities of €30,000, net of tax.

One Statement Approach

In this approach, the traditional net income is a subtotal, with total comprehensive income shown as a final total. The combined statement has the advantage of not requiring the creation of a new financial statement. However, burying net income as a subtotal on the statement is a disadvantage. Illustration 4-21 shows the one statement format for V. Gill.

V. GILL INC. STATEMENT OF COMPREHENSIVE INCOME FOR THE YEAR ENDED DECEMBER 31, 2015	
Sales revenue	€800,000
Cost of goods sold	600,000
Gross profit	200,000
Operating expenses	90,000
Net income	110,000
Other comprehensive income	
Unrealized holding gain, net of tax	30,000
Comprehensive income	€140,000

ILLUSTRATION 4-21
One Statement Format: Comprehensive Income

Two Statement Approach

Illustration 4-22 shows the two statement format for V. Gill. Reporting comprehensive income in a separate statement indicates that the gains and losses identified as other comprehensive income have the same status as traditional gains and losses.

V. GILL INC. INCOME STATEMENT FOR THE YEAR ENDED DECEMBER 31, 2015	
Sales revenue	€800,000
Cost of goods sold	600,000
Gross profit	200,000
Operating expenses	90,000
Net income	€110,000

V. GILL INC. COMPREHENSIVE INCOME STATEMENT FOR THE YEAR ENDED DECEMBER 31, 2015	
Net income	€110,000
Other comprehensive income	
Unrealized holding gain, net of tax	30,000
Comprehensive income	€140,000

ILLUSTRATION 4-22
Two Statement Format: Comprehensive Income

---

[16]A company must display the components of other comprehensive income either (1) net of related tax effects, or (2) before related tax effects, with one amount shown for the aggregate amount of tax related to the total amount of other comprehensive income. Both alternatives must show each component of other comprehensive income, net of related taxes either on the face of the statement or in the notes. **[7]**

As indicated in the chapter, information reported in the income statement is important to meeting the objective of financial reporting. However, there is debate over income reporting practices, be it the controversy over pro forma reporting or whether to report comprehensive income in a one statement or a two statement format. In response to these debates and to differences between income reporting under U.S. GAAP and IFRS, standard-setters are working on a project to improve the usefulness of the income statement.

Work to date has resulted in two core principles for financial statement presentation (for the income statement, balance sheet, and the statement of cash flows) based on the objective of financial reporting:

1. **Disaggregate information so that it is useful in predicting an entity's future cash flows.** Disaggregation means separating resources by the activity in which they are used and by their economic characteristics.

2. **Portray a cohesive financial picture of a company's activities.** A cohesive financial picture means that the relationship between items across financial statements is clear and that a company's financial statements complement each other as much as possible.

Cohesiveness will be addressed by using the same classifications across the three primary statements; the two classifications currently under consideration are referred to as business and financing. Thus, this proposal is consistent with some current income reporting practices. However, agreeing on a standard level of disaggregation in the income statement may be difficult, given the current controversies surrounding pro forma reporting, extraordinary items, and comprehensive income reporting.

The statement presentation project is currently inactive on the Boards' joint agenda (*http://www.ifrs.org/Current-Projects/IASB-Projects/Financial-Statement-Presentation/Pages/Financial-Statement-Presentation.aspx*), but it is expected to restart once the projects on financial instruments, revenue, and leases are completed.

Statement of Changes in Equity

In addition to a statement of comprehensive income, companies are also required to present a statement of changes in equity. Equity is generally comprised of share capital—ordinary, share premium—ordinary, retained earnings, and the accumulated balances in other comprehensive income. The statement reports the change in each equity account and in total equity for the period. The following items are disclosed in this statement.

1. Accumulated other comprehensive income for the period.
2. Contributions (issuances of shares) and distributions (dividends) to owners.
3. Reconciliation of the carrying amount of each component of equity from the beginning to the end of the period.

Companies often prepare the statement of changes in equity in column form. In this format, they use columns for each account and for total equity.

To illustrate, assume the same information for V. Gill as shown in Illustration 4-22 (on page 157). The company had the following equity account balances at the beginning of 2015: Share Capital—Ordinary €300,000, Retained Earnings €50,000, and Accumulated Other Comprehensive Income €60,000, related to unrealized gains on non-trading equity securities. No changes in the Share Capital—Ordinary account occurred during the year. Cash dividends during the period were €10,000. Illustration 4-23 shows a statement of changes in equity for V. Gill.

Total comprehensive income is comprised of net income of €110,000 added to retained earnings and €30,000 related to the unrealized gain. Separate columns are used to report each additional item of other comprehensive income.[17] Thus, this statement is useful for understanding how equity changed during the period.

---

[17]The other comprehensive income section shall present line items for amounts of other comprehensive income grouped into those that, in accordance with other IFRSs, (a) will not be reclassified subsequently to profit or loss, and (b) will be reclassified subsequently to profit or loss when specific conditions are met. If a company has non-controlling interest, an additional column would be added to report changes in non-controlling interest amounts. **[8]**

V. GILL INC.
STATEMENT OF CHANGES IN EQUITY
FOR THE YEAR ENDED DECEMBER 31, 2015

	Total	Retained Earnings	Accumulated Other Comprehensive Income	Share Capital— Ordinary
Beginning balance	€410,000	€ 50,000	€60,000	€300,000
Net income	110,000	110,000		
Dividends	(10,000)	(10,000)		
Other comprehensive income				
Unrealized holding gain, net of tax	30,000		30,000	
Ending balance	€540,000	€150,000	€90,000	€300,000

ILLUSTRATION 4-23
Statement of Changes in Equity

Regardless of the display format used, V. Gill reports the **accumulated other comprehensive income** of €90,000 in the equity section of the statement of financial position as follows.[18]

V. GILL INC.
STATEMENT OF FINANCIAL POSITION
AS OF DECEMBER 31, 2015
(EQUITY SECTION)

Equity	
Share capital—ordinary	€300,000
Retained earnings	150,000
Accumulated other comprehensive income	90,000
Total equity	€540,000

ILLUSTRATION 4-24
Presentation of Accumulated Other Comprehensive Income in the Statement of Financial Position

By providing information on the components of comprehensive income, as well as accumulated other comprehensive income, the company communicates information about all changes in net assets.[19] With this information, users will better understand the quality of the company's earnings.

[18]Many companies use the term Reserve to include all items in equity except for contributed capital. Contributed capital is comprised of Share Capital (ordinary and preference) and Share Premium (ordinary and preference). Rather than the term Reserve, we use Retained Earnings and Accumulated Other Comprehensive Income because these concepts are more descriptive of the items in the equity section.

[19]Corrections of errors and changes in accounting principle are not considered other comprehensive income items.

GLOBAL ACCOUNTING INSIGHTS

INCOME STATEMENT

Standards issued by the FASB (U.S. GAAP) are the primary global alternative to IFRS. As in IFRS, the income statement is a required statement for U.S. GAAP. In addition, the content and presentation of the U.S. GAAP income statement is similar to the one used for IFRS. A number of U.S. GAAP standards have been issued that provide guidance on issues related to income statement presentation.

Relevant Facts

Following are the key similarities and differences between U.S. GAAP and IFRS related to the income statement.

Similarities
- Both U.S. GAAP and IFRS require companies to indicate the amount of net income attributable to non-controlling interest.

- Both U.S. GAAP and IFRS follow the same presentation guidelines for discontinued operations, but IFRS defines a discontinued operation more narrowly. Both standard-setters have indicated a willingness to develop a similar definition to be used in the joint project on financial statement presentation.

- Both U.S. GAAP and IFRS have items that are recognized in equity as part of other comprehensive income but do not affect net income. Both U.S. GAAP and IFRS allow a one statement or two statement approach to preparing the statement of comprehensive income.

Differences
- Presentation of the income statement under U.S. GAAP follows either a single-step or multiple-step format. IFRS does not mention a single-step or multiple-step approach. In addition, under U.S. GAAP, companies must report an item as extraordinary if it is unusual in nature and infrequent in occurrence. Extraordinary-item reporting is prohibited under IFRS.

- The U.S. SEC requires companies to have a functional presentation of expenses. Under IFRS, companies must classify expenses by either nature *or* function. U.S. GAAP does not have that requirement.

- U.S. GAAP has no minimum information requirements for the income statement. However, the U.S. SEC rules have more rigorous presentation requirements. IFRS identifies certain minimum items that *should* be presented on the income statement.

- U.S. SEC regulations define many key measures and provide requirements and limitations on companies reporting non-U.S. GAAP information. IFRS does not define key measures like income from operations.

- U.S. GAAP does not permit revaluation accounting. Under IFRS, revaluation of property, plant, and equipment, and intangible assets is permitted and is reported as other comprehensive income. The effect of this difference is that application of IFRS results in more transactions affecting equity but not net income.

About the Numbers

The terminology used in the IFRS literature is sometimes different than what is used in U.S. GAAP. For example, here are some of the differences related to this chapter.

IFRS	U.S. GAAP
Equity or shareholders' equity	Shareholders' equity or stockholders' equity
Share capital—ordinary	Common stock
Share capital—preference	Preferred stock
Ordinary shares	Common shares
Preference shares	Preferred shares
Share premium—ordinary	Premium on common stock or Paid-in capital in excess of par—common
Share premium—preference	Premium on preferred stock or Paid-in capital in excess of par—preferred
Reserves	Retained earnings and accumulated other comprehensive income
Statement of financial position	Balance sheet or Statement of financial position
Profit or loss	Net income or Net loss

On the Horizon

The IASB and FASB are working on a project that would rework the structure of financial statements. One stage of this project will address the issue of how to classify various items in the income statement. A main goal of this new approach is to provide information that better represents how businesses are run. In addition, this approach draws attention away from just one number—net income.

SUMMARY OF LEARNING OBJECTIVES

1 **Understand the uses and limitations of an income statement.** The income statement provides investors and creditors with information that helps them predict the amounts, timing, and uncertainty of future cash flows. Also, the income statement helps users determine the risk (level of uncertainty) of not achieving particular cash flows. The limitations of an income statement are as follows. (1) The statement does not include many items that contribute to general growth and well-being of a company. (2) Income numbers are often affected by the accounting methods used. (3) Income measures are subject to estimates.

2 **Understand the content and format of the income statement.** Net income results from revenue, expense, gain, and loss transactions. This method of income measurement, the transaction approach, focuses on the income-related activities that have occurred during a given period. Instead of presenting only a net change in net assets, it discloses the components of the change.

The following sections are generally shown on an income statement: sales or revenue, cost of goods sold, selling expense, administrative or general expense, financing costs, and income tax. If present, a company also reports discontinued operations (net of tax). Earnings per share is reported, and an allocation of net income or loss to the non-controlling interest is also presented, where applicable.

3 **Prepare an income statement.** Companies determine net income by deducting expenses from revenues but also classify various revenues and expenses in order to report useful subtotals within the income statement. These subtotals are gross profit, income from operations, income before income tax, and a final total, net income.

4 **Explain how to report items in the income statement.** Companies generally provide some detail on revenues and expenses on the face of the income statement but may prepare a condensed income statement with details on various components presented in the notes to the financial statements. Companies are required to classify expense either by nature or by function. Unusual and non-recurring items should be reported in income from operations, but financing costs are reported separate from operating revenues and expenses. Companies report the effects of discontinued operations of a component of a business as a separate item, after income from continuing operations.

5 **Identify where to report earnings per share information.** Companies must disclose earnings per share on the face of the income statement. A company that reports a discontinued operation must report per share amounts for these line items either on the face of the income statement or in the notes to the financial statements.

6 **Explain intraperiod tax allocation.** Companies should relate the tax expense for the year to specific items on the income statement to provide a more informative disclosure to statement users. This procedure, intraperiod tax allocation, relates the income tax expense for the fiscal period to the following items that affect the amount of the tax provisions for (1) income from continuing operations and (2) discontinued operations.

7 **Understand the reporting of accounting changes and errors.** Changes in accounting principle and corrections of errors are adjusted through retained earnings. Changes in accounting estimates are a normal part of the accounting process. The effects of these changes are handled prospectively, with the effects recorded in income in the period of change and in future periods without adjustment to retained earnings.

KEY TERMS

accumulated other comprehensive income, *159*

Appropriated Retained Earnings, *156*

capital maintenance approach, *138 (n)*

changes in accounting estimates, *154*

changes in accounting principle, *153*

comprehensive income, *156*

discontinued operation, *148*

earnings management, *137*

earnings per share, *148*

function-of-expense method, *143*

income statement, *136*

intraperiod tax allocation, *150*

nature-of-expense method, *143*

other comprehensive income, *156*

Other income and expense, *146*

prior period adjustments, *154*

quality of earnings, *137*

statement of changes in equity, *158*

statement of comprehensive income, *136 (n)*

transaction approach, *138*

8 **Prepare a retained earnings statement.** The retained earnings statement should disclose net income (loss), dividends, adjustments due to changes in accounting principles, error corrections, and restrictions of retained earnings.

9 **Explain how to report other comprehensive income.** Companies report the components of other comprehensive income in one of two ways: (1) a combined statement of comprehensive income (one statement format) or (2) in a second statement (two statement format).

IFRS AUTHORITATIVE LITERATURE

Authoritative Literature References

[1] The Conceptual Framework for Financial Reporting, "Chapter 4: *The Framework* (1989): The Remaining Text" (London, U.K.: IASB, 2010), par. 4.25.

[2] International Accounting Standard 1, *Presentation of Financial Statements* (London, U.K.: IASB, 2007), par. 82.

[3] International Accounting Standard 33, *Earnings per Share* (London, U.K.: IASB, 2003).

[4] International Financial Reporting Standard 5, *Non-current Assets Held for Sale and Discontinued Operations* (London, U.K.: IASB, 2004).

[5] International Accounting Standard 33, *Earnings per Share* (London, U.K.: IASB, 2003).

[6] International Accounting Standard 8, *Accounting Policies, Changes in Accounting Estimates and Errors* (London, U.K.: IASB, 2003).

[7] International Accounting Standard 1, *Presentation of Financial Statements* (London, U.K.: International Accounting Standards Committee Foundation, 2007), paras. 90–91.

[8] International Accounting Standard 1, *Presentation of Financial Statements* (London, U.K.: International Accounting Standards Committee Foundation, 2007), paras. 81–82.

QUESTIONS

1. What kinds of questions about future cash flows do investors and creditors attempt to answer with information in the income statement?

2. How can information based on past transactions be used to predict future cash flows?

3. Identify at least two situations in which important changes in value are not reported in the income statement.

4. Identify at least two situations in which application of different accounting methods or accounting estimates results in difficulties in comparing companies.

5. Explain the transaction approach to measuring income. Why is the transaction approach to income measurement preferable to other ways of measuring income?

6. What is earnings management?

7. How can earnings management affect the quality of earnings?

8. Why should caution be exercised in the use of the net income figure derived in an income statement? What are the objectives of IFRS in their application to the income statement?

9. A *Wall Street Journal* article noted that **MicroStrategy** (USA) reported higher income than its competitors by using a more aggressive policy for recognizing revenue on future upgrades to its products. Some contend that MicroStrategy's quality of earnings is low. What does the term "quality of earnings" mean?

10. What is the major distinction between income and expenses under IFRS?

11. Do the elements of financial statements, income and expense, include gains and losses? Explain.

12. What are the sections of the income statement that comprise (1) gross profit and (2) income from operations?

13. **Ahold** (NLD), in its consolidated income statement, reported "settlement of securities class action" €803 million loss. In what section of the income statement is this amount reported?

14. Explain where the following items are reported on the income statement: (1) interest expense and (2) income tax.

15. Explain the difference between the "nature-of-expense" and "function-of-expense" classifications.

16. Discuss the appropriate treatment in the income statement for the following items:

    (a) Loss on discontinued operations.
    (b) Non-controlling interest allocation.
    (c) Earnings per share.
    (d) Gain on sale of equipment.

17. Discuss the appropriate treatment in the financial statements of each of the following.

    (a) Write-down of plant assets due to impairment.
    (b) A delivery expense on goods sold.
    (c) Additional depreciation on factory machinery because of an error in computing depreciation for the previous year.
    (d) Rent received from subletting a portion of the office space.
    (e) A patent infringement suit, brought 2 years ago against the company by another company, was settled this year by a cash payment of NT$725,000.
    (f) A reduction in the Allowance for Doubtful Accounts balance, because the account appears to be considerably in excess of the probable loss from uncollectible receivables.

18. Indicate where the following items would ordinarily appear on the financial statements of Boleyn, Inc. for the year 2015.

    (a) The service life of certain equipment was changed from 8 to 5 years. If a 5-year life had been used previously, additional depreciation of £425,000 would have been charged.
    (b) In 2015, a flood destroyed a warehouse that had a book value of £1,600,000.
    (c) In 2015, the company wrote off £1,000,000 of inventory that was considered obsolete.
    (d) Interest expense for the year was £45,000.
    (e) In 2012, a supply warehouse with an expected useful life of 7 years was erroneously expensed.
    (f) Boleyn, Inc. changed from weighted-average to FIFO inventory pricing.

19. Indicate the section of an income statement in which each of the following is shown.

    (a) Loss on inventory write-down.
    (b) Loss from strike.
    (c) Bad debt expense.
    (d) Loss on disposal of a component of the business.
    (e) Gain on sale of machinery.
    (f) Interest expense.
    (g) Depreciation expense.
    (h) Interest revenue.

20. Santo Corporation has eight expense accounts in its general ledger which could be classified as selling expenses. Should Santo report these eight expenses separately in its income statement or simply report one total amount for selling expenses? Explain.

21. Cooper Investments reported an unusual gain from the sale of certain assets in its 2015 income statement. How does intraperiod tax allocation affect the reporting of this unusual gain?

22. What effect does intraperiod tax allocation have on reported net income?

23. Neumann Company computed earnings per share as follows.

$$\frac{\text{Net income}}{\text{Shares outstanding at year-end}}$$

    Neumann has a simple capital structure. What possible errors might the company have made in the computation? Explain.

24. How should a loss on the disposal of a component of a business be disclosed in the income statement?

25. Qualls Corporation reported 2014 earnings per share of €7.21. In 2015, Qualls reported earnings per share as follows.

On income from continuing operations	€8.00
On loss on discontinued operations	.88
On net income	€7.12

    Is the decrease in earnings per share from €7.21 to €7.12 a negative trend? Explain.

26. What is meant by "tax allocation within a period"? What is the justification for such a practice?

27. When does tax allocation within a period become necessary? How should this allocation be handled?

28. Linus Paper Company decided to close two small pulp mills in Conway, New Hampshire, and Corvallis, Oregon. Would these closings be reported in a separate section entitled "Discontinued operations after income from continuing operations"? Discuss.

29. How should corrections of errors be reported in the financial statements?

30. Explain how a change in accounting principles affects the current year's net income.

31. What major types of items are reported in the retained earnings statement?

32. IFRS usually requires the use of accrual accounting to "fairly present" income. If the cash receipts and disbursements method of accounting will "clearly reflect" taxable income, why does this method also not usually "fairly present" income?

33. What are two ways that other comprehensive income may be displayed (reported)?

34. Gribble Company reported the following amounts in 2015: Net income, €150,000; Unrealized gain related to revaluation of buildings, €10,000; Unrealized loss related to non-trading equity securities, €(35,000). Determine Gribble's total comprehensive income for 2015.

35. What are U.S. GAAP's requirements with respect to expense classification?

36. Bradshaw Company experienced a loss that was deemed to be both unusual in nature and infrequent in occurrence. How should Bradshaw report this item in accordance with U.S. GAAP?

37. Explain the U.S. GAAP reporting guidelines for items recognized in comprehensive income that do not affect net income.

BRIEF EXERCISES

2 3 **BE4-1** Starr Co. had sales revenue of £540,000 in 2015. Other items recorded during the year were:

Cost of goods sold	£330,000
Selling expenses	120,000
Income tax	25,000
Increase in value of employees	15,000
Administrative expenses	10,000

Prepare an income statement for Starr for 2015. Starr has 100,000 shares outstanding.

2 3 **BE4-2** Brisky Corporation had net sales of $2,400,000 and interest revenue of $31,000 during 2015. Expenses for 2015 were cost of goods sold $1,450,000, administrative expenses $212,000, selling expenses $280,000, and interest expense $45,000. Brisky's tax rate is 30%. The corporation had 100,000 shares authorized and 70,000 shares issued and outstanding during 2015. Prepare an income statement for the year ended December 31, 2015.

3 4 **BE4-3** Presented below is some financial information related to Volaire Group, a service company.

Revenues	€800,000
Income from continuing operations	100,000
Comprehensive income	120,000
Net income	90,000
Income from operations	220,000
Selling and administrative expenses	500,000
Income before income tax	200,000

Compute the following: (a) other income and expense, (b) financing costs, (c) income tax, (d) discontinued operations, and (e) other comprehensive income.

3 4 **BE4-4** The following information is provided.

Sales revenue	HK$100,000	Cost of goods sold	HK$55,000
Gain on sale of plant assets	30,000	Interest expense	5,000
Selling and administrative expenses	10,000	Income tax rate	20%

Determine (a) income from operations, (b) income before income tax, and (c) net income.

3 4 **BE4-5** The following information is provided about Caltex Company: income from operations $430,000, loss on inventory write-downs $12,000, selling expenses $62,000, and interest expense $20,000. The tax rate is 30%. Determine net income.

3 4 **BE4-6** Indicate in what section (gross profit, income from operations, or income before income tax) the following items are reported: (a) interest revenue, (b) interest expense, (c) loss on impairment of goodwill, (d) sales revenue, and (e) administrative expenses.

3 4 **BE4-7** Finley Corporation had income from continuing operations of £10,600,000 in 2015. During 2015, it disposed of its restaurant division at an after-tax loss of £189,000. Prior to disposal, the division operated at a loss of £315,000 (net of tax) in 2015. Finley had 10,000,000 shares outstanding during 2015. Prepare a partial income statement for Finley beginning with income from continuing operations.

4 7 **BE4-8** During 2015, Williamson Company changed from FIFO to weighted-average inventory pricing. Pretax income in 2014 and 2013 (Williamson's first year of operations) under FIFO was $160,000 and $180,000, respectively. Pretax income using weighted-average pricing in the prior years would have been $145,000 in 2014 and $170,000 in 2013. In 2015, Williamson Company reported pretax income (using weighted-average pricing) of $180,000. Show comparative income statements for Williamson Company, beginning with "Income before income tax," as presented on the 2015 income statement. (The tax rate in all years is 30%.)

4 7 **BE4-9** Vandross Company has recorded bad debt expense in the past at a rate of 1½% of net sales. In 2015, Vandross decides to increase its estimate to 2%. If the new rate had been used in prior years, cumulative bad debt expense would have been €380,000 instead of €285,000. In 2015, bad debt expense will be €120,000 instead of €90,000. If Vandross's tax rate is 30%, what amount should it report as the cumulative effect of changing the estimated bad debt rate?

5 **BE4-10** In 2015, Hollis Corporation reported net income of $1,000,000. It declared and paid preference dividends of $250,000. During 2015, Hollis had a weighted average of 190,000 ordinary shares outstanding. Compute Hollis's 2015 earnings per share.

8 **BE4-11** Tsui Corporation has retained earnings of NT$675,000 at January 1, 2015. Net income during 2015 was NT$1,400,000, and cash dividends declared and paid during 2015 totaled NT$75,000. Prepare a retained earnings statement for the year ended December 31, 2015.

7 **8** **BE4-12** Using the information from BE4-11, prepare a retained earnings statement for the year ended December 31, 2015. Assume an error was discovered: Land costing NT$80,000 (net of tax) was charged to repairs expense in 2014.

9 **BE4-13** On January 1, 2015, Otano Inc. had cash and share capital of ¥60,000,000. At that date, the company had no other asset, liability, or equity balances. On January 2, 2015, it purchased for cash ¥20,000,000 of equity securities that it classified as non-trading. It received cash dividends of ¥3,000,000 during the year on these securities. In addition, it has an unrealized holding gain on these securities of ¥4,000,000 (net of tax). Determine the following amounts for 2015: (a) net income, (b) comprehensive income, (c) other comprehensive income, and (d) accumulated other comprehensive income (end of 2015).

EXERCISES

2 **8** **9** **E4-1 (Compute Income Measures)** Presented below is information related to Viel Company at December 31, 2015, the end of its first year of operations.

Sales revenue	€310,000
Cost of goods sold	140,000
Selling and administrative expenses	50,000
Gain on sale of plant assets	30,000
Unrealized gain on non-trading equity securities	10,000
Interest expense	6,000
Loss on discontinued operations	12,000
Allocation to non-controlling interest	40,000
Dividends declared and paid	5,000

Instructions

Compute the following: (a) income from operations, (b) net income, (c) net income attributable to Viel Company controlling shareholders, (d) comprehensive income, and (e) retained earnings balance at December 31, 2015.

2 **E4-2 (Computation of Net Income)** Presented below are changes in all account balances of Jackson Furniture Co. during the current year, except for retained earnings.

	Increase (Decrease)		Increase (Decrease)
Cash	£ 69,000	Accounts Payable	£ (51,000)
Accounts Receivable (net)	45,000	Bonds Payable	82,000
Inventory	127,000	Share Capital—Ordinary	138,000
Investments	(47,000)		

Instructions

Compute the net income for the current year, assuming that there were no entries in the Retained Earnings account except for net income and a dividend declaration of £24,000 which was paid in the current year.

2 **E4-3 (Income Statement Items)** Presented below are certain account balances of Wade Products Co.

Rent revenue	$ 6,500	Sales discounts	$ 7,800
Interest expense	12,700	Selling expenses	99,400
Beginning retained earnings	114,400	Sales revenue	400,000
Ending retained earnings	134,000	Income tax expense	26,600
Dividend revenue	71,000	Cost of goods sold	184,400
Sales returns and allowances	12,400	Administrative expenses	82,500

Instructions

From the foregoing, compute the following: (a) total net revenue, (b) net income, and (c) dividends declared during the current year.

2 **3** **E4-4 (Income Statement Presentation)** The financial records of Dunbar Inc. were destroyed by fire at the end of 2015. Fortunately, the controller had kept the following statistical data related to the income statement.

    1. The beginning merchandise inventory was $92,000 and decreased 20% during the current year.

    2. Sales discounts amount to $17,000.

3. 30,000 ordinary shares were outstanding for the entire year.

4. Interest expense was $20,000.

5. The income tax rate is 30%.

6. Cost of goods sold amounts to $500,000.

7. Administrative expenses are 18% of cost of goods sold but only 8% of gross sales.

8. Four-fifths of the operating expenses relate to sales activities.

Instructions

From the foregoing information, prepare an income statement for the year 2015.

3 4 E4-5 (Income Statement) Presented below is information related to Webster Company (amounts in thousands).

Administrative expenses	
Officers' salaries	£ 4,900
Depreciation of office furniture and equipment	3,960
Cost of goods sold	63,570
Rent revenue	17,230
Selling expenses	
Delivery expense	2,690
Sales commissions	7,980
Depreciation of sales equipment	6,480
Sales revenue	96,500
Income tax	7,580
Interest expense	1,860

Instructions

Prepare an income statement for the year 2015. Ordinary shares outstanding for 2015 total 40,550 (in thousands).

3 4 E4-6 (Income Statement Items) The following balances were taken from the books of Parnevik Corp. on December 31, 2015.

Interest revenue	€ 86,000	Accumulated depreciation—buildings	€ 28,000
Cash	51,000	Notes receivable	155,000
Sales revenue	1,280,000	Selling expenses	194,000
Accounts receivable	150,000	Accounts payable	170,000
Prepaid insurance	20,000	Bonds payable	100,000
Sales returns and allowances	150,000	Administrative and general expenses	97,000
Allowance for doubtful accounts	7,000	Accrued liabilities	32,000
Sales discounts	45,000	Interest expense	60,000
Land	100,000	Notes payable	100,000
Equipment	200,000	Loss from impairment of plant assets	120,000
Buildings	140,000	Share capital—ordinary	500,000
Cost of goods sold	621,000	Retained earnings	21,000
Accumulated depreciation—equipment	40,000		

Assume the total effective tax rate on all items is 34%.

Instructions

Prepare an income statement; 100,000 ordinary shares were outstanding during the year.

3 4 E4-7 (Income Statement) The accountant of Weatherspoon Shoe Co. has compiled the following information from the company's records as a basis for an income statement for the year ended December 31, 2015.

Rent revenue	£ 29,000
Interest expense	18,000
Unrealized gain on non-trading equity securities, net of tax	31,000
Selling expenses	140,000
Income tax	30,600
Administrative expenses	181,000
Cost of goods sold	516,000
Net sales	980,000
Cash dividends declared	16,000
Loss on sale of plant assets	15,000

There were 20,000 ordinary shares outstanding during the year.

Instructions

(a) Prepare a comprehensive income statement using the combined statement approach.

(b) Prepare a comprehensive income statement using the two statement approach.

(c) Which format do you prefer? Discuss.

2 3 4 5 6 **E4-8 (Income Statement, EPS)** Presented below are selected ledger accounts of McGraw Corporation as of December 31, 2015.

Cash	€ 50,000
Administrative expenses	100,000
Selling expenses	80,000
Net sales	540,000
Cost of goods sold	260,000
Cash dividends declared (2015)	20,000
Cash dividends paid (2015)	15,000
Discontinued operations (loss before income tax)	40,000
Depreciation expense, not recorded in 2014	30,000
Retained earnings, December 31, 2014	90,000
Effective tax rate 30%	

Instructions

(a) Compute net income for 2015.

(b) Prepare a partial income statement beginning with income before income tax, and including appropriate earnings per share information. Assume 20,000 ordinary shares were outstanding during 2015.

3 4 5 6 8 **E4-9 (Income Statement with Retained Earnings)** Presented below is information related to Tao Corp. for the year 2015 (amounts in thousands).

Net sales	HK$1,200,000	Write-off of inventory due to obsolescence	HK$ 80,000
Cost of goods sold	780,000	Depreciation expense omitted by accident in 2014	40,000
Selling expenses	65,000	Interest expense	50,000
Administrative expenses	48,000	Cash dividends declared	45,000
Dividend revenue	20,000	Retained earnings at December 31, 2014	980,000
Interest revenue	7,000	Effective tax rate of 34% on all items	

Instructions

(a) Prepare an income statement for 2015. Assume that 60,000 ordinary shares are outstanding.

(b) Prepare a retained earnings statement for 2015.

5 **E4-10 (Earnings per Share)** The equity section of Sosa Corporation appears below as of December 31, 2015.

Share capital—preference (6% preference shares, R$50 par value, authorized 100,000 shares, outstanding 90,000 shares)		R$ 4,500,000
Share capital—ordinary (R$1 par, authorized and issued 10 million shares)		10,000,000
Share premium—ordinary		20,500,000
Retained earnings	R$134,000,000	
Net income	33,000,000	167,000,000
		R$202,000,000

Net income for 2015 reflects a total effective tax rate of 20%. Included in the net income figure is a loss of R$12,000,000 (before tax) as a result of discontinued operations. Preference dividends of R$270,000 were declared and paid in 2015. Dividends of R$1,000,000 were declared and paid to ordinary shareholders in 2015.

Instructions

Compute earnings per share data as it should appear on the income statement of Sosa Corporation.

3 4 5 6 **E4-11 (Condensed Income Statement—Periodic Inventory Method)** Presented below are selected ledger accounts of Woods Corporation at December 31, 2015.

Cash	$ 185,000	Salaries and wages expense (sales)	$284,000
Inventory (beginning)	535,000	Salaries and wages expense (office)	346,000
Sales revenue	4,175,000	Purchase returns	15,000
Unearned sales revenue	117,000	Sales returns and allowance	79,000
Purchases	2,786,000	Freight-in	72,000
Sales discounts	34,000	Accounts receivable	142,500
Purchase discounts	27,000	Sales commissions	83,000
Selling expenses	69,000	Telephone and Internet expense (sales)	17,000
Accounting and legal services	33,000	Utilities expense (office)	32,000
Insurance expense (office)	24,000	Miscellaneous office expenses	8,000
Advertising expense	54,000	Rent revenue	240,000
Delivery expense	93,000	Loss on sale of division	60,000
Depreciation expense (office equipment)	48,000	Interest expense	176,000
Depreciation expense (sales equipment)	36,000	Share capital—ordinary ($10 par)	900,000

Woods's effective tax rate on all items is 30%. A physical inventory indicates that the ending inventory is $686,000.

Instructions

Prepare a 2015 income statement for Woods Corporation.

8 **E4-12 (Retained Earnings Statement)** McEntire Corporation began operations on January 1, 2012. During its first 3 years of operations, McEntire reported net income and declared dividends as follows.

	Net income	Dividends declared
2012	$ 40,000	$ –0–
2013	125,000	50,000
2014	160,000	50,000

The following information relates to 2015.

Income before income tax	$220,000
Prior period adjustment: understatement of 2013 depreciation expense (before taxes)	$ 25,000
Cumulative decrease in income from change in inventory methods (before taxes)	$ 45,000
Dividends declared (of this amount, $25,000 will be paid on Jan. 15, 2016)	$100,000
Effective tax rate	20%

Instructions

(a) Prepare a 2015 retained earnings statement for McEntire Corporation.

(b) Assume McEntire Corp. restricted retained earnings in the amount of $70,000 on December 31, 2015. After this action, what would McEntire report as total retained earnings in its December 31, 2015, statement of financial position?

4 5 6 **E4-13 (Earnings per Share)** At December 31, 2014, Schroeder Corporation had the following shares outstanding.

8% cumulative preference shares, €100 par, 107,500 shares	€10,750,000
Ordinary shares, €5 par, 4,000,000 shares	20,000,000

During 2015, Schroeder did not issue any additional shares. The following also occurred during 2015.

Income before income tax	€21,650,000
Discontinued operations (loss before taxes)	3,225,000
Preference dividends declared	860,000
Ordinary dividends declared	2,200,000
Effective tax rate	35%

Instructions

Compute earnings per share data as it should appear in the 2015 income statement of Schroeder Corporation. (Round to two decimal places.)

6 7 **E4-14 (Change in Accounting Principle)** Zehms Company began operations in 2013 and adopted weighted-average pricing for inventory. In 2015, in accordance with other companies in its industry, Zehms changed its inventory pricing to FIFO. The pretax income data is reported below.

Year	Weighted-Average	FIFO
2013	$370,000	$395,000
2014	390,000	420,000
2015	410,000	460,000

Instructions

(a) What is Zehms's net income in 2015? Assume a 35% tax rate in all years.

(b) Compute the cumulative effect of the change in accounting principle from weighted-average to FIFO inventory pricing.

(c) Show comparative income statements for Zehms Company, beginning with income before income tax, as presented on the 2015 income statement.

4 9 **E4-15 (Comprehensive Income)** Gaertner Corporation reported the following for 2015: net sales €1,200,000, cost of goods sold €720,000, selling and administrative expenses €320,000, and an unrealized holding gain on non-trading equity securities €15,000.

Instructions

Prepare a statement of comprehensive income, using the two statement format. Ignore income taxes and earnings per share.

8 9 **E4-16 (Comprehensive Income)** Bryant Co. reports the following information for 2015: sales revenue £750,000, cost of goods sold £500,000, operating expenses £80,000, and an unrealized holding loss on non-trading equity securities for 2015 of £50,000. It declared and paid a cash dividend of £10,000 in 2015.

Bryant Co. has January 1, 2015, balances in share capital—ordinary £350,000, accumulated other comprehensive income related to the unrealized holding gain of £80,000, and retained earnings £90,000. It issued no ordinary shares during 2015. Ignore income taxes.

Instructions
Prepare a statement of changes in equity.

3 4 5 6 8 9 E4-17 (Various Reporting Formats) The following information was taken from the records of Vega Inc. for the year 2015: income tax applicable to income from continuing operations R$119,000, income tax applicable to loss on discontinued operations R$25,500, and unrealized holding gain on non-trading equity securities R$15,000.

Gain on sale of plant assets	R$ 95,000	Cash dividends declared	R$ 150,000
Loss on discontinued operations	75,000	Retained earnings January 1, 2015	600,000
Administrative expenses	240,000	Cost of goods sold	850,000
Rent revenue	40,000	Selling expenses	300,000
Loss on impairment of land	60,000	Sales revenue	1,700,000

Ordinary shares outstanding during 2015 were 100,000.

Instructions
    (a) Prepare a comprehensive income statement for 2015 using the one statement approach.
    (b) Prepare a retained earnings statement for 2015.

9 E4-18 (Changes in Equity) The equity section of Hasbro Inc. at January 1, 2015, was as follows.

Share capital—ordinary	$300,000
Accumulated other comprehensive income	
Unrealized holding gain on non-trading equity securities	50,000
Retained earnings	20,000

During the year, the company had the following transactions.

  1. Issued 10,000 shares at $3 per share.

  2. Dividends of $9,000 were declared and paid.

  3. Net income for the year was $100,000.

  4. Unrealized holding loss of $5,000 occurred on its non-trading equity securities.

Instructions
Prepare a statement of changes in equity for Hasbro Inc.

PROBLEMS

4 8 9 P4-1 (Income Components) Presented below are financial statement classifications for the statement of comprehensive income and the retained earnings statement. For each transaction or account title, enter in the space provided a letter(s) to indicate the usual classification.

Statement of Comprehensive Income		**Retained Earnings Statement**	
A	Revenue	F	An addition or deduction from beginning balance
B	Operating expense	G	Additions to retained earnings
C	Other income or expense	H	Deduction from retained earnings
D	Discontinued operations	I	Note classification
E	Other comprehensive income		

Transactions

1. _____ Unrealized holding loss on non-trading equity securities.
2. _____ Gain on sale of non-trading equity securities.
3. _____ Sales revenue.
4. _____ Loss on impairment of goodwill.
5. _____ Sales salaries accrued.
6. _____ Net income for the period.
7. _____ Loss on sale of investments.
8. _____ Depreciation on equipment used in operations.
9. _____ Cash dividends declared and paid.
10. _____ Correction of an error due to expensing the cost of equipment in a previous year.
11. _____ Insurance gain on flood loss—insurance proceeds exceed the carrying amount of assets destroyed.
12. _____ The company has decided to stop production of its candy division and suffered a loss on the sale of this division.

3 4 5 6 8 **P4-2 (Income Statement, Retained Earnings)** Presented below is information related to Dickinson Company for 2015.

Retained earnings balance, January 1, 2015	€ 980,000
Sales revenue	25,000,000
Cost of goods sold	16,000,000
Interest expense	70,000
Selling and administrative expenses	4,700,000
Write-off of goodwill	820,000
Income taxes for 2015	1,244,000
Gain on the sale of investments	110,000
Loss due to flood damage	390,000
Loss on the disposition of the wholesale division (net of tax)	440,000
Loss on operations of the wholesale division (net of tax)	90,000
Dividends declared on ordinary shares	250,000
Dividends declared on preference shares	80,000

Instructions

Prepare an income statement and a retained earnings statement. Dickinson Company decided to discontinue its entire wholesale operations and to retain its manufacturing operations. On September 15, Dickinson sold the wholesale operations to Rogers Company. During 2015, there were 500,000 ordinary shares outstanding all year.

2 3 4 6 8 **P4-3 (Income Statement, Retained Earnings, Periodic Inventory)** Presented below is the trial balance of Thompson Corporation at December 31, 2015.

THOMPSON CORPORATION
TRIAL BALANCE
DECEMBER 31, 2015

	Debit	Credit
Purchase Discounts		£ 10,000
Cash	£ 189,700	
Accounts Receivable	105,000	
Rent Revenue		18,000
Retained Earnings		160,000
Salaries and Wages Payable		18,000
Sales Revenue		1,100,000
Notes Receivable	110,000	
Accounts Payable		49,000
Accumulated Depreciation—Equipment		28,000
Sales Discounts	14,500	
Sales Returns and Allowances	17,500	
Notes Payable		70,000
Selling Expenses	232,000	
Administrative Expenses	99,000	
Share Capital—Ordinary		300,000
Income Tax Expense	53,900	
Cash Dividends	45,000	
Allowance for Doubtful Accounts		5,000
Supplies	14,000	
Freight-In	20,000	
Land	70,000	
Equipment	140,000	
Bonds Payable		100,000
Gain on Sale of Land		30,000
Accumulated Depreciation—Buildings		19,600
Inventory	89,000	
Buildings	98,000	
Purchases	610,000	
Totals	£1,907,600	£1,907,600

A physical count of inventory on December 31 resulted in an inventory amount of £64,000; thus, cost of goods sold for 2015 is £645,000.

Instructions

Prepare an income statement and a retained earnings statement. Assume that the only changes in retained earnings during the current year were from net income and dividends. Thirty thousand ordinary shares were outstanding the entire year.

P4-4 (Income Statement Items) Maher Inc. reported income before income tax during 2015 of €790,000. Additional transactions occurring in 2015 but not considered in the €790,000 are as follows.

1. The corporation experienced an uninsured flood loss in the amount of €90,000 during the year.
2. At the beginning of 2013, the corporation purchased a machine for €54,000 (residual value of €9,000) that had a useful life of 6 years. The bookkeeper used straight-line depreciation for 2013, 2014, and 2015 but failed to deduct the residual value in computing the depreciation base.
3. Sale of securities held as a part of its portfolio resulted in a gain of €47,000.
4. The corporation disposed of its recreational division at a loss of €115,000 before taxes. Assume that this transaction meets the criteria for discontinued operations.
5. The corporation decided to change its method of inventory pricing from average-cost to the FIFO method. The effect of this change on prior years is to increase 2013 income by €60,000 and decrease 2014 income by €20,000 before taxes. The FIFO method has been used for 2015.

Instructions

Prepare an income statement for the year 2015, starting with income before income tax. Compute earnings per share as it should be shown on the face of the income statement. Ordinary shares outstanding for the year are 120,000 shares. (Assume a tax rate of 30% on all items.)

P4-5 (Income Statement, Retained Earnings) The following account balances were included in the trial balance of Twain Corporation at June 30, 2015.

Sales revenue	$1,578,500	Depreciation expense (office furniture	
Sales discounts	31,150	and equipment)	$ 7,250
Cost of goods sold	896,770	Property tax expense	7,320
Salaries and wages expense (sales)	56,260	Bad debt expense (selling)	4,850
Sales commissions	97,600	Maintenance and repairs expense	
Travel expense (salespersons)	28,930	(administration)	9,130
Delivery expense	21,400	Office expenses	6,000
Entertainment expense	14,820	Sales returns and allowances	62,300
Telephone and Internet expense		Dividend revenue	38,000
(sales)	9,030	Interest expense	18,000
Depreciation expense (sales		Income tax expense	102,000
equipment)	4,980	Depreciation understatement	
Maintenance and repairs expense (sales)	6,200	due to error—2013	17,700
Miscellaneous selling expenses	4,715	Dividends declared on	
Supplies expense	3,450	preference shares	9,000
Telephone and Internet expense		Dividends declared on	
(administration)	2,820	ordinary shares	37,000

The Retained Earnings account had a balance of $337,000 at July 1, 2014. There are 80,000 ordinary shares outstanding.

Instructions

Prepare an income statement and a retained earnings statement for the year ended June 30, 2015.

P4-6 (Statement Presentation) Presented below is a combined income and retained earnings statement for Sapporo Company for 2015 (amounts in thousands).

Net sales		¥640,000
Costs and expenses		
Cost of goods sold	¥500,000	
Selling, general, and administrative expenses	66,000	
Other, net	17,000	583,000
Income before income tax		57,000
Income tax		19,400
Net income		37,600
Retained earnings at beginning of period, as previously reported	141,000	
Adjustment required for correction of error	(7,000)	
Retained earnings at beginning of period, as restated		134,000
Dividends on ordinary shares		(12,200)
Retained earnings at end of period		¥159,400

Additional facts are as follows.

1. "Selling, general, and administrative expenses" for 2015 included a charge of ¥8,500,000 for impairment of intangibles.

2. "Other, net" for 2015 was a loss on sale of equipment of ¥17,000,000.

3. "Adjustment required for correction of an error" was a result of a change in estimate (useful life of certain assets reduced to 8 years and a catch-up adjustment made).

4. Sapporo Company disclosed earnings per share for net income in the notes to the financial statements.

Instructions

Determine from these additional facts whether the presentation of the facts in the Sapporo Company income and retained earnings statement is appropriate. If the presentation is not appropriate, describe the appropriate presentation and discuss its theoretical rationale. (Do not prepare a revised statement.)

4 7 8 P4-7 (Retained Earnings Statement, Prior Period Adjustment) The following is the retained earnings account for the year 2015 for Acadian Corp.

Retained earnings, January 1, 2015		$257,600
Add:		
Gain on sale of investments	$41,200	
Net income	84,500	
Refund on litigation with government	21,600	
Recognition of income earned in 2014, but omitted from income statement in that year	25,400	172,700
		430,300
Deduct:		
Loss on discontinued operations	35,000	
Write-off of goodwill	60,000	
Cumulative effect on income of prior years in changing from average-cost to FIFO inventory valuation in 2015	23,200	
Cash dividends declared	32,000	150,200
Retained earnings, December 31, 2015		$280,100

Instructions

(a) Prepare a corrected retained earnings statement. (Ignore income tax effects.) FIFO inventory was used in 2015 to compute net income.

(b) State where the items that do not appear in the corrected retained earnings statement should be shown.

4 5 6 P4-8 (Income Statement) Wade Corp. has 150,000 ordinary shares of outstanding. In 2015, the company reports income before income tax of €1,210,000. Additional transactions not considered in the €1,210,000 are as follows.

1. In 2015, Wade Corp. sold equipment for €40,000. The machine had originally cost €80,000 and had accumulated depreciation of €30,000.

2. The company discontinued operations of one of its subsidiaries during the current year at a loss of €190,000 before taxes. Assume that this transaction meets the criteria for discontinued operations. The loss from operations of the discontinued subsidiary was €90,000 before taxes; the loss from disposal of the subsidiary was €100,000 before taxes.

3. An internal audit discovered that amortization of intangible assets was understated by €35,000 (net of tax) in a prior period. The amount was charged against retained earnings.

4. The company had a gain of €125,000 on the condemnation of much of its property.

Instructions

Analyze the above information and prepare an income statement for the year 2015, starting with income before income tax. Compute earnings per share as it should be shown on the face of the income statement. (Assume a total effective tax rate of 20% on all items.)

CONCEPTS FOR ANALYSIS

CA4-1 (Identification of Income Statement Deficiencies) O'Malley Corporation was incorporated and began business on January 1, 2015. It has been successful and now requires a bank loan for additional working capital to finance expansion. The bank has requested an audited income statement for the year 2015. The accountant for O'Malley Corporation provides you with the following income statement, which O'Malley plans to submit to the bank.

O'MALLEY CORPORATION
INCOME STATEMENT

Sales revenue		£850,000
Dividends		32,300
Gain on recovery of insurance proceeds from earthquake loss		38,500
		920,800
Less:		
Selling expenses	£101,100	
Cost of goods sold	510,000	
Interest expense	13,700	
Loss on obsolescence of inventories	34,000	
Loss on discontinued operations	48,600	
Administrative expenses	73,400	780,800
Income before income tax		140,000
Income tax		56,000
Net income		£ 84,000

Instructions
Indicate the deficiencies in the income statement presented.

CA4-2 (Earnings Management) Bobek Inc. has recently reported steadily increasing income. The company reported income of €20,000 in 2012, €25,000 in 2013, and €30,000 in 2014. A number of market analysts have recommended that investors buy Bobek shares because the analysts expect the steady growth in income to continue. Bobek is approaching the end of its fiscal year in 2015, and it again appears to be a good year. However, it has not yet recorded warranty expense.

Based on prior experience, this year's warranty expense should be around €5,000, but some managers have approached the controller to suggest a larger, more conservative warranty expense should be recorded this year. Income before warranty expense is €43,000. Specifically, by recording a €7,000 warranty accrual this year, Bobek could report an increase in income for this year and still be in a position to cover its warranty costs in future years.

Instructions
  (a) What is earnings management?
  (b) Assume income before warranty expense is €43,000 for both 2015 and 2016 and that total warranty expense over the 2-year period is €10,000. What is the effect of the proposed accounting in 2015? In 2016?
  (c) What is the appropriate accounting in this situation?

CA4-3 (Earnings Management) Charlie Brown, controller for Kelly Corporation, is preparing the company's income statement at year-end. He notes that the company lost a considerable sum on the sale of some equipment it had decided to replace. Brown does not want to highlight it as a material loss since he feels that will reflect poorly on him and the company. He reasons that if the company had recorded more depreciation during the assets' lives, the losses would not be so great. Since depreciation is included among the company's operating expenses, he wants to report the losses along with the company's expenses, where he hopes it will not be noticed.

Instructions
  (a) What are the ethical issues involved?
  (b) What should Brown do?

CA4-4 (Income Reporting Items) Simpson Corp. is an entertainment firm that derives approximately 30% of its income from the Casino Knights Division, which manages gambling facilities. As auditor for Simpson Corp., you have recently overheard the following discussion between the controller and financial vice president.

VICE PRESIDENT: If we sell the Casino Knights Division, it seems ridiculous to segregate the results of the sale in the income statement. Separate categories tend to be absurd and confusing to the shareholders. I believe that we should simply report the gain on the sale as other income or expense without detail.

CONTROLLER:	IFRS would require that we disclose this information more fully in the income statement as a gain on discontinued operations.
VICE PRESIDENT:	What about the walkout we had last month when employees were upset about their commission income? We had a loss as a result of this walkout.
CONTROLLER:	I am not sure where this item would be reported.
VICE PRESIDENT:	Oh well, it doesn't make any difference because the net effect of all these items is immaterial, so no disclosure is necessary.

Instructions

(a) On the basis of the foregoing discussion, answer the following questions: Who is correct about handling the sale? What would be the correct income statement presentation for the sale of the Casino Knights Division?

(b) How should the walkout by the employees be reported?

(c) What do you think about the vice president's observation on materiality?

(d) What are the earnings per share implications of these topics?

CA4-5 (Identification of Income Statement Weaknesses) The following financial statement was prepared by employees of Walters Corporation.

WALTERS CORPORATION

INCOME STATEMENT

YEAR ENDED DECEMBER 31, 2015

Revenues	
Gross sales, including sales taxes	£1,044,300
Less: Returns, allowances, and cash discounts	56,200
Net sales	988,100
Dividends, interest, and purchase discounts	30,250
Recoveries of accounts written off in prior years	13,850
Total revenues	1,032,200
Costs and expenses	
Cost of goods sold, including sales taxes	465,900
Salaries and related payroll expenses	60,500
Rent	19,100
Delivery expense and freight-in	3,400
Bad debt expense	27,800
Total costs and expenses	576,700
Income before unusual items	455,500
Unusual items	
Loss on discontinued styles (Note 1)	71,500
Loss on sale of marketable securities (Note 2)	39,050
Loss on sale of warehouse (Note 3)	86,350
Total unusual items	196,900
Net income	£ 258,600
Net income per ordinary share	£2.30

Note 1: New styles and rapidly changing consumer preferences resulted in a £71,500 loss on the disposal of discontinued styles and related accessories.

Note 2: The corporation sold an investment in marketable securities at a loss of £39,050. The corporation normally sells securities of this nature.

Note 3: The corporation sold one of its warehouses at an £86,350 loss.

Instructions

Identify and discuss the weaknesses in classification and disclosure in the income statement above. You should explain why these treatments are weaknesses and what the proper presentation of the items would be in accordance with IFRS.

CA4-6 (Classification of Income Statement Items) As audit partner for Grupo and Rijo, you are in charge of reviewing the classification of unusual items that have occurred during the current year. The following material items have come to your attention.

1. A merchandising company incorrectly overstated its ending inventory 2 years ago. Inventory for all other periods is correctly computed.

2. An automobile dealer sells for $137,000 an extremely rare 1930 S type Invicta which it purchased for $21,000 10 years ago. The Invicta is the only such display item the dealer owns.

3. A drilling company during the current year extended the estimated useful life of certain drilling equipment from 9 to 15 years. As a result, depreciation for the current year was materially lowered.

4. A retail outlet changed its computation for bad debt expense from 1% to ½ of 1% of sales because of changes in its customer clientele.

5. A mining concern sells a foreign subsidiary engaged in uranium mining. It is the only uranium mine the company has.

6. A steel company changes from the average-cost method to the FIFO method for inventory costing purposes.

7. A construction company, at great expense, prepared a major proposal for a government loan. The loan is not approved.

8. A water pump manufacturer has had large losses resulting from a strike by its employees early in the year.

9. Depreciation for a prior period was incorrectly understated by $950,000. The error was discovered in the current year.

10. A large sheep rancher suffered a major loss because the state required that all sheep in the state be killed to halt the spread of a rare disease. Such a situation has not occurred in the state for 20 years.

11. A food distributor that sells wholesale to supermarket chains and to fast-food restaurants (two distinguishable classes of customers) decides to discontinue the division that sells to one of the two classes of customers.

Instructions
From the foregoing information, indicate in what section of the income statement or retained earnings statement these items should be classified. Provide a brief rationale for your position.

CA4-7 (Comprehensive Income) Willie Nelson, Jr., controller for Jenkins Corporation, is preparing the company's financial statements at year-end. Currently, he is focusing on the income statement and determining the format for reporting comprehensive income. During the year, the company earned net income of $400,000 and had unrealized gains on non-trading equity securities of $15,000. In the previous year, net income was $410,000, and the company had no unrealized gains or losses.

Instructions
(a) Show how income and comprehensive income will be reported on a comparative basis for the current and prior years, using the separate income statement format.
(b) Show how income and comprehensive income will be reported on a comparative basis for the current and prior years, using the combined comprehensive income statement format.
(c) Which format should Nelson recommend?

USING YOUR JUDGMENT

FINANCIAL REPORTING

Financial Reporting Problem

Marks and Spencer plc (M&S)
The financial statements of M&S (GBR) are presented in Appendix A. The company's complete annual report, including the notes to the financial statements, is available online.

Instructions

    (a) What type of income statement format does M&S use? Indicate why this format might be used to present income statement information.

    (b) What are M&S's primary revenue sources?

    (c) Compute M&S's gross profit for each of the years 2012 and 2013. Explain why gross profit increased in 2013.

    (d) Why does M&S make a distinction between operating and non-operating profit?

    (e) Does M&S report any non-IFRS measures? Explain.

Comparative Analysis Case

Adidas and Puma

The financial statements of adidas (DEU) and Puma (DEU) are presented in Appendices B and C, respectively. The complete annual reports, including the notes to the financial statements, are available online.

Instructions

Use the companies' financial information to answer the following questions.

    (a) Which company had the greater percentage increase in revenues from 2011 to 2012?

    (b) Did either company report the effect of a discontinued operation in its income statement? Briefly describe how the reporting of a discontinued operation can affect comparisons between two companies.

    (c) Which company had more depreciation and amortization expense, as a percentage of operating cash flow for 2012? What are some reasons that there would be a difference in these amounts between the two companies?

    (d) Did either company report profit attributed to minority interests? If so, which company has the more significant non-controlling (minority) interest?

Financial Statement Analysis Cases

Case 1: Bankruptcy Prediction

The Z-score bankruptcy prediction model uses statement of financial position and income information to arrive at a Z-Score, which can be used to predict financial distress:

$$Z = \frac{\text{Working capital}}{\text{Total assets}} \times 1.2 + \frac{\text{Retained earnings}}{\text{Total assets}} \times 1.4 + \frac{\text{EBIT}}{\text{Total assets}} \times 3.3 + \frac{\text{Sales}}{\text{Total assets}} \times .99 + \frac{\text{MV equity}}{\text{Total liabilities}} \times 0.6$$

EBIT is earnings before interest and taxes. MV equity is the market value of equity, which can be determined by multiplying share price by shares outstanding.

    Following extensive testing, it has been shown that companies with Z-scores above 3.0 are unlikely to fail; those with Z-scores below 1.81 are very likely to fail. While the original model was developed for publicly held manufacturing companies, the model has been modified to apply to companies in various industries, emerging companies, and companies not traded in public markets.

Instructions

    (a) Use information in the financial statements of a company like Vodafone (GBR) or Nokia (FIN) to compute the Z-score for the past 2 years.

    (b) Interpret your result. Where does the company fall in the financial distress range?

    (c) The Z-score uses EBIT as one of its elements. Why do you think this income measure is used?

Case 2: P/E Ratios

One of the more closely watched ratios by investors is the price/earnings or P/E ratio. By dividing price per share by earnings per share, analysts get insight into the value the market attaches to a company's earnings. More specifically, a high P/E ratio (in comparison to companies in the same industry) may suggest the shares are overpriced. Also, there is some evidence that companies with low P/E ratios are underpriced and tend to outperform the market. However, the ratio can be misleading.

P/E ratios are sometimes misleading because the E (earnings) is subject to a number of assumptions and estimates that could result in overstated earnings and a lower P/E. Some analysts conduct "revenue analysis" to evaluate the quality of an earnings number. Revenues are less subject to management estimates and all earnings must begin with revenues. These analysts also compute the price-to-sales ratio (PSR = price per share ÷ sales per share) to assess whether a company is performing well compared to similar companies. If a company has a price-to-sales ratio significantly higher than its competitors, investors may be betting on a company that has yet to prove itself. [*Source:* Janice Revell, "Beyond P/E," *Fortune* (May 28, 2001), p. 174.]

Instructions

(a) Identify some of the estimates or assumptions that could result in overstated earnings.

(b) Compute the P/E ratio and the PSR for **Puma** (DEU) and **adidas** (DEU) for 2012.

(c) Use these data to compare the quality of each company's earnings.

International Reporting Case

Presented below is the income statement for **Campbell Soup Company** (USA). Campbell prepares its financial statements in accordance with U.S. GAAP.

Campbell Soup Company

Consolidated Statements of Earnings
(millions, except per share amounts)

	2012	2011
Net sales	$ 7,707	$ 7,719
Costs and expenses		
Cost of products sold	4,715	4,616
Marketing and selling expenses	1,020	1,007
Administrative expenses	611	612
Research and development expenses	125	129
Other expenses/(income)	14	13
Restructuring charges	10	63
Total costs and expenses	6,495	6,440
Earnings before interest and taxes	1,212	1,279
Interest expense	114	122
Interest income	8	11
Earnings before taxes	1,106	1,168
Taxes on earnings	342	366
Net earnings	764	802
Less: Net earnings (loss) attributable to noncontrolling interests	(10)	(3)
Net earnings attributable to Campbell Soup Company	$ 774	$ 805
Per Share—Basic		
Net earnings attributable to Campbell Soup Company	$2.43	$2.44
Weighted average shares outstanding—basic	317	326
Per Share—Assuming Dilution		
Net earnings attributable to Campbell Soup Company	$2.41	$2.42
Weighted average shares outstanding—assuming dilution	319	329

Instructions

(a) Review the Campbell income statement and identify similarities and differences between the U.S. GAAP income statement and an income statement of an IFRS company as presented in the chapter.

(b) Identify any non-recurring items reported by Campbell, if any. Is the reporting of these non-recurring items in the income statement under U.S. GAAP similar to reporting of these items in IFRS companies' income statements? Explain.

Accounting, Analysis, and Principles

Counting Crows Inc. provided the following information for the year 2015.

Retained earnings, January 1, 2015	£ 600,000
Administrative expenses	240,000
Selling expenses	300,000
Sales revenue	1,900,000
Cash dividends declared	80,000
Cost of goods sold	850,000
Gain on sale of investments	62,700
Loss on discontinued operations	75,000
Rent revenue	40,000
Unrealized holding gain on non-trading equity securities	17,000
Income tax applicable to continuing operations	187,000
Income tax benefit applicable to loss on discontinued operations	25,500
Income tax applicable to unrealized holding gain on non-trading equity securities	2,000
Weighted-average shares outstanding	100,000

Accounting

Prepare (a) an income statement for 2015, (b) a retained earnings statement for 2015, and (c) a statement of comprehensive income using the two statement format.

Analysis

Explain how income statement subheads can provide useful information to financial statement readers.

Principles

In a recent meeting with its auditor, Counting Crows' management argued that the company should be able to prepare a pro forma income statement, with some one-time administrative expenses reported similar to discontinued operations. Is such reporting consistent with the qualitative characteristics of accounting information as discussed in the Conceptual Framework? Explain.

IFRS BRIDGE TO THE PROFESSION

Professional Research

Your client took accounting a number of years ago and was unaware of comprehensive income reporting. He is not convinced that any accounting standards exist for comprehensive income.

Instructions

Access the IFRS authoritative literature at the IASB website (*http://eifrs.iasb.org/*) (you may register for free eIFRS access at this site). When you have accessed the documents, you can use the search tool in your Internet browser to respond to the following questions. (Provide paragraph citations.)

(a) What IFRS addresses reporting in the statement of comprehensive income? When was it issued?
(b) Provide the definition of total comprehensive income.
(c) Explain the rationale for presenting additional line items, headings, and subtotals in the statement of comprehensive income.
(d) What items of income or expense may be presented either in the statement of comprehensive income or in the notes?

Professional Simulation

In this simulation, you are asked to compute various income amounts. Assume a tax rate of 30% and 100,000 ordinary shares outstanding during the year. Prepare responses to all parts.

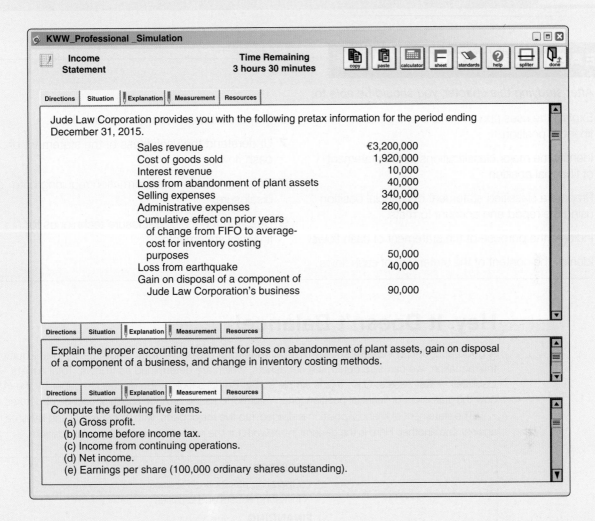

KWW_Professional _Simulation

| Income Statement | Time Remaining 3 hours 30 minutes | copy | paste | calculator | sheet | standards | help | splitter | done |

Directions | Situation | Explanation | Measurement | Resources

Jude Law Corporation provides you with the following pretax information for the period ending December 31, 2015.

Sales revenue	€3,200,000
Cost of goods sold	1,920,000
Interest revenue	10,000
Loss from abandonment of plant assets	40,000
Selling expenses	340,000
Administrative expenses	280,000
Cumulative effect on prior years of change from FIFO to average-cost for inventory costing purposes	50,000
Loss from earthquake	40,000
Gain on disposal of a component of Jude Law Corporation's business	90,000

Directions | Situation | Explanation | Measurement | Resources

Explain the proper accounting treatment for loss on abandonment of plant assets, gain on disposal of a component of a business, and change in inventory costing methods.

Directions | Situation | Explanation | Measurement | Resources

Compute the following five items.
(a) Gross profit.
(b) Income before income tax.
(c) Income from continuing operations.
(d) Net income.
(e) Earnings per share (100,000 ordinary shares outstanding).

Statement of Financial Position and Statement of Cash Flows

Hey, It Doesn't Balance!

A good accounting student knows by now that Total Assets = Total Liabilities + Total Equity. From this equation, we can also determine net assets, which are determined as follows: Total Assets − Total Liabilities = Net Assets. O.K., this is simple so far. But let's look at the discussion paper by the IASB on how the statement of financial position (often referred to as the balance sheet) should be structured.

The statement of financial position is divided into five major parts, with many assets and liabilities netted against one another. Here is the general framework for the new statement of financial position:

BUSINESS
　　Operating assets and liabilities
　　Investing assets and liabilities

FINANCING
　　Financing assets
　　Financing liabilities

INCOME TAXES

DISCONTINUED OPERATIONS

EQUITY

The statement does look a bit different than the traditional balance sheet. Let's put some numbers to the statement and see how it works. (See the example on the facing page.)

Well, it does balance—in that net assets equal equity—but isn't it important to know total assets and total liabilities? As some have observed, the statement of financial position will not balance the way we expect it to. That is, assets won't equal liabilities and equity. This is because the assets and liabilities are grouped into the business, financing, discontinued operations, and income taxes categories. This new model raises a number of questions, such as:

- Does separating "business activities" from "financing activities" provide information that is more decision-useful?

- Does information on income taxes and discontinued operations merit separate categories?

The IASB is working to get answers to these and other questions about this proposed model. One thing is for sure—adoption of the new financial statement will be a dramatic change but hopefully one for the better.

STATEMENT OF FINANCIAL POSITION		
BUSINESS		
Operating		
Inventories	€ 400,000	
Receivables	200,000	
Total short-term assets		€ 600,000
Property (net)	500,000	
Intangible assets	50,000	
Total long-term assets		550,000
Accounts payable	30,000	
Wages payable	40,000	
Total short-term liabilities		(70,000)
Lease liability	10,000	
Other long-term debt	35,000	
Total long-term liabilities		(45,000)
Net operating assets		**1,035,000**
Investing		
Trading securities	45,000	
Other securities	5,000	
Total investing assets		50,000
TOTAL NET BUSINESS ASSETS		**1,085,000**
FINANCING		
Financing assets		
Cash	30,000	
Total financing assets		30,000
Financing liabilities		
Short- and long-term borrowing	130,000	
Total financing liabilities		130,000
NET FINANCING LIABILITIES		**100,000**
INCOME TAXES		
Deferred income taxes		70,000
DISCONTINUED OPERATIONS		
Assets held for sale		420,000
NET ASSETS		**€1,475,000**
EQUITY		
Share capital—ordinary	€1,000,000	
Retained earnings	475,000	
TOTAL EQUITY		**€1,475,000**

CONCEPTUAL FOCUS

> See the **Underlying Concepts** on page 196.
> Read the **Evolving Issue** on pages 209–210 for a discussion of statement of financial position reporting.

INTERNATIONAL FOCUS

> Read the **Global Accounting Insights** on pages 210–211 for a discussion of convergence efforts in financial statement presentation.

Sources: Marie Leone and Tim Reason, "How Extreme Is the Makeover?" *CFO Magazine* (March 1, 2009); and *Preliminary Views on Financial Statement Presentation*, FASB/IASB Discussion Paper (October 2008).

PREVIEW OF CHAPTER 5

As the opening story indicates, the IASB is currently working to improve the presentation of financial information on the statement of financial position, as well as other financial statements. In this chapter, we examine the many different types of assets, liabilities, and equity items that affect the statement of financial position and the statement of cash flows. The content and organization of the chapter are as follows.

Statement of Financial Position and Statement of Cash Flows		
Statement of Financial Position	**Statement of Cash Flows**	**Additional Information**
• Usefulness	• Purpose	• Notes
• Limitations	• Content and format	• Techniques of disclosure
• Classification	• Preparation overview	• Other guidelines
• Format	• Usefulness	

STATEMENT OF FINANCIAL POSITION

LEARNING OBJECTIVE **1**

Explain the uses and limitations of a statement of financial position.

The statement of financial position, also referred to as the balance sheet, reports the assets, liabilities, and equity of a business enterprise at a specific date.[1] This financial statement provides information about the nature and amounts of investments in enterprise resources, obligations to creditors, and the equity in net resources. It therefore helps in predicting the amounts, timing, and uncertainty of future cash flows.

Usefulness of the Statement of Financial Position

Liquidity

How quickly will my assets convert to cash?

Solvency

S.O.S

Obligation Ocean

We are drowning in a sea of debt!

Hmm... I wonder if they will pay me back?

By providing information on assets, liabilities, and equity, the statement of financial position provides a basis for computing rates of return and evaluating the capital structure of the enterprise. Analysts also use information in the statement of financial position to assess a company's risk[2] and future cash flows. In this regard, analysts use the statement of financial position to assess a company's liquidity, solvency, and financial flexibility.

Liquidity describes "the amount of time that is expected to elapse until an asset is realized or otherwise converted into cash or until a liability has to be paid." Creditors are interested in short-term liquidity ratios, such as the ratio of cash (or near cash) to short-term liabilities. These ratios indicate whether a company, like adidas (DEU), will have the resources to pay its current and maturing obligations. Similarly, shareholders assess liquidity to evaluate the possibility of future cash dividends or the buyback of shares. In general, the greater adidas' liquidity, the lower its risk of failure.

Solvency refers to the ability of a company to pay its debts as they mature. For example, when a company carries a high level of long-term debt relative to assets, it has lower solvency than a similar company with a low level of long-term debt. Companies with higher debt are relatively more risky because they will need more of their assets to meet their fixed obligations (interest and principal payments).

Liquidity and solvency affect a company's financial flexibility, which measures the ability of a company to take effective actions to alter the amounts and timing of cash flows so it can respond to unexpected needs and opportunities. For example, a company may become so loaded with debt—so financially inflexible—that it has little or no sources of cash to finance expansion or to pay off maturing debt. A company with a high degree of financial flexibility is better able to survive bad times, to recover from unexpected setbacks, and to take advantage of profitable and unexpected investment opportunities. Generally, the greater an enterprise's financial flexibility, the lower its risk of failure.

Limitations of the Statement of Financial Position

Some of the major limitations of the statement of financial position are:

1. Most assets and liabilities are reported at **historical cost**. As a result, the information provided in the statement of financial position is often criticized for not reporting a more relevant fair value. For example, Pemex (MEX) owns crude oil and natural gas that may appreciate in value. Yet, it reports any increase only if and when it sells the assets.

I
F
R
S

See the Authoritative Literature section (page 215).

[1]The IASB indicates that the title "statement of financial position" better reflects the function of the statement and is consistent with the Conceptual Framework discussed in Chapter 2. The title "balance sheet" simply reflects the condition that double-entry bookkeeping requires all debits to equal all credits and does not identify the content or purpose of the statement. **[1]**

[2]Risk conveys the unpredictability of future events, transactions, circumstances, and results of the company.

2. Companies use **judgments and estimates** to determine many of the items reported in the statement of financial position. For example, in its statement of financial position, Lenovo (CHN) estimates the amount of receivables that it will collect, the useful life of its warehouses, and the number of computers that will be returned under warranty.

3. The statement of financial position necessarily **omits many items that are of financial value** but that a company cannot record objectively. For example, the knowledge and skill of Intel (USA) employees in developing new computer chips are arguably the company's most significant asset. However, because Intel cannot reliably measure the value of its employees and other intangible assets (such as customer base, research superiority, and reputation), it does not recognize these items in the statement of financial position. Similarly, many liabilities are reported in an "off-balance-sheet" manner, if at all.

Statement of
Financial Position

**Hey....we left out the
value of the employees!**

The bankruptcy of Enron (USA), the seventh-largest U.S. company at the time, highlights the omission of important items in the statement of financial position. In Enron's case, it failed to disclose certain off-balance-sheet financing obligations in its main financial statements.

Classification in the Statement of Financial Position

Statement of financial position accounts are **classified**. That is, a statement of financial position groups together similar items to arrive at significant subtotals. Furthermore, the material is arranged so that important relationships are shown.

The IASB indicates that the parts and subsections of financial statements are more informative than the whole. Therefore, the IASB discourages the reporting of summary accounts alone (total assets, net assets, total liabilities, etc.). Instead, companies should report and classify individual items in sufficient detail to permit users to assess the amounts, timing, and uncertainty of future cash flows. Such classification also makes it easier for users to evaluate the company's liquidity and financial flexibility, profitability, and risk.

To classify items in financial statements, companies group those items with similar characteristics and separate items with different characteristics. For example, companies should report separately:

2 LEARNING OBJECTIVE
Identify the major classifications of the statement of financial position.

1. Assets and liabilities with **different general liquidity characteristics**. For example, Nokia (FIN) reports cash separately from inventories.

2. Assets that differ in their **expected function** in the company's central operations or other activities. For example, Puma (DEU) reports merchandise inventories separately from property, plant, and equipment. Similarly, a company like Marks and Spencer plc (GBR) that uses assets in its operations should report these assets differently from assets held for investments and assets subject to restrictions, such as leased facilities.

3. Liabilities that differ in their **amounts, nature, and timing**. For example, Royal Ahold (NLD) should report accounts payable separately from its pension liability.

The three general classes of items included in the statement of financial position are assets, liabilities, and equity. We defined them in Chapter 2 as follows.[3]

---

[3]A company may classify the statement of financial position in some other manner, but in practice you see little departure from these major subdivisions. In some countries, such as Germany, companies often list current assets first. *IAS No. 1* requires companies to distinguish current assets and liabilities from non-current ones, except in limited situations. [2]

ELEMENTS OF THE STATEMENT OF FINANCIAL POSITION

1 ASSET. Resource controlled by the entity as a result of past events and from which future economic benefits are expected to flow to the entity.

2 LIABILITY. Present obligation of the entity arising from past events, the settlement of which is expected to result in an outflow from the entity of resources embodying economic benefits.

3 EQUITY. Residual interest in the assets of the entity after deducting all its liabilities.

Companies then further divide these items into several subclassifications. Illustration 5-1 indicates the general format of statement of financial position presentation.

ILLUSTRATION 5-1
Statement of Financial Position Classification

Assets	Equity and Liabilities
Non-current assets	Equity
Investments	Share capital
Property, plant, and equipment	Share premium
Intangible assets	Retained earnings
Other assets	Accumulated other comprehensive income
Current assets	Non-controlling interest (Minority interest)
	Non-current liabilities
	Current liabilities

What do the numbers mean? WHAT COMES FIRST?

There is much discussion involving the format of the financial statements. An interesting question is whether current assets or non-current assets should be shown first on the statement of financial position. Recently, a survey was done of 175 international companies which showed the following trends in the order in which assets are presented.

Format of Statement of Financial Position

Classified	2011	2010	2009
Current assets, non-current assets, current liabilities, non-current liabilities, equity	84	51	43
Non-current assets, current assets, equity, non-current liabilities, current liabilities	54	67	64
Non-current assets, current assets, current liabilities, non-current liabilities, equity	16	30	32
Non-current assets, current assets, non-current liabilities, current liabilities, equity	0	5	4

Source: P. Walters, "IFRS Financial Statements," *Accounting Trends and Techniques—2012* (New York: AICPA), p. 117.

This survey shows that companies are moving toward reporting current assets first on the statement of financial position, which is a change from a few years ago. Recognize that companies are required to present a classified statement of financial position except when one based on liquidity provides more relevant information. Therefore, either current assets or non-current assets can be shown first. The important point is that financial statement users have a good understanding of what is going to be realized in cash in the short-term versus the long-term.

Non-Current Assets

Current assets are cash and other assets a company expects to convert to cash, sell, or consume either in one year or the operating cycle, whichever is longer. **Non-current assets** are those not meeting the definition of current assets. They include a variety of items, as we discuss in the following sections.

Long-Term Investments. Long-term investments, often referred to simply as investments, normally consist of one of four types:

1. Investments in securities, such as bonds, ordinary shares, or long-term notes.
2. Investments in tangible assets not currently used in operations, such as land held for speculation.
3. Investments set aside in special funds, such as a sinking fund, pension fund, or plant expansion fund.
4. Investments in non-consolidated subsidiaries or associated companies.

Companies group investments in debt and equity securities into three separate portfolios for valuation and reporting purposes:

- Held-for-collection: Debt securities that a company manages to collect contractual principal and interest payments.
- Trading (also referred to as designated at fair value through profit or loss): Debt and equity securities bought and held primarily for sale in the near term to generate income on short-term price changes.
- Non-trading equity: Certain equity securities held for purposes other than trading (e.g., to meet a legal or contractual requirement).

We further discuss the held-for-collection and non-trading equity securities in Chapter 17.[4]

A company should report trading securities (whether debt or equity) as current assets. It classifies individual held-for-collection and non-trading equity securities as current or non-current, depending on the circumstances. It should report held-for-collection securities at amortized cost. All trading and non-trading equity securities are reported at fair value. [3]

Christian Dior (FRA) reported its investments as follows.

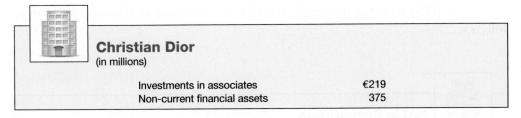

Christian Dior (in millions)	
Investments in associates	€219
Non-current financial assets	375

ILLUSTRATION 5-2
Statement of Financial Position Presentation of Long-Term Investments

Property, Plant, and Equipment. Property, plant, and equipment are tangible long-lived assets used in the regular operations of the business. These assets consist of physical property such as land, buildings, machinery, furniture, tools, and wasting resources (minerals). With the exception of land, a company either depreciates (e.g., buildings) or depletes (e.g., oil reserves) these assets.

ÆON Co. Ltd. (JPN) presented its property, plant, and equipment in its statement of financial position as shown in Illustration 5-3 (on page 186).

---

[4] Note that the IASB issued *IFRS 9, Financial Instruments*, which eliminated the available-for-sale and held-to-maturity classifications.

ILLUSTRATION 5-3
Statement of Financial
Position Presentation of
Property, Plant, and
Equipment

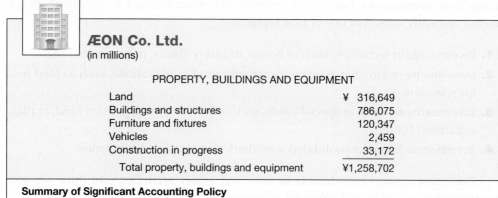

ÆON Co. Ltd.
(in millions)

PROPERTY, BUILDINGS AND EQUIPMENT

Land	¥ 316,649
Buildings and structures	786,075
Furniture and fixtures	120,347
Vehicles	2,459
Construction in progress	33,172
Total property, buildings and equipment	¥1,258,702

Summary of Significant Accounting Policy
Property, buildings and equipment—Property, buildings and equipment are stated at cost. Depreciation of property, buildings and equipment is computed under the straight-line method based on the estimated useful lives of the assets. The range of useful lives is principally from 20 to 39 years for store buildings, from 38 to 50 years for office buildings, from 3 to 20 years for structures, from 2 to 20 years for furniture and fixtures, and from 4 to 6 years for vehicles. Accumulated depreciation of property, buildings and equipment at year-end was ¥861,445 million.

A company discloses the basis it uses to value property, plant, and equipment; any liens against the properties; and accumulated depreciation—usually in the notes to the statements.

Intangible Assets. Intangible assets lack physical substance and are not financial instruments.[5] They include patents, copyrights, franchises, goodwill, trademarks, trade names, and customer lists. A company writes off (amortizes) limited-life intangible assets over their useful lives. It periodically assesses indefinite-life intangibles (such as goodwill) for impairment. Intangibles can represent significant economic resources, yet financial analysts often ignore them, because valuation is difficult. Research and development costs are expensed as incurred except for certain development costs, which are capitalized when it is probable that a development project will generate future economic benefits.

Nokia (FIN) reported intangible assets in its statement of financial position as follows.

ILLUSTRATION 5-4
Statement of Financial
Position Presentation
of Intangible Assets

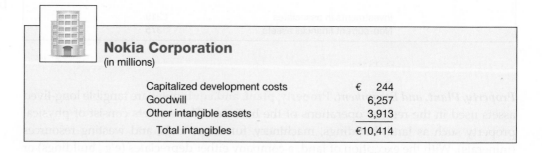

Nokia Corporation
(in millions)

Capitalized development costs	€ 244
Goodwill	6,257
Other intangible assets	3,913
Total intangibles	€10,414

Other Assets. The items included in the section "Other assets" vary widely in practice. Some include items such as long-term prepaid expenses and non-current receivables. Other items that might be included are assets in special funds, property

---

[5]A **financial instrument** is any contract that gives rise to a financial asset for one company and a financial liability or equity instrument for another company. **[4]**

held for sale, and restricted cash or securities. A company should limit this section to include only unusual items sufficiently different from assets included in specific categories.

Current Assets

As indicated earlier, current assets **are cash and other assets a company expects to convert into cash, sell, or consume either in one year or in the operating cycle, whichever is longer.** The operating cycle is the average time between when a company acquires materials and supplies and when it receives cash for sales of the product (for which it acquired the materials and supplies). The cycle operates from cash through inventory, production, receivables, and back to cash. When several operating cycles occur within one year (which is generally the case for service companies), a company uses the one-year period. If the operating cycle is more than one year, a company uses the longer period.

The five major items found in the current assets section, and their bases of valuation, are shown in Illustration 5-5. These assets are generally presented in the following order.

Item	Basis of Valuation
Inventories	Lower-of-cost-or-net realizable value
Prepaid expenses	Cost
Receivables	Estimated amount collectible
Short-term investments	Generally, fair value
Cash and cash equivalents	Fair value

ILLUSTRATION 5-5
Current Assets and Basis of Valuation

A company does not report these five items as current assets if it does not expect to realize them in one year or in the operating cycle, whichever is longer. For example, a company excludes from the current assets section cash restricted for purposes other than payment of current obligations or for use in current operations. **Generally, if a company expects to convert an asset into cash or to use it to pay a current liability within a year or the operating cycle, whichever is longer, it classifies the asset as current.**

This rule, however, is subject to interpretation. A company classifies an investment in non-trading equity securities as either a current asset or a non-current asset, depending on management's intent. When it has holdings of ordinary or preference shares or bonds that it will hold long-term, it should not classify them as current.

Although a current asset is well defined, certain theoretical problems also develop. For example, how is inclusion of prepaid expenses in the current assets section justified? The rationale is that if a company did not pay these items in advance, it would instead need to use other current assets during the operating cycle. If we follow this logic to its ultimate conclusion, however, any asset previously purchased saves the use of current assets during the operating cycle and would be considered current.

Another problem occurs in the current-asset definition when a company consumes plant assets during the operating cycle. Conceptually, it seems that a company should place in the current assets section an amount equal to the current depreciation charge on the plant assets, because it will consume them in the next operating cycle. However, this conceptual problem is ignored. This example illustrates that the formal distinction made between some current and non-current assets is somewhat arbitrary.

Inventories. To present inventories properly, a company discloses the basis of valuation (e.g., lower-of-cost-or-net realizable value) and the cost flow assumption used (e.g., FIFO or average-cost). Presented in Illustration 5-6 is how Royal Ahold (NLD) reports its inventories.

ILLUSTRATION 5-6
Statement of Financial
Position Presentation of
Inventories

Royal Ahold
(in millions)

CURRENT ASSETS
INVENTORIES (NOTE 16) €1,319

Note 16
Inventories are stated at cost or net realizable value, whichever is lower. Cost consists of all costs of purchase, cost of conversion and other costs incurred in bringing the inventories to their present location and condition, net of vendor allowances attributable to inventories. The cost of inventories is determined using either the first-in, first-out ("FIFO") method or the weighted average cost method, depending on their nature or use. For certain inventories, cost is measured using the retail method, whereby the sales value of the inventories is reduced by the appropriate percentage gross margin. Net realizable value is the estimated selling price in the ordinary course of business, less the estimated marketing, distribution and selling expenses.

A manufacturing company, like Acer Incorporated (TWN), also indicates the stage of completion for inventory, as shown in Illustration 5-7. Note that Acer shows amounts both in New Taiwan dollars (NT$) and U.S. dollars ($).

ILLUSTRATION 5-7
Statement of Financial
Position Presentation of
Inventories

Acer Incorporated
(in millions)

CURRENT ASSETS
INVENTORIES (NOTE 7) NT$ 40,028,195 $1,219,702

Note 7
Inventories

	NT$	US$
Raw materials	14,528,727	442,706
Work in process	49,437	1,506
Finished goods	16,907,906	515,202
Spare parts	4,544,547	138,477
Inventories in transit	9,233,802	281,364
Less: provision for inventory obsolescence and net realizable value	(5,236,224)	(159,553)
	40,028,195	1,219,702

Receivables. A company should clearly identify any anticipated loss due to uncollectibles, the amount and nature of any non-trade receivables, and any receivables used as collateral. Major categories of receivables should be shown in the statement of financial position or the related notes. For receivables arising from unusual transactions (such as sale of property, or a loan to associates or employees), companies should separately classify these as long-term, unless collection is expected within one year. Reed Elsevier (GBR) reported its receivables as shown in Illustration 5-8.

Reed Elsevier
(in millions)

CURRENT ASSETS
TRADE AND OTHER RECEIVABLES   NOTE 22   €1,685

Note 22 Trade and other receivables	
Trade receivables	€1,578
Allowance for doubtful debts	(77)
	1,501
Prepayments and accrued income	184
Total	**€1,685**

Trade receivables are predominantly non-interest bearing and their carrying amounts approximate their fair value.

ILLUSTRATION 5-8
Statement of Financial Position Presentation of Receivables

Prepaid Expenses. A company includes prepaid expenses in current assets if it will receive benefits (usually services) within one year or the operating cycle, whichever is longer. As we discussed earlier, these items are current assets because if they had not already been paid, they would require the use of cash during the next year or the operating cycle. A company reports prepaid expenses at the amount of the unexpired or unconsumed cost.

A common example is the prepayment for an insurance policy. A company classifies it as a prepaid expense because the payment precedes the receipt of the benefit of coverage. Other common prepaid expenses include prepaid rent, advertising, taxes, and office or operating supplies. adidas (DEU) reports prepaid expenses in other current assets, along with tax receivables other than income taxes and derivative financial assets, as shown in Illustration 5-9.

adidas
(in millions)

OTHER CURRENT ASSETS   NOTE 9   €789

Note 9 Other current assets	
Other current assets consist of the following:	
Prepaid expenses	€292
Tax receivables other than income taxes	82
Financial assets	
Interest rate derivatives	1
Currency options	22
Forward contracts	156
Security deposits	66
Other financial assets	43
Sundry	129
Other current assets, gross	**791**
Less: allowance	2
Other current assets, net	**€789**

ILLUSTRATION 5-9
Statement of Financial Position Presentation of Prepaid Expenses

Short-Term Investments. As indicated earlier, a company should report trading securities (whether debt or equity) as current assets. It classifies individual non-trading investments as current or non-current, depending on the circumstances. It should report held-for-collection (sometimes referred to as held-to-maturity) securities at amortized cost. All trading securities are reported at fair value.[6]

Illustration 5-10 provides an excerpt from the annual report of **AB InBev** (BEL) with respect to its short-term financial assets.

ILLUSTRATION 5-10
Statement of Financial Position Presentation of Short-Term Investments

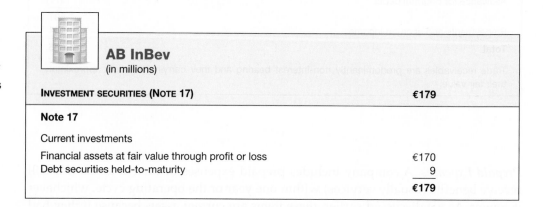

AB InBev (in millions)	
INVESTMENT SECURITIES (NOTE 17)	€179

Note 17

Current investments	
Financial assets at fair value through profit or loss	€170
Debt securities held-to-maturity	9
	€179

Cash. Cash is generally considered to consist of currency and demand deposits (monies available on demand at a financial institution). **Cash equivalents** are short-term, highly liquid investments that will mature within three months or less. Most companies use the caption "Cash and cash equivalents," and they indicate that this amount approximates fair value. As an example, see the excerpt from **adidas** (DEU) in Illustration 5-11.

ILLUSTRATION 5-11
Statement of Financial Position Presentation of Cash and Cash Equivalents

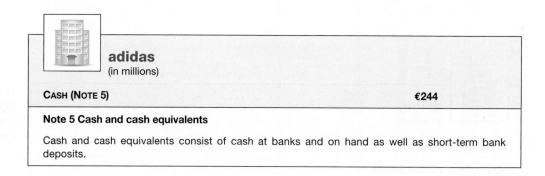

adidas (in millions)	
CASH (NOTE 5)	€244

Note 5 Cash and cash equivalents

Cash and cash equivalents consist of cash at banks and on hand as well as short-term bank deposits.

A company must disclose any restrictions or commitments related to the availability of cash. If a company restricts cash for purposes other than current obligations, it excludes the cash from current assets. Illustration 5-12 shows an example of this, from the annual report of **Vodafone plc** (GBR).

---

[6]Under the fair value option, companies may elect to use fair value as the measurement basis for selected financial assets and liabilities. For these companies, some of their financial assets (and liabilities) may be recorded at historical cost, while others are recorded at fair value. **[5]**

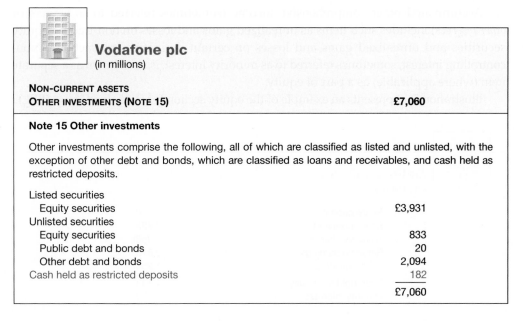

Equity

The **equity** (also referred to as **shareholders' equity**) section is one of the most difficult sections to prepare and understand. This is due to the complexity of ordinary and preference share agreements and the various restrictions on equity imposed by corporation laws, liability agreements, and boards of directors. Companies usually divide the section into six parts:

EQUITY SECTION

1. SHARE CAPITAL. The par or stated value of shares issued. It includes ordinary shares (sometimes referred to as *common shares*) and preference shares (sometimes referred to as *preferred shares*).

2. SHARE PREMIUM. The excess of amounts paid-in over the par or stated value.

3. RETAINED EARNINGS. The corporation's undistributed earnings.

4. ACCUMULATED OTHER COMPREHENSIVE INCOME. The aggregate amount of the other comprehensive income items.

5. TREASURY SHARES. Generally, the amount of ordinary shares repurchased.

6. NON-CONTROLLING INTEREST (MINORITY INTEREST). A portion of the equity of subsidiaries not owned by the reporting company.

For ordinary shares, companies must disclose the par value and the authorized, issued, and outstanding share amounts. The same holds true for preference shares. A company usually presents the share premium (for both ordinary and preference shares) in one amount although subtotals are informative if the sources of additional capital are varied and material. The retained earnings amount may be divided between the **unappropriated** (the amount that is usually available for dividend distribution) and **restricted** (e.g., by bond indentures or other loan agreements) amounts. In addition, companies show any shares reacquired (treasury shares) as a reduction of equity.

Accumulated other comprehensive income (sometimes referred to as *reserves* or *other reserves*) includes such items as unrealized gains and losses on non-trading equity securities and unrealized gains and losses on certain derivative transactions. Non-controlling interest, sometimes referred to as minority interest, is also shown as a separate item (where applicable) as a part of equity.

Illustration 5-13 presents an example of the equity section for Delhaize Group (BEL).

ILLUSTRATION 5-13
Statement of Financial
Position Presentation
of Equity

Delhaize Group
(in millions)

Share capital	€ 50
Share premium	2,725
Treasury shares	(56)
Retained earnings	2,678
Other reserves	(1,254)
Shareholders' equity	4,143
Minority interests	52
Total equity	€ 4,195

Many companies reporting under IFRS often use the term "reserve" as an all-inclusive catch-all for items such as retained earnings, share premium, and accumulated other comprehensive income. An example of such a presentation is shown for Lenovo Group Limited (CHN).

ILLUSTRATION 5-14
Statement of Financial
Position Presentation
of Reserves

Lenovo Group Limited
(in millions)

Share capital	$ 29,530
Reserves	1,281,208
Shareholders' funds	1,310,738
Minority interests	177
Total equity	$1,310,915

The equity accounts in a corporation differ considerably from those in a partnership or proprietorship. Partners show separately their permanent capital accounts and the balance in their temporary accounts (drawing accounts). Proprietorships ordinarily use a single capital account that handles all of the owner's equity transactions.

Non-Current Liabilities

Non-current liabilities are obligations that a company does not reasonably expect to liquidate within the longer of one year or the normal operating cycle. Instead, it expects to pay them at some date beyond that time. The most common examples are bonds payable, notes payable, some deferred income tax amounts, lease obligations, and pension obligations. **Companies classify non-current liabilities that mature within the current operating cycle or one year as current liabilities if payment of the obligation requires the use of current assets.**

Generally, non-current liabilities are of three types:

1. Obligations arising from specific financing situations, such as the issuance of bonds, long-term lease obligations, and long-term notes payable.

2. Obligations arising from the ordinary operations of the company, such as pension obligations and deferred income tax liabilities.

3. Obligations that depend on the occurrence or non-occurrence of one or more future events to confirm the amount payable, or the payee, or the date payable, such as service or product warranties, environmental liabilities, and restructurings, often referred to as *provisions*.

Companies generally provide a great deal of supplementary disclosure for non-current liabilities because most long-term debt is subject to various covenants and restrictions for the protection of lenders.

Companies frequently describe the terms of all non-current liability agreements (including maturity date or dates, rates of interest, nature of obligation, and any security pledged to support the debt) in notes to the financial statements. Illustration 5-15 provides an example of this, taken from an excerpt from Silver Fern Farms Limited's (NZL) financials.

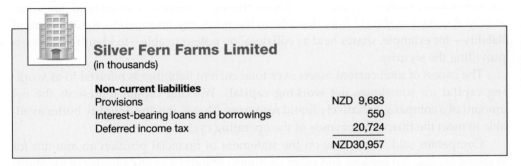

Silver Fern Farms Limited
(in thousands)

Non-current liabilities

Provisions	NZD 9,683
Interest-bearing loans and borrowings	550
Deferred income tax	20,724
	NZD30,957

ILLUSTRATION 5-15
Statement of Financial Position Presentation of Non-Current Liabilities

Current Liabilities

Current liabilities are the obligations that a company generally expects to settle in its normal operating cycle or one year, whichever is longer. This concept includes:

1. Payables resulting from the acquisition of goods and services: accounts payable, salaries and wages payable, income taxes payable, and so on.

2. Collections received in advance for the delivery of goods or performance of services, such as unearned rent revenue or unearned subscriptions revenue.

3. Other liabilities whose liquidation will take place within the operating cycle or one year, such as the portion of long-term bonds to be paid in the current period, short-term obligations arising from purchase of equipment, or estimated liabilities, such as a warranty liability. As indicated earlier, estimated liabilities are often referred to as provisions.

At times, a liability that is payable within the next year is not included in the current liabilities section. This occurs when the company refinances the debt on a long-term basis before the end of the reporting period. **[6]** This approach is used because liquidation does not result from the use of current assets or the creation of other current liabilities.

Companies do not report current liabilities in any consistent order. In general, though, companies most commonly list notes payable, accounts payable, or short-term debt as the first item. Income tax payables or other current liabilities are commonly listed last. For example, see Siemens AG's (DEU) current liabilities section in Illustration 5-16 (on page 194).

ILLUSTRATION 5-16
Statement of Financial
Position Presentation of
Current Liabilities

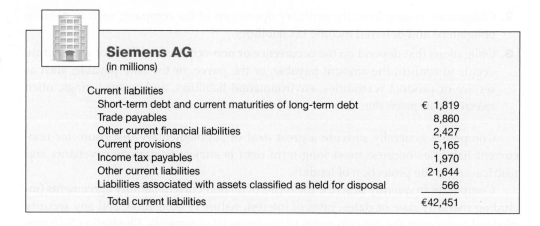

Siemens AG (in millions)	
Current liabilities	
Short-term debt and current maturities of long-term debt	€ 1,819
Trade payables	8,860
Other current financial liabilities	2,427
Current provisions	5,165
Income tax payables	1,970
Other current liabilities	21,644
Liabilities associated with assets classified as held for disposal	566
Total current liabilities	€42,451

Current liabilities include such items as trade and non-trade notes and accounts payable, advances received from customers, and current maturities of long-term debt. If the amounts are material, companies classify income taxes and other accrued items separately. A company should fully describe in the notes any information about a secured liability—for example, shares held as collateral on notes payable—to identify the assets providing the security.

The excess of total current assets over total current liabilities is referred to as **working capital** (or sometimes **net working capital**). Working capital represents the net amount of a company's relatively liquid resources. That is, it is the liquidity buffer available to meet the financial demands of the operating cycle.

Companies seldom disclose on the statement of financial position an amount for working capital. But bankers and other creditors compute it as an indicator of the short-run liquidity of a company. To determine the actual liquidity and availability of working capital to meet current obligations, however, requires analysis of the composition of the current assets and their nearness to cash.

Statement of Financial Position Format

LEARNING OBJECTIVE 3

Prepare a classified statement of financial position using the report and account formats.

As indicated earlier, IFRS does not specify the order or format in which a company presents items in the statement of financial position (see the "What do the numbers mean?" box on page 184). Thus, some companies present assets first, followed by equity, and then liabilities. Other companies report current assets first in the assets section, and current liabilities first in the liabilities section. Many companies report items such as receivables and property, plant, and equipment net and then disclose the additional information related to the contra accounts in the notes.

In general, companies use either the account form or the report form to present the statement of financial position information. The account form lists assets, by sections, on the left side, and equity and liabilities, by sections, on the right side. The main disadvantage is the need for a sufficiently wide space in which to present the items side by side. Often, the account form requires two facing pages.

To avoid this disadvantage, the report form lists the sections one above the other, on the same page. See, for example, Illustration 5-17, which lists assets, followed by equity and liabilities directly below, on the same page.

Infrequently, companies use other statement of financial position formats. For example, companies sometimes deduct current liabilities from current assets to arrive at working capital. Or, they deduct all liabilities from all assets.

ILLUSTRATION 5-17
Classified Report-Form
Statement of Financial
Position

SCIENTIFIC PRODUCTS, INC.
STATEMENT OF FINANCIAL POSITION
DECEMBER 31, 2015

Assets

Non-Current Assets

Long-term investments

Investments in held-for-collection securities	$ 82,000	
Land held for future development	5,500	$ 87,500

Property, plant, and equipment

Land		125,000	
Buildings	$975,800		
Less: Accumulated depreciation	341,200	634,600	
Total property, plant, and equipment			759,600

Intangible assets

Capitalized development costs	6,000	
Goodwill	66,000	
Other identifiable intangible assets	28,000	100,000
Total non-current assets		947,100

Current Assets

Inventory	489,713	
Prepaid expenses	16,252	
Accounts receivable	165,824	
Less: Allowance for doubtful accounts	1,850	163,974
Short-term investments	51,030	
Cash and cash equivalents	52,485	
Total current assets		773,454
Total assets		$1,720,554

Equity and Liabilities

Equity

Share capital—preference	$300,000	
Share capital—ordinary	400,000	
Share premium—preference	10,000	
Share premium—ordinary	27,500	
Retained earnings	170,482	
Accumulated other comprehensive income (loss)	(8,650)	
Less: Treasury shares	12,750	
Equity attributable to owners	$886,582	
Non-controlling interest	13,500	
Total equity		$ 900,082

Non-current liabilities

Bond liabilities due January 31, 2024	425,000	
Provisions related to pensions	75,000	
Total non-current liabilities		500,000

Current liabilities

Notes payable	80,000	
Accounts payable	197,532	
Interest payable	20,500	
Salaries and wages payable	5,560	
Provisions related to warranties	12,500	
Deposits received from customers	4,380	
Total current liabilities		320,472
Total liabilities		820,472
Total equity and liabilities		$1,720,554

Analysts use statement of financial position information in models designed to predict financial distress. Researcher E. I. Altman pioneered a bankruptcy-prediction model that derives a "Z-score" by combining statement of financial position and income measures in the following equation.

$$Z = \frac{\text{Working capital}}{\text{Total assets}} \times 1.2 + \frac{\text{Retained earnings}}{\text{Total assets}} \times 1.4 + \frac{\text{EBIT}}{\text{Total assets}} \times 3.3 + \frac{\text{Sales}}{\text{Total assets}} \times 0.99 + \frac{\text{MV equity}}{\text{Total liabilities}} \times 0.6$$

Following extensive testing, Altman found that companies with Z-scores above 3.0 are unlikely to fail. Those with Z-scores below 1.81 are very likely to fail.

Altman developed the original model for publicly held manufacturing companies. He and others have modified the model to apply to companies in various industries, emerging companies, and companies not traded in public markets.

At one time, the use of Z-scores was virtually unheard of among practicing accountants. Today, auditors, management consultants, and courts of law use this measure to help evaluate the overall financial position and trends of a firm. In addition, banks use Z-scores for loan evaluation. While a low score does not guarantee bankruptcy, the model has been proven accurate in many situations.

Source: Adapted from E. I. Altman and E. Hotchkiss, *Corporate Financial Distress and Bankruptcy,* Third Edition (New York: John Wiley and Sons, 2005).

STATEMENT OF CASH FLOWS

LEARNING OBJECTIVE **4**

Indicate the purpose of the statement of cash flows.

Chapter 2 indicated that an important element of the objective of financial reporting is "assessing the amounts, timing, and uncertainty of cash flows." The three financial statements we have looked at so far—the income statement (or statement of comprehensive income), the statement of changes in equity, and the statement of financial position—each present some information about the cash flows of an enterprise during a period. But they do so to a limited extent. For instance, the income statement provides information about resources provided by operations but not exactly cash. The statement of changes in equity shows the amount of cash used to pay dividends or purchase treasury shares. Comparative statements of financial position might show what assets the company has acquired or disposed of and what liabilities it has incurred or liquidated.

 Underlying Concepts

The statement of cash flows meets the objective of financial reporting—to help assess the amounts, timing, and uncertainty of future cash flows.

Useful as they are, none of these statements presents a detailed summary of all the cash inflows and outflows, or the sources and uses of cash during the period. To fill this need, the IASB requires the statement of cash flows (also called the **cash flow statement**). **[7]**

Purpose of the Statement of Cash Flows

The primary purpose of the statement of cash flows is to provide relevant information about the cash receipts and cash payments of an enterprise during a period. To achieve this purpose, the statement of cash flows reports the following: (1) the cash effects of operations during a period, (2) investing transactions, (3) financing transactions, and (4) the net increase or decrease in cash during the period.[7]

Reporting the sources, uses, and net increase or decrease in cash helps investors, creditors, and others know what is happening to a company's most liquid resource. Because most individuals maintain a checkbook and prepare a tax return on a cash basis, they can comprehend the information reported in the statement of cash flows.

[7]Cash is generally meant to be "cash and cash equivalents." **Cash equivalents** are liquid investments that mature within three months or less.

The statement of cash flows provides answers to the following simple but important questions:

1. Where did the cash come from during the period?

2. What was the cash used for during the period?

3. What was the change in the cash balance during the period?

What do the numbers mean? WATCH THAT CASH FLOW

Investors usually focus on net income measured on an accrual basis. However, information on cash flows can be important for assessing a company's liquidity, financial flexibility, and overall financial performance. The graph below shows a company's financial performance over 7 years.

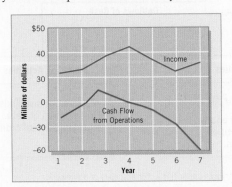

Although this company showed consistent profits and even some periods of earnings growth, its cash flow began to "go south" starting in about year 3. The company filed for bankruptcy shortly after year 7. Thus, financial statement readers who studied the company's cash flows would have found indications of this company's problems well before year 7. This case illustrates the importance of cash flows as an early-warning signal of financial problems.

Another retailer case is Target (USA). Although Target has shown good profits, some are concerned that a bit too much of its sales have been made on credit rather than cash. Why is this a problem? Like the example illustrated above, the earnings of profitable lenders can get battered in future periods if they have to start adding large amounts to their bad-loan reserve to catch up with credit losses. And if losses ramp up on Target-branded credit cards, Target may get hit in this way.

Source: Peter Eavis, "Is Target Corp.'s Credit Too Generous?" *Wall Street Journal* (March 11, 2008), p. C1.

Content and Format of the Statement of Cash Flows

Companies classify cash receipts and cash payments during a period into three different activities in the statement of cash flows—operating, investing, and financing activities, defined as follows.

5 LEARNING OBJECTIVE

Identify the content of the statement of cash flows.

1. Operating activities involve the cash effects of transactions that enter into the determination of net income.

2. Investing activities include making and collecting loans and acquiring and disposing of investments (both debt and equity) and property, plant, and equipment.

3. Financing activities involve liability and equity items. They include (a) obtaining resources from owners and providing them with a return on their investment, and (b) borrowing money from creditors and repaying the amounts borrowed.

Illustration 5-18 shows the basic format of the statement of cash flows.

STATEMENT OF CASH FLOWS	
Cash flows from operating activities	$XXX
Cash flows from investing activities	XXX
Cash flows from financing activities	XXX
Net increase (decrease) in cash	XXX
Cash at beginning of year	XXX
Cash at end of year	$XXX

ILLUSTRATION 5-18
Basic Format of Cash Flow Statement

Illustration 5-19 graphs the inflows and outflows of cash classified by activity.

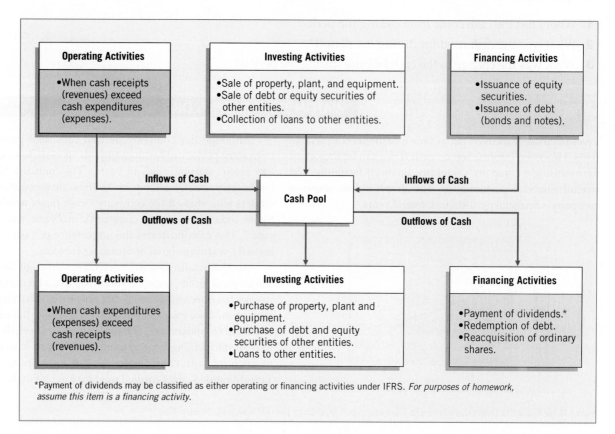

ILLUSTRATION 5-19
Cash Inflows and
Outflows

The statement's value is that it helps users evaluate liquidity, solvency, and financial flexibility. As stated earlier, **liquidity** refers to the "nearness to cash" of assets and liabilities. **Solvency** is the firm's ability to pay its debts as they mature. **Financial flexibility** is a company's ability to respond and adapt to financial adversity and unexpected needs and opportunities.

We have devoted Chapter 23 entirely to the detailed preparation and content of the statement of cash flows. The intervening chapters will cover several elements and complex topics that affect the content of a typical statement of cash flows. The presentation in this chapter is introductory—a reminder of the existence of the statement of cash flows and its usefulness.

Overview of the Preparation of the Statement of Cash Flows

Sources of Information

LEARNING OBJECTIVE **6**

Prepare a basic statement of
cash flows.

Companies obtain the information to prepare the statement of cash flows from several sources: (1) comparative statements of financial position, (2) the current income statement, and (3) selected transaction data.

The following simple example demonstrates how companies use these sources in preparing a statement of cash flows.

On January 1, 2015, in its first year of operations, Telemarketing Inc. issued 50,000 ordinary shares of $1 par value for $50,000 cash. The company rented its office space, furniture, and telecommunications equipment and performed marketing services throughout the first year. In June 2015, the company purchased land for $15,000.

Illustration 5-20 shows the company's comparative statements of financial position at the beginning and end of 2015.

TELEMARKETING INC. STATEMENTS OF FINANCIAL POSITION			
Assets	Dec. 31, 2015	Jan. 1, 2015	Increase/Decrease
Land	$15,000	$-0-	$15,000 Increase
Accounts receivable	41,000	-0-	41,000 Increase
Cash	31,000	-0-	31,000 Increase
Total	$87,000	$-0-	
Equity and Liabilities			
Share capital	$50,000	$-0-	50,000 Increase
Retained earnings	25,000	-0-	25,000 Increase
Accounts payable	12,000	-0-	12,000 Increase
Total	$87,000	$-0-	

ILLUSTRATION 5-20
Comparative Statements of Financial Position

Illustration 5-21 presents the income statement and additional information.

TELEMARKETING INC. INCOME STATEMENT FOR THE YEAR ENDED DECEMBER 31, 2015	
Revenues	$172,000
Operating expenses	120,000
Income before income tax	52,000
Income tax	13,000
Net income	$ 39,000

Additional information:
Dividends of $14,000 were paid during the year.

ILLUSTRATION 5-21
Income Statement Data

Preparing the Statement of Cash Flows

Preparing the statement of cash flows from these sources involves four steps:

1. Determine the net cash provided by (or used in) operating activities.
2. Determine the net cash provided by (or used in) investing and financing activities.
3. Determine the change (increase or decrease) in cash during the period.
4. Reconcile the change in cash with the beginning and the ending cash balances.

Net cash provided by operating activities is the excess of cash receipts over cash payments from operating activities. Companies determine this amount by converting net income on an accrual basis to a cash basis. To do so, they add to or deduct from net income those items in the income statement that do not affect cash. This procedure requires that a company analyze not only the current year's income statement but also the comparative statements of financial position and selected transaction data.

Analysis of Telemarketing's comparative statements of financial position reveals two items that will affect the computation of net cash provided by operating activities:

1. The increase in accounts receivable reflects a non-cash increase of $41,000 in revenues.
2. The increase in accounts payable reflects a non-cash increase of $12,000 in expenses.

Therefore, to arrive at net cash provided by operating activities, Telemarketing Inc. deducts from net income the increase in accounts receivable ($41,000), and it adds back to net income the increase in accounts payable ($12,000). As a result of these adjustments, the company determines net cash provided by operating activities to be $10,000, computed as shown in Illustration 5-22.

ILLUSTRATION 5-22
Computation of Net
Cash Provided by
Operating Activities

Net income		$39,000
Adjustments to reconcile net income		
to net cash provided by operating activities:		
Increase in accounts receivable	$(41,000)	
Increase in accounts payable	12,000	(29,000)
Net cash provided by operating activities		$10,000

Next, the company determines its investing and financing activities. Telemarketing Inc.'s only **investing activity** was the land purchase. It had two **financing activities**. (1) Share capital—ordinary increased $50,000 from the issuance of 50,000 ordinary shares for cash. (2) The company paid $14,000 cash in dividends. Knowing the amounts provided/used by operating, investing, and financing activities, the company determines the **net increase in cash**. Illustration 5-23 presents Telemarketing Inc.'s statement of cash flows for 2015.

ILLUSTRATION 5-23
Statement of Cash Flows

TELEMARKETING INC.
STATEMENT OF CASH FLOWS
FOR THE YEAR ENDED DECEMBER 31, 2015

Cash flows from operating activities		
Net income		$39,000
Adjustments to reconcile net income to		
net cash provided by operating activities:		
Increase in accounts receivable	$(41,000)	
Increase in accounts payable	12,000	(29,000)
Net cash provided by operating activities		10,000
Cash flows from investing activities		
Purchase of land	(15,000)	
Net cash used by investing activities		(15,000)
Cash flows from financing activities		
Issuance of ordinary shares	50,000	
Payment of cash dividends	(14,000)	
Net cash provided by financing activities		36,000
Net increase in cash		31,000
Cash at beginning of year		–0–
Cash at end of year		$31,000

The increase in cash of $31,000 reported in the statement of cash flows **agrees with** the increase of $31,000 in cash calculated from the comparative statements of financial position.[8]

---

[8]Companies are required either in the statement of cash flows or in the related notes to report the amounts paid for interest and income taxes. We assume here that the company is presenting this information in the notes to the financial statements. *Therefore, for homework purposes, you need not present this information in the statement.* In Chapter 23, we will explore this issue in more detail.

Significant Non-Cash Activities

Not all of a company's significant activities involve cash. Examples of significant non-cash activities are:

1. Issuance of ordinary shares to purchase assets.

2. Conversion of bonds into ordinary shares.

3. Issuance of debt to purchase assets.

4. Exchanges of long-lived assets.

Significant financing and investing activities that do not affect cash are not reported in the body of the statement of cash flows. Rather, these activities are reported in a separate note to the financial statements. Such reporting of these non-cash activities satisfies the full disclosure principle.

Illustration 5-24 shows an example of a comprehensive statement of cash flows. Note that the company purchased equipment through the issuance of €50,000 of bonds, which is a significant non-cash transaction. *For homework purposes, you should present significant non-cash activities in a separate note entitled "Cash Flow Note."*

ILLUSTRATION 5-24
Comprehensive Statement of Cash Flows

NESTOR COMPANY STATEMENT OF CASH FLOWS FOR THE YEAR ENDED DECEMBER 31, 2015		
Cash flows from operating activities		
Net income		€320,750
Adjustments to reconcile net income to net cash provided by operating activities:		
Depreciation expense	€88,400	
Amortization of intangibles	16,300	
Gain on sale of plant assets	(8,700)	
Increase in accounts receivable (net)	(11,000)	
Decrease in inventory	15,500	
Decrease in accounts payable	(9,500)	91,000
Net cash provided by operating activities		411,750
Cash flows from investing activities		
Sale of plant assets	90,500	
Purchase of equipment	(182,500)	
Purchase of land	(70,000)	
Net cash used by investing activities		(162,000)
Cash flows from financing activities		
Payment of cash dividend	(19,800)	
Issuance of ordinary shares	100,000	
Redemption of bonds	(50,000)	
Net cash provided by financing activities		30,200
Net increase in cash		279,950
Cash at beginning of year		135,000
Cash at end of year		€414,950[1]

[1]**Cash Flow Note**
A non-cash investing and financing activity was the purchase of equipment through issuance of €50,000 of bonds.

Usefulness of the Statement of Cash Flows

"Happiness is a positive cash flow" is certainly true. Although net income provides a long-term measure of a company's success or failure, cash is its lifeblood. Without cash, a company will not survive. For small and newly developing companies, cash flow is the single most important element for survival. Even medium and large companies must control cash flow.

7 LEARNING OBJECTIVE

Understand the usefulness of the statement of cash flows.

Creditors examine the cash flow statement carefully because they are concerned about being paid. They begin their examination by finding net cash provided by operating activities. A high amount indicates that a company is able to generate sufficient cash from operations to pay its bills without further borrowing. Conversely, a low or negative amount of net cash provided by operating activities indicates that a company may have to borrow or issue equity securities to acquire sufficient cash to pay its bills. Consequently, creditors look for answers to the following questions in the company's cash flow statements.

1. How successful is the company in generating net cash provided by operating activities?

2. What are the trends in net cash flow provided by operating activities over time?

3. What are the major reasons for the positive or negative net cash provided by operating activities?

You should recognize that companies can fail even though they report net income. The difference between net income and net cash provided by operating activities can be substantial. Companies sometimes report high net income numbers but negative net cash provided by operating activities. This type of situation can eventually lead to bankruptcy.

In addition, substantial increases in receivables and/or inventory can explain the difference between positive net income and negative net cash provided by operating activities. For example, in its first year of operations Hu Inc. reported a net income of HK$80,000. Its net cash provided by operating activities, however, was a negative HK$95,000, as shown in Illustration 5-25.

ILLUSTRATION 5-25
Negative Net Cash Provided by Operating Activities

HU INC.		
NET CASH FLOW FROM OPERATING ACTIVITIES		
Cash flows from operating activities		
Net income		HK$ 80,000
Adjustments to reconcile net income to net cash provided by operating activities:		
Increase in receivables	HK$ (75,000)	
Increase in inventory	(100,000)	(175,000)
Net cash provided by operating activities		HK$ (95,000)

Hu could easily experience a "cash crunch" because it has its cash tied up in receivables and inventory. If Hu encounters problems in collecting receivables, or if inventory moves slowly or becomes obsolete, its creditors may have difficulty collecting on their loans.

Financial Liquidity

Readers of financial statements often assess liquidity by using the current cash debt coverage. It indicates whether the company can pay off its current liabilities from its operations in a given year. Illustration 5-26 shows the formula for this ratio.

ILLUSTRATION 5-26
Formula for Current Cash Debt Coverage

$$\frac{\text{Net Cash Provided by Operating Activities}}{\text{Average Current Liabilities}} = \text{Current Cash Debt Coverage}$$

The higher the current cash debt coverage, the less likely a company will have liquidity problems. For example, a ratio near 1:1 is good. It indicates that the company can meet all of its current obligations from internally generated cash flow.

Financial Flexibility

The **cash debt coverage** provides information on financial flexibility. It indicates a company's ability to repay its liabilities from net cash provided by operating activities, without having to liquidate the assets employed in its operations. Illustration 5-27 shows the formula for this ratio. Notice its similarity to the current cash debt coverage. However, because it uses average total liabilities in place of average current liabilities, it takes a somewhat longer-range view.

$$\frac{\text{Net Cash Provided by Operating Activities}}{\text{Average Total Liabilities}} = \frac{\text{Cash Debt}}{\text{Coverage}}$$

ILLUSTRATION 5-27
Formula for Cash Debt Coverage

The higher this ratio, the less likely the company will experience difficulty in meeting its obligations as they come due. It signals whether the company can pay its debts and survive if external sources of funds become limited or too expensive.

Free Cash Flow

A more sophisticated way to examine a company's financial flexibility is to develop a free cash flow analysis. **Free cash flow** is the amount of discretionary cash flow a company has. It can use this cash flow to purchase additional investments, retire its debt, purchase treasury shares, or simply add to its liquidity. Financial statement users calculate free cash flow as shown in Illustration 5-28.

$$\begin{array}{c}\text{Net Cash Provided}\\\text{by Operating}\\\text{Activities}\end{array} - \begin{array}{c}\text{Capital}\\\text{Expenditures}\end{array} - \text{Dividends} = \begin{array}{c}\text{Free}\\\text{Cash Flow}\end{array}$$

ILLUSTRATION 5-28
Formula for Free Cash Flow

In a free cash flow analysis, we first deduct capital spending to indicate it is the least discretionary expenditure a company generally makes. (Without continued efforts to maintain and expand facilities, it is unlikely that a company can continue to maintain its competitive position.) We then deduct dividends. Although a company *can* cut its dividend, it usually will do so only in **a financial emergency**. The amount resulting after these deductions is the company's free cash flow. Obviously, the greater the amount of free cash flow, the greater the company's amount of financial flexibility.

Questions that a free cash flow analysis answers are:

1. Is the company able to pay its dividends without resorting to external financing?
2. If business operations decline, will the company be able to maintain its needed capital investment?
3. What is the amount of discretionary cash flow that can be used for additional investment, retirement of debt, purchase of treasury shares, or addition to liquidity?

Illustration 5-29 is a free cash flow analysis using the cash flow statement for Nestor Company (shown in Illustration 5-24 on page 201).

ILLUSTRATION 5-29
Free Cash Flow Computation

NESTOR COMPANY	
FREE CASH FLOW ANALYSIS	
Net cash provided by operating activities	€411,750
Capital expenditures	(252,500)
Dividends	(19,800)
Free cash flow	€139,450

This computation shows that Nestor has a positive, and substantial, net cash provided by operating activities of €411,750. Nestor's statement of cash flows reports that the company purchased equipment of €182,500 and land of €70,000 for total capital spending of €252,500. Nestor has more than sufficient cash flow to meet its dividend payment and therefore has satisfactory financial flexibility.

As you can see from looking back at Illustration 5-24 (on page 201), Nestor used its free cash flow to redeem bonds and add to its liquidity. If it finds additional investments that are profitable, it can increase its spending without putting its dividend or basic capital spending in jeopardy. Companies that have strong financial flexibility can take advantage of profitable investments even in tough times. In addition, strong financial flexibility frees companies from worry about survival in poor economic times. In fact, those with strong financial flexibility often fare better in a poor economy because they can take advantage of opportunities that other companies cannot.

ADDITIONAL INFORMATION

LEARNING OBJECTIVE **8**
Determine additional information requiring note disclosure.

IFRS requires that a complete set of financial statements be presented annually. Along with the current year's financial statements, companies must also provide **comparative information** from the previous period. In other words, two complete sets of financial statements and related notes must be reported.

A complete set of financial statements comprise the following.

1. A statement of financial position at the end of the period;

2. A statement of comprehensive income for the period to be presented either as:
   (a) One single statement of comprehensive income.
   (b) A separate income statement and statement of comprehensive income. In this situation, the income statement is presented first.

3. A statement of changes in equity;

4. A statement of cash flows; and

5. Notes, comprising a summary of significant accounting policies and other explanatory information. **[8]**

Chapters 4 and 5 discussed the first four items. However, the primary financial statements cannot provide the complete picture related to the financial position and financial performance of the company. Descriptive information is also required by IFRS in the notes to the financial statements to amplify or explain the items presented in the main body of the statements.

Notes to the Financial Statements

As indicated earlier, notes are an integral part of reporting financial statement information. Notes can explain in qualitative terms information related to specific financial statement items. In addition, they can provide supplemental data of a quantitative nature to expand the information in financial statements. Notes also can explain restrictions imposed by financial arrangements or basic contractual agreements. Although notes may be technical and difficult to understand in some cases, they provide meaningful information for the user of the financial statements.

Accounting Policies

Accounting policies are the specific principles, bases, conventions, rules, and practices applied by a company in preparing and presenting financial information. The IASB recommends disclosure for all significant accounting principles and methods that involve selection from among alternatives or those that are peculiar to a given industry. For instance, companies can compute inventories under several cost flow assumptions (e.g., average-cost and FIFO), depreciate plant and equipment under several accepted methods (e.g., double-declining balance and straight-line), and carry investments at different valuations (e.g., cost, equity, and fair value). Sophisticated users of financial statements know of these possibilities and examine the statements closely to determine the methods used.

Companies therefore present a "Summary of Significant Accounting Policies" generally as the first note to the financial statements. This disclosure is important because, under IFRS, alternative treatments of a transaction are sometimes permitted. If these policies are not understood, users of the financial statements are not able to use the financial statements to make comparisons among companies. Here are some examples of various accounting policies adapted from companies' annual reports.

LG Korea
(KOR)

ILLUSTRATION 5-30
Accounting Policies—
Inventory

Inventories

Inventories are stated at the lower of cost or market value, with cost being determined by the moving-average method or the weighted-average method, except for materials-in-transit for which cost is determined by the specific identification method. When the market value of inventories (net realizable value for finished goods or merchandise and current replacement cost for raw materials) is less than the carrying value, the carrying value is stated at the lower of cost or market. The Group applies the lower of cost or market method by group of inventories and loss on inventory valuation is presented as a deduction from inventories and charged to cost of sales. The valuation loss is recorded as cost of sales. If, however, the circumstances which cause the valuation loss cease to exist, causing the market value to rise above the carrying amount, the valuation loss is reversed limited to the original carrying amount before valuation. The reversal is a deduction from cost of sales.

Stora Enso
(FIN)

ILLUSTRATION 5-31
Accounting Policies—
Intangible Asset

Intangible assets are stated at historical cost and are amortized on a straight-line basis over their expected useful lives, which usually vary from 3 to 10 years and up to 20 years for patents.

JJB Sports
(GBR)

ILLUSTRATION 5-32
Accounting Policies—
Property, Plant, and
Equipment

Property, plant, and equipment

Property, plant, and equipment are stated at cost less accumulated depreciation and any recognised impairment loss.

Depreciation is charged so as to write off the cost of assets, other than land and properties under construction, over their estimated useful lives, using the straight-line method, as follows:

Freehold land and buildings	50 years
Leasehold improvements	over the period of the lease
Plant and equipment	5 to 25 years

Assets held under finance leases are depreciated over their expected useful lives on the same basis as owned assets or, where shorter, over the term of the relevant lease.

The gain or loss arising on the disposal or retirement of an asset is determined as the difference between the sales proceeds and the carrying amount of the asset and is recognized in the profit or loss.

ILLUSTRATION 5-33
Accounting Policies—
Financial Liabilities

Delhaize Group
(BEL)

Non-derivative Financial Liabilities

IAS 39 *Financial Instruments: Recognition and Measurement* contains two categories for non-derivative financial liabilities (hereafter "financial liabilities"): financial liabilities at fair value through profit or loss and financial liabilities measured at amortized cost. Delhaize Group holds only financial liabilities measured at amortized cost, which are included in "Debts," "Borrowings," "Accounts payable" and "Other liabilities."

Additional Notes to the Financial Statements

In addition to a note related to explanation of the companies' accounting policies, companies use specific notes to discuss items in the financial statements. Judgment must be exercised to identify the important aspects of financial information that need amplification in the notes. In many cases, IFRS requires specific disclosures. For example, using the statement of financial position as an example, note disclosures include:

1. Items of property, plant, and equipment are disaggregated into classes such as land, buildings, etc., in the notes, with related accumulated depreciation reported where applicable.

2. Receivables are disaggregated into amounts receivable from trade customers, receivables from related parties, prepayments, and other amounts.

3. Inventories are disaggregated into classifications such as merchandise, production supplies, work in process, and finished goods.

4. Provisions are disaggregated into provisions for employee benefits and other items.

In addition, there are often schedules and computations required by a specific standard. For example, for receivables, IFRS requires a maturity analysis for receivables. Illustration 5-34 shows a maturity analysis for **Cadbury plc** (GBR).

ILLUSTRATION 5-34
Maturity Analysis
for Receivables

Cadbury plc
(in millions)

	Current	Non-current
Trade receivables	£835	—
Less: provision for impairment of trade receivables	(46)	—
	£789	—

20. Trade and other receivables

The aged analysis of past due but not impaired receivables is as follows:

Total trade receivables	£835
Less: Provision for impairment of trade receivables	(46)
	£789
Of which:	
Not overdue	£657
Past due less than three months	123
Past due more than three months	9
	£789

Another maturity analysis is required for financial liabilities. Illustration 5-35 shows such an analysis for **Christian Dior** (FRA).

Christian Dior
(in millions)

Note 17.4
Analysis of gross borrowings by payment date before hedging

(*millions*)		2012			Maturing in 2013
Payment date	2013	€3,866	Payment date	First quarter	€3,356
	2014	1,440		Second quarter	78
	2015	2,152		Third quarter	66
	2016	449		Fourth quarter	366
	2017	307			
	Thereafter	788			
TOTAL		€9,002	TOTAL		€3,866

ILLUSTRATION 5-35
Maturity Analysis for
Financial Liabilities

Also, companies are required to reconcile the balances for many of the assets and liabilities reported in the financial statements from the beginning to the end of the year. For example, a reconciliation of the balances in property, plant, and equipment; intangible assets; and provisions are generally provided. An example for property, plant, and equipment for Nestlé (CHE) is shown in Illustration 5-36.

Nestlé
(in millions)

	Land and buildings	Machinery and equipment	Tools, furniture and other equipment	Vehicles	Total
Gross value					
At 1 January	CHF13,245	CHF25,455	CHF7,446	CHF931	CHF47,077
Currency retranslations	(156)	(478)	(171)	(86)	(891)
Capital expenditure	860	2,695	1,209	207	4,971
Disposals	(258)	(884)	(492)	(78)	(1,712)
Reclassified as held for sale	(30)	(38)	(3)	—	(71)
Modification of the scope of consolidation	90	51	3	(44)	100
At 31 December	CHF13,751	CHF26,801	CHF7,992	CHF930	CHF49,474

ILLUSTRATION 5-36
Reconciliation Schedule
for Property, Plant, and
Equipment

Note disclosure is extensive using IFRS. Many companies' annual reports are substantial in nature, and it is not unusual for a large company to have over 20 pages of notes to the financial statements.

Techniques of Disclosure

Companies should disclose as completely as possible the effect of various uncertainties on financial condition, the methods of valuing assets and liabilities, and the company's contracts and agreements. To disclose this pertinent information, companies may use parenthetical explanations and cross-reference and contra items.

9 LEARNING OBJECTIVE

Describe the major disclosure techniques
for financial statements.

Parenthetical Explanations

Companies often provide additional information by parenthetical explanations following the item. For example, Illustration 5-37 shows a parenthetical explanation of the number of shares issued by **Cadbury plc** (GBR) on the statement of financial position under "Equity."

ILLUSTRATION 5-37
Parenthetical Disclosure of Shares Issued

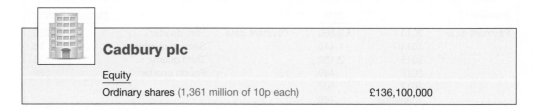

Cadbury plc

Equity

Ordinary shares (1,361 million of 10p each)   £136,100,000

This additional pertinent statement of financial position information adds clarity and completeness. It has an advantage over a note because it brings the additional information into the **body of the statement** where readers will less likely overlook it. Companies, however, should avoid lengthy parenthetical explanations, which might be distracting.

Cross-Reference and Contra Items

Companies "cross-reference" a direct relationship between an asset and a liability on the statement of financial position. For example, as shown in Illustration 5-38, on December 31, 2015, a company might show the following entries—one listed among the current assets, and the other listed among the current liabilities.

ILLUSTRATION 5-38
Cross-Referencing and Contra Items

Current Assets (in part)

Cash on deposit with sinking fund trustee for
  redemption of bonds payable—see Current liabilities $800,000

Current Liabilities (in part)

Bonds payable to be redeemed in 2015—see Current assets $2,300,000

This cross-reference points out that the company will redeem $2,300,000 of bonds payable currently, for which it has only set aside $800,000. Therefore, it needs additional cash from unrestricted cash, from sales of investments, from profits, or from some other source. Alternatively, the company can show the same information parenthetically.

Another common procedure is to establish contra or adjunct accounts. A **contra account** on a statement of financial position reduces either an asset, liability, or equity account. Examples include Accumulated Depreciation and Allowance for Doubtful Accounts. Contra accounts provide some flexibility in presenting the financial information. With the use of the Accumulated Depreciation account, for example, a reader of the statement can see the original cost of the asset as well as the depreciation to date.

An **adjunct account**, on the other hand, increases either an asset, liability, or equity account. An example is Fair Value Adjustment, which, when added to the Non-Trading Equity Investment account, describes the total investment asset of the company.

Other Guidelines

In addition to the specifics related to individual financial statements and notes to these statements, *IAS No. 1* also addresses important issues related to presentation. **[9]**

Offsetting

IAS No. 1 indicates that it is important that assets and liabilities, and income and expense, be reported separately. Otherwise, it may be difficult for users to understand the transactions or events that occurred at the company. Therefore, it is improper for a company like Sinopec (CHN) to offset accounts payable against cash. Similarly, it is improper for Sinopec to offset debt used to purchase buildings against the buildings on the statement of financial position. However, it is proper for Sinopec to measure assets net of valuation allowances, such as allowance for doubtful accounts or inventory net of impairment. In these cases, the company is simply reporting the appropriate value on the financial statement, and therefore it is not considered offsetting. In general, unless a specific IFRS permits offsetting, it is not permitted.

Consistency

The Conceptual Framework discussed in Chapter 2 notes that one of the enhancing qualitative characteristics is comparability. As part of comparability, the Conceptual Framework indicates that companies should follow consistent principles and methods from one period to the next. **[10]** As a result, accounting policies must be consistently applied for similar transactions and events unless an IFRS requires a different policy. Thus, Woolworths (AUS), which uses the straight-line method for depreciating property, plant, and equipment, reports on the straight-line method for all periods presented.

Fair Presentation

Companies must present fairly the financial position, financial performance, and cash flows of the company. Fair presentation means the faithful representation of transactions and events using the definitions and recognition criteria in the Conceptual Framework. It is presumed that the use of IFRS with appropriate disclosure results in financial statements that are fairly presented. In other words, inappropriate use of accounting policies cannot be overcome by explanatory notes to the financial statements.

In some rare cases, as indicated in Chapter 2, companies can use a "true and fair" override. This situation develops, for example, when the IFRS for a given company appears to conflict with the objective of financial reporting. This situation might occur when a regulatory body indicates that a specific IFRS may be misleading. As indicated earlier, a true and fair override is highly unlikely in today's reporting environment.[9]

 **Evolving Issue** STATEMENT OF FINANCIAL POSITION REPORTING: GROSS OR NET?

In addition to the issue of financial statement presentation discussed in the opening story, a second area of controversy for statement of financial position reporting is the issue of offsetting (or netting) of assets and liabilities. It is generally accepted that offsetting of recognized assets and recognized liabilities detracts from the ability of users both to understand the transactions and conditions that have occurred and to assess the company's future cash flows. In other words, providing information on assets, liabilities, and equity helps users to compute rates of return and evaluate capital structure.

However, netting assets and liabilities limits a user's ability to assess the future economic benefits and obligations.

That is, offsetting hides the existence of assets and liabilities, making it difficult to evaluate liquidity, solvency, and financial flexibility. As a result, U.S. GAAP does not permit the reporting of summary accounts alone (e.g., total assets, net assets, and total liabilities). Recently, the IASB and FASB have worked to develop common criteria for offsetting on the statement of financial position. Current offsetting rules under IFRS are more restrictive than under U.S. GAAP. The

---

[9]One highly publicized exception is the case of Société Générale (SocGen) (FRA). The bank used the true and fair rule to justify reporting losses that occurred in 2008 in the prior year. Although allowed under the true and fair rule, such reporting was questioned because it permitted the bank to "take a bath," that is, record as many losses as possible in 2007, which was already a bad year for the bank. As a result, SocGen's 2008 reports looked better. See F. Norris, "SocGen Changes Its Numbers," *The New York Times* (May 13, 2008).

rules proposed would allow offsetting only in rare circumstances (e.g., when right of offset is legally enforceable).

Implementation of these new rules in the United States would result in a dramatic "grossing up" of statements of financial position (particularly for financial institutions). For example, one study estimated that the new rules would gross up U.S. banks' statements of financial position by $900 billion (or an average of 68%, ranging from a 31.4% increase for Citigroup to 104.7% for Morgan Stanley).* Not surprisingly, the FASB received significant push-back from some of its constituents (particularly financial institutions) to the proposed rules. The U.S. banks feared the new rules could place them in a less-favorable light when compared to their international counterparts, such as Deutsche Bank (DEU) and BNP Paribas (FRA). As a result, to date the Boards have not been able to agree on a converged standard, thereby stalling this project.

However, the Boards have issued converged disclosure requirements. The disclosure rules require companies to disclose both gross information and net information about instruments and transactions that are eligible for offset in the statement of financial position. While the Boards have not been able to develop a converged set of criteria for offsetting, the information provided under the new converged disclosure rules should enable users of a company's financial statements to evaluate the effects of netting arrangements on its financial position. In doing so, the new rules support the full disclosure principle.

*See Y. N'Diaye, "S&P: Accounting Rule Could Boost Bank Balance Sheets by Average 68%," *https://mninews.deutsche-boerse.com* (September 22, 2011).

GLOBAL ACCOUNTING INSIGHTS

STATEMENT OF FINANCIAL POSITION AND STATEMENT OF CASH FLOWS

As in IFRS, the statement of financial position and the statement of cash flows are required statements for U.S. GAAP. In addition, the content and presentation of a U.S. GAAP statement of financial position and cash flow statement are similar to those used for IFRS.

Relevant Facts

Following are the key similarities and differences between U.S. GAAP and IFRS related to the statement of financial position.

Similarities
- Both U.S. GAAP and IFRS allow the use of the title "balance sheet" or "statement of financial position." IFRS recommends but does not require the use of the title "statement of financial position" rather than balance sheet.
- Both U.S. GAAP and IFRS require disclosures about (1) accounting policies followed, (2) judgments that management has made in the process of applying the entity's accounting policies, and (3) the key assumptions and estimation uncertainty that could result in a material adjustment to the carrying amounts of assets and liabilities within the next financial year. Comparative prior period information must be presented and financial statements must be prepared annually.
- U.S. GAAP and IFRS require presentation of non-controlling interests in the equity section of the statement of financial position.

Differences
- U.S. GAAP follows the same guidelines as presented in the chapter for distinguishing between current and non-current assets and liabilities. However, under U.S. GAAP, public companies must follow U.S. SEC regulations, which require specific line items. In addition, specific U.S. GAAP mandates certain forms of reporting for this information. IFRS requires a classified statement of financial position except in very limited situations.
- Under U.S. GAAP cash is listed first, but under IFRS it is many times listed last. That is, under IFRS, current assets are

usually listed in the reverse order of liquidity than under U.S. GAAP.

- U.S. GAAP has many differences in terminology that you will notice in this textbook. One example is the use of

common stock under U.S. GAAP, which is referred to as share capital—ordinary under IFRS.

- Use of the term "reserve" is discouraged in U.S. GAAP, but there is no such prohibition in IFRS.

About the Numbers

The order of presentation in the statement of financial position differs between U.S. GAAP and IFRS. As indicated in the following table, U.S. companies generally present current assets, non-current assets, current and non-current liabilities, and shareholders' equity.

In addition, within the current asset and liability classifications, items are presented in order of liquidity, as indicated in the following excerpt from **Hasbro, Inc.** (USA).

Assets	Liabilities and Owners' Equity
Current assets	Current liabilities
Long-term investments	Long-term debt
Property, plant, and equipment	Shareholders' equity
Intangible assets	Common stock
Other assets	Additional paid-in capital
	Retained earnings

Hasbro, Inc.
(in thousands)

Current assets	
Cash and cash equivalents	$ 715,400
Accounts receivable, less allowances of $27,700	556,287
Inventories	203,337
Prepaid expenses and other current assets	243,291
Total current assets	$1,718,315

On the Horizon

The IASB and the FASB are working on a project to converge their standards related to financial statement presentation. A key feature of the proposed framework is that each of the statements will be organized, in the same format, to separate an entity's financing activities from its operating and investing activities and, further, to separate financing activities into transactions with owners and creditors. Thus, the same

classifications used in the statement of financial position would also be used in the statement of comprehensive income and the statement of cash flows. The project has three phases. You can follow the joint financial presentation project at the following link: *http://www.ifrs.org/Current-Projects/IASB-Projects/Financial-Statement-Presentation/Pages/Financial-Statement-Presentation.aspx.*

SUMMARY OF LEARNING OBJECTIVES

KEY TERMS

1 **Explain the uses and limitations of a statement of financial position.** The statement of financial position provides information about the nature and amounts of investments in a company's resources, obligations to creditors, and equity. The statement of financial position contributes to financial reporting by providing a basis for (1) computing rates of return, (2) evaluating the capital structure of the enterprise, and (3) assessing the liquidity, solvency, and financial flexibility of the enterprise.

Three limitations of a statement of financial position are as follows. (1) The statement of financial position generally does not reflect fair value because accountants use a historical cost basis in valuing and reporting most assets and liabilities. (2) Companies must use judgments and estimates to determine certain amounts, such as the collectibility of receivables and the useful life of long-term tangible and intangible assets. (3) The statement of financial position omits many items that are of financial value to the business but cannot be recorded objectively, such as human resources, customer base, and reputation.

2 **Identify the major classifications of the statement of financial position.** The general elements of the statement of financial position are assets, equity, and liabilities. The major classifications of assets are non-current assets; long-term investments; property, plant, and equipment; intangible assets; other assets; and current assets. The major classifications of liabilities are non-current and current liabilities. The statement of financial position of a corporation generally classifies equity as share capital, share premium, and retained earnings.

3 **Prepare a classified statement of financial position using the report and account formats.** The report form lists equity and liabilities directly below assets on the same page. The account form lists assets, by sections, on the left side, and equity and liabilities, by sections, on the right side.

4 **Indicate the purpose of the statement of cash flows.** The primary purpose of a statement of cash flows is to provide relevant information about a company's cash receipts and cash payments during a period. Reporting the sources, uses, and net change in cash enables financial statement readers to know what is happening to a company's most liquid resource.

5 **Identify the content of the statement of cash flows.** In the statement of cash flows, companies classify the period's cash receipts and cash payments into three different activities. (1) *Operating activities*: Involve the cash effects of transactions that enter into the determination of net income. (2) *Investing activities*: Include making and collecting loans, and acquiring and disposing of investments (both debt and equity) and of property, plant, and equipment. (3) *Financing activities*: Involve liability and equity items. Financing activities include (a) obtaining capital from owners and providing them with a return on their investment, and (b) borrowing money from creditors and repaying the amounts borrowed.

6 **Prepare a basic statement of cash flows.** The information to prepare the statement of cash flows usually comes from comparative statements of financial position, the current income statement, and selected transaction data. Companies follow four steps to prepare the statement of cash flows from these sources. (1) Determine the net cash provided by (or used in) operating activities. (2) Determine the net cash provided by (or used in) investing and financing activities. (3) Determine the change (increase or decrease) in cash during the period. (4) Reconcile the change in cash with the beginning and ending cash balances.

7 **Understand the usefulness of the statement of cash flows.** Creditors examine the cash flow statement carefully because they are concerned about being paid. The net cash flow provided by operating activities in relation to the company's liabilities is helpful in making this assessment. Two ratios used in this regard are the current cash debt coverage and the cash debt coverage. In addition, the amount of free cash flow provides creditors and shareholders with a picture of the company's financial flexibility.

8 **Determine additional information requiring note disclosure.** In addition to a complete set of financial statements, IFRS also requires additional reporting in the notes to the financial statements. Disclosure in the notes includes (1) accounting policies and (2) expanded disclosures and detailed schedules related to such items as property, plant, and equipment; receivables; liabilities and provisions; and equity.

9 **Describe the major disclosure techniques for the statement of financial position.** Companies use two methods to disclose pertinent information in the statement of financial position. (1) *Parenthetical explanations:* Parenthetical information provides additional information or description following the item. (2) *Cross-reference and contra items:* Companies "cross-reference" a direct relationship between an asset and a liability on the statement of financial position. IFRS also provides guidelines related to offsetting amounts (generally not permitted), consistency in application of accounting policies, and "true and fair" presentation.

APPENDIX **5A**	RATIO ANALYSIS—A REFERENCE

USING RATIOS TO ANALYZE PERFORMANCE

Analysts and other interested parties can gather qualitative information from financial statements by examining relationships between items on the statements and identifying trends in these relationships. A useful starting point in developing this information is ratio analysis.

10 **LEARNING OBJECTIVE**
Identify the major types of financial ratios and what they measure.

A **ratio** expresses the mathematical relationship between one quantity and another. Ratio analysis expresses the relationship among pieces of selected financial statement data, in a **percentage**, a **rate**, or a simple **proportion**.

To illustrate, Acer Group (TWN) recently had current assets of NT$186,391 million and current liabilities of NT$149,315 million. We find the ratio between these two amounts by dividing current assets by current liabilities. The alternative means of expression are:

Percentage: Current assets are 125% of current liabilities.

Rate: Current assets are 1.25 times as great as current liabilities.

Proportion: The relationship of current assets to current liabilities is 1.25:1.

To analyze financial statements, we classify ratios into four types, as follows.

MAJOR TYPES OF RATIOS

LIQUIDITY RATIOS. Measures of the company's short-term ability to pay its maturing obligations.

ACTIVITY RATIOS. Measures of how effectively the company uses its assets.

PROFITABILITY RATIOS. Measures of the degree of success or failure of a given company or division for a given period of time.

COVERAGE RATIOS. Measures of the degree of protection for long-term creditors and investors.

In Chapter 5, we discussed three measures related to the statement of cash flows (current cash debt coverage, cash debt coverage, and free cash flow). Throughout the remainder of the textbook, we provide ratios to help you understand and interpret the information presented in financial statements. Illustration 5A-1 presents the ratios that we will use throughout the textbook. You should find this chart helpful as you examine these ratios in more detail in the following chapters. An appendix to Chapter 24 further discusses financial statement analysis.

ILLUSTRATION 5A-1
A Summary of Financial Ratios

Ratio	Formula	Purpose or Use
I. Liquidity		
1. Current ratio	$\dfrac{\text{Current assets}}{\text{Current liabilities}}$	Measures short-term debt-paying ability
2. Quick or acid-test ratio	$\dfrac{\text{Cash, short-term investments, and net receivables}}{\text{Current liabilities}}$	Measures immediate short-term liquidity
3. Current cash debt coverage	$\dfrac{\text{Net cash provided by operating activities}}{\text{Average current liabilities}}$	Measures a company's ability to pay off its current liabilities in a given year from its operations
II. Activity		
4. Accounts receivable turnover	$\dfrac{\text{Net sales}}{\text{Average trade receivables (net)}}$	Measures liquidity of receivables
5. Inventory turnover	$\dfrac{\text{Cost of goods sold}}{\text{Average inventory}}$	Measures liquidity of inventory
6. Asset turnover	$\dfrac{\text{Net sales}}{\text{Average total assets}}$	Measures how efficiently assets are used to generate sales
III. Profitability		
7. Profit margin on sales	$\dfrac{\text{Net income}}{\text{Net sales}}$	Measures net income generated by each dollar of sales
8. Return on assets	$\dfrac{\text{Net income}}{\text{Average total assets}}$	Measures overall profitability of assets
9. Return on share capital—ordinary	$\dfrac{\text{Net income minus preference dividends}}{\text{Average shareholders' equity—ordinary}}$	Measures profitability of owners' investment
10. Earnings per share	$\dfrac{\text{Net income minus preference dividends}}{\text{Weighted-average number of shares outstanding}}$	Measures net income earned on each ordinary share
11. Price-earnings ratio	$\dfrac{\text{Market price of share}}{\text{Earnings per share}}$	Measures the ratio of the market price per share to earnings per share
12. Payout ratio	$\dfrac{\text{Cash dividends}}{\text{Net income}}$	Measures percentage of earnings distributed in the form of cash dividends
IV. Coverage		
13. Debt to assets ratio	$\dfrac{\text{Total liabilities}}{\text{Total assets}}$	Measures the percentage of total assets provided by creditors
14. Times interest earned	$\dfrac{\text{Income before interest expense and taxes}}{\text{Interest expense}}$	Measures ability to meet interest payments as they come due
15. Cash debt coverage	$\dfrac{\text{Net cash provided by operating activities}}{\text{Average total liabilities}}$	Measures a company's ability to repay its total liabilities in a given year from its operations
16. Book value per share	$\dfrac{\text{Shareholders' equity—ordinary}}{\text{Outstanding shares}}$	Measures the amount each ordinary share would receive if the company were liquidated at the amounts reported on the statement of financial position
17. Free cash flow	Net cash provided by operating activities − Capital expenditures − Dividends	Measures the amount of discretionary cash flow

SUMMARY OF LEARNING OBJECTIVE FOR APPENDIX 5A

10 **Identify the major types of financial ratios and what they measure.**
Ratios express the mathematical relationship between one quantity and another, expressed as a percentage, a rate, or a proportion. *Liquidity* ratios measure the short-term ability to pay maturing obligations. *Activity* ratios measure the effectiveness of asset usage. *Profitability* ratios measure the success or failure of an enterprise. *Coverage* ratios measure the degree of protection for long-term creditors and investors.

IFRS AUTHORITATIVE LITERATURE

Authoritative Literature References

[1] International Accounting Standard 1, *Presentation of Financial Statements* (London, U.K.: International Accounting Standards Committee Foundation, 2005), par. BC 16.

[2] International Accounting Standard 1, *Presentation of Financial Statements* (London, U.K.: International Accounting Standards Committee Foundation, 2005), par. 60.

[3] International Accounting Standard 39, *Financial Instruments: Recognition and Measurement* (London, U.K.: International Accounting Standards Committee Foundation, 2003), paras. 43–46.

[4] International Accounting Standard 32, *Financial Instruments: Presentation* (London, U.K.: International Accounting Standards Committee Foundation, December 2003), par. 11.

[5] International Accounting Standard 39, *Financial Instruments: Recognition and Measurement* (London, U.K.: International Accounting Standards Committee Foundation, 2003), par. 9b.

[6] International Accounting Standard 1, *Presentation of Financial Statements* (London, U.K.: International Accounting Standards Committee Foundation, September 2005), par. 72.

[7] International Accounting Standard 1, *Presentation of Financial Statements* (London, U.K.: International Accounting Standards Committee Foundation, September 2005), par. 10d.

[8] International Accounting Standard 1, *Presentation of Financial Statements* (London, U.K.: International Accounting Standards Committee Foundation, September 2005), par. 10.

[9] International Accounting Standard 1, *Presentation of Financial Statements* (London, U.K.: International Accounting Standards Committee Foundation, December 2005).

[10] International Accounting Standard 8, *Accounting Policies, Changes in Accounting Estimates and Errors* (London, U.K.: International Accounting Standards Committee Foundation, 2003).

QUESTIONS

1. How does information from the statement of financial position help users of the financial statements?

2. What is meant by solvency? What information in the statement of financial position can be used to assess a company's solvency?

3. A financial magazine indicated that the airline industry has poor financial flexibility. What is meant by financial flexibility, and why is it important?

4. Discuss at least two situations in which estimates could affect the usefulness of information in the statement of financial position.

5. Perez Company reported an increase in inventories in the past year. Discuss the effect of this change on the current ratio (current assets ÷ current liabilities). What does this tell a statement user about Perez Company's liquidity?

6. What is meant by liquidity? Rank the following assets from one to five in order of liquidity.

   (a) Goodwill.
   (b) Inventory.
   (c) Buildings.
   (d) Short-term investments.
   (e) Accounts receivable.

7. What are the major limitations of the statement of financial position as a source of information?

8. Discuss at least two items that are important to the value of companies like **Louis Vuitton (LVMH Group)** (FRA) or **adidas** (DEU) but that are not recorded in their statements of financial position. What are some reasons why these items are not recorded in the statement of financial position?

9. How does separating current assets from property, plant, and equipment in the statement of financial position help analysts?

10. In its December 31, 2015, statement of financial position, Oakley Corporation reported as an asset, "Net notes and accounts receivable, €7,100,000." What other disclosures are necessary?

11. Should non-trading equity securities always be reported as a current asset? Explain.

12. What is the relationship between current assets and current liabilities?

13. Manchester United, Inc. sold 10,000 season tickets at £2,000 each. By December 31, 2015, 8 of the 20 home games had been played. What amount should be reported as a current liability at December 31, 2015?

14. What is working capital? How does working capital relate to the operating cycle?

15. In what section of the statement of financial position should the following items appear, and what statement of financial position terminology would you use?

    (a) Treasury shares (recorded at cost).
    (b) Checking account at bank.
    (c) Land (held as an investment).
    (d) Sinking fund.
    (e) Provision for warranties (short-term).
    (f) Copyrights.
    (g) Pension fund assets.
    (h) Share capital—ordinary.
    (i) Long-term investments (pledged against bank loans payable).
    (j) Non-controlling interest (minority interest).

16. Where should the following items be shown on the statement of financial position, if shown at all?

    (a) Allowance for doubtful accounts.
    (b) Merchandise held on consignment.
    (c) Advances received on sales contract.
    (d) Accumulated other comprehensive income.
    (e) Land.
    (f) Merchandise out on consignment.
    (g) Franchises.
    (h) Accumulated depreciation of plant and equipment.
    (i) Materials in transit—purchased f.o.b. destination.

17. State the usual basis of valuation of each of the following assets.

    (a) Trade accounts receivable.
    (b) Land.
    (c) Inventory.
    (d) Trading securities (ordinary shares of other companies).
    (e) Prepaid expenses.

18. Refer to the definition of assets on page 184. Discuss how a leased building might qualify as an asset of the lessee (tenant) under this definition.

19. Kathleen Battle says, "Retained earnings should be reported as an asset, since it is earnings which are reinvested in the business." How would you respond to Battle?

20. The creditors of Chan Ho Company agree to accept promissory notes for the amount of its indebtedness with a condition that two-thirds of the annual profits must be applied to their liquidation. How should these notes be reported on the statement of financial position of the issuing company? Give a reason for your answer.

21. What is the purpose of a statement of cash flows? How does it differ from a statement of financial position and a statement of comprehensive income?

22. The net income for the year for Genesis, Inc. is £750,000, but the statement of cash flows reports that net cash provided by operating activities is £640,000. What might account for the difference?

23. Net income for the year for Carrie, Inc. was $750,000, but the statement of cash flows reports that net cash provided by operating activities was $860,000. What might account for the difference?

24. Differentiate between operating activities, investing activities, and financing activities.

25. Each of the following items must be considered in preparing a statement of cash flows. Indicate where each item is to be reported in the statement, if at all. Assume that net income is reported as ¥90,000 (amounts in thousands).

    (a) Accounts receivable increased from ¥34,000 to ¥39,000 from the beginning to the end of the year.
    (b) During the year, 10,000 ordinary shares with a par value of ¥100 per share were issued at ¥115 per share.
    (c) Depreciation expense amounted to ¥14,000, and intangible asset amortization amounted to ¥5,000.
    (d) Land increased from ¥10,000 to ¥30,000 due to purchase through issuance of long-term debt.

26. Sergey Co. has net cash provided by operating activities of €1,200,000. Its average current liabilities for the period are €1,000,000, and its average total liabilities are €1,500,000. Comment on the company's liquidity and financial flexibility given this information.

27. Net income for the year for Tanizaki, Inc. was $750,000, but the statement of cash flows reports that net cash provided by operating activities was $860,000. Tanizaki also reported capital expenditures of $75,000 and paid dividends in the amount of $30,000. Compute Tanizaki's free cash flow.

28. What is the purpose of a free cash flow analysis?

29. What is a "Summary of Significant Accounting Policies"?

30. What are some of the techniques of disclosure for financial statement information?

31. Briefly describe some of the similarities and differences between IFRS and U.S. GAAP with respect to statement of financial position reporting.

32. Briefly describe the convergence efforts related to financial statement presentation.

33. Rainmaker Company prepares its financial statements in accordance with U.S. GAAP. Briefly discuss the differences in order of presentation in its statement of financial position compared to IFRS.

BRIEF EXERCISES

2 3 **BE5-1** Harding Corporation has the following accounts included in its December 31, 2015, trial balance: Accounts Receivable €110,000, Inventory €290,000, Allowance for Doubtful Accounts €8,000, Patents €72,000, Prepaid Insurance €9,500, Accounts Payable €77,000, and Cash €30,000. Prepare the current assets section of the statement of financial position, listing the accounts in the sequence shown in the chapter.

2 3 **BE5-2** Koch Corporation's adjusted trial balance contained the following asset accounts at December 31, 2015: Cash €7,000, Land €40,000, Patents €12,500, Accounts Receivable €90,000, Prepaid Insurance €5,200, Inventory €30,000, Allowance for Doubtful Accounts €4,000, and Trading Securities €11,000. Prepare the current assets section of the statement of financial position, listing the accounts in the sequence shown in the chapter.

2 3 **BE5-3** Included in Outkast Company's December 31, 2015, trial balance are the following accounts: Prepaid Rent $5,200, Held-for-Collection Securities $56,000, Unearned Service Revenue $17,000, Land Held for Investment $39,000, and Notes Receivable (long-term) $42,000. Prepare the long-term investments section of the statement of financial position.

2 3 **BE5-4** Lowell Company's December 31, 2015, trial balance includes the following accounts: Inventory $120,000, Buildings $207,000, Accumulated Depreciation–Equipment $19,000, Equipment $190,000, Land Held for Investment $46,000, Accumulated Depreciation–Buildings $45,000, and Land $71,000. Prepare the property, plant, and equipment section of the statement of financial position.

2 3 **BE5-5** Crane Corporation has the following accounts included in its December 31, 2015, trial balance: Trading Securities £21,000, Goodwill £150,000, Prepaid Insurance £12,000, Patents £220,000, and Franchises £130,000. Prepare the intangible assets section of the statement of financial position.

2 3 **BE5-6** Patrick Corporation's adjusted trial balance contained the following asset accounts at December 31, 2015: Capitalized Development Costs $18,000, Prepaid Rent $12,000, Goodwill $50,000, Franchise Fees Receivable $2,000, Franchises $47,000, Patents $33,000, and Trademarks $10,000. Prepare the intangible assets section of the statement of financial position.

2 3 **BE5-7** Thomas Corporation's adjusted trial balance contained the following liability accounts at December 31, 2015. Bonds Payable (due in 3 years) $100,000, Accounts Payable $72,000, Notes Payable (due in 90 days) $22,500, Salaries and Wages Payable $4,000, and Income Taxes Payable $7,000. Prepare the current liabilities section of the statement of financial position.

2 3 **BE5-8** Included in Arco Company's December 31, 2015, trial balance are the following accounts: Accounts Payable ₺220,000, Pension Liability ₺375,000, Advances from Customers ₺41,000, Bonds Payable ₺371,000, Salaries and Wages Payable ₺27,000, Interest Payable ₺12,000, Income Taxes Payable ₺29,000, and Provision for Warranties (current ₺3,000, non-current ₺6,000). Prepare the current liabilities section of the statement of financial position.

2 3 **BE5-9** Use the information presented in BE5-8 for Arco Company to prepare the non-current liabilities section of the statement of financial position.

2 3 **BE5-10** Hawthorn Corporation's adjusted trial balance contained the following accounts at December 31, 2015: Retained Earnings €120,000, Share Capital—Ordinary €750,000, Bonds Payable €100,000, Share Premium—Ordinary €200,000, Goodwill €55,000, Accumulated Other Comprehensive Income €(150,000), and Non-Controlling Interest €80,000. Prepare the equity section of the statement of financial position.

2 3 **BE5-11** Stowe Company's December 31, 2015, trial balance includes the following accounts: Share Capital— Ordinary €70,000, Retained Earnings €114,000, Trademarks €31,000, Share Capital—Preference €152,000, Trading Securities €55,000, Deferred Income Taxes €88,000, Share Premium—Ordinary €174,000, and Non-Controlling Interest €18,000. Prepare the equity section of the statement of financial position.

6 **BE5-12** Keyser Beverage Company reported the following items in the most recent year.

Net income	$40,000
Dividends paid	5,000
Increase in accounts receivable	10,000
Increase in accounts payable	7,000
Purchase of equipment (capital expenditure)	8,000
Depreciation expense	4,000
Issue of notes payable	20,000

Compute net cash provided by operating activities, the net change in cash during the year, and free cash flow.

6 **BE5-13** Ames Company reported 2015 net income of HK$151,000. During 2015, accounts receivable increased by HK$13,000 and accounts payable increased by HK$9,500. Depreciation expense was HK$44,000. Prepare the cash flows from operating activities section of the statement of cash flows (amounts in thousands).

6 **BE5-14** Martinez Corporation engaged in the following cash transactions during 2015.

Sale of land and building	R$191,000
Purchase of treasury shares	40,000
Purchase of land	37,000
Payment of cash dividend	95,000
Purchase of equipment	53,000
Issuance of ordinary shares	147,000
Retirement of bonds	100,000

Compute the net cash provided (used) by investing activities.

6 **BE5-15** Use the information presented in BE5-14 for Martinez Corporation to compute the net cash provided (used) by financing activities.

7 **BE5-16** Using the information in BE5-14, determine Martinez's free cash flow, assuming that it reported net cash provided by operating activities of R$400,000.

EXERCISES

2 **3** **E5-1 (Statement of Financial Position Classifications)** Presented below are a number of statement of financial position accounts of Cunningham, Inc.

(a) Investment in Preference Shares.
(b) Treasury Shares.
(c) Share Capital—Ordinary.
(d) Dividends Payable.
(e) Accumulated Depreciation—Equipment
(f) Construction in Process.
(g) Petty Cash.

(h) Interest Payable.
(i) Deficit.
(j) Trading Securities.
(k) Income Taxes Payable.
(l) Unearned Service Revenue.
(m) Work in Process.
(n) Salaries and Wages Payable.

Instructions

For each of the accounts above, indicate the proper statement of financial position classification. In the case of borderline items, indicate the additional information that would be required to determine the proper classification.

2 **3** **E5-2 (Classification of Statement of Financial Position Accounts)** Presented below are the captions of Nikos Company's statement of financial position.

(a) Non-current assets.

(1) Investments.

(2) Property, plant, and equipment.

(3) Intangible assets.

(4) Other assets.

(b) Current assets.

(c) Equity.
(d) Non-current liabilities.
(e) Current liabilities.

Instructions

Indicate by letter where each of the following items would be classified.

1. Share capital—preference.
2. Goodwill.
3. Salaries and wages payable.
4. Accounts payable.
5. Buildings.

6. Trading securities.
7. Current portion of long-term debt.
8. Patents.
9. Allowance for doubtful accounts.
10. Accounts receivable.

11. Accumulated other comprehensive income.

12. Notes payable (due next year).

13. Supplies.

14. Share capital—ordinary.

15. Land.

16. Bond sinking fund.

17. Inventory.

18. Prepaid insurance.

19. Bonds payable.

20. Income taxes payable.

E5-3 (Classification of Statement of Financial Position Accounts) Assume that Masters Enterprises uses the following headings on its statement of financial position.

(a) Investments.
(b) Property, plant, and equipment.
(c) Intangible assets.
(d) Other assets.
(e) Current assets.
(f) Non-current liabilities.
(g) Current liabilities.
(h) Share capital.
(i) Share premium.
(j) Retained earnings.
(k) Accumulated other comprehensive income.

Instructions

Indicate by letter how each of the following usually should be classified. If an item should appear in a note to the financial statements, use the letter "N" to indicate this fact. If an item need not be reported at all on the statement of financial position, use the letter "X."

1. Prepaid insurance.

2. Shares owned in associated companies.

3. Unearned service revenue.

4. Advances to suppliers.

5. Unearned rent revenue.

6. Share capital—preference.

7. Share premium—preference.

8. Copyrights.

9. Petty cash fund.

10. Sales taxes payable.

11. Interest on notes receivable.

12. Twenty-year bonds payable that will mature within the next year. (No sinking fund exists, and refunding is not planned.)

13. Accounts receivable.

14. Unrealized gain on non-trading equity securities.

15. Interest on bonds payable.

16. Salaries that company budget shows will be paid to employees within the next year.

17. Accumulated depreciation—equipment.

E5-4 (Preparation of a Classified Statement of Financial Position) Assume that Gulistan Inc. has the following accounts at the end of the current year.

1. Share Capital—Ordinary.
2. Notes Payable (long-term).
3. Treasury Shares (at cost).
4. Note Payable (short-term).
5. Raw Materials.
6. Long-Term Investment in Preference Shares.
7. Unearned Rent Revenue.
8. Work in Process.
9. Copyrights.
10. Buildings.
11. Notes Receivable (short-term).
12. Cash.
13. Salaries and Wages Payable.
14. Accumulated Depreciation—Buildings.
15. Cash Restricted for Plant Expansion.
16. Land Held for Future Plant Site.
17. Allowance for Doubtful Accounts (Accounts Receivable).
18. Retained Earnings.
19. Share Premium—Ordinary.
20. Unearned Service Revenue.
21. Receivables—Officers (due in 1 year).
22. Finished Goods.
23. Accounts Receivable.
24. Bonds Payable (due in 4 years).

Instructions

Prepare a classified statement of financial position in good form. (No monetary amounts are necessary.)

E5-5 (Preparation of a Corrected Statement of Financial Position) Bruno Company has decided to expand its operations. The bookkeeper recently completed the statement of financial position shown on the next page in order to obtain additional funds for expansion.

BRUNO COMPANY
STATEMENT OF FINANCIAL POSITION
DECEMBER 31, 2015

Current assets	
Cash	€260,000
Accounts receivable (net)	340,000
Inventory (at lower-of-average-cost-or-net realizable value)	401,000
Trading securities—at cost (fair value €120,000)	140,000
Property, plant, and equipment	
Buildings (net)	570,000
Equipment (net)	160,000
Land held for future use	175,000
Intangible assets	
Goodwill	80,000
Other identifiable assets	90,000
Prepaid expenses	12,000
Current liabilities	
Accounts payable	135,000
Notes payable (due next year)	125,000
Pension liability	82,000
Rent payable	49,000
Premium on bonds payable	53,000
Non-current liabilities	
Bonds payable	500,000
Equity	
Share capital—ordinary, €1.00 par, authorized	
400,000 shares, issued 290,000	290,000
Share premium—ordinary	180,000
Retained earnings	?

Instructions

Prepare a revised statement of financial position given the available information. Assume that the accumulated depreciation balance for the buildings is €160,000 and for the equipment, €105,000. The allowance for doubtful accounts has a balance of €17,000. The pension liability is considered a non-current liability.

3 **E5-6 (Corrections of a Statement of Financial Position)** The bookkeeper for Garfield Company has prepared the following statement of financial position as of July 31, 2015 (amounts in thousands).

LIBA COMPANY
STATEMENT OF FINANCIAL POSITION
AS OF JULY 31, 2015

Equipment (net)	¥ 84,000	Equity	¥155,500
Patents	21,000	Non-current liabilities	75,000
Inventory	60,000	Notes and accounts payable	44,000
Accounts receivable (net)	40,500		¥274,500
Cash	69,000		
	¥274,500		

The following additional information is provided.

1. Cash includes ¥1,200 in a petty cash fund and ¥12,000 in a bond sinking fund.

2. The net accounts receivable balance is comprised of the following three items: (a) accounts receivable—debit balances ¥52,000, (b) accounts receivable—credit balances ¥8,000, and (c) allowance for doubtful accounts ¥3,500.

3. Inventory costing ¥5,300 was shipped out on consignment on July 31, 2015. The ending inventory balance does not include the consigned goods. Receivables in the amount of ¥5,300 were recognized on these consigned goods.

4. Equipment had a cost of ¥112,000 and an accumulated depreciation balance of ¥28,000.

5. Income taxes payable of ¥9,000 were accrued on July 31. Liba Company, however, had set up a cash fund to meet this obligation. This cash fund was not included in the cash balance but was offset against the income taxes payable amount.

Instructions

Prepare a corrected classified statement of financial position as of July 31, 2015, from the available information, adjusting the account balances using the additional information.

2 **E5-7 (Current Assets Section of the Statement of Financial Position)** Presented below are selected accounts of Aramis Company at December 31, 2015.

Inventory (finished goods)	€ 52,000	Cost of Goods Sold	€2,100,000
Unearned Service Revenue	90,000	Notes Receivable	40,000
Equipment	253,000	Accounts Receivable	161,000
Inventory (work in process)	34,000	Inventory (raw materials)	187,000
Cash	42,000	Supplies Expense	60,000
Trading Securities	31,000	Allowance for Doubtful Accounts	12,000
Customer Advances	36,000	Licenses	18,000
Cash Restricted for Plant Expansion	50,000	Share Premium—Ordinary	88,000
		Treasury Shares	22,000

The following additional information is available.

1. Inventory is valued at lower-of-cost-or-net realizable value using FIFO.

2. Equipment is recorded at cost. Accumulated depreciation, computed on a straight-line basis, is €50,600.

3. The trading securities have a fair value of €29,000.

4. The notes receivable are due April 30, 2017, with interest receivable every April 30. The notes bear interest at 6%. (*Hint:* Accrue interest due on December 31, 2015.)

5. The allowance for doubtful accounts applies to the accounts receivable. Accounts receivable of €50,000 are pledged as collateral on a bank loan.

6. Licenses are recorded net of accumulated amortization of €14,000.

7. Treasury shares are recorded at cost.

Instructions

Prepare the current assets section of Aramis Company's December 31, 2015, statement of financial position, with appropriate disclosures.

2 **E5-8 (Current vs. Non-Current Liabilities)** Pascal Corporation is preparing its December 31, 2015, statement of financial position. The following items may be reported as either a current or non-current liability.

1. On December 15, 2015, Pascal declared a cash dividend of $2.00 per share to shareholders of record on December 31. The dividend is payable on January 15, 2016. Pascal has issued 1,000,000 ordinary shares of which 50,000 shares are held in treasury.

2. At December 31, bonds payable of $100,000,000 are outstanding. The bonds pay 8% interest every September 30 and mature in installments of $25,000,000 every September 30, beginning September 30, 2016.

3. At December 31, 2014, customer advances were $12,000,000. During 2015, Pascal collected $30,000,000 of customer advances, and advances of $25,000,000 were earned.

Instructions

For each item above, indicate the dollar amounts to be reported as a current liability and as a non-current liability, if any.

2 **3** **E5-9 (Current Assets and Current Liabilities)** The current assets and current liabilities sections of the statement of financial position of Jin Liu Company appear as follows (amounts in thousands).

JIN LIU COMPANY
STATEMENT OF FINANCIAL POSITION (PARTIAL)
DECEMBER 31, 2015

Inventory		¥171,000	Notes payable	¥ 67,000
Accounts receivable	¥89,000		Accounts payable	61,000
Less: Allowance for				¥128,000
doubtful accounts	7,000	82,000		
Prepaid expenses		9,000		
Cash		40,000		
		¥302,000		

The following errors in the corporation's accounting have been discovered:

1. January 2016 cash disbursements entered as of December 2015 included payments of accounts payable in the amount of ¥35,000, on which a cash discount of 2% was taken.

2. The inventory included ¥27,000 of merchandise that had been received at December 31 but for which no purchase invoices had been received or entered. Of this amount, ¥10,000 had been received on consignment; the remainder was purchased f.o.b. destination, terms 2/10, n/30.

3. Sales for the first four days in January 2016 in the amount of ¥30,000 were entered in the sales book as of December 31, 2015. Of these, ¥21,500 were sales on account and the remainder were cash sales.

4. Cash, not including cash sales, collected in January 2016 and entered as of December 31, 2015, totaled ¥35,324. Of this amount, ¥23,324 was received on account after cash discounts of 2% had been deducted; the remainder represented the proceeds of a bank loan.

Instructions
(a) Restate the current assets and current liabilities sections of the statement of financial position in accordance with good accounting practice. (Assume that both accounts receivable and accounts payable are recorded gross.)
(b) State the net effect of your adjustments on Jin Liu Company's retained earnings balance.

2 **E5-10 (Current Liabilities)** Mary Pierce is the controller of Arnold Corporation and is responsible for the preparation of the year-end financial statements. The following transactions occurred during the year.

(a) Bonuses to key employees based on net income for 2015 are estimated to be $150,000.
(b) On December 1, 2015, the company borrowed $900,000 at 8% per year. Interest is paid quarterly.
(c) Credit sales for the year amounted to $10,000,000. Arnold's expense provision for doubtful accounts is estimated to be 2% of credit sales.
(d) On December 15, 2015, the company declared a $2 per share dividend on the 40,000 ordinary shares outstanding, to be paid on January 5, 2016.
(e) During the year, customer advances of $160,000 were received; $50,000 of this amount was earned by December 31, 2015.

Instructions
For each item above, indicate the dollar amount to be reported as a current liability. If a liability is not reported, explain why.

3 **E5-11 (Statement of Financial Position Preparation)** Presented below is the adjusted trial balance of Abbey Corporation at December 31, 2015.

	Debit	Credit
Cash	£ ?	
Supplies	1,200	
Prepaid Insurance	1,000	
Equipment	48,000	
Accumulated Depreciation—Equipment		£ 9,000
Trademarks	950	
Accounts Payable		10,000
Salaries and Wages Payable		500
Unearned Service Revenue		2,000
Bonds Payable (due 2022)		9,000
Share Capital—Ordinary		10,000
Retained Earnings		20,000
Service Revenue		10,000
Salaries and Wages Expense	9,000	
Insurance Expense	1,400	
Rent Expense	1,200	
Interest Expense	900	
Total	£ ?	£ ?

Additional information:

1. Net loss for the year was £2,500.

2. No dividends were declared during 2015.

Instructions
Prepare a classified statement of financial position as of December 31, 2015.

3 **E5-12 (Preparation of a Statement of Financial Position)** Presented below is the trial balance of Vivaldi Corporation at December 31, 2015.

	Debit	Credit
Cash	€ 197,000	
Sales Revenue		€ 7,900,000
Trading Securities (at cost, €145,000)	153,000	
Cost of Goods Sold	4,800,000	
Long-term Investments in Bonds	299,000	
Long-term Investments in Shares	277,000	
Notes Payable (short-term)		90,000
Accounts Payable		455,000
Selling Expenses	2,000,000	
Investment Revenue		63,000
Land	260,000	
Buildings	1,040,000	
Dividends Payable		136,000
Accrued Liabilities		96,000
Accounts Receivable	435,000	
Accumulated Depreciation—Buildings		352,000
Allowance for Doubtful Accounts		25,000
Administrative Expenses	900,000	
Interest Expense	211,000	
Inventory	597,000	
Pension Liability (long-term)		80,000
Notes Payable (long-term)		900,000
Equipment	600,000	
Bonds Payable		1,000,000
Accumulated Depreciation—Equipment		60,000
Franchises	160,000	
Share Capital—Ordinary (€5 par)		1,000,000
Treasury Shares	191,000	
Patents	195,000	
Retained Earnings		78,000
Accumulated Other Comprehensive Income		80,000
Total	€12,315,000	€12,315,000

Instructions

Prepare a statement of financial position at December 31, 2015, for Vivaldi Corporation. (Ignore income taxes.)

5 **E5-13 (Statement of Cash Flows—Classifications)** The major classifications of activities reported in the statement of cash flows are operating, investing, and financing. Classify each of the transactions listed below as:

1. Operating activity—add to net income.

2. Operating activity—deduct from net income.

3. Investing activity.

4. Financing activity.

5. Reported as significant non-cash activity in the notes to the financial statements.

The transactions are as follows.

(a) Issuance of ordinary shares.
(b) Purchase of land and building.
(c) Redemption of bonds.
(d) Sale of equipment.
(e) Depreciation of machinery.
(f) Amortization of patent.
(g) Issuance of bonds for plant assets.

(h) Payment of cash dividends.
(i) Exchange of furniture for office equipment.
(j) Purchase of treasury shares.
(k) Loss on sale of equipment.
(l) Increase in accounts receivable during the year.
(m) Decrease in accounts payable during the year.

6 **E5-14 (Preparation of a Statement of Cash Flows)** The comparative statements of financial position of Lopez Inc. at the beginning and the end of the year 2015 appear on the next page.

LOPEZ INC.
STATEMENTS OF FINANCIAL POSITION

Assets	Dec. 31, 2015	Jan. 1, 2015	Inc./Dec.
Equipment	$ 39,000	$ 22,000	$17,000 Inc.
Less: Accumulated depreciation—equipment	(17,000)	(11,000)	6,000 Inc.
Accounts receivable	91,000	88,000	3,000 Inc.
Cash	45,000	13,000	32,000 Inc.
Total	$158,000	$112,000	
Equity and Liabilities			
Share capital—ordinary	$100,000	$ 80,000	20,000 Inc.
Retained earnings	38,000	17,000	21,000 Inc.
Accounts payable	20,000	15,000	5,000 Inc.
Total	$158,000	$112,000	

Net income of $34,000 was reported, and dividends of $13,000 were paid in 2015. New equipment was purchased and none was sold.

Instructions
Prepare a statement of cash flows for the year 2015.

6 7 E5-15 (Preparation of a Statement of Cash Flows) Presented below is a condensed version of the comparative statements of financial position for Yoon Corporation for the last two years at December 31 (amounts in millions).

	2015	2014
Investments	₩ 52,000	₩ 74,000
Equipment	298,000	240,000
Less: Accumulated depreciation—equipment	(106,000)	(89,000)
Accounts receivable	180,000	185,000
Cash	157,000	78,000
Share capital—ordinary	160,000	160,000
Retained earnings	287,000	177,000
Current liabilities	134,000	151,000

Additional information:

Investments were sold at a loss of ₩7,000; no equipment was sold; cash dividends paid were ₩50,000; and net income was ₩160,000.

Instructions
(a) Prepare a statement of cash flows for 2015 for Yoon Corporation.
(b) Determine Yoon Corporation's free cash flow.

6 7 E5-16 (Preparation of a Statement of Cash Flows) A comparative statement of financial position for Orozco Corporation is presented below.

	December 31	
Assets	2015	2014
Land	€ 71,000	€110,000
Equipment	270,000	200,000
Accumulated depreciation—equipment	(69,000)	(42,000)
Inventory	180,000	189,000
Accounts receivable	82,000	66,000
Cash	63,000	22,000
Total	€597,000	€545,000
Equity and Liabilities		
Share capital—ordinary (€1 par)	€214,000	€164,000
Retained earnings	199,000	134,000
Bonds payable	150,000	200,000
Accounts payable	34,000	47,000
Total	€597,000	€545,000

Additional information:

1. Net income for 2015 was €105,000.

2. Cash dividends of €40,000 were declared and paid.

3. Bonds payable amounting to €50,000 were retired through issuance of ordinary shares.

Instructions

    (a) Prepare a statement of cash flows for 2015 for Orozco Corporation.

    (b) Determine Orozco Corporation's current cash debt coverage, cash debt coverage, and free cash flow. Comment on its liquidity and financial flexibility.

3 6 E5-17 (Preparation of a Statement of Cash Flows and a Statement of Financial Position) Chekov Corporation's statement of financial position at the end of 2014 included the following items.

Land	$ 30,000	Bonds payable	$100,000
Buildings	120,000	Current liabilities	150,000
Equipment	90,000	Share capital—ordinary	180,000
Accum. depr.—buildings	(30,000)	Retained earnings	44,000
Accum. depr.—equipment	(11,000)	Total	$474,000
Patents	40,000		
Current assets	235,000		
Total	$474,000		

The following information is available for 2015.

1. Net income was $55,000.

2. Equipment (cost $20,000 and accumulated depreciation $8,000) was sold for $9,000.

3. Depreciation expense was $4,000 on the building and $9,000 on equipment.

4. Patent amortization was $2,500.

5. Current assets other than cash increased by $25,000. Current liabilities increased by $13,000.

6. An addition to the building was completed at a cost of $27,000.

7. A long-term investment in debt securities was purchased for $16,000.

8. Bonds payable of $50,000 were issued.

9. Cash dividends of $25,000 were declared and paid.

10. Treasury shares were purchased at a cost of $11,000.

Instructions

(Show only totals for current assets and current liabilities.)

    (a) Prepare a statement of cash flows for 2015.

    (b) Prepare a statement of financial position at December 31, 2015.

6 7 E5-18 (Preparation of a Statement of Cash Flows, Analysis) The comparative statements of financial position of Menachem Corporation at the beginning and end of the year 2015 appear below.

MENACHEM CORPORATION			
STATEMENTS OF FINANCIAL POSITION			
Assets	Dec. 31, 2015	Jan. 1, 2015	Inc./Dec.
Equipment	€ 37,000	€ 22,000	€15,000 Inc.
Less: Accumulated depreciation—equipment	(17,000)	(11,000)	6,000 Inc.
Accounts receivable	106,000	88,000	18,000 Inc.
Cash	22,000	13,000	9,000 Inc.
Total	€148,000	€112,000	
Equity and Liabilities			
Share capital—ordinary	€100,000	€ 80,000	20,000 Inc.
Retained earnings	28,000	17,000	11,000 Inc.
Accounts payable	20,000	15,000	5,000 Inc.
Total	€148,000	€112,000	

Net income of €34,000 was reported, and dividends of €23,000 were paid in 2015. New equipment was purchased and none was sold.

Instructions

(a) Prepare a statement of cash flows for the year 2015.

(b) Compute the current ratio (current assets ÷ current liabilities) as of January 1, 2015, and December 31, 2015, and compute free cash flow for the year 2015.

(c) In light of the analysis in (b), comment on Menachem's liquidity and financial flexibility.

PROBLEMS

3 **P5-1 (Preparation of a Classified Statement of Financial Position, Periodic Inventory)** Presented below is a list of accounts in alphabetical order.

Accounts Receivable	Land for Future Plant Site
Accumulated Depreciation—Buildings	Loss from Flood
Accumulated Depreciation—Equipment	Non-Controlling Interest
Advances to Employees	Notes Payable (due next year)
Advertising Expense	Patents
Allowance for Doubtful Accounts	Payroll Taxes Payable
Bond Sinking Fund	Pension Liability
Bonds Payable	Petty Cash
Buildings	Prepaid Rent
Cash (in bank)	Purchase Returns and Allowances
Cash (on hand)	Purchases
Commission Expense	Retained Earnings
Copyrights	Salaries and Wages Expense (sales)
Delivery Expense	Salaries and Wages Payable
Dividends Payable	Sales Discounts
Equipment	Sales Revenue
Gain on Sale of Equipment	Share Capital—Ordinary
Interest Receivable	Share Capital—Preference
Inventory (beginning)	Share Premium—Ordinary
Inventory (ending)	Trading Securities
Land	Treasury Shares (at cost)
	Unearned Service Revenue

Instructions

Prepare a classified statement of financial position in good form. (No monetary amounts are to be shown.)

3 **P5-2 (Statement of Financial Position Preparation)** Presented below are a number of statement of financial position items for Montoya, Inc., for the current year, 2015.

Goodwill	€ 125,000	Accumulated depreciation—equipment	€ 292,000
Payroll taxes payable	177,591	Inventory	239,800
Bonds payable	285,000	Rent payable (short-term)	45,000
Cash	360,000	Income taxes payable	98,362
Land	480,000	Long-term rental obligations	480,000
Notes receivable	445,700	Share capital—ordinary, €1 par value	200,000
Notes payable (to banks)	265,000	Share capital—preference, €10 par value	150,000
Accounts payable	490,000	Prepaid expenses	87,920
Retained earnings	?	Equipment	1,470,000
Income taxes receivable	97,630	Trading securities	121,000
Unsecured notes payable (long-term)	1,600,000	Accumulated depreciation—buildings	270,200
		Buildings	1,640,000

Instructions

Prepare a classified statement of financial position in good form. Share capital—ordinary shares authorized was 400,000 shares, and share capital—preference shares authorized was 20,000 shares. Assume that notes receivable and notes payable are short-term, unless stated otherwise. Cost and fair value of trading securities are the same.

3 P5-3 (Statement of Financial Position Adjustment and Preparation) The adjusted trial balance of Asian-Pacific Company and other related information for the year 2015 are presented below (amounts in thousands).

ASIAN-PACIFIC COMPANY
ADJUSTED TRIAL BALANCE
DECEMBER 31, 2015

	Debit	Credit
Cash	¥ 41,000	
Accounts Receivable	163,500	
Allowance for Doubtful Accounts		¥ 8,700
Prepaid Insurance	5,900	
Inventory	208,500	
Long-term Investments	339,000	
Land	85,000	
Construction in Process	124,000	
Patents	36,000	
Equipment	400,000	
Accumulated Depreciation—Equipment		240,000
Accounts Payable		148,000
Accrued Expenses		49,200
Notes Payable		94,000
Bonds Payable		180,000
Share Capital—Ordinary		500,000
Share Premium—Ordinary		45,000
Retained Earnings		138,000
	¥1,402,900	¥1,402,900

Additional information:

1. The average-cost method of inventory value is used.

2. The cost and fair value of the long-term investments that consist of ordinary shares and bonds is the same.

3. The amount of the Construction in Process account represents the costs expended to date on a building in the process of construction. (The company rents factory space at the present time.) The land on which the building is being constructed cost ¥85,000, as shown in the trial balance.

4. The patents were purchased by the company at a cost of ¥40,000 and are being amortized on a straight-line basis.

5. The notes payable represent bank loans that are secured by long-term investments carried at ¥120,000. These bank loans are due in 2016.

6. The bonds payable bear interest at 8% payable every December 31, and are due January 1, 2026.

7. 600,000 ordinary shares with a par value of ¥1 were authorized, of which 500,000 shares were issued and outstanding.

Instructions

Prepare a statement of financial position as of December 31, 2015, so that all important information is fully disclosed.

3 P5-4 (Preparation of a Corrected Statement of Financial Position) Presented on the next page is the statement of financial position of Kishwaukee Corporation as of December 31, 2015.

KISHWAUKEE CORPORATION
STATEMENT OF FINANCIAL POSITION
DECEMBER 31, 2015

Assets

Goodwill (Note 1)	£ 120,000
Buildings	1,640,000
Inventory	312,100
Land	950,000
Accounts receivable	170,000
Treasury shares (50,000 shares)	87,000
Cash on hand	175,900
Assets allocated to trustee for plant expansion	
Cash in bank	70,000
Treasury notes, at cost and fair value	138,000
	£3,663,000

Equities

Notes payable (Note 2)	£ 600,000
Share capital—ordinary, authorized and issued,	
1,000,000 shares, no par	1,150,000
Retained earnings	858,000
Non-controlling interest	570,000
Income taxes payable	75,000
Accumulated depreciation—buildings	410,000
	£3,663,000

Note 1: Goodwill in the amount of £120,000 was recognized because the company believed that book value was not an accurate representation of the fair value of the company. The gain of £120,000 was credited to Retained Earnings.

Note 2: Notes payable are non-current except for the current installment due of £100,000.

Instructions
Prepare a corrected classified statement of financial position in good form. The notes above are for information only.

 P5-5 (Statement of Financial Position Adjustment and Preparation) Presented below is the statement of financial position of Sargent Corporation for the current year, 2015.

SARGENT CORPORATION
STATEMENT OF FINANCIAL POSITION
DECEMBER 31, 2015

Investments	$ 640,000	Equity	$1,770,000
Property, plant, and equipment	1,720,000	Non-current liabilities	960,000
Intangible assets	265,000	Current liabilities	380,000
Current assets	485,000		$3,110,000
	$3,110,000		

The following information is presented.

1. The current assets section includes cash $150,000, accounts receivable $170,000 less $10,000 for allowance for doubtful accounts, inventory $180,000, and unearned service revenue $5,000. Inventory is stated at the lower-of-FIFO-cost-or net realizable value.

2. The investments section includes land held for speculation $40,000; investments in ordinary shares, short-term (trading) $80,000 and long-term (non-trading) $270,000; and bond sinking fund $250,000. The cost and fair value of investments in ordinary shares are the same.

3. Property, plant, and equipment includes buildings $1,040,000 less accumulated depreciation $360,000, equipment $450,000 less accumulated depreciation $180,000, land $500,000, and land held for future use $270,000.

4. Intangible assets include a franchise $165,000 and goodwill $100,000.

5. Current liabilities include accounts payable $140,000; notes payable—short-term $80,000 and long-term $120,000; and income taxes payable $40,000.

6. Non-current liabilities are composed solely of 7% bonds payable due 2023.

7. Equity has share capital—preference, $5 par value, authorized 200,000 shares, issued 90,000 shares for $450,000; and share capital—ordinary, $1 par value, authorized 400,000 shares, issued 100,000 shares at an average price of $10. In addition, the corporation has retained earnings of $320,000.

Instructions

Prepare a statement of financial position in good form, adjusting the amounts in each statement of financial position classification as affected by the information given above.

P5-6 (Preparation of a Statement of Cash Flows and a Statement of Financial Position) Lansbury Inc. had the statement of financial position shown below at December 31, 2014.

LANSBURY INC.
STATEMENT OF FINANCIAL POSITION
DECEMBER 31, 2014

Investments	$ 32,000	Share capital—ordinary	$100,000
Plant assets (net)	81,000	Retained earnings	23,200
Land	40,000	Long-term notes payable	41,000
Accounts receivable	21,200	Accounts payable	30,000
Cash	20,000		$194,200
	$194,200		

During 2015, the following occurred.

1. Lansbury Inc. sold part of its investment portfolio for $15,000. This transaction resulted in a gain of $3,400 for the firm. The company classifies its investments as non-trading equity.

2. A tract of land was purchased for $18,000 cash.

3. Long-term notes payable in the amount of $16,000 were retired before maturity by paying $16,000 cash.

4. An additional $20,000 in ordinary shares were issued at par.

5. Dividends totalling $8,200 were declared and paid to shareholders.

6. Net income for 2015 was $32,000 after allowing for depreciation of $11,000.

7. Land was purchased through the issuance of $30,000 in bonds.

8. At December 31, 2015, Cash was $32,000, Accounts Receivable was $41,600, and Accounts Payable remained at $30,000.

Instructions

(a) Prepare a statement of cash flows for 2015.

(b) Prepare a statement of financial position as it would appear at December 31, 2015.

(c) How might the statement of cash flows help the user of the financial statements? Compute free cash flow and two cash flow ratios.

P5-7 (Preparation of a Statement of Cash Flows and Statement of Financial Position) Luo Inc. had the following statement of financial position at December 31, 2014 (amounts in thousands).

LUO INC.
STATEMENT OF FINANCIAL POSITION
DECEMBER 31, 2014

Investments	¥ 32,000	Share capital—ordinary	¥100,000
Plant assets (net)	81,000	Retained earnings	23,200
Land	40,000	Bonds payable	41,000
Accounts receivable	21,200	Accounts payable	30,000
Cash	20,000		¥194,200
	¥194,200		

During 2015, the following occurred.

1. Luo liquidated its non-trading equity investment portfolio at a loss of ¥5,000.

2. A tract of land was purchased for ¥38,000.

3. An additional ¥30,000 in ordinary shares were issued at par.

4. Dividends totaling ¥10,000 were declared and paid to shareholders.

5. Net income for 2015 was ¥35,000, including ¥12,000 in depreciation expense.

6. Land was purchased through the issuance of ¥30,000 in additional bonds.

7. At December 31, 2015, Cash was ¥70,200, Accounts Receivable was ¥42,000, and Accounts Payable was ¥40,000.

Instructions

(a) Prepare a statement of cash flows for the year 2015 for Luo.

(b) Prepare the statement of financial position as it would appear at December 31, 2015.

(c) Compute Luo's free cash flow and the current cash debt coverage for 2015.

(d) Use the analysis of Luo to illustrate how information in the statement of financial position and statement of cash flows helps the user of the financial statements.

CONCEPTS FOR ANALYSIS

CA5-1 (Reporting the Financial Effects of Varied Transactions) In an examination of Arenes Corporation as of December 31, 2015, you have learned that the following situations exist. No entries have been made in the accounting records for these items.

1. The corporation erected its present factory building in 2000. Depreciation was calculated by the straight-line method, using an estimated life of 35 years. Early in 2015, the board of directors conducted a careful survey and estimated that the factory building had a remaining useful life of 25 years as of January 1, 2015.

2. When calculating the accrual for officers' salaries at December 31, 2015, it was discovered that the accrual for officers' salaries for December 31, 2014, had been overstated.

3. On December 15, 2015, Arenes Corporation declared a cash dividend on its ordinary shares outstanding, payable February 1, 2016, to the shareholders of record December 31, 2015.

Instructions

Describe fully how each of the items above should be reported in the financial statements of Arenes Corporation for the year 2015.

CA5-2 (Current Asset and Liability Classification) Below are the titles of a number of debit and credit accounts as they might appear on the statement of financial position of Hayduke Corporation as of October 31, 2015.

Debit	Credit
Interest Accrued on Government Securities	Share Capital—Preference
Notes Receivable	6% First Mortgage Bonds, due in 2022
Petty Cash Fund	Preference Dividend, payable Nov. 1, 2015
Government Securities	Allowance for Doubtful Accounts
Treasury Shares	Income Taxes Payable
Cash in Bank	Customers' Advances (on contracts to be completed next year)
Land	Provision for Warranties
Inventory of Operating Parts and Supplies	Officers' 2015 Bonus Accrued
Inventory of Raw Materials	Accrued Payroll
Patents	Notes Payable
Cash and Government Bonds Set Aside for Property Additions	Accrued Interest on Bonds
Investment in Subsidiary	Accumulated Depreciation
Accounts Receivable:	Accounts Payable
Government Contracts	Share Premium—Preference
Regular	Accrued Interest on Notes Payable
Goodwill	6½% First Mortgage Bonds, due in 2015 out of current assets
Inventory of Finished Goods	Non-Controlling Interest
Inventory of Work in Process	Accumulated Other Comprehensive Income (loss)
Deficit	

Instructions

Select the current asset and current liability items from among these debit and credit accounts. If there appear to be certain borderline cases that you are unable to classify without further information, mention them and explain your difficulty, or give your reasons for making questionable classifications, if any.

CA5-3 (Identifying Statement of Financial Position Deficiencies) The assets of Fonzarelli Corporation are presented on the next page (amounts in thousands).

FONZARELLI CORPORATION
STATEMENT OF FINANCIAL POSITION (PARTIAL)
DECEMBER 31, 2015

Assets

Current assets		
Cash		€ 100,000
Non-controlling interest		27,500
Trading securities (fair value €30,000) at cost		37,000
Accounts receivable (less bad debt reserve)		75,000
Inventory—at lower-of-cost (determined by the first-in, first-out method)-or-net realizable value		240,000
Total current assets		479,500
Tangible assets		
Land (less accumulated depreciation)		80,000
Buildings and equipment	€800,000	
Less: Accumulated depreciation	250,000	550,000
Net tangible assets		630,000
Investments		
Bonds		100,000
Treasury shares		70,000
Total investments		170,000
Other assets		
Land held for future factory site		19,400
Sinking fund		975,000
Total other assets		994,400
Total assets		€2,273,900

Instructions

Indicate the deficiencies, if any, in the foregoing presentation of Fonzarelli Corporation's assets.

CA5-4 (Critique of Statement of Financial Position Format and Content) The following is the statement of financial position of Rasheed Brothers Corporation (amounts in thousands).

RASHEED BROTHERS CORPORATION
STATEMENT OF FINANCIAL POSITION
DECEMBER 31, 2015

Assets

Current assets		
Cash	$26,000	
Short-term investments	18,000	
Accounts receivable	25,000	
Inventory	20,000	
Supplies	4,000	
Investment in associated company	20,000	$113,000
Investments		
Treasury shares		25,000
Property, plant, and equipment		
Buildings and land	91,000	
Less: Accumulated depreciation	31,000	60,000
Other assets		
Cash restricted for plant expansion		19,000
Total assets		$217,000

Liabilities and Equity

Current liabilities		
Accounts payable	$22,000	
Income taxes payable	15,000	$ 37,000
Deferred credits		
Unrealized gains on non-trading equity investments		2,000
Non-current liabilities		
Bonds payable		60,000
Total liabilities		99,000

Equity		
Share capital—ordinary, par $5	85,000	
Retained earnings	25,000	
Cash dividends declared	8,000	118,000
Total liabilities and equity		$217,000

Instructions

Evaluate the statement of financial position presented. State briefly the proper treatment of any item criticized.

CA5-5 (Presentation of Property, Plant, and Equipment) Carol Keene, corporate comptroller for Dumaine Industries, is trying to decide how to present "Property, plant, and equipment" in the statement of financial position. She realizes that the statement of cash flows will show that the company made a significant investment in purchasing new equipment this year, but overall she knows the company's plant assets are rather old. She feels that she can disclose one figure titled "Property, plant, and equipment, net of depreciation," and the result will be a low figure. However, it will not disclose the age of the assets. If she chooses to show the cost less accumulated depreciation, the age of the assets will be apparent. She proposes the following.

Property, plant, and equipment, net of depreciation	£ 10,000,000
rather than	
Property, plant, and equipment	£ 50,000,000
Less: Accumulated depreciation	(40,000,000)
Net book value	£ 10,000,000

Instructions

Answer the following questions.

(a) What are the ethical issues involved?

(b) What should Keene do?

CA5-6 (Cash Flow Analysis) The partner in charge of the Kappeler Corporation audit comes by your desk and leaves a letter he has started to the CEO and a copy of the cash flow statement for the year ended December 31, 2015. Because he must leave on an emergency, he asks you to finish the letter by explaining (1) the disparity between net income and cash flow, (2) the importance of operating cash flow, (3) the renewable source(s) of cash flow, and (4) possible suggestions to improve the cash position.

KAPPELER CORPORATION
STATEMENT OF CASH FLOWS
FOR THE YEAR ENDED DECEMBER 31, 2015

Cash flows from operating activities		
Net income		$100,000
Adjustments to reconcile net income to net cash provided by operating activities:		
Depreciation expense	$ 10,000	
Amortization expense	1,000	
Loss on sale of fixed assets	5,000	
Increase in accounts receivable (net)	(40,000)	
Increase in inventory	(35,000)	
Decrease in accounts payable	(41,000)	(100,000)
Net cash provided by operating activities		–0–
Cash flows from investing activities		
Sale of plant assets	25,000	
Purchase of equipment	(100,000)	
Purchase of land	(200,000)	
Net cash used by investing activities		(275,000)
Cash flows from financing activities		
Payment of dividends	(10,000)	
Redemption of bonds	(100,000)	
Net cash used by financing activities		(110,000)
Net decrease in cash		(385,000)
Cash balance, January 1, 2015		400,000
Cash balance, December 31, 2015		$ 15,000

Date

President Kappeler, CEO
Kappeler Corporation
125 Wall Street
Middleton, Kansas 67458

Dear Mr. Kappeler:

I have good news and bad news about the financial statements for the year ended December 31, 2015. The good news is that net income of $100,000 is close to what you predicted in the strategic plan last year, indicating strong performance this year. The bad news is that the cash balance is seriously low. Enclosed is the Statement of Cash Flows, which best illustrates how both of these situations occurred simultaneously . . .

Instructions
Complete the letter to the CEO, including the four components requested by your boss.

USING YOUR JUDGMENT

FINANCIAL REPORTING

Financial Reporting Problem

Marks and Spencer plc (M&S)
The financial statements of M&S (GBR) are presented in Appendix A. The company's complete annual report, including the notes to the financial statements, is available online.

Instructions
Refer to M&S's financial statements and the accompanying notes to answer the following questions.

- **(a)** What alternative formats could M&S have adopted for its statement of financial position? Which format did it adopt?
- **(b)** In what classifications are M&S's investments reported? What valuation basis does M&S use to report its investments? How much working capital did M&S have on 30 March 2013? On 31 March 2012?
- **(c)** What were M&S's cash flows from its operating, investing, and financing activities for 2013? What were its trends in net cash provided by operating activities over the period 2012 to 2013? Explain why the change in accounts payable and in accrued and other liabilities is added to net income to arrive at net cash provided by operating activities.
- **(d)** Compute M&S's: (1) current cash debt coverage, (2) cash debt coverage, and (3) free cash flow for 2013. What do these ratios indicate about M&S's financial conditions?

Comparative Analysis Case

adidas and Puma
The financial statements of adidas (DEU) and Puma (DEU) are presented in Appendices B and C, respectively. The complete annual reports, including the notes to the financial statements, are available online.

Instructions
Use the companies' financial information to answer the following questions.

- **(a)** What format(s) did these companies use to present their statements of financial position?
- **(b)** How much working capital did each of these companies have at the end of 2012? Speculate as to their rationale for the amount of working capital they maintain.
- **(c)** What are some of the significant differences in the asset structure of the two companies? What causes these differences?
- **(d)** What were these two companies' trends in net cash provided by operating activities over the period 2011 to 2012?
- **(e)** Compute both companies': (1) current cash debt coverage, (2) cash debt coverage, and (3) free cash flow. What do these ratios indicate about the financial condition of the two companies?

Financial Statement Analysis Cases

Case 1 Cathay Pacific Airlines
Cathay Pacific Airways (HKG) is an international airline offering scheduled passenger and cargo services to 116 destinations in 35 countries and territories. The company was founded in Hong Kong in 1946 and

remains deeply committed to its home base, making substantial investments to develop Hong Kong as one of the world's leading global transportation hubs. In addition to the fleet of 123 wide-bodied aircraft, these investments include catering, aircraft maintenance, ground-handling companies, and the corporate. The following titles were shown on Cathay's statement of financial position in a recent year.

Current portion of long-term liabilities	Non-controlling interest
Deferred taxation	Net non-current assets
Fixed assets	Other long-term receivables and investments
Funds attributable to owners of Cathay Pacific	Reserves
	Retirement benefit obligations
Intangible assets	Share capital—ordinary
Investments in associates	Taxation
Liquid funds	Trade and other payables
Long-term liabilities	Trade and other receivables
	Unearned transportation revenue

Instructions

(a) Organize the accounts in the general order in which they would be presented in a classified statement of financial position.

(b) When Cathay passengers purchase tickets for travel on future flights, what statement of financial position accounts are most likely affected? Do the balances in these accounts decrease or increase?

Case 2 Christian Dior

Presented below is information reported by Christian Dior (FRA) related to its off-balance-sheet commitments in its 2011 annual report. Christian Dior reported current assets of €13,679 and total current liabilities of €10,256 at 31 December 2011. (All amounts are in millions of euros.)

Christian Dior
2011 Annual Report

Note 29 (in part) Off-balance-sheet commitments

Purchase commitments

As of December 31, 2011, the maturity dates of these commitments break down as follows:

	Less than 1 Year	1 to 5 Years	More than 5 Years	Total
Grapes, wines and distilled alcohol	540	414	65	1,019
Other purchase commitments for raw materials	81	3	—	84
Industrial and commercial fixed assets	85	38	31	154
Investments in joint venture shares and non-current financial assets	40	16	34	90

Operating leases and concession fees
The fixed or minimum portion of commitments in respect of operating lease or concession contracts over the irrevocable period of the contracts were as follows as of December 31, 2011:

	2011	2010	2009
Less than one year	1,158	943	907
One to five years	2,977	2,338	2,162
More than five years	1,300	1,049	967
Commitments given for operating leases and concession fees	**5,435**	**4,330**	**4,036**

Instructions

(a) Compute Christian Dior's working capital and current ratio (current assets ÷ current liabilities) with and without the off-balance-sheet items reported in Note 29.

(b) Briefly discuss how the information provided in the off-balance-sheet note would be useful in evaluating Christian Dior for loans (1) due in one year, and (2) due in five years.

Case 3 LG Korea

The incredible growth of LG Korea (KOR) has put fear into the hearts of competing appliance makers. The following financial information is taken from LG's financial statements.

(Korean won in billions)	Current Year	Prior Year
Current assets	₩30,517	₩24,297
Total assets	64,782	54,080
Current liabilities	28,110	21,136
Total liabilities	39,048	32,152
Cash provided by operations	10,217	8,807
Capital expenditures	8,190	5,071
Dividends paid	659	423
Net income (loss)	2,967	3,632
Sales	90,222	76,228

Instructions

(a) Calculate free cash flow for LG for the current and prior years, and discuss its ability to finance expansion from internally generated cash. Assume that LG's major capital expenditures related to building manufacturing plants and that to date it has avoided purchasing large warehouses. Instead, it has used those of others. It is possible, however, that in order to continue its growth in international sales, the company may have to build its own warehouses. If this happens, how might your impression of its ability to finance expansion change?

(b) Discuss any potential implications of the change in LG's cash provided by operations from the prior year to the current year.

International Reporting Case

 Presented below is the balance sheet (statement of financial position) for **Nordstrom, Inc.** (USA).

(in millions)	February 2, 2013		January 28, 2012	
Assets				
Current assets:				
Cash and cash equivalents	$1,285		$1,877	
Accounts receivable, net	2,129		2,033	
Merchandise inventories	1,360		1,148	
Current deferred tax assets, net	227		220	
Prepaid expenses and other	80		282	
Total current assets		$5,081		$5,560
Land, buildings and equipment, net		2,579		2,469
Goodwill		175		175
Other assets		254		287
Total assets		**$8,089**		**$8,491**
Liabilities and Shareholders' Equity				
Current liabilities:				
Accounts payable	$1,011		$ 917	
Accrued salaries, wages and related benefits	404		388	
Other current liabilities	804		764	
Current portion of long-term debt	7		506	
Total current liabilities		$2,226		$2,575
Long-term debt, net		3,124		3,141
Deferred property incentives, net		485		500
Other liabilities		341		319
Commitments and contingencies				
Shareholders' equity:				
Common stock, no par value: 1,000 shares authorized 197.0 and 207.6 shares issued and outstanding	1,645		1,484	
Retained earnings	315		517	
Accumulated other comprehensive loss	(47)		(45)	
Total shareholders' equity		1,913		1,956
Total liabilities and shareholders' equity		**$8,089**		**$8,491**

Instructions

(a) Identify at least three differences in statement of financial position reporting between IFRS and U.S. GAAP, as shown in Nordstrom's balance sheet.

(b) Review Nordstrom's balance sheet and identify how the format of this financial statement provides useful information, as illustrated in the chapter.

Accounting, Analysis, and Principles

Early in January 2016, Hopkins Company is preparing for a meeting with its bankers to discuss a loan request. Its bookkeeper provided the following accounts and balances at December 31, 2015.

	Debit	Credit
Inventory	£ 65,300	
Accounts Receivable (net)	38,500	
Cash	75,000	
Equipment (net)	84,000	
Patents	15,000	
Notes and Accounts Payable		£ 52,000
Notes Payable (due 2017)		75,000
Share Capital—Ordinary		100,000
Retained Earnings		50,800
	£277,800	£277,800

Except for the following items, Hopkins has recorded all adjustments in its accounts.

1. Net accounts receivable is comprised of £52,000 in accounts receivable and £13,500 in allowance for doubtful accounts.

2. Cash includes £500 petty cash and £15,000 in a bond sinking fund.

3. Equipment had a cost of £112,000 and accumulated depreciation of £28,000.

4. On January 8, 2016, one of Hopkins' customers declared bankruptcy. At December 31, 2015, this customer owed Hopkins £9,000.

Accounting

Prepare a corrected December 31, 2015, statement of financial position for Hopkins Company.

Analysis

Hopkins' bank is considering granting an additional loan in the amount of £45,000, which will be due December 31, 2016. How can the information in the statement of financial position provide useful information to the bank about Hopkins' ability to repay the loan?

Principles

In the upcoming meeting with the bank, Hopkins plans to provide additional information about the fair value of its equipment and some internally generated intangible assets related to its customer lists. This information indicates that Hopkins has significant unrealized gains on these assets, which are not reflected on the statement of financial position. What objections are the bank likely to raise about the usefulness of this information in evaluating Hopkins for the loan renewal?

IFRS BRIDGE TO THE PROFESSION

Professional Research

In light of the full disclosure principle, investors and creditors need to know the balances for assets, liabilities, and equity, as well as the accounting policies adopted by management to measure the items reported in the statement of financial position.

Instructions

Access the IFRS authoritative literature at the IASB website (*http://eifrs.iasb.org/*) (you may register for free eIFRS access at the site). When you have accessed the documents, you can use the search tool in your Internet browser to respond to the following questions. (Provide paragraph citations.)

(a) Identify the literature that addresses the disclosure of accounting policies.

(b) How are accounting policies defined in the literature?

(c) What are the guidelines concerning consistency in applying accounting policies?

(d) What are some examples of common disclosures that are required under this statement?

Professional Simulation

In this simulation, you are asked to address questions related to the statement of financial position. Prepare responses to all parts.

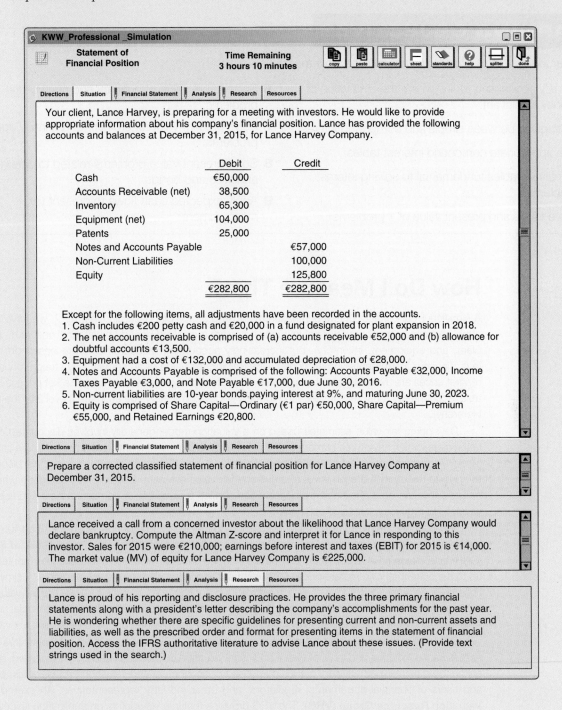

KWW_Professional _Simulation

| **Statement of Financial Position** | **Time Remaining** 3 hours 10 minutes | copy | paste | calculator | sheet | standards | help | splitter | done |

Directions | Situation | Financial Statement | Analysis | Research | Resources

Your client, Lance Harvey, is preparing for a meeting with investors. He would like to provide appropriate information about his company's financial position. Lance has provided the following accounts and balances at December 31, 2015, for Lance Harvey Company.

	Debit	Credit
Cash	€50,000	
Accounts Receivable (net)	38,500	
Inventory	65,300	
Equipment (net)	104,000	
Patents	25,000	
Notes and Accounts Payable		€57,000
Non-Current Liabilities		100,000
Equity		125,800
	€282,800	€282,800

Except for the following items, all adjustments have been recorded in the accounts.
1. Cash includes €200 petty cash and €20,000 in a fund designated for plant expansion in 2018.
2. The net accounts receivable is comprised of (a) accounts receivable €52,000 and (b) allowance for doubtful accounts €13,500.
3. Equipment had a cost of €132,000 and accumulated depreciation of €28,000.
4. Notes and Accounts Payable is comprised of the following: Accounts Payable €32,000, Income Taxes Payable €3,000, and Note Payable €17,000, due June 30, 2016.
5. Non-current liabilities are 10-year bonds paying interest at 9%, and maturing June 30, 2023.
6. Equity is comprised of Share Capital—Ordinary (€1 par) €50,000, Share Capital—Premium €55,000, and Retained Earnings €20,800.

Directions | Situation | Financial Statement | Analysis | Research | Resources

Prepare a corrected classified statement of financial position for Lance Harvey Company at December 31, 2015.

Directions | Situation | Financial Statement | Analysis | Research | Resources

Lance received a call from a concerned investor about the likelihood that Lance Harvey Company would declare bankruptcy. Compute the Altman Z-score and interpret it for Lance in responding to this investor. Sales for 2015 were €210,000; earnings before interest and taxes (EBIT) for 2015 is €14,000. The market value (MV) of equity for Lance Harvey Company is €225,000.

Directions | Situation | Financial Statement | Analysis | Research | Resources

Lance is proud of his reporting and disclosure practices. He provides the three primary financial statements along with a president's letter describing the company's accomplishments for the past year. He is wondering whether there are specific guidelines for presenting current and non-current assets and liabilities, as well as the prescribed order and format for presenting items in the statement of financial position. Access the IFRS authoritative literature to advise Lance about these issues. (Provide text strings used in the search.)

Accounting and the Time Value of Money

LEARNING OBJECTIVES

After studying this chapter, you should be able to:

1 Identify accounting topics where the time value of money is relevant.

2 Distinguish between simple and compound interest.

3 Use appropriate compound interest tables.

4 Identify variables fundamental to solving interest problems.

5 Solve future and present value of 1 problems.

6 Solve future value of ordinary and annuity due problems.

7 Solve present value of ordinary and annuity due problems.

8 Solve present value problems related to deferred annuities and bonds.

9 Apply expected cash flows to present value measurement.

How Do I Measure That?

A significant part of accounting is measurement. And as we discussed in Chapter 2, we have a mixed-attribute measurement model. That is, many items are measured based on historical cost (e.g., property, plant, and equipment, inventory), but increasingly accounting measurements are based on fair value (e.g., financial instruments, impairments). Determining fair value of an item is fairly straightforward when market prices are available (Level 1 in the fair value hierarchy). However, when a market price is not available, accountants must rely on valuation models to develop a fair value estimate (Level 3 of the fair value hierarchy).

Developing fair value estimates based on a valuation model generally involves discounted cash flow techniques, which have three primary elements: (1) estimating the amounts and timing of future cash flows, (2) developing probability estimates for those cash flows, and (3) determining the appropriate discount rate to apply to the expected cash flows to arrive at a fair value estimate. Seems pretty straightforward, right? Actually, this can be a challenging process when applied to a variety of complex assets and liabilities for which IFRS requires a fair value estimate.

For example, many European financial institutions faced this challenge when they had to deal with losses on Greek bond holdings. Major banks, such as **Crédit Agricole** (FRA), **Royal Bank of Scotland** (GBR), and **Dexia** (FRA–BEL), and many others incurred substantial losses after securities markets seized up to the point that valid market prices for investment and loans were not readily available. A similar valuation challenge arose for companies with investments in auction rates securities (ARS). The fair value of ARS is generally determined at quarterly auctions. However, these auctions failed during the financial crisis, and ARS investors were forced to use a valuation model rather than market prices to determine fair value.

The IASB provides fair value estimation guidance (*IFRS 13*), but the Board also performs ongoing assessment of whether and to what extent additional valuation guidance is needed. In this regard, standard-setters have established advisory groups comprised of accounting and valuation professionals, preparers and users of financial statements, regulators, and other industry representatives. An example is the **Valuation Resource Group (VRG)**. The VRG provides multiple viewpoints on application issues relating to fair value for financial reporting purposes. Here is a sampling of the issues discussed by the VRG:

- Measurement of contingent consideration in a business combination.
- Incorporating multi-period excess earnings in valuing intangible assets.
- Effects of premiums and discounts in fair value measurements.

- Determining the carrying amount of a reporting unit when performing the goodwill impairment test.
- Measurement uncertainty analysis disclosures.

As indicated, the list of topics is revealing as to the variety and complexity of the issues that must be addressed in implementing the fair value measurement principle. Discussion of these items by the VRG helped develop appropriate approaches for applying fair value guidance to specific examples. For example, with respect to the contingent consideration topic, the VRG noted that taxes must be considered when developing future cash flow estimates and that, in some cases, these tax effects are different for assets and liabilities.

The VRG provides good counsel to the standard-setters with respect to applying the fair value measurement principle. After studying this chapter, you should have a better understanding of time value of money principles and discounted cash flow techniques as they are applied in accounting measurements.

Sources: Ernst and Young, "Valuation Resource Group: Highlights of November 2010 Meeting," *Hot Topic—Update on Major Accounting and Auditing Activities, No. 2010-59* (5 November 2010).

CONCEPTUAL FOCUS

> See the **Underlying Concepts** on page 240.

INTERNATIONAL FOCUS

> The time value of money concept is universal and applied the same, regardless of whether a company follows IFRS or U.S. GAAP.

PREVIEW OF CHAPTER   6

As we indicated in the opening story, as a financial expert in today's accounting environment, you will be expected to make present and future value measurements and to understand their implications. The purpose of this chapter is to present the tools and techniques that will help you measure the present value of future cash inflows and outflows. The content and organization of the chapter are as follows.

Accounting and the Time Value of Money

Basic Time Value Concepts	Single-Sum Problems	Annuities	More Complex Situations	Present Value Measurement
• Applications • The nature of interest • Simple interest • Compound interest • Fundamental variables	• Future value of a single sum • Present value of a single sum • Solving for other unknowns	• Future value of ordinary annuity • Future value of annuity due • Examples of FV of annuity • Present value of ordinary annuity • Present value of annuity due • Examples of PV of annuity	• Deferred annuities • Valuation of long-term bonds • Effective-interest method of bond discount/premium amortization	• Choosing an appropriate interest rate • Example of expected cash flow

BASIC TIME VALUE CONCEPTS

LEARNING OBJECTIVE 1

Identify accounting topics where the time value of money is relevant.

In accounting (and finance), the phrase **time value of money** indicates a relationship between time and money—that a dollar received today is worth more than a dollar promised at some time in the future. Why? Because of the opportunity to invest today's dollar and receive interest on the investment. Yet, when deciding among investment or borrowing alternatives, it is essential to be able to compare today's dollar and tomorrow's dollar on the same footing—to "compare apples to apples." Investors do that by using the concept of **present value**, which has many applications in accounting.

Applications of Time Value Concepts

 Underlying Concepts

The time value of money is a fundamental element of any present value technique.

I F R S

See the Authoritative Literature section (page 270).

Financial reporting uses different measurements in different situations—historical cost for equipment, net realizable value for inventories, fair value for investments. As we discussed in Chapter 2, the IASB increasingly is requiring the use of fair values in the measurement of assets and liabilities. According to the IASB's recent guidance on fair value measurements, the most useful fair value measures are based on market prices in active markets. Within the fair value hierarchy, these are referred to as Level 1. Recall that Level 1 fair value measures are the most reliable because they are based on quoted prices, such as a closing share price.

However, for many assets and liabilities, market-based fair value information is not readily available. In these cases, fair value can be estimated based on the expected future cash flows related to the asset or liability. Such fair value estimates are generally considered Level 3 (least reliable) in the fair value hierarchy because they are based on unobservable inputs, such as a company's own data or assumptions related to the expected future cash flows associated with the asset or liability. As discussed in the fair value guidance, present value techniques are used to convert expected cash flows into present values, which represent an estimate of fair value. **[1]**

Because of the increased use of present values in this and other contexts, it is important to understand present value techniques.[1] We list some of the applications of present value-based measurements to accounting topics below; we discuss many of these in the following chapters.

PRESENT VALUE-BASED ACCOUNTING MEASUREMENTS

1. **NOTES.** Valuing long-term receivables and payables that carry no stated interest rate or a lower than market interest rate.

2. **LEASES.** Valuing assets and obligations to be capitalized under long-term leases and measuring the amount of the lease payments and annual leasehold amortization.

3. **PENSIONS AND OTHER POSTRETIREMENT BENEFITS.** Measuring service cost components of employers' postretirement benefits expense and postretirement benefits obligation.

4. **LONG-TERM ASSETS.** Evaluating alternative long-term investments by discounting future cash flows. Determining the value of assets acquired under deferred payment contracts. Measuring impairments of assets.

[1]IFRS addresses present value as a measurement basis for a broad array of transactions, such as accounts and loans receivable **[2]**, leases **[3]**, postretirement benefits **[4]**, asset impairments **[5]**, and share-based compensation **[6]**.

5. SHARE-BASED COMPENSATION. Determining the fair value of employee services in compensatory share-option plans.

6. BUSINESS COMBINATIONS. Determining the value of receivables, payables, liabilities, accruals, and commitments acquired or assumed in a "purchase."

7. DISCLOSURES. Measuring the value of future cash flows from oil and gas reserves for disclosure in supplementary information.

8. ENVIRONMENTAL LIABILITIES. Determining the fair value of future obligations for asset retirements.

In addition to accounting and business applications, compound interest, annuity, and present value concepts apply to personal finance and investment decisions. In purchasing a home or car, planning for retirement, and evaluating alternative investments, you will need to understand time value of money concepts.

The Nature of Interest

Interest is payment for the use of money. It is the excess cash received or repaid over and above the amount lent or borrowed (**principal**). For example, Corner Bank lends Hillfarm Company $10,000 with the understanding that it will repay $11,500. The excess over $10,000, or $1,500, represents interest expense.

The lender generally states the amount of interest as a rate over a specific period of time. For example, if Hillfarm borrowed $10,000 for one year before repaying $11,500, the rate of interest is 15% per year ($1,500 ÷ $10,000). The custom of expressing interest as a percentage rate is an established business practice.[2] In fact, business managers make investing and borrowing decisions on the basis of the rate of interest involved, rather than on the actual dollar amount of interest to be received or paid.

How is the interest rate determined? One important factor is the level of credit risk (risk of non-payment) involved. Other factors being equal, the higher the credit risk, the higher the interest rate. Low-risk borrowers like **Nokia** (FIN) or **adidas** (DEU) can probably obtain a loan at or slightly below the going market rate of interest. However, a bank would probably charge the neighborhood bakery several percentage points above the market rate, if granting the loan at all.

The amount of interest involved in any financing transaction is a function of three variables:

VARIABLES IN INTEREST COMPUTATION

1. PRINCIPAL. The amount borrowed or invested.

2. INTEREST RATE. A percentage of the outstanding principal.

3. TIME. The number of years or fractional portion of a year that the principal is outstanding.

Thus, the following three relationships apply:

- The larger the principal amount, the larger the dollar amount of interest.
- The higher the interest rate, the larger the dollar amount of interest.
- The longer the time period, the larger the dollar amount of interest.

---

[2]Many regulatory frameworks require the disclosure of interest rates on an annual basis in all contracts. That is, instead of stating the rate as "1% per month," contracts must state the rate as "12% per year" if it is simple interest or "12.68% per year" if it is compounded monthly.

Simple Interest

Companies compute **simple interest** on the amount of the principal only. It is the return on (or growth of) the principal for one time period. The following equation expresses simple interest.[3]

$$\text{Interest} = p \times i \times n$$

where

p = principal

i = rate of interest for a single period

n = number of periods

To illustrate, Barstow Electric Inc. borrows $10,000 for 3 years with a simple interest rate of 8% per year. It computes the total interest it will pay as follows.

$$\begin{aligned}
\text{Interest} &= p \times i \times n \\
&= \$10,000 \times .08 \times 3 \\
&= \$2,400
\end{aligned}$$

If Barstow borrows $10,000 for 3 months at 8%, the interest is $200, computed as follows.

$$\begin{aligned}
\text{Interest} &= \$10,000 \times .08 \times 3/12 \\
&= \$200
\end{aligned}$$

Compound Interest

John Maynard Keynes, the legendary English economist, supposedly called it magic. Mayer Rothschild, the founder of the famous European banking firm, proclaimed it the eighth wonder of the world. Today, people continue to extol its wonder and its power. The object of their affection? Compound interest.

We compute **compound interest** on principal **and** on any interest earned that has not been paid or withdrawn. It is the return on (or growth of) the principal for two or more time periods. Compounding computes interest not only on the principal but also on the interest earned to date on that principal, assuming the interest is left on deposit.

To illustrate the difference between simple and compound interest, assume that Vasquez Company deposits $10,000 in the Last National Bank, where it will earn simple interest of 9% per year. It deposits another $10,000 in the First State Bank, where it will earn compound interest of 9% per year compounded annually. In both cases, Vasquez will not withdraw any interest until 3 years from the date of deposit. Illustration 6-1 shows the computation of interest Vasquez will receive, as well as its accumulated year-end balance.

ILLUSTRATION 6-1
Simple vs. Compound Interest

Last National Bank				First State Bank		
Simple Interest Calculation	Simple Interest	Accumulated Year-End Balance		Compound Interest Calculation	Compound Interest	Accumulated Year-End Balance
Year 1 $10,000.00 × 9%	$ 900.00	$10,900.00		Year 1 $10,000.00 × 9%	$ 900.00	$10,900.00
Year 2 $10,000.00 × 9%	900.00	$11,800.00		Year 2 $10,900.00 × 9%	981.00	$11,881.00
Year 3 $10,000.00 × 9%	900.00	$12,700.00		Year 3 $11,881.00 × 9%	1,069.29	$12,950.29
	$2,700.00				$2,950.29	

$250.29 Difference

[3]Business mathematics and business finance textbooks traditionally state simple interest as I (interest) $= P$ (principal) $\times R$ (rate) $\times T$ (time).

Note in Illustration 6-1 that simple interest uses the initial principal of $10,000 to compute the interest in all 3 years. **Compound interest uses the accumulated balance (principal plus interest to date) at each year-end to compute interest in the succeeding year.** This explains the larger balance in the compound interest account.

Obviously, any rational investor would choose compound interest, if available, over simple interest. In the example above, compounding provides $250.29 of additional interest revenue. For practical purposes, compounding assumes that unpaid interest earned becomes a part of the principal. Furthermore, the accumulated balance at the end of each year becomes the new principal sum on which interest is earned during the next year.

Compound interest is the typical interest computation applied in business situations. This occurs particularly in our economy, where companies use and finance large amounts of long-lived assets over long periods of time. Financial managers view and evaluate their investment opportunities in terms of a series of periodic returns, each of which they can reinvest to yield additional returns. Simple interest usually applies only to short-term investments and debts that involve a time span of one year or less.

What do the numbers mean?   *A PRETTY GOOD START*

The continuing debate by governments as to how to provide retirement benefits to their citizens serves as a great context to illustrate the power of compounding. One proposed idea is for the government to give $1,000 to every citizen at birth. This gift would be deposited in an account that would earn interest tax-free until the citizen retires. Assuming the account earns a 5% annual return until retirement at age 65, the $1,000 would grow to $23,839. With monthly compounding, the $1,000 deposited at birth would grow to $25,617.

Why start so early? If the government waited until age 18 to deposit the money, it would grow to only $9,906 with annual compounding. That is, reducing the time invested by a third results in more than a 50% reduction in retirement money. This example illustrates the importance of starting early when the power of compounding is involved.

Compound Interest Tables (see pages 284–293)

We present five different types of compound interest tables at the end of this chapter. These tables should help you study this chapter as well as solve other problems involving interest.

INTEREST TABLES AND THEIR CONTENTS

1. **FUTURE VALUE OF 1** *TABLE.* Contains the amounts to which 1 will accumulate if deposited now at a specified rate and left for a specified number of periods (Table 6-1).

2. **PRESENT VALUE OF 1** *TABLE.* Contains the amounts that must be deposited now at a specified rate of interest to equal 1 at the end of a specified number of periods (Table 6-2).

3. **FUTURE VALUE OF AN ORDINARY ANNUITY OF 1** *TABLE.* Contains the amounts to which periodic rents of 1 will accumulate if the payments (rents) are invested at the **end** of each period at a specified rate of interest for a specified number of periods (Table 6-3).

4. **PRESENT VALUE OF AN ORDINARY ANNUITY OF 1** *TABLE.* Contains the amounts that must be deposited now at a specified rate of interest to permit withdrawals of 1 at the **end** of regular periodic intervals for the specified number of periods (Table 6-4).

5. **PRESENT VALUE OF AN ANNUITY DUE OF 1** *TABLE.* Contains the amounts that must be deposited now at a specified rate of interest to permit withdrawals of 1 at the **beginning** of regular periodic intervals for the specified number of periods (Table 6-5).

Illustration 6-2 presents the general format and content of these tables. It shows how much principal plus interest a dollar accumulates to at the end of each of five periods, at three different rates of compound interest.

ILLUSTRATION 6-2
Excerpt from Table 6-1

	FUTURE VALUE OF 1 AT COMPOUND INTEREST (EXCERPT FROM TABLE 6-1, PAGE 285)		
Period	9%	10%	11%
1	1.09000	1.10000	1.11000
2	1.18810	1.21000	1.23210
3	1.29503	1.33100	1.36763
4	1.41158	1.46410	1.51807
5	1.53862	1.61051	1.68506

The compound tables rely on basic formulas. For example, the formula to determine the future value factor (*FVF*) for 1 is:

$$FVF_{n,i} = (1 + i)^n$$

where

$FVF_{n,i}$ = future value factor for n periods at i interest

n = number of periods

i = rate of interest for a single period

Financial calculators include preprogrammed $FVF_{n,i}$ and other time value of money formulas.

To illustrate the use of interest tables to calculate compound amounts, assume an interest rate of 9%. Illustration 6-3 shows the future value to which 1 accumulates (the future value factor).

ILLUSTRATION 6-3
Accumulation of
Compound Amounts

Period	Beginning-of-Period Amount	×	Multiplier (1 + i)	=	End-of-Period Amount*	Formula (1 + i)ⁿ
1	1.00000		1.09		1.09000	$(1.09)^1$
2	1.09000		1.09		1.18810	$(1.09)^2$
3	1.18810		1.09		1.29503	$(1.09)^3$

*Note that these amounts appear in Table 6-1 in the 9% column.

Throughout our discussion of compound interest tables, note the intentional use of the term **periods** instead of **years**. Interest is generally expressed in terms of an annual rate. However, many business circumstances dictate a compounding period of less than one year. In such circumstances, a company must convert the annual interest rate to correspond to the length of the period. To convert the "annual interest rate" into the "compounding period interest rate," a company **divides the annual rate by the number of compounding periods per year**.

In addition, companies determine the number of periods by **multiplying the number of years involved by the number of compounding periods per year**. To illustrate, assume an investment of $1 for 6 years at 8% annual interest compounded **quarterly**. Using Table 6-1, page 284, read the factor that appears in the 2% column on the 24th row—6 years × 4 compounding periods per year, namely 1.60844, or approximately $1.61. Thus, all compound interest tables use the term **periods**, not **years**, to express the quantity of *n*. Illustration 6-4 shows how to determine (1) the interest rate per compounding period and (2) the number of compounding periods in four situations of differing compounding frequency.[4]

12% Annual Interest Rate over 5 Years Compounded	Interest Rate per Compounding Period	Number of Compounding Periods
Annually (1)	$.12 \div 1 = .12$	5 years × 1 compounding per year = 5 periods
Semiannually (2)	$.12 \div 2 = .06$	5 years × 2 compoundings per year = 10 periods
Quarterly (4)	$.12 \div 4 = .03$	5 years × 4 compoundings per year = 20 periods
Monthly (12)	$.12 \div 12 = .01$	5 years × 12 compoundings per year = 60 periods

ILLUSTRATION 6-4
Frequency of Compounding

How often interest is compounded can substantially affect the rate of return. For example, a 9% annual interest compounded **daily** provides a 9.42% yield, or a difference of 0.42%. The 9.42% is the **effective yield**.[5] The annual interest rate (9%) is the **stated, nominal,** or **face rate**. When the compounding frequency is greater than once a year, the effective-interest rate will always exceed the stated rate.

Illustration 6-5 shows how compounding for five different time periods affects the effective yield and the amount earned by an investment of $10,000 for one year.

Interest Rate	Compounding Periods				
	Annually	Semiannually	Quarterly	Monthly	Daily
8%	8.00% $800	8.16% $816	8.24% $824	8.30% $830	8.33% $833
9%	9.00% $900	9.20% $920	9.31% $931	9.38% $938	9.42% $942
10%	10.00% $1,000	10.25% $1,025	10.38% $1,038	10.47% $1,047	10.52% $1,052

ILLUSTRATION 6-5
Comparison of Different Compounding Periods

[4]Because interest is theoretically earned (accruing) every second of every day, it is possible to calculate interest that is **compounded continuously**. Using the natural, or Napierian, system of logarithms facilitates computations involving continuous compounding. As a practical matter, however, most business transactions assume interest to be compounded no more frequently than daily.

[5]The formula for calculating the **effective rate**, in situations where the compounding frequency (*n*) is greater than once a year, is as follows.

$$\text{Effective rate} = (1 + i)^n - 1$$

To illustrate, if the stated annual rate is 8% compounded quarterly (or 2% per quarter), the effective annual rate is:

$$\text{Effective rate} = (1 + .02)^4 - 1$$
$$= (1.02)^4 - 1$$
$$= 1.0824 - 1$$
$$= .0824$$
$$= 8.24\%$$

Fundamental Variables

The following four variables are fundamental to all compound interest problems.

FUNDAMENTAL VARIABLES

1. **RATE OF INTEREST.** This rate, unless otherwise stated, is an annual rate that must be adjusted to reflect the length of the compounding period if less than a year.
2. **NUMBER OF TIME PERIODS.** This is the number of compounding periods. (A period may be equal to or less than a year.)
3. **FUTURE VALUE.** The value at a future date of a given sum or sums invested assuming compound interest.
4. **PRESENT VALUE.** The value now (present time) of a future sum or sums discounted assuming compound interest.

Illustration 6-6 depicts the relationship of these four fundamental variables in a **time diagram**.

ILLUSTRATION 6-6
Basic Time Diagram

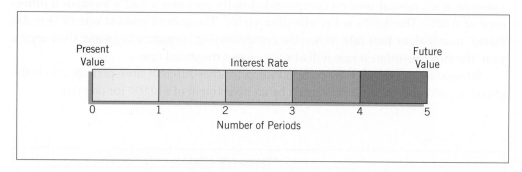

In some cases, all four of these variables are known. However, at least one variable is unknown in many business situations. To better understand and solve the problems in this chapter, we encourage you to sketch compound interest problems in the form of the preceding time diagram.

SINGLE-SUM PROBLEMS

Many business and investment decisions involve a single amount of money that either exists now or will in the future. Single-sum problems are generally classified into one of the following two categories.

1. Computing the **unknown** future value of a known single sum of money that is invested now for a certain number of periods at a certain interest rate.
2. Computing the **unknown** present value of a known single sum of money in the future that is discounted for a certain number of periods at a certain interest rate.

When analyzing the information provided, determine first whether the problem involves a future value or a present value. Then apply the following general rules, depending on the situation:

- **If solving for a future value,** *accumulate* all cash flows to a future point. In this instance, interest increases the amounts or values over time so that the future value exceeds the present value.

• **If solving for a present value**, *discount* all cash flows from the future to the present. In this case, **discounting** reduces the amounts or values, so that the present value is less than the future amount.

Preparation of time diagrams aids in identifying the unknown as an item in the future or the present. Sometimes the problem involves neither a future value nor a present value. Instead, the unknown is the interest or discount rate, or the number of compounding or discounting periods.

Future Value of a Single Sum

To determine the **future value** of a single sum, multiply the future value factor by its present value (principal), as follows.

$$FV = PV\,(FVF_{n,i})$$

where

FV = future value

PV = present value (principal or single sum)

$FVF_{n,i}$ = future value factor for n periods at i interest

To illustrate, Bruegger Co. wants to determine the future value of €50,000 invested for 5 years compounded annually at an interest rate of 11%. Illustration 6-7 shows this investment situation in time-diagram form.

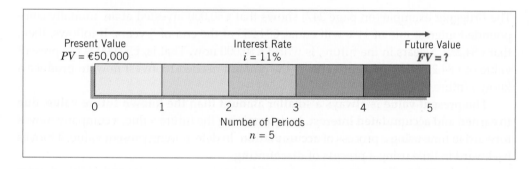

ILLUSTRATION 6-7
Future Value Time
Diagram ($n = 5, i = 11\%$)

Using the future value formula, Bruegger solves this investment problem as follows.

$$\text{Future value} = PV\,(FVF_{n,i})$$
$$= €50,000\,(FVF_{5,11\%})$$
$$= €50,000\,(1 + .11)^5$$
$$= €50,000\,(1.68506)$$
$$= €84,253$$

To determine the future value factor of 1.68506 in the formula above, Bruegger uses a financial calculator or reads the appropriate table, in this case Table 6-1 (11% column, 5-period row).

Companies can apply this time diagram and formula approach to routine business situations. To illustrate, assume that **Shanghai Electric Power** (CHN) deposited ¥250 million in an escrow account with **Industrial and Commercial Bank of China** (CHN) at the beginning of 2015 as a commitment toward a power plant to be completed December 31, 2018. How much will the company have on deposit at the end of 4 years if interest is 10%, compounded semiannually?

With a known present value of ¥250 million, a total of 8 compounding periods (4 × 2), and an interest rate of 5% per compounding period (.10 ÷ 2), the company can time-diagram this problem and determine the future value, as shown in Illustration 6-8.

ILLUSTRATION 6-8
Future Value Time
Diagram ($n = 8$, $i = 5\%$)

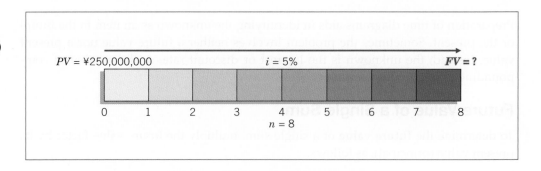

$$\text{Future value} = \yen250{,}000{,}000\ (FVF_{8,5\%})$$
$$= \yen250{,}000{,}000\ (1 + .05)^8$$
$$= \yen250{,}000{,}000\ (1.47746)$$
$$= \yen369{,}365{,}000$$

Using a future value factor found in Table 1 (5% column, 8-period row), we find that the deposit of ¥250 million will accumulate to ¥369,365,000 by December 31, 2018.

Present Value of a Single Sum

The Bruegger example (on page 247) shows that €50,000 invested at an annually compounded interest rate of 11% will equal €84,253 at the end of 5 years. It follows, then, that €84,253, 5 years in the future, is worth €50,000 now. That is, €50,000 is the present value of €84,253. The **present value** is the amount needed to invest now, to produce a known future value.

The present value is always a smaller amount than the known future value, due to earned and accumulated interest. In determining the future value, a company moves forward in time using a process of **accumulation**. In determining present value, it moves backward in time using a process of **discounting**.

As indicated earlier, a "present value of 1 table" appears at the end of this chapter as Table 6-2. Illustration 6-9 demonstrates the nature of such a table. It shows the present value of 1 for five different periods at three different rates of interest.

ILLUSTRATION 6-9
Excerpt from Table 6-2

	PRESENT VALUE OF 1 AT COMPOUND INTEREST (EXCERPT FROM TABLE 6-2, PAGE 287)		
Period	9%	10%	11%
1	0.91743	0.90909	0.90090
2	0.84168	0.82645	0.81162
3	0.77218	0.75132	0.73119
4	0.70843	0.68301	0.65873
5	0.64993	0.62092	0.59345

The following formula is used to determine the present value of 1 (present value factor).

$$PVF_{n,i} = \frac{1}{(1 + i)^n}$$

where

$$PVF_{n,i} = \text{present value factor for } n \text{ periods at } i \text{ interest}$$

To illustrate, assuming an interest rate of 9%, the present value of 1 discounted for three different periods is as shown in Illustration 6-10.

Discount Periods	$\frac{1}{}$	$\div$	$(1 + i)^n$	$=$	Present Value*	Formula $1/(1 + i)^n$
1	1.00000		1.09		.91743	$1/(1.09)^1$
2	1.00000		$(1.09)^2$		.84168	$1/(1.09)^2$
3	1.00000		$(1.09)^3$		.77218	$1/(1.09)^3$

*Note that these amounts appear in Table 6-2 in the 9% column.

ILLUSTRATION 6-10
Present Value of 1 Discounted at 9% for Three Periods

The present value of any single sum (future value), then, is as follows.

$$PV = FV\,(PVF_{n,i})$$

where

PV = present value

FV = future value

$PVF_{n,i}$ = present value factor for n periods at i interest

To illustrate, what is the present value of €84,253 to be received or paid in 5 years discounted at 11% compounded annually? Illustration 6-11 shows this problem as a time diagram.

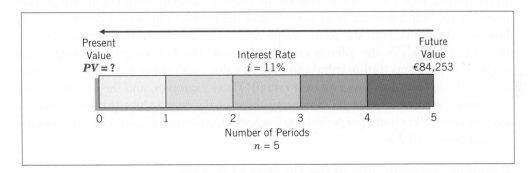

ILLUSTRATION 6-11
Present Value Time Diagram ($n = 5$, $i = 11\%$)

Using the formula, we solve this problem as follows.

$$\textbf{Present value} = FV\,(PVF_{n,i})$$
$$= €84{,}253\,(PVF_{5,11\%})$$
$$= €84{,}253 \left(\frac{1}{(1 + .11)^5} \right)$$
$$= €84{,}253\,(.59345)$$
$$= €50{,}000$$

To determine the present value factor of 0.59345, use a financial calculator or read the present value of a single sum in Table 6-2 (11% column, 5-period row).

The time diagram and formula approach can be applied in a variety of situations. For example, assume that your rich uncle decides to give you $2,000 for a vacation when you graduate from college 3 years from now. He proposes to finance the trip by investing a sum of money now at 8% compound interest that will provide you with $2,000 upon your graduation. The only conditions are that you graduate and that you tell him how much to invest now.

To impress your uncle, you set up the time diagram in Illustration 6-12 and solve this problem as follows.

ILLUSTRATION 6-12
Present Value Time
Diagram ($n = 3$, $i = 8\%$)

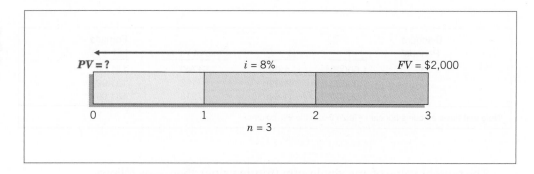

Present value = $2,000 (PVF_{3,8\%})$

$$= \$2,000 \left(\frac{1}{(1 + .08)^3} \right)$$

$$= \$2,000 (.79383)$$

$$= \$1,587.66$$

Advise your uncle to invest $1,587.66 now to provide you with $2,000 upon graduation. To satisfy your uncle's other condition, you must pass this course (and many more).

Solving for Other Unknowns in Single-Sum Problems

In computing either the future value or the present value in the previous single-sum illustrations, both the number of periods and the interest rate were known. In many business situations, both the future value and the present value are known, but the number of periods or the interest rate is unknown. The following two examples are single-sum problems (future value and present value) with either an unknown number of periods (n) or an unknown interest rate (i). These examples, and the accompanying solutions, demonstrate that knowing any three of the four values (future value, FV; present value, PV; number of periods, n; interest rate, i) allows you to derive the remaining unknown variable.

Example—Computation of the Number of Periods

The Village of Somonauk wants to accumulate $70,000 for the construction of a veterans monument in the town square. At the beginning of the current year, the Village deposited $47,811 in a memorial fund that earns 10% interest compounded annually. How many years will it take to accumulate $70,000 in the memorial fund?

In this illustration, the Village knows both the present value ($47,811) and the future value ($70,000), along with the interest rate of 10%. Illustration 6-13 depicts this investment problem as a time diagram.

ILLUSTRATION 6-13
Time Diagram to Solve
for Unknown Number
of Periods

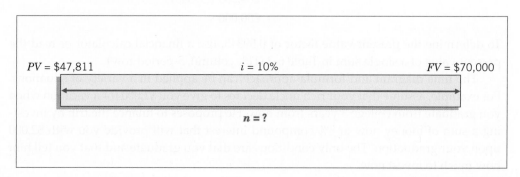

Knowing both the present value and the future value allows the Village to solve for the unknown number of periods. It may use either the future value or the present value formulas, as shown in Illustration 6-14.

Future Value Approach	Present Value Approach
$FV = PV\,(FVF_{n,10\%})$	$PV = FV\,(PVF_{n,10\%})$
$\$70{,}000 = \$47{,}811\,(FVF_{n,10\%})$	$\$47{,}811 = \$70{,}000\,(PVF_{n,10\%})$
$FVF_{n,10\%} = \dfrac{\$70{,}000}{\$47{,}811} = 1.46410$	$PVF_{n,10\%} = \dfrac{\$47{,}811}{\$70{,}000} = .68301$

ILLUSTRATION 6-14
Solving for Unknown
Number of Periods

Using the future value factor of 1.46410, refer to Table 6-1 and read down the 10% column to find that factor in the 4-period row. Thus, it will take 4 years for the $47,811 to accumulate to $70,000 if invested at 10% interest compounded annually. Or, using the present value factor of 0.68301, refer to Table 6-2 and read down the 10% column to find that factor in the 4-period row.

Example—Computation of the Interest Rate

Advanced Design, Inc. needs €1,409,870 for basic research 5 years from now. The company currently has €800,000 to invest for that purpose. At what rate of interest must it invest the €800,000 to fund basic research projects of €1,409,870, 5 years from now?

The time diagram in Illustration 6-15 depicts this investment situation.

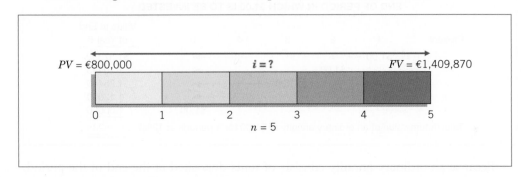

ILLUSTRATION 6-15
Time Diagram to Solve
for Unknown Interest
Rate

Advanced Design may determine the unknown interest rate from either the future value approach or the present value approach, as Illustration 6-16 shows.

Future Value Approach	Present Value Approach
$FV = PV\,(FVF_{5,i})$	$PV = FV\,(PVF_{5,i})$
$€1{,}409{,}870 = €800{,}000\,(FVF_{5,i})$	$€800{,}000 = €1{,}409{,}870\,(PVF_{5,i})$
$FVF_{5,i} = \dfrac{€1{,}409{,}870}{€800{,}000} = 1.76234$	$PVF_{5,i} = \dfrac{€800{,}000}{€1{,}409{,}870} = .56743$

ILLUSTRATION 6-16
Solving for Unknown
Interest Rate

Using the future value factor of 1.76234, refer to Table 6-1 and read across the 5-period row to find that factor in the 12% column. Thus, the company must invest the €800,000 at 12% to accumulate to €1,409,870 in 5 years. Or, using the present value factor of .56743 and Table 6-2, again find that factor at the juncture of the 5-period row and the 12% column.

ANNUITIES

The preceding discussion involved only the accumulation or discounting of a single principal sum. However, many situations arise in which a series of dollar amounts are paid or received periodically, such as installment loans or sales; regular, partially recovered invested funds; or a series of realized cost savings.

 **LEARNING OBJECTIVE**

Solve future value of ordinary and annuity due problems.

For example, a life insurance contract involves a series of equal payments made at equal intervals of time. Such a process of periodic payment represents the accumulation of a sum of money through an annuity. An **annuity**, by definition, requires the following: (1) periodic payments or receipts (called **rents**) of the same amount, (2) the same-length interval between such rents, and (3) compounding of **interest** once each interval. The **future value of an annuity** is the sum of all the rents plus the accumulated compound interest on them.

Note that the rents may occur at either the beginning or the end of the periods. If the rents occur at the end of each period, an annuity is classified as an **ordinary annuity**. If the rents occur at the beginning of each period, an annuity is classified as an **annuity due**.

Future Value of an Ordinary Annuity

One approach to determining the future value of an annuity computes the value to which **each** of the rents in the series will accumulate, and then totals their individual future values.

For example, assume that $1 is deposited at the **end** of each of 5 years (an ordinary annuity) and earns 12% interest compounded annually. Illustration 6-17 shows the computation of the future value, using the "future value of 1" table (Table 6-1) for each of the five $1 rents.

ILLUSTRATION 6-17
Solving for the Future Value of an Ordinary Annuity

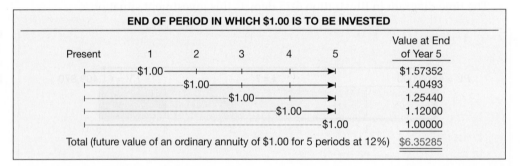

Because an ordinary annuity consists of rents deposited at the end of the period, those rents earn no interest during the period. For example, the third rent earns interest for only two periods (periods four and five). It earns no interest for the third period since it is not deposited until the end of the third period. When computing the future value of an ordinary annuity, the number of compounding periods will always be **one less than the number of rents**.

The foregoing procedure for computing the future value of an ordinary annuity always produces the correct answer. However, it can become cumbersome if the number of rents is large. A formula provides a more efficient way of expressing the future value of an ordinary annuity of 1. This formula sums the individual rents plus the compound interest, as follows.

$$FVF\text{-}OA_{n,i} = \frac{(1+i)^n - 1}{i}$$

where

$$FVF\text{-}OA_{n,i} = \text{future value factor of an ordinary annuity}$$

$$i = \text{rate of interest per period}$$

$$n = \text{number of compounding periods}$$

For example, $FVF\text{-}OA_{5,12\%}$ refers to the value to which an ordinary annuity of 1 will accumulate in 5 periods at 12% interest.

Using the formula above has resulted in the development of tables, similar to those used for the "future value of 1" and the "present value of 1" for both an ordinary annuity and an annuity due. Illustration 6-18 provides an excerpt from the "future value of an ordinary annuity of 1" table.

FUTURE VALUE OF AN ORDINARY ANNUITY OF 1 (EXCERPT FROM TABLE 6-3, PAGE 289)			
Period	10%	11%	12%
1	1.00000	1.00000	1.00000
2	2.10000	2.11000	2.12000
3	3.31000	3.34210	3.37440
4	4.64100	4.70973	4.77933
5	6.10510	6.22780	6.35285*

*Note that this annuity table factor is the same as the sum of the future values of 1 factors shown in Illustration 6-17.

ILLUSTRATION 6-18
Excerpt from Table 6-3

Interpreting the table, if $1 is invested at the end of each year for 4 years at 11% interest compounded annually, the value of the annuity at the end of the fourth year is $4.71 (4.70973 × $1.00). Now, multiply the factor from the appropriate line and column of the table by the dollar amount of **one rent** involved in an ordinary annuity. The result: the accumulated sum of the rents and the compound interest to the date of the last rent.

The following formula computes the future value of an ordinary annuity.

Future value of an ordinary annuity = R (FVF-OA$_{n,i}$)

where

$$R = \text{periodic rent}$$

$$FVF\text{-}OA_{n,i} = \text{future value of an ordinary annuity}$$
$$\text{factor for } n \text{ periods at } i \text{ interest}$$

To illustrate, what is the future value of five $5,000 deposits made at the end of each of the next 5 years, earning interest of 12%? Illustration 6-19 depicts this problem as a time diagram.

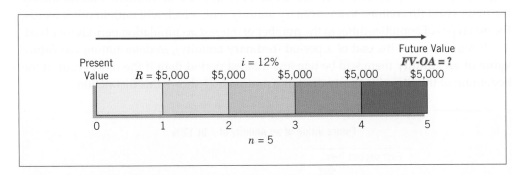

ILLUSTRATION 6-19
Time Diagram for Future Value of Ordinary Annuity ($n = 5, i = 12\%$)

Use of the formula solves this investment problem as follows.

$$\text{Future value of an ordinary annuity} = R \ (FVF\text{-}OA_{n,i})$$
$$= \$5,000 \ (FVF\text{-}OA_{5,12\%})$$
$$= \$5,000 \left(\frac{(1 + .12)^5 - 1}{.12} \right)$$
$$= \$5,000 \ (6.35285)$$
$$= \$31,764.25$$

To determine the future value of an ordinary annuity factor of 6.35285 in the formula above, use a financial calculator or read the appropriate table, in this case, Table 6-3 (12% column, 5-period row).

To illustrate these computations in a business situation, assume that Hightown Electronics deposits $75,000 at the end of each 6-month period for the next 3 years, to accumulate enough money to meet debts that mature in 3 years. What is the future value that the company will have on deposit at the end of 3 years if the annual interest rate is 10%? The time diagram in Illustration 6-20 depicts this situation.

ILLUSTRATION 6-20
Time Diagram for Future
Value of Ordinary
Annuity ($n = 6$, $i = 5\%$)

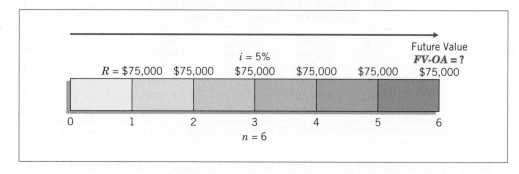

The formula solution for the Hightown Electronics situation is as follows.

$$\text{Future value of an ordinary annuity} = R\ (FVF\text{-}OA_{n,i})$$

$$= \$75{,}000\ (FVF\text{-}OA_{6,5\%})$$

$$= \$75{,}000 \left(\frac{(1 + .05)^6 - 1}{.05} \right)$$

$$= \$75{,}000\ (6.80191)$$

$$= \$510{,}143.25$$

Thus, six 6-month deposits of $75,000 earning 5% per period will grow to $510,143.25.

Future Value of an Annuity Due

The preceding analysis of an ordinary annuity assumed that the periodic rents occur at the **end** of each period. Recall that an **annuity due** assumes periodic rents occur at the **beginning** of each period. This means an annuity due will accumulate interest during the first period (in contrast to an ordinary annuity rent, which will not). In other words, the two types of annuities differ in the number of interest accumulation periods involved.

If rents occur at the end of a period (ordinary annuity), in determining the **future value of an annuity** there will be one less interest period than if the rents occur at the beginning of the period (annuity due). Illustration 6-21 shows this distinction.

ILLUSTRATION 6-21
Comparison of the
Future Value of an
Ordinary Annuity with
an Annuity Due

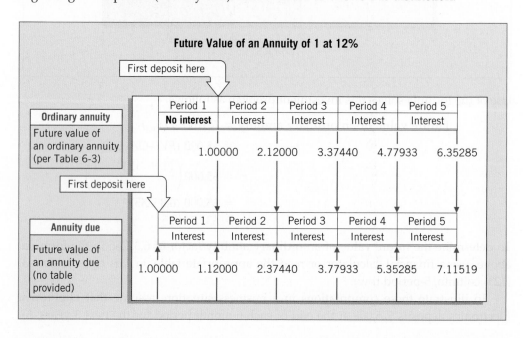

In this example, the cash flows from the annuity due come exactly one period earlier than for an ordinary annuity. As a result, the future value of the annuity due factor is exactly 12% higher than the ordinary annuity factor. For example, the value of an ordinary annuity factor at the end of period one at 12% is 1.00000, whereas for an annuity due it is 1.12000.

To find the future value of an annuity due factor, multiply the future value of an ordinary annuity factor by 1 plus the interest rate. For example, to determine the future value of an annuity due interest factor for 5 periods at 12% compound interest, simply multiply the future value of an ordinary annuity interest factor for 5 periods (6.35285), by one plus the interest rate (1 + .12), to arrive at 7.11519 (6.35285 × 1.12).

To illustrate the use of the ordinary annuity tables in converting to an annuity due, assume that Erin Berge plans to deposit £800 a year on each birthday of her son Venden. She makes the first deposit on his tenth birthday, at 6% interest compounded annually. Erin wants to know the amount she will have accumulated for college expenses by her son's eighteenth birthday.

If the first deposit occurs on Venden's tenth birthday, Erin will make a total of 8 deposits over the life of the annuity (assume no deposit on the eighteenth birthday), as shown in Illustration 6-22. Because all the deposits are made at the beginning of the periods, they represent an annuity due.

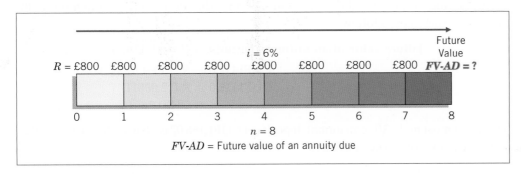

ILLUSTRATION 6-22
Annuity Due Time Diagram

Referring to the "future value of an ordinary annuity of 1" table for 8 periods at 6%, Erin finds a factor of 9.89747. She then multiplies this factor by (1 + .06) to arrive at the future value of an annuity due factor. As a result, the accumulated value on Venden's eighteenth birthday is £8,393.05, as calculated in Illustration 6-23.

1. Future value of an ordinary annuity of 1 for 8 periods at 6% (Table 6-3)	9.89747
2. Factor (1 + .06)	× 1.06
3. Future value of an annuity due of 1 for 8 periods at 6%	10.49132
4. Periodic deposit (rent)	× £800
5. Accumulated value on son's 18th birthday	£8,393.05

ILLUSTRATION 6-23
Computation of Accumulated Value of Annuity Due

Depending on the college he chooses, Venden may have enough to finance only part of his first year of school.

Examples of Future Value of Annuity Problems

The foregoing annuity examples relied on three known values—amount of each rent, interest rate, and number of periods. Using these values enables us to determine the unknown fourth value, future value.

The first two future value problems we present illustrate the computations of (1) the amount of the rents and (2) the number of rents. The third problem illustrates the computation of the future value of an annuity due.

Computation of Rent

Assume that you plan to accumulate CHF14,000 for a down payment on a condominium apartment 5 years from now. For the next 5 years, you earn an annual return of 8% compounded semiannually. How much should you deposit at the end of each 6-month period?

The CHF14,000 is the future value of 10 (5 × 2) semiannual end-of-period payments of an unknown amount, at an interest rate of 4% (8% ÷ 2). Illustration 6-24 depicts this problem as a time diagram.

ILLUSTRATION 6-24
Future Value of Ordinary Annuity Time Diagram
($n = 10, i = 4\%$)

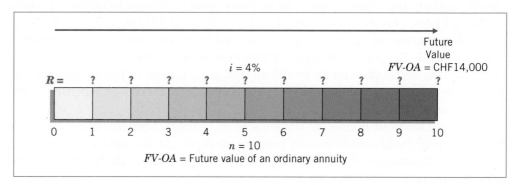

Using the formula for the future value of an ordinary annuity, you determine the amount of each rent as follows.

$$\text{Future value of an ordinary annuity} = R\,(FVF\text{-}OA_{n,i})$$
$$\text{CHF}14,000 = R\,(FVF\text{-}OA_{10,4\%})$$
$$\text{CHF}14,000 = R\,(12.00611)$$
$$R = \text{CHF}1,166.07$$

Thus, you must make 10 semiannual deposits of CHF1,166.07 each in order to accumulate CHF14,000 for your down payment.

Computation of the Number of Periodic Rents

Suppose that a company's goal is to accumulate $117,332 by making periodic deposits of $20,000 at the end of each year, which will earn 8% compounded annually while accumulating. How many deposits must it make?

The $117,332 represents the future value of n(?) $20,000 deposits, at an 8% annual rate of interest. Illustration 6-25 depicts this problem in a time diagram.

ILLUSTRATION 6-25
Future Value of Ordinary Annuity Time Diagram, to Solve for Unknown Number of Periods

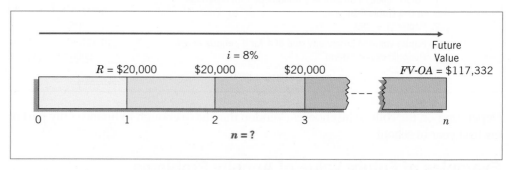

Using the future value of an ordinary annuity formula, the company obtains the following factor.

$$\text{Future value of an ordinary annuity} = R\,(FVF\text{-}OA_{n,i})$$
$$\$117,332 = \$20,000\,(FVF\text{-}OA_{n,8\%})$$
$$FVF\text{-}OA_{n,8\%} = \frac{\$117,332}{\$20,000} = 5.86660$$

Use Table 6-3 and read down the 8% column to find 5.86660 in the 5-period row. Thus, the company must make five deposits of $20,000 each.

Computation of the Future Value

To create his retirement fund, Walter Goodwrench, a mechanic, now works weekends. Mr. Goodwrench deposits $2,500 today in a savings account that earns 9% interest. He plans to deposit $2,500 every year for a total of 30 years. How much cash will Mr. Goodwrench accumulate in his retirement savings account, when he retires in 30 years? Illustration 6-26 depicts this problem in a time diagram.

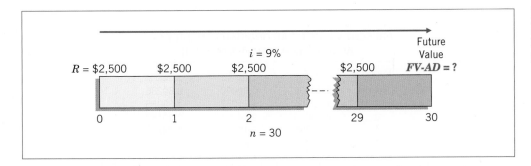

ILLUSTRATION 6-26
Future Value Annuity
Due Time Diagram
($n = 30, i = 9\%$)

Using the "future value of an ordinary annuity of 1" table, Mr. Goodwrench computes the solution as shown in Illustration 6-27.

1. Future value of an ordinary annuity of 1 for 30 periods at 9%	136.30754
2. Factor (1 + .09)	× 1.09
3. Future value of an annuity due of 1 for 30 periods at 9%	148.57522
4. Periodic rent	× $2,500
5. Accumulated value at end of 30 years	$371,438

ILLUSTRATION 6-27
Computation of
Accumulated Value
of an Annuity Due

Present Value of an Ordinary Annuity

The present value of an annuity is **the single sum** that, if invested at compound interest now, would provide for an annuity (a series of withdrawals) for a certain number of future periods. In other words, the present value of an ordinary annuity is the present value of a series of equal rents, to be withdrawn at equal intervals.

7 LEARNING OBJECTIVE
Solve present value of ordinary and annuity due problems.

One approach to finding the present value of an annuity determines the present value of each of the rents in the series and then totals their individual present values. For example, we may view an annuity of $1, to be received at the **end** of each of 5 periods, as separate amounts. We then compute each present value using the table of present values (see pages 286–287), assuming an interest rate of 12%. Illustration 6-28 shows this approach.

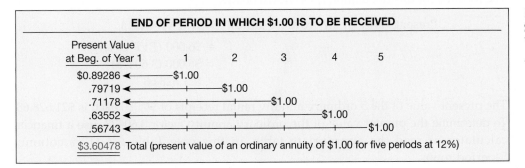

ILLUSTRATION 6-28
Solving for the Present
Value of an Ordinary
Annuity

This computation tells us that if we invest the single sum of $3.60 today at 12% interest for 5 periods, we will be able to withdraw $1 at the end of each period for 5 periods. We can summarize this cumbersome procedure by the following formula.

$$PVF\text{-}OA_{n,i} = \frac{1 - \dfrac{1}{(1 + i)^n}}{i}$$

The expression $PVF\text{-}OA_{n,i}$ refers to the present value of an ordinary annuity of 1 factor for n periods at i interest. Ordinary annuity tables base present values on this formula. Illustration 6-29 shows an excerpt from such a table.

ILLUSTRATION 6-29
Excerpt from Table 6-4

PRESENT VALUE OF AN ORDINARY ANNUITY OF 1 (EXCERPT FROM TABLE 6-4, PAGE 291)			
Period	10%	11%	12%
1	0.90909	0.90090	0.89286
2	1.73554	1.71252	1.69005
3	2.48685	2.44371	2.40183
4	3.16986	3.10245	3.03735
5	3.79079	3.69590	3.60478*

*Note that this annuity table factor is equal to the sum of the present value of 1 factors shown in Illustration 6-28.

The general formula for the present value of any ordinary annuity is as follows.

Present value of an ordinary annuity = R $(PVF\text{-}OA_{n,i})$

where

R = periodic rent (ordinary annuity)
$PVF\text{-}OA_{n,i}$ = present value of an ordinary annuity of 1 for n periods at i interest

To illustrate with an example, what is the present value of rental receipts of $6,000 each, to be received at the end of each of the next 5 years when discounted at 12%? This problem may be time-diagrammed and solved as shown in Illustration 6-30.

ILLUSTRATION 6-30
Present Value of Ordinary Annuity Time Diagram

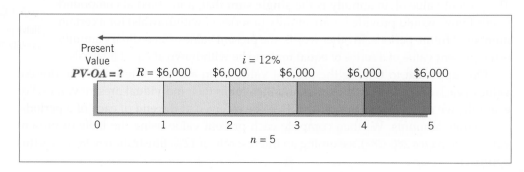

The formula for this calculation is as shown below.

Present value of an ordinary annuity = R $(PVF\text{-}OA_{n,i})$

= $6,000 $(PVF\text{-}OA_{5,12\%})$
= $6,000 (3.60478)
= $21,628.68

The present value of the 5 ordinary annuity rental receipts of $6,000 each is $21,628.68. To determine the present value of the ordinary annuity factor 3.60478, use a financial calculator or read the appropriate table, in this case Table 6-4 (12% column, 5-period row).

What do the numbers mean? UP IN SMOKE

Time value of money concepts also can be relevant to public policy debates. For example, many governments must evaluate the financial cost-benefit of selling to a private operator the future cash flows associated with government-run services, such as toll roads and bridges. In these cases, the policy-maker must estimate the present value of the future cash flows in determining the price for selling the rights. In another example, some governmental entities had to determine how to receive the payments from tobacco companies as settlement for a national lawsuit against the companies for the healthcare costs of smoking.

In one situation, a governmental entity was due to collect 25 years of payments totaling $5.6 billion. The government could wait to collect the payments, or it could sell the payments to an investment bank (a process called *securitization*). If it were to sell the payments, it would receive a lump-sum payment today of $1.26 billion. Is this a good deal for this governmental entity? Assuming a discount rate of 8% and that the payments will be received in equal

amounts (e.g., an annuity), the present value of the tobacco payment is:

$$\$5.6 \text{ billion} \div 25 = \$224 \text{ million}$$
$$\$224 \text{ million} \times 10.67478^* = \$2.39 \text{ billion}$$

$$^*PV\text{-}OA \ (i = 8\%, n = 25)$$

Why would the government be willing to take just $1.26 billion today for an annuity whose present value is almost twice that amount? One reason is that the governmental entity was facing a hole in its budget that could be plugged in part by the lump-sum payment. Also, some believed that the risk of not getting paid by the tobacco companies in the future makes it prudent to get the money earlier.

If this latter reason has merit, then the present value computation above should have been based on a higher interest rate. Assuming a discount rate of 15%, the present value of the annuity is $1.448 billion ($5.6 billion ÷ 25 = $224 million; $224 million × 6.46415), which is much closer to the lump-sum payment offered to the governmental entity.

Present Value of an Annuity Due

In our discussion of the present value of an ordinary annuity, we discounted the final rent based on the number of rent periods. In determining the present value of an annuity due, there is always one fewer discount period. Illustration 6-31 shows this distinction.

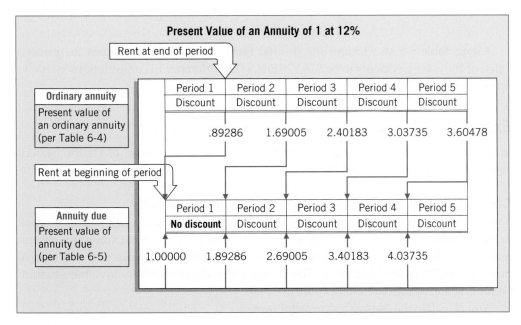

ILLUSTRATION 6-31
Comparison of Present Value of an Ordinary Annuity with an Annuity Due

Because each cash flow comes exactly one period sooner in the present value of the annuity due, the present value of the cash flows is exactly 12% higher than the present value of an ordinary annuity. Thus, **to find the present value of an annuity due factor, multiply the present value of an ordinary annuity factor by 1 plus the interest rate** (that is, $1 + i$).

To determine the present value of an annuity due interest factor for 5 periods at 12% interest, take the present value of an ordinary annuity for 5 periods at 12% interest (3.60478) and multiply it by 1.12 to arrive at the present value of an annuity due, 4.03735 (3.60478 × 1.12). We provide present value of annuity due factors in Table 6-5.

To illustrate, Space Odyssey, Inc., rents a communications satellite for 4 years with annual rental payments of $4.8 million to be made at the beginning of each year. If the relevant annual interest rate is 11%, what is the present value of the rental obligations? Illustration 6-32 shows the company's time diagram for this problem.

ILLUSTRATION 6-32
Present Value of Annuity
Due Time Diagram
($n = 4, i = 11\%$)

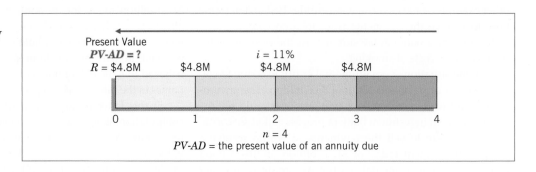

Illustration 6-33 shows the computations to solve this problem.

ILLUSTRATION 6-33
Computation of Present
Value of an Annuity Due

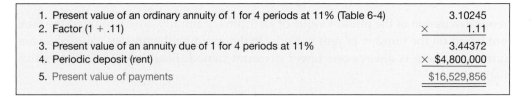

1. Present value of an ordinary annuity of 1 for 4 periods at 11% (Table 6-4)	3.10245
2. Factor (1 + .11)	× 1.11
3. Present value of an annuity due of 1 for 4 periods at 11%	3.44372
4. Periodic deposit (rent)	× $4,800,000
5. Present value of payments	$16,529,856

Using Table 6-5 also locates the desired factor 3.44371 and computes the present value of the lease payments to be $16,529,808. (The difference in computations is due to rounding.)

Examples of Present Value of Annuity Problems

In the following three examples, we demonstrate the computation of (1) the present value, (2) the interest rate, and (3) the amount of each rent.

Computation of the Present Value of an Ordinary Annuity

You have just won a lottery totaling $4,000,000. You learn that you will receive a check in the amount of $200,000 at the end of each of the next 20 years. What amount have you really won? That is, what is the present value of the $200,000 checks you will receive over the next 20 years? Illustration 6-34 shows a time diagram of this enviable situation (assuming an appropriate interest rate of 10%).

You calculate the present value as follows.

$$\text{Present value of an ordinary annuity} = R\ (PVF\text{-}OA_{n,i})$$

$$= \$200,000\ (PVF\text{-}OA_{20,10\%})$$
$$= \$200,000\ (8.51356)$$
$$= \$1,702,712$$

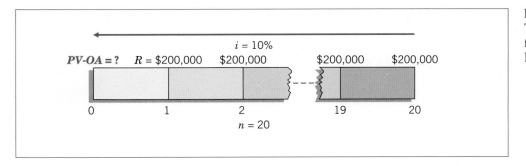

As a result, if the state deposits $1,702,712 now and earns 10% interest, it can withdraw $200,000 a year for 20 years to pay you the $4,000,000.

Computation of the Interest Rate

Many shoppers use credit cards to make purchases. When you receive the statement for payment, you may pay the total amount due or you may pay the balance in a certain number of payments. For example, assume you receive a statement from **MasterCard** with a balance due of €528.77. You may pay it off in 12 equal monthly payments of €50 each, with the first payment due one month from now. What rate of interest would you be paying?

The €528.77 represents the present value of the 12 payments of €50 each at an unknown rate of interest. The time diagram in Illustration 6-35 depicts this situation.

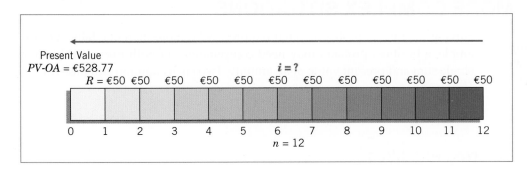

ILLUSTRATION 6-35
Time Diagram to Solve
for Effective-Interest Rate
on Loan

You calculate the rate as follows.

$$\text{Present value of an ordinary annuity} = R\ (PVF\text{-}OA_{n,i})$$

$$€528.77 = €50\ (PVF\text{-}OA_{12,i})$$

$$(PVF\text{-}OA_{12,i}) = \frac{€528.77}{€50} = 10.57540$$

Referring to Table 6-4 and reading across the 12-period row, you find 10.57534 in the 2% column. Since 2% is a monthly rate, the nominal annual rate of interest is 24% (12 × 2%). The effective annual rate is 26.82% $[(1 + .02)^{12} - 1]$. Obviously, you are better off paying the entire bill now if possible.

Computation of a Periodic Rent

Juan and Marcia Perez have saved $36,000 to finance their daughter Maria's college education. They deposited the money in the Santos Bank, where it earns 4% interest compounded semiannually. What equal amounts can their daughter withdraw at the end of every 6 months during her 4 college years, without exhausting the fund? Illustration 6-36 (on page 262) shows a time diagram of this situation.

ILLUSTRATION 6-36
Time Diagram for
Ordinary Annuity for a
College Fund

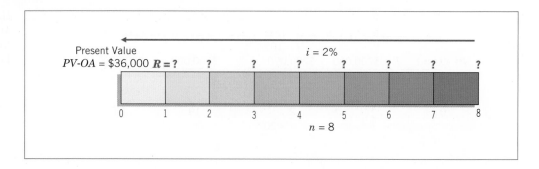

Determining the answer by simply dividing $36,000 by 8 withdrawals is wrong. Why? Because that ignores the interest earned on the money remaining on deposit. Maria must consider that interest is compounded semiannually at 2% (4% ÷ 2) for 8 periods (4 years × 2). Thus, using the same present value of an ordinary annuity formula, she determines the amount of each withdrawal that she can make as follows.

$$\text{Present value of an ordinary annuity} = R\,(PVF\text{-}OA_{n,i})$$

$$\$36{,}000 = R\,(PVF\text{-}OA_{8,2\%})$$
$$\$36{,}000 = R\,(7.32548)$$
$$R = \$4{,}914.35$$

MORE COMPLEX SITUATIONS

LEARNING OBJECTIVE 8
Solve present value problems related to deferred annuities and bonds.

Solving time value problems often requires using more than one table. For example, a business problem may need computations of both present value of a single sum and present value of an annuity. Two such common situations are:

1. Deferred annuities.

2. Bond problems.

Deferred Annuities

A **deferred annuity** is an annuity in which the rents begin after a specified number of periods. A deferred annuity does not begin to produce rents until two or more periods have expired. For example, "an **ordinary annuity** of six annual rents deferred 4 years" means that no rents will occur during the first 4 years and that the first of the six rents will occur at the end of the fifth year. "An **annuity due** of six annual rents deferred 4 years" means that no rents will occur during the first 4 years and that the first of six rents will occur at the beginning of the fifth year.

Future Value of a Deferred Annuity

Computing the future value of a deferred annuity is relatively straightforward. Because there is no accumulation or investment on which interest may accrue, the future value of a deferred annuity is the same as the future value of an annuity not deferred. That is, computing the future value simply ignores the deferred period.

To illustrate, assume that Sutton Corporation plans to purchase a land site in 6 years for the construction of its new corporate headquarters. Because of cash flow problems, Sutton budgets deposits of $80,000 on which it expects to earn 5% annually, only at the end of the fourth, fifth, and sixth periods. What future value will Sutton have accumulated at the end of the sixth year? Illustration 6-37 shows a time diagram of this situation.

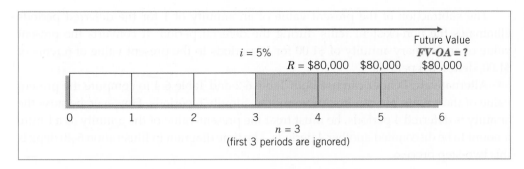

ILLUSTRATION 6-37
Time Diagram for Future
Value of Deferred
Annuity

Sutton determines the value accumulated by using the standard formula for the future value of an ordinary annuity:

$$\text{Future value of an ordinary annuity} = R \, (FVF\text{-}OA_{n,i})$$
$$= \$80,000 \, (FVF\text{-}OA_{3,5\%})$$
$$= \$80,000 \, (3.15250)$$
$$= \$252,200$$

Present Value of a Deferred Annuity

Computing the present value of a deferred annuity must recognize the interest that accrues on the original investment during the deferral period.

To compute the present value of a deferred annuity, we compute the present value of an ordinary annuity of 1 as if the rents had occurred for the entire period. We then subtract the present value of rents that were not received during the deferral period. We are left with the present value of the rents actually received subsequent to the deferral period.

To illustrate, Bob Bender has developed and copyrighted tutorial software for students in advanced accounting. He agrees to sell the copyright to Campus Micro Systems for 6 annual payments of $5,000 each. The payments will begin 5 years from today. Given an annual interest rate of 8%, what is the present value of the 6 payments?

This situation is an ordinary annuity of 6 payments deferred 4 periods. The time diagram in Illustration 6-38 depicts this sales agreement.

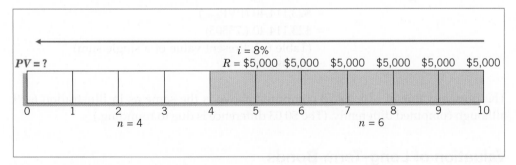

ILLUSTRATION 6-38
Time Diagram for
Present Value of Deferred
Annuity

Two options are available to solve this problem. The first is to use only Table 6-4, as shown in Illustration 6-39.

1. Each periodic rent		$5,000
2. Present value of an ordinary annuity of 1 for total periods (10) [number of rents (6) plus number of deferred periods (4)] at 8%	6.71008	
3. Less: Present value of an ordinary annuity of 1 for the number of deferred periods (4) at 8%	−3.31213	
4. Difference		× 3.39795
5. Present value of 6 rents of $5,000 deferred 4 periods		$16,989.75

ILLUSTRATION 6-39
Computation of the
Present Value of a
Deferred Annuity

The subtraction of the present value of an annuity of 1 for the deferred periods eliminates the non-existent rents during the deferral period. It converts the present value of an ordinary annuity of $1.00 for 10 periods to the present value of 6 rents of $1.00, deferred 4 periods.

Alternatively, Bender can use both Table 6-2 and Table 6-4 to compute the present value of the 6 rents. He can first discount the annuity 6 periods. However, because the annuity is deferred 4 periods, he must treat the present value of the annuity as a future amount to be discounted another 4 periods. The time diagram in Illustration 6-40 depicts this two-step process.

ILLUSTRATION 6-40
Time Diagram for
Present Value of Deferred
Annuity (2-Step Process)

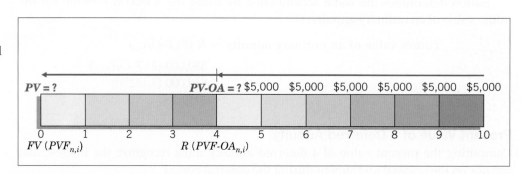

Calculation using formulas would be done in two steps, as follows.

Step 1: Present value of
an ordinary annuity $= R\ (PVF\text{-}OA_{n,i})$
$= \$5,000\ (PVF\text{-}OA_{6,8\%})$
$= \$5,000\ (4.62288)$
(Table 6-4, Present value of an ordinary annuity)
$= \$23,114.40$

Step 2: Present value of
a single sum $= FV\ (PVF_{n,i})$
$= \$23,114.40\ (PVF_{4,8\%})$
$= \$23,114.40\ (.73503)$
(Table 6-2, Present value of a single sum)
$= \$16,989.78$

The present value of $16,989.78 computed above is the same as in Illustration 6-39 although computed differently. (The $0.03 difference is due to rounding.)

Valuation of Long-Term Bonds

A long-term bond produces two cash flows: (1) periodic interest payments during the life of the bond, and (2) the principal (face value) paid at maturity. At the date of issue, bond buyers determine the present value of these two cash flows using the market rate of interest.

The periodic interest payments represent an annuity. The principal represents a single-sum problem. The current market value of the bonds is the combined present values of the interest annuity and the principal amount.

To illustrate, Alltech Corporation on January 1, 2015, issues $100,000 of 9% bonds due in 5 years with interest payable annually at year-end. The current market rate of interest for bonds of similar risk is 11%. What will the buyers pay for this bond issue?

The time diagram in Illustration 6-41 depicts both cash flows.

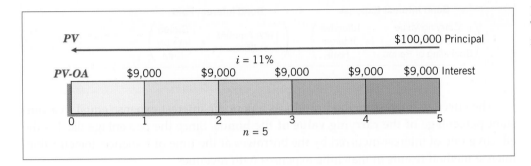

ILLUSTRATION 6-41
Time Diagram to Solve
for Bond Valuation

Alltech computes the present value of the two cash flows by discounting at 11% as follows.

1. Present value of the principal: FV ($PVF_{5,11\%}$) = $100,000 (.59345)	$59,345.00
2. Present value of the interest payments: R ($PVF\text{-}OA_{5,11\%}$) = $9,000 (3.69590)	33,263.10
3. Combined present value (market price)—carrying value of bonds	$92,608.10

ILLUSTRATION 6-42
Computation of the
Present Value of an
Interest-Bearing Bond

By paying $92,608.10 at date of issue, the buyers of the bonds will realize an effective yield of 11% over the 5-year term of the bonds. This is true because Alltech discounted the cash flows at 11%.

Effective-Interest Method of Amortization of Bond Discount or Premium

In the previous example (Illustration 6-42), Alltech Corporation issued bonds at a discount, computed as follows.

Maturity value (face amount) of bonds		$100,000.00
Present value of the principal	$59,345.00	
Present value of the interest	33,263.10	
Proceeds (present value and cash received)		92,608.10
Discount on bonds issued		$ 7,391.90

ILLUSTRATION 6-43
Computation of Bond
Discount

Alltech amortizes (writes off to interest expense) the amount of this discount over the life of the bond issue.

The procedure for amortization of a discount or premium is the **effective-interest method**. Under the effective-interest method:

1. The company issuing the bond first computes bond interest expense by multiplying the carrying value of the bonds at the beginning of the period by the effective-interest rate.

2. The company then determines the bond discount or premium amortization by comparing the bond interest expense with the interest to be paid.

Illustration 6-44 depicts the computation of bond amortization.

ILLUSTRATION 6-44
Amortization
Computation

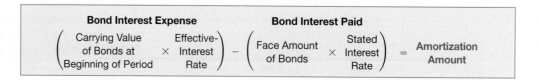

The effective-interest method produces a periodic interest expense equal to **a constant percentage of the carrying value of the bonds**. Since the percentage used is the effective rate of interest incurred by the borrower at the time of issuance, the effective-interest method results in matching expenses with revenues.

We can use the data from the Alltech Corporation example to illustrate the effective-interest method of amortization. Alltech issued $100,000 face value of bonds at a discount of $7,391.90, resulting in a carrying value of $92,608.10. Illustration 6-45 shows the effective-interest amortization schedule for Alltech's bonds.

ILLUSTRATION 6-45
Effective-Interest
Amortization Schedule

	SCHEDULE OF BOND DISCOUNT AMORTIZATION 5-YEAR, 9% BONDS SOLD TO YIELD 11%			
Date	Cash Interest Paid	Interest Expense	Bond Discount Amortization	Carrying Value of Bonds
1/1/15				$ 92,608.10
12/31/15	$ 9,000ᵃ	$10,186.89ᵇ	$1,186.89ᶜ	93,794.99ᵈ
12/31/16	9,000	10,317.45	1,317.45	95,112.44
12/31/17	9,000	10,462.37	1,462.37	96,574.81
12/31/18	9,000	10,623.23	1,623.23	98,198.04
12/31/19	9,000	10,801.96	1,801.96	100,000.00
	$45,000	$52,391.90	$7,391.90	

ᵃ$100,000 × .09 = $9,000   ᶜ$10,186.89 − $9,000 = $1,186.89
ᵇ$92,608.10 × .11 = $10,186.89   ᵈ$92,608.10 + $1,186.89 = $93,794.99

We use the amortization schedule illustrated above for note and bond transactions in Chapters 7 and 14.

PRESENT VALUE MEASUREMENT

LEARNING OBJECTIVE ⑨

Apply expected cash flows to present value measurement.

In the past, most accounting calculations of present value relied on the most likely cash flow amount. *IFRS 13* explains in detail a different approach called the **expected cash flow approach**. **[7]** It uses a range of cash flows and incorporates the probabilities of those cash flows to provide a more relevant measurement of present value.

To illustrate the expected cash flow model, assume that there is a 30% probability that future cash flows will be $100, a 50% probability that they will be $200, and a 20% probability that they will be $300. In this case, the expected cash flow would be $190 [($100 × 0.3) + ($200 × 0.5) + ($300 × 0.2)]. Traditional present value approaches would use the most likely estimate ($200). However, that estimate fails to consider the different probabilities of the possible cash flows.

Choosing an Appropriate Interest Rate

After determining expected cash flows, a company must then use the proper interest rate to discount the cash flows. The interest rate used for this purpose has three components:

THREE COMPONENTS OF INTEREST

1. **PURE RATE OF INTEREST (2%–4%).** This would be the amount a lender would charge if there were no possibilities of default and no expectation of inflation.

2. **EXPECTED INFLATION RATE OF INTEREST (0%–?).** Lenders recognize that in an inflationary economy, they are being paid back with less valuable dollars. As a result, they increase their interest rate to compensate for this loss in purchasing power. When inflationary expectations are high, interest rates are high.

3. **CREDIT RISK RATE OF INTEREST (0%–5%).** The government has little or no credit risk (i.e., risk of non-payment) when it issues bonds. A business enterprise, however, depending upon its financial stability, profitability, and liquidity, can have a low or a high credit risk.

The IASB takes the position that after computing the expected cash flows, a company should discount those cash flows by the risk-free rate of return. That rate is defined as **the pure rate of return plus the expected inflation rate**. The Board notes that the expected cash flow framework adjusts for credit risk because it incorporates the probability of receipt or payment into the computation of expected cash flows. Therefore, the rate used to discount the expected cash flows should consider only the pure rate of interest and the inflation rate.[6]

Example of Expected Cash Flow

To illustrate, assume that Juno's Appliance Outlet offers a 2-year warranty on all products sold. In 2015, Juno's Appliance sold $250,000 of a particular type of clothes dryer. Juno's Appliance entered into an agreement with Lorenzo's Repair to perform all warranty service on the dryers sold in 2015. To determine the warranty expense to record in 2015 and the amount of warranty liability to record on the December 31, 2015, statement of financial position, Juno's Appliance must measure the fair value of the agreement. Since there is not a ready market for these warranty contracts, Juno's Appliance uses expected cash flow techniques to value the warranty obligation.

Based on prior warranty experience, Juno's Appliance estimates the expected cash outflows associated with the dryers sold in 2015, as shown in Illustration 6-46 (on page 268).

---

[6]In other words, the interest rate(s) used to discount cash flows should reflect assumptions that are consistent with those inherent in the estimated cash flows. Otherwise, the effect of some assumptions will be double-counted or ignored. For example, a discount rate of 12% might be applied to contractual cash flows of a loan receivable. That rate reflects expectations about future defaults from loans with particular characteristics. That same 12% rate should not be used to discount expected cash flows because those cash flows already reflect assumptions about future defaults. **[8]**

ILLUSTRATION 6-46
Expected Cash
Outflows—Warranties

	Cash Flow Estimate	×	Probability Assessment	=	Expected Cash Flow
2015	$3,800		20%		$ 760
	6,300		50%		3,150
	7,500		30%		2,250
			Total		$6,160
2016	$5,400		30%		$1,620
	7,200		50%		3,600
	8,400		20%		1,680
			Total		$6,900

Applying expected cash flow concepts to these data, Juno's Appliance estimates warranty cash outflows of $6,160 in 2015 and $6,900 in 2016.

Illustration 6-47 shows the present value of these cash flows, assuming a risk-free rate of 5% and cash flows occurring at the end of the year.[7]

ILLUSTRATION 6-47
Present Value of Cash
Flows

Year	Expected Cash Flow	×	PV Factor, $i = 5\%$	=	Present Value
2015	$6,160		0.95238		$ 5,866.66
2016	6,900		0.90703		6,258.51
			Total		$12,125.17

KEY TERMS

annuity, 252

annuity due, 252

compound interest, 242

deferred annuity, 262

discounting, 247

effective-interest
  method, 265

effective yield, 245

expected cash flow
  approach, 266

face rate, 245

future value, 246

future value of an
  annuity, 252

interest, 241

nominal rate, 245

ordinary annuity, 252

present value, 246

principal, 241

risk-free rate of
  return, 267

simple interest, 242

stated rate, 245

time value of money, 240

SUMMARY OF LEARNING OBJECTIVES

1 **Identify accounting topics where the time value of money is relevant.** Some of the applications of present value–based measurements to accounting topics are (1) notes, (2) leases, (3) pensions and other postretirement benefits, (4) long-term assets, (5) sinking funds, (6) business combinations, (7) disclosures, and (8) installment contracts.

2 **Distinguish between simple and compound interest.** See items 1 and 2 in the Fundamental Concepts on page 269.

3 **Use appropriate compound interest tables.** In order to identify which of the five compound interest tables to use, determine whether you are solving for (1) the future value of a single sum, (2) the present value of a single sum, (3) the future value of a series of sums (an annuity), or (4) the present value of a series of sums (an annuity). In addition, when a series of sums (an annuity) is involved, identify whether these sums are received or paid (1) at the beginning of each period (annuity due) or (2) at the end of each period (ordinary annuity).

[7]As indicated in the beginning of the chapter, there are a number of situations where present value computations are needed. A common situation (and the one the IASB commented on specifically) is when a company is determining whether its assets are impaired. Impairment occurs when the carrying value of an asset such as equipment is not recoverable. One method used to determine the recoverable amount is the value-in-use approach. The **value-in-use approach** computes the present value of the expected cash flows to be generated using the asset. The discussion of this method will be examined in later chapters on non-current assets.

4 **Identify variables fundamental to solving interest problems.** The following four variables are fundamental to all compound interest problems. (1) *Rate of interest:* unless otherwise stated, an annual rate, adjusted to reflect the length of the compounding period if less than a year. (2) *Number of time periods:* the number of compounding periods (a period may be equal to or less than a year). (3) *Future value:* the value at a future date of a given sum or sums invested assuming compound interest. (4) *Present value:* the value now (present time) of a future sum or sums discounted assuming compound interest.

5 **Solve future and present value of 1 problems.** See items 5(a) and 6(a) in the Fundamental Concepts below and on page 270.

6 **Solve future value of ordinary and annuity due problems.** See item 5(b) in the Fundamental Concepts on page 270.

7 **Solve present value of ordinary and annuity due problems.** See item 6(b) in the Fundamental Concepts on page 270.

8 **Solve present value problems related to deferred annuities and bonds.** Deferred annuities are annuities in which rents begin after a specified number of periods. The future value of a deferred annuity is computed the same as the future value of an annuity not deferred. To find the present value of a deferred annuity, compute the present value of an ordinary annuity of 1 as if the rents had occurred for the entire period, and then subtract the present value of rents not received during the deferral period. The current market value of bonds combines the present values of the interest annuity and the principal amount.

9 **Apply expected cash flows to present value measurement.** The expected cash flow approach uses a range of cash flows and the probabilities of those cash flows to provide the most likely estimate of expected cash flows. The proper interest rate used to discount the cash flows is the risk-free rate of return.

FUNDAMENTAL CONCEPTS

1. SIMPLE INTEREST. Interest on principal only, regardless of interest that may have accrued in the past.

2. COMPOUND INTEREST. Interest accrues on the unpaid interest of past periods as well as on the principal.

3. RATE OF INTEREST. Interest is usually expressed as an annual rate, but when the compounding period is shorter than one year, the interest rate for the shorter period must be determined.

4. ANNUITY. A series of payments or receipts (called rents) that occur at equal intervals of time. Types of annuities:
  (a) **Ordinary Annuity.** Each rent is payable (receivable) at the end of the period.
  (b) **Annuity Due.** Each rent is payable (receivable) at the beginning of the period.

5. FUTURE VALUE. Value at a later date of a single sum that is invested at compound interest.
  (a) **Future Value of 1** (or value of a single sum). The future value of 1 (or a single given sum), FV, at the end of n periods at i compound interest rate (Table 6-1).

(b) Future Value of an Annuity. The future value of a series of rents invested at compound interest. In other words, the accumulated total that results from a series of equal deposits at regular intervals invested at compound interest. Both deposits and interest increase the accumulation.

(1) Future Value of an Ordinary Annuity. The future value on the date of the last rent (Table 6-3).

(2) Future Value of an Annuity Due. The future value one period after the date of the last rent. When an annuity due table is not available, use Table 6-3 with the following formula.

$$\text{Value of annuity due of 1 for } n \text{ rents} = \text{(Value of ordinary annuity for } n \text{ rents)} \times (1 + \text{interest rate})$$

6. PRESENT VALUE. The value at an earlier date (usually now) of a given future sum discounted at compound interest.

(a) Present Value of 1 (or present value of a single sum). The present value (worth) of 1 (or a given sum), due n periods hence, discounted at i compound interest (Table 6-2).

(b) Present Value of an Annuity. The present value (worth) of a series of rents discounted at compound interest. In other words, it is the sum when invested at compound interest that will permit a series of equal withdrawals at regular intervals.

(1) Present Value of an Ordinary Annuity. The value now of 1 to be received or paid at the end of each period (rents) for n periods, discounted at i compound interest (Table 6-4).

(2) Present Value of an Annuity Due. The value now of 1 to be received or paid at the beginning of each period (rents) for n periods, discounted at i compound interest (Table 6-5). To use Table 6-4 for an annuity due, apply this formula.

$$\text{Present value of annuity due of 1 for } n \text{ rents} = \text{(Present value of an ordinary annuity of } n \text{ rents)} \times (1 + \text{interest rate})$$

IFRS AUTHORITATIVE LITERATURE

Authoritative Literature References

[1] International Accounting Standard 36, *Impairment of Assets* (London, U.K.: International Accounting Standards Committee Foundation, March 2004), Appendix A and International Financial Reporting Standard 7, *Financial Instruments: Disclosures* (London, U.K.: International Accounting Standards Committee Foundation, 2005), par. 27.

[2] International Accounting Standard 39, *Financial Instruments: Recognition and Measurement* (London, U.K.: International Accounting Standards Committee Foundation, 2003).

[3] International Accounting Standard 17, *Leases* (London, U.K.: International Accounting Standards Committee Foundation, 2003).

[4] International Accounting Standard 19, *Employee Benefits* (London, U.K.: International Accounting Standards Committee Foundation, 2001).

[5] International Accounting Standard 36, *Impairment of Assets* (London, U.K.: International Accounting Standards Committee Foundation, 2004).

[6] International Financial Reporting Standard 2, *Share-Based Payment* (London, U.K.: International Accounting Standards Committee Foundation, 2004).

[7] International Financial Reporting Standard 13, *Fair Value Measurement* (London, U.K.: International Accounting Standards Committee Foundation, 2011), paras. B12–B30; and International Accounting Standard 36, *Impairment of Assets* (London, U.K.: International Accounting Standards Committee Foundation, 2004), Appendix A.

[8] International Financial Reporting Standard 13, *Fair Value Measurement* (London, U.K.: International Accounting Standards Committee Foundation, 2011), paras. B14–B19; and International Accounting Standard 36, *Impairment of Assets* (London, U.K.: International Accounting Standards Committee Foundation, 2004), par. A3.

QUESTIONS

1. What is the time value of money? Why should accountants have an understanding of compound interest, annuities, and present value concepts?

2. Identify three situations in which accounting measures are based on present values. Do these present value applications involve single sums or annuities, or both single sums and annuities? Explain.

3. What is the nature of interest? Distinguish between "simple interest" and "compound interest."

4. What are the components of an interest rate? Why is it important for accountants to understand these components?

5. Presented below are a number of values taken from compound interest tables involving the same number of periods and the same rate of interest. Indicate what each of these four values represents.

   (a) 6.71008   (c) .46319
   (b) 2.15892   (d) 14.48656

6. Jose Oliva is considering two investment options for a R$1,500 gift he received for graduation. Both investments have 8% annual interest rates. One offers quarterly compounding; the other compounds on a semiannual basis. Which investment should he choose? Why?

7. Regina Henry deposited $20,000 in a money market certificate that provides interest of 10% compounded quarterly if the amount is maintained for 3 years. How much will Regina Henry have at the end of 3 years?

8. Will Smith will receive $80,000 on December 31, 2020 (5 years from now), from a trust fund established by his father. Assuming the appropriate interest rate for discounting is 12% (compounded semiannually), what is the present value of this amount today?

9. What are the primary characteristics of an annuity? Differentiate between an "ordinary annuity" and an "annuity due."

10. Kehoe, Inc. owes €40,000 to Ritter Company. How much would Kehoe have to pay each year if the debt is retired through four equal payments (made at the end of the year), given an interest rate on the debt of 12%? (Round to two decimal places.)

11. The Wangs are planning for a retirement home. They estimate they will need ¥20,000,000 4 years from now to purchase this home. Assuming an interest rate of 10%, what amount must be deposited at the end of each of the 4 years to fund the home price? (Round to two decimal places.)

12. Assume the same situation as in Question 11, except that the four equal amounts are deposited at the beginning of the period rather than at the end. In this case, what amount must be deposited at the beginning of each period? (Round to two decimals.)

13. Explain how the future value of an ordinary annuity interest table is converted to the future value of an annuity due interest table.

14. Explain how the present value of an ordinary annuity interest table is converted to the present value of an annuity due interest table.

15. In a book named *Treasure*, the reader has to figure out where a 2.2 pound, 24 kt gold horse has been buried. If the horse is found, a prize of $25,000 a year for 20 years is provided. The actual cost to the publisher to purchase an annuity to pay for the prize is $245,000. What interest rate (to the nearest percent) was used to determine the amount of the annuity? (Assume end-of-year payments.)

16. Verma Enterprises leases property to Pandey, Inc. Because Pandey, Inc. is experiencing financial difficulty, Verma agrees to receive five rents of £20,000 at the end of each year, with the rents deferred 3 years. What is the present value of the five rents discounted at 12%?

17. Answer the following questions.

    (a) On May 1, 2015, Goldberg Company sold some machinery to Newlin Company on an installment contract basis. The contract required five equal annual payments, with the first payment due on May 1, 2015. What present value concept is appropriate for this situation?

    (b) On June 1, 2015, Lin Inc. purchased a new machine that it does not have to pay for until May 1, 2017. The total payment on May 1, 2017, will include both principal and interest. Assuming interest at a 12% rate, the cost of the machine would be the total payment multiplied by what time value of money concept?

    (c) Guha Company wishes to know how much money it will have available in 5 years if five equal amounts of $35,000 are invested, with the first amount invested immediately. What interest table is appropriate for this situation?

    (d) Jane Lindholm invests in a "jumbo" $200,000, 3-year certificate of deposit at ING Bank. What table would be used to determine the amount accumulated at the end of 3 years?

18. Recently, Glenda Estes was interested in purchasing a Honda Acura. The salesperson indicated that the price of the car was either R$27,600 cash or R$6,900 at the end of each of 5 years. Compute the effective-interest rate to the nearest percent that Glenda would pay if she chooses to make the five annual payments.

19. Recently, property/casualty insurance companies have been criticized because they reserve for the total loss as much as 5 years before it may happen. The taxing authority has joined the debate because it says the full reserve is unfair from a taxation viewpoint. What do you believe is the taxing authority's position?

BRIEF EXERCISES

---

5 ▸ **BE6-1** Victor Romano invested $15,000 today in a fund that earns 8% compounded annually. To what amount will the investment grow in 3 years? To what amount would the investment grow in 3 years if the fund earns 8% annual interest compounded semiannually?

5 ▸ **BE6-2** Tony Bautista needs R$25,000 in 4 years. What amount must he invest today if his investment earns 12% compounded annually? What amount must he invest if his investment earns 12% annual interest compounded quarterly?

5 ▸ **BE6-3** Candice Willis will invest €30,000 today. She needs €150,000 in 21 years. What annual interest rate must she earn?

5 ▸ **BE6-4** Bo Newman will invest $10,000 today in a fund that earns 5% annual interest. How many years will it take for the fund to grow to $17,100?

6 ▸ **BE6-5** Sally Medavoy will invest €8,000 a year for 20 years in a fund that will earn 12% annual interest. If the first payment into the fund occurs today, what amount will be in the fund in 20 years? If the first payment occurs at year-end, what amount will be in the fund in 20 years?

6 ▸ **BE6-6** Steve Madison needs $250,000 in 10 years. How much must he invest at the end of each year, at 11% interest, to meet his needs?

5 ▸ **BE6-7** Jose Garcia's lifelong dream is to own a fishing boat to use in his retirement. Jose has recently come into an inheritance of R$400,000. He estimates that the boat he wants will cost R$300,000 when he retires in 5 years. How much of his inheritance must he invest at an annual rate of 12% (compounded annually) to buy the boat at retirement?

5 ▸ **BE6-8** Refer to the data in BE6-7. Assuming quarterly compounding of amounts invested at 12%, how much of Jose Garcia's inheritance must be invested to have enough at retirement to buy the boat?

6 ▸ **BE6-9** Morgan Freeman is investing $16,380 at the end of each year in a fund that earns 10% interest. In how many years will the fund be at $100,000?

7 ▸ **BE6-10** Henry Quincy wants to withdraw £30,000 each year for 10 years from a fund that earns 8% interest. How much must he invest today if the first withdrawal is at year-end? How much must he invest today if the first withdrawal takes place immediately?

7 ▸ **BE6-11** Leon Tyler's VISA balance is $793.15. He may pay it off in 12 equal end-of-month payments of $75 each. What interest rate is Leon paying?

7 ▸ **BE6-12** Maria Alvarez is investing $300,000 in a fund that earns 8% interest compounded annually. What equal amounts can Maria withdraw at the end of each of the next 20 years?

6 ▸ **BE6-13** Gomez Inc. will deposit $30,000 in a 12% fund at the end of each year for 8 years beginning December 31, 2015. What amount will be in the fund immediately after the last deposit?

7 ▸ **BE6-14** Liv Diaz wants to create a fund today that will enable her to withdraw R$25,000 per year for 8 years, with the first withdrawal to take place 5 years from today. If the fund earns 8% interest, how much must Liv invest today?

8 ▸ **BE6-15** Wong Inc. issues HK$2,000,000 of 7% bonds due in 10 years with interest payable at year-end. The current market rate of interest for bonds of similar risk is 8%. What amount will Wong receive when it issues the bonds (amounts in thousands)?

7 ▸ **BE6-16** Zach Taylor is settling a £20,000 loan due today by making 6 equal annual payments of £4,727.53. Determine the interest rate on this loan if the payments begin one year after the loan is signed.

7 ▸ **BE6-17** Consider the loan in BE6-16. What payments must Zach Taylor make to settle the loan at the same interest rate but with the 6 payments beginning on the day the loan is signed?

EXERCISES

(Interest rates are per annum unless otherwise indicated.)

3 **E6-1 (Using Interest Tables)** For each of the following cases, indicate (a) to what rate columns, and (b) to what number of periods you would refer in looking up the interest factor.

1. In a future value of 1 table

Annual Rate	Number of Years Invested	Compounded
a. 9%	9	Annually
b. 8%	5	Quarterly
c. 10%	15	Semiannually

2. In a present value of an annuity of 1 table

Annual Rate	Number of Years Involved	Number of Rents Involved	Frequency of Rents
a. 9%	25	25	Annually
b. 8%	15	30	Semiannually
c. 12%	7	28	Quarterly

2 **5** **E6-2 (Simple and Compound Interest Computations)** Sue Ang invests HK$30,000 at 8% annual interest, leaving the money invested without withdrawing any of the interest for 8 years. At the end of the 8 years, Sue withdraws the accumulated amount of money.

Instructions
(a) Compute the amount Sue would withdraw assuming the investment earns simple interest.
(b) Compute the amount Sue would withdraw assuming the investment earns interest compounded annually.
(c) Compute the amount Sue would withdraw assuming the investment earns interest compounded semiannually.

5 **6** **7** **E6-3 (Computation of Future Values and Present Values)** Using the appropriate interest table, answer each of the following questions. (Each case is independent of the others.)
(a) What is the future value of €9,000 at the end of 5 periods at 8% compounded interest?
(b) What is the present value of €9,000 due 8 periods hence, discounted at 11%?
(c) What is the future value of 15 periodic payments of €9,000 each made at the end of each period and compounded at 10%?
(d) What is the present value of €9,000 to be received at the end of each of 20 periods, discounted at 5% compound interest?

6 **7** **E6-4 (Computation of Future Values and Present Values)** Using the appropriate interest table, answer the following questions. (Each case is independent of the others.)
(a) What is the future value of 20 periodic payments of $5,000 each made at the beginning of each period and compounded at 8%?
(b) What is the present value of $2,500 to be received at the beginning of each of 30 periods, discounted at 10% compound interest?
(c) What is the future value of 15 deposits of $2,000 each made at the beginning of each period and compounded at 10%? (Future value as of the end of the fifteenth period.)
(d) What is the present value of six receipts of $3,000 each received at the beginning of each period, discounted at 9% compounded interest?

7 **8** **E6-5 (Computation of Present Value)** Using the appropriate interest table, compute the present values of the following periodic amounts due at the end of the designated periods.
(a) £50,000 receivable at the end of each period for 8 periods compounded at 12%.
(b) £50,000 payments to be made at the end of each period for 16 periods at 9%.
(c) £50,000 payable at the end of the seventh, eighth, ninth, and tenth periods at 12%.

5 **6** **7** **E6-6 (Future Value and Present Value Problems)** Presented below are three unrelated situations (amounts in thousands).
(a) Li Chang Company recently signed a lease for a new office building, for a lease period of 10 years. Under the lease agreement, a security deposit of ¥1,200,000 is made, with the deposit to be returned at the expiration of the lease, with interest compounded at 10% per year. What amount will the company receive at the time the lease expires?

(b) Ron Wu Corporation, having recently issued a ₩20 million, 15-year bond issue, is committed to make annual sinking fund deposits of ₩620,000. The deposits are made on the last day of each year and yield a return of 10%. Will the fund at the end of 15 years be sufficient to retire the bonds? If not, what will the deficiency be?

(c) Under the terms of his salary agreement, president Juan Rivera has an option of receiving either an immediate bonus of R$40,000, or a deferred bonus of R$75,000 payable in 10 years. Ignoring tax considerations and assuming a relevant interest rate of 8%, which form of settlement should Rivera accept?

8 **E6-7 (Computation of Bond Prices)** What would you pay for a $100,000 debenture bond that matures in 15 years and pays $10,000 a year in interest if you wanted to earn a yield of:

    (a) 8%?   **(b)** 10%?   **(c)** 12%?

8 **E6-8 (Computations for a Retirement Fund)** Stephen Bosworth, a super salesman contemplating retirement on his fifty-fifth birthday, decides to create a fund on an 8% basis that will enable him to withdraw $25,000 per year on June 30, beginning in 2019 and continuing through 2022. To develop this fund, Stephen intends to make equal contributions on June 30 of each of the years 2015–2018.

Instructions

    (a) How much must the balance of the fund equal on June 30, 2018, in order for Stephen Bosworth to satisfy his objective?

    (b) What are each of Stephen's contributions to the fund?

5 **E6-9 (Unknown Rate)** Kross Company purchased a machine at a price of £100,000 by signing a note payable, which requires a single payment of £118,810 in 2 years. Assuming annual compounding of interest, what rate of interest is being paid on the loan?

5 **E6-10 (Unknown Periods and Unknown Interest Rate)** Consider the following independent situations.

    (a) R. Chopra wishes to become a millionaire. His money market fund has a balance of $148,644 and has a guaranteed interest rate of 10%. How many years must Chopra leave that balance in the fund in order to get his desired $1 million?

    (b) Assume that Elvira Lehman desires to accumulate $1 million in 15 years using her money market fund balance of $239,392. At what interest rate must Elvira's investment compound annually?

7 **E6-11 (Evaluation of Purchase Options)** Rossi Excavating Inc. is purchasing a bulldozer. The equipment has a price of €100,000. The manufacturer has offered a payment plan that would allow Rossi to make 10 equal annual payments of €15,582, with the first payment due one year after the purchase.

Instructions

    (a) How much total interest will Rossi pay on this payment plan?

    (b) Rossi could borrow €100,000 from its bank to finance the purchase at an annual rate of 8%. Should Rossi borrow from the bank or use the manufacturer's payment plan to pay for the equipment?

7 **E6-12 (Analysis of Alternatives)** Brubaker Inc., a manufacturer of high-sugar, low-sodium, low-cholesterol TV dinners, would like to increase its market share in the Sunbelt. In order to do so, Brubaker has decided to locate a new factory in the Panama City area. Brubaker will either buy or lease a site depending upon which is more advantageous. The site location committee has narrowed down the available sites to the following three buildings.

Building A: Purchase for a cash price of $610,000, useful life 25 years.

Building B: Lease for 25 years with annual lease payments of $70,000 being made at the beginning of the year.

Building C: Purchase for $650,000 cash. This building is larger than needed; however, the excess space can be sublet for 25 years at a net annual rental of $6,000. Rental payments will be received at the end of each year. Brubaker Inc. has no aversion to being a landlord.

Instructions

In which building would you recommend that Brubaker Inc. locate, assuming a 12% cost of funds?

8 **E6-13 (Computation of Bond Liability)** Messier Inc. manufactures cycling equipment. Recently, the vice president of operations of the company has requested construction of a new plant to meet the increasing demand for the company's bikes. After a careful evaluation of the request, the board of directors has decided to raise funds for the new plant by issuing €3,000,000 of 11% term corporate bonds on March 1, 2015, due on March 1, 2030, with interest payable each March 1 and September 1. At the time of issuance, the market interest rate for similar financial instruments is 10%.

Instructions

As the controller of the company, determine the selling price of the bonds.

8 **E6-14 (Computation of Pension Liability)** Calder, Inc. is a furniture manufacturing company with 50 employees. Recently, after a long negotiation with the local labor union, the company decided to initiate a pension plan as a part of its compensation plan. The plan will start on January 1, 2015. Each employee covered by the plan is entitled to a pension payment each year after retirement. As required by accounting standards, the controller of the company needs to report the pension obligation (liability). On the basis of a discussion with the supervisor of the Personnel Department and an actuary from an insurance company, the controller develops the following information related to the pension plan.

Average length of time to retirement	15 years
Expected life duration after retirement	10 years
Total pension payment expected each year after retirement	
for all employees. Payment made at the end of the year.	$800,000 per year

The interest rate to be used is 8%.

Instructions

On the basis of the information above, determine the present value of the pension liability.

5 **6** **E6-15 (Investment Decision)** Derek Lee just received a signing bonus of $1,000,000. His plan is to invest this payment in a fund that will earn 6%, compounded annually.

Instructions

    (a) If Lee plans to establish the DL Foundation once the fund grows to $1,898,000, how many years until he can establish the foundation?

    (b) Instead of investing the entire $1,000,000, Lee invests $300,000 today and plans to make 9 equal annual investments into the fund beginning one year from today. What amount should the payments be if Lee plans to establish the $1,898,000 foundation at the end of 9 years?

6 **E6-16 (Retirement of Debt)** Rual Fernandez borrowed $90,000 on March 1, 2013. This amount plus accrued interest at 12% compounded semiannually is to be repaid March 1, 2023. To retire this debt, Rual plans to contribute to a debt retirement fund five equal amounts starting on March 1, 2018, and for the next 4 years. The fund is expected to earn 10% per annum.

Instructions

How much must be contributed each year by Rual Fernandez to provide a fund sufficient to retire the debt on March 1, 2023?

7 **E6-17 (Computation of Amount of Rentals)** Your client, Wyeth Leasing Company, is preparing a contract to lease a machine to Souvenirs Corporation for a period of 25 years. Wyeth has an investment cost of £421,087 in the machine, which has a useful life of 25 years and no salvage value at the end of that time. Your client is interested in earning an 11% return on its investment and has agreed to accept 25 equal rental payments at the end of each of the next 25 years.

Instructions

You are requested to provide Wyeth with the amount of each of the 25 rental payments that will yield an 11% return on investment.

7 **E6-18 (Least Costly Payoff)** Assume that Aoki Company has a contractual debt outstanding. Aoki has available two means of settlement: It can either make immediate payment of ¥3,500,000, or it can make annual payments of ¥400,000 for 15 years, each payment due on the last day of the year (yen in thousands).

Instructions

Which method of payment do you recommend, assuming an expected effective-interest rate of 8% during the future period?

7 **E6-19 (Least Costly Payoff)** Assuming the same facts as those in E6-18 except that the payments must begin now and be made on the first day of each of the 15 years, what payment method would you recommend?

9 **E6-20 (Expected Cash Flows)** For each of the following, determine the expected cash flows.

	Cash Flow Estimate	Probability Assessment
(a)	£ 4,800	20%
	6,300	50%
	7,500	30%
(b)	£ 5,400	30%
	7,200	50%
	8,400	20%
(c)	£(1,000)	10%
	3,000	80%
	5,000	10%

9 **E6-21 (Expected Cash Flows and Present Value)** Angela Contreras is trying to determine the amount to set aside so that she will have enough money on hand in 2 years to overhaul the engine on her vintage used car. While there is some uncertainty about the cost of engine overhauls in 2 years, by conducting some research online, Angela has developed the following estimates.

Engine Overhaul Estimated Cash Outflow	Probability Assessment
$200	10%
450	30%
600	50%
750	10%

Instructions

How much should Angela Contreras deposit today in an account earning 6%, compounded annually, so that she will have enough money on hand in 2 years to pay for the overhaul?

9 **E6-22 (Fair Value Estimate)** Killroy Company owns a trade name that was purchased in an acquisition of McClellan Company. The trade name has a book value of $3,500,000, but according to IFRS, it is assessed for impairment on an annual basis. To perform this impairment test, Killroy must estimate the fair value of the trade name. (You will learn more about intangible asset impairments in Chapter 12.) It has developed the following cash flow estimates related to the trade name based on internal information. Each cash flow estimate reflects Killroy's estimate of annual cash flows over the next 8 years. The trade name is assumed to have no residual value after the 8 years. (Assume the cash flows occur at the end of each year.)

Cash Flow Estimate	Probability Assessment
$380,000	20%
630,000	50%
750,000	30%

Instructions

(a) What is the estimated fair value of the trade name? Killroy determines that the appropriate discount rate for this estimation is 8%. (Round calculations to the nearest dollar.)

(b) Is the estimate developed for part (a) a Level 1 or Level 3 fair value estimate? Explain.

PROBLEMS

(Interest rates are per annum unless otherwise indicated.)

5 **7** **P6-1 (Various Time Value Situations)** Answer each of these unrelated questions.

(a) On January 1, 2015, Yang Corporation sold a building that cost ¥25,000,000 and that had accumulated depreciation of ¥10,000,000 on the date of sale. Yang received as consideration a ¥24,000,000 non-interest-bearing note due on January 1, 2018. There was no established exchange price for the building, and the note had no ready market. The prevailing rate of interest for a note of this type on January 1, 2015, was 9%. At what amount should the gain from the sale of the building be reported?

(b) On January 1, 2015, Yang Corporation purchased 300 of the ¥100,000 face value, 9%, 10-year bonds of Walters Inc. The bonds mature on January 1, 2025, and pay interest annually beginning January 1, 2016. Yang purchased the bonds to yield 11%. How much did Yang pay for the bonds?

(c) Yang Corporation bought a new machine and agreed to pay for it in equal annual installments of ¥400,000 at the end of each of the next 10 years. Assuming that a prevailing interest rate of 8% applies to this contract, how much should Yang record as the cost of the machine?

(d) Yang Corporation purchased a special tractor on December 31, 2015. The purchase agreement stipulated that Yang should pay ¥2,000,000 at the time of purchase and ¥500,000 at the end of each of the next 8 years. The tractor should be recorded on December 31, 2015, at what amount, assuming an appropriate interest rate of 12%?

(e) Yang Corporation wants to withdraw ¥12,000,000 (including principal) from an investment fund at the end of each year for 9 years. What should be the required initial investment at the beginning of the first year if the fund earns 11%?

5 **6** **P6-2 (Various Time Value Situations)** Using the appropriate interest table, provide the solution to each of the following four questions by computing the unknowns.

(a) What is the amount of the payments that Ned Winslow must make at the end of each of 8 years to accumulate a fund of $90,000 by the end of the eighth year, if the fund earns 8% interest, compounded annually?

(b) Robert Hitchcock is 40 years old today and he wishes to accumulate $500,000 by his sixty-fifth birthday so he can retire to his summer place on Lake Hopatcong. He wishes to accumulate this amount by making equal deposits on his fortieth through his sixty-fourth birthdays. What annual deposit must Robert make if the fund will earn 12% interest compounded annually?

(c) Diane Ross has $20,000 to invest today at 9% to pay a debt of $47,347. How many years will it take her to accumulate enough to liquidate the debt?

(d) Cindy Houston has a $27,600 debt that she wishes to repay 4 years from today; she has $19,553 that she intends to invest for the 4 years. What rate of interest will she need to earn annually in order to accumulate enough to pay the debt?

5 **7** **P6-3 (Analysis of Alternatives)** Assume that Koh ShopMart has decided to surface and maintain for 10 years a vacant lot next to one of its stores to serve as a parking lot for customers. Management is considering the following bids involving two different qualities of surfacing for a parking area of 12,000 square yards (amounts in thousands).

Bid A: A surface that costs ₩5.75 per square yard to install. This surface will have to be replaced at the end of 5 years. The annual maintenance cost on this surface is estimated at 25 cents per square yard for each year except the last year of its service. The replacement surface will be similar to the initial surface.

Bid B: A surface that costs ₩10.50 per square yard to install. This surface has a probable useful life of 10 years and will require annual maintenance in each year except the last year, at an estimated cost of 9 cents per square yard.

Instructions
Prepare computations showing which bid should be accepted by Koh ShopMart. You may assume that the cost of capital is 9%, that the annual maintenance expenditures are incurred at the end of each year, and that prices are not expected to change during the next 10 years.

7 **P6-4 (Evaluating Payment Alternatives)** Ronald Long has just learned he has won a $500,000 prize in the lottery. The lottery has given him two options for receiving the payments. (1) If Ronald takes all the money today, the government will deduct taxes at a rate of 46% immediately. (2) The lottery offers Ronald a payout of 20 equal payments of $36,000 with the first payment occurring when Ronald turns in the winning ticket. Ronald will be taxed on each of these payments at a rate of 25%.

Instructions
Assuming Ronald can earn an 8% rate of return (compounded annually) on any money invested during this period, which payout option should he choose?

5 **7** **P6-5 (Analysis of Alternatives)** Julia Baker died, leaving to her husband Brent an insurance policy contract that provides that the beneficiary (Brent) can choose any one of the following four options.

(a) €55,000 immediate cash.

(b) €4,000 every 3 months payable at the end of each quarter for 5 years.

(c) €18,000 immediate cash and $1,800 every 3 months for 10 years, payable at the beginning of each 3-month period.

(d) €4,000 every 3 months for 3 years and $1,500 each quarter for the following 25 quarters, all payments payable at the end of each quarter.

Instructions

If money is worth 2½% per quarter, compounded quarterly, which option would you recommend that Brent exercise?

8 **P6-6 (Purchase Price of a Business)** During the past year, Stacy McGill planted a new vineyard on 150 acres of land that she leases for €30,000 a year. She has asked you as her accountant to assist her in determining the value of her vineyard operation.

The vineyard will bear no grapes for the first 5 years (1–5). In the next 5 years (6–10), Stacy estimates that the vines will bear grapes that can be sold for €60,000 each year. For the next 20 years (11–30) she expects the harvest will provide annual revenues of €110,000. But during the last 10 years (31–40) of the vineyard's life, she estimates that revenues will decline to €80,000 per year.

During the first 5 years the annual cost of pruning, fertilizing, and caring for the vineyard is estimated at €9,000; during the years of production, 6–40, these costs will rise to €12,000 per year. The relevant market rate of interest for the entire period is 12%. Assume that all receipts and payments are made at the end of each year.

Instructions

Dick Button has offered to buy Stacy's vineyard business by assuming the 40-year lease. On the basis of the current value of the business, what is the minimum price Stacy should accept?

5 **6** **P6-7 (Time Value Concepts Applied to Solve Business Problems)** Answer the following questions related **7** to Dubois Inc.

(a) Dubois Inc. has $600,000 to invest. The company is trying to decide between two alternative uses of the funds. One alternative provides $80,000 at the end of each year for 12 years, and the other is to receive a single lump-sum payment of $1,900,000 at the end of the 12 years. Which alternative should Dubois select? Assume the interest rate is constant over the entire investment.

(b) Dubois Inc. has completed the purchase of new iPad tablets. The fair value of the equipment is $824,150. The purchase agreement specifies an immediate down payment of $200,000 and semiannual payments of $76,952 beginning at the end of 6 months for 5 years. What is the interest rate, to the nearest percent, used in discounting this purchase transaction?

(c) Dubois Inc. loans money to John Kruk Corporation in the amount of $800,000. Dubois accepts an 8% note due in 7 years with interest payable semiannually. After 2 years (and receipt of interest for 2 years), Dubois needs money and therefore sells the note to Chicago National Bank, which demands interest on the note of 10% compounded semiannually. What is the amount Dubois will receive on the sale of the note?

(d) Dubois Inc. wishes to accumulate $1,300,000 by December 31, 2025, to retire bonds outstanding. The company deposits $200,000 on December 31, 2015, which will earn interest at 10% compounded quarterly, to help in the retirement of this debt. In addition, the company wants to know how much should be deposited at the end of each quarter for 10 years to ensure that $1,300,000 is available at the end of 2025. (The quarterly deposits will also earn at a rate of 10%, compounded quarterly.) (Round to even dollars.)

7 **P6-8 (Analysis of Alternatives)** Ellison Inc., a manufacturer of steel school lockers, plans to purchase a new punch press for use in its manufacturing process. After contacting the appropriate vendors, the purchasing department received differing terms and options from each vendor. The Engineering Department has determined that each vendor's punch press is substantially identical and each has a useful life of 20 years. In addition, Engineering has estimated that required year-end maintenance costs will be £1,000 per year for the first 5 years, £2,000 per year for the next 10 years, and £3,000 per year for the last 5 years. Following is each vendor's sale package.

Vendor A: £55,000 cash at time of delivery and 10 year-end payments of £18,000 each. Vendor A offers all its customers the right to purchase at the time of sale a separate 20-year maintenance service contract, under which Vendor A will perform all year-end maintenance at a one-time initial cost of £10,000.

Vendor B: Forty seminannual payments of £9,500 each, with the first installment due upon delivery. Vendor B will perform all year-end maintenance for the next 20 years at no extra charge.

Vendor C: Full cash price of £150,000 will be due upon delivery.

Instructions

Assuming that both Vendor A and B will be able to perform the required year-end maintenance, that Ellison's cost of funds is 10%, and the machine will be purchased on January 1, from which vendor should the press be purchased?

5 7 P6-9 (Analysis of Business Problems) James Kirk is a financial executive with McDowell Enterprises. Although James Kirk has not had any formal training in finance or accounting, he has a "good sense" for numbers and has helped the company grow from a very small company ($500,000 sales) to a large operation ($45 million in sales). With the business growing steadily, however, the company needs to make a number of difficult financial decisions in which James Kirk feels a little "over his head." He therefore has decided to hire a new employee with "numbers" expertise to help him. As a basis for determining whom to employ, he has decided to ask each prospective employee to prepare answers to questions relating to the following situations he has encountered recently. Here are the questions.

(a) In 2015, McDowell Enterprises negotiated and closed a long-term lease contract for newly constructed truck terminals and freight storage facilities. The buildings were constructed on land owned by the company. On January 1, 2016, McDowell took possession of the leased property. The 20-year lease is effective for the period January 1, 2016, through December 31, 2035. Advance rental payments of $800,000 are payable to the lessor (owner of facilities) on January 1 of each of the first 10 years of the lease term. Advance payments of $400,000 are due on January 1 for each of the last 10 years of the lease term. McDowell has an option to purchase all the leased facilities for $1 on December 31, 2035. At the time the lease was negotiated, the fair value of the truck terminals and freight storage facilities was approximately $7,200,000. If the company had borrowed the money to purchase the facilities, it would have had to pay 10% interest. Should the company have purchased rather than leased the facilities?

(b) Last year, the company exchanged a piece of land for a zero–interest-bearing note. The note is to be paid at the rate of $15,000 per year for 9 years, beginning one year from the date of disposal of the land. An appropriate rate of interest for the note was 11%. At the time the land was originally purchased, it cost $90,000. What is the fair value of the note?

(c) The company has always followed the policy to take any cash discounts on goods purchased. Recently the company purchased a large amount of raw materials at a price of $800,000 with terms 1/10, n/30 on which it took the discount. McDowell has recently estimated its cost of funds at 10%. Should McDowell continue this policy of always taking the cash discount?

5 7 P6-10 (Analysis of Lease vs. Purchase) Dunn Inc. owns and operates a number of hardware stores in the New England region. Recently, the company has decided to locate another store in a rapidly growing area of Maryland. The company is trying to decide whether to purchase or lease the building and related facilities.

Purchase: The company can purchase the site, construct the building, and purchase all store fixtures. The cost would be $1,850,000. An immediate down payment of $400,000 is required, and the remaining $1,450,000 would be paid off over 5 years at $350,000 per year (including interest; payments made at end of year). The property is expected to have a useful life of 12 years, and then it will be sold for $500,000. As the owner of the property, the company will have the following out-of-pocket expenses each period.

Property taxes (to be paid at the end of each year)	$40,000
Insurance (to be paid at the beginning of each year)	27,000
Other (primarily maintenance which occurs at the end of each year)	16,000
	$83,000

Lease: First Bank has agreed to purchase the site, construct the building, and install the appropriate fixtures for Dunn Inc. if Dunn will lease the completed facility for 12 years. The annual costs for the lease would be $270,000. Dunn would have no responsibility related to the facility over the 12 years. The terms of the lease are that Dunn would be required to make 12 annual payments (the first payment to be made at the time the store opens and then each following year). In addition, a deposit of $100,000 is required when the store is opened. This deposit will be returned at the end of the twelfth year, assuming no unusual damage to the building structure or fixtures.

Currently, the cost of funds for Dunn Inc. is 10%.

Instructions

Which of the two approaches should Dunn Inc. follow?

8 **P6-11 (Pension Funding)** You have been hired as a benefit consultant by Jean Barclay, the owner of Attic Angels. She wants to establish a retirement plan for herself and her three employees. Jean has provided the following information. The retirement plan is to be based upon annual salary for the last year before retirement and is to provide 50% of Jean's last-year annual salary and 40% of the last-year annual salary for each employee. The plan will make annual payments at the beginning of each year for 20 years from the date of retirement. Jean wishes to fund the plan by making 15 annual deposits beginning January 1, 2015. Invested funds will earn 12% compounded annually. Information about plan participants as of January 1, 2015, is as follows.

Jean Barclay, owner: Current annual salary of £48,000; estimated retirement date January 1, 2040.

Colin Davis, flower arranger: Current annual salary of £36,000; estimated retirement date January 1, 2045.

Anita Baker, sales clerk: Current annual salary of £18,000; estimated retirement date January 1, 2035.

Gavin Bryars, part-time bookkeeper: Current annual salary of £15,000; estimated retirement date January 1, 2030.

In the past, Jean has given herself and each employee a year-end salary increase of 4%. Jean plans to continue this policy in the future.

Instructions
(a) Based upon the above information, what will be the annual retirement benefit for each plan participant? (Round to the nearest pound.) (*Hint:* Jean will receive raises for 24 years.)
(b) What amount must be on deposit at the end of 15 years to ensure that all benefits will be paid? (Round to the nearest pound.)
(c) What is the amount of each annual deposit Jean must make to the retirement plan?

8 **P6-12 (Pension Funding)** Tim Buhl, newly appointed controller of STL, is considering ways to reduce his company's expenditures on annual pension costs. One way to do this is to switch STL's pension fund assets from First Security to NET Life. STL is a very well-respected computer manufacturer that recently has experienced a sharp decline in its financial performance for the first time in its 25-year history. Despite financial problems, STL still is committed to providing its employees with good pension and postretirement health benefits.

Under its present plan with First Security, STL is obligated to pay £43 million to meet the expected value of future pension benefits that are payable to employees as an annuity upon their retirement from the company. On the other hand, NET Life requires STL to pay only £35 million for identical future pension benefits. First Security is one of the oldest and most reputable insurance companies in Europe. NET Life has a much weaker reputation in the insurance industry. In pondering the significant difference in annual pension costs, Buhl asks himself, "Is this too good to be true?"

Instructions
Answer the following questions.

(a) Why might NET Life's pension cost requirement be £8 million less than First Security's requirement for the same future value?
(b) What ethical issues should Tim Buhl consider before switching STL's pension fund assets?
(c) Who are the stakeholders that could be affected by Buhl decision?

7 **9** **P6-13 (Expected Cash Flows and Present Value)** Danny's Lawn Equipment sells high-quality lawn mowers and offers a 3-year warranty on all new lawn mowers sold. In 2015, Danny sold $300,000 of new specialty mowers for golf greens for which Danny's service department does not have the equipment to do the service. Danny has entered into an agreement with Mower Mavens to perform all warranty service on the special mowers sold in 2015. Danny wishes to measure the fair value of the agreement to determine the warranty liability for sales made in 2015. The controller for Danny's Lawn Equipment estimates the following expected warranty cash outflows associated with the mowers sold in 2015.

Year	Cash Flow Estimate	Probability Assessment
2016	$2,500	20%
	4,000	60%
	5,000	20%
2017	$3,000	30%
	5,000	50%
	6,000	20%
2018	$4,000	30%
	6,000	40%
	7,000	30%

Instructions

Using expected cash flow and present value techniques, determine the value of the warranty liability for the 2015 sales. Use an annual discount rate of 5%. Assume all cash flows occur at the end of the year.

7 9 **P6-14 (Expected Cash Flows and Present Value)** At the end of 2015, Sawyer Company is conducting an impairment test and needs to develop a fair value estimate for machinery used in its manufacturing operations. Given the nature of Sawyer's production process, the equipment is for special use. (No second-hand market values are available.) The equipment will be obsolete in 2 years, and Sawyer's accountants have developed the following cash flow information for the equipment.

Year	Net Cash Flow Estimate	Probability Assessment
2016	€6,000	40%
	9,000	60%
2017	€ (500)	20%
	2,000	60%
	4,000	20%
	Residual Value	
2017	€500	50%
	900	50%

Instructions

Using expected cash flow and present value techniques, determine the fair value of the machinery at the end of 2015. Use a 6% discount rate. Assume all cash flows occur at the end of the year.

9 **P6-15 (Fair Value Estimate)** Murphy Mining Company recently purchased a quartz mine that it intends to work for the next 10 years. According to state environmental laws, Murphy must restore the mine site to its original natural prairie state after it ceases mining operations at the site. To properly account for the mine, Murphy must estimate the fair value of this environmental liability. This amount will be recorded as a liability and added to the value of the mine on Murphy's books. (You will learn more about these environmental liabilities in Chapters 10 and 13.)

There is no active market for environmental liabilities such as these, but Murphy has developed the following cash flow estimates based on its prior experience in mining-site restoration. It will take 3 years to restore the mine site when mining operations cease in 10 years. Each estimated cash outflow reflects an annual payment at the end of each year of the 3-year restoration period.

Restoration Estimated Cash Outflow	Probability Assessment
$15,000	10%
22,000	30%
25,000	50%
30,000	10%

Instructions

(a) What is the estimated fair value of Murphy's environmental liability? Murphy determines that the appropriate discount rate for this estimation is 5%. Round calculations to the nearest dollar.

(b) Is the estimate developed for part (a) a Level 1 or Level 3 fair value estimate? Explain.

USING YOUR JUDGMENT

FINANCIAL REPORTING

Financial Reporting Problem

Marks and Spencer plc (M&S)

The financial statements of M&S (GBR) are presented in Appendix A. The company's complete annual report, including the notes to the financial statements, is available online.

Instructions

Refer to M&S's financial statements and the accompanying notes to answer the following questions.

(a) Examining each item in M&S's statement of financial position, identify those items that require present value, discounting, or interest computations in establishing the amount reported. (The accompanying notes are an additional source for this information.)

(b) (1) What interest rates are disclosed by M&S as being used to compute interest and present values?
(2) Why are there so many different interest rates applied to M&S's financial statement elements (assets, liabilities, revenues, and expenses)?

Financial Statement Analysis Case

Assume the following information for Alta Gas (CAN). In 2014, Alta estimated the cash inflows from its oil and gas producing properties to be $375,000 per year. During 2015, a write-down caused the estimate to be decreased to $275,000 per year. Production costs (cash outflows) associated with all these properties were estimated to be $125,000 per year in 2014, but this amount was revised to $155,000 per year in 2015.

Instructions

(Assume that all cash flows occur at the end of the year.)

(a) Calculate the present value of net cash flows for 2014–2016 (three years), using the 2014 estimates and a 10% discount factor.

(b) Calculate the present value of net cash flows for 2015–2017 (three years), using the 2015 estimates and a 10% discount factor.

(c) Compare the results using the two estimates. Is information on future cash flows from oil- and gas-producing properties useful, considering that the estimates must be revised each year? Explain.

Accounting, Analysis, and Principles

Johnson Co. accepts a note receivable from a customer in exchange for some damaged inventory. The note requires the customer to make 10 semiannual installments of $50,000 each. The first installment begins six months from the date the customer took delivery of the damaged inventory. Johnson's management estimates that the fair value of the damaged inventory is $320,883.

Accounting

(a) What interest rate is Johnson implicitly charging the customer? Express the rate as an annual rate but assume semiannual compounding.

(b) At what dollar amount do you think Johnson should record the note receivable on the day the customer takes delivery of the damaged inventory?

Analysis

Assume the note receivable for damaged inventory makes up a significant portion of Johnson's assets. If interest rates increase, what happens to the fair value of the receivable? Briefly explain why.

Principles

The IASB has issued an accounting standard that allows companies to report assets such as notes receivable at fair value. Discuss how fair value versus historical cost potentially involves a trade-off of one desired quality of accounting information against another.

IFRS BRIDGE TO THE PROFESSION

Professional Research

At a recent meeting of the accounting staff in your company, the controller raised the issue of using present value techniques to conduct impairment tests for some of the company's fixed assets. Some of the more senior members of the staff admitted having little knowledge of present value concepts in this context, but they had heard about an appendix to an IFRS that provides some guidance. As the junior staff in the department, you have been asked to conduct some research of the authoritative literature on this topic and report back at the staff meeting next week.

Instructions

Access the IFRS authoritative literature at the IASB website (*http://eifrs.iasb.org/*) (you may register for free eIFRS access at this site). When you have accessed the documents, you can use the search tool in your Internet browser to respond to the following questions. (Provide paragraph citations.)

(a) Identify the components of present value measurement.

(b) Briefly describe the differences between the "traditional" and "expected cash flow" approaches to present value.

(c) What are the factors that should be taken into account when an asset-specific discount rate is not available from the market?

Professional Simulation

In this simulation, you are asked to address questions concerning the application of time value of money concepts to accounting problems. Prepare responses to all parts.

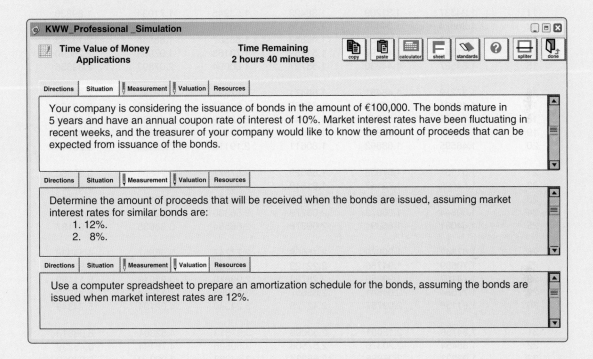

KWW_Professional _Simulation

Time Value of Money Applications

Time Remaining 2 hours 40 minutes

copy | paste | calculator | sheet | standards | ? | spliter | done

Directions | Situation | Measurement | Valuation | Resources

Your company is considering the issuance of bonds in the amount of €100,000. The bonds mature in 5 years and have an annual coupon rate of interest of 10%. Market interest rates have been fluctuating in recent weeks, and the treasurer of your company would like to know the amount of proceeds that can be expected from issuance of the bonds.

Directions | Situation | Measurement | Valuation | Resources

Determine the amount of proceeds that will be received when the bonds are issued, assuming market interest rates for similar bonds are:
1. 12%.
2. 8%.

Directions | Situation | Measurement | Valuation | Resources

Use a computer spreadsheet to prepare an amortization schedule for the bonds, assuming the bonds are issued when market interest rates are 12%.

TABLE 6-1   FUTURE VALUE OF 1 (FUTURE VALUE OF A SINGLE SUM)

$$FVF_{n,i} = (1 + i)^n$$

(n) Periods	2%	2½%	3%	4%	5%	6%
1	1.02000	1.02500	1.03000	1.04000	1.05000	1.06000
2	1.04040	1.05063	1.06090	1.08160	1.10250	1.12360
3	1.06121	1.07689	1.09273	1.12486	1.15763	1.19102
4	1.08243	1.10381	1.12551	1.16986	1.21551	1.26248
5	1.10408	1.13141	1.15927	1.21665	1.27628	1.33823
6	1.12616	1.15969	1.19405	1.26532	1.34010	1.41852
7	1.14869	1.18869	1.22987	1.31593	1.40710	1.50363
8	1.17166	1.21840	1.26677	1.36857	1.47746	1.59385
9	1.19509	1.24886	1.30477	1.42331	1.55133	1.68948
10	1.21899	1.28008	1.34392	1.48024	1.62889	1.79085
11	1.24337	1.31209	1.38423	1.53945	1.71034	1.89830
12	1.26824	1.34489	1.42576	1.60103	1.79586	2.01220
13	1.29361	1.37851	1.46853	1.66507	1.88565	2.13293
14	1.31948	1.41297	1.51259	1.73168	1.97993	2.26090
15	1.34587	1.44830	1.55797	1.80094	2.07893	2.39656
16	1.37279	1.48451	1.60471	1.87298	2.18287	2.54035
17	1.40024	1.52162	1.65285	1.94790	2.29202	2.69277
18	1.42825	1.55966	1.70243	2.02582	2.40662	2.85434
19	1.45681	1.59865	1.75351	2.10685	2.52695	3.02560
20	1.48595	1.63862	1.80611	2.19112	2.65330	3.20714
21	1.51567	1.67958	1.86029	2.27877	2.78596	3.39956
22	1.54598	1.72157	1.91610	2.36992	2.92526	3.60354
23	1.57690	1.76461	1.97359	2.46472	3.07152	3.81975
24	1.60844	1.80873	2.03279	2.56330	3.22510	4.04893
25	1.64061	1.85394	2.09378	2.66584	3.38635	4.29187
26	1.67342	1.90029	2.15659	2.77247	3.55567	4.54938
27	1.70689	1.94780	2.22129	2.88337	3.73346	4.82235
28	1.74102	1.99650	2.28793	2.99870	3.92013	5.11169
29	1.77584	2.04641	2.35657	3.11865	4.11614	5.41839
30	1.81136	2.09757	2.42726	3.24340	4.32194	5.74349
31	1.84759	2.15001	2.50008	3.37313	4.53804	6.08810
32	1.88454	2.20376	2.57508	3.50806	4.76494	6.45339
33	1.92223	2.25885	2.65234	3.64838	5.00319	6.84059
34	1.96068	2.31532	2.73191	3.79432	5.25335	7.25103
35	1.99989	2.37321	2.81386	3.94609	5.51602	7.68609
36	2.03989	2.43254	2.89828	4.10393	5.79182	8.14725
37	2.08069	2.49335	2.98523	4.26809	6.08141	8.63609
38	2.12230	2.55568	3.07478	4.43881	6.38548	9.15425
39	2.16474	2.61957	3.16703	4.61637	6.70475	9.70351
40	2.20804	2.68506	3.26204	4.80102	7.03999	10.28572

TABLE 6-1   FUTURE VALUE OF 1

8%	9%	10%	11%	12%	15%	(n) Periods
1.08000	1.09000	1.10000	1.11000	1.12000	1.15000	1
1.16640	1.18810	1.21000	1.23210	1.25440	1.32250	2
1.25971	1.29503	1.33100	1.36763	1.40493	1.52088	3
1.36049	1.41158	1.46410	1.51807	1.57352	1.74901	4
1.46933	1.53862	1.61051	1.68506	1.76234	2.01136	5
1.58687	1.67710	1.77156	1.87041	1.97382	2.31306	6
1.71382	1.82804	1.94872	2.07616	2.21068	2.66002	7
1.85093	1.99256	2.14359	2.30454	2.47596	3.05902	8
1.99900	2.17189	2.35795	2.55803	2.77308	3.51788	9
2.15892	2.36736	2.59374	2.83942	3.10585	4.04556	10
2.33164	2.58043	2.85312	3.15176	3.47855	4.65239	11
2.51817	2.81267	3.13843	3.49845	3.89598	5.35025	12
2.71962	3.06581	3.45227	3.88328	4.36349	6.15279	13
2.93719	3.34173	3.79750	4.31044	4.88711	7.07571	14
3.17217	3.64248	4.17725	4.78459	5.47357	8.13706	15
3.42594	3.97031	4.59497	5.31089	6.13039	9.35762	16
3.70002	4.32763	5.05447	5.89509	6.86604	10.76126	17
3.99602	4.71712	5.55992	6.54355	7.68997	12.37545	18
4.31570	5.14166	6.11591	7.26334	8.61276	14.23177	19
4.66096	5.60441	6.72750	8.06231	9.64629	16.36654	20
5.03383	6.10881	7.40025	8.94917	10.80385	18.82152	21
5.43654	6.65860	8.14028	9.93357	12.10031	21.64475	22
5.87146	7.25787	8.95430	11.02627	13.55235	24.89146	23
6.34118	7.91108	9.84973	12.23916	15.17863	28.62518	24
6.84847	8.62308	10.83471	13.58546	17.00000	32.91895	25
7.39635	9.39916	11.91818	15.07986	19.04007	37.85680	26
7.98806	10.24508	13.10999	16.73865	21.32488	43.53532	27
8.62711	11.16714	14.42099	18.57990	23.88387	50.06561	28
9.31727	12.17218	15.86309	20.62369	26.74993	57.57545	29
10.06266	13.26768	17.44940	22.89230	29.95992	66.21177	30
10.86767	14.46177	19.19434	25.41045	33.55511	76.14354	31
11.73708	15.76333	21.11378	28.20560	37.58173	87.56507	32
12.67605	17.18203	23.22515	31.30821	42.09153	100.69983	33
13.69013	18.72841	25.54767	34.75212	47.14252	115.80480	34
14.78534	20.41397	28.10244	38.57485	52.79962	133.17552	35
15.96817	22.25123	30.91268	42.81808	59.13557	153.15185	36
17.24563	24.25384	34.00395	47.52807	66.23184	176.12463	37
18.62528	26.43668	37.40434	52.75616	74.17966	202.54332	38
20.11530	28.81598	41.14479	58.55934	83.08122	232.92482	39
21.72452	31.40942	45.25926	65.00087	93.05097	267.86355	40

TABLE 6-2   PRESENT VALUE OF 1 (PRESENT VALUE OF A SINGLE SUM)

$$PVF_{n,i} = \frac{1}{(1 + i)^n} = (1 + i)^{-n}$$

(n) Periods	2%	2½%	3%	4%	5%	6%
1	.98039	.97561	.97087	.96154	.95238	.94340
2	.96117	.95181	.94260	.92456	.90703	.89000
3	.94232	.92860	.91514	.88900	.86384	.83962
4	.92385	.90595	.88849	.85480	.82270	.79209
5	.90573	.88385	.86261	.82193	.78353	.74726
6	.88797	.86230	.83748	.79031	.74622	.70496
7	.87056	.84127	.81309	.75992	.71068	.66506
8	.85349	.82075	.78941	.73069	.67684	.62741
9	.83676	.80073	.76642	.70259	.64461	.59190
10	.82035	.78120	.74409	.67556	.61391	.55839
11	.80426	.76214	.72242	.64958	.58468	.52679
12	.78849	.74356	.70138	.62460	.55684	.49697
13	.77303	.72542	.68095	.60057	.53032	.46884
14	.75788	.70773	.66112	.57748	.50507	.44230
15	.74301	.69047	.64186	.55526	.48102	.41727
16	.72845	.67362	.62317	.53391	.45811	.39365
17	.71416	.65720	.60502	.51337	.43630	.37136
18	.70016	.64117	.58739	.49363	.41552	.35034
19	.68643	.62553	.57029	.47464	.39573	.33051
20	.67297	.61027	.55368	.45639	.37689	.31180
21	.65978	.59539	.53755	.43883	.35894	.29416
22	.64684	.58086	.52189	.42196	.34185	.27751
23	.63416	.56670	.50669	.40573	.32557	.26180
24	.62172	.55288	.49193	.39012	.31007	.24698
25	.60953	.53939	.47761	.37512	.29530	.23300
26	.59758	.52623	.46369	.36069	.28124	.21981
27	.58586	.51340	.45019	.34682	.26785	.20737
28	.57437	.50088	.43708	.33348	.25509	.19563
29	.56311	.48866	.42435	.32065	.24295	.18456
30	.55207	.47674	.41199	.30832	.23138	.17411
31	.54125	.46511	.39999	.29646	.22036	.16425
32	.53063	.45377	.38834	.28506	.20987	.15496
33	.52023	.44270	.37703	.27409	.19987	.14619
34	.51003	.43191	.36604	.26355	.19035	.13791
35	.50003	.42137	.35538	.25342	.18129	.13011
36	.49022	.41109	.34503	.24367	.17266	.12274
37	.48061	.40107	.33498	.23430	.16444	.11579
38	.47119	.39128	.32523	.22529	.15661	.10924
39	.46195	.38174	.31575	.21662	.14915	.10306
40	.45289	.37243	.30656	.20829	.14205	.09722

TABLE 6-2   PRESENT VALUE OF 1

8%	9%	10%	11%	12%	15%	(n) Periods
.92593	.91743	.90909	.90090	.89286	.86957	1
.85734	.84168	.82645	.81162	.79719	.75614	2
.79383	.77218	.75132	.73119	.71178	.65752	3
.73503	.70843	.68301	.65873	.63552	.57175	4
.68058	.64993	.62092	.59345	.56743	.49718	5
.63017	.59627	.56447	.53464	.50663	.43233	6
.58349	.54703	.51316	.48166	.45235	.37594	7
.54027	.50187	.46651	.43393	.40388	.32690	8
.50025	.46043	.42410	.39092	.36061	.28426	9
.46319	.42241	.38554	.35218	.32197	.24719	10
.42888	.38753	.35049	.31728	.28748	.21494	11
.39711	.35554	.31863	.28584	.25668	.18691	12
.36770	.32618	.28966	.25751	.22917	.16253	13
.34046	.29925	.26333	.23199	.20462	.14133	14
.31524	.27454	.23939	.20900	.18270	.12289	15
.29189	.25187	.21763	.18829	.16312	.10687	16
.27027	.23107	.19785	.16963	.14564	.09293	17
.25025	.21199	.17986	.15282	.13004	.08081	18
.23171	.19449	.16351	.13768	.11611	.07027	19
.21455	.17843	.14864	.12403	.10367	.06110	20
.19866	.16370	.13513	.11174	.09256	.05313	21
.18394	.15018	.12285	.10067	.08264	.04620	22
.17032	.13778	.11168	.09069	.07379	.04017	23
.15770	.12641	.10153	.08170	.06588	.03493	24
.14602	.11597	.09230	.07361	.05882	.03038	25
.13520	.10639	.08391	.06631	.05252	.02642	26
.12519	.09761	.07628	.05974	.04689	.02297	27
.11591	.08955	.06934	.05382	.04187	.01997	28
.10733	.08216	.06304	.04849	.03738	.01737	29
.09938	.07537	.05731	.04368	.03338	.01510	30
.09202	.06915	.05210	.03935	.02980	.01313	31
.08520	.06344	.04736	.03545	.02661	.01142	32
.07889	.05820	.04306	.03194	.02376	.00993	33
.07305	.05340	.03914	.02878	.02121	.00864	34
.06763	.04899	.03558	.02592	.01894	.00751	35
.06262	.04494	.03235	.02335	.01691	.00653	36
.05799	.04123	.02941	.02104	.01510	.00568	37
.05369	.03783	.02674	.01896	.01348	.00494	38
.04971	.03470	.02430	.01708	.01204	.00429	39
.04603	.03184	.02210	.01538	.01075	.00373	40

TABLE 6-3   FUTURE VALUE OF AN ORDINARY ANNUITY OF 1

$$FVF\text{-}OA_{n,i} = \frac{(1 + i)^n - 1}{i}$$

(n) Periods	2%	2½%	3%	4%	5%	6%
1	1.00000	1.00000	1.00000	1.00000	1.00000	1.00000
2	2.02000	2.02500	2.03000	2.04000	2.05000	2.06000
3	3.06040	3.07563	3.09090	3.12160	3.15250	3.18360
4	4.12161	4.15252	4.18363	4.24646	4.31013	4.37462
5	5.20404	5.25633	5.30914	5.41632	5.52563	5.63709
6	6.30812	6.38774	6.46841	6.63298	6.80191	6.97532
7	7.43428	7.54743	7.66246	7.89829	8.14201	8.39384
8	8.58297	8.73612	8.89234	9.21423	9.54911	9.89747
9	9.75463	9.95452	10.15911	10.58280	11.02656	11.49132
10	10.94972	11.20338	11.46338	12.00611	12.57789	13.18079
11	12.16872	12.48347	12.80780	13.48635	14.20679	14.97164
12	13.41209	13.79555	14.19203	15.02581	15.91713	16.86994
13	14.68033	15.14044	15.61779	16.62684	17.71298	18.88214
14	15.97394	16.51895	17.08632	18.29191	19.59863	21.01507
15	17.29342	17.93193	18.59891	20.02359	21.57856	23.27597
16	18.63929	19.38022	20.15688	21.82453	23.65749	25.67253
17	20.01207	20.86473	21.76159	23.69751	25.84037	28.21288
18	21.41231	22.38635	23.41444	25.64541	28.13238	30.90565
19	22.84056	23.94601	25.11687	27.67123	30.53900	33.75999
20	24.29737	25.54466	26.87037	29.77808	33.06595	36.78559
21	25.78332	27.18327	28.67649	31.96920	35.71925	39.99273
22	27.29898	28.86286	30.53678	34.24797	38.50521	43.39229
23	28.84496	30.58443	32.45288	36.61789	41.43048	46.99583
24	30.42186	32.34904	34.42647	39.08260	44.50200	50.81558
25	32.03030	34.15776	36.45926	41.64591	47.72710	54.86451
26	33.67091	36.01171	38.55304	44.31174	51.11345	59.15638
27	35.34432	37.91200	40.70963	47.08421	54.66913	63.70577
28	37.05121	39.85980	42.93092	49.96758	58.40258	68.52811
29	38.79223	41.85630	45.21885	52.96629	62.32271	73.63980
30	40.56808	43.90270	47.57542	56.08494	66.43885	79.05819
31	42.37944	46.00027	50.00268	59.32834	70.76079	84.80168
32	44.22703	48.15028	52.50276	62.70147	75.29883	90.88978
33	46.11157	50.35403	55.07784	66.20953	80.06377	97.34316
34	48.03380	52.61289	57.73018	69.85791	85.06696	104.18376
35	49.99448	54.92821	60.46208	73.65222	90.32031	111.43478
36	51.99437	57.30141	63.27594	77.59831	95.83632	119.12087
37	54.03425	59.73395	66.17422	81.70225	101.62814	127.26812
38	56.11494	62.22730	69.15945	85.97034	107.70955	135.90421
39	58.23724	64.78298	72.23423	90.40915	114.09502	145.05846
40	60.40198	67.40255	75.40126	95.02552	120.79977	154.76197

TABLE 6-3   FUTURE VALUE OF AN ORDINARY ANNUITY OF 1

8%	9%	10%	11%	12%	15%	(n) Periods
1.00000	1.00000	1.00000	1.00000	1.00000	1.00000	1
2.08000	2.09000	2.10000	2.11000	2.12000	2.15000	2
3.24640	3.27810	3.31000	3.34210	3.37440	3.47250	3
4.50611	4.57313	4.64100	4.70973	4.77933	4.99338	4
5.86660	5.98471	6.10510	6.22780	6.35285	6.74238	5
7.33592	7.52334	7.71561	7.91286	8.11519	8.75374	6
8.92280	9.20044	9.48717	9.78327	10.08901	11.06680	7
10.63663	11.02847	11.43589	11.85943	12.29969	13.72682	8
12.48756	13.02104	13.57948	14.16397	14.77566	16.78584	9
14.48656	15.19293	15.93743	16.72201	17.54874	20.30372	10
16.64549	17.56029	18.53117	19.56143	20.65458	24.34928	11
18.97713	20.14072	21.38428	22.71319	24.13313	29.00167	12
21.49530	22.95339	24.52271	26.21164	28.02911	34.35192	13
24.21492	26.01919	27.97498	30.09492	32.39260	40.50471	14
27.15211	29.36092	31.77248	34.40536	37.27972	47.58041	15
30.32428	33.00340	35.94973	39.18995	42.75328	55.71747	16
33.75023	36.97371	40.54470	44.50084	48.88367	65.07509	17
37.45024	41.30134	45.59917	50.39593	55.74972	75.83636	18
41.44626	46.01846	51.15909	56.93949	63.43968	88.21181	19
45.76196	51.16012	57.27500	64.20283	72.05244	102.44358	20
50.42292	56.76453	64.00250	72.26514	81.69874	118.81012	21
55.45676	62.87334	71.40275	81.21431	92.50258	137.63164	22
60.89330	69.53194	79.54302	91.14788	104.60289	159.27638	23
66.76476	76.78981	88.49733	102.17415	118.15524	184.16784	24
73.10594	84.70090	98.34706	114.41331	133.33387	212.79302	25
79.95442	93.32398	109.18177	127.99877	150.33393	245.71197	26
87.35077	102.72314	121.09994	143.07864	169.37401	283.56877	27
95.33883	112.96822	134.20994	159.81729	190.69889	327.10408	28
103.96594	124.13536	148.63093	178.39719	214.58275	377.16969	29
113.28321	136.30754	164.49402	199.02088	241.33268	434.74515	30
123.34587	149.57522	181.94343	221.91317	271.29261	500.95692	31
134.21354	164.03699	201.13777	247.32362	304.84772	577.10046	32
145.95062	179.80032	222.25154	275.52922	342.42945	644.66553	33
158.62667	196.98234	245.47670	306.83744	384.52098	765.36535	34
172.31680	215.71076	271.02437	341.58955	431.66350	881.17016	35
187.10215	236.12472	299.12681	380.16441	484.46312	1014.34568	36
203.07032	258.37595	330.03949	422.98249	543.59869	1167.49753	37
220.31595	282.62978	364.04343	470.51056	609.83053	1343.62216	38
238.94122	309.06646	401.44778	523.26673	684.01020	1546.16549	39
259.05652	337.88245	442.59256	581.82607	767.09142	1779.09031	40

TABLE 6-4 PRESENT VALUE OF AN ORDINARY ANNUITY OF 1

$$PVF\text{-}OA_{n,i} = \frac{1 - \dfrac{1}{(1+i)^n}}{i}$$

(n) Periods	2%	2½%	3%	4%	5%	6%
1	.98039	.97561	.97087	.96154	.95238	.94340
2	1.94156	1.92742	1.91347	1.88609	1.85941	1.83339
3	2.88388	2.85602	2.82861	2.77509	2.72325	2.67301
4	3.80773	3.76197	3.71710	3.62990	3.54595	3.46511
5	4.71346	4.64583	4.57971	4.45182	4.32948	4.21236
6	5.60143	5.50813	5.41719	5.24214	5.07569	4.91732
7	6.47199	6.34939	6.23028	6.00205	5.78637	5.58238
8	7.32548	7.17014	7.01969	6.73274	6.46321	6.20979
9	8.16224	7.97087	7.78611	7.43533	7.10782	6.80169
10	8.98259	8.75206	8.53020	8.11090	7.72173	7.36009
11	9.78685	9.51421	9.25262	8.76048	8.30641	7.88687
12	10.57534	10.25776	9.95400	9.38507	8.86325	8.38384
13	11.34837	10.98319	10.63496	9.98565	9.39357	8.85268
14	12.10625	11.69091	11.29607	10.56312	9.89864	9.29498
15	12.84926	12.38138	11.93794	11.11839	10.37966	9.71225
16	13.57771	13.05500	12.56110	11.65230	10.83777	10.10590
17	14.29187	13.71220	13.16612	12.16567	11.27407	10.47726
18	14.99203	14.35336	13.75351	12.65930	11.68959	10.82760
19	15.67846	14.97889	14.32380	13.13394	12.08532	11.15812
20	16.35143	15.58916	14.87747	13.59033	12.46221	11.46992
21	17.01121	16.18455	15.41502	14.02916	12.82115	11.76408
22	17.65805	16.76541	15.93692	14.45112	13.16300	12.04158
23	18.29220	17.33211	16.44361	14.85684	13.48857	12.30338
24	18.91393	17.88499	16.93554	15.24696	13.79864	12.55036
25	19.52346	18.42438	17.41315	15.62208	14.09394	12.78336
26	20.12104	18.95061	17.87684	15.98277	14.37519	13.00317
27	20.70690	19.46401	18.32703	16.32959	14.64303	13.21053
28	21.28127	19.96489	18.76411	16.66306	14.89813	13.40616
29	21.84438	20.45355	19.18845	16.98371	15.14107	13.59072
30	22.39646	20.93029	19.60044	17.29203	15.37245	13.76483
31	22.93770	21.39541	20.00043	17.58849	15.59281	13.92909
32	23.46833	21.84918	20.38877	17.87355	15.80268	14.08404
33	23.98856	22.29188	20.76579	18.14765	16.00255	14.23023
34	24.49859	22.72379	21.13184	18.41120	16.19290	14.36814
35	24.99862	23.14516	21.48722	18.66461	16.37419	14.49825
36	25.48884	23.55625	21.83225	18.90828	16.54685	14.62099
37	25.96945	23.95732	22.16724	19.14258	16.71129	14.73678
38	26.44064	24.34860	22.49246	19.36786	16.86789	14.84602
39	26.90259	24.73034	22.80822	19.58448	17.01704	14.94907
40	27.35548	25.10278	23.11477	19.79277	17.15909	15.04630

TABLE 6-4   PRESENT VALUE OF AN ORDINARY ANNUITY OF 1

8%	9%	10%	11%	12%	15%	(n) Periods
.92593	.91743	.90909	.90090	.89286	.86957	1
1.78326	1.75911	1.73554	1.71252	1.69005	1.62571	2
2.57710	2.53130	2.48685	2.44371	2.40183	2.28323	3
3.31213	3.23972	3.16986	3.10245	3.03735	2.85498	4
3.99271	3.88965	3.79079	3.69590	3.60478	3.35216	5
4.62288	4.48592	4.35526	4.23054	4.11141	3.78448	6
5.20637	5.03295	4.86842	4.71220	4.56376	4.16042	7
5.74664	5.53482	5.33493	5.14612	4.96764	4.48732	8
6.24689	5.99525	5.75902	5.53705	5.32825	4.77158	9
6.71008	6.41766	6.14457	5.88923	5.65022	5.01877	10
7.13896	6.80519	6.49506	6.20652	5.93770	5.23371	11
7.53608	7.16073	6.81369	6.49236	6.19437	5.42062	12
7.90378	7.48690	7.10336	6.74987	6.42355	5.58315	13
8.24424	7.78615	7.36669	6.98187	6.62817	5.72448	14
8.55948	8.06069	7.60608	7.19087	6.81086	5.84737	15
8.85137	8.31256	7.82371	7.37916	6.97399	5.95424	16
9.12164	8.54363	8.02155	7.54879	7.11963	6.04716	17
9.37189	8.75563	8.20141	7.70162	7.24967	6.12797	18
9.60360	8.95012	8.36492	7.83929	7.36578	6.19823	19
9.81815	9.12855	8.51356	7.96333	7.46944	6.25933	20
10.01680	9.29224	8.64869	8.07507	7.56200	6.31246	21
10.20074	9.44243	8.77154	8.17574	7.64465	6.35866	22
10.37106	9.58021	8.88322	8.26643	7.71843	6.39884	23
10.52876	9.70661	8.98474	8.34814	7.78432	6.43377	24
10.67478	9.82258	9.07704	8.42174	7.84314	6.46415	25
10.80998	9.92897	9.16095	8.48806	7.89566	6.49056	26
10.93516	10.02658	9.23722	8.54780	7.94255	6.51353	27
11.05108	10.11613	9.30657	8.60162	7.98442	6.53351	28
11.15841	10.19828	9.36961	8.65011	8.02181	6.55088	29
11.25778	10.27365	9.42691	8.69379	8.05518	6.56598	30
11.34980	10.34280	9.47901	8.73315	8.08499	6.57911	31
11.43500	10.40624	9.52638	8.76860	8.11159	6.59053	32
11.51389	10.46444	9.56943	8.80054	8.13535	6.60046	33
11.58693	10.51784	9.60858	8.82932	8.15656	6.60910	34
11.65457	10.56682	9.64416	8.85524	8.17550	6.61661	35
11.71719	10.61176	9.67651	8.87859	8.19241	6.62314	36
11.77518	10.65299	9.70592	8.89963	8.20751	6.62882	37
11.82887	10.69082	9.73265	8.91859	8.22099	6.63375	38
11.87858	10.72552	9.75697	8.93567	8.23303	6.63805	39
11.92461	10.75736	9.77905	8.95105	8.24378	6.64178	40

TABLE 6-5   PRESENT VALUE OF AN ANNUITY DUE OF 1

$$PVF\text{-}AD_{n,i} = 1 + \dfrac{1 - \dfrac{1}{(1+i)^{n-1}}}{i}$$

(n) Periods	2%	2½%	3%	4%	5%	6%
1	1.00000	1.00000	1.00000	1.00000	1.00000	1.00000
2	1.98039	1.97561	1.97087	1.96154	1.95238	1.94340
3	2.94156	2.92742	2.91347	2.88609	2.85941	2.83339
4	3.88388	3.85602	3.82861	3.77509	3.72325	3.67301
5	4.80773	4.76197	4.71710	4.62990	4.54595	4.46511
6	5.71346	5.64583	5.57971	5.45182	5.32948	5.21236
7	6.60143	6.50813	6.41719	6.24214	6.07569	5.91732
8	7.47199	7.34939	7.23028	7.00205	6.78637	6.58238
9	8.32548	8.17014	8.01969	7.73274	7.46321	7.20979
10	9.16224	8.97087	8.78611	8.43533	8.10782	7.80169
11	9.98259	9.75206	9.53020	9.11090	8.72173	8.36009
12	10.78685	10.51421	10.25262	9.76048	9.30641	8.88687
13	11.57534	11.25776	10.95400	10.38507	9.86325	9.38384
14	12.34837	11.98319	11.63496	10.98565	10.39357	9.85268
15	13.10625	12.69091	12.29607	11.56312	10.89864	10.29498
16	13.84926	13.38138	12.93794	12.11839	11.37966	10.71225
17	14.57771	14.05500	13.56110	12.65230	11.83777	11.10590
18	15.29187	14.71220	14.16612	13.16567	12.27407	11.47726
19	15.99203	15.35336	14.75351	13.65930	12.68959	11.82760
20	16.67846	15.97889	15.32380	14.13394	13.08532	12.15812
21	17.35143	16.58916	15.87747	14.59033	13.46221	12.46992
22	18.01121	17.18455	16.41502	15.02916	13.82115	12.76408
23	18.65805	17.76541	16.93692	15.45112	14.16300	13.04158
24	19.29220	18.33211	17.44361	15.85684	14.48857	13.30338
25	19.91393	18.88499	17.93554	16.24696	14.79864	13.55036
26	20.52346	19.42438	18.41315	16.62208	15.09394	13.78336
27	21.12104	19.95061	18.87684	16.98277	15.37519	14.00317
28	21.70690	20.46401	19.32703	17.32959	15.64303	14.21053
29	22.28127	20.96489	19.76411	17.66306	15.89813	14.40616
30	22.84438	21.45355	20.18845	17.98371	16.14107	14.59072
31	23.39646	21.93029	20.60044	18.29203	16.37245	14.76483
32	23.93770	22.39541	21.00043	18.58849	16.59281	14.92909
33	24.46833	22.84918	21.38877	18.87355	16.80268	15.08404
34	24.98856	23.29188	21.76579	19.14765	17.00255	15.23023
35	25.49859	23.72379	22.13184	19.41120	17.19290	15.36814
36	25.99862	24.14516	22.48722	19.66461	17.37419	15.49825
37	26.48884	24.55625	22.83225	19.90828	17.54685	15.62099
38	26.96945	24.95732	23.16724	20.14258	17.71129	15.73678
39	27.44064	25.34860	23.49246	20.36786	17.86789	15.84602
40	27.90259	25.73034	23.80822	20.58448	18.01704	15.94907

TABLE 6-5   PRESENT VALUE OF AN ANNUITY DUE OF 1

8%	9%	10%	11%	12%	15%	(n) Periods
1.00000	1.00000	1.00000	1.00000	1.00000	1.00000	1
1.92593	1.91743	1.90909	1.90090	1.89286	1.86957	2
2.78326	2.75911	2.73554	2.71252	2.69005	2.62571	3
3.57710	3.53130	3.48685	3.44371	3.40183	3.28323	4
4.31213	4.23972	4.16986	4.10245	4.03735	3.85498	5
4.99271	4.88965	4.79079	4.69590	4.60478	4.35216	6
5.62288	5.48592	5.35526	5.23054	5.11141	4.78448	7
6.20637	6.03295	5.86842	5.71220	5.56376	5.16042	8
6.74664	6.53482	6.33493	6.14612	5.96764	5.48732	9
7.24689	6.99525	6.75902	6.53705	6.32825	5.77158	10
7.71008	7.41766	7.14457	6.88923	6.65022	6.01877	11
8.13896	7.80519	7.49506	7.20652	6.93770	6.23371	12
8.53608	8.16073	7.81369	7.49236	7.19437	6.42062	13
8.90378	8.48690	8.10336	7.74987	7.42355	6.58315	14
9.24424	8.78615	8.36669	7.98187	7.62817	6.72448	15
9.55948	9.06069	8.60608	8.19087	7.81086	6.84737	16
9.85137	9.31256	8.82371	8.37916	7.97399	6.95424	17
10.12164	9.54363	9.02155	8.54879	8.11963	7.04716	18
10.37189	9.75563	9.20141	8.70162	8.24967	7.12797	19
10.60360	9.95012	9.36492	8.83929	8.36578	7.19823	20
10.81815	10.12855	9.51356	8.96333	8.46944	7.25933	21
11.01680	10.29224	9.64869	9.07507	8.56200	7.31246	22
11.20074	10.44243	9.77154	9.17574	8.64465	7.35866	23
11.37106.	10.58021	9.88322	9.26643	8.71843	7.39884	24
11.52876	10.70661	9.98474	9.34814	8.78432	7.43377	25
11.67478	10.82258	10.07704	9.42174	8.84314	7.46415	26
11.80998	10.92897	10.16095	9.48806	8.89566	7.49056	27
11.93518	11.02658	10.23722	9.54780	8.94255	7.51353	28
12.05108	11.11613	10.30657	9.60162	8.98442	7.53351	29
12.15841	11.19828	10.36961	9.65011	9.02181	7.55088	30
12.25778	11.27365	10.42691	9.69379	9.05518	7.56598	31
12.34980	11.34280	10.47901	9.73315	9.08499	7.57911	32
12.43500	11.40624	10.52638	9.76860	9.11159	7.59053	33
12.51389	11.46444	10.56943	9.80054	9.13535	7.60046	34
12.58693	11.51784	10.60858	9.82932	9.15656	7.60910	35
12.65457	11.56682	10.64416	9.85524	9.17550	7.61661	36
12.71719	11.61176	10.67651	9.87859	9.19241	7.62314	37
12.77518	11.65299	10.70592	9.89963	9.20751	7.62882	38
12.82887	11.69082	10.73265	9.91859	9.22099	7.63375	39
12.87858	11.72552	10.75697	9.93567	9.23303	7.63805	40

Cash and Receivables

LEARNING OBJECTIVES

After studying this chapter, you should be able to:

1 Identify items considered cash.

2 Indicate how to report cash and related items.

3 Define receivables and identify the different types of receivables.

4 Explain accounting issues related to recognition of accounts receivable.

5 Explain accounting issues related to valuation of accounts receivable.

6 Explain accounting issues related to recognition of notes receivable.

7 Explain accounting issues related to valuation of notes receivable.

8 Understand special topics related to receivables.

9 Describe how to report and analyze receivables.

No-Tell Nortel

Nortel Networks (CAN) filed for bankruptcy in early 2009. Nortel's demise represents one of the biggest financial failures in Canadian history. At one time, it accounted for one-third of all equity traded on the Toronto Stock Exchange; in 2000, its shares were as high as $124.50. In 2009, however, those shares were worth just 1.2 cents. What happened to Nortel? First, competition was intense, and some bad business decisions were made. As a result, the company was hit very hard by the technology share price decline in the early 2000s. Second, it became involved in accounting scandals for which three of its executives eventually faced criminal charges.

In one loan accounting scheme, Nortel managed its bad debt allowance to ensure that executives received additional bonuses. For example, Nortel announced that it was necessary to restate its net income for 2003 to one-half of what it originally reported. In addition, the company had *understated* net income for 2002. How could this happen? Nortel executed a classic case of "cookie jar" earnings management by manipulating the allowance for doubtful accounts as the cookie jar.

As shown in the chart below, in 2002 Nortel overestimated the amount of bad debt expense (with a sizable allowance for doubtful accounts). Then, in 2003 Nortel slashed the amount of bad debt expense even though the total money owed by customers remained nearly unchanged. In 2002, its allowance was 19 percent of receivables compared to 10 percent in 2003—quite a difference.

It is difficult to determine if the allowance was too high in 2002, too low in 2003, or both. Whatever the case, the use of the allowance cookie jar permitted Nortel to report higher operating margins and net income in 2003. This analysis suggests the importance of looking carefully at the amount of bad debt expense that companies report. That is, an analysis of Nortel's bad debt accounting could have been used to help predict its slide into bankruptcy.

More recently, in the wake of the financial crisis of 2008, market analysts have raised the alarm on the bad debt allowances for receivables in the banking sector. In this case, the concern is that the allowances are not

	2003	2002
Amount customers owe, gross	$2.62 billion	$2.68 billion
Allowance for doubtful accounts	$256 million	$517 million
Allowance as % of gross	10%	19%

Source: Company reports.

high enough. That is, are the banks waiting too long to recognize bad debts? A classic example relates to many European banks that hold loans to countries like Greece, Spain, Ireland, and Portugal. Although these loans are clearly toxic (values overstated), some banks still contend that they should not be written down (partly because they can be held to maturity). However, this contention is suspect, and loan write-offs are rising. For example, **Bankia Group** (ESP), the country's third largest bank, recently restated its 2011 results to show a €3.3 billion loss rather than the previously reported €40.9 billion profit.

Given questionable bad debt accounting at both financial and non-financial companies, it is not surprising that the IASB is working on a project to improve the accounting for bad debts.

CONCEPTUAL FOCUS

> See the **Underlying Concepts** on pages 302, 312, and 322.
> Read the **Evolving Issue** on pages 319–320 for a discussion of accounting for loan losses.

INTERNATIONAL FOCUS

> Read the **Global Accounting Insights** on pages 322–323 for a discussion of non-IFRS financial reporting regarding cash and receivables.

PREVIEW OF CHAPTER 7

As our opening story indicates, estimating the collectibility of accounts receivable has important implications for accurate reporting of operating profits, net income, and assets. In this chapter, we discuss cash and receivables—two assets that are important to non-financial companies such as **Nortel** (CAN) and **Nokia** (FIN), and financial companies like **Bankia Group** (ESP) and **UBS** (CHE). The content and organization of the chapter are as follows.

Cash and Receivables

Cash	Accounts Receivable	Notes Receivable	Special Issues
• What is cash? • Reporting cash • Summary of cash-related items	• Recognition • Valuation • Impairment evaluation process	• Recognition • Valuation	• Fair value option • Derecognition of receivables • Presentation and analysis

CASH

What Is Cash?

LEARNING OBJECTIVE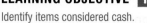

Identify items considered cash.

Cash is a financial asset—it is also a financial instrument. A **financial instrument** is defined as any contract that gives rise to a financial asset of one entity and a financial liability or equity interest of another entity. Examples of financial and non-financial assets are shown in Illustration 7-1.

ILLUSTRATION 7-1
Types of Assets

Financial Assets	Non-Financial Assets
Cash	Inventory
Loans and receivables	Prepaid expenses
Investments in debt securities	Property, plant, and equipment
Investments in equity securities	Intangible assets

See the Authoritative
Literature section
(page 332).

Cash, the most liquid of assets, is the standard medium of exchange and the basis for measuring and accounting for all other items. Companies generally classify cash as a current asset. Cash consists of coin, currency, and available funds on deposit at the bank. **[1]** Negotiable instruments such as money orders, certified checks, cashier's checks, personal checks, and bank drafts are also viewed as cash. What about savings accounts? Banks do have the legal right to demand notice before withdrawal. But, because banks rarely demand prior notice, savings accounts nevertheless are considered cash.

Some negotiable instruments provide small investors with an opportunity to earn interest. These items, more appropriately classified as temporary investments than as cash, include money market funds, money market savings certificates, certificates of deposit (CDs), and similar types of deposits and "short-term paper." These securities usually contain restrictions or penalties on their conversion to cash. Money market funds that provide checking account privileges, however, are usually classified as cash.

Certain items present classification problems: Companies treat **postdated checks and I.O.U.s** as receivables. They also treat **travel advances** as receivables if collected from employees or deducted from their salaries. Otherwise, companies classify the travel advance as a prepaid expense. **Postage stamps on hand** are classified as part of office supplies inventory or as a prepaid expense. Because **petty cash funds and change funds are used** to meet current operating expenses and liquidate current liabilities, companies include these funds in current assets as cash.

Reporting Cash

LEARNING OBJECTIVE 2

Indicate how to report cash and
related items.

Although the reporting of cash is relatively straightforward, a number of issues merit special attention. These issues relate to the reporting of:

1. Cash equivalents.
2. Restricted cash.
3. Bank overdrafts.

Cash Equivalents

A current classification that has become popular is "Cash and cash equivalents." **Cash equivalents** are short-term, highly liquid investments that are both (a) readily convertible to known amounts of cash, and (b) so near their maturity that they present insignificant risk of changes in value due to changes in interest rates. Generally, only investments with original maturities of three months or less qualify under these definitions. Examples of cash equivalents are Treasury bills, commercial paper, and money market funds. Some companies combine cash with temporary investments on the statement of financial position. In these cases, they describe the amount of the temporary investments either parenthetically or in the notes.

Most individuals think of cash equivalents as cash. Unfortunately, that is not always the case. Some companies found out the hard way and have taken sizable write-downs on cash equivalents. Their losses resulted because they purchased auction-rate notes that declined in value. These notes carry interest rates that usually reset weekly and often have long-maturity dates (as long as 30 years). Companies argued that such notes should be classified as cash equivalents because they can be routinely traded at auction on a daily basis. (In short, they are liquid and risk-free.) Auditors agreed and permitted cash-equivalent treatment even though maturities extended well beyond three months. But when the 2008 credit crunch hit, the auctions stopped and the value of these securities dropped because no market existed. In retrospect, the cash-equivalent classification was misleading.

It now appears likely that the cash-equivalent classification will be eliminated from financial statement presentations altogether. Companies will now report only cash. If an asset is not cash and is short-term in nature, it should be reported as a temporary investment. An interesting moral to this story is that when times are good, some sloppy accounting may work. But in bad times, it quickly becomes apparent that sloppy accounting can lead to misleading and harmful effects for users of the financial statements.

Restricted Cash

Petty cash, payroll, and dividend funds are examples of cash set aside for a particular purpose. In most situations, these fund balances are not material. Therefore, companies do not segregate them from cash in the financial statements. When material in amount, companies segregate **restricted cash** from "regular" cash for reporting purposes. Companies classify restricted cash either in the current assets or in the non-current assets section, depending on the date of availability or disbursement. Classification in the current section is appropriate if using the cash for payment of existing or maturing obligations (within a year or the operating cycle, whichever is longer). On the other hand, companies show the restricted cash in the non-current section of the statement of financial position if holding the cash for a longer period of time.

Cash classified in the non-current section is frequently set aside for plant expansion and retirement of long-term debt. **Infosys**'s (IND) restricted cash disclosure is shown in Illustration 7-2.

 Infosys

ILLUSTRATION 7-2
Disclosure of Restricted Cash

Cash and Cash Equivalents (000,000). Cash and cash equivalents as of March 31, 2013 and March 31, 2012 include restricted cash and bank balances of ₹3,050 and ₹2,680, respectively. The restrictions are primarily on account of cash and bank balances held as margin money deposits against guarantees, cash and bank balances held by irrevocable trusts controlled by the Company and unclaimed dividends.

Restricted Deposits (000,000). Deposits with financial institutions as at March 31, 2013 include ₹7,980 (₹5,500 as at March 31, 2012) deposited with Life Insurance Corporation of India to settle employee-related obligations as and when they arise during the normal course of business. This amount is considered as restricted cash and hence not considered "cash and cash equivalents."

Banks and other lending institutions often require customers to maintain minimum cash balances in checking or savings accounts. These minimum balances, called **compensating balances**, are "that portion of any demand deposit (or any time deposit or certificate of deposit) maintained by a corporation which constitutes support for existing borrowing arrangements of the corporation with a lending institution. Such arrangements would include both outstanding borrowings and the assurance of future credit availability." **[2]**

To avoid misleading investors about the amount of cash available to meet recurring obligations, companies should state separately **legally restricted deposits** held as compensating balances against **short-term** borrowing arrangements among the "Cash and cash equivalent items" in current assets. Companies should classify separately restricted deposits held as compensating balances against **long-term** borrowing arrangements as non-current assets in either the investments or other assets sections, using a caption such as "Cash on deposit maintained as compensating balance." In cases where compensating balance arrangements exist without agreements that restrict the use of cash amounts shown on the statement of financial position, companies should describe the arrangements and the amounts involved in the notes.

Bank Overdrafts

Bank overdrafts occur when a company writes a check for more than the amount in its cash account. Companies should report bank overdrafts in the current liabilities section, adding them to the amount reported as accounts payable. If material, companies should disclose these items separately, either on the face of the statement of financial position or in the related notes.[1]

Bank overdrafts are included as a component of cash if such overdrafts are repayable on demand and are an integral part of a company's cash management (such as the common practice of establishing offsetting arrangements against other accounts at the same bank). **[3]** Overdrafts not meeting these conditions should be reported as a current liability.

Summary of Cash-Related Items

Cash and cash equivalents include the medium of exchange and most negotiable instruments. If the item cannot be quickly converted to coin or currency, a company separately classifies it as an investment, receivable, or prepaid expense. Companies segregate and classify cash that is unavailable for payment of currently maturing liabilities in the non-current assets section. Illustration 7-3 summarizes the classification of cash-related items.

ILLUSTRATION 7-3
Classification of
Cash-Related Items

Classification of Cash, Cash Equivalents, and Non-Cash Items		
Item	Classification	Comment
Cash	Cash	If unrestricted, report as cash. If restricted, identify and classify as current and noncurrent assets.
Petty cash and change funds	Cash	Report as cash.
Short-term paper	Cash equivalents	Investments with maturity of less than 3 months, often combined with cash.
Short-term paper	Short-term investments	Investments with maturity of 3 to 12 months.
Postdated checks and I.O.U.s	Receivables	Assumed to be collectible.
Travel advances	Receivables	Assumed to be collected from employees or deducted from their salaries.
Postage on hand (as stamps or in postage meters)	Prepaid expenses	May also be classified as office supplies inventory.
Bank overdrafts	Cash	If no offsetting allowed, current liability.
Compensating balances	Cash separately classified as a deposit maintained as compensating balance	Classify as current or non-current in the statement of financial position. Disclose separately in notes details of the arrangement.

[1]Bank overdrafts usually occur because of a simple oversight by the company writing the check. Banks often expect companies to have overdrafts from time to time and therefore negotiate a fee as payment for this possible occurrence. However, at one time, one large brokerage firm began intentionally overdrawing its accounts by astronomical amounts—on some days exceeding $1 billion—thus obtaining interest-free loans that it could invest. Because the amounts were so large and fees were not negotiated in advance, the company came under criminal investigation for its actions.

What do the numbers mean? DEEP POCKETS

Many companies are loaded with cash. One major reason for hoarding cash is to make the company more secure in this credit-crunch environment, similar to that experienced in the post-credit-crunch environment of 2009. As one analyst noted, "At times like this, shareholder value goes out the window and it is all about survival. Liquidity is an absolute key component of any business." Another strategy is using the cash to look for deals. Centrica (GBR) indicates that it raises cash for the purpose of making acquisitions. Others point out that it enables them to continue investing even in the downturn. For example, the iPod was born during the last downturn related to the dot-com bubble. The following are some well-known companies that have substantial cash resources.

Company	Industry	Cash ($000,000)	Cash/Market Value
Nokia (FIN)	Technology hardware and equipment	$10,917	3.8%
Sony (JPN)	Technology hardware and equipment	8,646	4.6
Vale (BRA)	Materials	10,331	5.3
Siemens (DEU)	Conglomerate	8,450	6.1
Hewlett-Packard (USA)	Technology hardware and equipment	11,189	6.2
ExxonMobil (USA)	Oil and gas operations	31,437	10.5
Apple (USA)	Technology hardware and equipment	7,236	12.5

Source: Anonymous, "Cheap and Cash Rich," *Forbes* (April 27, 2009).

ACCOUNTS RECEIVABLE

Receivables are also financial assets—they are also a financial instrument. Receivables (often referred to as *loans and receivables*) are claims held against customers and others for money, goods, or services. An example of a loan is a financial institution like **HSBC** (GBR) providing funds to **Fiat** (ITA). An example of a receivable is a company like **Airbus** (FRA) recording an account receivable when it sells an airplane on account to **All Nippon Airways Co. Ltd.** (JPN). For purposes of discussion, we will simply use the term *receivables* to mean loans and receivables.

3 **LEARNING OBJECTIVE**
Define receivables and identify the different types of receivables.

For financial statement purposes, companies classify receivables as either **current** (short-term) or **non-current** (long-term). Companies expect to collect **current receivables** within a year or during the current operating cycle, whichever is longer. They classify all other receivables as **non-current**. Receivables are further classified in the statement of financial position as either trade or non-trade receivables.

Customers often owe a company amounts for goods bought or services rendered. A company may subclassify these **trade receivables**, usually the most significant item in its current assets, into accounts receivable and notes receivable. **Accounts receivable** are oral promises of the purchaser to pay for goods and services sold. They represent "open accounts" resulting from short-term extensions of credit. A company normally collects them within 30 to 60 days. **Notes receivable** are written promises to pay a certain sum of money on a specified future date. They may arise from sales, financing, or other transactions. Notes may be short-term or long-term.

Non-trade receivables arise from a variety of transactions. Some examples of non-trade receivables are:

1. Advances to officers and employees.

2. Advances to subsidiaries.

3. Deposits paid to cover potential damages or losses.

4. Deposits paid as a guarantee of performance or payment.

5. Dividends and interest receivable.

6. Claims against:

    (a) Insurance companies for casualties sustained.

    (b) Defendants under suit.

    (c) Governmental bodies for tax refunds.

    (d) Common carriers for damaged or lost goods.

    (e) Creditors for returned, damaged, or lost goods.

    (f) Customers for returnable items (crates, containers, etc.).

Because of the peculiar nature of non-trade receivables, companies generally report them as separate items in the statement of financial position. Illustration 7-4 shows the reporting of trade and non-trade receivables in the statements of financial position of **Heineken** (NLD) and **Nokia** (FIN).

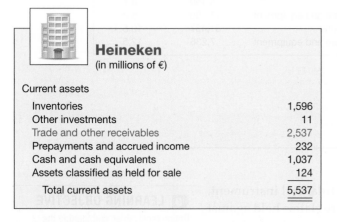

ILLUSTRATION 7-4
Receivables Statement of Financial Position Presentations

The basic issues in accounting for accounts and notes receivable are the same: **recognition** and **valuation**. We discuss these basic issues for accounts and notes receivable next.

Recognition of Accounts Receivable

LEARNING OBJECTIVE **4**
Explain accounting issues related to recognition of accounts receivable.

In most receivables transactions, the amount to be recognized is the exchange price between the two parties. **The exchange price is the amount due from the debtor** (a customer or a borrower). Some type of business document, often an invoice, serves as evidence of the exchange price. Two factors may complicate the measurement of the exchange price: (1) the availability of discounts (trade and cash discounts), and (2) the length of time between the sale and the due date of payments (the interest element).

Trade Discounts

Prices may be subject to a trade or quantity discount. Companies use such **trade discounts** to avoid frequent changes in catalogs, to alter prices for different quantities purchased, or to hide the true invoice price from competitors.

Trade discounts are commonly quoted in percentages. For example, say your textbook has a list price of $90, and the publisher sells it to college bookstores for list less a 30 percent trade discount. The publisher then records the receivable at $63 per textbook. The publisher, per normal practice, simply deducts the trade discount from the list price and bills the customer net.

As another example, a major coffee roaster at one time sold a 10-ounce package of its coffee listing at €5.85 to supermarkets for €5.05, a trade discount of approximately 14 percent. The supermarkets in turn sold the coffee for €5.20 per package. The roaster records the receivable and related sales revenue at €5.05 per package, not €5.85.

Cash Discounts (Sales Discounts)

Companies offer **cash discounts (sales discounts)** to induce prompt payment. Cash discounts generally presented in terms such as 2/10, n/30 (2 percent if paid within 10 days, gross amount due in 30 days), or 2/10, E.O.M., net 30, E.O.M. (2 percent if paid any time before the tenth day of the following month, with full payment received by the thirtieth of the following month).

Companies usually take sales discounts unless their cash is severely limited. Why? A company that receives a 1 percent reduction in the sales price for payment within 10 days, total payment due within 30 days, effectively earns 18.25 percent ($.01 \div [20/365]$), or at least avoids that rate of interest cost.

Companies usually record sales and related sales discount transactions by entering the receivable and sale at the gross amount. Under this method, companies recognize sales discounts only when they receive payment within the discount period. The income statement shows sales discounts as a deduction from sales to arrive at net sales.

Some contend that sales discounts not taken reflect penalties added to an established price to encourage prompt payment. That is, the seller offers sales on account at a slightly higher price than if selling for cash. The cash discount offered offsets the increase. Thus, customers who pay within the discount period actually purchase at the cash price. Those who pay after expiration of the discount period pay a penalty for the delay—an amount in excess of the cash price. Per this reasoning, companies record sales and receivables net. They subsequently debit any discounts not taken to Accounts Receivable and credit to Sales Discounts Forfeited. The entries in Illustration 7-5 show the difference between the gross and net methods.

Gross Method			Net Method		
Sales of $10,000, terms 2/10, n/30					
Accounts Receivable	10,000		Accounts Receivable	9,800	
Sales Revenue		10,000	Sales Revenue		9,800
Payment on $4,000 of sales received within discount period					
Cash	3,920		Cash	3,920	
Sales Discounts ($4,000 × .02)	80		Accounts Receivable		3,920
Accounts Receivable		4,000			
Payment on $6,000 of sales received after discount period					
Cash	6,000		Accounts Receivable	120	
Accounts Receivable		6,000	Sales Discounts		
			Forfeited ($6,000 × .02)		120
			Cash	6,000	
			Accounts Receivable		6,000

ILLUSTRATION 7-5
Entries under Gross and Net Methods of Recording Cash (Sales) Discounts

If using the gross method, a company reports sales discounts as a deduction from sales in the income statement. Proper expense recognition dictates that the company also reasonably estimates the expected discounts to be taken and charges that amount against sales. If using the net method, a company considers Sales Discounts Forfeited as an "Other income and expense" item.[2]

Theoretically, the recognition of Sales Discounts Forfeited (net method) is correct. The receivable is stated closer to its realizable value, and the net sales figure measures the revenue earned from the sale. As a practical matter, however, companies seldom use the net method because it requires additional analysis and bookkeeping. For example, the net method requires adjusting entries to record sales discounts forfeited on accounts receivable that have passed the discount period.

Non-Recognition of Interest Element

Ideally, a company should measure receivables in terms of their present value, that is, the discounted value of the cash to be received in the future. When expected cash receipts require a waiting period, the receivable face amount is not worth the amount that the company ultimately receives.

To illustrate, assume that **Carrefour** (FRA) makes a sale on account for €1,000 with payment due in four months. The applicable annual rate of interest is 12 percent, and payment is made at the end of four months. The present value of that receivable is not €1,000 but €961.54 (€1,000 × .96154). In other words, the €1,000 Carrefour receives four months from now is not the same as the €1,000 received today.

Theoretically, any revenue after the period of sale is interest revenue. In practice, companies ignore interest revenue related to accounts receivable because, for current assets, the amount of the discount is not usually material in relation to the net income for the period.

LEARNING OBJECTIVE 5
Explain accounting issues related to valuation of accounts receivable.

Valuation of Accounts Receivable

Reporting of receivables involves (1) classification and (2) valuation on the statement of financial position. Classification involves determining the length of time each receivable will be outstanding. Companies classify receivables intended to be collected within a year or the operating cycle, whichever is longer, as current. All other receivables are classified as non-current.

Companies value and report short-term receivables at cash realizable value—**the net amount they expect to receive in cash.**[3] Determining cash realizable value requires estimating both uncollectible receivables and any returns or allowances to be granted.

Uncollectible Accounts Receivable

As one revered accountant aptly noted, the credit manager's idea of heaven probably would be a place where everyone (eventually) paid his or her debts.[4] Unfortunately, this situation often does not occur. For example, a customer may not be able to pay because of a decline in its sales revenue due to a downturn in the economy. Similarly, individuals may be laid off from their jobs or faced with unexpected hospital bills. Companies record credit losses as debits to Bad Debt Expense (or Uncollectible Accounts Expense). Such losses are a normal and necessary risk of doing business on a credit basis.

---

[2]To the extent that discounts not taken reflect a short-term financing, some argue that companies could use an interest revenue account to record these amounts.

[3]Technically, the IASB indicates that receivables are reported at amortized cost. **Amortized cost** is the receivable amount measured at the date of acquisition, adjusted for any principal payments, amortization of premium or discount, and reduced by any impairment or estimated uncollectibility. **[4]** Given that this term has more relevance for long-term receivables, we defer discussion of this concept until later and use cash realizable value here. The reason is that generally there is no discounting of the principal amount or any discount or premium amortization related to the short-term receivables.

[4]William J. Vatter, *Managerial Accounting* (Englewood Cliffs, N.J.: Prentice-Hall, 1950), p. 60.

Two methods are used in accounting for uncollectible accounts: (1) the direct write-off method and (2) the allowance method. The following sections explain these methods.

Direct Write-Off Method for Uncollectible Accounts

Under the direct write-off method, when a company determines a particular account to be uncollectible, it charges the loss to Bad Debt Expense. Assume, for example, that on December 10 Cruz Co. writes off as uncollectible Yusado's NT$8,000 balance. The entry is:

December 10		
Bad Debt Expense	8,000	
Accounts Receivable (Yusado)		8,000
(To record write-off of Yusado account)		

Under this method, Bad Debt Expense will show only **actual losses** from uncollectibles. The company will report accounts receivable at its gross amount.

Supporters of the **direct write-off-method** (which is often used for tax purposes) contend that it records facts, not estimates. It assumes that a good account receivable resulted from each sale, and that later events revealed certain accounts to be uncollectible and worthless. From a practical standpoint, this method is simple and convenient to apply. But the direct write-off method is theoretically deficient: It usually fails to match costs with revenues of the period. Nor does it result in receivables being stated at cash realizable value on the statement of financial position. **As a result, using the direct write-off method is not considered appropriate, except when the amount uncollectible is immaterial.**

Allowance Method for Uncollectible Accounts

The allowance method of accounting for bad debts involves estimating uncollectible accounts at the end of each period. This provides a better measure of income. It also ensures that companies state receivables on the statement of financial position at their cash realizable value. **Cash realizable value** is the net amount the company expects to receive in cash. It excludes amounts that the company estimates it will not collect. Thus, this method reduces receivables in the statement of financial position by the amount of estimated uncollectible receivables.

IFRS requires the allowance method for financial reporting purposes when bad debts are material in amount. This method has three essential features:

1. Companies **estimate** uncollectible accounts receivable. They record this estimated expense in the same accounting period in which they record the revenues.

2. Companies debit estimated uncollectibles to Bad Debt Expense and credit them to Allowance for Doubtful Accounts (a contra asset account) through an adjusting entry at the end of each period.

3. When companies write off a specific account, they debit actual uncollectibles to Allowance for Doubtful Accounts and credit that amount to Accounts Receivable.

Recording Estimated Uncollectibles. To illustrate the allowance method, assume that Brown Furniture has credit sales of £1,800,000 in 2015. Of this amount, £150,000 remains uncollected at December 31. The credit manager estimates that £10,000 of these sales will never be collected. The adjusting entry to record the estimated uncollectibles is:

December 31, 2015		
Bad Debt Expense	10,000	
Allowance for Doubtful Accounts		10,000
(To record estimate of uncollectible accounts)		

Brown reports Bad Debt Expense in the income statement as an operating expense. Thus, the estimated uncollectibles are recorded with sales in 2015. That is, Brown records the expense in the same year it made the sales.

As Illustration 7-6 shows, the company deducts the allowance account from accounts receivable in the current assets section of the statement of financial position.

ILLUSTRATION 7-6
Presentation of Allowance for Doubtful Accounts

BROWN FURNITURE STATEMENT OF FINANCIAL POSITION (PARTIAL)		
Current assets		
Inventory		£300,000
Prepaid expense		25,000
Accounts receivable	£150,000	
Less: Allowance for doubtful accounts	10,000	140,000
Cash		15,000
Total current assets		£480,000

Allowance for Doubtful Accounts shows the estimated amount of claims on customers that the company expects will become uncollectible in the future. Companies use a contra account instead of a direct credit to Accounts Receivable because they do not know which customers will not pay. The credit balance in the allowance account will absorb the specific write-offs when they occur. The amount of £140,000 in Illustration 7-6 represents the **cash realizable value** of the accounts receivable at the statement date. **Companies do not close Allowance for Doubtful Accounts at the end of the fiscal year.**

Recording the Write-Off of an Uncollectible Account. When companies have exhausted all means of collecting a past-due account and collection appears impossible, the company should write off the account. In the credit card industry, for example, it is standard practice to write off accounts that are 210 days past due.

To illustrate a receivables write-off, assume that the financial vice president of Brown Furniture authorizes a write-off of the £1,000 balance owed by Randall Co. on March 1, 2016. The entry to record the write-off is:

March 1, 2016

Allowance for Doubtful Accounts	1,000	
Accounts Receivable (Randall Co.)		1,000
(Write-off of Randall Co. account)		

Bad Debt Expense does not increase when the write-off occurs. **Under the allowance method, companies debit every bad debt write-off to the allowance account rather than to Bad Debt Expense.** A debit to Bad Debt Expense would be incorrect because the company has already recognized the expense when it made the adjusting entry for estimated bad debts. Instead, the entry to record the write-off of an uncollectible account reduces both Accounts Receivable and Allowance for Doubtful Accounts.

Recovery of an Uncollectible Account. Occasionally, a company collects from a customer after it has written off the account as uncollectible. The company makes two entries to record the recovery of a bad debt: (1) It reverses the entry made in writing off the account. This reinstates the customer's account. (2) It journalizes the collection in the usual manner.

To illustrate, assume that on July 1, Randall Co. pays the £1,000 amount that Brown had written off on March 1. These are the entries:

July 1, 2016

Accounts Receivable (Randall Co.)	1,000	
Allowance for Doubtful Accounts		1,000
(To reverse write-off of account)		
Cash	1,000	
Accounts Receivable (Randall Co.)		1,000
(Collection of account)		

Note that the recovery of a bad debt, like the write-off of a bad debt, affects **only statement of financial position accounts**. The net effect of the two entries above is a debit to Cash and a credit to Allowance for Doubtful Accounts for £1,000.[5]

Bases Used for Allowance Method. To simplify the preceding explanation, we assumed we knew the amount of the expected uncollectibles. In "real life," companies must estimate that amount when they use the allowance method. Two bases are used to determine this amount: **(1) percentage of sales** and **(2) percentage of receivables**. Both bases are generally accepted. The choice is a management decision. It depends on the relative emphasis that management wishes to give to expenses and revenues on the one hand or to cash realizable value of the accounts receivable on the other. The choice is whether to emphasize income statement or statement of financial position relationships. Illustration 7-7 compares the two bases.

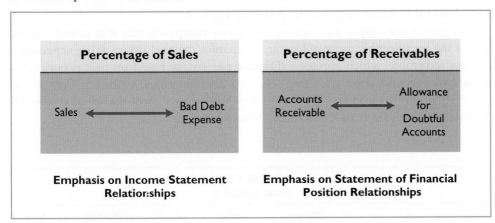

ILLUSTRATION 7-7
Comparison of Bases for
Estimating Uncollectibles

The percentage-of-sales basis results in a better matching of expenses with revenues—an income statement viewpoint. The percentage-of-receivables basis produces the better estimate of cash realizable value—a statement of financial position viewpoint. Under both bases, the company determines the amount of bad debt expense based on its past experience with bad debt losses.

Percentage-of-sales (income statement) approach. In the **percentage-of-sales approach**, management estimates what percentage of credit sales will be uncollectible. This percentage is based on past experience and anticipated credit policy.

The company applies this percentage to either total credit sales or net credit sales of the current year. To illustrate, assume that Gonzalez Company elects to use the percentage-of-sales basis. It concludes that 1% of net credit sales will become uncollectible. If net credit sales for 2015 are R$800,000, the estimated bad debts expense is R$8,000 (1% × R$800,000). The adjusting entry is:

December 31, 2015

Bad Debt Expense	8,000	
Allowance for Doubtful Accounts		8,000

After the adjusting entry is posted, assuming the allowance account already has a credit balance of R$1,723, the accounts of Gonzalez Company will show the following:

Bad Debt Expense		Allowance for Doubtful Accounts	
Dec. 31 Adj. 8,000		Jan. 1 Bal. 1,723	
		Dec. 31 Adj. 8,000	
		Dec. 31 Bal. 9,723	

ILLUSTRATION 7-8
Bad Debt Accounts
after Posting

[5]If using the direct write-off approach, the company debits the amount collected to Cash and credits a revenue account entitled Uncollectible Amounts Recovered, with proper notation in the customer's account.

The amount of bad debt expense and the related credit to the allowance account are unaffected by any balance currently existing in the allowance account. Because the bad debt expense estimate is related to a nominal account (Sales Revenue), any balance in the allowance is ignored. Therefore, the percentage-of-sales method achieves a better matching of cost and revenues. This method is frequently referred to as the **income statement approach**.

Percentage-of-receivables (statement of financial position) approach. Using past experience, a company can estimate the percentage of its outstanding receivables that will become uncollectible, without identifying specific accounts. This procedure provides a reasonably accurate estimate of the receivables' realizable value. But, it does not fit the concept of matching cost and revenues. Rather, it simply reports receivables in the statement of financial position at cash realizable value. Hence, it is referred to as the percentage-of-receivables (or statement of financial position) approach.

Companies may apply this method using one **composite rate** that reflects an estimate of the uncollectible receivables. Or, companies may set up an aging schedule of accounts receivable, which applies a different percentage based on past experience to the various age categories. An aging schedule also identifies which accounts require special attention by indicating the extent to which certain accounts are past due. The schedule of Wilson & Co. in Illustration 7-9 is an example.

ILLUSTRATION 7-9
Accounts Receivable
Aging Schedule

WILSON & CO.
AGING SCHEDULE

Name of Customer	Balance Dec. 31	Under 60 days	60–90 days	91–120 days	Over 120 days
Western Stainless Steel Corp.	€ 98,000	€ 80,000	€18,000		
Brockway Steel Company	320,000	320,000			
Freeport Sheet & Tube Co.	55,000				€55,000
Allegheny Iron Works	74,000	60,000		€14,000	
	€547,000	€460,000	€18,000	€14,000	€55,000

Summary

Age	Amount	Percentage Estimated to Be Uncollectible	Required Balance in Allowance
Under 60 days old	€460,000	4%	€18,400
60–90 days old	18,000	15%	2,700
91–120 days old	14,000	20%	2,800
Over 120 days	55,000	25%	13,750
Year-end balance of allowance for doubtful accounts			€37,650

Wilson reports bad debt expense of €37,650 for this year, assuming that no balance existed in the allowance account.

To change the illustration slightly, **assume that the allowance account had a credit balance of €800 before adjustment**. In this case, Wilson adds €36,850 (€37,650 − €800) to the allowance account, and makes the following entry.

| Bad Debt Expense | 36,850 | |
| Allowance for Doubtful Accounts | | 36,850 |

Wilson therefore states the balance in the allowance account at €37,650. **If the allowance balance before adjustment had a debit balance of €200**, then Wilson records bad debt expense of €37,850 (€37,650 desired balance + €200 debit balance). In the percentage-of-receivables method, Wilson **cannot ignore** the balance in the allowance account because the percentage is related to a real account (Accounts Receivable).

Impairment Evaluation Process

For many companies, making appropriate allowances for bad debts is relatively straight-forward. The IASB, however, provides detailed guidelines to be used to assess whether receivables should be considered uncollectible (often referred to as *impaired*).

Companies assess their receivables for impairment each reporting period and start the impairment assessment by considering whether objective evidence indicates that one or more loss events have occurred. Examples of possible loss events are:

1. Significant financial problems of the customer.
2. Payment defaults.
3. Renegotiation of terms of the receivable due to financial difficulty of the customer.
4. Measurable decrease in estimated future cash flows from a group of receivables since initial recognition, although the decrease cannot yet be identified with individual assets in the group.

A receivable is considered impaired when a loss event indicates a negative impact on the estimated future cash flows to be received from the customer. **[5]**

The IASB requires that the impairment assessment should be performed as follows.

1. Receivables that are individually significant should be considered for impairment separately. If impaired, the company recognizes it. Receivables that are not individually significant may also be assessed individually, but it is not necessary to do so.
2. Any receivable individually assessed that is not considered impaired should be included with a group of assets with similar credit-risk characteristics and collectively assessed for impairment.
3. Any receivables not **individually assessed** should be **collectively assessed** for impairment.

To illustrate, assume that Hector Company has the following receivables classified into individually significant and all other receivables.

Individually significant receivables		
Yaan Company	€ 40,000	
Randon Inc.	100,000	
Fernando Co.	60,000	
Blanchard Ltd.	50,000	€250,000
All other receivables		500,000
Total		€750,000

Hector determines that Yaan's receivable is impaired by €15,000, and Blanchard's receivable is totally impaired. Both Randon's and Fernando's receivables are not considered impaired. Hector also determines that a composite rate of 2% is appropriate to measure impairment on all other receivables. The total impairment is computed as follows.

ILLUSTRATION 7-10
Computation of
Impairment

Accounts Receivable Impairments		
Individually assessed receivables		
Yaan Company		€15,000
Blanchard Ltd.		50,000
Collectively assessed receivables	€500,000	
Add: Randon Inc.	100,000	
Fernando Co.	60,000	
Total collectively assessed receivables	€660,000	
Collectively assessed impairments (€660,000 × 2%)		13,200
Total impairment		€78,200

Hector therefore has an impairment related to its receivables of €78,200. The most controversial part of this computation is that Hector must include in the collective assessment the receivables from Randon and Fernando that were individually assessed and not considered impaired. The rationale for including Randon and Fernando in the collective assessment is that companies often do not have all the information at hand to make an informed decision for individual assessments.

NOTES RECEIVABLE

LEARNING OBJECTIVE 6

Explain accounting issues related to recognition of notes receivable.

A note receivable is supported by a formal **promissory note**, a written promise to pay a certain sum of money at a specific future date. Such a note is a negotiable instrument that a **maker** signs in favor of a designated **payee** who may legally and readily sell or otherwise transfer the note to others. Although all notes contain an interest element because of the time value of money, companies classify them as interest-bearing or non-interest-bearing. **Interest-bearing notes** have a stated rate of interest. **Zero-interest-bearing notes** (non-interest-bearing) include interest as part of their face amount. Notes receivable are considered fairly liquid, even if long-term, because companies may easily convert them to cash (although they might pay a fee to do so).

Companies frequently accept notes receivable from customers who need to extend the payment period of an outstanding receivable. Or, they require notes from high-risk or new customers. In addition, companies often use notes in loans to employees and subsidiaries, and in the sales of property, plant, and equipment. In some industries (e.g., the pleasure and sport boat industry) notes support all credit sales. The majority of notes, however, originate from lending transactions. The basic issues in accounting for notes receivable are the same as those for accounts receivable: **recognition and valuation**.

Recognition of Notes Receivable

Companies generally record short-term notes at face value (less allowances), ignoring the interest implicit in the maturity value. A general rule is that notes treated as cash equivalents (maturities of three months or less and easily converted to cash) are not subject to premium or discount amortization due to materiality considerations.

However, companies should record and report long-term notes receivable on a discounted basis. When the interest stated on an interest-bearing note equals the effective (market) rate of interest, the note sells at face value.[6] When the stated rate differs from the market rate, the cash exchanged (present value) differs from the face value of the

---

[6]The **stated interest rate**, also referred to as the face rate or the coupon rate, is the rate contracted as part of the note. The **effective-interest rate**, also referred to as the *market rate* or the *effective yield*, is the rate used in the market to determine the value of the note—that is, the discount rate used to determine present value.

note. Companies then record the note at present value and amortize any discount or premium over the life of a note to approximate the effective-interest (market) rate. This illustrates one of the many situations in which time value of money concepts are applied to accounting measurement.

Note Issued at Face Value

To illustrate the discounting of a note issued at face value, assume that Bigelow Corp. lends Scandinavian Imports €10,000 in exchange for a €10,000, three-year note bearing interest at 10 percent annually. The market rate of interest for a note of similar risk is also 10 percent. We show the time diagram depicting both cash flows in Illustration 7-11.

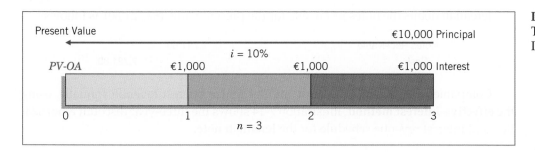

ILLUSTRATION 7-11
Time Diagram for Note Issued at Face Value

Bigelow computes the present value or exchange price of the note as follows.

Face value of the note		€10,000
Present value of the principal:		
€10,000 ($PVF_{3,10\%}$) = €10,000 × .75132	€7,513	
Present value of the interest:		
€1,000 ($PVF\text{-}OA_{3,10\%}$) = €1,000 × 2.48685	2,487	
Present value of the note		10,000
Difference		€ –0–

ILLUSTRATION 7-12
Present Value of Note—Stated and Market Rates the Same

In this case, the present value of the note equals its face value because the effective and stated rates of interest are the same. Bigelow records the receipt of the note as follows.

Notes Receivable	10,000	
Cash		10,000

Bigelow recognizes the interest earned each year as follows.

Cash	1,000	
Interest Revenue		1,000

Note Not Issued at Face Value

Zero-Interest-Bearing Notes. If a company receives a zero-interest-bearing note, its present value is the cash paid to the issuer. Because the company knows both the future amount and the present value of the note, it can compute the interest rate. This rate is often referred to as the **implicit interest rate**. Companies record the note at the present value (cash paid) and amortize the discount to interest revenue over the life of the note.

To illustrate, Jeremiah Company receives a three-year, $10,000 zero-interest-bearing note, the present value of which is $7,721.80. The implicit rate that equates the total cash to be received ($10,000 at maturity) to the present value of the future cash flows ($7,721.80) is 9 percent (the present value of 1 for three periods at 9 percent is .77218). We show the time diagram depicting the one cash flow in Illustration 7-13 (page 310).

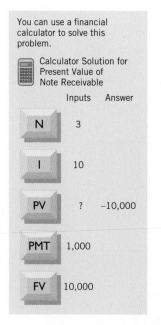

You can use a financial calculator to solve this problem.

Calculator Solution for Present Value of Note Receivable

	Inputs	Answer
N	3	
I	10	
PV	?	–10,000
PMT	1,000	
FV	10,000	

ILLUSTRATION 7-13
Time Diagram for Zero-
Interest-Bearing Note

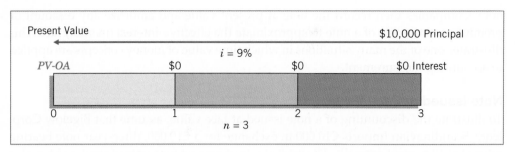

Calculator Solution for Effective-Interest Rate on Note

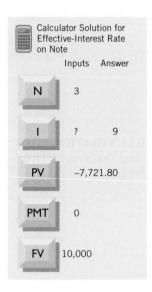

Inputs	Answer
N	3
I	? 9
PV	−7,721.80
PMT	0
FV	10,000

Jeremiah debits the notes receivable for the present value ($7,721.80) as follows.

Notes Receivable	7,721.80	
Cash		7,721.80

Companies amortize the discount, and recognize interest revenue annually, using the **effective-interest method**. Illustration 7-14 shows the three-year discount amortization and interest revenue schedule for the Jeremiah note.

ILLUSTRATION 7-14
Discount Amortization
Schedule—Effective-
Interest Method

SCHEDULE OF NOTE DISCOUNT AMORTIZATION
EFFECTIVE-INTEREST METHOD
0% NOTE DISCOUNTED AT 9%

	Cash Received	Interest Revenue	Discount Amortized	Carrying Amount of Note
Date of issue				$ 7,721.80
End of year 1	$ -0-	$ 694.96[a]	$ 694.96[b]	8,416.76[c]
End of year 2	-0-	757.51	757.51	9,174.27
End of year 3	-0-	825.73[d]	825.73	10,000.00
	$ -0-	$2,278.20	$2,278.20	

[a]$7,721.80 × .09 = $694.96   [c]$7,721.80 + $694.96 = $8,416.76
[b]$694.96 − 0 = $694.96   [d]5¢ adjustment to compensate for rounding

Jeremiah records interest revenue at the end of the first year using the effective-interest method as follows.

Notes Receivable	694.96	
Interest Revenue ($7,721.80 × 9%)		694.96

At the end of each year, Jeremiah increases notes receivable and interest revenue. At maturity, Jeremiah receives the face value of the note.

Interest-Bearing Notes. Often the stated rate and the effective rate differ. The zero-interest-bearing note is one example.

To illustrate a more common situation, assume that Morgan Corp. makes a loan to Marie Co. and receives in exchange a three-year, €10,000 note bearing interest at 10 percent annually. The market rate of interest for a note of similar risk is 12 percent. We show the time diagram depicting both cash flows in Illustration 7-15.

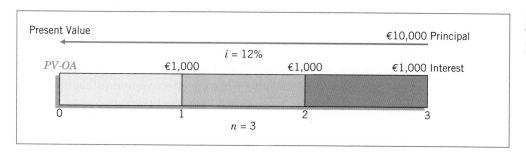

ILLUSTRATION 7-15
Time Diagram for
Interest-Bearing Note

Morgan computes the present value of the two cash flows as follows.

ILLUSTRATION 7-16
Computation of Present
Value—Effective Rate
Different from Stated
Rate

Face value of the note	€10,000
Present value of the principal:	
€10,000 ($PVF_{3,12\%}$) = €10,000 × .71178	€7,118
Present value of the interest:	
€1,000 ($PVF\text{-}OA_{3,12\%}$) = €1,000 × 2.40183	2,402
Present value of the note	9,520
Difference (Discount)	€ 480

In this case, because the effective rate of interest (12 percent) exceeds the stated rate (10 percent), the present value of the note is less than the face value. That is, Morgan exchanged the note at a **discount**. Morgan records the present value of the note as follows.

Notes Receivable	9,520	
Cash		9,520

Morgan then amortizes the discount and recognizes interest revenue annually using the **effective-interest method**. Illustration 7-17 shows the three-year discount amortization and interest revenue schedule.

ILLUSTRATION 7-17
Discount Amortization
Schedule—Effective-
Interest Method

SCHEDULE OF NOTE DISCOUNT AMORTIZATION
EFFECTIVE-INTEREST METHOD
10% NOTE DISCOUNTED AT 12%

	Cash Received	Interest Revenue	Discount Amortized	Carrying Amount of Note
Date of issue				€ 9,520
End of year 1	€1,000[a]	€1,142[b]	€142[c]	9,662[d]
End of year 2	1,000	1,159	159	9,821
End of year 3	1,000	1,179	179	10,000
	€3,000	€3,480	€480	

[a]€10,000 × 10% = €1,000   [c]€1,142 − €1,000 = €142
[b]€9,520 × 12% = €1,142   [d]€9,520 + €142 = €9,662

On the date of issue, the note has a present value of €9,520. As a result, additional interest revenue spread over the three-year life of the note is €480 (€10,000 − €9,520).

At the end of year 1, Morgan receives €1,000 in cash. But its interest revenue is €1,142 (€9,520 × 12%). The difference between €1,000 and €1,142 is the additional interest revenue (€142) using the effective-interest rate. Morgan records receipt of the annual interest and amortization of the discount for the first year as follows (amounts per amortization schedule).

Cash	1,000	
Notes Receivable	142	
Interest Revenue		1,142

Underlying Concepts

IFRS uses the terms book value, carrying value, and carrying amount interchangeably.

The carrying amount of the note is now €9,662 (€9,520 + €142). Morgan repeats this process until the end of year 3.

When the present value exceeds the face value, the note is exchanged at a premium. The premium increases the Notes Receivable account. The increase is then amortized over the life of the note using the effective-interest method. The amortization reduces both notes receivable and interest revenue.

Notes Received for Property, Goods, or Services. When a **note is received in exchange for property, goods, or services** in a bargained transaction entered into at arm's length, the stated interest rate is presumed to be fair unless:

1. No interest rate is stated, or

2. The stated interest rate is unreasonable, or

3. The face amount of the note is materially different from the current cash sales price for the same or similar items or from the current market value of the debt instrument.

In these circumstances, the company measures the present value of the note by the fair value of the property, goods, or services or by an amount that reasonably approximates the fair value of the note.

To illustrate, Oasis Development Co. sold a corner lot to Rusty Pelican as a restaurant site. Oasis accepted in exchange a five-year note having a maturity value of £35,247 and no stated interest rate. The land originally cost Oasis £14,000. At the date of sale, the land had a fair value of £20,000. Given the criterion above, Oasis uses the fair value of the land, £20,000, as the present value of the note. Oasis therefore records the sale as:

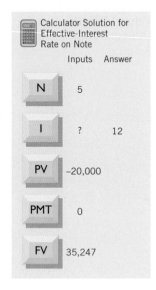

Calculator Solution for Effective-Interest Rate on Note

	Inputs	Answer
N	5	
I	?	12
PV	-20,000	
PMT	0	
FV	35,247	

Notes Receivable	20,000	
Land		14,000
Gain on Sale of Land (£20,000 − £14,000)		6,000

Oasis amortizes the discount to interest revenue over the five-year life of the note using the effective-interest method.

Choice of Interest Rate

In note transactions, other factors involved in the exchange, such as the fair value of the property, goods, or services, determine the effective or real interest rate. But, if a company cannot determine that fair value and if the note has no ready market, determining the present value of the note is more difficult. To estimate the present value of a note under such circumstances, the company must approximate an applicable interest rate that may differ from the stated interest rate. This process of interest-rate approximation is called **imputation**. The resulting interest rate is called an **imputed interest rate**.

The prevailing rates for similar instruments, from issuers with similar credit ratings, affect the choice of a rate. Restrictive covenants, collateral, payment schedule, and the existing prime interest rate also impact the choice. A company determines the imputed interest rate when it receives the note. It ignores any subsequent changes in prevailing interest rates.

Valuation of Notes Receivable

LEARNING OBJECTIVE 7

Explain accounting issues related to valuation of notes receivable.

The computations and estimations involved in valuing short-term notes receivable and in recording bad debt expense and the related allowance exactly parallel that for trade accounts receivable. As a result, **companies often use one of the collective assessment methods (percentage-of-sales or percentage-of-receivables) to measure possible impairments**.

Long-term receivables, however, often involve additional estimation problems. For example, the value of a note receivable may change over time as a discount or premium is amortized. In addition, because these receivables are outstanding for a number of periods, significant differences between fair value and amortized cost often result. In the case of long-term notes receivable, impairment tests are often done on an individual assessment basis rather than on a collective assessment basis. In this situation, impairment losses are measured as the difference between the carrying value of the receivable and the present value of the estimated future cash flows discounted at the original effective-interest rate.

For example, assume that Tesco Inc. has a note receivable with a carrying amount of €200,000. The debtor, Morganese Company, has indicated that it is experiencing financial difficulty. Tesco decides that Morganese's note receivable is therefore impaired. Tesco computes the present value of the future cash flows discounted at its original effective-interest rate to be €175,000. The computation of the loss on impairment is as follows.

Carrying amount of note receivable	€ 200,000
Present value of note receivable	(175,000)
Impairment loss	€ 25,000

The entry to record the impairment loss is as follows.

Bad Debt Expense	25,000	
Allowance for Doubtful Accounts		25,000

The present value of the note discounted at the **original effective-interest rate will generally not be equal** to the fair value of the receivable. That is, the market rate of interest used for discounting will generally be different than the original effective rate. The IASB indicates that this approach results in the receivable being reported at amortized cost. The accounting for interest-bearing receivables and impairment testing is discussed more fully in Appendix 7B of this chapter.

What do the numbers mean? ECONOMIC CONSEQUENCES AND WRITE-OFFS

As mentioned in the opening story, the write-downs that financial companies are posting are raising alarms among some investors. At the same time, executives are blaming accounting rules for exaggerating the losses and, as a result, are seeking new, more forgiving ways to value investments (including receivables and notes receivable). The rules being criticized require companies to value many of the securities they hold at fair value (generally, at the price that prevails in the market), no matter how sharply the fair values swing. Bank executives (and some analysts) argue such "mark to fair value" accounting triggers a domino effect. The market falls, forcing banks to take write-offs, pushing the market lower, and causing more write-offs.

Companies like **Barclays** (GBR) and **Société Générale** (FRA) argue that their write-downs may never actually result in a true charge to their company. It's a sore point because companies feel they are being forced to take big financial hits on holdings that they have no intention of actually selling at current prices. Companies believe they are strong enough to simply keep the holdings in their portfolios until the crisis passes. Therefore, forcing companies to value securities based on what they would fetch if sold today "is an attempt to apply liquidation accounting to a going concern," says one analyst.

One standard-setter acknowledges the difficulty but notes, "you tell me what a better answer is. . . . Is just pretending that things aren't decreasing in value a better answer? Should you just let everybody say they think it's going to recover?" Others who favor the use of fair values say that for all its imperfections, fair (market) value also imposes discipline on companies. Japan stands out as an example of how ignoring problems can lead to years-long stagnation. "Look at Japan, where they ignored write-downs at all their financial institutions when loans went bad," said Jeff Mahoney, general counsel at the Council for Institutional Investors. In addition, companies don't always have the luxury of waiting out a storm until assets recover the long-term value that executives believe exists.

A classic example relates to many European banks that hold loans to countries like Greece, Spain, Ireland, and Portugal. Although these loans were underwater, the banks still contended that they should not be written down (partly because they could be held to maturity). However, this contention was suspect, and impairment losses continued to rise. For example, **Bankia Group** (ESP) recently recorded a nearly €40 billion loss on problem loans. Similar concerns are being raised in the Asian loan market, where the proportion of unrated high-risk lending has increased from 8 percent to 11 percent in a recent annual period. Thus, investors must be on guard for possible loan impairment surprises if managers are optimistic in their loan and investment valuations.

Sources: Adapted from David Reilly, "Wave of Write-Offs Rattles Market: Accounting Rules Blasted as Dow Falls; A $600 Billion Toll?" *Wall Street Journal* (March 1, 2008), p. Al; J. Weil, "The E4 Smiled While Spain's Banks Cooked the Books," *Bloomberg* (June 14, 2012); and J. Grant, "Red Flags Waving Over Asian Corporate Debt," *Financial Times* (November 4, 2013).

SPECIAL ISSUES RELATED TO RECEIVABLES

Companies generally follow the recognition and valuation principles discussed in the previous section of this chapter. Additional issues related to receivables are:

1. Use of fair value option.

2. Derecognition of receivables.

3. Presentation and analysis.

Fair Value Option

As indicated earlier, receivables are generally measured at amortized cost. However, companies have the option to record fair value in their accounts for most financial assets and liabilities, including receivables. **[6]**[7] The IASB believes that fair value measurement for financial instruments provides more relevant and understandable information than historical cost. It considers fair value to be more relevant because it reflects the current cash equivalent value of financial instruments.

Fair Value Measurement

If companies choose the fair value option, receivables are recorded at fair value, with unrealized holding gains or losses reported as part of net income. An **unrealized holding gain or loss** is the net change in the fair value of the receivable from one period to another, exclusive of interest revenue recognized but not recorded. As a result, the company reports the receivable at fair value each reporting date. In addition, it reports the change in value as part of net income.

Companies may elect to use the fair value option at the time the receivable is originally recognized or when some event triggers a new basis of accounting (such as when a business acquisition occurs). If a company elects the fair value option for a receivable, it must continue to use fair value measurement for that receivable until the company no longer owns this receivable. If the company does not elect the fair value option for a given receivable at the date of recognition, it may not use this option on that specific receivable in subsequent periods.

Recording Fair Value Option

Assume that Escobar Company has notes receivable that have a fair value of R$810,000 and a carrying amount of R$620,000. Escobar decides on December 31, 2015, to use the fair value option for these receivables. This is the first valuation of these recently acquired receivables. Having elected to use the fair value option, Escobar must value these receivables **at fair value in all subsequent periods in which it holds these receivables**. Similarly, if Escobar elects *not* to use the fair value option, it must use its carrying amount (measured at amortized cost) for all future periods.

When using the fair value option, Escobar reports the receivables at fair value, with any unrealized holding gains and losses reported as part of net income. The **unrealized holding gain** is the difference between the fair value and the carrying amount at December 31, 2015, which for Escobar is R$190,000 (R$810,000 − R$620,000). At

---

[7]The IASB issued a narrow amendment to the rules for using the fair value option for liabilities. The change addresses the concern that when liabilities are measured at fair value under the fair value option, gains can be recorded in income if the company's own credit risk declines. Under the new rules, such gains are not recorded in income. **[7]**

December 31, 2015, Escobar makes an adjusting entry to record the increase in value of Notes Receivable and to record the unrealized holding gain, as follows.

December 31, 2015

Notes Receivable	190,000	
Unrealized Holding Gain or Loss—Income		190,000

As a result of this entry, Escobar reports the notes receivable at fair value on its statement of financial position, with the unrealized holding gain reported in "Other income and expense" on its income statement. In subsequent periods, the company will report **any change in fair value** as an unrealized holding gain or loss. For example, if at December 31, 2016, the fair value of the notes receivable is R$800,000, Escobar would recognize an unrealized holding loss of R$10,000 (R$810,000 − R$800,000) and reduce the Notes Receivable account.

Derecognition of Receivables

At what point should a receivable no longer be included as an asset of a company like Unilever (NLD)—that is, **derecognized?** One situation occurs when the receivable no longer has any value; that is, the contractual rights to the cash flows of the receivable no longer exist. For example, if Unilever has a receivable from a customer who declares bankruptcy, the value of this receivable has expired. Similarly, when Unilever collects a receivable when due, it removes this receivable from its books. In both cases, Unilever no longer has any contractual rights to these receivables. As a result, the receivables are derecognized.

A second situation often occurs if Unilever transfers (e.g., sells) a receivable to another company, thereby transferring the risks and rewards of ownership to this other company. As an example, if Garcia Company sells its receivables to Holt Inc. and transfers all the risks and rewards of ownership to Holt, the receivables are derecognized. Although this guideline is straightforward, it is sometimes difficult to assess whether some or all of the risks and rewards of ownership are transferred. The following discussion highlights the key issues related to transfers of receivables.

Transfers of Receivables

There are various reasons for the transfer of receivables to another party. For example, in order to accelerate the receipt of cash from receivables, companies may transfer receivables to other companies for cash. In addition, for competitive reasons, providing sales financing for customers is virtually mandatory in many industries. In the sale of durable goods, such as automobiles, trucks, industrial and farm equipment, computers, and appliances, most sales are on an installment contract basis. Many major companies in these industries have created wholly owned subsidiaries specializing in receivables financing. For example, Daimler (DEU) has Daimler Truck Financial (DEU), and Toyota (JPN) has Toyota Motor Credit (JPN).

Second, the **holder** may sell receivables because money is tight and access to normal credit is unavailable or too expensive. Also, a firm may sell its receivables, instead of borrowing, to avoid violating existing lending agreements.

Finally, billing and collection of receivables are often time-consuming and costly. Credit card companies such as MasterCard, Visa, American Express, and Discover take over the collection process and provide merchants with immediate cash.

Conversely, some **purchasers** of receivables buy them to obtain the legal protection of ownership rights afforded a purchaser of assets versus the lesser rights afforded a secured creditor. In addition, banks and other lending institutions may need to purchase receivables because of legal lending limits. That is, they cannot make any additional loans, but they can buy receivables and charge a fee for this service.

The transfer of receivables to a third party for cash happens in one of two ways:

1. Secured borrowing.

2. Sales of receivables.

Secured Borrowing

A company often uses receivables as collateral in a borrowing transaction. In fact, a creditor often requires that the debtor designate (assign) or pledge[8] receivables as security for the loan. If the loan is not paid when due, the creditor can convert the collateral to cash—that is, collect the receivables.

To illustrate, on March 1, 2015, Meng Mills, Inc. provides (assigns) NT$700,000 of its accounts receivable to Sino Bank as collateral for a NT$500,000 note. Meng Mills continues to collect the accounts receivable; the account debtors are not notified of the arrangement. Sino Bank assesses a finance charge of 1 percent of the accounts receivable and interest on the note of 12 percent. Meng Mills makes monthly payments to the bank for all cash it collects on the receivables. Illustration 7-18 shows the entries for the secured borrowing for Meng Mills and Sino Bank.

ILLUSTRATION 7-18
Entries for Transfer of Receivables—Secured Borrowing

Meng Mills, Inc.			Sino Bank		
Transfer of accounts receivable and issuance of note on March 1, 2015					
Cash	493,000		Notes Receivable	500,000	
Interest Expense	7,000*		Interest Revenue		7,000*
Notes Payable		500,000	Cash		493,000
*(NT$700,000 × .01)					
Collection in March of NT$440,000 of accounts less cash discounts of NT$6,000 plus receipt of NT$14,000 sales returns					
Cash	434,000				
Sales Discounts	6,000				
Sales Returns and Allowances	14,000		(No entry)		
Accounts Receivable		454,000*			
*(NT$440,000 + NT$14,000 = NT$454,000)					
Remitted March collections plus accrued interest to the bank on April 1, 2015					
Interest Expense	5,000*		Cash	439,000	
Notes Payable	434,000		Interest Revenue		5,000*
Cash		439,000	Notes Receivable		434,000
*(NT$500,000 × .12 × 1/12)					
Collection in April of the balance of accounts less NT$2,000 written off as uncollectible					
Cash	244,000				
Allowance for Doubtful Accounts	2,000		(No entry)		
Accounts Receivable		246,000*			
*(NT$700,000 − NT$454,000)					
Remitted the balance due of NT$66,000 (NT$500,000 − NT$434,000) on the note plus interest on May 1, 2015					
Interest Expense	660*		Cash	66,660	
Notes Payable	66,000		Interest Revenue		660*
Cash		66,660	Notes Receivable		66,000
*(NT$66,000 × .12 × 1/12)					

[8]If a company transfers the receivables for custodial purposes, the custodial arrangement is often referred to as a **pledge**.

In addition to recording the collection of receivables, Meng Mills must recognize all discounts, returns and allowances, and bad debts. Each month, Meng Mills uses the proceeds from the collection of the accounts receivable to retire the note obligation. In addition, it pays interest on the note.[9]

Sales of Receivables

Sales of receivables have increased substantially in recent years. A common type is a sale to a factor. **Factors** are finance companies or banks that buy receivables from businesses for a fee and then collect the remittances directly from the customers. **Factoring receivables** is traditionally associated with the textile, apparel, footwear, furniture, and home furnishing industries.[10] Illustration 7-19 shows a typical factoring arrangement.

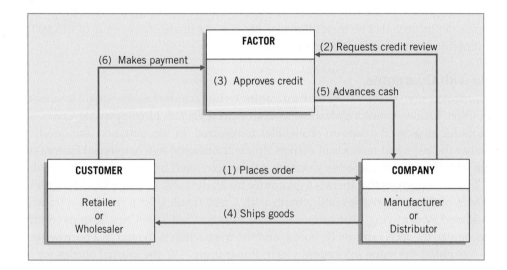

ILLUSTRATION 7-19
Basic Procedures in Factoring

Sale without Guarantee

When buying receivables, the purchaser generally assumes the risk of collectibility and absorbs any credit losses. A sale of this type is often referred to as a sale **without guarantee (without recourse)** against credit loss. The transfer of receivables in this case is an outright sale of the receivables both in form (transfer of title) and substance (transfer of risks and rewards). As in any sale of assets, the seller debits Cash for the proceeds and credits Accounts Receivable for the face value of the receivables. The seller recognizes the difference, reduced by any provision for probable adjustments (discounts, returns, allowances, etc.), as a Loss on Sale of Receivables. The seller uses a Due from Factor account (reported as a receivable) to account for the proceeds retained by the factor to cover probable sales discounts, sales returns, and sales allowances.

To illustrate, Crest Textiles, Inc. factors €500,000 of accounts receivable with Commercial Factors, Inc., on a **non-guarantee** (or **without recourse**) basis. Crest Textiles transfers the receivable records to Commercial Factors, which will receive the collections.

---

[9]What happens if Sino Bank collected the transferred accounts receivable rather than Meng Mills? Sino Bank would simply remit the cash proceeds to Meng Mills, and Meng Mills would make the same entries shown in Illustration 7-18. As a result, Meng Mills reports these "collaterized" receivables as an asset on the statement of financial position. The point here is that the risks and rewards of ownership have not been transferred to Sino Bank.

[10]Credit cards like **MasterCard** and **Visa** are a type of factoring arrangement. Typically, the purchaser of the receivable charges a ¾–1½ percent commission of the receivables purchased (the commission is 4–5 percent for credit card factoring).

ILLUSTRATION 7-20
Entries for Sale of
Receivables without
Guarantee

Commercial Factors assesses a finance charge of 3 percent of the amount of accounts receivable and retains an amount equal to 5 percent of the accounts receivable (for probable adjustments). Crest Textiles and Commercial Factors make the following journal entries for the receivables transferred without guarantee.

Crest Textiles, Inc.			Commercial Factors, Inc.		
Cash	460,000		Accounts (Notes) Receivable	500,000	
Due from Factor	25,000*		Due to Customer (Crest Textiles)		25,000
Loss on Sale of Receivables	15,000**		Interest Revenue		15,000
Accounts (Notes) Receivable		500,000	Cash		460,000
*(5% × €500,000) **(3% × €500,000)					

In recognition of the sale of receivables, Crest Textiles records a loss of €15,000. The factor's net income will be the difference between the financing revenue of €15,000 and the amount of any uncollectible receivables.

Sale with Guarantee

To illustrate a sale of receivables **with guarantee (with recourse)** against credit loss, assume that Crest Textiles issues a guarantee to Commercial Factors to compensate Commercial Factors for any credit losses on receivables transferred. In this situation, the question is whether the risks and rewards of ownership are transferred to Commercial Factors or remain with Crest Textile. In other words, is it to be accounted for as a sale or a borrowing?

In this case, given that there is a guarantee for all defaults, it appears that the risks and rewards of these receivables still remain with Crest Textiles. As a result, the transfer is considered a borrowing—sometimes referred to as a **failed sale**. Crest Textiles continues to recognize the receivable on its books, and the transaction is treated as a borrowing.[11]

Assuming the same information as in Illustration 7-20, the journal entries for both Crest Textiles and Commercial Factors are shown in Illustration 7-21.

ILLUSTRATION 7-21
Sale with Guarantee

Crest Textiles			Commercial Factors		
Cash	460,000		Accounts Receivable	500,000	
Due from Factor	25,000		Due to Customer		
Finance Charge	15,000		(Crest Textiles)		25,000
Recourse Liability		500,000	Interest Revenue		15,000
			Cash		460,000

In this case, Crest Textiles records a liability to Commercial Factors. Commercial Factors records an accounts receivable from Crest Textiles. That is, the accounting for a failed sale is similar to that for a secured borrowing. As the transferred receivables are collected, the Recourse Liability account on the books of Crest Textiles is reduced. Similarly, on the books of Commercial Factors, the accounts receivable from Crest Textiles is also reduced.

Summary of Transfers

The IASB uses the term **derecognition** when referring to the accounting for transfers of receivables. According to the IASB, determining whether receivables that are transferred can be derecognized and accounted for as a sale is based on an evaluation of whether the seller has transferred substantially all the risks and rewards of ownership

---

[11]In general, IFRS does not allow netting of assets and liabilities unless there is an explicit right of set-off. **[8]** Thus, Crest Textiles reports both a receivable and a liability of €500,000 in its statement of financial position.

of the financial asset. Illustration 7-22 summarizes the accounting guidelines for transfers of receivables. **[9]**

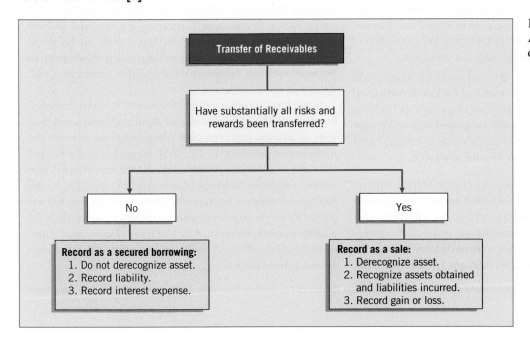

ILLUSTRATION 7-22
Accounting for Transfers
of Receivables

As indicated, if substantially all the risks and rewards of ownership of the receivable are transferred, then it is derecognized. However, if substantially all of the risks and rewards are not transferred, then the company treats the transfer as a secured borrowing. If sale accounting is appropriate, a company must still consider assets obtained and liabilities incurred in the transaction (e.g., a guarantee).[12]

Evolving Issue   A CURE FOR "TOO LITTLE, TOO LATE"?

A significant accounting weakness revealed during the financial crisis relates to the accounting for loan losses (or allowance for doubtful accounts). The concern is that the existing IFRS results in allowances for loan losses that tend to be at their lowest level when they are most needed—at the beginning of a downward-trending economic cycle (the "too little, too late" concern). In response, the IASB is developing a standard to ensure that the allowance for loan loss balance is sufficient to cover all estimated credit losses for the remaining life of a loan.

The Board has decided that a company should recognize in net income an impairment when it does not expect to collect all contractual amounts due for a loan. Furthermore, the IASB indicates that it is inappropriate to allocate

(defer) an impairment loss over the life of a loan. In other words, if a company does not expect to collect all amounts due, a loss exists and should be recognized immediately. This new model, referred to as the three-bucket approach, would classify loans (and other financial assets) according to three stages, which reflect increasing severity of impairment.

- Stage 1 includes only loans for which allowances reflecting expected credit losses for the next 12 months have been recorded. This initial allowance serves as a proxy for the initial expectations of credit losses that are priced into the loan at day 1. Interest revenue on loans in Stage 1 is accrued on the gross amount of the loans.

---

[12]In some situations, a company may continue to hold the receivable but does not retain substantially all the risks and rewards of the receivable. In this case, the company must determine whether it has retained control of the receivable. The primary indicator that the company has control of an asset is if it can sell the asset. If control has not been retained, the asset is derecognized and sale accounting is applied. In all other cases, the company has retained control and the arrangement is accounted for as a secured borrowing. As noted in Chapter 18, concepts of risks and rewards and control are relevant in determining revenue recognition. However, transfers of financial assets are outside the scope of the recently issued revenue standard.

- Stage 2 includes loans for which credit risk increases significantly, such that the loan has credit quality below "investment grade." Allowances for loans in Stage 2 are increased to reflect lifetime-expected credit losses. The calculation of interest revenue on loans in Stage 2 is unchanged.

- Stage 3 includes loans or financial assets for which credit quality deteriorates to the point that the loan is considered credit-impaired (e.g., the customer stops paying). Lifetime-expected credit losses are still recognized in the allowance for loans in Stage 3, but interest revenue is accrued based on the loan balance adjusted for the allowance.

In this model, financial assets start out in Stage 1 with reserves equal to 12 months of expected losses. Then, if assets move to Stages 2 or 3, allowances increase to reflect expected losses over the entire life of those assets, as the credit quality deteriorates. In addition, interest revenue on loans in Stage 3 is lower compared to the same loan in Stages 1 or 2. Importantly, the new model broadens the information that a company is required to consider when determining its expectations of credit losses. Specifically, companies are required to base measurement of expected credit losses both on historical information about past events and expanded information of future events (e.g., forecasts) that indicate contractual cash flows will not be collected.

Some have complained that the model is overly complex. In response, the IASB has sought input and conducted field tests to address concerns over complexity and to make the model more operational. The IASB hopes to issue a revised standard in 2014. The proposed model for impairments represents a significant change from current practice. The model has gained support because the allowance captures the expected losses on an asset in response to deterioration in credit quality. Further, based on consideration of expected future-oriented information on credit quality, estimated loan losses are recognized earlier.

Source: IASB Exposure Draft, *Financial Instruments: Expected Credit Losses* (March 2013); see *http://www.ifrs.org/Current-Projects/IASB-Projects/Pages/IASB-Work-Plan.aspx.*

Presentation and Analysis

Presentation of Receivables

LEARNING OBJECTIVE 9

Describe how to report and analyze receivables.

The general rules in classifying receivables are: [10]

1. Segregate and report the carrying amounts of the different categories of receivables.

2. Indicate the receivables classified as current and non-current in the statement of financial position.

3. Appropriately offset the valuation accounts for receivables that are impaired, including a discussion of individual and collectively determined impairments.

4. Disclose the fair value of receivables in such a way that permits it to be compared with its carrying amount.

5. Disclose information to assess the credit risk inherent in the receivables by providing information on:
   (a) Receivables that are neither past due nor impaired.
   (b) The carrying amount of receivables that would otherwise be past due or impaired, whose terms have been renegotiated.
   (c) For receivables that are either past due or impaired, disclose an analysis of the age of the receivables that are past due as of the end of the reporting period.

6. Disclose any receivables pledged as collateral.

7. Disclose all significant concentrations of credit risk arising from receivables.[13]

[13]Concentrations of credit risk exist when receivables have common characteristics that may affect their collection. These common characteristics might be companies in the same industry or same geographic region. For example, Abu Dhabi Aviation (ARE) recently reported nearly 61 percent of its trade receivables due from the United Arab Emirates (UAE) government and 16 percent from UAE's oil industry. Financial statement users want to know if a substantial amount of receivables from such sales are to customers facing similar uncertain economic conditions. No numerical guidelines are provided as to what is meant by a "concentration of credit risk." Information to be disclosed includes such items as (1) the carrying amounts of the concentration, (2) information on the characteristic that determines the concentration, (3) the amount of loss that could occur upon non-performance, and (4) information on any collateral related to the receivable. [11]

The assets section of Colton Company's statement of financial position in Illustration 7-23 shows many of the disclosures required for receivables.

ILLUSTRATION 7-23
Disclosure of Receivables

COLTON COMPANY
STATEMENT OF FINANCIAL POSITION (PARTIAL)
AT 31 DECEMBER 2015
(AMOUNTS IN 000)

Current assets		
Other receivables		€ 1,300
Receivables from associates		2,722
Trade receivables (Note 12)	€20,896	
Less: Provision for impairment of trade receivables	109	20,787
Total receivables		24,809
Less non-current portion		2,322
Total current receivables		22,487
Cash and cash equivalents		20,509
Total current assets		42,996
Non-current receivables		
Receivable from associates		2,126
Other receivables		196

Segregate different types of receivables

Classify receivables as current and non-current

Note 12 Trade and Other Receivables (partial)

All non-current receivables are due within five years from the statement of financial position date. Trade receivables that are less than three months past due are not considered impaired. At 31 December, the aging analysis of trade receivables is as follows:

		Neither Past		Past Due but Not Impaired			
Amounts		Due or	<30	30–60	60–90	90–120	>120
(€000)	Total	Impaired	days	days	days	days	days
2015	20,896	11,991	4,791	2,592	1,070	360	92

Disclose aging of receivables

As at 31 December 2015, trade receivables at initial value of €109 were impaired and fully provided for. The following table summarises movements in the provision for impairment of receivables.

	Individually Impaired (€000)	Collectively Impaired Total (€000)	Total (€000)
At 1 January 2015	29	69	98
Expense for the year	10	16	26
Written off	(3)	(6)	(9)
Recoveries	(2)	(4)	(6)
At 31 December 2015	34	75	109

Presentation of individually and collectively impaired receivables

The fair values of trade and other receivables are as follows:

	2015
Trade receivables	€20,896
Receivables from associates	2,776
Other receivables	1,300
	€24,972

Disclose fair value

Certain European subsidiaries transferred receivable balances amounting to €1,014 to a bank in exchange for cash during the year ended 31 December 2015. The transaction has been accounted for as a secured borrowing. In case of default under the loan agreement, the borrower has the right to receive the cash flows from the receivables transferred. Without default, the subsidiaries will collect the receivables and assign new receivables as collateral.

Disclose collateral arrangements

Analysis of Receivables

Accounts Receivable Turnover. Analysts frequently compute financial ratios to evaluate the liquidity of a company's accounts receivable. To assess the liquidity of the receivables, they use the accounts receivable turnover. This ratio measures the number of times, on average, a company collects receivables during the period. The ratio is computed by dividing net sales by average (net) receivables outstanding during the year.

Theoretically, the numerator should include only net credit sales, but this information is frequently unavailable. However, if the relative amounts of credit and cash sales remain fairly constant, the trend indicated by the ratio will still be valid. Barring significant seasonal factors, average receivables outstanding can be computed from the beginning and ending balances of net trade receivables.

To illustrate, **Louis Vuitton (LVMH Group) (FRA)** reported 2012 net sales of €28,103 million, its beginning and ending accounts receivable balances were €1,878 million and €1,985 million, respectively. Illustration 7-24 shows the computation of its accounts receivable turnover.

ILLUSTRATION 7-24
Computation of Accounts
Receivable Turnover

$$\frac{\text{Net Sales}}{\text{Average Trade Receivables (net)}} = \frac{\text{Accounts Receivable}}{\text{Turnover}}$$

$$\frac{€28,103}{(€1,878 + €1,985)/2} = 15 \text{ times, or every } 24.3 \text{ days } (365 \div 15)$$

Underlying Concepts

Providing information that will help users assess a company's current liquidity and prospective cash flows is a primary objective of accounting.

This information[14] shows how successful the company is in collecting its outstanding receivables. If possible, an aging schedule should also be prepared to help determine how long receivables have been outstanding. A satisfactory accounts receivable turnover may have resulted because certain receivables were collected quickly though others have been outstanding for a relatively long period. An aging schedule would reveal such patterns.

Often, the accounts receivable turnover is transformed to **days to collect accounts receivable or days outstanding**—an average collection period. In this case, 15 is divided into 365 days, resulting in 24.3 days. Companies frequently use the average collection period to assess the effectiveness of a company's credit and collection policies. The general rule is that the average collection period should not greatly exceed the credit term period. That is, if customers are given a 60-day period for payment, then the average collection period should not be too much in excess of 60 days.

[14]Several figures other than 365 could be used. A common alternative is 360 days because it is divisible by 30 (days) and 12 (months). *Use 365 days in any homework computations.*

GLOBAL ACCOUNTING INSIGHTS

CASH AND RECEIVABLES

IFRS and U.S. GAAP are very similar in accounting for cash and receivables. For example, the definition of cash and cash equivalents is similar, and both IFRS and U.S. GAAP have a fair value option. In the wake of the international credit crisis, the Boards are working together to improve the accounting for loan impairments.

Relevant Facts

Following are the key similarities and differences between IFRS and U.S. GAAP related to cash and receivables.

Similarities

• The accounting and reporting related to cash is essentially the same under both U.S. GAAP and IFRS. In addition, the definition used for cash equivalents is the same.

• Cash and receivables are generally reported in the current assets section of the balance sheet under U.S. GAAP, similar to IFRS.

• U.S. GAAP requires that loans and receivables be accounted for at amortized cost, adjusted for allowances for doubtful accounts, similar to IFRS.

Differences

- Under U.S. GAAP, cash and receivables are reported in order of liquidity. Under IFRS, companies may report cash and receivables as the last items in current assets.

- U.S. GAAP has explicit guidance concerning how receivables with different characteristics should be reported separately. There is no IFRS that mandates this segregation.

- The fair value option is similar under U.S. GAAP and IFRS but not identical. The international standard related to the fair value option is subject to certain qualifying criteria not in the U.S. standard. In addition, there is some difference in the financial instruments covered.

- Under U.S. GAAP, overdrafts are reported as liabilities. Under IFRS, bank overdrafts are generally reported as cash if such overdrafts are repayable upon demand and are an integral part of a company's cash management (offsetting arrangements against other accounts at the same bank).

- U.S. GAAP and IFRS differ in the criteria used to account for transfers of receivables. U.S. GAAP uses loss of control as the primary criterion. IFRS is a combination of an approach focused on risks and rewards and loss of control. In addition, U.S. GAAP does not permit partial transfers; IFRS generally does.

About the Numbers

In the accounting for loans and receivables, IFRS permits the reversal of impairment losses, with the reversal limited to the asset's amortized cost before the impairment. To illustrate, Zirbel Company has a loan receivable with a carrying value of $10,000 at December 31, 2014. On January 2, 2015, the borrower declares bankruptcy, and Zirbel estimates that it will collect only one-half of the loan balance. Zirbel makes the following entry to record the impairment.

Impairment Loss	5,000	
Loan Receivable		5,000

On January 10, 2016, Zirbel learns that the customer has emerged from bankruptcy. Zirbel now estimates that all but $1,000 will be repaid on the loan. Under IFRS, Zirbel records this reversal as follows.

Loan Receivable	4,000	
Recovery of Impairment Loss		4,000

Zirbel reports the recovery in 2016 income. Under U.S. GAAP, reversal of an impairment is not permitted. Rather, the balance on the loan after the impairment becomes the new basis for the loan.

On the Horizon

It appears likely that the question of recording fair values for financial instruments will continue to be an important issue to resolve as the Boards work toward convergence. Both the IASB and the FASB have indicated that they believe that financial statements would be more transparent and understandable if companies recorded and reported all financial instruments at fair value. The fair value option for recording financial instruments such as receivables is an important step in moving closer to fair value recording. We hope that this is only an intermediate step and that the Boards continue to work toward the adoption of comprehensive fair value accounting for financial instruments.

Finally, as discussed in the Evolving Issue box on page 319, the IASB is working on a new impairment model, which will be more forward-looking when evaluating financial instruments for impairment. The FASB is working on a similar impairment model. The final standards adopted, however, may not be fully converged in terms of the implementation details.

SUMMARY OF LEARNING OBJECTIVES

1 Identify items considered cash. To be reported as "cash," an asset must be readily available for the payment of current obligations and free from contractual restrictions that limit its use in satisfying debts. Cash consists of coin, currency, and available funds on deposit at the bank. Negotiable instruments such as money orders, certified checks, cashier's checks, personal checks, and bank drafts are also viewed as cash. Savings accounts are usually classified as cash.

2 Indicate how to report cash and related items. Companies report cash as a current asset in the statement of financial position. The reporting of other related items are as follows. (1) *Restricted cash:* Companies should state separately legally restricted deposits held as compensating balances against short-term borrowing among the "Cash and cash equivalent items" in current assets. Restricted deposits held against long-term borrowing arrangements should be separately classified as non-current assets in either the investments or other assets sections. (2) *Bank overdrafts:* Companies should include overdrafts as a component of cash if such overdrafts are payable on demand and are an integral part of a company's cash management; otherwise, report as a current liability. If material, these items should be separately disclosed either on the face of the statement of financial position or in the related notes. (3) *Cash equivalents:* Companies often report this item together with cash as "Cash and cash equivalents."

3 **Define receivables and identify the different types of receivables.**
Receivables are claims held against customers and others for money, goods, or services. Receivables are classified into three types: (1) current or non-current, (2) trade or non-trade, and (3) accounts receivable or notes receivable.

4 **Explain accounting issues related to recognition of accounts receivable.**
Two issues that may complicate the measurement of accounts receivable are (1) the availability of discounts (trade and cash discounts), and (2) the length of time between the sale and the payment due dates (the interest element).

Ideally, companies should measure receivables in terms of their present value—that is, the discounted value of the cash to be received in the future. The profession specifically excludes from the present-value considerations receivables arising from normal business transactions that are due in customary trade terms within approximately one year.

5 **Explain accounting issues related to valuation of accounts receivable.**
Companies value and report short-term receivables at amortized cost (cash realizable value). Amortized cost is the amount at which the receivable was measured at acquisition, adjusted for any principal payments, amortization of any discount of premium, and reduced by any impairment or uncollectibility. Impairments are evaluated using individual and collective assessment approaches.

6 **Explain accounting issues related to recognition of notes receivable.**
Companies record short-term notes at face value and long-term notes receivable at the present value of the cash they expect to collect. When the interest stated on an interest-bearing note equals the effective (market) rate of interest, the note sells at face value. When the stated rate differs from the effective rate, the notes are reported at more or less than their face value.

7 **Explain accounting issues related to valuation of notes receivable.**
Like accounts receivable, companies record and report short-term notes receivable at their cash realizable value. The same is also true of long-term receivables.

8 **Understand special topics related to receivables.** Special issues relate to use of the fair value option and derecognition. Companies have the option to record receivables at fair value. Once the fair value option is chosen, the receivable is reported on the statement of financial position at fair value, with the change in fair value recorded in income. To accelerate the receipt of cash from receivables, the owner may transfer the receivables to another company for cash in one of two ways. (1) *Secured borrowing:* A creditor often requires that the debtor designate or pledge receivables as security for the loan. (2) *Sales (factoring) of receivables:* Factors are finance companies or banks that buy receivables from businesses and then collect the remittances directly from the customers. Transferred receivables are derecognized and accounted for as a sale based on an evaluation of whether the seller has transferred the risks and rewards of ownership. If substantially all the risks and rewards of ownership are transferred, then the receivable is derecognized. Otherwise, the transfer is accounted for as a secured borrowing.

9 **Describe how to report and analyze receivables.** Companies should report receivables with appropriate offset of valuation accounts against receivables, classify receivables as current or non-current, identify pledged or designated receivables, provide fair value information, assess credit risk, and identify concentrations of risks arising from receivables. Analysts assess receivables based on turnover and the days outstanding.

APPENDIX **7A**	CASH CONTROLS

Cash is the asset most susceptible to improper diversion and use. Management faces two problems in accounting for cash transactions: (1) establishing proper controls to prevent any unauthorized transactions by officers or employees, and (2) providing information necessary to properly manage cash on hand and cash transactions. In this appendix, we discuss some of the basic control issues related to cash.

10 **LEARNING OBJECTIVE**
Explain common techniques employed to control cash.

USING BANK ACCOUNTS

To obtain desired control objectives, a company can vary the number and location of banks and the types of bank accounts. For large companies operating in multiple locations, the location of bank accounts can be important. Establishing collection accounts in strategic locations can accelerate the flow of cash into the company by shortening the time between a customer's mailing of a payment and the company's use of the cash. Multiple collection centers generally reduce the size of a company's **collection float**. This is the difference between the amount on deposit according to the company's records and the amount of collected cash according to the bank record.

Large, multilocation companies frequently use **lockbox accounts** to collect in cities with heavy customer billing. The company rents a local post office box and authorizes a local bank to pick up the remittances mailed to that box number. The bank empties the box at least once a day and immediately credits the company's account for collections. The greatest advantage of a lockbox is that it accelerates the availability of collected cash. Generally, in a lockbox arrangement the bank microfilms the checks for record purposes and provides the company with a deposit slip, a list of collections, and any customer correspondence. Thus, a lockbox system improves the control over cash and accelerates collection of cash. If the income generated from accelerating the receipt of funds exceeds the cost of the lockbox system, then it is a worthwhile undertaking.

The **general checking account** is the principal bank account in most companies and frequently the only bank account in small businesses. A company deposits in and disburses cash from this account. A company cycles all transactions through it. For example, a company deposits from and disburses to all other bank accounts through the general checking account.

Companies use **imprest bank accounts** to make a specific amount of cash available for a limited purpose. The account acts as a clearing account for a large volume of checks or for a specific type of check. To clear a specific and intended amount through the imprest account, a company transfers that amount from the general checking account or other source. Companies often use imprest bank accounts for disbursing payroll checks, dividends, commissions, bonuses, confidential expenses (e.g., officers' salaries), and travel expenses.

THE IMPREST PETTY CASH SYSTEM

Almost every company finds it necessary to pay small amounts for miscellaneous expenses such as taxi fares, minor office supplies, and employee's lunches. Disbursements by check for such items is often impractical, yet some control over them is important. A simple method of obtaining reasonable control, while adhering to the rule of disbursement by check, is the **imprest system for petty cash** disbursements. This is how the system works:

1. The company designates a petty cash custodian and gives the custodian a small amount of currency from which to make payments. It records transfer of funds to petty cash as:

Petty Cash	300	
Cash		300

2. The petty cash custodian obtains signed receipts from each individual to whom he or she pays cash, attaching evidence of the disbursement to the petty cash receipt. Petty cash transactions are not recorded until the fund is reimbursed; someone other than the petty cash custodian records those entries.

3. When the supply of cash runs low, the custodian presents to the controller or accounts payable cashier a request for reimbursement supported by the petty cash receipts and other disbursement evidence. The custodian receives a company check to replenish the fund. At this point, the company records transactions based on petty cash receipts.

Supplies Expense	42	
Postage Expense	53	
Miscellaneous Expense	76	
Cash Over and Short	2	
Cash		173

4. If the company decides that the amount of cash in the petty cash fund is excessive, it lowers the fund balance as follows.

Cash	50	
Petty Cash		50

Subsequent to establishment, a company makes entries to the Petty Cash account only to increase or decrease the size of the fund.

A company uses a **Cash Over and Short** account when the petty cash fund fails to prove out. That is, an error occurs such as incorrect change, overpayment of expense, or lost receipt. If cash proves out **short** (i.e., the sum of the receipts and cash in the fund is less than the imprest amount), the company debits the shortage to the Cash Over and Short account. If cash proves out **over**, it credits the overage to Cash Over and Short. The company closes Cash Over and Short only at the end of the year. It generally shows Cash Over and Short on the income statement as an "Other income and expense."

There are usually expense items in the fund except immediately after reimbursement. Therefore, to maintain accurate financial statements, a company must reimburse the funds at the end of each accounting period and also when nearly depleted.

Under the imprest system the petty cash custodian is responsible at all times for the amount of the fund on hand either as cash or in the form of signed receipts. These receipts provide the evidence required by the disbursing officer to issue a reimbursement check.

Further, a company follows two additional procedures to obtain more complete control over the petty cash fund:

1. A superior of the petty cash custodian makes surprise counts of the fund from time to time to determine that a satisfactory accounting of the fund has occurred.
2. The company cancels or mutilates petty cash receipts after they have been submitted for reimbursement, so that they cannot be used to secure a second reimbursement.

PHYSICAL PROTECTION OF CASH BALANCES

Not only must a company safeguard cash receipts and cash disbursements through internal control measures, but it must also protect the cash on hand and in banks. Because receipts become cash on hand and disbursements are made from cash in banks, adequate control of receipts and disbursements is part of the protection of cash balances, along with certain other procedures.

Physical protection of cash is so elementary a necessity that it requires little discussion. A company should make every effort to minimize the cash on hand in the office. It should only have on hand a petty cash fund, the current day's receipts, and perhaps funds for making change. Insofar as possible, it should keep these funds in a vault, safe, or locked cash drawer. The company should transmit intact each day's receipts to the bank as soon as practicable. Accurately stating the amount of available cash both in internal management reports and in external financial statements is also extremely important.

Every company has a record of cash received, disbursed, and the balance. Because of the many cash transactions, however, errors or omissions may occur in keeping this record. Therefore, a company must periodically prove the balance shown in the general ledger. It can count cash actually present in the office—petty cash, change funds, and undeposited receipts—for comparison with the company records. For cash on deposit, a company prepares a bank reconciliation—a reconciliation of the company's record and the bank's record of the company's cash.

RECONCILIATION OF BANK BALANCES

At the end of each calendar month, the bank supplies each customer with a **bank statement** (a copy of the bank's account with the customer) together with the customer's checks (or electronic images of the checks) that the bank paid during the month.[15] If neither the bank nor the customer made any errors, if all deposits made and all checks drawn by the customer reached the bank within the same month, and if no unusual transactions occurred that affected either the company's or the bank's record of cash, the balance of cash reported by the bank to the customer equals that shown in the customer's own records. This condition seldom occurs due to one or more of the reconciling items presented on the next page. Hence, a company expects differences between its record of cash and the bank's record. Therefore, it must reconcile the two to determine the nature of the differences between the two amounts.

---

[15]As we mentioned in Chapter 7, paper checks continue to be used as a means of payment. However, ready availability of desktop publishing software and hardware has created new opportunities for check fraud in the form of duplicate, altered, and forged checks. At the same time, new fraud-fighting technologies, such as ultraviolet imaging, high-capacity barcodes, and biometrics, are being developed. These technologies convert paper documents into electronically processed document files, thereby reducing the risk of fraud.

RECONCILING ITEMS

1. DEPOSITS IN TRANSIT. End-of-month deposits of cash recorded on the depositor's books in one month are received and recorded by the bank in the following month.

2. OUTSTANDING CHECKS. Checks written by the depositor are recorded when written but may not be recorded by (may not "clear") the bank until the next month.

3. BANK CHARGES. Charges recorded by the bank against the depositor's balance for such items as bank services, printing checks, **not-sufficient-funds (NSF) checks**, and safe-deposit box rentals. The depositor may not be aware of these charges until the receipt of the bank statement.

4. BANK CREDITS. Collections or deposits by the bank for the benefit of the depositor that may be unknown to the depositor until receipt of the bank statement. Examples are note collection for the depositor and interest earned on interest-bearing checking accounts.

5. BANK OR DEPOSITOR ERRORS. Errors on either the part of the bank or the part of the depositor cause the bank balance to disagree with the depositor's book balance.

A **bank reconciliation** is a schedule explaining any differences between the bank's and the company's records of cash. If the difference results only from transactions not yet recorded by the bank, the company's record of cash is considered correct. But, if some part of the difference arises from other items, either the bank or the company must adjust its records.

A company may prepare two forms of a bank reconciliation. One form reconciles from the bank statement balance to the book balance or vice versa. The other form reconciles both the bank balance and the book balance to a correct cash balance. Most companies use this latter form. Illustration 7A-1 shows a sample of that form and its common reconciling items.

ILLUSTRATION 7A-1
Bank Reconciliation
Form and Content

Balance per bank statement (end of period)		$$$
Add: Deposits in transit	$$	
Undeposited receipts (cash on hand)	$$	
Bank errors that understate the bank statement balance	$$	$$
		$$$
Deduct: Outstanding checks	$$	
Bank errors that overstate the bank statement balance	$$	$$
Correct cash balance		$$$
Balance per depositor's books		$$$
Add: Bank credits and collections not yet recorded in the books	$$	
Book errors that understate the book balance	$$	$$
		$$$
Deduct: Bank charges not yet recorded in the books	$$	
Book errors that overstate the book balance	$$	$$
Correct cash balance		$$$

This form of reconciliation consists of two sections: (1) "Balance per bank statement" and (2) "Balance per depositor's books." Both sections end with the same "Correct cash balance." The correct cash balance is the amount to which the books must be adjusted and is the amount reported on the statement of financial position. **Companies prepare adjusting journal entries for all the addition and deduction items appearing in the "Balance per depositor's books" section.** Companies should immediately call to the bank's attention any errors attributable to it.

To illustrate, Nugget Mining Company's books show a cash balance at the Melbourne Bank on November 30, 2015, of $20,502. The bank statement covering the month of

November shows an ending balance of $22,190. An examination of Nugget's accounting records and November bank statement identified the following reconciling items.

1. A deposit of $3,680 that Nugget mailed November 30 does not appear on the bank statement.

2. Checks written in November but not charged to the November bank statement are:

Check #7327	$ 150
#7348	4,820
#7349	31

3. Nugget has not yet recorded the $600 of interest collected by the bank November 20 on Sequoia Co. bonds held by the bank for Nugget.

4. Bank service charges of $18 are not yet recorded on Nugget's books.

5. The bank returned one of Nugget's customer's checks for $220 with the bank statement, marked "NSF." The bank deducted $220 from Nugget's account.

6. Nugget discovered that it incorrectly recorded check #7322, written in November for $131 in payment of an account payable, as $311.

7. A check for Nugent Oil Co. in the amount of $175 that the bank incorrectly charged to Nugget accompanied the statement.

Nugget reconciled the bank and book balances to the correct cash balance of $21,044 as shown in Illustration 7A-2.

NUGGET MINING COMPANY
BANK RECONCILIATION
MELBOURNE BANK, NOVEMBER 30, 2015

Balance per bank statement (end of period)			$22,190
Add: Deposit in transit	(1)	$3,680	
Bank error—incorrect check charged to account by bank	(7)	175	3,855
			26,045
Deduct: Outstanding checks	(2)		5,001
Correct cash balance			$21,044
Balance per books			$20,502
Add: Interest collected by the bank	(3)	$ 600	
Error in recording check #7322	(6)	180	780
			21,282
Deduct: Bank service charges	(4)	18	
NSF check returned	(5)	220	238
Correct cash balance			$21,044

ILLUSTRATION 7A-2
Sample Bank
Reconciliation

The journal entries required to adjust and correct Nugget's books in early December 2015 are taken from the items in the "Balance per books" section and are as follows.

Cash	600	
Interest Revenue		600
(To record interest on Sequoia Co. bonds, collected by bank)		
Cash	180	
Accounts Payable		180
(To correct error in recording amount of check #7322)		
Office Expense (bank charges)	18	
Cash		18
(To record bank service charges for November)		
Accounts Receivable	220	
Cash		220
(To record customer's check returned NSF)		

After posting the entries, Nugget's cash account will have a balance of $21,044. Nugget should return the Nugent Oil Co. check to Melbourne Bank, informing the bank of the error.

SUMMARY OF LEARNING OBJECTIVE FOR APPENDIX 7A

10 **Explain common techniques employed to control cash.** The common techniques employed to control cash are as follows. (1) *Using bank accounts:* A company can vary the number and location of banks and the types of accounts to obtain desired control objectives. (2) *The imprest petty cash system:* It may be impractical to require small amounts of various expenses be paid by check, yet some control over them is important. (3) *Physical protection of cash balances:* Adequate control of receipts and disbursements is a part of the protection of cash balances. Every effort should be made to minimize the cash on hand in the office. (4) *Reconciliation of bank balances:* Cash on deposit is not available for count and is proved by preparing a bank reconciliation.

APPENDIX **7B** | IMPAIRMENTS OF RECEIVABLES

LEARNING OBJECTIVE

Describe the accounting for a loan impairment.

As indicated in the chapter, companies assess their receivables for impairment each reporting period. Companies start the impairment assessment by considering whether objective evidence indicates that one or more loss events have occurred. Examples of possible loss events are significant financial problems of the customer, payment defaults, or renegotiation of terms of the receivable due to financial difficulty of the customer. A receivable is considered impaired when a loss event has a negative impact on the future cash flows to be received from the customer.[16] As shown in the chapter, the percentage-of-sales and -receivables approaches are examples of impairment testing using the **collective assessment approach**. In this appendix, we discuss impairments based on the **individual assessment approach** for long-term receivables.

IMPAIRMENT MEASUREMENT AND REPORTING

If a receivable is determined to be individually impaired, the company should measure the loss due to the **impairment**. This impairment loss is calculated as the difference between the carrying amount (generally the principal plus accrued interest) and the expected future cash flows discounted at the loan's historical effective-interest rate.[17] **When using the historical effective-interest loan rate, the value of the investment will change only**

---

[16]The impairment test discussed here applies only to receivables that are measured at amortized cost. **[12]** More complex rules arise when these loans are sold as part of the securitization process, especially when the original terms of the notes are modified. If the loans are bundled into a security (e.g., mortgage-backed securities), the impairment evaluation is different. We discuss this accounting in Chapter 17.

[17]The creditor may also, for the sake of expediency, use the market price of the loan (if such a price is available) or the fair value of the collateral if it is a collateralized loan. Recognize that if the value of the investment is based on the historical rate, generally the resultant value will not be equal to the fair value of the loan in subsequent periods. We consider this accounting inconsistent with fair value principles as applied to other financial instruments.

if some of the legally contracted cash flows are reduced. A company recognizes a loss in this case because the expected future cash flows are now lower. The company ignores interest rate changes caused by current economic events that affect the fair value of the loan. In estimating future cash flows, the creditor should use reasonable and supportable assumptions and projections.

Impairment Loss Example

At December 31, 2014, Ogden Bank recorded an investment of €100,000 in a loan to Carl King. The loan has an historical effective-interest rate of 10 percent, the principal is due in full at maturity in three years, and interest is due annually. Unfortunately, King is experiencing significant financial difficulty and indicates that he will have a difficult time making full payment. The loan officer performs a review of the loan's expected future cash flows and utilizes the present value method for measuring the required impairment loss. Illustration 7B-1 shows the cash flow schedule prepared by the loan officer.

Dec. 31	Contractual Cash Flow	Expected Cash Flow	Loss of Cash Flow
2015	€ 10,000	€ 5,000	€ 5,000
2016	10,000	5,000	5,000
2017	110,000	105,000	5,000
Total cash flows	€130,000	€115,000	€15,000

ILLUSTRATION 7B-1
Impaired Loan Cash Flows

As indicated, this loan is impaired. The expected cash flows of €115,000 are less than the contractual cash flows, including principal and interest, of €130,000. The amount of the impairment to be recorded equals the difference between the recorded investment of €100,000 and the present value of the expected cash flows, as shown in Illustration 7B-2.

Recorded investment		€100,000
Less: Present value of €100,000 due in 3 years at 10%		
(Table 6-2); *FV (PVF*$_{3,10\%}$); (€100,000 × .75132)	€75,132	
Present value of €5,000 interest receivable annually		
for 3 years at 10% R *(PVF-OA*$_{3,10\%}$); (€5,000 × 2.48685)	12,434	87,566
Loss on impairment		€ 12,434

ILLUSTRATION 7B-2
Computation of Impairment Loss

The loss due to the impairment is €12,434. Why isn't it €15,000 (€130,000 − €115,000)? Because Ogden Bank must measure the loss at a present value amount, not at an undiscounted amount, when it records the loss.

Recording Impairment Losses

Ogden Bank (the creditor) recognizes an impairment loss of €12,434 by debiting Bad Debt Expense for the expected loss. At the same time, it reduces the overall value of the receivable by crediting Allowance for Doubtful Accounts. The journal entry to record the loss is therefore as follows.[18]

Bad Debt Expense	12,434	
Allowance for Doubtful Accounts		12,434

[18]In the event of a receivable write-off, the company charges the loss against the allowance. In subsequent periods, if revising estimated expected cash flows based on new information, the company adjusts the allowance account and bad debt expense account (either increased or decreased depending on whether conditions improved or worsened) in the same fashion as the original impairment. We use the terms "loss" and "bad debt expense" interchangeably throughout this discussion. Companies may charge losses related to receivables transactions to Bad Debt Expense or the related Allowance for Doubtful Accounts because they use these accounts to recognize changes in values affecting receivables.

Recovery of Impairment Loss

Subsequent to recording an impairment, events or economic conditions may change such that the extent of the impairment loss decreases (e.g., due to an improvement in the debtor's credit rating). In this situation, some or all of the previously recognized impairment loss shall be reversed either directly, with a debit to Accounts Receivable, or by debiting the allowance account and crediting Bad Debt Expense.

To illustrate, assume that in the year following the impairment recorded by Ogden, Carl King has worked his way out of financial difficulty. Ogden now expects to receive all payments on the loan according to the original loan terms. Based on this new information, the present value of the expected payments is €100,000. Thus, Ogden makes the following entry to reverse the previously recorded impairment.

Allowance for Doubtful Accounts	12,434	
Bad Debt Expense		12,434

Note that the reversal of impairment losses shall not result in a carrying amount of the receivable that exceeds the amortized cost that would have been reported had the impairment not been recognized.[19]

KEY TERMS

collective assessment approach, *330*

impairment, *330*

individual assessment approach, *330*

SUMMARY OF LEARNING OBJECTIVE FOR APPENDIX 7B

11 **Describe the accounting for a loan impairment.** A creditor bases an impairment loan loss on the difference between the present value of the future cash flows (using the historical effective-interest rate) and the carrying amount of the note.

IFRS AUTHORITATIVE LITERATURE

Authoritative Literature References

[1] International Accounting Standard 7, *Statement of Cash Flows* (London, U.K.: International Accounting Standards Committee Foundation, 2001), paras. 6–7.

[2] FASB ASC 210-10-S99-1. [Predecessor literature: "Amendments to Regulations S-X and Related Interpretations and Guidelines Regarding the Disclosure of Compensating Balances and Short-Term Borrowing Arrangements," *Accounting Series Release No. 148*, Securities and Exchange Commission (November 13, 1973).]

[3] International Accounting Standard 7, *Statement of Cash Flows* (London, U.K.: International Accounting Standards Committee Foundation, 2001), par. 8.

[4] International Accounting Standard 39, *Financial Instruments: Recognition and Measurement* (London, U.K.: International Accounting Standards Committee Foundation, 2003), par. 9.

[5] International Accounting Standard 39, *Financial Instruments: Recognition and Measurement* (London, U.K.: International Accounting Standards Committee Foundation, 2003), paras. 58–70.

[6] International Accounting Standard 39, *Financial Instruments: Recognition and Measurement* (London, U.K.: International Accounting Standards Committee Foundation, 2003), paras. IN16 and 9.

[7] International Financial Reporting Standard 9, *Financial Instruments* (London, U.K.: IFRS Foundation, November 2013), par. 5.7.

[19]What entry does Carl King (the debtor) make? The debtor makes no entry because he still legally owes €100,000.

[8] International Accounting Standard 1, *Presentation of Financial Statements* (London, U.K.: International Accounting Standards Committee Foundation, 2003), paras. 32–35.

[9] International Financial Reporting Standard 9, *Financial Instruments* (London, U.K.: IFRS Foundation, 2010), par. 3.2.

[10] International Financial Reporting Standard 7, *Financial Instruments: Disclosure* (London, U.K.: International Accounting Standards Committee Foundation, 2005), paras. 1–19.

[11] International Financial Reporting Standard 7, *Financial Instruments: Disclosure* (London, U.K.: International Accounting Standards Committee Foundation, 2005), paras. 31–38.

[12] International Accounting Standard 39, *Financial Instruments: Recognition and Measurement* (London, U.K.: International Accounting Standards Committee Foundation, 2001), paras. 58, 63–65.

Note: All asterisked Questions, Exercises, and Problems relate to material in the appendices to the chapter.

QUESTIONS

1. What may be included under the heading of "cash"?

2. In what accounts should the following items be classified?

    (a) Coins and currency.
    (b) U.S. Treasury (government) bonds.
    (c) Certificate of deposit.
    (d) Cash in a bank that is in receivership.
    (e) Deposit in foreign bank (exchangeability limited).
    (f) Postdated checks.
    (g) Cash to be used for retirement of long-term bonds.
    (h) Deposits in transit.
    (i) 100 shares of Daimler (DEU) (intention is to sell in one year or less).
    (j) Savings and checking accounts.
    (k) Petty cash.
    (l) Stamps.
    (m) Travel advances.

3. Define a "compensating balance." How should a compensating balance be reported?

4. Springsteen Inc. reported in a recent annual report "Restricted cash for debt redemption." What section of the statement of financial position would report this item?

5. What are the reasons that a company gives trade discounts? Why are trade discounts not recorded in the accounts like cash discounts?

6. What are two methods of recording accounts receivable transactions when a cash discount situation is involved? Which is more theoretically correct? Which is used in practice more of the time? Why?

7. Define amortized cost.

8. What are the basic problems that occur in the valuation of accounts receivable?

9. What is the theoretical justification of the allowance method as contrasted with the direct write-off method of accounting for bad debts?

10. Indicate how well the percentage-of-sales method and the percentage-of-receivables method accomplish the objectives of the allowance method of accounting for bad debts.

11. Of what merit is the contention that the allowance method lacks the objectivity of the direct write-off method? Discuss in terms of accounting's measurement function.

12. Briefly describe the impairment evaluation process and assessment of receivables on an individual or collective basis.

13. Because of calamitous earthquake losses, Bernstein Company, one of your client's oldest and largest customers, suddenly and unexpectedly became bankrupt. Approximately 30% of your client's total sales have been made to Bernstein Company during each of the past several years. The amount due from Bernstein Company—none of which is collectible—equals 22% of total accounts receivable, an amount that is considerably in excess of what was determined to be an adequate provision for doubtful accounts at the close of the preceding year. How would your client record the write-off of the Bernstein Company receivable if it is using the allowance method of accounting for bad debts? Justify your suggested treatment.

14. What is the normal procedure for handling the collection of accounts receivable previously written off?

15. On January 1, 2015, Fong Co. sells property for which it had paid NT$690,000 to Chou Company, receiving in return Chou's zero-interest-bearing note for NT$1,000,000 payable in 5 years. What entry would Fong make to record the sale, assuming that Fong frequently sells similar items of property for a cash sales price of NT$640,000?

16. What is "imputed interest"? In what situations is it necessary to impute an interest rate for notes receivable? What are the considerations in imputing an appropriate interest rate?

17. What is the fair value option? Where do companies that elect the fair value option report unrealized holding gains and losses?

18. Indicate three reasons why a company might sell its receivables to another company.

19. What is the role of "risks and rewards" when accounting for a transfer of receivables?

20. Moon Hardware is planning to factor some of its receivables. The cash received will be used to pay for inventory purchases. The factor has indicated that it will require "full guarantee (with recourse)" on credit losses on the sold receivables. Explain to the controller of Moon Hardware what "full guarantee" on credit losses is and how the guarantee will be reflected in Moon's financial statements after the sale of the receivables.

21. Horizon Outfitters Company includes in its trial balance for December 31 an item for Accounts Receivable €789,000. This balance consists of the following items:

Due from regular customers	€523,000
Refund receivable on prior year's income taxes (an established claim)	15,500
Travel advance to employees	22,000
Loan to wholly owned subsidiary	45,500
Advances to suppliers for goods ordered	61,000
Accounts receivable assigned as security for loans payable	75,000
Notes receivable past due plus interest on these notes	47,000
Total	€789,000

Illustrate how these items should be shown in the statement of financial position as of December 31.

22. What is the accounts receivable turnover, and what type of information does it provide?

23. You are evaluating Woodlawn Racetrack for a potential loan. An examination of the notes to the financial statements indicates restricted cash at year-end amounts to $100,000. Explain how you would use this information in evaluating Woodlawn's liquidity.

24. What are some steps taken by both the FASB and IASB to move to fair value measurement for financial instruments?

25. Briefly describe some of the similarities and differences between U.S. GAAP and IFRS with respect to the accounting for cash and receivables.

26. Simonis Company, which uses IFRS, has a note receivable with a carrying value of $30,000 at December 31, 2015. On January 2, 2016, the borrower declares bankruptcy, and Simonis estimates that only $25,000 of the note will be collected. Prepare the journal entry to record this loss. Briefly describe the accounting for the loan subsequent to the bankruptcy under U.S. GAAP, assuming Simonis estimates that *more than* $25,000 can be repaid.

*27. Distinguish among the following: (1) a general checking account, (2) an imprest bank account, and (3) a lockbox account.

*28. What are the general rules for measuring and recognizing an impairment of a receivable?

BRIEF EXERCISES

1 **BE7-1** Kraft Enterprises owns the following assets at December 31, 2015.

Cash in bank—savings account	€68,000	Checking account balance	€17,000
Cash on hand	9,300	Postdated checks	750
Tax refund due	31,400	Certificates of deposit (180-day)	90,000

What amount should be reported as cash?

4 **BE7-2** Restin Co. uses the gross method to record sales made on credit. On June 1, 2015, it made sales of £50,000 with terms 3/15, n/45. On June 12, 2015, Restin received full payment for the June 1 sale. Prepare the required journal entries for Restin Co.

4 **BE7-3** Use the information from BE7-2, assuming Restin Co. uses the net method to account for cash discounts. Prepare the required journal entries for Restin Co.

5 **BE7-4** Wilton, Inc. had net sales in 2015 of €1,400,000. At December 31, 2015, before adjusting entries, the balances in selected accounts were Accounts Receivable €250,000 debit, and Allowance for Doubtful Accounts €2,400 credit. If Wilton estimates that 2% of its net sales will prove to be uncollectible, prepare the December 31, 2015, journal entry to record bad debt expense.

5 **BE7-5** Use the information presented in BE7-4 for Wilton, Inc.

(a) Instead of estimating the uncollectibles at 2% of net sales, assume that 10% of accounts receivable will prove to be uncollectible. Prepare the entry to record bad debt expense.

(b) Instead of estimating uncollectibles at 2% of net sales, assume Wilton prepares an aging schedule that estimates total uncollectible accounts at €24,600. Prepare the entry to record bad debt expense.

6 **BE7-6** Milner Family Importers sold goods to Tung Decorators for $30,000 on November 1, 2015, accepting Tung's $30,000, 6-month, 6% note. Prepare Milner's November 1 entry, December 31 annual adjusting entry, and May 1 entry for the collection of the note and interest.

6 **BE7-7** Deng Acrobats lent NT$16,529 to Donaldson, Inc., accepting Donaldson's 2-year, NT$20,000, zero-interest-bearing note. The implied interest rate is 10%. Prepare Deng's journal entries for the initial transaction, recognition of interest each year, and the collection of NT$20,000 at maturity.

5 **BE7-8** Modest Mouse Company had the following information related to an account receivable from Counting Crows Inc. Initial face value, €22,000; payments received, €3,000; provision for uncollectibility, €5,000. Determine the amortized cost for the Counting Crows receivable.

8 **BE7-9** Jack Sparrow Corporation has elected to use the fair value option for one of its notes receivable. The note, accepted from a customer in exchange for trade accounts receivable, has a carrying value of $16,000. At year-end, Sparrow estimates the fair value of the note to be $17,500. (1) Determine the unrealized gain or loss on the note. (2) Prepare the entry to record any unrealized gain or loss.

8 **BE7-10** On October 1, 2015, Chung, Inc. assigns ¥1,000,000 of its accounts receivable to Seneca National Bank as collateral for a ¥750,000 note. The bank assesses a finance charge of 2% of the receivables assigned and interest on the note of 9%. Prepare the October 1 journal entries for both Chung and Seneca.

8 **BE7-11** Wood Incorporated factored €150,000 of accounts receivable with Engram Factors Inc., without guarantee of credit loss. Engram assesses a 2% finance charge of the amount of accounts receivable and retains an amount equal to 6% of accounts receivable for possible adjustments. Prepare the journal entry for Wood Incorporated and Engram Factors to record the factoring of the accounts receivable to Engram.

8 **BE7-12** Use the information in BE7-11 for Wood Incorporated. Assume that the receivables are sold with recourse (guarantee). Prepare the journal entry for Wood to record the sale.

8 **BE7-13** Arness Woodcrafters sells $250,000 of receivables to Commercial Factors, Inc. on a without guarantee basis. Commercial assesses a finance charge of 5% and retains an amount equal to 4% of accounts receivable. Prepare the journal entry for Arness to record the sale.

8 **BE7-14** Use the information presented in BE7-13 for Arness Woodcrafters but assume that the receivables were sold with a full guarantee for credit losses. Prepare the journal entry and discuss the effects on Arness's financial statements.

9 **BE7-15** Recent financial statements of adidas (DEU) report net sales of €10,799 million. Accounts receivable are €1,459 million at the beginning of the year and €1,624 million at the end of the year. Compute adidas's accounts receivable turnover. Compute adidas's average collection period for accounts receivable in days.

10 *BE7-16** Finman Company designated Jill Holland as petty cash custodian and established a petty cash fund of £200. The fund is reimbursed when the cash in the fund is at £15. Petty cash receipts indicate funds were disbursed for office supplies £94 and miscellaneous expense £87. Prepare journal entries for the establishment of the fund and the reimbursement.

10 *BE7-17** Horton Corporation is preparing a bank reconciliation and has identified the following potential reconciling items. For each item, indicate if it is (1) added to balance per bank statement, (2) deducted from balance per bank statement, (3) added to balance per books, or (4) deducted from balance per books.

    (a) Deposit in transit $5,500.   **(d)** Outstanding checks $7,422.

    (b) Bank service charges $25.   **(e)** NSF check returned $377.

    (c) Interest credited to Horton's account $31.

10 *BE7-18** Use the information presented in BE7-17 for Horton Corporation. Prepare any entries necessary to make Horton's accounting records correct and complete.

11 *BE7-19** Assume that Toni Braxton Company has recently fallen into financial difficulties. By reviewing all available evidence on December 31, 2015, one of Toni Braxton's creditors, the National Bank, determined that Toni Braxton would pay back only 65% of the principal at maturity. As a result, the bank decided that the loan was impaired. If the loss is estimated to be £225,000, what entry(ies) should National Bank make to record this loss?

EXERCISES

1 **E 7-1 (Determine Cash Balance)** The controller for Wallaby Co. is attempting to determine the amount of cash and cash equivalents to be reported on its December 31, 2015, statement of financial position. The following information is provided.

    1. Commercial savings account of £600,000 and a commercial checking account balance of £800,000 are held at First National Bank of Olathe.

    2. Money market fund account held at Volonte Co. (a mutual fund organization) permits Wallaby to write checks on this balance, £5,000,000.

    3. Travel advances of £180,000 for executive travel for the first quarter of next year (employee to reimburse through salary reduction).

4. A separate cash fund in the amount of £1,500,000 is restricted for the retirement of long-term debt.

5. Petty cash fund of £1,000.

6. An I.O.U. from Marianne Koch, a company customer, in the amount of £150,000.

7. A bank overdraft of £110,000 has occurred at one of the banks the company uses to deposit its cash receipts. At the present time, the company has no deposits at this bank.

8. The company has two certificates of deposit, each totaling £500,000. These CDs have a maturity of 120 days.

9. Wallaby has received a check that is dated January 12, 2016, in the amount of £125,000.

10. Wallaby has agreed to maintain a cash balance of £500,000 at all times at First National Bank of Olathe to ensure future credit availability.

11. Wallaby has purchased £2,100,000 of commercial paper of Sergio Leone Co. which is due in 60 days.

12. Currency and coin on hand amounted to £7,700.

Instructions

(a) Compute the amount of cash (and cash equivalents) to be reported on Wallaby Co.'s statement of financial position at December 31, 2015.

(b) Indicate the proper reporting for items that are not reported as cash on the December 31, 2015, statement of financial position.

1 **E7-2** **(Determine Cash Balance)** Presented below are a number of independent situations.

Instructions

For each individual situation, determine the amount that should be reported as cash. If the item(s) is not reported as cash, explain the rationale.

1. Checking account balance $925,000; certificate of deposit $1,400,000; cash advance to subsidiary of $980,000; utility deposit paid to gas company $180.

2. Checking account balance $500,000; an overdraft in special checking account at same bank as normal checking account of $17,000; cash held in a bond sinking fund $200,000; petty cash fund $300; coins and currency on hand $1,350.

3. Checking account balance $590,000; postdated check from customer $11,000; cash restricted due to maintaining compensating balance requirement of $100,000; certified check from customer $9,800; postage stamps on hand $620.

4. Checking account balance at bank $42,000; money market balance at mutual fund (has checking privileges) $48,000; NSF check received from customer $800.

5. Checking account balance $700,000; cash restricted for future plant expansion $500,000; short-term Treasury bills $180,000; cash advance received from customer $900 (not included in checking account balance); cash advance of $7,000 to company executive, payable on demand; refundable deposit of $26,000 paid to the government to guarantee performance on construction contract.

3 **4** **E7-3** **(Financial Statement Presentation of Receivables)** Pique Company shows a balance of €241,140 in the Accounts Receivable account on December 31, 2015. The balance consists of the following.

Installment accounts due in 2016	€23,000
Installment accounts due after 2016	34,000
Overpayments to creditors	2,640
Due from regular customers, of which €40,000 represents	
accounts pledged as security for a bank loan	89,000
Advances to employees	1,500
Advance to subsidiary company (made in 2013)	91,000

Instructions

Illustrate how the information should be shown on the statement of financial position of Pique Company on December 31, 2015.

3 **4** **E7-4** **(Determine Ending Accounts Receivable)** Your accounts receivable clerk, Mary Herman, to whom you pay a salary of $1,500 per month, has just purchased a new Audi. You decided to test the accuracy of the accounts receivable balance of $117,000 as shown in the ledger.

The following information is available for your *first year* in business.

(1) Collections from customers	$198,000
(2) Merchandise purchased	320,000
(3) Ending merchandise inventory	70,000
(4) Goods are marked to sell at 40% above cost	

Instructions

Compute an estimate of the ending balance of accounts receivable from customers that should appear in the ledger and any apparent shortages. Assume that all sales are made on account.

4 E7-5 (Recording Sales Gross and Net) On June 3, Bolton Company sold to Arquette Company merchandise having a sales price of £2,000 with terms of 2/10, n/60. An invoice totaling £90, terms n/30, was received by Arquette on June 8 from John Booth Transport Service for the freight cost. On June 12, the company received a check for the balance due from Arquette Company.

Instructions

(a) Prepare journal entries on the Bolton Company books to record all the events noted above under each of the following bases.

    (1) Sales and receivables are entered at gross selling price.

    (2) Sales and receivables are entered at net of cash discounts.

(b) Prepare the journal entry under basis (a)(2), assuming that Arquette Company did not remit payment until July 29.

4 E7-6 (Recording Sales Transactions) Presented below is information from Lopez Computers Incorporated.

July 1	Sold R$30,000 of computers to Smallwood Company with terms 3/15, n/60. Lopez uses the gross method to record cash discounts.
10	Lopez received payment from Smallwood for the full amount owed from the July transactions.
17	Sold R$250,000 in computers and peripherals to The Hernandez Store with terms of 2/10, n/30.
30	The Hernandez Store paid Lopez for its purchase of July 17.

Instructions

Prepare the necessary journal entries for Lopez Computers.

5 E7-7 (Recording Bad Debts) Sandel Company reports the following financial information before adjustments.

	Dr.	Cr.
Accounts Receivable	€160,000	
Allowance for Doubtful Accounts		€ 2,000
Sales Revenue (all on credit)		800,000
Sales Returns and Allowances	50,000	

Instructions

Prepare the journal entry to record bad debt expense assuming Sandel Company estimates bad debts at (a) 1% of net sales and (b) 5% of accounts receivable.

5 E7-8 (Recording Bad Debts) At the end of 2015, Sorter Company has accounts receivable of £900,000 and an allowance for doubtful accounts of £40,000. On January 16, 2016, Sorter Company determined that its receivable from Ordonez Company of £8,000 will not be collected, and management authorized its write-off.

Instructions

(a) Prepare the journal entry for Sorter Company to write off the Ordonez receivable.

(b) What is the cash realizable value of Sorter Company's accounts receivable before the write-off of the Ordonez receivable?

(c) What is the cash realizable value of Sorter Company's accounts receivable after the write-off of the Ordonez receivable?

5 E7-9 (Computing Bad Debts and Preparing Journal Entries) The trial balance before adjustment of Estefan Inc. shows the following balances.

	Dr.	Cr.
Accounts Receivable	$80,000	
Allowance for Doubtful Accounts	1,750	
Sales Revenue (net, all on credit)		$580,000

Instructions

Give the entry for estimated bad debts assuming that the allowance is to provide for doubtful accounts on the basis of (a) 4% of gross accounts receivable and (b) 1% of net sales.

5 **E7-10 (Bad-Debt Reporting)** The chief accountant for Ballywood Corporation provides you with the following list of accounts receivable written off in the current year (amounts in thousands).

Date	Customer	Amount
March 31	E. L. Masters Company	₹7,800
June 30	Hocking Associates	9,700
September 30	Amy Lowell's Dress Shop	7,000
December 31	R. Bronson, Inc.	9,830

Ballywood Corporation follows the policy of debiting Bad Debt Expense as accounts are written off. The chief accountant maintains that this procedure is appropriate for financial statement purposes because the tax authority will not accept other methods for recognizing bad debts.

All of Ballywood Corporation's sales are on a 30-day credit basis. Sales for the current year total ₹2,400,000, and research has determined that bad debt losses approximate 2% of sales.

Instructions

(a) Do you agree or disagree with Ballywood's policy concerning recognition of bad debt expense? Why or why not?

(b) By what amount would net income differ if bad debt expense was computed using the percentage-of-sales approach?

5 **E7-11 (Bad Debts—Aging)** Puckett, Inc. includes the following account among its trade receivables.

Alstott Co.

1/1	Balance forward	700	1/28	Cash (#1710)	1,100
1/20	Invoice #1710	1,100	4/2	Cash (#2116)	1,350
3/14	Invoice #2116	1,350	4/10	Cash (1/1 Balance)	255
4/12	Invoice #2412	1,710	4/30	Cash (#2412)	1,000
9/5	Invoice #3614	490	9/20	Cash (#3614 and	
10/17	Invoice #4912	860		part of #2412)	890
11/18	Invoice #5681	2,000	10/31	Cash (#4912)	860
12/20	Invoice #6347	800	12/1	Cash (#5681)	1,250
			12/29	Cash (#6347)	800

Instructions

Age the balance and specify any items that apparently require particular attention at year-end.

4 **5** **8** **E7-12 (Journalizing Various Receivable Transactions)** Presented below is information related to Sanford Corp.

July 1   Sanford Corp. sold to Legler Co. merchandise having a sales price of €10,000 with terms 2/10, net/60. Sanford records its sales and receivables net.

5   Accounts receivable of €12,000 (gross) are factored with Rothchild Credit Corp. without guarantee at a financing charge of 9%. Cash is received for the proceeds; collections are handled by the finance company. (These accounts were all past the discount period.)

9   Specific accounts receivable of €9,000 (gross) are pledged to Rather Credit Corp. as security for a loan of €6,000 at a finance charge of 6% of the amount of the loan. The finance company will make the collections. (All the accounts receivable are past the discount period.)

Dec. 29   Legler Co. notifies Sanford that it is bankrupt and will pay only 10% of its account. Give the entry to write off the uncollectible balance using the allowance method. (*Note:* First record the increase in the receivable on July 11 when the discount period passed.)

31   Sanford conducts an individual assessment of a note receivable with a carrying value of €350,000. Sanford determines the present value of the note is €275,000.

Instructions

Prepare all necessary entries in general journal form for Sanford Corp.

8 **9** **E7-13 (Fair Value Option)** Kobiashi Company sells large store-rack systems and frequently accepts notes receivable from customers as payment. Kobiashi conducts a thorough credit check on its customers, and it charges a fairly low interest rate (½ of 1% payable monthly) on these notes. Kobiashi has elected to use the fair value option for one of these notes and has the following data related to the carrying and fair value for this note (amounts in thousands).

	Carrying Value	Fair Value
December 31, 2015	¥54,000	¥54,000
December 31, 2016	44,000	42,500
December 31, 2017	36,000	38,000

Instructions

(a) Prepare the journal entry at December 31 (Kobiashi's year-end) for 2015, 2016, and 2017, to record the fair value option for these notes.

(b) At what amount will the note be reported on Kobiashi's 2016 statement of financial position?

(c) What is the effect of recording the fair value option on this note on Kobiashi's 2017 income?

8 **E7-14 (Assigning Accounts Receivable)** On April 1, 2015, Prince Company assigns $500,000 of its accounts receivable to the Hibernia Bank as collateral for a $300,000 loan due July 1, 2015. The assignment agreement calls for Prince Company to continue to collect the receivables. Hibernia Bank assesses a finance charge of 2% of the accounts receivable, and interest on the loan is 10% (a realistic rate of interest for a note of this type).

Instructions

(a) Prepare the April 1, 2015, journal entry for Prince Company.

(b) Prepare the journal entry for Prince's collection of $350,000 of the accounts receivable during the period from April 1, 2015, through June 30, 2015.

(c) On July 1, 2015, Prince paid Hibernia all that was due from the loan it secured on April 1, 2015. Prepare the journal entry to record this payment.

5 **8** **E7-15 (Journalizing Various Receivable Transactions)** The trial balance before adjustment for Misumi Company shows the following balances (amounts in thousands).

	Dr.	Cr.
Accounts Receivable	¥82,000	
Allowance for Doubtful Accounts	1,750	
Sales Revenue		¥430,000

Instructions

Using the data above, give the journal entries required to record each of the following cases. (Each situation is independent.)

1. To obtain additional cash, Misumi factors without guarantee of credit loss ¥20,000 of accounts receivable with Stills Finance. The finance charge is 10% of the amount factored.

2. To obtain a one-year loan of ¥55,000, Misumi assigns ¥65,000 of specific receivable accounts to Obihiro Financial. The finance charge is 8% of the loan; the cash is received and the accounts turned over to Obihiro Financial.

3. The company wants to maintain Allowance for Doubtful Accounts at 5% of gross accounts receivable.

4. The company wishes to increase the allowance account by 1½% of net sales.

8 **E7-16 (Transfer of Receivables with Guarantee)** Bryant Inc. factors receivables with a carrying amount of £200,000 to Warren Company for £190,000 and guarantees all credit losses.

Instructions

Prepare the appropriate journal entry to record this transaction on the books of Bryant Inc.

8 **E7-17 (Transfer of Receivables with Guarantee)** Bohannon Corporation factors €250,000 of accounts receivable with Winkler Financing, Inc. on a without guarantee (no recourse) basis. Winkler Financing will collect the receivables. The receivables records are transferred to Winkler Financing on August 15, 2015. Winkler Financing assesses a finance charge of 2% of the amount of accounts receivable and also reserves an amount equal to 4% of accounts receivable to cover probable adjustments.

Instructions

(a) What conditions must be met for a transfer of receivables with recourse to be accounted for as a sale?

(b) Assume the conditions from part (a) are met. Prepare the journal entry on August 15, 2015, for Bohannon to record the sale of receivables.

8 **E7-18 (Transfer of Receivables without Guarantee)** SEK Corp. factors ¥400,000 of accounts receivable with Mays Finance Corporation, without guaranteeing any payment for possible credit losses (without recourse) on July 1, 2015. The receivables records are transferred to Mays Finance, which will receive the collections. Mays Finance assesses a finance charge of 1½% of the amount of accounts receivable and retains an amount equal to 4% of accounts receivable to cover sales discounts, returns, and allowances. The transaction is to be recorded as a sale.

Instructions

(a) Prepare the journal entry on July 1, 2015, for SEK Corp. to record the sale of receivables without recourse.

(b) Prepare the journal entry on July 1, 2015, for Mays Finance Corporation to record the purchase of receivables without recourse.

6 7 **E7-19 (Notes Transactions at Unrealistic Interest Rates)** On July 1, 2015, Rentoul Inc. made two sales.

1. It sold land having a fair value of £900,000 in exchange for a 4-year, zero-interest-bearing promissory note in the face amount of £1,416,163. The land is carried on Rentoul's books at a cost of £590,000.

2. It rendered services in exchange for a 3%, 8-year promissory note having a face value of £400,000 (interest payable annually).

Rentoul Inc. recently had to pay 8% interest for money that it borrowed from British National Bank. The customers in these two transactions have credit ratings that require them to borrow money at 12% interest.

Instructions
Record the two journal entries that should be recorded by Rentoul Inc. for the sales transactions above that took place on July 1, 2015.

6 7 **E7-20 (Notes Receivable with Unrealistic Interest Rate)** On December 31, 2014, Hurly Co. performed environmental consulting services for Cascade Co. Cascade was short of cash, and Hurly Co. agreed to accept a $300,000 zero-interest-bearing note due December 31, 2016, as payment in full. Cascade is somewhat of a credit risk and typically borrows funds at a rate of 10%. Hurly is much more creditworthy and has various lines of credit at 6%.

Instructions
(a) Prepare the journal entry to record the transaction of December 31, 2014, for Hurly Co.
(b) Assuming Hurly Co.'s fiscal year-end is December 31, prepare the journal entry for December 31, 2015.
(c) Assuming Hurly Co.'s fiscal year-end is December 31, prepare the journal entry for December 31, 2016.
(d) Assume that Hurly Co. elects the fair value option for this note. Prepare the journal entry at December 31, 2015, if the fair value of the note is $320,000.

9 **E7-21 (Analysis of Receivables)** Presented below is information for Grant Company.

1. Beginning-of-the-year Accounts Receivable balance was €15,000.

2. Net sales (all on account) for the year were €100,000. Grant does not offer cash discounts.

3. Collections on accounts receivable during the year were €80,000.

Instructions
(a) Prepare (summary) journal entries to record the items noted above.
(b) Compute Grant's accounts receivable turnover for the year. The company does not believe it will have any bad debts.
(c) Use the turnover ratio computed in (b) to analyze Grant's liquidity. The turnover ratio last year was 7.0.

8 9 **E7-22 (Transfer of Receivables)** Use the information for Grant Company as presented in E7-21. Grant is planning to factor some accounts receivable at the end of the year. Accounts totaling €10,000 will be transferred to Credit Factors, Inc. without guarantee. Credit Factors will retain 5% of the balances for probable adjustments and assesses a finance charge of 4%.

Instructions
(a) Prepare the journal entry to record the sale of the receivables.
(b) Compute Grant's accounts receivable turnover for the year, assuming the receivables are sold. Discuss how factoring of receivables affects the turnover ratio.

10 *E7-23 (Petty Cash)** McMann, Inc. decided to establish a petty cash fund to help ensure internal control over its small cash expenditures. The following information is available for the month of April.

1. On April 1, it established a petty cash fund in the amount of $200.

2. A summary of the petty cash expenditures made by the petty cash custodian as of April 10 is as follows.

Delivery charges paid on merchandise purchased	$60
Supplies purchased and used	25
Postage expense	40
I.O.U. from employees	17
Miscellaneous expense	36

The petty cash fund was replenished on April 10. The balance in the fund was $12.

3. The petty cash fund balance was increased $100 to $300 on April 20.

Instructions
Prepare the journal entries to record transactions related to petty cash for the month of April.

10 *E7-24 **(Petty Cash)** The petty cash fund of Teasdale's Auto Repair Service, a sole proprietorship, contains the following.

1. Coins and currency		$ 10.20
2. Postage stamps		7.90
3. An I.O.U. from Richie Cunningham, an employee, for cash advance		40.00
4. Check payable to Teasdale's Auto Repair from Pottsie Weber, an employee, marked NSF		34.00
5. Vouchers for the following:		
Stamps	$ 20.00	
Two Premier Cup tickets for Nick Teasdale	170.00	
Printer cartridge	14.35	204.35
		$296.45

The general ledger account Petty Cash has a balance of $300.

Instructions

Prepare the journal entry to record the reimbursement of the petty cash fund.

10 *E7-25 **(Bank Reconciliation and Adjusting Entries)** Kipling Company deposits all receipts and makes all payments by check. The following information is available from the cash records.

June 30 Bank Reconciliation

Balance per bank	£7,000
Add: Deposits in transit	1,540
Deduct: Outstanding checks	2,000
Balance per books	£6,540

Month of July Results

	Per Bank	Per Books
Balance July 31	£8,650	£9,250
July deposits	4,500	5,810
July checks	4,000	3,100
July note collected (not included in July deposits)	1,500	—
July bank service charge	15	—
July NSF check from a customer, returned by the bank (recorded by bank as a charge)	335	—

Instructions

(a) Prepare a bank reconciliation going from balance per bank and balance per book to correct the cash balance.

(b) Prepare the general journal entry or entries to correct the Cash account.

10 *E7-26 **(Bank Reconciliation and Adjusting Entries)** Aragon Company has just received the August 31, 2015, bank statement, which is summarized below.

County National Bank	Disbursements	Receipts	Balance
Balance, August 1			$ 9,369
Deposits during August		$32,200	41,569
Note collected for depositor, including $40 interest		1,040	42,609
Checks cleared during August	$34,500		8,109
Bank service charges	20		8,089
Balance, August 31			8,089

The general ledger Cash account contained the following entries for the month of August.

Cash			
Balance, August 1	10,050	Disbursements in August	35,403
Receipts during August	35,000		

Deposits in transit at August 31 are $3,800, and checks outstanding at August 31 total $1,550. Cash on hand at August 31 is $310. The bookkeeper improperly entered one check in the books at $146.50 which was written for $164.50 for supplies (expense); it cleared the bank during the month of August.

Instructions

(a) Prepare a bank reconciliation dated August 31, 2015, proceeding to a correct balance.

(b) Prepare any entries necessary to make the books correct and complete.

(c) What amount of cash should be reported in the August 31 statement of financial position?

11 *E7-27 (Impairments)** On December 31, 2015, Iva Majoli Company borrowed €62,092 from Paris Bank, signing a 5-year, €100,000 zero-interest-bearing note. The note was issued to yield 10% interest. Unfortunately, during 2017, Majoli began to experience financial difficulty. As a result, at December 31, 2017, Paris Bank determined that it was probable that it would receive back only €75,000 at maturity. The market rate of interest on loans of this nature is now 11%.

Instructions

(a) Prepare the entry to record the issuance of the loan by Paris Bank on December 31, 2015.

(b) Prepare the entry, if any, to record the impairment of the loan on December 31, 2017, by Paris Bank.

11 *E7-28 (Impairments)** On December 31, 2015, Conchita Martinez Company signed a $1,000,000 note to Sauk City Bank. The market interest rate at that time was 12%. The stated interest rate on the note was 10%, payable annually. The note matures in 5 years. Unfortunately, because of lower sales, Conchita Martinez's financial situation worsened. On December 31, 2017, Sauk City Bank determined that it was probable that the company would pay back only $600,000 of the principal at maturity. However, it was considered likely that interest would continue to be paid, based on the $1,000,000 loan.

Instructions

(a) Determine the amount of cash Conchita Martinez received from the loan on December 31, 2015.

(b) Prepare a note amortization schedule for Sauk City Bank up to December 31, 2017.

(c) Determine the loss on impairment that Sauk City Bank should recognize on December 31, 2017.

PROBLEMS

2 **P7-1 (Determine Proper Cash Balance)** Francis Equipment Co. closes its books regularly on December 31, but at the end of 2015 it held its cash book open so that a more favorable statement of financial position could be prepared for credit purposes. Cash receipts and disbursements for the first 10 days of January were recorded as December transactions. The information is given below.

1. January cash receipts recorded in the December cash book totaled €45,640, of which €28,000 represents cash sales, and €17,640 represents collections on account for which cash discounts of €360 were given.

2. January cash disbursements recorded in the December check register liquidated accounts payable of €22,450 on which discounts of €250 were taken.

3. The ledger has not been closed for 2015.

4. The amount shown as inventory was determined by physical count on December 31, 2015.

The company uses the periodic method of inventory.

Instructions

(a) Prepare any entries you consider necessary to correct Francis's accounts at December 31.

(b) To what extent was Francis Equipment Co. able to show a more favorable statement of financial position at December 31 by holding its cash book open? (Compute working capital and the current ratio.) Assume that the statement of financial position that was prepared by the company showed the following amounts:

	Dr.	Cr.
Cash	€39,000	
Accounts receivable	42,000	
Inventory	67,000	
Accounts payable		€45,000
Other current liabilities		14,200

 5 **P7-2 (Bad-Debt Reporting)** The following are a series of unrelated situations.

1. Halen Company's unadjusted trial balance at December 31, 2015, included the following accounts.

	Debit	Credit
Allowance for doubtful accounts	$4,000	
Net sales		$1,200,000

Halen Company estimates its bad debt expense to be 1½% of net sales. Determine its bad debt expense for 2015.

2. An analysis and aging of Stuart Corp. accounts receivable at December 31, 2015, disclosed the following.

Amounts estimated to be uncollectible	$ 180,000
Accounts receivable	1,750,000
Allowance for doubtful accounts (per books)	125,000

What is the cash realizable value of Stuart's receivables at December 31, 2015?

3. Shore Co. provides for doubtful accounts based on 3% of credit sales. The following data are available for 2015.

Credit sales during 2015	$2,400,000
Allowance for doubtful accounts 1/1/15	17,000
Collection of accounts written off in prior years	
(customer credit was reestablished)	8,000
Customer accounts written off as uncollectible during 2015	30,000

What is the balance in Allowance for Doubtful Accounts at December 31, 2015?

4. At the end of its first year of operations, December 31, 2015, Darden Inc. reported the following information.

Accounts receivable, net of allowance for doubtful accounts	$950,000
Customer accounts written off as uncollectible during 2015	24,000
Bad debt expense for 2015	84,000

What should be the balance in accounts receivable at December 31, 2015, before subtracting the allowance for doubtful accounts?

5. The following accounts were taken from Bullock Inc.'s trial balance at December 31, 2015.

	Debit	Credit
Net credit sales		$750,000
Allowance for doubtful accounts	$ 14,000	
Accounts receivable	310,000	

If doubtful accounts are 3% of accounts receivable, determine the bad debt expense to be reported for 2015.

Instructions

Answer the questions relating to each of the five independent situations as requested.

5 **P7-3 (Bad-Debt Reporting—Aging)** Manilow Corporation operates in an industry that has a high rate of bad debts. Before any year-end adjustments, the balance in Manilow's Accounts Receivable was $555,000 and Allowance for Doubtful Accounts had a credit balance of $40,000. The year-end balance reported in the statement of financial position for Allowance for Doubtful Accounts will be based on the aging schedule shown below.

Days Account Outstanding	Amount	Probability of Collection
Less than 16 days	$300,000	.98
16–30 days	100,000	.90
31–45 days	80,000	.85
46–60 days	40,000	.80
61–75 days	20,000	.55
Over 75 days	15,000	.00

Instructions

(a) What is the appropriate balance for Allowance for Doubtful Accounts at year-end?
(b) Show how accounts receivable would be presented on the statement of financial position.
(c) What is the dollar effect of the year-end bad debt adjustment on the before-tax income?

5 **P7-4 (Bad-Debt Reporting)** From inception of operations to December 31, 2015, Fortner Corporation provided for uncollectible accounts receivable under the allowance method: provisions were made monthly at 2% of credit sales; bad debts written off were charged to the allowance account; recoveries of bad debts previously written off were credited to the allowance account; and no year-end adjustments to the allowance account were made. Fortner's usual credit terms are net 30 days.

The balance in Allowance for Doubtful Accounts was £130,000 at January 1, 2015. During 2015, credit sales totaled £9,000,000, interim provisions for doubtful accounts were made at 2% of credit sales, £90,000 of bad debts were written off, and recoveries of accounts previously written off amounted to £15,000. Fortner installed a computer system in November 2015, and an aging of accounts receivable was prepared for the first time as of December 31, 2015. A summary of the aging is as follows.

Classification by Month of Sale	Balance in Each Category	Estimated % Uncollectible
November–December 2015	£1,080,000	2%
July–October	650,000	10%
January–June	420,000	25%
Prior to 1/1/15	150,000	80%
	£2,300,000	

Based on the review of collectibility of the account balances in the "prior to 1/1/15" aging category, additional receivables totaling £60,000 were written off as of December 31, 2015. The 80% uncollectible estimate applies to the remaining £90,000 in the category. Effective with the year ended December 31, 2015, Fortner adopted a different method for estimating the allowance for doubtful accounts at the amount indicated by the year-end aging analysis of accounts receivable.

Instructions

(a) Prepare a schedule analyzing the changes in Allowance for Doubtful Accounts for the year ended December 31, 2015. Show supporting computations in good form. (*Hint:* In computing the 12/31/15 allowance, subtract the £60,000 write-off.)

(b) Prepare the journal entry for the year-end adjustment to the Allowance for Doubtful Accounts balance as of December 31, 2015.

5 ▶ **P7-5 (Bad-Debt Reporting)** Presented below is information related to the Accounts Receivable accounts of Gulistan Inc. during the current year 2015.

1. An aging schedule of the accounts receivable as of December 31, 2015, is as follows.

Age	Net Debit Balance	% to Be Applied after Correction Is Made
Under 60 days	€172,342	1%
60–90 days	136,490	3%
91–120 days	39,924*	6%
Over 120 days	23,644	€3,700 definitely uncollectible;
	€372,400	estimated remainder uncollectible is 25%

*The €3,240 write-off of receivables is related to the 91-to-120 day category.

2. The Accounts Receivable account has a debit balance of €372,400 on December 31, 2015.

3. Two entries were made in the Bad Debt Expense account during the year: (1) a debit on December 31 for the amount credited to Allowance for Doubtful Accounts, and (2) a credit for €3,240 on November 3, 2015, and a debit to Allowance for Doubtful Accounts because of a bankruptcy.

4. Allowance for Doubtful Accounts is as follows for 2015.

	Allowance for Doubtful Accounts				
Nov. 3	Uncollectible accounts written off	3,240	Jan. 1	Beginning balance	8,750
			Dec. 31	5% of €372,400	18,620

5. A credit balance exists in Accounts Receivable (60–90 days) of €4,840, which represents an advance on a sales contract.

Instructions

Assuming that the books have not been closed for 2015, make the necessary correcting entries.

3 ▶ **4** **5** ▶ **P7-6 (Journalize Various Accounts Receivable Transactions)** The statement of financial position of Stancia Company at December 31, 2015, includes the following.

Notes receivable	R$ 36,000	
Accounts receivable	182,100	
Less: Allowance for doubtful accounts	17,300	R$200,800

Transactions in 2015 include the following.

1. Accounts receivable of R$138,000 were collected including accounts of R$60,000 on which 2% sales discounts were allowed.

2. R$5,300 was received in payment of an account which was written off the books as worthless in 2015. (*Hint:* Reestablish the receivable account.)

3. Customer accounts of R$17,500 were written off during the year.

4. At year-end, Allowance for Doubtful Accounts was estimated to need a balance of R$20,000. This estimate is based on an analysis of aged accounts receivable.

Instructions
Prepare all journal entries necessary to reflect the transactions above.

8 **P7-7 (Assigned Accounts Receivable—Journal Entries)** Salen Company finances some of its current operations by assigning accounts receivable to a finance company. On July 1, 2015, it assigned, under guarantee, specific accounts amounting to ¥150,000,000. The finance company advanced to Salen 80% of the accounts assigned (20% of the total to be withheld until the finance company has made its full recovery), less a finance charge of ½% of the total accounts assigned.

On July 31, Salen Company received a statement that the finance company had collected ¥80,000,000 of these accounts and had made an additional charge of ½% of the total accounts outstanding as of July 31. This charge is to be deducted at the time of the first remittance due Salen Company from the finance company. (*Hint:* Make entries at this time.) On August 31, 2015, Salen Company received a second statement from the finance company, together with a check for the amount due. The statement indicated that the finance company had collected an additional ¥50,000,000 and had made a further charge of ½% of the balance outstanding as of August 31.

Instructions
Make all entries on the books of Salen Company that are involved in the transactions above.

6 **P7-8 (Notes Receivable with Realistic Interest Rate)** On October 1, 2015, Arden Farm Equipment Company sold a pecan-harvesting machine to Valco Brothers Farm, Inc. In lieu of a cash payment Valco Brothers Farm gave Arden a 2-year, $120,000, 8% note (a realistic rate of interest for a note of this type). The note required interest to be paid annually on October 1. Arden's financial statements are prepared on a calendar-year basis.

Instructions
Assuming Valco Brothers Farm fulfills all the terms of the note, prepare the necessary journal entries for Arden Farm Equipment Company for the entire term of the note.

6 **P7-9 (Notes Receivable Journal Entries)** On December 31, 2015, Regent Inc. rendered services to Begin Corporation at an agreed price of £102,049, accepting £40,000 down and agreeing to accept the balance in four equal installments of £20,000 receivable each December 31. An assumed interest rate of 11% is imputed.

Instructions
Prepare the entries that would be recorded by Regent Inc. for the sale and for the receipts and interest on the following dates. (Assume that the effective-interest method is used for amortization purposes.)

(a) December 31, 2015.　　(c) December 31, 2017.　　(e) December 31, 2019.
(b) December 31, 2016.　　(d) December 31, 2018.

6 **7** **P7-10 (Comprehensive Receivables Problem)** Braddock Inc. had the following long-term receivable account balances at December 31, 2014.

Note receivable from sale of division	$1,500,000
Note receivable from officer	400,000

Transactions during 2015 and other information relating to Braddock's long-term receivables were as follows.

1. The $1,500,000 note receivable is dated May 1, 2014, bears interest at 9%, and represents the balance of the consideration received from the sale of Braddock's electronics division to New York Company. Principal payments of $500,000 plus appropriate interest are due on May 1, 2015, 2016, and 2017. The first principal and interest payment was made on May 1, 2015. Collection of the note installments is reasonably assured.

2. The $400,000 note receivable is dated December 31, 2014, bears interest at 8%, and is due on December 31, 2017. The note is due from Sean May, president of Braddock Inc. and is collateralized by 10,000 of Braddock's ordinary shares. Interest is payable annually on December 31, and all interest payments were paid on their due dates through December 31, 2015. The quoted market price of Braddock's ordinary shares was $45 per share on December 31, 2015.

3. On April 1, 2015, Braddock sold a patent to Pennsylvania Company in exchange for a $100,000 zero-interest-bearing note due on April 1, 2017. There was no established exchange price for the patent, and the note had no ready market. The prevailing rate of interest for a note of this type at April 1, 2015, was 12%. The present value of $1 for two periods at 12% is 0.797 (use this factor). The patent had a carrying value of $40,000 at January 1, 2015, and the amortization for the year ended December 31, 2015, would have been $8,000. The collection of the note receivable from Pennsylvania is reasonably assured.

4. On July 1, 2015, Braddock sold a parcel of land to Splinter Company for $200,000 under an installment sale contract. Splinter made a $60,000 cash down payment on July 1, 2015, and signed a 4-year 11% note for the $140,000 balance. The equal annual payments of principal and interest on the note will be $45,125 payable on July 1, 2016, through July 1, 2019. The land could have been sold at an established cash price of $200,000. The cost of the land to Braddock was $150,000. Circumstances are such that the collection of the installments on the note is reasonably assured.

Instructions

(a) Prepare the long-term receivables section of Braddock's statement of financial position at December 31, 2015.

(b) Prepare a schedule showing the current portion of the long-term receivables and accrued interest receivable that would appear in Braddock's statement of financial position at December 31, 2015.

(c) Prepare a schedule showing interest revenue from the long-term receivables that would appear on Braddock's income statement for the year ended December 31, 2015.

 8 9 P7-11 (Income Effects of Receivables Transactions) Sandburg Company requires additional cash for its business. Sandburg has decided to use its accounts receivable to raise the additional cash and has asked you to determine the income statement effects of the following contemplated transactions.

1. On July 1, 2015, Sandburg assigned €400,000 of accounts receivable to Keller Finance Company. Sandburg received an advance from Keller of 80% of the assigned accounts receivable less a commission of 3% on the advance. Prior to December 31, 2015, Sandburg collected €220,000 on the assigned accounts receivable, and remitted €232,720 to Keller, €12,720 of which represented interest on the advance from Keller.

2. On December 1, 2015, Sandburg sold €300,000 of net accounts receivable to Wunsch Company for €270,000. The receivables were sold outright on a without guarantee (recourse) basis.

3. On December 31, 2015, an advance of €120,000 was received from First Bank by pledging €160,000 of Sandburg's accounts receivable. Sandburg's first payment to First Bank is due on January 30, 2016.

Instructions

Prepare a schedule showing the income statement effects for the year ended December 31, 2015, as a result of the above facts.

10 ▸ *P7-12 (Petty Cash, Bank Reconciliation) Bill Jovi is reviewing the cash accounting for Nottleman, Inc., a local mailing service. Jovi's review will focus on the petty cash account and the bank reconciliation for the month ended May 31, 2015. He has collected the following information from Nottleman's bookkeeper for this task.

Petty Cash

1. The petty cash fund was established on May 10, 2015, in the amount of £250.
2. Expenditures from the fund by the custodian as of May 31, 2015, were evidenced by approved receipts for the following.

Postage expense	£33.00
Mailing labels and other supplies	65.00
I.O.U. from employees	30.00
Shipping charges	57.45
Newspaper advertising	22.80
Miscellaneous expense	15.35

On May 31, 2015, the petty cash fund was replenished and increased to £300; currency and coin in the fund at that time totaled £26.40.

Bank Reconciliation

SHIRE BANK **BANK STATEMENT**			
	Disbursements	Receipts	Balance
Balance, May 1, 2015			£8,769
Deposits		£28,000	
Note payment direct from customer (interest of £30)		930	
Checks cleared during May	£31,150		
Bank service charges	27		
Balance, May 31, 2015			6,522

Nottleman's Cash Account

Balance, May 1, 2015	£ 8,850
Deposits during May 2015	31,000
Checks written during May 2015	(31,835)

Deposits in transit are determined to be £3,000, and checks outstanding at May 31 total £850. Cash on hand (besides petty cash) at May 31, 2015, is £246.

Instructions

(a) Prepare the journal entries to record the transactions related to the petty cash fund for May.

(b) Prepare a bank reconciliation dated May 31, 2015, proceeding to a correct cash balance, and prepare the journal entries necessary to make the books correct and complete.

(c) What amount of cash should be reported in the May 31, 2015, statement of financial position?

10 *P7-13 (Bank Reconciliation and Adjusting Entries)** The Cash account of Aguilar Co. showed a ledger balance of $3,969.85 on June 30, 2015. The bank statement as of that date showed a balance of $4,150. Upon comparing the statement with the cash records, the following facts were determined.

1. There were bank service charges for June of $25.

2. A bank memo stated that Bao Dai's note for $1,200 and interest of $36 had been collected on June 29, and the bank had made a charge of $5.50 on the collection. (No entry had been made on Aguilar's books when Bao Dai's note was sent to the bank for collection.)

3. Receipts for June 30 for $3,390 were not deposited until July 2.

4. Checks outstanding on June 30 totaled $2,136.05.

5. The bank had charged the Aguilar Co.'s account for a customer's uncollectible check amounting to $253.20 on June 29.

6. A customer's check for $90 had been entered as $60 in the cash receipts journal by Aguilar on June 15.

7. Check no. 742 in the amount of $491 had been entered in the cash journal as $419, and check no. 747 in the amount of $58.20 had been entered as $582. Both checks had been issued to pay for purchases of equipment.

Instructions

(a) Prepare a bank reconciliation dated June 30, 2015, proceeding to a correct cash balance.

(b) Prepare any entries necessary to make the books correct and complete.

10 *P7-14 (Bank Reconciliation and Adjusting Entries)** Presented below is information related to Haselhof Inc.

Balance per books at October 31, $41,847.85; receipts $173,523.91; disbursements $164,893.54. Balance per bank statement November 30, $56,274.20.

The following checks were outstanding at November 30.

1224	$1,635.29
1230	2,468.30
1232	2,125.15
1233	482.17

Included with the November bank statement and not recorded by the company were a bank debit memo for $27.40 covering bank charges for the month, a debit memo for $372.13 for a customer's check returned and marked NSF, and a credit memo for $1,400 representing bond interest collected by the bank in the name of Haselhof Inc. Cash on hand at November 30 recorded and awaiting deposit amounted to $1,915.40.

Instructions

(a) Prepare a bank reconciliation (to the correct balance) at November 30, for Haselhof Inc. from the information above.

(b) Prepare any journal entries required to adjust the cash account at November 30.

11 *P7-15 (Loan Impairment Entries)** On January 1, 2015, Botosan Company issued a €1,200,000, 5-year, zero-interest-bearing note to National Organization Bank. The note was issued to yield 8% annual interest. Unfortunately, during 2016, Botosan fell into financial trouble due to increased competition. After reviewing all available evidence on December 31, 2016, National Organization Bank decided that the loan was impaired. Botosan will probably pay back only €800,000 of the principal at maturity.

Instructions

(a) Prepare journal entries for both Botosan Company and National Organization Bank to record the issuance of the note on January 1, 2015. (Round to the nearest €10.)

(b) Assuming that both Botosan Company and National Organization Bank use the effective-interest method to amortize the discount, prepare the amortization schedule for the note.

(c) Under what circumstances can National Organization Bank consider Botosan's note to be impaired?

(d) Compute the loss National Organization Bank will suffer from Botosan's financial distress on December 31, 2016. What journal entries should be made to record this loss?

CONCEPTS FOR ANALYSIS

CA7-1 (Bad-Debt Accounting) Simms Company has significant amounts of trade accounts receivable. Simms uses the allowance method to estimate bad debts instead of the direct write-off method. During the year, some specific accounts were written off as uncollectible, and some that were previously written off as uncollectible were collected.

Instructions

(a) What are the deficiencies of the direct write-off method?

(b) What are the two basic allowance methods used to estimate bad debts, and what is the theoretical justification for each?

(c) How should Simms account for the collection of the specific accounts previously written off as uncollectible?

CA7-2 (Various Receivable Accounting Issues) Kimmel Company uses the net method of accounting for sales discounts. Kimmel also offers trade discounts to various groups of buyers.

On August 1, 2015, Kimmel sold some accounts receivable on a without guarantee (recourse) basis. Kimmel incurred a finance charge.

Kimmel also has some notes receivable bearing an appropriate rate of interest. The principal and total interest are due at maturity. The notes were received on October 1, 2015, and mature on September 30, 2017. Kimmel's operating cycle is less than one year.

Instructions

(a) (1) Using the net method, how should Kimmel account for the sales discounts at the date of sale? What is the rationale for the amount recorded as sales under the net method?

(2) Using the net method, what is the effect on Kimmel's sales revenues and net income when customers do not take the sales discounts?

(b) What is the effect of trade discounts on sales revenues and accounts receivable? Why?

(c) How should Kimmel account for the accounts receivable factored on August 1, 2015? Why?

(d) How should Kimmel account for the note receivable and the related interest on December 31, 2015? Why?

CA7-3 (Bad-Debt Reporting Issues) Clark Pierce conducts a wholesale merchandising business that sells approximately 5,000 items per month with a total monthly average sales value of €250,000. Its annual bad debt rate has been approximately 1½% of sales. In recent discussions with his bookkeeper, Mr. Pierce has become confused by all the alternatives apparently available in handling the Allowance for Doubtful Accounts balance. The following information has been presented to Pierce.

1. An allowance can be set up (a) on the basis of a percentage of sales or (b) on the basis of a valuation of all past due or otherwise questionable accounts receivable. Those considered uncollectible can be charged to such allowance at the close of the accounting period, or specific items can be charged off directly against (1) Gross Sales or to (2) Bad Debt Expense in the year in which they are determined to be uncollectible.

2. Collection agency and legal fees, and so on, incurred in connection with the attempted recovery of bad debts can be charged to (a) Bad Debt Expense, (b) Allowance for Doubtful Accounts, (c) Legal Expense, or (d) General Expense.

3. Debts previously written off in whole or in part but currently recovered can be credited to (a) Other Revenue, (b) Bad Debt Expense, or (c) Allowance for Doubtful Accounts.

Instructions

Which of the above methods would you recommend to Mr. Pierce in regard to (1) allowances and charge-offs, (2) collection expenses, and (3) recoveries? State briefly and clearly the reasons supporting your recommendations.

CA7-4 (Basic Note and Accounts Receivable Transactions)

Part 1

On July 1, 2015, Wallace Company, a calendar-year company, sold special-order merchandise on credit and received in return an interest-bearing note receivable from the customer. Wallace Company will receive interest at the prevailing rate for a note of this type. Both the principal and interest are due in one lump sum on June 30, 2016.

Instructions

When should Wallace Company report interest revenue from the note receivable? Discuss the rationale for your answer.

Part 2

On December 31, 2015, Wallace Company had significant amounts of accounts receivable as a result of credit sales to its customers. Wallace uses the allowance method based on credit sales to estimate bad debts. Past experience indicates that 2% of credit sales normally will not be collected. This pattern is expected to continue.

Instructions

    (a) Discuss the rationale for using the allowance method based on credit sales to estimate bad debts. Contrast this method with the allowance method based on the balance in the trade receivables accounts.

    (b) How should Wallace Company report the allowance for doubtful accounts on its statement of financial position at December 31, 2015? Also, describe the alternatives, if any, for presentation of bad debt expense in Wallace Company's 2015 income statement.

CA7-5 (Bad-Debt Reporting Issues) Valasquez Company sells office equipment and supplies to many organizations in the city and surrounding area on contract terms of 2/10, n/30. In the past, over 75% of the credit customers have taken advantage of the discount by paying within 10 days of the invoice date.

    The number of customers taking the full 30 days to pay has increased within the last year. Current indications are that less than 60% of the customers are now taking the discount. Bad debts as a percentage of gross credit sales have risen from the 1.5% provided in past years to about 4% in the current year.

    The controller has responded to a request for more information on the deterioration in collections of accounts receivable with the report reproduced below.

VALASQUEZ COMPANY
FINANCE COMMITTEE REPORT—ACCOUNTS RECEIVABLE COLLECTIONS
MAY 31, 2015

The fact that some credit accounts will prove uncollectible is normal. Annual bad debt write-offs have been 1.5% of gross credit sales over the past five years. During the last fiscal year, this percentage increased to slightly less than 4%. The current Accounts Receivable balance is R$1,600,000. The condition of this balance in terms of age and probability of collection is as follows.

Proportion of Total	Age Categories	Probability of Collection
68%	not yet due	99%
15%	less than 30 days past due	96½%
8%	30 to 60 days past due	95%
5%	61 to 120 days past due	91%
2½%	121 to 180 days past due	70%
1½%	over 180 days past due	20%

Allowance for Doubtful Accounts had a credit balance of R$43,300 on June 1, 2014. Valasquez Company has provided for a monthly bad debt expense accrual during the current fiscal year based on the assumption that 4% of gross credit sales will be uncollectible. Total gross credit sales for the 2014–2015 fiscal year amounted to R$4,000,000. Write-offs of bad accounts during the year totaled R$145,000.

Instructions

    (a) Prepare an accounts receivable aging schedule for Valasquez Company using the age categories identified in the controller's report to the finance committee showing:
        (1) The amount of accounts receivable outstanding for each age category and in total.
        (2) The estimated amount that is uncollectible for each category and in total.

    (b) Compute the amount of the year-end adjustment necessary to bring Allowance for Doubtful Accounts to the balance indicated by the age analysis. Then, prepare the necessary journal entry to adjust the accounting records.

    (c) In a recessionary environment with tight credit and high interest rates:
        (1) Identify steps Valasquez Company might consider to improve the accounts receivable situation.
        (2) Then evaluate each step identified in terms of the risks and costs involved.

CA7-6 (Sale of Notes Receivable) Corrs Wholesalers Co. sells industrial equipment for a standard 3-year note receivable. Revenue is recognized at time of sale. Each note is secured by a lien on the equipment and has a face amount equal to the equipment's list price. Each note's stated interest rate is below the customer's market rate at date of sale. All notes are to be collected in three equal annual installments beginning one year after sale. Some of the notes are subsequently sold to a bank with guarantee (recourse), some are subsequently sold without guarantee (recourse), and some are retained by Corrs. At year-end, Corrs evaluates all outstanding notes receivable and provides for estimated losses arising from defaults.

Instructions

(a) What is the appropriate valuation basis for Corrs's notes receivable at the date it sells equipment?

(b) How should Corrs account for the sale, without guarantee (recourse), of a February 1, 2015, note receivable sold on May 1, 2015? Why is it appropriate to account for it in this way?

(c) At December 31, 2015, how should Corrs measure and account for the impact of estimated losses resulting from notes receivable that it
   (1) Retained and did **not** sell?
   (2) Sold to bank with guarantee (recourse)?

CA7-7 (Zero-Interest-Bearing Note Receivable) On September 30, 2015, Rolen Machinery Co. sold a machine and accepted the customer's zero-interest-bearing note. Rolen normally makes sales on a cash basis. Since the machine was unique, its sales price was not determinable using Rolen's normal pricing practices.

After receiving the first of two equal annual installments on September 30, 2016, Rolen immediately sold the note with guarantee. On October 9, 2017, Rolen received notice that the note was dishonored, and it paid all amounts due. At all times prior to default, the note was reasonably expected to be paid in full.

Instructions

(a) (1) How should Rolen determine the sales price of the machine?
   (2) How should Rolen report the effects of the zero-interest-bearing note on its income statement for the year ended December 31, 2015? Why is this accounting presentation appropriate?

(b) What are the effects of the sale of the note receivable with guarantee on Rolen's income statement for the year ended December 31, 2016, and its statement of financial position at December 31, 2016?

(c) How should Rolen account for the effects of the note being dishonored?

CA7-8 (Reporting of Notes Receivable, Interest, and Sale of Receivables) On July 1, 2015, Moresan Company sold special-order merchandise on credit and received in return an interest-bearing note receivable from the customer. Moresan will receive interest at the prevailing rate for a note of this type. Both the principal and interest are due in one lump sum on June 30, 2016.

On September 1, 2015, Moresan sold special-order merchandise on credit and received in return a zero-interest-bearing note receivable from the customer. The prevailing rate of interest for a note of this type is determinable. The note receivable is due in one lump sum on August 31, 2017.

Moresan also has significant amounts of accounts receivable as a result of credit sales to its customers. On October 1, 2015, some accounts receivable were assigned to Indigo Finance Company on a non-notification (Moresan handles collections) basis for an advance of 75% of their amount at an interest charge of 8% on the balance outstanding.

On November 1, 2015, other accounts receivable were sold on a without guarantee (recourse) basis. The factor withheld 5% of the accounts receivable factored as protection against sales returns and allowances and charged a finance charge of 3%.

Instructions

(a) How should Moresan determine the interest revenue for 2015 on the:
   (1) Interest-bearing note receivable? Why?
   (2) Zero-interest-bearing note receivable? Why?

(b) How should Moresan report the interest-bearing note receivable and the zero-interest-bearing note receivable on its statement of financial position at December 31, 2015?

(c) How should Moresan account for subsequent collections on the accounts receivable assigned on October 1, 2015, and the payments to Indigo Finance? Why?

(d) How should Moresan account for the accounts receivable factored on November 1, 2015? Why?

CA7-9 (Accounting for Zero-Interest-Bearing Note) Soon after beginning the year-end audit work on March 10 at Engone Company, the auditor has the following conversation with the controller.

CONTROLLER: The year ended March 31st should be our most profitable in history and, as a consequence, the board of directors has just awarded the officers generous bonuses.

AUDITOR: I thought profits were down this year in the industry, according to your latest interim report.

CONTROLLER: Well, they were down, but 10 days ago we closed a deal that will give us a substantial increase for the year.

AUDITOR: Oh, what was it?

CONTROLLER: Well, you remember a few years ago our former president bought shares in Henderson Enterprises because he had those grandiose ideas about becoming a conglomerate. For 6 years, we have not been able to sell these shares, which cost us £3,000,000 and has not paid anything in dividends. Thursday, we sold these shares to Bimini Inc. for £4,000,000. So, we will have a gain of £700,000 (£1,000,000 pretax) which will increase our net income for the year to £4,000,000, compared with last year's £3,800,000. As far as I know, we'll be the only company in the industry to register an increase in net income this year. That should help the market price of the shares!

AUDITOR: Do you expect to receive the £4,000,000 in cash by March 31st, your fiscal year-end?

CONTROLLER: No. Although Bimini Inc. is an excellent company, it is a little tight for cash because of its rapid growth. Consequently, we will receive a £4,000,000 zero-interest-bearing note with payments of £400,000 per year for the next 10 years. The first payment is due on March 31 of next year.

AUDITOR: Why is the note zero-interest-bearing?

CONTROLLER: Because that's what everybody agreed to. Since we don't have any interest-bearing debt, the funds invested in the note do not cost us anything. Besides, we were not getting any dividends on the Henderson Enterprises shares.

Instructions

Do you agree with the way the controller has accounted for the transaction? If not, how should the transaction be accounted for?

CA7-10 (Receivables Management) As the manager of the accounts receivable department for Beavis Leather Goods, Ltd., you recently noticed that Kelly Collins, your accounts receivable clerk who is paid $1,200 per month, has been wearing unusually tasteful and expensive clothing. (This is Beavis's first year in business.) This morning, Collins drove up to work in a brand new Lexus.

Naturally suspicious by nature, you decide to test the accuracy of the accounts receivable balance of $132,000 as shown in the ledger. The following information is available for your first year (precisely 9 months ended September 30, 2015) in business.

(1) Collections from customers	$188,000
(2) Merchandise purchased	360,000
(3) Ending merchandise inventory	90,000
(4) Goods are marked to sell at 40% above cost.	

Instructions

Assuming all sales were made on account, compute the ending accounts receivable balance that should appear in the ledger, noting any apparent shortage. Then, draft a memo dated October 3, 2015, to Mark Price, the branch manager, explaining the facts in this situation. Remember that this problem is serious, and you do not want to make hasty accusations.

CA7-11 (Bad-Debt Reporting) Marvin Company is a subsidiary of Hughes Corp. The controller believes that the yearly allowance for doubtful accounts for Marvin should be 2% of net credit sales. The president, nervous that the parent company might expect the subsidiary to sustain its 10% growth rate, suggests that the controller increase the allowance for doubtful accounts to 3% yearly. The president thinks that the lower net income, which reflects a 6% growth rate, will be a more sustainable rate for Marvin Company.

Instructions

(a) Should the controller be concerned with Marvin Company's growth rate in estimating the allowance? Explain your answer.

(b) Does the president's request pose an ethical dilemma for the controller? Give your reasons.

USING YOUR JUDGMENT

FINANCIAL REPORTING

Financial Reporting Problem

Marks and Spencer plc (M&S)

The financial statements of M&S (GBR) are presented in Appendix A. The company's complete annual report, including the notes to the financial statements, is available online.

Instructions

Refer to M&S's financial statements and the accompanying notes to answer the following questions.

(a) What criteria does M&S use to classify "Cash and cash equivalents" as reported in its statement of financial position?

(b) As of 3 April 2013, what balances did M&S have in cash and cash equivalents? What were the major uses of cash during the year?

(c) What amounts related to trade receivables does M&S report? Does M&S have any past due but not impaired receivables?

Comparative Analysis Case

adidas and Puma

The financial statements of adidas (DEU) and Puma (DEU) are presented in Appendices B and C, respectively. The complete annual reports, including the notes to the financial statements, are available online.

Instructions

Use the companies' financial information to answer the following questions.

(a) What were the cash and cash equivalents reported by adidas and Puma at the end of 2012? What does each company classify as cash equivalents?

(b) What were the accounts receivable (net) for adidas and Puma at the end of 2012? Which company reports the greater allowance for doubtful accounts receivable (amount and percentage of gross receivable) at the end of 2012?

(c) Assuming that all "Net sales" (adidas) and all "Sales" (Puma) were net *credit* sales, compute the accounts receivable turnovers for 2012 for adidas and Puma; also compute the days outstanding for receivables. What is your evaluation of the difference?

Financial Statement Analysis Cases

Case 1 PetroChina Company Limited

PetroChina Company Limited (CHN) reported the following information in a recent annual report.

PetroChina Company Limited
Consolidated Balance Sheets
(in RMB millions)

Assets at December 31,	Current Year	Prior Year
Current assets		
Cash at bank and on hand	49,953	64,299
Notes receivable	9,981	12,688
Accounts receivable	64,450	53,822
Advances to suppliers	32,813	39,296
Other receivables	14,165	8,576
Inventories	214,117	182,253
Other current assets	32,561	24,486
Total current assets	418,040	385,420

Notes to Consolidated Financial Statements

Cash and Cash Equivalents. Cash and cash equivalents refer to all cash on hand and deposit held at call with banks, short-term highly liquid investments that are readily convertible to known amounts of cash and which are subject to an insignificant risk of changes in value.

Notes Receivable. Notes receivable represents mainly bills of acceptance issued by banks for the sale of goods and products. All notes receivable of the Group are due within one year.

Instructions

(a) What items other than coin and currency may be included in "cash"?

(b) What items may be included in "cash equivalents"?

(c) What are compensating balance arrangements, and how should they be reported in financial statements?

(d) What are the possible differences between cash equivalents and short-term (temporary) investments?

(e) Assume that PetroChina has an agreement to transfer receivables to various banks. If the sale agreement meets the criteria for sale accounting, cash proceeds were RMB345 million, the carrying value of the receivables sold was RMB360 million, and the fair value of the recourse obligation was RMB15 million, what was the effect on income from the sale of receivables?

(f) Briefly discuss the impact of the transaction in (e) on PetroChina's liquidity.

Case 2 **Meriter Group**

Meriter Group is a sports manufacturer. To continue to be successful, Meriter must generate new products, which requires significant amounts of cash. The following current asset and current liability information is from a recent Meriter statement of financial position. Following the Meriter data is the current asset and current liability information for Monitor, another major sports manufacturer.

Meriter
Statements of Financial Position (partial)
As of December 31
(in millions)

Current assets	Current Year	Prior Year
Cash and equivalents	€ 244	€ 295
Short-term investments	141	86
Accounts receivable	1,624	1,459
Other	2,925	2,298
Total current assets	€4,934	€4,138
Total current liabilities	€3,645	€2,615

Monitor
Statements of Financial Position (partial)
As of December 31
(in millions)

Current assets	Current Year	Prior Year
Cash and equivalents	€ 375.0	€ 522.5
Receivables	396.5	389.6
Other current assets	590.6	483.3
Total current assets	€1,362.1	€1,395.4
Current liabilities	€ 614.8	€ 603.1

Part 1 (Cash and Cash Equivalents)

Instructions

(a) What is the definition of a cash equivalent? Give some examples of cash equivalents. How do cash equivalents differ from other types of short-term investments?

(b) Calculate (1) the current ratio and (2) working capital for each company for the current year and discuss your results.

(c) Is it possible to have too many liquid assets?

Part 2 (Accounts Receivable)

Meriter provided the following disclosure related to its accounts receivable.

(€ in millions)	Current Year	Prior Year
Accounts receivable, gross	1,743	1,570
Less: allowance for doubtful accounts	119	111
Accounts receivable, net	**1,624**	**1,459**

Movement in allowances for doubtful accounts	Current Year	Prior Year
Allowances at January 1	**111**	**112**
Additions	53	78
Write-offs and other	(45)	(79)
Allowances at December 31	**119**	**111**

Instructions

(a) Compute Meriter's accounts receivable turnover for the current year and discuss your results. Meriter had sales revenue of €10,799 million in the current year.

(b) Reconstruct the summary journal entries for the current year based on the information in the disclosure.

(c) Briefly discuss how the accounting for bad debts affects the analysis in Part 2 (a).

Accounting, Analysis, and Principles

The Flatiron Pub provides catering services to local businesses. The following information was available for Flatiron for the years ended December 31, 2014 and 2015.

	31-Dec-14	31-Dec-15
Cash	€ 2,000	€ 1,685
Accounts receivable	46,000	?
Allowance for doubtful accounts	550	?
Other current assets	8,500	7,925
Current liabilities	37,000	44,600
Total credit sales	205,000	255,000
Collections on accounts receivable	190,000	228,000

Flatiron management is preparing for a meeting with its bank concerning renewal of a loan and has collected the following information related to the above balances.

1. The cash reported at December 31, 2015, reflects the following items: petty cash €1,575 and postage stamps €110. The other current assets balance at 12/31/15 includes the checking account balance of €4,000.

2. On November 30, 2015, Flatiron agreed to accept a 6-month, €5,000 note bearing 12% interest, payable at maturity, from a major client in settlement of a €5,000 bill. The above balances do not reflect this transaction.

3. Flatiron factored some accounts receivable at the end of 2015. It transferred accounts totaling €10,000 to Final Factor, Inc. without guarantee (recourse). Final Factor will receive the collections from Flatiron's customers and will retain 2% of the balances. Final Factor assesses Flatiron a finance charge of 3% on this transfer. However, management has determined that the amount due from the factor has not been recorded and is not included in the balances above.

4. Flatiron wrote off uncollectible accounts with balances of €1,600. On the basis of the latest available information, the 2015 uncollectible accounts are estimated to be 2.5% of accounts receivable.

Accounting

(a) Based on the above transactions, determine the balance for (1) Accounts Receivable and (2) Allowance for Doubtful Accounts at December 31, 2015.

(b) Prepare the current assets section of Flatiron's statement of financial position at December 31, 2015.

Analysis

(a) Compute Flatiron's current ratio and accounts receivable turnover for December 31, 2015. Use these measures to analyze Flatiron's liquidity. The accounts receivable turnover in 2014 was 4.37.

(b) Discuss how the analysis you did above of Flatiron's liquidity would be affected if Flatiron had transferred the receivables in a secured borrowing transaction.

Principles

What is the conceptual basis for recording bad debt expense based on the percentage-of-receivables at December 31, 2015?

IFRS BRIDGE TO THE PROFESSION

Professional Research

As the new staff person in your company's treasury department, you have been asked to conduct research related to a proposed transfer of receivables. Your supervisor wants the authoritative sources for the following items that are discussed in the securitization agreement.

Instructions

Access the IFRS authoritative literature at the IASB website (*http://eifrs.iasb.org/*) (you may register for free eIFRS access at this site). When you have accessed the documents, you can use the search tool in your Internet browser to prepare responses to the following items. (Provide paragraph citations.)

(a) Identify relevant IFRSs that address transfers of receivables.

(b) What are the objectives for reporting transfers of receivables?

(c) Provide definitions for the following:

    (1) Derecognition.

    (2) Amortized cost.

(d) Provide other examples (besides recourse and collateral) that qualify as continuing involvement.

Professional Simulation

The professional simulation for this chapter asks you to address questions related to the accounting for receivables. Prepare responses for all parts.

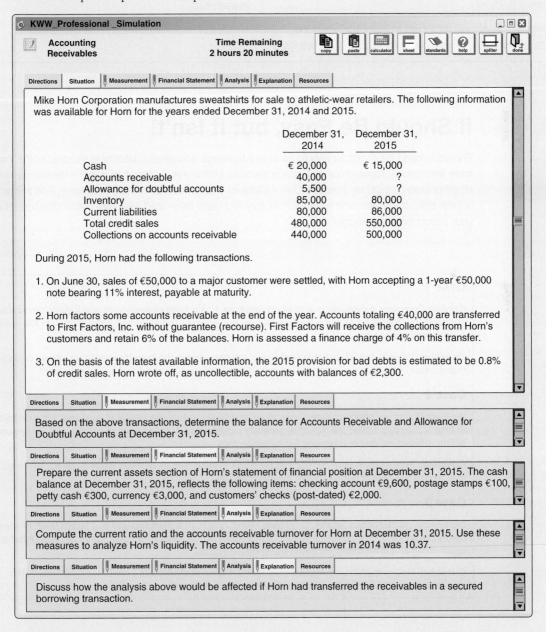

KWW_Professional_Simulation

Accounting Receivables

Time Remaining
2 hours 20 minutes

copy | paste | calculator | sheet | standards | help | splitter | done

Directions | Situation | Measurement | Financial Statement | Analysis | Explanation | Resources

Mike Horn Corporation manufactures sweatshirts for sale to athletic-wear retailers. The following information was available for Horn for the years ended December 31, 2014 and 2015.

	December 31, 2014	December 31, 2015
Cash	€ 20,000	€ 15,000
Accounts receivable	40,000	?
Allowance for doubtful accounts	5,500	?
Inventory	85,000	80,000
Current liabilities	80,000	86,000
Total credit sales	480,000	550,000
Collections on accounts receivable	440,000	500,000

During 2015, Horn had the following transactions.

1. On June 30, sales of €50,000 to a major customer were settled, with Horn accepting a 1-year €50,000 note bearing 11% interest, payable at maturity.

2. Horn factors some accounts receivable at the end of the year. Accounts totaling €40,000 are transferred to First Factors, Inc. without guarantee (recourse). First Factors will receive the collections from Horn's customers and retain 6% of the balances. Horn is assessed a finance charge of 4% on this transfer.

3. On the basis of the latest available information, the 2015 provision for bad debts is estimated to be 0.8% of credit sales. Horn wrote off, as uncollectible, accounts with balances of €2,300.

Directions | Situation | Measurement | Financial Statement | Analysis | Explanation | Resources

Based on the above transactions, determine the balance for Accounts Receivable and Allowance for Doubtful Accounts at December 31, 2015.

Directions | Situation | Measurement | Financial Statement | Analysis | Explanation | Resources

Prepare the current assets section of Horn's statement of financial position at December 31, 2015. The cash balance at December 31, 2015, reflects the following items: checking account €9,600, postage stamps €100, petty cash €300, currency €3,000, and customers' checks (post-dated) €2,000.

Directions | Situation | Measurement | Financial Statement | Analysis | Explanation | Resources

Compute the current ratio and the accounts receivable turnover for Horn at December 31, 2015. Use these measures to analyze Horn's liquidity. The accounts receivable turnover in 2014 was 10.37.

Directions | Situation | Measurement | Financial Statement | Analysis | Explanation | Resources

Discuss how the analysis above would be affected if Horn had transferred the receivables in a secured borrowing transaction.

Remember to check the book's companion website, at www.wiley.com/ college/kieso, to find additional resources for this chapter.

8 Valuation of Inventories: A Cost-Basis Approach

It Should Be Easy, but It Isn't!

The accounting for inventory should be straightforward. You simply determine the cost of the inventory and carry this amount forward until the goods are sold. Unfortunately, the devil is in the details. Questions about whether costs should be inventoried or expensed are sometimes difficult to answer. And in some cases, it is even difficult to determine whether inventory has really been sold. Here are some situations that may test your accounting knowledge.

Case 1

Chocola Company, a manufacturer of chocolate bars, has a sales promotion in which customers receive a free chocolate bar for each bar purchased—a two-for-one special. The sales price of a chocolate bar is €3, and the cost to produce one bar is €1.

Question: When a chocolate bar is sold to a customer, what is the inventory cost that should be assigned to that product? Is it €2 in inventory cost or is it €1 of inventory cost and €1 of selling expense?

Case 2

Wellness Pharmacy offers manufacturers more attractive product placement in its stores, for a defined period of time, if they pay a fixed fee (which is generally independent of the volume of goods sold) for this upgraded space. These fees are often referred to as slotting fees.

Question: Should Wellness Pharmacy report these slotting fees as revenue when received, or should these fees reduce the cost of goods sold of the merchandise?

Case 3

Digital Age, an electronics retailer, purchases computers from a manufacturer and stores them in warehouses before delivery to its various retail stores. Digital Age then transfers these computers between internal warehouses and retail stores, incurring transportation costs.

Question: How should Digital Age account for the transportation costs both between different internal warehouses and from the internal warehouses to its retail stores?

Here are the solutions to these questions.

Case 1: The purchase cost of the free chocolate bar is a component of inventory cost and should be reported as cost of goods sold at the time a chocolate bar is sold. The cost of goods sold of one chocolate bar is therefore €2, not €1. Chocola Company should not charge the free bar to selling expense, as the inventory of chocolate bars will be misstated.

Case 2: Wellness Pharmacy should record the slotting fees as a reduction of cost of goods sold (and therefore a reduction in inventory value). To recognize the fee revenue immediately is premature as Wellness Pharmacy has a performance obligation to provide space for a given period of time. The fee received is best associated with the inventory sold over the period of time allocated to the manufacturer.

Case 3: Intermediate transportation costs between different internal warehouses and to the retail stores should be included in the cost of inventory. These costs represent an unavoidable part of the supply chain in getting inventory to the first point of sale.

As indicated, the issues involving inventory are sometimes difficult and complex. Finding the appropriate answer is important because inventory is often the largest asset on a company's statement of financial position. Failure to record inventory correctly leads to misstatements of key measures of financial performance, such as gross profit and net income.

CONCEPTUAL FOCUS

> See the **Underlying Concepts** on pages 364, 366, and 369.

INTERNATIONAL FOCUS

> **Global Accounting Insights** related to inventory are presented in Chapter 9 on pages 421–422.

PREVIEW OF CHAPTER **8**

As our opening story indicates, the issues related to accounting and reporting for inventory are complex. Inappropriate recognition and measurement of inventory leads to misstatements of key measures of financial performance. The content and organization of the chapter are as follows.

Valuation of Inventories: A Cost-Basis Approach

Inventory Issues	Physical Goods Included in Inventory	Costs Included in Inventory	Cost Flow Assumptions
• Classification	• Goods in transit	• Product costs	• Specific identification
• Cost flow	• Consigned goods	• Period costs	• Average-cost
• Control	• Special sales agreements	• Purchase discounts	• FIFO
• Basic inventory valuation	• Inventory errors		• Summary analysis

INVENTORY ISSUES

Classification

LEARNING OBJECTIVE
Identify major classifications of inventory.

Inventories are asset items that a company holds for sale in the ordinary course of business, or goods that it will use or consume in the production of goods to be sold. The description and measurement of inventory require careful attention. The investment in inventories is frequently the largest current asset of merchandising (retail) and manufacturing businesses.

A **merchandising concern**, such as Carrefour (FRA), usually purchases its merchandise in a form ready for sale. It reports the cost assigned to unsold units left on hand as merchandise inventory. Only one inventory account, Inventory, appears in the financial statements.

Manufacturing concerns, on the other hand, produce goods to sell to merchandising firms. Many of the largest businesses are manufacturers, such as China Petroleum & Chemical Corp. (CHN), Toyota Motor Corp. (JPN), Royal Dutch Shell (NLD), Procter & Gamble (USA), George Weston Ltd. (CAN), and Nokia (FIN). Although the products they produce may differ, manufacturers normally have three inventory accounts—Raw Materials, Work in Process, and Finished Goods.

A company reports the cost assigned to goods and materials on hand but not yet placed into production as **raw materials inventory**. Raw materials include the wood to make a baseball bat or the steel to make a car. These materials can be traced directly to the end product.

At any point in a continuous production process, some units are only partially processed. The cost of the raw material for these unfinished units, plus the direct labor cost applied specifically to this material and a ratable share of manufacturing overhead costs, constitute the **work in process inventory**.

ILLUSTRATION 8-1
Comparison of Presentation of Current Assets for Merchandising and Manufacturing Companies

Companies report the costs identified with the completed but unsold units on hand at the end of the fiscal period as **finished goods inventory**. Illustration 8-1 contrasts the financial statement presentation of inventories of Carrefour (FRA) (a merchandising company) with those of CNH Global (NLD) (a manufacturing company). The remainder of the statement of financial position is essentially similar for the two types of companies.

Merchandising Company

Carrefour

Statement of Financial Position (Balance Sheet)
December 31, 2012

Current assets (in millions)	
Inventories	€ 5,658
Commercial receivables	2,144
Consumer credit from financial companies—short term	3,286
Other current financial assets	352
Tax receivables	520
Other assets	795
Cash and cash equivalents	6,573
Assets held for sale	465
Total current assets	€19,793

Manufacturing Company

CNH Global

Statement of Financial Position (Balance Sheet)
December 31, 2012

Current assets (in millions)		
Cash and cash equivalents		$ 2,008
Restricted cash		885
Deposits in Fiat affiliates cash management pools		4,232
Accounts and notes receivable, net		9,514
Inventories		
Raw materials	$1,027	
Work in process	226	
Finished goods	2,481	
Total inventories		3,734
Deferred income taxes		659
Prepayments and other		560
Total current assets		$21,592

A manufacturing company, like **CNH Global**, also might include a Manufacturing or Factory **Supplies Inventory** account. In it, CNH Global would include such items as machine oils, nails, cleaning material, and the like—supplies that are used in production but are not the primary materials being processed.

Illustration 8-2 shows the differences in the flow of costs through a merchandising company and a manufacturing company.

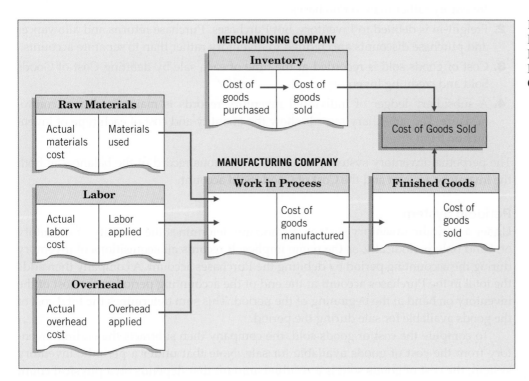

ILLUSTRATION 8-2
Flow of Costs through Manufacturing and Merchandising Companies

Inventory Cost Flow

Companies that sell or produce goods report inventory and cost of goods sold at the end of each accounting period. The flow of costs for a company is as follows. Beginning inventory plus the cost of goods purchased is the cost of goods available for sale. As goods are sold, they are assigned to cost of goods sold. Those goods that are not sold by the end of the accounting period represent ending inventory. Illustration 8-3 shows these relationships.

2 LEARNING OBJECTIVE
Distinguish between perpetual and periodic inventory systems.

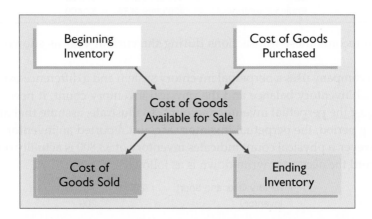

ILLUSTRATION 8-3
Inventory Cost Flow

Companies use one of two types of systems for maintaining accurate inventory records for these costs—the perpetual system or the periodic system.

Perpetual System

A **perpetual inventory system** continuously tracks changes in the Inventory account. That is, a company records all purchases and sales (issues) of goods directly in the Inventory account **as they occur**. The accounting features of a perpetual inventory system are as follows.

1. Purchases of merchandise for resale or raw materials for production are debited to Inventory rather than to Purchases.

2. Freight-in is debited to Inventory, not Purchases. Purchase returns and allowances and purchase discounts are credited to Inventory rather than to separate accounts.

3. Cost of goods sold is recorded at the time of each sale by debiting Cost of Goods Sold and crediting Inventory.

4. A subsidiary ledger of individual inventory records is maintained as a control measure. The subsidiary records show the quantity and cost of each type of inventory on hand.

The perpetual inventory system provides a continuous record of the balances in both the Inventory account and the Cost of Goods Sold account.

Periodic System

Under a **periodic inventory system**, a company determines the quantity of inventory on hand only periodically, as the name implies. It records all acquisitions of inventory during the accounting period by debiting the Purchases account. A company then adds the total in the Purchases account at the end of the accounting period to the cost of the inventory on hand at the beginning of the period. This sum determines the total cost of the goods available for sale during the period.

To compute the cost of goods sold, the company then subtracts the ending inventory from the cost of goods available for sale. Note that under a periodic inventory system, the cost of goods sold is a residual amount that depends on a physical count of ending inventory. This process is referred to as "taking a physical inventory." Companies that use the periodic system take a physical inventory at least once a year.

Comparing Perpetual and Periodic Systems

To illustrate the difference between a perpetual and a periodic system, assume that Fesmire Company had the following transactions during the current year.

Beginning inventory	100 units at $6	= $ 600
Purchases	900 units at $6	= $5,400
Sales	600 units at $12	= $7,200
Ending inventory	400 units at $6	= $2,400

Fesmire records these transactions during the current year as shown in Illustration 8-4.

When a company uses a perpetual inventory system and a difference exists between the perpetual inventory balance and the physical inventory count, it needs a separate entry to adjust the perpetual inventory account. To illustrate, assume that at the end of the reporting period, the perpetual inventory account reported an inventory balance of $4,000. However, a physical count indicates inventory of $3,800 is actually on hand. The entry to record the necessary write-down is as follows.

Inventory Over and Short	200	
Inventory		200

Perpetual inventory overages and shortages generally represent a misstatement of cost of goods sold. The difference results from normal and expected shrinkage, breakage,

ILLUSTRATION 8-4
Comparative Entries—
Perpetual vs. Periodic

Perpetual Inventory System		Periodic Inventory System	
Beginning inventory, 100 units at $6			
The Inventory account shows the inventory on hand at $600.		The Inventory account shows the inventory on hand at $600.	
Purchase 900 units at $6			
Inventory	5,400	Purchases	5,400
Accounts Payable	5,400	Accounts Payable	5,400
Sale of 600 units at $12			
Accounts Receivable	7,200	Accounts Receivable	7,200
Sales Revenue	7,200	Sales Revenue	7,200
Cost of Goods Sold		(No entry)	
(600 at $6)	3,600		
Inventory	3,600		
End-of-period entries for inventory accounts, 400 units at $6			
No entry necessary.		Inventory (ending, by count)	2,400
The Inventory account shows the ending		Cost of Goods Sold	3,600
balance of $2,400 ($600 + $5,400 − $3,600).		Purchases	5,400
		Inventory (beginning)	600

shoplifting, incorrect recordkeeping, and the like. Inventory Over and Short therefore adjusts Cost of Goods Sold. In practice, companies sometimes report Inventory Over and Short in the "Other income and expense" section of the income statement.

Note that a company using the periodic inventory system does not report the account Inventory Over and Short. The reason: The periodic method does not have accounting records against which to compare the physical count. As a result, a company buries inventory overages and shortages in cost of goods sold.

Inventory Control

For various reasons, management is vitally interested in inventory planning and control. Whether a company manufactures or merchandises goods, it needs an accurate accounting system with up-to-date records. It may lose sales and customers if it does not stock products in the desired style, quality, and quantity. Further, companies must monitor inventory levels carefully to limit the financing costs of carrying large amounts of inventory.

In a perfect world, companies would like a continuous record of both their inventory levels and their cost of goods sold. The popularity and affordability of accounting software make the perpetual system cost-effective for many kinds of businesses. Companies like **Loblaw Companies Ltd.** (CAN), **Woolworth Ltd.** (AUS), and **J. Sainsbury** (GBR) now incorporate the recording of sales with optical scanners at the cash register into perpetual inventory systems.

However, many companies cannot afford a complete perpetual system. But, most of these companies need current information regarding their inventory levels, to protect against stockouts or overpurchasing and to aid in preparation of monthly or quarterly financial data. As a result, these companies use a **modified perpetual inventory system**. This system provides detailed inventory records of increases and decreases in quantities only—not currency amounts. It is merely a memorandum device outside the double-entry system, which helps in determining the level of inventory at any point in time.

Whether a company maintains a complete perpetual inventory in quantities and currency amounts or a modified perpetual inventory system, it probably takes a physical inventory once a year. No matter what type of inventory records companies use, they all face the danger of loss and error. Waste, breakage, theft, improper entry, failure to prepare or record requisitions, and other similar possibilities may cause the inventory records to differ from the actual inventory on hand. Thus, **all companies** need periodic verification of the inventory records by actual count, weight, or measurement, with the counts compared with the detailed inventory records. As indicated earlier, a company corrects the records to agree with the quantities actually on hand.

Insofar as possible, companies should take the physical inventory near the end of their fiscal year, to properly report inventory quantities in their annual accounting reports. Because this is not always possible, however, physical inventories taken within two or three months of the year's end are satisfactory if a company maintains detailed inventory records with a fair degree of accuracy.[1]

Basic Issues in Inventory Valuation

Goods sold (or used) during an accounting period seldom correspond exactly to the goods bought (or produced) during that period. As a result, inventories either increase or decrease during the period. Companies must then allocate the cost of all the goods available for sale (or use) between the goods that were sold or used and those that are still on hand. The **cost of goods available for sale or use** is the *sum* of (1) the cost of the goods on hand at the beginning of the period, and (2) the cost of the goods acquired or produced during the period. The **cost of goods sold** is the *difference* between (1) the cost of goods available for sale during the period, and (2) the cost of goods on hand at the end of the period. Illustration 8-5 shows these calculations.

ILLUSTRATION 8-5
Computation of Cost of Goods Sold

Beginning inventory, Jan. 1	$100,000
Cost of goods acquired or produced during the year	800,000
Total cost of goods available for sale	900,000
Ending inventory, Dec. 31	(200,000)
Cost of goods sold during the year	$700,000

Valuing inventories can be complex. It requires determining the following.

1. **The physical goods to include in inventory** (who owns the goods?—goods in transit, consigned goods, special sales agreements).
2. **The costs to include in inventory** (product vs. period costs).
3. **The cost flow assumption to adopt** (specific identification, average-cost, FIFO, retail, etc.).

We explore these basic issues in the next three sections.

PHYSICAL GOODS INCLUDED IN INVENTORY

LEARNING OBJECTIVE 3
Determine the goods included in inventory and the effects of inventory errors on the financial statements.

Conceptually, a company should record purchases of inventory in the Inventory account when it has control of the asset. That is, the company has the ability to direct the use of and obtain substantially all the remaining benefits from the inventory purchased. Control also includes the company's ability to prevent other companies from directing the use of, or receiving the benefits from, the inventory

---

[1]Some companies have developed methods of determining inventories, including statistical sampling, that are sufficiently reliable to make unnecessary an annual physical count of each item of inventory.

purchased. A general rule is that a company should record inventory when it obtains legal title to the goods.[2]

In practice, however, a company generally records acquisitions when it receives the goods. Why? Because it is difficult to determine the exact time of legal passage of title for every purchase. In addition, no material error likely results from such a practice if consistently applied. Illustration 8-6 indicates the general guidelines companies use in evaluating whether the seller or buyer reports an item as inventory. Exceptions to the general guidelines can arise for goods in transit and consigned goods.

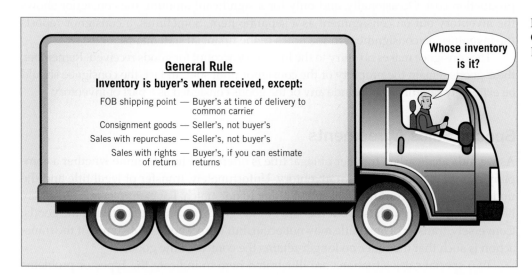

ILLUSTRATION 8-6
Guidelines for Determining Ownership

Goods in Transit

Sometimes purchased merchandise remains in transit—not yet received—at the end of a fiscal period. The accounting for these shipped goods depends on who owns them. For example, a company like **LG** (KOR) determines ownership by applying the "passage of title" rule. If a supplier ships goods to LG **f.o.b. shipping point**, title passes to LG when the supplier delivers the goods to the common carrier, who acts as an agent for LG. (The abbreviation f.o.b. stands for free on board.) If the supplier ships the goods **f.o.b. destination**, title passes to LG only when it receives the goods from the common carrier. "Shipping point" and "destination" are often designated by a particular location, for example, f.o.b. Seoul.

When LG obtains legal title to goods, it must record them as purchases in that fiscal period, assuming a periodic inventory system (or as inventory in a perpetual system). Thus, goods shipped to LG f.o.b. shipping point, but in transit at the end of the period, belong to LG. It should show the purchase in its records because legal title to these goods passed to LG upon shipment of the goods. To disregard such purchases results in understating inventories and accounts payable in the statement of financial position, and understating purchases and ending inventories in the income statement.

Consigned Goods

Companies market certain products through a **consignment** shipment. Under this arrangement, a company like Williams Art Gallery (the consignor) ships various art

---

[2]Indicators that the customer has obtained control are (1) the company has a right to payment for the asset, (2) the company has transferred legal title to the asset, (3) the company has transferred physical possession of the asset, (4) the customer has significant risks and rewards of ownership, and (5) the customer has accepted the asset.

merchandise to **Sotheby's Holdings** (USA) (the consignee), who acts as Williams' agent in selling the **consigned goods**. Sotheby's agrees to accept the goods without any liability, except to exercise due care and reasonable protection from loss or damage, until it sells the goods to a third party. When Sotheby's sells the goods, it remits the revenue, less a selling commission and expenses incurred in accomplishing the sale, to Williams.

Goods out on consignment remain the property of the consignor (Williams in the example above). Williams thus includes the goods in its inventory at purchase price or production cost. Occasionally, and only for a significant amount, the consignor shows the inventory out on consignment as a separate item. Sometimes, a consignor reports the inventory on consignment in the notes to the financial statements.

The consignee makes no entry to the Inventory account for goods received. Remember, these goods remain the property of the consignor until sold. In fact, the consignee should be extremely careful *not* to include any of the goods consigned as a part of inventory.

Special Sales Agreements

As we indicated earlier, transfer of legal title is often used to determine whether a company should include an item in inventory. Unfortunately, transfer of legal title and the underlying substance of the transaction often do not match. For example, legal title may have passed to the purchaser, but the seller of the goods retains the control of the goods. Conversely, transfer of legal title may not occur, but the economic substance of the transaction is such that the seller no longer retains the control of the goods.

Two special sales situations are illustrated here to indicate the types of problems companies encounter in practice. These are:

1. Sales with repurchase agreements.

2. Sales with rights of return.

Sales with Repurchase Agreements

Sometimes an enterprise finances its inventory without reporting either the liability or the inventory on its statement of financial position. This approach, often referred to as a **product financing arrangement**, usually involves a "sale" with either an implicit or explicit "buyback" agreement.

To illustrate, Hill Enterprises transfers ("sells") inventory to Chase, Inc. and simultaneously agrees to repurchase this merchandise at a specified price over a specified period of time. Chase then uses the inventory as collateral and borrows against it. Chase uses the loan proceeds to pay Hill, which repurchases the inventory in the future. Chase employs the proceeds from repayment to meet its loan obligation.

> **Underlying Concepts**
>
> Recognizing revenue at the time the inventory is "parked" violates the revenue recognition principle. That is, a performance obligation is met when the risks and rewards of ownership are transferred to the buyer.

The essence of this transaction is that Hill Enterprises is financing its inventory—and retains control of the inventory—even though it transferred to Chase technical legal title to the merchandise. By structuring a transaction in this manner, Hill often avoids personal property taxes. Other advantages of this transaction for Hill are the removal of the current liability from its statement of financial position and the ability to manipulate income. Chase may enter into a similar reciprocal agreement at a later date.

I
F See the Authoritative
R Literature section
S (page 378).

These arrangements are often described in practice as "**parking transactions**." In this situation, Hill simply parks the inventory on Chase's statement of financial position for a short period of time. When a repurchase agreement exists at a set price and this price covers all costs of the inventory plus related holding costs, Hill should report the inventory and related liability on its books. **[1]**

Sales with Rights of Return

In industries such as publishing, music, and retail, formal or informal agreements often exist that permit purchasers to return inventory for a full or partial refund.

To illustrate, Quality Publishing Company sells textbooks to Campus Bookstores with an agreement that Campus may return for full credit any books not sold. Historically, Campus Bookstores returned approximately 25 percent of the textbooks from Quality Publishing. How should Quality Publishing report its sales transactions?

To account for the sale, Quality Publishing should recognize:

(a) Revenue from the textbooks sold that it expects will not be returned.
(b) A refund liability for the estimated books to be returned.
(c) An asset for the books estimated to be returned which reduces the cost of goods sold.

If Quality Publishing is unable to estimate the level of returns with any reliability, it should not report any revenue until the returns become predictive.

As they relate to revenue recognition, sales with repurchase agreements and sales with rights of return are discussed in more detail in Chapter 18.

What do the numbers mean?　NO PARKING!

In one of the more elaborate accounting frauds, employees at Kurzweil Applied Intelligence Inc. (USA) booked millions of dollars in phony inventory sales during a two-year period that straddled two audits and an initial public offering. They dummied up phony shipping documents and logbooks to support bogus sales transactions. Then, they shipped high-tech equipment, not to customers, but to a public warehouse for "temporary" storage, where some of it sat for 17 months. (Kurzweil still had ownership.)

To foil auditors' attempts to verify the existence of the inventory, Kurzweil employees moved the goods from warehouse to warehouse. To cover the fraudulently recorded sales transactions as auditors closed in, the employees brought back the still-hidden goods, under the pretense that the goods were returned by customers. When auditors uncovered the fraud, the bottom dropped out of Kurzweil's shares.

Source: Adapted from "Anatomy of a Fraud," *Business Week* (September 16, 1996), pp. 90–94.

Effect of Inventory Errors

Items incorrectly included or excluded in determining cost of goods sold through inventory misstatements will result in errors in the financial statements. Let's look at two cases, assuming a periodic inventory system.

Ending Inventory Misstated

What would happen if Lenovo (CHN) correctly records its beginning inventory and purchases, but fails to include some items in ending inventory? In this situation, we would have the following effects on the financial statements at the end of the period.

Statement of Financial Position		Income Statement	
Inventory	Understated	Cost of goods sold	Overstated
Retained earnings	Understated		
Working capital	Understated	Net income	Understated
Current ratio	Understated		

ILLUSTRATION 8-7
Financial Statement Effects of Misstated Ending Inventory

If ending inventory is understated, working capital and the current ratio are understated. If cost of goods sold is overstated, then net income is understated.

Underlying Concepts

When inventory is misstated, its presentation lacks representational usefulness.

To illustrate the effect on net income over a two-year period (2015–2016), assume that Yei Chen Corp. understates its ending inventory by HK$10,000 in 2015; all other items are correctly stated. The effect of this error is to decrease net income in 2015 and to increase net income in 2016. The error is counterbalanced (offset) in 2016 because beginning inventory is understated and net income is overstated. As Illustration 8-8 shows, the income statement misstates the net income figures for both 2015 and 2016, although the *total* for the two years is correct.

ILLUSTRATION 8-8
Effect of Ending Inventory Error on Two Periods

	YEI CHEN CORP. (IN THOUSANDS)			
	Incorrect Recording		Correct Recording	
	2015	2016	2015	2016
Revenues	HK$100,000	HK$100,000	HK$100,000	HK$100,000
Cost of goods sold				
Beginning inventory	25,000	→ 20,000	25,000	→ 30,000
Purchased or produced	45,000	60,000	45,000	60,000
Goods available for sale	70,000	80,000	70,000	90,000
Less: Ending inventory	20,000* ←	40,000	30,000 ←	40,000
Cost of goods sold	50,000	40,000	40,000	50,000
Gross profit	50,000	60,000	60,000	50,000
Administrative and selling expenses	40,000	40,000	40,000	40,000
Net income	HK$ 10,000	HK$ 20,000	HK$ 20,000	HK$ 10,000
	Total income for two years = HK$30,000		Total income for two years = HK$30,000	

*Ending inventory understated by HK$10,000 in 2015.

If Chen *overstates* ending inventory in 2015, the reverse effect occurs. Inventory, working capital, current ratio, and net income are overstated and cost of goods sold is understated. The effect of the error on net income will be counterbalanced in 2016, but the income statement misstates both years' net income figures.

Purchases and Inventory Misstated

Suppose that Bishop Company does not record as a purchase certain goods that it owns and does not count them in ending inventory. The effect on the financial statements (assuming this is a purchase on account) is as follows.

ILLUSTRATION 8-9
Financial Statement Effects of Misstated Purchases and Inventory

Statement of Financial Position		Income Statement	
Inventory	Understated	Purchases	Understated
Retained earnings	No effect	Cost of goods sold	No effect
Accounts payable	Understated	Net income	No effect
Working capital	No effect	Inventory (ending)	Understated
Current ratio	Overstated		

Omission of goods from purchases and inventory results in an understatement of inventory and accounts payable in the statement of financial position; it also results in an understatement of purchases and ending inventory in the income statement. However, the omission of such goods does not affect net income for the period. Why not? Because Bishop understates both purchases and ending inventory by the same amount—the error is thereby offset in cost of goods sold. Total working capital is unchanged, but the current ratio is overstated because of the omission of equal amounts from inventory and accounts payable.

To illustrate the effect on the current ratio, assume that Bishop *understated* accounts payable and ending inventory by $40,000. Illustration 8-10 shows the understated and correct data.

Purchases and Ending Inventory Understated		Purchases and Ending Inventory Correct	
Current assets	$120,000	Current assets	$160,000
Current liabilities	$ 40,000	Current liabilities	$ 80,000
Current ratio	3 to 1	Current ratio	2 to 1

ILLUSTRATION 8-10
Effects of Purchases and Ending Inventory Errors

The understated data indicate a current ratio of 3 to 1, whereas the correct ratio is 2 to 1. Thus, understatement of accounts payable and ending inventory can lead to a "window dressing" of the current ratio. That is, Bishop can make the current ratio appear better than it is.

If Bishop *overstates* both purchases (on account) and ending inventory, then the effects on the statement of financial position are exactly the reverse. The financial statements overstate inventory and accounts payable, and understate the current ratio. The overstatement does not affect cost of goods sold and net income because the errors offset one another. Similarly, working capital is not affected.

We cannot overemphasize the importance of proper inventory measurement in presenting accurate financial statements. For example, one women's apparel maker had accounting irregularities that wiped out one year's net income and caused a restatement of the prior year's earnings. One reason: It inflated inventory and deflated cost of goods sold. In another case, a company had to restate its income by $1.7 million because an accountant in the antenna manufacturing division overstated the ending inventory, thereby reducing its cost of sales.

COSTS INCLUDED IN INVENTORY

One of the most important problems in dealing with inventories concerns the dollar amount at which to carry the inventory in the accounts. **Companies generally account for the acquisition of inventories, like other assets, on a cost basis.**

4 LEARNING OBJECTIVE
Understand the items to include as inventory cost.

Product Costs

Product costs are those costs that "attach" to the inventory. As a result, a company records product costs in the Inventory account. These costs are directly connected with bringing the goods to the buyer's place of business and converting such goods to a salable condition. Such charges generally include (1) costs of purchase, (2) costs of conversion, and (3) "other costs" incurred in bringing the inventories to the point of sale and in salable condition.

Cost of purchase includes all of:

1. The purchase price.
2. Import duties and other taxes.
3. Transportation costs.
4. Handling costs directly related to the acquisition of the goods. [2]

Conversion costs for a manufacturing company include direct materials, direct labor, and manufacturing overhead costs. Manufacturing overhead costs include indirect materials, indirect labor, and various costs, such as depreciation, taxes, insurance, and heat and electricity.[3]

[3]A separate IFRS addresses the accounting for agricultural inventories. [3] According to IFRS, agricultural inventories, such as wheat, oranges, etc., are recorded at their fair value less estimated selling costs at the point of harvest. This measure is deemed to be cost for purposes of applying the IFRS for inventory. [4]

"Other costs" include costs incurred to bring the inventory to its present location and condition ready to sell. An example of these other costs is the costs to design a product for specific customer needs. For example, if a customer of **Lenovo** (CHN) requests that computers to be sold in Europe have an additional power adapter that is compatible with European power sources, the cost to design a multisource-adapter would be included in the cost of the computer.

It seems proper also to allocate to inventories a share of any buying costs or expenses of a purchasing department, storage costs, and other costs incurred in storing or handling the goods before their sale. However, because of the practical difficulties involved in allocating such costs and expenses, companies usually exclude these items in valuing inventories.

Period Costs

Period costs are those costs that are indirectly related to the acquisition or production of goods. Period costs such as selling expenses and, under ordinary circumstances, general and administrative expenses are therefore not included as part of inventory cost.

Yet, conceptually, these expenses are as much a cost of the product as the initial purchase price and related freight charges attached to the product. Why then do companies exclude these costs from inventoriable items? Because companies generally consider selling expenses as more directly related to the cost of goods sold than to the unsold inventory. In addition, period costs, especially administrative expenses, are so unrelated or indirectly related to the immediate production process that any allocation is purely arbitrary. Companies should not record **abnormal** freight, handling costs, and amounts of wasted materials (spoilage) as inventory costs. If the costs associated with the actual level of spoilage or product defects are greater than the costs associated with normal spoilage or defects, the company should charge the excess as an expense in the current period. **[5]**

Interest is another period cost. Companies usually expense **interest costs** associated with getting inventories ready for sale. Supporters of this approach argue that interest costs are really a **cost of financing**. Others contend that interest costs incurred to finance activities associated with readying inventories for sale are as much a **cost of the asset** as materials, labor, and overhead. Therefore, they reason, companies should capitalize interest costs.

The IASB ruled that companies should capitalize interest costs related to assets constructed for internal use or assets produced as discrete projects (such as ships or real estate projects) for sale or lease. [6][4] The IASB emphasized that these discrete projects should take considerable time, entail substantial expenditures, and be likely to involve significant amounts of interest cost. Thus, a company **should not capitalize interest costs for inventories** that it routinely manufactures or otherwise produces in large quantities on a repetitive basis. In this case, the informational benefit does not justify the cost.

Treatment of Purchase Discounts

Purchase or trade discounts are reductions in the selling prices granted to customers. These discounts may be used to provide an incentive for a first-time purchase or as a reward for a large order. In some cases, incentives are provided to encourage early payment. There has been some diversity in practice regarding the accounting for these discounts, with some companies recording the discount as a reduction in inventory while others treated the discount as revenue. However, the IASB requires these discounts to be recorded as a reduction from the cost of inventories. **[7]**

With respect to the bookkeeping related to purchase discounts, the use of a **Purchase Discounts** account in a periodic inventory system indicates that the company is reporting

---

[4]The reporting rules related to interest cost capitalization have their greatest impact in accounting for non-current assets. We therefore discuss them in Chapter 10.

its purchases and accounts payable at the gross amount. If a company uses this gross method, it reports purchase discounts as a deduction from purchases on the income statement.

Another approach is to record the purchases and accounts payable at an amount net of the cash discount. In this approach, the company records failure to take a purchase discount within the discount period in a Purchase Discounts Lost account. If a company uses this net method, it considers purchase discounts lost as a financial expense and reports it in the "Other income and expense" section of the income statement. This treatment is considered better for two reasons. (1) It provides a correct reporting of the cost of the asset and related liability. (2) It can measure management inefficiency by holding management responsible for discounts not taken.

To illustrate the difference between the gross and net methods, assume the following transactions.

ILLUSTRATION 8-11
Entries under Gross and Net Methods

Gross Method			Net Method		
Purchase cost $10,000, terms 2/10, net 30					
Purchases	10,000		Purchases	9,800	
Accounts Payable		10,000	Accounts Payable		9,800
Invoices of $4,000 are paid within discount period					
Accounts Payable	4,000		Accounts Payable	3,920	
Purchase Discounts		80	Cash		3,920
Cash		3,920			
Invoices of $6,000 are paid after discount period					
Accounts Payable	6,000		Accounts Payable	5,880	
Cash		6,000	Purchase Discounts Lost	120	
			Cash		6,000

Underlying Concepts

Not using the net method because of resultant difficulties is an example of the application of the cost constraint.

Many believe that the somewhat more complicated net method is not justified by the resulting benefits. This could account for the widespread use of the less logical but simpler gross method. In addition, some contend that management is reluctant to report in the financial statements the amount of purchase discounts lost.

WHICH COST FLOW ASSUMPTION TO ADOPT?

5 LEARNING OBJECTIVE
Describe and compare the methods used to price inventories.

During any given fiscal period, companies typically purchase merchandise at several different prices. If a company prices inventories at cost and it made numerous purchases at different unit costs, which cost price should it use? Conceptually, a specific identification of the given items sold and unsold seems optimal. Therefore, the IASB requires use of the specific identification method in cases where inventories **are not ordinarily interchangeable or for goods and services produced or segregated for specific projects**. For example, an inventory of single-family homes is a good candidate for use of the specific identification method. Unfortunately, for most companies, the specific identification method is not practicable. Only in situations where inventory turnover is low, unit price is high, or inventory quantities are small are the specific identification criteria met. In other cases, the cost of inventory should be measured using one of two cost flow assumptions: (1) first-in, first-out (FIFO) or (2) average-cost. **[8]**

To illustrate these cost flow methods, assume that Call-Mart Inc. had the following transactions in its first month of operations.

Date	Purchases	Sold or Issued	Balance
March 2	2,000 @ €4.00		2,000 units
March 15	6,000 @ €4.40		8,000 units
March 19		4,000 units	4,000 units
March 30	2,000 @ €4.75		6,000 units

From this information, **Call-Mart computes the ending inventory of 6,000 units and the cost of goods available for sale (beginning inventory + purchases) of €43,900** [(2,000 @ €4.00) + (6,000 @ €4.40) + (2,000 @ €4.75)]. The question is, which price or prices should it assign to the 6,000 units of ending inventory? The answer depends on which cost flow assumption it uses.

Specific Identification

Specific identification calls for identifying each item sold and each item in inventory. A company includes in cost of goods sold the costs of the specific items sold. It includes in inventory the costs of the specific items on hand. This method may be used only in instances where it is practical to separate physically the different purchases made. As a result, most companies only use this method when handling a relatively small number of costly, easily distinguishable items. In the retail trade, this includes some types of jewelry, fur coats, automobiles, and some furniture. In manufacturing, it includes special orders and many products manufactured under a job cost system.

To illustrate, assume that Call-Mart Inc.'s 6,000 units of inventory consists of 1,000 units from the March 2 purchase, 3,000 from the March 15 purchase, and 2,000 from the March 30 purchase. Illustration 8-12 shows how Call-Mart computes the ending inventory and cost of goods sold.

ILLUSTRATION 8-12
Specific Identification
Method

Date	No. of Units	Unit Cost	Total Cost
March 2	1,000	€4.00	€ 4,000
March 15	3,000	4.40	13,200
March 30	2,000	4.75	9,500
Ending inventory	6,000		€26,700

Cost of goods available for sale (computed in previous section)	€43,900
Deduct: Ending inventory	26,700
Cost of goods sold	€17,200

This method appears ideal. Specific identification matches actual costs against actual revenue. Thus, a company reports ending inventory at actual cost. In other words, **under specific identification the cost flow matches the physical flow of the goods**. On closer observation, however, this method has certain deficiencies in addition to its lack of practicability in many situations.

Some argue that specific identification allows a company to manipulate net income. For example, assume that a wholesaler purchases identical plywood early in the year at three different prices. When it sells the plywood, the wholesaler can select either the lowest or the highest price to charge to expense. It simply selects the plywood from a specific lot for delivery to the customer. A business manager, therefore, can manipulate net income by delivering to the customer the higher- or lower-priced item, depending on whether the company seeks lower or higher reported earnings for the period.

Another problem relates to the arbitrary allocation of costs that sometimes occurs with specific inventory items. For example, a company often faces difficulty in relating freight charges, storage costs, and discounts directly to a given inventory item. This results in allocating these costs somewhat arbitrarily, leading to a "breakdown" in the precision of the specific identification method.[5]

Average-Cost

As the name implies, the **average-cost method** prices items in the inventory on the basis of the average cost of all similar goods available during the period. To illustrate use of the periodic inventory method (amount of inventory computed at the end of the period), Call-Mart computes the ending inventory and cost of goods sold using a **weighted-average method** as follows.

Date of Invoice	No. Units	Unit Cost	Total Cost
March 2	2,000	€4.00	€ 8,000
March 15	6,000	4.40	26,400
March 30	2,000	4.75	9,500
Total goods available	10,000		€43,900

Weighted-average cost per unit $\dfrac{€43,900}{10,000} = €4.39$

Inventory in units	6,000 units
Ending inventory	6,000 × €4.39 = €26,340

Cost of goods available for sale	€43,900
Deduct: Ending inventory	26,340
Cost of goods sold	€17,560

ILLUSTRATION 8-13
Weighted-Average Method—Periodic Inventory

In computing the average cost per unit, Call-Mart includes the beginning inventory, if any, both in the total units available and in the total cost of goods available.

Companies use the **moving-average method** with perpetual inventory records. Illustration 8-14 shows the application of the average-cost method for perpetual records.

Date	Purchased		Sold or Issued		Balance	
March 2	(2,000 @ €4.00)	€ 8,000			(2,000 @ €4.00)	€ 8,000
March 15	(6,000 @ 4.40)	26,400			(8,000 @ 4.30)	34,400
March 19			(4,000 @ €4.30)	€17,200	(4,000 @ 4.30)	17,200
March 30	(2,000 @ 4.75)	9,500			(6,000 @ 4.45)	26,700

ILLUSTRATION 8-14
Moving-Average Method—Perpetual Inventory

In this method, Call-Mart computes a **new average unit cost** each time it makes a purchase. For example, on March 15, after purchasing 6,000 units for €26,400, Call-Mart has 8,000 units costing €34,400 (€8,000 plus €26,400) on hand. The average unit cost is €34,400 divided by 8,000, or €4.30. Call-Mart uses this unit cost in costing withdrawals

---

[5]The motion picture industry provides a good illustration of the cost allocation problem. Often actors receive a percentage of net income for a given movie or television program. Some actors, however, have alleged that their programs have been extremely profitable to the motion picture studios but they have received little in the way of profit-sharing. Actors contend that the studios allocate additional costs to successful projects to avoid sharing profits.

until it makes another purchase. At that point, Call-Mart computes a new average unit cost. Accordingly, the company shows the cost of the 4,000 units withdrawn on March 19 at €4.30, for a total cost of goods sold of €17,200. On March 30, following the purchase of 2,000 units for €9,500, Call-Mart determines a new unit cost of €4.45, for an ending inventory of €26,700.

Companies often use average-cost methods for practical rather than conceptual reasons. These methods are simple to apply and objective. They are not as subject to income manipulation as some of the other inventory pricing methods. In addition, proponents of the average-cost methods reason that measuring a specific physical flow of inventory is often impossible. Therefore, it is better to cost items on an average-price basis. This argument is particularly persuasive when dealing with similar inventory items.

First-In, First-Out (FIFO)

The first-in, first-out (FIFO) method assumes that a company uses goods in the order in which it purchases them. In other words, the FIFO method assumes that **the first goods purchased are the first used** (in a manufacturing concern) **or the first sold** (in a merchandising concern). The inventory remaining must therefore represent the most recent purchases.

To illustrate, assume that Call-Mart uses the periodic inventory system. It determines its cost of the ending inventory by taking the cost of the most recent purchase and working back until it accounts for all units in the inventory. Call-Mart determines its ending inventory and cost of goods sold as shown in Illustration 8-15.

ILLUSTRATION 8-15
FIFO Method—Periodic Inventory

Date	No. Units	Unit Cost	Total Cost
March 30	2,000	€4.75	€ 9,500
March 15	4,000	4.40	17,600
Ending inventory	6,000		€27,100
Cost of goods available for sale		€43,900	
Deduct: Ending inventory		27,100	
Cost of goods sold		€16,800	

If Call-Mart instead uses a perpetual inventory system in quantities and euros, it attaches a cost figure to each withdrawal. Then, the cost of the 4,000 units removed on March 19 consists of the cost of the items purchased on March 2 and March 15. Illustration 8-16 shows the inventory on a FIFO basis perpetual system for Call-Mart.

ILLUSTRATION 8-16
FIFO Method—Perpetual Inventory

Date	Purchased		Sold or Issued		Balance	
March 2	(2,000 @ €4.00)	€ 8,000			2,000 @ €4.00	€ 8,000
March 15	(6,000 @ 4.40)	26,400			2,000 @ 4.00 } 6,000 @ 4.40 }	34,400
March 19			2,000 @ €4.00 } 2,000 @ 4.40 } (€16,800)		4,000 @ 4.40	17,600
March 30	(2,000 @ 4.75)	9,500			4,000 @ 4.40 } 2,000 @ 4.75 }	27,100

Here, the ending inventory is €27,100, and the cost of goods sold is €16,800 [(2,000 @ €4.00) + (2,000 @ €4.40)].

Notice that in these two FIFO examples, the cost of goods sold (€16,800) and ending inventory (€27,100) are the same. **In all cases where FIFO is used, the inventory and**

cost of goods sold would be the same at the end of the month whether a perpetual or periodic system is used. Why? Because the same costs will always be first in and, therefore, first out. This is true whether a company computes cost of goods sold as it sells goods throughout the accounting period (the perpetual system) or as a residual at the end of the accounting period (the periodic system).

One objective of FIFO is to approximate the physical flow of goods. When the physical flow of goods is actually first-in, first-out, the FIFO method closely approximates specific identification. At the same time, it prevents manipulation of income. With FIFO, a company cannot pick a certain cost item to charge to expense.

Another advantage of the FIFO method is that the ending inventory is close to current cost. Because the first goods in are the first goods out, the ending inventory amount consists of the most recent purchases. This is particularly true with rapid inventory turnover. This approach generally approximates replacement cost on the statement of financial position when price changes have not occurred since the most recent purchases.

However, the FIFO method fails to match current costs against current revenues on the income statement. A company charges the oldest costs against the more current revenue, possibly distorting gross profit and net income.

Companies often combine inventory methods. For example, Nestlé (CHE) uses FIFO for its raw materials inventories and prices the remainder using average-cost. For high inventory turnover in certain product lines, a company cannot justify FIFO's additional recordkeeping and expense. In such cases, a company often uses average-cost because it is easy to compute.

Although a company may use a variety of inventory methods to assist in accurate computation of net income, once it selects a pricing method, it must apply it consistently thereafter. If conditions indicate that the inventory pricing method in use is unsuitable, the company must seriously consider all other possibilities before selecting another method. It should clearly explain any change and disclose its effect in the financial statements.[6]

Inventory Valuation Methods—Summary Analysis

The preceding sections of this chapter described a number of inventory valuation methods. Here, we present a brief summary of the two commonly used inventory cost flow methods to show the effects these valuation methods have on the financial statements. This comparison assumes periodic inventory procedures and the following selected data.

Selected Data		
Beginning cash balance		€ 7,000
Beginning retained earnings		€10,000
Beginning inventory:	4,000 units @ €3	€12,000
Purchases:	6,000 units @ €4	€24,000
Sales:	5,000 units @ €12	€60,000
Operating expenses		€10,000
Income tax rate		40%

[6]A method which is used extensively in the United States is the **last-in, first-out (LIFO)** method. Under IFRS, LIFO is not permitted for financial reporting purposes because the IASB states it does not provide a reliable representation of actual inventory flow. **[9]** Appendix 8A discusses the basics of the LIFO method. A discussion of special issues related to the LIFO method is available at the book's companion website, *www.wiley.com/college/kieso*.

Illustration 8-17 shows the comparative results on net income of the use of average-cost and FIFO.

ILLUSTRATION 8-17
Comparative Results of
Average-Cost and FIFO
Methods

	Average-Cost	FIFO
Sales	€60,000	€60,000
Cost of goods sold	18,000[a]	16,000[b]
Gross profit	42,000	44,000
Operating expenses	10,000	10,000
Income before taxes	32,000	34,000
Income taxes (40%)	12,800	13,600
Net income	€19,200	€20,400

[a]4,000 @ €3 = €12,000
6,000 @ €4 = 24,000
€36,000

€36,000 ÷ 10,000 = €3.60
€3.60 × 5,000 = €18,000

[b]4,000 @ €3 = €12,000
1,000 @ €4 = 4,000
€16,000

Notice that gross profit and net income are higher under FIFO compared to average-cost because prices are increasing.

Illustration 8-18 shows the final balances of selected items at the end of the period.

ILLUSTRATION 8-18
Balances of Selected
Items under Alternative
Inventory Valuation
Methods

	Inventory	Gross Profit	Taxes	Net Income	Retained Earnings	Cash
Average-Cost	€18,000 (5,000 × €3.60)	€42,000	€12,800	€19,200	€29,200 (€10,000 + €19,200)	€20,200[a]
FIFO	€20,000 (5,000 × €4)	€44,000	€13,600	€20,400	€30,400 (€10,000 + €20,400)	€19,400[a]

[a]Cash at year-end = Beg. Balance + Sales − Purchases − Operating expenses − Taxes
Average-cost—€20,200 = €7,000 + €60,000 − €24,000 − €10,000 − €12,800
FIFO—€19,400 = €7,000 + €60,000 − €24,000 − €10,000 − €13,600

Average-cost results in the higher cash balance at year-end (because taxes are lower). This example assumes that prices are rising. The opposite result occurs if prices are declining.

SUMMARY OF LEARNING OBJECTIVES

1 Identify major classifications of inventory. Only one inventory account, Inventory, appears in the financial statements of a merchandising concern. A manufacturer normally has three inventory accounts: Raw Materials, Work in Process, and Finished Goods. Companies report the cost assigned to goods and materials on hand but not yet placed into production as raw materials inventory. They report the cost of the raw materials on which production has been started but not completed, plus the direct labor cost applied specifically to this material and a ratable share of manufacturing overhead costs, as work in process inventory. Finally, they report the costs identified with the completed but unsold units on hand at the end of the fiscal period as finished goods inventory.

2 Distinguish between perpetual and periodic inventory systems. A perpetual inventory system maintains a continuous record of inventory changes in the

Inventory account. That is, a company records all purchases and sales (issues) of goods directly in the Inventory account as they occur. Under a periodic inventory system, companies determine the quantity of inventory on hand only periodically. A company debits a Purchases account, but the Inventory account remains the same. It determines cost of goods sold at the end of the period by subtracting ending inventory from cost of goods available for sale. A company ascertains ending inventory by physical count.

3 **Determine the goods included in inventory and the effects of inventory errors on the financial statements.** Companies record purchases of inventory when they obtain legal title to the goods (generally when they receive the goods). Shipping terms must be evaluated to determine when legal title passes, and careful consideration must be made for cost of goods sold on consignment and sales with repurchase agreements and rights of return.

If the company misstates ending inventory: (1) In the statement of financial position, the inventory and retained earnings will be misstated, which will lead to miscalculation of the working capital and current ratio, and (2) in the income statement the cost of goods sold and net income will be misstated. *If the company misstates purchases (and related accounts payable) and inventory:* (1) In the statement of financial position, the inventory and accounts payable will be misstated, which will lead to miscalculation of the current ratio, and (2) in the income statement, purchases and ending inventory will be misstated.

4 **Understand the items to include as inventory cost.** Product costs are those costs that attach to the inventory and are recorded in the Inventory account. Such charges generally include (1) costs of purchase, (2) costs of conversion, and (3) "other costs" incurred in bringing the inventories to the point of sale and in salable condition. Period costs are those costs that are indirectly related to the acquisition or production of the goods. These charges, such as selling expenses and general and administrative expenses, are therefore not included as part of inventory cost.

5 **Describe and compare the methods used to price inventories.** The IASB requires use of the specific identification method in cases where inventories are not ordinarily interchangeable or for goods and services produced or segregated for specific projects. Only in situations where inventory turnover is low, unit price is high, or inventory quantities are small are the specific identification criteria met. In other cases companies use one of two cost flow assumptions. (1) Average-cost prices items in the inventory on the basis of the average cost of all similar goods available during the period. (2) First-in, first-out (FIFO) assumes that a company uses goods in the order in which it purchases them. The inventory remaining must therefore represent the most recent purchases.

APPENDIX **8A**	LIFO COST FLOW ASSUMPTION

As we discussed in the chapter, under IFRS, LIFO is not permitted for financial reporting purposes. In prohibiting LIFO, the IASB noted that use of LIFO results in inventories being recognized in the statement of financial position at amounts that may bear little relationship to recent cost levels of inventories. While some argued for use of LIFO because it may better match the costs of recently purchased inventory with current prices, the Board concluded that it is not appropriate to allow an approach that results in a measurement of profit or loss for the period that is inconsistent with the measurement of inventories in the statement of financial position. **[10]** Nonetheless, LIFO is permitted for financial reporting purposes in the United States, it is permitted for tax purposes in some countries, and its use can result in significant tax savings. In this appendix, we provide an expanded discussion of LIFO inventory procedures.

6 **LEARNING OBJECTIVE**
Describe the LIFO cost flow assumption.

LAST-IN, FIRST-OUT (LIFO)

The **last-in, first-out (LIFO) method** matches the cost of the last goods purchased against revenue. To illustrate, we extend the Call-Mart example introduced on page 370. Recall that Call-Mart Inc. had the following transactions in its first month of operations.

Date	Purchases	Sold or Issued	Balance
March 2	2,000 @ €4.00		2,000 units
March 15	6,000 @ €4.40		8,000 units
March 19		4,000 units	4,000 units
March 30	2,000 @ €4.75		6,000 units

If Call-Mart Inc. uses a periodic inventory system, it assumes that **the cost of the total quantity sold or issued during the month comes from the most recent purchases**. Call-Mart prices the ending inventory by using the total units as a basis of computation and disregards the exact dates of sales or issuances. For example, Call-Mart would assume that the cost of the 4,000 units withdrawn absorbed the 2,000 units purchased on March 30 and 2,000 of the 6,000 units purchased on March 15. Illustration 8A-1 shows how Call-Mart computes the inventory and related cost of goods sold, using the periodic inventory method.

ILLUSTRATION 8A-1
LIFO Method—Periodic Inventory

Date of Invoice	No. Units	Unit Cost	Total Cost
March 2	2,000	€4.00	€ 8,000
March 15	4,000	4.40	17,600
Ending inventory	6,000		€25,600
Goods available for sale		€43,900	
Deduct: Ending inventory		25,600	
Cost of goods sold		€18,300	

If Call-Mart keeps a perpetual inventory record in quantities and euros, use of the LIFO method results in **different ending inventory and cost of goods sold amounts than the amounts calculated under the periodic method**. Illustration 8A-2 shows these differences under the perpetual method.

ILLUSTRATION 8A-2
LIFO Method—Perpetual Inventory

Date	Purchased		Sold or Issued	Balance	
March 2	(2,000 @ €4.00)	€ 8,000		2,000 @ €4.00	€ 8,000
March 15	(6,000 @ 4.40)	26,400		2,000 @ 4.00	34,400
				6,000 @ 4.40	
March 19			(4,000 @ €4.40)	2,000 @ 4.00	16,800
			€17,600	2,000 @ 4.40	
March 30	(2,000 @ 4.75)	9,500		2,000 @ 4.00	26,300
				2,000 @ 4.40	
				2,000 @ 4.75	

The month-end periodic inventory computation presented in Illustration 8A-1 (inventory €25,600 and cost of goods sold €18,300) shows a different amount from the perpetual inventory computation (inventory €26,300 and cost of goods sold €17,600). The periodic system matches the total withdrawals for the month with the total purchases for the month in applying the last-in, first-out method. In contrast, the perpetual system matches each withdrawal with the immediately preceding purchases. In effect, the periodic computation assumed that Call-Mart included the cost of the goods that it purchased on March 30 in the sale or issue on March 19.

INVENTORY VALUATION METHODS—SUMMARY ANALYSIS

With the addition of the LIFO example, we can revisit the summary analysis presented in the chapter, which was based on the following data. Recall that this example assumes periodic inventory procedures.

Beginning cash balance		€ 7,000
Beginning retained earnings		€10,000
Beginning inventory:	4,000 units @ €3	€12,000
Purchases:	6,000 units @ €4	€24,000
Sales:	5,000 units @ €12	€60,000
Operating expenses		€10,000
Income tax rate		40%

Illustration 8A-3 shows the comparative results on net income of the use of average-cost, FIFO, and LIFO.

	Average-Cost	FIFO	LIFO
Sales	€60,000	€60,000	€60,000
Cost of goods sold	18,000[a]	16,000[b]	20,000[c]
Gross profit	42,000	44,000	40,000
Operating expenses	10,000	10,000	10,000
Income before taxes	32,000	34,000	30,000
Income taxes (40%)	12,800	13,600	12,000
Net income	€19,200	€20,400	€18,000

[a]4,000 @ €3 = €12,000
6,000 @ €4 = €24,000
€36,000

€36,000 ÷ 10,000 = €3.60
€3.60 × 5,000 = €18,000

[b]4,000 @ €3 = €12,000
1,000 @ €4 = € 4,000
€16,000

[c]5,000 @ €4 = €20,000

ILLUSTRATION 8A-3
Comparative Results of Average-Cost, FIFO, and LIFO Methods

Notice that gross profit and net income are lowest under LIFO, highest under FIFO, and somewhere in the middle under average-cost.

Illustration 8A-4 shows the final balances of selected items at the end of the period.

	Inventory	Gross Profit	Taxes	Net Income	Retained Earnings	Cash
Average-Cost	€18,000 (5,000 × €3.60)	€42,000	€12,800	€19,200	€29,200 (€10,000 + €19,200)	€20,200[a]
FIFO	€20,000 (5,000 × €4)	€44,000	€13,600	€20,400	€30,400 (€10,000 + €20,400)	€19,400[a]
LIFO	€16,000 (4,000 × €3) (1,000 × €4)	€40,000	€12,000	€18,000	€28,000 (€10,000 + €18,000)	€21,000[a]

[a]Cash at year-end = Beg. Balance + Sales − Purchases − Operating expenses − Taxes

Average-cost—€20,200	=	€7,000	+	€60,000	−	€24,000	−	€10,000	−	€12,800
FIFO—€19,400	=	€7,000	+	€60,000	−	€24,000	−	€10,000	−	€13,600
LIFO—€21,000	=	€7,000	+	€60,000	−	€24,000	−	€10,000	−	€12,000

ILLUSTRATION 8A-4
Balances of Selected Items under Alternative Inventory Valuation Methods

LIFO results in the highest cash balance at year-end (because taxes are lower). This example assumes that prices are rising. The opposite result occurs if prices are declining.

SUMMARY OF LEARNING OBJECTIVE FOR APPENDIX 8A

KEY TERM

last-in, first-out (LIFO) method, *376*

6 **Describe the LIFO cost flow assumption.** The LIFO method assumes that the last items purchased are the first items sold. This method matches the costs of the most recently purchased items with revenues in the period. In times of rising prices, use of the LIFO method results in lower net income and income taxes and higher cash flow.

IFRS AUTHORITATIVE LITERATURE

Authoritative Literature References

[1] International Accounting Standard 18, *Revenue* (London, U.K.: International Accounting Standards Committee Foundation, 2001), par. 16; Appendix, par. 5.

[2] International Accounting Standard 2, *Inventories* (London, U.K.: International Accounting Standards Committee Foundation, 2001), par. 11.

[3] International Accounting Standard 41, *Agriculture* (London, U.K.: International Accounting Standards Committee Foundation, 2001).

[4] International Accounting Standard 2, *Inventories* (London, U.K.: International Accounting Standards Committee Foundation, 2001), par. 20.

[5] International Accounting Standard 2, *Inventories* (London, U.K.: International Accounting Standards Committee Foundation, 2001), par. 16.

[6] International Accounting Standard 23, *Borrowing Costs* (London, U.K.: International Accounting Standards Committee Foundation, 2001).

[7] International Accounting Standard 2, *Inventories* (London, U.K.: International Accounting Standards Committee Foundation, 2001), par. 11.

[8] International Accounting Standard 2, *Inventories* (London, U.K.: International Accounting Standards Committee Foundation, 2001), paras. 23–25.

[9] International Accounting Standard 2, *Inventories* (London, U.K.: International Accounting Standards Committee Foundation, 2001), paras. BC9–BC10.

[10] International Accounting Standard 2, *Inventories* (London, U.K.: International Accounting Standards Committee Foundation, 2001), paras. BC13–BC14.

Note: All asterisked Questions, Exercises, and Problems relate to material in the appendix to the chapter.

QUESTIONS

1. In what ways are the inventory accounts of a retailing company different from those of a manufacturing company?

2. Why should inventories be included in (a) a statement of financial position and (b) the computation of net income?

3. What is the difference between a perpetual inventory and a physical inventory? If a company maintains a perpetual inventory, should its physical inventory at any date be equal to the amount indicated by the perpetual inventory records? Why?

4. Mishima, Inc. indicated in a recent annual report that approximately ¥19 million of merchandise was received on consignment. Should Mishima, Inc. report this amount on its statement of financial position? Explain.

5. What is a product financing arrangement? How should product financing arrangements be reported in the financial statements?

6. Where, if at all, should the following items be classified on a statement of financial position?

   (a) Goods out on approval to customers.
   (b) Goods in transit that were recently purchased f.o.b. destination.
   (c) Land held by a realty firm for sale.
   (d) Raw materials.
   (e) Goods received on consignment.
   (f) Manufacturing supplies.

7. Yang Specialty Products has a generous return policy. Yang gives customers a 30-day trial period, after which

they can return the product for a full refund if not satisfied. Under what conditions can Yang consider the inventory sold when the generous return policy is offered?

8. Holland Home Electronics transfers (sells) inventory to Oslo Company with right of return within the next 3 months. Advise Holland management on the conditions under which it can consider goods sold under this plan.

9. In the third quarter of 2016, David Beckham, the controller for Swiss Precision Company, discovers an error in ending inventory counts for the December 31, 2015, cutoff. After Beckham reports the error in a management meeting, the president for Swiss argues that this error in the prior year is of no consequence to the 2016 financial statements. How should Beckham respond to the president?

10. At the statement of financial position date, Clarkson Company held title to goods in transit amounting to $214,000. This amount was omitted from the purchases figure for the year and also from the ending inventory. What is the effect of this omission on the net income for the year as calculated when the books are closed? What is the effect on the company's statement of financial position? Is materiality a factor in determining whether an adjustment for this item should be made?

11. Define "cost" as applied to the valuation of inventories.

12. Distinguish between product costs and period costs as they relate to inventory.

13. Honda (JPN) is considering alternate methods of accounting for the cash discounts it takes when paying suppliers promptly. One method suggested was to report these discounts as financial income when payments are made. Comment on the propriety of this approach.

14. Wysocki Company has incurred borrowing costs as part of its manufacturing process of its inventory. Should these costs be included in the cost of the inventory? Explain.

15. Biestek Meat-Packing Company historically has experienced a 0.5% spoilage rate associated with production of its Polish sausage line of products. However, due to installation of new meat-grinding equipment, higher than usual spoilage of €45,000 was experienced on the Polish sausage line in a recent month. How should Biestek account for the usual and unusual spoilage in determining the cost of its sausage inventory?

16. Zonker Inc. purchases 500 units of an item at an invoice cost of €30,000. What is the cost per unit? If the goods are shipped f.o.b. shipping point and the freight bill was €1,500, what is the cost per unit if Zonker Inc. pays the freight charges? If these items were bought on 2/10, n/30 terms and the invoice and the freight bill were paid within the 10-day period, what would be the cost per unit?

17. Specific identification is sometimes said to be the ideal method of assigning cost to inventory and to cost of goods sold. Briefly indicate the arguments for and against this method of inventory valuation.

18. FIFO and weighted-average methods are often used instead of specific identification for inventory valuation purposes. Compare these methods with the specific identification method, discussing the theoretical propriety of each method in the determination of income and asset valuation.

*19. As compared with the FIFO method of costing inventories, does the LIFO method result in a larger or smaller net income in a period of rising prices? What is the comparative effect on net income in a period of falling prices?

BRIEF EXERCISES

1 **BE8-1** Included in the December 31 trial balance of Rivera Company are the following assets.

Cash	₺ 190,000	Work in process	₺200,000
Equipment (net)	1,100,000	Accounts receivable (net)	400,000
Prepaid insurance	41,000	Patents	110,000
Raw materials	335,000	Finished goods	170,000

Prepare the current assets section of the December 31 statement of financial position.

2 **BE8-2** Matlock Company uses a perpetual inventory system. Its beginning inventory consists of 50 units that cost €34 each. During June, the company purchased 150 units at €34 each, returned 6 units for credit, and sold 125 units at €50 each. Journalize the June transactions.

3 **BE8-3** Bienvenu Enterprises reported cost of goods sold for 2015 of $1,400,000 and retained earnings of $5,200,000 at December 31, 2015. Bienvenu later discovered that its ending inventories at December 31, 2014 and 2015, were overstated by $110,000 and $35,000, respectively. Determine the corrected amounts for 2015 cost of goods sold and December 31, 2015, retained earnings.

3 **BE8-4** Stallman Company took a physical inventory on December 31 and determined that goods costing $200,000 were on hand. Not included in the physical count were $25,000 of goods purchased from Pelzer Corporation, f.o.b. shipping point, and $22,000 of goods sold to Alvarez Company for $30,000, f.o.b. destination. Both the Pelzer purchase and the Alvarez sale were in transit at year-end. What amount should Stallman report as its December 31 inventory?

4 **BE8-5** Obihiro Company has the following information related to its inventory of embroidered baseball caps: purchase price, ¥45,000,000; import duties, ¥375,000; interest costs on inventory loan, ¥520,000; and transportation costs, ¥125,000. Determine the cost of the Obihiro inventory.

5 **BE8-6** Jakarta Company uses a periodic inventory system. For June, when the company sold 600 units, the following information is available.

	Units	Unit Cost	Total Cost
June 1 inventory	150	€5	€ 750
June 15 purchase	600	6	3,600
June 23 purchase	400	8	3,200
	1,150		€7,550

Compute the June 30 inventory and the June cost of goods sold using the average-cost method. (Round unit costs to two decimal points.)

5 **BE8-7** Data for Jakarta Company are presented in BE8-6. Compute the June 30 inventory and the June cost of goods sold using the FIFO method.

5 **BE8-8** Amsterdam Company uses a periodic inventory system. For April, when the company sold 600 units, the following information is available.

	Units	Unit Cost	Total Cost
April 1 inventory	250	$10	$ 2,500
April 15 purchase	400	12	4,800
April 23 purchase	350	13	4,550
	1,000		$11,850

Compute the April 30 inventory and the April cost of goods sold using the average-cost method.

5 **BE8-9** Data for Amsterdam Company are presented in BE8-8. Compute the April 30 inventory and the April cost of goods sold using the FIFO method.

6 *****BE8-10** Data for Amsterdam Company are presented in BE8-8. Compute the April 30 inventory and the April cost of goods sold using the LIFO method.

EXERCISES

3 **4** **E8-1 (Inventoriable Costs)** Presented below is a list of items that may or may not be reported as inventory in a company's December 31 statement of financial position.

1. Goods sold on an installment basis (bad debts can be reasonably estimated).
2. Goods out on consignment at another company's store.
3. Goods purchased f.o.b. shipping point that are in transit at December 31.
4. Goods purchased f.o.b. destination that are in transit at December 31.
5. Goods sold to another company, for which our company has signed an agreement to repurchase at a set price that covers all costs related to the inventory.
6. Goods sold where large returns are predictable.
7. Goods sold f.o.b. shipping point that are in transit at December 31.
8. Freight charges on goods purchased.
9. Interest costs incurred for inventories that are routinely manufactured.
10. Materials on hand not yet placed into production by a manufacturing firm.
11. Costs incurred to advertise goods held for resale.
12. Office supplies.
13. Raw materials on which a manufacturing firm has started production but which are not completely processed.
14. Factory supplies.
15. Goods held on consignment from another company.
16. Costs identified with units completed by a manufacturing firm but not yet sold.
17. Goods sold f.o.b. destination that are in transit at December 31.
18. Short-term investments in shares and bonds that will be resold in the near future.

Instructions

Indicate which of these items would typically be reported as inventory in the financial statements. If an item should **not** be reported as inventory, indicate how it should be reported in the financial statements.

3 **E8-2 (Inventoriable Costs)** In your audit of Garza Company, you find that a physical inventory on December 31, 2015, showed merchandise with a cost of $441,000 was on hand at that date. You also discover the following items were all excluded from the $441,000.

1. Merchandise of $61,000 which is held by Garza on consignment. The consignor is the Bontemps Company.
2. Merchandise costing $33,000 which was shipped by Garza f.o.b. destination to a customer on December 31, 2015. The customer was expected to receive the merchandise on January 6, 2016.
3. Merchandise costing $46,000 which was shipped by Garza f.o.b. shipping point to a customer on December 29, 2015. The customer was scheduled to receive the merchandise on January 2, 2016.
4. Merchandise costing $73,000 shipped by a vendor f.o.b. destination on December 30, 2015, and received by Garza on January 4, 2016.
5. Merchandise costing $51,000 shipped by a vendor f.o.b. shipping point on December 31, 2015, and received by Garza on January 5, 2016.

Instructions

Based on the above information, calculate the amount that should appear on Garza's statement of financial position at December 31, 2015, for inventory.

3 **E8-3 (Inventoriable Costs)** Assume that in an annual audit of Webber Inc. at December 31, 2015, you find the following transactions near the closing date.

1. A special machine, fabricated to order for a customer, was finished and specifically segregated in the back part of the shipping room on December 31, 2015. The customer was billed on that date and the machine excluded from inventory although it was shipped on January 4, 2016.
2. Merchandise costing €2,800 was received on January 3, 2016, and the related purchase invoice recorded January 5. The invoice showed the shipment was made on December 29, 2015, f.o.b. destination.
3. A packing case containing a product costing €3,400 was standing in the shipping room when the physical inventory was taken. It was not included in the inventory because it was marked "Hold for shipping instructions." Your investigation revealed that the customer's order was dated December 18, 2015, but that the case was shipped and the customer billed on January 10, 2016. The product was a stock item of your client.
4. Merchandise costing €720 was received on December 28, 2015, and the invoice was not recorded. You located it in the hands of the purchasing agent; it was marked "on consignment."
5. Merchandise received on January 6, 2016, costing €680 was entered in the purchase journal on January 7, 2016. The invoice showed shipment was made f.o.b. supplier's warehouse on December 31, 2015. Because it was not on hand at December 31, it was not included in inventory.

Instructions

Assuming that each of the amounts is material, state whether the merchandise should be included in the client's inventory, and give your reason for your decision on each item.

2 **3** **E8-4 (Inventoriable Costs—Perpetual)** Bradford Machine Company maintains a general ledger account for each class of inventory, debiting such accounts for increases during the period and crediting them for decreases. The transactions below relate to the Raw Materials inventory account, which is debited for materials purchased and credited for materials requisitioned for use.

1. An invoice for £8,100, terms f.o.b. destination, was received and entered January 2, 2016. The receiving report shows that the materials were received December 28, 2015.
2. Materials costing £7,300 were returned to the supplier on December 29, 2015, and were shipped f.o.b. shipping point. The return was entered on that date, even though the materials are not expected to reach the supplier's place of business until January 6, 2016.
3. Materials costing £28,000, shipped f.o.b. destination, were not entered by December 31, 2015, "because they were in a railroad car on the company's siding on that date and had not been unloaded."
4. An invoice for £7,500, terms f.o.b. shipping point, was received and entered December 30, 2015. The receiving report shows that the materials were received January 4, 2016, and the bill of lading shows that they were shipped January 2, 2016.

5. Materials costing £19,800 were received December 30, 2015, but no entry was made for them because "they were ordered with a specified delivery of no earlier than January 10, 2016."

Instructions
Prepare correcting general journal entries required at December 31, 2015, assuming that the books have not been closed.

E8-5 (Inventoriable Costs—Error Adjustments) Werth Company asks you to review its December 31, 2015, inventory values and prepare the necessary adjustments to the books. The following information is given to you.

1. Werth uses the periodic method of recording inventory. A physical count reveals $234,890 of inventory on hand at December 31, 2015.

2. Not included in the physical count of inventory is $10,420 of merchandise purchased on December 15 from Browser. This merchandise was shipped f.o.b. shipping point on December 29 and arrived in January. The invoice arrived and was recorded on December 31.

3. Included in inventory is merchandise sold to Bubbey on December 30, f.o.b. destination. This merchandise was shipped after it was counted. The invoice was prepared and recorded as a sale on account for $12,800 on December 31. The merchandise cost $7,350, and Bubbey received it on January 3.

4. Included in inventory was merchandise received from Dudley on December 31 with an invoice price of $15,630. The merchandise was shipped f.o.b. destination. The invoice, which has not yet arrived, has not been recorded.

5. Not included in inventory is $8,540 of merchandise purchased from Minsky Industries. This merchandise was received on December 31 after the inventory had been counted. The invoice was received and recorded on December 30.

6. Included in inventory was $10,438 of inventory held by Werth on consignment from Jackel Industries.

7. Included in inventory is merchandise sold to Sims f.o.b. shipping point. This merchandise was shipped after it was counted. The invoice was prepared and recorded as a sale for $18,900 on December 31. The cost of this merchandise was $11,520, and Sims received the merchandise on January 5.

8. Excluded from inventory was a carton labeled "Please accept for credit." This carton contains merchandise costing $1,500 which had been sold to a customer for $2,600. No entry had been made to the books to reflect the return, but none of the returned merchandise seemed damaged.

Instructions
(a) Determine the proper inventory balance for Werth Company at December 31, 2015.
(b) Prepare any correcting entries to adjust inventory and related accounts to their proper amounts at December 31, 2015. Assume the books have not been closed.

E8-6 (Determining Merchandise Amounts—Periodic) Two or more items are omitted in each of the tabulations of income statement data shown below.

	2014	2015	2016
Sales revenue	£290,000	£ ?	£410,000
Sales returns and allowances	6,000	13,000	?
Net sales	?	347,000	?
Beginning inventory	20,000	32,000	?
Ending inventory	?	?	?
Purchases	?	260,000	298,000
Purchase returns and allowances	5,000	8,000	10,000
Freight-in	8,000	9,000	12,000
Cost of goods sold	238,000	?	303,000
Gross profit on sales	46,000	91,000	97,000

Instructions
Fill in the amounts that are missing.

E8-7 (Purchases Recorded Net) Presented below are transactions related to Guillen, Inc.

May 10 Purchased goods billed at £20,000 subject to cash discount terms of 2/10, n/60.
    11 Purchased goods billed at £15,000 subject to terms of 1/15, n/30.
    19 Paid invoice of May 10.
    24 Purchased goods billed at £11,500 subject to cash discount terms of 2/10, n/30.

Instructions

(a) Prepare general journal entries for the transactions above under the assumption that purchases are to be recorded at net amounts after cash discounts and that discounts lost are to be treated as financial expense.

(b) Assuming no purchase or payment transactions other than those given above, prepare the adjusting entry required on May 31 if financial statements are to be prepared as of that date.

4 **E8-8 (Purchases Recorded, Gross Method)** Ohno Industries purchased ¥12,000 of merchandise on February 1, 2015, subject to a trade discount of 10% and with credit terms of 3/15, n/60. It returned ¥3,000 (gross price before trade or cash discount) on February 4. The invoice was paid on February 13. (All amounts in thousands.)

Instructions

(a) Assuming that Ohno uses the perpetual method for recording merchandise transactions, record the purchase, return, and payment using the gross method.

(b) Assuming that Ohno uses the periodic method for recording merchandise transactions, record the purchase, return, and payment using the gross method.

(c) At what amount would the purchase on February 1 be recorded if the net method were used?

2 5 **E8-9 (Periodic versus Perpetual Entries)** Chippewas Company sells one product. Presented below is information for January for Chippewas Company.

Jan.	1	Inventory	100 units at $6 each
	4	Sale	80 units at $8 each
	11	Purchase	150 units at $6.50 each
	13	Sale	120 units at $8.75 each
	20	Purchase	160 units at $7 each
	27	Sale	100 units at $9 each

Chippewas uses the FIFO cost flow assumption. All purchases and sales are on account.

Instructions

(a) Assume Chippewas uses a periodic system. Prepare all necessary journal entries, including the end-of-month closing entry, to record cost of goods sold. A physical count indicates that the ending inventory for January is 110 units.

(b) Compute gross profit using the periodic system.

(c) Assume Chippewas uses a perpetual system. Prepare all necessary journal entries.

(d) Compute gross profit using the perpetual system.

3 **E8-10 (Inventory Errors—Periodic)** Thomason Company makes the following errors during the current year. (In all cases, assume ending inventory in the following year is correctly stated.)

1. Both ending inventory and purchases and related accounts payable are understated. (Assume this purchase was recorded and paid for in the following year.)

2. Ending inventory is overstated, but purchases and related accounts payable are recorded correctly.

3. Ending inventory is correct, but a purchase on account was not recorded. (Assume this purchase was recorded and paid for in the following year.)

Instructions

Indicate the effect of each of these errors on working capital, current ratio (assume that the current ratio is greater than 1), retained earnings, and net income for the current year and the subsequent year.

3 **E8-11 (Inventory Errors)** At December 31, 2015, Dwight Corporation reported current assets of €390,000 and current liabilities of €200,000. The following items may have been recorded incorrectly. Dwight uses the periodic method.

1. Goods purchased costing €22,000 were shipped f.o.b. shipping point by a supplier on December 28. Dwight received and recorded the invoice on December 29, 2015, but the goods were not included in Dwight's physical count of inventory because they were not received until January 4, 2016.

2. Goods purchased costing €20,000 were shipped f.o.b. destination by a supplier on December 26. Dwight received and recorded the invoice on December 31, but the goods were not included in Dwight's 2015 physical count of inventory because they were not received until January 2, 2016.

3. Goods held on consignment from Kishi Company were included in Dwight's December 31, 2015, physical count of inventory at €13,000.

4. Freight-in of €3,000 was debited to advertising expense on December 28, 2015.

Instructions

(a) Compute the current ratio based on Dwight's statement of financial position.

(b) Recompute the current ratio after corrections are made.

(c) By what amount will income (before taxes) be adjusted up or down as a result of the corrections?

3 **E8-12 (Inventory Errors)** The net income per books of Wu Company was determined without knowledge of the following errors.

Year	Net Income per Books	Error in Ending Inventory	
2011	HK$50,000	Overstated	HK$ 5,000
2012	52,000	Overstated	9,000
2013	54,000	Understated	11,000
2014	56,000	No error	
2015	58,000	Understated	2,000
2016	60,000	Overstated	10,000

Instructions

Prepare a worksheet to show the adjusted net income figure for each of the 6 years after taking into account the inventory errors.

5 **E8-13 (FIFO and Average-Cost Determination)** LoBianco Company's record of transactions for the month of April was as follows.

Purchases			Sales		
April	1 (balance on hand)	600 @ $6.00	April	3	500 @ $10.00
	4	1,500 @ 6.08		9	1,300 @ 10.00
	8	800 @ 6.40		11	600 @ 11.00
	13	1,200 @ 6.50		23	1,200 @ 11.00
	21	700 @ 6.60		27	900 @ 12.00
	29	500 @ 6.79			4,500
		5,300			

Instructions

(a) Assuming that periodic inventory records are kept, compute the inventory at April 30 using (1) FIFO and (2) average-cost.

(b) Assuming that perpetual inventory records are kept in both units and dollars, determine the inventory at April 30 using (1) FIFO and (2) average-cost.

(c) In an inflationary period, which inventory method—FIFO or average-cost—will show the highest net income?

5 **E8-14 (FIFO and Average-Cost Inventory)** Esplanade Company was formed on December 1, 2014. The following information is available from Esplanade's inventory records for Product BAP.

	Units	Unit Cost
January 1, 2015 (beginning inventory)	600	R$ 8.00
Purchases:		
January 5, 2015	1,100	9.00
January 25, 2015	1,300	10.00
February 16, 2015	800	11.00
March 26, 2015	600	12.00

A physical inventory on March 31, 2015, shows 1,500 units on hand.

Instructions

Prepare schedules to compute the ending inventory at March 31, 2015, under each of the following inventory methods (round to two decimal places).

(a) Specific identification. (b) FIFO. (c) Weighted-average.

Under (a), 400 units from the beginning inventory are on hand and 1,100 units from the January 5 purchase are on hand.

5 **E8-15 (Compute FIFO and Average-Cost—Periodic)** Presented below is information related to radios for the Couples Company for the month of July.

Date	Transaction	Units In	Units Cost	Total	Units Sold	Selling Price	Total
July 1	Balance	100	$4.10	$ 410			
6	Purchase	800	4.30	3,440			
7	Sale				300	$7.00	$ 2,100
10	Sale				300	7.30	2,190
12	Purchase	400	4.51	1,804			
15	Sale				200	7.40	1,480
18	Purchase	300	4.60	1,380			
22	Sale				400	7.40	2,960
25	Purchase	500	4.58	2,290			
30	Sale				200	7.50	1,500
	Totals	2,100		$9,324	1,400		$10,230

Instructions

(a) Assuming that the periodic inventory method is used, compute the inventory cost at July 31 under each of the following cost flow assumptions.

   (1) FIFO.

   (2) Weighted-average.

(b) Answer the following questions.

   (1) Which of the methods used above will yield the highest figure for gross profit for the income statement? Explain why.

   (2) Which of the methods used above will yield the highest figure for ending inventory for the statement of financial position? Explain why.

5 **E8-16 (FIFO and Average-Cost, Income Statement Presentation)** The board of directors of Oksana Corporation is considering whether or not it should instruct the accounting department to change from a first-in, first-out (FIFO) basis of pricing inventories to an average-cost basis. The following information is available.

Sales	20,000 units @ €50
Inventory, January 1	6,000 units @ 20
Purchases	6,000 units @ 22
	10,000 units @ 25
	7,000 units @ 30
Inventory, December 31	9,000 units @ ?
Operating expenses	€200,000

Instructions

Prepare a condensed income statement for the year on both bases for comparative purposes (round to two decimal places).

5 **6** ***E8-17 (FIFO and LIFO—Periodic and Perpetual)** Inventory information for Part 311 of Seminole Corp. discloses the following information for the month of June.

June 1	Balance	300 units @ $10	June 10	Sold	200 units @ $24
11	Purchased	800 units @ $11	15	Sold	500 units @ $25
20	Purchased	500 units @ $13	27	Sold	250 units @ $27

Instructions

(a) Assuming that the periodic inventory method is used, compute the cost of goods sold and ending inventory under (1) LIFO and (2) FIFO.

(b) Assuming that the perpetual inventory method is used and costs are computed at the time of each withdrawal, what is the value of the ending inventory at LIFO?

(c) Assuming that the perpetual inventory method is used and costs are computed at the time of each withdrawal, what is the gross profit if the inventory is valued at FIFO?

(d) Why is it stated that LIFO usually produces a lower gross profit than FIFO?

5 **6** ***E8-18 (FIFO, LIFO, and Average-Cost Determination)** Keyser Company's record of transactions for the month of April is shown on page 386.

Purchases			Sales		
April	1 (balance on hand)	600 @ $6.00	April	3	500 @ $10.00
	4	1,500 @ 6.08		9	1,300 @ 10.00
	8	800 @ 6.40		11	600 @ 11.00
	13	1,200 @ 6.50		23	1,200 @ 11.00
	21	700 @ 6.60		27	900 @ 12.00
	29	500 @ 6.79			4,500
		5,300			

Instructions

(a) Assuming that periodic inventory records are kept, compute the inventory at April 30 using (1) LIFO and (2) average-cost.

(b) Assuming that perpetual inventory records are kept in both units and dollars, determine the inventory at April 30 using (1) FIFO and (2) LIFO.

(c) Compute cost of goods sold assuming periodic inventory procedures and inventory priced at FIFO.

(d) In an inflationary period, which inventory method—FIFO, LIFO, or average-cost—will show the highest net income?

5 6 *E8-19 (FIFO, LIFO, Average-Cost Inventory)** Mills Company was formed on December 1, 2014. The following information is available from Mills' inventory records for Product Zone.

	Units	Unit Cost
January 1, 2015 (beginning inventory)	600	$ 8.00
Purchases:		
January 5, 2015	1,100	9.00
January 25, 2015	1,300	10.00
February 16, 2015	800	11.00
March 26, 2015	600	12.00

A physical inventory on March 31, 2015, shows 1,500 units on hand.

Instructions

Prepare schedules to compute the ending inventory at March 31, 2015, under each of the following inventory methods (round to two decimal places).

(a) FIFO.

(b) LIFO.

(c) Weighted-average.

5 6 *E8-20 (FIFO and LIFO—Periodic and Perpetual)** The following is a record of Cannondale Company's transactions for Boston Teapots for the month of May 2015.

May	1	Balance 400 units @ $20	May 10	Sale 300 units @ $38
	12	Purchase 600 units @ $25	20	Sale 590 units @ $38
	28	Purchase 400 units @ $30		

Instructions

(a) Assuming that perpetual inventories are **not** maintained and that a physical count at the end of the month shows 510 units on hand, what is the cost of the ending inventory using (1) FIFO and (2) LIFO?

(b) Assuming that perpetual records are maintained and they tie into the general ledger, calculate the ending inventory using (1) FIFO and (2) LIFO.

5 6 *E8-21 (FIFO and LIFO, Income Statement Presentation)** The board of directors of Hayward Corporation is considering whether or not it should instruct the accounting department to change from a first-in, first-out (FIFO) basis of pricing inventories to a last-in, first-out (LIFO) basis. The following information is available.

Sales	20,000 units @ $50
Inventory, January 1	6,000 units @ 20
Purchases	6,000 units @ 22
	10,000 units @ 25
	7,000 units @ 30
Inventory, December 31	9,000 units @ ?
Operating expenses	$200,000

Instructions

Prepare a condensed income statement for the year on both bases for comparative purposes.

5 6 *E8-22 (FIFO and LIFO Effects)** You are the vice president of finance of Mickiewicz Corporation, a retail company that prepared two different schedules of gross margin for the first quarter ended March 31, 2015. These schedules appear below.

	Sales ($5 per unit)	Cost of Goods Sold	Gross Margin
Schedule 1	$150,000	$124,900	$25,100
Schedule 2	150,000	129,600	20,400

The computation of cost of goods sold in each schedule is based on the following data.

	Units	Cost per Unit	Total Cost
Beginning inventory, January 1	10,000	$4.00	$40,000
Purchase, January 10	8,000	4.20	33,600
Purchase, January 30	6,000	4.25	25,500
Purchase, February 11	9,000	4.30	38,700
Purchase, March 17	12,000	4.40	52,800

Peggy Fleming, the president of the corporation, cannot understand how two different gross margins can be computed from the same set of data. As the vice president of finance, you have explained to Ms. Fleming that the two schedules are based on different assumptions concerning the flow of inventory costs, i.e., FIFO and LIFO. Schedules 1 and 2 were not necessarily prepared in this sequence of cost flow assumptions.

Instructions
Prepare two separate schedules computing cost of goods sold and supporting schedules showing the composition of the ending inventory under both cost flow assumptions (assume periodic system).

5 6 *E8-23 (FIFO and LIFO—Periodic)** Tom Brady Shop began operations on January 2, 2015. The following stock record card for footballs was taken from the records at the end of the year.

Date	Voucher	Terms	Units Received	Unit Invoice Cost	Gross Invoice Amount
1/15	10624	Net 30	50	$20	$1,000
3/15	11437	1/5, net 30	65	16	1,040
6/20	21332	1/10, net 30	90	15	1,350
9/12	27644	1/10, net 30	84	12	1,008
11/24	31269	1/10, net 30	76	11	836
	Totals		365		$5,234

A physical inventory on December 31, 2015, reveals that 110 footballs were in stock. The bookkeeper informs you that all the discounts were taken. Assume that Tom Brady Shop uses the invoice price less discount for recording purchases.

Instructions
(a) Compute the December 31, 2015, inventory using the FIFO method. (Round all unit costs to two decimal places.)
(b) Compute the 2015 cost of goods sold using the LIFO method.
(c) What method would you recommend to the owner to minimize income taxes in 2015, using the inventory information for footballs as a guide?

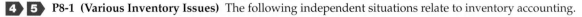

PROBLEMS

4 5 **P8-1 (Various Inventory Issues)** The following independent situations relate to inventory accounting.

1. Kim Co. purchased goods with a list price of €175,000, subject to trade discounts of 20% and 10%, with no cash discounts allowable. How much should Kim Co. record as the cost of these goods?

2. Keillor Company's inventory of €1,100,000 at December 31, 2015, was based on a physical count of goods priced at cost and before any year-end adjustments relating to the following items.
   (a) Goods shipped from a vendor f.o.b. shipping point on December 24, 2015, at an invoice cost of €69,000 to Keillor Company were received on January 4, 2016.
   (b) The physical count included €29,000 of goods billed to Sakic Corp. f.o.b. shipping point on December 31, 2015. The carrier picked up these goods on January 3, 2016.

What amount should Keillor report as inventory on its statement of financial position?

3. Zimmerman Corp. had 1,500 units of part M.O. on hand May 1, 2015, costing €21 each. Purchases of part M.O. during May were as follows.

	Units	Unit Cost
May 9	2,000	€22
17	3,500	23
26	1,000	24

A physical count on May 31, 2015, shows 2,000 units of part M.O. on hand. Using the FIFO method, what is the cost of part M.O. inventory at May 31, 2015? Using the average-cost method, what is the inventory cost?

4. Donovan Inc., a retail store chain, had the following information in its general ledger for the year 2015.

Merchandise purchased for resale	€909,400
Interest on notes payable to vendors	8,700
Purchase returns	16,500
Freight-in	22,000
Freight-out (delivery expense)	17,100
Cash discounts on purchases	6,800

What is Donovan's inventoriable cost for 2015?

Instructions

Answer each of the preceding questions about inventories, and explain your answers.

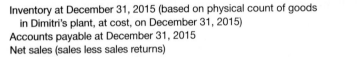 **P8-2 (Inventory Adjustments)** Dimitri Company, a manufacturer of small tools, provided the following information from its accounting records for the year ended December 31, 2015.

Inventory at December 31, 2015 (based on physical count of goods in Dimitri's plant, at cost, on December 31, 2015)	$1,520,000
Accounts payable at December 31, 2015	1,200,000
Net sales (sales less sales returns)	8,150,000

Additional information is as follows.

1. Included in the physical count were tools billed to a customer f.o.b. shipping point on December 31, 2015. These tools had a cost of $31,000 and were billed at $40,000. The shipment was on Dimitri's loading dock waiting to be picked up by the common carrier.

2. Goods were in transit from a vendor to Dimitri on December 31, 2015. The invoice cost was $76,000, and the goods were shipped f.o.b. shipping point on December 29, 2015.

3. Work in process inventory costing $30,000 was sent to an outside processor for plating on December 30, 2015.

4. Tools returned by customers and held pending inspection in the returned goods area on December 31, 2015, were not included in the physical count. On January 8, 2016, the tools costing $32,000 were inspected and returned to inventory. Credit memos totaling $47,000 were issued to the customers on the same date.

5. Tools shipped to a customer f.o.b. destination on December 26, 2015, were in transit at December 31, 2015, and had a cost of $26,000. Upon notification of receipt by the customer on January 2, 2016, Dimitri issued a sales invoice for $42,000.

6. Goods, with an invoice cost of $27,000, received from a vendor at 5:00 p.m. on December 31, 2015, were recorded on a receiving report dated January 2, 2016. The goods were not included in the physical count, but the invoice was included in accounts payable at December 31, 2015.

7. Goods received from a vendor on December 26, 2015, were included in the physical count. However, the related $56,000 vendor invoice was not included in accounts payable at December 31, 2015, because the accounts payable copy of the receiving report was lost.

8. On January 3, 2016, a monthly freight bill in the amount of $8,000 was received. The bill specifically related to merchandise purchased in December 2015, one-half of which was still in the inventory at December 31, 2015. The freight charges were not included in either the inventory or in accounts payable at December 31, 2015.

Instructions

Using the following format, prepare a schedule of adjustments as of December 31, 2015, to the initial amounts per Dimitri's accounting records. Show separately the effect, if any, of each of the eight transactions on the December 31, 2015, amounts. If the transactions would have no effect on the initial amount shown, enter NONE.

	Inventory	Accounts Payable	Net Sales
Initial amounts	$1,520,000	$1,200,000	$8,150,000
Adjustments—increase (decrease)			
1			
2			
3			
4			
5			
6			
7			
8			
Total adjustments			
Adjusted amounts	$	$	$

4 **P8-3 (Purchases Recorded Gross and Net)** Some of the transactions of Torres Company during August are listed below. Torres uses the periodic inventory method.

August 10   Purchased merchandise on account, £12,000, terms 2/10, n/30.
       13   Returned part of the purchase of August 10, £1,200, and received credit on account.
       15   Purchased merchandise on account, £16,000, terms 1/10, n/60.
       25   Purchased merchandise on account, £20,000, terms 2/10, n/30.
       28   Paid invoice of August 15 in full.

Instructions

(a) Assuming that purchases are recorded at gross amounts and that discounts are to be recorded when taken:

  (1) Prepare general journal entries to record the transactions.

  (2) Describe how the various items would be shown in the financial statements.

(b) Assuming that purchases are recorded at net amounts and that discounts lost are treated as financial expenses:

  (1) Prepare general journal entries to enter the transactions.

  (2) Prepare the adjusting entry necessary on August 31 if financial statements are to be prepared at that time.

  (3) Describe how the various items would be shown in the financial statements.

(c) Which of the two methods do you prefer and why?

2 5 **P8-4 (Compute Specific Identification, FIFO, and Average-Cost)** Silva Company's record of transactions concerning part X for the month of April was as follows.

Purchases		Sales	
April 1 (balance on hand)	100 @ R$5.00	April 5	300
4	400 @ 5.10	12	200
11	300 @ 5.30	27	800
18	200 @ 5.35	28	150
26	600 @ 5.60		
30	200 @ 5.80		

Instructions

(a) Compute the inventory at April 30 on each of the following bases. Assume that perpetual inventory records are kept in units only. (Carry unit costs to the nearest cent.)

  (1) Specific identification; ending inventory is comprised of 100 units from beginning inventory and 250 units from the April 26 purchase.

  (2) First-in, first-out (FIFO).

  (3) Average-cost.

(b) If the perpetual inventory record is kept in dollars, and costs are computed at the time of each withdrawal, what amount would be shown as ending inventory in 1, 2, and 3 above? (Carry average unit costs to four decimal places.)

2 5 **P8-5** **(Compute FIFO and Average-Cost)** Some of the information found on a detail inventory card for Cheng Inc. for the first month of operations is as follows (amounts in thousands).

| | Received | | Issued, | Balance, |
Date	No. of Units	Unit Cost	No. of Units	No. of Units
January 2	1,200	¥3.00		1,200
7			700	500
10	600	3.20		1,100
13			500	600
18	1,000	3.30	300	1,300
20			1,100	200
23	1,300	3.40		1,500
26			800	700
28	1,600	3.50		2,300
31			1,300	1,000

Instructions

(a) From these data compute the ending inventory on each of the following bases. Assume that perpetual inventory records are kept in units only. (Carry unit costs to two decimal places and ending inventory to the nearest 1,000 yen.)

(1) First-in, first-out (FIFO).

(2) Average-cost.

(b) If the perpetual inventory record is kept in yen, and costs are computed at the time of each withdrawal, would the amounts shown as ending inventory in 1 and 2 above be the same? Explain and compute.

2 5 **P8-6** **(Compute FIFO and Average-Cost—Periodic and Perpetual)** Ehlo Company is a multiproduct firm.

Presented below is information concerning one of its products, the Hawkeye.

Date	Transaction	Quantity	Price/Cost
1/1	Beginning inventory	1,000	€12
2/4	Purchase	2,000	18
2/20	Sale	2,500	30
4/2	Purchase	3,000	23
11/4	Sale	2,200	33

Instructions

Compute cost of goods sold, assuming Ehlo uses:

(a) Periodic system, FIFO cost flow.

(b) Perpetual system, FIFO cost flow.

(c) Periodic system, weighted-average cost flow.

(d) Perpetual system, moving-average cost flow.

5 6 *P8-7 **(Compute FIFO, LIFO, and Average-Cost)** Ronaldo Company's record of transactions concerning part VF5 for the month of September was as follows.

Purchases		Sales	
September 1 (balance on hand)	100 @ $5.00	September 5	300
4	400 @ 5.10	12	200
11	300 @ 5.30	27	800
18	200 @ 5.35	28	150
26	600 @ 5.60		
30	200 @ 5.80		

Instructions

(a) Compute the inventory at September 30 on each of the following bases. Assume that perpetual inventory records are kept in units only. (Carry unit costs to the nearest cent.)

(1) First-in, first-out (FIFO).

(2) Average-cost.

(3) Last-in, first-out (LIFO).

(b) If the perpetual inventory record is kept in dollars, and costs are computed at the time of each withdrawal, what amount would be shown as ending inventory in 1 and 2 above? (Carry average unit costs to four decimal places.)

5 6 *P8-8 **(Compute FIFO, LIFO, and Average-Cost)** Some of the information found on a detail inventory card for Slatkin Inc. for the first month of operations is as follows.

	Received		Issued,	Balance,
Date	No. of Units	Unit Cost	No. of Units	No. of Units
January 2	1,200	$3.00		1,200
7			700	500
10	600	3.20		1,100
13			500	600
18	1,000	3.30	300	1,300
20			1,100	200
23	1,300	3.40		1,500
26			800	700
28	1,600	3.50		2,300
31			1,300	1,000

Instructions

(a) From these data compute the ending inventory on each of the following bases. Assume that per-petual inventory records are kept in units only. (Carry unit costs to four decimal places and ending inventory to the nearest dollar.)

(1) First-in, first-out (FIFO).

(2) Last-in, first-out (LIFO).

(3) Average-cost.

(b) If the perpetual inventory record is kept in dollars, and costs are computed at the time of each withdrawal, would the amounts shown as ending inventory in 1, 2, and 3 above be the same? Explain and compute.

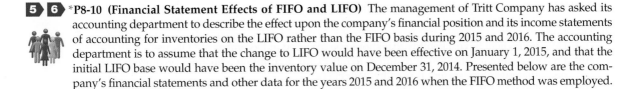

5 6 *P8-9 (Compute FIFO, LIFO, and Average-Cost—Periodic and Perpetual) Tsui Company is a multiproduct firm. Presented below is information concerning one of its products, the Jayhawk.

Date	Transaction	Quantity	Unit Cost
1/1	Beginning inventory	1,000	NT$12
2/4	Purchase	2,000	18
2/20	Sale	2,500	30
4/2	Purchase	3,000	23
11/4	Sale	2,200	33

Instructions

(Carry unit costs to the nearest cent.)

Compute cost of goods sold, assuming Tsui uses:

(a) Periodic system, FIFO cost flow.

(b) Perpetual system, FIFO cost flow.

(c) Periodic system, LIFO cost flow.

(d) Perpetual system, LIFO cost flow.

(e) Periodic system, weighted-average cost flow.

(f) Perpetual system, moving-average cost flow.

5 6 *P8-10 (Financial Statement Effects of FIFO and LIFO) The management of Tritt Company has asked its accounting department to describe the effect upon the company's financial position and its income statements of accounting for inventories on the LIFO rather than the FIFO basis during 2015 and 2016. The accounting department is to assume that the change to LIFO would have been effective on January 1, 2015, and that the initial LIFO base would have been the inventory value on December 31, 2014. Presented below are the com-pany's financial statements and other data for the years 2015 and 2016 when the FIFO method was employed.

	Financial Position as of		
	12/31/14	12/31/15	12/31/16
Inventory	$120,000	$140,000	$ 176,000
Other assets	160,000	170,000	200,000
Accounts receivable	80,000	100,000	120,000
Cash	90,000	130,000	154,000
Total assets	$450,000	$540,000	$ 650,000
Share capital—ordinary	$200,000	$200,000	$ 200,000
Retained earnings	140,000	200,000	260,000
Accounts payable	40,000	60,000	80,000
Other liabilities	70,000	80,000	110,000
Total equity and liabilities	$450,000	$540,000	$ 650,000

	Income for Years Ended	
	12/31/15	12/31/16
Sales revenue	$900,000	$1,350,000
Less: Cost of goods sold	505,000	756,000
Other expenses	205,000	304,000
	710,000	1,060,000
Income before income taxes	190,000	290,000
Income taxes (40%)	76,000	116,000
Net income	$114,000	$ 174,000

Other data:
1. Inventory on hand at December 31, 2014, consisted of 40,000 units valued at $3.00 each.
2. Sales (all units sold at the same price in a given year):

    2015—150,000 units @ $6.00 each   2016—180,000 units @ $7.50 each

3. Purchases (all units purchased at the same price in given year):

    2015—150,000 units @ $3.50 each   2016—180,000 units @ $4.40 each

4. Income taxes at the effective rate of 40% are paid on December 31 each year.

Instructions
Name the account(s) presented in the financial statements that would have different amounts for 2016 if LIFO rather than FIFO had been used, and state the new amount for each account that is named. Show computations.

CONCEPTS FOR ANALYSIS

CA8-1 (Inventoriable Costs) You are asked to travel to Vienna to observe and verify the inventory of the Vienna branch of one of your clients. You arrive on Thursday, December 30, and find that the inventory procedures have just been started. You spot a railway car on the sidetrack at the unloading door and ask the warehouse superintendent, Buck Rogers, how he plans to inventory the contents of the car. He responds, "We are not going to include the contents in the inventory."

Later in the day, you ask the bookkeeper for the invoice on the carload and the related freight bill. The invoice lists the various items, prices, and extensions of the goods in the car. You note that the carload was shipped December 24 from Berlin, f.o.b. Berlin, and that the total invoice price of the goods in the car was €35,300. The freight bill called for a payment of €1,500. Terms were net 30 days. The bookkeeper affirms the fact that this invoice is to be held for recording in January.

Instructions
(a) Does your client have a liability that should be recorded at December 31? Discuss.
(b) Prepare a journal entry(ies), if required, to reflect any accounting adjustment required. Assume a perpetual inventory system is used by your client.
(c) For what possible reason(s) might your client wish to postpone recording the transaction?

CA8-2 (Inventoriable Costs) Carlos Beltran, an inventory control specialist, is interested in improving his understanding of the accounting for inventories. Although Carlos understands the more sophisticated computer inventory control systems, he has little knowledge of how inventory cost is determined. In studying the records of Strider Enterprises, which sells normal brand-name goods from its own store and on consignment through Chavez Inc., he asks you to answer the following questions.

Instructions
(a) Should Strider Enterprises include in its inventory normal brand-name goods purchased from its suppliers but not yet received if the terms of purchase are f.o.b. shipping point (manufacturer's plant)? Why?
(b) Should Strider Enterprises include freight-in expenditures as an inventory cost? Why?

(c) If Strider Enterprises purchases its goods on terms 2/10, net 30, should the purchases be recorded gross or net? Why?

(d) What are products on consignment? How should they be reported in the financial statements?

CA8-3 (Inventoriable Costs) George Solti, the controller for Garrison Lumber Company, has recently hired you as assistant controller. He wishes to determine your expertise in the area of inventory accounting and therefore asks you to answer the following unrelated questions.

(a) A company is involved in the wholesaling and retailing of automobile tires for foreign cars. Most of the inventory is imported, and it is valued on the company's records at the actual inventory cost plus freight-in. At year-end, the warehousing costs are prorated over cost of goods sold and ending inventory. Are warehousing costs considered a product cost or a period cost?

(b) A certain portion of a company's "inventory" is composed of obsolete items. Should obsolete items that are not currently consumed in the production of "goods or services to be available for sale" be classified as part of inventory?

(c) A company purchases airplanes for sale to others. However, until they are sold, the company charters and services the planes. What is the proper way to report these airplanes in the company's financial statements?

(d) A company wants to buy coal deposits but does not want the financing for the purchase to be reported on its financial statements. The company therefore establishes a trust to acquire the coal deposits. The company agrees to buy the coal over a certain period of time at specified prices. The trust is able to finance the coal purchase and pay off the loan as it is paid by the company for the minerals. How should this transaction be reported?

CA8-4 (Accounting Treatment of Purchase Discounts) Feng Corp., a household appliances dealer, purchases its inventories from various suppliers.

Instructions

Feng is considering alternate methods of accounting for the cash discounts it takes when paying its suppliers promptly. From a theoretical standpoint, discuss the acceptability of each of the following methods.

(a) Financial income when payments are made.

(b) Reduction of cost of goods sold for the period when payments are made.

(c) Direct reduction of purchase cost.

CA8-5 (Average-Cost and FIFO) Draft written responses to the following items.

(a) Describe the cost flow assumptions used in average-cost and FIFO methods of inventory valuation.

(b) Distinguish between weighted-average cost and moving-average cost for inventory costing purposes.

(c) Identify the effects on both the statement of financial position and the income statement of using the average-cost method instead of the FIFO method for inventory costing purposes over a substantial time period when purchase prices of inventoriable items are rising. State why these effects take place.

CA8-6 (Inventory Choices) Wilkens Company uses the average-cost method for inventory costing. The company is having a very good year. In an effort to reduce income in the current year, company president Lenny Wilkens tells the plant accountant to take the unusual step of recommending to the purchasing department to make a large purchase of inventory at year-end. The price of the item to be purchased has nearly doubled during the year, and the item represents a major portion of inventory value.

Instructions

Answer the following questions.

(a) Identify the major stakeholders. If the plant accountant recommends the purchase, what are the consequences?

(b) If Wilkens Company were using the FIFO method of inventory costing, would Lenny Wilkens give the same order? Why or why not?

USING YOUR JUDGMENT

FINANCIAL REPORTING

Financial Statement Analysis Cases

Case 1 Lumber Supply International

Lumber Supply International is a manufacturer of specialty building products. The company, through its partnership in the Trus Joist MacMillan joint venture, develops and manufactures engineered lumber. This product is a high-quality substitute for structural lumber, and uses lower-grade wood and materials formerly considered waste. The company also is majority owner of the Outlook Window Partnership, which is a consortium of three wood and vinyl window manufacturers.

Following is Lumber Supply International's adapted income statement and information concerning inventories from its statement of financial position.

Lumber Supply International

Sales revenue	€618,876,000
Cost of goods sold	475,476,000
Gross profit	143,400,000
Selling and administrative expenses	102,112,000
Income from operations	41,288,000
Other expense	24,712,000
Income before income taxes	16,576,000
Income taxes	7,728,000
Net income	€ 8,848,000

Inventories. Inventories are valued at the lower-of-cost-or-net realizable value and include material, labor, and production overhead costs. Inventories consisted of the following:

	Current Year	Prior Year
Finished goods	€27,512,000	€23,830,000
Raw materials and work in progress	34,363,000	33,244,000
	61,875,000	57,074,000
Reduction to average-cost	(5,263,000)	(3,993,000)
	€56,612,000	€53,081,000

The average-cost (AC) method is used for determining the cost of lumber, veneer, Microllam lumber, LSI joists, and open web joists. Approximately 35 percent of total inventories at the end of the current year were valued using the AC method. The first-in, first-out (FIFO) method is used to determine the cost of all other inventories.

Instructions

(a) How much would income before taxes have been if FIFO costing had been used to value all inventories?

(b) If the income tax rate is 46.6%, what would income tax have been if FIFO costing had been used to value all inventories? In your opinion, is this difference in net income between the two methods material? Explain.

(c) Does the use of a different costing system for different types of inventory mean that there is a different physical flow of goods among the different types of inventory? Explain.

Case 2 Noven Pharmaceuticals, Inc.

Noven Pharmaceuticals, Inc. (USA), headquartered in Miami, Florida, describes itself in a recent annual report as follows.

Noven Pharmaceuticals, Inc.

Noven is a place of ideas—a company where scientific excellence and state-of-the-art manufacturing combine to create new answers to human needs. Our transdermal delivery systems speed drugs painlessly and effortlessly into the bloodstream by means of a simple skin patch. This technology has proven applications in estrogen replacement, but at Noven we are developing a variety of systems incorporating bestselling drugs that fight everything from asthma, anxiety and dental pain to cancer, heart disease and neurological illness. Our research portfolio also includes new technologies, such as iontophoresis, in which drugs are delivered through the skin by means of electrical currents, as well as products that could satisfy broad consumer needs, such as our anti-microbial mouthrinse.

Noven also reported in its annual report that its activities to date have consisted of product development efforts, some of which have been independent and some of which have been completed in conjunction with **Rhone-Poulenc Rorer (RPR)** (FRA) and **Ciba-Geigy** (USA). The revenues so far have consisted of money received from licensing fees, "milestone" payments (payments made under licensing agreements when certain stages of the development of a certain product have been completed), and interest on its investments. The company expects that it will have significant revenue in the upcoming fiscal year from the launch of its first product, a transdermal estrogen delivery system.

The current assets portion of Noven's statement of financial position follows.

Cash and cash equivalents	$12,070,272
Investment securities	23,445,070
Inventory of supplies	1,264,553
Prepaid and other current assets	825,159
Total current assets	$37,605,054

Inventory of supplies is recorded at the lower-of-cost (first-in, first-out)-or-net realizable value and consists mainly of supplies for research and development.

Instructions

(a) What would you expect the physical flow of goods for a pharmaceutical manufacturer to be most like, FIFO or random (flow of goods does not follow a set pattern)? Explain.

(b) What are some of the factors that Noven should consider as it selects an inventory measurement method?

(c) Suppose that Noven had $49,000 in an inventory of transdermal estrogen delivery patches. These patches are from an initial production run, and will be sold during the coming year. Why do you think that this amount is not shown in a separate inventory account? In which of the accounts shown is the inventory likely to be? At what point will the inventory be transferred to a separate inventory account?

*Case 3 SUPERSTORE

SUPERSTORE reported that its inventory turnover decreased from 17.1 times in 2015 to 15.8 times in 2016. The following data appear in SUPERSTORE's annual report.

	Feb. 26, 2014	Feb. 25, 2015	Feb. 24, 2016
Total revenues	$19,543	$19,864	$37,406
Cost of sales (using LIFO)	16,681	16,977	29,267
Year-end inventories using FIFO	1,181	1,114	2,927
Year-end inventories using LIFO	1,032	954	2,749

(a) Compute SUPERSTORE's inventory turnovers (see Appendix 5A for the inventory turnover formula) for 2015 and 2016 using:
   (1) Cost of sales and LIFO inventory.
   (2) Cost of sales and FIFO inventory.

(b) Some firms calculate inventory turnover using sales rather than cost of goods sold in the numerator. Calculate SUPERSTORE's 2015 and 2016 turnover using:
   (1) Sales and LIFO inventory.
   (2) Sales and FIFO inventory.

(c) Describe the method that SUPERSTORE appears to use.

(d) State which method you would choose to evaluate SUPERSTORE's performance. Justify your choice.

Accounting, Analysis, and Principles

Englehart Company sells two types of pumps. One is large and is for commercial use. The other is smaller and is used in residential swimming pools. The following inventory data is available for the month of March.

	Units	Price per Unit	Total
Residential Pumps			
Inventory at Feb. 28	200	£ 400	£ 80,000
Purchases:			
March 10	500	£ 450	£225,000
March 20	400	£ 475	£190,000
March 30	300	£ 500	£150,000
Sales:			
March 15	500	£ 540	£270,000
March 25	400	£ 570	£228,000
Inventory at Mar. 31	500		
Commercial Pumps			
Inventory at Feb. 28	600	£ 800	£480,000
Purchases:			
March 3	600	£ 900	£540,000
March 12	300	£ 950	£285,000
March 21	500	£1,000	£500,000
Sales:			
March 18	900	£1,080	£972,000
March 29	600	£1,140	£684,000
Inventory at Mar. 31	500		

Accounting

(a) Assuming Englehart uses a periodic inventory system, determine the cost of inventory on hand at March 31 and the cost of goods sold for March under first-in, first-out (FIFO).

(b) Assume Englehart uses average-cost. Determine the cost of inventory on hand at March 31 and the cost of goods sold for March.

Analysis

(a) Assume you need to compute a current ratio for Englehart. Which inventory method (FIFO or average-cost) do you think would give you a more meaningful current ratio?

(b) Some of Englehart's competitors use average-cost inventory costing and some use FIFO. How can an analyst compare the results of companies in an industry when some use average-cost and others use FIFO?

Principles

(a) Can companies change from one inventory accounting method to another? If a company changes to an inventory accounting method used by most of its competitors, what are the trade-offs in terms of the Conceptual Framework discussed in Chapter 2 of the textbook?

*(b) If a U.S. company decides to adopt IFRS, what inventory accounting methods could it choose from?

IFRS BRIDGE TO THE PROFESSION

Professional Research

In conducting year-end inventory counts, your audit team is debating the impact of the client's right of return policy both on inventory valuation and revenue recognition. The assistant controller argues that there is no need to worry about the return policies since they have not changed in a while. The audit senior wants a more authoritative answer and has asked you to conduct some research of the authoritative literature before she presses the point with the client.

Instructions

Access the IFRS authoritative literature at the IASB website (*http://eifrs.iasb.org/*) (you may register for free eIFRS access at this site). When you have accessed the documents, you can use the search tool in your Internet browser to respond to the following questions. (Provide paragraph citations if necessary.)

(a) Which statement addresses revenue recognition when right of return exists?

(b) When is this statement important for a company?

(c) Sales with rights of return can ultimately cause inventory to be misstated. Why are returns allowed? Should different industries be able to make different types of return policies?

(d) In what situations would a reasonable estimate of returns be difficult to make?

Professional Simulation

In this simulation, you are asked to address questions regarding inventory valuation and measurement. Prepare responses to all parts.

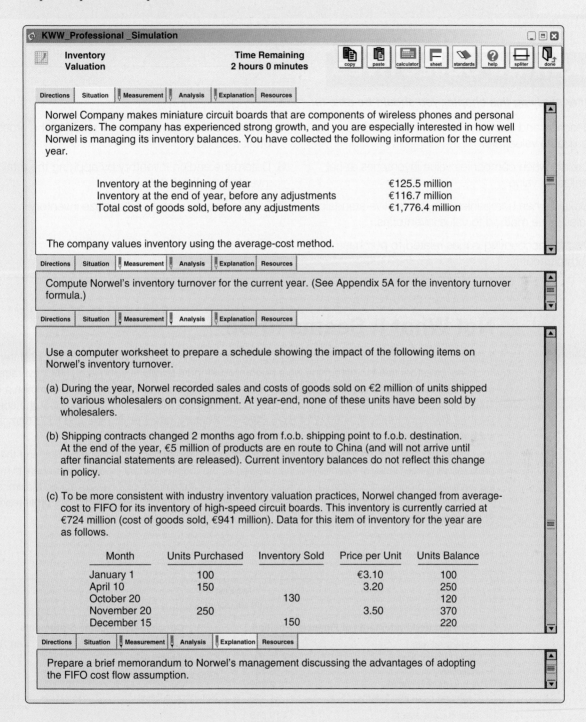

Inventories: Additional Valuation Issues

CHAPTER 9

LEARNING OBJECTIVES

After studying this chapter, you should be able to:

1 Describe and apply the lower-of-cost-or-net realizable value rule.

2 Explain when companies value inventories at net realizable value.

3 Explain when companies use the relative standalone sales value method to value inventories.

4 Discuss accounting issues related to purchase commitments.

5 Determine ending inventory by applying the gross profit method.

6 Determine ending inventory by applying the retail inventory method.

7 Explain how to report and analyze inventory.

Not What It Seems to Be

Investors need comparable information about inventory when evaluating a retailer's financial statements. To do so, investors need to determine what inventory method a retailer is using (e.g., FIFO, average-cost, or a combination of methods) and then adjust the company's financial information to a common method. That is a good start. What investors often then do is compute relevant information about the company such as inventory turnover, number of days sales in inventory, gross profit rate, and liquidity measures such as the acid-test ratio.

These calculations are critical. Inventory is a significant component of working capital, and the gross profit resulting from sales of inventory is often viewed as the most important income component in measuring a retailer's progress. For example, consider the financial statements of a typical retailer, Maxim, shown in the following table. Inventory comprises over 50 percent of current assets, and gross profit represents 25 percent of sales revenue.

MAXIM (IN MILLIONS)			
Consolidated Statements of Financial Position		**Consolidated Income Statements**	
<u>Current Assets</u>		Sales revenue	€50,705
Other current assets	€ 1,101	Cost of goods sold	38,132
Inventory	5,731	Gross profit	€12,573
Accounts receivable	2,288		
Cash and cash equivalents	1,199	Net income (loss)	€ (1,231)
Total current assets	€10,319		

Analysis is based on these numbers. However, there are often still questions about the reliability of the information reported in the financial statements. That is, subjective estimates are involved because of the possible impairment of the inventory. For example, Maxim provides disclosures related to inventory in its annual report, shown on the next page.

As indicated in the table below, subjective estimates concerning the measurement and valuation of inventory (related to markdowns and inventory losses) could have a significant impact on an investor's ability to compare inventory levels (and their impact on gross profit) at Maxim relative to other retailers. Thus, inventory balances may not be what they seem, not only due to the cost flow assumptions (e.g., FIFO/weighted-average) you learned about in Chapter 8 but also due to significant markdowns and losses that you will learn about in this chapter.

CONCEPTUAL FOCUS

> See the **Underlying Concepts** on pages 403, 405, and 408.

INTERNATIONAL FOCUS

> Read the **Global Accounting Insights** on pages 421–422 for a discussion of non-IFRS financial reporting related to inventory.

Critical Accounting Estimates in Preparation of the Financial Statements: Inventory	Judgments and Uncertainties
We value our inventory at the lower-of-cost-or-net realizable value through the establishment of markdown and inventory loss adjustments.	
Our inventory valuation reflects markdowns for the excess of the cost over the amount we expect to realize from the Ultimate sale or other disposal of the inventory. Markdowns establish a new cost basis for our inventory. Subsequent changes in facts or circumstances do not result in the reversal of previously recorded markdowns or an increase in that newly established cost basis.	Our markdown adjustment contains uncertainties because the calculation requires management to make assumptions and to apply judgment regarding inventory aging, forecast consumer demand, the promotional environment, and technological obsolescence.
Our inventory valuation also reflects adjustments for anticipated physical inventory losses (e.g., theft) that have occurred since the last physical inventory. Physical inventory counts are taken on a regular basis to ensure that the inventory reported in our consolidated financial statements is properly stated.	Our inventory loss adjustment contains uncertainties because the calculation requires management to make assumptions and to apply judgment regarding a number of factors, including historical results and current inventory loss trends.

PREVIEW OF CHAPTER 9

As our opening story indicates, information on inventories helps to predict financial performance—in particular, profits. In this chapter, we discuss some of the valuation and estimation concepts that companies use to develop relevant inventory information. The content and organization of the chapter are as follows.

Inventories: Additional Valuation Issues

Lower-of-Cost-or-Net Realizable Value (LCNRV)	Valuation Bases	Gross Profit Method	Retail Inventory Method	Presentation and Analysis
• Net realizable value • Illustration of LCNRV • Application of LCNRV • Recording net realizable value • Use of an allowance • Recovery of inventory loss • Evaluation of rule	• Special valuation situations • Relative standalone sales value • Purchase commitments	• Gross profit percentage • Evaluation of method	• Concepts • Conventional method • Special items • Evaluation of method	• Presentation • Analysis

LOWER-OF-COST-OR-NET REALIZABLE VALUE (LCNRV)

LEARNING OBJECTIVE
Describe and apply the lower-of-cost-or-net realizable value rule.

Inventories are recorded at their cost. However, if inventory declines in value below its original cost, a major departure from the historical cost principle occurs. Whatever the reason for a decline—obsolescence, price-level changes, or damaged goods—a company should write down the inventory to net realizable value to report this loss. **A company abandons the historical cost principle when the future utility (revenue-producing ability) of the asset drops below its original cost.**

Net Realizable Value

**I
F
R
S**

See the Authoritative Literature section (page 423).

Recall that **cost** is the acquisition price of inventory computed using one of the historical cost-based methods—specific identification, average-cost, or FIFO. The term **net realizable value (NRV)** refers to the net amount that a company expects to realize from the sale of inventory. Specifically, net realizable value is the estimated selling price in the normal course of business less estimated costs to complete and estimated costs to make a sale. **[1]**

To illustrate, assume that Mander Corp. has unfinished inventory with a cost of €950, a sales value of €1,000, estimated cost of completion of €50, and estimated selling costs of €200. Mander's net realizable value is computed as follows.

ILLUSTRATION 9-1
Computation of Net Realizable Value

Inventory value—unfinished		€1,000
Less: Estimated cost of completion	€ 50	
Estimated cost to sell	200	250
Net realizable value		€ 750

Mander reports inventory on its statement of financial position at €750. In its income statement, Mander reports a Loss on Inventory Write-Down of €200 (€950 − €750). A departure from cost is justified because inventories should not be reported at amounts higher than their expected realization from sale or use. In addition, a company like Mander should charge the loss of utility against revenues in the period in which the loss occurs, not in the period of sale.

Companies therefore report their inventories at the **lower-of-cost-or-net realizable value (LCNRV)** at each reporting date. Illustration 9-2 shows how two companies indicate measurement at LCNRV.

ILLUSTRATION 9-2
LCNRV Disclosures

Nokia (FIN)
Inventories are stated at the lower of cost or net realizable value. Cost is determined using standard cost, which approximates actual cost on a FIFO basis. Net realizable value is the amount that can be realized from the sale of the inventory in the normal course of business after allowing for the costs of realization. In addition to the cost of materials and direct labor, an appropriate proportion of production overhead is included in the inventory values. An allowance is recorded for excess inventory and obsolescence based on the lower-of-cost-or-net realizable value.

Kesa Electricals (GBR)
Inventories are stated at the lower-of-cost-and-net realisable value. Cost is determined using the weighted average method. Net realisable value represents the estimated selling price in the ordinary course of business, less applicable variable selling expenses.

Illustration of LCNRV

As indicated, a company values inventory at LCNRV. A company estimates net realizable value based on the most reliable evidence of the inventories' realizable amounts (expected selling price, expected costs of completion, and expected costs to sell). **[2]** To illustrate, Jinn-Feng Foods computes its inventory at LCNRV, as shown in Illustration 9-3 (amounts in thousands).

Food	Cost	Net Realizable Value	Final Inventory Value
Spinach	¥ 80,000	¥120,000	¥ 80,000
Carrots	100,000	110,000	100,000
Cut beans	50,000	40,000	40,000
Peas	90,000	72,000	72,000
Mixed vegetables	95,000	92,000	92,000
			¥384,000

Final Inventory Value:

Spinach	Cost (¥80,000) is selected because it is lower than net realizable value.
Carrots	Cost (¥100,000) is selected because it is lower than net realizable value.
Cut beans	Net realizable value (¥40,000) is selected because it is lower than cost.
Peas	Net realizable value (¥72,000) is selected because it is lower than cost.
Mixed vegetables	Net realizable value (¥92,000) is selected because it is lower than cost.

ILLUSTRATION 9-3
Determining Final Inventory Value

As indicated, the final inventory value of ¥384,000 equals the sum of the LCNRV for each of the inventory items. That is, Jinn-Feng applies the LCNRV rule to each individual type of food.

Methods of Applying LCNRV

In the Jinn-Feng Foods illustration, we assumed that the company applied the LCNRV rule to each individual type of food. However, companies may apply the LCNRV rule to a group of similar or related items, or to the total of the inventory. For example, in the textile industry, it may not be possible to determine selling price for each textile individually, and therefore it may be necessary to perform the net realizable value assessment on all textiles that will be used to produce clothing for a particular season.[1]

If a company follows a similar-or-related-items or total-inventory approach in determining LCNRV, increases in market prices tend to offset decreases in market prices. To illustrate, assume that Jinn-Feng Foods separates its food products into two major groups, frozen and canned, as shown in Illustration 9-4.

			LCNRV by:		
	Cost	LCNRV	Individual Items	Major Groups	Total Inventory
Frozen					
Spinach	¥ 80,000	¥120,000	¥ 80,000		
Carrots	100,000	110,000	100,000		
Cut beans	50,000	40,000	40,000		
Total frozen	230,000	270,000		¥230,000	
Canned					
Peas	90,000	72,000	72,000		
Mixed vegetables	95,000	92,000	92,000		
Total canned	185,000	164,000		164,000	
Total	¥415,000	¥434,000	¥384,000	¥394,000	¥415,000

ILLUSTRATION 9-4
Alternative Applications of LCNRV

[1]It may be necessary to write down an entire product line or a group of inventories in a given geographic area that cannot be practicably evaluated separately. However, it is not appropriate to write down an entire class of inventory, such as finished goods or all inventory of a particular industry. **[3]**

If Jinn-Feng applied the LCNRV rule to individual items, the amount of inventory is ¥384,000. If applying the rule to major groups, it jumps to ¥394,000. If applying LCNRV to the total inventory, it totals ¥415,000. Why this difference? When a company uses a major group or total-inventory approach, net realizable values higher than cost offset net realizable values lower than cost. For Jinn-Feng, using the similar-or-related-items approach partially offsets the high net realizable value for spinach. Using the total-inventory approach totally offsets it.[2]

In most situations, companies price inventory on an item-by-item basis. In fact, tax rules in some countries require that companies use an individual-item basis barring practical difficulties. In addition, the individual-item approach gives the lowest valuation for statement of financial position purposes. In some cases, a company prices inventory on a total-inventory basis when it offers only one end product (comprised of many different raw materials). If it produces several end products, a company might use a similar-or-related-items approach instead. **Whichever method a company selects, it should apply the method consistently from one period to another.**[3]

Recording Net Realizable Value Instead of Cost

One of two methods may be used to record the income effect of valuing inventory at net realizable value. One method, referred to as the cost-of-goods-sold method, debits cost of goods sold for the write-down of the inventory to net realizable value. As a result, the company does not report a loss in the income statement because the cost of goods sold already includes the amount of the loss. The second method, referred to as the loss method, debits a loss account for the write-down of the inventory to net realizable value. We use the following inventory data for Ricardo Company to illustrate entries under both methods.

Cost of goods sold (before adjustment to net realizable value)	€108,000
Ending inventory (cost)	82,000
Ending inventory (at net realizable value)	70,000

Illustration 9-5 shows the entries for both the cost-of-goods-sold and loss methods, assuming the use of a perpetual inventory system.

ILLUSTRATION 9-5
Accounting for the Reduction of Inventory to Net Realizable Value—Perpetual Inventory System

Cost-of-Goods-Sold Method		Loss Method	
To reduce inventory from cost to net realizable value			
Cost of Goods Sold 12,000		Loss Due to Decline of Inventory	
Inventory (€82,000 − €70,000)	12,000	to Net Realizable Value 12,000	
		Inventory (€82,000 − €70,000)	12,000

The cost-of-goods-sold method buries the loss in the Cost of Goods Sold account. The loss method, by identifying the loss due to the write-down, shows the loss separate from Cost of Goods Sold in the income statement.

Illustration 9-6 contrasts the differing amounts reported in the income statement under the two approaches, using data from the Ricardo example.

[2]The rationale for use of the individual-item approach whenever practicable is to avoid realization of unrealized gains, which can arise when applying LCNRV on a similar-or-related-items approach (e.g., unrealized gains on some items offset unrealized losses on other items). In general, IFRS prohibits recognition of unrealized gains in income.

[3]Materials and other supplies held for use in the production of inventories are not written down below cost if the finished products in which they will be incorporated are expected to be sold at or above cost. However, a decline in the price of materials may indicate that the cost of the finished products exceeds net realizable value. In this situation, the materials are written down to net realizable value.

Cost-of-Goods-Sold Method	
Sales revenue	€200,000
Cost of goods sold (after adjustment to net realizable value*)	120,000
Gross profit on sales	€ 80,000

Loss Method	
Sales revenue	€200,000
Cost of goods sold	108,000
Gross profit on sales	92,000
Loss due to decline of inventory to net realizable value	12,000
	€ 80,000

*Cost of goods sold (before adjustment to net realizable value)	€108,000
Difference between inventory at cost and net realizable value	
(€82,000 − €70,000)	12,000
Cost of goods sold (after adjustment to net realizable value)	€120,000

ILLUSTRATION 9-6
Income Statement
Presentation—Cost-of-Goods-Sold and Loss
Methods of Reducing
Inventory to Net
Realizable Value

IFRS does not specify a particular account to debit for the write-down. We believe the loss method presentation is preferable because it clearly discloses the loss resulting from a decline in inventory net realizable values.

Use of an Allowance

Instead of crediting the Inventory account for net realizable value adjustments, companies generally use an allowance account, often referred to as Allowance to Reduce Inventory to Net Realizable Value. For example, using an allowance account under the loss method, Ricardo Company makes the following entry to record the inventory write-down to net realizable value.

Loss Due to Decline of Inventory to Net Realizable Value	12,000	
Allowance to Reduce Inventory to Net Realizable Value		12,000

Use of the allowance account results in reporting both the cost and the net realizable value of the inventory. Ricardo reports inventory in the statement of financial position as follows.

Inventory (at cost)	€82,000
Allowance to reduce inventory to net realizable value	(12,000)
Inventory at net realizable value	€70,000

ILLUSTRATION 9-7
Presentation of Inventory
Using an Allowance
Account

> **Underlying Concepts** 🔍
>
> The income statement under the cost-of-goods-sold method presentation lacks *representational faithfulness.* The cost-of-goods-sold method does not represent what it purports to represent. However, allowing this presentation illustrates the concept of materiality.

The use of the allowance under the cost-of-goods-sold or loss method permits both the income statement and the statement of financial position to reflect inventory measured at €82,000, although the statement of financial position shows a net amount of €70,000. It also keeps subsidiary inventory ledgers and records in correspondence with the control account without changing prices. *For homework purposes, use an allowance account to record net realizable value adjustments, unless instructed otherwise.*

Recovery of Inventory Loss

In periods following the write-down, economic conditions may change such that the net realizable value of inventories previously written down may be *greater* than cost or there is clear evidence of an increase in the net realizable value. In this situation, the amount of the write-down is reversed, with the reversal limited to the amount of the original write-down. [4]

Continuing the Ricardo example, assume that in the subsequent period, market conditions change, such that the net realizable value increases to €74,000 (an increase of

€4,000). As a result, only €8,000 is needed in the allowance. Ricardo makes the following entry, using the loss method.

Allowance to Reduce Inventory to Net Realizable Value	4,000	
Recovery of Inventory Loss (€74,000 − €70,000)		4,000

The allowance account is then adjusted in subsequent periods, such that inventory is reported at the LCNRV. Illustration 9-8 shows the net realizable value evaluation for Vuko Company and the effect of net realizable value adjustments on income.

ILLUSTRATION 9-8
Effect on Net Income of Adjusting Inventory to Net Realizable Value

Date	Inventory at Cost	Inventory at Net Realizable Value	Amount Required in Allowance Account	Adjustment of Allowance Account Balance	Effect on Net Income
Dec. 31, 2015	₱188,000	₱176,000	₱12,000	₱12,000 inc.	Decrease
Dec. 31, 2016	194,000	187,000	7,000	5,000 dec.	Increase
Dec. 31, 2017	173,000	174,000	0	7,000 dec.	Increase
Dec. 31, 2018	182,000	180,000	2,000	2,000 inc.	Decrease

Thus, if prices are falling, the company records an additional write-down. If prices are rising, the company records an increase in income. We can think of the net increase as a recovery of a previously recognized loss. Under no circumstances should the inventory be reported at a value above original cost.

Evaluation of the LCNRV Rule

The LCNRV rule suffers some conceptual deficiencies:

1. A company recognizes decreases in the value of the asset and the charge to expense in the period in which the loss in utility occurs—not in the period of sale. On the other hand, it recognizes increases in the value of the asset (in excess of original cost) only at the point of sale. This inconsistent treatment can distort income data.

2. Application of the rule results in inconsistency because a company may value the inventory at cost in one year and at net realizable value in the next year.

3. LCNRV values the inventory in the statement of financial position conservatively, but its effect on the income statement may or may not be conservative. Net income for the year in which a company takes the loss is definitely lower. Net income of the subsequent period may be higher than normal if the expected reductions in sales price do not materialize.

Many financial statement users appreciate the LCNRV rule because they at least know that it prevents overstatement of inventory. In addition, recognizing all losses but anticipating no gains generally avoids overstatement of income.

VALUATION BASES

Special Valuation Situations

LEARNING OBJECTIVE 2

Explain when companies value inventories at net realizable value.

For the most part, companies record inventory at LCNRV.[4] However, there are some situations in which companies depart from the LCNRV rule. Such treatment may be justified in situations when cost is difficult to determine, the items

---

[4]Manufacturing companies frequently employ a standardized cost system that predetermines the unit costs for material, labor, and manufacturing overhead and that values raw materials, work in process, and finished goods inventories at their standard costs. Standard costs take into account normal levels of materials and supplies, labor, efficiency, and capacity utilization, and are regularly reviewed and, if necessary, revised in the light of current conditions. For financial reporting purposes, the standard cost method may be used for convenience if the results approximate cost. [5] Nokia (FIN) and Hewlett-Packard (USA) use standard costs for valuing at least a portion of their inventories.

are readily marketable at quoted market prices, and units of product are interchangeable. In this section, we discuss two common situations in which net realizable value is the general rule for valuing inventory:

- Agricultural assets (including biological assets and agricultural produce).
- Commodities held by broker-traders.

Agricultural Inventory

Under IFRS, net realizable value measurement is used for inventory when the inventory is related to agricultural activity. In general, agricultural activity results in two types of agricultural assets: (1) biological assets or (2) agricultural produce at the point of harvest. **[6]**

A **biological asset** (classified as a non-current asset) is a living animal or plant, such as sheep, cows, fruit trees, or cotton plants. **Agricultural produce** is the harvested product of a biological asset, such as wool from a sheep, milk from a dairy cow, picked fruit from a fruit tree, or cotton from a cotton plant. The accounting for these assets is as follows.

- Biological assets are measured on initial recognition and at the end of each reporting period at fair value less costs to sell (net realizable value). Companies record a gain or loss due to changes in the net realizable value of biological assets in income when it arises.[5]

- Agricultural produce (which are harvested from biological assets) are measured at fair value less costs to sell (net realizable value) at the point of harvest. Once harvested, the net realizable value of the agricultural produce becomes its cost, and this asset is accounted for similar to other inventories held for sale in the normal course of business.[6]

Illustration of Agricultural Accounting at Net Realizable Value

To illustrate the accounting at net realizable value for agricultural assets, assume that Bancroft Dairy produces milk for sale to local cheese-makers. Bancroft began operations on January 1, 2015, by purchasing 420 milking cows for €460,000. Bancroft provides the following information related to the milking cows.

ILLUSTRATION 9-9
Agricultural Assets—
Bancroft Dairy

Milking cows		
Carrying value, January 1, 2015*		€460,000
Change in fair value due to growth and price changes	€35,000	
Decrease in fair value due to harvest	(1,200)	
Change in carrying value		33,800
Carrying value, January 31, 2015		€493,800
Milk harvested during January**		€ 36,000

*The carrying value is measured at fair value less costs to sell (net realizable value). The fair value of milking cows is determined based on market prices of livestock of similar age, breed, and genetic merit.

**Milk is initially measured at its fair value less costs to sell (net realizable value) at the time of milking. The fair value of milk is determined based on market prices in the local area.

As indicated, the carrying value of the milking cows increased during the month. Part of the change is due to changes in market prices (less costs to sell) for milking cows. The change in market price may also be affected by growth—the increase in value as the cows mature and develop increased milking capacity.

Underlying Concepts

IFRS uses the terms book value, carrying value, and carrying amount interchangeably.

[5]A gain may arise on initial recognition of a biological asset, such as when a calf is born. A gain or loss may arise on initial recognition of agricultural produce as a result of harvesting. Losses may arise on initial recognition for agricultural assets because costs to sell are deducted in determining fair value less costs to sell.

[6]Measurement at fair value or selling price less point of sale costs corresponds to the net realizable value measure in the LCNRV test (selling price less estimated costs to complete and sell) since at harvest, the agricultural product is complete and is ready for sale. **[7]**

At the same time, as mature cows are milked, their milking capacity declines (fair value decrease due to harvest).[7]

Bancroft makes the following entry to record the change in carrying value of the milking cows.

Biological Asset (milking cows) (€493,800 − €460,000)	33,800	
Unrealized Holding Gain or Loss—Income		33,800

As a result of this entry, Bancroft's statement of financial position reports Biological Asset (milking cows) as a non-current asset at fair value less costs to sell (net realizable value). In addition, the unrealized gains and losses are reported as "Other income and expense" on the income statement. In subsequent periods at each reporting date, Bancroft continues to report Biological Asset at net realizable value and records any related unrealized gains or losses in income. Because there is a ready market for the biological assets (milking cows), valuation at net realizable value provides more relevant information about these assets.

In addition to recording the change in the biological asset, Bancroft makes the following summary entry to record the milk harvested for the month of January.

Inventory (milk)	36,000	
Unrealized Holding Gain or Loss—Income		36,000

The milk inventory is recorded at net realizable value at the time it is harvested and Unrealized Holding Gain or Loss—Income is recognized in income. As with the biological assets, net realizable value is considered the most relevant for purposes of valuation at harvest. What happens to the milk inventory that Bancroft recorded upon harvesting the milk from the cows? Assuming the milk harvested in January was sold to a local cheese-maker for €38,500, Bancroft records the sale as follows.

Cash	38,500	
Cost of Goods Sold	36,000	
Inventory (milk)		36,000
Sales Revenue		38,500

Thus, once harvested, the net realizable value of the harvested milk becomes its cost, and the milk is accounted for similar to other inventories held for sale in the normal course of business.

A final note: Some animals or plants may not be considered biological assets but would be classified and accounted for as other types of assets (not at net realizable value). For example, a pet shop may hold an inventory of dogs purchased from breeders that it then sells. Because the pet shop is not breeding the dogs, these dogs are not considered biological assets. As a result, the dogs are accounted for as inventory held for sale (at LCNRV).

Commodity Broker-Traders

Commodity broker-traders also generally measure their inventories at fair value less costs to sell (net realizable value), with changes in net realizable value recognized in income in the period of the change. Broker-traders buy or sell commodities (such as harvested corn, wheat, precious metals, heating oil) for others or on their own account. The primary purpose for holding these inventories is to sell the commodities in the near term and generate a profit from fluctuations in price. Thus, net realizable value is the most relevant measure in this industry because it indicates the amount that the broker-trader will receive from this inventory in the future.

---

[7]Changes in fair value arising from growth and harvesting from mature cows can be estimated based on changes in market prices of different age cows in the herd.

Assessing whether a company is acting in the role of a broker-trader requires judgment. Companies should consider the length of time they are likely to hold the inventory and the extent of additional services related to the commodity. If there are significant additional services, such as distribution, storage, or repackaging, the company is likely not acting as a broker-dealer. Thus, measurement of the commodity inventory at net realizable value is not appropriate. For example, Columbia Coffee Wholesalers buys coffee beans and resells the commodity in the same condition after a short period of time. Accounting for the coffee inventory at net realizable value appears appropriate. However, if Columbia expands the business to roast the beans and repackage them for resale to local coffee shops, the coffee inventory should be accounted for at LCNRV, similar to other inventory held for sale.[8]

Valuation Using Relative Standalone Sales Value

A special problem arises when a company buys a group of varying units in a single lump-sum purchase, also called a **basket purchase**.

> **3 LEARNING OBJECTIVE**
> Explain when companies use the relative standalone sales value method to value inventories.

To illustrate, assume that Woodland Developers purchases land for $1 million that it will subdivide into 400 lots. These lots are of different sizes and shapes but can be roughly sorted into three groups graded A, B, and C. As Woodland sells the lots, it apportions the purchase cost of $1 million among the lots sold and the lots remaining on hand.

Why would Woodland not simply divide the total cost of $1 million by 400 lots, to get a cost of $2,500 for each lot? This approach would not recognize that the lots vary in size, shape, and attractiveness. Therefore, to accurately value each unit, the common and most logical practice is to allocate the total among the various units on the basis of their **relative standalone sales value**.

Illustration 9-10 shows the allocation of relative standalone sales value for the Woodland Developers example.

Lots	Number of Lots	Sales Price per Lot	Total Sales Price	Relative Sales Price	Total Cost	Cost Allocated to Lots	Cost per Lot
A	100	$10,000	$1,000,000	100/250	$1,000,000	$ 400,000	$4,000
B	100	6,000	600,000	60/250	1,000,000	240,000	2,400
C	200	4,500	900,000	90/250	1,000,000	360,000	1,800
			$2,500,000			$1,000,000	

ILLUSTRATION 9-10
Allocation of Costs, Using Relative Standalone Sales Value

Using the amounts given in the "Cost per Lot" column, Woodland can determine the cost of lots sold and the gross profit as follows.

Lots	Number of Lots Sold	Cost per Lot	Cost of Lots Sold	Sales	Gross Profit
A	77	$4,000	$308,000	$ 770,000	$ 462,000
B	80	2,400	192,000	480,000	288,000
C	100	1,800	180,000	450,000	270,000
			$680,000	$1,700,000	$1,020,000

ILLUSTRATION 9-11
Determination of Gross Profit, Using Relative Standalone Sales Value

[8]Minerals and mineral products, such as coal or iron ore, may also be measured at net realizable value in accordance with well-established industry practices. In the mining industry, when minerals have been extracted, there is often an assured sale under a forward contract, government guarantee, or in an active market. Because there is negligible risk of failure to sell, measurement at net realizable value is justified. In these contexts, and similar to the accounting for agricultural assets, minerals and mineral products are recorded at net realizable value at the point of extraction, with a gain recorded in the period of extraction. In subsequent periods, changes in value of minerals and mineral products inventory are recognized in profit or loss in the period of the change.

The ending inventory is therefore $320,000 ($1,000,000 − $680,000).

Woodland also can compute this inventory amount another way. The ratio of cost to selling price for all the lots is $1 million divided by $2,500,000, or 40 percent. Accordingly, if the total sales price of lots sold is, say $1,700,000, then the cost of the lots sold is 40 percent of $1,700,000, or $680,000. The inventory of lots on hand is then $1 million less $680,000, or $320,000.

The petroleum industry widely uses the relative standalone sales value method to value (at cost) the many products and by-products obtained from a barrel of crude oil.

Purchase Commitments—A Special Problem

LEARNING OBJECTIVE 4

Discuss accounting issues related to purchase commitments.

In many lines of business, a company's survival and continued profitability depend on its having a sufficient stock of merchandise to meet customer demand. Consequently, it is quite common for a company to make **purchase commitments**, which are agreements to buy inventory weeks, months, or even years in advance. Generally, the seller retains title to the merchandise or materials covered in the purchase commitments. Indeed, the goods may exist only as natural resources as unplanted seed (in the case of agricultural commodities), or as work in process (in the case of a product).[9]

Usually, it is neither necessary nor proper for the buyer to make any entries to reflect commitments for purchases of goods that the seller has not shipped. Ordinary orders, for which the buyer and seller will determine prices at the time of shipment and **which are subject to cancellation**, do not represent either an asset or a liability to the buyer. Therefore, the buyer need not record such purchase commitments or report them in the financial statements.

What happens, though, if a buyer enters into a formal, non-cancelable purchase contract? Even then, the buyer recognizes no asset or liability at the date of inception **because the contract is "executory" in nature**: Neither party has fulfilled its part of the contract. However, if material, the buyer should disclose such contract details in a note to its financial statements. Illustration 9-12 shows an example of a purchase commitment disclosure.

ILLUSTRATION 9-12
Disclosure of Purchase Commitment

> **Note 1:** Contracts for the purchase of raw materials in 2016 have been executed in the amount of $600,000. The market price of such raw materials on December 31, 2015, is $640,000.

 Underlying Concepts

Reporting the loss is *conservative*. However, reporting the decline in market price is debatable because no asset is recorded. This area demonstrates the need for good definitions of assets and liabilities.

In the disclosure in Illustration 9-12, the contract price was less than the market price at the statement of financial position date. **If the contract price is greater than the market price and the buyer expects that losses will occur when the purchase is made, the buyer should recognize a liability and corresponding loss in the period during which such declines in market prices take place.**[10]

To illustrate the accounting problem, assume that Apres Paper Co. signed timber-cutting contracts with Galling Land Ltd. to be executed in 2016 at a price of €10,000,000. Assume further that the market price of the timber-cutting rights on December 31, 2015, dropped to €7,000,000. Apres would make the following entry on December 31, 2015.

Unrealized Holding Gain or Loss—Income	3,000,000	
Purchase Commitment Liability (€10,000,000 − €7,000,000)		3,000,000

---

[9]In a recent survey of 175 international companies, commitments to purchase goods and services were mentioned 83 times. See P. Walters, *IFRS Accounting Trends and Techniques* (AICPA, 2012), p. 64.

[10]Such a contract is deemed to be **onerous**, which is defined as a contract under which the unavoidable costs of satisfying the obligations exceed the economic benefits expected. **[8]** This concept is discussed in more detail in Chapter 13.

Apres reports this unrealized holding loss in the income statement under "Other income and expense." And because the contract is to be executed within the next fiscal year, Apres reports the Purchase Commitment Liability (often referred to as a provision) in the current liabilities section on the statement of financial position. When Apres cuts the timber at a cost of €10 million, it would make the following entry.

Purchases (Inventory)	7,000,000	
Purchase Commitment Liability	3,000,000	
Cash		10,000,000

The result of the purchase commitment was that Apres paid €10 million for a contract worth only €7 million. It recorded the loss in the previous period—when the price actually declined.

If Apres can partially or fully recover the contract price before it cuts the timber, it reduces the Purchase Commitment Liability. In that case, it then reports in the period of the price increase a resulting gain for the amount of the partial or full recovery. For example, assume that Galling Land Ltd. permits Apres to reduce its commitment from €10,000,000 to €9,000,000. The entry to record this transaction is as follows.

Purchase Commitment Liability (€10,000,000 − €9,000,000)	1,000,000	
Unrealized Holding Gain or Loss—Income		1,000,000

If the market price at the time Apres cuts the timber is more than €2,000,000 below the contract price, Apres will have to recognize an additional loss in the period of cutting and record the purchase at the LCNRV.

Are purchasers at the mercy of market price declines? Not totally. Purchasers can protect themselves against the possibility of market price declines of goods under contract by hedging. In **hedging**, the purchaser in the purchase commitment simultaneously enters into a contract in which it agrees to sell in the future the same quantity of the same (or similar) goods at a fixed price. Thus, the company holds a *buy position* in a purchase commitment and a *sell position* in a futures contract in the same commodity. The purpose of the hedge is to offset the price risk of the buy and sell positions: The company will be better off under one contract by approximately (maybe exactly) the same amount by which it is worse off under the other contract.

For example, Apres could have hedged its purchase commitment contract with a futures contract for timber rights of the same amount. In that case, its loss of €3,000,000 on the purchase commitment could have been offset by a €3,000,000 gain on the futures contract.[11]

As easy as this makes it sound, accounting for purchase commitments is controversial. Some argue that companies should report purchase commitments as assets and liabilities at the time they sign the contract. Others believe that delaying the recognition to the delivery date is more appropriate. Although the discussion in the Conceptual Framework does not exclude the possibility of recording assets and liabilities for purchase commitments, it contains no definitive conclusion about whether companies should record them. **[9]**

THE GROSS PROFIT METHOD OF ESTIMATING INVENTORY

Companies take a physical inventory to verify the accuracy of the perpetual inventory records or, if no records exist, to arrive at an inventory amount. Sometimes, however, taking a physical inventory is impractical. In such cases, companies use substitute measures to approximate inventory on hand.

5 LEARNING OBJECTIVE

Determine ending inventory by applying the gross profit method.

---

[11]Appendix 17A provides a complete discussion of hedging and the use of derivatives such as futures.

One substitute method of verifying or determining the inventory amount is the **gross profit method** (also called the **gross margin method**). Auditors widely use this method in situations where they need only an estimate of the company's inventory (e.g., interim reports). Companies also use this method when fire or other catastrophe destroys either inventory or inventory records. The gross profit method relies on three assumptions:

1. The beginning inventory plus purchases equal total goods to be accounted for.

2. Goods not sold must be on hand.

3. The sales, reduced to cost, deducted from the sum of the opening inventory plus purchases, equal ending inventory.

To illustrate, assume that Cetus Corp. has a beginning inventory of €60,000 and purchases of €200,000, both at cost. Sales at selling price amount to €280,000. The gross profit on selling price is 30 percent. Cetus applies the gross profit method as follows.

ILLUSTRATION 9-13
Application of Gross
Profit Method

Beginning inventory (at cost)		€ 60,000
Purchases (at cost)		200,000
Goods available (at cost)		260,000
Sales (at selling price)	€280,000	
Less: Gross profit (30% of €280,000)	84,000	
Sales (at cost)		196,000
Approximate inventory (at cost)		€ 64,000

The current period's records contain all the information Cetus needs to compute inventory at cost, except for the gross profit percentage. Cetus determines the gross profit percentage by reviewing company policies or prior period records. In some cases, companies must adjust this percentage if they consider prior periods unrepresentative of the current period.[12]

Computation of Gross Profit Percentage

In most situations, the **gross profit percentage** is stated as a percentage of selling price. The previous illustration, for example, used a 30 percent gross profit on sales. Gross profit on selling price is the common method for quoting the profit for several reasons.

[12]An alternative method of estimating inventory using the gross profit percentage is considered by some to be less complicated than the traditional method. This alternative method uses the standard income statement format as follows. (Assume the same data as in the Cetus example above.)

Relationships				Solution	
Sales revenue		€280,000			€280,000
Cost of sales					
Beginning inventory	€ 60,000			€ 60,000	
Purchases	200,000			200,000	
Goods available for sale	260,000			260,000	
Ending inventory	(3) ?			(3) 64,000 Est.	
Cost of goods sold		(2) ?			(2)196,000 Est.
Gross profit on sales (30%)		(1) ?			(1) 84,000 Est.

Compute the unknowns as follows: first the gross profit amount, then cost of goods sold, and finally the ending inventory, as shown below.

(1) €280,000 × 30% = €84,000 (gross profit on sales).
(2) €280,000 − €84,000 = €196,000 (cost of goods sold).
(3) €260,000 − €196,000 = €64,000 (ending inventory).

(1) Most companies state goods on a retail basis, not a cost basis. (2) A profit quoted on selling price is lower than one based on cost. This lower rate gives a favorable impression to the consumer. (3) The gross profit based on selling price can never exceed 100 percent.[13]

In Illustration 9-13, the gross profit was a given. But how did Cetus derive that figure? To see how to compute a gross profit percentage, assume that an article costs €15 and sells for €20, a gross profit of €5. As shown in the computations in Illustration 9-14, this markup is ¼ or 25 percent of retail, and ⅓ or 33⅓ percent of cost.

$$\frac{\text{Markup}}{\text{Retail}} = \frac{€5}{€20} = 25\% \text{ at retail} \qquad \frac{\text{Markup}}{\text{Cost}} = \frac{€5}{€15} = 33\frac{1}{2}\% \text{ on cost}$$

ILLUSTRATION 9-14
Computation of Gross Profit Percentage

Although companies normally compute the gross profit on the basis of selling price, you should understand the basic relationship between markup on cost and markup on selling price. For example, assume that a company marks up a given item by 25 percent on cost. What, then, is the **gross profit on selling price**? To find the answer, assume that the item sells for €1. In this case, the following formula applies.

$$\textbf{Cost + Gross profit = Selling price}$$
$$C + .25C = SP$$
$$(1 + .25)C = SP$$
$$1.25C = €1.00$$
$$C = €0.80$$

The gross profit equals €0.20 (€1.00 − €0.80). The rate of gross profit on selling price is therefore 20 percent (€0.20/€1.00).

Conversely, assume that the gross profit on selling price is 20 percent. What is the **markup on cost**? To find the answer, assume that the item sells for €1. Again, the same formula holds:

$$\textbf{Cost + Gross profit = Selling price}$$
$$C + .20SP = SP$$
$$C = (1 - .20)SP$$
$$C = .80SP$$
$$C = .80(€1.00)$$
$$C = €0.80$$

As in the previous example, the markup equals €0.20 (€1.00 − €0.80). The markup on cost is 25 percent (€0.20/€0.80).

Retailers use the following formulas to express these relationships:

1. $\text{Gross Profit on Selling Price} = \dfrac{\text{Percentage Markup on Cost}}{100\% + \text{Percentage Markup on Cost}}$

2. $\text{Percentage Markup on Cost} = \dfrac{\text{Gross Profit on Selling Price}}{100\% - \text{Gross Profit on Selling Price}}$

ILLUSTRATION 9-15
Formulas Relating to Gross Profit

To understand how to use these formulas, consider their application in the following calculations.

---

[13]The terms *gross margin percentage*, *rate of gross profit*, and *percentage markup* are synonymous, although companies more commonly use *markup* in reference to cost and *gross profit* in reference to sales.

ILLUSTRATION 9-16
Application of Gross
Profit Formulas

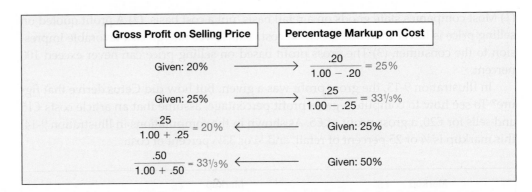

Because selling price exceeds cost, and with the gross profit amount the same for both, **gross profit on selling price will always be less than the related percentage based on cost**. Note that companies do not multiply sales by a cost-based markup percentage. Instead, they must convert the gross profit percentage to a percentage based on selling price.

Evaluation of Gross Profit Method

What are the major disadvantages of the gross profit method? One disadvantage is that **it provides an estimate**. As a result, companies must take a physical inventory once a year to verify the inventory. Second, the gross profit method **uses past percentages** in determining the markup. Although the past often provides answers to the future, a current rate is more appropriate. Note that whenever significant fluctuations occur, companies should adjust the percentage as appropriate. Third, companies must be **careful in applying a blanket gross profit rate**. Frequently, a store or department handles merchandise with widely varying rates of gross profit. In these situations, the company may need to apply the gross profit method by subsections, lines of merchandise, or a similar basis that classifies merchandise according to their respective rates of gross profit. **The gross profit method is normally unacceptable for financial reporting purposes because it provides only an estimate**. IFRS requires a physical inventory as additional verification of the inventory indicated in the records. Note that the gross profit method will follow closely the inventory method used (FIFO or average-cost) because it relies on historical records.

What do the numbers mean?   **THE SQUEEZE**

Managers and analysts closely follow gross profits. A small change in the gross profit rate can significantly affect the bottom line. For example, at one time, Apple Computer (USA) suffered a textbook case of shrinking gross profits. In response to pricing wars in the personal computer market, Apple had to quickly reduce the price of its signature Macintosh computers—reducing prices more quickly than it could reduce its costs. As a result, its gross profit rate fell from 44 percent in 1992 to 40 percent in 1993. Though the drop of 4 percent seems small, its impact on the bottom line caused Apple's share price to drop from $57 per share to $27.50 in just six weeks.

As another example, Debenham (GBR), the second largest department store in the United Kingdom, experienced a 14 percentage share price decline. The cause? Markdowns on slow-moving inventory reduced its gross margin.

On the positive side, an increase in the gross profit rate provides a positive signal to the market. For example, just a 1 percent boost in Dr. Pepper's (USA) gross profit rate cheered the market, indicating the company was able to avoid the squeeze of increased commodity costs by raising its prices.

Sources: Alison Smith, "Debenham's Shares Hit by Warning," *Financial Times* (July 24, 2002), p. 21; and D. Kardous, "Higher Pricing Helps Boost Dr. Pepper Snapple's Net," *Wall Street Journal Online* (June 5, 2008).

RETAIL INVENTORY METHOD

Accounting for inventory in a retail operation presents several challenges. Retailers with certain types of inventory may use the specific identification method to value their inventories. Such an approach makes sense when a retailer holds significant individual inventory units, such as automobiles, pianos, or fur coats. However, imagine attempting to use such an approach at **Carrefour** (FRA), **Debenham** (GBR), or **Bloomingdale's** (USA)—high-volume retailers and supermarkets that have many different types of merchandise. It would be extremely difficult to determine the cost of each sale, to enter cost codes on the tickets, to change the codes to reflect declines in value of the merchandise, to allocate costs such as transportation, and so on.

6 LEARNING OBJECTIVE

Determine ending inventory by applying the retail inventory method.

An alternative is to compile the inventories at retail prices. For most retailers, an observable pattern between cost and price exists. The retailer can then use a formula to convert retail prices to cost. This method is called the **retail inventory method**. **It requires that the retailer keep a record of (1) the total cost and retail value of goods purchased, (2) the total cost and retail value of the goods available for sale, and (3) the sales for the period.** Use of the retail inventory method is very common. For example, **Carrefour** supermarkets uses the retail inventory method, as does **Wal-Mart** (USA) and **Debenham** (GBR).

Here is how it works at a company like Debenham. Beginning with the retail value of the goods available for sale, Debenham deducts the sales for the period. This calculation determines an estimated inventory (goods on hand) at retail. It next computes the **cost-to-retail ratio** for all goods. The formula for this computation is to divide the total goods available for sale at cost by the total goods available at retail price. Finally, to obtain ending inventory at cost, Debenham applies the cost-to-retail ratio to the ending inventory valued at retail. Illustration 9-17 shows the retail inventory method calculations for Debenham using assumed data.

	Cost	Retail
Beginning inventory	£14,000	£ 20,000
Purchases	63,000	90,000
Goods available for sale	£77,000	110,000
Deduct: Sales		85,000
Ending inventory, at retail		£ 25,000

Ratio of cost to retail (£77,000 ÷ £110,000) = 70%
Ending inventory at cost (70% of £25,000) = £17,500

ILLUSTRATION 9-17
Retail Inventory Method Calculations

There are different versions of the retail inventory method. These include the **conventional** method (based on LCNRV) and the **cost** method. Regardless of which version a company uses, tax authorities, various retail associations, and the accounting profession all sanction use of the retail inventory method. One of its advantages is that a company like Debenham can approximate the inventory balance **without a physical count**. However, to avoid a potential overstatement of the inventory, Debenham makes periodic inventory counts. Such counts are especially important in retail operations where loss due to shoplifting or breakage is common.

The retail inventory method is particularly useful for any type of interim report because such reports usually need a fairly quick and reliable measure of the inventory. Also, insurance adjusters often use this method to estimate losses from fire, flood, or other type of casualty. This method also acts as a **control device** because a company will have to explain any discrepancies between the results of the retail method and a physical count at the end of the year. Finally, the retail method **expedites the physical inventory count** at the end of the year. The crew taking the physical inventory need record only the retail price of each item. The crew does not need to look up each item's invoice cost, thereby saving time and expense.

Retail-Method Concepts

The amounts shown in the "Retail" column of Illustration 9-17 (page 413) represent the original retail prices, assuming no price changes. In practice, though, retailers frequently mark up or mark down the prices they charge buyers.

For retailers, the term markup means an additional markup of the original retail price. (In another context, such as the gross profit discussion on pages 409–412, we often think of markup on the basis of cost.) Markup cancellations are decreases in prices of merchandise that the retailer had marked up above the original retail price.

In a competitive market, retailers often need to use markdowns, which are decreases in the original sales prices. Such cuts in sales prices may be necessary because of a decrease in the general level of prices, special sales, soiled or damaged goods, overstocking, and market competition. Markdowns are common in retailing these days. Markdown cancellations occur when the markdowns are later offset by increases in the prices of goods that the retailer had marked down—such as after a one-day sale. Neither a markup cancellation nor a markdown cancellation can exceed the original markup or markdown.

To illustrate these concepts, assume that Designer Clothing Store recently purchased 100 dress shirts from Marroway, Inc. The cost for these shirts was €1,500, or €15 a shirt. Designer Clothing established the selling price on these shirts at €30 a shirt. The shirts were selling quickly, so the manager added a markup of €5 per shirt. This markup made the price too high for customers, and sales slowed. The manager then reduced the price to €32. At this point, we would say that the shirts at Designer Clothing have had a markup of €5 and a markup cancellation of €3.

A month later, the manager marked down the remaining shirts to a sales price of €23. At this point, an additional markup cancellation of €2 has taken place, and a €7 markdown has occurred. If the manager later increases the price of the shirts to €24, a markdown cancellation of €1 would occur.

Retail Inventory Method with Markups and Markdowns—Conventional Method

Retailers use markup and markdown concepts in developing the proper inventory valuation at the end of the accounting period. To obtain the appropriate inventory figures, companies must give proper treatment to markups, markup cancellations, markdowns, and markdown cancellations.

To illustrate the different possibilities, consider the data for In-Fusion Inc., shown in Illustration 9-18. In-Fusion can calculate its ending inventory at cost under two assumptions, A and B. (We'll explain the reasons for the two later.)

Assumption A: Computes a cost ratio after markups (and markup cancellations) but before markdowns.

Assumption B: Computes a cost ratio after both markups and markdowns (and cancellations).

ILLUSTRATION 9-18
Retail Inventory Method
with Markups and
Markdowns

	Cost	Retail
Beginning inventory	€ 500	€ 1,000
Purchases (net)	20,000	35,000
Markups		3,000
Markup cancellations		1,000
Markdowns		2,500
Markdown cancellations		2,000
Sales (net)		25,000

IN-FUSION INC.

	Cost	Retail
Beginning inventory	€ 500	€ 1,000
Purchases (net)	20,000	35,000
Merchandise available for sale	20,500	36,000
Add: Markups	€3,000	
Less: Markup cancellations	1,000	
Net markups		2,000
	20,500	38,000

(A) Cost-to-retail ratio $= \dfrac{€20,500}{€38,000} = 53.9\%$

Deduct:		
Markdowns	2,500	
Less: Markdown cancellations	(2,000)	
Net markdowns		500
	€20,500	37,500

(B) Cost-to-retail ratio $= \dfrac{€20,500}{€37,500} = 54.7\%$

Deduct: Sales (net)		25,000
Ending inventory, at retail		€12,500

The computations for In-Fusion are:

Ending Inventory at Retail × Cost Ratio = Value of Ending Inventory

Assumption A: €12,500 × 53.9% = €6,737.50
Assumption B: €12,500 × 54.7% = €6,837.50

The question becomes: Which assumption and which percentage should In-Fusion use to compute the ending inventory valuation? The answer depends on which retail inventory method In-Fusion chooses.

One approach uses only Assumption A (a cost ratio using markups but not markdowns). It approximates the lower-of-average-cost-or-net realizable value. We will refer to this approach as the conventional retail inventory method or the **LCNRV**.

To understand why this method considers only the markups, not the markdowns, in the cost percentage, you must understand how a retail business operates. A markup normally indicates an increase in the sales value of the item. On the other hand, a markdown means a decline in the utility of that item. Therefore, to approximate the LCNRV, we would consider markdowns a current loss and so would not include them in calculating the cost-to-retail ratio. Omitting the markdowns would make the cost-to-retail ratio lower, which leads to an approximate LCNRV.

An example will make the distinction between the two methods clear. Assume In-Fusion purchased two items for €5 apiece; the original sales price was €10 each. One item was subsequently marked down to €2. Assuming no sales for the period, **if markdowns are considered** in the cost-to-retail ratio (Assumption B—the **cost method**), we compute the ending inventory in the following way.

ILLUSTRATION 9-19
Retail Inventory Method Including Markdowns—Cost Method

Markdowns Included in Cost-to-Retail Ratio		
	Cost	Retail
Purchases	€10	€20
Deduct: Markdowns (€10 − €2)		8
Ending inventory, at retail		€12

$$\text{Cost-to-retail ratio} = \frac{€10}{€12} = 83.3\%$$

Ending inventory at cost (€12 × .833) = €10

This approach (the cost method) reflects an **average cost** of the two items of the commodity without considering the loss on the one item. It values ending inventory at €10.

If markdowns are not considered in the cost-to-retail ratio (Assumption A—the **conventional retail method**), we compute the ending inventory as follows.

ILLUSTRATION 9-20
Retail Inventory Method Excluding Markdowns—Conventional Method (LCNRV)

Markdowns Not Included in Cost-to-Retail Ratio		
	Cost	Retail
Purchases	€10	€20

$$\text{Cost-to-retail ratio} = \frac{€10}{€20} = 50\%$$

Deduct: Markdowns		8
Ending inventory, at retail		€12

Ending inventory at cost (€12 × .50) = €6

Under this approach (the conventional retail method, in which markdowns are **not considered**), ending inventory would be €6. The inventory valuation of €6 reflects two inventory items, one inventoried at €5 and the other at €1. It reflects the fact that In-Fusion reduced the sales price from €10 to €2, and reduced the cost from €5 to €1.[14]

To approximate the LCNRV, In-Fusion must establish the **cost-to-retail ratio**. It does this by dividing the cost of goods available for sale by the sum of the original retail price of these goods plus the net markups. This calculation excludes markdowns and markdown cancellations. Illustration 9-21 shows the basic format for the retail inventory method using the LCNRV approach along with the In-Fusion Inc. information.

Because an averaging effect occurs, an exact LCNRV inventory valuation is ordinarily not obtained, but an adequate approximation can be achieved. In contrast, adding net markups **and** deducting net markdowns yields **approximate cost**.

---

[14]This figure is not really net realizable value, but it is net realizable value less the normal margin that is allowed. In other words, the sales price of the goods written down is €2, but subtracting a normal margin of 50 percent (€5 cost ÷ €10 price), the figure becomes €1. To the extent the profit margin approximates expected costs to complete and sell an item, this measure approximates net realizable value.

IN-FUSION INC.		
	Cost	Retail
Beginning inventory	€ 500	€ 1,000
Purchases (net)	20,000	35,000
Totals	20,500	36,000
Add: Net markups		
Markups	€3,000	
Markup cancellations	(1,000)	2,000
Totals	€20,500 ⟷	38,000
Deduct: Net markdowns		
Markdowns	2,500	
Markdown cancellations	(2,000)	500
Sales price of goods available		37,500
Deduct: Sales (net)		25,000
Ending inventory, at retail		€12,500

$$\text{Cost-to-retail ratio} = \frac{\text{Cost of goods available}}{\text{Original retail price of goods available, plus net markups}}$$

$$= \frac{€20,500}{€38,000} = 53.9\%$$

Ending inventory at LCNRV (53.9% × €12,500) = €6,737.50

ILLUSTRATION 9-21
Comprehensive
Conventional Retail
Inventory Method
Format

Special Items Relating to Retail Method

The retail inventory method becomes more complicated when we consider such items as freight-in, purchase returns and allowances, and purchase discounts. In the retail method, we treat such items as follows.

- **Freight costs** are part of the purchase cost.
- **Purchase returns** are ordinarily considered as a reduction of the price at both cost and retail.
- **Purchase discounts and allowances** usually are considered as a reduction of the cost of purchases.

In short, the treatment for the items affecting the cost column of the retail inventory approach follows the computation for cost of goods available for sale.[15]

Note also that **sales returns and allowances** are considered as proper adjustments to gross sales. However, when sales are recorded gross, companies do not recognize **sales discounts**. To adjust for the sales discount account in such a situation would provide an ending inventory figure at retail that would be overvalued.

In addition, a number of special items require careful analysis:

- **Transfers-in** from another department are reported in the same way as purchases from an outside enterprise.
- **Normal shortages** (breakage, damage, theft, shrinkage) should reduce the retail column because these goods are no longer available for sale. Such costs are reflected in the selling price because a certain amount of shortage is considered normal in a retail enterprise. As a result, companies do not consider this amount in computing the cost-to-retail percentage. Rather, to arrive at ending inventory at retail, they show normal shortages as a deduction similar to sales.
- **Abnormal shortages**, on the other hand, are deducted from both the cost and retail columns and reported as a special inventory amount or as a loss. To do otherwise distorts the cost-to-retail ratio and overstates ending inventory.

---

[15]When the purchase allowance is not reflected by a reduction in the selling price, no adjustment is made to the retail column.

• **Employee discounts** (given to employees to encourage loyalty, better performance, and so on) are deducted from the retail column in the same way as sales. These discounts should not be considered in the cost-to-retail percentage because they do not reflect an overall change in the selling price.[16]

Illustration 9-22 shows some of these concepts. The company, Extreme Sport Apparel, determines its inventory using the conventional retail inventory method.

ILLUSTRATION 9-22
Conventional Retail
Inventory Method—
Special Items Included

EXTREME SPORT APPAREL		
	Cost	Retail
Beginning inventory	€ 1,000	€ 1,800
Purchases	30,000	60,000
Freight-in	600	—
Purchase returns	(1,500)	(3,000)
Totals	30,100	58,800
Net markups		9,000
Abnormal shortage	(1,200)	(2,000)
Totals	€28,900 ⟷	65,800
Deduct:		
Net markdowns		1,400
Sales	€36,000	
Sales returns	(900)	35,100
Employee discounts		800
Normal shortage		1,300
Ending inventory, at retail		€27,200

$$\text{Cost-to-retail ratio} = \frac{€28,900}{€65,800} = 43.9\%$$

Ending inventory at LCNRV (43.9% × €27,200) = €11,940.80

Evaluation of Retail Inventory Method

Companies like **Carrefour** (FRA), **Marks and Spencer** (GBR), or your local department store use the retail inventory method of computing inventory for the following reasons: (1) to permit the computation of net income without a physical count of inventory, (2) as a control measure in determining inventory shortages, (3) in regulating quantities of merchandise on hand, and (4) for insurance information.

One characteristic of the retail inventory method is that it **has an averaging effect on varying rates of gross profit**. This can be problematic when companies apply the method to an entire business, where rates of gross profit vary among departments. There is no allowance for possible distortion of results because of such differences. Companies refine the retail method under such conditions by computing inventory separately by departments or by classes of merchandise with similar gross profits. In addition, the reliability of this method assumes that the distribution of items in inventory is similar to the "mix" in the total goods available for sale.

PRESENTATION AND ANALYSIS

Presentation of Inventories

LEARNING OBJECTIVE 7

Explain how to report and analyze inventory.

Accounting standards require financial statement disclosure of the following items related to inventories:

1. The accounting policies adopted in measuring inventories, including the cost formula used (weighted-average, FIFO).

---

[16]Note that if employee sales are recorded gross, no adjustment is necessary for employee discounts in the retail column.

2. The total carrying amount of inventories and the carrying amount in classifications (common classifications of inventories are merchandise, production supplies, raw materials, work in progress, and finished goods).

3. The carrying amount of inventories carried at fair value less costs to sell.

4. The amount of inventories recognized as an expense during the period.

5. The amount of any write-down of inventories recognized as an expense in the period and the amount of any reversal of write-downs recognized as a reduction of expense in the period.

6. The circumstances or events that led to the reversal of a write-down of inventories.

7. The carrying amount of inventories pledged as security for liabilities, if any.

This information can be disclosed in the statement of financial position or in a separate schedule in the notes. The relative mix of raw materials, work in process, and finished goods helps in assessing liquidity and in computing the stage of inventory completion. Significant or unusual financing arrangements relating to inventories may require note disclosure. Examples include transactions with related parties, product financing arrangements, firm purchase commitments, and pledging of inventories as collateral. **[10]** For example, the annual report of **Lectra SA** (FRA) contains the following disclosures.

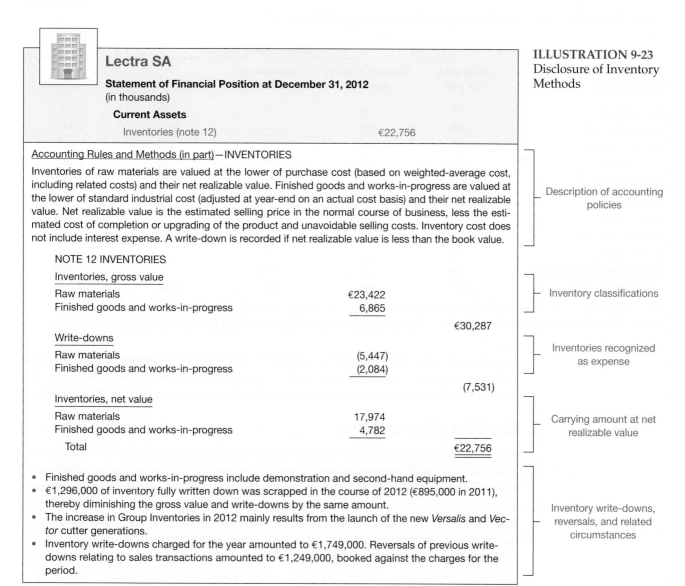

ILLUSTRATION 9-23
Disclosure of Inventory Methods

Lectra SA

Statement of Financial Position at December 31, 2012
(in thousands)

Current Assets

Inventories (note 12)   €22,756

Accounting Rules and Methods (in part)—INVENTORIES

Inventories of raw materials are valued at the lower of purchase cost (based on weighted-average cost, including related costs) and their net realizable value. Finished goods and works-in-progress are valued at the lower of standard industrial cost (adjusted at year-end on an actual cost basis) and their net realizable value. Net realizable value is the estimated selling price in the normal course of business, less the estimated cost of completion or upgrading of the product and unavoidable selling costs. Inventory cost does not include interest expense. A write-down is recorded if net realizable value is less than the book value.

Description of accounting policies

NOTE 12 INVENTORIES

Inventories, gross value		
Raw materials	€23,422	
Finished goods and works-in-progress	6,865	
		€30,287
Write-downs		
Raw materials	(5,447)	
Finished goods and works-in-progress	(2,084)	
		(7,531)
Inventories, net value		
Raw materials	17,974	
Finished goods and works-in-progress	4,782	
Total		€22,756

Inventory classifications

Inventories recognized as expense

Carrying amount at net realizable value

- Finished goods and works-in-progress include demonstration and second-hand equipment.
- €1,296,000 of inventory fully written down was scrapped in the course of 2012 (€895,000 in 2011), thereby diminishing the gross value and write-downs by the same amount.
- The increase in Group Inventories in 2012 mainly results from the launch of the new *Versalis* and *Vector* cutter generations.
- Inventory write-downs charged for the year amounted to €1,749,000. Reversals of previous write-downs relating to sales transactions amounted to €1,249,000, booked against the charges for the period.

Inventory write-downs, reversals, and related circumstances

If Lectra changes the method of pricing any of its inventory elements, it must report a change in accounting principle. For example, if Lectra changes its method of accounting for its finished goods from weighted-average to FIFO, it should separately report this change, along with the effect on income, in the current and prior periods (as discussed in Chapter 22). Changes in accounting principle require an explanatory paragraph in the auditor's report describing the change in method.

As another example of inventory disclosure practices, **Pernod Ricard** (FRA) reported its inventories in its annual report as follows (note the "trade practice" followed in classifying some long-cycle inventories among the current assets).

ILLUSTRATION 9-24
Disclosure of Trade Practice in Valuing Inventories

Pernod Ricard

Current assets

Inventories (Note 13)   €3,715

13. Inventories

Inventories are measured at the lowest of either cost (acquisition cost and cost of production, including indirect production overheads) or net realisable value. Net realisable value is the selling price less the estimated costs of completion and sale of the inventories. Most inventories are valued using the weighted average cost method. The cost of long-cycle inventories is calculated using a single method which includes distilling and ageing maturing costs but excludes finance costs. These inventories are classified in current assets, although a substantial part remains in inventory for more than one year before being sold in order to undergo the ageing process used for certain Wines and Spirits.

The breakdown of inventories and work-in-progress at the balance sheet date is as follows:

In euro million	Beginning of year	Movements in the year			End of year
		Changes in gross amounts	Changes in impairment	Other movements	
Raw materials	135	18	—	(3)	150
Work-in-progress	2,836	379	—	(254)	2,961
Goods in inventory	399	52	—	(38)	413
Finished products	253	15	—	(10)	258
GROSS VALUE	**3,623**	**464**	**—**	**(305)**	**3,782**
Raw materials	(12)	—	(3)	0	(15)
Work-in-progress	(20)	—	(6)	3	(23)
Goods in inventory	(12)	—	(2)	(1)	(15)
Finished products	(15)	—	0	1	(14)
VALUATION ALLOWANCES	**(59)**	**—**	**(11)**	**3**	**(67)**
INVENTORIES, NET	**3,564**	**464**	**(11)**	**(302)**	**3,715**

Other movements are mostly due to foreign currency gains and losses. At year-end, maturing inventories intended mainly for use in whisky and cognac production accounted for 84% of work-in-progress. Pernod Ricard is not significantly dependent on its suppliers.

As indicated in the prior illustration, companies also disclose inventory revaluations and valuation allowances to arrive at inventory recorded at net realizable value. Thus, for Pernod Ricard, its inventories at cost (or net realizable value) at year-end are €3,715 million.

Analysis of Inventories

The amount of inventory that a company carries can have significant economic consequences. As a result, companies must manage inventories. But, inventory management is a double-edged sword. It requires constant attention. On the one hand, management wants to stock a great variety and quantity of items. Doing so will provide customers with the greatest selection. However, such an inventory policy may incur excessive carrying costs (e.g., investment, storage, insurance, taxes, obsolescence, and damage). On the other hand, low inventory levels lead to stockouts, lost sales, and disgruntled customers.

Using financial ratios helps companies to chart a middle course between these two dangers. Common ratios used in the management and evaluation of inventory levels are inventory turnover and a related measure, average days to sell the inventory.

Inventory Turnover

The **inventory turnover** measures the number of times on average a company sells the inventory during the period. It measures the liquidity of the inventory. To compute inventory turnover, divide the cost of goods sold by the average inventory on hand during the period.

Barring seasonal factors, analysts compute average inventory from beginning and ending inventory balances. For example, in its 2013 annual report, **Tate & Lyle plc** (GBR) reported a beginning inventory of £450 million, an ending inventory of £510 million, and cost of goods sold of £2,066 million for the year. Illustration 9-25 shows the inventory turnover formula and Tate & Lyle's 2013 ratio computation.

$$\text{Inventory Turnover} = \frac{\text{Cost of Goods Sold}}{\text{Average Inventory}} = \frac{£2,066}{(£450 + £510)/2} = 4.30 \text{ times}$$

ILLUSTRATION 9-25
Inventory Turnover

Average Days to Sell Inventory

A variant of the inventory turnover ratio is the **average days to sell inventory**. This measure represents the average number of days' sales for which a company has inventory on hand. For example, the inventory turnover for **Tate & Lyle** of 4.30 times divided into 365 is approximately 85 days.

There are typical levels of inventory in every industry. However, companies that keep their inventory at lower levels with higher turnovers than those of their competitors, and that still can satisfy customer needs, are generally the most successful.

 # GLOBAL ACCOUNTING INSIGHTS

INVENTORIES

In most cases, IFRS and U.S. GAAP related to inventory are the same. The major differences are that IFRS prohibits the use of the LIFO cost flow assumption and records market in the LCNRV differently.

Relevant Facts

Following are the key similarities and differences between U.S. GAAP and IFRS related to inventories.

Similarities

- U.S. GAAP and IFRS account for inventory acquisitions at historical cost and evaluate inventory for lower-of-cost-or-net realizable value (market) subsequent to acquisition.

- Who owns the goods—goods in transit, consigned goods, special sales agreements—as well as the costs to include in inventory are essentially accounted for the same under U.S. GAAP and IFRS.

Differences

- U.S. GAAP provides more detailed guidelines in inventory accounting. The requirements for accounting for and reporting inventories are more principles-based under IFRS.

- A major difference between U.S. GAAP and IFRS relates to the LIFO cost flow assumption. U.S. GAAP permits the use of LIFO for inventory valuation. IFRS prohibits its use. FIFO and average-cost are the only two acceptable cost flow assumptions permitted under IFRS. Both sets of standards permit specific identification where appropriate.

- In the lower-of-cost-or-market test for inventory valuation, U.S. GAAP defines market as replacement cost subject to the constraints of net realizable value (the ceiling) and net realizable value less a normal markup (the floor). IFRS defines market as net realizable value and does not use a ceiling or a floor to determine market.

- Under U.S. GAAP, if inventory is written down under the lower-of-cost-or-market valuation, the new basis is now considered its cost. As a result, the inventory may not be written up back to its original cost in a subsequent period.

Under IFRS, the write-down may be reversed in a subsequent period up to the amount of the previous write-down. Both the write-down and any subsequent reversal should be reported on the income statement.

- IFRS requires both biological assets and agricultural produce at the point of harvest to be reported at net realizable value. U.S. GAAP does not require companies to account for all biological assets in the same way. Furthermore, these assets generally are not reported at net realizable value. Disclosure requirements also differ between the two sets of standards.

About the Numbers

Presented below is a disclosure under U.S. GAAP related to inventories for **Fortune Brands, Inc.** (USA), which reflects application of U.S. GAAP to its inventories.

Fortune Brands, Inc.

Current assets

Inventories (Note 2)

Leaf tobacco	$ 563,424,000
Bulk whiskey	232,759,000
Other raw materials, supplies and work in process	238,906,000
Finished products	658,326,000
	$1,693,415,000

Note 2: Inventories

Inventories are priced at the lower of cost (average; first-in, first-out; and minor amounts at last-in, first-out) or market. In accordance with generally recognized trade practice, the leaf tobacco and bulk whiskey inventories are classified as current assets, although part of such inventories due to the duration of the aging process, ordinarily will not be sold within one year.

On the Horizon

One convergence issue that will be difficult to resolve relates to the use of the LIFO cost flow assumption. As indicated, IFRS specifically prohibits its use. Conversely, the LIFO cost flow assumption is widely used in the United States because of its favorable tax advantages. In addition, many argue that LIFO from a financial reporting point of view provides a better matching of current costs against revenue and therefore enables companies to compute a more realistic income.

SUMMARY OF LEARNING OBJECTIVES

1 **Describe and apply the lower-of-cost-or-net realizable value rule.** If inventory declines in value below its original cost, for whatever reason, a company should write down the inventory to reflect this loss. The general rule is to abandon the historical cost principle when the future utility (revenue-producing ability) of the asset drops below its original cost.

2 **Explain when companies value inventories at net realizable value.** Companies value inventory at net realizable value when cost is difficult to determine, the items are readily marketable at quoted market prices, and units of product are interchangeable. Three common situations in which net realizable value is the general rule for valuing inventory are (1) agricultural inventory (including biological assets and agricultural produce), (2) minerals and mineral products, and (3) commodities held by broker-traders.

3 **Explain when companies use the relative standalone sales value method to value inventories.** When a company purchases a group of varying units at a single lump-sum price—a so-called basket purchase—the company may allocate the total purchase price to the individual items on the basis of relative standalone sales value.

4 **Discuss accounting issues related to purchase commitments.** Accounting for purchase commitments is controversial. Some argue that companies should report purchase commitment contracts as assets and liabilities at the time the contract is signed. Others believe that recognition at the delivery date is most appropriate. If a company has a firm purchase commitment and the price falls below the original cost, a loss should be recognized. IFRS refers to this situation as an onerous contract.

5 **Determine ending inventory by applying the gross profit method.** Companies follow these steps to determine ending inventory by the gross profit method. (1) Compute the gross profit percentage on selling price. (2) Compute gross profit by multiplying net sales by the gross profit percentage. (3) Compute cost of goods sold by subtracting gross profit from net sales. (4) Compute ending inventory by subtracting cost of goods sold from total goods available for sale.

6 **Determine ending inventory by applying the retail inventory method.** Companies follow these steps to determine ending inventory by the conventional retail method. (1) To estimate inventory at retail, deduct the sales for the period from the retail value of the goods available for sale. (2) To find the cost-to-retail ratio for all goods passing through a department or firm, divide the total goods available for sale at cost by the total goods available at retail. (3) Convert the inventory valued at retail to approximate cost by applying the cost-to-retail ratio.

7 **Explain how to report and analyze inventory.** IFRS inventory disclosure requirements are presented in the numbered list on pages 418–419, with examples in Illustrations 9-23 and 9-24. Accounting standards also require the consistent application of costing methods from one period to another. Common ratios used in the management and evaluation of inventory levels are inventory turnover and average days to sell the inventory.

IFRS AUTHORITATIVE LITERATURE

Authoritative Literature References

[1] International Accounting Standard 2, *Inventories* (London, U.K.: International Accounting Standards Committee Foundation, 2003), par. 6.

[2] International Accounting Standard 2, *Inventories* (London, U.K.: International Accounting Standards Committee Foundation, 2003), paras. 28–29.

[3] International Accounting Standard 2, *Inventories* (London, U.K.: International Accounting Standards Committee Foundation, 2003), par. 29.

[4] International Accounting Standard 2, *Inventories* (London, U.K.: International Accounting Standards Committee Foundation, 2003), par. 33.

[5] International Accounting Standard 2, *Inventories* (London, U.K.: International Accounting Standards Committee Foundation, 2003), par. 21.

[6] International Accounting Standard 41, *Agriculture* (London, U.K.: International Accounting Standards Committee Foundation, 2001).

[7] International Accounting Standard 2, *Inventories* (London, U.K.: International Accounting Standards Committee Foundation, 2003), paras. 3–4.

[8] International Accounting Standard 37, *Provisions, Contingent Liabilities and Contingent Assets* (London, U.K.: International Accounting Standards Committee Foundation, 2001), paras. 66–68.

[9] Conceptual Framework for Financial Reporting (London, U.K.: International Accounting Standards Committee Foundation, 2010), par. 4.46.

[10] International Accounting Standard 2, *Inventories* (London, U.K.: International Accounting Standards Committee Foundation, 2001), par. 36.

QUESTIONS

1. Where there is evidence that the utility of inventory goods, as part of their disposal in the ordinary course of business, will be less than cost, what is the proper accounting treatment?

2. Why are inventories valued at the lower-of-cost-or-net realizable value (LCNRV)? What are the arguments against the use of the LCNRV method of valuing inventories?

3. What approaches may be employed in applying the LCNRV procedure? Which approach is normally used and why?

4. In some instances, accounting principles require a departure from valuing inventories at cost alone. Determine the proper unit inventory price in the following cases.

	Cases				
	1	2	3	4	5
Cost	€15.90	€16.10	€15.90	€15.90	€15.90
Sales value	14.80	19.20	15.20	10.40	17.80
Estimated cost to complete	1.50	1.90	1.65	.80	1.00
Estimated cost to sell	.50	.70	.55	.40	.60

5. What method(s) might be used in the accounts to record a loss due to a price decline in the inventories? Discuss.

6. What factors might call for inventory valuation at net realizable value?

7. Briefly describe the valuation of (a) biological assets and (b) agricultural produce.

8. Under what circumstances is relative standalone sales value an appropriate basis for determining the price assigned to inventory?

9. At December 31, 2015, Ashley Co. has outstanding purchase commitments for purchase of 150,000 gallons, at £6.20 per gallon, of a raw material to be used in its manufacturing process. The company prices its raw material inventory at cost or net realizable value, whichever is lower. Assuming that the market price as of December 31, 2015, is £5.90, how would you treat this situation in the accounts?

10. What are the major uses of the gross profit method?

11. Distinguish between gross profit as a percentage of cost and gross profit as a percentage of sales price. Convert the following gross profit percentages based on cost to gross profit percentages based on sales price: 25% and 33⅓%. Convert the following gross profit percentages based on sales price to gross profit percentages based on cost: 33⅓% and 60%.

12. Adriana Co. with annual net sales of $5 million maintains a markup of 25% based on cost. Adriana's expenses average 15% of net sales. What is Adriana's gross profit and net profit in dollars?

13. A fire destroys all of the merchandise of Assante Company on February 10, 2015. The following is information compiled up to the date of the fire.

Inventory, January 1, 2015	$ 400,000
Sales to February 10, 2015	1,950,000
Purchases to February 10, 2015	1,140,000
Freight-in to February 10, 2015	60,000
Rate of gross profit on selling price	40%

What is the approximate inventory on February 10, 2015?

14. What conditions must exist for the retail inventory method to provide valid results?

15. The conventional retail inventory method yields results that are essentially the same as those yielded by the LCNRV method. Explain. Prepare an illustration of how the retail inventory method reduces inventory to market.

16. (a) Determine the ending inventory under the conventional retail method for the furniture department of Mayron Department Stores from the following data (amounts in thousands). (Round to nearest percent.)

	Cost	Retail
Inventory, Jan. 1	¥ 149,000	¥ 283,500
Purchases	1,400,000	2,160,000
Freight-in	70,000	
Markups, net		92,000
Markdowns, net		48,000
Sales		2,175,000

(b) If the results of a physical inventory indicated an inventory at retail of ¥295,000, what inferences would you draw?

17. Tesco (GBR) reported inventory in its statement of financial position as follows:

Inventories   £2,430,000,000

What additional disclosures might be necessary to present the inventory fairly?

18. Of what significance is inventory turnover to a retail store?

19. Briefly describe some of the similarities and differences between U.S. GAAP and IFRS with respect to the accounting for inventories.

20. LaTour Inc. is based in France and prepares its financial statements in accordance with IFRS. In 2015, it reported cost of goods sold of €578 million and average inventory of €154 million. Briefly discuss how analysis of LaTour's inventory turnover (and comparisons to a company using U.S. GAAP) might be affected by differences in inventory accounting between IFRS and U.S. GAAP.

21. Reed Pentak, a finance major, has been following globalization and made the following observation concerning accounting convergence: "I do not see many obstacles concerning development of a single accounting standard for inventories." Prepare a response to Reed to explain the main obstacle to achieving convergence in the area of inventory accounting.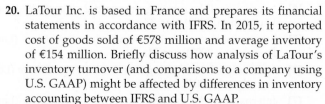

BRIEF EXERCISES

1 **BE9-1** Presented below is information related to Rembrandt Inc.'s inventory.

(per unit)	Skis	Boots	Parkas
Historical cost	$190.00	$106.00	$53.00
Selling price	212.00	145.00	73.75
Cost to sell	19.00	8.00	2.50
Cost to complete	32.00	29.00	21.25

Determine the following: (a) the net realizable value for each item, and (b) the carrying value of each item under LCNRV.

1 **BE9-2** Floyd Corporation has the following four items in its ending inventory.

Item	Cost	Net Realizable Value (NRV)
Jokers	€2,000	€2,100
Penguins	5,000	4,950
Riddlers	4,400	4,625
Scarecrows	3,200	3,830

Determine (a) the LCNRV for each item, and (b) the amount of write-down, if any, using (1) an item-by-item LCNRV evaluation and (2) a total-group LCNRV evaluation.

1 **BE9-3** Kumar Inc. uses a perpetual inventory system. At January 1, 2015, inventory was R$214,000,000 at both cost and net realizable value. At December 31, 2015, the inventory was R$286,000,000 at cost and R$265,000,000 at net realizable value. Prepare the necessary December 31 entry under (a) the cost-of-goods-sold method and (b) the loss method.

2 **BE9-4** Keyser's Fleece Inc. holds a drove of sheep. Keyser shears the sheep on a semiannual basis and then sells the harvested wool into the specialty knitting market. Keyser has the following information related to the shearing sheep at January 1, 2015, and during the first six months of 2015.

Shearing sheep	
Carrying value (equal to net realizable value), January 1, 2015	€74,000
Change in fair value due to growth and price changes	4,700
Change in fair value due to harvest	(575)
Wool harvested during the first 6 months (at NRV)	9,000

Prepare the journal entry(ies) for Keyser's biological asset (shearing sheep) for the first six months of 2015.

2 **BE9-5** Refer to the data in BE9-4 for Keyser's Fleece Inc. Prepare the journal entries for (a) the wool harvested in the first six months of 2015, and (b) when the wool harvested is sold for €10,500 in July 2015.

3 **BE9-6** Benke Inc. buys 1,000 computer game CDs from a distributor who is discontinuing those games. The purchase price for the lot is ¥8,000. Benke will group the CDs into three price categories for resale, as indicated below (yen in thousands).

Group	No. of CDs	Price per CD
1	100	¥ 5
2	800	10
3	100	15

Determine the cost per CD for each group, using the relative standalone sales value method.

4 **BE9-7** Kemper Company signed a long-term, non-cancelable purchase commitment with a major supplier to purchase raw materials in 2016 at a cost of $1,000,000. At December 31, 2015, the raw materials to be purchased have a fair value of $950,000. Prepare any necessary December 31 entry.

4 **BE9-8** Use the information for Kemper Company from BE9-7. In 2016, Kemper paid $1,000,000 to obtain the raw materials which were worth $950,000. Prepare the entry to record the purchase.

5 **BE9-9** Fosbre Corporation's April 30 inventory was destroyed by fire. January 1 inventory was €150,000, and purchases for January through April totaled €500,000. Sales for the same period were €700,000. Fosbre's normal gross profit percentage is 35% on sales. Using the gross profit method, estimate Fosbre's April 30 inventory that was destroyed by fire.

6 **BE9-10** Boyne Inc. had beginning inventory of $12,000 at cost and $20,000 at retail. Net purchases were $120,000 at cost and $170,000 at retail. Net markups were $10,000; net markdowns were $7,000; and sales were $147,000. Compute ending inventory at cost using the conventional retail method.

7 **BE9-11** In its 2013 annual report, Inditex (ESP) reported inventory of €1,581.297 on January 31, 2013, and €1,297.009 on January 31, 2012. For 2013, cost of sales was €6,486.825 and net sales were €15,946.143 (all amounts in millions). Compute Inditex's inventory turnover and average days to sell inventory for fiscal year 2013.

EXERCISES

1 **E9-1 (LCNRV)** The inventory of Oheto Company on December 31, 2015, consists of the following items.

Part No.	Quantity	Cost per Unit	Net Realizable Value per Unit
110	600	$ 95	$100
111	1,000	60	52
112	500	80	76
113	200	170	180
120	400	205	208
121ᵃ	1,600	16	1
122	300	240	235

ᵃPart No. 121 is obsolete and has a realizable value of $1 each as scrap.

Instructions
(a) Determine the inventory as of December 31, 2015, by the LCNRV method, applying this method to each item.
(b) Determine the inventory by the LCNRV method, applying the method to the total of the inventory.

1 **E9-2 (LCNRV)** Riegel Company uses the LCNRV method, on an individual-item basis, in pricing its inventory items. The inventory at December 31, 2015, consists of products D, E, F, G, H, and I. Relevant per-unit data for these products appear below.

	Item D	Item E	Item F	Item G	Item H	Item I
Estimated selling price	€120	€110	€95	€90	€110	€90
Cost	75	80	80	80	50	36
Cost to complete	30	30	25	35	30	30
Selling costs	10	18	10	20	10	20

Instructions
Using the LCNRV rule, determine the proper unit value for statement of financial position reporting purposes at December 31, 2015, for each of the inventory items above.

1 **E9-3 (LCNRV)** Sedato Company follows the practice of pricing its inventory at LCNRV, on an individual-item basis.

Item No.	Quantity	Cost per Unit	Estimated Selling Price	Cost to Complete and Sell
1320	1,200	$3.20	$4.50	$1.60
1333	900	2.70	3.40	1.00
1426	800	4.50	5.00	1.40
1437	1,000	3.60	3.20	1.35
1510	700	2.25	3.25	1.40
1522	500	3.00	3.90	0.80
1573	3,000	1.80	2.50	1.20
1626	1,000	4.70	6.00	1.50

Instructions
From the information above, determine the amount of Sedato Company inventory.

1 **E9-4 (LCNRV—Journal Entries)** Dover Company began operations in 2015 and determined its ending inventory at cost and at LCNRV at December 31, 2015, and December 31, 2016. This information is presented below.

	Cost	Net Realizable Value
12/31/15	£346,000	£322,000
12/31/16	410,000	390,000

Instructions

(a) Prepare the journal entries required at December 31, 2015, and December 31, 2016, assuming inventory is recorded at LCNRV and a perpetual inventory system using the cost-of-goods-sold method.

(b) Prepare journal entries required at December 31, 2015, and December 31, 2016, assuming inventory is recorded at cost and a perpetual system using the loss method.

(c) Which of the two methods above provides the higher net income in each year?

1 **E9-5 (LCNRV—Valuation Account)** Presented below is information related to Knight Enterprises.

	Jan. 31	Feb. 28	Mar. 31	Apr. 30
Inventory at cost	$15,000	$15,100	$17,000	$14,000
Inventory at LCNRV	14,500	12,600	15,600	13,300
Purchases for the month		17,000	24,000	26,500
Sales for the month		29,000	35,000	40,000

Instructions

(a) From the information, prepare (as far as the data permit) monthly income statements in columnar form for February, March, and April. The inventory is to be shown in the statement at cost; the gain or loss due to market fluctuations is to be shown separately (using a valuation account).

(b) Prepare the journal entry required to establish the valuation account at January 31 and entries to adjust it monthly thereafter.

1 **E9-6 (LCNRV—Error Effect)** LaGreca Company uses the LCNRV method, on an individual-item basis, in pricing its inventory items. The inventory at December 31, 2015, included product X. Relevant per-unit data for product X are as follows.

Estimated selling price	€50
Cost	40
Estimated selling expenses	14
Normal profit	9

There were 1,000 units of product X on hand at December 31, 2015. Product X was incorrectly valued at €38 per unit for reporting purposes. All 1,000 units were sold in 2016.

Instructions

Compute the effect of this error on net income for 2015 and the effect on net income for 2016, and indicate the direction of the misstatement for each year.

2 **E9-7 (Valuation at Net Realizable Value)** Matsumura Dairy began operations on April 1, 2015, with the purchase of 200 milking cows for ¥6,700,000. It has completed the first month of operations and has the following information for its milking cows at the end of April 2015 (yen in thousands).

Milking cows	
Change in fair value due to growth and price changes*	¥(200,000)
Decrease in fair value due to harvest	(12,000)
Milk harvested during April 2015 (at net realizable value)	72,000

*Due to a very high rate of calving in the past month, there is a glut of milking cows on the market.

Instructions

(a) Prepare the journal entries for Matsumura's biological asset (milking cows) for the month of April 2015.

(b) Prepare the journal entry for the milk harvested by Matsumura during April 2015.

(c) Matsumura sells the milk harvested in April on the local milk exchange and receives ¥74,000. Prepare the summary journal entry to record the sale of the milk.

2 **E9-8 (Valuation at Net Realizable Value)** Mt. Horeb Alpaca Co. has a herd of 150 alpaca. The alpaca are sheared once a quarter to harvest very valuable alpaca wool that is used in designer sweaters. Mt. Horeb has the following information related to the alpaca herd at July 1, 2015, and during the first quarter of the fiscal year.

Alpaca	
Carrying value (equal to net realizable value), July 1, 2015	$120,000
Change in fair value due to growth and price changes	7,700
Decrease in fair value due to harvest	(975)
Alpaca wool harvested during the first quarter (at net realizable value)	13,000

Instructions

(a) Prepare the journal entries for Mt. Horeb's biological asset (Alpaca herd) for the first quarter.
(b) Prepare the journal entries for the Alpaca wool harvested in the first quarter.
(c) Prepare the journal entry when the Alpaca wool is sold for $14,500.
(d) Briefly discuss the impact on income of the following events related to the alpaca biological asset: (1) a female alpaca gives birth to a baby alpaca, and (2) an older alpaca can only be sheared once every other quarter due to irritation caused by repeated shearing over its life.

3 **E9-9 (Relative Standalone Sales Value Method)** Larsen Realty Corporation purchased a tract of unimproved land for £55,000. This land was improved and subdivided into building lots at an additional cost of £30,000. These building lots were all of the same size. However, owing to differences in location, the lots were offered for sale at different prices as follows.

Group	No. of Lots	Price per Lot
1	9	£3,000
2	15	4,000
3	19	2,000

Operating expenses for the year allocated to this project total £18,200. Lots unsold at the year-end were as follows.

Group 1	5 lots
Group 2	7 lots
Group 3	2 lots

Instructions

At the end of the fiscal year, Larsen Realty Corporation instructs you to arrive at the net income realized on this operation to date.

2 **E9-10 (Relative Standalone Sales Value Method)** During 2015, Crawford Furniture Company purchases a carload of wicker chairs. The manufacturer sells the chairs to Crawford for a lump sum of £60,000 because it is discontinuing manufacturing operations and wishes to dispose of its entire stock. Three types of chairs are included in the carload. The three types and the estimated selling price for each are listed below.

Type	No. of Chairs	Estimated Selling Price Each
Lounge chairs	400	£90
Armchairs	300	80
Straight chairs	800	50

During 2015, Crawford sells 200 lounge chairs, 100 armchairs, and 120 straight chairs.

Instructions

What is the amount of gross profit realized during 2015? What is the amount of inventory of unsold straight chairs on December 31, 2015?

4 **E9-11 (Purchase Commitments)** Prater Company has been having difficulty obtaining key raw materials for its manufacturing process. The company therefore signed a long-term, non-cancelable purchase commitment with its largest supplier of this raw material on November 30, 2015, at an agreed price of $400,000. At December 31, 2015, the raw material had declined in price to $375,000.

Instructions

What entry would you make on December 31, 2015, to recognize these facts?

4 **E9-12 (Purchase Commitments)** At December 31, 2015, Volkan Company has outstanding non-cancelable purchase commitments for 40,000 gallons, at €3.00 per gallon, of raw material to be used in its manufacturing process. The company prices its raw material inventory at lower-of-cost-or-net realizable value.

Instructions
(a) Assuming that the market price as of December 31, 2015, is €3.30, how would this matter be treated in the accounts and statements? Explain.
(b) Assuming that the market price as of December 31, 2015, is €2.70 instead of €3.30, how would you treat this situation in the accounts and statements?
(c) Give the entry in January 2016, when the 40,000-gallon shipment is received, assuming that the situation given in (b) above existed at December 31, 2015, and that the market price in January 2016 was €2.70 per gallon. Give an explanation of your treatment.

5 **E9-13 (Gross Profit Method)** Each of the following gross profit percentages is expressed in terms of cost.

1. 20%.   **3.** 33$\frac{1}{3}$%.
2. 25%.   **4.** 50%.

Instructions
Indicate the gross profit percentage in terms of sales for each of the above.

5 **E9-14 (Gross Profit Method)** Astaire Company uses the gross profit method to estimate inventory for monthly reporting purposes. Presented below is information for the month of May.

Inventory, May 1	€ 160,000
Purchases (gross)	640,000
Freight-in	30,000
Sales	1,000,000
Sales returns	70,000
Purchase discounts	12,000

Instructions
(a) Compute the estimated inventory at May 31, assuming that the gross profit is 25% of sales.
(b) Compute the estimated inventory at May 31, assuming that the gross profit is 25% of cost.

5 **E9-15 (Gross Profit Method)** Zidek Corp. requires an estimate of the cost of goods lost by fire on March 9. Merchandise on hand on January 1 was $38,000. Purchases since January 1 were $92,000; freight-in, $3,400; purchase returns and allowances, $2,400. Sales are made at 33$\frac{1}{3}$% above cost and totaled $120,000 to March 9. Goods costing $10,900 were left undamaged by the fire; remaining goods were destroyed.

Instructions
(a) Compute the cost of goods destroyed.
(b) Compute the cost of goods destroyed, assuming that the gross profit is 33$\frac{1}{3}$% of sales.

5 **E9-16 (Gross Profit Method)** Castlevania Company lost most of its inventory in a fire in December just before the year-end physical inventory was taken. The corporation's books disclosed the following.

Beginning inventory	R$170,000	Sales	R$650,000
Purchases for the year	450,000	Sales returns	24,000
Purchase returns	30,000	Rate of gross margin on net sales	30%

Merchandise with a selling price of R$21,000 remained undamaged after the fire. Damaged merchandise with an original selling price of R$15,000 had a net realizable value of R$5,300.

Instructions
Compute the amount of the loss as a result of the fire, assuming that the corporation had no insurance coverage.

5 **E9-17 (Gross Profit Method)** You are called by Yao Ming of Rocket Co. on July 16 and asked to prepare a claim for insurance as a result of a theft that took place the night before. You suggest that an inventory be taken immediately. The following data are available (amounts in thousands).

Inventory, July 1	¥ 38,000
Purchases—goods placed in stock July 1–15	90,000
Sales—goods delivered to customers (gross)	116,000
Sales returns—goods returned to stock	4,000

Your client reports that the goods on hand on July 16 cost ¥30,500, but you determine that this figure includes goods of ¥6,000 received on a consignment basis. Your past records show that sales are made at approximately 25% over cost. Rocket's insurance covers only goods owned.

Instructions

Compute the claim against the insurance company.

5 **E9-18 (Gross Profit Method)** Sliver Lumber Company handles three principal lines of merchandise with these varying rates of gross profit on cost.

Lumber	25%
Millwork	30%
Hardware	40%

On August 18, a fire destroyed the office, lumber shed, and a considerable portion of the lumber stacked in the yard. To file a report of loss for insurance purposes, the company must know what the inventories were immediately preceding the fire. No detail or perpetual inventory records of any kind were maintained. The only pertinent information you are able to obtain are the following facts from the general ledger, which was kept in a fireproof vault and thus escaped destruction.

	Lumber	Millwork	Hardware
Inventory, Jan. 1, 2015	$ 250,000	$ 90,000	$ 45,000
Purchases to Aug. 18, 2015	1,500,000	375,000	160,000
Sales to Aug. 18, 2015	2,050,000	533,000	245,000

Instructions

Submit your estimate of the inventory amounts immediately preceding the fire.

5 **E9-19 (Gross Profit Method)** Presented below is information related to Jerrold Corporation for the current year.

Beginning inventory	£ 600,000	
Purchases	1,500,000	
Total goods available for sale		£2,100,000
Sales		2,300,000

Instructions

Compute the ending inventory, assuming that (a) gross profit is 40% of sales, (b) gross profit is 60% of cost, (c) gross profit is 35% of sales, and (d) gross profit is 25% of cost.

6 **E9-20 (Retail Inventory Method)** Presented below is information related to Luzon Company.

	Cost	Retail
Beginning inventory	R$ 58,000	R$100,000
Purchases (net)	122,000	200,000
Net markups		20,000
Net markdowns		30,000
Sales		186,000

Instructions

(a) Compute the ending inventory at retail.

(b) Compute a cost-to-retail percentage (round to two decimals) under the following conditions.

  (1) Excluding both markups and markdowns.

  (2) Excluding markups but including markdowns.

  (3) Excluding markdowns but including markups.

  (4) Including both markdowns and markups.

(c) Which of the methods in (b) above (1, 2, 3, or 4) does the following?

  (1) Provides the most conservative estimate of ending inventory.

  (2) Provides an approximation of LCNRV.

  (3) Is used in the conventional retail method.

(d) Compute ending inventory at LCNRV (round to nearest dollar).

(e) Compute cost of goods sold based on (d).

(f) Compute gross margin based on (d).

6 E9-21 (Retail Inventory Method) Presented below is information related to Kuchinsky Company.

	Cost	Retail
Beginning inventory	€ 200,000	€ 280,000
Purchases	1,425,000	2,140,000
Markups		95,000
Markup cancellations		15,000
Markdowns		35,000
Markdown cancellations		5,000
Sales		2,250,000

Instructions
Compute the inventory by the conventional retail inventory method.

6 E9-22 (Retail Inventory Method) The records of Mandy's Boutique report the following data for the month of April.

Sales	£95,000	Purchases (at cost)	£55,000
Sales returns	2,000	Purchases (at sales price)	88,000
Markups	10,000	Purchase returns (at cost)	2,000
Markup cancellations	1,500	Purchase returns (at sales price)	3,000
Markdowns	9,300	Beginning inventory (at cost)	30,000
Markdown cancellations	2,800	Beginning inventory (at sales price)	46,500
Freight on purchases	2,400		

Instructions
Compute the ending inventory by the conventional retail inventory method.

7 E9-23 (Analysis of Inventories) The financial statements of AB InBev's (BEL) 2012 annual report disclosed the following information.

(in millions)	31 December 2012	31 December 2011
Inventories	$2,500	$2,466

	Fiscal Year	
	2012	2011
Sales	$39,758	$39,046
Cost of sales	16,447	16,634
Net income	9,434	7,959

Instructions
Compute AB InBev's (a) inventory turnover and (b) average days to sell inventory for 2012.

PROBLEMS

1 P9-1 (LCNRV) Remmers Company manufactures desks. Most of the company's desks are standard models and are sold on the basis of catalog prices. At December 31, 2015, the following finished desks appear in the company's inventory.

Finished Desks	A	B	C	D
2015 catalog selling price	€450	€480	€900	€1,050
FIFO cost per inventory list 12/31/15	470	450	830	960
Estimated cost to complete and sell	50	110	260	200
2016 catalog selling price	500	540	900	1,200

The 2015 catalog was in effect through November 2015, and the 2016 catalog is effective as of December 1, 2015. All catalog prices are net of the usual discounts.

Instructions

At what amount should each of the four desks appear in the company's December 31, 2015, inventory, assuming that the company has adopted a lower-of-FIFO-cost-or-net realizable value approach for valuation of inventories on an individual-item basis?

P9-2 (LCNRV) Garcia Home Improvement Company installs replacement siding, windows, and louvered glass doors for single-family homes and condominium complexes. The company is in the process of preparing its annual financial statements for the fiscal year ended May 31, 2015. Jim Alcide, controller for Garcia, has gathered the following data concerning inventory.

At May 31, 2015, the balance in Garcia's Raw Materials Inventory account was £408,000, and Allowance to Reduce Inventory to NRV had a credit balance of £27,500. Alcide summarized the relevant inventory cost and market data at May 31, 2015, in the schedule below.

Alcide assigned Patricia Devereaux, an intern from a local college, the task of calculating the amount that should appear on Garcia's May 31, 2015, financial statements for inventory under the LCNRV rule as applied to each item in inventory. Devereaux expressed concern over departing from the historical cost principle.

	Cost	Sales Price	Net Realizable Value
Aluminum siding	£ 70,000	£ 64,000	£ 56,000
Cedar shake siding	86,000	94,000	84,800
Louvered glass doors	112,000	186,400	168,300
Thermal windows	140,000	154,800	140,000
Total	£408,000	£499,200	£449,100

Instructions

(a) (1) Determine the proper balance in Allowance to Reduce Inventory to Net Realizable Value at May 31, 2015.

   (2) For the fiscal year ended May 31, 2015, determine the amount of the gain or loss that would be recorded (using the loss method) due to the change in Allowance to Reduce Inventory to Net Realizable Value.

(b) Explain the rationale for the use of the LCNRV rule as it applies to inventories.

P9-3 (LCNRV—Cost-of-Goods-Sold and Loss) Malone Company determined its ending inventory at cost and at LCNRV at December 31, 2015, December 31, 2016, and December 31, 2017, as shown below.

	Cost	LCNRV
12/31/15	$650,000	$650,000
12/31/16	780,000	712,000
12/31/17	905,000	830,000

Instructions

(a) Prepare the journal entries required at December 31, 2016, and at December 31, 2017, assuming that a perpetual inventory system and the cost-of-goods-sold method of adjusting to LCNRV is used.

(b) Prepare the journal entries required at December 31, 2016, and at December 31, 2017, assuming that a perpetual inventory is recorded at cost and reduced to LCNRV using the loss method.

P9-4 (Valuation at Net Realizable Value) Finn Berge realized his lifelong dream of becoming a vineyard owner when he was able to purchase the Hillside Vineyard at an estate auction in August 2015 for €750,000. Finn retained the Hillside name for his new business. The purchase was risky because the growing season was coming to an end, the grapes must be harvested in the next several weeks, and Finn has limited experience in carrying off a grape harvest.

At the end of the first quarter of operations, Finn is feeling pretty good about his early results. The first harvest was a success; 300 bushels of grapes were harvested with a value of €30,000 (based on current local commodity prices at the time of harvest). And, given the strong yield from area vineyards during this season, the net realizable value of Finn's vineyard has increased by €15,000 at the end of the quarter. After storing the grapes for a short period of time, Finn was able to sell the entire harvest for €35,000.

Instructions

(a) Prepare the journal entries for the Hillside biological asset (grape vines) for the first quarter of operations (the beginning carrying and net realizable value is €750,000).

(b) Prepare the journal entry for the grapes harvested during the first quarter.

(c) Prepare the journal entry to record the sale of the grapes harvested in the first quarter.

(d) Determine the total effect on income for the quarter related to the Hillside biological asset and agricultural produce.

(e) Looking to the next growing season, Finn is doing some forecasting, based on the following two developments: (1) demand for the type of grapes his vineyard produces is expected to increase, and (2) there are new producing vineyards coming on line that will increase the supply of similar grapevines in the market. Briefly discuss how these developments are likely to affect the value of Hillside's biological assets and agricultural produce in the next growing season.

5 **P9-5 (Gross Profit Method)** Yu Company lost most of its inventory in a fire in December just before the year-end physical inventory was taken. Corporate records disclose the following (yen in thousands).

Inventory (beginning)	¥ 80,000	Sales	¥415,000
Purchases	290,000	Sales returns	21,000
Purchase returns	28,000	Gross profit % based on net selling price	35%

Merchandise with a selling price of ¥30,000 remained undamaged after the fire, and damaged merchandise has a residual value of ¥8,150. The company does not carry fire insurance on its inventory.

Instructions

Prepare a formal labeled schedule computing the fire loss incurred. (Do not use the retail inventory method.)

5 **P9-6 (Gross Profit Method)** On April 15, 2015, fire damaged the office and warehouse of Stanislaw Corporation. The only accounting record saved was the general ledger, from which the trial balance below was prepared.

STANISLAW CORPORATION TRIAL BALANCE MARCH 31, 2015		
Cash	€ 20,000	
Accounts receivable	40,000	
Inventory, December 31, 2014	75,000	
Land	35,000	
Equipment	110,000	
Accumulated depreciation—equipment		€ 41,300
Other assets	3,600	
Accounts payable		23,700
Other expense accruals		10,200
Share capital—ordinary		100,000
Retained earnings		52,000
Sales revenue		135,000
Purchases	52,000	
Miscellaneous expenses	26,600	
	€362,200	€362,200

The following data and information have been gathered.

1. The fiscal year of the corporation ends on December 31.

2. An examination of the April bank statement and canceled checks revealed that checks written during the period April 1–15 totaled €13,000: €5,700 paid to accounts payable as of March 31, €3,400 for April merchandise shipments, and €3,900 paid for other expenses. Deposits during the same period amounted to €12,950, which consisted of receipts on account from customers with the exception of a €950 refund from a vendor for merchandise returned in April.

3. Correspondence with suppliers revealed unrecorded obligations at April 15 of €15,600 for April merchandise shipments, including €2,300 for shipments in transit (f.o.b. shipping point) on that date.

4. Customers acknowledged indebtedness of €46,000 at April 15, 2015. It was also estimated that customers owed another €8,000 that will never be acknowledged or recovered. Of the acknowledged indebtedness, €600 will probably be uncollectible.

5. The companies insuring the inventory agreed that the corporation's fire-loss claim should be based on the assumption that the overall gross profit ratio for the past 2 years was in effect during the current year. The corporation's audited financial statements disclosed this information:

	Year Ended December 31	
	2014	2013
Net sales	€530,000	€390,000
Net purchases	280,000	235,000
Beginning inventory	50,000	66,000
Ending inventory	75,000	50,000

6. Inventory with a cost of €7,000 was salvaged and sold for €3,500. The balance of the inventory was a total loss.

Instructions
Prepare a schedule computing the amount of inventory fire loss. The supporting schedule of the computation of the gross profit should be in good form.

P9-7 (Retail Inventory Method) The records for the Clothing Department of Wei's Discount Store are summarized below for the month of January (HK$ in thousands).

Inventory, January 1: at retail HK$25,000; at cost HK$17,000
Purchases in January: at retail HK$137,000; at cost HK$82,500
Freight-in: HK$7,000
Purchase returns: at retail HK$3,000; at cost HK$2,300
Transfers-in from suburban branch: at retail HK$13,000; at cost HK$9,200
Net markups: HK$8,000
Net markdowns: HK$4,000
Inventory losses due to normal breakage, etc.: at retail HK$400
Sales at retail: HK$95,000
Sales returns: HK$2,400

Instructions
(a) Compute the inventory for this department as of January 31, at retail prices.
(b) Compute the ending inventory using lower-of-average-cost-or-net realizable value.

P9-8 (Retail Inventory Method) Presented below is information related to Waveland Inc.

	Cost	Retail
Inventory, 12/31/15	$250,000	$ 390,000
Purchases	914,500	1,460,000
Purchase returns	60,000	80,000
Purchase discounts	18,000	—
Gross sales (after employee discounts)	—	1,410,000
Sales returns	—	97,500
Markups	—	120,000
Markup cancellations	—	40,000
Markdowns	—	45,000
Markdown cancellations	—	20,000
Freight-in	42,000	—
Employee discounts granted	—	8,000
Loss from breakage (normal)	—	4,500

Instructions
Assuming that Waveland Inc. uses the conventional retail inventory method, compute the cost of its ending inventory at December 31, 2015.

6 **P9-9 (Retail Inventory Method)** Fuque Inc. uses the retail inventory method to estimate ending inventory for its monthly financial statements. The following data pertain to a single department for the month of October 2015.

Inventory, October 1, 2015	
At cost	£ 52,000
At retail	78,000
Purchases (exclusive of freight and returns)	
At cost	272,000
At retail	423,000
Freight-in	16,600
Purchase returns	
At cost	5,600
At retail	8,000
Markups	9,000
Markup cancellations	2,000
Markdowns (net)	3,600
Normal spoilage and breakage	10,000
Sales	390,000

Instructions

(a) Using the conventional retail method, prepare a schedule computing estimated LCNRV inventory for October 31, 2015.

(b) A department store using the conventional retail inventory method estimates the cost of its ending inventory as £60,000. An accurate physical count reveals only £47,000 of inventory at LCNRV. List the factors that may have caused the difference between the computed inventory and the physical count.

1 **4** **7** **P9-10 (Statement and Note Disclosure, LCNRV, and Purchase Commitment)** Maddox Specialty Company, a division of Lost World Inc., manufactures three models of gear shift components for bicycles that are sold to bicycle manufacturers, retailers, and catalog outlets. Since beginning operations in 1983, Maddox has used normal absorption costing and has assumed a first-in, first-out cost flow in its perpetual inventory system. The balances of the inventory accounts at the end of Maddox's fiscal year, November 30, 2015, are shown below. The inventories are stated at cost before any year-end adjustments.

Finished goods	$647,000
Work in process	112,500
Raw materials	264,000
Factory supplies	69,000

The following information relates to Maddox's inventory and operations.

1. The finished goods inventory consists of the items analyzed below.

	Cost	Net Realizable Value
Down tube shifter		
Standard model	$ 67,500	$ 67,000
Click adjustment model	94,500	89,000
Deluxe model	108,000	110,000
Total down tube shifters	270,000	266,000
Bar end shifter		
Standard model	83,000	90,050
Click adjustment model	99,000	97,550
Total bar end shifters	182,000	187,600
Head tube shifter		
Standard model	78,000	77,650
Click adjustment model	117,000	119,300
Total head tube shifters	195,000	196,950
Total finished goods	$647,000	$650,550

2. One-half of the head tube shifter finished goods inventory is held by catalog outlets on consignment.

3. Three-quarters of the bar end shifter finished goods inventory has been pledged as collateral for a bank loan.

4. One-half of the raw materials balance represents derailleurs acquired at a contracted price 20 percent above the current market price. The net realizable value of the rest of the raw materials is $127,400.

5. The net realizable value of the work in process inventory is $108,700.

6. Included in the cost of factory supplies are obsolete items with an historical cost of $4,200. The net realizable value of the remaining factory supplies is $65,900.

7. Maddox applies the LCNRV method to each of the three types of shifters in finished goods inventory. For each of the other three inventory accounts, Maddox applies the LCNRV method to the total of each inventory account.

8. Consider all amounts presented above to be material in relation to Maddox's financial statements taken as a whole.

Instructions

(a) Prepare the inventory section of Maddox's statement of financial position as of November 30, 2015, including any required note(s).

(b) Without prejudice to your answer to (a), assume that the net realizable value of Maddox's inventories is less than cost. Explain how this decline would be presented in Maddox's income statement for the fiscal year ended November 30, 2015.

(c) Assume that Maddox has a firm purchase commitment for the same type of derailleur included in the raw materials inventory as of November 30, 2015, and that the purchase commitment is at a contracted price 15% greater than the current market price. These derailleurs are to be delivered to Maddox after November 30, 2015. Discuss the impact, if any, that this purchase commitment would have on Maddox's financial statements prepared for the fiscal year ended November 30, 2015.

P9-11 (LCNRV) Taipai Co. follows the practice of valuing its inventory at the LCNRV. The following information is available from the company's inventory records as of December 31, 2015 (amounts in thousands).

Item	Quantity	Unit Cost	Estimated Selling Price/Unit	Completion & Selling Cost/Unit
A	1,100	NT$7.50	NT$10.50	NT$1.50
B	800	8.20	9.40	1.30
C	1,000	5.60	7.20	1.75
D	1,000	3.80	6.30	1.80
E	1,400	6.40	6.70	0.70

Instructions

Jay Shin is an accounting clerk in the accounting department of Taipai Co., and he cannot understand how completion and selling costs affect the determination of net realizable value. Jay is very confused, and he is the one who records inventory purchases and calculates ending inventory. You are the manager of the department and an accountant.

(a) Calculate the LCNRV using the "individual-item" approach.

(b) Show the journal entry he will need to make in order to write down the ending inventory from cost to market.

(c) Then, write a memo to Jay explaining what net realizable value is as well as how it is computed. Use your calculations to aid in your explanation.

CONCEPTS FOR ANALYSIS

CA9-1 (LCNRV) You have been asked by the financial vice president to develop a short presentation on the LCNRV method for inventory purposes. The financial VP needs to explain this method to the president because it appears that a portion of the company's inventory has declined in value.

Instructions

The financial vice president asks you to answer the following questions.

(a) What is the purpose of the LCNRV method?
(b) What is meant by "net realizable value"?
(c) Do you apply the LCNRV method to each individual item, to a category, or to the total of the inventory? Explain.
(d) What are the potential disadvantages of the LCNRV method?

CA9-2 (LCNRV) The net realizable value of Lake Corporation's inventory has declined below its cost. Allyn Conan, the controller, wants to use the loss method to write down inventory because it more clearly discloses the decline in the net realizable value and does not distort the cost of goods sold. His supervisor, financial vice president Bill Ortiz, prefers the cost-of-goods-sold method to write down inventory because it does not call attention to the decline in net realizable value.

Instructions

Answer the following questions.

(a) What, if any, is the ethical issue involved?
(b) Is any stakeholder harmed if Bill Ortiz's preference is used?
(c) What should Allyn Conan do?

CA9-3 (LCNRV) Ogala Corporation purchased a significant amount of raw materials inventory for a new product that it is manufacturing.

Ogala uses the LCNRV rule for these raw materials. The net realizable value of the raw materials is below the original cost.

Ogala uses the FIFO inventory method for these raw materials. In the last 2 years, each purchase has been at a lower price than the previous purchase, and the ending inventory quantity for each period has been higher than the beginning inventory quantity for that period.

Instructions

(a) (1) At which amount should Ogala's raw materials inventory be reported on the statement of financial position? Why?
    (2) In general, why is the LCNRV rule used to report inventory?
(b) What would have been the effect on ending inventory and cost of goods sold had Ogala used the average-cost inventory method instead of the FIFO inventory method for the raw materials? Why?

CA9-4 (Retail Inventory Method) Saurez Company, your client, manufactures paint. The company's president, Maria Saurez, has decided to open a retail store to sell Saurez paint as well as wallpaper and other supplies that would be purchased from other suppliers. She has asked you for information about the conventional retail method of pricing inventories at the retail store.

Instructions

Prepare a report to the president explaining the retail method of pricing inventories. Your report should include the following points.

(a) Description and accounting features of the method.
(b) The conditions that may distort the results under the method.
(c) A comparison of the advantages of using the retail method with those of using cost methods of inventory pricing.
(d) The accounting theory underlying the treatment of net markdowns and net markups under the method.

CA9-5 (Cost Determination, LCNRV, Retail Method) Olson Corporation, a retailer and wholesaler of brand-name household lighting fixtures, purchases its inventories from various suppliers.

Instructions

(a) (1) What criteria should be used to determine which of Olson's costs are inventoriable?
    (2) Are Olson's administrative costs inventoriable? Defend your answer.
(b) (1) Olson uses the LCNRV rule for its wholesale inventories. What are the theoretical arguments for that rule?
    (2) The net realizable value of the inventories is below the original cost. What amount should be used to value the inventories? Why?
(c) Olson calculates the estimated cost of its ending inventories held for sale at retail using the conventional retail inventory method. How would Olson treat the beginning inventories and net markdowns in calculating the cost ratio used to determine its ending inventories? Why?

CA9-6 (Purchase Commitments) Prophet Company signed a long-term purchase contract to buy timber from the government forest service at $300 per thousand board feet. Under these terms, Prophet must cut and pay $6,000,000 for this timber during the next year. Currently, the market governmental price is $250 per thousand board feet. At this rate, the market price is $5,000,000. Hu Cho, the controller, wants to recognize the loss in value on the year-end financial statements, but the financial vice president, Rondo Star, argues that the loss is temporary and should be ignored. Cho notes that market price has remained near $250 for many months, and he sees no sign of significant change.

Instructions
- **(a)** What are the ethical issues, if any?
- **(b)** Is any particular stakeholder harmed by the financial vice president's decision?
- **(c)** What should the controller do?

USING YOUR JUDGMENT

FINANCIAL REPORTING

Financial Reporting Problem

Marks and Spencer plc (M&S)

The financial statements of M&S (GBR) are presented in Appendix A. The company's complete annual report, including the notes to the financial statements, is available online.

Instructions

Refer to M&S's financial statements and the accompanying notes to answer the following questions.

- **(a)** How does M&S value its inventories? Which inventory costing method does M&S use as a basis for reporting its inventories?
- **(b)** How does M&S report its inventories in the statement of financial position? In the notes to its financial statements, what three descriptions are used to classify its inventories?
- **(c)** What costs does M&S include in Inventory and Cost of Sales?
- **(d)** What was M&S inventory turnover in 2013? What is its gross profit percentage? Evaluate M&S's inventory turnover and its gross profit percentage.

Comparative Analysis Case

adidas and Puma

The financial statements of adidas (DEU) and Puma (DEU) are presented in Appendices B and C, respectively. The complete annual reports, including the notes to the financial statements, are available online.

Instructions

Use the companies' financial information to answer the following questions.

- **(a)** What is the amount of inventory reported by adidas at December 31, 2012, and by Puma at December 31, 2012? What percent of total assets is invested in inventory by each company?
- **(b)** What inventory costing methods are used by adidas and Puma? How does each company value its inventories?
- **(c)** In the notes, what classifications (description) are used by adidas and Puma to categorize their inventories?
- **(d)** Compute and compare the inventory turnovers and days to sell inventory for adidas and Puma for 2012. Indicate why there might be a significant difference between the two companies.

Financial Statement Analysis Case

Barrick Gold Corporation

Barrick Gold Corporation (CAN) is the world's most profitable and largest gold mining company outside South Africa. Part of the key to Barrick's success has been due to its ability to maintain cash flow while improving production and increasing its reserves of gold-containing property. Recently, Barrick has achieved record growth in cash flow, production, and reserves.

The company maintains an aggressive policy of developing previously identified target areas that have the possibility of a large amount of gold ore and that have not been previously developed. Barrick limits the riskiness of this development by choosing only properties that are located in politically stable regions, and by the company's use of internally generated funds, rather than debt, to finance growth.

Barrick's inventories are as follows.

Barrick Gold Corporation

Inventories (in millions, U.S. dollars)

Current	
Gold in process	$133
Mine operating supplies	82
	$215
Non-current (included in Other assets)	
Ore in stockpiles	$ 65

Instructions

(a) Why do you think that there are no finished goods inventories? Why do you think the raw material, ore in stockpiles, is considered to be a non-current asset?

(b) Consider that Barrick has no finished goods inventories. What journal entries are made to record a sale?

(c) Suppose that gold bullion that cost $1.8 million to produce was sold for $2.4 million. The journal entry was made to record the sale, but no entry was made to remove the gold from the gold in process inventory. How would this error affect the following?

Statement of Financial Position		Income Statement	
Inventory	?	Cost of goods sold	?
Retained earnings	?	Net income	?
Accounts payable	?		
Working capital	?		
Current ratio	?		

Accounting, Analysis, and Principles

Englehart Company sells two types of pumps. One is large and is for commercial use. The other is smaller and is used in residential swimming pools. The following inventory data is available for the month of March.

	Units	Value per Unit	Total
Residential Pumps			
Inventory at Feb. 28:	200	$ 400	$ 80,000
Purchases:			
March 10	500	$ 450	$225,000
March 20	400	$ 475	$190,000
March 30	300	$ 500	$150,000
Sales:			
March 15	500	$ 540	$270,000
March 25	400	$ 570	$228,000
Inventory at Mar. 31:	500		
Commercial Pumps			
Inventory at Feb. 28:	600	$ 800	$480,000
Purchases:			
March 3	600	$ 900	$540,000
March 12	300	$ 950	$285,000
March 21	500	$1,000	$500,000
Sales:			
March 18	900	$1,080	$972,000
March 29	600	$1,140	$684,000
Inventory at Mar. 31:	500		

In addition to the above information, due to a downturn in the economy that has hit Englehart's commercial customers especially hard, Englehart expects commercial pump prices from March 31 onward to be considerably different (and lower) than at the beginning of and during March. Englehart has developed the following additional information.

	Commercial Pumps	Residential Pumps
Expected selling price (per unit, net of costs to sell)	$1,050	$580
Costs to complete	150	30

Englehart uses the FIFO accounting method.

Accounting

(a) Determine the dollar amount that Englehart should report on its March 31 statement of financial position for inventory. Assume Englehart applies LCNRV at the individual-product level.

(b) Repeat part (a) but assume Englehart applies LCNRV at the major-group level. Englehart places both commercial and residential pumps into the same (and only) group.

Analysis

Which of the two approaches above (individual-product or major-group level) for applying LCNRV do you think gives the financial statement reader better information?

Principles

Assume that during April, the net realizable value of commercial pumps rebounds to $1,060. Briefly describe how Englehart's April financial statements changed with respect to its inventory remaining from March 31 under IFRS.

IFRS BRIDGE TO THE PROFESSION

Professional Research

Jones Co. is in a technology-intensive industry. Recently, one of its competitors introduced a new product with technology that might render obsolete some of Jones's inventory. The accounting staff wants to follow the appropriate authoritative literature in determining the accounting for this significant market event.

Instructions

Access the IFRS authoritative literature at the IASB website (*http://eifrs.iasb.org/*) (you may register for free eIFRS access at this site). When you have accessed the documents, you can use the search tool in your Internet browser to respond to the following questions. (Provide paragraph citations.)

(a) Identify the authoritative literature addressing inventory pricing.

(b) List three types of goods that are classified as inventory. What characteristic will automatically exclude an item from being classified as inventory?

(c) Define "net realizable value" as used in the phrase "lower-of-cost-or-net realizable value."

(d) Explain when it is acceptable to state inventory above cost and which industries allow this practice.

Professional Simulation

The professional simulation for this chapter asks you to address questions related to inventory valuation and measurement. Prepare responses to all parts.

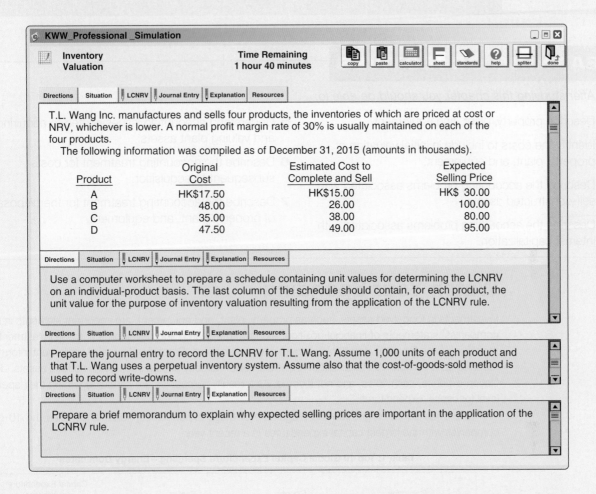

KWW_Professional _Simulation

Inventory
Valuation

Time Remaining
1 hour 40 minutes

copy | paste | calculator | sheet | standards | help | spliter | done

Directions | Situation | LCNRV | Journal Entry | Explanation | Resources

T.L. Wang Inc. manufactures and sells four products, the inventories of which are priced at cost or NRV, whichever is lower. A normal profit margin rate of 30% is usually maintained on each of the four products.

The following information was compiled as of December 31, 2015 (amounts in thousands).

Product	Original Cost	Estimated Cost to Complete and Sell	Expected Selling Price
A	HK$17.50	HK$15.00	HK$ 30.00
B	48.00	26.00	100.00
C	35.00	38.00	80.00
D	47.50	49.00	95.00

Directions | Situation | LCNRV | Journal Entry | Explanation | Resources

Use a computer worksheet to prepare a schedule containing unit values for determining the LCNRV on an individual-product basis. The last column of the schedule should contain, for each product, the unit value for the purpose of inventory valuation resulting from the application of the LCNRV rule.

Directions | Situation | LCNRV | Journal Entry | Explanation | Resources

Prepare the journal entry to record the LCNRV for T.L. Wang. Assume 1,000 units of each product and that T.L. Wang uses a perpetual inventory system. Assume also that the cost-of-goods-sold method is used to record write-downs.

Directions | Situation | LCNRV | Journal Entry | Explanation | Resources

Prepare a brief memorandum to explain why expected selling prices are important in the application of the LCNRV rule.

10 Acquisition and Disposition of Property, Plant, and Equipment

LEARNING OBJECTIVES

After studying this chapter, you should be able to:

1 Describe property, plant, and equipment.

2 Identify the costs to include in initial valuation of property, plant, and equipment.

3 Describe the accounting problems associated with self-constructed assets.

4 Describe the accounting problems associated with interest capitalization.

5 Understand accounting issues related to acquiring and valuing plant assets.

6 Describe the accounting treatment for costs subsequent to acquisition.

7 Describe the accounting treatment for the disposal of property, plant, and equipment.

Watch Your Spending

Investments in long-lived assets, such as property, plant, and equipment, are important elements in many companies' statements of financial position. Along with research and development, these investments are the driving force for many companies in generating cash flows. Property, plant, and equipment information reported on a company's statement of financial position directly affects such items as total assets, depreciation expense, cash flows, and net income. As a result, companies are careful regarding their spending level for capital expenditures.

To provide some insight into the magnitude of these expenditures, Table 1 identifies the 10 global companies with the largest capital expenditures in a recent year.

Table 1: Top 10 Global Capital Expenditure Spending—Energy Dominates

Company	Country	Sector	Capital Expenditure (in billions)
PetroChina Company	China	Energy	$50.0
Petrobras	Brazil	Energy	38.5
ExxonMobil	U.S.	Energy	34.3
Royal Dutch Shell	Netherlands	Energy	32.6
Chevron	U.S.	Energy	30.9
Total S.A.	France	Energy	26.2
China Petroleum & Chemical	China	Energy	25.2
BP plc	U.K.	Energy	23.1
Samsung Electronics	South Korea	IT	21.6
Toyota	Japan	Consumer discretionary	21.0

Source: S&P Capital IQ, Standard & Poor's Ratings Services' Calculations.

As indicated, not surprisingly, energy companies make up eight out of the top 10—with **Samsung** (KOR) and **Toyota** (JPN) the sole representatives from other industries (manufacturing).

Determining the proper level of capital expenditures in many companies is challenging. Expenditures that are too much or too little run the risk of decreasing cash flows, losing competitive position, and diminishing pricing power. The recession in Europe, the financial crisis in 2008 and its lingering effects, and China's reduced level of spending are now slowing down the level of capital expenditures. Western Europe, Latin America, and the Asian-Pacific countries are all showing signs of capital expenditure fatigue. Table 2 shows that global capital expenditure levels have stalled or become negative in the last few years.

To illustrate the concerns about the level of capital expenditures, take France as an example. Companies in France (the second largest economy in Europe) are taking a conservative approach to capital expenditures, despite low interest rates. Reasons for their reluctance to spend are higher taxes and foreign competition, which have pushed profit margins to their lowest level since 1985—reducing companies' abilities to stomach additional risk. As the CEO of the construction materials company **Compagnie de Saint-Gobain SA** (FRA) said, "We need as little uncertainty as possible, but instead there is more and more."

Even in good times, the issues related to capital expenditures are complex. The following areas and subsequent questions have led to many sleepless nights for company managers:

1. Spending volume—how much should be spent?

2. Capital allocation—what should it be spent on?

3. Project execution—how does spending transform into real returns?

Answers to these questions are not easy, and failure to answer them correctly can lead to loss of profitability. It also follows that these issues are of extreme interest to users of financial statements. As mentioned previously, too much or too little capital spending by companies can lead to decreased cash flows, loss of competitive position, and diminished pricing power. Relationships between capital expenditures to sales and capital expenditures to depreciation, as well as free cash flow, provide insight into the underlying financial flexibility of a company.

CONCEPTUAL FOCUS

> See the **Underlying Concepts** on pages 444, 448, and 463.

INTERNATIONAL FOCUS

> **Global Accounting Insights** related to property, plant, and equipment are presented in Chapter 11.

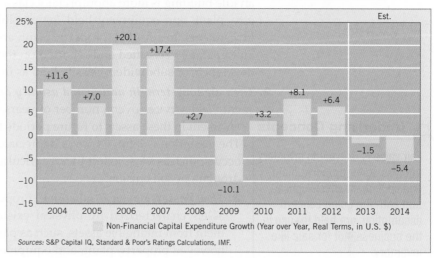

Table 2: Global Non-Financial Corporate Capital Expenditure Growth

Non-Financial Capital Expenditure Growth (Year over Year, Real Terms, in U.S. $)

Sources: S&P Capital IQ, Standard & Poor's Ratings Calculations, IMF.

Sources: W. Horobein and S. Schnechner, "Facing Uncertainty, French Firms Cut Back on Investments," *Wall Street Journal* (July 7, 2013); *Pulling the Capex Lever,* AT Kearney (2013); and G. Williams, *Global Capital Expenditures Survey 2013*, Standard and Poor's (July 10, 2013).

PREVIEW OF CHAPTER 10

As we indicate in the opening story, a company like **PetroChina Company** (CHN) has a substantial investment in property, plant, and equipment. Conversely, other companies, such as **Alcatel-Lucent** (FRA), have a minor investment in these types of assets. In this chapter, we discuss the proper accounting for the acquisition, use, and disposition of property, plant, and equipment. The content and organization of the chapter are as follows.

Acquisition and Disposition of Property, Plant, and Equipment

Acquisition	Valuation	Costs Subsequent to Acquisition	Disposition
• Acquisition costs: land, buildings, equipment • Self-constructed assets • Interest costs • Observations	• Cash discounts • Deferred contracts • Lump-sum purchases • Share issuance • Non-monetary exchanges • Government grants	• Additions • Improvements and replacements • Rearrangement and reorganization • Repairs • Summary	• Sale • Involuntary conversion

PROPERTY, PLANT, AND EQUIPMENT

**I
F
R
S**

See the Authoritative
Literature section
(page 469).

Companies like **Hon Hai Precision** (TWN), **Tata Steel** (IND), and **Royal Dutch Shell** (GBR and NLD) use assets of a durable nature. Such assets are called **property, plant, and equipment**. Other terms commonly used are **plant assets** and **fixed assets**. We use these terms interchangeably. Property, plant, and equipment is defined as tangible assets that are held for use in production or supply of goods and services, for rentals to others, or for administrative purposes; they are expected to be used during more than one period. **[1]** Property, plant, and equipment therefore includes land, building structures (offices, factories, warehouses), and equipment (machinery, furniture, tools). The major characteristics of property, plant, and equipment are as follows.

1. *They are acquired for use in operations and not for resale.* Only assets used in normal business operations are classified as property, plant, and equipment. For example, an idle building is more appropriately classified separately as an investment. Property, plant, and equipment held for possible price appreciation are classified as investments. In addition, property, plant, and equipment held for sale or disposal are separately classified and reported on the statement of financial position. Land developers or subdividers classify land as inventory.

2. *They are long-term in nature and usually depreciated.* Property, plant, and equipment yield services over a number of years. Companies allocate the cost of the investment in these assets to future periods through periodic depreciation charges. The exception is land, which is depreciated only if a material decrease in value occurs, such as a loss in fertility of agricultural land because of poor crop rotation, drought, or soil erosion.

🔍 **Underlying Concepts**

Fair value is relevant to inventory but less so for property, plant, and equipment which, consistent with the going concern assumption, are held for use in the business, not for sale like inventory.

3. *They possess physical substance.* Property, plant, and equipment are tangible assets characterized by physical existence or substance. This differentiates them from intangible assets, such as patents or goodwill. Unlike raw material, however, property, plant, and equipment do not physically become part of a product held for resale.

ACQUISITION OF PROPERTY, PLANT, AND EQUIPMENT

Most companies use historical cost as the basis for valuing property, plant, and equipment. **Historical cost** measures the cash or cash equivalent price of obtaining the asset and bringing it to the location and condition necessary for its intended use.

Companies recognize property, plant, and equipment when the cost of the asset can be **measured reliably** and it is probable that the company will **obtain future economic benefits**. **[2]** For example, when **Starbucks** (USA) purchases coffee makers for its operations, these costs are reported as an asset because they can be reliably measured and benefit future periods. However, when Starbucks makes ordinary repairs to its coffee machines, it expenses these costs because the primary period benefited is only the current period.

In general, companies report the following costs as part of property, plant, and equipment. **[3]**[1]

---

[1]Materiality considerations are important in considering items to capitalize. Assume, for example, that Cathay Company has spare parts on hand to service any breakdowns in its equipment. Unless the spare parts either separately or in combination are material in amount, expenditures related to spare parts are expensed as incurred even though they provide future benefit.

1. Purchase price, including import duties and non-refundable purchase taxes, less trade discounts and rebates. For example, **British Airways** (GBR) indicates that aircraft are stated at fair value of the consideration given after offsetting manufacturing credits.

2. Costs attributable to bringing the asset to the location and condition necessary for it to be used in a manner intended by the company. For example, when **Skanska AB** (SWE) purchases heavy machinery from **Caterpillar** (USA), it capitalizes the costs of purchase, including delivery costs.[2]

Companies value property, plant, and equipment in subsequent periods using either the cost method or fair value (revaluation) method. Companies can apply the cost or fair value method to all the items of property, plant, and equipment or to a single class(es) of property, plant, and equipment. For example, a company may value land (one class of asset) after acquisition using the fair value method and at the same time value buildings and equipment (other classes of assets) at cost.

Most companies use the cost method—it is less expensive to use because the cost of an appraiser is not needed. In addition, the fair value method generally leads to higher asset values, which means that companies report higher depreciation expense and lower net income. This chapter discusses the cost method; we illustrate the fair value method in Chapter 11.

Cost of Land

All expenditures made to acquire land and ready it for use are considered part of the land cost. Thus, when **Group Auchan** (FRA) or **ÆON** (JPN) purchases land on which to build a new store, land costs typically include (1) the purchase price; (2) closing costs, such as title to the land, attorney's fees, and recording fees; (3) costs incurred in getting the land in condition for its intended use, such as grading, filling, draining, and clearing; (4) assumption of any liens, mortgages, or encumbrances on the property; and (5) any additional land improvements that have an indefinite life.

For example, when ÆON purchases land for the purpose of constructing a building, it considers all costs incurred up to the excavation for the new building as land costs. **Removal of old buildings—clearing, grading, and filling—is a land cost because this activity is necessary to get the land in condition for its intended purpose.** ÆON treats any proceeds from getting the land ready for its intended use, such as salvage receipts on the demolition of an old building or the sale of cleared timber, as **reductions in the price of the land**.

In some cases, when ÆON purchases land, it may assume certain obligations on the land such as back taxes or liens. In such situations, the cost of the land is the cash paid for it, plus the encumbrances. In other words, if the purchase price of the land is ¥50,000,000 cash but ÆON assumes accrued property taxes of ¥5,000,000 and liens of ¥10,000,000, its land cost is ¥65,000,000.

ÆON also might incur **special assessments** for local improvements, such as pavements, street lights, sewers, and drainage systems. It should charge these costs to the Land account because they are relatively permanent in nature. That is, after installation, they are maintained by the local government. In addition, ÆON should charge

---

[2]Companies also recognize estimates of dismantling, removing, and site restoration if the company has an obligation that it incurs on acquisition of the asset. For example, **BP** (GBR) indicates that liabilities for decommissioning costs are recognized when the group has an obligation to dismantle or remove a facility or an item of plant and restore the site on which it is located. A corresponding item of property, plant, and equipment of an amount equivalent to the provision is also created. We discuss the recognition and measurement of these assets and related obligations in Chapter 13.

any permanent improvements it makes, such as landscaping, to the Land account. It records separately any **improvements with limited lives**, such as private driveways, walks, fences, and parking lots, to the Land Improvements account. These costs are depreciated over their estimated lives.

Generally, land is part of property, plant, and equipment. However, if the major purpose of acquiring and holding land is speculative, a company more appropriately classifies the land as an **investment**. If a real estate concern holds the land for resale, it should classify the land as **inventory**.

In cases where land is held as an investment, what accounting treatment should be given for taxes, insurance, and other direct costs incurred while holding the land? Many believe these costs should be capitalized. The reason: They are not generating revenue from the investment at this time. Companies generally use this approach except when the asset is currently producing revenue (such as rental property).

Cost of Buildings

The cost of buildings should include all expenditures related directly to their acquisition or construction. These costs include (1) materials, labor, and overhead costs incurred during construction, and (2) professional fees and building permits. Generally, companies contract others to construct their buildings. Companies consider all costs incurred, from excavation to completion, as part of the building costs.

But how should companies account for an old building that is on the site of a newly proposed building? Is the cost of removal of the old building a cost of the land or a cost of the new building? Recall that **if a company purchases land with an old building on it, then the cost of demolition less its residual value is a cost of getting the land ready for its intended use and relates to the land rather than to the new building.** In other words, all costs of getting an asset ready for its intended use are costs of that asset.

It follows that any costs that are not directly attributable to getting the building ready for its intended use should not be capitalized. For example, start-up costs, such as promotional costs related to the building's opening or operating losses incurred initially due to low sales, should not be capitalized. Also, general administrative expenses (such as the cost of the finance department) should not be allocated to the cost of the building.

Cost of Equipment

The term "equipment" in accounting includes delivery equipment, office equipment, machinery, furniture and fixtures, furnishings, factory equipment, and similar fixed assets. The cost of such assets includes the purchase price, freight and handling charges incurred, insurance on the equipment while in transit, cost of special foundations if required, assembling and installation costs, and costs of conducting trial runs. Any proceeds from selling any items produced while bringing the equipment to the location and condition for its intended use (such as samples produced when testing equipment) should reduce the cost of the equipment. Costs thus include all expenditures incurred in acquiring the equipment and preparing it for use.

Self-Constructed Assets

LEARNING OBJECTIVE ❸

Describe the accounting problems associated with self-constructed assets.

Occasionally, companies construct their own assets. Determining the cost of such machinery and other fixed assets can be a problem. Without a purchase price or contract price, the company must allocate costs and expenses to arrive at the cost of the **self-constructed asset**. Materials and direct labor used in construction pose no problem. A company can trace these costs directly to work and material orders related to the fixed assets constructed.

However, the assignment of indirect costs of manufacturing creates special problems. These indirect costs, called **overhead** or burden, include power, heat, light, insurance, property taxes on factory buildings and equipment, factory supervisory labor, depreciation of fixed assets, and supplies.

Companies can handle overhead in one of two ways:

1. *Assign no fixed overhead to the cost of the constructed asset.* The major argument for this treatment is that overhead is generally fixed in nature. As a result, this approach assumes that the company will have the same costs regardless of whether or not it constructs the asset. Therefore, to charge a portion of the overhead costs to the equipment will normally reduce current expenses and consequently overstate income of the current period. However, the company would assign to the cost of the constructed asset variable overhead costs that increase as a result of the construction.

2. *Assign a portion of all overhead to the construction process.* This approach, called a **full-costing approach**, assumes that costs attach to all products and assets manufactured or constructed. Under this approach, a company assigns a portion of all overhead to the construction process, as it would to normal production. Advocates say that failure to allocate overhead costs understates the initial cost of the asset and results in an inaccurate future allocation.

Companies should assign to the asset **a pro rata portion** of the fixed overhead to determine its cost. Companies use this treatment extensively because many believe that it results in a better matching of costs with revenues. Abnormal amounts of wasted material, labor, or other resources should not be added to the cost of the asset. **[4]**

If the allocated overhead results in recording construction costs in excess of the costs that an outside independent producer would charge, the company should record the excess overhead as a period loss rather than capitalize it. This avoids capitalizing the asset at more than its fair value. Under no circumstances should a company record a "profit on self-construction."

Interest Costs During Construction

The proper accounting for interest costs has been a long-standing controversy.[3] Three approaches have been suggested to account for the interest incurred in financing the construction of property, plant, and equipment:

LEARNING OBJECTIVE
Describe the accounting problems associated with interest capitalization.

1. *Capitalize no interest charges during construction.* Under this approach, interest is considered a cost of financing and not a cost of construction. Some contend that if a company had used equity financing rather than debt, it would not incur this cost. The major argument against this approach is that the use of cash, whatever its source, has an associated implicit interest cost, which should not be ignored.

2. *Charge construction with all costs of funds employed, whether identifiable or not.* This method maintains that the cost of construction should include the cost of financing, whether by cash, debt, or equity. Its advocates say that all costs necessary to get an asset ready for its intended use, including interest, are part of the asset's cost. Interest, whether actual or imputed, is a cost, just as are labor and materials. A major criticism of this approach is that imputing the cost of equity capital is subjective and outside the framework of an historical cost system.

---

[3]IFRS uses the term *borrowing costs* instead of interest costs. Borrowing costs include interest expense calculated using the effective-interest method. We use the term *interest costs* here to mean borrowing costs.

3. *Capitalize only the actual interest costs incurred during construction.* This approach agrees in part with the logic of the second approach—that interest is just as much a cost as are labor and materials. But this approach capitalizes only interest costs incurred through debt financing. (That is, it does not try to determine the cost of equity financing.) Under this approach, a company that uses debt financing will have an asset of higher cost than a company that uses equity financing. Some consider this approach unsatisfactory because they believe the cost of an asset should be the same whether it is financed with cash, debt, or equity.

Illustration 10-1 shows how a company might add interest costs (if any) to the cost of the asset under the three capitalization approaches.

ILLUSTRATION 10-1
Capitalization of Interest Costs

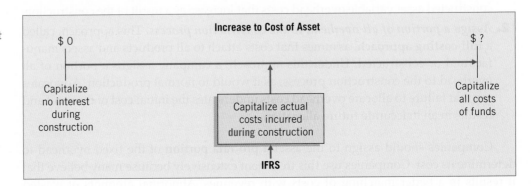

IFRS requires the third approach—capitalizing actual interest (with modification). This method follows the concept that the **historical cost of acquiring an asset includes all costs (including interest) incurred to bring the asset to the condition and location necessary for its intended use**. The rationale for this approach is that during construction, the asset is not generating revenues. Therefore, a company should defer (capitalize) interest costs. Once construction is complete, the asset is ready for its intended use and a company can earn revenues. At this point, the company should report interest as an expense and match it to these revenues. It follows that the company should expense any interest cost incurred in purchasing an asset that is ready for its intended use. **[5]**

To implement this general approach, companies consider three items:

Underlying Concepts

The objective of capitalizing interest is to obtain a measure of acquisition cost that reflects a company's total investment in the asset and to charge that cost to future periods benefitted.

1. Qualifying assets.
2. Capitalization period.
3. Amount to capitalize.

Qualifying Assets

To qualify for interest capitalization, assets must require a substantial period of time to get them ready for their intended use or sale. A company capitalizes interest costs starting with the first expenditure related to the asset. Capitalization continues until the company substantially readies the asset for its intended use.

Assets that qualify for interest cost capitalization include assets under construction for a company's own use (including buildings, plants, and large machinery) and assets intended for sale or lease that are constructed or otherwise produced as discrete projects (e.g., ships or real estate developments).

Examples of assets that do not qualify for interest capitalization are (1) assets that are in use or ready for their intended use, and (2) assets that the company does not use in its earnings activities and that are not undergoing the activities necessary to get them ready for use. Examples of this second type include land remaining undeveloped and assets not used because of obsolescence, excess capacity, or need for repair.

Capitalization Period

The **capitalization period** is the period of time during which a company must capitalize interest. It begins with the presence of three conditions:

1. Expenditures for the asset are being incurred.
2. Activities that are necessary to get the asset ready for its intended use or sale are in progress.
3. Interest cost is being incurred.

Interest capitalization **continues as long as these three conditions are present**. The capitalization period ends when the asset is substantially complete and ready for its intended use.

Amount to Capitalize

The amount of interest to capitalize is limited to the lower of actual interest cost incurred during the period or avoidable interest. **Avoidable interest** is the amount of interest cost during the period that a company could theoretically avoid if it had not made expenditures for the asset. If the actual interest cost for the period is $90,000 and the avoidable interest is $80,000, the company capitalizes only $80,000. Or, if the actual interest cost is $80,000 and the avoidable interest is $90,000, it still capitalizes only $80,000. In no situation should interest cost include a cost of capital charge for equity.

To apply the avoidable interest concept, a company determines the potential amount of interest that it may capitalize during an accounting period by multiplying the appropriate interest rate(s) by the **weighted-average accumulated expenditures** for qualifying assets during the period.

Weighted-Average Accumulated Expenditures. In computing the weighted-average accumulated expenditures, a company weights the construction expenditures by the amount of time (fraction of a year or accounting period) that it can incur interest cost on the expenditure.

To illustrate, assume that Han Ren Company decides to build a bridge, which is estimated to take 17 months to complete, starting in 2015. The company makes the following payments to the contractor in 2015: $240,000 on March 1, $480,000 on July 1, and $360,000 on November 1. The company computes the weighted-average accumulated expenditures for the year ended December 31, 2015, as follows.

Expenditures			Capitalization		Weighted-Average
Date	Amount	×	Period*	=	Accumulated Expenditures
March 1	$ 240,000		10/12		$200,000
July 1	480,000		6/12		240,000
November 1	360,000		2/12		60,000
	$1,080,000				$500,000

*Months between date of expenditure and date interest capitalization stops or end of year, whichever comes first (in this case December 31).

ILLUSTRATION 10-2
Computation of Weighted-Average Accumulated Expenditures

To compute the weighted-average accumulated expenditures, Han Ren weights the expenditures by the amount of time that it can incur interest cost on each one. For the March 1 expenditure, Han Ren associates 10 months' interest cost with the expenditure.

For the expenditure on July 1, it incurs only 6 months' interest costs. For the expenditure made on November 1, the company incurs only 2 months of interest cost.

Interest Rates. Companies follow these principles in selecting the appropriate interest rates to be applied to the weighted-average accumulated expenditures:

1. For the portion of weighted-average accumulated expenditures that is less than or equal to any amounts borrowed specifically to finance construction of the assets, **use the interest rate incurred on the specific borrowings**.

2. For the portion of weighted-average accumulated expenditures that is greater than any debt incurred specifically to finance construction of the assets, **use a weighted average of interest rates incurred on all other outstanding debt during the period**.

Illustration 10-3 shows the computation of a capitalization rate (weighted-average interest rate) for debt greater than the amount incurred specifically to finance construction of the assets.[4]

ILLUSTRATION 10-3
Computation of
Capitalization Rate

	Principal	Interest
12%, 2-year note	$ 600,000	$ 72,000
9%, 10-year bonds	2,000,000	180,000
7.5%, 20-year bonds	5,000,000	375,000
	$7,600,000	$627,000

$$\text{Capitalization Rate} = \frac{\text{Total Interest}}{\text{Total Principal}} = \frac{\$627,000}{\$7,600,000} = 8.25\%$$

Comprehensive Example of Interest Capitalization

To illustrate the issues related to interest capitalization, assume that on November 1, 2014, Shalla Company contracted Pfeifer Construction Co. to construct a building for $1,400,000 on land costing $100,000 (purchased from the contractor and included in the first payment). Shalla made the following payments to the construction company during 2015.

January 1	March 1	May 1	December 31	Total
$210,000	$300,000	$540,000	$450,000	$1,500,000

Pfeifer Construction completed the building, ready for occupancy, on December 31, 2015. Shalla had the following debt outstanding at December 31, 2015.

Specific Construction Debt

1. 15%, 3-year note to finance purchase of land and construction of the building, dated December 31, 2014, with interest payable annually on December 31 $750,000

Other Debt

2. 10%, 5-year note payable, dated December 31, 2011, with interest payable annually on December 31 $550,000

3. 12%, 10-year bonds issued December 31, 2010, with interest payable annually on December 31 $600,000

Shalla computed the weighted-average accumulated expenditures during 2015, as shown in Illustration 10-4.

---

[4]In considering possible interest costs not related to specific borrowings, companies must exercise judgment on other debt to use. Only debt that has a reasonable relationship to the possible funding of the qualifying asset should be considered.

ILLUSTRATION 10-4
Computation of
Weighted-Average
Accumulated
Expenditures

Expenditures			Current-Year Capitalization		Weighted-Average
Date	Amount	×	Period	=	Accumulated Expenditures
January 1	$ 210,000		12/12		$210,000
March 1	300,000		10/12		250,000
May 1	540,000		8/12		360,000
December 31	450,000		0		0
	$1,500,000				$820,000

Note that the expenditure made on December 31, the last day of the year, does not have any interest cost.

Shalla computes the avoidable interest, as shown in Illustration 10-5.

ILLUSTRATION 10-5
Computation of
Avoidable Interest

Weighted-Average Accumulated Expenditures	×	Interest Rate	=	Avoidable Interest
$750,000		.15 (construction note)		$112,500
70,000[a]		.1104 (capitalization rate)[b]		7,728
$820,000				$120,228

[a]The amount by which the weighted-average accumulated expenditures exceeds the specific construction loan.
[b]Capitalization rate computation:

	Principal	Interest
10%, 5-year note	$ 550,000	$ 55,000
12%, 10-year bonds	600,000	72,000
	$1,150,000	$127,000

$$\text{Capitalization Rate} = \frac{\text{Total Interest}}{\text{Total Principal}} = \frac{\$127,000}{\$1,150,000} = 11.04\%$$

The company determines the actual interest cost, which represents the maximum amount of interest that it may capitalize during 2015, as shown in Illustration 10-6.

ILLUSTRATION 10-6
Computation of Actual
Interest Cost

Construction note	$750,000 × .15	=	$112,500
5-year note	$550,000 × .10	=	55,000
10-year bonds	$600,000 × .12	=	72,000
Actual interest			$239,500

The interest cost that Shalla capitalizes is the lesser of $120,228 (avoidable interest) and $239,500 (actual interest), or $120,228.

Shalla records the following journal entries during 2015:

January 1

Land	100,000	
Buildings (or Construction in Process)	110,000	
Cash		210,000

March 1

Buildings	300,000	
Cash		300,000

May 1

Buildings	540,000	
Cash		540,000

December 31

Buildings	450,000	
Cash		450,000
Buildings (Capitalized Interest)	120,228	
Interest Expense ($239,500 − $120,228)	119,272	
Cash ($112,500 + $55,000 + $72,000)		239,500

Shalla should write off capitalized interest cost as part of depreciation over the useful life of the assets involved and not over the term of the debt. It should disclose the amount of interest cost capitalized during the period and the capitalization rate used to determine the amount of interest capitalized, with the portion charged to expense and the portion capitalized indicated.

At December 31, 2015, Shalla discloses the amount of interest capitalized either as part of the income statement or in the notes accompanying the financial statements. We illustrate both forms of disclosure, in Illustrations 10-7 and 10-8.

ILLUSTRATION 10-7
Capitalized Interest
Reported in the Income
Statement

Other income and expense		
Interest expense	$239,500	
Less: Capitalized interest	120,228	$119,272
Income before income taxes		XXXX
Income taxes		XXX
Net income		$ XXXX

ILLUSTRATION 10-8
Capitalized Interest
Disclosed in a Note

Note 1: Accounting Policies. *Capitalized Interest.* During 2015, total interest cost was $239,500, of which $120,228 was capitalized and $119,272 was charged to expense. The capitalization rate used was 11.04%.

Special Issues Related to Interest Capitalization

Two issues related to interest capitalization merit special attention:

1. Expenditures for land.

2. Interest revenue.

Expenditures for Land. When a company purchases land with the intention of developing it for a particular use, interest costs associated with those expenditures qualify for interest capitalization. If it purchases land as a site for a structure (such as a plant site), **interest costs capitalized during the period of construction are part of the cost of the plant, not the land**. Conversely, if the company develops land for lot sales, it includes any capitalized interest cost as part of the acquisition cost of the developed land. However, it should **not** capitalize interest costs involved in purchasing land held **for speculation** because the asset is ready for its intended use.

Interest Revenue. Companies frequently borrow money to finance construction of assets. They temporarily invest the excess borrowed funds in interest-bearing securities until they need the funds to pay for construction. During the early stages of construction, interest revenue earned may exceed the interest cost incurred on the borrowed funds.

Should companies offset interest revenue against interest cost when determining the amount of interest to capitalize as part of the construction cost of assets? IFRS requires that interest revenue earned on specific borrowings should offset interest costs capitalized. The rationale is that the interest revenue earned on specific borrowings is directly related to the interest cost incurred on that borrowing. To illustrate, assume that Shalla Company (see Illustration 10-7) earned $10,000 in interest revenue in 2015 related to its specific borrowings of $750,000. In that case, Shalla capitalizes interest costs of $110,228 ($120,228 − $10,000), not $120,228. As indicated, Shalla uses only interest revenue on its specific borrowings to reduce the amount capitalized. Offsetting interest revenue from other general borrowings is not appropriate as it leads to misleading reductions in capitalized interest.

Observations

The interest capitalization requirement is still debated. From a conceptual viewpoint, many believe that, for the reasons mentioned earlier, companies should either capitalize **no interest cost** or **all interest costs**, actual or imputed.

What do the numbers mean?　　WHAT'S IN YOUR INTEREST?

How do financial statement users determine the impact of interest capitalization on a company's bottom line? They examine the notes to the financial statements. Companies with material interest capitalization must disclose the amounts of capitalized interest relative to total interest costs. For example, Royal Dutch Shell (GBR and NLD) capitalized nearly 42 percent of its total interest costs in a recent year and provided the following footnote related to capitalized interest.

Interest Expense (in millions):	
Interest incurred	$2,051
Less: Interest capitalised	(870)
Total	$1,181

The interest rate applied in determining the amount of interest capitalised was 5.0%.

VALUATION OF PROPERTY, PLANT, AND EQUIPMENT

Like other assets, **companies should record property, plant, and equipment at the fair value of what they give up or at the fair value of the asset received, whichever is more clearly evident**. However, the process of asset acquisition sometimes obscures fair value. For example, if a company buys land and buildings together for one price, how does it determine separate values for the land and buildings? We examine these types of accounting problems in the following sections.

5 LEARNING OBJECTIVE
Understand accounting issues related to acquiring and valuing plant assets.

Cash Discounts

When a company purchases plant assets subject to cash discounts for prompt payment, how should it report the discount? If it takes the discount, the company should consider the discount as a reduction in the purchase price of the asset. But should the company reduce the asset cost even if it does not take the discount?

Two points of view exist on this question. One approach considers the discount—whether taken or not—as a reduction in the cost of the asset. The rationale for this approach is that the real cost of the asset is the cash or cash equivalent price of the asset. In addition, some argue that the terms of cash discounts are so attractive that failure to take them indicates management error or inefficiency.

With respect to the second approach, its proponents argue that failure to take the discount should not always be considered a loss. The terms may be unfavorable, or it might not be prudent for the company to take the discount. At present, companies use both methods, though most prefer the former method. (*For homework purposes, treat the discount as a reduction in the cost of the asset.*)

Deferred-Payment Contracts

Companies frequently purchase plant assets on long-term credit contracts, using notes, mortgages, bonds, or equipment obligations. **To properly reflect cost, companies account for assets purchased on long-term credit contracts at the present value of the consideration exchanged between the contracting parties at the date of the transaction.**

For example, Greathouse Company purchases an asset today in exchange for a $10,000 zero-interest-bearing note payable four years from now. The company would not record the asset at $10,000. Instead, the present value of the $10,000 note establishes the exchange price of the transaction (the purchase price of the asset). Assuming an appropriate interest rate of 9 percent at which to discount this single payment of $10,000 due four years from now, Greathouse records this asset at $7,084.30 ($10,000 × .70843). [See Table 6-2 for the present value of a single sum, $PV = \$10,000\ (PVF_{4,9\%})$.]

When no interest rate is stated or if the specified rate is unreasonable, the company imputes an appropriate interest rate. The objective is to approximate the interest rate that the buyer and seller would negotiate at arm's length in a similar borrowing transaction. In imputing an interest rate, companies consider such factors as the borrower's credit rating, the amount and maturity date of the note, and prevailing interest rates. **The company uses the cash exchange price of the asset acquired (if determinable) as the basis for recording the asset and measuring the interest element.**

To illustrate, Sutter Company purchases a specially built robot spray painter for its production line. The company issues a €100,000, five-year, zero-interest-bearing note to Wrigley Robotics, Inc. for the new equipment. The prevailing market rate of interest for obligations of this nature is 10 percent. Sutter is to pay off the note in five €20,000 installments, made at the end of each year. Sutter cannot readily determine the fair value of this specially built robot. Therefore, Sutter approximates the robot's value by establishing the fair value (present value) of the note. Entries for the date of purchase and dates of payments, plus computation of the present value of the note, are as follows.

Date of Purchase

Equipment	75,816*	
Notes Payable		75,816

*Present value of note = €20,000 $(PVF\text{-}OA_{5,10\%})$
  = €20,000 (3.79079); Table 6-4
  = €75,816

End of First Year

Interest Expense	7,582	
Notes Payable	12,418	
Cash		20,000

Interest expense in the first year under the effective-interest approach is €7,582 (€75,816 × 10%). The entry at the end of the second year to record interest and principal payment is as follows.

End of Second Year

Interest Expense	6,340	
Notes Payable	13,660	
Cash		20,000

Interest expense in the second year under the effective-interest approach is €6,340 [(€75,816 − €12,418) × 10%].

If Sutter did not impute an interest rate for deferred-payment contracts, it would record the asset at an amount greater than its fair value. In addition, Sutter would understate interest expense in the income statement for all periods involved.

Lump-Sum Purchases

A special problem of valuing fixed assets arises when a company purchases a group of assets at a single lump-sum price. When this common situation occurs, the company allocates the total cost among the various assets on the basis of their relative fair values.

The assumption is that costs will vary in direct proportion to fair value. This is the same principle that companies apply to allocate a lump-sum cost among different inventory items.

To determine fair value, a company should use valuation techniques that are appropriate in the circumstances. In some cases, a single valuation technique will be appropriate. In other cases, multiple valuation approaches might have to be used.[5]

To illustrate, Norduct Homes, Inc. decides to purchase several assets of a small heating concern, Comfort Heating, for $80,000. Comfort Heating is in the process of liquidation. Its assets sold are:

	Book Value	Fair Value
Inventory	$30,000	$ 25,000
Land	20,000	25,000
Building	35,000	50,000
	$85,000	$100,000

Norduct Homes allocates the $80,000 purchase price on the basis of the relative fair values (assuming specific identification of costs is impracticable) in the following manner.

ILLUSTRATION 10-9
Allocation of Purchase Price—Relative Fair Value Basis

$$\text{Inventory} \quad \frac{\$25,000}{\$100,000} \times \$80,000 = \$20,000$$

$$\text{Land} \quad \frac{\$25,000}{\$100,000} \times \$80,000 = \$20,000$$

$$\text{Building} \quad \frac{\$50,000}{\$100,000} \times \$80,000 = \$40,000$$

Issuance of Shares

When companies acquire property by issuing securities, such as ordinary shares, the par or stated value of such shares fails to properly measure the property cost. If trading of the shares is active, **the market price of the shares issued is a fair indication of the cost of the property acquired. The shares are a good measure of the current cash equivalent price.**

For example, Upgrade Living Co. decides to purchase some adjacent land for expansion of its carpeting and cabinet operation. In lieu of paying cash for the land, the company issues to Deedland Company 5,000 ordinary shares (par value $10) that have a market price of $12 per share. Upgrade Living Co. records the following entry.

Land (5,000 × $12)	60,000	
Share Capital—Ordinary		50,000
Share Premium—Ordinary		10,000

If the company cannot determine the fair value of the ordinary shares exchanged (based on a market price), it may estimate the fair value of the property. It then uses the value of the property as the basis for recording the asset and issuance of the ordinary shares.

---

[5]The valuation approaches that should be used are the market, income, or cost approach, or a combination of these approaches. The *market approach* uses observable prices and other relevant information generated by market transactions involving comparable assets. The *income approach* uses valuation techniques to convert future amounts (for example, cash flows or earnings) to a single present value amount (discounted). The *cost approach* is based on the amount that currently would be required to replace the service capacity of an asset (often referred to as current replacement cost).

Exchanges of Non-Monetary Assets

The proper accounting for exchanges of non-monetary assets, such as property, plant, and equipment, is controversial.[6] Some argue that companies should account for these types of exchanges based on the fair value of the asset given up or the fair value of the asset received, with a gain or loss recognized. Others believe that they should account for exchanges based on the recorded amount (book value) of the asset given up, with no gain or loss recognized. Still others favor an approach that recognizes losses in all cases but defers gains in special situations.

Ordinarily, companies account for the exchange of **non-monetary assets** on the basis of **the fair value of the asset given up or the fair value of the asset received, whichever is clearly more evident. [6]** Thus, companies **should recognize immediately** any gains or losses on the exchange. The rationale for immediate recognition is that most transactions have **commercial substance**, and therefore gains and losses should be recognized.

Meaning of Commercial Substance

As indicated above, fair value is the basis for measuring an asset acquired in a non-monetary exchange if the transaction has commercial substance. An exchange has **commercial substance** if the future cash flows change as a result of the transaction. That is, if the two parties' economic positions change, the transaction has commercial substance.

For example, Andrew Co. exchanges some of its equipment for land held by Roddick Inc. It is likely that the timing and amount of the cash flows arising for the land will differ significantly from the cash flows arising from the equipment. As a result, both Andrew Co. and Roddick Inc. are in different economic positions. Therefore, the exchange has commercial substance, and the companies recognize a gain or loss on the exchange.

What if companies exchange similar assets, such as one truck for another truck? Even in an exchange of similar assets, a change in the economic position of the company can result. For example, let's say the useful life of the truck received is significantly longer than that of the truck given up. The cash flows for the trucks can differ significantly. As a result, the transaction has commercial substance, and the company should use fair value as a basis for measuring the asset received in the exchange.

However, it is possible to exchange similar assets but not have a significant difference in cash flows. That is, the company is in the same economic position as before the exchange. In that case, the company recognizes a loss but generally defers a gain.

As we will see in the following examples, use of fair value generally results in recognizing a gain or loss at the time of the exchange. Consequently, companies must determine if the transaction has commercial substance. To make this determination, they must carefully evaluate the cash flow characteristics of the assets exchanged.[7]

---

[6]Non-monetary assets are items whose price in terms of the monetary unit may change over time. Monetary assets—cash and short- or long-term accounts and notes receivable—are fixed in terms of units of currency by contract or otherwise.

[7]The determination of the commercial substance of a transaction requires significant judgment. In determining whether future cash flows change, it is necessary to do one of two things.
(1) Determine whether the risk, timing, and amount of cash flows arising for the asset received differ from the cash flows associated with the outbound asset. Or, (2) evaluate whether cash flows are affected with the exchange versus without the exchange. Also, note that if companies cannot determine fair values of the assets exchanged, they should use recorded book values in accounting for the exchange.

Illustration 10-10 summarizes asset exchange situations and the related accounting.

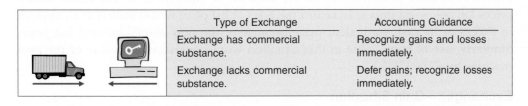

Type of Exchange	Accounting Guidance
Exchange has commercial substance.	Recognize gains and losses immediately.
Exchange lacks commercial substance.	Defer gains; recognize losses immediately.

ILLUSTRATION 10-10
Accounting for Exchanges

As Illustration 10-10 indicates, companies immediately recognize losses they incur on all exchanges. The accounting for gains depends on whether the exchange has commercial substance. If the exchange has commercial substance, the company recognizes the gain immediately. However, if the exchange lacks commercial substance, it defers recognition of a gain.

To illustrate the accounting for these different types of transactions, we examine various loss and gain exchange situations.

Exchanges—Loss Situation

When a company exchanges non-monetary assets and a loss results, the company recognizes the loss immediately. The rationale: Companies should not value assets at more than their cash equivalent price. If the loss were deferred, assets would be overstated. Therefore, companies recognize a loss immediately whether the exchange has commercial substance or not.

For example, Information Processing, Inc. trades its used machine for a new model at Jerrod Business Solutions Inc. The exchange has commercial substance. The used machine has a book value of €8,000 (original cost €12,000 less €4,000 accumulated depreciation) and a fair value of €6,000. The new model lists for €16,000. Jerrod gives Information Processing a trade-in allowance of €9,000 for the used machine. Information Processing computes the cost of the new asset as follows.

List price of new machine	€16,000
Less: Trade-in allowance for used machine	9,000
Cash payment due	7,000
Fair value of used machine	6,000
Cost of new machine	€13,000

ILLUSTRATION 10-11
Computation of Cost of New Machine

Information Processing records this transaction as follows.

Equipment	13,000	
Accumulated Depreciation—Equipment	4,000	
Loss on Disposal of Equipment	2,000	
Equipment		12,000
Cash		7,000

We verify the loss on the disposal of the used machine as follows.

Fair value of used machine	€6,000
Less: Book value of used machine	8,000
Loss on disposal of used machine	€2,000

ILLUSTRATION 10-12
Computation of Loss on Disposal of Used Machine

Why did Information Processing not use the trade-in allowance or the book value of the old asset as a basis for the new equipment? The company did not use the trade-in allowance because it included a price concession (similar to a price discount). Few individuals pay list price for a new car or other new equipment. Dealers such as Jerrod often inflate trade-in allowances on the used car or equipment so that actual selling prices fall below list prices. To record the asset at list price would state it at an amount in excess of its cash equivalent price because of the new asset's inflated list price. Similarly, use of book value in this situation would overstate the value of the new machine by €2,000.[8]

Exchanges—Gain Situation

Has Commercial Substance. Now let's consider the situation in which a non-monetary exchange has commercial substance and a gain is realized. In such a case, a company usually records the cost of a non-monetary asset acquired in exchange for another non-monetary asset at the **fair value of the asset given up**, and immediately recognizes a gain. The company should use the **fair value of the asset received** only if it is more clearly evident than the fair value of the asset given up.

To illustrate, Interstate Transportation Company exchanged a number of used trucks plus cash for a semi-truck. The used trucks have a combined book value of $42,000 (cost $64,000 less $22,000 accumulated depreciation). Interstate's purchasing agent, experienced in the secondhand market, indicates that the used trucks have a fair value of $49,000. In addition to the trucks, Interstate must pay $11,000 cash for the semi-truck. Interstate computes the cost of the semi-truck as follows.

ILLUSTRATION 10-13
Computation of
Semi-Truck Cost

Fair value of trucks exchanged	$49,000
Cash paid	11,000
Cost of semi-truck	$60,000

Interstate records the exchange transaction as follows.

Trucks (semi)	60,000	
Accumulated Depreciation—Trucks	22,000	
Trucks (used)		64,000
Gain on Disposal of Trucks		7,000
Cash		11,000

The gain is the difference between the fair value of the used trucks and their book value. We verify the computation as follows.

ILLUSTRATION 10-14
Computation of Gain on
Disposal of Used Trucks

Fair value of used trucks		$49,000
Cost of used trucks	$64,000	
Less: Accumulated depreciation	22,000	
Less: Book value of used trucks		42,000
Gain on disposal of used trucks		$ 7,000

In this case, Interstate is in a different economic position, and therefore the transaction has commercial substance. Thus, it **recognizes a gain**.

Lacks Commercial Substance. We now assume that the Interstate Transportation Company exchange lacks commercial substance. That is, the economic position of Interstate did not change significantly as a result of this exchange. In this case, Interstate defers the

[8]Recognize that for Jerrod (the dealer), the asset given up in the exchange is considered inventory. As a result, Jerrod records a sale and related cost of goods sold. The used machine received by Jerrod is recorded at fair value.

gain of $7,000 and reduces the basis of the semi-truck. Illustration 10-15 shows two different but acceptable computations to illustrate this reduction.

Fair value of semi-truck	$60,000		Book value of used trucks	$42,000	
Less: Gain deferred	7,000	OR	Plus: Cash paid	11,000	
Basis of semi-truck	$53,000		Basis of semi-truck	$53,000	

ILLUSTRATION 10-15
Basis of Semi-Truck—
Fair Value vs. Book Value

Interstate records this transaction as follows.

Trucks (semi)	53,000	
Accumulated Depreciation—Trucks	22,000	
Trucks (used)		64,000
Cash		11,000

If the exchange lacks commercial substance, the company recognizes the gain (reflected in the basis of the semi-truck) when it later sells the semi-truck, not at the time of the exchange.

Illustration 10-16 presents in summary form the accounting requirements for recognizing gains and losses on exchanges of non-monetary assets.

1. Compute the total gain or loss on the transaction. This amount is equal to the difference between the fair value of the asset given up and the book value of the asset given up.
2. If a loss is computed in Step 1, always recognize the entire loss.
3. If a gain is computed in Step 1:
   (a) And the exchange has commercial substance, recognize the entire gain.
   (b) And the exchange lacks commercial substance, no gain is recognized.

ILLUSTRATION 10-16
Summary of Gain and
Loss Recognition on
Exchanges of Non-
Monetary Assets

Companies disclose in their financial statements non-monetary exchanges during a period. Such disclosure indicates the nature of the transaction(s), the method of accounting for the assets exchanged, and gains or losses recognized on the exchanges.

Government Grants

Many companies receive government grants. **Government grants** are assistance received from a government in the form of transfers of resources to a company in return for past or future compliance with certain conditions relating to the operating activities of the company.[9] For example, **AB InBev NV (BEL)** received government grants related to fiscal incentives given by certain Brazilian states, based on the company's operations and investments in these states. **Danisco A/S (DEN)** notes that it receives government grants for such items as research, development, and carbon-dioxide (CO_2) allowances and investments.

In other words, a government grant is often some type of asset (such as cash; securities; property, plant, and equipment; or use of facilities) provided as a subsidy to a company. A government grant also occurs when debt is forgiven or borrowings are

---

[9]Recognize that there is a distinction between government grants and government assistance. Government assistance can take many forms, such as providing advice related to technical legal or product issues or being a supplier for the company's goods or services. Government grants are a special part of government assistance where financial resources are provided to the company. In rare situations, a company may receive a donation (gift). The accounting for grants and donations is essentially the same. IFRS does provide an option of recording property, plant, and equipment at zero cost although it appears this practice is rarely followed.

provided to the company at a below-market interest rate. The major accounting issues with government grants are to determine the proper method of accounting for these transfers on the company's books and how they should be presented in the financial statements.

Accounting Approaches

When companies acquire an asset such as property, plant, and equipment through a government grant, a strict cost concept dictates that the valuation of the asset should be zero. However, a departure from the historical cost principle seems justified because the only costs incurred (legal fees and other relatively minor expenditures) are not a reasonable basis of accounting for the assets acquired. To record nothing is to ignore the economic realities of an increase in wealth and assets. Therefore, most companies use the **fair value of the asset** to establish its value on the books.

What, then, is the proper accounting for the credit related to the government grant when the fair value of the asset is used? Two approaches are suggested—the capital (equity) approach and the income approach. Supporters of the equity approach believe the credit should go directly to equity because often no repayment of the grant is expected. In addition, these grants are an incentive by the government—they are not earned as part of normal operations and should not offset expenses of operations on the income statement.

Supporters of the income approach disagree—they believe that the credit should be reported as revenue in the income statement. Government grants should not go directly to equity because the government is not a shareholder. In addition, most government grants have conditions attached to them which likely affect future expenses. They should, therefore, be reported as grant revenue (or deferred grant revenue) and matched with the associated expenses that will occur in the future as a result of the grant.

Income Approach

IFRS requires the income approach and indicates that the general rule is that grants should be recognized in income on a systematic basis that matches them with the related costs that they are intended to compensate. **[7]** This is accomplished in one of two ways for an asset such as property, plant, and equipment:

1. Recording the grant as deferred grant revenue, which is recognized as income on a systematic basis over the useful life of the asset, or
2. Deducting the grant from the carrying amount of the assets received from the grant, in which case the grant is recognized in income as a reduction of depreciation expense.

To illustrate application of the income approach, consider the following three examples.

Example 1: Grant for Lab Equipment. AG Company received a €500,000 subsidy from the government to purchase lab equipment on January 2, 2015. The lab equipment cost is €2,000,000, has a useful life of five years, and is depreciated on the straight-line basis. As indicated, AG can record this grant in one of two ways. (1) Credit Deferred Grant Revenue for the subsidy and amortize the deferred grant revenue over the five-year period. (2) Credit the lab equipment for the subsidy and depreciate this amount over the five-year period.

If AG chooses to record deferred revenue of €500,000, it amortizes this amount over the five-year period to income (€100,000 per year). The effects on the financial statements at December 31, 2015, are shown in Illustration 10-17.

```
Statement of Financial Position
Non-current assets
    Equipment                                €2,000,000
    Less: Accumulated depreciation              400,000      €1,600,000

Non-current liabilities
    Deferred grant revenue                   €  300,000
Current liabilities
    Deferred grant revenue                      100,000

Income Statement
Grant revenue for the year                   €  100,000
Depreciation expense for the year               400,000
    Net income (loss) effect                 € (300,000)
```

ILLUSTRATION 10-17
Government Grant
Recorded as Deferred
Revenue

If AG chooses to reduce the cost of the lab equipment, AG reports the equipment at €1,500,000 (€2,000,000 − €500,000) and depreciates this amount over the five-year period. The effects on the financial statements at December 31, 2015, are shown in Illustration 10-18.

```
Statement of Financial Position
Non-current assets
    Equipment                                €1,500,000
    Less: Accumulated depreciation              300,000      €1,200,000

Income Statement
Depreciation expense for the year                           €  300,000
```

ILLUSTRATION 10-18
Government Grant
Adjusted to Asset

The amount of net expense is the same for both situations (€300,000), but the presentation on the financial statements is different.[10]

Example 2: Grant for Past Losses. Flyaway Airlines has incurred substantial operating losses over the last five years. The company now has little liquidity remaining and is considering bankruptcy. The City of Plentiville does not want to lose airline service and feels it has some responsibility related to the airlines losses. It therefore agrees to provide a cash grant of $1,000,000 to the airline to pay off its creditors so that it may continue service. Because the grant is given to pay amounts owed to creditors for past losses, Flyaway Airlines should record the income in the period it is received. The entry to record this grant is as follows.

```
Cash                                1,000,000
    Grant Revenue                                 1,000,000
```

If the conditions of the grant indicate that Flyaway must satisfy some future obligations related to this grant, then it is appropriate to credit Deferred Grant Revenue and amortize it over the appropriate periods in the future.

Example 3: Grant for Borrowing Costs. The City of Puerto Aloa is encouraging the high-tech firm TechSmart to move its plant to Puerto Aloa. The city has agreed to provide an interest-free loan of $10,000,000, with the loan payable at the end of 10 years,

---

[10]Both approaches have deficiencies. Reducing the cost of the asset for the grant means that the lab equipment's cost on the statement of financial position may be considered understated. Recording the deferred grant revenue on the credit side of the statement of financial position is problematic as many believe it is not a liability nor is it equity.

provided that TechSmart will employ at least 50 percent of its work force from the community of Puerto Aloa over the next 10 years. TechSmart's incremental borrowing rate is 9 percent. Therefore, the present value of the future loan payable ($10,000,000) is $6,499,300 ($10,000,000 × .64993$_{i=9\%, n=5}$). The entry to record the borrowing is as follows.

Cash	6,499,300	
Notes Payable		6,499,300

In addition, using the deferred revenue approach, the company records the grant as follows.

Cash	3,500,700	
Deferred Grant Revenue		3,500,700

TechSmart then uses the effective-interest rate to determine interest expense of $584,937 (9% × $6,499,300) in the first year. The company also decreases Deferred Grant Revenue and increases Grant Revenue for $584,937. As a result, the net expense related to the borrowing is zero in each year.

Unfortunately, the accounting for government grants is still somewhat unsettled. Companies are permitted to record grants at nominal values or at fair value. In addition, they may record grants to property, plant, and equipment either as a reduction of the asset or to deferred grant revenue. The key to these situations is to provide disclosures that highlight the accounting approaches. Presented below are examples of how grants are disclosed in the notes to the financial statements.

A company that adopted the deferred income approach is **AB Electrolux** (SWE), as shown in Illustration 10-19.

ILLUSTRATION 10-19
Deferred Income
Disclosure

AB Electrolux

Note 1. Accounting and valuation principles: Government grants

Government grants relate to financial grants from governments, public authorities, and similar local, national, or international bodies. These are recognized when there is a reasonable assurance that the Group will comply with the conditions attaching to them, and that the grants will be received. Government grants related to assets are included in the balance sheet as deferred income and recognized as income over the useful life of the assets.

Kazakhymys plc (GBR) is an example of a company adopting a policy of deducting grants related to assets from the cost of the assets, as shown in Illustration 10-20.

ILLUSTRATION 10-20
Reduction of Asset
Disclosure

Kazakhymys plc

Note 3. Summary of significant accounting policies: Government grants

Government grants are recognised at their fair value where there is reasonable assurance that the grant will be received and all attaching conditions will be complied with. When the grant relates to an expense item, it is recognised as income over the periods necessary to match the grant on a systematic basis to the costs that it is intended to compensate. Where the grant relates to an asset, the fair value is credited to the cost of the asset and is released to the income statement over the expected useful life in a consistent manner with the depreciation method for the relevant asset.

When a company **contributes** a non-monetary asset, it should record the amount of the donation as an expense at the fair value of the donated asset. If a difference exists between the fair value of the asset and its book value, the company should recognize a gain or loss. To illustrate, Kline Industries donates land to the City of São Paulo for a city park. The land cost R$80,000 and has a fair value of R$110,000. Kline Industries records this donation as follows.

Contribution Expense	110,000	
Land		80,000
Gain on Disposal of Land		30,000

The gain on disposal should be reported in the "Other income and expense" section of the income statement, not as revenue.

COSTS SUBSEQUENT TO ACQUISITION

After installing plant assets and readying them for use, a company incurs additional costs that range from ordinary repairs to significant additions. The major problem is allocating these costs to the proper time periods.

6 LEARNING OBJECTIVE
Describe the accounting treatment for costs subsequent to acquisition.

In determining how costs should be allocated subsequent to acquisition, companies follow the same criteria used to determine the initial cost of property, plant, and equipment. That is, they recognize costs subsequent to acquisition as an asset when the costs can be measured reliably and it is probable that the company will obtain future economic benefits. Evidence of future economic benefit would include increases in (1) useful life, (2) quantity of product produced, and (3) quality of product produced.

Underlying Concepts

Expensing long-lived waste baskets is an application of the materiality concept.

Generally, companies incur four types of major expenditures relative to existing assets.

MAJOR TYPES OF EXPENDITURES

ADDITIONS. Increase or extension of existing assets.

IMPROVEMENTS AND REPLACEMENTS. Substitution of a better or similar asset for an existing one.

REARRANGEMENT AND REORGANIZATION. Movement of assets from one location to another.

REPAIRS. Expenditures that maintain assets in condition for operation.

Additions

Additions should present no major accounting problems. By definition, **companies capitalize any addition to plant assets because a new asset is created**. For example, the addition of a wing to a hospital, or of an air conditioning system to an office, increases the service potential of that facility. Companies should capitalize such expenditures and match them against the revenues that will result in future periods.

One problem that arises in this area is the accounting for any changes related to the existing structure as a result of the addition. Is the cost incurred to tear down an old wall, to make room for the addition, a cost of the addition or an expense or loss of the period? The answer is that it depends on the original intent. If the company had anticipated building an addition later, then this cost of removal is a proper cost of the addition. But if the company had not anticipated this development, it should properly report the removal as a loss in the current period on the basis of inefficient planning. Conceptually, the company should remove the cost of the old wall and related depreciation and record a loss. It should then add the cost of the new wall to the cost of the building. In these situations, it is sometimes impracticable to determine a reasonable carrying amount for the old wall. Companies therefore assume the old asset to have a zero carrying amount and simply add the cost of the replacement to the overall cost.

What do the numbers mean?   DISCONNECTED

It all started with a check of the books by an internal auditor for WorldCom Inc. (USA). The telecom giant's newly installed chief executive had asked for a financial review, and the auditor was spot-checking records of capital expenditures. She found the company was using an unorthodox technique to account for one of its biggest expenses: charges paid to local telephone networks to complete long-distance calls.

Instead of recording these charges as operating expenses, WorldCom recorded a significant portion as capital expenditures. The maneuver was worth hundreds of millions of dollars to WorldCom's bottom line. It effectively turned a loss for all of 2001 and the first quarter of 2002 into a profit. The following illustration compares WorldCom's accounting to that under proper accounting principles. Soon after this discovery, WorldCom filed for bankruptcy.

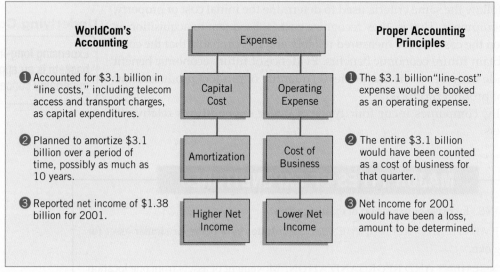

Source: Adapted from Jared Sandberg, Deborah Solomon, and Rebecca Blumenstein, "Inside WorldCom's Unearthing of a Vast Accounting Scandal," *Wall Street Journal* (June 27, 2002), p. A1.

Improvements and Replacements

Companies substitute one asset for another through **improvements** and **replacements**. What is the difference between an improvement and a replacement? An improvement (**betterment**) is the substitution of a **better asset** for the one currently used (say, a concrete floor for a wooden floor). A replacement, on the other hand, is the substitution of a **similar asset** (a wooden floor for a wooden floor).

Many times, improvements and replacements result from a general policy to modernize or rehabilitate an older building or piece of equipment. The problem is differentiating these types of expenditures from normal repairs. Does the expenditure increase the **future service potential** of the asset? Or, does it merely **maintain the existing level** of service? Frequently, the answer is not clear-cut. Good judgment is required to correctly classify these expenditures.

If the expenditure increases the future service potential of the asset, a company should capitalize it. The company should simply remove the cost of the old asset and related depreciation and recognize a loss, if any. It should then add the cost of the new substituted asset.

To illustrate, Instinct Enterprises decides to replace the pipes in its plumbing system. A plumber suggests that the company use plastic tubing in place of the cast iron pipes and copper tubing. The old pipe and tubing have a book value of £15,000 (cost of £150,000 less accumulated depreciation of £135,000), and a residual value of £1,000. The plastic tubing system costs £125,000. If Instinct pays £124,000 for the new tubing after exchanging the old tubing, it makes the following entry.

Equipment (plumbing system)	125,000	
Accumulated Depreciation—Equipment	135,000	
Loss on Disposal of Equipment	14,000	
Equipment (plumbing system)		150,000
Cash (£125,000 − £1,000)		124,000

One issue in any substitution is computing the cost and accumulated depreciation of the old asset. Fortunately, IFRS requires each significant component of an asset to be identified and its depreciation base to be determined and depreciated separately. This approach is referred to as component depreciation accounting. To illustrate, Hanoi Company has a tractor that it purchased at a cost of £50,000. Individual components of this tractor and useful life are as follows (all residual values are zero).

	Cost	Useful Life	Depreciation per Year
Tires	£ 6,000	2 years	£3,000
Transmission	10,000	5 years	2,000
Truck	34,000	10 years	3,400

Companies should keep accounting records based on the components of the asset. If the company does not have this information, estimation methods generally can provide a reasonable answer.

Rearrangement and Reorganization

As indicated earlier, a company may incur rearrangement or reorganization costs for some of its assets. The question is whether the costs incurred in this rearrangement or reorganization are capitalized or expensed. IFRS indicates that the recognition of costs ceases once the asset is in the location and condition necessary to begin operations as management intended. As a result, the costs of reorganizing or rearranging existing property, plant, and equipment are not capitalized but are expensed as incurred.

Repairs

Ordinary Repairs

A company makes ordinary repairs to maintain plant assets in operating condition. It charges ordinary repairs to an expense account in the period incurred on the basis that **it is the primary period benefited**. Maintenance charges that occur regularly include replacing minor parts, lubricating and adjusting equipment, repainting, and cleaning. A company treats these as ordinary operating expenses.

It is often difficult to distinguish a repair from an improvement or replacement. The major consideration is whether the expenditure benefits more than one year or one operating cycle, whichever is longer. If a major repair (such as an overhaul) occurs, several periods will benefit. A company should generally handle this cost as an improvement or replacement.

Major Repairs

Some companies, such as airlines **Ryanair** (IRL) or **Lufthansa** (DEU) or shipping companies such as **A.P. Moller—Maersk** (DEN) or **CMA CGM Group** (FRA), have substantial overhaul costs related to their airplanes or ships. For example, assume the Shipaway Company has just purchased a new ship for $200 million. The useful life of the ship is 20 years, but every 4 years it must be dry-docked and a major overhaul done. It is estimated that the overhaul will cost $4 million. The $4 million should be accounted for as a separate component of the cost of the ship (using component depreciation) and depreciated over 4 years. At the time of the major overhaul, the cost and related depreciation to date should be eliminated and replaced with the new cost incurred for the overhaul.

Summary of Costs Subsequent to Acquisition

Illustration 10-21 summarizes the accounting treatment for various costs incurred subsequent to the acquisition of capitalized assets.

ILLUSTRATION 10-21
Summary of Costs
Subsequent to
Acquisition of Property,
Plant, and Equipment

Type of Expenditure	Normal Accounting Treatment
Additions	Capitalize cost of addition to asset account.
Improvements and replacements	Remove cost of and accumulated depreciation on old asset, recognizing any gain or loss. Capitalize cost of improvement/replacement.
Rearrangement and reorganization	Expense costs of rearrangement and reorganization costs as expense.
Repairs	(a) **Ordinary:** Expense cost of repairs when incurred. (b) **Major:** Remove cost and accumulated depreciation of old asset, recognizing any gain or loss. Capitalize cost of major repair.

DISPOSITION OF PROPERTY, PLANT, AND EQUIPMENT

LEARNING OBJECTIVE 7

Describe the accounting treatment for the disposal of property, plant, and equipment.

A company, like **Nokia** (FIN), may retire plant assets voluntarily or dispose of them by sale, exchange, involuntary conversion, or abandonment. Regardless of the type of disposal, depreciation must be taken up to the date of disposition. Then, Nokia should remove all accounts related to the retired asset. Generally, the book value of the specific plant asset does not equal its disposal value. As a result, a gain or loss develops. The reason: Depreciation is an estimate of cost allocation and not a process of valuation. **The gain or loss is really a correction of net income** for the years during which Nokia used the fixed asset.

Nokia should report gains or losses on the disposal of plant assets in the income statement along with other items from customary business activities. However, if it sold, abandoned, spun off, or otherwise disposed of the "operations of a component of a business," then it should report the results separately in the discontinued operations section of the income statement. That is, Nokia should report any gain or loss from disposal of a business component with the related results of discontinued operations.

Sale of Plant Assets

Companies record depreciation for the period of time between the date of the last depreciation entry and the date of sale. To illustrate, assume that Barret Company recorded depreciation on a machine costing €18,000 for nine years at the rate of €1,200 per year. If it sells the machine in the middle of the tenth year for €7,000, Barret records depreciation to the date of sale as:

Depreciation Expense (€1,200 × $\frac{1}{2}$)	600	
Accumulated Depreciation—Machinery		600

The entry for the sale of the asset then is:

Cash	7,000	
Accumulated Depreciation—Machinery	11,400	
[(€1,200 × 9) + €600]		
Machinery		18,000
Gain on Disposal of Machinery		400

The book value of the machinery at the time of the sale is €6,600 (€18,000 − €11,400). Because the machinery sold for €7,000, the amount of the gain on the sale is €400 (€7,000 − €6,600).

Involuntary Conversion

Sometimes, an asset's service is terminated through some type of **involuntary conversion** such as fire, flood, theft, or condemnation. Companies report the difference between the amount recovered (e.g., from a condemnation award or insurance recovery), if any, and the asset's book value as a gain or loss. They treat these gains or losses like any other type of disposition.

To illustrate, Camel Transport Corp. had to sell a plant located on company property that stood directly in the path of a public highway. For a number of years, the government had sought to purchase the land on which the building stood, but the company resisted. The government ultimately exercised its right of eminent domain, which the courts upheld. In settlement, Camel received $500,000, which substantially exceeded the book value of the land of $150,000 and the book value of the building of $100,000 (cost $300,000 less accumulated depreciation $200,000). Camel made the following entry.

Cash	500,000	
Accumulated Depreciation—Buildings	200,000	
Buildings		300,000
Land		150,000
Gain on Disposal of Plant Assets		250,000

The gain on disposal should be reported in "Other income and expense" on the income statement and not as revenue. If there is a delay in the payment of the condemnation award or insurance recovery, a receivable is recorded at its cash equivalent price.

Some object to the recognition of a gain or loss in certain *involuntary* conversions. For example, governments often condemn forests for national parks. The paper companies that owned these forests must report a gain or loss on the condemnation. However, some companies contend that no gain or loss should be reported because they must replace the condemned forest land immediately and so are in the same economic position as they were before. The issue is whether condemnation and subsequent purchase should be viewed as one or two transactions. IFRS requires that a gain or loss be reported in this situation because the conversion is viewed as two transactions—a disposal and a subsequent event.

SUMMARY OF LEARNING OBJECTIVES

1 **Describe property, plant, and equipment.** The major characteristics of property, plant, and equipment are as follows. (1) They are acquired for use in operations and not for resale. (2) They are long-term in nature and usually subject to depreciation. (3) They possess physical substance.

2 **Identify the costs to include in initial valuation of property, plant, and equipment.** The costs included in initial valuation of property, plant, and equipment are as follows.

Cost of land: Includes all expenditures made to acquire land and to ready it for use. Land costs typically include (1) the purchase price; (2) closing costs, such as title to the land, attorney's fees, and recording fees; (3) costs incurred in getting the land in condition for its intended use, such as grading, filling, draining, and clearing; (4) assumption of any liens, mortgages, or encumbrances on the property; and (5) any additional land improvements that have an indefinite life.

Cost of buildings: Includes all expenditures related directly to their acquisition or construction. These costs include (1) materials, labor, and overhead costs incurred during construction, and (2) professional fees and building permits.

Cost of equipment: Includes the purchase price, freight and handling charges incurred, insurance on the equipment while in transit, cost of special foundations if required, assembling and installation costs, and costs of conducting trial runs.

3 **Describe the accounting problems associated with self-constructed assets.** Indirect costs of manufacturing create special problems because companies cannot easily trace these costs directly to work and material orders related to the constructed assets. Companies might handle these costs in one of two ways. (1) Assign no fixed overhead to the cost of the constructed asset. Or, (2) assign a portion of all overhead to the construction process. Companies should use the second method.

4 **Describe the accounting problems associated with interest capitalization.** Only actual interest (with modifications) should be capitalized. The rationale for this approach is that during construction, the asset is not generating revenue and therefore companies should defer (capitalize) interest cost. Once construction is completed, the asset is ready for its intended use and revenues can be earned. Any interest cost incurred in purchasing an asset that is ready for its intended use should be expensed.

5 **Understand accounting issues related to acquiring and valuing plant assets.** The following issues relate to acquiring and valuing plant assets. (1) *Cash discounts:* Whether taken or not, they are generally considered a reduction in the cost of the asset; the real cost of the asset is the cash or cash equivalent price of the asset. (2) *Deferred-payment contracts:* Companies account for assets purchased on long-term credit contracts at the present value of the consideration exchanged between the contracting parties. (3) *Lump-sum purchase:* Allocate the total cost among the various assets on the basis of their relative fair values. (4) *Issuance of shares:* If the shares are actively traded, the market price of the shares issued is a fair indication of the cost of the property acquired. If the market price of the ordinary shares exchanged is not determinable, establish the fair value of the property and use it as the basis for recording the asset and issuance of the ordinary shares. (5) *Exchanges of non-monetary assets.* The accounting for exchanges of non-monetary assets depends on whether the exchange has commercial substance. See Illustrations 10-10 (page 457) and 10-16 (page 459) for summaries of how to account for exchanges. (6) *Grants:* Record at the fair value of the asset received, and credit deferred revenue or the appropriate asset in most cases.

6 **Describe the accounting treatment for costs subsequent to acquisition.** Illustration 10-21 (page 466) summarizes how to account for costs subsequent to acquisition.

7 **Describe the accounting treatment for the disposal of property, plant, and equipment.** Regardless of the time of disposal, companies take depreciation up to the date of disposition and then remove all accounts related to the retired asset. Gains or losses on the retirement of plant assets are shown in the income statement along with other items that arise from customary business activities. Gains or losses on involuntary conversions are reported in "Other income and expense."

IFRS AUTHORITATIVE LITERATURE

Authoritative Literature References

[1] International Accounting Standard 16, *Property, Plant and Equipment* (London, U.K.: International Accounting Standards Committee Foundation, 2003), par. 6.

[2] International Accounting Standard 16, *Property, Plant and Equipment* (London, U.K.: International Accounting Standards Committee Foundation, 2003), par. 7.

[3] International Accounting Standard 16, *Property, Plant and Equipment* (London, U.K.: International Accounting Standards Committee Foundation, 2003), par. 16.

[4] International Accounting Standard 16, *Property, Plant and Equipment* (London, U.K.: International Accounting Standards Committee Foundation, 2003), par. 22.

[5] International Accounting Standard 23, *Borrowing Costs* (London, U.K.: International Accounting Standards Committee Foundation, 2007), paras. 20–25.

[6] International Accounting Standard 16, *Property, Plant and Equipment* (London, U.K.: International Accounting Standards Committee Foundation, 2003), paras. 24–26.

[7] International Accounting Standard 20, *Accounting for Government Grants and Disclosure of Government Assistance* (London, U.K.: International Accounting Standards Committee Foundation, 2001).

QUESTIONS

1. What are the major characteristics of plant assets?

2. Name the items, in addition to the amount paid to the former owner or contractor, that may properly be included as part of the acquisition cost of the following plant assets.

   (a) Land.
   (b) Machinery and equipment.
   (c) Buildings.

3. Indicate where the following items would be shown on a statement of financial position.

   (a) A lien that was attached to the land when purchased.
   (b) Landscaping costs.
   (c) Attorney's fees and recording fees related to purchasing land.
   (d) Variable overhead related to construction of machinery.
   (e) A parking lot servicing employees in the building.
   (f) Cost of temporary building for workers during construction of building.
   (g) Interest expense on bonds payable incurred during construction of a building.
   (h) Assessments for sidewalks that are maintained by the city.

   (i) The cost of demolishing an old building that was on the land when purchased.

4. Two positions have normally been taken with respect to the recording of fixed manufacturing overhead as an element of the cost of plant assets constructed by a company for its own use:

   (a) It should be excluded completely.
   (b) It should be included at the same rate as is charged to normal operations.

   What are the circumstances or rationale that support or deny the application of these methods?

5. The Buildings account of Postera Inc. includes the following items that were used in determining the basis for depreciating the cost of a building.

   (a) Promotion expenses.
   (b) Architect's fees.
   (c) Interest during construction.
   (d) Interest revenue on investments held to fund construction of a building.
   (e) First-year operating losses related to the building.

Do you agree with these charges? If not, how would you deal with each of these items in the corporation's books and in its annual financial statements?

6. Cruz Company has purchased two tracts of land. One tract will be the site of its new manufacturing plant, while the other is being purchased with the hope that it will be sold in the next year at a profit. How should these two tracts of land be reported in the statement of financial position?

7. One financial accounting issue encountered when a company constructs its own plant is whether the interest cost on funds borrowed to finance construction should be capitalized and then amortized over the life of the assets constructed. What is the justification for capitalizing such interest?

8. Provide examples of assets that do not qualify for interest capitalization.

9. What interest rates should be used in determining the amount of interest to be capitalized? How should the amount of interest to be capitalized be determined?

10. How should the amount of interest capitalized be disclosed in the notes to the financial statements? How should interest revenue from temporarily invested excess funds borrowed to finance the construction of assets be accounted for?

11. Discuss the basic accounting problem that arises in handling each of the following situations.

    (a) Assets purchased by issuance of ordinary shares.
    (b) Acquisition of plant assets by grant.
    (c) Purchase of a plant asset subject to a cash discount.
    (d) Assets purchased on a long-term credit basis.
    (e) A group of assets acquired for a lump sum.
    (f) An asset traded in or exchanged for another asset.

12. Magilke Industries acquired equipment this year to be used in its operations. The equipment was delivered by the suppliers, installed by Magilke, and placed into operation. Some of it was purchased for cash with discounts available for prompt payment. Some of it was purchased under long-term payment plans for which the interest charges approximated prevailing rates. What costs should Magilke capitalize for the new equipment purchased this year? Explain.

13. Ocampo Co. purchased for €2,200,000 property that included both land and a building to be used in operations. The seller's book value was €300,000 for the land and €900,000 for the building. By appraisal, the fair value was estimated to be €500,000 for the land and €2,000,000 for the building. At what amount should Ocampo record the land and the building?

14. Pueblo Co. acquires machinery by paying $10,000 cash and signing a $5,000, 2-year, zero-interest-bearing note payable. The note has a present value of $4,208, and Pueblo purchased a similar machine last month for $13,500. At what cost should the new equipment be recorded?

15. Stan Ott is evaluating two recent transactions involving exchanges of equipment. In one case, the exchange has commercial substance. In the second situation, the exchange lacks commercial substance. Explain to Stan the differences in accounting for these two situations.

16. Crowe Company purchased a heavy-duty truck on July 1, 2012, for €30,000. It was estimated that it would have a useful life of 10 years and then would have a residual value of €6,000. The company uses the straight-line method. It was traded on August 1, 2016, for a similar truck costing €42,000; €16,000 was allowed as trade-in value (also fair value) on the old truck and €26,000 was paid in cash. A comparison of expected cash flows for the trucks indicates the exchange lacks commercial substance. What is the entry to record the exchange?

17. Ito Company receives a local government grant to help defray the cost of its plant facilitates. The grant is provided to encourage Ito to move its operations to a certain area. Explain how the grant might be reported.

18. Once equipment has been installed and placed in operation, subsequent expenditures relating to this equipment are frequently thought of as repairs or general maintenance and, hence, chargeable to operations in the period in which the expenditure is made. Actually, determination of whether such an expenditure should be charged to operations or capitalized involves a much more careful analysis of the character of the expenditure. What are the factors that should be considered in making such a decision?

19. What accounting treatment is normally given to the following items in accounting for plant assets?

    (a) Additions.
    (b) Major repairs.
    (c) Improvements.
    (d) Replacements.

20. New machinery, which replaced a number of employees, was installed and put in operation in the last month of the fiscal year. The employees had been dismissed after payment of an extra month's wages, and this amount was added to the cost of the machinery. Discuss the propriety of the charge. If it was improper, describe the proper treatment.

21. To what extent do you consider the following items to be proper costs of property, plant, and equipment? Give reasons for your opinions.

    (a) Overhead of a business that builds its own equipment.
    (b) Cash discounts on purchases of equipment.
    (c) Interest paid during construction of a building.
    (d) Profit on self-construction.
    (e) Freight on equipment returned before installation, for replacement by other equipment of greater capacity.
    (f) Cost of moving machinery to a new location.
    (g) Cost of plywood partitions erected as part of the remodeling of the office.
    (h) Replastering of a section of the building.
    (i) Cost of a new motor for one of the trucks.

22. Neville Enterprises has a number of fully depreciated assets that are still being used in the main operations of the business. Because the assets are fully depreciated, the president of the company decides not to show them on the statement of financial position or disclose this information in the notes. Evaluate this procedure.

23. What are the general rules for how gains or losses on disposal of plant assets should be reported in income?

BRIEF EXERCISES

2 BE10-1 Previn Brothers Inc. purchased land at a price of $27,000. Closing costs were $1,400. An old building was removed at a cost of $10,200. What amount should be recorded as the cost of the land?

4 BE10-2 Zhang Company is constructing a building. Construction began on February 1 and was completed on December 31. Expenditures were HK$1,800,000 on March 1, HK$1,200,000 on June 1, and HK$3,000,000 on December 31. Compute Zhang's weighted-average accumulated expenditures for interest capitalization purposes.

4 BE10-3 Zhang Company (see BE10-2) borrowed HK$1,000,000 on March 1 on a 5-year, 12% note to help finance construction of the building. In addition, the company had outstanding all year a 10%, 5-year, HK$2,000,000 note payable and an 11%, 4-year, HK$3,500,000 note payable. Compute the capitalization rate used for interest capitalization purposes.

4 BE10-4 Use the information for Zhang Company from BE10-2 and BE10-3. Compute avoidable interest for Zhang Company.

5 BE10-5 Chopra Corporation purchased a truck by issuing an £80,000, 4-year, zero-interest-bearing note to Equinox Inc. The market rate of interest for obligations of this nature is 10%. Prepare the journal entry to record the purchase of this truck.

5 BE10-6 Mohave Inc. purchased land, building, and equipment from Laguna Corporation for a cash payment of $315,000. The estimated fair values of the assets are land $60,000, building $220,000, and equipment $80,000. At what amounts should each of the three assets be recorded?

5 BE10-7 Fielder Company obtained land by issuing 2,000 shares of its $10 par value ordinary shares. The land was recently appraised at $85,000. The ordinary shares are actively traded at $40 per share. Prepare the journal entry to record the acquisition of the land.

5 BE10-8 Navajo Corporation traded a used truck (cost €20,000, accumulated depreciation €18,000) for a small computer worth €3,300. Navajo also paid €500 in the transaction. Prepare the journal entry to record the exchange. (The exchange has commercial substance.)

5 BE10-9 Use the information for Navajo Corporation from BE10-8. Prepare the journal entry to record the exchange, assuming the exchange lacks commercial substance.

5 BE10-10 Mehta Company traded a used welding machine (cost €9,000, accumulated depreciation €3,000) for office equipment with an estimated fair value of €5,000. Mehta also paid €3,000 cash in the transaction. Prepare the journal entry to record the exchange. (The exchange has commercial substance.)

5 BE10-11 Cheng Company traded a used truck for a new truck. The used truck cost $30,000 and has accumulated depreciation of $27,000. The new truck is worth $37,000. Cheng also made a cash payment of $36,000. Prepare Cheng's entry to record the exchange. (The exchange lacks commercial substance.)

5 BE10-12 Slaton Corporation traded a used truck for a new truck. The used truck cost £20,000 and has accumulated depreciation of £17,000. The new truck is worth £35,000. Slaton also made a cash payment of £33,000. Prepare Slaton's entry to record the exchange. (The exchange has commercial substance.)

6 BE10-13 Indicate which of the following costs should be expensed when incurred.
   (a) €13,000 paid to rearrange and reorganize machinery.
   (b) €200,000 paid for addition to building.
   (c) €200 paid for tune-up and oil change on a delivery truck.
   (d) €7,000 paid to replace a wooden floor with a concrete floor.
   (e) €2,000 paid for a major overhaul on a truck.

5 BE10-14 In 2015, Sato Corporation received a grant for ¥2 million to defray the cost of purchasing research equipment for its manufacturing facility. The total cost of the equipment is ¥10 million. Prepare the journal entry to record this transaction if Sato uses (a) the deferred revenue approach, and (b) the reduction of asset approach.

7 BE10-15 Ottawa Corporation owns machinery that cost $20,000 when purchased on July 1, 2012. Depreciation has been recorded at a rate of $2,400 per year, resulting in a balance in accumulated depreciation of $8,400 at December 31, 2015. The machinery is sold on September 1, 2016, for $10,500. Prepare journal entries to (a) update depreciation for 2016 and (b) record the sale.

7 **BE10-16** Use the information presented for Ottawa Corporation in BE10-15, but assume the machinery is sold for $5,200 instead of $10,500. Prepare journal entries to (a) update depreciation for 2016 and (b) record the sale.

EXERCISES

2 **E10-1 (Acquisition Costs of Realty)** The expenditures and receipts below are related to land, land improvements, and buildings acquired for use in a business enterprise. The receipts are enclosed in parentheses.

(a)	Money borrowed to pay building contractor (signed a note)	€(275,000)
(b)	Payment for construction from note proceeds	275,000
(c)	Cost of land fill and clearing	10,000
(d)	Delinquent real estate taxes on property assumed by purchaser	7,000
(e)	Premium on 6-month insurance policy during construction	6,000
(f)	Refund of 1-month insurance premium because construction completed early	(1,000)
(g)	Architect's fee on building	25,000
(h)	Cost of real estate purchased as a plant site (land €200,000 and building €50,000)	250,000
(i)	Commission fee paid to real estate agency	9,000
(j)	Installation of fences around property	4,000
(k)	Cost of razing and removing building	11,000
(l)	Proceeds from residual value of demolished building	(5,000)
(m)	Interest paid during construction on money borrowed for construction	13,000
(n)	Cost of parking lots and driveways	19,000
(o)	Cost of trees and shrubbery planted (permanent in nature)	14,000
(p)	Excavation costs for new building	3,000

Instructions

Identify each item by letter and list the items in columnar form, using the headings shown below. All receipt amounts should be reported in parentheses. For any amounts entered in the Other Accounts column, also indicate the account title.

Item	Land	Land Improvements	Buildings	Other Accounts

2 **E10-2 (Acquisition Costs of Realty)** Pollachek Co. purchased land as a factory site for $450,000. The process of tearing down two old buildings on the site and constructing the factory required 6 months. The company paid $42,000 to raze the old buildings and sold salvaged lumber and brick for $6,300. Legal fees of $1,850 were paid for title investigation and drawing the purchase contract. Pollachek paid $2,200 to an engineering firm for a land survey, and $65,000 for drawing the factory plans. The land survey had to be made before definitive plans could be drawn. Title insurance on the property cost $1,500, and a liability insurance premium paid during construction was $900. The contractor's charge for construction was $2,740,000. The company paid the contractor in two installments: $1,200,000 at the end of 3 months and $1,540,000 upon completion. Interest costs of $170,000 were incurred to finance the construction.

Instructions

Determine the cost of the land and the cost of the building as they should be recorded on the books of Pollachek Co. Assume that the land survey was for the building.

2 **E10-3 (Acquisition Costs of Trucks)** Haddad Corporation operates a retail computer store. To improve delivery services to customers, the company purchases four new trucks on April 1, 2015. The terms of acquisition for each truck are described below.

1. Truck #1 has a list price of $15,000 and is acquired for a cash payment of $13,900.

2. Truck #2 has a list price of $20,000 and is acquired for a down payment of $2,000 cash and a zero-interest-bearing note with a face amount of $18,000. The note is due April 1, 2016. Haddad would normally have to pay interest at a rate of 10% for such a borrowing, and the dealership has an incremental borrowing rate of 8%.

3. Truck #3 has a list price of $16,000. It is acquired in exchange for a computer system that Haddad carries in inventory. The computer system cost $12,000 and is normally sold by Haddad for $15,200. Haddad uses a perpetual inventory system.

4. Truck #4 has a list price of $14,000. It is acquired in exchange for 1,000 ordinary shares in Haddad Corporation. The shares have a par value per share of $10 and a market price of $13 per share.

Instructions

Prepare the appropriate journal entries for the foregoing transactions for Haddad Corporation. (Round computations to the nearest dollar.)

2 3 **E10-4 (Purchase and Self-Constructed Cost of Assets)** Dane Co. both purchases and constructs various equipment it uses in its operations. The following items for two different types of equipment were recorded in random order during the calendar year 2015.

Purchase	
Cash paid for equipment, including sales tax of €5,000	€105,000
Freight and insurance cost while in transit	2,000
Cost of moving equipment into place at factory	3,100
Wage cost for technicians to test equipment	6,000
Insurance premium paid during first year of operation on this equipment	1,500
Special plumbing fixtures required for new equipment	8,000
Repair cost incurred in first year of operations related to this equipment	1,300

Construction	
Material and purchased parts (gross cost €200,000; failed to take 1% cash discount)	€200,000
Imputed interest on funds used during construction (share financing)	14,000
Labor costs	190,000
Allocated overhead costs (fixed—€20,000; variable—€30,000)	50,000
Profit on self-construction	30,000
Cost of installing equipment	4,400

Instructions

Compute the total cost for each of these two types of equipment. If an item is not capitalized as a cost of the equipment, indicate how it should be reported.

2 3 **4** **E10-5 (Treatment of Various Costs)** Allegro Supply Company, a newly formed corporation, incurred the following expenditures related to Land, to Buildings, and to Equipment.

Abstract company's fee for title search		£ 520
Architect's fees		3,170
Cash paid for land and dilapidated building thereon		92,000
Removal of old building	£20,000	
Less: Residual value	5,500	14,500
Interest on short-term loans during construction		7,400
Excavation before construction for basement		19,000
Equipment purchased (subject to 2% cash discount, which was not taken)		65,000
Freight on equipment purchased		1,340
Storage charges on equipment, necessitated by non-completion of building when equipment was delivered		2,180
New building constructed (building construction took 6 months from date of purchase of land and old building)		485,000
Assessment by city for drainage project		1,600
Hauling charges for delivery of equipment from storage to new building		620
Installation of equipment		2,000
Trees, shrubs, and other landscaping after completion of building (permanent in nature)		5,400

Instructions

Determine the amounts that should be debited to Land, to Buildings, and to Equipment. Assume the benefits of capitalizing interest during construction exceed the cost of implementation. Indicate how any costs not debited to these accounts should be recorded.

3 4 **E10-6 (Correction of Improper Cost Entries)** Plant acquisitions for selected companies are presented as follows.

1. Natchez Industries Inc. acquired land, buildings, and equipment from a bankrupt company, Vivace Co., for a lump-sum price of $680,000. At the time of purchase, Vivace's assets had the following book and appraisal values.

	Book Values	Appraisal Values
Land	$200,000	$150,000
Buildings	230,000	350,000
Equipment	300,000	300,000

To be conservative, the company decided to take the lower of the two values for each asset acquired. The following entry was made.

Land	150,000	
Buildings	230,000	
Equipment	300,000	
Cash		680,000

2. Arawak Enterprises purchased store equipment by making a $2,000 cash down payment and signing a 1-year, $23,000, 10% note payable. The purchase was recorded as follows.

Equipment	27,300	
Cash		2,000
Notes Payable		23,000
Interest Payable		2,300

3. Ace Company purchased office equipment for $20,000, terms 2/10, n/30. Because the company intended to take the discount, it made no entry until it paid for the acquisition. The entry was:

Equipment	20,000	
Cash		19,600
Purchase Discounts		400

4. Paunee Inc. recently received at zero cost a building from the Village of Cardassia as an inducement to locate its business in the village. The appraised value of the building is $270,000. The company made no entry to record the building because it had no cost basis.

5. Mohegan Company built a warehouse for $600,000. It could have purchased the building for $740,000. The controller made the following entry.

Buildings	740,000	
Cash		600,000
Profit on Construction		140,000

Instructions

Prepare the entry that should have been made at the date of each acquisition.

4 **E10-7 (Capitalization of Interest)** McPherson Furniture Company started construction of a combination office and warehouse building for its own use at an estimated cost of €5,000,000 on January 1, 2015. McPherson expected to complete the building by December 31, 2015. McPherson has the following debt obligations outstanding during the construction period.

Construction loan—12% interest, payable semiannually, issued	
December 31, 2014	€2,000,000
Short-term loan—10% interest, payable monthly, and principal	
payable at maturity on May 30, 2016	1,600,000
Long-term loan—11% interest, payable on January 1 of each	
year. Principal payable on January 1, 2019	1,000,000

Instructions

(Carry all computations to two decimal places.)

(a) Assume that McPherson completed the office and warehouse building on December 31, 2015, as planned at a total cost of €5,200,000, and the weighted-average accumulated expenditures was €3,800,000. Compute the avoidable interest on this project.

(b) Compute the depreciation expense for the year ended December 31, 2016. McPherson elected to depreciate the building on a straight-line basis and determined that the asset has a useful life of 30 years and a residual value of €300,000.

4 **E10-8 (Capitalization of Interest)** On December 31, 2014, Tsang Inc. borrowed HK$3,000,000 at 12% payable annually to finance the construction of a new building. In 2015, the company made the following expenditures related to this building: March 1, HK$360,000; June 1, HK$600,000; July 1, HK$1,500,000; December 1, HK$1,200,000. Additional information is provided as follows.

1. Other debt outstanding
    10-year, 11% bond, December 31, 2008, interest payable annually   HK$4,000,000
    6-year, 10% note, dated December 31, 2012, interest payable annually   HK$1,600,000

2. March 1, 2015, expenditure included land costs of HK$150,000

3. Interest revenue earned in 2015 on funds related to specific borrowing   HK$49,000

Instructions

(a) Determine the amount of interest to be capitalized in 2015 in relation to the construction of the building.

(b) Prepare the journal entry to record the capitalization of interest and the recognition of interest expense, if any, at December 31, 2015.

4 **E10-9 (Capitalization of Interest)** On July 31, 2015, Bismarck Company engaged Duval Tooling Company to construct a special-purpose piece of factory machinery. Construction began immediately and was completed on November 1, 2015. To help finance construction, on July 31 Bismarck issued a $400,000, 3-year, 12% note payable at Wellington National Bank, on which interest is payable each July 31. $300,000 of the proceeds of the note was paid to Duval on July 31. The remainder of the proceeds was temporarily invested in short-term marketable securities (trading securities) at 10% until November 1. On November 1, Bismarck made a final $100,000 payment to Duval. Other than the note to Wellington, Bismarck's only outstanding liability at December 31, 2015, is a $30,000, 8%, 6-year note payable, dated January 1, 2012, on which interest is payable each December 31.

Instructions

(a) Calculate the interest revenue, weighted-average accumulated expenditures, avoidable interest, and total interest cost to be capitalized during 2015. (Round all computations to the nearest dollar.)

(b) Prepare the journal entries needed on the books of Bismarck Company at each of the following dates.

(1) July 31, 2015.

(2) November 1, 2015.

(3) December 31, 2015.

4 **E10-10 (Capitalization of Interest)** The following three situations involve the capitalization of interest.

Situation I: On January 1, 2015, Columbia, Inc. signed a fixed-price contract to have Builder Associates construct a major plant facility at a cost of R$4,000,000. It was estimated that it would take 3 years to complete the project. Also on January 1, 2015, to finance the construction cost, Columbia borrowed R$4,000,000 payable in 10 annual installments of R$400,000, plus interest at the rate of 10%. During 2015, Columbia made deposit and progress payments totaling R$1,500,000 under the contract; the weighted-average amount of accumulated expenditures was R$900,000 for the year. The excess borrowed funds were invested in short-term securities, from which Columbia realized investment income of R$50,000.

Instructions

What amount should Columbia report as capitalized interest at December 31, 2015?

Situation II: During 2015, Evander Corporation constructed and manufactured certain assets and incurred the following interest costs in connection with those activities.

	Interest Costs Incurred
Warehouse constructed for Evander's own use	R$30,000
Special-order machine for sale to unrelated customer, produced according to customer's specifications	9,000
Inventories routinely manufactured, produced on a repetitive basis	8,000

All of these assets required an extended period of time for completion.

Instructions

Assuming the effect of interest capitalization is material, what is the total amount of interest costs to be capitalized?

Situation III: Antonio, Inc. has a fiscal year ending April 30. On May 1, 2015, Antonio borrowed R$10,000,000 at 11% to finance construction of its own building. Repayments of the loan are to commence the month following completion of the building. During the year ended April 30, 2016, expenditures for the partially completed structure totaled R$6,000,000. These expenditures were incurred evenly throughout the year. Interest earned on the unexpended portion of the loan amounted to R$150,000 for the year.

Instructions

How much should be shown as capitalized interest on Antonio's financial statements at April 30, 2016?

2 3 5 **E10-11 (Entries for Equipment Acquisitions)** Song Engineering Corporation purchased conveyor equipment with a list price of ₩15,000. Presented below are three independent cases related to the equipment (amounts in thousands).

(a) Song paid cash for the equipment 8 days after the purchase. The vendor's credit terms are 2/10, n/30. Assume that equipment purchases are initially recorded gross.

(b) Song traded in equipment with a book value of ₩2,000 (initial cost ₩8,000), and paid ₩14,200 in cash one month after the purchase. The old equipment could have been sold for ₩400 at the date of trade. (The exchange has commercial substance.)

(c) Song gave the vendor a ₩16,200, zero-interest-bearing note for the equipment on the date of purchase. The note was due in one year and was paid on time. Assume that the effective-interest rate in the market was 9%.

Instructions

Prepare the general journal entries required to record the acquisition and payment in each of the independent cases above. (Round to the nearest won.)

2 3 5 **E10-12 (Entries for Asset Acquisition, Including Self-Construction)** Below are transactions related to Impala Company.

(a) The City of Pebble Beach gives the company 5 acres of land as a plant site. The fair value of this land is determined to be $81,000.

(b) 14,000 ordinary shares with a par value of $50 per share are issued in exchange for land and buildings. The property has been appraised at a fair value of $810,000, of which $180,000 has been allocated to land and $630,000 to buildings. The shares of Impala Company are not listed on any exchange, but a block of 100 shares was sold by a shareholder 12 months ago at $65 per share, and a block of 200 shares was sold by another shareholder 18 months ago at $58 per share.

(c) No entry has been made to remove from the accounts for Materials, Direct Labor, and Overhead the amounts properly chargeable to plant asset accounts for machinery constructed during the year. The following information is given relative to costs of the machinery constructed.

Materials used	$12,500
Factory supplies used	900
Direct labor incurred	16,000
Additional overhead (over regular) caused by construction of machinery, excluding factory supplies used	2,700
Fixed overhead rate applied to regular manufacturing operations	60% of direct labor cost
Cost of similar machinery if it had been purchased from outside suppliers	44,000

Instructions

Prepare journal entries on the books of Impala Company to record these transactions.

2 5 **E10-13 (Entries for Acquisition of Assets)** The following information is related to Rommel Company.

1. On July 6, Rommel Company acquired the plant assets of Studebaker Company, which had discontinued operations. The appraised value of the property is:

Land	€ 400,000
Building	1,200,000
Machinery	800,000
Total	€2,400,000

Rommel Company gave 12,500 shares of its €100 par value ordinary shares in exchange. The shares had a market price of €180 per share on the date of the purchase of the property.

2. Rommel Company expended the following amounts in cash between July 6 and December 15, the date when it first occupied the building.

Repairs to building	€105,000
Construction of bases for machinery to be installed later	135,000
Driveways and parking lots	122,000
Remodeling of office space in building, including new partitions and walls	161,000
Special assessment by city on land	18,000

3. On December 20, the company paid cash for machinery, €280,000, subject to a 2% cash discount, and freight on machinery of €10,500.

Instructions

Prepare entries on the books of Rommel Company for these transactions.

5 **E10-14 (Purchase of Equipment with Zero-Interest-Bearing Debt)** Sterling Inc. has decided to purchase equipment from Central Industries on January 2, 2015, to expand its production capacity to meet customers' demand for its product. Sterling issues a $900,000, 5-year, zero-interest-bearing note to Central for the new equipment when the prevailing market rate of interest for obligations of this nature is 12%. The company will pay off the note in five $180,000 installments due at the end of each year over the life of the note.

Instructions

(a) Prepare the journal entry(ies) at the date of purchase. (Round to nearest dollar in all computations.)
(b) Prepare the journal entry(ies) at the end of the first year to record the payment and interest, assuming that the company employs the effective-interest method.
(c) Prepare the journal entry(ies) at the end of the second year to record the payment and interest.
(d) Assuming that the equipment had a 10-year life and no residual value, prepare the journal entry necessary to record depreciation in the first year. (Straight-line depreciation is employed.)

5 **E10-15 (Purchase of Computer with Zero-Interest-Bearing Debt)** Windsor Corporation purchased a computer on December 31, 2014, for £130,000, paying £30,000 down and agreeing to pay the balance in five equal installments of £20,000 payable each December 31 beginning in 2015. An assumed interest rate of 10% is implicit in the purchase price.

Instructions

(a) Prepare the journal entry(ies) at the date of purchase. (Round to two decimal places.)
(b) Prepare the journal entry(ies) at December 31, 2015, to record the payment and interest (effective-interest method employed).
(c) Prepare the journal entry(ies) at December 31, 2016, to record the payment and interest (effective-interest method employed).

5 **E10-16 (Asset Acquisition)** Logan Industries purchased the following assets and constructed a building as well. All this was done during the current year.

Assets 1 and 2: These assets were purchased as a lump sum for €104,000 cash. The following information was gathered.

Description	Initial Cost on Seller's Books	Depreciation to Date on Seller's Books	Book Value on Seller's Books	Appraised Value
Machinery	€100,000	€50,000	€50,000	€90,000
Equipment	60,000	10,000	50,000	30,000

Asset 3: This machine was acquired by making a €10,000 down payment and issuing a €30,000, 2-year, zero-interest-bearing note. The note is to be paid off in two €15,000 installments made at the end of the first and second years. It was estimated that the asset could have been purchased outright for €35,900.

Asset 4: This machinery was acquired by trading in used machinery. (The exchange lacks commercial substance.) Facts concerning the trade-in are as follows.

Cost of machinery traded	€100,000
Accumulated depreciation to date of sale	36,000
Fair value of machinery traded	80,000
Cash received	10,000
Fair value of machinery acquired	70,000

Asset 5: Equipment was acquired by issuing 100 shares of €8 par value ordinary shares. The shares have a market price of €11 per share.

Construction of Building: A building was constructed at a cost of €180,000. Construction began on February 1 and was completed on November 1. The payments to the contractor were as follows.

Date	Payment
2/1	€120,000
6/1	360,000
9/1	480,000
11/1	100,000

To finance construction of the building, a €600,000, 12% construction loan was taken out on February 1. The loan was repaid on November 1. The firm had €200,000 of other outstanding debt during the year at a borrowing rate of 8%.

Instructions

Record the acquisition of each of these assets.

5 **E10-17 (Non-Monetary Exchange)** Alatorre Corporation, which manufactures shoes, hired a recent college graduate to work in its accounting department. On the first day of work, the accountant was assigned to total a batch of invoices with the use of an adding machine. Before long, the accountant, who had never before seen such a machine, managed to break the machine. Alatorre Corporation gave the machine plus €320 to Mills Business Machine Company (dealer) in exchange for a new machine. Assume the following information about the machines.

	Alatorre Corp. (Old Machine)	Mills Co. (New Machine)
Machine cost	€290	€270
Accumulated depreciation	140	–0–
Fair value	85	405

Instructions

For each company, prepare the necessary journal entry to record the exchange. (The exchange has commercial substance.)

5 **E10-18 (Non-Monetary Exchange)** Montgomery Company purchased an electric wax melter on April 30, 2016, by trading in its old gas model and paying the balance in cash. The following data relate to the purchase.

List price of new melter	£15,800
Cash paid	10,000
Cost of old melter (5-year life, £700 residual value)	12,700
Accumulated depreciation (old melter—straight-line)	7,200
Fair value of old melter	5,200

Instructions

Prepare the journal entry(ies) necessary to record this exchange, assuming that the exchange (a) has commercial substance, and (b) lacks commercial substance. Montgomery's year ends on December 31, and depreciation has been recorded through December 31, 2015.

5 **E10-19 (Non-Monetary Exchange)** Santana Company exchanged equipment used in its manufacturing operations plus R$2,000 in cash for similar equipment used in the operations of Delaware Company. The following information pertains to the exchange.

	Santana Co.	Delaware Co.
Equipment (cost)	R$28,000	R$28,000
Accumulated depreciation	19,000	10,000
Fair value of equipment	13,500	15,500
Cash given up	2,000	

Instructions

(a) Prepare the journal entries to record the exchange on the books of both companies. Assume that the exchange lacks commercial substance.

(b) Prepare the journal entries to record the exchange on the books of both companies. Assume that the exchange has commercial substance.

5 **E10-20 (Non-Monetary Exchange)** Yintang Group has negotiated the purchase of a new piece of automatic equipment at a price of HK$7,000 plus trade-in, f.o.b. factory. Yintang paid HK$7,000 cash and traded in used equipment. The used equipment had originally cost HK$62,000; it had a book value of HK$42,000 and a secondhand fair value of HK$45,800, as indicated by recent transactions involving similar equipment. Freight and installation charges for the new equipment required a cash payment of HK$1,100.

Instructions

(a) Prepare the general journal entry to record this transaction, assuming that the exchange has commercial substance.

(b) Assuming the same facts as in (a) except that fair value information for the assets exchanged is not determinable, prepare the general journal entry to record this transaction.

5 **E10-21 (Government Grants)** Rialto Group received a grant from the government of £100,000 to acquire £500,000 of delivery equipment on January 2, 2015. The delivery equipment has a useful life of 5 years. Rialto uses the straight-line method of depreciation. The delivery equipment has a zero residual value.

Instructions

(a) If Rialto Group reports the grant as a reduction of the asset, answer the following questions.

(1) What is the carrying amount of the delivery equipment on the statement of financial position at December 31, 2015?

(2) What is the amount of depreciation expense related to the delivery equipment in 2016?

(3) What is the amount of grant revenue reported in 2015 on the income statement?

(b) If Rialto Group reports the grant as deferred grant revenue, answer the following questions.

(1) What is the balance in the deferred grant revenue account at December 31, 2015?

(2) What is the amount of depreciation expense related to the delivery equipment in 2016?

(3) What is the amount of grant revenue reported in 2015 on the income statement?

5 **E10-22 (Government Grants)** Yilmaz Company is provided a grant by the local government to purchase land for a building site. The grant is a zero-interest-bearing note for 5 years. The note is issued on January 2, 2015, for €5 million payable on January 2, 2020. Yilmaz's incremental borrowing rate is 6%. The land is not purchased until July 15, 2015.

Instructions

(a) Prepare the journal entry(ies) to record the grant and note payable on January 2, 2015.

(b) Determine the amount of interest expense and grant revenue to be reported on December 31, 2015.

6 **E10-23 (Analysis of Subsequent Expenditures)** Accardo Resources Group has been in its plant facility for 15 years. Although the plant is quite functional, numerous repair costs are incurred to maintain it in sound working order. The company's plant asset book value is currently R$800,000, as indicated below.

Original cost	R$1,200,000
Less: Accumulated depreciation	400,000
Book value	R$ 800,000

During the current year, the following expenditures were made to the plant facility.

(a) Because of increased demands for its product, the company increased its plant capacity by building a new addition at a cost of R$270,000.

(b) The entire plant was repainted at a cost of R$23,000.

(c) The roof was an asbestos cement slate. For safety purposes, it was removed and replaced with a wood shingle roof at a cost of R$61,000. Book value of the old roof was R$41,000.

(d) The electrical system was updated at a cost of R$12,000. The cost of the old electrical system was not known. It is estimated that the useful life of the building will not change as a result of this updating.

(e) A series of major repairs were made at a cost of R$75,000 because parts of the wood structure were rotting. The cost of the old wood structure was not known. These extensive repairs are estimated to increase the useful life of the building. The company believes the R$75,000 is representative of the parts for the wood structure at the date of purchase.

Instructions

Indicate how each of these transactions would be recorded in the accounting records.

6 **E10-24 (Analysis of Subsequent Expenditures)** The following transactions occurred during 2016. Assume that depreciation of 10% per year is charged on all machinery and 5% per year on buildings, on a straight-line basis, with no estimated residual value. Depreciation is charged for a full year on all fixed assets acquired during the year, and no depreciation is charged on fixed assets disposed of during the year.

Jan. 30   A building that cost $112,000 in 1999 is torn down to make room for a new building. The wrecking contractor was paid $5,100 and was permitted to keep all materials salvaged.

Mar. 10   Machinery that was purchased in 2009 for $16,000 is sold for $2,900 cash, f.o.b. purchaser's plant. Freight of $300 is paid on the sale of this machinery.

Mar. 20   A gear breaks on a machine that cost $9,000 in 2011. The gear is replaced at a cost of $3,000. The replacement does not extend the useful life of the machine.

May 18   A special base installed for a machine in 2010 when the machine was purchased has to be replaced at a cost of $5,500 because of defective workmanship on the original base. The cost of the machinery was $14,200 in 2010. The cost of the base was $4,000, and this amount was charged to the Machinery account in 2010.

June 23   One of the buildings is repainted at a cost of $6,900. It had not been painted since it was constructed in 2012.

Instructions

Prepare general journal entries for the transactions. (Round to the nearest dollar.)

6 **E10-25 (Analysis of Subsequent Expenditures)** Plant assets often require expenditures subsequent to acquisition. It is important that they be accounted for properly. Any errors will affect both the statements of financial position and income statements for a number of years.

Instructions
For each of the following items, indicate whether the expenditure should be capitalized (C) or expensed (E) in the period incurred.

(a) _____ Improvement.
(b) _____ Replacement of a minor broken part on a machine.
(c) _____ Expenditure that increases the useful life of an existing asset.
(d) _____ Expenditure that increases the efficiency and effectiveness of a productive asset but does not increase its residual value.
(e) _____ Expenditure that increases the efficiency and effectiveness of a productive asset and increases the asset's residual value.
(f) _____ Ordinary repairs.
(g) _____ Improvement to a machine that increased its fair value and its production capacity by 30% without extending the machine's useful life.
(h) _____ Expenditure that increases the quality of the output of the productive asset.

7 **E10-26 (Entries for Disposition of Assets)** On December 31, 2015, Mitsui Inc. has a machine with a book value of ¥940,000. The original cost and related accumulated depreciation at this date are as follows (all amounts in thousands).

Machine	¥1,300,000
Less: Accumulated depreciation	360,000
Book value	¥ 940,000

Depreciation is computed at ¥72,000 per year on a straight-line basis.

Instructions
Presented below is a set of independent situations. For each independent situation, indicate the journal entry to be made to record the transaction. Make sure that depreciation entries are made to update the book value of the machine prior to its disposal.

(a) A fire completely destroys the machine on August 31, 2016. An insurance settlement of ¥630,000 was received for this casualty. Assume the settlement was received immediately.
(b) On April 1, 2016, Mitsui sold the machine for ¥1,040,000 to Avanti Company.
(c) On July 31, 2016, the company donated this machine to the Mountain King City Council. The fair value of the machine at the time of the donation was estimated to be ¥1,100,000.

7 **E10-27 (Disposition of Assets)** On April 1, 2015, Pavlova Company received a condemnation award of $410,000 cash as compensation for the forced sale of the company's land and building, which stood in the path of a new highway. The land and building cost $60,000 and $280,000, respectively, when they were acquired. At April 1, 2015, the accumulated depreciation relating to the building amounted to $160,000. On August 1, 2015, Pavlova purchased a piece of replacement property for cash. The new land cost $90,000, and the new building cost $380,000.

Instructions
Prepare the journal entries to record the transactions on April 1 and August 1, 2015.

PROBLEMS

2 **P10-1 (Classification of Acquisition and Other Asset Costs)** At December 31, 2014, certain accounts included in the property, plant, and equipment section of Reagan Company's statement of financial position had the following balances.

Land	£230,000
Buildings	890,000
Leasehold improvements	660,000
Machinery and equipment	875,000

During 2015, the following transactions occurred.

1. Land site number 621 was acquired for £850,000. In addition, to acquire the land Reagan paid a £51,000 commission to a real estate agent. Costs of £35,000 were incurred to clear the land. During the course of clearing the land, timber and gravel were recovered and sold for £13,000.

2. A second tract of land (site number 622) with a building was acquired for £420,000. The closing statement indicated that the land value was £300,000 and the building value was £120,000. Shortly after acquisition, the building was demolished at a cost of £41,000. A new building was constructed for £330,000 plus the following costs.

Excavation fees	£38,000
Architectural design fees	11,000
Building permit fee	2,500
Imputed interest on funds used	
during construction (share financing)	8,500

The building was completed and occupied on September 30, 2015.

3. A third tract of land (site number 623) was acquired for £650,000 and was put on the market for resale.

4. During December 2015, costs of £89,000 were incurred to improve leased office space. The related lease will terminate on December 31, 2017, and is not expected to be renewed. (*Hint:* Leasehold improvements should be handled in the same manner as land improvements.)

5. A group of new machines was purchased under a royalty agreement that provides for payment of royalties based on units of production for the machines. The invoice price of the machines was £87,000, freight costs were £3,300, installation costs were £2,400, and royalty payments for 2015 were £17,500.

Instructions

(a) Prepare a detailed analysis of the changes in each of the following statement of financial position accounts for 2015.

Land	Leasehold improvements
Buildings	Machinery and equipment

Disregard the related accumulated depreciation accounts.

(b) List the items in the situation that were not used to determine the answer to (a) above, and indicate where, or if, these items should be included in Reagan's financial statements.

2 7 **P10-2 (Classification of Acquisition Costs)** Selected accounts included in the property, plant, and equipment section of Lobo Corporation's statement of financial position at December 31, 2014, had the following balances.

Land	$ 300,000
Land improvements	140,000
Buildings	1,100,000
Equipment	960,000

During 2015, the following transactions occurred.

1. A tract of land was acquired for $150,000 as a potential future building site.

2. A plant facility consisting of land and building was acquired from Mendota Company in exchange for 20,000 shares of Lobo's ordinary shares. On the acquisition date, Lobo's shares had a closing market price of $37 per share on a national exchange. The plant facility was carried on Mendota's books at $110,000 for land and $320,000 for the building at the exchange date. Current appraised values for the land and building, respectively, are $230,000 and $690,000.

3. Items of equipment were purchased at a total cost of $400,000. Additional costs were incurred as follows.

Freight and unloading	$13,000
Sales taxes	20,000
Installation	26,000

4. Expenditures totaling $95,000 were made for new parking lots, streets, and sidewalks at the corporation's various plant locations. These expenditures had an estimated useful life of 15 years.

5. Equipment costing $80,000 on January 1, 2007, was scrapped on June 30, 2015. Straight-line depreciation has been recorded on the basis of a 10-year life with no residual values.

6. Equipment was sold for $20,000 on July 1, 2015. Original cost of the equipment was $44,000 on January 1, 2012, and it was depreciated on the straight-line basis over an estimated useful life of 7 years and a residual value of $2,000.

Instructions

(a) Prepare a detailed analysis of the changes in each of the following statement of financial position accounts for 2015.

Land	Buildings
Land improvements	Equipment

(*Hint:* Disregard the related accumulated depreciation accounts.)

(b) List the items in the fact situation that were not used to determine the answer to (a), showing the pertinent amounts and supporting computations in good form for each item. In addition, indicate where, or if, these items should be included in Lobo's financial statements.

2 3 5 P10-3 (Classification of Land and Building Costs) Spitfire Company was incorporated on January 2, 2016, but was unable to begin manufacturing activities until July 1, 2016, because new factory facilities were not completed until that date.

The Land and Buildings account reported the following items during 2016.

January 31	Land and building	€160,000
February 28	Cost of removal of building	9,800
May 1	Partial payment of new construction	60,000
May 1	Legal fees paid	3,770
June 1	Second payment on new construction	40,000
June 1	Insurance premium	2,280
June 1	Special tax assessment	4,000
June 30	General expenses	36,300
July 1	Final payment on new construction	30,000
December 31	Asset write-up	53,800
		399,950
December 31	Depreciation—2016 at 1%	4,000
December 31, 2016	Account balance	€395,950

The following additional information is to be considered.

1. To acquire land and building, the company paid €80,000 cash and 800 shares of its 8% preference shares, par value €100 per share. The shares trade in an active market at €117 per share.

2. Cost of removal of old buildings amounted to €9,800, and the demolition company retained all materials of the building.

3. Legal fees covered the following.

Cost of organization	€ 610
Examination of title covering purchase of land	1,300
Legal work in connection with construction contract	1,860
	€3,770

4. Insurance premium covered the building for a 2-year term beginning May 1, 2016.

5. The special tax assessment covered street improvements that are permanent in nature.

6. General expenses covered the following for the period from January 2, 2016, to June 30, 2016.

President's salary	€32,100
Plant superintendent's salary—supervision of new building	4,200
	€36,300

7. Because of a general increase in construction costs after entering into the building contract, the board of directors increased the value of the building €53,800, believing that such an increase was justified to reflect the current market at the time the building was completed. Retained earnings was credited for this amount.

8. Depreciation for 2016—1% of asset value (1% of €400,000, or €4,000).

Instructions

    (a) Prepare entries to reflect correct land, buildings, and depreciation accounts at December 31, 2016.

    (b) Show the proper presentation of land, buildings, and depreciation on the statement of financial position at December 31, 2016.

 P10-4 (Dispositions, Including Condemnation, Demolition, and Trade-in) Presented below is a schedule of property dispositions for Hollerith Co.

	Cost	Accumulated Depreciation	Cash Proceeds	Fair Value	Nature of Disposition
		Schedule of Property Dispositions			
Land	$40,000	—	$31,000	$31,000	Condemnation
Building	15,000	—	3,600	—	Demolition
Warehouse	70,000	$16,000	74,000	74,000	Destruction by fire
Machine	8,000	2,800	900	7,200	Trade-in
Furniture	10,000	7,850	—	3,100	Contribution
Automobile	9,000	3,460	2,960	2,960	Sale

The following additional information is available.

    Land: On February 15, a condemnation award was received as consideration for unimproved land held primarily as an investment, and on March 31, another parcel of unimproved land to be held as an investment was purchased at a cost of $35,000.

    Building: On April 2, land and building were purchased at a total cost of $75,000, of which 20% was allocated to the building on the corporate books. The real estate was acquired with the intention of demolishing the building, and this was accomplished during the month of November. Cash proceeds received in November represent the net proceeds from demolition of the building.

    Warehouse: On June 30, the warehouse was destroyed by fire. The warehouse was purchased January 2, 2012, and had depreciated $16,000. On December 27, the insurance proceeds and other funds were used to purchase a replacement warehouse at a cost of $90,000.

    Machine: On December 26, the machine was exchanged for another machine having a fair value of $6,300 and cash of $900 was received. (The exchange lacks commercial substance.)

    Furniture: On August 15, furniture was contributed to a qualified charitable organization. No other contributions were made or pledged during the year.

    Automobile: On November 3, the automobile was sold to Jared Winger, a shareholder.

Instructions

Indicate how these items would be reported on the income statement of Hollerith Co.

P10-5 (Classification of Costs and Interest Capitalization) On January 1, 2015, Blair Corporation purchased for $500,000 a tract of land (site number 101) with a building. Blair paid a real estate broker's commission of $36,000, legal fees of $6,000, and title guarantee insurance of $18,000. The closing statement indicated that the land value was $500,000 and the building value was $100,000. Shortly after acquisition, the building was razed at a cost of $54,000.

    Blair entered into a $3,000,000 fixed-price contract with Slatkin Builders, Inc. on March 1, 2015, for the construction of an office building on land site number 101. The building was completed and occupied on September 30, 2016. Additional construction costs were incurred as follows.

Plans, specifications, and blueprints	$21,000
Architects' fees for design and supervision	82,000

The building is estimated to have a 40-year life from date of completion and will be depreciated using the 150% declining-balance method.

    To finance construction costs, Blair borrowed $3,000,000 on March 1, 2015. The loan is payable in 10 annual installments of $300,000 plus interest at the rate of 10%. Blair's weighted-average amounts of accumulated building construction expenditures were as follows.

For the period March 1 to December 31, 2015	$1,300,000
For the period January 1 to September 30, 2016	1,900,000

Instructions

(a) Prepare a schedule that discloses the individual costs making up the balance in the Land account in respect of land site number 101 as of September 30, 2016.

(b) Prepare a schedule that discloses the individual costs that should be capitalized in the Buildings account as of September 30, 2016. Show supporting computations in good form.

2 4 P10-6 (Interest During Construction) Cho Landscaping began construction of a new plant on December 1, 2015 (all amounts in thousands). On this date, the company purchased a parcel of land for ¥139,000 in cash. In addition, it paid ¥2,000 in surveying costs and ¥4,000 for a title insurance policy. An old dwelling on the premises was demolished at a cost of ¥3,000, with ¥1,000 being received from the sale of materials.

Architectural plans were also formalized on December 1, 2015, when the architect was paid ¥30,000. The necessary building permits costing ¥3,000 were obtained from the city and paid for on December 1 as well. The excavation work began during the first week in December with payments made to the contractor in 2016 as follows.

Date of Payment	Amount of Payment
March 1	¥240,000
May 1	330,000
July 1	60,000

The building was completed on July 1, 2016.

To finance construction of this plant, Cho borrowed ¥600,000 from the bank on December 1, 2015. Cho had no other borrowings. The ¥600,000 was a 10-year loan bearing interest at 8%.

Instructions

Compute the balance in each of the following accounts at December 31, 2015, and December 31, 2016. (Round amounts to the nearest 1,000 yen.)

(a) Land.

(b) Buildings.

(c) Interest Expense.

 4 P10-7 (Capitalization of Interest) Laserwords Inc. is a book distributor that had been operating in its original facility since 1985. The increase in certification programs and continuing education requirements in several professions has contributed to an annual growth rate of 15% for Laserwords since 2010. Laserwords' original facility became obsolete by early 2015 because of the increased sales volume and the fact that Laserwords now carries CDs in addition to books.

On June 1, 2015, Laserwords contracted with Black Construction to have a new building constructed for ₺4,000,000 on land owned by Laserwords. The payments made by Laserwords to Black Construction are shown in the schedule below.

Date	Amount
July 30, 2015	₺ 900,000
January 30, 2016	1,500,000
May 30, 2016	1,600,000
Total payments	₺4,000,000

Construction was completed, and the building was ready for occupancy on May 27, 2016. Laserwords had no new borrowings directly associated with the new building but had the following debt outstanding at May 31, 2016, the end of its fiscal year.

10%, 5-year note payable of ₺2,000,000, dated April 1, 2012, with interest payable annually on April 1.

12%, 10-year bond issue of ₺3,000,000 sold at par on June 30, 2008, with interest payable annually on June 30.

The new building qualifies for interest capitalization. The effect of capitalizing the interest on the new building, compared with the effect of expensing the interest, is material.

Instructions

(a) Compute the weighted-average accumulated expenditures on Laserwords' new building during the capitalization period.

(b) Compute the avoidable interest on Laserwords' new building.

(c) Some interest cost of Laserwords Inc. is capitalized for the year ended May 31, 2016.

(1) Identify the items relating to interest costs that must be disclosed in Laserwords' financial statements.

(2) Compute the amount of each of the items that must be disclosed.

5 **P10-8 (Non-Monetary Exchanges)** Holyfield Corporation wishes to exchange a machine used in its operations. Holyfield has received the following offers from other companies in the industry.

1. Dorsett Company offered to exchange a similar machine plus €23,000. (The exchange has commercial substance for both parties.)

2. Winston Company offered to exchange a similar machine. (The exchange lacks commercial substance for both parties.)

3. Liston Company offered to exchange a similar machine but wanted €3,000 in addition to Holyfield's machine. (The exchange has commercial substance for both parties.)

4. In addition, Holyfield contacted Greeley Corporation, a dealer in machines. To obtain a new machine, Holyfield must pay €93,000 in addition to trading in its old machine.

	Holyfield	Dorsett	Winston	Liston	Greeley
Machine cost	€160,000	€120,000	€152,000	€160,000	€130,000
Accumulated depreciation	60,000	45,000	71,000	75,000	–0–
Fair value	92,000	69,000	92,000	95,000	185,000

Instructions

For each of the four independent situations, prepare the journal entries to record the exchange on the books of each company.

5 **P10-9 (Non-Monetary Exchanges)** On August 1, Hyde, Inc. exchanged productive assets with Wiggins, Inc. Hyde's asset is referred to below as Asset A, and Wiggins' is referred to as Asset B. The following facts pertain to these assets.

	Asset A	Asset B
Original cost	£96,000	£110,000
Accumulated depreciation (to date of exchange)	40,000	47,000
Fair value at date of exchange	60,000	75,000
Cash paid by Hyde, Inc.	15,000	
Cash received by Wiggins, Inc.		15,000

Instructions

(a) Assuming that the exchange of Assets A and B has commercial substance, record the exchange for both Hyde, Inc. and Wiggins, Inc.

(b) Assuming that the exchange of Assets A and B lacks commercial substance, record the exchange for both Hyde, Inc. and Wiggins, Inc.

5 **P10-10 (Non-Monetary Exchanges)** During the current year, Marshall Construction trades an old crane that has a book value of €90,000 (original cost €140,000 less accumulated depreciation €50,000) for a new crane from Brigham Manufacturing Co. The new crane cost Brigham €165,000 to manufacture and is classified as inventory. The following information is also available.

	Marshall Const.	Brigham Mfg. Co.
Fair value of old crane	€ 82,000	
Fair value of new crane		€200,000
Cash paid	118,000	
Cash received		118,000

Instructions

(a) Assuming that this exchange is considered to have commercial substance, prepare the journal entries on the books of (1) Marshall Construction and (2) Brigham Manufacturing.

(b) Assuming that this exchange lacks commercial substance for Marshall, prepare the journal entries on the books of Marshall Construction.

(c) Assuming the same facts as those in (a) except that the fair value of the old crane is €98,000 and the cash paid is €102,000, prepare the journal entries on the books of (1) Marshall Construction and (2) Brigham Manufacturing.

(d) Assuming the same facts as those in (b) except that the fair value of the old crane is €97,000 and the cash paid €103,000, prepare the journal entries on the books of (1) Marshall Construction and (2) Brigham Manufacturing.

2 **5** **P10-11 (Purchases by Deferred Payment, Lump-Sum, and Non-Monetary Exchanges)** Kang Company,
7 a manufacturer of ballet shoes, is experiencing a period of sustained growth. In an effort to expand its production capacity to meet the increased demand for its product, the company recently made several

acquisitions of plant and equipment. Rob Joffrey, newly hired in the position of fixed-asset accountant, requested that Danny Nolte, Kang's controller, review the following transactions.

Transaction 1: On June 1, 2015, Kang Company purchased equipment from Wyandot Corporation. Kang issued a HK$28,000, 4-year, zero-interest-bearing note to Wyandot for the new equipment. Kang will pay off the note in four equal installments due at the end of each of the next 4 years. At the date of the transaction, the prevailing market rate of interest for obligations of this nature was 10%. Freight costs of HK$425 and installation costs of HK$500 were incurred in completing this transaction. The appropriate factors for the time value of money at a 10% rate of interest are given below.

Future value of HK$1 for 4 periods	1.46
Future value of an ordinary annuity for 4 periods	4.64
Present value of HK$1 for 4 periods	0.68
Present value of an ordinary annuity for 4 periods	3.17

Transaction 2: On December 1, 2015, Kang Company purchased several assets of Yakima Shoes Inc., a small shoe manufacturer whose owner was retiring. The purchase amounted to HK$220,000 and included the assets listed below. Kang engaged the services of Tennyson Appraisal Inc., an independent appraiser, to determine the fair values of the assets which are also presented below.

	Yakima Book Value	Fair Value
Inventory	HK$ 60,000	HK$ 50,000
Land	40,000	80,000
Buildings	70,000	120,000
	HK$170,000	HK$250,000

During its fiscal year ended May 31, 2016, Kang incurred HK$8,000 for interest expense in connection with the financing of these assets.

Transaction 3: On March 1, 2016, Kang Company exchanged a number of used trucks plus cash for vacant land adjacent to its plant site. (The exchange has commercial substance.) Kang intends to use the land for a parking lot. The trucks had a combined book value of HK$35,000, as Kang had recorded HK$20,000 of accumulated depreciation against these assets. Kang's purchasing agent, who has had previous dealings in the secondhand market, indicated that the trucks had a fair value of HK$46,000 at the time of the transaction. In addition to the trucks, Kang paid HK$19,000 cash for the land.

Instructions

(a) Plant assets such as land, buildings, and equipment receive special accounting treatment. Describe the major characteristics of these assets that differentiate them from other types of assets.

(b) For each of the three transactions described above, determine the value at which Kang Company should record the acquired assets. Support your calculations with an explanation of the underlying rationale.

(c) The books of Kang Company show the following additional transactions for the fiscal year ended May 31, 2016.

(1) Acquisition of a building for speculative purposes.

(2) Purchase of a 2-year insurance policy covering plant equipment.

(3) Purchase of the rights for the exclusive use of a process used in the manufacture of ballet shoes.

For each of these transactions, indicate whether the asset should be classified as a plant asset. If it is a plant asset, explain why it is. If it is not a plant asset, explain why not, and identify the proper classification.

CONCEPTS FOR ANALYSIS

CA10-1 (Acquisition, Improvements, and Sale of Realty) Tonkawa Company purchased land for use as its corporate headquarters. A small factory that was on the land when it was purchased was torn down before construction of the office building began. Furthermore, a substantial amount of rock blasting and removal had to be done to the site before construction of the building foundation began. Because the office building was set back on the land far from the public road, Tonkawa Company had the contractor construct a paved road that led from the public road to the parking lot of the office building.

Three years after the office building was occupied, Tonkawa Company added four stories to the office building. The four stories had an estimated useful life of 5 years more than the remaining estimated useful life of the original office building.

Ten years later, the land and building were sold at an amount more than their net book value, and Tonkawa Company had a new office building constructed at another site for use as its new corporate headquarters.

Instructions

(a) Which of the expenditures above should be capitalized? How should each be depreciated or amortized? Discuss the rationale for your answers.

(b) How would the sale of the land and building be accounted for? Include in your answer an explanation of how to determine the net book value at the date of sale. Discuss the rationale for your answer.

CA10-2 (Accounting for Self-Constructed Assets) Troopers Medical Labs, Inc. began operations 5 years ago producing stetrics, a new type of instrument it hoped to sell to doctors, dentists, and hospitals. The demand for stetrics far exceeded initial expectations, and the company was unable to produce enough stetrics to meet demand.

The company was manufacturing its product on equipment that it built at the start of its operations. To meet demand, more efficient equipment was needed. The company decided to design and build the equipment because the equipment currently available on the market was unsuitable for producing stetrics.

In 2015, a section of the plant was devoted to development of the new equipment and a special staff was hired. Within 6 months, a machine developed at a cost of €714,000 increased production dramatically and reduced labor costs substantially. Elated by the success of the new machine, the company built three more machines of the same type at a cost of €441,000 each.

Instructions

(a) In general, what costs should be capitalized for self-constructed equipment?

(b) Discuss the propriety of including in the capitalized cost of self-constructed assets:

(1) The increase in overhead caused by the self-construction of fixed assets.

(2) A proportionate share of overhead on the same basis as that applied to goods manufactured for sale.

(c) Discuss the proper accounting treatment of the €273,000 (€714,000 − €441,000) by which the cost of the first machine exceeded the cost of the subsequent machines. This additional cost should not be considered research and development costs.

CA10-3 (Capitalization of Interest) Langer Airline is converting from piston-type planes to jets. Delivery time for the jets is 3 years, during which substantial progress payments must be made. The multimillion-dollar cost of the planes cannot be financed from working capital; Langer must borrow funds for the payments.

Because of high interest rates and the large sum to be borrowed, management estimates that interest costs in the second year of the period will be equal to one-third of income before interest and taxes, and one-half of such income in the third year.

After conversion, Langer's passenger-carrying capacity will be doubled with no increase in the number of planes, although the investment in planes would be substantially increased. The jet planes have a 7-year service life.

Instructions

Give your recommendation concerning the proper accounting for interest during the conversion period. Support your recommendation with reasons and suggested accounting treatment. (Disregard income tax implications.)

CA10-4 (Capitalization of Interest) Vang Magazine Company started construction of a warehouse building for its own use at an estimated cost of ¥5,000,000 on January 1, 2014, and completed the building on December 31, 2014 (all amounts in thousands). During the construction period, Vang has the following debt obligations outstanding.

Construction loan—12% interest, payable semiannually, issued December 31, 2013	¥2,000,000
Short-term loan—10% interest, payable monthly, and principal payable at maturity, on May 30, 2015	1,400,000
Long-term loan—11% interest, payable on January 1 of each year. Principal payable on January 1, 2017	1,000,000

Total cost amounted to ¥5,200,000, and the weighted-average accumulated expenditures was ¥3,500,000.

Jane Edo, the president of the company, has been shown the costs associated with this construction project and capitalized on the statement of financial position. She is bothered by the "avoidable interest" included in the cost. She argues that, first, all the interest is unavoidable—no one lends money without expecting to be compensated for it. Second, why can't the company use all the interest on all the loans when computing this avoidable interest? Finally, why can't her company capitalize all the annual interest that accrued over the period of construction?

Instructions

You are the manager of accounting for the company. In a memo dated January 15, 2016, explain what avoidable interest is, how you computed it (being especially careful to explain why you used the interest rates that you did), and why the company cannot capitalize all its interest for the year. Attach a schedule supporting any computations that you use.

CA10-5 (Non-Monetary Exchanges) You have two clients that are considering trading machinery with each other. Although the machines are different from each other, you believe that an assessment of expected cash flows on the exchanged assets will indicate the exchange lacks commercial substance. Your clients would prefer that the exchange be deemed to have commercial substance, to allow them to record gains. Here are the facts:

	Client A	Client B
Original cost	£100,000	£150,000
Accumulated depreciation	40,000	80,000
Fair value	80,000	100,000
Cash received (paid)	(20,000)	20,000

Instructions

(a) Record the trade-in on Client A's books assuming the exchange has commercial substance.

(b) Record the trade-in on Client A's books assuming the exchange lacks commercial substance.

(c) Write a memo to the controller of Company A indicating and explaining the specific financial impact on current and future statements of treating the exchange as having versus lacking commercial substance.

(d) Record the entry on Client B's books assuming the exchange has commercial substance.

(e) Record the entry on Client B's books assuming the exchange lacks commercial substance.

(f) Write a memo to the controller of Company B indicating and explaining the specific financial impact on current and future statements of treating the exchange as having versus lacking commercial substance.

CA10-6 (Costs of Acquisition) The invoice price of a machine is €50,000. Various other costs relating to the acquisition and installation of the machine including transportation, electrical wiring, special base, and so on amount to €7,500. The machine has an estimated life of 10 years, with no residual value at the end of that period.

The owner of the business suggests that the incidental costs of €7,500 be charged to expense immediately for the following reasons.

1. If the machine should be sold, these costs cannot be recovered in the sales price.
2. The inclusion of the €7,500 in the machinery account on the books will not necessarily result in a closer approximation of the market price of this asset over the years because of the possibility of changing demand and supply levels.
3. Charging the €7,500 to expense immediately will reduce income taxes.

Instructions

Discuss each of the points raised by the owner of the business.

CA10-7 (Cost of Land vs. Building—Ethics) Tones Company purchased a warehouse in a downtown district where land values are rapidly increasing. Gerald Carter, controller, and Wilma Ankara, financial vice president, are trying to allocate the cost of the purchase between the land and the building. Noting that depreciation can be taken only on the building, Carter favors placing a very high proportion of the cost on the warehouse itself, thus reducing taxable income and income taxes. Ankara, his supervisor, argues that the allocation should recognize the increasing value of the land, regardless of the depreciation potential

of the warehouse. Besides, she says, net income is negatively impacted by additional depreciation and will cause the company's share price to go down.

Instructions

Answer the following questions.

- **(a)** What stakeholder interests are in conflict?
- **(b)** What ethical issues does Carter face?
- **(c)** How should these costs be allocated?

USING YOUR JUDGMENT

FINANCIAL REPORTING

Financial Statement Analysis Case

Unilever Group

Unilever Group (GBR and NLD) is ranked at 135 in the Fortune 500. It is a leading international company in the nutrition, hygiene, and personal-care product lines. Information related to Unilever's property, plant, and equipment in its 2012 annual report is shown in the notes to the financial statements as follows.

---

10. Property, Plant and Equipment

Property, plant and equipment is measured at cost including eligible borrowing costs less depreciation and accumulated impairment losses. Depreciation is provided on a straight-line basis over the expected average useful lives of the assets. Residual values are reviewed at least annually. Estimated useful lives by major class of assets are as follows:

- Freehold buildings [no depreciation on freehold land]   40 years
- Leasehold land and buildings   40 years [or life of lease if less]
- Plant and equipment   2-20 years

Property, plant and equipment is subject to review for impairment if triggering events or circumstances indicate that this is necessary. If an indication of impairment exists, the asset or cash generating unit recoverable amount is estimated and any impairment loss is charged to the income statement as it arises.

Movements during 2012	€ million Land and buildings	€ million Plant and equipment	€ million Total
Cost			
1 January 2012	3,875	12,592	16,467
Acquisitions	—	1	1
Disposals of group companies	—	(52)	(52)
Additions	293	1,694	1,987
Disposals	(65)	(516)	(581)
Currency retranslation	(52)	(181)	(233)
Reclassification as held for sale	(50)	(77)	(127)
Other adjustments	5	42	47
31 December 2012	4,006	13,503	17,509
Depreciation			
1 January 2012	(1,237)	(6,456)	(7,693)
Disposals of group companies	—	9	9
Depreciation charge for the year	(121)	(865)	(986)
Disposals	40	448	488
Currency retranslation	13	71	84
Reclassification as held for sale	22	64	86
Other adjustments	(3)	(49)	(52)
31 December 2012	(1,286)	(6,778)	(8,064)
Net book value 31 December 2012	2,720	6,725	9,445
Includes payments on account and assets in course of construction	188	1,343	1,531

Unilever provided the following selected information in its 2012 cash flow statement.

Unilever	€ million 2012
Cash flow from operating activities	8,516
Income tax paid	(1,680)
Net cash flow from operating activities	6,836
Interest received	146
Purchase of intangible assets	(405)
Purchase of land, buildings and equipment	(1,975)
Disposal of land, buildings and equipment	237
Acquisition of group companies, joint ventures and associates	(133)
Disposal of group companies, joint ventures and associates	246
Acquisition of other non-current investments	(91)
Disposal of other non-current investments	88
Dividends from joint ventures, associates and other non-current investments	128
(Purchase)/sale of financial assets	1,004
Net cash flow from/(used in) investing activities	(755)
Dividends paid on ordinary share capital	(2,699)
Interest and preference dividends paid	(506)
Net change in short-time borrowing	(870)
Additional financial liabilities	1,441
Repayment of financial liabilities	(3,565)
Capital element of finance lease rental payments	(15)
Other movements on treasury stock	48
Other financing activities	(456)
Net cash flow from/(used in) financing activities	(6,622)
Net increase/(decrease) in cash and cash equivalents	(541)
Cash and cash equivalents at the beginning of the year	2,978
Effect of foreign exchange rate changes	(220)
Cash and cash equivalents at the end of the year 17A	2,217

Instructions

(a) What was the carrying value of land, buildings, and equipment at the end of 2012?
(b) Does Unilever use a conservative or liberal method to depreciate its property, plant, and equipment?
(c) What was the actual interest expense and preference dividends paid by the company in 2012?
(d) What is Unilever's free cash flow? From the information provided, comment on Unilever's financial flexibility.

Accounting, Analysis, and Principles

Durler Company purchased equipment on January 2, 2011, for $112,000. The equipment had an estimated useful life of 5 years, with an estimated residual value of $12,000. Durler uses straight-line depreciation on all assets. On January 2, 2015, Durler exchanged this equipment, plus $12,000 in cash for newer equipment. The old equipment has a fair value of $50,000.

Accounting

Prepare the journal entry to record the exchange on the books of Durler Company. Assume that the exchange has commercial substance.

Analysis

How will this exchange affect comparisons of the return on assets ratio for Durler in the year of the exchange compared to prior years?

Principles

How does the concept of commercial substance affect the accounting and analysis of this exchange?

IFRS BRIDGE TO THE PROFESSION

Professional Research

Your client is in the planning phase for a major plant expansion, which will involve the construction of a new warehouse. The assistant controller does not believe that interest cost can be included in the cost of the warehouse because it is a financing expense. Others on the planning team believe that some interest cost can be included in the cost of the warehouse, but no one could identify the specific authoritative guidance for this issue. Your supervisor asks you to research this issue.

Instructions

Access the IFRS authoritative literature at the IASB website (*http://eifrs.iasb.org/*) (you may register for free eIFRS access at this site). When you have accessed the documents, you can use the search tool in your Internet browser to respond to the following questions. (Provide paragraph citations.)

(a) Is it permissible to capitalize interest into the cost of assets? Provide authoritative support for your answer.
(b) What are the objectives for capitalizing interest?
(c) Discuss which assets qualify for interest capitalization.
(d) Is there a limit to the amount of interest that may be capitalized in a period?
(e) If interest capitalization is allowed, what disclosures are required?

Professional Simulation

In this simulation, you are asked to address questions regarding the accounting for property, plant, and equipment. Prepare responses to all parts.

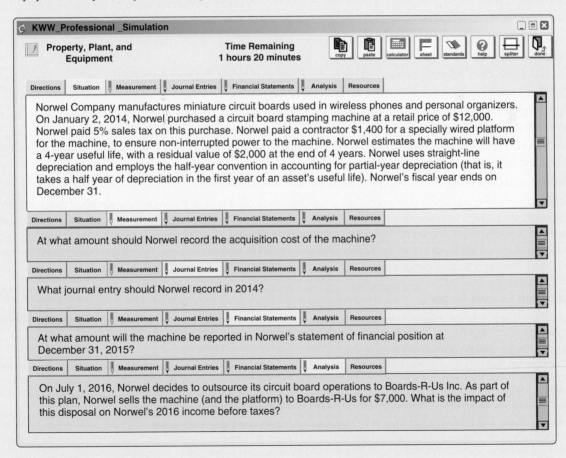

KWW_Professional _Simulation

Property, Plant, and Equipment

Time Remaining
1 hours 20 minutes

copy | paste | calculator | sheet | standards | help | splitter | done

Directions | Situation | Measurement | Journal Entries | Financial Statements | Analysis | Resources

Norwel Company manufactures miniature circuit boards used in wireless phones and personal organizers. On January 2, 2014, Norwel purchased a circuit board stamping machine at a retail price of $12,000. Norwel paid 5% sales tax on this purchase. Norwel paid a contractor $1,400 for a specially wired platform for the machine, to ensure non-interrupted power to the machine. Norwel estimates the machine will have a 4-year useful life, with a residual value of $2,000 at the end of 4 years. Norwel uses straight-line depreciation and employs the half-year convention in accounting for partial-year depreciation (that is, it takes a half year of depreciation in the first year of an asset's useful life). Norwel's fiscal year ends on December 31.

Directions | Situation | Measurement | Journal Entries | Financial Statements | Analysis | Resources

At what amount should Norwel record the acquisition cost of the machine?

Directions | Situation | Measurement | Journal Entries | Financial Statements | Analysis | Resources

What journal entry should Norwel record in 2014?

Directions | Situation | Measurement | Journal Entries | Financial Statements | Analysis | Resources

At what amount will the machine be reported in Norwel's statement of financial position at December 31, 2015?

Directions | Situation | Measurement | Journal Entries | Financial Statements | Analysis | Resources

On July 1, 2016, Norwel decides to outsource its circuit board operations to Boards-R-Us Inc. As part of this plan, Norwel sells the machine (and the platform) to Boards-R-Us for $7,000. What is the impact of this disposal on Norwel's 2016 income before taxes?

Remember to check the book's companion website, at www.wiley.com/college/kieso, to find additional resources for this chapter.

11 Depreciation, Impairments, and Depletion

Here Come the Write-Offs

The credit crisis starting in late 2008 affected many financial and non-financial institutions. Many of the statistics related to this crisis are sobering, as noted below.

- In October 2008, the FTSE 100 in the United Kingdom suffered its biggest one-day fall since October 1987. The index closed at its lowest level since October 2004.

- The U.S. Dow Jones Industrial Average fell below the 8,000 level for the first time since 2003.

- Germany's benchmark DAX tumbled after the collapse of the proposed rescue plan for **Hypo Real Estate** (DEU).

- Tightening credit and less disposable income led to Japanese electronic groups losing value; the Nikkei fell to its lowest point since February 2004.

- The Hong Kong Hang Seng dropped in line with the rest of Asia, closing below 17,000 points for the first time in two years in October and below 11,000 by November 2008.

- Governments have spent billions of dollars bailing out financial institutions.

Although some financial rebound has occurred since October 2008, it is clear that most economies of the world are now in a slower growth pattern. This slowdown raises many questions related to the proper accounting for many non-current assets, such as property, plant, and equipment; intangible assets; and many types of financial assets. One of the most difficult issues relates to the possibility of higher impairment charges related to these assets and the related disclosures that may be needed. The following is an example of a recent impairment charge taken by **Fujitsu Limited** (JPN).

Impairment Losses (in part)

Due to the worsening of the global business environment, Fujitsu recognized consolidated impairment losses of 58.9 billion yen in relation to property, plant and equipment of businesses with decreased profitability. The main losses are as follows:

(1) Property, Plant, and Equipment of LSI Business
Impairment losses related to the property, plant, and equipment of the LSI business of Fujitsu Microelectronics Limited totaled 49.9 billion yen. In January, Fujitsu Microelectronics announced business reforms in response to a sharp downturn in customer demand that began last autumn. Though the company continues to implement these reforms, since the business environment is unlikely to improve quickly, Fujitsu is taking a cautious approach to evaluating the expected future return from the LSI business assets.

(2) Property, Plant, and Equipment of Optical Transmission Systems and Other Businesses
Consolidated impairment losses of 8.9 billion yen were recognized in relation to the property, plant, and equipment of the optical transmission systems business, the electronic components business and other businesses due to their decreased profitability.

(3) Property, Plant, and Equipment of HDD Business (included in business restructuring expenses)
Impairment losses of 16.2 billion yen have been recognized in relation to the property, plant, and equipment of the reorganized HDD business. These losses are included in business restructuring expenses. The impairment loss includes 5.3 billion yen recognized in the third quarter for the discontinuation for the HDD head business.

Here are some of the questions that will need to be addressed regarding possible impairments.

1. How often should a company test for impairment?
2. What are key impairment indicators?
3. What types of disclosures are necessary for impairments?
4. What is the process that companies use to match their cash flows to the asset that is potentially impaired?

Assessing whether a company has impaired assets is difficult. For example, in addition to the technical accounting issues, the environment can change quickly. Reduced spending by consumers, lack of confidence in global economic decisions, and higher volatility in both share and commodity markets are factors to consider. Nevertheless, for investors and creditors to have assurance that the amounts reported on the statement of financial position for property, plant, and equipment are relevant and representationally faithful, appropriate impairment charges must be reported on a timely basis.

Source: A portion of this discussion is taken from "Top 10 Tips for Impairment Testing," PricewaterhouseCoopers (December 2008).

CONCEPTUAL FOCUS

> See the **Underlying Concepts** on pages 496, 497, and 504.

INTERNATIONAL FOCUS

> Read the **Global Accounting Insights** on pages 519–520 for a discussion of non-IFRS financial reporting for property, plant, and equipment.

PREVIEW OF CHAPTER | **11**

As noted in the opening story, many companies like Fujitsu (JPN) are affected by impairment rules. These rules recognize that when economic conditions deteriorate, companies may need to write off an asset's cost to indicate the decline in its usefulness. The purpose of this chapter is to examine the depreciation process and the methods of writing off the cost of property, plant, and equipment and mineral resources. The content and organization of the chapter are as follows.

Depreciation, Impairments, and Depletion

Depreciation	Impairments	Depletion	Revaluations	Presentation and Analysis
• Factors involved • Methods of depreciation • Component depreciation • Special issues	• Recognizing impairments • Impairment illustrations • Reversal of loss • Cash-generating units • Assets to be disposed of	• Establishing a base • Write-off of resource cost • Estimating reserves • Liquidating dividends • Presentation	• Recognition • Issues	• Presentation • Analysis

DEPRECIATION—A METHOD OF COST ALLOCATION

LEARNING OBJECTIVE

Explain the concept of depreciation.

Most individuals at one time or another purchase and trade in an automobile. The automobile dealer and the buyer typically discuss what the trade-in value of the old car is. Also, they may talk about what the trade-in value of the new car will be in several years. In both cases, a decline in value is considered to be an example of depreciation.

To accountants, however, depreciation is not a matter of valuation. Rather, **depreciation is a means of cost allocation**. Depreciation **is the accounting process of allocating the cost of tangible assets to expense in a systematic and rational manner to those periods expected to benefit from the use of the asset.** For example, a company like Enhance Electronics Co., Ltd. (TWN) does not depreciate assets on the basis of a decline in their fair value. Instead, it depreciates through systematic charges to expense.

This approach is employed because the value of the asset may fluctuate between the time the asset is purchased and the time it is sold or junked. Attempts to measure these interim value changes have not been well received because values are difficult to measure objectively. Therefore, Enhance Electronics charges the asset's cost to depreciation expense over its estimated life. It makes no attempt to value the asset at fair value between acquisition and disposition. Companies use the cost allocation approach because it matches costs with revenues and because fluctuations in fair value are uncertain and difficult to measure.

When companies write off the cost of long-lived assets over a number of periods, they typically use the term **depreciation**. They use the term depletion to describe the reduction in the cost of mineral resources (such as oil, gas, and coal) over a period of time. The expiration of intangible assets, such as patents or copyrights, is called amortization.

Factors Involved in the Depreciation Process

LEARNING OBJECTIVE

Identify the factors involved in the depreciation process.

Before establishing a pattern of charges to revenue, a company must answer three basic questions:

1. What depreciable base is to be used for the asset?
2. What is the asset's useful life?
3. What method of cost apportionment is best for this asset?

The answers to these questions involve combining several estimates into one single figure. Note the calculations assume perfect knowledge of the future, which is never attainable.

Depreciable Base for the Asset

The base established for depreciation is a function of two factors: the original cost and residual value. We discussed historical cost in Chapter 10. **Residual value** (often referred to as **salvage value**) is the estimated amount that a company will receive when it sells the asset or removes it from service.[1] It is the amount to which a company writes down or depreciates the asset during its useful life. If an asset has a cost of €10,000 and a residual value of €1,000, its **depreciation base** is €9,000.

ILLUSTRATION 11-1
Computation of Depreciation Base

I
F
R
S

See the Authoritative Literature section (page 529).

Original cost	€10,000
Less: Residual value	1,000
Depreciation base	€ 9,000

---

[1]Residual value does not include possible future inflation effects. **[1]**

From a practical standpoint, companies often assign a zero residual value. Some long-lived assets, however, have substantial residual values.

Estimation of Service Lives

The service life of an asset often differs from its physical life. A piece of machinery may be physically capable of producing a given product for many years beyond its service life. But, a company may not use the equipment for all that time because the cost of producing the product in later years may be too high.

Companies retire assets for two reasons: **physical factors** (such as casualty or expiration of physical life) and **economic factors** (obsolescence). Physical factors are the wear and tear, decay, and casualties that make it difficult for the asset to perform indefinitely. These physical factors set the outside limit for the service life of an asset.

We can classify the economic or functional factors into three categories:

1. Inadequacy results when an asset ceases to be useful to a company because the demands of the firm have changed. An example would be the need for a larger building to handle increased production. Although the old building may still be sound, it may have become inadequate for the company's purpose.

2. Supersession is the replacement of one asset with another more efficient and economical asset. Examples would be the replacement of the mainframe computer with a PC network, or the replacement of the Boeing 767 with the Boeing 787.

3. Obsolescence is the catchall for situations not involving inadequacy and supersession.

Because the distinction between these categories appears artificial, it is probably best to consider economic factors collectively instead of trying to make distinctions that are not clear-cut.

To illustrate the concepts of physical and economic factors, consider a new nuclear power plant. Which is more important in determining the useful life of a nuclear power plant—physical factors or economic factors? The limiting factors seem to be (1) ecological considerations, (2) competition from other power sources, and (3) safety concerns. Physical life does not appear to be the primary factor affecting useful life. Although the plant's physical life may be far from over, the plant may become obsolete in 10 years.

For a house, physical factors undoubtedly are more important than the economic or functional factors relative to useful life. Whenever the physical nature of the asset primarily determines useful life, maintenance plays an extremely vital role. The better the maintenance, the longer the life of the asset.[2]

Most companies estimate the useful life of an asset based on their past experiences with the same or similar assets. Others use sophisticated statistical methods to establish a useful life for accounting purposes. And, in some cases, companies select arbitrary service lives. In highly industrial economies, where research and innovation are so prominent, technological factors have as much effect, if not more, on service lives of tangible plant assets as physical factors do.

Methods of Depreciation

The third factor involved in the depreciation process is the **method** of cost apportionment. The profession requires that the depreciation method employed be "systematic and rational." To be systematic and rational, the depreciation

3 LEARNING OBJECTIVE

Compare activity, straight-line, and diminishing-charge methods of depreciation.

---

[2]The airline industry also illustrates the type of problem involved in estimation. In the past, aircraft were assumed not to wear out—they just became obsolete. However, some jets have been in service as long as 20 years, and maintenance of these aircraft has become increasingly expensive. As a result, some airlines now replace aircraft not because of obsolescence but because of physical deterioration.

method should reflect the pattern in which the asset's future economic benefits are expected to be consumed by the company. **[2]** Companies may use a number of depreciation methods, as follows.

Underlying Concepts

Depreciation attempts to match the cost of an asset to the periods that benefit from the use of that asset.

1. Activity method (units of use or production).

2. Straight-line method.

3. Diminishing (accelerated)-charge methods:
    (a) Sum-of-the-years'-digits.
    (b) Declining-balance method.[3]

To illustrate these depreciation methods, assume that Stanley Coal Mines recently purchased an additional crane for digging purposes. Illustration 11-2 contains the pertinent data concerning this purchase.

ILLUSTRATION 11-2
Data Used to Illustrate
Depreciation Methods

Cost of crane	$500,000
Estimated useful life	5 years
Estimated residual value	$ 50,000
Productive life in hours	30,000 hours

Activity Method

The **activity method** (also called the **variable-charge** or **units-of-production approach**) assumes that depreciation is **a function of use or productivity, instead of the passage of time**. A company considers the life of the asset in terms of either the **output** it provides (units it produces) or an **input** measure such as the number of hours it works. Conceptually, the proper cost association relies on output instead of hours used, but often the output is not easily measurable. In such cases, an input measure such as machine hours is a more appropriate method of measuring the dollar amount of depreciation charges for a given accounting period.

The crane poses no particular depreciation problem. Stanley can measure the usage (hours) relatively easily. If Stanley uses the crane for 4,000 hours the first year, the depreciation charge is:

ILLUSTRATION 11-3
Depreciation Calculation,
Activity Method—Crane
Example

$$\frac{(\text{Cost} - \text{Residual Value}) \times \text{Hours this Year}}{\text{Total Estimated Hours}} = \text{Depreciation Charge}$$

$$\frac{(\$500,000 - \$50,000) \times 4,000}{30,000} = \$60,000$$

The major limitation of this method is that it is inappropriate in situations in which depreciation is a function of time instead of activity. For example, a building steadily deteriorates due to the elements (time) regardless of its use. In addition, where economic or functional factors affect an asset, independent of its use, the activity method loses much of its significance. For example, if a company is expanding rapidly, a particular building may soon become obsolete for its intended purposes. In both cases, activity is irrelevant. Another problem in using an activity method is the difficulty of estimating units of output or service hours received.

---

[3]Companies use the straight-line method more than any other method of depreciation. In a survey of 200 international companies, straight-line depreciation was used 170 times, declining-balance 11 times, units-of-production (activity method) 18 times, and other (e.g., proportion of proven reserve) 8 times. In some cases, companies use two or more depreciation methods. See *IFRS Accounting Trends & Techniques, 2012–2013* (AICPA, 2012).

In cases where loss of services results from activity or productivity, the activity method matches costs and revenues the best. Companies that desire low depreciation during periods of low productivity, and high depreciation during high productivity, either adopt or switch to an activity method. In this way, a plant running at 40 percent of capacity generates 60 percent lower depreciation charges.

Straight-Line Method

The **straight-line method** considers depreciation as a **function of time rather than a function of usage**. Companies widely use this method because of its simplicity. The straight-line procedure is often the most conceptually appropriate, too. When creeping obsolescence is the primary reason for a limited service life, the decline in usefulness may be constant from period to period. Stanley computes the depreciation charge for the crane as follows.

Underlying Concepts

If benefits flow on a "straight-line" basis, then justification exists for matching the cost of the asset on a straight-line basis with these benefits.

$$\frac{\text{Cost} - \text{Residual Value}}{\text{Estimated Service Life}} = \text{Depreciation Charge}$$

$$\frac{\$500,000 - \$50,000}{5} = \$90,000$$

ILLUSTRATION 11-4
Depreciation Calculation, Straight-Line Method—Crane Example

The major objection to the straight-line method is that it rests on two tenuous assumptions: (1) the asset's economic usefulness is the same each year, and (2) the maintenance and repair expense is essentially the same each period.

One additional problem that occurs in using straight-line—as well as some other methods—is that distortions in the rate of return analysis (income/assets) develop. Illustration 11-5 indicates how the rate of return increases, given constant revenue flows, because the asset's book value decreases.

Year	Depreciation Expense	Undepreciated Asset Balance (book value)	Income (after depreciation expense)	Rate of Return (Income ÷ Assets)
0		$500,000		
1	$90,000	410,000	$100,000	24.4%
2	90,000	320,000	100,000	31.2%
3	90,000	230,000	100,000	43.5%
4	90,000	140,000	100,000	71.4%
5	90,000	50,000	100,000	200.0%

ILLUSTRATION 11-5
Depreciation and Rate of Return Analysis—Crane Example

Diminishing-Charge Methods

The **diminishing-charge methods** provide for a higher depreciation cost in the earlier years and lower charges in later periods. Because these methods allow for higher early-year charges than in the straight-line method, they are often called **accelerated depreciation methods**.

What is the main justification for this approach? The rationale is that companies should charge more depreciation in earlier years because the asset is most productive in its earlier years. Furthermore, the accelerated methods provide a constant cost because the depreciation charge is lower in the later periods, at the time when the maintenance and repair costs are often higher. Generally, companies use one of two diminishing-charge methods: the sum-of-the-years'-digits method or the declining-balance method.

Underlying Concepts

The expense recognition concept does not justify a constant charge to income. If the benefits from the asset decline as the asset ages, then a diminishing charge to income better matches cost to benefits.

Sum-of-the-Years'-Digits. The **sum-of-the-years'-digits method** results in a decreasing depreciation charge based on a decreasing fraction of depreciable cost (original cost less residual value). Each fraction uses the sum of the years as a denominator (5 + 4 + 3 + 2 + 1 = 15). The numerator is the number of years of estimated life remaining as of the beginning of the year. In this method, the numerator decreases year by year, and the denominator remains constant (5/15, 4/15, 3/15, 2/15, and 1/15). At the end of the asset's useful life, the balance remaining should equal the residual value. Illustration 11-6 shows this method of computation.[4]

ILLUSTRATION 11-6
Sum-of-the-Years'-Digits
Depreciation Schedule—
Crane Example

Year	Depreciation Base	Remaining Life in Years	Depreciation Fraction	Depreciation Expense	Book Value, End of Year
1	$450,000	5	5/15	$150,000	$350,000
2	450,000	4	4/15	120,000	230,000
3	450,000	3	3/15	90,000	140,000
4	450,000	2	2/15	60,000	80,000
5	450,000	1	1/15	30,000	50,000[a]
		15	15/15	$450,000	

[a]Residual value.

Declining-Balance Method. The **declining-balance method** (often referred to as the **reducing-balance method**) utilizes a depreciation rate (expressed as a percentage) that is some multiple of the straight-line method. For example, the double-declining rate for a 10-year asset is 20 percent (double the straight-line rate, which is 1/10 or 10 percent). Companies apply the constant rate to the declining book value each year.

Unlike other methods, the declining-balance method **does not deduct the residual value** in computing the depreciation base. The declining-balance rate is multiplied by the book value of the asset at the beginning of each period. Since the depreciation charge reduces the book value of the asset each period, applying the constant-declining-balance rate to a successively lower book value results in lower depreciation charges each year. This process continues until the book value of the asset equals its estimated residual value. At that time, the company discontinues depreciation.

Companies use various multiples in practice. For example, the **double-declining-balance method** depreciates assets at twice (200 percent) the straight-line rate. Illustration 11-7 shows Stanley's depreciation charges if using the double-declining approach.

ILLUSTRATION 11-7
Double-Declining
Depreciation Schedule—
Crane Example

Year	Book Value of Asset First of Year	Rate on Declining Balance[a]	Depreciation Expense	Balance Accumulated Depreciation	Book Value, End of Year
1	$500,000	40%	$200,000	$200,000	$300,000
2	300,000	40%	120,000	320,000	180,000
3	180,000	40%	72,000	392,000	108,000
4	108,000	40%	43,200	435,200	64,800
5	64,800	40%	14,800[b]	450,000	50,000

[a]Based on twice the straight-line rate of 20% ($90,000/$450,000 = 20%; 20% × 2 = 40%).
[b]Limited to $14,800 because book value should not be less than residual value.

[4]What happens if the estimated service life of the asset is, let us say, 51 years? How would we calculate the sum-of-the-years'-digits? Fortunately, mathematicians have developed the following formula that permits easy computation:

$$\frac{n(n+1)}{2} = \frac{51(51+1)}{2} = 1{,}326$$

Companies often switch from the declining-balance method to the straight-line method near the end of the asset's useful life to ensure that they depreciate the asset only to its residual value.[5]

Component Depreciation

As indicated in Chapter 10, companies are required to use **component depreciation**. IFRS requires that each part of an item of property, plant, and equipment that is significant to the total cost of the asset must be depreciated separately. Companies therefore have to exercise judgment to determine the proper allocations to the components. As an example, when a company like Nokia (FIN) purchases a building, it must determine how the various building components (e.g., the foundation, structure, roof, heating and cooling system, and elevators) should be segregated and depreciated.

4 LEARNING OBJECTIVE
Explain component depreciation.

To illustrate the accounting for component depreciation, assume that EuroAsia Airlines purchases an airplane for €100,000,000 on January 1, 2016. The airplane has a useful life of 20 years and a residual value of €0. EuroAsia uses the straight-line method of depreciation for all its airplanes. EuroAsia identifies the following components, amounts, and useful lives, as shown in Illustration 11-8.

Components	Component Amount	Component Useful Life
Airframe	€60,000,000	20 years
Engine components	32,000,000	8 years
Other components	8,000,000	5 years

ILLUSTRATION 11-8
Airplane Components

Illustration 11-9 shows the computation of depreciation expense for EuroAsia for 2016.

Components	Component Amount	÷	Useful Life	=	Component Depreciation
Airframe	€ 60,000,000		20		€3,000,000
Engine components	32,000,000		8		4,000,000
Other components	8,000,000		5		1,600,000
Total	€100,000,000				€8,600,000

ILLUSTRATION 11-9
Computation of Component Depreciation

As indicated, EuroAsia records depreciation expense of €8,600,000 in 2016, as follows.

Depreciation Expense	8,600,000	
Accumulated Depreciation—Equipment		8,600,000

On the statement of financial position at the end of 2016, EuroAsia reports the airplane as a single amount. The presentation is shown in Illustration 11-10.

Non-current assets	
Airplane	€100,000,000
Less: Accumulated depreciation—airplane	8,600,000
	€ 91,400,000

ILLUSTRATION 11-10
Presentation of Carrying Amount of Airplane

---

[5]A pure form of the declining-balance method (sometimes called the "fixed percentage of book value method") has also been suggested as a possibility. This approach uses a rate that depreciates the asset exactly to the residual value at the end of its expected useful life. The formula for determining the rate is as follows.

$$\text{Depreciation rate} = 1 - \sqrt[n]{\frac{\text{Residual value}}{\text{Acquisition cost}}}$$

The life in years is n. After computing the depreciation rate, a company applies it on the declining book value of the asset from period to period, which means that depreciation expense will be successively lower. This method is not used extensively in practice, and it is generally not permitted for tax purposes.

In many situations, a company may not have a good understanding of the cost of the individual components purchased. In that case, the cost of individual components should be estimated based on reference to current market prices (if available), discussion with experts in valuation, or use of other reasonable approaches.

Special Depreciation Issues

We still need to discuss several special issues related to depreciation:

1. How should companies compute depreciation for partial periods?

2. Does depreciation provide for the replacement of assets?

3. How should companies handle revisions in depreciation rates?

Depreciation and Partial Periods

Companies seldom purchase plant assets on the first day of a fiscal period or dispose of them on the last day of a fiscal period. A practical question is: How much depreciation should a company charge for the partial periods involved?

In computing depreciation expense for partial periods, companies must determine the depreciation expense for the full year and then prorate this depreciation expense between the two periods involved. This process should continue throughout the useful life of the asset.

Assume, for example, that Steeltex Company purchases an automated drill machine with a five-year life for £45,000 (no residual value) on June 10, 2015. The company's fiscal year ends December 31. Steeltex therefore charges depreciation for only 6⅔ months during that year. The total depreciation for a full year (assuming straight-line depreciation) is £9,000 (£45,000/5). The depreciation for the first, partial year is therefore:

$$\frac{6^2\!/_3}{12} \times £9,000 = £5,000$$

The partial-period calculation is relatively simple when Steeltex uses straight-line depreciation. But how is partial-period depreciation handled when it uses an accelerated method such as sum-of-the-years'-digits or double-declining-balance? As an illustration, assume that Steeltex purchased another machine for £10,000 on July 1, 2015, with an estimated useful life of five years and no residual value. Illustration 11-11 shows the depreciation figures for 2015, 2016, and 2017.

ILLUSTRATION 11-11
Calculation of Partial-Period Depreciation, Two Methods

	Sum-of-the-Years'-Digits	Double-Declining-Balance
1st full year	(5/15 × £10,000) = £3,333.33	(40% × £10,000) = £4,000
2nd full year	(4/15 × 10,000) = 2,666.67	(40% × 6,000) = 2,400
3rd full year	(3/15 × 10,000) = 2,000.00	(40% × 3,600) = 1,440

Depreciation from July 1, 2015, to December 31, 2015

6/12 × £3,333.33 = £1,666.67	6/12 × £4,000 = £2,000

Depreciation for 2016

6/12 × £3,333.33 = £1,666.67	6/12 × £4,000 = £2,000
6/12 × 2,666.67 = 1,333.33	6/12 × 2,400 = 1,200
£3,000.00	£3,200
	or (£10,000 − £2,000) × 40% = £3,200

Depreciation for 2017

6/12 × £2,666.67 = £1,333.33	6/12 × £2,400 = £1,200
6/12 × 2,000.00 = 1,000.00	6/12 × 1,440 = 720
£2,333.33	£1,920
	or (£10,000 − £5,200) × 40% = £1,920

Sometimes a company like Steeltex modifies the process of allocating costs to a partial period to handle acquisitions and disposals of plant assets more simply. One variation is to take no depreciation in the year of acquisition and a full year's depreciation in the year of disposal. Other variations charge one-half year's depreciation both in the year of acquisition and in the year of disposal (referred to as the **half-year convention**), or charge a full year in the year of acquisition and none in the year of disposal.

In fact, Steeltex may adopt any one of these several fractional-year policies in allocating cost to the first and last years of an asset's life so long as it applies the method consistently. However, **unless otherwise stipulated, companies normally compute depreciation on the basis of the nearest full month**.

Illustration 11-12 shows depreciation allocated under five different fractional-year policies using the straight-line method on the £45,000 automated drill machine purchased by Steeltex Company on June 10, 2015, discussed earlier.

Machine Cost = £45,000	Depreciation Allocated per Period Over 5-Year Life*					
Fractional-Year Policy	2015	2016	2017	2018	2019	2020
1. Nearest fraction of a year.	£5,000[a]	£9,000	£9,000	£9,000	£9,000	£4,000[b]
2. Nearest full month.	5,250[c]	9,000	9,000	9,000	9,000	3,750[d]
3. Half year in period of acquisition and disposal.	4,500	9,000	9,000	9,000	9,000	4,500
4. Full year in period of acquisition, none in period of disposal.	9,000	9,000	9,000	9,000	9,000	–0–
5. None in period of acquisition, full year in period of disposal.	–0–	9,000	9,000	9,000	9,000	9,000

[a]6.667/12 (£9,000) [b]5.333/12 (£9,000) [c]7/12 (£9,000) [d]5/12 (£9,000)
*Rounded to nearest pound.

ILLUSTRATION 11-12
Fractional-Year
Depreciation Policies

Depreciation and Replacement of Property, Plant, and Equipment

A common misconception about depreciation is that it provides funds for the replacement of property, plant, and equipment. Depreciation is like other expenses in that it reduces net income. It differs, though, in that **it does not involve a current cash outflow**.

To illustrate why depreciation does not provide funds for replacement of plant assets, assume that a business starts operating with plant assets of $500,000 that have a useful life of five years. The company's statement of financial position at the beginning of the period is:

Plant assets $500,000	Equity $500,000

If we assume that the company earns no revenue over the five years, the income statements are:

	Year 1	Year 2	Year 3	Year 4	Year 5
Revenue	$ –0–	$ –0–	$ –0–	$ –0–	$ –0–
Depreciation	(100,000)	(100,000)	(100,000)	(100,000)	(100,000)
Loss	$(100,000)	$(100,000)	$(100,000)	$(100,000)	$(100,000)

Total depreciation of the plant assets over the five years is $500,000. The statement of financial position at the end of the five years therefore is:

Plant assets –0–	Equity –0–

This extreme example illustrates that depreciation **in no way** provides funds for the replacement of assets. **The funds for the replacement of the assets come from the revenues** (generated through use of the asset). Without the revenues, no income materializes and no cash inflow results.

Revision of Depreciation Rates

When purchasing a plant asset, companies carefully determine depreciation rates based on past experience with similar assets and other pertinent information. The provisions for depreciation are only estimates, however. Companies may need to revise them during the life of the asset. Unexpected physical deterioration or unforeseen obsolescence may decrease the estimated useful life of the asset. Improved maintenance procedures, revision of operating procedures, or similar developments may prolong the life of the asset beyond the expected period.[6]

For example, assume that Nestlé (CHE) purchased machinery with an original cost of CHF90,000. It estimates a 20-year life with no residual value. However, during year 11, Nestlé estimates that it will use the machine for an additional 20 years. Its total life, therefore, will be 30 years instead of 20. Depreciation has been recorded at the rate of 1/20 of CHF90,000, or CHF4,500 per year by the straight-line method. On the basis of a 30-year life, Nestlé should have recorded depreciation as 1/30 of CHF90,000, or CHF3,000 per year. It has therefore overstated depreciation, and understated net income, by CHF1,500 for each of the past 10 years, or a total amount of CHF15,000. Illustration 11-13 shows this computation.

ILLUSTRATION 11-13
Computation of
Accumulated Difference
Due to Revisions

	Per Year	For 10 Years
Depreciation charged per books (1/20 × CHF90,000)	CHF4,500	CHF45,000
Depreciation based on a 30-year life (1/30 × CHF90,000)	(3,000)	(30,000)
Excess depreciation charged	CHF1,500	CHF15,000

Nestlé should report this change in estimate in the current and prospective periods. It should not make any changes in previously reported results. And it does not adjust opening balances nor attempt to "catch up" for prior periods. The reason? Changes in estimates are a continual and inherent part of any estimation process. Continual restatement of prior periods would occur for revisions of estimates unless handled prospectively. Therefore, no entry is made at the time the change in estimate occurs. Charges for depreciation in subsequent periods (assuming use of the straight-line method) are determined by **dividing the remaining book value less any residual value by the remaining estimated life.**

ILLUSTRATION 11-14
Computing Depreciation
after Revision of
Estimated Life

Machinery	CHF90,000
Less: Accumulated depreciation	45,000
Book value of machinery at end of 10th year	CHF45,000

Depreciation (future periods) = CHF45,000 book value ÷ 20 years remaining life = CHF2,250

---

[6]As an example of a change in operating procedures, General Motors (USA) used to write off its tools—such as dies and equipment used to manufacture car bodies—over the life of the body type. Through this procedure, it expensed tools twice as fast as Ford (USA) and three times as fast as Chrysler (USA). However, it slowed the depreciation process on these tools and lengthened the lives on its plant and equipment. These revisions reduced depreciation and amortization charges by approximately $1.23 billion, or $2.55 per share, in the year of the change. In Chapter 22, we provide a more complete discussion of changes in estimates.

The entry to record depreciation for each of the remaining 20 years is:

Depreciation Expense	2,250	
Accumulated Depreciation—Machinery		2,250

What do the numbers mean?   DEPRECIATION CHOICES

The amount of depreciation expense recorded depends on both the depreciation method used and estimates of service lives and residual values of the assets. Differences in these choices and estimates can significantly impact a company's reported results and can make it difficult to compare the depreciation numbers of different companies.

For example, Veolia Environment (FRA) provided information regarding useful lives of its assets in the note to its financial statements, as shown to the right.

With the information provided, an analyst determines the impact of these management choices and judgments on the amount of depreciation expense for classes of property, plant, and equipment.

1.7 Property, Plant, and Equipment

Property, plant, and equipment are recorded at historical acquisition cost to the Group, less accumulated depreciation and any accumulated impairment losses.

Property, plant, and equipment are recorded by component, with each component depreciated over its useful life. Useful lives are as follows:

	Range of Useful Lives in Number of Years*
Buildings	20 to 50
Technical systems	7 to 24
Vehicles	3 to 25
Other plant and equipment	3 to 12

*The range of useful lives is due to the diversity of property, plant and equipment concerned.

IMPAIRMENTS

The general accounting standard of **lower-of-cost-or-net realizable value for inventories does not apply to property, plant, and equipment**. Even when property, plant, and equipment has suffered partial obsolescence, accountants have been reluctant to reduce the asset's carrying amount. Why? Because, unlike inventories, it is difficult to arrive at a fair value for property, plant, and equipment that is not somewhat subjective and arbitrary.

> **5 LEARNING OBJECTIVE**
> Explain the accounting issues related to asset impairment.

For example, Falconbridge Ltd. Nickel Mines (CAN) had to decide whether to write off all or a part of its property, plant, and equipment in a nickel-mining operation in the Dominican Republic. The project had been incurring losses because nickel prices were low and operating costs were high. Only if nickel prices increased by approximately 33 percent would the project be reasonably profitable. Whether a write-off was appropriate depended on the future price of nickel. Even if the company decided to write off the asset, how much should be written off?

Recognizing Impairments

As discussed in the opening story, the credit crisis starting in late 2008 has affected many financial and non-financial institutions. As a result of this global slump, many companies are considering write-offs of some of their long-lived assets. These write-offs are referred to as impairments.

A long-lived tangible asset is impaired when a company is not able to recover the asset's carrying amount either through using it or by selling it. To determine whether an asset is impaired, **on an annual basis, companies review the asset for indicators of impairments**—that is, a decline in the asset's cash-generating ability through use or sale. This review should consider internal sources (e.g., adverse changes in performance) and external sources (e.g., adverse changes in the business or regulatory environment) of

Underlying Concepts

IFRS uses the terms carrying value, carrying amount, and book value interchangeably.

information. **If impairment indicators are present, then an** impairment test **must be conducted.** This test compares the asset's recoverable amount with its carrying amount. If the carrying amount is higher than the recoverable amount, the difference is an impairment loss. If the recoverable amount is greater than the carrying amount, no impairment is recorded. **[3]**

Recoverable amount is defined as the higher of fair value less costs to sell or value-in-use. Fair value less costs to sell means what the asset could be sold for after deducting costs of disposal. Value-in-use is the present value of cash flows expected from the future use and eventual sale of the asset at the end of its useful life. Illustration 11-15 highlights the nature of the impairment test.

ILLUSTRATION 11-15
Impairment Test

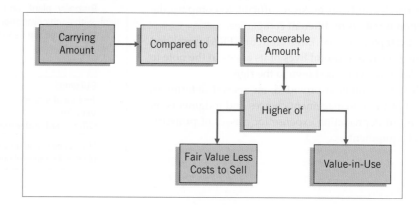

If either the fair value less costs to sell or value-in-use is higher than the carrying amount, there is no impairment. If both the fair value less costs to sell and value-in-use are lower than the carrying amount, a loss on impairment occurs.

Example: No Impairment

Assume that Cruz Company performs an impairment test for its equipment. The carrying amount of Cruz's equipment is €200,000, its fair value less costs to sell is €180,000, and its value-in-use is €205,000. In this case, the value-in-use of Cruz's equipment is higher than its carrying amount of €200,000. As a result, there is no impairment.[7]

Example: Impairment

Assume the same information for Cruz Company above except that the value-in-use of Cruz's equipment is €175,000 rather than €205,000. Cruz measures the impairment loss as the difference between the carrying amount of €200,000 and the higher of fair value less costs to sell (€180,000) or value-in-use (€175,000). Cruz therefore uses the fair value less cost of disposal to record an impairment loss of €20,000 (€200,000 − €180,000).

Cruz makes the following entry to record the impairment loss.

Loss on Impairment	20,000	
Accumulated Depreciation—Equipment		20,000

The Loss on Impairment is reported in the income statement in the "Other income and expense" section. The company then either credits Equipment or Accumulated Depreciation—Equipment to reduce the carrying amount of the equipment for the impairment. *For purposes of homework, credit accumulated depreciation when recording an impairment for a depreciable asset.*

---

[7]If a company can more readily determine value-in-use (or fair value less costs to sell) and it determines that no impairment is needed, it is not required to compute the other measure. **[4]**

Impairment Illustrations

Presented below are additional examples of impairments.

Case 1

At December 31, 2016, Hanoi Company has equipment with a cost of VND26,000,000, and accumulated depreciation of VND12,000,000. The equipment has a total useful life of four years with a residual value of VND2,000,000. The following information relates to this equipment.

1. The equipment's carrying amount at December 31, 2016, is VND14,000,000 (VND26,000,000 − VND12,000,000).

2. Hanoi uses straight-line depreciation. Hanoi's depreciation was VND6,000,000 [(VND26,000,000 − VND2,000,000) ÷ 4] for 2016 and is recorded.

3. Hanoi has determined that the recoverable amount for this asset at December 31, 2016, is VND11,000,000.

4. The remaining useful life of the equipment after December 31, 2016, is two years.

Hanoi records the impairment on its equipment at December 31, 2016, as follows.

Loss on Impairment (VND14,000,000 − VND11,000,000)	3,000,000	
Accumulated Depreciation—Equipment		3,000,000

Following the recognition of the impairment loss in 2016, the carrying amount of the equipment is now VND11,000,000 (VND14,000,000 − VND3,000,000). For 2017, Hanoi Company determines that the equipment's total useful life has not changed (thus, the equipment's remaining useful life is still two years). However, the estimated residual value of the equipment is now zero. Hanoi continues to use straight-line depreciation and makes the following journal entry to record depreciation for 2017.

Depreciation Expense (VND11,000,000/2)	5,500,000	
Accumulated Depreciation—Equipment		5,500,000

Hanoi records depreciation in the periods following the impairment using the carrying amount of the asset adjusted for the impairment. Hanoi then evaluates whether the equipment was further impaired at the end of 2017. For example, the carrying amount of Hanoi's equipment at December 31, 2017, is VND5,500,000 (VND26,000,000 − VND12,000,000 − VND3,000,000 − VND5,500,000). If Hanoi determines that the recoverable amount at December 31, 2017, is lower than VND5,500,000, then an additional impairment loss is recorded.

Case 2

At the end of 2015, Verma Company tests a machine for impairment. The machine has a carrying amount of $200,000. It has an estimated remaining useful life of five years. Because of the unique nature of the machine, there is little market-related information on which to base a recoverable amount based on fair value. As a result, Verma determines the machine's recoverable amount (i.e., the higher of value-in-use and fair value less costs to sell) should be based on value-in-use.

To determine value-in-use, Verma develops an estimate of future cash flows based on internal company cash budgets (and reflecting cash inflows from the machine and estimated costs necessary to maintain the machine in its current condition). [5] Verma uses a discount rate of 8 percent, which should be a pretax rate that approximates Verma's cost of borrowing.[8] Verma's analysis indicates that its future cash flows will be

---

[8]Specifically, the pretax rate is determined taking into account market- and company-specific borrowing rates, adjusted for any risks the market might attribute to expected cash flows for the asset. [6]

$40,000 each year for five years, and it will receive a residual value of $10,000 at the end of the five years. It is assumed that all cash flows occur at the end of the year. The computation of the value-in-use for Verma's machine is shown in Illustration 11-16.

ILLUSTRATION 11-16
Value-in-Use
Computation

Present value of 5 annual payments of $40,000 ($40,000 × 3.99271, Table 6-4)	$159,708.40
Present value of residual value of $10,000 ($10,000 × .68058, Table 6-1)	6,805.80
Value-in-use related to machine	$166,514.20

The computation of the impairment loss on the machine at the end of 2015 is shown in Illustration 11-17.

ILLUSTRATION 11-17
Impairment Loss
Calculation Based on
Value-in-Use

Carrying amount of machine before impairment loss	$200,000.00
Recoverable amount of machine	166,514.20
Loss on impairment	$ 33,485.80

The company therefore records an impairment loss at December 31, 2015, as follows.

Loss on Impairment	33,485.80	
Accumulated Depreciation—Machinery		33,485.80

The carrying amount of the machine after recording the loss is $166,514.20.

Reversal of Impairment Loss

After recording the impairment loss, the recoverable amount becomes the basis of the impaired asset. What happens if a review in a future year indicates that the asset is no longer impaired because the recoverable amount of the asset is higher than the carrying amount? In that case, the impairment loss may be reversed.

To illustrate, assume that Tan Company purchases equipment on January 1, 2015, for HK$300,000, with a useful life of three years and no residual value. Its depreciation and related carrying amount over the three years is as follows.

Year	Depreciation Expense	Carrying Amount
2015	HK$100,000 (HK$300,000/3)	HK$200,000
2016	HK$100,000 (HK$300,000/3)	HK$100,000
2017	HK$100,000 (HK$300,000/3)	0

At December 31, 2015, Tan determines it has an impairment loss of HK$20,000 and therefore makes the following entry.

Loss on Impairment	20,000	
Accumulated Depreciation—Equipment		20,000

Tan's depreciation expense and related carrying amount after the impairment is as indicated below.

Year	Depreciation Expense	Carrying Amount
2016	HK$90,000 (HK$180,000/2)	HK$90,000
2017	HK$90,000 (HK$180,000/2)	0

At the end of 2016, Tan determines that the recoverable amount of the equipment is HK$96,000, which is greater than its carrying amount of HK$90,000. In this case, Tan reverses the previously recognized impairment loss with the following entry.

Accumulated Depreciation—Equipment	6,000	
Recovery of Impairment Loss		6,000

The recovery of the impairment loss is reported in the "Other income and expense" section of the income statement. The carrying amount of Tan's equipment is now HK$96,000 (HK$90,000 + HK$6,000) at December 31, 2016.

The general rule related to reversals of impairments is as follows. The amount of the recovery of the loss is limited to the carrying amount that would result if the impairment had not occurred. For example, the carrying amount of Tan's equipment at the end of 2016 would be HK$100,000, assuming no impairment. The HK$6,000 recovery is therefore permitted because Tan's carrying amount on the equipment is now only HK$96,000. However, any recovery above HK$10,000 is not permitted. The reason is that any recovery above HK$10,000 results in Tan carrying the asset at a value above its historical cost.

Cash-Generating Units

In some cases, it may not be possible to assess a single asset for impairment because the single asset generates cash flows only in combination with other assets. In that case, companies should identify the smallest group of assets that can be identified that generates cash flows independently of the cash flows from other assets. Such a group is called a **cash-generating unit (CGU)**.

For example, Santos Company is reviewing its plant assets for indicators of impairment. However, it is finding that identifying cash flows for individual assets is very cumbersome and inaccurate because the cash flows related to a group of assets are interdependent. This situation can arise if Santos has one operating unit (machining division) that manufactures products that are transferred to another Santos business unit (packing division), which then markets the products to end customers. Because the cash flows to the assets in the machining division are dependent on the cash flows in the packing division, Santos should evaluate both divisions together as a cash-generating unit in its impairment assessments.

Impairment of Assets to Be Disposed Of

What happens if a company intends to dispose of the impaired asset, instead of holding it for use? Recently, Kroger (USA) recorded an impairment loss of $54 million on property, plant, and equipment it no longer needed due to store closures. In this case, Kroger reports the impaired asset at the **lower-of-cost-or-net realizable value** (fair value less costs to sell). Because Kroger intends to dispose of the assets in a short period of time, it uses net realizable value in order to provide a better measure of the net cash flows that it will receive from these assets.

Kroger does not depreciate or amortize assets held for disposal during the period it holds them. The rationale is that depreciation is inconsistent with the notion of assets to be disposed of and with the use of the lower-of-cost-or-net realizable value. In other words, **assets held for disposal are like inventory; companies should report them at the lower-of-cost-or-net realizable value**.

Because Kroger will recover assets held for disposal through sale rather than through operations, it continually revalues them. Each period, the assets are reported at the lower-of-cost-or-net realizable value. Thus, **Kroger can write up or down an asset held for disposal in future periods, as long as the carrying amount after the write-up never exceeds the carrying amount of the asset before the impairment**. Companies should report losses or gains related to these impaired assets as part of **operating income** in "Other income and expense."

Illustration 11-18 summarizes the key concepts in accounting for impairments.

ILLUSTRATION 11-18
Graphic of Accounting
for Impairments

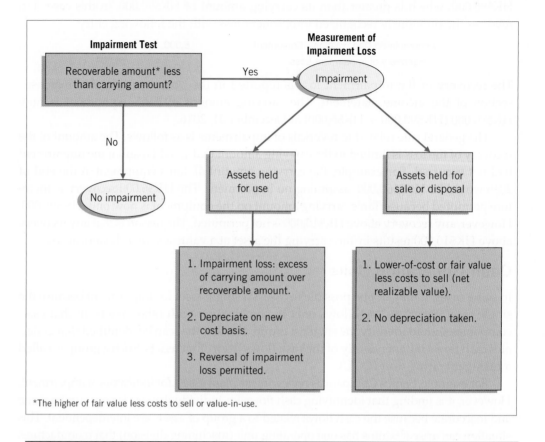

DEPLETION

LEARNING OBJECTIVE **6**

Explain the accounting procedures
for depletion of mineral resources.

Natural resources, often called wasting assets, include petroleum, minerals, and timberlands. Natural resources can be further subdivided into two categories: (1) biological assets such as timberlands, and (2) mineral resources such as oil, gas, and mineral mining. The accounting and reporting requirements for biological assets such as timberlands use a fair value approach and are discussed in Chapter 9. Here, we focus on **mineral resources**, which have two main features: (1) the complete removal (consumption) of the asset, and (2) replacement of the asset only by an act of nature.

Unlike plant and equipment, mineral resources are consumed physically over the period of use and do not maintain their physical characteristics. Still, the accounting problems associated with these resources are similar to those encountered with property, plant, and equipment. The questions to be answered are:

1. How do companies establish the cost basis for write-off?
2. What pattern of allocation should companies employ?

Recall that the accounting profession uses the term **depletion** for the process of allocating the cost of mineral resources.

Establishing a Depletion Base

How do we determine the depletion base for mineral resources? For example, a company like **Total S.A.** (FRA) makes sizable expenditures to find mineral resources. And, for every successful discovery, there are many failures. Furthermore, the company often encounters long delays between the time it incurs costs and the time it obtains the benefits from the extracted resources. As a result, a company in the extractive industries, like Total S.A., frequently adopts a conservative policy in accounting for the expenditures related to finding and extracting mineral resources.

Computation of the depletion base involves properly accounting for three types of expenditures:

1. Pre-exploratory costs.
2. Exploratory and evaluation costs.
3. Development costs.

Pre-Exploratory Costs

Pre-exploratory expenditures are costs incurred before the company has obtained the legal rights to explore a specific area. For example, Royal Dutch Shell (GBR and NLD) may perform seismic testing of possible oil-drilling sites before incurring any substantial costs of exploration. These costs (often referred to as prospecting costs) are generally considered speculative in nature and are expensed as incurred.

Exploratory and Evaluation (E&E) Costs

Examples of some types of exploratory and evaluation (E&E) costs are as follows.

- Acquisition of rights to explore.
- Topographical, geological, geochemical, and geophysical studies.
- Exploratory drilling.
- Sampling.
- Activities in relation to evaluating the technical feasibility and commercial viability of extracting a mineral resource.

Companies have a choice regarding E&E costs. They can either write off these costs as incurred or capitalize these costs pending evaluation. IFRS therefore provides companies with flexibility as how to account for E&E costs at inception. **[7]**

The reason for the flexibility is that the accounting for these types of expenditures is controversial. To illustrate, assume that Royal Dutch Shell is exploring for oil and determines that the area of exploration has oil reserves. It therefore drills a well to determine the amount of the reserves. Unfortunately, the well drilled results in a dry hole; that is, no reserves are found. Shell then drills more wells and finds some oil reserves, but some others are dry holes. The question is: Should the cost of the dry holes be capitalized? Or should only the cost of the wells that find reserves be capitalized?

Those who hold the full-cost concept (full capitalization) argue that the cost of drilling a dry hole is a cost needed to find the commercially profitable wells. Others believe that companies should capitalize only the costs of the successful wells. This is the successful-efforts concept. Its proponents believe that the only relevant measure for a project is the cost directly related to that project, and that companies should report any remaining costs as period charges. In addition, they argue that an unsuccessful company will end up capitalizing many costs that will make it, over a short period of time, show no less income than does one that is successful.

Development Costs

Once technical feasibility and commercial viability of production are demonstrated, E&E assets are reclassified as development costs. Generally, the development phase occurs when the company has determined that it has a reasonable level of mineral resources in the ground so that production will be profitable. At this time, any E&E assets recognized as assets are subsequently tested for impairment, to ensure that these assets are not carried at an amount above their recoverable amount.

Companies divide development costs into two parts: (1) tangible equipment costs and (2) intangible development costs. Tangible equipment costs include all of the transportation and other heavy equipment needed to extract the resource and get it ready for market. Because companies can move the heavy equipment from one extracting site to another, companies **do not normally include tangible equipment costs in the depletion base**. Instead, they use separate depreciation charges to allocate the costs of such equipment. However, some tangible assets (e.g., a drilling rig foundation) cannot be moved. Companies depreciate these assets over their useful life or the life of the resource, whichever is shorter.

Intangible development costs, on the other hand, are such items as drilling costs, tunnels, shafts, and wells. These costs have no tangible characteristics but are needed for the production of the mineral resource. **Intangible development costs are considered part of the depletion base.**

Companies sometimes incur substantial costs to restore property to its natural state after extraction has occurred. These are restoration costs. Companies consider **restoration costs part of the depletion base**. The amount included in the depletion base is the fair value of the obligation to restore the property after extraction. A more complete discussion of the accounting for restoration costs and related liabilities (sometimes referred to as environmental liability provisions) is provided in Chapter 13. Similar to other long-lived assets, companies deduct from the depletion base any residual value to be received on the property.

Write-Off of Resource Cost

Once the company establishes the depletion base, the next problem is determining how to allocate the cost of the mineral resource to accounting periods.

Normally, companies compute depletion (often referred to as cost depletion) on a **units-of-production method** (an activity approach). Thus, depletion is a function of the number of units extracted during the period. In this approach, the total cost of the mineral resource less residual value is divided by the number of units estimated to be in the resource deposit, to obtain a **cost per unit of product**. To compute depletion, the cost per unit is then multiplied by the number of units extracted.

For example, MaClede Co. acquired the right to use 1,000 acres of land in South Africa to mine for silver. The lease cost is €50,000, and the related exploration costs on the property are €100,000. Intangible development costs incurred in opening the mine are €850,000. Total costs related to the mine before the first ounce of silver is extracted are, therefore, €1,000,000. MaClede estimates that the mine will provide approximately 100,000 ounces of silver. Illustration 11-19 shows computation of the depletion cost per unit (depletion rate).

ILLUSTRATION 11-19
Computation of
Depletion Rate

$$\frac{\text{Total Cost} - \text{Residual Value}}{\text{Total Estimated Units Available}} = \text{Depletion Cost per Unit}$$

$$\frac{\text{€1,000,000}}{100,000} = \text{€10 per ounce}$$

If MaClede extracts 25,000 ounces in the first year, then the depletion for the year is €250,000 (25,000 ounces × €10). It records the depletion as follows.

Inventory	250,000	
Accumulated Depletion		250,000

MaClede debits Inventory for the total depletion for the year and credits Accumulated Depletion to reduce the carrying amount of the mineral resource. MaClede credits Inventory when it sells the inventory. The amount not sold remains in inventory and is reported in the current assets section of the statement of financial position.

Sometimes companies do not use an Accumulated Depletion account. In that case, the credit goes directly to the mineral resources asset account. MaClede's statement of financial position would present the cost of the mineral resource and the amount of accumulated depletion entered to date as follows.

Silver mine (at cost)	€1,000,000	
Less: Accumulated depletion	250,000	€750,000

ILLUSTRATION 11-20
Statement of Financial Position Presentation of Mineral Resource

In the income statement, the depletion cost related to the inventory sold is part of the cost of goods sold.

MaClede may also depreciate on a units-of-production basis the tangible equipment used in extracting the silver. This approach is appropriate if it can directly assign the estimated lives of the equipment to one given resource deposit. If MaClede uses the equipment on more than one job, other cost allocation methods such as straight-line or accelerated depreciation methods would be more appropriate.

Estimating Recoverable Reserves

Sometimes companies need to change the estimate of recoverable reserves. They do so either because they have new information or because more sophisticated production processes are available. Mineral resources such as oil and gas deposits and some rare metals have recently provided the greatest challenges. Estimates of these reserves are in large measure merely "knowledgeable guesses."[9]

This problem is the **same as accounting for changes in estimates for the useful lives of plant and equipment**. The procedure is to **revise the depletion rate on a prospective basis**: A company divides the remaining cost by the new estimate of the recoverable reserves. This approach has much merit because the required estimates are so uncertain.

Liquidating Dividends

A company often owns as its only major asset a property from which it intends to extract mineral resources. If the company does not expect to purchase additional properties, it may gradually distribute to shareholders their capital investments by paying liquidating dividends, which are dividends greater than the amount of accumulated net income.

The major accounting problem is to distinguish between dividends that are a return of capital and those that are not. Because the dividend is a return of the investor's original contribution, the company issuing a liquidating dividend should debit Share Premium—Ordinary for that portion related to the original investment, instead of debiting Retained Earnings.

To illustrate, at year-end, Callahan Mining had a retained earnings balance of £1,650,000, accumulated depletion on mineral properties of £2,100,000, and share premium of £5,435,493. Callahan's board declared a dividend of £3 per share on the 1,000,000 shares outstanding. It records the £3,000,000 cash dividend as follows.

[9]The IASB has conducted a research project on the extractive industry. The primary focus are the financial reporting issues associated with mineral and other natural resource reserves. The key question is whether and how to define, recognize, measure, and disclose reserves in the financial statements. At present, the Board is contemplating an agenda decision for a future standard. See *http://www.ifrs.org/Current-Projects/IASB-Projects/Extractive-Activities/DPA p10/Pages/DP.aspx.*

Retained Earnings	1,650,000	
Share Premium—Ordinary	1,350,000	
Cash		3,000,000

Callahan must inform shareholders that the £3 dividend per share represents a £1.65 (£1,650,000 ÷ 1,000,000 shares) per share return on investment and a £1.35 (£1,350,000 ÷ 1,000,000 shares) per share liquidating dividend.

Presentation on the Financial Statements

Companies should disclose the following related to E&E expenditures.

1. The accounting policies for exploration and evaluation expenditures, including the recognition of E&E assets.

2. The amounts of assets, liabilities, income and expense, and operating cash flow arising from the exploration for and evaluation of mineral resources.

The financial statement excerpts for **Tullow Oil plc** (GBR) in Illustration 11-21 highlight the nature of these disclosures.

ILLUSTRATION 11-21
Reporting of
Exploration Costs

Tullow Oil plc
(in thousands)

Income Statement

Exploration costs written off	£ 226,701

Statement of Financial Position

Intangible exploration and evaluation assets	£1,417,777

Statement of Cash Flows

Purchase of intangible exploration and evaluation of assets	£ 323,569

Accounting Policies

Exploration, evaluation, and production assets
The Group adopts the successful efforts method of accounting for exploration and appraisal costs. All license acquisition, exploration, and evaluation costs are initially capitalized in cost centers by well, field, or exploration area, as appropriate. Directly attributable administration costs and interest payable are capitalized insofar as they relate to specific development activities. Pre-license costs are expensed in the period in which they are incurred. These costs are then written off as exploration costs in the Income Statement unless commercial reserves have been established or the determination process has not been completed and there are no indications of impairment. All field development costs are capitalized as property, plant, and equipment. Property, plant, and equipment related to production activities are amortized in accordance with the Group's depletion and amortization accounting policy.

(k) Depletion and amortization—discovery fields

All expenditure carried within each field is amortized from the commencement of production on a unit of production basis, which is the ratio of oil and gas production in the period to the estimated quantities of commercial reserves at the end of the period plus the production in the period, generally on a field-by-field basis. Costs used in the unit of production calculation comprise the net book value of capitalized costs plus the estimated future field development costs. Changes in the estimates of commercial reserves or future field development costs are dealt with prospectively.

Where there has been a change in economic conditions that indicates a possible impairment in a discovery field, the recoverability of the net book value relating to that field is assessed by comparison with the estimated discounted future cash flows based on management's expectations of future oil and gas prices and future costs. Where there is evidence of economic interdependency between fields, such as common infrastructure, the fields are grouped as a single cash-generating unit for impairment purposes.

Any impairment identified is charged to the Income Statement as additional depletion and amortization. Where conditions giving rise to impairment subsequently reverse, the effect of the impairment charge is also reversed as a credit to the Income Statement, net of any depreciation that would have been charged since the impairment.

REVALUATIONS

Up to this point, we have assumed that companies use the historical cost principle to value long-lived tangible assets after acquisition. However, companies have a choice: They may value these assets at cost or at fair value. **[8]**

7 LEARNING OBJECTIVE

Explain the accounting for revaluations.

Recognizing Revaluations

Network Rail (GBR) is an example of a company that elected to use fair values to account for its railroad network. Its use of fair value led to an increase of £4,289 million to its long-lived tangible assets. When companies choose to fair value their long-lived tangible assets subsequent to acquisition, they account for the change in the fair value by adjusting the appropriate asset account and establishing an unrealized gain on the revalued long-lived tangible asset. This unrealized gain is often referred to as **revaluation surplus**.

Revaluation—Land

To illustrate revaluation of land, assume that Siemens Group (DEU) purchased land for €1,000,000 on January 5, 2015. The company elects to use revaluation accounting for the land in subsequent periods. At December 31, 2015, the land's fair value is €1,200,000. The entry to record the land at fair value is as follows.

Land	200,000	
Unrealized Gain on Revaluation—Land		200,000

The land is reported on the statement of financial position at €1,200,000, and the Unrealized Gain on Revaluation—Land increases other comprehensive income in the statement of comprehensive income. In addition, if this is the only revaluation adjustment to date, the statement of financial position reports accumulated other comprehensive income of €200,000.

Revaluation—Depreciable Assets

To illustrate the accounting for revaluations of depreciable assets, assume that Lenovo Group (CHN) purchases equipment for ¥500,000 on January 2, 2015. The equipment has a useful life of five years, is depreciated using the straight-line method of depreciation, and its residual value is zero. Lenovo chooses to revalue its equipment to fair value over the life of the equipment. Lenovo records depreciation expense of ¥100,000 (¥500,000 ÷ 5) at December 31, 2015, as follows.

December 31, 2015

Depreciation Expense	100,000	
Accumulated Depreciation—Equipment		100,000
(To record depreciation expense in 2015)		

After this entry, Lenovo's equipment has a carrying amount of ¥400,000 (¥500,000 − ¥100,000). Lenovo receives an independent appraisal for the fair value of equipment at December 31, 2015, which is ¥460,000. To report the equipment at fair value, Lenovo does the following.

1. Reduces the Accumulated Depreciation—Equipment account to zero.

2. Reduces the Equipment account by ¥40,000—it then is reported at its fair value of ¥460,000.

3. Records Unrealized Gain on Revaluation—Equipment for the difference between the fair value and carrying amount of the equipment, or ¥60,000 (¥460,000 − ¥400,000). The entry to record this revaluation at December 31, 2015, is as follows.

December 31, 2015		
Accumulated Depreciation—Equipment	100,000	
Equipment		40,000
Unrealized Gain on Revaluation—Equipment		60,000
(To adjust the equipment to fair value and record revaluation increase)		

The equipment is now reported at its fair value of ¥460,000 (¥500,000 − ¥40,000).[10] The increase in the fair value of ¥60,000 is reported on the statement of comprehensive income as other comprehensive income. In addition, the ending balance is reported in accumulated other comprehensive income on the statement of financial position in the equity section.

Illustration 11-22 shows the presentation of revaluation elements.

ILLUSTRATION 11-22
Financial Statement
Presentation—
Revaluations

Statement of Comprehensive Income	
Other comprehensive income	
Unrealized gain on revaluation—equipment	¥ 60,000
Statement of Financial Position	
Non-current assets	
Equipment (¥500,000 − ¥40,000)	¥460,000
Accumulated depreciation—equipment (¥100,000 − ¥100,000)	−0−
Carrying amount	¥460,000
Equity	
Accumulated other comprehensive income	¥ 60,000

As indicated, at December 31, 2015, the carrying amount of the equipment is now ¥460,000. Lenovo reports depreciation expense of ¥100,000 in the income statement and an Unrealized Gain on Revaluation—Equipment of ¥60,000 in "Other comprehensive income." Assuming no change in the useful life of the equipment, depreciation in 2016 is ¥115,000 (¥460,000 ÷ 4).

In summary, a revaluation increase generally goes to equity. A revaluation decrease is reported as an expense (as an impairment loss), unless it offsets previously recorded revaluation increases. If the revaluation increase offsets a revaluation decrease that went to expense, then the increase is reported in income. **Under no circumstances can the Accumulated Other Comprehensive Income account related to revaluations have a negative balance.**

Revaluation Issues

The use of revaluation accounting is not an "all or nothing" proposition. That is, a company can select to value only one class of assets, say buildings, and not revalue other assets such as land or equipment. However, if a company selects only buildings, revaluation applies to all assets in that class of assets. A class of assets is a grouping of items that have a similar nature and use in a company's operations. For example, a company like Siemens (DEU) may have the following classes of assets: land, equipment, and buildings. If Siemens chooses to fair value its land class, it must fair value all land. It cannot selectively apply revaluation accounting to certain parcels of land within the class and report them at fair value and keep the remainder at historical cost. To permit such

---

[10]When a depreciable asset is revalued, companies use one of two approaches to record the revaluation. As an alternative to the one shown here, companies restate on a proportionate basis the cost and accumulated depreciation of the asset, such that the carrying amount of the asset after revaluation equals its revalued amount.

"cherry-picking" not only leads to a misleading mixture of historical cost and fair value, but also permits a company to maximize its fair value through selective revaluation.

Companies using revaluation accounting must also make every effort to keep the assets' values up to date. Assets that are experiencing rapid price changes must be revalued on an annual basis. Otherwise, less frequent revaluation is acceptable. The fair value of items of property, plant, and equipment is usually determined by appraisal. Appendix 11A illustrates the accounting for revaluations in more detail both for land and depreciable assets.

What do the numbers mean? **TO REVALUE OR NOT**

Most companies do not use revaluation accounting. A major reason is the substantial and continuing costs associated with appraisals to determine fair value. In addition, the gains associated with revaluations above historical cost are not reported in net income but instead go directly to equity. On the other hand, losses associated with revaluations below historical cost decrease net income. In addition, for depreciable assets, the higher depreciation charges related to the revalued assets also reduce net income. The following table indicates the widespread use of the cost method over the revaluation method, based on a survey of 175 international companies.

	2011	2010	2009
Cost	172	163	155
Revaluation			
Land	1	2	3
Buildings	1	1	1
Property (land and buildings)	6	4	4
Other asset class	1	1	1
More than one asset class	1	0	0
All asset classes	3	3	1
Total companies using revaluation for at least one asset class	13	11	10
Companies not disclosing a model	0	3	3
Companies using more than one model	(10)	(7)	(8)
Total companies surveyed	175	170	160

Source: IFRS Accounting Trends & Techniques, 2012–2013 (AICPA, 2012).

Companies that choose revaluation accounting often are in highly inflationary environments where the historical cost numbers are badly out of date. In addition, some companies select the revaluation approach because they wish to increase their equity base. Increases in its equity base may help a company meet covenant requirements or provide additional assurances to investors and creditors that the company is solvent.

PRESENTATION AND ANALYSIS
Presentation of Property, Plant, Equipment, and Mineral Resources

A company should disclose the basis of valuation—usually historical cost—for property, plant, equipment, and mineral resources along with pledges, liens, and other commitments related to these assets. It should not offset any liability secured by property, plant, equipment, and mineral resources against these assets. Instead, this obligation should be reported in the liabilities section. The

8 LEARNING OBJECTIVE

Explain how to report and analyze property, plant, equipment, and mineral resources.

company should segregate property, plant, and equipment not currently employed as producing assets in the business (such as idle facilities or land held as an investment) from assets used in operations.

When depreciating assets, a company credits a valuation account, normally called Accumulated Depreciation. Using an accumulated depreciation account permits the user of the financial statements to see the original cost of the asset and the amount of depreciation that the company charged to expense in past years.

When depleting mineral resources, some companies use an accumulated depletion account. Many, however, simply credit the mineral resource account directly. The rationale for this approach is that the mineral resources are physically consumed, making direct reduction of the cost of the mineral resources appropriate.

Illustration 11-23 provides the reporting of property, plant, and equipment by **Nestlé Group** (CHE) in a recent annual report. Nestlé presents condensed statement of financial position data, supplemented with detail amounts and accounting policies provided in the notes to the financial statements.

ILLUSTRATION 11-23
Disclosures for Property, Plant, and Equipment

Nestlé Group
(in millions of CHF)

Non-current assets

Property, plant, and equipment	26,903	23,971
Investments in associates	9,846	8,629
Deferred tax assets	2,903	2,476
Current income tax assets	27	39
Financial assets	5,003	7,161
Employee benefits assets	84	127
Goodwill	32,615	29,008
Intangible assets	13,643	9,356
Total non-current assets	**91,024**	**80,767**

Note 1 Accounting Policies

Property, plant, and equipment

Property, plant, and equipment are shown in the balance sheet at their historical cost. Depreciation is provided on components that have homogenous useful lives by using the straight-line method so as to depreciate the initial cost down to the residual value over the estimated useful lives. The residual values are 30% on head offices and nil for all other asset types. The useful lives are as follows:

Buildings	20–40 years
Machinery and equipment	10–25 years
Tools, furniture, information technology, and sundry equipment	3–10 years
Vehicles	3–8 years
Land is not depreciated.	

Useful lives, components, and residual amounts are reviewed annually. Such a review takes into consideration the nature of the assets, their intended use including but not limited to the closure of facilities, and the evolution of the technology and competitive pressures that may lead to technical obsolescence.

Depreciation of property, plant, and equipment is allocated to the appropriate headings of expenses by function in the income statement.

Borrowing costs incurred during the course of construction are capitalised if the assets under construction are significant and if their construction requires a substantial period to complete (typically more than one year). The capitalisation rate is determined on the basis of the short-term borrowing rate for the period of construction. Premiums capitalised for leasehold land or buildings are amortised over the length of the lease. Government grants are recognised in accordance with the deferral method, whereby the grant is set up as deferred income which is released to the income statement over the useful life of the related assets. Grants that are not related to assets are credited to the income statement when they are received.

	Land and buildings	Machinery and equipment	Tools, furniture, and other equipment	Vehicles	Total
Gross value					
At 1 January	14,109	26,472	7,728	961	49,270
Currency retranslations	(156)	(622)	(34)	(29)	(841)
Capital expenditure	1,419	2,863	957	129	5,368
Disposals	(169)	(548)	(610)	(95)	(1,422)
Reclassified as held for sale	(17)	(14)	(1)	—	(32)
Modification of the scope of consolidation	484	342	(29)	(4)	793
At 31 December	**15,670**	**28,493**	**8,011**	**962**	**53,136**
Accumulated depreciation and impairments					
At 1 January	(5,068)	(14,449)	(5,278)	(504)	(25,299)
Currency retranslations	70	259	66	11	406
Depreciation	(393)	(1,434)	(782)	(102)	(2,711)
Impairments	4	(58)	(21)	—	(75)
Disposals	120	490	552	79	1,241
Reclassified as held for sale	12	11	1	—	24
Modification of the scope of consolidation	26	105	44	6	181
At 31 December	**(5,229)**	**(15,076)**	**(5,418)**	**(510)**	**(26,233)**
Net at 31 December	**10,441**	**13,417**	**2,593**	**452**	**26,903**

At 31 December, property, plant and equipment include CHF1,332 million of assets under construction. Net property, plant and equipment held under finance leases amount to CHF154 million. Net property, plant and equipment of CHF294 million are pledged as security for financial liabilities. Fire risks, reasonably estimated, are insured in accordance with domestic requirements.

Impairment
Impairment of property, plant, and equipment arises mainly from the plans to optimise industrial manu-facturing capacities by closing or selling inefficient production facilities.

Commitments for expenditure
At 31 December, the Group was committed to expenditure amounting to CHF650 million.

Analysis of Property, Plant, and Equipment

Analysts evaluate assets relative to activity (turnover) and profitability.

Asset Turnover

How efficiently a company uses its assets to generate sales is measured by the **asset turnover**. This ratio divides net sales by average total assets for the period. The resulting number is the dollars of sales produced by each dollar invested in assets. To illustrate, we use the following data from **adidas AG**'s (DEU) 2012 annual report.

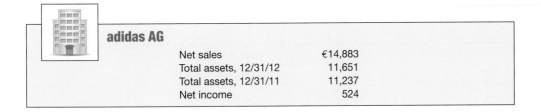

adidas AG

Net sales	€14,883
Total assets, 12/31/12	11,651
Total assets, 12/31/11	11,237
Net income	524

Illustration 11-24 (on page 518) shows computation of the asset turnover.

ILLUSTRATION 11-24
Asset Turnover

$$\text{Asset Turnover} = \frac{\text{Net Sales}}{\text{Average Total Assets}}$$

$$= \frac{\text{€14,883}}{\text{(€11,651 + €11,237)/2}}$$

$$= 1.30$$

The asset turnover shows that adidas generated sales of €1.30 per euro of assets in the year ended December 31, 2012.

Asset turnovers vary considerably among industries. For example, a large utility like Ameren (USA) has a ratio of 0.32 times. A large grocery chain like Morrisons (GBR) has a ratio of 1.86 times. Thus, in comparing performance among companies based on the asset turnover, you need to consider the ratio within the context of the industry in which a company operates.

Profit Margin on Sales

Another measure for analyzing the use of property, plant, and equipment is the profit margin on sales (return on sales). Calculated as net income divided by net sales, this profitability ratio does not, by itself, answer the question of how profitably a company uses its assets. But by relating the profit margin on sales to the asset turnover during a period of time, we can ascertain how profitably the company used assets during that period of time in a measure of the return on assets. Using the adidas data shown on page 517, we compute the profit margin on sales and the return on assets as follows.

ILLUSTRATION 11-25
Profit Margin on Sales

$$\text{Profit Margin on Sales} = \frac{\text{Net Income}}{\text{Net Sales}}$$

$$= \frac{\text{€524}}{\text{€14,883}}$$

$$= 3.5\%$$

$$\text{Return on Assets} = \text{Profit Margin on Sales} \times \text{Asset Turnover}$$

$$= 3.5\% \times 1.30$$

$$= 4.6\%$$

Return on Assets

The rate of return a company achieves through use of its assets is the return on assets (ROA). Rather than using the profit margin on sales, we can compute it directly by dividing net income by average total assets. Using adidas' data, we compute the ratio as follows.

ILLUSTRATION 11-26
Return on Assets

$$\text{Return on Assets} = \frac{\text{Net Income}}{\text{Average Total Assets}}$$

$$= \frac{\text{€524}}{\text{(€11,651 + €11,237)/2}}$$

$$= 4.6\%$$

The 4.6 percent rate of return computed in this manner equals the 4.6 percent rate computed by multiplying the profit margin on sales by the asset turnover. The return on assets measures profitability well because it combines the effects of profit margin and asset turnover.

 # GLOBAL ACCOUNTING INSIGHTS

PROPERTY, PLANT, AND EQUIPMENT

U.S. GAAP adheres to many of the same principles as IFRS in the accounting for property, plant, and equipment. Major differences relate to use of component depreciation, impairments, and revaluations.

Relevant Facts

Following are the key similarities and differences between U.S. GAAP and IFRS related to property, plant, and equipment.

Similarities
- The definition of property, plant, and equipment is essentially the same under U.S. GAAP and IFRS.
- Under both U.S. GAAP and IFRS, changes in depreciation method and changes in useful life are treated in the current and future periods. Prior periods are not affected.
- The accounting for plant asset disposals is the same under U.S. GAAP and IFRS.
- The accounting for the initial costs to acquire natural resources is similar under U.S. GAAP and IFRS.
- Under both U.S. GAAP and IFRS, interest costs incurred during construction must be capitalized. Recently, IFRS converged to U.S. GAAP.
- The accounting for exchanges of non-monetary assets is essentially the same between U.S. GAAP and IFRS. U.S. GAAP requires that gains on exchanges of non-monetary assets be recognized if the exchange has commercial substance. This is the same framework used in IFRS.

- U.S. GAAP and IFRS both view depreciation as allocation of cost over an asset's life. U.S. GAAP and IFRS permit the same depreciation methods (straight-line, diminishing-balance, units-of-production).

Differences
- Under U.S. GAAP, component depreciation is permitted but is rarely used. IFRS requires component depreciation.
- U.S. GAAP does not permit revaluations of property, plant, equipment, and mineral resources. Under IFRS, companies can use either the historical cost model or the revaluation model.
- In testing for impairments of long-lived assets, U.S. GAAP uses a different model than IFRS (details of the U.S. GAAP impairment test is presented in the About the Numbers discussion). Under U.S. GAAP, as long as future undiscounted cash flows exceed the carrying amount of the asset, no impairment is recorded. The IFRS impairment test is stricter. However, unlike U.S. GAAP, reversals of impairment losses are permitted under IFRS.

About the Numbers

As indicated, impairment testing under U.S. GAAP is a two-step process. The graphic on page 520 summarizes impairment measurement under U.S. GAAP. The key distinctions relative to IFRS relate to the use of a cash flow recovery test to determine if an impairment test should be performed. Also, U.S. GAAP does not permit reversal of impairment losses for assets held for use.

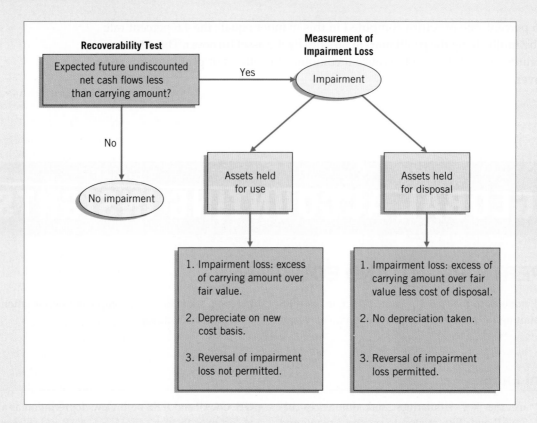

On the Horizon

With respect to revaluations, as part of the conceptual framework project, the Boards will examine the measurement bases used in accounting. It is too early to say whether a converged conceptual framework will recommend fair value measurement (and revaluation accounting) for property, plant, and equipment. However, this is likely to be one of the more contentious issues, given the long-standing use of historical cost as a measurement basis in U.S. GAAP.

KEY TERMS

accelerated depreciation
 methods, 497

activity method, *496*

amortization, *494*

asset turnover, *517*

cash-generating unit
 (CGU), *507*

component depreciation,
 499

cost depletion, *510*

declining (reducing)-
 balance method, *498*

depletion, *494, 508*

SUMMARY OF LEARNING OBJECTIVES

1 **Explain the concept of depreciation.** Depreciation allocates the cost of tangible assets to expense in a systematic and rational manner to those periods expected to benefit from the use of the asset.

2 **Identify the factors involved in the depreciation process.** Three factors involved in the depreciation process are (1) determining the depreciation base for the asset, (2) estimating service lives, and (3) selecting a method of cost apportionment (depreciation).

3 **Compare activity, straight-line, and diminishing-charge methods of depreciation.** (1) *Activity method:* Assumes that depreciation is a function of use or productivity instead of the passage of time. The life of the asset is considered in terms of either the output it provides, or an input measure such as the number of hours it works. (2) *Straight-line method:* Considers depreciation a function of time instead of a function of usage. The straight-line procedure is often the most conceptually appropriate when the decline in usefulness is constant from period to period. (3) *Diminishing-charge methods:* Provides for a higher depreciation cost in the earlier years and lower charges in later periods. The main justification for this approach is that the asset is the most productive in its early years.

4 **Explain component depreciation.** IFRS requires that each part of an item of property, plant, and equipment that is significant to the total cost of the asset must be depreciated separately.

5 **Explain the accounting issues related to asset impairment.** The process to determine an impairment loss is as follows. (1) Review events and changes in circumstances for indicators of impairment. (2) If impairment indicators are present, an impairment test must be conducted. The impairment test compares the asset's recoverable amount (the higher of fair value less costs to sell and value-in-use) with its carrying amount. If the carrying amount is higher than the recoverable amount, the difference is an impairment loss. If the recoverable amount is greater than the carrying amount, no impairment is recorded.

After a company records an impairment loss, the reduced carrying amount of the long-lived asset is its new cost basis. Impairment losses may be reversed as long as the write-up is never to an amount greater than the carrying amount before impairment. If the company expects to dispose of the asset, it should report the impaired asset at the lower-of-cost-or-net realizable value. Assets held for disposal are not depreciated.

6 **Explain the accounting procedures for depletion of mineral resources.** To account for depletion of mineral resources, companies (1) establish the depletion base and (2) write off resource cost. Three types of costs are considered in establishing the depletion base: (a) pre-exploratory costs, (b) exploration and evaluation costs, and (c) development costs. To write off resource cost, companies normally compute depletion on the units-of-production method. Thus, depletion is a function of the number of units withdrawn during the period. To obtain a cost per unit of product, the total cost of the mineral resource less residual value is divided by the number of units estimated to be in the resource deposit. To compute depletion, this cost per unit is multiplied by the number of units withdrawn.

7 **Explain the accounting for revaluations.** Under IFRS, companies may choose to value long-lived assets at cost or at fair value. When companies choose to fair value their long-lived tangible assets subsequent to acquisition, they account for the change in the fair value by adjusting the appropriate asset account and recording an unrealized gain on the revalued long-lived tangible asset, which is recorded in other comprehensive income.

8 **Explain how to report and analyze property, plant, equipment, and mineral resources.** The basis of valuation for property, plant, and equipment and for mineral resources should be disclosed along with pledges, liens, and other commitments related to these assets. Companies should not offset any liability secured by property, plant, and equipment or by mineral resources against these assets, but should report it in the liabilities section. When depreciating assets, credit a valuation account normally called Accumulated Depreciation. When depleting assets, use an accumulated depletion account, or credit the depletion directly to the mineral resource account. Analysis may be performed to evaluate the asset turnover, profit margin on sales, and return on assets.

| APPENDIX **11A** | REVALUATION OF PROPERTY, PLANT, AND EQUIPMENT |

LEARNING OBJECTIVE ❾

Explain revaluation accounting procedures.

As indicated in Chapter 11, companies can use revaluation accounting subsequent to acquisition. When companies choose to fair value their long-lived tangible assets subsequent to acquisition, they account for the change in the fair value by adjusting the appropriate asset account and recording an unrealized gain on the revalued long-lived tangible asset. This unrealized gain is often referred to as revaluation surplus.

The general rules for revaluation accounting are as follows.

1. When a company revalues its long-lived tangible assets above historical cost, it reports an unrealized gain that increases other comprehensive income. Thus, the unrealized gain bypasses net income, increases other comprehensive income, and increases accumulated other comprehensive income.

2. If a company experiences a loss on impairment (decrease of value below historical cost), the loss reduces income and retained earnings. Thus, gains on revaluation increase equity but not net income, whereas losses decrease income and retained earnings (and therefore equity).

3. If a revaluation increase reverses a decrease that was previously reported as an impairment loss, a company credits the revaluation increase to income using the account Recovery of Impairment Loss up to the amount of the prior loss. Any additional valuation increase above historical cost increases other comprehensive income and is credited to Unrealized Gain on Revaluation.

4. If a revaluation decrease reverses an increase that was reported as an unrealized gain, a company first reduces other comprehensive income by eliminating the unrealized gain. Any additional valuation decrease reduces net income and is reported as a loss on impairment.

In the following two sections, we explain revaluation procedures for land and depreciable assets in a multiple-year setting.

REVALUATION OF LAND

Revaluation—2015: Valuation Increase

To illustrate the accounting for a revaluation, assume that **Unilever Group** (GBR and NLD) purchased land on January 1, 2015, that cost €400,000. Unilever decides to report the land at fair value in subsequent periods. At December 31, 2015, an appraisal of the land indicates that its fair value is €520,000. Unilever makes the following entry to record the increase in fair value.

December 31, 2015

Land	120,000	
Unrealized Gain on Revaluation—Land (€520,000 − €400,000)		120,000
(To recognize increase in land value)		

Illustration 11A-1 provides a summary of the revaluation adjustments for Unilever in 2015.

ILLUSTRATION 11A-1
Summary of
Revaluation—2015

Date	Item	Land Fair Value	Retained Earnings	Accumulated Other Comprehensive Income (AOCI)
Jan. 1, 2015	Beginning balance	€400,000	€0	€ 0
Dec. 31, 2015	Revaluation	120,000	0	120,000
Dec. 31, 2015	**Ending balance**	**520,000**	**0**	**120,000**

The land is now reported at its fair value of €520,000. The increase in the fair value of €120,000 is reported on the statement of comprehensive income as other comprehensive income. In addition, the ending balance in Unrealized Gain on Revaluation—Land is reported as accumulated other comprehensive income in the statement of financial position in the equity section.

Revaluation—2016: Decrease below Historical Cost

What happens if the land's fair value at December 31, 2016, is €380,000, a decrease of €140,000 (€520,000 − €380,000)? In this case, the land's fair value is below its historical cost. Therefore, Unilever debits Unrealized Gain on Revaluation—Land for €120,000 to eliminate its balance. In addition, Unilever reports a Loss on Impairment of €20,000 (€400,000 − €380,000), reducing net income. Unilever makes the following entry to record the decrease in fair value of the land.

December 31, 2016

Unrealized Gain on Revaluation—Land	120,000	
Loss on Impairment	20,000	
Land (€520,000 − €380,000)		140,000
(To record decrease in value of land below historical cost)		

Illustration 11A-2 provides a summary of the revaluation adjustments for Unilever in 2016.

ILLUSTRATION 11A-2
Summary of
Revaluation—2016

Date	Item	Land Fair Value	Retained Earnings	Accumulated Other Comprehensive Income (AOCI)
Jan. 1, 2015	Beginning balance	€400,000	€ 0	€ 0
Dec. 31, 2015	Revaluation	120,000	0	120,000
Dec. 31, 2015	**Ending balance**	**520,000**	**0**	**120,000**
Jan. 1, 2016	Beginning balance	€520,000	€ 0	€ 120,000
Dec. 31, 2016	Revaluation	(140,000)	(20,000)	(120,000)
Dec. 31, 2016	**Ending balance**	**380,000**	**(20,000)**	**0**

The decrease to Unrealized Gain on Revaluation—Land of €120,000 reduces other comprehensive income, which then reduces the balance in accumulated other comprehensive income. The Loss on Impairment of €20,000 reduces net income and retained earnings. In this case, Unilever had a revaluation decrease which first reverses any increases that Unilever reported in prior periods as an unrealized gain. Any additional amount is reported as an impairment loss. **Under no circumstances can the revaluation decrease reduce accumulated other comprehensive income below zero.**

Revaluation—2017: Recovery of Impairment Loss

At December 31, 2017, Unilever's land value increases to €415,000, an increase of €35,000 (€415,000 − €380,000). In this case, the Loss on Impairment of €20,000 is reversed and the remaining increase of €15,000 is reported in other comprehensive income. Unilever makes the following entry to record this transaction.

December 31, 2017

Land	35,000	
Unrealized Gain on Revaluation—Land		15,000
Recovery of Impairment Loss		20,000
(Revaluation of land, recovery of impairment loss)		

Illustration 11A-3 provides a summary of the revaluation adjustments for Unilever in 2017.

ILLUSTRATION 11A-3
Summary of
Revaluation—2017

Date	Item	Land Fair Value	Retained Earnings	Accumulated Other Comprehensive Income (AOCI)
Jan. 1, 2015	Beginning balance	€ 400,000	€ 0	€ 0
Dec. 31, 2015	Revaluation	120,000	0	120,000
Dec. 31, 2015	**Ending balance**	**520,000**	**0**	**120,000**
Jan. 1, 2016	Beginning balance	€ 520,000	€ 0	€120,000
Dec. 31, 2016	Revaluation	(140,000)	(20,000)	(120,000)
Dec. 31, 2016	**Ending balance**	**380,000**	**(20,000)**	**0**
Jan. 1, 2017	Beginning balance	€ 380,000	€(20,000)	€ 0
Dec. 31, 2017	Revaluation	35,000	20,000	15,000
Dec. 31, 2017	**Ending balance**	**415,000**	**0**	**15,000**

The recovery of the impairment loss of €20,000 increases income (and retained earnings) only to the extent that it reverses previously recorded impairment losses.

On January 2, 2018, Unilever sells the land for €415,000. Unilever makes the following entry to record this transaction.

January 2, 2018

Cash	415,000	
Land		415,000
(To record sale of land)		

In this case, Unilever does not record a gain or loss because the carrying amount of the land is the same as its fair value. At this time, since the land is sold, Unilever has the option to transfer Accumulated Other Comprehensive Income (AOCI) to Retained Earnings. The entry to record the transfer is as follows.

January 2, 2018

Accumulated Other Comprehensive Income	15,000	
Retained Earnings		15,000
(To eliminate the remaining balance in AOCI)		

The purpose of this transfer is to eliminate the unrealized gain on the land that was sold. It should be noted that transfers from Accumulated Other Comprehensive Income cannot increase net income. This last entry illustrates why revaluation accounting is not popular. Even though the land has appreciated in value by €15,000, Unilever is not able to recognize this gain in net income over the periods that it held the land.

REVALUATION OF DEPRECIABLE ASSETS

To illustrate the accounting for revaluations using depreciable assets, assume that Nokia (FIN) purchases equipment for €1,000,000 on January 2, 2015. The equipment has a useful life of five years, is depreciated using the straight-line method of depreciation, and its residual value is zero.

Revaluation—2015: Valuation Increase

Nokia chooses to revalue its equipment to fair value over the life of equipment. Nokia records depreciation expense of €200,000 (€1,000,000 ÷ 5) as follows.

December 31, 2015

Depreciation Expense	200,000	
Accumulated Depreciation—Equipment		200,000
(To record depreciation expense at December 31, 2015)		

After this entry, Nokia's equipment has a carrying amount of €800,000 (€1,000,000 − €200,000). Nokia employs an independent appraiser, who determines that the fair value of equipment at December 31, 2015, is €950,000. To report the equipment at fair value, Nokia does the following.

1. Reduces the Accumulated Depreciation—Equipment account to zero.

2. Reduces the Equipment account by €50,000—it then is reported at its fair value of €950,000.

3. Records an Unrealized Gain on Revaluation—Equipment for the difference between the fair value and carrying amount of the equipment, or €150,000 (€950,000 − €800,000). The entry to record this revaluation at December 31, 2015, is as follows.

December 31, 2015

Accumulated Depreciation—Equipment	200,000	
Equipment		50,000
Unrealized Gain of Revaluation—Equipment		150,000
(To adjust the equipment to fair value and record unrealized gain)		

Illustration 11A-4 provides a summary of the revaluation adjustments for Nokia in 2015.

ILLUSTRATION 11A-4
Revaluation Summary—2015

Date	Item	Equipment Fair Value	Accumulated Depreciation	Retained Earnings	Accumulated Other Comprehensive Income (AOCI)
Jan. 1, 2015	Beginning balance	€1,000,000			€ 0
Dec. 31, 2015	Depreciation		€ 200,000	€(200,000)	
Dec. 31, 2015	Revaluation	(50,000)	(200,000)		150,000
Dec. 31, 2015	**Ending balance**	**950,000**	**0**	**(200,000)**	**150,000**

Following these revaluation adjustments, the carrying amount of the asset is now €950,000. Nokia reports depreciation expense of €200,000 in the income statement and Unrealized Gain on Revaluation—Equipment of €150,000 in other comprehensive income. This unrealized gain increases accumulated other comprehensive income (reported on the statement of financial position in the equity section).

Revaluation—2016: Decrease below Historical Cost

Assuming no change in the useful life of the equipment, depreciation expense for Nokia in 2016 is €237,500 (€950,000 ÷ 4), and the entry to record depreciation expense is as follows.

December 31, 2016

Depreciation Expense	237,500	
Accumulated Depreciation—Equipment		237,500
(To record depreciation expense at December 31, 2016)		

Under IFRS, Nokia may transfer from AOCI the difference between depreciation based on the revalued carrying amount of the equipment and depreciation based on the asset's original cost to retained earnings. Depreciation based on the original cost was €200,000 (€1,000,000 ÷ 5) and on fair value is €237,500, or a difference of €37,500 (€237,500 − €200,000). The entry to record this transfer is as follows.

December 31, 2016

Accumulated Other Comprehensive Income	37,500	
Retained Earnings		37,500
(To record transfer from AOCI to Retained Earnings)		

At this point, before revaluation in 2016, Nokia has the following amounts related to its equipment.

Equipment	€950,000
Less: Accumulated depreciation—equipment	237,500
Carrying amount	€712,500
Accumulated other comprehensive income	€112,500 (€150,000 − €37,500)[11]

Nokia determines through appraisal that the equipment now has a fair value of €570,000. To report the equipment at fair value, Nokia does the following.

1. Reduces the Accumulated Depreciation—Equipment account of €237,500 to zero.

2. Reduces the Equipment account by €380,000 (€950,000 − €570,000)—it then is reported at its fair value of €570,000.

3. Reduces Unrealized Gain on Revaluation—Equipment by €112,500, to offset the balance in the unrealized gain account (related to the revaluation in 2015).

4. Records a loss on impairment of €30,000.

The entry to record this transaction is as follows.

Accumulated Depreciation—Equipment	237,500	
Loss on Impairment	30,000	
Unrealized Gain on Revaluation—Equipment	112,500	
Equipment		380,000
(To adjust the equipment to fair value and record impairment loss)		

Illustration 11A-5 provides a summary of the revaluation adjustments for Nokia in 2016.

ILLUSTRATION 11A-5
Revaluation
Summary—2016

Date	Item	Equipment Fair Value	Accumulated Depreciation	Retained Earnings	Accumulated Other Comprehensive Income (AOCI)
Jan. 1, 2015	Beginning balance	€1,000,000			€ 0
Dec. 31, 2015	Depreciation		€200,000	€(200,000)	
Dec. 31, 2015	Revaluation	(50,000)	(200,000)		150,000
Dec. 31, 2015	**Ending balance**	**950,000**	**0**	**(200,000)**	**150,000**
Jan. 1, 2016	Beginning balance	€ 950,000	€ 0	€(200,000)	€150,000
Dec. 31, 2016	Depreciation		237,500	(237,500)	
Dec. 31, 2016	Transfer from AOCI			37,500	(37,500)
Dec. 31, 2016	Revaluation	(380,000)	(237,500)	(30,000)	(112,500)
Dec. 31, 2016	**Ending balance**	**570,000**	**0**	**(430,000)**	**0**

[11]The entry for the transfer recognizes that any depreciation on the revalued part of the asset's carrying amount has been realized by being charged to retained earnings. By making this entry, it should be noted that the historical cost carrying amount (as if no revaluations have been recorded) can be determined by deducting the AOCI balance from the revalued carrying amount. In this case, the historical cost carrying amount after two years is €600,000 (€1,000,000 − €200,000 − €200,000), which is equal to the revalued carrying amount of €712,500 less AOCI of €112,500.

Following the revaluation entry, the carrying amount of the equipment is now €570,000. Nokia reports depreciation expense of €237,500 and an impairment loss of €30,000 in the income statement (which reduces retained earnings).[12] Nokia reports the reversal of the previously recorded unrealized gain by recording the transfer to retained earnings of €37,500 and the entry to Unrealized Gain on Revaluation—Equipment of €112,500. These two entries reduce the balance in AOCI to zero.

Revaluation—2017: Recovery of Impairment Loss

Assuming no change in the useful life of the equipment, depreciation expense for Nokia in 2017 is €190,000 (€570,000 ÷ 3), and the entry to record depreciation expense is as follows.

December 31, 2017

Depreciation Expense	190,000	
Accumulated Depreciation—Equipment		190,000
(To record depreciation expense)		

Nokia transfers the difference between depreciation based on the revalued carrying amount of the equipment and depreciation based on the asset's original cost from AOCI to retained earnings. Depreciation based on the original cost was €200,000 (€1,000,000 ÷ 5) and on fair value is €190,000, or a difference of €10,000 (€200,000 − €190,000). The entry to record this transfer is as follows.

December 31, 2017

Retained Earnings	10,000	
Accumulated Other Comprehensive Income		10,000
(To record transfer from AOCI to Retained Earnings)		

At this point, before revaluation in 2017, Nokia has the following amounts related to its equipment.

Equipment	€570,000
Less: Accumulated depreciation—equipment	190,000
Carrying amount	€380,000
Accumulated other comprehensive income	€ 10,000

Nokia determines through appraisal that the equipment now has a fair value of €450,000. To report the equipment at fair value, Nokia does the following.

1. Reduces the Accumulated Depreciation—Equipment account of €190,000 to zero.

2. Reduces the Equipment account by €120,000 (€570,000 − €450,000)—it then is reported at its fair value of €450,000.

3. Records an Unrealized Gain on Revaluation—Equipment for €40,000.

4. Records a Recovery of Loss on Impairment for €30,000.

---

[12]Another way to compute the loss on impairment of €30,000 is to determine the historical cost carrying amount of the equipment at December 31, 2016, which is €600,000 (€1,000,000 − €200,000 − €200,000), and subtract the fair value of the equipment (€570,000).

The entry to record this transaction is as follows.

December 31, 2017

Accumulated Depreciation—Equipment	190,000	
Unrealized Gain on Revaluation—Equipment		40,000
Equipment		120,000
Recovery of Loss on Impairment		30,000
(To adjust the equipment to fair value and record mpairment recovery)		

Illustration 11A-6 provides a summary of the revaluation adjustments for Nokia in 2017.

ILLUSTRATION 11A-6
Revaluation
Summary—2017

Date	Item	Equipment Fair Value	Accumulated Depreciation	Retained Earnings	Accumulated Other Comprehensive Income (AOCI)
Jan. 1, 2015	Beginning balance	€1,000,000			€ 0
Dec. 31, 2015	Depreciation		€200,000	€(200,000)	
Dec. 31, 2015	Revaluation	(50,000)	(200,000)		150,000
Dec. 31, 2015	**Ending balance**	**950,000**	**0**	**(200,000)**	**150,000**
Jan. 1, 2016	Beginning balance	€ 950,000	€ 0	€(200,000)	€150,000
Dec. 31, 2016	Depreciation		237,500	(237,500)	
Dec. 31, 2016	Transfer from AOCI			37,500	(37,500)
Dec. 31, 2016	Revaluation	(380,000)	(237,500)	(30,000)	(112,500)
Dec. 31, 2016	**Ending balance**	**570,000**	**0**	**(430,000)**	**0**
Jan. 1, 2017	Beginning balance	€ 570,000	€ 0	€(430,000)	€ 0
Dec. 31, 2017	Depreciation		190,000	(190,000)	
Dec. 31, 2017	Transfer from AOCI			(10,000)	10,000
Dec. 31, 2017	Revaluation	(120,000)	(190,000)	30,000	40,000
Dec. 31, 2017	**Ending balance**	**450,000**	**0**	**(600,000)**	**50,000**

Following the revaluation entry, the carrying amount of the equipment is now €450,000. Nokia reports depreciation expense of €190,000 and an impairment loss recovery of €30,000 in the income statement. Nokia records €40,000 to Unrealized Gain on Revaluation—Equipment, which increases AOCI to €50,000.

On January 2, 2018, Nokia sells the equipment for €450,000. Nokia makes the following entry to record this transaction.

January 2, 2018

Cash	450,000	
Equipment		450,000
(To record sale of equipment)		

Nokia does not record a gain or loss because the carrying amount of the equipment is the same as its fair value. Nokia transfers the remaining balance in Accumulated Other Comprehensive Income to Retained Earnings because the equipment has been sold. The entry to record this transaction is as follows.

January 2, 2018

Accumulated Other Comprehensive Income	50,000	
Retained Earnings		50,000
(To eliminate the remaining balance in AOCI)		

The transfer from Accumulated Other Comprehensive Income does not increase net income. Even though the equipment has appreciated in value by €50,000, the company does not recognize this gain in net income over the periods that Nokia held the equipment.

SUMMARY OF LEARNING OBJECTIVE FOR APPENDIX 11A

9 **Explain revaluation accounting procedures.** The general rules for revaluation accounting are as follows. (1) Companies record unrealized gains in other comprehensive income (the unrealized gain bypasses income). (2) Companies record losses on impairment (decrease of value below historical cost) in net income. Thus, gains on revaluation increase equity but not net income, whereas losses decrease equity and net income. (3) If a revaluation increase reverses a decrease that was reported as an impairment loss, a company credits the revaluation increase in net income; any additional valuation increase beyond the recovery is credited to other comprehensive income.

IFRS AUTHORITATIVE LITERATURE

Authoritative Literature References

[1] International Accounting Standard 16, *Property, Plant and Equipment* (London, U.K.: International Accounting Standards Committee Foundation, 2003), par. BC29.

[2] International Accounting Standard 16, *Property, Plant and Equipment* (London, U.K.: International Accounting Standards Committee Foundation, 2003), par. 60.

[3] International Financial Reporting Standard 36, *Impairment of Assets* (London, U.K.: International Accounting Standards Committee Foundation, 2001).

[4] International Financial Reporting Standard 36, *Impairment of Assets* (London, U.K.: International Accounting Standards Committee Foundation, 2001), par. 19.

[5] International Financial Reporting Standard 36, *Impairment of Assets* (London, U.K.: International Accounting Standards Committee Foundation, 2001), par. 33.

[6] International Financial Reporting Standard 36, *Impairment of Assets* (London, U.K.: International Accounting Standards Committee Foundation, 2001), par. 55.

[7] International Financial Reporting Standard 6, *Exploration for and Evaluation of Natural Resources* (London, U.K.: International Accounting Standards Committee Foundation, 2004).

[8] International Accounting Standard 16, *Property, Plant and Equipment* (London, U.K.: International Accounting Standards Committee Foundation, 2003), paras. 31–42.

Note: All asterisked Questions, Exercises, and Problems relate to material in the appendix to the chapter.

QUESTIONS

1. Distinguish among depreciation, depletion, and amortization.

2. Identify the factors that are relevant in determining the annual depreciation charge, and explain whether these factors are determined objectively or whether they are based on judgment.

3. Some believe that accounting depreciation measures the decline in the value of property, plant, and equipment. Do you agree? Explain.

4. Explain how estimation of service lives can result in unrealistically high valuations of property, plant, and equipment.

5. The plant manager of a manufacturing firm suggested in a conference of the company's executives that accountants should speed up depreciation on the machinery in the finishing department because improvements were rapidly making those machines obsolete, and a depreciation fund big enough to cover their replacement is needed. Discuss the accounting concept of depreciation and the effect on a business concern of the depreciation recorded for plant assets, paying particular attention to the issues raised by the plant manager.

6. For what reasons are plant assets retired? Define inadequacy, supersession, and obsolescence.

7. What basic questions must be answered before the amount of the depreciation charge can be computed?

8. Workman Company purchased a machine on January 2, 2015, for €800,000. The machine has an estimated useful life of 5 years and a residual value of €100,000. Depreciation was computed by the 150% declining-balance method. What is the amount of accumulated depreciation at the end of December 31, 2016?

9. Silverman Company purchased machinery for $162,000 on January 1, 2015. It is estimated that the machinery will have a useful life of 20 years, residual value of $15,000, production of 84,000 units, and working hours of 42,000. During 2015, the company uses the machinery for 14,300 hours, and the machinery produces 20,000 units. Compute depreciation under the straight-line, units-of-output, working hours, sum-of-the-years'-digits, and double-declining-balance methods.

10. What are the major factors considered in determining what depreciation method to use?

11. What is component depreciation?

12. A building that was purchased December 31, 1991, for £2,500,000 was originally estimated to have a life of 50 years with no residual value at the end of that time. Depreciation has been recorded through 2015. During 2016, an examination of the building by an engineering firm discloses that its estimated useful life is 15 years after 2015. What should be the amount of depreciation for 2016?

13. Charlie Parker, president of Spinners Company, has recently noted that depreciation increases cash provided by operations and therefore depreciation is a good source of funds. Do you agree? Discuss.

14. Andrea Shen purchased a computer for €8,000 on July 1, 2015. She intends to depreciate it over 4 years using the double-declining-balance method. Residual value is €1,000. Compute depreciation for 2016.

15. Walkin Inc. is considering the write-down of its long-term plant because of a lack of profitability. Explain to the management of Walkin how to determine whether a write-down is permitted.

16. Last year, Wyeth Company recorded an impairment on an asset held for use. Recent appraisals indicate that the asset has increased in value. Should Wyeth record this recovery in value?

17. Toro Co. has equipment with a carrying amount of €700,000. The value-in-use of the equipment is €705,000, and its fair value less cost of disposal is €590,000. The equipment is expected to be used in operations in the future. What amount (if any) should Toro report as an impairment to its equipment?

18. Explain how gains or losses on impaired assets should be reported in income.

19. It has been suggested that plant and equipment could be replaced more quickly if depreciation rates for income tax and accounting purposes were substantially increased. As a result, business operations would receive the benefit of more modern and more efficient plant facilities. Discuss the merits of this proposition.

20. List (a) the similarities and (b) the differences in the accounting treatments of depreciation and cost depletion.

21. Describe cost depletion.

22. Explain the difference between exploration and development costs as used in the extractive industries.

23. In the extractive industries, businesses may pay dividends in excess of net income. What is the maximum permissible? How can this practice be justified?

24. Shumway Oil uses successful-efforts accounting for its exploration and evaluation costs but also provides full-cost results as well. Under full-cost, Shumway Oil would have reported retained earnings of $42 million and net income of $4 million. Under successful-efforts, retained earnings were $29 million and net income was $3 million. Explain the difference between full-costing and successful-efforts accounting.

25. Tanaka Company has land that cost ¥15,000,000. Its fair value on December 31, 2015, is ¥20,000,000. Tanaka chooses the revaluation model to report its land. Explain how the land and its related valuation should be reported.

26. Why might a company choose not to use revaluation accounting?

27. Vodafone (GBR) reported net income of £3 billion, net sales of £41 billion, and average total assets of £140 billion. What is Vodafone's asset turnover? What is Vodafone's return on assets?

28. Briefly describe some of the similarities and differences between IFRS and U.S. GAAP with respect to the accounting for property, plant, and equipment.

29. At a recent executive committee meeting, the controller for Ricardo Company remarked, "With only a single key difference between IFRS and U.S. GAAP for property, plant, and equipment, it should be smooth sailing for the IASB and FASB to converge their standards in this area." Prepare a response to the controller.

*30. Mandive Corp., in accordance with IFRS, applies revaluation accounting to plant assets with a carrying amount of $400,000, a useful life of 4 years, and no residual value. At the end of year 1, independent appraisers determine that the asset has a fair value of $360,000. Prepare the entries to record this revaluation and depreciation, assuming straight-line depreciation.

BRIEF EXERCISES

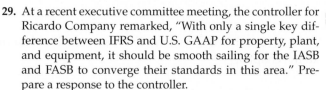

BE11-1 Fernandez Corporation purchased a truck at the beginning of 2015 for $50,000. The truck is estimated to have a residual value of $2,000 and a useful life of 160,000 miles. It was driven 23,000 miles in 2015 and 31,000 miles in 2016. Compute depreciation expense for 2015 and 2016.

2 **3** **BE11-2** Lockard Company purchased machinery on January 1, 2015, for €80,000. The machinery is estimated to have a residual value of €8,000 after a useful life of 8 years. (a) Compute 2015 depreciation expense using the straight-line method. (b) Compute 2015 depreciation expense using the straight-line method, assuming the machinery was purchased on September 1, 2015.

2 **3** **BE11-3** Use the information for Lockard Company given in BE11-2. (a) Compute 2015 depreciation expense using the sum-of-the-years'-digits method. (b) Compute 2015 depreciation expense using the sum-of-the-years'-digits method, assuming the machinery was purchased on April 1, 2015.

2 **3** **BE11-4** Use the information for Lockard Company given in BE11-2. (a) Compute 2015 depreciation expense using the double-declining-balance method. (b) Compute 2015 depreciation expense using the double-declining-balance method, assuming the machinery was purchased on October 1, 2015.

2 **BE11-5** Cominsky Company purchased a machine on July 1, 2016, for $28,000. Cominsky paid $200 in title fees and county property tax of $125 on the machine. In addition, Cominsky paid $500 shipping charges for delivery, and $475 was paid to a local contractor to build and wire a platform for the machine on the plant floor. The machine has an estimated useful life of 6 years with a residual value of $3,000. Determine the depreciation base of Cominsky's new machine. Cominsky uses straight-line depreciation.

4 **BE11-6** Ortiz purchased a piece of equipment that cost R$202,000 on January 1, 2015. The equipment has the following components.

Component	Cost	Residual Value	Estimated Useful Life
A	R$70,000	R$7,000	10 years
B	50,000	5,000	5 years
C	82,000	4,000	12 years

Compute the depreciation expense for this equipment at December 31, 2015.

2 **3** **BE11-7** Holt Company purchased a computer for £8,000 on January 1, 2014. Straight-line depreciation is used, based on a 5-year life and a £1,000 residual value. In 2016, the estimates are revised. Holt now feels the computer will be used until December 31, 2017, when it can be sold for £500. Compute the 2016 depreciation.

4 **BE11-8** Tan Chin Company purchases a building for HK$11,300,000 on January 2, 2015. An engineer's report shows that of the total purchase price, HK$11,000,000 should be allocated to the building (with a 40-year life, no residual value), HK$150,000 to 15-year property, and HK$150,000 to 5-year property. Compute depreciation expense for 2015 using component depreciation.

5 **BE11-9** Jurassic Company owns machinery that cost $900,000 and has accumulated depreciation of $380,000. The present value of expected future net cash flows from the use of the asset are expected to be $500,000. The fair value less cost of disposal of the equipment is $400,000. Prepare the journal entry, if any, to record the impairment loss.

6 **BE11-10** Everly Corporation acquires a coal mine at a cost of $400,000. Intangible development costs total $100,000. After extraction has occurred, Everly must restore the property (estimated fair value of the obligation is $80,000), after which it can be sold for $160,000. Everly estimates that 4,000 tons of coal can be extracted. If 700 tons are extracted the first year, prepare the journal entry to record depletion.

7 **9** *BE11-11 Obihiro Group has equipment with an original cost of ¥500,000,000 and related accumulated depreciation of ¥100,000,000 on December 31, 2015. The fair value of the equipment at December 31, 2015, is ¥650,000,000. The equipment has a useful life of 4 years remaining after December 31, 2015, with no residual value. Obihiro uses the straight-line method of depreciation. Prepare the entry to (a) record the revaluation of the equipment on December 31, 2015, and (b) record depreciation on the equipment at December 31, 2016.

8 **BE11-12** In its annual report, Campbell Soup Company (USA) reports beginning-of-the-year total assets of $7,745 million, end-of-the-year total assets of $6,445 million, total sales of $7,867 million, and net income of $854 million. Compute Campbell's (a) asset turnover and (b) profit margin on sales. (c) Compute Campbell's return on assets using (1) asset turnover and profit margin and (2) net income.

EXERCISES

2 3 E11-1 (Depreciation Computations—SL, SYD, DDB) Lansbury Company purchases equipment on January 1, Year 1, at a cost of £518,000. The asset is expected to have a service life of 12 years and a residual value of £50,000.

Instructions

(a) Compute the amount of depreciation for each of years 1 through 3 using the straight-line depreciation method.

(b) Compute the amount of depreciation for each of years 1 through 3 using the sum-of-the-years'-digits method.

(c) Compute the amount of depreciation for each of years 1 through 3 using the double-declining-balance method. (In performing your calculations, round constant percentage to the nearest one-hundredth of a point and round answers to the nearest pound.)

2 3 E11-2 (Depreciation—Conceptual Understanding) Hasselback Company acquired a plant asset at the beginning of year 1. The asset has an estimated service life of 5 years. An employee has prepared depreciation schedules for this asset using three different methods to compare the results of using one method with the results of using other methods. You are to assume that the following schedules have been correctly prepared for this asset using (1) the straight-line method, (2) the sum-of-the-years'-digits method, and (3) the double-declining-balance method.

Year	Straight-Line	Sum-of-the-Years'-Digits	Double-Declining-Balance
1	$ 9,000	$15,000	$20,000
2	9,000	12,000	12,000
3	9,000	9,000	7,200
4	9,000	6,000	4,320
5	9,000	3,000	1,480
Total	$45,000	$45,000	$45,000

Instructions

Answer the following questions.

(a) What is the cost of the asset being depreciated?

(b) What amount, if any, was used in the depreciation calculations for the residual value for this asset?

(c) Which method will produce the highest charge to income in year 1?

(d) Which method will produce the highest charge to income in year 4?

(e) Which method will produce the highest book value for the asset at the end of year 3?

(f) If the asset is sold at the end of year 3, which method would yield the highest gain (or lowest loss) on disposal of the asset?

2 3 E11-3 (Depreciation Computations—SYD, DDB—Partial Periods) Cosby Company purchased a new plant asset on April 1, 2015, at a cost of €774,000. It was estimated to have a service life of 20 years and a residual value of €60,000. Cosby's accounting period is the calendar year.

Instructions

(a) Compute the depreciation for this asset for 2015 and 2016 using the sum-of-the-years'-digits method.

(b) Compute the depreciation for this asset for 2015 and 2016 using the double-declining-balance method.

2 3 E11-4 (Depreciation Computations—Five Methods) Wenner Furnace Corp. purchased machinery for $279,000 on May 1, 2015. It is estimated that it will have a useful life of 10 years, residual value of $15,000, production of 240,000 units, and working hours of 25,000. During 2016, Wenner Corp. uses the machinery for 2,650 hours, and the machinery produces 25,500 units.

Instructions

From the information given, compute the depreciation charge for 2016 under each of the following methods. (Round to the nearest dollar.)

(a) Straight-line.

(b) Units-of-output.

(c) Working hours.

(d) Sum-of-the-years'-digits.

(e) Double-declining-balance.

2 3 **E11-5 (Depreciation Computations—Four Methods)** Maserati Corporation purchased a new machine for its assembly process on August 1, 2015. The cost of this machine was €150,000. The company estimated that the machine would have a residual value of €24,000 at the end of its service life. Its life is estimated at 5 years, and its working hours are estimated at 21,000 hours. Year-end is December 31.

Instructions

Compute the depreciation expense under the following methods. Each of the following should be considered unrelated.

    (a) Straight-line depreciation for 2015.
    (b) Activity method for 2015, assuming that machine usage was 800 hours.
    (c) Sum-of-the-years'-digits for 2016.
    (d) Double-declining-balance for 2016.

2 3 **E11-6 (Depreciation Computations—Five Methods, Partial Periods)** Agazzi Company purchased equipment for $304,000 on October 1, 2015. It is estimated that the equipment will have a useful life of 8 years and a residual value of $16,000. Estimated production is 40,000 units, and estimated working hours are 20,000. During 2015, Agazzi uses the equipment for 525 hours, and the equipment produces 1,000 units.

Instructions

Compute depreciation expense under each of the following methods. Agazzi is on a calendar-year basis ending December 31.

    (a) Straight-line method for 2015.
    (b) Activity method (units of output) for 2015.
    (c) Activity method (working hours) for 2015.
    (d) Sum-of-the-years'-digits method for 2017.
    (e) Double-declining-balance method for 2016.

2 3 **E11-7 (Different Methods of Depreciation)** Jeeter Industries presents you with the following information.

Description	Date Purchased	Cost	Residual Value	Life in Years	Depreciation Method	Accumulated Depreciation to 12/31/15	Depreciation for 2016
Machine A	2/12/14	$159,000	$16,000	10	**(a)**	$37,700	**(b)**
Machine B	8/15/13	**(c)**	21,000	5	SL	29,000	**(d)**
Machine C	7/21/12	88,000	28,500	8	DDB	**(e)**	**(f)**
Machine D	10/12/**(g)**	219,000	69,000	5	SYD	70,000	**(h)**

Instructions

Complete the table for the year ended December 31, 2016. The company depreciates all assets using the half-year convention.

2 3 **E11-8 (Depreciation Computation—Replacement, Non-Monetary Exchange)** Goldman Corporation bought a machine on June 1, 2013, for €31,800, f.o.b. the place of manufacture. Freight to the point where it was set up was €200, and €500 was expended to install it. The machine's useful life was estimated at 10 years, with a residual value of €2,500. On June 1, 2014, an essential part of the machine is replaced, at a cost of €2,700, with one designed to reduce the cost of operating the machine. The book value of the old part is estimated to be €900.

    On June 1, 2017, the company buys a new machine of greater capacity for €35,000, delivered, trading in the old machine which has a fair value and trade-in allowance of €20,000. To prepare the old machine for removal from the plant cost €75, and expenditures to install the new one were €1,500. It is estimated that the new machine has a useful life of 10 years, with a residual value of €4,000 at the end of that time. The exchange has commercial substance.

Instructions

Assuming that depreciation is to be computed on the straight-line basis, compute the annual depreciation on the new equipment that should be provided for the fiscal year beginning June 1, 2017.

2 3 4 **E11-9 (Component Depreciation)** Morrow Manufacturing has equipment that is comprised of five components (amounts in thousands).

Component	Cost	Estimated Residual	Estimated Life (in years)
A	¥40,500	¥5,500	10
B	33,600	4,800	9
C	36,000	3,600	8
D	19,000	1,500	7
E	23,500	2,500	6

Instructions

(a) Prepare the adjusting entry necessary at the end of the year to record depreciation for the year. Assume that Morrow uses straight-line depreciation.

(b) Prepare the entry to record the replacement of component B for cash of ¥40,000. It was used for 6 years.

E11-10 (Depreciation Computations, SYD) Pippen Company purchased a piece of equipment at the beginning of 2012. The equipment cost ₺502,000. It has an estimated service life of 8 years and an expected residual value of ₺70,000. The sum-of-the-years'-digits method of depreciation is being used. Someone has already correctly prepared a depreciation schedule for this asset. This schedule shows that ₺60,000 will be depreciated for a particular calendar year.

Instructions

Show calculations to determine for what particular year the depreciation amount for this asset will be ₺60,000.

E11-11 (Depreciation—Change in Estimate) Machinery purchased for $52,000 by Carver Co. in 2011 was originally estimated to have a life of 8 years with a residual value of $4,000 at the end of that time. Depreciation has been entered for 5 years on this basis. In 2016, it is determined that the total estimated life should be 10 years with a residual value of $4,500 at the end of that time. Assume straight-line depreciation.

Instructions

(a) Prepare the entry to correct the prior years' depreciation, if necessary.

(b) Prepare the entry to record depreciation for 2016.

E11-12 (Depreciation Computation—Addition, Change in Estimate) In 1988, Abraham Company completed the construction of a building at a cost of €1,900,000 and first occupied it in January 1989. It was estimated that the building will have a useful life of 40 years and a residual value of €60,000 at the end of that time.

Early in 1999, an addition to the building was constructed at a cost of €470,000. At that time it was estimated that the remaining life of the building would be, as originally estimated, an additional 30 years, and that the addition would have a life of 30 years and a residual value of €20,000.

In 2017, it is determined that the probable life of the building and addition will extend to the end of 2048, or 20 years beyond the original estimate.

Instructions

(a) Using the straight-line method, compute the annual depreciation that would have been charged from 1989 through 1998.

(b) Compute the annual depreciation that would have been charged from 1999 through 2016.

(c) Prepare the entry, if necessary, to adjust the account balances because of the revision of the estimated life in 2017.

(d) Compute the annual depreciation to be charged beginning with 2017.

E11-13 (Depreciation—Replacement, Change in Estimate) Peloton Company constructed a building at a cost of $2,400,000 and occupied it beginning in January 1996. It was estimated at that time that its life would be 40 years, with no residual value.

In January 2016, a new roof was installed at a cost of $300,000, and it was estimated then that the building would have a useful life of 25 years from that date. The cost of the old roof was $180,000.

Instructions

(a) What amount of depreciation should have been charged annually from the years 1996 to 2015? (Assume straight-line depreciation.)

(b) What entry should be made in 2016 to record the replacement of the roof?

(c) Prepare the entry in January 2016 to record the revision in the estimated life of the building, if necessary.

(d) What amount of depreciation should be charged for the year 2016?

E11-14 (Error Analysis and Depreciation, SL and SYD) Kawasaki Company shows the following entries in its Equipment account for 2016. All amounts (in yen, in thousands) are based on historical cost.

Equipment					
2016				2016		
Jan. 1	Balance	133,000		June 30	Cost of equipment sold	
Aug. 10	Purchases	32,000			(purchased prior	
12	Freight on equipment				to 2016)	23,000
	purchased	700				
25	Installation costs	2,500				
Nov. 10	Repairs	500				

Instructions

(a) Prepare any correcting entries necessary.

(b) Assuming that depreciation is to be charged for a full year on the ending balance in the asset account, compute the proper depreciation charge for 2016 under each of the methods listed below. Assume an estimated life of 10 years, with no residual value. The machinery included in the January 1, 2016, balance was purchased in 2014.

   (1) Straight-line.

   (2) Sum-of-the-years'-digits.

E11-15 (Depreciation for Fractional Periods) On March 10, 2017, No Doubt Company sells equipment that it purchased for $240,000 on August 20, 2010. It was originally estimated that the equipment would have a life of 12 years and a residual value of $21,000 at the end of that time, and depreciation has been computed on that basis. The company uses the straight-line method of depreciation.

Instructions

(a) Compute the depreciation charge on this equipment for 2010, for 2017, and the total charge for the period from 2011 to 2016, inclusive, under each of the six following assumptions with respect to partial periods.

   (1) Depreciation is computed for the exact period of time during which the asset is owned. (Use 365 days for the base.)

   (2) Depreciation is computed for the full year on the January 1 balance in the asset account.

   (3) Depreciation is computed for the full year on the December 31 balance in the asset account.

   (4) Depreciation for one-half year is charged on plant assets acquired or disposed of during the year.

   (5) Depreciation is computed on additions from the beginning of the month following acquisition and on disposals to the beginning of the month following disposal.

   (6) Depreciation is computed for a full period on all assets in use for over one-half year, and no depreciation is charged on assets in use for less than one-half year.

(b) Briefly evaluate the methods above, considering them from the point of view of basic accounting theory as well as simplicity of application.

E11-16 (Component Depreciation) Brazil Group purchases a tractor at a cost of €50,000 on January 2, 2015. Individual components of the tractor and useful lives are as follows (zero residual value).

	Cost	Useful Lives
Tires	€ 6,000	2 years
Transmission	10,000	5 years
Tractor	34,000	10 years

Instructions

(a) Compute depreciation expense for 2015, assuming Brazil depreciates the tractor as a single unit.

(b) Compute depreciation expense for 2015, assuming Brazil uses component depreciation.

(c) Why might a company want to use component depreciation to depreciate its assets?

E11-17 (Component Depreciation) Presented below are the components related to an office block that Veenman Company is considering purchasing for €10,000,000.

Component	Useful Life	Value
Land	Indefinite life	€3,000,000
Building structure	60-year life	4,200,000
Building engineering	30-year life	2,100,000
Building external works	30-year life	700,000

Instructions

(a) Compute depreciation expense for 2015, assuming that Veenman uses component depreciation (zero residual value).

(b) Assume that the building engineering was replaced in 20 years at a cost of €2,300,000. Prepare the entry to record the replacement of the old component with the new component.

E11-18 (Impairment) Presented below is information related to equipment owned by Pujols Company at December 31, 2015.

Cost	€9,000,000
Accumulated depreciation to date	1,000,000
Value-in-use	7,000,000
Fair value less cost of disposal	4,400,000

Assume that Pujols will continue to use this asset in the future. As of December 31, 2015, the equipment has a remaining useful life of 4 years.

Instructions

(a) Prepare the journal entry (if any) to record the impairment of the asset at December 31, 2015.

(b) Prepare the journal entry to record depreciation expense for 2016.

(c) The recoverable amount of the equipment at December 31, 2016, is €6,000,000. Prepare the journal entry (if any) necessary to record this increase.

5 **E11-19 (Impairment)** Assume the same information as E11-18, except that Pujols intends to dispose of the equipment in the coming year.

Instructions

(a) Prepare the journal entry (if any) to record the impairment of the asset at December 31, 2015.

(b) Prepare the journal entry (if any) to record depreciation expense for 2016.

(c) The asset was not sold by December 31, 2016. The fair value of the equipment on that date is €5,100,000. Prepare the journal entry (if any) necessary to record this increase. It is expected that the cost of disposal is €20,000.

5 **E11-20 (Impairment)** The management of Sprague Inc. was discussing whether certain equipment should be written off as a charge to current operations because of obsolescence. This equipment has a cost of $900,000 with depreciation to date of $400,000 as of December 31, 2015. On December 31, 2015, management projected the present value of future net cash flows from this equipment to be $300,000 and its fair value less cost of disposal to be $280,000. The company intends to use this equipment in the future. The remaining useful life of the equipment is 4 years.

Instructions

(a) Prepare the journal entry (if any) to record the impairment at December 31, 2015.

(b) Where should the gain or loss (if any) on the write-down be reported in the income statement?

(c) At December 31, 2016, the equipment's recoverable amount is $270,000. Prepare the journal entry (if any).

(d) What accounting issues did management face in accounting for this impairment?

6 **E11-21 (Depletion Computations—Oil)** Federer Drilling Company has leased property on which oil has been discovered. Wells on this property produced 18,000 barrels of oil during the past year that sold at an average sales price of €65 per barrel. Total oil resources of this property are estimated to be 250,000 barrels.

The lease provided for an outright payment of €600,000 to the lessor (owner) before drilling could be commenced and an annual rental of €31,500. A premium of 5% of the sales price of every barrel of oil removed is to be paid annually to the lessor. In addition, Federer (lessee) is to clean up all the waste and debris from drilling and to bear the costs of reconditioning the land for farming when the wells are abandoned. The estimated fair value, at the time of the lease, of this clean-up and reconditioning is €30,000.

Instructions

From the provisions of the lease agreement, compute the cost per barrel for the past year, exclusive of operating costs, to Federer Drilling Company.

6 **E11-22 (Depletion Computations—Mining)** Henrik Mining Company purchased land on February 1, 2015, at a cost of €1,250,000. It estimated that a total of 60,000 tons of mineral was available for mining. After it has removed all the mineral resources, the company will be required to restore the property to its previous state because of strict environmental protection laws. It estimates the fair value of this restoration obligation at €90,000. It believes it will be able to sell the property afterwards for €100,000. It incurred developmental costs of €200,000 before it was able to do any mining. In 2015, resources removed totaled 30,000 tons. The company sold 24,000 tons.

Instructions

Compute the following information for 2015.

(a) Per unit mineral cost.

(b) Total material cost of December 31, 2015, inventory.

(c) Total materials cost in cost of goods sold at December 31, 2015.

6 **E11-23 (Depletion Computations—Minerals)** At the beginning of 2015, Callaway Company acquired a mine for $850,000. Of this amount, $100,000 was ascribed to the land value and the remaining portion to the minerals in the mine. Surveys conducted by geologists have indicated that approximately 12,000,000 units of the ore appear to be in the mine. Callaway incurred $170,000 of development costs associated with this mine prior to any extraction of minerals. It also determined that the fair value of its obligation to prepare the land for an alternative use when all of the mineral has been removed was $40,000. During 2015, 2,500,000 units of ore were extracted and 2,200,000 of these units were sold.

Instructions

Compute the following.

    (a) The total amount of depletion for 2015.

    (b) The amount that is charged as an expense for 2015 for the cost of the minerals sold during 2015.

7 **E11-24 (Revaluation Accounting)** Croatia Company purchased land in 2015 for $300,000. The land's fair value at the end of 2015 is $320,000; at the end of 2016, $280,000; and at the end of 2017, $305,000. Assume that Croatia chooses to use revaluation accounting to account for its land.

Instructions

Prepare the journal entries to record the land using revaluation accounting for 2015–2017.

7 **E11-25 (Revaluation Accounting)** Pengo Company owns land that it purchased at a cost of ¥400 million in 2013. The company chooses to use revaluation accounting to account for the land. The land's value fluctuates as follows (all amounts in thousands as of December 31): 2013, ¥450,000; 2014, ¥360,000; 2015, ¥385,000; 2016, ¥410,000; and 2017, ¥460,000.

Instructions

Complete the following table below.

Value at December 31	Accumulated Other Comprehensive Income	Other Comprehensive Income	Recognized in Net Income
2013			
2014			
2015			
2016			
2017			

7 **E11-26 (Revaluation Accounting)** Use the information in E11-25.

Instructions

Prepare the journal entries to record the revaluation of the land in each year.

7 **E11-27 (Revaluation Accounting)** Falcetto Company acquired equipment on January 1, 2014, for €12,000. Falcetto elects to value this class of equipment using revaluation accounting. This equipment is being depreciated on a straight-line basis over its 6-year useful life. There is no residual value at the end of the 6-year period. The appraised value of the equipment approximates the carrying amount at December 31, 2014 and 2016. On December 31, 2015, the fair value of the equipment is determined to be €7,000.

Instructions

    (a) Prepare the journal entries for 2014 related to the equipment.

    (b) Prepare the journal entries for 2015 related to the equipment.

    (c) Determine the amount of depreciation expense that Falcetto will record on the equipment in 2016.

8 **E11-28 (Ratio Analysis)** A recent annual report of Eastman Company contains the following information.

(in millions)	Current Year-End	Prior Year-End
Total assets	£13,659	£14,320
Total liabilities	10,630	12,932
Net sales	10,301	10,568
Net income	676	(601)

Instructions

Compute the following ratios for Eastman Company for the current year.

    (a) Asset turnover.

    (b) Return on assets.

    (c) Profit margin on sales.

    (d) How can the asset turnover be used to compute the return on assets?

7 **9** *E11-29 (Revaluation Accounting)** Su Company acquired an excavator on January 1, 2013, for ¥10,000 (all amounts in thousands). This excavator represents the company's only piece of equipment, and Su chooses revaluation accounting. This excavator is being depreciated on a straight-line basis over its 10-year useful life. There is no residual value at the end of the 10-year period. The appraised value of the excavator approximates the carrying value at December 31, 2013 and 2015. On December 31, 2014, the fair value is determined to be ¥8,800; on December 31, 2016, the fair value is determined to be ¥5,000.

Instructions

(a) Show all journal entries for each year from 2013 through 2016.

(b) Su also owns some property and buildings for which revaluation accounting is not used. Briefly discuss why Su might not use revaluation accounting for these assets.

PROBLEMS

2 3 **P11-1 (Depreciation for Partial Period—SL, SYD, and DDB)** Alladin Company purchased Machine #201 on May 1, 2015. The following information relating to Machine #201 was gathered at the end of May.

Price	$85,000
Credit terms	2/10, n/30
Freight-in costs	$ 800
Preparation and installation costs	$ 3,800
Labor costs during regular production operations	$10,500

It was expected that the machine could be used for 10 years, after which the residual value would be zero. Alladin intends to use the machine for only 8 years, however, after which it expects to be able to sell it for $1,500. The invoice for Machine #201 was paid May 5, 2015. Alladin uses the calendar year as the basis for the preparation of financial statements.

Instructions

(a) Compute the depreciation expense for the years indicated using the following methods. (Round to the nearest dollar.)

(1) Straight-line method for 2015.

(2) Sum-of-the-years'-digits method for 2016.

(3) Double-declining-balance method for 2015.

(b) Suppose Kate Crow, the president of Alladin, tells you that because the company is a new organization, she expects it will be several years before production and sales reach optimum levels. She asks you to recommend a depreciation method that will allocate less of the company's depreciation expense to the early years and more to later years of the assets' lives. What method would you recommend?

2 3 **P11-2 (Depreciation for Partial Periods—SL, Act., SYD, and DDB)** The cost of equipment purchased by Charleston, Inc., on June 1, 2015, is €89,000. It is estimated that the machine will have a €5,000 residual value at the end of its service life. Its service life is estimated at 7 years; its total working hours are estimated at 42,000 and its total production is estimated at 525,000 units. During 2015, the machine was operated 6,000 hours and produced 55,000 units. During 2016, the machine was operated 5,500 hours and produced 48,000 units.

Instructions

Compute depreciation expense on the machine for the year ending December 31, 2015, and the year ending December 31, 2016, using the following methods.

(a) Straight-line.   (d) Sum-of-the-years'-digits.

(b) Units-of-output.   (e) Declining-balance (twice the straight-line rate).

(c) Working hours.

2 3 **P11-3 (Depreciation—SYD, Act., SL, and DDB)** The following data relate to the Plant Assets account of Eshkol, Inc. at December 31, 2015.

Plant Assets

	A	B	C	D
Original cost	£46,000	£51,000	£80,000	£80,000
Year purchased	2010	2011	2012	2014
Useful life	10 years	15,000 hours	15 years	10 years
Residual value	£ 3,100	£ 3,000	£ 5,000	£ 5,000
Depreciation method	Sum-of-the-years'-digits	Activity	Straight-line	Double-declining-balance
Accum. Depr. through 2015*	£31,200	£35,200	£15,000	£16,000

*In the year an asset is purchased, Eshkol, Inc. does not record any depreciation expense on the asset.

In the year an asset is retired or traded in, Eshkol, Inc. takes a full year's depreciation on the asset.

The following transactions occurred during 2016.

    (a) On May 5, Asset A was sold for £13,000 cash. The company's bookkeeper recorded this retirement in the following manner in the cash receipts journal.

Cash	13,000	
Plant Assets (Asset A)		13,000

    (b) On December 31, it was determined that Asset B had been used 2,100 hours during 2016.

    (c) On December 31, before computing depreciation expense on Asset C, the management of Eshkol, Inc. decided the useful life remaining from January 1, 2016, was 10 years.

    (d) On December 31, it was discovered that a plant asset purchased in 2015 had been expensed completely in that year. This asset cost £28,000 and has a useful life of 10 years and no residual value. Management has decided to use the double-declining-balance method for this asset, which can be referred to as "Asset E."

Instructions

Prepare the necessary correcting entries for the year 2016. Record the appropriate depreciation expense on the above-mentioned assets.

2 3 **P11-4 (Depreciation and Error Analysis)** A depreciation schedule for semi-trucks of Ichiro Manufacturing Company was requested by your auditor soon after December 31, 2016, showing the additions, retirements, depreciation, and other data affecting the income of the company in the 4-year period 2013 to 2016, inclusive. The following data were ascertained (amounts in thousands).

Balance of Trucks account, Jan. 1, 2013	
Truck No. 1 purchased Jan. 1, 2010, cost	¥18,000
Truck No. 2 purchased July 1, 2010, cost	22,000
Truck No. 3 purchased Jan. 1, 2012, cost	30,000
Truck No. 4 purchased July 1, 2012, cost	24,000
Balance, Jan. 1, 2013	¥94,000

    The Accumulated Depreciation—Trucks account previously adjusted to January 1, 2013, and entered in the ledger, had a balance on that date of ¥30,200 (depreciation on the four trucks from the respective dates of purchase, based on a 5-year life, no residual value). No charges had been made against the account before January 1, 2013.

    Transactions between January 1, 2013, and December 31, 2016, which were recorded in the ledger, are as follows.

July 1, 2013	Truck No. 3 was traded for a larger one (No. 5), the agreed purchase price of which was ¥40,000. Ichiro paid the automobile dealer ¥22,000 cash on the transaction. The entry was a debit to Trucks and a credit to Cash, ¥22,000. The transaction has commercial substance.
Jan. 1, 2014	Truck No. 1 was sold for ¥3,500 cash; entry debited Cash and credited Trucks, ¥3,500.
July 1, 2015	A new truck (No. 6) was acquired for ¥42,000 cash and was charged at that amount to the Trucks account. (Assume Truck No. 2 was not retired.)
July 1, 2015	Truck No. 4 was damaged in a wreck to such an extent that it was sold as junk for ¥700 cash. Ichiro received ¥2,500 from the insurance company. The entry made by the bookkeeper was a debit to Cash, ¥3,200, and credits to Miscellaneous Income ¥700 and Trucks ¥2,500.

Entries for depreciation had been made at the close of each year as follows: 2013, ¥21,000; 2014, ¥22,500; 2015, ¥25,050; and 2016, ¥30,400.

Instructions

    (a) For each of the 4 years, compute separately the increase or decrease in net income arising from the company's errors in determining or entering depreciation or in recording transactions affecting trucks, ignoring income tax considerations.

    (b) Prepare one compound journal entry as of December 31, 2016, for adjustment of the Trucks account to reflect the correct balances as revealed by your schedule, assuming that the books have not been closed for 2016.

2 3
7 **P11-5 (Comprehensive Property, Plant, and Equipment Problem)** Darby Sporting Goods Inc. has been experiencing growth in the demand for its products over the last several years. The last two Olympic Games greatly increased the popularity of basketball around the world. As a result, a European sports retailing consortium entered into an agreement with Darby's Roundball Division to purchase basketballs and other accessories on an increasing basis over the next 5 years.

    To be able to meet the quantity commitments of this agreement, Darby had to obtain additional manufacturing capacity. A real estate firm located an available factory in close proximity to Darby's Roundball manufacturing facility, and Darby agreed to purchase the factory and used machinery from Quay Athletic

Equipment Company on October 1, 2014. Renovations were necessary to convert the factory for Darby's manufacturing use.

The terms of the agreement required Darby to pay Quay £50,000 when renovations started on January 1, 2015, with the balance to be paid as renovations were completed. The overall purchase price for the factory and machinery was £400,000. The building renovations were contracted to Malone Construction at £100,000. The payments made, as renovations progressed during 2015, are shown below. The factory was placed in service on January 1, 2016.

	1/1	4/1	10/1	12/31
Quay	£50,000	£90,000	£110,000	£150,000
Malone		30,000	30,000	40,000

On January 1, 2015, Darby secured a £500,000 line-of-credit with a 12% interest rate to finance the purchase cost of the factory and machinery, and the renovation costs. Darby drew down on the line-of-credit to meet the payment schedule shown above; this was Darby's only outstanding loan during 2015.

Bob Sprague, Darby's controller, will capitalize the maximum allowable interest costs for this project. Darby's policy regarding purchases of this nature is to use the appraisal value of the land for book purposes and prorate the balance of the purchase price over the remaining items. The building had originally cost Quay £300,000 and had a net book value of £50,000, while the machinery originally cost £125,000 and had a net book value of £40,000 on the date of sale. The land was recorded on Quay's books at £40,000. An appraisal, conducted by independent appraisers at the time of acquisition, valued the land at £290,000, the building at £105,000, and the machinery at £45,000.

Angie Justice, chief engineer, estimated that the renovated plant would be used for 15 years, with an estimated residual value of £30,000. Justice estimated that the productive machinery would have a remaining useful life of 5 years and a residual value of £3,000. Darby's depreciation policy specifies the 200% declining-balance method for machinery and the 150% declining-balance method for the plant. One-half year's depreciation is taken in the year the plant is placed in service and one-half year is allowed when the property is disposed of or retired. Darby uses a 360-day year for calculating interest costs.

Instructions

(a) Determine the amounts to be recorded on the books of Darby Sporting Goods Inc. as of December 31, 2015, for each of the following properties acquired from Quay Athletic Equipment Company.
   (1) Land.   **(2)** Building.   **(3)** Machinery.

(b) Calculate Darby Sporting Goods Inc.'s 2016 depreciation expense, for book purposes, for each of the properties acquired from Quay Athletic Equipment Company.

(c) Discuss the arguments for and against the capitalization of interest costs.

(d) Given the enhancements to the building, Darby thinks it would make its financial position look better if it used revaluation accounting. Advise Darby management on whether the company can use revaluation accounting for this building. Should Darby management use revaluation accounting? Briefly discuss some of the reasons for and against use of revaluation accounting.

 P11-6 (Comprehensive Depreciation Computations) Kohlbeck Corporation, a manufacturer of steel products, began operations on October 1, 2014. The accounting department of Kohlbeck has started the plant asset and depreciation schedule presented on page 541. You have been asked to assist in completing this schedule. In addition to ascertaining that the data already on the schedule are correct, you have obtained the following information from the company's records and personnel.

1. Depreciation is computed from the first of the month of acquisition to the first of the month of disposition.

2. Land A and Building A were acquired from a predecessor corporation. Kohlbeck paid $800,000 for the land and building together. At the time of acquisition, the land had an appraised value of $90,000, and the building had an appraised value of $810,000.

3. Land B was acquired on October 2, 2014, in exchange for 2,500 newly issued shares of Kohlbeck's ordinary shares. At the date of acquisition, the shares had a par value of $5 per share and a fair value of $30 per share. During October 2014, Kohlbeck paid $16,000 to demolish an existing building on this land so it could construct a new building.

4. Construction of Building B on the newly acquired land began on October 1, 2015. By September 30, 2016, Kohlbeck had paid $320,000 of the estimated total construction costs of $450,000. It is estimated that the building will be completed and occupied by July 2017.

5. A grant for certain equipment was given to the corporation by the local community. An independent appraisal of the equipment when granted placed the fair value at $40,000 and the residual value at $3,000. The grant is recorded as deferred grant revenue.

6. Machinery A's total cost of $182,900 includes installation expense of $600 and normal repairs and maintenance of $14,900. Residual value is estimated at $6,000. Machinery A was sold on February 1, 2016.

7. On October 1, 2015, Machinery B was acquired with a down payment of $5,740 and the remaining payments to be made in 11 annual installments of $6,000 each beginning October 1, 2015. The prevailing interest rate was 8%. The following data were abstracted from present value tables (rounded).

Present value of $1.00 at 8%		Present value of an ordinary annuity of $1.00 at 8%	
10 years	.463	10 years	6.710
11 years	.429	11 years	7.139
15 years	.315	15 years	8.559

KOHLBECK CORPORATION
Plant Asset and Depreciation Schedule
For Fiscal Years Ended September 30, 2015, and September 30, 2016

Assets	Acquisition Date	Cost	Residual Value	Depreciation Method	Estimated Life in Years	Depreciation Expense Year Ended September 30 2015	Depreciation Expense Year Ended September 30 2016
Land A	October 1, 2014	$ (1)	N/A	N/A	N/A	N/A	N/A
Building A	October 1, 2014	(2)	$40,000	Straight-line	(3)	$13,600	(4)
Land B	October 2, 2014	(5)	N/A	N/A	N/A	N/A	N/A
Building B	Under Construction	320,000 to date	—	Straight-line	30	—	(6)
Donated Equipment	October 2, 2014	(7)	3,000	150% declining-balance	10	(8)	(9)
Machinery A	October 2, 2014	(10)	6,000	Sum-of-the-years'-digits	8	(11)	(12)
Machinery B	October 1, 2015	(13)	—	Straight-line	20	—	(14)

N/A—Not applicable

Instructions

For each numbered item on the schedule above, supply the correct amount. (Round each answer to the nearest dollar.)

2 3 **P11-7 (Depreciation for Partial Periods—SL, Act., SYD, and DDB)** On January 1, 2013, a machine was purchased for $90,000. The machine has an estimated residual value of $6,000 and an estimated useful life of 5 years. The machine can operate for 100,000 hours before it needs to be replaced. The company closed its books on December 31 and operates the machine as follows: 2013, 20,000 hours; 2014, 25,000 hours; 2015, 15,000 hours; 2016, 30,000 hours; and 2017, 10,000 hours.

Instructions

(a) Compute the annual depreciation charges over the machine's life assuming a December 31 year-end for each of the following depreciation methods.

  (1) Straight-line method.   (3) Sum-of-the-years'-digits method.

  (2) Activity method.   (4) Double-declining-balance method.

(b) Assume a fiscal year-end of September 30. Compute the annual depreciation charges over the asset's life applying each of the following methods.

  (1) Straight-line method.   (3) Double-declining-balance method.

  (2) Sum-of-the-years'-digits method.

2 3 **P11-8 (Depreciation Methods)** On January 1, 2014, Luis Company, a small machine-tool manufacturer, acquired for R$1,260,000 a piece of new industrial equipment. The new equipment had a useful life of 5 years, and the residual value was estimated to be R$60,000. Luis estimates that the new equipment can produce 12,000 machine tools in its first year and 50,000 units over its life. It estimates that production will decline by 1,000 units per year over the remaining useful life of the equipment.

The following depreciation methods may be used: (1) straight-line, (2) double-declining-balance, (3) sum-of-the-years'-digits, and (4) units-of-output.

Instructions

Which depreciation method would maximize net income for financial statement reporting for the 3-year period ending December 31, 2016? Prepare a schedule showing the amount of accumulated depreciation at

December 31, 2016, under the method selected. (Ignore present value, income tax, and deferred income tax considerations.)

5 **P11-9 (Impairment)** Roland Company uses special strapping equipment in its packaging business. The equipment was purchased in January 2014 for €10,000,000 and had an estimated useful life of 8 years with no residual value. At December 31, 2015, new technology was introduced that would accelerate the obsolescence of Roland's equipment. Roland's controller estimates that the present value of expected future net cash flows on the equipment will be €5,300,000 and that the fair value less costs to sell the equipment will be €5,600,000. Roland intends to continue using the equipment, but it is estimated that the remaining useful life is 4 years. Roland uses straight-line depreciation.

Instructions

(a) Prepare the journal entry (if any) to record the impairment at December 31, 2015 (depreciation for 2015 has been recorded).

(b) Prepare any journal entries for the equipment at December 31, 2016. The recoverable amount of the equipment at December 31, 2016, is estimated to be €4,900,000.

(c) Repeat the requirements for (a) and (b), assuming that Roland intends to dispose of the equipment and that it has not been disposed of as of December 31, 2016.

5 **P11-10 (Impairment)** At the end of 2015, Sapporo Group tests a machine for impairment. The machine is carried at depreciated historical cost, and its carrying amount is ¥150,000. It has an estimated remaining useful life of 10 years. The machine's recoverable amount is determined on the basis of a value-in-use calculation, using a pretax discount rate of 15%. Management-approved budgets reflect estimated costs necessary to maintain the level of economic benefit expected to arise from the machine in its current condition. The following information related to future cash flows is available at the end of 2015 (amounts in thousands).

Year	Future Cash Flow	Year	Future Cash Flow
2016	¥22,165	2021	¥24,825
2017	21,450	2022	24,123
2018	20,550	2023	25,533
2019	24,725	2024	24,234
2020	25,325	2025	22,850

Instructions

Part I

(a) Compute the amount of the impairment loss at December 31, 2015.

(b) Prepare the journal entry to record the impairment loss, if any, at December 31, 2015.

Part II

In the years 2016–2018, no event occurs that requires the machine's recoverable amount to be re-estimated. At the end of 2019, costs of ¥25,000 are incurred to enhance the machine's performance. Revised estimated cash flows in management's most recent budget are as follows.

Year	Future Cash Flow	Year	Future Cash Flow
2020	¥30,321	2023	¥31,950
2021	32,750	2024	33,100
2022	31,721	2025	27,999

(c) Prepare the journal entry for an impairment or reversal of an impairment at December 31, 2019.

6 **P11-11 (Mineral Resources)** Phelps Oil Wildcatters Group has leased property on which oil has been discovered. Wells on this property produced 36,000 barrels of oil during the past year, which sold at an average sales price of £65 per barrel. Total oil resources of this property are estimated to be 500,000 barrels. The lease provided for an outright payment of £1,200,000 to the lessor (owner) before drilling could be commenced and an annual rental of £62,000. A premium of 4% of the sales price of every barrel of oil removed is to be paid annually to the lessor. In addition, Phelps (lessee) is to clean up all the waste and debris from drilling and to bear the costs of reconditioning the land for farming when the wells are abandoned. The estimated fair value, at the time of the lease, of this clean-up and reconditioning is £50,000.

Instructions

(a) From the provisions of the lease agreement, compute the cost per barrel for the past year, exclusive of operating costs, to Phelps.

(b) Compute the impact on Phelps' current year profit and loss of the operation of the leased property.

(c) Phelps is considering putting in a bid to lease an adjacent tract of land for development, based on some preliminary geological surveys and exploratory drilling. Advise Phelps on how to account for these exploration and evaluation costs.

3 6 P11-12 (Depletion and Depreciation—Mining) Khamsah Mining Company has purchased a tract of mineral land for $900,000. It is estimated that this tract will yield 120,000 tons of ore with sufficient mineral content to make mining and processing profitable. It is further estimated that 6,000 tons of ore will be mined the first and last year and 12,000 tons every year in between. (Assume 11 years of mining operations.) The land will have a residual value of $30,000.

The company builds necessary structures and sheds on the site at a cost of $36,000. It is estimated that these structures can serve 15 years. But, because they must be dismantled if they are to be moved, they have no residual value. The company does not intend to use the buildings elsewhere. Mining machinery installed at the mine was purchased secondhand at a cost of $60,000. This machinery cost the former owner $150,000 and was 50% depreciated when purchased. Khamsah Mining estimates that about half of this machinery will still be useful when the present mineral resources have been exhausted but that dismantling and removal costs will just about offset its value at that time. The company does not intend to use the machinery elsewhere. The remaining machinery will last until about one-half the present estimated mineral ore has been removed and will then be worthless. Cost is to be allocated equally between these two classes of machinery.

Instructions
(a) As chief accountant for the company, you are to prepare a schedule showing estimated depletion and depreciation costs for each year of the expected life of the mine.
(b) Also compute the depreciation and depletion for the first year assuming actual production of 5,000 tons. Nothing occurred during the year to cause the company engineers to change their estimates of either the mineral resources or the life of the structures and equipment.

7 9 *P11-13 (Revaluations) Wang Company owns land (cost HK$200,000) for which it uses revaluation accounting. It has the following information related to this asset, the only land asset that Wang owns.

Date	Fair Value
January 1, 2014	HK$200,000
December 31, 2014	215,000
December 31, 2015	185,000
December 31, 2016	205,000

Instructions
(a) Prepare all entries related to the land for 2014.
(b) Determine the amounts to be reported by Wang at December 31, 2015 and 2016, as Land, Other Comprehensive Income, Impairment Loss, and Accumulated Other Comprehensive Income.
(c) Prepare the entry for any revaluation adjustments at December 31, 2015 and 2016.
(d) Prepare the entries for the sale of the property by Wang on January 15, 2017, for HK$220,000.

7 9 *P11-14 (Revaluations) Parnevik Group uses revaluation accounting for a class of equipment it uses in its golf club refurbishing business. The equipment was purchased on January 2, 2015, for €500,000; it has a 10-year useful life with no residual value. Parnevik has the following information related to the equipment. (Assume that estimated useful life and residual value does not change during the periods presented below.)

Date	Fair Value
January 2, 2015	€500,000
December 31, 2015	468,000
December 31, 2016	380,000
December 31, 2017	355,000

Instructions
(a) Prepare all entries related to the equipment for 2015.
(b) Determine the amounts to be reported by Parnevik at December 31, 2016 and 2017, as Equipment, Other Comprehensive Income, Depreciation Expense, Impairment Loss, and Accumulated Other Comprehensive Income.
(c) Prepare the entry for any revaluation adjustments at December 31, 2016 and 2017.
(d) Prepare the entries for the sale of the equipment by Parnevik on January 2, 2018, for €330,000.

CONCEPTS FOR ANALYSIS

CA11-1 (Depreciation Basic Concepts) Hakodat Manufacturing Company was organized January 1, 2015. During 2015, it has used in its reports to management the straight-line method of depreciating its plant assets.

On November 8, you are having a conference with Hakodat's officers to discuss the depreciation method to be used for income tax and shareholder reporting. Tao Chen, president of Hakodat, has suggested the use of a new method, which he feels is more suitable than the straight-line method for the needs of the company during the period of rapid expansion of production and capacity that he foresees. Following is an example in which the proposed method is applied to a fixed asset with an original cost of ¥248,000, an estimated useful life of 5 years, and a residual value of approximately ¥8,000 (amounts in thousands).

Year	Years of Life Used	Fraction Rate	Depreciation Expense	Accumulated Depreciation at End of Year	Book Value at End of Year
1	1	1/15	¥16,000	¥ 16,000	¥232,000
2	2	2/15	32,000	48,000	200,000
3	3	3/15	48,000	96,000	152,000
4	4	4/15	64,000	160,000	88,000
5	5	5/15	80,000	240,000	8,000

The president favors the new method because he has heard that:

1. It will increase the funds recovered during the years near the end of the assets' useful lives when maintenance and replacement disbursements are high.
2. It will result in increased write-offs in later years and thereby will reduce taxes.

Instructions

(a) What is the purpose of accounting for depreciation?

(b) Is the president's proposal within the scope of international financial reporting standards? In making your decision discuss the circumstances, if any, under which use of the method would be reasonable and those, if any, under which it would not be reasonable.

(c) The president wants your advice on the following issues.

(1) Do depreciation charges recover or create funds? Explain.

(2) Assume that the taxing authorities accept the proposed depreciation method in this case. If the proposed method were used for shareholder and tax reporting purposes, how would it affect the availability of cash flows generated by operations?

CA11-2 (Depreciation—Strike, Units-of-Production, Obsolescence) Presented below are three different and unrelated situations involving depreciation accounting. Answer the question(s) at the end of each situation.

Situation I: Recently, Nai Su Company experienced a strike that affected a number of its operating plants. The controller of this company indicated that it was not appropriate to report depreciation expense during this period because the equipment did not depreciate and an improper matching of costs and revenues would result. She based her position on the following points.

1. It is inappropriate to charge the period with costs for which there are no related revenues arising from production.
2. The basic factor of depreciation in this instance is wear and tear, and because equipment was idle, no wear and tear occurred.

Instructions

Comment on the appropriateness of the controller's comments.

Situation II: Etheridge Company manufactures electrical appliances, most of which are used in homes. Company engineers have designed a new type of blender which, through the use of a few attachments, will perform more functions than any blender currently on the market. Demand for the new blender can be projected with reasonable probability. In order to make the blenders, Etheridge needs a specialized machine that is not available from outside sources. It has been decided to make such a machine in Etheridge's own plant.

Instructions

(a) Discuss the effect of projected demand in units for the new blenders (which may be steady, decreasing, or increasing) on the determination of a depreciation method for the machine.

(b) What other matters should be considered in determining the depreciation method? Ignore income tax considerations.

Situation III: Haley Paper Company operates a 300-ton-per-day kraft pulp mill and four sawmills. The company is in the process of expanding its pulp mill facilities to a capacity of 1,000 tons per day and plans to replace three of its older, less efficient sawmills with an expanded facility. One of the mills to be replaced did not operate for most of 2015 (current year), and there are no plans to reopen it before the new sawmill facility becomes operational.

In reviewing the depreciation rates and in discussing the residual values of the sawmills that were to be replaced, it was noted that if present depreciation rates were not adjusted, substantial amounts of plant costs on these three mills would not be depreciated by the time the new mill came online.

Instructions

What is the proper accounting for the four sawmills at the end of 2015?

CA11-3 (Depreciation Concepts) As a cost accountant for San Francisco Cannery, you have been approached by Phil Perriman, canning room supervisor, about the 2015 costs charged to his department. In particular, he is concerned about the line item "depreciation." Perriman is very proud of the excellent condition of his canning room equipment. He has always been vigilant about keeping all equipment serviced and well oiled. He is sure that the huge charge to depreciation is a mistake; it does not at all reflect the cost of minimal wear and tear that the machines have experienced over the last year. He believes that the charge should be considerably lower.

The machines being depreciated are six automatic canning machines. All were put into use on January 1, 2015. Each cost $625,000, having a residual value of $55,000 and a useful life of 12 years. San Francisco depreciates this and similar assets using double-declining-balance depreciation. Perriman has also pointed out that if you used straight-line depreciation the charge to his department would not be so great.

Instructions

Write a memo to Phil Perriman to clear up his misunderstanding of the term "depreciation." Also, calculate year-1 depreciation on all machines using both methods. Explain the theoretical justification for double-declining-balance and why, in the long run, the aggregate charge to depreciation will be the same under both methods.

CA11-4 (Depreciation Choice) Jerry Prior, Beeler Corporation's controller, is concerned that net income may be lower this year. He is afraid upper-level management might recommend cost reductions by laying off accounting staff, including him.

Prior knows that depreciation is a major expense for Beeler. The company currently uses the double-declining-balance method for both financial reporting and tax purposes, and he's thinking of selling equipment that, given its age, is primarily used when there are periodic spikes in demand. The equipment has a carrying amount of €2,000,000 and a fair value of €2,180,000. The gain on the sale would be reported in the income statement. He doesn't want to highlight this method of increasing income. He thinks, "Why don't I increase the estimated useful lives and the residual values? That will decrease depreciation expense and require less extensive disclosure, since the changes are accounted for prospectively. I may be able to save my job and those of my staff."

Instructions

Answer the following questions.

(a) Who are the stakeholders in this situation?
(b) What are the ethical issues involved?
(c) What should Prior do?

USING YOUR JUDGMENT

FINANCIAL REPORTING

Financial Reporting Problem

Marks and Spencer plc (M&S)

The financial statements of M&S (GBR) are presented in Appendix A. The company's complete annual report, including the notes to the financial statements, is available online.

Instructions

Refer to M&S's financial statements and the accompanying notes to answer the following questions.

(a) What descriptions are used by M&S in its statement of financial position to classify its property, plant, and equipment?

(b) What method or methods of depreciation does M&S use to depreciate its property, plant, and equipment?

(c) Over what estimated useful lives does M&S depreciate its property, plant, and equipment?

(d) What amounts for depreciation expense did M&S charge to its income statement in 2013 and 2012?

(e) What were the capital expenditures for property, plant, and equipment made by M&S in 2013 and 2012?

Comparative Analysis Case

adidas and Puma

The financial statements of **adidas** (DEU) and **Puma** (DEU) are presented in Appendices B and C, respectively. The complete annual reports, including the notes to the financial statements, are available online.

Instructions

Use the companies' financial information to answer the following questions.

(a) What amount is reported in the statements of financial position as property, plant, and equipment (net) of adidas at year-end 2012 and of Puma at year-end 2012? What percentage of total assets is invested in property, plant, and equipment by each company?

(b) What depreciation methods are used by adidas and Puma for property, plant, and equipment? How much depreciation was reported by adidas and Puma in 2012 and 2011?

(c) Compute and compare the following ratios for adidas and Puma for 2012.
   (1) Asset turnover.
   (2) Profit margin on sales.
   (3) Return on assets.

(d) What amount was spent in 2012 for capital expenditures by adidas and Puma? What amount of interest was capitalized in 2012?

Financial Statement Analysis Case

Carrefour Group

Carrefour Group (FRA), the top retailer in Europe (second worldwide), recently had €108.629 billion in sales. It has more than 495,000 employees worldwide, with operations in 31 countries. It is the seventh largest employer worldwide, with 15,430 stores. Carrefour provided the following information in a recent annual report related to its property and equipment.

Carrefour Group
(in millions)

Notes to the Financial Statements (in part)

(3) Tangible fixed assets

In accordance with IAS 16 "Tangible Fixed Assets," land, buildings, equipment, fixtures and fittings are valued at their cost price at acquisition, or at production cost less depreciation and loss in value. The cost of borrowing is not included in the acquisition price of fixed assets. Tangible fixed assets in progress are posted at cost less any identified loss in value. Depreciation of these assets begins when the assets are ready for use. Tangible fixed assets are depreciated on a straight-line basis according to the following average useful lives:

- Construction: • Buildings 40 years
              • Grounds 10 years
              • Car parks 6-and-two-thirds years
- Equipment, fixtures, fittings and installations 6-and-two-thirds years to 8 years
- Other fixed assets 4 to 10 years

Note 8: Depreciation, amortization and provisions

	Current Year	Prior Year	Change
Depreciation of tangible fixed assets	€1,623	€1,484	9.4%

Note 15: Tangible fixed assets

	Current Year	Prior Year
Land	€ 2,913	€ 2,934
Buildings	9,838	9,628
Equipment, fixtures, fittings and installations	14,006	13,219
Other fixed assets	1,159	1,148
Fixed assets in progress	769	790
Leased land, buildings, fixtures	1,717	1,720
Gross tangible fixed assets	30,402	29,439
Accumulated Depreciation	(15,333)	(14,486)
Impairment	(260)	(202)
Net tangible fixed assets	€ 14,809	€ 14,751

Cash Provided by Operations

(euros in millions)	Current Year	Prior Year
Cash provided by operations	€4,887	€3,912
Capital expenditures	2,918	3,069
Cash provided by operations as a percent of capital expenditures	167%	127%

Instructions

(a) What method of depreciation does Carrefour use?

(b) Does depreciation and amortization expense cause cash flow from operations to increase? Explain.

(c) What do the schedule of cash flow measures indicate?

Accounting, Analysis, and Principles

Electroboy Enterprises, Inc. operates several stores throughout northern Belgium and the southern part of the Netherlands. As part of an operational and financial reporting review in a response to a downturn in it markets, the company's management has decided to perform an impairment test on five stores (combined). The five stores' sales have declined due to aging facilities and competition from a rival that opened new stores in the same markets. Management has developed the following information concerning the five stores as of the end of fiscal 2015.

Original cost	€36 million
Accumulated depreciation	€10 million
Estimated remaining useful life	4 years
Estimated expected future annual cash flows (not discounted)	€4.0 million per year
Appropriate discount rate	5%
Fair value less cost of disposal	€23 million

Accounting

(a) Determine the amount of impairment loss, if any, that Electroboy should report for fiscal 2015 and the carrying amount at which Electroboy should report the five stores on its fiscal year-end 2015 statement of financial position. Assume that the cash flows occur at the end of each year.

(b) Repeat part (a), but instead assume that (1) the estimated remaining useful life is 10 years, (2) the estimated annual cash flows are €2,720,000 per year, and (3) the appropriate discount rate is 6%.

Analysis

Assume that you are a financial analyst and you participate in a conference call with Electroboy management in early 2016 (before Electroboy closes the books on fiscal 2015). During the conference call, you learn that management is considering selling the five stores, but the sale will not likely be completed until the second quarter of fiscal 2016. Briefly discuss what implications this would have for Electroboy's 2015 financial statements. Assume the same facts as in part (b) above.

Principles

Electroboy management would like to know the accounting for the impaired asset in periods subsequent to the impairment.

(a) Suppose conditions improve in its markets. Can the assets be written back up? Briefly discuss the conceptual arguments for this accounting.

(b) Briefly describe how IFRS differs from U.S. GAAP with respect to accounting for impaired tangible, long-lived assets. Does U.S. accounting better align with the concept of neutrality? Explain.

International Reporting Case

Liberty International (GBR), a real estate company, follows IFRS. In a recent year, Liberty disclosed the following information on revaluations of its tangible fixed assets. The revaluation reserve measures the amount by which tangible fixed assets are recorded above historical cost and is reported in Liberty's equity.

Liberty International

Completed Investment Properties

Completed investment properties are professionally valued on a market value basis by external valuers at the balance sheet date. Surpluses and deficits arising during the year are reflected in the revaluation reserve.

Liberty reported the following additional data. Amounts for Kimco Realty (USA) (which follows U.S. GAAP) in the same year are provided for comparison.

	Liberty (pounds sterling, in thousands)	Kimco (dollars, in millions)
Total revenues	£ 741	$ 517
Average total assets	5,577	4,696
Net income	125	297

Instructions

(a) Compute the following ratios for Liberty and Kimco.
   (1) Return on assets.
   (2) Profit margin.
   (3) Asset turnover.
   How do these companies compare on these performance measures?

(b) Liberty reports a revaluation surplus in Accumulated Other Comprehensive Income of £1,952. Assume that £1,550 of this amount arose from an increase in the net replacement value of investment properties during the year. Prepare the journal entry to record this increase.

(c) Under IFRS, are Liberty's assets and equity overstated? If so, why? When comparing Liberty to U.S. companies, like Kimco, what adjustments would you need to make in order to have valid comparisons of ratios such as those computed in (a) above?

IFRS BRIDGE TO THE PROFESSION

Professional Research

Matt Holmes recently joined Klax Company as a staff accountant in the controller's office. Klax Company provides warehousing services for companies in several European cities.

The location in Koblenz, Germany, has not been performing well due to increased competition and the loss of several customers that have recently gone out of business. Matt's department manager suspects that the plant and equipment may be impaired and wonders whether those assets should be written down. Given the company's prior success, this issue has never arisen in the past, and Matt has been asked to conduct some research on this issue.

Instructions

Access the IFRS authoritative literature at the IASB website (*http://eifrs.iasb.org/*) (you may register for free eIFRS access at this site). When you have accessed the documents, you can use the search tool in your Internet browser to respond to the following questions. (Provide paragraph citations.)

(a) What is the authoritative guidance for asset impairments? Briefly discuss the scope of the standard (i.e., explain the types of transactions to which the standard applies).

(b) Give several examples of events that would cause an asset to be tested for impairment. Does it appear that Klax should perform an impairment test? Explain.

(c) What is the best evidence of fair value? Describe alternate methods of estimating fair value.

Professional Simulation

In this simulation, you are asked to address questions regarding the accounting for property, plant, and equipment. Prepare responses to all parts.

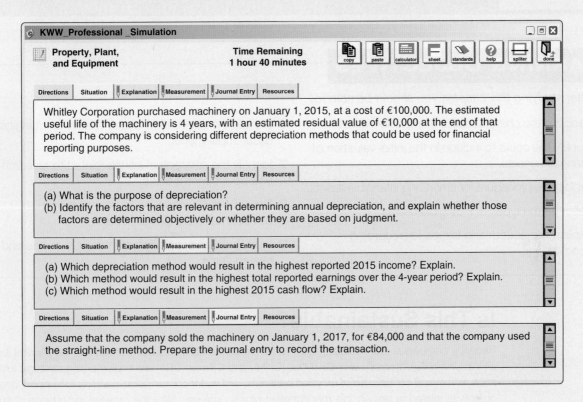

KWW_Professional _Simulation

| Property, Plant, and Equipment | Time Remaining 1 hour 40 minutes | copy paste calculator sheet standards help splitter done |

Directions | Situation | Explanation | Measurement | Journal Entry | Resources

Whitley Corporation purchased machinery on January 1, 2015, at a cost of €100,000. The estimated useful life of the machinery is 4 years, with an estimated residual value of €10,000 at the end of that period. The company is considering different depreciation methods that could be used for financial reporting purposes.

Directions | Situation | Explanation | Measurement | Journal Entry | Resources

(a) What is the purpose of depreciation?
(b) Identify the factors that are relevant in determining annual depreciation, and explain whether those factors are determined objectively or whether they are based on judgment.

Directions | Situation | Explanation | Measurement | Journal Entry | Resources

(a) Which depreciation method would result in the highest reported 2015 income? Explain.
(b) Which method would result in the highest total reported earnings over the 4-year period? Explain.
(c) Which method would result in the highest 2015 cash flow? Explain.

Directions | Situation | Explanation | Measurement | Journal Entry | Resources

Assume that the company sold the machinery on January 1, 2017, for €84,000 and that the company used the straight-line method. Prepare the journal entry to record the transaction.

Remember to check the book's companion website, at www.wiley.com/college/kieso, to find additional resources for this chapter.

12 Intangible Assets

Is This Sustainable?

Recently, companies are increasing their focus on sustainability issues. Companies like **Alcatel Lucent** (FRA), **China Southern Power Grid Co.** (CHN), and **Clorox** (USA) are implementing strategic initiatives such as fuel-spill control, use of recycled materials, and water conservation in efforts to support long-term objectives related to responsible management of resource use. Why the growing importance of sustainability? One important reason is that market participants are increasingly looking to invest in companies that are pursuing sustainability strategies.

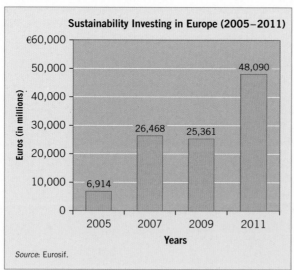

Source: Eurosif.

For example, as indicated in the adjacent graph, sustainability investments in Europe have increased from below €10 trillion in 2005 to nearly €50 trillion in 2011.

As a result of investor focus on sustainability, it is not surprising that some companies are expanding the amount of information provided about their sustainability efforts. This additional information, in turn, helps investors determine the value of these companies. However, rather than adding a line item in the income statement or statement of financial position, companies are instead providing more useful, "non-financial" information about the future cash flow consequences of sustainability strategies.

A good example is the disclosure of information about greenhouse gases. Regulators have recently issued guidance to public companies clarifying the circumstances in which public companies should disclose information related to climate change, as well as the impact on financial performance of their efforts to manage the consequences of greenhouse gas emissions. So here's the paradox: If non-financial data, such as greenhouse gas emissions per dollar of revenue, is included in a financial report for investors, how can it still be called non-financial?

As with the reporting of research and development expenditures and other intangible assets—many of which do not show up on a statement of financial position or income statement—companies are now exploring ways to combine the non-financial information with mandated disclosures in what is called an

integrated report. In such a report, a company discloses data on any of dozens of metrics beyond conventional financial statements, whether the data are "integrated" or released in a separate format. Practitioners collectively refer to sustainability reporting as ESG, for the three major categories of data: environmental, social, and corporate governance.

While a growing number of global companies are issuing sustainability reports, there is significant variation in the content and format. Only a handful, like those prepared by **Clorox** (USA), **SAP** (DEU), and **Polymer Group Inc.** (USA), are integrated with the financial statements. Perhaps sustainability reporting is in need of standards to ensure useful information on environmental, social, and corporate governance issues. Such standards are being proposed by the **International Integrated Reporting Council**.

Sources: S. Lopresti and P. Lilak, "Do Investors Care About Sustainability?" *PricewaterhouseCoopers* (March 2012); E. Rostin, "Non-Financial Data Is Material: The Sustainability Paradox," *www.bloombergnews.com* (April 13, 2012); *European SRI Study*, *http://www.eurosif.org/research/eurosif-sri-study/sri-study-2012* (2012); and E. Chasan, "Taking Corporate Sustainability Reporting to the Next Level," *Wall Street Journal* (November 1, 2013).

CONCEPTUAL FOCUS

> See the **Underlying Concepts** on pages 553, 554, and 562.
> Read the **Evolving Issue** on pages 571–572 for a discussion of recognition of R&D and internally generated intangibles.

INTERNATIONAL FOCUS

> Read the **Global Accounting Insights** on pages 576–577 for a discussion of non-IFRS financial reporting of intangible assets.

PREVIEW OF CHAPTER 12

As our opening story indicates, sustainability strategies are taking on increased importance for companies like **SAP** (DEU) and **Alcatel Lucent** (FRA). Reporting challenges for effective sustainability investments are similar to those for intangible assets. In this chapter, we explain the basic conceptual and reporting issues related to intangible assets. The content and organization of the chapter are as follows.

Intangible Assets

Intangible Asset Issues	Types of Intangibles	Impairment of Intangibles	Research and Development Costs	Presentation of Intangibles and Related Items
• **Characteristics** • **Valuation** • **Amortization**	• **Marketing-related** • **Customer-related** • **Artistic-related** • **Contract-related** • **Technology-related** • **Goodwill**	• **Limited-life intangibles** • **Reversal of impairment loss** • **Indefinite-life intangibles other than goodwill** • **Goodwill**	• **Identifying R&D** • **Accounting for R&D** • **Similar costs**	• **Intangible assets** • **R&D costs**

INTANGIBLE ASSET ISSUES

Characteristics

LEARNING OBJECTIVE ❶

Describe the characteristics of intangible assets.

Christian Dior's (FRA) most important asset is its brand image, not its store fixtures. The Coca-Cola Company's (USA) success comes from its secret formula for making Coca-Cola, not its plant facilities. The world economy is dominated by information and service providers. For these companies, their major assets are often intangible in nature.

What exactly are intangible assets? **Intangible assets** have three main characteristics. **[1]**

I F R S

See the Authoritative Literature section (page 579).

1. *They are identifiable.* To be identifiable, an intangible asset must either be separable from the company (can be sold or transferred), or it arises from a contractual or legal right from which economic benefits will flow to the company.

2. *They lack physical existence.* Tangible assets such as property, plant, and equipment have physical form. Intangible assets, in contrast, derive their value from the rights and privileges granted to the company using them.

3. *They are not monetary assets.* Assets such as bank deposits, accounts receivable, and long-term investments in bonds and shares also lack physical substance. However, monetary assets derive their value from the right (claim) to receive cash or cash equivalents in the future. Monetary assets are not classified as intangibles.

In most cases, intangible assets provide benefits over a period of years. Therefore, companies normally classify them as non-current assets.

Valuation

Purchased Intangibles

LEARNING OBJECTIVE ❷

Identify the costs to include in the initial valuation of intangible assets.

Companies **record at cost** intangibles purchased from another party. Cost includes all acquisition costs plus expenditures to make the intangible asset ready for its intended use. Typical costs include purchase price, legal fees, and other incidental expenses.

Sometimes companies acquire intangibles in exchange for shares or other assets. In such cases, **the cost of the intangible is the fair value of the consideration given or the fair value of the intangible received, whichever is more clearly evident.** What if a company buys several intangibles, or a combination of intangibles and tangibles? In such a "basket purchase," the company should allocate the cost on the basis of fair values. Essentially, the accounting treatment for purchased intangibles closely parallels that for purchased tangible assets.[1]

Internally Created Intangibles

Businesses frequently incur costs on a variety of intangible resources, such as scientific or technological knowledge, market research, intellectual property, and brand names. These costs are commonly referred to as research and development (R&D) costs. Intangible assets that might arise from these expenditures include patents, computer software, copyrights, and trademarks. For example, **Nokia** (FIN) incurred R&D costs to develop its communications equipment, resulting in patents related to its technology. In determining the accounting for these costs, Nokia must determine whether its R&D

---

[1]The accounting in this section relates to the acquisition of a single asset or group of assets. The accounting for intangible assets acquired in a **business combination** (transaction in which the purchaser obtains control of one or more businesses) is discussed later in this chapter.

project is at a sufficiently advanced stage to be considered economically viable. To perform this assessment, Nokia evaluates costs incurred during the **research phase** and the **development phase**.

Illustration 12-1 indicates the two stages of research and development activities, along with the accounting treatment for costs incurred during these phases.

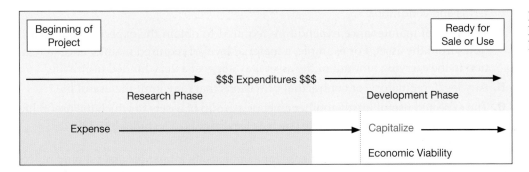

ILLUSTRATION 12-1
Research and
Development Stages

As indicated, all costs incurred in the research phase are expensed as incurred. Once a project moves to the development phase, certain development costs are capitalized. Specifically, development costs are capitalized when certain criteria are met, indicating that an economically viable intangible asset will result from the R&D project. In essence, **economic viability** indicates that the project is far enough along in the process such that the economic benefits of the R&D project will flow to the company. Therefore, development costs incurred from that point forward meet the recognition criteria and should be recorded as an intangible asset.

In summary, **companies expense all research phase costs and some development phase costs. Certain development costs are capitalized once economic viability criteria are met.** IFRS identifies several specific criteria that must be met before development costs are capitalized (which we discuss in more detail later in the chapter).[2]

Underlying Concepts

The controversy surrounding the accounting for R&D expenditures reflects a debate about whether such expenditures meet the definition of an asset. If so, then an "expense all R&D costs" policy results in overstated expenses and understated assets.

Amortization of Intangibles

The allocation of the cost of intangible assets in a systematic way is called **amortization**. Intangibles have either a **limited (finite) useful life** or an **indefinite useful life**. For example, a company like **Disney** (USA) has both types of intangibles. Disney **amortizes** its **limited-life** intangible assets (e.g., copyrights on its movies and licenses related to its branded products). It **does not amortize indefinite-life** intangible assets (e.g., the Disney trade name or its Internet domain name).

3 LEARNING OBJECTIVE
Explain the procedure for amortizing intangible assets.

Limited-Life Intangibles

Companies amortize their limited-life intangibles by systematic charges to expense over their useful life. The useful life should reflect the periods over which these assets will contribute to cash flows. Disney, for example, considers these factors in determining useful life:

1. The expected use of the asset by the company.

2. The effects of obsolescence, demand, competition, and other economic factors. Examples include the stability of the industry, known technological advances, legislative

---

[2]IFRS also prohibits recognition of intangible assets such as internally generated brands, mastheads, and customer lists. These expenditures are similar to other costs to develop the business as whole; therefore, they do not meet the separately identifiable criterion. **[2]**

action that results in an uncertain or changing regulatory environment, and expected changes in distribution channels.

3. Any provisions (legal, regulatory, or contractual) that enable renewal or extension of the asset's legal or contractual life without substantial cost. This factor assumes that there is evidence to support renewal or extension. Disney also must be able to accomplish renewal or extension without material modifications of the existing terms and conditions.

4. The level of maintenance expenditure required to obtain the expected future cash flows from the asset. For example, a material level of required maintenance in relation to the carrying amount of the asset may suggest a very limited useful life.

5. Any legal, regulatory, or contractual provisions that may limit the useful life.

6. The expected useful life of another asset or a group of assets to which the useful life of the intangible asset may relate (such as lease rights to a studio lot). **[3]**

The amount of amortization expense for a limited-life intangible asset should reflect the pattern in which the company consumes or uses up the asset, if the company can reliably determine that pattern. For example, assume that Second Wave, Inc. purchases a license to provide a specified quantity of a gene product called Mega. Second Wave should amortize the cost of the license following the pattern of use of Mega. If Second Wave's license calls for it to provide 30 percent of the total the first year, 20 percent the second year, and 10 percent per year until the license expires, it would amortize the license cost using that pattern. If it cannot determine the pattern of production or consumption, Second Wave should use the straight-line method of amortization. (*For homework problems, assume the use of the straight-line method unless stated otherwise.*) **When Second Wave amortizes this license, it should show the charges as expenses. It should credit either the appropriate asset accounts or separate accumulated amortization accounts.**

The amount of an intangible asset to be amortized should be its cost less residual value. The residual value is assumed to be zero, unless at the end of its useful life the intangible asset has value to another company. For example, if Hardy Co. commits to purchasing an intangible asset from U2D Co. at the end of the asset's useful life, U2D Co. should reduce the cost of its intangible asset by the residual value. Similarly, U2D Co. should consider fair values, if reliably determined, for residual values.

> ### Underlying Concepts
>
> The terms "carrying amount," "carrying value," and "book value" are all used to refer to the cost less accumulated amortization of intangible assets.

IFRS requires companies to assess the estimated residual values and useful lives of intangible assets at least annually. What happens if the life of a limited-life intangible asset changes? In that case, the remaining carrying amount should be amortized over the revised remaining useful life. Companies must also evaluate the limited-life intangibles annually to determine if there is an indication of impairment. If there is indication of impairment, an impairment test is performed.

An impairment loss should be recognized for the amount that the carrying amount of the intangible is greater than the recoverable amount. Recall that the recoverable amount is the greater of the fair value less costs to sell or value-in-use. (We will cover impairment of intangibles in more detail later in the chapter.)

Indefinite-Life Intangibles

If no factors (legal, regulatory, contractual, competitive, or other) limit the useful life of an intangible asset, a company considers its useful life indefinite. An **indefinite life** means that there is no foreseeable limit on the period of time over which the intangible asset is expected to provide cash flows. A company **does not amortize** an intangible asset with an indefinite life. To illustrate, assume that Double Clik Inc. acquired a trademark that it uses to distinguish a leading consumer product. It renews the trademark every 10 years. All evidence indicates that this trademark product will generate cash flows for an indefinite period of time. In this case, the trademark has an indefinite life; Double Clik does not record any amortization.

Companies also must test indefinite-life intangibles for **impairment** at least annually. The **impairment test** for indefinite-life intangibles is similar to the one for limited-life intangibles. That is, an impairment loss should be recognized for the amount that the carrying amount of the indefinite-life intangible asset is greater than the recoverable amount.[3]

Illustration 12-2 summarizes the accounting treatment for intangible assets.[4]

ILLUSTRATION 12-2
Accounting Treatment
for Intangibles

Type of Intangible	Manner Acquired		Amortization	Impairment Test
	Purchased	Internally Created		
Limited-life intangibles	Capitalize	Expense*	Over useful life	Compare recoverable amount to carrying value.
Indefinite-life intangibles	Capitalize	Expense*	Do not amortize	Compare recoverable amount to carrying value.
	* (Except for certain limited costs that meet recognition criteria.)			

TYPES OF INTANGIBLE ASSETS

There are many different types of intangibles, often classified into the following six major categories. **[5]**

4 LEARNING OBJECTIVE

Describe the types of intangible assets.

1. Marketing-related intangible assets.

2. Customer-related intangible assets.

3. Artistic-related intangible assets.

4. Contract-related intangible assets.

5. Technology-related intangible assets.

6. Goodwill.

Marketing-Related Intangible Assets

Companies primarily use **marketing-related intangible assets** in the marketing or promotion of products or services. Examples are trademarks or trade names, newspaper mastheads, Internet domain names, and non-competition agreements.

A **trademark** or **trade name** is a word, phrase, or symbol that distinguishes or identifies a particular company or product. Trade names like Mercedes-Benz, Pepsi-Cola, Honda, Cadbury Eggs, Wheaties, and Ikea create immediate product identification in

---

[3]For limited-life intangibles, the impairment test is performed only if there is indication of impairment. However, the impairment test for indefinite-life intangibles must be conducted annually. This more stringent test is required because indefinite-life intangibles are not amortized, and the recognized amounts may be subject to significant judgment.

[4]Similar to long-lived tangible assets, companies may revalue certain types of intangible assets subsequent to acquisition. The revaluation model can only be used for intangible assets that trade in active markets (e.g., taxi licenses or similar contracts). **[4]** This constraint, as well as the cost to perform the annual revaluation process, explains the limited use of the revaluation option for intangible assets. See I. von Kleits and KPMG IFRG Limited, *The Application of IFRS: Choices in Practice* (December 2006), p. 11.

our minds, thereby enhancing marketability. A recent expansion of Internet domain names will allow industries to use terms like .cars or even web slang like .lol. This expansion has led to a new wave of domain-name activity. For a fee of $185,000, companies can register their own domain names; applications received include company names such as Sony (JPN) (which would have the name .sony) and for city-based domains such as .NYC and .Berlin.

Under common law, the right to use a trademark or trade name, whether registered or not, rests exclusively with the original user as long as the original user continues to use it. For example, in the United States, registration with the U.S. Patent and Trademark Office provides legal protection for an **indefinite number of renewals for periods of 10 years each**.[5] Therefore, a company that uses an established trademark or trade name may properly consider it to have an indefinite life and does not amortize its cost.

If a company buys a trademark or trade name, it capitalizes the cost at the purchase price. If a company develops a trademark or trade name, it capitalizes costs related to securing it, such as attorney fees, registration fees, design costs, consulting fees, and successful legal defense costs. However, it excludes research costs and development costs that do not meet recognition criteria. When the total cost of a trademark or trade name is insignificant, a company simply expenses it.

What do the numbers mean?   *KEEP YOUR HANDS OFF MY INTANGIBLE!*

Companies go to great extremes to protect their valuable intangible assets. Consider how the creators of the highly successful game *Trivial Pursuit* protected their product. First, they copyrighted the 6,000 questions that are at the heart of the game. Then, they shielded the *Trivial Pursuit* name by applying for a registered trademark. As a third mode of protection, they obtained a design patent on the playing board's design as a unique graphic creation.

Another example is the iPhone trade name. Cisco Systems (USA) sued Apple (USA) for using the iPhone trade name when Apple introduced its hot new phone in 2007. Not so fast, said Cisco, which had held the iPhone trade name since 2000 and was using it on its own Voice over Internet Protocol (VoIP) products. The two companies came to an agreement for joint use of the name. It was not disclosed what Apple paid for this arrangement, but it is not surprising why Apple would want to settle—to avoid a costly delay to the launch of its highly anticipated iPhone.

Source: Nick Wingfield, "Apple, Cisco Reach Accord Over iPhone," *Wall Street Journal Online* (February 22, 2007).

Customer-Related Intangible Assets

Customer-related intangible assets result from interactions with outside parties. Examples include customer lists, order or production backlogs, and both contractual and non-contractual customer relationships.

To illustrate, assume that Green Market Inc. acquires the customer list of a large newspaper for €6,000,000 on January 1, 2015. This customer database includes name, contact details, order history, and demographic information. Green Market expects to benefit from the information evenly over a three-year period. In this case, the customer list is a limited-life intangible that Green Market should amortize on a straight-line basis.

---

[5]The legal life of trade names or trademarks may vary across countries. However, over 70 countries, including members of the European Union (EU), Australia, and the United States, are party to the Madrid Protocol, which recognizes the trade names and trademarks registered in other member countries (see *http://www.ipo.gov.uk/*).

Green Market records the purchase of the customer list and the amortization of the customer list at the end of each year as follows.

January 1, 2015

Customer List	6,000,000	
Cash		6,000,000
(To record purchase of customer list)		

December 31, 2015, 2016, 2017

Amortization Expense (customer list)	2,000,000	
Customer List (or Accumulated Customer List Amortization)		2,000,000
(To record amortization expense)		

The preceding example assumed no residual value for the customer list. But what if Green Market determines that it can sell the list for €60,000 to another company at the end of three years? In that case, Green Market should subtract this residual value from the cost in order to determine the amortization expense for each year. Amortization expense would be €1,980,000 per year, as shown in Illustration 12-3.

Cost	€6,000,000
Residual value	(60,000)
Amortization base	€5,940,000
Amortization expense per period: €1,980,000 (€5,940,000 ÷ 3)	

ILLUSTRATION 12-3
Calculation of Amortization Expense with Residual Value

Companies should assume a zero residual value unless the asset's useful life is less than the economic life and reliable evidence is available concerning the residual value. **[6]**

Artistic-Related Intangible Assets

Artistic-related intangible assets involve ownership rights to plays, literary works, musical works, pictures, photographs, and video and audiovisual material. Copyrights protect these ownership rights.

A **copyright** is a government-granted right that all authors, painters, musicians, sculptors, and other artists have in their creations and expressions. A copyright is granted for the **life of the creator plus 70 years**.[6] It gives the owner or heirs the exclusive right to reproduce and sell an artistic or published work. Copyrights are not renewable.

Copyrights can be valuable. In the late 1990s, Disney (USA) faced the loss of its copyright on Mickey Mouse, which could have affected sales of billions of dollars of Mickey-related goods and services (including theme parks). This copyright was so important that Disney and many other big entertainment companies fought all the way to the U.S. Supreme Court—and won an extension of copyright lives from 50 to 70 years.

---

[6]As with trademarks and trade names, the legal life of a copyright may vary across countries. However, the United Kingdom, the countries of the European Union, and the United States all have the same copyright length.

As another example, Really Useful Group (USA) owns copyrights on the musicals of Andrew Lloyd Webber—*Cats, Phantom of the Opera, Jesus Christ-Superstar,* and others. Really Useful Group has little in the way of tangible assets, yet analysts value the company at over $300 million.

Companies capitalize the costs of acquiring and defending a copyright. They amortize any capitalized costs over the useful life of the copyright if less than its legal life (life of the creator plus 70 years). For example, Really Useful Group should allocate the costs of its copyrights to the years in which it expects to receive the benefits. The difficulty of determining the number of years over which it will receive benefits typically encourages a company like Really Useful Group to write off these costs over a fairly short period of time. Companies must expense all research costs and any development costs not meeting recognition criteria that lead to a copyright as those costs are incurred.

Contract-Related Intangible Assets

Contract-related intangible assets represent the value of rights that arise from contractual arrangements. Examples are franchise and licensing agreements, construction permits, broadcast rights, and service or supply contracts.

A franchise is a contractual arrangement under which the franchisor grants the franchisee the right to sell certain products or services, to use certain trademarks or trade names, or to perform certain functions, usually within a designated geographical area. When you purchase a Prius from a Toyota (JPN) dealer, fill up your tank at the corner Shell (NLD) station, or eat lunch at a McDonald's (USA) restaurant, you are most likely dealing with franchises.

The franchisor, having developed a unique concept or product, protects its concept or product through a patent, copyright, or trademark or trade name. The franchisee acquires the right to exploit the franchisor's idea or product by signing a franchise agreement.

Another type of franchise arrangement, granted by a governmental body, permits a business to use public property in performing its services. Examples are the use of city streets for a bus line or taxi service; the use of public land for telephone, electric, or cable television lines; and the use of airwaves for radio or TV broadcasting. Such operating rights are referred to as licenses or permits.

Franchises and licenses may be for a definite period of time, for an indefinite period of time, or perpetual. The company securing the franchise or license carries an intangible asset account (entitled Franchises or Licenses) on its books, only when it can identify costs with the acquisition of the operating right. (Such costs might be legal fees or an advance lump-sum payment, for example.) **A company should amortize the cost of a franchise (or license) with a limited life as operating expense over the life of the franchise.** It should not amortize a franchise with an indefinite life nor a perpetual franchise; the company should instead carry such franchises at cost.

Annual payments made under a franchise agreement should be entered as operating expenses in the period in which they are incurred. These payments do not represent an asset since they do not relate to *future rights* to use the property.

Technology-Related Intangible Assets

Technology-related intangible assets relate to innovations or technological advances. Examples are patented technology and trade secrets granted by a governmental body.

In many countries, a **patent** gives the holder exclusive right to use, manufacture, and sell a product or process **for a period of 20 years** without interference or infringement by others.[7] Companies such as Merck (USA) and Canon (JPN) were founded on patents and built on the exclusive rights thus granted.[8] The two principal kinds of patents are **product patents**, which cover actual physical products, and **process patents**, which govern the process of making products.

If a company like Samsung (KOR) purchases a patent from an inventor, the purchase price represents its cost. Samsung can capitalize other costs incurred in connection with securing a patent, as well as attorneys' fees and other unrecovered costs of a successful legal suit to protect the patent, as part of the patent cost. However, it **must expense all research costs and any development costs incurred before achieving economic viability** related to the **development** of the product, process, or idea that it subsequently patents. (We discuss accounting for research and development costs in more detail on pages 569–570.)

Companies should amortize the cost of a patent over its legal life or its useful life (the period in which benefits are received), **whichever is shorter**. If Samsung owns a patent from the date it is granted and expects the patent to be useful during its entire legal life, the company should amortize it over 20 years. If it appears that the patent will be useful for a shorter period of time, say, for five years, it should amortize its cost over five years.

Changing demand, new inventions superseding old ones, inadequacy, and other factors often limit the useful life of a patent to less than the legal life. For example, the useful life of pharmaceutical patents is frequently less than the legal life because of the testing and approval period that follows their issuance. A typical drug patent has several years knocked off its 20-year legal life. Why? Because, in the United States, a drugmaker spends one to four years on animal tests, four to six years on human tests, and two to three years for the U.S. Food and Drug Administration to review the tests. All this time occurs *after* issuing the patent but *before* the product goes on pharmacists' shelves.

As mentioned earlier, companies capitalize the costs of defending copyrights. The accounting treatment for a patent defense is similar. **A company charges all legal fees and other costs incurred in successfully defending a patent suit to Patents**, an asset account. Such costs should be amortized along with acquisition cost over the remaining useful life of the patent.

Amortization expense should reflect the pattern, if reliably determined, in which a company uses up the patent.[9] A company may credit amortization of patents directly to the Patents account or to an Accumulated Patent Amortization account. To illustrate, assume that Harcott Co. incurs $180,000 in legal costs on January 1, 2015, to successfully defend a patent. The patent's useful life is 20 years, amortized on a

---

[7]While patent lives may vary across countries, the term of protection under most modern patent laws is 20 years from the filing date of the application. Over 140 countries are party to the Patent Cooperation Treaty (PCT), which was ratified in 1970 and most recently amended in 2001. The PCT makes it possible to seek patent protection for an invention simultaneously in each of a large number of countries by filing an "international" patent application (see *http://www.wipo.int/ patentscope/en/patents/*).

[8]Consider the opposite result: Sir Alexander Fleming, who discovered penicillin, decided not to use a patent to protect his discovery. He hoped that companies would produce it more quickly to help save sufferers. Companies, however, refused to develop it because they did not have the patent shield and, therefore, were afraid to make the investment.

[9]Companies may compute amortization using the activity method in a manner similar to that described for depreciation on property, plant, and equipment.

straight-line basis. Harcott records the legal fees and the amortization at the end of 2015 as follows.

January 1, 2015

Patents	180,000	
Cash		180,000
(To record legal fees related to patent)		

December 31, 2015

Patent Amortization Expense ($180,000 ÷ 20)	9,000	
Patents (or Accumulated Patent Amortization)		9,000
(To record amortization of patent)		

We've indicated that a patent's useful life should not extend beyond its legal life of 20 years. However, companies often make small modifications or additions that lead to a new patent. For example, **Astra Zeneca plc** (GBR) filed for additional patents on minor modifications to its heartburn drug, Prilosec. The effect may be to extend the life of the old patent. If the new patent provides essentially the same benefits, Astra Zeneca can apply the unamortized costs of the old patent to the new patent.

Alternatively, if a patent becomes impaired because demand drops for the product, the asset should be written down or written off immediately to expense.

What do the numbers mean?   PATENTS—STRATEGIC LIFEBLOOD

Are patents valuable assets, even though they are intangible? Let's take a look at **BASF** (DEU), a leading international chemical company. Here is the BASF strategy statement regarding innovation:

"... innovation is key to profitable growth in a competitive global marketplace. Therefore, we maintain our high level of investment in research and development, and network globally with universities, institutes, customers and industrial partners."

And BASF acts on this strategy through expenditures on research and development, which many times lead to valuable patents. For example, in a recent year, BASF spent €1,746 million on research and development (that's 35.8% of net income), and it expected product innovation alone (from products on the market less than 10 years) to generate annual sales of €30 billion. In that year alone, BASF filed 1,170 patents worldwide.

Because patented technology is so important to BASF's success, it is not surprising that it provides expansive disclosure of patent-related information in its financial statements. Here is an excerpt, from the note disclosure.

Assets	2012	2011
Intangible assets (000,000)	€12,241	€11,919

11—INTANGIBLE ASSETS (in part)

	Know-how, patents and production technology
Acquisition costs	
Balance as of January 1, 2012	€2,002
Additions	198
Disposals/Transfers	(249)
Exchange differences, other	(8)
Balance as of December 31, 2012	1,943
Accumulated amortization	(653)
Net carrying value	€1,290

This development schedule (sometimes referred to as a "roll-forward") provides reconciliation of the changes in the intangible asset account. This information is important for understanding the magnitude of this important intangible asset and how it changed during the period. Note that while BASF's total intangible assets increased during the year, there was a net decrease in its patent balance. This would be something to watch, given the importance of patented innovations in the BASF strategy.

Goodwill

Although companies may capitalize certain costs incurred in developing specifically identifiable assets such as patents and copyrights, the amounts capitalized are generally insignificant. But companies do record material amounts of intangible assets when purchasing intangible assets, particularly in situations involving a business combination (the purchase of another business).

5 LEARNING OBJECTIVE

Explain the accounting issues for recording goodwill.

To illustrate, assume that Portofino Company decides to purchase Aquinas Company. In this situation, Portofino measures the assets acquired and the liabilities assumed at fair value. In measuring these assets and liabilities, Portofino must identify all the assets and liabilities of Aquinas. As a result, Portofino may recognize some assets or liabilities not previously recognized by Aquinas. For example, Portofino may recognize intangible assets such as a brand name, patent, or customer list that were not recorded by Aquinas. In this case, Aquinas may not have recognized these assets because they were developed internally and charged to expense.[10]

In many business combinations, the purchasing company records goodwill. Goodwill is measured as the excess of the cost of the purchase over the fair value of the identifiable net assets (assets less liabilities) purchased. For example, if Portofino paid $2,000,000 to purchase Aquinas's identifiable net assets (with a fair value of $1,500,000), Portofino records goodwill of $500,000. Goodwill is therefore measured as a residual rather than measured directly. That is why goodwill is sometimes referred to as a *plug*, a **gap filler**, or a **master valuation account**.

Conceptually, goodwill represents the future economic benefits arising from the other assets acquired in a business combination that are not individually identified and separately recognized. It is often called "the most intangible of the intangible assets" because it is identified only with the business as a whole. The only way to sell goodwill is to sell the business.

Recording Goodwill

Internally Created Goodwill. **Goodwill generated internally should not be capitalized in the accounts.** The reason? Measuring the components of goodwill is simply too complex, and associating any costs with future benefits is too difficult. The future benefits of goodwill may have no relationship to the costs incurred in the development of that goodwill. To add to the mystery, goodwill may even exist in the absence of specific costs to develop it. Finally, because no objective transaction with outside parties takes place, a great deal of subjectivity—even misrepresentation—may occur.

---

[10]IFRS **[7]** provides detailed guidance regarding the recognition of identifiable intangible assets in a business combination. With this guidance, the IASB expected that companies would recognize more identifiable intangible assets, and less goodwill, in the financial statements as a result of business combinations.

Purchased Goodwill. As indicated earlier, **goodwill is recorded only when an entire business is purchased.** To record goodwill, a company compares the fair value of the net tangible and identifiable intangible assets with the purchase price (cost) of the acquired business. The difference is considered goodwill. **Goodwill is the residual—the excess of cost over fair value of the identifiable net assets acquired.**

To illustrate, Feng, Inc. decides that it needs a parts division to supplement its existing tractor distributorship. The president of Feng is interested in buying Tractorling S.A., a small concern in São Paulo, Brazil. Illustration 12-4 presents Tractorling's statement of financial position.

ILLUSTRATION 12-4
Tractorling Statement of Financial Position

TRACTORLING S.A.			
STATEMENT OF FINANCIAL POSITION			
AS OF DECEMBER 31, 2015			
Assets		**Equities**	
Property, plant, and equipment, net	$153,000	Share capital	$100,000
Inventory	42,000	Retained earnings	100,000
Accounts receivable	35,000	Current liabilities	55,000
Cash	25,000		
Total assets	$255,000	Total equities	$255,000

After considerable negotiation, Tractorling decides to accept Feng's offer of $400,000. What, then, is the value of the goodwill, if any?

The answer is not obvious. Tractorling's historical cost-based statement of financial position does not disclose the fair values of its identifiable assets. Suppose, though, that as the negotiations progress, Feng investigates Tractorling's underlying assets to determine their fair values. Such an investigation may be accomplished either through a purchase audit undertaken by Feng or by an independent appraisal from some other source. The investigation determines the valuations shown in Illustration 12-5.

ILLUSTRATION 12-5
Fair Value of Tractorling's Net Assets

Fair Values	
Property, plant, and equipment, net	$205,000
Patents	18,000
Inventory	122,000
Accounts receivable	35,000
Cash	25,000
Liabilities	(55,000)
Fair value of net assets	$350,000

Normally, differences between fair value and book value are more common among non-current assets than among current assets. Cash obviously poses no problems as to value. Receivables normally are fairly close to current valuation although they may at times need certain adjustments due to inadequate bad debt provisions. Liabilities usually are stated at book value. However, if interest rates have changed since the company incurred the liabilities, a different valuation (such as present value based on expected cash flows) is appropriate. Careful analysis must be made to determine that no unrecorded liabilities are present.

The $80,000 difference in Tractorling's inventories ($122,000 − $42,000) could result from a number of factors. The most likely is that the company uses the average-cost method. Recall that during periods of inflation, average-cost will result in lower inventory valuations than FIFO.

In many cases, the values of non-current assets such as property, plant, and equipment and intangibles may have increased substantially over the years. This difference could be due to inaccurate estimates of useful lives, continual expensing of small expenditures (say, less than $300), inaccurate estimates of residual values, and the discovery of some unrecorded assets. (For example, in Tractorling's case, analysis determines Patents have a fair value of $18,000.) Or, fair values may have substantially increased.

Since the investigation now determines the fair value of net assets to be $350,000, why would Feng pay $400,000? Undoubtedly, Tractorling points to its established reputation, good credit rating, top management team, well-trained employees, and so on. These factors make the value of the business greater than $350,000. Feng places a premium on the future earning power of these attributes as well as on the basic asset structure of the company today.

Feng labels the difference between the purchase price of $400,000 and the fair value of $350,000 as goodwill. Goodwill is viewed as one or a group of unidentifiable values (intangible assets), the cost of which "is measured by the difference between the cost of the group of assets or enterprise acquired and the sum of the assigned costs of individual tangible and identifiable intangible assets acquired less liabilities assumed."[11] This procedure for valuation is called a **master valuation approach**. It assumes goodwill covers all the values that cannot be specifically identified with any identifiable tangible or intangible asset. Illustration 12-6 shows this approach.

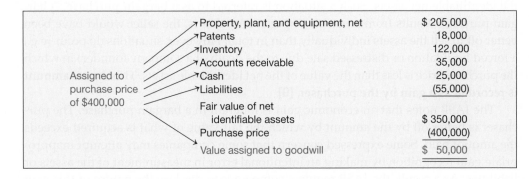

Assigned to purchase price of $400,000	Property, plant, and equipment, net	$ 205,000
	Patents	18,000
	Inventory	122,000
	Accounts receivable	35,000
	Cash	25,000
	Liabilities	(55,000)
	Fair value of net identifiable assets	$ 350,000
	Purchase price	(400,000)
	Value assigned to goodwill	$ 50,000

ILLUSTRATION 12-6
Determination of Goodwill—Master Valuation Approach

Feng records this transaction as follows.

Property, Plant, and Equipment	205,000	
Patents	18,000	
Inventory	122,000	
Accounts receivable	35,000	
Cash	25,000	
Goodwill	50,000	
Liabilities		55,000
Cash		400,000

[11]The IASB expressed concern about measuring goodwill as a residual but noted that there is no real measurement alternative since goodwill is not separable from the company as a whole. **[8]**

Companies often identify goodwill on the statement of financial position as the **excess of cost over the fair value** of the net assets acquired.

Goodwill Write-Off

Companies that recognize goodwill in a business combination **consider it to have an indefinite life and therefore should not amortize it**. Although goodwill may decrease in value over time, predicting the actual life of goodwill and an appropriate pattern of amortization is extremely difficult. In addition, investors find the amortization charge of little use in evaluating financial performance.

Furthermore, the investment community wants to know the amount invested in goodwill, which often is the largest intangible asset on a company's statement of financial position. Therefore, **companies adjust its carrying value only when goodwill is impaired**. This approach significantly impacts the income statements of some companies.

Some believe that goodwill's value eventually disappears. Therefore, they argue, companies should charge goodwill to expense over the periods affected, to better match expense with revenues. Others note that the accounting treatment for purchased goodwill and goodwill created internally should be consistent. They point out that companies immediately expense goodwill created internally and should follow the same treatment for purchased goodwill. Though these arguments may have some merit, non-amortization of goodwill combined with an adequate impairment test should provide the most useful financial information to the investment community. We discuss the accounting for goodwill impairments later in the chapter.

Bargain Purchase

In a few cases, the purchaser in a business combination pays *less than* the fair value of the identifiable net assets. Such a situation is referred to as a bargain purchase. A bargain purchase results from a market imperfection, that is, the seller would have been better off to sell the assets individually than in total. However, situations do occur (e.g., a forced liquidation or distressed sale due to the death of a company founder) in which the purchase price is less than the value of the net identifiable assets. **This excess amount is recorded as a gain by the purchaser. [9]**

The IASB notes that an economic gain is inherent in a bargain purchase. The purchaser is better off by the amount by which the fair value of what is acquired exceeds the amount paid. Some expressed concern that some companies may attempt inappropriate gain recognition by making an intentional error in measurement of the assets or liabilities. As a result, the IASB requires companies to disclose the nature of this gain transaction. Such disclosure will help users to better evaluate the quality of the earnings reported.

IMPAIRMENT OF INTANGIBLE ASSETS

LEARNING OBJECTIVE 6

Explain the accounting issues related to intangible asset impairments.

An intangible asset is impaired when a company is not able to recover the asset's carrying amount either through using it or by selling it. As discussed in Chapter 11, to determine whether a long-lived asset (property, plant, and equipment or intangible assets) is impaired, a review is made of the asset's cash-generating ability through use or sale. If the carrying amount is higher than the recoverable amount, the difference is an impairment loss. If the recoverable amount is greater than the carrying amount, no impairment is recorded. **[10]** The specific procedures for recording impairments depend on the type of intangible asset—limited-life or indefinite-life (including goodwill).

Impairment of Limited-Life Intangibles

The rules that apply to **impairments of property, plant, and equipment also apply to limited-life intangibles**. At each statement of financial position date, a company should review limited-life intangibles for impairment. Information indicating that an impairment test should be performed might be internal (e.g., physical damage or adverse changes in performance) or external (e.g., adverse changes in the business or regulatory environment, or technological or competitive developments). If there is an indication that an intangible asset is impaired, the company performs an impairment test: compare the carrying value of the intangible asset to the recoverable amount.

Recall that the **recoverable amount** is defined as the higher of fair value less costs to sell or value-in-use. Fair value less costs to sell means what the asset could be sold for after deducting costs of disposal. Value-in-use is the present value of cash flows expected from the future use and eventual sale of the asset at the end of its useful life. The **impairment loss** is the carrying amount of the asset less the recoverable amount of the impaired asset. As with other impairments, the loss is reported in profit or loss. Companies generally report the loss in the "Other income and expense" section.

To illustrate, assume that Lerch, Inc. has a patent on how to extract oil from shale rock, with a carrying value of €5,000,000 at the end of 2014. Unfortunately, several recent non-shale-oil discoveries adversely affected the demand for shale-oil technology, indicating that the patent is impaired. Lerch determines the recoverable amount for the patent, based on value-in-use (because there is no active market for the patent). Lerch estimates the patent's value-in-use at €2,000,000, based on the discounted expected net future cash flows at its market rate of interest. Illustration 12-7 shows the impairment loss computation (based on value-in-use).

Carrying value of patent	€5,000,000
Recoverable amount (based on value-in-use)	(2,000,000)
Loss on impairment	€3,000,000

ILLUSTRATION 12-7
Computation of Loss on Impairment of Patent

Lerch records this loss as follows.

Loss on Impairment	3,000,000	
Patents		3,000,000

After recognizing the impairment, the recoverable amount of €2,000,000 is the new cost basis of the patent. Lerch should amortize the patent's recoverable amount (new carrying amount) over its remaining useful life or legal life, whichever is shorter.

Reversal of Impairment Loss

What happens if a review in a future year indicates that an intangible asset is no longer impaired because the recoverable amount of the asset is higher than the carrying amount? In that case, the impairment loss may be reversed. To illustrate, continuing the Lerch patent example, assume that the remaining life of the patent is five years with zero residual value. Recall the carrying value of the patent after impairment is €2,000,000 (€5,000,000 − €3,000,000). Thus, Lerch's amortization is €400,000 (€2,000,000 ÷ 5) over the remaining five years of the patent's life. The amortization expense and related carrying amount after the impairment is shown in Illustration 12-8.

ILLUSTRATION 12-8
Post-Impairment
Carrying Value of Patent

Year	Amortization Expense	Carrying Amount	
2015	€400,000	€1,600,000	(€2,000,000 − €400,000)
2016	400,000	1,200,000	(€1,600,000 − €400,000)
2017	400,000	800,000	(€1,200,000 − €400,000)
2018	400,000	400,000	(€800,000 − €400,000)
2019	400,000	0	(€400,000 − €400,000)

Early in 2016, based on improving conditions in the market for shale-oil technology, Lerch remeasures the recoverable amount of the patent to be €1,750,000. In this case, Lerch reverses a portion of the recognized impairment loss with the following entry.

Patents (€1,750,000 − €1,600,000)	150,000	
Recovery of Impairment Loss		150,000

The recovery of the impairment loss is reported in the "Other income and expense" section of the income statement. The carrying amount of the patent is now €1,750,000 (€1,600,000 + €150,000).[12] Assuming the remaining life of the patent is four years, Lerch records €437,500 (€1,750,000 ÷ 4) of amortization expense in 2016.

Impairment of Indefinite-Life Intangibles Other Than Goodwill

Companies test indefinite-life intangibles (including goodwill) for impairment annually.[13] The impairment test for indefinite-life assets other than goodwill is the same as that for limited-life intangibles. That is, compare the recoverable amount of the intangible asset with the asset's carrying value. If the recoverable amount is less than the carrying amount, the company recognizes an impairment.

To illustrate, assume that Arcon Radio purchased a broadcast license for €2,000,000. The license is renewable every 10 years if the company provides appropriate service and does not violate Government Communications Commission (GCC) rules. Arcon Radio has renewed the license with the GCC twice, at a minimal cost. Because it expects cash flows to last indefinitely, Arcon reports the license as an indefinite-life intangible asset. Recently, the GCC decided to auction these licenses to the highest bidder instead of renewing them. Based on recent auctions of similar licenses, Arcon Radio estimates the fair value less costs to sell (the recoverable amount) of its license to be €1,500,000. Arcon therefore reports an impairment loss of €500,000, computed as shown in Illustration 12-9.

ILLUSTRATION 12-9
Computation of Loss on
Impairment of Broadcast
License

Carrying value of broadcast license	€2,000,000
Recoverable amount (based on fair value less costs to sell)	(1,500,000)
Loss on impairment	€ 500,000

Guidelines for reversal of impairments similar to those applied to limited-life intangible assets are applied to indefinite-life intangible assets other than goodwill.

[12]As with impairments of property, plant, and equipment, the amount of the recovery of the loss is limited to the carrying value amount that would result if the impairment had not occurred.

[13]Note that the impairment test is performed every year (not only when there is an impairment indicator). This more stringent impairment model for indefinite-life intangibles (and goodwill) is used because these assets are not amortized and the recognized amounts may be subject to significant judgment.

Impairment of Goodwill

The timing of the impairment test for goodwill is the same as that for other indefinite-life intangibles. That is, companies must test goodwill at least annually. However, because goodwill generates cash flows only in combination with other assets, the impairment test is conducted based on the cash-generating unit to which the goodwill is assigned. Recall from our discussion in Chapter 11 that companies identify a **cash-generating unit** based on the smallest identifiable group of assets that generate cash flows independently of the cash flows from other assets. Under IFRS, when a company records goodwill in a business combination, it must assign the goodwill to the cash-generating unit that is expected to benefit from the synergies and other benefits arising from the business combination.

To illustrate, assume that Kohlbuy Corporation has three divisions. It purchased one division, Pritt Products, four years ago for €2 million. Unfortunately, Pritt experienced operating losses over the last three quarters. Kohlbuy management is now reviewing the division (the cash-generating unit), for purposes of its annual impairment testing. Illustration 12-10 lists the Pritt Division's net assets, including the associated goodwill of €900,000 from the purchase.

Property, plant, and equipment (net)	€ 800,000
Goodwill	900,000
Inventory	700,000
Receivables	300,000
Cash	200,000
Accounts and notes payable	(500,000)
Net assets	€2,400,000

ILLUSTRATION 12-10
Net Assets of Pritt Division, Including Goodwill

Kohlbuy determines the recoverable amount for the Pritt Division to be €2,800,000, based on a value-in-use estimate.[14] **Because the fair value of the division exceeds the carrying amount of the net assets, Kohlbuy does not recognize any impairment.**

However, if the recoverable amount for the Pritt Division were less than the carrying amount of the net assets, then Kohlbuy must record an impairment. To illustrate, assume that the recoverable amount for the Pritt Division is €1,900,000 instead of €2,800,000. Illustration 12-11 computes the amount of the impairment loss to be recorded.

Recoverable amount of Pritt Division	€ 1,900,000
Net identifiable assets	(2,400,000)
Loss on impairment	€ 500,000

ILLUSTRATION 12-11
Determination of Impairment for the Pritt Division

Kohlbuy makes the following entry to record the impairment.

Loss on Impairment	500,000	
Goodwill		500,000

Following this entry, the carrying value of the goodwill is €400,000.

---

[14]Because there is rarely a market for cash-generating units, estimation of the recoverable amount for goodwill impairments is usually based on value-in-use estimates.

If conditions change in subsequent periods, such that the recoverable amount of the Pritt Division's assets other than goodwill exceeds their carrying value, Kohlbuy may reverse an impairment loss on the Pritt Division assets other than goodwill. **Goodwill impairment loss reversals are not permitted. [11]** [15]

RESEARCH AND DEVELOPMENT COSTS

Research and development (R&D) costs are not in themselves intangible assets. However, we present the accounting for R&D costs here because R&D activities frequently result in the development of patents or copyrights (such as a new product, process, idea, formula, composition, or literary work) that may provide future value.

As indicated in the opening story, many companies spend considerable sums on research and development. Illustration 12-12 shows the outlays for R&D made by selected companies.

ILLUSTRATION 12-12
R&D Outlays, as a Percentage of Sales

Company	Sales (in millions)	R&D/Sales
Canon (JPN)	¥3,479,788	8.52%
Daimler (DEU)	€114,297	3.66%
GlaxoSmithKline (GBR)	£26,431	15.01%
Johnson & Johnson (USA)	$67,224	13.13%
Nokia (FIN)	€30,176	15.85%
Roche (CHE)	CHF45,449	21.02%
Procter & Gamble (USA)	$83,680	2.42%
Samsung (KOR)	₩201,103,613	5.73%

As discussed earlier, IFRS requires that all research costs be expensed as incurred. Development costs may or may not be expensed as incurred. Once a project moves to the development phase, certain development costs are capitalized. Capitalization begins when the project is far enough along in the process such that the economic benefits of the R&D project will flow to the company (the project is economically viable). [16] *For purposes of homework, assume that all R&D costs are expensed as incurred unless stated otherwise.*

[15] In the Kohlbuy case, the entire impairment loss is allocated to goodwill. If the impairment loss exceeds the carrying value of the goodwill, Kohlbuy allocates the impairment loss to the goodwill and other assets as follows: (1) reduce the goodwill to zero and (2) allocate any remaining impairment loss to the other assets on the basis of their relative carrying amounts. In this case, Kohlbuy follows the impairment guidelines for long-lived assets, as discussed in Chapter 11. If these assets are evaluated for impairment on an individual basis, impairment losses may have been recorded on these assets as part of that process. Alternatively, the Kohlbuy example could represent a situation in which the other assets are evaluated at the cash-generating-unit level. These procedures are complex and beyond the scope of this textbook.

[16] All of the following criteria must be met to begin capitalizing development costs into the carrying value of the related intangible: (1) the project achieves technical feasibility of completing the intangible asset so that it will be available for use or sale; (2) the company intends, and has the ability, to complete the intangible asset and use or sell it; (3) the intangible asset will generate probable future economic benefits (there is a market for the asset or the output of the asset); (4) the company has adequate technical, financial, and other resources to complete the development of the intangible asset; and (5) the company can measure reliably the development costs associated with the intangible asset to be developed. **[12]**

Research and development investments are the lifeblood of product and process developments that lead to future cash flows and growth. Countries around the world understand this and as a result provide significant incentives in the form of tax credits, "superdeductions" (deductions greater than 100%), and corporate tax rate reductions, including "patent box" rates for companies that own and use patents registered in that country. Here is a summary for seven major economies.

Country	Statutory Tax Rate	R&D Incentives
China	25.00%	Offers a reduced corporate income tax rate for certain entities, along with a 150% superdeduction. China also offers several other indirect tax incentives for R&D.
France	33.33%	Offers a 30% tax credit for research expenses, as well as a patent box incentive reducing the corporate tax rate to 15% on qualifying intellectual property income.
Ireland	12.50%	Offers corporations a refundable 25% credit for research expenses and has implemented various government grants for expanding R&D activities in Ireland.
Japan	28.01%	Provides a non-refundable maximum credit of a percentage of R&D expenditures, up to 20% of the corporation's total tax liability.
Singapore	17.00%	Offers a productivity and innovation credit that allows a 400% superdeduction on certain qualifying R&D expenses and offers multiple grants covering multiple fields of innovation.
United Kingdom	20.00–23.00%	Offers a refundable tax credit of 9.1% of qualifying R&D expenditures and allows 100% tax depreciation of expenditures on assets used for R&D in the year of acquisition, a superdeduction of 130% to 225%, and a 10% patent rate for net income originating from qualifying intellectual property.
United States	35.00%	Offers an annual deduction for R&D spending and a non-refundable tax credit for incremental R&D spending and permits an incremental credit for "qualified research" and "basic research" equal to 20% of eligible expenses.

As indicated, there are wide variations in both statutory tax rates and R&D incentives. However, tax credits, government incentives, and corporate tax rates may constitute only a fraction of the relevant factors a corporation considers when evaluating development centers. In addition, depending on the politics of tax provisions, there can be year-to-year uncertainty in corporate tax planning, thereby weakening the effectiveness of such incentives.

Source: L. Cutler, D. Sayuk, and Camille Shoff, "Global R&D Incentives Compared," *Journal of Accountancy* (June 2013).

Identifying R&D Activities

Illustration 12-13 (on page 570) shows the definitions for research activities and development activities. These definitions differentiate research and development costs from other similar costs. **[13]**

R&D activities do not include routine or periodic alterations to existing products, production lines, manufacturing processes, and other ongoing operations, even though these alterations may represent improvements. For example, routine ongoing efforts to refine, enrich, or improve the qualities of an existing product are not considered R&D activities.

ILLUSTRATION 12-13
Research Activities
versus Development
Activities

Research Activities	Development Activities
Original and planned investigation undertaken with the prospect of gaining new scientific or technical knowledge and understanding.	Application of research findings or other knowledge to a plan or design for the production of new or substantially improved materials, devices, products, processes, systems, or services before the start of commercial production or use.
Examples	**Examples**
Laboratory research aimed at discovery of new knowledge; searching for applications of new research findings.	Conceptual formulation and design of possible product or process alternatives; construction of prototypes and operation of pilot plants.

Accounting for R&D Activities

LEARNING OBJECTIVE 8

Describe the accounting for research and development and similar costs.

The costs associated with R&D activities and the accounting treatments accorded them are as follows.

1. *Materials, equipment, and facilities.* Expense the entire costs, **unless the items have alternative future uses** (in other projects or otherwise). If there are alternative future uses, carry the items as inventory and allocate as consumed, or capitalize and depreciate as used.

2. *Personnel.* Expense as incurred salaries, wages, and other related costs of personnel engaged in R&D.

3. *Purchased intangibles.* Recognize and measure at fair value. After initial recognition, account for in accordance with their nature (as either limited-life or indefinite-life intangibles).[17]

4. *Contract services.* Expense the costs of services performed by others in connection with the R&D as incurred.

5. *Indirect costs.* Include a reasonable allocation of indirect costs in R&D costs, except for general and administrative costs, which must be clearly related in order to be included in R&D.

Consistent with item 1 above, if a company owns a research facility that conducts R&D activities and that has alternative future uses (in other R&D projects or otherwise), it should capitalize the facility as an operational asset. The company accounts for depreciation and other costs related to such research facilities as R&D expenses.

To illustrate, assume that Next Century Incorporated develops, produces, and markets laser machines for medical, industrial, and defense uses. Illustration 12-14 lists the types of expenditures related to its laser-machine activities, along with the recommended accounting treatment.

---

[17]If R&D-related intangibles (often referred to as *in-process R&D*) are also acquired in a business combination, they are also recognized and measured at fair value. After initial recognition, these intangible assets are accounted for in accordance with their nature (as either limited-life or indefinite-life intangibles). **[14]**

NEXT CENTURY INCORPORATED

Type of Expenditure	Accounting Treatment	Rationale
1. Construction of long-range research facility for use in current and future projects (three-story, 400,000-square-foot building).	Capitalize and depreciate as R&D expense.	Has alternative future use.
2. Acquisition of R&D equipment for use on current project only.	Expense immediately as R&D.	Research cost.
3. Acquisition of machinery for use on current and future R&D projects.	Capitalize and depreciate as R&D expense.	Has alternative future use.
4. Purchase of materials for use on current and future R&D projects.	Inventory and allocate to R&D projects; expense as consumed.	Has alternative future use.
5. Salaries of research staff designing new laser bone scanner.	Expense immediately as R&D.	Research cost.
6. Research costs incurred under contract with New Horizon, Inc., and billable monthly.	Record as a receivable.	Not R&D cost (reimbursable expense).
7. Material, labor, and overhead costs of prototype laser scanner (economic viability not achieved).	Expense immediately as R&D.	Does not meet recognition criteria.
8. Costs of testing prototype and design modifications (economic viability not achieved).	Expense immediately as R&D.	Does not meet recognition criteria.
9. Legal fees to obtain patent on new laser scanner.	Capitalize as patent and amortize to overhead as part of cost of goods manufactured.	Direct cost of patent.
10. Executive salaries.	Expense as operating expense.	Not R&D cost (general and administrative expense).
11. Cost of marketing research to promote new laser scanner.	Expense as operating expense.	Not R&D cost (selling expense).
12. Engineering costs incurred to advance the laser scanner to full production stage (economic viability achieved).	Capitalize as R&D.	Meets recognition criteria.
13. Costs of successfully defending patent on laser scanner.	Capitalize as patent and amortize to overhead as part of cost of goods manufactured.	Direct cost of patent.
14. Commissions to sales staff marketing new laser scanner.	Expense as operating expense.	Not R&D cost (selling expense).

ILLUSTRATION 12-14
Sample R&D
Expenditures and Their
Accounting Treatment

Evolving Issue — RECOGNITION OF R&D AND INTERNALLY GENERATED INTANGIBLES

The requirement that companies expense immediately all research and many development costs (as well as start-up costs) incurred internally is a practical solution. It ensures consistency in practice and uniformity among companies. But the practice of immediately writing off expenditures made in the expectation of benefiting future periods is conceptually incorrect.

Proponents of immediate expensing contend that from an income statement standpoint, long-run application of this standard frequently makes little difference. They argue that because of the ongoing nature of most companies' R&D activities, the amount of R&D cost charged to expense each accounting period is about the same, whether there is immediate expensing or capitalization and subsequent amortization.

Others criticize this practice. They believe that the statement of financial position should report an intangible asset related to expenditures that have future benefit. To preclude capitalization of all R&D expenditures removes from the statement of financial position what may be a company's most valuable asset.

Indeed, research findings indicate that capitalizing R&D costs may be helpful to investors. For example, one study showed a significant relationship between R&D outlays and subsequent benefits in the form of increased productivity, earnings, and shareholder value for R&D-intensive companies. Another study found that there was a significant decline in earnings usefulness for companies that were forced to switch from capitalizing to expensing R&D costs, and that the decline appears to persist over time.

The current accounting for R&D and other internally generated intangible assets represents one of the many trade-offs made among relevance, faithful representation, and cost-benefit considerations. The FASB and IASB have completed some limited-scope projects on the accounting for intangible assets, and the Boards have contemplated a joint project on the accounting for identifiable intangible assets (i.e., excluding goodwill). Such a project would address concerns that the current accounting requirements lead to inconsistent treatments for some types of intangible assets depending on how they arise. (See *http://www.ifrs.org/Current-Projects/IASB-Projects/Intangible-Assets/Pages/Intangible-Assets.aspx*.)

Sources for research studies: Baruch Lev and Theodore Sougiannis, "The Capitalization, Amortization, and Value-Relevance of R&D," *Journal of Accounting and Economics* (February 1996); and Martha L. Loudder and Bruce K. Behn, "Alternative Income Determination Rules and Earnings Usefulness: The Case of R&D Costs," *Contemporary Accounting Research* (Fall 1995).

Costs Similar to R&D Costs

Many costs have characteristics similar to research and development costs.[18] Examples are:

1. Start-up costs for a new operation.
2. Initial operating losses.
3. Advertising costs.

For the most part, these costs are expensed as incurred, similar to the accounting for research costs. We briefly explain these costs in the following sections.

Start-Up Costs

Start-up costs are incurred for one-time activities to start a new operation. Examples include opening a new plant, introducing a new product or service, or conducting business in a new territory. Start-up costs include organizational costs, such as legal and governmental fees incurred to organize a new business entity.

The accounting for start-up costs is straightforward: **Expense start-up costs as incurred.** The profession recognizes that companies incur start-up costs with the expectation of future revenues or increased efficiencies. However, determining the amount and timing of future benefits is so difficult that a conservative approach—expensing these costs as incurred—is required. **[16]**

To illustrate examples of start-up costs, assume that U.S.-based Hilo Beverage Company decides to construct a new plant in Brazil. This represents Hilo's first entry into the Brazilian market. Hilo plans to introduce the company's major U.S. brands into Brazil on a locally produced basis. The following costs might be involved:

1. Travel-related costs; costs related to employee salaries; and costs related to feasibility studies, accounting, tax, and government affairs.
2. Training of local employees related to product, maintenance, computer systems, finance, and operations.
3. Recruiting, organizing, and training related to establishing a distribution network.

Hilo Beverage should expense all these start-up costs as incurred.

---

[18]With the growth in online selling activities, internally developed websites represent a significant source of internally generated intangible assets. IFRS has specific criteria for determining whether the development costs associated with websites meet capitalization thresholds. In essence, these criteria assess whether the website is economically viable in generating sales for the company. **[15]**

Start-up activities commonly occur at the same time as activities involving the acquisition of assets. For example, as it is incurring start-up costs for the new plant, Hilo probably is also buying or building property, plant, equipment, and inventory. Hilo should not immediately expense the costs of these tangible assets. Instead, it should report them on the statement of financial position using appropriate IFRS reporting guidelines.

Initial Operating Losses

Some contend that companies should be allowed to capitalize initial operating losses incurred in the start-up of a business. They argue that such operating losses are an unavoidable cost of starting a business.

For example, assume that Hilo lost money in its first year of operations and wishes to capitalize this loss. Hilo's CEO argues that as the company becomes profitable, it will offset these losses in future periods. What do *you* think? We believe that this approach is unsound, since losses have no future service potential and therefore cannot be considered an asset.

IFRS requires that operating losses during the early years **should not be capitalized**. In short, **the accounting and reporting standards should be no different for an enterprise trying to establish a new business than they are for other enterprises. [17]**[19]

Advertising Costs

Over the years, **PepsiCo** (USA) has hired various pop stars, such as Justin Timberlake and Beyoncé, to advertise its products. How should it report such advertising costs related to its star spokespeople? PepsiCo could expense the costs in various ways:

1. When the pop stars have completed their singing assignments.
2. The first time the advertising runs.
3. Over the estimated useful life of the advertising.
4. In an appropriate fashion to each of the three periods identified above.
5. Over the period revenues are expected to result.

PepsiCo must expense these advertising costs as incurred. The IASB acknowledges that advertising and promotional activities may enhance or create customer relationships, which in turn generate revenues. However, those expenditures are no different than other internally generated intangible assets (e.g., brands, mastheads, and customer lists), which primarily contribute to the development of the business as a whole. Therefore, they do not meet the separately identifiable criterion and should be expensed as incurred. **[18]**

What do the numbers mean? | BRANDED

For many companies, developing a strong brand image is as important as developing the products they sell. Now more than ever, companies see the power of a strong brand, enhanced by significant and effective advertising investments.

As the following chart indicates, the value of brand investments is substantial. **Coca-Cola** (USA) heads the list with an estimated brand value of about $78 billion. Companies from around the globe are represented in the top 20 brands.

---

[19]A company is considered to be in the developing stages when it is directing its efforts toward establishing a new business and either the company has not started the principal operations or it has earned no significant revenue.

Valuable Global Brands			
(in billions)			
1 Coca-Cola (USA)	$77.8	9 Samsung (KOR)	$32.9
2 Apple (USA)	76.6	10 Toyota (JPN)	30.3
3 IBM (USA)	75.5	11 Mercedes-Benz (DEU)	30.1
4 Google (USA)	69.7	12 BMW (DEU)	29.1
5 Microsoft (USA)	57.9	17 Louis Vuitton (FRA)	23.6

Source: 2012 data, from Interbrand Corp.

Occasionally, you may find the value of a brand included in a company's financial statements under goodwill. But generally you will not find the estimated values of brands recorded in companies' statements of financial position. The reason? The subjectivity that goes into estimating a brand's value. In some cases, analysts base an estimate of brand value on opinion polls or on some multiple of advertising spending. For example, in estimating the brand values

shown above, Interbrand Corp. (USA) estimates the percentage of the overall future revenues the brand will generate and then discounts the net cash flows, to arrive at a present value. Some analysts believe that information on brand values is relevant. Others voice valid concerns about the reliability of brand value estimates due to subjectivity in the estimates for revenues, costs, and the risk component of the discount rate.

Source: Interbrand Corp., *Best Global Brands Report* (October 2, 2012).

PRESENTATION OF INTANGIBLES AND RELATED ITEMS

Presentation of Intangible Assets

LEARNING OBJECTIVE 9

Indicate the presentation of intangible assets and related items.

The reporting of intangible assets is similar to the reporting of property, plant, and equipment. However, contra accounts may not be shown for intangibles on the statement of financial position.

As indicated, on the statement of financial position, companies should report as a separate item all intangible assets other than goodwill. If goodwill is present, companies should report it separately. The IASB concluded that since goodwill and other intangible assets differ significantly from other types of assets, such disclosure benefits users of the statement of financial position.

On the income statement, companies should present amortization expense and impairment losses and reversals for intangible assets other than goodwill separately in net income (usually in the operating section), usually presented as a separate line item.

The notes to the financial statements should include information about acquired intangible assets, including the amortization expense for each type of asset. The notes should include information about changes in the carrying amount of each type of intangible asset during the period.

Illustration 12-15 shows an excerpt of the intangible asset reporting for Nestlé (CHE). Note that Nestlé uses the label "Balance Sheet" for its statement of financial position. Another example of an intangible asset disclosure is provided for BASF (DEU) in the "What do the numbers mean?" box on page 560.

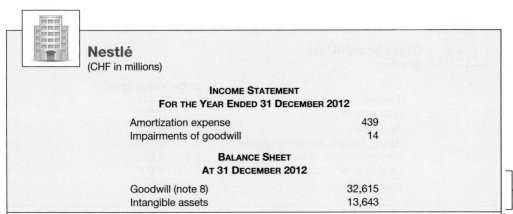

ILLUSTRATION 12-15
Nestlé's Intangible Asset
Disclosures

Nestlé
(CHF in millions)

INCOME STATEMENT
FOR THE YEAR ENDED 31 DECEMBER 2012

Amortization expense	439
Impairments of goodwill	14

BALANCE SHEET
AT 31 DECEMBER 2012

Goodwill (note 8)	32,615
Intangible assets	13,643

Separate reporting for goodwill and other intangible assets

1. Accounting policies (in part)

Intangible assets

This heading includes intangible assets that are acquired either separately or in a business combination when they are identifiable and can be reliably measured. Intangible assets comprise indefinite life intangible assets and finite life intangible assets. Indefinite life intangible assets are those for which there is no foreseeable limit to their useful economic life as they arise from contractual or other legal rights that can be renewed without significant cost and are the subject of continuous marketing support.

The depreciation period and depreciation method are reviewed annually by taking into account the risk of obsolescence. Depreciation of intangible assets is allocated to the appropriate headings of expenses by function in the income statement.

Impairment of goodwill and indefinite life intangible assets

Goodwill and indefinite life intangible assets are tested for impairment at least annually and upon the occurrence of an indication of impairment. The impairment tests are performed annually at the same time each year and at the cash generating unit (CGU) level. The Group defines its CGUs based on the way that it monitors and derives economic benefits from the acquired goodwill and intangibles. The impairment tests are performed by comparing the carrying value of the assets of these CGUs with their recoverable amount, based on their future projected cash flows discounted at an appropriate pre-tax rate of return.

8. Goodwill (in millions of CHF)	2012	
Gross value		
At 1 January	30,951	
Currency retranslations	(589)	
Goodwill from acquisitions	4,217	
Disposals	(263)	
At 31 December		**34,316**
Accumulated impairments		
At 1 January	(1,943)	
Currency retranslations	(7)	
Impairments	(14)	
Disposals	263	
At 31 December		**(1,701)**
Net at 31 December		**32,615**

Information on changes in carrying amounts of intangible assets

Presentation of Research and Development Costs

Companies should disclose in the financial statements (generally in the notes) the total R&D costs charged to expense each period for which they present an income statement. GlaxoSmithKline (GBR), a global research pharmaceutical company, reported research and development in its recent income statement, with related accounting policy discussion in the notes as shown in Illustration 12-16 (on page 576).

ILLUSTRATION 12-16
R&D Reporting

GlaxoSmithKline
(in millions)

	31 December 2012
Turnover	£26,431
Cost of Sales	(7,894)
Gross Profit	18,537
Selling, General, and Administrative	(8,739)
Research and Development	(3,968)
Other Operating Income	1,562
Operating Profit	£ 7,392

Note 1 (in part) Research and development

Research and development expenditure is charged to the income statement in the period in which it is incurred. Development expenditure is capitalised when the criteria for recognising an asset are met, usually when a regulatory filing has been made in a major market and approval is considered highly probable. Property, plant and equipment used for research and development is depreciated in accordance with the Group's policy.

GLOBAL ACCOUNTING INSIGHTS

INTANGIBLE ASSETS

There are some significant differences between IFRS and U.S. GAAP in the accounting for both intangible assets and impairments. U.S. GAAP related to intangible assets is presented in FASB literature addressing Goodwill and Other Intangible Assets and Business Combinations. The accounting for research and development, start-up costs, and advertising costs are prescribed in separate parts of the FASB literature.

Relevant Facts

Following are the key similarities and differences between U.S. GAAP and IFRS related to intangible assets.

Similarities

- Like IFRS, under U.S. GAAP intangible assets (1) lack physical substance and (2) are not financial instruments. In addition, under IFRS an intangible asset is identifiable. To be identifiable, an intangible asset must either be separable from the company (can be sold or transferred) or it arises from a contractual or legal right from which economic benefits will flow to the company. Fair value is used as the measurement basis for intangible assets under U.S. GAAP if it is more clearly evident.

- With the issuance of a recently converged statement on business combinations (*IFRS 3* and *SFAS No. 141—Revised*), U.S. GAAP and IFRS are very similar for intangibles acquired in a business combination. That is, companies recognize an intangible asset separately from goodwill if the intangible represents contractual or legal rights or is capable of being separated or divided and sold, transferred, licensed, rented, or exchanged. In addition, under both IFRS and U.S. GAAP, companies recognize acquired in-process research and development (IPR&D) as a separate intangible asset if it meets the definition of an intangible asset and its fair value can be measured reliably.

- As in IFRS, under U.S. GAAP the costs associated with research and development are segregated into the two components. Costs in the research phase are always expensed under both U.S. GAAP and IFRS.

Differences

- U.S. GAAP does not permit the revaluation basis of accounting. While under IFRS revaluations are not permitted for goodwill, revaluation of other indefinite-life intangible assets are rare because revaluations are not allowed unless there is an active market for the intangible asset.

- U.S. GAAP requires expensing of all costs associated with internally generated intangibles. IFRS permits some capitalization of internally generated intangible assets (e.g., brand value) if it is probable there will be a future benefit and the amount can be reliably measured.

- Under U.S. GAAP, impairment loss is measured as the excess of the carrying amount over the asset's fair value. IFRS requires an impairment test at each reporting date for long-lived assets and intangibles, and records an impairment if the asset's carrying amount exceeds its recoverable amount. The recoverable amount is the higher of the asset's fair value less costs to sell and its value-in-use. **Value-in-use** is the future cash flows to be derived from the particular asset, discounted to present value.

- U.S. GAAP gives companies the option to perform a qualitative assessment to determine whether it is more likely than not (i.e., a likelihood of more than 50 percent) that an indefinite-life intangible asset (including goodwill) is impaired. If the qualitative assessment indicates that the fair value of the reporting unit is more likely than not to be greater than the carrying value (i.e., the asset is not impaired), the company need not continue with the fair value test.

- Under U.S. GAAP, impairment losses cannot be reversed for assets to be held and used; the impairment loss results in a new cost basis for the asset. IFRS and U.S. GAAP are similar in the accounting for impairments of assets held for disposal. IFRS allows reversal of impairment losses when there has been a change in economic conditions or in the expected use of limited-life intangibles and indefinite-life intangibles other than goodwill.

- Under U.S. GAAP, all development costs are expensed as incurred. Under IFRS, costs in the development phase of a research and development project are capitalized once technological feasibility (referred to as **economic viability**) is achieved.

About the Numbers

To illustrate the effect of differences in the accounting for brands, consider the following disclosure by GlaxoSmithKline (GBR) in a recent annual report. Note that GlaxoSmithKline would report lower income by £1.3 billion if it accounted for its brands under U.S. GAAP.

Notes to the Financial Statements

Intangible assets (in part):
The following table sets out the IFRS to U.S. GAAP adjustments required to the IFRS income statement for amortisation of brands:

Income Statement

	(£ million)
Amortisation charge under IFRS	(139)
Amortisation charge under U.S. GAAP	1,454
IFRS to U.S. GAAP adjustment	1,315

On the Horizon

The IASB has identified a project, in a very preliminary stage, which would consider expanded recognition of internally generated intangible assets. As indicated, IFRS permits more recognition of intangibles compared to U.S. GAAP. Thus, it will be challenging to develop converged standards for intangible assets, given the long-standing prohibition on capitalizing internally generated intangible assets and research and development in U.S. GAAP. Learn more about the timeline for the intangible asset project at the IASB website: *http://www.ifrs.org/Current-Projects/IASB-Projects/Intangible-Assets/Pages/Intangible-Assets.aspx.*

SUMMARY OF LEARNING OBJECTIVES

1 Describe the characteristics of intangible assets. Intangible assets have three main characteristics: (1) they are identifiable, (2) they lack physical existence, and (3) they are not monetary assets. In most cases, intangible assets provide services over a period of years and so are normally classified as non-current assets.

2 Identify the costs to include in the initial valuation of intangible assets. Intangibles are recorded at cost. Cost includes all acquisition costs and expenditures needed to make the intangible asset ready for its intended use. If intangibles are acquired in exchange for shares or other assets, the cost of the intangible is the fair value of the consideration given or the fair value of the intangible received, whichever is more clearly evident. When a company makes a "basket purchase" of several intangibles or a combination of intangibles and tangibles, it should allocate the cost on the basis of relative fair values.

3 Explain the procedure for amortizing intangible assets. Intangibles have either a limited useful life or an indefinite useful life. Companies amortize limited-life intangibles. They do not amortize indefinite-life intangibles. Limited-life intangibles should be amortized by systematic charges to expense over their useful life. The useful life should reflect the period over which these assets will contribute to cash flows. The amount to report for amortization expense should reflect the pattern in which a company consumes or uses up the asset, if it can reliably determine that pattern. Otherwise, use a straight-line approach.

4 Describe the types of intangible assets. Major types of intangibles are (1) *marketing-related intangibles*, used in the marketing or promotion of products or services; (2) *customer-related intangibles*, resulting from interactions with outside parties; (3) *artistic-related intangibles*, giving ownership rights to such items as plays and literary works; (4) *contract-related intangibles*, representing the value of rights that arise from contractual arrangements; (5) *technology-related intangibles*, relating to innovations or technological advances; and (6) *goodwill*, arising from business combinations.

5 Explain the accounting issues for recording goodwill. Unlike receivables, inventories, and patents that a company can sell or exchange individually in the marketplace, goodwill can be identified only with the company as a whole. Goodwill is a "going concern" valuation and is recorded only when an entire business is purchased. A company should not capitalize goodwill generated internally. The future benefits of goodwill may have no relationship to the costs incurred in the development of that goodwill. Goodwill may exist even in the absence of specific costs to develop it.

To record goodwill, a company compares the fair value of the net tangible and identifiable intangible assets with the purchase price of the acquired business. The difference is considered goodwill. Goodwill is the residual. Goodwill is often identified on the statement of financial position as the excess of cost over the fair value of the net assets acquired.

6 Explain the accounting issues related to intangible asset impairments. An intangible asset is impaired when a company is not able to recover the asset's carrying amount either through using it or by selling it. Limited-life intangibles are reviewed annually to determine if there are impairment indicators; if so, the impairment test is performed. Indefinite-life intangibles, including goodwill, must be tested for impairment every year. An impairment loss is recorded in net income if the recoverable amount (the greater of fair value less costs to sell and value-in-use) of an intangible asset is less than the carrying value. Impairment losses on intangible assets (other than goodwill) may be reversed but only up to the carrying amount that would have been recorded in the absence of the impairment.

7 **Identify the conceptual issues related to research and development costs.** R&D costs are not in themselves intangible assets, but R&D activities frequently result in the development of something a company patents or copyrights. The difficulties in accounting for R&D expenditures are (1) identifying the costs associated with particular activities, projects, or achievements; and (2) determining the magnitude of the future benefits and length of time over which a company may realize such benefits. Because of these latter uncertainties, companies are required to expense all research costs when incurred. Certain costs incurred during the development phase of an R&D project are capitalized when an R&D project achieves economic viability.

8 **Describe the accounting for research and development and similar costs.** Illustration 12-14 (page 571) shows the costs associated with R&D activities and the accounting treatment accorded them. Many costs have characteristics similar to R&D costs. Examples are start-up costs, initial operating losses, and advertising costs. For the most part, these costs are expensed as incurred, similar to the accounting for all research and many development costs.

9 **Indicate the presentation of intangible assets and related items.** On the statement of financial position, companies should report all intangible assets other than goodwill as a separate item. Contra accounts are not normally shown. If goodwill is present, it too should be reported as a separate item. On the income statement, companies should report amortization expense and impairment losses in operating income. The notes to the financial statements have additional detailed information. Financial statements must disclose the total R&D costs charged to expense each period for which an income statement is presented.

IFRS AUTHORITATIVE LITERATURE

Authoritative Literature References

[1] International Accounting Standard 38, *Intangible Assets* (London, U.K.: International Accounting Standards Committee Foundation, 2004), paras. 8–17.

[2] International Accounting Standard 38, *Intangible Assets* (London, U.K.: International Accounting Standards Committee Foundation, 2004), paras. 48–67.

[3] International Accounting Standard 38, *Intangible Assets* (London, U.K.: International Accounting Standards Committee Foundation, 2004), par. 90.

[4] International Accounting Standard 38, *Intangible Assets* (London, U.K.: International Accounting Standards Committee Foundation, 2004), paras. 75–87.

[5] International Financial Reporting Standard 3, *Business Combinations* (London, U.K.: International Accounting Standards Committee Foundation, 2004), paras. IE16–IE44.

[6] International Accounting Standard 38, *Intangible Assets* (London, U.K.: International Accounting Standards Committee Foundation, 2004), par. 100.

[7] International Financial Reporting Standard 3, *Business Combinations* (London, U.K.: International Accounting Standards Committee Foundation, 2004), paras. 13 and BC157–BC158.

[8] International Financial Reporting Standard 3, *Business Combinations* (London, U.K.: International Accounting Standards Committee Foundation, 2004), par. BC328.

[9] International Financial Reporting Standard 3, *Business Combinations* (London, U.K.: International Accounting Standards Committee Foundation, 2004), paras. 34–36.

[10] International Accounting Standard 36, *Impairment of Assets* (London, U.K.: International Accounting Standards Committee Foundation, 2001).

[11] International Accounting Standard 36, *Impairment of Assets* (London, U.K.: International Accounting Standards Committee Foundation, 2001), par. 124.

[12] International Accounting Standard 38, *Intangible Assets* (London, U.K.: International Accounting Standards Committee Foundation, 2004), par. 57.

[13] International Accounting Standard 38, *Intangible Assets* (London, U.K.: International Accounting Standards Committee Foundation, 2004), paras. 56–59.

[14] International Accounting Standard 38, *Intangible Assets* (London, U.K.: International Accounting Standards Committee Foundation, 2004), paras. 42–43.

[15] International Accounting SIC Interpretation 32, *Intangible Assets—Web Site Costs* (London, U.K.: International Accounting Standards Committee Foundation, 2002).

[16] International Accounting Standard 38, *Intangible Assets* (London, U.K.: International Accounting Standards Committee Foundation, 2004), par. 69.

[17] International Accounting Standard 38, *Intangible Assets* (London, U.K.: International Accounting Standards Committee Foundation, 2004), par. 69(a).

[18] International Accounting Standard 38, *Intangible Assets* (London, U.K.: International Accounting Standards Committee Foundation, 2004), par. 69(c).

QUESTIONS

1. What are the three main characteristics of intangible assets?

2. If intangibles are acquired for shares, how is the cost of the intangible determined?

3. Intangibles have either a limited useful life or an indefinite useful life. How should these two different types of intangibles be amortized?

4. Why does IFRS make a distinction between internally created intangibles and purchased intangibles?

5. In 2015, Ghostbusters Corp. spent €420,000 for "goodwill" visits by sales personnel to key customers. The purpose of these visits was to build a solid, friendly relationship for the future and to gain insight into the problems and needs of the companies served. How should this expenditure be reported?

6. What are factors to be considered in estimating the useful life of an intangible asset?

7. What should be the pattern of amortization for a limited-life intangible?

8. Novartis (CHE) acquired a trademark that is helpful in distinguishing one of its new products. The trademark is renewable every 10 years at minimal cost. All evidence indicates that this trademark product will generate cash flows for an indefinite period of time. How should this trademark be amortized?

9. McNabb Company spent $190,000 developing a new process prior to achieving economic viability, $45,000 in legal fees to obtain a patent, and $91,000 to market the process that was patented, all in the year 2015. How should these costs be accounted for in 2015?

10. Izzy Inc. purchased a patent for £350,000 which has an estimated useful life of 10 years. Its pattern of use or consumption cannot be reliably determined. Prepare the entry to record the amortization of the patent in its first year of use.

11. Explain the difference between artistic-related intangible assets and contract-related intangible assets.

12. What is goodwill? What is a bargain purchase?

13. Under what circumstances is it appropriate to record goodwill in the accounts? How should goodwill, properly recorded on the books, be written off in order to conform with IFRS?

14. In examining financial statements, financial analysts often write off goodwill immediately. Comment on this procedure.

15. Braxton Inc. is considering the write-off of a limited-life intangible because of its lack of profitability. Explain to the management of Braxton how to determine whether a write-off is permitted.

16. Last year, Zeno Company recorded an impairment on an intangible asset. Recent appraisals indicate that the asset has increased in value. Should Zeno record this recovery in value?

17. Explain how losses on impaired intangible assets should be reported in income.

18. Shi Company determines that its goodwill is impaired. It finds that its recoverable amount is HK$3,600,000 and its recorded goodwill is HK$4,000,000. The fair value of its identifiable assets is HK$14,500,000. What is the amount of goodwill impaired?

19. What is the nature of research and development costs? Can development costs be capitalized? Explain.

20. Research and development activities may include (a) personnel costs, (b) materials and equipment costs, and (c) indirect costs. What is the recommended accounting treatment for these three types of R&D costs?

21. Which of the following activities should be expensed currently as R&D costs?
   (a) Testing in search for or evaluation of product or process alternatives.
   (b) Engineering follow-through in an early phase of commercial production.
   (c) Legal work in connection with patent applications or litigation, and the sale or licensing of patents.

22. Indicate the proper accounting for the following items.
   (a) Organization costs.
   (b) Advertising costs.
   (c) Operating losses.

23. In 2014, Jackie Chan Corporation developed a new product that will be marketed in 2016. In connection with the development of this product, the following costs were incurred in 2015: research and development costs ¥40,000,000; materials and supplies consumed ¥6,000,000; and compensation paid to research consultants ¥12,500,000. (¥23,000,000

of the development phase costs were incurred after the product became economically viable.) It is anticipated that these costs will be recovered in 2018. What is the amount of research and development costs that Chan should record in 2015 as a charge to expense?

24. Recently, a group of university students decided to incorporate for the purposes of selling a process to recycle the waste product from manufacturing cheese. Some of the initial costs involved were legal fees and office expenses incurred in starting the business, governmental incorporation fees, and stamp taxes. One student wishes to charge these costs against revenue in the current period. Another wishes to defer these costs and amortize them in the future. Which student is correct?

25. An intangible asset with an estimated useful life of 30 years was acquired on January 1, 2005, for $540,000. On January 1, 2015, a review was made of intangible assets and their expected service lives, and it was determined

that this asset had an estimated useful life of 30 more years from the date of the review. What is the amount of amortization for this intangible in 2015?

26. Briefly describe some of the similarities and differences between U.S. GAAP and IFRS with respect to the accounting for intangible assets.

27. Sophia Co., a cellular phone company based in Italy, prepares its financial statements in accordance with IFRS. In 2015, it reported average assets of €12,500 and net income €1,125. Included in net income is amortization expense of €120. Under U.S. GAAP, Sophia's amortization expense would have been €325. Briefly discuss how analysis of Sophia's 2015 return on assets (and comparisons to a company using U.S. GAAP) would be affected by differences in intangible asset amortization between IFRS and U.S. GAAP.

28. Briefly discuss the convergence efforts that are underway in the area of intangible assets.

BRIEF EXERCISES

BE12-1 Celine Dion Corporation purchases a patent from Salmon Company on January 1, 2015, for $54,000. The patent has a remaining legal life of 16 years. Celine Dion feels the patent will be useful for 10 years. Prepare Celine Dion's journal entries to record the purchase of the patent and 2015 amortization.

BE12-2 Use the information provided in BE12-1. Assume that at January 1, 2017, the carrying amount of the patent on Celine Dion's books is $43,200. In January, Celine Dion spends $24,000 successfully defending a patent suit. Celine Dion still feels the patent will be useful until the end of 2024. Prepare the journal entries to record the $24,000 expenditure and 2017 amortization.

BE12-3 Larry Lyon, Inc., spent €68,000 in attorney fees while developing the trade name of its new product, the Mean Bean Machine. Prepare the journal entries to record the €68,000 expenditure and the first year's amortization, using an 8-year life.

BE12-4 Gershwin Corporation obtained a franchise from Sonic Hedgehog Inc. for a cash payment of £120,000 on April 1, 2015. The franchise grants Gershwin the right to sell certain products and services for a period of 8 years. Prepare Gershwin's April 1 journal entry and December 31 adjusting entry.

BE12-5 On September 1, 2015, Winans Corporation acquired Aumont Enterprises for a cash payment of £700,000. At the time of purchase, Aumont's statement of financial position showed assets of £620,000, liabilities of £200,000, and equity of £420,000. The fair value of Aumont's assets is estimated to be £800,000. Compute the amount of goodwill acquired by Winans.

BE12-6 Kenoly Corporation owns a patent that has a carrying amount of $300,000. Kenoly expects future net cash flows from this patent to total $210,000 over its remaining life of 10 years. The recoverable amount of the patent is $110,000. Prepare Kenoly's journal entry, if necessary, to record the loss on impairment.

BE12-7 Use the information in BE12-6. Assume that at the end of the year following the impairment (after recording amortization expense), the estimated recoverable amount for the patent is $130,000. Prepare Kenoly's journal entry, if needed.

BE12-8 Waters Corporation purchased Jang Group 3 years ago and at that time recorded goodwill of HK$400,000. The Jang Division's net assets, including the goodwill, have a carrying amount of HK$800,000. The fair value of the division is estimated to be HK$1,000,000. Prepare Waters' journal entry, if necessary, to record impairment of the goodwill.

BE12-9 Use the information provided in BE12-8. Assume that the recoverable amount of the division is estimated to be HK$750,000. Prepare Waters' journal entry, if necessary, to record impairment of the goodwill.

BE12-10 Sujo Corporation commenced operations in early 2015. The corporation incurred HK$60,000,000 of costs such as fees to underwriters, legal fees, governmental fees, and promotional expenditures during its formation. Prepare journal entries to record the HK$60,000,000 expenditure and 2015 amortization, if any.

8 **BE12-11** Treasure Land Corporation incurred the following costs in 2015.

Cost of laboratory research aimed at discovery of new knowledge	£120,000
Cost of testing in search for product alternatives	100,000
Cost of engineering activity required to advance the design of a product to the manufacturing stage	210,000
Prototype testing subsequent to meeting economic viability	75,000
	£505,000

Prepare the necessary 2015 journal entry or entries for Treasure Land.

8 **BE12-12** Indicate whether the following items are capitalized or expensed in the current year.

(a) Purchase cost of a patent from a competitor.

(b) Research costs.

(c) Development costs (after achieving economic viability).

(d) Organizational costs.

(e) Costs incurred internally to create goodwill.

3 **9** **BE12-13** Nieland Industries had one patent recorded on its books as of January 1, 2015. This patent had a book value of $288,000 and a remaining useful life of 8 years. During 2015, Nieland incurred research costs of $96,000 and brought a patent infringement suit against a competitor. On December 1, 2015, Nieland received the good news that its patent was valid and that its competitor could not use the process Nieland had patented. The company incurred $85,000 to defend this patent. At what amount should the patent(s) be reported on the December 31, 2015, statement of financial position, assuming monthly amortization of patents?

3 **9** **BE12-14** Sinise Industries acquired two copyrights during 2015. One copyright related to a textbook that was developed internally at a cost of €9,900. This textbook is estimated to have a useful life of 3 years from September 1, 2015, the date it was published. The second copyright (a history research textbook) was purchased from University Press on December 1, 2015, for €24,000. This textbook has an indefinite useful life. How should these two copyrights be reported on Sinise's statement of financial position as of December 31, 2015?

EXERCISES

1 **4** **E12-1** **(Classification Issues—Intangibles)** Presented below is a list of items that could be included in the intangible assets section of the statement of financial position.

1. Investment in a subsidiary company.

2. Timberland.

3. Cost of engineering activity required to advance the design of a product to the manufacturing stage.

4. Lease prepayment (6 months' rent paid in advance).

5. Cost of equipment obtained.

6. Cost of searching for applications of new research findings.

7. Costs incurred in the formation of a corporation.

8. Operating losses incurred in the start-up of a business.

9. Training costs incurred in start-up of new operation.

10. Purchase cost of a franchise.

11. Goodwill generated internally.

12. Cost of testing in search for product alternatives.

13. Goodwill acquired in the purchase of a business.

14. Cost of developing a patent (before achieving economic viability).

15. Cost of purchasing a patent from an inventor.

16. Legal costs incurred in securing a patent.

17. Unrecovered costs of a successful legal suit to protect the patent.

18. Cost of conceptual formulation of possible product alternatives.

19. Cost of purchasing a copyright.

20. Development costs incurred after achieving economic viability.

21. Long-term receivables.

22. Cost of developing a trademark.

23. Cost of purchasing a trademark.

Instructions
(a) Indicate which items on the list above would generally be reported as intangible assets in the statement of financial position.
(b) Indicate how, if at all, the items not reportable as intangible assets would be reported in the financial statements.

E12-2 (Classification Issues—Intangibles) Presented below is selected account information related to Matt Perry Inc. as of December 21, 2015. All these accounts have debit balances.

Cable television franchises	Film contract rights
Music copyrights	Customer lists
Research and development costs	Prepaid expenses
Goodwill	Covenants not to compete
Cash	Brand names
Accounts receivable	Notes receivable
Property, plant, and equipment	Investments in associated companies
Internet domain name	Organization costs
Land	

Instructions
Identify which items should be classified as an intangible asset. For those items not classified as an intangible asset, indicate where they would be reported in the financial statements.

E12-3 (Classification Issues—Intangibles) Langrova Inc. has the following amounts reported in its general ledger at December 31, 2015.

Organization costs	€24,000
Trademarks	20,000
Bonds payable	35,000
Deposits with advertising agency for ads to promote goodwill of company	10,000
Excess of cost over fair value of net identifiable assets of acquired subsidiary	75,000
Cost of equipment acquired for research and development projects; the equipment has an alternative future use	90,000
Costs of developing a secret formula for a product that is expected to be marketed for at least 20 years (all research phase)	70,000

Instructions
(a) On the basis of the information above, compute the total amount to be reported by Langrova for intangible assets on its statement of financial position at December 31, 2015. As noted, the equipment has alternative future use.
(b) If an item is not to be included in intangible assets, explain its proper treatment for reporting purposes.

E12-4 (Intangible Amortization) Presented below is selected information for Palmiero Company.

1. Palmiero purchased a patent from Vania Co. for $1,500,000 on January 1, 2013. The patent is being amortized over its remaining legal life of 10 years, expiring on January 1, 2023. During 2015, Palmiero determined that the economic benefits of the patent would not last longer than 6 years from the date of acquisition. What amount should be reported in the statement of financial position for the patent, net of accumulated amortization, at December 31, 2015?

2. Palmiero bought a franchise from Dougherty Co. on January 1, 2014, for $350,000. The carrying amount of the franchise on Dougherty's books on January 1, 2014, was $500,000. The franchise agreement had an estimated useful life of 30 years. Because Palmiero must enter a competitive bidding at the end of 2023, it is unlikely that the franchise will be retained beyond 2023. What amount should be amortized for the year ended December 31, 2015?

3. On January 1, 2013, Palmiero incurred organization costs of $275,000. What amount of organization expense should be reported in 2015?

4. Palmiero purchased the license for distribution of a popular consumer product on January 1, 2015, for $150,000. It is expected that this product will generate cash flows for an indefinite period of time. The license has an initial term of 5 years but by paying a nominal fee, Palmiero can renew the license indefinitely for successive 5-year terms. What amount should be amortized for the year ended December 31, 2015?

Instructions

Answer the questions asked about each of the factual situations.

2 3 7 **E12-5 (Correct Intangible Assets Account)** As the recently appointed auditor for Ng Corporation, you have been asked to examine selected accounts before the 6-month financial statements of June 30, 2015, are prepared. The controller for Ng Corporation mentions that only one account is kept for intangible assets.

Intangible Assets

		Debit	Credit	Balance
Jan. 4	Research and development costs (prior to achieving economic viability)	HK$940,000		HK$ 940,000
Jan. 5	Legal costs to obtain patent	75,000		1,015,000
Jan. 31	Payment of 7 months' rent on property leased by Ng	91,000		1,106,000
Feb. 11	Share premium on ordinary shares		HK$250,000	856,000
March 31	Unamortized bond discount on bonds due March 31, 2035	84,000		940,000
April 30	Promotional expenses related to start-up of business	207,000		1,147,000
June 30	Operating losses for first 6 months	141,000		1,288,000

Instructions

Prepare the entry or entries necessary to correct this account. Assume that the patent has a useful life of 12 years.

3 8 **E12-6 (Recording and Amortization of Intangibles)** Powerglide Company, organized in 2014, has set up a single account for all intangible assets. The following summary discloses the debit entries that have been recorded during 2015.

1/2/15	Purchased patent (8-year life)	£ 380,000
4/1/15	Goodwill (indefinite life)	360,000
7/1/15	Purchased franchise with 10-year life; expiration date 7/1/25	450,000
8/1/15	Payment of copyright (5-year life)	156,000
9/1/15	Development costs to increase the value of the patent (£55,000 incurred after economic viability achieved)	215,000
		£1,561,000

Instructions

Prepare the necessary entries to clear the Intangible Assets account and to set up separate accounts for distinct types of intangibles. Make the entries as of December 31, 2015, recording any necessary amortization and reflecting all balances accurately as of that date. (Use straight-line amortization.)

2 3 6 **E12-7 (Accounting for Trade Name)** In early January 2014, Reymont Corporation applied for a trade name, incurring legal costs of $18,000. In January 2015, Reymont incurred $7,800 of legal fees in a successful defense of its trade name.

Instructions

(a) Compute 2014 amortization, 12/31/14 book value, 2015 amortization, and 12/31/15 book value if the company amortizes the trade name over 10 years.

(b) Compute the 2015 amortization and the 12/31/15 book value, assuming that at the beginning of 2015, Reymont determines that the trade name will provide no future benefits beyond December 31, 2018.

(c) Ignoring the response for part (b), compute the 2016 amortization and the 12/31/16 book value, assuming that at the beginning of 2016, based on new market research, Reymont determines that the recoverable amount of the trade name is $16,000.

8 **E12-8 (Accounting for Organization Costs)** Fontenot Corporation was organized in 2014 and began operations at the beginning of 2015. The company is involved in interior design consulting services. The following costs were incurred prior to the start of operations.

Attorney's fees in connection with organization of the company	€17,000
Purchase of drafting and design equipment	10,000
Costs of meetings of incorporators to discuss organizational activities	7,000
Government filing fees to incorporate	1,000
	€35,000

Instructions

(a) Compute the total amount of organization costs incurred by Fontenot.

(b) Prepare the journal entry to record organization costs for 2015.

E12-9 (Accounting for Patents, Franchises, and R&D) Devon Harris Company has provided information on intangible assets as follows.

A patent was purchased from Bradtke Company for $2,500,000 on January 1, 2014. Harris estimated the remaining useful life of the patent to be 10 years. The patent was carried in Bradtke's accounting records at a net book value of $2,000,000 when Bradtke sold it to Harris.

During 2015, a franchise was purchased from Greene Company for $580,000. In addition, 5% of revenue from the franchise must be paid to Greene. Revenue from the franchise for 2015 was $2,500,000. Harris estimates the useful life of the franchise to be 10 years and takes a full year's amortization in the year of purchase.

Harris incurred research and development costs in 2015 as follows.

Materials and equipment	$142,000
Personnel	189,000
Indirect costs	102,000
	$433,000

Harris estimates that these costs will be recouped by December 31, 2018, but due to uncertainty in the market, its process has not achieved economic viability. The materials and equipment purchased have no alternative uses.

On January 1, 2015, because of recent events in the field, Harris estimates that the remaining life of the patent purchased on January 1, 2014, is only 5 years from January 1, 2015.

Instructions

(a) Prepare a schedule showing the intangibles section of Harris's statement of financial position at December 31, 2015. Show supporting computations in good form.

(b) Prepare a schedule showing the income statement effect for the year ended December 31, 2015, as a result of the facts above. Show supporting computations in good form.

E12-10 (Accounting for Patents) During 2014, Matsumura Corporation spent ¥170,000 in research costs. As a result, a new product called the New Age Piano was patented. The patent was obtained on October 1, 2014, and had a legal life of 20 years and a useful life of 10 years. Legal costs of ¥24,000 related to the patent were incurred as of October 1, 2014. (Amounts are in thousands.)

Instructions

(a) Prepare all journal entries required in 2014 and 2015 as a result of the transactions above.

(b) On June 1, 2014, Matsumura spent ¥12,400 to successfully prosecute a patent infringement suit. As a result, the estimate of useful life was extended to 12 years from June 1, 2014. Prepare all journal entries required in 2014 and 2015.

(c) In 2016, Matsumura determined that a competitor's product would make the New Age Piano obsolete and the patent worthless by December 31, 2017. Prepare all journal entries required in 2016 and 2017.

E12-11 (Accounting for Patents) Yoon Industries has the following patents on its December 31, 2014, statement of financial position (amounts in thousands).

Patent Item	Initial Cost	Date Acquired	Useful Life at Date Acquired
Patent A	₩40,800	3/1/11	17 years
Patent B	₩15,000	7/1/12	10 years
Patent C	₩14,400	9/1/13	4 years

The following events occurred during the year ended December 31, 2015.

1. Research and development costs of ₩245,700 were incurred during the year. All of these costs (except for ₩28,000 incurred on May 1, 2015, for Patent C) were incurred prior to projects achieving economic viability.

2. Patent D was purchased on July 1 for ₩28,500. This patent has a useful life of 9½ years.

3. As a result of reduced demands for certain products protected by Patent B, a possible impairment of Patent B's value may have occurred at December 31, 2015. The controller for Yoon estimates the expected future cash flows from Patent B will be as follows.

Year	Expected Future Cash Flows
2016	₩2,000
2017	2,000
2018	2,000

The proper discount rate to be used for these cash flows is 8%. (Assume that the cash flows occur at the end of the year.)

Instructions
(a) Compute the total carrying amount of Yoon's patents on its December 31, 2014, statement of financial position.
(b) Compute the total carrying amount of Yoon's patents on its December 31, 2015, statement of financial position.

5 **E12-12 (Accounting for Goodwill)** Fred Graf, owner of Graf Interiors, is negotiating for the purchase of Terrell Galleries. The statement of financial position of Terrell is given in an abbreviated form below.

TERRELL GALLERIES
STATEMENT OF FINANCIAL POSITION
AS OF DECEMBER 31, 2015

Assets			Equity and Liabilities		
Buildings (net)	$200,000		Share capital—ordinary	$200,000	
Equipment (net)	175,000		Retained earnings	25,000	$225,000
Copyrights (net)	30,000		Accounts payable	50,000	
Land	70,000		Long-term notes payable	300,000	
Cash	100,000		Total liabilities		350,000
Total assets	$575,000		Total equity and liabilities		$575,000

Graf and Terrell agree that:
1. Land is undervalued by $50,000.
2. Equipment is overvalued by $5,000.

Terrell agrees to sell the gallery to Graf for $380,000.

Instructions
Prepare the entry to record the purchase of Terrell Galleries on Graf's books.

3 **5** **E12-13 (Accounting for Goodwill)** On July 1, 2015, Brandon Corporation purchased Mills Company by paying €250,000 cash and issuing a €150,000 note payable. At July 1, 2015, the statement of financial position of Mills Company was as follows.

Buildings (net)	€ 75,000	Equity	€235,000
Equipment (net)	70,000	Accounts payable	200,000
Trademarks	10,000		€435,000
Land	40,000		
Inventory	100,000		
Accounts receivable	90,000		
Cash	50,000		
	€435,000		

The recorded amounts all approximate current values except for land (fair value of €80,000), inventory (fair value of €125,000), and trademarks (fair value of €15,000).

Instructions
(a) Prepare the July 1 entry for Brandon Corporation to record the purchase.
(b) Prepare the December 31 entry for Brandon Corporation to record amortization of intangibles. The trademarks have an estimated useful life of 4 years with a residual value of €3,000.

6 **E12-14 (Copyright Impairment)** Presented below is information related to copyrights owned by Botticelli Company at December 31, 2015.

Cost	$8,600,000
Carrying amount	4,300,000
Recoverable amount	3,400,000

Assume that Botticelli Company will continue to use this copyright in the future. As of December 31, 2015, the copyright is estimated to have a remaining useful life of 10 years.

Instructions
(a) Prepare the journal entry (if any) to record the impairment of the asset at December 31, 2015. The company does not use accumulated amortization accounts.
(b) Prepare the journal entry to record amortization expense for 2016 related to the copyrights.

(c) The fair value of the copyright at December 31, 2016, is $3,500,000. Prepare the journal entry (if any) necessary to record the increase in fair value.

5 6 E12-15 (Goodwill Impairment) Presented below is net asset information related to the Ting Division of Santana, Inc.

TING DIVISION **NET ASSETS** **AS OF DECEMBER 31, 2015** **(IN MILLIONS)**	
Property, plant, and equipment (net)	HK$2,600
Goodwill	200
Accounts receivable	200
Cash	60
Less: Notes payable	(2,700)
Net assets	HK$ 360

The purpose of the Ting Division (cash-generating unit) is to develop a nuclear-powered aircraft. If successful, traveling delays associated with refueling could be substantially reduced. Many other benefits would also occur. To date, management has not had much success and is deciding whether a write-down at this time is appropriate. Management estimated its future net cash flows from the project to be HK$400 million. Management has also received an offer to purchase the division for HK$335 million (fair value less costs to sell). All identifiable assets' and liabilities' book and fair value amounts are the same.

Instructions
(a) Prepare the journal entry (if any) to record the impairment at December 31, 2015.
(b) At December 31, 2016, it is estimated that the division's recoverable amount increased to HK$345 million. Prepare the journal entry (if any) to record this increase in fair value.

8 E12-16 (Accounting for R&D Costs) Margaret Avery Company from time to time embarks on a research program when a special project seems to offer possibilities. In 2014, the company expends €325,000 on a research project, but by the end of 2014 it is impossible to determine whether any benefit will be derived from it.

Instructions
(a) What account should be charged for the €325,000, and how should it be shown in the financial statements?
(b) The project is completed in 2015, and a successful patent is obtained. The development costs to complete the project are €110,000 (€36,000 of these costs were incurred after achieving economic viability). Additional administrative and legal expenses incurred in obtaining patent number 472-1001-84 in 2015 total €24,000. The patent has an expected useful life of 5 years. Record these costs in journal entry form. Also, record patent amortization (full year) in 2015.
(c) In 2016, the company successfully defends the patent in extended litigation at a cost of €47,200, thereby extending the patent life to December 31, 2023. What is the proper way to account for this cost? Also, record patent amortization (full year) in 2016.
(d) Additional engineering and consulting costs incurred in 2016 required to advance the design of a product to the manufacturing stage total €60,000. These costs enhance the design of the product considerably, but it is highly uncertain if there will be a market for the new version of the product (it has not achieved economic viability). Discuss the proper accounting treatment for this cost.

8 E12-17 (Accounting for R&D Costs) Martinez Company incurred the following costs during 2015 in connection with its research and development activities.

Cost of equipment acquired that will have alternative uses in future R&D projects over the next 5 years (uses straight-line depreciation)	$330,000
Materials consumed in R&D projects	59,000
Consulting fees paid to outsiders for R&D projects	100,000
Personnel costs of persons involved in R&D projects	128,000
Indirect costs reasonably allocable to R&D projects	50,000
Materials purchased for future R&D projects	34,000

Instructions
Compute the amount to be reported as research and development expense by Martinez on its income statement for 2015. Assume equipment is purchased at the beginning of the year and economic viability has not been achieved.

PROBLEMS

2 3 **P12-1 (Correct Intangible Assets Account)** Reichenbach Co., organized in 2014, has set up a single account for all intangible assets. The following summary discloses the debit entries that have been recorded during 2014 and 2015.

Intangible Assets

7/1/14	8-year franchise; expiration date 6/30/22	€ 48,000
10/1/14	Advance payment on laboratory space (2-year lease)	24,000
12/31/14	Net loss for 2014 including governmental incorporation fee, €1,000, and related legal fees of organizing, €5,000 (all fees incurred in 2014)	16,000
1/2/15	Patent purchased (10-year life)	84,000
3/1/15	Cost of developing a secret formula (indefinite life)	75,000
4/1/15	Goodwill purchased (indefinite life)	278,400
6/1/15	Legal fee for successful defense of patent purchased above	12,650
9/1/15	Research and development costs (development costs of €45,000 incurred related to 1/2/15 patent, which has achieved economic viability)	160,000

Instructions

Prepare the necessary entries to clear the Intangible Assets account and to set up separate accounts for distinct types of intangibles. Make the entries as of December 31, 2015, recording any necessary amortization and reflecting all balances accurately as of that date. (Ignore income tax effects.)

2 3 **P12-2 (Accounting for Patents)** Choo Laboratories holds a valuable patent (No. 758-6002-1A) on a precipitator that prevents certain types of air pollution. Choo does not manufacture or sell the products and processes it develops. Instead, it conducts research and develops products and processes which it patents, and then assigns the patents to manufacturers on a royalty basis. Occasionally, it sells a patent. The history of Choo's patent number 758-6002-1A is as follows.

Date	Activity	Cost
2006–2007	Research conducted to develop precipitator	HK$384,000
Jan. 2008	Design and construction of a prototype	87,600
March 2008	Testing of models	42,000
Jan. 2009	Fees paid engineers and lawyers to prepare patent application; patent granted June 30, 2009	59,500
Nov. 2010	Engineering activity necessary to advance the design of the precipitator to the manufacturing stage	81,500
Dec. 2011	Legal fees paid to successfully defend precipitator patent	42,000
April 2012	Research aimed at modifying the design of the patented precipitator	49,000
July 2016	Legal fees paid in unsuccessful patent infringement suit against a competitor	34,000

Based on execution of a royalty contract in March 2012, the patent is deemed to be economically viable. Choo assumed a useful life of 17 years when it received the initial precipitator patent. On January 1, 2014, it revised its useful life estimate downward to 5 remaining years. Amortization is computed for a full year if the cost is incurred prior to July 1, and no amortization for the year if the cost is incurred after June 30. The company's year ends December 31.

Instructions

Compute the carrying value of patent No. 758-6002-1A on each of the following dates:

(a) December 31, 2009.
(b) December 31, 2013.
(c) December 31, 2016.

2 3 **P12-3 (Accounting for Franchise, Patents, and Trademark)** Information concerning Sandro Corporation's intangible assets is as follows.

1. On January 1, 2015, Sandro signed an agreement to operate as a franchisee of Hsian Copy Service, Inc. for an initial franchise fee of R$75,000. Of this amount, R$15,000 was paid when the agreement was signed, and the balance is payable in 4 annual payments of R$15,000 each, beginning January 1, 2016. The agreement provides that the down payment is not refundable and no future services are required of the franchisor. The present value at January 1, 2015, of the 4 annual payments discounted at 14%

(the implicit rate for a loan of this type) is R$43,700. The agreement also provides that 5% of the revenue from the franchise must be paid to the franchisor annually. Sandro's revenue from the franchise for 2015 was R$900,000. Sandro estimates the useful life of the franchise to be 10 years. (*Hint:* You may want to refer to Chapter 18 to determine the proper accounting treatment for the franchise fee and payments.)

2. Sandro incurred R$65,000 of experimental and development costs in its laboratory to develop a patent that was granted on January 2, 2015. Legal fees and other costs associated with registration of the patent totaled R$17,600. Sandro estimates that the useful life of the patent will be 8 years. The patent has yet to achieve economic viability.

3. A trademark was purchased from Shanghai Company for R$36,000 on July 1, 2012. Expenditures for successful litigation in defense of the trademark totaling R$10,200 were paid on July 1, 2015. Sandro estimates that the useful life of the trademark will be 20 years from the date of acquisition.

Instructions
(a) Prepare a schedule showing the intangible assets section of Sandro's statement of financial position at December 31, 2015. Show supporting computations in good form.
(b) Prepare a schedule showing all expenses resulting from the transactions that would appear on Sandro's income statement for the year ended December 31, 2015. Show supporting computations in good form.

8 9 **P12-4 (Accounting for R&D Costs)** During 2013, Robin Wright Tool Company purchased a building site for its proposed research and development laboratory at a cost of $60,000. Construction of the building was started in 2013. The building was completed on December 31, 2014, at a cost of $320,000 and was placed in service on January 2, 2015. The estimated useful life of the building for depreciation purposes was 20 years. The straight-line method of depreciation was to be employed, and there was no estimated residual value.

Management estimates that about 50% of the projects of the research and development group will result in long-term benefits (i.e., at least 10 years) to the corporation. The remaining projects either benefit the current period or are abandoned before completion. A summary of the number of projects and the direct costs incurred in conjunction with the research and development activities for 2015 appears below.

	Number of Projects	Salaries and Employee Benefits	Other Expenses (excluding Building Depreciation Charges)
Completed projects with long-term benefits (development costs incurred after achieving economic viability)	15	$ 90,000	$50,000
Abandoned projects or projects that benefit the current period	10	65,000	15,000
Projects in process—results indeterminate	5	40,000	12,000
Total	30	$195,000	$77,000

Upon recommendation of the research and development group, Robin Wright Tool Company acquired a patent for manufacturing rights at a cost of $88,000. The patent was acquired on April 1, 2014, and has an economic life of 10 years.

Instructions
Under IFRS, how would the items above relating to research and development activities be reported on the following financial statements?
(a) The company's income statement for 2015.
(b) The company's statement of financial position as of December 31, 2015.

Be sure to give account titles and amounts, and briefly justify your presentation.

5 6 **P12-5 (Goodwill, Impairment)** On July 31, 2015, Mexico Company paid $3,000,000 to acquire all of the common stock of Conchita Incorporated, which became a division (cash-generating unit) of Mexico. Conchita reported the following statement of financial position at the time of the acquisition.

Non-current assets	$2,700,000	Equity	$2,400,000
Current assets	800,000	Non-current liabilities	500,000
Total assets	$3,500,000	Current liabilities	600,000
		Total equity and liabilities	$3,500,000

It was determined at the date of the purchase that the fair value of the identifiable net assets of Conchita was $2,750,000. Over the next 6 months of operations, the newly purchased division experienced operating losses. In addition, it now appears that it will generate substantial losses for the foreseeable future. At December 31, 2015, Conchita reports the following statement of financial position information.

Current assets	$ 450,000
Non-current assets (including goodwill recognized in purchase)	2,400,000
Current liabilities	(700,000)
Non-current liabilities	(500,000)
Net assets	$1,650,000

It is determined that the recoverable amount of the Conchita Division is $1,850,000.

Instructions

(a) Compute the amount of goodwill recognized, if any, on July 31, 2015.
(b) Determine the impairment loss, if any, to be recorded on December 31, 2015.
(c) Assume that the recoverable amount of the Conchita Division is $1,600,000 instead of $1,850,000. Determine the impairment loss, if any, to be recorded on December 31, 2015.
(d) Prepare the journal entry to record the impairment loss, if any, and indicate where the loss would be reported in the income statement.

P12-6 (Comprehensive Intangible Assets) Montana Matt's Golf Inc. was formed on July 1, 2014, when Matt Magilke purchased the Old Master Golf Company. Old Master provides video golf instruction at kiosks in shopping malls. Magilke plans to integrate the instructional business into his golf equipment and accessory stores. Magilke paid £770,000 cash for Old Master. At the time, Old Master's statement of financial position reported assets of £650,000 and liabilities of £200,000 (thus equity was £450,000). The fair value of Old Master's assets is estimated to be £800,000. Included in the assets is the Old Master trade name with a fair value of £10,000 and a copyright on some instructional books with a fair value of £24,000. The trade name has a remaining life of 5 years and can be renewed at nominal cost indefinitely. The copyright has a remaining life of 40 years.

Instructions

(a) Prepare the intangible assets section of Montana Matt's Golf Inc. at December 31, 2014. How much amortization expense is included in Montana Matt's income for the year ended December 31, 2014? Show all supporting computations.
(b) Prepare the journal entry to record amortization expense for 2015. Prepare the intangible assets section of Montana Matt's Golf Inc. at December 31, 2015. (No impairments are required to be recorded in 2015.)
(c) At the end of 2016, Magilke is evaluating the results of the instructional business. Due to fierce competition from online and television (e.g., the Golf Channel), the Old Master cash-generating unit has been losing money. Its book value is now £500,000. The recoverable amount of the Old Master reporting unit is £420,000. Magilke has collected the following information related to the company's intangible assets.

Intangible Asset	Value-in-Use
Trade names	£ 3,000
Copyrights	25,000

Prepare the journal entries required, if any, to record impairments on Montana Matt's intangible assets. (Assume that any amortization for 2016 has been recorded.) Show supporting computations.

CONCEPTS FOR ANALYSIS

CA12-1 (Development Costs) Dogwood Electronics has been working to develop a patented technology for backing up computer hard drives. Dogwood had the following activities related to this project.

March 1	Dogwood incurred €10,000 in legal and processing fees to file and record a patent for the technology.
April 5	Laboratory and materials fees to identify a working system, €23,000.
May 15	Prototype development and testing, €34,000.
June 1	Dogwood meets the economic viability threshold, upon receiving a firm contract for the product.
June 30	Final development of product based on earlier tests, €45,000.

Instructions

(a) Prepare a schedule indicating Dogwood's R&D costs to be expensed and Dogwood's R&D costs to be capitalized.

(b) Briefly discuss how the accounting for these costs will impact the information presented in Dogwood's income statement and statement of financial position. Discuss the effects in current and future periods.

(c) Identify the criteria for determining "economic viability."

CA12-2 (Accounting for Pre-Opening Costs) After securing lease commitments from several major stores, Auer Shopping Center, Inc. was organized and built a shopping center in a growing suburb.

The shopping center would have opened on schedule on January 1, 2015, if it had not been struck by a severe tornado in December. Instead, it opened for business on October 1, 2015. All of the additional construction costs that were incurred as a result of the tornado were covered by insurance.

In July 2014, in anticipation of the scheduled January opening, a permanent staff had been hired to promote the shopping center, obtain tenants for the uncommitted space, and manage the property.

A summary of some of the costs incurred in 2014 and the first nine months of 2015 follows.

	2014	January 1, 2015 through September 30, 2015
Interest on mortgage bonds	$720,000	$540,000
Cost of obtaining tenants	300,000	360,000
Promotional advertising	540,000	557,000

The promotional advertising campaign was designed to familiarize shoppers with the center. Had it been known in time that the center would not open until October 2015, the 2014 expenditure for promotional advertising would not have been made. The advertising had to be repeated in 2015.

All of the tenants who had leased space in the shopping center at the time of the tornado accepted the October occupancy date on condition that the monthly rental charges for the first 9 months of 2015 be canceled.

Instructions

Explain how each of the costs for 2014 and the first 9 months of 2015 should be treated in the accounts of the shopping center corporation. Give the reasons for each treatment.

CA12-3 (Accounting for Patents) On June 30, 2015, your client, Ferry Company, was granted two patents covering plastic cartons that it had been producing and marketing profitably for the past 3 years. One patent covers the manufacturing process, and the other covers the related products.

Ferry's executives tell you that these patents represent the most significant breakthrough in the industry in the past 30 years. The products have been marketed under the registered trademarks Evertight, Duratainer, and Sealrite. Licenses under the patents have already been granted by your client to other manufacturers around the world and are producing substantial royalties.

On July 1, Ferry commenced patent infringement actions against several companies whose names you recognize as those of substantial and prominent competitors. Ferry's management is optimistic that these suits will result in a permanent injunction against the manufacture and sale of the infringing products as well as collection of damages for loss of profits caused by the alleged infringement.

The financial vice president has suggested that the patents be recorded at value-in-use, based on the discounted value of expected net royalty receipts.

Instructions

(a) What is the meaning of "discounted value of expected net receipts"? Explain.

(b) How would such a value be calculated for net royalty receipts?

(c) What basis of valuation for Ferry's patents would be used under IFRS? Give supporting reasons for this basis.

(d) Assuming no practical problems of implementation and ignoring IFRS, what is the preferable basis of valuation for patents? Explain.

(e) What would be the preferable theoretical basis of amortization? Explain.

(f) What recognition, if any, should be made of the infringement litigation in the financial statements for the year ending September 30, 2015? Discuss.

CA12-4 (Accounting for Research and Development Costs) Cuevas Co. is in the process of developing a revolutionary new product. A new division of the company was formed to develop, manufacture, and market this new product. As of year-end (December 31, 2015), the new product has not been manufactured for resale (economic viability has not been achieved). However, a prototype unit was built and is in operation.

Throughout 2015, the new division incurred certain costs. These costs include design and engineering studies, prototype manufacturing costs, administrative expenses (including salaries of administrative personnel), and market research costs. In addition, approximately €900,000 in equipment (with an estimated useful life of 10 years) was purchased for use in developing and manufacturing the new product. Approximately €315,000 of this equipment was built specifically for the design development of the new product. The remaining €585,000 of equipment was used to manufacture the pre-production prototype and will be used to manufacture the new product once it is in commercial production.

Instructions

(a) How are "research" and "development" defined in IFRS?

(b) Briefly indicate the practical and conceptual reasons for the conclusion reached by the IASB on accounting and reporting practices for research and development costs.

(c) In accordance with IFRS, how should the various costs of Cuevas described above be recorded on the financial statements for the year ended December 31, 2015?

(d) Discuss the importance of economic viability as it relates to research and development cost accounting.

 CA12-5 (Accounting for Research and Development Costs) Czeslaw Corporation's research and development department has an idea for a project it believes will culminate in a new product that would be very profitable for the company. Because the project will be very expensive, the department requests approval from the company's controller, Jeff Reid.

Reid recognizes that corporate profits have been down lately and is hesitant to approve a project that will incur significant expenses that cannot be capitalized due to IFRS requirements. He knows that if they hire an outside firm that does the work and obtains a patent for the process, Czeslaw Corporation can purchase the patent from the outside firm and record the expenditure as an asset. Reid knows that the company's own R&D department is first-rate, and he is confident they can do the work well.

Instructions

Answer the following questions.

(a) Who are the stakeholders in this situation?

(b) What are the ethical issues involved?

(c) What should Reid do?

USING YOUR JUDGMENT

FINANCIAL REPORTING

Financial Reporting Problem

Marks and Spencer plc (M&S)

The financial statements of M&S (GBR) are presented in Appendix A. The company's complete annual report, including the notes to the financial statements, is available online.

Instructions

Refer to M&S's financial statements and the accompanying notes to answer the following questions.

(a) Does M&S report any intangible assets and goodwill in its financial statements and accompanying notes? Briefly explain.

(b) How much selling and administrative expenses does M&S report in 2012 and 2013? Briefly discuss the significance of these expenses to M&S's operating results.

Comparative Analysis Case

adidas and Puma

The financial statements of adidas (DEU) and Puma (DEU) are presented in Appendices B and C, respectively. The complete annual reports, including the notes to the financial statements, are available online.

Instructions

Use the companies' financial information to answer the following questions.

   (a) **(1)** What amounts for intangible assets were reported in their respective statements of financial position by adidas and Puma?

        (2) What percentage of total assets is each of these reported amounts?

        (3) What was the change in the amount of intangibles from 2011 to 2012 for adidas and Puma?

   (b) **(1)** On what basis and over what periods of time did adidas and Puma amortize their intangible assets?

        (2) What were the amounts of accumulated amortization reported by adidas and Puma at the end of 2012 and 2011? Did either company record impairments on intangible assets? Explain.

        (3) What was the composition of the identifiable and unidentifiable intangible assets reported by adidas and Puma at the end of 2012?

Financial Statement Analysis Cases

Case 1: Merck and Johnson & Johnson

Merck & Co., Inc. (USA) and Johnson & Johnson (USA) are two leading producers of healthcare products. Each has considerable assets and each expends considerable funds each year toward the development of new products. The development of a new healthcare product is often very expensive and risky. New products frequently must undergo considerable testing before approval for distribution to the public. For example, it took Johnson & Johnson 4 years and $200 million to develop its 1-DAY ACUVUE contact lenses. The following are some basic data compiled from the financial statements of these two companies.

(all dollars in millions)	Johnson & Johnson	Merck
Total assets	$53,317	$42,573
Total revenue	47,348	22,939
Net income	8,509	5,813
Research and development expense	5,203	4,010
Intangible assets	11,842	2,765

Instructions

   (a) What kinds of intangible assets might a healthcare products company have? Does the composition of these intangibles matter to investors—that is, would it be perceived differently if all of Merck's intangibles were goodwill, than if all of its intangibles were patents?

   (b) Suppose the president of Merck has come to you for advice. He has noted that by eliminating all research and development expenditures the company could have reported $1.3 billion more in net income. He is frustrated because much of the research never results in a product, or the products take years to develop. He says shareholders are eager for higher returns, so he is considering eliminating research and development expenditures for at least a couple of years. What would you advise?

   (c) The notes to Merck's financial statements state that Merck has goodwill of $1.1 billion. Where does recorded goodwill come from? Is it necessarily a good thing to have a lot of goodwill on your books?

Case 2: Analysis of Goodwill

As a new intern for the local branch office of a national brokerage firm, you are excited to get an assignment that allows you to use your accounting expertise. Your supervisor provides you with the spreadsheet below, which contains data for the most recent quarter for three companies that the firm has been recommending to its clients as "buys." All of the companies' returns on assets have outperformed their industry cohorts in the past, but given recent challenges in their markets, there is concern that the companies may experience operating challenges and lower earnings. (All numbers in millions, except return on assets.)

	A	B	C	D	E
1	**Company**	**Market Value of Company**	**Book Value (Net Assets)**	**Carrying Value of Goodwill**	**Return on Assets**
2	Sprint Nextel	$36,361	$51,271	$30,718	3.5%
3	Washington Mutual	11,742	23,941	9,062	2.4%
4	E* Trade Financial	1,639	4,104	2,035	5.6%
5					

Instructions

(a) The market value for each of these companies is lower than the corresponding book value. What implications does this have for each company's future prospects?

(b) To date, none of these companies has recorded goodwill impairments. Your supervisor suspects that the companies will need to record impairments in the near future, but he is unsure about the goodwill impairment rules. Is it likely that these companies will recognize impairments? Explain.

(c) Using the above data, estimate the amount of goodwill impairment for each company and prepare the journal entry to record the impairment. For each company, you may assume that the book value less the carrying value of the goodwill approximates the fair value of the company's net assets.

(d) Discuss the effects of your entries in part (c) on your evaluation of these companies based on the return on assets ratio.

International Reporting Case

Bayer and Merck

Presented are data and accounting policy notes for the goodwill of two international drug companies. Bayer, a German company, prepares its statements in accordance with International Financial Reporting Standards (IFRS). Merck, a U.S. company, prepares its financial statements in accordance with U.S. GAAP.

Related Information	Bayer (€ millions)	Merck ($ millions)
Research and development expense	2,107	4,010
Amortization expense	0	0
Net income	603	5,813
Accumulated goodwill amortization	0	0
Shareholders' equity	12,268	17,288

Both U.S. GAAP and IFRS do not allow amortization of goodwill.

Instructions

(a) Compute the return on equity for each of these companies, and use this analysis to briefly discuss the relative profitability of the two companies.

(b) IFRS requires that development costs must be capitalized if technical and commercial feasibility (economic viability) of the resulting product has been established. Assume that Bayer recorded €1 million of development costs in the year reported above. Discuss briefly how this accounting affects your ability to compare the financial results of Bayer and Merck.

Accounting, Analysis, and Principles

On January 2, 2015, Raconteur Corp. reported the following intangible assets: (1) a copyright with a carrying value of €15,000, and (2) a trade name with a carrying value of €8,500. The trade name has a remaining life of 5 years and can be renewed at nominal cost indefinitely. The copyright has a remaining life of 10 years.

At December 31, 2015, Raconteur assessed the intangible assets for possible impairment and developed the following information.

	Estimated Undiscounted Expected Future Cash Flows	Estimated Recoverable Amount
Copyright	€20,000	€16,000
Trade name	10,000	5,000

Accounting

Prepare any journal entries required for Raconteur's intangible assets at December 31, 2015.

Analysis

Many securities analysts indicate a preference for less-volatile operating income measures. Such measures make it easier to predict future income and cash flows, using reported income measures. How does the accounting for impairments of intangible assets affect the volatility of operating income?

Principles

Many accounting issues involve a trade-off between the primary characteristics of relevance and faithful representation of information. How does the accounting for intangible asset impairments reflect this trade-off?

IFRS BRIDGE TO THE PROFESSION

Professional Research

King Company is contemplating the purchase of a smaller company, which is a distributor of King's products. Top management of King is convinced that the acquisition will result in significant synergies in its selling and distribution functions. The financial management group (of which you are a part) has been asked to analyze the effects of the acquisition on the combined company's financial statements. This is the first acquisition for King, and some of the senior staff insist that based on their recollection of goodwill accounting, any goodwill recorded on the acquisition will result in a "drag" on future earnings for goodwill amortization. Other younger members on the staff argue that goodwill accounting has changed. Your supervisor asks you to research this issue.

Instructions

Access the IFRS authoritative literature at the IASB website (*http://eifrs.iasb.org/*) (you may register for free eIFRS access at this site). When you have accessed the documents, you can use the search tool in your Internet browser to respond to the following questions. (Provide paragraph citations.)

(a) Identify the accounting literature that addresses goodwill and other intangible assets.
(b) Define goodwill.
(c) Is goodwill subject to amortization? Explain.
(d) When goodwill is recognized by a subsidiary, should it be tested for impairment at the consolidated level or the subsidiary level? Discuss.

Professional Simulation

In this simulation, you are asked to address questions related to intangible assets and similar costs. Prepare responses to all parts.

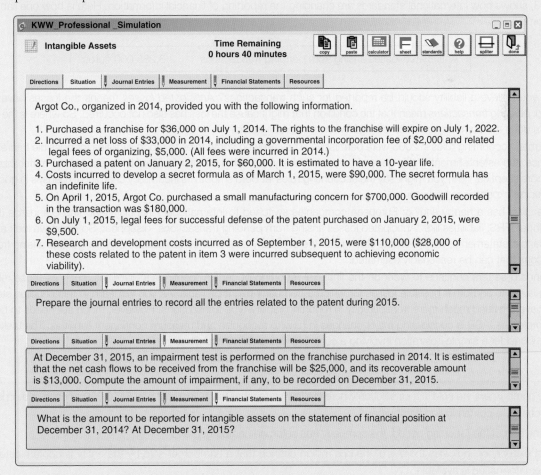

| KWW_Professional_Simulation |

Intangible Assets   **Time Remaining** **0 hours 40 minutes**   copy paste calculator sheet standards help splitter done

| Directions | Situation | Journal Entries | Measurement | Financial Statements | Resources |

Argot Co., organized in 2014, provided you with the following information.

1. Purchased a franchise for $36,000 on July 1, 2014. The rights to the franchise will expire on July 1, 2022.
2. Incurred a net loss of $33,000 in 2014, including a governmental incorporation fee of $2,000 and related legal fees of organizing, $5,000. (All fees were incurred in 2014.)
3. Purchased a patent on January 2, 2015, for $60,000. It is estimated to have a 10-year life.
4. Costs incurred to develop a secret formula as of March 1, 2015, were $90,000. The secret formula has an indefinite life.
5. On April 1, 2015, Argot Co. purchased a small manufacturing concern for $700,000. Goodwill recorded in the transaction was $180,000.
6. On July 1, 2015, legal fees for successful defense of the patent purchased on January 2, 2015, were $9,500.
7. Research and development costs incurred as of September 1, 2015, were $110,000 ($28,000 of these costs related to the patent in item 3 were incurred subsequent to achieving economic viability).

| Directions | Situation | Journal Entries | Measurement | Financial Statements | Resources |

Prepare the journal entries to record all the entries related to the patent during 2015.

| Directions | Situation | Journal Entries | Measurement | Financial Statements | Resources |

At December 31, 2015, an impairment test is performed on the franchise purchased in 2014. It is estimated that the net cash flows to be received from the franchise will be $25,000, and its recoverable amount is $13,000. Compute the amount of impairment, if any, to be recorded on December 31, 2015.

| Directions | Situation | Journal Entries | Measurement | Financial Statements | Resources |

What is the amount to be reported for intangible assets on the statement of financial position at December 31, 2014? At December 31, 2015?

Remember to check the book's companion website, at www.wiley.com/college/kieso, to find additional resources for this chapter.

13 Current Liabilities, Provisions, and Contingencies

Now You See It, Now You Don't

A look at the liabilities side of the statement of financial position of the company **Beru AG Corporation** (DEU), dated March 31, 2003, shows how international standards are changing the reporting of financial information. Here is how one liability was shown on this date:

Anticipated losses arising from pending transactions	3,285,000 euros

Do you believe a liability should be reported for such transactions? *Anticipated losses* means the losses have not yet occurred; *pending transactions* mean that the condition that might cause the loss has also not occurred. So where is the liability? To whom does the company owe something? Where is the obligation?

German accounting rules in 2003 were permissive. They allowed companies to report liabilities for possible future events. In essence, the establishment of this general-purpose "liability" provided a buffer for Beru if losses were to materialize. If you take a more skeptical view, you might say the accounting rules let Beru smooth its income by charging expenses in good years and reducing expenses in bad years.

The story has a happy ending: European companies switched to International Financial Reporting Standards (IFRS) in 2005. Under IFRS, liabilities like "Anticipated losses arising from pending transactions" disappear. So when we look at Beru's 2005 financial statements, we find a note stating that the company has reported as liabilities only obligations arising from past transactions that can be reasonably estimated.

Standard-setters continue to work on the financial reporting of certain "contingent" liabilities, such as those related to pending lawsuits and other possible losses for which a company might be liable. As you will learn in this chapter, standard-setters have provided much more transparency in reporting liability-type transactions. However, much still needs to be done. For example, the IASB is considering major changes in how to recognize and measure contingent liabilities. The task will not be easy. Consider a simple illustration involving a company that sells hamburgers:

- The hamburgers are sold in a jurisdiction where the law states that the seller must pay €100,000 to each customer that purchases a contaminated hamburger;
- At the end of the reporting period, the company has sold one hamburger; and
- Past experience indicates there is a one in a million chance that a hamburger sold by the entity is contaminated. No other information is available.

Does the company have a liability? What is the conceptual justification, if any, to record a liability or for that matter, not to record a liability? And if you conclude that the sale of the hamburger results in a liability, how do you measure it? Another way to ask the question is whether the hamburger issue is a recognition issue or a measurement issue. This example illustrates some of the difficult questions that the IASB faces in this area.

Thus, developing good standards for the reporting and disclosure of contingencies continues to be a challenge. One regulator recently proposed expanded disclosure about the nature of contingencies, more quantitative and qualitative background on contingencies, and, maybe most welcome of all, required tabular presentation of the changes in contingencies, including explanation of the changes. What's not to like about these enhanced disclosures? Well quite a bit, according to early responses by some companies and the legal profession. These parties are concerned that the information in these enhanced disclosures could be used against them in a lawsuit and they are voicing strong opposition to the proposed rules. We do not know the end of this liability story. However, the controversy over the proposed rules illustrates the challenges of developing accounting rules for liabilities that meet the needs of investors while avoiding harm to the companies reporting the information.

CONCEPTUAL FOCUS

> See the **Underlying Concepts** on pages 598, 603, and 622.
> Read the **Evolving Issue** on pages 627–628 for a discussion of how to account for greenhouse gases.

INTERNATIONAL FOCUS

> **Global Accounting Insights** related to liabilities are presented in Chapter 14 on pages 681–682.

PREVIEW OF CHAPTER 13

As our opening story indicates, the use of IFRS should lead to improved reporting of liabilities. In this chapter, we explain the basic issues related to accounting and reporting for current liabilities, provisions, and contingencies. The content and organization of the chapter are as follows.

Current Liabilities, Provisions, and Contingencies

Current Liabilities	Provisions	Contingencies	Presentation and Analysis
• Accounts payable • Notes payable • Current maturities of long-term debt • Short-term obligations • Dividends payable • Customer advances and deposits • Unearned revenues • Taxes payable • Employee-related liabilities	• Recognition • Measurement • Common types • Disclosures	• Contingent liabilities • Contingent assets	• Presentation of current liabilities • Analysis of current liabilities

CURRENT LIABILITIES

LEARNING OBJECTIVE
Describe the nature, type, and valuation of current liabilities.

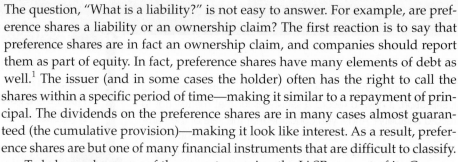

Underlying Concepts

To determine the appropriate classification of specific financial instruments, companies need proper definitions of assets, liabilities, and equities. They often use the Conceptual Framework definitions as the basis for resolving controversial classification issues.

See the Authoritative Literature section (page 629).

The question, "What is a liability?" is not easy to answer. For example, are preference shares a liability or an ownership claim? The first reaction is to say that preference shares are in fact an ownership claim, and companies should report them as part of equity. In fact, preference shares have many elements of debt as well.[1] The issuer (and in some cases the holder) often has the right to call the shares within a specific period of time—making it similar to a repayment of principal. The dividends on the preference shares are in many cases almost guaranteed (the cumulative provision)—making it look like interest. As a result, preference shares are but one of many financial instruments that are difficult to classify.

To help resolve some of these controversies, the IASB, as part of its Conceptual Framework, defines a **liability** as a present obligation of a company arising from past events, the settlement of which is expected to result in an outflow from the company of resources, embodying economic benefits. In other words, a liability has three essential characteristics:

1. It is a present obligation.

2. It arises from past events.

3. It results in an outflow of resources (cash, goods, services). **[1]**

Because liabilities involve future disbursements of assets or services, one of their most important features is the date on which they are payable. A company must satisfy currently maturing obligations in the ordinary course of business to continue operating. Liabilities with a more distant due date do not, as a rule, represent a claim on the company's current resources. They are therefore in a slightly different category. This feature gives rise to the basic division of liabilities into (1) current liabilities and (2) non-current liabilities.

Recall that current assets are cash or other assets that companies reasonably expect to convert into cash, sell, or consume in operations within a single operating cycle or within a year (if completing more than one cycle each year). Similarly, a **current liability** is reported if one of two conditions exists:[2]

1. The liability is expected to be settled within its normal operating cycle; or

2. The liability is expected to be settled within 12 months after the reporting date.

This definition has gained wide acceptance because it recognizes operating cycles of varying lengths in different industries.

The **operating cycle** is the period of time elapsing between the acquisition of goods and services involved in the manufacturing process and the final cash realization resulting from sales and subsequent collections. Industries that manufacture products

---

[1]This illustration is not just a theoretical exercise. In practice, a number of preference share issues have all the characteristics of a debt instrument, except that they are called and legally classified as preference shares. In some cases, taxing authorities have even permitted companies to treat the dividend payments as interest expense for tax purposes.

[2]The IASB also indicates two other conditions that do not normally occur. The first is that if the liability is held primarily for trading purposes, it should be reported as a current liability. Trading means that the liability is subject to selling or repurchasing in the short-term. These liabilities are recorded at fair value, and gains or losses are reported in income. In addition, if a liability is not subject to an unconditional right of the company to defer settlement of the liability for at least 12 months after the reporting date, it is classified as current. This condition is discussed more fully on page 602.

requiring an aging process as well as certain capital-intensive industries have an operating cycle of considerably more than one year. In these cases, companies classify operating items, such as accounts payable and accruals for wages and other expenses, as current liabilities, even if they are due to be settled more than 12 months after the reporting period.

Here are some typical current liabilities:

1. Accounts payable.
2. Notes payable.
3. Current maturities of long-term debt.
4. Short-term obligations expected to be refinanced.
5. Dividends payable.
6. Customer advances and deposits.
7. Unearned revenues.
8. Sales and value-added taxes payable.
9. Income taxes payable.
10. Employee-related liabilities.

Accounts Payable

Accounts payable, or **trade accounts payable**, are balances owed to others for goods, supplies, or services purchased on open account. Accounts payable arise because of the time lag between the receipt of services or acquisition of title to assets and the payment for them. The terms of the sale (e.g., 2/10, n/30 or 1/10, E.O.M.) usually state this period of extended credit, commonly 30 to 60 days.

Most companies record liabilities for purchases of goods upon receipt of the goods. If title has passed to the purchaser before receipt of the goods, the company should record the transaction at the time of title passage. A company must pay special attention to transactions occurring near the end of one accounting period and at the beginning of the next. It needs to ascertain that the record of goods received (the inventory) agrees with the liability (accounts payable), and that it records both in the proper period.

Measuring the amount of an account payable poses no particular difficulty. The invoice received from the creditor specifies the due date and the exact outlay in money that is necessary to settle the account. The only calculation that may be necessary concerns the amount of cash discount. See Chapter 8 for illustrations of entries related to accounts payable and purchase discounts.

Notes Payable

Notes payable are written promises to pay a certain sum of money on a specified future date. They may arise from purchases, financing, or other transactions. Some industries require notes (often referred to as **trade notes payable**) as part of the sales/purchases transaction in lieu of the normal extension of open account credit. Notes payable to banks or loan companies generally arise from cash loans. Companies classify notes as short-term or long-term, depending on the payment due date. Notes may also be interest-bearing or zero-interest-bearing.

Interest-Bearing Note Issued

Assume that Castle National Bank agrees to lend €100,000 on March 1, 2015, to Landscape Co. if Landscape signs a €100,000, 6 percent, four-month note. Landscape records the cash received on March 1 as follows.

March 1, 2015

Cash	100,000	
Notes Payable		100,000
(To record issuance of 6%, 4-month note to		
Castle National Bank)		

If Landscape prepares financial statements semiannually, it makes the following adjusting entry to recognize interest expense and interest payable of €2,000 (€100,000 × 6% × 4/12) at June 30, 2015.

June 30, 2015		
Interest Expense	2,000	
Interest Payable		2,000
(To accrue interest for 4 months on Castle National Bank note)		

If Landscape prepares financial statements monthly, its interest expense at the end of each month is €500 (€100,000 × 6% × 1/12).

At maturity (July 1, 2015), Landscape must pay the face value of the note (€100,000) plus €2,000 interest (€100,000 × 6% × 4/12). Landscape records payment of the note and accrued interest as follows.

July 1, 2015		
Notes Payable	100,000	
Interest Payable	2,000	
Cash		102,000
(To record payment of Castle National Bank interest-bearing note and accrued interest at maturity)		

Zero-Interest-Bearing Note Issued

A company may issue a zero-interest-bearing note instead of an interest-bearing note. A zero-interest-bearing note does not explicitly state an interest rate on the face of the note. **Interest is still charged**, however. At maturity, the borrower must pay back an amount greater than the cash received at the issuance date. In other words, the borrower receives in cash the present value of the note. The present value equals the face value of the note at maturity minus the interest or discount charged by the lender for the term of the note.

To illustrate, assume that Landscape issues a €102,000, four-month, zero-interest-bearing note to Castle National Bank on March 1, 2015. The present value of the note is €100,000. Landscape records this transaction as follows.

March 1, 2015		
Cash	100,000	
Notes Payable		100,000
(To record issuance of 4-month, zero-interest-bearing note to Castle National Bank)		

Landscape credits the Notes Payable account for the present value of the note, which is €100,000. If Landscape prepares financial statements semiannually, it makes the following adjusting entry to recognize the interest expense and the increase in the note payable of €2,000 at June 30, 2015.

June 30, 2015		
Interest Expense	2,000	
Notes Payable		2,000
(To accrue interest for 4 months on Castle National Bank note)		

At maturity (July 1, 2015), Landscape must pay the face value of the note, as follows.

July 1, 2015		
Notes Payable	102,000	
Cash		102,000
(To record payment of Castle National Bank zero-interest-bearing at maturity)		

In this case, the amount of interest expense recorded and the total cash outlay are exactly the same whether Landscape signed a loan agreement with a stated interest rate or used the zero-interest-rate approach. This circumstance rarely happens, as often the borrower on an interest-bearing note will have to make cash payments for interest during the term of the note on a monthly basis. We discuss additional accounting issues related to notes payable in Chapter 14.

Current Maturities of Long-Term Debt

Delhaize Group (BEL) reports as part of its current liabilities the portion of bonds, mortgage notes, and other long-term indebtedness that matures within the next fiscal year. It categorizes this amount as **current maturities of long-term debt**. Companies, like Delhaize, exclude long-term debts maturing currently as current liabilities if they are to be:

1. Retired by assets accumulated for this purpose that properly have not been shown as current assets;

2. Refinanced, or retired from the proceeds of a new long-term debt issue (discussed in the next section); or

3. Converted into ordinary shares.

When only a part of a long-term debt is to be paid within the next 12 months, as in the case of serial bonds that it retires through a series of annual installments, **the company reports the maturing portion of long-term debt as a current liability** and the remaining portion as a long-term debt.

However, a company should classify as current any liability that is **due on demand** (callable by the creditor) or will be due on demand within one year (or operating cycle, if longer). Liabilities often become callable by the creditor when there is a violation of the debt agreement. For example, most debt agreements specify a given level of equity to debt be maintained, or specify that working capital be of a minimum amount. If the company violates an agreement, it must classify the debt as current because it is a reasonable expectation that existing working capital will be used to satisfy the debt.

To illustrate a breach of a covenant, assume that Gyro Company on November 1, 2015, has a long-term note payable to Sanchez Inc., which is due on April 1, 2017. Unfortunately, Gyro breaches a covenant in the note, and the obligation becomes payable on demand. Gyro is preparing its financial statements at December 31, 2015. Given the breach in the covenant, Gyro must classify its obligation as current. However, Gyro can classify the liability as non-current if Sanchez agrees before December 31, 2015, to provide a grace period for the breach of the agreement. The grace period must end at least 12 months after December 31, 2015, to be reported as a non-current liability. If the agreement is not finalized by December 31, 2015, Gyro **must classify the note payable as a current liability**. [2]

Short-Term Obligations Expected to Be Refinanced

Short-term obligations are debts scheduled to mature within one year after the date of a company's statement of financial position or within its normal operating cycle. Some **short-term obligations** are **expected to be refinanced** on a long-term basis. These short-term obligations will not require the use of working capital during the next year (or operating cycle).[3]

---

[3]*Refinancing a short-term obligation on a long-term basis* means either replacing it with a long-term obligation or equity securities, or renewing, extending, or replacing it with short-term obligations for an uninterrupted period extending beyond one year (or the normal operating cycle) from the date of the company's statement of financial position.

At one time, the accounting profession generally supported the exclusion of short-term obligations from current liabilities if they were "expected to be refinanced." But the profession provided no specific guidelines, so companies determined whether a short-term obligation was "expected to be refinanced" based solely on management's **intent** to refinance on a long-term basis. Classification was not clear-cut. For example, a company might obtain a five-year bank loan but handle the actual financing with 90-day notes, which it must keep turning over (renewing). In this case, is the loan a long-term debt or a current liability? It depends on refinancing criteria.

What do the numbers mean? GOING, GOING, GONE

A classic example of the need for rules for liabilities expected to be refinanced is the case of Penn Central Railroad (USA) before it went bankrupt. The railroad was deep into short-term debt but classified it as long-term debt. Why? Because the railroad believed it had commitments from lenders to keep refinancing the short-term debt. When those commitments suddenly disappeared, it was "good-bye Pennsy." As the Greek philosopher Epictetus once said, "Some things in this world are not and yet appear to be."

Refinancing Criteria

To resolve these classification problems, the IASB has developed criteria for determining the circumstances under which short-term obligations may be properly excluded from current liabilities. Specifically, a company can exclude a short-term obligation from current liabilities if both of the following conditions are met:

1. It must intend to refinance the obligation on a long-term basis; and
2. It must have an unconditional right to defer settlement of the liability for at least 12 months after the reporting date.

Intention to refinance on a long-term basis means that the company intends to refinance the short-term obligation so that it will not require the use of working capital during the ensuing fiscal year (or operating cycle, if longer). Entering into a financing arrangement that clearly permits the company to refinance the debt on a long-term basis on terms that are readily determinable before the next reporting date is one way to satisfy the second condition. In addition, the fact that a company has the right to refinance at any time and intends to do so permits the company to classify the liability as non-current.

To illustrate, assume that Haddad Company provides the following information related to its note payable.

- Issued note payable of €3,000,000 on November 30, 2015, due on February 28, 2016. Haddad's reporting date is December 31, 2015.
- Haddad intends to extend the maturity date of the loan (refinance the loan) to June 30, 2017.
- Its December 31, 2015, financial statements are authorized for issue on March 15, 2016.
- The necessary paperwork to refinance the loan is completed on January 15, 2016. Haddad did not have an unconditional right to defer settlement of the obligation at December 31, 2015.

A graphical representation of the refinancing events is provided in Illustration 13-1.

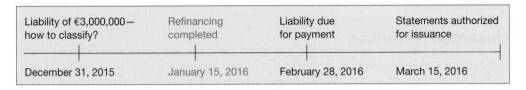

ILLUSTRATION 13-1
Refinancing Events

In this case, Haddad must classify its note payable as a current liability because the refinancing was not completed by December 31, 2015, the financial reporting date. Only if the refinancing was completed before December 31, 2015, can Haddad classify the note obligation as non-current. The rationale: Refinancing a liability after the statement of financial position date does not affect the liquidity or solvency at the date of the statement of financial position, the reporting of which should reflect contractual agreements in force on that date. **[3]**

What happens if Haddad has both the intention and the discretion (within the loan agreement) to refinance or roll over its €3,000,000 note payable to June 30, 2017? In this case, Haddad should classify the note payable as non-current because it has the ability to defer the payment to June 30, 2017.

Dividends Payable

A **cash dividend payable** is an amount owed by a corporation to its shareholders as a result of board of directors' authorization (or in other cases, vote of shareholders). At the date of declaration, the corporation assumes a liability that places the shareholders in the position of creditors in the amount of dividends declared. Because companies always pay cash dividends within one year of declaration (generally within three months), they classify them as current liabilities.

On the other hand, companies do not recognize accumulated but undeclared dividends on cumulative preference shares as a liability. Why? Because **preference dividends in arrears** are not an obligation until the board of directors authorizes the payment. Nevertheless, companies should disclose the amount of cumulative dividends unpaid in a note, or show it parenthetically in the share capital section.

Dividends payable in the form of additional shares are not recognized as a liability. Such **share dividends** (as we discuss in Chapter 15) do not require future outlays of assets or services. Companies generally report such undistributed share dividends in the equity section because they represent retained earnings in the process of transfer to share capital.

Underlying Concepts

> Preference dividends in arrears do represent a probable future economic sacrifice, but the expected sacrifice does not result from a past transaction or past event. The sacrifice will result from a future event (declaration by the board of directors). Note disclosure improves the predictive value of the financial statements.

Customer Advances and Deposits

Current liabilities may include **returnable cash deposits** received from customers and employees. Companies may receive deposits from customers to guarantee performance of a contract or service or as guarantees to cover payment of expected future obligations. For example, a company like **Alltel Corp.** (USA) often requires a deposit on equipment that customers use to connect to the Internet or to access its other services. Alltel also may receive deposits from customers as guarantees for possible damage to property. Additionally, some companies require their employees to make deposits for the return of keys or other company property.

The classification of these items as current or non-current liabilities depends on the time between the date of the deposit and the termination of the relationship that required the deposit.

Unearned Revenues

A magazine publisher such as Hachette (FRA) receives payment when a customer subscribes to its magazines. An airline company such as China Southern Airlines (CHN) sells tickets for future flights. And software companies like Microsoft (USA) issue coupons that allow customers to upgrade to the next version of their software. How do these companies account for **unearned revenues** that they receive before providing goods or performing services?

1. When a company receives an advance payment, it debits Cash and credits a current liability account identifying the source of the unearned revenue.

2. When a company recognizes revenue, it debits the unearned revenue account and credits a revenue account.

To illustrate, assume that Logo University sells 10,000 season soccer tickets at $50 each for its five-game home schedule. Logo University records the sales of season tickets as follows.

	August 6		
Cash		500,000	
Unearned Sales Revenue			500,000
(To record sale of 10,000 season tickets)			

After each game, Logo University makes the following entry.

	September 7		
Unearned Sales Revenue		100,000	
Sales Revenue			100,000
(To record soccer ticket revenue)			

The account Unearned Sales Revenue represents unearned revenue. Logo University reports it as a current liability in the statement of financial position because the school has a performance obligation. As ticket holders attend games, Logo recognizes revenue and reclassifies the amount from Unearned Sales Revenue to Sales Revenue. Unearned revenue is material for some companies: In the airline industry, for example, tickets sold for future flights represent almost 50 percent of total current liabilities.

Illustration 13-2 shows specific unearned revenue and revenue accounts sometimes used in selected types of businesses.

ILLUSTRATION 13-2
Unearned Revenue and
Revenue Accounts

Type of Business	Account Title	
	Unearned Revenue	Revenue
Airline	Unearned Passenger Ticket Revenue	Passenger Revenue
Magazine publisher	Unearned Subscription Revenue	Subscription Revenue
Hotel	Unearned Rental Revenue	Rental Revenue
Auto dealer	Unearned Warranty Revenue	Warranty Revenue
Retailers	Unearned Gift Card Revenue	Sales Revenue

The statement of financial position reports obligations for any commitments that are redeemable in goods and services. The income statement reports revenues related to performance obligations satisfied during the period.

Sales and Value-Added Taxes Payable

Most countries have a consumption tax. Consumption taxes are generally either a sales tax or a value-added tax (VAT). The purpose of these taxes is to generate revenue for the government similar to the corporate or personal income tax. These two taxes accomplish the same objective—to tax the final consumer of the good or service. However, the two systems use different methods to accomplish this objective.

Sales Taxes Payable

To illustrate the accounting for sales taxes, assume that Halo Supermarket sells loaves of bread to consumers on a given day for €2,400. Assuming a sales tax rate of 10 percent, Halo Supermarket makes the following entry to record the sale.

Cash	2,640	
Sales Revenue		2,400
Sales Taxes Payable		240

In this situation, Halo Supermarket records a liability to provide for taxes collected from customers but not yet remitted to the appropriate tax authority. At the proper time, Halo Supermarket remits the €240 to the tax authority.

Sometimes, the sales tax collections credited to the liability account are not equal to the liability as computed by the governmental formula. In such a case, companies make an adjustment of the liability account by recognizing a gain or a loss on sales tax collections. Many companies do not segregate the sales tax and the amount of the sale at the time of sale. Instead, the company credits both amounts in total in the Sales Revenue account. Then, to reflect correctly the actual amount of sales and the liability for sales taxes, the company debits the Sales Revenue account for the amount of the sales taxes due the government on these sales and credits the Sales Taxes Payable account for the same amount.

To illustrate, assume that the Sales Revenue account balance of €150,000 includes sales taxes of 4 percent. Thus, the amount recorded in the Sales Revenue account is comprised of the sales amount plus sales tax of 4 percent of the sales amount. Sales therefore are €144,230.77 (€150,000 ÷ 1.04) and the sales tax liability is €5,769.23 (€144,230.77 × 0.04, or €150,000 − €144,230.77). The following entry records the amount due to the tax authority.

Sales Revenue	5,769.23	
Sales Taxes Payable		5,769.23

Value-Added Taxes Payable

Value-added taxes (VAT) are used by tax authorities more than sales taxes (over 100 countries require that companies collect a value-added tax). As indicted earlier, a **value-added tax** is a consumption tax. This tax is placed on a product or service whenever value is added at a stage of production and at final sale. A VAT is a cost to the end user, normally a private individual, similar to a sales tax.

However, a VAT should not be confused with a sales tax. A sales tax is collected only once at the consumer's point of purchase. No one else in the production or supply chain is involved in the collection of the tax. In a VAT taxation system, the VAT is collected every time a business purchases products from another business in the product's supply chain. To illustrate, let's return to the Halo Supermarket example but now assume that a VAT is imposed rather than a sales tax. To understand how a VAT works, we need to understand how the loaves of bread were made ready for purchase. Here is what happened.

1. Hill Farms Wheat Company grows wheat and sells it to Sunshine Baking for €1,000. Hill Farms Wheat makes the following entry to record the sale, assuming the VAT is 10 percent.

Cash	1,100	
Sales Revenue		1,000
Value-Added Taxes Payable		100

Hill Farms Wheat then remits the €100 to the tax authority.

2. Sunshine Baking makes loaves of bread from this wheat and sells it to Halo Supermarket for €2,000. Sunshine Baking makes the following entry to record the sale, assuming the VAT is 10 percent.

Cash	2,200	
Sales Revenue		2,000
Value-Added Taxes Payable		200

Sunshine Baking then remits €100 to the government, not €200. The reason: Sunshine Baking has already paid €100 to Hill Farms Wheat. At this point, the tax authority is only entitled to €100. Sunshine Baking receives a credit for the VAT paid to Hill Farms Wheat, which reduces the VAT payable.

3. Halo Supermarket sells the loaves of bread to consumers for €2,400. Halo Supermarket makes the following entry to record the sale, assuming the VAT is 10 percent.

Cash	2,640	
Sales Revenue		2,400
Value-Added Taxes Payable		240

Halo Supermarket then sends only €40 to the tax authority as it deducts the €200 VAT already paid to Sunshine Baking.

Who then in this supply chain ultimately pays the VAT of €240? The consumers. A summary of the process is provided in Illustration 13-3.

ILLUSTRATION 13-3
Who Pays the VAT?

1. Hill Farms Wheat collected €100 of VAT and remitted this amount to the tax authority; it did not have a net cash outlay for these taxes.
2. Sunshine Baking collected €200 of VAT but only remitted €100 to the tax authority because it received credit for the €100 VAT that it paid to Hill Farms Wheat; it did not have a net cash outlay for these taxes.
3. Halo Supermarket collected €240 of VAT but only remitted €40 to the tax authority because it received credit for the €200 of VAT it paid to Sunshine Baking; it did not have a net cash outlay for these taxes.

In summary, the total VAT collected and remitted by the companies in the supply chain is as follows.

	VAT Collected	VAT Remitted	VAT Credited	VAT Owed
Hill Farms Wheat	€100	€100	€ 0	€0
Sunshine Baking	200	100	100	0
Halo Supermarket	240	40	200	0
Totals	€540	€240	€300	€0

So who actually pays the VAT? It is the consumers who bear the €240 VAT cost as part of their purchase price, not the companies that produced and distributed the bread.

An advantage of a VAT is that it is easier to collect than a sales tax because it has a self-correcting mechanism built into the tax system. For example, look again at Sunshine Baking in Illustration 13-3. If Sunshine Baking is considering not paying the VAT, it knows that Halo Supermarket will report its purchase from Sunshine Baking in order to claim its credit. As a result, the tax authority has records that a purchase was made and therefore could charge Sunshine Baking with fraud if it fails to remit the VAT. A sales tax does not have this self-correcting mechanism and is thus easier to avoid. For example, if the sales tax is high, consumers may use the Internet for purchases, buy goods in different jurisdictions than their residence, or pretend to be a business in the supply chain rather than the ultimate consumer. On the other hand, a disadvantage of a VAT is the increased amount of record-keeping involved in implementing the system.

Income Taxes Payable

Most income tax varies in proportion to the amount of annual income. Using the best information and advice available, a business must prepare an income tax return and compute the income taxes payable resulting from the operations of the current period. Corporations should classify as a current liability the taxes payable on net income, as computed per the tax return. Unlike a corporation, proprietorships and partnerships are not taxable entities. Because the individual proprietor and the members of a partnership are subject to personal income taxes on their share of the business's taxable income, income tax liabilities do not appear on the financial statements of proprietorships and partnerships.

Most corporations must make periodic tax payments throughout the year to the appropriate government agency. These payments are based upon estimates of the total annual tax liability. As the estimated total tax liability changes, the periodic contributions also change. If in a later year the taxing authority assesses an additional tax on the income of an earlier year, the company should credit Income Taxes Payable and charge the related debit to current operations.

Differences between taxable income under the tax laws and accounting income under IFRS sometimes occur. Because of these differences, the amount of income taxes payable to the government in any given year may differ substantially from income tax expense as reported on the financial statements. Chapter 19 is devoted solely to income tax matters and presents an extensive discussion of this complex topic.

Employee-Related Liabilities

Companies also report as a current liability amounts owed to employees for salaries or wages at the end of an accounting period. In addition, they often also report as current liabilities the following items related to employee compensation.

3 LEARNING OBJECTIVE

Identify types of employee-related liabilities.

1. Payroll deductions.
2. Compensated absences.
3. Bonuses.

Payroll Deductions

The most common types of payroll deductions are taxes, insurance premiums, employee savings, and union dues. **To the extent that a company has not remitted the amounts deducted to the proper authority at the end of the accounting period, it should recognize them as current liabilities.**

Social Security Taxes. Most governments provide a level of social benefits (for retirement, unemployment, income, disability, and medical benefits) to individuals and families. The benefits are generally funded from taxes assessed on both the employer and the employees. These taxes are often referred to as Social Security taxes or **Social Welfare taxes**. Funds for these payments generally come from taxes levied on both the employer and the employee. Employers collect the employee's share of this tax by deducting it from the employee's gross pay, and remit it to the government along with their share. The government often taxes both the employer and the employee at the same rate. **Companies should report the amount of unremitted employee and employer Social Security tax on gross wages paid as a current liability.**

Income Tax Withholding. Income tax laws generally require employers to withhold from each employee's pay the applicable income tax due on those wages. The employer computes the amount of income tax to withhold according to a government-prescribed formula or withholding tax table. That amount depends on the length of the pay period and each employee's taxable wages, marital status, and claimed dependents. Illustration 13-4 summarizes payroll deductions and liabilities.

ILLUSTRATION 13-4
Summary of Payroll
Liabilities

Item	Who Pays	
Income tax withholding		
Social Security taxes—employee share	Employee	Employer reports these amounts as liabilities until remitted.
Union dues		
Social Security taxes—employer share	Employer	

Payroll Deductions Example. Assume a weekly payroll of $10,000 entirely subject to Social Security taxes (8%), with income tax withholding of $1,320 and union dues of $88 deducted. The company records the wages and salaries paid and the **employee payroll deductions** as follows.

Salaries and Wages Expense	10,000	
Withholding Taxes Payable		1,320
Social Security Taxes Payable		800
Union Dues Payable		88
Cash		7,792

It records the **employer payroll taxes** as follows.

Payroll Tax Expense	800	
Social Security Taxes Payable		800

The employer must remit to the government its share of Social Security tax along with the amount of Social Security tax deducted from each employee's gross compensation. It should record all unremitted employer Social Security taxes as payroll tax expense and payroll tax payable.[4]

Compensated Absences

Compensated absences are paid absences from employment—such as vacation, illness, and maternity, paternity, and jury leaves.[5] The following considerations are relevant to the accounting for compensated absences.

---

[4]A manufacturing company allocates all of the payroll costs (wages, payroll taxes, and fringe benefits) to appropriate cost accounts such as Direct Labor, Indirect Labor, Sales Salaries, Administrative Salaries, and the like. This abbreviated and somewhat simplified discussion of payroll costs and deductions is not indicative of the volume of records and clerical work that may be involved in maintaining a sound and accurate payroll system.

[5]Companies provide **postemployment benefits** to past or inactive employees **after employment but prior to retirement**. Examples include salary continuation, supplemental unemployment benefits, severance pay, job training, and continuation of health and life insurance coverage.

Vested rights exist when an employer has an obligation to make payment to an employee even after terminating his or her employment. Thus, vested rights are not contingent on an employee's future service. **Accumulated rights** are those that employees can carry forward to future periods if not used in the period in which earned. For example, assume that you earn four days of vacation pay as of December 31, the end of your employer's fiscal year. Company policy is that you will be paid for this vacation time even if you terminate employment. In this situation, your four days of vacation pay are vested, and your employer must accrue the amount.

Now assume that your vacation days are not vested but that you can carry the four days over into later periods. Although the rights are not vested, they are accumulated rights for which the employer must make an accrual. However, the amount of the accrual is adjusted to allow for estimated forfeitures due to turnover.

Non-accumulating rights do not carry forward; they lapse if not used. As a result, a company does not recognize a liability or expense until the time of absence (benefit). Thus, if an employee takes a vacation day during a month and it is non-accumulating, the vacation day is an expense in that month. Similarly, a benefit such as a maternity or paternity leave is contingent upon a future event and does not accumulate. Therefore, these costs are recognized only when the absence commences. **[4]**

A modification of the general rules relates to the issue of **sick pay**. If sick pay benefits vest, a company must accrue them. If sick pay benefits accumulate but do not vest, a company may choose whether to accrue them. Why this distinction? Companies may administer compensation designated as sick pay in one of two ways. In some companies, employees receive sick pay only if illness causes their absence. Therefore, these companies may or may not accrue a liability because its payment depends on future employee illness. Other companies allow employees to accumulate unused sick pay and take compensated time off from work even when not ill. For this type of sick pay, a company must accrue a liability because the company will pay it, regardless of whether employees become ill.

Companies should recognize the expense and related liability for compensated absences in the year earned by employees. For example, if new employees receive rights to two weeks' paid vacation at the beginning of their second year of employment, a company considers the vacation pay to be earned during the first year of employment.

What rate should a company use to accrue the compensated absence cost—the current rate or an expected rate? IFRS recommends the use of the expected rate. However, companies will likely use the current rather than expected rates because future rates are not known. To illustrate, assume that Amutron Inc. began operations on January 1, 2015. The company employs 10 individuals and pays each €480 per week. Employees earned 20 unused vacation weeks in 2015. In 2016, the employees used the vacation weeks, but now they each earn €540 per week. Amutron accrues the accumulated vacation pay on December 31, 2015, as follows.

Salaries and Wages Expense	9,600	
Salaries and Wages Payable (€480 × 20)		9,600

At December 31, 2015, the company reports on its statement of financial position a liability of €9,600. In 2016, it records the payment of vacation pay as follows.

Salaries and Wages Payable	9,600	
Salaries and Wages Expense	1,200	
Cash (€540 × 20)		10,800

In 2016, the use of the vacation weeks extinguishes the liability. Note that Amutron records the difference between the amount of cash paid and the reduction in the liability account as an adjustment to Salaries and Wages Expense in the period when paid.

This difference arises because it accrues the liability account at the rates of pay in effect during the period when employees *earned* the compensated time. The cash paid, however, depends on the rates in effect during the period when employees *used* the compensated time. If Amutron used the future rates of pay to compute the accrual in 2015, then the cash paid in 2016 would equal the liability.[6]

Profit-Sharing and Bonus Plans

Many companies give a **bonus** to certain or all employees in addition to their regular salaries or wages. Frequently, the bonus amount depends on the company's yearly profit. A company may consider **bonus payments to employees** as additional salaries and wages and should include them as a deduction in determining the net income for the year.

To illustrate the entries for an employee bonus, assume that Palmer Inc. shows income for the year 2015 of $100,000. It will pay out bonuses of $10,700 in January 2016. Palmer makes an adjusting entry dated December 31, 2015, to record the bonuses as follows.

Salaries and Wages Expense	10,700	
Salaries and Wages Payable		10,700

In January 2016, when Palmer pays the bonus, it makes this journal entry:

Salaries and Wages Payable	10,700	
Cash		10,700

Palmer should show the expense account in the income statement as an operating expense. **The liability, Salaries and Wages Payable, is usually payable within a short period of time. Companies should include it as a current liability in the statement of financial position.** An obligation under a profit-sharing or bonus plan must be accounted for as an expense and not a distribution of profit since it results from employee service and not a transaction with owners.

Similar to bonus agreements are contractual agreements for **conditional expenses**. Examples would be agreements covering rents or royalty payments conditional on the amount of revenues recognized or the quantity of product produced or extracted. Conditional expenses based on revenues or units produced are usually less difficult to compute than bonus arrangements.

For example, assume that a lease calls for a fixed rent payment of $500 per month and 1 percent of all sales over $300,000 per year. The company's annual rent obligation would amount to $6,000 plus $0.01 of each dollar of revenue over $300,000. Or, a royalty agreement may give to a patent owner $1 for every ton of product resulting from the patented process, or give to a mineral rights owner $0.50 on every barrel of oil extracted. As the company produces or extracts each additional unit of product, it creates an additional obligation, usually a current liability.

PROVISIONS

A **provision** is a liability of uncertain timing or amount (sometimes referred to as an *estimated liability*). Provisions are very common and may be reported either as current or non-current depending on the date of expected payment. **[5]**

---

[6]Some companies have obligations for benefits paid to employees after they retire. The accounting and reporting standards for postretirement benefit payments are complex. These standards relate to two different types of **postretirement benefits:** (1) pensions, and (2) postretirement healthcare and life insurance benefits. We discuss these issues extensively in Chapter 20.

Common types of provisions are obligations related to litigation, warrantees or product guarantees, business restructurings, and environmental damage.[7]

For example, **Pretonas** (MYS) reported RM19,915 million related to a provision for decommissioning oil and gas properties. **Nokia** (FIN) reported €2,619 million for warranties, intellectual property infringement, and restructuring costs. And **Adecoagro SA** (BRA) reported R$2,635,000 for labor, legal, and other claims.

The difference between a provision and other liabilities (such as accounts or notes payable, salaries payable, and dividends payable) is that **a provision has greater uncertainty about the timing or amount of the future expenditure required to settle the obligation**. For example, when **Siemens AG** (DEU) reports an accounts payable, there is an invoice or formal agreement as to the existence and the amount of the liability. Similarly, when Siemens accrues interest payable, the timing and the amount are known.[8]

Recognition of a Provision

Companies accrue an expense and related liability for a provision only if the following three conditions are met.

1. A company has a present obligation (legal or constructive) as a result of a past event;

2. It is probable that an outflow of resources embodying economic benefits will be required to settle the obligation; and

3. A reliable estimate can be made of the amount of the obligation.

If these three conditions are not met, no provision is recognized. **[6]**

In applying the first condition, the past event (often referred to as the *past obligatory event*) must have occurred. In applying the second condition, the term **probable** is defined as "more likely than not to occur." This phrase is interpreted to mean the probability of occurrence is greater than 50 percent. If the probability is 50 percent or less, the provision is not recognized.

Recognition Examples

We provide three examples to illustrate when a provision should be recognized. It is assumed for each of these examples that a reliable estimate of the amount of the obligation can be determined. Illustration 13-5 presents the first example in which a company has a legal obligation to honor its warranties. A legal obligation generally results from a contract or legislation.

WARRANTY

Facts: Santos Company gives warranties to its customers related to the sale of its electrical products. The warranties are for three years from the date of sale. Based on past experience, it is probable (more likely than not) that there will be some claims under the warranties.

Question: **Should Santos recognize at the statement of financial position date a provision for the warranty costs yet to be settled?**

Solution: (1) The warranty is a present obligation as a result of a past obligating event—the past obligating event is the sale of the product with a warranty, which gives rise to a legal obligation. (2) The warranty results in the outflow of resources embodying benefits in settlement—it is probable that there will be some claims related to these warranties. Santos Company should recognize the provision based on past experience.

ILLUSTRATION 13-5
Recognition of a Provision—Warranty

---

[7]The term provision can be confusing because it can be used to describe a liability, a valuation account, or an expense. Its most common use is to describe a liability and therefore is used as such in this chapter. The IASB is now considering using the term non-financial liability instead to describe provisions for liabilities. However, until that change occurs, companies will continue to use the term provision to describe various liabilities.

[8]The distinction is important because provisions are subject to disclosure requirements that do not apply to other types of payables.

A **constructive obligation** is an obligation that derives from a company's actions where:

1. By an established pattern of past practice, published policies, or a sufficiently specific current statement, the company has indicated to other parties that it will accept certain responsibilities; and
2. As a result, the company has created a valid expectation on the part of those other parties that it will discharge those responsibilities.

The second example, presented in Illustration 13-6, demonstrates how a constructive obligation is reported.

ILLUSTRATION 13-6
Recognition of a
Provision—Refunds

REFUNDS

Facts: Christian Dior (FRA) has a policy of refunding purchases to dissatisfied customers even though it is under no legal obligation to do so. Its policy of making refunds is generally known.

Question: Should Christian Dior record a provision for these refunds?

Solution: (1) The refunds are a present obligation as a result of a past obligating event—the sale of the product. This sale gives rise to a constructive obligation because the conduct of the company has created a valid expectation on the part of its customers that it will refund purchases. (2) The refunds result in the outflow of resources in settlement—it is probable that a proportion of goods are returned for refund. A provision is recognized for the best estimate of the costs of refunds.

The third example, the case of Wm Morrison Supermarkets (GBR) in Illustration 13-7, presents a situation in which the recognition of the provision depends on the probability of future payment.

ILLUSTRATION 13-7
Recognition of a
Provision—Lawsuit

LAWSUIT

Facts: Assume that an employee filed a £1,000,000 lawsuit on November 30, 2015, against Wm Morrison Supermarkets for damages suffered when the employee slipped and suffered a serious injury at one of the company's facilities. Morrison's lawyers believe that Morrison will not lose the lawsuit, putting the probability at less than 50 percent.

Question: Should Morrison recognize a provision for legal claims at December 31, 2015?

Solution: Although a past obligating event has occurred (the injury leading to the filing of the lawsuit), **it is not probable (more likely than not)** that Morrison will have to pay any damages. Morrison therefore does not need to record a provision. If, on the other hand, Morrison's lawyer determined that it is probable that the company will lose the lawsuit, then Morrison should recognize a provision at December 31, 2015.

Measurement of Provisions

How does a company like Toyota (JPN), for example, determine the amount to report for its warranty cost on its automobiles? How does a company like Carrefour (FRA) determine its liability for customer refunds? Or, how does Novartis (CHE) determine the amount to report for a lawsuit that it probably will lose? And, how does a company like Total S.A. (FRA) determine the amount to report as a provision for its remediation costs related to environmental clean-up?

IFRS provides an answer: The amount recognized should be the **best estimate of the expenditure required to settle the present obligation**. Best estimate represents the amount that a company would pay to settle the obligation at the statement of financial position date. [7]

In determining the best estimate, the management of a company must use judgment, based on past or similar transactions, discussions with experts, and any other pertinent information. Here is how this judgment might be used in three different types of situations to arrive at best estimate:

- *Toyota warranties.* Toyota sells many cars and must make an estimate of the number of warranty repairs and related costs it will incur. Because it is dealing with a large population of automobiles, it is often best to weight all possible outcomes by associated probabilities. For example, it might determine that 80 percent of its cars will not have any warranty cost, 12 percent will have substantial costs, and 8 percent will have a much smaller cost. In this case, by weighting all the possible outcomes by their associated probabilities, Toyota **arrives at an expected value** for its warranty liability.

- *Carrefour refunds.* Carrefour sells many items at varying selling prices. Refunds to customers for products sold may be viewed as a continuous range of refunds, with each point in the range having the same probability of occurrence. In this case, the **midpoint in the range** can be used as the basis for measuring the amount of the refunds.

- *Novartis lawsuit.* Large companies like Novartis are involved in numerous litigation issues related to their products. Where a single obligation such as a lawsuit is being measured, **the most likely outcome** of the lawsuit may be the best estimate of the liability.

In each of these situations, the measurement of the liability should consider the time value of money, if material. In addition, future events that may have an impact on the measurement of the costs should be considered. For example, a company like Total S.A., which may have high remediation costs related to environmental clean-up, may consider future technological innovations that reduce future costs if reasonably certain of happening.

Common Types of Provisions

Here are some common areas for which provisions may be recognized in the financial statements:

1. Lawsuits   **4.** Environmental

2. Warranties   **5.** Onerous contracts

3. Consideration payable   **6.** Restructuring

Although companies generally report only one current and one non-current amount for provisions in the statement of financial position, IFRS also requires extensive disclosure related to provisions in the notes to the financial statements. Companies do not record or report in the notes to the financial statements general risk contingencies inherent in business operations (e.g., the possibility of war, strike, uninsurable catastrophes, or a business recession). **[8]**

Litigation Provisions

Companies must consider the following factors, among others, in determining whether to record a liability with respect to **pending or threatened** litigation and actual or possible claims and assessments.

1. The **time period** in which the underlying cause of action occurred.

2. The **probability** of an unfavorable outcome.

3. The ability to make a **reasonable estimate** of the amount of loss.

To report a loss and a liability in the financial statements, **the cause for litigation must have occurred on or before the date of the financial statements**. It does not matter that the company became aware of the existence or possibility of the lawsuit or claims after the date of the financial statements but before issuing them. To evaluate the probability of an unfavorable outcome, a company considers the following: the nature of the litigation, the progress of the case, the opinion of legal counsel, its own and others' experience in similar cases, and any management response to the lawsuit.

With respect to **unfiled suits** and **unasserted claims and assessments**, a company must determine (1) the degree of **probability** that a suit may be filed or a claim or assessment may be asserted, and (2) the **probability** of an unfavorable outcome. For example, assume that a regulatory body investigates the Nawtee Company for restraint of trade and institutes enforcement proceedings. Private claims of triple damages for redress often follow such proceedings. In this case, Nawtee must determine the probability of the claims being asserted **and** the probability of triple damages being awarded. If both are probable, if the loss is reasonably estimable, and if the cause for action is dated on or before the date of the financial statements, then Nawtee should accrue the liability.

Companies can seldom predict the outcome of pending litigation, however, with any assurance. And, even if evidence available at the statement of financial position date does not favor the company, it is hardly reasonable to expect the company to publish in its financial statements a dollar estimate of the probable negative outcome. Such specific disclosures might weaken the company's position in the dispute and encourage the plaintiff to intensify its efforts. As a result, many companies provide a general provision for the costs expected to be incurred without relating the disclosure to any specific lawsuit or set of lawsuits. Illustration 13-8 provides the disclosure by Nestlé Group (CHE) related to its litigation claims.

ILLUSTRATION 13-8
Litigation Disclosure

 Nestlé Group

Notes to the financial statements (partial)

Litigation

Litigation provisions have been set up to cover tax, legal and administrative proceedings that arise in the ordinary course of business. These provisions concern numerous cases whose detailed disclosure could seriously prejudice the interests of the Group. Reversal of such provisions refer to cases resolved in favor of the Group. The timing of cash outflows of litigation provisions is uncertain as it depends upon the outcome of the proceedings. These provisions are therefore not discounted because their present value would not represent meaningful information. Group Management does not believe it is possible to make assumptions on the evolution of the cases beyond the balance sheet date.

Warranty Provisions

A warranty **(product guarantee)** is a promise made by a seller to a buyer to make good on a deficiency of quantity, quality, or performance in a product. Manufacturers commonly use it as a sales promotion technique. Automakers, for instance, "hyped" their sales by extending their new-car warranty to seven years or 100,000 miles. For a specified period of time following the date of sale to the consumer, the manufacturer may promise to bear all or part of the cost of replacing defective parts, to perform any necessary repairs or servicing without charge, to refund the purchase price, or even to "double your money back."

Warranties and guarantees entail future costs. These additional costs, sometimes called "after costs" or "post-sale costs," frequently are significant. Although the future cost is indefinite as to amount, due date, and even customer, a liability is probable in most cases. Companies should recognize this liability in the accounts if they can reasonably estimate it. The estimated amount of the liability includes all the costs that the company will incur after sale and delivery and that are incident to the correction of defects or deficiencies required under the warranty provisions. Thus, warranty costs are a classic example of a provision.

Companies often provide one of two types of warranties to customers:

1. Warranty that the product meets agreed-upon specifications in the contract at the time the product is sold. This type of warranty is included in the sales price of a company's product and is often referred to as an assurance-type warranty.

2. Warranty that provides an additional service beyond the assurance-type warranty. This warranty is not included in the sales price of the product and is referred to as a service-type warranty. As a result, it is recorded as a separate performance obligation.

Assurance-Type Warranty. Companies do not record a separate performance obligation for assurance-type warranties. This type of warranty is nothing more than a quality guarantee that the good or service is free from defects at the point of sale. These types of obligations should be expensed in the period the goods are provided or services performed (in other words, at the point of sale). In addition, the company should record a warranty liability. The estimated amount of the liability includes all the costs that the company will incur after sale due to the correction of defects or deficiencies required under the warranty provisions. Illustration 13-9 provides an example of an assurance-type warranty.

ILLUSTRATION 13-9
Accounting for an
Assurance-Type
Warranty

ASSURANCE-TYPE WARRANTY

Facts: Denson Machinery Company begins production of a new machine in July 2015 and sells 100 of these machines for $5,000 cash by year-end. Each machine is under warranty for one year. Denson estimates, based on past experience with similar machines, that the warranty cost will average $200 per unit. Further, as a result of parts replacements and services performed in compliance with machinery warranties, it incurs $4,000 in warranty costs in 2015 and $16,000 in 2016.

Question: What are the journal entries for the sale and the related warranty costs for 2015 and 2016?

Solution: For the sale of the machines and related warranty costs in 2015 the entry is as follows.

1. To recognize sales of machines and accrual of warranty liability:

July–December 2015

Cash	500,000	
Warranty Expense	20,000	
Warranty Liability		20,000
Sales Revenue		500,000

2. To record payment for warranties incurred:

July–December 2015

Warranty Liability	4,000	
Cash, Inventory, Accrued Payroll		4,000

The December 31, 2015, statement of financial position reports Warranty Liability as a current liability of $16,000. The income statement for 2015 reports Warranty Expense of $20,000.

3. To record payment for warranty costs incurred in 2016 related to 2015 machinery sales:

January 1–December 31, 2016

Warranty Liability	16,000	
Cash, Inventory, Accrued Payroll		16,000

At the end of 2016, no warranty liability is reported for the machinery sold in 2015.

Service-Type Warranty. A warranty is sometimes sold separately from the product. For example, when you purchase a television, you are entitled to an assurance-type warranty. You also will undoubtedly be offered an extended warranty on the product at an additional cost, referred to as a service-type warranty. In most cases, service-type warranties provide the customer a service beyond fixing defects that existed at the time of sale.

Companies record a service-type warranty as a separate performance obligation. For example, in the case of the television, the seller recognizes the sale of the television with the assurance-type warranty separately from the sale of the service-type warranty. The sale of the service-type warranty is usually recorded in an Unearned Warranty Revenue account.

Companies then recognize revenue on a straight-line basis over the period the service-type warranty is in effect. Companies only defer and amortize costs that vary with and are directly related to the sale of the contracts (mainly commissions). Companies expense employees' salaries and wages, advertising, and general and administrative expenses because these costs occur even if the company did not sell the service-type warranty. Illustration 13-10 presents an example of both an assurance-type and service-type warranty.

ILLUSTRATION 13-10
Assurance-Type and
Service-Type Warranties

WARRANTIES

Facts: You purchase an automobile from Hamlin Auto for €30,000 on January 2, 2014. Hamlin estimates the assurance-type warranty costs on the automobile to be €700 (Hamlin will pay for repairs for the first 36,000 miles or three years, whichever comes first). You also purchase for €900 a service-type warranty for an additional three years or 36,000 miles. Hamlin incurs warranty costs related to the assurance-type warranty of €500 in 2014 and €200 in 2015. Hamlin records revenue on the service-type warranty on a straight-line basis.

Question: What entries should Hamlin make in 2014 and 2017?

Solution:

1. To record the sale of the automobile and related warranties:

January 2, 2014

Cash (€30,000 + €900)	30,900	
Warranty Expense	700	
Warranty Liability		700
Unearned Warranty Revenue		900
Sales Revenue		30,000

2. To record warranty costs incurred in 2014:

January 2–December 31, 2014

Warranty Liability	500	
Cash, Inventory, Accrued Payroll		500

3. To record revenue recognized in 2017 on the service-type warranty:

January 1–December 31, 2017

Unearned Warranty Revenue (€900 ÷ 3)	300	
Warranty Revenue		300

Consideration Payable

Companies often make payments (provide consideration) to their customers as part of a revenue arrangement. Consideration paid or payable may indicate discounts, volume rebates, free products, or services. For example, numerous companies offer premiums (either on a limited or continuing basis) to customers in return for box tops, certificates, coupons, labels, or wrappers. The **premium** may be silverware, dishes, a small appliance, a toy, or free transportation. Also, **printed coupons** that can be redeemed for a cash discount on items purchased are extremely popular. Another popular marketing innovation is the **cash rebate**, which the buyer can obtain by returning the store receipt, a rebate coupon, and Universal Product Code (UPC label) or "bar code" to the manufacturer.

Companies offer premiums, coupon offers, and rebates to stimulate sales. Thus, companies should charge the **costs of premiums and coupons to expense in the period of the sale** that benefits from the plan. The period that benefits is not necessarily the period in which the company pays the premium. At the end of the accounting period, many premium offers may be outstanding and must be redeemed when presented in subsequent periods. In order to reflect the existing current liability and to match costs with revenues, the company estimates the number of outstanding premium offers that customers will present for redemption. The company then charges the cost of premium offers to Premium Expense. It credits the outstanding obligations to an account titled Premium Liability. Illustration 13-11 provides an example of the accounting for consideration payable using premiums.

ILLUSTRATION 13-11
Accounting for
Consideration Payable

CONSIDERATION PAYABLE

Facts: Fluffy Cake Mix Company sells boxes of cake mix for £3 per box. In addition, Fluffy Cake Mix offers its customers a large durable mixing bowl in exchange for £1 and 10 box tops. The mixing bowl costs Fluffy Cake Mix £2, and the company estimates that customers will redeem 60 percent of the box tops. The premium offer began in June 2015. During 2015, Fluffy Cake Mix purchased 20,000 mixing bowls at £2, sold 300,000 boxes of cake mix for £3 per box, and redeemed 60,000 box tops.

Question: What entries should Fluffy Cake Mix record in 2015?

Solution:

1. To record purchase of 20,000 mixing bowls at £2 per bowl:

Premium Inventory (20,000 mixing bowls × £2)	40,000	
Cash		40,000

2. Before Fluffy Cake Mix makes the entry to record the sale of the cake mix boxes, it determines its premium expense and related premium liability. This computation is as follows.

Total box tops sold in 2015	300,000
Estimated redemptions (in percent)	60%
Total estimated redemptions	180,000
Cost of estimated redemptions	
[(180,000 box tops ÷ 10) × (£2 − £1)]	£18,000

The entry to record the sale of the cake mix boxes and premium expense and premium liability is as follows.

Cash (300,000 boxes of cake mix × £3)	900,000	
Premium Expense	18,000	
Sales Revenue		900,000
Premium Liability		18,000

3. To record the actual redemption of 60,000 box tops, the receipt of £1 per 10 box tops, and the delivery of the mixing bowls:

Cash [(60,000 ÷ 10) × £1]	6,000	
Premium Liability	6,000	
Premium Inventory [(60,000 ÷ 10) × £2]		12,000

The December 31, 2015, statement of financial position of Fluffy Cake Mix Company reports Premium Inventory of £28,000 (£40,000 − £12,000) as a current asset and Premium Liability of £12,000 (£18,000 − £6,000) as a current liability. The 2015 income statement reports £18,000 premium expense as a selling expense.

Numerous companies offer premiums to customers in the form of a promise of future goods or services as an incentive for purchases today. Premium plans that have widespread adoption are the frequent-flyer programs used by all major airlines. On the basis of mileage accumulated, frequent-flyer members receive discounted or free airline tickets. Airline customers can earn miles toward free travel by making long-distance phone calls, staying in hotels, and charging gasoline and groceries on a credit card. Those free tickets represent an enormous potential liability because people using them may displace paying passengers.

When airlines first started offering frequent-flyer bonuses, everyone assumed that they could accommodate the free-ticket holders with otherwise empty seats. That made the additional cost of the program so minimal that airlines didn't accrue it or report the small liability. But, as more and more paying passengers have been crowded off flights by frequent-flyer awardees, the loss of revenues has grown enormously. For example, Qantas Airways Limited (AUS) recently reported a liability of $4,508 million for advance ticket sales, including frequent-flyer obligations.

Environmental Provisions

Estimates to clean up existing toxic waste sites are substantial. In addition, cost estimates of cleaning up our air and preventing future deterioration of the environment run even higher.

In many industries, the construction and operation of long-lived assets involves obligations for the retirement of those assets. When a mining company opens up a strip mine, it may also commit to restore the land once it completes mining. Similarly, when an oil company erects an offshore drilling platform, it may be legally obligated to dismantle and remove the platform at the end of its useful life.

Accounting Recognition of Environmental Liabilities. As with other provisions, a company must recognize an environmental liability when it has an existing legal obligation associated with the retirement of a long-lived asset and when it can reasonably estimate the amount of the liability.

Obligating events. Examples of existing legal obligations that require recognition of a liability include but are not limited to:

- Decommissioning nuclear facilities.
- Dismantling, restoring, and reclamation of oil and gas properties.
- Certain closure, reclamation, and removal costs of mining facilities.
- Closure and postclosure costs of landfills.

In order to capture the benefits of these long-lived assets, **the company is generally legally obligated for the costs associated with retirement of the asset, whether the company hires another party to perform the retirement activities or performs the activities with its own workforce and equipment**. Environmental liabilities give rise to various recognition patterns. For example, the obligation may arise at the outset of the asset's use (e.g., erection of an oil rig), or it may build over time (e.g., a landfill that expands over time).

Measurement. A company initially measures an environmental liability at the best estimate of its future costs. The estimate should reflect the amount a company would pay in an active market to settle its obligation (essentially fair value). While active markets do not exist for many environmental liabilities, companies should estimate fair value based on the best information available. Such information could include market prices of similar liabilities, if available. Alternatively, companies may use present value techniques to estimate fair value.

Recognition and allocation. To record an environmental liability in the financial statements, a company includes the cost associated with the environmental liability in the carrying amount of the related long-lived asset, and records a liability for the same amount. It records the environmental costs as part of the related asset because these costs are tied to operating the asset and are necessary to prepare the asset for its intended use. Therefore, the specific asset (e.g., mine, drilling platform, nuclear power plant) should be increased because the future economic benefit comes from the use of this productive asset. **Companies should not record the capitalized environmental costs in a separate account because there is no future economic benefit that can be associated with these costs alone.**

In subsequent periods, companies allocate the cost of the asset to expense over the period of the related asset's useful life. Companies may use the straight-line method for this allocation, as well as other systematic and rational allocations.

Example of accounting provisions. To illustrate the accounting for these types of environmental liabilities, assume that on January 1, 2015, Wildcat Oil Company erected an oil platform in the Gulf of Mexico. Wildcat is legally required to dismantle and remove the platform at the end of its useful life, estimated to be five years. Wildcat estimates that dismantling and removal will cost $1,000,000. Based on a 10 percent discount rate, the fair value of the environmental liability is estimated to be $620,920 ($1,000,000 × .62092). Wildcat records this liability as follows.

January 1, 2015

Drilling Platform	620,920	
Environmental Liability		620,920

During the life of the asset, Wildcat allocates the asset cost to expense. Using the straight-line method, Wildcat makes the following entries to record this expense.

December 31, 2015, 2016, 2017, 2018

Depreciation Expense ($620,920 ÷ 5)	124,184	
Accumulated Depreciation—Plant Assets		124,184

In addition, Wildcat must accrue interest expense each period. Wildcat records interest expense and the related increase in the environmental liability on December 31, 2015, as follows.

December 31, 2015

Interest Expense ($620,920 × 10%)	62,092	
Environmental Liability		62,092

On January 10, 2020, Wildcat contracts with Rig Reclaimers, Inc. to dismantle the platform at a contract price of $995,000. Wildcat makes the following journal entry to record settlement of the liability.

January 10, 2020

Environmental Liability	1,000,000	
Gain on Settlement of Environmental Liability		5,000
Cash		995,000

As indicated, as a result of the discounting, Wildcat incurs two types of costs: (1) an operating cost related to depreciation expense, and (2) a finance cost related to interest expense. The recording of the interest expense is often referred to as "unwinding the discount," which refers to the fact that the obligation was discounted as a result of present value computations. This discount can be substantial. For example, when **BP plc** (GBR) changed its policy and started discounting its environmental provision, it decreased its initial obligation by £350 million.

A company like Wildcat can consider future events when considering the measurement of the liability. For example, a technological development that will make restoration less expensive and is virtually certain to happen should be considered. Generally, future events are limited to those that are virtually certain to happen, as well as technology advances or proposed legislation that will impact future costs.

Onerous Contract Provisions

Sometimes, companies have what are referred to as **onerous contracts**. These contracts are ones in which "the unavoidable costs of meeting the obligations exceed the economic benefits expected to be received." **[9]** An example of an onerous contract is a loss recognized on unfavorable non-cancelable purchase commitments related to inventory items (discussed in Chapter 9).

To illustrate another situation, assume that Sumart Sports operates profitably in a factory that it has leased and on which it pays monthly rentals. Sumart decides to relocate its operations to another facility. However, the lease on the old facility continues for the next three years. Unfortunately, Sumart cannot cancel the lease nor will it be able to sublet the factory to another party. The expected costs to satisfy this onerous contract are €200,000. In this case, Sumart makes the following entry.

Loss on Lease Contract	200,000	
Lease Contract Liability		200,000

The expected costs should reflect the least net cost of exiting from the contract, which is the lower of (1) the cost of fulfilling the contract, or (2) the compensation or penalties arising from failure to fulfill the contract.

To illustrate, assume the same facts as above for the Sumart example and the expected costs to fulfill the contract are €200,000. However, Sumart can cancel the lease by paying a penalty of €175,000. In this case, Sumart should record the liability at €175,000.

Illustration 13-12 indicates how **Nestlé Group** (CHE) discloses onerous contracts.

ILLUSTRATION 13-12
Onerous Contract
Disclosure

Nestlé Group

Notes to the financial statements (partial)

Other Provisions

Other provisions are mainly constituted by onerous contracts, liabilities for partial refund of selling prices of divested businesses and various damage claims having occurred during the period but not covered by insurance companies. Onerous contracts result from unfavorable leases or supply agreements above market prices in which the unavoidable costs of meeting the obligations under the contracts exceed the economic benefits expected to be received or for which no benefits are expected to be received. These agreements have been entered into as a result of selling and closing inefficient facilities.

Restructuring Provisions

The accounting for **restructuring** provisions is controversial. Once companies make a decision to restructure part of their operations, they have the temptation to charge as many costs as possible to this provision. The rationale: Many believe analysts often dismiss these costs as not part of continuing operations and therefore somewhat irrelevant in assessing the overall performance of the company. Burying as many costs as possible in a restructuring provision therefore permits companies to provide a more optimistic presentation of current operating results.

On the other hand, companies are continually in a state of flux, and what constitutes a restructuring is often difficult to assess. One thing is certain—companies should not be permitted to provide for future operating losses in the current period when accounting for restructuring costs. Nor should they be permitted to bury operating costs in the restructuring cost classification. **[10]**

As a consequence, IFRS is very restrictive regarding when a restructuring provision can be recorded and what types of costs may be included in a restructuring provision. Restructurings are defined as a "program that is planned and controlled by management and materially changes either (1) the scope of a business undertaken by the company; or (2) the manner in which that business is conducted." Examples of restructurings are the sale of a line of business, changes in management structures such as eliminating a layer of management, or closure of operations in a country.

For a company to record restructuring costs and a related liability, it must meet the general requirements for recording provisions discussed earlier. In addition, to assure that the restructuring is valid, companies are required to have a detailed formal plan for the restructuring and to have raised a valid expectation to those affected by implementation or announcement of the plan.

Only direct incremental costs associated with the restructuring may be included in the restructuring provision. At the same time, IFRS provides specific guidance related to certain costs and losses that should be excluded from the restructuring provision. Illustration 13-13 provides a summary of costs that may and may not be included in a restructuring provision.

Costs Included (direct, incremental)	Costs Excluded
• Employee termination costs related directly to the restructuring. • Contract termination costs, such as lease termination penalties. • Onerous contract provisions.	• Investment in new systems. • Lower utilization of facilities. • Costs of training or relocating staff. • Costs of moving assets or operations. • Administration or marketing costs. • Allocations of corporate overhead. • Expected future operating costs or expected operating losses unless they relate to an onerous contract.

ILLUSTRATION 13-13
Costs Included/Excluded from Restructuring Provision

In general, the costs-excluded list is comprised of expenditures that relate to the future operations of the business and are not liabilities associated with the restructuring as of the end of the reporting period. Therefore, such expenditures are recognized on the same basis as if they arose independently of a restructuring. **[11]**

The case of Rodea Group's solar panel division, presented in Illustration 13-14, provides an example of a restructuring.

ILLUSTRATION 13-14
Accounting for Restructuring

CLOSURE OF DIVISION

Facts: On December 12, 2015, the board of Rodea decided to close down a division making solar panels. On December 20, 2015, a detailed plan for closing down the division was agreed to by the board; letters were sent to customers warning them to seek an alternative source of supply and termination notices were sent to the staff of the division. Rodea estimates that it is probable that it will have €500,000 in restructuring costs.

Question: Should Rodea report a restructuring liability if it has costs related to the restructuring?

Solution: (1) The past obligating event for Rodea is the communication of the decision to the customers and employees, which gives rise to a constructive obligation on December 31, 2015, because it creates a valid expectation that the division will be closed. (2) An outflow of resources in settlement is probable and reliably estimated. A provision is recognized at December 31, 2015, for the best estimate of closing the division, in this case, €500,000.

Self-Insurance

As discussed earlier, liabilities are not recorded for general risks (e.g., losses that might arise due to poor expected economic conditions). Similarly, companies do not record liabilities for more specific future risks such as allowances for repairs. These items do not meet the definition of a liability because they do not arise from a past transaction but instead relate to future events.

Some companies take out insurance policies against the potential losses from fire, flood, storm, and accident. Other companies do not. The reasons: Some risks are not insurable, the insurance rates are prohibitive (e.g., earthquakes and riots), or the companies make a business decision to self-insure. Self-insurance is another item that is not recognized as a provision.

Despite its name, self-insurance is **not insurance but risk assumption**. Any company that assumes its own risks puts itself in the position of incurring expenses or losses as they occur. There is little theoretical justification for the establishment of a liability based on a hypothetical charge to insurance expense. This is "as if" accounting. The conditions for accrual stated in IFRS are not satisfied prior to the occurrence of the event. Until that time, there is no diminution in the value of the property. And unlike an insurance company, which has contractual obligations to reimburse policyholders for losses, a company can have no such obligation to itself and, hence, no liability either before or after the occurrence of damage.[9]

Exposure to **risks of loss resulting from uninsured past injury to others**, however, is an existing condition involving uncertainty about the amount and timing of losses that may develop. A company with a fleet of vehicles for example, would have to accrue uninsured losses resulting from injury to others or damage to the property of others that took place prior to the date of the financial statements (if the experience of the company or other information enables it to make a reasonable estimate of the liability).[10] However, it should not establish a liability for **expected future injury** to others or damage to the property of others, even if it can reasonably estimate the amount of losses.

Disclosures Related to Provisions

The disclosures related to provisions are extensive. A company must provide a reconciliation of its beginning to ending balance for each major class of provisions, identifying what caused the change during the period. In addition, the provision must be described and the expected timing of any outflows disclosed. Also, disclosure about uncertainties related to expected outflows as well as expected reimbursements should be provided. **[12]** Illustration 13-15 provides an example, based on the provisions note in Nokia's (FIN) annual report.

---

[9]A commentary in the financial magazine *Forbes* (June 15, 1974), p. 42, stated its position on this matter quite succinctly: "The simple and unquestionable fact of life is this: Business is cyclical and full of unexpected surprises. Is it the role of accounting to disguise this unpleasant fact and create a fairyland of smoothly rising earnings? Or, should accounting reflect reality, warts and all—floods, expropriations and all manner of rude shocks?"

[10]This type of situation is often referred to as "an incurred but not recorded" (IBNR) provision. A company may not be able to identify the claims giving rise to the obligation, but it knows a past obligating event has occurred.

Nokia

Notes to the Financial Statements (partial)

27. Provisions

(€ in millions)

	Warranty	Restructuring	IPR infringements	Material liability	Project losses	Tax	Other	Total
At January 1, 2012	688	459	431	125	205	299	420	2,627
Exchange differences	3	—	—	4	—	(11)	(7)	(11)
Acquisitions	—	—	—	—	—	—	—	—
Additional provisions	340	1,458	38	300	247	99	159	2,641
Changes in estimates	(28)	(112)	(63)	(85)	(65)	(45)	(73)	(471)
Charged to profit and loss account	312	1,346	(25)	215	182	54	86	2,170
Utilized during year	(596)	(1,152)	(18)	(102)	(238)	(15)	(46)	(2,167)
At December 31, 2012	**407**	**653**	**388**	**242**	**149**	**327**	**453**	**2,619**

	2012	2011
Analysis of total provisions at December 31:		
Non-current	971	1,175
Current	1,648	1,452

Outflows for the warranty provision are generally expected to occur within the next 18 months. Timing of outflows related to tax provisions is inherently uncertain.

The restructuring provision is mainly related to restructuring activities in Devices & Services and Nokia Siemens Networks businesses. The majority of outflows related to the restructuring is expected to occur during 2013.

In February 2012, Nokia announced planned changes at its factories in Komarom, Hungary, Reynosa, Mexico and Salo, Finland to increase efficiency in smartphone manufacturing. In June 2012, Nokia announced additional actions to align its workforce and operations. The planned actions was expected to lead to a total reduction of up to 10,000 positions globally by the end of 2013. As part of this Nokia planned to make significant reductions in certain R&D projects, which resulted in the closure of Ulm in Germany and Burnaby, Canada; reduce factory operations, including the closure of the factory in Salo; prioritize sales efforts around certain markets resulting in reducing headcount in certain other markets; align support functions around Nokia's focused strategy resulting in a significant reduction in the number of employees in corporate functions. As a result, Devices & Services recognized restructuring charges of €550 million in total.

The IPR provision is based on estimated potential future settlements for asserted past IPR infringements. Final resolution of IPR claims generally occurs over several periods.

Material liability provision relates to non-cancellable purchase commitments with suppliers. The outflows are expected to occur over the next 12 months.

Provisions for losses on projects in progress are related to Nokia Siemens Networks' onerous contracts. Utilization of provisions for project losses is generally expected to occur in the next 12 months.

Other provisions include provisions for various contractual obligations and provisions for pension and other social security costs on share-based awards.

ILLUSTRATION 13-15
Provisions Disclosure

CONTINGENCIES

In a general sense, all provisions are contingent because they are uncertain in timing or amount. However, IFRS uses the term "contingent" for liabilities and assets that are not recognized in the financial statements. **[13]**

5 LEARNING OBJECTIVE

Identify the criteria used to account for and disclose contingent liabilities and assets.

Contingent Liabilities

Contingent liabilities are not recognized in the financial statements because they are (1) a possible obligation (not yet confirmed as a present obligation), (2) a present obligation for which it is not probable that payment will be made, or (3) a present obligation for which a reliable estimate of the obligation cannot be made. Examples of contingent liabilities are:

- A lawsuit in which it is only possible that the company might lose.
- A guarantee related to collectibility of a receivable.

Illustration 13-16 presents the general guidelines for the accounting and reporting of contingent liabilities.

ILLUSTRATION 13-16
Contingent Liability
Guidelines

Outcome	Probability*	Accounting Treatment
Virtually certain	At least 90%	Report as liability (provision).
Probable (more likely than not)	51–89% probable	Report as liability (provision).
Possible but not probable	5–50%	Disclosure required.
Remote	Less than 5%	No disclosure required.

*In practice, the percentages for virtually certain and remote may deviate from those presented here.

Unless the possibility of any outflow in settlement is remote, companies should disclose the contingent liability at the end of the reporting period, providing a brief description of the nature of the contingent liability and, where practicable:

1. An estimate of its financial effect;
2. An indication of the uncertainties relating to the amount or timing of any outflow; and
3. The possibility of any reimbursement.

Illustration 13-17 provides a disclosure by Barloworld Limited (ZAF) related to its contingent liabilities.

ILLUSTRATION 13-17
Contingent Liability
Disclosure

Barloworld Limited

(R in millions)	2012	2011
Contingent liabilities (in part)		
Bills, lease and hire-purchase agreements discounted with recourse, other guarantees and claims	1,440	1,316
Buy-back and repurchase commitments not reflected on the balance sheet	131	161

The related assets are estimated to have a value at least equal to the repurchase commitment.

The group has given guarantees to the purchaser of the coatings Australian business relating to environmental claims. The guarantees are for a maximum period of eight years and are limited to the sales price received for the business. Freeworld Coatings Limited is responsible for the first AUD5 million of any claim in terms of the unbundling arrangement.

Warranties and guarantees have been given as a consequence of the various disposals completed during the year and prior years. None are expected to have a material impact on the financial results of the group.

There are no material contingent liabilities in joint venture companies. Litigation, current or pending, is not considered likely to have a material adverse effect on the group.

Contingent Assets

A **contingent asset** is a possible asset that arises from past events and whose existence will be confirmed by the occurrence or non-occurrence of uncertain future events not wholly within the control of the company. **[14]** Typical contingent assets are:

1. Possible receipts of monies from gifts, donations, and bonuses.
2. Possible refunds from the government in tax disputes.
3. Pending court cases with a probable favorable outcome.

Contingent assets are not recognized on the statement of financial position. If realization of the contingent asset is virtually certain, it is no longer considered a contingent asset and is recognized as an asset. **Virtually certain** is generally interpreted to be at least a probability of 90 percent or more.

The general rules related to contingent assets are presented in Illustration 13-18.

Outcome	Probability*	Accounting Treatment
Virtually certain	At least 90% probable	Report as asset (no longer contingent).
Probable (more likely than not)	51–90% probable	Disclose.
Possible but not probable	5–50%	No disclosure required.
Remote	Less than 5%	No disclosure required.

*In practice, the percentages for virtually certain and remote may deviate from those presented here.

ILLUSTRATION 13-18
Contingent Asset Guidelines

Contingent assets are disclosed when an inflow of economic benefits is considered more likely than not to occur (greater than 50 percent). However, it is important that disclosures for contingent assets avoid giving misleading indications of the likelihood of income arising. As a result, it is not surprising that the thresholds for allowing recognition of contingent assets are more stringent relative to those for liabilities.

What might be an example of a contingent asset that becomes an asset to be recorded? To illustrate, assume that Marcus Realty leases a property to **Marks and Spencer plc (M&S)** (GBR). The contract is non-cancelable for five years. On December 1, 2015, before the end of the contract, M&S withdraws from the contract and is required to pay £245,000 as a penalty. At the time M&S cancels the contract, a receivable and related income should be reported by Marcus. The disclosure includes the nature and, where practicable, the estimated financial effects of the asset.

PRESENTATION AND ANALYSIS
Presentation of Current Liabilities

In practice, current liabilities are usually recorded and reported in financial statements at their full maturity value. Because of the short time periods involved, frequently less than one year, the difference between the present value of a current liability and the maturity value is usually not large. The profession accepts as immaterial any slight overstatement of liabilities that results from carrying current liabilities at maturity value.

6 LEARNING OBJECTIVE
Indicate how to present and analyze liability-related information.

The current liabilities accounts are commonly presented after non-current liabilities in the statement of financial position. Within the current liabilities section, companies may list the accounts in order of maturity, in descending order of amount, or in order of liquidation preference. Illustration 13-19 presents an adapted excerpt of **Wilmar International Limited**'s (SGP) financial statements that is representative of the reports of large corporations.

ILLUSTRATION 13-19
Current Assets and
Current Liabilities

Wilmar International Limited
December 31
(in thousands)

Current assets	2012	2011
Inventories	$ 7,137,227	$ 7,265,300
Trade receivables	3,953,104	3,502,925
Other financial receivables	2,162,266	3,156,123
Other non-financial assets	1,432,703	1,368,955
Derivative financial instruments	254,126	239,354
Financial assets held for trading	317,887	333,715
Other bank deposits	6,981,163	6,521,570
Cash and bank balances	1,581,003	1,376,783
	$23,819,479	$23,764,725
Current liabilities		
Trade payables	$ 1,579,750	$ 1,710,004
Other financial payables	1,204,336	1,147,089
Other non-financial liabilities	494,796	469,834
Derivative financial instruments	271,924	263,402
Loans and borrowings	17,740,250	18,409,070
Tax payables	122,227	146,086
	$21,413,283	$22,145,485

Detail and supplemental information concerning current liabilities should be sufficient to meet the requirement of full disclosure. Companies should clearly identify secured liabilities, as well as indicate the related assets pledged as collateral. If the due date of any liability can be extended, a company should disclose the details. Companies should not offset current liabilities against assets that it will apply to their liquidation. Finally, current maturities of long-term debt are classified as current liabilities.

Analysis of Current Liabilities

The distinction between current and non-current liabilities is important. It provides information about the liquidity of the company. Liquidity regarding a liability is the expected time to elapse before its payment. In other words, a liability soon to be paid is a current liability. A liquid company is better able to withstand a financial downturn. Also, it has a better chance of taking advantage of investment opportunities that develop.

Analysts use certain basic ratios such as net cash flow provided by operating activities to current liabilities, and the turnover ratios for receivables and inventory, to assess liquidity. Two other ratios used to examine liquidity are the current ratio and the acid-test ratio.

Current Ratio

The current ratio is the ratio of total current assets to total current liabilities. Illustration 13-20 shows its formula.

ILLUSTRATION 13-20
Formula for Current
Ratio

$$\text{Current Ratio} = \frac{\text{Current Assets}}{\text{Current Liabilities}}$$

The ratio is frequently expressed as a coverage of so many times. Sometimes it is called the working capital ratio because working capital is the excess of current assets over current liabilities.

A satisfactory current ratio does not provide information on the portion of the current assets that may be tied up in slow-moving inventories. With inventories, especially raw materials and work in process, there is a question of how long it will take to transform them into the finished product and what ultimately will be realized in the sale of the merchandise. Eliminating the inventories, along with any prepaid expenses, from the amount of current assets might provide better information for short-term creditors. Therefore, some analysts use the acid-test ratio in place of the current ratio.

Acid-Test Ratio

Many analysts favor an **acid-test** or **quick ratio** that relates total current liabilities to cash, short-term investments, and receivables. Illustration 13-21 shows the formula for this ratio. As you can see, the acid-test ratio does not include inventories and prepaid expenses.

$$\text{Acid-Test Ratio} = \frac{\text{Cash} + \text{Short-Term Investments} + \text{Net Receivables}}{\text{Current Liabilities}}$$

ILLUSTRATION 13-21
Formula for Acid-Test Ratio

To illustrate the computation of these two ratios, we use the information for Wilmar International Limited (SGP) in Illustration 13-19 (on page 626). Illustration 13-22 shows the computation of the current and acid-test ratios for Wilmar.

$$\text{Current Ratio} = \frac{\text{Current Assets}}{\text{Current Liabilities}} = \frac{\$23,819,479}{\$21,413,283} = 1.11 \text{ times}$$

$$\text{Acid-Test Ratio} = \frac{\text{Cash} + \text{Short-Term Investments} + \text{Net Receivables}}{\text{Current Liabilities}} = \frac{\$16,682,252}{\$21,413,283} = 0.78 \text{ times}$$

ILLUSTRATION 13-22
Computation of Current and Acid-Test Ratios for Wilmar

Evolving Issue — GREENHOUSE GASES: LET'S BE STANDARD-SETTERS

Ok, here is your chance to determine what to do about a very fundamental issue—how to account for greenhouse gases (GHG), often referred to as carbon emissions. Many governments are trying a market-based system, in which companies pay for an excessive amount of carbon emissions put into the atmosphere. In this market-based system, companies are granted carbon allowance permits. Each permit allows them to discharge, as an example, one metric ton of carbon dioxide (CO_2). In some cases, companies may receive a number of these permits free—in other situations, they must pay for them. Other approaches require companies only to pay when they exceed a certain amount.

The question is, how to account for these permits and related liabilities? For example, what happens when the permits issued by the government are free? Should an asset and revenue be reported? And if an asset is recorded, should the debit be to an intangible asset or inventory? Also, should the company recognize a liability related to its pollution? And how do we account for companies that have to purchase permits because they have exceeded their allowance? Two views seem to have emerged. The first is referred to as the **net liability approach**. In this approach, a company does not recognize an asset or liability. A company only recognizes a liability once GHG exceed the permits granted.

To illustrate, Holton Refinery receives permits on January 1, 2015, representing the right to emit 10,000 tons of GHG for the year 2015. Other data:

• The market price of each permit at date of issuance is €10 per ton.

- During the year, Holton emits 12,000 tons.
- The market price for a permit is €16 per ton at December 31, 2015.

Under the net liability approach, Holton records only a liability of €32,000 for the additional amount that it must pay for the 2,000 permits it must purchase at €16 per ton.

Another approach is referred to as the **government grant approach**. In this approach, permits granted by the govern-

ment are recorded at their fair value based on the initial price of €10 per ton. The asset recorded is an intangible asset. At the same time, an unearned revenue account is credited, which is subsequently recognized in income over the 2015 year. During 2015, a liability and a related emission expense of €132,000 is recognized (10,000 tons × €10 + 2,000 tons × €16). The chart below compares the results of each approach on the financial statements.

	Net Liability Approach	Government Grant Approach
Income Statement		
Revenues	€ 0	€100,000
Emission expenses	32,000	132,000
Net loss	€32,000	€ 32,000
Statement of Financial Position		
Assets	€ 0	€100,000
Liabilities	32,000	132,000

So what do you think—net liability or government grant approach? As indicated, companies presently can report this information either way, plus some other variants which were not mentioned here. Please feel free to contact the IASB regarding your views.

SUMMARY OF LEARNING OBJECTIVES

KEY TERMS

accumulated rights, *609*
acid-test (quick) ratio, *627*
assessments, *613*
bonus, *610*
cash dividend payable, *603*
claims, *613*
compensated absences, *608*
constructive obligation, *612*
contingent assets, *625*
contingent liabilities, *623*
current liabilities, *598*
current maturity of long-term debt, *601*
current ratio, *626*
environmental liabilities, *618*
liability, *598*

1 **Describe the nature, type, and valuation of current liabilities.** A current liability is generally reported if one of two conditions exists: (1) the liability is expected to be settled within its normal operating cycle, or (2) the liability is expected to be settled within 12 months after the reporting date. This definition has gained wide acceptance because it recognizes operating cycles of varying lengths in different industries. Theoretically, liabilities should be measured by the present value of the future outlay of cash required to liquidate them. In practice, companies usually record and report current liabilities at their full maturity value.

There are several types of current liabilities, such as (1) accounts payable, (2) notes payable, (3) current maturities of long-term debt, (4) dividends payable, (5) customer advances and deposits, (6) unearned revenues, (7) taxes payable, and (8) employee-related liabilities.

2 **Explain the classification issues of short-term debt expected to be refinanced.** A short-term obligation is excluded from current liabilities if both of the following conditions are met: (1) the company must intend to refinance the obligation on a long-term basis, *and* (2) it must have an unconditional right to defer settlement of the liability for at least 12 months after the reporting date.

3 **Identify types of employee-related liabilities.** The employee-related liabilities are (1) payroll deductions, (2) compensated absences, and (3) bonus agreements.

4 **Explain the accounting for different types of provisions.** A provision is a liability of uncertain timing or amount (sometimes referred to as an estimated liability). Provisions are very common and may be reported either as current or non-current depending on the date of expected payment. Common types of provisions are (1) litigation obligations, (2) warranty obligations, (3) consideration payable, (4) environmental obligations, (5) onerous obligations, and (6) restructuring obligations. Companies accrue an expense and related liability for a provision only if the following three conditions are met: (1) a company has a present obligation (legal or constructive) as a result of a past event, (2) it is probable that an outflow of resources embodying economic benefits will be required to settle the obligation, and (3) a reliable estimate can be made of the amount of the obligation. If any of these three conditions is not met, no provision is recognized.

5 **Identify the criteria used to account for and disclose contingent liabilities and assets.** Contingent liabilities are not recognized in the financial statements because they are a possible obligation (not yet confirmed as a present obligation) or they are present obligations but it is not probable that payment will be necessary or a reliable estimate of the obligations cannot be made.

Contingent assets are not recognized on the statement of financial position. If realization of the contingent asset is virtually certain, it is no longer considered a contingent asset and is recognized as an asset. Virtually certain is generally interpreted to be at least a probability of 90 percent or more.

6 **Indicate how to present and analyze liability-related information.** Current liabilities are usually recorded and reported in financial statements at full maturity value. Current liabilities are commonly presented after non-current liabilities in the statement of financial position. Within the current liabilities section, companies may list the accounts in order of maturity, in descending order of amount, or in order of liquidation preference. Two ratios used to analyze liquidity are the current and acid-test ratio.

IFRS AUTHORITATIVE LITERATURE

Authoritative Literature References

[1] Conceptual Framework for Financial Reporting, "Chapter 4: *The Framework* (1989): The Remaining Text" (London, U.K.: IASB, 2010), paras. 4.15–4.19.

[2] International Accounting Standard 1, *Presentation of Financial Statements* (London, U.K.: IASB, 2007), par. BC48.

[3] International Accounting Standard 1, *Presentation of Financial Statements* (London, U.K.: IASB, 2007), par. BC44.

[4] International Accounting Standard 19, *Employee Benefits* (London, U.K.: IASB, 2001).

[5] International Accounting Standard 37, *Provisions, Contingent Liabilities and Contingent Assets* (London, U.K.: IASB, 2001).

[6] International Accounting Standard 37, *Provisions, Contingent Liabilities and Contingent Assets* (London, U.K.: IASB, 2001), par. 14.

[7] International Accounting Standard 37, *Provisions, Contingent Liabilities and Contingent Assets* (London, U.K.: IASB, 2001), par. 36.

[8] International Accounting Standard 37, *Provisions, Contingent Liabilities and Contingent Assets* (London, U.K.: IASB, 2001), paras. 63–65.

[9] International Accounting Standard 37, *Provisions, Contingent Liabilities and Contingent Assets* (London, U.K.: IASB, 2001), par. 68.

[10] International Accounting Standard 37, *Provisions, Contingent Liabilities and Contingent Assets* (London, U.K.: IASB, 2001), par. 82.

[11] International Accounting Standard 37, *Provisions, Contingent Liabilities and Contingent Assets* (London, U.K.: IASB, 2001), paras. 80–82.

[12] International Accounting Standard 37, *Provisions, Contingent Liabilities and Contingent Assets* (London, U.K.: IASB, 2001), paras. 84–92.

[13] International Accounting Standard 37, *Provisions, Contingent Liabilities and Contingent Assets* (London, U.K.: IASB, 2001), paras. 27–35.

[14] International Accounting Standard 37, *Provisions, Contingent Liabilities and Contingent Assets* (London, U.K.: IASB, 2001), par. 10.

QUESTIONS

1. Distinguish between a current liability and a non-current liability.

2. Assume that your friend Hans Jensen, who is a music major, asks you to define and discuss the nature of a liability. Assist him by preparing a definition of a liability and by explaining to him what you believe are the elements or factors inherent in the concept of a liability.

3. Why is the liabilities section of the statement of financial position of primary significance to bankers?

4. How are current liabilities related to a company's operating cycle?

5. Leong Hock, a newly hired loan analyst, is examining the current liabilities of a corporate loan applicant. He observes that unearned revenues have declined in the current year compared to the prior year. Is this a positive indicator about the client's liquidity? Explain.

6. How is present value related to the concept of a liability?

7. Explain how to account for a zero-interest-bearing note payable.

8. How should a debt callable by the creditor be reported in the debtor's financial statements?

9. Under what conditions should a short-term obligation be excluded from current liabilities?

10. What evidence is necessary to demonstrate the ability to defer settlement of short-term debt?

11. Discuss the accounting treatment or disclosure that should be accorded a declared but unpaid cash dividend; an accumulated but undeclared dividend on cumulative preference shares; and a share dividend distributable.

12. How does unearned revenue arise? Why can it be classified properly as a current liability? Give several examples of business activities that result in unearned revenues.

13. What are compensated absences?

14. Under what conditions must an employer accrue a liability for the cost of compensated absences?

15. What do the terms vested rights, accumulated rights, and non-accumulated rights mean in relation to compensated absences? Explain their accounting significance.

16. Faith Battle operates a health food store, and she has been the only employee. Her business is growing, and she is considering hiring some additional staff to help her in the store. Explain to her the various payroll deductions that she will have to account for, including their potential impact on her financial statements, if she hires additional staff.

17. Explain the difference between a value-added tax and a sales tax.

18. Define a provision, and give three examples of a provision.

19. Under what conditions should a provision be recorded?

20. Distinguish between a current liability, such as accounts payable, and a provision.

21. How are the terms "probable" and "virtually certain" related to provisions and contingencies?

22. Explain the difference between a legal obligation and a constructive obligation.

23. Explain the accounting for an assurance-type warranty.

24. Grant Company has had a record-breaking year in terms of growth in sales and profitability. However, market research indicates that it will experience operating losses in two of its major businesses next year. The controller has proposed that the company record a provision for these future losses this year since it can afford to take the charge and still show good results. Advise the controller on the appropriateness of this charge.

25. How does an assurance-type warranty differ from a service-type warranty?

26. What is an onerous contract? Give two examples of an onerous contract.

27. Define a restructuring. What costs should not be accrued in a restructuring?

28. When must a company recognize an environmental provision?

29. Should a liability be recorded for risk of loss due to lack of insurance coverage? Discuss.

30. What factors must be considered in determining whether or not to record a liability for pending litigation? For threatened litigation?

31. Within the current liabilities section, how do you believe the accounts should be listed? Defend your position.

32. How does the acid-test ratio differ from the current ratio? How are they similar?

33. When should liabilities for each of the following items be recorded on the books of an ordinary business corporation?

(a) Acquisition of goods by purchase on credit.

(b) Onerous contract.

(c) Special bonus to employees.

(d) Warranty.

(e) Profit-sharing payment.

BRIEF EXERCISES

1 **BE13-1** Roley Corporation uses a periodic inventory system and the gross method of accounting for purchase discounts. On July 1, Roley purchased €60,000 of inventory, terms 2/10, n/30, FOB shipping point. Roley paid freight costs of €1,200. On July 3, Roley returned damaged goods and received credit of €6,000. On July 10, Roley paid for the goods. Prepare all necessary journal entries for Roley.

1 **BE13-2** Upland Company borrowed $40,000 on November 1, 2014, by signing a $40,000, 9%, 3-month note. Prepare Upland's November 1, 2014, entry; the December 31, 2014, annual adjusting entry; and the February 1, 2015, entry.

1 **BE13-3** Takemoto Corporation borrowed ¥60,000,000 on November 1, 2014, by signing a ¥61,350,000 3-month, zero-interest-bearing note. Prepare Takemoto's November 1, 2014, entry; the December 31, 2014, annual adjusting entry; and the February 1, 2015, entry.

1 **2** **BE13-4** At December 31, 2014, Burr Corporation owes €500,000 on a note payable due February 15, 2015. (a) If Burr intends to refinance the obligation by issuing a long-term note on February 14 and using the proceeds to pay off the note due February 15, how much (if any) of the €500,000 should be reported as a current liability at December 31, 2014? (b) If Burr pays off the note on February 15, 2015, and then borrows €1,000,000 on a long-term basis on March 1, how much (if any) of the €500,000 should be reported as a current liability at December 31, 2014, the end of the fiscal year?

2 **BE13-5** Herzog Company has a long-term debt with a maturity date of November 2, 2016. On October 10, 2014, it breaches a covenant related to this debt and the loan becomes due on demand. Herzog reaches an agreement with the lender on January 5, 2015, to provide a waiver of the breach. The financial statement reporting date is December 31, 2014, and the financial statements are authorized for issue on March 16, 2015. Explain whether the debt obligation should be classified as current or non-current.

1 **BE13-6** Sport Pro Magazine sold 12,000 annual subscriptions on August 1, 2015, for €18 each. Prepare Sport Pro's August 1, 2015, journal entry and the December 31, 2015, annual adjusting entry.

1 **BE13-7** Dillons Corporation made credit sales of €30,000 which are subject to 6% VAT. The corporation also made cash sales which totaled €20,670 including the 6% VAT. (a) Prepare the entry to record Dillons' credit sales. (b) Prepare the entry to record Dillons' cash sales.

1 **BE13-8** Henning Company sells its products to Len Taylor, a private individual, for €5,000. The sale is subject to a VAT of 15%. Prepare the journal entry to record the sale by Henning Company.

3 **BE13-9** Lexington Corporation's weekly payroll of €24,000 included Social Security taxes withheld of €1,920, income taxes withheld of €2,990, and insurance premiums withheld of €250. Prepare the journal entry to record Lexington's payroll.

3 **BE13-10** Kasten Inc. provides paid vacations to its employees. At December 31, 2015, 30 employees have each earned 2 weeks of vacation time. The employees' average salary is €700 per week. Prepare Kasten's December 31, 2015, adjusting entry.

3 **BE13-11** Mayaguez Corporation provides its officers with bonuses based on net income. For 2014, the bonuses total £350,000 and are paid on February 15, 2015. Prepare Mayaguez's December 31, 2014, adjusting entry and the February 15, 2015, entry.

4 **5** **BE13-12** Scorcese Inc. is involved in a lawsuit at December 31, 2015. (a) Prepare the December 31 entry assuming it is probable that Scorcese will be liable for ₿900,000 as a result of this suit. (b) Prepare the December 31 entry, if any, assuming it is *not* probable that Scorcese will be liable for any payment as a result of this suit.

4 **5** **BE13-13** Buchanan Company recently was sued by a competitor for patent infringement. Attorneys have determined that it is probable that Buchanan will lose the case and that a reasonable estimate of damages to be paid by Buchanan is $300,000. In light of this case, Buchanan is considering establishing a $100,000 self-insurance allowance. What entry(ies), if any, should Buchanan record to recognize this provision.

4 BE13-14 Calaf's Drillers erects and places into service an off-shore oil platform on January 1, 2015, at a cost of £10,000,000. Calaf estimates it will cost £1,000,000 to dismantle and remove the platform at the end of its useful life in 10 years, which it is legally obligated to do. (The fair value at January 1, 2015, of the dismantle and removal costs is £450,000.) Prepare the entry to record the environmental liability.

4 BE13-15 Streep Factory provides a 2-year warranty with one of its products which was first sold in 2015 for ¥4,000,000. Streep estimates that ¥450,000 will be spent in the future to service warranty claims related to the 2015 sales. In 2015, Streep spent ¥130,000 servicing warranty claims. Prepare the journal entries to record the sale, warranty costs, and related warranty expenditures in 2015.

4 BE13-16 Main Company sells 100 televisions on June 1, 2015, at a total price of €35,000 with a warranty guarantee that the product was free of any defects. The assurance warranties extend for a 2-year period and are estimated to cost €1,000. Main also sold extended warranties for €800 related to the televisions covering 2 additional years beyond the assurance warranty period. Prepare the journal entries that Main should make in 2015 related to the sale of the televisions and related warranties. Warranty costs incurred in 2015 were €150.

4 BE13-17 Wynn Company offers a set of building blocks to customers who send in 3 UPC codes from Wynn cereal, along with 50¢. The blocks sets cost Wynn $1.10 each to purchase and 60¢ each to mail to customers. During 2015, Wynn sold 1,200,000 boxes of cereal at $3 per box. The company expects 30% of the UPC codes to be sent in. During 2015, 120,000 UPC codes were redeemed. Prepare the journal entries that Wynn should make to record the sale of the cereal in 2015 and the related cost of the premiums associated with the sale.

4 BE13-18 Cargo Company purchased land from Hazard Company for €20,000,000 on September 13, 2015. On October 31, 2015, it learned that the site was contaminated. As a result, Cargo Company sued Hazard Company for €4,000,000. Cargo's attorneys believe that their odds of winning the case are 75%. Indicate how Cargo should account for this lawsuit at December 31, 2015.

4 BE13-19 Management at Eli Company has decided to close one of its plants. It will continue to operate the plant for approximately one year. It anticipates the following costs will be incurred as a result of this closing: (1) termination compensation costs, (2) marketing costs to rebrand the company image, (3) future losses for keeping the plant open for another year, and (4) lease termination costs related to the closing. Indicate which, if any, of these costs should not be considered restructuring costs for purposes of establishing a provision.

4 BE13-20 Luckert Company decided to cancel an existing property lease in one of its divisions, as its operations in this area were no longer profitable. Unfortunately, Luckert has a non-cancelable lease and cannot sublease the property. The present value of future lease payments under the lease is €2,000,000. The penalty to break the lease is €1,450,000. Prepare the journal entry to record this cancelation.

EXERCISES

1 E13-1 (Statement of Financial Position Classification) Consider the following items.

(a) Accrued vacation pay.
(b) Income taxes payable.
(c) Service-type warranties on appliance sales.
(d) Social Security taxes payable.
(e) Personal injury claim pending.
(f) Unpaid bonus to officers.
(g) Deposit received from customer to guarantee performance of a contract.
(h) Value-added tax payable.
(i) Gift certificates sold to customers but not yet redeemed.

(j) Premium offers outstanding.
(k) Accounts payable.
(l) Employee payroll deductions unremitted.
(m) Current maturities of long-term debts to be paid from current assets.
(n) Cash dividends declared but unpaid.
(o) Dividends in arrears on preference shares.
(p) Loans from officers.

Instructions

How would each of the preceding items be reported on the statement of financial position?

1 **E13-2 (Accounts and Notes Payable)** The following are selected 2015 transactions of Darby Corporation.

Sept. 1   Purchased inventory from Orion Company on account for $50,000. Darby records purchases gross and uses a periodic inventory system.
Oct. 1   Issued a $50,000, 12-month, 8% note to Orion in payment of account.
Oct. 1   Borrowed $75,000 from the Shore Bank by signing a 12-month, zero-interest-bearing $81,000 note.

Instructions

    (a) Prepare journal entries for the selected transactions above.
    (b) Prepare adjusting entries at December 31.
    (c) Compute the total net liability to be reported on the December 31 statement of financial position for:
        (1) The interest-bearing note.
        (2) The zero-interest-bearing note.

2 **E13-3 (Refinancing of Short-Term Debt)** On December 31, 2014, Alexander Company had €1,200,000 of short-term debt in the form of notes payable due February 2, 2015. On January 21, 2015, the company issued 25,000 ordinary shares for €36 per share, receiving €900,000 proceeds after brokerage fees and other costs of issuance. On February 2, 2015, the proceeds from the share sale, supplemented by an additional €300,000 cash, are used to liquidate the €1,200,000 debt. The December 31, 2014, statement of financial position is authorized for issue on February 23, 2015.

Instructions

Show how the €1,200,000 of short-term debt should be presented on the December 31, 2014, statement of financial position.

2 **E13-4 (Refinancing of Short-Term Debt)** The CFO for Yong Corporation is discussing with the company's chief executive officer issues related to the company's short-term obligations. Presently, both the current ratio and the acid-test ratio for the company are quite low, and the chief executive officer is wondering if any of these short-term obligations could be reclassified as long-term. The financial reporting date is December 31, 2014. Two short-term obligations were discussed, and the following action was taken by the CFO.

Short-Term Obligation A: Yong has a $50,000 short-term obligation due on March 1, 2015. The CFO discussed with its lender whether the payment could be extended to March 1, 2017, provided Yong agrees to provide additional collateral. An agreement is reached on February 1, 2015, to change the loan terms to extend the obligation's maturity to March 1, 2017. The financial statements are authorized for issuance on April 1, 2015.

Short-Term Obligation B: Yong also has another short-term obligation of $120,000 due on February 15, 2015. In its discussion with the lender, the lender agrees to extend the maturity date to February 1, 2016. The agreement is signed on December 18, 2014. The financial statements are authorized for issuance on March 31, 2015.

Instructions

Indicate how these transactions should be reported at December 31, 2014, on Yong's statement of financial position.

2 **E13-5 (Debt Classifications)** Presented below are four different situations related to Mckee Corporation debt obligations. Mckee's next financial reporting date is December 31, 2014. The financial statements are authorized for issuance on March 1, 2015.

    1. Mckee has a debt obligation maturing on December 31, 2017. The debt is callable on demand by the lender at any time.

    2. Mckee also has a long-term obligation due on December 1, 2016. On November 10, 2014, it breaches a covenant on its debt obligation and the loan becomes due on demand. An agreement is reached to provide a waiver of the breach on December 8, 2014.

    3. Mckee has a long-term obligation of £400,000, which is maturing over 4 years in the amount of £100,000 per year. The obligation is dated November 1, 2014, and the first maturity date is November 1, 2015.

    4. Mckee has a short-term obligation due February 15, 2015. Its lender agrees to extend the maturity date of this loan to February 15, 2017. The agreement for extension is signed on January 15, 2015.

Instructions

Indicate how each of these debt obligations is reported on Mckee's statement of financial position on December 31, 2014.

3 **E13-6 (Compensated Absences)** Matthewson Company began operations on January 2, 2014. It employs 9 individuals who work 8-hour days and are paid hourly. Each employee earns 10 paid vacation days and 6 paid sick days annually. Vacation days may be taken after January 15 of the year following the year in which they are earned. Sick days may be taken as soon as they are earned; unused sick days accumulate. Additional information is as follows.

Actual Hourly Wage Rate		Vacation Days Used by Each Employee		Sick Days Used by Each Employee	
2014	2015	2014	2015	2014	2015
€12	€13	0	9	4	5

Matthewson Company has chosen to accrue the cost of compensated absences at rates of pay in effect during the period when earned and to accrue sick pay when earned.

Instructions

(a) Prepare journal entries to record transactions related to compensated absences during 2014 and 2015.

(b) Compute the amounts of any liability for compensated absences that should be reported on the statement of financial position at December 31, 2014 and 2015.

3 **E13-7 (Compensated Absences)** Assume the facts as in E13-6 except that Matthewson Company has chosen (1) not to accrue paid sick leave until used and (2) to accrue vacation time at expected future rates of pay without discounting. The company used the following projected rates to accrue vacation time.

Year in Which Vacation Time Was Earned	Projected Future Pay Rates Used to Accrue Vacation Pay
2014	€12.90
2015	13.70

Instructions

(a) Prepare journal entries to record transactions related to compensated absences during 2014 and 2015.

(b) Compute the amounts of any liability for compensated absences that should be reported on the statement of financial position at December 31, 2014, and 2015.

1 **E13-8 (Adjusting Entry for Sales Tax and VAT)** During the month of June, Danielle's Boutique had cash sales of R$265,000 and credit sales of R$153,700, both of which include the 6% sales tax that must be remitted to the government by July 15.

Instructions

(a) Prepare the adjusting entry that should be recorded to fairly present the June 30 financial statements.

(b) How would the adjusting entry change if the 6% tax was a VAT rather than a sales tax?

1 **E13-9 (Adjusting Entry for Sales Tax and VAT)** Eastwood Ranchers sells a herd of cattle to Rozo Meat Packers for €30,000 and the related VAT. Rozo Meat Packers sells the beef to Wrangler Supermarkets for €40,000 and the related VAT. Wrangler Supermarkets sells this beef to customers for €50,000 plus related VAT.

Instructions

(a) Assuming the VAT is 15% on all sales, prepare the journal entry to record the sale by Rozo Meat Packers to Wrangler Supermarkets.

(b) What is the net cash outlay that Eastwood Ranchers incurs related to the VAT?

3 **E13-10 (Payroll Tax Entries)** The payroll of Kee Company for September 2015 is as follows (amounts in thousands): total payroll was ¥340,000; income taxes in the amount of ¥80,000 were withheld, as was ¥9,000 in union dues; and the current Social Security tax is 8% of an employee's wages. The employer must also remit 8% for employees' wages.

Instructions
Prepare the necessary journal entries if the salaries and wages paid and the employer payroll taxes are recorded separately.

3 **E13-11 (Payroll Tax Entries)** Allison Hardware Company's payroll for November 2015 is as follows: factory, €140,000; sales, €32,000; and administrative, €36,000. The Social Security rate is 8% on an employee's wages. Income tax withheld amounts to €16,000 for factory, €7,000 for sales, and €6,000 for administrative.

Instructions
(a) Prepare a schedule showing the employer's total cost of salaries and wages for November by function.
(b) Prepare the journal entries to record the factory, sales, and administrative payrolls including the employer's payroll taxes.

4 **E13-12 (Warranties)** Winslow Company sold 150 color laser copiers in 2015 for £4,000 apiece, together with a one-year assurance-type warranty. Maintenance on each copier during the warranty period averages £300.

Instructions
Prepare entries to record the sale of the copiers and the related warranty costs. Actual warranty costs incurred in 2015 were £17,000.

4 **E13-13 (Warranties)** Selzer Equipment Company sold 500 Rollomatics during 2015 at $6,000 each. During 2015, Selzer spent $30,000 servicing the 2-year assurance-type warranties that accompany the Rollomatic.

Instructions
(a) Prepare 2015 entries for Selzer assuming that Selzer estimates the total cost of servicing the warranties will be $120,000 for 2 years.
(b) Prepare 2015 entries for Selzer assuming that the warranties are service-type warranties and are not considered part of the sale of the Rollomatics. Assume that of the sales total of the Rollomatics, $160,000 relates to sales of warranty contracts. Selzer estimates the total cost of servicing the warranties will be $120,000 for 2 years. Estimate revenue related to the service-type warranties.

4 **E13-14 (Premium Entries)** Moleski Company includes 1 coupon in each box of soap powder that it packs, and 10 coupons are redeemable for a premium (a kitchen utensil). In 2015, Moleski Company purchased 8,800 premiums at €.90 each and sold 120,000 boxes of soap powder at €3.30 per box; 44,000 coupons were presented for redemption in 2015. It is estimated that 60% of the coupons will eventually be presented for redemption.

Instructions
Prepare all the entries that would be made relative to sales of soap powder and to the premium plan in 2015.

4 **E13-15 (Restructuring Issues)** EADS Company is involved in a restructuring related to its energy division. The company controller and CFO are considering the following costs to accrue as part of the restructuring. The costs are as follows (amounts in thousands).

1. The company has a long-term lease on one of the facilities related to the division. It is estimated that it will have to pay a penalty cost of ¥400,000 to break the lease. The company estimates that the present value related to payments on the lease contract is ¥650,000.
2. The company's allocation of overhead costs to other divisions will increase by ¥1,500,000 as a result of restructuring these facilities.
3. Due to the restructuring, some employees will be shifted to some of the other divisions. The cost of retraining these individuals is estimated to be ¥2,000,000.
4. The company has hired an outplacement firm to help it in dealing with the number of terminations related to the restructuring. It is estimated the cost for this outplacement firm will be ¥600,000.
5. It is estimated that employee termination costs will be ¥3,000,000.
6. The company believes that it will cost ¥320,000 to move useable assets from the energy division to other divisions in the company.

Instructions

Indicate whether each of these costs should be included in the restructuring provision in the financial statements.

4 **E13-16 (Restructuring)** On December 31, 2015, the board of Dolman Group decided to close one of its divisions. On December 31, 2015, a detailed plan for closing the division was agreed to by the board, and letters were sent to customers and employees affected by this closure.

Instructions

(a) What is a restructuring? Provide two examples.

(b) To ensure that the restructuring is valid, what two conditions must take place?

(c) Possible costs that may be incurred during the restructuring are as follows: (1) investment in new software as a result of closing the division, (2) cost of moving some assets of the closed division to other parts of the company, (3) employee termination costs related to closing the division, (4) expected future operating losses in closing the division, and (5) onerous contract provisions related to the closing. Indicate which (if any) of these costs may be part of a restructuring provision.

4 **5** **E13-17 (Provisions and Contingencies)** Presented below are three independent situations.

1. During 2015, Maverick Inc. became involved in a tax dispute with the government. Maverick's attorneys have indicated that they believe it is probable that Maverick will lose this dispute. They also believe that Maverick will have to pay the government between €800,000 and €1,400,000. After the 2015 financial statements were issued, the case was settled with the government for €1,200,000. What amount, if any, should be reported as a liability for this tax dispute as of December 31, 2015?

2. On October 1, 2015, Holmgren Chemical was identified as a potentially responsible party by its Environmental Regulatory Agency. Holmgren's management along with its counsel have concluded that it is probable that Holmgren will be responsible for damages, and a reasonable estimate of these damages is €6,000,000. Holmgren's insurance policy of €9,000,000 has a deductible clause of €500,000. How should Holmgren Chemical report this information in its financial statements at December 31, 2015?

3. Shinobi Inc. had a manufacturing plant in Darfur, which was destroyed in the civil war. It is not certain who will compensate Shinobi for this destruction, but Shinobi has been assured by governmental officials that it will receive a definite amount for this plant. The amount of the compensation will be less than the fair value of the plant but more than its book value. How should the compensation be reported in the financial statements of Shinobi Inc.?

Instructions

Answer the question at the end of each situation.

4 **E13-18 (Environmental Liability)** Bassinger Company purchases an oil tanker depot on January 1, 2015, at a cost of $600,000. Bassinger expects to operate the depot for 10 years, at which time it is legally required to dismantle the depot and remove the underground storage tanks. It is estimated that it will cost $70,000 to dismantle the depot and remove the tanks at the end of the depot's useful life.

Instructions

(a) Prepare the journal entries to record the depot and the environmental liability for the depot on January 1, 2015. Based on an effective-interest rate of 6%, the fair value of the environmental liability on January 1, 2015, is $39,087.

(b) Prepare any journal entries required for the depot and the environmental liability at December 31, 2015. Bassinger uses straight-line depreciation; the estimated residual value for the depot is zero.

(c) On December 31, 2024, Bassinger pays a demolition firm to dismantle the depot and remove the tanks at a price of $80,000. Prepare the journal entry for the settlement of the environmental liability.

4 **E13-19 (Premiums)** Presented below and on page 637 are three independent situations.

1. Martin Stamp Company records stamp service revenue and provides for the cost of redemptions in the year stamps are sold to licensees. Martin's past experience indicates that only 80% of the stamps sold to licensees will be redeemed. Martin's liability for stamp redemptions was $13,000,000 at December 31, 2014. Additional information for 2015 is as follows.

Stamp service revenue from stamps sold to licensees	$9,500,000
Cost of redemptions (stamps sold prior to 1/1/15)	6,000,000

If all the stamps sold in 2015 were presented for redemption in 2016, the redemption cost would be $5,200,000. What amount should Martin report as a liability for stamp redemptions at December 31, 2015?

2. In packages of its products, Wiseman Inc. includes coupons that may be presented at retail stores to obtain discounts on other Wiseman products. Retailers are reimbursed for the face amount of coupons redeemed plus 10% of that amount for handling costs. Wiseman honors requests for coupon redemption by retailers up to 3 months after the consumer expiration date. Wiseman estimates that 60% of all coupons issued will ultimately be redeemed. Information relating to coupons issued by Wiseman during 2015 is as follows.

Consumer expiration date	12/31/15
Total face amount of coupons issued	$850,000
Total payments to retailers as of 12/31/15	330,000

What amount should Wiseman report as a liability for unredeemed coupons at December 31, 2015?

3. Newell Company sold 600,000 boxes of pie mix for $6,000,000 under a new sales promotional program. Each box contains one coupon, which when submitted with $4.00, entitles the customer to a baking pan. Newell pays $6.00 per pan and $0.50 for handling and shipping. Newell estimates that 70% of the coupons will be redeemed even though only 250,000 coupons had been processed during 2015. What amount should Newell report as a liability for unredeemed coupons at December 31, 2015?

Instructions
Answer the question at the end of each situation.

4 **E13-20 (Provisions)** Presented below are three independent situations.

1. Bruegger Transportation purchased a ship on January 1, 2015, for £20,000,000. The useful life of the ship is 40 years, but it is subject to a government-mandated major overhaul every 4 years with a total projected cost of £4,000,000. The present value related to these payments is £3,200,000. Explain how this transaction should be accounted for at January 1, 2015, and at December 31, 2015. Prepare the journal entries to record all appropriate entries related to the ship in 2015. Bruegger uses the straight-line method of depreciation and assumes no residual value for the ship.

2. Marquardt Company signs a 5-year lease related to office space at an annual rental of £30,000. At the end of the second year, the company decides to close its operation in this part of country. Its lease is non-cancelable, and the penalty for non-payment is £62,000. The present value of future payments on the lease is estimated to be £81,000. The company does not believe that it can sublet these facilities. Explain how this transaction should be accounted for at December 31, 2015. Prepare the journal entry to record this entry on December 31, 2015.

3. Powersurge Group operates a nuclear power plant. The plant cost £40,000,000 on January 2, 2016. It is estimated that the present value of dismantling the plant and the ensuing clean-up will be £1,000,000. Explain how this transaction should be accounted for on January 2, 2016. Prepare the journal entry to record this transaction on January 2, 2016.

Instructions
Prepare the explanation and journal entry required for each situation.

4 **E13-21 (Provisions)** The following situations relate to Bolivia Company.

1. Bolivia provides a warranty with all products sold. It estimates that it will sell 1,000,000 units of its product for the year ended December 31, 2015, and that its total revenue for the product will be $100,000,000. It also estimates that 60% of the product will have no defects, 30% will have major defects, and 10% will have minor defects. The cost of a minor defect is estimated to be $5 for each product sold, and the cost for a major defect is $15. The company also estimates that the minimum amount of warranty expense will be $2,000,000 and the maximum will be $10,000,000.

2. Bolivia is involved in a tax dispute with the tax authorities. The most likely outcome of this dispute is that Bolivia will lose and have to pay $400,000. The minimum it will lose is $20,000 and the maximum is $2,500,000.

Instructions

Determine the amount to record as provisions, if any, for Bolivia at December 31, 2015.

6 **E13-22 (Financial Statement Impact of Liability Transactions)** Presented below is a list of possible transactions.

1. Purchased inventory for €80,000 on account (assume perpetual system is used).

2. Issued an €80,000 note payable in payment on account (see item 1 above).

3. Recorded accrued interest on the note from item 2 above.

4. Borrowed €100,000 from the bank by signing a 6-month, €112,000, zero-interest-bearing note.

5. Recognized 4 months' interest expense on the note from item 4 above.

6. Recorded cash sales of €75,260, which includes 10% VAT.

7. Recorded wage expense of €35,000. The cash paid was €25,000; the difference was due to various amounts withheld.

8. Recorded employer's payroll taxes.

9. Accrued accumulated vacation pay.

10. Recorded an environmental liability and related asset.

11. Recorded bonuses due to employees.

12. Recorded sales of product and related warranties (assume both assurance-type warranty and service-type warranty).

13. Paid warranty costs that were accrued in item 12 above related to assurance-type warranty.

14. Recorded a liability on a lawsuit that the company will probably lose.

15. Paid service-type warranty costs under contracts from item 12.

16. Recognized warranty revenue (see item 12).

Instructions

Set up a table using the format shown below and analyze the effect of the 16 transactions on the financial statement categories indicated.

#	Assets	Liabilities	Equity	Net Income
1				

Use the following code:

   I: Increase   D: Decrease   NE: No net effect

6 **E13-23 (Ratio Computations and Discussion)** Chen Company has been operating for several years, and on December 31, 2015, presented the following statement of financial position (amounts in thousands).

CHEN COMPANY
STATEMENT OF FINANCIAL POSITION
DECEMBER 31, 2015

Plant assets (net)	¥220,000	Share capital—ordinary	¥160,000
Inventory	95,000	Retained earnings	60,000
Receivables	75,000	Mortgage payable	140,000
Cash	40,000	Accounts payable	70,000
	¥430,000		¥430,000

The net income for 2015 was ¥25,000. Assume that total assets are the same in 2014 and 2015.

Instructions

Compute each of the following ratios. For each of the four, indicate the manner in which it is computed and its significance as a tool in the analysis of the financial soundness of the company.

   (a) Current ratio.   **(c)** Debt to assets.

   (b) Acid-test ratio.   **(d)** Return on assets.

6 **E13-24 (Ratio Computations and Analysis)** EAN Company's condensed financial statements provide the following information (amounts in thousands).

EAN COMPANY
STATEMENT OF FINANCIAL POSITION

	Dec. 31, 2015		Dec. 31, 2014	
Property, plant, and equipment		¥ 897,000		¥ 853,000
Current assets				
Inventory	¥440,000		¥360,000	
Prepaid expenses	3,000		7,000	
Accounts receivable	158,000		80,000	
Short-term investments	80,000		40,000	
Cash	52,000	733,000	60,000	547,000
Total assets		¥1,630,000		¥1,400,000
Equity		¥ 990,000		¥ 840,000
Bonds payable		400,000		400,000
Current liabilities		240,000		160,000
		¥1,630,000		¥1,400,000

INCOME STATEMENT
FOR THE YEAR ENDED 2015

Sales revenue	¥1,640,000
Cost of goods sold	(800,000)
Gross profit	840,000
Selling and administrative expenses	(480,000)
Interest expense	(40,000)
Net income	¥ 320,000

Instructions
(a) Determine the following for 2015.
   (1) Current ratio at December 31.
   (2) Acid-test ratio at December 31.
   (3) Accounts receivable turnover.
   (4) Inventory turnover.
   (5) Return on assets.
   (6) Profit margin on sales.
(b) Prepare a brief evaluation of the financial condition of EAN Company and of the adequacy of its profits.

6 **E13-25 (Ratio Computations and Effect of Transactions)** Presented below and on page 640 is information related to Leland Inc.

LELAND INC.
STATEMENT OF FINANCIAL POSITION
DECEMBER 31, 2015

Equipment (net)		€150,000	Share capital—ordinary (par €5)	€260,000
Land		20,000	Retained earnings	141,000
Prepaid insurance		8,000	Notes payable (short-term)	50,000
Inventory		170,000	Accounts payable	32,000
Receivables	€110,000		Accrued liabilities	5,000
Less: Allowance	15,000	95,000		
Cash		45,000		
		€488,000		€488,000

LELAND INC.		
INCOME STATEMENT		
FOR THE YEAR ENDED DECEMBER 31, 2015		
Sales revenue		€1,400,000
Cost of goods sold		
Inventory, Jan. 1, 2015	€200,000	
Purchases	790,000	
Cost of goods available for sale	990,000	
Inventory, Dec. 31, 2015	(170,000)	
Cost of goods sold		820,000
Gross profit on sales		580,000
Operating expenses		370,000
Net income		€ 210,000

Instructions

(a) Compute the following ratios or relationships of Leland Inc. Assume that the ending account balances are representative unless the information provided indicates differently.

(1) Current ratio.

(2) Inventory turnover.

(3) Accounts receivable turnover.

(4) Earnings per share.

(5) Profit margin on sales.

(6) Return on assets on December 31, 2015.

(b) Indicate for each of the following transactions whether the transaction would improve, weaken, or have no effect on the current ratio of Leland Inc. at December 31, 2015.

(1) Write off an uncollectible account receivable, €2,200.

(2) Repurchase ordinary shares for cash.

(3) Pay €40,000 on notes payable (short-term).

(4) Collect €23,000 on accounts receivable.

(5) Buy equipment on account.

(6) Give an existing creditor a short-term note in settlement of account.

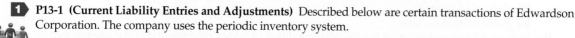

PROBLEMS

P13-1 (Current Liability Entries and Adjustments) Described below are certain transactions of Edwardson Corporation. The company uses the periodic inventory system.

1. On February 2, the corporation purchased goods from Martin Company for €70,000 subject to cash discount terms of 2/10, n/30. Purchases and accounts payable are recorded by the corporation at net amounts after cash discounts. The invoice was paid on February 26.

2. On April 1, the corporation bought a truck for €50,000, paying €4,000 in cash and signing a one-year, 12% note for the balance of the purchase price.

3. On August 1, the board of directors declared a €300,000 cash dividend that was payable on September 10 to shareholders of record on August 31.

Instructions

(a) Make all the journal entries necessary to record the transactions above using appropriate dates.

(b) Edwardson Corporation's year-end is December 31. Assuming that no adjusting entries relative to the transactions above have been recorded, prepare any adjusting journal entries concerning interest that are necessary to present fair financial statements at December 31.

P13-2 (Liability Entries and Adjustments) Listed below are selected transactions of Schultz Department Store for the current year ending December 31.

1. On December 5, the store received €500 from the Jackson Players as a deposit to be returned after certain furniture to be used in stage production was returned on January 15.

2. During December, cash sales totaled €798,000, which includes the 5% VAT that must be remitted to the tax authority by the fifteenth day of the following month.

3. On December 10, the store purchased for cash three delivery trucks for €120,000. The trucks were purchased in a jurisdiction that applies a 5% VAT.

4. The store determined it will cost €100,000 to restore the area surrounding one of its store parking lots, when the store is closed in 2 years. Schultz estimates the fair value of the obligation at December 31 is €84,000.

Instructions

Prepare all the journal entries necessary to record the transactions noted above as they occurred and any adjusting journal entries relative to the transactions that would be required to present fair financial statements at December 31. Date each entry. For simplicity, assume that adjusting entries are recorded only once a year on December 31.

P13-3 (Payroll Tax Entries) Cedarville Company pays its office employee payroll weekly. Below is a partial list of employees and their payroll data for August. Because August is their vacation period, vacation pay is also listed.

Employee	Earnings to July 31	Weekly Pay	Vacation Pay to Be Received in August
Mark Hamill	$4,200	$200	—
Karen Robbins	3,500	150	$300
Brent Kirk	2,700	110	220
Alec Guinness	7,400	250	—
Ken Sprouse	8,000	330	660

Assume that the income tax withheld is 10% of wages. Union dues withheld are 2% of wages. Vacations are taken the second and third weeks of August by Robbins, Kirk, and Sprouse. The Social Security rate is 8% on employee and employer.

Instructions

Make the journal entries necessary for each of the four August payrolls. The entries for the payroll and for the company's liability are made separately. Also make the entry to record the monthly payment of payroll liabilities.

P13-4 (Payroll Tax Entries) Below is a payroll sheet for Otis Import Company for the month of September 2015. Assume a 10% income tax rate for all employees and an 8% Social Security tax on employee and employer.

Name	Earnings to Aug. 31	September Earnings	Income Tax Withholding	Social Security
B.D. Williams	£ 6,800	£ 800		
D. Raye	6,500	700		
K. Baker	7,600	1,100		
F. Lopez	13,600	1,900		
A. Daniels	105,000	13,000		
B. Kingston	112,000	16,000		

Instructions

(a) Complete the payroll sheet and make the necessary entry to record the payment of the payroll.

(b) Make the entry to record the payroll tax expenses of Otis Import Company.

(c) Make the entry to record the payment of the payroll liabilities created. Assume that the company pays all payroll liabilities at the end of each month.

P13-5 (Warranties) Brooks Corporation sells computers under a 2-year warranty contract that requires the corporation to replace defective parts and to provide the necessary repair labor. During 2015, the corporation sells for cash 400 computers at a unit price of £2,500. On the basis of past experience, the 2-year warranty costs are estimated to be £155 for parts and £185 for labor per unit. (For simplicity, assume that all sales occurred on December 31, 2015.) The warranty is not sold separately from the computer.

Instructions

(a) Record any necessary journal entries in 2015.

(b) What liability relative to these transactions would appear on the December 31, 2015, statement of financial position and how would it be classified?

In 2016, the actual warranty costs to Brooks Corporation were £21,400 for parts and £39,900 for labor.

(c) Record any necessary journal entries in 2016.

P13-6 (Warranties) Dos Passos Company sells televisions at an average price of R$900 and also offers to each customer a separate 3-year service-type warranty contract for R$90 that requires the company to perform periodic services and to replace defective parts. During 2014, the company sold 300 televisions and 270 warranty contracts for cash. It estimates the 3-year warranty costs as R$20 for parts and R$40 for labor and accounts for warranties separately. Assume sales occurred on December 31, 2014, and straight-line recognition of warranty revenues occurs.

Instructions

(a) Record any necessary journal entries in 2014.

(b) What liability relative to these transactions would appear on the December 31, 2014, statement of financial position and how would it be classified?

In 2015, Dos Passos Company incurred actual costs relative to 2014 television warranty sales of R$2,000 for parts and R$4,000 for labor.

(c) Record any necessary journal entries in 2015 relative to 2014 television warranties.

(d) What amounts relative to the 2014 television warranties would appear on the December 31, 2015, statement of financial position and how would they be classified?

P13-7 (Warranties) Alvarado Company sells a machine for $7,400 under a 12-month warranty agreement that requires the company to replace all defective parts and to provide the repair labor at no cost to the customers. With sales being made evenly throughout the year, the company sells 600 machines in 2014 (warranty costs are incurred half in 2014 and half in 2015). As a result of product testing, the company estimates that the warranty cost is $390 per machine ($170 parts and $220 labor).

Instructions

(a) Assuming that actual warranty costs are incurred exactly as estimated, what journal entries would be made in 2014 and 2015?

(b) What amount, if any, is disclosed in the statement of financial position as a liability for warranty costs as of December 31, 2014?

P13-8 (Premium Entries) To stimulate the sales of its Alladin breakfast cereal, Loptien Company places 1 coupon in each box. Five coupons are redeemable for a premium consisting of a child's hand puppet. In 2015, the company purchases 40,000 puppets at €1.50 each and sells 480,000 boxes of Alladin at €3.75 a box. From its experience with other similar premium offers, the company estimates that 40% of the coupons issued will be mailed back for redemption. During 2015, 115,000 coupons are presented for redemption.

Instructions

Prepare the journal entries that should be recorded in 2015 relative to the premium plan.

P13-9 (Premium Entries and Financial Statement Presentation) Sycamore Candy Company offers an MP3 download (seven-single medley) as a premium for every five candy bar wrappers presented by customers together with $2.50. The candy bars are sold by the company to distributors for 30 cents each. The purchase price of each download code to the company is $2.25; in addition it costs 50 cents to distribute each code. The results of the premium plan for the years 2014 and 2015 are as follows. (All purchases and sales are for cash.)

	2014	2015
MP3 codes purchased	250,000	330,000
Candy bars sold	2,895,400	2,743,600
Wrappers redeemed	1,200,000	1,500,000
2014 wrappers expected to be redeemed in 2015	290,000	
2015 wrappers expected to be redeemed in 2016		350,000

Instructions

(a) Prepare the journal entries that should be made in 2014 and 2015 to record the transactions related to the premium plan of the Sycamore Candy Company.

(b) Indicate the account names, amounts, and classifications of the items related to the premium plan that would appear on the statement of financial position and the income statement at the end of 2014 and 2015.

4 5 P13-10 (Litigation Claim: Entries and Essay) On November 24, 2014, 26 passengers on Wong Airlines Flight No. 901 were injured upon landing when the plane skidded off the runway. Personal injury suits for damages totaling NT$9,000,000 were filed on January 11, 2015, against the airline by 18 injured passengers. The airline carries no insurance. Legal counsel has studied each suit and advised Wong that it can reasonably expect to pay 60% of the damages claimed. The financial statements for the year ended December 31, 2014, were authorized for issuance on February 27, 2015.

Instructions

(a) Prepare any disclosures and journal entries required by the airline in preparation of the December 31, 2014, financial statements.

(b) Ignoring the November 24, 2014, accident, what liability due to the risk of loss from lack of insurance coverage should Wong Airlines record or disclose? During the past decade the company has experienced at least one accident per year and incurred average damages of NT$3,200,000. Discuss fully.

4 5 P13-11 (Contingencies: Entries and Essays) Polska Corporation, in preparation of its December 31, 2015, financial statements, is attempting to determine the proper accounting treatment for each of the following situations.

1. As a result of uninsured accidents during the year, personal injury suits for €350,000 and €60,000 have been filed against the company. It is the judgment of Polska's legal counsel that an unfavorable outcome is unlikely in the €60,000 case but that an unfavorable verdict approximating €250,000 will probably result in the €350,000 case.

2. Polska Corporation owns a subsidiary in a foreign country that has a book value of €5,725,000 and an estimated fair value of €9,500,000. The foreign government has communicated to Polska its intention to expropriate the assets and business of all foreign investors. On the basis of settlements other firms have received from this same country, it is virtually certain that Polska will receive 40% of the fair value of its properties as final settlement.

3. Polska's chemical product division consisting of five plants is uninsurable because of the special risk of injury to employees and losses due to fire and explosion. The year 2015 is considered one of the safest (luckiest) in the division's history because no loss due to injury or casualty was suffered. Having suffered an average of three casualties a year during the rest of the past decade (ranging from €60,000 to €700,000), management is certain that next year the company will probably not be so fortunate.

4. Polska operates profitably from a factory it has leased. During 2015, Polska decides to relocate these operations to a new factory. The lease of the old factory continues for the next 5 years. The lease cannot be cancelled and the factory cannot be subleased. Polska determines that the cost to settle the old lease is €950,000.

5. Litigation is being pursued for the recovery of €1,300,000 consulting fees on a failed project. The directors believe it is more likely than not that their claim will be successful.

Instructions

(a) Prepare the journal entries that should be recorded as of December 31, 2015, to recognize each of the situations above.

(b) Indicate what should be reported relative to each situation in the financial statements and accompanying notes. Explain why.

4 P13-12 (Warranties and Premiums) Garison Music Emporium carries a wide variety of musical instruments, sound reproduction equipment, recorded music, and sheet music. Garison uses two sales promotion techniques—warranties and premiums—to attract customers.

Musical instruments and sound equipment are sold with a one-year assurance-type warranty for replacement of parts and labor. The estimated warranty cost, based on past experience, is 2% of sales.

The premium is offered on the recorded and sheet music. Customers receive a coupon for each dollar spent on recorded music or sheet music. Customers may exchange 200 coupons and $20 for an MP3 player. Garison pays $32 for each MP3 player and estimates that 60% of the coupons given to customers will be redeemed.

Garison's total sales for 2015 were $7,200,000—$5,700,000 from musical instruments and sound reproduction equipment and $1,500,000 from recorded music and sheet music. Replacement parts and labor for warranty work totaled $164,000 during 2015. A total of 6,500 MP3 players used in the premium program were purchased during the year and there were 1,200,000 coupons redeemed in 2015.

The balances in the accounts related to warranties and premiums on January 1, 2015, were as shown below.

Inventory of Premium MP3 Players	$ 37,600
Estimated Premium Claims Outstanding	44,800
Warranty Liability	136,000

Instructions

Garison Music Emporium is preparing its financial statements for the year ended December 31, 2015. Determine the amounts that will be shown on the 2015 financial statements for the following.

(a) Warranty Expense.
(b) Warranty Liability.
(c) Premium Expense.

(d) Inventory of Premium MP3 Players.
(e) Estimated Premium Claims Outstanding.

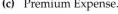

P13-13 (Liability Errors) You are the independent auditor engaged to audit Millay Corporation's December 31, 2015, financial statements. Millay manufactures household appliances. During the course of your audit, you discovered the following situations.

1. Millay began production of a new dishwasher in June 2015 and, by December 31, 2015, sold 120,000 to various retailers for £500 each. Each dishwasher is under a one-year warranty. The company estimates that its warranty expense per dishwasher will amount to £25. At year-end, the company had already paid out £1,000,000 in warranty expenses. Millay's income statement shows warranty expenses of £1,000,000 for 2015.

2. In response to your attorney's letter, Morgan Chye, Esq., has informed you that Millay has been cited for dumping toxic waste into the Loden River. Clean-up costs and fines amount to £2,750,000. Although the case is still being contested, Chye is certain that Millay will most probably have to pay the fine and clean-up costs. No disclosure of this situation was found in the financial statements.

3. Millay is the defendant in a patent infringement lawsuit by Megan Drabek over Millay's use of a hydraulic compressor in several of its products. Chye claims that, if the suit goes against Millay, the loss may be as much as £5,000,000. However, Chye believes the loss of this suit to be only possible. Again, no mention of this suit is made in the financial statements.

As presented, these situations are not reported in accordance with IFRS, which may create problems in issuing a favorable audit report. You feel the need to note these problems in the work papers.

Instructions

Heading each page with the name of the company, statement of financial position date, and a brief description of the problem, write a brief narrative for each of the above issues in the form of a **memorandum** to be incorporated in the audit work papers. Explain what led to the discovery of each problem, what the problem really is, and what you advised your client to do (along with any appropriate journal entries) in order to bring these situations in accordance with IFRS.

P13-14 (Warranty and Coupon Computation) Schmitt Company must make computations and adjusting entries for the following independent situations at December 31, 2015.

1. Its line of amplifiers carries a 3-year assurance-type warranty against defects. On the basis of past experience, the estimated warranty costs related to dollar sales are first year after sale—2% of sales; second year after sale—3% of sales; and third year after sale—5% of sales. Sales and actual warranty expenditures for the first 3 years of business were:

	Sales	Warranty Expenditures
2013	$ 800,000	$ 6,500
2014	1,100,000	17,200
2015	1,200,000	62,000

Instructions

Compute the amount that Schmitt Company should report as a liability in its December 31, 2015, statement of financial position. Assume that all sales are made evenly throughout each year with warranty expenses also evenly spaced relative to the rates above.

2. With some of its products, Schmitt Company includes coupons that are redeemable in merchandise. The coupons have no expiration date and, in the company's experience, 40% of them are redeemed. The liability for unredeemed coupons at December 31, 2014, was $9,000. During 2015, coupons worth $30,000 were issued, and merchandise worth $8,000 was distributed in exchange for coupons redeemed.

Instructions
Compute the amount of the liability that should appear on the December 31, 2015, statement of financial position.

CONCEPTS FOR ANALYSIS

CA13-1 (Nature of Liabilities) Presented below is the current liabilities section of Micro Corporation (amounts in thousands).

	2015	2014
Current liabilities		
Notes payable	€ 68,713	€ 7,700
Accounts payable	179,496	101,379
Compensation to employees	60,312	31,649
Accrued liabilities	158,198	77,621
Income taxes payable	10,486	26,491
Current maturities of long-term debt	16,592	6,649
Total current liabilities	€493,797	€251,489

Instructions
Answer the following questions.
   (a) What are the essential characteristics that make an item a liability?
   (b) What distinguishes a current liability from a non-current liability?
   (c) What are accrued liabilities? Give three examples of accrued liabilities that Micro might have.
   (d) What is the theoretically correct way to value liabilities? How are current liabilities usually valued?
   (e) Why are notes payable reported first in the current liabilities section?
   (f) What might be the items that comprise Micro's liability for "Compensation to employees"?

CA13-2 (Current versus Non-Current Classification) Rodriguez Corporation includes the following items in its liabilities at December 31, 2014.

   1. Notes payable, $25,000,000, due June 30, 2015.
   2. Deposits from customers on equipment ordered by them from Rodriguez, $6,250,000.
   3. Salaries payable, $3,750,000, due January 14, 2015.

Instructions
Indicate in what circumstances, if any, each of the three liabilities above would be excluded from current liabilities.

CA13-3 (Refinancing of Short-Term Debt) Kobayashi Corporation reports in the current liability section of its statement of financial position at December 31, 2014 (its year-end), short-term obligations of ¥15,000,000, which includes the current portion of 12% long-term debt in the amount of ¥10,000,000 (matures in March 2015). Management has stated its intention to refinance the 12% debt whereby no portion of it will mature during 2015. The date of issuance of the financial statements is March 25, 2015.

Instructions
   (a) Is management's intent enough to support long-term classification of the obligation in this situation?
   (b) Assume that Kobayashi Corporation issues ¥13,000,000 of 10-year debentures to the public in January 2015 and that management intends to use the proceeds to liquidate the ¥10,000,000 debt maturing in March 2015. Furthermore, assume that the debt maturing in March 2015 is paid from these proceeds prior to the authorization to issue the financial statements. Will this have any impact on the statement of financial position classification at December 31, 2014? Explain your answer.
   (c) Assume that Kobayashi Corporation issues ordinary shares to the public in January and that management intends to entirely liquidate the ¥10,000,000 debt maturing in March 2015 with the proceeds of this equity securities issue. In light of these events, should the ¥10,000,000 debt maturing in March 2015 be included in current liabilities at December 31, 2014?
   (d) Assume that Kobayashi Corporation, on February 15, 2015, entered into a financing agreement with a commercial bank that permits Kobayashi Corporation to borrow at any time through 2016 up to ¥15,000,000 at the bank's prime rate of interest. Borrowings under the financing agreement mature three years after the date of the loan. The agreement is not cancelable except for violation

of a provision with which compliance is objectively determinable. No violation of any provision exists at the date of issuance of the financial statements. Assume further that the current portion of long-term debt does not mature until August 2015. In addition, management may refinance the ¥10,000,000 obligation under the terms of the financial agreement with the bank, which is expected to be financially capable of honoring the agreement. Given these facts, should the ¥10,000,000 be classified as current on the statement of financial position at December 31, 2014?

CA13-4 (Contingencies) On February 1, 2015, one of the huge storage tanks of Viking Manufacturing Company exploded. Windows in houses and other buildings within a one-mile radius of the explosion were severely damaged, and a number of people were injured. As of February 15, 2015 (when the December 31, 2014, financial statements were completed and sent to the publisher for printing and public distribution), no suits had been filed or claims asserted against the company as a consequence of the explosion. The company fully anticipates that suits will be filed and claims asserted for injuries and damages. Because the casualty was uninsured and the company considered at fault, Viking Manufacturing will have to cover the damages from its own resources.

Instructions

Discuss fully the accounting treatment and disclosures that should be accorded the casualty and related contingent losses in the financial statements dated December 31, 2014.

CA13-5 (Possible Environmental Liability) Presented below is a note disclosure for Matsui Corporation.

> **Litigation and Environmental:** The Company has been notified, or is a named or a potentially responsible party in a number of governmental and private actions associated with environmental matters. These actions seek clean-up costs, penalties and/or damages for personal injury or to property or natural resources.
>
> In 2015, the Company recorded a pretax charge of ¥56,229,000, included in the "Other expense (income)—net" caption of the Company's consolidated income statements, as an additional provision for environmental matters. These expenditures are expected to take place over the next several years and are indicative of the Company's commitment to improve and maintain the environment in which it operates. At December 31, 2015, environmental accruals amounted to ¥69,931,000, of which ¥61,535,000 are considered non-current and are included in the "Non-current liability" caption of the Company's consolidated statements of financial position.
>
> While it is impossible at this time to determine with certainty the ultimate outcome of environmental matters, it is management's opinion, based in part on the advice of independent counsel (after taking into account accruals and insurance coverage applicable to such actions) that when the costs are finally determined they will not have a material adverse effect on the financial position of the Company.

Instructions

Answer the following questions.

(a) What conditions must exist before a provision can be recorded in the accounts?

(b) Suppose that Matsui Corporation could not reasonably estimate the amount of the loss, although it could establish with a high degree of probability the minimum and maximum loss possible. How should this information be reported in the financial statements?

(c) If the amount of the loss is uncertain, how would the potential liability be reported in the financial statements?

CA13-6 (Warranties and Litigation Provisions) The following two independent situations involve litigation provisions.

Part 1: Benson Company sells two products, Grey and Yellow. Each carries a one-year warranty.

1. Product Grey—Product warranty costs, based on past experience, will normally be 1% of sales.
2. Product Yellow—Product warranty costs cannot be reasonably estimated because this is a new product line. However, the chief engineer believes that product warranty costs are likely to be incurred.

Instructions

How should Benson report the estimated product warranty costs for each of the two types of merchandise above? Discuss the rationale for your answer. Do not discuss disclosures that should be made in Benson's financial statements or notes.

Part 2: Constantine Company is being sued for £4,000,000 for an injury caused to a child as a result of alleged negligence while the child was visiting the Constantine Company plant in March 2015. The suit was filed in July 2015. Constantine's lawyer states that it is probable that Constantine will lose the suit and be found liable for a judgment costing anywhere from £400,000 to £2,000,000. However, the lawyer states that the most probable judgment is £1,000,000.

Instructions

How should Constantine report the suit in its 2015 financial statements? Discuss the rationale for your answer. Include in your answer disclosures, if any, that should be made in Constantine's financial statements or notes.

CA13-7 (Ethics of Warranties) The Dotson Company, owner of Bleacher Mall, charges Rich Clothing Store a rental fee of $600 per month plus 5% of yearly profits over $500,000. Matt Rich, the owner of the store, directs his accountant, Ron Hamilton, to increase the estimate of bad debt expense and warranty costs in order to keep profits at $475,000.

Instructions

Answer the following questions.

- **(a)** Should Hamilton follow his boss's directive?
- **(b)** Who is harmed if the estimates are increased?
- **(c)** Is Matt Rich's directive ethical?

USING YOUR JUDGMENT

FINANCIAL REPORTING

Financial Reporting Problem

Marks and Spencer plc (M&S)

The financial statements of M&S (GBR) are presented in Appendix A. The company's complete annual report, including the notes to the financial statements, is available online.

Instructions

Refer to M&S's financial statements and the accompanying notes to answer the following questions.

- **(a)** What was the composition of M&S's borrowings and other financial liabilities shown in its current liability section at year-end 2013?
- **(b)** What was M&S's year-end 2013 working capital and current ratio? Comment on M&S's liquidity.
- **(c)** What types of commitments and contingencies has M&S reported in its financial statements? What is management's reaction to these contingencies?

Comparative Analysis Case

adidas and Puma

The financial statements of adidas (DEU) and Puma (DEU) are presented in Appendices B and C, respectively. The complete annual reports, including the notes to the financial statements, are available online.

Instructions

Use the companies' financial information to answer the following questions.

- **(a)** How much working capital do each of these companies have at the end of 2012?
- **(b)** Compute both companies' (a) current cash debt coverage, (b) cash debt coverage, (c) current ratio, (d) acid-test ratio, (e) accounts receivable turnover, and (f) inventory turnover for 2012. Comment on each company's overall liquidity.
- **(c)** What types of loss or gain contingencies do these two companies have at the end of 2012?

Financial Statement Analysis Cases

Case 1 Northland Cranberries

Despite being a publicly traded company only since 1987, Northland Cranberries (USA) of Wisconsin Rapids, Wisconsin, is one of the world's largest cranberry growers. Despite its short life as a publicly traded corporation, it has engaged in an aggressive growth strategy. As a consequence, the company has taken on significant amounts of both short-term and long-term debt. The following information is taken from recent annual reports of the company.

Northland Cranberries

	Current Year	Prior Year
Current assets	$ 6,745,759	$ 5,598,054
Total assets	107,744,751	83,074,339
Current liabilities	10,168,685	4,484,687
Total liabilities	73,118,204	49,948,787
Shareholders' equity	34,626,547	33,125,552
Net sales	21,783,966	18,051,355
Cost of goods sold	13,057,275	8,751,220
Interest expense	3,654,006	2,393,792
Income tax expense	1,051,000	1,917,000
Net income	1,581,707	2,942,954

Instructions

(a) Evaluate the company's liquidity by calculating and analyzing working capital and the current ratio.

(b) The following discussion of the company's liquidity was provided by the company in the Management Discussion and Analysis section of the company's annual report. Comment on whether you agree with management's statements, and what might be done to remedy the situation.

The lower comparative current ratio in the current year was due to $3 million of short-term borrowing then outstanding which was incurred to fund the Yellow River Marsh acquisitions last year. As a result of the extreme seasonality of its business, the company does not believe that its current ratio or its underlying stated working capital at the current, fiscal year-end is a meaningful indication of the Company's liquidity. As of March 31 of each fiscal year, the Company has historically carried no significant amounts of inventories and by such date all of the Company's accounts receivable from its crop sold for processing under the supply agreements have been paid in cash, with the resulting cash received from such payments used to reduce indebtedness. The Company utilizes its revolving bank credit facility, together with cash generated from operations, to fund its working capital requirements throughout its growing season.

Case 2 Suzuki Company

Presented below is the current liabilities section and related note of Suzuki Company.

	(yen in millions)	
	Current Year	Prior Year
Current liabilities		
Current portion of long-term debt	¥ 15,000	¥ 10,000
Short-term debt	2,668	405
Accounts payable	29,495	42,427
Accrued warranty	16,843	16,741
Accrued marketing programs	17,512	16,585
Other accrued liabilities	35,653	33,290
Accrued and deferred income taxes	16,206	17,348
Total current liabilities	¥133,377	¥136,796

Notes to Consolidated Financial Statements

Note 1 (in part): Summary of Significant Accounting Policies and Related Data

Accrued Warranty The company provides an accrual for future warranty costs based upon the relationship of prior years' sales to actual warranty costs.

Instructions

Answer the following questions.

(a) What type of warranty is Suzuki Company providing to customers?

(b) Under what circumstance, if any, would it be appropriate for Suzuki Company to recognize unearned revenue on warranty contracts?

(c) If Suzuki Company recognized unearned revenue on warranty contracts, how would it recognize this revenue in subsequent periods?

Case 3 BOP Clothing Co.

As discussed in the chapter, an important consideration in evaluating current liabilities is a company's operating cycle. The operating cycle is the average time required to go from cash to cash in generating revenue. To determine the length of the operating cycle, analysts use two measures: the average days to sell inventory (*inventory days*) and the average days to collect receivables (*receivable days*). The inventory-days computation measures the average number of days it takes to move an item from raw materials or purchase to final sale (from the day it comes in the company's door to the point it is converted to cash or an account receivable). The receivable-days computation measures the average number of days it takes to collect an account.

Most businesses must then determine how to finance the period of time when the liquid assets are tied up in inventory and accounts receivable. To determine how much to finance, companies first determine accounts payable days—how long it takes to pay creditors. Accounts payable days measures the number of days it takes to pay a supplier invoice. Consider the following operating cycle worksheet for BOP Clothing Co.

	2014	2015
Cash	$ 45,000	$ 30,000
Accounts receivable	250,000	325,000
Inventory	830,000	800,000
Accounts payable	720,000	775,000
Purchases	1,100,000	1,425,000
Cost of goods sold	1,145,000	1,455,000
Sales	1,750,000	1,950,000
Operating Cycle		
Inventory days[1]	264.6	200.7
Receivable days[2]	52.1	60.8
Operating cycle	316.7	261.5
Less: Accounts payable days[3]	238.9	198.5
Days to be financed	77.8	63.0
Working capital	$ 405,000	$ 380,000
Current ratio	1.56	1.49
Acid-test ratio	0.41	0.46

[1]Inventory days = (Inventory × 365) ÷ Cost of goods sold
[2]Receivable days = (Accounts receivable × 365) ÷ Sales
[3]Accounts payable days = (Accounts payable × 365) ÷ Purchases

Purchases = Cost of goods sold + Ending inventory − Beginning inventory.
The ratios above assume that other current assets and liabilities are negligible.

These data indicate that BOP has reduced its overall operating cycle (to 261.5 days) as well as the number of days to be financed with sources of funds other than accounts payable (from 78 to 63 days). Most businesses cannot finance the operating cycle with accounts payable financing alone, so working capital financing, usually short-term interest-bearing loans, is needed to cover the shortfall. In this case, BOP would need to borrow less money to finance its operating cycle in 2015 than in 2014.

Instructions

(a) Use the BOP analysis to briefly discuss how the operating cycle data relate to the amount of working capital and the current and acid-test ratios.

(b) Select two other real companies that are in the same industry and complete the operating cycle worksheet (similar to that prepared for BOP), along with the working capital and ratio analysis. Briefly summarize and interpret the results. To simplify the analysis, you may use ending balances to compute turnover ratios.

(Adapted from Operating Cycle Worksheet at *www.entrepreneur.com*)

Accounting, Analysis, and Principles

YellowCard Company manufactures accessories for iPods. It had the following selected transactions during 2015. (For any part of this problem requiring an interest or discount rate, use 10%.)

1. YellowCard provides a 2-year warranty on its docking stations, which it began selling in 2015. YellowCard estimates that €45,000 will be spent in the future to service warranties related to 2015 sales. During 2015, YellowCard spent €6,000 servicing warranty claims.

2. YellowCard has a one year €200,000 loan outstanding from UBS. The loan is set to mature on February 28, 2016. For several years, UBS has agreed to extend the loan, as long as YellowCard makes all of its quarterly interest payments (interest is due on the last days of each February, May, August, and November) and maintains an acid-test ratio (also called quick ratio) of at least 1.25. On December 10, 2015, UBS provided YellowCard a commitment letter indicating that UBS will extend the loan another 12 months, provided that YellowCard makes the interest payment due on May 31.

3. During 2014, YellowCard constructed a small manufacturing facility specifically to manufacture one particular accessory. YellowCard paid the construction contractor €5,000,000 cash (which was the total contract price) and placed the facility into service on January 1, 2015. Because of technological change, YellowCard anticipates that the manufacturing facility will be useful for no more than 10 years. The local government where the facility is located required that, at the end of the 10-year period, Yellow-Card remediate the facility so that it can be used as a community center. YellowCard estimates the cost of remediation in the future to be €500,000.

Accounting

Prepare all 2015 journal entries relating to (a) YellowCard's warranties, (b) YellowCard's loan from UBS, and (c) the new manufacturing facility that YellowCard opened on January 1, 2015.

Analysis

Describe how the transactions above affect ratios that might be used to assess YellowCard's liquidity. How important is the commitment letter that YellowCard has from UBS to these ratios?

Principles

YellowCard is contemplating offering an extended warranty. If customers pay an additional €50 at the time of product purchase, YellowCard would extend the warranty an additional 2 years. Would the extended warranty meet the definition of a liability under IFRS? Briefly explain.

IFRS BRIDGE TO THE PROFESSION

Professional Research

Hincapie Co. manufactures specialty bike accessories. The company is most well known for its product quality, and it has offered one of the best warranties in the industry on its higher-priced products—a lifetime guarantee. The warranty on these products is included in the sales price. Hincapie has a contract with a service company, which performs all warranty work on Hincapie products. Under the contract, Hincapie guarantees the service company at least €200,000 of warranty work for each year of the 3-year contract.

The recent economic recession has been hard on Hincapie's business, and sales for its higher-end products have been especially adversely impacted. As a result, Hincapie is planning to restructure its high-quality lines by moving manufacturing for those products into one of its other factories, shutting down assembly lines, and terminating workers. In order to keep some workers on-board, Hincapie plans to bring all warranty work in-house. It can terminate the current warranty contract by making a one-time termination payment of €75,000.

The restructuring plans have been discussed by management during November 2014; they plan to get approval from the board of directors at the December board meeting and execute the restructuring in early 2015. Given the company's past success, the accounting for restructuring activities has never come up. Hincapie would like you to do some research on how it should account for this restructuring according to IFRS.

Instructions

Access the IFRS authoritative literature at the IASB website (*http://eifrs.iasb.org/*) (you may register for free eIFRS access at this site). When you have accessed the documents, you can use the search tool in your Internet browser to respond to the following questions. (Provide paragraph citations.)

(a) Identify the accounting literature that addresses the accounting for the various restructuring costs that will be incurred in the restructuring.

(b) Advise Hincapie on the restructuring costs. When should Hincapie recognize liabilities arising from the restructuring? What costs can be included? What costs are excluded?

(c) Does Hincapie have a liability related to the service contract? Explain. If Hincapie has a liability, at what amount should it be recorded?

Professional Simulation

In this simulation, you are asked to address questions related to the accounting for current liabilities. Prepare responses to all parts.

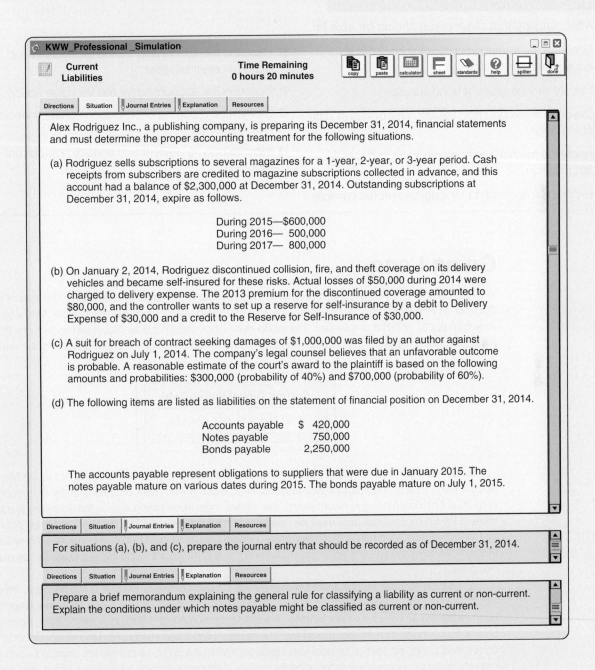

KWW_Professional_Simulation

Current
Liabilities

Time Remaining
0 hours 20 minutes

copy | paste | calculator | sheet | standards | help | splitter | done

Directions | Situation | Journal Entries | Explanation | Resources

Alex Rodriguez Inc., a publishing company, is preparing its December 31, 2014, financial statements and must determine the proper accounting treatment for the following situations.

(a) Rodriguez sells subscriptions to several magazines for a 1-year, 2-year, or 3-year period. Cash receipts from subscribers are credited to magazine subscriptions collected in advance, and this account had a balance of $2,300,000 at December 31, 2014. Outstanding subscriptions at December 31, 2014, expire as follows.

During 2015—$600,000
During 2016— 500,000
During 2017— 800,000

(b) On January 2, 2014, Rodriguez discontinued collision, fire, and theft coverage on its delivery vehicles and became self-insured for these risks. Actual losses of $50,000 during 2014 were charged to delivery expense. The 2013 premium for the discontinued coverage amounted to $80,000, and the controller wants to set up a reserve for self-insurance by a debit to Delivery Expense of $30,000 and a credit to the Reserve for Self-Insurance of $30,000.

(c) A suit for breach of contract seeking damages of $1,000,000 was filed by an author against Rodriguez on July 1, 2014. The company's legal counsel believes that an unfavorable outcome is probable. A reasonable estimate of the court's award to the plaintiff is based on the following amounts and probabilities: $300,000 (probability of 40%) and $700,000 (probability of 60%).

(d) The following items are listed as liabilities on the statement of financial position on December 31, 2014.

Accounts payable | $ 420,000
Notes payable | 750,000
Bonds payable | 2,250,000

The accounts payable represent obligations to suppliers that were due in January 2015. The notes payable mature on various dates during 2015. The bonds payable mature on July 1, 2015.

Directions | Situation | Journal Entries | Explanation | Resources

For situations (a), (b), and (c), prepare the journal entry that should be recorded as of December 31, 2014.

Directions | Situation | Journal Entries | Explanation | Resources

Prepare a brief memorandum explaining the general rule for classifying a liability as current or non-current. Explain the conditions under which notes payable might be classified as current or non-current.

LEARNING OBJECTIVES

After studying this chapter, you should be able to:

1 Describe the formal procedures associated with issuing long-term debt.

2 Identify various types of bond issues.

3 Describe the accounting valuation for bonds at date of issuance.

4 Apply the methods of bond discount and premium amortization.

5 Explain the accounting for long-term notes payable.

6 Describe the accounting for the extinguishment of non-current liabilities.

7 Describe the accounting for the fair value option.

8 Explain the reporting of off-balance-sheet financing arrangements.

9 Indicate how to present and analyze non-current liabilities.

Going Long

The clock is ticking. Every second, it seems, someone in the world takes on more debt. The idea of a debt clock for an individual nation is familiar to anyone who has been to Times Square in New York, where the American public shortfall is revealed. The world debt clock shown below (accessed in January 2014 at *www.nationaldebtclocks.org*) indicates the global figure for almost all government debts in dollar terms.

> **Current Global Public Debt**
>
> $ 52,521,833,443,124,156

Does it matter? After all, world governments owe the money to their own citizens, not to the Martians. But the rising total is important for two reasons. First, when government debt rises faster than economic output (as it has been doing in recent years), this implies more state interference in the economy and higher taxes in the future. Second, debt must be rolled over at regular intervals. This creates a recurring popularity test for individual governments, much like reality-TV contestants facing a public phone vote every week. Fail that vote, as various euro-zone governments have done, and the country (and its neighbors) can be plunged into crisis.

In addition to government debt, companies are issuing corporate debt at a record pace. Why this trend? For one thing, low interest rates and rising inflows into fixed-income funds have triggered record bond issuances as banks cut back lending. In addition, for some high-rated companies, it can be riskier to borrow from a bank than the bond markets. The reason: High-rated companies tend to rely on short-term commercial paper, backed up by undrawn loans, to fund working capital but are left stranded when these markets freeze up. Some are now financing themselves with longer-term bonds instead. In fact, non-financial companies are issuing 30-year bonds at a record pace as they look to increase long-term borrowings, lock in low interest rates, and take advantage of investor demand. The charts on the next page show the substantial increase in bond issues as interest rates have fallen.

Companies, like **Phillip Morris** (USA), **Sinopec** (CHN), and **Apple** (USA), have all sold 30-year bonds recently. Increases in the issuance of these bonds suggest confidence in the economy as investors appear comfortable holding such long-term investments. In addition, companies have a strong appetite

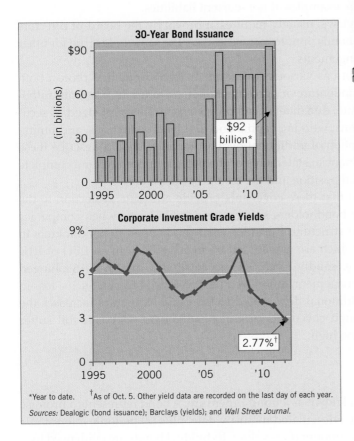

30-Year Bond Issuance

$92 billion*

Corporate Investment Grade Yields

2.77%†

*Year to date.   †As of Oct. 5. Other yield data are recorded on the last day of each year.

Sources: Dealogic (bond issuance); Barclays (yields); and *Wall Street Journal.*

CONCEPTUAL FOCUS

> See the **Underlying Concepts** on pages 660 and 676.
> Read the **Evolving Issue** on page 679 for a discussion of off-balance-sheet reporting.

INTERNATIONAL FOCUS

> Read the **Global Accounting Insights** on pages 681–682 for a discussion of non-IFRS financial reporting of liabilities.

for issuing these bonds because they provide a substantial cash infusion at a relatively low interest rate. Hopefully, it will work out for both the investor and the company in the long run.

Sources: A. Sakoui and N. Bullock, "Companies Choose Bonds for Cheap Funds," *Financial Times* (October 12, 2009); *http://www. economist.com/content/global_debt_clock*; V. Monga, "Companies Feast on Cheap Money Market for 30-Year Bonds, Priced at Stark Lows, Brings Out GE, UPS and Other Once-Shy Issuers," *Wall Street Journal* (October 8, 2012); and Josh Noble, "Sinopec Raises €550m from Euro Bond Sale," *Financial Times* (October 10, 2013).

PREVIEW OF CHAPTER **14**

As our opening story indicates, companies may rely on different forms of long-term borrowing, depending on market conditions and the features of various non-current liabilities. In this chapter, we explain the accounting issues related to non-current liabilities. The content and organization of the chapter are as follows.

Non-Current Liabilities

Bonds Payable	Long-Term Notes Payable	Special Issues
• Issuing bonds	• Notes issued at face value	• Extinguishments
• Types and ratings of bonds	• Notes not issued at face value	• Fair value option
• Valuation	• Special situations	• Off-balance-sheet financing
• Effective-interest method	• Mortgage notes payable	• Presentation and analysis

BONDS PAYABLE

 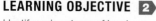
Non-current liabilities (sometimes referred to as long-term debt) consist of an expected outflow of resources arising from present obligations that are not payable within a year or the operating cycle of the company, whichever is longer. Bonds payable, long-term notes payable, mortgages payable, pension liabilities, and lease liabilities are examples of non-current liabilities.

A corporation, per its bylaws, usually requires approval by the board of directors and the shareholders before bonds or notes can be issued. The same holds true for other types of long-term debt arrangements.

Generally, long-term debt has various **covenants** or **restrictions** that protect both lenders and borrowers. The indenture or agreement often includes the amounts authorized to be issued, interest rate, due date(s), call provisions, property pledged as security, sinking fund requirements, working capital and dividend restrictions, and limitations concerning the assumption of additional debt. Companies should describe these features in the body of the financial statements or the notes if important for a complete understanding of the financial position and the results of operations.

Although it would seem that these covenants provide adequate protection to the long-term debtholder, many bondholders suffer considerable losses when companies add more debt to the capital structure. Consider what can happen to bondholders in leveraged buyouts (LBOs), which are usually led by management. In an LBO of RJR Nabisco (USA), for example, solidly rated 9⅜ percent bonds due in 2016 plunged 20 percent in value when management announced the leveraged buyout. Such a loss in value occurs because the additional debt added to the capital structure increases the likelihood of default. Although covenants protect bondholders, they can still suffer losses when debt levels get too high.

Issuing Bonds

A bond arises from a contract known as a **bond indenture**. A bond represents a promise to pay (1) a sum of money at a designated maturity date, plus (2) periodic interest at a specified rate on the maturity amount (face value). Individual bonds are evidenced by a paper certificate and typically have a €1,000 face value. Companies usually make bond interest payments semiannually although the interest rate is generally expressed as an annual rate. As discussed in the opening story, the main purpose of bonds is to borrow for the long term when the amount of capital needed is too large for one lender to supply. By issuing bonds in €100, €1,000, or €10,000 denominations, a company can divide a large amount of long-term indebtedness into many small investing units, thus enabling more than one lender to participate in the loan.

A company may sell an entire bond issue to an investment bank, which acts as a selling agent in the process of marketing the bonds. In such arrangements, investment banks may either underwrite the entire issue by guaranteeing a certain sum to the company, thus taking the risk of selling the bonds for whatever price they can get (firm underwriting). Or, they may sell the bond issue for a commission on the proceeds of the sale (best-efforts underwriting). Alternatively, the issuing company may sell the bonds directly to a large institution, financial or otherwise, without the aid of an underwriter (private placement).

Types and Ratings of Bonds

Presented on the next page, we define some of the more common types of bonds found in practice.

TYPES OF BONDS

SECURED AND UNSECURED BONDS. **Secured bonds** are backed by a pledge of some sort of collateral. Mortgage bonds are secured by a claim on real estate. Collateral trust bonds are secured by shares and bonds of other corporations. Bonds not backed by collateral are **unsecured**. A **debenture bond** is unsecured. A "junk bond" is unsecured and also very risky, and therefore pays a high interest rate. Companies often use these bonds to finance leveraged buyouts.

TERM, SERIAL BONDS, AND CALLABLE BONDS. Bond issues that mature on a single date are called **term bonds**; issues that mature in installments are called **serial bonds**. Serially maturing bonds are frequently used by school or sanitary districts, municipalities, or other local taxing bodies that receive money through a special levy. **Callable bonds** give the issuer the right to call and retire the bonds prior to maturity.

CONVERTIBLE, COMMODITY-BACKED, AND DEEP-DISCOUNT BONDS. If bonds are convertible into other securities of the corporation for a specified time after issuance, they are **convertible bonds**.

Two types of bonds have been developed in an attempt to attract capital in a tight money market—commodity-backed bonds and deep-discount bonds. **Commodity-backed bonds** (also called **asset-linked bonds**) are redeemable in measures of a commodity, such as barrels of oil, tons of coal, or ounces of rare metal. To illustrate, Sunshine Mining (USA), a silver-mining company, sold two issues of bonds redeemable with either $1,000 in cash or 50 ounces of silver, whichever is greater at maturity, and that have a stated interest rate of 8½ percent. The accounting problem is one of projecting the maturity value, especially since silver has fluctuated between $4 and $40 an ounce since issuance.

Deep-discount bonds, also referred to as **zero-interest debenture bonds**, are sold at a discount that provides the buyer's total interest payoff at maturity.

REGISTERED AND BEARER (COUPON) BONDS. Bonds issued in the name of the owner are **registered bonds** and require surrender of the certificate and issuance of a new certificate to complete a sale. A **bearer** or **coupon bond**, however, is not recorded in the name of the owner and may be transferred from one owner to another by mere delivery.

INCOME AND REVENUE BONDS. **Income bonds** pay no interest unless the issuing company is profitable. **Revenue bonds**, so called because the interest on them is paid from specified revenue sources, are most frequently issued by airports, school districts, counties, toll-road authorities, and governmental bodies.

What do the numbers mean? ALL ABOUT BONDS

How do investors monitor their bond investments? One way is to review the bond listings found in the newspaper or online. Corporate bond listings show the coupon (interest) rate, maturity date, and last price. However, because corporate bonds are more actively traded by large institutional investors, the listings also indicate the current yield. Corporate bond listings would look like this below.

Issuer	Coupon	Maturity	Price	Yield	Rating
Vodafone Group	5.00	2018/06/04	106.66	4.05	AA
Telecom Italia S.p.A.	5.25	2022/10/02	100.00	5.25	BB⁺

The companies issuing the bonds are listed in the first column, in this case, two telecommunications companies, **Vodafone Group** (GBR) and **Telecom Italia S.p.A** (ITA). In the second column is the interest rate paid by the bond as a percentage of its par value, followed by its maturity date. The Vodafone bonds, for example, pay 5 percent and mature on June 4, 2018. The Telecom Italia bonds pay 5.25 percent, a bit higher. The Vodafone bonds have a current yield of 4.05 percent, based on the price of 106.66 per £1,000. In contrast, the Telecom Italia bonds at 100.00 yield 5.25 percent. The final column gives the bond rating. Vodafone, with a rating of AA, is viewed as more creditworthy than Telecom Italia, which explains why Vodafone's bonds sell at a higher price and lower yield.

Also, as indicated in the chapter, interest rates and the bond's term to maturity have a real effect on bond prices. For example, an increase in interest rates will lead to a decline in bond values. Similarly, a decrease in interest rates will lead to a rise in bond values. The following data, based on three different bond funds, demonstrate these relationships between interest rate changes and bond values.

Bond Price Changes in Response to Interest Rate Changes	1% Interest Rate Increase	1% Interest Rate Decrease
Short-term fund (2–5 years)	−2.5%	+2.5%
Intermediate-term fund (5 years)	−5%	+5%
Long-term fund (10 years)	−10%	+10%

Source: The Vanguard Group.

Another factor that affects bond prices is the call feature, which decreases the value of the bond. Investors must be rewarded for the risk that the issuer will call the bond if interest rates decline, which would force the investor to reinvest at lower rates.

Valuation of Bonds Payable

LEARNING OBJECTIVE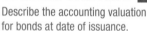

Describe the accounting valuation for bonds at date of issuance.

The issuance and marketing of bonds to the public does not happen overnight. It usually takes weeks or even months. First, the issuing company must arrange for underwriters that will help market and sell the bonds. Then, it must obtain regulatory approval of the bond issue, undergo audits, and issue a prospectus (a document that describes the features of the bond and related financial information). Finally, the company must generally have the bond certificates printed. Frequently, the issuing company establishes the terms of a bond indenture well in advance of the sale of the bonds. Between the time the company sets these terms and the time it issues the bonds, the market conditions and the financial position of the issuing corporation may change significantly. Such changes affect the marketability of the bonds and thus their selling price.

The selling price of a bond issue is set by the supply and demand of buyers and sellers, relative risk, market conditions, and the state of the economy. The investment community values a bond at the **present value of its expected future cash flows**, which consist of (1) interest and (2) principal. The rate used to compute the present value of these cash flows is the interest rate that provides an acceptable return on an investment commensurate with the issuer's risk characteristics.

The interest rate written in the terms of the bond indenture (and often printed on the bond certificate) is known as the **stated, coupon,** or **nominal rate**. The issuer of the bonds sets this rate. The stated rate is expressed as a percentage of the **face value** of the bonds (also called the **par value, principal amount,** or **maturity value**).

Bonds Issued at Par

If the rate employed by the investment community (buyers) is the same as the stated rate, the bond sells at par. That is, the par value equals the present value of the bonds computed by the buyers (and the current purchase price). To illustrate the computation of the **present value of a bond issue**, assume that Santos Company issues R$100,000 in bonds dated January 1, 2015, due in five years with 9 percent interest payable annually on January 1. At the time of issue, the market rate for such bonds is 9 percent. The time diagram in Illustration 14-1 depicts both the interest and the principal cash flows.

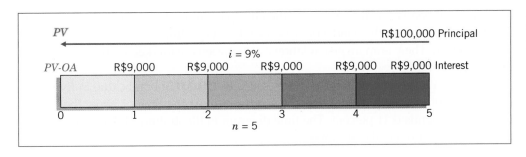

ILLUSTRATION 14-1
Time Diagram for Bonds
Issued at Par

The actual principal and interest cash flows are discounted at a 9 percent rate for five periods, as shown in Illustration 14-2.

Present value of the principal:	
R$100,000 × .64993 (Table 6-2)	R$ 64,993
Present value of the interest payments:	
R$9,000 × 3.88965 (Table 6-4)	35,007
Present value (selling price) of the bonds	R$100,000

ILLUSTRATION 14-2
Present Value
Computation of Bond
Selling at Par

By paying R$100,000 (the par value) at the date of issue, investors realize an effective rate or yield of 9 percent over the five-year term of the bonds. Santos makes the following entry when it issues the bonds.

January 1, 2015

Cash	100,000	
Bonds Payable		100,000

Santos records accrued interest expense of R$9,000 (R$100,000 × .09) at December 31, 2015 (year-end), as follows.

December 31, 2015

Interest Expense	9,000	
Interest Payable		9,000

It records the first interest payment as follows.

January 1, 2016

Interest Payable	9,000	
Cash		9,000

Bonds Issued at Discount or Premium

If the rate employed by the investment community (buyers) differs from the stated rate, the present value of the bonds computed by the buyers (and the current purchase price) will differ from the face value of the bonds. The difference between the face value and the present value of the bonds determines the actual price that buyers pay for the bonds. This difference is either a discount or premium.[1]

- If the bonds sell for less than face value, they sell at a **discount**.
- If the bonds sell for more than face value, they sell at a **premium**.

The rate of interest actually earned by the bondholders is called the **effective yield** or **market rate**. If bonds sell at a discount, the effective yield exceeds the stated rate.

[1]It is generally the case that the stated rate of interest on bonds is set in rather precise decimals (such as 10.875 percent). Companies usually attempt to align the stated rate as closely as possible with the market or effective rate at the time of issue.

Conversely, if bonds sell at a premium, the effective yield is lower than the stated rate. Several variables affect the bond's price while it is outstanding, most notably the market rate of interest. There is an inverse relationship between the market interest rate and the price of the bond.

To illustrate, assume now that Santos issues R$100,000 in bonds, due in five years with 9 percent interest payable annually at year-end. At the time of issue, the market rate for such bonds is 11 percent. The time diagram in Illustration 14-3 depicts both the interest and the principal cash flows.

ILLUSTRATION 14-3
Time Diagram for Bonds
Issued at a Discount

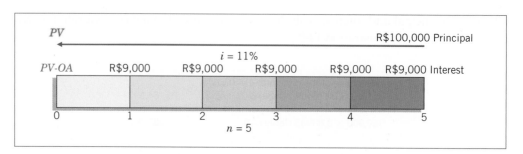

The actual principal and interest cash flows are discounted at an 11 percent rate for five periods, as shown in Illustration 14-4.

ILLUSTRATION 14-4
Present Value
Computation of Bond
Selling at a Discount

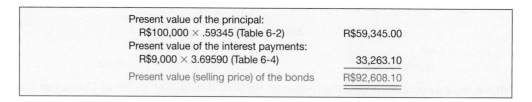

Present value of the principal:	
R$100,000 × .59345 (Table 6-2)	R$59,345.00
Present value of the interest payments:	
R$9,000 × 3.69590 (Table 6-4)	33,263.10
Present value (selling price) of the bonds	R$92,608.10

By paying R$92,608.10 at the date of issue, investors realize an effective rate or yield of 11 percent over the five-year term of the bonds. These bonds would sell at a discount of R$7,391.90 (R$100,000 − R$92,608.10). The price at which the bonds sell is typically stated as a percentage of the face or par value of the bonds. For example, the Santos bonds sold for 92.6 (92.6% of par). If Santos had received R$102,000, then the bonds sold for 102 (102% of par).

When bonds sell at less than face value, it means that investors demand a rate of interest **higher** than the stated rate. Usually, this occurs because the investors can earn a higher rate on alternative investments of equal risk. They cannot change the stated rate, so they refuse to pay face value for the bonds. Thus, by changing the amount invested, they alter the effective rate of return. The investors receive interest at the stated rate computed on the face value, but they actually earn at **an effective rate that exceeds the stated rate because they paid less than face value for the bonds**. (Later in the chapter, in Illustrations 14-8 and 14-9 on page 661, we show an illustration for a bond that sells at a premium.)

What do the numbers mean?   HOW ABOUT A 100-YEAR BOND?

Yes, some companies issue bonds with maturities that exceed a person's lifetime. For example, Électricité de France S.A. (FRA) in early 2014 sold 100-year bonds in Europe. The world's biggest operator of nuclear reactors priced £1.35 billion of notes to yield 6.125 percent. The Paris-based utility is the second company to sell century bonds in Europe, following GDF Suez S.A. (FRA) in March 2011.

Why do companies issue 100-year bonds? A number of investors, such as pension funds and insurance companies, have non-current liabilities. They need long-duration assets to reduce an asset-liability mismatch. While investing in a 100-year bond carries interest-rate risk, long-term debt has an offsetting effect against long-duration assets. Thus, this group of investors has a strong demand for these bonds.

Other multibillion-dollar companies, such as **Walt Disney Company** (USA) and **The Coca-Cola Company** (USA), have issued 100-year bonds in the past. Many of these bonds and debentures contain an option that lets the debt issuer partially or fully repay the debt long before the scheduled maturity. For example, the 100-year bond that Disney issued in 1993 is supposed to mature in 2093, but the company can start repaying the bonds any time after 30 years (2023).

You may be surprised to learn that *1,000-year* bonds also exist. A few issuers, such as the **Canadian Pacific Corporation** (CAN), have issued such bonds in the past. And, there have also been instances of bonds issued with no maturity date at all, meaning that the debt issuers continue fulfilling the coupon payments forever. These types of financial instruments are commonly referred to as perpetuities.

Sources: Albert Phung, "Why Do Companies Issue 100-Year Bonds?" *Investopedia* (February 2009); and K. Linsell, "EDF's Borrowing Exceeds $12 Billion This Week with 100-Year Bond," *Bloomberg* (January 17, 2014).

Effective-Interest Method

As discussed earlier, by paying more or less at issuance, investors earn a rate different than the coupon rate on the bond. Recall that the issuing company pays the contractual interest rate over the term of the bonds but also must pay the face value at maturity. If the bond is issued at a discount, the amount paid at maturity is more than the issue amount. If issued at a premium, the company pays less at maturity relative to the issue price.

> **4 LEARNING OBJECTIVE**
>
> Apply the methods of bond discount and premium amortization.

The company records this adjustment to the cost as **bond interest expense** over the life of the bonds through a process called amortization. **Amortization of a discount increases bond interest expense. Amortization of a premium decreases bond interest expense.**

The required procedure for amortization of a discount or premium is the **effective-interest method** (also called **present value amortization**). Under the effective-interest method, companies: **[1]**

> **I F R S**
>
> See the Authoritative Literature section (page 684).

1. Compute bond interest expense first by multiplying the **carrying value** (book value) of the bonds at the beginning of the period by the effective-interest rate.[2]

2. Determine the bond discount or premium amortization next by comparing the bond interest expense with the interest (cash) to be paid.

Illustration 14-5 depicts graphically the computation of the amortization.

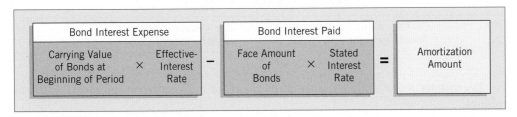

ILLUSTRATION 14-5
Bond Discount and Premium Amortization Computation

The effective-interest method produces a periodic interest expense equal to **a constant percentage of the carrying value of the bonds**.[3]

---

[2]The **carrying value** is the face amount minus any unamortized discount or plus any unamortized premium. The term *carrying value* is synonymous with *book value*.

[3]The issuance of bonds involves engraving and printing costs, legal and accounting fees, commissions, promotion costs, and other similar charges. These costs should be recorded as a reduction to the issue amount of the bond payable and then amortized into expense over the life of the bond, through an adjustment to the effective-interest rate. **[2]** For example, if the face value of the bond is €100,000 and issue costs are €1,000, then the bond payable (net of the bond issue costs) is recorded at €99,000. Thus, the effective-interest rate will be higher, based on the reduced carrying value.

Bonds Issued at a Discount

To illustrate amortization of a discount under the effective-interest method, Evermaster Corporation issued €100,000 of 8 percent term bonds on January 1, 2015, due on January 1, 2020, with interest payable each July 1 and January 1. Because the investors required an effective-interest rate of 10 percent, they paid €92,278 for the €100,000 of bonds, creating a €7,722 discount. Evermaster computes the €7,722 discount as follows.[4]

ILLUSTRATION 14-6
Computation of Discount on Bonds Payable

Maturity value of bonds payable		€100,000
Present value of €100,000 due in 5 years at 10%, interest payable semiannually (Table 6-2); $FV(PVF_{10,5\%})$; (€100,000 × .61391)	€61,391	
Present value of €4,000 interest payable semiannually for 5 years at 10% annually (Table 6-4); $R(PVF\text{-}OA_{10,5\%})$; (€4,000 × 7.72173)	30,887	
Proceeds from sale of bonds		(92,278)
Discount on bonds payable		€ 7,722

The five-year amortization schedule appears in Illustration 14-7.

ILLUSTRATION 14-7
Bond Discount Amortization Schedule

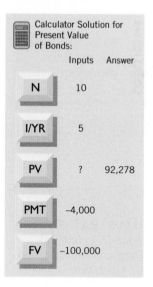

Calculator Solution for Present Value of Bonds:

	Inputs	Answer
N	10	
I/YR	5	
PV	?	92,278
PMT	−4,000	
FV	−100,000	

SCHEDULE OF BOND DISCOUNT AMORTIZATION
EFFECTIVE-INTEREST METHOD—SEMIANNUAL INTEREST PAYMENTS
5-YEAR, 8% BONDS SOLD TO YIELD 10%

Date	Cash Paid	Interest Expense	Discount Amortized	Carrying Amount of Bonds
1/1/15				€ 92,278
7/1/15	€ 4,000[a]	€ 4,614[b]	€ 614[c]	92,892[d]
1/1/16	4,000	4,645	645	93,537
7/1/16	4,000	4,677	677	94,214
1/1/17	4,000	4,711	711	94,925
7/1/17	4,000	4,746	746	95,671
1/1/18	4,000	4,783	783	96,454
7/1/18	4,000	4,823	823	97,277
1/1/19	4,000	4,864	864	98,141
7/1/19	4,000	4,907	907	99,048
1/1/20	4,000	4,952	952	100,000
	€40,000	€47,722	€7,722	

[a]€4,000 = €100,000 × .08 × 6/12   [c]€614 = €4,614 − €4,000
[b]€4,614 = €92,278 × .10 × 6/12   [d]€92,892 = €92,278 + €614

Evermaster records the issuance of its bonds at a discount on January 1, 2015, as follows.

Cash	92,278	
Bonds Payable		92,278

It records the first interest payment on July 1, 2015, and amortization of the discount as follows.

Interest Expense	4,614	
Bonds Payable		614
Cash		4,000

---

[4]Because companies pay interest semiannually, the interest rate used is 5% (10% × $^6/_{12}$). The number of periods is 10 (5 years × 2).

Evermaster records the interest expense accrued at December 31, 2015 (year-end), and amortization of the discount as follows.

Interest Expense	4,645	
Interest Payable		4,000
Bonds Payable		645

Bonds Issued at a Premium

Now assume that for the bond issue described above, investors are willing to accept an effective-interest rate of 6 percent. In that case, they would pay €108,530 or a premium of €8,530, computed as follows.

Maturity value of bonds payable		€100,000
Present value of €100,000 due in 5 years at 6%, interest payable semiannually (Table 6-2); $FV(PVF_{10,3\%})$; (€100,000 × .74409)	€74,409	
Present value of €4,000 interest payable semiannually for 5 years at 6% annually (Table 6-4); $R(PVF\text{-}OA_{10,3\%})$; (€4,000 × 8.53020)	34,121	
Proceeds from sale of bonds		(108,530)
Premium on bonds payable		€ 8,530

ILLUSTRATION 14-8
Computation of Premium on Bonds Payable

The five-year amortization schedule appears in Illustration 14-9.

ILLUSTRATION 14-9
Bond Premium Amortization Schedule

SCHEDULE OF BOND PREMIUM AMORTIZATION EFFECTIVE-INTEREST METHOD—SEMIANNUAL INTEREST PAYMENTS 5-YEAR, 8% BONDS SOLD TO YIELD 6%				
Date	Cash Paid	Interest Expense	Premium Amortized	Carrying Amount of Bonds
1/1/15				€108,530
7/1/15	€ 4,000[a]	€ 3,256[b]	€ 744[c]	107,786[d]
1/1/16	4,000	3,234	766	107,020
7/1/16	4,000	3,211	789	106,231
1/1/17	4,000	3,187	813	105,418
7/1/17	4,000	3,162	838	104,580
1/1/18	4,000	3,137	863	103,717
7/1/18	4,000	3,112	888	102,829
1/1/19	4,000	3,085	915	101,914
7/1/19	4,000	3,057	943	100,971
1/1/20	4,000	3,029	971	100,000
	€40,000	€31,470	€8,530	

[a]€4,000 = €100,000 × .08 × 6/12
[b]€3,256 = €108,530 × .06 × 6/12
[c]€744 = €4,000 − €3,256
[d]€107,786 = €108,530 − €744

Calculator Solution for Present Value of Bonds:

	Inputs	Answer
N	10	
I/YR	3	
PV	?	108,530
PMT	−4,000	
FV	−100,000	

Evermaster records the issuance of its bonds at a premium on January 1, 2015, as follows.

Cash	108,530	
Bonds Payable		108,530

Evermaster records the first interest payment on July 1, 2015, and amortization of the premium as follows.

Interest Expense	3,256	
Bonds Payable	744	
Cash		4,000

Evermaster should amortize the discount or premium as an adjustment to interest expense over the life of the bond in such a way as to result in a **constant rate of interest** when applied to the carrying amount of debt outstanding at the beginning of any given period.[5]

Accruing Interest

In our previous examples, the interest payment dates and the date the financial statements were issued were essentially the same. For example, when Evermaster sold bonds at a premium (page 661), the two interest payment dates coincided with the financial reporting dates. However, what happens if Evermaster prepares financial statements at the end of February 2015? In this case, the company **prorates** the premium by the appropriate number of months to arrive at the proper interest expense, as follows.

ILLUSTRATION 14-10
Computation of Interest Expense

Interest accrual (€4,000 × 2/6)	€1,333.33
Premium amortized (€744 × 2/6)	(248.00)
Interest expense (Jan.–Feb.)	€1,085.33

Evermaster records this accrual as follows.

Interest Expense	1,085.33	
Bonds Payable	248.00	
Interest Payable		1,333.33

If the company prepares financial statements six months later, it follows the same procedure. That is, the premium amortized would be as follows.

ILLUSTRATION 14-11
Computation of Premium Amortization

Premium amortized (March–June) (€744 × 4/6)	€496.00
Premium amortized (July–August) (€766 × 2/6)	255.33
Premium amortized (March–August 2015)	€751.33

Bonds Issued Between Interest Dates

Companies usually make bond interest payments semiannually, on dates specified in the bond indenture. When companies issue bonds on other than the interest payment dates, **bond investors will pay the issuer the interest accrued from the last interest payment date to the date of issue.** The bond investors, in effect, pay the bond issuer in advance for that portion of the full six-months' interest payment to which they are not entitled because they have not held the bonds for that period. **Then, on the next semi-annual interest payment date, the bond investors will receive the full six-months' interest payment.**

Bonds Issued at Par. To illustrate, assume that instead of issuing its bonds on January 1, 2015, Evermaster issued its five-year bonds, dated January 1, 2015, on May 1, 2015, at

---

[5]The issuer may call some bonds at a stated price after a certain date. This call feature gives the issuing corporation the opportunity to reduce its bonded indebtedness or take advantage of lower interest rates. Whether callable or not, a company must amortize any premium or discount over the bond's life to maturity because early redemption (call of the bond) is not a certainty.

par (€100,000). Evermaster records the issuance of the bonds between interest dates as follows.

May 1, 2015

Cash	100,000	
Bonds Payable		100,000
(To record issuance of bonds at par)		
Cash	2,667	
Interest Expense (€100,000 × .08 × 4/12)		2,667
(To record accrued interest; Interest Payable might be credited instead)		

Because Evermaster issues the bonds between interest dates, it records the bond issuance at **par (€100,000) plus accrued interest (€2,667)**. That is, the total amount paid by the bond investor includes four months of accrued interest.

On July 1, 2015, two months after the date of purchase, Evermaster pays the investors six months' interest, by making the following entry.

July 1, 2015

Interest Expense (€100,000 × .08 × 1/2)	4,000	
Cash		4,000
(To record first interest payment)		

The Interest Expense account now contains a debit balance of €1,333 (€4,000 − €2,667), which represents the proper amount of interest expense—two months at 8 percent on €100,000.

Interest Expense	
	5/1/15 2,667[a]
7/1/15 4,000[b]	
Balance 1,333	

[a]Accrued interest received.
[b]Cash paid.

Bonds Issued at Discount or Premium

The illustration above was simplified by having the January 1, 2015, bonds issued on May 1, 2015, **at par**. However, if the bonds are issued at a discount or premium between interest dates, Evermaster **must not only account for the partial cash interest payment but also the amount of effective amortization for the partial period**.

To illustrate, assume that the Evermaster 8-percent bonds were issued on May 1, 2015, to yield 6 percent. Thus, the bonds are issued at a premium; in this case, the price is €108,039.[6] Evermaster records the issuance of the bonds between interest dates as follows.

May 1, 2015

Cash	108,039	
Bonds Payable		108,039
(To record the present value of the cash flows)		
Cash	2,667	
Interest Expense (€100,000 × .08 × 4/12)		2,667
(To record accrued interest; Interest Payable might be credited instead)		

In this case, Evermaster receives a total of €110,706 at issuance, comprised of the bond price of €108,039 plus the accrued interest of €2,667. Following the effective-interest procedures, Evermaster then determines interest expense from the date of sale (May 1, 2015), not from the date of the bonds (January 1, 2015).

---

[6]Determination of the price of a bond between interest payment dates generally requires use of a financial calculator because the time value of money tables shown in this textbook do not have factors for all compounding periods. *For homework purposes, the price of a bond sold between interest dates will be provided.*

Illustration 14-12 provides the computation, using the effective-interest rate of 6 percent.

ILLUSTRATION 14-12
Partial Period Interest
Amortization

Interest Expense		
Carrying value of bonds	€108,039	
Effective-interest rate (6% × 2/12)	× 1%	
Interest expense for two months	€ 1,080	

The bond interest expense therefore for the two months (May and June) is €1,080.

The premium amortization of the bonds is also for only two months. It is computed by taking the difference between the net cash paid related to bond interest and the effective-interest expense of €1,080. Illustration 14-13 shows the computation of the partial amortization, using the effective-interest rate of 6 percent.

ILLUSTRATION 14-13
Partial Period Interest
Amortization

Cash interest paid on July 1, 2015 (€100,000 × 8% × 6/12)	€4,000
Less: Cash interest received on May 2, 2015	2,667
Net cash paid	€1,333
Bond interest expense (at the effective rate) for two months	(1,080)
Premium amortization	€ 253

As indicated, both the bond interest expense and amortization reflect the shorter two-month period between the issue date and the first interest payment. Evermaster therefore makes the following entries on July 1, 2015, to record the interest payment and the premium amortization.

Interest Expense		
	5/1/15 2,667[a]	
7/1/15 4,000[b]	7/1/15 253[c]	
Balance 1,080		

[a]Accrued interest received.
[b]Cash paid.
[c]2 months' amortization.

July 1, 2015

Interest Expense	4,000	
Cash		4,000
(To record first interest payment)		
Bonds Payable	253	
Interest Expense		253
(To record two-months' premium amortization)		

The Interest Expense account now contains a debit balance of €1,080 (€4,000 − €2,667 − €253), which represents the proper amount of interest expense—two months at an effective annual interest rate of 6 percent on €108,039.

What do the numbers mean?   YOUR DEBT IS KILLING MY EQUITY

Traditionally, investors in the equity and bond markets operate in their own separate worlds. However, in recent volatile markets, even quiet murmurs in the bond market have been amplified into movements (usually negative) in share prices. At one extreme, these gyrations heralded the demise of a company well before the investors could sniff out the problem.

The swift decline of Enron (USA) in late 2001 provided the ultimate lesson: A company with no credit is no company at all. As one analyst remarked, "You can no longer have an opinion on a company's shares without having an appreciation for its credit rating." Indeed, other energy companies also felt the effect of Enron's troubles as lenders tightened or closed down the credit supply and raised interest rates on already-high levels of debt. The result? Share prices took a hit.

Other industries are not immune from the negative shareholder effects of credit problems. For example, analysts at **TheStreet.com** compiled a list of companies with a focus on debt levels. Companies like Copel CIA (BRA) (an energy distribution company) were rewarded with improved share ratings, based on their manageable debt levels. In contrast, other companies with high debt levels and low ability to cover interest costs were not viewed very favorably. Among them is Goodyear Tire and Rubber (USA), which reported debt six times greater than its equity. Goodyear is a classic example of how swift and crippling a heavy debt-load can be. Not too long ago, Goodyear had a good credit rating and was paying a good dividend. But, with mounting operating losses, Goodyear's debt became a huge burden, its debt rating fell to junk status, the company cut its dividend, and its share price dropped 80 percent. This was yet another example of share prices taking a hit due to concerns about credit quality. Thus, even if your investment tastes are in equity, keep an eye on the liabilities.

Sources: Adapted from Steven Vames, "Credit Quality, Stock Investing Seem to Go Hand in Hand," *Wall Street Journal* (April 1, 2002), p. R4; Herb Greenberg, "The Hidden Dangers of Debt," *Fortune* (July 21, 2003), p. 153; and Christine Richard, "Holders of Corporate Bonds Seek Protection from Risk," *Wall Street Journal* (December 17–18, 2005), p. B4.

LONG-TERM NOTES PAYABLE

The difference between current notes payable and long-term notes payable is the maturity date. As discussed in Chapter 13, short-term notes payable are those that companies expect to pay within a year or the operating cycle—whichever is longer. Long-term notes are similar in substance to bonds in that both have fixed maturity dates and carry either a stated or implicit interest rate. However, notes do not trade as readily as bonds in the organized public securities markets. Non-corporate and small corporate enterprises issue notes as their long-term instruments. Larger corporations issue both long-term notes and bonds.

5 LEARNING OBJECTIVE
Explain the accounting for long-term notes payable.

Accounting for notes and bonds is quite similar. **Like a bond, a note is valued at the present value of its future interest and principal cash flows. The company amortizes any discount or premium over the life of the note**, just as it would the discount or premium on a bond. Companies compute the present value of an **interest-bearing note**, record its issuance, and amortize any discount or premium and accrual of interest in the same way that they do for bonds (as shown on pages 657–664 of this chapter).

As you might expect, accounting for long-term notes payable parallels accounting for long-term notes receivable, as was presented in Chapter 7.

Notes Issued at Face Value

In Chapter 7, we discussed the recognition of a €10,000, three-year note Scandinavian Imports issued at face value to Bigelow Corp. In this transaction, the stated rate and the effective rate were both 10 percent. The time diagram and present value computation on page 309 of Chapter 7 (see Illustration 7-12) for Bigelow Corp. would be the same for the issuer of the note, Scandinavian Imports, in recognizing a note payable. Because the present value of the note and its face value are the same, €10,000, Scandinavian would recognize no premium or discount. It records the issuance of the note as follows.

Cash	10,000	
Notes Payable		10,000

Scandinavian Imports would recognize the interest incurred each year as follows.

Interest Expense (€10,000 × .10)	1,000	
Cash		1,000

Notes Not Issued at Face Value

Zero-Interest-Bearing Notes

If a company issues a zero-interest-bearing (non-interest-bearing) note[7] solely for cash, it measures the note's present value by the cash received. The implicit interest rate is the **rate that equates the cash received with the amounts to be paid in the future.** The issuing

---

[7]Although we use the term "note" throughout this discussion, the basic principles and methodology apply equally to other long-term debt instruments.

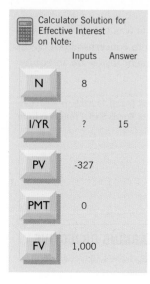

Calculator Solution for
Effective Interest
on Note:

	Inputs	Answer
N	8	
I/YR	?	15
PV	-327	
PMT	0	
FV	1,000	

company records the difference between the face amount and the present value (cash received) as **a discount and amortizes that amount to interest expense over the life of the note**.

An example of such a transaction is **Beneficial Corporation**'s (USA) offering of $150 million of zero-coupon notes (deep-discount bonds) having an eight-year life. With a face value of $1,000 each, these notes sold for $327—a deep discount of $673 each. The present value of each note is the cash proceeds of $327. We can calculate the interest rate by determining the rate that equates the amount the investor currently pays with the amount to be received in the future. Thus, Beneficial amortizes the discount over the eight-year life of the notes using an effective-interest rate of 15 percent.[8]

To illustrate the entries and the amortization schedule, assume that Turtle Cove Company issued the three-year, $10,000, zero-interest-bearing note to Jeremiah Company illustrated on page 309 of Chapter 7 (notes receivable). The implicit rate that equated the total cash to be paid ($10,000 at maturity) to the present value of the future cash flows ($7,721.80 cash proceeds at date of issuance) was 9 percent. (The present value of $1 for three periods at 9 percent is $0.77218.) Illustration 14-14 shows the time diagram for the single cash flow.

ILLUSTRATION 14-14
Time Diagram for
Zero-Interest Note

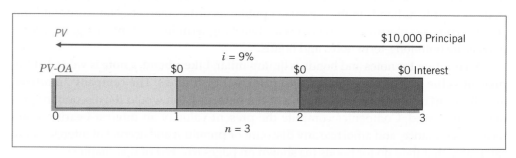

Turtle Cove records issuance of the note as follows.

Cash	7,721.80	
Notes Payable		7,721.80

Turtle Cove amortizes the discount and recognizes interest expense annually using the **effective-interest method**. Illustration 14-15 shows the three-year discount amortization and interest expense schedule. (This schedule is similar to the note receivable schedule of Jeremiah Company in Illustration 7-14.)

ILLUSTRATION 14-15
Schedule of Note
Discount Amortization

SCHEDULE OF NOTE DISCOUNT AMORTIZATION
EFFECTIVE-INTEREST METHOD
0% NOTE DISCOUNTED AT 9%

	Cash Paid	Interest Expense	Discount Amortized	Carrying Amount of Note
Date of issue				$ 7,721.80
End of year 1	$–0–	$ 694.96[a]	$ 694.96[b]	8,416.76[c]
End of year 2	–0–	757.51	757.51	9,174.27
End of year 3	–0–	825.73[d]	825.73	10,000.00
	$–0–	$2,278.20	$2,278.20	

[a]$7,721.80 × .09 = $694.96   [c]$7,721.80 + $694.96 = $8,416.76
[b]$694.96 − 0 = $694.96   [d]5¢ adjustment to compensate for rounding.

[8]$327 = $1,000(PVF_{8,i})$

$$PVF_{8,i} = \frac{\$327}{\$1,000} = .327$$

.327 = 15% (in Table 6-2 locate .32690).

Turtle Cove records interest expense at the end of the first year using the effective-interest method as follows.

Interest Expense ($7,721.80 × 9%)	694.96	
Notes Payable		694.96

The total amount of the discount, $2,278.20 in this case, represents the expense that Turtle Cove Company will incur on the note over the three years.

Interest-Bearing Notes

The zero-interest-bearing note above is an example of the extreme difference between the stated rate and the effective rate. In many cases, the difference between these rates is not so great.

Consider the example from Chapter 7 where Marie Co. issued for cash a €10,000, three-year note bearing interest at 10 percent to Morgan Corp. The market rate of interest for a note of similar risk is 12 percent. Illustration 7-15 (page 311) shows the time diagram depicting the cash flows and the computation of the present value of this note. In this case, because the effective rate of interest (12%) is greater than the stated rate (10%), the present value of the note is less than the face value. That is, the note is exchanged at a **discount**. Marie Co. records the issuance of the note as follows.

Cash	9,520	
Notes Payable		9,520

Marie Co. then amortizes the discount and recognizes interest expense annually using the **effective-interest method**. Illustration 14-16 shows the three-year discount amortization and interest expense schedule.

SCHEDULE OF NOTE DISCOUNT AMORTIZATION
EFFECTIVE-INTEREST METHOD
10% NOTE DISCOUNTED AT 12%

	Cash Paid	Interest Expense	Discount Amortized	Carrying Amount of Note
Date of issue				€ 9,520
End of year 1	€1,000[a]	€1,142[b]	€142[c]	9,662[d]
End of year 2	1,000	1,159	159	9,821
End of year 3	1,000	1,179	179	10,000
	€3,000	€3,480	€480	

[a]€10,000 × 10% = €1,000
[b]€9,520 × 12% = €1,142
[c]€1,142 − €1,000 = €142
[d]€9,520 + €142 = €9,662

ILLUSTRATION 14-16
Schedule of Note Discount Amortization

Marie Co. records payment of the annual interest and amortization of the discount for the first year as follows (amounts per amortization schedule).

Interest Expense	1,142	
Notes Payable		142
Cash		1,000

When the present value exceeds the face value, Marie Co. exchanges the note at a premium. It does so by recording the premium as a credit and amortizing it using the effective-interest method over the life of the note as annual reductions in the amount of interest expense recognized.

Special Notes Payable Situations

Notes Issued for Property, Goods, or Services

Sometimes, companies may receive property, goods, or services in exchange for a note payable. When exchanging the debt instrument for property, goods, or services in a bargained transaction entered into at arm's length, the stated interest rate is presumed to be fair unless:

1. No interest rate is stated, or

2. The stated interest rate is unreasonable, or

3. The stated face amount of the debt instrument is materially different from the current cash sales price for the same or similar items or from the current fair value of the debt instrument.

In these circumstances, the company measures the present value of the debt instrument by the fair value of the property, goods, or services or by an amount that reasonably approximates the fair value of the note. [3] If there is **no stated rate of interest, the amount of interest is the difference between the face amount of the note and the fair value of the property**.

For example, assume that Scenic Development Company sells land having a cash sale price of €200,000 to Health Spa, Inc. In exchange for the land, Health Spa gives a five-year, €293,866, zero-interest-bearing note. The €200,000 cash sale price represents the present value of the €293,866 note discounted at 8 percent for five years. Should both parties record the transaction on the sale date at the face amount of the note, which is €293,866? No—if they did, Health Spa's Land account and Scenic's sales would be overstated by €93,866 (the interest for five years at an effective rate of 8 percent). Similarly, interest revenue to Scenic and interest expense to Health Spa for the five-year period would be understated by €93,866.

Because the difference between the cash sale price of €200,000 and the €293,866 face amount of the note represents interest at an effective rate of 8 percent, the companies' transaction is recorded at the exchange date as follows.

ILLUSTRATION 14-17
Entries for Non-Cash
Note Transaction

Health Spa, Inc. (Buyer)			Scenic Development Company (Seller)		
Land	200,000		Notes Receivable	200,000	
Notes Payable		200,000	Sales Revenue		200,000

During the five-year life of the note, Health Spa amortizes annually a portion of the discount of €93,866 as a charge to interest expense. Scenic Development records interest revenue totaling €93,866 over the five-year period by also amortizing the discount. The effective-interest method is required, unless the results obtained from using another method are not materially different from those that result from the effective-interest method.

Choice of Interest Rate

In note transactions, the effective or market interest rate is either evident or determinable by other factors involved in the exchange, such as the fair value of what is given or received. But, if a company cannot determine the fair value of the property, goods, services, or other rights, and if the note has no ready market, the problem of determining the present value of the note is more difficult. To estimate the present value of a note under such circumstances, a company must approximate an applicable interest rate that may differ from the stated interest rate. This process of interest-rate approximation is called **imputation**, and the resulting interest rate is called an **imputed interest rate**.

The prevailing rates for similar instruments of issuers with similar credit ratings affect the choice of a rate. Other factors such as restrictive covenants, collateral, payment schedule, and the existing prime interest rate also play a part. Companies determine the imputed interest rate when they issue a note; any subsequent changes in prevailing interest rates are ignored.

To illustrate, assume that on December 31, 2015, Wunderlich Company issued a promissory note to Brown Interiors Company for architectural services. The note has a face value of £550,000, a due date of December 31, 2020, and bears a stated interest rate of 2 percent, payable at the end of each year. Wunderlich cannot readily determine the fair value of the architectural services, nor is the note readily marketable. On the basis of Wunderlich's credit rating, the absence of collateral, the prime interest rate at that date, and the prevailing interest on Wunderlich's other outstanding debt, the company imputes an 8 percent interest rate as appropriate in this circumstance. Illustration 14-18 shows the time diagram depicting both cash flows.

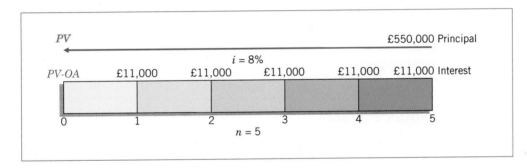

ILLUSTRATION 14-18
Time Diagram for Interest-Bearing Note

The present value of the note and the imputed fair value of the architectural services are determined as follows.

Face value of the note		£ 550,000
Present value of £550,000 due in 5 years at 8% interest payable annually (Table 6-2); $FV(PVF_{5,8\%})$; (£550,000 × .68058)	£374,319	
Present value of £11,000 interest payable annually for 5 years at 8%; $R(PVF\text{-}OA_{5,8\%})$; (£11,000 × 3.99271)	43,920	
Present value of the note		(418,239)
Discount on notes payable		£131,761

ILLUSTRATION 14-19
Computation of Imputed Fair Value and Note Discount

Wunderlich records issuance of the note in payment for the architectural services as follows.

December 31, 2015

Buildings (or Construction in Process)	418,239	
Notes Payable		418,239

The five-year amortization schedule appears below.

ILLUSTRATION 14-20
Schedule of Discount
Amortization Using
Imputed Interest Rate

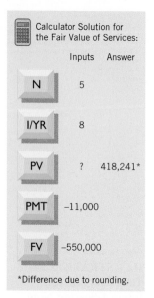

Calculator Solution for
the Fair Value of Services:

	Inputs	Answer
N	5	
I/YR	8	
PV	?	418,241*
PMT	–11,000	
FV	–550,000	

*Difference due to rounding.

SCHEDULE OF NOTE DISCOUNT AMORTIZATION				
EFFECTIVE-INTEREST METHOD				
2% NOTE DISCOUNTED AT 8% (IMPUTED)				
Date	Cash Paid (2%)	Interest Expense (8%)	Discount Amortized	Carrying Amount of Note
12/31/15				£418,239
12/31/16	£11,000[a]	£ 33,459[b]	£ 22,459[c]	440,698[d]
12/31/17	11,000	35,256	24,256	464,954
12/31/18	11,000	37,196	26,196	491,150
12/31/19	11,000	39,292	28,292	519,442
12/31/20	11,000	41,558[e]	30,558	550,000
	£55,000	£186,761	£131,761	

[a]£550,000 × 2% = £11,000
[b]£418,239 × 8% = £33,459
[c]£33,459 − £11,000 = £22,459

[d]£418,239 + £22,459 = £440,698
[e]£3 adjustment to compensate for rounding.

Wunderlich records payment of the first year's interest and amortization of the discount as follows.

December 31, 2016

Interest Expense	33,459	
Notes Payable		22,459
Cash		11,000

Mortgage Notes Payable

A common form of long-term notes payable is a mortgage note payable. A **mortgage note payable** is a promissory note secured by a document called a mortgage that pledges title to property as security for the loan. Individuals, proprietorships, and partnerships use mortgage notes payable more frequently than do corporations. (Corporations usually find that bond issues offer advantages in obtaining large loans.)

The borrower usually receives cash for the face amount of the mortgage note. In that case, the face amount of the note is the true liability, and no discount or premium is involved. When the lender assesses "points," however, the total amount received by the borrower is less than the face amount of the note.[9] Points raise the effective-interest rate above the rate specified in the note. A **point** is 1 percent of the face of the note.

For example, assume that Harrick Co. borrows $1,000,000, signing a 20-year mortgage note with a stated interest rate of 10.75 percent as part of the financing for a new plant. If Associated Savings demands 4 points to close the financing, Harrick will receive 4 percent less than $1,000,000—or $960,000—but it will be obligated to repay the entire $1,000,000 at the rate of $10,150 per month. Because Harrick received only $960,000 and must repay $1,000,000, its effective-interest rate is increased to approximately 11.3 percent on the money actually borrowed.

On the statement of financial position, Harrick should report the mortgage note payable as a liability using a title such as "Mortgage Notes Payable" or "Notes Payable—Secured," with a brief disclosure of the property pledged in notes to the financial statements.

Mortgages may be payable in full at maturity or in installments over the life of the loan. If payable at maturity, Harrick classifies its mortgage payable as a non-current liability

---

[9]Points, in mortgage financing, are analogous to the original issue discount of bonds.

on the statement of financial position until such time as the approaching maturity date warrants showing it as a current liability. If it is payable in installments, Harrick shows the current installments due as current liabilities, with the remainder as a non-current liability.

Lenders have partially replaced the traditional **fixed-rate mortgage** with alternative mortgage arrangements. Most lenders offer **variable-rate mortgages** (also called floating-rate or adjustable-rate mortgages) featuring interest rates tied to changes in the fluctuating market rate. Generally, the variable-rate lenders adjust the interest rate at either one- or three-year intervals, pegging the adjustments to changes in the prime rate or the London Interbank Offering (LIBOR) rate.

SPECIAL ISSUES RELATED TO NON-CURRENT LIABILITIES

Reporting of non-current liabilities is one of the most controversial areas in financial reporting. Because non-current liabilities have a significant impact on the cash flows of the company, reporting requirements must be substantive and informative. Four additional reporting issues related to non-current liabilities are addressed in this section:

6 LEARNING OBJECTIVE
Describe the accounting for extinguishment of non-current liabilities.

1. Extinguishment of non-current liabilities.
2. Fair value option.
3. Off-balance-sheet financing.
4. Presentation and analysis.

Extinguishment of Non-Current Liabilities

How do companies record the payment of non-current liabilities—often referred to as **extinguishment of debt**? If a company holds the bonds (or any other form of debt security) to maturity, the answer is straightforward: The company does not compute any gains or losses. It will have fully amortized any premium or discount and any issue costs at the date the bonds mature. As a result, the carrying amount, the maturity (face) value, and the fair value of the bond are the same. Therefore, no gain or loss exists.

In this section, we discuss extinguishment of debt under three common additional situations:

1. Extinguishment with cash before maturity,
2. Extinguishment by transferring assets or securities, and
3. Extinguishment with modification of terms.

Extinguishment with Cash before Maturity

In some cases, a company extinguishes debt before its maturity date.[10] The amount paid on extinguishment or redemption before maturity, including any call premium and expense of reacquisition, is called the **reacquisition price**. On any specified date, the **carrying**

---

[10]Some companies have attempted to extinguish debt through an in-substance defeasance. **In-substance defeasance** is an arrangement whereby a company provides for the future repayment of a long-term debt issue by placing purchased securities in an irrevocable trust. The company pledges the principal and interest of the securities in the trust to pay off the principal and interest of its own debt securities as they mature. However, it is not legally released from its primary obligation for the debt that is still outstanding. In some cases, debtholders are not even aware of the transaction and continue to look to the company for repayment. This practice is not considered an extinguishment of debt, and therefore the company does not record a gain or loss. **[4]**

amount of the bonds is the amount payable at maturity, adjusted for unamortized premium or discount. Any excess of the net carrying amount over the reacquisition price is a **gain from extinguishment**. The excess of the reacquisition price over the carrying amount is a **loss from extinguishment**. At the time of reacquisition, **the unamortized premium or discount must be amortized up to the reacquisition date**.

To illustrate, we use the Evermaster bonds issued at a discount on January 1, 2015. These bonds are due in five years. The bonds have a par value of €100,000, a coupon rate of 8 percent paid semiannually, and were sold to yield 10 percent. The amortization schedule for the Evermaster bonds is presented in Illustration 14-21.

ILLUSTRATION 14-21
Bond Premium
Amortization Schedule,
Bond Extinguishment

SCHEDULE OF BOND DISCOUNT AMORTIZATION
EFFECTIVE-INTEREST METHOD—SEMIANNUAL INTEREST PAYMENTS
5-YEAR, 8% BONDS SOLD TO YIELD 10%

Date	Cash Paid	Interest Expense	Discount Amortized	Carrying Amount of Bonds
1/1/15				€ 92,278
7/1/15	€ 4,000[a]	€ 4,614[b]	€ 614[c]	92,892[d]
1/1/16	4,000	4,645	645	93,537
7/1/16	4,000	4,677	677	94,214
1/1/17	4,000	4,711	711	94,925
7/1/17	4,000	4,746	746	95,671
1/1/18	4,000	4,783	783	96,454
7/1/18	4,000	4,823	823	97,277
1/1/19	4,000	4,864	864	98,141
7/1/19	4,000	4,907	907	99,048
1/1/20	4,000	4,952	952	100,000
	€40,000	€47,722	€7,722	

[a]€4,000 = €100,000 × .08 × 6/12   [c]€614 = €4,614 − €4,000
[b]€4,614 = €92,278 × .10 × 6/12   [d]€92,892 = €92,278 + €614

Two years after the issue date on January 1, 2017, Evermaster calls the entire issue at 101 and cancels it.[11] As indicated in the amortization schedule, the carrying value of the bonds on January 1, 2017, is €94,925. Illustration 14-22 indicates how Evermaster computes the loss on redemption (extinguishment).

ILLUSTRATION 14-22
Computation of Loss on
Redemption of Bonds

Reacquisition price (€100,000 × 1.01)	€101,000
Carrying amount of bonds redeemed	(94,925)
Loss on extinguishment	€ 6,075

Evermaster records the reacquisition and cancellation of the bonds as follows.

Bonds Payable	94,925	
Loss on Extinguishment of Debt	6,075	
Cash		101,000

[11]The issuer of callable bonds must generally exercise the call on an interest date. Therefore, the amortization of any discount or premium will be up to date, and there will be no accrued interest. However, early extinguishments through purchases of bonds in the open market are more likely to be on other than an interest date. If the purchase is not made on an interest date, the discount or premium must be amortized, and the interest payable must be accrued from the last interest date to the date of purchase.

Note that it is often advantageous for the issuer to acquire the **entire** outstanding bond issue and replace it with a new bond issue bearing a lower rate of interest. The replacement of an existing issuance with a new one is called refunding. Whether the early redemption or other extinguishment of outstanding bonds is a non-refunding or a refunding situation, a company should recognize the difference (gain or loss) between the reacquisition price and the carrying amount of the redeemed bonds in income of the period of redemption.

Extinguishment by Exchanging Assets or Securities

In addition to using cash, settling a debt obligation can involve either a transfer of non-cash assets (real estate, receivables, or other assets) or the issuance of the debtor's shares. In these situations, **the creditor should account for the non-cash assets or equity interest received at their fair value**.

The debtor must determine the excess of the carrying amount of the payable over the fair value of the assets or equity transferred (gain).[12] The debtor recognizes a gain equal to the amount of the excess. In addition, the debtor recognizes a gain or loss on disposition of assets to the extent that the fair value of those assets differs from their carrying amount (book value).

Transfer of Assets. Assume that Hamburg Bank loaned €20,000,000 to Bonn Mortgage Company. Bonn, in turn, invested these monies in residential apartment buildings. However, because of low occupancy rates, it cannot meet its loan obligations. Hamburg Bank agrees to accept from Bonn Mortgage real estate with a fair value of €16,000,000 in full settlement of the €20,000,000 loan obligation. The real estate has a carrying value of €21,000,000 on the books of Bonn Mortgage. Bonn (debtor) records this transaction as follows.

Notes Payable (to Hamburg Bank)	20,000,000	
Loss on Disposal of Real Estate (€21,000,000 − €16,000,000)	5,000,000	
Real Estate		21,000,000
Gain on Extinguishment of Debt (€20,000,000 − €16,000,000)		4,000,000

Bonn Mortgage has a loss on the disposition of real estate in the amount of €5,000,000 (the difference between the €21,000,000 book value and the €16,000,000 fair value). In addition, it has a gain on settlement of debt of €4,000,000 (the difference between the €20,000,000 carrying amount of the note payable and the €16,000,000 fair value of the real estate).

Granting of Equity Interest. Now assume that Hamburg Bank agrees to accept from Bonn Mortgage 320,000 ordinary shares (€10 par) that have a fair value of €16,000,000, in full settlement of the €20,000,000 loan obligation. Bonn Mortgage (debtor) records this transaction as follows.

Notes Payable (to Hamburg Bank)	20,000,000	
Share Capital—Ordinary		3,200,000
Share Premium—Ordinary		12,800,000
Gain on Extinguishment of Debt		4,000,000

It records the ordinary shares issued in the normal manner. It records the difference between the par value and the fair value of the shares as share premium.

---

[12]Likewise, the creditor must determine the excess of the receivable over the fair value of those same assets or equity interests transferred. The creditor normally charges the excess (loss) against Allowance for Doubtful Accounts. Creditor accounting for these transactions is addressed in Chapter 7.

Extinguishment with Modification of Terms

Practically every day, the *Wall Street Journal* or the *Financial Times* runs a story about some company in financial difficulty, such as **Nakheel** (ARE) or **Parmalat** (ITA). In many of these situations, the creditor may grant a borrower concessions with respect to settlement. The creditor offers these concessions to ensure the highest possible collection on the loan. For example, a creditor may offer one or a combination of the following modifications:

1. Reduction of the stated interest rate.
2. Extension of the maturity date of the face amount of the debt.
3. Reduction of the face amount of the debt.
4. Reduction or deferral of any accrued interest.

As with other extinguishments, when a creditor grants favorable concessions on the terms of a loan, the debtor has an economic gain. Thus, the accounting for modifications is similar to that for other extinguishments. That is, the original obligation is extinguished, the new payable is recorded at fair value, and a gain is recognized for the difference in the fair value of the new obligation and the carrying value of the old obligation.[13]

To illustrate, assume that on December 31, 2015, Morgan National Bank enters into a debt modification agreement with Resorts Development Company, which is experiencing financial difficulties. The bank restructures a ¥10,500,000 loan receivable issued at par (interest paid to date) by:

- Reducing the principal obligation from ¥10,500,000 to ¥9,000,000;
- Extending the maturity date from December 31, 2015, to December 31, 2019; and
- Reducing the interest rate from the historical effective rate of 12 percent to 8 percent. Given Resorts Development's financial distress, its market-based borrowing rate is 15 percent.

IFRS requires the modification to be accounted for as an extinguishment of the old note and issuance of the new note, measured at fair value. **[6]** Illustration 14-23 shows the calculation of the fair value of the modified note, using Resorts Development's market discount rate of 15 percent.

ILLUSTRATION 14-23
Fair Value of
Restructured Note

Present value of restructured cash flows:	
Present value of ¥9,000,000 due in 4 years at 15%, interest payable annually (Table 6-2); $FV(PVF_{4,15\%})$; (¥9,000,000 × .57175)	¥5,145,750
Present value of ¥720,000 interest payable annually for 4 years at 15% (Table 6-4); $R(PVF\text{-}OA_{4,15\%})$; (¥720,000 × 2.85498)	2,055,586
Fair value of note	¥7,201,336

[13]An exception to the general rule is when the modification of terms is not substantial. A **substantial modification** is defined as one in which the discounted cash flows under the terms of the new debt (using the historical effective-interest rate) differ by at least 10 percent of the carrying value of the original debt. If a modification is not substantial, the difference (gain) is deferred and amortized over the remaining life of the debt at the (historical) effective-interest rate. **[5]** In the case of a non-substantial modification, in essence, the new loan is a continuation of the old loan. Therefore, the debtor should record interest at the historical effective-interest rate.

The gain on the modification is ¥3,298,664, which is the difference between the prior carrying value (¥10,500,000) and the fair value of the restructured note, as computed in Illustration 14-23 (¥7,201,336). Given this information, Resorts Development makes the following entry to record the modification.

Notes Payable (old)	10,500,000	
Gain on Extinguishment of Debt		3,298,664
Notes Payable (new)		7,201,336

Illustration 14-24 shows the amortization schedule for the new note, following the modification.

Date	Cash Paid	Interest Expense	Amortization	Carrying Value
12/31/2015				¥7,201,336
12/31/2016	¥720,000[a]	¥1,080,200[b]	¥360,200[c]	7,561,536[d]
12/31/2017	720000	1,134,230	414,230	7,975,767
12/31/2018	720000	1,196,365	476,365	8,452,132
12/31/2019	720000	1,267,820	547,868	9,000,000

[a]¥9,000,000 × 8%   [c]¥1,080,200 − ¥720,000
[b]¥7,201,336 × 15%   [d]¥7,201,336 + ¥360,200

ILLUSTRATION 14-24
Schedule of Interest and Amortization after Debt Modification

Resorts Development recognizes interest expense on this note using the effective rate of 15 percent. Thus, on December 31, 2016 (date of first interest payment after restructure), Resorts Development makes the following entry.

December 31, 2016

Interest Expense	1,080,200	
Notes Payable		360,200
Cash		720,000

Resorts Development makes a similar entry (except for different amounts for credits to Notes Payable and debits to Interest Expense) each year until maturity. At maturity, Resorts Development makes the following entry.

December 31, 2019

Notes Payable	9,000,000	
Cash		9,000,000

In summary, following the modification, Resorts Development has extinguished the old note with an effective rate of 12 percent and now has a new loan with a much higher effective rate of 15 percent.

Fair Value Option

As indicated earlier, non-current liabilities such as bonds and notes payable are generally measured at amortized cost (face value of the payable, adjusted for any payments and amortization of any premium or discount). However, companies have the option to record fair value in their accounts for most financial assets and liabilities, including bonds and notes payable. **[7]** As discussed in Chapter 7 (pages 314–315), the IASB believes that fair value measurement for financial instruments, including financial liabilities, provides more relevant and understandable information than amortized cost. It considers fair value to be more relevant because it reflects the current cash equivalent value of financial instruments.

7 LEARNING OBJECTIVE
Describe the accounting for the fair value option.

Fair Value Measurement

If companies choose the fair value option, non-current liabilities such as bonds and notes payable are recorded at fair value, with unrealized holding gains or losses reported as part of net income. An **unrealized holding gain or loss** is the net change in the fair value of the liability from one period to another, exclusive of interest expense recognized but not recorded. As a result, the company reports the liability at fair value each reporting date. In addition, it reports the change in value as part of net income.

To illustrate, Edmonds Company has issued €500,000 of 6 percent bonds at face value on May 1, 2015. Edmonds chooses the fair value option for these bonds. At December 31, 2015, the value of the bonds is now €480,000 because interest rates in the market have increased to 8 percent. The value of the debt securities falls because the bond is paying less than market rate for similar securities. Under the fair value option, Edmonds makes the following entry.

Bonds Payable (€500,000 − €480,000)	20,000	
Unrealized Holding Gain or Loss—Income		20,000

As the journal entry indicates, the value of the bonds declined. This decline leads to a reduction in the bond liability and a resulting unrealized holding gain, which is reported as part of net income. The value of Edmonds' debt declined because interest rates increased. It should be emphasized that Edmonds must continue to value the bonds payable at fair value in all subsequent periods.

Fair Value Controversy

Underlying Concepts

The fair value controversy represents a classic trade-off between relevance and faithful representation.

With the Edmonds bonds, we assumed that the decline in value of the bonds was due to an interest rate increase. In other situations, the decline may occur because the bonds become more likely to default. That is, **if the creditworthiness of Edmonds Company declines, the value of its debt also declines**. If its creditworthiness declines, its bond investors are receiving a lower rate relative to investors with similar-risk investments. If Edmonds is using the fair value option, changes in the fair value of the bonds payable for a decline in creditworthiness are included as part of income. Some question how Edmonds can record a gain when its creditworthiness is becoming worse. As one writer observed, "It seems counterintuitive." However, the IASB notes that the debtholders' loss is the shareholders' gain. That is, the shareholders' claims on the assets of the company increase when the value of the debtholders' claims declines. In addition, the worsening credit position may indicate that the assets of the company are declining in value as well. Thus, the company may be reporting losses on the asset side, which will be offsetting gains on the liability side.

The IASB apparently agrees with this statement and requires that the effects of changes in a company's credit risk should not affect profit and loss unless the liability is held for trading. [8] Therefore, any change in the value of the liability due to credit risk changes should be reported in other comprehensive income. To illustrate, assume the change in the interest rate related to the Edmonds Company bonds described in the previous section changed from 6 percent to 8 percent due to a decrease in the credit quality of these bonds. Under the fair value option, Edmonds makes the following entry.

Bonds Payable	20,000	
Unrealized Holding Gain or Loss—Equity		20,000

This entry recognizes the decline in the fair value of the liability and a resulting unrealized holding gain, which is reported as part of other comprehensive income. The value of the Edmonds bonds declined because of the change in its credit risk, not because of general market conditions. Edmonds then continues to value the bonds payable at fair value in all subsequent periods.

Off-Balance-Sheet Financing

What do **Air Berlin** (DEU), **HSBC** (GBR), **China Construction Bank Corp.** (CHN), and **Enron** (USA) have in common? They all have been accused of using off-balance-sheet financing to minimize the reporting of debt on their statements of financial position.[14] **Off-balance-sheet financing** is an attempt to borrow monies in such a way to prevent recording the obligations. It has become an issue of extreme importance. Many allege that Enron, in one of the largest corporate failures on record, hid a considerable amount of its debt off the statement of financial position. As a result, any company that uses off-balance-sheet financing today risks investors dumping their shares. Consequently (as discussed in the "What Do the Numbers Mean?" box on page 664), their share price will suffer. Nevertheless, a considerable amount of off-balance-sheet financing continues to exist. As one writer noted, "The basic drives of humans are few: to get enough food, to find shelter, and to keep debt off the balance sheet."

> **8 LEARNING OBJECTIVE**
> Explain the reporting of off-balance-sheet financing arrangements.

Different Forms

Off-balance-sheet financing can take many different forms:

1. *Non-consolidated subsidiary.* Under IFRS, a parent company does not have to consolidate a subsidiary company that is less than 50 percent owned. In such cases, the parent therefore does not report the assets and liabilities of the subsidiary. All the parent reports on its statement of financial position is the investment in the subsidiary. As a result, users of the financial statements may not understand that the subsidiary has considerable debt for which the parent may ultimately be liable if the subsidiary runs into financial difficulty.

2. *Special purpose entity (SPE).* A company creates a **special purpose entity (SPE)** to perform a special project. To illustrate, assume that Clarke Company decides to build a new factory. However, management does not want to report the plant or the borrowing used to fund the construction on its statement of financial position. It therefore creates an SPE, the purpose of which is to build the plant. (This arrangement is called a **project financing arrangement**.) The SPE finances and builds the plant. In return, Clarke guarantees that it or some outside party will purchase all the products produced by the plant (sometimes referred to as a **take-or-pay contract**). As a result, Clarke might not report the asset or liability on its books.

3. *Operating leases.* Another way that companies keep debt off the statement of financial position is by leasing. Instead of owning the assets, companies lease them. Again, by meeting certain conditions, the company has to report only rent expense each period and to provide note disclosure of the transaction. Note that SPEs often use leases to accomplish off-balance-sheet treatment. We discuss accounting for lease transactions extensively in Chapter 21.

---

[14]Throughout the textbook, we use the label "statement of financial position" rather than "balance sheet" in referring to the financial statement that reports assets, liabilities, and equity. We use off-*balance-sheet* in the present context because of its common usage in financial markets.

Rationale

Why do companies engage in off-balance-sheet financing? A major reason is that many believe that **removing debt enhances the quality of the statement of financial position** and permits credit to be obtained more readily and at less cost.

Second, loan covenants often limit the amount of debt a company may have. As a result, the company uses off-balance-sheet financing because **these types of commitments might not be considered in computing debt limits**.

Third, some argue that the asset side of the statement of financial position is severely understated. For example, companies that depreciate assets on an accelerated basis will often have carrying amounts for property, plant, and equipment that are much lower than their fair values. As an offset to these lower values, some believe that part of the debt does not have to be reported. In other words, **if companies report assets at fair values**, less pressure would undoubtedly exist for off-balance-sheet financing arrangements.

Whether the arguments above have merit is debatable. The general idea of "out of sight, out of mind" may not be true in accounting. Many users of financial statements indicate that they attempt to factor these off-balance-sheet financing arrangements into their computations when assessing debt to equity relationships. Similarly, many loan covenants also attempt to account for these complex arrangements. Nevertheless, many companies still believe that benefits will accrue if they omit certain obligations from the statement of financial position.

As a response to off-balance-sheet financing arrangements, the IASB has increased disclosure (note) requirements. This response is consistent with an "efficient markets" philosophy: The important question is not whether the presentation is off-balance-sheet or not but whether the items are disclosed at all. In addition, the U.S. SEC now requires companies that it regulates to disclose (1) all contractual obligations in a tabular format and (2) contingent liabilities and commitments in either a textual or tabular format. An example of this disclosure appears in the "Evolving Issue" box on page 679.[15]

We believe that recording more obligations on the statement of financial position will enhance financial reporting. Given the problems with companies such as Enron, **Tiger Air** (AUS), **Petra Perdana** (MYS), and **Washington Mutual** (USA) and on-going efforts by the IASB and market regulators, we expect that less off-balance-sheet financing will occur in the future.[16]

---

[15]The IASB has issued consolidation guidance that looks beyond equity ownership as the primary criterion for determining whether an off-balance-sheet entity (and its assets and liabilities) should be on-balance-sheet (i.e., consolidated). Specifically, an investor controls an investee when it is exposed, or has rights, to variable returns from its involvement with the investee and has the ability to affect those returns through its power over the investee. Thus, the principle of control sets out the following three elements of control: (1) power over the investee; (2) exposure, or rights, to variable returns from involvement with the investee; and (3) the ability to use power over the investee to affect the amount of the investor's returns. In general, the control principle is applied in circumstances when voting rights are not the dominant factor in deciding who controls the investee, such as when any voting rights relate to administrative tasks only and the relevant activities are directed by means of contractual arrangements. **[9]** The details of consolidation accounting procedures are beyond the scope of this textbook and are usually addressed in an advanced accounting course.

[16]It is unlikely that the IASB will be able to stop all types of off-balance-sheet transactions. Financial engineering is the Holy Grail of securities markets. Developing new financial instruments and arrangements to sell and market to customers is not only profitable but also adds to the prestige of the investment firms that create them. Thus, new financial products will continue to appear that will test the ability of the IASB to develop appropriate accounting standards for them.

Evolving Issue   OFF-AND-ON REPORTING

The off-balance-sheet world is slowly but surely becoming more on-balance-sheet. New rules on guarantees and consolidation of SPEs are doing their part to increase the amount of debt reported on corporate statements of financial position. See footnote 15 (page 678) for a discussion of the IASB's consolidation guidance.

In addition, companies must disclose off-balance-sheet arrangements and contractual obligations that currently have, or are reasonably likely to have, a material future effect on the companies' financial condition. Presented below is **Novartis Group**'s (CHE) tabular disclosure of its contractual obligations. Because Novartis lists its securities in the United States, it is subject to U.S. SEC rules.

Novartis Group
Contractual Obligations

The following table summarizes the Group's contractual obligations and other commercial commitments as well as the effect these obligations and commitments are expected to have on the Group's liquidity and cash flow in future periods:

	Payments due by period				
	Total USD millions	Less than 1 year USD millions	2–3 years USD millions	4–5 years USD millions	After 5 years USD millions
Non-current financial debt	15,790	2,009	5,823	2,006	5,952
Operating leases	3,145	372	467	293	2,013
Unfunded pensions and other post-retirement obligations	2,144	97	195	207	1,645
Research & Development					
–Unconditional commitments	219	48	79	59	33
–Potential milestone commitments	2,014	456	526	766	266
Purchase commitments					
–Property, plant & equipment	755	508	236	11	
Total contractual cash obligations	**24,067**	**3,490**	**7,326**	**3,342**	**9,909**

The Group expects to fund the R&D and purchase commitments with internally generated resources.

Enron's (USA) abuse of off-balance-sheet financing to hide debt was shocking and inappropriate. One silver lining in the Enron debacle, however, is that the standard-setting bodies are now providing increased guidance on companies' reporting of contractual obligations. We believe the new U.S. SEC rule, which requires companies to report their obligations over a period of time, will be extremely useful to the investment community.

Presentation and Analysis

Presentation of Non-Current Liabilities

Companies that have large amounts and numerous issues of non-current liabilities frequently report only one amount in the statement of financial position, supported with comments and schedules in the accompanying notes. Long-term debt that **matures within one year** should be reported as a current liability, unless using non-current assets to accomplish retirement. If the company plans to refinance debt, convert it into shares, or retire it from a bond retirement fund, it should continue to report the debt as non-current if the refinancing agreement is completed by the end of the period. **[10]**

9 LEARNING OBJECTIVE
Indicate how to present and analyze non-current liabilities.

Note disclosures generally indicate the nature of the liabilities, maturity dates, interest rates, call provisions, conversion privileges, restrictions imposed by the creditors, and assets designated or pledged as security. Companies should show any assets pledged as security for the debt in the assets section of the statement of financial position. The fair value of the long-term debt should also be disclosed. Finally, companies must disclose future payments for sinking fund requirements and maturity amounts of long-term debt during each of the next five years. These disclosures aid financial statement users in evaluating the amounts and timing of future cash flows. Illustration 14-25 shows an example of the type of information provided for Novartis Group.

Novartis Group
(in millions)

	Dec. 31, 2012	Dec. 31, 2011
Total current assets	$28,004	$24,084
Non-current liabilities		
Financial debt	13,781	13,855
Deferred tax liabilities	7,286	6,761
Provisions and other non-current liabilities	9,879	7,792
Total non-current liabilities	**30,946**	**28,408**
Current liabilities		
Trade payables	5,593	4,989
Financial debts and derivative financial instruments	5,945	6,374
Current income tax liabilities	2,070	1,706
Provisions and other current liabilities	10,443	10,079
Total current liabilities	**24,051**	**23,148**
Total liabilities	**$54,997**	**$51,556**

19. Non-Current Financial Debts (in part)

	2012	2011
Straight bonds	$14,783	$13,483
Liabilities to banks and other financial institutions[1]	1,004	1,146
Finance lease obligations	3	4
Total (including current portion of non-current financial debt)	**15,790**	**14,633**
Less current portion of non-current financial debt	−2,009	−778
Total non-current financial debts	**$13,781**	**$13,855**

[1]Average interest rate 0.8% (2011: 0.9%)

Breakdown by maturity		2012	2011
	2012		$ 778
	2013	$ 2,009	2,029
	2014	2,713	2,789
	2015	3,110	3,108
	2016	1,987	1,948
	2017	19	3
	After 2017	5,952	3,978
Total		**$15,790**	**$14,633**

Breakdown by currency		2012	2011
	USD	$11,943	$ 9,962
	EUR	2,043	2,042
	JPY	929	1,031
	CHF	869	1,589
	Others	6	9
Total		**$15,790**	**$14,633**

Fair value comparison	2012 Balance sheet	2012 Fair values	2011 Balance sheet	2011 Fair values
Straight bonds	$14,783	$16,130	$13,483	$14,794
Others	1,007	1,007	1,150	1,150
Total	**$15,790**	**$17,137**	**$14,633**	**$15,944**

Collateralized non-current financial debt and pledged assets	2012	2011
Total amount of collateralized non-current financial debts	$ 12	$ 7
Total net book value of property, plant & equipment pledged as collateral for non-current financial debt	$136	$100

The Group's collateralized non-current financial debt consists of loan facilities at usual market conditions.

The percentage of fixed rate financial debt to total financial debt was 80% at December 31, 2012, and 72% at the end of 2011.

Financial debt, including current financial debt, contains only general default covenants. The Group is in compliance with these covenants.

The average interest rate on total financial debt in 2012 was 2.9% (2011: 2.7%, 2010: 3.1%).

ILLUSTRATION 14-25
Long-Term Debt
Disclosure

Analysis of Non-Current Liabilities

Long-term creditors and shareholders are interested in a company's long-run solvency, particularly its ability to pay interest as it comes due and to repay the face value of the debt at maturity. Debt to assets and times interest earned are two ratios that provide information about debt-paying ability and long-run solvency.

Debt to Assets Ratio. The **debt to assets ratio** measures the percentage of the total assets provided by creditors. To compute it, divide total debt (both current and non-current liabilities) by total assets, as Illustration 14-26 shows.

$$\text{Debt to Assets} = \frac{\text{Total Liabilities}}{\text{Total Assets}}$$

ILLUSTRATION 14-26
Computation of Debt to Assets Ratio

The higher the percentage of total liabilities to total assets, the greater the risk that the company may be unable to meet its maturing obligations.

Times Interest Earned. The **times interest earned** ratio indicates the company's ability to meet interest payments as they come due. As shown in Illustration 14-27, it is computed by dividing income before interest expense and income taxes by interest expense.

$$\text{Times Interest Earned} = \frac{\text{Income before Income Taxes and Interest Expense}}{\text{Interest Expense}}$$

ILLUSTRATION 14-27
Computation of Times Interest Earned

To illustrate these ratios, we use data from Novartis's 2012 annual report. Novartis has total liabilities of $54,997 million, total assets of $124,216 million, interest expense of $724 million, income taxes of $1,625 million, and net income of $9,618 million. We compute Novartis's debt to assets and times interest earned ratios as shown in Illustration 14-28.

$$\text{Debt to assets} = \frac{\$54,997}{\$124,216} = 44\%$$

$$\text{Times interest earned} = \frac{(\$9,618 + \$1,625 + \$724)}{\$724} = 16.5 \text{ times}$$

ILLUSTRATION 14-28
Computation of Long-Term Debt Ratios for Novartis

Even though Novartis has a relatively high debt to assets ratio of 44 percent, its interest coverage of 16.5 times indicates it can meet its interest payments as they come due.

GLOBAL ACCOUNTING INSIGHTS

LIABILITIES

U.S. GAAP and IFRS have similar definitions for liabilities. In addition, the accounting for current liabilities is essentially the same under both IFRS and U.S. GAAP. However, there are substantial differences in terminology related to non-current liabilities as well as some differences in the accounting for various types of long-term debt transactions.

Relevant Facts

Similarities

- As indicated above, U.S. GAAP and IFRS have similar liability definitions. Both also classify liabilities as current and non-current.

- Much of the accounting for bonds and long-term notes is the same under U.S. GAAP and IFRS.

- Both U.S. GAAP and IFRS require the best estimate of a probable loss. In U.S. GAAP, the minimum amount in a range is used. Under IFRS, if a range of estimates is predicted and no amount in the range is more likely than any other amount in the range, the midpoint of the range is used to measure the liability.

- Both U.S. GAAP and IFRS prohibit the recognition of liabilities for future losses.

Differences

- Under U.S. GAAP, companies must classify a refinancing as current only if it is completed before the financial statements are issued. IFRS requires that the current portion of long-term debt be classified as current unless an agreement to refinance on a long-term basis is completed before the reporting date.

- U.S. GAAP uses the term contingency in a different way than IFRS. A contingency under U.S. GAAP may be reported as a liability under certain situations. IFRS does not permit a contingency to be recorded as a liability.

- U.S. GAAP uses the term estimated liabilities to discuss various liability items that have some uncertainty related to timing or amount. IFRS generally uses the term provisions.

- U.S. GAAP and IFRS are similar in the treatment of environmental liabilities. However, the recognition criteria for environmental liabilities are more stringent under U.S. GAAP: Environmental liabilities are not recognized unless there is a present legal obligation and the fair value of the obligation can be reasonably estimated.

- U.S. GAAP uses the term troubled debt restructurings and develops recognition rules related to this category. IFRS generally assumes that all restructurings should be considered extinguishments of debt.

- Under U.S. GAAP, companies are permitted to use the straight-line method of amortization for bond discount or premium, provided that the amount recorded is not materially different than that resulting from effective-interest amortization. However, the effective-interest method is preferred and is generally used. Under IFRS, companies must use the effective-interest method.

- Under U.S. GAAP, companies record discounts and premiums in separate accounts (see the About the Numbers section). Under IFRS, companies do not use premium or discount accounts but instead show the bond at its net amount.

- Under U.S. GAAP, bond issue costs are recorded as an asset. Under IFRS, bond issue costs are netted against the carrying amount of the bonds.

- Under U.S. GAAP, losses on onerous contract are generally not recognized unless addressed by industry- or transaction-specific requirements. IFRS requires a liability and related expense or cost be recognized when a contract is onerous.

About the Numbers

Under IFRS, premiums and discounts are netted against the face value of the bonds for recording purposes. Under U.S. GAAP, discounts and premiums are recorded in separate accounts. To illustrate, consider the €100,000 of bonds dated January 1, 2015 (8 percent coupon, paid semiannually), issued by Evermaster to yield 6 percent on January 1, 2015. Recall from the discussion on page 661 that the price of these bonds was €108,530. Using U.S. GAAP procedures, Evermaster makes the following entry to record issuance of the bonds.

January 1, 2015

Cash	108,530	
Bonds Payable		100,000
Premium on Bonds Payable		8,530
(€108,530 − €100,000)		

As indicated, the bond premium is recorded in a separate account (the account, "Discount on Bonds Payable," has a debit

balance and is used for bonds issued at a discount). Evermaster makes the following entry on the first interest payment date.

July 1, 2015

Interest Expense (€108,530 × 6% × ½)	3,256	
Premium on Bonds Payable (€4,000 − €3,256)	744	
Cash (€100,000 × 8% × ½)		4,000

Following this entry, the net carrying value of the bonds is as follows.

Bonds payable	€100,000
Premium on bonds payable (€8,530 − €744)	7,786
Carrying value of bonds payable	€107,786

Thus, with a separate account for the premium, entries to record amortization are made to the premium account, which reduces the carrying value of the bonds to face value over the life of the bonds.

On the Horizon

As indicated in Chapter 2, the IASB and FASB are working on a conceptual framework project, part of which will examine the definition of a liability. In addition, the two Boards are attempting to clarify the accounting related to provisions and related contingencies.

SUMMARY OF LEARNING OBJECTIVES

1 Describe the formal procedures associated with issuing long-term debt. Incurring long-term debt is often a formal procedure. The bylaws of corporations usually require approval by the board of directors and the shareholders before corporations can issue bonds or can make other long-term debt arrangements. Generally, long-term debt has various covenants or restrictions. The covenants and other terms of the agreement between the borrower and the lender are stated in the bond indenture or note agreement.

2 Identify various types of bond issues. Various types of bond issues are (1) secured and unsecured bonds; (2) term, serial, and callable bonds; (3) convertible, commodity-backed, and deep-discount bonds; (4) registered and bearer (coupon) bonds; and (5) income and revenue bonds. The variety in the types of bonds results from attempts to attract capital from different investors and risk-takers and to satisfy the cash flow needs of the issuers.

3 Describe the accounting valuation for bonds at date of issuance. The investment community values a bond at the present value of its future cash flows, which consist of interest and principal. The rate used to compute the present value of these cash flows is the interest rate that provides an acceptable return on an investment commensurate with the issuer's risk characteristics. The interest rate written in the terms of the bond indenture and ordinarily appearing on the bond certificate is the stated, coupon, or nominal rate. The issuer of the bonds sets the rate and expresses it as a percentage of the face value (also called the par value, principal amount, or maturity value) of the bonds. If the rate employed by the buyers differs from the stated rate, the present value of the bonds computed by the buyers will differ from the face value of the bonds. The difference between the face value and the present value of the bonds is either a discount or premium.

4 Apply the methods of bond discount and premium amortization. The discount (premium) is amortized and charged (credited) to interest expense over the life of the bonds. Amortization of a discount increases bond interest expense, and amortization of a premium decreases bond interest expense. The procedure for amortization of a discount or premium is the effective-interest method. Under the effective-interest method, (1) bond interest expense is computed by multiplying the carrying value of the bonds at the beginning of the period by the effective-interest rate; then, (2) the bond discount or premium amortization is determined by comparing the bond interest expense with the interest to be paid.

5 Explain the accounting for long-term notes payable. Accounting procedures for notes and bonds are similar. Like a bond, a note is valued at the present value of its expected future interest and principal cash flows, with any discount or premium being similarly amortized over the life of the note. Whenever the face amount of the note does not reasonably represent the present value of the consideration in the exchange, a company must evaluate the entire arrangement in order to properly record the exchange and the subsequent interest.

6 Describe the accounting for the extinguishment of non-current liabilities. Non-current liabilities, such as bonds and notes payable, may be extinguished by (1) paying cash, (2) transferring non-cash assets and/or granting of an equity interest, and (3) modification of terms. At the time of extinguishment, any unamortized premium or discount must be amortized up to the reacquisition date. The reacquisition price is the amount paid on extinguishment or redemption before maturity, including

KEY TERMS

amortization, *659*

bearer (coupon)
  bonds, *655*

bond discount, *657*

bond indenture, *654*

bond premium, *657*

callable bonds, *655*

carrying value, *659*

commodity-backed
  bonds, *655*

convertible bonds, *655*

debenture bonds, *655*

debt to assets
  ratio, *681*

deep-discount (zero-
  interest debenture)
  bonds, *655*

effective-interest
  method, *659*

effective yield or market
  rate, *657*

extinguishment of
  debt, *671*

face, par, principal, or
  maturity value, *656*

fair value option, *676*

imputation, *669*

imputed interest rate, *669*

income bonds, *655*

long-term debt, *654*

long-term notes
  payable, *665*

mortgage notes
  payable, *670*

off-balance-sheet
  financing, *677*

refunding, *673*

registered bonds, *655*

revenue bonds, *655*

secured bonds, *655*

serial bonds, *655*

special purpose entity
  (SPE), *677*

stated, coupon, or
  nominal rate, *656*

substantial
  modification, *674 (n)*

term bonds, *655*

times interest earned, *681*

zero-interest debenture
  bonds, *655*

any call premium and expense of reacquisition. On any specified date, the carrying amount of the debt is the amount payable at maturity, adjusted for unamortized premium or discount. Any excess of the carrying amount over the reacquisition price is a gain from extinguishment. The excess of the reacquisition price over the carrying amount is a loss from extinguishment. Gains and losses on extinguishments are recognized currently in income. When debt is extinguished by transfer of non-cash assets or granting of equity interest, debtors record losses and gains on settlements based on fair values. The accounting for debt extinguished with modification is similar to that for other extinguishments. That is, the original obligation is extinguished, the new payable is recorded at fair value, and a gain or loss is recognized for the difference in the fair value of the new obligation and the carrying value of the old obligation.

7 **Describe the accounting for the fair value option.** Companies have the option to record fair value in their accounts for most financial assets and liabilities, including non-current liabilities. Fair value measurement for financial instruments, including financial liabilities, provides more relevant and understandable information than amortized cost. If companies choose the fair value option, non-current liabilities such as bonds and notes payable are recorded at fair value, with unrealized holding gains or losses reported as part of net income. An unrealized holding gain or loss is the net change in the fair value of the liability from one period to another, exclusive of interest expense recognized but not recorded.

8 **Explain the reporting of off-balance-sheet financing arrangements.** Off-balance-sheet financing is an attempt to borrow funds in such a way as to prevent recording obligations. Examples of off-balance-sheet arrangements are (1) non-consolidated subsidiaries, (2) special purpose entities, and (3) operating leases.

9 **Indicate how to present and analyze non-current liabilities.** Companies that have large amounts and numerous issues of non-current liabilities frequently report only one amount in the statement of financial position and support this with comments and schedules in the accompanying notes. Any assets pledged as security for the debt should be shown in the assets section of the statement of financial position. Long-term debt that matures within one year should be reported as a current liability, unless retirement is to be accomplished with other than current assets. If a company plans to refinance the debt, convert it into shares, or retire it from a bond retirement fund, it should continue to report it as non-current, as long as the refinancing is completed by the end of the period. Disclosure is required of future payments for sinking fund requirements and maturity amounts of long-term debt during each of the next five years. Debt to assets and times interest earned are two ratios that provide information about a company's debt-paying ability and long-run solvency.

IFRS AUTHORITATIVE LITERATURE

Authoritative Literature References

[1] International Accounting Standard 39, *Financial Instruments: Recognition and Measurement* (London, U.K.: International Accounting Standards Committee Foundation, 2003), par. 47.

[2] International Accounting Standard 39, *Financial Instruments: Recognition and Measurement* (London, U.K.: International Accounting Standards Committee Foundation, 2003), par. 43.

[3] International Accounting Standard 39, *Financial Instruments: Recognition and Measurement* (London, U.K.: International Accounting Standards Committee Foundation, 2003), paras. AG64–65.

[4] International Accounting Standard 39, *Financial Instruments: Recognition and Measurement* (London, U.K.: International Accounting Standards Committee Foundation, 2003), paras. AG59–61.

[5] International Accounting Standard 39, *Financial Instruments: Recognition and Measurement* (London, U.K.: International Accounting Standards Committee Foundation, 2003), par. AG62.

[6] International Accounting Standard 39, *Financial Instruments: Recognition and Measurement* (London, U.K.: International Accounting Standards Committee Foundation, 2003), par. 40.

[7] International Accounting Standard 39, *Financial Instruments: Recognition and Measurement* (London, U.K.: International Accounting Standards Committee Foundation, 2003), paras. IN16–17.

[8] International Financial Reporting Standard 9, *Financial Instruments* (London, U.K.: IFRS Foundation, November 2013), paras. 5.7.7–5.7.8.

[9] International Financial Reporting Standard 10, *Consolidated Financial Statements* (London, U.K.: International Accounting Standards Committee Foundation, May 2011), paras. IN8–IN9.

[10] International Accounting Standard 1, *Presentation of Financial Statements* (London, U.K.: International Accounting Standards Committee Foundation, 2003), paras. 69–76.

QUESTIONS

1. (a) From what sources might a corporation obtain funds through long-term debt? (b) What is a bond indenture? What does it contain? (c) What is a mortgage?

2. Novartis Group (CHE) has issued various types of bonds such as term bonds, income bonds, and debentures. Differentiate between term bonds, mortgage bonds, collateral trust bonds, debenture bonds, income bonds, callable bonds, registered bonds, bearer or coupon bonds, convertible bonds, commodity-backed bonds, and deep-discount bonds.

3. Distinguish between the following interest rates for bonds payable:

(a) Yield rate.   **(d)** Market rate.
(b) Nominal rate.   **(e)** Effective rate.
(c) Stated rate.

4. Distinguish between the following values relative to bonds payable:

(a) Maturity value.   **(c)** Market (fair) value.
(b) Face value.   **(d)** Par value.

5. Under what conditions of bond issuance does a discount on bonds payable arise? Under what conditions of bond issuance does a premium on bonds payable arise?

6. Briefly explain how bond premium or discount affects interest expense over the life of a bond.

7. What is the required method of amortizing discount and premium on bonds payable? Explain the procedures.

8. Zopf Company sells its bonds at a premium and applies the effective-interest method in amortizing the premium. Will the annual interest expense increase or decrease over the life of the bonds? Explain.

9. Vodafone (GBR) recently issued debt. How should the costs of issuing these bonds be accounted for?

10. Will the amortization of a bond discount increase or decrease bond interest expense? Explain.

11. What is done to record properly a transaction involving the issuance of a non-interest-bearing long-term note in exchange for property?

12. How is the present value of a non-interest-bearing note computed?

13. When is the stated interest rate of a debt instrument presumed to be fair?

14. What are the considerations in imputing an appropriate interest rate?

15. Differentiate between a fixed-rate mortgage and a variable-rate mortgage.

16. Identify the situations under which debt is extinguished.

17. What is the "call" feature of a bond issue? How does the call feature affect the amortization of bond premium or discount?

18. Why would a company wish to reduce its bond indebtedness before its bonds reach maturity? Indicate how this can be done and the correct accounting treatment for such a transaction.

19. What are the general rules for measuring a gain or a loss by a debtor in a debt extinguishment?

20. **(a)** In a debt modification situation, why might the creditor grant concessions to the debtor?

(b) What type of concessions might a creditor grant the debtor in a debt modification situation?

21. What are the general rules for measuring and recognizing gain or loss by a debt extinguishment with modification?

22. What is the fair value option? Briefly describe the controversy of applying the fair value option to financial liabilities.

23. Pierre Company has a 12% note payable with a carrying value of €20,000. Pierre applies the fair value option to this note; given an increase in market interest rates, the fair value of the note is €22,600. Prepare the entry to record the fair value option for this note.

24. What disclosures are required relative to long-term debt and sinking fund requirements?

25. What is off-balance-sheet financing? Why might a company be interested in using off-balance-sheet financing?

26. What are some forms of off-balance-sheet financing?

27. Explain how a non-consolidated subsidiary can be a form of off-balance-sheet financing.

28. Briefly describe some of the similarities and differences between U.S. GAAP and IFRS with respect to the accounting for liabilities.

29. Diaz Company issued $100,000 face value, 9% coupon bonds on January 1, 2014, for $92,608 to yield 11%. The bonds mature in 5 years and pay interest annually on December 31. Prepare the entries under U.S. GAAP for Diaz for (a) date of issue, (b) first interest payment date, and (c) January 1, 2016, when Diaz calls and extinguishes the bonds at 101.

30. Briefly discuss how accounting convergence efforts addressing liabilities are related to the IASB/FASB conceptual framework project.

BRIEF EXERCISES

(All calculations are to be rounded to nearest whole currency unit, unless otherwise stated.)

BE14-1 Whiteside Corporation issues ¥500,000 of 9% bonds, due in 10 years, with interest payable semi-annually. At the time of issue, the market rate for such bonds is 10%. Compute the issue price of the bonds.

BE14-2 The Colson Company issued €300,000 of 10% bonds on January 1, 2015. The bonds are due January 1, 2020, with interest payable each July 1 and January 1. The bonds are issued at face value. Prepare Colson's journal entries for (a) the January issuance, (b) the July 1 interest payment, and (c) the December 31 adjusting entry.

BE14-3 Assume the bonds in BE14-2 were issued at 108.11 to yield 8%. Prepare the journal entries for (a) January 1, (b) July 1, and (c) December 31.

BE14-4 Assume the bonds in BE14-2 were issued at 92.6393 to yield 12%. Prepare the journal entries for (a) January 1, (b) July 1, and (c) December 31.

BE14-5 Devers Corporation issued £400,000 of 6% bonds on May 1, 2015. The bonds were dated January 1, 2015, and mature January 1, 2017, with interest payable July 1 and January 1. The bonds were issued at face value plus accrued interest. Prepare Devers' journal entries for (a) the May 1 issuance, (b) the July 1 interest payment, and (c) the December 31 adjusting entry.

BE14-6 On January 1, 2015, JWS Corporation issued $600,000 of 7% bonds, due in 10 years. The bonds were issued for $559,224, and pay interest each July 1 and January 1. Prepare the company's journal entries for (a) the January 1 issuance, (b) the July 1 interest payment, and (c) the December 31 adjusting entry. Assume an effective-interest rate of 8%.

BE14-7 Assume the bonds in BE14-6 were issued for $644,636 with the effective-interest rate of 6%. Prepare the company's journal entries for (a) the January 1 issuance, (b) the July 1 interest payment, and (c) the December 31 adjusting entry.

BE14-8 Tan Corporation issued HK$600,000,000 of 7% bonds on November 1, 2015, for HK$644,636,000. The bonds were dated November 1, 2015, and mature in 10 years, with interest payable each May 1 and November 1. The effective-interest rate is 6%. Prepare Tan's December 31, 2015, adjusting entry.

BE14-9 Coldwell, Inc. issued a €100,000, 4-year, 10% note at face value to Flint Hills Bank on January 1, 2015, and received €100,000 cash. The note requires annual interest payments each December 31. Prepare Coldwell's journal entries to record (a) the issuance of the note and (b) the December 31 interest payment.

BE14-10 Samson Corporation issued a 4-year, £75,000, zero-interest-bearing note to Brown Company on January 1, 2015, and received cash of £47,664. The implicit interest rate is 12%. Prepare Samson's journal entries for (a) the January 1 issuance and (b) the December 31 recognition of interest.

BE14-11 McCormick Corporation issued a 4-year, $40,000, 5% note to Greenbush Company on January 1, 2015, and received a computer that normally sells for $31,495. The note requires annual interest payments each December 31. The market rate of interest for a note of similar risk is 12%. Prepare McCormick's journal entries for (a) the January 1 issuance and (b) the December 31 interest.

BE14-12 Shlee Corporation issued a 4-year, €60,000, zero-interest-bearing note to Garcia Company on January 1, 2015, and received cash of €60,000. In addition, Shlee agreed to sell merchandise to Garcia at an amount less than regular selling price over the 4-year period. The market rate of interest for similar notes is 12%. Prepare Shlee Corporation's January 1 journal entry.

BE14-13 On January 1, 2015, Henderson Corporation retired $500,000 of bonds at 99. At the time of retirement, the unamortized premium was $15,000. Prepare Henderson's journal entry to record the reacquisition of the bonds.

6 **BE14-14** Refer to the note issued by Coldwell, Inc. in BE14-9. During 2015, Coldwell experiences financial difficulties. On January 1, 2016, Coldwell negotiates a settlement of the note by issuing to Flint Hills Bank 20,000 €1 par Coldwell ordinary shares. The ordinary shares have a market price of €4.75 per share on the date of the settlement. Prepare Coldwell's entries to settle this note.

6 **BE14-15** Refer to the note issued by Coldwell, Inc. in BE14-9. During 2015, Coldwell experiences financial difficulties. On January 1, 2016, Coldwell negotiates a modification of the terms of the note. Under the modification, Flint Hills Bank agrees to reduce the face value of the note to €90,000 and to extend the maturity date to January 1, 2020. Annual interest payments on December 31 will be made at a rate of 8%. Coldwell's market interest rate at the time of the modification is 12%. Prepare Coldwell's entries for (a) the modification on January 1, 2016, and (b) the first interest payment date on December 31, 2016.

7 **BE14-16** Shonen Knife Corporation has elected to use the fair value option for one of its notes payable. The note was issued at an effective rate of 11% and has a carrying value of HK$16,000. At year-end, Shonen Knife's borrowing rate has declined; the fair value of the note payable is now HK$17,500. (a) Determine the unrealized gain or loss on the note. (b) Prepare the entry to record any unrealized gain or loss, assuming that the change in value was due to general market conditions.

9 **BE14-17** At December 31, 2015, Hyasaki Corporation has the following account balances:

Bonds payable, due January 1, 2023	$1,912,000
Interest payable	80,000

Show how the above accounts should be presented on the December 31, 2015, statement of financial position, including the proper classifications.

EXERCISES

(All calculations are to be rounded to nearest whole currency unit, unless otherwise stated.)

2 **E14-1 (Classification of Liabilities)** Presented below are various account balances.

   (a) Bank loans payable of a winery, due March 10, 2018. (The product requires aging for 5 years before sale.)
   (b) Serial bonds payable, €1,000,000, of which €250,000 are due each July 31.
   (c) Amounts withheld from employees' wages for income taxes.
   (d) Notes payable due January 15, 2017.
   (e) Credit balances in customers' accounts arising from returns and allowances after collection in full of account.
   (f) Bonds payable of €2,000,000 maturing June 30, 2016.
   (g) Overdraft of €1,000 in a bank account. (No other balances are carried at this bank.)
   (h) Deposits made by customers who have ordered goods.

Instructions
Indicate whether each of the items above should be classified on December 31, 2015, as a current liability, a non-current liability, or under some other classification. Consider each one independently from all others; that is, do not assume that all of them relate to one particular business. If the classification of some of the items is doubtful, explain why in each case.

2 **E14-2 (Classification)** The following items are found in the financial statements.

   (a) Interest expense (credit balance).
   (b) Bond issue costs.
   (c) Gain on repurchase of debt.
   (d) Mortgage payable (payable in equal amounts over next 3 years).
   (e) Debenture bonds payable (maturing in 5 years).
   (f) Notes payable (due in 4 years).
   (g) Income bonds payable (due in 3 years).

Instructions
Indicate how each of these items should be classified in the financial statements.

3 **4** **E14-3 (Entries for Bond Transactions)** Presented below are two independent situations.

1. On January 1, 2015, Divac Company issued €300,000 of 9%, 10-year bonds at par. Interest is payable quarterly on April 1, July 1, October 1, and January 1.

2. On June 1, 2015, Verbitsky Company issued €200,000 of 12%, 10-year bonds dated January 1 at par plus accrued interest. Interest is payable semiannually on July 1 and January 1.

Instructions

For each of these two independent situations, prepare journal entries to record the following.

(a) The issuance of the bonds.

(b) The payment of interest on July 1.

(c) The accrual of interest on December 31.

3 **4** **E14-4 (Entries for Bond Transactions)** Foreman Company issued €800,000 of 10%, 20-year bonds on January 1, 2015, at 119.792 to yield 8%. Interest is payable semiannually on July 1 and January 1.

Instructions

Prepare the journal entries to record the following.

(a) The issuance of the bonds.

(b) The payment of interest and the related amortization on July 1, 2015.

(c) The accrual of interest and the related amortization on December 31, 2015.

3 **4** **E14-5 (Entries for Bond Transactions)** Assume the same information as in E14-4, except that the bonds were issued at 84.95 to yield 12%.

Instructions

Prepare the journal entries to record the following. (Round to the nearest euro.)

(a) The issuance of the bonds.

(b) The payment of interest and related amortization on July 1, 2015.

(c) The accrual of interest and the related amortization on December 31, 2015.

3 **4** **E14-6 (Amortization Schedule)** Spencer Company sells 10% bonds having a maturity value of £3,000,000 for £2,783,724. The bonds are dated January 1, 2015, and mature January 1, 2020. Interest is payable annually on January 1.

Instructions

Set up a schedule of interest expense and discount amortization. (*Hint:* The effective-interest rate must be computed.)

3 **4** **E14-7 (Determine Proper Amounts in Account Balances)** Presented below are three independent situations.

Instructions

(a) McEntire Co. sold $2,500,000 of 11%, 10-year bonds at 106.231 to yield 10% on January 1, 2015. The bonds were dated January 1, 2015, and pay interest on July 1 and January 1. Determine the amount of interest expense to be reported on July 1, 2015, and December 31, 2015.

(b) Cheriel Inc. issued $600,000 of 9%, 10-year bonds on June 30, 2015, for $562,500. This price provided a yield of 10% on the bonds. Interest is payable semiannually on December 31 and June 30. Determine the amount of interest expense to record if financial statements are issued on October 31, 2015.

(c) On October 1, 2015, Chinook Company sold 12% bonds having a maturity value of $800,000 for $853,382 plus accrued interest, which provides the bondholders with a 10% yield. The bonds are dated January 1, 2015, and mature January 1, 2020, with interest payable December 31 of each year. Prepare the journal entries at the date of the bond issuance and for the first interest payment.

3 **4** **E14-8 (Entries and Questions for Bond Transactions)** On June 30, 2014, Macias Company issued R$5,000,000 face value of 13%, 20-year bonds at R$5,376,150 to yield 12%. The bonds pay semiannual interest on June 30 and December 31.

Instructions

(a) Prepare the journal entries to record the following transactions.

(1) The issuance of the bonds on June 30, 2014.

(2) The payment of interest and the amortization of the premium on December 31, 2014.

(3) The payment of interest and the amortization of the premium on June 30, 2015.

(4) The payment of interest and the amortization of the premium on December 31, 2015.

(b) Show the proper statement of financial position presentation for the liability for bonds payable on the December 31, 2015, statement of financial position.

(c) Provide the answers to the following questions.

(1) What amount of interest expense is reported for 2015?

(2) Determine the total cost of borrowing over the life of the bond.

3 4 E14-9 (Entries for Bond Transactions) On January 1, 2015, Osborn Company sold 12% bonds having a maturity value of £800,000 for £860,651.79, which provides the bondholders with a 10% yield. The bonds are dated January 1, 2015, and mature January 1, 2020, with interest payable December 31 of each year.

Instructions
(a) Prepare the journal entry at the date of the bond issuance.
(b) Prepare a schedule of interest expense and bond amortization for 2015–2017.
(c) Prepare the journal entry to record the interest payment and the amortization for 2015.
(d) Prepare the journal entry to record the interest payment and the amortization for 2017.

3 4 E14-10 (Information Related to Various Bond Issues) Pawnee Inc. has issued three types of debt on January 1, 2015, the start of the company's fiscal year.

(a) $10 million, 10-year, 13% unsecured bonds, interest payable quarterly. Bonds were priced to yield 12%.
(b) $25 million par of 10-year, zero-coupon bonds at a price to yield 12% per year.
(c) $15 million, 10-year, 10% mortgage bonds, interest payable annually to yield 12%.

Instructions
Prepare a schedule that identifies the following items for each bond: (1) maturity value, (2) number of interest periods over life of bond, (3) stated rate per each interest period, (4) effective-interest rate per each interest period, (5) payment amount per period, and (6) present value of bonds at date of issue.

5 E14-11 (Entries for Zero-Interest-Bearing Notes) On January 1, 2015, McLean Company makes the two following acquisitions.

1. Purchases land having a fair value of €300,000 by issuing a 5-year, zero-interest-bearing promissory note in the face amount of €505,518.

2. Purchases equipment by issuing a 6%, 8-year promissory note having a maturity value of €400,000 (interest payable annually).

The company has to pay 11% interest for funds from its bank.

Instructions
(a) Record the two journal entries that should be recorded by McLean Company for the two purchases on January 1, 2015.
(b) Record the interest at the end of the first year on both notes.

5 E14-12 (Imputation of Interest) Presented below are two independent situations.

Instructions
(a) On January 1, 2015, Spartan Inc. purchased land that had an assessed value of $390,000 at the time of purchase. A $600,000, zero-interest-bearing note due January 1, 2018, was given in exchange. There was no established exchange price for the land, nor a ready market price for the note. The interest rate charged on a note of this type is 12%. Determine at what amount the land should be recorded at January 1, 2015, and the interest expense to be reported in 2015 related to this transaction.
(b) On January 1, 2015, Geimer Furniture Co. borrowed $4,000,000 (face value) from Aurora Co., a major customer, through a zero-interest-bearing note due in 4 years. Because the note was zero-interest-bearing, Geimer Furniture agreed to sell furniture to this customer at lower than market price. A 10% rate of interest is normally charged on this type of loan. Prepare the journal entry to record this transaction and determine the amount of interest expense to report for 2015.

5 E14-13 (Imputation of Interest with Right) On January 1, 2015, Durdil Co. borrowed and received ₹500,000 from a major customer evidenced by a zero-interest-bearing note due in 3 years. As consideration for the zero-interest-bearing feature, Durdil agrees to supply the customer's inventory needs for the loan period at lower than the market price. The appropriate rate at which to impute interest is 8%.

Instructions

(a) Prepare the journal entry to record the initial transaction on January 1, 2015.
(b) Prepare the journal entry to record any adjusting entries needed at December 31, 2015. Assume that the sales of Durdil's product to this customer occur evenly over the 3-year period.

3 4 6 **E14-14 (Entry for Retirement of Bond; Bond Issue Costs)** On January 2, 2012, Prebish Corporation issued $1,500,000 of 10% bonds to yield 11% due December 31, 2021. Interest on the bonds is payable annually each December 31. The bonds are callable at 101 (i.e., at 101% of face amount), and on January 2, 2015, Prebish called $1,000,000 face amount of the bonds and retired them.

Instructions

(a) Determine the price of the Prebish bonds when issued on January 2, 2012.
(b) Prepare an amortization schedule for 2012–2016 for the bonds.
(c) Ignoring income taxes, compute the amount of loss, if any, to be recognized by Prebish as a result of retiring the $1,000,000 of bonds in 2015 and prepare the journal entry to record the retirement.

3 4 6 **E14-15 (Entries for Retirement and Issuance of Bonds)** On June 30, 2007, Mendenhal Company issued 8% bonds with a par value of £600,000 due in 20 years. They were issued at 82.8414 to yield 10% and were callable at 104 at any date after June 30, 2015. Because of lower interest rates and a significant change in the company's credit rating, it was decided to call the entire issue on June 30, 2016, and to issue new bonds. New 6% bonds were sold in the amount of £800,000 at 112.5513 to yield 5%; they mature in 20 years. Interest payment dates are December 31 and June 30 for both old and new bonds.

Instructions

(a) Prepare journal entries to record the retirement of the old issue and the sale of the new issue on June 30, 2016. Unamortized discount is £78,979.
(b) Prepare the entry required on December 31, 2016, to record the payment of the first 6 months' interest and the amortization of premium on the bonds.

3 4 6 **E14-16 (Entries for Retirement and Issuance of Bonds)** Kobiachi Company had bonds outstanding with a maturity value of ¥5,000,000. On April 30, 2016, when these bonds had an unamortized discount of ¥100,000, they were called in at 104. To pay for these bonds, Kobiachi had issued other bonds a month earlier bearing a lower interest rate. The newly issued bonds had a life of 10 years. The new bonds were issued at 103 (face value ¥5,000,000).

Instructions

Ignoring interest, compute the gain or loss and record this refunding transaction.

6 **E14-17 (Settlement of Debt)** Strickland Company owes $200,000 plus $18,000 of accrued interest to Moran State Bank. The debt is a 10-year, 10% note. During 2015, Strickland's business deteriorated due to a faltering regional economy. On December 31, 2015, Moran State Bank agrees to accept an old machine and cancel the entire debt. The machine has a cost of $390,000, accumulated depreciation of $221,000, and a fair value of $180,000.

Instructions

(a) Prepare journal entries for Strickland Company to record this debt settlement.
(b) How should Strickland report the gain or loss on the disposition of machine and on restructuring of debt in its 2015 income statement?
(c) Assume that, instead of transferring the machine, Strickland decides to grant 15,000 of its ordinary shares ($10 par), which have a fair value of $180,000 in full settlement of the loan obligation. Prepare the entries to record the transaction.

6 **E14-18 (Loan Modification)** On December 31, 2015, Sterling Bank enters into a debt restructuring agreement with Barkley Company, which is now experiencing financial trouble. The bank agrees to restructure a 12%, issued at par, £3,000,000 note receivable by the following modifications:

1. Reducing the principal obligation from £3,000,000 to £2,400,000.
2. Extending the maturity date from December 31, 2015, to January 1, 2019.
3. Reducing the interest rate from 12% to 10%. Barkley's market rate of interest is 15%.

Barkley pays interest at the end of each year. On January 1, 2019, Barkley Company pays £2,400,000 in cash to Sterling Bank.

Instructions

   (a) Can Barkley Company record a gain under the term modification mentioned above? Explain.

   (b) Prepare the amortization schedule of the note for Barkley Company after the debt modification.

   (c) Prepare the interest payment entry for Barkley Company on December 31, 2017.

   (d) What entry should Barkley make on January 1, 2019?

6 **E14-19 (Loan Modification)** Use the same information as in E14-18 except that Sterling Bank reduced the principal to £1,900,000 rather than £2,400,000. On January 1, 2019, Barkley pays £1,900,000 in cash to Sterling Bank for the principal.

Instructions

   (a) Prepare the journal entries to record the loan modification for Barkley.

   (b) Prepare the amortization schedule of the note for Barkley Company after the debt modification.

   (c) Prepare the interest payment entries for Barkley Company on December 31 of 2016, 2017, and 2018.

   (d) What entry should Barkley make on January 1, 2019?

6 **E14-20 (Entries for Settlement of Debt)** Consider the following independent situations.

Instructions

   (a) Gottlieb Co. owes €199,800 to Ceballos Inc. The debt is a 10-year, 11% note. Because Gottlieb Co. is in financial trouble, Ceballos Inc. agrees to accept some land and cancel the entire debt. The land has a book value of €90,000 and a fair value of €140,000. Prepare the journal entry on Gottlieb's books for debt settlement.

   (b) Vargo Corp. owes $270,000 to First Trust. The debt is a 10-year, 12% note due December 31, 2015. Because Vargo Corp. is in financial trouble, First Trust agrees to extend the maturity date to December 31, 2017, reduce the principal to $220,000, and reduce the interest rate to 5%, payable annually on December 31. Vargo's market rate of interest is 8%. Prepare the journal entries on Vargo's books on December 31, 2015, 2016, and 2017.

7 **E14-21 (Fair Value Option)** Fallen Company commonly issues long-term notes payable to its various lenders. Fallen has had a pretty good credit rating such that its effective borrowing rate is quite low (less than 8% on an annual basis). Fallen has elected to use the fair value option for the long-term notes issued to Barclay's Bank and has the following data related to the carrying and fair value for these notes. (Assume that changes in fair value are due to general market interest rate changes).

	Carrying Value	Fair Value
December 31, 2015	€54,000	€54,000
December 31, 2016	44,000	42,500
December 31, 2017	36,000	38,000

Instructions

   (a) Prepare the journal entry at December 31 (Fallen's year-end) for 2015, 2016, and 2017, to record the fair value option for these notes.

   (b) At what amount will the note be reported on Fallen's 2016 statement of financial position?

   (c) What is the effect of recording the fair value option on these notes on Fallen's 2017 income?

   (d) Assuming that general market interest rates have been stable over the period, does the fair value data for the notes indicate that Fallen's creditworthiness has improved or declined in 2017? Explain.

   (e) Assuming the conditions that exist in (d), what is the effect of recording the fair value option on these notes in Fallen's income statement in 2015, 2016, and 2017?

9 **E14-22 (Long-Term Debt Disclosure)** At December 31, 2015, Redmond Company has outstanding three long-term debt issues. The first is a $2,000,000 note payable which matures June 30, 2018. The second is a $6,000,000 bond issue which matures September 30, 2019. The third is a $12,500,000 sinking fund debenture with annual sinking fund payments of $2,500,000 in each of the years 2017 through 2021.

Instructions

Prepare the required note disclosure for the long-term debt at December 31, 2015.

PROBLEMS

(All calculations are to be rounded to nearest whole currency unit, unless otherwise stated.)

3 **4** **P14-1 (Analysis of Amortization Schedule and Interest Entries)** The amortization and interest schedule on page 692 reflects the issuance of 10-year bonds by Capulet Corporation on January 1, 2009, and the subsequent interest payments and charges. The company's year-end is December 31, and financial statements are prepared once yearly.

Amortization Schedule

Year	Cash	Interest	Amount Unamortized	Book Value
1/1/2009			€5,651	€ 94,349
2009	€11,000	€11,322	5,329	94,671
2010	11,000	11,361	4,968	95,032
2011	11,000	11,404	4,564	95,436
2012	11,000	11,452	4,112	95,888
2013	11,000	11,507	3,605	96,395
2014	11,000	11,567	3,038	96,962
2015	11,000	11,635	2,403	97,597
2016	11,000	11,712	1,691	98,309
2017	11,000	11,797	894	99,106
2018	11,000	11,894		100,000

Instructions

(a) Indicate whether the bonds were issued at a premium or a discount and how you can determine this fact from the schedule.

(b) Determine the stated interest rate and the effective-interest rate.

(c) On the basis of the schedule, prepare the journal entry to record the issuance of the bonds on January 1, 2009.

(d) On the basis of the schedule, prepare the journal entry or entries to reflect the bond transactions and accruals for 2009. (Interest is paid January 1.)

(e) On the basis of the schedule, prepare the journal entry or entries to reflect the bond transactions and accruals for 2016. Capulet Corporation does not use reversing entries.

3 4 6 P14-2 (Issuance and Retirement of Bonds) Venzuela Co. is building a new hockey arena at a cost of $2,500,000. It received a down payment of $500,000 from local businesses to support the project and now needs to borrow $2,000,000 to complete the project. It therefore decides to issue $2,000,000 of 10.5%, 10-year bonds. These bonds were issued on January 1, 2014, and pay interest annually on each January 1. The bonds yield 10%.

Instructions

(a) Prepare the journal entry to record the issuance of the bonds on January 1, 2014.

(b) Prepare a bond amortization schedule up to and including January 1, 2018.

(c) Assume that on July 1, 2017, Venzuela Co. retires half of the bonds at a cost of $1,065,000 plus accrued interest. Prepare the journal entry to record this retirement.

3 4 P14-3 (Negative Amortization) Good-Deal Inc. developed a new sales gimmick to help sell its inventory of new automobiles. Because many new car buyers need financing, Good-Deal offered a low down payment and low car payments for the first year after purchase. It believes that this promotion will bring in some new buyers.

On January 1, 2015, a customer purchased a new €33,000 automobile, making a down payment of €1,000. The customer signed a note indicating that the annual rate of interest would be 8% and that quarterly payments would be made over 3 years. For the first year, Good-Deal required a €400 quarterly payment to be made on April 1, July 1, October 1, and January 1, 2016. After this one-year period, the customer was required to make regular quarterly payments that would pay off the loan as of January 1, 2018.

Instructions

(a) Prepare a note amortization schedule for the first year.

(b) Indicate the amount the customer owes on the contract at the end of the first year.

(c) Compute the amount of the new quarterly payments.

(d) Prepare a note amortization schedule for these new payments for the next 2 years.

(e) What do you think of the new sales promotion used by Good-Deal?

4 P14-4 (Effective-Interest Method) Samantha Cordelia, an intermediate accounting student, is having difficulty amortizing bond premiums and discounts using the effective-interest method. Furthermore, she cannot understand why IFRS requires that this method be used. She has come to you with the following problem, looking for help.

On June 30, 2015, Hobart Company issued R$2,000,000 face value of 11%, 20-year bonds at R$2,171,600, a yield of 10%. Hobart Company uses the effective-interest method to amortize bond premiums or discounts. The bonds pay semiannual interest on June 30 and December 31. Compute the amortization schedule for four periods.

Instructions
Using the data above for illustrative purposes, write a short memo (1–1.5 pages double-spaced) to Samantha, explaining what the effective-interest method is, why it is preferable, and how it is computed. (Do not forget to include an amortization schedule, referring to it whenever necessary.)

5 **P14-5 (Entries for Zero-Interest-Bearing Note)** On December 31, 2015, Faital Company acquired a computer from Plato Corporation by issuing a £600,000 zero-interest-bearing note, payable in full on December 31, 2019. Faital Company's credit rating permits it to borrow funds from its several lines of credit at 10%. The computer is expected to have a 5-year life and a £70,000 residual value.

Instructions
(a) Prepare the journal entry for the purchase on December 31, 2015.
(b) Prepare any necessary adjusting entries relative to depreciation (use straight-line) and amortization on December 31, 2016.
(c) Prepare any necessary adjusting entries relative to depreciation and amortization on December 31, 2017.

5 **P14-6 (Entries for Zero-Interest-Bearing Note; Payable in Installments)** Sabonis Cosmetics Co. purchased machinery on December 31, 2014, paying $50,000 down and agreeing to pay the balance in four equal installments of $40,000 payable each December 31. An assumed interest of 8% is implicit in the purchase price.

Instructions
Prepare the journal entries that would be recorded for the purchase and for the payments and interest on the following dates.
(a) December 31, 2014.   (d) December 31, 2017.
(b) December 31, 2015.   (e) December 31, 2018.
(c) December 31, 2016.

3 **4** **6** **9** **P14-7 (Issuance and Retirement of Bonds; Income Statement Presentation)** Chen Company issued its 9%, 25-year mortgage bonds in the principal amount of ¥30,000,000 on January 2, 2001, at a discount of ¥2,722,992 (effective rate of 10%). The indenture securing the issue provided that the bonds could be called for redemption in total but not in part at any time before maturity at 104% of the principal amount, but it did not provide for any sinking fund.

On December 18, 2015, the company issued its 11%, 20-year debenture bonds in the principal amount of ¥40,000,000 at 102, and the proceeds were used to redeem the 9%, 25-year mortgage bonds on January 2, 2016. The indenture securing the new issue did not provide for any sinking fund or for retirement before maturity. The unamortized discount at retirement was ¥1,842,888.

Instructions
(a) Prepare journal entries to record the issuance of the 11% bonds and the retirement of the 9% bonds.
(b) Indicate the income statement treatment of the gain or loss from retirement and the note disclosure required.

3 **4** **6** **P14-8 (Comprehensive Bond Problem)** In each of the following independent cases, the company closes its books on December 31.

1. Sanford Co. sells $500,000 of 10% bonds on March 1, 2015. The bonds pay interest on September 1 and March 1. The due date of the bonds is September 1, 2018. The bonds yield 12%. Give entries through December 31, 2016.

2. Titania Co. sells $400,000 of 12% bonds on June 1, 2015. The bonds pay interest on December 1 and June 1. The due date of the bonds is June 1, 2019. The bonds yield 10%. On October 1, 2016, Titania buys back $120,000 worth of bonds for $126,000 (includes accrued interest). Give entries through December 1, 2017.

Instructions
For the two cases, prepare all of the relevant journal entries from the time of sale until the date indicated. (Construct amortization tables where applicable.) Amortize premium or discount on interest dates and at year-end. (Assume that no reversing entries were made; round to the nearest dollar.)

3 4 6 **P14-9 (Issuance of Bonds Between Interest Dates, Retirement)** Presented below are selected transactions on the books of Simonson Corporation.

July 1, 2015	Bonds payable with a par value of €900,000, which are dated January 1, 2015, are sold at 119.219 plus accrued interest to yield 10%. They are coupon bonds, bear interest at 12% (payable annually at January 1), and mature January 1, 2025. (Use interest expense account for accrued interest.)
Dec. 31	Adjusting entries are made to record the accrued interest on the bonds, and the amortization of the proper amount of premium.
Jan. 1, 2016	Interest on the bonds is paid.
Jan. 2	Bonds of par value of €360,000 are called at 102 and extinguished.
Dec. 31	Adjusting entries are made to record the accrued interest on the bonds, and the proper amount of premium amortized.

Instructions

Prepare journal entries for the transactions above.

3 4 6 **P14-10 (Entries for Life Cycle of Bonds)** On April 1, 2015, Sarkar Company sold 15,000 of its 11%, 15-year, R$1,000 face value bonds to yield 12%. Interest payment dates are April 1 and October 1. On April 2, 2016, Sarkar took advantage of favorable prices of its shares to extinguish 6,000 of the bonds by issuing 200,000 of its R$10 par value ordinary shares. At this time, the accrued interest was paid in cash. The company's shares were selling for R$31 per share on April 2, 2016.

Instructions

Prepare the journal entries needed on the books of Sarkar Company to record the following.

    (a) April 1, 2015: issuance of the bonds.
    (b) October 1, 2015: payment of semiannual interest.
    (c) December 31, 2015: accrual of interest expense.
    (d) April 2, 2016: extinguishment of 6,000 bonds. (No reversing entries made.)

5 6 **P14-11 (Modification of Debt)** Daniel Perkins is the sole shareholder of Perkins Inc., which is currently under protection of the U.S. bankruptcy court. As a "debtor in possession," he has negotiated the following revised loan agreement with United Bank. Perkins Inc.'s $600,000, 12%, 10-year note was refinanced with a $600,000, 5%, 10-year note. Perkins has a market rate of interest of 15%.

Instructions

    (a) What is the accounting nature of this transaction?
    (b) Prepare the journal entry to record this refinancing on the books of Perkins Inc.

5 6 **P14-12 (Modification of Note under Different Circumstances)** Halvor Corporation is having financial difficulty and therefore has asked Frontenac National Bank to restructure its $5 million note outstanding. The present note has 3 years remaining and pays a current rate of interest of 10%. The present market rate for a loan of this nature is 12%. The note was issued at its face value.

Instructions

Presented below are three independent situations. Prepare the journal entry that Halvor would make for each of these restructurings.

    (a) Frontenac National Bank agrees to take an equity interest in Halvor by accepting ordinary shares valued at $3,700,000 in exchange for relinquishing its claim on this note. The ordinary shares have a par value of $1,700,000.
    (b) Frontenac National Bank agrees to accept land in exchange for relinquishing its claim on this note. The land has a book value of $3,250,000 and a fair value of $4,000,000.
    (c) Frontenac National Bank agrees to modify the terms of the note, indicating that Halvor does not have to pay any interest on the note over the 3-year period.

6 **P14-13 (Debtor/Creditor Entries for Continuation of Debt with New Effective Interest)** Crocker Corp. owes D. Yaeger Corp. a 10-year, 10% note in the amount of £330,000 plus £33,000 of accrued interest. The note is due today, December 31, 2015. Because Crocker Corp. is in financial trouble, D. Yaeger Corp. agrees to forgive the accrued interest, £30,000 of the principal and to extend the maturity date to December 31, 2018. Interest at 10% of revised principal will continue to be due on 12/31 each year. Given Crocker's financial difficulties, the market rate for its loans is 12%.

Instructions

    (a) Prepare the amortization schedule for the years 2015 through 2018.
    (b) Prepare all the necessary journal entries on the books of Crocker Corp. for the years 2015, 2016, and 2017.

P14-14 (Comprehensive Problem: Issuance, Classification, Reporting) Presented below are three independent situations.

Instructions

(a) On January 1, 2015, Langley Co. issued 9% bonds with a face value of $700,000 for $656,992 to yield 10%. The bonds are dated January 1, 2015, and pay interest annually. What amount is reported for interest expense in 2015 related to these bonds?

(b) Tweedie Building Co. has a number of long-term bonds outstanding at December 31, 2015. These long-term bonds have the following sinking fund requirements and maturities for the next 6 years.

	Sinking Fund	Maturities
2016	$300,000	$100,000
2017	100,000	250,000
2018	100,000	100,000
2019	200,000	—
2020	200,000	150,000
2021	200,000	100,000

Indicate how this information should be reported in the financial statements at December 31, 2015.

(c) In the long-term debt structure of Beckford Inc., the following three bonds were reported: mortgage bonds payable $10,000,000; collateral trust bonds $5,000,000; bonds maturing in installments, secured by plant equipment $4,000,000. Determine the total amount, if any, of debenture bonds outstanding.

CONCEPTS FOR ANALYSIS

CA14-1 (Bond Theory: Statement of Financial Position Presentations, Interest Rate, Premium) On January 1, 2016, Nichols Company issued for $1,085,800 its 20-year, 11% bonds that have a maturity value of $1,000,000 and pay interest semiannually on January 1 and July 1. Bond issue costs were not material in amount. Below are three presentations of the non-current liability section of the statement of financial position that might be used for these bonds at the issue date.

1. Bonds payable (maturing January 1, 2036)	$1,085,800
2. Bonds payable—principal (face value $1,000,000 maturing January 1, 2036)	$ 142,050[a]
Bonds payable—interest (semiannual payment $55,000)	943,750[b]
Total bond liability	$1,085,800
3. Bonds payable—principal (maturing January 1, 2036)	$1,000,000
Bonds payable—interest ($55,000 per period for 40 periods)	2,200,000
Total bond liability	$3,200,000

[a]The present value of $1,000,000 due at the end of 40 (6-month) periods at the yield rate of 5% per period.
[b]The present value of $55,000 per period for 40 (6-month) periods at the yield rate of 5% per period.

Instructions

(a) Discuss the conceptual merit(s) of each of the date-of-issue statement of financial position presentations shown above for these bonds.

(b) Explain why investors would pay $1,085,800 for bonds that have a maturity value of only $1,000,000.

(c) Assuming that a discount rate is needed to compute the carrying value of the obligations arising from a bond issue at any date during the life of the bonds, discuss the conceptual merit(s) of using for this purpose:
   (1) The coupon or nominal rate.
   (2) The effective or yield rate at date of issue.

(d) If the obligations arising from these bonds are to be carried at their present value computed by means of the current market rate of interest, how would the bond valuation at dates subsequent to the date of issue be affected by an increase or a decrease in the market rate of interest?

CA14-2 (Various Non-Current Liability Conceptual Issues) Schrempf Company has completed a number of transactions during 2015. In January, the company purchased under contract a machine at a total price of €1,200,000, payable over 5 years with installments of €240,000 per year. The seller has considered the transaction as an installment sale with the title transferring to Schrempf at the time of the final payment.

On March 1, 2015, Schrempf issued €10 million of general revenue bonds priced at 99 with a coupon of 10% payable July 1 and January 1 of each of the next 10 years. The July 1 interest was paid and on December 30, the company transferred €1,000,000 to the trustee, Flagstad Company, for payment of the January 1, 2016, interest.

As the accountant for Schrempf Company, you have prepared the statement of financial position as of December 31, 2015, and have presented it to the president of the company. You are asked the following questions about it.

1. Why has depreciation been charged on equipment being purchased under contract? Title has not passed to the company as yet and, therefore, it is not our asset. Why should the company not show on the left side of the statement of financial position only the amount paid to date instead of showing the full contract price on the left side and the unpaid portion on the right side? After all, the seller considers the transaction an installment sale.

2. Bond interest is shown as a current liability. Did we not pay our trustee, Flagstad Company, the full amount of interest due this period?

Instructions

Outline your answers to these questions by writing a brief paragraph that will justify your treatment.

CA14-3 (Bond Theory: Price, Presentation, and Retirement) On March 1, 2016, Sealy Company sold its 5-year, £1,000 face value, 9% bonds dated March 1, 2016, at an effective annual interest rate (yield) of 11%. Interest is payable semiannually, and the first interest payment date is September 1, 2016. Sealy uses the effective-interest method of amortization. The bonds can be called by Sealy at 101 at any time on or after March 1, 2017.

Instructions

(a) (1) How would the selling price of the bond be determined?
   (2) Specify how all items related to the bonds would be presented in a statement of financial position prepared immediately after the bond issue was sold.
(b) What items related to the bond issue would be included in Sealy's 2016 income statement, and how would each be determined?
(c) Would the amount of bond discount amortization using the effective-interest method of amortization be lower in the second or third year of the life of the bond issue? Why?
(d) Assuming that the bonds were called in and extinguished on March 1, 2017, how should Sealy report the retirement of the bonds on the 2017 income statement?

CA14-4 (Bond Theory: Amortization and Gain or Loss Recognition)
Part I: The required method of amortizing a premium or discount on issuance of bonds is the effective-interest method.

Instructions

How is amortization computed using the effective-interest method, and why and how do amounts obtained using the effective-interest method provide financial statement readers useful information about the cost of borrowing?

Part II: Gains or losses from the early extinguishment of debt that is refunded can theoretically be accounted for in three ways:

1. Amortized over remaining life of old debt.
2. Amortized over the life of the new debt issue.
3. Recognized in the period of extinguishment.

Instructions

(a) Develop supporting arguments for each of the three theoretical methods of accounting for gains and losses from the early extinguishment of debt.
(b) Which of the methods above is generally accepted under IFRS and how should the appropriate amount of gain or loss be shown in a company's financial statements?

CA14-5 (Off-Balance-Sheet Financing) Matt Ryan Corporation is interested in building its own soda can manufacturing plant adjacent to its existing plant in Partyville, Kansas. The objective would be to ensure a steady supply of cans at a stable price and to minimize transportation costs. However, the company has been experiencing some financial problems and has been reluctant to borrow any additional cash to fund the project. The company is not concerned with the cash flow problems of making payments but rather with the impact of adding ladditional long-term debt to its statement of financial position.

The president of Ryan, Andy Newlin, approached the president of the Aluminum Can Company (ACC), its major supplier, to see if some agreement could be reached. ACC was anxious to work out an arrangement since it seemed inevitable that Ryan would begin its own can production. Aluminum Can Company could not afford to lose the account.

After some discussion, a two-part plan was worked out. First, ACC was to construct the plant on Ryan's land adjacent to the existing plant. Second, Ryan would sign a 20-year purchase agreement. Under the purchase agreement, Ryan would express its intention to buy all of its cans from ACC, paying a unit price which at normal capacity would cover labor and material, an operating management fee, and the debt service requirements on the plant. The expected unit price, if transportation costs are taken into consideration, is lower than current market. If Ryan did not take enough production in any one year and if the excess cans could not be sold at a high enough price on the open market, Ryan agrees to make up any cash shortfall so that ACC could make the payments on its debt. The bank will be willing to make a 20-year loan for the plant, taking the plant and the purchase agreement as collateral. At the end of 20 years, the plant is to become the property of Ryan.

Instructions

    (a) What are project financing arrangements using special purpose entities?

    (b) What are take-or-pay contracts?

    (c) Should Ryan record the plant as an asset together with the related obligation? If not, should Ryan record an asset relating to the future commitment?

    (d) What is meant by off-balance-sheet financing?

CA14-6 (Bond Issue) Donald Lennon is the president, founder, and majority owner of Wichita Medical Corporation, an emerging medical technology products company. Wichita is in dire need of additional capital to keep operating and to bring several promising products to final development, testing, and production. Donald, as owner of 51% of the outstanding shares, manages the company's operations. He places heavy emphasis on research and development and long-term growth. The other principal shareholder is Nina Friendly who, as a non-employee investor, owns 40% of the shares. Nina would like to deemphasize the R & D functions and emphasize the marketing function to maximize short-run sales and profits from existing products. She believes this strategy would raise the market price of Wichita's shares.

All of Donald's personal capital and borrowing power is tied up in his 51% share ownership. He knows that any offering of additional shares will dilute his controlling interest because he won't be able to participate in such an issuance. But, Nina has money and would likely buy enough shares to gain control of Wichita. She then would dictate the company's future direction, even if it meant replacing Donald as president and CEO.

The company already has considerable debt. Raising additional debt will be costly, will adversely affect Wichita's credit rating, and will increase the company's reported losses due to the growth in interest expense. Nina and the other minority shareholders express opposition to the assumption of additional debt, fearing the company will be pushed to the brink of bankruptcy. Wanting to maintain his control and to preserve the direction of "his" company, Donald is doing everything to avoid a share issuance and is contemplating a large issuance of bonds, even if it means the bonds are issued with a high effective-interest rate.

Instructions

    (a) Who are the stakeholders in this situation?

    (b) What are the ethical issues in this case?

    (c) What would you do if you were Donald?

USING YOUR JUDGMENT

Financial Reporting Problem

Marks and Spencer plc (M&S)

The financial statements of M&S (GBR) are presented in Appendix A. The company's complete annual report, including the notes to the financial statements, is available online.

Instructions

Refer to M&S's financial statements and the accompanying notes to answer the following questions.

(a) What cash outflow obligations related to the repayment of long-term debt does M&S have over the next 5 years?

(b) M&S indicates that it believes that it has the ability to meet business requirements in the foreseeable future. Prepare an assessment of its liquidity, solvency, and financial flexibility using ratio analysis.

Comparative Analysis Case

adidas and Puma

The financial statements of **adidas** (DEU) and **Puma** (DEU) are presented in Appendices B and C, respectively. The complete annual reports, including the notes to the financial statements, are available online.

Instructions

Use the companies' financial information to answer the following questions.

(a) Compute the debt to assets ratio and the times interest earned for these two companies. Comment on the quality of these two ratios for both adidas and Puma.

(b) What is the difference between the fair value and the historical cost (carrying amount) of each company's borrowings at year-end 2012? Why might a difference exist in these two amounts?

(c) Do these companies have debt issued in foreign countries? Speculate as to why these companies may use foreign debt to finance their operations. What risks are involved in this strategy, and how might they adjust for this risk?

Financial Statement Analysis Cases

Case 1 Commonwealth Edison Co.

The following article about **Commonwealth Edison Co.** (USA) appeared in the *Wall Street Journal*.

> **Bond Markets**
> *Giant Commonwealth Edison Issue Hits Resale Market With $70 Million Left Over*
> NEW YORK—Commonwealth Edison Co.'s slow-selling new 9¼% bonds were tossed onto the resale market at a reduced price with about $70 million still available from the $200 million offered Thursday, dealers said.
>
> The Chicago utility's bonds, rated double-A by Moody's and double-A-minus by Standard & Poor's, originally had been priced at 99.803, to yield 9.3% in 5 years. They were marked down yesterday the equivalent of about $5.50 for each $1,000 face amount, to about 99.25, where their yield jumped to 9.45%.

Instructions

(a) How will the development above affect the accounting for Commonwealth Edison's bond issue?

(b) Provide several possible explanations for the markdown and the slow sale of Commonwealth Edison's bonds.

Case 2 Eurotec

Consider the following events relating to Eurotec's long-term debt in a recent year.

1. The company decided on February 1 to refinance €500 million in short-term 7.4% debt to make it long-term 6%.

2. €780 million of long-term zero-coupon bonds with an effective-interest rate of 10.1% matured July 1 and were paid.

3. On October 1, the company issued €250 million in Australian dollars 6.3% bonds at 102 and €95 million in Italian lira 11.4% bonds at 99.

4. The company holds €100 million in perpetual foreign interest payment bonds that were issued in 1989 and presently have a rate of interest of 5.3%. These bonds are called perpetual because they have no stated due date. Instead, at the end of every 10-year period after the bond's issuance, the bondholders and Eurotec have the option of redeeming the bonds. If either party desires to redeem the bonds, the bonds must be redeemed. If the bonds are not redeemed, a new interest rate is set, based on the

then-prevailing interest rate for 10-year bonds. The company does not intend to cause redemption of the bonds but will reclassify this debt to current next year since the bondholders could decide to redeem the bonds.

Instructions

(a) Consider event 1. What are some of the reasons the company may have decided to refinance this short-term debt, besides lowering the interest rate?

(b) What do you think are the benefits to the investor in purchasing zero-coupon bonds, such as those described in event 2? What journal entry would be required to record the payment of these bonds? If financial statements are prepared each December 31, in which year would the bonds have been included in current liabilities?

(c) Make the journal entry to record the bond issue described in event 3. Note that the bonds were issued on the same day, yet one was issued at a premium and the other at a discount. What are some of the reasons that this may have happened?

(d) What are the benefits to Eurotec in having perpetual bonds as described in event 4? Suppose that in the current year, the bonds are not redeemed and the interest rate is adjusted to 6% from 7.5%. Make all necessary journal entries to record the renewal of the bonds and the change in rate.

Accounting, Analysis, and Principles

The following information is taken from the 2015 annual report of Bugant, Inc. Bugant's fiscal year ends December 31 of each year.

Bugant, Inc.
Statement of Financial Position
December 31, 2015

Assets

Plant and equipment (net of accumulated depreciation of €160)		€1,840
Inventory	€1,800	
Cash	450	
Total current assets		2,250
Total assets		**€4,090**

Equity

Share capital	€1,500
Retained earnings	1,164

Liabilities

Bonds payable (net of discount)	1,426
Total equity and liabilities	**€4,090**

Note X: Long-Term Debt
On January 1, 2014, Bugant issued bonds with face value of €1,500 and coupon rate equal to 10%. The bonds were issued to yield 12% and mature on January 1, 2019.

Additional information concerning 2016 is as follows.

1. Sales were €2,922, all for cash.

2. Purchases were €2,000, all paid in cash.

3. Salaries were €700, all paid in cash.

4. Plant and equipment was originally purchased for €2,000 and is depreciated on a straight-line basis over a 25-year life with no residual value.

5. Ending inventory was €1,900.

6. Cash dividends of €100 were declared and paid by Bugant.

7. Ignore taxes.

8. The market rate of interest on bonds of similar risk was 16% during all of 2016.

9. Interest on the bonds is paid semiannually each June 30 and December 31.

Accounting

Prepare an income statement for Bugant, Inc. for the year ending December 31, 2016, and a statement of financial position at December 31, 2016. Assume semiannual compounding.

Analysis

Use common ratios for analysis of long-term debt to assess Bugant's long-run solvency. Has Bugant's solvency changed much from 2015 to 2016? Bugant's net income in 2015 was €550 and interest expense was €169.39.

Principles

Recently, the FASB and the IASB allowed companies the option of recognizing in their financial statements the fair values of their long-term debt. That is, companies have the option to change the statement of financial position value of their long-term debt to the debt's fair (or market) value and report the change in statement of financial position value as a gain or loss in income. In terms of the qualitative characteristics of accounting information (Chapter 2), briefly describe the potential trade-off(s) involved in reporting long-term debt at its fair value.

IFRS BRIDGE TO THE PROFESSION

Professional Research

Wie Company has been operating for just 2 years, producing specialty golf equipment for women golfers. To date, the company has been able to finance its successful operations with investments from its principal owner, Michelle Wie, and cash flows from operations. However, current expansion plans will require some borrowing to expand the company's production line.

As part of the expansion plan, Wie is contemplating a borrowing on a note payable or issuance of bonds. In the past, the company has had little need for external borrowing so the management team has a number of questions concerning the accounting for these new non-current liabilities. They have asked you to conduct some research on this topic.

Instructions

Access the IFRS authoritative literature at the IASB website (*http://eifrs.iasb.org/*) (you may register for free eIFRS access at this site). When you have accessed the documents, you can use the search tool in your Internet browser to respond to the following questions. (Provide paragraph citations.)

(a) With respect to a decision of issuing notes or bonds, management is aware of certain costs (e.g., printing, marketing, and selling) associated with a bond issue. How will these costs affect Wie's reported earnings in the year of issue and while the bonds are outstanding?

(b) If all goes well with the plant expansion, the financial performance of Wie Company could dramatically improve. As a result, Wie's market rate of interest (which is currently around 12%) could decline. This raises the possibility of retiring or exchanging the debt, in order to get a lower borrowing rate. How would such a debt extinguishment be accounted for?

Professional Simulation

In this simulation, you are asked to address questions related to the accounting for non-current liabilities. Prepare responses to all parts.

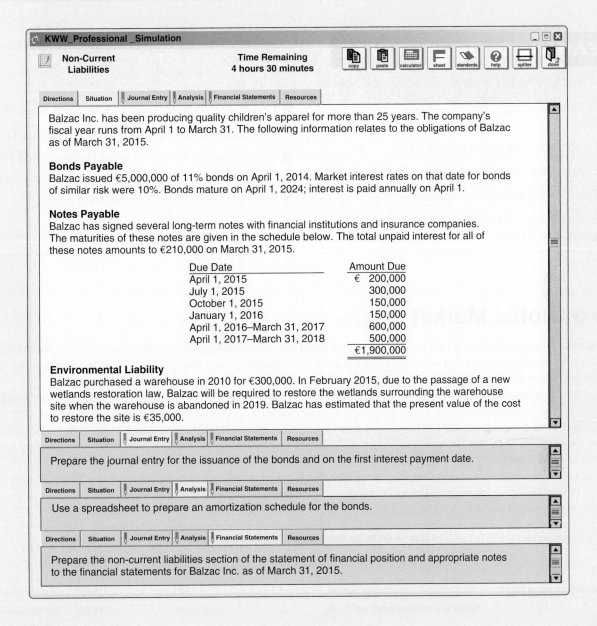

KWW_Professional _Simulation

| Non-Current Liabilities | Time Remaining 4 hours 30 minutes | copy paste calculator sheet standards help splitter done |

| Directions | Situation | Journal Entry | Analysis | Financial Statements | Resources |

Balzac Inc. has been producing quality children's apparel for more than 25 years. The company's fiscal year runs from April 1 to March 31. The following information relates to the obligations of Balzac as of March 31, 2015.

Bonds Payable
Balzac issued €5,000,000 of 11% bonds on April 1, 2014. Market interest rates on that date for bonds of similar risk were 10%. Bonds mature on April 1, 2024; interest is paid annually on April 1.

Notes Payable
Balzac has signed several long-term notes with financial institutions and insurance companies. The maturities of these notes are given in the schedule below. The total unpaid interest for all of these notes amounts to €210,000 on March 31, 2015.

Due Date	Amount Due
April 1, 2015	€ 200,000
July 1, 2015	300,000
October 1, 2015	150,000
January 1, 2016	150,000
April 1, 2016–March 31, 2017	600,000
April 1, 2017–March 31, 2018	500,000
	€1,900,000

Environmental Liability
Balzac purchased a warehouse in 2010 for €300,000. In February 2015, due to the passage of a new wetlands restoration law, Balzac will be required to restore the wetlands surrounding the warehouse site when the warehouse is abandoned in 2019. Balzac has estimated that the present value of the cost to restore the site is €35,000.

| Directions | Situation | Journal Entry | Analysis | Financial Statements | Resources |

Prepare the journal entry for the issuance of the bonds and on the first interest payment date.

| Directions | Situation | Journal Entry | Analysis | Financial Statements | Resources |

Use a spreadsheet to prepare an amortization schedule for the bonds.

| Directions | Situation | Journal Entry | Analysis | Financial Statements | Resources |

Prepare the non-current liabilities section of the statement of financial position and appropriate notes to the financial statements for Balzac Inc. as of March 31, 2015.

Remember to check the book's companion website, at www.wiley.com/ college/kieso, to find additional resources for this chapter.

15 Equity

It's a Global Market

As discussed in earlier chapters, we are moving toward one set of global financial reporting standards and one "common language" for financial information. This change will probably lead to more consolidation of our capital markets. To understand how quickly the global financial world is changing, let's examine a few trends occurring on securities exchanges around the world.

In 2007, the New York Stock Exchange (NYSE) merged with Paris-based Euronext, creating the world's first transatlantic securities exchange. Since the merger, NYSE Euronext has grown to be the world's largest exchange group, with over 8,000 listed issuers representing over 30 percent of the world's trading volume. Similarly, NASDAQ, the world's largest electronic securities market, merged with OMX, the Nordic market operator. This electronic exchange has 3,300 listed issuers, with a market value of approximately $5.9 trillion.

Another reason behind the strong impetus for international financial reporting standards can be found in recent initial public offerings (IPOs). The emerging markets are driving the global IPO market, as shown in the following table.

		Top 10 IPOs by Amount of Capital Raised, 2012			
Ranking	Issue Month	Issuer Name	Industry	Capital Raised (US$b)	Exchange(s)
1	May	Glencore International plc (CHE)	Materials	10.0	London, Hong Kong
2	March	Hutchison Port Holdings Trust (CHN)	Industrials	5.5	Singapore
3	July	Bankia (ESP)	Financials	4.4	Madrid
4	March	HCA Holdings Inc. (USA)	Healthcare	4.4	NYSE
5	February	Kinder Morgan Inc. (USA)	Energy	3.3	NYSE
6	June	Prada SpA (ITA)	Retail	2.5	NYSE
7	October	Sinohydro Group Ltd. (CHN)	Energy	2.1	Shanghai
8	May	Shanghai Pharmaceuticals Holding Co. Ltd. (CHN)	Healthcare	2.1	Hong Kong
9	December	Chow Tai Fook Jewellery Co. Ltd. (HKG)	Consumer products	2.0	Hong Kong
10	July	JSW SA (POL)	Materials	1.9	Warsaw

As another example, Brazil, Russia, India, and China—often referred to as the *BRIC countries*—generated 48 percent of total IPO proceeds in 2011, compared to 41 percent for the BRIC countries in 2007.

Finally, consider the international sales of some large corporations: **Bombardier** (CAN) now has 96 percent of its sales overseas, **Boeing** (USA) in a recent year sold more planes overseas than in the United States, and **Hyundai**'s (KOR) vehicle revenues are over 88 percent in overseas markets.

Source: Ernst and Young, *Global IPO Trends Report* (2012).

CONCEPTUAL FOCUS

> See the **Underlying Concepts** on pages 706 and 711.

INTERNATIONAL FOCUS

> Read the **Global Accounting Insights** on pages 729–730 for a discussion of non-IFRS financial reporting for equity.

PREVIEW OF CHAPTER 15

As our opening story indicates, the growth of global equity capital markets indicates that investors around the world need useful information. In this chapter, we explain the accounting issues related to the equity of a corporation. The content and organization of the chapter are as follows.

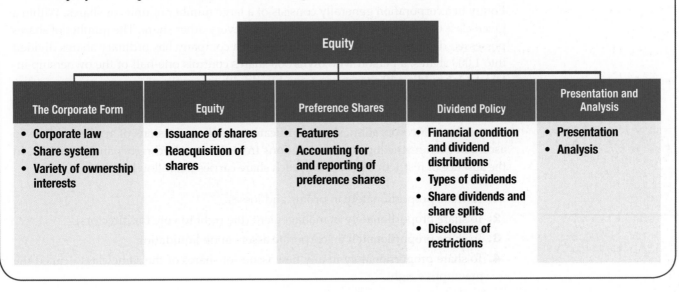

Equity				
The Corporate Form	**Equity**	**Preference Shares**	**Dividend Policy**	**Presentation and Analysis**
• **Corporate law** • **Share system** • **Variety of ownership interests**	• **Issuance of shares** • **Reacquisition of shares**	• **Features** • **Accounting for and reporting of preference shares**	• **Financial condition and dividend distributions** • **Types of dividends** • **Share dividends and share splits** • **Disclosure of restrictions**	• **Presentation** • **Analysis**

THE CORPORATE FORM OF ORGANIZATION

LEARNING OBJECTIVE **1**
Discuss the characteristics of the corporate form of organization.

Of the three **primary forms of business organization**—the proprietorship, the partnership, and the corporation—the corporate form dominates. The corporation is by far the leader in terms of the aggregate amount of resources controlled, goods and services produced, and people employed. Although the corporate form has a number of advantages (as well as disadvantages) over the other two forms, its principal benefit is its facility for attracting and accumulating large amounts of capital.

The special characteristics of the corporate form that affect accounting include:

1. Influence of corporate law.

2. Use of the share system.

3. Development of a variety of ownership interests.

Corporate Law

Anyone who wishes to establish a corporation must generally submit **articles of incorporation** to the appropriate governmental agency for the country in which incorporation is desired. After fulfilling requirements, the governmental agency issues a corporation charter, thereby recognizing the company as a legal entity. Regardless of the number of countries in which a corporation has operating divisions, it is incorporated in only one country. It is to the company's advantage to incorporate where laws favor the corporate form of business organization.

Many governments have their own business incorporation act. The accounting for equity follows the provisions of these acts. In many cases, the laws are complex and vary both in their provisions and in their definitions of certain terms. Some laws fail to define technical terms. As a result, terms often have one meaning in one country and another meaning in a different country. These problems may be further compounded because legal authorities often interpret the effects and restrictions of the laws differently.

Share System

Equity in a corporation generally consists of a large number of units or shares. Within a given class of shares, each share exactly equals every other share. The number of shares possessed determines each owner's interest. If a company has ordinary shares divided into 1,000 shares, a person who owns 500 shares controls one-half of the ownership interest. One holding 10 shares has a one-hundredth interest.

Each share has certain rights and privileges. Only by special contract can a company restrict these rights and privileges at the time it issues the shares. Owners must examine the articles of incorporation, share certificates, and the provisions of applicable laws to ascertain such restrictions on or variations from the standard rights and privileges. In the absence of restrictive provisions, each share carries the following rights:

1. To share proportionately in profits and losses.

2. To share proportionately in management (the right to vote for directors).

3. To share proportionately in corporate assets upon liquidation.

4. To share proportionately in any new issues of shares of the same class—called the preemptive right.[1]

---

[1]This privilege is referred to as a **share right** or **warrant**. The warrants issued in these situations are of short duration, unlike the warrants issued with other securities.

The first three rights are self-explanatory. The last right is used to protect each shareholder's proportional interest in the company. **The preemptive right protects an existing shareholder from involuntary dilution of ownership interest.** Without this right, shareholders might find their interest reduced by the issuance of additional shares without their knowledge and at prices unfavorable to them. However, many corporations have eliminated the preemptive right. Why? Because this right makes it inconvenient for corporations to issue large amounts of additional shares, as they frequently do in acquiring other companies.

The share system easily allows one individual to transfer an interest in a company to another investor. For example, individuals owning shares in Páo de Acucar (BRA) **may sell them to others at any time and at any price without obtaining the consent of the company or other shareholders**. Each share is personal property of the owner, who may dispose of it at will. Páo de Acucar simply maintains a list or subsidiary ledger of shareholders as a guide to dividend payments, issuance of share rights, voting proxies, and the like. Because owners freely and frequently transfer shares, Páo de Acucar must revise the subsidiary ledger of shareholders periodically, generally in advance of every dividend payment or shareholders' meeting.

In addition, the major securities exchanges require ownership controls that the typical corporation finds uneconomic to provide. Thus, corporations often use **registrars and transfer agents** who specialize in performing services for recording and transferring shares.

Variety of Ownership Interests

In every corporation, one class of shares must represent the basic ownership interest. That class of shares is called ordinary. Ordinary shares represent the residual corporate interest that bears the ultimate risks of loss and receives the benefits of success. They are guaranteed neither dividends nor assets upon dissolution. But ordinary shareholders generally control the management of the corporation and tend to profit most if the company is successful. In the event that a corporation has only one authorized issue of shares, that issue is by definition ordinary shares, whether so designated in the charter or not.

In an effort to broaden investor appeal, corporations may offer two or more classes of shares, each with different rights or privileges. In the preceding section, we pointed out that each share of a given issue has the same four inherent rights as other shares of the same issue. By special contracts between the corporation and its shareholders, however, the shareholder may sacrifice certain of these rights in return for other special rights or privileges. Thus special classes of shares, usually called preference shares, are created. In return for any special preference, the preference shareholder always sacrifices some of the inherent rights of ordinary shareholders.

A common type of preference is to give preference shareholders a prior claim on earnings. The corporation thus assures them a dividend, usually at a stated rate, before it distributes any amount to the ordinary shareholders. In return for this preference, the preference shareholders may sacrifice their right to a voice in management or their right to share in profits beyond the stated rate.

What do the numbers mean? A CLASS (B) ACT

Some companies grant preferences to different shareholders by issuing different classes of ordinary shares. For a family-controlled company, issuing newer classes of lower or non-voting shares (referred to as B shares) effectively creates currency for acquisitions, increases liquidity, or puts a public value on the company without diluting the family's powers. For example, the B shareholders at Vodafone (GBR) only get a vote if the company is to be dissolved. The following are some notable companies with two-tiered shares.

Company	Votes Controlled by Class B Shareholders
Vodafone (GBR)	0%
Google (USA)	78%
Air Canada (CAN)	(Only Canadian citizens can vote)
Ford (USA)	40%
Facebook (USA)	43%
Bombardier (CAN)	0%

Some trading exchanges impose rules to protect minority investors. For example, the FTSE requires family owners to hold no more than 50 percent of voting shares. The Hong Kong exchange prohibits dual-share structures. As a result of these rules, companies like **Alibaba Group** (CHN) and **Manchester United** (GBR) that wanted to trade on the Hong Kong exchange are looking to other markets on which to list their shares. For most retail investors, voting rights are not that important. But, investors must carefully compare the apparent bargain prices for some classes of shares—they may end up as second-class citizens with no voting rights.

Sources: Adapted from Andy Serwer, "Dual-Listed Companies Aren't Fair or Balanced," *Fortune* (September 20, 2004), p. 83; Alex Halperin, "A Class (B) Act," *BusinessWeek* (May 28, 2007), p. 12; and R. Sullivan, "Dual Share Structure Goes under Spotlight," *Financial Times* (November 1, 2011).

EQUITY

LEARNING OBJECTIVE 2

Identify the key components of equity.

IFRS

See the Authoritative Literature section (page 735).

Equity is the residual interest in the assets of the company after deducting all liabilities. **[1]** Equity is often referred to as shareholders' equity, stockholders' equity, or corporate capital. Equity is often subclassified on the statement of financial position into the following categories (as discussed in Chapter 5).

1. Share capital.
2. Share premium.
3. Retained earnings.
4. Accumulated other comprehensive income.
5. Treasury shares.
6. Non-controlling interest (minority interest).

Such classifications help financial statement users to better understand the legal or other restrictions related to the ability of the company to pay dividends or otherwise use its equity for certain defined purposes.

Underlying Concepts

According to the Conceptual Framework, equity is defined as a residual, based on the net of assets minus liabilities.

Companies often make a distinction between contributed capital (paid-in capital) and earned capital. **Contributed (paid-in) capital** is the total amount paid in on capital shares—the amount provided by shareholders to the corporation for use in the business. Contributed capital includes items such as the par value of all outstanding shares and premiums less discounts on issuance. **Earned capital** is the capital that develops from profitable operations. It consists of all undistributed income that remains invested in the company. **Retained earnings** represents the earned capital of the company.

As indicated above, equity is a **residual interest** and therefore its value is derived from the amount of the corporations' assets and liabilities. Only in unusual cases will a company's equity equal the total fair value of its shares. For example, **BMW** (DEU) recently had total equity of €30,295 million and a market capitalization of €45,000 million. BMW's equity represents the net contributions from shareholders (from both majority and minority shareholders) plus retained earnings and accumulated other comprehensive income. As a residual interest, its equity has no existence apart from the assets and liabilities of BMW—equity equals net assets. Equity is not a claim to specific assets but a claim against a portion of the total assets. Its amount is not specified or fixed; it depends on BMW's profitability. Equity grows if the company is profitable. It shrinks, or may disappear entirely, if BMW loses money.

Issuance of Shares

In issuing shares, companies follow these procedures. First, the applicable governmental agency must authorize the shares, generally in a certificate of incorporation or charter. Next, the corporation offers shares for sale, entering into contracts to sell these shares. Then, after receiving amounts for the shares, the corporation issues the shares. The corporation generally makes no entry in the general ledger accounts when it receives its share authorization from the jurisdiction of incorporation.

◀3 LEARNING OBJECTIVE

Explain the accounting procedures for issuing shares.

We discuss the accounting problems involved in the issuance of shares under the following topics.

1. Accounting for par value shares.

2. Accounting for no-par shares.

3. Accounting for shares issued in combination with other securities (lump-sum sales).

4. Accounting for shares issued in non-cash transactions.

5. Accounting for costs of issuing shares.

Par Value Shares

The par value of a share has no relationship to its fair value. At present, the par value associated with most ordinary share issuances is very low. For example, par value for **China Railway Construction Corporation** (CHN) is ¥1.00, and for **Nestlé S.A.** (CHE) is CHF1. Low par values help companies avoid the contingent liability associated with shares sold below par.[2]

To show the required information for issuance of par value shares, corporations maintain accounts for each class of shares as follows.

1. *Preference Shares or Ordinary Shares.* Together, these two share accounts reflect the par value of the corporation's issued shares. The company credits these accounts when it originally issues the shares. It makes no additional entries in these accounts unless it issues additional shares or retires them.

2. *Share Premium.* The **Share Premium** account indicates any excess over par value paid in by shareholders in return for the shares issued to them. Once paid in, the excess over par becomes a part of the corporation's share premium. The individual shareholder has no greater claim on the excess paid in than all other holders of the same class of shares.

No-Par Shares

Many countries permit the issuance of shares without par value, called **no-par shares**. The reasons for issuance of no-par shares are twofold. First, issuance of no-par shares **avoids the contingent liability** (see footnote 2) that might occur if the corporation issued par value shares at a discount. Second, some confusion exists over the relationship (or rather the absence of a relationship) between the par value and fair value. If shares have no par value, **the questionable treatment of using par value as a basis for fair value never arises**. This is particularly advantageous whenever issuing shares for property items such as tangible or intangible fixed assets.

---

[2]Companies rarely, if ever, issue shares at a value below par value. The reason: The corporation may call on the original purchaser or the current holder of the shares issued below par to pay in the amount of the discount to prevent creditors from sustaining a loss upon liquidation of the corporation.

A major disadvantage of no-par shares is that some countries levy a high tax on these issues. In addition, in some countries the total issue price for no-par shares may be considered legal capital, which could reduce the flexibility in paying dividends.

Corporations sell no-par shares, like par value shares, for whatever price they will bring. However, unlike par value shares, corporations issue them without a premium or a discount. The exact amount received represents the credit to ordinary or preference shares. For example, Video Electronics Corporation is organized with 10,000 ordinary shares authorized without par value. Video Electronics makes only a memorandum entry for the authorization, inasmuch as no amount is involved. If Video Electronics then issues 500 shares for cash at €10 per share, it makes the following entry:

Cash	5,000	
Share Capital—Ordinary		5,000

If it issues another 500 shares for €11 per share, Video Electronics makes this entry:

Cash	5,500	
Share Capital—Ordinary		5,500

True no-par shares should be carried in the accounts at issue price without any share premium reported. But some countries require that no-par shares have a **stated value**. The stated value is a minimum value below which a company cannot issue it. Thus, instead of being no-par shares, such stated-value shares become, in effect, shares with a very low par value. Therefore, such shares with very low stated values are open to all the criticism and abuses that first encouraged the development of no-par shares.

If no-par shares have a stated value of €5 per share but sell for €11, all such amounts in excess of €5 are recorded as share premium, which in many jurisdictions is fully or partially available for dividends. Thus, no-par value shares, with a low stated value, permit a new corporation to commence its operations with share premium that may exceed its stated capital. For example, if a company issued 1,000 of the shares with a €5 stated value at €15 per share for cash, it makes the following entry.

Cash	15,000	
Share Capital—Ordinary		5,000
Share Premium—Ordinary		10,000

Most corporations account for no-par shares with a stated value as if they were par value shares with par equal to the stated value.

Shares Issued with Other Securities (Lump-Sum Sales)

Generally, corporations sell classes of shares separately from one another. The reason to do so is to track the proceeds relative to each class as well as relative to each lot. Occasionally, a corporation issues two or more classes of securities for a single payment or lump sum, in the acquisition of another company. The accounting problem in such lump-sum sales is how to allocate the proceeds among the several classes of securities. Companies use one of two methods of allocation: (1) the proportional method and (2) the incremental method.

Proportional Method. If the fair value or other sound basis for determining relative value is available for each class of security, **the company allocates the lump sum received among the classes of securities on a proportional basis**. For instance, assume a company issues 1,000 shares of $10 stated value ordinary shares having a fair value of $20 a share and 1,000 shares of $10 par value preference shares having a fair value of $12 a share for a lump sum of $30,000. Illustration 15-1 shows how the company allocates the $30,000 to the two classes of shares.

Fair value of ordinary (1,000 × $20) =	$20,000
Fair value of preference (1,000 × $12) =	12,000
Aggregate fair value	$32,000
Allocated to ordinary: $\dfrac{\$20,000}{\$32,000} \times \$30,000 = \$18,750$	
Allocated to preference: $\dfrac{\$12,000}{\$32,000} \times \$30,000 = \$11,250$	
Total allocation	$30,000

Incremental Method. In instances where a company cannot determine the fair value of all classes of securities, it may use the incremental method. It uses the fair value of the securities as a basis for those classes that it knows, and allocates the remainder of the lump sum to the class for which it does not know the fair value. For instance, if a company issues 1,000 shares of $10 stated value ordinary shares having a fair value of $20 and 1,000 shares of $10 par value preference shares having no established fair value for a lump sum of $30,000, it allocates the $30,000 to the two classes as shown in Illustration 15-2.

Lump-sum receipt	$30,000
Allocated to ordinary (1,000 × $20)	(20,000)
Balance allocated to preference	$10,000

If a company cannot determine the fair value for any of the classes of shares involved in a lump-sum exchange, it may need to use other approaches. It may rely on an expert's appraisal. Or, if the company knows that one or more of the classes of securities issued will have a determinable fair value in the near future, it may use a best-estimate basis with the intent to adjust later upon establishment of the future fair value.

Shares Issued in Non-Cash Transactions

Accounting for the issuance of shares for property or services involves an issue of valuation. **The general rule is companies should record shares issued for services or property other than cash at the fair value of the goods or services received, unless that fair value cannot be measured reliably. If the fair value of the goods or services cannot be measured reliably, use the fair value of the shares issued. [2]**

If a company can readily determine both and the transaction results from an arm's-length exchange, there will probably be little difference in their fair values. In such cases, the basis for valuing the exchange should not matter.

If a company cannot readily determine either the fair value of the shares it issues or the property or services it receives, it should employ an appropriate valuation technique. Depending on available data, the valuation may be based on market transactions involving comparable assets or the use of discounted expected future cash flows. Companies should avoid the use of book, par, or stated values as a basis of valuation for these transactions.

A company may exchange unissued shares or treasury shares (issued shares that it has reacquired but not retired) for property or services. If it uses treasury shares and the fair value of the property or services cannot be reliably estimated, the cost of the treasury shares should not be considered the decisive factor in establishing the fair value of the property or services. Instead, it should use the fair value of the treasury shares to value the property or services.

The series of transactions shown in Illustration 15-3 indicate the procedure for recording the issuance of 10,000 shares of €10 par value ordinary shares for a patent for Marlowe Company, in various circumstances.

ILLUSTRATION 15-3
Treasury Share
Transactions

Marlowe cannot readily determine the fair value of the patent, but it knows the fair value of the shares is €140,000.		
Patents	140,000	
Share Capital—Ordinary (10,000 shares × €10 per share)		100,000
Share Premium—Ordinary		40,000

Marlowe cannot readily determine the fair value of the shares, but it determines the fair value of the patent is €150,000.		
Patents	150,000	
Share Capital—Ordinary (10,000 shares × €10 per share)		100,000
Share Premium—Ordinary		50,000

Marlowe cannot readily determine the fair value of the shares nor the fair value of the patent. An independent consultant values the patent at €125,000 based on discounted expected cash flows.		
Patents	125,000	
Share Capital—Ordinary (10,000 shares × €10 per share)		100,000
Share Premium—Ordinary		25,000

Generally, the board of directors has the power to set the value of non-cash transactions. However, boards sometimes abuse this power. The issuance of shares for property or services has resulted in cases of overstated corporate capital through intentional overvaluation of the property or services received. The overvaluation of equity resulting from inflated asset values creates **watered shares**. The corporation should eliminate the "water" by simply writing down the overvalued assets.

If, as a result of the issuance of shares for property or services, a corporation undervalues the recorded assets, it creates **secret reserves**. An understated corporate structure (secret reserve) may also result from other methods: excessive depreciation or amortization charges, expensing capital expenditures, excessive write-downs of inventories or receivables, or any other understatement of assets or overstatement of liabilities. An example of a liability overstatement is an excessive provision for estimated product warranties that ultimately results in an understatement of equity, thereby creating a secret reserve.

Costs of Issuing Shares

When a company like **Wesfarmers** (AUS) issues shares, it should report direct costs incurred to sell shares, such as underwriting costs, accounting and legal fees, printing costs, and taxes, as a reduction of the amounts paid in. Wesfarmers therefore debits issue costs to Share Premium because they are unrelated to corporate operations. In effect, **issue costs are a cost of financing**. As such, issue costs should reduce the proceeds received from the sale of the shares.

Wesfarmers should expense management salaries and other indirect costs related to the share issue because it is difficult to establish a relationship between these costs and the sale proceeds. In addition, Wesfarmers expenses recurring costs, primarily registrar and transfer agents' fees, as incurred.

Reacquisition of Shares

Companies often buy back their own shares. Corporations purchase their outstanding shares for several reasons:

4 **LEARNING OBJECTIVE**
Describe the accounting for treasury shares.

1. *To provide tax-efficient distributions of excess cash to shareholders.* Tax rates on sales of shares to the company by the shareholders are often much lower than the ordinary tax rate for many investors.

2. *To increase earnings per share and return on equity.* Reducing both shares outstanding and equity often enhances certain performance ratios. For example, Siemens (DEU) announced its €4 billion buyback as part of its efforts to improve profitability. However, strategies to hype performance measures might increase performance in the short-run, but these tactics add no real long-term value.

3. *To provide shares for employee compensation contracts or to meet potential merger needs.* Honeywell Inc. (USA) reported that it would use part of its purchase of one million ordinary shares for employee share option contracts. Other companies acquire shares to have them available for business acquisitions.

4. *To thwart takeover attempts or to reduce the number of shareholders.* By reducing the number of shares held by the public, existing owners and managements bar "outsiders" from gaining control or significant influence.

5. *To make a market in the shares.* As one company executive noted, "Our company is trying to establish a floor for its shares." Purchasing shares in the marketplace creates a demand. This may stabilize the share price or, in fact, increase it. For example, HTC (TWN) indicated its recent treasury share transaction was one of the options for boosting its sagging share price.

Some publicly held corporations have chosen to "go private," that is, to eliminate public (outside) ownership entirely by purchasing all of their outstanding shares. Companies often accomplish such a procedure through a **leveraged buyout (LBO)**, in which the company borrows money to finance the share repurchases.

After reacquiring shares, a company may either retire them or hold them in the treasury for reissue. If not retired, such shares are referred to as **treasury shares**. Technically, treasury shares are a corporation's own shares, reacquired after having been issued and fully paid.

Treasury shares are not an asset. When a company purchases treasury shares, a reduction occurs in both assets and equity. It is inappropriate to imply that a corporation can own a part of itself. A corporation may sell treasury shares to obtain funds, but that does not make treasury shares a statement of financial position asset. When a corporation buys back some of its own outstanding shares, it has not acquired an asset; the buyback reduces net assets.

The possession of treasury shares does not give the corporation the right to vote, to exercise preemptive rights as a shareholder, to receive cash dividends, or to receive assets upon corporate liquidation. **Treasury shares are essentially the same as unissued ordinary shares.** No one advocates classifying unissued ordinary shares as an asset in the statement of financial position.[3]

Underlying Concepts

As we indicated in Chapter 2, an asset should have probable future economic benefits. Treasury shares simply reduce ordinary shares outstanding.

---

[3]The possible justification for classifying these shares as assets is that the company will use them to liquidate a specific liability that appears on the statement of financial position.

Few company announcements are more beloved by investors than those that indicate a share buyback is in the offing. Following a lull in buybacks during the financial crisis, companies recently are increasing their buyback programs. For example, buybacks by the companies in the FTSE 100 increased 40 percent in 2007 before the crisis (spending £764.3 million to buy 4.7 percent of their own shares in a single week), with major companies such as BP (GBR), Royal Dutch Shell (NLD and GBR), and Burberry (GBR) making some of the bigger repurchases. In 2009, just £593 million was returned to shareholders through buyback schemes. But in 2012, U.K.-listed companies spent £12.4 billion on buying back shares, compared to the £5.9 billion they raised from the securities market through IPOs and rights issues.

Increases in buybacks are music to investors' ears because it indicates that executives at some of the companies have confidence that better times are ahead. The buys also show that cash reserves are healthy enough for companies to believe they not only have enough cash to cover their day-to-day functions but also enough to spare to allow for generous buybacks.

In fact, market experts often look to share buybacks as a buy signal. That strategy is not that surprising if you look at the performance of the companies that did buybacks. For example, in one study, buyback companies outperformed similar companies without buybacks by an average of 23 percent. In a recent three-year period, companies followed by BuybackLetter.com (USA) were up 16.4 percent, while the broader market index was up just 7.1 percent. Why the premium? Well, the conventional wisdom is that companies that buy back shares believe their shares are undervalued. Thus, analysts view the buyback announcement as an important piece of inside information about future company prospects.

Sources: "FTSE 100 Buy-Backs Leap 40%," *www.marketwatch.com* (August 22, 2007); and G. Howes, "FTSE 100 Share Buy-Backs on the Increase: Is This a Good Sign?" *Director of Finance Online* (05 February 2013).

Purchase of Treasury Shares

Companies use two general methods of handling treasury shares in the accounts: the cost method and the par value method. Both methods are generally acceptable.

- The **cost method** results in debiting the Treasury Shares account for the reacquisition cost and in reporting this account as a deduction from equity on the statement of financial position.
- The **par (stated) value method** records all transactions in treasury shares at their par value and reports the treasury shares as a deduction from share capital only.

No matter which method a company uses, most jurisdictions consider the cost of the treasury shares acquired as a restriction on retained earnings.

Because just about all companies use the cost method to account for treasury shares, we illustrate its use here. This method derives its name from the fact that a company maintains the Treasury Shares account at the cost of the shares purchased.[4] Under the cost method, the company debits the Treasury Shares account for the cost of the shares acquired. Upon reissuance of the shares, it credits the account for this same cost. The original price received for the shares does not affect the entries to record the acquisition and reissuance of the treasury shares.

To illustrate, assume that Pacific Company issued 100,000 shares of $1 par value ordinary shares at a price of $10 per share. In addition, it has retained earnings of $300,000. Illustration 15-4 shows the equity section on December 31, 2014, before purchase of treasury shares.

---

[4]If making numerous acquisitions of blocks of treasury shares at different prices, a company may use inventory costing methods—such as specific identification, average-cost, or FIFO—to identify the cost at date of reissuance.

ILLUSTRATION 15-4
Equity with No Treasury
Shares

Equity	
Share capital—ordinary, $1 par, 100,000 shares	
issued and outstanding	$ 100,000
Share premium—ordinary	900,000
Retained earnings	300,000
Total equity	$1,300,000

On January 20, 2015, Pacific acquires 10,000 of its shares at $11 per share. Pacific records the reacquisition as follows.

January 20, 2015

Treasury Shares	110,000	
Cash		110,000

Note that Pacific debits Treasury Shares for the cost of the shares purchased. The original account, Share Capital—Ordinary, is not affected because the number of issued shares does not change. The same is true for the Share Premium—Ordinary account. Pacific then deducts treasury shares to determine total equity.

Illustration 15-5 shows the equity section for Pacific after purchase of the treasury shares.

ILLUSTRATION 15-5
Equity with Treasury
Shares

Equity	
Share capital—ordinary, $1 par value, 100,000 shares	
issued and 90,000 outstanding	$ 100,000
Share premium—ordinary	900,000
Retained earnings	300,000
Less: Cost of treasury shares (10,000 shares)	110,000
Total equity	$1,190,000

Pacific subtracts the cost of the treasury shares from the total of share capital—ordinary, share premium—ordinary, and retained earnings. It therefore reduces equity. Many jurisdictions require a corporation to restrict retained earnings for the cost of treasury shares purchased. The restriction keeps intact the corporation's capital. When the corporation sells the treasury shares, it lifts the restriction.

Pacific discloses both the number of shares issued (100,000) and the number in the treasury (10,000). The difference is the number of shares outstanding (90,000). The term **outstanding shares** means the number of issued shares that shareholders own.

Sale of Treasury Shares

Companies usually reissue or retire treasury shares. When selling treasury shares, the accounting for the sale depends on the price. If the selling price of the treasury shares equals its cost, the company records the sale of the shares by debiting Cash and crediting Treasury Shares. In cases where the selling price of the treasury shares is not equal to cost, then accounting for treasury shares sold **above cost** differs from the accounting for treasury shares sold **below cost**. However, the sale of treasury shares either above or below cost increases both total assets and equity.

Sale of Treasury Shares above Cost. When the selling price of the treasury shares exceeds its cost, a company credits the difference to Share Premium—Treasury. To illustrate, assume that Pacific acquired 10,000 treasury shares at $11 per share. It now sells 1,000 shares at $15 per share on March 10. Pacific records the entry as follows.

March 10, 2015

Cash	15,000	
Treasury Shares		11,000
Share Premium—Treasury		4,000

There are two reasons why Pacific does not credit $4,000 to Gain on Sale of Treasury Shares. (1) Gains on sales occur when selling **assets**; treasury shares are not an asset. (2) A gain or loss should not be recognized from share transactions with its own shareholders. Thus, Pacific should not include share premium arising from the sale of treasury shares in the measurement of net income. Instead, it lists share premium from treasury shares separately on the statement of financial position.

Sale of Treasury Shares below Cost. When a corporation sells treasury shares below its cost, it usually debits the excess of the cost over selling price to Share Premium—Treasury. Thus, if Pacific sells an additional 1,000 treasury shares on March 21 at $8 per share, it records the sale as follows.

March 21, 2015

Cash	8,000	
Share Premium—Treasury	3,000	
Treasury Shares		11,000

We can make several observations based on the two sale entries (sale above cost and sale below cost). (1) Pacific credits Treasury Shares at cost in each entry. (2) Pacific uses Share Premium—Treasury for the difference between the cost and the resale price of the shares. (3) Neither entry affects Share Capital—Ordinary.

After eliminating the credit balance in Share Premium—Treasury, the corporation debits any additional excess of cost over selling price to Retained Earnings. To illustrate, assume that Pacific sells an additional 1,000 shares at $8 per share on April 10. Illustration 15-6 shows the balance in the Share Premium—Treasury account (before the April 10 purchase).

ILLUSTRATION 15-6
Treasury Share Transactions in Share Premium—Treasury Account

		Share Premium—Treasury			
Mar. 21	3,000		Mar. 10	4,000	
			Balance	1,000	

In this case, Pacific debits $1,000 of the excess to Share Premium—Treasury. It debits the remainder to Retained Earnings. The entry is:

April 10, 2015

Cash	8,000	
Share Premium—Treasury	1,000	
Retained Earnings	2,000	
Treasury Shares		11,000

Retiring Treasury Shares

The board of directors may approve the retirement of treasury shares. This decision results in cancellation of the treasury shares and a reduction in the number of issued shares. Retired treasury shares have the status of authorized and unissued shares. The accounting effects are similar to the sale of treasury shares except that corporations debit **applicable equity accounts related to the retired shares** instead of cash. For example, if a corporation originally sells the shares at par, it debits Share Capital—Ordinary for the par value per share. If it originally sells the shares at $3 above par value, it also debits Share Premium—Ordinary for $3 per share at retirement.

What do the numbers mean?   **BUYBACK VOLATILITY**

As indicated in the "What do the numbers mean?" box on page 712, we have seen wide swings in share repurchase activity. That is, following a long run of high buyback activity, share repurchases tumbled in 2008–2009 and since then have bounced back. Why the ups and downs? When times are good, companies are optimistic and can spare the cash needed for the buybacks. What about in bad times? One experienced analyst reasoned that many companies cut back on buybacks in a bid to boost liquidity and preserve cash in the face of tight credit markets. Indeed, while cash levels can rise to record levels as companies cut spending in a host of areas, the reluctance of many companies to spend money on share repurchases reflects what another analyst called a "storm-center mentality." Financial officers, watching companies teeter because of arid credit conditions and slowing business, have prioritized cash preservation above all else. And, from a corporate perspective, share repurchases are considered more "discretionary" than quarterly dividends.

Sources: K. Grace and R. Curran, "Stock Buybacks Plummet," *Wall Street Journal* (March 27, 2009), p. C9; and L. Pleven and J. Light, "Leading Indicators for Investors: Corporate Spinoffs, Share Buybacks, Insider Buying and Stock Splits Can All Signal What Insiders Think Lies Ahead for Their Company's Share Price," *Wall Street Journal* (September 6, 2013).

PREFERENCE SHARES

As noted earlier, **preference shares** are a special class of shares that possess certain preferences or features not possessed by ordinary shares. The following features are those most often associated with preference share issues.

5 LEARNING OBJECTIVE
Explain the accounting for and reporting of preference shares.

1. Preference as to dividends.
2. Preference as to assets in the event of liquidation.
3. Convertible into ordinary shares.
4. Callable at the option of the corporation.
5. Non-voting.

The features that distinguish preference from ordinary shares may be of a more restrictive and negative nature than preferences. For example, the preference shares may be non-voting, non-cumulative, and non-participating.

Companies usually issue preference shares with a par value, expressing the dividend preference as a **percentage of the par value**. Thus, holders of 8 percent preference shares with a $100 par value are entitled to an annual dividend of $8 per share ($100 × 8%). This share is commonly referred to as an 8 percent preference share. In the case of no-par preference shares, a corporation expresses a dividend preference as a **specific dollar amount** per share, for example, $7 per share. This share is commonly referred to as a $7 preference share.

A preference as to dividends does not assure the payment of dividends. It merely assures that the corporation must pay the stated dividend rate or amount applicable to the preference shares before paying any dividends on the ordinary shares.

A company often issues preference shares (instead of debt) because of a high debt to equity ratio. In other instances, it issues preference shares through private placements with other corporations at a lower-than-market dividend rate because the acquiring corporation often receives largely tax-free dividends in certain countries.

Features of Preference Shares

A corporation may attach whatever preferences or restrictions, in whatever combination it desires, to a preference share issue, as long as it does not specifically violate its country's incorporation law. Also, it may issue more than one class of preference shares. We discuss the most common features attributed to preference shares below.

Cumulative Preference Shares

Cumulative preference shares require that if a corporation fails to pay a dividend in any year, it must make it up in a later year before paying any dividends to ordinary shareholders. If the directors fail to declare a dividend at the normal date for dividend action, the dividend is said to have been "passed." Any passed dividend on cumulative preference shares constitutes a dividend in arrears. Because no liability exists until the board of directors declares a dividend, a corporation does not record a dividend in arrears as a liability but discloses it in a note to the financial statements. A corporation seldom issues non-cumulative preference shares because a passed dividend is lost forever to the preference shareholder. As a result, this type of share issue would be less marketable.

Participating Preference Shares

Holders of participating preference shares share ratably with the ordinary shareholders in any profit distributions beyond the prescribed rate. That is, 5 percent preference shares, if fully participating, will receive not only its 5 percent return, but also dividends at the same rates as those paid to ordinary shareholders if paying amounts in excess of 5 percent of par or stated value to ordinary shareholders. Note that participating preference shares may be only partially participating.

Convertible Preference Shares

Convertible preference shares allow shareholders, at their option, to exchange preference shares for ordinary shares at a predetermined ratio. The convertible preference shareholder not only enjoys a preference claim on dividends but also has the option of converting into an ordinary shareholder with unlimited participation in earnings.

Callable Preference Shares

Callable preference shares permit the corporation at its option to call or redeem the outstanding preference shares at specified future dates and at stipulated prices. Many preference issues are callable. The corporation usually sets the call or redemption price slightly above the original issuance price and commonly states it in terms related to the par value. The callable feature permits the corporation to use the capital obtained through the issuance of such shares until the need has passed or it is no longer advantageous.

The existence of a call price or prices tends to set a ceiling on the market price of the preference shares unless they are convertible into ordinary shares. When a corporation redeems preference shares, it must pay any dividends in arrears.

Redeemable Preference Shares

Recently, more and more issuances of preference shares have features that make the securities more like debt (legal obligation to pay) than an equity instrument. For example, redeemable preference shares have a mandatory redemption period or a redemption feature that the issuer cannot control.

Previously, public companies were not permitted to report these debt-like preference share issues in equity, but they were not required to report them as a liability either.

There were concerns about classification of these debt-like securities, which may have been reported as equity or in the "mezzanine" section of statements of financial position between equity and debt. There also was diversity in practice as to how dividends on these securities were reported. IFRS requires debt-like securities, like redeemable preference shares, to be classified as liabilities and be measured and accounted for similar to liabilities. **[3]**

Accounting for and Reporting of Preference Shares

The accounting for preference shares at issuance is similar to that for ordinary shares. A corporation allocates proceeds between the par value of the preference shares and share premium. To illustrate, assume that Bishop Co. issues 10,000 shares of £10 par value preference shares for £12 cash per share. Bishop records the issuance as follows.

Cash	120,000	
Share Capital—Preference		100,000
Share Premium—Preference		20,000

Thus, Bishop maintains separate accounts for these different classes of shares.

Corporations consider convertible preference shares as a part of equity. In addition, when exercising convertible preference shares, there is no theoretical justification for recognition of a gain or loss. A company recognizes no gain or loss when dealing with shareholders in their capacity as business owners. Instead, the company **employs the book value method**: debit Share Capital—Preference, along with any related Share Premium—Preference; credit Share Capital—Ordinary and Share Premium— Ordinary (if an excess exists).

Preference shares generally have no maturity date. Therefore, no legal obligation exists to pay the preference shareholder. As a result, companies classify preference shares as part of equity. Companies generally report preference shares at par value as the first item in the equity section. They report any excess over par value as part of share premium. They also consider dividends on preference shares as a distribution of income and not an expense. Companies must disclose the pertinent rights of the preference shares outstanding. **[4]**

DIVIDEND POLICY

Determining the proper amount of dividends to pay is a difficult financial management decision. Companies that are paying dividends are extremely reluctant to reduce or eliminate their dividend. They fear that the securities market might view this action negatively. As a consequence, companies that have been paying cash dividends will make every effort to continue to do so. In addition, the type of shareholder the company has (taxable or non-taxable, retail investor or institutional investor) plays a large role in determining dividend policy.[5]

6 LEARNING OBJECTIVE
Describe the policies used in distributing dividends.

Very few companies pay dividends in amounts equal to their legally available retained earnings. The major reasons are as follows.

1. To maintain agreements (bond covenants) with specific creditors, to retain all or a portion of the earnings, in the form of assets, to build up additional protection against possible loss.

---

[5]One recent study of large international companies showed that in the decade ending in March 2013, companies with the highest dividend payouts showed the highest share price increases. See "Rising Corporate Cash: What It Means for Investors," *T. Rowe Price Report* (Summer 2013).

2. To meet corporation requirements, that earnings equivalent to the cost of treasury shares purchased be restricted against dividend declarations.

3. To retain assets that would otherwise be paid out as dividends, to finance growth or expansion. This is sometimes called internal financing, reinvesting earnings, or "plowing" the profits back into the business.

4. To smooth out dividend payments from year to year by accumulating earnings in good years and using such accumulated earnings as a basis for dividends in bad years.

5. To build up a cushion or buffer against possible losses or errors in the calculation of profits.

The reasons above are self-explanatory except for the second. The laws of some jurisdictions require that the corporation restrict its contributed capital from distribution to shareholders, to protect against loss for creditors.[6] The applicable law determines the legality of a dividend.

Financial Condition and Dividend Distributions

Effective management of a company requires attention to more than the legality of dividend distributions. Management must also consider economic conditions, most importantly, liquidity. Assume an extreme situation as shown in Illustration 15-7.

ILLUSTRATION 15-7
Statement of Financial Position, Showing a Lack of Liquidity

STATEMENT OF FINANCIAL POSITION			
Plant assets	€500,000	Share capital	€400,000
	€500,000	Retained earnings	100,000
			€500,000

The depicted company has a retained earnings credit balance. Unless restricted, it can declare a dividend of €100,000. But because all its assets are plant assets used in operations, payment of a cash dividend of €100,000 would require the sale of plant assets or borrowing.

Even if a statement of financial position shows current assets, as in Illustration 15-8, the question remains as to whether the company needs those cash assets for other purposes.

ILLUSTRATION 15-8
Statement of Financial Position, Showing Cash but Minimal Working Capital

STATEMENT OF FINANCIAL POSITION				
Plant assets	€460,000	Share capital	€400,000	
Cash	100,000	Retained earnings	100,000	€500,000
	€560,000	Current liabilities		60,000
				€560,000

The existence of current liabilities strongly implies that the company needs some of the cash to meet current debts as they mature. In addition, day-to-day cash requirements for payrolls and other expenditures not included in current liabilities also require cash.

Thus, before declaring a dividend, management must consider **availability of funds to pay the dividend**. A company should not pay a dividend unless both the present and future financial position warrant the distribution.

---

[6]If the corporation buys its own outstanding shares, it reduces its contributed capital and distributes assets to shareholders. If permitted, the corporation could, by purchasing treasury shares at any price desired, return to the shareholders their investments and leave creditors with little or no protection against loss.

Types of Dividends

Companies generally base dividend distributions either on accumulated profits (that is, retained earnings) or on some other equity item such as share premium. Dividends are of the following types.

1. Cash dividends.

2. Property dividends.

3. Liquidating dividends.

4. Share dividends.

Although commonly paid in cash, companies occasionally pay dividends in shares or some other asset. **All dividends, except for share dividends, reduce the total equity in the corporation.** When declaring a share dividend, the corporation does not pay out assets or incur a liability. It issues additional shares to each shareholder and nothing more.

The natural expectation of any shareholder who receives a dividend is that the corporation has operated successfully. As a result, he or she is receiving a share of its profits. A company should disclose a liquidating dividend—that is, a dividend not based on retained earnings—to the shareholders so that they will not misunderstand its source.

Cash Dividends

The board of directors votes on the declaration of cash dividends. Upon approval of the resolution, the board declares a dividend. Before paying it, however, the company must prepare a current list of shareholders. For this reason, there is usually a time lag between declaration and payment. For example, the board of directors might approve a resolution at the January 10 (**date of declaration**) meeting and declare it payable February 5 (**date of payment**) to all shareholders of record January 25 (**date of record**).[7] In this example, the period from January 10 to January 25 gives time for the company to complete and register any transfers in process. The time from January 25 to February 5 provides an opportunity for the transfer agent or accounting department, depending on who does this work, to prepare a list of shareholders as of January 25 and to prepare and mail dividend checks.

A declared cash dividend is a liability. Because payment is generally required very soon, it is usually a current liability. Companies use the following entries to record the declaration and payment of an ordinary dividend payable in cash. For example, Roadway Freight Corp. on June 10 declared a cash dividend of 50 cents a share on 1.8 million shares payable July 16 to all shareholders of record June 24. The entries for this dividend are shown in Illustration 15-9.

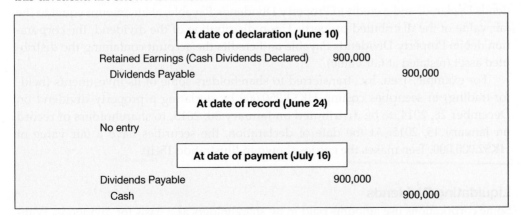

At date of declaration (June 10)		
Retained Earnings (Cash Dividends Declared)	900,000	
Dividends Payable		900,000
At date of record (June 24)		
No entry		
At date of payment (July 16)		
Dividends Payable	900,000	
Cash		900,000

ILLUSTRATION 15-9
Cash Dividend Entries

[7]Theoretically, the ex-dividend date is the day after the date of record. However, to allow time for transfer of the shares, the securities exchanges generally advance the ex-dividend date two to four days. Therefore, the party who owns the shares on the day prior to the expressed ex-dividend date receives the dividends. The party who buys the shares on and after the ex-dividend date does not receive the dividend. Between the declaration date and the ex-dividend date, the market price of the shares includes the dividend.

To set up a ledger account that shows the amount of dividends declared during the year, Roadway Freight might debit Cash Dividends Declared instead of Retained Earnings at the time of declaration. It then closes this account to Retained Earnings at year-end.

A company may declare dividends either as a certain percentage of par, such as a 6 percent dividend on preference shares, or as an amount per share, such as 60 cents per share on no-par ordinary shares. In the first case, the rate multiplied by the par value of outstanding shares equals the total dividend. In the second, the dividend equals the amount per share multiplied by the number of shares outstanding. **Companies do not declare or pay cash dividends on treasury shares.**

Dividend policies vary among corporations. Some companies take pride in a long, unbroken string of quarterly dividend payments. They would lower or pass the dividend only if forced to do so by a sustained decline in earnings or a critical shortage of cash.

"Growth" companies, on the other hand, pay little or no cash dividends because their policy is to expand as rapidly as internal and external financing permit. For example, Salamander Energy plc (GBR) does not pay cash dividends to its ordinary shareholders so that the cash can be used in exploration and production. Investors in these growth companies hope that the price of their shares will appreciate in value. The investors will then realize a profit when they sell their shares. Many companies focus more on increasing share price, share repurchase programs, and corporate earnings than on dividend payout.

Property Dividends

Dividends payable in assets of the corporation other than cash are called property dividends or **dividends in kind**. Property dividends may be merchandise, real estate, or investments, or whatever form the board of directors designates. Gold Bullion Development Corporation (CAN) has a long-standing practice of paying dividends in gold instead of cash. Because of the obvious difficulties of divisibility of units and delivery to shareholders, the usual property dividend is in the form of securities of other companies that the distributing corporation holds as an investment.

When declaring a property dividend, the corporation should **restate at fair value the property it will distribute**, **recognizing any gain or loss** as the difference between the property's fair value and carrying value at date of declaration. The corporation may then record the declared dividend as a debit to Retained Earnings (or Property Dividends Declared) and a credit to Property Dividends Payable, at an amount equal to the fair value of the distributed property. Upon distribution of the dividend, the corporation debits Property Dividends Payable and credits the account containing the distributed asset (restated at fair value).

For example, Tsen, Inc. transferred to shareholders some of its investments (held-for-trading) in securities costing HK$1,250,000 by declaring a property dividend on December 28, 2014, to be distributed on January 30, 2015, to shareholders of record on January 15, 2015. At the date of declaration, the securities have a fair value of HK$2,000,000. Tsen makes the entries shown in Illustration 15-10.

Liquidating Dividends

Some corporations use amounts paid in by shareholders as a basis for dividends. Without proper disclosure of this fact, shareholders may erroneously believe the corporation has been operating at a profit. To avoid this type of deception, intentional or unintentional, a clear statement of the source of every dividend should accompany the dividend check.

ILLUSTRATION 15-10
Property Dividend
Entries

At date of declaration (December 28, 2014)		
Equity Investments	750,000	
Unrealized Holding Gain or Loss—Income		750,000
Retained Earnings (Property Dividends Declared)	2,000,000	
Property Dividends Payable		2,000,000

At date of distribution (January 30, 2015)		
Property Dividends Payable	2,000,000	
Equity Investments		2,000,000

ILLUSTRATION 15-10
Property Dividend
Entries

Dividends based on other than retained earnings are sometimes described as liquidating dividends. This term implies that such dividends are a return of the shareholder's investment rather than of profits. In other words, **any dividend not based on earnings reduces amounts paid-in by shareholders and to that extent, it is a liquidating dividend**. Companies in the extractive industries may pay dividends equal to the total of accumulated income and depletion. The portion of these dividends in excess of accumulated income represents a return of part of the shareholder's investment.

For example, McChesney Mines Inc. issued a "dividend" to its ordinary shareholders of £1,200,000. The cash dividend announcement noted that shareholders should consider £900,000 as income and the remainder a return of capital. McChesney Mines records the dividend as shown in Illustration 15-11.

At date of declaration		
Retained Earnings	900,000	
Share Premium—Ordinary	300,000	
Dividends Payable		1,200,000

At date of payment		
Dividends Payable	1,200,000	
Cash		1,200,000

ILLUSTRATION 15-11
Liquidating Dividend
Entries

In some cases, management simply decides to cease business and declares a liquidating dividend. In these cases, liquidation may take place over a number of years to ensure an orderly and fair sale of assets. For example, when Overseas National Airways (USA) dissolved, it agreed to pay a liquidating dividend to its shareholders over a period of years equivalent to $8.60 per share. Each liquidating dividend payment in such cases reduces the amount paid-in by shareholders.

Share Dividends and Share Splits

Share Dividends

Companies sometimes issue a share dividend. In this case, **the company distributes no assets**. Each shareholder maintains exactly the same proportionate interest in the corporation and the same total book value after the company issues the share dividend. Of course, the book value per share is lower because each shareholder holds more shares.

8 LEARNING OBJECTIVE

Explain the accounting for share dividends and share splits.

A share dividend therefore is the issuance by a corporation of its own shares to its shareholders on a pro rata basis, without receiving any consideration. In recording a share dividend, some believe that the company should transfer the **par value of the shares issued** as a dividend from retained earnings to share capital.[8]

To illustrate a share dividend, assume that Vine Corporation has outstanding 100,000 shares of £1 par value ordinary shares and retained earnings of £50,000. If Vine declares a 10 percent share dividend, it issues 10,000 additional shares to current share-holders. The fair value of the shares at the time of the share dividend is £8. Given this information, the entry is:

At date of declaration

Retained Earnings (Share Dividend Declared)	10,000	
Ordinary Share Dividend Distributable		10,000

Two important points should be noted about this entry. First, the par value, not the fair value, is used to record the share dividend. Second, the share dividend does not affect any asset or liability. The entry merely reflects a reclassification of equity. If Vine prepares a statement of financial position between the dates of declaration and distribution, it should show the ordinary share dividend distributable in the equity section as an addition to share capital—ordinary (whereas it shows cash or property dividends payable as current liabilities).

When issuing the shares, the entry is:

At date of distribution

Ordinary Share Dividend Distributable	10,000	
Share Capital—Ordinary		10,000

No matter what the fair value is at the time of the share dividend, each shareholder retains the same proportionate interest in the corporation.

Some applicable laws and exchange rules specifically prohibit the issuance of share dividends on treasury shares. In those jurisdictions that permit treasury shares to participate in the distribution accompanying a share dividend or share split, the planned use of the treasury shares influences corporate practice. For example, if a corporation issues treasury shares in connection with employee share options, the treasury shares may participate in the distribution because the corporation usually adjusts the number of shares under option for any share dividends or splits. But no useful purpose is served by issuing additional shares to the treasury shares without a specific purpose, since they are essentially equivalent to authorized but unissued shares.

To continue with our example of the effect of the share dividend, note in Illustration 15-12 that the share dividend does not change the total equity. Also note that it does not change the proportion of the total shares outstanding held by each shareholder.

---

[8] An alternative approach (required in the United States) is the fair value approach. Under this approach, for small share dividends (defined as those less than 20–25%) companies transfer the fair value of the shares issued from retained earnings. This approach was adopted, at least in part, to influence the share dividend policies of corporations—some of which were possibly misleading investors as to the real impact of the share dividend. That is, some argued that "many recipients of share dividends look upon them as distributions of corporate earnings and usually in an amount equivalent to the fair value of the additional shares received." (See Stephen A. Zeff, "The Rise of 'Economic Consequences,'" *The Journal of Accountancy* (December 1978), pp. 53–66 for a complete discussion of the evolution of this issue.) IFRS is silent on the accounting for share dividends under either the par value or fair value method. We show the par value method because it is more conceptually sound, as it is generally accepted that share dividends are not income for investors.

ILLUSTRATION 15-12
Effects of Share
Dividends

Before dividend	
Share capital—ordinary, 100,000 shares of £1 par	£100,000
Retained earnings	50,000
Total equity	£150,000
Shareholders' interests:	
A. 40,000 shares, 40% interest, book value	£ 60,000
B. 50,000 shares, 50% interest, book value	75,000
C. 10,000 shares, 10% interest, book value	15,000
	£150,000
After declaration but before distribution of 10% share dividend	
Share capital—ordinary, 100,000 shares at £1 par	£100,000
Ordinary share dividend distributable, 10,000 shares at £1 par	10,000
Retained earnings (£50,000 − £10,000)	40,000
Total equity	£150,000
After declaration and distribution of 10% share dividend	
Share capital—ordinary, 110,000 shares at £1 par	£110,000
Retained earnings (£50,000 − £10,000)	40,000
Total equity	£150,000
Shareholders' interest:	
A. 44,000 shares, 40% interest, book value	£ 60,000
B. 55,000 shares, 50% interest, book value	75,000
C. 11,000 shares, 10% interest, book value	15,000
	£150,000

Share Splits

If a company has undistributed earnings over several years, and accumulates a sizable balance in retained earnings, the market value of its outstanding shares likely increases. Shares issued at prices less than £50 a share can easily attain a market price in excess of £200 a share. The higher the market price of a share, however, the less readily some investors can purchase it.

The managements of many corporations believe that better public relations depend on wider ownership of the corporation shares. They therefore target a market price sufficiently low to be within range of the majority of potential investors. To reduce the market price of each share, they use the common device of a share split. For example, after its share price increased significantly, Arcam AB (SWE) announced a split of its shares 4-for-1. The split should reduce the share price, leading to wider distribution of shares at lower trading prices.

From an accounting standpoint, **Arcam records no entry for a share split**. However, it enters a memorandum note to indicate the changed par value of the shares and the increased number of shares. Illustration 15-13 shows the lack of change in equity for a 2-for-1 share split on 100,000 shares of €1 par value, with the par being halved upon issuance of the additional shares.

ILLUSTRATION 15-13
Effects of a Share Split

Equity before 2-for-1 Split		Equity after 2-for-1 Split	
Share capital—ordinary, 100,000 shares at €1 par	€100,000	Share capital—ordinary, 200,000 shares at €.50 par	€100,000
Retained earnings	50,000	Retained earnings	50,000
	€150,000		€150,000

Share Split and Share Dividend Differentiated

From a legal standpoint, a share split differs from a share dividend. How? A share split increases the number of shares outstanding and decreases the par or stated value per share. **A share dividend, although it increases the number of shares outstanding, does not decrease the par value; thus, it increases the total par value of outstanding shares.**

The reasons for issuing a share dividend are numerous and varied. Share dividends can be primarily a publicity gesture **because many consider share dividends as dividends**. Another reason is that the corporation may simply wish to retain profits in the business by capitalizing a part of retained earnings. In such a situation, it makes a transfer on declaration of a share dividend from earned capital to contributed capital.

A corporation may also use a share dividend, like a share split, to increase the marketability of the shares, although marketability is often a secondary consideration. That is, a share dividend has the same effect on market price as a share split. However, as discussed earlier, a share dividend does not alter the par value per share.

Illustration 15-14 summarizes and compares the effects in the statement of financial position and related items of various types of dividends and share splits.

ILLUSTRATION 15-14
Effects of Dividends and Share Splits on Financial Statement Elements

Effect on:	Declaration of Cash Dividend	Payment of Cash Dividend	Declaration and Distribution of	
			Share Dividend	Share Split
Retained earnings	Decrease	–0–	Decrease[a]	–0–
Share capital	–0–	–0–	Increase[a]	–0–
Share premium	–0–	–0–	–0–	–0–
Total equity	Decrease	–0–	–0–	–0–
Working capital	Decrease	–0–	–0–	–0–
Total assets	–0–	Decrease	–0–	–0–
Number of shares outstanding	–0–	–0–	Increase	Increase

[a]Par or stated value of shares.

What do the numbers mean? DIVIDENDS UP, DIVIDENDS DOWN

As the economy continues to recover from the financial crisis of 2009, a number of companies are increasing their dividend payouts in a sign of growing confidence and rising cash balances. For example, Nestlé (CHE), L'Oréal (FRA), and Novo Nordisk (DEN) all increased their dividends in 2013. In fact, the overall number of dividend increases has been on the rise, even as some have concerns that dividend payouts would level off if economic growth stalls.

A focus on dividends makes sense. Consider that in a slow-growth environment, with interest rates persistently low and the tax treatment of dividends still favorable, an investment strategy focusing on equity shares (rather than bonds) with the potential of *increasing* dividends may be particularly timely. Said one market watcher, "Investors too often overlook the importance of dividends, particularly the contribution to total return from reinvested dividends. . . . Dividends also can provide a good hedge against inflation in the form of a growing stream of income." A look at the returns for "dividend growers" compared to "dividend cutters" in the following chart supports the advice to keep an eye on dividend growth.

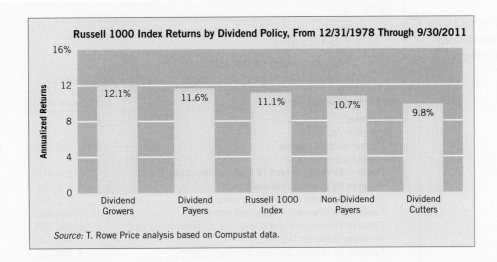

Russell 1000 Index Returns by Dividend Policy, From 12/31/1978 Through 9/30/2011

Source: T. Rowe Price analysis based on Compustat data.

As indicated, from 1979 through the end of 2011, shares in the Russell 1000 Index that were growing their dividends outperformed dividend-paying shares, the index itself, non-dividend-paying shares, and shares that cut their dividends. During that time, an investment of $100 in dividend growers would have risen to $4,018 compared with $3,134 based on the index return. Dividend payers outperformed non-dividend payers during down and flat markets, and offered lower volatility of returns in all market environments.

Furthermore, the best performers are shares with the combination of a relatively high yield—though not always the very highest—and a high dividend growth rate. This is because high yields sometimes are a function of beaten down share prices due to poor corporate earnings prospects or other issues. Indeed, in such cases, dividend cuts could be in the offing. By contrast, shares that have performed best historically have been those in which the company's true growth potential has been undervalued by investors. Thus, companies with growing dividends are signaling confidence about their future earnings and are most likely to perform well throughout market cycles, which make them good candidates for long-term growth.

Sources: "Dividend Growth Stocks May Be Timely as the Economy Sputters," *T. Rowe Price Report* (Fall 2011); and R. Evans, "Here Are the American and European Companies with Incredible Track Records of Raising Their Dividends," *The Telegraph* (November 4, 2013).

Disclosure of Restrictions on Retained Earnings

Many corporations restrict retained earnings or dividends, without any formal journal entries. Such restrictions are **best disclosed by note**. Parenthetical notations are sometimes used, but restrictions imposed by bond indentures and loan agreements commonly require an extended explanation. Notes provide a medium for more complete explanations and free the financial statements from abbreviated notations. The note disclosure should reveal the source of the restriction, pertinent provisions, and the amount of retained earnings subject to restriction or the amount not restricted.

Restrictions may be based on the retention of a certain retained earnings balance, the ability to maintain certain working capital requirements, additional borrowing, and other considerations. The example from the annual report of Samsung (KOR) in Illustration 15-15 (on page 726) shows a note disclosing potential restrictions on retained earnings and dividends.

Samsung

21. RETAINED EARNINGS

Retained earnings as of December 31 consist of the following:

(in millions of Korean won)	Current Year	Prior Year
Appropriated		
Legal reserve:		
Earned surplus reserve[1]	₩ 450,789	₩ 450,789
Discretionary reserve:		
Reserve for improvement of financial structure	204,815	204,815
Reserve for business rationalization	9,512,101	8,512,101
Reserve for overseas market development	510,750	510,750
Reserve for overseas investment losses	164,962	164,982
Reserve for research and human resource development	26,936,458	22,936,458
Reserve for export losses	167,749	167,749
Reserve for loss on disposal of treasury stock	3,100,000	2,550,000
Reserve for capital expenditure	8,816,905	8,216,439
	49,864,549	**43,714,083**
Unappropriated	5,555,022	7,351,091
Total	**₩55,419,571**	**₩51,065,174**

[1]The Commercial Code of the Republic of Korea requires the Company to appropriate as a legal reserve, an amount equal to a minimum of 10% of annual cash dividends declared, until the reserve equals 50% of its issued capital stock. The reserve is not available for the payment of cash dividends, but may be transferred to capital stock through a resolution of the Board of Directors or used to reduce accumulated deficit, if any, with the ratification of the shareholders.

PRESENTATION AND ANALYSIS OF EQUITY

Presentation of Equity

Statement of Financial Position

Illustration 15-16 shows a comprehensive equity section from the statement of financial position of Frost Company that includes the equity items we discussed in this chapter.[9]

FROST COMPANY EQUITY DECEMBER 31, 2015		
Share capital—preference, €100 par value, 7% cumulative, 100,000 shares authorized, 30,000 shares issued and outstanding	€3,000,000	
Share capital—ordinary, no par, stated value €10 per share, 500,000 shares authorized, 400,000 shares issued	4,000,000	
Ordinary share dividend distributable	200,000	€ 7,200,000
Share premium—preference	150,000	
Share premium—ordinary	840,000	990,000
Retained earnings		4,360,000
Treasury shares (2,000 ordinary shares)		(190,000)
Accumulated other comprehensive loss		(360,000)
Total equity		€12,000,000

[9]Looking at Illustration 15-16, note that companies may include a number of items in "Accumulated other comprehensive loss" or "Accumulated other comprehensive income." Among these items are "Foreign currency translation adjustments" (covered in advanced accounting), "Unrealized holding gains and losses for non-trading equity investments" (covered in Chapter 17), and "Unrealized holding gains or losses on property, plant, and equipment" (covered in Chapter 11), often referred to as revaluation surplus.

Frost should disclose the pertinent rights and privileges of the various securities outstanding. For example, companies must disclose all of the following: dividend and liquidation preferences, participation rights, call prices and dates, conversion or exercise prices and pertinent dates, sinking fund requirements, unusual voting rights, and significant terms of contracts to issue additional shares. Liquidation preferences should be disclosed in the equity section of the statement of financial position, rather than in the notes to the financial statements, to emphasize the possible effect of this restriction on future cash flows.

Presentation of Statement of Changes in Equity

Companies are also required to present a **statement of changes in equity**. The statement of changes in equity includes the following.

1. Total comprehensive income for the period, showing separately the total amounts attributable to owners of the parent and to non-controlling interests.

2. For each component of equity, the effects of retrospective application or retrospective restatement.

3. For each component of equity, a reconciliation between the carrying amount at the beginning and the end of the period, separately disclosing changes resulting from:
   (a) Profit or loss;
   (b) Each item of other comprehensive income; and
   (c) Transactions with owners in their capacity as owners, showing separately contributions by and distributions to owners and changes in ownership interests in subsidiaries that do not result in a loss of control.

A statement of changes in equity for **BASF Group** (DEU) is presented in Illustration 15-17.

BASF Group
Statement of Equity
(in millions of euros)

	Number of Subscribed Shares Out-standing	Subscribed Capital	Capital Surplus	Retained Earnings	Other Comprehensive Income[1]	Equity of Shareholders of BASF SE	Minority Interests	Total Equity
January 1, 2012	918,478,694	1,176	3,203	19,446	314	24,139	1,246	25,385
Effects of acquisitions achieved in stages	—	—	—	—	—	—	(5)	(5)
Dividend paid	—	—	—	(2,296)	—	(2,296)	(345)	(2,641)
Net income	—	—	—	4,879	—	4,879	343	5,222
Income and expense recognized directly in equity	—	—	—	(1,939)	(204)	(2,143)	(9)	(2,152)
Changes in scope of consolidation and other changes	—	—	(15)	16	—	1	(6)	(5)
December 31, 2012	918,478,694	1,176	3,188	20,106	110	24,580	1,224	25,804

In addition, BASF is required to present, either in the statement of changes in equity or in the notes, the amount of dividends recognized as distributions to owners during the period and the related amount per share. **[5]**

ILLUSTRATION 15-17
Statement of Changes in Equity

Analysis

Analysts use equity ratios to evaluate a company's profitability and long-term solvency. We discuss and illustrate the following three ratios below.

1. Return on ordinary share equity.

2. Payout ratio.

3. Book value per share.

Return on Ordinary Share Equity

The **return on ordinary share equity** (or return on equity) measures profitability from the ordinary shareholders' viewpoint. This ratio shows how many dollars of net income the company earned for each dollar invested by the owners. Return on equity (ROE) also helps investors judge the worthiness of a share when the overall market is not doing well.

Return on equity equals net income less preference dividends, divided by average ordinary shareholders' equity. For example, assume that Gerber's Inc. had net income of $360,000, declared and paid preference dividends of $54,000, and average ordinary shareholders' equity of $2,550,000. Illustration 15-18 shows how to compute Gerber's ratio.

ILLUSTRATION 15-18
Computation of Return on Ordinary Share Equity

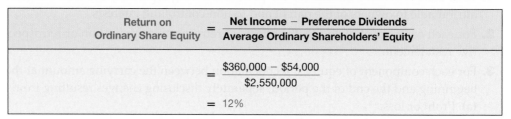

As shown in Illustration 15-18, when preference shares are present, income available to ordinary shareholders equals net income less preference dividends.

A company can improve its return on ordinary share equity through the prudent use of debt or preference share financing. **Trading on the equity** describes the practice of using borrowed money or issuing preference shares in hopes of obtaining a higher rate of return on the money used. Ordinary shareholders win if return on the assets is higher than the cost of financing these assets. When this happens, the return on ordinary share equity will exceed the return on total assets. In short, the company is "trading on the equity at a gain." In this situation, the money obtained from bondholders or preference shareholders earns enough to pay the interest or preference dividends and leaves a profit for the ordinary shareholders. On the other hand, if the cost of the financing is higher than the rate earned on the assets, the company is trading on equity at a loss and shareholders lose.

Payout Ratio

Another ratio of interest to investors, the **payout ratio**, is the ratio of cash dividends to net income. If preference shares are outstanding, this ratio equals cash dividends paid to ordinary shareholders, divided by net income available to ordinary shareholders. For example, assume that Troy Co. has cash dividends of €100,000 and net income of €500,000, and no preference shares outstanding. Illustration 15-19 shows the payout ratio computation.

ILLUSTRATION 15-19
Computation of Payout Ratio

	Cash Dividends	
Payout Ratio =	Net income − Preference Dividends	

$$= \frac{€100,000}{€500,000}$$

$$= 20\%$$

Recently, the payout ratio has plummeted. In 2000, more than half of earnings were converted to dividends. In 2011, just 37 percent of the earnings of global public companies was distributed via dividends.[10]

[10]Andrew Blackman, "How Well Do You Know . . . Dividends?" *Wall Street Journal* (September 10, 2007), p. R5. Also, see payout data at *http://pages.stern.nyu.edu/~%20adamodar/New_Home_Page/ data.html*.

Book Value per Share

Another basis for evaluating net worth is found in the book value or equity value per share. **Book value per share** is the amount each share would receive if the company were liquidated **on the basis of amounts reported on the statement of financial position**. However, the figure loses much of its relevance if the valuations on the statement of financial position fail to approximate fair value of the assets. Book value per share equals ordinary shareholders' equity divided by outstanding ordinary shares. Assume that Chen Corporation's ordinary shareholders' equity is HK$1,000,000 and it has 100,000 shares of ordinary shares outstanding. Illustration 15-20 shows its book value per share computation.

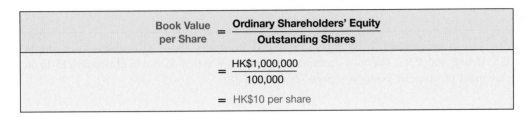

ILLUSTRATION 15-20
Computation of Book
Value per Share

GLOBAL ACCOUNTING INSIGHTS

EQUITY

The accounting for transactions related to equity, such as issuance of shares, purchase of treasury shares, and declaration and payment of dividends, are similar under both IFRS and U.S. GAAP. Major differences relate to terminology used and presentation of equity information.

Relevant Facts

Following are the key similarities and differences between U.S. GAAP and IFRS related to equity.

Similarities
• The accounting for the issuance of shares and purchase of treasury shares are similar under both U.S. GAAP and IFRS.

• The accounting for declaration and payment of dividends and the accounting for share splits are similar under both U.S. GAAP and IFRS.

Differences
• U.S. GAAP requires that small share dividends (referred to as stock dividends) should be recorded by transferring an amount equal to the fair value of the shares issued from retained earnings to share capital accounts. IFRS is silent on the accounting for share dividends.

• Major differences relate to terminology used, introduction of concepts such as revaluation surplus, and presentation of equity information.

• In the United States and the United Kingdom, many companies rely on substantial investments from private investors. Other countries have different investor groups. For example, in Germany, financial institutions such as banks are not only the major creditors but often are the largest shareholders as well.

• The accounting for treasury share retirements differs between U.S. GAAP and IFRS. Under U.S. GAAP, a company has three options: (1) charge the excess of the cost of treasury shares over par value to retained earnings, (2) allocate the difference between paid-in capital and retained earnings, or (3) charge the entire amount to paid-in capital. Under IFRS, the excess may have to be charged to paid-in capital, depending on the original transaction related to the issuance of the shares.

• The statement of changes in equity is usually referred to as the statement of stockholders' equity (or shareholders' equity) under U.S. GAAP.

• Both U.S. GAAP and IFRS use the term retained earnings. However, U.S. GAAP uses the account Accumulated Other Comprehensive Income (Loss). Use of this account is gaining prominence within the IFRS literature, which

traditionally has relied on the term "reserve" as a dumping ground for other types of equity transactions, such as other comprehensive income items as well as various types of unusual transactions related to convertible debt and share option contracts.

• The term surplus is generally not used in U.S. GAAP, as the standards do not allow revaluation accounting. Under IFRS, it is common to report "revaluation surplus" related to increases or decreases in items such as property, plant, and equipment; mineral resources; and intangible assets.

About the Numbers

As indicated, numerous differences in terminology exist in comparing equity under U.S. GAAP and IFRS. The following excerpt from a U.S. statement of financial position (balance sheet) illustrates these distinctions (you might compare the presentation here to that in Illustration 15-16 on page 726 under IFRS).

FROST COMPANY
STOCKHOLDERS' EQUITY
DECEMBER 31, 2015

Capital stock		
Preferred stock, $100 par value, 7% cumulative,		
100,000 shares authorized, 30,000 shares issued		
and outstanding		$ 3,000,000
Common stock, no par, stated value $10 per share,		
500,000 shares authorized, 400,000 shares issued		4,000,000
Common stock dividend distributable, 20,000 shares		200,000
Total capital stock		7,200,000
Additional paid-in capital		
Excess over par—preferred	$150,000	
Excess over stated value—common	840,000	990,000
Total paid-in capital		8,190,000
Retained earnings		4,360,000
Total paid-in capital and retained earnings		12,550,000
Less: Cost of treasury stock		
(2,000 shares, common)		190,000
Accumulated other comprehensive		
loss		360,000
Total stockholders' equity		$12,000,000

On the Horizon

As indicated in earlier discussions, the IASB and the FASB have completed some work on a project related to financial statement presentation. An important part of this study is to determine whether certain line items, subtotals, and totals should be clearly defined and required to be displayed in the financial statements. For example, it is likely that the statement of changes in equity and its presentation will be examined closely. In addition, the options of how to present other comprehensive income under U.S. GAAP will change in any converged standard.

SUMMARY OF LEARNING OBJECTIVES

1 **Discuss the characteristics of the corporate form of organization.**
Among the specific characteristics of the corporate form that affect accounting are the
(1) influence of corporate law, (2) use of the share system, and (3) development of a variety of ownership interests. In the absence of restrictive provisions, each ordinary share
carries the right to share proportionately in (1) profits and losses, (2) management (the
right to vote for directors), (3) corporate assets upon liquidation, and (4) any new issues
of shares of the same class (called the preemptive right).

2 **Identify the key components of equity.** Equity is classified into two categories:
contributed capital and earned capital. Contributed capital (paid-in capital) describes the
total amount paid in as share capital. Put another way, it is the amount that shareholders
advance to the corporation for use in the business. Contributed capital includes items
such as the par value of all outstanding shares and premiums less any discounts on
issuance. Earned capital is the capital that develops if the business operates profitably; it
consists of all undistributed income that remains invested in the company.

3 **Explain the accounting procedures for issuing shares.** Accounts are kept
for the following different types of shares. *Par value shares:* (a) Share Capital—Preference
or Share Capital—Ordinary, (b) Share Premium—Preference and Share Premium—
Ordinary. *No-par shares:* Share Capital—Ordinary or Share Capital—Ordinary and Share
Premium—Ordinary if stated value used. For shares issued in combination with other
securities (lump-sum sales), the two methods of allocation available are (a) the proportional method and (b) the incremental method. When issuing shares for services or
property other than cash, the company should record the exchange at the fair value of
the property or services received unless that fair value cannot be reliably measured.
Otherwise, use the fair value of the shares issued.

4 **Describe the accounting for treasury shares.** The cost method is generally
used in accounting for treasury shares. This method derives its name from the fact that
a company maintains the Treasury Shares account at the cost of the shares purchased.
Under the cost method, a company debits the Treasury Shares account for the cost of the
shares acquired and credits it for this same cost upon reissuance. The price received for
the shares when originally issued does not affect the entries to record the acquisition
and reissuance of the treasury shares.

5 **Explain the accounting for and reporting of preference shares.** Preference shares are a special class of shares that possess certain preferences or features not
possessed by the ordinary shares. The features that are most often associated with preference share issues are (1) preference as to dividends, (2) preference as to assets in the
event of liquidation, (3) convertible into ordinary shares, (4) callable at the option of the
corporation, and (5) non-voting. At issuance, the accounting for preference shares is
similar to that for ordinary shares. When convertible preference shares are converted, a
company uses the book value method. It debits Share Capital—Preference, along with
any related Share Premium—Preference, and credits Share Capital—Ordinary and
Share Premium— Ordinary (if an excess exists).

6 **Describe the policies used in distributing dividends.** The incorporation laws
normally provide information concerning the legal restrictions related to the payment of

dividends. Corporations rarely pay dividends in an amount equal to the legal limit. This is due, in part, to the fact that companies use assets represented by undistributed earnings to finance future operations of the business. If a company is considering declaring a dividend, it must ask two preliminary questions. (1) Is the condition of the corporation such that the dividend is **legally permissible**? (2) Is the condition of the corporation such that a dividend is **economically sound**?

7 **Identify the various forms of dividend distributions.** Dividends are of the following types: (1) cash dividends, (2) property dividends, (3) liquidating dividends (dividends based on other than retained earnings), and (4) share dividends (the issuance by a corporation of its own shares to its shareholders on a pro rata basis but without receiving consideration).

8 **Explain the accounting for share dividends and share splits.** When declaring a share dividend, a company debits Retained Earnings at the par value of the shares it distributes. The entry includes a credit to Ordinary Share Dividend Distributable at par value times the number of shares. A share dividend is a capitalization of retained earnings that reduces retained earnings. The par value per share and total equity remain unchanged with a share dividend, and all shareholders retain their same proportionate share of ownership. A share split results in an increase or decrease in the number of shares outstanding, with a corresponding decrease or increase in the par or stated value per share. No accounting entry is required for a share split.

9 **Indicate how to present and analyze equity.** The equity section of a statement of financial position includes share capital, share premium, and retained earnings. A company may also have additional items such as treasury shares, accumulated other comprehensive income (loss), and minority interest. Companies are required to present a statement of changes in equity. Ratios that use equity amounts are return on ordinary share equity, payout ratio, and book value per share.

APPENDIX **15A**	DIVIDEND PREFERENCES AND BOOK VALUE PER SHARE

DIVIDEND PREFERENCES

LEARNING OBJECTIVE **10**
Explain the different types of preference share dividends and their effect on book value per share.

Illustrations 15A-1 to 15A-4 indicate the **effects of** various **dividend preferences** on dividend distributions to ordinary and preference shareholders. Assume that in 2015, Mason Company is to distribute €50,000 as cash dividends, its outstanding ordinary shares have a par value of €400,000, and its 6 percent preference shares have a par value of €100,000. Mason would distribute dividends to each class, employing the assumptions given, as follows.

1. If the preference shares are non-cumulative and non-participating:

ILLUSTRATION 15A-1
Dividend Distribution, Non-Cumulative and Non-Participating Preference

	Preference	Ordinary	Total
6% of €100,000	€6,000		€ 6,000
The remainder to ordinary		€44,000	44,000
Totals	€6,000	€44,000	€50,000

2. If the preference shares are cumulative and non-participating, and Mason Company did not pay dividends on the preference shares in the preceding two years:

	Preference	Ordinary	Total
Dividends in arrears, 6% of €100,000 for 2 years	€12,000		€12,000
Current year's dividend, 6% of €100,000	6,000		6,000
The remainder to ordinary		€32,000	32,000
Totals	€18,000	€32,000	€50,000

ILLUSTRATION 15A-2
Dividend Distribution, Cumulative and Non-Participating Preference Shares, with Dividends in Arrears

3. If the preference shares are non-cumulative and are fully participating:[11]

	Preference	Ordinary	Total
Current year's dividend, 6%	€ 6,000	€24,000	€30,000
Participating dividend of 4%	4,000	16,000	20,000
Totals	€10,000	€40,000	€50,000

ILLUSTRATION 15A-3
Dividend Distribution, Non-Cumulative and Fully Participating Preference Shares

The participating dividend was determined as follows:
Current year's dividend:
Preference, 6% of €100,000 = € 6,000		
Ordinary, 6% of €400,000 = 24,000	€30,000	
Amount available for participation (€50,000 − €30,000)	€20,000	
Par value of shares that are to participate (€100,000 + €400,000)	€500,000	
Rate of participation (€20,000 ÷ €500,000)	4%	
Participating dividend:		
Preference, 4% of €100,000	€ 4,000	
Ordinary, 4% of €400,000	16,000	
	€20,000	

4. If the preference shares are cumulative and are fully participating, and Mason Company did not pay dividends on the preference shares in the preceding two years:

	Preference	Ordinary	Total
Dividends in arrears, 6% of €100,000 for 2 years	€12,000		€12,000
Current year's dividend, 6%	6,000	€24,000	30,000
Participating dividend, 1.6% (€8,000 ÷ €500,000)	1,600	6,400	8,000
Totals	€19,600	€30,400	€50,000

ILLUSTRATION 15A-4
Dividend Distribution, Cumulative and Fully Participating Preference Shares, with Dividends in Arrears

BOOK VALUE PER SHARE

Book value per share in its simplest form is computed as net assets divided by outstanding shares at the end of the year. The computation of book value per share becomes more complicated if a company has preference shares in its capital structure. For

---

[11]When preference shares are participating, there may be different agreements as to how the participation feature is to be executed. However, in the absence of any specific agreement the following procedure is recommended:

a. After the preference shares are assigned the current year's dividend, the ordinary shares will receive a "like" percentage of par value outstanding. In example (3), this amounts to 6 percent of €400,000.

b. In example (3), shown in Illustration 15A-3, the remainder of the declared dividend is €20,000. We divide this amount by total par value (€500,000) to find the rate of participation to be applied to each class of shares. In this case, the rate of participation is 4% (€20,000 ÷ €500,000), which we then multiply by the par value of each class of shares to determine the amount of participation.

example, if preference dividends are in arrears, if the preference shares are participating, or if preference shares have a redemption or liquidating value higher than its carrying amount, the company must allocate retained earnings between the preference and ordinary shareholders in computing book value.

To illustrate, assume that the following situation exists.

ILLUSTRATION 15A-5
Computation of Book Value per Share—No Dividends in Arrears

Equity	Preference	Ordinary
Preference shares, 5%	€300,000	
Ordinary shares		€400,000
Share premium—ordinary		37,500
Retained earnings		162,582
Totals	€300,000	€600,082
Shares outstanding		4,000
Book value per share		€150.02

The situation in Illustration 15A-5 assumes that no preference dividends are in arrears and that the preference shares are not participating. Now assume that the same facts exist except that the 5 percent preference shares are cumulative, participating up to 8 percent, and that dividends for three years before the current year are in arrears. Illustration 15A-6 shows how to compute the book value of the ordinary shares, assuming that no action has yet been taken concerning dividends for the current year.

ILLUSTRATION 15A-6
Computation of Book Value per Share—with Dividends in Arrears, Participating

Equity	Preference	Ordinary
Preference shares, 5%	€300,000	
Ordinary shares		€400,000
Share premium—ordinary		37,500
Retained earnings:		
Dividends in arrears (3 years at 5% a year)	45,000	
Current year requirement at 5%	15,000	20,000
Participating—additional 3%	9,000	12,000
Remainder to ordinary		61,582
Totals	€369,000	€531,082
Shares outstanding		4,000
Book value per share		€132.77

As indicated, retained earnings is allocated between preference and ordinary shareholders in computing book value per share.

In connection with the book value computation, the analyst must know how to handle the following items: the number of authorized and unissued shares, the number of treasury shares on hand, any commitments with respect to the issuance of unissued shares or the reissuance of treasury shares, and the relative rights and privileges of the various types of shares authorized. As an example, if the liquidating value of the preference shares is higher than its carrying amount, the liquidating amount should be used in the book value computation.

SUMMARY OF LEARNING OBJECTIVE FOR APPENDIX 15A

10 **Explain the different types of preference share dividends and their effect on book value per share.** The dividend preferences of preference shares affect the dividends paid to shareholders. Preference shares can be (1) cumulative or non-cumulative, and (2) fully participating, partially participating, or non-participating. If preference dividends are in arrears, if the preference shares are participating, or if preference shares have a redemption or liquidation value higher than its carrying amount, allocate retained earnings between preference and ordinary shareholders in computing book value per share.

IFRS AUTHORITATIVE LITERATURE

Authoritative Literature References

[1] Conceptual Framework for Financial Reporting, "Chapter 4, *The Framework* (1989): The Remaining Text" (London, U.K.: IASB, September 2010), par. 4.20.

[2] International Financial Reporting Standard 2, *Share-Based Payment* (London, U.K.: International Accounting Standards Committee Foundation, 2004), par. 10.

[3] International Accounting Standard 32, *Financial Instruments: Presentation* (London, U.K.: International Accounting Standards Committee Foundation, 2003), paras. 18–20.

[4] International Accounting Standard 1, *Presentation of Financial Statements* (London, U.K.: International Accounting Standards Committee Foundation, 2003), par. 79.

[5] International Accounting Standard 1, *Presentation of Financial Statements* (London, U.K.: International Accounting Standards Committee Foundation, 2003), paras. 106–107.

Note: All asterisked Questions, Exercises, and Problems relate to material in the appendix to the chapter.

QUESTIONS

1. In the absence of restrictive provisions, what are the basic rights of shareholders of a corporation?

2. Why is a preemptive right important?

3. Distinguish between ordinary and preference shares.

4. Why is the distinction between contributed capital (paid-in capital) and retained earnings important?

5. Explain each of the following terms: authorized ordinary shares, unissued ordinary shares, issued ordinary shares, outstanding ordinary shares, and treasury shares.

6. What is meant by par value, and what is its significance to shareholders?

7. Describe the accounting for the issuance for cash of no-par value ordinary shares at a price in excess of the stated value of the ordinary shares.

8. Explain the difference between the proportional method and the incremental method of allocating the proceeds of lump-sum sales of share capital.

9. What are the different bases for share valuation when assets other than cash are received for issued shares?

10. Explain how underwriting costs and accounting and legal fees associated with the issuance of shares should be recorded.

11. For what reasons might a corporation purchase its own shares?

12. Discuss the propriety of showing:
    (a) Treasury shares as an asset.
    (b) "Gain" or "loss" on sale of treasury shares as additions to or deductions from income.
    (c) Dividends received on treasury shares as income.

13. What features or rights may alter the character of preference shares?

14. Kim Inc. recently noted that its 4% preference shares and 4% participating preference shares are both cumulative and have priority as to dividends up to 4% of their par value. Its participating preference shares participate equally with the ordinary shares in any dividends in excess of 4%. What is meant by the term participating? Cumulative?

15. Where in the financial statements are preference shares normally reported?

16. List five elements included in equity.

17. BMG Inc. purchases 10,000 shares of its own previously issued €10 par ordinary shares for €290,000. Assuming the shares are held in the treasury with intent to reissue, what effect does this transaction have on (a) net income, (b) total assets, (c) retained earnings, and (d) total equity?

18. Indicate how each of the following accounts should be classified in the equity section.
    (a) Share Capital—Ordinary
    (b) Retained Earnings
    (c) Share Premium—Ordinary
    (d) Treasury Shares
    (e) Share Premium—Treasury
    (f) Accumulated Other Comprehensive Income
    (g) Share Capital—Preference

19. What factors influence the dividend policy of a company?

20. What are the principal considerations of a board of directors in making decisions involving dividend declarations? Discuss briefly.

21. Dividends are sometimes said to have been paid "out of retained earnings." What is the error, if any, in that statement?

22. Distinguish among cash dividends, property dividends, liquidating dividends, and share dividends.

23. Describe the accounting entry for a share dividend, if any. Describe the accounting entry for a share split, if any.

24. Share splits and share dividends may be used by a corporation to change the number of its shares outstanding.
    (a) From an accounting viewpoint, explain how the share split differs from an ordinary share dividend.
    (b) How should a share dividend that has been declared but not yet issued be classified in a statement of financial position? Why?

25. The following comment appeared in the notes of Mona Corporation's annual report: "Such distributions, representing proceeds from the sale of Sarazan, Inc. were paid in the form of partial liquidating dividends and were in lieu of a portion of the Company's ordinary cash dividends." How would a partial liquidating dividend be accounted for in the financial records?

26. This comment appeared in the annual report of Christensen Inc.: "The Company could pay cash or property dividends on the Class A ordinary shares without paying cash or property dividends on the Class B ordinary shares. But if the Company pays any cash or property dividends on the Class B ordinary shares, it would be required to pay at least the same dividend on the Class A ordinary shares." How is a property dividend accounted for in the financial records?

27. For what reasons might a company restrict a portion of its retained earnings?

28. How are restrictions of retained earnings reported?

29. Mary Tokar is comparing a U.S. GAAP-based company to a company that uses IFRS. Both companies report non-trading equity investments. The IFRS company reports unrealized losses on these investments under the heading "Reserves" in its equity section. However, Mary can find no similar heading in the U.S. GAAP company financial statements. Can Mary conclude that the U.S. GAAP company has no unrealized gains or losses on its non-trading equity investments? Explain.

30. Briefly describe some of the similarities and differences between U.S. GAAP and IFRS with respect to the accounting for equity.

31. Briefly discuss the implications of the financial statement presentation project for the reporting of equity.

*32. Wang Corp. had $100,000 of 7%, $20 par value preference shares and 12,000 shares of $25 par value ordinary shares outstanding throughout 2015.
    (a) Assuming that total dividends declared in 2015 were $64,000 and that the preference shares are not cumulative but are fully participating, ordinary shareholders should receive 2015 dividends totaling what amount?
    (b) Assuming that total dividends declared in 2015 were $64,000 and that the preference shares are fully participating and cumulative with preference dividends in arrears for 2014, preference shareholders should receive 2015 dividends totaling what amount?
    (c) Assuming that total dividends declared in 2015 were $30,000; that the preference shares are cumulative, non-participating, and were issued on January 1, 2014; and that $5,000 of preference dividends were declared and paid in 2014, the ordinary shareholders should receive 2015 dividends totaling what amount?

BRIEF EXERCISES

BE15-1 Kaymer Corporation issued 300 shares of €10 par value ordinary shares for €4,500. Prepare Kaymer's journal entry.

BE15-2 Swarten Corporation issued 600 shares of no-par ordinary shares for €8,200. Prepare Swarten's journal entry if (a) the shares have no stated value, and (b) the shares have a stated value of €2 per share.

BE15-3 Wilco Corporation has the following equity balances at December 31, 2015.

Share capital—ordinary, €5 par value	€ 510,000
Treasury shares	90,000
Retained earnings	2,340,000
Share premium—ordinary	1,320,000

Prepare Wilco's December 31, 2015, equity section in the statement of financial position.

BE15-4 Ravonette Corporation issued 300 shares of $10 par value ordinary shares and 100 shares of $50 par value preference shares for a lump sum of $13,500. The ordinary shares have a market price of $20 per share, and the preference shares have a market price of $90 per share. Prepare the journal entry to record the issuance.

BE15-5 On February 1, 2015, Gruber Corporation issued 3,000 shares of its £5 par value ordinary shares for land worth £31,000. Prepare the February 1, 2015, journal entry.

BE15-6 Moonwalker Corporation issued 2,000 shares of its $10 par value ordinary shares for $60,000. Moonwalker also incurred $1,500 of costs associated with issuing the shares. Prepare Moonwalker's journal entry to record the issuance of the company's shares.

BE15-7 Sprinkle Inc. has outstanding 10,000 shares of €10 par value ordinary shares. On July 1, 2015, Sprinkle reacquired 100 shares at €87 per share. On September 1, Sprinkle reissued 60 shares at €90 per share. On November 1, Sprinkle reissued 40 shares at €83 per share. Prepare Sprinkle's journal entries to record these transactions using the cost method.

4 **BE15-8** Arantxa Corporation has outstanding 20,000 shares of R$5 par value ordinary shares. On August 1, 2015, Arantxa reacquired 200 shares at R$80 per share. On November 1, Arantxa reissued the 200 shares at R$70 per share. Arantxa had no previous treasury share transactions. Prepare Arantxa's journal entries to record these transactions using the cost method.

5 **BE15-9** Hinges Corporation issued 500 shares of €100 par value preference shares for €61,500. Prepare Hinges's journal entry.

6 **BE15-10** Woolford Inc. declared a cash dividend of $1 per share on its 2 million outstanding shares. The dividend was declared on August 1, payable on September 9 to all shareholders of record on August 15. Prepare all journal entries necessary on those three dates.

6 **7** **BE15-11** Silva Inc. owns shares of Costa Corporation classified as a trading equity investment. At December 31, 2015, the trading equity investment was carried in Silva's accounting records at its cost of R$875,000, which equals its fair value. On September 21, 2016, when the fair value of the investment was R$1,200,000, Silva declared a property dividend whereby the Costa securities are to be distributed on October 23, 2016, to shareholders of record on October 8, 2016. Prepare all journal entries necessary on those three dates.

6 **7** **BE15-12** Zhang Mining Company declared, on April 20, a dividend of ¥500,000,000 payable on June 1. Of this amount, ¥125,000,000 is a return of capital. Prepare the April 20 and June 1 entries for Zhang.

8 **BE15-13** Green Day Corporation has outstanding 400,000 shares of $10 par value ordinary shares. The corporation declares a 5% share dividend when the fair value is $65 per share. Prepare the journal entries for Green Day Corporation for both the date of declaration and the date of distribution.

8 **BE15-14** Use the information from BE15-13 but assume Green Day Corporation declared a 100% share dividend rather than a 5% share dividend. Prepare the journal entries for both the date of declaration and the date of distribution.

10 *BE15-15** Nottebart Corporation has outstanding 10,000 shares of €100 par value, 6% preference shares and 60,000 shares of €10 par value ordinary shares. The preference shares were issued in January 2015, and no dividends were declared in 2015 or 2016. In 2017, Nottebart declares a cash dividend of €300,000. How will the dividend be shared by ordinary and preference shareholders if the preference is (a) non-cumulative and (b) cumulative?

EXERCISES

3 **E15-1 (Recording the Issuances of Ordinary Shares)** During its first year of operations, Sitwell Corporation had the following transactions pertaining to its ordinary shares.

Jan.	10	Issued 80,000 shares for cash at €6 per share.
Mar.	1	Issued 5,000 shares to attorneys in payment of a bill for €35,000 for services rendered in helping the company to incorporate.
July	1	Issued 30,000 shares for cash at €8 per share.
Sept.	1	Issued 60,000 shares for cash at €10 per share.

Instructions

(a) Prepare the journal entries for these transactions, assuming that the ordinary shares have a par value of €3 per share.

(b) Briefly discuss how the entries in part (a) will change if the shares are no-par with a stated value of €2 per share.

3 **E15-2 (Recording the Issuance of Ordinary and Preference Shares)** Abernathy Corporation was organized on January 1, 2015. It is authorized to issue 10,000 shares of 8%, $50 par value preference shares, and 500,000 shares of no-par ordinary shares with a stated value of $2 per share. The following share transactions were completed during the first year.

Jan.	10	Issued 80,000 ordinary shares for cash at $5 per share.
Mar.	1	Issued 5,000 preference shares for cash at $108 per share.
Apr.	1	Issued 24,000 ordinary shares for land. The asking price of the land was $90,000; the fair value of the land was $80,000.
May	1	Issued 80,000 ordinary shares for cash at $7 per share.
Aug.	1	Issued 10,000 ordinary shares to attorneys in payment of their bill of $50,000 for services rendered in helping the company organize.
Sept.	1	Issued 10,000 ordinary shares for cash at $9 per share.
Nov.	1	Issued 1,000 preference shares for cash at $112 per share.

Instructions
Prepare the journal entries to record the above transactions.

3 **E15-3 (Shares Issued for Land)** Twenty-five thousand shares reacquired by Pierce Corporation for £48 per share were exchanged for undeveloped land that has an appraised value of £1,700,000. At the time of the exchange, the ordinary shares were trading at £60 per share on an organized exchange.

Instructions

  (a) Prepare the journal entry to record the acquisition of land, assuming that the purchase of the shares was originally recorded using the cost method.

  (b) Briefly identify the possible alternatives (including those that are totally unacceptable) for quantifying the cost of the land and briefly support your choice.

3 **E15-4 (Lump-Sum Sale of Shares with Bonds)** Fogelberg Corporation is a regional company, whose securities are thinly traded. Fogelberg has issued 10,000 units. Each unit consists of a CHF500 par, 12% subordinated debenture and 10 shares of CHF5 par ordinary shares. The investment banker has retained 400 units as the underwriting fee. The other 9,600 units were sold to outside investors for cash at CHF850 per unit. Prior to this sale, the 2-week ask price of ordinary shares was CHF40 per share. Twelve percent is a reasonable market yield for the debentures, and therefore the par value of the bonds is equal to the fair value.

Instructions

  (a) Prepare the journal entry to record Fogelberg's transaction, under the following conditions. (Round to the nearest CHF.)

    (1) Employing the incremental method.

    (2) Employing the proportional method, assuming the recent price quote on the ordinary shares reflects fair value.

  (b) Briefly explain which method is, in your opinion, the better method.

3 **5** **E15-5 (Lump-Sum Sales of Ordinary and Preference Shares)** Hartman Inc. issues 500 shares of €10 par value ordinary shares and 100 shares of €100 par value preference shares for a lump sum of €100,000.

Instructions

  (a) Prepare the journal entry for the issuance when the fair value of the ordinary shares is €168 each and fair value of the preference shares is €210 each. (Round to the nearest euro.)

  (b) Prepare the journal entry for the issuance when only the fair value of the ordinary shares (€170 per share) is known.

3 **4** **E15-6 (Share Issuances and Repurchase)** Loxley Corporation is authorized to issue 50,000 shares of $10 par value ordinary shares. During 2015, Loxley took part in the following selected transactions.

  1. Issued 5,000 shares at $45 per share, less costs related to the issuance of the shares totaling $7,000.

  2. Issued 1,000 shares for land appraised at $50,000. The shares were actively traded on a national securities exchange at approximately $46 per share on the date of issuance.

  3. Purchased 500 treasury shares at $44 per share. The treasury shares purchased were issued in 2014 at $40 per share.

Instructions

  (a) Prepare the journal entry to record item 1.
  (b) Prepare the journal entry to record item 2.
  (c) Prepare the journal entry to record item 3 using the cost method.

4 **E15-7 (Effect of Treasury Share Transactions on Financials)** Goosen Company has outstanding 40,000 shares of €5 par ordinary shares which had been issued at €30 per share. Goosen then entered into the following transactions.

  1. Purchased 5,000 treasury shares at €45 per share.

  2. Resold 500 of the treasury shares at €40 per share.

  3. Resold 2,000 of the treasury shares at €49 per share.

Instructions

Use the following code to indicate the effect each of the three transactions has on the financial statement categories listed in the table below, assuming Goosen Company uses the cost method: I = Increase; D = Decrease; and NE = No effect.

#	Assets	Liabilities	Equity	Share Premium	Retained Earnings	Net Income
1						
2						
3						

3 5 E15-8 (Preference Share Entries and Dividends) Weisberg Corporation has 10,000 shares of $100 par
10 value, 6%, preference shares and 50,000 ordinary shares of $10 par value outstanding at December 31, 2015.

Instructions

Answer the questions in each of the following independent situations.

(a) If the preference shares are cumulative and dividends were last paid on the preference shares on
December 31, 2012, what are the dividends in arrears that should be reported on the December 31,
2015, statement of financial position? How should these dividends be reported?

(b) If the preference shares are convertible into seven shares of $10 par value ordinary shares and
3,000 shares are converted, what entry is required for the conversion, assuming the preference
shares were issued at par value?

(c) If the preference shares were issued at $107 per share, how should the preference shares be
reported in the equity section?

3 4 E15-9 (Correcting Entries for Equity Transactions) Davison plc recently hired a new accountant with
extensive experience in accounting for partnerships. Because of the pressure of the new job, the accountant
was unable to review what he had learned earlier about corporation accounting. During the first month, he
made the following entries for the corporation's ordinary shares.

May	2	Cash	192,000	
		Share Capital—Ordinary		192,000
		(Issued 12,000 shares of £10 par value ordinary shares at £16 per share)		
	10	Cash	600,000	
		Share Capital—Ordinary		600,000
		(Issued 10,000 shares of £30 par value preference shares at £60 per share)		
	15	Share Capital—Ordinary	14,000	
		Cash		14,000
		(Purchased 1,000 ordinary shares for the treasury at £14 per share)		
	31	Cash	8,500	
		Share Capital—Ordinary		5,000
		Gain on Sale of Shares		3,500
		(Sold 500 treasury shares at £17 per share)		

Instructions

On the basis of the explanation for each entry, prepare the entries that should have been made for the
ordinary share transactions.

3 4 E15-10 (Analysis of Equity Data and Equity Section Preparation) For a recent 2-year period, the statement
of financial position of Jiang Group showed the following equity data at December 31 (amounts in millions).

	2016	2015
Share premium—ordinary	HK$ 891	HK$ 817
Share capital—ordinary	545	540
Retained earnings	7,167	5,226
Treasury shares	(1,428)	(918)
Total equity	HK$7,175	HK$5,665
Ordinary shares issued	218	216
Ordinary shares authorized	500	500
Treasury shares	34	27

Instructions

(a) Answer the following questions.

(1) What is the par value of the ordinary shares?

(2) What is the cost per treasury share at December 31, 2016, and at December 31, 2015?

(b) Prepare the equity section of the statement of financial position at December 31, 2016.

7 8 E15-11 (Equity Items on the Statement of Financial Position) The following are selected transactions that
may affect equity.

1. Recorded accrued interest earned on a note receivable.
2. Declared and distributed a share split.
3. Declared a cash dividend.
4. Recorded a retained earnings restriction.

5. Recorded the expiration of insurance coverage that was previously recorded as prepaid insurance.

6. Paid the cash dividend declared in item 3 above.

7. Recorded accrued interest expense on a note payable.

8. Declared a share dividend.

9. Distributed the share dividend declared in item 8.

Instructions

In the following table, indicate the effect each of the nine transactions has on the financial statement elements listed. Use the following code:

I = Increase   D = Decrease   NE = No effect

Item	Assets	Liabilities	Equity	Share Premium	Retained Earnings	Net Income

7 **E15-12 (Cash Dividend and Liquidating Dividend)** Addison Corporation has 10 million shares of ordinary shares issued and outstanding. On June 1, the board of directors voted a 60 cents per share cash dividend to shareholders of record as of June 14, payable June 30.

Instructions

(a) Prepare the journal entry for each of the dates above, assuming the dividend represents a distribution of earnings.

(b) How would the entry differ if the dividend were a liquidating dividend?

8 **E15-13 (Share Split and Share Dividend)** The ordinary shares of Otuk Inc. are currently selling at ₺110 per share. The directors wish to reduce the share price and increase share volume prior to a new issue. The per share par value is ₺10; book value is ₺70 per share. Five million shares are issued and outstanding.

Instructions

Prepare the necessary journal entries assuming the following.

(a) The board votes a 2-for-1 share split.

(b) The board votes a 100% share dividend.

(c) Briefly discuss the accounting and securities market differences between these two methods of increasing the number of shares outstanding.

8 **E15-14 (Entries for Share Dividends and Share Splits)** The equity accounts of Lawrence Company have the following balances on December 31, 2015.

Share Capital—Ordinary, €10 par, 200,000 shares issued and outstanding	€2,000,000
Share Premium—Ordinary	1,200,000
Retained Earnings	5,600,000

Shares of Lawrence Company are currently selling at €37.

Instructions

Prepare the appropriate journal entries for each of the following cases.

(a) A share dividend of 5% is declared and issued.

(b) A share dividend of 100% is declared and issued.

(c) A 2-for-1 share split is declared and issued.

7 **8** **E15-15 (Dividend Entries)** The following data were taken from the statement of financial position accounts of Murless Corporation on December 31, 2015.

Current Assets	R$540,000
Investments	624,000
Share Capital—Ordinary (par value R$10)	600,000
Share Premium—Ordinary	150,000
Retained Earnings	840,000

Instructions

Prepare the required journal entries for the following unrelated items.

    (a) A 5% share dividend is declared and distributed at a time when the market price of the shares is R$39 per share.

    (b) The par value of the ordinary shares is reduced to R$2 with a 5-for-1 share split.

    (c) A dividend is declared January 5, 2016, and paid January 25, 2016, in bonds held as an investment. The bonds have a book value of R$90,000 and a fair value of R$125,000.

6 7
8 **E15-16 (Computation of Retained Earnings)** The following information has been taken from the ledger accounts of Choi Corporation (all amounts in thousands).

Total Income since Incorporation	₩287,000
Total Cash Dividends Paid	60,000
Total Value of Share Dividends Distributed	40,000
Gains on Treasury Share Transactions	18,000
Accumulated Other Comprehensive Income	32,000

Instructions

Determine the current balance of retained earnings.

9 **E15-17 (Equity Section)** Teller Corporation's post-closing trial balance at December 31, 2015, was as follows.

TELLER CORPORATION
POST-CLOSING TRIAL BALANCE
DECEMBER 31, 2015

	Dr.	Cr.
Accounts payable		€ 310,000
Accounts receivable	€ 480,000	
Accumulated depreciation—buildings		185,000
Allowance for doubtful accounts		30,000
Bonds payable		700,000
Buildings	1,450,000	
Cash	190,000	
Dividends payable (preference shares—cash)		4,000
Inventory	560,000	
Land	400,000	
Prepaid expenses	40,000	
Retained earnings		201,000
Share capital—ordinary (€1 par value)		200,000
Share capital—preference (€50 par value)		500,000
Share premium—ordinary		1,000,000
Share premium—treasury		160,000
Treasury shares (ordinary at cost)	170,000	
Total	€3,290,000	€3,290,000

At December 31, 2015, Teller had the following number of ordinary and preference shares.

	Ordinary	Preference
Authorized	600,000	60,000
Issued	200,000	10,000
Outstanding	190,000	10,000

The dividends on preference shares are €4 cumulative. In addition, the preference shares have a preference in liquidation of €50 per share.

Instructions

Prepare the equity section of Teller's statement of financial position at December 31, 2015.

4 7
8 **E15-18 (Dividends and Equity Section)** Elizabeth Company reported the following amounts in the equity section of its December 31, 2015, statement of financial position.

Share capital—preference, 8%, $100 par (10,000 shares authorized, 2,000 shares issued)	$200,000
Share capital—ordinary, $5 par (100,000 shares authorized, 20,000 shares issued)	100,000
Share premium—preference	125,000
Retained earnings	450,000
Total	$875,000

During 2016, Elizabeth took part in the following transactions concerning equity.

1. Paid the annual 2015 $8 per share dividend on preference shares and a $2 per share dividend on ordinary shares. These dividends had been declared on December 31, 2015.

2. Purchased 2,700 shares of its own outstanding ordinary shares for $40 per share. Elizabeth uses the cost method.

3. Reissued 700 treasury shares for land valued at $30,000.

4. Issued 500 preference shares at $105 per share.

5. Declared a 10% share dividend on the outstanding ordinary shares when the shares are selling for $45 per share.

6. Issued the share dividend.

7. Declared the annual 2016 $8 per share dividend on preference shares and the $2 per share dividend on ordinary shares. These dividends are payable in 2017.

Instructions

(a) Prepare journal entries to record the transactions described above.

(b) Prepare the December 31, 2016, equity section of the statement of financial position. Assume 2016 net income was $330,000.

9 **E15-19 (Comparison of Alternative Forms of Financing)** Shown below is the equity and liabilities section of the statement of financial position for Ingalls Company and Wilder Company. Each has assets totaling £4,200,000.

Ingalls Co.			Wilder Co.	
Share capital—ordinary (£20 par)	£2,000,000		Share capital—ordinary (£20 par)	£2,900,000
Retained earnings (Cash			Retained earnings (Cash	
dividends, £220,000)	700,000		dividends, £328,000)	700,000
Non-current liabilities, 10%	1,200,000		Current liabilities	600,000
Current liabilities	300,000			
	£4,200,000			£4,200,000

For the year, each company has earned the same income before interest and taxes.

	Ingalls Co.	Wilder Co.
Income from operations	£1,200,000	£1,200,000
Interest expense	120,000	–0–
Income before income tax	1,080,000	1,200,000
Income tax (40%)	432,000	480,000
Net income	£ 648,000	£ 720,000

At year-end, the market price of an Ingalls' share was £101, and Wilder's was £63.50. Assume statement of financial position amounts are representative for the entire year.

Instructions

(a) Which company is more profitable in terms of return on total assets?

(b) Which company is more profitable in terms of return on ordinary share equity?

(c) Which company has the greater net income per share? Neither company issued or reacquired shares during the year.

(d) From the point of view of net income, is it advantageous to the shareholders of Ingalls Co. to have the non-current liabilities outstanding? Why?

(e) What is the book value per share for each company?

9 **E15-20 (Trading on the Equity Analysis)** Presented below is information from the annual report of DeVries Plastics, Inc.

Operating income	€ 532,150
Bond interest expense	135,000
Income before income tax	397,150
Income tax	183,432
Net income	€ 213,718
Bonds payable	€1,500,000
Share capital—ordinary	875,000
Retained earnings	575,000

Instructions

   (a) Compute the return on ordinary share equity and the rate of interest paid on bonds. (Assume balances for debt and equity accounts approximate averages for the year.)

   (b) Is DeVries Plastics, Inc. trading on the equity successfully? Explain.

10 *E15-21 **(Preference Dividends)** The outstanding share capital of Pennington Corporation consists of 2,000 shares of $100 par value, 6% preference, and 5,000 shares of $50 par value ordinary.

Instructions

Assuming that the company has retained earnings of $70,000, all of which is to be paid out in dividends, and that preference dividends were not paid during the 2 years preceding the current year, determine how much each class of shares should receive under each of the following conditions.

   (a) The preference shares are non-cumulative and non-participating.

   (b) The preference shares are cumulative and non-participating.

   (c) The preference shares are cumulative and participating. (Round dividend rate percentages to four decimal places.)

10 *E15-22 **(Preference Dividends)** Martinez Company's ledger shows the following balances on December 31, 2015.

Share Capital—Preference, 5%—€10 par value, outstanding 20,000 shares	€ 200,000
Share Capital—Ordinary—€100 par value, outstanding 30,000 shares	3,000,000
Retained Earnings	630,000

Instructions

Assuming that the directors decide to declare total dividends in the amount of €266,000, determine how much each class of shares should receive under each of the conditions stated below. One year's dividends are in arrears on the preference shares.

   (a) The preference shares are cumulative and fully participating.

   (b) The preference shares are non-cumulative and non-participating.

   (c) The preference shares are non-cumulative and are participating in distributions in excess of a 7% dividend rate on the ordinary shares.

10 *E15-23 **(Preference Share Dividends)** Hagar Company has outstanding 2,500 shares of £100 par, 6% preference shares and 15,000 shares of £10 par value ordinary. The schedule below shows the amount of dividends paid out over the last 4 years.

Instructions

Allocate the dividends to each type of shares under assumptions (a) and (b). Express your answers in per share amounts using the format shown below.

		Assumptions			
		(a) Preference, non-cumulative, and non-participating		(b) Preference, cumulative, and fully participating	
Year	Paid-out	Preference	Ordinary	Preference	Ordinary
2014	£12,000				
2015	£26,000				
2016	£52,000				
2017	£76,000				

10 *E15-24 **(Computation of Book Value per Share)** Johnstone Inc. began operations in January 2014 and reported the following results for each of its 3 years of operations.

2014 $260,000 net loss   2015 $40,000 net loss   2016 $700,000 net income

At December 31, 2016, Johnstone Inc. share capital accounts were as follows.

Share Capital—Preference, 6% cumulative, par value $100; authorized, issued, and outstanding 5,000 shares	$500,000
Share Capital—Ordinary, par value $1.00; authorized 1,000,000 shares; issued and outstanding 750,000 shares	$750,000

Johnstone Inc. has never paid a cash or share dividend. There has been no change in the share capital accounts since Johnstone began operations. The country law permits dividends only from retained earnings.

Instructions

(a) Compute the book value of the ordinary shares at December 31, 2016.

(b) Compute the book value of the ordinary shares at December 31, 2016, assuming that the preference shares have a liquidating value of $106 per share.

PROBLEMS

P15-1 (Equity Transactions and Statement Preparation) On January 5, 2015, Phelps Corporation received a charter granting the right to issue 5,000 shares of $100 par value, 8% cumulative and non-participating preference shares, and 50,000 shares of $10 par value ordinary shares. It then completed these transactions.

Jan. 11 Issued 20,000 ordinary shares at $16 per share.

Feb. 1 Issued to Sanchez Corp. 4,000 preference shares for the following assets: machinery with a fair value of $50,000; a factory building with a fair value of $160,000; and land with an appraised value of $270,000.

July 29 Purchased 1,800 ordinary shares at $17 per share. (Use cost method.)

Aug. 10 Sold the 1,800 treasury shares at $14 per share.

Dec. 31 Declared a $0.25 per share cash dividend on the ordinary shares and declared the preference dividend.

Dec. 31 Closed the Income Summary account. There was $175,700 net income.

Instructions

(a) Record the journal entries for the transactions listed above.

(b) Prepare the equity section of Phelps Corporation's statement of financial position as of December 31, 2015.

P15-2 (Treasury Share Transactions and Presentation) Clemson Company had the following equity as of January 1, 2015.

Share capital—ordinary, €5 par value, 20,000 shares issued	€100,000
Share premium—ordinary	300,000
Retained earnings	320,000
Total equity	€720,000

During 2015, the following transactions occurred.

Feb. 1 Clemson repurchased 2,000 treasury shares at a price of €19 per share.

Mar. 1 800 shares of treasury shares repurchased above were reissued at €17 per share.

Mar. 18 500 shares of treasury shares repurchased above were reissued at €14 per share.

Apr. 22 600 shares of treasury shares repurchased above were reissued at €20 per share.

Instructions

(a) Prepare the journal entries to record the treasury share transactions in 2015, assuming Clemson uses the cost method.

(b) Prepare the equity section of the statement of financial position as of April 30, 2015. Net income for the first 4 months of 2015 was €130,000.

P15-3 (Equity Transactions and Statement Preparation) Hatch Company has two classes of share capital outstanding: 8%, £20 par preference and £5 par ordinary. At December 31, 2014, the following accounts were included in equity.

Share Capital—Preference, 150,000 shares	£ 3,000,000
Share Capital—Ordinary, 2,000,000 shares	10,000,000
Share Premium—Preference	200,000
Share Premium—Ordinary	27,000,000
Retained Earnings	4,500,000

The following transactions affected equity during 2015.

Jan. 1 30,000 preference shares issued at £22 per share.

Feb. 1 50,000 ordinary shares issued at £20 per share.

June 1 2-for-1 share split (par value reduced to £2.50).

July 1 30,000 ordinary treasury shares purchased at £10 per share. Hatch uses the cost method.

Sept. 15 10,000 treasury shares reissued at £11 per share.

Dec. 31 The preference dividend is declared, and an ordinary dividend of 50 pence per share is declared.

Dec. 31 Net income is £2,100,000.

Instructions

Prepare the equity section of the statement of financial position for Hatch Company at December 31, 2015. Show all supporting computations.

3 5 P15-4 (Share Transactions—Lump Sum) Seles Corporation's charter authorized issuance of 100,000 ordinary shares of €10 par value and 50,000 shares of €50 preference shares. The following transactions involving the issuance of shares were completed. Each transaction is independent of the others.

1. Issued a €10,000, 9% bond payable at par and gave as a bonus one preference share, which at that time was selling for €106 a share.
2. Issued 500 ordinary shares for machinery. The machinery had been appraised at €7,100; the seller's book value was €6,200. The most recent market price of the ordinary shares is €16 a share.
3. Issued 375 ordinary shares and 100 preference shares for a lump sum amounting to €10,800. The ordinary had been selling at €14 and the preference at €65.
4. Issued 200 shares of ordinary and 50 shares of preference for furniture and fixtures. The ordinary shares had a fair value of €16 per share; the furniture and fixtures have a fair value of €6,500.

Instructions
Record the transactions listed above in journal entry form.

4 P15-5 (Treasury Shares—Cost Method) Before Smith Corporation engages in the treasury share transactions listed below, its general ledger reflects, among others, the following account balances (par value is £30 per share).

Share Premium—Ordinary	Share Capital—Ordinary	Retained Earnings
£99,000	£270,000	£80,000

Instructions
Record the treasury share transactions (given below) under the cost method of handling treasury shares; use the FIFO method for purchase-sale purposes.

   (a) Bought 380 treasury shares at £40 per share.
   (b) Bought 300 treasury shares at £45 per share.
   (c) Sold 350 treasury shares at £42 per share.
   (d) Sold 110 treasury shares at £38 per share.

4 7 9 P15-6 (Treasury Shares—Cost Method—Equity Section Preparation) Washington Company has the following equity accounts at December 31, 2015.

Share Capital—Ordinary—$100 par value, authorized 8,000 shares	$480,000
Retained Earnings	294,000

Instructions
   (a) Prepare entries in journal form to record the following transactions, which took place during 2016.

      (1) 280 ordinary shares were purchased at $97 per share. (These are to be accounted for using the cost method.)
      (2) A $20 per share cash dividend was declared.
      (3) The dividend declared in No. 2 above was paid.
      (4) The treasury shares purchased in No. 1 above were resold at $102 per share.
      (5) 500 shares were purchased at $105 per share.
      (6) 350 of the shares purchased in No. 5 above were resold at $96 per share.

   (b) Prepare the equity section of Washington Company's statement of financial position after giving effect to these transactions, assuming that the net income for 2016 was $94,000. Country law requires restriction of retained earnings for the amount of treasury shares.

4 7 P15-7 (Cash Dividend Entries) The books of Conchita Corporation carried the following account balances as of December 31, 2015.

Cash	R$ 195,000
Share Capital—Preference (6% cumulative, non-participating, R$50 par)	300,000
Share Capital—Ordinary (no-par value, 300,000 shares issued)	1,500,000
Share Premium—Preference	150,000
Treasury Shares (ordinary 2,800 shares at cost)	33,600
Retained Earnings	105,000

The company decided not to pay any dividends in 2015.

The board of directors, at their annual meeting on December 21, 2016, declared the following: "The current year dividends shall be 6% on the preference and R$0.30 per share on the ordinary. The dividends in arrears shall be paid by issuing 1,500 treasury shares." At the date of declaration, the preference is selling at R$80 per share, and the ordinary at R$12 per share. Net income for 2016 is estimated at R$77,000.

Instructions
   (a) Prepare the journal entries required for the dividend declaration and payment, assuming that they occur simultaneously.
   (b) Could Conchita Corporation give the preference shareholders 2 years' dividends and ordinary shareholders a 30 cents per share dividend, all in cash?

P15-8 (Dividends and Splits) Myers Company provides you with the following condensed statement of financial position information.

Assets		Equity and Liabilities		
Equipment (net)	€250,000	Equity		
Intangibles	60,000	Share capital—ordinary (€5 par)	€ 20,000	
Investments in ABC shares		Share premium—ordinary	110,000	
(10,000 shares at cost)	70,000	Retained earnings	180,000	€310,000
Current assets	40,000	Non-current and current liabilities		110,000
Total assets	€420,000	Total equity and liabilities		€420,000

Instructions

For each transaction below, indicate the euro impact (if any) on the following five items: (1) total assets, (2) share capital—ordinary, (3) share premium—ordinary, (4) retained earnings, and (5) equity. (Each situation is independent.)

(a) Myers declares and pays a €1 per share cash dividend.

(b) Myers declares and issues a 10% share dividend when the market price is €14 per share.

(c) Myers declares and issues a 100% share dividend when the market price is €15 per share.

(d) Myers declares and distributes a property dividend. Myers gives one ABC share for every two shares held of Myers Company. ABC is selling for €10 per share on the date the property dividend is declared.

(e) Myers declares a 2-for-1 share split and issues new shares.

P15-9 (Equity Section of Statement of Financial Position) The following is a summary of all relevant transactions of Vicario Corporation since it was organized in 2015.

In 2015, 15,000 shares were authorized and 7,000 ordinary shares ($50 par value) were issued at a price of $57. In 2016, 1,000 shares were issued as a share dividend when a share was selling for $60. Three hundred ordinary shares were bought in 2017 at a cost of $64 per share. These 300 shares are still in the company treasury.

In 2016, 10,000 preference shares were authorized and the company issued 5,000 of them ($100 par value) at $113. Some of the preference shares were reacquired by the company and later reissued for $4,700 more than it cost the company.

The corporation has earned a total of $610,000 in net income and paid out a total of $312,600 in cash dividends since incorporation.

Instructions

Prepare the equity section of the statement of financial position in proper form for Vicario Corporation as of December 31, 2017. Account for treasury shares using the cost method.

P15-10 (Share Dividends and Share Split) Ortago S.A.'s €10 par ordinary shares are selling for €110 per share. Four million shares are currently issued and outstanding. The board of directors wishes to stimulate interest in Ortago S.A. ordinary shares before a forthcoming share issue but does not wish to distribute cash at this time. The board also believes that too many adjustments to the equity section, especially retained earnings, might discourage potential investors.

The board has considered three options for stimulating interest in the shares:

1. A 20% share dividend.

2. A 100% share dividend.

3. A 2-for-1 share split.

Instructions

Acting as financial advisor to the board, you have been asked to report briefly on each option and, considering the board's wishes, make a recommendation. Discuss the effects of each of the foregoing options.

P15-11 (Share and Cash Dividends) Earnhart Corporation has outstanding 3,000,000 ordinary shares with a par value of $10 each. The balance in its retained earnings account at January 1, 2015, was $24,000,000, and it then had Share Premium of $5,000,000. During 2015, the company's net income was $4,700,000. A cash dividend of $0.60 per share was declared on May 5, 2015, and was paid June 30, 2015, and a 6% share dividend was declared on November 30, 2015, and distributed to shareholders of record at the close of business on December 31, 2015. You have been asked to advise on the proper accounting treatment of the share dividend.

The existing shares of the company are quoted on a national securities exchange. The market price of the shares has been as follows.

October 31, 2015	$31
November 30, 2015	$34
December 31, 2015	$38

Instructions

(a) Prepare the journal entry to record the declaration and payment of the cash dividend.

(b) Prepare the journal entry to record the declaration and distribution of the share dividend.

(c) Prepare the equity section (including schedules of retained earnings and share premium) of the statement of financial position of Earnhart Corporation for the year 2015 on the basis of the foregoing information. Draft a note to the financial statements setting forth the basis of the accounting for the share dividend, and add separately appropriate comments or explanations regarding the basis chosen.

P15-12 (Analysis and Classification of Equity Transactions) Penzi Company was formed on July 1, 2013. It was authorized to issue 300,000 shares of £10 par value ordinary shares and 100,000 shares of 8% £25 par value, cumulative and non-participating preference shares. Penzi Company has a July 1–June 30 fiscal year. The following information relates to the equity accounts of Penzi Company.

Ordinary Shares

Prior to the 2015–2016 fiscal year, Penzi Company had 110,000 ordinary shares outstanding issued as follows.

1. 85,000 shares were issued for cash on July 1, 2013, at £31 per share.

2. On July 24, 2013, 5,000 shares were exchanged for a plot of land which cost the seller £70,000 in 2007 and had an estimated fair value of £220,000 on July 24, 2013.

3. 20,000 shares were issued on March 1, 2014, for £42 per share.

During the 2015–2016 fiscal year, the following transactions regarding ordinary shares took place.

November 30, 2015	Penzi purchased 2,000 of its own shares on the open market at £39 per share. Penzi uses the cost method for treasury shares.
December 15, 2015	Penzi declared a 5% share dividend for shareholders of record on January 15, 2016, to be issued on January 31, 2016. Penzi was having a liquidity problem and could not afford a cash dividend at the time. Penzi's ordinary shares were selling at £52 per share on December 15, 2015.
June 20, 2016	Penzi sold 500 of its own ordinary shares that it had purchased on November 30, 2015, for £21,000.

Preference Shares

Penzi issued 40,000 preference shares at £44 per share on July 1, 2014.

Cash Dividends

Penzi has followed a schedule of declaring cash dividends in December and June, with payment being made to shareholders of record in the following month. The cash dividends which have been declared since inception of the company through June 30, 2016, are shown below.

Declaration Date	Ordinary Shares	Preference Shares
12/15/14	£0.30 per share	£1.00 per share
6/15/15	£0.30 per share	£1.00 per share
12/15/15	—	£1.00 per share

No cash dividends were declared during June 2016 due to the company's liquidity problems.

Retained Earnings

As of June 30, 2015, Penzi's retained earnings account had a balance of £690,000. For the fiscal year ending June 30, 2016, Penzi reported net income of £40,000.

Instructions

Prepare the equity section of the statement of financial position, including appropriate notes, for Penzi Company as of June 30, 2016, as it should appear in its annual report to the shareholders.

CONCEPTS FOR ANALYSIS

CA15-1 (Preemptive Rights and Dilution of Ownership) Wallace Computer Company is a small, closely held corporation. Eighty percent of the shares are held by Derek Wallace, president. Of the remainder, 10% are held by members of his family and 10% by Kathy Baker, a former officer who is now retired. The statement of financial position of the company at June 30, 2015, was substantially as shown on page 748.

Assets		Equity and Liabilities	
Cash	£ 22,000	Share capital—ordinary	£250,000
Other	450,000	Retained earnings	172,000
	£472,000	Current liabilities	50,000
			£472,000

Additional authorized ordinary shares of £300,000 par value have never been issued. To strengthen the cash position of the company, Wallace issued ordinary shares with a par value of £100,000 to himself at par for cash. At the next shareholders' meeting, Baker objected and claimed that her interests had been injured.

Instructions

(a) Which shareholder's right was ignored in the issue of shares to Derek Wallace?

(b) How may the damage to Baker's interests be repaired most simply?

(c) If Derek Wallace offered Baker a personal cash settlement and they agreed to employ you as an impartial arbitrator to determine the amount, what settlement would you propose? Present your calculations with sufficient explanation to satisfy both parties.

CA15-2 (Issuance of Shares for Land) Martin Corporation is planning to issue 3,000 shares of its own $10 par value ordinary shares for two acres of land to be used as a building site.

Instructions

(a) What general rule should be applied to determine the amount at which the land should be recorded?

(b) Under what circumstances should this transaction be recorded at the fair value of the land?

(c) Under what circumstances should this transaction be recorded at the fair value of the shares issued?

(d) Assume Martin intentionally records this transaction at an amount greater than the fair value of the land and the shares. Discuss this situation.

CA15-3 (Conceptual Issues—Equity) The IASB has set forth the Conceptual Framework that it will use in developing standards. As part of this Conceptual Framework, the IASB defines various elements of financial statements.

Instructions

Answer the following questions based on the Conceptual Framework.

(a) Define and discuss the term "equity."

(b) What transactions or events change equity?

(c) What financial statement element other than equity is typically affected by owner investments?

(d) What financial statement element other than equity is typically affected by distributions to owners?

(e) What are examples of changes within equity that do not change the total amount of equity?

CA15-4 (Share Dividends and Splits) The directors of Merchant Corporation are considering the issuance of a share dividend. They have asked you to discuss the proposed action by answering the following questions.

Instructions

(a) What is a share dividend? How is a share dividend distinguished from a share split (1) from a legal standpoint, and (2) from an accounting standpoint?

(b) For what reasons does a corporation usually declare a share dividend? A share split?

(c) Discuss the amount, if any, of retained earnings to be capitalized in connection with a share dividend.

CA15-5 (Share Dividends) Yamada Inc., a client, is considering the authorization of a 10% ordinary share dividend to ordinary shareholders. The financial vice president of Yamada wishes to discuss the accounting implications of such an authorization with you before the next meeting of the board of directors.

Instructions

(a) The first topic the vice president wishes to discuss is the nature of the share dividend to the recipient. Discuss the case against considering the share dividend as income to the recipient.

(b) The other topic for discussion is the propriety of issuing the share dividend to all "shareholders of record" or to "shareholders of record exclusive of shares held in the name of the corporation as treasury shares." Discuss the case against issuing share dividends on treasury shares.

CA15-6 (Share Dividend, Cash Dividend, and Treasury Shares) Mask Company has 30,000 shares of €10 par value ordinary shares authorized and 20,000 shares issued and outstanding. On August 15, 2015, Mask purchased 1,000 shares of treasury shares for €18 per share. Mask uses the cost method to account for treasury shares. On September 14, 2015, Mask sold 500 shares of the treasury shares for €20 per share.

In October 2015, Mask declared and distributed 1,950 shares as a share dividend from unissued shares when the market price of the ordinary shares was €21 per share.

On December 20, 2015, Mask declared a €1 per share cash dividend, payable on January 10, 2016, to shareholders of record on December 31, 2015.

Instructions

(a) How should Mask account for the purchase and sale of the treasury shares, and how should the treasury shares be presented in the statement of financial position at December 31, 2015?

(b) How should Mask account for the share dividend, and how would it affect equity at December 31, 2015? Why?

(c) How should Mask account for the cash dividend, and how would it affect the statement of financial position at December 31, 2015? Why?

 CA15-7 (Treasury Shares) Lois Kenseth, president of Sycamore Corporation, is concerned about several large shareholders who have been very vocal lately in their criticisms of her leadership. She thinks they might mount a campaign to have her removed as the corporation's CEO. She decides that buying them out by purchasing their shares could eliminate them as opponents, and she is confident they would accept a "good" offer. Kenseth knows the corporation's cash position is decent, so it has the cash to complete the transaction. She also knows the purchase of these shares will increase earnings per share, which should make other investors quite happy. (Earnings per share is calculated by dividing net income available for the ordinary shareholders by the weighted-average number of shares outstanding. Therefore, if the number of shares outstanding is decreased by purchasing treasury shares, earnings per share increases.)

Instructions

Answer the following questions.

(a) Who are the stakeholders in this situation?

(b) What are the ethical issues involved?

(c) Should Kenseth authorize the transaction?

USING YOUR JUDGMENT

FINANCIAL REPORTING

Financial Reporting Problem

Marks and Spencer plc (M&S)

The financial statements of M&S (GBR) are presented in Appendix A. The company's complete annual report, including the notes to the financial statements, is available online.

Instructions

Refer to M&S's financial statements and the accompanying notes to answer the following questions.

(a) What is the par or stated value of M&S's preference shares?

(b) What is the par or stated value of M&S's ordinary shares?

(c) What percentage of M&S's authorized ordinary shares was issued at year-end 2013?

(d) How many ordinary shares were outstanding at year-end 2012 and 2013?

(e) What was the pound amount effect of the cash dividends on M&S's equity?

(f) What is M&S's return on ordinary share equity for 2013 and 2012?

(g) What is M&S's payout ratio for 2013 and 2012?

Comparative Analysis Case

adidas and Puma

The financial statements of adidas (DEU) and Puma (DEU) are presented in Appendices B and C, respectively. The complete annual reports, including the notes to the financial statements, are available online.

Instructions

Use the companies' financial statements to answer the following questions.

(a) What is the par or stated value of adidas's and Puma's ordinary shares?

(b) How many shares were issued by adidas and Puma at December 31, 2012?

(c) How many shares are held as treasury shares by adidas at December 31, 2012, and by Puma at December 31, 2012?

(d) How many adidas ordinary shares are outstanding at December 31, 2012? How many Puma ordinary shares are outstanding at December 29, 2012?

(e) What amounts of cash dividends per share were declared by adidas and Puma in 2012? What were the monetary amount effects of the cash dividends on each company's equity?

(f) What are adidas's and Puma's return on equity for 2012 and 2011? Which company gets the higher return on the equity of its shareholders?

(g) What are adidas's and Puma's payout ratios for 2012?

Financial Statement Analysis Case

Case 1: BHP Billiton

BHP Billiton (GBR) is the world's largest diversified natural resources company. The company extracts and processes minerals, oil, and gas from its production operations located primarily in Australia, the Americas, and southern Africa. BHP Billiton sells its products globally, with sales and marketing taking place through its principal hubs of The Hague and Singapore. Presented below are some basic facts for BHP Billiton.

Billiton (in thousands)	2013	2012
Sales	$ 65,986	$ 72,226
Net earnings	11,075	15,532
Total assets	138,109	129,273
Total liabilities	66,074	62,188
Share capital	2,255	2,255
Reserves	1,970	1,912
Retained earnings	66,979	62,236
Treasury shares	(540)	(533)
Number of shares outstanding (millions)	5,322	5,323

Instructions

(a) What are some of the reasons that management purchases its own shares?

(b) Explain how earnings per share might be affected by treasury share transactions.

(c) Calculate the ratio of debt to assets for 2012 and 2013, and discuss the implications of the change.

Case 2: Jinpain International Ltd.

The following note related to equity was reported in Jinpain International's (CHN) annual report.

On February 1, the Board of Directors declared a 2-for-1 share split, distributed on February 25 to shareholders of record on February 10. Accordingly, all numbers of common (ordinary) shares, except unissued shares and treasury shares, and all per share data have been restated to reflect this share split.

Instructions

(a) What is the significance of the date of record and the date of distribution?

(b) Why might Jinpain have declared a 2-for-1 for share split?

(c) What impact does Jinpain's share split have on (1) total equity, (2) total par value, (3) outstanding shares, and (4) book value per share?

Accounting, Analysis, and Principles

On January 1, 2015, Nadal Corporation had the following equity accounts.

Share Capital—Ordinary (€10 par value, 60,000 shares issued and outstanding)	€600,000
Share Premium—Ordinary	500,000
Retained Earnings	620,000

During 2015, the following transactions occurred.

Jan. 15	Declared and paid a €1.05 cash dividend per share to shareholders.
Apr. 15	Declared and issued a 10% share dividend. The market price of the shares was €14 per share.
May 15	Reacquired 2,000 ordinary shares at a market price of €15 per share.
Nov. 15	Reissued 1,000 shares held in treasury at a price of €18 per share.
Dec. 31	Determined that net income for the year was €370,000.

Accounting

Journalize the above transactions. (Include entries to close net income to Retained Earnings.) Determine the ending balances to be reported for Share Capital—Ordinary, Retained Earnings, and Equity.

Analysis

Calculate the payout ratio and the return on equity ratio.

Principles

The Federer Group is examining Nadal's financial statements and wonders whether the "gains" or "losses" on Nadal's treasury share transactions should be included in income for the year. Briefly explain whether, and the conceptual reasons why, gains or losses on treasury share transactions should be recorded in income.

IFRS   BRIDGE TO THE PROFESSION

Professional Research

Recall from Chapter 13 that Hincapie Co. (a specialty bike-accessory manufacturer) is expecting growth in sales of some products targeted to the low-price market. Hincapie is contemplating a preference share issue to help finance this expansion in operations. The company is leaning toward preference shares because ownership will not be diluted, but the investors will get an extra dividend if the company does well. The company management wants to be certain that its reporting of this transaction is transparent to its current shareholders and wants you to research the disclosure requirements related to its capital structure.

Instructions

Access the IFRS authoritative literature at the IASB website (*http://eifrs.iasb.org/*) (you may register for free eIFRS access at this site). When you have accessed the documents, you can use the search tool in your Internet browser to respond to the following questions. (Provide paragraph citations.)

(a) Identify the authoritative literature that addresses disclosure of information about capital structure.

(b) What information about share capital must companies disclose? Discuss how Hincapie should report the proposed preference share issue.

Professional Simulation

In this simulation, you are asked to address equations related to the accounting for equity. Prepare responses to all parts.

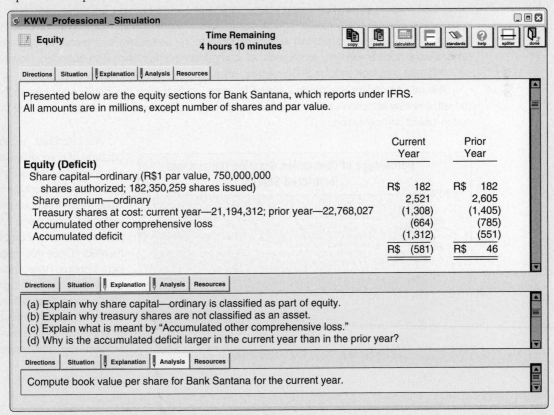

KWW_Professional _Simulation

Equity   Time Remaining   4 hours 10 minutes

Directions | Situation | Explanation | Analysis | Resources

Presented below are the equity sections for Bank Santana, which reports under IFRS. All amounts are in millions, except number of shares and par value.

	Current Year	Prior Year
Equity (Deficit)		
Share capital—ordinary (R$1 par value, 750,000,000 shares authorized; 182,350,259 shares issued)	R$ 182	R$ 182
Share premium—ordinary	2,521	2,605
Treasury shares at cost: current year—21,194,312; prior year—22,768,027	(1,308)	(1,405)
Accumulated other comprehensive loss	(664)	(785)
Accumulated deficit	(1,312)	(551)
	R$ (581)	R$ 46

Directions | Situation | Explanation | Analysis | Resources

(a) Explain why share capital—ordinary is classified as part of equity.
(b) Explain why treasury shares are not classified as an asset.
(c) Explain what is meant by "Accumulated other comprehensive loss."
(d) Why is the accumulated deficit larger in the current year than in the prior year?

Directions | Situation | Explanation | Analysis | Resources

Compute book value per share for Bank Santana for the current year.

Remember to check the book's companion website, at www.wiley.com/ college/kieso, to find additional resources for this chapter.

Kicking the Habit

Some habits die hard. Take share options—called by some "the crack cocaine of incentives." Share options are a form of compensation that gives key employees the choice to purchase shares at a given (usually lower-than-market) price. For many years, companies were hooked on these products. Why? The combination of a hot equity market and favorable accounting treatment made share options the incentive of choice. They were compensation with no expense to the companies that granted them, and the share options were popular with key employees, so companies granted them with abandon. However, the accounting rules that took effect in 2005 required *expensing* the fair value of share options.

This new treatment has made it easier for companies to kick this habit. As shown in the chart on the left, a review of option use for over 250 companies around the world indicates a decline in the use of option-based compensation.

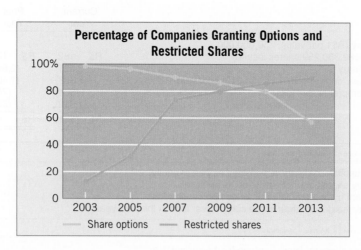

Percentage of Companies Granting Options and Restricted Shares

Share options   Restricted shares

As indicated, a smaller percentage of companies are granting share options, following implementation of share-option expensing, while there is an upward trend for restricted-share plans. As a spokesperson at one company commented, "Once you begin expensing options, the attractiveness significantly drops." Indeed, in the 1990s, executives with huge option stockpiles had an almost irresistible incentive to do whatever it took to increase the share price and cash in their options.

By reining in options, many companies are taking steps toward curbing both out-of-control executive pay and the era of corporate corruption that it spawned. Some of the ways that companies are curbing option grants include replacing options with restricted shares. As indicated in the chart on the right, in addition to the increase in the percentage of companies granting restricted shares, there is also a marked trend in the value of restricted shares granted relative to options in recent years. Some companies in the information technology industry, such as **Microsoft** (USA) and **Yahoo!** (USA), have switched to restricted-share plans completely.

Is this a good trend? Most believe it is. The requirement to expense share-based compensation similar to other forms of compensation has changed the focus of compensation plans to rewarding talent and performance without breaking the bank. The positive impact on corporate behavior, while hard to measure, should benefit investors in years to come.

Sources: Adapted from Louis Lavelle, "Kicking the Stock-Options Habit," *BusinessWeek Online* (February 16, 2005). Graphs from J. Doyle and S. Sussman, "Global Long-Term Incentives: Trends and Predictions," Buck Consultants (October 8, 2013); and J. Ciesielski, "S&P 500 Executive Pay: The Bread Keeps Rising," *The Analyst's Accounting Observer* (June 25, 2012).

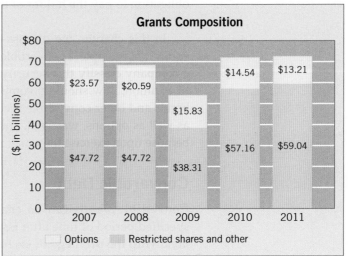

CONCEPTUAL FOCUS

> See the **Underlying Concepts** on pages 770 and 781.

INTERNATIONAL FOCUS

> Read the **Global Accounting Insights** on pages 783–784 for a discussion of non-IFRS financial reporting for dilutive securities and EPS.

PREVIEW OF CHAPTER 16

As the opening story indicates, companies are rethinking the use of various forms of share-based compensation. The purpose of this chapter is to discuss the proper accounting for share-based compensation. In addition, the chapter examines issues related to other types of financial instruments, such as convertible securities, warrants, and contingent shares, including their effects on reporting earnings per share. The content and organization of the chapter are as follows.

Dilutive Securities and Earnings per Share

Dilutive Securities and Compensation Plans	Computing Earnings per Share
• **Debt and equity**	• **Simple capital structure**
• **Convertible debt**	• **Complex capital structure**
• **Convertible preference shares**	
• **Share warrants**	
• **Accounting for share compensation**	
• **Debate over share-option accounting**	

DILUTIVE SECURITIES AND COMPENSATION PLANS

Debt and Equity

Many of the controversies related to the accounting for financial instruments such as share options, convertible securities, and preference shares relate to whether companies should report these instruments as a liability or as equity. For example, companies should classify non-redeemable ordinary shares as equity because the issuer has no **obligation** to pay dividends or repurchase the shares. Declaration of dividends is at the issuer's discretion, as is the decision to repurchase the shares. Similarly, preference shares that are not redeemable do not require the issuer to pay dividends or repurchase the shares. Thus, non-redeemable ordinary or preference shares lack an important characteristic of a liability—an obligation to pay the holder of the ordinary or preference shares at some point in the future.[1]

In this chapter, we discuss securities that have characteristics of *both* debt and equity. For example, a convertible bond has both debt and equity characteristics. Should a company classify this security as debt, as equity, or as part debt and part equity? In addition, how should a company compute earnings per share if it has convertible bonds and other convertible securities in its capital structure? Convertible securities, as well as options, warrants, and other securities, are often called dilutive securities because upon exercise they may reduce (dilute) earnings per share.

Convertible Debt

Convertible bonds can be changed into other corporate securities during some specified period of time after issuance. A convertible bond combines the benefits of a bond with the privilege of exchanging it for shares at the holder's option. Investors who purchase it desire the security of a bond holding (guaranteed interest and principal) plus the added option of conversion if the value of the shares appreciates significantly.

Corporations issue convertibles for two main reasons. One is to raise equity capital without giving up more ownership control than necessary. To illustrate, assume a company wants to raise $1 million; its ordinary shares are selling at $45 a share. To raise the $1 million, the company would have to sell 22,222 shares (ignoring issue costs). By selling 1,000 bonds at $1,000 par, each convertible into 20 ordinary shares, the company could raise $1 million by committing only 20,000 ordinary shares.

A second reason to issue convertibles is to obtain debt financing at cheaper rates. Many companies could issue debt only at high interest rates unless they attach a conversion option. The conversion privilege entices the investor to accept a lower interest rate than would normally be the case on a straight debt issue. For example,

---

[1]Presently, the IASB is working to develop a standard that will improve the financial reporting requirements for financial instruments with characteristics of debt and equity. It recognizes that the line between debt and equity is sometimes blurred and therefore classification of these instruments is inconsistent. At this point, the Board has identified certain securities that indicate equity classification. For example, a perpetual instrument is one that is not required to be redeemed unless the company decides to, or is forced to, liquidate. Without a specific limit to perpetual instruments' lives, the Board agrees that perpetual instruments should be classified as equity. Similarly, it requires that convertible debt should be split into a debt and an equity component if it is exchanged for a specified number of shares. If not exchangeable for a specified number of shares, the instrument would be classified entirely as debt.

China Minsheng Bank (CHN) recently issued convertible bonds that pay interest at an effective yield of 1.5 percent. This rate was much lower than China Minsheng would have had to pay by issuing straight debt. For this lower interest rate, the investor receives the right to buy China Minsheng's ordinary shares at a fixed price until the bond's maturity.[2]

Accounting for Convertible Debt

Convertible debt is accounted for as a compound instrument because it contains both a liability and an equity component. IFRS requires that compound instruments be separated into their liability and equity components for purposes of accounting. [1] Companies use the "with-and-without" method to value compound instruments.

Illustration 16-1 identifies the components used in the with-and-without method.

I F R S

See the Authoritative Literature section (page 794).

Fair value of convertible debt at date of issuance **(with both debt and equity components)**	−	Fair value of liability component at date of issuance, based on present value of cash flows	=	Equity component at date of issuance **(without the debt component)**

ILLUSTRATION 16-1
Convertible Debt Components

As indicated, the equity component is the residual amount after subtracting the liability component. IFRS does not permit companies to assign a value to the equity amount first and then determine the liability component. To do so would be inconsistent with the definition of equity, which is considered a residual amount. [2]

To implement the with-and-without approach, a company does the following:

1. First, determine the total fair value of the convertible debt *with both* the liability and equity component. **This is straightforward, as this amount is the proceeds received upon issuance.**

2. Second, determine the liability component by computing the net present value of all contractual future cash flows discounted at the market rate of interest. This market rate is the rate the company would pay on similar non-convertible debt.

3. Finally, subtract the liability component estimated in the second step from the fair value of the convertible debt (issue proceeds) to arrive at the equity component. That is, the equity component is the fair value of the convertible debt *without* the liability component.

Accounting at Time of Issuance. To illustrate the accounting for convertible debt, assume that Roche Group (CHE) issues 2,000 convertible bonds at the beginning of 2015. The bonds have a four-year term with a stated rate of interest of 6 percent and are issued at par with a face value of €1,000 per bond (the total proceeds received from issuance of the bonds are €2,000,000). Interest is payable annually at December 31. Each bond is convertible into 250 ordinary shares with a par value of €1. The market rate of interest on similar non-convertible debt is 9 percent.

[2]As with any investment, a buyer has to be careful. For example, Wherehouse Entertainment Inc. (USA), which had 6¼ percent convertibles outstanding, was taken private in a leveraged buyout. As a result, the convertible was suddenly as risky as a junk bond of a highly leveraged company with a coupon of only 6¼ percent. As one holder of the convertibles noted, "What's even worse is that the company will be so loaded down with debt that it probably won't have enough cash flow to make its interest payments. And the convertible debt we hold is subordinated to the rest of Wherehouse's debt." These types of situations have made convertibles less attractive and have led to the introduction of takeover protection covenants in some convertible bond offerings. Or, sometimes convertibles are permitted to be called at par, and therefore the conversion premium may be lost.

The time diagram in Illustration 16-2 depicts both the interest and principal cash flows.

ILLUSTRATION 16-2
Time Diagram for
Convertible Bond

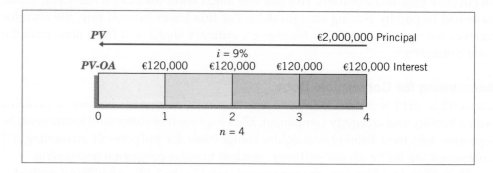

The liability component of the convertible debt is computed as shown in Illustration 16-3.

ILLUSTRATION 16-3
Fair Value of Liability
Component of
Convertible Bond

Present value of principal: €2,000,000 × .70843 (Table 6-2; $n = 4$, $i = 9\%$)	€1,416,860
Present value of the interest payments: €120,000 × 3.23972 (Table 6-4; $n = 4$, $i = 9\%$)	388,766
Present value of the liability component	€1,805,626

The equity component of Roche's convertible debt is then computed as shown in Illustration 16-4.

ILLUSTRATION 16-4
Equity Component of
Convertible Bond

Fair value of convertible debt at date of issuance	€2,000,000
Less: Fair value of liability component at date of issuance	1,805,626
Fair value of equity component at date of issuance	€ 194,374

The journal entry to record this transaction is as follows.

Cash	2,000,000	
Bonds Payable		1,805,626
Share Premium—Conversion Equity		194,374

The liability component of Roche's convertible debt issue is recorded as Bonds Payable. As shown in Chapter 14, the amount of the discount relative to the face value of the bond is amortized at each reporting period. So at maturity, the Bonds Payable account is reported at €2,000,000 (face value). The equity component of the convertible bond is recorded in the Share Premium—Conversion Equity account and is reported in the equity section of the statement of financial position. Because this amount is considered part of contributed capital, it does not change over the life of the convertible.[3]

Settlement of Convertible Bonds. We illustrate four settlement situations: (1) repurchase at maturity, (2) conversion at maturity, (3) conversion before maturity, and (4) repurchase before maturity.

Repurchase at maturity. If the bonds are not converted at maturity, Roche makes the following entry to pay off the convertible debtholders.

Bonds Payable	2,000,000	
Cash		2,000,000
(To record the redemption of bonds at maturity)		

[3]Transaction costs related to the liability and equity components are allocated in proportion to the proceeds received from the two components. *For purposes of homework, use the Share Premium—Conversion Equity account to record the equity component.* In practice, there may be considerable variance in the accounts used to record this component.

Because the carrying value of the bonds equals the face value, there is no gain or loss on repurchase at maturity. The amount originally allocated to equity of €194,374 either remains in the Share Premium—Conversion Equity account or is transferred to Share Premium—Ordinary.

Conversion of bonds at maturity. If the bonds are converted at maturity, Roche makes the following entry.

Share Premium—Conversion Equity	194,374	
Bonds Payable	2,000,000	
Share Capital—Ordinary		500,000
Share Premium—Ordinary		1,694,374
(To record the conversion of bonds at maturity)		

As indicated, Roche records a credit to Share Capital—Ordinary for €500,000 (2,000 bonds × 250 shares × €1 par) and the remainder to Share Premium—Ordinary for €1,694,374. There is no gain or loss on conversion at maturity. The original amount allocated to equity (€194,374) is transferred to the Share Premium—Ordinary account. As a result, Roche's equity has increased by a total of €2,194,374 through issuance and conversion of the convertible bonds. This accounting approach is often referred to as the **book value method** in that the carrying amount (book value) of the bond and related conversion equity determines the amount in the ordinary equity accounts.

Conversion of bonds before maturity. What happens if bonds are converted before maturity? To understand the accounting, we again use the Roche Group example. A schedule of bond amortization related to Roche's convertible bonds is shown in Illustration 16-5.

ILLUSTRATION 16-5
Convertible Bond Amortization Schedule

	SCHEDULE OF BOND AMORTIZATION			
	EFFECTIVE-INTEREST METHOD			
	6% BOND DISCOUNTED AT 9%			
Date	Cash Paid	Interest Expense	Discount Amortized	Carrying Amount of Bonds
1/1/15				€1,805,626
12/31/15	€120,000	€162,506	€42,505	1,848,132
12/31/16	120,000	166,332	46,330	1,894,464
12/31/17	120,000	170,502	50,500	1,944,966
12/31/18	120,000	175,034*	55,059	2,000,000

*€13 difference due to rounding.

Assuming that Roche converts its bonds into ordinary shares on December 31, 2016, Roche debits the Bonds Payable account for its carrying value of €1,894,464 (see Illustration 16-5). In addition, Roche credits Share Capital—Ordinary for €500,000 (2,000 × 250 × €1) and credits Share Premium—Ordinary for €1,588,838. The entry to record this conversion is as follows.

Share Premium—Conversion Equity	194,374	
Bonds Payable	1,894,464	
Share Capital—Ordinary		500,000
Share Premium—Ordinary		1,588,838
(To record the conversion of bonds before maturity)		

There is no gain or loss on conversion before maturity: The original amount allocated to equity (€194,374) is transferred to the Share Premium—Ordinary account.

Repurchase before maturity. In some cases, companies decide to repurchase the convertible debt before maturity. The approach used for allocating the amount paid upon repurchase follows the approach used when the convertible bond was originally issued. That is, Roche determines the fair value of the liability component of the convertible bonds at December 31, 2016, and then subtracts this amount from the fair value of the convertible bond issue (including the equity component) to arrive at the value for the equity. After this allocation is completed:

1. The difference between the consideration allocated to the liability component and the carrying amount of the liability is recognized as a gain or loss, and

2. The amount of consideration relating to the equity component is recognized (as a reduction) in equity. **[3]**

To illustrate, instead of converting the bonds on December 31, 2016, assume that Roche repurchases the convertible bonds from the bondholders. Pertinent information related to this conversion is as follows.

- Fair value of the convertible debt (including both liability and equity components), based on market prices at December 31, 2016, is €1,965,000.

- The fair value of the liability component is €1,904,900. This amount is based on computing the present value of a non-convertible bond with a two-year term (which corresponds to the shortened time to maturity of the repurchased bonds).

Roche first determines the gain or loss on the liability component, as computed in Illustration 16-6.

ILLUSTRATION 16-6
Gain or Loss on Debt
Repurchase

Present value of liability component at December 31, 2016 (given above)	€ 1,904,900
Carrying value of liability component at December 31, 2016 (per Illustration 16-5)	(1,894,464)
Loss on repurchase	€ 10,436

Roche has a loss on this repurchase because the fair value of the debt extinguished is greater than its carrying amount. To determine any adjustment to the equity, Roche computes the value of the equity as shown in Illustration 16-7.

ILLUSTRATION 16-7
Equity Adjustment on
Repurchase of
Convertible Bonds

Fair value of convertible debt at December 31, 2016 (**with equity component**)	€1,965,000
Less: Fair value of liability component at December 31, 2016 (similar 2-year non-convertible debt)	1,904,900
Fair value of equity component at December 31, 2016 (without debt component)	€ 60,100

Roche makes the following compound journal entry to record the entire repurchase transaction.

Bonds Payable	1,894,464	
Share Premium—Conversion Equity	60,100	
Loss on Repurchase	10,436	
Cash		1,965,000
(To record the repurchase of convertible bonds)		

In summary, the repurchase results in a loss related to the liability component and a reduction in Share Premium—Conversion Equity. The remaining balance in Share Premium—Conversion Equity of €134,274 (€194,374 − €60,100) is often transferred to Share Premium—Ordinary upon the repurchase.

Induced Conversions

Sometimes, the issuer wishes to encourage prompt conversion of its convertible debt to equity securities in order to reduce interest costs or to improve its debt to equity ratio. In this situation, the issuer may offer some form of additional consideration (such as cash or ordinary shares), called a "sweetener," to **induce conversion**. The issuing company reports the sweetener as an expense of the current period. Its amount is the fair value of the additional securities or other consideration given.

Assume that Helloid, Inc. has outstanding $1,000,000 par value convertible debentures convertible into 100,000 ordinary shares ($1 par value). When issued, Helloid recorded Share Premium—Conversion Equity of $15,000. Helloid wishes to reduce its annual interest cost. To do so, Helloid agrees to pay the holders of its convertible debentures an additional $80,000 if they will convert. Assuming conversion occurs, Helloid makes the following entry.

Conversion Expense	80,000	
Share Premium—Conversion Equity	15,000	
Bonds Payable	1,000,000	
Share Capital—Ordinary		100,000
Share Premium—Ordinary		915,000
Cash		80,000

Helloid records the additional $80,000 as **an expense of the current period** and not as a reduction of equity. **[4]**

Some argue that the cost of a conversion inducement is a cost of obtaining equity capital. As a result, they contend that companies should recognize the cost of conversion as a cost of (a reduction of) the equity capital acquired and not as an expense. However, the IASB indicated that when an issuer makes an additional payment to encourage conversion, the payment is for a service (bondholders converting at a given time) and should be reported as an expense.

Convertible Preference Shares

Convertible preference shares include an option for the holder to convert preference shares into a fixed number of ordinary shares. The major difference between accounting for a convertible bond and a convertible preference share is their classification. Convertible bonds are compound instruments because they have both a liability and an equity component. Convertible preference shares (unless mandatory redemption exists) are not compound instruments because they have only an equity component. As a result, convertible preference shares are reported as part of equity. When preference shares are converted or repurchased, there is no gain or loss recognized. The rationale is that a company does not recognize a gain or loss involving transactions with its existing shareholders.

2 LEARNING OBJECTIVE

Explain the accounting for convertible preference shares.

To illustrate, assume that Morse Company issues 1,000 convertible preference shares that have a par value of €1 per share. The shares were issued at a price of €200 per share. The journal entry to record this transaction is as follows.

Cash (1,000 × €200)	200,000	
Share Capital—Preference (1,000 × €1)		1,000
Share Premium—Conversion Equity		199,000
(To record the issuance of convertible		
preference shares)		

If each share is subsequently converted into 25 each ordinary shares (€2 par value) that have a fair value of €410,000, the journal entry to record the conversion is as follows.

Share Capital—Preference	1,000	
Share Premium—Conversion Equity	199,000	
Share Capital—Ordinary (1,000 × 25 × €2)		50,000
Share Premium—Ordinary		150,000
(To record the conversion of convertible		
preference shares)		

As indicated (and similar to the treatment for convertible bonds), Morse uses the book value method and does not recognize a gain or loss on the conversion. The fair value of the ordinary shares is therefore ignored in this computation. If the convertible preference shares are repurchased at their fair value instead of converted, Morse makes the following entry.

Share Capital—Preference	1,000	
Share Premium—Conversion Equity	199,000	
Retained Earnings	210,000	
Cash		410,000
(To record the repurchase of convertible preference shares)		

Morse does not report a gain or loss on the repurchase. Any excess paid above the book value of the convertible preference shares is often debited to Retained Earnings on the theory that an excess dividend is being paid to the preference shareholders to facilitate the repurchase.

What do the numbers mean?   **HOW LOW CAN YOU GO?**

Financial engineers are always looking for the next innovation in security design to meet the needs of both issuers and investors. Consider the convertible bonds issued by **Sony** (JPN). Sony's 5-year bonds have a zero coupon and are convertible into Sony ordinary shares at an exercise price of 957 yen. When issued, the bonds sold at an effective yield of 0 percent. That's right—a yield of zero.

How could this happen? When Sony issued the bonds, investors thought the options to convert were so valuable that they were willing to take zero interest payments. In essence,

the investors are paying interest to Sony, and Sony records interest revenue. Why would investors do this? If the share price rises, as many thought it would for Sony and many other tech companies at this time, these bond investors could convert and get a big gain in the shares.

Other Asian companies are on the convertible bandwagon, with **Qihoo 360 Technology** (CHN) and semiconductor maker **ASE** (TWN) issuing convertible bonds to meet investor demand for the potential gains from share appreciation.

Sources: Mariko Yasu, "Sony Shares Plunge after Convertible Bond Offering: Tokyo Mover," *Bloomberg* (November 14, 2012); and P. Davies, "Asia Turns Bullish on Convertible Bonds," *Financial Times* (September 1, 2013).

Share Warrants

Warrants are certificates entitling the holder to acquire shares at a certain price within a stated period. This option is similar to the conversion privilege: Warrants, if exercised, become ordinary shares and usually have a dilutive effect (reduce earnings per share) similar to that of the conversion of convertible securities. However, a substantial difference between convertible securities and share warrants is that upon exercise of the warrants, the holder has to pay a certain amount of money to obtain the shares.

The issuance of warrants or options to buy additional shares normally arises under three situations:

1. When issuing different types of securities, such as bonds or preference shares, companies often include warrants **to make the security more attractive**—by providing an "equity kicker."

2. Upon the issuance of additional ordinary shares, existing shareholders have a **preemptive right to purchase ordinary shares** first. Companies may issue warrants to evidence that right.

3. Companies give warrants, often referred to as *share options*, **to executives and employees** as a form of **compensation**.

The problems in accounting for share warrants are complex and present many difficulties—some of which remain unresolved. The following sections address the accounting for share warrants in the three situations listed on page 760.

Share Warrants Issued with Other Securities

Warrants issued with other securities are basically long-term options to buy ordinary shares at a fixed price. Generally, the life of warrants is five years, occasionally 10 years; very occasionally, a company may offer perpetual warrants.

A share warrant works like this. Assume that **Bohai Pharmaceutical Group** (CHN) offers a unit comprising one ordinary share and one share warrant. In this case, Bohai's warrants are detachable; that is, they can be detached (separated) from the ordinary shares and traded as a separate security. Companies may also issue non-detachable warrants with debt, which means the warrant cannot be separated from the debt. In either case, debt issued with warrants is considered a compound instrument for accounting purposes. The Bohai warrant in this example is exercisable at ¥24.25 per share and good for five years. The unit (share plus detachable warrant) sells for 22.75 (¥22.75). Since the price of the ordinary share the day before the sale was 19.88 (¥19.88), the difference suggests a price of 2.87 (¥2.87) for the warrant.

The investor pays for the warrant in order to receive the right to buy ordinary shares, at a fixed price of ¥24.25, sometime in the future. It would not be profitable at present for the purchaser to exercise the warrant and buy the share because the price of the share is much below the exercise price. But if, for example, the price of the share rises to ¥30, the investor gains ¥2.88 (¥30 − ¥24.25 − ¥2.87) on an investment of ¥2.87, a 100 percent increase! If the price never rises, the investor loses the full ¥2.87 per warrant.[4]

Thus, debt issued with share warrants is a compound instrument that has a debt and an equity component. As a result, the company should use the with-and-without method to allocate the proceeds between the two components.

Illustration. At one time, **Siemens AG** (DEU) issued bonds with detachable five-year warrants. Assume that the five-year warrants provide the option to buy one ordinary share (par value €5) at €25. At the time, an ordinary share of Siemens was selling for approximately €30. These warrants enabled Siemens to price its bond offering (with a €10,000,000 face value) at par with an 8¾ percent yield (quite a bit lower than prevailing rates at that time). In this example, Siemens was able to sell the bonds plus the warrants for €10,200,000.

To account for the proceeds from this sale, Siemens uses the with-and-without method. Using this approach, Siemens determines the present value of the future cash flows related to the bonds, which is €9,707,852. It then subtracts this amount from €10,200,000 to determine the equity component. Determination of the equity component, using the with-and-without method, is shown in Illustration 16-8.

Fair value of bonds with warrants	€10,200,000
Less: Fair value of liability component at date of issuance	9,707,852
Equity component at date of issuance	€ 492,148

ILLUSTRATION 16-8
Equity Component of Security Issue

In this situation, the bonds sell at a discount. Siemens records the sale as follows.

Cash	9,707,852	
Bonds Payable		9,707,852

In addition, Siemens sells warrants that it credits to Share Premium—Share Warrants. It makes the following entry.

Cash	492,148	
Share Premium—Share Warrants		492,148

[4]From the illustration, it is apparent that buying warrants can be an "all or nothing" proposition.

Siemens may combine the entries if desired. Here, we show them separately, to indicate that the purchaser of the bond is buying not only a bond but also a possible future claim on ordinary shares.

Assuming investors exercise all 10,000 warrants (one warrant per one ordinary share), Siemens makes the following entry.

Cash (10,000 × €25)	250,000	
Share Premium—Share Warrants	492,148	
Share Capital—Ordinary (10,000 × €5)		50,000
Share Premium—Ordinary		692,148

What if investors fail to exercise the warrants? In that case, Siemens debits Share Premium—Share Warrants for €492,148 and credits Share Premium—Expired Share Warrants for a like amount. The Share Premium—Expired Share Warrants reverts to the former shareholders.

Summary Analysis. The IASB indicates that companies should separate the debt and equity components of securities, such as convertible debt or bonds issued with warrants. We agree with this position. In both situations (convertible debt and debt issued with warrants), the investor has made a payment to the company for an equity feature—the right to acquire an equity instrument in the future. The only real distinction between them is that the additional payment made when the equity instrument is formally acquired takes different forms. The warrant holder pays additional cash to the issuing company; the convertible debtholder pays for shares by forgoing the receipt of interest from the conversion date until maturity and by forgoing the receipt of the maturity value itself. Thus, the difference is one of method or form of payment only, rather than one of substance.

Rights to Subscribe to Additional Shares

If the directors of a corporation decide to issue new ordinary shares, the old shareholders generally have the right (**preemptive privilege**) to purchase newly issued shares in proportion to their holdings. This privilege, referred to as a share right, saves existing shareholders from suffering a dilution of voting rights without their consent. Also, it may allow them to purchase shares somewhat below their market price. Unlike the warrants issued with other securities, the warrants issued for share rights are of short duration.

The certificate representing the share right states the number of shares the holder of the right may purchase. Each share owned ordinarily gives the owner one share right. The certificate also states the price at which the new shares may be purchased. The price is normally less than the current market price of such shares, which gives the rights a value in themselves. From the time they are issued until they expire, holders of share rights may purchase and sell them like any other security.

Companies make only a memorandum entry when they issue rights to existing shareholders. This entry indicates the number of rights issued to existing shareholders in order to ensure that the company has additional unissued shares registered for issuance in case the rights are exercised. Companies make no formal entry at this time because they have not yet issued shares nor received cash.

If holders exercise the share rights, a cash payment of some type usually is involved. If the company receives cash equal to the par value, it makes an entry crediting Share Capital—Ordinary at par value. If the company receives cash in excess of par value, it credits Share Premium—Ordinary. If it receives cash less than par value, a debit to Share Premium—Ordinary is appropriate.

Share Compensation Plans

The third form of warrant arises in share compensation plans to pay and motivate employees. This warrant is a share option, which gives key employees the option to purchase ordinary shares at a given price over an extended period of time.

A consensus of opinion is that effective compensation programs are ones that do the following:

1. Base compensation on employee and company performance.

2. Motivate employees to high levels of performance.

3. Help retain executives and allow for recruitment of new talent.

4. Maximize the employee's after-tax benefit and minimize the employer's after-tax cost.

5. Use performance criteria over which the employee has control.

Straight cash-compensation plans (salary and perhaps a bonus), though important, are oriented to the short run. Many companies recognize that they need a longer-term compensation plan in addition to the cash component.

Long-term compensation plans attempt to develop company loyalty among key employees by giving them "a piece of the action"—that is, an equity or ownership interest. These plans, generally referred to as **share-based compensation plans**, come in many forms. Essentially, they provide the employee with the opportunity to receive shares if the performance of the company (by whatever measure) is satisfactory. Typical performance measures focus on long-term improvements that are readily measurable and that benefit the company as a whole, such as increases in earnings per share, revenues, share price, or market share.

The data reported in Illustration 16-9 reinforce the point that the fair value of equity grants is significant and increasing. The study documents that compensation increased 7.7 percent for top executives, with equity grants (like restricted shares) being the biggest source of growth.

($ in millions)	2011	% Change from 2010
Salary	$ 1,781.3	0.2%
Bonus	648.8	−2.8
Fair value of equity grants	8,389.1	13.8
Non-equity incentive compensation	2,719.2	−2.9
Pension benefits	1,309.2	11.9
All other	590.6	7.8
Total executive compensation	$15,438.2	7.7

Source: J. Ciesielski, "S&P 500 Executive Pay: The Bread Keeps Rising," *The Analyst's Accounting Observer* (June 25, 2012).

ILLUSTRATION 16-9
Compensation Elements

Illustration 16-9 shows that cash compensation is less than 20 percent of total compensation. The fair value of equity grants comprised approximately 54 percent of total compensation.

As indicated in our opening story, companies are changing the way they use share-based compensation. That is, recent data indicate that share-option use is on the decline and that another form of share-based compensation, **restricted shares**, is on the rise. The major reasons for this change are two-fold. Critics often cited the indiscriminate use of share options as a reason why company executives manipulated accounting numbers in an attempt to achieve higher share price, thereby increasing the value of their options. As a result, many responsible companies decided to cut back on the issuance of options, both to avoid such accounting manipulations and to head off investor doubts. In addition, IFRS now results in companies recording a higher expense when share options are granted.

The Major Reporting Issue. Suppose that, as an employee for Hurdle Inc., you receive options to purchase 10,000 shares of the firm's ordinary shares as part of your compensation. The date you receive the options is referred to as the **grant date**. The options are good for 10 years. The market price and the exercise price for the shares are both $20 at the grant date. **What is the value of the compensation you just received?**

Some believe that what you have received has no value. They reason that because the difference between the market price and the exercise price is zero, no compensation results. Others argue these options do have value. If the share price goes above $20 any time in the next 10 years and you exercise the options, you may earn substantial compensation. For example, if at the end of the fourth year the share market price is $30 and you exercise your options, you earn $100,000 [10,000 options × ($30 − $20)], ignoring income taxes.

The question for Hurdle is how to report the granting of these options. One approach measures compensation cost by the excess of the market price of the shares over their exercise price at the grant date. This approach is referred to as the intrinsic-value method. It measures what the holder would receive today if the option was immediately exercised. The intrinsic value is **the difference between the market price of the shares and the exercise price of the options at the grant date**. Using the intrinsic-value method, Hurdle would not recognize any compensation expense related to your options because at the grant date the market price equaled the exercise price. (In the preceding paragraph, those who answered that the options had no value were looking at the question from the intrinsic-value approach.)

The second way to look at the question of how to report the granting of these options bases the cost of employee share options on the **fair value** of the share options granted. Under this fair value method, companies use acceptable option-pricing models to value the options at the date of grant. These models take into account the many factors that determine an option's underlying value.[5]

The IASB guidelines require that companies recognize compensation cost using the fair value method. [5] The IASB position is that companies should base the accounting for the cost of employee services on the fair value of compensation paid. This amount is presumed to be a measure of the value of the services received. We will discuss more about the politics of IFRS in this area later (see "Debate over Share-Option Accounting," page 770). Let's first describe the procedures involved.

Accounting for Share Compensation

Share-Option Plans

LEARNING OBJECTIVE 4

Describe the accounting for share compensation plans.

Share-option plans involve two main accounting issues:

1. How to determine compensation expense.

2. Over what periods to allocate compensation expense.

Determining Expense. **Under the fair value method**, companies compute total compensation expense based on the fair value of the options expected to vest on the date they grant the options to the employee(s) (i.e., the **grant date**).[6] Public companies estimate fair value by using an option-pricing model, with some adjustments for the unique factors of employee share options. No adjustments occur after the grant date in response to subsequent changes in the share price—either up or down.

Allocating Compensation Expense. In general, a company recognizes compensation expense in the periods in which its employees perform the service—the service period.

---

[5]These factors include the volatility of the underlying shares, the expected life of the options, the risk-free rate during the option life, and the expected dividends during the option life.

[6]"To vest" means "to earn the rights to." An employee's award becomes vested at the date that the employee's right to receive or retain shares or cash under the award is no longer contingent on remaining in the service of the employer.

Unless otherwise specified, the service period is the vesting period—the time between the grant date and the vesting date. Thus, the company determines total compensation cost at the grant date and allocates it to the periods benefited by its employees' services.

Share Compensation Example. An example will help show the accounting for a share-option plan. Assume that on November 1, 2014, the shareholders of Chen Company approve a plan that grants the company's five executives options to purchase 2,000 shares each of the company's ¥100 par value ordinary shares. The company grants the options on January 1, 2015. The executives may exercise the options at any time within the next 10 years. The option price per share is ¥6,000, and the market price of the shares at the date of grant is ¥7,000 per share.

Under the fair value method, the company computes total compensation expense by applying an acceptable fair value option-pricing model (such as the Black-Scholes option-pricing model). To keep this illustration simple, we assume that the fair value option-pricing model determines Chen's total compensation expense to be ¥22,000,000.

Basic entries. Under the fair value method, a company recognizes the value of the options as an expense in the periods in which the employee performs services. In the case of Chen Company, assume that the expected period of benefit is two years, starting with the grant date. Chen would record the transactions related to this option contract as follows.

At date of grant (January 1, 2015)

No entry.

To record compensation expense for 2015 (December 31, 2015)

Compensation Expense	11,000,000	
Share Premium—Share Options (¥22,000,000 ÷ 2)		11,000,000

To record compensation expense for 2016 (December 31, 2016)

Compensation Expense	11,000,000	
Share Premium—Share Options		11,000,000

As indicated, Chen allocates compensation expense evenly over the two-year service period.

Exercise. If Chen's executives exercise 2,000 of the 10,000 options (20 percent of the options) on June 1, 2018 (three years and five months after date of grant), the company records the following journal entry.

June 1, 2018

Cash (2,000 × ¥6,000)	12,000,000	
Share Premium—Share Options (20% × ¥22,000,000)	4,400,000	
Share Capital—Ordinary (2,000 × ¥100)		200,000
Share Premium—Ordinary		16,200,000

Expiration. If Chen's executives fail to exercise the remaining share options before their expiration date, the company transfers the balance in the Share Premium—Share Options account to a more properly titled share premium account, such as Share Premium—Expired Share Options. Chen records this transaction at the date of expiration as follows.

January 1, 2025 (expiration date)

Share Premium—Share Options	17,600,000	
Share Premium—Expired Share Options		17,600,000
(80% × ¥22,000,000)		

Adjustment. An unexercised share option does not nullify the need to record the costs of services received from executives and attributable to the share-option plan. Under IFRS, a company therefore does not adjust compensation expense upon expiration of the options.

Once the total compensation is measured at the date of grant, can it be changed in future periods? The answer is that it depends on whether the adjustment is caused by a service or market condition. A service condition requires employees to complete a specified period of service to receive the award. If a service condition exists, the company is permitted to adjust the number of share options expected to the actual number of instruments vested. **Thus, compensation can be adjusted.** The company should adjust the estimate of compensation expense recorded in the current period (as a change in estimate). A company records this change in estimate by debiting Share Premium—Share Options and crediting Compensation Expense for the amount of cumulative compensation expense recorded to date (thus decreasing compensation expense in the period of forfeiture).

A market condition results when vesting or exercisability of the share option depends on a performance condition, such as a rise in the market price of the company's ordinary shares. Because market conditions are reflected in the determination of fair value at the grant date, **no adjustment to compensation expense is permitted**.

Many question this accounting treatment. The practice of not reversing share-option awards due to market conditions (share price stays below exercise price) means that a company may recognize an expense for an option that is never exercised. However, if the reason the option is not exercised relates to a service condition (**failure to stay as an employee and perform services**), the compensation expense related to the option is adjusted. In summary, estimates of the number of share options that are expected to vest are adjusted to the actual number that do vest. Cancellations due to market conditions are not adjusted.[7]

Restricted Shares

As indicated earlier, many companies are also using restricted shares (or replacing options altogether) to compensate employees. Restricted-share plans transfer shares to employees, subject to an agreement that the shares cannot be sold, transferred, or pledged until vesting occurs. Similar to share options, these shares are subject to forfeiture if the conditions for vesting are not met.[8]

Major advantages of restricted-share plans are:

1. *Restricted shares never become completely worthless.* In contrast, if the share price does not exceed the exercise price for a share option, the options are worthless. The restricted shares, however, still have value.

2. *Restricted shares generally result in less dilution to existing shareholders.* Restricted-share awards are usually one-half to one-third the size of share options. For example, if a company issues share options on 1,000 shares, an equivalent restricted-share offering might be 333 to 500 shares. The reason for the difference is that at the end of the vesting period, the restricted shares will have value, whereas the share options may not. As a result, fewer shares are involved in restricted-share plans, and therefore less dilution results if the share price rises.

---

[7]Companies sometimes modify the terms and conditions on which the share options were granted, to reward outstanding performance or provide a morale boost for some or all employees. Modifications may reduce the exercise period, extend the term of the options, or increase the number of shares issuable upon exercise. Modifications to share-based arrangements that decrease the fair value of the grant are basically ignored. However, if the fair value of the grant increases due to a modification, then the incremental fair value of the modified grant should be accounted for as additional compensation expense over the remaining vesting period.

[8]Most companies base vesting on future service for a period of generally three to five years. Vesting may also be conditioned on some performance target such as revenue, net income, cash flows, or some combination of these three factors. The employee also collects dividends on the restricted shares. These dividends generally must be repaid if forfeiture occurs.

3. *Restricted shares better align the employee incentives with the companies' incentives.* The holder of restricted shares is essentially a shareholder and should be more interested in the long-term objectives of the company. In contrast, the recipients of share options often have a short-run focus, which leads to taking risks to hype the share price for short-term gain to the detriment of the long-term.

The accounting for restricted shares follows the same general principles as accounting for share options at the date of grant. That is, the company determines the fair value of the restricted shares at the date of grant (usually the fair value of a share) and then expenses that amount over the service period. Subsequent changes in the fair value of the shares are ignored for purposes of computing compensation expense.

Restricted Shares Example. Assume that on January 1, 2015, Ogden Company issues 1,000 restricted shares to its CEO, Christie DeGeorge. Ogden's shares have a fair value of $20 per share on January 1, 2015. Additional information is as follows.

- The service period related to the restricted shares is five years.
- Vesting occurs if DeGeorge stays with the company for a five-year period.
- The par value is $1 per share.

Ogden makes the following entry on the grant date (January 1, 2015).

Unearned Compensation	20,000	
Share Capital—Ordinary (1,000 × $1)		1,000
Share Premium—Ordinary (1,000 × $19)		19,000

The credits to Share Capital—Ordinary and Share Premium—Ordinary indicate that Ogden has issued shares. The debit to Unearned Compensation (often referred to as Deferred Compensation Expense) identifies the total compensation expense the company will recognize over the five-year period. **Unearned Compensation represents the cost of services yet to be performed, which is not an asset.** Consequently, the company reports Unearned Compensation in equity in the statement of financial position, as a contra equity account (similar to the reporting of treasury shares at cost).

At December 31, 2015, Ogden records compensation expense of $4,000 (1,000 shares × $20 × 20%) as follows.

Compensation Expense	4,000	
Unearned Compensation		4,000

Ogden records compensation expense of $4,000 for each of the next four years (2016, 2017, 2018, and 2019).

What happens if DeGeorge leaves the company before the five years has elapsed (that is, she does not fulfill a service condition)? In this situation, DeGeorge forfeits her rights to the shares, and Ogden reverses the compensation expense already recorded.

For example, assume that DeGeorge leaves on February 3, 2017 (before any expense has been recorded during 2017). The entry to record this forfeiture is as follows.

Share Capital—Ordinary	1,000	
Share Premium—Ordinary	19,000	
Compensation Expense ($4,000 × 2)		8,000
Unearned Compensation		12,000

In this situation, Ogden reverses the compensation expense of $8,000 recorded through 2016. In addition, the company debits Share Capital—Ordinary and Share Premium—Ordinary, reflecting DeGeorge's forfeiture. It credits the balance of Unearned Compensation since none remains when DeGeorge leaves Ogden.

This accounting is similar to accounting for share options when employees do not fulfill vesting requirements. Recall that once compensation expense is recorded for share options, it is not reversed. The only exception is if the employee does not fulfill a service condition by leaving the company early.

In Ogden's restricted-share plan, vesting never occurred because DeGeorge left the company before she met the service requirement. Because DeGeorge was never vested, she had to forfeit her shares. Therefore, the company must reverse compensation expense recorded to date.[9]

Employee Share-Purchase Plans

Employee share-purchase plans (ESPPs) generally permit all employees to purchase shares at a discounted price for a short period of time. The company often uses such plans to secure equity capital or to induce widespread ownership of its ordinary shares among employees. **These plans are considered compensatory and should be recorded as expense over the service period.**

To illustrate, assume that Masthead Company offers all its 1,000 employees the opportunity to participate in an employee share-purchase plan. Under the terms of the plan, the employees are entitled to purchase 100 ordinary shares (par value £1 per share) at a 20 percent discount. The purchase price must be paid immediately upon acceptance of the offer. In total, 800 employees accept the offer, and each employee purchases on average 80 shares. That is, the employees purchase a total of 64,000 shares. The weighted-average market price of the shares at the purchase date is £30 per share, and the weighted-average purchase price is £24 per share. The entry to record this transaction is as follows.

Cash (64,000 × £24)	1,536,000	
Compensation Expense [64,000 × (£30 − £24)]	384,000	
Share Capital—Ordinary (64,000 × £1)		64,000
Share Premium—Ordinary		1,856,000
(Issue shares in an employee share-purchase plan)		

The IASB indicates that there is no reason to treat broad-based employee share plans differently from other employee share plans. Some have argued that because these plans are used to raise capital, they should not be compensatory. However, IFRS requires recording expense for these arrangements. The Board notes that because these arrangements are available only to employees, it is sufficient to conclude that the benefits provided represent employee compensation.[10] **[6]**

Disclosure of Compensation Plans

Companies must fully disclose the status of their compensation plans at the end of the periods presented. To meet these objectives, companies must make extensive disclosures. Specifically, a company with one or more share-based payment arrangements must disclose information that enables users of the financial statements to understand:

1. The nature and extent of share-based payment arrangements that existed during the period.

2. How the fair value of the goods and services received, or the fair value of the equity instruments granted during the period, was determined.

3. The effect of share-based payment transactions on the company's net income (loss) during the period and on its financial position. **[7]**

---

[9]There are numerous variations on restricted-share plans, including restricted-share units (for which the shares are issued at the end of the vesting period) and restricted-share plans with performance targets, such as EPS or share price growth.

[10]As indicated, employee share-purchase plans offer company shares to workers through payroll deduction, often at significant discounts. Unfortunately, many employees do not avail themselves of this benefit. Hopefully, if you have the opportunity to purchase your company's shares at a significant discount, you will take advantage of the plan. By not participating, you are "leaving money on the table."

Illustration 16-10 presents the type of information disclosed for compensation plans.

ILLUSTRATION 16-10
Share-Option Plan
Disclosure

Share-Option Plan

The Company has a share-based compensation plan. The compensation cost that has been charged against income for the plan was $29.4 million, and $28.7 million for 2015 and 2014, respectively.

Total expense for share-based plans

The Company's 2015 Employee Share-Option Plan (the Plan), which is shareholder-approved, permits the grant of share options and shares to its employees for up to 8 million shares of ordinary shares. The Company believes that such awards better align the interests of its employees with those of its shareholders. Option awards are generally granted with an exercise price equal to the market price of the Company's shares at the date of grant; those option awards generally vest based on 5 years of continuous service and have 10-year contractual terms. Share awards generally vest over five years. Certain option and share awards provide for accelerated vesting if there is a change in control (as defined by the Plan).

Description of share-option plan

The fair value of each option award is estimated on the date of grant using an option valuation model based on the assumptions noted in the following table.

	2015	2014
Expected volatility	25%–40%	24%–38%
Weighted-average volatility	33%	30%
Expected dividends	1.5%	1.5%
Expected term (in years)	5.3–7.8	5.5–8.0
Risk-free rate	6.3%–11.2%	6.0%–10.0%

Explanation of valuation model

A summary of option activity under the Plan as of December 31, 2015, and changes during the year then ended are presented below.

Options	Shares (000)	Weighted-Average Exercise Price	Weighted-Average Remaining Contractual Term	Aggregate Intrinsic Value ($000)
Outstanding at January 1, 2015	4,660	42		
Granted	950	60		
Exercised	(800)	36		
Forfeited or expired	(80)	59		
Outstanding at December 31, 2015	4,730	47	6.5	85,140
Exercisable at December 31, 2015	3,159	41	4.0	75,816

Number and weighted-average exercise prices for share options

The weighted-average grant-date fair value of options granted during the years 2015 and 2014 was $19.57 and $17.46, respectively. The total intrinsic value of options exercised during the years ended December 31, 2015 and 2014, was $25.2 million, and $20.9 million, respectively.

As of December 31, 2015, there was $25.9 million of total unrecognized compensation cost related to non-vested share-based compensation arrangements granted under the Plan. That cost is expected to be recognized over a weighted-average period of 4.9 years. The total fair value of shares vested during the years ended December 31, 2015 and 2014, was $22.8 million and $21 million, respectively.

Restricted-Share Awards

The Company also has a restricted-share plan. The Plan is intended to retain and motivate the Company's Chief Executive Officer over the term of the award and to bring his total compensation package closer to median levels for Chief Executive Officers of comparable companies. The fair value of grants during the year was $1,889,000, or $35.68 per share, equivalent to 92% of the market price of a share of the Company's Ordinary Shares on the date the award was granted.

Restricted-share activity for the year ended 2015 is as follows.

	Shares	Price
Outstanding at December 31, 2014	57,990	—
Granted	149,000	$12.68
Vested	(19,330)	—
Forfeited	—	—
Outstanding at December 31, 2015	187,660	

Description of restricted-share plan

Debate over Share-Option Accounting

LEARNING OBJECTIVE 5

Discuss the controversy involving share compensation plans.

The IASB faced considerable opposition when it proposed the fair value method for accounting for share options. This is not surprising, given that the fair value method results in greater compensation costs relative to the intrinsic-value model.

Many small high-technology companies have been especially vocal in their opposition, arguing that only through offering share options can they attract top professional management. They contend that recognizing large amounts of compensation expense under these plans places them at a competitive disadvantage against larger companies that can withstand higher compensation charges. As one high-tech executive stated, "If your goal is to attack fat-cat executive compensation in multi-billion dollar firms, then please do so! But not at the expense of the people who are 'running lean and mean,' trying to build businesses and creating jobs in the process."

Underlying Concepts

The share-option controversy involves economic-consequence issues. The IASB believes companies should follow the neutrality concept. Others disagree, noting that factors other than accounting theory should be considered.

The share-option saga is a classic example of the difficulty the IASB faces in issuing new accounting guidance. Many powerful interests aligned against the Board. Even some who initially appeared to support the Board's actions later reversed themselves. These efforts undermine the authority of the IASB at a time when it is essential that we restore faith in our financial reporting system.

Transparent financial reporting—including recognition of share-based expense—should not be criticized because companies will report lower income. We may not like what the financial statements say, but we are always better off when the statements are representationally faithful to the underlying economic substance of transactions.

By leaving share-based compensation expense out of income, reported income is biased. Biased reporting not only raises concerns about the credibility of companies' reports but also of financial reporting in general. Even good companies get tainted by the biased reporting of a few "bad apples." If we write standards to achieve some social, economic, or public policy goal, financial reporting loses its credibility.

COMPUTING EARNINGS PER SHARE

LEARNING OBJECTIVE 6

Compute earnings per share in a simple capital structure.

The financial press frequently reports earnings per share data. Further, shareholders and potential investors widely use this data in evaluating the profitability of a company. **Earnings per share** indicates the income earned by each ordinary share. Thus, **companies report earnings per share only for ordinary shares**. For example, if Oscar Co. has net income of €300,000 and a weighted average of 100,000 ordinary shares outstanding for the year, earnings per share is €3 (€300,000 ÷ 100,000). Because of the importance of earnings per share information, companies must report this information on the face of the income statement. **[8]** The exception, due to the cost constraint, is non-public companies.[11] Generally, companies report earnings per share information below net income in the income statement. Illustration 16-11 shows Oscar Co.'s income statement presentation of earnings per share.

ILLUSTRATION 16-11
Income Statement
Presentation of EPS

Net income	€300,000
Earnings per share	€3.00

[11]In general, a non-public enterprise is an enterprise whose debt or equity securities are not traded in a public market on a foreign or domestic securities exchange or in the over-the-counter market (including securities quoted locally or regionally). An enterprise is not considered a non-public enterprise when its financial statements are issued in preparation for the sale of any class of securities in a public market.

When the income statement contains discontinued operations, companies are required to report earnings per share from continuing operations and net income on the face of the income statement. The presentation in Illustration 16-12 is representative.

Earnings per share:	
Income from continuing operations	€4.00
Loss from discontinued operations, net of tax	0.60
Net income	€3.40

ILLUSTRATION 16-12
Income Statement
Presentation of EPS
Components

These disclosures enable the user of the financial statements to compare performance between different companies in the same reporting period and between different reporting periods for the same company. Even though earnings per share data have limitations because of the different accounting policies that may be used for determining "earnings," a consistently determined denominator enhances financial reporting. **[9]**

Earnings per Share—Simple Capital Structure

A company's capital structure is simple if it consists only of ordinary shares or includes no potential ordinary shares that upon conversion or exercise could dilute earnings per ordinary share. In this case, a company reports basic earnings per share. A capital structure is complex if it includes securities (potential ordinary shares) that could have a dilutive effect on earnings per ordinary share.[12] In this situation, a company reports both basic and diluted earnings per share.

The computation of basic earnings per share for a simple capital structure involves two items (other than net income): (1) preference share dividends and (2) weighted-average number of shares outstanding.

Preference Share Dividends

As we indicated earlier, earnings per share relates to earnings per ordinary share. When a company has both ordinary and preference shares outstanding, **it subtracts the current-year preference share dividend from net income to arrive at** income available to ordinary shareholders. Illustration 16-13 shows the formula for computing earnings per share.

$$\text{Earnings per Share} = \frac{\text{Net Income} - \text{Preference Dividends}}{\text{Weighted-Average Number of Shares Outstanding}}$$

ILLUSTRATION 16-13
Formula for Computing
Earnings per Share

In reporting earnings per share information, a company must calculate income available to ordinary shareholders. To do so, the company subtracts dividends on preference shares from income from continuing operations and net income. If a company declares dividends on preference shares and a net loss occurs, **the company adds the preference dividend to the loss** for purposes of computing the loss per share.

If the preference shares are cumulative and the company declares no dividend in the current year, it subtracts (or adds) **an amount equal to the dividend that it should**

---

[12]A potential ordinary share is a financial instrument or other contract that may entitle its holder to ordinary shares. Examples of potential ordinary shares are (1) convertible debt and convertible preference shares that are convertible into ordinary shares, (2) options and warrants, and (3) shares that would be issued upon the satisfaction of conditions resulting from contractual arrangements, such as the purchase of a business or other assets. These concepts are discussed later in this chapter.

have declared for the current year only from net income (or to the loss). The company should have included dividends in arrears for previous years in the previous years' computations.[13]

Weighted-Average Number of Shares Outstanding

In all computations of earnings per share, the **weighted-average number of shares outstanding** during the period constitutes the basis for the per share amounts reported. Shares issued or purchased during the period affect the amount outstanding. Companies must **weight the shares by the fraction of the period they are outstanding**. The rationale for this approach is to find the equivalent number of whole shares outstanding for the year.

To illustrate, assume that Franks Inc. has changes in its ordinary shares outstanding for the period, as shown in Illustration 16-14.

ILLUSTRATION 16-14
Shares Outstanding, Ending Balance— Franks Inc.

Date	Share Changes	Shares Outstanding
January 1	Beginning balance	90,000
April 1	Issued 30,000 shares for cash	30,000
		120,000
July 1	Purchased 39,000 shares	(39,000)
		81,000
November 1	Issued 60,000 shares for cash	60,000
December 31	Ending balance	141,000

Franks computes the weighted-average number of shares outstanding as follows.

ILLUSTRATION 16-15
Weighted-Average Number of Shares Outstanding

Dates Outstanding	(A) Shares Outstanding	(B) Fraction of Year	(C) Weighted Shares (A × B)
Jan. 1–Apr. 1	90,000	3/12	22,500
Apr. 1–July 1	120,000	3/12	30,000
July 1–Nov. 1	81,000	4/12	27,000
Nov. 1–Dec. 31	141,000	2/12	23,500
Weighted-average number of shares outstanding			103,000

As Illustration 16-15 shows, 90,000 shares were outstanding for three months, which translates to 22,500 whole shares for the entire year. Because Franks issued additional shares on April 1, it must weight these shares for the time outstanding. When the company purchased 39,000 shares on July 1, it reduced the shares outstanding. Therefore, from July 1 to November 1, only 81,000 shares were outstanding, which is equivalent to 27,000 shares. The issuance of 60,000 shares increases shares outstanding for the last two months of the year. Franks then makes a new computation to determine the proper weighted shares outstanding.

Share Dividends and Share Splits. When **share dividends** or **share splits** occur, companies need to restate the shares outstanding before the share dividend or split, in order to compute the weighted-average number of shares. For example, assume that Vijay Corporation had 100,000 shares outstanding on January 1 and issued a 25 percent share dividend on June 30. For purposes of computing a weighted-average for the current year, it assumes the additional 25,000 shares outstanding as a result of the share dividend

---

[13]Recall that an ordinary share is an equity instrument that is subordinate to all other classes of equity instruments. In addition, we assume that ordinary shares relate only to the controlling (majority) interest. As a result, the earnings per share computation does not include earnings related to the non-controlling (minority) interest.

to be **outstanding since the beginning of the year**. Thus, the weighted-average for the year for Vijay is 125,000 shares.

Companies restate the issuance of a share dividend or share split, but not the issuance or repurchase of shares for cash. Why? Because share splits and share dividends do not increase or decrease the net assets of the company. The company merely issues additional shares. Because of the added shares, it must restate the weighted-average shares. Restating allows valid comparisons of earnings per share between periods before and after the share split or share dividend. Conversely, the issuance or purchase of shares for cash **changes the amount of net assets**. As a result, the company either earns more or less in the future as a result of this change in net assets. Stated another way, **a share dividend or split does not change the shareholders' total investment**—it only increases (unless it is a reverse share split) the number of ordinary shares representing this investment.

To illustrate how a share dividend affects the computation of the weighted-average number of shares outstanding, assume that Sabrina Company has the following changes in its ordinary shares during the year.

Date	Share Changes	Shares Outstanding
January 1	Beginning balance	100,000
March 1	Issued 20,000 shares for cash	20,000
		120,000
June 1	60,000 additional shares (50% share dividend)	60,000
		180,000
November 1	Issued 30,000 shares for cash	30,000
December 31	Ending balance	210,000

ILLUSTRATION 16-16
Shares Outstanding, Ending Balance—Sabrina Company

Sabrina computes the weighted-average number of shares outstanding as follows.

Dates Outstanding	(A) Shares Outstanding	(B) Restatement	(C) Fraction of Year	(D) Weighted Shares (A × B × C)
Jan. 1–Mar. 1	100,000	1.50	2/12	25,000
Mar. 1–June 1	120,000	1.50	3/12	45,000
June 1–Nov. 1	180,000		5/12	75,000
Nov. 1–Dec. 31	210,000		2/12	35,000
Weighted-average number of shares outstanding				180,000

ILLUSTRATION 16-17
Weighted-Average Number of Shares Outstanding—Share Issue and Share Dividend

Sabrina must restate the shares outstanding prior to the share dividend. The company adjusts the shares outstanding from January 1 to June 1 for the share dividend, so that it now states these shares on the same basis as shares issued subsequent to the share dividend. Sabrina does not restate shares issued after the share dividend because they are on the new basis. The share dividend simply restates existing shares. **The same type of treatment applies to a share split**.

If a share dividend or share split occurs after the end of the year but before the financial statements are authorized for issuance, a company must restate the weighted-average number of shares outstanding for the year (and any other years presented in comparative form). For example, assume that Hendricks Company computes its weighted-average number of shares as 100,000 for the year ended December 31, 2015. On January 15, 2016, before authorizing the issuance of the financial statements, the company splits its shares 3 for 1. In this case, the weighted-average number of shares used in computing earnings per share for 2015 is now 300,000 shares. If providing earnings per share information for 2014 as comparative information, Hendricks must also adjust it for the share split.

Comprehensive Example

Let's study a comprehensive illustration for a simple capital structure. Diaz Corporation has income from continuing operations of R$580,000 and a gain on discontinued operations, net of tax, of R$240,000. In addition, it has declared preference dividends of R$1 per share on 100,000 shares of preference shares outstanding. Diaz also has the following changes in its ordinary shares outstanding during 2015.

ILLUSTRATION 16-18
Shares Outstanding, Ending Balance— Diaz Corp.

Date	Share Changes	Shares Outstanding
January 1	Beginning balance	180,000
May 1	Purchased 30,000 treasury shares	30,000
		150,000
July 1	300,000 additional shares (3-for-1 share split)	300,000
		450,000
December 31	Issued 50,000 shares for cash	50,000
December 31	Ending balance	500,000

To compute the earnings per share information, Diaz determines the weighted-average number of shares outstanding as follows.

ILLUSTRATION 16-19
Weighted-Average Number of Shares Outstanding

Dates Outstanding	(A) Shares Outstanding	(B) Restatement	(C) Fraction of Year	(D) Weighted Shares (A × B × C)
Jan. 1–May 1	180,000	3	4/12	180,000
May 1–July 1	150,000	3	2/12	75,000
July 1–Dec. 31	450,000		6/12	225,000
Weighted-average number of shares outstanding				480,000

In computing the weighted-average number of shares, the company ignores the shares sold on December 31, 2015, because they have not been outstanding during the year. Diaz then divides the weighted-average number of shares into income from continuing operations and net income to determine earnings per share. It subtracts its preference dividends of R$100,000 from income from continuing operations (R$580,000) to arrive at income from continuing operations available to ordinary shareholders of R$480,000 (R$580,000 − R$100,000).

Deducting the preference dividends from the income from continuing operations also reduces net income without affecting the gain on discontinued operations. The final amount is referred to as **income available to ordinary shareholders**, as shown in Illustration 16-20.

ILLUSTRATION 16-20
Computation of Income Available to Ordinary Shareholders

	(A) Income Information	(B) Weighted Shares	(C) Earnings per Share (A ÷ B)
Income from continuing operations available to ordinary shareholders	R$480,000*	480,000	R$1.00
Gain on discontinued operations (net of tax)	240,000	480,000	0.50
Income available to ordinary shareholders	R$720,000	480,000	R$1.50

*R$580,000 − R$100,000

Diaz must disclose the per share amount for gain on discontinued operations (net of tax) either on the face of the income statement or in the notes to the financial statements.

Illustration 16-21 shows the income and per share information reported on the face of Diaz's income statement.

Income from continuing operations	R$580,000
Gain on discontinued operations, net of tax	240,000
Net income	R$820,000
Earnings per share:	
Income from continuing operations	R$1.00
Gain on discontinued operations, net of tax	0.50
Net income	R$1.50

ILLUSTRATION 16-21
Earnings per Share, with Gain on Discontinued Operations

Earnings per Share—Complex Capital Structure

The EPS discussion to this point applies to **basic EPS** for a simple capital structure. One problem with a **basic EPS** computation is that it fails to recognize the potential impact of a corporation's dilutive securities. As discussed at the beginning of the chapter, **dilutive securities** are securities that can be converted to ordinary shares.[14] Upon conversion or exercise by the holder, the dilutive securities reduce (dilute) earnings per share. This adverse effect on EPS can be significant and, more importantly, *unexpected* unless financial statements call attention to their potential dilutive effect.

As indicated earlier, a complex capital structure exists when a corporation has convertible securities, options, warrants, or other rights that upon conversion or exercise could dilute earnings per share. When a company has a complex capital structure, **it reports both basic and diluted earnings per share**.

Computing **diluted EPS** is similar to computing basic EPS. The difference is that diluted EPS includes the effect of all potential dilutive ordinary shares that were outstanding during the period. The formula in Illustration 16-22 shows the relationship between basic EPS and diluted EPS.

7 **LEARNING OBJECTIVE**
Compute earnings per share in a complex capital structure.

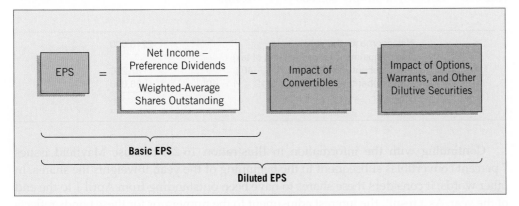

ILLUSTRATION 16-22
Relation between Basic and Diluted EPS

Some securities are antidilutive. **Antidilutive securities** are securities that upon conversion or exercise **increase** earnings per share (or reduce the loss per share). Companies with complex capital structures will not report diluted EPS if the securities in their capital structure are antidilutive. The purpose of presenting both basic and diluted EPS is to inform financial statement users of situations that will likely occur (basic EPS) and also to provide "worst case" dilutive situations (dilutive EPS). If the securities are antidilutive, the likelihood of conversion or exercise is considered remote. Thus, companies that have

[14]Issuance of these types of securities is typical in mergers and compensation plans.

only antidilutive securities must report only the basic EPS number. We illustrated the computation of basic EPS in the prior section. In the following sections, we address the effects of convertible and other dilutive securities on EPS calculations.

Diluted EPS—Convertible Securities

At conversion, companies exchange convertible securities for ordinary shares. Companies measure the dilutive effects of potential conversion on EPS using the **if-converted method**. This method for a convertible bond assumes (1) the conversion of the convertible securities at the beginning of the period (or at the time of issuance of the security, if issued during the period), and (2) the elimination of related interest, net of tax. Thus, the additional shares assumed issued increase the **denominator**—the weighted-average number of shares outstanding. The amount of interest expense, net of tax, increases the **numerator**—net income.

Comprehensive Example—If-Converted Method. As an example, Mayfield Corporation has net income of £210,000 for the year and a weighted-average number of ordinary shares outstanding during the period of 100,000 shares. The basic earnings per share is therefore £2.10 (£210,000 ÷ 100,000). The company has two convertible debenture bond issues outstanding. One is a 6 percent issue sold at 100 (total £1,000,000) in a prior year and convertible into 20,000 ordinary shares. Interest expense for the current year related to the liability component of this convertible bond is £62,000. The other is a 7 percent issue sold at 100 (total £1,000,000) on April 1 of the current year and convertible into 32,000 ordinary shares. Interest expense for the current year related to the liability component of this convertible bond is £80,000.[15] The tax rate is 40 percent.

As Illustration 16-23 shows, to determine the numerator for diluted earnings per share, Mayfield adds back the interest on the if-converted securities, less the related tax effect. Because the if-converted method assumes conversion as of the beginning of the year, Mayfield assumes that it pays no interest on the convertibles during the year. The effective interest on the 6 percent convertibles is £62,000 for the year. The increased tax expense is £24,800 (£62,000 × 0.40). The interest added back net of taxes is £37,200 (£62,000 − £24,800) or simply £62,000 × (1 − 0.40).

ILLUSTRATION 16-23
Computation of Adjusted Net Income

Net income for the year	£210,000
Add: Adjustment for interest (net of tax)	
6% debentures (£62,000 × [1 −.40])	37,200
7% debentures (£80,000 × 9/12 × [1 −.40])	36,000
Adjusted net income	£283,200

Continuing with the information in Illustration 16-23, because Mayfield issues 7 percent convertibles subsequent to the beginning of the year, it weights the shares. In other words, it considers these shares to have been outstanding from April 1 to the end of the year. As a result, the interest adjustment to the numerator for these bonds reflects the interest for only nine months. Thus, the interest added back on the 7 percent convertible is £36,000 [£80,000 × 9/12 year × (1 − 0.4)]. The final item in Illustration 16-23 shows the adjusted net income. This amount becomes the numerator for Mayfield's computation of diluted earnings per share.

---

[15]As indicated earlier, a convertible bond is a compound instrument that has both a liability and an equity component. As a result, the interest expense reported on the income statement will not equal the interest paid in cash during the period. The interest adjustment in the numerator is based on interest expense reported on the income statement. That is, interest expense, net of tax, is added back to net income.

Mayfield then calculates the weighted-average number of shares outstanding, as shown in Illustration 16-24. This number of shares becomes the denominator for Mayfield's computation of diluted earnings per share.

Weighted-average number of shares outstanding	100,000
Add: Shares assumed to be issued:	
6% debentures (as of beginning of year)	20,000
7% debentures (as of date of issue, April 1; 9/12 × 32,000)	24,000
Weighted-average number of shares adjusted for dilutive securities	144,000

ILLUSTRATION 16-24
Computation of Weighted-Average Number of Shares

In its income statement, Mayfield reports basic and diluted earnings per share.[16] Illustration 16-25 shows this dual presentation.

Net income for the year		£210,000
Earnings per Share (Note X)		
Basic earnings per share (£210,000 ÷ 100,000)	£2.10	
Diluted earnings per share (£283,200 ÷ 144,000)	£1.97	

ILLUSTRATION 16-25
Earnings per Share Disclosure

Other Factors. The conversion rate on a dilutive security may change during the period in which the security is outstanding. For the diluted EPS computation in such a situation, the **company uses the most dilutive conversion rate available. [10]** For example, assume that a company issued a convertible bond on January 1, 2013, with a conversion rate of 10 ordinary shares for each bond starting January 1, 2015. Beginning January 1, 2016, the conversion rate is 12 ordinary shares for each bond. Beginning January 1, 2022, it is 15 ordinary shares for each bond. In computing diluted EPS in 2013, the company uses the conversion rate of 15 shares to one bond.

Another issue relates to preference shares. For example, assume that Mayfield's 6 percent convertible debentures were instead 6 percent convertible *preference shares.* In that case, Mayfield considers the convertible preference shares as potential ordinary shares. Thus, it includes them in its diluted EPS calculations as shares outstanding. The company does not subtract preference dividends from net income in computing the numerator. Why not? Because for purposes of computing EPS, it assumes conversion of the convertible preference shares to outstanding ordinary shares. The company uses net income as the numerator—it computes **no tax effect** because preference dividends generally are not tax-deductible.

Diluted EPS—Options and Warrants

A company includes in diluted earnings per share all share options and warrants outstanding (whether or not presently exercisable), unless they are antidilutive. Companies use the **treasury-share method** to include options and warrants and their equivalents in EPS computations.

The treasury-share method assumes that the options or warrants are exercised at the beginning of the year (or date of issue if later) and that the company uses those proceeds to purchase ordinary shares for the treasury. If the exercise price is lower than the market price of the shares, then the proceeds from exercise are insufficient to buy back all the shares. The company then adds the incremental shares remaining to the

---

[16]Conversion of bonds is dilutive because EPS with conversion (£1.97) is less than basic EPS (£2.10). See Appendix 16B for a comprehensive evaluation of antidilution with multiple securities.

weighted-average number of shares outstanding for purposes of computing diluted earnings per share.

For example, if the exercise price of a warrant is €5 and the fair value of the shares is €15, the treasury-share method increases the shares outstanding. Exercise of the warrant results in one additional share outstanding, but the €5 received for the one share issued is insufficient to purchase one share in the market at €15. The company needs to exercise three warrants (and issue three additional shares) to produce enough money (€15) to acquire one share in the market. Thus, a net increase of two shares outstanding results.

To see this computation using larger numbers, assume 1,500 options outstanding at an exercise price of €30 for an ordinary share and a market price per ordinary share of €50. Through application of the treasury-share method, the company would have 600 incremental shares outstanding, computed as shown in Illustration 16-26.[17]

ILLUSTRATION 16-26
Computation of
Incremental Shares

Proceeds from exercise of 1,500 options (1,500 × €30)	€45,000
Shares issued upon exercise of options	1,500
Treasury shares purchasable with proceeds (€45,000 ÷ €50)	(900)
Incremental shares outstanding (potential ordinary shares)	600

Thus, if the exercise price of the option or warrant is **lower** than the market price of the shares, dilution occurs. An exercise price of the option or warrant **higher** than the market price of the shares reduces ordinary shares. In this case, the options or warrants are **antidilutive** because their assumed exercise leads to an increase in earnings per share.

For both options and warrants, exercise is assumed only if the average market price of the share exceeds the exercise price during the reported period.[18] As a practical matter, a simple average of the weekly or monthly prices is adequate, so long as the prices do not fluctuate significantly.

Comprehensive Example—Treasury-Share Method. To illustrate application of the treasury-share method, assume that Kubitz Industries, Inc. has net income for the period of ₴220,000. The average number of shares outstanding for the period was 100,000 shares. Hence, basic EPS—ignoring all dilutive securities—is ₴2.20. The average number of shares related to options outstanding (although not exercisable at this time), at an option price of ₴20 per share, is 5,000 shares. The average market price of the ordinary shares during the year was ₴28. Illustration 16-27 shows the computation of EPS using the treasury-share method.

Contingently Issuable Shares

Contingently issuable ordinary shares are defined as ordinary shares issuable for little or no cash consideration upon satisfaction of specified conditions in a contingent share agreement. For example, in business combinations, the acquirer may agree to issue additional shares—contingently issuable shares—under certain circumstances. Companies generally issue these contingent shares based on a measure, such as attainment of a

---

[17]The incremental number of shares may be more simply computed:

$$\frac{\text{Market price} - \text{Option price}}{\text{Market price}} \times \text{Number of options} = \text{Number of shares}$$

$$\frac{€50 - €30}{€50} \times 1{,}500 \text{ options} = 600 \text{ shares}$$

[18]Options and warrants have essentially the same assumptions and computational problems although the warrants may allow or require the tendering of some other security, such as debt, in lieu of cash upon exercise. This subject is beyond the scope of this textbook.

ILLUSTRATION 16-27
Computation of Earnings
per Share—Treasury-
Share Method

	Basic Earnings per Share	Diluted Earnings per Share
Average number of shares related to options outstanding:		5,000
Option price per share		× ₽20
Proceeds upon exercise of options		₽100,000
Average market price of ordinary shares		₽28
Treasury shares that could be repurchased with proceeds (₽100,000 ÷ ₽28)		3,571
Excess of shares under option over the treasury shares that could be repurchased (5,000 − 3,571)—potential ordinary incremental shares		1,429
Average number of ordinary shares outstanding	100,000	100,000
Total average number of ordinary shares outstanding and potential ordinary shares	100,000 (A)	101,429 (C)
Net income for the year	₽220,000 (B)	₽220,000 (D)
Earnings per share	₽2.20 (B ÷ A)	₽2.17 (D ÷ C)

certain earnings or market price level. The basic rule is that the number of contingent shares to be included in diluted earnings per share is based on the number of shares that would be issuable as if the end of the period were the end of the contingency period.[19] **[11]**

For example, assume that Watts Corporation purchased Cardoza Company in 2014 and agreed to give Cardoza's shareholders 20,000 additional shares in 2017 if Cardoza's net income in 2016 is R$90,000. Here is what happened in the next two years:

1. In 2015, Cardoza's net income is R$100,000. Cardoza therefore has met the net income test in 2015 and **should include** the 20,000 shares in diluted earnings per share for 2015.

2. In 2016, Cardoza's net income is R$80,000. Cardoza therefore does not meet the earnings test in 2016 and **should not** include the shares in diluted earnings per share in 2016.

Because Cardoza's earnings in 2015 may change in 2016, the calculation of basic EPS does not include contingent shares until the end of the contingency period because not all conditions have been satisfied.

Antidilution Revisited

In computing diluted EPS, a company must consider the aggregate of all dilutive securities. But first it must determine which potentially dilutive securities are in fact individually dilutive and which are antidilutive. **A company should exclude any security that is antidilutive**, nor can the company use such a security to offset dilutive securities.

Recall that including antidilutive securities in earnings per share computations increases earnings per share (or reduces net loss per share). With options or warrants, whenever the exercise price exceeds the market price, the security is antidilutive. Convertible debt is antidilutive if the addition to income of the interest (net of tax) causes a greater percentage increase in income (numerator) than conversion of the bonds causes a percentage increase in ordinary and potentially dilutive shares (denominator). In other words, convertible debt is antidilutive if conversion of the security causes ordinary share earnings to increase by a greater amount per additional ordinary share than earnings per share was before the conversion.

[19]In addition to contingent issuances of shares, other situations that might lead to dilution are the issuance of participating securities and two-class ordinary shares. The reporting of these types of securities in EPS computations is beyond the scope of this textbook.

To illustrate, assume that Martin Corporation has a $1,000,000 debt issue that is convertible into 10,000 ordinary shares. Interest expense on the liability component of this convertible bond is $60,000. Net income for the year is $210,000, the weighted-average number of ordinary shares outstanding is 100,000 shares, and the tax rate is 40 percent. In this case, assumed conversion of the debt into ordinary shares at the beginning of the year requires the following adjustments of net income and the weighted-average number of shares outstanding.

ILLUSTRATION 16-28
Test for Antidilution

Net income for the year	$210,000	Average number of shares outstanding	100,000
Add: Adjustment for interest (net of tax) on bonds $60,000 × (1 − .40)	36,000	Add: Shares issued upon assumed conversion of debt	10,000
Adjusted net income	$246,000	Average number of ordinary and potential ordinary shares	110,000

Basic EPS = $210,000 ÷ 100,000 = $2.10
Diluted EPS = $246,000 ÷ 110,000 = $2.24 = **Antidilutive**

As a shortcut, Martin can also identify the convertible debt as antidilutive by comparing the EPS resulting from conversion, $3.60 ($36,000 additional earnings ÷ 10,000 additional shares), with EPS before inclusion of the convertible debt, $2.10.

Companies should ignore antidilutive securities in all calculations and in computing diluted earnings per share. This approach is reasonable. The accounting profession's intent was to inform the investor of the possible dilution that might occur in reported earnings per share and not to be concerned with securities that, if converted or exercised, would result in an increase in earnings per share. Appendix 16B to this chapter provides an extended example of how companies consider antidilution in a complex situation with multiple securities.

EPS Presentation and Disclosure

A company should present both basic and diluted EPS information as follows.

ILLUSTRATION 16-29
EPS Presentation—
Complex Capital
Structure

Earnings per ordinary share	
Basic earnings per share	$3.30
Diluted earnings per share	$2.70

When the earnings of a period include discontinued operations, a company should show per share amounts for the following: income from continuing operations, discontinued operations, and net income. Companies that report a discontinued operation should present per share amounts **for those line items** either on the face of the income statement or in the notes to the financial statements. Illustration 16-30 shows a presentation reporting discontinued operations.

ILLUSTRATION 16-30
EPS Presentation, with
Discontinued Operations

Basic earnings per share	
Income from continuing operations	$3.80
Discontinued operations (loss)	(0.80)
Net income	$3.00
Diluted earnings per share	
Income from continuing operations	$3.35
Discontinued operations (loss)	(0.65)
Net income	$2.70

The following information should also be disclosed.

1. The amounts used as the numerators in calculating basic and diluted earnings per share, and a reconciliation of those amounts to net income or loss. The reconciliation should include the individual effect of each class of instruments that affects earnings per share.

2. The weighted-average number of ordinary shares used as the denominator in calculating basic and diluted earnings per share, and a reconciliation of these denominators to each other. The reconciliation shall include the individual effect of each class of instruments that affects earnings per share.

3. Instruments (including contingently issuable shares) that could potentially dilute basic earnings per share in the future but were not included in the calculation of diluted earnings per share because they are antidilutive for the period(s) presented.

4. A description of ordinary share transactions or potential ordinary share transactions that occur after the reporting period and that would have significantly changed the number of ordinary shares or potential ordinary shares outstanding at the end of the period if those transactions had occurred before the end of the reporting period.

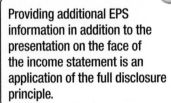

Underlying Concepts

Providing additional EPS information in addition to the presentation on the face of the income statement is an application of the full disclosure principle.

Note that if the number of ordinary or potential ordinary shares outstanding increases as a result of a share dividend or share split, or decreases as a result of diluted EPS calculations, such changes in the number of shares shall be disclosed.

Illustration 16-31 presents the reconciliation and the related disclosure to meet the requirements of this standard. **[12]**

ILLUSTRATION 16-31
Reconciliation for Basic and Diluted EPS

	Income (Numerator)	Shares (Denominator)	Per Share Amount	
		For the Year Ended 2015		
Income from continued operations	$7,500,000			Numerator amounts
Less: Preference share dividends	(45,000)			
Basic EPS	7,455,000	3,991,666	$1.87	Per share calculation
Warrants		30,768		Potentially dilutive securities shares
Convertible preference shares	45,000	308,333		
Convertible bonds (net of tax)	60,000	50,000		
Diluted EPS	$7,560,000	4,380,767	$1.73	Reconciliation schedule

Share options to purchase 1,000,000 shares of ordinary shares at $85 per share were outstanding during the second half of 2015 but were not included in the computation of diluted EPS because the options' exercise price was greater than the average market price of the ordinary shares. The options were still outstanding at the end of year 2015 and expire on June 30, 2025.

Summary of EPS Computation

Computation of earnings per share is a complex issue. It is also a controversial area because many securities, although technically not ordinary shares, have many of their basic characteristics. Indeed, some companies have issued these other securities rather than ordinary shares in order to avoid an adverse dilutive effect on earnings per share. Illustrations 16-32 and 16-33 (on page 782) display the elementary points of calculating earnings per share in a simple capital structure and in a complex capital structure.

ILLUSTRATION 16-32
Calculating EPS, Simple
Capital Structure

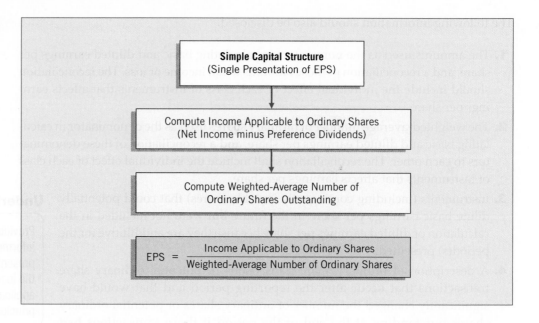

ILLUSTRATION 16-33
Calculating EPS, Complex
Capital Structure

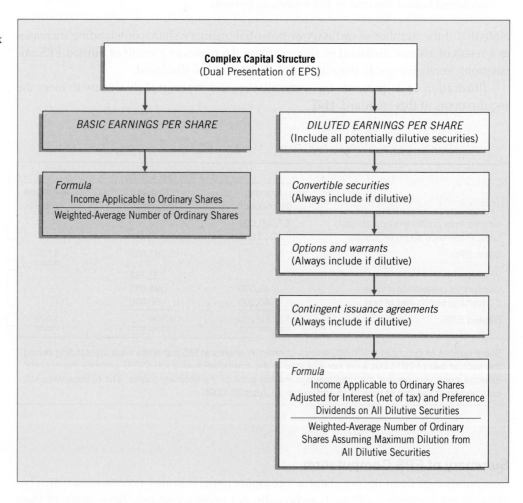

GLOBAL ACCOUNTING INSIGHTS

DILUTIVE SECURITIES AND EARNINGS PER SHARE

Both the FASB and the IASB are working on a standard related to the distinction between liabilities and equity. The U.S. GAAP approach to account for certain dilutive securities, such as convertible debt and debt issued with share warrants, is different than IFRS. The accounting and disclosure requirements for accounting for share options and EPS computations are similar between U.S. GAAP and IFRS.

Relevant Facts

Similarities

- U.S. GAAP and IFRS follow the same model for recognizing share-based compensation: The fair value of shares and options awarded to employees is recognized over the period to which the employees' services relate.

- Although the calculation of basic and diluted earnings per share is similar between U.S. GAAP and IFRS, the Boards are working to resolve the few minor differences in EPS reporting. One proposal in the FASB project concerns contracts that can be settled in either cash or shares. IFRS requires that share settlement must be used, while U.S. GAAP gives companies a choice. The FASB project proposes adopting the IFRS approach, thus converging U.S. GAAP and IFRS in this regard.

Differences

- A significant difference between U.S. GAAP and IFRS is the accounting for securities with characteristics of debt and equity, such as convertible debt. Under U.S. GAAP, all of the proceeds of convertible debt are recorded as long-term debt. Under IFRS, convertible bonds are "bifurcated"—

separated into the equity component (the value of the conversion option) of the bond issue and the debt component.

- Related to employee share-purchase plans, these plans under U.S. GAAP are often considered non-compensatory and therefore no compensation is recorded. However, certain conditions must exist before a plan can be considered non-compensatory (see the discussion below in the About the Numbers section for U.S. GAAP treatment). Under IFRS, all employee share-purchase plans are deemed to be compensatory; that is, compensation expense is recorded for the amount of the discount.

- Modification of a share option results in the recognition of any incremental fair value under both U.S. GAAP and IFRS. However, if the modification leads to a reduction, U.S. GAAP permits the reduction. IFRS does not.

- Other EPS differences relate to (1) the treasury-share method and how the proceeds from extinguishment of a liability should be accounted for, and (2) how to compute the weighted average of contingently issuable shares.

About the Numbers

Accounting for Convertible Bonds

As indicated, a significant difference in U.S. GAAP and IFRS is the accounting for convertible debt. To illustrate, assume PepsiCo (USA) issued, at par, $10 million of 10-year convertible bonds with a coupon rate of 4.75%. Assuming the conversion is settled in shares, PepsiCo makes the following entry to record the issuance under U.S. GAAP.

Cash	10,000,000	
Bonds Payable		10,000,000

Under IFRS, PepsiCo must split out the liability and equity component—the value of the conversion option—of the bond issue.

Thus, IFRS records separately the bond issue's debt and equity components. Many believe this provides a more faithful representation of the impact of the bond issue. However,

there are concerns about reliability of the method used to estimate the liability component of the bond.

Employee Stock-Purchase Plans Under U.S. GAAP

Employee stock-purchase plans (ESPPs) generally permit all employees to purchase shares at a discounted price for a short period of time. The company often uses such plans to secure equity capital or to induce widespread ownership of its common stock (ordinary shares) among employees. Under U.S. GAAP, these plans are considered compensatory unless they satisfy **all three** conditions presented below.

1. Substantially all full-time employees may participate on an equitable basis.

2. The discount relative to the market price is small. That is, the discount does not exceed the per share amount of costs

avoided by not having to raise cash in a public offering. If the amount of the discount is 5% or less, no compensation needs to be recorded.

3. The plan offers no substantive option feature.

For example, Masthead Company's stock-purchase plan allowed employees who met minimal employment qualifications to purchase its shares at a 5% reduction from market price for a short period of time. The reduction from market price is not considered compensatory. Why? Because the per share amount of the costs avoided by not having to raise the cash in a public offering equals 5%. Companies that offer their employees a compensatory ESPP should record the compensation expense over the service life of the employees.

It is difficult for some companies to claim that their ESPPs are non-compensatory (and therefore not record compensation expense) unless they change their discount policy, which in the past often was 15%. If they change their discount policy to 5%, participation in these plans will undoubtedly be lower. As a result, it is likely that some U.S. companies will end up dropping these plans.

On the Horizon

The FASB has been working on a standard that will likely converge to IFRS in the accounting for convertible debt. Similar to the IASB, the FASB is examining the classification of hybrid securities; the IASB is seeking comment on a discussion document similar to the FASB Preliminary Views document, "Financial Instruments with Characteristics of Equity."

It is hoped that the Boards will develop a converged standard in this area. While U.S. GAAP and IFRS are similar as to the presentation of EPS, the Boards have been considering a project to resolve remaining differences related to earnings per share computations.

KEY TERMS

antidilutive securities, *775*

basic EPS, *771, 775*

complex capital
  structure, *771*

compound
  instrument, *755*

contingently issuable
  ordinary shares, *778*

convertible bonds, *754*

convertible preference
  shares, *759*

diluted EPS, *771, 775*

dilutive securities,
  754, 775

earnings per share, *770*

fair value method, *764*

grant date, *763*

if-converted method, *776*

income available
  to ordinary
  shareholders, *771*

induce (induced)
  conversion, *759*

intrinsic-value
  method, *764*

market condition, *766*

restricted-share plans, *766*

SUMMARY OF LEARNING OBJECTIVES

1 **Describe the accounting for the issuance, conversion, and retirement of convertible securities.** Convertible debt is accounted for as a compound instrument because it contains both a liability and an equity component. IFRS requires that compound instruments be separated into their liability and equity components for purposes of accounting. Companies use the with-and-without method to value compound instruments. If companies convert bonds into other securities, the principal accounting problem is to determine the amount at which to record the securities exchanged for the bonds; the book value method is considered IFRS. The retirement of convertible debt is considered a debt extinguishment, and the difference between the carrying amount of the retired convertible debt and the cash paid should result in a gain or loss.

2 **Explain the accounting for convertible preference shares.** When convertible preference shares are converted, a company uses the book value approach. It debits Share Capital—Preference, along with the related Share Premium—Conversion Equity, and credits Share Capital—Ordinary and Share Premium—Ordinary (if any excess exists).

3 **Contrast the accounting for share warrants and for share warrants issued with other securities.** *Share warrants*: Companies should allocate the proceeds from the sale of debt with warrants between the two securities using the with-and-without method. *Share rights*: No entry is required when a company issues rights to existing shareholders. The company needs only to make a memorandum entry to indicate the number of rights issued to existing shareholders and to ensure that the company has additional unissued shares registered for issuance in case the shareholders exercise the rights.

4 **Describe the accounting for share compensation plans.** Companies must use the fair value approach to account for share-based compensation. Under this approach, a company computes total compensation expense based on the fair value of the options that it expects to vest on the grant date. Companies recognize compensation expense in the periods in which the employee performs the services. Restricted-share plans follow the same general accounting principles as those for share options. Companies estimate total compensation cost at the grant date based on the fair value of the restricted share; they expense that cost over the service period.

5 **Discuss the controversy involving share compensation plans.** When first proposed, there was considerable opposition to the recognition provisions contained in the fair value approach. The reason: That approach could result in substantial, previously unrecognized compensation expense. Many small companies believed that the standard would place them at a competitive disadvantage with larger companies that can withstand higher compensation charges. Offsetting such opposition is the need for greater transparency in financial reporting, on which our capital markets depend.

6 **Compute earnings per share in a simple capital structure.** When a company has both ordinary and preference shares outstanding, it subtracts the current-year preference shares dividend from net income to arrive at income available to ordinary shareholders. The formula for computing earnings per share is net income less preference share dividends, divided by the weighted-average number of shares outstanding.

7 **Compute earnings per share in a complex capital structure.** A complex capital structure requires a dual presentation of earnings per share, each with equal prominence on the face of the income statement. These two presentations are referred to as basic earnings per share and diluted earnings per share. Basic earnings per share relies on the number of weighted-average ordinary shares outstanding (i.e., equivalent to EPS for a simple capital structure). Diluted earnings per share indicates the dilution of earnings per share that will occur if all potential issuances of ordinary shares that would reduce earnings per share takes place. Companies with complex capital structures should exclude antidilutive securities when computing earnings per share.

APPENDIX **16A** ACCOUNTING FOR SHARE-APPRECIATION RIGHTS

A major disadvantage of many share-option plans is that an executive must pay income tax on the difference between the market price of the share and the option price at the **date of exercise**. This feature of share-option plans (those referred to as **non-qualified**) can be a financial hardship for an executive who wishes to keep the shares (rather than sell them immediately) because he or she would have to pay not only income tax but the option price as well. In another type of plan (an **incentive plan**), the executive pays no taxes at exercise but may need to borrow to finance the exercise price, which leads to related interest cost.

8 **LEARNING OBJECTIVE**

Explain the accounting for share-appreciation rights plans.

One solution to this problem was the creation of **share-appreciation rights (SARs)**. In this type of plan, the company gives an executive the right to receive compensation equal to the share appreciation. **Share appreciation** is the excess of the market price of the shares at the date of exercise over a pre-established price. The company may pay the share appreciation in cash, shares, or a combination of the two.

The major advantage of SARs is that the executive often does not have to make a cash outlay at the date of exercise but receives a payment for the share appreciation. Unlike shares acquired under a share-option plan, the company does not issue the shares that constitute the basis for computing the appreciation in a SARs plan. Rather, the company simply awards the executive cash or shares having a fair value equivalent to the appreciation. The accounting for share-appreciation rights depends on whether the company classifies the rights as equity or as a liability.

SARS—SHARE-BASED EQUITY AWARDS

Companies classify SARs as **equity awards** if at the date of exercise the holder receives shares from the company upon exercise. In essence, SARs are essentially equivalent to a share option. The major difference relates to the form of payment. With the share option, the holder pays the exercise price and then receives the shares. In an equity SAR, the holder receives shares in an amount equal to the **share-price appreciation** (the difference between the market price and the pre-established price). The accounting for SARs when they are equity awards follows the accounting used for share options. At the date of grant, the company determines a fair value for the SAR and then allocates this amount to compensation expense over the service period of the employees.

SARS—SHARE-BASED LIABILITY AWARDS

Companies classify SARs as liability awards if at the date of exercise the holder receives a cash payment. In this case, the holder is not receiving additional shares but a cash payment equal to the amount of share-price appreciation. The company's compensation expense therefore changes as the value of the liability changes.

A company uses the following approach to record share-based liability awards:

1. Measure the fair value of the award at the grant date and accrue compensation over the service period.

2. Remeasure the fair value each reporting period until the award is settled; adjust the compensation cost each period for changes in fair value prorated for the portion of the service period completed.

3. Once the service period is completed, determine compensation expense each subsequent period by reporting the full change in market price as an adjustment to compensation expense.

For liability awards, the company estimates the fair value of the SARs using an option-pricing model. The company then allocates this total estimated compensation cost over the service period, recording expense (or a decrease in expense if fair value declines) in each period. At the end of each period, total compensation expense reported to date should equal the percentage of the total service period that has elapsed, multiplied by the total estimated compensation cost.

For example, assume that the service period is 40 percent complete, and total estimated compensation is $100,000. The company reports cumulative compensation expense to date of $40,000 ($100,000 × .40).

The method of allocating compensation expense is called the **percentage approach**. In this method, in the first year of, say, a four-year plan, the company charges one-fourth of the estimated cost to date. In the second year, it charges off two-fourths, or 50 percent, of the estimated cost to date, less the amount already recognized in the first year. In the third year, it charges off three-fourths of the estimated cost to date, less the amount recognized previously. In the fourth year, it charges off the remaining compensation expense.

A special problem arises when the exercise date is past the service period. In the previous example, if the share-appreciation rights were not exercised at the end of four years, in the fifth year the company would have to account for the difference in the market price and the pre-established price. In this case, the company adjusts compensation expense whenever a change in the market price of the shares **occurs in subsequent reporting periods until the rights expire or are exercised,** whichever **comes first**.

Increases or decreases in the fair value of the SAR between the date of grant and the exercise date, therefore, result in a change in the measure of compensation. Some periods will have credits to compensation expense if the fair value decreases from one period to the next. The credit to compensation expense, however, cannot exceed previously recognized compensation expense. In other words, **cumulative compensation expense cannot be negative**.

SHARE-APPRECIATION RIGHTS EXAMPLE

Assume that Brazil Hotels, Inc. establishes a share-appreciation rights plan on January 1, 2015. The plan entitles executives to receive cash at the date of exercise for the difference between the share's market price and the pre-established price of R$10 on 10,000 SARs. The fair value of the SARs on December 31, 2015, is R$3, and the service period runs for two years (2015–2016). Illustration 16A-1 indicates the amount of compensation expense to be recorded each period, assuming that the executives hold the SARs for three years, at which time they exercise the rights.

SHARE-APPRECIATION RIGHTS
SCHEDULE OF COMPENSATION EXPENSE

(1) Date	(2) Fair Value	(3) Cumulative Compensation Recognizable[a]	(4) Percentage Accrued[b]	(5) Cumulative Compensation Accrued to Date	Expense 2015	Expense 2016	Expense 2017
12/31/15	R$3	R$30,000	50%	R$ 15,000	R$15,000		
				55,000		R$55,000	
12/31/16	7	70,000	100%	70,000			
				(20,000)			R$(20,000)
12/31/17	5	50,000	100%	R$ 50,000			

[a]Cumulative compensation for unexercised SARs to be allocated to periods of service.
[b]The percentage accrued is based upon a two-year service period (2015–2016).

ILLUSTRATION 16A-1
Compensation Expense, Share-Appreciation Rights

In 2015, Brazil Hotels records compensation expense of R$15,000 because 50 percent of the R$30,000 total compensation cost estimated at December 31, 2015, is allocable to 2015. In 2016, the fair value increased to R$7 per right (R$70,000 total). The company recorded additional compensation expense of R$55,000 (R$70,000 minus R$15,000).

The executives held the SARs through 2017, during which time the fair value declined to R$5 (and the obligation to the executives equals R$50,000). Brazil Hotels recognizes the decrease by recording a R$20,000 credit to compensation expense and a debit to Liability under Share-Appreciation Plan. Note that after the service period ends, since the rights are still outstanding, the company adjusts the rights to market at December 31, 2017. Any such credit to compensation expense cannot exceed previous charges to expense attributable to that plan.

As the company records the compensation expense each period, the corresponding credit is to a liability account, because the company will pay the share appreciation in cash. Brazil Hotels records compensation expense in the first year as follows.

Compensation Expense	15,000	
Liability under Share-Appreciation Plan		15,000

The company would credit the liability account for R$55,000 again in 2016. In 2017, when it records negative compensation expense, Brazil would debit the account for R$20,000. The entry to record the negative compensation expense is as follows.

Liability under Share-Appreciation Plan	20,000	
Compensation Expense		20,000

At December 31, 2017, the executives receive R$50,000 (which equals the market price of the shares less the pre-established price). Brazil would remove the liability with the following entry.

Liability under Share-Appreciation Plan	50,000	
Cash		50,000

Compensation expense can increase or decrease substantially from one period to the next. The reason is that compensation expense is remeasured each year, which can lead to large swings in compensation expense.

SUMMARY OF LEARNING OBJECTIVE FOR APPENDIX 16A

8 **Explain the accounting for share-appreciation rights plans.** The accounting for share-appreciation rights depends on whether the rights are classified as equity- or liability-based. If equity-based, the accounting is similar to that used for share options. If liability-based, companies remeasure compensation expense each period and allocate it over the service period using the percentage approach.

APPENDIX 16B — COMPREHENSIVE EARNINGS PER SHARE EXAMPLE

LEARNING OBJECTIVE 9

Compute earnings per share in a complex situation.

This appendix illustrates the method of computing dilution when many securities are involved. We present the following section of the statement of financial position of Webster Corporation for analysis. Assumptions related to the capital structure follow the statement of financial position.

WEBSTER CORPORATION
STATEMENT OF FINANCIAL POSITION (PARTIAL)
AT DECEMBER 31, 2015

Equity	
10% cumulative, convertible preference shares, par value $100;	
100,000 shares authorized, 25,000 shares issued and outstanding	$ 2,500,000
Share capital—ordinary, par value $1, 5,000,000 shares authorized,	
500,000 shares issued and outstanding	500,000
Share premium	2,000,000
Retained earnings	9,000,000
Total equity	$14,000,000
Long-term debt	
Notes payable, 14%	$ 1,000,000
Convertible bonds payable (Issue A)	2,500,000
Convertible bonds payable (Issue B)	2,500,000
Total long-term debt	$ 6,000,000

Notes and Assumptions
December 31, 2015

1. Options were granted in July 2013 to purchase 50,000 ordinary shares at $20 per share. The average market price of Webster's ordinary shares during 2016 was $30 per share. All options are still outstanding at the end of 2015.
2. Both convertible bonds were issued in 2014. Each convertible bond is convertible into 40 shares of ordinary shares. (Each bond has a face value of $1,000.) In 2015, interest expense of $200,000 on the liability component of convertible bonds (Issue A) is recorded, and interest expense of $250,000 is recorded on the liability component of convertible bonds (Issue B).
3. The 10 percent cumulative, convertible preference shares were issued at the beginning of 2015 at par. Each preference share is convertible into four ordinary shares.
4. The average income tax rate is 40 percent.
5. The 500,000 ordinary shares were outstanding during the entire year.
6. Preference dividends were not declared in 2015.
7. Net income was $1,750,000 in 2015.
8. No bonds or preference shares were converted during 2015.

ILLUSTRATION 16B-1
Statement of Financial Position for Comprehensive Illustration

The computation of basic earnings per share for 2015 starts with the amount based upon the weighted-average of ordinary shares outstanding, as shown in Illustration 16B-2.

Net income	$1,750,000
Less: 10% cumulative, convertible preference share dividend requirements	250,000
Income applicable to ordinary shareholders	$1,500,000
Weighted-average number of ordinary shares outstanding	500,000
Earnings per ordinary share	$3.00

ILLUSTRATION 16B-2
Computation of Earnings per Share—Simple Capital Structure

Note the following points concerning this calculation.

1. When preference shares are cumulative, the company subtracts the preference dividend to arrive at income applicable to ordinary shares, whether the dividend is declared or not.
2. The company must compute earnings per share of $3 as a starting point because it is the per share amount that is subject to reduction due to the existence of convertible securities and options.

DILUTED EARNINGS PER SHARE

The steps for computing diluted earnings per share are:

1. Determine, for each dilutive security, the per share effect assuming exercise/conversion.

2. Rank the results from Step 1 from smallest to largest earnings effect per share. That is, rank the results from most dilutive to least dilutive.

3. Beginning with the earnings per share based upon the weighted-average of ordinary shares outstanding ($3), recalculate earnings per share by adding the smallest per share effects from Step 2. If the results from this recalculation are less than $3, proceed to the next smallest per share effect and recalculate earnings per share. Continue this process so long as each recalculated earnings per share is smaller than the previous amount. The process will end either because there are no more securities to test or a particular security maintains or increases earnings per share (is antidilutive).

We'll now apply the three steps to Webster Corporation. (Note that net income and income available to ordinary shareholders are not the same if preference dividends are declared or cumulative.) Webster Corporation has four securities that could reduce EPS: options, convertible bonds (Issue A), convertible bonds (Issue B), and the convertible preference shares.

The first step in the computation of diluted earnings per share is to determine a per share effect for each potentially dilutive security. Illustrations 16B-3 through 16B-6 illustrate these computations.

ILLUSTRATION 16B-3
Per Share Effect of
Options (Treasury-Share
Method), Diluted
Earnings per Share

Number of shares under option	50,000
Option price per share	× $20
Proceeds upon assumed exercise of options	$1,000,000
Average 2015 market price ordinary shares	$30
Treasury shares that could be acquired with proceeds ($1,000,000 ÷ $30)	33,333
Excess of shares under option over treasury shares that could be repurchased (50,000 − 33,333)	16,667

Per share effect:
$$\frac{\text{Incremental Numerator Effect}}{\text{Incremental Denominator Effect}} = \frac{\text{None}}{16,667 \text{ shares}} = \$0$$

ILLUSTRATION 16B-4
Per Share Effect of Issue
A Bonds (If-Converted
Method), Diluted
Earnings per Share

Interest expense on bonds (Issue A) for year	$200,000
Income tax reduction due to interest (40% × $200,000)	80,000
Interest expense avoided (net of tax)	$120,000
Number of ordinary shares issued assuming conversion of bonds (2,500 bonds × 40 shares)	100,000

Per share effect:
$$\frac{\text{Incremental Numerator Effect}}{\text{Incremental Denominator Effect}} = \frac{\$120,000}{100,000 \text{ shares}} = \$1.20$$

ILLUSTRATION 16B-5
Per Share Effect of Issue B
Bonds (If-Converted
Method), Diluted
Earnings per Share

Interest expense on bonds (Issue B) for year	$250,000
Income tax reduction due to interest (40% × $250,000)	100,000
Interest expense avoided (net of tax)	$150,000
Number of ordinary shares issued assuming conversion of bonds (2,500 bonds × 40 shares)	100,000

Per share effect:
$$\frac{\text{Incremental Numerator Effect}}{\text{Incremental Denominator Effect}} = \frac{\$150,000}{100,000 \text{ shares}} = \$1.50$$

Dividend requirement on cumulative preference share (25,000 shares × $10)	$250,000
Income tax effect (dividends not a tax deduction)	none
Dividend requirement avoided	$250,000
Number of ordinary shares issued assuming conversion of preference shares (4 × 25,000 shares)	100,000
Per share effect:	

$$\frac{\text{Incremental Numerator Effect}}{\text{Incremental Denominator Effect}} = \frac{\$250,000}{100,000 \text{ shares}} = \quad \$2.50$$

ILLUSTRATION 16B-6
Per Share Effect of 10%
Convertible Preference
Shares (If-Converted
Method), Diluted
Earnings per Share

Illustration 16B-7 shows the ranking of all four potentially dilutive securities.

	Effect per Share
1. Options	$ 0
2. Convertible bonds (Issue A)	1.20
3. Convertible bonds (Issue B)	1.50
4. 10% convertible preference	2.50

ILLUSTRATION 16B-7
Ranking of Per Share
Effects (Smallest to
Largest), Diluted
Earnings per Share

The next step is to determine earnings per share giving effect to the ranking in Illustration 16B-7. Starting with the earnings per share of $3 computed previously, add the incremental effects of the options to the original calculation, as follows.

Options	
Income applicable to ordinary shareholders	$1,500,000
Add: Incremental numerator effect of options	none
Total	$1,500,000
Weighted-average number of ordinary shares outstanding	500,000
Add: Incremental denominator effect of options (Illustration 16B-3)	16,667
Total	516,667
Recomputed earnings per share ($1,500,000 ÷ 516,667 shares)	$2.90

ILLUSTRATION 16B-8
Recomputation of EPS
Using Incremental Effect
of Options

Since the recomputed earnings per share is reduced (from $3 to $2.90), the effect of the options is dilutive. Again, we could have anticipated this effect because the average market price ($30) exceeded the option price ($20).

Assuming that Webster converts the bonds (Issue A), recomputed earnings per share is as shown below.

Convertible Bonds (Issue A)	
Numerator from previous calculation	$1,500,000
Add: Interest expense avoided (net of tax)	120,000
Total	$1,620,000
Denominator from previous calculation (shares)	516,667
Add: Number of ordinary shares assumed issued upon conversion of bonds	100,000
Total	616,667
Recomputed earnings per share ($1,620,000 ÷ 616,667 shares)	$2.63

ILLUSTRATION 16B-9
Recomputation of EPS
Using Incremental Effect
of Convertible Bonds
(Issue A)

Since the recomputed earnings per share is reduced (from $2.90 to $2.63), the effect of the bonds (Issue A) is dilutive.

Next, assuming Webster converts the bonds (Issue B), the company recomputes earnings per share as shown in Illustration 16B-10.

ILLUSTRATION 16B-10
Recomputation of EPS Using Incremental Effect of Convertible Bonds (Issue B)

Convertible Bonds (Issue B)	
Numerator from previous calculation	$1,620,000
Add: Interest expense avoided (net of tax)	150,000
Total	$1,770,000
Denominator from previous calculation (shares)	616,667
Add: Number of ordinary shares assumed issued upon conversion of bonds	100,000
Total	716,667
Recomputed earnings per share ($1,770,000 ÷ 716,667 shares)	$2.47

Since the recomputed earnings per share is reduced (from $2.63 to $2.47), the effect of the convertible bonds (Issue B) is dilutive.

The final step is the recomputation that includes the 10 percent preference shares. This is shown in Illustration 16B-11.

ILLUSTRATION 16B-11
Recomputation of EPS Using Incremental Effect of 10% Convertible Preference Shares

10% Convertible Preference	
Numerator from previous calculation	$1,770,000
Add: Dividend requirement avoided	250,000
Total	$2,020,000
Denominator from previous calculation (shares)	716,667
Add: Number of ordinary shares assumed issued upon conversion of preference shares	100,000
Total	816,667
Recomputed earnings per share ($2,020,000 ÷ 816,667 shares)	$2.47

Since the recomputed earnings per share is not reduced, the effect of the 10 percent convertible preference shares are not dilutive. Diluted earnings per share is $2.47. The per share effects of the preference shares are not used in the computation.

Finally, Illustration 16B-12 shows Webster Corporation's disclosure of earnings per share on its income statement.

ILLUSTRATION 16B-12
Income Statement Presentation, EPS

Net income	$1,750,000
Basic earnings per ordinary share (Note X)	$3.00
Diluted earnings per ordinary share	$2.47

A company uses income from continuing operations (adjusted for preference dividends) to determine whether potential ordinary shares are dilutive or antidilutive. Some refer to this measure as the **control number**. To illustrate, assume that Barton Company provides the following information.

Income from continuing operations	$2,400,000
Loss from discontinued operations	3,600,000
Net loss	$1,200,000
Weighted-average shares of ordinary shares outstanding	1,000,000
Potential ordinary shares	200,000

ILLUSTRATION 16B-13
Barton Company Data

Barton reports basic and dilutive earnings per share as follows.

Basic earnings per share	
Income from continuing operations	$2.40
Loss from discontinued operations	3.60
Net loss	$1.20
Diluted earnings per share	
Income from continuing operations	$2.00
Loss from discontinued operations	3.00
Net loss	$1.00

ILLUSTRATION 16B-14
Basic and Diluted EPS

As Illustration 16B-14 shows, basic earnings per share from continuing operations is higher than the diluted earnings per share from continuing operations. The reason: The diluted earnings per share from continuing operations includes an additional 200,000 shares of potential ordinary shares in its denominator.[20]

Companies use income from continuing operations as the control number because many of them show income from continuing operations (or a similar line item above net income if it appears on the income statement), but report a final net loss due to a loss on discontinued operations. If a company uses final net loss as the control number, basic and diluted earnings per share would be the same because the potential ordinary shares are antidilutive.[21]

SUMMARY OF LEARNING OBJECTIVE FOR APPENDIX 16B

KEY TERMS

control number, 792

9 **Compute earnings per share in a complex situation.** For diluted EPS, make the following computations. (1) For each potentially dilutive security, determine the per share effect assuming exercise/conversion. (2) Rank the results from most dilutive to least dilutive. (3) Recalculate EPS starting with the most dilutive and continue adding securities until EPS does not change or becomes larger.

---

[20]A company that does not report a discontinued operation uses net income as the control number.

[21]If a company reports a loss from continuing operations, basic and diluted earnings per share will be the same because potential ordinary shares will be antidilutive even if the company reports final net income. The IASB believes that comparability of EPS information will be improved by using income from continuing operations as the control number.

IFRS AUTHORITATIVE LITERATURE

Authoritative Literature References

[1] International Accounting Standard 32, *Financial Instruments: Presentation* (London, U.K.: International Accounting Standards Committee Foundation, 2003), paras. 28–32.

[2] International Accounting Standard 32, *Financial Instruments: Presentation* (London, U.K.: International Accounting Standards Committee Foundation, 2003), par. BC29.

[3] International Accounting Standard 32, *Financial Instruments: Presentation* (London, U.K.: International Accounting Standards Committee Foundation, 2003), par. AG34.

[4] International Accounting Standard 32, *Financial Instruments: Presentation* (London, U.K.: International Accounting Standards Committee Foundation, 2003), par. 36.

[5] International Financial Reporting Standard 2, *Share-Based Payment* (London, U.K.: International Accounting Standards Committee Foundation, 2004), par. 16.

[6] International Financial Reporting Standard 2, *Share-Based Payment* (London, U.K.: International Accounting Standards Committee Foundation, 2004), par. BC11.

[7] International Financial Reporting Standard 2, *Share-Based Payment* (London, U.K.: International Accounting Standards Committee Foundation, 2004), par. IN8.

[8] International Accounting Standard 33, *Earnings per Share* (London, U.K.: International Accounting Standards Committee Foundation, 2003), par. 66.

[9] International Accounting Standard 33, *Earnings per Share* (London, U.K.: International Accounting Standards Committee Foundation, 2003), par. 1.

[10] International Accounting Standard 33, *Earnings per Share* (London, U.K.: International Accounting Standards Committee Foundation, 2003), par. 39.

[11] International Accounting Standard 33, *Earnings per Share* (London, U.K.: International Accounting Standards Committee Foundation, 2003), par. 56.

[12] International Accounting Standard 33, *Earnings per Share* (London, U.K.: International Accounting Standards Committee Foundation, 2003), par. 66.

Note: All asterisked Questions, Exercises, and Problems relate to material in the appendices to the chapter.

QUESTIONS

1. What is meant by a dilutive security?

2. Briefly explain why corporations issue convertible securities.

3. Discuss the similarities between convertible debt and debt issued with share warrants.

4. Bridgewater Corp. offered holders of its 1,000 convertible bonds a premium of €160 per bond to induce conversion into ordinary shares. Upon conversion of all the bonds, Bridgewater Corp. recorded the €160,000 premium as a reduction of Share Premium—Ordinary. Comment on Bridgewater's treatment of the €160,000 "sweetener."

5. Explain how the conversion feature of convertible debt has a value (a) to the issuer and (b) to the purchaser.

6. What are the arguments for giving separate accounting recognition to the conversion feature of debentures?

7. Four years after issue, debentures with a face value of £1,000,000 and book value of £960,000 are tendered for conversion into 80,000 ordinary shares immediately after an interest payment date. At that time, the market price of the debentures is 104, and the ordinary shares are selling at £14 per share (par value £10). The company records the conversion as follows.

Bonds Payable	960,000	
Share Premium—Conversion Equity		10,000
Share Capital—Ordinary		800,000
Share Premium—Ordinary		150,000

Discuss the propriety of this accounting treatment.

8. On July 1, 2015, Roberts Corporation issued €3,000,000 of 9% bonds payable in 20 years. The bonds include warrants giving the bondholder the right to purchase for €30 one ordinary share of €1 par value at any time during the next 10 years. The bonds were sold for €3,000,000. The net present value of the debt at the time of issuance was €2,900,000. Prepare the journal entry to record this transaction.

9. What are share rights? How does the issuing company account for them?

10. Briefly explain the accounting requirements for share compensation plans under IFRS.

11. Cordero Corporation has an employee share-purchase plan which permits all full-time employees to purchase 10 ordinary shares on the third anniversary of their employment and an additional 15 shares on each subsequent anniversary date. The purchase price is set at the market price on the date purchased less a 10% discount. How is this discount accounted for by Cordero?

12. What date or event does the profession believe should be used in determining the value of a share option? What arguments support this position?

13. Over what period of time should compensation cost for a share-option plan be allocated?

14. How is compensation expense for a share-option plan computed using the fair value approach?

15. What are the advantages of using restricted shares to compensate employees?

16. At December 31, 2015, Ruiz Company had 600,000 ordinary shares issued and outstanding, 400,000 of which had been issued and outstanding throughout the year and 200,000 of which were issued on October 1, 2015. Net income for 2015 was R$1,750,000, and dividends declared on preference shares were R$400,000. Compute Ruiz's earnings per ordinary share.

17. What effect do share dividends or share splits have on the computation of the weighted-average number of shares outstanding?

18. Define the following terms.
   (a) Basic earnings per share.
   (b) Potentially dilutive security.
   (c) Diluted earnings per share.
   (d) Complex capital structure.
   (e) Potential ordinary shares.

19. What are the computational guidelines for determining whether a convertible security is to be reported as part of diluted earnings per share?

20. Discuss why options and warrants may be considered potentially dilutive ordinary shares for the computation of diluted earnings per share.

21. Explain how convertible securities are determined to be potentially dilutive ordinary shares and how those convertible securities that are not considered to be potentially dilutive ordinary shares enter into the determination of earnings per share data.

22. Explain the treasury-share method as it applies to options and warrants in computing dilutive earnings per share data.

23. Earnings per share can affect market prices of ordinary shares. Can market prices affect earnings per share? Explain.

24. What is meant by the term antidilution? Give an example.

25. What type of earnings per share presentation is required in a complex capital structure?

26. Briefly describe some of the similarities and differences between U.S. GAAP and IFRS with respect to the accounting for share-based compensation.

27. Norman Co., a fast-growing golf equipment company, uses IFRS. It is considering the issuance of convertible bonds. The bonds mature in 10 years, have a face value of €400,000, and pay interest annually at a rate of 4%. The net present value of the liability component is €365,000. Greg Shark is curious as to the difference in accounting **for these bonds if the company were to use U.S. GAAP.** (a) Prepare the entry to record issuance of the bonds at par under IFRS. (b) Repeat the requirement for part (a), assuming application of U.S. GAAP to the bond issuance. (c) Which approach provides the better accounting? Explain.

*28. How is antidilution determined when multiple securities are involved?

BRIEF EXERCISES

➊ **BE16-1** Archer Company issued £4,000,000 par value, 7% convertible bonds at 99 for cash. The net present value of the debt without the conversion feature is £3,800,000. Prepare the journal entry to record the issuance of the convertible bonds.

➊ **BE16-2** Petrenko Corporation has outstanding 2,000 €1,000 bonds, each convertible into 50 shares of €10 par value ordinary shares. The bonds are converted on December 31, 2015. The bonds payable have a carrying value of €1,950,000, and there is conversion equity of €20,000. Record the conversion using the book value method.

➋ **BE16-3** Pechstein Corporation issued 2,000 shares of $10 par value ordinary shares upon conversion of 1,000 shares of $50 par value preference shares. The preference shares were originally issued at $60 per share. The ordinary shares are trading at $26 per share at the time of conversion. Record the conversion of the convertible preference shares.

➌ **BE16-4** Eisler Corporation issued 2,000 $1,000 bonds at 101. Each bond was issued with one detachable share warrant. At issuance, the net present value of the bonds without the warrants was $1,970,000. Prepare the journal entry to record the issuance of the bonds and the share warrants.

3 **BE16-5** Parsons Corporation issued 3,000 €1,000 bonds at 98. Each bond was issued with one detachable share warrant. At issuance, the net present value of the bonds without the warrants was €2,910,000. Prepare the journal entry to record the issuance of the bonds and the share warrants.

4 **BE16-6** On January 1, 2015, Barwood Corporation granted 5,000 options to executives. Each option entitles the holder to purchase one share of Barwood's £5 par value ordinary shares at £50 per share at any time during the next 5 years. The market price of the shares is £65 per share on the date of grant. The fair value of the options at the grant date is £150,000. The period of benefit is 2 years. Prepare Barwood's journal entries for January 1, 2015, and December 31, 2015 and 2016.

4 **BE16-7** Refer to the data for Barwood Corporation in BE16-6. Repeat the requirements, assuming that instead of options, Barwood granted 2,000 restricted shares.

4 **BE16-8** On January 1, 2015 (the date of grant), Lutz Corporation issues 2,000 restricted shares to its executives. The fair value of these shares is $75,000, and their par value is $10,000. The shares are forfeited if the executives do not complete 3 years of employment with the company. Prepare the journal entry (if any) on January 1, 2015, and on December 31, 2015, assuming the service period is 3 years.

6 **BE16-9** Kalin Corporation had 2015 net income of €1,000,000. During 2015, Kalin paid a dividend of €2 per share on 100,000 preference shares. During 2015, Kalin had outstanding 250,000 ordinary shares. Compute Kalin's 2015 earnings per share.

6 **BE16-10** Douglas Corporation had 120,000 ordinary shares outstanding on January 1, 2015. On May 1, 2015, Douglas issued 60,000 ordinary shares. On July 1, Douglas purchased 10,000 treasury shares, which were reissued on October 1. Compute Douglas's weighted-average number of ordinary shares outstanding for 2015.

6 **BE16-11** Tomba Corporation had 300,000 ordinary shares outstanding on January 1, 2015. On May 1, Tomba issued 30,000 ordinary shares. (a) Compute the weighted-average number of shares outstanding if the 30,000 shares were issued for cash. (b) Compute the weighted-average number of shares outstanding if the 30,000 shares were issued in a share dividend.

7 **BE16-12** Rockland Corporation earned net income of R$300,000 in 2015 and had 100,000 ordinary shares outstanding throughout the year. Also outstanding all year was R$800,000 of 10% bonds, which are convertible into 16,000 ordinary shares. The interest expense on the liability component of the convertible bonds was R$64,000. Rockland's tax rate is 40%. Compute Rockland's 2015 diluted earnings per share.

7 **BE16-13** DiCenta Corporation reported net income of €270,000 in 2015 and had 50,000 ordinary shares outstanding throughout the year. Also outstanding all year were 5,000 shares of cumulative preference shares, each convertible into 2 ordinary shares. The preference shares pay an annual dividend of €5 per share. DiCenta's tax rate is 40%. Compute DiCenta's 2015 diluted earnings per share.

7 **BE16-14** Bedard Corporation reported net income of ₺300,000 in 2015 and had 200,000 ordinary shares outstanding throughout the year. Also outstanding all year were 45,000 options to purchase ordinary shares at ₺10 per share. The average market price of the shares during the year was ₺15. Compute diluted earnings per share.

6 **BE16-15** The 2015 income statement of Wasmeier Corporation showed net income of €480,000 and a loss from discontinued operations of €120,000. Wasmeier had 100,000 shares of ordinary shares outstanding all year. Prepare Wasmeier's income statement presentation of earnings per share.

8 *****BE16-16** Ferraro, Inc. established a share-appreciation rights (SARs) program on January 1, 2015, which entitles executives to receive cash at the date of exercise for the difference between the market price of the shares and the pre-established price of $20 on 5,000 SARs. The required service period is 2 years. The fair value of the SARs are determined to be $4 on December 31, 2015, and $9 on December 31, 2016. Compute Ferraro's compensation expense for 2015 and 2016.

EXERCISES

1 **E16-1 (Issuance and Repurchase of Convertible Bonds)** Angela Corporation issues 2,000 convertible bonds at January 1, 2015. The bonds have a 3-year life and are issued at par with a face value of €1,000 per bond, giving total proceeds of €2,000,000. Interest is payable annually at 6%. Each bond is convertible into 250 ordinary shares (par value of €1). When the bonds are issued, the market rate of interest for similar debt without the conversion option is 8%.

Instructions

    (a) Compute the liability and equity component of the convertible bond on January 1, 2015.

    (b) Prepare the journal entry to record the issuance of the convertible bond on January 1, 2015.

    (c) Prepare the journal entry to record the repurchase of the convertible bond for cash at January 1, 2018, its maturity date.

1 ▶ **E16-2 (Issuance and Repurchase of Convertible Bonds)** Assume the same information in E16-1, except that Angela Corporation converts its convertible bonds on January 1, 2016.

Instructions

(a) Compute the carrying value of the bond payable on January 1, 2016.

(b) Prepare the journal entry to record the conversion on January 1, 2016.

(c) Assume that the bonds were repurchased on January 1, 2016, for €1,940,000 cash instead of being converted. The net present value of the liability component of the convertible bonds on January 1, 2016, is €1,900,000. Prepare the journal entry to record the repurchase on January 1, 2016.

1 ▶ **E16-3 (Issuance and Repurchase of Convertible Bonds)** On January 1, 2015, Cai Company issued a 10% convertible bond at par, with a face value of ¥100,000, maturing on January 1, 2025. The bond is convertible into ordinary shares of Cai at a conversion price of ¥2,500 per share. Interest is payable annually. At date of issue, Cai could have issued at par non-convertible debt with a 10-year term bearing an interest rate of 11%.

Instructions

(a) Prepare the journal entry to record the issuance of the convertible debt on January 1, 2015.

(b) On January 1, 2018, Cai makes a tender offer to the holder of the convertible debt to repurchase the bond for ¥112,000, which the holder accepts. At the date of repurchase, Cai could have issued non-convertible debt with a 7-year term at an effective-interest rate of 8%. Prepare the journal entry to record this repurchase on January 1, 2018.

1 ▶ **E16-4 (Issuance, Conversion, Repurchase of Convertible Bonds)** On January 1, 2015, Lin Company issued a convertible bond with a par value of £50,000 in the market for £60,000. The bonds are convertible into 6,000 ordinary shares of £1 per share par value. The bond has a 5-year life and has a stated interest rate of 10% payable annually. The market interest rate for a similar non-convertible bond at January 1, 2015, is 8%. The liability component of the bond is computed to be £53,993. The following bond amortization schedule is provided for this bond.

	EFFECTIVE-INTEREST METHOD			
	10% BOND DISCOUNTED AT 8%			
Date	Cash Paid	Interest Expense	Premium Amortized	Carrying Amount of Bonds
1/1/15				£53,993
12/31/15	£5,000	£4,319	£681	53,312
12/31/16	5,000	4,265	735	52,577
12/31/17	5,000	4,206	794	51,783
12/31/18	5,000	4,143	857	50,926
12/31/19	5,000	4,074	926	50,000

Instructions

(a) Prepare the journal entry to record the issuance of the convertible bond on January 1, 2015.

(b) Prepare the journal entry to record the payment of interest on December 31, 2016.

(c) Assume that the bonds were converted on December 31, 2017. The fair value of the liability component of the bond is determined to be £54,000 on December 31, 2017. Prepare the journal entry to record the conversion on December 31, 2017. Assume that the accrual of interest related to 2017 has been recorded.

(d) Assume that the convertible bonds were repurchased on December 31, 2017, for £55,500 instead of being converted. As indicated, the liability component of the bond is determined to be £54,000 on December 31, 2017. Assume that the accrual of interest related to 2017 has been recorded.

(e) Assume that the bonds matured on December 31, 2019, and Lin repurchased the bonds. Prepare the entry(ies) to record this transaction.

1 ▶ **E16-5 (Conversion of Bonds)** Schuss Inc. issued €3,000,000 of 10%, 10-year convertible bonds on April 1, 2015, at 98. The bonds were dated April 1, 2015, with interest payable April 1 and October 1. Bond discount is amortized semiannually using the effective-interest method. The net present value of the bonds without the conversion feature discounted at 12% (its market rate) was €2,655,888.

On April 1, 2016, €1,000,000 of these bonds were converted into 30,000 shares of €20 par value ordinary shares. Accrued interest was paid in cash at the time of conversion.

Instructions

(a) Prepare the entry to record the issuance of the convertible bond on April 1, 2015.

(b) Prepare the entry to record the interest expense at October 1, 2015.

(c) Prepare the entry(ies) to record the conversion on April 1, 2016. (The book value method is used.)

1 **E16-6 (Conversion of Bonds)** Gabel Company has bonds payable outstanding with a carrying value of $406,000. When issued, Gabel recorded $3,500 of conversion equity. Each $1,000 bond is convertible into 20 shares of preference shares with par value of $50 per share. All bonds are converted into preference shares.

Instructions
Assuming that the book value method was used, what entry would be made?

1 **3** **E16-7 (Issuance and Conversion of Bonds)** For each of the unrelated transactions described below, present the entry(ies) required to record each transaction.

1. Coyle Corp. issued €10,000,000 par value 10% convertible bonds at 99. If the bonds had not been convertible, the company's investment banker determines that they would have been sold at 95.

2. Lambert Company issued €10,000,000 par value 10% bonds at 98. One share warrant was issued with each €100 par value bond. At the time of issuance, the warrants were selling for €4. The net present value of the bonds without the warrants was €9,600,000.

3. Sepracor, Inc. called its convertible debt in 2015. Assume the following related to the transaction. The 11%, €10,000,000 par value bonds were converted into 1,000,000 shares of €1 par value ordinary shares on July 1, 2015. The carrying amount of the debt on July 1 was €9,700,000. The Share Premium—Conversion Equity account had a balance of €200,000, and the company paid an additional €75,000 to the bondholders to induce conversion of all the bonds. The company records the conversion using the book value method.

3 **E16-8 (Issuance of Bonds with Share Warrants)** Sun Inc. has decided to raise additional capital by issuing HK$175,000 face value of bonds with a coupon rate of 10%. In discussions with investment bankers, it was determined that to help the sale of the bonds, share warrants should be issued at the rate of one warrant for each HK$100 bond sold. The fair value of the bonds without the warrants is HK$136,000, and the estimated value of the warrants is HK$18,000. The proceeds upon issuance of the bonds and warrants was HK$150,000.

Instructions
(a) What entry should be made at the time of the issuance of the bonds and warrants?
(b) If the warrants were non-detachable, would the entries be different? Discuss.

3 **E16-9 (Issuance of Bonds with Share Warrants)** On September 1, 2015, Tokachi Company sold at 104 (plus accrued interest) 30,000 of its 8%, 10-year, ¥10,000 face value, non-convertible bonds with detachable share warrants. Each bond carried two detachable warrants. Each warrant was for one ordinary share at a specified option price of ¥1,500 per share. The net present value of bonds is determined to be ¥290,000,000. Interest is payable on December 1 and June 1.

Instructions
Prepare in general journal format the entry to record the issuance of the bonds.

3 **E16-10 (Issuance of Bonds with Share Warrants)** On May 1, 2015, Barkley Company issued 3,000 €1,000 bonds at 102. Each bond was issued with one detachable share warrant. The fair value of the bonds on May 1, 2015, was €2,940,000.

Instructions
(a) Prepare the entry to record the issuance of the bonds and warrants.
(b) Assume the same facts as part (a), except that the warrants had an estimated fair value of €20. Prepare the entry to record the issuance of the bonds and warrants.

4 **E16-11 (Issuance and Exercise of Share Options)** On November 1, 2014, Olympic Company adopted a share-option plan that granted options to key executives to purchase 40,000 shares of the company's £10 par value ordinary shares. The options were granted on January 2, 2015, and were vested 2 years after the date of grant if the grantee was still an employee of the company. The options expired 6 years from date of grant. The option price was set at £40, and the fair value option-pricing model determines the total compensation expense to be £600,000.

All of the options were exercised during the year 2017: 30,000 on January 3 when the market price was £67, and 10,000 on May 1 when the market price was £77 a share.

Instructions
Prepare journal entries relating to the share-option plan for the years 2015, 2016, and 2017. Assume that the employees perform services equally in 2015 and 2016.

4 **E16-12 (Issuance, Exercise, and Forfeiture of Share Options)** On January 1, 2015, Magilla Inc. granted share options to officers and key employees for the purchase of 20,000 of the company's €10 par ordinary shares at €25 per share. The options were exercisable within a 5-year period beginning January 1, 2017, by grantees still in the employ of the company, and expiring December 31, 2021. The service period for this award is 2 years. Assume that the fair value option-pricing model determines total compensation expense to be €400,000.

On April 1, 2016, 3,000 options were forfeited when the employees resigned from the company. The market price of the ordinary shares was €35 per share on this date.

On March 31, 2017, 12,000 options were exercised when the market price of the ordinary shares was €40 per share.

Instructions

Prepare journal entries to record issuance of the share options, forfeiture of the share options, exercise of the share options, and charges to compensation expense, for the years ended December 31, 2015, 2016, and 2017.

4 E16-13 (Issuance, Exercise, and Expiration of Share Options) On January 1, 2014, Tsang Corporation granted 10,000 options to key executives. Each option allows the executive to purchase one share of Tsang's HK$5 par value ordinary shares at a price of HK$20 per share. The options were exercisable within a 2-year period beginning January 1, 2016, if the grantee is still employed by the company at the time of the exercise. On the grant date, Tsang's shares were trading at HK$25 per share, and a fair value option-pricing model determines total compensation to be HK$450,000.

On May 1, 2016, 9,000 options were exercised when the market price of Tsang's shares were HK$30 per share. The remaining options lapsed in 2018 because executives decided not to exercise their options.

Instructions

Prepare the necessary journal entries related to the share-option plan for the years 2014 through 2018.

4 E16-14 (Accounting for Restricted Shares) Derrick Company issues 4,000 restricted shares to its CFO, Dane Yaping, on January 1, 2015. The shares have a fair value of £120,000 on this date. The service period related to these restricted shares is 4 years. Vesting occurs if Yaping stays with the company for 4 years. The par value of the shares is £5. At December 31, 2016, the fair value of the shares is £145,000.

Instructions

(a) Prepare the journal entries to record the restricted shares on January 1, 2015 (the date of grant), and December 31, 2016.

(b) On March 4, 2017, Yaping leaves the company. Prepare the journal entry (if any) to account for this forfeiture.

4 E16-15 (Accounting for Restricted Shares) Lopez Company issues 10,000 restricted shares to its CFO, Juan Carlos, on January 1, 2015. The shares have a fair value of €500,000 on this date. The service period related to the restricted shares is 5 years. Vesting occurs if Carlos stays with the company for 6 years. The par value of the shares is €10. At December 31, 2015, the fair value of the shares is €450,000.

Instructions

(a) Prepare the journal entries to record the restricted shares on January 1, 2015 (the date of grant), and December 31, 2016.

(b) On January 1, 2020, Carlos leaves the company. Prepare the journal entry (if any) to account for this forfeiture.

6 E16-16 (Weighted-Average Number of Shares) Portillo Inc. uses a calendar year for financial reporting. The company is authorized to issue 9,000,000 R$10 par ordinary shares. At no time has Portillo issued any potentially dilutive securities. Listed below is a summary of Portillo's ordinary share activities.

1. Number of ordinary shares issued and outstanding at December 31, 2014	2,400,000
2. Shares issued as a result of a 10% share dividend on September 30, 2015	240,000
3. Shares issued for cash on March 31, 2016	2,000,000
Number of ordinary shares issued and outstanding at December 31, 2016	4,640,000
4. A 2-for-1 share split of Portillo's ordinary shares took place on March 31, 2017	

Instructions

(a) Compute the weighted-average number of ordinary shares used in computing earnings per ordinary share for 2015 on the 2016 comparative income statement.

(b) Compute the weighted-average number of ordinary shares used in computing earnings per ordinary share for 2016 on the 2016 comparative income statement.

(c) Compute the weighted-average number of ordinary shares to be used in computing earnings per ordinary share for 2016 on the 2017 comparative income statement.

(d) Compute the weighted-average number of ordinary shares to be used in computing earnings per ordinary share for 2017 on the 2017 comparative income statement.

6 **E16-17 (EPS: Simple Capital Structure)** On January 1, 2015, Chang Corp. had 480,000 ordinary shares outstanding. During 2015, it had the following transactions that affected the ordinary share account.

February 1	Issued 120,000 shares
March 1	Issued a 20% share dividend
May 1	Acquired 100,000 treasury shares
June 1	Issued a 3-for-1 share split
October 1	Reissued 60,000 treasury shares

Instructions

(a) Determine the weighted-average number of shares outstanding as of December 31, 2015.

(b) Assume that Chang Corp. earned net income of ¥3,256,000,000 during 2015. In addition, it had 100,000 shares of 9%, ¥100 par, non-convertible, non-cumulative preference shares outstanding for the entire year. Because of liquidity considerations, however, the company did not declare and pay a preference dividend in 2015. Compute earnings per share for 2015, using the weighted-average number of shares determined in part (a).

(c) Assume the same facts as in part (b), except that the preference shares were cumulative. Compute earnings per share for 2015.

(d) Assume the same facts as in part (b), except that net income included a loss from discontinued operations of ¥432,000,000. The loss from discontinued operations is net of applicable income taxes. Compute earnings per share for 2015.

6 **E16-18 (EPS: Simple Capital Structure)** Ott Company had 210,000 ordinary shares outstanding on December 31, 2015. During the year 2016, the company issued 8,000 shares on May 1 and retired 14,000 shares on October 31. For the year 2016, Ott Company reported net income of £229,690 after a loss on discontinued operations of £40,600 (net of tax).

Instructions

What earnings per share data should be reported at the bottom of its income statement?

6 **E16-19 (EPS: Simple Capital Structure)** Huang Company presented the following data (yen in thousands).

Net income	¥2,200,000
Preference shares: 50,000 shares outstanding,	
¥100 par, 8% cumulative, not convertible	5,000,000
Ordinary shares: Shares outstanding 1/1	600,000
Issued for cash, 5/1	300,000
Acquired treasury shares for cash, 8/1	150,000
2-for-1 share split, 10/1	

Instructions

Compute earnings per share.

6 **E16-20 (EPS: Simple Capital Structure)** A portion of the statement of income and retained earnings of Pierson Inc. for the current year follows.

Income from continuing operations		$15,000,000
Loss on discontinued operations, net of applicable income tax (Note 1)		1,340,000
Net income		13,660,000
Retained earnings at the beginning of the year		83,250,000
		96,910,000
Dividends declared:		
On preference shares—$6.00 per share	$ 300,000	
On ordinary shares—$1.75 per share	14,875,000	15,175,000
Retained earnings at the end of the year		$81,735,000

Note 1. During the year, Pierson Inc. had a loss from discontinued operations of $1,340,000 after applicable income tax reduction of $1,200,000.

At the end of the current year, Pierson Inc. has outstanding 8,000,000 shares of $10 par ordinary shares and 50,000 shares of 6% preference shares.

On April 1 of the current year, Pierson Inc. issued 1,000,000 ordinary shares for $32 per share to help finance the loss on discontinued operations.

Instructions

Compute the earnings per share on ordinary shares for the current year as it should be reported to shareholders.

6 **E16-21 (EPS: Simple Capital Structure)** On January 1, 2015, Bailey Industries had shares outstanding as follows.

6% cumulative preference shares, €100 par value, issued and outstanding 10,000 shares	€1,000,000
Ordinary shares €10 par value, issued and outstanding 200,000 shares	2,000,000

To acquire the net assets of three smaller companies, Bailey authorized the issuance of an additional 170,000 ordinary shares. The acquisitions took place as shown below.

Date of Acquisition	Shares Issued
Company A: April 1, 2015	60,000
Company B: July 1, 2015	80,000
Company C: October 1, 2015	30,000

On May 14, 2015, Bailey realized a €90,000 (before taxes) gain from discontinued operations. On December 31, 2015, Bailey recorded net income of €300,000 before tax and exclusive of the gain.

Instructions
Assuming a 40% tax rate, compute the earnings per share data that should appear on the financial statements of Bailey Industries as of December 31, 2015.

6 **E16-22 (EPS: Simple Capital Structure)** At January 1, 2015, Cameron Company's outstanding shares included the following.

280,000 shares of R$50 par value, 7% cumulative preference shares
800,000 shares of R$1 par value ordinary shares

Net income for 2015 was R$2,830,000. No cash dividends were declared or paid during 2015. On February 15, 2016, however, all preference dividends in arrears were paid, together with a 5% share dividend on ordinary shares. There were no dividends in arrears prior to 2015.

On April 1, 2015, 450,000 ordinary shares were sold for R$10 per share. On October 1, 2015, 110,000 ordinary shares were purchased for R$20 per share and held as treasury shares.

Instructions
Compute earnings per share for 2015. Assume that financial statements for 2015 were issued in March 2016.

7 **E16-23 (EPS with Convertible Bonds, Various Situations)** In 2015, Buraka Enterprises issued, at par, 75 ₺1,000, 8% bonds, each convertible into 100 ordinary shares. The liability component of convertible bonds was ₺950 per bond, based on a market rate of interest of 10%. Buraka had revenues of ₺17,500 and expenses other than interest and taxes of ₺8,400 for 2016. (Assume that the tax rate is 40%.) Throughout 2016, 2,000 ordinary shares were outstanding; none of the bonds was converted or redeemed.

Instructions
(a) Compute diluted earnings per share for 2016.
(b) Assume the same facts as those assumed for part (a), except that the 75 bonds were issued on September 1, 2016 (rather than in 2015), and none have been converted or redeemed.
(c) Assume the same facts as assumed for part (a), except that 25 of the 75 bonds were actually converted on July 1, 2016.

7 **E16-24 (EPS with Convertible Bonds)** On June 1, 2014, Bluhm Company and Amanar Company merged to form Davenport Inc. A total of 800,000 shares were issued to complete the merger. The new corporation reports on a calendar-year basis.

On April 1, 2016, the company issued an additional 600,000 shares for cash. All 1,400,000 shares were outstanding on December 31, 2016.

Davenport Inc. also issued €600,000 of 20-year, 8% convertible bonds at par on July 1, 2016. Each €1,000 bond converts to 40 ordinary shares at any interest date. None of the bonds have been converted to date. The interest expense on the liability component of convertible bonds for 2016 was €30,000.

Davenport Inc. is preparing its annual report for the fiscal year ending December 31, 2016. The annual report will show earnings per share figures based upon a reported after-tax net income of €1,540,000. (The tax rate is 40%.)

Instructions

Determine the following for 2016.

(a) The number of shares to be used for calculating:

(1) Basic earnings per share.

(2) Diluted earnings per share.

(b) The earnings figures to be used for calculating:

(1) Basic earnings per share.

(2) Diluted earnings per share.

2 7 E16-25 (EPS with Convertible Bonds and Preference Shares) The Ottey Corporation issued 10-year, $4,000,000 par, 7% callable convertible subordinated debentures on January 2, 2015. The bonds have a par value of $1,000, with interest payable annually. The interest expense recorded on the liability component of the convertible bond for 2015 was $320,000. The current conversion ratio is 14:1, and in 2 years it will increase to 18:1. At the date of issue, the bonds were sold at 98. Ottey's effective tax was 35%. Net income in 2015 was $7,500,000, and the company had 2,000,000 shares outstanding during the entire year.

Instructions

(a) Prepare a schedule to compute both basic and diluted earnings per share.

(b) Discuss how the schedule would differ if the security was convertible preference shares.

2 7 E16-26 (EPS with Convertible Bonds and Preference Shares) On January 1, 2015, Lund Company issued 10-year, €3,000,000 face value, 6% bonds, at par. Each €1,000 bond is convertible into 15 ordinary shares of Lund. Lund's net income in 2016 was €240,000, and its tax rate was 40%. Interest expense on the liability component in 2016 was €210,000. The company had 100,000 ordinary shares outstanding throughout 2015. None of the bonds were converted in 2015.

Instructions

(a) Compute diluted earnings per share for 2015.

(b) Compute diluted earnings per share for 2015, assuming the same facts as above, except that €1,000,000 of 6% convertible preference shares were issued instead of the bonds. Each €100 preference share is convertible into 5 ordinary shares of Lund.

7 E16-27 (EPS with Options, Various Situations) Zambrano Company's net income for 2015 is £40,000. The only potentially dilutive securities outstanding were 1,000 options issued during 2014, each exercisable for one share at £8. None has been exercised, and 10,000 ordinary shares were outstanding during 2015. The average market price of Zambrano's shares during 2015 was £20.

Instructions

(a) Compute diluted earnings per share. (Round to two decimal places.)

(b) Assume the same facts as those assumed for part (a), except that the 1,000 options were issued on October 1, 2015 (rather than in 2014). The average market price during the last 3 months of 2015 was £20.

7 E16-28 (EPS with Contingent Issuance Agreement) Brooks Inc. recently purchased Donovan Corp., a large midwestern home painting corporation. One of the terms of the merger was that if Donovan's income for 2016 was $110,000 or more, 10,000 additional shares would be issued to Donovan's shareholders in 2017. Donovan's income for 2015 was $125,000.

Instructions

(a) Would the contingent shares have to be considered in Brooks' 2015 earnings per share computations?

(b) Assume the same facts, except that the 10,000 shares are contingent on Donovan's achieving a net income of $130,000 in 2016. Would the contingent shares have to be considered in Brooks' earnings per share computations for 2015?

7 E16-29 (EPS with Warrants) Werth Corporation earned €260,000 during a period when it had an average of 100,000 ordinary shares outstanding. The ordinary shares sold at an average market price of €15 per share during the period. Also outstanding were 30,000 warrants that could be exercised to purchase one ordinary share for €10 for each warrant exercised.

Instructions

(a) Are the warrants dilutive?

(b) Compute basic earnings per share.

(c) Compute diluted earnings per share.

8 *E16-30 (Share-Appreciation Rights) On December 31, 2012, Flessel Company issues 120,000 share-appreciation rights to its officers entitling them to receive cash for the difference between the market price of its shares and a pre-established price of £10. The fair value of the SARs is estimated to be £4 per SAR on December 31, 2013; £1 on December 31, 2014; £11 on December 31, 2015; and £9 on December 31, 2016. The service period is 4 years, and the exercise period is 7 years.

Instructions

(a) Prepare a schedule that shows the amount of compensation expense allocable to each year affected by the share-appreciation rights plan.

(b) Prepare the entry at December 31, 2016, to record compensation expense, if any, in 2016.

(c) Prepare the entry on December 31, 2016, assuming that all 120,000 SARs are exercised.

8 *E16-31 (Share-Appreciation Rights) Dominquez Company establishes a share-appreciation rights program that entitles its new president Dan Scott to receive cash for the difference between the market price of the shares and a pre-established price of R$30 (also market price) on December 31, 2013, on 40,000 SARs. The date of grant is December 31, 2013, and the required employment (service) period is 4 years. Scott exercises all of the SARs in 2019. The fair value of the SARs is estimated to be R$6 per SAR on December 31, 2014; R$9 on December 31, 2015; R$15 on December 31, 2016; R$8 on December 31, 2017; and R$18 on December 31, 2018.

Instructions

(a) Prepare a 5-year (2014–2018) schedule of compensation expense pertaining to the 40,000 SARs granted to Scott.

(b) Prepare the journal entry for compensation expense in 2014, 2017, and 2018 relative to the 40,000 SARs.

PROBLEMS

1 3 4 P16-1 (Entries for Various Dilutive Securities) The equity section of Martino Inc. at the beginning of the current year appears below.

Share capital—ordinary, €10 par value, authorized 1,000,000 shares, 300,000 shares issued and outstanding	€3,000,000
Share premium—ordinary	600,000
Retained earnings	570,000

During the current year, the following transactions occurred.

1. The company issued to the shareholders 100,000 rights. Ten rights are needed to buy one share at €32. The rights were void after 30 days. The market price of the shares at this time was €34 per share.

2. The company sold to the public a €200,000, 10% bond issue at 104. The company also issued with each €100 bond one detachable share-purchase warrant, which provided for the purchase of ordinary shares at €30 per share. The net present value of the bonds without the warrants was €192,000.

3. All but 5,000 of the rights issued in (1) were exercised in 30 days.

4. At the end of the year, 80% of the warrants in (2) had been exercised, and the remaining were outstanding and in good standing.

5. During the current year, the company granted share options for 10,000 ordinary shares to company executives. The company using a fair value option-pricing model determines that each option is worth €10. The option price is €30. The options were to expire at year-end and were considered compensation for the current year.

6. All but 1,000 shares related to the share-option plan were exercised by year-end. The expiration resulted because one of the executives failed to fulfill an obligation related to the employment contract.

Instructions

(a) Prepare general journal entries for the current year to record the transactions listed above.

(b) Prepare the equity section of the statement of financial position at the end of the current year. Assume that retained earnings at the end of the current year is €750,000.

4 P16-2 (Share-Option Plan) Berg Company adopted a share-option plan on November 30, 2014, that provided that 70,000 shares of $5 par value ordinary shares be designated as available for the granting of options to officers of the corporation at a price of $9 a share. The market price was $12 a share on November 30, 2014.

On January 2, 2015, options to purchase 28,000 shares were granted to president Tom Winter—15,000 for services to be rendered in 2015 and 13,000 for services to be rendered in 2016. Also on that date, options to purchase 14,000 shares were granted to vice president Michelle Bennett—7,000 for services to be rendered in 2015 and 7,000 for services to be rendered in 2016. The market price of the shares was $14 a share on January 2, 2015. The options were exercisable for a period of one year following the year in which the services were rendered. The fair value of the options on the grant date was $4 per option.

In 2016, neither the president nor the vice president exercised their options because the market price of the shares was below the exercise price. The market price was $8 a share on December 31, 2016, when the options for 2015 services lapsed.

On December 31, 2017, both Winter and Bennett exercised their options for 13,000 and 7,000 shares, respectively, when the market price was $16 a share.

Instructions

Prepare the necessary journal entries in 2014 when the share-option plan was adopted, in 2015 when options were granted, in 2016 when options lapsed, and in 2017 when options were exercised.

4 P16-3 (Share-Based Compensation) Assume that Sarazan Company has a share-option plan for top management. Each share option represents the right to purchase a R$1 par value ordinary share in the future at a price equal to the fair value of the shares at the date of the grant. Sarazan has 5,000 share options outstanding, which were granted at the beginning of 2015. The following data relate to the option grant.

Exercise price for options	R$40
Market price at grant date (January 1, 2015)	R$40
Fair value of options at grant date (January 1, 2015)	R$6
Service period	5 years

Instructions

(a) Prepare the journal entry(ies) for the first year of the share-option plan.

(b) Prepare the journal entry(ies) for the first year of the plan assuming that, rather than options, 700 shares of restricted shares were granted at the beginning of 2015.

(c) Now assume that the market price of Sarazan shares on the grant date was R$45 per share. Repeat the requirements for (a) and (b).

(d) Sarazan would like to implement an employee share-purchase plan for rank-and-file employees, but it would like to avoid recording expense related to this plan. Explain how employee share-purchase plans are recorded.

 7 P16-4 (EPS with Complex Capital Structure) Amy Dyken, controller at Fitzgerald Pharmaceutical Industries, a public company, is currently preparing the calculation for basic and diluted earnings per share and the related disclosure for Fitzgerald's financial statements. Selected financial information for the fiscal year ended June 30, 2015, is shown below.

FITZGERALD PHARMACEUTICAL INDUSTRIES
SELECTED STATEMENT OF FINANCIAL POSITION INFORMATION
JUNE 30, 2015

Equity	
Share capital—preference, 6% cumulative, €50 par value,	
100,000 shares authorized, 25,000 shares issued	
and outstanding	€ 1,250,000
Share capital—ordinary, €1 par, 10,000,000 shares authorized,	
1,000,000 shares issued and outstanding	1,000,000
Share premium—ordinary (includes any amounts for options	
and conversions)	4,000,000
Retained earnings	6,000,000
Total equity	€12,250,000
Long-term debt	
Notes payable, 10%	€ 1,000,000
Convertible bonds payable	5,000,000
10% bonds payable	6,000,000
Total long-term debt	€12,000,000

The following transactions have also occurred at Fitzgerald.

1. Options were granted on July 1, 2014, to purchase 200,000 shares at €15 per share. Although no options were exercised during fiscal year 2015, the average price per ordinary share during fiscal year 2015 was €20 per share.

2. Each bond was issued at face value. The convertible bonds will convert into ordinary shares at 50 shares per €1,000 bond. It is exercisable after 5 years and was issued in 2013. The interest on the liability component of the convertible bonds payable for the fiscal year ending June 30, 2015, was €450,000.

3. The preference shares were issued in 2013.

4. There are no preference dividends in arrears; however, preference dividends were not declared in fiscal year 2015.

5. The 1,000,000 ordinary shares were outstanding for the entire 2015 fiscal year.

6. Net income for fiscal year 2015 was €1,500,000, and the average income tax rate is 40%.

Instructions

For the fiscal year ended June 30, 2015, calculate the following for Fitzgerald Pharmaceutical Industries.

  (a) Basic earnings per share.
  (b) Diluted earnings per share.

6 **P16-5 (Basic EPS: Two-Year Presentation)** Meng Group is preparing the comparative financial statements for the annual report to its shareholders for fiscal years ended May 31, 2015, and May 31, 2016 (yen in thousands). The income from continuing operations for each year was ¥1,800,000 and ¥2,500,000, respectively. In both years, the company incurred a 10% interest expense on ¥2,400,000 of debt, an obligation that requires interest-only payments for 5 years. In 2016, the company experienced a loss from discontinued operations, net of tax, of ¥360,000. The company uses a 40% effective tax rate for income taxes.

The capital structure of Meng Group on June 1, 2014, consisted of 1 million ordinary shares outstanding and 20,000 shares of ¥50 par value, 6%, cumulative preference shares. There were no preference dividends in arrears, and the company had not issued any convertible securities, options, or warrants.

On October 1, 2014, Meng sold an additional 500,000 ordinary shares at ¥20 per share. Meng distributed a 20% share dividend on the ordinary shares outstanding on January 1, 2015. On December 1, 2015, Meng was able to sell an additional 800,000 ordinary shares at ¥22 per share. These were the only ordinary share transactions that occurred during the two fiscal years.

Instructions

  (a) Identify whether the capital structure at Meng Group is a simple or complex capital structure, and explain why.
  (b) Determine the weighted-average number of shares that Meng Group would use in calculating earnings per share for the fiscal year ended:

  (1) May 31, 2015.

  (2) May 31, 2016.

  (c) Prepare, in good form, a comparative income statement, beginning with income from operations, for Meng Group for the fiscal years ended May 31, 2015, and May 31, 2016. This statement will be included in Meng's annual report and should display the appropriate earnings per share presentations.

 7 **P16-6 (Computation of Basic and Diluted EPS)** Charles Austin of the controller's office of Thompson Corporation was given the assignment of determining the basic and diluted earnings per share values for the year ending December 31, 2016. Austin has compiled the information listed below.

1. The company is authorized to issue 8,000,000 $10 par value ordinary shares. As of December 31, 2015, 2,000,000 shares had been issued and were outstanding.

2. The per share market prices of the ordinary shares on selected dates were as follows.

	Price per Share
July 1, 2015	$20.00
January 1, 2016	21.00
April 1, 2016	25.00
July 1, 2016	11.00
August 1, 2016	10.50
November 1, 2016	9.00
December 31, 2016	10.00

3. A total of 700,000 shares of an authorized 1,200,000 shares of convertible preference shares have been issued on July 1, 2015. Each share had a par value of $25 and a cumulative dividend of $3 per share. The shares are convertible into ordinary shares at the rate of one convertible preference share for one ordinary share. The rate of conversion is to be automatically adjusted for share splits and share dividends. Dividends are paid quarterly on September 30, December 31, March 31, and June 30.

4. Thompson Corporation is subject to a 40% income tax rate.

5. The after-tax net income for the year ended December 31, 2016, was $11,550,000.

The following specific activities took place during 2016.

1. January 1—A 5% ordinary share dividend was issued. The dividend had been declared on December 1, 2015, to all shareholders of record on December 29, 2015.

2. April 1—A total of 400,000 shares of the $3 convertible preference shares were converted into ordinary shares. The company issued new ordinary shares and retired the preference shares. This was the only conversion of the preference shares during 2016.

3. July 1—A 2-for-1 split of the ordinary shares became effective on this date. The board of directors had authorized the split on June 1.

4. August 1—A total of 300,000 ordinary shares were issued to acquire a factory building.

5. November 1—A total of 24,000 ordinary shares were purchased on the open market at $9 per share. These shares were to be held as treasury shares and were still in the treasury as of December 31, 2016.

6. Ordinary share cash dividends—Cash dividends to ordinary shareholders were declared and paid as follows.
   April 15—$0.30 per share.
   October 15—$0.20 per share.

7. Preference share cash dividends—Cash dividends to preference shareholders were declared and paid as scheduled.

Instructions

(a) Determine the number of shares used to compute basic earnings per share for the year ended December 31, 2016.

(b) Determine the number of shares used to compute diluted earnings per share for the year ended December 31, 2016.

(c) Compute the adjusted net income to be used as the numerator in the basic earnings per share calculation for the year ended December 31, 2016.

7 **P16-7 (Computation of Basic and Diluted EPS)** The information below pertains to Barkley Company for 2015.

Net income for the year	£1,200,000
8% convertible bonds issued at par (£1,000 per bond); each bond is convertible into 30 shares of ordinary shares; the liability component of the bonds is £1,800,000 based on a market rate of 9%	2,000,000
6% convertible, cumulative preference shares, £100 par value; each share is convertible into 3 shares of ordinary shares	4,000,000
Ordinary shares, £10 par value	6,000,000
Tax rate for 2015	40%
Average market price of ordinary shares	£25 per share

There were no changes during 2015 in the number of ordinary shares, preference shares, or convertible bonds outstanding. There are no treasury shares. The company also has ordinary share options (granted in a prior year) to purchase 75,000 ordinary shares at £20 per share.

Instructions

(a) Compute basic earnings per share for 2015.

(b) Compute diluted earnings per share for 2015.

6 **P16-8 (EPS with Share Dividend and Discontinued Operations)** Agassi Corporation is preparing the comparative financial statements to be included in the annual report to shareholders. Agassi employs a fiscal year ending May 31.

Income before income tax for Agassi was €1,400,000 and €660,000, respectively, for fiscal years ended May 31, 2016 and 2015. Agassi experienced a loss from discontinued operations of €400,000 in March 2016. A 40% combined income tax rate pertains to any and all of Agassi Corporation's profits, gains, and losses.

Agassi's capital structure consists of preference shares and ordinary shares. The company has not issued any convertible securities or warrants, and there are no outstanding share options.

Agassi issued 40,000 shares of €100 par value, 6% cumulative preference shares in 2012. All of these shares are outstanding, and no preference dividends are in arrears.

There were 1,000,000 shares of €1 par ordinary shares outstanding on June 1, 2014. On September 1, 2014, Agassi sold an additional 400,000 ordinary shares at €17 per share. Agassi distributed a 20% share dividend on the ordinary shares outstanding on December 1, 2015. These were the only ordinary share transactions during the past 2 fiscal years.

Instructions

(a) Determine the weighted-average number of ordinary shares that would be used in computing earnings per share on the current comparative income statement for:

(1) The year ended May 31, 2015.

(2) The year ended May 31, 2016.

(b) Starting with income before income tax, prepare a comparative income statement for the years ended May 31, 2016 and 2015. The statement will be part of Agassi Corporation's annual report to shareholders and should include appropriate earnings per share presentation.

(c) The capital structure of a corporation is the result of its past financing decisions. Furthermore, the earnings per share data presented on a corporation's financial statements is dependent upon the capital structure.

(1) Explain why Agassi Corporation is considered to have a simple capital structure.

(2) Describe how earnings per share data would be presented for a corporation that has a complex capital structure.

CONCEPTS FOR ANALYSIS

CA16-1 (Dilutive Securities, EPS) Two students are discussing the current chapter on dilutive securities and earnings per share. Here are some of the points raised in their discussion.

1. Is there a difference between issuing convertible debt versus issuing debt with share warrants? Also does it make a difference whether the share warrants are detachable or non-detachable?

2. Why is it that companies are not permitted to adjust compensation expense for share options when the options become worthless because the share price does not increase in value?

3. What is the rationale for using the treasury-share method in earnings per share computations?

4. Why do companies have to report compensation expense for employee share-purchase plans? After the employee receives the shares, the price can go up or down, so what is the benefit that the employee is receiving?

Instructions

Prepare a response to each of the questions asked by the students.

CA16-2 (Ethical Issues—Compensation Plan) The executive officers of Rouse Corporation have a performance-based compensation plan. The performance criteria of this plan is linked to growth in earnings per share. When annual EPS growth is 12%, the Rouse executives earn 100% of the shares; if growth is 16%, they earn 125%. If EPS growth is lower than 8%, the executives receive no additional compensation.

In 2015, Gail Devers, the controller of Rouse, reviews year-end estimates of bad debt expense and warranty expense. She calculates the EPS growth at 15%. Kurt Adkins, a member of the executive group, remarks over lunch one day that the estimate of bad debt expense might be decreased, increasing EPS growth to 16.1%. Devers is not sure she should do this because she believes that the current estimate of bad debts is sound. On the other hand, she recognizes that a great deal of subjectivity is involved in the computation.

Instructions

Answer the following questions.

(a) What, if any, is the ethical dilemma for Devers?

(b) Should Devers' knowledge of the compensation plan be a factor that influences her estimate?

(c) How should Devers respond to Adkins' request?

CA16-3 (Share Warrants—Various Types) For various reasons a corporation may issue warrants to purchase its ordinary shares at specified prices that, depending on the circumstances, may be less than, equal to, or greater than the current market price. For example, warrants may be issued:

1. To existing shareholders on a pro rata basis.

2. To certain key employees under an incentive share-option plan.

3. To purchasers of the corporation's bonds.

Instructions

For each of the three examples of how share warrants are used:

(a) Explain why they are used.

(b) Discuss the significance of the price (or prices) at which the warrants are issued (or granted) in relation to (1) the current market price of the company's shares, and (2) the length of time over which they can be exercised.

(c) Describe the information that should be disclosed in financial statements, or notes thereto, that are prepared when share warrants are outstanding in the hands of the three groups listed above.

 CA16-4 (Share Compensation Plans) The following item appeared on the Internet concerning the requirement to expense share options.

"Here We Go Again!" by Jack Ciesielski (2/21/2005, *http://www.accountingobserver.com/blog/2005/02/here-we-go-again*) On February 17, Congressman David Dreier (R–CA), and Congresswoman Anna Eshoo (D–CA), officially entered Silicon Valley's bid to gum up the launch of honest reporting of share option compensation: They co-sponsored a bill to "preserve broad-based employee share option plans and give investors critical information they need to understand how employee share options impact the value of their shares." You know what "critical information" they mean: stuff like the share compensation for the top five officers in a company, with a rigged value set as close to zero as possible. Investors *crave* this kind of information. Other ways the good Congresspersons want to "help" investors: The bill "also requires the SEC to study the effectiveness of those disclosures over three years, during which time, no new accounting standard related to the treatment of share options could be recognized. Finally, the bill requires the Secretary of Commerce to conduct a study and report to Congress on the impact of broad-based employee share option plans on expanding employee corporate ownership, skilled worker recruitment and retention, research and innovation, economic growth, and international competitiveness."

It's the old "four corners" basketball strategy: stall, stall, stall. In the meantime, hope for regime change at your opponent, the FASB.

Instructions

(a) What are the accounting requirements related to share-based compensation?

(b) How do the provisions of IFRS in this area differ from the bill introduced by members of the U.S. Congress (Dreier and Eshoo), which would require expensing for options issued to only the top five officers in a company? Which approach do you think would result in more useful information? (Focus on comparability.)

(c) The bill in the U.S. Congress urges a standard that preserves "the ability of companies to use this innovative tool to attract talented employees." Write a response to these congresspeople explaining the importance of neutrality in financial accounting and reporting.

CA16-5 (EPS: Preference Dividends, Options, and Convertible Debt) Earnings per share (EPS) is the most featured, single financial statistic about modern corporations. Daily published quotations of share prices have recently been expanded to include for many securities a "times earnings" figure that is based on EPS. Securities analysts often focus their discussions on the EPS of the corporations they study.

Instructions

(a) Explain how dividends or dividend requirements on any class of preference shares that may be outstanding affect the computation of EPS.

(b) One of the technical procedures applicable in EPS computations is the treasury-share method. Briefly describe the circumstances under which it might be appropriate to apply the treasury-share method.

(c) Convertible debentures are considered potentially dilutive ordinary shares. Explain how convertible debentures are handled for purposes of EPS computations.

CA16-6 (EPS Concepts and Effect of Transactions on EPS) Chorkina Corporation, a new audit client of yours, has not reported earnings per share data in its annual reports to shareholders in the past. The treasurer, Beth Botsford, requested that you furnish information about the reporting of earnings per share data in the current year's annual report in accordance with IFRS.

Instructions

(a) Define the term "earnings per share" as it applies to a corporation with a capitalization structure composed of only one class of ordinary shares. Explain how earnings per share should be computed and how the information should be disclosed in the corporation's financial statements.

(b) Discuss the treatment, if any, that should be given to each of the following items in computing earnings per share of ordinary shares for financial statement reporting.

(1) Outstanding preference shares issued at a premium with a par value liquidation right.

(2) The exercise at a price below market price but above book value of an ordinary share option issued during the current fiscal year to officers of the corporation.

(3) The replacement of a machine immediately prior to the close of the current fiscal year at a cost 20% above the original cost of the replaced machine. The new machine will perform the same function as the old machine that was sold for its book value.

(4) The declaration of current dividends on cumulative preference shares.

(5) The acquisition of some of the corporation's outstanding ordinary shares during the current fiscal year. The shares were classified as treasury shares.

(6) A 2-for-1 share split of ordinary shares during the current fiscal year.

(7) A provision created out of retained earnings for a contingent liability from a possible lawsuit.

CA16-7 (EPS, Antidilution) Brad Dolan, a shareholder of Rhode Corporation, has asked you, the firm's accountant, to explain why his share warrants were not included in diluted EPS. In order to explain this situation, you must briefly explain what dilutive securities are, why they are included in the EPS calculation, and why some securities are antidilutive and thus not included in this calculation.

Instructions

Write Mr. Dolan a 1–1.5 page letter explaining why the warrants are not included in the calculation. Use the following data to help you explain this situation.

Rhode Corporation earned $228,000 during the period, when it had an average of 100,000 ordinary shares outstanding. The ordinary shares sold at an average market price of $25 per share during the period. Also outstanding were 30,000 warrants that could be exercised to purchase one ordinary share at $30 per warrant.

USING YOUR JUDGMENT

FINANCIAL REPORTING

Financial Reporting Problem

Marks and Spencer plc (M&S)

The financial statements of M&S (GBR) are presented in Appendix A. The company's complete annual report, including the notes to the financial statements, is available online.

Instructions

Refer to M&S's financial statements and the accompanying notes to answer the following questions.

(a) Under M&S's share-based compensation plan, share options are granted annually to key managers and directors.

(1) How many options were granted during 2013 under the plan?

(2) How many options were exercisable at year-end 2013?

(3) How many options were exercised in 2013, and what was the average price of those exercised?

(4) How many years from the grant date do the options expire?

(5) To what accounts are the proceeds from these option exercises credited?

(6) What was the number of outstanding options at year-end 2013, and at what average exercise price?

(b) What number of diluted weighted-average shares outstanding was used by M&S in computing earnings per share for 2013 and 2012? What was M&S's diluted earnings per share in 2013 and 2012?

(c) What other share-based compensation plans does M&S have?

Comparative Analysis Case

adidas and Puma

The financial statements of adidas (DEU) and Puma (DEU) are presented in Appendices B and C, respectively. The complete annual reports, including the notes to the financial statements, are available online.

Instructions

Use the companies' financial information to answer the following questions.

(a) What employee share-option compensation plans are offered by adidas and Puma?

(b) What are the weighted-average number of shares used by adidas and Puma in 2012 and 2011 to compute diluted EPS?

(c) What was the diluted net income per share for adidas and Puma for 2012 and 2011?

International Reporting Case

Sepracor, Inc., a U.S. drug company, reported the following information in a recent annual report (amounts in thousands). The company prepares its financial statements in accordance with U.S. GAAP.

Current liabilities	$ 554,114
Convertible subordinated debt	648,020
Total liabilities	1,228,313
Stockholders' equity	176,413
Net income	58,333

Analysts attempting to compare Sepracor to international drug companies may face a challenge due to differences in accounting for convertible debt under IFRS. Under *IAS 32*, "Financial Instruments," convertible bonds, at issuance, must be classified separately into their debt and equity components based on estimated fair value.

Instructions

(a) Compute the following ratios for Sepracor, Inc. (Assume that year-end balances approximate annual averages.)
   (1) Return on assets.
   (2) Return on shareholders' equity.
   (3) Debt to assets ratio.

(b) Briefly discuss the operating performance and financial position of Sepracor. Industry averages for these ratios were ROA 3.5%, return on equity 16%, and debt to assets 75%. Based on this analysis, would you make an investment in the company's 5% convertible bonds? Explain.

(c) Assume you want to compare Sepracor to a company like Bayer (DEU), which prepares its financial statements in accordance with IFRS. Assuming that the fair value of the liability component of Sepracor's convertible bonds is $398,020, how would you adjust the analysis above to make valid comparisons between Sepracor and Bayer?

Accounting, Analysis, and Principles

On January 1, 2015, Garner issued 10-year, €200,000 face value, 6% bonds at par. Each €1,000 bond is convertible into 30 shares of Garner €2, par value, ordinary shares. Interest on the bonds is paid annually on December 31. The market rate for Garner's non-convertible debt is 9%. The company has had 10,000 ordinary shares (and no preference shares) outstanding throughout its life. None of the bonds have been converted as of the end of 2016. (Ignore all tax effects.)

Accounting

(a) Prepare the journal entry Garner would have made on January 1, 2015, to record the issuance of the bonds and prepare an amortization table for the first three years of the bonds.

(b) Garner's net income in 2016 was €30,000 and was €27,000 in 2015. Compute basic and diluted earnings per share for Garner for 2016 and 2015.

(c) Assume that all of the holders of Garner's convertible bonds convert their bonds to shares on January 2, 2017, when Garner's shares are trading at €32 per share. Garner pays €50 per bond to induce bondholders to convert. Prepare the journal entry to record the conversion, using the book value method.

Analysis

Show how Garner Company will report income and EPS for 2016 and 2015. Briefly discuss the importance of IFRS for EPS to analysts evaluating companies based on price-earnings ratios. Consider comparisons for a company over time, as well as comparisons between companies at a point in time.

Principles

In order to converge U.S. GAAP and IFRS, U.S. standard-setters (the FASB) are considering whether the equity element of a convertible bond should be reported as equity. Describe how the journal entry you made in part (a) above would differ under U.S. GAAP. In terms of the accounting principles discussed in Chapter 2, what does IFRS for convertible debt accomplish that U.S. GAAP potentially sacrifices? What does U.S. GAAP for convertible debt accomplish that IFRS potentially sacrifices?

IFRS BRIDGE TO THE PROFESSION

Professional Research

Richardson Company is contemplating the establishment of a share-based compensation plan to provide long-run incentives for its top management. However, members of the compensation committee of the board of directors have voiced some concerns about adopting these plans, based on news accounts related to a recent accounting standard in this area. They would like you to conduct some research on this recent standard so they can be better informed about the accounting for these plans.

Instructions

Access the IFRS authoritative literature at the IASB website (*http://eifrs.iasb.org/*) (you may register for free eIFRS access at this site). When you have accessed the documents, you can use the search tool in your Internet browser to respond to the following questions. (Provide paragraph citations.)

(a) Identify the authoritative literature that addresses the accounting for share-based payment compensation plans.

(b) Briefly discuss the objectives for the accounting for share-based compensation. What is the role of fair value measurement?

(c) The Richardson Company board is also considering an employee share-purchase plan, but the Board does not want to record expense related to the plan. What are the IFRS requirements for the accounting for an employee share-purchase plan?

Professional Simulation

In this simulation, you are asked to address questions related to the accounting for share options and earnings per share computations. Prepare responses to all parts.

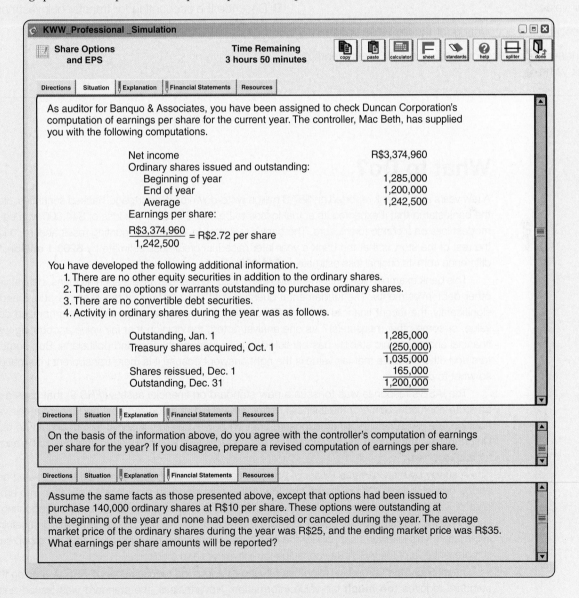

KWW_Professional_Simulation

Share Options and EPS

Time Remaining 3 hours 50 minutes

copy | paste | calculator | sheet | standards | help | splitter | done

Directions | Situation | Explanation | Financial Statements | Resources

As auditor for Banquo & Associates, you have been assigned to check Duncan Corporation's computation of earnings per share for the current year. The controller, Mac Beth, has supplied you with the following computations.

Net income	R$3,374,960
Ordinary shares issued and outstanding:	
Beginning of year	1,285,000
End of year	1,200,000
Average	1,242,500
Earnings per share:	

$$\frac{R\$3,374,960}{1,242,500} = R\$2.72 \text{ per share}$$

You have developed the following additional information.
1. There are no other equity securities in addition to the ordinary shares.
2. There are no options or warrants outstanding to purchase ordinary shares.
3. There are no convertible debt securities.
4. Activity in ordinary shares during the year was as follows.

Outstanding, Jan. 1	1,285,000
Treasury shares acquired, Oct. 1	(250,000)
	1,035,000
Shares reissued, Dec. 1	165,000
Outstanding, Dec. 31	1,200,000

Directions | Situation | Explanation | Financial Statements | Resources

On the basis of the information above, do you agree with the controller's computation of earnings per share for the year? If you disagree, prepare a revised computation of earnings per share.

Directions | Situation | Explanation | Financial Statements | Resources

Assume the same facts as those presented above, except that options had been issued to purchase 140,000 ordinary shares at R$10 per share. These options were outstanding at the beginning of the year and none had been exercised or canceled during the year. The average market price of the ordinary shares during the year was R$25, and the ending market price was R$35. What earnings per share amounts will be reported?

Remember to check the book's companion website, at www.wiley.com/college/kieso, to find additional resources for this chapter.

17 Investments

After studying this chapter, you should be able to:

1 Describe the accounting framework for financial assets.

2 Understand the accounting for debt investments at amortized cost.

3 Understand the accounting for debt investments at fair value.

4 Describe the accounting for the fair value option.

5 Understand the accounting for equity investments at fair value.

6 Explain the equity method of accounting and compare it to the fair value method for equity investments.

7 Discuss the accounting for impairments of debt investments.

8 Describe the accounting for transfer of investments between categories.

What to Do?

A few years ago, a bank reported an $87.3 million write-down on its mortgage-backed securities. However, the bank stated that it expected its actual losses to be only $44,000. The loss of $44,000 was equal to a modest loss on a condo foreclosure. The bank's regulator found "the accounting result absurd." However, the rest of the story is that the bank a year later raised its credit-loss estimate by **$263.1 million**, quite a difference from its original loss estimate of **$44,000**.

This bank example highlights the challenge of valuing financial assets such as loans, derivatives, and other debt investments. The fundamental question that emerged out of the example above and, more significantly, the recent financial crisis is: Should financial instruments be valued at amortized cost, fair value, or some other measure(s)? As one analyst noted, the opinion that fair value accounting weakens financial and economic stability has persisted among many regulators and politicians. But, some investors and others believe that fair value is the right answer because it is more transparent information. OK, so what to do?

The IASB's response was to issue a new standard on financial assets (*IFRS 9*) that uses a mixed-attribute approach. Some of the financial assets are valued at amortized cost and others at fair value. In addition, the FASB has issued an exposure draft on how it believes financial assets should be reported. Unfortunately, at this point the two bodies do not agree as to how these instruments should be accounted for and reported.

A survey by the Chartered Financial Analysts association on *IFRS 9* contained the following question on the new standard: "Do you agree that the IASB's new standard requiring classification into amortized cost or fair value will improve the decision-usefulness of overall financial instrument accounting?" The survey results indicate that 47 percent believe the IASB's approach improves the decision-usefulness of information. This lukewarm support for the new rules is somewhat troubling given that the group surveyed is representative of the IASB's key constituency—investors and creditors.

Interestingly, the European Union has refused to adopt the requirements of *IFRS 9*, arguing that this standard requires **too much** fair value information. Nevertheless, the standard was issued and other

countries that follow IFRS will soon be implementing the new standard. Thus, the early reaction to *IFRS 9* indicates that, unfortunately, once again politics is raising its ugly head on an accounting issue. Some European regulators have suggested that the IASB's future funding may even depend on the Board putting more regulators on it. Such an intrusion could lead to the end of the convergence efforts between the IASB and the FASB.

Sources: Adapted from Jonathan Weil, "Suing Wall Street Banks Never Looked So Shady," *http://www.bloomberg.com/apps/news?pid= 20601039&sid=7ZeWzn42KX4* (February 28, 2010); Rachel Sanderson and Jennifer Hughes, "Carried Forward," *Financial Times Online* (April 20, 2010); and CFA Institute, *Survey on Proposed Financial Instrument Accounting Changes and International Convergence* (November 2009).

CONCEPTUAL FOCUS

> See the **Underlying Concepts** on page 831.
> Read the **Evolving Issue** on page 834 for a discussion of the fair value controversy.

INTERNATIONAL FOCUS

> Read the **Global Accounting Insights** on pages 836–837 for a discussion of non-IFRS financial reporting for investments.

PREVIEW OF CHAPTER 17

As indicated in the opening story, the accounting for financial assets is highly controversial. How to measure, recognize, and disclose this information is now being debated and discussed extensively. In this chapter, we address the accounting for debt and equity investments. Appendices to this chapter discuss the accounting for derivative instruments and fair value disclosures. The content and organization of the chapter are as follows.

Investments			
Accounting for Financial Assets	**Debt Investments**	**Equity Investments**	**Other Reporting Issues**
• Measurement basis	• Amortized cost • Fair value • Fair value option • Summary of debt investment accounting	• Holdings of less than 20% • Holdings between 20% and 50% • Holdings of more than 50%	• Impairment of value • Transfers between categories • Summary

ACCOUNTING FOR FINANCIAL ASSETS

LEARNING OBJECTIVE ❶
Describe the accounting framework
for financial assets.

**I
F
R
S**

See the Authoritative
Literature section
(page 861).

A **financial asset** is cash, an equity investment of another company (e.g., ordinary or preference shares), or a contractual right to receive cash from another party (e.g., loans, receivables, and bonds). **[1]** The accounting for cash is relatively straightforward and is discussed in Chapter 7. The accounting and reporting for equity and debt investments, as discussed in the opening story, is extremely contentious, particularly in light of the credit crisis in the latter part of 2008.

Some users of financial statements support a single measurement—fair value—for all financial assets. They view fair value as more relevant than other measurements in helping investors assess the effect of current economic events on the future cash flows of a financial asset. In addition, they believe that the use of a single method promotes consistency in valuation and reporting on the asset, thereby improving the usefulness of the financial statements. Others disagree. These financial statement users note that many investments are not held for sale but rather for the income they will generate over the life of the investment. They believe cost-based information (referred to as amortized cost) provides the most relevant information for predicting future cash flows in these cases. Finally, some express concern that using fair value information to measure financial assets is unreliable when markets for the investments are not functioning in an ordinary fashion.

After much discussion, the IASB decided that reporting all financial assets at fair value is not the most appropriate approach for providing relevant information to financial statement users. **The IASB noted that both fair value and a cost-based approach can provide useful information to financial statement readers for particular types of financial assets in certain circumstances.** As a result, the IASB requires that companies classify financial assets into two measurement categories—**amortized cost and fair value**—depending on the circumstances.

Measurement Basis—A Closer Look

In general, IFRS requires that companies determine how to measure their financial assets based on two criteria:

- The company's business model for managing its financial assets; and
- The contractual cash flow characteristics of the financial asset.

If a company has (1) a business model whose objective is to hold assets in order to collect contractual cash flows and (2) the contractual terms of the financial asset provides specified dates to cash flows that are solely payments of principal and interest on the principal amount outstanding, then the company should use amortized cost. **[2]**[1]

For example, assume that Mitsubishi (JPN) purchases a bond investment that it intends to hold to maturity. Its business model for this type of investment is to collect interest and then principal at maturity. The payment dates for the interest rate and principal are stated on the bond. In this case, Mitsubishi accounts for the investment at amortized cost. If, on the other hand, Mitsubishi purchased the bonds as part of a trading strategy to speculate on interest rate changes (a trading investment), then the debt investment is reported at fair value. As a result, only debt investments such as receivables, loans, and bond investments that meet the two criteria above are recorded at amortized cost. All other debt investments are recorded and reported at fair value.

[1]The IASB indicates that the business model should be considered first. And, that the contractual cash flow characteristics should be considered only for financial assets (e.g., debt investments) that are eligible to be measured at amortized cost. It states that both classification conditions are essential to ensure that amortized cost provides useful information about debt investments. **[3]**

Equity investments are generally recorded and reported at fair value. Equity investments do not have a fixed interest or principal payment schedule and therefore cannot be accounted for at amortized cost. In summary, companies account for investments based on the type of security, as indicated in Illustration 17-1.

Type of Investment	Assessment of Accounting Criteria	Valuation Approach
Debt	Meets business model (held-for-collection) and contractual cash flow tests.	Amortized cost
	Does not meet the business model test (not held-for-collection).	Fair value
Equity	Does not meet contractual cash flow test.	Fair value*

*For some equity investments for which the investor exercises some control over the investee, use the equity method.

ILLUSTRATION 17-1
Summary of Investment Accounting Approaches

We organize our study of investments by type of investment security. Within each section, we explain how the accounting for investments in debt and equity securities varies according to how the investment is managed and the contractual cash flow characteristics of the investment.

DEBT INVESTMENTS

Debt investments are characterized by contractual payments on specified dates of principal and interest on the principal amount outstanding. Companies measure debt investments at amortized cost if the objective of the company's business model is to hold the financial asset to collect the contractual cash flows (**held-for-collection**). **Amortized cost** is the initial recognition amount of the investment minus repayments, plus or minus cumulative amortization and net of any reduction for uncollectibility. If the criteria for measurement at amortized cost are not met, then the debt investment is valued and accounted for at fair value. **Fair value** is the amount for which an asset could be exchanged between knowledgeable willing parties in an arm's length transaction. **[4]**

2 LEARNING OBJECTIVE
Understand the accounting for debt investments at amortized cost.

Debt Investments—Amortized Cost

Only debt investments can be measured at amortized cost. If a company like **Carrefour** (FRA) makes an investment in the bonds of **Nokia** (FIN), it will receive contractual cash flows of interest over the life of the bonds and repayment of the principal at maturity. If it is Carrefour's strategy to hold this investment in order to receive these cash flows over the life of the bond, it has a held-for-collection strategy and it will measure the investment at amortized cost.[2]

Example: Debt Investment at Amortized Cost

To illustrate the accounting for a debt investment at amortized cost, assume that Robinson Company purchased €100,000 of 8 percent bonds of Evermaster Corporation

[2]Classification as held-for-collection does not mean the security must be held to maturity. For example, a company may sell an investment before maturity if (1) the security does not meet the company's investment strategy (e.g., the company has a policy to invest in only AAA-rated bonds but the bond investment has a decline in its credit rating), (2) a company changes its strategy to invest only in securities within a certain maturity range, or (3) the company needs to sell a security to fund certain capital expenditures. However, if a company begins trading held-for-collection investments on a regular basis, it should assess whether such trading is consistent with the held-for-collection classification. **[5]**

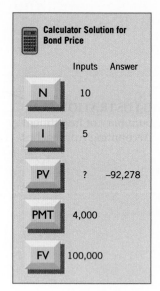

Calculator Solution for Bond Price

	Inputs	Answer
N	10	
I	5	
PV	?	−92,278
PMT	4,000	
FV	100,000	

on January 1, 2015, at a discount, paying €92,278. The bonds mature January 1, 2020, and yield 10 percent; interest is payable each July 1 and January 1. Robinson records the investment as follows.

January 1, 2015

Debt Investments	92,278	
Cash		92,278

As indicated in Chapter 14, companies must amortize premiums or discounts using the **effective-interest method**. They apply the effective-interest method to bond investments in a way similar to that for bonds payable. To compute interest revenue, companies compute the effective-interest rate or yield at the time of investment and apply that rate to the beginning carrying amount (book value) for each interest period. The investment carrying amount is increased by the amortized discount or decreased by the amortized premium in each period.

Illustration 17-2 shows the effect of the discount amortization on the interest revenue that Robinson records each period for its investment in Evermaster bonds.

ILLUSTRATION 17-2
Schedule of Interest Revenue and Bond Discount Amortization—Effective-Interest Method

		8% BONDS PURCHASED TO YIELD 10%		
Date	Cash Received	Interest Revenue	Bond Discount Amortization	Carrying Amount of Bonds
1/1/15				€ 92,278
7/1/15	€ 4,000ᵃ	€ 4,614ᵇ	€ 614ᶜ	92,892ᵈ
1/1/16	4,000	4,645	645	93,537
7/1/16	4,000	4,677	677	94,214
1/1/17	4,000	4,711	711	94,925
7/1/17	4,000	4,746	746	95,671
1/1/18	4,000	4,783	783	96,454
7/1/18	4,000	4,823	823	97,277
1/1/19	4,000	4,864	864	98,141
7/1/19	4,000	4,907	907	99,048
1/1/20	4,000	4,952	952	100,000
	€40,000	€47,722	€7,722	

ᵃ€4,000 = €100,000 × .08 × ⁶/₁₂   ᶜ€614 = €4,614 − €4,000
ᵇ€4,614 = €92,278 × .10 × ⁶/₁₂   ᵈ€92,892 = €92,278 + €614

Robinson records the receipt of the first semiannual interest payment on July 1, 2015 (using the data in Illustration 17-2), as follows.

July 1, 2015

Cash	4,000	
Debt Investments	614	
Interest Revenue		4,614

Because Robinson is on a calendar-year basis, it accrues interest and amortizes the discount at December 31, 2015, as follows.

December 31, 2015

Interest Receivable	4,000	
Debt Investments	645	
Interest Revenue		4,645

Again, Illustration 17-2 shows the interest and amortization amounts.

Robinson reports its investment in Evermaster bonds in its December 31, 2015, financial statements, as follows.[3]

ILLUSTRATION 17-3
Reporting of Bond
Investments at
Amortized Cost

Statement of Financial Position	
Long-term investments	
Debt investments	€93,537
Current assets	
Interest receivable	€ 4,000
Income Statement	
Other income and expense	
Interest revenue (€4,614 + €4,645)	€ 9,259

Sometimes, a company sells a bond investment before its maturity. For example, Robinson Company may sell securities as part of a change in its investment strategy to move away from five-year debt investments, like the Evermaster bonds, to invest in shorter-term bonds. Such a strategy would allow the bonds to reprice more frequently in response to interest rate changes. Let's assume that Robinson Company sells its investment in Evermaster bonds on November 1, 2017, at 99¾ plus accrued interest. The discount amortization from July 1, 2017, to November 1, 2017, is €522 (⁴⁄₆ × €783). Robinson records this discount amortization as follows.

November 1, 2017

Debt Investments	522	
Interest Revenue		522

Illustration 17-4 shows the computation of the realized gain on the sale.

ILLUSTRATION 17-4
Computation of Gain on
Sale of Bonds

Selling price of bonds (exclusive of accrued interest)		€99,750
Less: Book value of bonds on November 1, 2017:		
Amortized cost, July 1, 2017	€95,671	
Add: Discount amortized for the period July 1, 2017, to November 1, 2017	522	96,193
Gain on sale of bonds		€ 3,557

Robinson records the sale of the bonds as:

November 1, 2017

Cash	102,417	
Interest Revenue (4/6 × €4,000)		2,667
Debt Investments		96,193
Gain on Sale of Investments		3,557

The credit to Interest Revenue represents accrued interest for four months, for which the purchaser pays cash. The debit to Cash represents the selling price of the bonds plus accrued interest (€99,750 + €2,667). The credit to Debt Investments represents the book value of the bonds on the date of sale. The credit to Gain on Sale of Investments represents the excess of the selling price over the book value of the bonds.

---

[3]Although the example here is based on a single investment, the IASB indicates that companies evaluate the investment strategy (or business model for managing the investments) at a higher level of aggregation than the individual security. As a result, a company may have more than one investment strategy. That is, a company may hold a portfolio of investments that is managed to collect contractual cash flows and another portfolio of investments that is managed to realize gains and losses on fair value changes. **[6]**

Debt Investments—Fair Value

LEARNING OBJECTIVE 3
Understand the accounting for debt investments at fair value.

In some cases, companies both manage and evaluate investment performance on a fair value basis. In these situations, these investments are managed and evaluated based on a documented risk-management or investment strategy based on fair value information. For example, some companies often hold debt investments with the intention of selling them in a short period of time. These debt investments are often referred to as **trading investments** because companies frequently buy and sell these investments to generate profits from short-term differences in price.

Companies that account for and report debt investments at fair value follow the same accounting entries as debt investments held-for-collection during the reporting period. That is, they are recorded at amortized cost. However, **at each reporting date, companies adjust the amortized cost to fair value, with any unrealized holding gain or loss reported as part of net income** (fair value method). An **unrealized holding gain or loss** is the net change in the fair value of a debt investment from one period to another.

Example: Debt Investment at Fair Value (Single Security)

To illustrate the accounting for debt investments using the fair value approach, assume the same information as in our previous example for Robinson Company. Recall that Robinson Company purchased €100,000 of 8 percent bonds of Evermaster Corporation on January 1, 2015, at a discount, paying €92,278.[4] The bonds mature January 1, 2020, and yield 10 percent; interest is payable each July 1 and January 1.

The journal entries in 2015 are exactly the same as those for amortized cost. These entries are as follows.

January 1, 2015

Debt Investments	92,278	
Cash		92,278

July 1, 2015

Cash	4,000	
Debt Investments	614	
Interest Revenue		4,614

December 31, 2015

Interest Receivable	4,000	
Debt Investments	645	
Interest Revenue		4,645

Again, Illustration 17-2 shows the interest and amortization amounts. If the debt investment is held-for-collection, no further entries are necessary. To apply the fair value approach, Robinson determines that, due to a decrease in interest rates, the fair value of the debt investment increased to €95,000 at December 31, 2015. Comparing the fair value with the carrying amount of these bonds at December 31, 2015, Robinson has an unrealized holding gain of €1,463, as shown in Illustration 17-5.

ILLUSTRATION 17-5
Computation of Unrealized Gain on Fair Value Debt Investment (2015)

Fair value at December 31, 2015	€95,000
Amortized cost at December 31, 2015 (per Illustration 17-2)	93,537
Unrealized holding gain or (loss)	€ 1,463

[4]Companies may incur brokerage and transaction costs in purchasing securities. For investments accounted for at fair value (both debt and equity), IFRS requires that these costs be recorded in net income as other income and expense and not as an adjustment to the carrying value of the investment. **[7]**

Robinson therefore makes the following entry to record the adjustment of the debt investment to fair value at December 31, 2015.

Fair Value Adjustment	1,463	
Unrealized Holding Gain or Loss—Income		1,463

Robinson uses a valuation account (**Fair Value Adjustment**) instead of debiting Debt Investments to record the investment at fair value. The use of the Fair Value Adjustment account enables Robinson to maintain a record at amortized cost in the accounts. Because the valuation account has a debit balance, in this case the fair value of Robinson's debt investment is higher than its amortized cost.

The Unrealized Holding Gain or Loss—Income account is reported in the "Other income and expense" section of the income statement as part of net income. This account is closed to net income each period. The Fair Value Adjustment account is not closed each period and is simply adjusted each period to its proper valuation. The Fair Value Adjustment balance is not shown on the statement of financial position but is simply used to restate the debt investment account to fair value.

Robinson reports its investment in Evermaster bonds in its December 31, 2015, financial statements as shown in Illustration 17-6.

<table>
<tr><td colspan="2" align="center">**Statement of Financial Position**</td></tr>
<tr><td>Investments</td><td></td></tr>
<tr><td>   Debt investments</td><td>€95,000</td></tr>
<tr><td>Current assets</td><td></td></tr>
<tr><td>   Interest receivable</td><td>€ 4,000</td></tr>
<tr><td colspan="2" align="center">**Income Statement**</td></tr>
<tr><td>Other income and expense</td><td></td></tr>
<tr><td>   Interest revenue (€4,614 + €4,645)</td><td>€ 9,259</td></tr>
<tr><td>   Unrealized holding gain or (loss)</td><td>1,463</td></tr>
</table>

ILLUSTRATION 17-6
Financial Statement Presentation of Debt Investments at Fair Value

Continuing with our example, at December 31, 2016, assume that the fair value of the Evermaster debt investment is €94,000. In this case, Robinson records an unrealized holding loss of €2,388, as shown in Illustration 17-7.

	DEBT INVESTMENTS **DECEMBER 31, 2016**		
Investment	Amortized Cost	Fair Value	Unrealized Gain (Loss)
Evermaster Corporation 10% bonds	€94,925	€94,000	€ (925)
Less: Previous fair value adjustment balance (Dr.)			1,463
Fair value adjustment (Cr.)			€(2,388)

ILLUSTRATION 17-7
Computation of Unrealized Gain on Debt Investment (2016)

As indicated in Illustration 17-7, the fair value of the debt investment is now less than the amortized cost by €925. However, Robinson had recorded an unrealized gain in 2015. Therefore, Robinson records a loss of €2,388 (€925 + €1,463), which offsets the gain recorded in 2015, resulting in a credit in the Fair Value Adjustment account of €925. Robinson makes the following journal entry.

Unrealized Holding Gain or Loss—Income	2,388	
Fair Value Adjustment		2,388

A credit balance in the Fair Value Adjustment account of €925 (€2,388 − €1,463) reduces the amortized cost amount to fair value. Robinson reports its investment in

Evermaster bonds in its December 31, 2016, financial statements as shown in Illustration 17-8.

ILLUSTRATION 17-8
Financial Statement
Presentation of Debt
Investments at Fair
Value (2016)

Statement of Financial Position	
Investments	
Debt investments	€94,000
Current assets	
Interest receivable	€ 4,000
Income Statement	
Other income and expense	
Interest revenue (€4,677 + €4,711)	€ 9,388
Unrealized holding gain or (loss)	€ (2,388)

Assume now that Robinson sells its investment in Evermaster bonds on November 1, 2017, at 99¾ plus accrued interest, similar to our earlier illustration on page 817. All the entries and computations are the same as the amortized cost example. The only difference occurs on December 31, 2017. In that case, since the bonds are no longer owned by Robinson, the Fair Value Adjustment account should now be reported at zero. Robinson makes the following entry to record the elimination of the valuation account.

December 31, 2017

Fair Value Adjustment	925	
Unrealized Holding Gain or Loss—Income		925

ILLUSTRATION 17-9
Income Effects on Debt
Investment (2015–2017)

At December 31, 2017, the income related to the Evermaster bonds is as shown in Illustration 17-9.

	Amortized Cost				Fair Value			
Years	Interest	Gain on Sale	Unrealized Gain (Loss)	Total	Interest	Gain on Sale	Unrealized Gain (Loss)	Total
2015	€ 9,259	€ 0	€0	€ 9,259	€ 9,259	€ 0	€1,463	€10,722
2016	9,388	0	0	9,388	9,388	0	(2,388)	7,000
2017	7,935	3,557	0	11,492	7,935	3,557	925	12,417
Total	€26,582	€3,557	€0	€30,139	€26,582	€3,557	€ 0	€30,139

As indicated, over the life of the bond investment, interest revenue and the gain on sale are the same using either amortized cost or fair value measurement. However, under the fair value approach, an unrealized gain or loss is recorded in income in each year as the fair value of the investment changes. Overall, the gains or losses net out to zero.

What do the numbers mean?   WHAT IS FAIR VALUE?

In a recent letter to market regulators, the International Accounting Standards Board said some European financial institutions should have booked bigger losses on their Greek government bond holdings. The IASB criticized inconsistencies in the way financial institutions wrote down the value of their Greek sovereign debt in their quarterly earnings.

The IASB said "some companies" were not using market prices to calculate the fair value of their Greek bond holdings, relying instead on internal models. While some claimed this was because the market for Greek debt had become illiquid, the IASB disagreed. "Although the level of trading activity in Greek government bonds has decreased, transactions are still taking place," IASB chair Hans Hoogervorst wrote.

European banks, taking a €3 billion hit on their Greek bond holdings earlier, employed markedly different approaches to valuing the debt. The write-downs disclosed in their quarterly results varied from 21 to 50 percent, showing a wide range of views on what they expect to get back from their holdings. Jacques Chahine, head of J. Chahine Capital (LUX) which manages €320 billion in assets, noted that "the Greek debt issue has been treated lightly. And it's not just Greek debt—all of it needs to be written down, Spain, Italy."

Many other issues of determining fair value have developed as well. For example, in the fall of 2000, Wall Street brokerage firm Morgan Stanley (USA) told investors that the rumor of big losses in its bond portfolio were "greatly exaggerated." As it turns out, Morgan Stanley was also exaggerating. As a result, the U.S. SEC accused Morgan Stanley of violating securities laws by overstating the value of certain bonds by $75 million. The SEC said that the overvaluations

stemmed more from wishful thinking than reality, in violation of accounting standards. The SEC wrote, "In effect, Morgan Stanley valued its positions at the price at which it thought a willing buyer and seller should enter into an exchange, rather than at a price at which a willing buyer and a willing seller would enter into a **current** exchange."

Especially egregious, stated one accounting expert, were the findings that Morgan Stanley in some instances used its own more optimistic assumptions as a substitute for external pricing sources. "What that is saying is: 'Fair value is what you want the value to be. Pick a number. . . .' That's especially troublesome."

Sources: Adapted from "Accounting Board Criticizes European Banks on Greek Debt," *The New York Times* (August 30, 2011); and Susanne Craig and Jonathan Weil, "SEC Targets Morgan Stanley Values," *Wall Street Journal* (November 8, 2004), p. C3.

Example: Debt Investment at Fair Value (Portfolio)

To illustrate the accounting for a portfolio of debt investments, assume that Wang Corporation has two debt investments accounted for at fair value. Illustration 17-10 identifies the amortized cost, fair value, and the amount of the unrealized gain or loss (amounts in thousands).

DEBT INVESTMENT PORTFOLIO
DECEMBER 31, 2015

Investments	Amortized Cost	Fair Value	Unrealized Gain (Loss)
Watson Corporation 8% bonds	¥ 93,537	¥103,600	¥ 10,063
Anacomp Corporation 10% bonds	200,000	180,400	(19,600)
Total of portfolio	¥293,537	¥284,000	(9,537)
Previous fair value adjustment balance			–0–
Fair value adjustment—Cr.			¥ (9,537)

ILLUSTRATION 17-10
Computation of Fair Value Adjustment—Fair Value Debt Investments (2015)

The fair value of Wang's debt investment portfolio totals ¥284,000. The gross unrealized gains are ¥10,063, and the gross unrealized losses are ¥19,600, resulting in a net unrealized loss of ¥9,537. That is, the fair value of the portfolio is ¥9,537 lower than its amortized cost. Wang makes an adjusting entry to the Fair Value Adjustment account to record the decrease in value and to record the loss as follows.

December 31, 2015

Unrealized Holding Gain or Loss—Income	9,537	
Fair Value Adjustment		9,537

Wang reports the unrealized holding loss of ¥9,537 in income.

Sale of Debt Investments

If a company sells bonds carried as fair value investments before the maturity date, it must make entries to remove from the Debt Investments account the amortized cost of bonds sold. To illustrate, assume that Wang Corporation sold the Watson bonds (from

Illustration 17-10) on July 1, 2016, for ¥90,000, at which time it had an amortized cost of ¥94,214. Illustration 17-11 shows the computation of the realized loss.

ILLUSTRATION 17-11
Computation of Loss on Sale of Bonds

Amortized cost (Watson bonds)	¥94,214
Less: Selling price of bonds	90,000
Loss on sale of bonds	¥ 4,214

Wang records the sale of the Watson bonds as follows.

July 1, 2016

Cash	90,000	
Loss on Sale of Investments	4,214	
Debt Investments		94,214

Wang reports this realized loss in the "Other income and expense" section of the income statement. Assuming no other purchases and sales of bonds in 2016, Wang on December 31, 2016, has the information shown in Illustration 17-12.

ILLUSTRATION 17-12
Computation of Fair Value Adjustment (2016)

DEBT INVESTMENT PORTFOLIO			
DECEMBER 31, 2016			
Investments	Amortized Cost	Fair Value	Unrealized Gain (Loss)
Anacomp Corporation 10% bonds (total portfolio)	¥200,000	¥195,000	¥(5,000)
Previous fair value adjustment balance—Cr.			(9,537)
Fair value adjustment—Dr.			¥ 4,537

Wang has an unrealized holding loss of ¥5,000. However, the Fair Value Adjustment account already has a credit balance of ¥9,537. To reduce the adjustment account balance to ¥5,000, Wang debits it for ¥4,537, as follows.

December 31, 2016

Fair Value Adjustment	4,537	
Unrealized Holding Gain or Loss—Income		4,537

Financial Statement Presentation

Wang's December 31, 2016, statement of financial position and the 2016 income statement include the following items and amounts (the Anacomp bonds are current assets because they are held for trading).

ILLUSTRATION 17-13
Reporting of Debt Investments at Fair Value

Statement of Financial Position		
Investments		
Debt Investments, at fair value		¥ 195,000
Current assets		
Interest receivable	¥	XXX
Income Statement		
Other income and expense		
Interest revenue	¥	XXX
Loss on sale of investments		4,214
Unrealized gain or loss		4,537

Fair Value Option

In some situations, a company meets the criteria for accounting for a debt investment at amortized cost, but it would rather account for the investment at fair value, with all gains and losses related to changes in fair value reported in income. The most common reason is to address a measurement or recognition "mismatch." For example, assume that **Pirelli** (ITA) purchases debt investments that it plans to manage on a held-for-collection basis (and account for at amortized cost). Pirelli also manages and evaluates this investment in conjunction with a related liability that is measured at fair value. Pirelli has a mismatch on these related financial assets because, even though the fair value of the investment may change, no gains and losses are recognized, while gains and losses on the liability are recorded in income.

To address this mismatch, **companies have the option to report most financial assets at fair value**. This option is applied on an instrument-by-instrument basis and is generally available only at the time a company first purchases the financial asset or incurs a financial liability. If a company chooses to use the fair value option, it measures this instrument at fair value until the company no longer has ownership. **[8]** By choosing the fair value option for the debt investment, Pirelli records gains and losses in income, which will offset the gains and losses recorded on the liability, thereby providing more relevant information about these related financial assets.

To illustrate, assume that Hardy Company purchases bonds issued by the German Central Bank. Hardy plans to hold the debt investment until it matures in five years. At December 31, 2015, the amortized cost of this investment is €100,000; its fair value at December 31, 2015, is €113,000. If Hardy chooses the fair value option to account for this investment, it makes the following entry at December 31, 2015.

December 31, 2015

Debt Investment (German bonds)	13,000	
Unrealized Holding Gain or Loss—Income		13,000

In this situation, Hardy uses an account titled Debt Investment to record the change in fair value at December 31. It does not use the Fair Value Adjustment account because the accounting for the fair value option is on an investment-by-investment basis rather than on a portfolio basis. Because Hardy selected the fair value option, the unrealized gain or loss is recorded as part of net income even though it is managing the investment on a held-for-collection basis. Hardy must continue to use the fair value method to record this investment until it no longer has ownership of the security.

Summary of Debt Investment Accounting

The following chart summarizes the basic accounting for debt investments.

ILLUSTRATION 17-14
Summary of Debt Investment Accounting

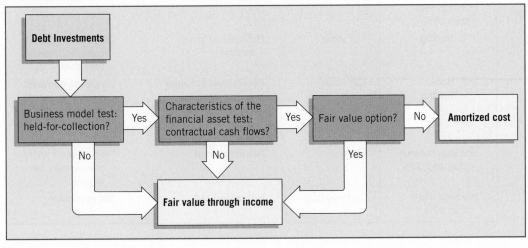

EQUITY INVESTMENTS

An **equity investment** represents ownership interest, such as ordinary, preference, or other capital shares. It also includes rights to acquire or dispose of ownership interests at an agreed-upon or determinable price, such as in warrants and rights. The cost of equity investments is measured at the purchase price of the security. Broker's commissions and other fees incidental to the purchase are recorded as expense. **[9]**

The degree to which one corporation (**investor**) acquires an interest in the shares of another corporation (**investee**) generally determines the accounting treatment for the investment subsequent to acquisition. The classification of such investments depends on the percentage of the investee voting shares that is held by the investor:

1. Holdings of less than 20 percent (**fair value method**)—investor has passive interest.
2. Holdings between 20 percent and 50 percent (**equity method**)—investor has significant influence.
3. Holdings of more than 50 percent (**consolidated statements**)—investor has controlling interest.

Illustration 17-15 lists these levels of interest or influence and the corresponding valuation and reporting method that companies must apply to the investment.

ILLUSTRATION 17-15
Levels of Influence
Determine Accounting
Methods

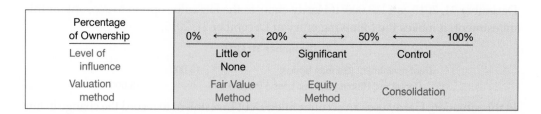

The accounting and reporting for equity investments therefore depend on the level of influence and the type of security involved, as shown in Illustration 17-16.

ILLUSTRATION 17-16
Accounting and
Reporting for Equity
Investments by Category

Category	Valuation	Unrealized Holding Gains or Losses	Other Income Effects
Holdings less than 20%			
1. Trading	Fair value	Recognized in net income	Dividends declared; gains and losses from sale.
2. Non-Trading	Fair value	Recognized in "Other comprehensive income" and as separate component of equity	Dividends declared; gains and losses from sale.
Holdings between 20% and 50%	Equity	Not recognized	Proportionate share of investee's net income.
Holdings more than 50%	Consolidation	Not recognized	Not applicable.

Holdings of Less Than 20%

When an investor has an interest of less than 20 percent, it is presumed that the investor has little or no influence over the investee. As indicated in Illustration 17-16, there are two classifications for holdings less than 20 percent. Under IFRS, the presumption is that equity investments are held-for-trading. That is, companies hold these securities to profit from price changes. As with debt investments that are held-for-trading, the general accounting and reporting rule for these investments is to value the securities at fair value and record unrealized gains and losses in net income (**fair value method**).[5]

However, some equity investments are held for purposes other than trading. For example, a company may be required to hold an equity investment in order to sell its products in a particular area. In this situation, the recording of unrealized gains and losses in income, as is required for trading investments, is not indicative of the company's performance with respect to this investment. As a result, IFRS allows companies to classify some equity investments as non-trading. **Non-trading equity investments** are recorded at fair value on the statement of financial position, with unrealized gains and losses reported in other comprehensive income. **[11]**

Equity Investments—Trading (Income)

Upon acquisition, companies record equity investments at fair value.[6] To illustrate, assume that on November 3, 2015, Republic Corporation purchased ordinary shares of three companies, each investment representing less than a 20 percent interest. These shares are held-for-trading.

	Cost
Burberry	€259,700
Nestlé	317,500
St. Regis Pulp Co.	141,350
Total cost	€718,550

Republic records these investments as follows.

November 3, 2015

Equity Investments	718,550	
Cash		718,550

On December 6, 2015, Republic receives a cash dividend of €4,200 on its investment in the ordinary shares of Nestlé. It records the cash dividend as follows.

December 6, 2015

Cash	4,200	
Dividend Revenue		4,200

---

[5]Fair value at initial recognition is the transaction price (exclusive of brokerage and other transaction costs). Subsequent fair value measurements should be based on market prices, if available. For non-trading investments, a valuation technique based on discounted expected cash flows can be used to develop a fair value estimate. While IFRS requires that all equity investments be measured at fair value, cost may be an appropriate estimate of fair value for an equity investment in certain limited cases. **[10]**

[6]Companies should record equity investments acquired in **exchange for non-cash consideration** (property or services) at the fair value of the consideration given, if the fair value can be measured reliably. Otherwise, the value of the exchange can be determined with reference to the fair value of the equity investment. Accounting for numerous purchases of securities requires the preservation of information regarding the cost of individual purchases, as well as the dates of purchases and sales. If **specific identification** is not possible, companies may use **average-cost** for multiple purchases of the same class of security. The **first-in, first-out** (FIFO) method of assigning costs to investments at the time of sale is also acceptable and normally employed.

All three of the investee companies reported net income for the year, but only Nestlé declared and paid a dividend to Republic. But, recall that when an investor owns less than 20 percent of the shares of another corporation, it is presumed that the investor has relatively little influence on the investee. As a result, **net income earned by the investee is not a proper basis for recognizing income from the investment by the investor**. Why? Because the increased net assets resulting from profitable operations may be permanently retained for use in the investee's business. Therefore, **the investor earns net income only when the investee declares cash dividends**.

At December 31, 2015, Republic's equity investment portfolio has the carrying value and fair value shown in Illustration 17-17.

ILLUSTRATION 17-17
Computation of Fair Value Adjustment—Equity Investment Portfolio (2015)

EQUITY INVESTMENT PORTFOLIO			
DECEMBER 31, 2015			
Investments	Carrying Value	Fair Value	Unrealized Gain (Loss)
Burberry	€259,700	€275,000	€ 15,300
Nestlé	317,500	304,000	(13,500)
St. Regis Pulp Co.	141,350	104,000	(37,350)
Total of portfolio	€718,550	€683,000	(35,550)
Previous fair value adjustment balance			–0–
Fair value adjustment—Cr.			€(35,550)

For Republic's equity investment portfolio, the gross unrealized gains are €15,300, and the gross unrealized losses are €50,850 (€13,500 + €37,350), resulting in a net unrealized loss of €35,550. The fair value of the equity investment portfolio is below cost by €35,550.

Republic records the net unrealized gains and losses related to changes in the fair value of **equity** investments in an Unrealized Holding Gain or Loss—Income account. Republic reports this amount as "Other income and expense." In this case, Republic prepares an adjusting entry debiting the Unrealized Holding Gain or Loss—Income account and crediting the Fair Value Adjustment account to record the decrease in fair value and to record the loss as follows.

December 31, 2015

Unrealized Holding Gain or Loss—Income	35,550	
Fair Value Adjustment		35,550

On January 23, 2016, Republic sold all of its Burberry ordinary shares, receiving €287,220. Illustration 17-18 shows the computation of the realized gain on the sale.

ILLUSTRATION 17-18
Computation of Gain on Sale of Burberry Shares

Net proceeds from sale	€287,220
Cost of **Burberry** shares	259,700
Gain on sale of shares	€ 27,520

Republic records the sale as follows.

January 23, 2016

Cash	287,220	
Equity Investments		259,700
Gain on Sale of Investments		27,520

In addition, assume that on February 10, 2016, Republic purchased €255,000 of Continental Trucking ordinary shares (20,000 shares × €12.75 per share), plus brokerage commissions of €1,850.

Illustration 17-19 lists Republic's equity investment portfolio as of December 31, 2016.

		EQUITY INVESTMENT PORTFOLIO DECEMBER 31, 2016	
Investments	Carrying Value	Fair Value	Unrealized Gain (Loss)
Continental Trucking	€255,000ᵃ	€278,350	€ 23,350
Nestlé	317,500	362,550	45,050
St. Regis Pulp Co.	141,350	139,050	(2,300)
Total of portfolio	€713,850	€779,950	66,100
Previous fair value adjustment balance—Cr.			(35,550)
Fair value adjustment—Dr.			€101,650

ᵃThe brokerage commissions are expensed.

At December 31, 2016, the fair value of Republic's equity investment portfolio exceeds carrying value by €66,100 (unrealized gain). The Fair Value Adjustment account had a credit balance of €35,550 at December 31, 2016. To adjust its December 31, 2016, equity investment portfolio to fair value, the company debits the Fair Value Adjustment account for €101,650 (€35,550 + €66,100). Republic records this adjustment as follows.

December 31, 2016

Fair Value Adjustment	101,650	
Unrealized Holding Gain or Loss—Income		101,650

Equity Investments—Non-Trading (OCI)

The accounting entries to record non-trading equity investments are the same as for trading equity investments, except for recording the unrealized holding gain or loss. For non-trading equity investments, companies **report the unrealized holding gain or loss as other comprehensive income**. Thus, the account titled Unrealized Holding Gain or Loss—Equity is used.

To illustrate, assume that on December 10, 2015, Republic Corporation purchased 1,000 ordinary shares of Hawthorne Company for €20.75 per share (total cost €20,750). The investment represents less than a 20 percent interest. Hawthorne is a distributor for Republic products in certain locales, the laws of which require a minimum level of share ownership of a company in that region. The investment in Hawthorne meets this regulatory requirement. As a result, Republic accounts for this investment at fair value, with unrealized gains and losses recorded in other comprehensive income (OCI).[7] Republic records this investment as follows.

December 10, 2015

Equity Investments	20,750	
Cash		20,750

[7]The classification of an equity investment as non-trading is irrevocable. This approach is designed to provide some discipline to the application of the non-trading classification, which allows unrealized gains and losses to bypass net income. **[12]**

On December 27, 2015, Republic receives a cash dividend of €450 on its investment in the ordinary shares of Hawthorne Company. It records the cash dividend as follows.

December 27, 2015

Cash	450	
Dividend Revenue		450

Similar to the accounting for trading investments, when an investor owns less than 20 percent of the ordinary shares of another corporation, it is presumed that the investor has relatively little influence on the investee. Therefore, **the investor earns income when the investee declares cash dividends**.

At December 31, 2015, Republic's investment in Hawthorne has the carrying value and fair value shown in Illustration 17-20.

ILLUSTRATION 17-20
Computation of Fair Value Adjustment—Non-Trading Equity Investment (2015)

Non-Trading Equity Investment	Carrying Value	Fair Value	Unrealized Gain (Loss)
Hawthorne Company	€20,750	€24,000	€3,250
Previous fair value adjustment balance			0
Fair value adjustment (Dr.)			€3,250

For Republic's non-trading investment, the unrealized gain is €3,250. That is, the fair value of the Hawthorne investment exceeds cost by €3,250. Because Republic has classified this investment as non-trading, Republic records the unrealized gains and losses related to changes in the fair value of this non-trading **equity** investment in an Unrealized Holding Gain or Loss—Equity account. Republic reports this amount as **a part of other comprehensive income and as a component of other accumulated comprehensive income (reported in equity)**. In this case, Republic prepares an adjusting entry crediting the Unrealized Holding Gain or Loss—Equity account and debiting the Fair Value Adjustment account to record the increase in fair value and to record the gain as follows.

December 31, 2015

Fair Value Adjustment	3,250	
Unrealized Holding Gain or Loss—Equity		3,250

Republic reports its equity investments in its December 31, 2015, financial statements as shown in Illustration 17-21.

ILLUSTRATION 17-21
Financial Statement Presentation of Equity Investments at Fair Value (2015)

Statement of Financial Position	
Investments	
Equity investments	€24,000
Equity	
Accumulated other comprehensive gain	€ 3,250
Statement of Comprehensive Income	
Other income and expense	
Dividend revenue	€ 450
Other comprehensive income	
Unrealized holding gain	€ 3,250

During 2016, sales of Republic products through Hawthorne as a distributor did not meet management's goals. As a result, Republic withdrew from these markets. On December 20, 2016, Republic sold all of its Hawthorne Company ordinary shares, receiving proceeds of €22,500. Republic determines the unrealized gain and loss on the investment at the time of the disposition as shown in Illustration 17-22.

Non-Trading Equity Investment	Cost	Fair Value	Unrealized Gain (Loss)
Hawthorne Company at 12/20/2016	€20,750	€22,500	€ 1,750
Previous fair value adjustment balance (Dr.)			(3,250)
Change in the Fair Value Adjustment account (loss)			€(1,500)

ILLUSTRATION 17-22
Adjustment to Carrying
Value of Investment

Republic makes the following entry to adjust the carrying value of the non-trading investment.

December 20, 2016

Unrealized Holding Gain or Loss—Equity	1,500	
Fair Value Adjustment		1,500

The following entry is then made to record the sale of the investment.

December 20, 2016

Cash	22,500	
Fair Value Adjustment		1,750
Equity Investments		20,750

As a result of these entries, the Fair Value Adjustment account is eliminated. Note that all gains and losses on the non-trading investment are recorded in equity.[8]

In summary, the accounting for non-trading equity investments deviates from the general provisions for equity investments. The IASB noted that while fair value provides the most useful information about investments in equity investments, recording unrealized gains or losses in other comprehensive income is more representative for non-trading equity investments. **[14]**

Holdings Between 20% and 50%

An investor corporation may hold an interest of less than 50 percent in an investee corporation and thus not possess legal control. However, an investment in voting shares of less than 50 percent can still give an investor the ability to exercise significant influence over the operating and financial policies of an investee. **[15]** For example, **Siemens AG** (DEU) owns 34 percent of **Areva** (FRA) (which constructs power plants). Areva is very important to Siemens because the power industry is a key customer for its generators and other power-related products. Thus, Siemens has a significant (but not controlling) ownership stake in a power plant construction company, which helps Siemens push its products into the market. **Significant influence** may be indicated in several ways. Examples include representation on the board of directors, participation in policy-making processes, material intercompany transactions, interchange of managerial personnel, or technological dependency.

Another important consideration is the extent of ownership by an investor in relation to the concentration of other shareholdings. To achieve a reasonable degree of uniformity in application of the "significant influence" criterion, the profession concluded that an investment (direct or indirect) of 20 percent or more of the voting shares of an

6 LEARNING OBJECTIVE
Explain the equity method of accounting
and compare it to the fair value method
for equity investments.

---

[8]Once non-trading equity investments are sold, companies may transfer the balance of unrealized holding gains or losses in accumulated other comprehensive income to retained earnings. Transferring the balance to retained earnings has merit, as these gains or losses would have been recorded in net income in a prior period if these securities were accounted for as trading securities. Some contend that these unrealized gains or losses should be "recycled"; that is, these amounts should be recorded in net income when a non-trading investment is sold. The IASB rejected this approach because it would increase the complexity of the accounting for these investments. **[13]**

investee should lead to a presumption that in the absence of evidence to the contrary, an investor has the ability to exercise significant influence over an investee.[9]

In instances of "significant influence" (generally an investment of 20 percent or more), the investor must account for the investment using the **equity method**.

Equity Method

Under the equity method, the investor and the investee acknowledge a substantive economic relationship. The company originally records the investment at the cost of the shares acquired but subsequently adjusts the amount each period for changes in the investee's net assets. That is, **the investor's proportionate share of the earnings (losses) of the investee periodically increases (decreases) the investment's carrying amount. All dividends received by the investor from the investee also decrease the investment's carrying amount.** The equity method recognizes that the investee's earnings increase the investee's net assets, and that the investee's losses and dividends decrease these net assets.

To illustrate the equity method and compare it with the fair value method, assume that Maxi Company purchases a 20 percent interest in Mini Company. To apply the fair value method in this example, assume that Maxi does not have the ability to exercise significant influence and classifies the investment as trading. Where this example applies the equity method, assume that the 20 percent interest permits Maxi to exercise significant influence. Illustration 17-23 shows the entries.

ILLUSTRATION 17-23
Comparison of Fair Value Method and Equity Method

ENTRIES BY MAXI COMPANY			
Fair Value Method		**Equity Method**	
On January 2, 2015, Maxi Company acquired 48,000 shares (20% of Mini Company ordinary shares) at a cost of $10 a share.			
Equity Investments	480,000	Equity Investments	480,000
Cash	480,000	Cash	480,000
For the year 2015, Mini Company reported net income of $200,000; Maxi Company's share is 20%, or $40,000.			
No entry		Equity Investments	40,000
		Investment Income	40,000
At December 31, 2015, the Mini Company 48,000 shares have a fair value (market price) of $12 a share, or $576,000.			
Fair Value Adjustment	96,000	No entry	
Unrealized Holding Gain or Loss—Income	96,000		
On January 28, 2016, Mini Company announced and paid a cash dividend of $100,000; Maxi Company received 20%, or $20,000.			
Cash	20,000	Cash	20,000
Dividend Revenue	20,000	Equity Investments	20,000
For the year 2016, Mini reported a net loss of $50,000; Maxi Company's share is 20%, or $10,000.			
No entry		Investment Loss	10,000
		Equity Investments	10,000
At December 31, 2016, the Mini Company 48,000 shares have a fair value (market price) of $11 a share, or $528,000.			
Unrealized Holding Gain or Loss—Income	48,000	No entry	
Fair Value Adjustment			
[($480,000 + $96,000) − $528,000]	48,000		

[9]Cases in which an investment of 20 percent or more might not enable an investor to exercise significant influence include (1) the investee opposes the investor's acquisition of its shares, (2) the investor and investee sign an agreement under which the investor surrenders significant shareholder rights, (3) the investor's ownership share does not result in "significant influence" because majority ownership of the investee is concentrated among a small group of shareholders who operate the investee without regard to the views of the investor, and (4) the investor tries and fails to obtain representation on the investee's board of directors. **[16]**

Note that under the **fair value method**, Maxi reports as revenue only the cash dividends received from Mini. **The earning of net income by Mini (the investee) is not considered a proper basis for recognition of income from the investment by Maxi (the investor).** Why? Mini may permanently retain in the business any increased net assets resulting from its profitable operation. Therefore, Maxi only recognizes revenue when it receives dividends from Mini.

Under the **equity method**, Maxi reports as revenue its share of the net income reported by Mini. Maxi records the cash dividends received from Mini as a decrease in the investment carrying value. As a result, Maxi records its share of the net income of Mini in the year when it is recognized. With significant influence, Maxi can ensure that Mini will pay dividends, if desired, on any net asset increases resulting from net income. To wait until receiving a dividend ignores the fact that Maxi is better off if the investee has earned income.

Using dividends as a basis for recognizing income poses an additional problem. For example, assume that the investee reports a net loss. However, the investor exerts influence to force a dividend payment from the investee. In this case, the investor reports income even though the investee is experiencing a loss. **In other words, using dividends as a basis for recognizing income fails to report properly the economics of the situation.**

For some companies, equity accounting can be a real pain to the bottom line. For example, **Amazon.com** (USA), the pioneer of Internet retailing, at one time struggled to turn a profit. Furthermore, some of Amazon's equity investments had resulted in Amazon's earnings performance going from bad to worse. At one time, Amazon disclosed equity stakes in such companies as **Altera International** (USA), **Basis Technology** (USA), **Drugstore.com** (USA), and **Eziba.com** (USA). These equity investees reported losses that made Amazon's already bad bottom line even worse, accounting for up to 22 percent of its reported loss in one year alone.

Investee Losses Exceed Carrying Amount. If an investor's share of the investee's losses exceeds the carrying amount of the investment, should the investor recognize additional losses? Ordinarily, the investor should discontinue applying the equity method and not recognize additional losses.

If the investor's potential loss is not limited to the amount of its original investment (by guarantee of the investee's obligations or other commitment to provide further financial support) or if imminent return to profitable operations by the investee appears to be assured, the investor should recognize additional losses. **[17]**

> **Underlying Concepts** 🔍
>
> A low level of ownership indicates that a company should defer the income from an investee until cash is received because such revenue may not meet recognition criteria.

Holdings of More Than 50%

When one corporation acquires a voting interest of more than 50 percent in another corporation, it is said to have a **controlling interest**. In such a relationship, the investor corporation is referred to as the **parent** and the investee corporation as the **subsidiary**. Companies present the investment in the ordinary shares of the subsidiary as a long-term investment on the separate financial statements of the parent.

When the parent treats the subsidiary as an investment, the parent generally prepares **consolidated financial statements**. Consolidated financial statements treat the parent and subsidiary corporations as a single economic entity. (Advanced accounting courses extensively discuss the subject of when and how to prepare consolidated financial statements.) Whether or not consolidated financial statements are prepared, the parent company generally accounts for the investment in the subsidiary **using the equity method** as explained in the previous section of this chapter.

Lenovo Group (CHN) owns a significant percentage (23 percent) of the shares of IGRS Engineering Lab Limited (CHN). The core business of IGRS Engineering Lab is to grant advanced technologies and solutions to companies (like Lenovo); launch intelligent terminals to the market; and offer efficient, green, and energy-saving total solutions to the industry, based on IGRS standards.

As you have learned, because Lenovo owns less than 50 percent of the shares, Lenovo does not consolidate IGRS Engineering Lab but instead accounts for its investment using the *equity method*. Under the equity method, Lenovo reports a single income item for its profits from IGRS Engineering Lab and only the net amount of its investment in the statement of financial position. Equity method accounting gives Lenovo a pristine statement of financial position and income statement, by separating the assets and liabilities and the profit margins of the related companies from its laptop-computer businesses.

Lenovo also owns a 49 percent interest in Chengdu Lenovo Rongjin (CHN), which is a property development company. In addition, it owns a 49 percent interest in Shanghai Shiyun Network (CHN), which distributes and develops information technology and software. In both these cases, Lenovo uses the equity method of accounting.

Some are critical of equity method accounting; they argue that some investees, like the 49 percent-owned companies, should be consolidated. The IASB has been working to tighten up consolidation rules, so that companies will be more likely to consolidate more of their 20 to 50 percent-owned investments. Consolidation of entities, such as for Chengdu Lenovo Rongjin and Shanghai Shiyun Network, is warranted if Lenovo effectively controls its equity method investments. See *http://www.iasb.org/Current+Projects/ IASB+Projects/Consolidation/Consolidation.htm* for more information on the consolidation project.

OTHER REPORTING ISSUES

LEARNING OBJECTIVE **7**
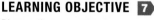
Discuss the accounting for impairments of debt investments.

We have identified the basic issues involved in accounting for investments in debt and equity securities. In addition, the following issues relate to the accounting for investments.

1. Impairment of value.
2. Transfers between categories.

Impairment of Value

A company should evaluate every held-for-collection investment, at each reporting date, to determine if it has suffered **impairment**—a loss in value such that the fair value of the investment is below its carrying value.[10] For example, if an investee experiences a bankruptcy or a significant liquidity crisis, the investor may suffer a permanent loss. **If the company determines that an investment is impaired, it writes down the amortized cost basis of the individual security to reflect this loss in value.** The company accounts for the write-down as a realized loss, and it includes the amount in net income.

For debt investments, a company uses the impairment test to determine whether "it is probable that the investor will be unable to collect all amounts due according to the contractual terms." If an investment is impaired, the company should measure the loss due to the impairment. This impairment loss is calculated as the difference between the carrying amount plus accrued interest and the expected future cash flows discounted at the investment's historical effective-interest rate. **[18]**

---

[10]Note that impairment tests are conducted only for debt investments that are held-for-collection (which are accounted for at amortized cost). Other debt and equity investments are measured at fair value each period; thus, an impairment test is not needed.

Example: Impairment Loss

At December 31, 2014, Mayhew Company has a debt investment in Bao Group, purchased at par for ¥200,000 (amounts in thousands). The investment has a term of four years, with annual interest payments at 10 percent, paid at the end of each year (the historical effective-interest rate is 10 percent). This debt investment is classified as held-for-collection. Unfortunately, Bao is experiencing significant financial difficulty and indicates that it will be unable to make all payments according to the contractual terms. Mayhew uses the present value method for measuring the required impairment loss. Illustration 17-24 shows the cash flow schedule prepared for this analysis.

December 31	Contractual Cash Flows	Expected Cash Flows	Loss of Cash Flows
2015	¥ 20,000	¥ 16,000	¥ 4,000
2016	20,000	16,000	4,000
2017	20,000	16,000	4,000
2018	220,000	216,000	4,000
Total cash flows	¥280,000	¥264,000	¥16,000

ILLUSTRATION 17-24
Investment Cash Flows

As indicated, the expected cash flows of ¥264,000 are less than the contractual cash flows of ¥280,000. The amount of the impairment to be recorded equals the difference between the recorded investment of ¥200,000 and the present value of the expected cash flows, as shown in Illustration 17-25.

Recorded investment		¥200,000
Less: Present value of ¥200,000 due in 4 years at 10%		
(Table 6-2); $FV(PVF_{4,10\%})$; (¥200,000 × .68301)	¥136,602	
Present value of ¥16,000 interest receivable annually		
for 4 years at 10% (Table 6-4); $R(PVF\text{-}OA_{4,10\%})$;		
(¥16,000 × 3.16986)	50,718	187,320
Loss on impairment		¥ 12,680

ILLUSTRATION 17-25
Computation of Impairment Loss

The loss due to the impairment is ¥12,680.[11] Why isn't it ¥16,000 (¥280,000 − ¥264,000)? A loss of ¥12,680 is recorded because Mayhew must measure the loss at a present value amount, not at an undiscounted amount. Mayhew recognizes an impairment loss of ¥12,680 by debiting Loss on Impairment for the expected loss. At the same time, it reduces the overall value of the investment. The journal entry to record the loss is therefore as follows.

December 31, 2014

Loss on Impairment	12,680	
Debt Investments		12,680

Recovery of Impairment Loss

Subsequent to recording an impairment, events or economic conditions may change such that the extent of the impairment loss decreases (e.g., due to an improvement in the debtor's credit rating). In this situation, some or all of the previously recognized impairment loss shall be reversed with a debit to the Debt Investments account and crediting Recovery of Impairment Loss. Similar to the accounting for impairments of receivables shown in Chapter 7, the reversal of impairment losses shall not result in a carrying amount of the investment that exceeds the amortized cost that would have been reported had the impairment not been recognized.

---

[11]Many question this present value calculation because it uses the investment's historical effective-interest rate—not the current market rate. As a result, the present value computation does not reflect the fair value of the debt investment, and many believe the impairment loss is misstated.

Transfers Between Categories

LEARNING OBJECTIVE **8**

Describe the accounting for transfer
of investments between categories.

Transferring an investment from one classification to another should occur only when the business model for managing the investment changes. The IASB expects such changes to be rare. **[19]** Companies account for transfers between classifications prospectively, at the beginning of the accounting period after the change in the business model.[12]

To illustrate, assume that **British Sky Broadcasting Group plc** (GBR) has a portfolio of debt investments that are classified as trading; that is, the debt investments are not held-for-collection but managed to profit from interest rate changes. As a result, it accounts for these investments at fair value. At December 31, 2014, British Sky has the following balances related to these securities.

Debt investments	£1,200,000
Fair value adjustment	125,000
Carrying value	£1,325,000

As part of its strategic planning process, completed in the fourth quarter of 2014, British Sky management decides to move from its prior strategy—which requires active management—to a held-for-collection strategy for these debt investments. British Sky makes the following entry to transfer these securities to the held-for-collection classification.

January 1, 2015

Debt Investments	125,000	
Fair Value Adjustment		125,000

Therefore, at January 1, 2015, the debt investments are stated at fair value. However, in subsequent periods, British Sky will account for the investment at amortized cost. The effective-interest rate used in the amortized cost model is the rate used to discount the future cash flows to the fair value of British Sky's debt investment of £1,325,000 on January 1, 2015.

Evolving Issue   FAIR VALUE CONTROVERSY

The reporting of investments is controversial. Some favor the present approach, which reflects a mixed-attribute model based on a company's business model for managing the investment and the type of security. Under this model, some debt investments are accounted for at amortized cost and others at fair value. Others call for fair value measurement for all financial assets, with gains and losses recorded in income. In this section, we look at some of the major unresolved issues.

• *Measurement based on business model.* Companies value debt investments at fair value or amortized cost,

depending on the business model and cash flow tests for managing the investments. Some believe that this framework provides the most relevant information about the performance of these investments. Others disagree; they note that two identical debt investments could be reported in different ways in the financial statements. They argue that this approach increases complexity and reduces the understandability of financial statements. Furthermore, the held-for-collection classification relies on management's plans, which can change. In other words, the classifications are subjective, resulting in arbitrary and non-comparable classifications.

[12]The Board rejected retrospective application because recasting prior periods according to the new investment model would not reflect how the investments were managed in the prior periods. The IASB indicates that a change in a company's investment business model is a significant and demonstrable event, and it is likely that this change will be disclosed when the change occurs. Note that other types of transfers are also permitted, such as non-trading to held-for-collection and vice versa, but these situations should be rare. **[20]**

- *Gains trading.* Debt investments classified as held-for-collection are reported at amortized cost; unrealized gains and losses on these investments are not recognized in income. Similarly, the unrealized gains or losses on non-trading equity investments also bypass income. Although significant trading out of these classifications might call into question management's business model assertions with respect to these classifications, a company can engage in "gains trading" (also referred to as "cherry picking," "snacking," or "sell the best and keep the rest"). In **gains trading**, companies sell their "winners," reporting the gains in income, and hold on to the losers. Furthermore, as one IASB member noted, in the recent financial crisis some of the most significant losses were recorded on investments that qualify for accounting in which unrealized gains or losses were not reported in income. That is, fair value accounting would have provided much more timely information on these investments when the markets needed it the most.

- *Liabilities not fairly valued.* Many argue that if companies report investments at fair value, they also should report liabilities at fair value. Why? By recognizing changes in value on only one side of the statement of financial position (the asset side), a high degree of volatility can occur in the income and equity amounts. Further, financial institutions are involved in asset and liability management (not just asset management). Viewing only one side may lead managers to make uneconomic decisions as a result of the accounting. As we discussed in Chapter 14, there is debate on the usefulness of fair value estimates for liabilities.

The IASB (and the FASB) believe that fair value information for many financial assets and financial liabilities provides more useful and relevant information than a cost-based system. The Boards take this position because fair value reflects the current cash equivalent of the financial instrument rather than the cost of a past transaction. As a consequence, only fair value provides an understanding of the current worth of the investment. Under *IFRS 9*, companies must report fair values for more types of financial assets relative to prior standards in this area. However, an exception is allowed for some debt investments. Whether this approach results in an improvement in the reporting for debt and equity investments remains to be seen.

Summary of Reporting Treatment of Investments

Illustration 17-26 summarizes the major debt and equity investment classifications and their reporting treatment.

ILLUSTRATION 17-26
Summary of Investment Accounting Approaches

Classification	Valuation Approach and Reporting on the Statement of Financial Position	Income Effects
Debt Investment		
1. Meets business model (held-for-collection) and contractual cash flow tests.	Amortized cost. Current or Non-current assets.	Interest is recognized as revenue.
2. Does not meet the business model test (not held-for-collection).	Fair value. Current assets.	Interest is recognized as revenue. Unrealized holding gains and losses are included in income.
3. Fair value option.	Fair value. Current or Non-current assets.	Interest is recognized as revenue. Unrealized holding gains and losses are included in income.
Equity Investment		
1. Does not meet contractual cash flow test; holdings less than 20 percent (trading).	Fair value. Current assets.	Dividends are recognized as revenue. Unrealized holding gains and losses are included in income.
2. Does not meet contractual cash flow test; holdings less than 20 percent (non-trading).	Fair value. Non-current assets.	Dividends are recognized as revenue. Unrealized holding gains and losses are not included in income but in other comprehensive income.
3. Holdings greater than 20 percent (significant influence or control).	Investments originally recorded at cost with periodic adjustment for the investor's share of the investee's income or loss, and decreased by all dividends received from the investee. Non-current assets.	Revenue is recognized to the extent of the investee's income or loss reported subsequent to the date of the investment.

GLOBAL ACCOUNTING INSIGHTS

INVESTMENTS

Before the IASB issued *IFRS 9*, the accounting and reporting for investments under IFRS and U.S. GAAP were for the most part very similar. However, *IFRS 9* introduces new investment classifications and increases the situations when investments are accounted for at fair value.

Relevant Facts

Following are the key similarities and differences between U.S. GAAP and IFRS related to investments.

Similarities

- U.S. GAAP and IFRS use similar classifications for trading investments.
- The accounting for trading investments is the same between U.S. GAAP and IFRS. Held-to-maturity (U.S. GAAP) and held-for-collection investments are accounted for at amortized cost. Gains and losses on some investments are reported in other comprehensive income.
- U.S. GAAP and IFRS use the same test to determine whether the equity method of accounting should be used, that is, significant influence with a general guide of over 20 percent ownership.
- U.S. GAAP and IFRS are similar in the accounting for the fair value option. That is, the option to use the fair value method must be made at initial recognition, the selection is irrevocable, and gains and losses are reported as part of income.
- The measurement of impairments is similar under U.S. GAAP and IFRS.

Differences

- While U.S. GAAP classifies investments as trading, available-for-sale (both debt and equity investments), and held-to-maturity (only for debt investments), IFRS uses held-for-collection (debt investments), trading (both debt and equity investments), and non-trading equity investment classifications.
- Under U.S. GAAP, a bipolar approach is used to determine consolidation, which is a risk-and-reward model (often referred to as a variable-entity approach) and a voting-interest approach. The basis for consolidation under IFRS is control. However, under both systems, for consolidation to occur, the investor company must generally own 50 percent of another company.
- While the measurement of impairments is similar under U.S. GAAP and IFRS, U.S. GAAP does not permit the reversal of an impairment charge related to available-for-sale debt and equity investments. IFRS allows reversals of impairments of held-for-collection investments.
- While U.S. GAAP and IFRS are similar in the accounting for the fair value option, one difference is that U.S. GAAP permits the fair value option for equity method investments; IFRS does not.

About the Numbers

The following example illustrates the accounting for investment impairments under IFRS. Belerus Company has a held-for-collection investment in the 8 percent, 10-year bonds of Wimbledon Company. The investment has a carrying value of €2,300,000 at December 31, 2015. Early in January 2016, Belerus learns that Wimbledon has lost a major customer. As a result, Belerus determines that this investment is impaired and now has a fair value of €1,500,000. Belerus makes the following entry to record the impairment.

Loss on Impairment (€2,300,000 − €1,500,000)	800,000	
Debt Investments (HFC)		800,000

Early in 2017, Wimbledon secures several new customers, and its prospects have improved considerably. Belerus determines the fair value of its investment is now €2,000,000 and makes the following entry under IFRS.

Debt Investments (HFC)		
(€2,000,000 − €1,500,000)	500,000	
Recovery of Investment Loss		500,000

Under U.S. GAAP, Belerus is prohibited from recording the recovery in value of the impaired investment. That is, once an investment is impaired, the impaired value becomes the new basis for the investment.

On the Horizon

At one time, both the FASB and IASB indicated that they believed that all financial instruments should be reported at fair value and that changes in fair value should be reported as part of net income. However, *IFRS 9* indicates that the IASB believes that certain debt investments should not be reported at fair value. The IASB's decision to issue new rules on investments, earlier than the FASB has completed its deliberations on financial instrument accounting, could create obstacles for the Boards in converging the accounting in this area.

SUMMARY OF LEARNING OBJECTIVES

1 **Describe the accounting framework for financial assets.** Financial assets (debt and equity investments) are accounted for either at amortized cost or fair value. If a company has (1) a business model whose objective is to hold assets in order to collect contractual cash flows and (2) the contractual terms of the financial asset give specified dates to cash flows that are solely payments of principal and interest on the principal amount outstanding, then the company should use amortized cost. Thus, only debt investments can be accounted for at amortized cost. Equity investments are generally recorded and reported at fair value. Equity investments do not have a fixed interest or principal payment schedule and therefore cannot be accounted for at amortized cost. In general, equity investments are valued at fair value, with all gains and losses reported in income.

2 **Understand the accounting for debt investments at amortized cost.** Similar to bonds payable, companies should amortize discounts or premiums on debt investments using the effective-interest method. They apply the effective-interest rate or yield to the beginning carrying value of the investment for each interest period in order to compute interest revenue.

3 **Understand the accounting for debt investments at fair value.** Companies that account for and report debt investments at fair value follow the same accounting entries as debt investments held-for-collection during the reporting period. That is, they are recorded at amortized cost. However, at each reporting date, companies adjust the amortized cost to fair value, with any unrealized holding gain or loss reported as part of net income.

4 **Describe the accounting for the fair value option.** Companies have the option to report most financial instruments at fair value, with all gains and losses related to changes in fair value reported in the income statement. This option is applied on an instrument-by-instrument basis. The fair value option is generally available only at the time a company first purchases the financial asset or incurs a financial liability. If a company chooses to use the fair value option, it must measure this instrument at fair value until the company no longer has ownership.

5 **Understand the accounting for equity investments at fair value.** For equity investment holdings less than 20 percent, it is presumed that companies hold the investment to profit from price changes. The accounting and reporting rule for these investments is to value the investments at fair value and record unrealized gains and losses in net income (the fair value method). Dividends received are recorded in income. Equity investments held for purposes other than trading are recorded at fair value on the statement of financial position, with unrealized gains and losses reported in other comprehensive income.

6 **Explain the equity method of accounting and compare it to the fair value method for equity investments.** The equity method is used when an investor

KEY TERMS

amortized cost, *815*

consolidated financial statements, *831*

controlling interest, *831*

debt investments, *815*

effective-interest method, *816*

equity investments, *824*

equity method, *830*

exchange for non-cash consideration, *825 (n)*

fair value, *815*

Fair Value Adjustment, *819*

fair value method, *818, 825*

financial assets, *814*

held-for-collection, *815*

impairment, *832*

investee, *824*

investor, *824*

non-trading equity investments, *825*

parent, *831*

significant influence, *829*

subsidiary, *831*

trading investments, *818*

unrealized holding gain, *818*

unrealized holding loss, *818*

company acquires ordinary shares of another company (investee), such that the investor has significant influence—a holding between 20 and 50 percent. Under the equity method, the investor and the investee acknowledge a substantive economic relationship. The company originally records the investment at cost but subsequently adjusts the amount each period for changes in the net assets of the investee. That is, the investor's proportionate share of the earnings (losses) of the investee periodically increases (decreases) the investment's carrying amount. In contrast to the fair value method, all dividends received by the investor from the investee decrease the investment's carrying amount.

7 **Discuss the accounting for impairments of debt investments.** Companies use the impairment test to determine whether it is probable that the investor will be unable to collect all amounts due according to the contractual terms. This impairment loss is reported in income, calculated as the difference between the carrying amount plus accrued interest and the expected future cash flows discounted at the investment's historical effective-interest rate.

8 **Describe the accounting for transfer of investments between categories.** Transfers of securities between categories of investments occur when a company changes it business model for managing the investments. The transfers are accounted for prospectively, at the beginning of the period following the business model change.

APPENDIX **17A**	ACCOUNTING FOR DERIVATIVE INSTRUMENTS

LEARNING OBJECTIVE

Explain who uses derivatives and why.

Until the early 1970s, most financial managers worked in a cozy, if unthrilling, world. Since then, constant change caused by volatile markets, new technology, and deregulation has increased the risks to businesses. In response, the financial community developed products to manage these risks.

These products—called **derivative financial instruments** or simply **derivatives**—are useful for managing risk. Companies use the fair values or cash flows of these instruments to offset the changes in fair values or cash flows of the at-risk assets. The development of powerful computing and communication technology has aided the growth in derivative use. This technology provides new ways to analyze information about markets as well as the power to process high volumes of payments.

DEFINING DERIVATIVES

In order to understand derivatives, consider the following examples.

Example 1—Forward Contract. Assume that a company like Lenovo (CHN) believes that the price of Yahoo!'s (USA) shares will increase substantially in the next three months. Unfortunately, it does not have the cash resources to purchase the shares today. Lenovo therefore enters into a contract with a broker for delivery of 1,000,000 Yahoo! shares in three months at the price of $37 per share.

Lenovo has entered into a **forward contract**, a type of derivative. As a result of the contract, Lenovo **has received the right** to receive 1,000,000 Yahoo! shares in three months. Further, it **has an obligation** to pay $37 per share at that time. What is the benefit of this derivative contract? Lenovo can buy Yahoo! shares today and take delivery in three months. If the price goes up, as it expects, Lenovo profits. If the price goes down, Lenovo loses.

Example 2—Option Contract. Now suppose that Lenovo needs two weeks to decide whether to purchase Yahoo! shares. It therefore enters into a different type of contract, one that gives it the right to purchase Yahoo! shares at its current price any time within the next two weeks. As part of the contract, the broker charges $30,000 for holding the contract open for two weeks at a set price.

Lenovo has now entered into an option contract, another type of derivative. As a result of this contract, **it has received the right**, **but not the obligation**, to purchase these shares. If the price of the Yahoo! shares increases in the next two weeks, Lenovo exercises its option. In this case, the cost of the shares is the price of the shares stated in the contract, plus the cost of the option contract. If the price does not increase, Lenovo does not exercise the contract but still incurs the cost for the option.

The forward contract and the option contract both involve a future delivery of shares. The value of the contract relies on the underlying asset—the Yahoo! shares. Thus, these financial instruments are known as derivatives because they **derive their value from** values of other assets (e.g., ordinary shares, bonds, or commodities). Or, put another way, their value relates to a market-determined indicator (e.g., share price, interest rates, or the London Stock Exchange composite index).

In this appendix, we discuss the accounting for three different types of derivatives:

1. Financial forwards or financial futures.
2. Options.
3. Swaps.

WHO USES DERIVATIVES, AND WHY?

Whether to protect for changes in interest rates, the weather, share prices, oil prices, or foreign currencies, derivative contracts help to smooth the fluctuations caused by various types of risks. A company that wants to ensure against certain types of business risks often uses derivative contracts to achieve this objective.[13]

Producers and Consumers

To illustrate, assume that Heartland Ag is a large producer of potatoes for the consumer market. The present price for potatoes is excellent. Unfortunately, Heartland needs two months to harvest its potatoes and deliver them to the market. Because Heartland expects the price of potatoes to drop in the coming months, it signs a forward contract. It agrees to sell its potatoes today at the current market price for delivery in two months. Who would buy this contract? Suppose on the other side of the contract is **McDonald's Corporation** (USA). McDonald's wants to have potatoes (for French fries) in two months and believes that prices will increase. McDonald's is therefore agreeable to accepting delivery in two months at current prices. It knows that it will need potatoes in two months and that it can make an acceptable profit at this price level.

In this situation, if the price of potatoes increases before delivery, Heartland loses and McDonald's wins. Conversely, if the price decreases, Heartland wins and McDonald's loses. However, the objective is not to gamble on the outcome. Regardless of which way the price moves, both Heartland and McDonald's have received a price at which they obtain an acceptable profit. In this case, although Heartland is a **producer** and McDonald's is a **consumer**, both companies are **hedgers**. They both **hedge their positions** to ensure an acceptable financial result.

---

[13]Derivatives are traded on many exchanges throughout the world. In addition, many derivative contracts (primarily interest rate swaps) are privately negotiated.

Commodity prices are volatile. They depend on weather, crop production, and general economic conditions. For the producer and the consumer to plan effectively, it makes good sense to lock in specific future revenues or costs in order to run their businesses successfully.

Speculators and Arbitrageurs

In some cases, instead of McDonald's taking a position in the forward contract, a speculator may purchase the contract from Heartland. The speculator bets that the price of potatoes will rise, thereby increasing the value of the forward contract. The speculator, who may be in the market for only a few hours, will then sell the forward contract to another speculator or to a company like McDonald's.

Arbitrageurs also use derivatives. These market players attempt to exploit inefficiencies in markets. They seek to lock in profits by simultaneously entering into transactions in two or more markets. For example, an arbitrageur might trade in a futures contract. At the same time, the arbitrageur will also trade in the commodity underlying the futures contract, hoping to achieve small price gains on the difference between the two. Markets rely on speculators and arbitrageurs to keep the market liquid on a daily basis.

In these illustrations, we explained why Heartland (the producer) and McDonald's (the consumer) would become involved in a derivative contract. Consider other types of situations that companies face.

1. Airlines, like **Japan Airlines** (JPN), **British Airways** (GBR), and **Delta** (USA), are affected by changes in the price of jet fuel.
2. Financial institutions, such as **Barclays** (GBR), **Deutsche Bank** (DEU), and **ING** (NLD), are involved in borrowing and lending funds that are affected by changes in interest rates.
3. Multinational corporations, like **Nokia** (FIN), **Coca-Cola** (USA), and **Siemens** (DEU), are subject to changes in foreign exchange rates.

In fact, most corporations are involved in some form of derivatives transactions. Companies give these reasons (in their annual reports) as to why they use derivatives:

1. **ExxonMobil** (USA) uses derivatives to hedge its exposure to fluctuations in interest rates, foreign currency exchange rates, and hydrocarbon prices.
2. **HSBC** (GBR) uses derivatives to manage foreign currency exchange rates and interest rates.
3. **GlaxoSmithKline** (GBR) uses derivatives to manage the impact of interest rate and foreign exchange rate changes on earnings and cash flows.

Many corporations use derivatives extensively and successfully. However, derivatives can be dangerous. All parties involved must understand the risks and rewards associated with these contracts.[14]

---

[14]There are some well-publicized examples of companies that have suffered considerable losses using derivatives. For example, companies such as **Fannie Mae** (USA), **Enron** (USA), **Showa Shell Sekiyu** (JPN), **Metallgesellschaft** (DEU), **Procter & Gamble** (USA), and **Air Products & Chemicals** (USA) incurred significant losses from investments in derivative instruments.

BASIC PRINCIPLES IN ACCOUNTING FOR DERIVATIVES

The IASB concluded that derivatives such as forwards and options are assets and liabilities. It also concluded that companies should report them in the statement of financial position **at fair value**.[15] The Board believes that fair value will provide statement users the best information about derivatives. Relying on some other basis of valuation for derivatives, such as historical cost, does not make sense. Why? Because many derivatives have a historical cost of zero. Furthermore, the markets for derivatives, and the assets upon which derivatives' values rely, are well developed. As a result, the Board believes that companies can determine reliable fair value amounts for derivatives.[16]

> **10 LEARNING OBJECTIVE**
> Understand the basic guidelines for accounting for derivatives.

On the income statement, a company should recognize any unrealized gain or loss in income if it uses the derivative for speculation purposes. If using the derivative for hedging purposes, the accounting for any gain or loss depends on the type of hedge used. We discuss the accounting for hedged transactions later in the appendix.

In summary, companies follow these guidelines in accounting for derivatives.

1. Recognize derivatives in the financial statements as assets and liabilities.

2. Report derivatives at fair value.

3. Recognize gains and losses resulting from speculation in derivatives immediately in income.

4. Report gains and losses resulting from hedge transactions differently, depending on the type of hedge.

Derivative Financial Instrument (Speculation)

To illustrate the measurement and reporting of a derivative for speculative purposes, we examine a derivative whose value depends on the market price of Laredo Inc. ordinary shares. A company can realize a gain from the increase in the value of the Laredo shares with the use of a derivative, such as a call option.[17] A **call option** gives the holder the right, but not the obligation, to buy shares at a preset price. This price is often referred to as the **strike price** or the **exercise price**.

> **11 LEARNING OBJECTIVE**
> Describe the accounting for derivative financial instruments.

For example, assume a company enters into a call option contract with Baird Investment Co., which gives it the option to purchase Laredo shares at €100 per share.[18] If the

---

[15]IFRS covers accounting and reporting for all derivative instruments, whether financial or not. In this appendix, we focus on derivative financial instruments because of their widespread use in practice. **[21]**

[16]As discussed in earlier chapters, fair value is defined as "the amount for which an asset could be exchanged or a liability settled between knowledgeable, willing parties in an arm's length transaction." Fair value is therefore a market-based measure. The IASB has also developed a fair value hierarchy, which indicates the reporting of valuation techniques to use to determine fair value. *Level 1* fair value measures are based on observable inputs that reflect quoted prices for identical assets or liabilities in active markets. *Level 2* measures are based on inputs other than quoted prices included in Level 1 but that can be corroborated with observable data. *Level 3* fair values are based on unobservable inputs (e.g., a company's own data or assumptions). Thus, Level 1 is the most reliable because it is based on quoted prices, like a closing share price in the *Financial Times*. Level 2 is the next most reliable and would rely on evaluating similar assets or liabilities in active markets. For Level 3 (the least reliable), much judgment is needed, based on the best information available, to arrive at a relevant and reliable fair value measurement. **[22]**

[17]Investors can use a different type of option contract—a **put option**—to realize a gain if anticipating a decline in the value of Laredo shares. A put option gives the holder the option to sell shares at a preset price. Thus, a put option **increases** in value when the underlying asset **decreases** in value.

[18]Baird Investment Co. is referred to as the **counterparty**. Counterparties frequently are investment bankers or other companies that hold inventories of financial instruments.

price of Laredo shares increases above €100, the company can exercise this option and purchase the shares for €100 per share. If Laredo's shares never increase above €100 per share, the call option is worthless.

Accounting Entries. To illustrate the accounting for a call option, assume that the company purchases a call option contract on January 2, 2015, when Laredo shares are trading at €100 per share. The contract gives it the option to purchase 1,000 shares (referred to as the **notional amount**) of Laredo shares at an option price of €100 per share. The option expires on April 30, 2015. The company purchases the call option for €400 and makes the following entry.

January 2, 2015

Call Option	400	
Cash		400

This payment is referred to as the **option premium**. It is generally much less than the cost of purchasing the shares directly. The option premium consists of two amounts: (1) intrinsic value and (2) time value. Illustration 17A-1 shows the formula to compute the option premium.

ILLUSTRATION 17A-1
Option Premium
Formula

Option Premium = Intrinsic Value + Time Value

Intrinsic value is the difference between the market price and the preset strike price at any point in time. It represents the amount realized by the option holder, if exercising the option immediately. On January 2, 2015, the intrinsic value is zero because the market price equals the preset strike price.

Time value refers to the option's value over and above its intrinsic value. Time value reflects the possibility that the option has a fair value greater than zero. How? Because there is some expectation that the price of Laredo shares will increase above the strike price during the option term. As indicated, the time value for the option is €400.[19]

The following additional data are available with respect to the call option.

Date	Market Price of Laredo Shares	Time Value of Call Option
March 31, 2015	€120 per share	€100
April 16, 2015	€115 per share	€60

As indicated, on March 31, 2015, the price of Laredo shares increases to €120 per share. The intrinsic value of the call option contract is now €20,000. That is, the company can exercise the call option and purchase 1,000 shares from Baird Investment for €100 per share. It can then sell the shares in the market for €120 per share. This gives the company a gain of €20,000 (€120,000 − €100,000) on the option contract.[20] It records the increase in the intrinsic value of the option as follows.

March 31, 2015

Call Option	20,000	
Unrealized Holding Gain or Loss—Income		20,000

---

[19]This cost is estimated using option-pricing models, such as that based on the Black-Scholes equation. The volatility of the underlying shares, the expected life of the option, the risk-free rate of interest, and expected dividends on the underlying shares during the option term affect the Black-Scholes fair value estimate.

[20]In practice, investors generally do not have to actually buy and sell the Laredo shares to settle the option and realize the gain. This is referred to as the **net settlement** feature of option contracts.

A market appraisal indicates that the time value of the option at March 31, 2015, is €100.[21] The company records this change in value of the option as follows.

March 31, 2015

Unrealized Holding Gain or Loss—Income	300	
Call Option (€400 − €100)		300

At March 31, 2015, the company reports the call option in its statement of financial position at fair value of €20,100.[22] The unrealized holding gain increases net income for the period. The loss on the time value of the option decreases net income.

On April 16, 2015, the company settles the option before it expires. To properly record the settlement, it updates the value of the option for the decrease in the intrinsic value of €5,000 ([€20 − €15]) × 1,000) as follows.

April 16, 2015

Unrealized Holding Gain or Loss—Income	5,000	
Call Option		5,000

The decrease in the time value of the option of €40 (€100 − €60) is recorded as follows.

April 16, 2015

Unrealized Holding Gain or Loss—Income	40	
Call Option		40

Thus, at the time of the settlement, the call option's carrying value is as follows.

Call Option

January 2, 2015	400	March 31, 2015	300
March 31, 2015	20,000	April 16, 2015	5,000
		April 16, 2015	40
Balance, April 16, 2015	15,060		

The company records the settlement of the option contract with Baird as follows.

April 16, 2015

Cash	15,000	
Loss on Settlement of Call Option	60	
Call Option		15,060

Illustration 17A-2 summarizes the effects of the call option contract on net income.

Date	Transaction	Income (Loss) Effect
March 31, 2015	Net increase in value of call option (€20,000 − €300)	€19,700
April 16, 2015	Decrease in value of call option (€5,000 + €40)	(5,040)
April 16, 2015	Settle call option	(60)
	Total net income	€14,600

ILLUSTRATION 17A-2
Effect on Income—
Derivative Financial
Instrument

The accounting summarized in Illustration 17A-2 is in accord with IFRS. That is, because the call option meets the definition of an asset, the company records it in the statement of financial position on March 31, 2015. Furthermore, it reports the call option at fair value, with any gains or losses reported in income.

---

[21]The decline in value reflects both the decreased likelihood that the Laredo shares will continue to increase in value over the option period and the shorter time to maturity of the option contract.

[22]As indicated earlier, the total value of the option at any point in time equals the intrinsic value plus the time value.

Differences between Traditional and Derivative Financial Instruments

How does a traditional financial instrument differ from a derivative one? A derivative financial instrument has the following three basic characteristics. **[23]**

1. *The instrument has (1) one or more underlyings and (2) an identified payment provision.* An underlying is a specified interest rate, security price, commodity price, index of prices or rates, or other market-related variable. The interaction of the underlying, with the face amount or the number of units specified in the derivative contract (the notional amounts), determines payment. For example, the value of the call option increased in value when the value of the Laredo shares increased. In this case, the underlying is the share price. To arrive at the payment provision, multiply the change in the share price by the number of shares (notional amount).

2. *The instrument requires little or no investment at the inception of the contract.* To illustrate, the company paid a small premium to purchase the call option—an amount much less than if purchasing the Laredo shares as a direct investment.

3. *The instrument requires or permits net settlement.* As indicated in the call option example, the company could realize a profit on the call option without taking possession of the shares. This **net settlement** feature reduces the transaction costs associated with derivatives.

Illustration 17A-3 summarizes the differences between traditional and derivative financial instruments. Here, we use an equity investment (trading) for the traditional financial instrument and a call option as an example of a derivative one.

ILLUSTRATION 17A-3
Features of Traditional and Derivative Financial Instruments

Feature	Traditional Financial Instrument Equity Investment (Trading)	Derivative Financial Instrument (Call Option)
Payment provision	Share price times the number of shares.	Change in share price (underlying) times number of shares (notional amount).
Initial investment	Investor pays full cost.	Initial investment is much less than full cost.
Settlement	Deliver shares to receive cash.	Receive cash equivalent, based on changes in share price times the number of shares.

DERIVATIVES USED FOR HEDGING

Flexibility in use, and the low-cost features of derivatives relative to traditional financial instruments, explain the popularity of derivatives. An additional use for derivatives is in risk management. For example, companies such as **Coca-Cola** (USA), **BP** (GBR), and **Siemens** (DEU) borrow and lend substantial amounts in credit markets. In doing so, they are exposed to significant **interest rate risk**. That is, they face substantial risk that the fair values or cash flows of interest-sensitive assets or liabilities will change if interest rates increase or decrease. These same companies also have significant international operations. As such, they are also exposed to **exchange rate risk**—the risk that changes in foreign currency exchange rates will negatively impact the profitability of their international businesses.

Companies can use derivatives to offset the negative impacts of changes in interest rates or foreign currency exchange rates. This use of derivatives is referred to as hedging.

The IASB established accounting and reporting standards for derivative financial instruments used in hedging activities. IFRS allows special accounting for two types of hedges—fair value and cash flow hedges.[23]

What do the numbers mean?   RISKY BUSINESS

In 2008, nearly *$500 trillion* (in notional amounts) in derivative contracts were in play. As shown in the graph below, use of derivatives has grown but declined slightly in recent years. The primary players in the market for derivatives are large companies and various financial institutions, which continue to find new uses for derivatives for speculation and risk management.

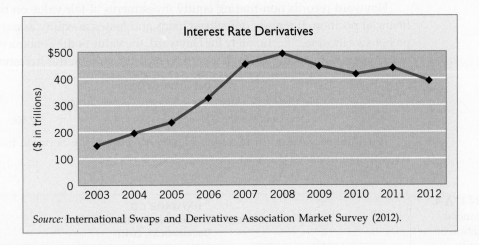

Source: International Swaps and Derivatives Association Market Survey (2012).

Financial engineers continue to develop new uses for derivatives, many times through the use of increasingly complex webs of transactions, spanning a number of markets. As new uses for derivatives appear, the financial system as a whole can be dramatically affected. As a result, some market-watchers are concerned about the risk that a crisis in one company or sector could bring the entire financial system to its knees.

This was the case recently when credit default swaps were used to facilitate the sales of mortgage-backed securities (MBS).

However, when the real estate market went south, the MBS defaulted, exposing large international financial institutions, like **Barclays** (GBR), **AIG** (USA), and **Bank of America** (USA), to massive losses. The losses were so widespread that government bailouts were required to prevent international securities markets from collapsing. In response, market regulators are proposing new rules to mitigate risks to broader markets from derivatives trading.

Source: P. Eavis, "Bill on Derivatives Overhaul Is Long Overdue," *Wall Street Journal* (April 14, 2010).

Fair Value Hedge

In a **fair value hedge**, a company uses a derivative to hedge (offset) the exposure to changes in the fair value of a recognized asset or liability or of an unrecognized commitment. In a perfectly hedged position, the gain or loss on the fair value of the derivative equals and offsets that of the hedged asset or liability.

12 LEARNING OBJECTIVE

Explain how to account for a fair value hedge.

---

[23]IFRS also addresses the accounting for certain foreign currency hedging transactions. In general, these transactions are special cases of the two hedges we discuss here. **[24]** Understanding of foreign currency hedging transactions requires knowledge related to consolidation of multinational entities, which is beyond the scope of this textbook.

Companies commonly use several types of fair value hedges. For example, companies use interest rate swaps to hedge the risk that changes in interest rates will impact the fair value of debt obligations. Or, they use put options to hedge the risk that an equity investment will decline in value.

To illustrate a fair value hedge, assume that on April 1, 2015, Hayward Co. purchases 100 ordinary shares of Sonoma Company at a market price of €100 per share. Due to a legal requirement, Hayward does not intend to actively trade this investment. It consequently classifies the Sonoma investment as a non-trading equity investment. Hayward records this investment as follows.

April 1, 2015

Equity Investments	10,000	
Cash		10,000

Hayward records non-trading equity investments at fair value on the statement of financial position. It reports unrealized gains and losses in equity as part of other comprehensive income.[24] Fortunately for Hayward, the value of the Sonoma shares increases to €125 per share during 2015. Hayward records the gain on this investment as follows.

December 31, 2015

Fair Value Adjustment	2,500	
Unrealized Holding Gain or Loss—Equity		2,500

Illustration 17A-4 indicates how Hayward reports the Sonoma investment in its statement of financial position.

ILLUSTRATION 17A-4
Statement of Financial Position Presentation of Non-Trading Equity Investment

HAYWARD CO.
STATEMENT OF FINANCIAL POSITION (PARTIAL)
DECEMBER 31, 2015

Assets	
Equity investment	€12,500
Equity	
Accumulated other comprehensive income	
Unrealized holding gain	€2,500

While Hayward benefits from an increase in the price of Sonoma shares, it is exposed to the risk that the price of the Sonoma shares will decline. To hedge this risk, Hayward locks in its gain on the Sonoma investment by purchasing a put option on 100 Sonoma shares.

Hayward enters into the put option contract on January 2, 2016, and designates the option as a fair value hedge of the Sonoma investment. This put option (which expires in two years) gives Hayward the option to sell Sonoma shares at a price of €125. Since the exercise price equals the current market price, no entry is necessary at inception of the put option.[25]

January 2, 2016

No entry required. A memorandum entry indicates the signing of the put option contract and its designation as a fair value hedge for the Sonoma investment.

At December 31, 2016, the price of the Sonoma shares has declined to €120 per share. Hayward records the following entry for the Sonoma investment.

---

[24]We discussed the distinction between trading and non-trading equity investments in the chapter.

[25]To simplify the example, we assume no premium is paid for the option.

December 31, 2016

Unrealized Holding Gain or Loss—Equity	500	
Fair Value Adjustment		500

The following journal entry records the increase in value of the put option on Sonoma shares.

December 31, 2016

Put Option	500	
Unrealized Holding Gain or Loss—Equity		500

The decline in the price of Sonoma shares results in an increase in the fair value of the put option. That is, Hayward could realize a gain on the put option by purchasing 100 shares in the open market for €120 and then exercise the put option, selling the shares for €125. This results in a gain to Hayward of €500 (100 shares × [€125 − €120]).[26]

Note that upon designation of the hedge, the accounting for the put option changes from regular IFRS. That is, Hayward records the unrealized holding loss in equity, not in income. If Hayward had not followed this accounting, a mismatch of gains and losses in the income statement would result. Thus, special accounting for the hedging instrument (in this case, a put option) is necessary in a fair value hedge. **[25]**

Illustration 17A-5 indicates how Hayward reports the amounts related to the Sonoma investment and the put option.

HAYWARD CO.
STATEMENT OF FINANCIAL POSITION (PARTIAL)
DECEMBER 31, 2016

Assets	
Equity investment (non-trading)	€12,000
Put option	500

ILLUSTRATION 17A-5
Statement of Financial Position Presentation of Fair Value Hedge

The increase in fair value on the option offsets or hedges the decline in value on Hayward's non-trading investment. The financial statements reflect the underlying substance of Hayward's net exposure to the risks of holding Sonoma shares. By using fair value accounting for both these financial instruments, the statement of financial position reports the amount that Hayward would receive on the investment and the put option contract if Hayward sold and settled them, respectively.

Illustration 17A-6 illustrates the reporting of the effects of the hedging transaction on income for the year ended December 31, 2016.

HAYWARD CO.
STATEMENT OF COMPREHENSIVE INCOME (PARTIAL)
FOR THE YEAR ENDED DECEMBER 31, 2016

Other income and expense	
Unrealized holding gain—put option	€ 500
Unrealized holding loss—equity investment	(500)

ILLUSTRATION 17A-6
Income Statement Presentation of Fair Value Hedge

The statement of comprehensive income indicates that the gain on the put option offsets the loss on the equity investment.[27] The reporting for these financial instruments,

[26]In practice, Hayward generally does not have to actually buy and sell the Sonoma shares to realize this gain. Rather, unless the counterparty wants to hold Hayward shares, Hayward can "close out" the contract by having the counterparty pay it €500 in cash. This is an example of the net settlement feature of derivatives.

[27]Note that the fair value changes in the option contract will not offset **increases** in the value of the Hayward investment. Should the price of Sonoma shares increase above €125 per share, Hayward would have no incentive to exercise the put option.

even when they reflect a hedging relationship, illustrates why the IASB argued that fair value accounting provides the most relevant information about financial instruments, including derivatives.

Cash Flow Hedge

LEARNING OBJECTIVE

Explain how to account for a cash flow hedge.

Companies use cash flow hedges to hedge exposures to **cash flow risk**, which results from the variability in cash flows. The IASB allows special accounting for cash flow hedges. Generally, companies measure and report derivatives at fair value on the statement of financial position. They report gains and losses directly in net income. However, companies account for derivatives used in cash flow hedges at fair value on the statement of financial position, but they **record gains or losses in equity, as part of other comprehensive income**.

To illustrate, assume that in September 2015 Allied Can Co. anticipates purchasing 1,000 metric tons of aluminum in January 2016. Concerned that prices for aluminum will increase in the next few months, Allied wants to hedge the risk that it might pay higher prices for inventory in January 2016. As a result, Allied enters into an aluminum futures contract.

A futures contract gives the holder the right and the obligation to purchase an asset at a preset price for a specified period of time.[28] In this case, the aluminum futures contract gives Allied the right and the obligation to purchase 1,000 metric tons of aluminum for ¥1,550 per ton (amounts in thousands). This contract price is good until the contract expires in January 2016. The underlying for this derivative is the price of aluminum. If the price of aluminum rises above ¥1,550, the value of the futures contract to Allied increases. Why? Because Allied will be able to purchase the aluminum at the lower price of ¥1,550 per ton.[29]

Allied enters into the futures contract on September 1, 2015. Assume that the price to be paid today for inventory to be delivered in January—the spot price—equals the contract price. With the two prices equal, the futures contract has no value. Therefore, no entry is necessary.

September 1, 2015

No entry required. A memorandum entry indicates
the signing of the futures contract.

At December 31, 2015, the price for January delivery of aluminum increases to ¥1,575 per metric ton. Allied makes the following entry to record the increase in the value of the futures contract.

December 31, 2015

Futures Contract	25,000	
Unrealized Holding Gain or Loss—Equity		
([¥1,575 − ¥1,550] × 1,000 tons)		25,000

Allied reports the futures contract in the statement of financial position as a current asset. It reports the gain on the futures contract as part of other comprehensive income.

Since Allied has not yet purchased and sold the inventory, this gain arises from an anticipated transaction. In this type of transaction, a company accumulates in equity gains or losses on the futures contract as part of other comprehensive income until the period in which it sells the inventory, thereby affecting earnings.

---

[28]A **futures contract** is a firm contractual agreement between a buyer and seller for a specified asset on a fixed date in the future. The contract also has a standard specification so both parties know exactly what is being traded. A **forward** is similar but is not traded on an exchange and does not have standardized conditions.

[29]As with the earlier call option example, the actual aluminum does not have to be exchanged. Rather, the parties to the futures contract settle by paying the cash difference between the futures price and the price of aluminum on each settlement date.

In January 2016, Allied purchases 1,000 metric tons of aluminum for ¥1,575 and makes the following entry.[30]

January 2016

Aluminum Inventory	1,575,000	
Cash (¥1,575 × 1,000 tons)		1,575,000

At the same time, Allied makes final settlement on the futures contract. It records the following entry.

January 2016

Cash	25,000	
Futures Contract (¥1,575,000 − ¥1,550,000)		25,000

Through use of the futures contract derivative, Allied fixes the cost of its inventory. The ¥25,000 futures contract settlement offsets the amount paid to purchase the inventory at the prevailing market price of ¥1,575,000. The result: net cash outflow of ¥1,550 per metric ton, as desired. As Illustration 17A-7 shows, Allied has therefore effectively hedged the cash flow for the purchase of inventory.

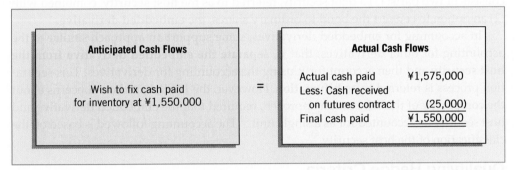

ILLUSTRATION 17A-7
Effect of Hedge on Cash Flows

There are no income effects at this point. Allied accumulates in equity the gain on the futures contract as part of other comprehensive income until the period when it sells the inventory, affecting earnings through cost of goods sold.

For example, assume that Allied processes the aluminum into finished goods (cans). The total cost of the cans (including the aluminum purchases in January 2016) is ¥1,700,000. Allied sells the cans in July 2016 for ¥2,000,000, and records this sale as follows.

July 2016

Cash	2,000,000	
Sales Revenue		2,000,000
Cost of Goods Sold	1,700,000	
Inventory (cans)		1,700,000

Since the effect of the anticipated transaction has now affected earnings, Allied makes the following entry related to the hedging transaction.

July 2016

Unrealized Holding Gain or Loss—Equity	25,000	
Cost of Goods Sold		25,000

The gain on the futures contract, which Allied reported as part of other comprehensive income, now reduces cost of goods sold. As a result, the cost of aluminum included in the overall cost of goods sold is ¥1,550,000. The futures contract has worked as planned. Allied has managed the cash paid for aluminum inventory and the amount of cost of goods sold.[31]

---

[30]In practice, futures contracts are settled on a daily basis. For our purposes, we show only one settlement for the entire amount.

[31]Recently, the IASB published an amendment to *IFRS 9* related to hedging. The main changes relate to determining when a hedge occurs and the eligibility of items as hedged items and hedging instruments. A key change allows components of non-financial items to be hedged as long as these components are separately identifiable and reliably measurable.

OTHER REPORTING ISSUES

The preceding examples illustrate the basic reporting issues related to the accounting for derivatives. Next, we discuss the following additional issues:

1. The accounting for embedded derivatives.

2. Qualifying hedge criteria.

Embedded Derivatives

As we indicated at the beginning of this appendix, rapid innovation in the development of complex financial instruments drove efforts toward unifying and improving the accounting standards for derivatives. In recent years, this innovation has led to the development of **hybrid securities**. These securities have characteristics of both debt and equity. They often combine traditional and derivative financial instruments.

For example, a convertible bond (discussed in Chapter 16) is a hybrid instrument. It consists of two parts: (1) a debt security, referred to as the **host security**, combined with (2) an option to convert the bond to ordinary shares, the **embedded derivative**.

In accounting for embedded derivatives, some support an approach similar to the accounting for other derivatives; that is, **separate the embedded derivative from the host security** and then account for it using the accounting for derivatives. This separation process is referred to as **bifurcation**. However, the IASB, based on concerns about the complexity of the bifurcation approach, required that the embedded derivative and host security be accounted for as a single unit.[32] The accounting followed is based on the classification of the host security.[33]

Qualifying Hedge Criteria

The IASB identified certain criteria that hedging transactions must meet before requiring the special accounting for hedges. The IASB designed these criteria to ensure the use of hedge accounting in a consistent manner across different hedge transactions. The general criteria relate to the following areas.

1. *Documentation, risk management, and designation.* At inception of the hedge, there must be formal **documentation** of the hedging relationship, the company's **risk management** objective, and the strategy for undertaking the hedge. **Designation** refers to identifying the hedging instrument, the hedged item or transaction, the nature of the risk being hedged, and how the hedging instrument will offset changes in the fair value or cash flows attributable to the hedged risk. **[26]**

The IASB decided that documentation and designation are critical to the implementation of the special accounting for hedges. Without these requirements, companies might try to apply the hedge accounting provisions retroactively, only in response to negative changes in market conditions, to offset the negative impact of a transaction on the financial statements. Allowing special hedge accounting in such a setting could mask the speculative nature of the original transaction.

2. *Effectiveness of the hedging relationship.* At inception and on an ongoing basis, the hedging relationship should be **effective** in achieving offsetting changes in fair value or cash flows. Companies must assess effectiveness whenever preparing financial statements. **[27]**

---

[32]A company can also designate such a derivative as a hedging instrument. The company would apply the hedge accounting provisions outlined earlier in the chapter.

[33]As discussed in Chapter 16, the **issuer** of the convertible bonds would bifurcate the option component of the convertible bonds payable.

The general guideline for effectiveness is that the fair values or cash flows of the hedging instrument (the derivative) and the hedged item exhibit a high degree of correlation. In our earlier hedging examples (put option and the futures contract on aluminum inventory), the fair values and cash flows are perfectly correlated. That is, when the cash payment for the inventory purchase increased, it offset, euro for euro, the cash received on the futures contract.

If the effectiveness criterion is not met, either at inception or because of changes following inception of the hedging relationship, IFRS no longer allows special hedge accounting. The company should then account for the derivative or the part of the derivative that is not effective in the hedging relationship as a free-standing derivative.[34]

3. *Effect on reported earnings of changes in fair values or cash flows.* A change in the fair value of a hedged item or variation in the cash flow of a hedged forecasted transaction must have the potential to change the amount recognized in reported earnings. There is no need for special hedge accounting if a company accounts for both the hedging instrument and the hedged item at fair value under existing IFRS. In this case, earnings will properly reflect the offsetting gains and losses.[35]

For example, special accounting is not needed for a fair value hedge of a trading security because a company accounts for both the investment and the derivative at fair value on the statement of financial position with gains or losses reported in earnings. Thus, "special" hedge accounting is necessary only when there is a mismatch of the accounting effects for the hedging instrument and the hedged item under IFRS.[36]

Summary of Derivatives Accounting

Illustration 17A-8 summarizes the accounting provisions for derivatives and hedging transactions.

ILLUSTRATION 17A-8
Summary of Derivative Accounting under IFRS

Derivative Use	Accounting for Derivative	Accounting for Hedged Item	Common Example
Speculation	At fair value with unrealized holding gains and losses recorded in income.	Not applicable.	Call or put option on an equity security.
Hedging Fair value	At fair value with holding gains and losses recorded in income.	At fair value with gains and losses recorded in income.	Put option to hedge a non-trading equity investment.
Cash flow	At fair value with unrealized holding gains and losses from the hedge recorded in other comprehensive income, and reclassified in income when the hedged transaction's cash flows affect earnings.	Use other IFRS for the hedged item.	Use of a futures contract to hedge a forecasted purchase of inventory.

---

[34]The accounting for the part of a derivative that is not effective in a hedge is at fair value, with gains and losses recorded in income.

[35]IFRS gives companies the option to measure most types of financial instruments—from equity investments to debt issued by the company—at fair value. Changes in fair value are recognized in net income each reporting period. Thus, IFRS provides companies with the opportunity to hedge their financial instruments without the complexity inherent in applying hedge accounting provisions. **[28]**

[36]An important criterion specific to cash flow hedges is that the forecasted transaction in a cash flow hedge "is likely to occur." A company should support this probability (defined as significantly greater than the term "more likely than not") by observable facts such as frequency of similar past transactions and its financial and operational ability to carry out the transaction.

As indicated, the general accounting for derivatives relies on fair values. IFRS also establishes special accounting guidance when companies use derivatives **for hedging purposes**. For example, when a company uses a put option to hedge price changes in a non-trading equity investment in a fair value hedge (see the Hayward example earlier), it records unrealized gains on the investment in earnings, which is not IFRS for these investments without such a hedge. This special accounting is justified in order to accurately report the nature of the hedging relationship in the statement of financial position (recording both the put option and the investment at fair value) and in the statement of comprehensive income (reporting offsetting gains and losses in the same period).

Special accounting also is used for cash flow hedges. Companies account for derivatives used in qualifying cash flow hedges at fair value on the statement of financial position but record unrealized holding gains or losses in other comprehensive income until selling or settling the hedged item. In a cash flow hedge, a company continues to record the hedged item at its historical cost.

Disclosure requirements for derivatives are complex. Recent pronouncements on fair value information and financial instruments provide a helpful disclosure framework for reporting derivative instruments. In general, companies that have derivatives are required to disclose the objectives for holding or issuing those instruments (speculation or hedging), the hedging context (fair value or cash flow), and the strategies for achieving risk-management objectives.

COMPREHENSIVE HEDGE ACCOUNTING EXAMPLE

To provide a comprehensive example of hedge accounting, we examine the use of an interest rate swap. First, let's consider how swaps work and why companies use them.

Options and futures trade on organized securities exchanges. Because of this, options and futures have standardized terms. Although that standardization makes the trading easier, it limits the flexibility needed to tailor contracts to specific circumstances. In addition, most types of derivatives have relatively short time horizons, thereby excluding their use for reducing long-term risk exposure.

As a result, many corporations instead turn to the swap, a very popular type of derivative. A swap is a transaction between two parties in which the first party promises to make a payment to the second party. Similarly, the second party promises to make a simultaneous payment to the first party.

The most common type of swap is the interest rate swap. In this type, one party makes payments based on a fixed or floating rate, and the second party does just the opposite. In most cases, large money-center banks bring together the two parties. These banks handle the flow of payments between the parties, as shown in Illustration 17A-9.

ILLUSTRATION 17A-9
Swap Transaction

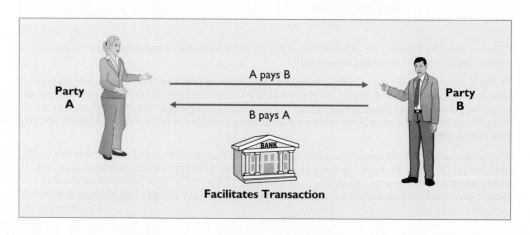

Party A — A pays B → Party B
B pays A

BANK

Facilitates Transaction

Fair Value Hedge

To illustrate the use of a swap in a fair value hedge, assume that Jones Company issues €1,000,000 of five-year, 8 percent bonds on January 2, 2015. Jones records this transaction as follows.

January 2, 2015

Cash	1,000,000	
Bonds Payable		1,000,000

Jones offered a fixed interest rate to appeal to investors. But Jones is concerned that if market interest rates decline, the fair value of the liability will increase. The company will then suffer an economic loss.[37] To protect against the risk of loss, Jones hedges the risk of a decline in interest rates by entering into a five-year interest rate swap contract. Jones agrees to the following terms:

1. Jones will receive fixed payments at 8 percent (based on the €1,000,000 amount).
2. Jones will pay variable rates, based on the market rate in effect for the life of the swap contract. The variable rate at the inception of the contract is 6.8 percent.

As Illustration 17A-10 shows, this swap allows Jones to change the interest on the bonds payable from a fixed rate to a variable rate.

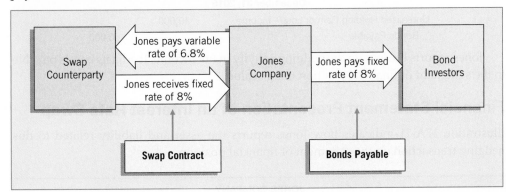

ILLUSTRATION 17A-10
Interest Rate Swap

The settlement dates for the swap correspond to the interest payment dates on the debt (December 31). On each interest payment (settlement) date, Jones and the counterparty compute the difference between current market interest rates and the fixed rate of 8 percent, and determine the value of the swap.[38] If interest rates decline, the value of the swap contract to Jones increases (Jones has a gain), while at the same time Jones's fixed-rate debt obligation increases (Jones has an economic loss).

The swap is an effective risk-management tool in this setting. Its value relates to the same underlying (interest rates) that will affect the value of the fixed-rate bond payable. Thus, if the value of the swap goes up, it offsets the loss related to the debt obligation.

Assuming that Jones enters into the swap on January 2, 2015 (the same date as the issuance of the debt), the swap at this time has no value. Therefore, no entry is necessary.

January 2, 2015

No entry required. A memorandum entry indicates the signing of the swap contract.

At the end of 2015, Jones makes the interest payment on the bonds. It records this transaction as follows.

December 31, 2015

Interest Expense	80,000	
Cash (8% × €1,000,000)		80,000

---

[37]This economic loss arises because Jones is locked into the 8 percent interest payments even if rates decline.

[38]The underlying for an interest rate swap is some index of market interest rates. The most commonly used index is the London Interbank Offer Rate, or LIBOR. In this example, we assume the LIBOR is 6.8 percent.

At the end of 2015, market interest rates have declined substantially. Therefore, the value of the swap contract increases. Recall (see Illustration 17A-9) that in the swap, Jones receives a fixed rate of 8 percent, or €80,000 (€1,000,000 × 8%), and pays a variable rate (6.8%), or €68,000. Jones therefore receives €12,000 (€80,000 − €68,000) as a settlement payment on the swap contract on the first interest payment date. Jones records this transaction as follows.

December 31, 2015

Cash	12,000	
Interest Expense		12,000

In addition, a market appraisal indicates that the value of the interest rate swap has increased €40,000. Jones records this increase in value as follows.[39]

December 31, 2015

Swap Contract	40,000	
Unrealized Holding Gain or Loss—Income		40,000

Jones reports this swap contract in the statement of financial position. It reports the gain on the hedging transaction in the income statement. Because interest rates have declined, the company records a loss and a related increase in its liability as follows.

December 31, 2015

Unrealized Holding Gain or Loss—Income	40,000	
Bonds Payable		40,000

Jones reports the loss on the hedging activity in net income. It adjusts bonds payable in the statement of financial position to fair value.

Financial Statement Presentation of an Interest Rate Swap

Illustration 17A-11 indicates how Jones reports the asset and liability related to this hedging transaction on the statement of financial position.

ILLUSTRATION 17A-11
Statement of Financial Position Presentation of Fair Value Hedge

JONES COMPANY
STATEMENT OF FINANCIAL POSITION (PARTIAL)
DECEMBER 31, 2015

Current assets	
Swap contract	€40,000
Non-current liabilities	
Bonds payable	€1,040,000

The effect on Jones's statement of financial position is the addition of the swap asset and an increase in the carrying value of the bonds payable. Illustration 17A-12 indicates how Jones reports the effects of this swap transaction in the income statement.

ILLUSTRATION 17A-12
Income Statement Presentation of Fair Value Hedge

JONES COMPANY
INCOME STATEMENT (PARTIAL)
FOR THE YEAR ENDED DECEMBER 31, 2015

Interest expense (€80,000 − €12,000)		€68,000
Other income and expense		
Unrealized holding gain—swap contract	€40,000	
Unrealized holding loss—bonds payable	(40,000)	
Net gain (loss)		€–0–

[39]Theoretically, this fair value change reflects the present value of expected future differences in variable and fixed interest rates.

On the income statement, Jones reports interest expense of €68,000. Jones has effectively changed the debt's interest rate from fixed to variable. That is, by receiving a fixed rate and paying a variable rate on the swap, the company converts the fixed rate on the bond payable to variable. This results in an effective interest rate of 6.8 percent in 2015.[40] Also, the gain on the swap offsets the loss related to the debt obligation. Therefore, the net gain or loss on the hedging activity is zero.

Illustration 17A-13 shows the overall impact of the swap transaction on the financial statements.

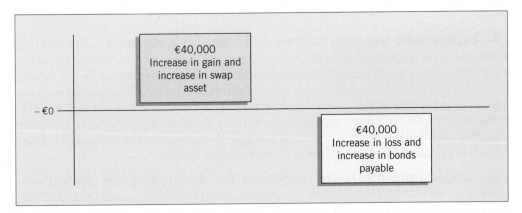

ILLUSTRATION 17A-13
Impact on Financial
Statements of Fair
Value Hedge

In summary, to account for fair value hedges (as illustrated in the Jones example) **record the derivative at its fair value in the statement of financial position, and record any gains and losses in income**. Thus, the gain on the swap offsets or hedges the loss on the bond payable, due to the decline in interest rates.

By adjusting the hedged item (the bond payable in the Jones case) to fair value, with the gain or loss recorded in earnings, the accounting for the Jones bond payable deviates from amortized cost. This special accounting is justified in order to report accurately the nature of the hedging relationship between the swap and the bond payable in the statement of financial position (both the swap and the debt obligation are recorded at fair value) and in the income statement (offsetting gains and losses are reported in the same period).[41]

CONTROVERSY AND CONCLUDING REMARKS

Companies need rules to properly measure and report derivatives in financial statements. However, some argue that reporting derivatives at fair value results in unrealized gains and losses that are difficult to interpret. Still, others raise concerns about the complexity and cost of implementing IFRS in this area.

However, we believe that the benefits of using fair value and reporting derivatives at fair value will far outweigh any implementation costs. As the volume and complexity of derivatives and hedging transactions continue to grow, so does the risk that investors and creditors will be exposed to unexpected losses arising from

---

[40]Jones will apply similar accounting and measurement at future interest payment dates. Thus, if interest rates increase, Jones will continue to receive 8 percent on the swap (records a loss) but will also be locked into the fixed payments to the bondholders at an 8 percent rate (records a gain).

[41]An interest rate swap can also be used in a cash flow hedge. A common setting is the cash flow risk inherent in having variable rate debt as part of a company's debt structure. In this situation, the variable debt issuer can hedge the cash flow risk by entering into a swap contract to receive variable rate cash flows but pay a fixed rate. The cash received on the swap contract will offset the variable cash flows to be paid on the debt obligation.

derivative transactions. Statement readers must have comprehensive information concerning many derivative financial instruments and the effects of hedging transactions using derivatives.

SUMMARY OF LEARNING OBJECTIVES FOR APPENDIX 17A

9 Explain who uses derivatives and why. Any company or individual that wants to ensure against different types of business risks may use derivative contracts to achieve this objective. In general, these transactions involve some type of hedge. Speculators also use derivatives, attempting to find an enhanced return. Speculators are very important to the derivatives market because they keep it liquid on a daily basis. Arbitrageurs attempt to exploit inefficiencies in various derivative contracts. A company primarily uses derivatives for purposes of hedging its exposure to fluctuations in interest rates, foreign currency exchange rates, and commodity prices.

10 Understand the basic guidelines for accounting for derivatives. Companies should recognize derivatives in the financial statements as assets and liabilities, and report them at fair value. Companies should recognize gains and losses resulting from speculation immediately in income. They report gains and losses resulting from hedge transactions in different ways, depending on the type of hedge.

11 Describe the accounting for derivative financial instruments. Companies report derivative financial instruments in the statement of financial position and record them at fair value. Except for derivatives used in hedging, companies record realized and unrealized gains and losses on derivative financial instruments in income.

12 Explain how to account for a fair value hedge. A company records the derivative used in a qualifying fair value hedge at its fair value in the statement of financial position, recording any gains and losses in income. In addition, the company also accounts for the item being hedged with the derivative at fair value. By adjusting the hedged item to fair value, with the gain or loss recorded in earnings, the accounting for the hedged item may deviate from IFRS in the absence of a hedge relationship. This special accounting is justified in order to report accurately the nature of the hedging relationship between the derivative hedging instruments and the hedged item. A company reports both in the statement of financial position, reporting offsetting gains and losses in income in the same period.

13 Explain how to account for a cash flow hedge. Companies account for derivatives used in qualifying cash flow hedges at fair value on the statement of financial position but record gains or losses in equity as part of other comprehensive income. Companies accumulate these gains or losses, and reclassify them in income when the hedged transaction's cash flows affect earnings. Accounting is according to IFRS for the hedged item.

14 Identify special reporting issues related to derivative financial instruments that cause unique accounting problems. A company should, based on the classification of the host security, account for a hybrid security containing a host security and an embedded derivative as a single unit. Special hedge accounting is allowed only for hedging relationships that meet certain criteria. The main criteria are as follows. (1) There is formal documentation of the hedging relationship, the company's risk management objective, and the strategy for undertaking the hedge, and the company designates the derivative as either a cash flow or fair value hedge. (2) The company expects the hedging relationship to be highly effective in achieving offsetting changes in fair value or cash flows. (3) "Special" hedge accounting is necessary only when there is a mismatch of the accounting effects for the hedging instrument and the hedged item under IFRS.

APPENDIX **17B**	FAIR VALUE DISCLOSURES

As indicated in the chapter, the IASB believes that fair value information is relevant for making effective business decisions. However, others express concern about fair value measurements for two reasons: (1) the lack of reliability related to the fair value measurements in certain cases, and (2) the ability to manipulate fair value measurements to achieve financial results inconsistent with the underlying economics of the situation.

15 **LEARNING OBJECTIVE**
Describe required fair value disclosures.

The Board recognizes these concerns and has attempted to develop a sound conceptual basis for measuring and reporting fair value information. In addition, it has placed emphasis on developing guidelines for reporting fair value information for financial instruments because many of these instruments have relatively active markets for which valuations can be reliably determined. The purpose of this appendix is to explain the disclosure requirements for financial instruments related to fair value information.

DISCLOSURE OF FAIR VALUE INFORMATION: FINANCIAL INSTRUMENTS

One requirement related to fair value disclosure is that both the cost and the fair value of all financial instruments be reported in the notes to the financial statements. This enables financial statement users to understand the fair value of the company's financial instruments and the potential gains and losses that might occur in the future as a result of these instruments.

The Board also decided that companies should disclose information that enables users to determine the extent of usage of fair value and the inputs used to implement fair value measurement. Two reasons for additional disclosure beyond the simple itemization of fair values are:

1. *Differing levels of reliability exist in the measurement of fair value information.* It therefore is important to understand the varying risks involved in measurement. It is difficult to incorporate these levels of uncertainty into the financial statements. Disclosure provides a framework for addressing the qualitative aspects related to risk and measurement.

2. *Changes in the fair value of financial instruments are reported differently in the financial statements, depending on the type of financial instrument involved and whether the fair value option is employed.* Note disclosure provides an opportunity to explain more precisely the impact that changes in the value of financial instruments have on financial results. In assessing the inputs, the Board recognizes that the reliability of the fair value measurement is of extreme importance. Many financial instruments are traded in active markets, and their valuation is not difficult. Other instruments are complex/illiquid, and their valuation is difficult.

To highlight these levels of reliability in valuation, the IASB established a fair value hierarchy. As discussed in Chapter 2 (page 41), this hierarchy identifies three broad levels—1, 2, and 3—related to the measurement of fair values. Level 1 is the most reliable measurement because fair value is based on quoted prices in active markets *for identical assets or liabilities.* Level 2 is less reliable; it is not based on quoted market prices for identical assets and liabilities but instead may be based on *similar assets or liabilities.* Level 3 is least reliable; it uses unobservable inputs that reflect the company's assumption as to the value of the financial instrument.

Illustration 17B-1 is an example of a fair value note disclosure for Sabathia Company. It includes both the fair value amounts and the reliability level. (A similar disclosure would be presented for liabilities.)

ILLUSTRATION 17B-1
Example of Fair Value Hierarchy

(amounts in thousands)		Fair Value Measurements at Reporting Data Using		
Description	Fair Value 12/31/15	Quoted Prices in Active Markets for Identical Assets (Level 1)	Significant Other Observable Inputs (Level 2)	Significant Unobservable Inputs (Level 3)
SABATHIA COMPANY				
NOTES TO THE FINANCIAL STATEMENTS				
Trading securities	$115	$105	$10	
Non-trading securities	75	75		
Derivatives	60	25	15	$20
Venture capital investments	10			10
Total	$260	$205	$25	$30

For assets and liabilities measured at fair value and classified as Level 3, a reconciliation of Level 3 changes for the period is required. In addition, companies should report an analysis of how Level 3 changes in fair value affect total gains and losses and their impact on net income. Illustration 17B-2 is an example of this disclosure.

ILLUSTRATION 17B-2
Reconciliation of Level 3 Inputs

SABATHIA COMPANY
NOTES TO THE FINANCIAL STATEMENTS

(amounts in thousands)	Fair Value Measurements Using Significant Unobservable Inputs (Level 3)		
	Derivatives	Venture Capital Investments	Total
Beginning balance	$14	$11	$25
Total gains or losses (realized/unrealized)			
Included in earnings (or changes in net assets)	11	(3)	8
Included in other comprehensive income	4		4
Purchases, issuances, and settlements	(7)	2	(5)
Transfers in and/or out of Level 3	(2)		(2)
Ending balance	$20	$10	$30
The amount of total gains or losses for the period included in earnings (or changes in net assets) attributable to the change in unrealized gains or losses relating to assets still held at the reporting date	$7	$2	$9

Gains and losses (realized and unrealized) included in earnings (or changes in net assets) for the period (above) are reported in trading revenues and in other revenues as follows.

	Trading Revenues	Other Revenues
Total gains or losses included in earnings (or changes in net assets) for the period (as shown in the table above)	$11	$(3)
Change in unrealized gains or losses relating to assets still held at reporting date	$7	$2

Sabathia Company's disclosure provides to the user of the financial statements an understanding of the following:

1. The carrying amount and the fair value of the company's financial instruments segregated by level of reliability. Thus, financial statement users have a basis for judging what credence should be given to the fair value amounts.

2. For Level 3 financial instruments, a reconciliation of the balance from the beginning to the end of the period. This reconciliation enables users to understand the composition of the change. It is important because these calculations are most affected by subjective estimates and could be subject to manipulation.

3. The impact of changes in fair value on the net assets of the company from one period to the next.

For companies that choose to use the fair value option for some or all of their financial instruments, they are permitted to incorporate the entire guidelines related to fair value measurement into one master schedule, or they can provide in a separate schedule information related solely to the fair value option.

Finally, companies must provide the following (with special emphasis on Level 3 measurements):

1. Quantitative information about significant unobservable inputs used for all Level 3 measurements.

2. A qualitative discussion about the sensitivity of recurring Level 3 measurements to changes in the unobservable inputs disclosed, including interrelationships between inputs.

3. A description of the company's valuation process.

4. Any transfers between Levels 1 and 2 of the fair value hierarchy.

5. Information about non-financial assets measured at fair value at amounts that differ from the assets' highest and best use.

6. The proper hierarchy classification for items that are not recognized on the statement of financial position but are disclosed in the notes to the financial statements.

A typical disclosure related to Level 3 fair value measurements is presented in Illustration 17B-3.

ILLUSTRATION 17B-3
Quantitative Information about Level 3 Fair Value Measurements

(amounts in millions)	Fair Value at 12/31/2015	Valuation Technique(s)	Unobservable Input	Range (Weighted-Average)
Residential mortgage-backed securities	125	Discounted cash flow	Constant prepayment rate Probability of default Loss severity	3.5%–5.5% (4.5%) 5%–50% (10%) 40%–100% (60%)
Collateralized debt obligations	35	Consensus pricing	Offered quotes Comparability adjustments (%)	20–45 −10%–+15% (+5%)
Direct venture capital investments: Healthcare	53	Discounted cash flow	Weighted-average cost of capital Long-term revenue growth rate Long-term pretax operating margin Discount for lack of marketability[a] Control premium[a]	7%–16% (12.1%) 2%–5% (4.2%) 3%–20% (10.3%) 5%–20% (17%) 10%–30% (20%)
		Market-comparable companies	EBITDA multiple[b] Revenue multiple[b] Discount for lack of marketability[a] Control premium[a]	6.5–12 (9.5) 1.0–3.0 (2.0) 5%–20% (10%) 10%–20% (12%)
Credit contracts	38	Option model	Annualized volatility of credit[c] Counterparty credit risk[d] Own credit risk[d]	10%–20% 0.5–3.5% 0.3–2.0%

[a]Represents amounts used when the reporting entity has determined that market participants would take into account these premiums and discounts when pricing the investments.
[b]Represents amounts used when the reporting entity has determined that market participants would use such multiples when pricing the investments.
[c]Represents the range of the volatility curves used in the valuation analysis that the reporting entity has determined market participants would use when pricing the contracts.
[d]Represents the range of the credit default swap spread curves used in the valuation analysis that the reporting entity has determined market participants would use when pricing the contracts.

(*Note:* For liabilities, a similar table should be presented.)

DISCLOSURE OF FAIR VALUES: IMPAIRED ASSETS OR LIABILITIES

In addition to financial instruments, companies often have assets or liabilities that are remeasured on a non-recurring basis due to impairment. In this case, the fair value hierarchy can highlight the reliability of the measurement, coupled with the related gain or loss for the period. Illustration 17B-4 highlights this disclosure for McClung Company.

ILLUSTRATION 17B-4
Disclosure of Fair Value, with Impairment

		McCLUNG COMPANY NOTES TO THE FINANCIAL STATEMENTS		
(amounts in millions)		Fair Value Measurements Using:		
Description	Year Ended 12/31/15	Quoted Prices in Active Markets for Identical Assets (Level 1)	Significant Other Observable Inputs (Level 2)	Significant Unobservable Inputs (Level 3)
Long-lived assets held and used	$75	—	$75	—
Goodwill	30	—	—	$30
Long-lived assets held for sale	26	—	26	—

Long-lived assets held and used with a carrying amount of $100 million were written down to their fair value of $75 million, resulting in an impairment charge of $25 million, which was included in earnings for the period.

Goodwill with a carrying amount of $65 million was written down to its fair value of $30 million, resulting in an impairment charge of $35 million, which was included in earnings for the period.

Long-lived assets held for sale with a carrying amount of $35 million were written down to their fair value of $26 million, less cost to sell of $6 million (or $20 million), resulting in a loss of $15 million, which was included in earnings for the period.

CONCLUSION

With recent joint IASB and FASB standard-setting efforts, we now have convergence with respect to fair value measurement, both in terms of the definition and measurement guidelines when fair value is the measurement approach in IFRS and U.S. GAAP. In addition, IFRS and U.S. GAAP have the same fair value disclosure requirements, as illustrated in this appendix. As the former chair of the IASB noted, this "marks the completion of a major convergence project and is a fundamentally important element of our joint response to the global crisis. The result is clearer and more consistent guidance on measuring fair value, where its use is already required."

SUMMARY OF LEARNING OBJECTIVE FOR APPENDIX 17B

15 **Describe required fair value disclosures.** The IASB has developed required fair value disclosures in response to concerns about the reliability of fair value measures. Disclosure elements include fair value amounts and reliability levels as well as impaired assets and liabilities.

IFRS AUTHORITATIVE LITERATURE

Authoritative Literature References

[1] International Accounting Standard 32, *Financial Instruments: Presentation* (London, U.K.: IASB Foundation, 2003), par. 11.

[2] International Financial Reporting Standard 9, *Financial Instruments* (London, U.K.: IFRS Foundation, 2009), par. 4.1.

[3] International Financial Reporting Standard 9, *Financial Instruments* (London, U.K.: IFRS Foundation, 2010), paras. 4.19–4.21.

[4] International Financial Reporting Standard 9, *Financial Instruments* (London, U.K.: IFRS Foundation, 2011), par. 9.

[5] International Financial Reporting Standard 9, *Financial Instruments* (London, U.K.: IFRS Foundation, 2010), par. BC4.19.

[6] International Financial Reporting Standard 9, *Financial Instruments* (London, U.K.: IFRS Foundation, 2010), par. BC4.21.

[7] International Financial Reporting Standard 9, *Financial Instruments* (London, U.K.: IFRS Foundation, 2009), par. 4.1.5.

[8] International Financial Reporting Standard 9, *Financial Instruments* (London, U.K.: IFRS Foundation, 2009), par. 4.5.

[9] International Financial Reporting Standard 9, *Financial Instruments* (London, U.K.: IFRS Foundation, 2009), par. B5.1.1.

[10] International Financial Reporting Standard 9, *Financial Instruments* (London, U.K.: IFRS Foundation, 2010), par. B5.4.14.

[11] International Financial Reporting Standard 9, *Financial Instruments* (London, U.K.: IFRS Foundation, 2010), par. 5.7.1.

[12] International Financial Reporting Standard 9, *Financial Instruments* (London, U.K.: IFRS Foundation, 2010), par. BC5.25(d).

[13] International Financial Reporting Standard 9, *Financial Instruments* (London, U.K.: IFRS Foundation, 2010), paras. BC5.25(b) and BC5.26.

[14] International Financial Reporting Standard 9, *Financial Instruments* (London, U.K.: IFRS Foundation, 2010), par. BC5.23.

[15] International Accounting Standard 28, *Investments in Associates* (London, U.K.: IASB Foundation, 2003).

[16] International Accounting Standard 28, *Investments in Associates* (London, U.K.: IASB Foundation, 2003), paras. 6–9.

[17] International Accounting Standard 28, *Investments in Associates* (London, U.K.: IASB Foundation, 2003), paras. 29–30.

[18] International Accounting Standard 39, *Financial Instruments: Recognition and Measurement* (London, U.K.: IASB Foundation, London (March 1999), paras. 58–65 and AG84–AG93.

[19] International Financial Reporting Standard 9, *Financial Instruments* (London, U.K.: IFRS Foundation, 2010), paras. BC4.116–BC4.117.

[20] International Financial Reporting Standard 9, *Financial Instruments* (London, U.K.: IFRS Foundation, 2010), par. BC4.118.

[21] International Financial Reporting Standard 9, *Financial Instruments*, "Chapter 6: Hedge Accounting" (London, U.K.: IFRS Foundation, 2013).

[22] International Financial Reporting Standard 13, *Fair Value Measurements* (London, U.K.: IFRS Foundation, 2011), paras. 72–90.

[23] International Financial Reporting Standard 9, *Financial Instruments*, "Appendix A" (London, U.K.: IFRS Foundation, 2010).

[24] International Financial Reporting Standard 9, *Financial Instruments* (London, U.K.: IFRS Foundation, 2013), paras. 6.5.13–6.5.16.

[25] International Financial Reporting Standard 9, *Financial Instruments* (London, U.K.: IFRS Foundation, 2013), paras. 6.5.8–6.5.9.

[26] International Financial Reporting Standard 9, *Financial Instruments* (London, U.K.: IFRS Foundation, 2013), par. 6.4.

[27] International Financial Reporting Standard 9, *Financial Instruments* (London, U.K.: IFRS Foundation, 2013), par. 6.4.16c.

[28] International Financial Reporting Standard 9, *Financial Instruments* (London, U.K.: IFRS Foundation, 2009), paras. 4.1.5 and 4.2,2.

Note: All asterisked Questions, Exercises, and Problems relate to material in the appendices to the chapter.

QUESTIONS

1. Describe the two criteria for determining the valuation of financial assets.

2. Which types of investments are valued at amortized cost? Explain the rationale for this accounting.

3. What is amortized cost? What is fair value?

4. Lady Gaga Co. recently made an investment in the bonds issued by Chili Peppers Inc. Lady Gaga's business model for this investment is to profit from trading in response to changes in market interest rates. How should this investment be classified by Lady Gaga? Explain.

5. Consider the bond investment by Lady Gaga in Question 4. Discuss the accounting for this investment if Lady Gaga's business model is to hold the investment to collect interest while outstanding and to receive the principal at maturity.

6. On July 1, 2015, Wheeler Company purchased €4,000,000 of Duggen Company's 8% bonds, due on July 1, 2022. The bonds, which pay interest semiannually on January 1 and July 1, were purchased for €3,500,000 to yield 10%. Determine the amount of interest revenue Wheeler should report on its income statement for year ended December 31, 2015, assuming Wheeler plans to hold this investment to collect contractual cash flows.

7. If the bonds in Question 6 are classified as trading and they have a fair value at December 31, 2015, of €3,604,000, prepare the journal entry (if any) at December 31, 2015, to record this transaction.

8. Indicate how unrealized holding gains and losses should be reported for investments classified as trading and held-for-collection.

9. (a) Assuming no Fair Value Adjustment account balance at the beginning of the year, prepare the adjusting entry at the end of the year if Laura Company's trading bond investment has a fair value €60,000 below carrying value.
(b) Assume the same information as part (a), except that Laura Company has a debit balance in its Fair Value Adjustment account of €10,000 at the beginning of the year. Prepare the adjusting entry at year-end.

10. What is the fair value option? Briefly describe its application to debt investments.

11. Franklin Corp. has an investment that it has held for several years. When it purchased the investment, Franklin accounted for the investment at amortized cost. Can Franklin use the fair value option for this investment? Explain.

12. Identify and explain the different types of classifications for equity investments.

13. Why is the held-for-collection classification not applicable to equity investments?

14. Hayes Company purchased 10,000 ordinary shares of Kenyon Co., paying $26 per share plus $1,500 in broker fees. Hayes plans to actively trade this investment. Prepare the entry to record this investment.

15. Hayes Company sold 10,000 shares of Kenyon Co. that it bought in Question 14 for $27.50 per share, incurring $1,770 in brokerage commissions. The carrying value of the investment is $260,000. Prepare the entry to record the sale of this investment.

16. Distinguish between the accounting treatment for non-trading equity investments and trading equity investments.

17. What constitutes "significant influence" when an investor's financial interest is below the 50% level?

18. Explain how the investment account is affected by investee activities under the equity method.

19. When the equity method is applied, what amounts relate to the investment, and where will these amounts be reported in the financial statements?

20. Hiram Co. uses the equity method to account for investments in ordinary shares. What accounting should be made for dividends received from these investments subsequent to the date of investment?

21. Raleigh Corp. has an investment with a carrying value (equity method) on its books of £170,000 representing a 30% interest in Borg Company, which suffered a £620,000 loss this year. How should Raleigh Corp. handle its proportionate share of Borg's loss?

22. Where on the asset side of the statement of financial position are amounts related to equity investments classified as trading and non-trading reported? Explain.

23. When is a debt investment considered impaired? Explain how to account for the impairment of a held-for-collection debt investment.

24. Briefly discuss how a transfer of investments from the trading category to the held-for-collection category affects the financial statements.

25. Briefly describe the unresolved issues related to fair value accounting.

26. Briefly describe some of the similarities and differences between U.S. GAAP and IFRS with respect to the accounting for investments.

27. Ramirez Company has a held-for-collection investment in the 6%, 20-year bonds of Soto Company. The investment was originally purchased for R$1,200,000 in 2013. Early in 2014, Ramirez recorded an impairment of R$300,000 on the Soto investment, due to Soto's financial distress. In 2015, Soto returned to profitability and the Soto investment was no longer impaired. What entry does Ramirez make in 2015 under (a) U.S. GAAP and (b) IFRS?

28. Discuss how recent IFRS developments in the accounting for investments might affect convergence with U.S. GAAP.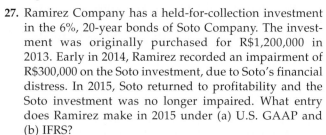

*29. What is meant by the term underlying as it relates to derivative financial instruments?

*30. What are the main distinctions between a traditional financial instrument and a derivative financial instrument?

*31. What is the purpose of a fair value hedge?

*32. In what situation will the unrealized holding gain or loss on a non-trading equity investment be reported in income?

*33. Why might a company become involved in an interest rate swap contract to receive fixed interest payments and pay variable?

*34. What is the purpose of a cash flow hedge?

*35. Where are gains and losses related to cash flow hedges involving anticipated transactions reported?

*36. What are hybrid securities? Give an example of a hybrid security.

BRIEF EXERCISES

2 **BE17-1** Garfield Company made an investment in €80,000 of the 9%, 5-year bonds of Chester Corporation for €74,086, which provides an 11% return. Garfield plans to hold these bonds to collect contractual cash flows. Prepare Garfield's journal entries for (a) the purchase of the investment, and (b) the receipt of annual interest and discount amortization.

2 **3** **BE17-2** Use the information from BE17-1 but assume Garfield plans to actively trade the bonds to profit from market interest rates changes. Prepare Garfield's journal entries for (a) the purchase of the investment, (b) the receipt of annual interest and discount amortization, and (c) the year-end fair value adjustment. The bonds have a year-end fair value of €75,500.

2 **BE17-3** Carow Corporation purchased, as a held-for-collection investment, €60,000 of the 8%, 5-year bonds of Harrison, Inc. for €65,118, which provides a 6% return. The bonds pay interest semiannually. Prepare Carow's journal entries for (a) the purchase of the investment, and (b) the receipt of semiannual interest and premium amortization.

3 **BE17-4** Hendricks Corporation purchased $50,000 of bonds at par. Hendricks has an active trading business model for this investment. At December 31, Hendricks received annual interest of $2,000, and the fair value of the bonds was $47,400. Prepare Hendricks' journal entries for (a) the purchase of the investment, (b) the interest received, and (c) the fair value adjustment.

4 **BE17-5** Refer to the information in BE17-3. Assume that, to address a measurement mismatch, Carow elects the fair value option for this debt investment. Prepare the journal entry at year-end, assuming the fair value of the bonds is €64,000.

5 **BE17-6** Fairbanks Corporation purchased 400 ordinary shares of Sherman Inc. as a trading investment for £13,200. During the year, Sherman paid a cash dividend of £3.25 per share. At year-end, Sherman shares were selling for £34.50 per share. Prepare Fairbanks' journal entries to record (a) the purchase of the investment, (b) the dividends received, and (c) the fair value adjustment.

5 **BE17-7** Use the information from BE17-6 but assume the shares were purchased to meet a non-trading regulatory requirement. Prepare Fairbanks' journal entries to record (a) the purchase of the investment, (b) the dividends received, and (c) the fair value adjustment.

5 **BE17-8** Cleveland Company has a non-trading equity investment portfolio valued at $4,000. Its cost was $3,300. If the Fair Value Adjustment account has a debit balance of $200, prepare the journal entry at year-end.

6 **BE17-9** Zoop Corporation purchased for $300,000 a 30% interest in Murphy, Inc. This investment enables Zoop to exert significant influence over Murphy. During the year, Murphy earned net income of $180,000 and paid dividends of $60,000. Prepare Zoop's journal entries related to this investment.

7 **BE17-10** Hillsborough Co. has a held-for-collection investment in the bonds of Schuyler Corp. with a carrying (and fair) value of $70,000. Due to poor economic prospects for Schuyler, Hillsborough determined that it will not be able to collect all contractual cash flows and the bonds have decreased in value to $60,000. It is determined that this is a permanent loss in value. Prepare the journal entry, if any, to record the reduction in value.

8 **BE17-11** Cameron Company has a portfolio of debt investments that it has managed as a trading investment. At December 31, 2015, Cameron had the following balances related to this portfolio: debt investments, £250,000; fair value adjustment, £10,325 (Dr). Cameron management decides to change its business model for these investments to a held-for-collection strategy, beginning in January 2016. Prepare the journal entry to transfer these investments to the held-for-collection classification.

EXERCISES

1 **3** **E17-1 (Investment Classifications)** For the following investments, identify whether they are:

1. Debt investments at amortized cost.
2. Debt investments at fair value.
3. Trading equity investments.
4. Non-trading equity investments.

Each case is independent of the other.

    (a) A bond that will mature in 4 years was bought 1 month ago when the price dropped. As soon as the value increases, which is expected next month, it will be sold.

    (b) 10% of the outstanding shares of Farm-Co was purchased. The company is planning on eventually getting a total of 30% of its outstanding shares.

    (c) 10-year bonds were purchased this year. The bonds mature at the first of next year, and the company plans to sell the bonds if interest rates fall.

    (d) Bonds that will mature in 5 years are purchased. The company has a strategy to hold them to collect the contractual cash flows on the bonds.

    (e) A bond that matures in 10 years was purchased. The company is investing money set aside for an expansion project planned 10 years from now.

    (f) Ordinary shares in a distributor are purchased to meet a regulatory requirement for doing business in the distributor's region. The investment will be held indefinitely.

2 **E17-2 (Debt Investments)** On January 1, 2015, Jennings Company purchased at par 10% bonds having a maturity value of €300,000. They are dated January 1, 2015, and mature January 1, 2020, with interest receivable December 31 of each year. The bonds are held to collect contractual cash flows.

Instructions

    (a) Prepare the journal entry at the date of the bond purchase.

    (b) Prepare the journal entry to record the interest received for 2015.

    (c) Prepare the journal entry to record the interest received for 2016.

2 **E17-3 (Debt Investments)** On January 1, 2015, Roosevelt Company purchased 12% bonds having a maturity value of $500,000 for $537,907.40. The bonds provide the bondholders with a 10% yield. They are dated January 1, 2015, and mature January 1, 2020, with interest receivable December 31 of each year. Roosevelt's business model is to hold these bonds to collect contractual cash flows.

Instructions

    (a) Prepare the journal entry at the date of the bond purchase.

    (b) Prepare a bond amortization schedule.

    (c) Prepare the journal entry to record the interest received and the amortization for 2015.

    (d) Prepare the journal entry to record the interest received and the amortization for 2016.

2 **E17-4 (Debt Investments)** On January 1, 2015, Morgan Company acquires $300,000 of Nicklaus, Inc., 9% bonds at a price of $278,384. The interest is payable each December 31, and the bonds mature December 31, 2017. The investment will provide Morgan Company a 12% yield. The bonds are classified as held-for-collection.

Instructions

    (a) Prepare a 3-year schedule of interest revenue and bond discount amortization. (Round to nearest cent.)

    (b) Prepare the journal entry for the interest receipt of December 31, 2016, and the discount amortization.

3 **E17-5 (Debt Investments)** Assume the same information as in E17-3 except that Roosevelt has an active trading strategy for these bonds. The fair value of the bonds at December 31 of each year-end is as follows.

2015	$534,200	2018	$517,000
2016	$515,000	2019	$500,000
2017	$513,000		

Instructions

    (a) Prepare the journal entry at the date of the bond purchase.

    (b) Prepare the journal entries to record the interest received and recognition of fair value for 2015.

    (c) Prepare the journal entry to record the recognition of fair value for 2016.

4 **E17-6 (Fair Value Option)** Refer to the information in E17-3 and assume that Roosevelt elected the fair value option for this held-for-collection investment.

Instructions

    (a) Prepare any entries necessary at December 31, 2015, assuming the fair value of the bonds is $540,000.

    (b) Prepare any entries necessary at December 31, 2016, assuming the fair value of the bonds is $525,000.

4 **E17-7 (Fair Value Option)** Presented on page 865 is selected information related to the financial instruments of Dawson Company at December 31, 2015 (amounts in thousands). This is Dawson Company's first year of operations.

	Carrying Amount	Fair Value (at December 31)
Debt investments (intent is to hold for collection)	¥ 40,000	¥ 41,000
Bonds payable	220,000	195,000

Instructions

(a) Dawson elects to use the fair value option whenever possible. Assuming that Dawson's net income is ¥100,000 in 2015 before reporting any financial instrument gains or losses, determine Dawson's net income for 2015.

(b) Record the journal entry, if any, necessary at December 31, 2015, to record the fair value option for the bonds payable.

E17-8 (Entries for Equity Investments) The following information is available for Kinney Company at December 31, 2015, regarding its investments.

Investments	Cost	Fair Value
3,000 ordinary shares of Petty Corporation	£40,000	£46,000
1,000 preference shares of Dowe Incorporated	25,000	22,000
	£65,000	£68,000

Instructions

(a) Prepare the adjusting entry (if any) for 2015, assuming the investments are classified as trading.

(b) Prepare the adjusting entry (if any) for 2015, assuming the investments are classified as non-trading.

(c) Discuss how the amounts reported in the financial statements are affected by the entries in (a) and (b).

E17-9 (Equity Investments) On December 21, 2015, Zurich Company provided you with the following information regarding its trading investments.

December 31, 2015

Investments (Trading)	Cost	Fair Value	Unrealized Gain (Loss)
Stargate Corp. shares	€20,000	€19,000	€(1,000)
Carolina Co. shares	10,000	9,000	(1,000)
Vectorman Co. shares	20,000	20,600	600
Total of portfolio	€50,000	€48,600	(1,400)
Previous fair value adjustment balance			–0–
Fair value adjustment—Cr.			€(1,400)

During 2016, Carolina Co. shares were sold for €9,500. The fair value of the shares on December 31, 2016, was Stargate Corp. shares—€19,300; Vectorman Co. shares—€20,500.

Instructions

(a) Prepare the adjusting journal entry needed on December 31, 2015.

(b) Prepare the journal entry to record the sale of the Carolina Co. shares during 2016.

(c) Prepare the adjusting journal entry needed on December 31, 2016.

E17-10 (Equity Investment Entries and Reporting) Player Corporation makes an equity investment costing $73,000 and classifies it as non-trading. At December 31, the fair value of the investment is $67,000.

Instructions

Prepare the adjusting entry to report the investment properly. Indicate the statement presentation of the accounts in your entry.

E17-11 (Equity Investment Entries and Financial Statement Presentation) At December 31, 2015, the equity investment portfolio for Wenger, Inc. is as follows.

Investment	Cost	Fair Value	Unrealized Gain (Loss)
A	$17,500	$15,000	($2,500)
B	12,500	14,000	1,500
C	23,000	25,500	2,500
Total	$53,000	$54,500	1,500
Previous fair value adjustment balance—Dr.			200
Fair value adjustment—Dr.			$1,300

On January 20, 2016, Wenger, Inc. sold investment A for $15,300. The sale proceeds are net of brokerage fees.

Instructions

    (a) Prepare the adjusting entry at December 31, 2015, to report the portfolio at fair value.

    (b) Show the statement of financial position presentation of the investment-related accounts at December 31, 2015. (Ignore notes presentation.)

    (c) Prepare the journal entry(ies) for the 2016 sale of investment A.

    (d) Repeat requirement (a), assuming the portfolio of investments is non-trading.

5 **E17-12 (Equity Investment Entries)** Capriati Corporation made the following cash investments during 2015, which is the first year in which Capriati invested in securities.

    1. On January 15, purchased 9,000 ordinary shares of Gonzalez Company at $33.50 per share plus commission $1,980.

    2. On April 1, purchased 5,000 ordinary shares of Belmont Co. at $52.00 per share plus commission $3,370.

    3. On September 10, purchased 7,000 preference shares of Thep Co. at $26.50 per share plus commission $4,910.

On May 20, 2015, Capriati sold 3,000 shares of Gonzalez Company at a market price of $35 per share less brokerage commissions, taxes, and fees of $2,850. The year-end fair values per share were Gonzalez $30, Belmont $55, and Thep $28. In addition, the chief accountant of Capriati told you that Capriati Corporation plans to actively trade these investments.

Instructions

    (a) Prepare the journal entries to record the above three investment purchases.

    (b) Prepare the journal entry for the investment sale on May 20.

    (c) Compute the unrealized gains or losses and prepare the adjusting entries for Capriati on December 31, 2015.

5 6 **E17-13 (Journal Entries for Fair Value and Equity Methods)** Presented below are two independent situations.

Situation 1: Hatcher Cosmetics acquired 10% of the 200,000 ordinary shares of Ramirez Fashion at a total cost of $14 per share on March 18, 2015. On June 30, Ramirez declared and paid a $75,000 cash dividend. On December 31, Ramirez reported net income of $122,000 for the year. At December 31, the market price of Ramirez Fashion was $15 per share. The investment is classified as trading.

Situation 2: Holmes, Inc. obtained significant influence over Nadal Corporation by buying 25% of Nadal's 30,000 outstanding ordinary shares at a total cost of $9 per share on January 1, 2015. On June 15, Nadal declared and paid a cash dividend of $36,000. On December 31, Nadal reported a net income of $85,000 for the year.

Instructions

Prepare all necessary journal entries in 2015 for both situations.

6 **E17-14 (Equity Method)** Gator Co. invested £1,000,000 in Demo Co. for 25% of its outstanding shares. Demo Co. pays out 40% of net income in dividends each year.

Instructions

Use the information in the following T-account for the investment in Demo to answer the following questions.

Investment in Demo Co.

1,000,000	
130,000	
	52,000

    (a) How much was Gator Co.'s share of Demo Co.'s net income for the year?

    (b) How much was Gator Co.'s share of Demo Co.'s dividends for the year?

    (c) What was Demo Co.'s total net income for the year?

    (d) What was Demo Co.'s total dividends for the year?

5 **E17-15 (Equity Investments—Trading)** Feiner Co. had purchased 300 shares of Guttman Co. for £40 each this year and classified the investment as a trading investment. Feiner Co. sold 100 shares for £43 each. At year-end, the price per share had dropped to £35.

Instructions

Prepare the journal entries for these transactions and any year-end adjustments.

5 **E17-16 (Equity Investments—Trading)** Swanson Company has the following trading investment portfolio on December 31, 2015.

Investments (Trading)	Cost	Fair Value
1,500 ordinary shares of Parker, Inc.	£ 71,500	£ 69,000
5,000 ordinary shares of Beilman Corp.	180,000	175,000
400 preference shares of Duncan, Inc.	60,000	61,600
	£311,500	£305,600

All of the investments were purchased in 2015. In 2016, Swanson completed the following investment transactions.

March 1	Sold the 1,500 ordinary shares of Parker, Inc., @ £45 less fees of £1,200.
April 1	Bought 700 ordinary shares of McDowell Corp., @ £75 plus fees of £1,300.

Swanson Company's portfolio of trading investments appeared as follows on December 31, 2016.

Investments (Trading)	Cost	Fair Value
5,000 ordinary shares of Beilman Corp.	£180,000	£175,000
700 ordinary shares of McDowell Corp.	52,500	50,400
400 preference shares of Duncan, Inc.	60,000	58,000
	£292,500	£283,400

Instructions

Prepare the general journal entries for Swanson Company for:

(a) The 2015 adjusting entry.
(b) The sale of the Parker shares.
(c) The purchase of the McDowell shares.
(d) The 2016 adjusting entry for the trading portfolio.

5 **6** **E17-17 (Fair Value and Equity Method Compared)** Chen Inc. acquired 20% of the outstanding ordinary shares of Cho Corp. on December 31, 2015. The purchase price was ¥125,000,000 for 50,000 shares. Cho Corp. declared and paid an ¥80 per share cash dividend on June 30 and on December 31, 2016. Cho reported net income of ¥73,000,000 for 2016. The fair value of Cho's shares was ¥2,700 per share at December 31, 2016.

Instructions

(a) Prepare the journal entries for Chen Inc. for 2015 and 2016, assuming that Chen cannot exercise significant influence over Cho. The investments should be classified as trading.
(b) Prepare the journal entries for Chen Inc. for 2015 and 2016, assuming that Chen can exercise significant influence over Cho.
(c) At what amount is the investment reported on the statement of financial position under each of these methods at December 31, 2016? What is the total net income reported in 2016 under each of these methods?

6 **E17-18 (Equity Method)** On January 1, 2015, Meredith Corporation purchased 25% of the ordinary shares of Pirates Company for £200,000. During the year, Pirates earned net income of £80,000 and paid dividends of £20,000.

Instructions

Prepare the entries for Meredith to record the purchase and any additional entries related to this investment in Pirates Company in 2015.

7 **E17-19 (Impairment)** Cairo Corporation has government bonds classified as held-for-collection at December 31, 2015. These bonds have a par value of $800,000, an amortized cost of $800,000, and a fair value of $740,000. In evaluating the bonds, Cairo determines the bonds have a $60,000 permanent decline in value. That is, the company believes that impairment accounting is now appropriate for these bonds.

Instructions

(a) Prepare the journal entry to recognize the impairment.
(b) What is the new cost basis of the bonds? Given that the maturity value of the bonds is $800,000, should Cairo Corporation amortize the difference between the carrying amount and the maturity value over the life of the bonds?
(c) At December 31, 2016, the fair value of the municipal bonds is $760,000. Prepare the entry (if any) to record this information.

7 **E17-20 (Impairment)** Komissarov Company has a debt investment in the bonds issued by Keune Inc. The bonds were purchased at par for €400,000 and, at the end of 2015, have a remaining life of 3 years with annual interest payments at 10%, paid at the end of each year. This debt investment is classified as held-for-collection. Keune is facing a tough economic environment and informs its investors that it will be unable to make all payments according to the contractual terms. The controller of Komissarov has prepared the following revised expected cash flow forecast for this bond investment.

Dec. 31	Expected Cash Flows
2016	€ 35,000
2017	35,000
2018	385,000
Total cash flows	€455,000

Instructions

(a) Determine the impairment loss for Komissarov at December 31, 2015.

(b) Prepare the entry to record the impairment loss for Komissarov at December 31, 2015.

(c) On January 15, 2016, Keune receives a major capital infusion from a private equity investor. It informs Komissarov that the bonds now will be paid according to the contractual terms. Briefly describe how Komissarov would account for the bond investment in light of this new information.

11 *E17-21 (Derivative Transaction)** On January 2, 2015, Jones Company purchases a call option for $300 on Merchant ordinary shares. The call option gives Jones the option to buy 1,000 shares of Merchant at a strike price of $50 per share. The market price of a Merchant share is $50 on January 2, 2015 (the intrinsic value is therefore $0). On March 31, 2015, the market price for Merchant shares is $53 per share, and the time value of the option is $200.

Instructions

(a) Prepare the journal entry to record the purchase of the call option on January 2, 2015.

(b) Prepare the journal entry(ies) to recognize the change in the fair value of the call option as of March 31, 2015.

(c) What was the effect on net income of entering into the derivative transaction for the period January 2 to March 31, 2015? (Ignore tax effects.)

12 *E17-22 (Fair Value Hedge)** On January 2, 2015, MacCloud Co. issued a 4-year, €100,000 note at 6% fixed interest, interest payable semiannually. MacCloud now wants to change the note to a variable-rate note.

As a result, on January 2, 2015, MacCloud Co. enters into an interest rate swap where it agrees to receive 6% fixed and pay LIBOR of 5.7% for the first 6 months on €100,000. At each 6-month period, the variable rate will be reset. The variable rate is reset to 6.7% on June 30, 2015.

Instructions

(a) Compute the net interest expense to be reported for this note and related swap transaction as of June 30, 2015.

(b) Compute the net interest expense to be reported for this note and related swap transaction as of December 31, 2015.

13 *E17-23 (Cash Flow Hedge)** On January 2, 2015, Parton Company issues a 5-year, $10,000,000 note at LIBOR, with interest paid annually. The variable rate is reset at the end of each year. The LIBOR rate for the first year is 5.8%.

Parton Company decides it prefers fixed-rate financing and wants to lock in a rate of 6%. As a result, Parton enters into an interest rate swap to pay 6% fixed and receive LIBOR based on $10 million. The variable rate is reset to 6.6% on January 2, 2016.

Instructions

(a) Compute the net interest expense to be reported for this note and related swap transactions as of December 31, 2015.

(b) Compute the net interest expense to be reported for this note and related swap transactions as of December 31, 2016.

12 *E17-24 (Fair Value Hedge)** Sarazan Company issues a 4-year, 7.5% fixed-rate interest only, non-prepayable £1,000,000 note payable on December 31, 2015. It decides to change the interest rate from a fixed rate to variable rate and enters into a swap agreement with M&S Corp. The swap agreement specifies that Sarazan will receive a fixed rate at 7.5% and pay variable with settlement dates that match the interest payments on the debt. Assume that interest rates have declined during 2016 and that Sarazan received £13,000 as an adjustment to interest expense for the settlement at December 31, 2016. The loss related to the debt (due to interest rate changes) was £48,000. The value of the swap contract increased £48,000.

Instructions

(a) Prepare the journal entry to record the payment of interest expense on December 31, 2016.
(b) Prepare the journal entry to record the receipt of the swap settlement on December 31, 2016.
(c) Prepare the journal entry to record the change in the fair value of the swap contract on December 31, 2016.
(d) Prepare the journal entry to record the change in the fair value of the debt on December 31, 2016.

11 *E17-25 (Call Option)** On August 15, 2015, Outkast Co. invested idle cash by purchasing a call option on Counting Crows Inc. ordinary shares for $360. The notional value of the call option is 400 shares, and the option price is $40. (Market price of a Counting Crows share is $40.) The option expires on January 31, 2016. The following data are available with respect to the call option.

Date	Market Price of Counting Crows Shares	Time Value of Call Option
September 30, 2015	$48 per share	$180
December 31, 2015	46 per share	65
January 15, 2016	47 per share	30

Instructions

Prepare the journal entries for Outkast for the following dates.

(a) Investment in call option on Counting Crows shares on August 15, 2015.
(b) September 30, 2015—Outkast prepares financial statements.
(c) December 31, 2015—Outkast prepares financial statements.
(d) January 15, 2016—Outkast settles the call option on the Counting Crows shares.

13 *E17-26 (Cash Flow Hedge)** Choi Golf Co. uses titanium in the production of its specialty drivers. Choi anticipates that it will need to purchase 200 ounces of titanium in October 2015, for clubs that will be shipped in the holiday shopping season. However, if the price of titanium increases, this will increase the cost to produce the clubs, which will result in lower profit margins.

To hedge the risk of increased titanium prices, on May 1, 2015, Choi enters into a titanium futures contract and designates this futures contract as a cash flow hedge of the anticipated titanium purchase. The notional amount of the contract is 200 ounces, and the terms of the contract give Choi the right and the obligation to purchase titanium at a price of ¥50,000 per ounce. The price will be good until the contract expires on November 30, 2015.

Assume the following data with respect to the price of the call options and the titanium inventory purchase.

Date	Spot Price for November Delivery
May 1, 2015	¥50,000 per ounce
June 30, 2015	52,000 per ounce
September 30, 2016	52,500 per ounce

Instructions

Present the journal entries for the following dates/transactions.

(a) May 1, 2015—Inception of futures contract, no premium paid.
(b) June 30, 2015—Choi prepares financial statements.
(c) September 30, 2015—Choi prepares financial statements.
(d) October 5, 2015—Choi purchases 200 ounces of titanium at ¥52,500 per ounce and settles the futures contract.
(e) December 15, 2015—Choi sells clubs containing titanium purchased in October 2015 for ¥25,000,000. The cost of the finished goods inventory is ¥14,000,000.
(f) Indicate the amount(s) reported in the income statement related to the futures contract and the inventory transactions on December 31, 2015.

PROBLEMS

2 3 **P17-1 (Debt Investments)** Presented below is an amortization schedule related to Spangler Company's 5-year, $100,000 bond with a 7% interest rate and a 5% yield, purchased on December 31, 2012, for $108,660.

Date	Cash Received	Interest Revenue	Bond Premium Amortization	Carrying Amount of Bonds
12/31/12				$108,660
12/31/13	$7,000	$5,433	$1,567	107,093
12/31/14	7,000	5,354	1,646	105,447
12/31/15	7,000	5,272	1,728	103,719
12/31/16	7,000	5,186	1,814	101,905
12/31/17	7,000	5,095	1,905	100,000

The following schedule presents a comparison of the amortized cost and fair value of the bonds at year-end.

	12/31/13	12/31/14	12/31/15	12/31/16	12/31/17
Amortized cost	$107,093	$105,447	$103,719	$101,905	$100,000
Fair value	106,500	107,500	105,650	103,000	100,000

Instructions

(a) Prepare the journal entry to record the purchase of these bonds on December 31, 2012, assuming the bonds are classified as held-for-collection investments.

(b) Prepare the journal entry(ies) related to the held-for-collection bonds for 2013.

(c) Prepare the journal entry(ies) related to the held-for-collection bonds for 2015.

(d) Prepare the journal entry(ies) to record the purchase of these bonds, assuming they are classified as trading.

(e) Prepare the journal entry(ies) related to the trading bonds for 2013.

(f) Prepare the journal entry(ies) related to the trading bonds for 2015.

2 4 **P17-2 (Debt Investments, Fair Value Option)** On January 1, 2015, Novotna Company purchased €400,000, 8% bonds of Aguirre Co. for €369,114. The bonds were purchased to yield 10% interest. Interest is payable semiannually on July 1 and January 1. The bonds mature on January 1, 2020. Novotna Company plans to hold the bonds to collect contractual cash flows. On January 1, 2017, after receiving interest, Novotna Company sold the bonds for €370,726 after receiving interest to meet its liquidity needs.

Instructions

(a) Prepare the journal entry to record the purchase of bonds on January 1.

(b) Prepare the amortization schedule for the bonds.

(c) Prepare the journal entries to record the semiannual interest on July 1, 2015, and December 31, 2015.

(d) Prepare the journal entry to record the sale of the bonds on January 1, 2017.

(e) Assume that Novotna elected the fair value option for this investment. If the fair value of Aguirre bonds is €368,000 on December 31, 2015, prepare the necessary adjusting entry.

3 5 **P17-3 (Debt and Equity Investments)** Cardinal Paz Corp. carries an account in its general ledger called Investments, which contained debits for investment purchases, and no credits, with the following descriptions.

Feb. 1, 2015	Sharapova Company ordinary shares, $100 par, 200 shares	$ 37,400
April 1	Government bonds, 11%, due April 1, 2025, interest payable April 1 and October 1, 110 bonds of $1,000 par each	110,000
July 1	McGrath Company 12% bonds, par $50,000, dated March 1, 2015 purchased at 104, plus accrued interest payable annually on March 1, due March 1, 2035	54,000

Instructions

(Round all computations to the nearest dollar.)

(a) Prepare entries necessary to classify the amounts into proper accounts, assuming that Paz plans to actively manage these investments.

(b) Prepare the entry to record the accrued interest on December 31, 2015.

(c) The fair values of the investments on December 31, 2015, were:

Sharapova Company shares	$ 31,800
Government bonds	124,700
McGrath Company bonds	58,600

What entry or entries, if any, would you recommend be made?

(d) The government bonds were sold on July 1, 2016, for $119,200 plus accrued interest. Give the proper entry.

3 **P17-4 (Debt Investments)** Presented below is information taken from a bond investment amortization schedule with related fair values provided. These bonds are managed to profit from changes in market interest rates.

	12/31/15	12/31/16	12/31/17
Amortized cost	€491,150	€519,442	€550,000
Fair value	497,000	509,000	550,000

Instructions

    (a) Indicate whether the bonds were purchased at a discount or at a premium.

    (b) Prepare the adjusting entry to record the bonds at fair value at December 31, 2015. The Fair Value Adjustment account has a debit balance of €1,000 prior to adjustment.

    (c) Prepare the adjusting entry to record the bonds at fair value at December 31, 2016.

5 **P17-5 (Equity Investment Entries and Disclosures)** Parnevik Company has the following investments in its investment portfolio on December 31, 2015 (all investments were purchased in 2015): (1) 3,000 ordinary shares of Anderson Co. which cost $58,500, (2) 10,000 ordinary shares of Munter Ltd. which cost $580,000, and (3) 6,000 preference shares of King Company which cost $255,000. The Fair Value Adjustment account shows a credit of $10,100 at the end of 2015.

In 2016, Parnevik completed the following investment transactions.

    1. On January 15, sold 3,000 ordinary shares of Anderson at $22 per share less fees of $2,150.

    2. On April 17, purchased 1,000 ordinary shares of Castle at $33.50 per share plus fees of $1,980.

On December 31, 2016, the fair values per share of these investments were: Munter $61, King $40, and Castle $29. Parnevik classifies these investments as trading.

Instructions

    (a) Prepare the entry for the sale on January 15, 2016.

    (b) Prepare the journal entry to record the purchase on April 17, 2016.

    (c) Compute the unrealized gains or losses and prepare the adjusting entry for Parnevik on December 31, 2016.

    (d) How should the unrealized gains or losses be reported on Parnevik's financial statements?

    (e) Assuming the investment in King Company preference shares is classified as non-trading, briefly describe the accounting and reporting of this investment.

6 **P17-6 (Equity Investments)** McElroy Company has the following portfolio of investments at September 30, 2015, its last reporting date.

Trading Investments	Cost	Fair Value
Horton, Inc. ordinary (5,000 shares)	£215,000	£200,000
Monty, Inc. preference (3,500 shares)	133,000	140,000
Oakwood Corp. ordinary (1,000 shares)	180,000	179,000

On October 10, 2015, the Horton shares were sold at a price of £54 per share. In addition, 3,000 ordinary shares of Patriot were acquired at £54.50 per share on November 2, 2015. The December 31, 2015, fair values were Monty £106,000, Patriot £132,000, and Oakwood £193,000. All the investments are classified as trading.

Instructions

    (a) Prepare the journal entries to record the sale, purchase, and adjusting entries related to the trading investments in the last quarter of 2015.

    (b) How would the entries in part (a) change if the investments were classified as non-trading?

2 **3** **4** **P17-7 (Debt Investment Entries)** The following information relates to the debt investments of Wildcat Company.

    1. On February 1, the company purchased 10% bonds of Gibbons Co. having a par value of £300,000 at 100 plus accrued interest. Interest is payable April 1 and October 1.

    2. On April 1, semiannual interest is received.

    3. On July 1, 9% bonds of Sampson, Inc. were purchased. These bonds with a par value of £200,000 were purchased at 100 plus accrued interest. Interest dates are June 1 and December 1.

    4. On September 1, bonds with a par value of £60,000, purchased on February 1, are sold at 99 plus accrued interest.

    5. On October 1, semiannual interest is received.

    6. On December 1, semiannual interest is received.

    7. On December 31, the fair value of the bonds purchased February 1 and July 1 are 95 and 93, respectively.

Instructions

(a) Prepare any journal entries you consider necessary, including year-end entries (December 31), assuming these investments are managed to profit from changes in market interest rates.

(b) If Wildcat classified these as held-for-collection investments, explain how the journal entries would differ from those in part (a).

(c) Assume that Wildcat elects the fair value option for these investments under the part (b) conditions. Briefly discuss how the accounting will change.

5 6 P17-8 (Fair Value and Equity Methods) Brooks Corp. is a medium-sized corporation specializing in quarrying stone for building construction. The company has long dominated the market, at one time achieving a 70% market penetration. During prosperous years, the company's profits, coupled with a conservative dividend policy, resulted in funds available for outside investment. Over the years, Brooks has had a policy of investing idle cash in equity investments. In particular, Brooks has made periodic investments in the company's principal supplier, Norton Industries. Although the firm currently owns 12% of the outstanding ordinary shares of Norton Industries, Brooks does not have significant influence over the operations of Norton Industries.

Cheryl Thomas has recently joined Brooks as assistant controller, and her first assignment is to prepare the 2015 year-end adjusting entries for the accounts that are valued by the "fair value" rule for financial reporting purposes. Thomas has gathered the following information about Brooks' pertinent accounts.

1. Brooks has trading equity investments related to Delaney Motors and Patrick Electric. During this fiscal year, Brooks purchased 100,000 shares of Delaney Motors for $1,400,000; these shares currently have a fair value of $1,600,000. Brooks' investment in Patrick Electric has not been profitable; the company acquired 50,000 shares of Patrick in April 2015 at $20 per share, a purchase that currently has a value of $720,000.

2. Prior to 2015, Brooks invested $22,500,000 in Norton Industries and has not changed its holdings this year. This investment in Norton Industries was valued at $21,500,000 on December 31, 2014. Brooks' 12% ownership of Norton Industries has a current fair value of $22,225,000.

Instructions

(a) Prepare the appropriate adjusting entries for Brooks as of December 31, 2015, to reflect the application of the "fair value" rule for both classes of investments described above.

(b) For both classes of investments presented above, describe how the results of the valuation adjustments made in (a) would be reflected in Brooks' 2015 financial statements.

(c) Prepare the entries for the Norton investment, assuming that Brooks owns 25% of Norton's shares. Norton reported income of $500,000 in 2015 and paid cash dividends of $100,000.

5 P17-9 (Financial Statement Presentation of Equity Investments) Kennedy Company has the following portfolio of trading investments at December 31, 2015.

Investment	Quantity	Percent Interest	Per Share Cost	Per Share Market
Frank, Inc.	2,000 shares	8%	$11	$16
Ellis Corp.	5,000 shares	14%	23	19
Mendota Company	4,000 shares	2%	31	24

On December 31, 2016, Kennedy's portfolio of trading investments consisted of the following investments.

Investment	Quantity	Percent Interest	Per Share Cost	Per Share Market
Ellis Corp.	5,000 shares	14%	$23	$28
Mendota Company	4,000 shares	2%	31	23
Mendota Company	2,000 shares	1%	25	23

At the end of year 2016, Kennedy Company changed the classification of its investment in Frank, Inc. to non-trading when the shares were selling for $8 per share.

Instructions

(a) What should be reported on Kennedy's December 31, 2015, statement of financial position relative to these equity investments?

(b) What should be reported on the face of Kennedy's December 31, 2016, statement of financial position relative to the trading investments? What should be reported to reflect the transactions above in Kennedy's 2016 income statement?

5 P17-10 (Equity Investments) Castleman Holdings, Inc. had the following investment portfolio at January 1, 2015.

Evers Company	1,000 shares @ £15 each	£15,000
Rogers Company	900 shares @ £20 each	18,000
Chance Company	500 shares @ £9 each	4,500
Non-trading investments at cost		37,500
Fair value adjustment		(7,500)
Non-trading investments at fair value		£30,000

During 2015, the following transactions took place.

1. On March 1, Rogers Company paid a £2 per share dividend.
2. On April 30, Castleman Holdings, Inc. sold 300 shares of Chance Company for £11 per share.
3. On May 15, Castleman Holdings, Inc. purchased 100 more shares of Evers Co. at £16 per share.
4. At December 31, 2015, the shares had the following price per share values: Evers £17, Rogers £19, and Chance £8.

During 2016, the following transactions took place.

5. On February 1, Castleman Holdings, Inc. sold the remaining Chance shares for £8 per share.
6. On March 1, Rogers Company paid a £2 per share dividend.
7. On December 21, Evers Company declared a cash dividend of £3 per share to be paid in the next month.
8. At December 31, 2016, the shares had the following price per shares values: Evers £19 and Rogers £21.

Instructions

(a) Prepare journal entries for each of the above transactions.
(b) Prepare a partial statement of financial position showing the Investments account at December 31, 2015 and 2016.
(c) Briefly describe how the accounting would change if the Evers investment was classified as trading.

5 P17-11 (Investments—Statement Presentation) Fernandez Corp. invested its excess cash in equity investments during 2015. The business model for these investments is to profit from trading on price changes.

Instructions

(a) As of December 31, 2015, the equity investment portfolio consisted of the following.

Investment	Quantity	Cost	Fair Value
Lindsay Jones, Inc.	1,000 shares	€ 15,000	€ 21,000
Poley Corp.	2,000 shares	40,000	42,000
Arnold Aircraft	2,000 shares	72,000	60,000
	Totals	€127,000	€123,000

What should be reported on Fernandez's December 31, 2015, statement of financial position relative to these investments? What should be reported on Fernandez's 2015 income statement?

(b) During the year 2016, Fernandez Corp. sold 2,000 shares of Poley Corp. for €38,200 and purchased 2,000 more shares of Lindsay Jones, Inc. and 1,000 shares of Duff Company. On December 31, 2016, Fernandez's equity investment portfolio consisted of the following.

Investment	Quantity	Cost	Fair Value
Lindsay Jones, Inc.	1,000 shares	€ 15,000	€20,000
Lindsay Jones, Inc.	2,000 shares	33,000	40,000
Duff Company	1,000 shares	16,000	12,000
Arnold Aircraft	2,000 shares	72,000	22,000
	Totals	€136,000	€94,000

What should be reported on Fernandez's December 31, 2016, statement of financial position? What should be reported on Fernandez's 2016 income statement?

(c) During the year 2017, Fernandez Corp. sold 3,000 shares of Lindsay Jones, Inc. for €39,900 and 500 shares of Duff Company at a loss of €2,700. On December 31, 2017, Fernandez's equity investment portfolio consisted of the following.

Investment	Quantity	Cost	Fair Value
Arnold Aircraft	2,000 shares	€72,000	€82,000
Duff Company	500 shares	8,000	6,000
Totals		€80,000	€88,000

What should be reported on the face of Fernandez's December 31, 2017, statement of financial position? What should be reported on Fernandez's 2017 income statement?

11 *P17-12 (Derivative Financial Instrument)** The treasurer of Miller Co. has read on the Internet that the price of Wade Inc. ordinary shares is about to take off. In order to profit from this potential development, Miller Co. purchased a call option on Wade shares on July 7, 2015, for €240. The call option is for 200 shares (notional value), and the strike price is €70. (The market price of a Wade share on that date is €70.) The option expires on January 31, 2016. The following data are available with respect to the call option.

Date	Market Price of Wade Shares	Time Value of Call Option
September 30, 2015	€77 per share	€180
December 31, 2015	75 per share	65
January 4, 2016	76 per share	30

Instructions

Prepare the journal entries for Miller Co. for the following dates.

(a) July 7, 2015—Investment in call option on Wade shares.
(b) September 30, 2015—Miller prepares financial statements.
(c) December 31, 2015—Miller prepares financial statements.
(d) January 4, 2016—Miller settles the call option on the Wade shares.

11 *P17-13 (Derivative Financial Instrument)** Johnstone Co. purchased a put option on Ewing ordinary shares on July 7, 2015, for €240. The put option is for 200 shares, and the strike price is €70. (The market price of an ordinary share of Ewing on that date is €70.) The option expires on January 31, 2016. The following data are available with respect to the put option.

Date	Market Price of Ewing Shares	Time Value of Put Option
September 30, 2015	€77 per share	€125
December 31, 2015	75 per share	50
January 31, 2016	78 per share	0

Instructions

Prepare the journal entries for Johnstone Co. for the following dates.

(a) July 7, 2015—Investment in put option on Ewing shares.
(b) September 30, 2015—Johnstone prepares financial statements.
(c) December 31, 2015—Johnstone prepares financial statements.
(d) January 31, 2016—Put option expires.

11 *P17-14 (Free-Standing Derivative)** Warren Co. purchased a put option on Echo ordinary shares on January 7, 2015, for $360. The put option is for 400 shares, and the strike price is $85 (which equals the price of an Echo share on the purchase date). The option expires on July 31, 2015. The following data are available with respect to the put option.

Date	Market Price of Echo Shares	Time Value of Put Option
March 31, 2015	$80 per share	$200
June 30, 2015	82 per share	90
July 6, 2015	77 per share	25

Instructions

Prepare the journal entries for Warren Co. for the following dates.

    (a) January 7, 2015—Investment in put option on Echo shares.

    (b) March 31, 2015—Warren prepares financial statements.

    (c) June 30, 2015—Warren prepares financial statements.

    (d) July 6, 2015—Warren settles the put option on the Echo shares.

12 ▶ ***P17-15 (Fair Value Hedge Interest Rate Swap)** On December 31, 2015, Mercantile Corp. had a $10,000,000, 8% fixed-rate note outstanding, payable in 2 years. It decides to enter into a 2-year swap with Chicago First Bank to convert the fixed-rate debt to variable-rate debt. The terms of the swap indicate that Mercantile will receive interest at a fixed rate of 8.0% and will pay a variable rate equal to the 6-month LIBOR rate, based on the $10,000,000 amount. The LIBOR rate on December 31, 2015, is 7%. The LIBOR rate will be reset every 6 months and will be used to determine the variable rate to be paid for the following 6-month period.

    Mercantile Corp. designates the swap as a fair value hedge. Assume that the hedging relationship meets all the conditions necessary for hedge accounting. The 6-month LIBOR rate and the swap and debt fair values are as follows.

Date	6-Month LIBOR Rate	Swap Fair Value	Debt Fair Value
December 31, 2015	7.0%	—	$10,000,000
June 30, 2016	7.5%	$(200,000)	9,800,000
December 31, 2016	6.0%	60,000	10,060,000

Instructions

    (a) Present the journal entries to record the following transactions.

        (1) The entry, if any, to record the swap on December 31, 2015.

        (2) The entry to record the semiannual debt interest payment on June 30, 2016.

        (3) The entry to record the settlement of the semiannual swap amount receivables at 8%, less amount payable at LIBOR, 7%.

        (4) The entry to record the change in the fair value of the debt on June 30, 2016.

        (5) The entry to record the change in the fair value of the swap at June 30, 2016.

    (b) Indicate the amount(s) reported on the statement of financial position and income statement related to the debt and swap on December 31, 2015.

    (c) Indicate the amount(s) reported on the statement of financial position and income statement related to the debt and swap on June 30, 2016.

    (d) Indicate the amount(s) reported on the statement of financial position and income statement related to the debt and swap on December 31, 2016.

13 ▶ ***P17-16 (Cash Flow Hedge)** Suzuki Jewelry Co. uses gold in the manufacture of its products. Suzuki anticipates that it will need to purchase 500 ounces of gold in October 2015, for jewelry that will be shipped for the holiday shopping season. However, if the price of gold increases, Suzuki's cost to produce its jewelry will increase, which would reduce its profit margins.

    To hedge the risk of increased gold prices, on April 1, 2015, Suzuki enters into a gold futures contract and designates this futures contract as a cash flow hedge of the anticipated gold purchase. The notional amount of the contract is 500 ounces, and the terms of the contract give Suzuki the right and the obligation to purchase gold at a price of ¥30,000 per ounce. The price will be good until the contract expires on October 31, 2015.

    Assume the following data with respect to the price of the gold inventory purchase.

Date	Spot Price for October Delivery
April 1, 2015	¥30,000 per ounce
June 30, 2015	31,000 per ounce
September 30, 2015	31,500 per ounce

Instructions

Prepare the journal entries for the following transactions.

    (a) April 1, 2015—Inception of the futures contract, no premium paid.

    (b) June 30, 2015—Suzuki Co. prepares financial statements.

    (c) September 30, 2015—Suzuki Co. prepares financial statements.

(d) October 10, 2015—Suzuki Co. purchases 500 ounces of gold at ¥31,500 per ounce and settles the futures contract.

(e) December 20, 2015—Suzuki sells jewelry containing gold purchased in October 2015 for ¥35,000,000. The cost of the finished goods inventory is ¥20,000,000.

(f) Indicate the amount(s) reported on the statement of financial position and income statement related to the futures contract on June 30, 2015.

(g) Indicate the amount(s) reported in the income statement related to the futures contract and the inventory transactions on December 31, 2015.

12 *P17-17 **(Fair Value Hedge)** On November 3, 2015, Sprinkle Co. invested €200,000 in 4,000 ordinary shares of Pratt Co. Sprinkle classified this investment as non-trading equity. Sprinkle Co. is considering making a more significant investment in Pratt Co. at some point in the future but has decided to wait and see how the shares do over the next several quarters.

To hedge against potential declines in the value of Pratt shares during this period, Sprinkle also purchased a put option on the Pratt shares. Sprinkle paid an option premium of €600 for the put option, which gives Sprinkle the option to sell 4,000 Pratt shares at a strike price of €50 per share. The option expires on July 31, 2016. The following data are available with respect to the values of the Pratt shares and the put option.

Date	Market Price of Pratt Shares	Time Value of Put Option
December 31, 2015	€50 per share	€375
March 31, 2016	45 per share	175
June 30, 2016	43 per share	40

Instructions

(a) Prepare the journal entries for Sprinkle Co. for the following dates.

(1) November 3, 2015—Investment in Pratt shares and the put option on Pratt shares.

(2) December 31, 2015—Sprinkle Co. prepares financial statements.

(3) March 31, 2016—Sprinkle prepares financial statements.

(4) June 30, 2016—Sprinkle prepares financial statements.

(5) July 1, 2016—Sprinkle settles the put option and sells the Pratt shares for €43 per share.

(b) Indicate the amount(s) reported on the statement of financial position and income statement related to the Pratt investment and the put option on December 31, 2015.

(c) Indicate the amount(s) reported on the statement of financial position and income statement related to the Pratt investment and the put option on June 30, 2016.

CONCEPTS FOR ANALYSIS

CA17-1 (Issues Raised about Investments) You have just started work for Warren Co. as part of the controller's group involved in current financial reporting problems. Jane Henshaw, controller for Warren, is interested in your accounting background because the company has experienced a series of financial reporting surprises over the last few years. Recently, the controller has learned from the company's auditors that there is authoritative literature that may apply to its debt and equity investments. She assumes that you are familiar with literature in this area and asks how the following situations should be reported in the financial statements.

Situation 1: Investments that are actively traded are reported in the current assets section and have a fair value that is €4,200 lower than cost.

Situation 2: A debt investment whose fair value is currently less than cost is transferred to the held-for-collection category.

Situation 3: A debt investment whose fair value is currently less than cost is classified as non-current but is to be reclassified as current.

Situation 4: A company's portfolio of debt investments at fair value consists of the bonds of one company. At the end of the prior year, the fair value of the bonds was 50% of original cost, and this reduction in value was reported as an impairment. However, at the end of the current year, the fair value of the bonds had appreciated to twice the original cost.

Situation 5: The company has purchased some convertible debentures that it plans to sell if the price increases. The fair value of the convertible debentures is €7,700 below its cost.

Instructions

What is the effect upon carrying value and earnings for each of the situations above? Assume that these situations are unrelated.

CA17-2 (Equity Investments) Lexington Co. has the following equity investments on December 31, 2015 (its first year of operations).

	Cost	Fair Value
Greenspan Corp. ordinary shares	$20,000	$19,000
Summerset Company ordinary shares	9,500	8,800
Tinkers Company ordinary shares	20,000	20,600
	$49,500	$48,400

During 2016, Summerset Company shares were sold for $9,200, the difference between the $9,200 and the "fair value" of $8,800 being recorded as a "Gain on Sale of Investments." The market price of the shares on December 31, 2016, was Greenspan Corp. shares $19,900, Tinkers Company shares $20,500.

Instructions

    (a) What justification is there for valuing these investments at fair value and reporting the unrealized gain or loss in income?

    (b) How should Lexington Company apply this rule on December 31, 2015? Explain.

    (c) Did Lexington Company properly account for the sale of the Summerset Company shares? Explain.

    (d) Are there any additional entries necessary for Lexington Company at December 31, 2016, to reflect the facts on the financial statements in accordance with IFRS? Explain.

CA17-3 (Financial Statement Effect of Investments) Presented below are three unrelated situations involving investments.

Situation 1: A debt investment portfolio, whose fair value is currently less than cost, is classified as trading but is to be reclassified as held-for-collection.

Situation 2: A debt investment portfolio with an aggregate fair value in excess of cost includes one particular debt investment whose fair value has declined to less than one-half of the original cost. The decline in value is considered to be permanent.

Situation 3: The portfolio of trading equity investments has a cost in excess of fair value of £13,500. The portfolio of non-trading equity investments has a fair value in excess of cost of £28,600.

Instructions

What is the effect upon carrying value and earnings for each of the situations above?

CA17-4 (Equity Investments) The IASB issued accounting guidance to clarify accounting methods and procedures with respect to debt and equity investments. An important part of the statement concerns the distinction between held-for-collection debt investments, trading debt and equity investments, and non-trading equity investments.

Instructions

    (a) Why does a company maintain investment portfolios for these different types of investments?

    (b) What factors should be considered in determining whether investments should be classified as held-for-collection, trading, or non-trading? How do these factors affect the accounting treatment for unrealized losses?

CA17-5 (Investment Accounted for under the Equity Method) On July 1, 2016, Fontaine Company purchased for cash 40% of the outstanding ordinary shares of Knoblett Company. Both Fontaine Company and Knoblett Company have a December 31 year-end. Knoblett Company, whose shares are actively traded in the over-the-counter market, reported its total net income for the year to Fontaine Company and also paid cash dividends on November 15, 2016, to Fontaine Company and its other shareholders.

Instructions

How should Fontaine Company report the above facts in its December 31, 2016, statement of financial position and its income statement for the year then ended? Discuss the rationale for your answer.

 CA17-6 (Equity Investments) On July 1, 2015, Selig Company purchased for cash 40% of the outstanding ordinary shares of Spoor Corporation. Both Selig and Spoor have a December 31 year-end. Spoor Corporation, whose shares are actively traded on the American Stock Exchange, paid a cash dividend on November 15, 2015, to Selig Company and its other shareholders. It also reported its total net income for the year of $920,000 to Selig Company.

Instructions

Prepare a one-page memorandum of instructions on how Selig Company should report the above facts in its December 31, 2015, statement of financial position and its 2015 income statement. In your memo, identify and describe the method of valuation you recommend. Provide rationale where you can. Address your memo to the chief accountant at Selig Company.

CA17-7 (Fair Value) Addison Manufacturing holds a large portfolio of debt and equity investments. The fair value of the portfolio is greater than its original cost, even though some investments have decreased in value. Sam Beresford, the financial vice president, and Angie Nielson, the controller, are near year-end in the process of classifying for the first time this investment portfolio in accordance with IFRS. Beresford wants to classify those investments that have increased in value during the period as trading investments in order to increase net income this year. He wants to classify all the investments that have decreased in value as non-trading (the equity investments) and as held-for-collection (the debt investments).

Nielson disagrees. She wants to classify those investments that have decreased in value as trading and those that have increased in value as non-trading (equity) and held-for-collection (debt). She contends that the company is having a good earnings year and that recognizing the losses will help to smooth the income this year. As a result, the company will have built-in gains for future periods when the company may not be as profitable.

Instructions

Answer the following questions.

(a) Will classifying the portfolio as each proposes actually have the effect on earnings that each says it will?

(b) Is there anything unethical in what each of them proposes? Who are the stakeholders affected by their proposals?

(c) Assume that Beresford and Nielson properly classify the entire portfolio into trading, non-trading, and held-for-collection categories. But then each proposes to sell just before year-end the investments with gains or with losses, as the case may be, to accomplish their effect on earnings. Is this unethical?

USING YOUR JUDGMENT

FINANCIAL REPORTING

Financial Reporting Problem

Marks and Spencer plc (M&S)

The financial statements of M&S (GBR) are presented in Appendix A. The company's complete annual report, including the notes to the financial statements, is available online.

Instructions

Refer to M&S's financial statements and the accompanying notes to answer the following questions.

(a) What investments does M&S report in fiscal year 2013, and where are these investments reported in its financial statements?

(b) How are M&S's investments valued? How does M&S determine fair value?

(c) How does M&S use derivative financial instruments?

Comparative Analysis Case

adidas and Puma

The financial statements of **adidas** (DEU) and **Puma** (DEU) are presented in Appendices B and C, respectively. The complete annual reports, including the notes to the financial statements, are available online.

Instructions

Based on the information contained in these financial statements, determine each of the following for each company.

(a) Cash used in (for) investing activities during 2012 (from the statement of cash flows).

(b) Cash used for acquisitions and investments in unconsolidated affiliates during 2012.

(c) Total investment in unconsolidated affiliates (or investments and other assets) at the end of 2012.

(d) What information do adidas and Puma provide on the classifications of their investments?

Financial Statement Analysis Case

Union Planters

Union Planters is a bank holding company (that is, a corporation that owns banks). Union Planters manages $32 billion in assets, the largest of which is its loan portfolio of $19 billion. In addition to its loan portfolio, however, like other banks it has significant debt investments. These investments vary from short-term to long-term in nature. As a consequence, consistent with the requirements of accounting rules, Union Planters reports both the fair value and amortized cost of its investments. The following facts were found in a recent Union Planters' annual report.

(amounts in millions)	Amortized Cost	Gross Unrealized Gains	Gross Unrealized Losses	Fair Value
Trading account assets	$ 275	—	—	$ 275
Non-trading equity investments	8,209	$108	$15	8,302
Net income				224
Net investment gains (losses)				(9)

Instructions

(a) Why do you suppose Union Planters purchases investments, rather than simply making loans? Why does it purchase investments that vary both in terms of their maturities and in type (debt versus equity)?

(b) How must Union Planters account for its investments at fair value and amortized cost?

(c) In what ways does classifying investments into two different categories assist investors in evaluating the profitability of a company like Union Planters?

(d) Could Union Planters adjust its investment portfolio to increase reported profit? If so, how much could it have increased reported profit? Why do you suppose it chose not to do this?

Accounting, Analysis, and Principles

Instar Company has several investments in other companies. The following information regarding these investments is available at December 31, 2015.

1. Instar holds bonds issued by Dorsel Corp. The bonds have an amortized cost of $320,000 (which is par value) and their fair value at December 31, 2015, is $400,000. Instar plans to hold the bonds to collect

contractual cash flows until they mature on December 31, 2025. The bonds pay interest at 10%, payable annually on December 31.

2. Instar has invested idle cash in the equity investments of several publicly traded companies. Instar intends to sell these investments during the first quarter of 2016, when it will need the cash to acquire seasonal inventory. These equity investments have a cost basis of $800,000 and a fair value of $920,000 at December 31, 2015.

3. Instar has an ownership stake in one of the companies that supplies Instar with various components that Instar uses in its products. Instar owns 6% of the ordinary shares of the supplier, does not have any representation on the supplier's board of directors, does not exchange any personnel with the supplier, and does not consult with the supplier on any of the supplier's operating, financial, or strategic decisions. The cost basis of the investment in the supplier is $1,200,000, and the fair value of the investment at December 31, 2015, is $1,550,000. Instar may sell the investment if it needs cash. The supplier reported net income of $80,000 for 2015 and paid no dividends.

4. Instar owns 1% of Forter Corp. ordinary shares. The cost basis of the investment in Forter is $200,000, and the fair value at December 31, 2015, is $187,000. Instar does not intend to trade the investment because it helps it meet regulatory requirements to sell its products in Forter's market area. The investment is not considered impaired.

5. Instar purchased 25% of the shares of Slobbaer Co. for $900,000. Instar has significant influence over the operating activities of Slobbaer Co. During 2015, Slobbaer Co. reported net income of $300,000 and paid a dividend of $100,000.

Accounting

(a) Determine whether each of the investments described above should be classified as held-for-collection, trading, or non-trading equity.

(b) Prepare any December 31, 2015, journal entries needed for Instar relating to Instar's various investments in other companies. Assume 2015 is Instar's first year of operations.

Analysis

What is the effect on Instar's 2015 net income (as reported on Instar's income statement) of its investments in other companies?

Principles

Briefly explain the different rationales for the different accounting and reporting rules for different types of investments in other companies.

IFRS BRIDGE TO THE PROFESSION

Professional Research

Your client, Cascade Company, is planning to invest some of its excess cash in 5-year revenue bonds issued by the county and in the shares of one of its suppliers, Teton Co. Teton's shares trade on the over-the-counter market but trading activity is quite low. Cascade plans to classify these investments as trading. The company would like you to conduct some research on the accounting for these investments.

Instructions

Access the IFRS authoritative literature at the IASB website (*http://eifrs.iasb.org/*) (you may register for free eIFRS access at this site). When you have accessed the documents, you can use the search tool in your Internet browser to respond to the following questions. (Provide paragraph citations.)

(a) Since the Teton shares are not actively traded, Cascade argues that this investment's market prices do not provide a good fair value measurement. According to the authoritative literature, what factors should be evaluated to conclude that a market price cannot be used as an estimate of fair value?

(b) To avoid volatility in their financial statements due to fair value adjustments, Cascade debated whether the bond investment could be classified as held-for-collection; Cascade is pretty sure it will hold the bonds for 5 years. What criteria must be met for Cascade to classify it as held-for-collection?

Professional Simulation

In this simulation, you are asked to address questions related to investments. Provide responses to all parts.

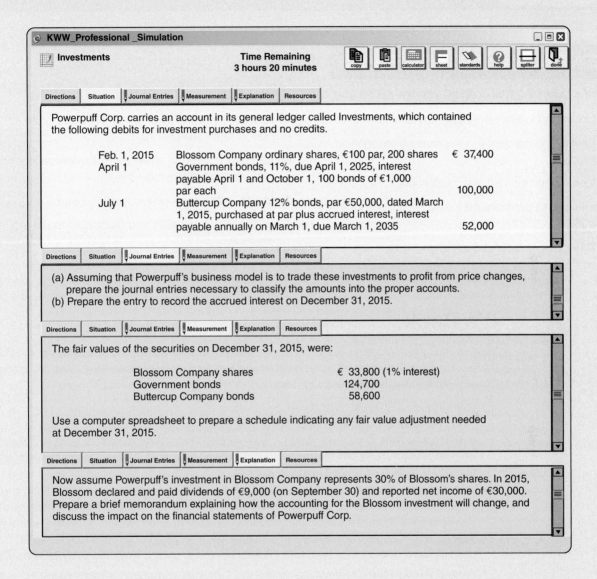

After studying this chapter, you should be able to:

1 Understand revenue recognition issues.

2 Identify the five steps in the revenue recognition process.

3 Identify the contract with customers.

4 Identify the separate performance obligations in the contract.

5 Determine the transaction price.

6 Allocate the transaction price to the separate performance obligations.

7 Recognize revenue when the company satisfies its performance obligation.

8 Identify other revenue recognition issues.

9 Describe presentation and disclosure regarding revenue.

It's Back

Revenue recognition practices are the most prevalent reasons for accounting restatements. A number of the revenue recognition issues relate to possible fraudulent behavior by company executives and employees. Consider the following situations.

- **Rolls-Royce** (GBR) was questioned by investors about the revenue recognition practices for its "Totalcare" contracts, where engines are sold at little or no profit but tie the customer into long-term servicing and parts purchases. When it was revealed that market regulators were exploring these revenue practices and changes in how Rolls booked fees from its risk-sharing partnerships, the company's share price slipped to a one-year low.

- The former co-chairman and CEO of **Qwest Communications International Inc.** (USA) and eight other former Qwest officers and employees were charged with fraud and other violations of U.S. securities laws. Three of these people fraudulently characterized non-recurring revenue from one-time sales as revenue from recurring data and Internet services. Internal correspondence likened Qwest's dependence on these transactions to fill the gap between actual and projected revenue to an addiction.

- **Sinovel Wind Group** (CHN) was scrutinized by Chinese regulators over accounting problems related to its turbine business. The accounting irregularities led to an overstatement of revenue by 10 percent and profits by 20 percent in 2011—its first year as a public company. Sinovel attributed the error to incorrectly recognizing revenue for uncompleted projects. Following the investigation, Sinovel's founder resigned as chairman but remained on the board of directors.

- Three former senior officers of **iGo Corp.** (USA) caused the company to improperly recognize revenue on consignment sales and products that were not shipped or that were shipped after the end of a fiscal quarter.

Though the cases cited involved fraud and irregularity, not all revenue recognition errors are intentional. For example, **Turquoise Hill Resources** (CAN) restated its financial results for three years due to revenue recognition irregularities. The restatement corrected errors in the accounting treatment for sales contracts, which provide for transfer of title—and revenue recognition—upon loading the coal onto customers' trucks. It was determined that, due to the changing nature of the contracts, revenue should not be recognized until customers pay.

Revenue numbers are attracting more attention from investors these days. A concern expressed recently is that revenue growth is not robust, and increases in net income (the bottom line) are caused by

factors such as low financing costs and lower labor costs which in the long run may not be sustainable. So more focus is now being given to a company's top-line revenue number as many believe strong revenue growth suggests a more profitable company in the future.

Recently, the IASB issued a new standard on revenue recognition that hopefully will improve the reporting of revenue transactions. This new standard provides a set of guidelines to follow in determining when revenue should be reported and how it should be measured. The new standard is comprehensive and applies to all companies. As a result, comparability and consistency in reporting revenue should be enhanced. After studying this chapter, you should have a good understanding of the new revenue recognition concepts.

CONCEPTUAL FOCUS

> See the **Underlying Concepts** on pages 885 and 891.
> Read the **Evolving Issue** on page 912 for a discussion of the implementation of the recently issued revenue recognition standard.

INTERNATIONAL FOCUS

> With the issuance of the new standard ("Revenue from Contracts with Customers"), the accounting for revenue recognition is now converged under IFRS and U.S. GAAP.

Sources: Cheryl de Mesa Graziano, "Revenue Recognition: A Perennial Problem," *Financial Executive* (July 14, 2005), *www.fei.org/mag/articles/7-2005_revenue.cfm;* S. Taub, "SEC Accuses Ex-CFO of Channel Stuffing," *CFO.com* (September 30, 2006)*;* B.Elder, "Rolls-Royce Hit by Accounting Concerns," *Financial Times* (February 18, 2014); W. Ma, "China Securities Regulator Probes Sinovel Wind Group," *Wall Street Journal* (January 13, 2014); and "Turquoise Hill Announces Restatement of Previously Reported Financial Results," *http://www.marketwired.com* (November 8, 2013).

PREVIEW OF CHAPTER 18

As indicated in the opening story, the issue of when revenue should be recognized is complex. The many methods of marketing products and services make it difficult to develop guidelines that will apply to all situations. This chapter provides you with general guidelines used in most business transactions. The content and organization of the chapter are as follows.

Revenue Recognition

Overview of Revenue Recognition	The Five-Step Process	Other Revenue Recognition Issues	Presentation and Disclosure
• Background • New revenue recognition standard	• Contract with customers • Separate performance obligations • Determining the transaction price • Allocating the transaction price • Satisfying performance obligations	• Right of return • Repurchase agreements • Bill-and-hold arrangements • Principal-agent relationships • Consignments • Warranties • Non-refundable upfront fees	• Presentation • Disclosure

OVERVIEW OF REVENUE RECOGNITION
Background

LEARNING OBJECTIVE
Understand revenue recognition issues.

Most revenue transactions pose few problems for revenue recognition. This is because, in many cases, the transaction is initiated and completed at the same time. However, not all transactions are that simple. For example, consider a cell phone contract between a company such as **Vodafone** (GBR) and a customer. The customer is often provided with a package that may include a handset, free minutes of talk time, data downloads, and text messaging service. In addition, some providers will bundle that with a fixed-line broadband service. At the same time, the customer may pay for these services in a variety of ways, possibly receiving a discount on the handset and then paying higher prices for connection fees and so forth. In some cases, depending on the package purchased, the company may provide free applications in subsequent periods. How, then, should the various pieces of this sale be reported by Vodafone? The answer is not obvious.

It is therefore not surprising that a recent survey of financial executives noted that the revenue recognition process is increasingly more complex to manage, more prone to error, and more material to financial statements compared to any other area in financial reporting. The report went on to note that revenue recognition is a top fraud risk and that regardless of the accounting rules followed (IFRS or U.S. GAAP), the risk of errors and inaccuracies in revenue reporting is significant.[1]

The IASB (and FASB) has indicated that the state of reporting for revenue was unsatisfactory. IFRS was criticized because it lacked guidance in a number of areas. For example, IFRS had one basic standard on revenue recognition—*IAS 18*—plus some limited guidance related to certain minor topics. In contrast, U.S. GAAP had numerous standards related to revenue recognition (by some counts, well over 100), but many believed the standards were often inconsistent with one another. Thus, the accounting for revenues provided a most fitting contrast of the principles-based (IFRS) and rules-based (U.S. GAAP) approaches. While both sides had their advocates, the IASB and FASB recognized a number of deficiencies in this area.[2]

Recently, the IASB and FASB issued a converged standard on revenue recognition entitled *Revenue from Contracts with Customers*. **[1]** To address the inconsistencies and weaknesses of the previous approaches, a comprehensive revenue recognition standard now applies to a wide range of transactions and industries. The Boards believe this new standard will improve IFRS and U.S. GAAP by:

(a) Providing a more robust framework for addressing revenue recognition issues.
(b) Improving comparability of revenue recognition practices across entities, industries, jurisdictions, and capital markets.

I
F See the Authoritative
R Literature section
S (page 930).

---

[1]See *www.prweb.com/releases/RecognitionRevenue/IFRS/prweb1648994.htm*.

[2]See, for example, "Preliminary Views on Revenue Recognition in Contracts with Customers," *IASB/FASB Discussion Paper* (December 19, 2008). Some noted that U.S. GAAP has so many standards that at times they are inconsistent with each other in applying basic principles. In addition, even with the many standards, no comprehensive guidance was provided for service transactions. Conversely, IFRS lacked guidance in certain fundamental areas such as multiple-deliverable arrangements. In addition, there were inconsistencies in applying revenue recognition principles to long-term contracts versus other elements of revenue recognition.

(c) Simplifying the preparation of financial statements by reducing the number of requirements to which companies must refer.

(d) Requiring enhanced disclosures to help financial statement users better understand the amount, timing, and uncertainty of revenue that is recognized. **[2]**

New Revenue Recognition Standard

The new standard, *Revenue from Contracts with Customers*, adopts an **asset-liability approach** as the basis for revenue recognition. The asset-liability approach recognizes and measures revenue based on changes in assets and liabilities. The Boards decided that focusing on (a) the recognition and measurement of assets and liabilities and (b) changes in those assets or liabilities over the life of the contract brings more discipline to the measurement of revenue, compared to the "risk and rewards" criteria in prior standards.

Under the asset-liability approach, companies account for revenue based on the asset or liability arising from contracts with customers. Companies are required to analyze contracts with customers because these contracts are the lifeblood of most companies. Contracts indicate the terms of the transaction and the measurement of the consideration. Without contracts, companies cannot know whether promises will be met.

Illustration 18-1 shows the key concepts related to this new standard on revenue recognition. The new standard first identifies the key objective of revenue recognition, followed by a five-step process that companies should use to ensure that revenue is measured and reported correctly. The culmination of the process is the **revenue recognition principle**, that is, recognition of revenue when the performance obligation is satisfied. We examine all steps in more detail in the following section.

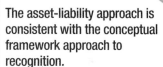

Underlying Concepts

The asset-liability approach is consistent with the conceptual framework approach to recognition.

KEY OBJECTIVE

Recognize revenue to depict the transfer of goods or services to customers in an amount that reflects the consideration that the company receives, or expects to receive, in exchange for these goods or services.

FIVE-STEP PROCESS FOR REVENUE RECOGNITION

1. Identify the contract with customers.
2. Identify the separate performance obligations in the contract.
3. Determine the transaction price.
4. Allocate the transaction price to the separate performance obligations.
5. Recognize revenue when each performance obligation is satisfied.

REVENUE RECOGNITION PRINCIPLE

Recognize revenue in the accounting period when the performance obligation is satisfied.

ILLUSTRATION 18-1
Key Concepts of Revenue Recognition

THE FIVE-STEP PROCESS

Assume that **Airbus** (FRA) signs a contract to sell airplanes to **Cathay Pacific Airlines** (HKG) for €100 million. Illustration 18-2 (on page 886) shows the five steps that Airbus follows to recognize revenue.

2 LEARNING OBJECTIVE
Identify the five steps in the revenue recognition process.

ILLUSTRATION 18-2
Five Steps of Revenue
Recognition

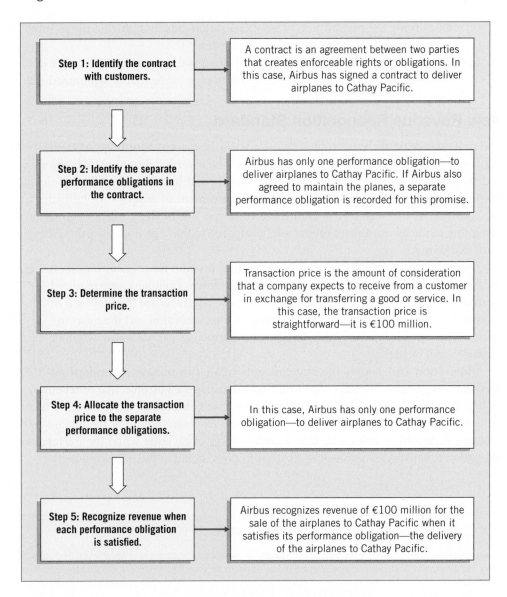

Illustration 18-2 highlights the five-step process used to recognize revenue. Step 5 is when Airbus recognizes revenue related to the sale of the airplanes to Cathay Pacific. At this point, Airbus delivers the airplanes to Cathay Pacific and satisfies its performance obligation. **[3]** In essence, a change in control from Airbus to Cathay Pacific occurs. Cathay Pacific now controls the assets because it has the ability to direct the use of and obtain substantially all the remaining benefits from the airplanes. Control also includes Cathay Pacific's ability to prevent other companies from directing the use of, or receiving the benefits from, the airplanes. In the following sections, we provide an expanded discussion of this five-step process.

Identifying the Contract with Customers—Step 1

LEARNING OBJECTIVE 3

Identify the contract with customers.

A **contract** is an agreement between two or more parties that creates enforceable rights or obligations. Contracts can be written, oral, or implied from customary business practice. A company applies the revenue guidance to a contract according to the following criteria in Illustration 18-3.

In some cases, there are multiple contracts related to the transaction, and accounting for each contract may or may not occur, depending on the circumstances. These situations often develop when not only a product is provided but some type of service is performed as well.

ILLUSTRATION 18-3
Contract Criteria for
Revenue Guidance

Apply Revenue Guidance to Contracts If:	Disregard Revenue Guidance to Contracts If:
• The contract has commercial substance; • The parties to the contract have approved the contract and are committed to perform their respective obligations; • The company can identify each party's rights regarding the goods or services to be transferred; and • The company can identify the payment terms for the goods and services to be transferred. • It is probable that the company will collect the consideration to which it will be entitled.[3]	• The contract is wholly unperformed, and • Each party can unilaterally terminate the contract without compensation.

In some cases, a company should combine contracts and account for them as one contract.

Basic Accounting

Revenue from a contract with a customer cannot be recognized until a contract exists. On entering into a contract with a customer, a company obtains rights to receive consideration from the customer and assumes obligations to transfer goods or services to the customer (performance obligations). The combination of those rights and performance obligations gives rise to an (net) asset or (net) liability. If the measure of the remaining rights exceeds the measure of the remaining performance obligations, the contract is an asset (a contract asset). Conversely, if the measure of the remaining performance obligations exceeds the measure of the remaining rights, the contract is a liability (a contract liability). However, **a company does not recognize contract assets or liabilities until one or both parties to the contract perform.** The basic accounting for a contract in which both parties perform is shown in Illustration 18-4.

ILLUSTRATION 18-4
Basic Revenue
Transaction

CONTRACTS AND RECOGNITION

Facts: On March 1, 2015, Margo Company enters into a contract to transfer a product to Soon Yoon on July 31, 2015. The contract is structured such that Soon Yoon is required to pay the full contract price of HK$5,000 on August 31, 2015. The cost of the goods transferred is HK$3,000. Margo delivers the product to Soon Yoon on July 31, 2015.

Question: What journal entries should Margo Company make in regards to this contract in 2015?

Solution: No entry is required on March 1, 2015, because neither party has performed on the contract. On July 31, 2015, Margo delivers the product and therefore should recognize revenue on that date as it satisfies its performance obligation by delivering the product to Soon Yoon.

The journal entry to record the sale and related cost of goods sold is as follows.

July 31, 2015

Accounts Receivable	5,000	
Sales Revenue		5,000
Cost of Goods Sold	3,000	
Inventory		3,000

After receiving the cash payment on August 31, 2015, Margo makes the following entry.

August 31, 2015

Cash	5,000	
Accounts Receivable		5,000

[3]The IASB included this criterion (which acts like a collectibility threshold) because the Board concluded that the assessment of a customer's credit risk was an important part of determining whether a contract is valid. That is, under the revenue standard (and discussed later in the chapter), collectibility is not a consideration for determining whether revenue is recognized. However, collectibility may be a consideration in assessing whether parties to the contract are committed to perform. In determining whether it is probable that a company will collect the amount of consideration to which it is entitled, the company assesses both the customer's ability and intent to pay as amounts become due. **[4]**

A key feature of the revenue arrangement is that the signing of the contract by the two parties is not recorded until one or both of the parties *perform under the contract*. **Until performance occurs, no net asset or net liability occurs.**

Contract Modifications

Companies sometimes change the contract terms while it is ongoing; this is referred to as a contract modification. When a contract modification occurs, companies determine whether a new contract (and performance obligations) results or whether it is a modification of the existing contract.

Separate Performance Obligation. A company accounts for a contract modification as a new contract if **both** of the following conditions are satisfied:

- The promised **goods or services are distinct** (i.e., the company sells them separately and they are not interdependent with other goods and services), and
- The company has the right to receive an amount of **consideration that reflects the standalone selling price** of the promised goods or services. **[5]**

For example, Crandall Co. has a contract to sell 100 products to a customer for €10,000 (€100 per product) at various points in time over a six-month period. After 60 products have been delivered, Crandall modifies the contract by promising to deliver 20 more products for an additional €1,900, or €95 per product (which is the standalone selling price of the products at the time of the contract modification). Crandall regularly sells the products separately. In this situation, the contract modification for the additional 20 products is, in effect, a **new and separate contract**, which does not affect the accounting for the original contract.

Given a new contract, Crandall recognizes an additional €4,000 [(100 units − 60 units) × €100] related to the original contract terms and €1,900 (20 units × €95) related to the new products. Total revenue after the modification is therefore €5,900 (€4,000 + €1,900).

Prospective Modification. What if Crandall Co. determines that the additional products are not a separate performance obligation? This might arise if the new products are not priced at the proper standalone selling price or if they are not distinct. In this situation, companies generally account for the modification using a prospective approach.

Under the prospective approach, Crandall should account for the effect of the change in the period of change as well as future periods if the change affects both. Crandall should not change previously reported results. Thus, for Crandall, the amount recognized as revenue for each of the remaining products would be a blended price of €98.33, computed as shown in Illustration 18-5.

ILLUSTRATION 18-5
Revenue Under
Prospective Modification

Consideration for products not yet delivered under original contract (€100 × 40)	€4,000
Consideration for products to be delivered under the contract modification (€95 × 20)	1,900
Total remaining revenue	€5,900
Revenue per remaining unit (€5,900 ÷ 60) = €98.33.	

Therefore, under the prospective approach, this computation differs from that in the separate performance obligation approach in that revenue on the remaining units is recognized at the blended price. Total revenue after the modification is therefore €5,900

(60 units × €98.33). Illustration 18-6 shows the revenue reported under the two contract modification approaches for Crandall Co.

ILLUSTRATION 18-6
Comparison of Contract
Modification Approaches

	Revenue Recognized Prior to Modification	Revenue Recognized After Modification	Total Revenue Recognized
Separate performance obligation	€6,000	€5,900	€11,900
No separate performance obligation—prospectively	€6,000	€5,900	€11,900

ILLUSTRATION 18-6
Comparison of Contract
Modification Approaches

As indicated, whether a modification is treated as a separate performance obligation or prospectively, the same amount of revenue is recognized before and after the modification. However, under the prospective approach, a blended price (€98.33) is used for sales in the periods after the modification.[4]

Identifying Separate Performance Obligations—Step 2

A **performance obligation** is a promise in a contract to provide a product or service to a customer. This promise may be explicit, implicit, or possibly based on customary business practice. To determine whether a performance obligation exists, **the company must provide a distinct product or service**. Illustration 18-7 summarizes some classic situations when revenue is recognized as a result of providing a distinct product or service, therefore satisfying its performance obligation.

4 LEARNING OBJECTIVE
Identify the separate performance obligations in the contract.

ILLUSTRATION 18-7
Revenue Recognition
Situations

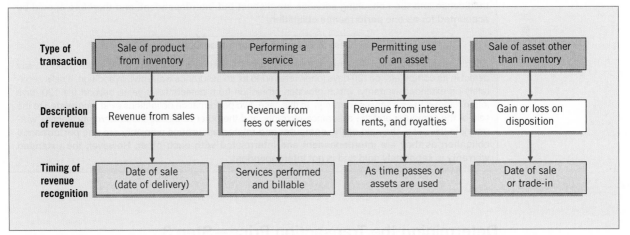

[4]Another approach to account for a contract modification is to report the information in a cumulative catch-up manner. In other words, assuming that these new products are part of the original contract, companies adjust the revenue account to reflect the cumulative effect for periods prior to when the modification occurred. An example of a catch-up situation is a long-term construction contract, which is discussed in more detail in Appendix 18A. Use of the prospective approach avoids the complexity of opening up the accounting for previously satisfied performance obligations. However, it ignores any adjustments to revenue that have already been recognized. **[6]** *For homework purposes, unless instructed otherwise, use the prospective approach for modifications that do not result in a separate performance obligation.* Expanded discussion of the prospective and cumulative catch-up (retrospective) approaches to accounting changes is provided in Chapter 22.

The accounting for the transactions in Illustration 18-7 is straightforward as only one performance obligation exists. However, many revenue arrangements may have more than one performance obligation. To determine whether a company has to account for multiple performance obligations, it evaluates a second condition: **whether the product is distinct within the contract**. In other words, if the performance obligation is not highly dependent on, or interrelated with, other promises in the contract, then each performance obligation should be accounted for separately. Conversely, if each of these services is interdependent and interrelated, these services are combined and reported as one performance obligation.

To illustrate, assume that Tata Motors (IND) sells an automobile to Marquart Auto Dealers at a price that includes six months of telematics services such as navigation and remote diagnostics. These telematics services are regularly sold on a standalone basis by Tata for a monthly fee. After the six-month period, the consumer can renew these services on a fee basis with Tata. In this case, two performance obligations exist, one related to providing the automobile and the other related to the telematics services. **Both are distinct (they can be sold separately) and are not interdependent**.

Illustration 18-8 provides additional case examples of issues related to identifying performance obligations.

ILLUSTRATION 18-8
Identifying Performance
Obligations

Case 1: Single Performance Obligation

SoftTech Inc. licenses customer-relationship software to Lopez Company. In addition to providing the software itself, SoftTech promises to perform consulting services by extensively customizing the software to Lopez's information technology environment, for a total consideration of $600,000. In this case, SoftTech is providing a significant service by integrating the goods and services (the license and the consulting service) into one combined item for which Lopez has contracted. In addition, the software is significantly customized by SoftTech in accordance with specifications negotiated by Lopez. As a result, **the license and the consulting services are distinct but interdependent, and therefore should be accounted for as one performance obligation.**

Case 2: Separate Performance Obligation

Chen Computer Inc. manufactures and sells computers that include a warranty to make good on any defect in its computers for 120 days (often referred to as an assurance warranty). In addition, it sells separately an extended warranty, which provides protection from defects for 3 years beyond the 120 days (often referred to as a service warranty). In this case, two performance obligations exist, one related to the sale of the computer and the assurance warranty, and the other to the extended warranty (service warranty). In this case, **the sale of the computer and related assurance warranty are one performance obligation as they are interdependent and interrelated with each other. However, the extended warranty is separately sold and is not interdependent.**

Determining the Transaction Price—Step 3

LEARNING OBJECTIVE 5
Determine the transaction price.

The transaction price is the amount of consideration that a company expects to receive from a customer in exchange for transferring goods and services. The transaction price in a contract is often easily determined because the customer agrees to pay a fixed amount to the company over a short period of time. In other contracts, companies must consider the following factors. **[7]**

- Variable consideration
- Time value of money
- Non-cash consideration
- Consideration paid or payable to customers

Variable Consideration

In some cases, the price of a good or service is dependent on future events. These future events might include discounts, rebates, credits, performance bonuses, or royalties. In these cases, the company estimates the amount of variable consideration it will receive from the contract to determine the amount of revenue to recognize. Companies use either the expected value, which is a probability-weighted amount, or the most likely amount in a range of possible amounts to estimate variable consideration. Companies select among these two methods based on which approach better predicts the amount of consideration to which a company is entitled. Illustration 18-9 highlights the issues to be considered in selecting the appropriate method. **[8]**

> **Underlying Concepts**
>
> The expected value approach is also illustrated in Chapter 6 to determine the liability for warranties.

Expected Value: Probability-weighted amount in a range of possible consideration amounts.	**Most Likely Amount:** The single most likely amount in a range of possible consideration outcomes.
• May be appropriate if a company has a large number of contracts with similar characteristics. • Can be based on a limited number of discrete outcomes and probabilities.	• May be appropriate if the contract has only two possible outcomes.

ILLUSTRATION 18-9
Estimating Variable Consideration

Illustration 18-10 provides an application of the two estimation methods.

ILLUSTRATION 18-10
Transaction Price—
Variable Consideration

ESTIMATING VARIABLE CONSIDERATION

Facts: Peabody Construction Company enters into a contract with a customer to build a warehouse for $100,000, with a performance bonus of $50,000 that will be paid based on the timing of completion. The amount of the performance bonus decreases by 10% per week for every week beyond the agreed-upon completion date. The contract requirements are similar to contracts that Peabody has performed previously, and management believes that such experience is predictive for this contract. Management estimates that there is a 60% probability that the contract will be completed by the agreed-upon completion date, a 30% probability that it will be completed 1 week late, and only a 10% probability that it will be completed 2 weeks late.

Question: How should Peabody account for this revenue arrangement?

Solution: The transaction price should include management's estimate of the amount of consideration to which Peabody will be entitled. Management has concluded that the **probability-weighted method** is the most predictive approach for estimating the variable consideration in this situation:

$$
\begin{array}{ll}
60\% \text{ chance of } \$150,000 \ [\$100,000 + (\$50,000 \times 1.0)] = & \$\ 90,000 \\
30\% \text{ chance of } \$145,000 \ [\$100,000 + (\$50,000 \times .90)] = & 43,500 \\
10\% \text{ chance of } \$140,000 \ [\$100,000 + (\$50,000 \times .80)] = & \underline{14,000} \\
& \$147,500
\end{array}
$$

Thus, the total transaction price is $147,500 based on the probability-weighted estimate. Management should update its estimate at each reporting date. Using a most likely outcome approach may be more predictive if a performance bonus is binary (Peabody either will or will not earn the performance bonus), such that Peabody earns either $50,000 for completion on the agreed-upon date or nothing for completion after the agreed-upon date. In this scenario, if management believes that Peabody will meet the deadline and estimates the consideration using the **most likely outcome**, the total transaction price would be $150,000 (the outcome with 60% probability).

A word of caution—a company only **allocates variable consideration if it is reasonably assured that it will be entitled to that amount.** Companies therefore may only recognize variable consideration if (1) they have experience with similar contracts and are able to estimate the cumulative amount of revenue, and (2) based on experience, it is highly probable that there will not be a significant reversal of revenue previously recognized.[5] If these criteria are not met, revenue recognition is constrained. Illustration 18-11 provides an example of how the revenue constraint works. **[10]**

ILLUSTRATION 18-11
Transaction Price—
Revenue Constraint

REVENUE CONSTRAINT

Facts: On January 1, Shera Company enters into a contract with Hornung Inc. to perform asset-management services for 1 year. Shera receives a quarterly management fee based on a percentage of Hornung's assets under management at the end of each quarter. In addition, Shera receives a performance-based incentive fee of 20% of the fund's return in excess of the return of an observable index at the end of the year.

Shera accounts for the contract as a single performance obligation to perform investment-management services for 1 year because the services are interdependent and interrelated. To recognize revenue for satisfying the performance obligation over time, Shera selects an output method of measuring progress toward complete satisfaction of the performance obligation. Shera has had a number of these types of contracts with customers in the past.

Question: At what point should Shera recognize the management fee and the performance-based incentive fee related to Hornung?

Solution: Shera should record the management fee each quarter as it performs the management of the fund over the year. However, Shera should not record the incentive fee until the end of the year. Although Shera has experience with similar contracts, that experience is not predictive of the outcome of the current contract because the amount of consideration is highly susceptible to volatility in the market. In addition, the incentive fee has a large number and high variability of possible consideration amounts. Thus, revenue related to the incentive fee is constrained (not recognized) until the incentive fee is known at the end of the year.

Time Value of Money

Timing of payment to the company sometimes does not match the transfer of the goods or services to the customer. In most situations, companies receive consideration after the product is provided or the service performed. In essence, the company provides financing for the customer.

Companies account for the time value of money if the contract **involves a significant financing component**. When a sales transaction involves a significant financing component (i.e., interest is accrued on consideration to be paid over time), the fair value is determined either by measuring the consideration received or by discounting the payment using an imputed interest rate. The imputed interest rate is the more clearly determinable of either (1) the prevailing rate for a similar instrument of an issuer with a similar credit rating, or (2) a rate of interest that discounts the nominal amount of the instrument to the current sales price of the goods or services. The company

---

[5]Conditions such as one of the following would indicate that the revenue is constrained (or not recognized):

1. The amount of consideration is highly susceptible to factors outside the company's influence. Factors include volatility in a market, the judgment of third parties, weather conditions, and a high risk of obsolescence of the promised good or service.
2. The uncertainty about the amount of consideration is not expected to be resolved for a long period of time.
3. The company's experience (or other evidence) with similar types of performance obligations is limited.
4. The contract has a large number and broad range of possible consideration amounts. **[9]**

will report the effects of the financing either as interest expense or interest revenue. Illustration 18-12 provides an example of a financing transaction.

ILLUSTRATION 18-12
Transaction Price—
Extended Payment Terms

EXTENDED PAYMENT TERMS

Facts: On July 1, 2015, SEK Company sold goods to Silva Company for R$900,000 in exchange for a 4-year, zero-interest-bearing note with a face amount of R$1,416,163. The goods have an inventory cost on SEK's books of R$590,000.

Questions: (a) How much revenue should SEK Company record on July 1, 2015? (b) How much revenue should it report related to this transaction on December 31, 2015?

Solution:
(a) SEK should record revenue of R$900,000 on July 1, 2015, which is the fair value of the inventory in this case.

(b) SEK is also financing this purchase and records interest revenue on the note over the 4-year period. In this case, the interest rate is imputed and is determined to be 12%. SEK records interest revenue of R$54,000 (12% × ½ × R$900,000) at December 31, 2015.

The entry to record SEK's sale to Silva Company is as follows.

July 1, 2015

Notes Receivable	1,416,163	
Sales Revenue		900,000
Discount on Notes Receivable		516,163

The related entry to record the cost of goods sold is as follows.

July 1, 2015

Cost of Goods Sold	590,000	
Inventory		590,000

SEK makes the following entry to record interest revenue at the end of the year.

December 31, 2015

Discount on Notes Receivable	54,000	
Interest Revenue (12% × ½ × R$900,000)		54,000

As a practical expedient, companies are not required to reflect the time value of money to determine the transaction price if the time period for payment is less than a year. **[11]**

Non-Cash Consideration

Companies sometimes receive consideration in the form of goods, services, or other non-cash consideration. When these situations occur, **companies generally recognize revenue on the basis of the fair value of what is received.** For example, assume that Raeylinn Company receives ordinary shares of Monroe Company in payment for consulting services. In that case, Raeylinn Company recognizes revenue in the amount of the fair value of the ordinary shares received. If Raeylinn cannot determine this amount, then it should estimate the selling price of the services performed and recognize this amount as revenue.

In addition, companies sometimes receive contributions (e.g., donations and gifts). A contribution is often some type of asset (e.g., securities, land, buildings, or use of facilities) but it could be the forgiveness of debt. In these cases, companies recognize revenue for the fair value of the consideration received. Similarly, customers sometimes contribute goods or services, such as equipment or labor, as consideration for goods provided or services performed. This consideration should be recognized as revenue based on the fair value of the consideration received.

Consideration Paid or Payable to Customers

Companies often make payments to their customers as part of a revenue arrangement. Consideration paid or payable may include discounts, volume rebates, coupons, free products, or services. In general, these elements reduce the consideration received and the revenue to be recognized. Illustration 18-13 provides an example of this type of transaction.

ILLUSTRATION 18-13
Transaction Price—
Volume Discount

VOLUME DISCOUNT

Facts: Sansung Company offers its customers a 3% volume discount if they purchase at least ¥2 million of its product during the calendar year. On March 31, 2015, Sansung has made sales of ¥700,000 to Artic Co. In the previous 2 years, Sansung sold over ¥3,000,000 to Artic in the period April 1 to December 31.

Question: How much revenue should Sansung recognize for the first 3 months of 2015?

Solution: In this case, Sansung should reduce its revenue by ¥21,000 (¥700,000 × 3%) because it is probable that it will provide this rebate. Revenue is therefore ¥679,000 (¥700,000 − ¥21,000). To not recognize this volume discount overstates Sansung's revenue for the first 3 months of 2015. In other words, the appropriate revenue is ¥679,000, not ¥700,000.

Given these facts, Sansung makes the following entry on March 31, 2015, to recognize revenue.

Accounts Receivable	679,000	
Sales Revenue		679,000

Assuming that Sansung's customer **meets the discount threshold**, Sansung makes the following entry.

Cash	679,000	
Accounts Receivable		679,000

If Sansung's customer **fails to meet the discount threshold**, Sansung makes the following entry upon payment.

Cash	700,000	
Accounts Receivable		679,000
Sales Discounts Forfeited		21,000

As indicated in Chapter 7 (pages 301–302), Sales Discounts Forfeited is reported in the "Other income and expense" section of the income statement.

In many cases, companies provide cash discounts to customers for a short period of time (often referred to as prompt settlement discounts). For example, assume that terms are payment due in 60 days, but if payment is made within five days, a two percent discount is given (referred to as 2/5, net 60). These prompt settlement discounts should reduce revenues, if material. In most cases, companies record the revenue at full price (gross) and record a sales discount if payment is made within the discount period.

Allocating the Transaction Price to Separate Performance Obligations—Step 4

LEARNING OBJECTIVE 6
Allocate the transaction price to the separate performance obligations.

Companies often have to allocate the transaction price to more than one performance obligation in a contract. If an allocation is needed, the transaction price allocated to the various performance obligations is based on their relative fair values. The best measure of fair value is what the company could sell the good or service for on a standalone basis, referred to as the **standalone selling price**. If this information is not available, companies should use their best estimate of what the good or service might sell for as a standalone unit. Illustration 18-14 summarizes the approaches that companies follow.

Allocation Approach	Implementation
Adjusted market assessment approach	Evaluate the market in which it sells goods or services and estimate the price that customers in that market are willing to pay for those goods or services. That approach also might include referring to prices from the company's competitors for similar goods or services and adjusting those prices as necessary to reflect the company's costs and margins.
Expected cost plus a margin approach	Forecast expected costs of satisfying a performance obligation and then add an appropriate margin for that good or service.
Residual approach	If the standalone selling price of a good or service is highly variable or uncertain, then a company may estimate the standalone selling price by reference to the total transaction price less the sum of the observable standalone selling prices of other goods or services promised in the contract.[6]

ILLUSTRATION 18-14
Transaction Price
Allocation

Illustrations 18-15 and 18-16 (on page 896) are examples of the measurement issues involved in allocating the transaction price.

MULTIPLE PERFORMANCE OBLIGATIONS—EXAMPLE 1

Facts: Lonnie Company enters into a contract to build, run, and maintain a highly complex piece of electronic equipment for a period of 5 years, commencing upon delivery of the equipment. There is a fixed fee for each of the build, run, and maintenance deliverables, and any progress payments made are non-refundable. All the deliverables have a standalone value. There is verifiable evidence of the selling price for the building and maintenance but not for running the equipment. It is determined that the transaction price must be allocated to the three performance obligations: building, running, and maintaining the equipment.

Question: What procedure should Lonnie Company use to allocate the transaction price to the three performance obligations?

Solution: The performance obligations relate to building the equipment, running the equipment, and maintaining the equipment. As indicated, Lonnie can determine standalone values for the equipment and the maintenance agreements. The company then can make a best estimate of the selling price for running the equipment, using the adjusted market assessment approach or expected cost plus a margin approach. Lonnie next applies the relative fair value method at the inception of the transaction to determine the proper allocation to each performance obligation. Once the allocation is performed, Lonnie recognizes revenue independently for each performance obligation using regular revenue recognition criteria.

If, on the other hand, the standalone selling price for running the equipment is highly variable or uncertain, Lonnie may use a residual approach. In this case, Lonnie uses the fair values of the equipment and maintenance agreements and subtracts their fair value from the total transaction price to arrive at a residual value for running the equipment.

ILLUSTRATION 18-15
Allocation—Multiple
Performance Obligations

[6]A selling price is highly variable when a company sells the same good or service to different customers (at or near the same time) for a broad range of amounts. A selling price is uncertain when a company has not yet established a price for a good or service and the good or service has not previously been sold. **[12]**

MULTIPLE PERFORMANCE OBLIGATIONS—EXAMPLE 2

Facts: Handler Company is an experienced manufacturer of equipment used in the construction industry. Handler's products range from small to large individual pieces of automated machinery to complex systems containing numerous components. Unit selling prices range from $600,000 to $4,000,000 and are quoted inclusive of installation and training. The installation process does not involve changes to the features of the equipment and does not require proprietary information about the equipment in order for the installed equipment to perform to specifications. Handler has the following arrangement with Chai Company.

- Chai purchases equipment from Handler for a price of $2,000,000 and chooses Handler to do the installation. Handler charges the same price for the equipment irrespective of whether it does the installation or not. (Some companies do the installation themselves because they either prefer their own employees to do the work or because of relationships with other customers.) The price of the installation service is estimated to have a fair value of $20,000.
- The fair value of the training sessions is estimated at $50,000. Other companies can also perform these training services.
- Chai is obligated to pay Handler the $2,000,000 upon the delivery and installation of the equipment.
- Handler delivers the equipment on September 1, 2015, and completes the installation of the equipment on November 1, 2015. Training related to the equipment starts once the installation is completed and lasts for 1 year. The equipment has a useful life of 10 years.

Questions: **(a) What are the performance obligations for purposes of accounting for the sale of the equipment? (b) If there is more than one performance obligation, how should the payment of $2,000,000 be allocated to various components?**

Solution:
(a) The first condition for separation into a standalone unit for the equipment is met. That is, the equipment, installation, and training are distinct and not interdependent—they are three separate products or services, and each of these items has a standalone selling price.
(b) The total revenue of $2,000,000 should be allocated to the three components based on their relative fair values. In this case, the fair value of the equipment should be considered $2,000,000, the installation fee is $20,000, and the training is $50,000. The total fair value to consider is $2,070,000 ($2,000,000 + $20,000 + $50,000). The allocation is as follows.

Equipment	$1,932,367	[($2,000,000 ÷ $2,070,000) × $2,000,000]
Installation	$19,324	[($20,000 ÷ $2,070,000) × $2,000,000]
Training	$48,309	[($50,000 ÷ $2,070,000) × $2,000,000]

Handler makes the following entry on November 1, 2015, to record both sales revenue and service revenue on the installation, as well as unearned service revenue.

November 1, 2015

Cash	2,000,000	
Service Revenue (installation)		19,324
Unearned Service Revenue		48,309
Sales Revenue		1,932,367

Assuming the cost of the equipment is $1,500,000, the entry to record cost of goods sold is as follows.

November 1, 2015

Cost of Goods Sold	1,500,000	
Inventory		1,500,000

As indicated by these entries, Handler recognizes revenue from the sale of the equipment once the installation is completed on November 1, 2015. In addition, it recognizes revenue for the installation fee because these services have been performed.

Handler recognizes the training revenues on a straight-line basis starting on November 1, 2015, or $4,026 ($48,309 ÷ 12) per month for one year (unless a more appropriate method such as the percentage-of-completion method is warranted). The journal entry to recognize the training revenue for 2 months in 2015 is as follows.

December 31, 2015

Unearned Service Revenue	8,052	
Service Revenue (training) ($4,026 × 2)		8,052

Therefore, Handler recognizes revenue at December 31, 2015, in the amount of $1,959,743 ($1,932,367 + $19,324 + $8,052). Handler makes the following journal entry to recognize the training revenue in 2016, assuming adjusting entries are made at year-end.

December 31, 2016

Unearned Service Revenue	40,257	
Service Revenue (training) ($48,309 − $8,052)		40,257

When a company sells a bundle of goods or services, the selling price of the bundle is often less than the sum of the individual standalone prices. In this case, the company should allocate the discount to the product (or products) that is causing the discount and not to the entire bundle. Illustration 18-17 indicates how a discount should be allocated.

ILLUSTRATION 18-17
Allocating Transaction
Price with a Discount

DISCOUNTED TRANSACTION PRICE

Facts: Java Joe's Golf Shop provides the following information related to three items that are often sold as a package.

Item	Standalone Selling Price	Price When Bundled
Lessons (per session)	€100	€100
Custom irons	525	500
Putter	125	25
Total	€750	€625

Question: How should the discount be allocated to the elements of the revenue arrangement?

Solution: As indicated, the standalone price for the lesson, custom irons, and putter is €750, but the bundled price for all three is €625. In this case, the discount applies to the performance obligations related to providing the custom irons and putter. As a result, Java Joe's allocates the discount solely to the custom irons and putter, and not to the lessons, as follows.

	Allocated Amounts
Lessons	€100
Custom irons and putter	525
Total	€625

Recognizing Revenue When (or as) Each Performance Obligation Is Satisfied—Step 5

A company satisfies its performance obligation when the customer obtains control of the good or service. As indicated earlier, the concept of change in control is the deciding factor in determining when a performance obligation is satisfied. The customer controls the product or service when it has the ability to direct the use of and obtain substantially all the remaining benefits from the asset or service. Control also includes the customer's ability to prevent other companies from directing the use of, or receiving the benefits, from the asset or service. Illustration 18-18 summarizes the indicators that the customer has obtained control. [13]

7 LEARNING OBJECTIVE
Recognize revenue when the company satisfies its performance obligation.

ILLUSTRATION 18-18
Change in Control
Indicators

1. The company has a right to payment for the asset.
2. The company has transferred legal title to the asset.
3. The company has transferred physical possession of the asset.
4. The customer has significant risks and rewards of ownership.
5. The customer has accepted the asset.

Companies satisfy performance obligations either at a point in time or over a period of time. Companies recognize revenue over a period of time if the customer receives and consumes the benefits as the seller performs and one of the following two criteria is met.

1. The customer controls the asset as it is created or enhanced (e.g., a builder constructs a building on a customer's property).

2. The company does not have an alternative use for the asset created or enhanced (e.g., an aircraft manufacturer builds specialty jets to a customer's specifications) and either (a) the customer receives benefits as the company performs and therefore the task would not need to be re-performed, or (b) the company has a right to payment and this right is enforceable.

Illustration 18-19 provides an example of the point in time when revenue should be recognized.

ILLUSTRATION 18-19
Satisfying a Performance
Obligation

TIMING OF REVENUE RECOGNITION

Facts: Gomez Software Company enters into a contract with Hurly Company to develop and install customer relationship management (CRM) software. Progress payments are made upon completion of each stage of the contract. If the contract is terminated, then the partly completed CRM software passes to Hurly Company. Gomez Software is prohibited from redirecting the software to another customer.

Question: **At what point should Gomez Software Company recognize revenue related to its contract with Hurly Company?**

Solution: Gomez Software does not create an asset with an alternative use because it is prohibited from redirecting the software to another customer. In addition, Gomez Software is entitled to payments for performance to date and expects to complete the project. Therefore, Gomez Software concludes that the contract meets the criteria for recognizing revenue over time.

A company recognizes revenue from a performance obligation over time by measuring the progress toward completion. The method selected for measuring progress should depict the transfer of control from the company to the customer. Companies use various methods to determine the extent of progress toward completion. The most common are the cost-to-cost and units-of-delivery methods. The objective of all these methods is to measure the extent of progress in terms of costs, units, or value added. Companies identify the various measures (costs incurred, labor hours worked, tons produced, floors completed, etc.) and classify them as input or output measures.

Input measures (e.g., costs incurred and labor hours worked) are efforts devoted to a contract. Output measures (with units of delivery measured as tons produced, floors of a building completed, miles of a highway completed, etc.) track results. Neither is universally applicable to all long-term projects. Their use requires the exercise of judgment and careful tailoring to the circumstances.

The most popular input measure used to determine the progress toward completion is the cost-to-cost basis. Under this basis, a company measures the percentage of completion by comparing costs incurred to date with the most recent estimate of the total costs required to complete the contract. The percentage-of-completion method is discussed more fully in Appendix 18A, which examines the accounting for long-term contracts.

Summary

Illustration 18-20 provides a summary of the five-step revenue recognition process.

Step in Process	Description	Implementation
1. Identify the contract with customers.	A contract is an agreement that creates enforceable rights or obligations.	A company applies the revenue guidance to contracts with customers and must determine if new performance obligations are created by a contract modification.
2. Identify the separate performance obligations in the contract.	A performance obligation is a promise in a contract to provide a product or service to a customer. A performance obligation exists if the customer can benefit from the good or service on its own or together with other readily available resources.	A contract may be comprised of multiple performance obligations. The accounting for multiple performance obligations is based on evaluation of whether the product or service is distinct within the contract. If each of the goods or services is distinct, but is interdependent and interrelated, these goods and services are combined and reported as one performance obligation.
3. Determine the transaction price.	The transaction price is the amount of consideration that a company expects to receive from a customer in exchange for transferring goods and services.	In determining the transaction price, companies must consider the following factors: (1) variable consideration, (2) time value of money, (3) non-cash consideration, and (4) consideration paid or payable to customer.
4. Allocate the transaction price to the separate performance obligations.	If more than one performance obligation exists, allocate the transaction price based on relative fair values.	The best measure of fair value is what the good or service could be sold for on a standalone basis (standalone selling price). Estimates of standalone selling price can be based on (1) adjusted market assessment, (2) expected cost plus a margin approach, or (3) a residual approach.
5. Recognize revenue when each performance obligation is satisfied.	A company satisfies its performance obligation when the customer obtains control of the good or service.	Companies satisfy performance obligations either at a point in time or over a period of time. Companies recognize revenue over a period of time if (1) the customer controls the asset as it is created or (2) the company does not have an alternative use for the asset.

ILLUSTRATION 18-20
Summary of the Five-Step Revenue Recognition Process

OTHER REVENUE RECOGNITION ISSUES

The revenue recognition principle and the concept of control are illustrated for the following situations.

8 **LEARNING OBJECTIVE**
Identify other revenue recognition issues.

- Right of return
- Repurchase agreements
- Bill and hold
- Principal-agent relationships
- Consignments
- Warranties
- Non-refundable upfront fees

Right of Return

Sales with rights of return have long been a challenge in the area of revenue recognition. For example, assume that Hogland Glass Works transfers control of hurricane glass to Henlo Builders. Hogland grants Henlo the **right of return** for the product for various reasons (e.g., dissatisfaction with the product) and to receive any combination of the following.

1. A full or partial refund of any consideration paid.
2. A credit that can be applied against amounts owed, or that will be owed, to the seller.
3. Another product in exchange.

To account for the transfer of this glass with a right of return (and for some services that are performed subject to a refund), Hogland should recognize all of the following.

(a) Revenue for the transferred products in the amount of consideration to which Hogland is reasonably assured to be entitled (considering the products expected to be returned).

(b) A refund liability.

(c) An asset (and corresponding adjustment to cost of sales) for its right to recover glass from Henlo on settling the refund liability.

An example of a return situation is presented in Illustration 18-21.[7]

ILLUSTRATION 18-21
Recognition—Right of Return

RIGHT OF RETURN

Facts: Venden Company sells 100 products for €100 each to Amaya Inc. for cash. Venden allows Amaya to return any unused product within 30 days and receive a full refund. The cost of each product is €60. To determine the transaction price, Venden decides that the approach that is most predictive of the amount of consideration to which it will be entitled is the most likely amount. Using the most likely amount, Venden estimates that:

1. Three products will be returned.
2. The costs of recovering the products will be immaterial.
3. The returned products are expected to be resold at a profit.

Question: How should Venden record this sale?

Solution: Upon transfer of control of the products, Venden recognizes (a) revenue of €9,700 (€100 × 97 products expected not to be returned), (b) a refund liability for €300 (€100 × 3 products expected to be returned), and (c) an asset of €180 (€60 × 3 products) for its right to recover products from customers on settling the refund liability. Hence, the amount recognized in cost of sales for 97 products is €5,820 (€60 × 97).

Venden records the sale as follows.

Cash	10,000	
Sales Revenue		9,700
Refund Liability		300

Venden also records the related cost of goods sold with the following entry.

Cost of Goods Sold	5,820	
Estimated Inventory Returns	180	
Inventory		6,000

When a return occurs, Venden should reduce the Refund Liability and Estimated Inventory Returns accounts. In addition, Venden recognizes the returned inventory in a Returned Inventory account as shown in the following entries for the return of two products.

Refund Liability (2 × €100)	200	
Accounts Payable		200
Returned Inventory (2 × €60)	120	
Estimated Inventory Returns		120

Companies record the returned asset in a separate account from inventory to provide transparency. The carrying value of the returned asset is subject to impairment testing, separate from the inventory. If a company is unable to estimate the level of returns with any reliability, it should not report any revenue until the returns become predictive.

[7]Adapted from "Revenue from Contracts with Customers," *Illustrative Examples (Revised)* (London, U.K.: IASB, November 14, 2011), p. 26.

Repurchase Agreements

In some cases, companies enter into **repurchase agreements**, which allow them to transfer control of (sell) an asset to a customer but have an obligation or right to repurchase the asset at a later date. In these situations, the question is whether the company sold the asset.[8] Generally, companies report these transactions as a financing (borrowing). That is, if the company has an obligation or right to repurchase the asset for an amount **greater than or equal to its selling price**, then the transaction is a financing transaction by the company. Illustration 18-22 examines the issues related to a repurchase agreement.

ILLUSTRATION 18-22
Recognition—
Repurchase Agreement

REPURCHASE AGREEMENT

Facts: Morgan Inc., an equipment dealer, sells equipment on January 1, 2015, to Lane Company for £100,000. It agrees to repurchase this equipment from Lane Company on December 31, 2016, for a price of £121,000.

Question: Should Morgan Inc. record a sale for this transaction?

Solution: For a sale and repurchase agreement, the terms of the agreement need to be analyzed to determine whether the seller has transferred control to the customer, Lane Company. As indicated earlier, control of an asset refers to the ability to direct the use of and obtain substantially all the benefits from the asset. Control also includes the ability to prevent other companies from directing the use of and receiving the benefit from a good or service. In this case, Morgan Inc. continues to have control of the asset. Therefore, this agreement is a financing transaction and not a sale. Thus, the asset is not removed from the books of Morgan Inc.

Assuming that an interest rate of 10% is imputed from the agreement, Morgan Inc. makes the following entries to record this agreement. Morgan Inc. records the financing on January 1, 2015, as follows.

January 1, 2015

Cash	100,000	
Liability to Lane Company		100,000

Morgan Inc. records interest on December 31, 2015, as follows.

December 31, 2015

Interest Expense	10,000	
Liability to Lane Company		10,000
(£100,000 × 10%)		

Morgan Inc. records interest and retirement of its liability to Lane Company as follows.

December 31, 2015

Interest Expense	11,000	
Liability to Lane Company		11,000
(£110,000 × 10%)		
Liability to Lane Company	121,000	
Cash (£100,000 + £10,000 + £11,000)		121,000

Rather than Morgan Inc. having the obligation or right to repurchase the asset, assume that Lane Company **has the option** to require Morgan Inc. to repurchase the asset at December 31, 2016. This option is a put option; that is, Lane Company has the option to put the asset back to Morgan Inc. Recall from the discussion in Appendix 17A

---

[8]Beyond financing motivations, a company may transfer inventory to another party on a short-term basis to avoid inventory taxes. If the counterparty is able to use the inventory during the transfer period, the transaction may more appropriately be accounted for as a rental agreement.

that the value of a put option increases when the value of the underlying asset (in this case, the equipment) decreases. In determining how to account for this transaction, Morgan Inc. has to determine whether Lane Company will have an economic incentive to exercise this put option at the end of 2016.

Specifically, Lane Company has a significant economic incentive to exercise its put option if the value of the equipment declines. In this case, the transaction is reported as a financing transaction as shown above. That is, Lane Company will return (put) the equipment back to Morgan Inc. if the repurchase price exceeds the fair value of the equipment. For example, if the repurchase price of the equipment is £150,000 but its fair value is £125,000, Lane Company is better off returning the equipment to Morgan Inc.

Conversely, if Lane Company does not have a significant economic incentive to exercise its put option, then the transaction should be reported as a sale of a product with a right of return.

What do the numbers mean? NO TAKE-BACKS

Investors in **Lucent Technologies** (USA) were negatively affected when Lucent violated one of the fundamental criteria for revenue recognition—the "no take-back" rule. This rule holds that revenue should not be booked on inventory that is shipped if the customer can return it at some point in the future. In this particular case, Lucent agreed to take back shipped inventory from its distributors if the distributors were unable to sell the items to their customers.

In essence, Lucent was "stuffing the channel." By booking sales when goods were shipped, even though they most likely would get them back, Lucent was able to report continued sales growth. However, Lucent investors got a nasty surprise when distributors returned those goods and Lucent had to restate its financial results. The restatement erased $679 million in revenues, turning an operating profit into a loss. In response to this bad news, Lucent's share price declined $1.31 per share, or 8.5 percent. Lucent is not alone in this practice. **Nortel** (CAN) got caught stuffing the sales channel with circuit boards and other electronic components, which contributed to its troubles when it was forced to restate its earnings.

Investors can be tipped off to potential channel stuffing by carefully reviewing a company's revenue recognition policy for generous return policies or use of cash incentives to encourage distributors to buy products (as was done at **Monsanto** (USA)) and by watching inventory and receivables levels. When sales increase along with receivables, that's one sign that customers are not paying for goods shipped on credit. And growing inventory levels are an indicator that customers have all the goods they need. Both scenarios suggest a higher likelihood of goods being returned and revenues and income being restated. So remember, no take-backs!

Sources: Adapted from S. Young, "Lucent Slashes First Quarter Outlook, Erases Revenue from Latest Quarter," *Wall Street Journal Online* (December 22, 2000); Tracey Byrnes, "Too Many Thin Mints: Spotting the Practice of Channel Stuffing," *Wall Street Journal Online* (February 7, 2002); and H. Weitzman, "Monsanto to Restate Results After SEC Probe," *Financial Times* (October 5, 2011).

Bill-and-Hold Arrangements

A **bill-and-hold arrangement** is a contract under which an entity bills a customer for a product but the entity retains physical possession of the product until it is transferred to the customer at a point in time in the future. Bill-and-hold sales result when the buyer is not yet ready to take delivery but does take title and accepts billing. For example, a customer may request a company to enter into such an arrangement because of (1) lack of available space for the product, (2) delays in its production schedule, or (3) more than sufficient inventory in its distribution channel.[9] Illustration 18-23 provides an example of a bill-and-hold arrangement.

[9]"Revenue from Contracts with Customers," *Exposure Draft* (London, U.K.: IASB, June 24, 2010), pp. 63–64.

ILLUSTRATION 18-23
Recognition—Bill and
Hold

BILL AND HOLD

Facts: Kaya Company sells ₺450,000 (cost ₺280,000) of fireplaces on March 1, 2015, to a local coffee shop, Baristo, which is planning to expand its locations around the city. Under the agreement, Baristo asks Kaya to retain these fireplaces in its warehouses until the new coffee shops that will house the fireplaces are ready. Title passes to Baristo at the time the agreement is signed.

Question: When should Kaya recognize the revenue from this bill-and-hold arrangement?

Solution: When to recognize revenue in a bill-and-hold arrangement depends on the circumstances. Kaya determines when it has satisfied its performance obligation to transfer a product by evaluating when Baristo obtains control of that product. For Baristo to have obtained control of a product in a bill-and-hold arrangement, all of the following criteria should be met:

(a) The reason for the bill-and-hold arrangement must be substantive.
(b) The product must be identified separately as belonging to Baristo.
(c) The product currently must be ready for physical transfer to Baristo.
(d) Kaya cannot have the ability to use the product or to direct it to another customer.

In this case, it appears that the above criteria were met, and therefore revenue recognition should be permitted at the time the contract is signed. Kaya has transferred control to Baristo; that is, Kaya has a right to payment for the fireplaces and legal title has transferred.

Kaya makes the following entry to record the bill-and-hold sale and related cost of goods sold.

March 1, 2015

Accounts Receivable	450,000	
Sales Revenue		450,000
Cost of Goods Sold	280,000	
Inventory		280,000

Principal-Agent Relationships

In a **principal-agent relationship**, the principal's performance obligation is to provide goods or perform services for a customer. The agent's performance obligation is to arrange for the principal to provide these goods or services to a customer. Examples of principal-agent relationships are as follows.

- Preferred Travel Company (agent) facilitates the booking of cruise excursions by finding customers for Regency Cruise Company (principal).
- Priceline (USA) (agent) facilitates the sale of various services such as car rentals at Hertz (USA) (principal).

In these types of situations, amounts collected on behalf of the principal are not revenue of the agent. Instead, revenue for the agent is the amount of the commission it receives (usually a percentage of total revenue). Illustration 18-24 provides an example of the issues related to principal-agent relationships.

ILLUSTRATION 18-24
Recognition—Principal-
Agent Relationship

PRINCIPAL-AGENT RELATIONSHIP

Facts: Fly-Away Travel sells airplane tickets for **British Airways (BA)** (GBR) to various customers.

Question: What are the performance obligations in this situation and how should revenue be recognized for both the principal and agent?

Solution: The principal in this case is BA and the agent is Fly-Away Travel. Because BA has the performance obligation to provide air transportation to the customer, it is the principal. Fly-Away Travel facilitates the sale of the airline ticket to the customer in exchange for a fee or commission. Its performance obligation is to arrange for BA to provide air transportation to the customer.

Although Fly-Away collects the full airfare from the customer, it then remits this amount to BA less the commission. Fly-Away therefore should not record the full amount of the fare as revenue on its books—to do so overstates revenue. Its revenue is the commission, not the full price. Control of performing the air transportation is with BA, not Fly-Away Travel.

Some might argue that there is no harm in letting Fly-Away record revenue for the full price of the ticket and then charging the cost of the ticket against the revenue (often referred to as the **gross method** of recognizing revenue). Others note that this approach overstates the agent's revenue and is misleading. The revenue received is the commission for providing the travel services, not the full fare price (often referred to as the **net approach**). The profession believes the net approach is the correct method for recognizing revenue in a principal-agent relationship. As a result, there are specific criteria to determine when a principal-agent relationship exists.[10] An important feature in deciding whether Fly-Away is acting as an agent is whether the amount it earns is predetermined, being either a fixed fee per transaction or a stated percentage of the amount billed to the customer.

What do the numbers mean?   GROSSED OUT

As you learned in Chapter 4, many corporate executives obsess over the bottom line. However, analysts on the outside look at the big picture, which includes examination of both the top line and the important subtotals in the income statement, such as gross profit. Recently, the top line is causing some concern, with nearly all companies in a global 500 index reporting a 2 percent decline in the bottom line while the top line saw revenue decline by 1 percent. This is troubling because it is the first decline in revenues since we crawled out of the recession following the financial crisis of 2008. McDonald's (USA) gave an ominous preview—it saw its first monthly sales decline in nine years.

What about income subtotals like gross margin? These metrics too have been under pressure. There is concern that struggling companies may employ a number of manipulations to mask the impact of gross margin declines on the bottom line. In fact, Marks and Spencer (GBR) prepares an income statement that omits the gross margin subtotal. While the gross margin is reported in the notes to the financial statements, a number of other items, such as impairments and fair value adjustments, are added back, offsetting a weak operating profit number.

Or, consider the classic case of Priceline.com (USA), the company made famous by William Shatner's ads about "naming your own price" for airline tickets and hotel rooms. In one quarter, Priceline reported that it earned $152 million in revenues. But, that included the full amount customers paid for tickets, hotel rooms, and rental cars. Traditional travel agencies call that amount "gross bookings," not revenues. And, much like regular travel agencies, Priceline keeps only a small portion of gross bookings—namely, the spread between the customers' accepted bids and the price Priceline paid for the merchandise. The rest, which Priceline calls "product costs," it pays to the airlines and hotels that supply the tickets and rooms.

However, Priceline's product costs came to $134 million, leaving Priceline just $18 million of what it calls "gross profit" and what most other companies would call revenues. And that's before all of Priceline's other costs—like advertising and salaries—which netted out to a loss of $102 million. The difference isn't academic. Priceline shares traded at about 23 times its reported revenues but at a mind-boggling 214 times its "gross profit." This and other aggressive recognition practices explain the stricter revenue recognition guidance, indicating that if a company performs as an agent or broker without assuming the risks and rewards of ownership of the goods, the company should report sales on a net (fee) basis.

Sources: Jeremy Kahn, "Presto Chango! Sales Are Huge," *Fortune* (March 20, 2000), p. 44; and S. Jakab, "Weak Revenue Is New Worry for Investors," *Wall Street Journal* (November 25, 2012).

Consignments

A common principal-agent relationship involves consignments. In these cases, manufacturers (or wholesalers) deliver goods but retain title to the goods until they are sold. This specialized method of marketing certain types of products makes use of an

---

[10]Indicators that the company's performance obligation is to arrange for the providing of goods or the performing of services by another party (i.e., the company is an agent and should recognize revenue in the net amount) include the following: (a) the other party is primarily responsible for fulfilling the contract; (b) the company does not have inventory risk before or after the customer order, during shipping, or on return; (c) the company does not have latitude in establishing prices for the other party's goods or services and, hence, the benefit that the company can receive from those goods or services is constrained; (d) the company's consideration is in the form of a commission; and (e) the company does not have customer credit risk for the amount receivable in exchange for the other party's goods or services. **[14]**

agreement known as a **consignment**. Under this arrangement, the **consignor** (manufacturer or wholesaler) ships merchandise to the **consignee** (dealer), who is to act as an agent for the consignor in selling the merchandise. Both consignor and consignee are interested in selling—the former to make a profit or develop a market, the latter to make a commission on the sale.

The consignee accepts the merchandise and agrees to exercise due diligence in caring for and selling it. The consignee remits to the consignor cash received from customers, after deducting a sales commission and any chargeable expenses. In consignment sales, the consignor uses a modified version of the point-of-sale basis of revenue recognition. That is, the consignor recognizes revenue only after receiving notification of the sale and the cash remittance from the consignee.

The consignor carries the merchandise as inventory throughout the consignment, separately classified as Inventory (consignments). **The consignee does not record the merchandise as an asset on its books**. Upon sale of the merchandise, the consignee has **a liability for the net amount due the consignor**. The consignor periodically receives from the consignee a report called **account sales** that shows the merchandise received, merchandise sold, expenses chargeable to the consignment, and the cash remitted. Revenue is then recognized by the consignor. Analysis of a consignment arrangement is provided in Illustration 18-25.

ILLUSTRATION 18-25
Recognition—Sales on Consignment

SALES ON CONSIGNMENT

Facts: Garcia Manufacturing Co. ships merchandise costing €36,000 on consignment to Best Value Stores. Garcia pays €3,750 of freight costs, and Best Value pays €2,250 for local advertising costs that are reimbursable from Garcia. By the end of the period, Best Value has sold two-thirds of the consigned merchandise for €40,000 cash. Best Value notifies Garcia of the sales, retains a 10% commission, and remits the cash due Garcia.

Question: What are the journal entries that the consignor (Garcia) and the consignee (Best Value) make to record this transaction?

Solution:

GARCIA MFG. CO. (CONSIGNOR)		BEST VALUE STORES (CONSIGNEE)	
Shipment of consigned merchandise			
Inventory (consignments)	36,000	No entry (record memo of merchandise received).	
Finished Goods Inventory	36,000		
Payment of freight costs by consignor			
Inventory (consignments)	3,750	No entry.	
Cash	3,750		
Payment of advertising by consignee			
No entry until notified.		Receivable from Consignor	2,250
		Cash	2,250
Sales of consigned merchandise			
No entry until notified.		Cash	40,000
		Payable to Consignor	40,000
Notification of sales and expenses and remittance of amount due			
Cash	33,750	Payable to Consignor	40,000
Advertising Expense	2,250	Receivable from	
Commission Expense	4,000	Consignor	2,250
Revenue from		Commission Revenue	
Consignment Sales	40,000	(€40,000 × 10%)	4,000
		Cash	33,750
Adjustment of inventory on consignment for cost of sales			
Cost of Goods Sold	26,500	No entry.	
Inventory (consignments)	26,500		
[2/3 (€36,000 + €3,750) = €26,500]			

Under the consignment arrangement, the consignor accepts the risk that the merchandise might not sell and relieves the consignee of the need to commit part of its working capital to inventory. Consignors use a variety of systems and account titles to record consignments, but they all share the common goal of postponing the recognition of revenue until it is known that a sale to a third party has occurred. **Consignees only recognize revenue associated with commissions.**

Warranties

Companies often provide one of two types of warranties to customers:

1. Warranties that the product **meets agreed-upon specifications in the contract at the time the product is sold**. This type of warranty is included in the sales price of a company's product and is often referred to as an **assurance-type warranty**.

2. Warranties that provide an **additional service beyond the assurance-type warranty**. This warranty is not included in the sales price of the product and is referred to as a **service-type warranty**. As a consequence, it is recorded as a separate performance obligation.

Companies do not record a separate performance obligation for assurance-type warranties. This type of warranty is nothing more than a quality guarantee that the good or service is free from defects at the point of sale. These types of obligations should be expensed in the period the goods are provided or services performed (in other words, at the point of sale). In addition, the company should record a warranty liability. The estimated amount of the liability includes all the costs that the company will incur after sale due to the correction of defects or deficiencies required under the warranty provisions.

In addition, companies sometimes provide customers with an option to purchase a warranty separately. In most cases, these extended warranties provide the customer a service beyond fixing defects that existed at the time of sale. For example, when you purchase a TV, you are entitled to the company's warranty. You will also undoubtedly be offered an extended warranty on the product at an additional cost. These service-type warranties represent a **separate service and are an additional performance obligation**. As a result, companies should allocate a portion of the transaction price to this performance obligation. The company recognizes revenue in the period that the service-type warranty is in effect. Illustration 18-26 presents an example of both an assurance-type and a service-type warranty.

ILLUSTRATION 18-26
Recognition—
Performance Obligations
and Warranties

WARRANTIES

Facts: Maverick Company sold 1,000 Rollomatics during 2015 at a total price of $6,000,000, with a warranty guarantee that the product was free of any defects. The cost of Rollomatics sold is $4,000,000. The term of the assurance warranty is 2 years, with an estimated cost of $30,000. In addition, Maverick sold extended warranties related to 400 Rollomatics for 3 years beyond the 2-year period for $12,000.

Question: **What are the journal entries that Maverick Company should make in 2015 related to the sale and the related warranties?**

Solution: To record the revenue and liabilities related to the warranties:

Cash ($6,000,000 + $12,000)	6,012,000	
Warranty Expense	30,000	
Warranty Liability		30,000
Unearned Warranty Revenue		12,000
Sales Revenue		6,000,000

To reduce inventory and recognize cost of goods sold:

Cost of Goods Sold	4,000,000	
Inventory		4,000,000

Similar to that illustrated in Chapter 13 (pages 615–616), Maverick Company reduces the Warranty Liability account over the first two years as the actual warranty costs are incurred. The company also recognizes revenue related to the service-type warranty over the three-year period that extends beyond the assurance warranty period (two years). In most cases, the unearned warranty revenue is recognized on a straight-line basis. The costs associated with the service-type warranty are expensed as incurred.

Non-Refundable Upfront Fees

Companies sometimes receive payments (**upfront fees**) from customers before they deliver a product or perform a service. Upfront payments generally relate to the initiation, activation, or setup of a good or service to be provided or performed in the future. In most cases, these upfront payments are non-refundable. Examples include fees paid for membership in a health club or buying club, and activation fees for phone, Internet, or cable.

Companies must determine whether these non-refundable advance payments are for products or services in the current period. In most situations, these payments are for future delivery of products and services and should therefore not be recorded as revenue at the time of payment. In some cases, the upfront fee is viewed similar to a renewal option for future products and services at a reduced price. An example would be a health club where once the initiation fee is paid, no additional fee is necessary upon renewal. Illustration 18-27 provides an example of an upfront fee payment.

ILLUSTRATION 18-27
Transaction Price—
Upfront Fee
Considerations

UPFRONT FEE CONSIDERATIONS

Facts: Erica Felise signs a 1-year contract with Bigelow Health Club. The terms of the contract are that Erica is required to pay a non-refundable initiation fee of £200 and an annual membership fee of £50 per month. Bigelow determines that its customers, on average, renew their annual membership two times before terminating their membership.

Question: What is the amount of revenue Bigelow Health Club should recognize in the first year?

Solution: In this case, the membership fee arrangement may be viewed as a single performance obligation (similar services are provided in all periods). That is, Bigelow is providing a discounted price in the second and third years for the same services, and this should be reflected in the revenue recognized in those periods. Bigelow determines the total transaction price to be £2,000—the upfront fee of £200 and the 3 years of monthly fees of £1,800 (£50 × 36)—and allocates it over the 3 years. In this case, Bigelow would report revenue of £55.56 (£2,000 ÷ 36) each month for 3 years. *Unless otherwise instructed, use this approach for homework problems.*[11]

Summary

Illustration 18-28 (page 908) provides a summary of the additional issues related to transfer of control and revenue recognition.

---

[11] The initiation fee might be viewed as a separate performance obligation (it provides a renewal option at a lower price than normally charged, perhaps with different services). In this situation, in the first period, Bigelow would report revenue of £600 (£50 × 12). The initiation fee would then be allocated to years two and three (£100 in each year) unless forfeited earlier.

Issue	Description	Implementation
Right of return	Return of product by customer (e.g., due to dissatisfaction with the product) in exchange for refunds, a credit against amounts owed or that will be owed, and/or another product in exchange.	Seller may recognize (a) an adjustment to revenue for the products expected to be returned, (b) a refund liability, and (c) an asset for the right to recover the product.
Repurchase agreements	Seller has an obligation or right to repurchase the asset at a later date.	Generally, if the company has an obligation or right to repurchase the asset for an amount greater than its selling price, then the transaction is a financing transaction.
Bill and hold	Result when the buyer is not yet ready to take delivery but does take title and accept billing.	Revenue is recognized depending on when the customer obtains control of that product.
Principal-agent	Arrangement in which the principal's performance obligation is to provide goods or perform services for a customer. The agent's performance obligation is to arrange for the principal to provide these goods or services to a customer.	Amounts collected on behalf of the principal are not revenue of the agent. Instead, revenue for the agent is the amount of the commission it receives. The principal recognizes revenue when the goods or services are sold to a third-party customer.
Consignments	A principal-agent relationship in which the consignor (manufacturer or wholesaler) ships merchandise to the consignee (dealer), who is to act as an agent for the consignor in selling the merchandise.	The consignor recognizes revenue only after receiving notification of the sale and the cash remittance from the consignee (consignor carries the merchandise as inventory throughout the consignment). The consignee records commission revenue (usually some percentage of the selling price).
Warranties	Warranties can be assurance-type (product meets agreed-upon specifications) or service-type (provides additional service beyond the assurance-type warranty).	A separate performance obligation is not recorded for assurance-type warranties (considered part of the product). Service-type warranties are recorded as a separate performance obligation. Companies should allocate a portion of the transaction price to service type-warranties, when present.
Non-refundable upfront fees	Upfront payments generally relate to initiation, activation, or setup activities for a good or service to be delivered in the future.	The upfront payment should be allocated over the periods benefited.

ILLUSTRATION 18-28
Summary—Other
Revenue Recognition
Issues

PRESENTATION AND DISCLOSURE

Presentation

Companies now use an asset-liability approach to recognize revenue. For example, when **Cereal Partners** (GBR) delivers cereal to **Carrefour** (FRA) (satisfying its performance obligation), it has a right to consideration from Carrefour and therefore has a contract asset. If, on the other hand, Carrefour performs first, by prepaying for this cereal, Cereal Partners has a contract liability. Companies must present these contract assets and contract liabilities on their statements of financial position.

Contract Assets and Liabilities

Contract assets are of two types: (1) unconditional rights to receive consideration because the company has satisfied its performance obligation with a customer, and (2) conditional rights to receive consideration because the company has satisfied one performance obligation but must satisfy another performance obligation in the contract before it can bill the customer. Companies should report unconditional rights to receive consideration as a receivable on the statement of financial position. Conditional rights on the statement of financial position should be reported separately as contract assets. Illustration 18-29 provides an example of the accounting and reporting for a contract asset.

ILLUSTRATION 18-29
Contract Asset
Recognition and
Presentation

CONTRACT ASSET

Facts: On January 1, 2015, Finn Company enters into a contract to transfer Product A and Product B to Obermine Co. for €100,000. The contract specifies that payment of Product A will not occur until Product B is also delivered. In other words, payment will not occur until both Product A and Product B are transferred to Obermine. Finn determines that standalone prices are €30,000 for Product A and €70,000 for Product B. Finn delivers Product A to Obermine on February 1, 2015. On March 1, 2015, Finn delivers Product B to Obermine.

Question: What journal entries should Finn Company make in regards to this contract in 2015?

Solution: No entry is required on January 1, 2015, because neither party has performed on the contract. On February 1, 2015, Finn records the following entry.

February 1, 2015

Contract Asset	30,000	
Sales Revenue		30,000

On February 1, Finn has satisfied its performance obligation and therefore reports revenue of €30,000. However, it does not record an accounts receivable at this point because it does not have an unconditional right to receive the €100,000 unless it also transfers Product B to Obermine. In other words, a contract asset occurs generally when a company must satisfy another performance obligation before it is entitled to bill the customer. When Finn transfers Product B on March 1, 2015, it makes the following entry.

March 1, 2015

Accounts Receivable	100,000	
Contract Asset		30,000
Sales Revenue		70,000

As indicated above, a **contract liability** is a company's obligation to transfer goods or services to a customer for which the company has received consideration from the customer. A contract liability is generally referred to as Unearned Sales Revenue, Unearned Service Revenue, or another appropriate account title. Illustration 18-30 provides an example of the recognition and presentation of a contract liability.

ILLUSTRATION 18-30
Contract Liability
Recognition and
Presentation

CONTRACT LIABILITY

Facts: On March 1, 2015, Henly Company enters into a contract to transfer a product to Propel Inc. on July 31, 2015. It is agreed that Propel will pay the full price of $10,000 in advance on April 1, 2015. The contract is non-cancelable. Propel, however, does not pay until April 15, 2015, and Henly delivers the product on July 31, 2015. The cost of the product is $7,500.

Question: What journal entries are required in 2015?

Solution: No entry is required on March 1, 2015, because neither party has performed on the contract. On receiving the cash on April 15, 2015, Henly records the following entry.

April 15, 2015

Cash	10,000	
Unearned Sales Revenue		10,000

On satisfying the performance obligation on July 31, 2015, Henly records the following entry to record the sale.

July 31, 2015

Unearned Sales Revenue	10,000	
Sales Revenue		10,000

In addition, Henly records cost of goods sold as follows.

Cost of Goods Sold	7,500	
Inventory		7,500

Companies are not required to use the terms "contract assets" and "contract liabilities" on the statement of financial position. For example, contract liabilities are performance obligations. Therefore, more descriptive titles (as noted earlier) such as unearned service revenue, unearned sales revenue, repurchase liability, and return liability may be used where appropriate. For contract assets, it is important that financial statement users can differentiate between unconditional and conditional rights through appropriate account presentation.

Costs to Fulfill a Contract

Companies may also report assets associated with fulfillment costs related to a revenue arrangement. Companies divide fulfillment costs (contract acquisition costs) into two categories:

1. Those that give rise to an asset.

2. Those that are expensed as incurred.

Companies recognize an asset for the incremental costs if these costs are incurred to obtain a contract with a customer. In other words, incremental costs are those that a company would not incur if the contract had not been obtained (e.g., selling commissions). Additional examples are (a) direct labor, direct materials, and allocation of costs that relate directly to the contract (e.g., costs of contract management and supervision, insurance, and depreciation of tools and equipment); and (b) costs that generate or enhance resources of the company that will be used in satisfying performance obligations in the future. Such costs include intangible design or engineering costs that will continue to give rise to benefits in the future.

Other costs that are expensed as incurred include general and administrative costs (unless those costs are explicitly chargeable to the customer under the contract) as well as costs of wasted materials, labor, or other resources to fulfill the contract that were not reflected in the price of the contract. That is, **companies only capitalize costs that are direct, incremental, and recoverable** (assuming that the contract period is more than one year). Illustration 18-31 provides an example of costs capitalized to fulfill a contract.

ILLUSTRATION 18-31
Recognition—Contract Costs

CONTRACT COSTS

Facts: Rock Integrators enters into a contract to operate Dello Company's information technology data center for 5 years. Rock Integrators incurs selling commission costs of R$10,000 to obtain the contract. Before performing the services, Rock Integrators designs and builds a technology platform that interfaces with Dello's systems. That platform is not transferred to Dello. Dello promises to pay a fixed fee of R$20,000 per month. Rock Integrators incurs the following costs: design services for the platform R$40,000, hardware for the platform R$120,000, software R$90,000, and migration and testing of data center R$100,000.

Question: What are Rock Integrators' costs for fulfilling the contract to Dello Company?

Solution: The R$10,000 selling commission costs related to obtaining the contract are recognized as an asset. The design services cost of R$40,000 and the hardware for the platform of R$120,000 are also capitalized. As the technology platform is independent of the contract, the pattern of amortization of this platform may not be related to the terms of the contract. The migration and testing costs are expensed as incurred; in general, these costs are not recoverable.

As a practical expedient, a company recognizes the incremental costs of obtaining a contract as an expense when incurred if the amortization period of the asset that the company otherwise would have recognized is one year or less.

Collectibility

As indicated earlier, if it is probable that the transaction price will not be collected, this is an indication that the parties are not committed to their obligations. As a result, one of the criteria for the existence of a contract is not met and therefore revenue is not recognized.

Any time a company sells a product or performs a service on account, a collectibility issue occurs. **Collectibility** refers to a customer's credit risk, that is, the risk that a customer will be unable to pay the amount of consideration in accordance with the contract. Under the revenue guidance—as long as a contract exists (it is probable that the customer will pay)—the amount recognized as revenue is not adjusted for customer credit risk.

Thus, companies report the revenue gross (without consideration of credit risk) and then present an allowance for any impairment due to bad debts (recognized initially and subsequently in accordance with the respective bad debt guidance). An impairment related to bad debts is reported as an operating expense in the income statement. Whether a company will get paid for satisfying a performance obligation is not a consideration in determining revenue recognition. **[15]**

Disclosure

The disclosure requirements for revenue recognition are designed to help financial statement users understand the nature, amount, timing, and uncertainty of revenue and cash flows arising from contracts with customers. To achieve that objective, companies disclose qualitative and quantitative information about all of the following:

- *Contracts with customers.* These disclosures include the disaggregation of revenue, presentation of opening and closing balances in contract assets and contract liabilities, and significant information related to their performance obligations.
- *Significant judgments.* These disclosures include judgments and changes in these judgments that affect the determination of the transaction price, the allocation of the transaction price, and the determination of the timing of revenue.
- *Assets recognized from costs incurred to fulfill a contract.* These disclosures include the closing balances of assets recognized to obtain or fulfill a contract, the amount of amortization recognized, and the method used for amortization.

To implement these requirements and meet the disclosure objectives, companies provide a range of disclosures, as summarized in Illustration 18-32.[12]

ILLUSTRATION 18-32
Revenue Disclosures

Disclosure Type	Requirements
Disaggregation of revenue	Disclose disaggregated revenue information in categories that depict how the nature, amount, timing, and uncertainty of revenue and cash flows are affected by economic factors. Reconcile disaggregated revenue to revenue for reportable segments.
Reconciliation of contract balances	Disclose opening and closing balances of contract assets (e.g., unbilled receivables) and liabilities (e.g., deferred revenue) and provide a qualitative description of significant changes in these amounts. Disclose the amount of revenue recognized in the current period relating to performance obligations satisfied in a prior period (e.g., from contracts with variable consideration). Disclose the opening and closing balances of trade receivables if not presented elsewhere.
Remaining performance obligations	Disclose the amount of the transaction price allocated to performance obligations of any remaining performance obligations not subject to significant revenue reversal. Provide a narrative discussion of potential additional revenue in constrained arrangements.
Costs to obtain or fulfill contracts	Disclose the closing balances of capitalized costs to obtain and fulfill a contract and the amount of amortization in the period. Disclose the method used to determine amortization for each reporting period.
Other qualitative disclosures	Disclose significant judgments and changes in judgments that affect the amount and timing of revenue from contracts with customers. Disclose how management determines the minimum amount of revenue not subject to the variable consideration constraint.

---

[12]See *PricewaterhouseCoopers Dataline 2013–2014.* **[16]**

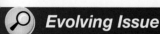

Evolving Issue   CH, CH, CH CHANGES IN REVENUE RECOGNITION

As you have learned in this chapter, the recently issued revenue recognition standard provides a comprehensive and general framework for recognizing revenue and should result in improvements in the reporting of revenue. However, these new rules reflect significant change relative to the prior revenue guidance and are expected to create implementation challenges, especially for companies that:

- Currently recognize revenue using industry-specific guidance.
- Have customer contracts with diverse terms and conditions.
- Have arrangements with goods or services delivered over long periods.
- Have systems or processes that do not easily provide new data requirements.

Among the companies that are likely to experience significant changes are those in the telecommunications, aerospace, construction, asset management, real estate, and software industries.

In the months after issuance of the new guidance, the IASB (and FASB) plans to issue documents that will address common questions posed by these industries. In addition, the Boards have created a joint transition resource group that is responsible for informing the IASB and FASB about interpretive issues that could arise when companies, institutions, and other organizations implement the revenue recognition standard. The transition group is comprised of specialists representing financial statement preparers, auditors, regulators, users, and other stakeholders, as well as members of the IASB and FASB.

The resource group solicits, analyzes, and discusses stakeholder issues that apply to common transactions that could reasonably create diversity in practice. In addition to providing a forum to discuss the application of the requirements, the transition group provides information that will help the Boards determine what, if any, action will be needed to resolve that diversity. The group itself will not issue guidance.

As noted by Hans Hoogervorst, chairman of the IASB:

"Revenue is a key performance indicator and is important to every business. Our joint transition group will help to ensure that stakeholders are reading the words in the new revenue standard in the way that we intend that they be read."

So change is necessary to achieve improvements in revenue recognition accounting. Hopefully, the extended transition period and expanded support by the transition group will make the change a bit less painful.

Sources: Executive Accounting Update: "Changes to Revenue Recognition," KPMG (January 22, 2014); and *Defining Issues No. 14-9:* "Implementing the Forthcoming Revenue Recognition Standard," KPMG (February 2014).

SUMMARY OF LEARNING OBJECTIVES

KEY TERMS

asset-liability approach, 885

assurance-type warranty, 906

bill-and-hold arrangement, 902

collectibility, 911

consignee, 905

consignment, 905

consignor, 905

contract, 886

contract assets, 908

contract liability, 909

contract modification, 888

performance obligation, 889

principal-agent relationship, 903

1 **Understand revenue recognition issues.** Most revenue transactions pose few problems for revenue recognition. This is because, in many cases, the transaction is initiated and completed at the same time. Increasing complexity of business and revenue arrangements have resulted in revenue recognition practices being identified as the most prevalent reasons for accounting restatements. A number of the revenue recognition issues relate to possible fraudulent behavior by company executives and employees, but are also due to sometimes incomplete and inconsistent accounting guidelines for revenue recognition. A recent new standard provides a set of guidelines to follow in determining when revenue should be reported and how it should be measured. The standard is comprehensive and applies to all companies. As a result, comparability and consistency in reporting revenue should be enhanced.

2 **Identify the five steps in the revenue recognition process.** The five steps in the revenue recognition process are (1) identify the contract with customers, (2) identify the separate performance obligations in the contract, (3) determine the transaction price, (4) allocate the transaction price to the separate performance obligations, and (5) recognize revenue when each performance obligation is satisfied.

3 **Identify the contract with customers.** A contract is an agreement that creates enforceable rights or obligations. A company applies the revenue guidance to contracts with customers and must determine if new performance obligations are created by a contract modification.

4 **Identify the separate performance obligations in the contract.** A performance obligation is a promise in a contract to provide a product or service to a customer. A contract may be comprised of multiple performance obligations. The accounting for multiple performance obligations is based on evaluation of whether the product or service is distinct within the contract. If each of the goods or services is distinct but is interdependent and interrelated, these goods and services are combined and reported as one performance obligation.

5 **Determine the transaction price.** The transaction price is the amount of consideration that a company expects to receive from a customer in exchange for transferring goods and services. In determining the transaction price, companies must consider the following factors: (1) variable consideration, (2) time value of money, (3) non-cash consideration, and (4) consideration paid or payable to a customer.

6 **Allocate the transaction price to the separate performance obligations.** If more than one performance obligation exists in a contract, allocate the transaction price based on relative fair values. The best measure of fair value is what the good or service could be sold for on a standalone basis (standalone selling price). Estimates of standalone selling price can be based on (1) adjusted market assessment, (2) expected cost plus a margin approach, or (3) a residual approach.

7 **Recognize revenue when the company satisfies its performance obligation.** A company satisfies its performance obligation when the customer obtains control of the good or service. Companies satisfy performance obligations either at a point in time or over a period of time. Companies recognize revenue over a period of time if (1) the customer controls the asset as it is created or (2) the company does not have an alternative use for the asset.

8 **Identify other revenue recognition issues.** Refer to Illustration 18-28 (page 908) for a summary of the accounting for (a) right of return, (b) repurchase agreements, (c) bill-and-hold arrangements, (d) principal-agent relationships, (e) consignments, (f) warranties, and (g) non-refundable upfront fees.

9 **Describe presentation and disclosure regarding revenue.** Under the asset-liability approach, to recognize revenue, companies present contract assets and contract liabilities on their statements of financial position. Contract assets are rights to receive consideration. A contract liability is a company's obligation to transfer goods or services to a customer for which the company has received consideration from the customer. Companies may also report assets associated with fulfillment costs and contract acquisition costs related to a revenue arrangement. Companies disclose qualitative and quantitative information about (a) contracts with customers with disaggregation of revenue, presentation of opening and closing balances in contract assets and contract liabilities, and significant information related to their performance obligations; (b) significant judgments that affect the determination of the transaction price, the allocation of the transaction price, and the determination of the timing of revenue; and (c) assets recognized from costs incurred to fulfill a contract.

APPENDIX **18A** LONG-TERM CONSTRUCTION CONTRACTS

REVENUE RECOGNITION OVER TIME

For the most part, companies recognize revenue at the point of sale because that is when the performance obligation is satisfied. However, as indicated in the chapter, under certain circumstances companies recognize revenue over time. The most notable context in which revenue may be recognized over time is long-term construction contract accounting.

10 LEARNING OBJECTIVE
Apply the percentage-of-completion method for long-term contracts.

Long-term contracts frequently provide that the seller (builder) may bill the purchaser at intervals, as the builder reaches various points in the project. Examples of long-term contracts are construction-type contracts, development of military and commercial aircraft, weapons-delivery systems, and space exploration hardware. When the project consists of separable units, such as a group of buildings or miles of roadway, contract provisions may provide for delivery in installments. In that case, the seller would bill the buyer and transfer title at stated stages of completion, such as the completion of each building unit or every 10 miles of road. The accounting records should record sales when installments are "delivered."

A company satisfies a performance obligation and recognizes revenue over time if at least one of the following two criteria is met: **[17]**

1. The company's performance creates or enhances an asset (e.g., work in process) that the customer controls as the asset is created or enhanced; or

2. The company's performance does not create an asset with an alternative use. For example, the asset cannot be used by another customer. In addition to this alternative-use element, at least *one* of the following criteria must be met:

   (a) The customer simultaneously receives and consumes the benefits of the entity's performance as the entity performs.

   (b) Another company would not need to substantially re-perform the work the company has completed to date if that other company were to fulfill the remaining obligation to the customer.

   (c) The company has a right to payment for its performance completed to date, and it expects to fulfill the contract as promised.[13]

Therefore, if criterion 1 or 2 is met, then a company recognizes revenue over time *if* it can reasonably estimate its progress toward satisfaction of the performance obligations. That is, the company recognizes revenues and gross profits each period based upon the progress of the construction—referred to as the **percentage-of-completion method**. The company accumulates construction costs plus gross profit recognized to date in an inventory account (Construction in Process), and it accumulates progress billings in a contra inventory account (Billings on Construction in Process).

The rationale for using percentage-of-completion accounting is that under most of these contracts, the buyer and seller have enforceable rights. The buyer has the legal right to require specific performance on the contract. The seller has the right to require progress payments that provide evidence of the buyer's ownership interest. As a result, a continuous sale occurs as the work progresses. Companies should recognize revenue according to that progression.

Alternatively, if the criteria for recognition over time are not met, the company recognizes revenues and gross profit at a point in time, that is, when the contract is completed. In these cases, contract revenue is recognized only to the extent of costs incurred that are expected to be recoverable. Once all costs are recognized, profit is recognized. This approach is referred to as the **cost-recovery (zero-profit) method**. The company accumulates construction costs in an inventory account (Construction in Process), and it accumulates progress billings in a contra inventory account (Billings on Construction in Process).

---

[13]The right to payment for performance completed to date does not need to be for a fixed amount. However, the company must be entitled to an amount that would compensate the company for performance completed to date (even if the customer can terminate the contract for reasons other than the company's failure to perform as promised). Compensation for performance completed to date includes payment that approximates the selling price of the goods or services transferred to date (e.g., recovery of the company's costs plus a reasonable profit margin).

Percentage-of-Completion Method

The **percentage-of-completion method** recognizes revenues, costs, and gross profit as a company makes progress toward completion on a long-term contract. To defer recognition of these items until completion of the entire contract is to misrepresent the efforts (costs) and accomplishments (revenues) of the accounting periods during the contract. In order to apply the percentage-of-completion method, a company must have some basis or standard for measuring the progress toward completion at particular interim dates.

Measuring the Progress Toward Completion

As one practicing accountant wrote, "The big problem in applying the percentage-of-completion method . . . has to do with the ability to make reasonably accurate estimates of completion and the final gross profit." Companies use various methods to determine the **extent of progress toward completion**. The most common are the *cost-to-cost* and *units-of-delivery* methods.

As indicated in the chapter, the objective of all these methods is to measure the extent of progress in terms of costs, units, or value added. Companies identify the various measures (costs incurred, labor hours worked, tons produced, floors completed, etc.) and classify them as input or output measures. **Input measures** (costs incurred, labor hours worked) are efforts devoted to a contract. **Output measures** (with units of delivery measured as tons produced, floors of a building completed, miles of a highway completed, etc.) track results. Neither measure is universally applicable to all long-term projects. Their use requires the exercise of judgment and careful tailoring to the circumstances.

Both input and output measures have certain disadvantages. The input measure is based on an established relationship between a unit of input and productivity. If inefficiencies cause the productivity relationship to change, inaccurate measurements result. Another potential problem is front-end loading, in which significant upfront costs result in higher estimates of completion. To avoid this problem, companies should disregard some early-stage construction costs—for example, costs of uninstalled materials or costs of subcontracts not yet performed—if they do not relate to contract performance.

Similarly, output measures can produce inaccurate results if the units used are not comparable in time, effort, or cost to complete. For example, using floors (stories) completed can be deceiving. Completing the first floor of an eight-story building may require more than one-eighth the total cost because of the substructure and foundation construction.

The most popular input measure used to determine the progress toward completion is the **cost-to-cost basis**. Under this basis, a company like **Ultra Electronics Holdings (UEH)** (GBR) measures the percentage of completion by comparing costs incurred to date with the most recent estimate of the total costs required to complete the contract. Illustration 18A-1 shows the formula for the cost-to-cost basis.

$$\frac{\text{Costs Incurred to Date}}{\text{Most Recent Estimate of Total Costs}} = \text{Percent Complete}$$

ILLUSTRATION 18A-1
Formula for Percentage-of-Completion, Cost-to-Cost Basis

Once UEH knows the percentage that costs incurred bear to total estimated costs, it applies that percentage to the total revenue or the estimated total gross profit on the contract. The resulting amount is the revenue or the gross profit to be recognized to date. Illustration 18A-2 shows this computation.

$$\text{Percent Complete} \times \begin{array}{c}\text{Estimated} \\ \text{Total Revenue} \\ \text{(or Gross Profit)}\end{array} = \begin{array}{c}\text{Revenue (or Gross} \\ \text{Profit) to Be} \\ \text{Recognized to Date}\end{array}$$

ILLUSTRATION 18A-2
Formula for Total Revenue (or Gross Profit) to Be Recognized to Date

To find the amounts of revenue and gross profit recognized each period, UEH subtracts total revenue or gross profit recognized in prior periods, as shown in Illustration 18A-3.

ILLUSTRATION 18A-3
Formula for Amount of Current-Period Revenue (or Gross Profit), Cost-to-Cost Basis

Revenue (or Gross Profit) to Be Recognized to Date	−	Revenue (or Gross Profit) Recognized in Prior Periods	=	Current-Period Revenue (or Gross Profit)

Because **the cost-to-cost method is widely used** (without excluding other bases for measuring progress toward completion), we have adopted it for use in our examples.

Example of Percentage-of-Completion Method—Cost-to-Cost Basis

To illustrate the percentage-of-completion method, assume that Hardhat Construction Company has a contract to construct a £4,500,000 bridge at an estimated cost of £4,000,000. The contract is to start in July 2015, and the bridge is to be completed in October 2017. The following data pertain to the construction period. (Note that by the end of 2016, Hardhat has revised the estimated total cost from £4,000,000 to £4,050,000.)

	2015	2016	2017
Costs to date	£1,000,000	£2,916,000	£4,050,000
Estimated costs to complete	3,000,000	1,134,000	–
Progress billings during the year	900,000	2,400,000	1,200,000
Cash collected during the year	750,000	1,750,000	2,000,000

Hardhat would compute the percent complete as shown in Illustration 18A-4.

ILLUSTRATION 18A-4
Application of Percentage-of-Completion Method, Cost-to-Cost Basis

	2015	2016	2017
Contract price	£4,500,000	£4,500,000	£4,500,000
Less estimated cost:			
Costs to date	1,000,000	2,916,000	4,050,000
Estimated costs to complete	3,000,000	1,134,000	–
Estimated total costs	4,000,000	4,050,000	4,050,000
Estimated total gross profit	£ 500,000	£ 450,000	£ 450,000
Percent complete	25% $\left(\dfrac{£1,000,000}{£4,000,000}\right)$	72% $\left(\dfrac{£2,916,000}{£4,050,000}\right)$	100% $\left(\dfrac{£4,050,000}{£4,050,000}\right)$

On the basis of the data above, Hardhat would make the following entries to record (1) the costs of construction, (2) progress billings, and (3) collections. These entries appear as summaries of the many transactions that would be entered individually as they occur during the year.

ILLUSTRATION 18A-5
Journal Entries—Percentage-of-Completion Method, Cost-to-Cost Basis

	2015		2016		2017	
To record costs of construction:						
Construction in Process	1,000,000		1,916,000		1,134,000	
Materials, Cash, Payables, etc.		1,000,000		1,916,000		1,134,000
To record progress billings:						
Accounts Receivable	900,000		2,400,000		1,200,000	
Billings on Construction in Process		900,000		2,400,000		1,200,000
To record collections:						
Cash	750,000		1,750,000		2,000,000	
Accounts Receivable		750,000		1,750,000		2,000,000

In this example, the costs incurred to date are a measure of the extent of progress toward completion. To determine this, Hardhat evaluates the costs incurred to date as a proportion of the estimated total costs to be incurred on the project. The estimated revenue and gross profit that Hardhat will recognize for each year are calculated as shown in Illustration 18A-6.

	To Date	Recognized in Prior Years	Recognized in Current Year
2015			
Revenues (£4,500,000 × 25%)	£1,125,000		£1,125,000
Costs	1,000,000		1,000,000
Gross profit	£ 125,000		£ 125,000
2016			
Revenues (£4,500,000 × 72%)	£3,240,000	£1,125,000	£2,115,000
Costs	2,916,000	1,000,000	1,916,000
Gross profit	£ 324,000	£ 125,000	£ 199,000
2017			
Revenues (£4,500,000 × 100%)	£4,500,000	£3,240,000	£1,260,000
Costs	4,050,000	2,916,000	1,134,000
Gross profit	£ 450,000	£ 324,000	£ 126,000

ILLUSTRATION 18A-6
Percentage-of-Completion Revenue, Costs, and Gross Profit by Year

Illustration 18A-7 shows Hardhat's entries to recognize revenue and gross profit each year and to record completion and final approval of the contract.

	2015		2016		2017	
To recognize revenue and gross profit:						
Construction in Process (gross profit)	125,000		199,000		126,000	
Construction Expenses	1,000,000		1,916,000		1,134,000	
Revenue from Long-Term Contracts		1,125,000		2,115,000		1,260,000
To record completion of the contract:						
Billings on Construction in Process					4,500,000	
Construction in Process						4,500,000

ILLUSTRATION 18A-7
Journal Entries to Recognize Revenue and Gross Profit and to Record Contract Completion—Percentage-of-Completion Method, Cost-to-Cost Basis

Note that **Hardhat debits gross profit (as computed in Illustration 18A-6) to Construction in Process**. Similarly, it credits Revenue from Long-Term Contracts for the amounts computed in Illustration 18A-6. Hardhat then debits the difference between the amounts recognized each year for revenue and gross profit to a nominal account, Construction Expenses (similar to Cost of Goods Sold in a manufacturing company). It reports that amount in the income statement as the actual cost of construction incurred in that period. For example, in 2015 Hardhat uses the actual costs of £1,000,000 to compute both the gross profit of £125,000 and the percent complete (25 percent).

Hardhat continues to accumulate costs in the Construction in Process account, in order to maintain a record of total costs incurred (plus recognized gross profit) to date. Although theoretically a series of "sales" takes place using the percentage-of-completion method, the selling company cannot remove the inventory cost until the construction is completed and transferred to the new owner. Hardhat's Construction in Process account for the bridge would include the following summarized entries over the term of the construction project.

ILLUSTRATION 18A-8
Content of Construction in Process Account—Percentage-of-Completion Method

Construction in Process				
2015 Construction costs	£1,000,000	12/31/17	To close	
2015 Recognized gross profit	125,000		completed	
2016 Construction costs	1,916,000		project	£4,500,000
2016 Recognized gross profit	199,000			
2017 Construction costs	1,134,000			
2017 Recognized gross profit	126,000			
Total	£4,500,000	Total		£4,500,000

Recall that the Hardhat Construction Company example contained a **change in estimated costs**: In the second year, 2016, it increased the estimated total costs from £4,000,000 to £4,050,000. The change in estimate is accounted for in a **cumulative catch-up manner**. This is done by first adjusting the percent completed to the new estimate of total costs. Next, Hardhat deducts the amount of revenues and gross profit recognized in prior periods from revenues and gross profit computed for progress to date. That is, it accounts for the change in estimate in the period of change. That way, the statement of financial position at the end of the period of change and the accounting in subsequent periods are as they would have been if the revised estimate had been the original estimate.

Financial Statement Presentation—Percentage-of-Completion

Generally, when a company records a receivable from a sale, it reduces the Inventory account. Under the percentage-of-completion method, however, the company continues to carry both the receivable and the inventory. Subtracting the balance in the **Billings account** from Construction in Process avoids double-counting the inventory. During the life of the contract, Hardhat reports in the statement of financial position the difference between the Construction in Process and the Billings on Construction in Process accounts. If that amount is a debit, Hardhat reports it **as a current asset**; if it is a credit, it reports it **as a current liability**.

At times, the costs incurred plus the gross profit recognized to date (the balance in Construction in Process) exceed the billings. In that case, Hardhat reports this excess as a current asset entitled "Costs and recognized profit in excess of billings." Hardhat can at any time calculate the unbilled portion of revenue recognized to date by subtracting the billings to date from the revenue recognized to date, as shown for 2015 for Hardhat Construction in Illustration 18A-9.

ILLUSTRATION 18A-9
Computation of Unbilled Contract Price at 12/31/15

Contract revenue recognized to date: £4,500,000 × $\dfrac{£1,000,000}{£4,000,000}$		£1,125,000
Billings to date		(900,000)
Unbilled revenue		£ 225,000

At other times, the billings exceed costs incurred and gross profit to date. In that case, Hardhat reports this excess as a current liability entitled "Billings in excess of costs and recognized profit."

What happens, as is usually the case, when companies have more than one project going at a time? When a company has a number of projects, costs exceed billings on some contracts and billings exceed costs on others. In such a case, the company segregates the contracts. The asset side includes only those contracts on which costs and recognized profit exceed billings. The liability side includes only those on which billings exceed costs and recognized profit. Separate disclosures of the dollar (or other currency) volume of billings and costs are preferable to a summary presentation of the net difference.

Using data from the bridge example, Hardhat Construction Company would report the status and results of its long-term construction activities under the percentage-of-completion method as shown in Illustration 18A-10.

HARDHAT CONSTRUCTION COMPANY

Income Statement (from Illustration 18A-6)	2015
Revenue from long-term contracts	£1,125,000
Costs of construction	1,000,000
Gross profit	£ 125,000

Statement of Financial Position (12/31)		2015
Current assets		
Accounts receivable (£900,000 − £750,000)		£ 150,000
Inventory		
Construction in process	£1,125,000	
Less: Billings	900,000	
Costs and recognized profit in excess of billings		225,000

ILLUSTRATION 18A-10
Financial Statement Presentation—Percentage-of-Completion Method (2015)

In 2016, its financial statement presentation is as follows.

HARDHAT CONSTRUCTION COMPANY

Income Statement (from Illustration 18A-6)	2016
Revenue from long-term contracts	£2,115,000
Costs of construction	1,916,000
Gross profit	£ 199,000

Statement of Financial Position (12/31)		2016
Current assets		
Accounts receivable (£150,000 + £2,400,000 − £1,750,000)		£ 800,000
Current liabilities		
Billings	£3,300,000	
Less: Construction in process	3,240,000	
Billings in excess of costs and recognized profits		60,000

ILLUSTRATION 18A-11
Financial Statement Presentation—Percentage-of-Completion Method (2016)

In 2017, Hardhat's financial statements only include an income statement because the bridge project was completed and settled.

HARDHAT CONSTRUCTION COMPANY

Income Statement (from Illustration 18A-6)	2017
Revenue from long-term contracts	£1,260,000
Costs of construction	1,134,000
Gross profit	£ 126,000

ILLUSTRATION 18A-12
Financial Statement Presentation—Percentage-of-Completion Method (2017)

In addition, Hardhat should disclose the following information in each year.

ILLUSTRATION 18A-13
Percentage-of-
Completion Method
Note Disclosure

> **Note 1.   Summary of significant accounting policies.**
> **Long-Term Construction Contracts.**   The company recognizes revenues and reports profits from long-term construction contracts, its principal business, under the percentage-of-completion method of accounting. These contracts generally extend for periods in excess of one year. The amounts of revenues and profits recognized each year are based on the ratio of costs incurred to the total estimated costs. Costs included in construction in process include direct materials, direct labor, and project-related overhead. Corporate general and administrative expenses are charged to the periods as incurred and are not allocated to construction contracts.

Cost-Recovery (Zero-Profit) Method

LEARNING OBJECTIVE 11

Apply the cost-recovery method for long-term contracts.

During the early stages of a contract, a company like **Alcatel-Lucent** (FRA) may not be able to estimate reliably the outcome of a long-term construction contract. Nevertheless, Alcatel-Lucent is confident that it will recover the contract costs incurred. In this case, Alcatel-Lucent uses the **cost-recovery method (zero-profit method)**. This method recognizes revenue only to the extent of costs incurred that are expected to be recoverable. Only after all costs are incurred is gross profit recognized.

To illustrate the cost-recovery method for the bridge project illustrated on the preceding pages, Hardhat Construction would report the following revenues and costs for 2015–2017, as shown in Illustration 18A-14.

ILLUSTRATION 18A-14
Cost-Recovery Method
Revenue, Costs, and
Gross Profit by Year

	To Date	Recognized in Prior Years	Recognized in Current Year
2015			
Revenues (costs incurred)	£1,000,000		£1,000,000
Costs	1,000,000		1,000,000
Gross profit	£ 0		£ 0
2016			
Revenues (costs incurred)	£2,916,000	£1,000,000	£1,916,000
Costs	2,916,000	1,000,000	1,916,000
Gross profit	£ 0	£ 0	£ 0
2017			
Revenues (£4,500,000 × 100%)	£4,500,000	£2,916,000	£1,584,000
Costs	4,050,000	2,916,000	1,134,000
Gross profit	£ 450,000	£ 0	£ 450,000

ILLUSTRATION 18A-15
Journal Entries—
Cost-Recovery Method

Illustration 18A-15 shows Hardhat's entries to recognize revenue and gross profit each year and to record completion and final approval of the contract.

	2015		2016		2017	
Construction Expenses	1,000,000		1,916,000			
Revenue from Long-Term Contracts		1,000,000		1,916,000		
(To recognize costs and related expenses)						
Construction in Process (Gross Profit)					450,000	
Construction Expenses					1,134,000	
Revenue from Long-Term Contracts						1,584,000
(To recognize costs and related expenses)						
Billings on Construction in Process					4,500,000	
Construction in Process						4,500,000
(To record completion of the contract)						

As indicated, no gross profit is recognized in 2015 and 2016. In 2017, Hardhat then recognizes gross profit and closes the Billings and Construction in Process accounts.

Illustration 18A-16 compares the amount of gross profit that Hardhat Construction Company would recognize for the bridge project under the two revenue recognition methods.

	Percentage-of-Completion	Cost-Recovery
2015	£125,000	£ 0
2016	199,000	0
2017	126,000	450,000

ILLUSTRATION 18A-16
Comparison of Gross Profit Recognized under Different Methods

Under the cost-recovery method, Hardhat Construction would report its long-term construction activities as shown in Illustration 18A-17.

HARDHAT CONSTRUCTION COMPANY

Income Statement		2015	2016	2017
Revenue from long-term contracts		£1,000,000	£1,916,000	£1,584,000
Costs of construction		1,000,000	1,916,000	1,134,000
Gross profit		£ 0	£ 0	£ 450,000

Statement of Financial Position (12/31)		2015	2016	2017
Current assets				
Inventories				
Construction in process	£1,000,000			
Less: Billings	900,000			
Costs in excess of billings		£ 100,000		£ –0–
Accounts receivable		150,000	£ 800,000	–0–
Current liabilities				
Billings	£3,300,000			
Less: Construction in process	2,916,000			
Billings in excess of costs and recognized profits			£ 384,000	£ –0–

Note 1. Summary of significant accounting policies.
Long-Term Construction Contracts. The company recognizes revenues and reports profits from long-term construction contracts, its principal business, under the cost-recovery method. These contracts generally extend for periods in excess of one year. Contract costs and billings are accumulated during the periods of construction, and revenues are recognized only to the extent of costs incurred that are expected to be recoverable. Only after all costs are incurred is net income recognized. Costs included in construction in process include direct material, direct labor, and project-related overhead. Corporate general and administrative expenses are charged to the periods as incurred.

ILLUSTRATION 18A-17
Financial Statement Presentation—Cost-Recovery Method

Long-Term Contract Losses

Two types of losses can become evident under long-term contracts:

12 LEARNING OBJECTIVE
Identify the proper accounting for losses on long-term contracts.

1. *Loss in the current period on a profitable contract.* This condition arises when, during construction, there is a significant increase in the estimated total contract costs but the increase does not eliminate all profit on the contract. Under the percentage-of-completion method only, the estimated cost increase requires a current-period adjustment of excess gross profit recognized on the project in prior periods. The company records this adjustment as a loss in the current period because it is a change in accounting estimate (discussed in Chapter 22).

2. *Loss on an unprofitable contract.* Cost estimates at the end of the current period may indicate that a loss will result on completion of the *entire* contract. Under both the percentage-of-completion and the cost-recovery methods, the company must recognize in the current period the entire expected contract loss.

The treatment described for unprofitable contracts is consistent with the accounting custom of anticipating foreseeable losses to avoid overstatement of current and future income (conservatism).[14]

Loss in Current Period

To illustrate a loss in the current period on a contract expected to be profitable upon completion, we'll continue with the Hardhat Construction Company bridge project. Assume that on December 31, 2016, Hardhat estimates the costs to complete the bridge contract at £1,468,962 instead of £1,134,000 (refer to page 916). Assuming all other data are the same as before, Hardhat would compute the percentage complete and recognize the loss as shown in Illustration 18A-18. Compare these computations with those for 2016 in Illustration 18A-4 (page 916). The "percent complete" has dropped, from 72 percent to 66½ percent, due to the increase in estimated future costs to complete the contract.

ILLUSTRATION 18A-18
Computation of Recognizable Loss, 2016—Loss in Current Period

Cost to date (12/31/16)	£2,916,000
Estimated costs to complete (revised)	1,468,962
Estimated total costs	£4,384,962
Percent complete (£2,916,000 ÷ £4,384,962)	66½%
Revenue recognized in 2016	
(£4,500,000 × 66½%) − £1,125,000	£1,867,500
Costs incurred in 2016	1,916,000
Loss recognized in 2016	£ (48,500)

The 2016 loss of £48,500 is a cumulative adjustment of the "excessive" gross profit recognized on the contract in 2015. Instead of restating the prior period, the company absorbs the prior period misstatement entirely in the current period. In this illustration, the adjustment was large enough to result in recognition of a loss.

Hardhat Construction would record the loss in 2016 as follows.

Construction Expenses	1,916,000	
Construction in Process (loss)		48,500
Revenue from Long-Term Contracts		1,867,500

Hardhat will report the loss of £48,500 on the 2016 income statement as the difference between the reported revenue of £1,867,500 and the costs of £1,916,000.[15] **Under the cost-recovery method, the company does not recognize a loss in 2016.** Why not? Because the company still expects the contract **to result in a profit**, to be recognized in the year of completion.

Loss on an Unprofitable Contract

To illustrate the accounting for an **overall loss on a long-term contract**, assume that at December 31, 2016, Hardhat Construction Company estimates the costs to complete the

---

[14]The accounting for losses reflects application of the accounting for onerous contracts. **[18]**

[15]In 2017, Hardhat Construction will recognize the remaining 33½ percent of the revenue (£1,507,500), with costs of £1,468,962 as expected, and will report a gross profit of £38,538. The total gross profit over the three years of the contract would be £115,038 [£125,000 (2015) − £48,500 (2016) + £38,538 (2017)]. This amount is the difference between the total contract revenue of £4,500,000 and the total contract costs of £4,384,962.

bridge contract at £1,640,250 instead of £1,134,000. Revised estimates for the bridge contract are as follows.

	2015	2016
	Original Estimates	Revised Estimates
Contract price	£4,500,000	£4,500,000
Estimated total cost	4,000,000	4,556,250*
Estimated gross profit	£ 500,000	
Estimated loss		£ (56,250)

*(£2,916,000 + £1,640,250)

Under the percentage-of-completion method, Hardhat recognized £125,000 of gross profit in 2015 (see Illustration 18A-18 on page 922). This amount must be offset in 2016 because it is no longer expected to be realized. In addition, since losses must be recognized as soon as estimable, the company must recognize the total estimated loss of £56,250 in 2016. Therefore, Hardhat must recognize a total loss of £181,250 (£125,000 + £56,250) in 2016.

Illustration 18A-19 shows Hardhat's computation of the revenue to be recognized in 2016.

Revenue recognized in 2016:	
Contract price	£4,500,000
Percent complete	× 64%*
Revenue recognizable to date	2,880,000
Less: Revenue recognized prior to 2016	1,125,000
Revenue recognized in 2016	£1,755,000
*Cost to date (12/31/16)	£2,916,000
Estimated cost to complete	1,640,250
Estimated total costs	£4,556,250
Percent complete: £2,916,000 ÷ £4,556,250 = 64%	

ILLUSTRATION 18A-19
Computation of Revenue Recognizable, 2016—Unprofitable Contract

To compute the construction costs to be expensed in 2016, Hardhat adds the total loss to be recognized in 2016 (£125,000 + £56,250) to the revenue to be recognized in 2016. Illustration 18A-20 shows this computation.

Revenue recognized in 2016 (computed above)		£1,755,000
Total loss recognized in 2016:		
Reversal of 2015 gross profit	£125,000	
Total estimated loss on the contract	56,250	181,250
Construction cost expensed in 2016		£1,936,250

ILLUSTRATION 18A-20
Computation of Construction Expense, 2016—Unprofitable Contract

Hardhat Construction would record the long-term contract revenues, expenses, and loss in 2016 as follows.

Construction Expenses	1,936,250	
Construction in Process (loss)		181,250
Revenue from Long-Term Contracts		1,755,000

At the end of 2016, Construction in Process has a balance of £2,859,750 as shown below.[16]

ILLUSTRATION 18A-21
Content of Construction in Process Account at End of 2016—Unprofitable Contract

Construction in Process			
2015 Construction costs	1,000,000		
2015 Recognized gross profit	125,000		
2016 Construction costs	1,916,000	2016 Recognized loss	181,250
Balance	**2,859,750**		

Under the cost-recovery method, Hardhat also would recognize the contract loss of £56,250 through the following entry in 2016 (the year in which the loss first became evident).

Loss from Long-Term Contracts	56,250	
Construction in Process (loss)		56,250

Just as the Billings account balance cannot exceed the contract price, neither can the balance in Construction in Process exceed the contract price. In circumstances where the Construction in Process balance exceeds the billings, the company can deduct the recognized loss from such accumulated costs on the statement of financial position. That is, under both the percentage-of-completion and the cost-recovery methods, the provision for the loss (the credit) may be combined with Construction in Process, thereby reducing the inventory balance. In those circumstances, however (as in the 2016 example above), where the billings exceed the accumulated costs, Hardhat must report separately on the statement of financial position, as a current liability, the amount of the estimated loss. That is, under both the percentage-of-completion and the cost-recovery methods, Hardhat would take the £56,250 loss, as estimated in 2016, from the Construction in Process account and report it separately as a current liability titled "Estimated liability from long-term contracts."

SUMMARY OF LEARNING OBJECTIVES FOR APPENDIX 18A

KEY TERMS

Billings account, *918*
cost-recovery (zero-profit) method, *914*
cost-to-cost basis, *915*
input measures, *915*
output measures, *915*
percentage-of-completion method, *914*

10 **Apply the percentage-of-completion method for long-term contracts.** To apply the percentage-of-completion method to long-term contracts, a company must have some basis for measuring the progress toward completion at particular interim dates. One of the most popular input measures used to determine the progress toward completion is the cost-to-cost basis. Using this basis, a company measures the percentage of completion by comparing costs incurred to date with the most recent estimate of the total costs to complete the contract. The company applies that percentage to the total revenue or the estimated total gross profit on the contract, to arrive at the amount of revenue or gross profit to be recognized to date.

11 **Apply the cost-recovery method for long-term contracts.** Under this method, companies recognize revenue and gross profit only at the point of sale, that is, when the company completes the contract. The company accumulates costs of long-term contracts in process and current billings. This method (sometimes referred to as the

---

[16]If the costs in 2017 are £1,640,250 as projected, at the end of 2017 the Construction in Process account will have a balance of £1,640,250 + £2,859,750, or £4,500,000, equal to the contract price. When the company matches the revenue remaining to be recognized in 2017 of £1,620,000 [£4,500,000 (total contract price) − £1,125,000 (2015) − £1,755,000 (2016)] with the construction expense to be recognized in 2017 of £1,620,000 [total costs of £4,556,250 less the total costs recognized in prior years of £2,936,250 (2015, £1,000,000; 2016, £1,936,250)], a zero profit results. Thus, the total loss has been recognized in 2016, the year in which it first became evident.

zero-profit method) recognizes revenue only to the extent of costs incurred that are expected to be recoverable. Only after all costs are incurred is gross profit recognized.

12 **Identify the proper accounting for losses on long-term contracts.**
Two types of losses can become evident under long-term contracts. (1) *Loss in current period on a profitable contract:* Under the percentage-of-completion method only, the estimated cost increase requires a current-period adjustment of excess gross profit recognized on the project in prior periods. The company records this adjustment as a loss in the current period because it is a change in accounting estimate. (2) *Loss on an unprofitable contract:* Under both the percentage-of-completion and the cost-recovery methods, the company must recognize the entire expected contract loss in the current period.

APPENDIX 18B   REVENUE RECOGNITION FOR FRANCHISES

In this appendix, we cover a common yet unique type of business transaction—franchises. As indicated throughout this chapter, companies recognize revenue when performance obligations in a revenue arrangement are satisfied. **Franchises** represent a challenging area because a variety of performance obligations may exist in a given franchise agreement. As a result, companies must carefully analyze franchise agreements to identify the separate performance obligations, determine when performance obligations are met, and, therefore, when revenue should be recognized.[17]

13 **LEARNING OBJECTIVE**
Explain revenue recognition for franchises.

Four types of franchising arrangements have evolved: (1) manufacturer-retailer, (2) manufacturer-wholesaler, (3) service sponsor-retailer, and (4) wholesaler-retailer. The fastest-growing category of franchising, and the one that has given rise to accounting challenges, is the third category, **service sponsor-retailer**. Included in this category are such industries and businesses as food drive-ins, restaurants, motels, and car rentals.

Franchise companies derive their revenue from one or both of two sources: (1) from the sale of initial franchises and related assets or services, and (2) from continuing fees based on the operations of franchises. The **franchisor** (the party who grants business rights under the franchise) normally provides the **franchisee** (the party who operates the franchised business) with the following services.

1. Assistance in site selection: (a) analyzing location and (b) negotiating lease.
2. Evaluation of potential income.
3. Supervision of construction activity: (a) obtaining financing, (b) designing building, and (c) supervising contractor while building.
4. Assistance in the acquisition of signs, fixtures, and equipment.
5. Bookkeeping and advisory services: (a) setting up franchisee's records; (b) advising on income, real estate, and other taxes; and (c) advising on local regulations of the franchisee's business.
6. Employee and management training.
7. Quality control.
8. Advertising and promotion.

---

[17]Franchises are an example of a license or similar rights to use intellectual property. In such arrangements, a company grants a customer the right to use, but not own, intellectual property of the company. Other examples of intellectual property include (1) software and technology; (2) motion pictures, music, and other forms of media and entertainment; and (3) patents, trademarks, and copyrights. Generally, revenue is recognized in these situations when the customer obtains control of the rights. In some cases, a license is a promise to provide a right, which transfers to the customer at a point in time. In other cases, a license is a promise to provide access to an entity's intellectual property, which transfers benefits to the customer over time. **[19]**

In the past, it was standard practice for franchisors to recognize the entire franchise fee at the date of sale, whether the fee was received then or was collectible over a long period of time. Frequently, franchisors recorded the entire amount as revenue in the year of sale even though many of the services were yet to be performed and uncertainty existed regarding the collection of the entire fee. (In effect, the franchisors were counting their fried chickens before they were hatched.) However, a **franchise agreement** may provide for refunds to the franchisee if certain conditions are not met, and franchise fee profit can be reduced sharply by future costs of obligations and services to be rendered by the franchisor.

FRANCHISE ACCOUNTING

As indicated, the performance obligations in a franchise arrangement relate to the right to open a business, use of the trade name or other intellectual property of the franchisor, and continuing services, such as marketing help, training, and in some cases supplying inventory and inventory management. Franchisors commonly charge an initial franchise fee as well as continuing franchise fees. The **initial franchise fee** is payment for establishing the franchise relationship and providing some initial services. **Continuing franchise fees** are received in return for the continuing rights granted by the franchise agreement and for providing such services as management training, advertising and promotion, legal assistance, and other support. Illustration 18B-1 provides an example of a franchise arrangement.

ILLUSTRATION 18B-1
Recognition—Franchise
Arrangement

FRANCHISE

Facts: Tum's Pizza Inc. enters into a franchise agreement on December 31, 2015, giving Food Fight Corp. the right to operate as a franchisee of Tum's Pizza for 5 years. Tum's charges Food Fight an initial franchise fee of $50,000 for the right to operate as a franchisee. Of this amount, $20,000 is payable when Food Fight signs the agreement, and the note balance is payable in five annual payments of $6,000 each on December 31. As part of the arrangement, Tum's helps locate the site, negotiate the lease or purchase of the site, supervise the construction activity, and provide employee training and the equipment necessary to be a distributor of its products. Similar training services and equipment are sold separately.

Food Fight also promises to pay ongoing royalty payments of 1% of its annual sales (payable each January 31 of the following year) and is obliged to purchase products from Tum's at its current standalone selling prices at the time of purchase. The credit rating of Food Fight indicates that money can be borrowed at 8%. The present value of an ordinary annuity of five annual receipts of $6,000 each discounted at 8% is $23,957. The discount of $6,043 represents the interest revenue to be accrued by Tum's over the payment period.

> **Question: What are the performance obligations in this arrangement and the point in time at which the performance obligations for Tum's are satisfied and revenue is recognized?**

Solution: To identify the performance obligations, Tum's must determine whether the promised rights, site selection and construction services, training services, and equipment are distinct.

- Rights to the trade name, market area, and proprietary know-how for 5 years are not individually distinct because each one is not sold separately and cannot be used with other goods or services that are readily available to the franchisee. Therefore, those combined rights give rise to a single performance obligation. Tum's satisfies the performance obligation to grant those rights at the point in time when Food Fight obtains control of the rights. That is, once Food Fight begins operating the store, Tum's has no further obligation with respect to these rights.
- Training services and equipment are distinct because similar services and equipment are sold separately. Tum's satisfies those performance obligations when it transfers the services and equipment to Food Fight.
- Tum's cannot recognize revenue for the royalty payments because it is not reasonably assured to be entitled to those sales-based royalty amounts. That is, these payments represent variable consideration. Therefore, Tum's recognizes revenue for the royalties when (or as) the uncertainty is resolved.

Tum's promise to stand ready to provide products to the franchisee in the future at standalone selling prices is not accounted for as a separate performance obligation in the contract because it does not provide Food Fight with a material right. Thus, revenue from those sales is recorded in the future when the sales are made.

To illustrate the accounting for this franchise, consider the following values for allocation of the transaction price at December 31, 2015.

Rights to the trade name, market area, and proprietary know-how	$20,000
Training services	9,957
Equipment (cost of $10,000)	14,000
Total transaction price	$43,957

Training is completed in January 2016, the equipment is installed in January 2016, and Food Fight holds a grand opening on February 2, 2016. The entries for the Tum's franchise arrangement are summarized in Illustration 18B-2.

ILLUSTRATION 18B-2
Franchise Entries—
Inception and
Commencement of
Operations

Tum's signs the agreement and receives upfront payment and note.		
December 31, 2015		
Cash	20,000	
Notes Receivable	30,000	
Discount on Notes Receivable		6,043
Unearned Franchise Revenue		20,000
Unearned Service Revenue (training)		9,957
Unearned Sales Revenue (equipment)		14,000

Franchise opens. Tum's satisfies the performance obligations related to the franchise rights, training, and equipment. That is, Tum's has no further obligations related to these elements of the franchise.		
February 2, 2016		
Unearned Franchise Revenue	20,000	
Franchise Revenue		20,000
Unearned Service Revenue (training)	9,957	
Service Revenue (training)		9,957
Unearned Sales Revenue (equipment)	14,000	
Sales Revenue		14,000
Cost of Goods Sold	10,000	
Inventory		10,000

As indicated, when Food Fight begins operations, Tum's satisfies the performance obligations related to the franchise rights, training, and equipment under the franchise agreement. That is, Tum's has no further obligations related to these elements of the franchise.

During 2016, Food Fight does well, recording $525,000 of sales in its first year of operations. The entries for Tum's related to the first year of operations of the franchise are summarized in Illustration 18B-3.

ILLUSTRATION 18B-3
Franchise Entries—First Year of Franchise Operations

To record continuing franchise fees		
December 31, 2016		
Accounts Receivable ($525,000 × 1%)	5,250	
Franchise Revenue		5,250

To record payment received and interest revenue on note		
December 31, 2016		
Cash	6,000	
Notes Receivable		6,000
Discount on Notes Receivable ($23,957 × 8%)	1,917	
Interest Revenue		1,917

Tum's will make similar entries in subsequent years of the franchise agreement.

RECOGNITION OF FRANCHISE RIGHTS REVENUE OVER TIME

In the franchise example presented in Illustration 18B-1, Tum's transferred control of the franchise rights at a point in time—that is, when the franchisee began operations and could benefit from control of the rights—with no further involvement by Tum's. In other situations, depending on the economic substance of the rights, the franchisor may be providing *access to the right* rather than transferring control of the franchise rights. In this case, **the franchise revenue is recognized over time**, rather than at a point in time. The franchise arrangement presented in Illustration 18B-4 provides an example of a franchise agreement with revenue recognized over time.

ILLUSTRATION 18B-4
Revenue Recognition over Time—Franchise

FRANCHISE REVENUE OVER TIME

Facts: Tech Solvers Corp. is a franchisor in the emerging technology consulting service business. Tech Solvers' stores perform a range of computing services (hardware/software installation, repairs, data backup, device syncing, and network solutions) on popular Apple and PC devices. Each franchise agreement gives a franchisee the right to open a Tech Solvers store and sell Tech Solvers' products and services in the area for 5 years. Under the contract, Tech Solvers also provides the franchisee with a number of services to support and enhance the franchise brand, including (a) advising and consulting on the operations of the store, (b) communicating new hardware and software developments and service techniques, (c) providing business and training manuals, and (d) advertising programs and training. As an almost entirely service operation (all parts and other supplies are purchased as needed by customers), Tech Solvers performs few upfront services to franchisees. Instead, the franchisee recruits service technicians, who are given Tech Solvers' training materials (online manuals and tutorials), which are updated for technology changes on a monthly basis at a minimum.

Tech Solvers enters into a franchise agreement on December 15, 2015, giving a franchisee the rights to operate a Tech Solvers franchise in eastern Bavaria for 5 years. Tech Solvers charges an initial franchise fee of €5,000 for the right to operate as a franchisee, payable upon signing the contract. Tech Solvers also receives ongoing royalty payments of 7% of the franchisee's annual sales (payable each January 15 of the following year).

> **Question:** What are the performance obligations in this arrangement and the point in time at which the performance obligations will be satisfied and revenue will be recognized?
>
> *Solution:* To identify the performance obligations, Tech Solvers must determine whether the promised rights and the ongoing franchisee technology support and training services are distinct.
>
> - Rights to the trade name, market area, and proprietary know-how for 5 years are not individually distinct because each one is not sold separately and cannot be used with other goods or services that are readily available to the franchisee. In addition, these licensed rights have a close connection with the underlying Tech Solvers' intellectual property (its ability to keep its service and training materials up-to-date). Therefore, those combined rights and the ongoing training materials are a single performance obligation. Tech Solvers satisfies the performance obligation over time. That is, once the franchisee begins operating a Tech Solvers franchise, Tech Solvers is providing access to the rights and must continue to perform updates and services.
> - Tech Solvers cannot recognize revenue for the royalty payments because it is not reasonably assured to be entitled to those revenue-based royalty amounts. That is, these payments represent variable consideration. Therefore, Tech Solvers recognizes revenue for the royalties when (or as) the uncertainty is resolved.

The entries for Tech Solvers related to the franchise are summarized in Illustration 18B-5.

ILLUSTRATION 18B-5
Franchise Entries—
Revenue Recognized
over Time

Franchise agreement signed and receipt of upfront payment and note		
December 15, 2015		
Cash	5,000	
Unearned Franchise Revenue		5,000
Franchise begins operations in January 2016 and records €85,000 of revenue for the year ended December 31, 2016		
December 31, 2016		
Unearned Franchise Revenue	1,000	
Franchise Revenue (€5,000 ÷ 5)		1,000
Accounts Receivable	5,950	
Franchise Revenue (€85,000 × 7%)		5,950
To record payment received from franchisee		
January 15, 2017		
Cash	5,950	
Accounts Receivable		5,950

As indicated, Tech Solvers satisfies the performance obligation related to access to the franchise rights and training materials over time (in this case, on a straight-line basis). Continuing franchise fees are recognized when uncertainty related to the variable consideration is resolved.

In summary, analysis of the characteristics of the Tech Solvers' franchise indicates that it does not reflect a right that is transferred at a point in time. That is, Tech Solvers has a continuing obligation to provide updated materials and ongoing support, suggesting the control of the right has not been transferred to the franchisee. Thus, revenue from the franchise rights is recognized over time.

```
╔══════════════════════════════════════════════════╗
║        SUMMARY OF LEARNING OBJECTIVE               ║
║            FOR APPENDIX 18B                        ║
╚══════════════════════════════════════════════════╝
```

KEY TERMS

continuing franchise
fees, *926*

franchisee, *925*

franchises, *925*

franchisor, *925*

initial franchise fee, *926*

13 **Explain revenue recognition for franchises.** In a franchise arrangement, the franchisor satisfies its performance obligation for a franchise license when control of the franchise rights is transferred, generally when the franchisee begins operations of the franchise. In situations where the franchisor provides *access to the rights* rather than transferring control of the franchise rights, the franchise rights' revenue is recognized over time rather than at a point in time. Franchisors recognize continuing franchise fees as uncertainty related to the variable consideration is resolved, that is, over time.

IFRS AUTHORITATIVE LITERATURE

Authoritative Literature References

[1] International Financial Reporting Standard 15, *Revenue from Contracts with Customers* (London, U.K.: IFRS Foundation, May 2014.

[2] International Financial Reporting Standard 15, *Revenue from Contracts with Customers* (London, U.K.: IFRS Foundation, May 2014), Introduction.

[3] International Financial Reporting Standard 15, *Revenue from Contracts with Customers* (London, U.K.: IFRS Foundation, May 2014), par. IN7e.

[4] International Financial Reporting Standard 15, *Revenue from Contracts with Customers* (London, U.K.: IFRS Foundation, May 2014), par. 9e.

[5] International Financial Reporting Standard 15, *Revenue from Contracts with Customers* (London, U.K.: IFRS Foundation, May 2014), par. 20.

[6] International Financial Reporting Standard 15, *Revenue from Contracts with Customers* (London, U.K.: IFRS Foundation, May 2014), par. 21.

[7] International Financial Reporting Standard 15, *Revenue from Contracts with Customers* (London, U.K.: IFRS Foundation, May 2014), paras. 47–48

[8] International Financial Reporting Standard 15, *Revenue from Contracts with Customers* (London, U.K.: IFRS Foundation, May 2014), par. 53.

[9] International Financial Reporting Standard 15, *Revenue from Contracts with Customers* (London, U.K.: IFRS Foundation, May 2014), par. 57.

[10] International Financial Reporting Standard 15, *Revenue from Contracts with Customers* (London, U.K.: IFRS Foundation, May 2014), par. 56.

[11] International Financial Reporting Standard 15, *Revenue from Contracts with Customers* (London, U.K.: IFRS Foundation, May 2014), par. 63.

[12] International Financial Reporting Standard 15, *Revenue from Contracts with Customers* (London, U.K.: IFRS Foundation, May 2014), as updated in Staff Paper, "Effects of Joint IASB and FASB Redeliberations on the November 2011 Exposure Draft Revenue from Contracts with Customers" (February 2013), par. 79c.

[13] International Financial Reporting Standard 15, *Revenue from Contracts with Customers* (London, U.K.: IFRS Foundation, May 2014), paras. 32–34.

[14] International Financial Reporting Standard 15, *Revenue from Contracts with Customers* (London, U.K.: IFRS Foundation, May 2014), par. B37.

[15] International Financial Reporting Standard 15, *Revenue from Contracts with Customers* (London, U.K.: IFRS Foundation, May 2014), paras. 107–108.

[16] International Financial Reporting Standard 15, *Revenue from Contracts with Customers* (London, U.K.: IFRS Foundation, May 2014), paras. 110–129.

[17] International Financial Reporting Standard 15, *Revenue from Contracts with Customers* (London, U.K.: IFRS Foundation, May 2014), paras. 35 and 38.

[18] International Financial Reporting Standard 15, *Revenue from Contracts with Customers* (London, U.K.: IFRS Foundation, May 2014), par. BC296.

[19] International Financial Reporting Standard 15, *Revenue from Contracts with Customers* (London, U.K.: IFRS Foundation, May 2014), paras. B52–B56.

Note: All asterisked Questions, Exercises, and Problems relate to material in the appendices to the chapter.

QUESTIONS

1. Explain the current environment regarding revenue recognition.

2. What was viewed as a major criticism of IFRS as regards revenue recognition?

3. Describe the revenue recognition principle.

4. Identify the five steps in the revenue recognition process.

5. Describe the critical factor in evaluating whether a performance obligation is satisfied.

6. When is revenue recognized in the following situations? (a) Revenue from selling products, (b) revenue from services performed, (c) revenue from permitting others to use company assets, and (d) revenue from disposing of assets other than products.

7. Explain the importance of a contract in the revenue recognition process.

8. On October 10, 2015, Executor Co. entered into a contract with Belisle Inc. to transfer Executor's specialty products (sales value of €10,000, cost of €6,500) on December 15, 2015. Belisle agrees to make a payment of €5,000 upon delivery and signs a promissory note to pay the remaining balance on January 15, 2016. What entries does Executor make in 2015 on this contract? Ignore time value of money considerations.

9. Explain the accounting for contract modifications.

10. What is a performance obligation? Under what conditions does a performance obligation exist?

11. When must multiple performance obligations in a revenue arrangement be accounted for separately?

12. Engelhart Implements Inc. sells tractors to area farmers. The price for each tractor includes GPS positioning service for 9 months (which facilitates field settings for planting and harvesting equipment). The GPS service is regularly sold on a standalone basis by Engelhart for a monthly fee. After the 9-month period, the consumer can renew the service on a fee basis. Does Engelhart have one or multiple performance obligations? Explain.

13. What is the transaction price? What additional factors related to the transaction price must be considered in determining the transaction price?

14. What are some examples of variable consideration? What are the two approaches for estimating variable consideration?

15. Allee Corp. is evaluating a revenue arrangement to determine proper revenue recognition. The contract is for construction of 10 speedboats for a contract price of £400,000. The customer needs the boats in its showrooms by February 1, 2015, for the boat purchase season; the customer provides a bonus payment of £21,000 if all boats are delivered by the February 1 deadline. The bonus is reduced by £7,000 each week that the boats are delivered after the deadline until no bonus is paid if the boats are delivered after February 15, 2015. Allee frequently includes such bonus terms in it contracts and thus has good historical data for estimating the probabilities of completion at different dates. It estimates an equal probability (25%) for each full delivery outcome. What approach should Allee use to determine the transaction price for this contract? Explain.

16. Refer to the information in Question 15. Assume that Allee has limited experience with a construction project on the same scale as the 10 speedboats. How does this affect the accounting for the variable consideration?

17. In measuring the transaction price, explain the accounting for (a) time value of money, and (b) non-cash consideration.

18. What is the proper accounting for volume discounts on sales of products?

19. On what basis should the transaction price be allocated to various performance obligations? Identify the approaches for allocating the transaction price.

20. Fuhremann Co. is a full-service manufacturer of surveillance equipment. Customers can purchase any combination of equipment, installation services, and training as part of Fuhremann's security services. Thus, each of these performance obligations are separate with individual standalone values. Laplante Inc. purchased cameras, installation, and training at a total price of $80,000. Estimated standalone fair values of the equipment, installation, and training are $90,000, $7,000, and $3,000, respectively. How should the transaction price be allocated to the equipment, installation, and training?

21. When does a company satisfy a performance obligation? Identify the indicators of satisfaction of a performance obligation.

22. Under what conditions does a company recognize revenue over a period of time?

23. How do companies recognize revenue from a performance obligation over time?

24. Explain the accounting for sales with right of return.

25. What are the reporting issues in a sale with a repurchase agreement?

26. Explain a bill-and-hold sale. When is revenue recognized in these situations?

27. Explain a principal-agent relationship and its significance to revenue recognition.

28. What is the nature of a sale on consignment?

29. What are the two types of warranties? Explain the accounting for each type.

30. Kwon Cellular provides cell phones and 1 year of cell service to students for an upfront, non-refundable fee of HK$300 and a usage fee of HK$5 per month. Students may renew the service for each year they are on campus (on average, students renew their service one time). What amount of revenue should Kwon Cellular recognize in the first year of the contract?

31. Describe the conditions when contract assets and liabilities are recognized and presented in financial statements.

32. Explain the reporting for (a) costs to fulfill a contract and (b) collectibility.

33. What qualitative and quantitative disclosures are required related to revenue recognition?

*34. What are the two basic methods of accounting for long-term construction contracts? Indicate the circumstances that determine when one or the other of these methods should be used.

*35. For what reasons should the percentage-of-completion method be used over the cost-recovery method whenever possible?

*36. What methods are used in practice to determine the extent of progress toward completion? Identify some "input measures" and some "output measures" that might be used to determine the extent of progress.

*37. What are the two types of losses that can become evident in accounting for long-term contracts? What is the nature of each type of loss? How is each type accounted for?

*38. Why in franchise arrangements may it not be proper to recognize the entire franchise fee as revenue at the date of sale?

*39. How should a franchisor account for continuing franchise fees and routine sales of equipment and supplies to franchisees?

BRIEF EXERCISES

3 **BE18-1** On May 10, 2015, Cosmo Co. enters into a contract to deliver a product to Greig Inc. on June 15, 2015. Greig agrees to pay the full contract price of €2,000 on July 15, 2015. The cost of the goods is €1,300. Cosmo delivers the product to Greig on June 15, 2015, and receives payment on July 15, 2015. Prepare the journal entries for Cosmo related to this contract.

3 **BE18-2** Stengel Co. enters into a 3-year contract to perform maintenance services to Laplante Inc. Laplante promises to pay $100,000 at the beginning of each year (the standalone selling price of the service at contract inception is $100,000 per year). At the end of the second year, the contract is modified and the fee for third year of service, which reflects a reduced menu of maintenance services to be performed at Laplante locations, is reduced to $80,000 (the standalone selling price of the services at the beginning of the third year is $80,000 per year). Briefly describe the accounting for this contract modification.

4 **BE18-3** Ismail Construction enters into a contract to design and build a hospital. Ismail is responsible for the overall management of the project and identifies various goods and services to be provided, including engineering, site clearance, foundation, procurement, construction of the structure, piping and wiring, installation of equipment, and finishing. Does Ismail have a single performance obligation to the customer in this revenue arrangement? Explain.

4 **BE18-4** Mauer Company licenses customer-relationship software to Hedges Inc. for 3 years. In addition to providing the software, Mauer promises to perform consulting services over the life of the license to maintain operability within Hedges' computer system. The total transaction price is £200,000. Based on standalone values, Mauer estimates the consulting services have a value of £75,000 and the software license has a value of £125,000. Upon installation of the software on July 1, 2015, Hedges pays £100,000; the contract balance is due on December 31, 2015. Identify the performance obligations and the revenue in 2015, assuming (a) the performance obligations are interdependent and (b) the performance obligations are not interdependent.

5 **BE18-5** Nair Corp. enters into a contract with a customer to build an apartment building for $1,000,000. The customer hopes to rent apartments at the beginning of the school year and provides a performance bonus of $150,000 to be paid if the building is ready for rental beginning August 1, 2015. The bonus is reduced by $50,000 each week that completion is delayed. Nair commonly includes these completion bonuses in its contracts and, based on prior experience, estimates the following completion outcomes:

Completed by	Probability
August 1, 2015	70%
August 8, 2015	20
August 15, 2015	5
After August 15, 2015	5

Determine the transaction price for this contract.

5 **BE18-6** Referring to the revenue arrangement in BE18-5, determine the transaction price for the contract, assuming (a) Nair is only able to estimate whether the building can be completed by August 1, 2015, or not (Nair estimates that there is a 70% chance that the building will be completed by August 1, 2015), and (b) Nair has limited information with which to develop a reliable estimate of completion by the August 1, 2015, deadline.

5 **BE18-7** On January 2, 2015, Adani Inc. sells goods (cost R$6,000) to Geo Company in exchange for a zero-interest-bearing note with face value of R$11,000, with payment due in 12 months. The fair value of the goods at the date of sale is R$10,000. Prepare the journal entry to record this transaction on January 2, 2015. How much total revenue should be recognized on this sale in 2015?

5 **BE18-8** On March 1, 2015, Parnevik Company sold goods to Goosen Inc. for €660,000 in exchange for a 5-year, zero-interest-bearing note in the face amount of €1,062,937. The goods have an inventory cost on Parnevik's books of €400,000. Prepare the journal entries for Parnevik on (a) March 1, 2015, and (b) December 31, 2015.

5 **BE18-9** Telephone Sellers Inc. sells prepaid telephone cards to customers. Telephone Sellers then pays the telecommunications company, TeleExpress, for the actual use of its telephone lines related to the prepaid telephone cards. Assume that Telephone Sellers sells $4,000 of prepaid cards in January 2015. It then pays TeleExpress based on usage, which turns out to be 50% in February, 30% in March, and 20% in April. The total payment by Telephone Sellers for TeleExpress lines over the 3 months is $3,000. Indicate how much income Telephone Sellers should recognize in January, February, March, and April.

5 **BE18-10** Manual Company sells goods to Nolan Company during 2015. It offers Nolan the following rebates based on total sales to Nolan. If total sales to Nolan are 10,000 units, it will grant a rebate of 2%. If it sells up to 20,000 units, it will grant a rebate of 4%. If it sells up to 30,000 units, it will grant a rebate of 6%. In the first quarter of the year, Manual sells 11,000 units to Nolan at a sales price of $110,000. Manual, based on past experience, has sold over 40,000 units to Nolan, and these sales normally take place in the third quarter of the year. Prepare the journal entry that Manual should make to record the sale of the 11,000 units in the first quarter of the year.

6 **BE18-11** Geraths Windows manufactures and sells custom storm windows for three-season porches. Geraths also provides installation service for the windows. The installation process does not involve changes in the windows, so this service can be performed by other vendors. Geraths enters into the following contract on July 1, 2015, with a local homeowner. The customer purchases windows for a price of £2,400 and chooses Geraths to do the installation. Geraths charges the same price for the windows irrespective of whether it does the installation or not. The price of the installation service is estimated to have a fair value of £600. The customer pays Geraths £2,000 (which equals the fair value of the windows, which have a cost of £1,100) upon delivery and the remaining balance upon installation of the windows. The windows are delivered on September 1, 2015, Geraths completes installation on October 15, 2015, and the customer pays the balance due. Prepare the journal entries for Geraths in 2015. (Round amounts to nearest pound.)

6 7 **BE18-12** Refer to the revenue arrangement in BE18-11. Repeat the requirements, assuming (a) Geraths estimates the standalone value of the installation based on an estimated cost of £400 plus a margin of 20% on cost, and (b) given uncertainty of finding skilled labor, Geraths is unable to develop a reliable estimate for the fair value of the installation. (Round amounts to nearest pound.)

8 **BE18-13** On July 10, 2015, Amodt Music sold CDs to retailers on account and recorded sales revenue of €700,000 (cost €560,000). Amodt grants the right to return CDs that do not sell in 3 months following delivery. Past experience indicates that the normal return rate is 15%. By October 11, 2015, retailers returned CDs to Amodt and were granted credit of €78,000. Prepare Amodt's journal entries to record (a) the sale on July 10, 2015, and (b) €78,000 of returns on October 11, 2015.

8 **BE18-14** Kristin Company sells 300 units of its products for $20 each to Logan Inc. for cash. Kristin allows Logan to return any unused product within 30 days and receive a full refund. The cost of each product is $12. To determine the transaction price, Kristin decides that the approach that is most predictive of the amount of consideration to which it will be entitled is the probability-weighted amount. Using the probability-weighted amount, Kristin estimates that (1) 10 products will be returned and (2) the returned products are expected to be resold at a profit. Prepare the journal entry for Kristin at the time of the sale to Logan.

8 **BE18-15** On June 1, 2015, Mills Company sells $200,000 of shelving units to a local retailer, ShopBarb, which is planning to expand its stores in the area. Under the agreement, ShopBarb asks Mills to retain the shelving units at its factory until the new stores are ready for installation. Title passes to ShopBarb at the time the agreement is signed. The shelving units are delivered to the stores on September 1, 2015, and ShopBarb pays in full. Prepare the journal entries for this bill-and-hold arrangement (assuming that conditions for recognizing the sale have been met) for Mills on June 1 and September 1, 2015. The cost of the shelving units to Mills is $110,000.

8 **BE18-16** Travel Inc. sells tickets for a Caribbean cruise on ShipAway Cruise Lines to Carmel Company employees. The total cruise package price to Carmel Company employees is R$70,000. Travel Inc. receives a commission of 6% of the total price. Travel Inc. therefore remits R$65,800 to ShipAway. Prepare the journal entry to record the remittance and revenue recognized by Travel Inc. on this transaction.

8 **BE18-17** Jansen Corporation shipped $20,000 of merchandise on consignment to Gooch Company. Jansen paid freight costs of $2,000. Gooch Company paid $500 for local advertising, which is reimbursable from Jansen. By year-end, 60% of the merchandise had been sold for $21,500. Gooch notified Jansen, retained a 10% commission, and remitted the cash due to Jansen. Prepare Jansen's journal entry when the cash is received.

8 **BE18-18** Talarczyk Company sold 10,000 Super-Spreaders on July 1, 2015, at a total price of €1,000,000, with a warranty guarantee that the product was free of any defects. The cost of the spreaders sold is €550,000. The assurance warranties extend for a 2-year period and are estimated to cost €40,000. Talarczyk also sold extended warranties (service-type warranties) related to 2,000 spreaders for 2 years beyond the 2-year period for €12,000. Prepare the journal entries that Talarczyk should make in 2015 related to the sale and the related warranties.

9 **BE18-19** On May 1, 2015, Mount Company enters into a contract to transfer a product to Eric Company on September 30, 2015. It is agreed that Eric will pay the full price of $25,000 in advance on June 15, 2015. Eric pays on June 15, 2015, and Mount delivers the product on September 30, 2015. Prepare the journal entries required for Mount in 2015.

8 **BE18-20** Nate Beggs signs a 1-year contract with BlueBox Video. The terms of the contract are that Nate is required to pay a non-refundable initiation fee of $100 and an annual membership fee of $5 per month. BlueBox determines that its customers, on average, renew their annual membership three times after the first year before terminating their membership. What amount of revenue should BlueBox recognize in its first year?

10 *BE18-21** Turner, Inc. began work on a £7,000,000 contract in 2015 to construct an office building. During 2015, Turner, Inc. incurred costs of £1,700,000, billed its customers for £1,200,000, and collected £960,000. At December 31, 2015, the estimated future costs to complete the project total £3,300,000. Prepare Turner's 2015 journal entries using the percentage-of-completion method.

11 *BE18-22** Guillen, Inc. began work on a $7,000,000 contract in 2015 to construct an office building. Guillen uses the cost-recovery method. At December 31, 2015, the balances in certain accounts were Construction in Process $1,715,000, Accounts Receivable $240,000, and Billings on Construction in Process $1,000,000. Indicate how these accounts would be reported in Guillen's December 31, 2015, statement of financial position.

12 *BE18-23** Archer Construction Company began work on a $420,000 construction contract in 2015. During 2015, Archer incurred costs of $278,000, billed its customer for $215,000, and collected $175,000. At December 31, 2015, the estimated future costs to complete the project total $162,000. Prepare Archer's journal entry to record profit or loss, if any, using (a) the percentage-of-completion method and (b) the cost-recovery method.

13 *BE18-24** Frozen Delight, Inc. charges an initial franchise fee of $75,000 for the right to operate as a franchisee of Frozen Delight. Of this amount, $25,000 is collected immediately. The remainder is collected in four equal annual installments of $12,500 each. These installments have a present value of $41,402. As part of the total franchise fee, Frozen Delight also provides training (with a fair value of $2,000) to help franchisees get the store ready to open. The franchise agreement is signed on April 1, 2015, training is completed, and the store opens on July 1, 2015. Prepare the journal entries required by Frozen Delight in 2015.

EXERCISES

3 **5** **E18-1 (Sales with Discounts)** Jupiter Company sells goods to Danone Inc. on account on January 1, 2015. The goods have a sales price of €610,000 (cost €500,000). The terms of the sale are net 30. If Danone pays within 5 days, it receives a cash discount of €10,000. Past history indicates the cash discount will be taken.

Instructions
(a) Prepare the journal entries for Jupiter for January 1, 2015.
(b) Prepare the journal entries for Jupiter for January 31, 2015, assuming Danone does not make payment until January 31, 2015.

3 5 **E18-2 (Transaction Price)** Presented below are three revenue recognition situations.

(a) Grupo sells goods to MTN for $1,000,000, payment due at delivery.

(b) Grupo sells goods on account to Grifols for $800,000, payment due in 30 days.

(c) Grupo sells goods to Magnus for $500,000, payment due in two installments: the first installment payable in 18 months and the second payment due 6 months later. The present value of the future payments is $464,000.

Instructions

Indicate the transaction price for each of these transactions and when revenue will be recognized.

3 **E18-3 (Contract Modification)** In September 2015, Gaertner Corp. commits to selling 150 of its iPhone-compatible docking stations to Better Buy Co. for R$15,000 (R$100 per product). The stations are delivered to Better Buy over the next 6 months. After 90 stations are delivered, the contract is modified and Gaertner promises to deliver 45 more products for an additional R$4,275 (R$95 per station). All sales are cash on delivery.

Instructions

(a) Prepare the journal entry for Gaertner for the sale of the first 90 stations. The cost of each station is R$54.

(b) Prepare the journal entry for the sale of 10 more stations after the contract modification, assuming that the price for the additional stations reflects the standalone selling price at the time of the contract modification. In addition, the additional stations are distinct from the original products as Gaertner regularly sells the products separately.

(c) Prepare the journal entry for the sale of 10 more stations (as in (b)), assuming that the pricing for the additional products *does not* reflect the standalone selling price of the additional products and the prospective method is used.

3 **E18-4 (Contract Modification)** Tyler Financial Services performs bookkeeping and tax-reporting services to startup companies in the Oconomowoc area. On January 1, 2015, Tyler entered into a 3-year service contract with Walleye Tech. Walleye promises to pay $10,000 at the beginning of each year, which at contract inception is the standalone selling price for these services. At the end of the second year, the contract is modified and the fee for the third year of services is reduced to $8,000. In addition, Walleye agrees to pay an additional $20,000 at the beginning of the third year to cover the contract for 3 additional years (i.e., 4 years remain after the modification). The extended contract services are similar to those provided in the first 2 years of the contract.

Instructions

(a) Prepare the journal entries for Tyler in 2015 and 2016 related to this service contract.

(b) Prepare the journal entries for Tyler in 2017 related to the modified service contract, assuming a prospective approach.

(c) Repeat the requirements for part (b), assuming Tyler and Walleye agree on a revised set of services (fewer bookkeeping services but more tax services) in the extended contract period and the modification results in a separate performance obligation.

5 **E18-5 (Variable Consideration)** Bai Biotech enters into a licensing agreement with Pang Pharmaceutical for a drug under development. Bai will receive a payment of ¥10,000,000 if the drug receives regulatory approval. Based on prior experience in the drug-approval process, Bai determines it is 90% likely that the drug will gain approval and a 10% chance of denial.

Instructions

(a) Determine the transaction price of the arrangement for Bai Biotech.

(b) Assuming that regulatory approval was granted on December 20, 2015, and that Bai received the payment from Pang on January 15, 2016, prepare the journal entries for Bai.

5 **E18-6 (Trailing Commission)** Aaron's Agency sells an insurance policy offered by Capital Insurance Company for a commission of $100. In addition, Aaron will receive an additional commission of $10 each year for as long as the policyholder does not cancel the policy. After selling the policy, Aaron does not have any remaining performance obligations. Based on Aaron's significant experience with these types of policies, it estimates that policyholders on average renew the policy for 4.5 years. It has no evidence to suggest that previous policyholder behavior will change.

Instructions

(a) Determine the transaction price of the arrangement for Aaron, assuming 100 policies are sold.

(b) Prepare the journal entries, assuming that the 100 policies are sold in January 2015 and that Aaron receives commissions from Capital.

5 **E18-7 (Sales with Discounts)** On June 3, 2015, Hunt Company sold to Ann Mount merchandise having a sales price of £8,000 (cost £5,600) with terms of 2/10, n/60, f.o.b. shipping point. Hunt estimates that merchandise with a sales value of £800 will be returned. An invoice totaling £120, terms n/30, was received by Mount on June 8 from Olympic Transport Service for the freight cost. Upon receipt of the goods, on June 5, Mount notified Hunt that £300 of merchandise contained flaws. The same day, Hunt issued a credit memo covering the defective merchandise and asked that it be returned at Hunt's expense. Hunt estimates the returned items to have a fair value of £120. The freight on the returned merchandise was £24, paid by Hunt on June 7. On June 12, the company received a check for the balance due from Mount.

Instructions

(a) Prepare journal entries for Hunt Company to record all the events noted above assuming sales and receivables are entered at gross selling price.

(b) Prepare the journal entry assuming that Ann Mount did not remit payment until August 5.

5 **E18-8 (Sales with Discounts)** Taylor Marina has 300 available slips that rent for €800 per season. Payments must be made in full at the start of the boating season, April 1, 2015. The boating season ends October 31, and the marina has a December 31 year-end. Slips for future seasons may be reserved if paid for by December 31, 2015. Under a new policy, if payment for 2016 season slips is made by December 31, 2015, a 5% discount is allowed. If payment for 2017 season slips is made by December 31, 2015, renters get a 20% discount (this promotion hopefully will provide cash flow for major dock repairs).

On December 31, 2014, all 300 slips for the 2015 season were rented at full price. On December 31, 2015, 200 slips were reserved and paid for the 2016 boating season, and 60 slips were reserved and paid for the 2017 boating season.

Instructions

(a) Prepare the appropriate journal entries for December 31, 2015, and December 31, 2016.

(b) Assume the marina operator is unsophisticated in business. Explain the managerial significance of the above accounting to this person.

5 **6** **E18-9 (Allocate Transaction Price)** Sanchez Co. enters into a contract to sell Product A and Product B on January 2, 2015, for an upfront cash payment of R$150,000. Product A will be delivered in 2 years (January 2, 2017) and Product B will be delivered in 5 years (January 2, 2020). Sanchez Co. allocates the R$150,000 to Products A and B on a relative standalone selling price basis as follows.

	Standalone Selling Prices	Percent Allocated	Allocated Amounts
Product A	R$ 40,000	25%	R$ 37,500
Product B	120,000	75%	112,500
	R$160,000		R$150,000

Sanchez Co. uses an interest rate of 6%, which is its incremental borrowing rate.

Instructions

(a) Prepare the journal entries necessary on January 2, 2015, and December 31, 2015.

(b) Prepare the journal entries necessary on December 31, 2016.

(c) Prepare the journal entries necessary on January 2, 2017.

6 **E18-10 (Allocate Transaction Price)** Shaw Company sells goods that cost $300,000 to Ricard Company for $410,000 on January 2, 2015. The sales price includes an installation fee, which is valued at $40,000. The fair value of the goods is $370,000. The installation is considered a separate performance obligation and is expected to take 6 months to complete.

Instructions

(a) Prepare the journal entries (if any) to record the sale on January 2, 2015.

(b) Shaw prepares an income statement for the first quarter of 2015, ending on March 31, 2015 (installation was completed on June 18, 2015). How much revenue should Shaw recognize related to its sale to Ricard?

6 **E18-11 (Allocate Transaction Price)** Crankshaft Company manufactures equipment. Crankshaft's products range from simple automated machinery to complex systems containing numerous components. Unit selling prices range from $200,000 to $1,500,000 and are quoted inclusive of installation. The installation process does not involve changes to the features of the equipment and does not require proprietary information about the equipment in order for the installed equipment to perform to specifications. Crankshaft has the following arrangement with Winkerbean Inc.

- Winkerbean purchases equipment from Crankshaft for a price of $1,000,000 and contracts with Crankshaft to install the equipment. Crankshaft charges the same price for the equipment irrespective of whether it does the installation or not. Using market data, Crankshaft determines installation service is estimated to have a fair value of $50,000. The cost of the equipment is $600,000.
- Winkerbean is obligated to pay Crankshaft the $1,000,000 upon the delivery and installation of the equipment.

Crankshaft delivers the equipment on June 1, 2015, and completes the installation of the equipment on September 30, 2015. The equipment has a useful life of 10 years. Assume that the equipment and the installation are two distinct performance obligations which should be accounted for separately.

Instructions

(a) How should the transaction price of $1,000,000 be allocated among the service obligations?

(b) Prepare the journal entries for Crankshaft for this revenue arrangement in 2015 assuming Crankshaft receives payment when installation is completed.

6 **E18-12 (Allocate Transaction Price)** Refer to the revenue arrangement in E18-11.

Instructions

Repeat requirements (a) and (b) assuming Crankshaft does not have market data with which to determine the standalone selling price of the installation services. As a result, an expected cost plus margin approach is used. The cost of installation is $36,000; Crankshaft prices these services with a 25% margin relative to cost.

6 **E18-13 (Allocate Transaction Price)** Appliance Center is an experienced home appliance dealer. Appliance Center also offers a number of services together with the home appliances that it sells. Assume that Appliance Center sells ovens on a standalone basis. Appliance Center also sells installation services and maintenance services for ovens. However, Appliance Center does not offer installation or maintenance services to customers who buy ovens from other vendors. Pricing for ovens is as follows.

Oven only	€ 800
Oven with installation service	850
Oven with maintenance services	975
Oven with installation and maintenance services	1,000

In each instance in which maintenance services are provided, the maintenance service is separately priced within the arrangement at €175. Additionally, the incremental amount charged by Appliance Center for installation approximates the amount charged by independent third parties. Ovens are sold subject to a general right of return. If a customer purchases an oven with installation and/or maintenance services, in the event Appliance Center does not complete the service satisfactorily, the customer is only entitled to a refund of the portion of the fee that exceeds €800.

Instructions

(a) Assume that a customer purchases an oven with both installation and maintenance services for €1,000. Based on its experience, Appliance Center believes that it is probable that the installation of the equipment will be performed satisfactorily to the customer. Assume that the maintenance services are priced separately. Identify the separate performance obligations related to the Appliance Center revenue arrangement.

(b) Indicate the amount of revenue that should be allocated to the oven, the installation, and to the maintenance contract.

8 **E18-14 (Sales with Returns)** Organic Growth Company is presently testing a number of new agricultural seeds that it has recently harvested. To stimulate interest, it has decided to grant to five of its largest customers the unconditional right of return to these products if not fully satisfied. The right of return extends for 4 months. Organic Growth sells these seeds on account for £1,500,000 (cost £800,000) on January 2, 2015. Customers are required to pay the full amount due by March 15, 2015.

Instructions

(a) Prepare the journal entry for Organic Growth at January 2, 2015, assuming Organic Growth estimates returns of 20% based on prior experience.

(b) Assume that one customer returns the seeds on March 1, 2015, due to unsatisfactory performance. Prepare the journal entry to record this transaction, assuming this customer purchased £100,000 of seeds from Organic Growth.

(c) Briefly describe the accounting for these sales if Organic Growth is unable to reliably estimate returns.

8 **E18-15 (Sales with Returns)** Uddin Publishing Co. publishes college textbooks that are sold to bookstores on the following terms. Each title has a fixed wholesale price, terms f.o.b. shipping point, and payment is due 60 days after shipment. The retailer may return a maximum of 30% of an order at the retailer's expense. Sales are made only to retailers who have good credit ratings. Past experience indicates that the normal return rate is 12%, and the average collection period is 72 days.

Instructions

(a) Identify alternative revenue recognition criteria that Uddin could employ concerning textbook sales.

(b) Briefly discuss the reasoning for your answers in (a) above.

(c) On July 1, 2015, Uddin shipped books invoiced at €15,000,000 (cost €12,000,000). Prepare the journal entry to record this transaction.

(d) On October 3, 2015, €1.5 million of the invoiced July sales were returned according to the return policy, and the remaining €13.5 million was paid. Prepare the journal entries for the return and payment.

8 **E18-16 (Sales with Repurchase)** Cramer Corp. sells idle machinery to Enyart Company on July 1, 2015, for $40,000. Cramer agrees to repurchase this equipment from Enyart on June 30, 2016, for a price of $42,400 (an imputed interest rate of 6%).

Instructions

(a) Prepare the journal entry for Cramer for the transfer of the asset to Enyart on July 1, 2015.

(b) Prepare any other necessary journal entries for Cramer in 2015.

(c) Prepare the journal entry for Cramer when the machinery is repurchased on June 30, 2016.

8 **E18-17 (Repurchase Agreement)** Zagat Inc. enters into an agreement on March 1, 2015, to sell Werner Metal Company aluminum ingots in 2 months. As part of the agreement, Zagat also agrees to repurchase the ingots in 60 days at the original sales price of ₺200,000 plus 2%. (Because Zagat has an unconditional obligation to repurchase the ingots at an amount greater than the original sales price, the transaction is treated as a financing.)

Instructions

(a) Prepare the journal entry necessary on March 1, 2015.

(b) Prepare the journal entry for the repurchase of the ingots on May 1, 2015.

8 **E18-18 (Bill and Hold)** Wood-Mode Company is involved in the design, manufacture, and installation of various types of wood products for large construction projects. Wood-Mode recently completed a large contract for Stadium Inc., which consisted of building 35 different types of concession counters for a new soccer arena under construction. The terms of the contract are that upon completion of the counters, Stadium would pay $2,000,000. Unfortunately, due to the depressed economy, the completion of the new soccer arena is now delayed. Stadium has therefore asked Wood-Mode to hold the counters for 2 months at its manufacturing plant until the arena is completed. Stadium acknowledges in writing that it ordered the counters and that they now have ownership. The time that Wood-Mode Company must hold the counters is totally dependent on when the arena is completed. Because Wood-Mode has not received additional progress payments for the arena due to the delay, Stadium has provided a deposit of $300,000.

Instructions

(a) Explain this type of revenue recognition transaction.

(b) What factors should be considered in determining when to recognize revenue in this transaction?

(c) Prepare the journal entry(ies) that Wood-Mode should make, assuming it signed a valid sales contract to sell the counters and received at the time the $300,000 deposit.

8 **E18-19 (Consignment Sales)** On May 3, 2015, Eisler Company consigned 80 freezers, costing €500 each, to Remmers Company. The cost of shipping the freezers amounted to €840 and was paid by Eisler Company. On December 30, 2015, a report was received from the consignee, indicating that 40 freezers had been sold for €750 each. Remittance was made by the consignee for the amount due after deducting a commission of 6%, advertising of €200, and total installation costs of €320 on the freezers sold.

Instructions

(a) Compute the inventory value of the units unsold in the hands of the consignee.

(b) Compute the profit for the consignor for the units sold.

(c) Compute the amount of cash that will be remitted by the consignee.

8 **E18-20 (Warranty Arrangement)** On December 31, 2015, Grando Company sells production equipment to Feliz Inc. for R$50,000. Grando includes a 1-year assurance warranty service with the sale of all its equipment. The customer receives and pays for the equipment on December 31, 2015. Grando estimates the prices to be R$48,800 for the equipment and R$1,200 for the cost of the warranty.

Instructions

(a) Prepare the journal entry to record this transaction on December 31, 2015.

(b) Repeat the requirements for (a), assuming that in addition to the assurance warranty, Grando sold an extended warranty (service-type warranty) for an additional 2 years (2017–2018) for R$800.

8 ▶ **E18-21 (Warranties)** Celic Inc. manufactures and sells computers that include an assurance-type warranty for the first 90 days. Celic offers an optional extended coverage plan under which it will repair or replace any defective part for 3 years from the expiration of the assurance-type warranty. Because the optional extended coverage plan is sold separately, Celic determines that the 3 years of extended coverage represent a separate performance obligation. The total transaction price for the sale of a computer and the extended warranty is $3,600 on October 1, 2015, and Celic determines the standalone selling price of each is $3,200 and $400, respectively. Further, Celic estimates, based on historical experience, it will incur $200 in costs to repair defects that arise within the 90-day coverage period for the assurance-type warranty. The cost of the equipment is $1,440.

Instructions

(a) Prepare the journal entry(ies) to record the sale of the computer, cost of goods sold, and liabilities related to the warranties.

(b) Briefly describe the accounting for the service-type warranty after the 90-day assurance-type warranty period.

9 ▶ **E18-22 (Existence of a Contract)** On January 1, 2015, Gordon Co. enters into a contract to sell a customer a wiring base and shelving unit that sits on the base in exchange for $3,000. The contract requires delivery of the base first but states that payment for the base will not be made until the shelving unit is delivered. Gordon identifies two performance obligations and allocates $1,200 of the transaction price to the wiring base and the remainder to the shelving unit. The cost of the wiring base is $700; the shelves have a cost of $320.

Instructions

(a) Prepare the journal entry on January 1, 2015, for Gordon.

(b) Prepare the journal entry on February 5, 2015, for Gordon when the wiring base is delivered to the customer.

(c) Prepare the journal entry on February 25, 2015, for Gordon when the shelving unit is delivered to the customer and Gordon receives full payment.

9 ▶ **E18-23 (Existence of a Contract)** On May 1, 2015, Richardson Inc. entered into a contract to deliver one of its specialty mowers to Kickapoo Landscaping Co. The contract requires Kickapoo to pay the contract price of $900 in advance on May 15, 2015. Kickapoo pays Richardson on May 15, 2015, and Richardson delivers the mower (with cost of $575) on May 31, 2015.

Instructions

(a) Prepare the journal entry on May 1, 2015, for Richardson.

(b) Prepare the journal entry on May 15, 2015, for Richardson.

(c) Prepare the journal entry on May 31, 2015, for Richardson.

9 ▶ **E18-24 (Contract Costs)** Rex's Reclaimers entered into a contract with Dan's Demolition to manage the processing of recycled materials on Dan's various demolition projects. Services for the 3-year contract include collecting, sorting, and transporting reclaimed materials to recycling centers or contractors who will reuse them. Rex's incurs selling commission costs of £2,000 to obtain the contract. Before performing the services, Rex's also designs and builds specialty receptacles and loading equipment that interfaces with Dan's demolition equipment at a cost of £27,000. These receptacles and equipment are retained by Rex's. Dan's promises to pay a fixed fee of £12,000 per year, payable every 6 months for the services under the contract. Rex's incurs the following costs: design services for the receptacles to interface with Dan's equipment £3,000, loading equipment controllers £6,000, and special testing and government inspection fees £2,000 (some of Dan's projects are on government property).

Instructions

(a) Determine the costs that should be capitalized as part of Rex's Reclaimers revenue arrangement with Dan's Demolition.

(b) Dan's also expects to incur general and administrative costs related to this contract, as well as costs of wasted materials and labor that likely cannot be factored into the contract price. Can these costs be capitalized? Explain.

9 ▶ **E18-25 (Contract Costs, Collectibility)** Refer to the information in E18-24.

Instructions

(a) Does the accounting for capitalized costs change if the contract is for 1 year rather than 3 years? Explain.

(b) Dan's Demolition is a startup company. As a result, there is more than insignificant uncertainty about Dan's ability to make the 6-month payments on time. Does this uncertainty affect the amount of revenue to be recognized under the contract? Explain.

10 *E18-26 (Recognition of Profit on Long-Term Contracts) During 2015, Nilsen Company started a construc-
11 tion job with a contract price of €1,600,000. The job was completed in 2017. The following information is available.

	2015	2016	2017
Costs incurred to date	€400,000	€825,000	€1,070,000
Estimated costs to complete	600,000	275,000	–0–
Billings to date	300,000	900,000	1,600,000
Collections to date	270,000	810,000	1,425,000

Instructions

(a) Compute the amount of gross profit to be recognized each year, assuming the percentage-of-completion method is used.
(b) Prepare all necessary journal entries for 2016.
(c) Compute the amount of gross profit to be recognized each year, assuming the cost-recovery method is used.

10 *E18-27 (Analysis of Percentage-of-Completion Financial Statements) In 2015, Steinrotter Construction Corp. began construction work under a 3-year contract. The contract price was €1,000,000. Steinrotter uses the percentage-of-completion method for financial accounting purposes. The income to be recognized each year is based on the proportion of cost incurred to total estimated costs for completing the contract. The financial statement presentations relating to this contract at December 31, 2015, are shown below.

Statement of Financial Position

Construction in process	€65,000
Less: Billings	61,500
Costs and recognized profit in excess of billings	3,500
Accounts receivable	18,000

Income Statement

Income (before tax) on the contract recognized in 2015	€19,500

Instructions

(a) How much cash was collected in 2015 on this contract?
(b) What was the initial estimated total income before tax on this contract?

10 *E18-28 (Gross Profit on Uncompleted Contract) On April 1, 2015, Dougherty Inc. entered into a cost plus fixed fee contract to construct an electric generator for Altom Corporation. At the contract date, Dougherty estimated that it would take 2 years to complete the project at a cost of $2,000,000. The fixed fee stipulated in the contract is $450,000. Dougherty appropriately accounts for this contract under the percentage-of-completion method. During 2015, Dougherty incurred costs of $800,000 related to the project. The estimated cost at December 31, 2015, to complete the contract is $1,200,000. Altom was billed $600,000 under the contract.

Instructions

Prepare a schedule to compute the amount of gross profit to be recognized by Dougherty under the contract for the year ended December 31, 2015. Show supporting computations in good form.

10 *E18-29 (Recognition of Revenue on Long-Term Contract and Entries) Hamilton Construction Company
11 uses the percentage-of-completion method of accounting. In 2015, Hamilton began work under contract #E2-D2, which provided for a contract price of £2,200,000. Other details follow:

	2015	2016
Costs incurred during the year	£640,000	£1,425,000
Estimated costs to complete, as of December 31	960,000	–0–
Billings during the year	420,000	1,680,000
Collections during the year	350,000	1,500,000

Instructions

(a) What portion of the total contract price would be recognized as revenue in 2015? In 2016?

(b) Assuming the same facts as those above except that Hamilton uses the cost-recovery method of accounting, what portion of the total contract price would be recognized as gross profit in 2016?

(c) Prepare a complete set of journal entries for 2015 (using the percentage-of-completion method).

10 **11** *E18-30 **(Recognition of Profit and Statement of Financial Position Amounts for Long-Term Contracts)** Yanmei Construction Company began operations on January 1, 2015. During the year, Yanmei Construction entered into a contract with Lundquist Corp. to construct a manufacturing facility. At that time, Yanmei estimated that it would take 5 years to complete the facility at a total cost of ¥4,500,000. The total contract price for construction of the facility is ¥6,000,000. During the year, Yanmei incurred ¥1,185,800 in construction costs related to the construction project. The estimated cost to complete the contract is ¥4,204,200. Lundquist Corp. was billed and paid 25% of the contract price.

Instructions

Prepare schedules to compute the amount of gross profit to be recognized for the year ended December 31, 2015, and the amount to be shown as "costs and recognized profit in excess of billings" or "billings in excess of costs and recognized profit" at December 31, 2015, under each of the following methods. Show supporting computations in good form.

(a) Cost-recovery method.

(b) Percentage-of-completion method.

13 *E18-31 **(Franchise Entries)** Pacific Crossburgers Inc. charges an initial franchise fee of $70,000. Upon the signing of the agreement (which covers 3 years), a payment of $28,000 is due. Thereafter, three annual payments of $14,000 are required. The credit rating of the franchisee is such that it would have to pay interest at 10% to borrow money. The franchise agreement is signed on May 1, 2015, and the franchise commences operation on July 1, 2015.

Instructions

Prepare the journal entries in 2015 for the franchisor under the following assumptions. (Round to the nearest dollar.)

(a) No future services are required by the franchisor once the franchise starts operations.

(b) The franchisor has substantial services to perform, once the franchise begins operations, to maintain the value of the franchise.

(c) The total franchise fee includes training services (with a value of $2,400) for the period leading up to the franchise opening and for 2 months following opening.

13 *E18-32 **(Franchise Fee, Initial Down Payment)** On January 1, 2015, Lesley Benjamin signed an agreement (covering 5 years) to operate as a franchisee of Campbell Inc. for an initial franchise fee of €50,000. The amount of €10,000 was paid when the agreement was signed, and the balance is payable in five annual payments of €8,000 each, beginning January 1, 2016. The agreement provides that the down payment is non-refundable and that no future services are required of the franchisor once the franchise commences operations on April 1, 2015. Lesley Benjamin's credit rating indicates that she can borrow money at 11% for a loan of this type.

Instructions

(a) Prepare journal entries for Campbell for 2015-related revenue for this franchise arrangement.

(b) Prepare journal entries for Campbell for 2015-related revenue for this franchise arrangement, assuming that in addition to the franchise rights, Campbell also provides 1 year of operational consulting and training services, beginning on the signing date. These services have a value of €3,600.

(c) Repeat the requirements for part (a), assuming that Campbell must provide services to Benjamin throughout the franchise period to maintain the franchise value.

PROBLEMS

4 **5** **6** **7** **P18-1 (Allocate Transaction Price, Upfront Fees)** Tablet Tailors sells tablet PCs combined with Internet service (Tablet Bundle A) that permits the tablet to connect to the Internet anywhere (set up a Wi-Fi hot spot). The price for the tablet and a 4-year Internet connection service contract is €500. The standalone selling price of the tablet is €250 (cost to Tablet Tailors €175). Tablet Tailors sells the Internet access service independently for an upfront payment of €100, plus €72 payments at the beginning of years 2–4 of the contract. With an imputed interest rate of 8%, the standalone value of the service is €286. On January 2, 2015, Tablet Tailors signed 100 contracts, receiving a total of €31,445 in cash (full payment of €500 each in cash, less the upfront fee for Internet service, less the present value of the note for the future service plan payments), delivered tablets, and started service for 100 tablet packages.

Instructions

    (a) Prepare any journal entries to record this revenue arrangement on January 2, 2015.

    (b) Prepare any journal entries to record this revenue arrangement on December 31, 2016.

    (c) Prepare any journal entries to record this revenue arrangement on December 31, 2017.

    (d) Repeat the requirements for part (a), assuming that Tablet Tailors has no reliable data with which to estimate the standalone selling price for the Internet service.

P18-2 **(Modification of Contract, Allocate Transaction Price)** Refer to the revenue arrangement in P18-1.

Instructions

Consider the following information and respond to the requirements indicated.

    (a) In response to competitive pressures for the Internet access service for Bundle A, at the end of the second year of the 4-year contract, Tablet Tailors offers a modified contract and extension incentive. The extended contract services are similar to those provided in the first 2 years of the contract. Signing the extension and paying €120 (which equals the fair value of the revised service package) extends access for 2 more years of Internet connection. Assuming 40 Bundle A customers sign up for this offer, prepare the journal entries when the contract is signed in January 2, 2017, and at December 31, 2017, for those contracts. Assume the modification does not result in a separate performance obligation.

    (b) Tablet Tailors offers a second package (Tablet Bundle B) which includes a service plan for the tablet PC covering the 4-year contract period. That product bundle sells for €600. Tablet Tailors provides the tablet service as a separate product with a standalone selling price of €160. Prepare any journal entries to record the sale of 200 of these packages on January 2, 2015.

P18-3 **(Allocate Transaction Price, Discounts, Time Value)** Grill Master Company sells total outdoor grilling solutions, providing gas and charcoal grills, accessories, and installation services for custom patio grilling stations.

Instructions

Respond to the requirements related to the following independent revenue arrangements for Grill Master products and services.

    (a) Grill Master offers contract GM205, which is comprised of a free-standing gas grill for small patio use plus installation to a customer's gas line for a total price £800. On a standalone basis, the grill sells for £700 (cost £425), and Grill Master estimates that the fair value of the installation service (based on cost-plus estimation) is £150. Grill Master signed 10 GM205 contracts on April 20, 2015, and customers paid the contract price in cash. The grills were delivered and installed on May 15, 2015. Prepare journal entries for Grill Master for GM205 in April and May 2015.

    (b) A local shire is planning major renovations in its parks during 2015 and enters into a contract with Grill Master to purchase 400 durable, easy maintenance, standard charcoal grills during 2015. The grills are priced at £200 each (with a cost of £160 each), and Grill Master provides a 6% volume discount if the shire purchases at least 300 grills during 2015. On April 17, 2015, Grill Master delivered and received payment for 280 grills. Based on prior experience with the shire's renovation projects, the delivery of this many grills makes it certain that the shire will meet the discount threshold. Prepare the journal entries for Grill Master for grills sold on April 17, 2015.

    (c) Grill Master sells its specialty combination gas/wood-fired grills to local restaurants. Each grill is sold for £1,000 (cost £550) on credit with terms 3/30, net/90. Prepare the journal entries for the sale of 20 grills on September 1, 2015, and upon payment, assuming the customer paid on (1) September 25, 2015, and (2) October 15, 2015. Assume the company records sales net.

    (d) On October 1, 2015, Grill Master sold one of its super deluxe combination gas/charcoal grills to a local builder. The builder plans to install it in one of its "Parade of Homes" houses. Grill Master accepted a 3-year, zero-interest-bearing note with face amount of £5,324. The grill has an inventory cost of £2,700. An interest rate of 10% is an appropriate market rate of interest for this customer. Prepare the journal entries on October 1, 2015, and December 31, 2015.

P18-4 **(Allocate Transaction Price, Discounts, Time Value)** Economy Appliance Co. manufactures low-price, no-frills appliances that are in great demand for rental units. Pricing and cost information on Economy's main products are as shown on page 943.

Item	Standalone Selling Price (Cost)
Refrigerator	$500 ($260)
Range	560 ($275)
Stackable washer/dryer unit	700 ($400)

Customers can contract to purchase either individually at the stated prices or a three-item bundle with a price of $1,800. The bundle price includes delivery and installation. Economy provides delivery and installation as a standalone service for any of its products for a price of $100.

Instructions

Respond to the requirements related to the following independent revenue arrangements for Economy Appliance Co.

(a) On June 1, 2015, Economy sold 100 washer/dryer units without installation to Laplante Rentals for $70,000. Laplante is a newer customer and is unsure how this product will work in its older rental units. Economy offers a 60-day return privilege and estimates, based on prior experience with sales on this product, 4% of the units will be returned. Prepare the journal entries for the sale and related cost of goods sold on June 1, 2015.

(b) YellowCard Property Managers operates upscale student apartment buildings. On May 1, 2015, Economy signs a contract with YellowCard for 300 appliance bundles to be delivered and installed in one of its new buildings. YellowCard pays 20% cash at contract signing and will pay the balance upon delivery and installation no later than August 1, 2015. Prepare journal entries for Economy on (1) May 1, 2015, and (2) August 1, 2015, when all appliances are delivered and installed.

(c) Refer to the arrangement in part (b). It would help YellowCard secure lease agreements with students if the delivery and installation of the appliance bundles can be completed by July 1, 2015. YellowCard offers a 10% bonus payment if Economy can complete delivery and installation by July 1, 2015. Economy estimates its chances of meeting the bonus deadline to be 60%, based on a number of prior contracts of similar scale. Repeat the requirement for part (b), given this bonus provision. Assume installation is completed by July 1, 2015.

(d) Epic Rentals would like to take advantage of the bundle price for its 400-unit project. On February 1, 2015, Economy signs a contract with Epic for delivery and installation of 400 bundles. Under the agreement, Economy will hold the appliance bundles in its warehouses until the new rental units are ready for installation. Epic pays 10% cash at contract signing. On April 1, 2015, Economy completes manufacture of the appliances in the Epic bundle order and places them in the warehouse. Economy and Epic have documented the warehouse arrangement and identified the units designated for Epic. The units are ready to ship, and Economy may not sell these units to other customers. Prepare journal entries for Economy on (1) February 1, 2015, and (2) April 1, 2015.

6 8 P18-5 (Allocate Transaction Price, Returns, and Consignments) Ritt Ranch & Farm is a distributor of ranch and farm equipment. Its products range from small tools, power equipment for trench-digging and fencing, grain dryers, and barn winches. Most products are sold direct via its company catalog and Internet site. However, given some of its specialty products, select farm implement stores carry Ritt's products. Pricing and cost information on three of Ritt's most popular products are as follows.

Item	Standalone Selling Price (Cost)
Mini-trencher	$ 3,600 ($2,000)
Power fence hole auger	1,200 ($800)
Grain/hay dryer	14,000 ($11,000)

Instructions

Respond to the requirements related to the following independent revenue arrangements for Ritt Ranch & Farm.

(a) On January 1, 2015, Ritt sells augers to Mills Farm & Fleet for $48,000. Mills signs a 6-month note at an annual interest rate of 12%. Ritt allows Mills to return any auger that it cannot use within 60 days and receive a full refund. Based on prior experience, Ritt estimates that 5% of units sold to customers like Mills will be returned (using the most likely outcome approach). Ritt's costs to recover the products will be immaterial, and the returned augers are expected to be resold at a profit. Prepare the journal entry for Ritt on January 1, 2015.

(b) On August 10, 2015, Ritt sells 16 mini-trenchers to a farm co-op in western Minnesota. Ritt provides a 4% volume discount on the mini-trenchers if the co-op has a 15% increase in purchases from Ritt compared to the prior year. Given the slowdown in the farm economy, sales to the co-op have been flat, and it is highly uncertain that the benchmark will be met. Prepare the journal entry for Ritt on August 10, 2015.

(c) Ritt sells three grain/hay dryers to a local farmer at a total contract price of $45,200. In addition to the dryers, Ritt provides installation, which has a standalone sales value of $1,000 per unit installed. The contract payment also includes a $1,200 maintenance plan for the dryers for 3 years after installation. Ritt signs the contract on June 20, 2015, and receives a 20% down payment from the farmer. The dryers are delivered and installed on October 1, 2015, and full payment is made to Ritt. Prepare the journal entries for Ritt in 2015 related to this arrangement.

(d) On April 25, 2015, Ritt ships 100 augers to Farm Depot, a farm supply dealer in Nebraska, on consignment. By June 30, 2015, Farm Depot has sold 60 of the consigned augers at the listed price of $1,200 per unit. Farm Depot notifies Ritt of the sales, retains a 10% commission, and remits the cash due Ritt. Prepare the journal entries for Ritt and Farm Depot for the consignment arrangement.

8 **P18-6 (Warranty, Customer Loyalty Program)** Hui Hardware takes pride as the "shop around the corner" that can compete with the big-box home improvement stores by providing good service from knowledgeable sales associates (many of whom are retired local handymen). Hui has developed the following two revenue arrangements to enhance its relationships with customers and increase its bottom line (HK$ in thousands).

1. Hui sells a specialty portable winch that is popular with many of the local customers for use at their lake homes (putting docks in and out, launching boats, etc.). The Hui winch is a standard manufacture winch that Hui modifies so the winch can be used for a variety of tasks. Hui sold 70 of these winches during 2015 at a total price of HK$21,000, with a warranty guarantee that the product was free of any defects. The cost of winches sold is HK$16,000. The assurance warranties extend for a 3-year period with an estimated cost of HK$2,100. In addition, Hui sold extended warranties related to 20 Hui winches for 2 years beyond the 3-year period for HK$400 each.

2. To bolster its already strong customer base, Hui implemented a customer loyalty program that rewards a customer with 1 loyalty point for every HK$10 of purchases on a select group of Hui products. Each point is redeemable for a HK$1 discount on any purchases of Hui merchandise in the following 2 years. During 2015, customers purchased select group products for HK$100,000 (all products are sold to provide a 45% gross profit) and earned 10,000 points redeemable for future purchases. The standalone selling price of the purchased products is HK$100,000. Based on prior experience with incentives programs like this, Hui expects 9,500 points to be redeemed related to these sales (Hui appropriately uses this experience to estimate the value of future consideration related to bonus points).

Instructions

(a) Identify the separate performance obligations in the Hui warranty and bonus point programs, and briefly explain the point in time when the performance obligations are satisfied.

(b) Prepare the journal entries for Hui related to the sales of Hui winches with warranties.

(c) Prepare the journal entries for the bonus point sales for Hui in 2015.

(d) How much additional sales revenue is recognized by Hui in 2016, assuming 4,500 bonus points are redeemed?

8 **P18-7 (Customer Loyalty Program)** Martz Inc. has a customer loyalty program that rewards a customer with 1 customer loyalty point for every €10 of purchases. Each point is redeemable for a €3 discount on any future purchases. On July 2, 2015, customers purchase products for €300,000 (with a cost of €171,000) and earn 30,000 points redeemable for future purchases. Martz expects 25,000 points to be redeemed (based on its past experience, which is predictive of the amount of consideration to which it will be entitled). Martz estimates a standalone selling price of €2.50 per point (or €75,000 total) on the basis of the likelihood of redemption. The points provide a material right to customers that they would not receive without entering into a contract. As a result, Martz concludes that the points are a separate performance obligation.

Instructions

(a) Determine the transaction price for the product and the customer loyalty points.

(b) Prepare the journal entries to record the sale of the product and related points on July 2, 2015.

(c) At the end of the first reporting period (July 31, 2015), 10,000 loyalty points are redeemed. Martz continues to expect 25,000 loyalty points to be redeemed in total. Determine the amount of loyalty point revenue to be recognized at July 31, 2015.

P18-8 (Comprehensive Three-Part Revenue Recognition) Van Hatten Consolidated has three operating divisions: DeMent Publishing Division, Ankiel Securities Division, and Depp Advisory Division. Each division maintains its own accounting system.

DeMent Publishing Division

The DeMent Publishing Division sells large volumes of novels to a few book distributors, which in turn sell to several national chains of bookstores. DeMent allows distributors to return up to 30% of sales, and distributors give the same terms to bookstores. While returns from individual titles fluctuate greatly, the returns from distributors have averaged 20% in each of the past 5 years. A total of $7,000,000 of paperback novel sales were made to distributors during fiscal 2015. On November 30, 2015 (the end of the fiscal year), $1,500,000 of fiscal 2015 sales were still subject to return privileges over the next 6 months. The remaining $5,500,000 of fiscal 2015 sales had actual returns of 21%. Sales from fiscal 2014 totaling $2,000,000 were collected in fiscal 2015 less 18% returns. This division records revenue according to the revenue recognition method when the right of return exists.

Ankiel Securities Division

The Ankiel Securities Division works through manufacturers' agents in various cities. Orders for alarm systems and down payments are forwarded from agents, and the division ships the goods f.o.b. factory directly to customers (usually police departments and security guard companies). Customers are billed directly for the balance due plus actual shipping costs. The company received orders for $6,000,000 of goods during the fiscal year ended November 30, 2015. Down payments of $600,000 were received, and $5,200,000 of goods were billed and shipped. Actual freight costs of $100,000 were also billed. Commissions of 10% on product price are paid to manufacturing agents after goods are shipped to customers. Such goods are warranted for 90 days after shipment, and warranty returns have been about 1% of sales. Revenue is recognized at the point of sale by this division.

Depp Advisory Division

The Depp Advisory Division performs asset management services. This division grew out of Van Hatten's own treasury and asset management operations that several of its customers asked to have access to. On January 1, 2015, Depp entered into a contract with Scutaro Co. to perform asset management services for 1 year. Depp receives a quarterly management fee of 0.25% of Scutaro's assets under management at the end of each quarter. In addition, Depp receives a performance-based incentive fee of 20% of the fund's return in excess of the return of the S&P 500 index at the end of the quarter (multiplied by the assets under management at quarter-end). At the end of the first quarter of 2015, Depp was managing $2,400,000 of Scutaro assets. The annualized return on the portfolio was 6.2% (the S&P 500 index had an annualized return of 5.7%).

Instructions

(a) For each division's revenue arrangements, identify the separate performance obligations, briefly explain allocation of the transaction process to each performance obligation, and indicate when the performance obligations are satisfied.

(b) Compute the revenue to be recognized in fiscal year 2015 for each of the three operating divisions of Van Hatten in accordance with IFRS.

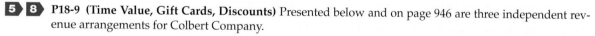

P18-9 (Time Value, Gift Cards, Discounts) Presented below and on page 946 are three independent revenue arrangements for Colbert Company.

Instructions

Respond to the requirements related to each revenue arrangement.

(a) Colbert sells 3-D printer systems. Recently, Colbert provided a special promotion of zero-interest financing for 2 years on any new 3-D printer system. Assume that Colbert sells Lyle Cartright a 3-D system receiving a £5,000 zero-interest-bearing note on January 1, 2015. The cost of the 3-D printer system is £4,000. Colbert imputes a 6% interest rate on this zero-interest-bearing note transaction. Prepare the journal entry to record the sale on January 1, 2015, and compute the total amount of revenue to be recognized in 2015.

(b) Colbert sells 20 non-refundable £100 gift cards for 3-D printer paper on March 1, 2015. The paper has a standalone selling price of £100 (cost £80). The gift cards expiration date is June 30, 2015. Colbert estimates that customers will not redeem 15% of these gift cards. The pattern of redemption is as follows.

	Redemption Total
March 31	50%
April 30	80%
June 30	85%

Prepare the 2015 journal entries related to the gift cards at March 1, March 31, April 30, and June 30.

(c) Colbert sells 3-D printers along with a number of retail items. The package price and standalone selling prices of each item are as follows

Item	Standalone Selling Price	Price When Bundled	Bundling Discount
3-D printer (cost £4,000)	£5,000	£4,500	£500
Custom stand (cost £200)	450	450	0
Special 3-D paper (cost £135)	175	175	0
Total for bundle	£5,625	£5,125	£500

Due to the timing of delivery—the paper is delivered 6 months after the printer is delivered to the customer—Colbert chooses to account for two performance obligations: (1) the printer and stand, and (2) the paper. Prepare the journal entries for Colbert on (a) March 1, 2015, when Colbert receives £51,250 for the sale of 10 printer bundles, and (b) September 1, 2015, when the paper is delivered to customers.

10 11 *P18-10 (Recognition of Profit on Long-Term Contract) Shanahan Construction Company has entered into a contract beginning January 1, 2015, to build a parking complex. It has been estimated that the complex will cost $600,000 and will take 3 years to construct. The complex will be billed to the purchasing company at $900,000. The following data pertain to the construction period.

	2015	2016	2017
Costs to date	$270,000	$450,000	$610,000
Estimated costs to complete	330,000	150,000	–0–
Progress billings to date	270,000	550,000	900,000
Cash collected to date	240,000	500,000	900,000

Instructions

(a) Using the percentage-of-completion method, compute the estimated gross profit that would be recognized during each year of the construction period.

(b) Using the cost-recovery method, compute the estimated gross profit that would be recognized during each year of the construction period.

10 11 12 *P18-11 (Long-Term Contract with Interim Loss) On March 1, 2015, Pechstein Construction Company contracted to construct a factory building for Fabrik Manufacturing Inc. for a total contract price of €8,400,000. The building was completed by October 31, 2017. The annual contract costs incurred, estimated costs to complete the contract, and accumulated billings to Fabrik for 2015, 2016, and 2017 are given below.

	2015	2016	2017
Contract costs incurred during the year	€2,880,000	€2,230,000	€2,190,000
Estimated costs to complete the contract at 12/31	3,520,000	2,190,000	–0–
Billings to Fabrik during the year	3,200,000	3,500,000	1,700,000

Instructions

(a) Using the percentage-of-completion method, prepare schedules to compute the profit or loss to be recognized as a result of this contract for the years ended December 31, 2015, 2016, and 2017. (Ignore income taxes.)

(b) Using the cost-recovery method, prepare schedules to compute the profit or loss to be recognized as a result of this contract for the years ended December 31, 2015, 2016, and 2017. (Ignore incomes taxes.)

10 **11** **12** *P18-12 (Long-Term Contract with an Overall Loss)* On July 1, 2015, Torvill Construction Company Inc. contracted to build an office building for Gumbel Corp. for a total contract price of $1,900,000. On July 1, Torvill estimated that it would take between 2 and 3 years to complete the building. On December 31, 2017, the building was deemed substantially completed. Following are accumulated contract costs incurred, estimated costs to complete the contract, and accumulated billings to Gumbel for 2015, 2016, and 2017.

	At 12/31/15	At 12/31/16	At 12/31/17
Contract costs incurred to date	$ 300,000	$1,200,000	$2,100,000
Estimated costs to complete the contract	1,200,000	800,000	–0–
Billings to Gumbel	300,000	1,100,000	1,850,000

Instructions

(a) Using the percentage-of-completion method, prepare schedules to compute the profit or loss to be recognized as a result of this contract for the years ended December 31, 2015, 2016, and 2017. (Ignore income taxes.)

(b) Using the cost-recovery method, prepare schedules to compute the profit or loss to be recognized as a result of this contract for the years ended December 31, 2015, 2016, and 2017. (Ignore income taxes.)

13 *P18-13 (Franchise Revenue)* Amigos Burrito Inc. sells franchises to independent operators throughout the northwestern part of Brazil. The contract with the franchisee includes the following provisions.

1. The franchisee is charged an initial fee of R$120,000. Of this amount, R$20,000 is payable when the agreement is signed, and a R$20,000 zero-interest-bearing note is payable at the end of each of the 5 subsequent years.

2. All of the initial franchise fee collected by Amigos is to be refunded and the remaining obligation canceled if, for any reason, the franchisee fails to open his or her franchise.

3. In return for the initial franchise fee, Amigos agrees to (a) assist the franchisee in selecting the location for the business, (b) negotiate the lease for the land, (c) obtain financing and assist with building design, (d) supervise construction, (e) establish accounting and tax records, and (f) provide expert advice over a 5-year period relating to such matters as employee and management training, quality control, and promotion. This continuing involvement by Amigos helps maintain the brand value of the franchise.

4. In addition to the initial franchise fee, the franchisee is required to pay to Amigos a monthly fee of 2% of sales for menu planning, recipe innovations, and the privilege of purchasing ingredients from Amigos at or below prevailing market prices.

Management of Amigos Burrito estimates that the value of the services rendered to the franchisee at the time the contract is signed amounts to at least R$20,000. All franchisees to date have opened their locations at the scheduled time, and none have defaulted on any of the notes receivable. The credit ratings of all franchisees would entitle them to borrow at the current interest rate of 10%. The present value of an ordinary annuity of five annual receipts of R$20,000 each discounted at 10% is R$75,816.

Instructions

(a) Discuss the alternatives that Amigos Burrito Inc. might use to account for the franchise fees.

(b) Prepare the journal entries for the initial and continuing franchise fees, assuming:

   (1) Franchise agreement is signed on January 5, 2015.

   (2) Amigos completes franchise startup tasks and the franchise opens on July 1, 2015.

   (3) The franchisee records R$260,000 in sales in the first 6 months of operations and remits the monthly franchise fee on December 31, 2015.

(c) Briefly describe the accounting for any unearned franchise fees, assuming that Amigos has little or no involvement with the franchisee related to expert advice on employee and management training, quality control, and promotion, once the franchise opens.

CONCEPTS FOR ANALYSIS

CA18-1 (Five-Step Revenue Process) Revenue is recognized based on a five-step process that is applied to a company's revenue arrangements.

Instructions
- **(a)** Briefly describe the five-step process.
- **(b)** Explain the importance of contracts when analyzing revenue arrangements.
- **(c)** How are fair value measurement concepts applied in implementation of the five-step process?
- **(d)** How does the five-step process reflect application of the definitions of assets and liabilities?

CA18-2 (Satisfying Performance Obligations) Judy Schaeffer is getting up to speed on the new guidance on revenue recognition. She is trying to understand the revenue recognition principle as it relates to the five-step revenue recognition process.

Instructions
- **(a)** Describe the revenue recognition principle.
- **(b)** Briefly discuss how the revenue recognition principle relates to the definitions of assets and liabilities. What is the importance of control?
- **(c)** Judy recalls that previous revenue recognition guidance required that revenue not be recognized unless the revenue was realized or realizable (also referred to as collectibility). Is collectibility a consideration in the recognition of revenue? Explain.

CA18-3 (Recognition of Revenue—Theory) Revenue is usually recognized at the point of sale (a point in time). Under special circumstances, however, bases other than the point of sale are used for the timing of revenue recognition.

Instructions
- **(a)** Why is the point of sale usually used as the basis for the timing of revenue recognition?
- **(b)** Disregarding the special circumstances when bases other than the point of sale are used, discuss the merits of each of the following objections to the sale basis of revenue recognition:
  - **(1)** It is too conservative because revenue is earned throughout the entire process of production.
  - **(2)** It is not conservative enough because accounts receivable do not represent disposable funds, sales returns and allowances may be made, and collection and bad debt expenses may be incurred in a later period.
- **(c)** Revenue may also be recognized over time. Give an example of the circumstances in which revenue is recognized over time and accounting merits of its use instead of the point-of-sale basis.

CA18-4 (Recognition of Revenue—Theory) Revenue is recognized for accounting purposes when a performance obligation is satisfied. In some situations, revenue is recognized over time as the fair values of assets and liabilities change. In other situations, however, accountants have developed guidelines for recognizing revenue at the point of sale.

Instructions
(Ignore income taxes.)
- **(a)** Explain and justify why revenue is often recognized at the time of sale.
- **(b)** Explain in what situations it would be appropriate to recognize revenue over time.

CA18-5 (Discounts) Fahey Company sells Stairmasters to a retailer, Physical Fitness, Inc., for €2,000,000. Fahey has a history of providing price concessions on this product if the retailer has difficulty selling the Stairmasters to customers. Fahey has experience with sales like these in the past and estimates that the maximum amount of price concessions is €300,000.

Instructions
- **(a)** Determine the amount of revenue that Fahey should recognize at the date of the sale of Stairmasters to Physical Fitness, Inc.
- **(b)** According to IFRS, in some situations, the amount of revenue recognized may be constrained. Explain how the accounting for the Stairmasters sales might be affected by the revenue constraint due to variable consideration or returns.
- **(c)** Some believe that revenue recognition should be constrained by collectibility. Is such a view consistent with IFRS? Explain.

CA18-6 (Recognition of Revenue from Subscriptions) *Cutting Edge* is a monthly magazine that has been on the market for 18 months. It currently has a circulation of 1.4 million copies. Negotiations are underway to obtain a bank loan in order to update the magazine's facilities. *Cutting Edge* is producing close to capacity and expects to grow at an average of 20% per year over the next 3 years.

After reviewing the financial statements of *Cutting Edge*, Andy Rich, the bank loan officer, had indicated that a loan could be offered to *Cutting Edge* only if it could increase its current ratio and decrease its debt to equity ratio to a specified level. Jonathan Embry, the marketing manager of *Cutting Edge*, has devised a plan to meet these requirements. Embry indicates that an advertising campaign can be initiated to immediately increase circulation. The potential customers would be contacted after the purchase of another magazine's mailing list. The campaign would include:

1. An offer to subscribe to *Cutting Edge* at three-fourths the normal price.
2. A special offer to all new subscribers to receive the most current world atlas whenever requested at a guaranteed price of $2.
3. An unconditional guarantee that any subscriber will receive a full refund if dissatisfied with the magazine.

Although the offer of a full refund is risky, Embry claims that few people will ask for a refund after receiving half of their subscription issues. Embry notes that other magazine companies have tried this sales promotion technique and experienced great success. Their average cancellation rate was 25%. On average, each company increased its initial circulation threefold and in the long run increased circulation to twice that which existed before the promotion. In addition, 60% of the new subscribers are expected to take advantage of the atlas premium. Embry feels confident that the increased subscriptions from the advertising campaign will increase the current ratio and decrease the debt to equity ratio.

You are the controller of *Cutting Edge* and must give your opinion of the proposed plan.

Instructions
(a) When should revenue from the new subscriptions be recognized?
(b) How would you classify the estimated sales returns stemming from the unconditional guarantee?
(c) How should the atlas premium be recorded? Is the estimated premium claims a liability? Explain.
(d) Does the proposed plan achieve the goals of increasing the current ratio and decreasing the debt to equity ratio?

CA18-7 (Recognition of Revenue—Bonus Points) Griseta & Dubel Inc. was formed early this year to sell merchandise credits to merchants, who distribute the credits free to their customers. For example, customers can earn additional credits based on the money they spend with a merchant (e.g., airlines and hotels). Accounts for accumulating the credits and catalogs illustrating the merchandise for which the credits may be exchanged are maintained online. Centers with inventories of merchandise premiums have been established for redemption of the credits. Merchants may not return unused credits to Griseta & Dubel.

The following schedule expresses Griseta & Dubel's expectations as to the percentages of a normal month's activity that will be attained. For this purpose, a "normal month's activity" is defined as the level of operations expected when expansion of activities ceases or tapers off to a stable rate. The company expects that this level will be attained in the third year and that sales of credits will average £6,000,000 per month throughout the third year.

Month	Actual Credit Sales Percent	Merchandise Premium Purchases Percent	Credit Redemptions Percent
6th	30%	40%	10%
12th	60	60	45
18th	80	80	70
24th	90	90	80
30th	100	100	95

Griseta & Dubel plans to adopt an annual closing date at the end of each 12 months of operation.

Instructions
(a) Discuss the factors to be considered in determining when revenue should be recognized.
(b) Apply the revenue recognition factors to the Griseta & Dubel Inc. revenue arrangement.
(c) Provide statement of financial position accounts that should be used and indicate how each should be classified.

CA18-8 (Revenue Recognition—Membership Fees) Midwest Health Club (MHC) offers 1-year memberships. Membership fees are due in full at the beginning of the individual membership period. As an incentive to new customers, MHC advertised that any customers not satisfied for any reason could receive a refund of the remaining portion of unused membership fees. As a result of this policy, Richard Nies, corporate controller, recognized revenue ratably over the life of the membership. MHC is in the process of preparing its year-end financial statements. Rachel Avery, MHC's treasurer, is concerned about the company's lackluster performance this year. She reviews the financial statements Nies prepared and tells Nies to recognize membership revenue when the fees are received.

Instructions
Answer the following questions.

(a) What are the ethical issues involved?
(b) What should Nies do?

*CA18-9 (Long-Term Contract—Percentage-of-Completion)** Widjaja Company is accounting for a long-term construction contract using the percentage-of-completion method. It is a 4-year contract that is currently in its second year. The latest estimates of total contract costs indicate that the contract will be completed at a profit to Widjaja Company.

Instructions
(a) What theoretical justification is there for Widjaja Company's use of the percentage-of-completion method?
(b) How would progress billings be accounted for? Include in your discussion the classification of progress billings in Widjaja Company financial statements.
(c) How would the income recognized in the second year of the 4-year contract be determined using the cost-to-cost method of determining percentage of completion?
(d) What would be the effect on earnings per share in the second year of the 4-year contract of using the cost-recovery method instead of the percentage-of-completion method? Discuss.

USING YOUR JUDGMENT

As the new revenue recognition guidance is not yet implemented, note that the financial statements and notes for Marks and Spencer, adidas, Puma, and British Airways reflect revenue recognition under prior standards.

FINANCIAL REPORTING

Financial Reporting Problem

Marks and Spencer plc (M&S)
The financial statements of M&S (GBR) are presented in Appendix A. The company's complete annual report, including the notes to the financial statements, is available online.

Instructions
Refer to M&S's financial statements and the accompanying notes to answer the following questions.

(a) What were M&S's sales for 2013?
(b) What was the percentage of increase or decrease in M&S's sales from 2012 to 2013?
(c) In its notes to the financial statements, what criteria does M&S use to recognize revenue?
(d) How does M&S account for discounts and loyalty schemes? Does the accounting conform to accrual-accounting concepts? Explain.

Comparative Analysis Case

adidas and Puma

The financial statements of adidas (DEU) and Puma (DEU) are presented in Appendices B and C, respectively. The complete annual reports, including the notes to the financial statements, are available online.

Instructions

Use the companies' financial information to answer the following questions.

(a) What were adidas's and Puma's net revenues (sales) for the year 2012? Which company increased its revenues more (amounts and percentage) from 2011 to 2012?

(b) Are the revenue recognition policies of adidas and Puma similar? Explain.

(c) In which foreign countries (geographic areas) did adidas (see Note) and Puma experience significant revenues in 2012?

Financial Statement Analysis Case

British Airways

The following note appears in the "Summary of Significant Accounting Policies" section of the annual report of British Airways (GBR).

Summary of significant accounting policies (in part)

Revenue

Passenger and cargo revenue is recognised when the transportation service is provided. Passenger tickets net of discounts are recorded as current liabilities in the 'sales in advance of carriage' account until recognised as revenue. Unused tickets are recognised as revenue using estimates regarding the timing of recognition based on the terms and conditions of the ticket and historical trends. Other revenue is recognised at the time the service is provided. Commission costs are recognised at the same time as the revenue to which they relate and are charged to operating expenditure.

Key Accounting Estimates and Judgments

Passenger revenue recognition

Passenger revenue is recognised when the transportation is provided. Ticket sales that are not expected to be used for transportation ('unused tickets') are recognised as revenue using estimates regarding the timing of recognition based on the terms and conditions of the ticket and historical trends. During the current year, changes in estimates regarding the timing of revenue recognition primarily for unused flexible tickets were made, resulting in increased revenue in the current year of £109 million. During the prior year, changes in estimates regarding the timing of revenue recognition for unused restricted tickets were made, resulting in increased revenue in the prior year of £36 million. Both the above changes reflect more accurate and timely data obtained through the increased use of electronic tickets.

Instructions

(a) Identify the revenue recognition policies used by British Airways as discussed in its note on significant accounting policies.

(b) Under what conditions are the revenue recognition methods identified in the first paragraph of British Airways' note above acceptable?

(c) From the information provided in the second paragraph of British Airways' note, identify the type of operation being described and defend the acceptability of the revenue recognition method.

Accounting, Analysis, and Principles

Diversified Industries manufactures sump-pumps. Its most popular product is called the Super Soaker, which has a retail price of $1,200 and costs $540 to manufacture. It sells the Super Soaker on a standalone basis directly to businesses. Diversified also provides installation services for these commercial customers, who want an emergency pumping capability (with regular and back-up generator power) at their businesses. Diversified also distributes the Super Soaker through a consignment agreement with Menards. Income data for the first quarter of 2015 from operations other than the Super Soaker are as follows.

Revenues	$9,500,000
Expenses	7,750,000

Diversified has the following information related to two Super Soaker revenue arrangements during the first quarter of 2015.

1. Diversified sells 30 Super Soakers to businesses in flood-prone areas for a total contract price of $54,600. In addition to the pumps, Diversified also provides installation (at a cost of $150 per pump). On a standalone basis, the fair value of this service is $200 per unit installed. The contract payment also includes a $10 per month service plan for the pumps for 3 years after installation (Diversified's cost to perform this service is $7 per month). The Super Soakers are delivered and installed on March 1, 2015, and full payment is made to Diversified. Any discount is applied to the pump/installation bundle.

2. Diversified ships 300 Super Soakers to Menards on consignment. By March 31, 2015, Menards has sold two-thirds of the consigned merchandise at the listed price of $1,200 per unit. Menards notifies Diversified of the sales, retains a 5% commission, and remits the cash due Diversified.

Accounting

Determine Diversified Industries' 2015 first-quarter net income. (Ignore taxes.)

Analysis

Determine free cash flow (see Chapter 5) for Diversified Industries for the first quarter of 2015. In the first quarter, Diversified had depreciation expense of $175,000 and a net increase in working capital (change in accounts receivable and accounts payable) of $250,000. In the first quarter, capital expenditures were $500,000; Diversified paid dividends of $120,000.

Principles

Explain how the five-step revenue recognition process, when applied to Diversified's two revenue arrangements, reflects the concept of control in the definition of an asset and trade-offs between relevance and faithful representation.

IFRS BRIDGE TO THE PROFESSION

Professional Research

Employees at your company disagree about the accounting for sales returns. The sales manager believes that granting more generous return provisions and allowing customers to order items on a bill-and-hold basis can give the company a competitive edge and increase sales revenue. The controller cautions that, depending on the terms granted, loose return or bill-and-hold provisions might lead to non-IFRS revenue recognition. The company CFO would like you to research the issue to provide an authoritative answer.

Instructions

Access the IFRS authoritative literature at the IASB website (*http://eifrs.iasb.org/*) (you may register for free eIFRS access at this site). Under the Standards Development tab, click on Work plan for IFRS and go to Revenue Recognition. Click on "Summary of Board Deliberations." When you have accessed the documents, you can use the search tool in your Internet browser to respond to the following questions. (Provide paragraph citations.)

(a) What is the authoritative literature addressing revenue recognition when right of return exists?
(b) What is meant by "right of return"? "Bill and hold"?
(c) Describe the accounting when there is a right of return.
(d) When goods are sold on a bill-and-hold basis, what conditions must be met to recognize revenue upon receipt of the order?

Professional Simulation

In this simulation, you are asked to address questions related to revenue recognition issues. Prepare responses to all parts.

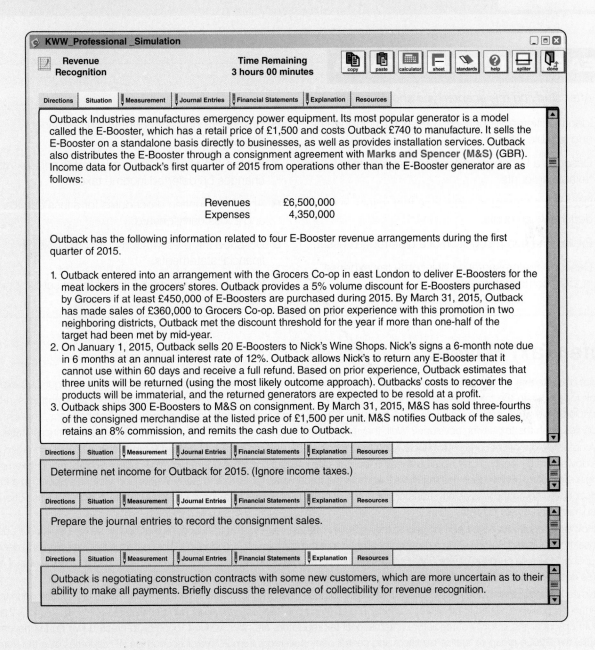

KWW_Professional _Simulation

Revenue Recognition

Time Remaining
3 hours 00 minutes

copy paste calculator sheet standards help spliter done

Directions | Situation | Measurement | Journal Entries | Financial Statements | Explanation | Resources

Outback Industries manufactures emergency power equipment. Its most popular generator is a model called the E-Booster, which has a retail price of £1,500 and costs Outback £740 to manufacture. It sells the E-Booster on a standalone basis directly to businesses, as well as provides installation services. Outback also distributes the E-Booster through a consignment agreement with **Marks and Spencer (M&S)** (GBR). Income data for Outback's first quarter of 2015 from operations other than the E-Booster generator are as follows:

Revenues	£6,500,000
Expenses	4,350,000

Outback has the following information related to four E-Booster revenue arrangements during the first quarter of 2015.

1. Outback entered into an arrangement with the Grocers Co-op in east London to deliver E-Boosters for the meat lockers in the grocers' stores. Outback provides a 5% volume discount for E-Boosters purchased by Grocers if at least £450,000 of E-Boosters are purchased during 2015. By March 31, 2015, Outback has made sales of £360,000 to Grocers Co-op. Based on prior experience with this promotion in two neighboring districts, Outback met the discount threshold for the year if more than one-half of the target had been met by mid-year.
2. On January 1, 2015, Outback sells 20 E-Boosters to Nick's Wine Shops. Nick's signs a 6-month note due in 6 months at an annual interest rate of 12%. Outback allows Nick's to return any E-Booster that it cannot use within 60 days and receive a full refund. Based on prior experience, Outback estimates that three units will be returned (using the most likely outcome approach). Outbacks' costs to recover the products will be immaterial, and the returned generators are expected to be resold at a profit.
3. Outback ships 300 E-Boosters to M&S on consignment. By March 31, 2015, M&S has sold three-fourths of the consigned merchandise at the listed price of £1,500 per unit. M&S notifies Outback of the sales, retains an 8% commission, and remits the cash due to Outback.

Directions | Situation | Measurement | Journal Entries | Financial Statements | Explanation | Resources

Determine net income for Outback for 2015. (Ignore income taxes.)

Directions | Situation | Measurement | Journal Entries | Financial Statements | Explanation | Resources

Prepare the journal entries to record the consignment sales.

Directions | Situation | Measurement | Journal Entries | Financial Statements | Explanation | Resources

Outback is negotiating construction contracts with some new customers, which are more uncertain as to their ability to make all payments. Briefly discuss the relevance of collectibility for revenue recognition.

Remember to check the book's companion website, at www.wiley.com/ college/kieso, to find additional resources for this chapter.

19 Accounting for Income Taxes

Safe (Tax) Haven?

One set of costs that companies manage are those related to taxes. In fact, in today's competitive markets, managers are expected to look for places in the tax code that a company can exploit to pay less tax to various tax authorities. By paying less in taxes, companies have more cash available to fund operations, finance expansion, and create new jobs. What happens, though, when companies push the tax-saving envelope? Well, they may face a tax audit, the results of which could hurt their financial statements.

A notable example of corporate maneuvering to reduce taxable income involved **Limited Brands Inc.** (USA). It managed its tax costs downward by locating part of its business in low-tax-rate jurisdictions while operating retail outlets elsewhere. For example, by basing a subsidiary (which does nothing more than hold the trademarks for Bath and Body Works and Victoria's Secret) in a low-tax jurisdiction, the company was able to transfer hundreds of millions of dollars from Limited's retail outlets in high-tax jurisdictions into a jurisdiction with a zero tax rate.

However, regulators have been increasing their scrutiny of these tax-evasion transactions that do not serve a legitimate business purpose. In the Limited Brands case, a prosecutor alleged that the company ". . . engaged in hocus pocus bookkeeping and deceptive accounting," the sole purpose of which was to reduce its tax bill. The court agreed, and Limited Brands had to pay millions of dollars in taxes dating back to 1994.

Limited Brands' shareholders likely got an unpleasant surprise when they learned the company also had a big tax obligation from its "uncertain tax position" related to off-shore locations. The same can be said for many other companies that take tax deductions that may not hold up under the scrutiny of regulators. International tax regulators are now working together to crack down on tax havens. For example, the **G20**, a group of finance ministers and central bank governors from 20 major economies (19 countries plus the European Union), has been at the forefront of efforts to establish a more effective, efficient, and fair international tax system since they declared the era of bank secrecy over at the G20 London Summit in April 2009. Here are some key elements identified by this group for implementation.

1. In an increasingly borderless world, ***strengthening international cooperation in tax matters*** is essential to ensuring the integrity of national tax systems and maintaining trust in governments.

2. ***The development of a new global tax standard with automatic exchange of information***. Recent developments involving undisclosed foreign bank accounts have highlighted the urgent need to move to this new standard. The **Global Forum** (an international body for ensuring the implementation of the internationally agreed-upon standards of transparency and exchange of information on request in the tax area) will establish a mechanism to monitor and review the effective implementation of the new tax standard.

3. ***International collective efforts to address the tax base erosion resulting from international tax planning***. Base erosion and profit shifting (BEPS) relates chiefly to instances where the interaction of different tax rules result in tax planning that

INTERNATIONAL FOCUS

> Read the **Global Accounting Insights** on pages 982–983 for a discussion of non-IFRS financial reporting for income taxes.

may be used by multinational enterprises to artificially shift profits out of the countries where they are earned, resulting in very low taxes or even double non-taxation. These practices, if left unchecked, undermine the fairness and integrity of our tax systems. They fundamentally distort competition because businesses that engage in cross-border BEPS strategies gain a competitive advantage compared with enterprises that operate mostly at the domestic level. Fair, transparent, and efficient tax systems are not only key pillars for sound public finances, they also provide a sustainable framework for dynamic economies.

4. ***Encouraging countries to examine how their domestic tax laws contribute to BEPS***. Such efforts help ensure that international and domestic tax rules do not allow or encourage multinational enterprises to reduce overall taxes paid by artificially shifting profits to low-tax jurisdictions. International tax rules, which date back to the 1920s, have not kept pace with the changing business environment, including the growing importance of intangibles and the digital economy.

Hopefully, through the efforts of these organizations and others, a more balanced and fair international tax system will emerge.

Sources: See Glenn Simpson, "A Tax Maneuver in Delaware Puts Squeeze on States," *Wall Street Journal* (August 9, 2002), p. A1; and *Tax Annex to the St. Petersburg G20 Leaders' Declaration* (September 2013).

PREVIEW OF CHAPTER   19

As our opening story indicates, companies spend a considerable amount of time and effort to minimize their income tax payments. And with good reason, as income taxes are a major cost of doing business for most corporations. Yet, at the same time, companies must present financial information to the investment community that provides a clear picture of present and potential tax obligations and tax benefits. In this chapter, we discuss the basic guidelines that companies must follow in reporting income taxes. The content and organization of the chapter are as follows.

Accounting for Income Taxes

Fundamentals of Accounting for Income Taxes	Accounting for Net Operating Losses	Financial Statement Presentation	Review of Asset-Liability Method
• Future taxable amounts and deferred taxes • Future deductible amounts and deferred taxes • Non-recognition of deferred tax asset • Income statement presentation • Specific differences • Rate considerations	• Loss carryback • Loss carryforward • Loss carryback example • Loss carryforward example	• Statement of financial position • Income statement • Tax reconciliation	

FUNDAMENTALS OF ACCOUNTING FOR INCOME TAXES

LEARNING OBJECTIVE **1**

Identify differences between pretax financial income and taxable income.

Up to this point, you have learned the basic guidelines that corporations use to report information to investors and creditors. Corporations also must file income tax returns following the guidelines developed by the appropriate tax authority. Because IFRS and tax regulations differ in a number of ways, so frequently do pretax financial income and taxable income. Consequently, the amount that a company reports as tax expense will differ from the amount of taxes payable to the tax authority. Illustration 19-1 highlights these differences.

ILLUSTRATION 19-1
Fundamental Differences between Financial and Tax Reporting

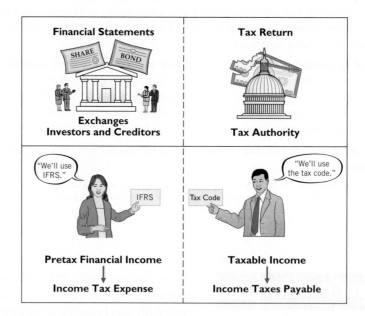

Pretax financial income is a *financial reporting* term. It also is often referred to as *income before taxes, income for financial reporting purposes,* or *income for book purposes.* Companies determine pretax financial income according to IFRS. They measure it with the objective of providing useful information to investors and creditors.

Taxable income (income for tax purposes) is a *tax accounting* term. It indicates the amount used to compute income taxes payable. Companies determine taxable income according to the tax regulations. Income taxes provide money to support government operations.

To illustrate how differences in IFRS and tax rules affect financial reporting and taxable income, assume that Chelsea Inc. reported revenues of $130,000 and expenses of $60,000 in each of its first three years of operations. Illustration 19-2 shows the (partial) income statement over these three years.

ILLUSTRATION 19-2
Financial Reporting Income

CHELSEA INC. IFRS REPORTING				
	2015	2016	2017	Total
Revenues	$130,000	$130,000	$130,000	
Expenses	60,000	60,000	60,000	
Pretax financial income	$ 70,000	$ 70,000	$ 70,000	$ 210,000
Income tax expense (40%)	$ 28,000	$ 28,000	$ 28,000	$ 84,000

For tax purposes (following the tax rules), Chelsea reported the same expenses to the tax authority in each of the years. But, as Illustration 19-3 shows, Chelsea reported taxable revenues of $100,000 in 2015, $150,000 in 2016, and $140,000 in 2017.

CHELSEA INC. TAX REPORTING				
	2015	2016	2017	Total
Revenues	$100,000	$150,000	$140,000	
Expenses	60,000	60,000	60,000	
Taxable income	$ 40,000	$ 90,000	$ 80,000	$ 210,000
Income taxes payable (40%)	$ 16,000	$ 36,000	$ 32,000	$ 84,000

ILLUSTRATION 19-3
Tax Reporting Income

Income tax expense and income taxes payable differed over the three years but were equal **in total**, as Illustration 19-4 shows.

CHELSEA INC. INCOME TAX EXPENSE AND INCOME TAXES PAYABLE				
	2015	2016	2017	Total
Income tax expense	$28,000	$28,000	$28,000	$84,000
Income taxes payable	16,000	36,000	32,000	84,000
Difference	$12,000	$ (8,000)	$ (4,000)	$ 0

ILLUSTRATION 19-4
Comparison of Income Tax Expense to Income Taxes Payable

The differences between income tax expense and income taxes payable in this example arise for a simple reason. For financial reporting, companies use the full accrual method to report revenues. For tax purposes, they generally use a modified cash basis. As a result, Chelsea reports pretax financial income of $70,000 and income tax expense of $28,000 for each of the three years. However, taxable income fluctuates. For example, in 2015 taxable income is only $40,000, so Chelsea owes just $16,000 to the tax authority that year. Chelsea classifies the income taxes payable as a current liability on the statement of financial position.

As Illustration 19-4 indicates, for Chelsea the $12,000 ($28,000 − $16,000) difference between income tax expense and income taxes payable in 2015 reflects taxes that it will pay in future periods. This $12,000 difference is often referred to as a **deferred tax amount**. In this case, it is a **deferred tax liability**. In cases where taxes will be lower in the future, Chelsea records a **deferred tax asset**. We explain the measurement and accounting for deferred tax liabilities and assets in the following two sections.[1]

Future Taxable Amounts and Deferred Taxes

The example summarized in Illustration 19-4 shows how income taxes payable can differ from income tax expense. This can happen when there are temporary differences between the amounts reported for tax purposes and those reported for book purposes. A **temporary difference** is the difference between the tax basis of an asset or liability and its reported (carrying or book) amount in the financial statements, which will result in taxable amounts or deductible amounts in future years.

2 LEARNING OBJECTIVE
Describe a temporary difference that results in future taxable amounts.

[1]Determining the amount of tax to pay the tax authority is a costly exercise for both individuals and companies. Individuals and businesses must pay not only the taxes owed but also the costs of their own time spent filing and complying with the tax code, including (1) the tax collection costs of the tax authority, and (2) the tax compliance outlays that individuals and businesses pay to help them file their taxes. One study estimated this cost to be 30 cents on every dollar sent to the government. Another study noted how big the tax-compliance industry has become. See A. Laffer, "The 30-Cent Tax Premium," *Wall Street Journal* (April 18, 2011).

Taxable amounts increase taxable income in future years. **Deductible amounts** decrease taxable income in future years.

In Chelsea's situation, the only difference between the book basis and tax basis of the assets and liabilities relates to accounts receivable that arose from revenue recognized for book purposes. Illustration 19-5 indicates that Chelsea reports accounts receivable at $30,000 in the December 31, 2015, IFRS-basis statement of financial position. However, the receivables have a zero tax basis.

ILLUSTRATION 19-5
Temporary Difference,
Accounts Receivable

Per Books	12/31/15	Per Tax Return	12/31/15
Accounts receivable	$30,000	Accounts receivable	$–0–

What will happen to the $30,000 temporary difference that originated in 2015 for Chelsea? Assuming that Chelsea expects to collect $20,000 of the receivables in 2016 and $10,000 in 2017, this collection results in future taxable amounts of $20,000 in 2016 and $10,000 in 2017. These future taxable amounts will cause taxable income to exceed pretax financial income in both 2016 and 2017.

An assumption inherent in a company's IFRS statement of financial position is that companies recover and settle the assets and liabilities at their reported amounts (carrying amounts). This assumption creates a requirement under accrual accounting to recognize *currently* the deferred tax consequences of temporary differences. That is, companies recognize the amount of income taxes that are payable (or refundable) when they recover and settle the reported amounts of the assets and liabilities, respectively. Illustration 19-6 shows the reversal of the temporary difference described in Illustration 19-5 and the resulting taxable amounts in future periods.

ILLUSTRATION 19-6
Reversal of Temporary
Difference, Chelsea Inc.

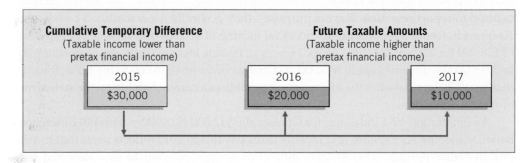

Chelsea assumes that it will collect the accounts receivable and report the $30,000 collection as taxable revenues in future tax returns. A payment of income tax in both 2016 and 2017 will occur. Chelsea should therefore record in its books in 2015 the deferred tax consequences of the revenue and related receivables reflected in the 2015 financial statements. Chelsea does this by recording a deferred tax liability.

Deferred Tax Liability

A **deferred tax liability** is the deferred tax consequences attributable to taxable temporary differences. In other words, **a deferred tax liability represents the increase in taxes payable in future years as a result of taxable temporary differences existing at the end of the current year.**

Recall from the Chelsea example that income taxes payable is $16,000 ($40,000 × 40%) in 2015 (Illustration 19-4 on page 957). In addition, a temporary difference exists at year-end because Chelsea reports the revenue and related accounts receivable differently for book and tax purposes. The book basis of accounts receivable is $30,000, and the tax basis is zero. Thus, the total deferred tax liability at the end of 2015 is $12,000, computed as shown in Illustration 19-7.

Book basis of accounts receivable	$30,000
Tax basis of accounts receivable	–0–
Cumulative temporary difference at the end of 2015	30,000
Tax rate	× 40%
Deferred tax liability at the end of 2015	$12,000

ILLUSTRATION 19-7
Computation of Deferred
Tax Liability, End of 2015

Companies may also compute the deferred tax liability by preparing a schedule that indicates the future taxable amounts due to existing temporary differences. Such a schedule, as shown in Illustration 19-8, is particularly useful when the computations become more complex.

	Future Years		
	2016	2017	Total
Future taxable amounts	$20,000	$10,000	$30,000
Tax rate	× 40%	× 40%	
Deferred tax liability at the end of 2015	$ 8,000	$ 4,000	$12,000

ILLUSTRATION 19-8
Schedule of Future
Taxable Amounts

Because it is the first year of operations for Chelsea, there is no deferred tax liability at the beginning of the year. Chelsea computes the income tax expense for 2015 as shown in Illustration 19-9.

Deferred tax liability at end of 2015	$12,000
Deferred tax liability at beginning of 2015	–0–
Deferred tax expense for 2015	12,000
Current tax expense for 2015 (income taxes payable)	16,000
Income tax expense (total) for 2015	$28,000

ILLUSTRATION 19-9
Computation of Income
Tax Expense, 2015

This computation indicates that income tax expense has two components—**current tax expense** (the amount of income taxes payable for the period) and deferred tax expense. **Deferred tax expense** is the increase in the deferred tax liability balance from the beginning to the end of the accounting period.

Companies credit taxes due and payable to Income Taxes Payable and credit the increase in deferred taxes to Deferred Tax Liability. They then debit the sum of those two items to Income Tax Expense. For Chelsea, it makes the following entry at the end of 2015.

Income Tax Expense	28,000	
Income Taxes Payable		16,000
Deferred Tax Liability		12,000

At the end of 2016 (the second year), the difference between the book basis and the tax basis of the accounts receivable is $10,000. Chelsea multiplies this difference by the applicable tax rate to arrive at the deferred tax liability of $4,000 ($10,000 × 40%), which it reports at the end of 2016. Income taxes payable for 2016 is $36,000 (Illustration 19-3 on page 957), and the income tax expense for 2016 is as shown in Illustration 19-10.

Deferred tax liability at end of 2016	$ 4,000
Deferred tax liability at beginning of 2016	12,000
Deferred tax expense (benefit) for 2016	(8,000)
Current tax expense for 2016 (income taxes payable)	36,000
Income tax expense (total) for 2016	$28,000

ILLUSTRATION 19-10
Computation of Income
Tax Expense, 2016

Chelsea records income tax expense, the change in the deferred tax liability, and income taxes payable for 2016 as follows.

Income Tax Expense	28,000	
Deferred Tax Liability	8,000	
Income Taxes Payable		36,000

The entry to record income taxes at the end of 2017 reduces the Deferred Tax Liability by $4,000. The Deferred Tax Liability account appears as follows at the end of 2017.

ILLUSTRATION 19-11
Deferred Tax Liability
Account after Reversals

Deferred Tax Liability			
2016	8,000	2015	12,000
2017	4,000		

The Deferred Tax Liability account has a zero balance at the end of 2017.

What do the numbers mean? "REAL LIABILITIES"

Some analysts dismiss deferred tax liabilities when assessing the financial strength of a company. But the IASB indicates that the deferred tax liability meets the definition of a liability established in the IASB Conceptual Framework because:

1. **It is a present obligation.** Taxable income in future periods will exceed pretax financial income as a result of this temporary difference. Thus, a present obligation exists.

2. **It results from a past transaction.** In the Chelsea example, the company performed services for customers and recognized revenue in 2015 for financial reporting purposes but deferred it for tax purposes.

3. **It represents a future outflow of resources.** Taxable income and taxes due in future periods will result from past events. The payment of these taxes when they come due is the future outflow of resources.

A study by B. Ayers indicates that the market views deferred tax assets and liabilities similarly to other assets and liabilities. Further, the study concludes that the accounting rules in this area increased the usefulness of deferred tax amounts in financial statements.

Source: B. Ayers, "Deferred Tax Accounting Under *SFAS No. 109*: An Empirical Investigation of Its Incremental Value-Relevance Relative to *APB No. 11*," *The Accounting Review* (April 1998).

Summary of Income Tax Accounting Objectives

I F R S

See the Authoritative Literature section (page 992).

One objective of accounting for income taxes is to recognize the amount of taxes payable or refundable for the current year. In Chelsea's case, income taxes payable is $16,000 for 2015.

A **second objective** is to recognize deferred tax liabilities and assets for the future tax consequences of events already recognized in the financial statements or tax returns. **[1]** For example, Chelsea sold services to customers that resulted in accounts receivable of $30,000 in 2015. It reported that amount on the 2015 income statement but not on the tax return as income. That amount will appear on future tax returns as income for the period **when collected**. As a result, a $30,000 temporary difference exists at the end of 2015, which will cause future taxable amounts. Chelsea reports a deferred tax liability of $12,000 on the statement of financial position at the end of 2015, which represents the increase in taxes payable in future years ($8,000 in 2016 and $4,000 in 2017) as a result of a temporary difference existing at the end of the current year. The related deferred tax liability is reduced by $8,000 at the end of 2016 and by another $4,000 at the end of 2017.

In addition to affecting the statement of financial position, deferred taxes impact income tax expense in each of the three years affected. In 2015, taxable income ($40,000) is less than pretax financial income ($70,000). Income taxes payable for 2015 is therefore $16,000 (based on taxable income). Deferred tax expense of $12,000 results from the increase in the Deferred Tax Liability account on the statement of financial position. Income tax expense is then $28,000 for 2015.

In 2016 and 2017, however, taxable income will exceed pretax financial income due to the reversal of the temporary difference ($20,000 in 2016 and $10,000 in 2017). Income taxes payable will therefore exceed income tax expense in 2016 and 2017. Chelsea will debit the Deferred Tax Liability account for $8,000 in 2016 and $4,000 in 2017. It records credits for these amounts in Income Tax Expense. These credits are often referred to as a **deferred tax benefit** (which we discuss again later on).

Future Deductible Amounts and Deferred Taxes

Assume that during 2015, Cunningham Inc. estimated its warranty costs related to the sale of microwave ovens to be $500,000, paid evenly over the next two years. For book purposes, in 2015 Cunningham reported warranty expense and a related estimated liability for warranties of $500,000 in its financial statements. For tax purposes, **the warranty tax deduction is not allowed until paid**. Therefore, Cunningham recognizes no warranty liability on a tax-basis statement of financial position. Illustration 19-12 shows the statement of financial position difference at the end of 2015.

3 LEARNING OBJECTIVE
Describe a temporary difference that results in future deductible amounts.

Per Books	12/31/15	Per Tax Return	12/31/15
Estimated liability for warranties	$500,000	Estimated liability for warranties	$–0–

ILLUSTRATION 19-12
Temporary Difference, Warranty Liability

When Cunningham pays the warranty liability, it reports an expense (deductible amount) for tax purposes. Because of this temporary difference, Cunningham should recognize in 2015 the tax benefits (positive tax consequences) for the tax deductions that will result from the future settlement of the liability. Cunningham reports this future tax benefit in the December 31, 2015, statement of financial position as a **deferred tax asset**.

We can think about this situation another way. Deductible amounts occur in future tax returns. These **future deductible amounts** cause taxable income to be less than pretax financial income in the future as a result of an existing temporary difference. Cunningham's temporary difference originates (arises) in one period (2015) and reverses over two periods (2016 and 2017). Illustration 19-13 diagrams this situation.

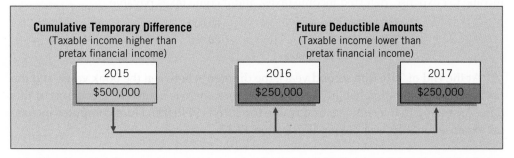

ILLUSTRATION 19-13
Reversal of Temporary Difference, Cunningham Inc.

A **deferred tax asset** is the deferred tax consequence attributable to deductible temporary differences. In other words, a **deferred tax asset represents the increase in taxes refundable (or saved) in future years as a result of deductible temporary differences existing at the end of the current year**.

To illustrate, assume that Hunt Co. accrues a loss and a related liability of $50,000 in 2015 for financial reporting purposes because of pending litigation. Hunt cannot deduct this amount for tax purposes until the period it pays the liability, expected in 2016. As a result, a deductible amount will occur in 2016 when Hunt settles the liability, causing taxable income to be lower than pretax financial income. Illustration 19-14 (on page 962) shows the computation of the deferred tax asset at the end of 2015 (assuming a 40 percent tax rate).

ILLUSTRATION 19-14
Computation of Deferred
Tax Asset, End of 2015

Book basis of litigation liability	$50,000
Tax basis of litigation liability	–0–
Cumulative temporary difference at the end of 2015	50,000
Tax rate	× 40%
Deferred tax asset at the end of 2015	$20,000

Hunt can also compute the deferred tax asset by preparing a schedule that indicates the future deductible amounts due to deductible temporary differences. Illustration 19-15 shows this schedule.

ILLUSTRATION 19-15
Schedule of Future
Deductible Amounts

	Future Years
Future deductible amounts	$50,000
Tax rate	× 40%
Deferred tax asset at the end of 2015	$20,000

Assuming that 2015 is Hunt's first year of operations, and income taxes payable is $100,000, Hunt computes its income tax expense as follows.

ILLUSTRATION 19-16
Computation of Income
Tax Expense, 2015

Deferred tax asset at end of 2015	$ 20,000
Deferred tax asset at beginning of 2015	–0–
Deferred tax expense (benefit) for 2015	(20,000)
Current tax expense for 2015 (income taxes payable)	100,000
Income tax expense (total) for 2015	$ 80,000

The **deferred tax benefit** results from the increase in the deferred tax asset from the beginning to the end of the accounting period (similar to the Chelsea deferred tax liability example earlier). The deferred tax benefit is a negative component of income tax expense. The total income tax expense of $80,000 on the income statement for 2015 thus consists of two elements—current tax expense of $100,000 and a deferred tax benefit of $20,000. For Hunt, it makes the following journal entry at the end of 2015 to record income tax expense, deferred income taxes, and income taxes payable.

Income Tax Expense	80,000	
Deferred Tax Asset	20,000	
Income Taxes Payable		100,000

At the end of 2016 (the second year), the difference between the book value and the tax basis of the litigation liability is zero. Therefore, there is no deferred tax asset at this date. Assuming that income taxes payable for 2016 is $140,000, Hunt computes income tax expense for 2016 as shown in Illustration 19-17.

ILLUSTRATION 19-17
Computation of Income
Tax Expense, 2016

Deferred tax asset at the end of 2016	$ –0–
Deferred tax asset at the beginning of 2016	20,000
Deferred tax expense (benefit) for 2016	20,000
Current tax expense for 2016 (income taxes payable)	140,000
Income tax expense (total) for 2016	$160,000

The company records income taxes for 2016 as follows.

Income Tax Expense	160,000	
Deferred Tax Asset		20,000
Income Taxes Payable		140,000

The total income tax expense of $160,000 on the income statement for 2016 thus consists of two elements—current tax expense of $140,000 and deferred tax expense of $20,000. Illustration 19-18 shows the Deferred Tax Asset account at the end of 2016.

Deferred Tax Asset			
2015	20,000	2016	20,000

ILLUSTRATION 19-18
Deferred Tax Asset
Account after Reversals

What do the numbers mean? "REAL ASSETS"

A key issue in accounting for income taxes is whether a company should recognize a deferred tax asset in the financial records. Based on the conceptual definition of an asset, a deferred tax asset meets the three main conditions for an item to be recognized as an asset:

1. **The entity controls access to the benefits.** In the Hunt example, the company can obtain the benefit of existing deductible temporary differences by reducing its taxes payable in the future. Hunt has the exclusive right to that benefit and can control others' access to it.

2. **It results from a past transaction.** For Hunt, the accrual of the loss contingency is the past event that gives rise to a future deductible temporary difference.

3. **It gives rise to a probable benefit in the future.** Taxable income exceeds Hunt's pretax financial income in the current year (2015). However, in the next year the exact opposite occurs. That is, taxable income is lower than pretax financial income. Because this deductible temporary difference reduces taxes payable in the future, a probable future benefit exists at the end of the current period.

Market analysts' reactions to the **write-off** of deferred tax assets also supports their treatment as assets. For example, many believe **MF Global**'s (USA) recent bankruptcy was precipitated by the large write-off of its deferred tax assets. In essence, the company was saying that it was highly unlikely that it would have future taxable profits with which to match these deferred tax deductions. As a result, investors lost total confidence in the firm.

Sources: J. Weil and S. Liesman, "Stock Gurus Disregard Most Big Write-Offs But They Often Hold Vital Clues to Outlook," *Wall Street Journal Online* (December 31, 2001); and Tim Worstall, "Why MF Global Really Went Bankrupt," *Forbes* (December 16, 2011).

Deferred Tax Asset (Non-Recognition)

Companies recognize a deferred tax asset for all deductible temporary differences. However, based on available evidence, a company should reduce a deferred tax asset if it is probable that it **will not realize** some portion or all of the deferred tax asset. "**Probable**" means a level of likelihood of at least slightly more than 50 percent.

4 LEARNING OBJECTIVE
Explain the non-recognition of a deferred tax asset.

Assume that Jensen Co. has a deductible temporary difference of €1,000,000 at the end of its first year of operations. Its tax rate is 40 percent, which means it records a deferred tax asset of €400,000 (€1,000,000 × 40%). Assuming €900,000 of income taxes payable, Jensen records income tax expense, the deferred tax asset, and income taxes payable as follows.

Income Tax Expense	500,000	
Deferred Tax Asset	400,000	
Income Taxes Payable		900,000

After careful review of all available evidence, Jensen determines that it is probable that it will not realize €100,000 of this deferred tax asset. Jensen records this reduction in asset value as follows.

Income Tax Expense	100,000	
Deferred Tax Asset		100,000

This journal entry increases income tax expense in the current period because Jensen does not expect to realize a favorable tax benefit for a portion of the deductible temporary difference. Jensen **simultaneously recognizes a reduction in the carrying amount**

of the deferred tax asset. Jensen then reports a deferred tax asset of €300,000 in its statement of financial position.

Jensen evaluates the deferred tax asset account at the end of each accounting period. If, at the end of the next period, it expects to realize €350,000 of this deferred tax asset, Jensen makes the following entry to adjust this account.

Deferred Tax Asset (€350,000 − €300,000)	50,000	
Income Tax Expense		50,000

Jensen should consider all available evidence, both positive and negative, to determine whether, based on the weight of available evidence, it needs to adjust the deferred tax asset. For example, if Jensen has been experiencing a series of loss years, it reasonably assumes that these losses will continue. Therefore, Jensen will lose the benefit of the future deductible amounts.

Generally, sufficient taxable income arises from temporary taxable differences that will reverse in the future or from a tax-planning strategy that will generate taxable income in the future. Illustration 19-19 shows how **Ahold** (NLD) describes its reporting of deferred assets.

ILLUSTRATION 19-19
Deferred Tax Asset
Disclosure

Ahold

Note 11. Significant judgment is required in determining whether deferred tax assets are realizable. Ahold determines this on the basis of expected taxable profits arising from recognized deferred tax liabilities and on the basis of budgets, cash flow forecasts, and impairment models. Where utilization is not considered probable, deferred taxes are not recognized.

Income Statement Presentation

LEARNING OBJECTIVE
Describe the presentation of income tax expense in the income statement.

Circumstances dictate whether a company should add or subtract the change in deferred income taxes to or from income taxes payable in computing income tax expense. For example, a company adds an increase in a deferred tax liability to income taxes payable. On the other hand, it subtracts an increase in a deferred tax asset from income taxes payable. The formula in Illustration 19-20 is used to compute income tax expense (benefit).

ILLUSTRATION 19-20
Formula to Compute
Income Tax Expense

Income Taxes Payable or Refundable	±	Change in Deferred Income Taxes	=	Total Income Tax Expense or Benefit

In the income statement or in the notes to the financial statements, a company should disclose the significant components of income tax expense attributable to continuing operations. Given the information related to Chelsea on page 959, the company reports its income statement as follows.

ILLUSTRATION 19-21
Income Statement
Presentation of Income
Tax Expense

CHELSEA INC.		
INCOME STATEMENT		
FOR THE YEAR ENDING DECEMBER 31, 2015		
Revenues		$130,000
Expenses		60,000
Income before income taxes		70,000
Income tax expense		
Current	$16,000	
Deferred	12,000	28,000
Net income		$ 42,000

As illustrated, Chelsea reports both the current portion (amount of income taxes payable for the period) and the deferred portion of income tax expense. Another option is to simply report the total income tax expense on the income statement and then indicate in the notes to the financial statements the current and deferred portions. Income tax expense is often referred to as "Provision for income taxes." Using this terminology, the current provision is $16,000, and the provision for deferred taxes is $12,000.

Specific Differences

Numerous items create differences between pretax financial income and taxable income. For purposes of accounting recognition, these differences are of two types: (1) temporary, and (2) permanent.

Temporary Differences

Taxable temporary differences are temporary differences that will result in taxable amounts in future years when the related assets are recovered. **Deductible temporary differences** are temporary differences that will result in deductible amounts in future years, when the related book liabilities are settled. Taxable temporary differences give rise to recording deferred tax liabilities. Deductible temporary differences give rise to recording deferred tax assets. Illustration 19-22 provides examples of temporary differences.

ILLUSTRATION 19-22
Examples of Temporary Differences

Revenues or gains are taxable after they are recognized in financial income (deferred tax liability).

An asset (e.g., accounts receivable or investment) may be recognized for revenues or gains that will result in **taxable amounts in future years** when the asset is recovered. Examples:
1. Sales accounted for on the accrual basis for financial reporting purposes and on the installment (cash) basis for tax purposes.
2. Contracts accounted for under the percentage-of-completion method for financial reporting purposes and the cost-recovery method (zero-profit method) for tax purposes.
3. Investments accounted for under the equity method for financial reporting purposes and under the cost method for tax purposes.
4. Gain on involuntary conversion of non-monetary asset which is recognized for financial reporting purposes but deferred for tax purposes.
5. Unrealized holding gains for financial reporting purposes (including use of the fair value option) but deferred for tax purposes.

Expenses or losses are deductible after they are recognized in financial income (deferred tax asset).

A liability (or contra asset) may be recognized for expenses or losses that will result in **deductible amounts in future years** when the liability is settled. Examples:
1. Product warranty liabilities.
2. Estimated liabilities related to discontinued operations or restructurings.
3. Litigation accruals.
4. Bad debt expense recognized using the allowance method for financial reporting purposes; direct write-off method used for tax purposes.
5. Share-based compensation expense.
6. Unrealized holding losses for financial reporting purposes (including use of the fair value option) but deferred for tax purposes.

Revenues or gains are taxable before they are recognized in financial income (deferred tax asset).

A liability may be recognized for an advance payment for goods or services to be provided or performed in future years. For tax purposes, the advance payment is included in taxable income upon the receipt of cash. Future sacrifices to provide goods or perform services (or future refunds to those who cancel their orders) that settle the liability will result in **deductible amounts in future years**. Examples:
1. Subscriptions received in advance.
2. Advance rental receipts.
3. Sales and leasebacks for financial reporting purposes (income deferral) but reported as sales for tax purposes.
4. Prepaid contracts and royalties received in advance.

Expenses or losses are deductible before they are recognized in financial income (deferred tax liability).

The cost of an asset may have been deducted for tax purposes faster than it was expensed for financial reporting purposes. Amounts received upon future recovery of the amount of the asset for financial reporting (through use or sale) will exceed the remaining tax basis of the asset and thereby result in **taxable amounts in future years**. Examples:
1. Depreciable property, depletable resources, and intangibles.
2. Deductible pension funding exceeding expense.
3. Prepaid expenses that are deducted on the tax return in the period paid.
4. Development costs that are deducted on the tax return in the period paid.

Determining a company's temporary differences may prove difficult. A company should prepare a statement of financial position for tax purposes that it can compare with its IFRS statement of financial position. Many of the differences between the two statements of financial position are temporary differences.

Originating and Reversing Aspects of Temporary Differences. An **originating temporary difference** is the initial difference between the book basis and the tax basis of an asset or liability, regardless of whether the tax basis of the asset or liability exceeds or is exceeded by the book basis of the asset or liability. A **reversing difference**, on the other hand, occurs when eliminating a temporary difference that originated in prior periods and then removing the related tax effect from the deferred tax account.

For example, assume that Sharp Co. has tax depreciation in excess of book depreciation of £2,000 in 2013, 2014, and 2015. Further, it has an excess of book depreciation over tax depreciation of £3,000 in 2016 and 2017 for the same asset. Assuming a tax rate of 30 percent for all years involved, the Deferred Tax Liability account reflects the following.

ILLUSTRATION 19-23
Tax Effects of Originating and Reversing Differences

	Deferred Tax Liability				
Tax Effects	2016	900	2013	600	Tax Effects
of	2017	900	2014	600	of
Reversing Differences			2015	600	Originating Differences

The originating differences for Sharp in each of the first three years are £2,000. The related tax effect of each originating difference is £600. The reversing differences in 2016 and 2017 are each £3,000. The related tax effect of each is £900.

Permanent Differences

Some differences between taxable income and pretax financial income are permanent. **Permanent differences** result from items that (1) enter into pretax financial income but **never** into taxable income, or (2) enter into taxable income but **never** into pretax financial income.

Governments enact a variety of tax law provisions to attain certain political, economic, and social objectives. Some of these provisions exclude certain revenues from taxation, limit the deductibility of certain expenses, and permit the deduction of certain other expenses in excess of costs incurred. A corporation that has tax-free income, non-deductible expenses, or allowable deductions in excess of cost has an effective tax rate that differs from its statutory (regular) tax rate.

Since permanent differences affect only the period in which they occur, they do not give rise to future taxable or deductible amounts. As a result, **companies recognize no deferred tax consequences**. Illustration 19-24 shows examples of permanent differences, given typical country laws.

ILLUSTRATION 19-24
Examples of Permanent Differences

Items are recognized for financial reporting purposes but not for tax purposes.

Examples:
1. Interest received on certain types of government obligations.
2. Expenses incurred in obtaining tax-exempt income.
3. Fines and expenses resulting from a violation of law.
4. Charitable donations recognized as expense but sometimes not deductible for tax purposes.

Items are recognized for tax purposes but not for financial reporting purposes.

Examples:
1. "Percentage depletion" of natural resources in excess of their cost.
2. The deduction for dividends received from other corporations, sometimes considered tax-exempt.

Examples of Temporary and Permanent Differences

To illustrate the computations used when both temporary and permanent differences exist, assume that Bio-Tech Company reports pretax financial income of €200,000 in each of the years 2013, 2014, and 2015. The company is subject to a 30 percent tax rate and has the following differences between pretax financial income and taxable income.

1. Bio-Tech reports an installment sale of €18,000 in 2013 for tax purposes over an 18-month period at a constant amount per month beginning January 1, 2014. It recognizes the entire sale for book purposes in 2013.

2. It pays life insurance premiums for its key officers of €5,000 in 2014 and 2015. Although not tax-deductible, Bio-Tech expenses the premiums for book purposes.

The installment sale is a temporary difference, whereas the life insurance premium is a permanent difference. Illustration 19-25 shows the reconciliation of Bio-Tech's pretax financial income to taxable income and the computation of income taxes payable.

	2013	2014	2015
Pretax financial income	€200,000	€200,000	€200,000
Permanent difference			
Non-deductible expense		5,000	5,000
Temporary difference			
Installment sale	(18,000)	12,000	6,000
Taxable income	182,000	217,000	211,000
Tax rate	× 30%	× 30%	× 30%
Income taxes payable	€ 54,600	€ 65,100	€ 63,300

ILLUSTRATION 19-25
Reconciliation and Computation of Income Taxes Payable

Note that Bio-Tech **deducts** the installment sales revenue from pretax financial income to arrive at taxable income. The reason: Pretax financial income includes the installment sales revenue; taxable income does not. Conversely, it **adds** the €5,000 insurance premium to pretax financial income to arrive at taxable income. The reason: Pretax financial income records an expense for this premium, but for tax purposes the premium is not deductible. As a result, pretax financial income is lower than taxable income. Therefore, the life insurance premium must be added back to pretax financial income to reconcile to taxable income.

Bio-Tech records income taxes for 2013, 2014, and 2015 as follows.

December 31, 2013

Income Tax Expense (€54,600 + €5,400)	60,000	
Deferred Tax Liability (€18,000 × 30%)		5,400
Income Taxes Payable (€182,000 × 30%)		54,600

December 31, 2014

Income Tax Expense (€65,100 − €3,600)	61,500	
Deferred Tax Liability (€12,000 × 30%)	3,600	
Income Taxes Payable (€217,000 × 30%)		65,100

December 31, 2015

Income Tax Expense (€63,300 − €1,800)	61,500	
Deferred Tax Liability (€6,000 × 30%)	1,800	
Income Taxes Payable (€211,000 × 30%)		63,300

Bio-Tech has one temporary difference, which originates in 2013 and reverses in 2014 and 2015. It recognizes a deferred tax liability at the end of 2013 because the temporary difference causes future taxable amounts. As the temporary difference reverses, Bio-Tech reduces the deferred tax liability. There is no deferred tax amount associated with the difference caused by the non-deductible insurance expense because it is a permanent difference.

Although an enacted tax rate of 30 percent applies for all three years, the effective rate differs from the enacted rate in 2014 and 2015. Bio-Tech computes the **effective tax rate** by dividing total income tax expense for the period by pretax financial income. The effective rate is 30 percent for 2013 (€60,000 ÷ €200,000 = 30%) and 30.75 percent for 2014 and 2015 (€61,500 ÷ €200,000 = 30.75%).

Tax Rate Considerations

LEARNING OBJECTIVE 7

Explain the effect of various tax rates and tax rate changes on deferred income taxes.

In our previous illustrations, the enacted tax rate did not change from one year to the next. Thus, to compute the deferred income tax amount to report on the statement of financial position, a company simply multiplies the cumulative temporary difference by the current tax rate. Using Bio-Tech as an example, it multiplies the cumulative temporary difference of €18,000 by the enacted tax rate, 30 percent in this case, to arrive at a deferred tax liability of €5,400 (€18,000 × 30%) at the end of 2013.

Future Tax Rates

What happens if tax rates are expected to change in the future? In this case, a company should use the **substantially enacted tax rate** expected to apply.[2] Therefore, a company must consider presently enacted changes in the tax rate that become effective for a particular future year(s) when determining the tax rate to apply to existing temporary differences. For example, assume that Wang Group at the end of 2012 has the following cumulative temporary difference of ¥300,000, computed as shown in Illustration 19-26.

ILLUSTRATION 19-26
Computation of Cumulative Temporary Difference

Book basis of depreciable assets	¥1,000,000
Tax basis of depreciable assets	700,000
Cumulative temporary difference	¥ 300,000

Furthermore, assume that the ¥300,000 will reverse and result in taxable amounts in the future, with the enacted tax rates shown in Illustration 19-27.

ILLUSTRATION 19-27
Deferred Tax Liability Based on Future Rates

	2013	2014	2015	2016	2017	Total
Future taxable amounts	¥80,000	¥70,000	¥60,000	¥50,000	¥40,000	¥300,000
Tax rate	×40%	×40%	×35%	×30%	×30%	
Deferred tax liability	¥32,000	¥28,000	¥21,000	¥15,000	¥12,000	¥108,000

The total deferred tax liability at the end of 2012 is ¥108,000. Wang may only use tax rates other than the current rate when the future tax rates have been enacted, as is the case in this example. **If new rates are not yet enacted for future years, Wang should use the current rate.**

In some countries, the applicable tax rate depends on how the carrying amount of an asset or liability is recovered or settled. For example, a company could be operating a plant that it intends to hold for continued use. The tax rate on normal operations is 35 percent. On the other hand, if the company wishes to sell the plant and the related capital gain or loss is subject to a tax rate of 15 percent, then the applicable tax rate may change. **[3]**

Revision of Future Tax Rates

When a change in the tax rate is enacted, companies should record its effect on the existing deferred income tax accounts immediately. **A company reports the effect as an adjustment to income tax expense in the period of the change.**

Assume that on December 10, 2014, a new income tax act is signed into law that lowers the corporate tax rate from 40 percent to 35 percent, effective January 1, 2016. If

---

[2]Substantially enacted generally means "virtually certain." The IASB provides guidelines as to how to interpret substantially enacted. **[2]** *For purposes of discussion and homework, assume that the term "enacted" is interchangeable with "substantially enacted."*

Hostel Co. has one temporary difference at the beginning of 2014 related to $3 million of excess tax depreciation, then it has a Deferred Tax Liability account with a balance of $1,200,000 ($3,000,000 × 40%) at January 1, 2014. If taxable amounts related to this difference are scheduled to occur equally in 2015, 2016, and 2017, the deferred tax liability at the end of 2014 is $1,100,000, computed as follows.

	2015	2016	2017	Total
Future taxable amounts	$1,000,000	$1,000,000	$1,000,000	$3,000,000
Tax rate	× 40%	× 35%	× 35%	
Deferred tax liability	$ 400,000	$ 350,000	$ 350,000	$1,100,000

ILLUSTRATION 19-28
Schedule of Future Taxable Amounts and Related Tax Rates

Hostel, therefore, recognizes the decrease of $100,000 ($1,200,000 − $1,100,000) at the end of 2014 in the deferred tax liability as follows.

Deferred Tax Liability	100,000	
Income Tax Expense		100,000

Corporate tax rates do not change often. Therefore, companies usually employ the current rate. However, tax rates in some jurisdictions change more frequently, and they require adjustments in deferred income taxes accordingly.[3]

What do the numbers mean? GLOBAL TAX RATES

If you are concerned about your tax rate and the taxes you pay, you might want to consider moving to the Cayman Islands or the Bahamas, which have a personal tax rate of zero percent. You don't want to move to Denmark though. Yes, the people of Denmark are regularly voted to be the happiest people on Earth but it's uncertain how many of these polls take place at tax time. The government in Denmark charges income tax rates up to 55.4 percent. So, taxes are a major item to many individuals, wherever they reside.

Taxes are also a big deal to corporations. For example, the Organisation for Economic Co-operation and Development (OECD) is an international organization of 38 countries that accepts the principles of a free-market economy. Most OECD members are high-income economies and are regarded as developed countries. However, companies in the OECD can be subject to significant tax levies, as indicated in the following list of the 10 highest corporate income tax rates for the OECD countries.

United States	40.0%	Germany	29.5%
Japan	38.0	Luxembourg	28.8
Belgium	33.9	New Zealand	28.0
France	33.3	Spain	28.0
Australia	30.0	Canada	26.0

On the low end of the tax rate spectrum are Iceland and Ireland, with tax rates of 15 percent and 12.5 percent, respectively. Indeed, corporate tax rates have been dropping around the world as countries attempt to spur capital investment, which in turn encourages international tax competition. However, with stagnant global economic growth, there is concern that governments will target increases in corporate tax rates as a source of revenues to address budget shortfalls. In addition, further expansion of value-added taxes (VAT) is being considered. Indirect taxes such as the VAT are charged on consumption of goods and services, which is much more stable than the corporate tax.

If these tax proposals result in changes in the tax rates applied to future deductible and taxable amounts, be prepared for significant remeasurement of deferred tax assets and liabilities.

Source: The rates reported reflect the base corporate rate in effect in 2012. Effective rates paid may vary depending on country-specific additional levies for such items as unemployment and local taxes, and, in the case of Japan, earthquake damage assessments. Effective rates may be lower due to credits for investments and capital gains. See *http://www.kpmg.com/global/en/services/tax/tax-tools-and-resources/pages/tax-rates-online.aspx.* See also P. Toscano, "The World's Highest Tax Rates," *http://www.cnbc.com/id/30727913* (May 13, 2009).

[3]Tax rate changes nearly always will substantially impact income numbers and the reporting of deferred income taxes on the statement of financial position. As a result, you can expect to hear an economic consequences argument every time that a government decides to change the tax rates. For example, when one country raised the corporate rate from 34 percent to 35 percent, companies took an additional "hit" to earnings if they were in a deferred tax liability position.

ACCOUNTING FOR NET OPERATING LOSSES

Every management hopes its company will be profitable. But hopes and profits may not materialize. For a start-up company, it is common to accumulate operating losses while expanding its customer base but before realizing economies of scale. For an established company, a major event such as a labor strike, a rapidly changing regulatory environment, or a competitive situation can cause expenses to exceed revenues—a net operating loss.

A **net operating loss (NOL)** occurs for tax purposes in a year when tax-deductible expenses exceed taxable revenues. An inequitable tax burden would result if companies were taxed during profitable periods without receiving any tax relief during periods of net operating losses. Under certain circumstances, therefore, tax laws permit taxpayers to use the losses of one year to offset the profits of other years.

Companies accomplish this income-averaging provision through the **carryback and carryforward of net operating losses**. Under this provision, a company pays no income taxes for a year in which it incurs a net operating loss. In addition, it may select one of the two options discussed below and on the following pages.[4]

Loss Carryback

Through use of a **loss carryback**, a company may carry the net operating loss back two years and receive refunds for income taxes paid in those years. The company must apply the loss to the earlier year first and then to the second year. It may **carry forward** any loss remaining after the two-year carryback up to 20 years to offset future taxable income. Illustration 19-29 diagrams the loss carryback procedure, assuming a loss in 2015.

ILLUSTRATION 19-29
Loss Carryback
Procedure

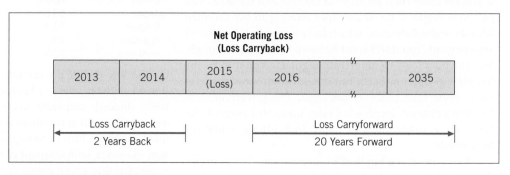

Loss Carryforward

A company may forgo the loss carryback and use only the **loss carryforward** option, offsetting future taxable income for up to 20 years. Illustration 19-30 shows this approach.

ILLUSTRATION 19-30
Loss Carryforward
Procedure

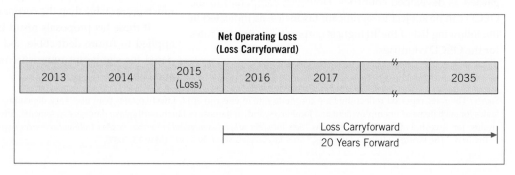

[4]Countries differ as to the years that operating losses can be carried back and forward. In our discussion, we assume that companies can carry their operating losses back two years and can carry them forward 20 years. *For homework purposes, use these periods as the basis for carrybacks and carryforwards.*

Loss Carryback Example

To illustrate the accounting procedures for a net operating loss carryback, assume that Groh Inc. has no temporary or permanent differences. Groh experiences the following.

Year	Taxable Income or Loss	Tax Rate	Tax Paid
2011	$ 50,000	35%	$17,500
2012	100,000	30%	30,000
2013	200,000	40%	80,000
2014	(500,000)	—	–0–

In 2014, Groh incurs a net operating loss that it decides to carry back. Under the law, Groh must apply the carryback first to the **second year preceding the loss year**. Therefore, it carries the loss back first to 2012. Then, Groh carries back any unused loss to 2013. Accordingly, Groh files amended tax returns for 2012 and 2013, receiving refunds for the $110,000 ($30,000 + $80,000) of taxes paid in those years.

For accounting as well as tax purposes, the $110,000 represents the **tax effect (tax benefit)** of the loss carryback. Groh should recognize this tax effect in 2014, the loss year. Since the tax loss gives rise to a refund that is both measurable and currently realizable, Groh should recognize the associated tax benefit in this loss period.

Groh makes the following journal entry for 2014.

Income Tax Refund Receivable	110,000	
Benefit Due to Loss Carryback (Income Tax Expense)		110,000

Groh reports the account debited, **Income Tax Refund Receivable**, on the statement of financial position as a current asset at December 31, 2014. It reports the account credited on the income statement for 2014 as shown in Illustration 19-31.

GROH INC.	
INCOME STATEMENT (PARTIAL) FOR 2014	
Operating loss before income taxes	$(500,000)
Income tax benefit	
Benefit due to loss carryback	110,000
Net loss	$(390,000)

ILLUSTRATION 19-31
Recognition of Benefit of the Loss Carryback in the Loss Year

Since the $500,000 net operating loss for 2014 exceeds the $300,000 total taxable income from the two preceding years, Groh carries forward the remaining $200,000 loss.

Loss Carryforward Example

If a carryback fails to fully absorb a net operating loss or if the company decides not to carry the loss back, then it can carry forward the loss for up to 20 years. Because companies use carryforwards to offset future taxable income, the **tax effect of a loss carryforward** represents **future tax savings**. Realization of the future tax benefit depends on future earnings, an uncertain prospect.

The key accounting issue is whether there should be different requirements for recognition of a deferred tax asset for (a) deductible temporary differences, and (b) operating loss carryforwards. The IASB's position is that in substance these items are the same—both are tax-deductible amounts in future years. As a result, the Board concluded that there **should not be different requirements** for recognition of a deferred tax asset from deductible temporary differences and operating loss carryforwards.[5]

Carryforward (Recognition)

To illustrate the accounting for an operating loss carryforward, return to the Groh example from the preceding section. In 2014, the company records the tax effect of the $200,000 loss carryforward as a deferred tax asset of $80,000 ($200,000 × 40%), assuming that the enacted future tax rate is 40 percent. Groh records the benefits of the carryback and the carryforward in 2014 as follows.

To recognize benefit of loss carryback

Income Tax Refund Receivable	110,000	
Benefit Due to Loss Carryback (Income Tax Expense)		110,000

To recognize benefit of loss carryforward

Deferred Tax Asset	80,000	
Benefit Due to Loss Carryforward (Income Tax Expense)		80,000

Groh realizes the income tax refund receivable of $110,000 immediately as a refund of taxes paid in the past. It establishes a Deferred Tax Asset for the benefits of future tax savings. The two accounts credited are contra income tax expense items, which Groh presents on the 2014 income statement shown in Illustration 19-32.

ILLUSTRATION 19-32
Recognition of the Benefit of the Loss Carryback and Carryforward in the Loss Year

GROH INC.		
INCOME STATEMENT (PARTIAL) FOR 2014		
Operating loss before income taxes		$(500,000)
Income tax benefit		
Benefit due to loss carryback	$110,000	
Benefit due to loss carryforward	80,000	190,000
Net loss		$(310,000)

The **current tax benefit** of $110,000 is the income tax refundable for the year. Groh determines this amount by applying the carryback provisions of the tax law to the taxable loss for 2014. The $80,000 is the **deferred tax benefit** for the year, which results from an increase in the deferred tax asset.

For 2015, assume that Groh returns to profitable operations and has taxable income of $250,000 (prior to adjustment for the NOL carryforward), subject to a 40 percent tax rate. Groh then realizes the benefits of the carryforward for tax purposes in 2015, which it recognized for accounting purposes in 2014. Groh computes the income taxes payable for 2015 as shown in Illustration 19-33.

ILLUSTRATION 19-33
Computation of Income Taxes Payable with Realized Loss Carryforward

Taxable income prior to loss carryforward	$ 250,000
Loss carryforward deduction	(200,000)
Taxable income for 2015	50,000
Tax rate	× 40%
Income taxes payable for 2015	$ 20,000

[5]This requirement is controversial because some believe that companies should never recognize deferred tax assets for loss carryforwards until realizing the income in the future.

Groh records income taxes in 2015 as follows.

Income Tax Expense	100,000	
Deferred Tax Asset		80,000
Income Taxes Payable		20,000

The benefits of the NOL carryforward, realized in 2015, reduce the Deferred Tax Asset account to zero.

The 2015 income statement that appears in Illustration 19-34 does **not report** the tax effects of either the loss carryback or the loss carryforward because Groh had reported both previously.

<table>
<tr><td colspan="3" align="center">GROH INC.
INCOME STATEMENT (PARTIAL) FOR 2015</td></tr>
<tr><td>Income before income taxes</td><td></td><td>$250,000</td></tr>
<tr><td>Income tax expense</td><td></td><td></td></tr>
<tr><td> Current</td><td>$20,000</td><td></td></tr>
<tr><td> Deferred</td><td>80,000</td><td>100,000</td></tr>
<tr><td>Net income</td><td></td><td>$150,000</td></tr>
</table>

ILLUSTRATION 19-34
Presentation of the Benefit of Loss Carryforward Realized in 2015, Recognized in 2014

Carryforward (Non-Recognition)

Let us continue with the Groh example. Assume now that it is probable that Groh will *not* realize the entire NOL carryforward in future years. In this situation, Groh records the tax benefits of $110,000 associated with the $300,000 NOL carryback, as we previously described. It does not recognize a deferred tax asset for the loss carryforward because it is probable that it will not realize the carryforward. Groh makes the following journal entry in 2014.

To recognize benefit of loss carryback		
Income Tax Refund Receivable	110,000	
Benefit Due to Loss Carryback (Income Tax Expense)		110,000

Illustration 19-35 shows Groh's 2014 income statement presentation.

<table>
<tr><td colspan="2" align="center">GROH INC.
INCOME STATEMENT (PARTIAL) FOR 2014</td></tr>
<tr><td>Operating loss before income taxes</td><td>$(500,000)</td></tr>
<tr><td>Income tax benefit</td><td></td></tr>
<tr><td> Benefit due to loss carryback</td><td>110,000</td></tr>
<tr><td>Net loss</td><td>$(390,000)</td></tr>
</table>

ILLUSTRATION 19-35
Recognition of Benefit of Loss Carryback Only

In 2015, assuming that Groh has taxable income of $250,000 (before considering the carryforward), subject to a tax rate of 40 percent, it realizes the deferred tax asset. Groh records the following entries.

To recognize deferred tax asset and loss carryforward		
Deferred Tax Asset	80,000	
Benefit Due to Loss Carryforward (Income Tax Expense)		80,000

To record current and deferred income taxes		
Income Tax Expense	100,000	
Deferred Tax Asset		80,000
Income Taxes Payable		20,000

Groh reports the $80,000 Benefit Due to the Loss Carryforward on the 2015 income statement. The company did not recognize it in 2014 because it was probable that it would not be realized. Assuming that Groh derives the income for 2015 from continuing operations, it prepares the income statement as shown in Illustration 19-36.

ILLUSTRATION 19-36
Recognition of Benefit of
Loss Carryforward When
Realized

GROH INC.		
INCOME STATEMENT (PARTIAL) FOR 2015		
Income before income taxes		$250,000
Income tax expense		
Current	$ 20,000	
Deferred	80,000	
Benefit due to loss carryforward	(80,000)	20,000
Net income		$230,000

Another method is to report only one line for total income tax expense of $20,000 on the face of the income statement and disclose the components of income tax expense in the notes to the financial statements.

Non-Recognition Revisited

Whether the company will realize a deferred tax asset depends on whether sufficient taxable income exists or will exist within the carryforward period available under tax law. Illustration 19-37 shows possible sources of taxable income and related factors that companies can consider in assessing the probability that taxable income will be available against which the unused tax losses or unused tax credits can be utilized.[6]

ILLUSTRATION 19-37
Possible Sources of
Taxable Income

Taxable Income Sources
a. Whether the company has sufficient taxable temporary differences relating to the same tax authority, which will result in taxable amounts against which the unused tax losses or unused tax credits can be utilized before they expire;
b. Whether it is probable that the company will have taxable profits before the unused tax losses or unused tax credits expire;
c. Whether the unused tax losses result from identifiable causes, which are unlikely to recur; and
d. Whether tax-planning opportunities are available to the company that will create taxable profit in the period in which the unused tax losses or unused tax credits can be utilized. [4]

To the extent that it is not probable that taxable profit will be available against which the unused tax losses or unused tax credits can be utilized, the deferred tax asset is not recognized.

Forming a conclusion that recognition of a loss carryforward is probable is difficult when there is negative evidence (such as cumulative losses in recent years). However, companies often cite positive evidence indicating that recognition of the carryforward is warranted.[7]

---

[6]Companies implement a tax-planning strategy to realize a tax benefit for an operating loss or tax carryforward before it expires. Companies consider tax-planning strategies when assessing the need of a deferred tax asset to recognize.

[7]**Sony Corp.** (JPN) announced a $3.2 billion net loss, blaming a $4.4 billion write-off on a certain portion of deferred tax assets in Japan, in what would be the company's third straight year of red ink. The write-off is an admission that the March 2011 earthquake and tsunami have shattered its expectations for a robust current fiscal year. In the wake of the disaster, Sony temporarily shut 10 plants in and around the quake-hit region. Like other Japanese auto and electronics makers, Sony faced uncertainties because its recovery prospects are partially dependent on parts and materials suppliers, many of which have also been affected by the quake. Thus, the post-quake outlook put Sony in a position where it had to set aside reserves of approximately $3 billion on certain deferred tax assets in its fiscal fourth quarter. See J. Osawa, "Sony Expects Hefty Loss: Electronics Giant Reverses Prediction for Full-Year Profit, Blaming Earthquake," *Wall Street Journal* (May 24, 2011).

Unfortunately, the subjective nature of determining an impairment for a deferred tax asset provides a company with an opportunity to manage its earnings. As one accounting expert notes, "The 'probable' provision is perhaps the most judgmental clause in accounting." Some companies may recognize the loss carryforward immediately and then use it to increase income as needed. Others may take the income immediately to increase capital or to offset large negative charges to income.

FINANCIAL STATEMENT PRESENTATION
Statement of Financial Position

Companies classify taxes receivable or payable as current assets or current liabilities. Although current tax assets and liabilities are separately recognized and measured, they are often offset in the statement of financial position. The offset occurs because companies normally have a legally enforceable right to set off a current tax asset (Income Taxes Receivable) against a current tax liability (Income Taxes Payable) when they relate to income taxes levied by the same taxation authority. **[5]** Deferred tax assets and deferred tax liabilities are also separately recognized and measured but may be offset in the statement of financial position.[8] The net deferred tax asset or net deferred tax liability is reported in the non-current section of the statement of financial position.[9]

9 LEARNING OBJECTIVE
Describe the presentation of income taxes in financial statements.

To illustrate, assume that K. Scott Company has four deferred tax items at December 31, 2015, as shown in Illustration 19-38.

Temporary Difference	Resulting Deferred Tax	
	(Asset)	Liability
1. Rent collected in advance: recognized when performance obligation satisfied for accounting purposes and when received for tax purposes.	$(42,000)	
2. Use of straight-line depreciation for accounting purposes and accelerated depreciation for tax purposes.		$214,000
3. Recognition of profits on installment sales during period of sale for accounting purposes and during period of collection for tax purposes.		45,000
4. Warranty liabilities: recognized for accounting purposes at time of sale; for tax purposes at time paid.	(12,000)	
Totals	$(54,000)	$259,000

ILLUSTRATION 19-38
Classification of Temporary Differences

As indicated, K. Scott has a total deferred tax asset of $54,000 and a total deferred tax liability of $259,000. Assuming these two items can be offset, K. Scott reports a deferred tax liability of $205,000 ($259,000 − $54,000) in the non-current liability section of its statement of financial position.

To provide another illustration, **Wm Morrison Supermarkets plc** (GBR) reports its information related to income taxes on its consolidated balance sheet (statement of financial position) and related note on defined income taxes as shown in Illustration 19-39 (on page 976).

---

[8]Companies are permitted to offset deferred tax assets and deferred tax liabilities if, and only if: (1) the company has a legally enforceable right to set off current tax assets against current tax liabilities, and (2) the deferred tax assets and the deferred tax liabilities relate to income taxes levied by the same tax authority and for the same company. **[6]**

[9]Deferred tax amounts should not be discounted. The IASB apparently considers discounting to be an unnecessary complication even if the effects are material. **[7]**

Wm Morrison Supermarkets plc
Consolidated Balance Sheet
3 February 2013
(£ in millions)

		2013	2012
Current liabilities			
Current tax liabilities		(149)	(163)
Non-current liabilities			
Deferred tax liabilities	(Note 19)	(471)	(464)

19 Deferred tax	2013	2012
Deferred tax liability	(519)	(509)
Deferred tax asset	48	45
Net deferred tax liability	(471)	(464)

IAS 12 'Income taxes' permits the offsetting of balances within the same tax jurisdiction. All of the deferred tax assets are available for offset against deferred tax liabilities.

The movements in deferred tax (liabilities)/assets during the period are shown below:

	Property, plant and equipment	Pensions	Share-based payments	Other short term temporary differences	**Total**
Current period					
At 29 January 2012	(509)	2	6	37	(464)
(Charged)/credited to profit for the period	(10)	5	(4)	6	(3)
Charged to other comprehensive expense and equity	—	(2)	(2)	—	(4)
At 3 February 2013	(519)	5	—	43	(471)
Prior period					
At 30 January 2011	(534)	(10)	3	42	(499)
Credited/(charged) to profit for the period	25	(1)	2	(11)	15
Credited to other comprehensive expense and equity	—	13	1	6	20
At 29 January 2012	(509)	2	6	37	(464)

Included within the total (charged)/credited to profit for the period is an amount credited of £41m (2012: £42m), and within the total charged to other comprehensive expense a charge of £4m (2012: £2m) in respect of the change in the tax rate at which deferred tax balances are expected to reverse.

ILLUSTRATION 19-39
Income Tax Reporting

In Note 19, Morrison Supermarkets explains how the net deferred tax liability is computed as well as the composition of the liability. A user of the financial statements and related notes therefore understands what comprises the net deferred tax liability of £471 million, which provides insight into the likelihood of future cash outflows related to the net deferred tax liability.

Income Statement

Companies allocate income tax expense (or benefit) to continuing operations, discontinued operations, other comprehensive income, and prior period adjustments. This approach is referred to as **intraperiod tax allocation**. In addition, the components of income tax expense (benefit) may include:

1. Current tax expense (benefit).

2. Any adjustments recognized in the period for current tax of prior periods.

3. The amount of deferred tax expense (benefit) relating to the origination and reversal of temporary differences.

4. The amount of deferred tax expense (benefit) relating to changes in tax rates or the imposition of new taxes.

5. The amount of the benefit arising from a previously unrecognized tax loss, tax credit, or temporary difference of a prior period that is used to reduce current and deferred tax expense.[10]

To illustrate, the relevant portion of the consolidated statement of comprehensive income of Morrison Supermarkets is presented in Illustration 19-40.

ILLUSTRATION 19-40
Taxes on Income
Statement

Wm Morrison Supermarkets plc
Consolidated Statement of Comprehensive Income (Partial)
53 Weeks Ended 3 February 2013
(£ in millions)

	Note	2013	2012
Profit before taxation		879	947
Taxation	7	(232)	(257)
Profit for the period attributable to the owners of the Company		647	690
Other comprehensive expense			
Actuarial loss arising in the pension scheme		(6)	(65)
Cash flow hedging movement		(2)	(23)
Tax in relation to components of other comprehensive expense	7	(2)	19
Other comprehensive expense for the period, net of tax		(10)	(69)
Total comprehensive income for the period attributable to the owners of the Company		637	621

Illustration 19-41 presents Note 7, which is the explanation of the composition of the taxes charged to Morrison Supermarkets.

Wm Morrison Supermarkets plc
(£ in millions)

7 Taxation
a) Analysis of charge in the period

	2013	2012
Corporation tax		
– current period	261	292
– adjustment in respect of prior period	(32)	(20)
	229	272
Deferred tax		
– origination and reversal of timing differences	(3)	5
– adjustment in respect of prior period	47	22
– impact of change in tax rate	(41)	(42)
	3	(15)
Tax charge for the period	232	257

b) Tax on items charged/(credited) in other comprehensive expense and equity

	2013	2012
Actuarial gain/(loss) arising in the pension scheme	2	(13)
Cash flow hedges	–	(6)
Total tax on items included in other comprehensive expense	2	(19)
Share-based payments	2	(1)
Total tax on items included in other comprehensive expense and equity	4	(20)
Analysis of items charged/(credited) to other comprehensive expense and equity: Deferred tax (note 19)	4	(20)

ILLUSTRATION 19-41
Components of
Income Tax

[10]Other components that should be reported are the deferred tax expense arising from the write-down, or reversal of a previous write-down, of a deferred tax asset, as well as the amount of tax expense (benefit) relating to those changes in accounting policies and errors that are included in profit or loss in accordance with *IAS 8*. **[8]**

As shown in Illustration 19-41, income taxes reduced profit by £232 million. In addition, taxes related to other comprehensive expense and equity are shown net of tax. Illustration 19-41 also provides information that identifies the components of the tax charge of €232 million. In addition, the individual tax effects related to other comprehensive expense and equity of £4 million are explained.

Tax Reconciliation

Another important disclosure is the reconciliation between actual tax expense and the applicable tax rate. Companies either provide:

- A numerical reconciliation between tax expense (benefit) and the product of accounting profit multiplied by the applicable tax rate(s), disclosing also the basis on which the applicable tax rate(s) is (are) computed; or
- A numerical reconciliation between the average effective tax rate and the applicable tax rate, disclosing also the basis on which the applicable tax rate is computed.

Morrison Supermarket provides the first type of reconciliation but also notes that the effective tax rate is higher than the applicable (standard) rate, as shown in a continuation of its tax note in Illustration 19-42.

ILLUSTRATION 19-42
Tax Reconciliation
Disclosure

Wm Morrison Supermarkets plc
(£ in millions)

c) Tax reconciliation

The tax for the period is higher (2012: higher) than the standard rate of corporation tax in the UK of 24.3% (2012: 26.3%). The differences are explained below:

	2013	2012
Profit before tax	879	947
Profit before tax at 24.3% (2012: 26.3%)	214	249
Effects of:		
Expenses not deductible for tax purposes	10	12
Non-qualifying depreciation	39	38
Deferred tax on Safeway acquisition assets	(10)	(12)
Effect of change in tax rate	(41)	(42)
Other	5	10
Prior period adjustments	15	2
Tax charge for the period	232	257

Factors affecting current and future tax charges

Legislation to reduce the rate of corporation tax from 24% to 23% was included in the Finance Act 2012, and as it had been substantively enacted at the balance sheet date the deferred tax balances as at 3 February 2013 have been measured at this rate. The impact of this change in tax rate is a credit of £41m to the income statement. In addition, further changes to the UK corporation tax system were announced in the Autumn Statement 2012. This includes a further reduction to the main rate to reduce the rate to 21% from 1 April 2014. This change had not been substantively enacted at the balance sheet date, and, therefore, is not included in these financial statements.

The proposed reduction of the main rate of corporation tax to 21% from 1 April 2014 will be enacted separately. The overall effect of this further change, if it applied to the deferred tax balance at 3 February 2013, would be to further reduce the deferred tax liability by an additional £40m.

In explaining the relationship between tax expense (benefit) and accounting income, companies use an applicable tax rate that provides the most meaningful information to the users of its financial statements.[11]

[11]Often, the most meaningful rate is the domestic rate of tax in the country in which the company is located, aggregating the tax rate applied for national taxes, with the rates applied for any local taxes, which are computed on a substantially similar level of taxable profit (tax loss). However, for a company operating in several jurisdictions, it may be more meaningful to aggregate separate reconciliations prepared using the domestic rate in each individual jurisdiction.

These income tax disclosures are required for several reasons:

1. *Assessing quality of earnings.* Many investors seeking to assess the quality of a company's earnings are interested in the relation between pretax financial income and taxable income. Analysts carefully examine earnings that are enhanced by a favorable tax effect, particularly if the tax effect is non-recurring. For Morrison Supermarkets, it is interesting to note that its applicable tax rate is greater than the effective tax rate (taxes paid divided by income before income taxes). Non-qualifying depreciation charges for tax purposes, as well as a prior period adjustment, are the primary reasons for this situation.

2. *Making better predictions of future cash flows.* Examination of the deferred portion of income tax expense provides information as to whether taxes payable are likely to be higher or lower in the future. In Morrison Supermarkets' case, analysts expect future taxable amounts and higher tax payments, due to lower depreciation in the future. It also appears that Morrison Supermarkets is generating other deductible amounts related to pensions, share-based payments, and other short-term temporary differences. These deferred tax items indicate that actual tax payments for Morrison Supermarkets will be lower than the tax expense reported on the income statement in the future. Conversely, the tax rate is expected to drop to as low as 21 percent, which will lead to lower current and deferred taxes.

3. *Predicting future cash flows for operating loss carryforwards.* Companies should disclose the amounts and expiration dates of any operating loss carryforwards for tax purposes. From this disclosure, analysts determine the amount of income that the company may recognize in the future on which it will pay no income tax. Morrison Supermarkets has no loss carryforwards.[12]

What do the numbers mean? THE TAX TWIST

As indicated in the information related to the tax reconciliation at **Wm Morrison Supermarkets plc** (GBR), a favorable development for the company is that tax rates decreased from 26.3 percent in 2012 to 24.3 percent in 2013. In addition, it is likely that rates will drop to 21 percent in the near future. As indicated in Illustration 19-41, this may lead to an additional reduction of deferred income taxes of £41 million, which will result in income tax expense also being decreased.

However, the reduction in rates can be a double-edged sword for companies that have large deferred tax asset balances. A tax rate decrease means that deferred tax assets are worth less since lower tax bills mean fewer opportunities to use deferred tax assets before they expire. **Citigroup** (USA), for example, indicated recently that a reduction in its tax rate could lead to a deferred tax write-off of $4 billion to $5 billion. The following graphic illustrates how that might happen if U.S. rates dropped from 35 percent to 20 percent, which has recently been proposed by some politicians.

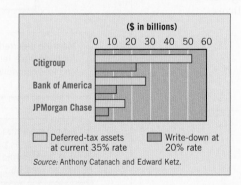

Source: Anthony Catanach and Edward Ketz.

So there is a tax twist in a tax rate reduction, which may not be positive for some companies that have large deferred tax asset balances.

Source: "Double-Edged Deferral: How Lower Taxes Could Hurt America's Big Banks," *The Economist* (December 10, 2011).

---

[12]P. McConnell, J. Pegg, C. Senyak, and D. Mott, "The ABCs of NOLs," *Accounting Issues*, Bear Stearns Equity Research (June 2005). Regulators frown on acquisitions done solely to obtain operating loss carryforwards. If they determine that the merger is solely tax-motivated, the regulators generally disallow the deductions. But, because it is very difficult to determine whether a merger is or is not tax-motivated, the "purchase of operating loss carryforwards" continues.

REVIEW OF THE ASSET-LIABILITY METHOD

LEARNING OBJECTIVE 10

Indicate the basic principles of the asset-liability method.

The IASB believes that the asset-liability method (sometimes referred to as the liability approach) is the most consistent method for accounting for income taxes. One objective of this approach is to recognize the amount of taxes payable or refundable for the current year. A second objective is to recognize **deferred tax liabilities and assets** for the **future tax consequences** of events that have been recognized in the financial statements or tax returns.

To implement the objectives, companies apply some basic principles in accounting for income taxes at the date of the financial statements, as listed in Illustration 19-43.

ILLUSTRATION 19-43
Basic Principles of the Asset-Liability Method

Basic Principles
a. A current tax liability or asset is recognized for the estimated taxes payable or refundable on the tax return for the current year.
b. A deferred tax liability or asset is recognized for the estimated future tax effects attributable to temporary differences and carryforwards.
c. The measurement of current and deferred tax liabilities and assets is based on provisions of the enacted tax law; the effects of future changes in tax laws or rates are not anticipated.
d. The measurement of deferred tax assets is reduced, if necessary, by the amount of any tax benefits that, based on available evidence, are not expected to be realized.

Illustration 19-44 diagrams the procedures for implementing the asset-liability method.

ILLUSTRATION 19-44
Procedures for Computing and Reporting Deferred Income Taxes

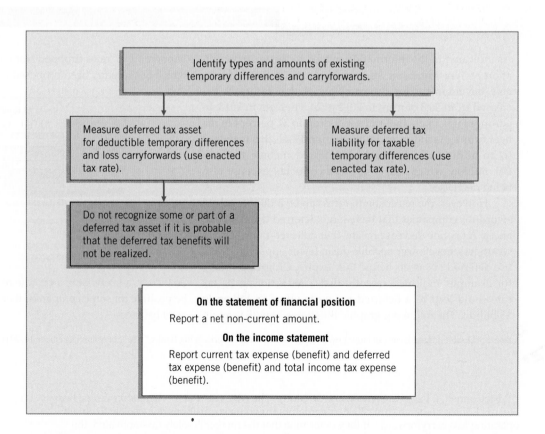

As an aid to understanding deferred income taxes, we provide the following glossary.

KEY DEFERRED INCOME TAX TERMS

CARRYBACKS. Deductions or credits that cannot be utilized on the tax return during a year and that may be carried back to reduce taxable income or taxes paid in a prior year. An **operating loss carryback** is an excess of tax deductions over gross income in a year. A **tax carryback** is the amount by which tax credits available for utilization exceed statutory limitations.

CARRYFORWARDS. Deductions or credits that cannot be utilized on the tax return during a year and that may be carried forward to reduce taxable income or taxes payable in a future year. An **operating loss carryforward** is an excess of tax deductions over gross income in a year. A **tax carryforward** is the amount by which tax credits available for utilization exceed statutory limitations.

CURRENT TAX EXPENSE (BENEFIT). The amount of income taxes paid or payable (or refundable) for a year as determined by applying the provisions of the enacted tax law to the taxable income or excess of deductions over revenues for that year.

DEDUCTIBLE TEMPORARY DIFFERENCE. Temporary differences that result in deductible amounts in future years when recovering or settling the related asset or liability, respectively.

DEFERRED TAX ASSET. The deferred tax consequences attributable to deductible temporary differences and carryforwards.

DEFERRED TAX CONSEQUENCES. The future effects on income taxes as measured by the enacted tax rate and provisions of the enacted tax law resulting from temporary differences and carryforwards at the end of the current year.

DEFERRED TAX EXPENSE (BENEFIT). The change during the year in a company's deferred tax liabilities and assets.

DEFERRED TAX LIABILITY. The deferred tax consequences attributable to taxable temporary differences.

INCOME TAXES. Domestic and foreign federal (national), state, and local (including franchise) taxes based on income.

INCOME TAXES CURRENTLY PAYABLE (REFUNDABLE). Refer to current tax expense (benefit).

INCOME TAX EXPENSE (BENEFIT). The sum of current tax expense (benefit) and deferred tax expense (benefit).

TAXABLE INCOME. The excess of taxable revenues over tax-deductible expenses and exemptions for the year as defined by the governmental tax authority.

TAXABLE TEMPORARY DIFFERENCE. Temporary differences that result in taxable amounts in future years when recovering or settling the related asset or liability, respectively.

TAX-PLANNING STRATEGY. An action that meets certain criteria and that a company implements to realize a tax benefit for an operating loss or tax carryforward before it expires. Companies consider tax-planning strategies when assessing whether to recognize a deferred tax asset.

TEMPORARY DIFFERENCE. A difference between the tax basis of an asset or liability and its reported amount in the financial statements that will result in taxable or deductible amounts in future years when recovering or settling the reported amount of the asset or liability, respectively.

GLOBAL ACCOUNTING INSIGHTS

INCOME TAXES

Similar to IFRS, U.S. GAAP uses the asset and liability approach for recording deferred taxes. The differences between IFRS and U.S. GAAP involve a few exceptions to the asset-liability approach; some minor differences in the recognition, measurement, and disclosure criteria; and differences in implementation guidance.

Relevant Facts

Following are the key similarities and differences between U.S. GAAP and IFRS related to accounting for taxes.

Similarities
- As indicated above, U.S. GAAP and IFRS both use the asset and liability approach for recording deferred taxes.

Differences
- Under U.S. GAAP, deferred tax assets and liabilities are classified based on the classification of the asset or liability to which it relates (see discussion in About the Numbers below). The classification of deferred taxes under IFRS is always non-current.
- U.S. GAAP uses an impairment approach to assess the need for a valuation allowance. In this approach, the deferred tax asset is recognized in full. It is then reduced by a valuation account if it is more likely than not that all or a portion of the deferred tax asset will not be realized. Under IFRS, an affirmative judgment approach is used, by which a deferred tax asset is recognized up to the amount that is probable to be realized.

- Under U.S. GAAP, the enacted tax rate must be used in measuring deferred tax assets and liabilities. IFRS uses the enacted tax rate or substantially enacted tax rate ("substantially enacted" means virtually certain).
- Under U.S. GAAP, charges or credits for all tax items are recorded in income. That is not the case under IFRS, in which the charges or credits related to certain items are reported in equity.
- U.S. GAAP requires companies to assess the likelihood of uncertain tax positions being sustainable upon audit. Potential liabilities must be accrued and disclosed if the position is more likely than not to be disallowed. Under IFRS, all potential liabilities must be recognized. With respect to measurement, IFRS uses an expected-value approach to measure the tax liability, which differs from U.S. GAAP.

About the Numbers

Classification of Deferred Tax Assets and Liabilities
Under U.S. GAAP, deferred tax accounts are reported on the balance sheet (statement of financial position) as assets and liabilities. Companies should classify these accounts as a net current amount and a net non-current amount. **An individual deferred tax liability or asset is classified as current or non-current based on the classification of the related asset or liability for financial reporting purposes.**

A company considers a deferred tax asset or liability to be related to an asset or liability if reduction of the asset or liability causes the temporary difference to reverse or turn around. A company should classify a deferred tax liability or asset that is unrelated to an asset or liability for financial reporting, including a deferred tax asset related to a loss carryforward, according to the expected reversal date of the temporary difference.

To illustrate, assume that PepsiCo, Inc. (USA) records bad debt expense using the allowance method for accounting purposes and the direct write-off method for tax purposes. It currently has Accounts Receivable and Allowance for Doubtful Accounts balances of $2 million and $100,000,

respectively. In addition, given a 40 percent tax rate, PepsiCo has a debit balance in the Deferred Tax Asset account of $40,000 (40% × $100,000). It considers the $40,000 debit balance in the Deferred Tax Asset account to be related to the Accounts Receivable and the Allowance for Doubtful Accounts balances because collection or write-off of the receivables will cause the temporary difference to reverse. Therefore, PepsiCo classifies the Deferred Tax Asset account as current, the same as the Accounts Receivable and Allowance for Doubtful Accounts balances.

In practice, most companies engage in a large number of transactions that give rise to deferred taxes. Companies should classify the balances in the deferred tax accounts on the balance sheet in two categories: one for the **net current amount** and one for the **net non-current amount**.

As we indicated earlier, a deferred tax asset or liability may not be related to an asset or liability for financial reporting purposes. One example is an operating loss carryforward. In this case, a company records a deferred tax asset, but there is no related identifiable asset or liability for financial reporting purposes. In these limited situations, deferred income taxes are classified according to the expected reversal date of the temporary difference. That is, a company should report the tax effect of any temporary difference reversing next year as current and the remainder as non-current. If a deferred tax asset is non-current, a company should classify it in the "Other assets" section.

The total of all deferred tax liabilities, the total of all deferred tax assets, and the total valuation allowance should be disclosed. In addition, companies should disclose the following: (1) any net change during the year in the total valuation allowance, and (2) the types of temporary differences, carryforwards, or carrybacks that give rise to significant portions of deferred tax liabilities and assets. Income taxes payable is reported as a current liability on the balance sheet.

U.S. GAAP/IFRS Differences

The following schedule taken from a recent annual report of **Glaxo-SmithKline plc** (GBR) indicates the impact of differences in IFRS and U.S. GAAP for deferred taxes.

Reconciliation to U.S. accounting principles	
(e) Deferred taxation (in part):	
Total tax expense (in millions of British pounds)	
IFRS:	
Current tax expense	2,710
Deferred tax (credit)/expense	(409)
Total tax expense	2,301
U.S. GAAP:	
Current tax expense	2,735
Deferred tax credit	(685)
Total tax expense	2,050
Total tax expense difference	(251)

Thus, due to the differences highlighted above, Glaxo's income tax expense under IFRS is £251 million higher than that reported under U.S. GAAP.

On the Horizon

The IASB and the FASB have been working to address some of the differences in the accounting for income taxes. One of the issues under discussion is the term "probable" under IFRS for recognition of a deferred tax asset, which might be interpreted to mean "more likely than not." If the term is changed, the reporting for impairments of deferred tax assets will be essentially the same between U.S. GAAP and IFRS. In addition, the IASB is considering adoption of the classification approach used in U.S. GAAP for deferred assets and liabilities. Also, U.S. GAAP will likely continue to use the enacted tax rate in computing deferred taxes, except in situations where the U.S. taxing jurisdiction is not involved. In that case, companies should use IFRS, which is based on enacted rates or substantially enacted tax rates. Finally, the issue of allocation of deferred income taxes to equity for certain transactions under IFRS must be addressed in order to converge with U.S. GAAP, which allocates the effects to income. At the time of this printing, deliberations on the income tax project have been suspended indefinitely.

SUMMARY OF LEARNING OBJECTIVES

KEY TERMS

1 **Identify differences between pretax financial income and taxable income.** Companies compute pretax financial income (or income for book purposes) in accordance with IFRS. They compute taxable income (or income for tax purposes) in accordance with prescribed tax regulations. Because tax regulations and IFRS differ in many ways, so frequently do pretax financial income and taxable income. Differences may exist, for example, in the timing of revenue recognition and the timing of expense recognition.

2 **Describe a temporary difference that results in future taxable amounts.** Revenue recognized for book purposes in the period when the performance obligation is satisfied but deferred and reported as revenue for tax purposes when collected results in future taxable amounts. The future taxable amounts will occur in the periods the company recovers the receivable and reports the collections as revenue for tax purposes. This results in a deferred tax liability.

3 **Describe a temporary difference that results in future deductible amounts.** An accrued warranty expense that a company pays for and deducts for tax purposes, in a period later than the period in which it incurs and recognizes it for book purposes, results in future deductible amounts. The future deductible amounts will occur in the periods during which the company settles the related liability for book purposes. This results in a deferred tax asset.

4 **Explain the non-recognition of a deferred tax asset.** A deferred tax asset should be reduced if it is probable that the company will not realize some portion or all of the deferred tax asset. The company should carefully consider possible sources of taxable income and related factors to assess the probability that taxable income will be available against which the unused tax losses or unused tax credits can be utilized. To the extent that it is not probable that taxable profit will be available against which the unused tax losses or unused tax credits can be utilized, the deferred tax asset is not recognized.

5 **Describe the presentation of income tax expense in the income statement.** Significant components of income tax expense should be disclosed in the income statement or in the notes to the financial statements. The most commonly encountered components are the current expense (or benefit) and the deferred expense (or benefit).

6 **Describe various temporary and permanent differences.** Examples of temporary differences are (1) revenue or gains that are taxable after recognition in financial income, (2) expenses or losses that are deductible after recognition in financial income, (3) revenues or gains that are taxable before recognition in financial income, and (4) expenses or losses that are deductible before recognition in financial income. Examples of permanent differences are (1) items recognized for financial reporting purposes but not for tax purposes, and (2) items recognized for tax purposes but not for financial reporting purposes.

7 **Explain the effect of various tax rates and tax rate changes on deferred income taxes.** Companies may use tax rates other than the current rate only after enactment or substantial enactment of the future tax rates. When a change in the tax rate is enacted, a company should immediately recognize its effect on the deferred income tax accounts. The company reports the effects as an adjustment to income tax expense in the period of the change.

8 **Apply accounting procedures for a loss carryback and a loss carryforward.** A company may carry a net operating loss back two years and receive refunds for income taxes paid in those years. The loss is applied to the earlier year first and then to the second year. Any loss remaining after the two-year carryback may be carried forward up to 20 years to offset future taxable income. A company may forgo the loss carryback and use the loss carryforward, offsetting future taxable income for up to 20 years.

9 **Describe the presentation of income taxes in financial statements.** Companies report deferred tax accounts on the statement of financial position as assets and liabilities. Companies classify taxes receivable or payable as current assets or current liabilities, and these items may be offset in the statement of financial position. Deferred tax assets and deferred tax liabilities are also separately recognized and measured, and may be offset in the statement of financial position. The net deferred tax asset or net deferred tax liability is reported in the non-current section of the statement of financial position. In the income statement, companies allocate income tax expense (or benefit) to continuing operations, discontinued operations, other comprehensive income, and prior period adjustments (intraperiod tax allocation), and indicate current tax expense (benefit) and deferred tax expense (benefit). An important disclosure is the reconciliation between actual tax expense and the applicable tax rate.

10 **Indicate the basic principles of the asset-liability method.** Companies apply the following basic principles in accounting for income taxes at the date of the financial statements. (1) Recognize a current tax liability or asset for the estimated taxes payable or refundable on the tax return for the current year. (2) Recognize a deferred tax liability or asset for the estimated future tax effects attributable to temporary differences and carryforwards using the enacted tax rate. (3) Base the measurement of current and deferred tax liabilities and assets on provisions of the enacted (or substantially enacted) tax law. (4) Reduce the measurement of deferred tax assets, if necessary, by the amount of any tax benefits that, based on available evidence, companies do not expect to realize.

APPENDIX **19A**	COMPREHENSIVE EXAMPLE OF INTERPERIOD TAX ALLOCATION

This appendix presents a comprehensive illustration of a deferred income tax problem with several temporary and permanent differences. The example follows one company through two complete years (2014 and 2015). **Study it carefully.** It should help you understand the concepts and procedures presented in the chapter.

◀11 LEARNING OBJECTIVE
Understand and apply the concepts and procedures of interperiod tax allocation.

FIRST YEAR—2014

Akai Company, which began operations at the beginning of 2014, produces various products on a contract basis. Each contract generates an income of ¥80,000 (amounts in thousands). Some of Akai's contracts provide for the customer to pay on an installment basis. Under these contracts, Akai collects one-fifth of the contract revenue in each of the following four years. For financial reporting purposes, the company recognizes income in the year of completion (accrual basis); for tax purposes, Akai recognizes income in the year cash is collected (installment basis).

Presented below is information related to Akai's operations for 2014.

1. In 2014, the company completed seven contracts that allow for the customer to pay on an installment basis. Akai recognized the related income of ¥560,000 for financial reporting purposes. It reported only ¥112,000 of income on installment sales on the 2014 tax return. The company expects future collections on the related receivables to result in taxable amounts of ¥112,000 in each of the next four years.

2. At the beginning of 2014, Akai purchased depreciable assets with a cost of ¥540,000. For financial reporting purposes, Akai depreciates these assets using the straight-line method over a six-year service life. The depreciation schedules for both financial reporting and tax purposes are shown as follows.

Year	Depreciation for Financial Reporting Purposes	Depreciation for Tax Purposes	Difference
2014	¥ 90,000	¥108,000	¥(18,000)
2015	90,000	172,800	(82,800)
2016	90,000	103,680	(13,680)
2017	90,000	62,208	27,792
2018	90,000	62,208	27,792
2019	90,000	31,104	58,896
	¥540,000	¥540,000	¥ –0–

3. The company warrants its product for two years from the date of completion of a contract. During 2014, the product warranty liability accrued for financial reporting purposes was ¥200,000, and the amount paid for the satisfaction of warranty liability was ¥44,000. Akai expects to settle the remaining ¥156,000 by expenditures of ¥56,000 in 2015 and ¥100,000 in 2016.

4. In 2014, non-taxable governmental bond interest revenue was ¥28,000.

5. During 2014, non-deductible fines and penalties of ¥26,000 were paid.

6. Pretax financial income for 2014 amounts to ¥412,000.

7. Tax rates enacted before the end of 2014 were:

2014	50%
2015 and later years	40%

8. The accounting period is the calendar year.

9. The company is expected to have taxable income in all future years.

Taxable Income and Income Taxes Payable—2014

The first step is to determine Akai's income taxes payable for 2014 by calculating its taxable income. Illustration 19A-1 shows this computation.

ILLUSTRATION 19A-1
Computation of Taxable Income, 2014

Pretax financial income for 2014	¥412,000
Permanent differences:	
Non-taxable revenue—governmental bond interest	(28,000)
Non-deductible expenses—fines and penalties	26,000
Temporary differences:	
Excess contract income per books (¥560,000 − ¥112,000)	(448,000)
Excess depreciation per tax (¥108,000 − ¥90,000)	(18,000)
Excess warranty expense per books (¥200,000 − ¥44,000)	156,000
Taxable income for 2014	¥100,000

Akai computes income taxes payable on taxable income for ¥100,000 as follows.

ILLUSTRATION 19A-2
Computation of Income Taxes Payable, End of 2014

Taxable income for 2014	¥100,000
Tax rate	× 50%
Income taxes payable (current tax expense) for 2014	¥ 50,000

Computing Deferred Income Taxes—End of 2014

The schedule in Illustration 19A-3 summarizes the temporary differences and the resulting future taxable and deductible amounts.

ILLUSTRATION 19A-3
Schedule of Future Taxable and Deductible Amounts, End of 2014

	Future Years					
	2015	2016	2017	2018	2019	Total
Future taxable (deductible) amounts:						
Installment sales	¥112,000	¥112,000	¥112,000	¥112,000		¥448,000
Depreciation	(82,800)	(13,680)	27,792	27,792	¥58,896	18,000
Warranty costs	(56,000)	(100,000)				(156,000)

Akai computes the amounts of deferred income taxes to be reported at the end of 2014 as shown in Illustration 19A-4.

ILLUSTRATION 19A-4
Computation of Deferred Income Taxes, End of 2014

Temporary Difference	Future Taxable (Deductible) Amounts	Tax Rate	Deferred Tax (Asset)	Liability
Installment sales	¥448,000	40%		¥179,200
Depreciation	18,000	40%		7,200
Warranty costs	(156,000)	40%	¥(62,400)	
Totals	¥310,000		¥(62,400)	¥186,400*

*Because only a single tax rate is involved in all relevant years, these totals can be reconciled:
¥310,000 × 40% = (¥62,400) + ¥186,400.

A temporary difference is caused by the use of the accrual basis for financial reporting purposes and the installment method for tax purposes. This temporary difference will result in future taxable amounts and hence a deferred tax liability. Because of the installment contracts completed in 2014, a temporary difference of ¥448,000 originates that will reverse in equal amounts over the next four years. The company expects to have taxable income in all future years, and there is only one enacted tax rate applicable to all future years. Akai uses that rate (40 percent) to compute the entire deferred tax liability resulting from this temporary difference.

The temporary difference caused by different depreciation policies for books and for tax purposes originates over three years and then reverses over three years. This difference will cause deductible amounts in 2015 and 2016 and taxable amounts in 2017, 2018, and 2019. These amounts sum to a net future taxable amount of ¥18,000 (which is the cumulative temporary difference at the end of 2014). Because the company expects to have taxable income in all future years and because there is only one tax rate enacted for all of the relevant future years, Akai applies that rate to the net future taxable amount to determine the related net deferred tax liability.

The third temporary difference is caused by different methods of accounting for warranties. This difference will result in deductible amounts in each of the two future years it takes to reverse. Because the company expects to report a positive income on all future tax returns and because there is only one tax rate enacted for each of the relevant future years, Akai uses that 40 percent rate to calculate the resulting deferred tax asset.

Deferred Tax Expense (Benefit) and the Journal Entry to Record Income Taxes—2014

To determine the deferred tax expense (benefit), Akai needs to compare the beginning and ending balances of the deferred income tax accounts. Illustration 19A-5 shows that computation.

Deferred tax asset at the end of 2014	¥ 62,400
Deferred tax asset at the beginning of 2014	–0–
Deferred tax expense (benefit)	¥ (62,400)
Deferred tax liability at the end of 2014	¥186,400
Deferred tax liability at the beginning of 2014	–0–
Deferred tax expense (benefit)	¥186,400

ILLUSTRATION 19A-5
Computation of Deferred Tax Expense (Benefit), 2014

The ¥62,400 increase in the deferred tax asset causes a deferred tax benefit to be reported in the income statement. The ¥186,400 increase in the deferred tax liability during 2014 results in a deferred tax expense. These two amounts **net** to a deferred tax expense of ¥124,000 for 2014.

Deferred tax expense (benefit)	¥ (62,400)
Deferred tax expense (benefit)	186,400
Net deferred tax expense for 2014	¥124,000

ILLUSTRATION 19A-6
Computation of Net Deferred Tax Expense, 2014

Akai then computes the total income tax expense as follows.

Current tax expense for 2014	¥ 50,000
Deferred tax expense for 2014	124,000
Income tax expense (total) for 2014	¥174,000

ILLUSTRATION 19A-7
Computation of Total Income Tax Expense, 2014

Akai records income taxes payable, deferred income taxes, and income tax expense as follows.

Income Tax Expense	174,000	
Deferred Tax Asset	62,400	
Income Taxes Payable		50,000
Deferred Tax Liability		186,400

Financial Statement Presentation—2014

Companies should classify deferred tax assets and liabilities as non-current on the statement of financial position. Deferred tax assets are therefore netted against deferred tax liabilities to compute a net deferred asset (liability). Illustration 19A-8 shows the classification of Akai's deferred tax accounts at the end of 2014.

ILLUSTRATION 19A-8
Classification of Deferred Tax Accounts, End of 2014

Temporary Difference	Resulting Deferred Tax (Asset)	Liability
Installment sales		¥179,200
Depreciation		7,200
Warranty costs	¥(62,400)	
Totals	¥(62,400)	¥186,400

The statement of financial position at the end of 2014 reports the following amounts.

ILLUSTRATION 19A-9
Statement of Financial Position Presentation of Deferred Taxes, 2014

Non-current liabilities	
Deferred tax liability (¥186,400 − ¥62,400)	¥124,000
Current liabilities	
Income taxes payable	¥ 50,000

Akai's income statement for 2014 reports the following.

ILLUSTRATION 19A-10
Income Statement Presentation of Income Tax Expense, 2014

Income before income taxes		¥412,000
Income tax expense		
Current	¥ 50,000	
Deferred	124,000	174,000
Net income		¥238,000

SECOND YEAR—2015

1. During 2015, Akai collected ¥112,000 from customers for the receivables arising from contracts completed in 2014. The company expects recovery of the remaining receivables to result in taxable amounts of ¥112,000 in each of the following three years.

2. In 2015, the company completed four new contracts that allow for the customer to pay on an installment basis. These installment sales created new installment receivables. Future collections of these receivables will result in reporting income of ¥64,000 for tax purposes in each of the next four years.

3. During 2015, Akai continued to depreciate the assets acquired in 2014 according to the depreciation schedules appearing on page 985. Thus, depreciation amounted to ¥90,000 for financial reporting purposes and ¥172,800 for tax purposes.

4. An analysis at the end of 2015 of the product warranty liability account shows the following details.

Balance of liability at beginning of 2015	¥156,000
Expense for 2015 income statement purposes	180,000
Amount paid for contracts completed in 2014	(56,000)
Amount paid for contracts completed in 2015	(50,000)
Balance of liability at end of 2015	¥230,000

The balance of the liability is expected to require expenditures in the future as follows.

¥100,000 in 2016 due to 2014 contracts
¥ 50,000 in 2016 due to 2015 contracts
¥ 80,000 in 2017 due to 2015 contracts
¥230,000

5. During 2015, non-taxable governmental bond interest revenue was ¥24,000.

6. Akai accrued a loss of ¥172,000 for financial reporting purposes because of pending litigation. This amount is not tax-deductible until the period the loss is realized, which the company estimates to be 2023.

7. Pretax financial income for 2015 amounts to ¥504,800.

8. The enacted tax rates still in effect are:

2014	50%
2015 and later years	40%

Taxable Income and Income Taxes Payable—2015

Akai computes taxable income for 2015 as follows.

Pretax financial income for 2015	¥504,800
Permanent difference:	
Non-taxable revenue—governmental bond interest	(24,000)
Reversing temporary differences:	
Collection on 2014 installment sales	112,000
Payments on warranties from 2014 contracts	(56,000)
Originating temporary differences:	
Excess contract income per books—2015 contracts	(256,000)
Excess depreciation per tax	(82,800)
Excess warranty expense per books—2015 contracts	130,000
Loss accrual per books	172,000
Taxable income for 2015	¥500,000

ILLUSTRATION 19A-11
Computation of Taxable Income, 2015

Income taxes payable for 2015 is as follows.

Taxable income for 2015	¥500,000
Tax rate	× 40%
Income taxes payable (current tax expense) for 2015	¥200,000

ILLUSTRATION 19A-12
Computation of Income Taxes Payable, End of 2015

Computing Deferred Income Taxes—End of 2015

ILLUSTRATION 19A-13
Schedule of Future
Taxable and Deductible
Amounts, End of 2015

The schedule in Illustration 19A-13 summarizes the temporary differences existing at the end of 2015 and the resulting future taxable and deductible amounts.

	Future Years					
	2016	2017	2018	2019	2023	Total
Future taxable (deductible) amounts:						
Installment sales—2014	¥112,000	¥112,000	¥112,000			¥336,000
Installment sales—2015	64,000	64,000	64,000	¥64,000		256,000
Depreciation	(13,680)	27,792	27,792	58,896		100,800
Warranty costs	(150,000)	(80,000)				(230,000)
Loss accrual					¥(172,000)	(172,000)

Akai computes the amounts of deferred income taxes to be reported at the end of 2015 as follows.

ILLUSTRATION 19A-14
Computation of Deferred
Income Taxes, End of
2015

Temporary Difference	Future Taxable (Deductible) Amounts	Tax Rate	Deferred Tax (Asset)	Liability
Installment sales	¥592,000*	40%		¥236,800
Depreciation	100,800	40%		40,320
Warranty costs	(230,000)	40%	¥ (92,000)	
Loss accrual	(172,000)	40%	(68,800)	
Totals	¥290,800		¥(160,800)	¥277,120**

*Cumulative temporary difference = ¥336,000 + ¥256,000
**Because of a flat tax rate, these totals can be reconciled: ¥290,800 × 40% = ¥(160,800) + ¥277,120

Deferred Tax Expense (Benefit) and the Journal Entry to Record Income Taxes—2015

To determine the deferred tax expense (benefit), Akai must compare the beginning and ending balances of the deferred income tax accounts, as shown in Illustration 19A-15.

ILLUSTRATION 19A-15
Computation of Deferred
Tax Expense (Benefit),
2015

Deferred tax asset at the end of 2015	¥160,800
Deferred tax asset at the beginning of 2015	62,400
Deferred tax expense (benefit)	¥ (98,400)
Deferred tax liability at the end of 2015	¥277,120
Deferred tax liability at the beginning of 2015	186,400
Deferred tax expense (benefit)	¥ 90,720

The deferred tax expense (benefit) and the total income tax expense for 2015 are therefore as follows.

ILLUSTRATION 19A-16
Computation of Total
Income Tax Expense,
2015

Deferred tax expense (benefit)	¥ (98,400)
Deferred tax expense (benefit)	90,720
Deferred tax benefit for 2015	(7,680)
Current tax expense for 2015	200,000
Income tax expense (total) for 2015	¥192,320

The deferred tax expense of ¥90,720 and the deferred tax benefit of ¥98,400 net to a deferred tax benefit of ¥7,680 for 2015.

Akai records income taxes for 2015 with the following journal entry.

Income Tax Expense	192,320	
Deferred Tax Asset	98,400	
Income Taxes Payable		200,000
Deferred Tax Liability		90,720

Financial Statement Presentation—2015

Illustration 19A-17 shows the classification of Akai's deferred tax accounts at the end of 2015.

Temporary Difference	Resulting Deferred Tax (Asset)	Liability
Installment sales		¥236,800
Depreciation		40,320
Warranty costs	¥ (92,000)	
Loss accrual	(68,800)	
Totals	¥(160,800)	¥277,120

ILLUSTRATION 19A-17
Classification of Deferred Tax Accounts, End of 2015

Akai's statement of financial position at the end of 2015 reports the following amounts.

Non-current liabilities	
Deferred tax liability (¥277,120 − ¥160,800)	¥116,320
Current liabilities	
Income taxes payable	¥200,000

ILLUSTRATION 19A-18
Statement of Financial Position Presentation of Deferred Taxes, End of 2015

The income statement for 2015 reports the following.

Income before income taxes		¥504,800
Income tax expense		
Current	¥200,000	
Deferred	(7,680)	192,320
Net income		¥312,480

ILLUSTRATION 19A-19
Income Statement Presentation of Income Tax Expense, 2015

SUMMARY OF LEARNING OBJECTIVE FOR APPENDIX 19A

11 **Understand and apply the concepts and procedures of interperiod tax allocation.** Accounting for deferred taxes involves the following steps. (1) Calculate taxable income and income taxes payable for the year. (2) Compute deferred income taxes at the end of the year. (3) Determine deferred tax expense (benefit) and make the journal entry to record income taxes. (4) Classify deferred tax assets and liabilities and report a net deferred tax asset or liability.

IFRS AUTHORITATIVE LITERATURE

Authoritative Literature References

[1] International Accounting Standard 12, *Income Taxes* (London, U.K.: International Accounting Standards Committee Foundation, 2001).

[2] International Accounting Standard 12, *Income Taxes* (London, U.K.: International Accounting Standards Committee Foundation, 2001), par. 48.

[3] International Accounting Standard 12, *Income Taxes* (London, U.K.: International Accounting Standards Committee Foundation, 2001), par. 49.

[4] International Accounting Standard 12, *Income Taxes* (London, U.K.: International Accounting Standards Committee Foundation, 2001), par. 36.

[5] International Accounting Standard 12, *Income Taxes* (London, U.K.: International Accounting Standards Committee Foundation, 2001), par. 72.

[6] International Accounting Standard 12, *Income Taxes* (London, U.K.: International Accounting Standards Committee Foundation, 2001), par. 74.

[7] International Accounting Standard 12, *Income Taxes* (London, U.K.: International Accounting Standards Committee Foundation, 2001), paras. 53–54.

[8] International Accounting Standard 12, *Income Taxes* (London, U.K.: International Accounting Standards Committee Foundation, 2001), par. 80(h).

QUESTIONS

1. Explain the difference between pretax financial income and taxable income.

2. What are the two objectives of accounting for income taxes?

3. Interest on governmental bonds is often referred to as a permanent difference when determining the proper amount to report for deferred taxes. Explain the meaning of permanent differences, and give two other examples.

4. Explain the meaning of a temporary difference as it relates to deferred tax computations, and give three examples.

5. Differentiate between an originating temporary difference and a reversing difference.

6. The book basis of depreciable assets for Erwin Co. is €900,000 and the tax basis is €700,000 at the end of 2015. The enacted tax rate is 34% for all periods. Determine the amount of deferred taxes to be reported on the statement of financial position at the end of 2015.

7. Roth Inc. has a deferred tax liability of €68,000 at the beginning of 2015. At the end of 2015, it reports accounts receivable on the books at €90,000 and the tax basis at zero (its only temporary difference). If the enacted tax rate is 34% for all periods and income taxes payable for the period is €230,000, determine the amount of total income tax expense to report for 2015.

8. What is the difference between a future taxable amount and a future deductible amount? When is it not appropriate to recognize a portion or all of a deferred tax asset?

9. Pretax financial income for Lake Inc. is £300,000, and its taxable income is £100,000 for 2015. Its only temporary difference at the end of the period relates to a £70,000 difference due to excess depreciation for tax purposes. If the tax rate is 40% for all periods, compute the amount of income tax expense to report in 2015. No deferred income taxes existed at the beginning of the year.

10. How are deferred tax assets and deferred tax liabilities reported on the statement of financial position?

11. Describe the procedure(s) involved in classifying deferred tax amounts on the statement of financial position.

12. At the end of the year, Falabella Co. has pretax financial income of $550,000. Included in the $550,000 is $70,000 interest income on governmental bonds, a $25,000 fine for dumping hazardous waste, and depreciation of $60,000. Depreciation for tax purposes is $45,000. Compute income taxes payable, assuming the tax rate is 30% for all periods.

13. Addison Co. has one temporary difference at the beginning of 2014 of £500,000. The deferred tax liability established for this amount is £150,000, based on a tax rate of 30%. The temporary difference will provide the following taxable amounts: £100,000 in 2015, £200,000 in 2016, and £200,000 in 2017. If a new tax rate for 2017 of 20% is enacted into law at the end of 2014, what is the journal entry necessary in 2014 (if any) to adjust deferred taxes?

14. What are some of the reasons that the components of income tax expense should be disclosed and a reconciliation between the statutory tax rate and the effective rate be provided?

15. Differentiate between "loss carryback" and "loss carryforward." Which can be accounted for with the greater certainty when it arises? Why?

16. What are the possible treatments for tax purposes of a net operating loss? What are the circumstances that determine the option to be applied? What is the proper treatment of a net operating loss for financial reporting purposes?

17. What controversy relates to the accounting for net operating loss carryforwards?

18. Briefly describe some of the similarities and differences between IFRS and U.S. GAAP with respect to income tax accounting.

19. Describe the current convergence efforts of the IASB and FASB in the area of accounting for taxes.

BRIEF EXERCISES

1 2 BE19-1 In 2015, Amirante Corporation had pretax financial income of $168,000 and taxable income of $120,000. The difference is due to the use of different depreciation methods for tax and accounting purposes. The effective tax rate is 40%. Compute the amount to be reported as income taxes payable at December 31, 2015.

1 2 BE19-2 Oxford Corporation began operations in 2015 and reported pretax financial income of €225,000 for the year. Oxford's tax depreciation exceeded its book depreciation by €40,000. Oxford's tax rate for 2015 and years thereafter is 30%. In its December 31, 2015, statement of financial position, what amount of deferred tax liability should be reported?

9 BE19-3 Using the information from BE19-2, assume this is the only difference between Oxford's pretax financial income and taxable income. Prepare the journal entry to record the income tax expense, deferred income taxes, and income taxes payable, and show how the deferred tax liability will be classified on the December 31, 2015, statement of financial position.

2 5 BE19-4 At December 31, 2014, Appaloosa Corporation had a deferred tax liability of $25,000. At December 31, 2015, the deferred tax liability is $42,000. The corporation's 2015 current tax expense is $48,000. What amount should Appaloosa report as total 2015 tax expense?

1 3 BE19-5 At December 31, 2015, Suffolk Corporation had an estimated warranty liability of £105,000 for accounting purposes and £0 for tax purposes. (The warranty costs are not deductible until paid.) The effective tax rate is 40%. Compute the amount Suffolk should report as a deferred tax asset at December 31, 2015.

3 5 BE19-6 At December 31, 2014, Percheron Inc. had a deferred tax asset of $30,000. At December 31, 2015, the deferred tax asset is $59,000. The corporation's 2015 current tax expense is $61,000. What amount should Percheron report as total 2015 tax expense?

4 BE19-7 At December 31, 2015, Hillyard Corporation has a deferred tax asset of £200,000. After a careful review of all available evidence, it is determined that it is probable that £60,000 of this deferred tax asset will not be realized. Prepare the necessary journal entry.

5 BE19-8 Mitchell Corporation had income before income taxes of $195,000 in 2015. Mitchell's current income tax expense is $48,000, and deferred income tax expense is $30,000. Prepare Mitchell's 2015 income statement, beginning with income before income taxes.

2 3 BE19-9 Shetland Inc. had pretax financial income of $154,000 in 2015 in its first year of operations. Included in the computation of that amount is insurance expense of $4,000, which is not deductible for tax purposes. In addition, depreciation for tax purposes exceeds accounting depreciation by $10,000. Prepare Shetland's journal entry to record 2015 taxes, assuming a tax rate of 45%.

2 BE19-10 Clydesdale Corporation has a cumulative temporary difference related to depreciation of $580,000 at December 31, 2014. This difference will reverse as follows: 2015, $42,000; 2016, $244,000; and 2017, $294,000. Enacted tax rates are 34% for 2015 and 2016, and 40% for 2017. Compute the amount Clydesdale should report as a deferred tax liability at December 31, 2014.

7 BE19-11 At December 31, 2015, Takeshi Corporation had a deferred tax liability of ¥680,000,000 resulting from future taxable amounts of ¥2,000,000,000 and an enacted tax rate of 34%. In May 2016, a new income tax act is signed into law that raises the tax rate to 40% for 2016 and future years. Prepare the journal entry for Takeshi to adjust the deferred tax liability.

8 BE19-12 Conlin Corporation had the following tax information.

Year	Taxable Income	Tax Rate	Taxes Paid
2012	€300,000	35%	€105,000
2013	€325,000	30%	€ 97,500
2014	€400,000	30%	€120,000

In 2015, Conlin suffered a net operating loss of €480,000, which it elected to carry back. The 2015 enacted tax rate is 29%. Prepare Conlin's entry to record the effect of the loss carryback.

8 **BE19-13** Rode Inc. incurred a net operating loss of €500,000 in 2015. Combined income for 2013 and 2014 was €350,000. The tax rate for all years is 40%. Rode elects the carryback option. Prepare the journal entries to record the benefits of the loss carryback and the loss carryforward.

4 8 **BE19-14** Use the information for Rode Inc. given in BE19-13. Assume that it is probable that the entire net operating loss carryforward will not be realized in future years. Prepare the journal entry(ies) necessary at the end of 2015.

9 **BE19-15** Youngman Corporation has temporary differences at December 31, 2015, that result in the following deferred taxes.

Deferred tax asset	HK$24,000
Deferred tax liability	HK$69,000

Indicate how these balances would be presented in Youngman's December 31, 2015, statement of financial position.

EXERCISES

2 5 **E19-1 (One Temporary Difference, Future Taxable Amounts, One Rate, No Beginning Deferred Taxes)** Starfleet Corporation has one temporary difference at the end of 2014 that will reverse and cause taxable amounts of $55,000 in 2015, $60,000 in 2016, and $75,000 in 2017. Starfleet's pretax financial income for 2014 is $400,000, and the tax rate is 30% for all years. There are no deferred taxes at the beginning of 2014.

Instructions
(a) Compute taxable income and income taxes payable for 2014.
(b) Prepare the journal entry to record income tax expense, deferred income taxes, and income taxes payable for 2014.
(c) Prepare the income tax expense section of the income statement for 2014, beginning with the line "Income before income taxes."

2 **E19-2 (Two Differences, No Beginning Deferred Taxes, Tracked through 2 Years)** The following information is available for McKee Corporation for 2015.

1. Excess of tax depreciation over book depreciation, £40,000. This £40,000 difference will reverse equally over the years 2016–2019.
2. Deferral, for book purposes, of £25,000 of rent received in advance. The rent will be recorded as revenue in 2016.
3. Pretax financial income, £350,000.
4. Tax rate for all years, 40%.

Instructions
(a) Compute taxable income for 2015.
(b) Prepare the journal entry to record income tax expense, deferred income taxes, and income taxes payable for 2015.
(c) Prepare the journal entry to record income tax expense, deferred income taxes, and income taxes payable for 2016, assuming taxable income of £325,000.

2 5 **E19-3 (One Temporary Difference, Future Taxable Amounts, One Rate, Beginning Deferred Taxes)** Brennan Corporation began 2015 with a $90,000 balance in the Deferred Tax Liability account. At the end of 2015, the related cumulative temporary difference amounts to $350,000, and it will reverse evenly over the next 2 years. Pretax accounting income for 2015 is $525,000, the tax rate for all years is 40%, and taxable income for 2015 is $400,000.

Instructions
(a) Compute income taxes payable for 2015.
(b) Prepare the journal entry to record income tax expense, deferred income taxes, and income taxes payable for 2015.
(c) Prepare the income tax expense section of the income statement for 2015, beginning with the line "Income before income taxes."

2 3 5 6 **E19-4 (Three Differences, Compute Taxable Income, Entry for Taxes)** Havaci Company reports pretax financial income of €80,000 for 2015. The following items cause taxable income to be different than pretax financial income.

1. Depreciation on the tax return is greater than depreciation on the income statement by €16,000.
2. Rent collected on the tax return is greater than rent revenue reported on the income statement by €27,000.
3. Fines for pollution appear as an expense of €11,000 on the income statement.

Havaci's tax rate is 30% for all years, and the company expects to report taxable income in all future years. There are no deferred taxes at the beginning of 2015.

Instructions
(a) Compute taxable income and income taxes payable for 2015.
(b) Prepare the journal entry to record income tax expense, deferred income taxes, and income taxes payable for 2015.
(c) Prepare the income tax expense section of the income statement for 2015, beginning with the line "Income before income taxes."
(d) Compute the effective income tax rate for 2015.

2 3 5 **E19-5 (Two Temporary Differences, One Rate, Beginning Deferred Taxes)** The following facts relate to Alschuler Corporation.

1. Deferred tax liability, January 1, 2015, £40,000.
2. Deferred tax asset, January 1, 2015, £0.
3. Taxable income for 2015, £115,000.
4. Pretax financial income for 2015, £200,000.
5. Cumulative temporary difference at December 31, 2015, giving rise to future taxable amounts, £220,000.
6. Cumulative temporary difference at December 31, 2015, giving rise to future deductible amounts, £35,000.
7. Tax rate for all years, 40%.
8. The company is expected to operate profitably in the future.

Instructions
(a) Compute income taxes payable for 2015.
(b) Prepare the journal entry to record income tax expense, deferred income taxes, and income taxes payable for 2015.
(c) Prepare the income tax expense section of the income statement for 2015, beginning with the line "Income before income taxes."

6 **E19-6 (Identify Temporary or Permanent Differences)** Listed below and on page 996 are items that are commonly accounted for differently for financial reporting purposes than they are for tax purposes.

Instructions
For each item below, indicate whether it involves:

(1) A temporary difference that will result in future deductible amounts and therefore will usually give rise to a deferred income tax asset.
(2) A temporary difference that will result in future taxable amounts and therefore will usually give rise to a deferred income tax liability.
(3) A permanent difference.

Use the appropriate number to indicate your answer for each.

(a) _____ An accelerated depreciation system is used for tax purposes, and the straight-line depreciation method is used for financial reporting purposes for some plant assets.
(b) _____ A landlord collects some rents in advance. Rents received are taxable in the period when they are received.
(c) _____ Expenses are incurred in obtaining tax-exempt income.
(d) _____ Costs of guarantees and warranties are estimated and accrued for financial reporting purposes.
(e) _____ Installment sales of investments are accounted for by the accrual method for financial reporting purposes and the installment method for tax purposes.
(f) _____ Interest is received on an investment in tax-exempt governmental obligations.

(g) _____ For some assets, straight-line depreciation is used for both financial reporting purposes and tax purposes, but the assets' lives are shorter for tax purposes.

(h) _____ The tax return reports a deduction for 80% of the dividends received from various corporations. The cost method is used in accounting for the related investments for financial reporting purposes.

(i) _____ Estimated losses on pending lawsuits and claims are accrued for books. These losses are tax-deductible in the period(s) when the related liabilities are settled.

(j) _____ Expenses on share options are accrued for financial reporting purposes.

2 3 4 6 **E19-7 (Terminology, Relationships, Computations, Entries)**

Instructions

Complete the following statements by filling in the blanks.

(a) In a period in which a taxable temporary difference reverses, the reversal will cause taxable income to be _____ (less than, greater than) pretax financial income.

(b) If a $68,000 balance in Deferred Tax Asset was computed by use of a 40% rate, the underlying cumulative temporary difference amounts to $_____.

(c) Deferred taxes _____ (are, are not) recorded to account for permanent differences.

(d) If a taxable temporary difference originates in 2015, it will cause taxable income for 2015 to be _____ (less than, greater than) pretax financial income for 2015.

(e) If total tax expense is $50,000 and deferred tax expense is $65,000, then the current portion of the expense computation is referred to as current tax _____ (expense, benefit) of $_____.

(f) If a corporation's tax return shows taxable income of $105,000 for Year 2 and a tax rate of 40%, how much will appear on the December 31, Year 2, statement of financial position for "Income taxes payable" if the company has made estimated tax payments of $36,500 for Year 2? $_____.

(g) An increase in the Deferred Tax Liability account on the statement of financial position is recorded by a _____ (debit, credit) to the Income Tax Expense account.

(h) An income statement that reports current tax expense of $82,000 and deferred tax benefit of $23,000 will report total income tax expense of $_____.

(i) A reduction in a deferred tax asset is needed whenever it is judged to be _____ that a portion of a deferred tax asset _____ (will be, will not be) realized.

(j) If the tax return shows total taxes due for the period of $75,000 but the income statement shows total income tax expense of $55,000, the difference of $20,000 is referred to as a deferred tax _____ (expense, benefit).

2 3 5 9 **E19-8 (Two Temporary Differences, One Rate, 3 Years)** Jeonbuk Company has two temporary differences between its income tax expense and income taxes payable. The information is shown below.

	2014	2015	2016
Pretax financial income	₩840,000,000	₩910,000,000	₩945,000,000
Excess depreciation expense on tax return	(30,000,000)	(40,000,000)	(20,000,000)
Excess warranty expense in financial income	20,000,000	10,000,000	8,000,000
Taxable income	₩830,000,000	₩880,000,000	₩933,000,000

The income tax rate for all years is 40%.

Instructions

(a) Prepare the journal entry to record income tax expense, deferred income taxes, and income taxes payable for 2014, 2015, and 2016.

(b) Assuming there were no temporary differences prior to 2014, indicate how deferred taxes will be reported on the 2016 statement of financial position. Jeonbuk's product warranty is for 12 months.

(c) Prepare the income tax expense section of the income statement for 2016, beginning with the line "Pretax financial income."

8 **E19-9 (Carryback and Carryforward of NOL, No Temporary Differences)** The pretax financial income (or loss) figures for Synergetics Company are as follows.

2010	$160,000
2011	250,000
2012	90,000
2013	(160,000)
2014	(350,000)
2015	120,000
2016	100,000

Pretax financial income (or loss) and taxable income (loss) were the same for all years involved. Assume a 45% tax rate for 2010 and 2011 and a 40% tax rate for the remaining years.

Instructions

Prepare the journal entries for the years 2012 to 2016 to record income tax expense and the effects of the net operating loss carrybacks and carryforwards, assuming Synergetics Company uses the carryback provision. All income and losses relate to normal operations. (In recording the benefits of a loss carryforward, assume that it is probable the loss carryforward will be realized.)

8 **E19-10 (Two NOLs, No Temporary Differences, Entries and Income Statement)** Lanier Corporation has pretax financial income (or loss) equal to taxable income (or loss) from 2007 through 2015 as follows.

	Income (Loss)	Tax Rate
2007	€ 29,000	30%
2008	40,000	30%
2009	22,000	35%
2010	48,000	50%
2011	(150,000)	40%
2012	90,000	40%
2013	30,000	40%
2014	105,000	40%
2015	(50,000)	45%

Pretax financial income (loss) and taxable income (loss) were the same for all years since Lanier has been in business. Assume the carryback provision is employed for net operating losses. In recording the benefits of a loss carryforward, assume that it is probable that the related benefits will be realized.

Instructions

(a) What entry(ies) for income taxes should be recorded for 2011?
(b) Indicate what the income tax expense portion of the income statement for 2011 should look like. Assume all income (loss) relates to continuing operations.
(c) What entry for income taxes should be recorded in 2012?
(d) How should the income tax expense section of the income statement for 2012 appear?
(e) What entry for income taxes should be recorded in 2015?
(f) How should the income tax expense section of the income statement for 2015 appear?

2 3 9 **E19-11 (Three Differences, Classify Deferred Taxes)** At December 31, 2014, Cascade Company had the following deferred tax items.

Temporary Differences	Resulting Balances in Deferred Taxes
1. Excess of tax depreciation over book depreciation.	€200,000
2. Accrual, for book purposes, of estimated loss contingency from pending lawsuit that is expected to be settled in 2015. The loss will be deducted on the tax return when paid.	(50,000)
3. Accrual method used for book purposes and installment method used for tax purposes for an isolated installment sale of an investment.	300,000

In analyzing the temporary differences, you find that €30,000 of the depreciation temporary difference will reverse in 2015, and €120,000 of the temporary difference due to the installment sale will reverse in 2015. The tax rate for all years is 40%.

Instructions

Indicate the manner in which deferred taxes should be presented on Cascade Company's December 31, 2014, statement of financial position.

2 3 5 **E19-12 (Two Temporary Differences, One Rate, Beginning Deferred Taxes, Compute Pretax Financial Income)** The following facts relate to McKane Corporation.

1. Deferred tax liability, January 1, 2015, $60,000.
2. Deferred tax asset, January 1, 2015, $20,000.
3. Taxable income for 2015, $115,000.

4. Cumulative temporary difference at December 31, 2015, giving rise to future taxable amounts, $210,000.

5. Cumulative temporary difference at December 31, 2015, giving rise to future deductible amounts, $95,000.

6. Tax rate for all years, 40%. No permanent differences exist.

7. The company is expected to operate profitably in the future.

Instructions

(a) Compute the amount of pretax financial income for 2015.

(b) Prepare the journal entry to record income tax expense, deferred income taxes, and income taxes payable for 2015.

(c) Prepare the income tax expense section of the income statement for 2015, beginning with the line "Income before income taxes."

(d) Compute the effective tax rate for 2015.

2 7 **E19-13 (One Difference, Multiple Rates, Effect of Beginning Balance versus No Beginning Deferred Taxes)** At the end of 2015, Wasicsko Company has €180,000 of cumulative temporary differences that will result in reporting future taxable amounts as follows.

2016	€ 70,000
2017	50,000
2018	40,000
2019	20,000
	€180,000

Tax rates enacted as of the beginning of 2014 are:

2014 and 2015	40%
2016 and 2017	30%
2018 and later	25%

Wasicsko's taxable income for 2015 is €340,000. Taxable income is expected in all future years.

Instructions

(a) Prepare the journal entry for Wasicsko to record income taxes payable, deferred income taxes, and income tax expense for 2015, assuming that there were no deferred taxes at the end of 2014.

(b) Prepare the journal entry for Wasicsko to record income taxes payable, deferred income taxes, and income tax expense for 2015, assuming that there was a balance of €22,000 in a Deferred Tax Liability account at the end of 2014.

3 4 **E19-14 (Deferred Tax Asset)** Callaway Corp. has a deferred tax asset account with a balance of €150,000 at the end of 2014 due to a single cumulative temporary difference of €375,000. At the end of 2015, this same temporary difference has increased to a cumulative amount of €500,000. Taxable income for 2015 is €850,000. The tax rate is 40% for all years.

Instructions

(a) Record income tax expense, deferred income taxes, and income taxes payable for 2015, assuming that it is probable that the deferred tax asset will be realized.

(b) Assuming that it is probable that €30,000 of the deferred tax asset will not be realized, prepare the journal entry at the end of 2015 to recognize this probability.

3 4 **E19-15 (Deferred Tax Asset)** Assume the same information as in E19-14 for Callaway Corp.

5 **Instructions**

(a) Record income tax expense, deferred income taxes, and income taxes payable for 2015, assuming that it is probable that €20,000 of the deferred tax asset will be realized in full.

(b) Record income tax expense, deferred income taxes, and income taxes payable for 2015, assuming that it is probable that none of the deferred tax asset will be realized.

2 5 **E19-16 (Deferred Tax Liability, Change in Tax Rate, Prepare Section of Income Statement)** Sharrer Inc.'s
7 9 only temporary difference at the beginning and end of 2015 is caused by a $2 million deferred gain for tax purposes for an installment sale of a plant asset, and the related receivable is due in equal installments in 2016 and 2017. The related deferred tax liability at the beginning of the year is $800,000. In the third quarter of 2015, a new tax rate of 34% is enacted into law and is scheduled to become effective for 2017. Taxable income for 2015 is $5,000,000, and taxable income is expected in all future years.

Instructions

(a) Determine the amount reported as a deferred tax liability at the end of 2015. Indicate proper classification(s).

(b) Prepare the journal entry (if any) necessary to adjust the deferred tax liability when the new tax rate is enacted into law.

(c) Draft the income tax expense portion of the income statement for 2015. Begin with the line "Income before income taxes." Assume no permanent differences exist.

2 3 7 E19-17 (Two Temporary Differences, Tracked through 3 Years, Multiple Rates) Taxable income and pretax financial income would be identical for Jiang Group except for its treatments of gross profit on installment sales and estimated costs of warranties. The following income computations have been prepared (amounts in thousands).

Taxable income	2014	2015	2016
Excess of revenues over expenses (excluding two temporary differences)	¥160,000	¥210,000	¥90,000
Installment income collected	8,000	8,000	8,000
Expenditures for warranties	(5,000)	(5,000)	(5,000)
Taxable income	¥163,000	¥213,000	¥93,000

Pretax financial income	2014	2015	2016
Excess of revenues over expenses (excluding two temporary differences)	¥160,000	¥210,000	¥90,000
Installment gross profit earned	24,000	–0–	–0–
Estimated cost of warranties	(15,000)	–0–	–0–
Income before taxes	¥169,000	¥210,000	¥90,000

The tax rates in effect are 2014, 45%; 2015 and 2016, 40%. All tax rates were enacted into law on January 1, 2014. No deferred income taxes existed at the beginning of 2014. Taxable income is expected in all future years.

Instructions

Prepare the journal entry to record income tax expense, deferred income taxes, and income taxes payable for 2014, 2015, and 2016.

2 3 7 E19-18 (Three Differences, Multiple Rates, Future Taxable Income) During 2015, Graham Co.'s first year of operations, the company reports pretax financial income of £250,000. Graham's enacted tax rate is 40% for 2015 and 35% for all later years. Graham expects to have taxable income in each of the next 5 years. The effects on future tax returns of temporary differences existing at December 31, 2015, are summarized below.

	Future Years					
	2016	2017	2018	2019	2020	Total
Future taxable (deductible) amounts:						
Installment sales	£32,000	£32,000	£32,000			£ 96,000
Depreciation	6,000	6,000	6,000	£6,000	£6,000	30,000
Unearned rent	(50,000)	(50,000)				(100,000)

Instructions

(a) Complete the schedule below to compute deferred taxes at December 31, 2015.

(b) Compute taxable income for 2015.

(c) Prepare the journal entry to record income taxes payable, deferred taxes, and income tax expense for 2015.

	Future Taxable (Deductible) Amounts	Tax Rate	December 31, 2015 Deferred Tax (Asset)	Liability
Temporary Difference				
Installment sales	£ 96,000			
Depreciation	30,000			
Unearned rent	(100,000)			
Totals	£____			

2 3 **E19-19 (Two Differences, One Rate, Beginning Deferred Balance, Compute Pretax Financial Income)**
9 Luo Co. establishes a ¥90 million liability at the end of 2015 for the estimated litigation settlement for manufacturing defects. All related costs will be paid and deducted on the tax return in 2016. Also, at the end of 2015, the company has ¥50 million of temporary differences due to excess depreciation for tax purposes, ¥7 million of which will reverse in 2016.

The enacted tax rate for all years is 40%, and the company pays taxes of ¥64 million on ¥160 million of taxable income in 2015. Luo expects to have taxable income in 2016.

Instructions

(a) Determine the deferred taxes to be reported at the end of 2015.
(b) Indicate how the deferred taxes computed in (a) are to be reported on the statement of financial position.
(c) Assuming that the only deferred tax account at the beginning of 2015 was a deferred tax liability of ¥10,000,000, draft the income tax expense portion of the income statement for 2015, beginning with the line "Income before income taxes." (*Hint:* You must first compute (1) the amount of temporary difference underlying the beginning ¥10,000,000 deferred tax liability, then (2) the amount of temporary differences originating or reversing during the year, and then (3) the amount of pretax financial income.)

2 3 **E19-20 (Two Differences, No Beginning Deferred Taxes, Multiple Rates)** Macinski Inc., in its first year
9 of operations, has the following differences between the book basis and tax basis of its assets and liabilities at the end of 2015.

	Book Basis	Tax Basis
Equipment (net)	$400,000	$340,000
Estimated warranty liability	150,000	–0–

It is estimated that the warranty liability will be settled in 2016. The difference in equipment (net) will result in taxable amounts of $20,000 in 2016, $30,000 in 2017, and $10,000 in 2018. The company has taxable income of $550,000 in 2015. As of the beginning of 2015, the enacted tax rate is 34% for 2015–2017, and 30% for 2018. Macinski expects to report taxable income through 2018.

Instructions

(a) Prepare the journal entry to record income tax expense, deferred income taxes, and income taxes payable for 2015.
(b) Indicate how deferred income taxes will be reported on the statement of financial position at the end of 2015.

2 3 **E19-21 (Two Temporary Differences, Multiple Rates, Future Taxable Income)** Flynn Inc. has two tempo-
7 9 rary differences at the end of 2015. The first difference stems from installment sales, and the second one results from the accrual of a loss contingency. Flynn's accounting department has developed a schedule of future taxable and deductible amounts related to these temporary differences as follows.

	2016	2017	2018	2019
Taxable amounts	$40,000	$50,000	$60,000	$90,000
Deductible amounts		(15,000)	(19,000)	
	$40,000	$35,000	$41,000	$90,000

As of the beginning of 2015, the enacted tax rate is 34% for 2015 and 2016, and 38% for 2017–2020. At the beginning of 2015, the company had no deferred income taxes on its statement of financial position. Taxable income for 2015 is $400,000. Taxable income is expected in all future years.

Instructions

(a) Prepare the journal entry to record income tax expense, deferred income taxes, and income taxes payable for 2015.
(b) Indicate how deferred income taxes would be classified on the statement of financial position at the end of 2015.

2 3 **E19-22 (Two Differences, One Rate, First Year)** The differences between the book basis and tax basis of
9 the assets and liabilities of Morgan Corporation at the end of 2015 are presented below.

	Book Basis	Tax Basis
Accounts receivable	$50,000	$–0–
Litigation liability	20,000	–0–

It is estimated that the litigation liability will be settled in 2016. The difference in accounts receivable will result in taxable amounts of $30,000 in 2016 and $20,000 in 2017. The company has taxable income of $300,000 in 2015 and is expected to have taxable income in each of the following 2 years. Its enacted tax rate is 34% for all years. This is the company's first year of operations.

Instructions

(a) Prepare the journal entry to record income tax expense, deferred income taxes, and income taxes payable for 2015.

(b) Indicate how deferred income taxes will be reported on the statement of financial position at the end of 2015.

4 7 8 E19-23 (NOL Carryback and Carryforward, Recognition versus Non-Recognition) Sondgeroth Inc. reports the following pretax income (loss) for both financial reporting purposes and tax purposes. (Assume the carryback provision is used for a net operating loss.)

Year	Pretax Income (Loss)	Tax Rate
2013	£110,000	34%
2014	90,000	34%
2015	(260,000)	38%
2016	220,000	38%

The tax rates listed were all enacted by the beginning of 2013.

Instructions

(a) Prepare the journal entries for the years 2013–2016 to record income tax expense (benefit) and income taxes payable (refundable) and the tax effects of the loss carryback and carryforward, assuming that at the end of 2015 it is probable that the benefits of the loss carryforward will be realized in the future.

(b) Using the assumption in (a), prepare the income tax section of the 2015 income statement, beginning with the line "Operating loss before income taxes."

(c) Prepare the journal entries for 2015 and 2016, assuming that based on the weight of available evidence at 12/31/15, it is probable that one-fourth of the benefits of the loss carryforward will not be realized.

(d) Using the assumption in (c), prepare the income tax section of the 2015 income statement, beginning with the line "Operating loss before income taxes."

4 7 8 E19-24 (NOL Carryback and Carryforward, Non-Recognition) Nielson Inc. reports the following pretax income (loss) for both book and tax purposes. (Assume the carryback provision is used where possible for a net operating loss.)

Year	Pretax Income (Loss)	Tax Rate
2013	€100,000	40%
2014	90,000	40%
2015	(240,000)	45%
2016	120,000	45%

The tax rates listed were all enacted by the beginning of 2013.

Instructions

(a) Prepare the journal entries for years 2013–2016 to record income tax expense (benefit) and income taxes payable (refundable) and the tax effects of the loss carryback and loss carryforward, assuming that based on the weight of available evidence it is probable that one-half of the benefits of the loss carryforward will not be realized.

(b) Prepare the income tax section of the 2015 income statement, beginning with the line "Operating loss before income taxes."

(c) Prepare the income tax section of the 2016 income statement, beginning with the line "Income before income taxes."

4 7 8 E19-25 (NOL Carryback and Carryforward, Non-Recognition) Hayes Co. reported the following pretax financial income (loss) for the years 2013–2017.

2013	$240,000
2014	350,000
2015	90,000
2016	(550,000)
2017	180,000

Pretax financial income (loss) and taxable income (loss) were the same for all years involved. The enacted tax rate was 34% for 2013 and 2014, and 40% for 2015–2017. Assume the carryback provision is used first for net operating losses.

Instructions

(a) Prepare the journal entries for the years 2015–2017 to record income tax expense, income taxes payable (refundable), and the tax effects of the loss carryback and loss carryforward, assuming that based on the weight of available evidence it is probable that one-fifth of the benefits of the loss carryforward will not be realized.

(b) Prepare the income tax section of the 2016 income statement, beginning with the line "Income (loss) before income taxes."

PROBLEMS

2 3 5 **P19-1 (Three Differences, No Beginning Deferred Taxes, Multiple Rates)** The following information is available for Remmers Corporation for 2015.

1. Depreciation reported on the tax return exceeded depreciation reported on the income statement by $120,000. This difference will reverse in equal amounts of $30,000 over the years 2016–2019.
2. Interest received on governmental bonds was $10,000.
3. Rent collected in advance on January 1, 2015, totaled $60,000 for a 3-year period. Of this amount, $40,000 was reported as unearned at December 31 for book purposes.
4. The tax rates are 40% for 2015 and 35% for 2016 and subsequent years.
5. Income taxes of $320,000 are due per the tax return for 2015.
6. No deferred taxes existed at the beginning of 2015.

Instructions

(a) Compute taxable income for 2015.

(b) Compute pretax financial income for 2015.

(c) Prepare the journal entries to record income tax expense, deferred income taxes, and income taxes payable for 2015 and 2016. Assume taxable income was $980,000 in 2016.

(d) Prepare the income tax expense section of the income statement for 2015, beginning with "Income before income taxes."

3 5 6 **P19-2 (One Temporary Difference, Tracked for 4 Years, One Permanent Difference, Change in Rate)** The pretax financial income of Truttman Company differs from its taxable income throughout each of 4 years as follows.

Year	Pretax Financial Income	Taxable Income	Tax Rate
2014	€290,000	€180,000	35%
2015	320,000	225,000	40%
2016	350,000	260,000	40%
2017	420,000	560,000	40%

Pretax financial income for each year includes a non-deductible expense of €30,000 (never deductible for tax purposes). The remainder of the difference between pretax financial income and taxable income in each period is due to one depreciation temporary difference. No deferred income taxes existed at the beginning of 2014.

Instructions

(a) Prepare journal entries to record income taxes in all 4 years. Assume that the change in the tax rate to 40% was not enacted until the beginning of 2015.

(b) Prepare the income statement for 2015, beginning with income before income taxes.

2 5 6 9 **P19-3 (Second Year of Depreciation Difference, Two Differences, Single Rate)** The following information has been obtained for the Gocker Corporation.

1. Prior to 2014, taxable income and pretax financial income were identical.
2. Pretax financial income is €1,700,000 in 2014 and €1,400,000 in 2015.
3. On January 1, 2014, equipment costing €1,200,000 is purchased. It is to be depreciated on a straight-line basis over 5 years for tax purposes and over 8 years for financial reporting purposes. (Under applicable tax law, a half-year of tax depreciation is recorded in 2014 and 2019.)
4. Interest of €60,000 was earned on tax-exempt governmental obligations in 2015.

5. Included in 2015 pretax financial income is a gain on discontinued operations of €200,000, which is fully taxable.

6. The tax rate is 35% for all periods.

7. Taxable income is expected in all future years.

Instructions

    (a) Compute taxable income and income taxes payable for 2015.

    (b) Prepare the journal entry to record 2015 income tax expense, income taxes payable, and deferred taxes.

    (c) Prepare the bottom portion of Gocker's 2015 income statement, beginning with "Income before income taxes."

    (d) Indicate how deferred income taxes should be presented on the December 31, 2015, statement of financial position.

2 3 5 P19-4 (Permanent and Temporary Differences, One Rate) The accounting records of Shinault Inc. show the following data for 2015.

    1. Equipment was acquired in early January for $300,000. Straight-line depreciation over a 5-year life is used, with no residual value. For tax purposes, Shinault used a 30% rate to calculate depreciation.

    2. Interest revenue on governmental bonds totaled $4,000.

    3. Product warranties were estimated to be $50,000 in 2015. Actual repair and labor costs related to the warranties in 2015 were $10,000. The remainder is estimated to be paid evenly in 2016 and 2017.

    4. Sales on an accrual basis were $100,000. For tax purposes, $75,000 was recorded on the installment-sales method.

    5. Fines incurred for pollution violations were $4,200.

    6. Pretax financial income was $750,000. The tax rate is 30%.

Instructions

    (a) Prepare a schedule starting with pretax financial income in 2015 and ending with taxable income in 2015.

    (b) Prepare the journal entry for 2015 to record income taxes payable, income tax expense, and deferred income taxes.

5 7 8 9 P19-5 (Recognition of NOL) Jennings Inc. reported the following pretax income (loss) and related tax rates during the years 2010–2016.

	Pretax Income (loss)	Tax Rate
2010	£ 40,000	30%
2011	25,000	30%
2012	50,000	30%
2013	80,000	40%
2014	(180,000)	45%
2015	70,000	40%
2016	100,000	35%

Pretax financial income (loss) and taxable income (loss) were the same for all years since Jennings began business. The tax rates from 2013–2016 were enacted in 2013.

Instructions

    (a) Prepare the journal entries for the years 2014–2016 to record income taxes payable (refundable), income tax expense (benefit), and the tax effects of the loss carryback and carryforward. Assume that Jennings elects the carryback provision where possible and it is probable that it will realize the benefits of any loss carryforward in the year that immediately follows the loss year.

    (b) Indicate the effect the 2014 entry(ies) has on the December 31, 2014, statement of financial position.

    (c) Prepare the portion of the income statement, starting with "Operating loss before income taxes," for 2014.

    (d) Prepare the portion of the income statement, starting with "Income before income taxes," for 2015.

2 3 9 P19-6 (Two Differences, Two Rates, Future Income Expected) Presented below and on page 1004 are two independent situations related to future taxable and deductible amounts resulting from temporary differences existing at December 31, 2014.

    1. Mooney Co. has developed the following schedule of future taxable and deductible amounts.

	2015	2016	2017	2018	2019
Taxable amounts	$300	$300	$300	$ 300	$300
Deductible amount	—	—	—	(1,600)	—

2. Roesch Co. has the following schedule of future taxable and deductible amounts.

	2015	2016	2017	2018
Taxable amounts	$300	$300	$ 300	$300
Deductible amount	—	—	(2,300)	—

Both Mooney Co. and Roesch Co. have taxable income of $4,000 in 2014 and expect to have taxable income in all future years. The tax rates enacted as of the beginning of 2014 are 30% for 2014–2017 and 35% for years thereafter.

Instructions

For each of these two situations, compute the net amount of deferred income taxes to be reported at the end of 2014, and indicate how it should be classified on the statement of financial position.

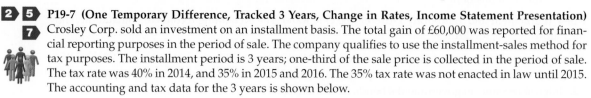

P19-7 (One Temporary Difference, Tracked 3 Years, Change in Rates, Income Statement Presentation) Crosley Corp. sold an investment on an installment basis. The total gain of £60,000 was reported for financial reporting purposes in the period of sale. The company qualifies to use the installment-sales method for tax purposes. The installment period is 3 years; one-third of the sale price is collected in the period of sale. The tax rate was 40% in 2014, and 35% in 2015 and 2016. The 35% tax rate was not enacted in law until 2015. The accounting and tax data for the 3 years is shown below.

	Financial Accounting	Tax Return
2014 (40% tax rate)		
Income before temporary difference	£ 70,000	£70,000
Temporary difference	60,000	20,000
Income	£130,000	£90,000
2015 (35% tax rate)		
Income before temporary difference	£ 70,000	£70,000
Temporary difference	–0–	20,000
Income	£ 70,000	£90,000
2016 (35% tax rate)		
Income before temporary difference	£ 70,000	£70,000
Temporary difference	–0–	20,000
Income	£ 70,000	£90,000

Instructions

(a) Prepare the journal entries to record the income tax expense, deferred income taxes, and the income taxes payable at the end of each year. No deferred income taxes existed at the beginning of 2014.

(b) Explain how the deferred taxes will appear on the statement of financial position at the end of each year.

(c) Draft the income tax expense section of the income statement for each year, beginning with "Income before income taxes."

P19-8 (Two Differences, 2 Years, Compute Taxable Income and Pretax Financial Income) The following information was disclosed during the audit of Zheng Inc.

1.

Year	Amount Due per Tax Return
2014	¥130,000,000
2015	104,000,000

2. On January 1, 2014, equipment costing ¥600,000,000 is purchased. For financial reporting purposes, the company uses straight-line depreciation over a 5-year life. For tax purposes, the company uses the double-declining balance method over 5 years.

3. In January 2015, ¥225,000,000 is collected in advance rental of a building for a 3-year period. The entire ¥225,000,000 is reported as taxable income in 2015, but ¥150,000,000 of the ¥225,000,000 is reported as unearned revenue in 2015 for financial reporting purposes. The remaining amount of unearned revenue is to be recognized equally in 2016 and 2017.

4. The tax rate is 40% in 2014 and all subsequent periods. (*Hint:* To find taxable income in 2014 and 2015, the related income taxes payable amounts will have to be "grossed up.")

5. No temporary differences existed at the end of 2013. Zheng expects to report taxable income in each of the next 5 years.

Instructions

(a) Determine the amount to report for deferred income taxes at the end of 2014, and indicate how it should be classified on the statement of financial position.

(b) Prepare the journal entry to record income taxes for 2014.

(c) Draft the income tax section of the income statement for 2014, beginning with "Income before income taxes." (*Hint:* You must compute taxable income and then combine that with changes in cumulative temporary differences to arrive at pretax financial income.)

(d) Determine the deferred income taxes at the end of 2015, and indicate how they should be classified on the statement of financial position.

(e) Prepare the journal entry to record income taxes for 2015.

(f) Draft the income tax section of the income statement for 2015, beginning with "Income before income taxes."

  P19-9 (Five Differences, Compute Taxable Income and Deferred Taxes, Draft Income Statement) Wise Company began operations at the beginning of 2015. The following information pertains to this company.

1. Pretax financial income for 2015 is €100,000.

2. The tax rate enacted for 2015 and future years is 40%.

3. Differences between the 2015 income statement and tax return are listed below:

(a) Warranty expense accrued for financial reporting purposes amounts to €7,000. Warranty deductions per the tax return amount to €2,000.

(b) Income on construction contracts using the percentage-of-completion method per books amounts to €92,000. Income on construction contracts for tax purposes amounts to €67,000.

(c) Depreciation of property, plant, and equipment for financial reporting purposes amounts to €60,000. Depreciation of these assets amounts to €80,000 for the tax return.

(d) A €3,500 fine paid for violation of pollution laws was deducted in computing pretax financial income.

(e) Interest revenue recognized on an investment in tax-exempt bonds amounts to €1,500.

4. Taxable income is expected for the next few years.

Instructions

(a) Compute taxable income for 2015.

(b) Compute the deferred taxes at December 31, 2015, that relate to the temporary differences described above. Clearly label them as deferred tax asset or liability.

(c) Prepare the journal entry to record income tax expense, deferred taxes, and income taxes payable for 2015.

(d) Draft the income tax expense section of the income statement, beginning with "Income before income taxes."

CONCEPTS FOR ANALYSIS

CA19-1 (Objectives and Principles for Accounting for Income Taxes) The amount of income taxes due to the government for a period of time is rarely the amount reported on the income statement for that period as income tax expense.

Instructions

(a) Explain the objectives of accounting for income taxes in general-purpose financial statements.

(b) Explain the basic principles that are applied in accounting for income taxes at the date of the financial statements to meet the objectives discussed in (a).

(c) List the steps in the annual computation of deferred tax liabilities and assets.

CA19-2 (Basic Accounting for Temporary Differences) Dexter Company appropriately uses the asset-liability method to record deferred income taxes. Dexter reports depreciation expense for certain machinery purchased this year using an accelerated method for income tax purposes and the straight-line basis for financial reporting purposes. The tax deduction is the larger amount this year.

Dexter received rent revenues in advance this year. These revenues are included in this year's taxable income. However, for financial reporting purposes, these revenues are reported as unearned revenues, a current liability.

Instructions

(a) What are the principles of the asset-liability approach?

(b) How would Dexter account for the temporary differences?

(c) How should Dexter classify the deferred tax consequences of the temporary differences on its statement of financial position?

CA19-3 (Identify Temporary Differences and Classification Criteria) The asset-liability approach for recording deferred income taxes is an integral part of IFRS.

Instructions

    (a) Indicate whether each of the following independent situations should be treated as a temporary difference or as a permanent difference, and explain why.

        (1) Estimated warranty costs (covering a 3-year warranty) are expensed for financial reporting purposes at the time of sale but deducted for income tax purposes when paid.

        (2) Depreciation for book and income tax purposes differs because of different bases of carrying the related property, which was acquired in a trade-in. The different bases are a result of different rules used for book and tax purposes to compute the basis of property acquired in a trade-in.

        (3) A company properly uses the equity method to account for its 30% investment in another company. The investee pays dividends that are about 10% of its annual earnings.

        (4) A company reports a gain on an involuntary conversion of a non-monetary asset to a monetary asset. The company elects to replace the property within the statutory period using the total proceeds so the gain is not reported on the current year's tax return.

    (b) Discuss the nature of the deferred income tax accounts and possible classifications in a company's statement of financial position. Indicate the manner in which these accounts are to be reported.

CA19-4 (Accounting for Deferred Income Taxes)

This year, Gumowski Company has each of the following items in its income statement.

    1. Income on installment sales.

    2. Revenues on long-term construction contracts.

    3. Estimated costs of product warranty contracts.

    4. Interest on tax-exempt bonds.

Instructions

    (a) Under what conditions would deferred income taxes need to be reported in the financial statements?

    (b) Specify when deferred income taxes would need to be recognized for each of the items above, and indicate the rationale for such recognition.

CA19-5 (Explain Computation of Deferred Tax Liability for Multiple Tax Rates) At December 31, 2014, Higley Corporation has one temporary difference which will reverse and cause taxable amounts in 2015. In 2014, a new tax act set taxes equal to 45% for 2014, 40% for 2015, and 34% for 2016 and years thereafter.

Instructions

Explain what circumstances would call for Higley to compute its deferred tax liability at the end of 2014 by multiplying the cumulative temporary difference by:

    (a) 45%.

    (b) 40%.

    (c) 34%.

CA19-6 (Explain Future Taxable and Deductible Amounts, How Carryback and Carryforward Affects Deferred Taxes) Maria Rodriquez and Lynette Kingston are discussing accounting for income taxes. They are currently studying a schedule of taxable and deductible amounts that will arise in the future as a result of existing temporary differences. The schedule is as follows.

| | Current Year | Future Years | | | |
	2015	2016	2017	2018	2019
Taxable income	€850,000				
Taxable amounts		€375,000	€375,000	€ 375,000	€375,000
Deductible amounts				(2,400,000)	
Enacted tax rate	50%	45%	40%	35%	30%

Instructions

    (a) Explain the concept of future taxable amounts and future deductible amounts as illustrated in the schedule.

    (b) How do the carryback and carryforward provisions affect the reporting of deferred tax assets and deferred tax liabilities?

CA19-7 (Deferred Taxes, Income Effects) Stephanie Delaney, a public accountant, is the newly hired director of corporate taxation for Acme Incorporated, which is a publicly traded corporation. Ms. Delaney's first job with Acme was the review of the company's accounting practices on deferred income taxes. In

doing her review, she noted differences between tax and book depreciation methods that permitted Acme to realize a sizable deferred tax liability on its statement of financial position. As a result, Acme paid very little in income taxes at that time.

Delaney also discovered that Acme has an explicit policy of selling off plant assets before they reversed in the deferred tax liability account. This policy, coupled with the rapid expansion of its plant asset base, allowed Acme to "defer" all income taxes payable for several years, even though it always has reported positive earnings and an increasing EPS. Delaney confirmed with the legal department that the policy is legal, but she is uncomfortable with the ethics of it.

Instructions
Answer the following questions.

(a) Why would Acme have an explicit policy of selling plant assets before the temporary differences reversed in the deferred tax liability account?
(b) What are the ethical implications of Acme's "deferral" of income taxes?
(c) Who could be harmed by Acme's ability to "defer" income taxes payable for several years, despite positive earnings?
(d) In a situation such as this, what are Ms. Delaney's professional responsibilities as a public accountant?

USING YOUR JUDGMENT

FINANCIAL REPORTING

Financial Reporting Problem

Marks and Spencer plc (M&S)
The financial statements of **M&S** (GBR) are presented in Appendix A. The company's complete annual report, including the notes to the financial statements, is available online.

Instructions
Refer to M&S's financial statements and the accompanying notes to answer the following questions.

(a) What amounts relative to income taxes does M&S report in its:
  (1) 2013 income statement?
  (2) 30 March 2013 statement of financial position?
  (3) 2013 statement of cash flows?
(b) M&S's provision for income taxes in 2012 and 2013 was computed at what effective tax rates? (See the notes to the financial statements.)
(c) How much of M&S's 2013 total provision for income taxes was current tax expense, and how much was deferred tax expense?
(d) What did M&S report as the significant components (the details) of its 30 March 2013 deferred tax assets and liabilities?

Comparative Analysis Case

adidas and Puma
The financial statements of **adidas** (DEU) and **Puma** (DEU) are presented in Appendices B and C, respectively. The complete annual reports, including the notes to the financial statements, are available online.

Instructions
Use the companies' financial information to answer the following questions.

(a) What are the amounts of adidas's and Puma's provision for income taxes for the year 2012? Of each company's 2012 provision for income taxes, what portion is current expense and what portion is deferred expense?
(b) What amount of cash was paid in 2012 for income taxes by adidas and by Puma?
(c) What was the effective tax rate in 2012 for adidas and Puma? Why might their effective tax rates differ?
(d) For year-end 2012, what amounts were reported by adidas and Puma as (1) gross deferred tax assets and (2) gross deferred tax liabilities?
(e) Do either adidas or Puma disclose any net operating loss carrybacks and/or carryforwards at year-end 2012? What are the amounts, and when do the carryforwards expire?

Financial Statement Analysis Case

Homestake Mining Company

Homestake Mining Company (USA) is a 120-year-old international gold mining company with substantial gold mining operations and exploration in the United States, Canada, and Australia. At year-end, Homestake reported the following items related to income taxes (thousands of dollars).

Total current taxes	$ 26,349
Total deferred taxes	(39,436)
Total income and mining taxes (the provision for taxes per its income statement)	(13,087)
Deferred tax liabilities	$303,050
Deferred tax assets, net of an unrecognized amount of $207,175	95,275
Net deferred tax liability	$207,775

Note 6 (partial):

Tax loss carryforwards (U.S., Canada, Australia, and Chile)	$71,151
Tax credit carryforwards	$12,007

Instructions

(a) What is the significance of Homestake's disclosure of "Current taxes" of $26,349 and "Deferred taxes" of $(39,436)?

(b) Explain the concept behind Homestake's disclosure of deferred tax liabilities (future taxable amounts) and deferred tax assets (future deductible amounts).

(c) Homestake reported tax loss carryforwards of $71,151 and tax credit carryforwards of $12,007. How do the carryback and carryforward provisions affect the reporting of deferred tax assets and deferred tax liabilities?

Accounting, Analysis, and Principles

Adler Company, which began operations at the beginning of 2013, produces various products on a contract basis. Each contract generates income of €80,000. Some of Adler's contracts provide for the customer to pay on an installment basis. Under these contracts, Adler collects one-fifth of the contract revenue in each of the following 4 years. For financial reporting purposes, the company recognizes income on an accrual basis; for tax purposes, Adler recognizes income in the year cash is collected (installment basis).

Presented below is information related to Adler's operations for 2015.

1. In 2015, the company completed seven contracts that allow for the customer to pay on an installment basis. Adler recognized the related income of €560,000 for financial reporting purposes. It reported only €112,000 of income on installment sales on the 2015 tax return. The company expects future collections on the related installment receivables to result in taxable amounts of €112,000 in each of the next 4 years.

2. Non-taxable government bond interest revenue was €28,000.

3. Non-deductible fines and penalties of €26,000 were paid.

4. Pretax financial income amounts to €500,000.

5. Tax rates (enacted before the end of 2015) are 50% for 2015 and 40% for 2016 and later.

6. The accounting period is the calendar year.

7. The company is expected to have taxable income in all future years.

8. The company had a deferred tax liability balance of €40,000 related to prior year installment sales at the end of 2014. None of this temporary difference reversed in 2015.

Accounting

Prepare the journal entry to record income taxes for 2015.

Analysis

Classify deferred income taxes on the statement of financial position at December 31, 2015, and indicate, starting with income before income taxes, how income taxes are reported on the income statement. What is Adler's effective tax rate?

Principles

Explain how the IASB Conceptual Framework is used as a basis for determining the proper accounting for deferred income taxes.

IFRS BRIDGE TO THE PROFESSION

Professional Research

Kleckner Company started operations in 2011. Although it has grown steadily, the company reported accumulated operating losses of $450,000 in its first four years in business. In the most recent year (2015), Kleckner appears to have turned the corner and reported modest taxable income of $30,000. In addition to a deferred tax asset related to its net operating loss, Kleckner has recorded a deferred tax asset related to product warranties and a deferred tax liability related to accelerated depreciation.

Given its past operating results, Kleckner has determined that it is not probable that it will realize any of the deferred tax assets. However, given its improved performance, Kleckner management wonders whether there are any accounting consequences for its deferred tax assets. They would like you to conduct some research on the accounting for recognition of its deferred tax asset.

Instructions

Access the IFRS authoritative literature at the IASB website (*http://eifrs.iasb.org/*) (you may register for free eIFRS access at this site). When you have accessed the documents, you can use the search tool in your Internet browser to respond to the following questions. (Provide paragraph citations.)

(a) Briefly explain to Kleckner management the importance of future taxable income as it relates to the recognition of deferred tax assets.

(b) What are the sources of income that may be relied upon in assessing realization of a deferred tax asset?

(c) What are tax-planning strategies? From the information provided, does it appear that Kleckner could employ a tax-planning strategy in evaluating its deferred tax asset?

Professional Simulation

In this simulation, you are asked to address questions related to the accounting for income taxes. Prepare responses to all parts.

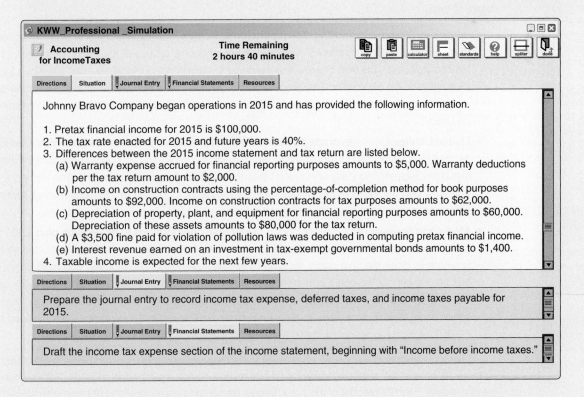

KWW_Professional_Simulation

| Accounting for IncomeTaxes | Time Remaining 2 hours 40 minutes | copy | paste | calculator | sheet | standards | help | splitter | done |

Directions | Situation | Journal Entry | Financial Statements | Resources

Johnny Bravo Company began operations in 2015 and has provided the following information.

1. Pretax financial income for 2015 is $100,000.
2. The tax rate enacted for 2015 and future years is 40%.
3. Differences between the 2015 income statement and tax return are listed below.
   (a) Warranty expense accrued for financial reporting purposes amounts to $5,000. Warranty deductions per the tax return amount to $2,000.
   (b) Income on construction contracts using the percentage-of-completion method for book purposes amounts to $92,000. Income on construction contracts for tax purposes amounts to $62,000.
   (c) Depreciation of property, plant, and equipment for financial reporting purposes amounts to $60,000. Depreciation of these assets amounts to $80,000 for the tax return.
   (d) A $3,500 fine paid for violation of pollution laws was deducted in computing pretax financial income.
   (e) Interest revenue earned on an investment in tax-exempt governmental bonds amounts to $1,400.
4. Taxable income is expected for the next few years.

Directions | Situation | Journal Entry | Financial Statements | Resources

Prepare the journal entry to record income tax expense, deferred taxes, and income taxes payable for 2015.

Directions | Situation | Journal Entry | Financial Statements | Resources

Draft the income tax expense section of the income statement, beginning with "Income before income taxes."

Remember to check the book's companion website, at www.wiley.com/ college/kieso, to find additional resources for this chapter.

20 Accounting for Pensions and Postretirement Benefits

LEARNING OBJECTIVES

After studying this chapter, you should be able to:

1 Distinguish between accounting for the employer's pension plan and accounting for the pension fund.

2 Identify types of pension plans and their characteristics.

3 Explain measures for valuing the pension obligation.

4 Identify amounts reported in financial statements.

5 Use a worksheet for employer's pension plan entries.

6 Explain the accounting for past service costs.

7 Explain the accounting for remeasurements.

8 Describe the requirements for reporting pension plans in financial statements.

9 Explain the accounting for other postretirement benefits.

Pension Peril

The effects of the financial crisis of 2008 and the resultant economic downturn continue to ripple through global markets. Pension plans, both those sponsored by governments and private companies, are now feeling the effects. Consider the following actions by private companies to deal with the effects of the financial crisis.

- Britain's employers are **shutting down pension schemes** at a rapid rate. A new study has concluded that traditional final salary pension benefits will soon become a thing of the past. The study found that total service cost—the cost of providing the current year's pension promises—had fallen by 15 percent as a result of the shutdown. The drop reflects a decline in the number of workers who are earning pension benefits. At this rate, final salary pensions in the private sector will no longer be available within six years.

- **United Utilities** (GBR) has **made its defined benefit pension schemes less generous** to employees as the United Kingdom's biggest listed water company looks to cut costs in the face of a harsher regulatory regime. The utility announced that the move was backed by unions. The company said it had amended the terms of its defined benefit schemes to increase contributions made by members, while also increasing the retirement age and capping increases in pensionable salaries.

- **Marks and Spencer plc** (GBR) is planning to **increase contributions to its pension plan** (£800 million) to address a deficit in the plan assets relative to its pension obligations. The retailer insisted that it had no plans to close the final salary scheme to existing members. The clothing and food chain, which has 20,000 current members in its defined benefits scheme, said it would not be following the growing band of companies—such as **BP** (GBR) and **Vodafone** (GBR)—which are closing their final salary schemes to existing members. In fact, recent data indicate that 88 percent of U.K. defined benefit pension plans have closed the door to new participants.

Just as market declines create challenges for companies and their pension plans, market recoveries can quickly reverse the negative consequences of market downturns for pension plans. This is what we are seeing recently, with 27 percent of the 1,000 largest global companies reporting pension plan funded status (which is defined as pension assets minus pension liabilities) of greater than 100 percent in 2013. That means these companies had more assets than liabilities, which is quite a change in two years when just 4.4 percent of these companies reported fully funded or overfunded pension plans. A good example is **Marks and Spencer**. As discussed above, it reported a net pension liability or deficit of £283.3 million at the

height of the financial crisis in 2008. In 2013, the company reported a pension *surplus* of £193.3 million—quite a swing in a five-year period.

Why are pension plans so vulnerable to the effects of swings in financial markets? As you will learn in this chapter, pensions are a form of deferred compensation. When a pension is included in a salary and benefit package, employees may accept lower pay while working in exchange for pension benefits that will be paid in the future at retirement. Companies and governments must set aside assets to meet these future obligations. However, when economic times are tough, assets in the funds (shares and bonds) lose value, and companies and governments may not have the resources to contribute to the funds. As a result, a pension deficit arises and employees' pensions may be in peril. Given the need for good information about the impact of these continuing pension perils on companies, the IASB has issued new rules to improve the accounting for pensions and other postretirement benefit plans.

Sources: Adapted from Norma Cohen, "Study Sees End for Final Salary Pensions," *Financial Times* (May 17, 2010); J. Raife, "Time to Talk Real Public Sector Pension Costs," *Financial Times* (June 27, 2010); S. Johnson, "Sea Change in the Pipeline for BP's Pension Fund," *Financial Times* (January 12, 2014); and Towers and Watson, "Funded Status of Fortune 1000 Pension Plans Estimated to Have Improved," *Insider* (January 2014).

CONCEPTUAL FOCUS

> See the **Underlying Concepts** on page 1033.

INTERNATIONAL FOCUS

> Read the **Global Accounting Insights** on pages 1036–1037 for a discussion of non-IFRS financial reporting of postretirement benefits.

PREVIEW OF CHAPTER 20

As our opening story indicates, the financial crisis of 2008 has put pension plans in peril and the cost of retirement benefits is getting steep. For example, **British Airways'** (GBR) pension and healthcare costs for retirees in a recent year totaled £149 million, or approximately £4 per passenger carried. Many other companies have substantial pension and other postretirement expenses and obligations as well. The content and organization of the chapter are as follows.

Accounting for Pensions and Postretirement Benefits

Nature of Pension Plans	Accounting for Pensions	Using a Pension Worksheet	Reporting Pension Plans in Financial Statements
• Defined contribution plan • Defined benefit plan • Role of actuaries	• Measures of the pension liability • Net defined benefit obligation (asset) • Changes in the defined benefit obligation (asset) • Plan assets and actual return	• 2015 entries and worksheet • Past service cost • 2016 entries and worksheet • Remeasurements • 2017 entries and worksheet	• Within the financial statements • Within the notes to the financial statements • Other postretirement benefits

NATURE OF PENSION PLANS

A **pension plan** is an arrangement whereby an employer provides benefits (payments) to retired employees for services they performed in their working years. Pension accounting may be divided and separately treated as **accounting for the employer** and **accounting for the pension fund**. The *company* or *employer* is the organization sponsoring the pension plan. It incurs the cost and makes contributions to the pension fund. The *fund* or *plan* is the entity that receives the contributions from the employer, administers the pension assets, and makes the benefit payments to the retired employees (pension recipients). Illustration 20-1 shows the three entities involved in a pension plan and indicates the flow of cash among them.

ILLUSTRATION 20-1
Flow of Cash among
Pension Plan Participants

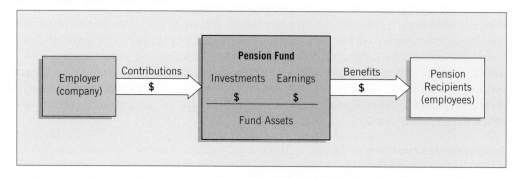

A pension plan is **funded** when the employer makes payments to a funding agency.[1] That agency accumulates the assets of the pension fund and makes payments to the recipients as the benefits come due.

Some pension plans are **contributory**. In these, the employees bear part of the cost of the stated benefits or voluntarily make payments to increase their benefits. Other plans are **non-contributory**. In these plans, the employer bears the entire cost. In some countries, companies design their pension plans so as to take advantage of certain income tax benefits. Plans that offer tax benefits are often called **qualified pension plans**. They permit **deductibility of the employer's contributions to the pension fund and tax-free status of earnings from pension fund assets**.

The pension fund should be a separate legal and accounting entity. The pension fund, as a separate entity, maintains a set of books and prepares financial statements. Maintaining records and preparing financial statements for the fund, an activity known as "accounting for employee benefit plans," is not the subject of this chapter.[2] Instead, this chapter explains the pension accounting and reporting problems **of the employer** as the sponsor of a pension plan.

The need to properly administer and account for pension funds becomes apparent when you understand the size of these funds. Listed in Illustration 20-2 are the pension fund assets and pension expenses of six major companies in a recent year. The two most common types of pension plans are **defined contribution plans** and **defined benefit plans**. We look at each of them in the following sections.

[1]When used as a verb, fund means to pay to a funding agency (as to fund future pension benefits or to fund pension cost). Used as a noun, it refers to assets accumulated in the hands of a funding agency (trustee) for the purpose of meeting pension benefits when they become due.

[2]The IASB issued a separate standard covering the accounting and reporting for employee benefit plans. **[1]**

ILLUSTRATION 20-2
Pension Funds and
Pension Expense

Company	Size of Pension Fund*	2012 Pension Expense*	Pension Expense as % of Pretax Income (Loss)
Siemens (DEU)	€24,052	€332	4.56%
AB InBev (BEL)	€5,704	€86	0.77%
BASF (DEU)	€16,739	€427	5.12%
Cathay Pacific (CHN)	$8,119	$231	14.95%
Dairy Farm International (CHN)	$191	$13	2.42%
Unilever (GBR)	£17,665	£353	5.28%

*Amounts in millions.

Defined Contribution Plan

In a **defined contribution plan**, the employer agrees to contribute to a pension trust a certain sum each period, based on a formula. This formula may consider such factors as age, length of employee service, employer's profits, and compensation level. **The plan defines only the employer's contribution.** It makes no promise regarding the ultimate benefits paid out to the employees.

2 **LEARNING OBJECTIVE**
Identify types of pension plans and their characteristics.

The size of the pension benefits that the employee finally collects under the plan depends on several factors: the amounts originally contributed to the pension trust, the income accumulated in the trust, and the treatment of forfeitures of funds caused by early terminations of other employees. A company usually turns over to an **independent third-party trustee** the amounts originally contributed. The trustee, acting on behalf of the beneficiaries (the participating employees), assumes ownership of the pension assets and is accountable for their investment and distribution. The trust is separate and distinct from the employer.

The accounting for a defined contribution plan is straightforward. The employee gets the benefit of gain (or the risk of loss) from the assets contributed to the pension plan. The employer simply contributes each year based on the formula established in the plan. As a result, the employer's annual cost (pension expense) is simply the amount that it is obligated to contribute to the pension trust. The employer reports a liability on its statement of financial position only if it does not make the contribution in full. The employer reports an asset only if it contributes more than the required amount and must disclose the amount of expense recorded for the defined contribution plan. **[2]**

Defined Benefit Plan

A **defined benefit plan** outlines the benefits that employees will receive when they retire. These benefits typically are a function of an employee's years of service and of the compensation level in the years approaching retirement.

To meet the defined benefit commitments that will arise at retirement, a company must determine what the contribution should be today (a time value of money computation). Companies may use many different contribution approaches. However, the funding method should provide enough money at retirement to meet the benefits defined by the plan.

The **employees** are the beneficiaries of a defined **contribution** trust, but the **employer** is the beneficiary of a defined **benefit** trust. Under a defined benefit plan, the trust's primary purpose is to safeguard and invest assets so that there will be enough to pay the employer's obligation to the employees. **In form**, the trust is a separate entity.

In substance, the trust assets and liabilities belong to the employer. That is, **as long as the plan continues, the employer is responsible for the payment of the defined benefits (without regard to what happens in the trust)**. The employer must make up any short-fall in the accumulated assets held by the trust. On the other hand, the employer can recapture any excess accumulated in the trust, either through reduced future funding or through a reversion of funds.

Because a defined benefit plan specifies benefits in terms of uncertain future variables, a company must establish an appropriate funding pattern to ensure the availability of funds at retirement in order to provide the benefits promised. This funding level depends on a number of factors such as turnover, mortality, length of employee service, compensation levels, and interest earnings.

Employers are at risk with defined benefit plans because they must contribute enough to meet the cost of benefits that the plan defines. The expense recognized each period is not necessarily equal to the cash contribution. Similarly, the liability is contro-versial because its measurement and recognition relate to unknown future variables. Thus, the accounting issues related to this type of plan are complex. **Our discussion in the following sections deals primarily with defined benefit plans.**[3]

What do the numbers mean?   WHICH PLAN IS RIGHT FOR YOU?

Defined contribution plans are more popular with employers than defined benefit plans. One reason is that they are cheaper. Defined contribution plans often cost no more than 3 percent of payroll, whereas defined benefit plans can cost 5 to 6 percent of payroll.

In the late 1970s, approximately 15 million individuals had defined contribution plans. Today, over 62 million do. The follow-ing chart reflects this significant change. It shows the percentage of companies in one country using various types of plans, based on a survey of over 650,000 single-employer pension plans.

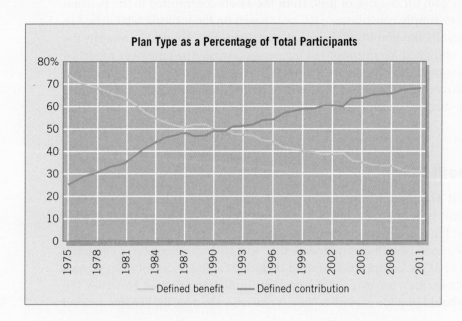

Plan Type as a Percentage of Total Participants

—— Defined benefit   —— Defined contribution

---

[3]In many cases, companies offer a defined contribution plan in combination with a defined benefit plan.

Although many companies are changing to defined contribution plans, the number of existing defined benefit plans and benefits paid from these plans are substantial. Further, while the balance between defined benefit and defined contribution plans has been shifting over time, there is also significant variation in the types of plans across countries, as shown in the chart below.

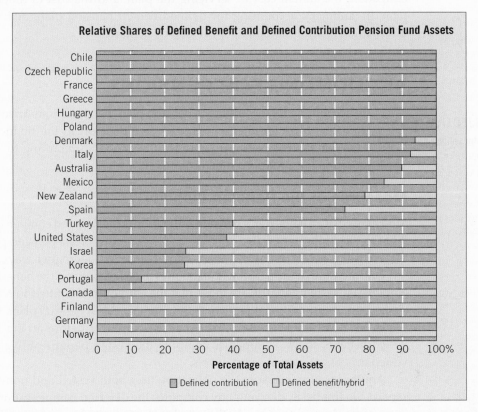

As indicated, for 12 of the 21 countries, assets in defined contribution plans outweighed those in defined benefit plans. In six countries, namely Chile, the Czech Republic, France, Greece, Hungary, and Poland, defined benefit plans did not exist at all. Defined benefit funds dominate the pension markets in Canada, Finland, Germany, Israel, Korea, Norway, Portugal, Turkey, and the United States.

Sources: Private Pension Plan Bulletin (2011), *http://www.dol.gov/ebsa/publications/form5500dataresearch.html#statisticalsummaries*; and "Pension Markets in Focus," OECD (2013).

The Role of Actuaries in Pension Accounting

The problems associated with pension plans involve complicated mathematical considerations. Therefore, companies engage **actuaries** to ensure that a pension plan is appropriate for the employee group covered.[4] Actuaries are individuals trained through a long and rigorous certification program to assign probabilities to future events and their financial effects. The insurance industry employs actuaries to assess risks and to advise on the setting of premiums and other aspects of insurance policies. Employers rely heavily on actuaries for assistance in developing, implementing, and funding pension funds.

[4]An actuary's primary purpose is to ensure that the company has established an appropriate funding pattern to meet its pension obligations. This computation involves developing a set of assumptions and continued monitoring of these assumptions to ensure their realism. IFRS encourages, but does not require, companies to use actuaries in the measurement of the pension amounts. **[3]** That the general public has little understanding of what an actuary does is illustrated by the following excerpt from the *Wall Street Journal*: "A polling organization once asked the general public what an actuary was, and received among its more coherent responses the opinion that it was a place where you put dead actors."

Actuaries make predictions (called *actuarial assumptions*) of mortality rates, employee turnover, interest and earnings rates, early retirement frequency, future salaries, and any other factors necessary to operate a pension plan. They also compute the various pension measures that affect the financial statements, such as the pension obligation, the annual cost of servicing the plan, and the cost of amendments to the plan. In summary, accounting for defined benefit pension plans relies heavily upon information and measurements provided by actuaries.

ACCOUNTING FOR PENSIONS

LEARNING OBJECTIVE **3**

Explain measures for valuing the pension obligation.

In accounting for a company's pension plan, two questions arise. (1) What is the pension obligation that a company should report in the financial statements? (2) What is the pension expense for the period? Attempting to answer the first question has produced much controversy.

Measures of the Pension Liability

Most agree that an employer's **pension obligation** is the deferred compensation obligation it has to its employees for their service under the terms of the pension plan. Measuring that obligation is not so simple, though, because there are alternative ways of measuring it.

One measure of the pension obligation is to base it only on the benefits vested to the employees. **Vested benefits** are those that the employee is entitled to receive even if he or she renders no additional services to the company. Most pension plans require a certain minimum number of years of service to the employer before an employee achieves vested benefits status. Companies compute the **vested benefit obligation** using only vested benefits at current salary levels.

Another way to measure the obligation uses both vested and non-vested years of service. On this basis, the company computes the deferred compensation amount on all years of employees' service—**both vested and non-vested**—using current salary levels. This measurement of the pension obligation is called the **accumulated benefit obligation**.

A third measure bases the deferred compensation amount on both vested and non-vested service **using future salaries**. This measurement of the pension obligation is called the **defined benefit obligation**. Because future salaries are expected to be higher than current salaries, this approach results in the largest measurement of the pension obligation.

The choice between these measures is critical. The choice affects the amount of a company's pension liability and the annual pension expense reported. The diagram in Illustration 20-3 (page 1017) presents the differences in these three measurements.

Which of these alternative measures of the pension liability does the profession favor? **The profession adopted the defined benefit obligation—the present value (without deducting any plan assets) of the expected future payments required to settle the obligation resulting from employee service in current and prior periods.**[5] **[4]** Those in favor of the defined benefit obligation contend that a promise by an employer to pay benefits based on a percentage of the employees' future salaries is far greater than a promise to pay a percentage of their current salary, and such a difference should be reflected in the pension liability and pension expense.

---

[5]When we use the term "present value of benefits" throughout this chapter, we really mean the *actuarial* present value of benefits. **Actuarial present value** is the amount payable adjusted to reflect the time value of money *and* the probability of payment (by means of decrements for events such as death, disability, withdrawals, or retirement) between the present date and the expected date of payment. For simplicity, though, we use the term "present value" instead of "actuarial present value" in our discussion.

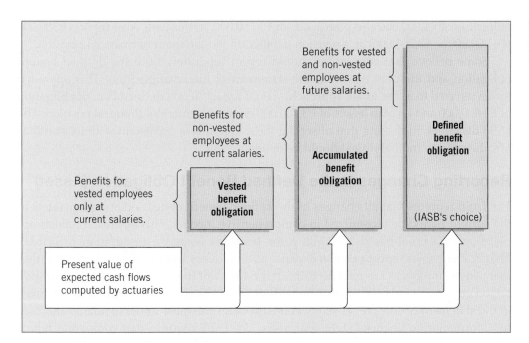

ILLUSTRATION 20-3
Different Measures of the
Pension Obligation

Moreover, companies discount to present value the estimated future benefits to be paid. Minor changes in the interest rate used to discount pension benefits can dramatically affect the measurement of the employer's obligation. For example, a 1 percent decrease in the discount rate can increase pension liabilities 15 percent. Accounting rules require that, at each measurement date, a company must determine the appropriate discount rate used to measure the pension liability, based on current interest rates. **[5]**

Net Defined Benefit Obligation (Asset)

The **net defined benefit obligation (asset)** (also referred to as the **funded status**) is the deficit or surplus related to a defined pension plan. The deficit or surplus is measured as follows.

4 LEARNING OBJECTIVE
Identify amounts reported in financial statements.

Defined Benefit Obligation	−	**Fair Value of Plan Assets (if any)**

The deficit or surplus is often referred to as the funded status of the plan.

If the defined benefit obligation is greater than the plan assets, the pension plan has a deficit. Conversely, if the defined benefit obligation is less than the plan assets, the pension plan has a surplus. Illustration 20-4 shows these relationships.

Deficit		Surplus	
Defined benefit obligation	€(1,000,000)	Defined benefit obligation	€(150,000)
Plan assets	900,000	Plan assets	200,000
Net defined benefit obligation	€ (100,000)	Net defined benefit asset	€ 50,000

ILLUSTRATION 20-4
Presentation of Funded Status

The net defined benefit obligation (asset) is often referred to simply as the pension liability or the pension asset on the statement of financial position.

As indicated, companies should report either a pension asset or pension liability related to a pension plan on the statement of financial position (often referred to as the **net approach**). To illustrate, assume that at year-end Acer Company has a defined benefit obligation of €4,000,000 and plan assets of €3,700,000. In this case, Acer reports €300,000 (€4,000,000 − €3,700,000) as a pension liability on its statement of financial position.

Some believe that companies should report separately both the defined benefit obligation and the plan assets on the statement of financial position. This approach (often referred to as the **gross approach**) would report Acer's defined benefit obligation of €4,000,000 and its plan assets of €3,700,000 on the statement of financial position. The IASB disagrees, indicating that offsetting these amounts is consistent with its standard on when assets and liabilities should be netted.[6]

Reporting Changes in the Defined Benefit Obligation (Asset)

The IASB requires that all changes in the defined benefit obligation and plan assets in the current period be recognized in comprehensive income. This approach reflects application of accrual-based accounting for pensions (expense recognition principle). That is, companies report pension expense as employees work and earn benefits rather than when employees are paid benefits after retirement (referred to as cash basis or pay as you go). The Board believes that immediate recognition of the effects of these changes in the statement of comprehensive income provides the most understandable and useful information to financial statement users. The IASB requires that companies report changes arising from different elements of pension liabilities and assets in different sections of the statement of comprehensive income, depending on their nature.

In the past, companies often reported only a single pension expense number in the comprehensive income statement. Disclosing additional segmentation of the **components of pension cost** provides additional transparency about the nature of these costs. **[7]** The three components are as follows.

- *Service cost.* **Service cost** is either current service cost or past service cost. Current service cost is the increase in the present value of the defined benefit obligation from employee service in the current period. Past service cost is the change in the present value of the defined benefit obligation for employee service for prior periods—generally resulting from a plan amendment (e.g., changes to the plan). This component is reported in the statement of comprehensive income in the operating section of the statement and affects net income.

- *Net interest.* Net interest is computed by multiplying the discount rate by the defined benefit obligation and the plan assets. If the plan has a net defined benefit obligation at the end of the period, the company reports interest expense. Conversely, if it has a net defined benefit asset, it reports interest revenue. This approach is justified on the basis of its simplicity and that any financing costs should be based on the funded status of the plan. This amount is often shown below the operating section of the income statement in the financing section and affects net income.

- *Remeasurements.* Remeasurements are gains and losses related to the defined benefit obligation (changes in discount rate or other actuarial assumptions) and gains or losses on the fair value of the plan assets (actual rate of return less interest revenue included in the finance component). This component is reported in other comprehensive income, net of tax. **These remeasurement gains or losses therefore affect comprehensive income but not net income.**

Illustration 20-5 (page 1019) shows the components of changes in the pension liability (asset) and their placement on the statement of comprehensive income.

---

[6]*IAS 32* states that a financial asset and a financial liability should be offset and the net amount reported in the statement of financial position when a company (a) has a legally enforceable right to set off the recognized amounts and (b) intends either to settle on a net basis, or to realize the asset and settle it simultaneously. **[6]**

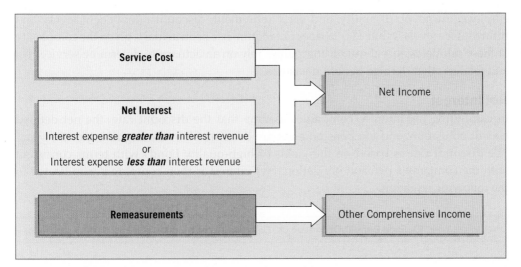

ILLUSTRATION 20-5
Reporting Changes in the
Pension Obligation
(Assets)

As indicated in Illustration 20-5, service cost and net interest are reported in net income. We discuss determination of each of these components in the following section. Remeasurements, which are reported in other comprehensive income, are discussed in a later section.

Service Cost

To determine current service cost and the related increase in the defined benefit obligation, companies must:

1. Apply an actuarial valuation method.
2. Assign benefits to period of service.
3. Make actuarial assumptions.[7]

In applying an actuarial valuation method, the IASB concluded that **companies must consider future compensation levels in measuring the present obligation and periodic pension expense if the plan benefit formula incorporates them**. In other words, the present obligation resulting from a promise to pay a benefit of 1 percent of an employee's **final pay** differs from the promise to pay 1 percent of **current pay**. To overlook this fact is to ignore an important aspect of pension expense. Thus, the Board adopts the **projected unit credit method (often referred to as the benefits/years-of-service method), which determines pension expense based on future salary levels**.

Some object to this determination, arguing that a company should have more freedom to select an expense recognition pattern. Others believe that incorporating future salary increases into current pension expense is accounting for events that have not yet happened. They argue that if a company terminates the plan today, it pays only liabilities for accumulated benefits. **Nevertheless, the IASB indicates that the defined benefit obligation provides a more realistic measure of the employer's obligation under the plan on a going concern basis. Therefore, companies should use it as the basis for determining service cost.**

The assignment of benefits to periods of service is based on the actuarial valuation method. The actuary then allocates the cost of the pension benefits over the expected service life of the company's employees. In determining the proper service cost for a period, the actuary makes assumptions related to such factors as mortality; rates of

---

[7]As indicated earlier, service cost is comprised of current and past service cost. Determination of past service cost is based on the same actuarial valuation model as that used for current service cost. We discuss recognition of past service cost in a later section.

employee turnover, disability, and early retirement; discount rate; benefit levels; and future salary levels. While *IAS 19* does not require use of an actuary, given the complexity of these estimates, just about all companies rely on an actuary to determine service cost and related other defined benefit measures.

Net Interest

In computing net interest, companies assume that the discount rate, the net defined benefit obligation, and the pension asset are determined at the beginning of the year.[8] The **discount rate** is based on the yields of high-quality bonds with terms consistent with the company's pension obligation. Net interest is then computed as indicated in the following equation.

Net Interest = (Defined Benefit Obligation × Discount Rate) − (Plan Assets × Discount Rate)

That is, net interest is determined by multiplying the net defined benefit obligation (asset) by the discount rate. **[9]**

Because payment of the pension obligation is deferred, companies record the pension liability on a discounted basis. As a result, the liability accrues interest over the service life of the employee (passage of time), which is essentially interest expense (**interest on the liability**). Similarly, companies earn a return on their plan assets. That is, a company assumes that it earns interest based on multiplying the discount rate by the plan assets. While the IASB recognizes that the actual return on plan assets may differ from the assumed interest revenue computed, it believes that the change in plan assets can be divided into an amount that arises from the passage of time and amounts that arise from other changes. As we discuss in the next section, changes not related to the passage of time are reported in other comprehensive income as remeasurements. Thus, the growth in the plan assets should mirror the growth in the defined benefit obligation. In other words, the assumed interest revenue on the plan assets based on the passage of time offsets the interest expense on the defined benefit obligation.

In summary, pension expense is comprised of two components: (1) service cost and (2) net interest. Companies report each of these components in the statement of comprehensive income. In some cases, companies may choose to report these components in one section of the statement of comprehensive income as a single amount of total pension expense. Other companies may choose to report the service cost component in operating income and the net interest in a separate section related to financing.[9]

Plan Assets and Actual Return

Pension **plan assets** are usually investments in shares, bonds, other securities, and real estate that a company holds to earn a reasonable rate of return. Plan assets are reported at fair value. Companies generally hold these assets in a separate legal entity (a pension fund) that exists only to administer the employee benefit plan. These assets held by the pension fund are therefore not available to the company's own creditors (even in bankruptcy). Employer contributions and the actual return on plan assets increase pension plan assets. **Actual return on plan assets** is the increase in the pension fund assets arising

---

[8]The IASB indicates that if the beginning of the year amount changes materially (due to contributions to or payments out of the plan), an adjustment to the beginning balances should be made. **[8]** *For homework purposes, unless information indicates that balances have changed materially, use the beginning of the year balances.*

[9]The IASB does not provide guidance on which of these two approaches is preferred. **[10]** *For homework purposes, report pension expense as a single total in income from operations in the statement of comprehensive income.*

from interest, dividends, and realized and unrealized changes in the fair value of the plan. Benefits paid to retired employees decrease plan assets.

To illustrate, assume that Hasbro Company has pension plan assets of €4,200,000 on January 1, 2015. During 2015, Hasbro contributed €300,000 to the plan and paid out retirement benefits of €250,000. Its actual return on plan assets was €210,000 for the year. Hasbro's plan assets at December 31, 2015, are €4,460,000, computed as shown in Illustration 20-6.

Plan assets, January 1, 2015	€4,200,000
Contributions by Hasbro to plan	300,000
Actual return	210,000
Benefits paid to employees	(250,000)
Plan assets, December 31, 2015	€4,460,000

ILLUSTRATION 20-6
Determination of Pension Assets

In some cases, companies compute that actual return by adjusting the change in plan assets for the effect of contributions during the year and benefits paid during the year. The equation in Illustration 20-7, or a variation thereof, can be used to compute the actual return.

$$\text{Actual Return} = \left(\begin{array}{c} \text{Plan Assets Ending Balance} \end{array} - \begin{array}{c} \text{Plan Assets Beginning Balance} \end{array} \right) - (\text{Contributions} - \text{Benefits Paid})$$

ILLUSTRATION 20-7
Equation for Computing Actual Return

Stated another way, the actual return on plan assets is the difference between the fair value of the plan assets at the beginning of the period and the end of the period, adjusted for contributions and benefit payments. Illustration 20-8 uses the equation above to compute actual return, using the information provided in Illustration 20-6.

Plan assets, December 31, 2015		€4,460,000
Plan assets, January 1, 2015		(4,200,000)
Increase in fair value of plan assets		260,000
Deduct: Contributions to plan	€300,000	
Add: Benefit payments to employees	250,000	(50,000)
Actual return		€ 210,000

ILLUSTRATION 20-8
Computation of Actual Return on Plan Assets

In this case, Hasbro has a positive actual return on plan assets. Recently, some pension plans have experienced negative actual returns due to the increased volatility in global securities markets.

USING A PENSION WORKSHEET

We will now illustrate the basic computation of pension expense using the first two components: (1) service cost and (2) net interest. We discuss remeasurements in later sections.

Companies often use a worksheet to record pension-related information. As its name suggests, the worksheet is a working tool. A worksheet is **not** a permanent accounting record. It is neither a journal nor part of the general ledger. The worksheet is merely a device to make it easier to prepare entries and the financial statements.[10] Illustration 20-9 (on page 1022) shows the format of the **pension worksheet**.

5 LEARNING OBJECTIVE
Use a worksheet for employer's pension plan entries.

[10]The use of a pension entry worksheet is recommended and illustrated by Paul B. W. Miller, "The New Pension Accounting (Part 2)," *Journal of Accountancy* (February 1987), pp. 86–94.

ILLUSTRATION 20-9
Basic Format of
Pension Worksheet

	A	B	C	D	E	F
		Pension Worksheet.xls				
		Home Insert Page Layout Formulas Data Review View				
	P18	fx				
	Items	General Journal Entries			Memo Record	
		Annual Pension Expense	Cash	Pension Asset/ Liability	Defined Benefit Obligation	Plan Assets

The "General Journal Entries" columns of the worksheet (near the left side) determine the entries to record in the formal general ledger accounts. The "Memo Record" columns (on the right side) maintain balances in the defined benefit obligation and the plan assets. The difference between the defined benefit obligation and the fair value of the plan assets is the **pension asset/liability**, which is shown in the statement of financial position. If the defined benefit obligation is greater than the plan assets, a pension liability occurs. If the defined benefit obligation is less than the plan assets, a pension asset occurs.

On the first line of the worksheet, a company enters the beginning balances (if any). It then records subsequent transactions and events related to the pension plan using debits and credits, using both sets of columns as if they were one. For each transaction or event, the debits must equal the credits. **The ending balance in the Pension Asset/ Liability column should equal the net balance in the memo record.**

2015 Entries and Worksheet

To illustrate the use of a worksheet and how it helps in accounting for a pension plan, assume that Zarle Company provides the following information related to its pension plan for the year 2015.

- Plan assets, January 1, 2015, are €100,000.
- Defined benefit obligation, January 1, 2015, is €100,000.
- Annual service cost is €9,000.
- Discount rate is 10 percent.
- Funding contributions are €8,000.
- Benefits paid to retirees during the year are €7,000.

Using this data, the worksheet in Illustration 20-10 presents the beginning balances and all of the pension entries recorded by Zarle in 2015. Zarle records the beginning balances for the defined benefit obligation and the pension plan assets on the first line of the worksheet in the memo record. Because the defined benefit obligation and the plan assets are the same at January 1, 2015, the Pension Asset/Liability account has a zero balance at January 1, 2015.

Entry (a) in Illustration 20-10 records the service cost component, which increases pension expense by €9,000 and increases the liability (defined benefit obligation) by €9,000. Entry (b) accrues the interest expense component, which increases both the liability and the pension expense by €10,000 (the beginning defined benefit obligation multiplied by the discount rate of 10 percent). Entry (c) records the interest revenue component, which increases plan assets and decreases pension expense by €10,000. This is computed by multiplying the beginning plan assets by the discount rate of 10 percent. As a result,

ILLUSTRATION 20-10
Pension
Worksheet—2015

	General Journal Entries			Memo Record	
Items	Annual Pension Expense	Cash	Pension Asset/ Liability	Defined Benefit Obligation	Plan Assets
Balance, Jan. 1, 2015			—	100,000 Cr.	100,000 Dr.
(a) Service cost	9,000 Dr.			9,000 Cr.	
(b) Interest expense	10,000 Dr.			10,000 Cr.	
(c) Interest revenue	10,000 Cr.				10,000 Dr.
(d) Contributions		8,000 Cr.			8,000 Dr.
(e) Benefits				7,000 Dr.	7,000 Cr.
Journal entry for 2015	9,000 Dr.	8,000 Cr.	1,000 Cr.*		
Balance, Dec. 31, 2015			1,000 Cr.**	112,000 Cr.	111,000 Dr.
*€9,000 – €8,000 = €1,000					
**€112,000 – €111,000 = €1,000					

interest expense (income) is zero in 2015. Entry (d) records Zarle's contribution (funding) of assets to the pension fund, thereby decreasing cash by €8,000 and increasing plan assets by €8,000. Entry (e) records the benefit payments made to retirees, which results in equal €7,000 decreases to the plan assets and the defined benefit obligation.

Zarle makes the "formal journal entry" on December 31, which records the pension expense in 2015 as follows.

2015

Pension Expense	9,000	
Cash		8,000
Pension Asset/Liability		1,000

The credit to Pension Asset/Liability for €1,000 represents the difference between the 2015 pension expense of €9,000 and the amount funded of €8,000. Pension Asset/ Liability (credit) is a liability because Zarle underfunds the plan by €1,000. The Pension Asset/Liability account balance of €1,000 also equals the net of the balances in the memo accounts. Illustration 20-11 shows that the defined benefit obligation exceeds the plan assets by €1,000, which reconciles to the pension liability reported in the statement of financial position.

Defined benefit obligation (Credit)	€(112,000)
Plan assets at fair value (Debit)	111,000
Pension asset/liability (Credit)	€ (1,000)

ILLUSTRATION 20-11
Pension Reconciliation
Schedule—December 31,
2015

If the net of the memo record balances is a credit, the reconciling amount in the Pension Asset/Liability column will be a credit equal in amount. If the net of the memo record balances is a debit, the Pension Asset/Liability amount will be a debit equal in amount. The worksheet is designed to produce this reconciling feature, which is useful later in the preparation of the financial statements and required note disclosure related to pensions.

In this illustration (for 2015), the debit to Pension Expense exceeds the credit to Cash, resulting in a credit to Pension Asset/Liability—the recognition of a liability. If the credit to Cash exceeded the debit to Pension Expense, Zarle would debit Pension Asset/ Liability—the recognition of an asset.[11]

Past Service Cost

LEARNING OBJECTIVE 6
Explain the accounting for past service costs.

Past service cost (PSC) is the change in the present value of the defined benefit obligation resulting from a plan amendment or a curtailment.[12] For example, a plan amendment arises when a company decides to provide additional benefits to existing employees for past service. Conversely, the company may decide that it is necessary to reduce its benefit package retroactively for existing employees, thereby reducing their pension benefit. A **curtailment** occurs when the company has a significant reduction in the number of employees covered by the plan. Because a curtailment has the same effect as a reduction in benefits due to an amendment to the plan, these situations are accounted for in the same way. Illustration 20-12 summarizes the nature of past service costs.

ILLUSTRATION 20-12
Types of Past Service Costs

PAST SERVICE COSTS (EXPENSE IN CURRENT PERIOD)	
Plan Amendments	Curtailments
• Introduction of a plan. • Withdrawal of a plan. • Changes to a plan.	• Significant reduction in the number of employees covered by the plan.

The accounting for past service cost is straightforward—expense past service cost in the period of the amendment or curtailment. As a result, a substantial increase (decrease) in pension expense and the defined benefit obligation often results when a plan amendment or curtailment occurs. Because current and past service costs relate directly to employment, they are reported in the operating section of the statement of comprehensive income.

Some disagree with the IASB position of expensing these costs in the year a plan is amended or curtailed. They argue that a company would not provide these additional benefits for past years of service unless it expects to receive benefits in the future. According to this reasoning, a company should not recognize the full past service cost in the year of the amendment. Instead, the past service cost should be spread out over the remaining service life of employees who are expected to benefit from the changes in the plan. Others believe that if they are truly past service costs, they should be treated retroactively as an adjustment made to prior periods.

However, the IASB decided that any changes in the defined benefit obligation or plan assets should be recognized in the current period. To do otherwise is not informative and leads to delayed recognition of costs or reduced benefits that are neither assets nor liabilities. **[13]**

It is also possible to decrease past service costs by decreasing the defined benefit obligation (referred to as negative past service cost). Negative past service cost arises when an entity changes the benefits attributable to past service cost so that the present value of the defined benefit obligation decreases. In that case, pension expense is decreased. Both positive (increased pension expense) and negative (decreased pension

[11]The IASB in *IAS 19* limits the amount of a pension asset that is recognized, based on a recoverability test. This test, which has been further clarified in *IFRIC 14*, limits the amount of the pension asset to the sum of unrecognized actuarial gains and losses (discussed later in this chapter) and amounts that will be received by the company in the form of refunds or reduction of future contributions. **[11]** *For purposes of homework, assume that a pension asset, if present, meets the criteria for full recognition.*

[12]The IASB also indicates that gains and losses on non-routine settlements are considered past service costs. **[12]** A **settlement** is a payment of benefits that is not set out in the terms of the plan.

expense) past service cost adjustments are handled in the same manner; that is, adjust pension expense immediately.

2016 Entries and Worksheet

Continuing the Zarle Company illustration into 2016, we note that the company amends the pension plan on January 1, 2016, to grant employees past service benefits with a present value of €81,600. The following additional facts apply to the pension plan for the year 2016.

- Annual service cost is €9,500.
- Discount rate is 10 percent.
- Annual funding contributions are €20,000.
- Benefits paid to retirees during the year are €8,000.

Illustration 20-13 presents a worksheet of all the pension entries and information recorded by Zarle in 2016.

ILLUSTRATION 20-13
Pension Worksheet—2016

	General Journal Entries			Memo Record	
Items	Annual Pension Expense	Cash	Pension Asset/ Liability	Defined Benefit Obligation	Plan Assets
Balance, Dec. 31, 2015			1,000 Cr.	112,000 Cr.	111,000 Dr.
(f) Additional PSC, 1/1/2016	81,600 Dr.			81,600 Cr.	
Balance, Jan. 1, 2016				193,600 Cr.	
(g) Service cost	9,500 Dr.			9,500 Cr.	
(h) Interest expense	19,360 Dr.			19,360 Cr.	
(i) Interest revenue	11,100 Cr.				11,100 Dr.
(j) Contributions		20,000 Cr.			20,000 Dr.
(k) Benefits				8,000 Dr.	8,000 Cr.
Journal entry for 2016	99,360 Dr.	20,000 Cr.	79,360 Cr.		
Balance, Dec. 31, 2016			80,360 Cr.	214,460 Cr.	134,100 Dr.

The first line of the worksheet shows the beginning balances of the Pension Asset/ Liability account and the memo accounts. Entry (f) records Zarle's granting of past service cost, by adding €81,600 to the defined benefit obligation and to Pension Expense. Entry (g) records the current service cost; entry (h) records interest expense for the period. Because the past service cost occurred at the beginning of the year, interest is computed on the January 1, 2016, balance of the defined benefit obligation, adjusted for the past service cost. Interest expense is therefore €19,360 (€193,600 × 10%). Entry (i) records interest revenue for the period of €11,100 (€111,000 × 10%). Entries (j) and (k) are similar to the corresponding entries in 2015.

Zarle makes the following journal entry on December 31 to formally record the 2016 pension expense—the sum of the annual pension expense column.

2016

Pension Expense	99,360	
Cash		20,000
Pension Asset/Liability		79,360

Because the expense exceeds the funding, Zarle credits the Pension Asset/Liability account for the €79,360 difference. That account is a liability. In 2016, as in 2015, the balance of the Pension Asset/Liability account (€80,360) is equal to the net of the balances in the memo accounts, as shown in Illustration 20-14.

ILLUSTRATION 20-14
Pension Reconciliation
Schedule—December 31,
2016

Defined benefit obligation (Credit)	€(214,460)
Plan assets at fair value (Debit)	134,100
Pension asset/liability (Credit)	€ (80,360)

The **reconciliation** is the formula that makes the worksheet work. It relates the components of pension accounting, recorded and unrecorded, to one another.

Remeasurements

LEARNING OBJECTIVE 7

Explain the accounting for remeasurements.

Of great concern to companies that have pension plans are the uncontrollable and unexpected swings that can result from (1) sudden and large changes in the fair value of plan assets and (2) changes in actuarial assumptions that affect the amount of the defined benefit obligation. How should these changes (referred to as **remeasurements**) affect the financial statements, most notably pension expense? The IASB believes that the most informative way is to recognize the remeasurement in other comprehensive income. The rationale for this reporting is that the predictive nature of remeasurements is much different than the other two components of pension benefit cost—service cost and net interest. **[14]**

Remeasurements are generally of two types:

1. Gains and losses on plan assets.
2. Gains and losses on the defined benefit obligation.

Asset Gains and Losses

The gains and losses on plan assets (referred to as **asset gains and losses**) is the difference between the actual return and the interest revenue computed in determining net interest. Asset gains occur when actual returns exceed the interest revenue. Asset losses occur when the actual returns are less than interest revenue. To illustrate, assume that Shopbob Company has plan assets at January 1, 2015, of €100,000. The discount rate for the year is 6 percent, and the actual return on the plan assets for 2015 is €8,000. In 2015, Shopbob should record an asset gain of €2,000, computed as follows.

ILLUSTRATION 20-15
Computation of Asset
Gain

Actual return	€8,000
Less: Interest revenue (€100,000 × 6%)	6,000
Asset gain	€2,000

Shopbob therefore debits plan assets for the asset gain of €2,000 and credits Other Comprehensive Income (G/L) for the same amount. If interest revenue exceeds the actual return, Shopbob debits Other Comprehensive Income (G/L) for the asset loss and credits plan assets.

Liability Gains and Losses

In estimating the defined benefit obligation (the liability), actuaries make assumptions about such items as mortality rate, retirement rate, turnover rate, disability rate, and salary amounts. Any change in these actuarial assumptions affects the amount of the defined benefit obligation. Seldom does actual experience coincide exactly with actuarial predictions. These gains or losses from changes in the defined benefit obligation are called **liability gains and losses**.

Companies report liability gains (resulting from unexpected decreases in the liability balance) and liability losses (resulting from unexpected increases in the liability balance) in Other Comprehensive Income (G/L). Companies combine the liability gains and losses in the same Other Comprehensive Income (G/L) account used for asset gains and losses. They accumulate the asset and liability gains and losses from year to year in Accumulated Other Comprehensive Income.[13] This amount is reported on the statement of financial position in the equity section.

2017 Entries and Worksheet

Continuing the Zarle Company illustration, the following facts apply to the pension plan for 2017.

- Annual service cost is €13,000.
- Discount rate is 10 percent.
- Actual return on plan assets is €12,000.
- Annual funding contributions are €24,000.
- Benefits paid to retirees during the year are €10,500.
- Changes in actuarial assumptions establish the end-of-year defined benefit obligation at €265,000.

The worksheet in Illustration 20-16 presents all of Zarle's 2017 pension entries and related information. The first line of the worksheet records the beginning balances that relate to the pension plan. In this case, Zarle's beginning balances are the ending balances from its 2016 pension worksheet in Illustration 20-13 (page 1025).

ILLUSTRATION 20-16
Pension Worksheet—2017

Pension Worksheet—2017.xls

Home | Insert | Page Layout | Formulas | Data | Review | View

P18   *fx*

	A	B	C	D	E	F	G
1							
2				**General Journal Entries**			**Memo Record**	
3			Annual			Pension	Defined	
4			Pension		OCI—	Asset/	Benefit	
5		Items	Expense	Cash	Gain/Loss	Liability	Obligation	Plan Assets
6	Balance, Jan. 1, 2017					80,360 Cr.	214,460 Cr.	134,100 Dr.
7	(l) Service cost	13,000 Dr.					13,000 Cr.	
8	(m) Interest expense	21,446 Dr.					21,446 Cr.	
9	(n) Interest revenue	13,410 Cr.						13,410 Dr.
10	(o) Contributions		24,000 Cr.					24,000 Dr.
11	(p) Benefits						10,500 Dr.	10,500 Cr.
12	(q) Asset loss			1,410 Dr.				1,410 Cr.
13	(r) Liability loss			26,594 Dr.			26,594 Cr.	
14	Journal entry for 2017	21,036 Dr.	24,000 Cr.	28,004 Dr.	25,040 Cr.			
15								
16	Accumulated OCI, Dec. 31, 2016			0				
17	Balance, Dec. 31, 2017			28,004 Dr.	105,400 Cr.		265,000 Cr.	159,600 Dr.
18								

---

[13]The IASB is silent as to whether the Accumulated Other Comprehensive Income account should be used instead of another equity account, like Retained Earnings. *For homework purposes, use the Accumulated Other Comprehensive Income account.* The IASB also permits the transfer of the balance in the Accumulated Other Comprehensive Income account to other equity accounts at a later date.

Entries (l), (m), (n), (o), and (p) are similar to the corresponding entries in 2015 or 2016. Entries (m) and (n) are related. Entry (m) records the interest expense of €21,446 (€214,460 × 10%). Entry (n) records interest revenue of €13,410 (€134,100 × 10%). Therefore, net interest expense is €8,036 (€21,446 − €13,410.) Entries (o) and (p) are recorded similarly in 2017 as those in 2015 and 2016.

Entries (q) and (r) need additional explanation. As indicated, the actual return on plan assets for 2017 was €12,000. However, as indicated in entry (n), pension expense was decreased €13,410 as a result of multiplying the beginning plan assets by the discount rate to arrive at an assumed interest revenue of €13,410. As a result, Zarle has an asset loss of €1,410 (€13,410 − €12,000) because the assumed interest revenue is greater than the actual return. This asset loss is debited to Other Comprehensive Income (G/L) and credited to plan assets. Pension plan assets are then properly stated at their fair value.

Entry (r) records the change in the defined benefit obligation resulting from the changes in the actuarial assumptions related to this obligation. As indicated in the facts above, the actuary has determined that the ending balance in the defined benefit obligation should be €265,000 at December 31, 2017. However, the balance at December 31, 2017, before any adjustment for actuarial gains and losses related to the defined benefit obligation is €238,406, as shown in Illustration 20-17.

ILLUSTRATION 20-17
Defined Benefit
Obligation Balance
(Unadjusted)

December 31, 2016, DBO balance	€214,460
Service cost [entry (l)]	13,000
Interest expense [entry (m)]	21,446
Benefits paid	(10,500)
December 31, 2017, DBO balance (before liability increases)	€238,406

The difference between the ending balance of €265,000 as determined by the actuary and the present balance of €238,406 is €26,594 (a liability loss on the defined benefit liability). As shown on the worksheet, this liability loss is debited to Other Comprehensive Income (G/L) and credited to the defined benefit obligation. After this worksheet adjustment, the defined benefit obligation is stated at its actuarial value of €265,000. The journal entry to record the information related to the pension plan at December 31, 2017, based on the pension worksheet in Illustration 20-16, is as follows.

Pension Expense	21,036	
Other Comprehensive Income (G/L)	28,004	
Cash		24,000
Pension Asset/Liability		25,040

As the 2017 worksheet indicates, the €105,400 balance in the Pension Asset/Liability account at December 31, 2017, is equal to the net of the balances in the memo accounts. Illustration 20-18 shows this computation.

ILLUSTRATION 20-18
Pension Reconciliation
Schedule—December 31,
2017

Defined benefit obligation (Credit)	€(265,000)
Plan assets at fair value (Debit)	159,600
Pension asset/liability	€(105,400)

Zarle carries the 2017 ending balances for Pension Asset/Liability and Accumulated Other Comprehensive Income forward as the beginning balances for pension plan accounting in 2018. These balances will be adjusted by changes in the defined benefit obligation and plan assets as shown in the prior examples. For example, assume that Zarle's pension plan had the following activity in 2018:

Pension expense	€17,450
Contributions	32,000
Asset gain	13,150
Decrease in Pension Asset/Liability	27,700

The ending balances for the defined benefit obligation and plan assets are €303,560 and €225,860, respectively. These elements are summarized in the partial 2018 pension worksheet shown in Illustration 20-19.

ILLUSTRATION 20-19
Partial Pension
Worksheet—2018

Partial Pension Worksheet—2018.xls

Home | Insert | Page Layout | Formulas | Data | Review | View

P18   *fx*

	A	B	C	D	E	F	G
1			**General Journal Entries**				**Memo Record**	
2							
3		Annual			Pension	Defined	
4		Pension		OCI—	Asset/	Benefit	
5	Items	Expense	Cash	Gain/Loss	Liability	Obligation	Plan Assets
6	Balance, Jan. 1, 2018			28,004 Dr.	105,400 Cr.	265,000 Cr.	159,600 Dr.
7							
8							
9	Journal entry for 2018	17,450 Dr.	32,000 Cr.	13,150 Cr.	27,700 Dr.		
10							
11	Accumulated OCI, Jan. 1, 2018			28,004 Dr.			
12	Balance, Dec. 31, 2018			14,854 Dr.	77,700 Cr.	303,560 Cr.	225,860 Dr.
13							

Focusing on the "Journal Entry" row, in 2018 Zarle records pension expense of €17,450 and a decrease in Pension Asset/Liability of €27,700. The reduction in Pension Asset/Liability is due in part to the asset gain of €13,150 recorded in 2018. As a result, Zarle's 2018 ending balances (which become the 2019 beginning balances) are €77,700 for Pension Asset/Liability and Accumulated Other Comprehensive Income €14,854 (beginning Accumulated OCI of €28,004 − gain of €13,150).

What do the numbers mean?   ROLLER COASTER

The chart below shows what has happened to the financial health of pension plans over the last few years. It is a real roller coaster.

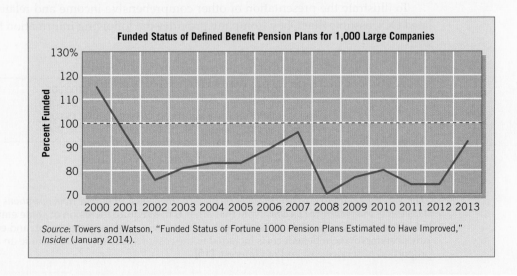

Funded Status of Defined Benefit Pension Plans for 1,000 Large Companies

Source: Towers and Watson, "Funded Status of Fortune 1000 Pension Plans Estimated to Have Improved," *Insider* (January 2014).

At the turn of the century, when the securities market was strong, pension plans were overfunded. However, the bubble burst. By 2002, companies saw their pension plans funded at just 76 percent of reported liabilities. As discussed in the opening story, the funded status of plans bounced back in 2007, declined in the wake of the financial crisis of 2008, and recently is trending up toward fully funded status again.

A number of factors cause a fund to change from being overfunded to underfunded. First, low interest rates decimate returns on pension plan assets. As a result, pension fund assets have not grown; in some cases, they have declined in value. Second, using low interest rates to discount the projected benefit payments leads to a higher pension liability. Finally, more individuals are retiring, which leads to a depletion of the pension plan assets.

Source: D. Zion and A. Varshay, "Strong Returns Didn't Close Pension Funding Gaps Last Year; But So Far So Good This Year," *Credit Suisse Equity Research* (February 5, 2013).

REPORTING PENSION PLANS IN FINANCIAL STATEMENTS

LEARNING OBJECTIVE
Describe the requirements for reporting pension plans in financial statements.

As you might suspect, a phenomenon as significant and complex as pensions involves extensive reporting and disclosure requirements. We will cover these requirements in two categories: (1) those within the financial statements and (2) those within the notes to the financial statements.

Within the Financial Statements

Pension Expense

As indicated earlier, pension expense (service cost and net interest) affects net income and is reported in the statement of comprehensive income. Companies may choose to report these components in one section of the statement of comprehensive income and report total pension expense. Other companies may choose to report the service cost component in operating income and the net interest in a separate section related to financing.[14]

Gains and Losses (Remeasurements)

Asset and liability gains and losses are recognized in other comprehensive income. By recognizing these gains and losses as part of other comprehensive income but not net income, the Board believes that the usefulness of financial statements is enhanced.

To illustrate the presentation of other comprehensive income and related accumulated OCI, assume that Obey Company provides the following information for the year 2015.

Net income for 2015	€100,000
Liability loss for 2015	60,000
Asset loss for 2015	15,000
Accumulated OCI, January 1, 2015	40,000

[14]*For homework purposes, report pension expense as a single total in income from operations in the statement of comprehensive income.* Note that other IFRSs require inclusion of some employee benefit costs within the costs of assets, such as inventories and property, plant, and equipment. Any postemployment benefit costs included in the cost of such assets will include an appropriate proportion of service cost and net interest. **[15]**

Both the liability loss and the asset loss decrease the funded status of the plan on the statement of financial position. This results because the defined benefit obligation increases and the plan assets decrease. However, neither the liability loss nor the asset loss affects pension expense in 2015.

For Obey Company, the computation of "Other comprehensive loss" for 2015 is as follows.

Liability loss	€60,000
Asset loss	15,000
Other comprehensive loss	€75,000

ILLUSTRATION 20-20
Computation of Other Comprehensive Income

The computation of "Comprehensive income" for 2015 is as follows.

Net income	€100,000
Other comprehensive loss	75,000
Comprehensive income	€ 25,000

ILLUSTRATION 20-21
Computation of Comprehensive Income

The components of other comprehensive income must be reported using one of two formats: (1) a two statement approach or (2) a one statement approach (a combined statement of comprehensive income). Regardless of the format used, net income must be added to other comprehensive income to arrive at comprehensive income. *For homework purposes, use the two statement approach unless stated otherwise.* Earnings per share information related to comprehensive income is not required.

To illustrate the two statement approach, assume that Obey Company has reported a traditional income statement. The comprehensive income statement is shown in Illustration 20-22.

OBEY COMPANY		
COMPREHENSIVE INCOME STATEMENT		
FOR THE YEAR ENDED DECEMBER 31, 2015		
Net income		€100,000
Other comprehensive loss		
Liability loss	€60,000	
Asset loss	15,000	75,000
Comprehensive income		€ 25,000

ILLUSTRATION 20-22
Comprehensive Income Reporting

The computation of "Accumulated other comprehensive income" as reported in equity at December 31, 2015, is as follows.

Accumulated other comprehensive income, January 1, 2015	€40,000
Other comprehensive loss	75,000
Accumulated other comprehensive loss, December 31, 2015	€35,000

ILLUSTRATION 20-23
Computation of Accumulated Other Comprehensive Income

Regardless of the display format for the income statement, the accumulated other comprehensive loss is reported in the equity section of the statement of financial position of Obey Company as shown in Illustration 20-24. (Illustration 20-24 uses assumed data for the share capital—ordinary and retained earnings information.)

ILLUSTRATION 20-24
Reporting of
Accumulated OCI

OBEY COMPANY		
STATEMENT OF FINANCIAL POSITION		
AS OF DECEMBER 31, 2015		
(EQUITY SECTION)		
Equity		
Share capital—ordinary	€100,000	
Retained earnings	60,000	
Accumulated other comprehensive loss	35,000	
Total equity	€125,000	

By providing information on the components of comprehensive income as well as total accumulated other comprehensive income, the company communicates all changes in net assets.

The IASB prohibits recycling of other comprehensive income items. Recycling means that other comprehensive income items are reclassified (through amortization) to net income over a period of time. Recycling, for example, is used under U.S. GAAP. The IASB notes that it is difficult to establish a reasonable basis for making these transfers. **[16]** In addition, not adjusting these amounts over time into net income signals that these items have characteristics different than normal revenues and expenses.

Recognition of the Net Funded Status of the Pension Plan

Companies must recognize on their statement of financial position the overfunded (pension asset) or underfunded (pension liability) status of their defined benefit pension plan. The overfunded or underfunded status is measured as the difference between the fair value of the plan assets and the defined benefit obligation.

Classification of Pension Asset or Pension Liability

The IASB does not indicate whether a company should distinguish current and noncurrent portions of assets and liabilities arising from pension benefits. *For homework purposes, assume that no portion of a pension asset is reported as a current asset.* The excess of the fair value of the plan assets over the defined benefit obligation is classified as a non-current asset. The rationale for non-current classification is that the pension plan assets are restricted. That is, these assets are used to fund the defined benefit obligation, and therefore non-current classification is appropriate.

The current portion of a net pension liability represents the amount of benefit payments to be paid in the next 12 months (or operating cycle, if longer) if that amount cannot be funded from existing plan assets. Otherwise, the pension liability is classified as a non-current liability.

Aggregation of Pension Plans

Some companies have two or more pension plans. In such instances, a question arises as to whether these multiple plans should be combined and shown as one amount on the statement of financial position. The Board takes the position that in general pension plans should not be combined. The only situation in which offsetting is permitted is when a company:

(a) Has a legally enforceable right to use a surplus in one plan to settle obligations in the other plan, and

(b) Intends either to settle the obligation on a net basis, or to realize the surplus in one plan and settle its obligations under the other plan simultaneously.

Within the Notes to the Financial Statements

Information on pension plans is frequently important to understanding a company's financial position, results of operations, and cash flows. To increase understanding of pension plans, a company is required to disclose information that: **[17]**

(a) Explains characteristics of its defined benefit plans and risks associated with them.

(b) Identifies and explains the amounts in its financial statements arising from its defined benefit plans.

(c) Describes how its defined benefit plans may affect the amount, timing, and uncertainty of the company's future cash flows.

To meet these requirements, companies provide extensive disclosures related to their defined benefit plans. We focus our discussion on the second objective that requires identifying and explaining the amounts in financial statements arising from defined pension plans. These requirements are summarized in Illustration 20-25.

ILLUSTRATION 20-25
Pension Disclosure Requirements

Amounts reported in the financial statements:

Companies should provide reconciliation from the beginning balance to the ending balance for each of the following:

1. Plan assets.
2. Defined benefit obligation.
3. Funded status of the plan.

This reconciliation should report the following, where appropriate.

- Current service cost.
- Interest revenue or expense.
- Remeasurements of the net defined benefit liability (asset) showing separately (a) the return on plan assets, excluding amounts of interest revenue computed in (2); and (b) actuarial gains and losses arising from changes in the defined benefit obligation.
- Past service cost and curtailments.
- Contributions and payments to the plan.

Information on how the defined benefit plan may affect the amount, timing, and uncertainty of future cash flows:

1. Sensitivity analysis for each significant actuarial assumption, showing how the defined benefit obligation would have been affected by changes in the relevant actuarial assumption that were reasonably possible at the reporting date.
2. Methods and assumptions used in preparing the sensitivity analyses required by (1) and the limitations of those methods.
3. Changes from the previous period in the methods and assumptions used in preparing the sensitivity analyses and the reasons for such changes.
4. Description of any funding arrangements and funding policy that affect future contributions.
5. Expected contributions to the plan for the next annual reporting period.
6. Information about the maturity profile of the defined benefit obligation, including information about the distribution of the timing of benefit payments, such as a maturity analysis of the benefit payments.

Underlying Concepts

This represents another compromise between relevance and faithful representation. Disclosure attempts to balance these objectives.

The reconciliation is a key element of the pension disclosure package. By having a reconciliation of the changes in the assets and liabilities from the beginning of the year to the end of the year, statement readers can better understand the underlying economics of the plan. In essence, this disclosure contains the information in the pension worksheet for the defined benefit obligation and plan asset columns in accordance with *IAS 19* requirements. Using the information for Zarle presented earlier in the chapter, the schedule in Illustration 20-26 provides an example of the reconciliation.

ILLUSTRATION 20-26
Pension Disclosure for
Zarle Company—2015,
2016, 2017

ZARLE COMPANY PENSION DISCLOSURE			
	2015	2016	2017
Change in benefit obligation			
Benefit obligation at beginning of year	€100,000	€112,000	€ 214,460
Service cost	9,000	9,500	13,000
Interest expense	10,000	19,360	21,446
Amendments (Past service cost)	0	81,600	0
Benefits paid	(7,000)	(8,000)	(10,500)
Actuarial loss	0	0	26,594
Benefit obligation at end of year	(112,000)	(214,460)	(265,000)
Change in plan assets			
Fair value of plan assets at beginning of year	100,000	111,000	134,100
Interest revenue	10,000	11,100	13,410
Contributions	8,000	20,000	24,000
Benefits paid	(7,000)	(8,000)	(10,500)
Asset loss	0	0	(1,410)
Fair value of plan assets at end of year	111,000	134,100	159,600
Funded status (Pension asset/liability)	€ (1,000)	€ (80,360)	€(105,400)

The 2015 column reveals that Zarle underfunds the defined benefit obligation by €1,000. The 2016 column reveals that Zarle reports the underfunded liability of €80,360 in the statement of financial position. Finally, the 2017 column indicates that Zarle recognizes the underfunded liability of €105,400 in the statement of financial position.

Other Postretirement Benefits

LEARNING OBJECTIVE 9

Explain the accounting for other postretirement benefits.

In addition to pensions, companies often promise other types of postretirement benefits. The benefits include life insurance outside a pension plan; medical, dental, and eye care; legal and tax services; and so on. Because healthcare benefits are the largest of other postretirement benefits, we provide a general description of how they differ from a traditional pension plan. Illustration 20-27 shows these differences.

ILLUSTRATION 20-27
Differences between
Pensions and
Postretirement
Healthcare Benefits

Item	Pensions	Healthcare Benefits
Funding	Generally funded.	Generally not funded.
Benefit	Well-defined and level dollar amount.	Generally uncapped and great variability.
Beneficiary	Retiree (maybe some benefit to surviving spouse).	Retiree, spouse, and other dependents.
Benefit payable	Monthly.	As needed and used.
Predictability	Variables are reasonably predictable.	Utilization difficult to predict. Level of cost varies geographically and fluctuates over time.

Two of the differences in Illustration 20-27 highlight why measuring the future payments for healthcare benefit plans is so much more difficult than for pension plans.

1. *Many postretirement plans do not set a limit on healthcare benefits.* No matter how serious the illness or how long it lasts, the benefits continue to flow. (Even if the employer uses an insurance company plan, the premiums will escalate according to the increased benefits provided.)

2. *The levels of healthcare benefit use and healthcare costs are difficult to predict.* Increased longevity, unexpected illnesses (e.g., AIDS, SARS, and H1N1 flu), along with new medical technologies and cures, cause changes in healthcare utilization.

Additionally, although the fiduciary and reporting standards for employee benefit funds under government regulations generally cover healthcare benefits, the stringent minimum vesting, participation, and funding standards that apply to pensions do not apply to healthcare benefits. Nevertheless, the basic concepts of pension accounting apply to other postretirement benefits. As a result, the IASB indicates that the accounting and reporting of these other types of postretirement benefits should be the same as that used for pension plan reporting. However, companies with both pension and other postretirement benefit plans must separately disclose the plan details when the plans are subject to materially different risks. **[18]**

Concluding Observations

Hardly a day goes by without the financial press analyzing in depth some issue related to pension plans around the world. This is not surprising since pension funds now hold trillions of dollars, euros, pounds, and yen in assets. As you have seen, the accounting issues related to pension plans are complex. Recent changes to IFRS have clarified many of these issues and should help users understand the financial implications of a company's pension plans on its financial position, results of operations, and cash flows.

What do the numbers mean?	HOW'S YOUR VOLATILITY?

Companies were not required to adopt the changes arising from the amendments to *IAS 19* until 2013. In the period leading up to adoption, many were analyzing the impact on financial statements and the implications for users of financial statements. The following table summarizes some of the key accounting impacts and their consequences—some good, some bad.

Accounting/Financial Reporting Impact	Consequences of the Changes
Potentially **higher pension expense** due to use of a single (usually lower) discount rate to determine return on assets (interest revenue) and recognition of all past service costs in net income.	Could lead to violation of loan covenants or increased bonus payments for performance plans based on net income.
Increased volatility in statement of financial position and shareholders' equity due to recognition of all remeasurements in other comprehensive income.	Could lead to violation of loan covenants based on shareholders' equity and affect regulatory oversight based on share capital.
Reduced net income volatility for companies that previously recognized all gains and losses in net income.	Companies may realize lower cost of capital because less volatility is associated with lower risk.

The reduced net income volatility could be a significant benefit when companies adopt the new rules. For example, the chart on page 1036 indicates that if the new rules would have been applied in the years 1998–2009 (black line), changes in net income would have been much less volatile, compared to net income changes reported under the prior rules (red line). Change can be painful. However, in this case the change to the new rules will likely result in less pain associated with net income volatility.

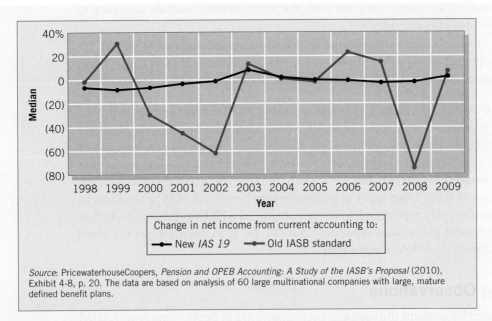

Change in net income from current accounting to:
●— New *IAS 19*   ●— Old IASB standard

Source: PricewaterhouseCoopers, *Pension and OPEB Accounting: A Study of the IASB's Proposal* (2010), Exhibit 4-8, p. 20. The data are based on analysis of 60 large multinational companies with large, mature defined benefit plans.

Not surprisingly, the biggest differences in income under the new and old rules emerge in periods of market decline (e.g., 2000–2002 and 2007–2008). In more stable market periods, there is expected to be minimal difference in reported pension expense. For example, in 2012 **Roche Group** (CHE) indicated that the effect on income would be CHF164 million or just 1 percent of operating profits. The company expects the ongoing impact for 2013 and beyond to be of a similar magnitude.

GLOBAL ACCOUNTING INSIGHTS

POSTRETIREMENT BENEFITS

The underlying concepts for the accounting for postretirement benefits are similar between U.S. GAAP and IFRS—both U.S. GAAP and IFRS view pensions and other postretirement benefits as forms of deferred compensation. At present, there are significant differences in the specific accounting provisions as applied to these plans.

Relevant Facts

Following are the key similarities and differences between U.S. GAAP and IFRS related to pensions.

Similarities

- U.S. GAAP and IFRS separate pension plans into defined contribution plans and defined benefit plans. The accounting for defined contribution plans is similar.

- U.S. GAAP and IFRS recognize a pension asset or liability as the funded status of the plan (i.e., defined benefit obligation minus the fair value of plan assets). (Note that defined benefit obligation is referred to as the projected benefit obligation in U.S. GAAP.)

- U.S. GAAP and IFRS compute unrecognized past service cost (PSC) (referred to as prior service cost in U.S. GAAP) in the same manner.

Differences

- U.S. GAAP includes an asset return component based on the expected return on plan assets. While both U.S. GAAP and IFRS include interest expense on the liability in pension expense, under IFRS for asset returns, pension expense is reduced by the amount of interest revenue (based on the discount rate times the beginning value of pension assets).

- U.S. GAAP amortizes PSC over the remaining service lives of employees, while IFRS recognizes past service cost as a component of pension expense in income immediately.

- U.S. GAAP recognizes liability and asset gains and losses in "Accumulated other comprehensive income" and amortizes these amounts to income over remaining service lives (generally using the "corridor approach"). Under IFRS, companies recognize both liability and asset gains and losses (referred to as remeasurements) in other comprehensive income. These gains and losses are not "recycled" into income in subsequent periods.

- U.S. GAAP has separate standards for pensions and post-retirement benefits, and significant differences exist in the accounting. The accounting for pensions and other postretirement benefit plans is the same under IFRS.

About the Numbers

As indicated, U.S. GAAP and IFRS differ in the amounts included in pension expense. Consider the following pension expense elements for Altidore Company, as measured under U.S. GAAP and IFRS.

	U.S. GAAP	IFRS
Current service cost	€28,000	€28,000
Past service cost	—	30,000
Interest expense	21,000	21,000
Interest revenue	—	(18,000)
Expected return on plan assets	(28,800)	—
Amortization of past service cost (10-year service lives)	3,000	—
Amortization of liability and asset gain/loss	500	—
Pension expense	€23,700	€61,000

Under U.S. GAAP, in determining pension expense, Altidore includes only current service cost, expected return on plan assets (which includes unexpected gains and losses). Gains and losses and past service costs are amortized to income over the service lives of employees. Under IFRS, Altidore includes all service costs and net interest elements in pension expense. Thus, depending on the features of the pension plan (e.g., in a year when past service costs are granted), pension expense can be significantly different between U.S. GAAP and IFRS.

On the Horizon

The IASB and the FASB have been working collaboratively on a postretirement benefit project. The recent amendments issued by the IASB moves IFRS closer to U.S. GAAP with respect to recognition of the funded status on the statement of financial position. However, as illustrated in the "About the Numbers" section above, significant differences remain in the components of pension expense. If the FASB restarts a project to reexamine expense measurement of postretirement benefit plans, it likely will consider the recent IASB amendments in this area.

SUMMARY OF LEARNING OBJECTIVES

1 **Distinguish between accounting for the employer's pension plan and accounting for the pension fund.** The company or employer is the organization sponsoring the pension plan. It incurs the cost and makes contributions to the pension fund. The fund or plan is the entity that receives the contributions from the employer, administers the pension assets, and makes the benefit payments to the pension recipients (retired employees). The fund should be a separate legal and accounting entity; it maintains a set of books and prepares financial statements.

2 **Identify types of pension plans and their characteristics.** The two most common types of pension arrangements are as follows. (1) *Defined contribution plans:* The employer agrees to contribute to a pension trust a certain sum each period based on a formula. This formula may consider such factors as age, length of employee service, employer's profits, and compensation level. Only the employer's contribution is defined; no promise is made regarding the ultimate benefits paid out to the employees. (2) *Defined benefit plans:* These plans define the benefits that the employee will receive at the time of retirement. The formula typically provides for the benefits to be a function of the employee's years of service and the compensation level when he or she nears retirement.

KEY TERMS

accumulated benefit obligation, *1016*

actual return on plan assets, *1020*

actuarial present value, *1016 (n)*

actuaries, *1015*

asset gains and losses, *1026*

benefits/years-of-service method, *1019*

components of pension cost, *1018*

contributory pension plan, *1012*

curtailment, *1024*

defined benefit obligation, *1016*

3 **Explain measures for valuing the pension obligation.** One measure bases the pension obligation only on the benefits vested to the employees. Vested benefits are those that the employee is entitled to receive even if he or she renders no additional services under the plan. Companies compute the *vested benefits pension obligation* using current salary levels; this obligation includes only vested benefits. Another measure of the obligation, called the *accumulated benefit obligation*, computes the deferred compensation amount based on all years of service performed by employees under the plan—both vested and non-vested—using current salary levels. A third measure, called the *defined benefit obligation*, bases the computation of the deferred compensation amount on both vested and non-vested service using future salaries.

4 **Identify amounts reported in financial statements.** In the statement of financial position, companies report the net defined benefit obligation/asset (funded status), which is the defined benefit obligation less the fair value of plan assets (if any). Changes in the net defined benefit obligation (asset) are reported in comprehensive income. Service cost (current and past) and net interest (computed by multiplying the discount rate by the funded status of the plan) are reported in the operating section of comprehensive income. Remeasurements are gains and losses related to the defined benefit obligation (changes in discount rate or other actuarial assumptions) and gains or losses on the fair value of the plan assets. Remeasurements are reported in other comprehensive income.

5 **Use a worksheet for employer's pension plan entries.** Companies may use a worksheet unique to pension accounting. This worksheet records both the formal entries and the memo entries to keep track of all the employer's relevant pension plan items and components.

6 **Explain the accounting for past service costs.** Past service cost is the change in the value of the defined benefit obligation resulting from a plan amendment or a curtailment. Past service costs are expensed in the period of the amendment or curtailment. As a result, a substantial increase (decrease) in pension expense and the defined benefit obligation often results when a plan amendment or curtailment occurs.

7 **Explain the accounting for remeasurements.** Remeasurements arise from (1) gains and losses on plan assets and (2) gains and losses on the defined benefit obligation. The gains and losses on plan assets (asset gain or loss) is the difference between the actual return and the interest revenue computed in determining net interest. Asset gains occur when actual returns exceed the interest revenue. Asset losses occur when the actual returns are less than interest revenue. The gains or losses on the defined benefit obligation (liability gain/loss) are due to changes in actuarial assumptions that affect the amount of the defined benefit obligation. All remeasurements are reported in other comprehensive income. These amounts are not recycled into income in subsequent periods.

8 **Describe the requirements for reporting pension plans in financial statements.** A company reports the pension asset/liability as an asset or a liability in the statement of financial position at the end of a reporting period. The classification as non-current or current follows the general guidelines used for classification of other assets or liabilities. On the income statement (or related notes), the company must report the amount of pension expense for the period. In addition, any actuarial gains or losses charged or credited to other comprehensive income should be reported in the statement of comprehensive income.

In the notes, a company is required to disclose information that (a) explains characteristics of its defined benefit plans and risks associated with them, (b) identifies and explains the amounts in its financial statements arising from its defined benefit plans, and (c) describes how its defined benefit plans may affect the amount, timing, and uncertainty of the company's future cash flows. Important note disclosures are summarized in Illustration 20-25 (page 1033). The reconciliation of the changes in the pension assets and liabilities is a key element of the pension disclosure package.

9 **Explain the accounting for other postretirement benefits.** Companies often provide other types of non-pension postretirement benefits, such as life insurance outside a pension plan, medical care, and legal and tax services. The accounting for these other types of postretirement benefits is the same as that used for pension plan reporting. Companies with both pension and other postretirement benefit plans must separately disclose the plan details when the plans are subject to materially different risks.

IFRS AUTHORITATIVE LITERATURE

Authoritative Literature References

[1] International Accounting Standard 26, *Accounting and Reporting by Retirement Benefit Plans* (London, U.K.: International Accounting Standards Committee Foundation, 2001).

[2] International Accounting Standard 19, *Employee Benefits* (London, U.K.: International Accounting Standards Committee Foundation, 2011), paras. 50–54.

[3] International Accounting Standard 19, *Employee Benefits* (London, U.K.: International Accounting Standards Committee Foundation, 2011), par. 59.

[4] International Accounting Standard 19, *Employee Benefits* (London, U.K.: International Accounting Standards Committee Foundation, 2011), par. 8.

[5] International Accounting Standard 19, *Employee Benefits* (London, U.K.: International Accounting Standards Committee Foundation, 2011), paras. 83–86.

[6] International Accounting Standard 19, *Employee Benefits* (London, U.K.: International Accounting Standards Committee Foundation, 2011), par. 131.

[7] International Accounting Standard 19, *Employee Benefits* (London, U.K.: International Accounting Standards Committee Foundation, 2011), paras. BC70–71 and BC89–90.

[8] International Accounting Standard 19, *Employee Benefits* (London, U.K.: International Accounting Standards Committee Foundation, 2011), par. 123.

[9] International Accounting Standard 19, *Employee Benefits* (London, U.K.: International Accounting Standards Committee Foundation, 2011), paras. 123–124.

[10] International Accounting Standard 19, *Employee Benefits* (London, U.K.: International Accounting Standards Committee Foundation, 2011), par. 134.

[11] International Accounting Standard 19, *Employee Benefits* (London, U.K.: International Accounting Standards Committee Foundation, 2011), par. 64; and IFRIC Interpretation 14, *IAS 19—The Limit on a Defined Benefit Asset, Minimum Funding Requirements and Their Interaction* (2007).

[12] International Accounting Standard 19, *Employee Benefits* (London, U.K.: International Accounting Standards Committee Foundation, 2011), par. BC163.

[13] International Accounting Standard 19, *Employee Benefits* (London, U.K.: International Accounting Standards Committee Foundation, 2011), par. BC70.

[14] International Accounting Standard 19, *Employee Benefits* (London, U.K.: International Accounting Standards Committee Foundation, 2011), par. BC90.

[15] International Accounting Standard 19, *Employee Benefits* (London, U.K.: International Accounting Standards Committee Foundation, 2011), par. 121.

[16] International Accounting Standard 19, *Employee Benefits* (London, U.K.: International Accounting Standards Committee Foundation, 2011), par. BC99.

[17] International Accounting Standard 19, *Employee Benefits* (London, U.K.: International Accounting Standards Committee Foundation, 2011), paras. 135–144.

[18] International Accounting Standard 19, *Employee Benefits* (London, U.K.: International Accounting Standards Committee Foundation, 2011), par. 138.

QUESTIONS

1. What is a pension plan? How does a contributory pension plan differ from a non-contributory plan?

2. Differentiate between a defined contribution pension plan and a defined benefit pension plan. Explain how the employer's obligation differs between the two types of plans.

3. Differentiate between "accounting for the employer" and "accounting for the pension fund."

4. The meaning of the term "fund" depends on the context in which it is used. Explain its meaning when used as a noun. Explain its meaning when used as a verb.

5. What is the role of an actuary relative to pension plans? What are actuarial assumptions?

6. What factors must be considered by the actuary in measuring the amount of pension benefits under a defined benefit plan?

7. Name three approaches to measuring benefits from a pension plan and explain how they differ.

8. Explain how cash-basis accounting for pension plans differs from accrual-basis accounting for pension plans. Why is cash-basis accounting generally considered unacceptable for pension plan accounting?

9. What is the net benefit obligation (asset)? How is the net benefit obligation (asset) reported in the financial statements?

10. What elements comprise changes in the net benefit obligation (asset)? How are these changes reported in the financial statements?

11. Identify the components of pension expense. Briefly explain the nature of each component.

12. What is service cost, and what is the basis of its measurement?

13. What is net interest? Identify the elements of net interest and explain how they are computed.

14. Given the following items and amounts, compute the actual return on plan assets: fair value of plan assets at the beginning of the period $9,200,000; benefits paid during the period $1,400,000; contributions made during the period $1,000,000; and fair value of the plan assets at the end of the period $10,150,000.

15. Explain the difference between service cost and past service cost.

16. What is meant by "past service cost"? When is past service cost recognized as pension expense?

17. What is a pension plan curtailment? Explain the accounting for pension plan curtailments.

18. Sarah is a finance major who has only taken one accounting course. She asserts that pension remeasurements, like many other accounting adjustments, are recorded in net income. Is Sarah correct? Explain.

19. How does an "asset gain or loss" develop in pension accounting?

20. What are "liability gains and losses," and how are they accounted for?

21. If pension expense recognized in a period exceeds the current amount funded by the employer, what kind of account arises, and how should it be reported in the financial statements? If the reverse occurs—that is, current funding by the employer exceeds the amount recognized as pension expense—what kind of account arises, and how should it be reported?

22. Bill Haley is learning about pension accounting. He is convinced that in years when companies record liability gains and losses, total comprehensive income will not be affected. Is Bill correct? Explain.

23. At the end of the current period, Jacob Inc. has a defined benefit obligation of €125,000 and pension plan assets with a fair value of €98,000. The amount of the vested benefits for the plan is €95,000. What amount and account(s) related to its pension plan will be reported on the company's statement of financial position?

24. At the end of the current year, Joshua Co. has a defined benefit obligation of £335,000 and pension plan assets with a fair value of £345,000. The amount of the vested benefits for the plan is £225,000. Joshua has a liability gain of £8,300. What amount and account(s) related to its pension plan will be reported on the company's statement of financial position?

25. Explain the meaning of the following terms.
    (a) Contributory plan.
    (b) Vested benefits.
    (c) Retroactive benefits.

26. Of what value to the financial statement reader is the schedule reconciling the funded status of the plan with amounts reported in the employer's statement of financial position?

27. What are postretirement benefits other than pensions?

28. What are the major differences between postretirement healthcare benefits and pension benefits?

29. Briefly describe some of the similarities and differences between U.S. GAAP and IFRS with respect to the accounting for pensions and other postretirement benefits.

30. Briefly discuss the convergence efforts that are underway with respect to the accounting for pensions and other postretirement benefits.

BRIEF EXERCISES

BE20-1 Assume that **Cathay Pacific Airlines** (CHN) reported the following in a recent annual report (in millions).

Service cost	HK$316
Interest on DBO	342
Interest revenue on plan assets	371

Compute Cathay Pacific's pension expense.

4 **BE20-2** For Becker Corporation, year-end plan assets were €2,000,000. At the beginning of the year, plan assets were €1,680,000. During the year, contributions to the pension fund were €120,000, and benefits paid were €200,000. Compute Becker's actual return on plan assets.

5 **BE20-3** At January 1, 2015, Uddin Company had plan assets of $250,000 and a defined benefit obligation of the same amount. During 2015, service cost was $27,500, the discount rate was 10%, actual return on plan assets was $25,000, contributions were $20,000, and benefits paid were $17,500. Prepare a pension worksheet for Uddin Company for 2015.

4 **BE20-4** For 2015, assume that Wm Morrison Supermarkets plc (GBR) had pension expense of £61 million and contributed £52 million to the pension fund. Prepare Morrison's journal entry to record pension income and funding.

6 **BE20-5** Duesbury Corporation amended its pension plan on January 1, 2015, and granted $120,000 of past service costs to its employees. The employees have an average time to vesting of 4 years. Current service cost for 2015 is $23,000, and net interest expense is $8,000. Compute pension expense for Duesbury in 2015.

6 **BE20-6** Villa Company has experienced tough competition, leading it to seek concessions from its employees in the company's pension plan. In exchange for promises to avoid layoffs and wage cuts, the employees agreed to receive lower pension benefits in the future. As a result, Villa amended its pension plan on January 1, 2015, and recorded negative past service cost of €125,000. The average period to vesting for the benefits affected by this plan is 5 years. Current service cost for 2015 is €26,000. Interest expense is €9,000, and interest revenue is €2,500. Actual return on assets in 2015 is €1,500. Compute pension expense for Villa in 2015.

7 **BE20-7** Refer to the information for Villa Company in BE20-6. Compute the gain or loss on pension plan assets for Villa Company and indicate the accounting and reporting for the asset gains or losses.

7 8 **BE20-8** Hemera Corporation had a defined benefit obligation of R$3,100,000 and plan assets of R$2,900,000 at January 1, 2015. Hemera's discount rate is 6%. In 2015, actual return on plan assets is R$160,000. Hemera contributed R$200,000 to the pension fund and paid benefits of R$150,000. Service cost for 2015 is R$50,000; Hemera reports that the defined benefit obligation at December 31, 2015, is R$3,600,000. Determine (a) pension expense for 2015; (b) pension assets at December 31, 2015; and (c) pension asset and liability gains and losses. Indicate how pension gains and losses will be reported by Hemera in the statement of comprehensive income and the statement of financial position.

8 **BE20-9** Tevez Company experienced an actuarial loss of €750 in its defined benefit plan in 2015. For 2015, Tevez's revenues are €125,000, and expenses (excluding pension expense of €14,000) are €85,000. Prepare Tevez's statement of comprehensive income for 2015.

8 **BE20-10** At December 31, 2015, Conway Corporation had a defined benefit obligation of €510,000 and plan assets of €322,000. Prepare a pension reconciliation schedule for Conway.

9 **BE20-11** Caleb Corporation has the following information available concerning its postretirement medical benefit plan for 2015.

Service cost	$40,000
Interest expense	52,400
Interest revenue	26,900

Compute Caleb's 2015 postretirement expense.

9 **BE20-12** For 2015, Benjamin Inc. computed its annual postretirement expense as £240,900. Benjamin's contribution to the plan during 2015 was £160,000. Prepare Benjamin's 2015 entry to record postretirement expense.

EXERCISES

4 **E20-1 (Pension Expense, Journal Entry)** The following information is available for the pension plan of Radcliffe Company for the year 2015.

Interest revenue on plan assets	$ 15,000
Benefits paid to retirees	40,000
Contributions (funding)	90,000
Discount (interest) rate	10%
Defined benefit obligation, January 1, 2015	500,000
Service cost	60,000

Instructions

(a) Compute pension expense for the year 2015.

(b) Prepare the journal entry to record pension expense and the employer's contribution to the pension plan in 2015.

4 **E20-2 (Computation of Pension Expense)** Veldre Company provides the following information about its defined benefit pension plan for the year 2015.

Service cost	€ 90,000
Contribution to the plan	105,000
Benefits paid	40,000
Plan assets at January 1, 2015	640,000
Defined benefit obligation at January 1, 2015	700,000
Discount (interest) rate	10%

Instructions

Compute the pension expense for the year 2015.

5 **E20-3 (Preparation of Pension Worksheet)** Using the information in E20-2, prepare a pension worksheet inserting January 1, 2015, balances, showing December 31, 2015, balances, and the journal entry recording pension expense.

5 **E20-4 (Basic Pension Worksheet)** The following facts apply to the pension plan of Boudreau Inc. for the year 2015.

Plan assets, January 1, 2015	£490,000
Defined benefit obligation, January 1, 2015	490,000
Discount (interest) rate	8%
Service cost	40,000
Contributions (funding)	25,000
Actual return on plan assets	39,200
Benefits paid to retirees	33,400

Instructions

Using the preceding data, compute pension expense for the year 2015. As part of your solution, prepare a pension worksheet that shows the journal entry for pension expense for 2015 and the year-end balances in the related pension accounts.

4 **E20-5 (Computation of Actual Return)** Gingrich Importers provides the following pension plan information.

Fair value of pension plan assets, January 1, 2015	₺2,400,000
Fair value of pension plan assets, December 31, 2015	2,725,000
Contributions to the plan in 2015	280,000
Benefits paid retirees in 2015	350,000
Discount (interest) rate	7%

Instructions

(a) From the data above, compute the actual return on the plan assets for 2015.

(b) Compute asset gain or loss, and indicate how the gain or loss will be reported.

5 **6** **E20-6 (Basic Pension Worksheet)** The following defined pension data of Yang Corp. apply to the year 2015 (amounts in thousands).

Defined benefit obligation, 1/1/15 (before amendment)	¥560,000
Plan assets, 1/1/15	546,200
Pension liability	13,800
On January 1, 2015, Yang Corp., through plan amendment,	
grants past service benefits having a present value of	120,000
Discount (interest) rate	9%
Service cost	58,000
Contributions (funding)	65,000
Actual return on plan assets	49,158
Benefits paid to retirees	40,000

Instructions

For 2015, prepare a pension worksheet for Yang Corp. that shows the journal entry for pension expense and the year-end balances in the related pension accounts.

5 **8** **E20-7 (Pension Worksheet, Gains and Losses)** Kennedy Company had a defined benefit obligation of $6,300,000 and plan assets of $4,900,000 at January 1, 2015. Kennedy has the following data related to the plan during 2015.

Discount (interest) rate	7%
Service cost	$120,000
Actual return on plan assets	295,000
Contributions	400,000
Benefits paid	300,000

Defined benefit obligation at December 31, 2015, is $6,650,000. There are no accumulated gains or losses at December 31, 2015.

Instructions
   (a) Prepare a pension worksheet for Kennedy Company for 2015.
   (b) Prepare the journal entry to record 2015 pension expense.
   (c) Indicate how pension gains and losses (if any) will be reported by Kennedy in the statement of comprehensive income and the statement of financial position.

8 **E20-8 (Disclosures: Pension Expense and Other Comprehensive Income)** Taveras Enterprises provides the following information related to its defined benefit pension plan.

Balances or Values at December 31, 2015

Defined benefit obligation	€2,737,000
Fair value of plan assets	2,278,329
Accumulated OCI—Net loss (1/1/15 balance, –0–)	34,220
Other pension plan data:	
Service cost for 2015	94,000
Actual return on plan assets in 2015	130,000
Interest on January 1, 2015, defined benefit obligation	164,220
Contributions to plan in 2015	93,329
Benefits paid	140,000
Discount (interest) rate	6%

Instructions
   (a) Prepare the note disclosing the components of pension expense for the year 2015.
   (b) Determine the amounts of other comprehensive income and comprehensive income for 2015. Net income for 2015 is €35,000.
   (c) Compute the amount of accumulated other comprehensive income reported at December 31, 2015.

5 **E20-9 (Pension Worksheet)** Webb Corp. sponsors a defined benefit pension plan for its employees. On January 1, 2015, the following balances relate to this plan.

Plan assets	$480,000
Defined benefit obligation	600,000
Pension asset/liability	120,000
Accumulated OCI	–0–

As a result of the operation of the plan during 2015, the following additional data are provided by the actuary.

Service cost for 2015	$90,000
Discount (interest) rate	6%
Actual return on plan assets in 2015	55,000
Unexpected loss from change in defined benefit obligation, due to change in actuarial predictions	76,000
Contributions in 2015	99,000
Benefits paid retirees in 2015	85,000

Instructions
   (a) Using the data above, compute pension expense for Webb Corp. for the year 2015 by preparing a pension worksheet.
   (b) Prepare the journal entry for pension expense for 2015.

4 **8** **E20-10 (Pension Expense, Journal Entries, Statement Presentation)** Henning Company sponsors a defined benefit pension plan for its employees. The following data relate to the operation of the plan for the year 2015.

   1. The actuarial present value of future benefits earned by employees for services rendered in 2015 amounted to £56,000.

2. The company's funding policy requires a contribution to the pension trustee amounting to £145,000 for 2015.

3. As of January 1, 2015, the company had a defined benefit obligation of £900,000, an accumulated benefit obligation of £800,000, and a balance of £40,000 in accumulated OCI (Loss). The fair value of pension plan assets amounted to £600,000 at the beginning of the year. The discount rate was 9%. Actual return on plan assets was £60,000, and no benefits were paid.

Instructions

(a) Determine the amounts of the components of pension expense that should be recognized by the company in 2015.

(b) Prepare the journal entry or entries to record pension expense and the employer's contribution to the pension trustee in 2015.

(c) Indicate the amounts that would be reported on the income statement and the statement of financial position for the year 2015.

4 6 7 8 E20-11 (Pension Expense, Journal Entries, Statement Presentation) Ferreri Company received the following selected information from its pension plan trustee concerning the operation of the company's defined benefit pension plan for the year ended December 31, 2015.

	January 1, 2015	December 31, 2015
Defined benefit obligation	€1,500,000	€1,527,000
Fair value of plan assets	800,000	1,130,000
Accumulated benefit obligation	1,600,000	1,720,000
Accumulated OCI (G/L)—Net gain	–0–	200,000

The service cost component of pension expense for employee services rendered in the current year amounted to €77,000. The company's actual funding (contributions) of the plan in 2015 amounted to €250,000. The discount (interest) rate was 10%. Assume no benefits paid in 2015.

Instructions

(a) Determine the amounts of the components of pension expense that should be recognized by the company in 2015.

(b) Prepare the journal entry to record pension expense and the employer's contribution to the pension plan in 2015.

(c) Indicate the pension-related amounts that would be reported on the income statement and the statement of financial position for Ferreri Company for the year 2015.

4 7 8 E20-12 (Computation of Actual Return, Gains and Losses, and Pension Expense) Erickson Company sponsors a defined benefit pension plan. The corporation's actuary provides the following information about the plan.

	January 1, 2015	December 31, 2015
Vested benefit obligation	£1,500	£1,900
Accumulated benefit obligation	1,900	2,730
Defined benefit obligation	2,500	3,300
Plan assets (fair value)	1,700	2,620
Discount (interest) rate		10%
Pension asset/liability	800	?
Service cost for the year 2015		400
Contributions (funding in 2015)		700
Benefits paid in 2015		200

Instructions

(a) Compute the actual return on the plan assets in 2015.

(b) Compute the amount of net gain or loss for 2015.

(c) Compute the amount of the other comprehensive income (G/L) as of December 31, 2015. (Assume the January 1, 2015, balance was zero.)

5 E20-13 (Worksheet for E20-12) Using the information in E20-12 about Erickson Company's defined benefit pension plan, prepare a 2015 pension worksheet with supplementary schedules of computations. Prepare the journal entries at December 31, 2015, to record pension expense and related pension transactions. Also, indicate the pension amounts reported in the statement of financial position.

4 **E20-14 (Pension Expense, Journal Entries)** Latoya Company provides the following selected information related to its defined benefit pension plan for 2015.

Pension asset/liability (January 1)	$ 25,000 Cr.
Accumulated benefit obligation (December 31)	400,000
Actual return on plan assets	67,500
Contributions (funding) in 2015	50,000
Discount (interest) rate	10%
Defined benefit obligation (January 1)	700,000
Service cost	80,000

Instructions

(a) Compute pension expense and prepare the journal entry to record pension expense and the employer's contribution to the pension plan in 2015. Preparation of a pension worksheet is not required. Benefits paid in 2015 were $35,000.

(b) Indicate the pension-related amounts that would be reported in the company's statement of comprehensive income and statement of financial position for 2015.

5 **8** **E20-15 (Pension Worksheet—Missing Amounts)** The accounting staff of Usher Inc. has prepared the following pension worksheet. Unfortunately, several entries in the worksheet are not decipherable. The company has asked for your assistance in completing the worksheet and the accounting tasks related to the pension plan for 2015.

	Pension Worksheet—Usher Inc.xls						
Home Insert Page Layout Formulas Data Review View							
P18 fx							
	A	B	C	D	E	F	G
1							
2			**General Journal Entries**			**Memo Record**	
3		Annual			Pension	Defined	
4		Pension		OCI—	Asset/	Benefit	
5	Items	Expense	Cash	Gain/Loss	Liability	Obligation	Plan Assets
6	Balance, Jan. 1, 2015				1,100 Cr.	2,800	1,700
7	Service cost	(1)				500	
8	Interest expense	(2)				280	
9	Interest revenue	(3)					170
10	Contributions		800				800
11	Benefits					200	200
12	Asset gain			(4)			50
13	Liability loss			(5)		365	
14	Journal entry	(6)	(7)	(8)	(9)		
15							
16	Accumulated OCI, Dec. 31, 2014			0			
17	Balance, Dec. 31, 2015			315	1,225	3,745	2,520
18							

Instructions

(a) Determine the missing amounts in the 2015 pension worksheet, indicating whether the amounts are debits or credits.

(b) Prepare the journal entry to record 2015 pension expense for Usher Inc.

9 **E20-16 (Postretirement Benefit Expense Computation)** Kreter Co. provides the following information about its postretirement benefit plan for the year 2015.

Service cost	₱ 45,000
Contribution to the plan	10,000
Actual return on plan assets (at 8%)	8,800
Benefits paid	20,000
Plan assets at January 1, 2015	110,000
Defined postretirement benefit obligation	
at January 1, 2015	330,000
Discount (interest) rate	8%

Instructions

Compute the postretirement benefit expense for 2015.

9 ▶ **E20-17 (Postretirement Benefit Worksheet)** Using the information in E20-16, prepare a worksheet inserting January 1, 2015, balances, and showing December 31, 2015, balances. Prepare the journal entry recording postretirement benefit expense.

9 ▶ **E20-18 (Postretirement Benefit Expense Computation)** Garner Inc. provides the following information related to its postretirement benefits for the year 2015.

Defined postretirement benefit obligation at January 1, 2015	$710,000
Actual return on plan assets (at 10%)	34,000
Discount (interest) rate	10%
Service cost	83,000

Instructions

Compute postretirement benefit expense for 2015.

9 ▶ **E20-19 (Postretirement Benefit Expense Computation)** Englehart Co. provides the following information about its postretirement benefit plan for the year 2015.

Service cost	€ 90,000
Contribution to the plan	56,000
Actual return on plan assets	62,000
Benefits paid	40,000
Plan assets at January 1, 2015	710,000
Defined postretirement benefit obligation at January 1, 2015	760,000
Accumulated OCI (Loss) at January 1, 2015	100 Dr.
Discount (interest) rate	9%

Instructions

Compute the postretirement benefit expense for 2015.

9 ▶ **E20-20 (Postretirement Benefit Worksheet)** Using the information in E20-19, prepare a worksheet inserting January 1, 2015, balances, showing December 31, 2015, balances, and the journal entry recording postretirement benefit expense.

9 ▶ **E20-21 (Postretirement Benefit Worksheet—Missing Amounts)** The accounting staff of Holder Inc. has prepared the following postretirement benefit worksheet. Unfortunately, several entries in the worksheet are not decipherable. The company has asked your assistance in completing the worksheet and completing the accounting tasks related to the pension plan for 2015.

			Postretirement Benefit Worksheet—Holder Inc.xls			
				General Journal Entries		Memo Record

	A	B	C	D	E	F	G
1				**General Journal Entries**		**Memo Record**	
2							
3				Other			
4		Annual		Comprehensive	Postretirement		
5	Items	Expense	Cash	Income—(G/L)	Asset/Liability	DPBO	Plan Assets
6	Balance, Jan. 1, 2015				290,000	410,000	120,000
7	Service cost	(1)				56,000	
8	Interest expense	(2)				36,900	
9	Interest revenue	(3)					10,800
10	Contributions		66,000				(4)
11	Benefits					5,000	5,000
12	Asset loss			8,800			(5)
13	Journal entry for 2015	(6)	(7)	(8)	(9)		
14							
15	Accumulated OCI, Dec. 31, 2014			18,200 Dr.			
16	Balance, Dec. 31, 2015			27,000 Dr.	314,900 Cr.	497,900 Cr.	183,000 Dr.
17							

Instructions

(a) Determine the missing amounts in the 2015 postretirement worksheet, indicating whether the amounts are debits or credits.

(b) Prepare the journal entry to record 2015 postretirement expense for Holder Inc.

(c) What discount rate is Holder using in accounting for the interest on its other postretirement benefit plan? Explain.

PROBLEMS

5 7 8 **P20-1 (2-Year Worksheet)** On January 1, 2015, Harrington Company has the following defined benefit pension plan balances.

Defined benefit obligation	€4,500,000
Fair value of plan assets	4,200,000

The interest (settlement) rate applicable to the plan is 10%. On January 1, 2016, the company amends its pension agreement so that past service costs of €500,000 are created. Other data related to the pension plan are as follows.

	2015	2016
Service cost	€150,000	€180,000
Contributions (funding) to the plan	240,000	285,000
Benefits paid	200,000	280,000
Actual return on plan assets	420,000	260,000

Instructions

(a) Prepare a pension worksheet for the pension plan for 2015 and 2016.

(b) For 2016, prepare the journal entry to record pension-related amounts.

5 6 7 8 **P20-2 (3-Year Worksheet, Journal Entries, and Reporting)** Jackson Company adopts acceptable accounting for its defined benefit pension plan on January 1, 2014, with the following beginning balances: plan assets $200,000 and defined benefit obligation $250,000. Other data relating to 3 years' operation of the plan are shown below.

	2014	2015	2016
Annual service cost	$16,000	$19,000	$26,000
Discount (interest) rate	10%	10%	10%
Actual return on plan assets	20,000	22,000	24,000
Annual funding (contributions)	16,000	40,000	48,000
Benefits paid	14,000	16,400	21,000
Past service cost (plan amended, 1/1/15)		160,000	
Change in actuarial assumptions establishes a December 31, 2016, defined benefit obligation of:			520,000

Instructions

(a) Prepare a pension worksheet presenting all 3 years' pension balances and activities.

(b) Prepare the journal entries (from the worksheet) to reflect all pension plan transactions and events at December 31 of each year.

(c) Indicate the pension-related amounts reported in the financial statements for 2016.

6 7 8 **P20-3 (Pension Expense, Journal Entries)** Gottschalk Company sponsors a defined benefit plan for its 100 employees. On January 1, 2015, the company's actuary provided the following information.

Pension plan assets (fair value and market-related asset value)	£200,000
Accumulated benefit obligation	260,000
Defined benefit obligation	380,000

The average remaining service period for the participating employees is 10 years. All employees are expected to receive benefits under the plan. On December 31, 2015, the actuary calculated that the present value of future benefits earned for employee services rendered in the current year amounted to £52,000; the defined benefit obligation was £490,000, fair value of pension assets was £276,000, and the accumulated benefit obligation amounted to £365,000. The discount (interest) rate is 10%. The actual return on plan assets is £11,000. The company's current year's contribution to the pension plan amounted to £65,000. No benefits were paid during the year.

Instructions

(a) Determine the components of pension expense that the company would recognize in 2015. (With only one year involved, you need not prepare a worksheet.)

(b) Prepare the journal entry to record the pension expense and the company's funding of the pension plan in 2015.

(c) Compute the amount of the 2015 increase/decrease in gains or losses.

(d) Indicate the pension amounts reported in the financial statement as of December 31, 2015.

5 7 P20-4 (Pension Expense, Journal Entries for 2 Years) Gordon Company sponsors a defined benefit pension plan. The following information related to the pension plan is available for 2015 and 2016.

	2015	2016
Plan assets (fair value), December 31	$699,000	$849,000
Defined benefit obligation, January 1	700,000	800,000
Pension asset/liability, January 1	140,000 Cr.	?
Service cost	60,000	90,000
Actual return on plan assets	24,000	30,000
Contributions (funding)	115,000	120,000
Accumulated benefit obligation, December 31	500,000	550,000
Discount (interest) rate	9%	9%

Instructions

(a) Compute pension expense for 2015 and 2016.

(b) Prepare the journal entries to record the pension expense and the company's funding of the pension plan for both years.

7 P20-5 (Computation of Pension Expense, Journal Entries for 3 Years) Hiatt Toothpaste Company initiates a defined benefit pension plan for its 50 employees on January 1, 2015. The insurance company which administers the pension plan provided the following selected information for the years 2015, 2016, and 2017.

	For Year Ended December 31,		
	2015	2016	2017
Plan assets (fair value)	€50,000	€ 85,000	€180,000
Vested benefit obligation	45,000	165,000	292,000
Defined benefit obligation	60,000	200,000	324,000
Net (gain) loss	–0–	78,900	5,800
Employer's funding contribution (made at end of year)	50,000	60,000	105,000

There were no balances as of January 1, 2015, when the plan was initiated. The actual return on plan assets was 10% over the 3-year period, but the discount (interest) rate was 13% in 2015, 11% in 2016, and 8% in 2017. The service cost component of net periodic pension expense amounted to the following: 2015, €60,000; 2016, €85,000; and 2017, €119,000. No benefits were paid in 2015, €30,000 of benefits were paid in 2016, and €18,500 of benefits were paid in 2017 (all benefits paid at end of year).

Instructions

(Round to the nearest euro.)

(a) Calculate the amount of net periodic pension expense that the company would recognize in 2015, 2016, and 2017.

(b) Prepare the journal entries to record net periodic pension expense, employer's funding contribution, and related pension amounts for the years 2015, 2016, and 2017.

4 7 P20-6 (Pension Expense, Journal Entries, and Net Gain or Loss) Aykroyd Inc. has sponsored a non-contributory, defined benefit pension plan for its employees since 1989. Prior to 2015, cumulative net pension expense recognized equaled cumulative contributions to the plan. Other relevant information about the pension plan on January 1, 2015, is as follows.

1. The company has 200 employees. All these employees are expected to receive benefits under the plan.

2. The defined benefit obligation amounted to $5,000,000 and the fair value of pension plan assets was $3,000,000. The market-related asset value was also $3,000,000.

On December 31, 2015, the defined benefit obligation and the vested benefit obligation were $4,850,000 and $4,025,000, respectively. The fair value of the pension plan assets amounted to $4,100,000 at the end of the year. A 10% discount rate was used in the actuarial present value computations in the pension plan. The present value of benefits attributed by the pension benefit formula to employee service in 2015 amounted to $200,000. The employer's contribution to the plan assets amounted to $775,000 in 2015. This problem assumes no payment of pension benefits.

Instructions

(Round all amounts to the nearest dollar.)

(a) Compute pension expense for the year 2015.
(b) Prepare the journal entries required to report the accounting for the company's pension plan for 2015.
(c) Compute the amount of the 2015 increase/decrease in net gains or losses in 2015.

P20-7 (Pension Worksheet) Hanson Corp. sponsors a defined benefit pension plan for its employees. On January 1, 2015, the following balances related to this plan.

Plan assets (fair value)	£520,000
Defined benefit obligation	700,000
Pension asset/liability	180,000 Cr.
Accumulated net gain (loss)	91,000

As a result of the operation of the plan during 2015, the actuary provided the following additional data on December 31, 2015.

Service cost for 2015	£108,000
Discount (interest) rate	9%
Actual return on plan assets in 2015	48,000
Contributions in 2015	133,000
Benefits paid retirees in 2015	85,000

Instructions

Using the preceding data, compute pension expense for Hanson Corp. for the year 2015 by preparing a pension worksheet that shows the journal entry for pension expense.

P20-8 (Comprehensive 2-Year Worksheet) Lemke Company sponsors a defined benefit pension plan for its employees. The following data relate to the operation of the plan for the years 2015 and 2016.

	2015	2016
Defined benefit obligation, January 1	R600,000	
Plan assets (fair value), January 1	410,000	
Pension asset/liability, January 1	190,000 Cr.	
Service cost	40,000	R 59,000
Discount (interest) rate	10%	10%
Actual return on plan assets	36,000	61,000
Annual contributions	97,000	81,000
Benefits paid retirees	31,500	54,000
Increase in defined benefit obligation due to changes in actuarial assumptions	87,000	–0–
Accumulated benefit obligation at December 31	721,800	789,000
Vested benefit obligation at December 31		464,000

Instructions

(a) Prepare a pension worksheet presenting both years 2015 and 2016.
(b) Prepare the journal entries (from the worksheet) to reflect all pension plan transactions and events at December 31 of each year.
(c) For 2016, indicate the pension amounts reported in the financial statements.

P20-9 (Comprehensive 2-Year Worksheet) Hobbs Co. has the following defined benefit pension plan balances on January 1, 2015.

Defined benefit obligation	€4,600,000
Fair value of plan assets	4,600,000

The discount (interest) rate applicable to the plan is 10%. On January 1, 2016, the company amends its pension agreement so that past service costs of €600,000 are created. Other data related to the pension plan are as follows.

	2015	2016
Service cost	€150,000	€170,000
Contributions (funding) to the plan	200,000	184,658
Benefits paid	220,000	280,000
Actual return on plan assets	252,000	350,000

Instructions

(a) Prepare a pension worksheet for the pension plan in 2015.

(b) Prepare any journal entries related to the pension plan that would be needed at December 31, 2015.

(c) Prepare a pension worksheet for 2016 and any journal entries related to the pension plan as of December 31, 2016.

(d) Indicate the pension-related amounts reported in the 2016 financial statements.

5 7 **P20-10 (Pension Worksheet—Missing Amounts)** Kramer Co. has prepared the following pension worksheet. Unfortunately, several entries in the worksheet are not decipherable. The company has asked your assistance in completing the worksheet and completing the accounting tasks related to the pension plan for 2015.

Pension Worksheet—Kramer Co.xls

Home   Insert   Page Layout   Formulas   Data   Review   View

P18   fx

	A	B	C	D	E	F	G
1							
2			General Journal Entries			Memo Record	
3		Annual			Pension	Defined	
4		Pension		OCI—	Asset/	Benefit	
5	Items	Expense	Cash	Gain/Loss	Liability	Obligation	Plan Assets
6	Balance, Jan. 1, 2015				120,000 Cr.	325,000 Cr.	205,000 Dr.
7	Service cost	(1)				20,000 Cr.	
8	Interest expense	(2)				26,000 Cr.	
9	Interest revenue	(3)					16,400 Dr.
10	Contributions		41,000 Cr.				41,000 Dr.
11	Benefits					15,000 Dr.	15,000 Cr.
12	Asset gain			(4)			1,600 Dr.
13	Liability loss			(5)		43,500 Cr.	
14	Journal entry for 2015	(6)	(7)	(8)	(9)		
15	Accumulated OCI, Dec. 31, 2014			0			
16	Balance, Dec. 31, 2015			41,900	150,500 Cr.	399,500 Cr.	249,000 Dr.
17							

Instructions

(a) Determine the missing amounts in the 2015 pension worksheet, indicating whether the amounts are debits or credits.

(b) Prepare the journal entry to record 2015 pension expense for Kramer Co.

(c) Determine for Kramer for 2015 the discount rate used to determine interest expense/revenue.

5 7 **P20-11 (Pension Worksheet)** The following data relate to the operation of Kramer Co.'s pension plan in **8** 2016. The pension worksheet for 2015 is provided in P20-10.

Service cost	$59,000
Actual return on plan assets	32,000
Annual contributions	51,000
Benefits paid retirees	27,000

For 2016, Kramer will use a discount rate of 8%.

Instructions

(a) Prepare a pension worksheet for 2016.

(b) Prepare the journal entries (from the worksheet) to reflect all pension plan transactions and events at December 31.

(c) Indicate the pension amounts reported in the financial statements.

P20-12 (Pension Worksheet) Chen Corp. sponsors a defined benefit pension plan for its employees. On January 1, 2015, the following balances related to this plan (amounts in thousands).

Plan assets (market-related value)	¥270,000
Defined benefit obligation	340,000
Pension asset/liability	70,000 Cr.
OCI—Loss	39,000

As a result of the operation of the plan during 2015, the actuary provided the following additional data at December 31, 2015.

Service cost for 2015	¥45,000
Actual return on plan assets in 2015	27,000
Contributions in 2015	65,000
Benefits paid retirees in 2015	41,000
Discount (interest) rate	7%

Instructions

(a) Compute pension expense for Chen Corp. for the year 2015 by preparing a pension worksheet that shows the journal entry for pension expense.

(b) Indicate the pension amounts reported in the financial statements.

 P20-13 (Postretirement Benefit Worksheet) Hollenbeck Foods Inc. sponsors a postretirement medical and dental benefit plan for its employees. The following balances relate to this plan on January 1, 2015.

Plan assets	$200,000
Defined postretirement benefit obligation	200,000

As a result of the plan's operation during 2015, the following additional data are provided by the actuary.

Service cost for 2015 is $70,000
Discount (interest) rate is 10%
Contributions to plan in 2015 are $65,000
Actual return on plan assets is $15,000
Benefits paid to employees are $44,000

Instructions

(a) Using the preceding data, compute the net periodic postretirement benefit cost for 2015 by preparing a worksheet that shows the journal entry for postretirement expense and the year-end balances in the related postretirement benefit memo accounts. (Assume that contributions and benefits are paid at the end of the year.)

(b) Prepare any journal entries related to the postretirement plan for 2015 and indicate the postretirement amounts reported in the financial statements for 2015.

P20-14 (Postretirement Benefit Worksheet—2 Years) Elton Co. has the following postretirement benefit plan balances on January 1, 2015.

Defined postretirement benefit obligation	€2,250,000
Fair value of plan assets	2,250,000

The discount (interest) rate applicable to the plan is 10%. On January 1, 2016, the company amends the plan so that past service costs of €175,000 are created. Other data related to the plan are as follows.

	2015	2016
Service costs	€ 75,000	€ 85,000
Contributions (funding) to the plan	45,000	35,000
Benefits paid	40,000	45,000
Actual return on plan assets	140,000	120,000

Instructions

(a) Prepare a worksheet for the postretirement plan in 2015.

(b) Prepare any journal entries related to the postretirement plan that would be needed at December 31, 2015.

(c) Prepare a worksheet for 2016 and any journal entries related to the postretirement plan as of December 31, 2016.

(d) Indicate the postretirement-benefit–related amounts reported in the 2016 financial statements.

CONCEPTS FOR ANALYSIS

CA20-1 (Pension Terminology and Theory) Since the late 1800s, many business organizations have been concerned with providing for the retirement of their employees. During recent decades, a marked increase in this concern has resulted in the establishment of pension plans in most large companies and in many medium- and small-sized ones.

The substantial growth of these plans, both in numbers of employees covered and in amounts of retirement benefits, has increased the significance of pension cost in relation to the financial position, results of operations, and cash flows of many companies. In examining the costs of pension plans, a public accountant encounters certain terms. The components of pension costs that the terms represent must be dealt with appropriately if IFRS is to be reflected in the financial statements of entities with pension plans.

Instructions
- **(a)** Define a pension plan. How does a contributory pension plan differ from a non-contributory plan?
- **(b)** Differentiate between "accounting for the employer" and "accounting for the pension fund."
- **(c)** Explain the terms "funded" and "pension liability" as they relate to:
  - **(1)** The pension fund.
  - **(2)** The employer.
- **(d)** **(1)** Discuss the theoretical justification for accrual recognition of pension costs.
  - **(2)** Discuss the relative objectivity of the measurement process of accrual versus cash (pay-as-you-go) accounting for annual pension costs.
- **(e)** Distinguish among the following as they relate to pension plans.
  - **(1)** Service cost.
  - **(2)** Past service costs.
  - **(3)** Vested benefits.

CA20-2 (Pension Terminology) The following items appear on Hollingsworth Company's financial statements.

1. Under the caption Assets:
   Pension asset/liability.

2. Under the caption Liabilities:
   Pension asset/liability.

3. Under the caption Equity:
   Asset loss as a component of Accumulated Other Comprehensive Income.

4. On the income statement:
   Pension expense.

Instructions
Explain the significance of each of the items above on corporate financial statements. (*Note:* All items set forth above are not necessarily to be found on the statements of a single company.)

CA20-3 (Basic Terminology) In examining the costs of pension plans, Leah Hutcherson, public accountant, encounters certain terms. The components of pension costs that the terms represent must be dealt with appropriately if IFRS is to be reflected in the financial statements of entities with pension plans.

Instructions
- **(a)** **(1)** Explain the application of accrual concepts to recognition of pension costs.
  - **(2)** Discuss the relative verifiability and neutrality of the measurement process of accrual versus cash (pay-as-you-go) accounting for annual pension costs.
- **(b)** Explain the following terms as they apply to accounting for pension plans.
  - **(1)** Fair value of pension assets.
  - **(2)** Defined benefit obligation.
  - **(3)** Net interest.
- **(c)** What information should be disclosed about a company's pension plans in its financial statements and its notes?

CA20-4 (Major Pension Concepts) Lyons Corporation is a medium-sized manufacturer of paperboard containers and boxes. The corporation sponsors a non-contributory, defined benefit pension plan that covers its 250 employees. Tim Shea has recently been hired as president of Lyons Corporation. While reviewing last year's financial statements with Anita Kroll, controller, Shea expressed confusion about several of the items in the footnote to the financial statements relating to the pension plan. In part, the footnote reads as follows.

> **Note J.** The company has a defined benefit pension plan covering substantially all of its employees. The benefits are based on years of service and the employee's compensation during the last four years of employment. The company's funding policy is to contribute annually the maximum amount allowed under the tax law. Contributions are intended to provide for benefits expected to be earned in the future as well as those earned to date.

The net periodic pension expense on Lyons Corporation's comparative income statement was £72,000 in 2016 and £57,680 in 2015.

The following are selected figures from the plan's funded status and amounts recognized in the Lyons Corporation's statement of financial position at December 31, 2016 (amounts in thousands).

Defined benefit obligation	£(1,200)
Plan assets at fair value	1,050
Defined benefit obligation in excess of plan assets	£ (150)

Given that Lyons Corporation's workforce has been stable for the last 6 years, Shea could not understand the increase in the net periodic pension expense. Kroll explained that the net periodic pension expense consists of several elements, some of which may increase or decrease the net expense.

Instructions
  (a) The determination of the net periodic pension expense is a function of two elements. List and briefly describe each of the elements.
  (b) Describe the major difference and the major similarity between the vested benefit obligation and the defined benefit obligation.
  (c) (1) Explain why pension gains and losses are not recognized in net income in the period in which they arise.
      (2) Briefly describe how pension gains and losses are recognized.

CA20-5 (Implications of *International Accounting Standard No. 19*) Ruth Moore and Carl Nies have to do a class presentation on the pension pronouncement "Employee Benefits." In developing the class presentation, they decided to provide the class with a series of questions related to pensions and then discuss the answers in class. Given that the class has all read *IAS 19*, they felt this approach would provide a lively discussion. Here are the situations:

  1. In an article prior to the recent amendments to *IAS 19*, it was reported that the discount rates used by the largest 200 companies for pension reporting ranged from 5% to 11%. How can such a situation exist, and does the pension pronouncement alleviate this problem?

  2. An article indicated that when *IAS 19* was issued, it caused an increase in the liability for pensions for a significant number of companies. Why might this situation occur?

  3. A recent article noted that most gains and losses are recognized in net income. However, pension accounting has long been recognized as an exception—an area of accounting in which at least some dampening of market swings is appropriate. This is because pension funds are managed so that their performance is insulated from the extremes of short-term market swings. A pension expense that reflects the volatility of market swings might, for that reason, convey information of little relevance. Are these statements true?

  4. Many companies held assets twice as large as they needed to fund their pension plans at one time. Are these assets reported on the statement of financial position of these companies per the pension pronouncement? If not, where are they reported?

  5. Understanding the impact of the changes required in pension reporting requires detailed information about its pension plan(s) and an analysis of the relationship of many factors, particularly:
     (a) The type of plan(s) and any significant amendments.
     (b) The plan participants.
     (c) The funding status.
     (d) The actuarial funding method and assumptions currently used.
     What impact does each of these items have on financial statement presentation?

Instructions

What answers do you believe Ruth and Carl gave to each of these questions?

CA20-6 (Non-Vested Employees—An Ethical Dilemma) Cardinal Technology recently merged with College Electronix (CE), a computer graphics manufacturing firm. In performing a comprehensive audit of CE's accounting system, Richard Nye, internal audit manager for Cardinal Technology, discovered that the new subsidiary did not capitalize pension assets and liabilities, subject to the requirements of IFRS.

The fair value of CE's pension assets was $15.5 million, the vested benefit obligation was $12.9 million, and the defined benefit obligation was $17.4 million. Nye reported this audit finding to Renée Selma, the newly appointed controller of CE. A few days later, Selma called Nye for his advice on what to do. Selma started her conversation by asking, "Can't we eliminate the negative income effect of our pension dilemma simply by terminating the employment of non-vested employees before the end of our fiscal year?"

Instructions

How should Nye respond to Selma's remark about firing non-vested employees?

USING YOUR JUDGMENT

FINANCIAL REPORTING PROBLEM

Marks and Spencer plc (M&S)

The financial statements of M&S (GBR) are presented in Appendix A. The company's complete annual report, including the notes to the financial statements, is available online.

Instructions

Refer to M&S's financial statements and the accompanying notes to answer the following questions.

(a) What kind of pension plan does M&S provide its employees?
(b) What was M&S's pension expense for 2013 and 2012?
(c) What is the impact of M&S's pension plans for 2013 on its financial statements?
(d) What information does M&S provide on the target allocation of its pension assets? How do the allocations relate to the expected returns on these assets?

Comparative Analysis Case

adidas and Puma

The financial statements of adidas (DEU) and Puma (DEU) are presented in Appendices B and C, respectively. The complete annual reports, including the notes to the financial statements, are available online.

Instructions

Use the companies' financial information to answer the following questions related to adidas and Puma.

(a) What kind of pension plans do adidas and Puma provide their employees?
(b) What net periodic pension expense (cost) did adidas and Puma report in 2012?
(c) What is the year-end 2012 funded status of adidas's and Puma's plans?
(d) What relevant rates were used by adidas and Puma in computing their pension amounts?
(e) Compare the expected benefit payments and contributions for adidas and Puma.

International Reporting Case

Walgreens (USA) is the leading drug store chain in the United States. The company provided the following disclosures related to its retirement benefits in its 2013 annual report.

Walgreens

15. Retirement Benefits (in part)

The principal retirement plan for employees is the Walgreen Profit-Sharing Retirement Plan, to which both the Company and the employees contribute.

The Company provides certain health insurance benefits for retired employees who meet eligibility requirements, including age, years of service and date of hire. The costs of these benefits are accrued over the service life of the employee. The Company's postretirement health benefit plans are not funded.

Components of net periodic benefit costs (*In millions*):

	2013	2012
Service cost	9	13
Interest cost	14	22
Amortization of actuarial loss	12	8
Amortization of prior service cost	−22	−10
Total postretirement benefit cost	13	33

Change in benefit obligation (*In millions*):

	2013	2012
Benefit obligation at September 1	342	407
Service cost	9	13
Interest cost	14	22
Amendments	0	−139
Actuarial (gain)/loss	−1	52
Benefit payments	−20	−18
Participants contributions	6	5
Benefit obligation at August 31	350	342

Change in plan assets (*In millions*):

	2013	2012
Plan assets at fair value at September 1	0	0
Plan participants contributions	6	5
Employer contributions	14	13
Benefits paid	−20	−18
Plan assets at fair value at August 31	0	0

Funded status (*In millions*):

	2013	2012
Funded status	−350	−342
Unrecognized actuarial gain	0	0
Unrecognized prior service cost	0	0
Accrued benefit cost at August 31	−350	−342

Amounts recognized in the Consolidated Balance Sheets (*In millions*):

	2013	2012
Current liabilities (present value of expected 2014 net benefit payments)	−10	−10
Non-current liabilities	−340	−332
Net liability recognized at August 31	−350	−342

Amounts recognized in accumulated other comprehensive loss (*In millions*):

	2013	2012
Prior service credit	−228	−250
Net actuarial loss	148	161

Amounts expected to be recognized as components of net periodic costs for fiscal year 2014 (*In millions*):

	2014
Prior service credit	−22
Net actuarial loss	11

The discount rate assumption used to compute the postretirement benefit obligation at year-end was 5.2% for 2013 and 4.15% for 2012. The discount rate assumption used to determine net periodic benefit cost was 4.15%, 5.40% and 4.95% for fiscal years ending 2013, 2012 and 2011, respectively.

Instructions

Use the information on Walgreens to respond to the following requirements.

(a) What are the key differences in accounting for pensions under U.S. GAAP and IFRS?

(b) Briefly explain how differences in U.S. GAAP and IFRS for pensions would affect the amounts reported in the financial statements.

(c) In light of the differences identified in (b), would Walgreens' income and equity be higher or lower under U.S. GAAP compared to IFRS standards? Explain.

Accounting, Analysis, and Principles

PENCOMP's statement of financial position at December 31, 2014, is as follows.

PENCOMP, INC.
STATEMENT OF FINANCIAL POSITION
AS OF DECEMBER 31, 2014

Assets			Equity		
Plant and equipment	€2,000		Share capital		€2,000
Accumulated depreciation	(240)		Retained earnings		896
		1,760	**Total equity**		**2,896**
Inventory	€ 1,800		Liabilities		
Cash	438		Notes payable	€ 1,000	
Total current assets		**2,238**	Pension liability	102	
Total assets		**€3,998**	**Total liabilities**		**1,102**
			Total equity and liabilities		**€3,998**

Additional information concerning PENCOMP's defined benefit pension plan is as follows.

Defined benefit obligation at 12/31/15	€ 820.5
Plan assets (fair value) at 12/31/15	718.5
Service cost for 2015	42.0
Discount (interest) rate	10%
Actual return on plan assets in 2015	60.6
Contributions to pension fund in 2015	70.0
Benefits paid during 2015	40.0
Accumulated OCI (net **loss** due to changes in actuarial assumptions and deferred net losses on plan assets) at 12/31/15; included in retained earnings balance	92.0

Other information about PENCOMP is as follows.

Salary expense, all paid with cash during 2015	€ 700.0
Sales, all for cash	3,000.0
Purchases, all for cash	2,000.0
Inventory at 12/31/2015	1,800.0

Property originally cost €2,000 and is depreciated on a straight-line basis over 25 years with no residual value.

Interest on the note payable is 10% annually and is paid in cash on 12/31 of each year. Dividends declared and paid are €200 in 2015.

Accounting

Prepare an income statement for 2015 and a statement of financial position as of December 31, 2015. Also, prepare the pension expense journal entry for the year ended December 31, 2015. Round to the nearest tenth (e.g., round 2.87 to 2.9).

Analysis

Compute return on equity for PENCOMP for 2015 (assume equity is equal to year-end equity). Do you think an argument can be made for including some or even all of the asset/liability gains and losses in the numerator of return on equity? Illustrate that calculation.

Principles

Explain a rationale for why the IASB has (so far) decided to exclude from the current-period income statement the effects of gains and losses due to changes in actuarial assumptions.

IFRS BRIDGE TO THE PROFESSION

Professional Research

Jack Kelly Company has grown rapidly since its founding in 2002. To instill loyalty in its employees, Kelly is contemplating establishment of a defined benefit plan. Kelly knows that lenders and potential investors will pay close attention to the impact of the pension plan on the company's financial statements, particularly any gains or losses that develop in the plan. Kelly has asked you to conduct some research on the accounting for gains and losses in a defined benefit plan.

Instructions

Access the IFRS authoritative literature at the IASB website (*http://eifrs.iasb.org/*) (you may register for free eIFRS access at this site). When you have accessed the documents, you can use the search tool in your Internet browser to respond to the following questions. (Provide paragraph citations.)

(a) Briefly describe how pension gains and losses are accounted for.

(b) Explain the rationale behind the accounting method described in part (a).

(c) What is the related pension asset or liability that may show up on the statement of financial position? When will each of these situations occur?

Professional Simulation

In this simulation, you are asked to address questions related to the accounting for pensions. Prepare responses to all parts.

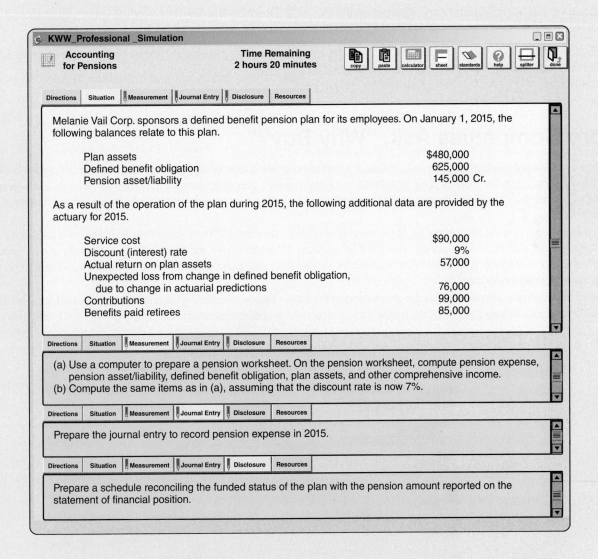

KWW_Professional_Simulation

Accounting for Pensions

Time Remaining
2 hours 20 minutes

| copy | paste | calculator | sheet | standards | help | splitter | done |

Directions | Situation | Measurement | Journal Entry | Disclosure | Resources

Melanie Vail Corp. sponsors a defined benefit pension plan for its employees. On January 1, 2015, the following balances relate to this plan.

Plan assets	$480,000
Defined benefit obligation	625,000
Pension asset/liability	145,000 Cr.

As a result of the operation of the plan during 2015, the following additional data are provided by the actuary for 2015.

Service cost	$90,000
Discount (interest) rate	9%
Actual return on plan assets	57,000
Unexpected loss from change in defined benefit obligation, due to change in actuarial predictions	76,000
Contributions	99,000
Benefits paid retirees	85,000

Directions | Situation | Measurement | Journal Entry | Disclosure | Resources

(a) Use a computer to prepare a pension worksheet. On the pension worksheet, compute pension expense, pension asset/liability, defined benefit obligation, plan assets, and other comprehensive income.

(b) Compute the same items as in (a), assuming that the discount rate is now 7%.

Directions | Situation | Measurement | Journal Entry | Disclosure | Resources

Prepare the journal entry to record pension expense in 2015.

Directions | Situation | Measurement | Journal Entry | Disclosure | Resources

Prepare a schedule reconciling the funded status of the plan with the pension amount reported on the statement of financial position.

Remember to check the book's companion website, at www.wiley.com/college/kieso, to find additional resources for this chapter.

21 Accounting for Leases

More Companies Ask, "Why Buy?"

Leasing has grown tremendously in popularity. Today, it is the fastest growing form of capital investment. Instead of borrowing money to buy an airplane, computer, nuclear core, or satellite, a company makes periodic payments to lease these assets. Even gambling casinos lease their slot machines. Companies that lease tend to be smaller, high growth, and in technology-oriented industries (see *www.techlease.com*).

A classic example is the airline industry. Many travelers on **British Airways** (GBR), **Cathay Pacific** (CHN), and **Japan Airlines** (JPN) believe these airlines own the planes on which they are flying. Often, this is not the case. Airlines lease many of their airplanes due to the favorable accounting treatment they receive if they lease rather than purchase. Presented below are the lease percentages for the major international airlines.

What about other companies? They are also exploiting the existing lease-accounting rules to keep assets and liabilities off the books. For example, **Krispy Kreme** (USA), a chain of 217 doughnut shops, had been showing good growth and profitability using

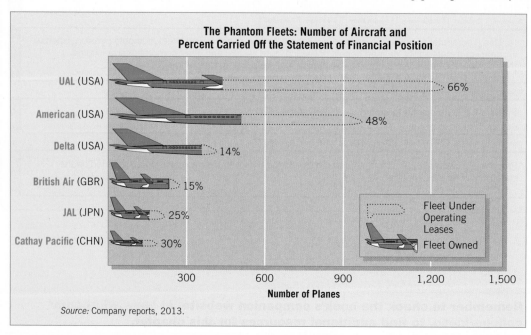

The Phantom Fleets: Number of Aircraft and Percent Carried Off the Statement of Financial Position

Source: Company reports, 2013.

CONCEPTUAL FOCUS

> See the **Underlying Concepts** on pages 1064 and 1102.
> Read the **Evolving Issue** on pages 1093–1094 for a discussion of off-balance-sheet reporting of leases.

INTERNATIONAL FOCUS

> Read the **Global Accounting Insights** on pages 1094–1095 for a discussion of non-IFRS financial reporting for leases.

a relatively small bit of capital. That's an impressive feat if you care about return on capital. But, there's a hole in this doughnut. The company explained that it was building a $30 million new mixing plant and warehouse. Yet, the financial statements failed to disclose the investments and obligations associated with that $30 million.

By financing through a synthetic lease, Krispy Kreme kept the investment and obligation off the books. In a synthetic lease, a financial institution like **Credit Suisse** (CHE) sets up a *special-purpose entity* (SPE) that borrows money to build the plant and then leases it to Krispy Kreme. For accounting purposes, Krispy Kreme reports only rent expense. But, for tax purposes, Krispy Kreme can be considered the owner of the asset and gets depreciation tax deductions. However, in response to negative publicity about the use of SPEs to get favorable financial reporting and tax benefits, Krispy Kreme announced it would change its method of financing construction of its doughnut-making plant.

As you will learn in this chapter, due to lease accounting rules, financial statement users must make an educated guess on the real-but-hidden leverage of leasing by using only the information disclosed in the notes and by applying a rule-of-thumb multiple. As the chairperson for the IASB noted, "It seems odd to expect an analyst to guess the liabilities associated with leases when management already has this information at its fingertips." This concern explains why the IASB (and FASB) is working on a new standard on leasing so that assets and liabilities avoid on-balance-sheet treatment simply by calling a loan a "lease."

Sources: Adapted from Seth Lubore and Elizabeth MacDonald, "Debt? Who, Me?" *Forbes* (February 18, 2002), p. 56; A. Catanach and E. Ketz, "Still Searching for the 'Rite' Stuff," *Grumpy Old Accountants* (April 30, 2012), *http://blogs.smeal.psu.edu/grumpyoldaccountants/archives/643*; and Hans Hoogervorst, "Harmonisation and Global Economic Consequences," public lecture at the London School of Economics (November 6, 2012).

PREVIEW OF CHAPTER **21**

Our opening story indicates the increased significance and prevalence of lease arrangements. As a result, the need for uniform accounting and informative reporting of these transactions has intensified. In this chapter, we look at the accounting issues related to leasing. The content and organization of this chapter are as follows.

Accounting for Leases

The Leasing Environment	Accounting by the Lessee	Accounting by the Lessor	Special Accounting Problems
• Who are the players? • Advantages of leasing • Conceptual nature of a lease	• Capitalization criteria • Accounting differences • Finance lease method • Operating method • Comparison of finance and operating leases	• Economics of leasing • Classification of leases • Direct-financing method • Operating method	• Residual values • Sales-type leases • Bargain-purchase option • Initial direct costs • Current versus non-current • Disclosure • Unresolved problems

THE LEASING ENVIRONMENT

LEARNING OBJECTIVE **1**

Explain the nature, economic substance, and advantages of lease transactions.

Aristotle once said, "Wealth does not lie in ownership but in the use of things!" Clearly, many companies have decided that Aristotle is right, as they have become heavily involved in leasing assets rather than owning them. For example, according to the 2014 *Global Leasing Report* by the White Clarke Group, the global leasing market is a $658 billion business. White Clarke estimates that 38 percent of lease volume is in Europe, 19 percent in Asia, and 37 percent in North America. Bouncing back from the financial-crisis-induced global recession, leasing activity grew by nearly 9 percent. Remember that these statistics are just for equipment leasing; add in real estate leasing, which is probably larger, and we are talking about a very large and growing business, one that is at least in part driven by the accounting.

What types of assets are being leased? As the opening story indicated, any type of equipment can be leased, such as railcars, helicopters, bulldozers, barges, CT scanners, computers, and so on.

Illustration 21-1 summarizes, in their own words, what several major companies are leasing.

ILLUSTRATION 21-1
What Do Companies Lease?

Company	Description
Carrefour (FRA)	"Stores not fully owned are rented under leasing agreements. The Group also owns shopping centres, mainly anchored by its hypermarkets and supermarkets, that are rented out."
Delhaize Group (BEL)	"Delhaize Group operates a significant number of its stores under finance and operating lease arrangements. Various properties leased are (partially or in full) subleased to third parties, where the Group is therefore acting as a lessor (see further below). Lease terms (including reasonably certain renewal options) generally range from 1 to 36 years with renewal options ranging from 3 to 30 years."
Diageo (GBR)	"The company owns or leases land and buildings throughout the world. Diageo's largest individual facility, in terms of net book value of property, is St James's Gate brewery in Dublin. Approximately 96% by value of the group's properties are owned and approximately 3% are held under leases running for 50 years or longer."
Marks and Spencer plc (GBR)	"The Group leases various stores, offices, warehouses and equipment under non-cancellable operating lease agreements. The leases have varying terms, escalation clauses and renewal rights."
McDonald's Corp. (USA)	"The Company was the lessee at 15,235 restaurant locations through ground leases (the Company leases the land and the Company or franchisee owns the building) and through improved leases (the Company leases land and buildings)."
Reed Elsevier (NLD)	"The company leases various properties, principally offices and warehouses, which have varying terms and renewal rights that are typical to the territory in which they are located."

The largest group of leased equipment involves information technology equipment, followed by assets in the transportation area (trucks, aircraft, rail), and then construction and agriculture.

Who Are the Players?

A **lease** is a contractual agreement between a lessor and a lessee. This arrangement gives the **lessee** the right to use specific property, owned by the **lessor**, for an agreed period of time. In return for the use of the property, the lessee makes rental payments over the lease term to the lessor.

Who are the lessors that own this property? They generally fall into one of three categories:

1. Banks.

2. Captive leasing companies.

3. Independents.

Banks

Banks are the largest players in the leasing business. They have low-cost funds, which give them the advantage of being able to purchase assets at less cost than their competitors. Banks also have been more aggressive in the leasing markets. They have decided that there is money to be made in leasing, and as a result they have expanded their product lines in this area. Finally, leasing transactions are now more standardized, which gives banks an advantage because they do not have to be as innovative in structuring lease arrangements. Thus, banks like **Credit Suisse** (CHE), **Chase** (USA), **Barclays** (GBR), and **Deutsche Bank** (DEU) have substantial leasing subsidiaries.

Captive Leasing Companies

Captive leasing companies are subsidiaries whose primary business is to perform leasing operations for the parent company. Companies like **CNH Capital** (NLD) (for CNH Global), **BMW Financial Services** (DEU) (for BMW), and **IBM Global Financing** (USA) (for IBM) facilitate the sale of products to consumers. For example, suppose that **Ivanhoe Mines Ltd.** (CAN) wants to acquire a number of earthmovers from CNH Global. In this case, CNH Capital will offer to structure the transaction as a lease rather than as a purchase. Thus, CNH Capital provides the financing rather than an outside financial institution.

Captive leasing companies have the point-of-sale advantage in finding leasing customers. That is, as soon as CNH Global receives a possible order, its leasing subsidiary can quickly develop a lease-financing arrangement. Furthermore, the captive lessor has product knowledge that gives it an advantage when financing the parent's product.

The current trend is for captives to focus primarily on their companies' products rather than do general lease financing. For example, **Boeing Capital** (USA) and **UPS Capital** (USA) are two captives that have left the general finance business to focus exclusively on their parent companies' products.

Independents

Independents are the final category of lessors. Independents have not done well over the last few years. Their market share has dropped fairly dramatically as banks and captive leasing companies have become more aggressive in the lease-financing area. Independents do not have point-of-sale access, nor do they have a low cost of funds advantage. What they *are* often good at is developing innovative contracts for lessees. In addition, they are starting to act as captive finance companies for some companies that do not have a leasing subsidiary.

According to recent data at *www.ficinc.com* on new business volume by lessor type, banks hold about 44 percent of the market, followed by independents at 30 percent. Captives had the remaining 26 percent of new business. Data on changes in market share show that both banks and captives have increased business at the expense of the independents. That is, banks' and captives' market shares had grown by 58 percent and 36 percent, respectively, while the independents' market share declined by 44 percent.

Advantages of Leasing

The growth in leasing indicates that it often has some genuine advantages over owning property, such as:

1. *100% financing at fixed rates.* Leases are often signed without requiring any money down from the lessee. This helps the lessee conserve scarce cash—an especially desirable feature for new and developing companies. In addition, lease payments often remain fixed, which protects the lessee against inflation and increases in the cost of money. The following comment explains why companies choose a lease instead of a conventional loan: "Our local bank finally came up to 80 percent of the purchase price but wouldn't go any higher, and they wanted a floating interest rate. We just couldn't afford the down payment, and we needed to lock in a final payment rate we knew we could live with."

2. *Protection against obsolescence.* Leasing equipment reduces risk of obsolescence to the lessee, and in many cases passes the risk of residual value to the lessor. For example, **Elan** (IRL) (a pharmaceutical maker) leases computers. Under the lease agreement, Elan may turn in an old computer for a new model at any time, canceling the old lease and writing a new one. The lessor adds the cost of the new lease to the balance due on the old lease, less the old computer's trade-in value. As one treasurer remarked, "Our instinct is to purchase." But if a new computer is likely to come along in a short time, "then leasing is just a heck of a lot more convenient than purchasing." Naturally, the lessor also protects itself by requiring the lessee to pay higher rental payments or provide additional payments if the lessee does not maintain the asset.

3. *Flexibility.* Lease agreements may contain less restrictive provisions than other debt agreements. Innovative lessors can tailor a lease agreement to the lessee's special needs. For instance, the duration of the lease—the **lease term**—may be anything from a short period of time to the entire expected economic life of the asset. The rental payments may be level from year to year, or they may increase or decrease in amount. The payment amount may be predetermined or may vary with sales, the prime interest rate, a price index, or some other factor. In most cases, the rent is set to enable the lessor to recover the cost of the asset plus a fair return over the life of the lease.

4. *Less costly financing.* Some companies find leasing cheaper than other forms of financing. For example, start-up companies in depressed industries or companies in low tax brackets may lease to claim tax benefits that they might otherwise lose. Depreciation deductions offer no benefit to companies that have little if any taxable income. Through leasing, the leasing companies or financial institutions use these tax benefits. They can then pass some of these tax benefits back to the user of the asset in the form of lower rental payments.

5. *Tax advantages.* In some cases, companies can "have their cake and eat it too" with tax advantages that leases offer. That is, for financial reporting purposes, companies do not report an asset or a liability for the lease arrangement. For tax purposes, however, companies can capitalize and depreciate the leased asset. As a result, a company takes deductions earlier rather than later and also reduces its taxes. A common vehicle for this type of transaction is a "synthetic lease" arrangement, such as that described in the opening story for **Krispy Kreme** (USA).

6. *Off-balance-sheet financing.* Certain leases do not add debt on a statement of financial position or affect financial ratios. In fact, they may add to borrowing capacity.[1] Such **off-balance-sheet financing** is critical to some companies.

---

[1]As demonstrated later in this chapter, certain types of lease arrangements are not capitalized on the statement of financial position. The liabilities section is thereby relieved of large future lease commitments that, if recorded, would adversely affect the debt to equity ratio. The reluctance to record lease obligations as liabilities is one of the primary reasons some companies resist capitalized lease accounting.

What do the numbers mean?   OFF-BALANCE-SHEET FINANCING

As shown in our opening story, airlines use lease arrangements extensively. This results in a great deal of off-balance-sheet financing. The following chart indicates that many airlines that lease aircraft understate debt levels by a substantial amount.

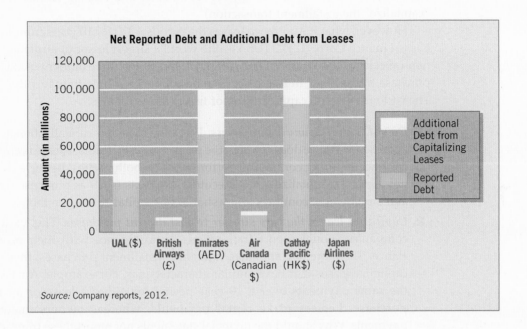

Source: Company reports, 2012.

Airlines are not the only ones playing the off-balance-sheet game. As indicated in Illustration 21-1, retailers like **Marks and Spencer plc** and **Carrefour**, and publisher **Reed Elsevier** employ leases in their businesses. Thus, analysts must adjust reported debt levels for the effects of non-capitalized leases. A methodology for making this adjustment is discussed in D. Zion and A. Varshney, "Leases Landing on Balance Sheets, Appendix: HOLT's Capitalization of Operating Leases," *Credit Suisse Equity Research* (August 17, 2010).

As also discussed in the opening story, the IASB is working on new rules to bring more leases on-balance-sheet. A PricewaterhouseCoopers survey of 3,000 international companies indicated the following impacts of leasing for several industries.

	Average Increase in Interest-Bearing Debt	Companies with over 25% Increase	Average Increase in Leverage
Retail and trade	213%	71%	64%
Other services	51	35	34
Transportation and warehousing	95	38	31
Professional services	158	52	19
Accommodation	101	41	18
All companies	58%	4%	13%

As indicated, the expected effects are significant, with all companies expecting a 58 percent increase in their debt levels and a 13 percent increase in leverage ratios. This is not a pretty picture, but investors need to see it if they are to fully understand a company's lease obligations.

Sources: Nanette Byrnes, "You May Be Liable for That Lease," *BusinessWeek* (June 5, 2006), p. 76; PricewaterhouseCoopers, *The Future of Leasing: Research of Impact on Companies' Financial Ratios* (2009); and J. E. Ketz, "Operating Lease Obligations to Be Capitalized," *Smartpros* (August 2010), http://accounting.smartpros.com/x70304.xml.

Conceptual Nature of a Lease

If **Air France—KLM** (FRA) borrows €47 million on a 10-year note from **UBS** (CHE) to purchase an Airbus A330 jet plane, Air France should clearly report an asset and related liability at that amount on its statement of financial position. Similarly, if Air France purchases the A330 for €47 million directly from Airbus through an installment purchase over 10 years, it should obviously report an asset and related liability (i.e., it should "capitalize" the installment transaction).

However, what if Air France **leases** the Airbus A330 for 10 years from **International Lease Finance Corp. (ILFC)** (USA)—the world's largest lessor of airplanes—through a non-cancelable lease transaction with payments of the same amount as the installment purchase transaction? In that case, opinion differs over how to report this transaction. The various views on **capitalization of leases** are as follows.

1. *Do not capitalize any leased assets.* This view considers capitalization inappropriate because Air France does not own the property. Furthermore, a lease is an **"executory" contract** requiring continuing performance by both parties. Because companies do not currently capitalize other executory contracts (such as purchase commitments and employment contracts), they should not capitalize leases either.

2. *Capitalize leases that are similar to installment purchases.* This view holds that companies should report transactions in accordance with their economic substance. Therefore, if companies capitalize installment purchases, they should also capitalize leases that have similar characteristics. For example, Air France makes the same payments over a 10-year period for either a lease or an installment purchase. Lessees make rental payments, whereas owners make mortgage payments. Why should the financial statements not report these transactions in the same manner?

3. *Capitalize all long-term leases.* This approach requires only the long-term right to use the property in order to capitalize. This property-rights approach capitalizes all long-term leases.

4. *Capitalize non-cancelable leases where the penalty for non-performance is substantial.* A final approach advocates capitalizing only non-cancelable contractual rights and obligations. Non-cancelable means that it is unlikely to avoid performance under the lease without a severe penalty.[2]

🔍 **Underlying Concepts**

The issue of how to report leases is the classic case of substance versus form. Although legal title does not technically pass in lease transactions, the benefits from the use of the property do transfer.

In short, the various viewpoints range from no capitalization to capitalization of all leases. The IASB apparently agrees with the capitalization approach when the lease is similar to an installment purchase: It notes that Air France **should capitalize a lease that transfers substantially all of the benefits and risks of property ownership, provided the lease is non-cancelable.**[3] **Non-cancelable** means that Air France can cancel the lease contract only upon the outcome of some remote contingency, or that the cancellation provisions and penalties of the contract are so costly to Air France that cancellation probably will not occur.

---

[2]Capitalization of most leases (based on either a right of use or on non-cancelable rights and obligations) has the support of financial analysts. As discussed in the Evolving Issue box on pages 1093–1094, the joint IASB/FASB project on lease accounting is based on a right of use model, which will require expanded capitalization of lease assets and liabilities.

[3]Benefits may be represented by the expectation of profitable operations over the asset's economic life and from appreciation in residual value. Risks include the possibility of losses from idle capacity or technological obsolescence and variation in return because of changing economic conditions. [1]

IFRS
See the Authoritative Literature section (page 1104).

This viewpoint leads to three basic conclusions. (1) Companies must identify the characteristics that indicate the transfer of substantially all of the benefits and risks of ownership. (2) The same characteristics should apply consistently to the lessee and the lessor. (3) Those leases that do **not** transfer substantially all the benefits and risks of ownership are operating leases. Companies should not capitalize operating leases. Instead, companies should account for them as rental payments and receipts.

ACCOUNTING BY THE LESSEE

If Air France (the lessee) **capitalizes** a lease, it records an asset and a liability generally equal to the present value of the rental payments. ILFC (the lessor), having transferred substantially all the benefits and risks of ownership, recognizes a sale by removing the asset from the statement of financial position and replacing it with a receivable. The typical journal entries for Air France and ILFC, assuming leased and capitalized equipment, appear as shown in Illustration 21-2.

2 LEARNING OBJECTIVE

Describe the accounting criteria and procedures for capitalizing leases by the lessee.

Air France (Lessee)			ILFC (Lessor)		
Leased Equipment	XXX		Lease Receivable	XXX	
Lease Liability		XXX	Equipment		XXX

ILLUSTRATION 21-2
Journal Entries for Capitalized Lease

Having capitalized the asset, Air France records depreciation on the leased asset. Both ILFC and Air France treat the lease rental payments as consisting of interest and principal.

If Air France does not capitalize the lease, it does not record an asset, nor does ILFC remove one from its books. When Air France makes a lease payment, it records rental expense; ILFC recognizes rental revenue.

A lease is classified as a **finance lease** if it transfers substantially all the risks and rewards incidental to ownership. In order to record a lease as a finance lease, the lease must be non-cancelable. The IASB identifies the four criteria listed in Illustration 21-3 for assessing whether the risks and rewards have been transferred in the lease arrangement.

Capitalization Criteria (Lessee)
1. The lease transfers ownership of the property to the lessee.
2. The lease contains a bargain-purchase option.[4]
3. The lease term is for the major part of the economic life of the asset.
4. The present value of the minimum lease payments amounts to substantially all of the fair value of the leased asset. [2]

ILLUSTRATION 21-3
Capitalization Criteria for Lessee

Air France classifies and accounts for leases that **do not meet any of the four criteria** as **operating leases**. Illustration 21-4 (on page 1066) shows that a lease meeting any one of the four criteria results in the lessee having a finance lease.[5]

[4]We define a bargain-purchase option in the next section.

[5]A fifth criterion applies to the relatively less common setting in which the leased asset is of such a specialized nature that only the lessee can use it without major modifications. If a lease involves an asset with these characteristics, then the risks and rewards of ownership are likely to transfer. In addition to the determinative criteria, lessees and lessors should also consider the following indicators of situations that individually or in combination could also lead to a lease being classified as a finance lease: (1) the lessee can cancel the lease, and the lessor's losses associated with the cancellation are borne by the lessee; (2) gains or losses from the fluctuation in the fair value of the residual accrue to the lessee (e.g., in the form of a rent rebate equaling most of the sales proceeds at the end of the lease); and (3) the lessee has the ability to continue the lease for a secondary period at a rent that is substantially lower than market rent. [3]

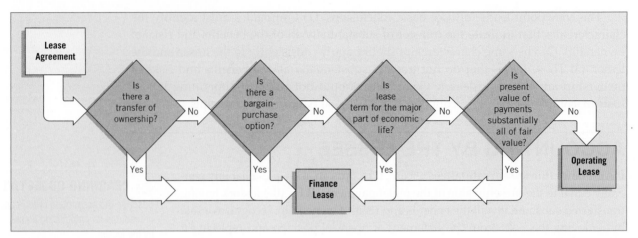

ILLUSTRATION 21-4
Diagram of Lessee's
Criteria for Lease
Classification

Thus, the proper classification of a lease is determined based on the substance of the lease transaction, rather than on its mere form. This determination often requires the use of professional judgment of whether the risks and rewards of ownership are transferred.

Capitalization Criteria

Three of the four capitalization criteria that apply to lessees are controversial and can be difficult to apply in practice. We discuss each of the criteria in detail on the following pages.

Transfer of Ownership Test

If the lease transfers ownership of the asset to the lessee, it is a finance lease. This criterion is not controversial and easily implemented in practice.

Bargain-Purchase Option Test

A bargain-purchase option allows the lessee to purchase the leased property for a price that is **significantly lower** than the property's expected fair value at the date the option becomes exercisable. At the inception of the lease, the difference between the option price and the expected fair value must be large enough to make exercise of the option reasonably assured.

For example, assume that Brett's Delivery Service was to lease a Honda Accord for $599 per month for 40 months, with an option to purchase for $100 at the end of the 40-month period. If the estimated fair value of the Honda Accord is $3,000 at the end of the 40 months, the $100 option to purchase is clearly a bargain. Therefore, Brett must capitalize the lease. In other cases, the criterion may not be as easy to apply, and determining *now* that a certain *future* price is a bargain can be difficult.

Economic Life Test

If the lease period is for a major part of the asset's economic life, the lessor transfers most of the risks and rewards of ownership to the lessee. Capitalization is therefore appropriate. However, determining the lease term and what constitutes the major part of the economic life of the asset can be troublesome.

The IASB has not defined what is meant by the "major part" of an asset's economic life. In practice, following the IASB hierarchy, it has been customary to look to U.S. GAAP, which has a 75 percent of economic life threshold for evaluating the economic life test. While the 75 percent guideline may be a useful reference point, it does not represent an automatic cutoff point. Rather, lessees and lessors should consider all relevant factors when assessing whether substantially all the risks and rewards of ownership have been transferred in the lease.[6] *For purposes of homework, assume a 75 percent threshold for the economic life test, unless otherwise stated.*

The **lease term** is generally considered to be the fixed, non-cancelable term of the lease. However, a bargain-renewal option, if provided in the lease agreement, can extend this period. A **bargain-renewal option** allows the lessee to renew the lease for a rental that is lower than the expected fair rental at the date the option becomes exercisable. At the inception of the lease, the difference between the renewal rental and the expected fair rental must be great enough to make exercise of the option to renew reasonably assured. **[4]**

For example, assume that **Carrefour** (FRA) leases **Lenovo** (CHN) PCs for two years at a rental of €100 per month per computer and subsequently can lease them for €10 per month per computer for another two years. The lease clearly offers a bargain-renewal option; the lease term is considered to be four years. However, with bargain-renewal options, as with bargain-purchase options, it is sometimes difficult to determine what is a bargain.

Determining estimated economic life can also pose problems, especially if the leased item is a specialized item or has been used for a significant period of time. For example, determining the economic life of a nuclear core is extremely difficult. It is subject to much more than normal "wear and tear."

Recovery of Investment Test

If the present value of the minimum lease payments equals or exceeds substantially all of the fair value of the asset, then a lessee like Air France should capitalize the leased asset. Why? If the present value of the minimum lease payments is reasonably close to the fair value of the aircraft, Air France is effectively purchasing the asset.

As with the economic life test, the IASB has not defined what is meant by "substantially all" of an asset's fair value. In practice, it has been customary to look to U.S. GAAP, which has a 90 percent of fair value threshold for assessing the recovery of investment test. Again, rather than focusing on any single element of the lease classification indicators, lessees and lessors should consider all relevant factors when evaluating lease classification criteria.[7] *For purposes of homework, assume a 90 percent threshold for the recovery of investment test.*

Determining the present value of the minimum lease payments involves three important concepts: (1) minimum lease payments, (2) executory costs, and (3) discount rate.

Minimum Lease Payments. Air France is obligated to make, or expected to make, **minimum lease payments** in connection with the leased property. These payments include the following. **[5]**

1. *Minimum rental payments.* Minimum rental payments are those that Air France must make to ILFC under the lease agreement. In some cases, the minimum rental payments may equal the minimum lease payments. However, the minimum lease payments may also include a guaranteed residual value (if any), penalty for failure to renew, or a bargain-purchase option (if any), as we note below.

---

[6]The International Financial Reporting Group of Ernst and Young, *International GAAP, 2013* (John Wiley and Sons: New York, 2013), p. 1669.

[7]*Ibid.* The 75 percent of useful life and 90 percent of fair value "bright-line" cutoffs in U.S. GAAP have been criticized. Many believe that lessees structure leases so as to just miss the 75 and 90 percent cutoffs, avoiding classifying leases as finance leases, thereby keeping leased assets and the related liabilities off the statement of financial position.

2. *Guaranteed residual value.* The residual value is the estimated fair value of the leased property at the end of the lease term. ILFC may transfer the risk of loss to Air France or to a third party by obtaining a guarantee of the estimated residual value. The **guaranteed residual value** is either (1) the certain or determinable amount that Air France will pay ILFC at the end of the lease to purchase the aircraft at the end of the lease, or (2) the amount Air France guarantees that ILFC will realize if the aircraft is returned. If not guaranteed in full, the **unguaranteed residual value** is the estimated residual value exclusive of any portion guaranteed.[8]

3. *Penalty for failure to renew or extend the lease.* The amount Air France must pay if the agreement specifies that it must extend or renew the lease, and it fails to do so.

4. *Bargain-purchase option.* As we indicated earlier (in item 1), an option given to Air France to purchase the aircraft at the end of the lease term at a price that is fixed sufficiently below the expected fair value, so that, at the inception of the lease, purchase is reasonably assured.

Air France excludes executory costs (defined below) from its computation of the present value of the minimum lease payments.

Executory Costs. Like most assets, leased tangible assets incur insurance, maintenance, and tax expenses—called **executory costs**—during their economic life. If ILFC retains responsibility for the payment of these "ownership-type costs," **it should exclude**, in computing the present value of the minimum lease payments, the portion of each lease payment that represents executory costs. Executory costs do not represent payment on or reduction of the obligation.

Many lease agreements specify that the lessee directly pays executory costs to the appropriate third parties. In these cases, the lessor can use the rental payment **without adjustment** in the present value computation.

Discount Rate. A lessee, like Air France, computes the present value of the minimum lease payments using the **implicit interest rate**. [7] This rate is defined as the discount rate that, at the inception of the lease, causes the aggregate present value of the minimum lease payments and the unguaranteed residual value to be equal to the fair value of the leased asset. [8]

While Air France may argue that it cannot determine the implicit rate of the lessor, in most cases Air France can approximate the implicit rate used by ILFC. In the event that it is impracticable to determine the implicit rate, Air France should use its incremental borrowing rate. The **incremental borrowing rate** is the rate of interest the lessee would have to pay on a similar lease or the rate that, at the inception of the lease, the lessee would incur to borrow over a similar term the funds necessary to purchase the asset.

If known or practicable to estimate, use of the implicit rate is preferred. This is because **the implicit rate of ILFC is generally a more realistic rate** to use in determining the amount (if any) to report as the asset and related liability for Air France. In addition, use of the implicit rate avoids use of **an artificially high incremental borrowing rate**

---

[8]If the residual value is guaranteed by a third party, it is not included in the minimum lease payments. (**Third-party guarantors** are, in essence, insurers who for a fee assume the risk of deficiencies in leased asset residual value.) A lease provision requiring the lessee to make up a residual value deficiency that is attributable to damage, extraordinary wear and tear, or excessive usage is not included in the minimum lease payments. Lessees recognize such costs as period costs when incurred. As noted earlier, such a provision could be an indicator that a lease should be classified as a finance lease. [6]

that would cause the present value of the minimum lease payments to be lower, supporting an argument that the lease does not meet the recovery of investment test. Use of such a rate would thus make it more likely that the lessee avoids capitalization of the leased asset and related liability.

The determination of whether or not a reasonable estimate of the implicit rate could be made will require judgment, particularly where the result from using the incremental borrowing rate comes close to meeting the fair value test. Because Air France **may not capitalize the leased property at more than its fair value** (as we discuss later), it cannot use an excessively low discount rate.

Asset and Liability Accounted for Differently

In a finance lease transaction, Air France uses the lease as a source of financing. ILFC finances the transaction (provides the investment capital) through the leased asset. Air France makes rent payments, which actually are installment payments. Therefore, over the life of the aircraft rented, **the rental payments to ILFC constitute a payment of principal plus interest**.

Asset and Liability Recorded

Under the finance lease method, Air France treats the lease transaction as if it purchases the aircraft in a financing transaction. That is, Air France acquires the aircraft and creates an obligation. Therefore, it records a finance lease as an asset and a liability at the lower of (1) the present value of the minimum lease payments (excluding executory costs) or (2) the fair value of the leased asset at the inception of the lease. The rationale for this approach is that companies should not record a leased asset for more than its fair value.

Depreciation Period

One troublesome aspect of accounting for the depreciation of the capitalized leased asset relates to the period of depreciation. If the lease agreement transfers ownership of the asset to Air France (criterion 1) or contains a bargain-purchase option (criterion 2), Air France depreciates the aircraft consistent with its normal depreciation policy for other aircraft, **using the economic life of the asset**.

On the other hand, if the lease does not transfer ownership or does not contain a bargain-purchase option, then Air France depreciates it over the **term of the lease**. In this case, the aircraft reverts to ILFC after a certain period of time.

Effective-Interest Method

Throughout the term of the lease, Air France uses the **effective-interest method** to allocate each lease payment between principal and interest. This method produces a periodic interest expense equal to a constant percentage of the carrying value of the lease obligation. When applying the effective-interest method to finance leases, Air France must use the same discount rate that determines the present value of the minimum lease payments.

Depreciation Concept

Although Air France computes the amounts initially capitalized as an asset and recorded as an obligation at the same present value, the **depreciation of the aircraft and the discharge of the obligation are independent accounting processes** during the term of the lease. It should depreciate the leased asset by applying conventional depreciation methods: straight-line, sum-of-the-years' digits, declining-balance, units of production, etc.

Finance Lease Method (Lessee)

To illustrate a finance lease, assume that **CNH Capital** (NLD) (a subsidiary of CNH Global) and **Ivanhoe Mines Ltd.** (CAN) sign a lease agreement dated January 1, 2015, that calls for CNH to lease a front-end loader to Ivanhoe beginning January 1, 2015. The terms and provisions of the lease agreement and other pertinent data are as follows.

- The term of the lease is five years. The lease agreement is non-cancelable, requiring equal rental payments of $25,981.62 at the beginning of each year (annuity-due basis).
- The loader has a fair value at the inception of the lease of $100,000, an estimated economic life of five years, and no residual value.
- Ivanhoe pays all of the executory costs directly to third parties except for the property taxes of $2,000 per year, which is included as part of its annual payments to CNH.
- The lease contains no renewal options. The loader reverts to CNH at the termination of the lease.
- Ivanhoe's incremental borrowing rate is 11 percent per year.
- Ivanhoe depreciates similar equipment that it owns on a straight-line basis.
- CNH sets the annual rental to earn a rate of return on its investment of 10 percent per year; Ivanhoe knows this fact.

The lease meets the criteria for classification as a finance lease for the following reasons.

1. The lease term of five years, being equal to the equipment's estimated economic life of five years, satisfies the economic life test.
2. The present value of the minimum lease payments ($100,000 as computed below) equals the fair value of the loader ($100,000).

The minimum lease payments are $119,908.10 ($23,981.62 × 5). Ivanhoe computes the amount capitalized as leased assets as the present value of the minimum lease payments (excluding executory costs—property taxes of $2,000) as shown in Illustration 21-5.

ILLUSTRATION 21-5
Computation of
Capitalized Lease
Payments

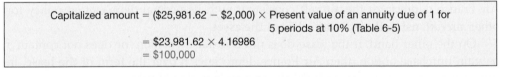

Capitalized amount = ($25,981.62 − $2,000) × Present value of an annuity due of 1 for
5 periods at 10% (Table 6-5)
= $23,981.62 × 4.16986
= $100,000

Ivanhoe uses CNH's implicit interest rate of 10 percent instead of its incremental borrowing rate of 11 percent because it knows about it.[9] Ivanhoe records the finance lease on its books on January 1, 2015, as follows.

Leased Equipment	100,000	
Lease Liability		100,000

Note that the entry records the obligation at the net amount of $100,000 (the present value of the future rental payments) rather than at the gross amount of $119,908.10 ($23,981.62 × 5).

Ivanhoe records the **first lease payment on January 1, 2015**, as follows.

Property Tax Expense	2,000.00	
Lease Liability	23,981.62	
Cash		25,981.62

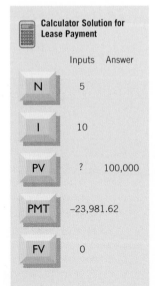

Calculator Solution for Lease Payment

	Inputs	Answer
N	5	
I	10	
PV	?	100,000
PMT	−23,981.62	
FV	0	

[9]If it is impracticable for Ivanhoe to determine the implicit rate and it has an incremental borrowing rate of, say, 9 percent (lower than the 10 percent rate used by CNH), the present value computation would yield a capitalized amount of $101,675.35 ($23,981.62 × 4.23972). Thus, use of an unrealistically low discount rate could lead to a lessee recording a leased asset at an amount exceeding the fair value of the equipment, which is generally prohibited in IFRS. This explains why the implicit rate should be used to capitalize the minimum lease payments.

Each lease payment of $25,981.62 consists of three elements: (1) a reduction in the lease liability, (2) a financing cost (interest expense), and (3) executory costs (property taxes). The total financing cost (interest expense) over the term of the lease is $19,908.10. This amount is the difference between the present value of the lease payments ($100,000) and the actual cash disbursed, net of executory costs ($119,908.10). The annual interest expense, applying the effective-interest method, is a function of the outstanding liability, as Illustration 21-6 shows.

ILLUSTRATION 21-6
Lease Amortization Schedule for Lessee—Annuity-Due Basis

IVANHOE MINES
LEASE AMORTIZATION SCHEDULE
ANNUITY-DUE BASIS

Date	Annual Lease Payment	Executory Costs	Interest (10%) on Liability	Reduction of Lease Liability	Lease Liability
	(a)	(b)	(c)	(d)	(e)
1/1/15					$100,000.00
1/1/15	$ 25,981.62	$ 2,000	$ –0–	$ 23,981.62	76,018.38
1/1/16	25,981.62	2,000	7,601.84	16,379.78	59,638.60
1/1/17	25,981.62	2,000	5,963.86	18,017.76	41,620.84
1/1/18	25,981.62	2,000	4,162.08	19,819.54	21,801.30
1/1/19	25,981.62	2,000	2,180.32*	21,801.30	–0–
	$129,908.10	$10,000	$19,908.10	$100,000.00	

(a) Lease payment as required by lease.
(b) Executory costs included in rental payment.
(c) Ten percent of the preceding balance of (e) except for 1/1/15; since this is an annuity due, no time has elapsed at the date of the first payment and no interest has accrued.
(d) (a) minus (b) and (c).
(e) Preceding balance minus (d).

*Rounded by 19 cents.

At the end of its fiscal year, December 31, 2015, Ivanhoe records **accrued interest** as follows.

Interest Expense	7,601.84	
Interest Payable		7,601.84

Depreciation of the leased equipment over its five-year lease term, applying Ivanhoe's normal depreciation policy (straight-line method), results in the following entry on December 31, 2015.

Depreciation Expense	20,000	
Accumulated Depreciation—Leased Equipment		20,000
($100,000 ÷ 5 years)		

At December 31, 2015, Ivanhoe separately identifies the assets recorded under finance leases on its statement of financial position. Similarly, it separately identifies the related obligations. Ivanhoe classifies the portion due within one year or the operating cycle, whichever is longer, with current liabilities, and the rest with non-current liabilities. For example, the current portion of the December 31, 2015, total obligation of $76,018.38 in Ivanhoe's amortization schedule is the amount of the reduction in the obligation in 2016, or $16,379.78. Illustration 21-7 shows the liabilities section as it relates to lease transactions at December 31, 2015.

ILLUSTRATION 21-7
Reporting Current and Non-Current Lease Liabilities

Non-current liabilities	
Lease liability ($76,018.38 − $16,379.78)	$59,638.60
Current liabilities	
Interest payable	$ 7,601.84
Lease liability	16,379.78

Ivanhoe records the lease payment of January 1, 2016, as follows.

Property Tax Expense	2,000.00	
Interest Payable	7,601.84	
Lease Liability	16,379.78	
Cash		25,981.62

Entries through 2017 would follow the pattern above. Ivanhoe records its other executory costs (insurance and maintenance) in a manner similar to how it records any other operating costs incurred on assets it owns.

Upon expiration of the lease, Ivanhoe has fully depreciated the amount capitalized as leased equipment. It also has fully discharged its lease obligation. If Ivanhoe does not purchase the loader, it returns the equipment to CNH. Ivanhoe then removes the leased equipment and related accumulated depreciation accounts from its books.

If Ivanhoe purchases the equipment at termination of the lease, at a price of $5,000 and the estimated life of the equipment changes from five to seven years, it makes the following entry.

Equipment ($100,000 + $5,000)	105,000	
Accumulated Depreciation—Leased Equipment	100,000	
Leased Equipment		100,000
Accumulated Depreciation—Equipment		100,000
Cash		5,000

Operating Method (Lessee)

Under the **operating method**, rent expense (and the associated liability) accrues day by day to the lessee as it uses the property. **The lessee assigns rent to the periods benefiting from the use of the asset and ignores, in the accounting, any commitments to make future payments.** The lessee makes appropriate accruals or deferrals if the accounting period ends between cash payment dates.

For example, assume that the finance lease illustrated in the previous section did not qualify as a finance lease. Ivanhoe therefore accounts for it as an operating lease. The first-year charge to operations is now $25,981.62, the amount of the rental payment. Ivanhoe records this payment on January 1, 2015, as follows.

Rent Expense	25,981.62	
Cash		25,981.62

Ivanhoe does not report the front-end loader, as well as any long-term liability for future rental payments, on the statement of financial position. Ivanhoe reports rent expense on the income statement. And, as discussed later in the chapter, **Ivanhoe must disclose all operating leases that have non-cancelable lease terms in excess of one year.**

Comparison of Finance Lease with Operating Lease

LEARNING OBJECTIVE

Contrast the operating and capitalization methods of recording leases.

As we indicated above for Ivanhoe, if accounting for the lease as an operating lease, the first-year charge to operations is $25,981.62, the amount of the rental payment. Treating the transaction as a finance lease, however, results in a first-year charge of $29,601.84: depreciation of $20,000 (assuming straight-line), interest expense of $7,601.84 (per Illustration 21-6 on page 1071), and executory costs of $2,000. Illustration 21-8 shows that **while the total charges to operations are the same over the lease term whether accounting for the lease as a finance lease or as an operating lease, under the finance lease treatment the charges are higher in the earlier years and lower in the later years.**[10]

[10]The higher charges in the early years is one reason lessees are reluctant to adopt the finance lease accounting method. Lessees (especially those of real estate) claim that it is really no more costly to operate the leased asset in the early years than in the later years. Thus, they advocate an even charge similar to that provided by the operating method.

ILLUSTRATION 21-8
Comparison of Charges
to Operations—Finance
vs. Operating Leases

IVANHOE MINES
SCHEDULE OF CHARGES TO OPERATIONS
FINANCE LEASE VERSUS OPERATING LEASE

	Finance Lease				Operating Lease Charge	Difference
Year	Depreciation	Executory Costs	Interest	Total Charge		
2015	$ 20,000	$ 2,000	$ 7,601.84	$ 29,601.84	$ 25,981.62	$3,620.22
2016	20,000	2,000	5,963.86	27,963.86	25,981.62	1,982.24
2017	20,000	2,000	4,162.08	26,162.08	25,981.62	180.46
2018	20,000	2,000	2,180.32	24,180.32	25,981.62	(1,801.30)
2019	20,000	2,000	—	22,000.00	25,981.62	(3,981.62)
	$100,000	$10,000	$19,908.10	$129,908.10	$129,908.10	$ –0–

If using an accelerated method of depreciation, the differences between the amounts charged to operations under the two methods would be even larger in the earlier and later years.

In addition, using the finance lease approach results in an asset and related liability of $100,000 initially reported on the statement of financial position. The lessee would not report any asset or liability under the operating method. Therefore, the following differences occur if using a finance lease instead of an operating lease:

1. An increase in the amount of reported debt (both short-term and long-term).

2. An increase in the amount of total assets (specifically long-lived assets).

3. A lower income early in the life of the lease and, therefore, lower retained earnings.

Thus, many companies believe that finance leases negatively impact their financial position: Their debt to total equity ratio increases, and their rate of return on total assets decreases. As a result, the business community resists capitalizing leases.

Whether this resistance is well founded is debatable. From a cash flow point of view, the company is in the same position whether accounting for the lease as an operating or a finance lease. Managers often argue against capitalization because it can more easily lead to **violation of loan covenants**. Capitalization also can affect the **amount of compensation received by managers** (for example, a share compensation plan tied to earnings). Finally, capitalization can **lower rates of return** and **increase debt to equity relationships**, making the company less attractive to present and potential investors.[11]

ACCOUNTING BY THE LESSOR

Earlier in this chapter, we discussed leasing's advantages to the lessee. Three important benefits are available to the lessor:

1. *Interest revenue.* Leasing is a form of financing. Banks, captives, and independent leasing companies find leasing attractive because it provides competitive interest margins.

4 **LEARNING OBJECTIVE**

Explain the advantages and economics of leasing to lessors and identify the classifications of leases for the lessor.

[11]One study indicates that management's behavior did change as a result of lease accounting rules. For example, many companies restructure their leases to avoid capitalization. Others increase their purchases of assets instead of leasing. Still others, faced with capitalization, postpone their debt offerings or issue shares instead. However, note that the study found no significant effect on share or bond prices as a result of capitalization of leases. See A. Rashad Abdel-khalik, "The Economic Effects on Lessees of *FASB Statement No. 13,* Accounting for Leases," Research Report (Stamford, Conn.: FASB, 1981).

2. *Tax incentives.* In many cases, companies that lease cannot use the tax benefit of the asset, but leasing allows them to transfer such tax benefits to another party (the lessor) in return for a lower rental rate on the leased asset. To illustrate, Airbus (FRA) might sell one of its Airbus 330 jet planes to a wealthy investor who needed only the tax benefit. The investor then leased the plane to a foreign airline, for whom the tax benefit was of no use. Everyone gained. Airbus sold its airplane, the investor received the tax benefit, and the foreign airline cheaply acquired a 330.[12]

3. *Residual value profits.* Another advantage to the lessor is the return of the property at the end of the lease term. Residual values can produce very large profits. Citigroup (USA) at one time assumed that the commercial aircraft it was leasing to the airline industry would have a residual value of 5 percent of their purchase price. It turned out that they were worth 150 percent of their cost—a handsome profit. At the same time, if residual values decline, lessors can suffer losses when less valuable leased assets are returned at the conclusion of the lease. At one time, automaker Ford (USA) took a $2.1 billion write-down on its lease portfolio when rising gas prices spurred dramatic declines in the resale values of leased trucks and SUVs.

Economics of Leasing

A lessor, such as CNH Capital in our earlier example, determines the amount of the rental, basing it on the rate of return—the implicit rate—needed to justify leasing the front-end loader. In establishing the rate of return, CNH considers the credit standing of Ivanhoe, the length of the lease, and the status of the residual value (guaranteed versus unguaranteed).

In the CNH/Ivanhoe example on pages 1070–1072, CNH's implicit rate was 10 percent, the cost of the equipment to CNH was $100,000 (also fair value), and the estimated residual value was zero. CNH determines the amount of the lease payment as follows.

ILLUSTRATION 21-9
Computation of Lease Payments

Fair value of leased equipment	$100,000.00
Less: Present value of the residual value	–0–
Amount to be recovered by lessor through lease payments	$100,000.00
Five beginning-of-the-year lease payments to yield a 10% return ($100,000 ÷ 4.16986[a])	$ 23,981.62

[a]PV of an annuity due of 1 for 5 years at 10% (Table 6-5).

If a residual value is involved (whether guaranteed or not), CNH would not have to recover as much from the lease payments. Therefore, the lease payments would be less. (Illustration 21-16, on page 1080, shows this situation.)

Classification of Leases by the Lessor

For accounting purposes, the **lessor** also classifies leases as operating or finance leases. Finance leases may be further subdivided into direct-financing and sales-type leases.

As with lessee accounting, if the lease transfers substantially all the risks and rewards incidental to ownership, the lessor shall classify and account for the arrangement as a finance lease. Lessors evaluate the same criteria shown in Illustration 21-3 (on page 1065) to make this determination.

The distinction for the lessor between a direct-financing lease and a sales-type lease is the presence or absence of a manufacturer's or dealer's profit (or loss). A sales-type lease involves a manufacturer's or dealer's profit, and a direct-financing lease does

[12]Some would argue that there is a loser—the tax authorities. The tax benefits enable the profitable investor to reduce or eliminate taxable income.

not. The profit (or loss) to the lessor is evidenced by the difference between the fair value of the leased property at the inception of the lease and the lessor's cost or carrying amount (book value).

Normally, sales-type leases arise when manufacturers or dealers use leasing as a means of marketing their products. For example, a computer manufacturer will lease its computer equipment (possibly through a captive) to businesses and institutions. Direct-financing leases generally result from arrangements with lessors that are primarily engaged in financing operations (e.g., banks).

Lessors classify and account for all leases that do not qualify as direct-financing or sales-type leases as operating leases. Illustration 21-10 shows the circumstances under which a lessor classifies a lease as operating, direct-financing, or sales-type.

ILLUSTRATION 21-10
Diagram of Lessor's Criteria for Lease Classification

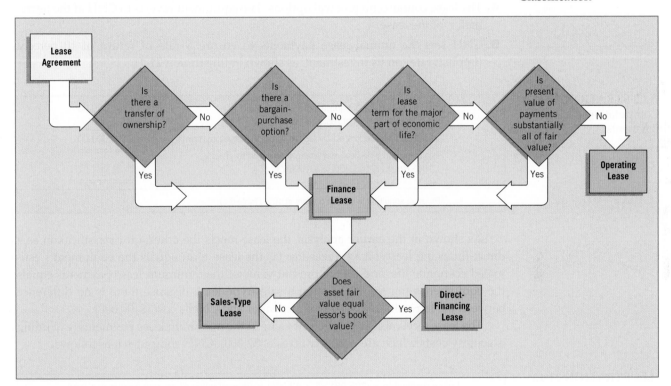

For purposes of comparison with the lessee's accounting, we will illustrate only the operating and direct-financing leases in the following section. We will discuss the more complex sales-type lease later in the chapter.

Direct-Financing Method (Lessor)

Direct-financing leases are in substance the financing of an asset purchase by the lessee. In this type of lease, the lessor records a **lease receivable** instead of a leased asset. The lease receivable is the present value of the minimum lease payments plus the present value of the unguaranteed residual value. Remember that "minimum lease payments" include (1) rental payments (excluding executory costs), (2) bargain-purchase option (if any), (3) guaranteed residual value (if any), and (4) penalty for failure to renew (if any).

Thus, the lessor records the residual value, whether guaranteed or not. Also, recall that if the lessor pays any executory costs, then it should reduce the rental payment by that amount in computing minimum lease payments.

5 LEARNING OBJECTIVE
Describe the lessor's accounting for direct-financing leases.

The following presentation, using the data from the preceding CNH/Ivanhoe example on pages 1070–1072, illustrates the accounting treatment for a direct-financing lease. We repeat here the information relevant to CNH in accounting for this lease transaction.

1. The term of the lease is five years beginning January 1, 2015, non-cancelable, and requires equal rental payments of $25,981.62 at the beginning of each year. Payments include $2,000 of executory costs (property taxes).
2. The equipment (front-end loader) has a cost of $100,000 to CNH, a fair value at the inception of the lease of $100,000, an estimated economic life of five years, and no residual value.
3. CNH incurred no initial direct costs in negotiating and closing the lease transaction.
4. The lease contains no renewal options. The equipment reverts to CNH at the termination of the lease.
5. CNH sets the annual lease payments to ensure a rate of return of 10 percent (implicit rate) on its investment, as shown in Illustration 21-11.

ILLUSTRATION 21-11
Computation of Lease Payments

Fair value of leased equipment	$100,000.00
Less: Present value of residual value	–0–
Amount to be recovered by lessor through lease payments	$100,000.00
Five beginning-of-the-year lease payments to yield a 10% return ($100,000 ÷ 4.16986[a])	$ 23,981.62

[a]PV of an annuity due of 1 for 5 years at 10% (Table 6-5).

As shown in the earlier analysis, the lease meets the criteria for classification as a direct-financing lease for two reasons: (1) the lease term equals the equipment's estimated economic life, and (2) the present value of the minimum lease payments equals the equipment's fair value. It is not a sales-type lease because there is no difference between the fair value ($100,000) of the loader and CNH's cost ($100,000).

The lease receivable is the present value of the minimum lease payments (excluding executory costs which are property taxes of $2,000). CNH computes it as follows.

ILLUSTRATION 21-12
Computation of Lease Receivable

Lease receivable = ($25,981.62 − $2,000) × Present value of an annuity due of 1 for 5 periods at 10% (Table 6-5)
= $23,981.62 × 4.16986
= $100,000

CNH records the lease of the asset and the resulting receivable on January 1, 2015 (the inception of the lease), as follows.

Lease Receivable	100,000	
Equipment		100,000

Companies often **report** the lease receivable in the statement of financial position as "Net investment in finance leases." Companies classify it either as current or non-current, depending on when they recover the net investment.[13]

[13]In the notes to the financial statements (see Illustration 21-31, page 1091), the lease receivable is reported at its gross amount (minimum lease payments plus the unguaranteed residual value). In addition, the lessor also reports total unearned interest related to the lease. As a result, some lessors record lease receivable on a gross basis and record the unearned interest in a separate account. We illustrate the net approach here because it is consistent with the accounting for the lessee.

CNH replaces its investment (the leased front-end loader, a cost of $100,000) with a lease receivable. In a manner similar to Ivanhoe's treatment of interest, CNH applies the effective-interest method and recognizes interest revenue as a function of the lease receivable balance, as Illustration 21-13 shows.

ILLUSTRATION 21-13
Lease Amortization Schedule for Lessor—Annuity-Due Basis

CNH CAPITAL
LEASE AMORTIZATION SCHEDULE
ANNUITY-DUE BASIS

Date	Annual Lease Payment	Executory Costs	Interest (10%) on Lease Receivable	Lease Receivable Recovery	Lease Receivable
	(a)	(b)	(c)	(d)	(e)
1/1/15					$100,000.00
1/1/15	$ 25,981.62	$ 2,000.00	$ –0–	$ 23,981.62	76,018.38
1/1/16	25,981.62	2,000.00	7,601.84	16,379.78	59,638.60
1/1/17	25,981.62	2,000.00	5,963.86	18,017.76	41,620.84
1/1/18	25,981.62	2,000.00	4,162.08	19,819.54	21,801.30
1/1/19	25,981.62	2,000.00	2,180.32*	21,801.30	–0–
	$129,908.10	$10,000.00	$19,908.10	$100,000.00	

(a) Annual rental that provides a 10% return on net investment.
(b) Executory costs included in rental payment.
(c) Ten percent of the preceding balance of (e) except for 1/1/15.
(d) (a) minus (b) and (c).
(e) Preceding balance minus (d).

*Rounded by 19 cents.

On January 1, 2015, CNH records receipt of the first year's lease payment as follows.

Cash	25,981.62	
Lease Receivable		23,981.62
Property Tax Expense/Property Taxes Payable		2,000.00

On December 31, 2015, CNH recognizes the interest revenue earned during the first year through the following entry.

Interest Receivable	7,601.84	
Interest Revenue		7,601.84

At December 31, 2015, CNH reports the lease receivable in its statement of financial position among current assets or non-current assets, or both. It classifies the portion due within one year or the operating cycle, whichever is longer, as a current asset, and the rest with non-current assets.

Illustration 21-14 shows the assets section as it relates to lease transactions at December 31, 2015.

ILLUSTRATION 21-14
Reporting Lease Transactions by Lessor

Non-current assets (investments)	
Lease receivable ($76,018.38 − $16,379.78)	$59,638.60
Current assets	
Interest receivable	$ 7,601.84
Lease receivable	16,379.78

The following entries record receipt of the second year's lease payment and recognition of the interest earned.

January 1, 2016

Cash	25,981.62	
Lease Receivable		16,379.78
Interest Receivable		7,601.84
Property Tax Expense/Property Taxes Payable		2,000.00

December 31, 2016

Interest Receivable	5,963.86	
Interest Revenue		5,963.86

Journal entries through 2019 follow the same pattern except that CNH records no entry in 2019 (the last year) for interest revenue. Because the company fully collects the receivable by January 1, 2019, no balance (investment) is outstanding during 2019. If Ivanhoe buys the loader for $5,000 upon expiration of the lease, CNH recognizes disposition of the equipment as follows.

Cash	5,000	
Gain on Disposal of Equipment		5,000

Operating Method (Lessor)

Under the **operating method**, the lessor records each rental receipt as rental revenue. It **depreciates the leased asset in the normal manner**, with the depreciation expense of the period matched against the rental revenue. The amount of revenue recognized in each accounting period is a level amount (straight-line basis) regardless of the lease provisions, unless another systematic and rational basis better represents the time pattern in which the lessor derives benefit from the leased asset.

In addition to the depreciation charge, the lessor expenses maintenance costs and the cost of any other services performed under the provisions of the lease that pertain to the current accounting period. The lessor **amortizes over the life of the lease** any costs paid to independent third parties, such as appraisal fees, finder's fees, and costs of credit checks, usually on a straight-line basis.

To illustrate the operating method, assume that the direct-financing lease illustrated in the previous section does not qualify as a finance lease. Therefore, CNH accounts for it as an operating lease. It records the cash rental receipt as follows.

Cash	25,981.62	
Rent Revenue		25,981.62

CNH records depreciation as follows (assuming a straight-line method, a cost basis of $100,000, and a five-year life).

Depreciation Expense	20,000	
Accumulated Depreciation—Equipment		20,000

If CNH pays property taxes, insurance, maintenance, and other operating costs during the year, it records them as expenses chargeable against the gross rental revenues.

If CNH owns plant assets that it uses in addition to those leased to others, the company **separately classifies the leased equipment and accompanying accumulated depreciation** as Equipment Leased to Others or Investment in Leased Property. If significant in amount or in terms of activity, CNH separates the rental revenues and accompanying expenses in the income statement from sales revenue and cost of goods sold.

SPECIAL ACCOUNTING PROBLEMS

LEARNING OBJECTIVE **6**

Identify special features of lease arrangements that cause unique accounting problems.

The features of lease arrangements that cause unique accounting problems are:

1. Residual values.

2. Sales-type leases (lessor).

3. Bargain-purchase options.

4. Initial direct costs.

5. Current versus non-current classification.

6. Disclosure.

We discuss each of these features on the following pages.

Residual Values

Up to this point, in order to develop the basic accounting issues related to lessee and lessor accounting, we have generally ignored residual values. Accounting for residual values is complex and will probably provide you with the greatest challenge in understanding lease accounting.

7 LEARNING OBJECTIVE
Describe the effect of residual values, guaranteed and unguaranteed, on lease accounting.

Meaning of Residual Value

The **residual value** is the estimated fair value of the leased asset at the end of the lease term. Frequently, a significant residual value exists at the end of the lease term, especially when the economic life of the leased asset exceeds the lease term. If title does not pass automatically to the lessee (criterion 1) and a bargain-purchase option does not exist (criterion 2), the lessee returns physical custody of the asset to the lessor at the end of the lease term.

Guaranteed versus Unguaranteed

The residual value may be unguaranteed or guaranteed by the lessee. Sometimes, the lessee agrees to make up any deficiency below a stated amount that the lessor realizes in residual value at the end of the lease term. In such a case, that stated amount is the **guaranteed residual value**.

The parties to a lease use guaranteed residual value in lease arrangements for two reasons. The first is a business reason: It protects the lessor against any loss in estimated residual value, thereby ensuring the lessor of the desired rate of return on investment. The second reason is an accounting benefit that we will discuss at the end of this chapter.

Lease Payments

A guaranteed residual value—by definition—has more assurance of realization than does an unguaranteed residual value. As a result, the lessor may adjust lease payments because of the increased certainty of recovery. After the lessor establishes the payments, it makes no difference from an accounting point of view whether the residual value is guaranteed or unguaranteed. The net investment that the lessor records (once the payments are set) will be the same.

Assume the same data as in the CNH/Ivanhoe illustrations except that CNH estimates a residual value of $5,000 at the end of the five-year lease term. In addition, CNH assumes a 10 percent return on investment (ROI),[14] whether the residual value is guaranteed or unguaranteed. CNH would compute the amount of the lease payments as follows.

CNH's COMPUTATION OF LEASE PAYMENTS (10% ROI) GUARANTEED OR UNGUARANTEED RESIDUAL VALUE ANNUITY-DUE BASIS, INCLUDING RESIDUAL VALUE	
Fair value of leased asset to lessor	$100,000.00
Less: Present value of residual value ($5,000 × .62092, Table 6-2)	3,104.60
Amount to be recovered by lessor through lease payments	$ 96,895.40
Five periodic lease payments ($96,895.40 ÷ 4.16986, Table 6-5)	$ 23,237.09

ILLUSTRATION 21-15
Lessor's Computation of Lease Payments

Contrast the foregoing lease payment amount to the lease payments of $23,981.62 as computed in Illustration 21-9 (on page 1074), where no residual value existed. In the

[14]Technically, the rate of return CNH demands would differ depending upon whether the residual value was guaranteed or unguaranteed. To simplify the illustrations, we are ignoring this difference in subsequent sections.

second example, the payments are less because the present value of the residual value reduces CNH's total recoverable amount from $100,000 to $96,895.40.

Lessee Accounting for Residual Value

Whether the estimated residual value is guaranteed or unguaranteed has both economic and accounting consequence to the lessee. We saw the economic consequence—lower lease payments—in the preceding example. The accounting consequence is that the **minimum lease payments**, the basis for capitalization, include the guaranteed residual value but exclude the unguaranteed residual value.

Guaranteed Residual Value (Lessee Accounting). A guaranteed residual value affects the lessee's computation of minimum lease payments. Therefore, it also affects the amounts capitalized as a leased asset and a lease obligation. In effect, the guaranteed residual value **is an additional lease payment that the lessee will pay in property or cash, or both, at the end of the lease term**.

Using the rental payments as computed by the lessor in Illustration 21-15, the minimum lease payments are $121,185.45 ([$23,237.09 × 5] + $5,000). Illustration 21-16 shows the capitalized present value of the minimum lease payments (excluding executory costs) for Ivanhoe.

ILLUSTRATION 21-16
Computation of Lessee's Capitalized Amount— Guaranteed Residual Value

IVANHOE'S CAPITALIZED AMOUNT (10% RATE)
ANNUITY-DUE BASIS, INCLUDING GUARANTEED RESIDUAL VALUE

Present value of five annual rental payments ($23,237.09 × 4.16986, Table 6-5)	$ 96,895.40
Present value of guaranteed residual value of $5,000 due five years after date of inception ($5,000 × .62092, Table 6-2)	3,104.60
Lessee's capitalized amount	$100,000.00

Ivanhoe prepares a schedule of interest expense and amortization of the $100,000 lease liability. That schedule, shown in Illustration 21-17, is based on a $5,000 final guaranteed residual value payment at the end of five years.

ILLUSTRATION 21-17
Lease Amortization Schedule for Lessee— Guaranteed Residual Value

IVANHOE MINES
LEASE AMORTIZATION SCHEDULE
ANNUITY-DUE BASIS, GUARANTEED RESIDUAL VALUE—GRV

Date	Lease Payment Plus GRV (a)	Executory Costs (b)	Interest (10%) on Liability (c)	Reduction of Lease Liability (d)	Lease Liability (e)
1/1/15					$100,000.00
1/1/15	$ 25,237.09	$ 2,000	$ –0–	$ 23,237.09	76,762.91
1/1/16	25,237.09	2,000	7,676.29	15,560.80	61,202.11
1/1/17	25,237.09	2,000	6,120.21	17,116.88	44,085.23
1/1/18	25,237.09	2,000	4,408.52	18,828.57	25,256.66
1/1/19	25,237.09	2,000	2,525.67	20,711.42	4,545.24
12/31/19	5,000.00*		454.76**	4,545.24	–0–
	$131,185.45	$10,000	$21,185.45	$100,000.00	

(a) Annual lease payment as required by lease.
(b) Executory costs included in rental payment.
(c) Preceding balance of (e) × 10%, except 1/1/15.
(d) (a) minus (b) and (c).
(e) Preceding balance minus (d).

*Represents the guaranteed residual value.
**Rounded by 24 cents.

Ivanhoe records the leased asset (front-end loader) and liability, depreciation, interest, property tax, and lease payments on the basis of a guaranteed residual value. (These journal entries are shown in Illustration 21-22, on page 1083.) The format of these entries is the same as illustrated earlier although the amounts are different because of the guaranteed residual value. Ivanhoe records the loader at $100,000 and depreciates it over five years. To compute depreciation, it subtracts the guaranteed residual value from the cost of the loader. Assuming that Ivanhoe uses the straight-line method, the depreciation expense each year is $19,000 ([$100,000 − $5,000] ÷ 5 years).

At the end of the lease term, before the lessee transfers the asset to CNH, the lease asset and liability accounts have the following balances.

Leased equipment (under capital leases)	$100,000.00	Interest payable	$ 454.76
Less: Accumulated depreciation—		Lease liability	4,545.24
leased equipment	95,000.00		
	$ 5,000.00		$5,000.00

ILLUSTRATION 21-18
Account Balances on Lessee's Books at End of Lease Term—Guaranteed Residual Value

If, at the end of the lease, the fair value of the residual value is less than $5,000, Ivanhoe will have to record a loss. Assume that Ivanhoe depreciated the leased asset down to its residual value of $5,000 but that the fair value of the residual value at December 31, 2019, was $3,000. In this case, Ivanhoe would have to report a loss of $2,000. Assuming that it pays cash to make up the residual value deficiency, Ivanhoe would make the following journal entry.

Loss on Disposal of Equipment	2,000.00	
Interest Expense (or Interest Payable)	454.76	
Lease Liability	4,545.24	
Accumulated Depreciation—Leased Equipment	95,000.00	
Leased Equipment		100,000.00
Cash		2,000.00

If the fair value *exceeds* $5,000, a gain may be recognized. CNH and Ivanhoe may apportion gains on guaranteed residual values in whatever ratio the parties initially agree.

When there is a guaranteed residual value, the lessee must be careful not to depreciate the total cost of the asset. For example, if Ivanhoe mistakenly depreciated the total cost of the loader ($100,000), a misstatement would occur. That is, the carrying amount of the asset at the end of the lease term would be zero, but Ivanhoe would show the liability under the finance lease at $5,000. In that case, if the asset was worth $5,000, Ivanhoe would end up reporting a gain of $5,000 when it transferred the asset back to CNH. As a result, Ivanhoe would overstate depreciation and would understate net income in 2015–2018; in the last year (2019), net income would be overstated.

Unguaranteed Residual Value (Lessee Accounting). From the lessee's viewpoint, an **unguaranteed residual value** is the same as no residual value in terms of its effect upon the lessee's method of computing the minimum lease payments and the capitalization of the leased asset and the lease liability.

Assume the same facts as those above except that the $5,000 residual value is **unguaranteed** instead of guaranteed. The amount of the annual lease payments would be the same—$23,237.09. Whether the residual value is guaranteed or unguaranteed, CNH will recover the same amount through lease rentals—that is, $96,895.40. The minimum lease payments are $116,185.45 ($23,237.09 × 5). Ivanhoe would capitalize the amount shown in Illustration 21-19 (on page 1082).

ILLUSTRATION 21-19
Computation of Lessee's
Capitalized Amount—
Unguaranteed Residual
Value

IVANHOE'S CAPITALIZED AMOUNT (10% RATE) ANNUITY-DUE BASIS, INCLUDING UNGUARANTEED RESIDUAL VALUE	
Present value of 5 annual rental payments of $23,237.09 × 4.16986 (Table 6-5)	$96,895.40
Unguaranteed residual value of $5,000 (not capitalized by lessee)	–0–
Lessee's capitalized amount	$96,895.40

Illustration 21-20 shows Ivanhoe's schedule of interest expense and amortization of the lease liability of $96,895.40, assuming an unguaranteed residual value of $5,000 at the end of five years.

ILLUSTRATION 21-20
Lease Amortization
Schedule for Lessee—
Unguaranteed Residual
Value

IVANHOE MINES LEASE AMORTIZATION SCHEDULE (10%) ANNUITY-DUE BASIS, UNGUARANTEED RESIDUAL VALUE					
Date	Annual Lease Payments	Executory Costs	Interest (10%) on Liability	Reduction of Lease Liability	Lease Liability
	(a)	(b)	(c)	(d)	(e)
1/1/15					$96,895.40
1/1/15	$ 25,237.09	$ 2,000	$ –0–	$23,237.09	73,658.31
1/1/16	25,237.09	2,000	7,365.83	15,871.26	57,787.05
1/1/17	25,237.09	2,000	5,778.71	17,458.38	40,328.67
1/1/18	25,237.09	2,000	4,032.87	19,204.22	21,124.45
1/1/19	25,237.09	2,000	2,112.64*	21,124.45	–0–
	$126,185.45	$10,000	$19,290.05	$96,895.40	

(a) Annual lease payment as required by lease.
(b) Executory costs included in rental payment.
(c) Preceding balance of (e) × 10%.
(d) (a) minus (b) and (c).
(e) Preceding balance minus (d).

*Rounded by 19 cents.

Ivanhoe records the leased asset and liability, depreciation, interest, property tax, and lease payments on the basis of an unguaranteed residual value. (These journal entries are shown in Illustration 21-22, on page 1083.) The format of these finance lease entries is the same as illustrated earlier. Note that Ivanhoe records the leased asset at $96,895.40 and depreciates it over five years. Assuming that the company uses the straight-line method, the depreciation expense each year is $19,379.08 ($96,895.40 ÷ 5 years). At the end of the lease term, before Ivanhoe transfers the asset to CNH, the lease asset and liability accounts have the following balances.

ILLUSTRATION 21-21
Account Balances on
Lessee's Books at
End of Lease Term—
Unguaranteed Residual
Value

Leased equipment	$96,895	Lease liability	$–0–
Less: Accumulated depreciation— leased equipment	96,895		
	$ –0–		

Assuming that Ivanhoe has fully depreciated the leased asset and has fully amortized the lease liability, no entry is required at the end of the lease term except to remove the asset from the books.

If Ivanhoe depreciated the asset down to its unguaranteed residual value, a misstatement would occur. That is, the carrying amount of the leased asset would be $5,000 at the end of the lease, but the liability under the finance lease would be stated at zero before the transfer of the asset. Thus, Ivanhoe would end up reporting a loss of $5,000 when it transferred the asset back to CNH. Ivanhoe would understate depreciation and would overstate net income in 2015–2018; in the last year (2019), net income would be understated because of the recorded loss.

Lessee Entries Involving Residual Values. Illustration 21-22 shows, in comparative form, Ivanhoe's entries for both a guaranteed and an unguaranteed residual value.

ILLUSTRATION 21-22
Comparative Entries for Guaranteed and Unguaranteed Residual Values, Lessee Company

Guaranteed Residual Value			Unguaranteed Residual Value		
Capitalization of lease (January 1, 2015):					
Leased Equipment	100,000.00		Leased Equipment	96,895.40	
Lease Liability		100,000.00	Lease Liability		96,895.40
First payment (January 1, 2015):					
Property Tax Expense	2,000.00		Property Tax Expense	2,000.00	
Lease Liability	23,237.09		Lease Liability	23,237.09	
Cash		25,237.09	Cash		25,237.09
Adjusting entry for accrued interest (December 31, 2015):					
Interest Expense	7,676.29		Interest Expense	7,365.83	
Interest Payable		7,676.29	Interest Payable		7,365.83
Entry to record depreciation (December 31, 2015):					
Depreciation Expense	19,000.00		Depreciation Expense	19,379.08	
Accumulated Depreciation—			Accumulated Depreciation—		
Leased Equipment		19,000.00	Leased Equipment		19,379.08
([$100,000 − $5,000] ÷ 5 years)			($96,895.40 ÷ 5 years)		
Second payment (January 1, 2016):					
Property Tax Expense	2,000.00		Property Tax Expense	2,000.00	
Lease Liability	15,560.80		Lease Liability	15,871.26	
Interest Expense			Interest Expense		
(or Interest Payable)	7,676.29		(or Interest Payable)	7,365.83	
Cash		25,237.09	Cash		25,237.09

Lessor Accounting for Residual Value

As we indicated earlier, the lessor will recover the same net investment whether the residual value is guaranteed or unguaranteed. That is, the lessor works on the assumption that it will realize **the residual value at the end of the lease term whether guaranteed or unguaranteed**. The lease payments required in order for the company to earn a certain return on investment are the same (e.g., $23,237.09 in our example) whether the residual value is guaranteed or unguaranteed.

To illustrate, we again use the CNH/Ivanhoe data and assume classification of the lease as a direct-financing lease. With a residual value (either guaranteed or unguaranteed) of $5,000, CNH determines the payments as follows.

ILLUSTRATION 21-23
Computation of Direct-Financing Lease Payments

Fair value of leased equipment	$100,000.00
Less: Present value of residual value ($5,000 × .62092, Table 6-2)	3,104.60
Amount to be recovered by lessor through lease payments	$ 96,895.40
Five beginning-of-the-year lease payments to yield a 10% return ($96,895.40 ÷ 4.16986, Table 6-5)	$ 23,237.09

The amortization schedule is the same for guaranteed or unguaranteed residual value, as Illustration 21-24 shows.

ILLUSTRATION 21-24
Lease Amortization Schedule, for Lessor—Guaranteed or Unguaranteed Residual Value

CNH CAPITAL
LEASE AMORTIZATION SCHEDULE
ANNUITY-DUE BASIS, GUARANTEED OR UNGUARANTEED RESIDUAL VALUE

Date	Annual Lease Payment Plus Residual Value (a)	Executory Costs (b)	Interest (10%) on Lease Receivable (c)	Lease Receivable Recovery (d)	Lease Receivable (e)
1/1/15					$100,000.00
1/1/15	$ 25,237.09	$ 2,000.00	$ –0–	$ 23,237.09	76,762.91
1/1/16	25,237.09	2,000.00	7,676.29	15,560.80	61,202.11
1/1/17	25,237.09	2,000.00	6,120.21	17,116.88	44,085.23
1/1/18	25,237.09	2,000.00	4,408.52	18,828.57	25,256.66
1/1/19	25,237.09	2,000.00	2,525.67	20,711.42	4,545.24
12/31/19	5,000.00	–0–	454.76*	4,545.24	–0–
	$131,185.45	$10,000.00	$21,185.45	$100,000.00	

(a) Annual lease payment as required by lease.
(b) Executory costs included in rental payment.
(c) Preceding balance of (e) × 10%, except 1/1/15.
(d) (a) minus (b) and (c).
(e) Preceding balance minus (d).

*Rounded by 24 cents.

Using the amounts computed above, CNH would make the entries shown in Illustration 21-25 for this direct-financing lease in the first year. Note the similarity to Ivanhoe's entries in Illustration 21-22 (on page 1083).

ILLUSTRATION 21-25
Entries for Either Guaranteed or Unguaranteed Residual Value, Lessor Company

Inception of lease (January 1, 2015):		
Lease Receivable	100,000.00	
Equipment		100,000.00

First payment received (January 1, 2015):		
Cash	25,237.09	
Lease Receivable		23,237.09
Property Tax Expense/Property Taxes Payable		2,000.00

Adjusting entry for accrued interest (December 31, 2015):		
Interest Receivable	7,676.29	
Interest Revenue		7,676.29

Sales-Type Leases (Lessor)

As already indicated, the primary difference between a direct-financing lease and a **sales-type lease** is the manufacturer's or dealer's gross profit (or loss). The diagram in Illustration 21-26 presents the distinctions between direct-financing and sales-type leases.

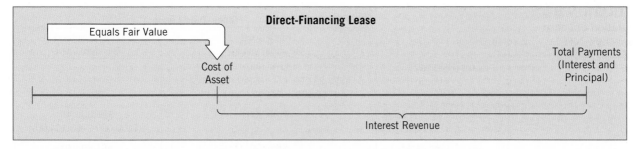

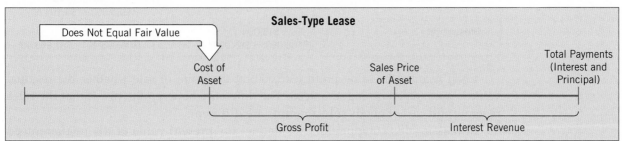

ILLUSTRATION 21-26
Direct-Financing versus
Sales-Type Leases

In a sales-type lease, the lessor records the sales price of the asset, the cost of goods sold and related inventory reduction, and the lease receivable. The information necessary to record the sales-type lease is as follows.

SALES-TYPE LEASE TERMS

LEASE RECEIVABLE (also referred to as **NET INVESTMENT**). The present value of the minimum lease payments plus the present value of any unguaranteed residual value. The lease receivable therefore includes the present value of the residual value, whether guaranteed or not.

SALES PRICE OF THE ASSET. The present value of the minimum lease payments.

COST OF GOODS SOLD. The cost of the asset to the lessor, less the present value of any unguaranteed residual value.

When recording sales revenue and cost of goods sold, there is a difference in the accounting for guaranteed and unguaranteed residual values. The guaranteed residual value can be considered part of sales revenue because the lessor knows that the entire asset has been sold. But, there is less certainty that the unguaranteed residual portion of the asset has been "sold" (i.e., will be realized). Therefore, the lessor recognizes sales and cost of goods sold only for the portion of the asset for which realization is assured. However, **the gross profit amount on the sale of the asset is the same whether a guaranteed or unguaranteed residual value is involved**.

To illustrate a sales-type lease with a guaranteed residual value and with an unguaranteed residual value, assume the same facts as in the preceding direct-financing lease situation (pages 1080–1081). The estimated residual value is $5,000 (the present value of which is $3,104.60), and the leased equipment has an $85,000 cost to the dealer (CNH). Assume that the fair value of the residual value is $3,000 at the end of the lease term.

Illustration 21-27 (on page 1086) shows the computation of the amounts relevant to a sales-type lease.

ILLUSTRATION 21-27
Computation of Lease
Amounts by CNH
Capital—Sales-Type
Lease

	Sales-Type Lease	
	Guaranteed Residual Value	Unguaranteed Residual Value
Lease receivable	$100,000 [$23,237.09 × 4.16986 (Table 6-5) + $5,000 ×.62092 (Table 6-2)]	Same
Sales price of the asset	$100,000	$96,895.40 ($100,000 − $3,104.60)
Cost of goods sold	$85,000	$81,895.40 ($85,000 − $3,104.60)
Gross profit	$15,000 ($100,000 − $85,000)	$15,000 ($96,895.40 − $81,895.40)

CNH records the same profit ($15,000) at the point of sale whether the residual value is guaranteed or unguaranteed. The difference between the two is that **the sales revenue and cost of goods sold amounts are different**.

In making this computation, we deduct the present value of the unguaranteed residual value from sales revenue and cost of goods sold. The reason—the revenue recognition criteria have not been met **because of the uncertainty surrounding the realization of the unguaranteed residual value**. That is, the gross profit recognized is the same as the amount recognized in an outright sale. **[9]**[15]

ILLUSTRATION 21-28
Entries for Guaranteed
and Unguaranteed
Residual Values, Lessor
Company—Sales-Type
Lease

CNH makes the entries shown in Illustration 21-28 to record this transaction on January 1, 2015, and the receipt of the residual value at the end of the lease term.

Guaranteed Residual Value			Unguaranteed Residual Value		
To record sales-type lease at inception (January 1, 2015):					
Cost of Goods Sold	85,000.00		Cost of Goods Sold	81,895.40	
Lease Receivable	100,000.00		Lease Receivable	100,000.00	
Sales Revenue		100,000.00	Sales Revenue		96,895.40
Inventory		85,000.00	Inventory		85,000.00
To record receipt of the first lease payment (January 1, 2015):					
Cash	25,237.09		Cash	25,237.09	
Lease Receivable		23,237.09	Lease Receivable		23,237.09
Property Tax Exp./Pay.		2,000.00	Property Tax Exp./Pay.		2,000.00
To recognize interest revenue earned during the first year (December 31, 2015):					
Interest Receivable	7,676.29		Interest Receivable	7,676.29	
Interest Revenue		7,676.29	Interest Revenue		7,676.29
(see lease amortization schedule, Illustration 21-17 on page 1080)					
To record receipt of the second lease payment (January 1, 2016):					
Cash	25,237.09		Cash	25,237.09	
Interest Receivable		7,676.29	Interest Receivable		7,676.29
Lease Receivable		15,560.80	Lease Receivable		15,560.80
Property Tax Exp./Pay.		2,000.00	Property Tax Exp./Pay.		2,000.00
To recognize interest revenue earned during the second year (December 31, 2016):					
Interest Receivable	6,120.21		Interest Receivable	6,120.21	
Interest Revenue		6,120.21	Interest Revenue		6,120.21
To record receipt of residual value at end of lease term (December 31, 2019):					
Inventory	3,000		Inventory	3,000	
Cash	2,000		Loss on Disposal of Equipment	2,000	
Lease Receivable		5,000	Lease Receivable		5,000

[15]Thus, in accounting for sales-type leases, lessors must also look to IFRS to apply revenue recognition guidelines. Recall (in Chapter 18) that revenue is recognized when a performance obligation is satisfied.

Companies must periodically review the **estimated unguaranteed residual value in a sales-type lease**. If the estimate of the unguaranteed residual value declines, the company must revise the accounting for the transaction using the changed estimate. The decline represents a reduction in the lessor's lease receivable (net investment). The lessor recognizes the decline as a loss in the period in which it reduces the residual estimate. Companies do not recognize upward adjustments in estimated residual value.

Bargain-Purchase Option (Lessee)

As stated earlier, a bargain-purchase option allows the lessee to purchase the leased property for a future price that is substantially lower than the property's expected future fair value. The price is so favorable at the lease's inception that the future exercise of the option appears to be reasonably assured. If a bargain-purchase option exists, **the lessee must increase the present value of the minimum lease payments by the present value of the option price**.

For example, assume that Ivanhoe Mines in Illustration 21-17 (on page 1080) had an option to buy the leased equipment for $5,000 at the end of the five-year lease term. At that point, Ivanhoe and CNH expect the fair value to be $18,000. The significant difference between the option price and the fair value creates a bargain-purchase option, and the exercise of that option is reasonably assured.

A bargain-purchase option affects the accounting for leases in essentially the same way as a guaranteed residual value. In other words, with a guaranteed residual value, the lessee must pay the residual value at the end of the lease. Similarly, a purchase option that is a bargain will almost certainly be paid by the lessee. Therefore, the computations, amortization schedule, and entries that would be prepared for this $5,000 bargain-purchase option are identical to those shown for the $5,000 guaranteed residual value (see Illustrations 21-15, 21-16, and 21-17 on pages 1079 and 1080).

The only difference between the accounting treatment for a bargain-purchase option and a guaranteed residual value of identical amounts and circumstances is in the **computation of the annual depreciation**. In the case of a guaranteed residual value, Ivanhoe depreciates the asset over the lease term; in the case of a bargain-purchase option, it uses the **economic life** of the asset.

Initial Direct Costs (Lessor)

Initial direct costs are of two types: incremental and internal. **Incremental direct costs** are paid to independent third parties for originating a lease arrangement. Examples include the cost of independent appraisal of collateral used to secure a lease, the cost of an outside credit check of the lessee, or a broker's fee for finding the lessee.

Internal direct costs are directly related to specified activities performed **by the lessor** on a given lease. Examples are evaluating the prospective lessee's financial condition; evaluating and recording guarantees, collateral, and other security arrangements; negotiating lease terms and preparing and processing lease documents; and closing the transaction. The costs directly related to an employee's time spent on a specific lease transaction are also considered initial direct costs.

However, initial direct costs should **not** include **internal indirect costs**. Such costs are related to activities the lessor performs for advertising, servicing existing leases, and establishing and monitoring credit policies. Nor should the lessor include the costs for supervision and administration or for expenses such as rent and depreciation.

The accounting for initial direct costs depends on the type of lease: [10]

- For **operating leases**, the lessor should defer initial direct costs and **allocate them over the lease term** in proportion to the recognition of rental revenue.[16]
- For **sales-type leases**, the lessor expenses the initial direct costs **in the period** in which it recognizes the profit on the sale.
- For a **direct-financing lease**, the lessor adds initial direct costs to the net investment in the lease and **amortizes them over the life of the lease as a yield adjustment**.

In a direct-financing lease, the lessor must disclose the unamortized deferred initial direct costs that are part of its investment in the direct-financing lease. For example, if the carrying value of the asset in the lease is $4,000,000 and the lessor incurs initial direct costs of $35,000, then the lease receivable (net investment in the lease) would be $4,035,000. The yield would be lower than the initial rate of return, and the lessor would adjust the yield to ensure proper amortization of the amount over the life of the lease.

Current versus Non-Current

Earlier in the chapter, we presented the classification of the lease liability/receivable in an annuity-due situation. Illustration 21-7 (on page 1071) indicated that Ivanhoe's current liability is the payment of $23,981.62 (excluding $2,000 of executory costs) to be made on January 1 of the next year. Similarly, as shown in Illustration 21-14 (on page 1077), CNH's current asset is the $23,981.62 (excluding $2,000 of executory costs) it will collect on January 1 of the next year. In these annuity-due instances, the statement of financial position date is December 31 and the due date of the lease payment is January 1 (less than one year), so the present value ($23,981.62) of the payment due the following January 1 is the same as the rental payment ($23,981.62).

What happens if the situation is an ordinary annuity rather than an annuity due? For example, assume that the rent is due at the **end of the year** (December 31) rather than at the beginning (January 1). Lease liabilities should be classified into current and non-current amounts. [11] However, IFRS does not indicate how to measure the current and non-current amounts. **A common method of measuring the current liability portion in ordinary annuity leases is the change-in-the-present-value method.**

To illustrate the change-in-the-present-value method, assume an ordinary-annuity situation with the same facts as the CNH/Ivanhoe case, excluding the $2,000 of executory costs. Because Ivanhoe pays the rents at the end of the period instead of at the beginning, CNH sets the five rents at $26,379.73, to have an effective-interest

---

[16]Technically, initial direct costs for operating leases are reported as an addition to the carrying amount of the leased asset. Because the deferred costs may be amortized on a different basis that used for depreciation expense, it is common for lessors to present these amounts as follows (assumed amounts).

Leased assets	€100,000
Less: Accumulated depreciation—leased assets	20,000
	80,000
Deferred initial direct costs	10,000
	€ 90,000

rate of 10 percent. Illustration 21-29 shows the ordinary-annuity amortization schedule.

IVANHOE/CNH LEASE AMORTIZATION SCHEDULE ORDINARY-ANNUITY BASIS				
Date	Annual Lease Payment	Interest 10%	Reduction of Lease Liability/Receivable	Balance of Lease Liability/Receivable
1/1/15				$100,000.00
12/31/15	$ 26,379.73	$10,000.00	$ 16,379.73	83,620.27
12/31/16	26,379.73	8,362.03	18,017.70	65,602.57
12/31/17	26,379.73	6,560.26	19,819.47	45,783.10
12/31/18	26,379.73	4,578.31	21,801.42	23,981.68
12/31/19	26,379.73	2,398.05*	23,981.68	–0–
	$131,898.65	$31,898.65	$100,000.00	

*Rounded by 12 cents.

ILLUSTRATION 21-29
Lease Amortization Schedule—Ordinary-Annuity Basis

The current portion of the lease liability/receivable under the **change-in-the-present-value method** as of December 31, 2015, would be $18,017.70 ($83,620.27 − $65,602.57). As of December 31, 2016, the current portion would be $19,819.47 ($65,602.57 − $45,783.10). At December 31, 2015, CNH classifies $65,602.57 of the receivable as non-current.

Thus, both the annuity-due and the ordinary-annuity situations report the reduction of principal for the next period as a current liability/current asset. In the annuity-due situation, CNH accrues interest during the year but is not paid until the next period. As a result, **a current asset arises for the receivable reduction and for the interest** that was earned in the preceding period.

In the ordinary-annuity situation, the interest accrued during the period is also paid in the same period. Consequently, the lessor shows as a current asset only the principal reduction due in the next period.

Disclosing Lease Data

In addition to the amounts reported in the financial statements related to lease assets and liabilities, the IASB requires **lessees** and **lessors** to disclose certain information about leases. These requirements vary based upon the type of lease (finance or operating) and whether the issuer is the lessor or lessee. These disclosure requirements provide investors with the following information:

9 LEARNING OBJECTIVE
List the disclosure requirements for leases.

For lessees: [12]

• A general description of material leasing arrangements.

• A reconciliation between the total of future minimum lease payments at the end of the reporting period and their present value.

• The total of future minimum lease payments at the end of the reporting period, and their present value for periods (1) not later than one year, (2) later than one year and not later than five years, and (3) later than five years.

For lessors: [13]

• A general description of material leasing arrangements.

- A reconciliation between the gross investment in the lease at the end of the reporting period, and the present value of minimum lease payments receivable at the end of the reporting period.
- Unearned finance income.
- The gross investment in the lease and the present value of minimum lease payments receivable at the end of the reporting period for periods (1) not later than one year, (2) later than one year and not later than five years, and (3) later than five years.

Illustration 21-30 presents financial statement excerpts from the 2012 annual report of **Delhaize Group** (BEL). These excerpts represent the statement and note disclosures typical of a lessee having both finance leases and operating leases.

ILLUSTRATION 21-30
Disclosure of Leases
by Lessee

Delhaize Group
(in millions)

	2012
Non-Current Liabilities	
Long-term obligations under finance leases, less current portion	€612
Current Liabilities	
Current obligations under finance leases	€62

18.3 Leases

General description

Delhaize Group operates a significant number of its stores under finance and operating lease arrangements. Various properties leased are (partially or fully) subleased to third parties, where the Group is therefore acting as a lessor (see further below). Lease terms (including reasonably certain renewal options) generally range from 1 to 45 years with renewal options ranging from 3 to 30 years.

The schedule below provides the future minimum lease payments, which were not reduced by expected minimum sublease income of €35 million, due over the term of non-cancellable subleases, as of December 31, 2012:

Reconciliation, timing, and amounts of cash outflows

(in millions of €)	2013	2014	2015	2016	2017	Thereafter	Total
Finance leases							
Future minimum lease payments	129	115	111	101	90	772	**1,318**
Less amount representing interest	(67)	(64)	(59)	(54)	(48)	(352)	**(644)**
Present value of minimum lease payments	62	51	52	47	42	420	**674**
Of which related to closed store lease obligations	6	5	5	5	4	33	**58**
Operating leases							
Future minimum lease payments (for non-cancellable leases)	312	260	231	195	164	754	**1,916**
Of which related to closed store lease obligations	21	18	15	14	12	49	**129**

Additional information

The average effective interest rate for finance leases was 11.6% at December 31, 2012. The fair value of the Group's finance lease obligations using an average market rate of 5.1% at December 31, 2012 was €842 million.

Rent payments, including scheduled rent increases, are recognized on a straight-line basis over the minimum lease term. Total rent expense under operating leases was €300 million in 2012, being included predominately in "Selling, general and administrative expenses."

Illustration 21-31 presents the lease note disclosure from the 2012 annual report of **Trinity Biotech plc** (IRL). The disclosure highlights required lessor disclosures.

Trinity Biotech
Notes to Financial Statements
(in millions)

ILLUSTRATION 21-31
Disclosure of Leases
by Lessor

Note 16: Trade and Other Receivables (in part)

Finance Lease Commitments

The Group leases instruments as part of its business. Future minimum finance lease receivables with non-cancellable terms are as follows:

General description

	December 31, 2012 US$'000		
	Gross Investment	Unearned Income	Minimum Payments Receivable
Less than one year	604	213	391
Between one and five years	1,341	509	832
	1,945	722	1,223

Reconciliation and timing of amounts receivable and unearned revenue

Operating Lease Commitments

The Group has leased a facility consisting of 9,000 square feet in Dublin, Ireland. This property has been sublet by the Group. The lease contains a clause to enable upward revision of the rent charge on a periodic basis. The Group also leases instruments under operating leases as part of its business. Future minimum rentals receivable under non-cancellable operating leases are as follows:

Description of leased assets

	December 31, 2012 US$'000		
	Land and Buildings	Instruments	Total
Less than one year	232	4,641	4,873
Between one and five years	636	2,323	2,959
More than five years	—	—	—
	868	6,964	7,832

Nature, timing, and amounts of future rentals

Unresolved Lease Accounting Problems

As we indicated at the beginning of this chapter, lease accounting is subject to abuse. Companies make strenuous efforts to circumvent IFRS in this area. In practice, the strong desires of lessees to resist capitalization have rendered the accounting rules for capitalizing leases partially ineffective. Leasing generally involves large monetary amounts that, when capitalized, materially increase reported liabilities and adversely affect the debt to equity ratio. Lessees also resist lease capitalization because charges to expense made in the early years of the lease term are higher under the finance lease method than under the operating method, frequently without tax benefit. As a consequence, "let's beat the lease standard" is one of the most popular games in town.

To avoid leased asset capitalization, companies design, write, and interpret lease agreements to prevent satisfying any of the four finance lease criteria. Companies can easily devise lease agreements in such a way, by meeting the following specifications.

1. Ensure that the lease does not specify the transfer of title of the property to the lessee.

2. Do not write in a bargain-purchase option.

3. Set the lease term sufficiently below the estimated economic life of the leased property such that the economic life test is not met.

4. Arrange for the present value of the minimum lease payments to be sufficiently less than the fair value of the leased property.

The real challenge lies in disqualifying the lease as a finance lease to the lessee, while having the same lease qualify as a finance (sales or financing) lease to the lessor. Unlike lessees, lessors try to avoid having lease arrangements classified as operating leases.[17]

Avoiding the first three criteria is relatively simple, but it takes a little ingenuity to avoid the recovery of investment test for the lessee while satisfying it for the lessor. Two of the factors involved in this effort are (1) the use of the incremental borrowing rate by the lessee when it is higher than the implicit interest rate of the lessor, by making information about the implicit rate unavailable to the lessee; and (2) residual value guarantees.

The lessee's use of the higher interest rate is probably the more popular subterfuge. Lessees are knowledgeable about the fair value of the leased property and, of course, the rental payments. However, they generally are unaware of the estimated residual value used by the lessor. Therefore, the lessee who does not know exactly the lessor's implicit interest rate might use a different (higher) incremental borrowing rate.

The residual value guarantee is the other unique, yet popular, device used by lessees and lessors. In fact, a whole new industry has emerged to circumvent symmetry between the lessee and the lessor in accounting for leases. The residual value guarantee has spawned numerous companies whose principal, or even sole, function is to guarantee the residual value of leased assets.

Because the minimum lease payments include the guaranteed residual value for the lessor, this satisfies the recovery of investment test. The lease is a non-operating lease to the lessor. **But because a third-party guarantees the residual value, the minimum lease payments of the lessee exclude the guarantee.** Thus, by merely transferring some of the risk to a third party, lessees can alter substantially the accounting treatment by converting what would otherwise be finance leases to operating leases.[18]

The nature of the criteria encourages much of this circumvention, stemming from weaknesses in the basic objective of the lease accounting guidelines to determine whether the lease qualifies as an operating or finance lease. This is often a very blurry line. The IASB has recognized that the existing lease accounting does not meet investors' needs and has proposed new rules to improve lease accounting.

Based on a right of use model, the proposed rules require that all leases, regardless of their terms, be accounted for in a manner similar to how finance leases are treated today. That is, the notion of an operating lease will be eliminated. In addition, the rules call for including not only the contractual amounts due over the lease term but also the lessee's best estimate of contingent rents due over that period. The lease term is not just the term of the initial lease but includes renewal periods that are more likely than not to occur.

Some believe that a more workable solution is to require capitalization of all leases that have non-cancelable payment terms in excess of one year. Under this approach, the lessee acquires an asset (a property right) and a corresponding liability, rather than on the basis that the lease transfers substantially all the risks and rewards of ownership.

---

[17]The reason is that most lessors are banks, which are not permitted to hold these assets on their statements of financial position except for relatively short periods of time. Furthermore, the finance lease transaction from the lessor's standpoint provides higher income flows in the earlier periods of the lease life.

[18]As an aside, third-party guarantors have experienced some difficulty. **Lloyd's of London** (GBR) at one time insured the fast-growing U.S. computer-leasing industry in the amount of $2 billion against revenue losses, and losses in residual value, for canceled leases. Because of "overnight" technological improvements and the successive introductions of more efficient and less expensive computers, lessees in abundance canceled their leases. As the market for second-hand computers became flooded, residual values plummeted, and third-party guarantor Lloyd's of London projected a loss of $400 million. The lessees' and lessors' desire to circumvent accounting rules stimulated much of the third-party guarantee business.

Many believe that if the lease accounting rules were to be reconsidered, they would support a property right approach in which all leases are included as "rights to use property" and as "lease obligations" in the lessee's statement of financial position. The IASB (with the FASB) has issued a proposal on lease accounting to address off-balance-sheet reporting of leases. As summarized in the table below, early analysis of the potential impact of the proposed leasing rules indicates significant impacts.

As indicated, over $1.3 trillion of operating leases will come on-balance-sheet if the rules are adopted. In addition, there will be a significant negative impact on lessee income statements in the early years of leases.

A quick look at the current leasing market, and some possible effects of the proposed rules:

- *$600 billion.* Annual volume of leased equipment.
- *70%.* Volume of real estate leases as a percentage of all leases held by public companies.
- *$1.3 trillion.* Amount of operating lease payments that public companies will bring back on-balance-sheet as capital leases under the proposed rule.
- *7%.* Potential first-year average increase in lease expense for a 3-year lease.
- *21%.* Potential first-year average increase in lease expense for a 10-year lease.

Source: Equipment Leasing and Finance Association, 2009; PricewaterhouseCoopers and Rotterdam School of Management, 2009.

As shown below, the frontloading of lease expenses will be felt by lessees in several industry sectors.

Lease Expense Impacts by Industry Sector			
Sector	Typical Lease Term (Years)	First-Year % Increase Prompted by New Rules*	Cumulative % Increase Through Peak Year*
Airline	17	26%	128%/yr. 9
Automotive fleet	3	4	N/A
Banking	10	21	64%/yr. 5
Copier/office equipment	3	7	7%/yr. 3
Equipment manufacturers	5	11	17%/yr. 2
Healthcare equipment	5	11	17%/yr. 2
Information technology	3	7	7%/yr. 2
Rail	22	26	200%/yr. 12
Real estate	10	21	64%/yr. 5
Trucking	7	16	33%/yr. 4

*As compared with the straight-line method of accounting.
Source: Equipment Leasing and Finance Association, 2009.

Given these effects—increased reported debt and lower income—as a consequence of these proposed rules, it is not surprising that the IASB (and FASB) is receiving numerous comments opposing changes in lease accounting rules. For example, a recent survey of analysts indicates fairly strong support for bringing operating leases out of the notes and onto the statement of financial position. At the same time, an analysis of the new rules and how they might impact the advantages of leasing (presented in the following table) suggests that many of the advantages of leases will remain after implementation of the new rules.

Reason for Leasing	Details	Status After Proposed New Rules Implemented
Funding source	Additional capital source, 100% financing, fixed rate, level payments, longer terms.	Still a major benefit versus a purchase—money loan financing, fixed rate, level payments—especially for smaller companies with limited sources of capital.
Low-cost capital	Low payments/rate due to tax benefits, residual and lessor's comparatively low cost of funds.	Still a benefit versus a loan.
Tax benefits	Lessee cannot use tax benefits and lease versus buy shows lease option offers lowest after tax cost.	Still a benefit.
Manage need for assets/ residual risk transfer	Lessee has flexibility to return asset.	Still a benefit.
Convenience	Quick and convenient financing process often available at point-of-sale.	Still a benefit.
Regulatory	Can help in meeting capital requirements.	Still a partial benefit if the capitalized amount is less than the cost of the asset as it is in many leases due to residuals assumed and tax benefits.
Accounting	Asset and liability off-balance-sheet.	Still a partial benefit if the capitalized amount is less than the cost of the asset as it is in many leases due to residuals assumed and tax benefits.

Source: Equipment Leasing & Finance Foundation, *2011 State of the Equipment Finance Industry Report.*

So while concerns about changes in lease accounting may be valid, accounting standard-setters are resolved to address lease accounting deficiencies. As the chairperson of the IASB remarked, ". . . a financing, in the form of a loan to purchase an asset, then it would be recorded. Call it a lease and miraculously it does not show up in your books. In my book, if it looks like a duck, swims like a duck, and quacks like a duck, then it probably is a duck. So is the case with debt—leasing or otherwise."

We hope that new accounting rules can be developed so that financial statements provide relevant and representationally faithful information about leasing arrangements.

Sources: M. Leone, "Taking the 'Ease' Out of 'Lease'?" *CFO Magazine* (December 1, 2010); and Hans Hoogervorst, "Harmonisation and Global Economic Consequences," public lecture at the London School of Economics (November 6, 2012). Survey results from *Lease Accounting Survey Report,* CFA Institute (October 2013).

GLOBAL ACCOUNTING INSIGHTS

LEASE ACCOUNTING

Leasing is a global business. Lessors and lessees enter into arrangements with one another without regard to national boundaries. Although U.S. GAAP and IFRS for leasing are similar, both the FASB and the IASB have decided that the existing accounting does not provide the most useful, transparent, and complete information about leasing transactions that should be provided in the financial statements.

Relevant Facts

Following are the key similarities and differences between U.S. GAAP and IFRS related to the accounting for leases.

Similarities

• Both U.S. GAAP and IFRS share the same objective of recording leases by lessees and lessors according to their economic substance, that is, according to the definitions of assets and liabilities.

- Much of the terminology for lease accounting in U.S. GAAP and IFRS is the same.

- Under U.S. GAAP and IFRS, lessees and lessors use the same general lease capitalization criteria to determine if the risks and rewards of ownership have been transferred in the lease.

Differences

- One difference in lease terminology is that finance leases are referred to as capital leases in U.S. GAAP.

- U.S. GAAP for leases uses bright-line criteria to determine if a lease arrangement transfers the risks and rewards of ownership; IFRS is more general in its provisions.

- U.S. GAAP has additional lessor criteria: payments are collectible, and there are no additional costs associated with a lease.

- U.S. GAAP requires use of the incremental rate unless the implicit rate is known by the lessee and the implicit

rate is lower than the incremental rate. IFRS requires that lessees use the implicit rate to record a lease unless it is impractical to determine the lessor's implicit rate.

- Under U.S. GAAP, extensive disclosure of future non-cancelable lease payments is required for each of the next five years and the years thereafter. IFRS does not require it although some companies (e.g., **Nokia** (FIN)) provide a year-by-year breakout of payments due in years 1 through 5.

- The FASB standard for leases was originally issued in 1976. The standard (*SFAS No. 13*) has been the subject of more than 30 interpretations since its issuance. The IFRS leasing standard is *IAS 17*, first issued in 1982. This standard is the subject of only three interpretations. One reason for this small number of interpretations is that IFRS does not specifically address a number of leasing transactions that are covered by U.S. GAAP. Examples include lease agreements for natural resources, sale-leasebacks, real estate leases, and leveraged leases.

About the Numbers

Under U.S. GAAP, extensive disclosure of future non-cancelable lease payments is required for each of the next five years and the years thereafter, as shown in disclosure below by **Wal-Mart Stores, Inc.** (USA).

Note 12: Commitments

The Company and certain of its subsidiaries have long-term leases for stores and equipment. Aggregate minimum annual rentals at January 31, 2012, under non-cancelable leases are as follows (amounts in millions):

	Operating Leases	Capital Leases
2013	$1,644	$ 608
2014	1,590	580
2015	1,525	532
2016	1,428	497
2017	1,312	457
Thereafter	8,916	3,261
Total minimum rentals		$5,935
Less estimated executory costs		50
Net minimum lease payments		$5,885
Less imputed interest		2,550
Present value of minimum lease payments		$3,335

Rental expense was approximately $2.4 billion in 2012 and $2 billion in 2011.

On the Horizon

Lease accounting is one of the areas identified in the IASB/FASB Memorandum of Understanding. The Boards have issued proposed rules based on "right of use," which requires that all leases, regardless of their terms, be accounted for in a manner similar to how finance leases are treated today. That is, the notion of an operating lease

will be eliminated, which will address the concerns under current rules in which no asset or liability is recorded for many operating leases. A final standard is expected in 2015. You can follow the lease project at the IASB website (*http://www.iasb.org*).

SUMMARY OF LEARNING OBJECTIVES

1 Explain the nature, economic substance, and advantages of lease transactions. A lease is a contractual agreement between a lessor and a lessee that conveys to the lessee the right to use specific property (real or personal), owned by the lessor, for a specified period of time. In return, the lessee periodically pays cash (rent) to the lessor. The advantages of lease transactions are (1) 100 percent financing, (2) protection against obsolescence, (3) flexibility, (4) less costly financing, (5) possible tax advantages, and (6) off-balance-sheet financing.

2 Describe the accounting criteria and procedures for capitalizing leases by the lessee. A lease is a finance lease if it meets one or more of the following criteria. (1) The lease transfers ownership of the property to the lessee. (2) The lease contains a bargain-purchase option. (3) The lease term is for a major part of the estimated economic life of the leased property. (4) The present value of the minimum lease payments (excluding executory costs) amounts to subtantially all of the fair value of the leased property. For a finance lease, the lessee records an asset and a liability at the present value of the minimum lease payments at the inception of the lease.

3 Contrast the operating and capitalization methods of recording leases. The total charges to operations are the same over the lease term whether accounting for the lease as a finance lease or as an operating lease. Under the finance lease treatment, the charges are higher in the earlier years and lower in the later years. If using an accelerated method of depreciation, the differences between the amounts charged to operations under the two methods would be even larger in the earlier and later years. If using a finance lease instead of an operating lease, the following occurs: (1) an increase in the amount of reported debt (both short-term and long-term), (2) an increase in the amount of total assets (specifically long-lived assets), and (3) lower income early in the life of the lease and, therefore, lower retained earnings.

4 Explain the advantages and economics of leasing to lessors and identify the classifications of leases for the lessor. Three important benefits available to the lessor are (1) interest revenue, (2) tax incentives, and (3) residual value profits. Lessors are essentially renting or selling assets, and in many cases are providing financing for the purchase of the asset. The lessor determines the amount of the rental, basing it on the rate of return—the implicit rate—needed to justify leasing the asset, taking into account the credit standing of the lessee, the length of the lease, and the status of the residual value (guaranteed versus unguaranteed).

A lessor may classify leases for accounting purposes as follows: (1) operating leases, (2) direct-financing leases, and (3) sales-type leases. The lessor should classify and account for an arrangement as a direct-financing lease or a sales-type lease if, at the date of the lease agreement, the lease meets one or more of the lease capitalization criteria (as shown in learning objective 2 for lessees). The lessor classifies and accounts for all leases that fail to meet the criteria as operating leases.

5 Describe the lessor's accounting for direct-financing leases. Leases that are in substance the financing of an asset purchase by a lessee require the lessor to substitute a "lease receivable" for the leased asset. "Lease receivable" is the present value of the minimum lease payments plus the present value of the unguaranteed residual value. Therefore, lessors include the residual value, whether guaranteed or unguaranteed, as part of lease receivable.

6 **Identify special features of lease arrangements that cause unique accounting problems.** The features of lease arrangements that cause unique accounting problems are (1) residual values, (2) sales-type leases (lessor), (3) bargain-purchase options, (4) initial direct costs, (5) current versus non-current, and (6) disclosure.

7 **Describe the effect of residual values, guaranteed and unguaranteed, on lease accounting.** Whether the estimated residual value is guaranteed or unguaranteed is of both economic and accounting consequence to the lessee. The accounting consequence is that the minimum lease payments, the basis for capitalization, include the guaranteed residual value but exclude the unguaranteed residual value. A guaranteed residual value affects the lessee's computation of minimum lease payments and the amounts capitalized as a leased asset and a lease obligation. In effect, the guaranteed residual value is an additional lease payment that the lessee will pay in property or cash, or both, at the end of the lease term. An unguaranteed residual value from the lessee's viewpoint is the same as no residual value in terms of its effect upon the lessee's method of computing the minimum lease payments and the capitalization of the leased asset and the lease liability.

8 **Describe the lessor's accounting for sales-type leases.** A sales-type lease recognizes interest revenue like a direct-financing lease. It also recognizes a manufacturer's or dealer's profit. In a sales-type lease, the lessor records at the inception of the lease the sales price of the asset, the cost of goods sold and related inventory reduction, and the lease receivable. Sales-type leases differ from direct-financing leases in terms of the cost and fair value of the leased asset, which results in gross profit. Lease receivable and interest revenue are the same whether a guaranteed or an unguaranteed residual value is involved. The accounting for guaranteed and for unguaranteed residual values requires recording sales revenue and cost of goods sold differently. The guaranteed residual value can be considered part of sales revenue because the lessor knows that the entire asset has been sold. There is less certainty that the unguaranteed residual portion of the asset has been "sold"; therefore, lessors recognize sales and cost of goods sold only for the portion of the asset for which realization is assured. However, the gross profit amount on the sale of the asset is the same whether a guaranteed or unguaranteed residual value is involved.

9 **List the disclosure requirements for leases.** The disclosure requirements for lessees and lessors vary based upon the type of lease (finance or operating) and whether the issuer is the lessor or lessee. These disclosure requirements provide investors with the following information: (1) general description of the nature of leasing arrangements; (2) the nature, timing, and amount of cash inflows and outflows associated with leases, including payments to be paid or received in the next year, in years 2–5, and years thereafter; and (3) amounts receivable and unearned revenues under lease agreements.

APPENDIX **21A**	EXAMPLES OF LEASE ARRANGEMENTS

To illustrate concepts discussed in this chapter, assume that Morgan Bakeries is involved in four different lease situations. Each of these leases is non-cancelable, and in no case does Morgan receive title to the properties leased during or at the end of the lease term. All leases start on January 1, 2015, with the first rental due at the beginning of the year. The additional information is shown in Illustration 21A-1 (on page 1098).

10 **LEARNING OBJECTIVE**
Understand and apply lease accounting concepts to various lease arrangements.

	Harmon, Inc.	Arden's Oven Co.	Mendota Truck Co.	Appleland Computer
Type of property	Cabinets	Oven	Truck	Computer
Yearly rental	€6,000	€15,000	€5,582.62	€3,557.25
Lease term	20 years	10 years	3 years	3 years
Estimated economic life	30 years	25 years	7 years	5 years
Purchase option	None	€75,000 at end of 10 years €4,000 at end of 15 years	None	€3,000 at end of 3 years, which approximates fair value
Renewal option	None	5-year renewal option at €15,000 per year	None	1 year at €1,500; no penalty for non-renewal; standard renewal clause
Fair value at inception of lease	€70,000	€120,000	€20,000	€10,000
Cost of asset to lessor	€70,000	€120,000	€15,000	€10,000
Residual value Guaranteed/Unguaranteed	–0– € 5,000	–0– –0–	€ 7,000 –0–	–0– € 3,000
Incremental borrowing rate of lessee	12%	12%	12%	12%
Executory costs paid by	Lessee €300 per year	Lessee €1,000 per year	Lessee €500 per year	Lessor Estimated to be €500 per year
Present value of minimum lease payments Using incremental borrowing rate of lessee	€50,194.68	€115,153.35	€20,000	€8,224.16
Using implicit rate of lessor	Impracticable to determine	Impracticable to determine	Known by lessee, €20,000	Known by lessee, €8,027.45
Estimated fair value at end of lease	€5,000	€80,000 at end of 10 years €60,000 at end of 15 years	Not available	€3,000

ILLUSTRATION 21A-1
Illustrative Lease
Situations, Lessors

EXAMPLE 1: HARMON, INC.

The following is an analysis of the Harmon, Inc. lease.

1. **Transfer of title?** No.

2. **Bargain-purchase option?** No.

3. **Economic life test:** The lease term is 20 years and the estimated economic life is 30 years. Thus, it **does not** meet the economic life test.

4. **Recovery of investment test:**

Rental payments	€ 6,000
PV of annuity due for 20 years at 12%	× 8.36578
PV of rental payments	€50,194.68

Because the present value of the minimum lease payments is just 72 percent (€50,195 ÷ €70,000) of the fair value of the asset, it does not appear that this is a substantial part of the fair value of the asset. Thus, the lease does not meet the recovery of investment test.

Both Morgan and Harmon should account for this lease as an operating lease, as indicated by the January 1, 2015, entries shown in Illustration 21A-2.

Morgan Bakeries (Lessee)			Harmon, Inc. (Lessor)		
Rent Expense	6,000		Cash	6,000	
Cash		6,000	Rent Revenue		6,000

ILLUSTRATION 21A-2
Comparative Entries for
Operating Lease

EXAMPLE 2: ARDEN'S OVEN CO.

The following is an analysis of the Arden's Oven Co. lease.

1. **Transfer of title?** No.
2. **Bargain-purchase option?** The €75,000 option at the end of 10 years does not appear to be sufficiently lower than the expected fair value of €80,000 to make it reasonably assured that it will be exercised. However, the €4,000 at the end of 15 years when the fair value is €60,000 does appear to be a bargain. From the information given, criterion 2 is therefore met. Note that both the guaranteed and the unguaranteed residual values are assigned zero values because the lessor does not expect to repossess the leased asset.
3. **Economic life test:** Given that a bargain-purchase option exists, the lease term is the initial lease period of 10 years plus the five-year renewal option since it precedes a bargain-purchase option. Even though the lease term is now considered to be 15 years, this test is still not met because the term of the lease is just 60 percent (15 years ÷ 25 years).
4. **Recovery of investment test:**

Rental payments	€ 15,000.00
PV of annuity due for 15 years at 12%	× 7.62817
PV of rental payments	€114,422.55

PV of bargain-purchase option = €4,000 × (PVF$_{15,12\%}$) = €4,000 × .18270 = €730.80

PV of rental payments	€114,422.55
PV of bargain-purchase option	730.80
PV of minimum lease payments	€115,153.35

The present value of the minimum lease payments is 96 percent (€115,153 ÷ €120,000) of the fair value of the asset. Thus, the recovery of investment test appears to be met since substantially all of the fair value of the asset will be recovered in the lease payments. Note that the incremental borrowing rate is used here because it is impracticable to determine the implicit rate of the lessor.

Morgan Bakeries should account for this as a finance lease because the lease meets both criteria 2 and 4. Assuming that Arden's implicit rate is less than Morgan's incremental borrowing rate, the following entries are made on January 1, 2015.

Morgan Bakeries (Lessee)			Arden's Oven Co. (Lessor)		
Leased Equipment	115,153.35		Lease Receivable	120,000	
Lease Liability		115,153.35	Asset (oven)		120,000

ILLUSTRATION 21A-3
Comparative Entries for
Finance Lease—Bargain-
Purchase Option

Morgan Bakeries would depreciate the leased asset over its economic life of 25 years, given the bargain-purchase option. Arden's Oven Co. does not use sales-type accounting because the fair value and the cost of the asset are the same at the inception of the lease.

EXAMPLE 3: MENDOTA TRUCK CO.

The following is an analysis of the Mendota Truck Co. lease.

1. **Transfer of title?** No.
2. **Bargain-purchase option?** No.
3. **Economic life test:** The lease term is three years and is just 43 percent of the estimated economic life of seven years. Thus, it **does not** meet the economic life test.
4. **Recovery of investment test:**

Rental payments	€ 5,582.62
PV of annuity due for 3 years at 12%	× 2.69005
PV of rental payments	€15,017.54

(Note: Adjusted for €0.01 due to rounding)

PV of guaranteed residual value = €7,000 × (PVF$_{3,12\%}$) = €7,000 × .71178 = €4,982.46

PV of rental payments	€15,017.54
PV of guaranteed residual value	4,982.46
PV of minimum lease payments	€20,000.00

The present value of the minimum lease payments is equal to the fair value; therefore, the lease meets the recovery of investment.

Assuming that Mendota's implicit rate is the same as Morgan's incremental borrowing rate, the following entries are made on January 1, 2015.

ILLUSTRATION 21A-4
Comparative Entries for
Finance Lease

Morgan Bakeries (Lessee)			Mendota Truck Co. (Lessor)		
Leased Equipment	20,000		Lease Receivable	20,000	
Lease Liability		20,000	Cost of Goods Sold	15,000	
			Inventory (truck)		15,000
			Sales Revenue		20,000

Morgan depreciates the leased asset over three years to its guaranteed residual value.

EXAMPLE 4: APPLELAND COMPUTER

The following is an analysis of the Appleland Computer lease.

1. **Transfer of title?** No.
2. **Bargain-purchase option?** No. The option to purchase at the end of three years at approximate fair value is clearly not a bargain.
3. **Economic life test:** The lease term is three years, which is just 60 percent (3 years ÷ 5 years) of the economic life of the asset, and no bargain-renewal period exists. Therefore, the economic life test **is not** met.
4. **Recovery of investment test:**

Rental payments	€3,557.25
Less executory costs	500.00
	3,057.25
PV of annuity-due factor for 3 years at 12%	× 2.69005
PV of minimum lease payments using incremental borrowing rate	€8,224.16

The present value of the minimum lease payments using the incremental borrowing rate is €8,224.16 (see Illustration 21A-1 on page 1098). However, the higher implicit rate used by the lessor is known by Morgan. Given this situation, the lessee uses the implicit rate, which results in a present value of €8,027.45. Because the present value of the minimum lease payments is just 80 percent (€8,027 ÷ €10,000) of the fair value, the lease does **not** meet the recovery of investment test.

The following entries are made on January 1, 2015, indicating an operating lease.

Morgan Bakeries (Lessee)		Appleland Computer (Lessor)	
Rent Expense	3,557.25	Cash	3,557.25
Cash	3,557.25	Rent Revenue	3,557.25

ILLUSTRATION 21A-5
Comparative Entries for Operating Lease

SUMMARY OF LEARNING OBJECTIVE FOR APPENDIX 21A

10 **Understand and apply lease accounting concepts to various lease arrangements.** The classification of leases by lessees and lessors is based on criteria that assess whether the lessor has transferred to the lessee substantially all of the risks and benefits of ownership of the asset. Lessees capitalize leases that meet any of the criteria, recording a lease asset and related lease liability. For leases that are in substance a financing of an asset purchase, lessors substitute a lease receivable for the leased asset. In a sales-type lease, the fair value of the leased asset is greater than the cost, and lessors record gross profit. Leases that do not meet capitalization criteria are classified as operating leases, on which rent expense (revenue) is recognized by lessees (lessors) for lease payments.

APPENDIX 21B   **SALE-LEASEBACKS**

The term **sale-leaseback** describes a transaction in which the owner of the property (seller-lessee) sells the property to another and simultaneously leases it back from the new owner. The use of the property is generally continued without interruption.

11 LEARNING OBJECTIVE
Describe the lessee's accounting for sale-leaseback transactions.

    Sale-leasebacks are common. Financial institutions (e.g., **HSBC** (GBR) and **BBVA** (ESP)) have used this technique for their administrative offices, retailers (**Liberty** (GBR)) for their stores, and hospitals (**Healthscope** (AUS)) for their facilities. The advantages of a sale-leaseback from the seller's viewpoint usually involve two primary considerations:

1. *Financing*. If the purchase of equipment has already been financed, a sale-leaseback can allow the seller to refinance at lower rates, assuming rates have dropped. In addition, a sale-leaseback can provide another source of working capital, particularly when liquidity is tight.

2. *Taxes*. At the time a company purchased equipment, it may not have known that it would be subject to certain tax laws and that ownership might increase its minimum tax liability. By selling the property, the seller-lessee may deduct the entire lease payment, which is not subject to these tax considerations.

DETERMINING ASSET USE

Underlying Concepts

A sale-leaseback is similar in substance to the parking of inventories (discussed in Chapter 8). The ultimate economic benefits remain under the control of the "seller," thus satisfying the definition of an asset.

To the extent the **seller-lessee continues to use** the asset after the sale, the sale-leaseback is really a form of financing. Therefore, the lessor **should not recognize a gain or loss** on the transaction. In short, the seller-lessee is simply borrowing funds.

On the other hand, if the **seller-lessee gives up the right to the use** of the asset, the transaction is in substance a sale. In that case, **gain or loss recognition** is appropriate. Trying to ascertain when the lessee has given up the use of the asset is difficult, however, and the IASB has formulated complex rules to identify this situation.[19] To understand the profession's position in this area, we discuss the basic accounting for the lessee and lessor below.

Lessee

If the lease meets one of the four criteria for treatment as a finance lease (see Illustration 21-3 on page 1065), the **seller-lessee accounts for the transaction as a sale and the lease as a finance lease**. The seller-lessee should defer any profit or loss it experiences from the sale of the assets that are leased back under a finance lease; it should **amortize that profit over the lease term** (or the economic life if either criterion 1 or 2 is satisfied) in proportion to the depreciation of the leased assets.

For example, assume **Stora Enso** (FIN) sells equipment having a book value of €580,000 and a fair value of €623,110 to **Deutsche Bank** (DEU) for €623,110 and leases the equipment back for €50,000 a year for 20 years. Assuming the lease meets one of the criteria for capitalization, Stora Enso should amortize the profit of €43,110 over the 20-year period at the same rate that it depreciates the €623,110. **[14]** It credits the €43,110 (€623,110 − €580,000) to **Unearned Profit on Sale-Leaseback**.

If none of the finance lease criteria are satisfied, **the seller-lessee accounts for the transaction as a sale and the lease as an operating lease**. Under an operating lease, as long as the sale-leaseback transaction is established at fair value, any gain or loss is recognized immediately.[20]

Lessor

If the lease meets one of the lease capitalization criteria, the **purchaser-lessor** records the transaction as a purchase and a direct-financing lease. If the lease does not meet the criteria, the purchaser-lessor records the transaction as a purchase and an operating lease.

SALE-LEASEBACK EXAMPLE

To illustrate the accounting treatment accorded a sale-leaseback transaction, assume that **Japan Airlines (JAL)** (JPN) on January 1, 2015, sells a used Boeing 757 having a carrying amount on its books of $75,500,000 to **CitiCapital** (USA) for $80,000,000. JAL immediately leases the aircraft back under the following conditions:

1. The term of the lease is 15 years, non-cancelable, and requires equal rental payments of $10,487,443 at the beginning of each year.

---

[19]Sales and leasebacks of real estate are often accounted for differently. A discussion of the issues related to these transactions is beyond the scope of this textbook.

[20]If the sales price is not at fair value and the loss is compensated for by reduced future lease payments (below market rates), the loss shall be deferred and amortized in proportion to the lease payments over the period for which the asset is expected to be used. If the sales price is above fair value, the excess over fair value shall be deferred and amortized over the period for which the asset is expected to be used. **[15]**

2. The aircraft has a fair value of $80,000,000 on January 1, 2015, and an estimated economic life of 15 years.

3. JAL pays all executory costs.

4. JAL depreciates similar aircraft that it owns on a straight-line basis over 15 years.

5. The annual payments assure the lessor a 12 percent return.

6. JAL knows the implicit rate.

This lease is a finance lease to JAL because the lease term is equal to the estimated life of the aircraft and because the present value of the lease payments is equal to the fair value of the aircraft to CitiCapital. CitiCapital should classify this lease as a direct-financing lease.

Illustration 21B-1 presents the typical journal entries to record the sale-leaseback transactions for JAL and CitiCapital for the first year.

ILLUSTRATION 21B-1
Comparative Entries for Sale-Leaseback for Lessee and Lessor

JAL (Lessee)		CitiCapital (Lessor)	
Sale of aircraft by JAL to CitiCapital (January 1, 2015):			
Cash	80,000,000	Aircraft	80,000,000
Aircraft	75,500,000	Cash	80,000,000
Unearned Profit on Sale-Leaseback	4,500,000	Lease Receivable	80,000,000
Leased Aircraft	80,000,000	Aircraft	80,000,000
Lease Liability	80,000,000		
First lease payment (January 1, 2015):			
Lease Liability	10,487,443	Cash	10,487,443
Cash	10,487,443	Lease Receivable	10,487,443
Incurrence and payment of executory costs by JAL throughout 2015:			
Insurance, Maintenance, Taxes, etc.	XXX	(No entry)	
Cash or Accounts Payable	XXX		
Depreciation expense on the aircraft (December 31, 2015):			
Depreciation Expense	5,333,333	(No entry)	
Accumulated Depr.— Leased Equipment ($80,000,000 ÷ 15)	5,333,333		
Amortization of profit on sale-leaseback by JAL (December 31, 2015):			
Unearned Profit on Sale-Leaseback	300,000	(No entry)	
Depreciation Expense* ($4,500,000 ÷ 15)	300,000		
*A case might be made for crediting Sales Revenue instead of Depreciation Expense.			
Interest for 2015 (December 31, 2015):			
Interest Expense	8,341,507[a]	Interest Receivable	8,341,507
Interest Payable	8,341,507	Interest Revenue	8,341,507[a]

[a]Partial Lease Amortization Schedule:

Date	Annual Rental Payment	Interest 12%	Reduction of Balance	Balance
1/1/15				$80,000,000
1/1/15	$10,487,443	$ –0–	$10,487,443	69,512,557
1/1/16	10,487,443	8,341,507	2,145,936	67,366,621

SUMMARY OF LEARNING OBJECTIVE FOR APPENDIX 21B

11 **Describe the lessee's accounting for sale-leaseback transactions.**
If the lease meets one of the criteria for treatment as a finance lease, the seller-lessee accounts for the transaction as a sale and the lease as a finance lease. The seller-lessee defers any profit it experiences from the sale of the assets that are leased back under a finance lease. The seller-lessee amortizes any profit over the lease term (or the economic life if either criterion 1 or 2 is satisfied) in proportion to the amortization of the leased assets. If the lease satisfies none of the finance lease criteria, the seller-lessee accounts for the transaction as a sale and the lease as an operating lease. Under an operating lease, the lessee recognizes any gain or loss immediately if the sale-leaseback is at fair value.

IFRS AUTHORITATIVE LITERATURE

Authoritative Literature References

[1] International Accounting Standard 17, *Leases* (London, U.K.: International Accounting Standards Committee Foundation, 2003), par. 7.

[2] International Accounting Standard 17, *Leases* (London, U.K.: International Accounting Standards Committee Foundation, 2003), par. 10.

[3] International Accounting Standard 17, *Leases* (London, U.K.: International Accounting Standards Committee Foundation, 2003), paras. 10(e) and 11.

[4] International Accounting Standard 17, *Leases* (London, U.K.: International Accounting Standards Committee Foundation, 2003), par. 11.

[5] International Accounting Standard 17, *Leases* (London, U.K.: International Accounting Standards Committee Foundation, 2003), par. 4.

[6] International Accounting Standard 17, *Leases* (London, U.K.: International Accounting Standards Committee Foundation, 2003), par. 11(b).

[7] International Accounting Standard 17, *Leases* (London, U.K.: International Accounting Standards Committee Foundation, 2003), par. 20.

[8] International Accounting Standard 17, *Leases* (London, U.K.: International Accounting Standards Committee Foundation, 2003), par. 4.

[9] International Accounting Standard 17, *Leases* (London, U.K.: International Accounting Standards Committee Foundation, 2003), par. 44.

[10] International Accounting Standard 17, *Leases* (London, U.K.: International Accounting Standards Committee Foundation, 2003), paras. 38 and 52.

[11] International Accounting Standard 17, *Leases* (London, U.K.: International Accounting Standards Committee Foundation, 2003), par. 23.

[12] International Accounting Standard 17, *Leases* (London, U.K.: International Accounting Standards Committee Foundation, 2003), paras. 31 and 35.

[13] International Accounting Standard 17, *Leases* (London, U.K.: International Accounting Standards Committee Foundation, 2003), paras. 47 and 56.

[14] International Accounting Standard 17, *Leases* (London, U.K.: International Accounting Standards Committee Foundation, 2003), par. 59.

[15] International Accounting Standard 17, *Leases* (London, U.K.: International Accounting Standards Committee Foundation, 2003), par. 61.

Note: All asterisked Questions, Exercises, and Problems relate to material in the appendices to the chapter.

QUESTIONS

1. What are the major lessor groups? What advantage does a captive have in a leasing arrangement?

2. Bradley Co. is expanding its operations and is in the process of selecting the method of financing this program. After some investigation, the company determines that it may (1) issue bonds and with the proceeds purchase the needed assets or (2) lease the assets on a long-term basis. Without knowing the comparative costs involved, answer these questions:

    (a) What might be the advantages of leasing the assets instead of owning them?

    (b) What might be the disadvantages of leasing the assets instead of owning them?

    (c) In what way will the statement of financial position be differently affected by leasing the assets as opposed to issuing bonds and purchasing the assets?

3. Identify the two recognized lease-accounting methods for lessees and distinguish between them.

4. Ballard Company rents a warehouse on a month-to-month basis for the storage of its excess inventory. The company periodically must rent space whenever its production greatly exceeds actual sales. For several years, the company officials have discussed building their own storage facility, but this enthusiasm wavers when sales increase sufficiently to absorb the excess inventory. What is the nature of this type of lease arrangement, and what accounting treatment should be accorded it?

5. Distinguish between minimum rental payments and minimum lease payments, and indicate what is included in minimum lease payments.

6. Explain the distinction between a direct-financing lease and a sales-type lease for a lessor.

7. Outline the accounting procedures involved in applying the operating method by a lessee.

8. Outline the accounting procedures involved in applying the finance lease method by a lessee.

9. Identify the lease classifications for lessors and the criteria that must be met for each classification.

10. Outline the accounting procedures involved in applying the direct-financing method.

11. Outline the accounting procedures involved in applying the operating method by a lessor.

12. Walker Company is a manufacturer and lessor of computer equipment. What should be the nature of its lease arrangements with lessees if the company wishes to account for its lease transactions as sales-type leases?

13. Metheny Corporation's lease arrangements qualify as sales-type leases at the time of entering into the transactions. How should the corporation recognize revenues and costs in these situations?

14. Dr. Alice Foyle (lessee) has a non-cancelable 20-year lease with Brownback Realty, Inc. (lessor) for the use of a medical building. Taxes, insurance, and maintenance are paid by the lessee in addition to the fixed annual payments, of which the present value is equal to the fair value of the leased property. At the end of the lease period, title becomes the lessee's at a nominal price. Considering the terms of the lease described above, comment on the nature of the lease transaction and the accounting treatment that should be accorded it by the lessee.

15. The residual value is the estimated fair value of the leased property at the end of the lease term.

    (a) Of what significance is (1) an unguaranteed and (2) a guaranteed residual value in the lessee's accounting for a finance lease transaction?

    (b) Of what significance is (1) an unguaranteed and (2) a guaranteed residual value in the lessor's accounting for a direct-financing lease transaction?

16. How should changes in the estimated unguaranteed residual value be handled by the lessor?

17. Describe the effect of a "bargain-purchase option" on accounting for a finance lease transaction by a lessee.

18. What are "initial direct costs" and how are they accounted for?

19. What disclosures should be made by lessees and lessors related to future lease payments?

20. Briefly describe some of the similarities and differences between U.S. GAAP and IFRS with respect to the accounting for leases.

21. Both U.S. GAAP and IFRS require footnote disclosure of operating lease payments. Are there any differences in the information provided to statement readers in these disclosures? Explain.

22. Briefly discuss the IASB and FASB's efforts to converge their accounting guidelines for leases.

*23. What is the nature of a "sale-leaseback" transaction?

BRIEF EXERCISES

2 **BE21-1** Mizuno Corp. (JPN) leases telecommunication equipment. Assume the following data for equipment leased from Photon Company. The lease term is 5 years and requires equal rental payments of ¥3,100,000 at the beginning of each year. The equipment has a fair value at the inception of the lease of ¥13,800,000, an estimated useful life of 8 years, and no residual value. Mizuno pays all executory costs directly to third parties. Photon set the annual rental to earn a rate of return of 10%, and this fact is known to Mizuno. The lease does not transfer title or contain a bargain-purchase option. How should Mizuno classify this lease?

2 **BE21-2** Waterworld Company leased equipment from Costner Company. The lease term is 4 years and requires equal rental payments of $43,019 at the beginning of each year. The equipment has a fair value at the inception of the lease of $150,000, an estimated useful life of 4 years, and no residual value. Waterworld pays all executory costs directly to third parties. The appropriate interest rate is 10%. Prepare Waterworld's January 1, 2015, journal entries at the inception of the lease.

2 **BE21-3** Rick Kleckner Corporation recorded a finance lease at €300,000 on January 1, 2015. The interest rate is 12%. Kleckner Corporation made the first lease payment of €53,920 on January 1, 2015. The lease requires eight annual payments. The equipment has a useful life of 8 years with no residual value. Prepare Kleckner Corporation's December 31, 2015, adjusting entries.

2 **BE21-4** Use the information for Rick Kleckner Corporation from BE21-3. Assume that at December 31, 2015, Kleckner made an adjusting entry to accrue interest expense of €29,530 on the lease. Prepare Kleckner's January 1, 2016, journal entry to record the second lease payment of €53,920.

3 **BE21-5** Jana Kingston Corporation enters into a lease on January 1, 2015, that does not transfer ownership or contain a bargain-purchase option. It covers 3 years of the equipment's 8-year useful life, and the present value of the minimum lease payments is less than 80% of the fair value of the asset leased. Prepare Jana Kingston's journal entry to record its January 1, 2015, annual lease payment of €35,000.

4 **5** **BE21-6** Assume that Lenovo (CHN) leased equipment that was carried at a cost of ¥150,000,000 to Sharon Swander Company. The term of the lease is 6 years beginning January 1, 2015, with equal rental payments of ¥30,044,000 at the beginning of each year. All executory costs are paid by Swander directly to third parties. The fair value of the equipment at the inception of the lease is ¥150,000,000. The equipment has a useful life of 6 years with no residual value. The lease has an implicit interest rate of 8%, no bargain-purchase option, and no transfer of title. Prepare Lenovo's January 1, 2015, journal entries at the inception of the lease.

4 **5** **BE21-7** Use the information for Lenovo from BE21-6. Assume the direct-financing lease was recorded at a present value of ¥150,000,000. Prepare Lenovo's December 31, 2015, entry to record interest.

4 **BE21-8** Jennifer Brent Corporation owns equipment that cost €80,000 and has a useful life of 8 years with no residual value. On January 1, 2015, Jennifer Brent leases the equipment to Lopez Inc. for one year with one rental payment of €15,000 on January 1. Prepare Jennifer Brent Corporation's 2015 journal entries.

6 **7** **BE21-9** Cortez Corporation enters into a 6-year lease of equipment on January 1, 2015, which requires 6 annual payments of R$40,000 each, beginning January 1, 2015. In addition, Cortez guarantees the lessor a residual value of R$20,000 at lease-end. The equipment has a useful life of 6 years. Prepare Cortez's January 1, 2015, journal entries assuming an interest rate of 10%.

6 **7** **BE21-10** Use the information for Cortez Corporation from BE21-9. Assume that for Lost Ark Company, the lessor, the carrying amount of the equipment is R$202,921. Prepare Lost Ark's January 1, 2015, journal entries.

8 **BE21-11** Buzz Lightyear Corporation manufactures replicators. On January 1, 2015, it leased to BoPeep Company a replicator that had cost £110,000 to manufacture. The lease agreement covers the 5-year useful life of the replicator and requires 5 equal annual rentals of £40,800 payable each January 1, beginning January 1, 2015. An interest rate of 12% is implicit in the lease agreement. Prepare Lightyear's January 1, 2015, journal entries.

11 *BE21-12** On January 1, 2015, Iniesta Animation sold a truck to Robben Finance for €33,000 and immediately leased it back. The truck was carried on Iniesta's books at €28,000. The term of the lease is 5 years, and title transfers to Iniesta at lease-end. The lease requires five equal rental payments of €8,705 at the end of each year. The appropriate rate of interest is 10%, and the truck has a useful life of 5 years with no residual value. Prepare Iniesta's 2015 journal entries.

EXERCISES

2 **E21-1 (Lessee Entries, Finance Lease with Unguaranteed Residual Value)** On January 1, 2015, Adams Corporation signed a 5-year, non-cancelable lease for a machine. The terms of the lease called for Adams to make annual payments of $9,968 at the beginning of each year, starting January 1, 2015. The machine has an estimated useful life of 6 years and a $5,000 unguaranteed residual value. The machine reverts back to the lessor at the end of the lease term. Adams uses the straight-line method of depreciation for all of its plant assets. Adams's incremental borrowing rate is 10%, and the lessor's implicit rate is unknown (it is impracticable to determine).

Instructions
- **(a)** What type of lease is this? Explain.
- **(b)** Compute the present value of the minimum lease payments.
- **(c)** Prepare all necessary journal entries for Adams for this lease through January 1, 2016.

2 **E21-2 (Lessee Computations and Entries, Finance Lease with Guaranteed Residual Value)** Brecker Company leases an automobile with a fair value of €10,906 from Emporia Motors, Inc., on the following terms:

1. Non-cancelable term of 50 months.
2. Rental of €250 per month (at end of each month). (The present value at 1% per month is €9,800.)
3. Estimated residual value after 50 months is €1,180. (The present value at 1% per month is €715.) Brecker Company guarantees the residual value of €1,180.
4. Estimated economic life of the automobile is 60 months.
5. Brecker Company's incremental borrowing rate is 12% a year (1% a month). It is impracticable to determine Emporia's implicit rate.

Instructions
- **(a)** What is the nature of this lease to Brecker Company?
- **(b)** What is the present value of the minimum lease payments?
- **(c)** Record the lease on Brecker Company's books at the date of inception.
- **(d)** Record the first month's depreciation on Brecker Company's books (assume straight-line).
- **(e)** Record the first month's lease payment.

2 **7** **E21-3 (Lessee Entries, Finance Lease with Executory Costs and Unguaranteed Residual Value)** Assume that on January 1, 2015, **Stora Enso** (FIN) signs a 10-year, non-cancelable lease agreement to lease a storage building from Balesteros Storage Company. The following information pertains to this lease agreement.

1. The agreement requires equal rental payments of €90,000 beginning on January 1, 2015.
2. The fair value of the building on January 1, 2015, is €550,000.
3. The building has an estimated economic life of 12 years, with an unguaranteed residual value of €10,000. Stora Enso depreciates similar buildings on the straight-line method.
4. The lease is non-renewable. At the termination of the lease, the building reverts to the lessor.
5. Stora Enso's incremental borrowing rate is 12% per year. It is impracticable to determine the lessor's implicit rate.
6. The yearly rental payment includes €3,088.14 of executory costs related to taxes on the property.

Instructions
Prepare the journal entries on the lessee's books to reflect the signing of the lease agreement and to record the payments and expenses related to this lease for the years 2015 and 2016. Stora Enso's corporate year-end is December 31.

5 **E21-4 (Lessor Entries, Direct-Financing Lease with Option to Purchase)** Krauss Leasing Company signs a lease agreement on January 1, 2015, to lease electronic equipment to Stewart Company. The term of the non-cancelable lease is 2 years, and payments are required at the end of each year. The following information relates to this agreement.

1. Stewart has the option to purchase the equipment for £16,000 upon termination of the lease.
2. The equipment has a cost and fair value of £240,000 to Krauss Leasing Company. The useful economic life is 2 years, with a residual value of £16,000.
3. Stewart Company is required to pay £7,000 each year to the lessor for executory costs.
4. Krauss Leasing Company desires to earn a return of 10% on its investment.

Instructions

(a) Prepare the journal entries on the books of Krauss Leasing to reflect the payments received under the lease and to recognize income for the years 2015 and 2016.

(b) Assuming that Stewart Company exercises its option to purchase the equipment on December 31, 2016, prepare the journal entry to reflect the sale on Krauss's books.

2 3 E21-5 (Type of Lease, Amortization Schedule) Jacobsen Leasing Company leases a new machine that has a cost and fair value of ₩75,000,000 to K. J. Choi Corporation on a 3-year, non-cancelable contract. K. J. Choi Corporation agrees to assume all risks of normal ownership, including costs such as insurance, taxes, and maintenance. The machine has a 3-year useful life and no residual value. The lease was signed on January 1, 2015. Jacobsen Leasing Company expects to earn a 9% return on its investment. The annual rentals are payable on each December 31.

Instructions

(a) Discuss the nature of the lease arrangement and the accounting method that each party to the lease should apply.

(b) Prepare an amortization schedule that would be suitable for both the lessor and the lessee and that covers all the years involved.

8 E21-6 (Lessor Entries, Sales-Type Lease) Wadkins Company, a machinery dealer, leased a machine to Aoki Corporation on January 1, 2015. The lease is for an 8-year period and requires equal annual payments of ¥38,514,000 at the beginning of each year. The first payment is received on January 1, 2015. Wadkins had purchased the machine during 2014 for ¥170,000,000. Wadkins set the annual rental to ensure an 11% rate of return. The machine has an economic life of 8 years with no residual value and reverts to Wadkins at the termination of the lease.

Instructions

(a) Compute the amount of the lease receivable.

(b) Prepare all necessary journal entries for Wadkins for 2015.

8 E21-7 (Lessee-Lessor Entries, Sales-Type Lease) On January 1, 2015, Palmer Company leased equipment to Immelman Corporation. The following information pertains to this lease.

1. The term of the non-cancelable lease is 6 years, with no renewal option. The equipment reverts to the lessor at the termination of the lease.

2. Equal rental payments are due on January 1 of each year, beginning in 2015.

3. The fair value of the equipment on January 1, 2015, is $200,000, and its cost is $150,000.

4. The equipment has an economic life of 8 years, with an unguaranteed residual value of $10,000. Immelman depreciates all of its equipment on a straight-line basis.

5. Palmer sets the annual rental to ensure an 11% rate of return. Immelman's incremental borrowing rate is 12%, and it is impracticable for Immelman to determine the implicit rate.

Instructions

(Both the lessor and the lessee's accounting period ends on December 31.)

(a) Discuss the nature of this lease to Palmer and Immelman.

(b) Calculate the amount of the annual rental payment.

(c) Prepare all the necessary journal entries for Immelman for 2015.

(d) Prepare all the necessary journal entries for Palmer for 2015.

6 7 E21-8 (Lessee Entries with Bargain-Purchase Option) The following facts pertain to a non-cancelable lease agreement between Lennox Leasing Company and Gill Company, a lessee.

Inception date:	May 1, 2015
Annual lease payment due at the beginning of	
each year, beginning with May 1, 2015	€18,829.49
Bargain-purchase option price at end of lease term	€ 4,000.00
Lease term	5 years
Economic life of leased equipment	10 years
Lessor's cost	€65,000.00
Fair value of asset at May 1, 2015	€81,000.00
Lessor's implicit rate	10%
Lessee's incremental borrowing rate	10%

The lessee assumes responsibility for all executory costs.

Instructions

(Round all numbers to the nearest cent.)

(a) Discuss the nature of this lease to Gill Company.

(b) Discuss the nature of this lease to Lennox Company.

(c) Prepare a lease amortization schedule for Gill Company for the 5-year lease term.

(d) Prepare the journal entries on the lessee's books to reflect the signing of the lease agreement and to record the payments and expenses related to this lease for the years 2015 and 2016. Gill's annual accounting period ends on December 31. Reversing entries are used by Gill.

8 **E21-9 (Lessor Entries with Bargain-Purchase Option)** A lease agreement between Lennox Leasing Company and Gill Company is described in E21-8.

Instructions

Refer to the data in E21-8 and do the following for the lessor. (Round all numbers to the nearest cent.)

(a) Compute the amount of the lease receivable at the inception of the lease.

(b) Prepare a lease amortization schedule for Lennox Leasing Company for the 5-year lease term.

(c) Prepare the journal entries to reflect the signing of the lease agreement and to record the receipts and income related to this lease for the years 2015, 2016, and 2017. The lessor's accounting period ends on December 31. Reversing entries are not used by Lennox.

5 **E21-10 (Computation of Rental, Journal Entries for Lessor)** Fieval Leasing Company signs an agreement on January 1, 2015, to lease equipment to Reid Company. The following information relates to this agreement.

1. The term of the non-cancelable lease is 6 years with no renewal option. The equipment has an estimated economic life of 6 years.

2. The cost and fair value of the asset at January 1, 2015, is £343,000.

3. The asset will revert to the lessor at the end of the lease term, at which time the asset is expected to have a residual value of £61,071, none of which is guaranteed.

4. Reid Company assumes direct responsibility for all executory costs.

5. The agreement requires equal annual rental payments, beginning on January 1, 2015.

Instructions

(Round all numbers to the nearest pound.)

(a) Assuming the lessor desires a 10% rate of return on its investment, calculate the amount of the annual rental payment required. (Round to the nearest pound.)

(b) Prepare an amortization schedule that would be suitable for the lessor for the lease term.

(c) Prepare all of the journal entries for the lessor for 2015 and 2016 to record the lease agreement, the receipt of lease payments, and the recognition of income. Assume the lessor's annual accounting period ends on December 31.

2 **E21-11 (Amortization Schedule and Journal Entries for Lessee)** Demir Leasing Company signs an agreement on January 1, 2015, to lease equipment to Azure Company. The following information relates to this agreement.

1. The term of the non-cancelable lease is 5 years with no renewal option. The equipment has an estimated economic life of 5 years.

2. The fair value of the asset at January 1, 2015, is ₺90,000.

3. The asset will revert to the lessor at the end of the lease term, at which time the asset is expected to have a residual value of ₺7,000, none of which is guaranteed.

4. Azure Company assumes direct responsibility for all executory costs, which include the following annual amounts: (1) ₺900 to Frontier Insurance Company for insurance and (2) ₺1,600 for property taxes.

5. The agreement requires equal annual rental payments of ₺20,541.11 to the lessor, beginning on January 1, 2015.

6. The lessee's incremental borrowing rate is 12%. The lessor's implicit rate is 10% and is known to the lessee.

7. Azure Company uses the straight-line depreciation method for all equipment.

8. Azure uses reversing entries when appropriate.

Instructions

(Round all numbers to two decimal places.)

(a) Prepare an amortization schedule that would be suitable for the lessee for the lease term.

(b) Prepare all of the journal entries for the lessee for 2015 and 2016 to record the lease agreement, the lease payments, and all expenses related to this lease. Assume the lessee's annual accounting period ends on December 31.

3 **4** **E21-12 (Accounting for an Operating Lease)** On January 1, 2015, Secada Co. leased a building to Ryker Inc. The relevant information related to the lease is as follows.

1. The lease arrangement is for 10 years.

2. The leased building cost €3,600,000 and was purchased for cash on January 1, 2015.

   3. The building is depreciated on a straight-line basis. Its estimated economic life is 50 years with no residual value.

   4. Lease payments are €220,000 per year and are made at the end of the year.

   5. Property tax expense of €85,000 and insurance expense of €10,000 on the building were incurred by Secada in the first year. Payment on these two items was made at the end of the year.

   6. Both the lessor and the lessee are on a calendar-year basis.

Instructions

   (a) Prepare the journal entries that Secada Co. should make in 2015.
   (b) Prepare the journal entries that Ryker Inc. should make in 2015.
   (c) If Secada paid €30,000 to a real estate broker on January 1, 2015, as a fee for finding the lessee, how much should be reported as an expense for this item in 2015 by Secada Co.?

3 4 **E21-13 (Accounting for an Operating Lease)** On January 1, 2015, a machine was purchased for $900,000 by Floyd Co. The machine is expected to have an 8-year life with no residual value. It is to be depreciated on a straight-line basis. The machine was leased to Crampton Inc. on January 1, 2015, at an annual rental of $180,000. Other relevant information is as follows.

   1. The lease term is for 3 years.

   2. Floyd Co. incurred maintenance and other executory costs of $25,000 in 2015 related to this lease.

   3. The machine could have been sold by Floyd Co. for $940,000 instead of leasing it.

   4. Crampton is required to pay a rent security deposit of $35,000 and to prepay the last month's rent of $15,000.

Instructions

   (a) How much should Floyd Co. report as income before income tax on this lease for 2015?
   (b) What amount should Crampton Inc. report for rent expense for 2015 on this lease?

3 4 **E21-14 (Operating Lease for Lessee and Lessor)** On February 20, 2015, Marcos Group purchased a machine for R$1,200,000 for the purpose of leasing it. The machine is expected to have a 10-year life, no residual value, and will be depreciated on the straight-line basis. The machine was leased to Sage Company on March 1, 2015, for a 4-year period at a monthly rental of R$15,600. There is no provision for the renewal of the lease or purchase of the machine by the lessee at the expiration of the lease term. Marcos paid R$30,000 of commissions associated with negotiating the lease in February 2015.

Instructions

   (a) What expense should Sage Company record as a result of the facts above for the year ended December 31, 2015? Show supporting computations in good form.
   (b) What income or loss before income taxes should Marcos record as a result of the facts above for the year ended December 31, 2015? (*Hint:* Amortize commissions over the life of the lease.)

11 *E21-15 (Sale-Leaseback)** Assume that on January 1, 2015, Peking Duck Co. sells a computer system to Liquidity Finance Co. for ¥510,000 and immediately leases the computer system back. The relevant information is as follows.

   1. The computer system was carried on Peking's books at a value of ¥450,000.

   2. The term of the non-cancelable lease is 10 years; title will transfer to Peking.

   3. The lease agreement requires equal rental payments of ¥83,000.11 at the end of each year.

   4. The incremental borrowing rate for Peking is 12%. Peking is aware that Liquidity Finance Co. set the annual rental to ensure a rate of return of 10%.

   5. The computer system has a fair value of ¥510,000 on January 1, 2015, and an estimated economic life of 10 years.

   6. Peking pays executory costs of ¥9,000 per year.

Instructions

Prepare the journal entries for both the lessee and the lessor for 2015 to reflect the sale-leaseback agreement.

11 *E21-16 (Lessee-Lessor, Sale-Leaseback)** Presented below and on page 1111 are four independent situations.

   (a) On December 31, 2015, Beard Inc. sold computer equipment to Barber Co. and immediately leased it back for 10 years. The sales price of the equipment was $560,000, its carrying amount is $400,000, and its estimated remaining economic life is 12 years. Determine the amount of deferred revenue to be reported from the sale of the computer equipment on December 31, 2015.

   (b) On December 31, 2015, Mikkelson Co. sold a machine to Ozaki Co. and simultaneously leased it back for one year. The sales price of the machine was $480,000, the carrying amount is $420,000, and it had an estimated remaining useful life of 14 years. The present value of the rental payments for the one year is $35,000. At December 31, 2015, how much should Mikkelson report as deferred revenue from the sale of the machine? Assume that the sale was at fair value.

(c) On January 1, 2015, Barone Corp. sold an airplane with an estimated useful life of 10 years. At the same time, Barone leased back the plane for 10 years. The sales price of the airplane was $500,000, the carrying amount $401,000, and the annual rental $73,975.22. Barone Corp. intends to depreciate the leased asset using the sum-of-the-years'-digits depreciation method. Discuss how the gain on the sale should be reported at the end of 2015 in the financial statements.

(d) On January 1, 2015, Durocher Co. sold equipment with an estimated useful life of 5 years. At the same time, Durocher leased back the equipment for 2 years under a lease classified as an operating lease. The sales price (fair value) of the equipment was $212,700, the carrying amount is $300,000, the monthly rental under the lease is $6,000, and the present value of the rental payments is $115,753. For the year ended December 31, 2015, determine which items would be reported on its income statement for the sale-leaseback transaction.

PROBLEMS

2 8 **P21-1 (Lessee-Lessor Entries, Sales-Type Lease)** Glaus Leasing Company agrees to lease machinery to Jensen Corporation on January 1, 2015. The following information relates to the lease agreement.

1. The term of the lease is 7 years with no renewal option, and the machinery has an estimated economic life of 9 years.

2. The cost of the machinery is €525,000, and the fair value of the asset on January 1, 2015, is €700,000.

3. At the end of the lease term, the asset reverts to the lessor. At the end of the lease term, the asset has a guaranteed residual value of €100,000. Jensen depreciates all of its equipment on a straight-line basis.

4. The lease agreement requires equal annual rental payments, beginning on January 1, 2015.

5. Glaus desires a 10% rate of return on its investments. Jensen's incremental borrowing rate is 11%, and it is impracticable to determine the lessor's implicit rate.

Instructions
(Assume the accounting period ends on December 31.)

(a) Discuss the nature of this lease for both the lessee and the lessor.
(b) Calculate the amount of the annual rental payment required.
(c) Compute the present value of the minimum lease payments.
(d) Prepare the journal entries Jensen would make in 2015 and 2016 related to the lease arrangement.
(e) Prepare the journal entries Glaus would make in 2015 and 2016.

3 4 **P21-2 (Lessee-Lessor Entries, Operating Lease)** Cancun Inc. leased a new crane to Abriendo Construction under a 5-year, non-cancelable contract starting January 1, 2015. Terms of the lease require payments of R$33,000 each January 1, starting January 1, 2015. Cancun will pay insurance, taxes, and maintenance charges on the crane, which has an estimated life of 12 years, a fair value of R$240,000, and a cost to Cancun of R$240,000. The estimated fair value of the crane is expected to be R$45,000 at the end of the lease term. No bargain-purchase or -renewal options are included in the contract. Both Cancun and Abriendo adjust and close books annually at December 31. Abriendo's incremental borrowing rate is 10%, and Cancun's implicit interest rate of 9% is known to Abriendo.

Instructions
(a) Identify the type of lease involved and give reasons for your classification. Discuss the accounting treatment that should be applied by both the lessee and the lessor.
(b) Prepare all the entries related to the lease contract and leased asset for the year 2015 for the lessee and lessor, assuming the following amounts.

   (1) Insurance R$500.
   (2) Taxes R$2,000.
   (3) Maintenance R$650.
   (4) Straight-line depreciation and residual value R$15,000.

(c) Discuss what should be presented in the statement of financial position, the income statement, and the related notes of both the lessee and the lessor at December 31, 2015.

2 8 P21-3 (Lessee-Lessor Entries, Financial Statement Presentation, Sales-Type Lease) Labron Industries and
9 Ewing Inc. enter into an agreement that requires Ewing Inc. to build three diesel-electric engines to Labron's
specifications. Upon completion of the engines, Labron has agreed to lease them for a period of 10 years and
to assume all costs and risks of ownership. The lease is non-cancelable, becomes effective on January 1, 2015,
and requires annual rental payments of $413,971 each January 1, starting January 1, 2015.

Labron's incremental borrowing rate is 10%. The implicit interest rate used by Ewing Inc. and
known to Labron is 8%. The total cost of building the three engines is $2,600,000. The economic life of
the engines is estimated to be 10 years, with residual value set at zero. Labron depreciates similar
equipment on a straight-line basis. At the end of the lease, Labron assumes title to the engines.

Instructions
(Round all numbers to the nearest dollar.)

(a) Discuss the nature of this lease transaction from the viewpoints of both lessee and lessor.
(b) Prepare the journal entry or entries to record the transaction on January 1, 2015, on the books of
Labron Industries.
(c) Prepare the journal entry or entries to record the transaction on January 1, 2015, on the books of
Ewing Inc.
(d) Prepare the journal entries for both the lessee and lessor to record the first rental payment on
January 1, 2015.
(e) Prepare the journal entries for both the lessee and lessor to record interest expense (revenue) at
December 31, 2015. (Prepare a lease amortization schedule for 2 years.)
(f) Show the items and amounts that would be reported on the statement of financial position (not
notes) at December 31, 2015, for both the lessee and the lessor.

2 6 P21-4 (Statement of Financial Position and Income Statement Disclosure—Lessee) The following facts
9 pertain to a non-cancelable lease agreement between Alschuler Leasing Company and McKee Electronics,
a lessee, for a computer system.

Inception date	October 1, 2015
Lease term	6 years
Economic life of leased equipment	6 years
Fair value of asset at October 1, 2015	£300,383
Residual value at end of lease term	–0–
Lessor's implicit rate	10%
Lessee's incremental borrowing rate	10%
Annual lease payment due at the beginning of each year, beginning with October 1, 2015	£62,700

The lessee assumes responsibility for all executory costs, which amount to £5,500 per year and are to be
paid each October 1, beginning October 1, 2015. (This £5,500 is not included in the rental payment of
£62,700.) The asset will revert to the lessor at the end of the lease term. The straight-line depreciation
method is used for all equipment.

The following amortization schedule has been prepared correctly for use by both the lessor and the
lessee in accounting for this lease. The lease is to be accounted for properly as a finance lease by the lessee
and as a direct-financing lease by the lessor.

Date	Annual Lease Payment/ Receipt	Interest (10%) on Unpaid Liability/Receivable	Reduction of Lease Liability/Receivable	Balance of Lease Liability/Receivable
10/01/15				£300,383
10/01/15	£ 62,700		£ 62,700	237,683
10/01/16	62,700	£23,768	38,932	198,751
10/01/17	62,700	19,875	42,825	155,926
10/01/18	62,700	15,593	47,107	108,819
10/01/19	62,700	10,822	51,818	57,001
10/01/20	62,700	5,699*	57,001	–0–
	£376,200	£75,817	£300,383	

*Rounding error is £1.

Instructions
(Round all numbers to the nearest pound.)

(a) Assuming the lessee's accounting period ends on September 30, answer the following questions
with respect to this lease agreement.

(1) What items and amounts will appear on the lessee's income statement for the year ending September 30, 2016?

(2) What items and amounts will appear on the lessee's statement of financial position at September 30, 2016?

(3) What items and amounts will appear on the lessee's income statement for the year ending September 30, 2017?

(4) What items and amounts will appear on the lessee's statement of financial position at September 30, 2017?

(b) Assuming the lessee's accounting period ends on December 31, answer the following questions with respect to this lease agreement.

(1) What items and amounts will appear on the lessee's income statement for the year ending December 31, 2015?

(2) What items and amounts will appear on the lessee's statement of financial position at December 31, 2015?

(3) What items and amounts will appear on the lessee's income statement for the year ending December 31, 2016?

(4) What items and amounts will appear on the lessee's statement of financial position at December 31, 2016?

5 **9** **P21-5 (Statement of Financial Position and Income Statement Disclosure—Lessor)** Assume the same information as in P21-4.

Instructions

(Round all numbers to the nearest pound.)

(a) Assuming the lessor's accounting period ends on September 30, answer the following questions with respect to this lease agreement.

(1) What items and amounts will appear on the lessor's income statement for the year ending September 30, 2016?

(2) What items and amounts will appear on the lessor's statement of financial position at September 30, 2016?

(3) What items and amounts will appear on the lessor's income statement for the year ending September 30, 2017?

(4) What items and amounts will appear on the lessor's statement of financial position at September 30, 2017?

(b) Assuming the lessor's accounting period ends on December 31, answer the following questions with respect to this lease agreement.

(1) What items and amounts will appear on the lessor's income statement for the year ending December 31, 2015?

(2) What items and amounts will appear on the lessor's statement of financial position at December 31, 2015?

(3) What items and amounts will appear on the lessor's income statement for the year ending December 31, 2016?

(4) What items and amounts will appear on the lessor's statement of financial position at December 31, 2016?

2 **7** **P21-6 (Lessee Entries with Residual Value)** The following facts pertain to a non-cancelable lease agreement between Faldo Leasing Company and Shigeki Company, a lessee.

Inception date	January 1, 2015
Annual lease payment due at the beginning of each year, beginning with January 1, 2015	€124,798
Residual value of equipment at end of lease term, guaranteed by the lessee	€50,000
Lease term	6 years
Economic life of leased equipment	6 years
Fair value of asset at January 1, 2015	€600,000
Lessor's implicit rate	12%
Lessee's incremental borrowing rate	12%

The lessee assumes responsibility for all executory costs, which are expected to amount to €5,000 per year. The asset will revert to the lessor at the end of the lease term. The lessee has guaranteed the lessor a residual value of €50,000. The lessee uses the straight-line depreciation method for all equipment.

Instructions

(Round all numbers to the nearest euro.)

(a) Prepare an amortization schedule that would be suitable for the lessee for the lease term.

(b) Prepare all of the journal entries for the lessee for 2015 and 2016 to record the lease agreement, the lease payments, and all expenses related to this lease. Assume the lessee's annual accounting period ends on December 31 and reversing entries are used when appropriate.

P21-7 (Lessee Entries and Statement of Financial Position Presentation, Finance Lease) Ludwick Steel Company as lessee signed a lease agreement for equipment for 5 years, beginning December 31, 2015. Annual rental payments of $40,000 are to be made at the beginning of each lease year (December 31). The taxes, insurance, and the maintenance costs are the obligation of the lessee. The interest rate used by the lessor in setting the payment schedule is 9%; Ludwick's incremental borrowing rate is 10%. It is impracticable for Ludwick to determine the rate being used by the lessor. At the end of the lease, Ludwick has the option to buy the equipment for $1, considerably below its estimated fair value at that time. The equipment has an estimated useful life of 7 years, with no residual value. Ludwick uses the straight-line method of depreciation on similar owned equipment.

Instructions

(Round all numbers to the nearest dollar.)

(a) Prepare the journal entry or entries, with explanations, that should be recorded on December 31, 2015, by Ludwick.

(b) Prepare the journal entry or entries, with explanations, that should be recorded on December 31, 2016, by Ludwick. (Prepare the lease amortization schedule for all five payments.)

(c) Prepare the journal entry or entries, with explanations, that should be recorded on December 31, 2017, by Ludwick.

(d) What amounts would appear on Ludwick's December 31, 2017, statement of financial position relative to the lease arrangement?

P21-8 (Lessee Entries and Statement of Financial Position Presentation, Finance Lease) On January 1, 2015, Singh Company contracts to lease equipment for 5 years, agreeing to make a payment of ₹137,899 (including the executory costs of ₹6,000) at the beginning of each year, starting January 1, 2015. The taxes, the insurance, and the maintenance, estimated at ₹6,000 a year, are the obligations of the lessee. The leased equipment is to be capitalized at ₹550,000. The asset is to be depreciated on a double-declining-balance basis, and the obligation is to be reduced on an effective-interest basis. Singh's incremental borrowing rate is 12%, and the implicit rate in the lease is 10%, which is known by Singh. Title to the equipment transfers to Singh when the lease expires. The asset has an estimated useful life of 5 years and no residual value.

Instructions

(Round all numbers to the nearest rupee.)

(a) Explain the probable relationship of the ₹550,000 amount to the lease arrangement.

(b) Prepare the journal entry or entries that should be recorded on January 1, 2015, by Singh Company.

(c) Prepare the journal entry to record depreciation of the leased asset for the year 2015.

(d) Prepare the journal entry to record the interest expense for the year 2015.

(e) Prepare the journal entry to record the lease payment of January 1, 2016, assuming reversing entries are not made.

(f) What amounts will appear on the lessee's December 31, 2015, statement of financial position relative to the lease contract?

P21-9 (Lessee Entries, Finance Lease with Monthly Payments) Shapiro Inc. was incorporated in 2015 to operate as a computer software service firm with an accounting fiscal year ending August 31. Shapiro's primary product is a sophisticated online inventory-control system; its customers pay a fixed fee plus a usage charge for using the system.

Shapiro has leased a large, Alpha-3 computer system from the manufacturer. The lease calls for a monthly rental of €40,000 for the 144 months (12 years) of the lease term. The estimated useful life of the computer is 15 years.

Each scheduled monthly rental payment includes €3,000 for full-service maintenance on the computer to be performed by the manufacturer. All rentals are payable on the first day of the month beginning with August 1, 2016, the date the computer was installed and the lease agreement was signed. The lease is non-cancelable for its 12-year term, and it is secured only by the manufacturer's chattel lien on the Alpha-3 system.

This lease is to be accounted for as a finance lease by Shapiro, and it will be depreciated by the straight-line method with no expected residual value. Borrowed funds for this type of transaction would cost Shapiro 12% per year (1% per month). Following is a schedule of the present value of €1 for selected periods discounted at 1% per period when payments are made at the beginning of each period.

Periods (months)	Present Value of €1 per Period Discounted at 1% per Period
1	1.000
2	1.990
3	2.970
143	76.658
144	76.899

Instructions

Prepare, in general journal form, all entries Shapiro should have made in its accounting records during August 2016 relating to this lease. Give full explanations and show supporting computations for each entry. Remember, August 31, 2016, is the end of Shapiro's fiscal accounting period and it will be preparing financial statements on that date. Do not prepare closing entries.

P21-10 (Lessor Computations and Entries, Sales-Type Lease with Unguaranteed Residual Value) Moonstruck Company manufactures a reservation system with an estimated economic life of 12 years and leases it to National Airlines for a period of 10 years. The normal selling price of the equipment is £278,072, and its unguaranteed residual value at the end of the lease term is estimated to be £20,000. National will pay annual payments of £40,000 at the beginning of each year and all maintenance, insurance, and taxes. Moonstruck incurred costs of £180,000 in manufacturing the equipment and £4,000 in negotiating and closing the lease. Moonstruck has determined that the implicit interest rate is 10%.

Instructions

(Round all numbers to the nearest pound.)

(a) Discuss the nature of this lease in relation to the lessor and compute the amount of each of the following items.

    (1) Lease receivable.

    (2) Sales price.

    (3) Cost of sales.

(b) Prepare a 10-year lease amortization schedule.

(c) Prepare all of the lessor's journal entries for the first year.

P21-11 (Lessee Computations and Entries, Finance Lease with Unguaranteed Residual Value) Assume the same data as in P21-10 with National Airlines having an incremental borrowing rate of 10%.

Instructions

(Round all numbers to the nearest pound.)

(a) Discuss the nature of this lease in relation to the lessee, and compute the amount of the initial obligation under finance leases.

(b) Prepare a 10-year lease amortization schedule.

(c) Prepare all of the lessee's journal entries for the first year.

P21-12 (Basic Lessee Accounting with Difficult PV Calculation) In 2014, Grishell Shipping Company negotiated and closed a long-term lease contract for newly constructed truck terminals and freight storage facilities. The buildings were erected to the company's specifications on land owned by the company. On January 1, 2015, Grishell Shipping Company took possession of the lease properties. On January 1, 2015 and 2016, the company made cash payments of £948,000 that were recorded as rental expenses.

Although the terminals have a composite useful life of 40 years, the non-cancelable lease runs for 20 years from January 1, 2015, with a bargain-purchase option available upon expiration of the lease.

The 20-year lease is effective for the period January 1, 2015, through December 31, 2034. Advance rental payments of £800,000 are payable to the lessor on January 1 of each of the first 10 years of the lease term. Advance rental payments of £320,000 are due on January 1 for each of the last 10 years of the lease. The company has an option to purchase all of these leased facilities for £1 on December 31, 2034. It also must make annual payments to the lessor of £125,000 for property taxes and £23,000 for insurance. The lease was negotiated to assure the lessor a 6% rate of return.

Instructions

(Round all numbers to the nearest pound.)

(a) Prepare a schedule to compute for Grishell Shipping Company the discounted present value of the terminal facilities and related obligation at January 1, 2015.

(b) Assuming that the discounted present value of terminal facilities and related obligation at January 1, 2015, was £7,600,000, prepare journal entries for Grishell Shipping Company to record the:

(1) Cash payment to the lessor on January 1, 2017.

(2) Amortization of the cost of the leased properties for 2017 using the straight-line method and assuming a zero residual value.

(3) Accrual of interest expense at December 31, 2017.

Selected present value factors are as follows.

Periods	For an Ordinary Annuity of £1 at 6%	For £1 at 6%
1	.943396	.943396
2	1.833393	.889996
8	6.209794	.627412
9	6.801692	.591898
10	7.360087	.558395
19	11.158117	.330513
20	11.469921	.311805

4 7 8 P21-13 (Lessor Computations and Entries, Sales-Type Lease with Guaranteed Residual Value) Amirante Inc. manufactures an X-ray machine with an estimated life of 12 years and leases it to Chambers Medical Center for a period of 10 years. The normal selling price of the machine is $411,324, and its guaranteed residual value at the end of the non-cancelable lease term is estimated to be $15,000. The hospital will pay rents of $60,000 at the beginning of each year and all maintenance, insurance, and taxes. Amirante Inc. incurred costs of $250,000 in manufacturing the machine and $14,000 in negotiating and closing the lease. Amirante Inc. has determined that the implicit interest rate is 10%.

Instructions

(Round all numbers to the nearest dollar.)

(a) Discuss the nature of this lease in relation to the lessor and compute the amount of each of the following items.

(1) Lease receivable at inception of the lease.	(2) Sales price.
	(3) Cost of sales.

(b) Prepare a 10-year lease amortization schedule.

(c) Prepare all of the lessor's journal entries for the first year.

2 7 P21-14 (Lessee Computations and Entries, Finance Lease with Guaranteed Residual Value) Assume the same data as in P21-13 and that Chambers Medical Center has an incremental borrowing rate of 10%.

Instructions

(Round all numbers to the nearest dollar.)

(a) Discuss the nature of this lease in relation to the lessee, and compute the amount of the initial obligation under finance leases.

(b) Prepare a 10-year lease amortization schedule.

(c) Prepare all of the lessee's journal entries for the first year.

2 3 7 P21-15 (Operating Lease vs. Finance Lease) You are auditing the December 31, 2015, financial statements of Hockney, Inc., manufacturer of novelties and party favors. During your inspection of the company garage, you discovered that a 2015 Shirk automobile not listed in the equipment subsidiary ledger is parked in the company garage. You ask Stacy Reeder, plant manager, about the vehicle, and she tells you that the company did not list the automobile because the company was only leasing it. The lease agreement was entered into on January 1, 2015, with Crown New and Used Cars.

You decide to review the lease agreement to ensure that the lease should be afforded operating lease treatment, and you discover the following lease terms.

1. Non-cancelable term of 4 years.

2. Rental of £3,240 per year (at the end of each year). (The present value at 8% per year is £10,731.)

Concepts for Analysis **1117**

3. Estimated residual value after 4 years is £1,100. (The present value at 8% per year is £809.) Hockney guarantees the residual value of £1,100.

4. Estimated economic life of the automobile is 5 years.

5. The implicit rate and Hockney's incremental borrowing rate is 8% per year.

Instructions

You are a senior auditor writing a memo to your supervisor, the audit partner in charge of this audit, to discuss the above situation. Be sure to include **(a)** why you inspected the lease agreement, **(b)** what you determined about the lease, and **(c)** how you advised your client to account for this lease. Explain every journal entry that you believe is necessary to record this lease properly on the client's books. (It is also necessary to include the fact that you communicated this information to your client.)

 P21-16 (Lessee-Lessor Accounting for Residual Values) Goring Dairy leases its milking equipment from King Finance Company under the following lease terms.

1. The lease term is 10 years, non-cancelable, and requires equal rental payments of €30,300 due at the beginning of each year starting January 1, 2015.

2. The equipment has a fair value and cost at the inception of the lease (January 1, 2015) of €220,404, an estimated economic life of 10 years, and a residual value (which is guaranteed by Goring Dairy) of €20,000.

3. The lease contains no renewable options, and the equipment reverts to King Finance Company upon termination of the lease.

4. Goring Dairy's incremental borrowing rate is 9% per year. The implicit rate is also 9%.

5. Goring Dairy depreciates similar equipment that it owns on a straight-line basis.

Instructions

(a) Evaluate the criteria for classification of the lease, and describe the nature of the lease. In general, discuss how the lessee and lessor should account for the lease transaction.

(b) Prepare the journal entries for the lessee and lessor at January 1, 2015, and December 31, 2015 (the lessee's and lessor's year-end). Assume no reversing entries.

(c) What would have been the amount capitalized by the lessee upon the inception of the lease if:

   (1) The residual value of €20,000 had been guaranteed by a third party, not the lessee?

   (2) The residual value of €20,000 had not been guaranteed at all?

(d) On the lessor's books, what would be the amount recorded as the Net Investment (Lease Receivable) at the inception of the lease, assuming:

   (1) The residual value of €20,000 had been guaranteed by a third party?

   (2) The residual value of €20,000 had not been guaranteed at all?

(e) Suppose the useful life of the milking equipment is 20 years. How large would the residual value have to be at the end of 10 years in order for the lessee to qualify for the operating method? (Assume that the residual value would be guaranteed by a third party.) (*Hint*: The lessee's annual payments will be appropriately reduced as the residual value increases.)

CONCEPTS FOR ANALYSIS

CA21-1 (Lessee Accounting and Reporting) On January 1, 2015, Evans Company entered into a non-cancelable lease for a machine to be used in its manufacturing operations. The lease transfers ownership of the machine to Evans by the end of the lease term. The term of the lease is 8 years. The minimum lease payment made by Evans on January 1, 2015, was one of eight equal annual payments. At the inception of the lease, the criteria established for classification as a finance lease by the lessee were met.

Instructions

(a) What is the theoretical basis for the accounting standard that requires certain long-term leases to be capitalized by the lessee? Do not discuss the specific criteria for classifying a specific lease as a finance lease.

(b) How should Evans account for this lease at its inception and determine the amount to be recorded?

(c) What expenses related to this lease will Evans incur during the first year of the lease, and how will they be determined?

(d) How should Evans report the lease transaction on its December 31, 2015, statement of financial position?

CA21-2 (Lessor and Lessee Accounting and Disclosure) Sylvan Inc. entered into a non-cancelable lease arrangement with Breton Leasing Corporation for a certain machine. Breton's primary business is leasing; it is not a manufacturer or dealer. Sylvan will lease the machine for a period of 3 years, which is 50% of the machine's economic life. Breton will take possession of the machine at the end of the initial 3-year lease and lease it to another, smaller company that does not need the most current version of the machine. Sylvan does not guarantee any residual value for the machine and will not purchase the machine at the end of the lease term.

Sylvan's incremental borrowing rate is 10%, and the implicit rate in the lease is 9%. Sylvan has no practicable way to determine the implicit rate used by Breton. Using either rate, the present value of the minimum lease payments is between 90% and 100% of the fair value of the machine at the date of the lease agreement.

Sylvan has agreed to pay all executory costs directly, and no allowance for these costs is included in the lease payments.

Assume that no indirect costs are involved.

Instructions

(a) With respect to Sylvan (the lessee), answer the following.

(1) What type of lease has been entered into? Explain the reason for your answer.

(2) How should Sylvan compute the appropriate amount to be recorded for the lease or asset acquired?

(3) What accounts will be created or affected by this transaction, and how will the lease or asset and other costs related to the transaction be recorded in earnings?

(4) What disclosures must Sylvan make regarding this leased asset?

(b) With respect to Breton (the lessor), answer the following.

(1) What type of leasing arrangement has been entered into? Explain the reason for your answer.

(2) How should this lease be recorded by Breton, and how are the appropriate amounts determined?

(3) How should Breton determine the appropriate amount of earnings to be recognized from each lease payment?

(4) What disclosures must Breton make regarding this lease?

CA21-3 (Lessee Capitalization Criteria) On January 1, Santiago Company, a lessee, entered into three non-cancelable leases for brand-new equipment, Lease L, Lease M, and Lease N. None of the three leases transfers ownership of the equipment to Santiago at the end of the lease term. For each of the three leases, the present value at the beginning of the lease term of the minimum lease payments, excluding that portion of the payments representing executory costs such as insurance, maintenance, and taxes to be paid by the lessor, is 75% of the fair value of the equipment.

The following information is peculiar to each lease.

1. Lease L does not contain a bargain-purchase option. The lease term is equal to 85% of the estimated economic life of the equipment.

2. Lease M contains a bargain-purchase option. The lease term is equal to 50% of the estimated economic life of the equipment.

3. Lease N does not contain a bargain-purchase option. The lease term is equal to 50% of the estimated economic life of the equipment.

Instructions

(a) How should Santiago Company classify each of the three leases above, and why? Discuss the rationale for your answer.

(b) What amount, if any, should Santiago record as a liability at the inception of the lease for each of the three leases above?

(c) Assuming that the minimum lease payments are made on a straight-line basis, how should Santiago record each minimum lease payment for each of the three leases above?

CA21-4 (Comparison of Different Types of Accounting by Lessee and Lessor)

Part 1: Finance leases and operating leases are the two classifications of leases described in IFRS from the standpoint of the **lessee**.

Instructions

    (a) Describe how a finance lease would be accounted for by the lessee both at the inception of the lease and during the first year of the lease, assuming the lease transfers ownership of the property to the lessee by the end of the lease.

    (b) Describe how an operating lease would be accounted for by the lessee both at the inception of the lease and during the first year of the lease, assuming equal monthly payments are made by the lessee at the beginning of each month of the lease.

Do **not** discuss the criteria for distinguishing between finance leases and operating leases.

Part 2: Sales-type leases and direct-financing leases are two of the classifications of leases described in IFRS from the standpoint of the **lessor**.

Instructions

Compare and contrast a sales-type lease with a direct-financing lease as follows.

    (a) Lease receivable.
    (b) Recognition of interest revenue.
    (c) Manufacturer's or dealer's profit.

Do **not** discuss the criteria for distinguishing between the leases described above and operating leases.

CA21-5 (Lessee Capitalization of Bargain-Purchase Option) Albertsen Corporation is a diversified company with nationwide interests in commercial real estate developments, banking, copper mining, and metal fabrication. The company has offices and operating locations in major cities throughout the United Kingdom. Corporate headquarters for Albertsen Corporation is located in a metropolitan area of The Lake District, and executives connected with various phases of company operations travel extensively. Corporate management is currently evaluating the feasibility of acquiring a business aircraft that can be used by company executives to expedite business travel to areas not adequately served by commercial airlines. Proposals for either leasing or purchasing a suitable aircraft have been analyzed, and the leasing proposal was considered to be more desirable.

    The proposed lease agreement involves a twin-engine turboprop Viking that has a fair value of £1,000,000. This plane would be leased for a period of 10 years beginning January 1, 2015. The lease agreement is cancelable only upon accidental destruction of the plane. An annual lease payment of £141,780 is due on January 1 of each year; the first payment is to be made on January 1, 2015. Maintenance operations are strictly scheduled by the lessor, and Albertsen Corporation will pay for these services as they are performed. Estimated annual maintenance costs are £6,900. The lessor will pay all insurance premiums and local property taxes, which amount to a combined total of £4,000 annually and are included in the annual lease payment of £141,780. Upon expiration of the 10-year lease, Albertsen Corporation can purchase the Viking for £44,440. The estimated useful life of the plane is 15 years, and its residual value in the used plane market is estimated to be £100,000 after 10 years. The residual value probably will never be less than £75,000 if the engines are overhauled and maintained as prescribed by the manufacturer. If the purchase option is not exercised, possession of the plane will revert to the lessor, and there is no provision for renewing the lease agreement beyond its termination on December 31, 2024.

    Albertsen Corporation can borrow £1,000,000 under a 10-year term loan agreement at an annual interest rate of 12%. The lessor's implicit interest rate is not expressly stated in the lease agreement, but this rate appears to be approximately 8% based on 10 net rental payments of £137,780 per year and the initial fair value of £1,000,000 for the plane. On January 1, 2015, the present value of all net rental payments and the purchase option of £44,440 is £888,890 using the 12% interest rate. The present value of all net rental payments and the £44,440 purchase option on January 1, 2015, is £1,022,226 using the 8% interest rate implicit in the lease agreement. The financial vice president of Albertsen Corporation has established that this lease agreement is a finance lease as defined in IFRS.

Instructions

    (a) What is the appropriate amount that Albertsen Corporation should recognize for the leased aircraft on its statement of financial position after the lease is signed?

    (b) Disregarding your answer in part (a), assume that the annual lease payment is £141,780 as stated in the case, that the appropriate capitalized amount for the leased aircraft is £1,000,000 on January 1, 2015, and that the interest rate is 9%. How will the lease be reported in the December 31, 2015, statement of financial position and related income statement? (Ignore any tax implications.)

CA21-6 (Lease Capitalization, Bargain-Purchase Option) Baden Corporation entered into a lease agreement for 10 photocopy machines for its corporate headquarters. The lease agreement qualifies as an operating lease in all terms except there is a bargain-purchase option. After the 5-year lease term, the corporation can purchase each copier for €1,000, when the anticipated fair value is €2,500.

    Jerry Suffolk, the financial vice president, thinks the financial statements must recognize the lease agreement as a finance lease because of the bargain-purchase agreement. The controller, Diane Buchanan, disagrees: "Although I don't know much about the copiers themselves, there is a way to avoid recording the lease liability." She argues that the corporation might claim that copier technology advances rapidly and that by the end of the lease term the machines will most likely not be worth the €1,000 bargain price.

Instructions

Answer the following questions.

(a) What ethical issue is at stake?

(b) Should the controller's argument be accepted if she does not really know much about copier technology? Would it make a difference if the controller were knowledgeable about the pace of change in copier technology?

(c) What should Suffolk do?

*CA21-7 **(Sale-Leaseback)** On January 1, 2015, Perriman Company sold equipment for cash and leased it back. As seller-lessee, Perriman retained the right to substantially all of the remaining use of the equipment.

The term of the lease is 8 years. There is a gain on the sale portion of the transaction. The lease portion of the transaction is classified appropriately as a finance lease.

Instructions

(a) What is the theoretical basis for requiring lessees to capitalize certain long-term leases? **Do not discuss the specific criteria for classifying a lease as a finance lease.**

(b) (1) How should Perriman account for the sale portion of the sale-leaseback transaction at January 1, 2015?

(2) How should Perriman account for the leaseback portion of the sale-leaseback transaction at January 1, 2015?

(c) How should Perriman account for the gain on the sale portion of the sale-leaseback transaction during the first year of the lease? Why?

*CA21-8 **(Sale-Leaseback)** On December 31, 2015, Shellhammer Co. sold 6-month-old equipment at fair value and leased it back. There was a loss on the sale. Shellhammer pays all insurance, maintenance, and taxes on the equipment. The lease provides for 8 equal annual payments, beginning December 31, 2016, with a present value equal to 80% of the equipment's fair value and sales price. The lease's term is 85% of the equipment's useful life. There is no provision for Shellhammer to reacquire ownership of the equipment at the end of the lease term.

Instructions

(a) (1) Why is it important to compare an equipment's fair value to its lease payments' present value and its useful life to the lease term?

(2) Evaluate Shellhammer's leaseback of the equipment in terms of each of the four criteria for determination of a finance lease.

(b) How should Shellhammer account for the sale portion of the sale-leaseback transaction at December 31, 2015?

(c) How should Shellhammer report the leaseback portion of the sale-leaseback transaction on its December 31, 2016, statement of financial position?

USING YOUR JUDGMENT

FINANCIAL REPORTING

Financial Reporting Problem

Marks and Spencer plc (M&S)

The financial statements of **M&S** (GBR) are presented in Appendix A. The company's complete annual report, including the notes to the financial statements, is available online.

Instructions

Refer to M&S's financial statements and the accompanying notes to answer the following questions.

(a) What types of leases are used by M&S?

(b) What amount of finance leases was reported by M&S in total and for less than one year?

(c) What minimum annual rental commitments under all non-cancelable leases at year-end 2013 did M&S disclose?

Comparative Analysis Case

British Airways and Air France—KLM

Instructions

Go to the British Airways (GBR) and Air France—KLM (FRA) (Air France) company websites and use information found there to answer the following questions related to these airlines.

   (a) What types of leases are used by Air France and on what assets are these leases primarily used?
   (b) How long-term are some of Air France's leases? What are some of the characteristics or provisions of Air France's (as lessee) leases?
   (c) What did Air France report in 2012 as its future minimum annual rental commitments under non-cancelable leases for aircraft and flight equipment?
   (d) At year-end 2012, what was the present value of the minimum rental payments under Air France's finance leases in part (c)? How much imputed interest was deducted from the future minimum annual rental commitments to arrive at the present value?
   (e) What were the amounts and details reported by Air France for rental expense in 2012 and 2011?
   (f) How does British Airways' use of leases compare with Air France's?

Financial Statement Analysis Case

Delhaize Group

Presented in Illustration 21-30 (page 1090) are the financial statement disclosures from the 2012 annual report of Delhaize Group (BEL).

Instructions

Answer the following questions related to these disclosures.

   (a) What is the total obligation under finance leases at year-end 2012 for Delhaize?
   (b) What is the total rental expense reported for leasing activity for the year ended December 31, 2012, for Delhaize?
   (c) Estimate the off-balance-sheet liability due to Delhaize operating leases at fiscal year-end 2012.

Accounting, Analysis, and Principles

Salaur Company is evaluating a lease arrangement being offered by TSP Company for use of a computer system. The lease is non-cancelable, and in no case does Salaur receive title to the computers during or at the end of the lease term. The lease starts on January 1, 2015, with the first rental due at the beginning of the year. Additional information related to the lease is as follows.

Yearly rental	$3,557.25
Lease term	3 years
Estimated economic life	5 years
Purchase option	$3,000 at end of 3 years, which approximates fair value
Renewal option	1 year at $1,500; no penalty for non-renewal; standard renewal clause
Fair value at inception of lease	$10,000
Cost of asset to lessor	$10,000
Residual value	
Guaranteed	–0–
Unguaranteed	$3,000
Lessor's implicit rate (known by lessee)	12%
Executory costs paid by:	Lessee; estimated to be $500 per year, included in payments
Estimated fair value at end of lease	$3,000

Accounting

Analyze the lease capitalization criteria for this lease for Salaur Company. Prepare the journal entry for Salaur on January 1, 2015.

Analysis

Briefly discuss the impact of the accounting for this lease for two common ratios: return on assets and debt to assets.

Principles

What fundamental quality of the conceptual framework is being addressed when a company like Salaur evaluates lease capitalization criteria?

IFRS BRIDGE TO THE PROFESSION

Professional Research

Daniel Hardware Co. is considering alternative financing arrangements for equipment used in its warehouses. Besides purchasing the equipment outright, Daniel is also considering a lease. Accounting for the outright purchase is fairly straightforward, but because Daniel has not used equipment leases in the past, the accounting staff is less informed about the specific accounting rules for leases.

The staff is aware of some general lease rules related to "risks and rewards," but they are unsure about the meanings of these terms in lease accounting. Daniel has asked you to conduct some research on these items related to lease capitalization criteria.

Instructions

Access the IFRS authoritative literature at the IASB website (*http://eifrs.iasb.org/*) (you may register for free eIFRS access at this site). When you have accessed the documents, you can use the search tool in your Internet browser to respond to the following questions. (Provide paragraph citations.)

(a) What is the objective of lease classification criteria?

(b) An important element of evaluating leases is determining whether substantially all of the risks and rewards of ownership are transferred in the lease. How is "substantially all" defined in the authoritative literature?

(c) Besides the non-cancelable term of the lease, name at least three other considerations in determining the "lease term."

Professional Simulations

Simulation 1

In this simulation, you are asked to address questions related to the accounting for leases. Prepare responses to all parts.

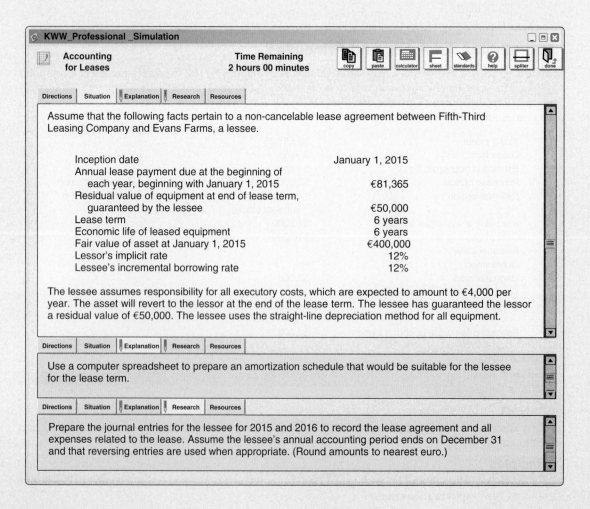

Assume that the following facts pertain to a non-cancelable lease agreement between Fifth-Third Leasing Company and Evans Farms, a lessee.

Inception date	January 1, 2015
Annual lease payment due at the beginning of each year, beginning with January 1, 2015	€81,365
Residual value of equipment at end of lease term, guaranteed by the lessee	€50,000
Lease term	6 years
Economic life of leased equipment	6 years
Fair value of asset at January 1, 2015	€400,000
Lessor's implicit rate	12%
Lessee's incremental borrowing rate	12%

The lessee assumes responsibility for all executory costs, which are expected to amount to €4,000 per year. The asset will revert to the lessor at the end of the lease term. The lessee has guaranteed the lessor a residual value of €50,000. The lessee uses the straight-line depreciation method for all equipment.

Use a computer spreadsheet to prepare an amortization schedule that would be suitable for the lessee for the lease term.

Prepare the journal entries for the lessee for 2015 and 2016 to record the lease agreement and all expenses related to the lease. Assume the lessee's annual accounting period ends on December 31 and that reversing entries are used when appropriate. (Round amounts to nearest euro.)

Simulation 2

In this simulation, you are asked to address questions related to the accounting for leases. Prepare responses to all parts.

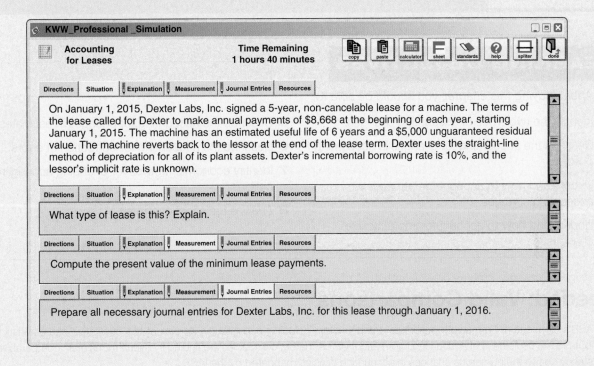

KWW_Professional _Simulation

| Accounting for Leases | Time Remaining 1 hours 40 minutes | copy paste calculator sheet standards help splitter done |

Directions | Situation | Explanation | Measurement | Journal Entries | Resources

On January 1, 2015, Dexter Labs, Inc. signed a 5-year, non-cancelable lease for a machine. The terms of the lease called for Dexter to make annual payments of $8,668 at the beginning of each year, starting January 1, 2015. The machine has an estimated useful life of 6 years and a $5,000 unguaranteed residual value. The machine reverts back to the lessor at the end of the lease term. Dexter uses the straight-line method of depreciation for all of its plant assets. Dexter's incremental borrowing rate is 10%, and the lessor's implicit rate is unknown.

Directions | Situation | Explanation | Measurement | Journal Entries | Resources

What type of lease is this? Explain.

Directions | Situation | Explanation | Measurement | Journal Entries | Resources

Compute the present value of the minimum lease payments.

Directions | Situation | Explanation | Measurement | Journal Entries | Resources

Prepare all necessary journal entries for Dexter Labs, Inc. for this lease through January 1, 2016.

22 Accounting Changes and Error Analysis

Needed: Valid Comparisons

The IASB's Conceptual Framework describes comparability (including consistency) as one of the qualitative characteristics that contribute to the usefulness of accounting information. Unfortunately, companies are finding it difficult to maintain comparability and consistency due to the numerous changes in accounting policies mandated by the IASB.

Presented below is a condensed version of the change in accounting policy note of **United Business Media (UBM)** (IRL) in a recent annual report.

Changes in accounting policies (in part)

The accounting policies adopted are consistent with those of the previous financial year except as follows:

IAS 1 — Presentation of Financial Statements (revised) The Group adopted this revised standard. The revision separates owner and non-owner changes in equity. The statement of changes in equity includes only details of transactions with owners, with non-owner changes in equity presented as a single line. In addition, the standard introduces the statement of comprehensive income to be presented either as a single statement, or as two linked statements. The Group has elected to present two statements.

IAS 36 — Impairment of Assets When discounted cash flows are used to estimate "fair value less costs to sell," additional disclosure is required about the discount rate, consistent with disclosures required when discounted cash flows are used to estimate "value in use." For those cash-generating units where the Group is required to compute the recoverable amount, fair value less costs to sell is used on an earnings multiples approach. Additional disclosures will be included in the future where applicable.

IFRS 7 — Financial Instruments Disclosures: The Group adopted this amendment which requires increased disclosures about fair value measurements and liquidity risk. Fair value measurements related to items recorded at fair value are to be disclosed by source of inputs using a three-level fair value hierarchy, by class, for all financial instruments recognized at fair value.

IFRS 8 — Operating Segments The Group adopted IFRS 8, which requires disclosure of information about the Group's operating segments and replaces the requirement to determine primary (business) and secondary (geographical) reporting segments of the Group. Adoption of this Standard did not have any effect on the financial position or performance of the Group. The Group determined that the four operating and reportable segments are Events, Data, Services and Online, Print — Magazines and Targeting, Distribution and Monitoring. Additional disclosures about each of these segments are shown in Note 3.

What these excerpts indicate is that the IASB is constantly attempting to improve financial reporting as conditions change in the financial world.

In addition, a number of companies have faced restatements due to errors in their financial statements. Presented on the next page is a chart that shows the total restatements per year since 2004. There is much good news in the chart. In 2007, restatements declined by 31.5 percent (from 1,771 to 1,213). In 2008, restatements declined another 24 percent (from 1,213 to 922). Although the

Total Restatements by Year

declining trend continued in 2009, from 2010–2012, restatements seem to have stabilized. The overall decline is attributed to improved reliability of internal controls, but some observers suspect that the drop may also be due to relaxed enforcement by market regulators.

The trend in restatements is a positive development. However, when restatements and accounting changes arise, financial statement users still need high-quality accounting information to make valid comparisons of financial performance to periods before the accounting change or restatement.

Source: 2009 Financial Restatements: A Nine Year Comparison, Audit Analytics (March 2013), p. 3.

PREVIEW OF CHAPTER 22

As our opening story indicates, changes in accounting policies and errors in financial information are significant. When these changes occur, companies must follow specific accounting and reporting requirements. In addition, to ensure comparability among companies, the IASB has standardized reporting of accounting changes, changes in accounting estimates, error corrections, and related earnings per share information. In this chapter, we discuss these reporting standards, which help investors better understand a company's financial condition. The content and organization of the chapter are as follows.

Accounting Changes and Error Analysis

Accounting Changes	Changes in Policy	Changes in Estimates	Accounting Errors	Error Analysis
	• Retrospective • Direct and indirect effects • Impracticability	• Prospective • Disclosure	• Example • Summary • Motivations	• Statement of financial position errors • Income statement errors • Statement of financial position and income statement errors • Comprehensive example • Preparation of statements with error corrections

ACCOUNTING CHANGES

LEARNING OBJECTIVE 1

Identify the two types of accounting changes.

See the Authoritative Literature section (page 1158).

Accounting alternatives diminish the comparability of financial information between periods and between companies; they also obscure useful historical trend data. For example, if Toyota (JPN) revises its estimates for equipment useful lives, depreciation expense for the current year will not be comparable to depreciation expense reported by Toyota in prior years. Similarly, if Tesco (GBR) changes to FIFO inventory pricing while Marks and Spencer plc (GBR) uses the retail method, it will be difficult to compare these companies' reported results. A reporting framework helps preserve comparability when there is an accounting change.

The IASB has established a reporting framework that involves two types of accounting changes. [1] The two types of accounting changes are:

1. *Change in accounting policy.* A change from one accepted accounting policy to another one. For example, Alcatel-Lucent (FRA) changed its method of accounting for actuarial gains and losses from using the corridor approach to immediate recognition.

2. *Change in accounting estimate.* A change that occurs as the result of new information or additional experience. As an example, Daimler AG (DEU) revised its estimates of the useful lives of its depreciable property recently due to modifications in its productive processes.

A third category necessitates changes in accounting, though it is not classified as an accounting change.

3. *Errors in financial statements.* Errors result from mathematical mistakes, mistakes in applying accounting policies, or oversight or misuse of facts that existed when preparing the financial statements. For example, a company may incorrectly apply the retail inventory method for determining its final inventory value.

The IASB classifies changes in these categories because each category involves different methods of recognizing changes in the financial statements. In this chapter, we discuss these classifications. We also explain how to report each item in the accounts and how to disclose the information in comparative statements.

CHANGES IN ACCOUNTING POLICY

LEARNING OBJECTIVE 2

Describe the accounting for changes in accounting policies.

By definition, a change in accounting policy involves a change from one accepted accounting policy to another. For example, a company might change the basis of inventory pricing from average-cost to FIFO. Or, it might change its method of revenue recognition for long-term construction contracts from the cost-recovery to the percentage-of-completion method.

Companies must carefully examine each circumstance to ensure that a change in policy has actually occurred. **Adoption of a new policy** in recognition of events that have occurred for the first time or that were previously immaterial is not a change in accounting policy. For example, a change in accounting policy has not occurred when a company adopts an inventory method (e.g., FIFO) for **newly** acquired items of inventory, even if FIFO differs from that used for **previously recorded** inventory. Another example is certain marketing expenditures that were previously immaterial and expensed in the period incurred. It would not be considered a change in accounting policy if they become material and so may be acceptably deferred and amortized.

Finally, what if a company previously followed an accounting policy that was not acceptable? Or, what if the company applied a policy incorrectly? In such cases, this type of change is **a correction of an error**. For example, a switch from the cash (income tax) basis of accounting to the accrual basis is a correction of an error. Or, if a company deducted residual value when computing double-declining depreciation on plant assets and later recomputed depreciation without deducting estimated residual value, it has corrected an error.

There are three possible approaches for reporting changes in accounting policies:

- *Report changes currently.* In this approach, companies report the cumulative effect of the change in the current year's income statement. The **cumulative effect** is the difference in prior years' income between the newly adopted and prior accounting policy. Under this approach, the effect of the change on prior years' income appears only in the current-year income statement. The company does not change **prior-year financial statements**.

  Advocates of this position argue that changing prior years' financial statements results in a loss of confidence in financial reports. How do investors react when told that the earnings computed three years ago are now entirely different? Changing prior periods, if permitted, also might upset contractual arrangements based on the old figures. For example, profit-sharing arrangements computed on the old basis might have to be recomputed and completely new distributions made, creating numerous legal problems. Many practical difficulties also exist: The cost of changing prior period financial statements may be excessive, or determining the amount of the prior period effect may be impossible on the basis of available data.

- *Report changes retrospectively.* **Retrospective application** refers to the application of a different accounting policy to recast previously issued financial statements—**as if the new policy had always been used**. In other words, the company "goes back" and adjusts **prior years' statements** on a basis consistent with the newly adopted policy. The company shows any cumulative effect of the change as an adjustment to beginning retained earnings of the earliest year presented.

  Advocates of this position argue that retrospective application ensures comparability. Think for a moment what happens if this approach is not used: The year *previous* to the change will be on the old method; the year *of the change* will report the entire cumulative adjustment; and the *following* year will present financial statements on the new basis without the cumulative effect of the change. Such lack of consistency fails to provide meaningful earnings-trend data and other financial relationships necessary to evaluate the business.

- *Report changes prospectively (in the future).* In this approach, previously reported results remain. As a result, companies do not adjust opening balances to reflect the change in policy. Advocates of this position argue that once management presents financial statements based on acceptable accounting policies, they are final; management cannot change prior periods by adopting a new policy. According to this line of reasoning, the current-period cumulative adjustment is not appropriate because that approach includes amounts that have little or no relationship to the current year's income or economic events.

Given these three possible approaches, which does the accounting profession prefer? The IASB **requires that companies use the retrospective approach**. Why? Because it provides financial statement users with more useful information than the cumulative-effect or prospective approaches. **[2]** The rationale is that changing the prior statements to be on the same basis as the newly adopted policy results in greater consistency across accounting periods. Users can then better compare results from one period to the next.

Underlying Concepts

Use of the retrospective approach contributes to the enhancing characteristic of consistency.

What do the numbers mean? COMPARISON CHALLENGES—SQUARED

As discussed in the opening story, accounting changes create comparability challenges when evaluating a company over time. This explains the importance of accounting rules that ensure investors have the information to understand accounting reports prepared under different sets of rules across time. However, the comparability challenges can be compounded by both the number of required accounting changes as well as the variation in implementation dates. The table below provides a summary of recent accounting standards and their effective dates.

Effective Date, Year Ending	Standards
June 30, 2013	*Presentation of Items of Other Comprehensive Income (Amendments to IAS 1)* *Disclosures: Offsetting Financial Assets and Financial Liabilities (Amendments to IFRS 7)*
December 31, 2013	IFRS 13 *Fair Value Measurement* IAS 19 *Employee Benefits*
December 31, 2014	*Recoverable Amount Disclosures for Non-Financial Assets (Amendments to IAS 36)*

Given the range of new standards coming online (the list above is a sampling of 18 new standards that became effective in 2013–2014), it is easy to understand why financial statement users would find it difficult to compare accounting results, to the extent that companies are differentially affected by these new standards. Furthermore, implementation guidance for some standards allows companies to adopt early if they wish. This is the case for the changes in rules for offsetting and recoverable amounts disclosure in the table above. This early-adoption option further magnifies the comparability challenges in the wake of new standards.

Source: "IFRS: New Standards—Are You Prepared?" *In the Headlines* (Issue 2014/4), KPMG (March 2014).

Retrospective Accounting Change Approach

A presumption exists that once a company adopts an accounting policy, it should not change. That presumption is understandable, given the idea that consistent use of an accounting policy enhances the usefulness of financial statements. **[3]** However, the environment continually changes, and companies change in response. Recent standards, such as borrowing costs and operating segments, and proposed standards on revenue recognition and financial instruments indicate that changes in accounting policies will continue to exist.

As a consequence, the IASB permits companies to change an accounting policy if:

1. It is required by IFRS (e.g., the new IFRS on financial instruments will be subject to the proper accounting for changes in accounting policy); or

2. It results in the financial statements providing more reliable and relevant information about a company's financial position, financial performance, and cash flows. For example, a company may determine that changing from the average-cost method of inventory valuation to the FIFO method provides more reliable and relevant information on the current value of its inventory.[1]

[1]In some cases, a particular transaction is not specifically addressed by IFRS. In this situation, *IAS 8* sets out a hierarchy of guidance to be considered in the selection of an accounting policy. The primary requirement is that management must use judgment to develop information that is relevant and reliable. In making that judgment, it should use the following sources in descending order: (1) the requirements and guidance in IFRS dealing with similar and related issues; (2) the definitions, recognition criteria, and measurement concepts for the elements in the Conceptual Framework; and (3) other materials such as standards from other countries that use a similar conceptual framework. **[4]**

When a company changes an accounting policy, it should report the change using retrospective application. In general terms, here is what the company must do:

1. Adjust (recast) its financial statements for each prior period presented. Thus, financial statement information about prior periods is on the same basis as the new accounting policy.

2. Adjust the carrying amounts of assets and liabilities as of the beginning of the first year presented. By doing so, these accounts reflect the cumulative effect on periods prior to those presented of the change to the new accounting policy. The company also makes an offsetting adjustment to the opening balance of retained earnings or other appropriate component of equity or net assets as of the beginning of the first year presented.

For example, assume that **Carrefour** (FRA) decides to change its inventory valuation method in 2015 from FIFO to average-cost. It provides comparative information for 2013 and 2014 based on the new method. Carrefour would adjust its assets, liabilities, and retained earnings for periods prior to 2013 and report these amounts in the 2013 financial statements, when it prepares comparative financial statements.

Retrospective Accounting Change: Long-Term Contracts

To illustrate the retrospective approach, assume that Denson Company has accounted for its income from long-term construction contracts using the cost-recovery (zero-profit) method. In 2015, the company changed to the percentage-of-completion method. Management believes this approach provides a more appropriate measure of the income earned. For tax purposes, the company uses the cost-recovery method and plans to continue doing so in the future. (We assume a 40 percent enacted tax rate.)

Illustration 22-1 shows portions of three income statements for 2013–2015—for both the cost-recovery and percentage-of-completion methods. (There were no differences in income between the old and new accounting methods before 2013.)

ILLUSTRATION 22-1
Comparative Income Statements for Cost-Recovery versus Percentage-of-Completion Methods

COST-RECOVERY METHOD
DENSON COMPANY
INCOME STATEMENT (PARTIAL)
FOR THE YEAR ENDED DECEMBER 31

	2013	2014	2015
Income before income tax	€400,000	€160,000	€190,000
Income tax (40%)	160,000	64,000	76,000
Net income	€240,000	€ 96,000	€114,000

PERCENTAGE-OF-COMPLETION METHOD
DENSON COMPANY
INCOME STATEMENT (PARTIAL)
FOR THE YEAR ENDED DECEMBER 31

	2013	2014	2015
Income before income tax	€600,000	€180,000	€200,000
Income tax (40%)	240,000	72,000	80,000
Net income	€360,000	€108,000	€120,000

To record a change from the cost-recovery to the percentage-of-completion method, we analyze the various effects, as Illustration 22-2 (on page 1130) shows.

ILLUSTRATION 22-2
Data for Retrospective
Change Example

	Pretax Income from		Difference in Income		
Year	Percentage-of-Completion	Cost-Recovery	Difference	Tax Effect 40%	Income Effect (net of tax)
Prior to 2014	€600,000	€400,000	€200,000	€80,000	€120,000
In 2014	180,000	160,000	20,000	8,000	12,000
Total at beginning of 2015	€780,000	€560,000	€220,000	€88,000	€132,000
Total in 2015	€200,000	€190,000	€ 10,000	€ 4,000	€ 6,000

The entry to record the change at the beginning of 2015 would be:

Construction in Process	220,000	
Deferred Tax Liability		88,000
Retained Earnings		132,000

The Construction in Process account increases by €220,000 (as indicated in the first column under "Difference in Income" in Illustration 22-2). The credit to Retained Earnings of €132,000 reflects the cumulative income effects prior to 2015 (third column under "Difference in Income" in Illustration 22-2). The company credits Retained Earnings because prior years' income is closed to this account each year. The credit to Deferred Tax Liability represents the adjustment to prior years' tax expense. The company now recognizes that amount, €88,000, as a tax liability for future taxable amounts. That is, in future periods, taxable income will be higher than book income as a result of current temporary differences. Therefore, Denson must report a deferred tax liability in the current year.

Reporting a Change in Policy. The disclosure of changes in accounting policies is particularly important. Financial statement users want consistent information from one period to the next. Such consistency ensures the usefulness of financial statements. The major disclosure requirements are as follows.

1. The nature of the change in accounting policy;
2. The reasons why applying the new accounting policy provides reliable and more relevant information;
3. For the current period and each prior period presented, to the extent practicable, the amount of the adjustment:
   (a) For each financial statement line item affected; and
   (b) Basic and diluted earnings per share.
4. The amount of the adjustment relating to periods before those presented, to the extent practicable.[2]

The disclosure here relates to a voluntary change in accounting policy, such as a change from the average-cost to FIFO method of inventory measurement. The requirements for disclosure are slightly different if the change is mandated by the issuance of a new IFRS. In that case, transitional adjustments are also considered, as required by the standard.

To illustrate, Denson will prepare comparative financial statements for 2014 and 2015 using the percentage-of-completion method (the new-construction accounting method). Illustration 22-3 indicates how Denson presents this information.

As Illustration 22-3 shows, Denson Company reports net income under the newly adopted percentage-of-completion method for both 2014 and 2015. The company retrospectively adjusted the 2014 income statement to report the information on a percentage-of-completion basis. Also, the note to the financial statements indicates the nature of the change, why the company made the change, and the years affected.

---

[2]Financial statements of subsequent periods need not repeat these disclosures. **[5]**

DENSON COMPANY
INCOME STATEMENT (PARTIAL)
FOR THE YEAR ENDED

	2015	2014
		As adjusted (Note A)
Income before income tax	€200,000	€180,000
Income tax (40%)	80,000	72,000
Net income	€120,000	€108,000

Note A: Change in Method of Accounting for Long-Term Contracts. The company has accounted for revenue and costs for long-term construction contracts by the percentage-of-completion method in 2015, whereas in all prior years revenue and costs were determined by the cost-recovery method. The new method of accounting for long-term contracts was adopted to recognize . . . [state justification for change in accounting policy] . . . , and financial statements of prior years have been restated to apply the new method retrospectively. For income tax purposes, the cost-recovery method has been continued. The effect of the accounting change on income of 2015 was an increase of €6,000 net of related taxes and on income of 2014 as previously reported was an increase of €12,000 net of related taxes. The balances of retained earnings for 2014 and 2015 have been adjusted for the effect of applying retrospectively the new method of accounting. As a result of the accounting change, retained earnings as of January 1, 2014, increased by €120,000 compared to that reported using the cost-recovery method.

ILLUSTRATION 22-3
Comparative Information Related to Accounting Change (Percentage-of-Completion)

In addition, companies are required to provide data on important differences between the amounts reported under percentage-of-completion versus cost-recovery. When identifying the significant differences, some companies show the *entire* financial statements and line-by-line differences between percentage-of-completion and cost-recovery. However, most companies will show only line-by-line differences. For example, Denson would show the differences in construction in process, retained earnings, gross profit, and net income for 2014 and 2015 under the cost-recovery and percentage-of-completion methods.

Retained Earnings Adjustment. As indicated earlier, one of the disclosure requirements is to show the cumulative effect of the change on retained earnings as of the beginning of the earliest period presented. For Denson Company, that date is January 1, 2014. Denson disclosed that information by means of a narrative description (see Note A in Illustration 22-3). Denson also would disclose this information in its retained earnings statement. Assuming a retained earnings balance of €1,360,000 at the beginning of 2013, Illustration 22-4 shows Denson's retained earnings statement under the cost-recovery method—that is, before giving effect to the change in accounting policy. (The income information comes from Illustration 22-1 on page 1129.)

DENSON COMPANY
RETAINED EARNINGS STATEMENT
FOR THE YEAR ENDED

	2015	2014	2013
Retained earnings, January 1	€1,696,000	€1,600,000	€1,360,000
Net income	114,000	96,000	240,000
Retained earnings, December 31	€1,810,000	€1,696,000	€1,600,000

ILLUSTRATION 22-4
Retained Earnings Statement before Retrospective Change

If Denson presents comparative statements for 2014 and 2015 under percentage-of-completion, then it must change the beginning balance of retained earnings at January 1, 2014. The difference between the retained earnings balances under cost-recovery and percentage-of-completion is computed as follows.

Retained earnings, January 1, 2014 (percentage-of-completion)	€1,720,000
Retained earnings, January 1, 2014 (cost-recovery)	1,600,000
Cumulative-effect difference	€ 120,000

The €120,000 difference is the cumulative effect. Illustration 22-5 shows a comparative retained earnings statement for 2014 and 2015, giving effect to the change in accounting policy to percentage-of-completion.

ILLUSTRATION 22-5
Retained Earnings
Statement after
Retrospective Application

DENSON COMPANY RETAINED EARNINGS STATEMENT FOR THE YEAR ENDED		
	2015	2014
Retained earnings, January 1, as reported	—	€1,600,000
Add: Adjustment for the cumulative effect on prior years of applying retrospectively the new method of accounting for construction contracts		120,000
Retained earnings, January 1, as adjusted	€1,828,000	1,720,000
Net income	120,000	108,000
Retained earnings, December 31	€1,948,000	€1,828,000

Denson adjusted the beginning balance of retained earnings on January 1, 2014, for the excess of percentage-of-completion net income over cost-recovery net income in 2013. This comparative presentation indicates the type of adjustment that a company needs to make. It follows that this adjustment would be much larger if a number of prior periods were involved.

Retrospective Accounting Change: Inventory Methods

As a second illustration of the retrospective approach, assume that Lancer Company has accounted for its inventory using the average-cost method. In 2015, the company changes to the FIFO method because management believes this approach provides a more appropriate measure of its inventory costs. Illustration 22-6 provides additional information related to Lancer Company.

ILLUSTRATION 22-6
Lancer Company
Information

1. Lancer Company started its operations on January 1, 2013. At that time, shareholders invested $100,000 in the business in exchange for ordinary shares.

2. All sales, purchases, and operating expenses for the period 2013–2015 are cash transactions. Lancer's cash flows over this period are as follows.

	2013	2014	2015
Sales	$300,000	$300,000	$300,000
Purchases	90,000	110,000	125,000
Operating expenses	100,000	100,000	100,000
Cash flow from operations	$110,000	$ 90,000	$ 75,000

3. Lancer has used the average-cost method for financial reporting since its inception.

4. Inventory determined under average-cost and FIFO for the period 2013–2015 is as follows.

	Average-Cost Method	FIFO Method	Difference
January 1, 2013	$ 0	$ 0	$ 0
December 31, 2013	10,000	12,000	2,000
December 31, 2014	20,000	25,000	5,000
December 31, 2015	32,000	39,000	7,000

5. Cost of goods sold under average-cost and FIFO for the period 2013–2015 is as follows.

	Cost of Goods Sold		
	Average-Cost	FIFO	Difference
2013	$ 80,000	$ 78,000	$2,000
2014	100,000	97,000	3,000
2015	113,000	111,000	2,000

6. Earnings per share information is not required on the income statement.

7. All tax effects for this illustration should be ignored.

Given the information about Lancer Company, Illustration 22-7 shows its income statement, retained earnings statement, statement of financial position, and statement of cash flows for 2013–2015 under average-cost.

ILLUSTRATION 22-7
Lancer Financial
Statements (Average-Cost)

LANCER COMPANY
INCOME STATEMENT
FOR THE YEAR ENDED DECEMBER 31

	2013	2014	2015
Sales	$300,000	$300,000	$300,000
Cost of goods sold (average-cost)	80,000	100,000	113,000
Operating expenses	100,000	100,000	100,000
Net income	$120,000	$100,000	$ 87,000

LANCER COMPANY
RETAINED EARNINGS STATEMENT
FOR THE YEAR ENDED DECEMBER 31

	2013	2014	2015
Retained earnings (beginning)	$ 0	$120,000	$220,000
Add: Net income	120,000	100,000	87,000
Retained earnings (ending)	$120,000	$220,000	$307,000

LANCER COMPANY
STATEMENT OF FINANCIAL POSITION
AT DECEMBER 31

	2013	2014	2015
Inventory (average-cost)	$ 10,000	$ 20,000	$ 32,000
Cash	210,000	300,000	375,000
Total assets	$220,000	$320,000	$407,000
Share capital	$100,000	$100,000	$100,000
Retained earnings	120,000	220,000	307,000
Total equity	$220,000	$320,000	$407,000

LANCER COMPANY
STATEMENT OF CASH FLOWS
FOR THE YEAR ENDED DECEMBER 31

	2013	2014	2015
Cash flows from operating activities			
Sales	$300,000	$300,000	$300,000
Purchases	90,000	110,000	125,000
Operating expenses	100,000	100,000	100,000
Net cash provided by operating activities	110,000	90,000	75,000
Cash flows from financing activities			
Issuance of ordinary shares	100,000	—	—
Net increase in cash	210,000	90,000	75,000
Cash at beginning of year	0	210,000	300,000
Cash at end of year	$210,000	$300,000	$375,000

As Illustration 22-7 indicates, under average-cost Lancer Company reports $120,000 net income in 2013, $100,000 net income in 2014, and $87,000 net income in 2015. The amount of inventory reported on Lancer's statement of financial position reflects average-cost inventory accounting.

Illustration 22-8 (page 1134) shows Lancer's income statement, retained earnings statement, statement of financial position, and statement of cash flows for 2013–2015 under **FIFO**. You can see that **the cash flow statement under FIFO is the same as under average-cost**. Although the net incomes are different in each period, there is no cash flow effect from these differences in net income. (If we considered income taxes, a cash flow effect would result.)

ILLUSTRATION 22-8
Lancer Financial
Statements (FIFO)

LANCER COMPANY
INCOME STATEMENT
FOR THE YEAR ENDED DECEMBER 31

	2013	2014	2015
Sales	$300,000	$300,000	$300,000
Cost of goods sold (FIFO)	78,000	97,000	111,000
Operating expenses	100,000	100,000	100,000
Net income	$122,000	$103,000	$ 89,000

LANCER COMPANY
RETAINED EARNINGS STATEMENT
FOR THE YEAR ENDED DECEMBER 31

	2013	2014	2015
Retained earnings (beginning)	$ 0	$122,000	$225,000
Add: Net income	122,000	103,000	89,000
Retained earnings (ending)	$122,000	$225,000	$314,000

LANCER COMPANY
STATEMENT OF FINANCIAL POSITION
AT DECEMBER 31

	2013	2014	2015
Inventory (FIFO)	$ 12,000	$ 25,000	$ 39,000
Cash	210,000	300,000	375,000
Total assets	$222,000	$325,000	$414,000
Share capital	$100,000	$100,000	$100,000
Retained earnings	122,000	225,000	314,000
Total equity	$222,000	$325,000	$414,000

LANCER COMPANY
STATEMENT OF CASH FLOWS
FOR THE YEAR ENDED DECEMBER 31

	2013	2014	2015
Cash flows from operating activities			
Sales	$300,000	$300,000	$300,000
Purchases	90,000	110,000	125,000
Operating expenses	100,000	100,000	100,000
Net cash provided by operating activities	110,000	90,000	75,000
Cash flows from financing activities			
Issuance of ordinary shares	100,000	—	—
Net increase in cash	210,000	90,000	75,000
Cash at beginning of year	0	210,000	300,000
Cash at end of year	$210,000	$300,000	$375,000

Compare the financial statements reported in Illustration 22-7 and Illustration 22-8. You can see that, under retrospective application, the change to FIFO inventory valuation affects reported inventories, cost of goods sold, net income, and retained earnings. In the following sections, we discuss the accounting and reporting of Lancer's accounting change from average-cost to FIFO.

Given the information provided in Illustrations 22-6, 22-7, and 22-8, we now are ready to account for and report on the accounting change.

Our first step is to adjust the financial records for the change from average-cost to FIFO. To do so, we perform the analysis in Illustration 22-9.

Year	Net Income Average-Cost	FIFO	Difference in Income
2013	$120,000	$122,000	$2,000
2014	100,000	103,000	3,000
Total at beginning of 2015	$220,000	$225,000	$5,000
Total in 2015	$ 87,000	$ 89,000	$2,000

ILLUSTRATION 22-9
Data for Recording Change in Accounting Policy

The entry to record the change to the FIFO method at the beginning of 2015 is as follows.

Inventory	5,000	
Retained Earnings		5,000

The change increases the inventory account by $5,000. This amount represents the difference between the ending inventory at December 31, 2014, under average-cost ($20,000) and the ending inventory under FIFO ($25,000). The credit to Retained Earnings indicates the amount needed to change prior-year's income, assuming that Lancer had used FIFO in previous periods.

Reporting a Change in Policy. Lancer Company will prepare comparative financial statements for 2014 and 2015 using FIFO (the new inventory method). Illustration 22-10 indicates how Lancer might present this information.

LANCER COMPANY
INCOME STATEMENT
FOR THE YEAR ENDED DECEMBER 31

	2015	2014 As adjusted (Note A)
Sales	$300,000	$300,000
Cost of goods sold	111,000	97,000
Operating expenses	100,000	100,000
Net income	$ 89,000	$103,000

ILLUSTRATION 22-10
Comparative Information Related to Accounting Change (FIFO)

Note A: *Change in Method of Accounting for Inventory Valuation.* On January 1, 2015, Lancer Company elected to change its method of valuing its inventory to the FIFO method; in all prior years inventory was valued using the average-cost method. The Company adopted the new method of accounting for inventory to better report cost of goods sold in the year incurred. Comparative financial statements of prior years have been adjusted to apply the new method retrospectively. The following financial statement line items for years 2015 and 2014 were affected by the change in accounting policy.

Nature and reason for change and description of prior period information adjusted

Statement of Financial Position	2015 Average-Cost	FIFO	Difference	2014 Average-Cost	FIFO	Difference
Inventory	$ 32,000	$ 39,000	$7,000	$ 20,000	$ 25,000	$5,000
Retained earnings	307,000	314,000	7,000	220,000	225,000	5,000
Income Statement						
Cost of goods sold	$113,000	$111,000	$2,000	$100,000	$ 97,000	$3,000
Net income	87,000	89,000	2,000	100,000	103,000	3,000

Effect of change on each financial statement affected

Statement of Cash Flows
(no effect)

As a result of the accounting change, retained earnings as of January 1, 2014, increased from $120,000, as originally reported using the average-cost method, to $122,000 using the FIFO method.

Cumulative effect on retained earnings

As Illustration 22-10 shows, Lancer Company reports net income under the newly adopted FIFO method for both 2014 and 2015. The company retrospectively adjusted the 2014 income statement to report the information on a FIFO basis. In addition, the note to the financial statements indicates the nature of the change, why the company made the change, and the years affected. The note also provides data on important differences between the amounts reported under average-cost versus FIFO. (When identifying the significant differences, some companies show the *entire* financial statements and line-by-line differences between average-cost and FIFO.)

Retained Earnings Adjustment. As indicated earlier, one of the disclosure requirements is to show the cumulative effect of the change on retained earnings as of the beginning of the earliest period presented. For Lancer Company, that date is January 1, 2014. Lancer disclosed that information by means of a narrative description (see Note A in Illustration 22-10). Lancer also would disclose this information in its retained earnings statement. Illustration 22-11 shows Lancer's retained earnings statement under average-cost—that is, before giving effect to the change in accounting policy. (This information comes from Illustration 22-7 on page 1133.)

ILLUSTRATION 22-11
Retained Earnings
Statements
(Average-Cost)

	2015	2014	2013
Retained earnings, January 1	$220,000	$120,000	$ 0
Net income	87,000	100,000	120,000
Retained earnings, December 31	$307,000	$220,000	$120,000

If Lancer presents comparative statements for 2014 and 2015 under FIFO, then it must change the beginning balance of retained earnings at January 1, 2014. The difference between the retained earnings balances under average-cost and FIFO is computed as follows.

Retained earnings, January 1, 2014 (FIFO)	$122,000
Retained earnings, January 1, 2014 (average-cost)	120,000
Cumulative effect difference	$ 2,000

The $2,000 difference is the cumulative effect. Illustration 22-12 shows a comparative retained earnings statement for 2014 and 2015, giving effect to the change in accounting policy to FIFO.

ILLUSTRATION 22-12
Retained Earnings
Statements after
Retrospective Application

	2015	2014
Retained earnings, January 1, as reported		$120,000
Add: Adjustment for the cumulative effect on prior years of applying retrospectively the new method of accounting for inventory		2,000
Retained earnings, January 1, as adjusted	$225,000	122,000
Net income	89,000	103,000
Retained earnings, December 31	$314,000	$225,000

Lancer adjusted the beginning balance of retained earnings on January 1, 2014, for the excess of FIFO net income over average-cost net income in 2013. This comparative presentation indicates the type of adjustment that a company needs to make. It follows that the amount of this adjustment would be much larger if a number of prior periods were involved.

Direct and Indirect Effects of Changes

Are there other effects that a company should report when it makes a change in accounting policy? For example, what happens when a company like Lancer has a bonus plan based on net income and the prior year's net income changes when FIFO is retrospectively applied? Should Lancer also change the reported amount of bonus expense? Or, what happens if we had not ignored income taxes in the Lancer example? Should Lancer adjust net income, given that taxes will be different under average-cost and FIFO in prior periods? The answers depend on whether the effects are direct or indirect.

Direct Effects

The IASB takes the position that companies should retrospectively apply the **direct effects of a change in accounting policy**. An example of a **direct effect** is an adjustment to an inventory balance as a result of a change in the inventory valuation method. For example, Lancer Company should change the inventory amounts in prior periods to indicate the change to the FIFO method of inventory valuation. Another inventory-related example would be an impairment adjustment resulting from applying the lower-of-cost-or-net realizable value test to the adjusted inventory balance. Related changes, such as deferred income tax effects of the impairment adjustment, are also considered direct effects. This entry was illustrated in the Denson example, in which the change to percentage-of-completion accounting resulted in recording a deferred tax liability.

Indirect Effects

In addition to direct effects, companies can have **indirect effects related to a change in accounting policy**. An **indirect effect** is any change to current or future cash flows of a company that result from making a change in accounting policy that is applied retrospectively. An example of an indirect effect is a change in profit-sharing or royalty payment that is based on a reported amount such as revenue or net income. The IASB is silent on what to do in this situation. U.S. GAAP (likely because its standard in this area was issued after *IAS 8*) requires that indirect effects do not change prior period amounts.

For example, let's assume that Lancer has an employee profit-sharing plan based on net income. As Illustration 22-9 (on page 1135) showed, Lancer would report higher income in 2014 and 2015 if it used the FIFO method. In addition, let's assume that the profit-sharing plan requires that Lancer pay the incremental amount due based on the FIFO income amounts. In this situation, Lancer reports this additional expense **in the current period**; it would not change prior periods for this expense. If the company prepares comparative financial statements, it follows that it does not recast the prior periods for this additional expense.[3]

If the terms of the profit-sharing plan indicate that *no payment is necessary* in the current period due to this change, then the company need not recognize additional profit-sharing expense in the current period. Neither does it change amounts reported for prior periods.

When a company recognizes the indirect effects of a change in accounting policy, it includes in the financial statements a description of the indirect effects. In doing so, it discloses the amounts recognized in the current period and related per share information.

---

[3]The rationale for this approach is that companies should recognize, in the period the adoption occurs (not the prior period), the effect on the cash flows that is caused by the adoption of the new accounting policy. That is, the accounting change is a necessary "past event" in the definition of an asset or liability that gives rise to the accounting recognition of the indirect effect in the current period.

Impracticability

It is not always possible for companies to determine how they would have reported prior periods' financial information under retrospective application of an accounting policy change. Retrospective application is considered **impracticable** if a company cannot determine the prior period effects using every reasonable effort to do so.

Companies should not use retrospective application if one of the following conditions exists:

1. The company cannot determine the effects of the retrospective application.
2. Retrospective application requires assumptions about management's intent in a prior period.
3. Retrospective application requires significant estimates for a prior period, and the company cannot objectively verify the necessary information to develop these estimates.

If any of the above conditions exists, it is deemed impracticable to apply the retrospective approach. In this case, the company **prospectively applies** the new accounting policy as of the earliest date it is practicable to do so. **[6]**

For example, assume that Williams Company changed its accounting policy for depreciable assets so as to more fully apply component depreciation under revaluation accounting. Unfortunately, the company does not have detailed accounting records to establish a basis for the components of these assets. As a result, Williams determines it is not practicable to account for the change to full component depreciation using the retrospective application approach. It therefore applies the policy prospectively, starting at the beginning of the current year.

Williams must disclose only the effect of the change on the results of operations in the period of change. Also, the company should explain the reasons for omitting the computations of the cumulative effect for prior years. Finally, it should disclose the justification for the change to component depreciation. **[7]**

CHANGES IN ACCOUNTING ESTIMATES

To prepare financial statements, companies must estimate the effects of future conditions and events. For example, the following items require estimates.

1. Bad debts.
2. Inventory obsolescence.
3. Useful lives and residual values of assets.
4. Periods benefited by deferred costs.
5. Liabilities for warranty costs and income taxes.
6. Recoverable mineral reserves.
7. Change in depreciation estimates.
8. Fair value of financial assets or financial liabilities.

A company cannot perceive future conditions and events and their effects with certainty. Therefore, estimating requires the exercise of judgment. Accounting estimates will change as new events occur, as a company acquires more experience, or as it obtains additional information.

Prospective Reporting

Companies report prospectively changes in accounting estimates. That is, companies should not adjust previously reported results for changes in estimates. Instead, they account for the effects of all changes in estimates in (1) the period of change if the change affects that period only (e.g., a change in the estimate of the amount of bad debts affects only the current period's income), or (2) the period of change and future periods if the change affects both (e.g., a change in the estimated useful life of a depreciable asset affects depreciation expense in the current and future periods). **[8]** The IASB views changes in estimates as **normal recurring corrections and adjustments**, the natural result of the accounting process. It prohibits retrospective treatment.

The circumstances related to a change in estimate differ from those for a change in accounting policy. If companies reported changes in estimates retrospectively, continual adjustments of prior years' income would occur. It seems proper to accept the view that, because new conditions or circumstances exist, the revision fits the new situation (not the old one). Companies should therefore handle such a revision in the current and future periods.

To illustrate, Lao Labs Inc. purchased for ¥3,000,000 a building that it originally estimated to have a useful life of 15 years and no residual value. It recorded depreciation for 5 years on a straight-line basis. On January 1, 2015, Lao Labs revises the estimate of the useful life. It now considers the asset to have a total life of 25 years. (Assume that the useful life for financial reporting and tax purposes and depreciation method are the same.) Illustration 22-13 shows the accounts at the beginning of the sixth year.

Buildings	¥3,000,000
Less: Accumulated depreciation—buildings (5 × ¥200,000)	1,000,000
Book value of building	¥2,000,000

ILLUSTRATION 22-13
Book Value after Five Years' Depreciation

Lao Labs records depreciation for the year 2015 as follows.

Depreciation Expense	100,000	
Accumulated Depreciation—Building		100,000

The company computes the ¥100,000 depreciation charge as shown in Illustration 22-14.

$$\text{Depreciation Charge} = \frac{\text{Book Value of Asset}}{\text{Remaining Service Life}} = \frac{¥2,000,000}{25 \text{ years} - 5 \text{ years}} = ¥100,000$$

ILLUSTRATION 22-14
Depreciation after Change in Estimate

Companies sometime find it difficult to differentiate between a change in estimate and a change in accounting policy. Is it a change in policy or a change in estimate when a company changes from deferring and amortizing marketing costs to expensing them as incurred because future benefits of these costs have become doubtful? **If it is impossible to determine whether a change in policy or a change in estimate has occurred, the rule is this: Consider the change as a change in estimate.**

Another example is a change in depreciation (as well as amortization or depletion) methods. Because companies change depreciation methods based on changes in estimates about future benefits from long-lived assets, it is not possible to separate the effect of the accounting policy change from that of the estimates. **As a result, companies account for a change in depreciation methods as a change in estimate.**

A similar problem occurs in differentiating between a change in estimate and a correction of an error, although here the answer is more clear-cut. How does a company determine whether it overlooked the information in earlier periods (an error) or whether it obtained new information (a change in estimate)? Proper classification is important because the accounting treatment differs for corrections of errors versus changes in estimates. The general rule is this: **Companies should consider careful estimates that later prove to be incorrect as changes in estimate.** Only when a company obviously computed the estimate incorrectly because of lack of expertise or in bad faith should it consider the adjustment an error. There is no clear demarcation line here. Companies must use good judgment in light of all the circumstances.

Disclosures

A company should disclose the nature and amount of a change in an accounting estimate that has an effect in the current period or is expected to have an effect in future periods (unless it is impracticable to estimate that effect). **[9]** Illustration 22-15 shows disclosure of a change in estimated useful lives, which appeared in a recent annual report of **Portugal Telecom, SGPS, S.A. (PRT).**

ILLUSTRATION 22-15
Disclosure of Change in Estimated Useful Lives

Portugal Telecom, SGPS, S.A.

Note 4 (in Part): Changes in Accounting Policies and Estimates

The change in estimate of the useful life of the UMTS license was effective as at 30 June. According to IAS 8 this change should be applicable on a prospective basis and, on an annual basis, the impact of this change will be a reduction in depreciation and amortisation costs by €26 million.

For the most part, companies need not disclose changes in accounting estimate made as part of normal operations, such as bad debt allowances or inventory obsolescence, unless such changes are material.

ACCOUNTING ERRORS

LEARNING OBJECTIVE

Describe the accounting for correction of errors.

No business, large or small, is immune from errors. As the opening story discussed, the number of accounting errors that lead to restatement has stabilized. However, without accounting and disclosure guidelines for the reporting of errors, investors can be left in the dark about the effects of errors.

Certain errors, such as misclassifications of balances within a financial statement, are not as significant to investors as other errors. Significant errors would be those resulting in overstating assets or income, for example. However, investors should know the potential impact of all errors. Even "harmless" misclassifications can affect important ratios. Also, some errors could signal important weaknesses in internal controls that could lead to more significant errors.

In general, accounting errors include the following types:

1. A change from an accounting policy that is **not** generally accepted to an accounting policy that is acceptable. The rationale is that the company incorrectly presented prior periods because of the application of an improper accounting policy. For example, a company may change from the cash (income tax) basis of accounting to the accrual basis.

2. Mathematical mistakes, such as incorrectly totaling the inventory count sheets when computing the inventory value.

3. Changes in estimates that occur because a company did not prepare the estimates in good faith. For example, a company may have adopted a clearly unrealistic depreciation rate.

4. An oversight, such as the failure to accrue or defer certain expenses and revenues at the end of the period.

5. A misuse of facts, such as the failure to use residual value in computing the depreciation base for the straight-line approach.

6. The incorrect classification of a cost as an expense instead of an asset, and vice versa.

Accounting errors occur for a variety of reasons. Illustration 22-16 indicates 11 major categories of accounting errors that drive restatements.

Accounting Category	Type of Restatement
Expense recognition	Recording expenses in the incorrect period or for an incorrect amount.
Revenue recognition	Improper revenue accounting, including instances in which revenue was improperly recognized, questionable revenues were recognized, or any other number of related errors that led to misreported revenue.
Misclassification	Misclassifying significant accounting items on the statement of financial position, income statement, or statement of cash flows. These include restatements due to misclassification of current or non-current accounts or those that impact cash flows from operations.
Equity—other	Improper accounting for EPS, restricted shares, warrants, and other equity instruments.
Reserves/Contingencies	Errors involving accounts receivables' bad debts, inventory reserves, income tax allowances, and loss contingencies.
Long-lived assets	Asset impairments of property, plant, and equipment; goodwill; or other related items.
Taxes	Errors involving correction of tax provision, improper treatment of tax liabilities, and other tax-related items.
Equity—other comprehensive income	Improper accounting for comprehensive income equity transactions including foreign currency items, revaluations of plant assets, unrealized gains and losses on certain investments in debt, equity securities, and derivatives.
Inventory	Inventory costing valuations, quantity issues, and cost of sales adjustments.
Equity—share options	Improper accounting for employee share options.
Other	Any restatement not covered by the listed categories, including those related to improper accounting for acquisitions or mergers.

Sources: T. Baldwin and D. Yoo, "Restatements—Traversing Shaky Ground," *Trend Alert*, Glass Lewis & Co. (June 2, 2005), p. 8; and "2012 Financial Restatements," *Audit Analytics* (March 2013).

ILLUSTRATION 22-16
Accounting-Error Types

As soon as a company discovers an error, it must correct the error. Companies record **corrections of errors** from prior periods as an adjustment to the beginning balance of retained earnings in the current period. Such corrections are called **prior period adjustments**.

If it presents comparative statements, a company should restate the prior statements affected, to correct for the error.[4] The company need not repeat the disclosures in the financial statements of subsequent periods.

Example of Error Correction

To illustrate, in 2016 the bookkeeper for Selectro Company discovered an error: In 2015, the company failed to record £20,000 of depreciation expense on a newly constructed building. This building is the only depreciable asset Selectro owns. The company correctly included the depreciation expense in its tax return and correctly reported its income taxes payable. Illustration 22-17 (on page 1142) presents Selectro's income statement for 2015 (starting with income before depreciation expense) with and without the error.

---

[4]The term **retrospective restatement** is used for the process of revising previously issued financial statements to reflect a correction of an error. This term distinguishes an error correction from a change in accounting policy, referred to as retrospective application.

ILLUSTRATION 22-17
Error Correction
Comparison

SELECTRO COMPANY				
INCOME STATEMENT				
FOR THE YEAR ENDED, DECEMBER 31, 2015				
		Without Error		With Error
Income before depreciation expense		£100,000		£100,000
Depreciation expense		20,000		0
Income before income tax		80,000		100,000
Current	£32,000		£32,000	
Deferred	–0–	32,000	8,000	40,000
Net income		£ 48,000		£ 60,000

Illustration 22-18 shows the entries that Selectro should have made and did make for recording depreciation expense and income taxes.

ILLUSTRATION 22-18
Error Entries

Entries Company Should Have Made (Without Error)			Entries Company Did Make (With Error)		
Depreciation Expense	20,000		No entry made for depreciation		
Accumulated					
Depreciation—Buildings		20,000			
Income Tax Expense	32,000		Income Tax Expense	40,000	
Income Taxes Payable		32,000	Deferred Tax Liability		8,000
			Income Taxes Payable		32,000

As Illustration 22-18 indicates, the £20,000 omission error in 2015 results in the following effects.

Income Statement Effects

Depreciation expense (2015) is understated £20,000.
Income tax expense (2015) is overstated £8,000 (£20,000 × 40%).
Net income (2015) is overstated £12,000 (£20,000 − £8,000).

Statement of Financial Position Effects

Accumulated depreciation—buildings is understated £20,000.
Deferred tax liability is overstated £8,000 (£20,000 × 40%).

To make the proper correcting entry in 2016, Selectro should recognize that net income in 2015 is overstated by £12,000, the Deferred Tax Liability is overstated by £8,000, and Accumulated Depreciation—Buildings is understated by £20,000. The entry to correct this error in 2016 is as follows.

Retained Earnings	12,000	
Deferred Tax Liability	8,000	
Accumulated Depreciation—Buildings		20,000

The debit to Retained Earnings results because net income for 2015 is overstated. The debit to the Deferred Tax Liability is made to remove this account, which was caused by the error. The credit to Accumulated Depreciation—Buildings reduces the book value of the building to its proper amount. Selectro will make the same journal entry to record the correction of the error in 2016 whether it prepares single-period (noncomparative) or comparative financial statements.

Single-Period Statements

To demonstrate how to show this information in a single-period statement, assume that Selectro Company has a beginning retained earnings balance at January 1, 2016, of £350,000. The company reports net income of £400,000 in 2016. Illustration 22-19 shows Selectro's retained earnings statement for 2016.

SELECTRO COMPANY RETAINED EARNINGS STATEMENT FOR THE YEAR ENDED DECEMBER 31, 2016		
Retained earnings, January 1, as reported		£350,000
Correction of an error (depreciation)	£20,000	
Less: Applicable income tax reduction	8,000	(12,000)
Retained earnings, January 1, as adjusted		338,000
Add: Net income		400,000
Retained earnings, December 31		£738,000

ILLUSTRATION 22-19
Reporting an Error—Single-Period Financial Statement

The statement of financial position in 2016 would not have any deferred tax liability related to the building, and Accumulated Depreciation—Buildings is now restated at a higher amount. The income statement would not be affected.

Comparative Statements

If preparing comparative financial statements, a company should make adjustments to correct the amounts for all affected accounts reported in the statements for **all periods** reported. The company should restate the data to the correct basis for each year presented. It should **show any catch-up adjustment as a prior period adjustment to retained earnings for the earliest period it reported**. These requirements are essentially the same as those for reporting a change in accounting policy.

For example, in the case of Selectro, the error of omitting the depreciation of £20,000 in 2015, discovered in 2016, results in the restatement of the 2015 financial statements. Illustration 22-20 shows the accounts that Selectro restates in the 2015 financial statements.

In the statement of financial position:	
Accumulated depreciation—buildings	£20,000 increase
Deferred tax liability	£ 8,000 decrease
Retained earnings, ending balance	£12,000 decrease
In the income statement:	
Depreciation expense—buildings	£20,000 increase
Income tax expense	£ 8,000 decrease
Net income	£12,000 decrease
In the retained earnings statement:	
Retained earnings, ending balance (due to lower net income for the period)	£12,000 decrease

ILLUSTRATION 22-20
Reporting an Error—Comparative Financial Statements

Selectro prepares the 2016 financial statements in comparative form with those of 2015 **as if the error had not occurred**. In addition, Selectro must disclose that it has restated its previously issued financial statements, and it describes the nature of the error. Selectro also must disclose the following:

1. The effect of the correction on each financial statement line item and any per share amounts affected for each prior period presented.

2. The cumulative effect of the change on retained earnings or other appropriate components of equity or net assets in the statement of financial position, as of the beginning of the earliest period presented.

As indicated earlier, it is sometimes impracticable to adjust comparative information for one or more prior periods for changes in accounting policies. It is also sometimes impracticable to correct a prior period error through retrospective restatement. For example, the company may have made errors in computing fringe-benefit amounts in prior years but is unable to now reconstruct this information fully. As a result, any adjustment is made at the beginning of the earliest period for which retrospective application is applicable.

What do the numbers mean?   *GUARD THE FINANCIAL STATEMENTS!*

Restatements sometimes occur because of financial fraud. Financial frauds involve the intentional misstatement or omission of material information in the organization's financial reports. Common methods of financial fraud manipulation include recording fictitious revenues, concealing liabilities or expenses, and artificially inflating reported assets. Financial frauds made up around 8 percent of the frauds in a recent study on occupational fraud but caused a median loss of more than $1 million in 2012 ($4 million in 2010)—by far the most costly category of fraud. The following chart compares loss amounts for 2012 versus 2010 for financial statement fraud, corruption, and asset misappropriation.

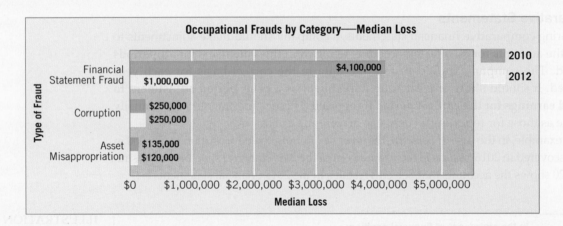

While the trend in the dollar amount of losses is going in the right direction, another study indicates that the number of fraud reports at 1,400 companies in the "Quarterly Corporate Fraud Index" is on the climb—with 2,348 reported frauds in the second quarter of 2005 to over 7,800 in the second quarter of 2012. While there is some debate about whether the reporting of fraud has increased with regulation that provides whistleblower protections (i.e., the incidence of fraud is not increasing as much as the reporting of fraud), companies must increase their efforts to protect their statements from the negative effects of fraud.

Sources: Report to the Nations on Occupational Fraud and Abuse, 2012 Global Fraud Study, Association of Certified Fraud Examiners (2012), p. 11; and C. McDonald, "Fraud Reports Climb Still Higher," *CFO.com* (September 26, 2012).

Summary of Accounting Changes and Correction of Errors

Having guidelines for reporting accounting changes and corrections has helped resolve several significant and long-standing accounting problems. Yet, because of diversity in situations and characteristics of the items encountered in practice, use of professional judgment is of paramount importance. In applying these guidelines, the primary objective is to serve the users of the financial statements. Achieving this objective requires accuracy, full disclosure, and an absence of misleading inferences.

Illustration 22-21 summarizes the main distinctions and treatments presented in the discussion in this chapter.

ILLUSTRATION 22-21
Summary of Guidelines for Accounting Changes and Errors

Changes in accounting policy

Employ the retrospective approach by:

a. Changing the financial statements of all prior periods presented.

b. Disclosing in the year of the change the effect on net income and earnings per share for all prior periods presented.

c. Reporting an adjustment to the beginning retained earnings balance in the statement of retained earnings in the earliest year presented.

If impracticable to determine the prior period effect:

a. Do not change prior years' income.

b. Use opening asset balance in the year the method is adopted as the base-year balance for all subsequent computations.

c. Disclose the effect of the change on the current year, and the reasons for omitting the computation of the cumulative effect and amounts for prior years.

Changes in accounting estimate

Employ the current and prospective approach by:

a. Reporting current and future financial statements on the new basis.

b. Presenting prior period financial statements as previously reported.

c. Making no adjustments to current-period opening balances for the effects in prior periods.

Changes due to error

Employ the restatement approach by:

a. Correcting all prior period statements presented.

b. Restating the beginning balance of retained earnings for the first period presented when the error effects occur in a period prior to the first period presented.

Changes in accounting policy are appropriate **only** when a company demonstrates that the newly adopted generally accepted accounting policy is more reliable and relevant than the existing one. Companies and accountants determine reliability and relevance on the basis of whether the new policy constitutes an **improvement in financial reporting**, not on the basis of the income tax effect alone.

But, it is not always easy to determine an improvement in financial reporting. **How does one measure preferability or improvement**? For example, a change from average-cost to FIFO because the accounting system is now computerized and has scanning capabilities seems justifiable. However, a change from immediate recognition of actuarial gains and losses (which is the method preferred by the IASB) to the corridor approach does not appear to be an improvement. Determining an improved method requires some "standard" or "objective." Because no universal standard or objective is generally accepted, the problem of determining improvement continues to be difficult and requires good judgment.

Motivations for Change of Accounting Policy

Difficult as it is to determine which accounting standards have the strongest conceptual support, other complications make the process even more complex. These complications stem from the fact that managers have self-interest in how the financial statements make the company look. They naturally wish to show their financial performance in the best light. A **favorable profit picture** can influence investors, and a strong liquidity position can influence creditors. **Too favorable a profit picture**, however, can provide union negotiators and government regulators with ammunition during bargaining talks. Hence, managers might have varying motives for reporting income numbers.

7 LEARNING OBJECTIVE

Identify economic motives for changing accounting policies.

Research has provided additional insight into why companies may prefer certain accounting policies.[5] Some of these reasons are as follows.

1. *Political costs.* As companies become larger and more politically visible, politicians and regulators devote more attention to them. The larger the firm, the more likely it is to become subject to regulation, such as antitrust, and the more likely it is to be required to pay higher taxes. Therefore, companies that are politically visible may seek to report low income numbers, to avoid the scrutiny of regulators. In addition, other constituents, such as labor unions, may be less willing to ask for wage increases if reported income is low. Researchers have found that the larger the company, the more likely it is to adopt income-decreasing approaches in selecting accounting policies.

2. *Capital structure.* A number of studies have indicated that the capital structure of the company can affect the selection of accounting policies. For example, a company with a high debt to equity ratio is more likely to be constrained by debt covenants. The debt covenant may indicate that the company cannot pay dividends if retained earnings fall below a certain level. As a result, such a company is more likely to select accounting policies that will increase net income.

3. *Bonus payments.* Studies have found that if compensation plans tie managers' bonus payments to income, management will select accounting policies that maximize their bonus payments.

4. *Smooth earnings.* Substantial earnings increases attract the attention of politicians, regulators, and competitors. In addition, large increases in income are difficult to achieve in following years. Further, executive compensation plans would use these higher numbers as a baseline and make it difficult for managers to earn bonuses in subsequent years. Conversely, investors and competitors might view large decreases in earnings as a signal that the company is in financial trouble. Also, substantial decreases in income raise concerns on the part of shareholders, lenders, and other interested parties about the competency of management. For all these reasons, companies have an incentive to "manage" or "smooth" earnings. In general, management tends to believe that a steady 10 percent growth a year is much better than a 30 percent growth one year and a 10 percent decline the next.[6] In other words, managers usually prefer a gradually increasing income report and sometimes change accounting policies to ensure such a result.

 Underlying Concepts

When accounting changes are motivated by reasons other than providing more useful information to investors and creditors, this can detract from both relevance and faithful representation.

Management pays careful attention to the accounting it follows and often changes accounting policies, not for conceptual reasons, but for economic reasons. As indicated throughout this textbook, such arguments have come to be known as **economic consequences** arguments. These arguments focus on the supposed impact of the accounting policy on the behavior of investors, creditors, competitors, governments, or managers of the reporting companies themselves.[7]

---

[5]See Ross L. Watts and Jerold L. Zimmerman, "Positive Accounting Theory: A Ten-Year Perspective," *The Accounting Review* (January 1990) for an excellent review of research findings related to management incentives in selecting accounting policies.

[6]O. Douglas Moses, "Income Smoothing and Incentives: Empirical Tests Using Accounting Changes," *The Accounting Review* (April 1987). The findings provide evidence that earnings smoothing is associated with firm size, the existence of bonus plans, and the divergence of actual earnings from expectations.

[7]Lobbyists use economic consequences arguments—and there are many of them—to put pressure on standard-setters. We have seen examples of these arguments in the oil and gas industry about successful-efforts versus full-cost, and in the technology area with the issue of mandatory expensing of research costs and share options.

To counter these pressures, the IASB has declared, as part of its Conceptual Framework, that it will assess the merits of proposed standards from a position of **neutrality**. That is, the IASB evaluates the soundness of standards on the basis of conceptual soundness, not on the grounds of possible impact on behavior. It is not the IASB's place to choose standards according to the kinds of behavior it wishes to promote and the kinds it wishes to discourage. At the same time, it must be admitted that some standards often **will have** the effect of influencing behavior. Yet, their justification should be conceptual and not viewed in terms of their economic impact.

ERROR ANALYSIS

In this section, we show some additional types of accounting errors. Companies generally do not correct for errors that do not have a significant effect on the presentation of the financial statements. For example, should a company with a total annual payroll of $1,750,000 and net income of $940,000 correct its financial statements if it finds it failed to record accrued wages of $500? No—it would not consider this error significant.

> **8 LEARNING OBJECTIVE**
> Analyze the effect of errors.

Obviously, defining materiality is difficult, and managers and auditors must use experience and judgment to determine whether adjustment is necessary for a given error. We assume **all errors discussed in this section to be material and to require adjustment**. (Also, we ignore all tax effects in this section.)

Companies must answer three questions in error analysis:

1. What type of error is involved?

2. What entries are needed to correct for the error?

3. After discovery of the error, how are financial statements to be restated?

As indicated earlier, companies treat errors **as prior period adjustments and report them in the current year as adjustments to the beginning balance of Retained Earnings**. If a company presents comparative statements, it restates the prior affected statements to correct for the error.

Statement of Financial Position Errors

Statement of financial position errors affect only the presentation of an asset, liability, or equity account. Examples are the classification of a short-term receivable as part of the investment section, the classification of a note payable as an account payable, and the classification of plant assets as inventory.

When the error is discovered, the company reclassifies the item to its proper position. If the company prepares comparative statements that include the error year, it should correctly restate the statement of financial position for the error year.

Income Statement Errors

Income statement errors involve the improper classification of revenues or expenses. Examples include recording interest revenue as part of sales, purchases as bad debt expense, and depreciation expense as interest expense. An income statement classification error has no effect on the statement of financial position and **no effect on net income**.

A company must make a reclassification entry when it discovers the error if it makes the discovery in the same year in which the error occurs. If the error occurred in prior periods, the company does not need to make a reclassification entry at the date of discovery because the accounts for the current year are correctly stated. (Remember that the company has closed the income statement accounts from the prior period to retained earnings.) If the company prepares comparative statements that include the error year, it restates the income statement for the error year.

Statement of Financial Position and Income Statement Errors

The third type of error involves both the statement of financial position and income statement. For example, assume that the bookkeeper overlooked accrued wages payable at the end of the accounting period. The effect of this error is to understate expenses, understate liabilities, and overstate net income for that period of time. This type of error affects both the statement of financial position and the income statement. We classify this type of error in one of two ways—counterbalancing or non-counterbalancing.

Counterbalancing errors are those that will be offset or corrected over two periods. For example, the failure to record accrued wages is a counterbalancing error because over a two-year period the error will no longer be present. In other words, the failure to record accrued wages in the previous period means (1) net income for the first period is overstated, (2) accrued wages payable (a liability) is understated, and (3) wages expense is understated. In the next period, net income is understated, accrued wages payable (a liability) is correctly stated, and wages expense is overstated. For the two **years combined** (1) net income is correct, (2) wages expense is correct, and (3) accrued wages payable at the end of the second year is correct. Most errors in accounting that affect both the statement of financial position and income statement are counterbalancing errors.

Non-counterbalancing errors are those that are not offset in the next accounting period. An example would be the failure to capitalize equipment that has a useful life of five years. If we expense this asset immediately, expenses will be overstated in the first period but understated in the next four periods. At the end of the second period, the effect of the error is not fully offset. Net income is correct in the aggregate only at the end of five years because the asset is fully depreciated at this point. Thus, **non-counterbalancing errors are those that take longer than two periods to correct themselves**.

Only in rare instances is an error never reversed. An example would be if a company initially expenses land. Because land is not depreciable, theoretically the error is never offset, unless the land is sold.

Counterbalancing Errors

We illustrate the usual types of counterbalancing errors on the following pages. In studying these illustrations, keep in mind a couple of points, discussed below.

First, determine whether the company has closed the books for the period in which the error is found:

1. **If the company has closed the books in the current year:**
   (a) If the error is already counterbalanced, no entry is necessary.
   (b) If the error is not yet counterbalanced, make an entry to adjust the present balance of retained earnings.

2. If the company has not closed the books in the current year:

    (a) If the error is already counterbalanced, make an entry to correct the error in the current period and to adjust the beginning balance of Retained Earnings.

    (b) If the error is not yet counterbalanced, make an entry to adjust the beginning balance of Retained Earnings.

    Second, if the company presents comparative statements, it must restate the amounts for comparative purposes. **Restatement is necessary even if a correcting journal entry is not required.**

    To illustrate, assume that Sanford's Cement Co. failed to accrue revenue in 2013 when it fulfilled its performance obligation but recorded the revenue in 2014 when it received payment. The company discovered the error in 2016. It does not need to make an entry to correct for this error because the effects have been counterbalanced by the time Sanford discovered the error in 2016. However, if Sanford presents comparative financial statements for 2013 through 2016, it must **restate the accounts and related amounts for the years 2013 and 2014 for financial reporting purposes**.

    The examples that follow demonstrate the accounting for the usual types of counterbalancing errors.

ILLUSTRATION 22-22
Errors—Accrued Wages

FAILURE TO RECORD ACCRUED WAGES

Facts: On December 31, 2015, Hurley Enterprises did not accrue wages in the amount of $1,500.

Question: What is the entry on December 31, 2016, to correct this error, assuming Hurley has not closed the books?

Solution: The entry to correct this error is as follows.

Retained Earnings	1,500	
Salaries and Wages Expense		1,500

The rationale for this entry is:

1. When Hurley pays the 2015 accrued wages in 2016, it makes an additional debit of $1,500 to 2016 Salaries and Wages Expense.
2. Salaries and Wages Expense in 2016 is overstated by $1,500.
3. Because the company did not record 2015 accrued wages as Salaries and Wages Expense in 2015, the net income for 2015 is overstated by $1,500.
4. Because 2015 net income is overstated by $1,500, the Retained Earnings account is overstated by $1,500 (because net income is closed to Retained Earnings).

    If Hurley has closed the books for 2016, it makes no entry because the error is counterbalanced.

ILLUSTRATION 22-23
Errors—Prepaid Expenses

FAILURE TO RECORD PREPAID EXPENSES

Facts: In January 2015, Hurley Enterprises purchased a 2-year insurance policy costing $1,000. It debited Insurance Expense and credited Cash. The company made no adjusting entries at the end of 2015.

Question: What is the entry on December 31, 2016, to correct this error, assuming Hurley has not closed the books for 2016?

Solution: The entry to correct this error on December 31, 2016, is as follows.

Insurance Expense	500	
Retained Earnings		500

> If Hurley has closed the books for 2016, it makes no entry because the error is counterbalanced.

ILLUSTRATION 22-24
Errors—Unearned
Revenues

UNDERSTATEMENT OF UNEARNED REVENUE

Facts: On December 31, 2015, Hurley Enterprises received $50,000 as a prepayment for renting certain office space for the following year. At the time of receipt of the rent payment, the company recorded a debit to Cash and a credit to Rent Revenue. It made no adjusting entry as of December 31, 2015.

Question: **What is the entry on December 31, 2016, to correct this error, assuming Hurley has not closed the books for 2016?**

Solution: The entry to correct this error on December 31, 2016, is as follows.

Retained Earnings	50,000	
Rent Revenue		50,000

> If Hurley has closed the books for 2016, it makes no entry because the error is counterbalanced.

ILLUSTRATION 22-25
Errors—Accrued
Revenue

OVERSTATEMENT OF ACCRUED REVENUE

Facts: On December 31, 2015, Hurley Enterprises accrued as interest revenue $8,000 that applied to 2016. On that date, the company recorded a debit to Interest Receivable and a credit to Interest Revenue.

Question: **What is the entry on December 31, 2016, to correct this error, assuming Hurley has not closed the books for 2016?**

Solution: The entry to correct this error on December 31, 2016, is as follows.

Retained Earnings	8,000	
Interest Revenue		8,000

> If Hurley has closed the books for 2016, it makes no entry because the error is counterbalanced.

ILLUSTRATION 22-26
Errors—Purchases

OVERSTATEMENT OF PURCHASES

Facts: Hurley's accountant recorded a purchase of merchandise for $9,000 in 2015 that applied to 2016. The physical inventory for 2015 was correctly stated. The company uses the periodic inventory method.

Question: **What is the entry on December 31, 2016, to correct this error, assuming Hurley has not closed the books for 2016?**

Solution: The entry to correct this error on December 31, 2016, is as follows.

Purchases	9,000	
Retained Earnings		9,000

> If Hurley has closed the books for 2016, it makes no entry because the error is counterbalanced.

Non-Counterbalancing Errors

The entries for non-counterbalancing errors are more complex. Companies must make correcting entries, even if they have closed the books.

FAILURE TO RECORD DEPRECIATION

ILLUSTRATION 22-27
Non-Counterbalancing
Errors—Depreciation

Facts: Assume that on January 1, 2015, Hurley Enterprises purchased a machine for $10,000 that had an estimated useful life of 5 years. The accountant incorrectly expensed this machine in 2015 but discovered the error in 2016.

Question: What is the entry on December 31, 2016, to correct this error, assuming Hurley has not closed the books for 2016?

Solution: If we assume that Hurley uses straight-line depreciation on this asset, the entry to correct this error on December 31, 2016, is as follows.

Equipment	10,000	
Depreciation Expense	2,000	
Retained Earnings		8,000*
Accumulated Depreciation—Equipment (20% × $10,000 × 2)		4,000

*Computations:
  Retained Earnings

Overstatement of expense in 2015	$10,000
Proper depreciation for 2015 (20% × $10,000)	(2,000)
Retained earnings understated as of Dec. 31, 2015	$ 8,000

If Hurley has closed the books for 2016, the entry is:

Equipment	10,000	
Retained Earnings		6,000*
Accumulated Depreciation—Equipment		4,000

*Computations:
  Retained Earnings

Retained earnings understated as of Dec. 31, 2015	$ 8,000
Proper depreciation for 2016 (20% × $10,000)	(2,000)
Retained earnings understated as of Dec. 31, 2016	$ 6,000

FAILURE TO ADJUST FOR BAD DEBTS

ILLUSTRATION 22-28
Non-Counterbalancing
Errors—Bad Debts

Facts: Companies sometimes use a specific charge-off method in accounting for bad debt expense when a percentage-of-sales method is more appropriate. They then make adjustments to change from the specific write-off to some type of allowance method. For example, assume that Hurley Enterprises has recognized bad debt expense when it has the following uncollectible debts.

	2015	2016
From 2015 sales	$550	$690
From 2016 sales		700

Hurley estimates that it will charge off an additional $1,400 in 2017, of which $300 is applicable to 2015 sales and $1,100 to 2016 sales.

Question: What is the entry on December 31, 2016, to correct this error, assuming Hurley has not closed the books for 2016?

Solution: The entry to correct this error on December 31, 2016, is as follows.

Bad Debt Expense	410	
Retained Earnings	990	
Allowance for Doubtful Accounts		1,400

Allowance for doubtful accounts: Additional $300 for 2015 sales and $1,100 for 2016 sales.
Bad debts and retained earnings balance:

	2015	2016
Bad debts charged for	$1,240*	$ 700
Additional bad debts anticipated in 2017	300	1,100
Proper bad debt expense	1,540	1,800
Charges currently made to each period	(550)	(1,390)
Bad debt adjustment	$ 990	$ 410

*$550 + $690 = $1,240

If Hurley has closed the books for 2016, the entry is:

Retained Earnings	1,400	
Allowance for Doubtful Accounts		1,400

Comprehensive Example: Numerous Errors

In some circumstances, a combination of errors occurs. The company therefore prepares a worksheet to facilitate the analysis. The following problem demonstrates use of the worksheet. The mechanics of its preparation should be obvious from the solution format. The income statements of Hudson Company for the years ended December 31, 2014, 2015, and 2016, indicate the following net incomes.

2014	€17,400
2015	20,200
2016	11,300

An examination of the accounting records for these years indicates that Hudson Company made several errors in arriving at the net income amounts reported:

1. The company consistently omitted from the records wages earned by workers but not paid at December 31. The amounts omitted were:

December 31, 2014	€1,000
December 31, 2015	€1,400
December 31, 2016	€1,600

   When paid in the year following that in which they were earned, Hudson recorded these amounts as expenses.

2. The company overstated merchandise inventory on December 31, 2014, by €1,900 as the result of errors made in the footings and extensions on the inventory sheets.

3. On December 31, 2015, Hudson expensed unexpired insurance of €1,200, applicable to 2016.

4. The company did not record on December 31, 2015, interest receivable in the amount of €240.

5. On January 2, 2015, Hudson sold for €1,800 a piece of equipment costing €3,900. At the date of sale, the equipment had accumulated depreciation of €2,400. The company recorded the cash received as Miscellaneous Income in 2015. In addition, the company continued to record depreciation for this equipment in both 2015 and 2016 at the rate of 10 percent of cost.

The first step in preparing the worksheet is to prepare a schedule showing the corrected net income amounts for the years ended December 31, 2014, 2015, and 2016. Each correction of the amount originally reported is clearly labeled. The next step is to indicate the statement of financial position accounts affected as of December 31, 2016. Illustration 22-29 shows the completed worksheet for Hudson Company.

Assuming that Hudson Company **has not closed the books**, correcting entries on December 31, 2016, are:

Retained Earnings	1,400	
Salaries and Wages Expense		1,400
(To correct improper charge to Salaries and Wages Expense for 2016)		

Salaries and Wages Expense	1,600	
Salaries and Wages Payable		1,600
(To record proper wages expense for 2016)		

Insurance Expense	1,200	
Retained Earnings		1,200
(To record proper insurance expense for 2016)		

Interest Revenue	240	
Retained Earnings		240
(To correct improper credit to Interest Revenue in 2016)		

Retained Earnings	1,500	
Accumulated Depreciation—Equipment	2,400	
Equipment		3,900
(To record write-off of equipment in 2015 and adjustment of Retained Earnings)		

Accumulated Depreciation—Equipment	780	
Depreciation Expense		390
Retained Earnings		390
(To correct improper charge for depreciation expense in 2015 and 2016)		

ILLUSTRATION 22-29
Worksheet to Correct Income and Statement of Financial Position Errors

HUDSON COMPANY.xls

Home   Insert   Page Layout   Formulas   Data   Review   View

P18   fx

HUDSON COMPANY
Worksheet to Correct Income and Statement of
Financial Position Errors

	A	B	C	D	E	F	G	H
4		Worksheet Analysis of Changes in Net Income				Statement of Financial Position Correction at December 31, 2016		
5		2014	2015	2016	Totals	Debit	Credit	Account
6	Net income as reported	€17,400	€20,200	€11,300	€48,900			
7	Wages unpaid, 12/31/14	(1,000)	1,000		–0–			
8	Wages unpaid, 12/31/15		(1,400)	1,400	–0–			
9	Wages unpaid, 12/31/16			(1,600)	(1,600)		€1,600	Salaries and Wages Payable
10	Inventory overstatement, 12/31/14	(1,900)	1,900		–0–			
11	Unexpired insurance, 12/31/15		1,200	(1,200)	–0–			
12	Interest receivable, 12/31/15		240	(240)	–0–			
13	Correction for entry made upon sale of equipment, 1/2/15ª		(1,500)		(1,500)	€2,400		Accumulated Depreciation—Equipment
							3,900	Equipment
14	Overcharge of depreciation, 2015		390		390	390		Accumulated Depreciation—Equipment
15	Overcharge of depreciation, 2016			390	390	390		Accumulated Depreciation—Equipment
16	Corrected net income	€14,500	€22,030	€10,050	€46,580			
17	ªCost	€ 3,900						
18	Accumulated depreciation	2,400						
19	Book value	1,500						
20	Proceeds from sale	1,800						
21	Gain on sale	300						
22	Income reported	(1,800)						
23	Adjustment	€(1,500)						

If Hudson Company **has closed the books** for 2016, the correcting entries are:

Retained Earnings	1,600	
Salaries and Wages Payable		1,600
(To record proper wages expense for 2016)		
Retained Earnings	1,500	
Accumulated Depreciation—Equipment	2,400	
Equipment		3,900
(To record write-off of equipment in 2015 and		
adjustment of Retained Earnings)		
Accumulated Depreciation—Equipment	780	
Retained Earnings		780
(To correct improper charge for depreciation expense		
in 2015 and 2016)		

Preparation of Financial Statements with Error Corrections

Up to now, our discussion of error analysis has focused on identifying the type of error involved and accounting for its correction in the records. We have noted that companies must present the correction of the error on comparative financial statements.

The following example illustrates how a company would restate a typical year's financial statements, given many different errors.

Dick & Wally's Outlet is a small retail outlet in the town of Holiday. Lacking expertise in accounting, the company does not keep adequate records, and numerous errors occurred in recording accounting information.

1. The bookkeeper inadvertently failed to record a cash receipt of $1,000 on the sale of merchandise in 2016.

2. Accrued wages expense at the end of 2015 was $2,500; at the end of 2016, $3,200. The company does not accrue for wages; all wages are charged to Administrative Expenses.

3. The company had not set up an allowance for estimated uncollectible receivables. Dick and Wally decided to set up such an allowance for the estimated probable losses, as of December 31, 2016, for 2015 accounts of $700, and for 2016 accounts of $1,500. They also decided to correct the charge against each year so that it shows the losses (actual and estimated) relating to that year's sales. The company has written off accounts to bad debt expense (selling expense) as follows.

	In 2015	In 2016
2015 accounts	$400	$2,000
2016 accounts		1,600

4. Unexpired insurance not recorded at the end of 2015 was $600, and at the end of 2016, $400. All insurance is charged to Administrative Expenses.

5. An account payable of $6,000 should have been a note payable.

6. During 2015, the company sold for $7,000 an asset that cost $10,000 and had a book value of $4,000. At the time of sale, Cash was debited and Miscellaneous Income was credited for $7,000.

7. As a result of the last transaction, the company overstated depreciation expense (an administrative expense) in 2015 by $800 and in 2016 by $1,200.

Illustration 22-30 presents a worksheet that begins with the unadjusted trial balance of Dick & Wally's Outlet. You can determine the correcting entries and their effect on the financial statements by examining the worksheet.

DICK & WALLY'S OUTLET.xls

Home | Insert | Page Layout | Formulas | Data | Review | View

P18

DICK & WALLY'S OUTLET
Worksheet Analysis to Adjust Financial Statements for the Year 2016

	Trial Balance Unadjusted		Adjustments				Income Statement Adjusted		Statement of Financial Position Adjusted	
	Dr.	Cr.		Dr.		Cr.	Dr.	Cr.	Dr.	Cr.
8 Cash	3,100		(1)	1,000					4,100	
9 Accounts Receivable	17,600								17,600	
10 Notes Receivable	8,500								8,500	
11 Inventory	34,000								34,000	
12 Property, Plant, and Equipment	112,000				(6)	10,000[a]			102,000	
13 Accumulated Depreciation—		83,500	(6)	6,000[a]						75,500
14 Equipment			(7)	2,000						
15 Investments	24,300								24,300	
16 Accounts Payable		14,500	(5)	6,000						8,500
17 Notes Payable		10,000			(5)	6,000				16,000
18 Share Capital		43,500								43,500
19 Retained Earnings		20,000	(3)	2,700[b]						
20			(6)	4,000[a]	(4)	600				
21			(2)	2,500	(7)	800				12,200
22 Sales Revenue		94,000			(1)	1,000		95,000		
23 Cost of Goods Sold	21,000						21,000			
24 Selling Expenses	22,000				(3)	500[b]	21,500			
25 Administrative Expenses	23,000		(2)	700	(4)	400	22,700			
26			(4)	600	(7)	1,200				
27 Totals	265,500	265,500								
29 Salaries and Wages Payable					(2)	3,200				3,200
30 Allowance for Doubtful					(3)	2,200[b]				2,200
31 Accounts										
32 Unexpired Insurance			(4)	400					400	
33 Net Income							29,800			29,800
34 Totals				25,900		25,900	95,000	95,000	190,900	190,900

Computations:

[a]Machinery

Proceeds from sale	$ 7,000
Book value of machinery	4,000
Gain on sale	3,000
Income credited	7,000
Retained earnings adjustment	$ 4,000

[b]Bad Debts

	2015	2016
Bad debts charged for	$2,400	$1,600
Additional bad debts anticipated	700	1,500
	3,100	3,100
Charges currently made to each year	(400)	(3,600)
Bad debt adjustment	$2,700	$ (500)

ILLUSTRATION 22-30
Worksheet to Analyze Effect of Errors in Financial Statements

GLOBAL ACCOUNTING INSIGHTS

ACCOUNTING CHANGES AND ERRORS

The FASB has issued guidance on changes in accounting policies, changes in estimates, and corrections of errors, which essentially converges U.S. GAAP to *IAS 8*.

Relevant Facts

Following are the key similarities and differences between U.S. GAAP and IFRS related to the accounting for accounting changes.

Similarities

• The accounting for changes in estimates is similar between U.S. GAAP and IFRS.

• Under U.S. GAAP and IFRS, if determining the effect of a change in accounting policy is considered impracticable, then a company should report the effect of the change in the period in which it believes it practicable to do so, which may be the current period.

Differences

• One area in which U.S. GAAP and IFRS differ is the reporting of error corrections in previously issued financial statements. While both sets of standards require restatement, U.S. GAAP is an absolute standard—there is no exception to this rule.

• Under U.S. GAAP, the impracticality exception applies only to changes in accounting principle. Under IFRS, this exception applies both to changes in accounting principles and to the correction of errors.

• U.S. GAAP has detailed guidance on the accounting and reporting of indirect effects. As indicated in the chapter, IFRS (*IAS 8*) does not specifically address the accounting and reporting for indirect effects of changes in accounting principles.

About the Numbers

An interesting sidelight to our discussion of accounting changes involves how companies that follow IFRS report financial information related to the equity method of accounting. Under the equity method of accounting, the investor increases its investment for the pro-rata share of the net income of the investee (often referred to as an associated company under IFRS). On the other hand, the investor reduces its investment for any dividends received from the investee. Both IFRS and U.S. GAAP follow this accounting approach.

However, there is a subtle difference between IFRS and U.S. GAAP related to how the investor evaluates the accounting policies of the investee. To illustrate, assume that Kirkland Company (the investor company) uses the FIFO inventory method, and Margo Company (the investee company) uses average-cost for its inventory valuation. If Kirkland follows IFRS, Kirkland must conform the accounting policies of Margo to its own accounting policies. Therefore, Kirkland adjusts the net income of Margo so its net income is reported on the FIFO basis.

This procedure is not used under U.S. GAAP. Under U.S. GAAP, Kirkland ignores the fact that Margo uses a different method of inventory valuation. Kirkland records its pro-rata share of the net income of Margo without adjusting for the fact that Margo uses a different inventory valuation method. As a result, there is a lack of comparability in the inventory methods used to report net income for Kirkland Company under U.S. GAAP.

On the Horizon

For the most part, U.S. GAAP and IFRS are similar in the area of accounting changes and reporting the effects of errors. Thus, there is no active project in this area. A related development involves the presentation of comparative data. U.S. GAAP requires comparative information for a three-year period. Under IFRS, when a company prepares financial statements on a new basis, two years of comparative data are reported. Use of the shorter comparative data period must be addressed before U.S. companies can adopt IFRS.

SUMMARY OF LEARNING OBJECTIVES

1 **Identify the two types of accounting changes.** The two different types of accounting changes are as follows. (1) *Change in accounting policy:* a change from one accepted accounting policy to another accepted accounting policy. (2) *Change in accounting estimate:* a change that occurs as the result of new information or as additional experience is acquired.

2 **Describe the accounting for changes in accounting policies.** A change in accounting policy involves a change from one accepted accounting policy to another. A change in accounting policy is not considered to result from the adoption of a new policy in recognition of events that have occurred for the first time or that were previously immaterial. If the accounting policy previously followed was not acceptable or if the policy was applied incorrectly, a change to an accepted accounting policy is considered a correction of an error.

3 **Understand how to account for retrospective accounting changes.** The general requirement for changes in accounting policy is retrospective application. Under retrospective application, companies change prior years' financial statements on a basis consistent with the newly adopted policy. They treat any part of the effect attributable to years prior to those presented as an adjustment of the earliest retained earnings presented.

4 **Understand how to account for impracticable changes.** Retrospective application is impracticable if the prior period effect cannot be determined using every reasonable effort to do so. For example, in changing to average-cost, the base-year inventory for all subsequent average-cost calculations may be the opening inventory in the year the company adopts the method. There is no restatement of prior years' income because it is often too impractical to do so.

5 **Describe the accounting for changes in estimates.** Companies report changes in estimates prospectively. That is, companies should make no changes in previously reported results. They do not adjust opening balances nor change financial statements of prior periods.

6 **Describe the accounting for correction of errors.** Companies must correct errors as soon as they discover them, by proper entries in the accounts, and report them in the financial statements. The profession requires that a company treat corrections of errors as prior period adjustments, record them in the year in which it discovered the errors, and report them in the financial statements in the proper periods. If presenting comparative statements, a company should restate the prior statements affected to correct for the errors. The company need not repeat the disclosures in the financial statements of subsequent periods.

7 **Identify economic motives for changing accounting policies.** Managers might have varying motives for income reporting, depending on economic times and whom they seek to impress. Some of the reasons for changing accounting policies are (1) political costs, (2) capital structure, (3) bonus payments, and (4) smoothing of earnings.

8 **Analyze the effect of errors.** Three types of errors can occur. (1) *Statement of financial position errors*, which affect only the presentation of an asset, liability, or equity account. (2) *Income statement errors*, which affect only the presentation of revenue, expense, gain, or loss accounts in the income statement. (3) *Statement of financial position and income statement errors*, which involve both the statement of financial position and income statement. Errors are classified into two types. (1) *Counterbalancing errors* are offset or corrected over two periods. (2) *Non-counterbalancing errors* are not offset in the next accounting period and take longer than two periods to correct themselves.

As an aid to understanding accounting changes, we provide the following glossary. **[10]**

KEY TERMS RELATED TO ACCOUNTING CHANGES

ACCOUNTING POLICIES. The specific principles, bases, conventions, rules, and practices applied by an entity in preparing and presenting financial statements.

CHANGE IN ACCOUNTING ESTIMATE. An adjustment of the carrying amount of an asset or a liability, or the amount of the periodic consumption of an asset, that results from the assessment of the present status of, and expected future benefits and obligations associated with, assets and liabilities. Changes in accounting estimates result from new information or new developments and, accordingly, are not corrections of errors.

DIRECT EFFECTS OF A CHANGE IN ACCOUNTING POLICY. Those recognized changes in assets or liabilities necessary to effect a change in accounting policy.

ERRORS. Omissions from, and misstatements in, the entity's financial statements for one or more prior periods arising from a failure to use, or misuse of, reliable information that (1) was available when financial statements for those periods were authorized for issue, and (2) could reasonably be expected to have been obtained and taken into account in the preparation and presentation of those financial statements. Such errors include the effects of mathematical mistakes, mistakes in applying accounting policies, oversights or misinterpretations of facts, and fraud.

IMPRACTICABLE. Applying a requirement is impracticable when the entity cannot apply it after making every reasonable effort to do so. For a particular prior period, it is impracticable to apply a change in an accounting policy retrospectively or to make a retrospective restatement to correct an error if (1) the effects of the retrospective application or retrospective restatement are not determinable, (2) the retrospective application or retrospective restatement requires assumptions about what management's intent would have been in that period, or (3) the retrospective application or retrospective restatement requires significant estimates of amounts and it is impossible to distinguish objectively information about those estimates.

INDIRECT EFFECTS OF A CHANGE IN ACCOUNTING POLICY. Any changes to current or future cash flows of an entity that result from making a change in accounting policy that is applied retrospectively.

PROSPECTIVE APPLICATION. Change in accounting policy requires (1) applying the new accounting policy to transactions, other events, and conditions occurring after the date as at which the policy is changed; and (2) recognizing the effect of the change in the accounting estimate in the current and future periods affected by the change.

RETROSPECTIVE APPLICATION. Applying a new accounting policy to transactions, other events, and conditions as if that policy had always been applied.

RETROSPECTIVE RESTATEMENT. Correcting the recognition, measurement, and disclosure of amounts of elements of financial statements as if a prior period error had never occurred.

IFRS AUTHORITATIVE LITERATURE

Authoritative Literature References

[1] International Accounting Standard 8, *Accounting Policies, Changes in Accounting Estimates, and Errors* (London, U.K.: International Accounting Standards Committee Foundation, 2003).

[2] International Accounting Standard 8, *Accounting Policies, Changes in Accounting Estimates, and Errors* (London, U.K.: International Accounting Standards Committee Foundation, 2003), paras. 19–22.

[3] International Accounting Standard 8, *Accounting Policies, Changes in Accounting Estimates, and Errors* (London, U.K.: International Accounting Standards Committee Foundation, 2003), par. 13.

[4] International Accounting Standard 8, *Accounting Policies, Changes in Accounting Estimates, and Errors* (London, U.K.: International Accounting Standards Committee Foundation, 2003), paras. 11–12.

[5] International Accounting Standard 8, *Accounting Policies, Changes in Accounting Estimates, and Errors* (London, U.K.: International Accounting Standards Committee Foundation, 2003), par. 29.

[6] International Accounting Standard 8, *Accounting Policies, Changes in Accounting Estimates, and Errors* (London, U.K.: International Accounting Standards Committee Foundation, 2003), par. 24.

[7] International Accounting Standard 8, *Accounting Policies, Changes in Accounting Estimates, and Errors* (London, U.K.: International Accounting Standards Committee Foundation, 2003), par. 29(e).

[8] International Accounting Standard 8, *Accounting Policies, Changes in Accounting Estimates, and Errors* (London, U.K.: International Accounting Standards Committee Foundation, 2003), paras. 37–38.

[9] International Accounting Standard 8, *Accounting Policies, Changes in Accounting Estimates, and Errors* (London, U.K.: International Accounting Standards Committee Foundation, 2003), par. 39.

[10] International Accounting Standard 8, *Accounting Policies, Changes in Accounting Estimates, and Errors* (London, U.K.: International Accounting Standards Committee Foundation, 2003), par. 5.

QUESTIONS

1. In recent years, the financial press has indicated that many companies have changed their accounting policies. What are the major reasons why companies change accounting policies?

2. State how each of the following items is reflected in the financial statements.
   (a) Change from FIFO to average-cost method for inventory valuation purposes.
   (b) Charge for failure to record depreciation in a previous period.
   (c) Litigation won in current year, related to prior period.
   (d) Change in the realizability of certain receivables.
   (e) Write-off of receivables.
   (f) Change from the percentage-of-completion to the cost-recovery method for reporting net income.

3. Discuss briefly the three approaches that have been suggested for reporting changes in accounting policies.

4. Identify and describe the approach the IASB requires for reporting changes in accounting policies.

5. What is the indirect effect of a change in accounting policy? Briefly describe the approach to reporting the indirect effects of a change in accounting policy.

6. Define a change in estimate and provide an illustration.

7. Lenexa State Bank has followed the practice of capitalizing certain marketing costs and amortizing these costs over their expected life. In the current year, the bank determined that the future benefits from these costs were doubtful. Consequently, the bank adopted the policy of expensing these costs as incurred. How should the bank report this accounting change in the comparative financial statements?

8. Indicate how the following items are recorded in the accounting records in the current year of Coronet Co.
   (a) Impairment of goodwill.
   (b) A change in depreciating plant assets from accelerated to the straight-line method.
   (c) Large write-off of inventories because of obsolescence.
   (d) Change from the cash basis to accrual basis of accounting.
   (e) Change from average-cost to FIFO method for inventory valuation purposes.
   (f) Change in the estimate of service lives for plant assets.

9. Whittier Construction Co. had followed the practice of expensing all materials assigned to a construction job without recognizing any residual inventory. On December 31, 2015, it was determined that residual inventory should be valued at CHF52,000. Of this amount, CHF29,000 arose during the current year. How does this information affect the financial statements to be prepared at the end of 2015?

10. Parsons Inc. wishes to change from the cost-recovery to the percentage-of-completion method for financial reporting purposes. The auditor indicates that a change would be permitted only if it is to a preferable method. What difficulties develop in assessing preferability?

11. Discuss how a change in accounting policy is handled when it is impracticable to determine previous amounts.

12. What relevance do political costs have to accounting changes?

13. What are some of the key motivations that managers might have to change accounting policies?

14. Distinguish between counterbalancing and non-counterbalancing errors. Give an example of each.

15. Discuss and illustrate how a correction of an error in previously issued financial statements should be handled.

16. Prior to 2015, Heberling Inc. excluded manufacturing overhead costs from work in process and finished goods inventory. These costs have been expensed as incurred. In 2015, the company decided to change its accounting methods for manufacturing inventories to full costing by including these costs as product costs. Assuming that these costs are material, how should this change be reflected in the financial statements for 2014 and 2015?

17. Elliott Corp. failed to record accrued salaries for 2013, €2,000; 2014, €2,100; and 2015, €3,900. What is the amount of the overstatement or understatement of Retained Earnings at December 31, 2016?

18. In January 2014, installation costs of £6,000 on new equipment were charged to Maintenance and Repairs Expense. Other costs of this equipment of £30,000 were correctly recorded and have been depreciated using the straight-line method with an estimated life of 10 years and no residual value. At December 31, 2015, it is decided that the equipment has a remaining useful life of 20 years, starting with January 1, 2015. What entry(ies) should be made in 2015 to correctly record transactions related to equipment, assuming the equipment has no residual value? The books have not been closed for 2015 and depreciation expense has not yet been recorded for 2015.

19. An entry to record Purchases and related Accounts Payable of ¥130,000 for merchandise purchased on December 23, 2015, was recorded in January 2016. This merchandise was not included in inventory at December 31, 2015. What

effect does this error have on reported net income for 2015? What entry should be made to correct for this error, assuming that the books are not closed for 2015?

20. Equipment was purchased on January 2, 2015, for $24,000, but no portion of the cost has been charged to depreciation. The corporation wishes to use the straight-line method for these assets, which have been estimated to have a life of 10 years and no residual value. What effect does this error have on net income in 2015? What entry is necessary to correct for this error, assuming that the books are not closed for 2015?

21. What is the major difference in accounting for errors under IFRS versus U.S. GAAP?

22. How are direct and indirect changes in accounting policy reported under U.S. GAAP?

23. What is the difference in approach between U.S. GAAP and IFRS in regards to the equity method of accounting for the investor?

BRIEF EXERCISES

3 BE22-1 Wertz Construction Company decided at the beginning of 2015 to change from the cost-recovery method to the percentage-of-completion method for financial reporting purposes. The company will continue to use the cost-recovery method for tax purposes. For years prior to 2015, pretax income under the two methods was as follows: percentage-of-completion $120,000, and cost-recovery $80,000. The tax rate is 35%. Prepare Wertz's 2015 journal entry to record the change in accounting policy.

3 BE22-2 Refer to the accounting change by Wertz Construction Company in BE22-1. Wertz has a profit-sharing plan, which pays all employees a bonus at year-end based on 1% of pretax income. Compute the indirect effect of Wertz's change in accounting policy that will be reported in the 2015 income statement, assuming that the profit-sharing contract explicitly requires adjustment for changes in income numbers.

3 BE22-3 Shannon, Inc., changed from the average-cost to the FIFO cost flow assumption in 2015. The increase in the prior year's income before taxes is €1,200,000. The tax rate is 40%. Prepare Shannon's 2015 journal entry to record the change in accounting policy.

5 BE22-4 Tedesco Company changed depreciation methods in 2015 from double-declining-balance to straight-line. Depreciation prior to 2015 under double-declining-balance was $90,000, whereas straight-line depreciation prior to 2015 would have been $50,000. Tedesco's depreciable assets had a cost of $250,000 with a $40,000 residual value, and an 8-year remaining useful life at the beginning of 2015. Prepare the 2015 journal entry, if necessary, related to Tedesco's depreciable assets.

5 BE22-5 Sesame Company purchased a computer system for £74,000 on January 1, 2013. It was depreciated based on a 7-year life and an £18,000 residual value. On January 1, 2015, Sesame revised these estimates to a total useful life of 4 years and a residual value of £10,000. Prepare Sesame's entry to record 2015 depreciation expense.

6 BE22-6 In 2015, Bailey Corporation discovered that equipment purchased on January 1, 2013, for €50,000 was expensed at that time. The equipment should have been depreciated over 5 years, with no residual value. The effective tax rate is 30%. Prepare Bailey's 2015 journal entry to correct the error.

6 BE22-7 At January 1, 2015, Cheng Company reported retained earnings of ¥20,000,000. In 2015, Cheng discovered that 2014 depreciation expense was understated by ¥4,000,000. In 2015, net income was ¥9,000,000 and dividends declared were ¥2,500,000. The tax rate is 40%. Prepare a 2015 retained earnings statement for Cheng Company.

6 BE22-8 Indicate the effect—**Understate, Overstate, No Effect**—that each of the following errors has on 2014 net income and 2015 net income.

	2014	2015
(a) Equipment purchased in 2013 was expensed.	___	___
(b) Wages payable were not recorded at 12/31/14.	___	___
(c) Equipment purchased in 2014 was expensed.	___	___
(d) 2014 ending inventory was overstated.	___	___
(e) Patent amortization was not recorded in 2015.	___	___

3 5 **BE22-9** Roundtree Manufacturing Co. is preparing its year-end financial statements and is considering the accounting for the following items.

1. The vice president of sales had indicated that one product line has lost its customer appeal and will be phased out over the next 3 years. Therefore, a decision has been made to lower the estimated lives on related production equipment from the remaining 5 years to 3 years.

2. The Hightone Building was converted from a sales office to offices for the Accounting Department at the beginning of this year. Therefore, the expense related to this building will now appear as an administrative expense rather than a selling expense on the current year's income statement.

3. Estimating the lives of new products in the Leisure Products Division has become very difficult because of the highly competitive conditions in this market. Therefore, the practice of deferring and amortizing preproduction costs has been abandoned in favor of expensing such costs as they are incurred.

Identify and explain whether each of the above items is a change in policy, a change in estimate, or an error.

3 6 **BE22-10** Palmer Co. is evaluating the appropriate accounting for the following items.

1. Management has decided to switch from the FIFO inventory valuation method to the average-cost inventory valuation method for all inventories.

2. When the year-end physical inventory adjustment was made for the current year, the controller discovered that the prior year's physical inventory sheets for an entire warehouse were mislaid and excluded from last year's count.

3. Palmer's Custom Division manufactures large-scale, custom-designed machinery on a contract basis. Management decided to switch from the cost-recovery method to the percentage-of-completion method of accounting for long-term contracts.

Identify and explain whether each of the above items is a change in accounting policy, a change in estimate, or an error.

EXERCISES

3 **E22-1 (Change in Policy—Long-Term Contracts)** Cherokee Construction Company changed from the cost-recovery to the percentage-of-completion method of accounting for long-term construction contracts during 2015. For tax purposes, the company employs the cost-recovery method and will continue this approach in the future. (*Hint:* Adjust all tax consequences through the Deferred Tax Liability account.) The appropriate information related to this change is as follows.

| | Pretax Income from | | |
	Percentage-of-Completion	Cost-Recovery	Difference
2014	$780,000	$610,000	$170,000
2015	700,000	480,000	220,000

Instructions
(a) Assuming that the tax rate is 35%, what is the amount of net income that would be reported in 2015?
(b) What entry(ies) is necessary to adjust the accounting records for the change in accounting policy?

3 **E22-2 (Change in Policy—Inventory Methods)** Whitman Company began operations on January 1, 2012, and uses the average-cost method of pricing inventory. Management is contemplating a change in inventory methods for 2015. The following information is available for the years 2012–2014.

| | Net Income Computed Using | |
	Average-Cost Method	FIFO Method
2012	€16,000	€19,000
2013	18,000	21,000
2014	20,000	25,000

Instructions

(Ignore all tax effects.)

(a) Prepare the journal entry necessary to record a change from the average-cost method to the FIFO method in 2015.

(b) Determine net income to be reported for 2012, 2013, and 2014, after giving effect to the change in accounting policy.

3 **E22-3 (Accounting Change)** Ramirez Co. decides at the beginning of 2015 to adopt the FIFO method of inventory valuation. Ramirez had used the average-cost method for financial reporting since its inception on January 1, 2013, and had maintained records adequate to apply the FIFO method retrospectively. Ramirez concluded that FIFO is the preferable inventory method because it reflects the current cost of inventory on the statement of financial position. The following table presents the effects of the change in accounting policy on inventory and cost of goods sold.

	Inventory Determined by		Cost of Goods Sold Determined by	
Date	Average-Cost Method	FIFO Method	Average-Cost Method	FIFO Method
January 1, 2013	$ 0	$ 0	$ 0	$ 0
December 31, 2013	100	80	800	820
December 31, 2014	200	240	1,000	940
December 31, 2015	320	390	1,130	1,100

Retained earnings reported under average-cost are as follows.

	Retained Earnings Balance
December 31, 2013	$2,200
December 31, 2014	4,200
December 31, 2015	6,070

Other information:

1. For each year presented, sales are $4,000 and operating expenses are $1,000.

2. Ramirez provides two years of financial statements. Earnings per share information is not required.

Instructions

(a) Prepare income statements under average-cost and FIFO for 2013, 2014, and 2015.

(b) Prepare income statements reflecting the retrospective application of the accounting change from the average-cost method to the FIFO method for 2015 and 2014.

(c) Prepare the note to the financial statements describing the change in method of inventory valuation. In the note, indicate the income statement line items for 2015 and 2014 that were affected by the change in accounting policy.

(d) Prepare comparative retained earnings statements for 2014 and 2015 under FIFO.

3 **E22-4 (Accounting Change)** Linden Company started operations on January 1, 2010, and has used the FIFO method of inventory valuation since its inception. In 2015, it decides to switch to the average-cost method. You are provided with the following information.

	Net Income		Retained Earnings (ending balance)
	Under FIFO	Under Average-Cost	Under FIFO
2010	£100,000	£ 92,000	£100,000
2011	70,000	65,000	160,000
2012	90,000	80,000	235,000
2013	120,000	130,000	340,000
2014	300,000	293,000	590,000
2015	305,000	310,000	780,000

Instructions

(a) What is the beginning retained earnings balance at January 1, 2012, if Linden prepares comparative financial statements starting in 2012?

(b) What is the beginning retained earnings balance at January 1, 2015, if Linden prepares comparative financial statements starting in 2015?

(c) What is the beginning retained earnings balance at January 1, 2016, if Linden prepares single-period financial statements for 2016?

(d) What is the net income reported by Linden in the 2015 income statement if it prepares comparative financial statements starting with 2013?

3 E22-5 (Accounting Change) Presented below are income statements prepared on an average-cost and FIFO basis for Carlton Company, which started operations on January 1, 2014. The company presently uses the average-cost method of pricing its inventory and has decided to switch to the FIFO method in 2015. The FIFO income statement is computed in accordance with IFRS. Carlton's profit-sharing agreement with its employees indicates that the company will pay employees 5% of income before profit sharing. Income taxes are ignored.

	Average-Cost Basis		FIFO Basis	
	2015	2014	2015	2014
Sales	€3,000	€3,000	€3,000	€3,000
Cost of goods sold	1,130	1,000	1,100	940
Operating expenses	1,000	1,000	1,000	1,000
Income before profit sharing	870	1,000	900	1,060
Profit-sharing expense	44	50	45	53
Net income	€ 826	€ 950	€ 855	€1,007

Instructions

Answer the following questions.

(a) If comparative income statements are prepared, what net income should Carlton report in 2014 and 2015?

(b) Explain why, under the FIFO basis, Carlton reports €50 in 2014 and €48 in 2015 for its profit-sharing expense.

(c) Assume that Carlton has a beginning balance of retained earnings at January 1, 2015, of €8,000 using the average-cost method. The company declared and paid dividends of €2,500 in 2015. Prepare the retained earnings statement for 2015, assuming that Carlton has switched to the FIFO method.

5 E22-6 (Accounting Changes—Depreciation) Robillard Inc. acquired the following assets in January 2012.

Equipment, estimated service life, 5 years; residual value, €15,000   €465,000
Building, estimated service life, 30 years; no residual value   €780,000

The equipment has been depreciated using the sum-of-the-years'-digits method for the first 3 years for financial reporting purposes. In 2015, the company decided to change the method of computing depreciation to the straight-line method for the equipment, but no change was made in the estimated service life or residual value. It was also decided to change the total estimated service life of the building from 30 years to 40 years, with no change in the estimated residual value. The building is depreciated on the straight-line method.

Instructions

(a) Prepare the journal entry to record depreciation expense for the equipment in 2015.

(b) Prepare the journal entry to record depreciation expense for the building in 2015. (Round to nearest euro.)

5 6 E22-7 (Change in Estimate and Error; Financial Statements) Presented below are the comparative income statements for Pannebecker Inc. for the years 2014 and 2015.

	2015	2014
Sales	$340,000	$270,000
Cost of sales	200,000	142,000
Gross profit	140,000	128,000
Expenses	88,000	50,000
Net income	$ 52,000	$ 78,000
Retained earnings (Jan. 1)	$125,000	$ 72,000
Net income	52,000	78,000
Dividends	(30,000)	(25,000)
Retained earnings (Dec. 31)	$147,000	$125,000

The following additional information is provided.

1. In 2015, Pannebecker Inc. decided to switch its depreciation method from sum-of-the-years'-digits to the straight-line method. The assets were purchased at the beginning of 2014 for $90,000 with an estimated useful life of 4 years and no residual value. (The 2015 income statement contains depreciation expense of $27,000 on the assets purchased at the beginning of 2014.)

2. In 2015, the company discovered that the ending inventory for 2014 was overstated by $20,000; ending inventory for 2015 is correctly stated.

Instructions

Prepare the revised retained earnings statement for 2014 and 2015, assuming comparative statements. (Ignore income taxes.)

E22-8 (Accounting for Accounting Changes and Errors) Listed below are various types of accounting changes and errors.

_____ 1. Change from FIFO to average-cost inventory method.

_____ 2. Change due to overstatement of inventory.

_____ 3. Change from an accelerated to straight-line method of depreciation.

_____ 4. Change from average-cost to FIFO inventory method.

_____ 5. Change in the rate used to compute warranty costs.

_____ 6. Change from an unacceptable accounting policy to an acceptable accounting policy.

_____ 7. Change in a patent's amortization period.

_____ 8. Change from cost-recovery to percentage-of-completion method on construction contracts.

_____ 9. Change in a plant asset's residual value.

Instructions

For each change or error, indicate how it would be accounted for using the following code letters:

(a) Accounted for prospectively.

(b) Accounted for retrospectively.

(c) Neither of the above.

E22-9 (Error and Change in Estimate—Depreciation) Yoon Co. purchased a machine on January 1, 2012, for ₩44,000,000. At that time, it was estimated that the machine would have a 10-year life and no residual value. On December 31, 2015, the firm's accountant found that the entry for depreciation expense had been omitted in 2013. In addition, management has informed the accountant that the company plans to switch to straight-line depreciation, starting with the year 2015. At present, the company uses the sum-of-the-years'-digits method for depreciating equipment.

Instructions

Prepare the general journal entries that should be made at December 31, 2015, to record these events. (Ignore tax effects.)

E22-10 (Depreciation Changes) On January 1, 2011, McElroy Company purchased a building and equipment that have the following useful lives, residual values, and costs.

Building, 40-year estimated useful life, £50,000 residual value, £1,200,000 cost
Equipment, 12-year estimated useful life, £10,000 residual value, £130,000 cost

The building has been depreciated under the double-declining-balance method through 2014. In 2015, the company decided to switch to the straight-line method of depreciation. McElroy also decided to change the total useful life of the equipment to 9 years, with a residual value of £5,000 at the end of that time. The equipment is depreciated using the straight-line method.

Instructions

(a) Prepare the journal entry(ies) necessary to record the depreciation expense on the building in 2015.

(b) Compute depreciation expense on the equipment for 2015.

E22-11 (Change in Estimate—Depreciation) Thurber Co. purchased equipment for $710,000 which was estimated to have a useful life of 10 years with a residual value of $10,000 at the end of that time. Depreciation has been entered for 7 years on a straight-line basis. In 2015, it is determined that the total estimated life should be 15 years with a residual value of $4,000 at the end of that time.

Instructions

(a) Prepare the entry (if any) to correct the prior years' depreciation.

(b) Prepare the entry to record depreciation for 2015.

5 **E22-12 (Change in Estimate—Depreciation)** Frederick Industries changed from the double-declining-balance to the straight-line method in 2015 on all its plant assets. There was no change in the assets' residual values or useful lives. Plant assets, acquired on January 2, 2012, had an original cost of €2,400,000, with a €100,000 residual value and an 8-year estimated useful life. Income before depreciation expense was €370,000 in 2014 and €300,000 in 2015.

Instructions

(a) Prepare the journal entry(ies) to reflect the change in depreciation method in 2015.

(b) Starting with income before depreciation expense, prepare the remaining portion of the income statement for 2014 and 2015.

3 **E22-13 (Change in Policy—Long-Term Contracts)** Bryant Construction Company changed from the cost-recovery to the percentage-of-completion method of accounting for long-term construction contracts during 2015. For tax purposes, the company employs the cost-recovery method and will continue this approach in the future. The information related to this change is as follows.

	Pretax Income from		
	Percentage-of-Completion	Cost-Recovery	Difference
2014	$980,000	$730,000	$250,000
2015	900,000	480,000	420,000

Instructions

(a) Assuming that the tax rate is 40%, what is the amount of net income that would be reported in 2015?

(b) What entry(ies) are necessary to adjust the accounting records for the change in accounting policy?

3 **E22-14 (Various Changes in Policy—Inventory Methods)** Below is the net income of Benchley Instrument Co., a private corporation, computed under the two inventory methods using a periodic system.

	FIFO	Average-Cost
2012	€26,000	€23,000
2013	30,000	25,000
2014	29,000	27,000
2015	34,000	30,000

Instructions

(Ignore tax considerations.)

(a) Assume that in 2015 Benchley decided to change from the FIFO method to the average-cost method of pricing inventories. Prepare the journal entry necessary for the change that took place during 2015, and show net income reported for 2012, 2013, 2014, and 2015.

(b) Assume that in 2015 Benchley, which had been using the average-cost method since incorporation in 2012, changed to the FIFO method of pricing inventories. Prepare the journal entry necessary to record the change in 2015, and show net income reported for 2012, 2013, 2014, and 2015.

6 **E22-15 (Error Correction Entries)** The first audit of the books of Fenimore Company was made for the year ended December 31, 2015. In examining the books, the auditor found that certain items had been overlooked or incorrectly handled in the last 3 years. These items are:

1. At the beginning of 2013, the company purchased a machine for $510,000 (residual value of $51,000) that had a useful life of 5 years. The bookkeeper used straight-line depreciation but failed to deduct the residual value in computing the depreciation base for the 3 years.

2. At the end of 2014, the company failed to accrue sales salaries of $45,000.

3. A tax lawsuit that involved the year 2013 was settled late in 2015. It was determined that the company owed an additional $85,000 in taxes related to 2013. The company did not record a liability in 2013 or 2014 because the possibility of loss was considered remote, and debited the $85,000 to a loss account in 2015 and credited Cash for the same amount.

4. Fenimore Company purchased a copyright from another company early in 2013 for $50,000. Fenimore had not amortized the copyright because its value had not diminished. The copyright has a useful life at purchase of 20 years.

5. In 2015, the company wrote off $87,000 of inventory considered to be obsolete; this loss was charged directly to Retained Earnings and credited to Inventory.

Instructions

Prepare the journal entries necessary in 2015 to correct the books, assuming that the books have not been closed. Disregard effects of corrections on income tax.

6 **E22-16 (Error Analysis and Correcting Entry)** You have been engaged to review the financial statements of Longfellow Corporation. In the course of your examination, you conclude that the bookkeeper hired during the current year is not doing a good job. You notice a number of irregularities, as follows.

1. Year-end salaries and wages payable of €3,400 were not recorded because the bookkeeper thought that "they were immaterial."

2. Accrued vacation pay for the year of €31,100 was not recorded because the bookkeeper "never heard that you had to do it."

3. Insurance for a 12-month period purchased on November 1 of this year was charged to insurance expense in the amount of €3,300 because "the amount of the check is about the same every year."

4. Reported sales revenue for the year is €1,908,000. This includes all sales taxes collected for the year. The sales tax rate is 6%. Because the sales tax is forwarded to the Department of Revenue, the Sales Tax Expense account is debited. The bookkeeper thought that "the sales tax is a selling expense." At the end of the current year, the balance in the Sales Tax Expense account is €103,400.

Instructions

Prepare the necessary correcting entries, assuming that Longfellow uses a calendar-year basis.

6 **E22-17 (Error Analysis and Correcting Entry)** The reported net incomes for the first 2 years of Sinclair Products, Inc., were as follows: 2014, $147,000; 2015, $185,000. Early in 2016, the following errors were discovered.

1. Depreciation of equipment for 2014 was overstated $19,000.

2. Depreciation of equipment for 2015 was understated $38,500.

3. December 31, 2014, inventory was understated $50,000.

4. December 31, 2015, inventory was overstated $14,200.

Instructions

Prepare the correcting entry necessary when these errors are discovered. Assume that the books for 2015 are closed. (Ignore income tax considerations.)

6 **8** **E22-18 (Error Analysis)** Emerson Tool Company's December 31 year-end financial statements contained the following errors.

	December 31, 2014	December 31, 2015
Ending inventory	£9,600 understated	£7,100 overstated
Depreciation expense	£2,300 understated	—

An insurance premium of £60,000 was prepaid in 2014 covering the years 2014, 2015, and 2016. The entire amount was charged to expense in 2014. In addition, on December 31, 2015, fully depreciated machinery was sold for £15,000 cash, but the entry was not recorded until 2016. There were no other errors during 2014 or 2015, and no corrections have been made for any of the errors. (Ignore income tax considerations.)

Instructions

(a) Compute the total effect of the errors on 2015 net income.

(b) Compute the total effect of the errors on the amount of Emerson's working capital at December 31, 2015.

(c) Compute the total effect of the errors on the balance of Emerson's retained earnings at December 31, 2015.

6 **8** **E22-19 (Error Analysis and Correcting Entries)** A partial trial balance of Dickinson Corporation is as follows on December 31, 2015.

	Dr.	Cr.
Supplies	R 2,500	
Salaries and wages payable		R 1,500
Interest receivable	5,100	
Prepaid insurance	90,000	
Unearned rent		–0–
Accrued interest payable		15,000

Additional adjusting data:

1. A physical count of supplies on hand on December 31, 2015, totaled R1,100.

2. Through oversight, the Salaries and Wages Payable account was not changed during 2015. Accrued salaries and wages on December 31, 2015, amounted to R4,400.

3. The Interest Receivable account was also left unchanged during 2015. Accrued interest on investments amounts to R4,350 on December 31, 2015.

4. The unexpired portions of the insurance policies totaled R65,000 as of December 31, 2015.

5. R24,000 was received on January 1, 2015, for the rent of a building for both 2015 and 2016. The entire amount was credited to rental income.

6. Depreciation for the year on equipment was erroneously recorded as R5,000 rather than the correct figure of R50,000.

7. A further review of depreciation calculations of prior years revealed that depreciation of R7,200 was not recorded. It was decided that this oversight should be corrected by a prior period adjustment.

Instructions

(a) Assuming that the books have not been closed, what are the adjusting entries necessary at December 31, 2015? (Ignore income tax considerations.)

(b) Assuming that the books have been closed, what are the adjusting entries necessary at December 31, 2015? (Ignore income tax considerations.)

6 **8** **E22-20 (Error Analysis)** The before-tax income for Fitzgerald Co. for 2014 was $101,000, and for 2015 was $77,400. However, the accountant noted that the following errors had been made.

1. Sales for 2014 included amounts of $38,200 which had been received in cash during 2014, but for which the related products were delivered in 2015. Title did not pass to the purchaser until 2015.

2. The inventory on December 31, 2014, was understated by $8,640.

3. The bookkeeper in recording interest expense for both 2014 and 2015 on bonds payable made the following entry on an annual basis.

Interest Expense	15,000	
Cash		15,000

The bonds have a face value of $250,000 and pay a stated interest rate of 6%. They were issued at a discount of $10,000 on January 1, 2014, to yield an effective-interest rate of 7%. (Assume that the effective-interest method should be used.)

4. Ordinary repairs to equipment had been erroneously charged to the Equipment account during 2014 and 2015. Repairs in the amount of $8,000 in 2014 and $9,400 in 2015 were so charged. The company applies a rate of 10% to the balance in the Equipment account at the end of the year in its determination of depreciation charges.

Instructions

Prepare a schedule showing the determination of corrected income before taxes for 2014 and 2015.

6 **8** **E22-21 (Error Analysis)** When the records of Aoki Corporation were reviewed at the close of 2015, the errors listed on page 1168 were discovered. For each item, indicate by a check mark in the appropriate column whether the error resulted in an overstatement, an understatement, or had no effect on net income for the years 2014 and 2015.

| | 2014 | | | 2015 | | |
Item	Over-statement	Under-statement	No Effect	Over-statement	Under-statement	No Effect
1. Failure to reflect supplies on hand on statement of financial position at end of 2014.						
2. Failure to record the correct amount of ending 2014 inventory. The amount was understated because of an error in calculation.						
3. Failure to record, until 2015, merchandise purchased in 2014. Merchandise was also omitted from ending inventory in 2014 but was not yet sold.						
4. Failure to record accrued interest on notes payable in 2014; that amount was recorded when paid in 2015.						
5. Failure to record amortization of patent in 2015.						

PROBLEMS

P22-1 (Change in Estimate and Error Correction) Holtzman Company is in the process of preparing its financial statements for 2015. Assume that no entries for depreciation have been recorded in 2015. The following information related to depreciation of fixed assets is provided to you.

1. Holtzman purchased equipment on January 2, 2012, for $85,000. At that time, the equipment had an estimated useful life of 10 years with a $5,000 residual value. The equipment is depreciated on a straight-line basis. On January 2, 2015, as a result of additional information, the company determined that the equipment has a remaining useful life of 4 years with a $3,000 residual value.

2. During 2015, Holtzman changed from the double-declining-balance method for its building to the straight-line method. The building originally cost $300,000. It had a useful life of 10 years and a residual value of $30,000. The following computations present depreciation on both bases for 2013 and 2014.

	2014	2013
Straight-line	$27,000	$27,000
Declining-balance	48,000	60,000

3. Holtzman purchased a machine on July 1, 2013, at a cost of $120,000. The machine has a residual value of $16,000 and a useful life of 8 years. Holtzman's bookkeeper recorded straight-line depreciation in 2013 and 2014 but failed to consider the residual value.

Instructions

(a) Prepare the journal entries to record depreciation expense for 2015 and correct any errors made to date related to the information provided.

(b) Show comparative net income for 2014 and 2015. Income before depreciation expense was $300,000 in 2015, and was $310,000 in 2014. (Ignore taxes.)

3 5 **P22-2 (Comprehensive Accounting Change and Error Analysis Problem)** Botticelli Inc. was organized in
6 late 2012 to manufacture and sell hosiery. At the end of its fourth year of operation, the company has been
fairly successful, as indicated by the following reported net incomes.

2012	€140,000ª		2014	€205,000
2013	160,000		2015	276,000

ªIncludes a €10,000 increase because of change in bad debt experience rate.

The company has decided to expand operations and has applied for a sizable bank loan. The bank officer
has indicated that the records should be audited and presented in comparative statements to facilitate
analysis by the bank. Botticelli Inc. therefore hired the auditing firm of Check & Doublecheck Co. and has
provided the following additional information.

1. In early 2013, Botticelli Inc. changed its estimate from 2% to 1% on the amount of bad debt expense to
   be charged to operations. Bad debt expense for 2012, if a 1% rate had been used, would have been
   €10,000. The company therefore restated its net income for 2012.

2. In 2015, the auditor discovered that the company had changed its method of inventory pricing from
   average-cost to FIFO. The effect on the income statements for the previous years is as follows.

	2012	2013	2014	2015
Net income unadjusted—average-cost basis	€140,000	€160,000	€205,000	€276,000
Net income unadjusted—FIFO basis	155,000	165,000	215,000	260,000
	€ 15,000	€ 5,000	€ 10,000	(€ 16,000)

3. In 2015, the auditor discovered that:
   a. The company incorrectly overstated the ending inventory by €14,000 in 2014.
   b. A dispute developed in 2013 with the tax authorities over the deductibility of entertainment ex-
      penses. In 2012, the company was not permitted these deductions, but a tax settlement was reached
      in 2015 that allowed these expenses. As a result of the court's finding, tax expenses in 2015 were
      reduced by €60,000.

Instructions
   (a) Indicate how each of these changes or corrections should be handled in the accounting records.
       (Ignore income tax considerations.)
   (b) Present comparative net income numbers for the years 2012 to 2015. (Ignore income tax consider-
       ations.)

3 5 **P22-3 (Error Corrections and Accounting Changes)** Chen Company is in the process of adjusting and
6 correcting its books at the end of 2015. In reviewing its records, the following information is compiled.

1. Chen has failed to accrue sales commissions payable at the end of each of the last 2 years, as follows.

December 31, 2014	¥3,500,000
December 31, 2015	¥2,500,000

2. In reviewing the December 31, 2015, inventory, Chen discovered errors in its inventory-taking procedures that have caused inventories for the last 3 years to be incorrect, as follows.

December 31, 2013	Understated	¥16,000,000
December 31, 2014	Understated	¥19,000,000
December 31, 2015	Overstated	¥ 6,700,000

   Chen has already made an entry that established the incorrect December 31, 2015, inventory amount.

3. At December 31, 2015, Chen decided to change the depreciation method on its office equipment
   from double-declining-balance to straight-line. The equipment had an original cost of ¥100,000,000
   when purchased on January 1, 2013. It has a 10-year useful life and no residual value. Depreciation
   expense recorded prior to 2015 under the double-declining-balance method was ¥36,000,000. Chen
   has already recorded 2015 depreciation expense of ¥12,800,000 using the double-declining-balance
   method.

4. Before 2015, Chen accounted for its income from long-term construction contracts on the cost-recovery
   basis. Early in 2015, Chen changed to the percentage-of-completion basis for accounting purposes. It
   continues to use the cost-recovery method for tax purposes. Income for 2015 has been recorded using
   the percentage-of-completion method. The information on page 1170 is available.

	Pretax Income from	
	Percentage-of-Completion	Cost-Recovery
Prior to 2015	¥150,000,000	¥105,000,000
2015	60,000,000	20,000,000

Instructions

Prepare the journal entries necessary at December 31, 2015, to record the above corrections and changes. The books are still open for 2015. The income tax rate is 40%. Chen has not yet recorded its 2015 income tax expense and payable amounts so current-year tax effects may be ignored. Prior-year tax effects must be considered in item 4.

P22-4 (Accounting Changes) Aston Corporation performs year-end planning in November of each year before its calendar year ends in December. The preliminary estimated net income is £3 million. The CFO, Rita Warren, meets with the company president, J. B. Aston, to review the projected numbers. She presents the following projected information.

ASTON CORPORATION
PROJECTED INCOME STATEMENT
FOR THE YEAR ENDED DECEMBER 31, 2015

Sales		£29,000,000
Cost of goods sold	£14,000,000	
Depreciation	2,600,000	
Operating expenses	6,400,000	23,000,000
Income before income tax		6,000,000
Income tax		3,000,000
Net income		£ 3,000,000

ASTON CORPORATION
SELECTED STATEMENT OF FINANCIAL POSITION INFORMATION
AT DECEMBER 31, 2015

Estimated cash balance	£ 5,000,000
Debt investments (held-for-collection)	10,000,000
Security fair value adjustment account (1/1/15)	200,000

Estimated fair value at December 31, 2015:

Investment	Cost	Estimated Fair Value
A	£ 2,000,000	£ 2,200,000
B	4,000,000	3,900,000
C	3,000,000	3,000,000
D	1,000,000	1,800,000
Total	£10,000,000	£10,900,000

Other information at December 31, 2015:

Equipment	£3,000,000
Accumulated depreciation (5-year SL)	1,200,000
New robotic equipment (purchased 1/1/15)	5,000,000
Accumulated depreciation (5-year DDB)	2,000,000

The corporation has never used robotic equipment before, and Warren assumed an accelerated method because of the rapidly changing technology in robotic equipment. The company normally uses straight-line depreciation for production equipment.

Aston explains to Warren that it is important for the corporation to show a £7,000,000 income before taxes because Aston receives a £1,000,000 bonus if the income before taxes and bonus reaches £7,000,000. Aston also does not want the company to pay more than £3,000,000 in income taxes to the government.

Instructions

    (a) What can Warren do within IFRS to accommodate the president's wishes to achieve £7,000,000 in income before taxes and bonus? Present the revised income statement based on your decision.

    (b) Are the actions ethical? Who are the stakeholders in this decision, and what effect do Warren's actions have on their interests?

3 **P22-5 (Change in Policy—Inventory—Periodic)** The management of Utrillo Instrument Company had concluded, with the concurrence of its independent auditors, that results of operations would be more fairly presented if Utrillo changed its method of pricing inventory from FIFO to average-cost in 2015. Given below is the 5-year summary of income under FIFO and a schedule of what the inventories would be if stated on the average-cost method (amounts in millions, except earnings per share).

UTRILLO INSTRUMENT COMPANY
STATEMENT OF INCOME AND RETAINED EARNINGS
FOR THE YEARS ENDED MAY 31

	2011	2012	2013	2014	2015
Sales—net	¥13,964	¥15,506	¥16,673	¥18,221	¥18,898
Cost of goods sold					
Beginning inventory	1,000	1,100	1,000	1,115	1,237
Purchases	13,000	13,900	15,000	15,900	17,100
Ending inventory	(1,100)	(1,000)	(1,115)	(1,237)	(1,369)
Total	12,900	14,000	14,885	15,778	16,968
Gross profit	1,064	1,506	1,788	2,443	1,930
Administrative expenses	700	763	832	907	989
Income before taxes	364	743	956	1,536	941
Income taxes (50%)	182	372	478	768	471
Net income	182	371	478	768	470
Retained earnings—beginning	1,206	1,388	1,759	2,237	3,005
Retained earnings—ending	¥ 1,388	¥ 1,759	¥ 2,237	¥ 3,005	¥ 3,475
Earnings per share	¥1.82	¥3.71	¥4.78	¥7.68	¥4.70

SCHEDULE OF INVENTORY BALANCES USING AVERAGE-COST METHOD
FOR THE YEAR ENDED MAY 31

2010	2011	2012	2013	2014	2015
¥1,010	¥1,124	¥1,101	¥1,270	¥1,500	¥1,720

Instructions

Prepare comparative statements for the 5 years, assuming that Utrillo changed its method of inventory pricing to average-cost. Indicate the effects on net income and earnings per share for the years involved. Utrillo Instruments started business in 2010. (All amounts except EPS are rounded up to the nearest yen.)

5 **6** **8** **P22-6 (Accounting Change and Error Analysis)** On December 31, 2015, before the books were closed, the management and accountants of Madrasa Inc. made the following determinations about three depreciable assets.

    1. Depreciable asset A was purchased January 2, 2012. It originally cost €540,000 and, for depreciation purposes, the straight-line method was originally chosen. The asset was originally expected to be useful for 10 years and have a zero residual value. In 2015, the decision was made to change the depreciation method from straight-line to sum-of-the-years'-digits, and the estimates relating to useful life and residual value remained unchanged.

    2. Depreciable asset B was purchased January 3, 2011. It originally cost €180,000 and, for depreciation purposes, the straight-line method was chosen. The asset was originally expected to be useful for 15 years and have a zero residual value. In 2015, the decision was made to shorten the total life of this asset to 9 years and to estimate the residual value at €3,000.

    3. Depreciable asset C was purchased January 5, 2011. The asset's original cost was €160,000, and this amount was entirely expensed in 2011. This particular asset has a 10-year useful life and no residual value. The straight-line method was chosen for depreciation purposes.

Additional data:

1. Income in 2015 before depreciation expense amounted to €400,000.

2. Depreciation expense on assets other than A, B, and C totaled €55,000 in 2015.

3. Income in 2014 was reported at €370,000.

4. Ignore all income tax effects.

5. 100,000 ordinary shares were outstanding in 2014 and 2015.

Instructions

(a) Prepare all necessary entries in 2015 to record these determinations.

(b) Prepare comparative retained earnings statements for Madrasa Inc. for 2014 and 2015. The company had retained earnings of €200,000 at December 31, 2013.

 P22-7 (Error Corrections) You have been assigned to examine the financial statements of Zarle Company for the year ended December 31, 2015. You discover the following situations.

1. Depreciation of $3,200 for 2015 on delivery vehicles was not recorded.

2. The physical inventory count on December 31, 2014, improperly excluded merchandise costing $19,000 that had been temporarily stored in a public warehouse. Zarle uses a periodic inventory system.

3. A collection of $5,600 on account from a customer received on December 31, 2015, was not recorded until January 2, 2016.

4. In 2015, the company sold for $3,700 fully depreciated equipment that originally cost $25,000. The company credited the proceeds from the sale to the Equipment account.

5. During November 2015, a competitor company filed a patent-infringement suit against Zarle claiming damages of $220,000. The company's legal counsel has indicated that an unfavorable verdict is probable and a reasonable estimate of the court's award to the competitor is $125,000. The company has not reflected or disclosed this situation in the financial statements.

6. Zarle has a portfolio of investments that it manages to profit from short-term price changes. No entry has been made to adjust to fair value. Information on cost and fair value is as follows.

	Cost	Fair Value
December 31, 2014	$95,000	$95,000
December 31, 2015	$84,000	$82,000

7. At December 31, 2015, an analysis of payroll information shows salaries and wages of $12,200. The Salaries and Wages Payable account had a balance of $16,000 at December 31, 2015, which was unchanged from its balance at December 31, 2014.

8. A large piece of equipment was purchased on January 3, 2015, for $40,000 and was charged to Maintenance and Repairs Expense. The equipment is estimated to have a service life of 8 years and no residual value. Zarle normally uses the straight-line depreciation method for this type of equipment.

9. A $12,000 insurance premium paid on July 1, 2014, for a policy that expires on June 30, 2017, was charged to insurance expense.

10. A trademark was acquired at the beginning of 2014 for $50,000. No amortization has been recorded since its acquisition. The maximum allowable amortization period is 10 years.

Instructions

Assume the trial balance has been prepared but the books have not been closed for 2015. Assuming all amounts are material, prepare journal entries showing the adjustments that are required. (Ignore income tax considerations.)

 P22-8 (Comprehensive Error Analysis) On March 5, 2016, you were hired by Hemingway Inc., a closely held company, as a staff member of its newly created internal auditing department. While reviewing the company's records for 2014 and 2015, you discover that no adjustments have yet been made for the items listed below.

Items

1. Interest income of £14,100 was not accrued at the end of 2014. It was recorded when received in February 2015.

2. A computer costing £4,000 was expensed when purchased on July 1, 2014. It is expected to have a 4-year life with no residual value. The company typically uses straight-line depreciation for all fixed assets.

3. Research costs of £33,000 were incurred early in 2014. They were capitalized and were to be amortized over a 3-year period. Amortization of £11,000 was recorded for 2014 and £11,000 for 2015.

4. On January 2, 2014, Hemingway leased a building for 5 years at a monthly rental of £8,000. On that date, the company paid the following amounts, which were expensed when paid.

Security deposit	£20,000
First month's rent	8,000
Last month's rent	8,000
	£36,000

5. The company received £36,000 from a customer at the beginning of 2014 for services that it is to perform evenly over a 3-year period beginning in 2014. None of the amount received was reported as unearned revenue at the end of 2014.

6. Merchandise inventory costing £18,200 was in the warehouse at December 31, 2014, but was incorrectly omitted from the physical count at that date. The company uses the periodic inventory method.

Instructions

Indicate the effect of any errors on the net income figure reported on the income statement for the year ending December 31, 2014, and the retained earnings figure reported on the statement of financial position at December 31, 2015. Assume all amounts are material and ignore income tax effects. Using the following format, enter the appropriate dollar amounts in the appropriate columns. Consider each item independent of the other items. It is not necessary to total the columns on the grid.

	Net Income for 2014		Retained Earnings at 12/31/15	
Item	Understated	Overstated	Understated	Overstated

6 8 **P22-9 (Error Analysis)** Lowell Corporation has used the accrual basis of accounting for several years. A review of the records, however, indicates that some expenses and revenues have been handled on a cash basis because of errors made by an inexperienced bookkeeper. Income statements prepared by the bookkeeper reported €29,000 net income for 2014 and €37,000 net income for 2015. Further examination of the records reveals that the following items were handled improperly.

1. Rent was received from a tenant in December 2014. The amount, €1,000, was recorded as income at that time even though the rental pertained to 2015.

2. Salaries and wages payable on December 31 have been consistently omitted from the records of that date and have been entered as expenses when paid in the following year. The amounts of the accruals recorded in this manner were:

December 31, 2013	€1,100
December 31, 2014	1,200
December 31, 2015	940

3. Invoices for office supplies purchased have been charged to expense accounts when received. Inventories of supplies on hand at the end of each year have been ignored, and no entry has been made for them.

December 31, 2013	€1,300
December 31, 2014	940
December 31, 2015	1,420

Instructions

Prepare a schedule that will show the corrected net income for the years 2014 and 2015. All items listed should be labeled clearly. (Ignore income tax considerations.)

6 8 **P22-10 (Error Analysis and Correcting Entries)** You have been asked by a client to review the records of Roberts Company, a small manufacturer of precision tools and machines. Your client is interested in buying the business, and arrangements have been made for you to review the accounting records. Your examination reveals the following information.

1. Roberts Company commenced business on April 1, 2012, and has been reporting on a fiscal year ending March 31. The company has never been audited, but the annual statements prepared by the bookkeeper reflect the following income before closing and before deducting income taxes.

Year Ended March 31	Income Before Taxes
2013	$ 71,600
2014	111,400
2015	103,580

2. A relatively small number of machines have been shipped on consignment. These transactions have been recorded as ordinary sales and billed as such. On March 31 of each year, machines billed and in the hands of consignees amounted to:

2013	$6,500
2014	none
2015	5,590

Sales price was determined by adding 25% to cost. Assume that the consigned machines are sold the following year.

3. On March 30, 2014, two machines were shipped to a customer on a C.O.D. basis. The sale was not entered until April 5, 2014, when cash was received for $6,100. The machines were not included in the inventory at March 31, 2014. (Title passed on March 30, 2014.)

4. All machines are sold subject to a 5-year warranty. It is estimated that the expense ultimately to be incurred in connection with the warranty will amount to ½ of 1% of sales. The company has charged an expense account for warranty costs incurred.

Sales per books and warranty costs were as follows.

Year Ended March 31	Sales	Warranty Expense for Sales Made in			Total
		2013	2014	2015	
2013	$ 940,000	$760			$ 760
2014	1,010,000	360	$1,310		1,670
2015	1,795,000	320	1,620	$1,910	3,850

5. Bad debts have been recorded on a direct write-off basis. Experience of similar enterprises indicates that losses will approximate ¼ of 1% of sales. Bad debts written off were:

	Bad Debts Incurred on Sales Made in			
	2013	2014	2015	Total
2013	$750			$ 750
2014	800	$ 520		1,320
2015	350	1,800	$1,700	3,850

6. The bank deducts 6% on all contracts financed. Of this amount, ½% is placed in a reserve to the credit of Roberts Company, which is refunded to Roberts as finance contracts are paid in full. The reserve established by the bank has not been reflected in the books of Roberts. The excess of credits over debits (net increase) to the Dealer Fund Reserve account with Roberts on the books of the bank for each fiscal year were as follows.

2013	$ 3,000
2014	3,900
2015	5,100
	$12,000

7. Commissions on sales have been entered when paid. Commissions payable on March 31 of each year were as follows.

2013	$1,400
2014	900
2015	1,120

8. A review of the corporate minutes reveals the manager is entitled to a bonus of 1% of the income before deducting income taxes and the bonus. The bonuses have never been recorded or paid. (Use Salaries and Wages accounts.)

Instructions

(a) Present a schedule showing the revised income before income taxes for each of the years ended March 31, 2013, 2014, and 2015. (Make computations to the nearest whole dollar.)

(b) Prepare the journal entry or entries you would give the bookkeeper to correct the books. Assume the books have not yet been closed for the fiscal year ended March 31, 2015. Disregard correction of income taxes.

CONCEPTS FOR ANALYSIS

CA22-1 (Analysis of Various Accounting Changes and Errors) Joblonsky Inc. has recently hired a new independent auditor, Karen Ogleby, who says she wants "to get everything straightened out." Consequently, she has proposed the following accounting changes in connection with Joblonsky Inc.'s 2015 financial statements.

1. At December 31, 2014, the client had a receivable of €820,000 from Hendricks Inc. on its statement of financial position. Hendricks Inc. has gone bankrupt, and no recovery is expected. The client proposes to write off the receivable as a prior period item.

2. The client proposes the following changes in depreciation policies.
   (a) For office furniture and fixtures, it proposes to change from a 10-year useful life to an 8-year life. If this change had been made in prior years, retained earnings at December 31, 2014, would have been €250,000 less. The effect of the change on 2015 income alone is a reduction of €60,000.
   (b) For its equipment in the leasing division, the client proposes to adopt the sum-of-the-years'-digits depreciation method. The client had never used SYD before. The first year the client operated a leasing division was 2015. If straight-line depreciation were used, 2015 income would be €110,000 greater.

3. In preparing its 2014 statements, one of the client's bookkeepers overstated ending inventory by €235,000 because of a mathematical error. The client proposes to treat this item as a prior period adjustment.

4. In the past, the client has spread preproduction costs in its furniture division over 5 years. Because its latest furniture is of the "fad" type, it appears that the largest volume of sales will occur during the first 2 years after introduction. Consequently, the client proposes to amortize preproduction costs on a per-unit basis, which will result in expensing most of such costs during the first 2 years after the furniture's introduction. If the new accounting method had been used prior to 2015, retained earnings at December 31, 2014, would have been €375,000 less.

5. For the nursery division, the client proposes to switch from FIFO to average-cost inventories because it believes that average-cost will provide a better matching of current costs with revenues. The effect of making this change on 2015 earnings will be an increase of €320,000. The client says that the effect of the change on December 31, 2014, retained earnings cannot be determined.

6. To achieve a better matching of revenues and expenses in its building construction division, the client proposes to switch from the cost-recovery method of accounting to the percentage-of-completion method. Had the percentage-of-completion method been employed in all prior years, retained earnings at December 31, 2014, would have been €1,075,000 greater.

Instructions
(a) For each of the changes described above, decide whether:
   (1) The change involves an accounting policy, accounting estimate, or correction of an error.
   (2) Restatement of opening retained earnings is required.
(b) What would be the proper adjustment to the December 31, 2014, retained earnings?

CA22-2 (Analysis of Various Accounting Changes and Errors) Various types of accounting changes can affect the financial statements of a business differently. Assume that the following list describes changes that have a material effect on the financial statements for the current year of your business.

1. A change from the cost-recovery method to the percentage-of-completion method of accounting for long-term construction-type contracts.

2. A change in the estimated useful life of previously recorded fixed assets as a result of newly acquired information.

3. A change from deferring and amortizing preproduction costs to recording such costs as an expense when incurred because future benefits of the costs have become doubtful. The new accounting method was adopted in recognition of the change in estimated future benefits.

4. A change from including the employer share of taxes with payroll tax expenses to including it with "Retirement benefits" on the income statement.

5. Correction of a mathematical error in inventory pricing made in a prior period.

6. A change in the method of accounting for leases for tax purposes to conform with the financial accounting method. As a result, both deferred and current taxes payable changed substantially.

7. A change from the FIFO method of inventory pricing to the average-cost method of inventory pricing.

Instructions

Identify the type of change that is described in each item above and indicate whether the prior year's financial statements should be retrospectively adjusted or restated when presented in comparative form with the current year's financial statements.

CA22-3 (Analysis of Three Accounting Changes and Errors) Listed below are three independent, unrelated sets of facts relating to accounting changes.

Situation 1: Sanford Company is in the process of having its first audit. The company has used the cash basis of accounting for revenue recognition. Sanford president, B. J. Jimenez, is willing to change to the accrual method of revenue recognition.

Situation 2: Hopkins Co. decides in January 2015 to change from FIFO to weighted-average pricing for its inventories.

Situation 3: Marshall Co. determined that the depreciable lives of its fixed assets are too long at present to fairly match the cost of the fixed assets with the revenue produced. The company decided at the beginning of the current year to reduce the depreciable lives of all of its existing fixed assets by 5 years.

Instructions

For each of the situations described, provide the information indicated below.

(a) Type of accounting change.
(b) Manner of reporting the change under IFRS, including a discussion, where applicable, of how amounts are computed.
(c) Effect of the change on the statement of financial position and income statement.

CA22-4 (Analysis of Various Accounting Changes and Errors) Katherine Irving, controller of Lotan Corp., is aware that a pronouncement on accounting changes has been issued. After reading the pronouncement, she is confused about what action should be taken on the following items related to Lotan Corp. for the year 2015.

1. In 2015, Lotan decided to change its policy on accounting for certain marketing costs. Previously, the company had chosen to defer and amortize all marketing costs over at least 5 years because Lotan believed that a return on these expenditures did not occur immediately. Recently, however, the time differential has considerably shortened, and Lotan is now expensing the marketing costs as incurred.

2. In 2015, the company examined its entire policy relating to the depreciation of plant equipment. Plant equipment had normally been depreciated over a 15-year period, but recent experience has indicated that the company was using too short a period in its estimates and that the assets should be depreciated over a 20-year period.

3. One division of Lotan Corp., Hawthorne Co., has consistently shown an increasing net income from period to period. On closer examination of its operating statement, it is noted that bad debt expense and inventory obsolescence charges are much lower than in other divisions. In discussing this with the controller of this division, it has been learned that the controller has increased his net income each period by knowingly making low estimates related to the write-off of receivables and inventory.

4. In 2015, the company purchased new machinery that should increase production dramatically. The company has decided to depreciate this machinery on an accelerated basis even though other machinery is depreciated on a straight-line basis.

5. All equipment sold by Lotan is subject to a 3-year warranty. It has been estimated that the expense ultimately to be incurred on these machines is 1% of sales. In 2015, because of a production breakthrough, it is now estimated that ½ of 1% of sales is sufficient. In 2013 and 2014, warranty expense was computed as $64,000 and $70,000, respectively. The company now believes that these warranty costs should be reduced by 50%.

6. In 2015, the company decided to change its method of inventory pricing from average-cost to the FIFO method. The effect of this change on prior years is to increase 2013 income by $65,000 and increase 2014 income by $20,000.

Instructions

Katherine Irving has come to you, as her accountant, for advice about the situations above. Prepare a report, indicating the appropriate accounting treatment that should be given each of these situations.

CA22-5 (Changes in Estimate) As a public accountant, you have been contacted by Joe Davison, CEO of Sports-Pro Athletics, Inc., a manufacturer of a variety of athletic equipment. He has asked you how to account for the following changes.

1. Sports-Pro appropriately changed its depreciation method for its production machinery from the double-declining-balance method to the production method effective January 1, 2015.

2. Effective January 1, 2015, Sports-Pro appropriately changed the residual values used in computing depreciation for its office equipment.

Instructions

Write a 1–1.5 page letter to Joe Davison, explaining how each of the above changes should be presented in the December 31, 2015, financial statements.

CA22-6 (Change in Estimate) Mike Crane, audit senior of a large public accounting firm, has just been assigned to the Frost Corporation's annual audit engagement. Frost has been a client of Crane's firm for many years. Frost is a fast-growing business in the commercial construction industry. In reviewing the fixed asset ledger, Crane discovered a series of unusual accounting changes, in which the useful lives of assets, depreciated using the straight-line method, were substantially lowered near the midpoint of the original estimate. For example, the useful life of one dump truck was changed from 10 to 6 years during its fifth year of service. Upon further investigation, Mike was told by Kevin James, Frost's accounting manager, "I don't really see your problem. After all, it's perfectly legal to change an accounting estimate. Besides, our CEO likes to see big earnings!"

Instructions

Answer the following questions.

(a) What are the ethical issues concerning Frost's practice of changing the useful lives of fixed assets?
(b) Who could be harmed by Frost's unusual accounting changes?
(c) What should Crane do in this situation?

USING YOUR JUDGMENT

FINANCIAL REPORTING

Financial Reporting Problem

Marks and Spencer plc (M&S)

The financial statements of **M&S** (GBR) are presented in Appendix A. The complete annual report, including the notes to the financial statements, is available online.

Instructions

Refer to M&S's financial statements and the accompanying notes to answer the following questions.

(a) Were there changes in accounting policies reported by M&S during the two years covered by its income statements (2012–2013)? If so, describe the nature of the change and the year of change.
(b) What types of estimates did M&S discuss in 2013?

Comparative Analysis Case

adidas and Puma

The financial statements of **adidas** (DEU) and **Puma** (DEU) are presented in Appendices B and C, respectively. The complete annual reports, including the notes to the financial statements, are available online.

Instructions

Use the companies' financial information to answer the following questions.

(a) Identify the changes in accounting policies reported by Puma during the 2 years covered by its income statements (2011–2012). Describe the nature of the change and the year of change.
(b) Identify the changes in accounting policies reported by adidas during the 2 years covered by its income statements (2011–2012). Describe the nature of the change and the year of change.
(c) For each change in accounting policy by adidas and Puma, identify, if possible, the cumulative effect of each change on prior years and the effect on operating results in the year of change.

Accounting, Analysis, and Principles

In preparation for significant international operations, ABC Co. has adopted a plan to gradually shift to the same accounting policies as used by its international competitors. Part of this plan includes a switch from average-cost inventory accounting to FIFO. ABC decides to make the switch to FIFO at January 1, 2015. The following data pertains to ABC's 2015 financial statements.

Sales	$550
Inventory purchases	350
12/31/15 inventory (using FIFO)	580
Compensation expense	17

All sales and purchases were with cash as were all of 2015's compensation expense (ignore taxes). ABC's plant, property, and equipment cost $400 and has an estimated useful life of 10 years with no residual value.

ABC Co. reported the following for fiscal 2014 (amounts are in millions).

ABC CO.
STATEMENT OF FINANCIAL POSITION
AT DECEMBER 31, 2014

	2014	2013		2014	2013
Plant, property, and equipment	$ 400	$ 400	Retained earnings	$ 685	$ 540
Accumulated depreciation	(80)	(40)	Share capital	500	500
Inventory	500	480			
Cash	365	200			
Total assets	$1,185	$1,040	Total equity	$1,185	$1,040

ABC CO.
INCOME STATEMENT
FOR THE YEAR ENDED DECEMBER 31, 2014

	2014
Sales	$ 500
Cost of goods sold	(300)
Depreciation expense	(40)
Compensation expense	(15)
Net income	$145

Summary of Significant Accounting Policies

Inventory: The company accounts for inventory by the average-cost method. The current cost of the company's inventory, which approximates FIFO, was $60 and $50 higher at the end of fiscal 2014 and 2013, respectively, than those reported in the statement of financial position.

Accounting

Prepare ABC's December 31, 2015, statement of financial position and an income statement for the year ended December 31, 2015. In columns beside 2015's numbers, include 2014's numbers *as they would appear in the 2015 financial statements* for comparative purposes.

Analysis

Compute ABC's inventory turnover for 2014 under both average-cost and FIFO. Assume averages are equal to year-end balances. What causes the differences in this ratio between average-cost and FIFO?

Principles

Briefly explain, in terms of the policies discussed in Chapter 22, why IFRS requires that companies that change accounting policies present restated prior year's financial statement data.

IFRS BRIDGE TO THE PROFESSION

Professional Research

As part of the year-end accounting process and review of operating policies, Cullen Co. is considering a change in the accounting for its equipment from the straight-line method to an accelerated method. Your supervisor wonders how the company will report this change in accounting. It has been a few years since he took intermediate accounting, and he cannot remember whether this change would be treated in a retrospective or prospective manner. Your supervisor wants you to research the authoritative guidance on a change in accounting policy related to depreciation methods.

Instructions

Access the IFRS authoritative literature at the IASB website (*http://eifrs.iasb.org/*) (you may register for free eIFRS access at this site). When you have accessed the documents, you can use the search tool in your Internet browser to respond to the following questions. (Provide paragraph citations.)

    (a) What are the accounting and reporting guidelines for a change in accounting related to depreciation methods?

    (b) What are the conditions that justify a change in depreciation method, as contemplated by Cullen Co.?

Professional Simulation

In this simulation, you are asked questions about changes in accounting policy. Prepare responses to all parts.

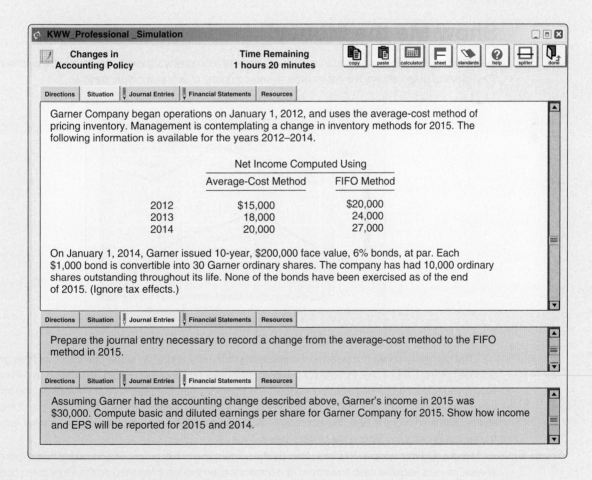

KWW_Professional _Simulation

Changes in Accounting Policy | Time Remaining 1 hours 20 minutes

copy | paste | calculator | sheet | standards | help | spliter | done

Directions | Situation | Journal Entries | Financial Statements | Resources

Garner Company began operations on January 1, 2012, and uses the average-cost method of pricing inventory. Management is contemplating a change in inventory methods for 2015. The following information is available for the years 2012–2014.

	Net Income Computed Using	
	Average-Cost Method	FIFO Method
2012	$15,000	$20,000
2013	18,000	24,000
2014	20,000	27,000

On January 1, 2014, Garner issued 10-year, $200,000 face value, 6% bonds, at par. Each $1,000 bond is convertible into 30 Garner ordinary shares. The company has had 10,000 ordinary shares outstanding throughout its life. None of the bonds have been exercised as of the end of 2015. (Ignore tax effects.)

Directions | Situation | Journal Entries | Financial Statements | Resources

Prepare the journal entry necessary to record a change from the average-cost method to the FIFO method in 2015.

Directions | Situation | Journal Entries | Financial Statements | Resources

Assuming Garner had the accounting change described above, Garner's income in 2015 was $30,000. Compute basic and diluted earnings per share for Garner Company for 2015. Show how income and EPS will be reported for 2015 and 2014.

Remember to check the book's companion website, at www.wiley.com/college/kieso, to find additional resources for this chapter.

23 | Statement of Cash Flows

LEARNING OBJECTIVES

After studying this chapter, you should be able to:

1 Describe the purpose of the statement of cash flows.

2 Identify the major classifications of cash flows.

3 Prepare a statement of cash flows.

4 Differentiate between net income and net cash flow from operating activities.

5 Determine net cash flows from investing and financing activities.

6 Identify sources of information for a statement of cash flows.

7 Contrast the direct and indirect methods of calculating net cash flow from operating activities.

8 Discuss special problems in preparing a statement of cash flows.

9 Explain the use of a worksheet in preparing a statement of cash flows.

Show Me the Money!

Investors usually look to net income as a key indicator of a company's financial health and future prospects. The following graph shows the net income of one company over a seven-year period.

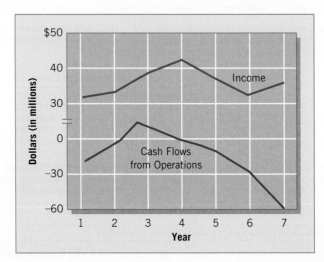

The company showed a pattern of consistent profitability and even some periods of income growth. Between years 1 and 4, net income for this company grew by 32 percent, from $31 million to $41 million. Would you expect its profitability to continue? The company had consistently paid dividends and interest. Would you expect it to continue to do so? Investors answered these questions by buying the company's shares. Eighteen months later, this company—**W. T. Grant** (USA)—filed for bankruptcy, in what was then the largest bankruptcy filing in the United States.

How could this happen? As indicated by the bottom line in the graph, the company had experienced several years of negative cash flows from its operations even though it reported profits. How can a company have negative cash flows while reporting profits? The answer lays partly in the fact that W. T. Grant was having trouble collecting the receivables from its credit sales, causing cash flow to be less than net income. Investors who analyzed the cash flows would have been likely to find an early warning signal of W. T. Grant's operating problems.

Investors can also look to cash flow information to sniff out companies that can be good buys. As one analyst stated when it comes to valuing shares: "Show me the money!" Here's the thinking behind that statement. Start with the "cash flows from operations" reported in the statement of cash flows, which (as you will learn in this chapter) consists of net income with non-cash charges (like depreciation and deferred taxes) added back and cash-draining events (like an inventory pile-up) taken out. Now subtract capital expenditures and dividends. What you're left with is free cash flow (as discussed in Chapter 5).

Many analysts like companies trading at low multiples of their free cash flow—low, that is, in relation to rivals today or the same company in past years. Why? They know that reported earnings can be misleading. Case in point: Computer-game firm **Activision Blizzard** (USA) reported net income of $113 million in a recent year. But it did better than that. It took in an additional $300 million, mostly for subscriptions to online multiplayer games. It gets the cash now but records the revenue only over time, as the subscriptions run out. A couple of investment houses put these shares on their buy list on the strength of its cash flows. So watch cash flow—to get an indicator of companies headed for trouble, as well as companies that may be undervalued.

Sources: Adapted from James A. Largay III and Clyde P. Stickney, "Cash Flows, Ratio Analysis, and the W. T. Grant Company Bankruptcy," *Financial Analysts Journal* (July–August 1980), p. 51; and D. Fisher, "Cash Doesn't Lie," *Forbes* (April 12, 2010), pp. 52–55.

CONCEPTUAL FOCUS

> See the **Underlying Concepts** on pages 1182 and 1210.
> Read the **Evolving Issue** on page 1203 for a discussion of the direct versus indirect method.

INTERNATIONAL FOCUS

> Read the **Global Accounting Insights** on pages 1220–1221 for a discussion of non-IFRS requirements for the statement of cash flows.

PREVIEW OF CHAPTER 23

As the opening story indicates, examination of **W. T. Grant**'s cash flows from operations would have shown the financial inflexibility that eventually caused the company's bankruptcy. This chapter explains the main components of a statement of cash flows and the types of information it provides. The content and organization of the chapter are as follows.

Statement of Cash Flows

Preparation of the Statement	Illustrations—Tax Consultants Inc.	Special Problems in Statement Preparation	Use of a Worksheet
• Usefulness of statement • Classification of cash flows • Cash and cash equivalents • Format of statement • Steps in preparation	• Change in cash • Operating cash flows • Cash flows from investing and financing • Statement of cash flows—2015 • Illustrations—2016 and 2017 • Sources of information • Direct method	• Adjustments to net income • Accounts receivable (net) • Other working capital changes • Net losses • Disclosures	• Preparation of worksheet • Analysis of transactions • Preparation of final statement

PREPARATION OF THE STATEMENT OF CASH FLOWS

LEARNING OBJECTIVE 1

Describe the purpose of the statement of cash flows.

I F R S

See the Authoritative Literature section (page 1223).

The primary purpose of the **statement of cash flows** is to provide information about a company's cash receipts and cash payments during a period. A secondary objective is to provide cash-basis information about the company's operating, investing, and financing activities. **[1]** The statement of cash flows therefore reports cash receipts, cash payments, and net change in cash resulting from a company's operating, investing, and financing activities during a period. Its format reconciles the beginning and ending cash balances for the period.

Usefulness of the Statement of Cash Flows

The statement of cash flows provides information to help investors, creditors, and others assess the following:

 Underlying Concepts

Reporting information in the statement of cash flows contributes to meeting the objective of financial reporting.

1. *The entity's ability to generate future cash flows.* A primary objective of financial reporting is to provide information with which to predict the amounts, timing, and uncertainty of future cash flows. By examining relationships between items such as sales and net cash flow from operating activities, or net cash flow from operating activities and increases or decreases in cash, it is possible to better predict the future cash flows than is possible using accrual-basis data alone.

2. *The entity's ability to pay dividends and meet obligations.* Simply put, cash is essential. Without adequate cash, a company cannot pay employees, settle debts, pay out dividends, or acquire equipment. A statement of cash flows indicates where the company's cash comes from and how the company uses its cash. Employees, creditors, shareholders, and customers should be particularly interested in this statement because it alone shows the flows of cash in a business.

3. *The reasons for the difference between net income and net cash flow from operating activities.* The net income number is important: It provides information on the performance of a company from one period to another. But some people are critical of accrual-basis net income because companies must make estimates to arrive at it. Such is not the case with cash. Thus, as the opening story showed, financial statement readers can benefit from knowing why a company's net income and net cash flow from operating activities differ and can assess for themselves the reliability of the income number.

4. *The cash and non-cash investing and financing transactions during the period.* Besides operating activities, companies undertake investing and financing transactions. *Investing* activities include the purchase and sale of assets other than a company's products or services. *Financing* activities include borrowings and repayments of borrowings, investments by owners, and distributions to owners. By examining a company's investing and financing activities, a financial statement reader can better understand why assets and liabilities increased or decreased during the period. For example, by reading the statement of cash flows, the reader might find answers to following questions:

   • Why did cash decrease for **Aixtron Aktiengesellschaft** (DEU) when it reported net income for the year?

   • How much did **Telefónica, S.A.** (ESP) spend on property, plant, and equipment, and intangible assets last year?

- Did dividends paid by **BP plc** (GBR) increase last year?
- How much money did **Coca-Cola** (USA) borrow last year?
- How much cash did **Delhaize Group** (BEL) use to repurchase ordinary shares?

Classification of Cash Flows

The statement of cash flows classifies cash receipts and cash payments by operating, investing, and financing activities. Transactions and other events characteristic of each kind of activity are as follows. **[2]**

2 **LEARNING OBJECTIVE**
Identify the major classifications of cash flows.

1. **Operating activities** involve the cash effects of transactions that enter into the determination of net income, such as cash receipts from sales of goods and services, and cash payments to suppliers and employees for acquisitions of inventory and expenses. The amount of cash flows arising from operating activities is a key indicator of the extent to which the operations of the entity have generated sufficient cash flows to repay loans, maintain the operating capability of the entity, pay dividends, and make new investments without recourse to external sources of financing.

2. **Investing activities** generally involve non-current assets and include (a) making and collecting loans, and (b) acquiring and disposing of investments and productive long-lived assets. The separate disclosure of cash flows arising from investing activities is important because the cash flows represent the extent to which expenditures have been made for resources intended to generate future income and cash flows.

3. **Financing activities** involve liability and equity items and include (a) obtaining cash from creditors and repaying the amounts borrowed, and (b) obtaining capital from owners and providing them with a return on, and a return of, their investment. The separate disclosure of cash flows arising from financing activities is important because it is useful in predicting claims on future cash flows by providers of capital to a company.

Illustration 23-1 (page 1184) classifies the typical cash receipts and payments of a company according to operating, investing, and financing activities. The operating activities category is the most important. It shows the cash provided by company operations. This source of cash is generally considered to be the best measure of a company's ability to generate enough cash to continue as a going concern.

Note the following general guidelines about the classification of cash flows.

1. Operating activities involve income statement items.
2. Investing activities involve cash flows resulting from changes in investments and other non-current asset items.
3. Financing activities involve cash flows resulting from changes in equity and non-current liability items.

IFRS allows some flexibility regarding the classification of certain items. Interest and dividends paid can be classified as either operating or financing, depending on what treatment the company thinks is most appropriate. Similarly, interest and dividends received can be classified as either operating or investing. Taxes paid are classified as operating except in circumstances where they can be identified with specific investing or financing activities. In order to limit the complexity of our presentation and to avoid ambiguity in assignment material, in Illustration 23-1 we have identified specific

ILLUSTRATION 23-1
Classification of Typical
Cash Inflows and
Outflows

Operating	
Cash inflows	
From sales of goods or services.	
From returns on loans (interest) and on equity securities (dividends).	Income Statement Items
Cash outflows	
To suppliers for inventory.	
To employees for services.	
To government for taxes.	
To lenders for interest.	
To others for expenses.	
Investing	
Cash inflows	
From sale of property, plant, and equipment.	
From sale of debt or equity securities of other entities.	Generally Long-Term Asset Items
From collection of principal on loans to other entities.	
Cash outflows	
To purchase property, plant, and equipment.	
To purchase debt or equity securities of other entities.	
To make loans to other entities.	
Financing	
Cash inflows	
From sale of equity securities.	Generally Long-Term Liability and Equity Items
From issuance of debt (bonds and notes).	
Cash outflows	
To shareholders as dividends.	
To redeem long-term debt or reacquire share capital.	

treatment for each of these items rather than allowing choices. *All assignment material is based on this treatment.*[1]

Also, companies classify some cash flows relating to operating activities as investing or financing activities. For example, a company classifies the total cash received from the sale of property, plant, and equipment as an investing activity. Therefore, sales of those assets are not considered operating activities. Because of this (as is discussed more fully later in the chapter), companies must eliminate any gains or losses arising from the disposal of these assets to arrive at net cash flow from operating activities. Likewise, the payment to extinguish debt is a financing cash flow and should be classified as such. Any gain or loss related to the extinguishment is eliminated from net cash provided by operating activities.

Cash and Cash Equivalents

The basis recommended by the IASB for the statement of cash flows is actually "cash and cash equivalents." **Cash equivalents** are short-term, highly liquid investments that are both:

• Readily convertible to known amounts of cash, and
• So near their maturity that they present insignificant risk of changes in value (e.g., due to changes in interest rates).

Generally, only investments with original maturities of three months or less qualify under this definition. Examples of cash equivalents are Treasury bills, commercial paper, and money market funds purchased with cash that is in excess of immediate needs.

---

[1]*IFRS Accounting Trends and Techniques—2012–2013* indicates that most companies surveyed report income taxes paid or received, interest received and paid, and dividends received as operating activities. However, most companies show dividends paid as a financing activity. These results are consistent with how this information is reported in Illustration 23-1.

Equity investments are excluded from cash equivalents unless they are, in substance, cash equivalents. Although we use the term "cash" throughout our discussion and illustrations, we mean cash and cash equivalents when reporting the cash flows and the net increase or decrease in cash. **[3]**

What do the numbers mean? HOW'S MY CASH FLOW?

To evaluate overall cash flows, it is useful to understand where in the product life cycle a company is. Generally, companies move through several stages of development, which have implications for cash flows. As the graph below shows, the pattern of cash flows from operating, financing, and investing activities will vary depending on the stage of the product life cycle.

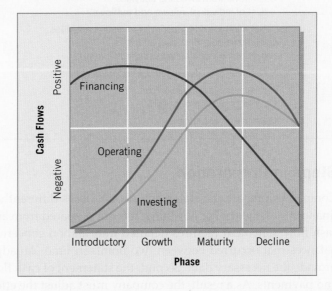

In the introductory phase, the product is likely not generating much revenue (net operating cash flow is negative). Because the company is making heavy investments to get a product off the ground, cash flow from investment is negative, and financing cash flows are positive.

As the product moves to the growth and maturity phases, these cash flow relationships reverse. The product generates more cash flows from operations, which can be used to cover investments needed to support the product, and less cash is needed from financing. So are negative operating cash flows bad? Not always. It depends on the product life cycle.

Source: Adapted from Paul D. Kimmel, Jerry J. Weygandt, and Donald E. Kieso, *Financial Accounting: Tools for Business Decision Making*, 7th ed. (New York: John Wiley & Sons, 2013), p. 631.

Format of the Statement of Cash Flows

The three activities we discussed above constitute the general format of the statement of cash flows. The operating activities section always appears first. It is followed by the investing activities section and then the financing activities section.

A company reports the individual inflows and outflows from investing and financing activities separately. That is, a company reports them gross, not netted against one another. Thus, a cash outflow from the purchase of property is reported separately from the cash inflow from the sale of property. Similarly, a cash inflow from the issuance of debt is reported separately from the cash outflow from its retirement.

The net increase or decrease in cash reported during the period should reconcile the beginning and ending cash balances as reported in the comparative statements of financial position. The general format of the statement of cash flows presents the results of the three activities discussed previously—operating, investing, and financing. Illustration 23-2 shows a widely used form of the statement of cash flows.

ILLUSTRATION 23-2
Format of the Statement
of Cash Flows

COMPANY NAME
STATEMENT OF CASH FLOWS
PERIOD COVERED

Cash flows from operating activities		
Net income		XXX
Adjustments to reconcile net income to net		
cash provided (used) by operating activities:		
(List of individual items)	XX	XX
Net cash provided (used) by operating activities		XXX
Cash flows from investing activities		
(List of individual inflows and outflows)	XX	
Net cash provided (used) by investing activities		XXX
Cash flows from financing activities		
(List of individual inflows and outflows)	XX	
Net cash provided (used) by financing activities		XXX
Net increase (decrease) in cash		XXX
Cash at beginning of period		XXX
Cash at end of period		XXX

Steps in Preparation

Companies prepare the statement of cash flows differently from the three other basic financial statements. For one thing, it is not prepared from an adjusted trial balance. The cash flow statement requires detailed information concerning the changes in account balances that occurred between two points in time. An adjusted trial balance will not provide the necessary data. Second, the statement of cash flows deals with cash receipts and payments. As a result, the company must adjust the effects of the use of accrual accounting to determine cash flows. The information to prepare this statement usually comes from three sources:

1. **Comparative statements of financial position** provide the amount of the changes in assets, liabilities, and equities from the beginning to the end of the period.
2. **Current income statement** data help determine the amount of net cash provided by or used by operations during the period.
3. **Selected transaction data** from the general ledger provide additional detailed information needed to determine how the company provided or used cash during the period.

Preparing the statement of cash flows from the data sources above involves three major steps:

Step 1. *Determine the change in cash.* This procedure is straightforward. A company can easily compute the difference between the beginning and the ending cash balance from examining its comparative statements of financial position.

Step 2. *Determine the net cash flow from operating activities.* This procedure is complex. It involves analyzing not only the current year's income statement but also comparative statements of financial position as well as selected transaction data.

Step 3. *Determine net cash flows from investing and financing activities.* A company must analyze all other changes in the statement of financial position accounts to determine their effects on cash.

On the following pages, we work through these three steps in the process of preparing the statement of cash flows for Tax Consultants Inc. over several years.

ILLUSTRATIONS—TAX CONSULTANTS INC.

We show the steps in preparing the statement of cash flows using data for Tax Consultants Inc. To begin, we use the **first year of operations** for Tax Consultants Inc. The company started on January 1, 2015, when it issued 60,000 ordinary shares of $1 par value for $60,000 cash. The company rented its office space, furniture, and equipment, and performed tax consulting services throughout the first year. The comparative statements of financial position at the beginning and end of the year 2015 appear in Illustration 23-3.

3 LEARNING OBJECTIVE

Prepare a statement of cash flows.

TAX CONSULTANTS INC. COMPARATIVE STATEMENTS OF FINANCIAL POSITION			
Assets	Dec. 31, 2015	Jan. 1, 2015	Change Increase/Decrease
Accounts receivable	$36,000	$-0-	$36,000 Increase
Cash	49,000	-0-	49,000 Increase
Total	$85,000	$-0-	
Equity and Liabilities			
Ordinary shares ($1 par)	$60,000	$-0-	$60,000 Increase
Retained earnings	20,000	-0-	20,000 Increase
Accounts payable	5,000	-0-	5,000 Increase
Total	$85,000	$-0-	

ILLUSTRATION 23-3
Comparative Statements of Financial Position, Tax Consultants Inc., Year 1

Illustration 23-4 shows the income statement and additional information for Tax Consultants.

TAX CONSULTANTS INC. INCOME STATEMENT FOR THE YEAR ENDED DECEMBER 31, 2015	
Revenues	$125,000
Operating expenses	85,000
Income before income taxes	40,000
Income tax expense	6,000
Net income	$ 34,000

Additional Information:
Examination of selected data indicates that a dividend of $14,000 was declared and paid during the year.

ILLUSTRATION 23-4
Income Statement, Tax Consultants Inc., Year 1

Step 1: Determine the Change in Cash

To prepare a statement of cash flows, the first step is to **determine the change in cash**. This is a simple computation. Tax Consultants had no cash on hand at the beginning of the year 2015. It had $49,000 on hand at the end of 2015. Thus, cash changed (increased) in 2015 by $49,000.

Step 2: Determine Net Cash Flow from Operating Activities

To determine net cash flow from operating activities,[2] companies adjust net income in numerous ways. A useful starting point is to understand why net income must be converted to net cash provided by operating activities.

Under IFRS, most companies use the accrual basis of accounting. As you have learned, this basis requires that companies record revenue when they satisfy performance obligations and record expenses when incurred. Revenues may include credit sales for which the company has not yet collected cash. Expenses incurred may include some items that the company has not yet paid in cash. Thus, under the accrual basis of accounting, net income is not the same as net cash flow from operating activities.

To arrive at net cash flow from operating activities, a company must determine revenues and expenses on a **cash basis**. **It does this by eliminating the effects of income statement transactions that do not result in an increase or decrease in cash.** Illustration 23-5 shows the relationship between net income and net cash flow from operating activities.

ILLUSTRATION 23-5
Net Income versus
Net Cash Flow from
Operating Activities

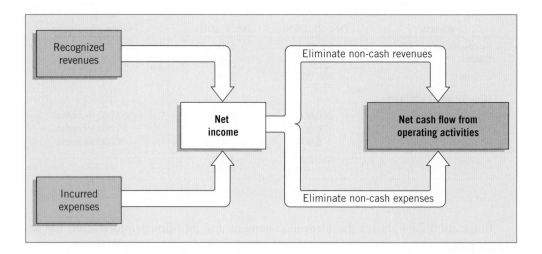

In this chapter, we use the term net income to refer to accrual-based net income. A company may convert net income to net cash flow from operating activities through either a direct method or an indirect method. Due to its widespread use in practice, in the following sections we illustrate use of the indirect method. Later in the chapter, we describe the direct method and discuss the advantages and disadvantages of the two methods.

The indirect method (or reconciliation method) starts with net income and converts it to net cash flow from operating activities. In other words, **the indirect method adjusts net income for items that affected reported net income but did not affect cash.** To compute net cash flow from operating activities, a company adds back non-cash charges in the income statement to net income and deducts non-cash credits. We explain the two adjustments to net income for Tax Consultants, namely, the increases in accounts receivable and accounts payable, as follows.

Increase in Accounts Receivable—Indirect Method

Tax Consultants' accounts receivable increased by $36,000 (from $0 to $36,000) during the year. For Tax Consultants, this means that cash receipts were $36,000 lower than

---

[2]"Net cash flow from operating activities" is a generic phrase, replaced in the statement of cash flows with either "Net cash provided by operating activities" if operations increase cash, or "Net cash used by operating activities" if operations decrease cash.

revenues. The Accounts Receivable account in Illustration 23-6 shows that Tax Consultants had $125,000 in revenues (as reported on the income statement), but it collected only $89,000 in cash.

ILLUSTRATION 23-6
Analysis of Accounts
Receivable

Accounts Receivable			
1/1/15	Balance	–0–	Receipts from customer	89,000
	Revenues	125,000		
12/31/15	Balance	36,000		

As shown in Illustration 23-7, to adjust net income to net cash provided by operating activities, Tax Consultants must deduct the increase of $36,000 in accounts receivable from net income. When the Accounts Receivable balance *decreases*, cash receipts are higher than revenue recognized under the accrual basis. Therefore, the company adds to net income the amount of the decrease in accounts receivable to arrive at net cash provided by operating activities.

Increase in Accounts Payable—Indirect Method

When accounts payable increase during the year, expenses on an accrual basis exceed those on a cash basis. Why? Because Tax Consultants incurred expenses, but some of the expenses are not yet paid. To convert net income to net cash flow from operating activities, Tax Consultants must add back the increase of $5,000 in accounts payable to net income.

As a result of the accounts receivable and accounts payable adjustments, Tax Consultants determines net cash provided by operating activities is $3,000 for the year 2015. Illustration 23-7 shows this computation.

Net income		$ 34,000
Adjustments to reconcile net income to net cash provided by operating activities:		
Increase in accounts receivable	$(36,000)	
Increase in accounts payable	5,000	(31,000)
Net cash provided by operating activities		$ 3,000

Step 3: Determine Net Cash Flows from Investing and Financing Activities

After Tax Consultants has computed the net cash provided by operating activities, the next step is to determine whether any other changes in the statement of financial position accounts caused an increase or decrease in cash.

For example, an examination of the remaining statement of financial position accounts for Tax Consultants shows increases in both ordinary shares and retained earnings. The Share Capital—Ordinary increase of $60,000 resulted from the issuance of ordinary shares for cash. The issuance of ordinary shares is reported in the statement of cash flows as a receipt of cash from a financing activity.

Two items caused the retained earnings increase of $20,000:

1. Net income of $34,000 increased retained earnings.
2. Declaration of $14,000 of dividends decreased retained earnings.

5 LEARNING OBJECTIVE
Determine net cash flows from investing and financing activities.

Tax Consultants has converted net income into net cash flow from operating activities, as explained earlier. The additional data indicate that it paid the dividend. Thus, the company reports the dividend payment as a cash outflow, classified as a financing activity.

Statement of Cash Flows—2015

We are now ready to prepare the statement of cash flows. The statement starts with the operating activities section. Tax Consultants may use either the direct or indirect method to report net cash flow from operating activities.

The IASB **encourages** the use of the direct method over the indirect method. **[4]** If a company uses the indirect method, it can either report the reconciliation within the statement of cash flows or can provide it in a separate schedule, with the statement of cash flows reporting only the **net** cash flow from operating activities. Throughout this chapter, we use the indirect method, which is also used more extensively in practice.[3]

Illustration 23-8 shows the statement of cash flows for Tax Consultants Inc., for year 1 (2015).

ILLUSTRATION 23-8
Statement of Cash Flows,
Tax Consultants Inc.,
Year 1

TAX CONSULTANTS INC.
STATEMENT OF CASH FLOWS
FOR THE YEAR ENDED DECEMBER 31, 2015
INCREASE (DECREASE) IN CASH

Cash flows from operating activities		
Net income		$ 34,000
Adjustments to reconcile net income to net cash provided by operating activities:		
Increase in accounts receivable	$(36,000)	
Increase in accounts payable	5,000	(31,000)
Net cash provided by operating activities		3,000
Cash flows from financing activities		
Issuance of ordinary shares	60,000	
Payment of cash dividends	(14,000)	
Net cash provided by financing activities		46,000
Net increase in cash		49,000
Cash, January 1, 2015		–0–
Cash, December 31, 2015		$ 49,000

As indicated, the $60,000 increase in ordinary shares results in a financing-activity cash inflow. The payment of $14,000 in cash dividends is a financing-activity outflow of cash. The $49,000 increase in cash reported in the statement of cash flows agrees with the increase of $49,000 shown in the comparative statements of financial position (in Illustration 23-3 on page 1187) as the change in the Cash account.

Illustration—2016

Tax Consultants Inc. continued to grow and prosper in its second year of operations. The company purchased land, building, and equipment, and revenues and net income increased substantially over the first year. Illustrations 23-9 and 23-10 present information related to the second year of operations for Tax Consultants Inc.

---

[3]*IFRS Accounting Trends and Techniques—2012–2013* reports that out of its 175 surveyed companies, 151 used the indirect method and 23 used the direct method. One company did not provide a statement of cash flows. *In doing homework assignments, you should follow instructions for use of either the direct or indirect method.*

ILLUSTRATION 23-9
Comparative Statements
of Financial Position, Tax
Consultants Inc., Year 2

TAX CONSULTANTS INC.
COMPARATIVE STATEMENTS OF FINANCIAL POSITION
AS OF DECEMBER 31

Assets	2016	2015	Change Increase/Decrease
Land	$ 70,000	$ –0–	$ 70,000 Increase
Buildings	200,000	–0–	200,000 Increase
Accumulated depreciation—buildings	(11,000)	–0–	11,000 Increase
Equipment	68,000	–0–	68,000 Increase
Accumulated depreciation—equipment	(10,000)	–0–	10,000 Increase
Accounts receivable	26,000	36,000	10,000 Decrease
Prepaid expenses	6,000	–0–	6,000 Increase
Cash	37,000	49,000	12,000 Decrease
Total	$386,000	$ 85,000	
Equity and Liabilities			
Share capital—ordinary ($1 par)	$ 60,000	$ 60,000	$ –0–
Retained earnings	136,000	20,000	116,000 Increase
Bonds payable	150,000	–0–	150,000 Increase
Accounts payable	40,000	5,000	35,000 Increase
Total	$386,000	$ 85,000	

ILLUSTRATION 23-10
Income Statement, Tax
Consultants Inc., Year 2

TAX CONSULTANTS INC.
INCOME STATEMENT
FOR THE YEAR ENDED DECEMBER 31, 2016

Revenues		$492,000
Operating expenses (excluding depreciation)	$269,000	
Depreciation expense	21,000	290,000
Income from operations		202,000
Income tax expense		68,000
Net income		$134,000

Additional Information
(a) The company declared and paid an $18,000 cash dividend.
(b) The company obtained $150,000 cash through the issuance of long-term bonds.
(c) Land, building, and equipment were acquired for cash.

Step 1: Determine the Change in Cash

To prepare a statement of cash flows from the available information, the first step is to determine the change in cash. As indicated from the information presented, cash decreased $12,000 ($49,000 − $37,000).

Step 2: Determine Net Cash Flow from Operating Activities—Indirect Method

Using the indirect method, we adjust net income of $134,000 on an accrual basis to arrive at net cash flow from operating activities. Explanations for the adjustments to net income follow.

Decrease in Accounts Receivable. Accounts receivable decreased during the period because cash receipts (cash-basis revenues) are higher than revenues reported on an accrual basis. To convert net income to net cash flow from operating activities, the decrease of $10,000 in accounts receivable must be added to net income.

Increase in Prepaid Expenses. When prepaid expenses (assets) increase during a period, expenses on an accrual-basis income statement are lower than they are on a cash-basis income statement. The reason: Tax Consultants has made cash payments in the current period, but expenses (as charges to the income statement) have been deferred to future periods. To convert net income to net cash flow from operating activities, the company must deduct from net income the increase of $6,000 in prepaid expenses. An increase in prepaid expenses results in a decrease in cash during the period.

Increase in Accounts Payable. Like the increase in 2015, Tax Consultants must add the 2016 increase of $35,000 in accounts payable to net income, to convert to net cash flow from operating activities. The company incurred a greater amount of expense than the amount of cash it disbursed.

Depreciation Expense (Increase in Accumulated Depreciation). The purchase of depreciable assets is a use of cash, shown in the investing section in the year of acquisition. Tax Consultants' depreciation expense of $21,000 (also represented by the increase in accumulated depreciation) is a non-cash charge; the company adds it back to net income, to arrive at net cash flow from operating activities. The $21,000 is the sum of the $11,000 depreciation on the building plus the $10,000 depreciation on the equipment.

Certain other periodic charges to expense do not require the use of cash. Examples are the amortization of intangible assets and depletion expense. Such charges are treated in the same manner as depreciation. Companies frequently list depreciation and similar non-cash charges as the first adjustments to net income in the statement of cash flows.

As a result of the foregoing items, net cash provided by operating activities is $194,000, as shown in Illustration 23-11.

ILLUSTRATION 23-11
Computation of Net
Cash Flow from
Operating Activities,
Year 2—Indirect Method

Net income		$134,000
Adjustments to reconcile net income to		
net cash provided by operating activities:		
Depreciation expense	$21,000	
Decrease in accounts receivable	10,000	
Increase in prepaid expenses	(6,000)	
Increase in accounts payable	35,000	60,000
Net cash provided by operating activities		$194,000

Step 3: Determine Net Cash Flows from Investing and Financing Activities

After you have determined the items affecting net cash provided by operating activities, the next step involves analyzing the remaining changes in the statement of financial position accounts. Tax Consultants Inc. analyzed the following accounts.

Increase in Land. As indicated from the change in the Land account, the company purchased land of $70,000 during the period. This transaction is an investing activity, reported as a use of cash.

Increase in Buildings and Related Accumulated Depreciation. As indicated in the additional data, and from the change in the Buildings account, Tax Consultants acquired an office building using $200,000 cash. This transaction is a cash outflow, reported in the investing section. The $11,000 increase in accumulated depreciation results from recording depreciation expense on the building. As indicated earlier, the reported depreciation expense has no effect on the amount of cash.

Increase in Equipment and Related Accumulated Depreciation. An increase in equipment of $68,000 resulted because the company used cash to purchase equipment. This transaction is an outflow of cash from an investing activity. The depreciation expense entry for the period explains the increase in Accumulated Depreciation—Equipment.

Increase in Bonds Payable. The Bonds Payable account increased $150,000. Cash received from the issuance of these bonds represents an inflow of cash from a financing activity.

Increase in Retained Earnings. Retained earnings increased $116,000 during the year. Two factors explain this increase: (1) net income of $134,000 increased retained earnings, and (2) dividends of $18,000 decreased retained earnings. As indicated earlier, the company adjusts net income to net cash provided by operating activities in the operating activities section. Payment of the dividends is a financing activity that involves a cash outflow.

Statement of Cash Flows—2016

Combining the foregoing items, we get a statement of cash flows for 2016 for Tax Consultants Inc., using the indirect method to compute net cash flow from operating activities.

<table>
<tr><td colspan="3" align="center">**TAX CONSULTANTS INC.**
STATEMENT OF CASH FLOWS
FOR THE YEAR ENDED DECEMBER 31, 2016
INCREASE (DECREASE) IN CASH</td></tr>
<tr><td>Cash flows from operating activities</td><td></td><td></td></tr>
<tr><td>Net income</td><td></td><td>$ 134,000</td></tr>
<tr><td>Adjustments to reconcile net income to</td><td></td><td></td></tr>
<tr><td>net cash provided by operating activities:</td><td></td><td></td></tr>
<tr><td>Depreciation expense</td><td>$ 21,000</td><td></td></tr>
<tr><td>Decrease in accounts receivable</td><td>10,000</td><td></td></tr>
<tr><td>Increase in prepaid expenses</td><td>(6,000)</td><td></td></tr>
<tr><td>Increase in accounts payable</td><td>35,000</td><td>60,000</td></tr>
<tr><td>Net cash provided by operating activities</td><td></td><td>194,000</td></tr>
<tr><td>Cash flows from investing activities</td><td></td><td></td></tr>
<tr><td>Purchase of land</td><td>(70,000)</td><td></td></tr>
<tr><td>Purchase of building</td><td>(200,000)</td><td></td></tr>
<tr><td>Purchase of equipment</td><td>(68,000)</td><td></td></tr>
<tr><td>Net cash used by investing activities</td><td></td><td>(338,000)</td></tr>
<tr><td>Cash flows from financing activities</td><td></td><td></td></tr>
<tr><td>Issuance of bonds</td><td>150,000</td><td></td></tr>
<tr><td>Payment of cash dividends</td><td>(18,000)</td><td></td></tr>
<tr><td>Net cash provided by financing activities</td><td></td><td>132,000</td></tr>
<tr><td>Net decrease in cash</td><td></td><td>(12,000)</td></tr>
<tr><td>Cash, January 1, 2016</td><td></td><td>49,000</td></tr>
<tr><td>Cash, December 31, 2016</td><td></td><td>$ 37,000</td></tr>
</table>

ILLUSTRATION 23-12
Statement of Cash Flows, Tax Consultants Inc., Year 2

Illustration—2017

Our third example, covering the 2017 operations of Tax Consultants Inc., is more complex. It again uses the indirect method to compute and present net cash flow from operating activities.

Tax Consultants Inc. experienced continued success in 2017 and expanded its operations to include the sale of computer software used in tax-return preparation and tax planning. Thus, inventory is a new asset appearing in the company's December 31, 2017, statement of financial position. Illustrations 23-13 and 23-14 (on page 1194) show the comparative statements of financial position, income statements, and selected data for 2017.

Step 1: Determine the Change in Cash

The first step in the preparation of the statement of cash flows is to determine the change in cash. As the comparative statements of financial position show, cash increased $17,000 in 2017.

ILLUSTRATION 23-13
Comparative Statements
of Financial Position, Tax
Consultants Inc., Year 3

TAX CONSULTANTS INC.
COMPARATIVE STATEMENTS OF FINANCIAL POSITION
AS OF DECEMBER 31

Assets	2017	2016	Change Increase/Decrease
Land	$ 45,000	$ 70,000	$ 25,000 Decrease
Buildings	200,000	200,000	–0–
Accumulated depreciation—buildings	(21,000)	(11,000)	10,000 Increase
Equipment	193,000	68,000	125,000 Increase
Accumulated depreciation—equipment	(28,000)	(10,000)	18,000 Increase
Inventory	54,000	–0–	54,000 Increase
Accounts receivable	68,000	26,000	42,000 Increase
Prepaid expenses	4,000	6,000	2,000 Decrease
Cash	54,000	37,000	17,000 Increase
Totals	$569,000	$386,000	
Equity and Liabilities			
Share capital—ordinary ($1 par)	$220,000	$ 60,000	$160,000 Increase
Retained earnings	206,000	136,000	70,000 Increase
Bonds payable	110,000	150,000	40,000 Decrease
Accounts payable	33,000	40,000	7,000 Decrease
Totals	$569,000	$386,000	

ILLUSTRATION 23-14
Income Statement, Tax
Consultants Inc., Year 3

TAX CONSULTANTS INC.
INCOME STATEMENT
FOR THE YEAR ENDED DECEMBER 31, 2017

Revenues		$890,000
Cost of goods sold	$465,000	
Operating expenses	221,000	
Interest expense	12,000	
Loss on sale of equipment	2,000	700,000
Income from operations		190,000
Income tax expense		65,000
Net income		$125,000

Additional Information
(a) Operating expenses include depreciation expense of $33,000 and expiration of prepaid expenses of $2,000.
(b) Land was sold at its book value for cash.
(c) Cash dividends of $55,000 were declared and paid.
(d) Interest expense of $12,000 was paid in cash.
(e) Equipment with a cost of $166,000 was purchased for cash. Equipment with a cost of $41,000 and a book value of $36,000 was sold for $34,000 cash.
(f) Bonds were redeemed at their book value for cash.
(g) Ordinary shares ($1 par) were issued for cash.

Step 2: Determine Net Cash Flow from Operating Activities—Indirect Method

We explain the adjustments to net income of $125,000 as follows.

Increase in Accounts Receivable. The increase in accounts receivable of $42,000 represents recorded accrual-basis revenues in excess of cash collections in 2017. The company deducts this increase from net income to convert from the accrual basis to the cash basis.

Increase in Inventories. The $54,000 increase in inventories represents an operating use of cash, not an expense. Tax Consultants therefore deducts this amount from net income, to arrive at net cash flow from operations. In other words, when inventory purchased exceeds inventory sold during a period, cost of goods sold on an accrual basis is lower than on a cash basis.

Decrease in Prepaid Expenses. The $2,000 decrease in prepaid expenses represents a charge to the income statement for which Tax Consultants made no cash payment in the current period. The company adds back the decrease to net income, to arrive at net cash flow from operating activities.

Decrease in Accounts Payable. When accounts payable decrease during the year, cost of goods sold and expenses on a cash basis are higher than they are on an accrual basis. To convert net income to net cash flow from operating activities, the company must deduct the $7,000 in accounts payable from net income.

Depreciation Expense (Increase in Accumulated Depreciation). Accumulated Depreciation—Buildings increased $10,000 ($21,000 − $11,000). The Buildings account did not change during the period, which means that Tax Consultants recorded depreciation expense of $10,000 in 2017.

Accumulated Depreciation—Equipment increased by $18,000 ($28,000 − $10,000) during the year. But Accumulated Depreciation—Equipment decreased by $5,000 as a result of the sale during the year. Thus, depreciation for the year was $23,000. The company reconciled Accumulated Depreciation—Equipment as follows.

Beginning balance	$10,000
Add: Depreciation for 2017	23,000
	33,000
Deduct: Sale of equipment	5,000
Ending balance	$28,000

The company must add back to net income the total depreciation of $33,000 ($10,000 + $23,000) charged to the income statement, to determine net cash flow from operating activities.

Loss on Sale of Equipment. Tax Consultants sold for $34,000 equipment that cost $41,000 and had a book value of $36,000. As a result, the company reported a loss of $2,000 on its sale. To arrive at net cash flow from operating activities, it must add back to net income the loss on the sale of the equipment. The reason is that the loss is a non-cash charge to the income statement. The loss did not reduce cash, but it did reduce net income.

From the foregoing items, the company prepares the operating activities section of the statement of cash flows, as shown in Illustration 23-15.

Cash flows from operating activities		
Net income		$125,000
Adjustments to reconcile net income to		
net cash provided by operating activities:		
Depreciation expense	$ 33,000	
Loss on sale of equipment	2,000	
Increase in accounts receivable	(42,000)	
Increase in inventories	(54,000)	
Decrease in prepaid expenses	2,000	
Decrease in accounts payable	(7,000)	(66,000)
Net cash provided by operating activities		59,000

ILLUSTRATION 23-15
Operating Activities Section of Cash Flow Statement

Step 3: Determine Net Cash Flows from Investing and Financing Activities

By analyzing the remaining changes in the statement of financial position accounts, Tax Consultants identifies cash flows from investing and financing activities.

Land. Land decreased $25,000 during the period. As indicated from the information presented, the company sold land for cash at its book value. This transaction is an investing activity, reported as a $25,000 source of cash.

Equipment. An analysis of the Equipment account indicates the following.

Beginning balance	$ 68,000
Purchase of equipment	166,000
	234,000
Sale of equipment	41,000
Ending balance	$193,000

The company used cash to purchase equipment with a fair value of $166,000—an investing transaction reported as a cash outflow. The sale of the equipment for $34,000 is also an investing activity, but one that generates a cash inflow.

Bonds Payable. Bonds payable decreased $40,000 during the year. As indicated from the additional information, the company redeemed the bonds at their book value. This financing transaction used $40,000 of cash.

Share Capital—Ordinary. The Share Capital—Ordinary account increased $160,000 during the year. As indicated from the additional information, Tax Consultants issued ordinary shares of $160,000 at par. This financing transaction provided cash of $160,000.

Retained Earnings. Retained earnings changed $70,000 ($206,000 − $136,000) during the year. The $70,000 change in retained earnings results from net income of $125,000 from operations and the financing activity of paying cash dividends of $55,000.

Statement of Cash Flows—2017

Tax Consultants Inc. combines the foregoing items to prepare the statement of cash flows shown in Illustration 23-16.

ILLUSTRATION 23-16
Statement of Cash Flows,
Tax Consultants Inc.,
Year 3

TAX CONSULTANTS INC.
STATEMENT OF CASH FLOWS
FOR THE YEAR ENDED DECEMBER 31, 2017
INCREASE (DECREASE) IN CASH

Cash flows from operating activities		
Net income		$ 125,000
Adjustments to reconcile net income to		
net cash provided by operating activities:		
Depreciation expense	$ 33,000	
Loss on sale of equipment	2,000	
Increase in accounts receivable	(42,000)	
Increase in inventories	(54,000)	
Decrease in prepaid expenses	2,000	
Decrease in accounts payable	(7,000)	(66,000)
Net cash provided by operating activities		59,000
Cash flows from investing activities		
Sale of land	25,000	
Sale of equipment	34,000	
Purchase of equipment	(166,000)	
Net cash used by investing activities		(107,000)
Cash flows from financing activities		
Redemption of bonds	(40,000)	
Sale of ordinary shares	160,000	
Payment of dividends	(55,000)	
Net cash provided by financing activities		65,000
Net increase in cash		17,000
Cash, January 1, 2017		37,000
Cash, December 31, 2017		$ 54,000

Sources of Information for the Statement of Cash Flows

Important points to remember in the preparation of the statement of cash flows are these:

6 **LEARNING OBJECTIVE**

Identify sources of information for a statement of cash flows.

1. Comparative statements of financial position provide the basic information from which to prepare the report. Additional information obtained from analyses of specific accounts is also included.

2. An analysis of the Retained Earnings account is necessary. The net increase or decrease in Retained Earnings without any explanation is a meaningless amount in the statement. Without explanation, it might represent the effect of net income, dividends declared, or prior period adjustments.

3. The statement includes all changes that have passed through cash or have resulted in an increase or decrease in cash.

4. Write-downs, amortization charges, and similar "book" entries, such as depreciation of plant assets, represent neither inflows nor outflows of cash because they have no effect on cash. To the extent that they have entered into the determination of net income, however, the company must add them back to or subtract them from net income, to arrive at net cash provided (used) by operating activities.

Indirect Method—Additional Adjustments

For consistency and comparability and because it is the most widely used method in practice, we used the indirect method in the Tax Consultants' illustrations. We determined net cash flow from operating activities by adding back to or deducting from net income those items that had no effect on cash. Illustration 23-17 presents a more complete set of common types of adjustments that companies make to net income to arrive at net cash flow from operating activities.

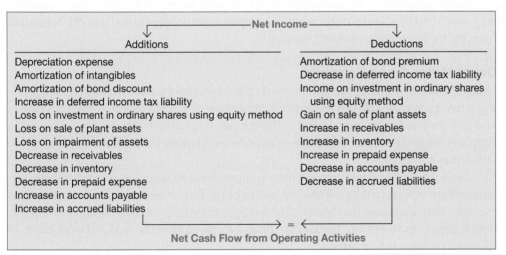

ILLUSTRATION 23-17
Adjustments Needed to Determine Net Cash Flow from Operating Activities—Indirect Method

The additions and deductions in Illustration 23-17 reconcile net income to net cash flow from operating activities, illustrating why the indirect method is also called the reconciliation method.

Net Cash Flow from Operating Activities—Direct Method

Two different methods are available to adjust income from operations on an accrual basis to net cash flow from operating activities. We showed the indirect method in the Tax Consultants' illustrations in the prior sections.

7 **LEARNING OBJECTIVE**

Contrast the direct and indirect methods of calculating net cash flow from operating activities.

The **direct method** reports cash receipts and cash disbursements from operating activities. The difference between these two amounts is the net cash flow from operating activities. In other words, the direct method deducts operating cash disbursements from operating cash receipts. The direct method results in the presentation of a condensed cash receipts and cash disbursements statement.

As indicated from the accrual-based income statement (see Illustration 23-4 on page 1187), Tax Consultants reported revenues of $125,000. However, because the company's accounts receivable increased during 2015 by $36,000, the company collected only $89,000 ($125,000 − $36,000) in cash from these revenues. Similarly, Tax Consultants reported operating expenses of $85,000. However, accounts payable increased during the period by $5,000. Assuming that these payables relate to operating expenses, cash operating expenses were $80,000 ($85,000 − $5,000). Because no taxes payable exist at the end of the year, the company must have paid $6,000 income tax expense for 2015 in cash during the year. Tax Consultants computes net cash flow from operating activities as shown in Illustration 23-18.

ILLUSTRATION 23-18
Computation of Net
Cash Flow from
Operating Activities,
Year 1—Direct Method

Cash collected from revenues	$89,000
Cash payments for expenses	80,000
Income before income taxes	9,000
Cash payments for income taxes	6,000
Net cash provided by operating activities	$ 3,000

"Net cash provided by operating activities" is the equivalent of cash basis net income. ("Net cash used by operating activities" is equivalent to cash basis net loss.)

The IASB encourages use of the direct method and permits use of the indirect method. Yet, if the direct method is used, the Board requires that companies provide in a separate schedule a reconciliation of net income to net cash flow from operating activities. Therefore, under either method, companies must prepare and report information from the indirect (reconciliation) method.

Direct Method—An Example

Under the direct method, the statement of cash flows reports net cash flow from operating activities as major classes of *operating cash receipts* (e.g., cash collected from customers and cash received from interest and dividends) and *cash disbursements* (e.g., cash paid to suppliers for goods, to employees for services, to creditors for interest, and to government authorities for taxes).

We illustrate the direct method here in more detail to help you understand the difference between accrual-based income and net cash flow from operating activities. This example also illustrates the data needed to apply the direct method. Drogba Company, which began business on January 1, 2015, has the following selected statement of financial position information.

ILLUSTRATION 23-19
Statement of Financial
Position Accounts,
Drogba Co.

	December 31, 2015	January 1, 2015
Property, plant, and equipment (net)	€ 90,000	€-0-
Inventory	160,000	-0-
Accounts payable	60,000	-0-
Accrued expenses payable	20,000	-0-
Accounts receivable	15,000	-0-
Prepaid expenses	8,000	-0-
Cash	159,000	-0-

Drogba's December 31, 2015, income statement and additional information are as follows.

Sales revenue		€780,000
Cost of goods sold		450,000
Gross profit		330,000
Operating expenses	€160,000	
Depreciation	10,000	170,000
Income before income taxes		160,000
Income tax expense		48,000
Net income		€112,000

Additional Information
(a) Dividends of €70,000 were declared and paid in cash.
(b) The accounts payable increase resulted from the purchase of merchandise.
(c) Prepaid expenses and accrued expenses payable relate to operating expenses.

ILLUSTRATION 23-20
Income Statement,
Drogba Co.

Under the **direct method**, companies compute net cash provided by operating activities by **adjusting each item in the income statement** from the accrual basis to the cash basis. To simplify and condense the operating activities section, only major classes of operating cash receipts and cash payments are reported. As Illustration 23-21 shows, the difference between these major classes of cash receipts and cash payments is the net cash provided by operating activities.

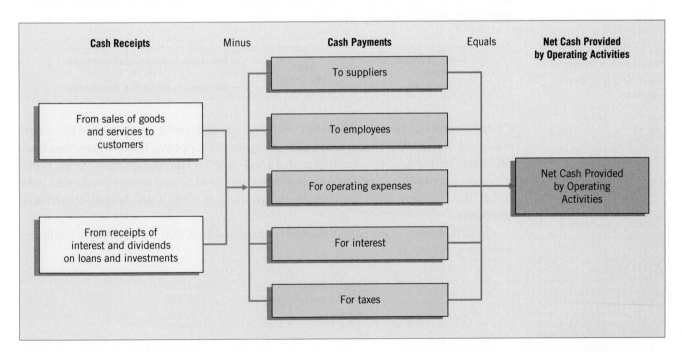

ILLUSTRATION 23-21
Major Classes of Cash
Receipts and Payments

An efficient way to apply the direct method is to analyze the revenues and expenses reported in the income statement in the order in which they are listed. The company then determines cash receipts and cash payments related to these revenues and expenses. In the following sections, we present the direct method adjustments for Drogba Company in 2016, to determine net cash provided by operating activities.

Cash Receipts from Customers. The income statement for Drogba Company reported revenues from customers of €780,000. To determine cash receipts from customers, the company considers the change in accounts receivable during the year.

When accounts receivable increase during the year, revenues on an accrual basis are higher than cash receipts from customers. In other words, operations led to increased revenues, but not all of these revenues resulted in cash receipts. To determine the amount of cash receipts, deduct the amount of the increase in accounts receivable from the total sales revenues. Conversely, a decrease in accounts receivable is added to sales revenues because cash receipts from customers then exceed sales revenues.

For Drogba, accounts receivable increased €15,000. Thus, cash receipts from customers were €765,000, computed as follows.

Sales revenue	€780,000
Deduct: Increase in accounts receivable	15,000
Cash receipts from customers	€765,000

Drogba could also determine cash receipts from customers by analyzing the Accounts Receivable account, as shown below.

Accounts Receivable				
1/1/16	Balance	–0–	Receipts from customers	765,000
	Sales revenue	780,000		
12/31/16	Balance	15,000		

Illustration 23-22 shows the relationships between cash receipts from customers, revenues from sales, and changes in accounts receivable.

ILLUSTRATION 23-22
Formula to Compute
Cash Receipts from
Customers

Cash Receipts from Customers	=	Sales Revenue	{ + Decrease in Accounts Receivable
			or
			− Increase in Accounts Receivable

Cash Payments to Suppliers. Drogba Company reported cost of goods sold on its income statement of €450,000. To determine cash payments to suppliers, the company first finds purchases for the year, by adjusting cost of goods sold for the change in inventory. When inventory increases during the year, purchases this year exceed cost of goods sold. As a result, the company adds the increase in inventory to cost of goods sold, to arrive at purchases.

In 2016, Drogba Company's inventory increased €160,000. The company computes purchases as follows.

Cost of goods sold	€450,000
Add: Increase in inventory	160,000
Purchases	€610,000

After computing purchases, Drogba determines cash payments to suppliers by adjusting purchases for the change in accounts payable. When accounts payable increase during the year, purchases on an accrual basis are higher than they are on a cash basis. As a result, it deducts from purchases the increase in accounts payable to arrive at cash payments to suppliers. Conversely, if cash payments to suppliers exceed purchases, Drogba adds to purchases the decrease in accounts payable. Cash payments to suppliers were €550,000, computed as follows.

Purchases			€610,000	
Deduct: Increase in accounts payable			60,000	
Cash payments to suppliers			€550,000	

Drogba also can determine cash payments to suppliers by analyzing Accounts Payable, as shown below.

Accounts Payable

Payments to suppliers	550,000	1/1/16	Balance	–0–
			Purchases	610,000
		12/31/16	Balance	60,000

Illustration 23-23 shows the relationships between cash payments to suppliers, cost of goods sold, changes in inventory, and changes in accounts payable.

Cash Payments to Suppliers	=	Cost of Goods Sold	{ + Increase in Inventory or − Decrease in Inventory	{ + Decrease in Accounts Payable or − Increase in Accounts Payable

ILLUSTRATION 23-23
Formula to Compute Cash Payments to Suppliers

Cash Payments for Operating Expenses. Drogba reported operating expenses of €160,000 on its income statement. To determine the cash paid for operating expenses, it must adjust this amount for any changes in prepaid expenses and accrued expenses payable.

For example, when prepaid expenses increased €8,000 during the year, cash paid for operating expenses was €8,000 higher than operating expenses reported on the income statement. To convert operating expenses to cash payments for operating expenses, the company adds to operating expenses the increase of €8,000. Conversely, if prepaid expenses decrease during the year, Drogba deducts from operating expenses the amount of the decrease.

Drogba also must adjust operating expenses for changes in accrued expenses payable. When accrued expenses payable increase during the year, operating expenses on an accrual basis are higher than they are on a cash basis. As a result, the company deducts from operating expenses an increase in accrued expenses payable, to arrive at cash payments for operating expenses. Conversely, it adds to operating expenses a decrease in accrued expenses payable because cash payments exceed operating expenses.

Drogba's cash payments for operating expenses were €148,000, computed as follows.

Operating expenses		€160,000
Add: Increase in prepaid expenses		8,000
Deduct: Increase in accrued expenses payable		20,000
Cash payments for operating expenses		€148,000

The relationships among cash payments for operating expenses, changes in prepaid expenses, and changes in accrued expenses payable are shown in Illustration 23-24.

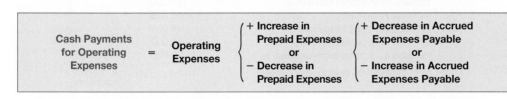

Cash Payments for Operating Expenses	=	Operating Expenses	{ + Increase in Prepaid Expenses or − Decrease in Prepaid Expenses	{ + Decrease in Accrued Expenses Payable or − Increase in Accrued Expenses Payable

ILLUSTRATION 23-24
Formula to Compute Cash Payments for Operating Expenses

Note that the company did not consider depreciation expense because it is a non-cash charge.

Cash Payments for Income Taxes. The income statement for Drogba shows income tax expense of €48,000. This amount equals the cash paid. How do we know that? Because the comparative statement of financial position indicated no income taxes payable at either the beginning or end of the year.

Summary of Net Cash Flow from Operating Activities—Direct Method

The following schedule summarizes the computations illustrated above.

ILLUSTRATION 23-25
Accrual Basis to Cash
Basis

Accrual Basis			Adjustment	Add (Subtract)	Cash Basis
Sales revenue	€780,000	−	Increase in accounts receivable	€ (15,000)	€765,000
Cost of goods sold	450,000	+	Increase in inventory	160,000	
		−	Increase in accounts payable	(60,000)	550,000
Operating expenses	160,000	+	Increase in prepaid expenses	8,000	
		−	Increase in accrued expenses payable	(20,000)	148,000
Depreciation expense	10,000	−	Depreciation expense	(10,000)	–0–
Income tax expense	48,000				48,000
Total expense	668,000				746,000
Net income	€112,000		Net cash provided by operating activities		€ 19,000

Illustration 23-26 shows the presentation of the direct method for reporting net cash flow from operating activities for the Drogba Company example.

ILLUSTRATION 23-26
Operating Activities
Section—Direct
Method, 2016

DROGBA COMPANY
STATEMENT OF CASH FLOWS (PARTIAL)

Cash flows from operating activities		
Cash received from customers		€765,000
Cash payments:		
To suppliers	€550,000	
For operating expenses	148,000	
For income taxes	48,000	746,000
Net cash provided by operating activities		€ 19,000

If Drogba uses the direct method to present the net cash flow from operating activities, it is required to provide in a separate schedule the reconciliation of net income to net cash provided by operating activities. The reconciliation assumes the identical form and content of the indirect method of presentation, as shown below.

ILLUSTRATION 23-27
Reconciliation of Net
Income to Net Cash
Provided by Operating
Activities, 2016

DROGBA COMPANY
RECONCILIATION

Net income		€112,000
Adjustments to reconcile net income to net cash provided by operating activities:		
Depreciation expense	€ 10,000	
Increase in accounts receivable	(15,000)	
Increase in inventory	(160,000)	
Increase in prepaid expenses	(8,000)	
Increase in accounts payable	60,000	
Increase in accrued expense payable	20,000	(93,000)
Net cash provided by operating activities		€ 19,000

A contentious decision that the IASB faced related to cash flow reporting was choosing between the direct method and the indirect method of determining net cash flow from operating activities. Companies lobbied *against* the direct method, urging adoption of the indirect method. Commercial lending officers expressed to the IASB a strong preference in favor of the direct method. What are the arguments in favor of each of the methods?

In Favor of the Direct Method

The principal advantage of the direct method is that it shows operating cash receipts and payments. Thus, it is more consistent with the objective of a statement of cash flows—to provide information about cash receipts and cash payments—than the indirect method, which does not report operating cash receipts and payments.

Supporters of the direct method contend that knowledge of the specific sources of operating cash receipts and the purposes for which operating cash payments were made in past periods is useful in estimating future operating cash flows. Furthermore, information about amounts of major classes of operating cash receipts and payments is more useful than information only about their arithmetic sum (the net cash flow from operating activities). Such information is more revealing of a company's ability (1) to generate sufficient cash from operating activities to pay its debts, (2) to reinvest in its operations, and (3) to make distributions to its owners.

Many companies indicate that they do not currently collect information in a manner that allows them to determine amounts such as cash received from customers or cash paid to suppliers directly from their accounting systems. But supporters of the direct method contend that the incremental cost of determining operating cash receipts and payments is not significant.

In Favor of the Indirect Method

The principal advantage of the indirect method is that it focuses on the differences between net income and net cash flow from operating activities. That is, it provides a useful link between the statement of cash flows and the income statement and statement of financial position.

Many companies contend that it is less costly to adjust net income to net cash flow from operating activities (indirect) than it is to report gross operating cash receipts and payments (direct). Supporters of the indirect method also state that the direct method, which effectively reports income statement information on a cash rather than an accrual basis, may erroneously suggest that net cash flow from operating activities is as good as, or better than, net income as a measure of performance.

In their joint financial statement presentation project, the IASB and the FASB have proposed to allow only the direct method. However, there has been significant pushback on this proposal, which suggests that the choice of either the direct or indirect method will continue to be available.

Source: See http:/www.fasb.org; click on Projects and then on Inactive Joint FASB/IASB Projects.

SPECIAL PROBLEMS IN STATEMENT PREPARATION

We discussed some of the special problems related to preparing the statement of cash flows in connection with the preceding illustrations. Other problems that arise with some frequency in the preparation of this statement include the following.

8 LEARNING OBJECTIVE
Discuss special problems in preparing a statement of cash flows.

1. Adjustments to net income.

2. Accounts receivable (net).

3. Other working capital changes.

4. Net loss.

5. Disclosures.

Adjustments to Net Income

Depreciation and Amortization

Depreciation expense is the most common adjustment to net income that companies make to arrive at net cash flow from operating activities. But there are numerous other non-cash expense or revenue items. Examples of expense items that companies must add back to net income are the **amortization of limited-life intangible assets**, such as patents, and **depletion of mineral resources**. These charges to expense involve expenditures made in prior periods that a company amortizes currently. These charges reduce net income without affecting cash in the current period.

Also, **amortization of bond discount or premium** on long-term bonds payable affects the amount of interest expense. However, neither changes cash. As a result, a company should add back discount amortization and subtract premium amortization from net income to arrive at net cash flow from operating activities.

Postretirement Benefit Costs

If a company has postretirement costs such as an employee pension plan, chances are that the pension expense recorded during a period will either be higher or lower than the cash funded. It will be higher when there is an unfunded liability and will be lower when there is a prepaid pension cost. When the expense is higher or lower than the cash paid, **the company must adjust net income by the difference between cash paid and the expense reported** in computing net cash flow from operating activities.

Change in Deferred Income Taxes

Changes in deferred income taxes affect net income but have no effect on cash. For example, **Baytex Energy Corp.** (CAN) reported an increase in its liability for deferred taxes of approximately $107,598,000. This change in the liability increased tax expense and decreased net income, but did not affect cash. Therefore, Baytex added back $107,598,000 to net income on its statement of cash flows.

Equity Method of Accounting

Another common adjustment to net income is **a change related to an investment in ordinary shares** when recording income or loss under the equity method. Recall that under the equity method, the investor (1) debits the investment account and credits revenue for its share of the investee's net income, and (2) credits dividends received to the investment account. Therefore, the net increase in the investment account does not affect cash flows. A company must deduct the net increase from net income to arrive at net cash flow from operating activities.

Assume that Victor Co. owns 40 percent of Milo Inc. During the year, Milo reports net income of $100,000 and pays a cash dividend of $30,000. Victor reports this in its statement of cash flows as a deduction from net income in the following manner— Equity in earnings of Milo, net of dividends, $28,000 [($100,000 − $30,000) × 40%].

Losses and Gains

Realized Losses and Gains. In the illustration for Tax Consultants, the company experienced a loss of $2,000 from the sale of equipment. The company added this loss to net income to compute net cash flow from operating activities because **the loss is a non-cash charge in the income statement**.

If Tax Consultants experiences a **gain** from a sale of equipment, it too requires an adjustment to net income. Because a company reports the gain in the statement of cash flows as part of the cash proceeds from the sale of equipment under investing activities, **it deducts the gain from net income to avoid double-counting**—once as part of net income and again as part of the cash proceeds from the sale.

To illustrate, assume that Tax Consultants had land with a carrying value of $200,000, which was condemned by the provincial government for a highway project. The condemnation proceeds received were $205,000, resulting in a gain of $5,000. In the statement of cash flows (indirect method), the company would deduct the $5,000 gain from net income in the operating activities section. It would report the $205,000 cash inflow from the condemnation as an investing activity, as follows.

Cash flows from investing activities	
Condemnation of land	$205,000

Unrealized Losses and Gains. Unrealized losses and gains generally occur for debt investments not held for collection and for equity investments. For example, assume that **AB InBev** (BEL) purchases the following two security investments on January 10, 2015.

1. Debt investment for €1 million that is classified as trading. During 2015, the debt investment has an unrealized holding gain of €110,000 (recorded in net income).

2. Equity investment for €600,000 that is non-trading in nature. During 2015, the non-trading equity investment has an unrealized holding loss of €50,000 (recorded in other comprehensive income).

For AB InBev, the unrealized holding gain of €110,000 on the debt investment increases net income but does not increase net cash flow from operating activities. As a result, the unrealized holding gain of €110,000 is deducted from net income to compute net cash flow from operating activities.

On the other hand, the unrealized holding loss of €50,000 that AB InBev incurs on the non-trading equity investment does not affect net income or cash flows—this loss is reported in the other comprehensive income section. As a result, no adjustment to net income is necessary in computing net cash flow from operating activities.

Thus, the general rule is that unrealized holding gains or losses that affect net income must be adjusted to determine net cash flow from operating activities. Conversely, unrealized holding gains or losses that do not affect net income are not adjusted to determine net cash flow from operating activities.[4]

Share-Based Compensation

Recall for share-based compensation plans that companies are required to use the fair value method to determine total compensation cost. The compensation cost is then recognized as an expense in the periods in which the employee provides services. When Compensation Expense is debited, Share Premium—Options is often credited. Cash is not affected by recording the expense. **Therefore, the company must increase net income by the amount of compensation expense from share options in computing net cash flow from operating activities.**

To illustrate how this information should be reported on a statement of cash flows, assume that First Wave Inc. grants 5,000 options to its CEO, Ann Johnson. Each option entitles Johnson to purchase one share of First Wave's £1 par value ordinary shares at

[4]Other unrealized holding gains or losses, such as revaluations on property, plant, and equipment, or intangible assets, are also reported as part of other comprehensive income. As a result, net income is not adjusted in computing cash flows from operating activities for any type of unrealized holding gains or losses that are reported in other comprehensive income.

£50 per share at any time in the next two years (the service period). The fair value of the options is £200,000. First Wave records compensation expense in the first year as follows.

Compensation Expense (£200,000 ÷ 2)	100,000	
Share Premium—Options		100,000

In addition, if we assume that First Wave has a 35 percent tax rate, it would recognize a deferred tax asset of £35,000 (£100,000 × 35%) in the first year, as follows.

Deferred Tax Asset	35,000	
Income Tax Expense		35,000

Therefore, on the statement of cash flows for the first year, First Wave reports the following (assuming a net income of £600,000).

Net income	£600,000
Adjustments to reconcile net income to net cash provided by operating activities:	
Share-based compensation expense	100,000
Increase in deferred tax asset	(35,000)

As shown in First Wave's statement of cash flows, it adds the share-based compensation expense to net income because it is a non-cash expense. The increase in the deferred tax asset and the related reduction in income tax expense increase net income. Although the negative income tax expense increases net income, it does not increase cash. Therefore, it should be deducted. Subsequently, if Ann Johnson exercises her options, Third Wave reports "Cash provided by exercise of share options" in the financing section of the statement of cash flows.[5]

Accounts Receivable (Net)

Up to this point, we assumed no allowance for doubtful accounts—a contra account—to offset accounts receivable. However, if a company needs an allowance for doubtful accounts, how does that allowance affect the company's determination of net cash flow from operating activities? For example, assume that Redmark Co. reports net income of €40,000. It has the accounts receivable balances, as shown in Illustration 23-28.

ILLUSTRATION 23-28
Accounts Receivable Balances, Redmark Co.

	2015	2014	Change Increase/Decrease
Accounts receivable	€105,000	€90,000	€15,000 Increase
Allowance for doubtful accounts	(10,000)	(4,000)	6,000 Increase
Accounts receivable (net)	€ 95,000	€86,000	9,000 Increase

Indirect Method

Because an increase in Allowance for Doubtful Accounts results from a charge to bad debt expense, a company should add back an increase in Allowance for Doubtful Accounts to

[5]In some countries, companies receive a tax deduction related to share-based compensation plans at the time employees exercise their options. The amount of the deduction is equal to the difference between the market price of the share and the exercise price at the date the employee purchases the shares, which in most cases is much larger than the total compensation expense recorded. When the tax deduction exceeds the total compensation recorded, this provides an additional cash inflow to the company. Under IFRS, this tax-related cash inflow should be reported in the financing section of the statement of cash flows. [5]

net income to arrive at net cash flow from operating activities. Illustration 23-29 shows one method for presenting this information in a statement of cash flows.

REDMARK CO.
STATEMENT OF CASH FLOWS (PARTIAL)
FOR THE YEAR 2015

Cash flows from operating activities		
Net income		€40,000
Adjustments to reconcile net income to net		
cash provided by operating activities:		
Increase in accounts receivable	€(15,000)	
Increase in allowance for doubtful accounts	6,000	(9,000)
		€31,000

As we indicated, the increase in the Allowance for Doubtful Accounts balance results from a charge to bad debt expense for the year. Because bad debt expense is a non-cash charge, a company must add it back to net income in arriving at net cash flow from operating activities.

Instead of separately analyzing the allowance account, a short-cut approach is to net the allowance balance against the receivable balance and compare the change in accounts receivable on a net basis. Illustration 23-30 shows this presentation.

REDMARK CO.
STATEMENT OF CASH FLOWS (PARTIAL)
FOR THE YEAR 2015

Cash flows from operating activities	
Net income	€40,000
Adjustments to reconcile net income to	
net cash provided by operating activities:	
Increase in accounts receivable (net)	(9,000)
	€31,000

This short-cut procedure works also if the change in the allowance account results from a write-off of accounts receivable. This reduces both Accounts Receivable and Allowance for Doubtful Accounts. No effect on cash flows occurs. Because of its simplicity, *use the net approach for your homework assignments.*

Direct Method

If using the direct method, a company **should not net** Allowance for Doubtful Accounts against Accounts Receivable. To illustrate, assume that Redmark Co.'s net income of €40,000 consisted of the following items.

ILLUSTRATION 23-31
Income Statement,
Redmark Co.

REDMARK CO.
INCOME STATEMENT
FOR THE YEAR 2015

Sales revenue		€100,000
Expenses		
Salaries	€46,000	
Utilities	8,000	
Bad debts	6,000	60,000
Net income		€ 40,000

If Redmark deducts the €9,000 increase in accounts receivable (net) from sales for the year, it would report cash sales at €91,000 (€100,000 − €9,000) and cash payments for operating expenses at €60,000. Both items would be misstated: Cash sales should be reported at €85,000 (€100,000 − €15,000), and total cash payments for operating expenses should be reported at €54,000 (€60,000 − €6,000). Illustration 23-32 shows the proper presentation.

ILLUSTRATION 23-32
Bad Debts—Direct
Method

REDMARK CO. STATEMENT OF CASH FLOWS (PARTIAL) FOR THE YEAR 2015		
Cash flows from operating activities		
Cash received from customers		€85,000
Salaries paid	€46,000	
Utilities paid	8,000	54,000
Net cash provided by operating activities		€31,000

An added complication develops when a company writes off accounts receivable. Simply adjusting sales for the change in accounts receivable will not provide the proper amount of cash sales. The reason is that the write-off of the accounts receivable is not a cash collection. Thus, an additional adjustment is necessary.

Other Working Capital Changes

Up to this point, we showed how companies handled all of the changes in working capital items (current asset and current liability items) as adjustments to net income in determining net cash flow from operating activities. You must be careful, however, because **some changes in working capital, although they affect cash, do not affect net income**. Generally, these are investing or financing activities of a current nature.

One activity is the purchase of **short-term non-trading equity investments**. For example, the purchase of short-term non-trading equity investments for ¥5,000,000 cash has no effect on net income, but it does cause a ¥5,000,000 decrease in cash. A company reports this transaction as a cash flow from investing activities as follows.

Cash flows from investing activities
Purchase of short-term non-trading equity investments   ¥5,000,000

Another example is the issuance of a **short-term non-trade note payable** for cash. This change in a working capital item has no effect on income from operations, but it increases cash by the amount of the note payable. For example, a company reports the issuance of a ¥10,000,000 short-term, non-trade note payable for cash in the statement of cash flows as follows.

Cash flows from financing activities
Issuance of short-term note   ¥10,000,000

Another change in a working capital item that has no effect on income from operations or on cash is a **cash dividend payable**. Although a company will report the cash dividends when paid as a financing activity, it does not report the declared but unpaid dividend on the statement of cash flows.

Net Losses

If a company reports a net loss instead of a net income, it must adjust the net loss for those items that do not result in a cash inflow or outflow. The net loss, after adjusting for the charges or credits not affecting cash, may result in a negative or a positive cash flow from operating activities.

For example, if the net loss is £50,000 and the total amount of charges to add back is £60,000, then net cash provided by operating activities is £10,000. Illustration 23-33 shows this computation.

Net income (loss)		£(50,000)
Adjustments to reconcile net income to net cash provided by operating activities:		
Depreciation of plant assets	£55,000	
Amortization of patents	5,000	60,000
Net cash provided by operating activities		£ 10,000

ILLUSTRATION 23-33
Computation of Net Cash Flow from Operating Activities—Cash Inflow

If the company experiences a net loss of £80,000 and the total amount of the charges to add back is £25,000, the presentation appears as follows.

Net income (loss)	£(80,000)
Adjustments to reconcile net income to net cash used by operating activities:	
Depreciation of plant assets	25,000
Net cash used by operating activities	£(55,000)

ILLUSTRATION 23-34
Computation of Net Cash Flow from Operating Activities—Cash Outflow

Although not illustrated in this chapter, a negative cash flow may result even if the company reports a net income.

Disclosures

Significant Non-Cash Transactions

Because the statement of cash flows reports only the effects of operating, investing, and financing activities in terms of cash flows, it omits some **significant non-cash transactions** and other events that are investing or financing activities. Among the more common of these non-cash transactions that a company should report or disclose in some manner are the following.

1. Acquisition of assets by assuming liabilities (including finance lease obligations) or by issuing equity securities.

2. Exchanges of non-monetary assets.

3. Refinancing of long-term debt.

4. Conversion of debt or preference shares to ordinary shares.

5. Issuance of equity securities to retire debt.

Investing and financing transactions that do not require the use of cash are excluded from the statement of cash flows. **[6]** If material in amount, these disclosures may be either narrative or summarized in a separate schedule. This schedule may appear in a separate note or supplementary schedule to the financial statements.[6] Illustration 23-35 (on page 1210) shows the presentation of these significant non-cash transactions or other events in a separate schedule in the notes to the financial statements.

---

[6]Some non-cash investing and financing activities are part cash and part non-cash. Companies should report only the cash portion on the statement of cash flows. The non-cash component should be reported in a separate note.

ILLUSTRATION 23-35
Note Presentation of
Non-Cash Investing and
Financing Activities

Note G: Significant non-cash transactions. During the year, the company engaged in the following significant non-cash investing and financing transactions:

Issued 250,000 ordinary shares to purchase land and building	€1,750,000
Exchanged land in New York, New York, for land in Berlin, Germany	€2,000,000
Converted 12% bonds to 50,000 ordinary shares	€ 500,000

Companies do not generally report certain other significant non-cash transactions or other events in conjunction with the statement of cash flows. Examples of these types of transactions are **share dividends, share splits, and restrictions on retained earnings**. Companies generally report these items, neither financing nor investing activities, in conjunction with the statement of changes in equity or schedules and notes pertaining to changes in equity accounts.

Special Disclosures

Underlying Concepts

Additional requirements for disclosures of interest, dividends, and taxes reflect application of the full disclosure principle.

IAS 7 indicates that cash flows related to interest received and paid, and dividends received and paid, should be separately disclosed in the statement of cash flows. **[7]** Each item should be classified in a consistent manner from period to period as operating, investing, or financing cash flows. As indicated earlier, *for homework purposes classify interest received and paid and dividends received as part of cash flows from operating activities and dividends paid as cash flows from financing activities.* The justification for reporting the first three items in cash flows from operating activities is that each item affects net income. Dividends paid, however, do not affect net income and are often considered a cost of financing.

Companies should also disclose income taxes paid separately in the cash flows from operating activities unless they can be separately identified as part of investing or financing activities. While tax expense may be readily identifiable with investing or financing activities, the related tax cash flows are often impracticable to identify and may arise in a different period from the cash flows of the underlying transaction. Therefore, taxes paid are usually classified as cash flows from operating activities. IFRS requires that the cash paid for taxes, as well as cash flows from interest and dividends received and paid, be disclosed. The category (operating, investing, or financing) in which each item was included must be disclosed as well.

An example of such a disclosure from the notes to **Daimler**'s (DEU) financial statement is provided in Illustration 23-36.

ILLUSTRATION 23-36
Note Disclosure of
Interest, Taxes, and
Dividends

Daimler

Cash provided by operating activities includes the following cash flows:

(in millions of €)	2012	2011
Interest paid	(561)	(489)
Interest received	192	243
Dividends received	192	140

Other companies choose to report these items directly in the statement of cash flows. In many cases, companies start with income before income taxes and then show income taxes paid as a separate item. In addition, they often add back interest expense on an accrual basis and then subtract interest paid. Reporting these items in the operating activites section is shown for Wáng Company in Illustration 23-37.

ILLUSTRATION 23-37
Reporting of Interest, Taxes, and Dividends in the Operating Section

WÁNG COMPANY STATEMENT OF CASH FLOWS (IN MILLIONS) (OPERATING ACTIVITIES SECTION ONLY)		
Income before income tax		¥4,000
Adjustments to reconcile income before income tax to net cash provided by operating activities		
Depreciation expense	¥1,000	
Interest expense	500	
Investment revenue	(650)	
Decrease in inventories	1,050	
Increase in trade receivables	(310)	1,590
Cash generated from operations		5,590
Interest paid	(300)	
Income taxes paid	(760)	(1,060)
Net cash provided by operating activities		¥4,530

Companies often provide a separate section to identify interest and income taxes paid.

What do the numbers mean?   BETTER THAN ROA?

As you have learned in your study of accounting, both accounting income (measured under accrual-accounting principles) and cash flow from operations can provide useful information. However, both measures are sometimes criticized. Accounting income is sometimes faulted for the multitude of judgments required to determine revenues and expenses. In addition, many companies can boost an earnings-based metric, return on equity, by piling on debt which also makes the company riskier, not better. On the other hand, cash flow performance metrics are criticized because they do not follow the revenue and expense recognition principles.

So what's a better way to measure how profitable companies really are? Or, adopting master investor Warren Buffett's view of investing: How do you find companies that consistently generate big returns on invested capital? Recently, a new measure of profitability, "COROA"—for cash operating return on assets—has been proposed to provide a better performance metric. The idea is to measure management's ability to generate pure cash returns, not cash expected in the future, on every dollar invested in property, plant, and equipment; R&D centers; inventories; and all other assets.

Specifically, COROA is computed by starting with the cash flow from operations amount and then adding back cash taxes and cash interest to calculate pure operating cash flows. That's the dollar amount that the company actually puts in its coffers during the year—and which could be used to pay dividends, make "investments" by purchasing companies or divisions, and fund capital expenditures, especially those that propel growth. That's the numerator. Adjustments for taxes and interest are fundamental to this COROA measure. This is because falling taxes can create the illusion of ongoing progress. Interest is added back because it primarily reflects the level of leverage but has nothing to do with how well management is managing their assets.

The denominator consists of every dollar spent on the assets that produce those operating cash flows. To calculate that figure, take "total assets" from the statement of financial position and add "accumulated depreciation" to account for operating assets that are still being used to make cars, semiconductors, or other products that, for accounting purposes, are fully expensed.

Thus, COROA—adjusted cash flow from operations as a percentage of total assets—is the ratio to keep an eye on. It's the best measure of pure profitability. If the number has been high for a while and is either staying high or improving, evidence is strong that the company is generating strong returns from its new investments. That's the quality that Buffett looks for. And according to accounting guru Jack Ciesielski, it's all about cash. "What's more important in the world than cash?" he asks. "Why, it's *more* cash, of course."

Source: S. Tully, "A Top Accounting Guru's Compelling New Measure for Profitability," *Fortune* (March 10, 2014).

USE OF A WORKSHEET

LEARNING OBJECTIVE **9**

Explain the use of a worksheet in preparing a statement of cash flows.

When numerous adjustments are necessary or other complicating factors are present, companies often use **a worksheet to assemble and classify the data that will appear on the statement of cash flows**. The worksheet is merely a device that aids in the preparation of the statement. Its use is optional. Illustration 23-38 shows the skeleton format of the worksheet for preparation of the statement of cash flows using the indirect method.

ILLUSTRATION 23-38
Format of Worksheet for
Preparation of Statement
of Cash Flows

	A	B	C	D	E
	🔲 ⟲ • ⟳ • 🔻		XYZ COMPANY.xls		
	Home Insert Page Layout Formulas Data Review View				
	P18 ⟨ ⟩ *fx*				
	XYZ COMPANY				
	Statement of Cash Flows for the Year Ended...				
1	Statement of Financial Position Accounts	End of Prior Year Balances	Reconciling Items — Debits	Reconciling Items — Credits	End of Current Year Balances
2	Debit balance accounts	XX	XX	XX	XX
3		XX	XX	XX	XX
4	Totals	XXX			XXX
5	Credit balance accounts	XX	XX	XX	XX
6		XX	XX	XX	XX
7	Totals	XXX			XXX
8	Statement of Cash Flows Effects				
9	Operating activities				
10	Net income		XX		
11	Adjustments		XX	XX	
12	Investing activities				
13	Receipts and payments		XX	XX	
14	Financing activities				
15	Receipts and payments		XX	XX	
16	Totals		XXX	XXX	
17	Increase (decrease) in cash		(XX)	XX	
18	Totals		XXX	XXX	

The following guidelines are important in using a worksheet.

1. In the statement of financial position accounts section, **list accounts with debit balances separately from those with credit balances**. This means, for example, that Accumulated Depreciation is listed under credit balances and not as a contra account under debit balances. Enter the beginning and ending balances of each account in the appropriate columns. Then, enter the transactions that caused the change in the account balance during the year as reconciling items in the two middle columns.

After all reconciling items have been entered, each line pertaining to a statement of financial position account should foot across. That is, the beginning balance plus or minus the reconciling item(s) must equal the ending balance. When this agreement exists for all statement of financial position accounts, all changes in account balances have been reconciled.

2. The bottom portion of the worksheet consists of the operating, investing, and financing activities sections. Accordingly, it provides the information necessary to prepare the formal statement of cash flows. **Enter inflows of cash as debits in the reconciling columns, and outflows of cash as credits in the reconciling columns.** Thus, in this section, a company would enter the sale of equipment for cash at book value as a debit under inflows of cash from investing activities. Similarly, it would enter the purchase of land for cash as a credit under outflows of cash from investing activities.

3. **Do not enter in any journal or post to any account the reconciling items shown in the worksheet.** These items do not represent either adjustments or corrections of the statement of financial position accounts. They are used only to facilitate the preparation of the statement of cash flows.

Preparation of the Worksheet

The preparation of a worksheet involves the following steps.

Step 1. Enter the statement of financial position accounts and their beginning and ending balances in the statement of financial position accounts section.

Step 2. Enter the data that explain the changes in the statement of financial position accounts (other than cash) and their effects on the statement of cash flows in the reconciling columns of the worksheet.

Step 3. Enter the increase or decrease in cash on the cash line and at the bottom of the worksheet. This entry should enable the totals of the reconciling columns to be in agreement.

To illustrate the preparation and use of a worksheet and to illustrate the reporting of some of the special problems discussed in the prior section, we present a comprehensive example for Satellite Corporation. Again, the indirect method serves as the basis for the computation of net cash provided by operating activities. Illustrations 23-39 and 23-40 (on pages 1214 and 1215) present the statement of financial position, combined statement of income and retained earnings, and additional information for Satellite Corporation. The discussion that follows these financial statements provides additional explanations related to the preparation of the worksheet.

Analysis of Transactions

The following discussion explains the individual adjustments that appear on the worksheet in Illustration 23-41 (page 1219). Because cash is the basis for the analysis, Satellite reconciles the cash account last. Because income is the first item that appears on the statement of cash flows, it is handled first.

Change in Retained Earnings

Net income for the period is HK$117,000. The entry for it on the worksheet is as follows.

(1)

Operating—Net Income	117,000	
Retained Earnings		117,000

Satellite reports net income on the bottom section of the worksheet. This **is the starting point for preparation of the statement of cash flows (under the indirect method).**

A share dividend and a cash dividend also affected retained earnings. The retained earnings statement reports a share dividend of HK$15,000. The worksheet entry for this transaction is as follows.

ILLUSTRATION 23-39
Comparative Statement
of Financial Position,
Satellite Corporation

	SATELLITE CORPORATION.xls

Home Insert Page Layout Formulas Data Review View

P18

SATELLITE CORPORATION
Comparative Statement of Financial
Position–December 31, 2016 and 2015
(in thousands)

	A	B	C	D
1		2016	2015	Increase or (Decrease)
2	Assets			
3	Equity investment in Porter Co. (equity method)	HK$ 18,500	HK$ 15,000	HK$ 3,500
4	Land	131,500	82,000	49,500
5	Equipment	198,000	142,000	56,000
6	Accumulated depreciation—equipment	(40,000)	(31,000)	9,000
7	Buildings	262,000	262,000	—
8	Accumulated depreciation—buildings	(74,100)	(71,000)	3,100
9	Trademarks	7,600	10,000	(2,400)
10	Inventory	493,000	341,000	152,000
11	Prepaid expenses	16,500	17,000	(500)
12	Accounts receivable (net)	104,000	51,000	53,000
13	Cash	59,000	66,000	(7,000)
14	Total assets	HK$1,176,000	HK$884,000	
15	Equity			
16	Share capital—ordinary (HK$1 par)	HK$ 60,000	HK$ 50,000	HK$ 10,000
17	Share premium—ordinary	187,000	38,000	149,000
18	Retained earnings	592,000	496,000	96,000
19	Treasury shares	(17,000)	—	17,000
20	Total equity	822,000	584,000	
21	Liabilities			
22	Notes payable (long-term)	60,000	—	60,000
23	Bonds payable	107,000	108,000	(1,000)
24	Deferred tax liability (long-term)	9,000	6,000	3,000
25	Accounts payable	132,000	131,000	1,000
26	Accrued liabilities	43,000	39,000	4,000
27	Income taxes payable	3,000	16,000	(13,000)
28	Total liabilities	354,000	300,000	
29	Total equity and liabilities	HK$1,176,000	HK$884,000	

(2)

Retained Earnings	15,000	
Share Capital—Ordinary		1,000
Share Premium—Ordinary		14,000

The issuance of share dividends is not a cash operating, investing, or financing item. Therefore, **although the company enters this transaction on the worksheet for reconciling purposes, it does not report it in the statement of cash flows**.

The HK$6,000 cash dividend paid represents a financing activity cash outflow. Satellite makes the following worksheet entry:

(3)

Retained Earnings	6,000	
Financing—Cash Dividends		6,000

Retained Earnings

(2)	15,000	Bal.	496,000
(3)	6,000	(1)	117,000
		Bal.	592,000

The company reconciles the beginning and ending balances of retained earnings by entry of the three items above.

SATELLITE CORPORATION
COMBINED STATEMENT OF INCOME AND RETAINED EARNINGS
FOR THE YEAR ENDED DECEMBER 31, 2016
(IN THOUSANDS)

Net sales		HK$526,500
Other revenue		3,500
Total revenues		530,000
Expense		
Cost of goods sold		310,000
Selling and administrative expenses		47,000
Other income and expense		4,000
Total expenses		361,000
Income before income tax		169,000
Income tax		
Current	HK$49,000	
Deferred	3,000	52,000
Net income		117,000
Retained earnings, January 1		496,000
Less:		
Cash dividends	6,000	
Share dividend	15,000	21,000
Retained earnings, December 31		HK$592,000
Per share:		
Net income		HK$2.13

Additional Information

(a) Other income of HK$3,500 represents Satellite's equity share in the net income of Porter Co., an equity investee. Satellite owns 22% of Porter Co.

(b) An analysis of the Equipment account and related Accumulated Depreciation—Equipment account indicates the following.

	Equipment Dr./(Cr.)	Accum. Dep. Dr./(Cr.)	Gain or (Loss)
Balance at end of 2015	HK$142,000	HK$(31,000)	
Purchases of equipment	53,000		
Sale of equipment	(8,000)	2,500	HK$(1,500)
Depreciation for the period		(11,500)	
Major repair charged to equipment	11,000		
Balance at end of 2016	HK$198,000	HK$(40,000)	

(c) Land in the amount of HK$60,000 was purchased through the issuance of a long-term note; in addition, certain parcels of land costing HK$10,500 were condemned. The government paid Satellite HK$18,500, resulting in an HK$8,000 gain.

(d) The change in the Accumulated Depreciation—Buildings, Trademarks, and Bonds Payable accounts resulted from depreciation and amortization entries.

(e) An analysis of the share capital and premium accounts in equity discloses the following:

	Share Capital— Ordinary	Share Premium— Ordinary
Balance at end of 2015	HK$50,000	HK$ 38,000
Issuance of 2% share dividend	1,000	14,000
Sale of shares for cash	9,000	135,000
Balance at end of 2016	HK$60,000	HK$187,000

(f) Interest paid is HK$9,000; income taxes paid is HK$62,000.

ILLUSTRATION 23-40
Income and Retained Earnings Statements, Satellite Corporation

Accounts Receivable (Net)

The increase in accounts receivable (net) of HK$53,000 represents adjustments that did not result in cash inflows during 2016. As a result, the company would deduct from net income the increase of HK$53,000. Satellite makes the following worksheet entry.

(4)

Accounts Receivable (net)	53,000	
Operating—Increase in Accounts Receivable (net)		53,000

Inventory

The increase in inventory of HK$152,000 represents an operating use of cash. The incremental investment in inventory during the year reduces cash without increasing the cost of goods sold. Satellite makes the following worksheet entry.

(5)

Inventory	152,000	
Operating—Increase in Inventory		152,000

Prepaid Expense

The decrease in prepaid expenses of HK$500 represents a charge in the income statement for which there was no cash outflow in the current period. Satellite should add that amount back to net income through the following entry.

(6)

Operating—Decrease in Prepaid Expenses	500	
Prepaid Expenses		500

Equity Investment in Porter Co. (Equity Method)

Satellite's investment in the shares of Porter Co. increased HK$3,500. This amount reflects Satellite's share of net income earned by Porter (its equity investee) during the current year. Although Satellite's revenue, and therefore its net income, increased HK$3,500 by recording Satellite's share of Porter Co.'s net income, no cash (dividend) was provided. Satellite makes the following worksheet entry.

(7)

Equity Investment in Porter Co.	3,500	
Operating—Equity in Earnings of Porter Co.		3,500

Land

Satellite purchased land in the amount of HK$60,000 through the issuance of a long-term note payable. This transaction did not affect cash. It is a significant non-cash investing/financing transaction that the company would disclose in the accompanying notes. Satellite makes the following entry to reconcile the worksheet.

(8)

Land	60,000	
Notes Payable		60,000

In addition to the non-cash transaction involving the issuance of a note to purchase land, the Land account was decreased by the condemnation proceedings. The following worksheet entry records the receipt of HK$18,500 for land having a book value of HK$10,500.

Land			
Bal.	82,000	(9)	10,500
(8)	60,000		
Bal.	131,500		

(9)

Investing—Proceeds from Condemnation of Land	18,500	
Land		10,500
Operating—Gain on Condemnation of Land		8,000

In reconciling net income to net cash flow from operating activities, Satellite deducts from net income the gain of HK$8,000. The reason is that the transaction that gave rise to the gain is an item whose cash effect is already classified as an investing cash inflow. The Land account is now reconciled.

Equipment and Accumulated Depreciation—Equipment

An analysis of Equipment and Accumulated Depreciation—Equipment shows that a number of transactions have affected these accounts. The company purchased equipment in the amount of HK$53,000 during the year. Satellite records this transaction on the worksheet as follows.

(10)

Equipment	53,000	
Investing—Purchase of Equipment		53,000

In addition, Satellite sold at a loss of HK$1,500 equipment with a book value of HK$5,500. It records this transaction as follows.

(11)

Investing—Sale of Equipment	4,000	
Operating—Loss on Sale of Equipment	1,500	
Accumulated Depreciation—Equipment	2,500	
Equipment		8,000

The proceeds from the sale of the equipment provided cash of HK$4,000. In addition, the loss on the sale of the equipment has reduced net income but did not affect cash. Therefore, the company adds back to net income the amount of the loss, in order to accurately report cash provided by operating activities.

Satellite reported depreciation on the equipment at HK$11,500 and recorded it on the worksheet as follows.

(12)

Operating—Depreciation Expense—Equipment	11,500	
Accumulated Depreciation—Equipment		11,500

The company adds depreciation expense back to net income because that expense reduced income but did not affect cash.

Finally, the company made a major repair to the equipment. It charged this expenditure, in the amount of HK$11,000, to the Equipment account. This expenditure required cash, and so Satellite makes the following worksheet entry.

(13)

Equipment	11,000	
Investing—Major Repairs of Equipment		11,000

After adjusting for the foregoing items, Satellite has reconciled the balances in the Equipment and related Accumulated Depreciation—Equipment accounts.

Equipment

Bal.	142,000	(11)	8,000
(10)	53,000		
(13)	11,000		
Bal.	198,000		

Accumulated Depreciation—Equipment

(11)	2,500	Bal.	31,000
		(12)	11,500
		Bal.	40,000

Building Depreciation and Amortization of Trademarks

Depreciation expense on the buildings of HK$3,100 and amortization of trademarks of HK$2,400 are both expenses in the income statement that reduced net income but did not require cash outflows in the current period. Satellite makes the following worksheet entry.

(14)

Operating—Depreciation Expense—Buildings	3,100	
Operating—Amortization of Trademarks	2,400	
Accumulated Depreciation—Buildings		3,100
Trademarks		2,400

Other Non-Cash Charges or Credits

Analysis of the remaining accounts indicates that changes in the Accounts Payable, Accrued Liabilities, Income Taxes Payable, Bonds Payable, and Deferred Tax Liability balances resulted from charges or credits to net income that did not affect cash. The company should individually analyze each of these items and enter them in the worksheet. The following compound entry summarizes these non-cash, income-related items.

	(15)		
Income Taxes Payable	13,000	
Bonds Payable	1,000	
Operating—Increase in Accounts Payable	1,000	
Operating—Increase in Accrued Liabilities	4,000	
Operating—Increase in Deferred Tax Liability	3,000	
Operating—Decrease in Income Taxes Payable		13,000
Operating—Amortization of Bond Premium		1,000
Accounts Payable		1,000
Accrued Liabilities		4,000
Deferred Tax Liability		3,000

Share Capital—Ordinary and Related Accounts

Comparison of the Share Capital—Ordinary and the Share Premium—Ordinary balances shows that transactions during the year affected these accounts. First, Satellite issues a share dividend of 2 percent to shareholders. As the discussion of worksheet entry (2) indicated, no cash was provided or used by the share dividend transaction. In addition to the shares issued via the share dividend, Satellite sold ordinary shares at HK$16 per share. The company records this transaction as follows.

Share Capital—Ordinary

Bal.	50,000
(2)	1,000
(16)	9,000
Bal.	60,000

Share Premium—Ordinary

Bal.	38,000
(2)	14,000
(16)	135,000
Bal.	187,000

	(16)		
Financing—Sale of Ordinary Shares	144,000	
Share Capital—Ordinary		9,000
Share Premium—Ordinary		135,000

Also, the company purchased its ordinary shares in the amount of HK$17,000. It records this transaction on the worksheet as follows.

	(17)		
Treasury Shares	17,000	
Financing—Purchase of Treasury Shares		17,000

Final Reconciling Entry

The final entry to reconcile the change in cash and to balance the worksheet is shown below. The HK$7,000 amount is the difference between the beginning and ending cash balance.

	(18)		
Decrease in Cash	7,000	
Cash		7,000

Once the company has determined that the differences between the beginning and ending balances per the worksheet columns have been accounted for, it can total the reconciling transactions columns, and they should balance. Satellite can prepare the statement of cash flows entirely from the items and amounts that appear at the bottom of the worksheet under "Statement of Cash Flows Effects," as shown in Illustration 23-41.

SATELLITE CORPORATION.xls

Home Insert Page Layout Formulas Data Review View

P18

SATELLITE CORPORATION
Worksheet for Preparation of Statement of Cash Flows
for the Year Ended December 31, 2016 (in thousands)

	Balance 12/31/15		Reconciling Items—2016 Dr.		Cr.	Balance 12/31/16
Debits						
Cash	HK$ 66,000			(18)	HK$ 7,000	HK$ 59,000
Accounts receivable (net)	51,000	(4)	HK$ 53,000			104,000
Inventory	341,000	(5)	152,000			493,000
Prepaid expenses	17,000			(6)	500	16,500
Investment (equity method)	15,000	(7)	3,500			18,500
Land	82,000	(8)	60,000	(9)	10,500	131,500
Equipment	142,000	(10)	53,000	(11)	8,000	198,000
		(13)	11,000			
Buildings	262,000					262,000
Trademarks	10,000			(14)	2,400	7,600
Treasury shares		(17)	17,000			17,000
Total debits	HK$986,000					HK$1,307,100
Credits						
Accum. depr.–equipment	HK$ 31,000	(11)	2,500	(12)	11,500	HK$ 40,000
Accum. depr.–buildings	71,000			(14)	3,100	74,100
Accounts payable	131,000			(15)	1,000	132,000
Accrued liabilities	39,000			(15)	4,000	43,000
Income taxes payable	16,000	(15)	13,000			3,000
Notes payable	-0-			(8)	60,000	60,000
Bonds payable	108,000	(15)	1,000			107,000
Deferred tax liability	6,000			(15)	3,000	9,000
Share capital—ordinary	50,000			(2)	1,000	
				(16)	9,000	60,000
Share premium—ordinary	38,000			(2)	14,000	
				(16)	135,000	187,000
Retained earnings	496,000	(2)	15,000	(1)	117,000	
		(3)	6,000			592,000
Total credits	HK$986,000					HK$1,307,100
Statement of Cash Flows Effects						
Operating activities						
Net income		(1)	117,000			
Increase in accounts receivable (net)				(4)	53,000	
Increase in inventory				(5)	152,000	
Decrease in prepaid expenses		(6)	500			
Equity in earnings of Porter Co.				(7)	3,500	
Gain on condemnation of land				(9)	8,000	
Loss on sale of equipment		(11)	1,500			
Depr. expense–equipment		(12)	11,500			
Depr. expense–buildings		(14)	3,100			
Amortization of trademarks		(14)	2,400			
Increase in accounts payable		(15)	1,000			
Increase in accrued liabilities		(15)	4,000			
Increase in deferred tax liability		(15)	3,000			
Decrease in income taxes payable				(15)	13,000	
Amortization of bond premium				(15)	1,000	
Investing activities						
Proceeds from condemnation of land		(9)	18,500			
Purchase of equipment				(10)	53,000	
Sale of equipment		(11)	4,000			
Major repairs of equipment				(13)	11,000	
Financing activities						
Payment of cash dividend				(3)	6,000	
Issuance of ordinary shares		(16)	144,000			
Purchase of treasury shares				(17)	17,000	
Totals			697,500		704,500	
Decrease in cash		(18)	7,000			
Totals			HK$704,500		HK$704,500	

ILLUSTRATION 23-41
Completed Worksheet for Preparation of Statement of Cash Flows, Satellite Corporation

Preparation of Final Statement

Illustration 23-42 presents a formal statement of cash flows prepared from the data compiled in the lower portion of the worksheet.

ILLUSTRATION 23-42
Statement of Cash Flows,
Satellite Corporation

SATELLITE CORPORATION
STATEMENT OF CASH FLOWS
FOR THE YEAR ENDED DECEMBER 31, 2016
INCREASE (DECREASE) IN CASH
(IN THOUSANDS)

Cash flows from operating activities		
Net income		HK$117,000
Adjustments to reconcile net income to net		
cash used by operating activities:		
Depreciation expense	HK$ 14,600	
Amortization of trademarks	2,400	
Amortization of bond premium	(1,000)	
Equity in earnings of Porter Co.	(3,500)	
Gain on condemnation of land	(8,000)	
Loss on sale of equipment	1,500	
Increase in deferred tax liability	3,000	
Increase in accounts receivable (net)	(53,000)	
Increase in inventory	(152,000)	
Decrease in prepaid expenses	500	
Increase in accounts payable	1,000	
Increase in accrued liabilities	4,000	
Decrease in income taxes payable	(13,000)	(203,500)
Net cash used by operating activities		(86,500)
Cash flows from investing activities		
Proceeds from condemnation of land	18,500	
Purchase of equipment	(53,000)	
Sale of equipment	4,000	
Major repairs of equipment	(11,000)	
Net cash used by investing activities		(41,500)
Cash flows from financing activities		
Payment of cash dividend	(6,000)	
Issuance of ordinary shares	144,000	
Purchase of treasury shares	(17,000)	
Net cash provided by financing activities		121,000
Net decrease in cash		(7,000)
Cash, January 1, 2016		66,000
Cash, December 31, 2016		HK$ 59,000

In addition, a supplemental note of Non-Cash Investing and Financing Activities is as follows.

Supplemental Note of Non-Cash Investing and Financing Activities
Purchase of land for HK$60,000 in exchange for a HK$60,000 long-term note.

GLOBAL ACCOUNTING INSIGHTS

STATEMENT OF CASH FLOWS

As in IFRS, the statement of cash flows is a required statement for U.S. GAAP. In addition, the content and presentation of a U.S. GAAP statement of cash flows is similar to one used for IFRS. However, the disclosure requirements related to the statement of cash flows are more extensive under U.S. GAAP.

Relevant Facts

Following are the key similarities and differences between U.S. GAAP and IFRS related to the statement of cash flows.

Similarities

• Both U.S. GAAP and IFRS require that companies prepare a statement of cash flows.

• Both U.S. GAAP and IFRS require that the statement of cash flows should have three major sections—operating, investing, and financing—along with changes in cash and cash equivalents.

• Similar to U.S. GAAP, the cash flow statement can be prepared using either the indirect or direct method under IFRS. For both U.S. GAAP and IFRS, most companies use the indirect method for reporting net cash flow from operating activities.

• The definition of cash equivalents used in U.S. GAAP is similar to that used in IFRS.

Differences

• Under U.S. GAAP, bank overdrafts are classified as financing activities. A major difference in the definition of cash and cash equivalents is that in certain situations, bank overdrafts are considered part of cash and cash equivalents under IFRS.

• Under U.S. GAAP, companies may present non-cash investing and financing activities in the cash flow statement. IFRS requires that non-cash investing and financing activities be excluded from the statement of cash flows. As indicated in the chapter, these non-cash activities should be reported elsewhere. This requirement is interpreted to mean that non-cash investing and financing activities should be disclosed in the notes to the financial statements instead of in the financial statements.

• One area where there can be substantive differences between U.S. GAAP and IFRS relates to the classification of interest, dividends, and taxes. U.S. GAAP requires that except for dividends paid (which are classified as a financing activity), these items are all reported as operating activities. IFRS provides more alternatives for disclosing these items.

About the Numbers

One area where there can be substantive differences between U.S. GAAP and IFRS relates to the classification of interest, dividends, and taxes. The following table indicates the differences between the two approaches.

Item	IFRS	U.S. GAAP
Interest paid	Operating or financing	Operating
Interest received	Operating or investing	Operating
Dividends paid	Operating or financing	Financing
Dividends received	Operating or investing	Operating
Taxes paid	Operating—unless specific identification with financing or investing	Operating[1, 2]

[1]U.S. GAAP has additional disclosure rules.
[2]U.S. GAAP has specific rules regarding the classification of the benefit associated with share-based compensation arrangements and the classification of derivatives that contain a financing element.

Source: PricewaterhouseCoopers, *Similarities and Difference–A Comparison of IFRS and U.S. GAAP* (October 2013).

As indicated, the major difference is that IFRS provides more alternatives for disclosing certain items.

On the Horizon

Presently, the IASB and the FASB are involved in a joint project on the presentation and organization of information in the financial statements. With respect to the cash flow statement specifically, the notion of *cash equivalents* will probably not be retained. The definition of cash in the existing literature would be retained, and the statement of cash flows would present information on changes in cash only. In addition, the IASB and FASB favor presentation of operating cash flows using the direct method only.

SUMMARY OF LEARNING OBJECTIVES

1 Describe the purpose of the statement of cash flows. The primary purpose of the statement of cash flows is to provide information about cash receipts and cash payments of an entity during a period. A secondary objective is to report the entity's operating, investing, and financing activities during the period.

2 Identify the major classifications of cash flows. Companies classify cash flows as follows. (1) *Operating activities*—transactions that result in the revenues, expenses, gains, and losses that determine net income. (2) *Investing activities*—lending money and collecting on those loans, and acquiring and disposing of investments, plant assets, and intangible assets. (3) *Financing activities*—obtaining cash from creditors and repaying loans, issuing and reacquiring share capital, and paying cash dividends.

3 Prepare a statement of cash flows. Preparing the statement involves three major steps. (1) *Determine the change in cash.* This is the difference between the beginning and the ending cash balance shown on the comparative statements of financial position. (2) *Determine the net cash flow from operating activities.* This procedure is complex; it involves analyzing not only the current year's income statement but also the comparative statements of financial position and the selected transaction data. (3) *Determine cash flows from investing and financing activities.* Analyze all other changes in the statement of financial position accounts to determine the effects on cash.

4 Differentiate between net income and net cash flow from operating activities. Companies must adjust net income on an accrual basis to determine net cash flow from operating activities because some expenses and losses do not cause cash outflows, and some revenues and gains do not provide cash inflows.

5 Determine net cash flows from investing and financing activities. Once a company has computed the net cash flow from operating activities, the next step is to determine whether any other changes in statement of financial position accounts caused an increase or decrease in cash. Net cash flows from investing and financing activities can be determined by examining the changes in non-current statement of financial position accounts.

6 Identify sources of information for a statement of cash flows. The information to prepare the statement usually comes from three sources. (1) *Comparative statements of financial position.* Information in these statements indicates the amount of the changes in assets, liabilities, and equities during the period. (2) *Current income statement.* Information in this statement is used in determining the cash provided by operations during the period. (3) *Selected transaction data.* These data from the general ledger provide additional detailed information needed to determine how cash was provided or used during the period.

7 Contrast the direct and indirect methods of calculating net cash flow from operating activities. Under the direct approach, companies calculate the major classes of operating cash receipts and cash disbursements. Presentation of the direct approach of reporting net cash flow from operating activities takes the form of a condensed cash-basis income statement. The indirect method adds back to net income the non-cash expenses and losses and subtracts the non-cash revenues and gains.

8 Discuss special problems in preparing a statement of cash flows. These special problems are (1) adjustments to net income, (2) accounts receivable (net), (3) other working capital changes, (4) net loss, and (5) disclosures.

9 **Explain the use of a worksheet in preparing a statement of cash flows.**
When numerous adjustments are necessary or other complicating factors are present, companies often use a worksheet to assemble and classify the data that will appear on the statement of cash flows. The worksheet is merely a device that aids in the preparation of the statement. Its use is optional.

IFRS AUTHORITATIVE LITERATURE

Authoritative Literature References

[1] International Accounting Standard 7, *Statement of Cash Flows* (London, U.K.: International Accounting Standards Committee Foundation, 2001).

[2] International Accounting Standard 7, *Statement of Cash Flows* (London, U.K.: International Accounting Standards Committee Foundation, 2001), paras. 13–17.

[3] International Accounting Standard 7, *Statement of Cash Flows* (London, U.K.: International Accounting Standards Committee Foundation, 2001), par. 7.

[4] International Accounting Standard 7, *Statement of Cash Flows* (London, U.K.: International Accounting Standards Committee Foundation, 2001), par. 19.

[5] International Accounting Standard 7, *Statement of Cash Flows* (London, U.K.: International Accounting Standards Committee Foundation, 2001), par. 36.

[6] International Accounting Standard 7, *Statement of Cash Flows* (London, U.K.: International Accounting Standards Committee Foundation, 2001), par. 43.

[7] International Accounting Standard 7, *Statement of Cash Flows* (London, U.K.: International Accounting Standards Committee Foundation, 2001), par. 31.

QUESTIONS

1. What is the purpose of the statement of cash flows? What information does it provide?

2. Of what use is the statement of cash flows?

3. Differentiate between investing activities, financing activities, and operating activities.

4. What are the major sources of cash (inflows) in a statement of cash flows? What are the major uses (outflows) of cash?

5. Identify and explain the major steps involved in preparing the statement of cash flows.

6. Identify the following items as (1) operating, (2) investing, or (3) financing activities: purchase of land, payment of dividends, cash sales, and purchase of treasury shares.

7. Unlike the other major financial statements, the statement of cash flows is not prepared from the adjusted trial balance. From what sources does the information to prepare this statement come, and what information does each source provide?

8. Why is it necessary to convert accrual-based net income to a cash basis when preparing a statement of cash flows?

9. Differentiate between the direct method and the indirect method by discussing each method.

10. Broussard Company reported net income of $3.5 million in 2015. Depreciation for the year was $520,000, accounts receivable increased $500,000, and accounts payable increased $300,000. Compute net cash flow from operating activities using the indirect method.

11. Collinsworth Co. reported sales on an accrual basis of £100,000. If accounts receivable increased £30,000 and the allowance for doubtful accounts increased £9,000 after a write-off of £2,000, compute cash sales.

12. Your roommate is puzzled. During the last year, the company in which she is a shareholder reported a net loss of $675,000, yet its cash increased $321,000 during the same period of time. Explain to your roommate how this situation could occur.

13. The board of directors of Gifford Corp. declared cash dividends of £260,000 during the current year. If dividends payable was £85,000 at the beginning of the year and £90,000 at the end of the year, how much cash was paid in dividends during the year?

14. Explain how the amount of cash payments to suppliers is computed under the direct method.

15. The net income for Letterman Company for 2015 was €320,000. During 2015, depreciation on plant assets was €124,000, amortization of patent was €40,000, and the company incurred a loss on sale of plant assets of €21,000. Compute net cash flow from operating activities.

16. Each of the following items must be considered in preparing a statement of cash flows for Blackwell Inc. for the year ended December 31, 2015. Indicate how each item is to be shown in the statement, if at all.

(a) Plant assets that had cost $18,000 6½ years before and were being depreciated on a straight-line basis over 10 years with no estimated residual value were sold for $4,000.

(b) During the year, 10,000 ordinary shares with a stated value of $20 a share were issued for $41 a share.

(c) Uncollectible accounts receivable in the amount of $22,000 were written off against Allowance for Doubtful Accounts.

(d) The company sustained a net loss for the year of $50,000. Depreciation amounted to $22,000, and a gain of $9,000 was realized on the sale of non-trading equity investments for $38,000 cash.

17. Classify the following items as (1) operating, (2) investing, (3) financing, or (4) significant non-cash investing and financing activities, using the direct method.

(a) Cash payments to employees.
(b) Redemption of bonds payable.
(c) Sale of building at book value.
(d) Cash payments to suppliers.
(e) Exchange of equipment for furniture.
(f) Issuance of preference shares.
(g) Cash received from customers.
(h) Purchase of treasury shares.

(i) Issuance of bonds for land.
(j) Payment of dividends.
(k) Purchase of equipment.
(l) Cash payments for operating expenses.

18. Silva Rojas and Hans Jensen were discussing the statement of cash flows of Liu Co. In the notes to the statement of cash flows was a schedule entitled "Non-cash investing and financing activities." Give three examples of significant non-cash transactions that would be reported in this schedule.

19. During 2015, Simms Company redeemed ¥2,000,000 of bonds payable for ¥1,880,000 cash. Indicate how this transaction would be reported on a statement of cash flows, if at all.

20. What are some of the arguments in favor of using the indirect (reconciliation) method as opposed to the direct method for reporting a statement of cash flows?

21. Why is it desirable to use a worksheet when preparing a statement of cash flows? Is a worksheet required to prepare a statement of cash flows?

22. Briefly describe some of the similarities and differences between IFRS and U.S. GAAP with respect to cash flow reporting.

23. Explain how the accounting for interest received and paid in a statement of cash flows may differ between IFRS and U.S. GAAP.

24. What are some of the key obstacles for the IASB and FASB in their convergence project for the statement of cash flows?

BRIEF EXERCISES

5 BE23-1 Wainwright Corporation had the following activities in 2015.

1. Sale of land $180,000.
2. Purchase of inventory $845,000.
3. Purchase of treasury shares $72,000.
4. Purchase of equipment $415,000.
5. Issuance of ordinary shares $320,000.
6. Purchase of investments—equity $59,000.

Compute the amount Wainwright should report as net cash provided (used) by investing activities in its statement of cash flows.

5 BE23-2 Stansfield Corporation had the following activities in 2015.

1. Payment of accounts payable €770,000.
2. Issuance of ordinary shares €250,000.
3. Payment of dividends €350,000.
4. Collection of note receivable €100,000.
5. Issuance of bonds payable €510,000.
6. Purchase of treasury shares €46,000.

Compute the amount Stansfield should report as net cash provided (used) by financing activities in its 2015 statement of cash flows.

2 BE23-3 Novak Corporation is preparing its 2015 statement of cash flows, using the indirect method. The following is a list of items that may affect the statement. Using the code letters provided, indicate how each item will affect Novak's 2015 statement of cash flows.

Code Letter	Effect
A	Added to net income in the operating section
D	Deducted from net income in the operating section
R-I	Cash receipt in investing section
P-I	Cash payment in investing section
R-F	Cash receipt in financing section
P-F	Cash payment in financing section
N	Non-cash investing and/or financing activity in notes

Items

(a) Purchase of land and building.
(b) Decrease in accounts receivable.
(c) Issuance of shares.
(d) Depreciation expense.
(e) Sale of land at book value.
(f) Sale of land at a gain.
(g) Payment of dividends.
(h) Increase in accounts receivable.
(i) Purchase of an equity investment.
(j) Increase in accounts payable.
(k) Decrease in accounts payable.
(l) Loan from bank by signing note.
(m) Purchase of equipment using a note.
(n) Increase in inventory.
(o) Issuance of bonds.
(p) Retirement of bonds payable.
(q) Sale of equipment at a loss.
(r) Purchase of treasury shares.

4 7 BE23-4 Bloom Corporation had the following 2015 income statement.

Sales revenue	€200,000
Cost of goods sold	120,000
Gross profit	80,000
Operating expenses (includes depreciation of €21,000)	50,000
Net income	€ 30,000

The following accounts increased during 2015: accounts receivable €12,000, inventory €11,000, and accounts payable €13,000. Prepare the cash flows from operating activities section of Bloom's 2015 statement of cash flows using the direct method.

4 7 BE23-5 Use the information from BE23-4 for Bloom Corporation. Prepare the cash flows from operating activities section of Bloom's 2015 statement of cash flows using the indirect method.

7 BE23-6 At January 1, 2015, Eikenberry Inc. had accounts receivable of $72,000. At December 31, 2015, accounts receivable is $54,000. Sales for 2015 total $420,000. Compute Eikenberry's 2015 cash receipts from customers.

7 BE23-7 Moxley Corporation had January 1 and December 31 balances as follows.

	1/1/15	12/31/15
Inventory	€95,000	€113,000
Accounts payable	61,000	69,000

For 2015, cost of goods sold was €500,000. Compute Moxley's 2015 cash payments to suppliers.

3 BE23-8 In 2015, Elbert Corporation had net cash provided by operating activities of £531,000, net cash used by investing activities of £963,000, and net cash provided by financing activities of £585,000. At January 1, 2015, the cash balance was £333,000. Compute December 31, 2015, cash.

4 7 BE23-9 Loveless Corporation had the following 2015 income statement.

Revenues	$100,000
Expenses	60,000
	$ 40,000

In 2015, Loveless had the following activity in selected accounts.

Accounts Receivable

1/1/15	20,000			
Revenues	100,000	1,000	Write-offs	
		90,000	Collections	
12/31/15	29,000			

Allowance for Doubtful Accounts

		1,200	1/1/15
Write-offs	1,000	1,840	Bad debt expense
		2,040	12/31/15

Prepare Loveless's cash flows from operating activities section of the statement of cash flows using (a) the direct method and (b) the indirect method.

4 **BE23-10** Hendrickson Corporation reported net income of $50,000 in 2015. Depreciation expense was $17,000. The following working capital accounts changed.

Accounts receivable	$11,000 increase
Non-trading equity investment	16,000 increase
Inventory	7,400 increase
Non-trade notes payable	15,000 decrease
Accounts payable	12,300 increase

Compute net cash provided by operating activities.

4 **BE23-11** In 2015, Shaw Corporation reported a net loss of €70,000. Shaw's only net income adjustments were depreciation expense €81,000, and increase in accounts receivable €8,100. Compute Shaw's net cash provided (used) by operating activities.

8 **BE23-12** In 2015, Leppard Inc. issued 1,000 ordinary shares of $10 par value for land worth $40,000.

   (a) Prepare Leppard's journal entry to record the transaction.
   (b) Indicate the effect the transaction has on cash.
   (c) Indicate how the transaction is reported on the statement of cash flows.

9 **BE23-13** Indicate in general journal form how the items below would be entered in a worksheet for the preparation of the statement of cash flows.

   (a) Net income is ¥317,000,000.
   (b) Cash dividends declared and paid totaled ¥120,000,000.
   (c) Equipment was purchased for ¥114,000,000.
   (d) Equipment that originally cost ¥40,000,000 and had accumulated depreciation of ¥32,000,000 was sold for ¥10,000,000.

EXERCISES

2 **E23-1 (Classification of Transactions)** Springsteen Co. had the following activity in its most recent year of operations.

   (a) Pension expense exceeds amount funded.
   (b) Redemption of bonds payable.
   (c) Sale of building at book value.
   (d) Depreciation.
   (e) Exchange of equipment for furniture.
   (f) Issuance of ordinary shares.
   (g) Amortization of intangible assets.
   (h) Purchase of treasury shares.
   (i) Issuance of bonds for land.
   (j) Payment of dividends.
   (k) Increase in interest receivable on notes receivable.
   (l) Purchase of equipment.

Instructions
Classify the items as (1) operating—add to net income, (2) operating—deduct from net income, (3) investing, (4) financing, or (5) significant non-cash investing and financing activities. Use the indirect method.

2 **4** **E23-2 (Statement Presentation of Transactions—Indirect Method)** Each of the following items must be considered in preparing a statement of cash flows (indirect method) for Granderson Inc. for the year ended December 31, 2015.

   (a) Plant assets that had cost €25,000 6 years before and were being depreciated on a straight-line basis over 10 years with no estimated residual value were sold at the beginning of the year for €5,300.
   (b) During the year, 10,000 ordinary shares with a stated value of €10 a share were issued for €33 a share.
   (c) Uncollectible accounts receivable in the amount of €27,000 were written off against Allowance for Doubtful Accounts.
   (d) The company sustained a net loss for the year of €50,000. Depreciation amounted to €22,000, and a gain of €9,000 was realized on the sale of land for €39,000 cash.
   (e) A 3-month certificate of deposit was purchased for €100,000. The company uses a cash and cash-equivalent basis for its cash flow statement.
   (f) Patent amortization for the year was €20,000.
   (g) The company exchanged ordinary shares for a 70% interest in Plumlee Co. for €900,000.
   (h) During the year, treasury shares costing €47,000 were purchased.
   (i) The company recognized an unrealized holding gain on a debt investment not held for collection.

Instructions

State where each item is to be shown in the statement of cash flows, if at all.

4 7 E23-3 (Preparation of Operating Activities Section—Indirect Method, Periodic Inventory) The income statement of Rodriquez Company is shown below.

RODRIQUEZ COMPANY
INCOME STATEMENT
FOR THE YEAR ENDED DECEMBER 31, 2015

Sales revenue		R$6,900,000
Cost of goods sold		
Beginning inventory	R$1,900,000	
Purchases	4,400,000	
Goods available for sale	6,300,000	
Ending inventory	1,600,000	
Cost of goods sold		4,700,000
Gross profit		2,200,000
Operating expenses		
Selling expenses	450,000	
Administrative expenses	700,000	1,150,000
Net income		R$1,050,000

Additional information:

1. Accounts receivable decreased R$310,000 during the year.
2. Prepaid expenses increased R$170,000 during the year.
3. Accounts payable to suppliers of merchandise decreased R$275,000 during the year.
4. Accrued expenses payable decreased R$120,000 during the year.
5. Administrative expenses include depreciation expense of R$60,000.

Instructions

Prepare the operating activities section of the statement of cash flows for the year ended December 31, 2015, for Rodriquez Company, using the indirect method.

4 7 E23-4 (Preparation of Operating Activities Section—Direct Method) Data for the Rodriquez Company are presented in E23-3.

Instructions

Prepare the operating activities section of the statement of cash flows using the direct method.

4 7 E23-5 (Preparation of Operating Activities Section—Direct Method) Norman Company's income statement for the year ended December 31, 2015, contained the following condensed information.

Service revenue		€840,000
Operating expenses (excluding depreciation)	€624,000	
Depreciation expense	60,000	
Loss on sale of equipment	26,000	710,000
Income before income taxes		130,000
Income tax expense		40,000
Net income		€ 90,000

Norman's statement of financial position contained the following comparative data at December 31.

	2015	2014
Accounts receivable	€37,000	€59,000
Accounts payable	46,000	31,000
Income taxes payable	4,000	8,500

(Accounts payable pertains to operating expenses.)

Instructions

Prepare the operating activities section of the statement of cash flows using the direct method.

4 7 E23-6 (Preparation of Operating Activities Section—Indirect Method) Data for Norman Company are presented in E23-5.

Instructions

Prepare the operating activities section of the statement of cash flows using the indirect method.

4 7 E23-7 (Computation of Operating Activities—Direct Method) Presented below are two independent situations.

Situation A: Chenowith Co. reports revenues of €200,000 and operating expenses of €110,000 in its first year of operations, 2015. Accounts receivable and accounts payable at year-end were €71,000 and €39,000, respectively. Assume that the accounts payable related to operating expenses. (Ignore income taxes.)

Instructions

Using the direct method, compute net cash provided (used) by operating activities.

Situation B: The income statement for Edgebrook Company shows cost of goods sold €310,000 and operating expenses (exclusive of depreciation) €230,000. The comparative statements of financial position for the year show that inventory increased €21,000, prepaid expenses decreased €8,000, accounts payable (related to merchandise) decreased €17,000, and accrued expenses payable increased €11,000.

Instructions

Compute (a) cash payments to suppliers and (b) cash payments for operating expenses.

4 7 E23-8 (Schedule of Net Cash Flow from Operating Activities—Indirect Method) Messner Co. reported €145,000 of net income for 2015. The accountant, in preparing the statement of cash flows, noted several items occurring during 2015 that might affect cash flows from operating activities. These items are listed below.

1. Messner purchased 100 treasury shares at a cost of €20 per share. These shares were then resold at €25 per share.

2. Messner sold 100 ordinary shares of Nokia at €200 per share. The acquisition cost of these shares was €165 per share. This investment was shown on Messner's December 31, 2014, statement of financial position as a non-trading equity investment.

3. Messner revised its estimate for bad debts. Before 2015, Messner's bad debt expense was 1% of its net sales. In 2015, this percentage was increased to 2%. Net sales for 2015 were €500,000, and net accounts receivable decreased by €12,000 during 2015.

4. Messner issued 500 ordinary shares with a €10 par value for a patent. The fair value of the shares on the date of the transaction was €23 per share.

5. Depreciation expense is €39,000.

6. Messner Co. holds 30% of the Sanchez Company's ordinary shares as a long-term investment. Sanchez Company reported €27,000 of net income for 2015.

7. Sanchez Company paid a total of €2,000 of cash dividends to all investees in 2015.

8. Messner declared a 10% share dividend. One thousand ordinary shares with a €10 par value were distributed. The market price at date of issuance was €20 per share.

Instructions

Prepare a schedule that shows the net cash flow from operating activities using the indirect method. Assume no items other than those listed above affected the computation of 2015 net cash flow from operating activities.

7 E23-9 (SCF—Direct Method) Costa Corp. uses the direct method to prepare its statement of cash flows. Costa's trial balances at December 31, 2015 and 2014, are as follows.

	December 31	
	2015	2014
Debits		
Cash	R$ 35,000	R$ 32,000
Accounts receivable	33,000	30,000
Inventory	31,000	47,000
Property, plant, and equipment	100,000	95,000
Cost of goods sold	250,000	380,000
Selling expenses	141,500	172,000
General and administrative expenses	137,000	151,300
Interest expense	4,300	2,600
Income tax expense	20,400	61,200
	R$752,200	R$971,100
Credits		
Allowance for doubtful accounts	R$ 1,300	R$ 1,100
Accumulated depreciation	16,500	13,500
Accounts payable	25,000	17,000
Income taxes payable	21,000	29,100
Deferred income taxes	5,300	4,600
8% callable bonds payable	40,500	15,000
Share capital—ordinary	50,000	40,000
Share premium—ordinary	9,100	7,500
Retained earnings	44,700	64,600
Sales revenue	538,800	778,700
	R$752,200	R$971,100

Additional information:

1. Costa purchased R$5,000 in equipment during 2015.
2. Costa allocated one-third of its depreciation expense to selling expenses and the remainder to general and administrative expenses.
3. Bad debt expense for 2015 was R$5,000, and write-offs of uncollectible accounts totaled R$3,800.
4. Interest expense includes R$500 of discount amortization.

Instructions

Determine what amounts Costa should report in its statement of cash flows for the year ended December 31, 2015, for the following items.

(a) Cash collected from customers.
(b) Cash paid to suppliers.
(c) Cash paid for interest.
(d) Cash paid for income taxes.
(e) Cash paid for selling expenses.

2 8 **E23-10 (Classification of Transactions)** Following are selected statement of financial position accounts of Sander Bros. Corp. at December 31, 2015 and 2014, and the increases or decreases in each account from 2014 to 2015. Also presented is selected income statement information for the year ended December 31, 2015, and additional information.

Selected statement of financial position accounts	2015	2014	Increase (Decrease)
Assets			
Property, plant, and equipment	$ 277,000	$247,000	$ 30,000
Accumulated depreciation	(178,000)	(167,000)	(11,000)
Accounts receivable	34,000	24,000	10,000
Equity and liabilities			
Share capital—ordinary, $1 par	$ 22,000	$ 19,000	$ 3,000
Share premium—ordinary	9,000	3,000	6,000
Retained earnings	104,000	91,000	13,000
Bonds payable	49,000	46,000	3,000
Dividends payable	8,000	5,000	3,000

Selected income statement information for the year ended December 31, 2015

Sales revenue	$ 155,000
Depreciation	38,000
Gain on sale of equipment	14,500
Net income	31,000

Additional information:

1. During 2015, equipment costing $45,000 was sold for cash.

2. Accounts receivable relate to sales of merchandise.

3. During 2015, $25,000 of bonds payable were issued in exchange for property, plant, and equipment. There was no amortization of bond discount or premium.

Instructions

Determine the category (operating, investing, or financing) and the amount that should be reported in the statement of cash flows for the following items.

   (a) Payments for purchase of property, plant, and equipment.
   (b) Proceeds from the sale of equipment.
   (c) Cash dividends paid.
   (d) Redemption of bonds payable.

3 **E23-11 (SCF—Indirect Method)** Condensed financial data of Fairchild Company for 2015 and 2014 are presented below.

FAIRCHILD COMPANY
COMPARATIVE STATEMENTS OF FINANCIAL POSITION
AS OF DECEMBER 31, 2015 AND 2014

	2015	2014
Debt investments (held-for-collection)	€1,300	€1,470
Plant assets	1,900	1,700
Accumulated depreciation	(1,200)	(1,170)
Inventory	1,600	1,900
Accounts receivable	1,750	1,300
Cash	1,800	1,100
	€7,150	€6,300
Share capital—ordinary	€1,900	€1,700
Retained earnings	2,450	1,900
Bonds payable	1,400	1,650
Accounts payable	1,200	800
Accrued liabilities	200	250
	€7,150	€6,300

FAIRCHILD COMPANY
INCOME STATEMENT
FOR THE YEAR ENDED DECEMBER 31, 2015

Sales revenue		€6,900
Cost of goods sold		4,700
Gross margin		2,200
Selling and administrative expense		930
Income from operations		1,270
Other income and expense		
Gain on sale of investments		80
Income before tax		1,350
Income tax expense		540
Net income		€ 810

Additional information:

During the year, €70 of ordinary shares were issued in exchange for plant assets. No plant assets were sold in 2015. Cash dividends were €260.

Instructions
Prepare a statement of cash flows using the indirect method.

E23-12 (SCF—Direct Method) Data for Fairchild Company are presented in E23-11.

Instructions
Prepare a statement of cash flows using the direct method.

E23-13 (SCF—Direct Method) Andrews Inc., a greeting card company, had the following statements prepared as of December 31, 2015.

ANDREWS INC.
COMPARATIVE STATEMENT OF FINANCIAL POSITION
AS OF DECEMBER 31, 2015 AND 2014

	12/31/15	12/31/14
Equipment	€154,000	€130,000
Accumulated depr.—equipment	(35,000)	(25,000)
Copyrights	46,000	50,000
Inventory	40,000	60,000
Prepaid rent	5,000	4,000
Accounts receivable	62,000	49,000
Short-term investments (trading)	35,000	18,000
Cash	6,000	9,000
Total assets	€313,000	€295,000
Share capital—ordinary, €10 par	€100,000	€100,000
Share premium—ordinary	30,000	30,000
Retained earnings	57,000	36,000
Long-term loans payable	60,000	67,000
Accounts payable	46,000	42,000
Income taxes payable	4,000	6,000
Salaries and wages payable	8,000	4,000
Short-term loans payable	8,000	10,000
Total equity and liabilities	€313,000	€295,000

ANDREWS INC.
INCOME STATEMENT
FOR THE YEAR ENDING DECEMBER 31, 2015

Sales revenue		€338,150
Cost of goods sold		175,000
Gross margin		163,150
Operating expenses		120,000
Operating income		43,150
Interest expense	€11,400	
Gain on sale of equipment	2,000	9,400
Income before tax		33,750
Income tax expense		6,750
Net income		€ 27,000

Additional information:
1. Dividends in the amount of €6,000 were declared and paid during 2015.
2. Depreciation expense and amortization expense are included in operating expenses.
3. No unrealized gains or losses have occurred on the investments during the year.
4. Equipment that had a cost of €30,000 and was 70% depreciated was sold during 2015.

Instructions
Prepare a statement of cash flows using the direct method.

3 **E23-14** **(SCF—Indirect Method)** Data for Andrews Inc. are presented in E23-13.

Instructions
Prepare a statement of cash flows using the indirect method.

3 **E23-15** **(SCF—Indirect Method)** The following are data taken from the records of Durand Company.

	December 31, 2015	December 31, 2014
Cash	€ 15,000	€ 10,000
Current assets other than cash	85,000	58,000
Long-term investments	10,000	53,000
Plant assets	335,000	215,000
	€445,000	€336,000
Accumulated depreciation	€ 20,000	€ 40,000
Current liabilities	40,000	22,000
Bonds payable	75,000	–0–
Share capital—ordinary	254,000	254,000
Retained earnings	56,000	20,000
	€445,000	€336,000

Additional information:

1. Held-for-collection investments carried at a cost of €43,000 on December 31, 2014, were sold in 2015 for €34,000. The loss was incorrectly charged directly to Retained Earnings.

2. Plant assets that cost €60,000 and were 80% depreciated were sold during 2015 for €8,000. The loss was incorrectly charged directly to Retained Earnings.

3. Net income as reported on the income statement for the year was €59,000.

4. Dividends paid amounted to €10,000.

5. Depreciation charged for the year was €28,000.

Instructions
Prepare a statement of cash flows for the year 2015 using the indirect method.

2 **4** **5** **E23-16** **(Cash Provided by Operating, Investing, and Financing Activities)** The statement of financial position data of Yang Company at the end of 2015 and 2014 follow (amounts in thousands).

	2015	2014
Equipment	¥ 90,000	¥ 75,000
Accumulated depreciation—equipment	(18,000)	(8,000)
Land	70,000	40,000
Inventory	65,000	45,000
Accounts receivable (net)	55,000	45,000
Prepaid expenses	15,000	25,000
Cash	30,000	35,000
	¥307,000	¥257,000
Share capital—ordinary, $10 par	¥189,000	¥159,000
Retained earnings	8,000	5,000
Notes payable—bank, long-term	–0–	23,000
Bonds payable	30,000	–0–
Accounts payable	65,000	52,000
Accrued expenses	15,000	18,000
	¥307,000	¥257,000

Land was acquired for ¥30,000 in exchange for ordinary shares, par ¥30,000, during the year; all equipment purchased was for cash. Equipment costing ¥13,000 was sold for ¥3,000; book value of the equipment was ¥6,000. Cash dividends of ¥9,000 were declared and paid during the year.

Instructions
Compute net cash provided (used) by:
   (a) Operating activities (indirect).
   (b) Investing activities.
   (c) Financing activities.

3 **E23-17 (SCF—Indirect Method and Statement of Financial Position)** Ochoa Inc., had the following condensed statement of financial position at the end of operations for 2014 (¥ in thousands).

OCHOA INC. STATEMENT OF FINANCIAL POSITION DECEMBER 31, 2014			
Investments	¥ 20,000	Share capital—ordinary	¥ 75,000
Land	40,000	Retained earnings	24,500
Plant assets (net)	67,500	Long-term notes payable	25,500
Current assets other than cash	29,000	Bonds payable	25,000
Cash	8,500	Current liabilities	15,000
	¥165,000		¥165,000

During 2015, the following occurred.

1. A tract of land was purchased for ¥11,000.
2. Bonds payable in the amount of ¥20,000 were retired at par.
3. An additional ¥10,000 in ordinary shares were issued at par.
4. Dividends totaling ¥9,375 were paid to shareholders.
5. Net income was ¥30,250 after deducting depreciation of ¥13,500.
6. Land was purchased through the issuance of ¥22,500 in bonds.
7. Ochoa Inc. sold part of its investment portfolio for ¥12,875. This transaction resulted in a gain of ¥2,000 for the company. The company classifies them as non-trading equity investments.
8. Both current assets (other than cash) and current liabilities remained at the same amount.

Instructions
(a) Prepare a statement of cash flows for 2015 using the indirect method.
(b) Prepare the condensed statement of financial position for Ochoa Inc. as it would appear at December 31, 2015.

3 **8** **E23-18 (Partial SCF—Indirect Method)** The accounts below appear in the ledger of Popovich Company.

Retained Earnings		Dr.	Cr.	Bal.
Jan. 1, 2015	Credit Balance			€ 42,000
Aug. 15	Dividends (cash)	€15,000		27,000
Dec. 31	Net Income for 2015		€50,000	77,000

Equipment		Dr.	Cr.	Bal.
Jan. 1, 2015	Debit Balance			€140,000
Apr. 8	Major Repairs	€21,000		161,000
Aug. 3	Purchase of Equipment	62,000		223,000
Sept. 10	Cost of Equipment Constructed	48,000		271,000
Nov. 15	Equipment Sold		€66,000	205,000

Accumulated Depreciation— Equipment		Dr.	Cr.	Bal.
Jan. 1, 2015	Credit Balance			€ 84,000
Nov. 15	Accum. Depreciation on Equipment Sold	€25,200		58,800
Dec. 31	Depreciation for 2015		€16,800	75,600

Instructions
From the postings in the accounts above, indicate how the information is reported on a statement of cash flows by preparing a partial statement of cash flows using the indirect method. The loss on sale of equipment (November 15) was €5,800.

9 **E23-19 (Worksheet Analysis of Selected Accounts)** Data for Popovich Company are presented in E23-18.

Instructions

Prepare entries in journal form for all adjustments that should be made on a worksheet for a statement of cash flows.

9 E23-20 **(Worksheet Analysis of Selected Transactions)** The transactions below took place during the year 2015.

1. Convertible bonds payable with a par value of $300,000 were exchanged for unissued ordinary shares with a par value of $300,000. The market price of both types of securities was par.

2. The net income for the year was $360,000.

3. Depreciation expense for the building was $90,000.

4. Some old equipment was traded in on the purchase of some newer equipment and the following entry was made. (The exchange has commercial substance.)

Equipment	45,000	
Accum. Depreciation—Equipment	30,000	
Equipment		40,000
Cash		34,000
Gain on Disposal of Plant Assets		1,000

The Gain on Disposal of Plant Assets was credited to current operations as ordinary income.

5. Dividends in the amount of $123,000 were declared. They are payable in January of next year.

Instructions

Show by journal entries the adjustments that would be made on a worksheet for a statement of cash flows.

9 E23-21 **(Worksheet Preparation)** Below are the comparative statements of financial position for Lowenstein Corporation.

	Dec. 31, 2015	Dec. 31, 2014
Land	$ 50,000	$ 50,000
Buildings	125,000	78,500
Accumulated depreciation—buildings	(30,000)	(23,000)
Equipment	53,000	46,000
Accumulated depreciation—equipment	(19,000)	(15,500)
Delivery equipment	39,000	39,000
Accumulated depreciation—delivery equipment	(22,000)	(20,500)
Patents	15,000	–0–
Inventory	81,500	57,000
Prepaid expenses	4,200	2,500
Accounts receivable	43,000	45,000
Allowance for doubtful accounts	(1,800)	(2,000)
Equity investments	25,000	19,000
Cash	16,500	24,000
	$379,400	$300,000
Share capital—ordinary	$140,000	$102,000
Share premium—ordinary	10,000	4,000
Retained earnings	73,400	51,500
Mortgage payable	73,000	53,400
Bonds payable	50,000	62,500
Accounts payable	26,000	16,000
Short-term notes payable (trade)	4,000	6,000
Accrued payables	3,000	4,600
	$379,400	$300,000

Dividends in the amount of $10,000 were declared and paid in 2015.

Instructions

From this information, prepare a worksheet for a statement of cash flows. Make reasonable assumptions as appropriate. The equity investments are considered trading, and no unrealized gains or losses have occurred on these securities.

PROBLEMS

3 **4** **P23-1 (SCF—Indirect Method)** The following is Sullivan Corp.'s comparative statement of financial posi-
8 tion accounts at December 31, 2015 and 2014, with a column showing the increase (decrease) from 2014 to
2015.

COMPARATIVE STATEMENTS OF FINANCIAL POSITION			
	2015	2014	Increase (Decrease)
Property, plant and equipment	$3,307,000	$2,967,000	$340,000
Accumulated depreciation	(1,165,000)	(1,040,000)	(125,000)
Equity investment (Myers Co.)	310,000	275,000	35,000
Inventory	1,850,000	1,715,000	135,000
Accounts receivable	1,128,000	1,168,000	(40,000)
Debt investment	250,000	—	250,000
Cash	815,000	700,000	115,000
Total assets	$6,495,000	$5,785,000	$710,000
Share capital—ordinary, $1 par	$ 500,000	$ 500,000	—
Share premium—ordinary	1,500,000	1,500,000	—
Retained earnings	2,970,000	2,680,000	$290,000
Finance lease obligation	400,000	—	400,000
Accounts payable	1,015,000	955,000	60,000
Income taxes payable	30,000	50,000	(20,000)
Dividends payable	80,000	100,000	(20,000)
Total equity and liabilities	$6,495,000	$5,785,000	$710,000

Additional information:

1. On December 31, 2013, Sullivan acquired 25% of Myers Co.'s ordinary shares for $275,000. On that
   date, the carrying value of Myers' assets and liabilities, which approximated their fair values, was
   $1,100,000. Myers reported income of $140,000 for the year ended December 31, 2015. No dividend
   was paid on Myers' ordinary shares during the year.

2. During 2015, Sullivan loaned $300,000 to TLC Co., an unrelated company. TLC made the first semi-
   annual principal repayment of $50,000, plus interest at 10%, on December 31, 2015.

3. On January 2, 2015, Sullivan sold equipment costing $60,000, with a carrying amount of $38,000, for
   $40,000 cash.

4. On December 31, 2015, Sullivan entered into a finance lease for an office building. The present value
   of the annual rental payments is $400,000, which equals the fair value of the building. Sullivan made
   the first rental payment of $60,000 when due on January 2, 2016.

5. Net income for 2015 was $370,000.

6. Sullivan declared and paid cash dividends for 2015 and 2014 as shown below.

	2015	2014
Declared	December 15, 2015	December 15, 2014
Paid	February 28, 2016	February 28, 2015
Amount	$80,000	$100,000

Instructions
Prepare a statement of cash flows for Sullivan Corp. for the year ended December 31, 2015, using the indirect method.

3 **4** **P23-2 (SCF—Indirect Method)** The comparative statements of financial position for Hinckley Corpora-
8 tion include the information shown on page 1236.

	December 31	
	2015	2014
Investments	€ –0–	€ 3,000
Buildings	–0–	29,750
Equipment	45,000	20,000
Patents	5,000	6,250
Inventory	12,000	9,000
Accounts receivable	12,250	10,000
Cash	33,500	13,000
	€107,750	€91,000
Share capital—ordinary	€ 43,000	€33,000
Retained earnings	20,750	6,000
Allowance for doubtful accounts	3,000	4,500
Accumulated depreciation—equipment	2,000	4,500
Accumulated depreciation—buildings	–0–	6,000
Accounts payable	5,000	3,000
Dividends payable	–0–	5,000
Long-term notes payable	31,000	25,000
Notes payable, short-term (non-trade)	3,000	4,000
	€107,750	€91,000

Additional data related to 2015 are as follows.

1. Equipment that had cost €11,000 and was 40% depreciated at time of disposal was sold for €2,500.
2. €10,000 of the long-term note payable was paid by issuing ordinary shares.
3. Cash dividends paid were €5,000.
4. On January 1, 2015, the building was completely destroyed by a flood. Insurance proceeds on the building were €32,000.
5. Equity investments were sold at €1,700 above their cost.
6. Cash was paid for the acquisition of equipment.
7. A long-term note for €16,000 was issued for the acquisition of equipment.
8. Interest of €2,000 and income taxes of €6,500 were paid in cash.

Instructions
Prepare a statement of cash flows using the indirect method.

3 7 **P23-3 (SCF—Direct Method)** Mortonson Company has not yet prepared a formal statement of cash flows for the 2015 fiscal year. Comparative statements of financial position as of December 31, 2014 and 2015, and a statement of income and retained earnings for the year ended December 31, 2015, are presented as follows.

MORTONSON COMPANY
STATEMENT OF INCOME AND RETAINED EARNINGS
FOR THE YEAR ENDED DECEMBER 31, 2015
(IN THOUSANDS)

Sales revenue		£3,800
Expenses		
Cost of goods sold	£1,200	
Salaries and benefits	725	
Heat, light, and power	75	
Depreciation	80	
Property taxes	19	
Patent amortization	25	
Miscellaneous expenses	10	
Interest	30	2,164
Income before income taxes		1,636
Income taxes		818
Net income		818
Retained earnings—Jan. 1, 2015		310
		1,128
Share dividend declared and issued		600
Retained earnings—Dec. 31, 2015		£ 528

MORTONSON COMPANY
COMPARATIVE STATEMENTS OF FINANCIAL POSITION
AS OF DECEMBER 31
(IN THOUSANDS)

Assets	2015	2014
Equity investments (non-trading)	£ 10	£ 50
Land	150	70
Buildings and equipment	910	600
Accumulated depreciation	(200)	(120)
Patents (less amortization)	105	130
Inventory	720	560
Accounts receivable	780	500
Cash	333	100
Total assets	£2,808	£1,890

Equity and Liabilities	2015	2014
Share capital—ordinary	£1,300	£ 700
Retained earnings	528	310
Total equity	1,828	1,010
Long-term notes payable—due 2017	200	200
Accounts payable	420	330
Income taxes payable	40	30
Notes payable	320	320
Total liabilities	980	880
Total equity and liabilities	£2,808	£1,890

Instructions
Prepare a statement of cash flows using the direct method. Changes in accounts receivable and accounts payable relate to sales and cost of goods sold.

3 6 7 8 **P23-4 (SCF—Direct Method)** Michaels Company had available at the end of 2015 the following information.

MICHAELS COMPANY
COMPARATIVE STATEMENTS OF FINANCIAL POSITION
AS OF DECEMBER 31, 2015 AND 2014

	2015	2014
Land	£125,000	£175,000
Buildings	350,000	350,000
Accumulated depreciation—buildings	(105,000)	(87,500)
Equipment	525,000	400,000
Accumulated depreciation—equipment	(130,000)	(112,000)
Patents	45,000	50,000
Inventory	42,000	35,000
Prepaid rent	3,000	12,000
Prepaid insurance	2,100	900
Supplies	1,000	750
Accounts receivable	20,500	12,950
Short-term equity investments	22,000	30,000
Cash	10,000	4,000
Total assets	£910,600	£871,100
Share capital—ordinary	£240,000	£220,000
Share premium—ordinary	25,000	17,500
Retained earnings	123,297	88,747
Long-term notes payable	60,000	70,000
Bonds payable	420,303	425,853
Accounts payable	22,000	32,000
Income taxes payable	5,000	4,000
Salaries and wages payable	5,000	3,000
Short-term notes payable	10,000	10,000
Total equity and liabilities	£910,600	£871,100

MICHAELS COMPANY
INCOME STATEMENT
FOR THE YEAR ENDED DECEMBER 31, 2015

Sales revenue		£1,160,000
Cost of goods sold		(748,000)
Gross margin		412,000
Operating expenses		
Selling expenses	£ 79,200	
Administrative expenses	156,700	
Depreciation/Amortization expense	40,500	
Total operating expenses		(276,400)
Income from operations		135,600
Other income and expense		
Gain on sale of land	8,000	
Gain on sale of short-term investment	4,000	
Dividend revenue	2,400	
Interest expense	(51,750)	(37,350)
Income before taxes		98,250
Income tax expense		(39,400)
Net income		58,850
Dividends to ordinary shareholders		(24,300)
To retained earnings		£ 34,550

Instructions

Prepare a statement of cash flows for Michaels Company using the direct method. Assume the short-term investments are non-trading. Bond premium amortized was £5,550.

 P23-5 (SCF—Indirect Method, and Net Cash Flow from Operating Activities, Direct Method) Comparative statement of financial position accounts of Marcus Inc. are presented below.

MARCUS INC.
COMPARATIVE STATEMENT OF FINANCIAL POSITION ACCOUNTS
AS OF DECEMBER 31, 2015 AND 2014

	December 31	
Debit Accounts	2015	2014
Cash	€ 42,000	€ 33,750
Accounts Receivable	70,500	60,000
Inventory	30,000	24,000
Equity Investments (non-trading)	22,250	38,500
Machinery	30,000	18,750
Buildings	67,500	56,250
Land	7,500	7,500
	€269,750	€238,750
Credit Accounts		
Allowance for Doubtful Accounts	€ 2,250	€ 1,500
Accumulated Depreciation—Machinery	5,625	2,250
Accumulated Depreciation—Buildings	13,500	9,000
Accounts Payable	35,000	24,750
Accrued Payables	3,375	2,625
Long-Term Notes Payable	21,000	31,000
Share Capital—Ordinary, no par	150,000	125,000
Retained Earnings	39,000	42,625
	€269,750	€238,750

Additional data (ignoring taxes):

1. Net income for the year was €42,500.
2. Cash dividends declared and paid during the year were €21,125.

3. A 20% share dividend was declared during the year. €25,000 of retained earnings was capitalized.

4. Equity investments that cost €25,000 were sold during the year for €28,750.

5. Machinery that cost €3,750, on which €750 of depreciation had accumulated, was sold for €2,200.

Marcus's 2015 income statement follows (ignoring taxes).

Sales revenue		€540,000
Less: Cost of goods sold		380,000
Gross margin		160,000
Less: Operating expenses (includes €8,625 depreciation and €5,400 bad debts)		120,450
Income from operations		39,550
Other: Gain on sale of equity investments (non-trading)	€3,750	
Loss on sale of machinery	(800)	2,950
Net income		€ 42,500

Instructions

(a) Compute net cash flow from operating activities using the direct method.

(b) Prepare a statement of cash flows using the indirect method.

 P23-6 (SCF—Direct and Indirect Methods from Comparative Financial Statements) Chapman Company, a major retailer of bicycles and accessories, operates several stores and is a publicly traded company. The comparative statement of financial position and income statement for Chapman as of May 31, 2015, are as follows. The company is preparing its statement of cash flows.

CHAPMAN COMPANY
COMPARATIVE STATEMENTS OF FINANCIAL POSITION
AS OF MAY 31

	2015	2014
Plant assets		
Plant assets	$600,000	$502,000
Less: Accumulated depreciation—plant assets	150,000	125,000
	450,000	377,000
Current assets		
Inventory	220,000	250,000
Prepaid expenses	9,000	7,000
Accounts receivable	75,000	58,000
Cash	28,250	20,000
Total current assets	332,250	335,000
Total assets	$782,250	$712,000
Equity		
Share capital—ordinary, $10 par	$370,000	$280,000
Retained earnings	145,000	120,000
Total equity	515,000	400,000
Non-current liabilities		
Bonds payable	70,000	100,000
Current liabilities		
Accounts payable	123,000	115,000
Salaries and wages payable	47,250	72,000
Interest payable	27,000	25,000
Total current liabilities	197,250	212,000
Total liabilities	267,250	312,000
Total equity and liabilities	$782,250	$712,000

CHAPMAN COMPANY
INCOME STATEMENT
FOR THE YEAR ENDED MAY 31, 2015

Sales revenue	$1,255,250
Cost of merchandise sold	722,000
Gross profit	533,250
Expenses	
Salaries and wages expense	252,100
Interest expense	75,000
Other expenses	8,150
Depreciation expense	25,000
Total expenses	360,250
Operating income	173,000
Income tax expense	43,000
Net income	$ 130,000

The following is additional information concerning Chapman's transactions during the year ended May 31, 2015.

1. All sales during the year were made on account.
2. All merchandise was purchased on account, comprising the total accounts payable account.
3. Plant assets costing $98,000 were purchased by paying $28,000 in cash and issuing 7,000 ordinary shares.
4. The "other expenses" are related to prepaid items.
5. All income taxes incurred during the year were paid during the year.
6. In order to supplement its cash, Chapman issued 2,000 ordinary shares at par value.
7. There were no penalties assessed for the retirement of bonds.
8. Cash dividends of $105,000 were declared and paid at the end of the fiscal year.

Instructions

(a) Compare and contrast the direct method and the indirect method for reporting cash flows from operating activities.
(b) Prepare a statement of cash flows for Chapman Company for the year ended May 31, 2015, using the direct method. Be sure to support the statement with appropriate calculations.
(c) Using the indirect method, calculate only the net cash flow from operating activities for Chapman Company for the year ended May 31, 2015.

3 6 7 8 **P23-7 (SCF—Direct and Indirect Methods)** Comparative statement of financial position accounts of Shi Group are presented below.

SHI GROUP
COMPARATIVE STATEMENT OF FINANCIAL POSITION ACCOUNTS
AS OF DECEMBER 31
(IN THOUSANDS)

Debit Balances	2015	2014
Cash	HK$ 70,000	HK$ 51,000
Accounts Receivable	155,000	130,000
Inventory	75,000	61,000
Equity Investments (non-trading)	55,000	85,000
Equipment	70,000	48,000
Buildings	145,000	145,000
Land	40,000	25,000
Totals	HK$610,000	HK$545,000
Credit Balances		
Allowance for Doubtful Accounts	HK$ 10,000	HK$ 8,000
Accumulated Depreciation—Equipment	21,000	14,000
Accumulated Depreciation—Buildings	37,000	28,000
Accounts Payable	66,000	60,000
Income Taxes Payable	12,000	10,000
Long-Term Notes Payable	62,000	70,000
Share Capital—Ordinary	310,000	260,000
Retained Earnings	92,000	95,000
Totals	HK$610,000	HK$545,000

Additional data:

1. Equipment that cost HK$10,000 and was 60% depreciated was sold in 2015.
2. Cash dividends were declared and paid during the year.
3. Ordinary shares were issued in exchange for land.
4. Equity investments that cost HK$35,000 were sold during the year.
5. There were no write-offs of uncollectible accounts during the year.

Shi's 2015 income statement is as follows.

Sales revenue		HK$950,000
Less: Cost of goods sold		600,000
Gross profit		350,000
Less: Operating expenses (includes depreciation expense and bad debt expense)		250,000
Income from operations		100,000
Other income and expense		
Gain on sale of investments	HK$15,000	
Loss on sale of equipment	(3,000)	12,000
Income before taxes		112,000
Income taxes		45,000
Net income		HK$ 67,000

Instructions

(a) Compute net cash provided by operating activities under the direct method.
(b) Prepare a statement of cash flows using the indirect method.

 P23-8 (Indirect SCF) Greco Corporation has contracted with you to prepare a statement of cash flows. The controller has provided the following trial balance information.

	December 31	
	2015	2014
Cash	$ 38,500	$13,000
Accounts receivable	12,250	10,000
Inventory	12,000	10,000
Equity investments (non-trading)	–0–	3,000
Buildings	–0–	29,750
Equipment	40,000	20,000
Copyright	5,000	5,250
Totals	$107,750	$91,000
Allowance for doubtful accounts	$ 3,000	$ 4,500
Accumulated depreciation—equipment	2,000	4,500
Accumulated depreciation—buildings	–0–	6,000
Accounts payable	5,000	4,000
Dividends payable	–0–	5,000
Notes payable, short-term (non-trade)	3,000	4,000
Long-term notes payable	36,000	25,000
Share capital—ordinary	38,000	33,000
Retained earnings	20,750	5,000
	$107,750	$91,000

Additional data related to 2015 are as follows.

1. Equipment that had cost $11,000 and was 30% depreciated at time of disposal was sold for $2,500.
2. $5,000 of the long-term note payable was paid by issuing ordinary shares.
3. Cash dividends paid were $5,000.
4. On January 1, 2015, the building was completely destroyed by a flood. Insurance proceeds on the building were $33,000 (net of $4,000 taxes).
5. Equity investments (non-trading) were sold at $1,500 above their cost. The company has made similar sales and investments in the past.

6. Cash and a long-term note for $16,000 were given for the acquisition of equipment.

7. Interest of $2,000 and income taxes of $5,000 were paid in cash.

Instructions

(a) Use the indirect method to analyze the above information and prepare a statement of cash flows for Greco.

(b) What would you expect to observe in the operating, investing, and financing sections of a statement of cash flows of:

(1) A severely financially troubled firm?

(2) A recently formed firm that is experiencing rapid growth?

CONCEPTS FOR ANALYSIS

CA23-1 (Analysis of Improper SCF) The following statement was prepared by Maloney Corporation's accountant.

MALONEY CORPORATION STATEMENT OF SOURCES AND USES OF CASH FOR THE YEAR ENDED SEPTEMBER 30, 2015	
Sources of cash	
Net income	$111,000
Depreciation and depletion	70,000
Increase in long-term debt	179,000
Changes in current receivables and inventories, less current	
liabilities (excluding current maturities of long-term debt)	14,000
	$374,000
Application of cash	
Cash dividends	$ 60,000
Expenditure for property, plant, and equipment	214,000
Investments and other uses	20,000
Change in cash	80,000
	$374,000

The following additional information relating to Maloney Corporation is available for the year ended September 30, 2015.

1. Salaries and wages expense attributable to share-option plans was $25,000 for the year.

2. Expenditures for property, plant, and equipment $250,000
   Proceeds from retirements of property, plant, and equipment   36,000
   Net expenditures $214,000

3. A share dividend of 10,000 Maloney Corporation ordinary shares was distributed to ordinary shareholders on April 1, 2015, when the per share market price was $7 and par value was $1.

4. On July 1, 2015, when its market price was $6 per share, 16,000 of Maloney Corporation ordinary shares were issued in exchange for 4,000 preference shares.

5. Depreciation expense $ 65,000
   Depletion expense   5,000
            $ 70,000

6. Increase in long-term debt $620,000
   Retirement of debt   441,000
   Net increase $179,000

Instructions

    (a) In general, what are the objectives of a statement of the type shown above for Maloney Corporation? Explain.

    (b) Identify the weaknesses in the form and format of Maloney Corporation's statement of cash flows without reference to the additional information. (Assume adoption of the indirect method.)

    (c) For each of the six items of additional information for the statement of cash flows, indicate the preferable treatment and explain why the suggested treatment is preferable.

 CA23-2 (SCF Theory and Analysis of Improper SCF) Teresa Ramirez and Lenny Traylor are examining the following statement of cash flows for Panaka Clothing Store's first year of operations.

PANAKA CLOTHING STORE
STATEMENT OF CASH FLOWS
FOR THE YEAR ENDED JANUARY 31, 2015

Sources of cash	
From sales of merchandise	€ 382,000
From sale of ordinary shares	380,000
From sale of debt investment	120,000
From depreciation	80,000
From issuance of note for truck	30,000
From interest on investments	8,000
Total sources of cash	1,000,000
Uses of cash	
For purchase of fixtures and equipment	330,000
For merchandise purchased for resale	253,000
For operating expenses (including depreciation)	170,000
For purchase of debt investment	95,000
For purchase of truck by issuance of note	30,000
For purchase of treasury shares	10,000
For interest on note	3,000
Total uses of cash	891,000
Net increase in cash	€ 109,000

Teresa claims that Panaka's statement of cash flows is an excellent portrayal of a superb first year, with cash increasing €109,000. Lenny replies that it was not a superb first year—that the year was an operating failure, the statement was incorrectly presented, and €109,000 is not the actual increase in cash.

Instructions

    (a) With whom do you agree, Teresa or Lenny? Explain your position.

    (b) Using the data provided, prepare a statement of cash flows in proper indirect method form. The only non-cash items in income are depreciation and the gain from the sale of the investment (purchase and sale are related).

CA23-3 (SCF Theory and Analysis of Transactions) Ashley Company is a young and growing producer of electronic measuring instruments and technical equipment. You have been retained by Ashley to advise it in the preparation of a statement of cash flows using the indirect method. For the fiscal year ended October 31, 2015, you have obtained the following information concerning certain events and transactions of Ashley.

    1. The amount of reported earnings for the fiscal year was $700,000, which included a deduction for a loss of $110,000 (see item 5 below).

    2. Depreciation expense of $315,000 was included in the income statement.

    3. Uncollectible accounts receivable of $40,000 were written off against the allowance for doubtful accounts. Also, $51,000 of bad debt expense was included in determining income for the fiscal year, and the same amount was added to the allowance for doubtful accounts.

    4. A gain of $6,000 was realized on the sale of a machine. It originally cost $75,000, of which $30,000 was undepreciated on the date of sale.

    5. On April 1, 2015, lightning caused an uninsured building loss of $110,000 ($180,000 loss, less reduction in income taxes of $70,000). This loss was included in determining income as indicated in item 1 above.

6. On July 3, 2015, building and land were purchased for $700,000. Ashley gave in payment $75,000 cash, $200,000 fair value of its unissued ordinary shares, and signed a $425,000 mortgage note payable.

7. On August 3, 2015, $800,000 face value of Ashley's 10% convertible preference shares was converted into $150,000 par value of its ordinary shares.

Instructions

Explain whether each of the seven numbered items above is a source or use of cash, and explain how each should be disclosed in Ashley's statement of cash flows for the fiscal year ended October 31, 2015. If any item is neither a source nor a use of cash, explain why it is not, and indicate the disclosure, if any, that should be made of the item for the fiscal year ended October 31, 2015.

 CA23-4 (Analysis of Transactions' Effect on SCF) Each of the following items must be considered in preparing a statement of cash flows for Boer Fashions Inc. for the year ended December 31, 2015.

1. Fixed assets that had cost R20,000 6½ years before and were being depreciated on a 10-year basis, with no estimated residual value, were sold for R4,750.

2. During the year, goodwill of R15,000 was considered impaired and was completely written off to expense.

3. During the year, 500 ordinary shares with a stated value of R25 a share were issued for R32 a share.

4. The company sustained a net loss for the year of R2,100. Depreciation amounted to R2,000 and patent amortization was R400.

5. Uncollectible accounts receivable in the amount of R2,000 were written off against Allowance for Doubtful Accounts.

6. Equity investments (non-trading) that cost R12,000 when purchased 4 years earlier were sold for R10,600.

7. Bonds payable with a par value of R24,000 on which there was an unamortized bond premium of R2,000 were redeemed at 101.

Instructions

For each item, state where it is to be shown in the statement and then how you would present the necessary information, including the amount. Consider each item to be independent of the others. Assume that correct entries were made for all transactions as they took place.

CA23-5 (Purpose and Elements of SCF) IFRS requires the statement of cash flows be presented when financial statements are prepared.

Instructions

(a) Explain the purposes of the statement of cash flows.

(b) List and describe the three categories of activities that must be reported in the statement of cash flows.

(c) Identify and describe the two methods that are allowed for reporting cash flows from operations.

(d) Describe the presentation of non-cash investing and financing transactions. Include in your description an example of a non-cash investing and financing transaction.

 CA23-6 (Cash Flow Reporting) Brockman Guitar Company is in the business of manufacturing top-quality, steel-string folk guitars. In recent years, the company has experienced working capital problems resulting from the procurement of factory equipment, the unanticipated buildup of receivables and inventories, and the payoff of a balloon mortgage on a new manufacturing facility. The founder and president of the company, Barbara Brockman, has attempted to raise cash from various financial institutions, but to no avail because of the company's poor performance in recent years. In particular, the company's lead bank, First Financial, is especially concerned about Brockman's inability to maintain a positive cash position. The commercial loan officer from First Financial told Barbara, "I can't even consider your request for capital financing unless I see that your company is able to generate positive cash flows from operations."

Thinking about the banker's comment, Barbara came up with what she believes is a good plan: With a more attractive statement of cash flows, the bank might be willing to provide long-term financing. To "window dress" cash flows, the company can sell its accounts receivables to factors and liquidate its raw materials inventories. These rather costly transactions would generate lots of cash. As the chief accountant for Brockman Guitar, it is your job to tell Barbara what you think of her plan.

Instructions

Answer the following questions.

(a) What are the ethical issues related to Barbara Brockman's idea?

(b) What would you tell Barbara Brockman?

USING YOUR JUDGMENT

FINANCIAL REPORTING

Financial Reporting Problem

Marks and Spencer plc (M&S)

The financial statements of M&S (GBR) are presented in Appendix A. The complete annual report, including the notes to the financial statements, is available online.

Instructions

Refer to M&S's financial statements and the accompanying notes to answer the following questions.

(a) Which method of computing net cash provided by operating activities does M&S use? What were the amounts of net cash provided by operating activities for the years 2012 and 2013? What were the two most significant items in the cash generated from operations in 2013?

(b) What was the most significant item in the cash flows used for investing activities section in 2013? What was the most significant item in the cash flows used for financing activities section in 2013?

(c) Where is "deferred income taxes" reported in M&S's statement of cash flows? Why does it appear in that section of the statement of cash flows?

(d) Where is depreciation reported in M&S's statement of cash flows? Why is depreciation added to net income in the statement of cash flows?

Comparative Analysis Case

adidas and Puma

The financial statements of adidas (DEU) and Puma (DEU) are presented in Appendices B and C, respectively. The complete annual reports, including the notes to the financial statements, are available online.

Instructions

Use the companies' financial information to answer the following questions.

(a) What method of computing net cash provided by operating activities does adidas use? What method does Puma use? What were the amounts of cash provided by operating activities reported by adidas and Puma in 2012?

(b) What was the most significant item reported by adidas and Puma in 2012 in their investing activities sections? What is the most significant item reported by adidas and Puma in 2012 in their financing activities sections?

(c) What were these two companies' trends in net cash provided by operating activities over the period 2010 to 2012?

(d) Where is "depreciation and amortization" reported by adidas and Puma in their statements of cash flows? What is the amount and why does it appear in that section of the statement of cash flows?

(e) Based on the information contained in adidas's and Puma's financial statements, compute the following 2012 ratios for each company. These ratios require the use of statement of cash flows data. (These ratios were covered in Chapter 5.)

(1) Current cash debt coverage.

(2) Cash debt coverage.

(f) What conclusions concerning the management of cash can be drawn from the ratios computed in (e)?

Financial Statement Analysis Case

The consolidated statement of cash flows for Telefónica, S.A. (ESP) for the year ended December 31, 2011 and 2012, is presented on page 1246.

(millions of euros)	2012	2011
Cash flows from operating activities		
Cash received from customers	75,962	77,222
Cash paid to suppliers and employees	(55,858)	(55,769)
Dividends received	85	82
Net interest and other financial expenses paid	(2,952)	(2,093)
Taxes paid	(2,024)	(1959)
Net cash from operating activities	15,213	17,483
Cash flows from investing activities		
Proceeds on disposals of property, plant and equipment and intangible assets	939	811
Payments on investments in property, plant and equipment and intangible assets	(9,481)	(9,085)
Proceeds on disposals of companies, net of cash and cash equivalents disposed	1,823	4
Payments on investments in companies, net of cash and cash equivalents acquired	(37)	(2,948)
Proceeds on financial investments not included under cash equivalents	30	23
Payments made on financial investments not included under cash equivalents	(834)	(669)
Payments from cash surpluses not included under cash equivalents	(318)	(646)
Government grants received	1	13
Net cash used in investing activities	(7,877)	(12,497)
Cash flows from financing activities		
Dividends paid	(3,273)	(7,567)
Transactions with equity holders	656	(399)
Proceeds on issue of debentures and bonds	8,090	4,582
Proceeds on loans, borrowings and promissory notes	6,002	4,387
Cancellation of debentures and bonds	(4,317)	(3,235)
Repayments of loans, borrowings and promissory notes	(8,401)	(2,680)
Net cash used in financing activities	(1,243)	(4,912)
Effect of foreign exchange rate changes on collections and payments	(382)	(169)
Effect of changes in consolidation methods	1	10
Net increase (decrease) in cash and cash equivalents during the year	5,712	(85)
Cash and cash equivalents at January 1	4,135	4,220
Cash and cash equivalents at December 31	9,847	4,135

Instructions

(a) What method does Telefónica use to prepare the operating cash flows section of its statement of cash flows? Briefly discuss how you can determine this.

(b) Telefónica reported net income of €4,403 in 2012 and €6,187 in 2011 (in millions). Briefly discuss some of the adjustments that would explain such a difference in its income and operating cash flows.

(c) IFRS requires disclosure of interest, taxes, and dividends. Briefly describe how Telefónica has complied with these requirements. What other approach could a company take to comply with the reporting requirement?

International Reporting Case

Vermont Teddy Bear Co.

Founded in the early 1980s, the **Vermont Teddy Bear Co.** (USA) designs and manufactures American-made teddy bears and markets them primarily as gifts called Bear-Grams or Teddy Bear-Grams. Bear-Grams are personalized teddy bears delivered directly to the recipient for special occasions such as birthdays and anniversaries. The Shelburne, Vermont, company's primary markets are New York, Boston, and Chicago. Sales have jumped dramatically in recent years. Such dramatic growth has significant implications for cash flows. Provided below are the cash flow statements for two recent years for the company.

	Current Year	Prior Year
Cash flows from operating activities:		
Net income	$ 17,523	$ 838,955
Adjustments to reconcile net income to net cash provided by operating activities		
Deferred income taxes	(69,524)	(146,590)
Depreciation and amortization	316,416	181,348
Changes in assets and liabilities:		
Accounts receivable, trade	(38,267)	(25,947)
Inventories	(1,599,014)	(1,289,293)
Prepaid and other current assets	(444,794)	(113,205)
Deposits and other assets	(24,240)	(83,044)
Accounts payable	2,017,059	(284,567)
Accrued expenses	61,321	170,755
Accrued interest payable, debentures	—	(58,219)
Other	—	(8,960)
Income taxes payable	—	117,810
Net cash provided by (used for) operating activities	236,480	(700,957)
Net cash used for investing activities	(2,102,892)	(4,422,953)
Net cash (used for) provided by financing activities	(315,353)	9,685,435
Net change in cash and cash equivalents	(2,181,765)	4,561,525

Other information:

Current liabilities	$ 4,055,465	$ 1,995,600
Total liabilities	4,620,085	2,184,386
Net sales	20,560,566	17,025,856

Instructions

(a) Briefly describe any similarities or differences in Vermont's U.S. GAAP-based statement of cash flows compared to the requirements of IFRS.

(b) Note that net income in the current year was only $17,523 compared to prior-year income of $838,955, but cash flows from operations was $236,480 in the current year and a negative $700,957 in the prior year. Explain the causes of this apparent paradox.

(c) Evaluate Vermont Teddy Bear's liquidity, solvency, and profitability for the current year using cash flow-based ratios (as covered in Chapter 5).

Accounting, Analysis, and Principles

The income statement for the year ended December 31, 2015, for Laskowski Manufacturing Company contains the following condensed information.

LASKOWSKI CO. INCOME STATEMENT		
Revenues		€6,583,000
Operating expenses (excluding depreciation)	€4,920,000	
Depreciation expense	880,000	5,800,000
Income before income tax		783,000
Income tax expense		353,000
Net income		€ 430,000

Included in operating expenses is a €24,000 loss resulting from the sale of machinery for €270,000 cash. The company purchased machinery at a cost of €750,000.

Laskowski reports the following balances on its comparative statements of financial position at December 31.

LASKOWSKI CO. COMPARATIVE STATEMENTS OF FINANCIAL POSITION (PARTIAL)		
	2015	2014
Inventories	€834,000	€867,000
Accounts receivable	775,000	610,000
Cash	672,000	130,000
Accounts payable	521,000	501,000

Income tax expense of €353,000 represents the amount paid in 2015. Dividends declared and paid in 2015 totaled €200,000.

Accounting

Prepare the statement of cash flows using the indirect method.

Analysis

Laskowski has an aggressive growth plan, which will require significant investments in plant and equipment over the next several years. Preliminary plans call for an investment of over €500,000 in the next year. Compute Laskowski's free cash flow and use it to evaluate the investment plans with the use of only internally generated funds.

Principles

How does the statement of cash flows contribute to achieving the objective of financial reporting?

 **BRIDGE TO THE PROFESSION**

Professional Research

As part of the year-end accounting process for your company, you are preparing the statement of cash flows according to IFRS. One of your team, a finance major, believes the statement should be prepared to report the change in working capital because analysts many times use working capital in ratio analysis. Your supervisor would like research conducted to verify the basis for preparing the statement of cash flows.

Instructions

Access the IFRS authoritative literature at the IASB website (*http://eifrs.iasb.org/*) (you may register for free eIFRS access at this site). When you have accessed the documents, you can use the search tool in your Internet browser to respond to the following questions. (Provide paragraph citations.)

(a) What is the primary objective for the statement of cash flows? Is working capital the basis for meeting this objective?

(b) What information is provided in a statement of cash flows?

(c) List some of the typical cash inflows and outflows from operations.

Professional Simulation

The professional simulation for this chapter asks you to address questions related to the accounting for the statement of cash flows.

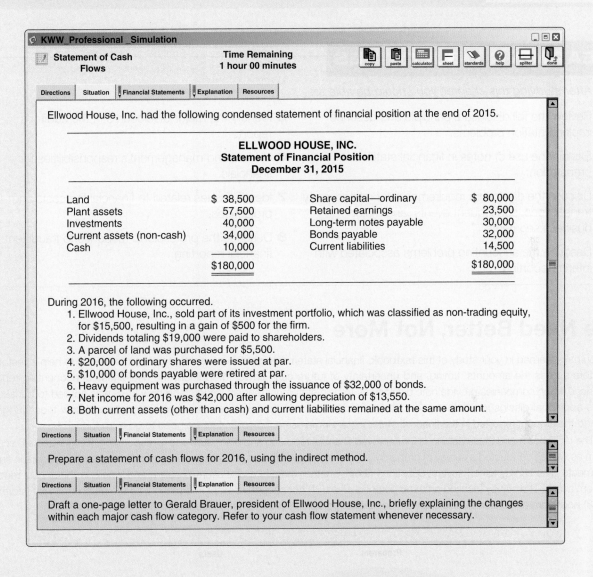

KWW_Professional _Simulation

| Statement of Cash Flows | Time Remaining 1 hour 00 minutes | copy paste calculator sheet standards help splitter done |

Directions | Situation | Financial Statements | Explanation | Resources

Ellwood House, Inc. had the following condensed statement of financial position at the end of 2015.

ELLWOOD HOUSE, INC.
Statement of Financial Position
December 31, 2015

Land	$ 38,500	Share capital—ordinary	$ 80,000
Plant assets	57,500	Retained earnings	23,500
Investments	40,000	Long-term notes payable	30,000
Current assets (non-cash)	34,000	Bonds payable	32,000
Cash	10,000	Current liabilities	14,500
	$180,000		$180,000

During 2016, the following occurred.
1. Ellwood House, Inc., sold part of its investment portfolio, which was classified as non-trading equity, for $15,500, resulting in a gain of $500 for the firm.
2. Dividends totaling $19,000 were paid to shareholders.
3. A parcel of land was purchased for $5,500.
4. $20,000 of ordinary shares were issued at par.
5. $10,000 of bonds payable were retired at par.
6. Heavy equipment was purchased through the issuance of $32,000 of bonds.
7. Net income for 2016 was $42,000 after allowing depreciation of $13,550.
8. Both current assets (other than cash) and current liabilities remained at the same amount.

Directions | Situation | Financial Statements | Explanation | Resources

Prepare a statement of cash flows for 2016, using the indirect method.

Directions | Situation | Financial Statements | Explanation | Resources

Draft a one-page letter to Gerald Brauer, president of Ellwood House, Inc., briefly explaining the changes within each major cash flow category. Refer to your cash flow statement whenever necessary.

Remember to check the book's companion website, at www.wiley.com/ college/kieso, to find additional resources for this chapter.

24 Presentation and Disclosure in Financial Reporting

We Need Better, Not More

As you have learned in your study of this textbook, financial statements contain a wealth of useful information to help investors and creditors assess the amounts, timing, and uncertainty of future cash flows. In addition, the usefulness of accounting reports is enhanced when companies provide note disclosures to help statement readers understand how IFRS was applied to transactions. These additional disclosures help readers understand both the judgments that management made and how those judgments affected the amount reported in the financial statements. Some users, however, feel we need to go even further.

The IASB has heard these demands for improved financial reporting and disclosure and is responding. It organized a Discussion Forum as well as conducted a survey of preparers and users to get input on the effectiveness of reporting and disclosure in financial statements. The survey asked several questions about whether there is a disclosure problem and where in the annual report the problem arises. The survey focused on three potential areas: (1) not enough relevant information, (2) too much irrelevant information, and (3) poor communication of disclosures. The following graphic summarizes the feedback.

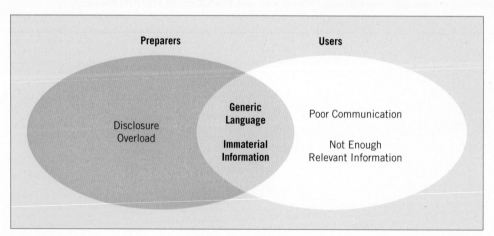

As indicated, preparers viewed the disclosure problem as primarily one of information overload; that is, they are being required to provide too much data. Users, on the other hand, complained that some of the information they get is poorly communicated and not that relevant. The message that emerged from the Discussion Forum was similar. Specifically, increases in the volume of financial disclosures has resulted in a perceived reduction in their quality and usefulness. More importantly, there was broad consensus that collective action was required in order for improvements to be made.

As a result, the IASB is taking action in three main areas:

1. ***Amendments to IAS 1.*** The IASB will make amendments to *IAS 1* ("Presentation of Financial Statements") to address perceived impediments to preparers exercising their judgment in presenting their financial reports.

2. ***Materiality.*** The IASB will seek to develop educational material on materiality with input from an advisory group.

3. ***Separate project on disclosure.*** The IASB will consider as part of its research agenda the broader challenges associated with disclosure effectiveness.

Hans Hoogervorst, chairman of the IASB, summarized the IASB's response as follows: "It is undoubtedly true that we and others can improve our [disclosure] requirements. However, material improvements will require behavioural change to ensure that financial statements are regarded as tools of communication rather than compliance. That means addressing the root causes of why preparers may err on the side of caution and 'kitchen-sink' their disclosures." The bottom line: We need better, not necessarily more, disclosure.

Source: "Discussion Forum—Financial Reporting Disclosure," *Feedback Statement* (London, U.K.: IASB, May 2013), *http://www.ifrs.org/Current-Projects/IASB-Projects/Disclosure-Initiative/Pages/Disclosure-Initiative.aspx.* See also "Disclosure Initiative: Proposed Amendments to IAS 1," *Exposure Draft ED/2014/1* (London, U.K.: IASB, March 2014).

CONCEPTUAL FOCUS

> See the **Underlying Concepts** on pages 1252, 1253, 1260, 1261, 1265, 1266, 1275, 1283, 1288, and 1290.
> Read the **Evolving Issue** on page 1283 for a discussion of IFRS and U.S. GAAP convergence.

INTERNATIONAL FOCUS

> Read the **Global Accounting Insights** on pages 1284–1286 for a discussion of non-IFRS disclosure requirements.

PREVIEW OF CHAPTER 24

As the opening story indicates, investors and other interested parties are concerned about the quality of information for all aspects of financial reporting—the financial statements, the notes, the president's letter, and management commentary. In this chapter, we cover the full disclosure principle in more detail and examine disclosures that must accompany financial statements so that they are not misleading. The content and organization of this chapter are as follows.

Presentation and Disclosure in Financial Reporting

Full Disclosure Principle	Notes to Financial Statements	Disclosure Issues	Auditor's and Management's Reports	Current Reporting Issues
• Increase in reporting requirements • Differential disclosure	• Accounting policies • Common notes	• Special transactions or events • Events after the reporting period • Diversified companies • Interim reports	• Auditor's report • Management's reports	• Reporting on forecasts and projections • Internet financial reporting • Fraudulent financial reporting • Criteria for accounting and reporting choices

FULL DISCLOSURE PRINCIPLE

LEARNING OBJECTIVE **1**

Review the full disclosure principle and describe implementation problems.

I
F
R
S

See the Authoritative Literature section (pages 1301–1302).

The IASB Conceptual Framework notes that while some useful information is best provided in the financial statements, some is best provided by other means. For example, net income and cash flows are readily available in financial statements, but investors might do better to look at comparisons to other companies in the same industry, found in news articles or brokerage house reports.

IASB rules directly affect financial statements, notes to the financial statements, and supplementary information. These accounting standards provide guidance on recognition and measurement of amounts reported in the financial statements. However, due to the many judgments involved in applying IFRS, note disclosures provide important information about the application of IFRS. Supplementary information includes items such as disclosures about the risks and uncertainties, resources and obligations not recognized in the statement of financial position (such as mineral reserves), and information about geographical and industry segments. Other types of information found in the annual report, such as management commentary and the letters to shareholders, are not subject to IASB rules. **[1]** Illustration 24-1 indicates the various types of financial information.

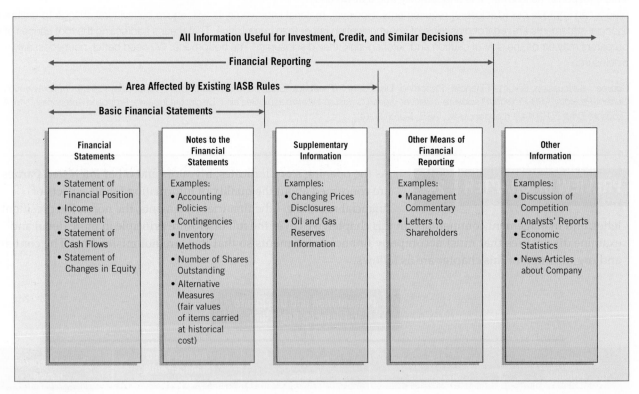

ILLUSTRATION 24-1
Types of Financial Information

As Chapter 2 indicated, the profession has adopted a **full disclosure principle**. The full disclosure principle calls for financial reporting of **any financial facts significant enough to influence the judgment of an informed reader**. In some situations, the benefits of disclosure may be apparent but the costs uncertain. In other instances, the costs may be certain but the benefits of disclosure not as apparent.

🔍 **Underlying Concepts**

> Here is a good example of the trade-off between cost considerations and the benefits of full disclosure.

For example, the IASB requires companies to provide expanded disclosures about their contractual obligations. In light of the accounting frauds at companies like **Parmalat** (ITA), the benefits of these expanded disclosures seem fairly obvious to the investing public. While no one has documented the exact costs of disclosure in these situations, they would appear to be relatively small.

On the other hand, the cost of disclosure can be substantial in some cases and the benefits difficult to assess. For example, at one time the financial press reported that if segment reporting were adopted, a company like Fruehauf (USA) would have had to increase its accounting staff 50 percent, from 300 to 450 individuals. In this case, the cost of disclosure can be measured, but the benefits are less well defined.

Some even argue that the reporting requirements are so detailed and substantial that users have a difficult time absorbing the information. These critics charge the profession with engaging in **information overload**.

Financial disasters at Mahindra Satyam (IND) and Société Générale (FRA) highlight the difficulty of implementing the full disclosure principle. They raise the issue of why investors were not aware of potential problems: Was the information these companies presented not comprehensible? Was it buried? Was it too technical? Was it properly presented and fully disclosed as of the financial statement date, but the situation later deteriorated? Or was it simply not there? In the following sections, we describe the elements of high-quality disclosure that will enable companies to avoid these disclosure pitfalls.

Increase in Reporting Requirements

Disclosure requirements have increased substantially. One survey showed that the size of many companies' annual reports is growing in response to demands for increased transparency. For example, annual report page counts ranged from 92 pages for Wm Morrison Supermarkets plc (GBR) up to a whopping 268 pages in Telefónica's (ESP) annual report. This result is not surprising; as illustrated throughout this textbook, the IASB has issued many pronouncements in the last 10 years that have substantial disclosure provisions.

The reasons for this increase in disclosure requirements are varied. Some of them are:

- *Complexity of the business environment.* The increasing complexity of business operations magnifies the difficulty of distilling economic events into summarized reports. Areas such as derivatives, leasing, business combinations, pensions, financing arrangements, revenue recognition, and deferred taxes are complex. As a result, companies extensively use **notes to the financial statements** to explain these transactions and their future effects.

- *Necessity for timely information.* Today, more than ever before, users are demanding information that is current and predictive. For example, users want more complete **interim data**.

- *Accounting as a control and monitoring device.* Regulators have recently sought public disclosure of such phenomena as management compensation, off-balance-sheet financing arrangements, and related-party transactions. Many of these newer disclosure requirements enlist accountants and auditors as the agents to assist in controlling and monitoring these concerns.

Underlying Concepts

Surveys indicate that to meet users' changing needs, business reporting must (1) provide more forward-looking information; (2) focus more on the factors that create longer-term value, including non-financial measures; and (3) better align information reported externally with the information reported internally.

Differential Disclosure

A trend toward **differential disclosure** is also occurring.[1] The IASB has developed IFRS for small- and medium-sized entities (SMEs). SMEs are entities that publish general-purpose financial statements for external users but do not issue shares or other securities

---

[1]The IASB is evaluating disclosure issues such as those related to management commentary. However, as noted by one standard-setter, the usefulness of expanded required disclosure also depends on users' ability to distinguish between disclosed versus recognized items in financial statements. Research to date is inconclusive on this matter. See Katherine Schipper, "Required Disclosures in Financial Reports," Presidential Address to the American Accounting Association Annual Meeting (San Francisco, Calif.: August 2005).

in a public market. SMEs are estimated to account for over 95 percent of all companies around the world. Many believe a simplified set of standards makes sense for these companies because they do not have the resources to implement full IFRS.

Simplified IFRS for SMEs is designed to meet their needs and capabilities. Compared with full IFRS (and many national accounting standards), simplified IFRS for SMEs is less complex in a number of ways:

- Topics not relevant for SMEs are omitted. Examples are earnings per share, interim financial reporting, and segment reporting.
- Simplified IFRS for SMEs allows fewer accounting policy choices. For example, there is no option to revalue property, equipment, or intangibles.
- Many principles for recognizing and measuring assets, liabilities, revenue, and expenses are simplified. For example, goodwill is amortized (as a result, there is no annual impairment test) and all borrowing and R&D costs are expensed.
- Significantly fewer disclosures are required (roughly 300 versus 3,000).
- To further reduce standard overload, revisions to the IFRS for SMEs will be limited to once every three years.

Thus, the option of using simplified IFRS helps SMEs meet the needs of their financial statement users while balancing the costs and benefits from a preparer perspective. **[2]**

NOTES TO THE FINANCIAL STATEMENTS

LEARNING OBJECTIVE
Explain the use of notes in financial statement preparation.

As you know from your study of this textbook, notes are an integral part of the financial statements of a business enterprise. However, readers of financial statements often overlook them because they are highly technical and often appear in small print. **Notes are the means of amplifying or explaining the items presented in the main body of the statements.** They can explain in qualitative terms information pertinent to specific financial statement items. In addition, they can provide supplementary data of a quantitative nature to expand the information in the financial statements. Notes also can explain restrictions imposed by financial arrangements or basic contractual agreements. Although notes may be technical and difficult to understand, they provide meaningful information for the user of the financial statements.

Accounting Policies

Accounting policies are the specific principles, bases, conventions, rules, and practices applied by a company in preparing and presenting financial statements. IFRS states that information about the accounting policies adopted by a reporting entity is essential for financial statement users in making economic decisions. It recommends that companies should present **as an integral part of the financial statements a statement identifying the accounting policies adopted and followed by the reporting entity**. Companies should present the disclosure as the first note or in a separate Summary of Significant Accounting Policies section preceding the notes to the financial statements.

The Summary of Significant Accounting Policies answers such questions as: What method of depreciation is used on plant assets? What valuation method is employed on inventories? What amortization policy is followed in regard to intangible assets? How are marketing costs handled for financial reporting purposes? You can see a good example of note disclosure for **Marks and Spencer plc** (GBR) (which accompany the financial statements presented in Appendix A) at the company's website, *www.marksandspencer.com*.

Analysts examine carefully the summary of accounting policies to determine whether a company is taking a conservative or a liberal approach to accounting practices. For example, depreciating plant assets over an unusually long period of time is considered liberal. Using weighted-average inventory valuation in a period of inflation is generally viewed as conservative.

In addition to disclosure of significant accounting policies, companies must:

1. Identify the judgments that management made in the process of applying the accounting policies and that have the most significant effect on the amounts recognized in the financial statements, and

2. Disclose information about the assumptions they make about the future, and other major sources of estimation uncertainty at the end of the reporting period, that have a significant risk of resulting in a material adjustment to the carrying amounts of assets and liabilities within the next financial year. In respect of those assets and liabilities, the notes shall include details of (a) their nature and (b) their carrying amount as of the end of the reporting period.

These disclosures are many times presented with the accounting policy note or may be provided in a specific policy note. The disclosures should identify the estimates that require management's most difficult, subjective, or complex judgments. **[3]** An example of this disclosure is presented in Illustration 24-2 for **British Airways** (GBR).

ILLUSTRATION 24-2
Accounting Estimate and Judgment Disclosure

British Airways

Key accounting estimates and judgements (in part)
The preparation of financial statements requires management to make judgements, estimates and assumptions that affect the application of policies and reported amounts of assets and liabilities, income and expenses. These estimates and associated assumptions are based on historical experience and various other factors believed to be reasonable under the circumstances. Actual results could differ from these estimates. These underlying assumptions are reviewed on an ongoing basis. Revisions to accounting estimates are recognised in the period in which the estimate is revised if the revision affects only that period, or in the period of the revision and future periods if these are also affected. The estimates and assumptions that have a significant risk of causing a material adjustment to the carrying amounts of assets and liabilities within the next financial year are discussed below.

a Impairment of non-financial assets
The Group assesses whether there are any indicators of impairment for all non-financial assets at each reporting date. Goodwill and intangible assets with indefinite economic lives are tested for impairment annually and at other times when such indicators exist. The recoverable amounts of cash-generating units have been

determined based on value-in-use calculations. These calculations require the use of estimates as disclosed in note 16.

Other non-financial assets are tested for impairment when there are indicators that the carrying amounts may not be recoverable.

d Passenger revenue recognition
Passenger revenue is recognised when the transportation is provided. Ticket sales that are not expected to be used for transportation (unused tickets) are recognised as revenue using estimates regarding the timing of recognition based on the terms and conditions of the ticket and historical trends.

e Frequent flyer revenue
The amount deferred as a liability is measured based on the fair value of the awarded Avios. The fair value is measured by reference to the amount that the award credit could have been sold for separately. The amount deferred is recognised as revenue on redemption of the points including a portion of the points that the Group does not expect to be redeemed by the customers ('breakage'). Both fair value and breakage used are estimates that management exercises judgement on.

Collectively, these disclosures help statement readers evaluate the quality of a company's accounting policies in providing information in the financial statements for assessing future cash flows. Companies that fail to adopt high-quality reporting policies may be heavily penalized by the market. For example, when **Isoft** (GBR) disclosed that it would restate prior-year results due to use of aggressive revenue recognition policies, its share price dropped over 39 percent in one day. Investors viewed Isoft's quality of earnings as low.

Common Notes

We have discussed many of the **notes to the financial statements** throughout this textbook and will discuss others more fully in this chapter. The more common are as follows.

MAJOR DISCLOSURES

INVENTORY. Companies should report the basis upon which inventory amounts are stated (lower-of-cost-or-net realizable value) and the method used in determining cost (FIFO, average-cost, etc.). Manufacturers should report, either in the statement of financial position or in a separate schedule in the notes, the inventory composition (finished goods, work in process, raw materials). Unusual or significant financing arrangements relating to inventories that may require disclosure include transactions with related parties, product financing arrangements, firm purchase commitments, and pledging of inventories as collateral. Chapter 9 (pages 418–420) illustrates these disclosures.

PROPERTY, PLANT, AND EQUIPMENT. Companies should state the basis of valuation for property, plant, and equipment (e.g., revaluation or historical cost). It is usually historical cost. Companies also should disclose pledges, liens, and other commitments related to these assets. In the presentation of depreciation, companies should disclose the following in the financial statements or in the notes: (1) depreciation expense for the period; (2) balances of major classes of depreciable assets, by nature and function, at the statement date; (3) accumulated depreciation, either by major classes of depreciable assets or in total, at the statement date; and (4) a general description of the method or methods used in computing depreciation with respect to major classes of depreciable assets. Finally, companies should explain any major impairments. Chapter 11 (pages 515–517) illustrates these disclosures.

CREDITOR CLAIMS. Investors normally find it extremely useful to understand the nature and cost of creditor claims. However, the liabilities section in the statement of financial position can provide the major types of liabilities only in the aggregate. Note schedules regarding such obligations provide additional information about how a company is financing its operations, the costs that it will bear in future periods, and the timing of future cash outflows. Financial statements must disclose for each of the five years following the date of the statements the aggregate amount of maturities and sinking fund requirements for all long-term borrowings. Chapter 14 (pages 679–680) illustrates these disclosures.

EQUITYHOLDERS' CLAIMS. Many companies present in the body of the statement of financial position information about equity securities: the number of shares authorized, issued, and outstanding and the par value for each type of security. Or, companies may present such data in a note. Beyond that, a common equity note disclosure relates to contracts and senior securities outstanding that might affect the various claims of the residual equityholders. An example would be the existence of outstanding share options, outstanding convertible debt, redeemable preference shares, and convertible preference shares. In addition, it is necessary to disclose certain types of restrictions currently in force. Generally, these types of restrictions involve the amount of earnings available for dividend distribution. Examples of these types of disclosures are illustrated in Chapter 15 (pages 726–727) and Chapter 16 (page 769).

CONTINGENCIES AND COMMITMENTS. A company may have gain or loss contingencies that are not disclosed in the body of the financial statements. These contingencies include litigation, debt and other guarantees, possible tax assessments, renegotiation of government contracts, and sales of receivables with recourse. In addition, companies should disclose in the notes commitments that relate to dividend restrictions, purchase agreements (through-put and take-or-pay), hedge contracts, and employment contracts. Disclosures of such items are illustrated in Chapter 7 (pages 320–321), Chapter 9 (pages 418–420), and Chapter 13 (pages 623, 625–626).

FAIR VALUES. Companies that have assets or liabilities measured at fair value generally disclose both the cost and the fair value in the notes to the financial statements. Fair value measurements may be used for many financial assets and liabilities; investments; revaluations for property, plant, and equipment; impairments of long-lived assets; and some contingencies. Companies also provide disclosure of information that enables users to determine the extent of usage of fair value and the inputs used to implement fair value measurement. This fair value hierarchy identifies three broad levels related to the measurement of fair values (Levels 1, 2, and 3). The levels indicate the reliability of the measurement of fair value information. Chapter 17 (pages 857–860) discusses in detail fair value disclosures.

DEFERRED TAXES, PENSIONS, AND LEASES. The IASB also requires extensive disclosure in the areas of deferred taxes, pensions, and leases. Chapter 19 (pages 975–978), Chapter 20 (pages 1033–1034), and Chapter 21 (pages 1089–1091) discuss in detail each of these disclosures. Users of financial statements should carefully read notes to the financial statements for information about off-balance-sheet commitments, future financing needs, and the quality of a company's earnings.

CHANGES IN ACCOUNTING POLICIES. The profession defines various types of accounting changes and establishes guides for reporting each type. Companies discuss, either in the summary of significant accounting policies or in the other notes, changes in accounting policies (as well as material changes in estimates and corrections of errors). See Chapter 22 (pages 1135 and 1040).

In earlier chapters, we discussed the disclosures listed above. The following sections of this chapter illustrate four additional disclosures of significance—special transactions or events, subsequent events, segment reporting, and interim reporting.

What do the numbers mean?   FOOTNOTE SECRETS

Often, note disclosures are needed to give a complete picture of a company's financial position. A good example is the required disclosure of collateral arrangements in repurchase agreements. Such arrangements gained front-page coverage when it was revealed that **Lehman Brothers** (USA)—and many other U.S. and European financial institutions—employed specialized repurchase agreements, referred to as Repo 105 (or Repo 108 in Europe), to "window-dress" their statements of financial positions. Here's how it works.

A repurchase agreement amounts to a short-term loan, exchanging collateral for cash upfront and then unwinding the trade as soon as overnight. The Repo 105 that Lehman employed used a variety of holdings as the collateral. Lehman made the exchanges with major global financial institutions, such as **Barclays** (GBR), **UBS** (CHE), **Mitsubishi UFJ Financial Group** (JPN), and **KBC Bank** (BEL). What was special about the Repo 105/108 is that the value of the securities that Lehman pledged in the transactions were worth 105 percent of the cash it received. That is, the firm was taking a

haircut on the transactions. And when Lehman eventually repaid the cash it received from its counterparties, it did so with interest, making this a rather expensive technique. Under accounting guidance at that time, Lehman could book the transactions as a "sale" rather than a "financing," as most repos are regarded. That meant that for a few days, Lehman could shuffle off tens of billions of dollars in assets to appear more financially healthy than it really was.

How can you get better informed about note disclosures that may contain important information related to your investments, like Repo 105? Beyond your study in this class, a good online resource for understanding the contents of note disclosures is *http://www.footnoted.org/*. This site highlights "the things companies bury" in their annual reports. It notes that company reports are more complete of late, but only the largest companies are preparing documents that are readable. As the editor of the site noted, "[some companies] are being dragged kicking and screaming into plain English."

Sources: Gretchen Morgenson, "Annual Reports: More Pages, but Better?" *The New York Times* (March 17, 2002); D. Stead, "The Secrets in SEC Filings," *BusinessWeek* (August 25, 2008), p. 12; and M. de la Merced and J. Werdigier, "The Origins of Lehman's 'Repo 105'," *The New York Times* (March 12, 2010).

DISCLOSURE ISSUES
Disclosure of Special Transactions or Events

LEARNING OBJECTIVE **3**

Discuss the disclosure requirements for related-party transactions, subsequent events, and major business segments.

Related-party transactions, errors, and fraud pose especially sensitive and difficult problems. The accountant/auditor who has responsibility for reporting on these types of transactions must take care to properly balance the rights of the reporting company and the needs of financial statement users.

Related-party transactions arise when a company engages in transactions in which one of the parties has the ability to significantly influence the policies of the other. They may also occur when a non-transacting party has the ability to influence the policies of the two transacting parties.[2] Competitive, free-market dealings may not exist in related-party transactions, and so an "arm's-length" basis cannot be assumed. Transactions such as borrowing or lending money at abnormally low or high interest rates, real estate sales at amounts that differ significantly from appraised value, exchanges of non-monetary assets, and transactions involving companies that have no economic substance ("shell corporations") suggest that related parties may be involved.

In order to make adequate disclosure, companies should report the economic substance, rather than the legal form, of these transactions. IFRS requires the following minimum disclosures of material related-party transactions. **[5]**

1. The nature of the related-party relationship;
2. The amount of the transactions and the amount of outstanding balances, including commitments, the nature of consideration, and details of any guarantees given or received;
3. Provisions for doubtful debts related to the amount of outstanding balances; and
4. The expense recognized during the period in respect of bad or doubtful debts due from related parties.

Illustration 24-3, from the annual report of **Volvo Group** (SWE), shows disclosure of related-party transactions.

ILLUSTRATION 24-3
Disclosure of Related-Party Transactions

 Volvo Group

Note 25. Transactions with related parties (in part)

The Volvo Group engages in transactions with some of its associated companies. The transactions consist mainly of sales of vehicles to dealers and purchases of engines.

	2012	2011
Sales to associated companies	1,670	1,296
Purchases from associated companies	702	60
Receivables from associated companies, Dec. 31	242	186
Liabilities to associated companies, Dec. 31	632	129

The increase in purchases and liabilities is explained by Deutz AG, which is an associated company from September 2012. Commercial terms and market prices apply for the supply of goods and services to/from associated companies.

Until December 2012 Renault s.a.s was a related party to the Volvo Group due to its holding in AB Volvo. In December 2012 Renault s.a.s. sold their Volvo shares. Sales to and purchases from Renault s.a.s. and its subsidiaries amounted to 29 (53) and 1,719 (2,321). Receivables from and liabilities to Renault s.a.s. is not included for 2012 and totalled 11 and 372, respectively, as of December 31, 2011. Sales were mainly from Renault Trucks to Renault s.a.s. and comprised components and spare parts. Purchases were mainly made by Renault Trucks from Renault s.a.s. and primarily comprised light trucks. Renault Trucks has a license from Renault s.a.s. for the use of the trademark Renault.

[2]Examples of related-party transactions include transactions between (a) a parent company and its subsidiaries, (b) subsidiaries of a common parent, (c) a company and trusts for the benefit of employees (controlled or managed by the enterprise), and (d) a company and its principal owners, management, or members of immediate families, and affiliates. **[4]**

Many companies are involved in related-party transactions. However, another type of special event, errors and fraud (sometimes referred to as irregularities), is the exception rather than the rule. Accounting **errors** are **unintentional** mistakes, whereas **fraud** (misappropriation of assets and fraudulent financial reporting) involves **intentional** distortions of financial statements.[3] As indicated earlier, companies should correct the financial statements when they discover errors. The same treatment should be given fraud. The discovery of fraud, however, gives rise to a different set of procedures and responsibilities for the accountant/auditor.

Disclosure plays a very important role in these types of transactions because the events are many times more qualitative than quantitative and involve more subjective than objective evaluation. Users of the financial statements need some indication of the existence and nature of these transactions, through disclosures, modifications in the auditor's report, or reports of changes in auditors.

Events after the Reporting Period (Subsequent Events)

Notes to the financial statements should explain any significant financial events that took place after the formal statement of financial position date, but before the statements are authorized for issuance (hereafter referred to as the authorization date). These events are referred to as **events after the reporting date** or **subsequent events**. Illustration 24-4 shows a time diagram of the subsequent events period.

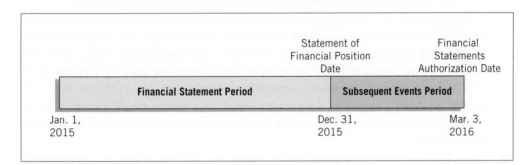

ILLUSTRATION 24-4
Time Periods for
Subsequent Events

A period of several weeks or sometimes months may elapse after the end of the fiscal year but before the management or the board of directors authorizes issuance of the financial statements.[4] Various activities involved in closing the books for the period and issuing the statements all take time: taking and pricing the inventory, reconciling subsidiary ledgers with controlling accounts, preparing necessary adjusting entries, ensuring that all transactions for the period have been entered, obtaining an audit of the financial statements by independent certified public accountants, and printing the annual report. During the period between the statement of financial position date and

---

[3]International Standard on Auditing 240, "The Auditor's Responsibilities Related to Fraud in an Audit of Financial Statements," *Handbook of International Quality Control, Auditing, Review, Other Assurance, and Other Related Services Pronouncements* (New York: International Federation of Accountants (IFAC), April 2010). We have an expanded discussion of fraud later in this chapter. Requirements for company audits vary according to the jurisdiction and market listing. Most public international companies outside the United States comply with the international auditing standards issued by the International Auditing and Assurance Standards Board (IAASB).

[4]In many jurisdictions, management is required to issue its financial statements to a supervisory board (made up solely of non-executives) for approval. In such cases, the financial statements are authorized for issue—the end of the subsequent events period—when the management authorizes them for issue to the supervisory board. In other jurisdictions, companies are required to submit the financial statements to their shareholders for approval after the financial statements have been made public. In such cases, the subsequent events period ends on the date of issue, not the date when shareholders approve the financial statements. **[6]**

its authorization date, important transactions or other events may occur that materially affect the company's financial position or operating situation.

Many who read a statement of financial position believe the financial condition is constant, and they project it into the future. However, readers must be told if the company has experienced a significant change—e.g., sold one of its plants, acquired a subsidiary, suffered unusual losses, settled significant litigation, or experienced any other important event in the post-statement of financial position period. Without an explanation in a note, the reader might be misled and draw inappropriate conclusions.

Two types of events or transactions occurring after the statement of financial position date may have a material effect on the financial statements or may need disclosure so that readers interpret these statements accurately:

 Underlying Concepts

The periodicity or time period assumption implies that economic activities of an enterprise can be divided into artificial time periods for purpose of analysis.

1. Events that provide additional evidence about conditions **that existed** at the statement of financial position date, including the estimates inherent in the process of preparing financial statements. These events are referred to as **adjusted subsequent events** and require adjustments to the financial statements. All information available prior to the authorization date of the financial statements helps investors and creditors evaluate estimates previously made. To ignore these subsequent events is to pass up an opportunity to improve the accuracy of the financial statements. This first type of event encompasses information that an accountant would have recorded in the accounts had the information been known at the statement of financial position date.

   For example, if a loss on an account receivable results from a customer's bankruptcy subsequent to the statement of financial position date, the company adjusts the financial statements before their issuance. The bankruptcy stems from the customer's poor financial health existing at the statement of financial position date.

   The same criterion applies to settlements of litigation. The company must adjust the financial statements if the events that gave rise to the litigation, such as personal injury or patent infringement, took place prior to the statement of financial position date.

2. Events that provide evidence about conditions that **did not exist** at the statement of financial position date but arise subsequent to that date. These events are referred as **non-adjusted subsequent events** and do not require adjustment of the financial statements. To illustrate, a loss resulting from a customer's fire or flood *after* the statement of financial position date does not reflect conditions existing at that date. Thus, adjustment of the financial statements is not necessary. A company should not recognize subsequent events that provide evidence about conditions that did not exist at the date of the statement of financial position but that arose after the statement of financial position date.

The following are examples of non-adjusted subsequent events:

- A major business combination after the reporting period or disposing of a major subsidiary.
- Announcing a plan to discontinue an operation or commencing the implementation of a major restructuring.
- Major purchases of assets, other disposals of assets, or expropriation of major assets by government.
- The destruction of a major production plant or inventories by a fire or natural disaster after the reporting period.
- Major ordinary share transactions and potential ordinary share transactions after the reporting period.

- Abnormally large changes after the reporting period in asset prices, foreign exchange rates, or taxes.
- Entering into significant commitments or contingent liabilities, for example, by issuing significant guarantees after the statement date. **[7]**[5]

Underlying Concepts

A company also should consider supplementing the historical financial statements with pro forma financial data. Occasionally, a non-adjusted subsequent event may be so significant that disclosure can best be made by means of pro forma financial data.

Some non-adjusted subsequent events may have to be disclosed to keep the financial statements from being misleading. For such events, a company discloses the nature of the event and an estimate of its financial effect.

Illustration 24-5 presents an example of subsequent events disclosure, excerpted from the annual report of **Tieto** (FIN).

Tieto

ILLUSTRATION 24-5
Disclosure of Subsequent Events

Note 32. Events After the Balance Sheet Date

In February, Tieto agreed to sell the majority of its operations in Germany and Netherlands to the German industrial group Aurelius. Closing is expected to take place during the second quarter of 2013. Net sales of the divested business amounted to over EUR 110 million in 2012. German businesses were loss-making in 2012 and the divestment will improve Tieto's operating margin of underlying business by some 0.5 percentage points based on 2012 performance. Tieto booked about EUR 30 million in impairment in the fourth-quarter 2012. The divested business operations, including around 900 employees in total, will be transferred to the new owner at the time of closing. The divestment excludes Tieto's global businesses and customers, i.e. the forest industry business in Germany, the energy industry business in Netherlands, Product Engineering resources for global customers and selective other global roles.

Between 7 December and 31 December 2012, a total of 111,846 Tieto Corporation new shares have been subscribed for with the company's stock options 2006C, and a total of 3,500 shares with stock options 2009A. As a result of the subscriptions, the number of Tieto shares increased to 72,492,559 and the share capital to EUR 76,064,020.00. The shares subscribed for under the stock options were registered in the Trade Register on 18 January 2013.

Many subsequent events or developments do not require adjustment of or disclosure in the financial statements. Typically, these are non-accounting events or conditions that management normally communicates by other means. These events include legislation, product changes, management changes, strikes, unionization, marketing agreements, and loss of important customers.

Reporting for Diversified (Conglomerate) Companies

In certain business climates, companies have a tendency to diversify their operations. Take the case of **Siemens AG** (DEU), whose products include energy technologies, consumer products, and financial services. When businesses are so diversified, investors and investment analysts want more information about the details behind conglomerate financial statements. Particularly, they want income statement, statement of financial position, and cash flow information on the **individual segments** that compose the total income figure.

---

[5]The effects from natural disasters, like the eruption of the Icelandic volcano, which occurred after the year-end for companies with March fiscal years, require disclosure in order to keep the statements from being misleading. Some companies may have to consider whether these disasters affect their ability to continue as going concerns.

Much information is hidden in the aggregated totals. With only the consolidated figures, the analyst cannot tell the extent to which the differing product lines **contribute to the company's profitability, risk, and growth potential**. For example, in Illustration 24-6, the office equipment segment looks like a risky venture. Segmented reporting would provide useful information about the two business segments and would be useful for making an informed investment decision regarding the whole company.

ILLUSTRATION 24-6
Segmented Income
Statement

OFFICE EQUIPMENT AND AUTO PARTS COMPANY INCOME STATEMENT DATA (IN MILLIONS)			
	Consolidated	Office Equipment	Auto Parts
Net sales	$78.8	$18.0	$60.8
Manufacturing costs			
Inventories, beginning	12.3	4.0	8.3
Materials and services	38.9	10.8	28.1
Wages	12.9	3.8	9.1
Inventories, ending	(13.3)	(3.9)	(9.4)
	50.8	14.7	36.1
Selling and administrative expenses	12.1	1.6	10.5
Total operating expenses	62.9	16.3	46.6
Income before taxes	15.9	1.7	14.2
Income taxes	(9.3)	(1.0)	(8.3)
Net income	$ 6.6	$ 0.7	$ 5.9

A classic situation that demonstrates the need for segmented data involved **Caterpillar, Inc. (USA)**. Market regulators cited Caterpillar because it failed to tell investors that nearly a quarter of its income in one year came from a Brazilian unit and was non-recurring in nature. The company knew that different economic policies in the next year would probably greatly affect earnings of the Brazilian unit. But Caterpillar presented its financial results on a consolidated basis, not disclosing the Brazilian operations. Caterpillar's failure to include information about Brazil left investors with an incomplete picture of the company's financial results and denied investors the opportunity to see the company "through the eyes of management."

Companies have always been somewhat hesitant to disclose segmented data for various reasons:

1. Without a thorough knowledge of the business and an understanding of such important factors as the competitive environment and capital investment requirements, the investor may find the segmented information meaningless or may even draw improper conclusions about the reported earnings of the segments.

2. Additional disclosure may be helpful to competitors, labor unions, suppliers, and certain government regulatory agencies, and thus harm the reporting company.

3. Additional disclosure may discourage management from taking intelligent business risks because segments reporting losses or unsatisfactory earnings may cause shareholder dissatisfaction with management.

4. The wide variation among companies in the choice of segments, cost allocation, and other accounting problems limits the usefulness of segmented information.

5. The investor is investing in the company as a whole and not in the particular segments, and it should not matter how any single segment is performing if the overall performance is satisfactory.

6. Certain technical problems, such as classification of segments and allocation of segment revenues and costs (especially "common costs"), are formidable.

On the other hand, the advocates of segmented disclosures offer these reasons in support of the practice:

1. Investors need segmented information to make an intelligent investment decision regarding a diversified company.
   (a) Sales and earnings of individual segments enable investors to evaluate the differences between segments in growth rate, risk, and profitability, and to forecast consolidated profits.
   (b) Segmented reports help investors evaluate the company's investment worth by disclosing the nature of a company's businesses and the relative size of the components.
2. The absence of segmented reporting by a diversified company may put its unsegmented, single product-line competitors at a competitive disadvantage because the conglomerate may obscure information that its competitors must disclose.

The advocates of segmented disclosures appear to have a much stronger case. Many users indicate that segmented data are the most useful financial information provided, aside from the basic financial statements. As a result, the IASB has issued extensive reporting guidelines in this area.

Objective of Reporting Segmented Information

The objective of reporting segmented financial data is to provide information about the **different types of business activities** in which an enterprise engages and the **different economic environments** in which it operates. Meeting this objective will help users of financial statements do the following.

(a) Better understand the enterprise's performance.
(b) Better assess its prospects for future net cash flows.
(c) Make more informed judgments about the enterprise as a whole.

Basic Principles

Financial statements can be disaggregated in several ways. For example, they can be disaggregated by products or services, by geography, by legal entity, or by type of customer. However, it is not feasible to provide all of that information in every set of financial statements. IFRS requires that general-purpose financial statements include selected information on a single basis of segmentation. Thus, a company can meet the segmented reporting objective by providing financial statements segmented based on how the company's operations are managed. The method chosen is referred to as the management approach. **[8] The management approach reflects how management segments the company for making operating decisions.** The segments are evident from the components of the company's organization structure. These components are called **operating segments**.

Identifying Operating Segments

An **operating segment** is a component of an enterprise:

(a) That engages in business activities from which it earns revenues and incurs expenses.
(b) Whose operating results are regularly reviewed by the company's chief operating decision-maker to assess segment performance and allocate resources to the segment.
(c) For which discrete financial information is available that is generated by or based on the internal financial reporting system.

Companies may aggregate information about two or more operating segments only if the segments have the same basic characteristics in each of the following areas.

(a) The nature of the products and services provided.

(b) The nature of the production process.

(c) The type or class of customer.

(d) The methods of product or service distribution.

(e) If applicable, the nature of the regulatory environment.

After the company decides on the possible segments for disclosure, it makes a quantitative materiality test. This test determines whether the segment is significant enough to warrant actual disclosure. An operating segment is deemed significant and therefore a reportable segment if it satisfies **one or more** of the following quantitative thresholds.

1. Its **revenue** (including both sales to external customers and intersegment sales or transfers) is 10 percent or more of the combined revenue of all the company's operating segments.

2. The absolute amount of its **profit or loss** is 10 percent or more of the greater, in absolute amount, of **(a)** the combined operating profit of all operating segments that did not incur a loss, or **(b)** the combined loss of all operating segments that did report a loss.

3. Its **identifiable assets** are 10 percent or more of the combined assets of all operating segments.

In applying these tests, the company must consider two additional factors. First, segment data must explain a significant portion of the company's business. Specifically, the segmented results must equal or exceed 75 percent of the combined sales to unaffiliated customers for the entire company. This test prevents a company from providing limited information on only a few segments and lumping all the rest into one category.

Second, the profession recognizes that reporting too many segments may overwhelm users with detailed information. The IASB decided that 10 is a reasonable upper limit for the number of segments that a company must disclose. **[9]**

To illustrate these requirements, assume a company has identified six possible reporting segments, as shown in Illustration 24-7 (euros in thousands).

ILLUSTRATION 24-7
Data for Different Possible Reporting Segments

Segments	Total Revenue (Unaffiliated)	Operating Profit (Loss)	Identifiable Assets
A	€ 100	€10	€ 60
B	50	2	30
C	700	40	390
D	300	20	160
E	900	18	280
F	100	(5)	50
	€2,150	€85	€970

The company would apply the respective tests as follows.

Revenue test: 10% × €2,150 = €215; C, D, and E meet this test.

Operating profit (loss) test: 10% × €90 = €9 (note that the €5 loss is ignored, because the test is based on non-loss segments); A, C, D, and E meet this test.

Identifiable assets tests: 10% × €970 = €97; C, D, and E meet this test.

The reporting segments are therefore A, C, D, and E, assuming that these four segments have enough sales to meet the 75 percent of combined sales test. The 75 percent test is computed as follows.

> **75% of combined sales test:** 75% × €2,150 = €1,612.50. The sales of A, C, D, and E total €2,000 (€100 + €700 + €300 + €900); therefore, the 75 percent test is met.

Measurement Principles

The accounting principles that companies use for segment disclosure need not be the same as the principles they use to prepare the consolidated statements. This flexibility may at first appear inconsistent. But, preparing segment information in accordance with IFRS would be difficult because some IFRS are not expected to apply at a segment level. Examples are accounting for the cost of company-wide employee benefit plans and accounting for income taxes in a company that files a consolidated tax return with segments in different tax jurisdictions.

The IASB does not require allocations of joint, common, or company-wide costs solely for external reporting purposes. **Common costs** are those incurred for the benefit of more than one segment and whose interrelated nature prevents a completely objective division of costs among segments. For example, the company president's salary is difficult to allocate to various segments. Allocations of common costs are inherently arbitrary and may not be meaningful. There is a presumption that if companies allocate common costs to segments, these allocations are either directly attributable or reasonably allocable to the segments.

Segmented Information Reported

The IASB requires that an enterprise report the following.

1. *General information about its operating segments.* This includes factors that management considers most significant in determining the company's operating segments and the types of products and services from which each operating segment derives its revenues.

2. *Segment profit and loss and related information.* Specifically, companies must report the following information about each operating segment if the amounts are included in determining segment profit or loss.
   (a) Revenues from transactions with external customers.
   (b) Revenues from transactions with other operating segments of the same enterprise.
   (c) Interest revenue.
   (d) Interest expense.
   (e) Depreciation and amortization expense.
   (f) Unusual items.
   (g) Equity in the net income of investees accounted for by the equity method.
   (h) Income tax expense or benefit.
   (i) Significant non-cash items other than depreciation, depletion, and amortization expense.

3. *Segment assets and liabilities.* A company must report each operating segment's total assets and liabilities.

4. *Reconciliations.* A company must provide a reconciliation of the total of the segments' revenues to total revenues, a reconciliation of the total of the operating segments' profits and losses to its income before income taxes, and a reconciliation of the total of the operating segments' assets and liabilities to total assets and liabilities.

5. *Information about products and services and geographic areas.* For each operating segment not based on geography, the company must report (unless it is impracticable): (1) revenues from external customers, (2) long-lived assets, and (3) expenditures during the period for long-lived assets. This information, if material, must be reported (a) in the enterprise's country of domicile and (b) in each other country.

6. *Major customers.* If 10 percent or more of company revenue is derived from a single customer, the company must disclose the total amount of revenue from each such customer by segment.

ILLUSTRATION 24-8
Segment Disclosure

Illustration of Disaggregated Information

Illustration 24-8 shows the segment disclosure for Statoil (NOR).

Statoil

Note 5. Segments (in part)
Segment data for the year ended 31 December is presented below:

(in NOK million)	Exploration and Production Norway	International Exploration and Production	Natural Gas	Manufacturing and Marketing	Other	Eliminations	Total
Year ended 31 December							
Revenues third party and Other income	4,153	12,301	96,973	348,941	1,287	0	463,655
Revenues inter-segment	154,431	28,459	1,241	2,014	2,295	(188,440)	0
Net income from associated companies	79	1,075	399	280	(55)	0	1,778
Total revenues and other income	158,663	41,835	98,613	351,235	3,527	(188,440)	465,433
Net operating income	104,318	2,599	18,488	(541)	(1,146)	(2,078)	121,640
Significant non-cash items recognised in segment profit or loss							
- Depreciation and amortisation	25,653	16,231	1,778	2,390	687	0	46,739
- Impairment losses	0	873	1,001	5,369	74	0	7,317
- Inventory valuation	0	0	(24)	(5,171)	0	1,377	(3,818)
- Commodity based derivatives	(1,781)	0	(2,814)	1,072	(122)	0	(3,645)
- Exploration expenditure written off	1,177	5,821	0	0	0	0	6,998
Investments in associated companies	214	4,962	2,829	917	1,134	0	10,056
Other segment non-current assets	175,998	152,678	34,797	28,587	3,028	0	395,088
Non-current assets, not allocated to segments*							41,312
Total non-current assets							446,456
Additions to PP&E and intangible assets**	34,875	39,354	2,528	7,618	1,340	0	85,715

*Deferred tax assets, post employment benefit assets and non-current financial instruments are not allocated to segments.
**Excluding movements due to changes in abandonment and removal obligations.

Interim Reports

LEARNING OBJECTIVE ❹

Describe the accounting problems associated with interim reporting.

 Underlying Concepts

For information to be relevant, it must be available to decision-makers before it loses its capacity to influence their decisions (timeliness). Interim reporting is an excellent example of this concept.

Another source of information for the investor is interim reports. As noted earlier, interim reports cover periods of less than one year. The securities exchanges, market regulators, and the accounting profession have an active interest in the presentation of interim information.

Because of the short-term nature of the information in these reports, there is considerable controversy as to the general approach companies should employ. One group, which favors the discrete approach, believes that companies should treat each interim period as a separate accounting period. Using that treatment, companies would follow the principles for deferrals and accruals used for annual reports. In this view, companies should report accounting transactions as they occur, and expense recognition should not change with the period of time covered.

Another group, which favors the integral approach, believes that the interim report is an integral part of the annual report and that deferrals and accruals should take into consideration what will happen for the entire year. In this approach, companies should assign estimated expenses to parts of a year on the basis of sales volume or some other activity base. In general, IFRS requires companies to follow the discrete approach. **[10]**

Interim Reporting Requirements

Generally, companies should use the same accounting policies for interim reports and for annual reports. They should recognize revenues in interim periods on the same basis as they are for annual periods. For example, if Cedars Corp. uses the percentage-of-completion method as the basis for recognizing revenue on an annual basis, then it should use the percentage-of-completion method for interim reports as well. Also, Cedars should treat costs directly associated with revenues (product costs, such as materials, labor and related fringe benefits, and manufacturing overhead) in the same manner for interim reports as for annual reports.

Companies should use the same inventory pricing methods (FIFO, average-cost, etc.) for interim reports and for annual reports. However, companies may use the gross profit method for interim inventory pricing. But, they must disclose the method and adjustments to reconcile with annual inventory.

Discrete Approach. Following the discrete approach, companies record in interim reports revenues and expenses according to the revenue and expense recognition principles. This includes costs and expenses other than product costs (often referred to as period costs). No accruals or deferrals in anticipation of future events during the year should be reported. For example, the cost of a planned major periodic maintenance or overhaul for a company like **Airbus** (FRA) or other seasonal expenditure that is expected to occur late in the year is not anticipated for interim reporting purposes. The mere intention or necessity to incur expenditure related to the future is not sufficient to give rise to an obligation.

Or, a company like **Carrefour** (FRA) may budget certain costs expected to be incurred irregularly during the financial year, such as advertising and employee training costs. Those costs generally are discretionary even though they are planned and tend to recur from year to year. However, recognizing an obligation at the end of an interim financial reporting period for such costs that have not yet been incurred generally is not consistent with the definition of a liability.

While year-to-date measurements may involve changes in estimates of amounts reported in prior interim periods of the current financial year, the principles for recognizing assets, liabilities, income, and expenses for interim periods are the same as in annual financial statements. For example, **Wm Morrison Supermarkets plc** (GBR) records losses from inventory write-downs, restructurings, or impairments in an interim period similar to how it would treat these items in the annual financial statements (when incurred). However, if an estimate from a prior interim period changes in a subsequent interim period of that year, the original estimate is adjusted in the subsequent interim period.

Interim Disclosures. IFRS does not require a complete set of financial statements at the interim reporting date. Rather, companies may comply with the requirements by providing condensed financial statements and selected explanatory notes. Because users of interim financial reports also have access to the most recent annual financial report, companies only need provide explanation of significant events and transactions since the end of the last annual reporting period. Companies should report the following interim data at a minimum.

1. Statement that the same accounting policies and methods of computation are followed in the interim financial statements as compared with the most recent annual financial statements or, if those policies or methods have been changed, a description of the nature and effect of the change.

2. Explanatory comments about the seasonality or cyclicality of interim operations.

3. The nature and amount of items affecting assets, liabilities, equity, net income, or cash flows that are unusual because of their nature, size, or incidence.

4. The nature and amount of changes in accounting policies and estimates of amounts previously reported.

5. Issuances, repurchases, and repayments of debt and equity securities.

6. Dividends paid (aggregate or per share) separately for ordinary shares and other shares.

7. Segment information, as required by *IFRS 8*, "Operating Segments."

8. Changes in contingent liabilities or contingent assets since the end of the last annual reporting period.

9. Effect of changes in the composition of the company during the interim period, such as business combinations, obtaining or losing control of subsidiaries and long-term investments, restructurings, and discontinued operations.

10. Other material events subsequent to the end of the interim period that have not been reflected in the financial statements for the interim period.

If a complete set of financial statements is provided in the interim report, companies comply with the provisions of *IAS 1*, "Presentation of Financial Statements."

Unique Problems of Interim Reporting

IFRS reflects a preference for the discrete approach. However, within this broad guideline, a number of unique reporting problems develop related to the following items.

Income Taxes. Not every dollar of corporate taxable income may be taxed at the same rate if the tax rate is progressive. This aspect of business income taxes poses a problem in preparing interim financial statements. Should the company use the **annualized approach**, which is to annualize income to date and accrue the proportionate income tax for the period to date? Or should it follow the **marginal principle approach**, which is to apply the lower rate of tax to the first amount of income earned? At one time, companies generally followed the latter approach and accrued the tax applicable to each additional dollar of income.

IFRS requires use of the annualized approach. Income tax expense is recognized in each interim period based on the best estimate of the weighted-average annual income tax rate expected for the full financial year. This approach is consistent with applying the same principles in interim reports as applied to annual report; that is, income taxes are assessed on an annual basis. However, amounts accrued for income tax expense in one interim period may have to be adjusted in a subsequent interim period of that financial year if the estimate of the annual income tax rate changes. **[11]**[6]

Seasonality. Seasonality occurs when most of a company's sales occur in one short period of the year, while certain costs are fairly evenly spread throughout the year. For example, the natural gas industry has its heavy sales in the winter months. In contrast, the beverage industry has its heavy sales in the summer months.

The problem of seasonality is related to the expense recognition principle in accounting. Generally, expenses are associated with the revenues they create. In a seasonal business, wide fluctuations in profits occur because off-season sales do not absorb the company's fixed costs (for example, manufacturing, selling, and administrative costs that tend to remain fairly constant regardless of sales or production).

---

[6]The estimated annual effective tax rate should reflect anticipated tax credits, foreign tax rates, percentage depletion, capital gains rates, and other available tax-planning alternatives.

To illustrate why seasonality is a problem, assume the following information.

Selling price per unit	$1
Annual sales for the period (projected and actual)	
100,000 units @ $1	$100,000
Manufacturing costs	
Variable	10¢ per unit
Fixed	20¢ per unit or $20,000 for the year
Non-manufacturing costs	
Variable	10¢ per unit
Fixed	30¢ per unit or $30,000 for the year

ILLUSTRATION 24-9
Data for Seasonality Example

Sales for four quarters and the year (projected and actual) were as follows.

		Percent of Sales
1st Quarter	$ 20,000	20%
2nd Quarter	5,000	5
3rd Quarter	10,000	10
4th Quarter	65,000	65
Total for the year	$100,000	100%

ILLUSTRATION 24-10
Sales Data for Seasonality Example

Under the present accounting framework, the income statements for the quarters might be as shown in Illustration 24-11.

	1st Qtr	2nd Qtr	3rd Qtr	4th Qtr	Year
Sales	$20,000	$ 5,000	$10,000	$65,000	$100,000
Manufacturing costs					
Variable	(2,000)	(500)	(1,000)	(6,500)	(10,000)
Fixed[a]	(4,000)	(1,000)	(2,000)	(13,000)	(20,000)
	14,000	3,500	7,000	45,500	70,000
Non-manufacturing costs					
Variable	(2,000)	(500)	(1,000)	(6,500)	(10,000)
Fixed[b]	(7,500)	(7,500)	(7,500)	(7,500)	(30,000)
Net income	$ 4,500	$(4,500)	$ (1,500)	$31,500	$ 30,000

ILLUSTRATION 24-11
Interim Net Income for Seasonal Business—Discrete Approach

[a]The fixed manufacturing costs are inventoried, so that equal amounts of fixed costs do not appear during each quarter.
[b]The fixed non-manufacturing costs are not inventoried, so equal amounts of fixed costs appear during each quarter.

An investor who uses the first quarter's results might be misled. If the first quarter's earnings are $4,500, should this figure be multiplied by four to predict annual earnings of $18,000? Or, if first-quarter sales of $20,000 are 20 percent of the predicted sales for the year, would the net income for the year be $22,500 ($4,500 × 5)? Both figures are obviously wrong. And, after the second quarter's results occur, the investor may become even more confused.

The problem with the conventional approach is that the fixed non-manufacturing costs are not charged in proportion to sales. Some enterprises have adopted a way of avoiding this problem by making all fixed non-manufacturing costs follow the sales pattern, as shown in Illustration 24-12.

	1st Qtr	2nd Qtr	3rd Qtr	4th Qtr	Year
Sales	$20,000	$ 5,000	$10,000	$65,000	$100,000
Manufacturing costs					
Variable	(2,000)	(500)	(1,000)	(6,500)	(10,000)
Fixed	(4,000)	(1,000)	(2,000)	(13,000)	(20,000)
	14,000	3,500	7,000	45,500	70,000
Non-manufacturing costs					
Variable	(2,000)	(500)	(1,000)	(6,500)	(10,000)
Fixed	(6,000)	(1,500)	(3,000)	(19,500)	(30,000)
Net income	$ 6,000	$ 1,500	$ 3,000	$19,500	$ 30,000

ILLUSTRATION 24-12
Interim Net Income for Seasonal Business—Integral Approach

This approach solves some of the problems of interim reporting: Sales in the first quarter are 20 percent of total sales for the year, and net income in the first quarter is 20 percent of total income. In this case, as in the previous example, the investor cannot rely on multiplying any given quarter by four but can use comparative data or rely on some estimate of sales in relation to income for a given period.

The greater the degree of seasonality experienced by a company, the greater the possibility of distortion. Because there are no definitive guidelines for handling such items as the fixed non-manufacturing costs, variability in income can be substantial. To alleviate this problem, IFRS requires companies subject to material seasonal variations to disclose the seasonal nature of their business and consider supplementing their interim reports with information for 12-month periods ended at the interim date for the current and preceding years.

The two illustrations highlight the difference between the **discrete** and **integral** approaches. Illustration 24-11 (page 1269) represents the discrete approach, in which the fixed non-manufacturing expenses are expensed as incurred. Illustration 24-12 (page 1269) shows the integral approach, in which expenses are charged to expense on the basis of some measure of activity.

Continuing Controversy. While IFRS has developed some rules for interim reporting, additional issues remain. For example, there is continuing debate on the independent auditor's involvement in interim reports. Many auditors are reluctant to express an opinion on interim financial information, arguing that the data are too tentative and subjective. On the other hand, more people are advocating some examination of interim reports. Generally, auditors perform a review of interim financial information. Such a review, which is much more limited in its procedures than the annual audit, provides some assurance that the interim information appears to be in accord with IFRS.[7]

Analysts and investors want financial information as soon as possible, before it is old news. We may not be far from a continuous database system in which corporate financial records can be accessed online. Investors might be able to access a company's financial records whenever they wish and put the information in the format they need. Thus, they could learn about sales slippage, cost increases, or earnings changes as they happen, rather than waiting until after the quarter has ended.

A steady stream of information from the company to the investor could be very positive because it might alleviate management's continual concern with short-run interim numbers. Today, many contend that management is too oriented to the short-term. The truth of this statement is echoed by the words of the president of a large company who decided to retire early: "I wanted to look forward to a year made up of four seasons rather than four quarters."

AUDITOR'S AND MANAGEMENT'S REPORTS

Auditor's Report

Another important source of information that is often overlooked is the **auditor's report**. An **auditor** is an accounting professional who conducts an independent examination of a company's accounting data.

---

[7]These are referred to as review engagements, which are less extensive than an audit. See International Standards on Review Engagements (ISRE) 2410, "Review of Interim Financial Information Performed by the Independent Auditor of the Entity," *Handbook of International Quality Control, Auditing, Review, Other Assurance, and Other Related Services Pronouncements* (April 2010).

If satisfied that the financial statements present the financial position, results of operations, and cash flows fairly in accordance with IFRS, the auditor expresses an **unmodified opinion**. An example is shown in Illustration 24-13.[8]

ILLUSTRATION 24-13
Auditor's Report

Wm Morrison Supermarkets plc

Independent auditors' report to the members of Wm Morrison Supermarkets plc

We have audited the financial statements of Wm Morrison Supermarkets plc for the 53 weeks ended 3 February 2013 set out on pages 60–108. The financial reporting framework that has been applied in the preparation of the Group financial statements is applicable law and International Financial Reporting Standards (IFRS) as adopted by the EU. The financial reporting framework that has been applied in the preparation of the Parent Company financial statements is applicable law and UK Accounting Standards (UK Generally Accepted Accounting Practice).

This report is made solely to the Company's members, as a body, in accordance with chapter 3 of part 16 of the Companies Act 2006. Our audit work has been undertaken so that we might state to the Company's members those matters we are required to state to them in an auditors' report and for no other purpose. To the fullest extent permitted by law, we do not accept or assume responsibility to anyone other than the Company and the Company's members, as a body, for our audit work, for this report, or for the opinions we have formed.

Respective responsibilities of directors and auditors

As explained more fully in the Directors' Responsibilities Statement set out on page 58, the Directors are responsible for the preparation of the financial statements and for being satisfied that they give a true and fair view. Our responsibility is to audit the financial statements in accordance with applicable law and International Standards on Auditing (UK and Ireland). Those standards require us to comply with the Auditing Practices Board's (APB) Ethical Standards for Auditors.

Scope of the audit of the financial statements

A description of the scope of an audit of financial statements is provided on the APB's website at www.frc.org.uk/apb/scope/UKP

Opinion on financial statements

In our opinion:

- The financial statements give a true and fair view of the state of the Group's and of the Parent Company's affairs as at 3 February 2013 and of the Group's profit for the year then ended;
- The Group financial statements have been properly prepared in accordance with IFRS as adopted by the EU;
- The Parent Company financial statements have been properly prepared in accordance with UK Generally Accepted Accounting Practice; and
- The financial statements have been prepared in accordance with the requirements of the Companies Act 2006; and, as regards the Group financial statements, Article 4 of the IAS Regulation.

Opinion on other matters prescribed by the companies Act 2006

In our opinion:

- The part of the Directors' remuneration report to be audited has been properly prepared in accordance with the Companies Act 2006; and
- The information given in the Directors' report for the financial year for which the financial statements are prepared is consistent with the financial statements.

Matters on which we are required to report by exception

We have nothing to report in respect of the following:

Under the Companies Act 2006 we are required to report to you if, in our opinion:

- Adequate accounting records have not been kept by the Parent Company, or returns adequate for our audit have not been received from branches not visited by us; or
- The Parent Company financial statements and the part of the Directors' remuneration report to be audited are not in agreement with the accounting records and returns; or
- Certain disclosures of Directors' remuneration specified by law are not made; or
- We have not received all the information and explanations we require for our audit.

Under the Listing Rules we are required to review:

- The Directors' statement, set out on page 56, in relation to going concern; and
- The part of the Corporate governance statement relating to the Company's compliance with the nine provisions of the June 2008 Combined Code specified for our review.
- Certain elements of the report to shareholders by the Board on directors' remuneration.

Adrian Stone
(Senior Statutory Auditor)
for and on behalf of KPMG Audit Plc, Statutory Auditor

Chartered Accountants
1 The Embankment
Neville Street
Leeds
L51 4DW
10 March 2013

---

[8]This auditor's report and the following discussion follow international auditing standards. See International Standard on Auditing 700, "Forming an Opinion and Reporting on Financial Statements" and International Standard on Auditing 705, "Modifications to the Opinion in the Independent Auditor's Report," *Handbook of International Quality Control, Auditing, Review, Other Assurance, and Other Related Services Pronouncements* (New York: International Federation of Accountants (IFAC), April 2010). They are also similar to the specifications for U.S. auditors contained in "Reports on Audited Financial Statements," *Statement on Auditing Standards No. 58* (New York: AICPA, 1988). U.S. standards differ due to the required audit opinion on the company's internal controls, as required by the U.S. SEC.

In preparing the report, the auditor follows these reporting standards.

1. The report states whether the financial statements are in accordance with the financial reporting framework (IFRS) and describes the responsibilities of the directors and auditors with respect to the financial statements.
2. The report identifies those circumstances in which the company has not consistently observed such policies in the current period in relation to the preceding period.
3. Users are to regard the informative disclosures in the financial statements as reasonably adequate unless the report states otherwise.
4. The report contains either an expression of opinion regarding the financial statements taken as a whole or an assertion to the effect that an opinion cannot be expressed. When the auditor cannot express an overall opinion, the report should state the reasons. In all cases where an auditor's name is associated with financial statements, the report should contain a clear-cut indication of the character of the auditor's examination, if any, and the degree of responsibility being taken.

In most cases, the auditor issues a standard **unmodified or clean opinion**, as shown in Illustration 24-13. That is, the auditor expresses the opinion that the financial statements present fairly, in all material respects, the financial position, results of operations, and cash flows of the entity in conformity with accepted accounting principles.

Certain circumstances, although they do not affect the auditor's unmodified opinion, may require the auditor to add an explanatory paragraph to the audit report. Some of the more important circumstances are as follows.

1. *Going concern.* The auditor must evaluate whether there is substantial doubt about the entity's **ability to continue as a going concern** for a reasonable period of time, taking into consideration all available information about the future. (Generally, the future is at least, but not limited to, 12 months from the end of the reporting period.) If substantial doubt exists about the company continuing as a going concern, the auditor adds to the report an explanatory note describing the potential problem.
2. *Lack of consistency.* If a company has changed accounting policies or the method of their application in a way that has a material effect on the comparability of its financial statements, the auditor should refer to the change in an explanatory paragraph of the report. Such an explanatory paragraph should identify the nature of the change and refer readers to the note in the financial statements that discusses the change in detail. The auditor's concurrence with a change is implicit unless the auditor takes exception to the change in expressing an opinion as to fair presentation in conformity with accepted accounting principles (IFRS).
3. *Emphasis of a matter.* The auditor may wish to emphasize a matter regarding the financial statements but nevertheless intends to express an unqualified opinion. For example, the auditor may wish to emphasize that the entity is a component of a larger business enterprise or that it has had significant transactions with related parties. The auditor presents such explanatory information in a separate paragraph of the report.

In some situations, however, the auditor expresses a **modified opinion**. A modified opinion can be either (1) a **qualified** opinion, (2) an **adverse** opinion, or (3) a **disclaimed** opinion.

A **qualified opinion** contains an exception to the standard opinion. Ordinarily, the exception is not of sufficient magnitude to invalidate the statements as a whole; if it were, an adverse opinion would be rendered. The usual circumstances in which the auditor may deviate from the standard unqualified report on financial statements are as follows.

1. The scope of the examination is limited or affected by conditions or restrictions.
2. The statements do not fairly present financial position or results of operations because of:
   (a) Lack of conformity with accepted accounting principles and standards.
   (b) Inadequate disclosure.

If confronted with one of the situations noted above, the auditor must offer a qualified opinion. A qualified opinion states that, except for the effects of the matter to which the qualification relates, the financial statements present fairly, in all material respects, the financial position, results of operations, and cash flows in conformity with accepted accounting principles.

Illustration 24-14 shows an example of an auditor's report with a modified opinion—in this case, a qualified opinion of **Helio Company** (USA). The auditor modified the opinion because the company used an accounting policy at variance with accepted accounting principles.

Helio Company

Independent Auditor's Report

(Same first and second paragraphs as the standard report)

Helio Company has excluded, from property and debt in the accompanying balance sheets, certain lease obligations that, in our opinion, should be capitalized in order to conform with accepted accounting principles. If these lease obligations were capitalized, property would be increased by $1,500,000 and $1,300,000, long-term debt by $1,400,000 and $1,200,000, and retained earnings by $100,000 and $50,000 as of December 31, in the current and prior year, respectively. Additionally, net income would be decreased by $40,000 and $30,000 and earnings per share would be decreased by $.06 and $.04, respectively, for the years then ended.

In our opinion, except for the effects of not capitalizing certain lease obligations as discussed in the preceding paragraph, the financial statements referred to above present fairly, in all material respects, the financial position of Helio Company, and the results of its operations and its cash flows for the years then ended in conformity with accepted accounting principles.

ILLUSTRATION 24-14
Auditor's Report with
Qualified Opinion

An **adverse opinion** is required in any report in which the exceptions to fair presentation are so material that in the independent auditor's judgment, a qualified opinion is not justified. In such a case, the financial statements taken as a whole are not presented in accordance with IFRS. Adverse opinions are rare because most companies change their accounting to conform with IFRS. Market regulators will not permit a company listed on an exchange to have an adverse opinion.

A **disclaimer of an opinion** is appropriate when the auditor has gathered so little information on the financial statements that no opinion can be expressed.

The audit report should provide useful information to the investor. One investment banker noted, "Probably the first item to check is the auditor's opinion to see whether or not it is a clean one—'in conformity with accepted accounting principles'—or is qualified in regard to differences between the auditor and company management in the accounting treatment of some major item, or in the outcome of some major litigation."

Financial disclosure is one of a number of institutional features that contribute to healthy security markets. In fact, a recent study of disclosure and other mechanisms (such as civil lawsuits and criminal sanctions) found that good disclosure is the most important contributor to a vibrant market. The study, which compared disclosure and other legal and regulatory elements across 49 countries, found that countries with the best disclosure laws have the biggest securities markets.

Countries with more successful market environments also tend to have regulations that make it relatively easy for private investors to sue corporations that provide bad information. That is, while criminal sanctions can be effective in some circumstances, disclosure and other legal and regulatory elements encouraging good disclosure are the most important determinants of highly liquid and deep securities markets.

These findings hold for nations in all stages of economic development, with particular importance for nations that are in the early stages of securities regulation. In addition, countries with fewer market protections likely will benefit the most from adoption of international standards for market regulation and disclosure. The lesson: Disclosure is good for your market.

Sources: Rebecca Christie, "Study: Disclosure at Heart of Effective Securities Laws," *Wall Street Journal Online* (August 11, 2003); and L. Hail, C. Leuz, and P. Wysocki, "Global Accounting Convergence and the Potential Adoption of IFRS by the U.S. (Part I): Conceptual Underpinnings and Economic Analysis," *Accounting Horizons* (September 2010).

Management's Reports

Management Commentary

LEARNING OBJECTIVE
Understand management's
responsibilities for financials.

Management commentary helps in the interpretation of the financial position, financial performance, and cash flows of a company. For example, a company like **Delhaize Group** (BEL) may present, outside the financial statements, a financial review by management that describes and explains the main features of the company's financial performance and financial position, and the principal uncertainties it faces. Such a report may include a review of:

- The main factors and influences determining financial performance, including changes in the environment in which the entity operates, the entity's response to those changes and their effect, and the company's policy for investment to maintain and enhance financial performance, including its dividend policy;
- The company's sources of funding and its targeted ratio of liabilities to equity; and
- The company's resources not recognized in the statement of financial position in accordance with IFRS.

Such commentary also provides an opportunity to understand management's objectives and its strategies for achieving those objectives. Users of financial reports, in their capacity as capital providers, routinely use the type of information provided in management commentary as a tool for evaluating an entity's prospects and its general risks, as well as the success of management's strategies for achieving its stated objectives.

For many companies, management commentary is already an important element of their communication with the capital markets, supplementing as well as complementing the financial statements. Management commentary encompasses reporting that is described in various jurisdictions as management's discussion and analysis (MD&A), operating and financial review (OFR), or management's report.

Illustration 24-15 presents an excerpt from the MD&A section of **Lectra**'s (FRA) annual report.

Lectra

ILLUSTRATION 24-15
Management's
Discussion and Analysis

Management Discussion and Analysis (in part)

4. RISK FACTORS—MANAGEMENT OF RISKS

This chapter describes the main risks facing the company having regard to the specific characteristics of its business, its structure and organization. It further describes how the company manages and prevents these risks, depending on their nature.

Identification of Risks

For internal controls to be effective, the company needs to identify and assess the risks to which it is subject. These risks are identified by means of a continuous process of analyzing the Group's external environment together with the organizational changes rendered necessary by the evolving nature of its markets. This process is overseen by the Finance department and the Legal Affairs department, with input from all Group operating and corporate departments. The key risks that could prevent the Group from achieving its objectives are described below.

The key factor protecting the Group against risks is its business model, which comprises two types of revenue streams:

- revenues from new systems sales (new software licenses and CAD/CAM equipment, and related services), the company's growth driver;
- recurring revenues, consisting partly of recurring contracts (e.g., software evolution, CAD/CAM equipment maintenance, and online support contracts), and partly of other statistically recurring revenues generated by the installed base (sales of spare parts and consumables, per-call maintenance and support interventions). These recurring revenues are a key factor in the company's stability, acting as a cushion in periods of slow overall economic growth.

The gross profit generated by recurring revenues alone covers more than 75% of annual fixed overhead costs. In addition, the business model is geared to generating free cash flow in excess of net income—assuming utilization or receipt of the annual research tax credit and tax credit for encouraging competitiveness and jobs applicable in France—enabling the Group to finance its future growth out of its own cash, with a practically zero working capital requirement.

Finally, uncompromising ethics in conducting business and respect for each individual are part of the company's core values.

4.1. Macroeconomic Environment Risks

The solutions marketed by the Group represent a sometimes sizable investment for its customers. Decisions depend in part on the general macroeconomic environment and on the state of the sectors of activity in which the customers operate. They could scale back or defer their investment decisions when global economic growth slows or when a particular sector suffers a downturn or is in crisis. The Group is consequently exposed to the global economic cycle.

4.2. Economic and Operational Risks Specific to the Company's Business

Lectra designs, produces, and markets full-line technological solutions—comprising software, CAD/CAM equipment, and associated services—specifically designed for industries that use large volumes of fabrics, leather, technical textiles, and composite materials.

It addresses a broad array of major global markets, including fashion (apparel, accessories, and footwear), automotive (car seats and interiors, airbags), furniture and a wide variety of other industries, such as the aeronautical and marine industries, wind power, etc.

4.3. Market Risks

Because of its international presence, foreign exchange risk is the principal market risk to which the Group is exposed.

There is little significant exposure to interest rate risk at present.

It is Group policy to manage these risks conservatively, refraining from any form of speculation, by means of hedging instruments.

4.4. Customer Dependency Risks

Each year, revenues from new systems, accounting for 42% of total revenues in 2012, are generated by around 2,000 customers, and comprise both sales to new customers and extensions to or the renewal of existing customers' installed bases. Revenues from recurring contracts, accounting for around 34% of total revenues, are generated on almost 5,000 of Lectra's customers. Finally, sales of spare parts and consumables, which account for 23% of total revenues, are generated on a large proportion of the installed CAD/CAM equipment.

There is no material risk of dependence on any particular customer or group of customers, as no individual customer represented more than 6% of consolidated revenues in 2012, as was the case in previous years, and the company's 10 largest customers represented less than 20% of revenues combined, and the top 20 customers less than 25%.

Underlying Concepts

The IASB Conceptual Framework notes that management knows more about the company than users and therefore can increase the usefulness of financial information by identifying significant transactions that affect the company and by explaining their financial impact.

Some companies use the management commentary section of the annual report to disclose company efforts in the area of sustainability. An excerpt from the annual report of **Marks and Spencer plc** (GBR) is presented in Illustration 24-16.

ILLUSTRATION 24-16
Sustainability Reporting

Marks and Spencer plc

Plan A
We aim to become the world's most sustainable retailer and Plan A, our eco and ethical programme, is at the very heart of how we do business. More than five years since launch, we continue to extend the influence of Plan A – engaging our employees, suppliers and customers.

Total Plan A commitments	Commitments achieved	Commitments on plan
180	139	31

How we do business
The founders of M&S understood clearly the importance of 'doing the right thing' to create long-term value. We continue their tradition of responsible behavior through our comprehensive environmental and ethical programme, **Plan A**. To succeed over the long term businesses need to make connections with society and Plan A is our manifestation of that. It also makes sound economic, as well as moral sense.

How Plan A helps us respond
Plan A – our eco and ethical programme – sets us apart as a leader in the marketplace and helps us tackle the sustainability issues that face all major retailers. With key raw materials and natural resources under increasing pressure, we continued to develop a more sustainable supply chain, focusing on areas such as cotton and sustainable fishing. Our long-established strict sourcing standards meant M&S did not need to withdraw any products as a result of the supply chain issues.
In a challenging economic environment, Plan A also helps us to run a more efficient business, through reducing waste and energy use. We continued to share our experiences with suppliers – enabling them to reduce their own manufacturing costs and create a more sustainable future.
This year we launched new ways to engage our customers in Plan A, with exciting initiatives such as Shwopping and our Big Beach Clean-Up.

Additional reporting on sustainability is important because it indicates the company's social responsibility and can provide insights about potential obligations that are reported in the financial statements.

While there are no formal IFRS requirements for management commentary, the IASB has initiated a project that offers a non-binding framework and limited guidance on its application, which could be adapted to the legal and economic circumstances of individual jurisdictions. While the proposal is focused on publicly traded entities, to the extent that the framework is deemed applicable, it may be a useful tool for non-exchange traded entities, for example, privately held and state-owned enterprises.[9]

Management's Responsibilities for Financial Statements

Management is responsible for preparing the financial statements and establishing and maintaining an effective system of internal controls. The auditor provides an independent assessment of whether the financial statements are prepared in accordance with IFRS (see the audit opinion in Illustration 24-13 on page 1271). An example of the type of disclosure that public companies are now making is shown in Illustration 24-17.

[9]See *http://www.ifrs.org/Current+Projects/IASB+Projects/Management+Commentary/Management+Commentary.htm*. The proposal will not result in an IFRS. Accordingly, it would not be a requirement for an entity to comply with the framework for the preparation and presentation of management commentary as a condition for asserting compliance with IFRS.

Wm Morrison Supermarkets plc

Statement of Directors' responsibilities in respect of the Annual report and financial statements

The Directors are responsible for preparing the Annual report and the Group and Parent Company financial statements in accordance with applicable law and regulations.

Company law requires the Directors to prepare Group and Parent Company financial statements for each financial year. Under that law they are required to prepare the Group financial statements in accordance with IFRS as adopted by the EU and applicable law and have elected to prepare the Parent Company financial statements in accordance with UK Accounting Standards and applicable law (UK Generally Accepted Accounting Practice).

Under company law the Directors must not approve the financial statements unless they are satisfied that they give a true and fair view of the state of affairs of the Group and Parent Company and of their profit or loss for that period. In preparing each of the Group and Parent Company financial statements, the Directors are required to:

- select suitable accounting policies and then apply them consistently:
- make judgements and estimates that are reasonable and prudent:
- for the Group financial statements, state whether they have been prepared in accordance with IFRS as adopted by the EU:
- for the Parent Company financial statements, state whether applicable UK Accounting Standards have been followed, subject to

any material departures disclosed and explained in the Parent Company financial statements; and

- prepare the financial statements on the going concern basis unless it is inappropriate to presume that the Group and the Parent Company will continue in business.

The Directors are responsible for keeping adequate accounting records that are sufficient to show and explain the Parent Company's transactions and disclose with reasonable accuracy at any time the financial positions of the Parent Company and enable them to ensure that its financial statements comply with the Companies Act 2006. They have general responsibility for taking such steps as are reasonably open to them to safeguard the assets of the Group and to prevent and detect fraud and other irregularities.

Under applicable law and regulations, the Directors are also responsible for preparing a Directors' report, Directors' remuneration report and Corporate governance statement that complies with that law and those regulations.

The Directors are responsible for the maintenance and integrity of the corporate and financial information included on the company's website. Legislation in the UK governing the preparation and dissemination of financial statements may differ from legislation in other jurisdictions.

Responsibility statement We confirm that to the best of our knowledge:

- the financial statements, prepared in accordance with the applicable set of accounting standards, give a true and fair review of the assets, liabilities, financial position and profit or loss of the Company and its subsidiaries included in the consolidation as a whole; and
- the Directors' report includes a fair review of the development of the business and the position of the Company and its

subsidiaries included in the consolidation taken as a whole, together with a description of the principal risks and uncertainties that they face.

By order of the Board
13 March 2013

ILLUSTRATION 24-17
Report on Management's
Responsibilities

CURRENT REPORTING ISSUES

Reporting on Financial Forecasts and Projections

In recent years, the investing public's demand for more and better information has focused on disclosure of corporate expectations for the future.[10] These disclosures take one of two forms:[11]

7 LEARNING OBJECTIVE
Identify issues related to financial
forecasts and projections.

- *Financial forecasts.* A **financial forecast** is a set of prospective financial statements that present, to the best of the responsible party's knowledge and belief, a company's expected financial position, results of operations, and cash flows. The

---

[10]Some areas in which companies are using financial information about the future are equipment lease-versus-buy analysis, analysis of a company's ability to successfully enter new markets, and examination of merger and acquisition opportunities. In addition, companies also prepare forecasts and projections for use by third parties in public offering documents (requiring financial forecasts), tax-oriented investments, and financial feasibility studies. Use of forward-looking data has been enhanced by the increased capability of computers to analyze, compare, and manipulate large quantities of data.

[11]There is not a specific international standard in this area. In the United States, see "Financial Forecasts and Projections" and "Guide for Prospective Financial Information," *Codification of Statements on Standards for Attestation Engagements* (New York: AICPA 2006), paras. 3.04 and 3.05.

responsible party bases a financial forecast on conditions it expects to exist and the course of action it expects to take.

- *Financial projections.* Financial projections are prospective financial statements that present, to the best of the responsible party's knowledge and belief, given one or more *hypothetical assumptions,* an entity's expected financial position, results of operations, and cash flows. The responsible party bases a financial projection on conditions it expects *would* exist and the course of action it expects *would* be taken, given one or more hypothetical assumptions.

The difference between a financial forecast and a financial projection is clear-cut: A forecast provides information on what is **expected** to happen, whereas a projection provides information on what **might** take place but is not necessarily expected to happen.

Whether companies should be required to provide financial forecasts is the subject of intensive discussion with journalists, corporate executives, market regulators, financial analysts, accountants, and others. Predictably, there are strong arguments on either side. Listed below are some of the arguments.

Arguments for requiring published forecasts:

1. Investment decisions are based on future expectations. Therefore, information about the future facilitates better decisions.

2. Companies already circulate forecasts informally. This situation should be regulated to ensure that the forecasts are available to all investors.

3. Circumstances now change so rapidly that historical information is no longer adequate for prediction.

Arguments against requiring published forecasts:

1. No one can foretell the future. Therefore, forecasts will inevitably be wrong. Worse, they may mislead if they convey an impression of precision about the future.

2. Companies may strive only to meet their published forecasts, thereby failing to produce results that are in the shareholders' best interest.

3. If forecasts prove inaccurate, there will be recriminations and probably legal actions.[12]

4. Disclosure of forecasts will be detrimental to organizations because forecasts will inform competitors (foreign and domestic), as well as investors.

Auditing standards establish guidelines for the preparation and presentation of financial forecasts and projections.[13] They require accountants to provide (1) a summary of significant assumptions used in the forecast or projection and (2) guidelines for minimum presentation.

To encourage management to disclose prospective financial information, some market regulators have established a **safe harbor rule**. It provides protection to a company that presents an erroneous forecast, as long as the company prepared the forecast on a reasonable basis and disclosed it in good faith.[14] However, many companies note that the

---

[12]The issue is serious. Over a recent three-year period, 8 percent of the companies on the New York Stock Exchange (NYSE) were sued because of an alleged lack of financial disclosure. Companies complain that they are subject to lawsuits whenever the share price drops. And as one executive noted, "You can even be sued if the share price goes up—because you did not disclose the good news fast enough."

[13]*Op cit.,* par. 1.02.

[14]For example, the U.S. SEC Issued "Safe-Harbor Rule for Projections," *Release No. 5993* (Washington: SEC, 1979). The U.S. Private Securities Litigation Reform Act of 1995 recognizes that some information that is useful to investors is inherently subject to less certainty or reliability than other information. By providing safe harbor for forward-looking statements, this should facilitate access to this information by investors.

safe harbor rule does not work in practice, since it does not cover oral statements, nor has it kept them from investor lawsuits.

What do the numbers mean?   GLOBAL FORECASTS

Great Britain permits financial forecasts, and the results have been fairly successful. Some significant differences do exist between the English and other business and legal environments. The British system, for example, does not permit litigation on forecasted information, and the solicitor (lawyer) is not permitted to work on a contingent-fee basis. A typical British forecast adapted from a construction company's report to support a public offering of shares is as follows.

> Profits have grown substantially over the past 10 years and directors are confident of being able to continue this expansion. . . . While the rate of expansion will be dependent on the level of economic activity in Ireland and England, the group is well structured to avail itself of opportunities as they arise, particularly in the field of property development, which is expected to play an increasingly important role in the group's future expansion.
>
> Profits before taxation for the half year ended 30th June were 402,000 pounds. On the basis of trading experiences since that date and the present level of sales and completions, the directors expect that in the absence of unforeseen circumstances, the group's profits before taxation for the year to 31st December will be not less than 960,000 pounds.
>
> No dividends will be paid in respect of the current year. In a full financial year, on the basis of above forecasts (not including full year profits) it would be the intention of the board, assuming current rates of tax, to recommend dividends totaling 40% (of after-tax profits), which will be payable in the next two years.

A general narrative-type forecast might appear as follows.

> On the basis of promotions planned by the company for the second half of the fiscal year, net earnings for that period are expected to be approximately the same as those for the first half of the fiscal year, with net earnings for the third quarter expected to make the predominant contribution to net earnings for the second half of the year.

As indicated, the general version is much less specific in its forecasted information.

But such differences probably could be overcome if influential interests cooperated to produce an atmosphere conducive to quality forecasting. What do you think? As an investor, would you prefer the more specific forecast?

Source: See "A Case for Forecasting—The British Have Tried It and Find That It Works," *World* (New York: Peat, Marwick, Mitchell & Co., Autumn 1978), pp. 10–13. In a recent survey, U.K. companies remain stubbornly backward-looking. Just 5 percent of FTSE 100 companies address the future of the business in their discussion and analysis. See PricewaterhouseCoopers, "Guide to Forward-looking Information: Don't Fear the Future" (2006).

Questions of Liability

What happens if a company does not meet its forecasts? Can the company and the auditor be sued? If a company, for example, projects an earnings increase of 15 percent and achieves only 5 percent, should shareholders be permitted to have some judicial recourse against the company?

One court case involving **Monsanto Chemical Corporation** (USA) set a precedent. In this case, Monsanto predicted that sales would increase 8 to 9 percent and that earnings would rise 4 to 5 percent. In the last part of the year, the demand for Monsanto's products dropped as a result of a business turndown. Instead of increasing, the company's earnings declined. Investors sued the company because the projected earnings figure was erroneous, but a judge dismissed the suit because the forecasts were the best estimates of qualified people whose intents were honest.

As indicated earlier, safe harbor rules are intended to protect companies that provide good-faith projections. However, much concern exists as to how market regulators and the courts will interpret such terms as "good faith" and "reasonable assumptions" when erroneous forecasts mislead users of this information.

Internet Financial Reporting

Most companies now use the power and reach of the Internet to provide more useful information to financial statement readers. All large companies have Internet sites, and a large proportion of companies' websites contain links to their financial statements and other disclosures. The popularity of such reporting is not surprising as companies can reduce the costs of printing and disseminating paper reports with the use of Internet reporting.

Does Internet financial reporting improve the usefulness of a company's financial reports? Yes, in several ways. First, dissemination of reports via the Web allows firms **to communicate more easily and quickly with users** than do traditional paper reports. In addition, **Internet reporting allows users to take advantage of tools** such as search engines and hyperlinks to quickly find information about the firm and, sometimes, to download the information for analysis, perhaps in computer spreadsheets. Finally, **Internet reporting can help make financial reports more relevant** by allowing companies to report expanded disaggregated data and more timely data than is possible through paper-based reporting. For example, some companies voluntarily report weekly sales data and segment operating data on their websites.

Given the widespread use of the Internet by investors and creditors, it is not surprising that organizations are developing new technologies and standards to further enable Internet financial reporting. An example is the increasing use of Extensible Business Reporting Language (XBRL). **XBRL** is a computer language adapted from the code of the Internet. It "tags" accounting data to correspond to financial reporting items that are reported in the statement of financial position, income statement, and the cash flow statement. Once tagged, any company's XBRL data can be easily processed using spreadsheets and other computer programs. In fact, XBRL is a global language with common tags across countries. As more companies prepare their financial reports using XBRL, users will be able to easily search a company's reports, extract and analyze data, and perform financial comparisons within industries and across countries.[15]

Fraudulent Financial Reporting

LEARNING OBJECTIVE **8**

Describe the profession's response to fraudulent financial reporting.

Economic crime is on the rise around the world. A recent global survey of over 3,000 executives from 54 countries documented the types of economic crimes, as shown in Illustration 24-18.[16]

ILLUSTRATION 24-18
Types of Economic Crime

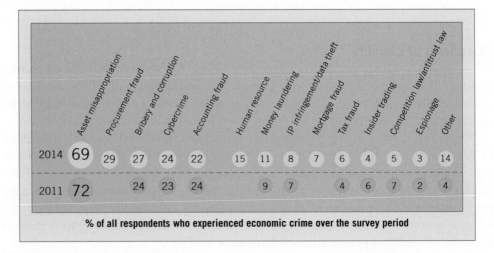

% of all respondents who experienced economic crime over the survey period

---

[15]See *www.sec.gov/rules/final/2009/33-9002.pdf* and C. Twarowski, "Financial Data 'on Steroids'," *Washington Post* (August 19, 2008), p. D01. See also *www.xbrl.org/us/us/BusinessCaseForXBRL.pdf* for additional information on XBRL.

[16]PricewaterhouseCoopers, *The Global Economic Crime Survey: Economic Crime in a Downturn* (2014).

As indicated, a wide range of economic crimes are reported. Unfortunately, for the top three areas, the trend is not good. As shown in Illustration 24-19, there has been a steady upward trend of economic crime.

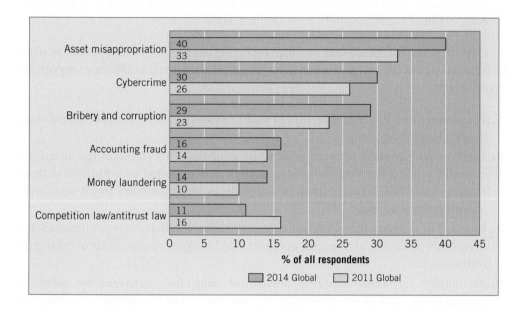

ILLUSTRATION 24-19
Trends in Reported
Frauds

Important and troubling, note that accounting frauds have also increased since 2011.

Fraudulent financial reporting is defined as "intentional or reckless conduct, whether act or omission, that results in materially misleading financial statements."[17] Fraudulent reporting can involve gross and deliberate distortion of corporate records (such as inventory count tags), or misapplication of accounting policies (failure to disclose material transactions). The frauds reported above and recent events involving such well-known companies as **Parmalat** (ITA), **Mahindra Satyam** (IND), and **Société Générale** (FRA) indicate that more must be done to address this issue.

Causes of Fraudulent Financial Reporting

Fraudulent financial reporting usually occurs because of conditions in a company's internal or external environment. Influences in the **internal environment** relate to poor internal control systems, management's poor attitude toward ethics, or perhaps a company's liquidity or profitability. Those in the **external environment** may relate to industry conditions, overall business environment, or legal and regulatory considerations.

General incentives for fraudulent financial reporting vary. Common ones are the desire to obtain a higher share price, avoid default on a loan covenant, or make a personal gain of some type (additional compensation, promotion). Situational pressures on the company or an individual manager also may lead to fraudulent financial reporting. Examples of these situational pressures include the following.

- *Sudden decreases in revenue or market share* for a single company or an entire industry.

---

[17]"Report of the National Commission on Fraudulent Financial Reporting" (Washington, D.C., 1987), p. 2. Unintentional errors as well as corporate improprieties (such as tax fraud, employee embezzlements, and so on) that do not cause the financial statements to be misleading are excluded from the definition of fraudulent financial reporting.

- *Unrealistic budget pressures* may occur when headquarters arbitrarily determines profit objectives (particularly for short-term results) and budgets without taking actual conditions into account.
- *Financial pressure resulting from bonus plans* that depend on short-term economic performance. This pressure is particularly acute when the bonus is a significant component of the individual's total compensation.

Opportunities for fraudulent financial reporting are present in circumstances when the fraud is easy to commit and when detection is difficult. Frequently, these opportunities arise from:

1. *The absence of a board of directors or audit committee* that vigilantly oversees the financial reporting process.
2. *Weak or non-existent internal accounting controls.* This situation can occur, for example, when a company's revenue system is overloaded as a result of a rapid expansion of sales, an acquisition of a new division, or the entry into a new, unfamiliar line of business.
3. *Unusual or complex transactions* such as the consolidation of two companies, the divestiture or closing of a specific operation, and the purchase and sale of derivative instruments.
4. *Accounting estimates requiring significant subjective judgment* by company management, such as the allowance for loan losses and the estimated liability for warranty expense.
5. *Ineffective internal audit staffs* resulting from inadequate staff size and severely limited audit scope.

A weak corporate ethical climate contributes to these situations. Opportunities for fraudulent financial reporting also increase dramatically when the accounting policies followed in reporting transactions are non-existent, evolving, or subject to varying interpretations.[18]

As discussed earlier, auditing regulators have issued numerous auditing standards in response to concerns of the accounting profession, the media, and the public.[19] For example, the recent standard on fraudulent financial reporting "raises the bar" on the performance of financial statement audits by explicitly requiring auditors to assess the risk of material financial misstatement due to fraud.[20]

Criteria for Making Accounting and Reporting Choices

Throughout this textbook, we have stressed the need to provide information that is useful to predict the amounts, timing, and uncertainty of future cash flows. To achieve

---

[18]The discussion in this section is based on "Report of the National Commission on Fraudulent Financial Reporting," (2004), pp. 23–24. See also "2012 Report to the Nation on Occupational Fraud and Abuse, Association of Certified Fraud Examiners," *http://www.acfe.com/uploadedFiles/ ACFE_Website/Content/rttn/2012-report-to-nations.pdf*, for fraudulent financial reporting causes and consequences.

[19]Because the profession believes that the role of the auditor is not well understood outside the profession, much attention has been focused on the expectation gap. The expectation gap is the gap between (1) the expectation of financial statement users concerning the level of assurance they believe the independent auditor provides, and (2) the assurance that the independent auditor actually does provide under generally accepted auditing standards.

[20]See International Standard on Auditing 240, "The Auditor's Responsibilities Relating to Fraud in an Audit of Financial Statements," *Handbook of International Quality Control, Auditing, Review, Other Assurance, and Other Related Services Pronouncements* (April 2010).

this objective, companies must make judicious choices between alternative accounting concepts, methods, and means of disclosure. You are probably surprised by the large number of choices that exist among acceptable alternatives.

You should recognize, however, as indicated in Chapter 1, that accounting is greatly influenced by its environment. It does not exist in a vacuum. Therefore, it is unrealistic to assume that the profession can entirely eliminate alternative presentations of certain transactions and events. Nevertheless, we are hopeful that the profession, by adhering to the Conceptual Framework, will be able to focus on the needs of financial statement users and eliminate diversity where appropriate. The IASB's focus on principles-based standards are directed at these very issues. It seeks to develop guidance that will result in accounting and financial reporting that reflects the economic substance of the transactions, not the desired financial result of management. The profession must continue its efforts to develop a sound foundation upon which to build financial standards and practice. As Aristotle said, "The correct beginning is more than half the whole."

Underlying Concepts

> The IASB statements on the objective of financial reporting, elements of financial statements, and qualitative characteristics of accounting information are important steps in the right direction.

Evolving Issue DISCLOSURE OVERLOAD?

As we discussed in Chapter 1 and throughout the textbook, IFRS is gaining popularity around the world. The U.S. Securities and Exchange Commission continues to evaluate whether U.S. publicly traded companies will be required or given the option to adopt IFRS. There is some debate on U.S. readiness to make the switch. For example, there are several areas in which the FASB and the IASB must iron out a number of technical accounting issues before they reach a substantially converged set of accounting standards. Here is a list of six important areas yet to be converged.

1. *Error correction.* According to *IAS 8*, it is not always necessary to retrospectively restate financial results when a company corrects errors, especially if the adjustment is impractical or too costly. U.S. GAAP, on the other hand, requires restatements in many error-correction cases.

2. *Death of LIFO.* Last-in, first-out (LIFO) inventory accounting is prohibited under *IAS 2*, so any U.S. company using the method will have to abandon it (and the tax benefits) and move to another methodology. Although LIFO is permitted under U.S. GAAP, the repeal of LIFO for tax purposes is an ongoing debate.

3. *Reversal of impairments.* *IAS 36* permits companies to reverse impairment losses up to the amount of the original impairment when the reason for the charge decreases or no longer exists. However, U.S. GAAP bans reversal.

4. *PP&E valuation.* *IAS 16* allows for the revaluation of property, plant, and equipment, but the entire asset class must be revalued. That means a company can choose to use the revaluation model if the asset class's fair value can be measured reliably. But, it must choose to use one model or the other; both cannot be used at the same time. U.S. GAAP does not allow revaluation.

5. *Component depreciation.* Also under *IAS 16*, companies must recognize and depreciate equipment components separately if the components can be physically separated from the asset and have different useful life spans. In practical terms, that means controllers will have to rely on the operations side of the business to help assess equipment components. U.S. GAAP allows component depreciation, but it is not required.

6. *Development costs.* Based on *IAS 38*, companies are permitted to capitalize development costs as long as they meet six criteria. However, research costs are still expensed. U.S. GAAP requires that all R&D costs be charged to expense when incurred.

Some are already debating what will happen if and when U.S. companies adopt these new standards. It is almost certain that expanded disclosure will be needed to help users navigate accounting reports upon adoption of IFRS. As one accounting analyst remarked, "get ready for an avalanche of footnotes." Since using IFRS requires more judgment than using U.S. GAAP, two to three times as many footnotes will be needed to explain the rationales for accounting approaches. So while principles-based standards should promote more comparability, they require investors to dig into the disclosures in the footnotes.

Source: Marie Leone, "GAAP and IFRS: Six Degrees of Separation," *CFO.com* (June 30, 2010).

GLOBAL ACCOUNTING INSIGHTS

DISCLOSURE

U.S. GAAP and IFRS disclosure requirements are similar in many regards. The IFRS addressing various disclosure issues are *IAS 24* ("Related Party Disclosures"), disclosure and recognition of post-statement of financial position events in *IAS 10* ("Events after the Balance Sheet Date"), segment reporting IFRS provisions in *IFRS 8* ("Operating Segments"), and interim reporting requirements in *IAS 34* ("Interim Financial Reporting").

Relevant Facts

Following are the key similarities and differences between U.S. GAAP and IFRS related to disclosures.

Similarities

- U.S. GAAP and IFRS have similar standards on post-statement of financial position (subsequent) events. That is, under both sets of standards, events that occurred after the statement of financial position date, and which provide additional evidence of conditions that existed at the statement of financial position date, are recognized in the financial statements.

- Like U.S. GAAP, IFRS requires that for transactions with related parties, companies disclose the amounts involved in a transaction; the amount, terms, and nature of the outstanding balances; and any doubtful amounts related to those outstanding balances for each major category of related parties.

- Following the recent issuance of *IFRS 8*, "Operating Segments," the requirements under U.S. GAAP and IFRS are very similar. That is, both standards use the management approach to identify reportable segments, and similar segment disclosures are required.

- Neither U.S. GAAP nor IFRS require interim reports. Rather, the U.S. SEC and securities exchanges outside the United States establish the rules. In the United States, interim reports generally are provided on a quarterly basis; outside the United States, six-month interim reports are common.

Differences

- Due to the narrower range of judgments allowed in more rules-based U.S. GAAP, note disclosures generally are less expansive under U.S. GAAP compared to IFRS.

- In the United States, there is a preference for one set of accepted accounting principles except in unusual situations. The FASB issues alternative guidance (within U.S. GAAP) for privately held companies with input from the Private Company Council. As indicated in the chapter, the IASB has developed a separate set of standards for small- and medium-sized entities (SMEs), which are designed to meet the needs of privately held companies.

- As indicated in the About the Numbers section below, U.S. GAAP uses the date when financial statements are "issued" when determining the reporting of subsequent events. Subsequent (or post-statement of financial position) events under IFRS are evaluated through the date that financial instruments are "authorized for issue." Also, for share dividends and splits in the subsequent period, U.S. GAAP adjusts but IFRS does not.

- U.S. GAAP has specific requirements to disclose the name of a related party; under IFRS, there is no specific requirement to disclose the name of the related party.

- Under U.S. GAAP, interim reports are prepared on an integral basis; IFRS generally follows the discrete approach.

About the Numbers

Post-Balance-Sheet Events (Subsequent Events)
Under U.S. GAAP (similar to IFRS), notes to the financial statements should explain any significant financial events that took place after the formal balance sheet (statement of financial position) date, but before the statement is issued. These events are referred to as **post-balance-sheet events** or just plain **subsequent events**. The illustration below shows a time diagram of the subsequent events period under U.S. GAAP.

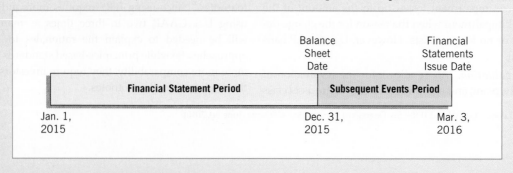

A period of several weeks and sometimes months may elapse after the end of the fiscal year but before the company issues financial statements. Various activities involved in closing the books for the period and issuing the statements all take time: taking and pricing the inventory, reconciling subsidiary ledgers with controlling accounts, preparing necessary adjusting entries, ensuring that all transactions for the period have been entered, obtaining an audit of the financial statements by independent public accountants, and printing the annual report. During the period between the balance sheet date and its distribution to shareholders and creditors, important transactions or other events may occur that materially affect the company's financial position or operating situation.

Many who read a balance sheet believe the balance sheet condition is constant, and they project it into the future.

However, readers must be told if the company has experienced a significant change—e.g., sold one of its plants, acquired a subsidiary, suffered extraordinary losses, settled significant litigation, or experienced any other important event in the post-balance-sheet period. Without an explanation in a note, the reader might be misled and draw inappropriate conclusions.

Relative to IFRS, which defines the subsequent-event period to end on the date the statements are authorized, under U.S. GAAP, the subsequent-event period is longer. Therefore, financial statement users generally receive more information about subsequent events. However, U.S. GAAP and IFRS define recognized and non-recognized subsequent events similarly. The following illustration presents an example of subsequent events disclosure, excerpted from the annual report of Commercial Metals Company.

Commercial Metals Company

NOTE 22. SUBSEQUENT EVENTS (August 31 Fiscal Year End)
On October 7, 2011, The Company announced its decision to exit the business in CMCS by way of sale and/or closure. During 2011, the Company made operational improvements in the business but not to a level which would restore profitability for the long run. Additionally, delayed entry in the European Union, cyclical demand for tubular products, unsustainable losses and increased demand for capital resources resulted in the decision to exit the business. The operation will service any existing customer commitments and the Company expects to wind down operations and liquidate inventory over the next several months. In connection with this decision, the Company expects to incur severance and other closure costs between $25 million and $40 million in fiscal 2012.

Many subsequent events or developments do not require adjustment of or disclosure in the financial statements. Typically, these are non-accounting events or conditions that management normally communicates by other means. These events include legislation, product changes, management changes, strikes, unionization, marketing agreements, and loss of important customers.

Summary Observations
Because U.S. GAAP and IFRS are quite similar in their disclosure provisions, we provide some observations on the application of IFRS by foreign companies listing securities in the United States. Recently, the staff of the U.S. SEC reviewed the financial statements filed with the SEC by 100 foreign issuers, prepared for the first time using IFRS. The staff did not make any statements regarding the overall *quality* of the reports but did identify areas where additional questions might be asked. Here are some of the items that warranted staff comment:

1. Revenue recognition, especially where a company provided generic policy disclosure but did not provide disclosure specific to its circumstances.

2. Intangible assets and goodwill, including the factors that led a company to recognize them in a business combination.

3. Companies' policies for identifying and evaluating impairment, the circumstances resulting in impairment recognition, or the circumstances surrounding impairment reversals of long-lived assets including goodwill.

4. Leases, including their terms and the future minimum payments under operating and financial leases.

5. Contingent liabilities, including their nature and estimated financial effects.

6. The significant terms of financial instruments, including derivatives, their effects on future cash flow, and the recognition and measurement criteria the company applied in accounting for financial instruments.

7. Additional issues related to income statement and cash flow statement formats and related notes.

On the Horizon

Hans Hoogervorst, chairman of the IASB, recently noted: "High quality financial information is the lifeblood of market-based economies. If the blood is of poor quality, then the body shuts down and the patient dies. It is the same with financial reporting. If investors cannot trust the numbers, then financial

markets stop working. For market-based economies, that is really bad news. It is an essential public good for market-based economies. . . . And in the past 10 years, most of the world's economies—developed and emerging—have embraced IFRSs." While the United States has yet to adopt IFRS, there is no question that IFRS and U.S. GAAP are converging quickly.

We have provided expanded discussion in the *Global Accounting Insights* to help you understand the issues surrounding convergence as they relate to intermediate accounting. After reading these discussions, you should realize that IFRS and U.S. GAAP are very similar in many areas, with differences in those areas revolving around some minor technical points. In other situations, the differences are major; for example, IFRS does not permit LIFO inventory accounting. Our hope is that the FASB and IASB can quickly complete their convergence efforts, resulting in a single set of high-quality accounting standards for use by companies around the world.

SUMMARY OF LEARNING OBJECTIVES

1 **Review the full disclosure principle and describe implementation problems.** The full disclosure principle calls for financial reporting of any financial facts significant enough to influence the judgment of an informed reader. Implementing the full disclosure principle is difficult because the cost of disclosure can be substantial and the benefits difficult to assess. Disclosure requirements have increased because of (1) the growing complexity of the business environment, (2) the necessity for timely information, and (3) the use of accounting as a control and monitoring device.

2 **Explain the use of notes in financial statement preparation.** Notes are the accountant's means of amplifying or explaining the items presented in the main body of the statements. Notes can explain in qualitative terms information pertinent to specific financial statement items and can provide supplementary data of a quantitative nature. Common note disclosures relate to such items as accounting policies; inventories; property, plant, and equipment; creditor claims; contingencies and commitments; and subsequent events.

3 **Discuss the disclosure requirements for related-party transactions, subsequent events, and major business segments.** In related-party transactions, one party has the ability to significantly influence the actions of the other. As a result, IFRS requires disclosure of the relationship, a description of the transactions including amounts, provisions for doubtful debts, and expenses recognized. For events after the reporting date, a company should disclose any transactions that materially affect its financial position or operating situation. Finally, aggregated figures hide much information about the composition of these consolidated figures. There is no way to tell from the consolidated data the extent to which the differing product lines contribute to the company's profitability, risk, and growth potential. As a result, the profession requires segment information in certain situations.

4 **Describe the accounting problems associated with interim reporting.** Interim reports cover periods of less than one year. Two viewpoints exist regarding interim reports. The discrete approach holds that each interim period should be treated as a separate accounting period. The integral approach is that the interim report is an integral part of the annual report and that deferrals and accruals should take into consideration what will happen for the entire year. IFRS requires use of the discrete approach.

Companies should use the same accounting policies for interim reports that they use for annual reports. A number of unique reporting problems develop related to the following items: (1) income taxes and (2) seasonality.

5 **Identify the major disclosures in the auditor's report.** The auditor expresses an unmodified or clean opinion if satisfied that the financial statements present the financial position, results of operations, and cash flows fairly in accordance with IFRS. A qualified opinion contains an exception to the standard opinion; ordinarily, the exception is not of sufficient magnitude to invalidate the statements as a whole.

An adverse opinion is required when the exceptions to fair presentation are so material that a qualified opinion is not justified. A disclaimer of an opinion is appropriate when the auditor has so little information on the financial statements that no opinion can be expressed.

6 **Understand management's responsibilities for financials.** Management commentary complements information reported in the financial statements. This commentary frequently discusses financial aspects of an enterprise's business, such as liquidity, capital resources, results of operations, important risks, and sustainability. Management's responsibility for the financial statements is often indicated in a letter to shareholders in the annual report.

7 **Identify issues related to financial forecasts and projections.** Companies are permitted (not required) to include profit forecasts in their reports. To encourage management to disclose such information, market regulators have issued a safe harbor rule. The rule provides protection to a company that presents an erroneous forecast, as long as it prepared the projection on a reasonable basis and disclosed it in good faith. However, the safe harbor rule has not worked well in practice.

8 **Describe the profession's response to fraudulent financial reporting.** Fraudulent financial reporting is intentional or reckless conduct, whether through act or omission, that results in materially misleading financial statements. Fraudulent financial reporting usually occurs because of poor internal control, management's poor attitude toward ethics, poor performance, and so on.

APPENDIX 24A   BASIC FINANCIAL STATEMENT ANALYSIS

What would be important to you in studying a company's financial statements? The answer depends on your particular interest—whether you are a creditor, shareholder, potential investor, manager, government agency, or labor leader. For example, **short-term creditors** such as banks are primarily interested in the ability of the firm to pay its currently maturing obligations. In that case, you would examine the current assets and their relation to short-term liabilities to evaluate the short-run solvency of the firm.

9 LEARNING OBJECTIVE

Understand the approach to financial statement analysis.

Bondholders, on the other hand, look more to long-term indicators, such as the enterprise's capital structure, past and projected earnings, and changes in financial position. **Shareholders**, present or prospective, also are interested in many of the features considered by a long-term creditor. As a shareholder, you would focus on the earnings picture because changes in it greatly affect the market price of your investment. You also would be concerned with the financial position of the company because it affects indirectly the stability of earnings.

The **managers** of a company are concerned about the composition of its capital structure and about the changes and trends in earnings. This financial information has a direct influence on the type, amount, and cost of external financing that the company can obtain. In addition, the company managers find financial information useful on a day-to-day operating basis in such areas as capital budgeting, break-even analysis, variance analysis, gross margin analysis, and for internal control purposes.

PERSPECTIVE ON FINANCIAL STATEMENT ANALYSIS

Readers of financial statements can gather information by examining relationships between items on the statements and identifying trends in these relationships. The relationships are expressed numerically in ratios and percentages, and trends are identified through comparative analysis.

A problem with learning how to analyze statements is that the means may become an end in itself. Analysts could identify and calculate thousands of possible relationships and trends. But knowing only how to calculate ratios and trends without understanding how such information can be used accomplishes little. Therefore, a logical approach to financial statement analysis is necessary, consisting of the following steps.

 Underlying Concepts

Because financial statements report on the past, they emphasize the *qualitative characteristic of feedback value*. This feedback value is useful because it can be used to better achieve the *qualitative characteristic of predictive value*.

1. *Know the questions for which you want to find answers.* As indicated earlier, various groups have different types of interest in a company.
2. *Know the questions that particular ratios and comparisons are able to help answer.* These will be discussed in this appendix.
3. *Match 1 and 2 above.* By such a matching, the statement analysis will have a logical direction and purpose.

Several caveats must be mentioned. **Financial statements report on the past.** Thus, analysis of these data is an examination of the past. When using such information in a decision-making (future-oriented) process, analysts assume that the past is a reasonable basis for predicting the future. This is usually a reasonable approach, but its limitations should be recognized.

Also, ratio and trend analyses will help identify a company's present strengths and weaknesses. They may serve as "red flags" indicating problem areas. In many cases, however, such analyses will not reveal **why** things are as they are. Finding answers about "why" usually requires an in-depth analysis and an awareness of many factors about a company that are not reported in the financial statements.

Another caveat is that a **single ratio by itself is not likely to be very useful.** For example, analysts may generally view a current ratio of 2 to 1 (current assets are twice current liabilities) as satisfactory. However, if the industry average is 3 to 1, such a conclusion may be invalid. Even given this industry average, you may conclude that the particular company is doing well if you know the previous year's ratio was 1.5 to 1. Consequently, to derive meaning from ratios, analysts need some standard against which to compare them. Such a standard may come from industry averages, past years' amounts, a particular competitor, or planned levels.

Finally, **awareness of the limitations of accounting numbers used in an analysis** is important. We will discuss some of these limitations and their consequences later in this appendix.

RATIO ANALYSIS

LEARNING OBJECTIVE **10**

Identify major analytic ratios and describe their calculation.

In analyzing financial statement data, analysts use various devices to bring out the comparative and relative significance of the financial information presented. These devices include ratio analysis, comparative analysis, percentage analysis, and examination of related data. No one device is more useful than another. Every situation is different, and analysts often obtain the needed answers only upon close examination of the interrelationships among all the data provided. Ratio analysis is the starting point. Ratios can be classified as follows.

MAJOR TYPES OF RATIOS

LIQUIDITY RATIOS. Measures of the company's short-run ability to pay its maturing obligations.

ACTIVITY RATIOS. Measures of how effectively the company is using the assets employed.

PROFITABILITY RATIOS. Measures of the degree of success or failure of a given company or division for a given period of time.

COVERAGE RATIOS. Measures of the degree of protection for long-term creditors and investors.[21]

We have integrated discussions and illustrations about the computation and use of these financial ratios throughout this textbook. Illustration 24A-1 summarizes all of the ratios presented in the textbook and identifies the specific chapters that presented that material.

ILLUSTRATION 24A-1
Summary of Financial Ratios

SUMMARY OF RATIOS PRESENTED IN EARLIER CHAPTERS

Ratio	Formula for Computation	Reference
I. Liquidity		
1. **Current ratio**	$\dfrac{\text{Current assets}}{\text{Current liabilities}}$	Chapter 13, p. 626
2. **Quick or acid-test ratio**	$\dfrac{\text{Cash, short-term investments, and net receivables}}{\text{Current liabilities}}$	Chapter 13, p. 627
3. **Current cash debt coverage**	$\dfrac{\text{Net cash provided by operating activities}}{\text{Average current liabilities}}$	Chapter 5, p. 202
II. Activity		
4. **Accounts receivable turnover**	$\dfrac{\text{Net sales}}{\text{Average trade receivables (net)}}$	Chapter 7, p. 322
5. **Inventory turnover**	$\dfrac{\text{Cost of goods sold}}{\text{Average inventory}}$	Chapter 9, p. 421
6. **Asset turnover**	$\dfrac{\text{Net sales}}{\text{Average total assets}}$	Chapter 11, p. 518
III. Profitability		
7. **Profit margin on sales**	$\dfrac{\text{Net income}}{\text{Net sales}}$	Chapter 11, p. 518
8. **Return on assets**	$\dfrac{\text{Net income}}{\text{Average total assets}}$	Chapter 11, p. 518
9. **Return on ordinary share capital— equity**	$\dfrac{\text{Net income minus preference dividends}}{\text{Average shareholders' equity—ordinary}}$	Chapter 15, p. 728

---

[21]Some analysts use other terms to categorize these ratios. For example, liquidity ratios are sometimes referred to as *solvency* ratios; activity ratios as *turnover* or *efficiency* ratios; and coverage ratios as *leverage* or *capital structure* ratios.

ILLUSTRATION 24A-1
(*Continued*)

Ratio	Formula for Computation	Reference
10. **Earnings per share**	$\dfrac{\text{Net income minus preference dividends}}{\text{Weighted-average number of shares outstanding}}$	Chapter 16, p. 771
11. **Payout ratio**	$\dfrac{\text{Cash dividends}}{\text{Net income}}$	Chapter 15, p. 728
IV. Coverage		
12. **Debt to assets ratio**	$\dfrac{\text{Total liabilities}}{\text{Total assets}}$	Chapter 14, p. 681
13. **Times interest earned**	$\dfrac{\text{Income before interest expense and taxes}}{\text{Interest expense}}$	Chapter 14, p. 681
14. **Cash debt coverage**	$\dfrac{\text{Net cash provided by operating activities}}{\text{Average total liabilities}}$	Chapter 5, p. 203
15. **Book value per share**	$\dfrac{\text{Shareholders' equity—ordinary}}{\text{Outstanding shares}}$	Chapter 15, p. 729

You can find additional coverage of these ratios, accompanied by assignment material, at the book's companion website, at **www.wiley.com/college/kieso**. This supplemental coverage takes the form of a comprehensive case adapted from the annual report of a large international chemical company that we have disguised under the name of Anetek Chemical Corporation.

Limitations of Ratio Analysis

LEARNING OBJECTIVE 11

Explain the limitations of ratio analysis.

The reader of financial statements must understand the basic limitations associated with ratio analysis. As analytical tools, ratios are attractive because they are simple and convenient. But too frequently decision-makers base their decisions on only these simple computations. The ratios are only as good as the data upon which they are based and the information with which they are compared.

One important limitation of ratios is that they generally are **based on historical cost, which can lead to distortions in measuring performance**. Inaccurate assessments of the enterprise's financial condition and performance can result from failing to incorporate fair value information.

Also, investors must remember that **where estimated items (such as depreciation and amortization) are significant, income ratios lose some of their credibility**. For example, income recognized before the termination of a company's life is an approximation. In analyzing the income statement, users should be aware of the uncertainty surrounding the computation of net income. As one analyst aptly noted, "The physicist has long since conceded that the location of an electron is best expressed by a probability curve. Surely an abstraction like earnings per share is even more subject to the rules of probability and risk."[22]

Probably the greatest limitation of ratio analysis is the **difficult problem of achieving comparability among firms in a given industry**. Achieving comparability requires that the analyst (1) identify basic differences in companies' accounting policies and procedures, and (2) adjust the balances to achieve comparability. Basic differences in accounting usually involve one of the following areas.

 Underlying Concepts

Consistency and comparability are important concepts for financial statement analysis. If the principles and assumptions used to prepare the financial statements are continually changing, accurate assessments of a company's progress become difficult.

---

[22]Richard E. Cheney, "How Dependable Is the Bottom Line?" *The Financial Executive* (January 1971), p. 12.

1. Inventory valuation (FIFO, average-cost).
2. Depreciation methods, particularly the use of straight-line versus accelerated depreciation.
3. Capitalization versus expensing of certain costs.
4. Capitalization of leases versus non-capitalization.
5. Investments in ordinary shares carried under the equity method versus fair value.
6. Differing treatments of postretirement benefit costs.
7. Questionable practices of defining discontinued operations, impairments, and unusual items.

The use of these different alternatives can make a significant difference in the ratios computed. For example, at one time **Anheuser-Busch** (now **AB InBev** (BEL)) (USA) noted that if it had used a different inventory method, inventories would have increased approximately $33,000,000. Such an increase would have a substantive impact on the current ratio. Several studies have analyzed the impact of different accounting methods on financial statement analysis. The differences in income that can develop are staggering in some cases. Investors must be aware of the potential pitfalls if they are to be able to make the proper adjustments.[23]

Finally, analysts should recognize that a **substantial amount of important information** is not included in a company's financial statements. Events such as industry changes, management changes, competitors' actions, technological developments, government actions, and union activities are often critical to a company's successful operation. These events occur continuously, and information about them must come from careful analysis of financial reports in the media and other sources. Indeed, many argue in what is known as the **efficient-market hypothesis** that financial statements contain "no surprises" to those engaged in market activities. They contend that the effect of these events is known in the marketplace—and the price of the company's shares adjusts accordingly—well before the issuance of such reports.

COMPARATIVE ANALYSIS

Comparative analysis presents the same information for two or more different dates or periods, so that like items may be compared. Ratio analysis provides only a single snapshot, for one given point or period in time. In a comparative analysis, an investment analyst can concentrate on a given item and determine whether it appears to be growing or diminishing year by year and the proportion of such change to related items. Generally, companies present comparative financial statements. They typically include two years of statement of financial position information and three years of income statement information.

12 LEARNING OBJECTIVE
Describe techniques of comparative analysis.

In addition, many companies include in their annual reports five- or 10-year summaries of pertinent data that permit readers to examine and analyze trends. As indicated in IFRS, "the presentation of comparative financial statements in annual and other reports enhances the usefulness of such reports and brings out more clearly the nature and trends of current changes affecting the enterprise." Illustration 24A-2 (page 1292) presents a five-year condensed statement, with additional supporting data, of Anetek Chemical Corporation.

---

[23]See for example, Eugene A. Imhoff, Jr., Robert C. Lipe, and David W. Wright, "Operating Leases: Impact of Constructive Capitalization," *Accounting Horizons* (March 1991).

ANETEK CHEMICAL CORPORATION
CONDENSED COMPARATIVE STATEMENTS
(IN MILLIONS)

	2015	2014	2013	2012	2011	10 Years Ago 2005	20 Years Ago 1995
Sales and other revenue:							
Net sales	$1,600.0	$1,350.0	$1,309.7	$1,176.2	$1,077.5	$636.2	$170.7
Other revenue	75.0	50.0	39.4	34.1	24.6	9.0	3.7
Total	1,675.0	1,400.0	1,349.1	1,210.3	1,102.1	645.2	174.4
Costs and other charges:							
Cost of sales	1,000.0	850.0	827.4	737.6	684.2	386.8	111.0
Depreciation and amortization	150.0	150.0	122.6	115.6	98.7	82.4	14.2
Selling and administrative expenses	225.0	150.0	144.2	133.7	126.7	66.7	10.7
Interest expense	50.0	25.0	28.5	20.7	9.4	8.9	1.8
Income taxes	100.0	75.0	79.5	73.5	68.3	42.4	12.4
Total	1,525.0	1,250.0	1,202.2	1,081.1	987.3	587.2	150.1
Net income for the year	$ 150.0	$ 150.0	$ 146.9	$ 129.2	$ 114.8	$ 58.0	$ 24.3

Other Statistics							
Earnings per share on ordinary shares (in dollars)[a]	$ 5.00	$ 5.00	$ 4.90	$ 3.58	$ 3.11	$ 1.66	$ 1.06
Cash dividends per share on ordinary shares (in dollars)[a]	2.25	2.15	1.95	1.79	1.71	1.11	0.25
Cash dividends declared on ordinary shares	67.5	64.5	58.5	64.6	63.1	38.8	5.7
Share dividend at approximate market value				46.8		27.3	
Taxes (major)	144.5	125.9	116.5	105.6	97.8	59.8	17.0
Wages paid	389.3	325.6	302.1	279.6	263.2	183.2	48.6
Cost of employee benefits	50.8	36.2	32.9	28.7	27.2	18.4	4.4
Number of employees at year end (thousands)	47.4	36.4	35.0	33.8	33.2	26.6	14.6
Additions to property	306.3	192.3	241.5	248.3	166.1	185.0	49.0

[a]Adjusted for share splits and share dividends.

ILLUSTRATION 24A-2
Condensed Comparative
Financial Information

PERCENTAGE (COMMON-SIZE) ANALYSIS

LEARNING OBJECTIVE 13
Describe techniques of percentage analysis.

Analysts also use percentage analysis to help them evaluate and compare companies. **Percentage analysis** consists of reducing a series of related amounts to a series of percentages of a given base. For example, analysts frequently express all items in an income statement as a percentage of sales or sometimes as a percentage of cost of goods sold. They may analyze a statement of financial position on the basis of total assets. Percentage analysis facilitates comparison and is helpful in evaluating the relative size of items or the relative change in items. A conversion of absolute dollar amounts to percentages may also facilitate comparison between companies of different size.

Illustration 24A-3 shows a comparative analysis of the expense section of Anetek Chemical for the last two years.

ANETEK CHEMICAL CORPORATION
HORIZONTAL COMPARATIVE ANALYSIS
(IN MILLIONS)

	2015	2014	Difference	% Change Inc. (Dec.)
Cost of sales	$1,000.0	$850.0	$150.0	17.6%
Depreciation and amortization	150.0	150.0	0	0
Selling and administrative expenses	225.0	150.0	75.0	50.0
Interest expense	50.0	25.0	25.0	100.0
Income taxes	100.0	75.0	25.0	33.3

This approach, normally called **horizontal analysis**, indicates the proportionate change over a period of time. It is especially useful in evaluating trends because absolute changes are often deceiving.

Another comparative approach, called **vertical analysis**, is the proportional expression of each financial statement item in a given period to a base figure. For example, Anetek Chemical's income statement using this approach appears in Illustration 24A-4.

ANETEK CHEMICAL CORPORATION
INCOME STATEMENT
(IN MILLIONS)

	Amount	Percentage of Total Revenue
Net sales	$1,600.0	96%
Other revenue	75.0	4
Total revenue	1,675.0	100
Less:		
Cost of sales	1,000.0	60
Depreciation and amortization	150.0	9
Selling and administrative expenses	225.0	13
Interest expense	50.0	3
Income taxes	100.0	6
Total expenses	1,525.0	91
Net income	$ 150.0	9%

Vertical analysis is frequently called **common-size analysis** because it reduces all of the statement items to a "common size." That is, all of the elements within each statement are expressed in percentages of some common number and always add up to 100 percent. Common-size (percentage) analysis reveals the composition of each of the financial statements.

In the analysis of the statement of financial position, common-size analysis answers such questions as: What percentage of the capital structure is equity, current liabilities, and long-term debt? What is the mix of assets (percentage-wise) with which the company has chosen to conduct business? What percentage of current assets is in inventory, receivables, and so forth?

Common-size analysis of the income statement typically relates each item to sales. It is instructive to know what proportion of each sales dollar is absorbed by various costs and expenses incurred by the enterprise.

Analysts may use common-size statements to compare one company's statements from different years, to detect trends not evident from comparing absolute amounts. Also, common-size statements provide intercompany comparisons regardless of size because they recast financial statements into a comparable common-size format.

SUMMARY OF LEARNING OBJECTIVES FOR APPENDIX 24A

9 **Understand the approach to financial statement analysis.** Basic financial statement analysis involves examining relationships between items on the statements (ratio and percentage analysis) and identifying trends in these relationships (comparative analysis). Analysis is used to predict the future, but ratio analysis is limited because the data are from the past. Also, ratio analysis identifies present strengths and weaknesses of a company, but it may not reveal *why* they are as they are. Although single ratios are helpful, they are not conclusive. For maximum usefulness, analysts must compare them with industry averages, past years, planned amounts, and the like.

10 **Identify major analytic ratios and describe their calculation.** Ratios are classified as liquidity ratios, activity ratios, profitability ratios, and coverage ratios. (1) *Liquidity ratio analysis* measures the short-run ability of a company to pay its currently maturing obligations. (2) *Activity ratio analysis* measures how effectively a company is using its assets. (3) *Profitability ratio analysis* measures the degree of success or failure of a company to generate revenues adequate to cover its costs of operation and provide a return to the owners. (4) *Coverage ratio analysis* measures the degree of protection afforded long-term creditors and investors.

11 **Explain the limitations of ratio analysis.** Ratios are based on historical cost, which can lead to distortions in measuring performance. Also, where estimated items are significant, income ratios lose some of their credibility. In addition, comparability problems exist because companies use different accounting policies and procedures. Finally, analysts must recognize that a substantial amount of important information is not included in a company's financial statements.

12 **Describe techniques of comparative analysis.** Companies present comparative data, which generally includes two years of statement of financial position information and three years of income statement information. In addition, many companies include in their annual reports five- to 10-year summaries of pertinent data that permit the reader to analyze trends.

13 **Describe techniques of percentage analysis.** Percentage analysis consists of reducing a series of related amounts to a series of percentages of a given base. Analysts use two approaches. *Horizontal analysis* indicates the proportionate change in financial statement items over a period of time; such analysis is most helpful in evaluating trends. *Vertical analysis* (common-size analysis) is a proportional expression of each item on the financial statements in a given period to a base amount. It analyzes the composition of each of the financial statements from different years (a) to detect trends not evident from the comparison of absolute amounts and (b) to make intercompany comparisons of different-sized enterprises.

APPENDIX **24B**	FIRST-TIME ADOPTION OF IFRS

LEARNING OBJECTIVE **14**

Describe the guidelines for first-time adoption of IFRS.

As discussed in Chapter 1, IFRS is growing in acceptance around the world. For example, recent statistics indicate 40 percent of the Global Fortune 500 companies use IFRS. And the chair of the IASB predicts that IFRS adoption will grow from more than 115 countries to nearly 150 countries in the near future.

When countries accept IFRS for use as accepted accounting policies, companies need guidance to ensure that their first IFRS financial statements contain high-quality information. Specifically, *IFRS 1* requires that information in a company's first IFRS statements (1) be transparent, (2) provide a suitable starting point, and (3) have a cost that does not exceed the benefits. **[12]**

The overriding principle in converting from national GAAP (e.g., U.S., Chinese, or Russian) to IFRS (the conversion process) is full retrospective application of all IFRS. Retrospective application—recasting prior financial statements on the basis of IFRS—provides financial statement users with comparable information. However, the IASB recognizes that full retrospective application may be difficult in some situations, particularly when information related to past periods is not readily available. In response, the IASB has established guidelines to ensure that financial statement users have high-quality comparable information while balancing the costs and benefits of providing comparable data.

GENERAL GUIDELINES

The objective of the conversion process is to present a set of IFRS financial statements as if the company always reported on IFRS. To achieve this objective, a company must:

1. Identify the timing for its first IFRS statements.

2. Prepare an opening statement of financial position at the date of transition to IFRS.

3. Select accounting policies that comply with IFRS and apply these policies retrospectively.

4. Consider whether to apply any optional exemptions and apply mandatory exceptions.

5. Make extensive disclosure to explain the transition to IFRS.

Relevant Dates

Once a company decides to convert to IFRS, it must decide on the transition date and the reporting date. The **transition date** is the beginning of the earliest period for which full comparative IFRS information is presented. The **reporting date** is the closing statement of financial position date for the first IFRS financial statements.

To illustrate, assume that FirstChoice Company plans to provide its first IFRS statements for the year ended December 31, 2016. FirstChoice decides to present comparative information for one year only. Therefore, its date of transition to IFRS is January 1, 2015, and its reporting date is December 31, 2016. The timeline for first-time adoption is presented in Illustration 24B-1.

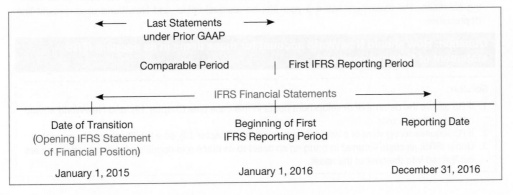

ILLUSTRATION 24B-1
First-Time Adoption Timeline

Illustration 24B-1 shows the following.

1. The **opening IFRS statement of financial position** for FirstChoice on January 1, 2015, serves as the starting point (date of transition) for the company's accounting under IFRS.

2. The first full IFRS statements are shown for FirstChoice for December 31, 2016. In other words, a minimum of two years of IFRS statements must be presented before a conversion to IFRS occurs. As a result, FirstChoice must prepare at least one year of comparative financial statements (for 2015) using IFRS.

3. FirstChoice presents financial statements in accordance with its national GAAP annually to December 31, 2015.

Following this conversion process, FirstChoice provides users of the financial statements with comparable IFRS statements for 2015 and 2016.

IMPLEMENTATION STEPS
Opening IFRS Statement of Financial Position

LEARNING OBJECTIVE 15

Describe the implementation steps for preparing the opening IFRS statement of financial position.

As indicated, to start the conversion process, companies first prepare an opening IFRS statement of financial position. This process involves the following steps.

1. Include all assets and liabilities that IFRS requires.
2. Exclude any assets and liabilities that IFRS does not permit.
3. Classify all assets, liabilities, and equity in accordance with IFRS.
4. Measure all assets and liabilities according to IFRS. **[13]**

Completing this process requires knowledge of both the prior GAAP used and IFRS (which you have obtained by your study of this textbook). To illustrate, the following facts for NewWorld Company are presented in Illustration 24B-2.

ILLUSTRATION 24B-2
Policy Changes—
Opening Statement
of Financial Position

OPENING STATEMENT OF FINANCIAL POSITION

Facts: NewWorld Company is preparing to adopt IFRS. It is preparing its opening statement of financial position on January 1, 2015. NewWorld identified the following accounting policy differences between IFRS and the national GAAP it currently uses. Under national GAAP, NewWorld:

1. Expenses development costs of €500,000 on a project that had met economic viability.
2. Does not make a provision for a warranty of €100,000 because the concept of a "constructive obligation" was not recognized.
3. Does not capitalize design fees of €150,000 into the cost of machinery that was put into service at the beginning of 2013 even though those costs were necessary to bring the asset to its working condition. The machinery has a 5-year life, no residual value, and NewWorld uses straight-line depreciation.

Question: How should NewWorld account for these items in its opening IFRS statement of financial position?

Solution:

1. IFRS allows the deferral of development costs in this case (see Chapter 12), and NewWorld should capitalize these costs.
2. IFRS requires recognition of a warranty provision (see Chapter 13), so a liability should be recorded.
3. Under IFRS, all costs incurred in bringing an asset to its place and condition for its intended use are capitalized into the cost of the asset.

Adjustments as a result of applying IFRS for the first time are generally recorded in retained earnings. NewWorld makes the following entries on January 1, 2015, to adjust the accounts to IFRS treatment.

Development Costs (or related intangible asset)	500,000	
Retained Earnings		500,000
(To capitalize development costs)		
Retained Earnings	100,000	
Warranty Liability		100,000
(To recognize warranty liability)		
Equipment	150,000	
Accumulated Depreciation—Equipment		60,000
Retained Earnings		90,000
(To recognize cost of machinery)		

In each of these situations, NewWorld adjusts retained earnings for the differences between IFRS and national GAAP to ensure that the opening statement of financial position is reported in accordance with IFRS.

After recording these adjustments, NewWorld prepares its opening IFRS statement of financial position. The January 1, 2015, statement of financial position is the starting point (the date of transition). Subsequently, in 2015 and 2016, NewWorld prepares IFRS financial statements internally. At December 31, 2016, it will formally adopt IFRS.[24]

Exemptions from Retrospective Treatment

In some cases, adjustments relating to prior periods cannot be reasonably determined. In other cases, it is "impracticable" to provide comparable information because the cost of generating the information exceeds the benefits. The IASB therefore targeted exemptions from the general retrospective treatment where it appeared appropriate. Two types of exemptions are provided—required and elective.

16 LEARNING OBJECTIVE
Describe the exemptions to retrospective application in first-time adoption of IFRS.

Required Exemptions
The Board identified three areas in which companies are prohibited from retrospective application in first-time adoption of IFRS:

1. Estimates.
2. Hedge accounting.
3. Non-controlling interests.

These required exemptions are imposed because implementation of retrospective application in these areas generally requires companies to obtain information that may not be readily available. In these cases, companies may have to re-create information about past transactions with the benefit of hindsight. **[15]** For example, retrospective application with respect to non-controlling interests requires information about conditions and estimates made at the time of a business combination—an often difficult task. In addition, this exception provides relief for companies that otherwise might have to determine the allocation of transactions between owners and non-controlling interests in periods prior to the transition period.

---

[24]To maintain comparisons in the transition year, companies may present comparative information in accordance with previous GAAP as well as the comparative information required by IFRS. Companies must (a) label the previous GAAP information prominently as not being prepared in accordance with IFRS, and (b) disclose the nature of the main adjustments that would make it comply with IFRS. Companies need not quantify those adjustments. **[14]**

Elective Exemptions

In addition to the required exemptions for retrospective treatment, the **IASB identified specific additional areas in which companies may elect exemption from retrospective treatment.** These exemptions provide companies some relief from full retrospective application. This simplifies the preparation of the first-time IFRS statements. Areas addressed in the textbook are presented in Illustration 24B-3.[25]

ILLUSTRATION 24B-3
Elective Exemption from Retrospective Treatment

Companies may elect an exemption from retrospective application for one or more of the following areas.

(a) Share-based payment transactions.
(b) Fair value or revaluation as deemed cost.
(c) Leases.
(d) Employee benefits.
(e) Compound financial instruments.
(f) Fair value measurement of financial assets or financial liabilities at initial recognition.
(g) Decommissioning liabilities included in the cost of property, plant, and equipment.
(h) Borrowing costs.

Optional exemption from retrospective treatment is understandable for certain situations. The accounting for the areas identified above generally requires a number of estimates and assumptions at initial recognition and in subsequent accounting. Depending on the accounting under previous GAAP, the information necessary for retrospective application may not be available, or may be obtained only at a high cost. We discuss two examples.[26]

Exemption Example: Compound Securities. As discussed in Chapter 16, IFRS requires splitting the debt and equity components of convertible debt, using the "with and without" approach. The subsequent accounting for the debt element reflects effective-interest amortization on the estimated debt component. However, if the liability component is no longer outstanding at the date of first-time adoption, retrospective application involves separating two portions of equity. The first portion is in retained earnings and represents the cumulative interest accredited on the liability component. The other portion represents the original equity component. Since the company would not have records on the debt once it is no longer outstanding, it would be costly to re-create that information for retrospective application. As a result, a first-time adopter need not separate these two portions if the liability component is no longer outstanding at the date of transition to IFRS.

Exemption Example: Fair Value or Revaluation as Deemed Cost. Companies can elect to measure property, plant, and equipment at fair value at the transition date and use that fair value as their **deemed cost** in accounting for those assets subsequent to the adoption of IFRS. This exemption may also be applied to intangible assets in certain situations. By using the exemption, companies avoid re-creating depreciation records for property, plant, and equipment, which is a costly exercise for many companies. In fact, in providing this exemption, the IASB noted that reconstructed cost data might be less relevant to users, and less reliable, than current fair value data. The Board therefore

[25]Other areas subject to the option are (1) business combinations; (2) insurance contracts; (3) investments in subsidiaries, jointly controlled entities, and associates; (4) designation of previously recognized financial instruments; (5) financial assets or intangible assets accounted for as Service Concession Arrangements; and (6) transfers of assets from customers. **[16]**

[26]Specific implementation guidance for other areas is provided in *IFRS 1.* **[17]**

concluded that it would allow companies to use fair value as deemed cost. A company that applies the fair value as deemed cost exemption is not required to revalue the assets subsequent to first-time adoption. **[18]**[27]

Presentation and Disclosure

Upon first-time adoption of IFRS, a company must present at least one year of comparative information under IFRS. **[19]** To comply with *IAS 1*, an entity's first IFRS financial statements shall include at least three statements of financial position, two statements of comprehensive income, two separate income statements (if presented), two statements of cash flows, and two statements of changes in equity and related notes, including comparative information. Companies must explain how the transition from previous GAAP to IFRS affected its reported financial position, financial performance, and cash flows.

> **17 LEARNING OBJECTIVE**
>
> Describe the presentation and disclosure requirements for first-time adoption of IFRS.

A company's first IFRS financial statements shall include reconciliations of:

- Its equity reported in accordance with previous GAAP to its equity in accordance with IFRS at the transition date.
- Its total comprehensive income in accordance with IFRS to total comprehensive income in accordance with previous GAAP for the same period. The reconciliation should be prepared for latest period in the company's most recent annual financial statements under the previous GAAP. **[20]**

For example, Jones plc first adopted IFRS in 2016, with a date of transition to IFRS January 1, 2015. Its last financial statements in accordance with previous GAAP were for the year ended December 31, 2015. An example of Jones plc's reconciliations for first-time adoption is provided in Illustration 24B-4 for the non-current assets section of the statement of financial position.

ILLUSTRATION 24B-4
Reconciliation of Equity for 2015

Jones plc
(amounts in thousands)

The first IFRS financial statements include the reconciliations and related notes shown below.

Reconciliation of equity at January 1, 2015 (date of transition to IFRS)

Note		Previous GAAP	Effect of Transition to IFRS	IFRS
1	Property, plant, and equipment	£ 8,299	£100	£ 8,399
2	Goodwill	1,220	150	1,370
2	Intangible assets	208	(150)	58
3	Financial assets	3,471	420	3,891
	Total non-current assets	£13,198	£520	£13,718

[27]In addition, IFRS does not restrict the use of fair value as deemed cost to an entire class of assets, as is done for revaluation accounting (see discussion in Chapter 11). For example, a company can use fair value for deemed cost for some buildings and not for others. However, if a company uses fair value as deemed cost for assets whose fair value is above cost, it cannot ignore indications that the recoverable amount of other assets may have fallen below their carrying amount. Thus, an impairment may need to be recorded.

Notes to the reconciliation at January 1, 2015:

1. Depreciation was influenced by tax requirements in accordance with previous GAAP, but in accordance with IFRS reflects the useful life of the assets. The cumulative adjustment increased the carrying amount of property, plant, and equipment by £100.
2. Intangible assets in accordance with previous GAAP included £150 for items that are transferred to goodwill because they do not qualify for recognition as intangible assets in accordance with IFRS.
3. Financial assets are all classified as non-trading equity investments in accordance with IFRS and are carried at their fair value of £3,891. They were carried at cost of £3,471 in accordance with previous GAAP. The resulting gains of £294 (£420, less related deferred tax of £126) are included in the accumulated other comprehensive income.

Through this reconciliation, statement users are provided information to evaluate the impact of the adoption of IFRS on the statement of financial position. In practice, it may be helpful to include cross-references to accounting policies and supporting analyses that give further explanation of the adjustments shown in the reconciliations.

The reconciliation for total comprehensive income for Jones with respect to the gross profit section of the income statement is presented in Illustration 24B-5.

ILLUSTRATION 24B-5
Reconciliation of Total
Comprehensive Income
for 2015

Jones plc
(amounts in thousands)

Note		Previous GAAP	Effect of Transition to IFRS	IFRS
	Revenue	£20,910	£ 0	£20,910
1, 2, 3	Cost of sales	(15,283)	(97)	(15,380)
	Gross profit	£ 5,627	£(97)	£ 5,530

Notes to the reconciliation of total comprehensive income for 2015:

1. A pension liability is recognized in accordance with IFRS but was not recognized in accordance with previous GAAP. The pension liability increased by £130 during 2015, which caused increases in cost of sales (£50), distribution costs (£30), and administrative expenses (£50).
2. Cost of sales is higher by £47 in accordance with IFRS because inventories include fixed and variable production overhead in accordance with IFRS but not in accordance with previous GAAP.
3. Depreciation was influenced by tax requirements in accordance with previous GAAP but reflects the useful life of the assets in accordance with IFRS. The effect on the profit for 2015 was not material.

Explanation of material adjustments to the statement of cash flows for 2015:
Income taxes of £133 paid during 2015 are classified as operating cash flows in accordance with IFRS but were included in a separate category of tax cash flows in accordance with previous GAAP. There are no other material differences between the statement of cash flows presented in accordance with IFRS and the statement of cash flows presented in accordance with previous GAAP.

SUMMARY

When companies adopt IFRS, they must ensure that financial statement users receive high-quality information in order to compare financial statements prepared under IFRS and previous GAAP. IFRS guidelines are designed to ensure that upon first-time adoption, financial statements are comparable and that the costs and benefits of first-time adoption are effectively managed.

SUMMARY OF LEARNING OBJECTIVES FOR APPENDIX 24B	KEY TERMS

KEY TERMS

deemed cost, *1298*
opening IFRS statement of financial position, *1296*
reporting date, *1295*
transition date, *1295*

14 **Describe the guidelines for first-time adoption of IFRS.** Upon first-time adoption of IFRS, a company must prepare and present an opening IFRS statement of financial position at the date of transition to IFRS. This is the starting point for its accounting in accordance with IFRS. The general rule for first-time adoption of IFRS is retrospective application. That is, recast prior financial statements on the basis of IFRS and using the same accounting policies in its opening IFRS statement of financial position and throughout all periods presented in its first IFRS financial statements. Those accounting policies shall comply with each IFRS effective at the end of its first IFRS reporting period. Companies provide at least one year of comparative statements prepared in accordance with IFRS.

15 **Describe the implementation steps for preparing the opening IFRS statement of financial position.** Companies must first prepare the opening IFRS statement of financial position by (1) including all assets and liabilities that IFRS requires; (2) excluding any assets and liabilities that IFRS does not permit; (3) classifying all assets, liabilities, and equity in accordance with IFRS; and (4) measuring all assets and liabilities according to IFRS. Companies must make entries through retrospective application. After recording these adjustments, an opening IFRS statement of financial position is prepared, which will reflect application of the same policies that will be applied in the first IFRS financial statements.

16 **Describe the exemptions to retrospective application in first-time adoption of IFRS.** Given the range of changes that might be required for first-time adoption, the IASB considered the cost-benefit of retrospective application and developed targeted exemptions from retrospective treatment when the amount of the adjustment relating to prior periods cannot be reasonably determined and when it is "impracticable" to provide comparable information. These exemptions are classified as required (in which a company is prohibited from retrospective application) and optional.

17 **Describe the presentation and disclosure requirements for first-time adoption of IFRS.** Upon first-time adoption of IFRS, a company presents at least one year of comparative information under IFRS. A company's first IFRS financial statements shall include at least three statements of financial position, two statements of comprehensive income, two separate income statements (if presented), two statements of cash flows, and two statements of changes in equity and related notes, including comparative information. Companies also must explain how the transition from previous GAAP to IFRS affected its reported financial position, financial performance, and cash flows. A company's first IFRS financial statements shall include reconciliations of its equity and total comprehensive income in accordance with previous GAAP to its equity and comprehensive income in accordance with IFRS.

IFRS AUTHORITATIVE LITERATURE

Authoritative Literature References

[1] "Framework for the Preparation and Presentation of Financial Statements" (London, U.K.: IASB, 2001), par. 21.

[2] *International Financial Reporting Standard for Small and Medium-sized Entities (IFRS for SMEs)* (London, U.K.: IASB, 2009).

[3] International Accounting Standard 1, *Presentation of Financial Statements* (London, U.K.: International Accounting Standards Committee Foundation, 2007).

[4] International Accounting Standard 24, *Related Party Disclosures* (London, U.K.: International Accounting Standards Committee Foundation, 2009), par. 9.

[5] International Accounting Standard 24, *Related Party Disclosures* (London, U.K.: International Accounting Standards Committee Foundation, 2009), par. 17.

[6] International Accounting Standard 10, *Events after the Reporting Period* (London, U.K.: International Accounting Standards Committee Foundation, 2007).

[7] International Accounting Standard 10, *Events after the Reporting Period* (London, U.K.: International Accounting Standards Committee Foundation, 2007), par. 22.

[8] International Financial Reporting Standard 8, *Operating Segments* (London, U.K.: International Accounting Standards Committee Foundation, 2006), par. BC15.

[9] International Financial Reporting Standard 8, *Operating Segments* (London, U.K.: International Accounting Standards Committee Foundation, 2006), par. 19.

[10] International Accounting Standard 34, *Interim Financial Reporting* (London, U.K.: International Accounting Standards Committee Foundation, 2001).

[11] International Accounting Standard 34, *Interim Financial Reporting* (London, U.K.: International Accounting Standards Committee Foundation, 2001), paras. B12–B19.

[12] International Financial Reporting Standard 1, *First-time Adoption of International Financial Reporting Standards* (London, U.K.: IASB, 2003), par. 1.

[13] International Financial Reporting Standard 1, *First-time Adoption of International Financial Reporting Standards* (London, U.K.: IASB, 2003), par. 10.

[14] International Financial Reporting Standard 1, *First-time Adoption of International Financial Reporting Standards* (London, U.K.: IASB, 2003), par. 22.

[15] International Financial Reporting Standard 1, *First-time Adoption of International Financial Reporting Standards* (London, U.K.: IASB, 2003), par. BC 22B.

[16] International Financial Reporting Standard 1, *First-time Adoption of International Financial Reporting Standards* (London, U.K.: IASB, 2003), App. C and D.

[17] International Financial Reporting Standard 1, *First-time Adoption of International Financial Reporting Standards* (London, U.K.: IASB, 2003), App. B–E.

[18] International Financial Reporting Standard 1, *First-time Adoption of International Financial Reporting Standards* (London, U.K.: IASB, 2003), paras. D5–D8 and BC41–BC47.

[19] International Financial Reporting Standard 1, *First-time Adoption of International Financial Reporting Standards* (London, U.K.: IASB, 2003), par. 19.

[20] International Financial Reporting Standard 1, *First-time Adoption of International Financial Reporting Standards* (London, U.K.: IASB, 2003), par. 24.

Note: All asterisked Questions, Exercises, and Problems relate to material in the appendices to the chapter.

QUESTIONS

1. What are the major advantages of notes to the financial statements? What types of items are usually reported in notes?

2. What is the full disclosure principle in accounting? Why has disclosure increased substantially in the last 10 years?

3. The IASB requires a reconciliation between the effective tax rate and the government's statutory rate. Of what benefit is such a disclosure requirement?

4. What type of disclosure or accounting do you believe is necessary for the following items?

   (a) Because of a general increase in the number of labor disputes and strikes, both within and outside the industry, there is an increased likelihood that a company will suffer a costly strike in the near future.

   (b) A company reports a loss on a discontinued operation (net of tax) correctly on the income statement. No other mention is made of this item in the annual report.

   (c) A company expects to recover a substantial amount in connection with a pending refund claim for a prior year's taxes. Although the claim is being contested, counsel for the company has confirmed the client's expectation of recovery.

5. The following information was described in a note of Canon Packing Co.

   "During August, Holland Products Corporation purchased 311,003 ordinary shares of the Company, which constitutes approximately 35% of the shares outstanding. Holland has since obtained representation on the Board of Directors."

"An affiliate of Holland Products Corporation acts as a food broker for Canon Packing in the greater Amsterdam marketing area. The commissions for such services after August amounted to approximately €20,000." Why is this information disclosed?

6. What are the major types of subsequent events? Indicate how each of the following "subsequent events" would be reported.

   (a) Collection of a note written off in a prior period.
   (b) Issuance of a large preference share offering.
   (c) Acquisition of a company in a different industry.
   (d) Destruction of a major plant in a flood.
   (e) Death of the company's chief executive officer (CEO).
   (f) Additional wage costs associated with settlement of a 4-week strike.
   (g) Settlement of an income tax case at considerably more tax than anticipated at year-end.
   (h) Change in the product mix from consumer goods to industrial goods.

7. What are diversified companies? What accounting problems are related to diversified companies?

8. What quantitative materiality test is applied to determine whether a segment is significant enough to warrant separate disclosure?

9. Identify the segment information that is required to be disclosed by IFRS.

10. What is an operating segment, and when can information about two operating segments be aggregated?

11. The controller for Lafayette Inc. recently commented, "If I have to disclose our segments individually, the only people who will gain are our competitors and the only people that will lose are our present shareholders." Evaluate this comment.

12. What are interim reports? Why is a complete set of financial statements often not provided with interim data?

13. What are the accounting problems related to the presentation of interim data?

14. Dierdorf Inc., a closely held corporation, has decided to go public. The controller, Ed Floyd, is concerned with presenting interim data when an inventory write-down is recorded. What problems are encountered with inventories when quarterly data are presented?

15. What approaches have been suggested to overcome the seasonality problem related to interim reporting?

16. An article in the financial press entitled "Important Information in Annual Reports This Year" noted that annual reports include a management commentary section. What would this section contain?

17. "The financial statements of a company are management's, not the accountant's." Discuss the implications of this statement.

18. Olga Conrad, a financial writer, noted recently, "There are substantial arguments for including earnings projections in annual reports and the like. The most compelling is that it would give anyone interested something now available to only a relatively select few—like large shareholders, creditors, and attentive bartenders." Identify some arguments against providing earnings projections.

19. The following comment appeared in the financial press: "Inadequate financial disclosure, particularly with respect to how management views the future and its role in the marketplace, has always been a stone in the shoe. After all, if you don't know how a company views the future, how can you judge the worth of its corporate strategy?" What are some arguments for reporting earnings forecasts?

20. What is the difference between an auditor's unmodified opinion or "clean" opinion and a modified one?

21. Jane Ellerby and Sam Callison are discussing the recent fraud that occurred at LowRental Leasing, Inc. The fraud involved the improper reporting of revenue to ensure that the company would have income in excess of $1 million. What is fraudulent financial reporting, and how does it differ from an embezzlement of company funds?

22. Briefly describe some of the similarities and differences between disclosure rules under U.S. GAAP and IFRS.

23. Bill Novak is working on an audit of a U.S. GAAP client. In his review of the client's interim reports, he notes that the reports are prepared on an integral basis. That is, each interim report is viewed as a part of the annual period. Is this acceptable under U.S. GAAP? If so, explain how that treatment could affect comparisons to an IFRS company.

*24. "The significance of financial statement data is not in the amount alone." Discuss the meaning of this statement.

*25. A close friend of yours, who is a history major and who has not had any college courses or any experience in business, is receiving the financial statements from companies in which he has minor investments (acquired for him by his now-deceased father). He asks you what he needs to know to interpret and to evaluate the financial statement data that he is receiving. What would you tell him?

*26. Distinguish between ratio analysis and percentage analysis relative to the interpretation of financial statements. What is the value of these two types of analyses?

*27. In calculating inventory turnover, why is cost of goods sold used as the numerator? As the inventory turnover increases, what increasing risk does the business assume?

*28. What is the relationship of the asset turnover to the return on assets?

*29. Explain the meaning of the following terms: (a) common-size analysis, (b) vertical analysis, (c) horizontal analysis, and (d) percentage analysis.

*30. Briefly explain the need for a standard on first-time adoption of IFRS.

*31. How is the date of transition and the date of reporting determined in first-time adoption of IFRS?

*32. What are the characteristics of high-quality information in a company's first IFRS financial statements?

*33. What are the steps to be completed in preparing the opening IFRS statement of financial position?

*34. What is the rationale for exemptions to retrospective application at first-time adoption of IFRS?

*35. Briefly describe the required exemptions to retrospective application at first-time adoption of IFRS.

*36. What are three elective exemptions to retrospective application at first-time adoption of IFRS?

*37. Briefly describe the deemed cost exemption to retrospective application at first-time adoption of IFRS.

*38. If a company elects the deemed cost exemption, must it continue to use revaluation accounting subsequent to first-time adoption? Explain.

*39. Briefly describe the presentation and disclosure requirements for first-time adoption of IFRS.

BRIEF EXERCISES

BE24-1 An annual report of Crestwood Industries states, "The company and its subsidiaries have long-term leases expiring on various dates after December 31, 2015. Amounts payable under such commitments, without reduction for related rental income, are expected to average approximately €5,711,000 annually for the next 3 years. Related rental income from certain subleases to others is estimated to average €3,094,000 annually for the next 3 years." What information is provided by this note?

BE24-2 An annual report of Barclays Company states, "Net income per share is computed based upon the average number of shares of all classes outstanding. Additional shares of ordinary shares may be issued or delivered in the future on conversion of outstanding convertible debentures, exercise of outstanding employee share options, and for payment of defined supplemental compensation. Had such additional shares been outstanding, net income per share would have been reduced by 10¢ in the current year and 3¢ in the previous year. . . . As a result of share transactions by the company during the current year (primarily the purchase of Class A shares from Barclays Foundation), net income per share was increased by 6¢." What information is provided by this note?

BE24-3 Morlan Corporation is preparing its December 31, 2015, financial statements. Two events that occurred between December 31, 2015, and March 10, 2016, when the statements were authorized for issue, are described below.

1. A liability, estimated at €160,000 at December 31, 2015, was settled on February 26, 2016, at €170,000.

2. A flood loss of €80,000 occurred on March 1, 2016.

What effect do these subsequent events have on 2015 net income?

BE24-4 Tina Bailey, an intermediate accounting student, was heard to remark after a class discussion on segment reporting, "All this is very confusing to me. First we are told that there is merit in presenting the consolidated results, and now we are told that it is better to show segmental results. I wish they would make up their minds." Evaluate this comment.

BE24-5 Foley Corporation has seven operating segments with total revenues as follows (in millions).

Penley	¥600	Cheng	¥225
Konami	650	Takuhi	200
KSC	250	Molina	700
Red Moon	275		

Based only on the revenues test, which operating segments are reportable?

BE24-6 Operating profits (losses) for the seven operating segments of Foley Corporation are as follows (in millions).

Penley	¥ 90	Cheng	¥ (20)
Konami	(40)	Takuhi	34
KSC	25	Molina	150
Red Moon	50		

Based only on the operating profit (loss) test, which industry segments are reportable?

BE24-7 Identifiable assets for the seven industry segments of Foley Corporation are as follows (in millions).

Penley	¥500	Cheng	¥200
Konami	550	Takuhi	150
KSC	250	Molina	475
Red Moon	400		

Based only on the identifiable assets test, which industry segments are reportable?

10 *BE24-8 Answer each of the questions in the following unrelated situations.

    (a) The current ratio of a company is 5:1 and its acid-test ratio is 1:1. If the inventories and prepaid items amount to $500,000, what is the amount of current liabilities?

    (b) A company had an average inventory last year of $200,000 and its inventory turnover was 5. If sales volume and unit cost remain the same this year as last and inventory turnover is 8 this year, what will average inventory have to be during the current year?

    (c) A company has current assets of $90,000 (of which $40,000 is inventory and prepaid items) and current liabilities of $40,000. What is the current ratio? What is the acid-test ratio? If the company borrows $15,000 cash from a bank on a 120-day loan, what will its current ratio be? What will the acid-test ratio be?

    (d) A company has current assets of $600,000 and current liabilities of $240,000. The board of directors declares a cash dividend of $180,000. What is the current ratio after the declaration but before payment? What is the current ratio after the payment of the dividend?

10 *BE24-9 Heartland Company's budgeted sales and budgeted cost of goods sold for the coming year are £144,000,000 and £99,000,000, respectively. Short-term interest rates are expected to average 10%. If Heartland can increase inventory turnover from its present level of 9 times a year to a level of 12 times per year, compute its expected cost savings for the coming year.

15 *BE24-10 Becker Ltd. is planning to adopt IFRS and prepare its first IFRS financial statements at December 31, 2016. What is the date of Becker's opening statement of financial position, assuming one year of comparative information? What periods will be covered in Becker's first IFRS financial statements?

15 *BE24-11 Bohmann Company is preparing its opening IFRS statement of financial position on January 1, 2015. Under its previous GAAP, Bohmann had capitalized all development costs of $50,000. Under IFRS, only $10,000 of the costs related to a patent were incurred after the project met economic viability thresholds. Prepare the entry (if any) needed to record this adjustment at the date of transition.

15 *BE24-12 Stengel plc is preparing its opening IFRS statement of financial position on January 1, 2015. Under its previous GAAP, Stengel used the LIFO inventory method. Under LIFO, its inventory is reported at £250,000; under FIFO, which Stengel will use upon adoption of IFRS, the inventory is valued at £265,000. Prepare the entry (if any) needed to record this adjustment at the date of issuance.

15 *BE24-13 Latta Inc. is preparing its opening IFRS statement of financial position on January 1, 2015. Under its previous GAAP, Latta had deferred certain advertising costs amounting to $37,000. Prepare the entry (if any) needed to record this adjustment at the date of issuance.

15 *BE24-14 Smitz Company is preparing its opening IFRS statement of financial position on January 1, 2015. Under its previous GAAP, Smitz did not record a provision for litigation in the amount of €85,000 that would be recognized under IFRS. Prepare the entry (if any) needed to record this adjustment at the date of issuance.

16 *BE24-15 Porter Company is evaluating the following assets to determine whether it can use fair value as deemed cost in first-time adoption of IFRS.

    1. Biological assets related to agricultural activity for which there is *no* active market.

    2. Intangible assets for which there is *no* active market.

    3. Any individual item of property, plant, and equipment.

    4. Financial liabilities that are *not* held for trading.

For each asset type, indicate if the deemed cost exemption can be used.

EXERCISES

2 **E24-1 (Subsequent Events)** Keystone Corporation issued its financial statements for the year ended December 31, 2015, on March 10, 2016. The following events took place before the statements were authorized for issue early in 2016.

    (a) On January 10, 10,000 ordinary shares of $5 par value were issued at $66 per share.

    (b) On March 1, Keystone determined after negotiations with the taxing authorities that income taxes payable for 2015 should be $1,320,000. At December 31, 2015, income taxes payable were recorded at $1,100,000.

Instructions

Discuss how the preceding subsequent events should be reflected in the 2015 financial statements.

2 **E24-2 (Subsequent Events)** Consider the following subsequent events.

_____ **1.** Settlement of a tax case at a cost considerably in excess of the amount expected at year-end.

_____ **2.** Introduction of a new product line.

_____ **3.** Loss of assembly plant due to fire.

_____ **4.** Sale of a significant portion of the company's assets.

_____ **5.** Retirement of the company president.

_____ **6.** Issuance of a significant number of ordinary shares.

_____ **7.** Loss of a significant customer.

_____ **8.** Prolonged employee strike.

_____ **9.** Material loss on a year-end receivable because of a customer's bankruptcy.

_____ **10.** Hiring of a new president.

_____ **11.** Settlement of prior year's litigation against the company.

_____ **12.** Merger with another company of comparable size.

Instructions

For each event, indicate whether a company should (a) adjust the financial statements, (b) disclose in notes to the financial statements, or (c) neither adjust nor disclose.

3 **E24-3 (Segmented Reporting)** LaGreca Company is involved in four separate industries. The following information is available for each of the four segments.

Operating Segment	Total Revenue	Operating Profit (Loss)	Identifiable Assets
W	€ 60,000	€15,000	€167,000
X	10,000	1,500	83,000
Y	23,000	(2,000)	21,000
Z	9,000	1,000	19,000
	€102,000	€15,500	€290,000

Instructions

Determine which of the operating segments are reportable based on the:

    (a) Revenue test.
    (b) Operating profit (loss) test.
    (c) Identifiable assets test.

10 *E24-4 (Ratio Computation and Analysis; Liquidity)** As loan analyst for Murray Bank, you have been presented the following information.

	Plunkett Co.	Herring Co.
Assets		
Other assets	£ 500,000	£ 612,000
Current assets		
Inventories	570,000	518,000
Receivables	220,000	302,000
Cash	120,000	320,000
Total current assets	910,000	1,140,000
Total assets	£1,410,000	£1,752,000
Equity and Liabilities		
Share capital and retained earnings	£ 710,000	£ 902,000
Non-current liabilities	400,000	500,000
Current liabilities	300,000	350,000
Total equity and liabilities	£1,410,000	£1,752,000
Annual sales	£ 930,000	£1,500,000
Rate of gross profit on sales	30%	40%

    Each of these companies has requested a loan of £50,000 for 6 months with no collateral offered. Inasmuch as your bank has reached its quota for loans of this type, only one of these requests is to be granted.

Instructions

Which of the two companies, as judged by the information given above, would you recommend as the better risk and why? Assume that the ending account balances are representative of the entire year.

10 *E24-5 **(Analysis of Given Ratios)** Robbins Company is a wholesale distributor of professional equipment and supplies. The company's sales have averaged about $900,000 annually for the 3-year period 2013–2015. The firm's total assets at the end of 2015 amounted to $850,000.

The president of Robbins Company has asked the controller to prepare a report that summarizes the financial aspects of the company's operations for the past 3 years. This report will be presented to the board of directors at their next meeting.

In addition to comparative financial statements, the controller has decided to present a number of relevant financial ratios which can assist in the identification and interpretation of trends. At the request of the controller, the accounting staff has calculated the following ratios for the 3-year period 2013–2015.

	2013	2014	2015
Current ratio	1.80	1.89	1.96
Acid-test (quick) ratio	1.04	0.99	0.87
Accounts receivable turnover	8.75	7.71	6.42
Inventory turnover	4.91	4.32	3.72
Debt to assets ratio	51.0%	46.0%	41.0%
Long-term debt to assets ratio	31.0%	27.0%	24.0%
Sales to fixed assets (fixed asset turnover)	1.58	1.69	1.79
Sales as a percent of 2013 sales	1.00	1.03	1.05
Gross margin percentage	36.0%	35.1%	34.6%
Net income to sales	6.9%	7.0%	7.2%
Return on assets	7.7%	7.7%	7.8%
Return on equity	13.6%	13.1%	12.7%

In preparation of the report, the controller has decided first to examine the financial ratios independent of any other data to determine if the ratios themselves reveal any significant trends over the 3-year period.

Instructions
(a) The current ratio is increasing while the acid-test (quick) ratio is decreasing. Using the ratios provided, identify and explain the contributing factor(s) for this apparently divergent trend.
(b) In terms of the ratios provided, what conclusion(s) can be drawn regarding the company's use of financial leverage during the 2013–2015 period?
(c) Using the ratios provided, what conclusion(s) can be drawn regarding the company's net investment in plant and equipment?

10 *E24-6 **(Ratio Analysis)** Howser Inc. is a manufacturer of electronic components and accessories with total assets of £20,000,000. Selected financial ratios for Howser and the industry averages for firms of similar size are presented below.

	Howser			2015 Industry Average
	2013	2014	2015	
Current ratio	2.09	2.27	2.51	2.24
Quick ratio	1.15	1.12	1.19	1.22
Inventory turnover	2.40	2.18	2.02	3.50
Net sales to equity	2.75	2.80	2.95	2.85
Net income to equity	0.14	0.15	0.17	0.11
Total liabilities to equity	1.41	1.37	1.44	0.95

Howser is being reviewed by several entities whose interests vary, and the company's financial ratios are a part of the data being considered. Each of the parties listed below must recommend an action based on its evaluation of Howser's financial position.

Citizens National Bank. The bank is processing Howser's application for a new 5-year term note. Citizens National has been Howser's banker for several years but must reevaluate the company's financial position for each major transaction.

Charleston Company. Charleston is a new supplier to Howser and must decide on the appropriate credit terms to extend to the company.

Shannon Financial. A brokerage firm specializing in the shares of electronics firms that are sold over-the-counter, Shannon Financial must decide if it will include Howser in a new fund being established for sale to Shannon Financial's clients.

Working Capital Management Committee. This is a committee of Howser's management personnel chaired by the chief operating officer. The committee is charged with the responsibility of periodically reviewing the company's working capital position, comparing actual data against budgets, and recommending changes in strategy as needed.

Instructions

(a) Describe the analytical use of each of the six ratios presented above.

(b) For each of the four entities described above, identify two financial ratios, from those ratios presented in Illustration 24A-1 (on pages 1289–1290), that would be most valuable as a basis for its decision regarding Howser.

(c) Discuss what the financial ratios presented in the question reveal about Howser. Support your answer by citing specific ratio levels and trends as well as the interrelationships between these ratios.

15 16 *E24-7 (Opening Statement of Financial Position) Goodman Company is preparing to adopt IFRS. In preparing its opening statement of financial position on January 1, 2015, Goodman identified the following accounting policy differences between IFRS and its previous GAAP.

1. Under its previous GAAP, Goodman classified proposed dividends of €45,000 as a current liability.

2. Goodman had deferred advertising costs of €500,000.

Instructions

(a) Prepare the journal entries (if any) needed before preparation of Goodman's opening statement of financial position.

(b) Determine the net change in equity from these adjustments.

15 16 17 *E24-8 (Opening Statement of Financial Position, Disclosure) Lombardo Group is preparing to adopt IFRS. It is preparing its opening statement of financial position on January 1, 2015. Lombardo identified the following accounting policy differences between IFRS and its previous GAAP.

1. Lombardo had not made a provision for a warranty of €75,000 under previous GAAP because the concept of a "constructive obligation" was not recognized.

2. Under previous GAAP, €60,000 paid for certain architect fees was not capitalized into the cost of a building that was put into service at the beginning of 2014, even though those costs were necessary to bring the asset to its working condition. The building has a 40-year life, no residual value, and Lombardo uses straight-line depreciation.

Instructions

(a) Prepare the journal entries (if any) needed before preparation of Lombardo's opening statement of financial position.

(b) Determine the net change in equity from these adjustments.

(c) Briefly describe the disclosures that Lombardo will make related to the adjustments in it first IFRS financial statements.

PROBLEMS

2 P24-1 (Subsequent Events) Your firm has been engaged to examine the financial statements of Almaden Corporation for the year 2015. The bookkeeper who maintains the financial records has prepared all the unaudited financial statements for the corporation since its organization on January 2, 2010. The client provides you with the following information.

ALMADEN CORPORATION
STATEMENT OF FINANCIAL POSITION
DECEMBER 31, 2015

Assets		Liabilities	
		Equity	€4,650,600
Other assets	€5,171,400	Non-current liabilities	1,439,500
Current assets	1,881,100	Current liabilities	962,400
	€7,052,500		€7,052,500

Current assets include:

Cash (restricted in the amount of €300,000 for plant expansion)	€ 571,000
Investments in land	185,000
Accounts receivable less allowance of €30,000	480,000
Inventories (weighted-average)	645,100
	€1,881,100

Other assets include:

Prepaid expenses	€ 62,400
Plant and equipment less accumulated depreciation of €1,430,000	4,130,000
Notes receivable (short-term)	162,300
Goodwill	252,000
Land	564,700
	€5,171,400

Current liabilities include:

Accounts payable	€ 510,000
Notes payable (due 2018)	157,400
Estimated income taxes payable	145,000
Share premium—ordinary	150,000
	€ 962,400

Non-current liabilities include:

Unearned revenue	€ 489,500
Dividends payable (cash)	200,000
8% bonds payable (due May 1, 2020)	750,000
	€1,439,500

Equity includes:

Retained earnings	€2,810,600
Share capital—ordinary, par value €10; authorized 200,000 shares, 184,000 shares issued	1,840,000
	€4,650,600

The supplementary information below is also provided.

1. On May 1, 2015, the corporation issued at par €750,000 of bonds to finance plant expansion. The long-term bond agreement provided for the annual payment of interest every May 1. The existing plant was pledged as security for the loan.

2. The bookkeeper made the following mistakes.
   (a) In 2013, the ending inventory was overstated by €183,000. The ending inventories for 2014 and 2015 were correctly computed.
   (b) In 2015, accrued wages in the amount of €225,000 were omitted from the statement of financial position, and these expenses were not charged on the income statement.
   (c) In 2015, a gain of €175,000 (net of tax) on the sale of certain plant assets was credited directly to retained earnings.

3. A major competitor has introduced a line of products that will compete directly with Almaden's primary line, now being produced in a specially designed new plant. Because of manufacturing innovations, the competitor's line will be of comparable quality but priced 50% below Almaden's line. The competitor announced its new line on January 14, 2016. Almaden indicates that the company will meet the lower prices that are high enough to cover variable manufacturing and selling expenses, but permit recovery of only a portion of fixed costs.

4. You learned on January 28, 2016, prior to completion of the audit, of heavy damage because of a recent fire to one of Almaden's two plants; the loss will not be reimbursed by insurance. The newspapers described the event in detail.

Instructions
Analyze the preceding information to prepare a corrected statement of financial position for Almaden in accordance with IFRS. Prepare a description of any notes that might need to be prepared. The books are closed, and adjustments to income are to be made through retained earnings.

3 **P24-2 (Segmented Reporting)** Cineplex Corporation is a diversified company that operates in five different industries: A, B, C, D, and E. The following information relating to each segment is available for 2015.

	A	B	C	D	E
Sales revenue	$40,000	$ 75,000	$580,000	$35,000	$55,000
Cost of goods sold	19,000	50,000	270,000	19,000	30,000
Operating expenses	10,000	40,000	235,000	12,000	18,000
Total expenses	29,000	90,000	505,000	31,000	48,000
Operating profit (loss)	$11,000	$(15,000)	$ 75,000	$ 4,000	$ 7,000
Identifiable assets	$35,000	$ 80,000	$500,000	$65,000	$50,000

Sales of segments B and C included intersegment sales of $20,000 and $100,000, respectively.

Instructions

(a) Determine which of the segments are reportable based on the:
   (1) Revenue test.
   (2) Operating profit (loss) test.
   (3) Identifiable assets test.
(b) Prepare the necessary disclosures required by IFRS.

10 **12** *P24-3 (Ratio Computations and Additional Analysis)* Bradburn Corporation was formed 5 years ago through a public subscription of ordinary shares. Daniel Brown, who owns 15% of the ordinary shares, was one of the organizers of Bradburn and is its current president. The company has been successful but it currently is experiencing a shortage of funds. On June 10, Daniel Brown approached the Hibernia Bank, asking for a 24-month extension on two £35,000 notes, which are due on June 30, 2015, and September 30, 2015. Another note of £6,000 is due on March 31, 2016, but he expects no difficulty in paying this note on its due date. Brown explained that Bradburn's cash flow problems are due primarily to the company's desire to finance a £300,000 plant expansion over the next 2 fiscal years through internally generated funds.

The commercial loan officer of Hibernia Bank requested financial reports for the last 2 fiscal years. These reports are reproduced below.

BRADBURN CORPORATION
STATEMENT OF FINANCIAL POSITION
MARCH 31

Assets	2015	2014
Plant and equipment (net of depreciation)	£1,449,000	£1,420,500
Inventories (at cost)	105,000	50,000
Accounts receivable (net)	131,800	125,500
Notes receivable	148,000	132,000
Cash	18,200	12,500
Total assets	£1,852,000	£1,740,500

Equity and Liabilities	2015	2014
Share capital—ordinary (130,000 shares, £10 par)	£1,300,000	£1,300,000
Retained earnings[a]	388,000	282,000
Accrued liabilities	9,000	6,000
Notes payable	76,000	61,500
Accounts payable	79,000	91,000
Total equity and liabilities	£1,852,000	£1,740,500

[a]Cash dividends were paid at the rate of £1 per share in fiscal year 2014 and £2 per share in fiscal year 2015.

BRADBURN CORPORATION
INCOME STATEMENT
FOR THE FISCAL YEARS ENDED MARCH 31

	2015	2014
Sales revenue	£3,000,000	£2,700,000
Cost of goods sold[a]	1,530,000	1,425,000
Gross margin	1,470,000	1,275,000
Operating expenses	860,000	780,000
Income before income taxes	610,000	495,000
Income taxes (40%)	244,000	198,000
Net income	£ 366,000	£ 297,000

[a]Depreciation charges on the plant and equipment of £100,000 and £102,500 for fiscal years ended March 31, 2014 and 2015, respectively, are included in cost of goods sold.

Instructions

(a) Compute the following items for Bradburn Corporation.
 (1) Current ratio for fiscal years 2014 and 2015.
 (2) Acid-test (quick) ratio for fiscal years 2014 and 2015.
 (3) Inventory turnover for fiscal year 2015.
 (4) Return on assets for fiscal years 2014 and 2015. (Assume total assets were £1,688,500 at 3/31/13.)
 (5) Percentage change in sales, cost of goods sold, gross margin, and net income after taxes from fiscal year 2014 to 2015.

(b) Identify and explain what other financial reports and/or financial analyses might be helpful to the commercial loan officer of Hibernia Bank in evaluating Daniel Brown's request for a time extension on Bradburn's notes.

(c) Assume that the percentage changes experienced in fiscal year 2015 as compared with fiscal year 2014 for sales and cost of goods sold will be repeated in each of the next 2 years. Is Bradburn's desire to finance the plant expansion from internally generated funds realistic? Discuss.

(d) Should Hibernia Bank grant the extension on Bradburn's notes considering Daniel Brown's statement about financing the plant expansion through internally generated funds? Discuss.

13 *P24-4 (Horizontal and Vertical Analysis)** Presented below are comparative statements of financial position for the Ozturk Company.

OZTURK COMPANY
COMPARATIVE STATEMENTS OF FINANCIAL POSITION
AS OF DECEMBER 31, 2015 AND 2014

	December 31	
	2015	2014
Assets		
Fixed assets	₺2,585,000	₺1,950,000
Accumulated depreciation	(1,000,000)	(750,000)
Prepaid expenses	25,000	25,000
Inventories	1,060,000	980,000
Accounts receivable (net)	220,000	155,000
Short-term investments	270,000	150,000
Cash	180,000	275,000
	₺3,340,000	₺2,785,000
Equity and Liabilities		
Share capital—ordinary	₺2,100,000	₺1,770,000
Retained earnings	570,000	550,000
Bonds payable	450,000	190,000
Accrued expenses	170,000	200,000
Accounts payable	50,000	75,000
	₺3,340,000	₺2,785,000

Instructions

(Round to two decimal places.)

(a) Prepare a comparative statement of financial position of Ozturk Company showing the percent each item is of the total assets or total equity and liabilities.

(b) Prepare a comparative statement of financial position of Ozturk Company showing the Turkish lira change and the percent change for each item.

(c) Of what value is the additional information provided in part (a)?

(d) Of what value is the additional information provided in part (b)?

10 *P24-5 **(Dividend Policy Analysis)** Matheny Inc. went public 3 years ago. The board of directors will be meeting shortly after the end of the year to decide on a dividend policy. In the past, growth has been financed primarily through the retention of earnings. A share or a cash dividend has never been declared. Presented below is a brief financial summary of Matheny Inc. operations (euros in thousands).

	2015	2014	2013	2012	2011
Sales revenue	€20,000	€16,000	€14,000	€6,000	€4,000
Net income	2,400	1,400	800	700	250
Average total assets	22,000	19,000	11,500	4,200	3,000
Current assets	8,000	6,000	3,000	1,200	1,000
Working capital	3,600	3,200	1,200	500	400
Ordinary shares:					
Number of shares					
outstanding (in thousands)	2,000	2,000	2,000	20	20
Average market price	€9	€6	€4	—	—

Instructions

(a) Suggest factors to be considered by the board of directors in establishing a dividend policy.

(b) Compute the return on assets, profit margin on sales, earnings per share, price-earnings ratio, and current ratio for each of the 5 years for Matheny Inc.

(c) Comment on the appropriateness of declaring a cash dividend at this time, using the ratios computed in part (b) as a major factor in your analysis.

CONCEPTS FOR ANALYSIS

CA24-1 (General Disclosures; Inventories; Property, Plant, and Equipment) Koch Corporation is in the process of preparing its annual financial statements for the fiscal year ended April 30, 2015. The company manufactures plastic, glass, and paper containers for sale to food and drink manufacturers and distributors.

Koch Corporation maintains separate control accounts for its raw materials, work in process, and finished goods inventories for each of the three types of containers. The inventories are valued at the lower-of-cost-or-net realizable value.

The company's property, plant, and equipment are classified in the following major categories: land, office buildings, furniture and fixtures, manufacturing facilities, manufacturing equipment, and leasehold improvements. All fixed assets are carried at cost. The depreciation methods employed depend on the type of asset (its classification) and when it was acquired.

Koch Corporation plans to present the inventory and fixed asset amounts in its April 30, 2015, statement of financial position as shown below.

Inventories	$4,814,200
Property, plant, and equipment (net of depreciation)	6,310,000

Instructions

What information regarding inventories and property, plant, and equipment must be disclosed by Koch Corporation in the audited financial statements issued to shareholders, either in the body or the notes, for the 2014–2015 fiscal year?

Instructions

Determine which of the segments must be reported separately and which can be combined under the category "Other." Then, write a one-page memo to the company's accountant, Anthony Reese, explaining the following.

(a) What segments must be reported separately and what segments can be combined.
(b) What criteria you used to determine reportable segments.
(c) What major items for each must be disclosed.

CA24-6 (Interim Reporting) Sino Corporation, a publicly traded company, is preparing the interim financial data which it will issue to its shareholders at the end of the first quarter of the 2014–2015 fiscal year. Sino's financial accounting department has compiled the following summarized revenue and expense data for the first quarter of the year.

Sales revenue	¥60,000,000
Cost of goods sold	36,000,000
Variable selling expenses	1,000,000
Fixed selling expenses	3,000,000

Included in the fixed selling expenses was the single lump-sum payment of ¥2,000,000 for television advertisements for the entire year.

Instructions

(a) Sino Corporation must issue its quarterly financial statements in accordance with IFRS regarding interim financial reporting.
  (1) Explain whether Sino should report its operating results for the quarter as if the quarter were a separate reporting period in and of itself, or as if the quarter were an integral part of the annual reporting period.
  (2) State how the sales revenue, cost of goods sold, and fixed selling expenses would be reflected in Sino Corporation's quarterly report prepared for the first quarter of the 2014–2015 fiscal year. Briefly justify your presentation.
(b) What financial information, as a minimum, must Sino Corporation disclose to its shareholders in its quarterly reports?

 CA24-7 (Treatment of Various Interim Reporting Situations) The following are six independent cases on how accounting facts might be reported on an individual company's interim financial reports.

Instructions

For each of these cases, state whether the method proposed to be used for interim reporting would be acceptable under IFRS applicable to interim financial data. Support each answer with a brief explanation.

(a) J. D. Long Company takes a physical inventory at year-end for annual financial statement purposes. Inventory and cost of sales reported in the interim quarterly statements are based on estimated gross profit rates because a physical inventory would result in a cessation of operations. Long Company does have reliable perpetual inventory records.
(b) Rockford Company is planning to report one-fourth of its pension expense each quarter.
(c) Republic Company wrote inventory down to reflect lower-of-cost-or-net realizable value in the first quarter. At year-end, the net realizable value exceeds the original acquisition cost of this inventory. Consequently, management plans to write the inventory back up to its original cost as a year-end adjustment.
(d) Gansner Company realized a large gain on the sale of investments at the beginning of the second quarter. The company wants to report one-third of the gain in each of the remaining quarters.
(e) Fredonia Company has estimated its annual audit fee. It plans to pro rate this expense equally over all four quarters.
(f) LaBrava Company was reasonably certain it would have an employee strike in the third quarter. As a result, it shipped heavily during the second quarter but plans to defer the recognition of the sales in excess of the normal sales volume. The deferred sales will be recognized as sales in the third quarter when the strike is in progress. LaBrava Company management thinks this is more representative of normal second- and third-quarter operations.

CA24-8 (Financial Forecasts) An article in *Barron's* noted the following.

Okay. Last fall, someone with a long memory and an even longer arm reached into that bureau drawer and came out with a moldy cheese sandwich and the equally moldy notion of corporate forecasts. However, the forecast proposal was dusted off, polished up and found quite serviceable. The U.S. SEC, indeed, lost no time in running it up the old flagpole—but no one was very eager to salute. Even after some of the more objectionable features—compulsory corrections and detailed explanations of why the estimates went awry—were peeled off the original proposal.

Seemingly, despite the Commission's smiles and sweet talk, those craven corporations were still afraid that an honest mistake would lead them down the primrose path to consent decrees and class action suits. To lay to rest such qualms, the Commission last week approved a "Safe Harbor" rule that, providing the forecasts were made on a reasonable basis and in good faith, protected corporations from litigation should the projections prove wide of the mark (as only about 99% are apt to do).

Instructions

(a) What are the arguments for preparing profit forecasts?
(b) What is the purpose of the "safe harbor" rule?
(c) Why are corporations concerned about presenting profit forecasts?

CA24-9 (Disclosure of Estimates) Nancy Tercek, the financial vice president, and Margaret Lilly, the controller, of Romine Manufacturing Company are reviewing the financial ratios of the company for the years 2015 and 2016. The financial vice president notes that the profit margin on sales has increased from 6% to 12%, a hefty gain for the 2-year period. Tercek is in the process of issuing a media release that emphasizes the efficiency of Romine Manufacturing in controlling costs. Margaret Lilly knows that the difference in ratios is due primarily to an earlier company decision to reduce the estimates of warranty and bad debt expense for 2016. The controller, not sure of her supervisor's motives, hesitates to suggest to Tercek that the company's improvement is unrelated to efficiency in controlling costs. To complicate matters, the media release is scheduled in a few days.

Instructions

(a) What, if any, is the ethical dilemma in this situation?
(b) Should Lilly, the controller, remain silent? Give reasons.
(c) What stakeholders might be affected by Tercek's media release?
(d) Give your opinion on the following statement and cite reasons: "Because Tercek, the vice president, is most directly responsible for the media release, Lilly has no real responsibility in this matter."

CA24-10 (Reporting of Subsequent Events) In June 2015, the board of directors for McElroy Enterprises Inc. authorized the sale of £10,000,000 of corporate bonds. Jennifer Grayson, treasurer for McElroy Enterprises Inc., is concerned about the date when the bonds are issued. The company really needs the cash, but she is worried that if the bonds are issued before the company's year-end (December 31, 2015) the additional liability will have an adverse effect on a number of important ratios. In July, she explains to company president, William McElroy, that if they delay issuing the bonds until after December 31, the bonds will not affect the ratios until December 31, 2016. They will have to report the issuance as a subsequent event which requires only footnote disclosure. Grayson expects that with expected improved financial performance in 2016 ratios should be better.

Instructions

(a) What are the ethical issues involved?
(b) Should McElroy agree to the delay?

*CA24-11 (Effect of Transactions on Financial Statements and Ratios) The transactions listed on page 1317 relate to Wainwright Inc. You are to assume that on the date on which each of the transactions occurred, the corporation's accounts showed only ordinary shares ($100 par) outstanding, a current ratio of 2.7:1, and a substantial net income for the year to date (before giving effect to the transaction concerned). On that date, the book value per share was $151.53.

Each numbered transaction is to be considered completely independent of the others, and its related answer should be based on the effect(s) of that transaction alone. Assume that all numbered transactions occurred during 2015 and that the amount involved in each case is sufficiently material to distort reported net income if improperly included in the determination of net income. Assume further that each transaction was recorded in accordance with IFRS and, where applicable, in conformity with the all-inclusive concept of the income statement.

For each of the numbered transactions you are to decide whether it:

(a) Increased the corporation's 2015 net income.
(b) Decreased the corporation's 2015 net income.
(c) Increased the corporation's total retained earnings directly (i.e., not via net income).
(d) Decreased the corporation's total retained earnings directly.

   (e) Increased the corporation's current ratio.
   (f) Decreased the corporation's current ratio.
   (g) Increased each shareholder's proportionate share of total equity.
   (h) Decreased each shareholder's proportionate share of total equity.
   (i) Increased each shareholder's equity per share (book value).
   (j) Decreased each shareholder's equity per share (book value).
   (k) Had none of the foregoing effects.

Instructions

List the numbers 1 through 9. Select as many letters as you deem appropriate to reflect the effect(s) of each transaction as of the date of the transaction by printing beside the transaction number the letter(s) that identifies that transaction's effect(s).

Transactions

   1. In January, the board directed the write-off of certain patent rights that had suddenly and unexpectedly become worthless.

   2. The corporation sold at a profit land and a building that had been idle for some time. Under the terms of the sale, the corporation received a portion of the sales price in cash immediately, the balance maturing at 6-month intervals.

   3. Treasury shares originally repurchased and carried at $127 per share was sold for cash at $153 per share.

   4. The corporation wrote off all of the unamortized discount and issue expense applicable to bonds that it refinanced in 2015.

   5. The corporation called in all its outstanding ordinary shares and exchanged them for new shares on a 2-for-1 basis, reducing the par value at the same time to $50 per share.

   6. The corporation paid a cash dividend that had been recorded in the accounts at time of declaration.

   7. Litigation involving Wainwright Inc. as defendant was settled in the corporation's favor, with the plaintiff paying all court costs and legal fees. In 2012, the corporation had appropriately established a special contingency for this court action. (Indicate the effect of reversing the contingency only.)

   8. The corporation received a check for the proceeds of an insurance policy from the company with which it is insured against theft of trucks. No entries concerning the theft had been made previously, and the proceeds reduce but do not cover completely the loss.

   9. Treasury shares, which had been repurchased at and carried at $127 per share, were issued as a share dividend. In connection with this distribution, the board of directors of Wainwright Inc. had authorized a transfer from retained earnings to permanent share capital of an amount equal to the aggregate market price ($153 per share) of the shares issued. No entries relating to this dividend had been made previously.

USING YOUR JUDGMENT

FINANCIAL REPORTING

Financial Reporting Problem

Marks and Spencer plc (M&S)

As stated in the chapter, notes to the financial statements are the means of explaining the items presented in the main body of the statements. Common note disclosures relate to such items as accounting policies, segmented information, and interim reporting. The financial statements of **M&S** (GBR) are presented in Appendix A. The company's complete annual report, including the notes to the financial statements, is available online.

Instructions

Refer to M&S's financial statements and the accompanying notes to answer the following questions.

(a) What specific items does M&S discuss in its **Note 1—Summary of Significant Accounting Policies**? (List the headings only.)

(b) For what segments did M&S report segmented information? Which segment is the largest? Who is M&S's largest customer?

(c) What interim information was reported by M&S?

Comparative Analysis Case

adidas and Puma

The financial statements of **adidas** (DEU) and **Puma** (DEU) are presented in Appendices B and C, respectively. The complete annual reports, including the notes to the financial statements, are available online.

Instructions

Use the companies' financial information to answer the following questions.

(a) (1) What specific items does Puma discuss in its **Note 2—Significant Consolidation, Accounting, and Valuation Principles**? (Prepare a list of the headings only.)

(2) What specific items does adidas discuss in its **Note 2—Our Summary of Significant Accounting Policies**? (Prepare a list of the headings only.)

(b) For what lines of business or segments do adidas and Puma present segmented information?

(c) Note and comment on the similarities and differences between the auditors' reports submitted by the independent auditors of adidas and Puma for the year 2012.

*Financial Statement Analysis Case

RNA Inc. manufactures a variety of consumer products. The company's founders have run the company for 30 years and are now interested in retiring. Consequently, they are seeking a purchaser who will continue its operations, and a group of investors, Morgan Inc., is looking into the acquisition of RNA. To evaluate its financial stability and operating efficiency, RNA was requested to provide the latest financial statements and selected financial ratios. The following is summary information provided by RNA.

RNA
INCOME STATEMENT
FOR THE YEAR ENDED NOVEMBER 30, 2015
(IN THOUSANDS)

Sales (net)	€30,500
Interest income	500
Total revenue	31,000
Costs and expenses	
Cost of goods sold	17,600
Selling and administrative expenses	3,550
Depreciation and amortization expense	1,890
Interest expense	900
Total costs and expenses	23,940
Income before taxes	7,060
Income taxes	2,800
Net income	€ 4,260

RNA
STATEMENT OF FINANCIAL POSITION
AS OF NOVEMBER 30
(IN THOUSANDS)

	2015	2014
Property, plant, & equipment (net)	€ 7,100	€ 7,000
Inventory	6,000	5,400
Accounts receivable (net)	3,200	2,900
Marketable securities (at cost)	300	200
Cash	400	500
Total current assets	9,900	9,000
Total assets	€17,000	€16,000
Share capital—ordinary (€1 par value)	€ 2,700	€ 2,700
Share premium—ordinary	1,000	1,000
Retained earnings	5,000	4,900
Total equity	8,700	8,600
Long-term debt	2,000	1,800
Accrued expenses	1,700	1,400
Income taxes payable	900	800
Accounts payable	3,700	3,400
Total current liabilities	6,300	5,600
Total equity and liabilities	€17,000	€16,000

SELECTED FINANCIAL RATIOS

	RNA		Current Industry Average
	2014	2013	
Current ratio	1.61	1.62	1.63
Acid-test ratio	.64	.63	.68
Times interest earned	8.55	8.50	8.45
Profit margin on sales	13.2%	12.1%	13.0%
Asset turnover	1.84	1.83	1.84
Inventory turnover	3.17	3.21	3.18

Instructions

(a) Calculate a new set of ratios for fiscal year 2015 for RNA based on the financial statements presented.

(b) Explain the analytical use of each of the six ratios presented, describing what the investors can learn about RNA's financial stability and operating efficiency.

(c) Identify two limitations of ratio analysis.

Accounting, Analysis, and Principles

Savannah, Inc. is a manufacturing company that manufactures and sells a single product. Unit sales for each of the four quarters of 2015 are projected as follows.

Quarter	Units
First	80,000
Second	150,000
Third	550,000
Fourth	120,000
Annual Total	900,000

Savannah incurs variable manufacturing costs of £0.40 per unit and variable non-manufacturing costs of £0.35 per unit. Savannah will incur fixed manufacturing costs of £720,000 and fixed non-manufacturing costs of £1,080,000. Savannah will sell its product for £4.00 per unit.

Accounting

Determine the amount of net income Savannah will report in each of the four quarters of 2015, assuming actual sales are as projected and employing (a) the integral approach to interim financial reporting and (b) the discrete approach to interim financial reporting. Ignore income taxes.

Analysis

Compute Savannah's profit margin on sales for each of the four quarters of 2015. What effect does employing the integral approach instead of the discrete approach have on the degree to which Savannah's profit margin on sales varies from quarter to quarter?

Principles

Should Savannah implement the integral or discrete approach under IFRS? Do you agree? That is, explain the conceptual rationale behind the integral approach to interim financial reporting.

IFRS BRIDGE TO THE PROFESSION

Professional Research

As part of the year-end audit, you are discussing the disclosure checklist with your client. The checklist identifies the items that must be disclosed in a set of IFRS financial statements. The client is surprised by the disclosure item related to accounting policies. Specifically, since the audit report will attest to the statements being prepared in accordance with IFRS, the client questions the accounting policy checklist item. The client has asked you to conduct some research to verify the accounting policy disclosures.

Instructions

Access the IFRS authoritative literature at the IASB website (*http://eifrs.iasb.org/*) (you may register for free eIFRS access at this site). When you have accessed the documents, you can use the search tool in your Internet browser to respond to the following questions. (Provide paragraph citations.)

(a) In general, what should disclosures of accounting policies encompass?
(b) List some examples of the most commonly required disclosures.

*Professional Simulation

In this simulation, you are asked to evaluate a company's solvency and going concern potential by analyzing a set of ratios. You also are asked to indicate possible limitations of ratio analysis. Prepare responses to all parts.

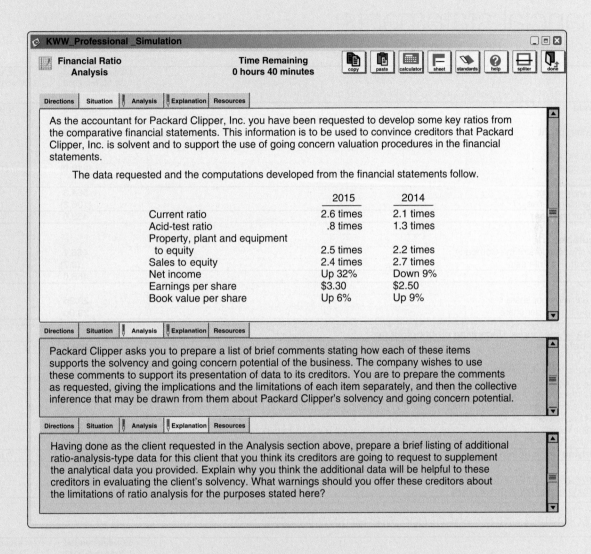

Financial statements

Consolidated income statement

	Notes	52 weeks ended 30 March 2013 £m	52 weeks ended 31 March 2012 £m
Revenue	2, 3	**10,026.8**	9,934.3
Operating profit	2, 3	**756.0**	746.5
Finance income	6	**26.5**	48.3
Finance costs	6	**(218.2)**	(136.8)
Profit before tax	4	**564.3**	658.0
Income tax expense	7	**(106.3)**	(168.4)
Profit for the year		**458.0**	489.6
Attributable to:			
Equity shareholders of the Company		**466.7**	513.1
Non-controlling interests		**(8.7)**	(23.5)
		458.0	489.6
Basic earnings per share	8	**29.2p**	32.5p
Diluted earnings per share	8	**29.0p**	32.2p

Non-GAAP measures: Underlying profit before tax			
Profit before tax		**564.3**	658.0
Adjusted for:			
Strategic programme costs	5	**6.6**	18.4
Restructuring costs	5	**9.3**	—
IAS 36 Impairment of assets	5	**—**	44.9
IAS 39 Fair value movement of put option over non-controlling interest in Czech business	5	**—**	(15.6)
IAS 39 Fair value movement of embedded derivative	5	**(5.8)**	0.2
Fair value movement on buy back of the Puttable Callable Reset medium-term notes	5	**75.3**	—
Reduction in M&S Bank income for the impact of the financial product mis-selling provision	5	**15.5**	—
Underlying profit before tax	1	**665.2**	705.9
Underlying basic earnings per share	8	**32.7p**	34.9p
Underlying diluted earnings per share	8	**32.5p**	34.6p

Consolidated statement of comprehensive income

	Notes	52 weeks ended 30 March 2013 £m	52 weeks ended 31 March 2012 £m
Profit for the year		**458.0**	489.6
Other comprehensive income:			
Foreign currency translation differences		**7.9**	(15.1)
Actuarial gains/(losses) on retirement benefit schemes	11	**90.7**	(189.9)
Tax on retirement benefit schemes		**(19.9)**	50.4
Cash flow and net investment hedges			
– fair value movements in other comprehensive income		**33.6**	53.0
– reclassified and reported in net profit		**(26.0)**	(23.0)
– amount recognised in inventories		**(13.6)**	13.7
Tax on cash flow hedges and net investment hedges		**(0.4)**	(7.3)
Other comprehensive income/(loss) for the year, net of tax		**72.3**	(118.2)
Total comprehensive income for the year		**530.3**	371.4
Attributable to:			
Equity shareholders of the Company		**539.0**	394.9
Non-controlling interests		**(8.7)**	(23.5)
		530.3	371.4

The accompanying notes, which are an integral part of these consolidated financial statements, are included in Marks and Spencer's 2013 annual report, available in the Corporate Site section of the company's website, *http://www.marksandspencer.com/*.

Consolidated statement of financial position

	Notes	As at 30 March 2013 £m	As at 31 March 2012 £m
Assets			
Non-current assets			
Intangible assets	14	695.0	584.3
Property, plant and equipment	15	5,033.7	4,789.9
Investment property		15.8	15.9
Investment in joint ventures		15.5	14.4
Other financial assets	16	3.0	3.0
Retirement benefit asset	11	206.1	91.3
Trade and other receivables	17	265.4	270.2
Derivative financial instruments	21	65.3	44.2
		6,299.8	5,813.2
Current assets			
Inventories		767.3	681.9
Other financial assets	16	16.9	260.5
Trade and other receivables	17	245.0	253.0
Derivative financial instruments	21	42.5	67.0
Current tax assets		3.1	1.6
Cash and cash equivalents	18	193.1	196.1
		1,267.9	1,460.1
Total assets		7,567.7	7,273.3
Liabilities			
Current liabilities			
Trade and other payables	19	1,503.8	1,449.1
Partnership liability to the Marks & Spencer UK Pension Scheme	12	71.9	71.9
Borrowings and other financial liabilities	20	558.7	327.7
Derivative financial instruments	21	13.7	60.5
Provisions	22	19.2	8.4
Current tax liabilities		71.0	87.8
		2,238.3	2,005.4
Non-current liabilities			
Retirement benefit deficit	11	13.1	13.3
Trade and other payables	19	292.1	280.8
Partnership liability to the Marks & Spencer UK Pension Scheme	12	550.7	—
Borrowings and other financial liabilities	20	1,727.3	1,948.1
Derivative financial instruments	21	13.1	27.2
Provisions	22	16.0	24.0
Deferred tax liabilities	23	230.7	195.7
		2,843.0	2,489.1
Total liabilities		5,081.3	4,494.5
Net assets		2,486.4	2,778.8
Equity			
Issued share capital	24	403.5	401.4
Share premium account		315.1	294.3
Capital redemption reserve		2,202.6	2,202.6
Hedging reserve		9.2	14.8
Other reserve		(6,542.2)	(6,114.3)
Retained earnings		6,117.2	5,991.4
Total shareholders' equity		2,505.4	2,790.2
Non-controlling interests in equity		(19.0)	(11.4)
Total equity		2,486.4	2,778.8

The financial statements were approved by the Board and authorised for issue on 20 May 2013. The financial statements also comprise the notes on pages 82 to 109.

Marc Bolland Chief Executive Officer

Alan Stewart Chief Finance Officer

Consolidated statement of changes in equity

	Ordinary share capital £m	Share premium account £m	Capital redemption reserve £m	Hedging reserve £m	Other reserve[1] £m	Retained earnings[2] £m	Total £m	Non-controlling interest £m	Total £m
At 3 April 2011	396.2	255.2	2,202.6	(11.3)	(6,042.4)	5,873.2	2,673.5	3.9	2,677.4
Profit/(loss) for the year	–	–	–	–	–	513.1	513.1	(23.5)	489.6
Other comprehensive income:									
Foreign currency translation	–	–	–	(1.1)	–	(14.0)	(15.1)	–	(15.1)
Actuarial losses on retirement benefit schemes	–	–	–	–	–	(189.9)	(189.9)	–	(189.9)
Tax on retirement benefit schemes	–	–	–	–	–	50.4	50.4	–	50.4
Cash flow and net investment hedges									
– fair value movements in other comprehensive income	–	–	–	43.8	–	9.2	53.0	–	53.0
– reclassified and reported in net profit[3]	–	–	–	(23.0)	–	–	(23.0)	–	(23.0)
– amount recognised in inventories	–	–	–	13.7	–	–	13.7	–	13.7
Tax on cash flow hedges and net investment hedges	–	–	–	(7.3)	–	–	(7.3)	–	(7.3)
Other comprehensive income	–	–	–	26.1	–	(144.3)	(118.2)	–	(118.2)
Total comprehensive income/(expenses)	–	–	–	26.1	–	368.8	394.9	(23.5)	371.4
Transactions with owners:									
Dividends	–	–	–	–	–	(267.8)	(267.8)	–	(267.8)
Transactions with non-controlling shareholders	–	–	–	–	–	(6.4)	(6.4)	8.2	1.8
Recognition of financial liability	–	–	–	–	(71.9)	–	(71.9)	–	(71.9)
Shares issued on exercise of employee share options	5.2	39.1	–	–	–	–	44.3	–	44.3
Purchase of own shares held by employee trusts	–	–	–	–	–	(13.2)	(13.2)	–	(13.2)
Credit for share-based payments	–	–	–	–	–	32.5	32.5	–	32.5
Deferred tax on share schemes	–	–	–	–	–	4.3	4.3	–	4.3
At 31 March 2012	401.4	294.3	2,202.6	14.8	(6,114.3)	5,991.4	2,790.2	(11.4)	2,778.8
At 1 April 2012	401.4	294.3	2,202.6	14.8	(6,114.3)	5,991.4	2,790.2	(11.4)	2,778.8
Profit/(loss) for the year	–	–	–	–	–	466.7	466.7	(8.7)	458.0
Other comprehensive income:									
Foreign currency translation	–	–	–	(1.5)	–	9.4	7.9	–	7.9
Actuarial gain on retirement benefit schemes	–	–	–	–	–	90.7	90.7	–	90.7
Tax on retirement benefit schemes	–	–	–	–	–	(19.9)	(19.9)	–	(19.9)
Cash flow and net investment hedges									
– fair value movements in other comprehensive income	–	–	–	35.9	–	(2.3)	33.6	–	33.6
– reclassified and reported in net profit[3]	–	–	–	(26.0)	–	–	(26.0)	–	(26.0)
– amount recognised in inventories	–	–	–	(13.6)	–	–	(13.6)	–	(13.6)
Tax on cash flow hedges and net investment hedges	–	–	–	(0.4)	–	–	(0.4)	–	(0.4)
Other comprehensive income	–	–	–	(5.6)	–	77.9	72.3	–	72.3
Total comprehensive income/(expenses)	–	–	–	(5.6)	–	544.6	539.0	(8.7)	530.3
Transactions with owners:									
Dividends	–	–	–	–	–	(271.3)	(271.3)	–	(271.3)
Transactions with non-controlling shareholders	–	–	–	–	–	–	–	1.1	1.1
Recognition of financial liability	–	–	–	–	(427.9)	(178.1)	(606.0)	–	(606.0)
Shares issued on exercise of employee share options	2.1	20.8	–	–	–	–	22.9	–	22.9
Credit for share-based payments	–	–	–	–	–	28.0	28.0	–	28.0
Deferred tax on share schemes	–	–	–	–	–	2.6	2.6	–	2.6
At 30 March 2013	403.5	315.1	2,202.6	9.2	(6,542.2)	6,117.2	2,505.4	(19.0)	2,486.4

1. The 'Other reserve' was originally created as part of the capital restructuring that took place in 2002. It represents the difference between the nominal value of the shares issued prior to the capital reduction by the Company (being the carrying value of the investment in Marks and Spencer plc) and the share capital, share premium and capital redemption reserve of Marks and Spencer plc at the date of the transaction. Last year the reserve also included discretionary distributions to the Marks & Spencer UK Pension Scheme, which following the Group's payment of an interim dividend in relation to 2011/12 and the resultant recognition of the annual distribution of £71.9m as a financial liability was £427.9m. On 21 May 2012 the Group changed the terms of the Marks and Spencer Scottish Limited Partnership and the total equity instrument of £427.9m was derecognised and the fair value of the remaining distributions of £606.0m was recognised as a financial liability (see note 12).

2. The 'Retained earnings reserve' includes a cumulative £14.5m gain (last year £5.1m gain) in the currency reserve.

3. Amounts reclassified and reported in net profit have all been recorded in cost of sales.

Consolidated cash flow information

	Notes	52 weeks ended 30 March 2013 £m	52 weeks ended 31 March 2012 £m
Cash flows from operating activities			
Cash generated from operations	26	**1,246.2**	1,352.1
Income tax paid		**(106.0)**	(149.1)
Net cash generated from operating activities		**1,140.2**	1,203.0
Cash flows from investing activities			
Purchase of property, plant and equipment		**(642.6)**	(564.3)
Purchase of intangible assets		**(187.1)**	(156.4)
Sale/(purchase) of current financial assets		**243.4**	(44.8)
Interest received		**5.9**	7.7
Net cash used in investing activities		**(580.4)**	(757.8)
Cash flows from financing activities			
Interest paid		**(135.2)**	(135.9)
Cash inflow/(outflow) from borrowings		**0.5**	(41.4)
Drawdown of syndicated loan notes		**81.0**	—
Issue of medium-term notes		**395.6**	295.5
Redemption of medium-term notes		**(606.4)**	(307.6)
Decrease in obligations under finance leases		**(11.0)**	(13.0)
Payment of liability to the Marks & Spencer UK Pension Scheme		**(71.9)**	(71.9)
Equity dividends paid		**(271.3)**	(267.8)
Shares issued on exercise of employee share options		**22.9**	44.3
Purchase of own shares by employee trust		**—**	(13.2)
Net cash used in financing activities		**(595.8)**	(511.0)
Net cash outflow from activities		**(36.0)**	(65.8)
Effects of exchange rate changes		**0.9**	(1.9)
Opening net cash		**195.8**	263.5
Closing net cash	27	**160.7**	195.8

	Notes	52 weeks ended 30 March 2013 £m	52 weeks ended 31 March 2012 £m
Reconciliation of net cash flow to movement in net debt			
Opening net debt		**(1,857.1)**	(1,900.9)
Net cash outflow from activities		**(36.0)**	(65.8)
(Decrease)/increase in current financial assets		**(243.4)**	44.8
Decrease in debt financing		**132.7**	138.4
Partnership liability to the Marks & Spencer UK Pension Scheme (non-cash)		**(606.0)**	(71.9)
Exchange and other non-cash movements		**(4.5)**	(1.7)
Movement in net debt		**(757.2)**	43.8
Closing net debt	27	**(2,614.3)**	(1,857.1)

Specimen Financial Statements: adidas AG

Consolidated Statement of Financial Position

.. / adidas AG Consolidated Statement of Financial Position (IFRS) (€ in millions)

	Note	Dec. 31, 2012	Dec. 31, 2011[1]	Change in %	Jan. 1, 2011[1]
ASSETS					
Cash and cash equivalents	5	1,670	906	84.4	1,150
Short-term financial assets	6	265	465	(42.9)	233
Accounts receivable	7	1,688	1,595	5.8	1,620
Other current financial assets	8	192	289	(33.7)	178
Inventories	9	2,486	2,502	(0.6)	2,135
Income tax receivables	34	76	77	(0.9)	71
Other current assets	10	489	469	4.0	390
Assets classified as held for sale	11	11	25	(55.0)	47
Total current assets		**6,877**	**6,328**	**8.7**	**5,824**
Property, plant and equipment	12	1,095	963	13.6	855
Goodwill	13	1,281	1,553	(17.5)	1,512
Trademarks	14	1,484	1,503	(1.3)	1,447
Other intangible assets	14	167	160	4.8	142
Long-term financial assets	15	112	97	14.7	93
Other non-current financial assets	16	21	42	(49.1)	54
Deferred tax assets	34	528	484	9.0	501
Other non-current assets	17	86	107	(19.2)	100
Total non-current assets		**4,774**	**4,909**	**(2.7)**	**4,704**
Total assets		**11,651**	**11,237**	**3.7**	**10,528**

1) Restated according to IAS 8, see Note 03.
Rounding differences may arise in percentages and totals.
The accompanying notes are an integral part of these consolidated financial statements.

The accompanying notes, which are an integral part of these consolidated financial statements, are included in adidas' 2012 annual report, available in the Corporate Information section of the company's website, *http://www.adidas-group.com*.

.. / adidas AG Consolidated Statement of Financial Position (IFRS) (€ in millions)

	Note	Dec. 31, 2012	Dec. 31, 2011[1]	Change in %	Jan. 1, 2011[1]
LIABILITIES AND EQUITY					
Short-term borrowings	18	280	289	(3.2)	284
Accounts payable		1,790	1,887	(5.1)	1,697
Other current financial liabilities	19	83	66	24.4	132
Income taxes	34	275	252	9.1	265
Other current provisions	20	563	549	2.6	485
Current accrued liabilities	21	1,084	992	9.3	842
Other current liabilities	22	299	303	(1.2)	241
Liabilities classified as held for sale	11	—	0	(100.0)	0
Total current liabilities		**4,374**	**4,338**	**0.8**	**3,946**
Long-term borrowings	18	1,207	991	21.8	1,337
Other non-current financial liabilities	23	17	9	92.3	17
Pensions and similar obligations	24	251	205	22.3	180
Deferred tax liabilities	34	368	430	(14.4)	451
Other non-current provisions	20	69	55	26.5	61
Non-current accrued liabilities	21	40	45	(9.0)	39
Other non-current liabilities	25	34	36	(9.5)	36
Total non-current liabilities		**1,986**	**1,771**	**12.2**	**2,121**
Share capital		209	209	—	209
Reserves		641	791	(18.9)	563
Retained earnings		4,454	4,137	7.7	3,691
Shareholders' equity	26	**5,304**	**5,137**	**3.3**	**4,463**
Non-controlling interests	27	(13)	(9)	(54.4)	(2)
Total equity		**5,291**	**5,128**	**3.2**	**4,461**
Total liabilities and equity		**11,651**	**11,237**	**3.7**	**10,528**

1) Restated according to IAS 8, see Note 03.
Rounding differences may arise in percentages and totals.
The accompanying notes are an integral part of these consolidated financial statements.

Consolidated Income Statement
.. / adidas AG Consolidated Income Statement (IFRS) (€ in millions)

	Note	Year ending Dec. 31, 2012	Year ending Dec. 31, 2011[1]	Change
Net sales	36	14,883	13,322	11.7%
Cost of sales		7,780	6,993	11.3%
Gross profit		**7,103**	**6,329**	**12.2%**
(% of net sales)		47.7%	47.5%	0.2pp
Royalty and commission income		105	93	13.0%
Other operating income	30	127	98	28.7%
Other operating expenses	12, 14, 31	6,150	5,567	10.5%
(% of net sales)		41.3%	41.8%	(0.5pp)
Goodwill impairment losses	13	265	–	100.0%
Operating profit		**920**	**953**	**(3.4%)**
(% of net sales)		6.2%	7.2%	(1.0pp)
Financial income	33	36	31	17.4%
Financial expenses	33	105	115	(7.8%)
Income before taxes		**851**	**869**	**(2.1%)**
(% of net sales)			6.5%	(0.8pp)
Income taxes	34	327	261	25.3%
(% of income before taxes)		38.4%	30.0%	8.4pp
Net income		**524**	**608**	**(13.8%)**
(% of net sales)		3.5%	4.6%	(1.0pp)
Net income attributable to shareholders		**526**	**613**	**(14.2%)**
(% of net sales)		3.5%	4.6%	(1.1pp)
Net income attributable to non-controlling interests		**(2)**	**(5)**	**54.8%**
Basic earnings per share (in €)	35	2.52	2.93	(14.2%)
Diluted earnings per share (in €)	35	2.52	2.93	(14.2%)

1) Restated according to IAS 8, see Note 03.
Rounding differences may arise in percentages and totals.
The accompanying notes are an integral part of these consolidated financial statements.

Consolidated Statement of Comprehensive Income

.. / adidas AG Consolidated Statement of Comprehensive Income (IFRS) (€ in millions)

	Note	Year ending Dec. 31, 2012	Year ending Dec. 31, 2011[1]
Net income after taxes		**524**	**608**
Net loss/gain on cash flow hedges, net of tax	29	(134)	123
Actuarial loss of defined benefit plans (IAS 19), net of tax	24	(26)	(10)
Asset ceiling effect (IAS 19), net of tax	24	0	0
Currency translation differences		(43)	116
Other comprehensive income		**(203)**	**229**
Total comprehensive income		**321**	**837**
Attributable to shareholders of adidas AG		321	841
Attributable to non-controlling interests		(0)	(4)

1) Restated according to IAS 8, see Note 03.
Rounding differences may arise in percentages and totals.
The accompanying notes are an integral part of these consolidated financial statements

Consolidated Statement of Changes in Equity
.. / adidas AG Consolidated Statement of Changes in Equity (IFRS) (€ in millions)

	Note	Share capital	Capital reserve
Balance at December 31, 2010		**209**	**722**
Adjustments according to IAS 8	3		
Balance at January 1, 2011[2]		**209**	**722**
Net income recognised directly in equity			
Net income			
Total comprehensive income			
Dividend payment	26		
Reclassifications of non-controlling interests in accordance with IAS 32	27		
Balance at December 31, 2011[2]		**209**	**722**
Net income recognised directly in equity			
Net income			
Total comprehensive income			
Dividend payment	26		
Acquisition of shares from non-controlling interest shareholders	4		
Convertible bond	18, 26		55
Reclassifications of non-controlling interests in accordance with IAS 32	27		
Balance at December 31, 2012		**209**	**777**

1) Reserves for actuarial gains/losses, share option plans and acquisition of shares from non-controlling interest shareholders.
2) Restated according to IAS 8, see Note 03.
3) Including € 17 million according to IAS 8.
Rounding differences may arise in percentages and totals.
The accompanying notes are an integral part of these consolidated financial statements.

Cumulative translation adjustments	Hedging reserves	Other reserves[1]	Retained earnings	Total share-holders' equity	Non-controlling interests	Total equity
(121)	**(10)**	**(28)**	**3,844**	**4,616**	**7**	**4,623**
			(153)	(153)	(9)	(162)
(121)	**(10)**	**(28)**	**3,691**	**4,463**	**(2)**	**4,461**
115[3]	123	(10)		228	1	229
			613	613	(5)	608
115	**123**	**(10)**	**613**	**841**	**(4)**	**837**
			(167)	(167)	(3)	(170)
			0	0		0
(6)	**113**	**(38)**	**4,137**	**5,137**	**(9)**	**5,128**
(45)	(134)	(26)		(205)	2	(203)
			526	526	(2)	524
(45)	**(134)**	**(26)**	**526**	**321**	**(0)**	**321**
			(209)	(209)	(3)	(212)
		(0)		(0)	(1)	(1)
				55		55
			0	0		0
(51)	**(21)**	**(64)**	**4,454**	**5,304**	**(13)**	**5,291**

Consolidated Statement of Cash Flows
.. / adidas AG Consolidated Statement of Cash Flows (IFRS) (€ in millions)

	Note	Year ending Dec. 31, 2012	Year ending Dec. 31, 2011[1]
Operating activities:			
Income before taxes		851	869
Adjustments for:			
Depreciation, amortisation and impairment losses	12, 13,15, 31	536	253
Reversals of impairment losses		(2)	(2)
Unrealised foreign exchange gains, net		(26)	(31)
Interest income	33	(35)	(30)
Interest expense	33	97	108
Losses on sale of property, plant and equipment, net		12	12
Other non-cash income	30, 31	(3)	(0)
Operating profit before working capital changes		**1,430**	**1,179**
Increase in receivables and other assets		(135)	(41)
Decrease/increase in inventories		23	(353)
Increase in accounts payable and other liabilities		94	449
Cash generated from operations before interest and taxes		**1,412**	**1,234**
Interest paid		(90)	(113)
Income taxes paid		(380)	(314)
Net cash generated from operating activities		**942**	**807**
Investing activities:			
Purchase of trademarks and other intangible assets		(58)	(58)
Proceeds from sale of trademarks and other intangible assets		1	0
Purchase of property, plant and equipment		(376)	(318)
Proceeds from sale of property, plant and equipment		19	2
Acquisition of subsidiaries and other business units net of cash acquired	4	(57)	(20)
Proceeds from disposal of subsidiaries net of cash	4	14	–
Proceeds from sale/purchase of short-term financial assets		195	(192)
Proceeds from sale/purchase of investments and other long-term assets		10	(10)
Interest received		35	30
Net cash used in investing activities		**(217)**	**(566)**
Financing activities:			
Repayments of long-term borrowings		(3)	(57)
Proceeds from issue of a convertible bond	18	496	–
Dividend paid to shareholders of adidas AG	26	(209)	(167)
Dividend paid to non-controlling interest shareholders		(3)	(3)
Acquisition of non-controlling interests	4	(8)	–
Cash repayments of short-term borrowings		(231)	(273)
Net cash used in financing activities		**42**	**(500)**
Effect of exchange rates on cash		**(3)**	**15**
Net increase/decrease of cash and cash equivalents		764	(244)
Cash and cash equivalents at beginning of the year	5	906	1,150
Cash and cash equivalents at end of the year	5	**1,670**	**906**

1) Restated according to IAS 8, see Note 03.
Rounding differences may arise in percentages and totals.
The accompanying notes are an integral part of these consolidated financial statements

Specimen Financial Statements: Puma Group

Consolidated Statement of Financial Position	Notes	31.12.2012 € million	31.12.2011 € million
ASSETS			
Cash and cash equivalents	3	407,3	448,2
Inventories	4	552,5	536,8
Trade receivables	5	507,0	533,1
Income tax receivables	22	58,1	72,6
Other current financial assets	6	32,9	44,8
Other current assets	7	84,8	79,0
Current assets		**1.642,6**	**1.714,5**
Deferred taxes	8	152,0	109,1
Property, plant and equipment	9	226,8	234,9
Intangible assets	10	463,4	452,2
Investments in associates	11	24,0	24,8
Other non-current financial assets	12	16,9	18,9
Other non-current assets	12	4,5	27,4
Non-current assets		**887,6**	**867,3**
Total assets		**2.530,3**	**2.581,8**
LIABILITIES AND SHAREHOLDERS' EQUITY			
Current bank liabilities	13	44,1	35,1
Trade payables	13	376,1	431,4
Income taxes	23	54,7	82,5
Other current provisions	16	118,1	43,8
Liabilities from acquisitions	17	2,6	93,6
Other current financial liabilities	13	114,1	56,4
Other current liabilities	13	93,8	96,4
Current liabilities		**803,5**	**839,2**
Deferred taxes	8	54,1	63,6
Pension provisions	15	30,7	29,8
Other non-current provisions	16	38,3	26,3
Liabilities from acquisitions	17	3,3	6,8
Other non-current financial liabilities	13	0,2	0,3
Other non-current liabilities	13	2,9	10,6
Non-current liabilities		**129,4**	**137,5**
Subscribed capital	18	38,6	38,6
Group reserves	18	223,8	281,2
Retained earnings	18	1.357,6	1.317,3
Treasury stock	18	−31,6	−32,6
Equity attributable to the shareholders of the parent	18	**1.588,5**	**1.604,5**
Non-controlling interest	18	8,9	0,7
Shareholders' equity	18	**1.597,4**	**1.605,2**
Total liabilities and shareholders' equity		**2.530,3**	**2.581,8**

The accompanying notes, which are an integral part of these consolidated financial statements, are included in Puma's 2012 annual report, available in the About Puma section of the company's website, *www.puma.com*.

Consolidated Income Statement

	Notes	2012 € million	2011 € million
Sales	25	**3.270,7**	**3.009,0**
Cost of sales	25	−1.691,7	−1.515,6
Gross profit	25	**1.579,0**	**1.493,4**
Royalty and commission income		19,2	17,6
Other operating income and expenses	20	−1.485,0	−1.177,8
Operating income (EBIT)		**113,2**	**333,2**
Result from associated companies	21	0,6	1,1
Financial income	21	6,9	5,2
Financial expenses	21	−8,4	−19,1
Financial result		**−0,9**	**−12,8**
Earnings before taxes (EBT)		**112,3**	**320,4**
Taxes on income	22	−32,5	−90,0
Consolidated net earnings for the year		**79,8**	**230,4**
attributable to: Non-controlling interest	18	−9,6	−0,3
Equity holders of the parent (net earnings)		**70,2**	**230,1**
Earnings per share (€)	23	4,69	15,36
Earnings per share (€) - diluted	23	4,69	15,36
Weighted average shares outstanding	23	14,967	14,981
Weighted average shares outstanding, diluted	23	14,968	14,985

Consolidated Statement of Comprehensive Income

	After tax 2012 € Mio.	Tax impact 2012 € Mio.	Before tax 2012 € Mio.	After tax 2011 € Mio.	Tax impact 2011 € Mio.	Before tax 2011 € Mio.
Net earnings before attribution	**79,8**		**79,8**	**230,4**		**230,4**
Unrecognized net actuarial gain/loss	−1,6	0,4	−1,9	−2,8	1,0	−3,8
Currency changes	−31,5	0,4	−31,9	6,4	−1,511	7,9
Cash flow hedge						
Release to the income statement	−19,8	7,0	−26,8	11,1	−5,5	16,6
Market value for cashflow hedges	−6,4	0,1	−6,5	19,8	−7,0	26,8
Share in the other comprehensive income of at equity accounted investments	−0,7	0,0	−0,7	0,7	0,0	0,7
Other result	**−59,9**	**8,0**	**−67,8**	**35,2**	**−13,0**	**48,2**
Comprehensive income	**19,9**	**8,0**	**12,0**	**265,6**	**−13,0**	**278,6**
attributable to: Non-controlling interest	9,4		9,4	0,4		0,4
Equity holder of the parent	10,6	8,0	2,6	265,2	−13,0	278,3

Consolidated Statement of Cashflows	Notes	2012 € million	2011 € million
Operating activities			
Earnings before tax (EBT)		112,3	320,4
Adjustments for:			
Depreciation	9,10	76,1	63,4
Non-realized currency gains/losses, net		1,1	0,3
Result from associated companies	13	−0,6	−1,1
Financial income	21	−4,4	−5,2
Financial expenses	21	8,4	19,1
Changes from the sale of fixed assets		−1,3	0,2
Changes to pension accruals	15	−2,3	−1,5
Other cash effected expenses/incomes		138,4	−13,9
Gross Cashflow	26	**327,6**	**381,5**
Changes in receivables and other current assets	5, 6, 7	−5,7	−96,7
Changes in inventories	4	−24,0	−97,2
Changes in trade payables and other current liabilities	13	−61,8	88,0
Cash inflow from operating activities		236,1	275,6
Interest paid	21	−6,4	−7,2
Income taxes paid		−73,0	−141,6
Net cash from operating activities	26	**156,7**	**126,8**
Investing activities			
Payment for acquisitions	17	−91,7	−44,2
Purchase of property and equipment	9, 10	−81,2	−71,1
Proceeds from sale of property and equipment		4,3	2,6
Changes in other non-current assets	12	−0,8	−2,5
Interest received	21	4,6	5,2
Cash outflow from investing activities		**−164,9**	**−110,0**
Financing activities			
Changes in non-current liabilities	13	−0,2	−0,3
Changes in current bank liabilities	13	10,1	−5,1
Dividend payments to equity holders of the parent	18	−29,9	−26,8
Dividend payments to non-controlling interests	18	−1,1	0,0
Purchase of treasury stock	18	0,0	−26,6
Cash outflow from financing activities	26	**−21,2**	**−58,8**
Exchange rate-related changes in cash flow		−11,7	10,7
Change in cash and cash equivalents		**−41,0**	**−31,4**
Cash and cash equivalents at beginning of the financial year		448,2	479,6
Cash and cash equivalents at the end of the financial year	3, 26	**407,3**	**448,2**

Statement of Changes in Equity in € million	Subscribed capital	Reserves					Retained earnings	Treasury stock	Equity before non-controlling interests	Non-controlling interests	Total equity
		Capital reserve	Revenue reserves	Difference from currency conversion	Cash Flow hedges	At equity accounted investments					
Dec. 31, 2010	**38,6**	**198,2**	**69,5**	**0,0**	**−11,1**		**1114,0**	**−23,2**	**1386,2**	**0,2**	**1386,4**
Net Earnings							230,1		230,1	0,3	230,4
Actuarial gain/loss from pension commitments			−2,8						−2,8		−2,8
Currency changes/others				6,4		0,6			7,0	0,1	7,0
Release to the income Statement					11,1				11,1		11,1
Market value for cashflow hedges					19,8				19,8		19,8
Total comprehensive income			−2,8	6,4	30,9	0,6	230,1		265,2	0,4	265,6
Dividend payment							−26,8		−26,8		−26,8
Valuation from option programs		6,5							6,5		6,5
Purchase of treasury stock								−26,6	−26,6		−26,6
Conversion of options		−17,3						17,3	0,0		0,0
Changes in the group of consolidated companies		0,1							0,1	0,1	0,3
Dec. 31, 2011	**38,6**	**187,6**	**66,7**	**6,4**	**19,8**	**0,8**	**1317,3**	**−32,6**	**1604,5**	**0,7**	**1605,2**
Net Earnings							70,2		70,2	9.6	79,8
Actuarial gain/loss from pension commitments			−1,6						−1,6		−1,6
Currency changes/others				−31,2		−0,7			−31,9	−0,2	−32,1
Release to the income statement					−19,8				−19,8		−19,8
Market valuation of cashflow hedges					−6,4				−6,4		−6,4
Total comprehensive income			−1,6	−31,2	−26,2	−0,7	70,2		10,6	9,4	19,9
Dividend payment							−29,9		−29,9	−1,1	−31,0
Valuation from option programs		3,2							3,3		3,3
Conversion of options		−1,0						1,0	0,0		0,0
Dec. 31, 2012	**38,6**	**189,8**	**65,1**	**−24,9**	**−6,4**	**0,2**	**1357,6**	**−31,6**	**1588,5**	**8,9**	**1597,4**